The *South Carolina* Encyclopedia

South Carolina Encyclopedia Editorial Advisory Board

Humanities Council Board of Directors

members during the encyclopedia project

Donors

Special thanks go to the following individuals, corporations, foundations, and organizations whose substantial financial support made this encyclopedia possible.

LEADERSHIP GIFTS ($25,000 OR MORE)
Lucy Hampton Bostick Residuary Charitable Trust
Mr. and Mrs. Alester G. (Mary Simms Oliphant) Furman III
Mills B. Lane Memorial Foundation
V. Kann Rasmussen Foundation
Self Family Foundation
South Carolina Department of Education

MAJOR GIFTS ($15,000 – $24,999)
Mr. and Mrs. Stanley W. (Paula Black) Baker
Mr. and Mrs. Roger A. F. (Marianna Black) Habisreutinger
John S. and James L. Knight Foundation
George E. and Sissy Stone
Betty and James K. Stone Foundation
The Post and Courier Foundation, Charleston

PATRONS ($10,000 – $14,999)
Blue Cross Blue Shield of South Carolina
Carolina First Foundation
Mr. and Mrs. Wayne Q. (Susan) Justesen, Jr.
Mr. and Mrs. S. C. (Cal) (Francis) McMeekin, Jr.
Santee Cooper
D. L. Scurry Foundation

BENEFACTORS ($5,000 – $9,999)
Bank of America
Betty and Walter Edgar
Greenwood Development Corporation
The Liberty Corporation Foundation
Piedmont Natural Gas
George M. and Carolyn Reeves
Olin and Muffet Sansbury
Scripps Howard Foundation
South Carolina State Fair
University South Caroliniana Society
The Wachovia Foundation, Inc.

CONTRIBUTORS ($1,000 – $4,999)
Randy L. and Mary Alice Akers
Herbert F., Herbert F. Jr., and Jane Ames
Judith T. and Robert W. Bainbridge
LaNelle and Robert Barber
Bill and Valerie Barnet
The Barnet Foundation Trust
Barbara L. Bellows
BellSouth
Mary and Clinch Belser
Mr. and Mrs. James McDuffie Bruce III
Jim and Jo Byrd
Maria A. Cordova and Carlos Salinas
John and Dulcie Creech
Duke Energy Foundation
Bettie and Van Edwards
Robert and Jan Figueira
Elaine T. Freeman
Nancy and John Garman
Robert D. Hazel
Carlanna H. Hendrick
Kate and A. V. Huff
Sig and Judy Huitt
Jason and Mary Murphey Hyman
Barbara and Larry Jackson
George Dean and Susan Johnson
William Light Kinney, Jr.
Hugh C. Lane
Alison W. Lockhart
John F. and Evelyn K. Lomax
S. E. (Gene) and Nancy Longbrake
William C. and Wendy Mayrose
B. Palmer and Mary McArthur
Mr. and Mrs. Joseph H. McGee
Governor and Mrs. Robert E. (Josephine) McNair
Betty Ann and Stephen Mead
Stephen and Gail Morrison
Mr. and Mrs. Julian J. Nexsen, Jr.
Suzanne Ozment
Phifer/Johnson Foundation
Bettis C. Rainsford
Peggy S. and Roosevelt Ratliff, Jr.
David E. Rison
Ardis M. Savory
Alan Schaffer
Sisters of Charity Foundation
Snelling Personnel Services
South Carolina Arts Commission
South Carolina Press Association Foundation
The Springs Close Foundation
Joseph D. and Bobbi Swann

Mr. and Mrs. H. Simmons (Elizabeth Anne Coker) Tate, Jr.
Washington Group International
William B. Watkins
Earl J. and Elizabeth H. Wilcox

Gifts in Honor or Memory of
John E. Eck
Margaret M. Hazel
Mr. and Mrs. Claudius M. Lide, Sr.
Franklin S. Lumpkin, Jr.
Mr. and Mrs. Laurin C. McArthur, Sr.
Robert L. Meriwether
Mary C. Simms Oliphant
Clithiel Ratliff and Roosevelt Ratliff, Sr.
Horace Fraser Rudisill
Jerold J. Savory
Martin David Watkins
John and Madge Gandy Wise

Spoleto Festival USA
WOOLEN FABRICS
ESTABLISHED 1840-

The *South Carolina* Encyclopedia

Edited by Walter Edgar

A Project of The Humanities Council[SC]

The University of South Carolina Press

Published by the University of South Carolina Press
Columbia, South Carolina 29208

www.sc.edu/uscpress

Manufactured in the United States of America

15 14 13 12 11 10 09 08 07 06 10 9 8 7 6 5 4 3 2 1

Library of Congress Cataloging-in-Publication Data

The South Carolina encyclopedia / edited by Walter Edgar.
p. cm.
"A project of the Humanities Council SC."
Includes bibliographical references and index.
ISBN-13: 978-1-57003-598-2 (cloth : alk. paper)
ISBN-10: 1-57003-598-9 (cloth : alk. paper)
1. South Carolina—Encyclopedias. 2. South Carolina—History—Encyclopedias. I. Edgar, Walter B., 1943– II. Humanities Council SC.
F269.S764 2006
975.7003—dc22 2006010320

Photographs on previous spread (left to right):
1 (*detail*) Spoleto Festival in Charleston, S.C., photo by Bill Murtin, courtesy, City of Charleston; 2 (*detail*) horse racing in Aiken, courtesy, South Caroliniana Library, University of South Carolina; 3 Anna Heyward Taylor, *Sea Turtle No. 1*, courtesy, Gibbes Museum of Art / Carolina Art Association; 4 (*detail*) Jenkins Orphanage Band, courtesy, South Carolina Historical Society; 5 (*detail*) an aerial view of Middleton Place, courtesy, South Carolina Department of Archives and History; 6 (*detail*) the silver matrix for the State Seal, courtesy, South Carolina Department of Archives and History; 7 (*detail*) reconstructed bell tower from the old Furman campus on the new campus, courtesy, Furman University; 8 (*detail*) some two thousand Marines at Parris Island form the Marine Corps emblem, 1918, courtesy, South Caroliniana Library, University of South Carolina

Photograph facing contents page: sand dunes at Myrtle Beach, circa 1930s; courtesy, South Caroliniana Library, University of South Carolina

Editorial Staff

Contents

Foreword

In the 1990s there was a movement in the Southeast toward state encyclopedias, sparked by the success of *The Kentucky Encyclopedia* (1992), published in celebration of the Kentucky bicentennial. Several other states had encyclopedias underway or in the planning stage. I first learned of these activities at a meeting of state humanities councils in Nashville, and it struck me that South Carolina could certainly use a comprehensive source of information such as an encyclopedia. Back in Columbia I telephoned my longtime colleague Walter Edgar, director of the Institute for Southern Studies at the University of South Carolina, to ask whether he would be interested in editing a South Carolina encyclopedia—assuming that the Humanities Council^SC^ would sponsor it. The next day he called to say that he would be available if the Humanities Council^SC^ decided to undertake the project. We then checked with Catherine Fry, director of the University of South Carolina Press at that time, and she said that the press would be pleased to enter into discussions with the Humanities Council^SC^.

Upon learning about these apparently auspicious circumstances, the council appointed an Encyclopedia Planning Committee, and in July 1998 the Humanities Council Board voted to undertake the sponsorship of the proposed encyclopedia in cooperation with the Institute for Southern Studies and USC Press. It would be a multiyear project, by far the largest and costliest ever undertaken by the council. After many discussions the separate roles of the three cooperating units were defined and contracts were prepared. The press would have autonomy in publishing and distributing the book. The Institute for Southern Studies would house the editorial staff, and Walter Edgar with his advisory board of specialists would have sole discretion in selecting the fields to be covered, the authors, and the entries. The Humanities Council^SC^, the contractual author of the work, would fund the project.

There were no deep pockets available to the council in Washington or in South Carolina, but a professional feasibility study indicated that the project could be funded by a multiyear effort in the state. The Encyclopedia Finance Committee was established with a majority membership of prominent businesspersons who were serving on the board. As a first step this committee secured pledges totaling more than $100,000 from current and former board members. With professional guidance the Finance Committee began its statewide campaign around the turn of the new century and continued for several years until success was assured. Approximately eight years have passed between the decision to proceed and the finished product—not a bad span as encyclopedias go.

The encyclopedia project, which began so fortuitously, could have faltered without the extraordinary efforts of a number of dedicated participants. Special recognition is due to Cal McMeekin, Wayne Justesen, George Stone, Olin Sansbury, and John Lomax for their informed leadership in the work of the Encyclopedia Finance Committee; to Walter Edgar for participating in fund-raising events in various parts of the state despite the demands of his heavy schedule; and to Randy Akers, executive director of the Humanities Council^SC^, for managing the logistics and paperwork, writing numerous grant applications, and in general keeping the multiyear endeavor on track.

The South Carolina Encyclopedia is intended as a resource for various constituencies. Copies will be placed in all the public schools in the state. The scope of the entries and the bibliographies that accompany them will make the work indispensable to libraries. It will be useful to businesses, colleges and universities, and other organizations that recruit at the national and international level. Finally, the price has been deliberately held at an affordable level with the hopes that the book will be widely available to all readers with an interest in the complex tapestry of the history and culture of the Palmetto State.

George M. Reeves
Chairman of the Encyclopedia
Planning Committee

Preface

The Beginning. In late 1998 I received a telephone call from my longtime friend George Reeves, who said he wanted to meet with me to talk about an interesting project. Several days later he ambled into my office with a copy of *The Kentucky Encyclopedia* under his arm. He had just returned from a regional meeting of state humanities councils, and one of the topics discussed was the compiling of encyclopedias in the various states. George asked me if I would be willing to undertake the overseeing of a similar effort in South Carolina. After having just finished ten years' work on *South Carolina: A History,* I was not sure I wanted to get involved in what would surely be a multiyear commitment. However, the more that I thought about the project, the more enthusiastic I became.

The proposed encyclopedia would be a handy one-volume reference tool for discovering just about everything you wanted to know about the Palmetto State but didn't know where to go to find the answers. There had never been a true encyclopedia of South Carolina. In the eighteenth and nineteenth centuries there were gazetteers and various collected biographies. The most famous of these was John Belton O'Neall's *Biographical Sketches of the Bench and Bar of South Carolina.* In the twentieth century Claude and Irene Neuffer's thirty-volume *Names in South Carolina* is the best known and the most useful. There were other reference works, such as the fourth volume of David Duncan Wallace's *The History of South Carolina* and *South Carolina: The WPA Guide to the Palmetto State.* While these were and are still invaluable reference tools, there was no single source to which someone could go to find out about a variety of topics such as the Boykin spaniel, John C. Calhoun, hoppin' john, Edwin Harleston, joggling boards, Matthew Perry, the Venus flytrap, Julia Peterkin, and Beaufort County. For general readers, schoolchildren, college students, and business professionals, the encyclopedia could provide the answers.

The Humanities Council[SC] decided, after thoughtful discussion, that it would adopt the encyclopedia as its major project—and would raise private funds to help underwrite its cost. From the outset, the people of South Carolina have responded enthusiastically to the project. In small towns and large, they opened their homes for meetings and their checkbooks for financial support. They asked questions and made suggestions for entries. Individuals, foundations, and businesses have contributed nearly a half-million dollars. It's a sum that amazes individuals in other states where either a large wealthy foundation or the state government underwrote their efforts. In South Carolina it was, as someone in Greenwood said, a "people's encyclopedia." And, as it has evolved and come to completion, it truly is just that.

The Organization. Before getting started, I examined many other encyclopedias. Once that was done, I contacted fifty-two individuals from around the country and asked them to serve on an advisory board to give advice on subject areas, individual entries, and potential authors. When you examine the list you will find very busy people who took the time to provide advice and counsel. All have some tie, either personal or professional, to South Carolina.

It was decided to create nineteen general subject areas and to have an associate editor in charge of each one. Each associate editor agreed to prepare a list of potential entries for his or her area and, once the list was finalized, to recruit authors. In addition to being responsible for her or his area, the associate editors—as a group—served as a sounding board for the managing editor and for me. When the entries were submitted, the associate editors were the first reviewers of an author's work before it was passed on to the managing editor.

Following a national search, Thomas Downey was chosen as the managing editor. With a background in South Carolina history and editorial experience from having worked on the Papers of Henry Laurens, he was a wonderful choice. For four years Tom dealt with the day-to-day operations of compiling the encyclopedia and directed a small team of dedicated researchers. When he left the project in August 2004 to become an associate editor of the Papers of Thomas Jefferson, one of our senior researchers, Aaron Marrs, assumed the position. Aaron did a superb job in the final stages of assembling the entries and in proofreading the text.

In planning the project, we decided to place most of the budget into the compilation process itself. Since work began, the support staff has consisted of only one person. For three and a half years Heather Buggy was the administrative assistant, kept track of 598 authors, 52 advisory board members, and 19 associate editors, and handled the financial records. Robert L. Ellis, Jr., assumed that position in 2004 and also compiled the index.

The University of South Carolina provided office space and, through its office of Sponsored Programs and Research (SPAR), assisted with the fiscal operation of the project. Patricia Hatcher of SPAR made sure that budgets, reports, and other necessary financial and administrative matters were attended to in a timely fashion.

The Content. Getting to know South Carolina is not an easy task, even for native sons and daughters. Over the nearly five hundred years of its recorded history—and the ten to fifteen millennia more of known human occupation—those who have lived in the 31,000 or so square miles of what is now the Palmetto State have presented a variety of faces to the outside world. South Carolina is a state that defies the stereotyping that would have made compiling this encyclopedia a breeze.

South Carolina *is* different. And, despite its small size, it has had more of an impact on the history of empires and nations than many larger American states. "South Carolina is the stormy petrel of the Union," wrote Kelly Miller. "She arouses the nation's wrath and rides upon the storm. There is not a dull period in her history." His contemporary Benjamin Brawley agreed: "The little triangle on the map known as South Carolina represents a portion of our country whose influence has been incalculable." These two black expatriate South Carolinians were writing in the 1920s, but their comments are just as valid nearly a century later.

Over the course of its history, South Carolina has been home to what is arguably one of the most diverse populations in what is now the United States. Prior to European settlement there were perhaps as many as forty different Indian nations living within its boundaries. By the end of the eighteenth century, in addition to the Native Americans, there were at least twenty-five identifiable West African ethnicities and nine European ethnic groups. Among the Europeans, these nine could be further subdivided by nationality and experience. For example, Carolinians of French ancestry could be from France itself, the French-speaking cantons of Switzerland, French Canada, or Haiti. And English settlers were from old England, New England, and the English Caribbean. Thus South Carolina's population is a rich mosaic, a variety of people from three continents. Over the centuries the interaction of these peoples produced a culture that made South Carolina a special place. Since World War II, migration and immigration have brought many new and different faces to the state. According to the 2000 census, there are individuals from over eighty different countries and six continents who call South Carolina home.

Capturing the richness of South Carolina past and present was the challenge I presented to the associate editors. There could not be an unlimited number of entries. It would not be possible to have an entry for every person, place, thing, or event that appeared in the quite literally thousands of books that have been published about the state since the late seventeenth century.

Each associate editor was tasked with drafting a list of "the one hundred fifty to two hundred *absolutely necessary* entries" for her or his subject area. The resulting list was far larger than we would be able to use, but it was a starting point. The lists were circulated to all other associate editors, and then the group met for an all-day session in Columbia. Each had been asked to make suggestions on whittling down the list to about 2,500. It was a fascinating exercise, and editors defended their selections or agreed that some could go. Naturally, there was some overlap, as an individual or event might fall into more than one category. At the conclusion of the meeting, the suggestions and recommendations were consolidated into a revised list. This list was circulated to the editors, who once again met in an all-day discussion session. There was a consensus that the resulting list of some 2,100 entries, as an entity, was representative of South Carolina and its people, and that it gave a fair depiction of the state, past and present. The list, however, was not carved in stone. Over time, there were additions and deletions. There are entries for every county, every incorporated municipality with a population of at least 2,500 (as of the 2000 census), every elected governor, and every elected United States senator. One of the last entries had to await the voters' choice in the U.S. Senate race in November 2004 before it could be completed.

Who was or is a South Carolinian was debated at length in general meetings and in individual conversations. In the end, some native Carolinians who achieved fame elsewhere have been included (Mary McLeod Bethune and Kary Mullis) as well as nonnatives who made significant contributions to the state or identified themselves as South Carolinians (Pierce Butler and Mark Sanford). As Georgia O'Keeffe, who taught briefly at Columbia College, said: "Where I was born and where and how I have lived is unimportant. It is what I have done with where I have been that should be of interest." Living persons are included.

Not every topic that we would have liked to have in the encyclopedia is contained in it. In some instances promised entries did not appear, and deadlines had to be met. In other instances, we simply could not find the appropriate person to write on a particular topic.

We did, however, find 598 willing and capable individuals to write the 1,927 entries contained herein. Entries range in length from 250 words for Blenheim Ginger Ale and Sheldon Church to 2,000 words for the Revolutionary War and the General Assembly. Each entry has a standardized format, and most have a brief bibliography.

When you examine the list of 598 authors you will find that it contains the names of men and women who care very deeply about the Palmetto State and its people. Some are academics; some are museum or historical society personnel; some are public officials; and some are interested citizens. A majority of the authors live in South Carolina, but the rest come from thirty-four other states and five foreign countries. Without their willingness to participate, there would have been no encyclopedia.

Every entry submitted was checked and rechecked at least six times for accuracy. Once an author finished an entry, it was forwarded to the appropriate associate editor, who made comments and either passed it on to the managing editor or returned it to the author for revision. Then the managing editor took his cut at the entry. If it passed muster, then it landed on my desk—and I read every single entry, many more than one time. At this stage it either was sent to our team of researchers for confirmation (every entry submitted had to have a source listed for every fact included in the text) or returned to the author for revision. If the entry was returned to an author for revision, the process was repeated with the revised entry.

The time-consuming, but vital, task of research checking was undertaken by Matthew Lockhart, Aaron Marrs, Benjamin Peterson, and Michael Reynolds. Once references had been verified, the entry went back to the managing editor for a final draft. At this stage, an entry was almost ready for publication. However, before an entry could be filed as "completed," it received a final, true blue-pencil edit from Thomas N. McLean. Tom, a seasoned South Carolina journalist and student of the state's history and culture, was our *volunteer* consulting editor. Every one of the entries in the encyclopedia went through this process—some more than once at various stages.

Once entries were in hand, then began the task of assembling illustrations. One of the joys of researching and writing about South Carolina is that I have found that across the state people are always willing to lend a hand. That's particularly true in the area of illustrations. Museums, individuals, and municipalities responded with alacrity when asked.

Not unexpectedly, there are a large number of illustrations from the two largest and richest collections in the state, the South Carolina Historical Society in Charleston and the South Caroliniana Library at the University of South Carolina. Mike Coker of the South Carolina Historical Society and Henry Fulmer of the South Caroliniana Library served as image consultants for the project. With their knowledge not only of their collections but of others, their advice and counsel were invaluable in assembling the final selection of illustrations. A number of the illustrations in the encyclopedia have not been previously published; some, however, are well known, but their inclusion was necessary to tell the story of South Carolina. In the last phases of locating and obtaining illustrations, Adam Hark was my research assistant. The individuals and depositories from which the illustrations are drawn are acknowledged separately with each one where it appears in the encyclopedia.

In addition to the illustrations, which like the entries themselves reflect the richness and diversity of our state, the encyclopedia contains seventy-eight originally drawn maps. Theodore Steinke of the Department of Geography of the University of South Carolina served as the project's cartographer.

The South Carolina Encyclopedia. This publication is intended to provide a ready reference to a number of different audiences. With that in mind, from the beginning, it was decided to make the encyclopedia as reader-friendly as possible. To that end, the encyclopedia is lavishly illustrated with 439 illustrations and 80 maps (approximately one illustration for every four entries) and contains bibliographical references with most entries to provide readers with resources for further research and an index that contains the name of individuals, events, items, and places that appear in the entries.

In a project of this magnitude—nearly two thousand entries containing more than one million words—there will likely be some errors. Every effort has been made to eliminate errors, but *The South Carolina Encyclopedia* was written and edited by human beings. No matter how carefully each entry was read, no matter how thoroughly each fact was checked, something will have slipped past us all. As the editor in chief, that is a responsibility that I accept, and I request that you send any corrections or suggestions to me.

Walter Edgar

Authors

The following authors have contributed entries to this encyclopedia:

Robert K. Ackerman
Rhett A. Adams
Randy L. Akers
Jane M. Aldrich
William Shaun Alexander
Louise Allen
Eugene Alvarez
Jo Anne Anderson
Paul Christopher Anderson
William D. Anderson, Jr.
Rod Andrew, Jr.
Steven W. Angell
Ronald W. Anthony
Donald S. Armentrout
Julia Arrants
Ken Autrey
Lawrence E. Babits
Hurley E. Badders
M. Alpha Bah
Judith T. Bainbridge
Robert W. Bainbridge
Bruce E. Baker
Laura Barfield
John Barnwell
Jacqueline Prior Bartley
Don Barton
Jack Bass
Frank Beacham
Ed Beardsley
Tony Bebber
Paul R. Begley
Posey Belcher
Daniel Bell
Michael Everette Bell
Barbara L. Bellows
Freeman Belser
Timothy J. Bergen, Jr.
Robert Black
Kay J. Blalock
Sidney R. Bland
Thomas J. Blumer
Gregory Z. Boling
Jackie R. Booker
David F. Boone
Carl Borick
Jackson C. Boswell
Carol Sears Botsch
Rick D. Boulware
David K. Bowden
W. R. Braddy
Solomon Breibart
Pat Brennan
Ronald E. Bridwell
Samuel I. Britt
Lee G. Brockington
William S. Brockington, Jr.
Richard D. Brooks
Albert S. Broussard
David S. Brown
James W. Brown
Jane McCutchen Brown
Linda Meggett Brown
Micheline Brown
Millicent Ellison Brown
Dickson D. Bruce, Jr.
Charles S. Bryan
Heather Buggy
W. Lewis Burke
William E. Burns
Beatrice Burton
Orville Vernon Burton
Sean R. Busick
Lindley S. Butler
Nicholas Michael Butler
Matthew A. Byron
Richard Calhoun
Sister Anne Francis Campbell
Kathy A. Campbell
Katherine Cann
Marvin L. Cann
David L. Carlton
James C. Carper
Tony W. Cawthon
Katherine Reynolds Chaddock
Ellen Chamberlain
Andrew W. Chandler
Allan D. Charles
Tommy Charles
Eric A. Cheezum
Matthew Cheney
Ron Chepesiuk
Diana Churchill
Thelma Chiles Clark
Erskine Clarke
Sallie D. Clarkson
Robert Ashton Cobb
Peter A. Coclanis
Nadine Cohodas
J. Bryan Collars
Thorne Compton
Hope Cooper
Peter Cooper
Rose Marie Cooper
William Copeland Cooper
William J. Cooper, Jr.
Roberta V. H. Copp
Curt Cottle
M. Reid Counts
Janson L. Cox
Mike Creel
Stephen Criswell
Ruth W. Cupp
Michael N. Danielson
Jayne Darke
Phebe Davidson
Hugh Davis
Larry Davis
Robert S. Davis
Kevin Dawson
Louis De Vorsey
Lewis S. Dean
Vennie Deas-Moore
Kendra Debany
Lauren Coflin Decker
Chester B. DePratter
Patricia Diamond
Dennis C. Dickerson
Lisa J. Dimitriadis
Bobby J. Donaldson
Amy Donnelly
Tom Downey
Barbara Doyle
Patricia Davis Doyle
Edmund L. Drago
Sonny DuBose
Meaghan N. Duff
W. Marvin Dulaney
James A. Dunlap III
Nathalie Dupree
Kristina Anne DuRocher
Walter Edgar
John T. Edge
Mary W. Edmonds
Pamela C. Edwards
Bruce W. Eelman
Douglas R. Egerton
Katie Eichler
Robert L. Ellis, Jr.
W. Eric Emerson
Lisa Ennis
Gwendolyn Gosney Erickson
Steve Estes
Carl D. Evans
Parker Evatt
Allison Faix
James O. Farmer, Jr.
J. Terrence Farris
Kevin Fellner
Leland Ferguson
Sarah Fick
Paul Figueroa
Catherine Fitzgerald
Suzanne Flandreau
Joseph M. Flora
Davis Folsom
Bob Ford
Lacy Ford
Damon Fordham
Samuel K. Fore
Caroline Foster
Leigh Fought
Donald L. Fowler
Rusty E. Frank
David Franklin
Herb Frazier
Kari Frederickson
Gemma K. Frock
James R. Frysinger
Jane S. Gabin
Kevin M. Gannon

Belinda F. Gergel
Richard Mark Gergel
Lindsey Gertz
Bryan A. Giemza
Michele Gillespie
David T. Gleeson
Barbara Owens Goggans
Rickie A. Good
Abby Gail Goodnite
Queen Quet Marquetta L. Goodwine
John W. Gordon
Cole Blease Graham, Jr.
Glennon Graham
H. Roger Grant
Robert P. Green, Jr.
Harlan Greene
Darren Grem
Jan Nordby Gretlund
D. Jonathan Grieser
Mark D. Groover
Philip G. Grose, Jr.
James Guignard
Gilbert S. Guinn
Robert Gurley
Aaron L. Haberman
Cantey Haile
Fritz Hamer
Richard F. Hamm
Tonya Bordeaux Hamm
James T. Hammond
Mary Taylor Haque
Nancy A. Hardesty
Kristin M. Harkey
Carmen V. Harris
Eliza Cope Harrison
Sarah Georgia Harrison
Stanley Harrold
T. Robert Hart
Herbert J. Hartsook
Bruce G. Harvey
Richard W. Hatcher III
James Haw
Jack Irby Hayes
Marguerite Hays
Steven W. Hays
J. Cantey Heath, Jr.
Natalie Harvey Hefter
Malie Heider
David C. R. Heisser
Alexia Jones Helsley
Terry Lynn Helsley
A. Scott Henderson
Alice H. Henderson
Carlanna H. Hendrick
Bela P. Herlong
Al Hester
Robert M. Hicklin, Jr.
David P. Hill
Patricia Evridge Hill
William C. Hine
Susan Giaimo Hiott
William D. Hiott
Trenton Hizer
Peter H. Hobbie
David Hodges
Brent Holcomb
Robert Holcombe, Jr.
Linda Hollandsworth
George W. Hopkins
Paul A. Horne, Jr.
Laurel Horton
Thomas B. Horton
Linda Howe
Janet G. Hudson
A. V. Huff, Jr.
Dan Huntley
James M. Hutchisson
John L. Idol, Jr.
Joan A. Inabinet
Ned L. Irwin
Charles Israel
Rhett Jackson
Elizabeth Jacoway
John F. Jakubs
David Marshall James
Edward Janak
Robert L. Janiskee
Rhonda Jeffries
Virginia Jelatis
Ellen Bush Jenkins
Matthew H. Jennings
Paul Jersild
Daniel McDonald Johnson
Joan Marie Johnson
Lloyd Johnson
Thomas L. Johnson
Cherisse R. Jones
Robert S. Jones, Jr.
Laylon Wayne Jordan
Hannah Joyner
Christopher Judge
Clara Juncker
Henry Kamerling
Stephen Kantrowitz
Robert F. Karachuk
Willis J. Keith
Susan A. Kelley
Stephen C. Kenny
Lawrence J. Kent
Marilyn Kern-Foxworth
Carolyn L. Kimbrell
Martha J. King
Susan King
William Light Kinney, Jr.
Rachel N. Klein
James Knight
Laura E. Koser
Charles F. Kovacik
Jill Beute Koverman
Palmer Krantz
Keith Krawczynski
Craig Kridel
Ethan J. Kytle
Elaine C. Lacy
Dennis Lambries
Ernest McPherson Lander, Jr.
Robert H. Landrum
Bruce Lane
John C. Larson
Peter F. Lau
John Laurens
James Walton Lawrence, Sr.
Desmond R. Layne
Malcolm W. Leaphart, Jr.
Joseph Edward Lee
Henry H. Lesesne
Charles H. Lesser
James A. Lewis
Suzanne Linder
Charles H. Lippy
Rhodri Windsor Liscombe
Daniel C. Littlefield
Dean B. Livingston
Matthew A. Lockhart
Thomas W. Lollis
John Wesley Lowery
Marion B. Lucas
Maxine Lutz
John Allen Macaulay
Adam Mack
Angela D. Mack
Michelle Maher
Ellen Malphrus
Wofford Malphrus
Theresa Mann
Aaron W. Marrs
John F. Marszalek
Sandy Dwayne Martin
William Martin
Gregory D. Massey
Paul E. Matheny III
Marty D. Matthews
Marko Maunula
Amy Thompson McCandless
Peter McCandless
John M. McCardell, Jr.
Patrick McCawley
Veronica Bruce McConnell
Sarah McCoy
Anne M. McCulloch
Kay W. McCutcheon
George McDaniel
John T. McGrath
Preston L. McKever-Floyd
Shephard W. McKinley
Russ McKinney, Jr.
Tom McLean
Patrick McMillan
Patricia G. McNeely
Margaret Meggs
Jack Allen Meyer
Edward A. Miller, Jr.
Mary S. Miller
Randall M. Miller
Whitney Miller
Lisle S. Mitchell
W. K. Mitchell
Anne M. Moise
Alexander Moore
John H. Moore
Sandra Barrett Moore
William V. Moore
Michael P. Morris
William P. Morris
Mary Mac Ogden Motley
Michael Robert Mounter
Ralph Muldrow
Hugh Munn
Carolyn H. Murphy
John E. Murray
Andrew H. Myers
Jerome J. Nadelhaft
Brian Nance
John L. Napier
David Nelson
John Nelson
Larry E. Nelson
Marie H. Nelson
Marilyn M. Nelson
Francis Neuffer
Caryn E. Neumann
Patricia Causey Nichols
W. Gary Nichols
Karen Nickless
Steven Noll
David Hoogland Noon
J. Eugene Norris
Kelly Obernuefemann
Farrell O'Gorman
Robert T. Oliver
R. Nicholas Olsberg
Jennifer Ottervik
Jason S. Overby
Karen L. Paar
Craig S. Pascoe
Jane H. Pease
William H. Pease
Kenneth E. Peters
Benjamin Peterson
Louise Pettus
Daniel S. Pierce
Jon B. Pierce
Robert A. Pierce
Elise Pinckney
Eric W. Plaag
Beth Pleming
Eli A. Poliakoff
Marsha Poliakoff
W. Scott Poole

William Post
Tamara S. Powell
J. Tracy Power
Bernard E. Powers, Jr.
Barry A. Price
Rulinda Price
Eldred E. Prince, Jr.
Mona Prufer
Philip N. Racine
Leo Redmond
Dale Volberg Reed
John Shelton Reed
David H. Rembert, Jr.
Catherine Collins Reynolds
Michael S. Reynolds
Robert D. Reynolds, Jr.
Nancy Rhyne
Alan Richard
Jeremy Richards
Miles S. Richards
Dorothy Fludd Richardson
Steve Richardson
Lyn Riddle
David E. Rison
Jacob Rivers
Carey M. Roberts
Giselle Roberts
Elizabeth Robeson
W. Stitt Robinson
Aida Rogers
George A. Rogers
Debbie Roland
Ronald Romine
Donna K. Roper
L. H. Roper
Robert N. Rosen
Dale Rosengarten
Ted Rosengarten
Nancy G. Rosoff
Julie Rotholz
Lawrence S. Rowland
Hyman S. Rubin III
Horace Fraser Rudisill
Dan G. Ruff
Stephen M. Russell, Jr.
Peter M. Rutkoff
William Ryan
Albert E. Sanders
Margaret Sankey
Marshall Sasser
Bradley S. Sauls
Nathania K. Sawyer
Elizabeth D. Schafer
James D. Schmidt
Brenda Thompson Schoolfield
Susan L. Schramm
Michael C. Scoggins
William B. Scott
Cleveland L. Sellers, Jr.
Ben H. Severance
Martha R. Severens
Margaret A. Shannon
Harry Shealy, Jr.
G. Anne Sheriff
John M. Sherrer III
Mary Sherrer
David E. Shi
David S. Shields
Bryant Simon
Patricia H. Simpson
Manisha Sinha
John S. Sledge
C. E. Smith
David C. Smith
Mark M. Smith
Matthew C. Smith
Samuel C. Smith
Selden K. Smith
Stephen D. Smith
W. Calvin Smith
T. Jason Soderstrum
Roberta Kefalos Sokolitz
Doug Southard
James Spady
Gerhard Spieler
Michael Sponhour
Stuart R. Sprague
John G. Sproat
Sarah Cain Spruill
Jane W. Squires
Nathan E. Stalvey
R. F. Stalvey
Rebecca Starr
Paula Stathakis
Elizabeth Dozier Steedly
Lester D. Stephens
Robert Stevens
Donald O. Stewart
Allen Stokes
Barbara Stokes
Jennifer A. Stollman
DeWitt Boyd Stone, Jr.
R. Phillip Stone II
Marian Elizabeth Strobel
Willard Strong
Rodger E. Stroup
Elsie Rast Stuart
Marion B. Sullivan
Carolyn Sung
Karen Swager
Deborah M. Switzer
Marcia G. Synnott
Roy Talbert, Jr.
H. Simmons Tate, Jr.
C. James Taylor
D. S. Taylor
John Martin Taylor
Saddler Taylor
Stephen Wallace Taylor
Rosalyn Terborg-Penn
Tom Terrill
Betsy Teter
Donald Tetreault
Monica Maria Tetzlaff
Neal D. Thigpen
Sam Thomas
Robert Tinkler
Rebecca Tolley-Stokes
Courtney L. Tollison
Charles W. Toth
Louis P. Towles
W. Stuart Towns
Ivan M. Tribe
Helen Lee Turner
James H. Tuten
Charlie B. Tyer
Zan Peters Tyler
James L. Underwood
Bertrand Van Ruymbeke
Daniel J. Vivian
John Michael Vlach
Jon L. Wakelyn
Melissa Walker
Ford Walpole
Becky Walton
Ashby Ward
Lowry Ware
Mary Baskin Waters
Harry L. Watson II
Ritchie Devon Watson
Robert M. Weir
Donald West
Elizabeth Cassidy West
Amy L. White
John W. White
C. N. Willborn
George C. Williams
Jay Williams
Rose-Marie Eltzroth Williams
Susan Millar Williams
Jeffrey R. Willis
Jim Wilson
Mark Winchell
Stephen R. Wise
Ellen Woodoff
Stan Woodward
W. Curtis Worthington
Deborah Wright
Scott Wyatt
Charles E. Wynes
Tomoko Yagyu
Tinsley E. Yarbrough
James Harvey Young
Benjamin T. Zeigler
Martha A. Zierden
Gary Phillip Zola
Richard Zuczek
South Carolina Forestry Commission
South Carolina State Climatology Office

The *South Carolina* Encyclopedia

Abbeville (Abbeville County; 2000 pop. 5,840). The initial site of Abbeville was a spring used to supply the blockhouse, or fortified post, built by Andrew Pickens in the late 1760s. The courthouse town derived its name from the county in which it is located. In 1792 South Carolina placed its upcountry powder magazine and arsenal in Abbeville, and the town was incorporated in 1832. The most prominent early residents were lawyers, merchants, and planters, many of whom built elegant town houses in addition to their plantation homes. The Abbeville Bar was particularly distinguished and included John C. Calhoun, who began his law practice in Abbeville and made his maiden political speech there in 1807. In 1861 the Bank of the State of South Carolina opened a branch in Abbeville, its first in the upcountry.

Although removed from the fighting during the Civil War, Abbeville nevertheless played a noteworthy role in the conflict. On November 22, 1860, Abbeville hosted one of the first secession meetings in the state at a site later known as Secession Hill. An Abbevillian, J. Clark Allen, was killed accidentally on Sullivan's Island on February 13, 1861, arguably the first casualty of the war. In addition, five men who had resided on the town's North Main Street were killed by the summer of 1863; they were referred to as "The Five Lost Colonels." The most celebrated events in Abbeville history occurred when Varina Davis, wife of the Confederate president, arrived on April 18, 1865, followed shortly by a wagon train carrying the remainder of the Confederate treasury. For twelve days she was a guest of former congressman Armistead Burt, a family friend. On May 2, two days after she left Abbeville, her husband arrived with his remaining cabinet members and elements of five brigades of cavalry. Davis held the last "war cabinet" meeting in Abbeville, where the decision was made to abandon armed resistance to Union forces. Thus, as host to the "Secession Hill" gathering and the final meeting of the Confederate cabinet, Abbeville claims to be "the cradle and grave of the Confederacy."

Most of the antebellum wealth of Abbeville evaporated with the emancipation of its slaves. Fires in the 1870s destroyed many antebellum houses and did irreparable damage to public buildings and public records. In the 1890s, however, the town experienced an economic revival. In 1892 Abbeville welcomed the arrival of the Georgia, Carolina and Northern Railroad (which later became the Seaboard Air Line). The Abbeville Cotton Mill Company was organized three years later and commenced operations in 1897. The Seaboard later chose Abbeville to locate its shops for maintaining rail lines between Hamlet, North Carolina, and Atlanta, Georgia.

In the twentieth century Abbeville erected an industrial park that attracted medium-sized industries. During the 1970s and 1980s the town became best known for the restoration of its public square and opera house, which attracted tourists to peruse Abbeville's antique shops and admire its well-preserved architecture. LOWRY WARE

Ferguson, Lester W. *Abbeville County: Southern Life-Styles Lost in Time.* Spartanburg, S.C.: Reprint Company, 1993.

Pursley, Larry E. *Abbeville, South Carolina: A Backward Glance.* Alpharetta, Ga.: W. H. Wolfe, 1993.

Ware, Lowry. *Old Abbeville: Scenes of the Past of a Town Where Old Time Things Are Not Forgotten.* Columbia, S.C.: SCMAR, 1992.

Abbeville County (508 sq. miles; 2000 pop. 26,167). Abbeville County was one of the six counties created in 1785 out of Ninety Six District. Its border to the north was the pre–Revolutionary War Indian boundary line. The Savannah and Saluda Rivers marked its eastern and western borders. The boundary with Edgefield County was surveyed from the mouth of Little River to Island Ford on the Saluda. Abbeville lost much of its area to Greenwood County in 1897 and gave up further territory in 1916 to McCormick County.

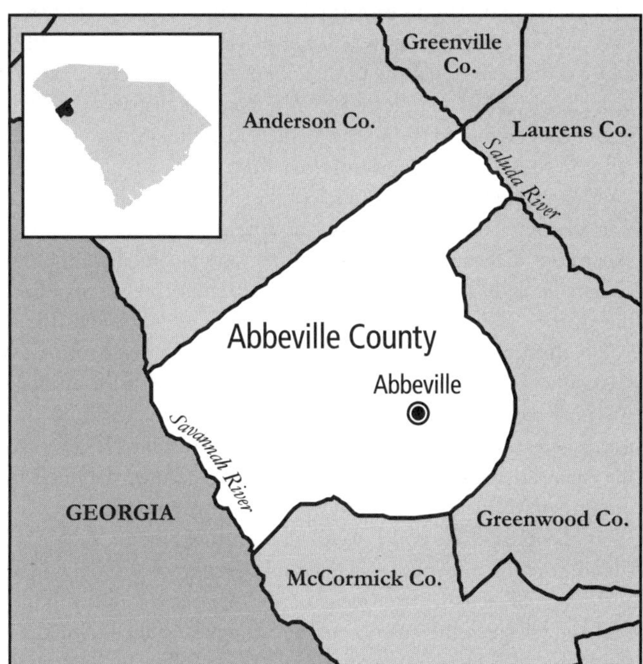

Before the Revolutionary War, the most significant early settlement in this area was in the Long Canes, the name early given to the watershed of Little River and its main tributary, Long Cane Creek. Beginning in 1756, the Calhoun family and other settlers from Virginia took up land grants along these streams. In the 1760s, under the direction of Governor Thomas Boone, colonies of "poor Protestants" (Scots-Irish) settled the township of Boonesborough at the headwaters of Long Cane Creek.

Most settlers joined the Whig or patriot cause in the Revolution. The best-known patriot leader was Andrew Pickens, who was aided by such neighbors and friends as Andrew Hamilton and Robert Anderson. Pickens resided near the center of what later became Abbeville County, and it was through his influence and that of Andrew Hamilton, who bought his land, that the site of a courthouse for the new county was located near Pickens's blockhouse, or fortified post. Dr. John de la Howe, one of the commissioners appointed to choose the location, was given the honor of naming the county. Some surmise that he may have been born in Abbeville, France, but it is known only that he was a native of France.

Robert Mills later called Abbeville "the original seat of learning in the upper country," and it quickly distinguished itself as the mother of some very famous Carolinians. The most notable of these native sons was John C. Calhoun, but there were others who won acclaim, such as Langdon Cheves, Patrick Noble, James L. Petigru, as well as adopted sons George McDuffie and Moses Waddel, whose Willington Academy drew students from throughout the South. Schools in Cokesbury and Due West also attracted students from a wide area.

The coming of cotton planting to the upcountry after the 1790s accelerated the introduction of slavery to Abbeville District and increased migration westward of small farmers. In 1790 one-fourth of the white families owned slaves. By 1850 two-thirds owned slaves and slaves comprised two-thirds of the population. Ten planters owned more than one hundred slaves, and one planter, George McDuffie, owned more than two hundred. This wealth manifested itself in the fine homes on plantations and in the town of Abbeville, which flourished in the 1850s.

Following the election of Abraham Lincoln in November 1860, Abbeville held one of the earliest public meetings in support of secession, and an Abbeville native, Francis H. Wardlaw, is considered by many to have authored the Ordinance of Secession. The Civil War brought bitter losses. At least 349 men from the district died in the war. Safely removed from the battlefields, the district attracted refugees from the coast and from the West.

Emancipation destroyed much of the planters' wealth. The postwar economy chiefly rested upon small farmers, largely through the expansion of tenant farming and sharecropping. In the 1850s the Greenville and Columbia Railroad ran through the eastern end of the district with a branchline from Hodges to Abbeville. In the 1880s the Savannah Valley Railroad connected the western part of the county with Augusta and Anderson. In the 1890s the Seaboard Air Line connected Abbeville and Greenwood with cities to their north and south. In 1895 the businessmen of Abbeville organized the Abbeville Cotton Mill Company and later secured the financing of northern textile magnate S. M. Milliken, which ensured its success.

In the first decade of the twentieth century, Calhoun Mills, a textile corporation under the experienced leadership of James P. Gossett and Judge W. F. Cox, from neighboring Anderson County, built a mill and village at the junction of the Savannah Valley Railroad and the Seaboard. The resulting town of Calhoun Falls soon became the second largest town in the county. The town of Due West ranked third with its male and female colleges, respectively Erskine College and Due West Female College.

During the twentieth century Abbeville County's agriculture experienced a transition from cotton to cattle, and its dependence on textiles gave way to more diversified industry and small businesses. In later years its population stabilized, with most concentrated in and around the city of Abbeville. By 1990 whites were a two-thirds majority of the county residents.

The creation of an industrial park and the aggressive pursuit of new investments resulted in the arrival of industries such as Pirelli Cable Corp., Flexible Technologies, Karistan-Bigelow, and West Point Pepperell. However, the absence of an interstate highway limited industrial expansion.

Despite a century of change, Abbeville County still managed to retain its rural character. The Long Cane District of the Sumter National Forest was established in 1936, featuring a recreation area around Parsons Mountain with a lake, trails, and camping as well as hunting and swimming. Lake Secession on Rocky River was completed in the 1940s and is owned by the city of Abbeville. Lake Russell, a Corps of Engineers hydroelectric project on the Savannah River, was completed in 1984 and is mostly in the county. The Calhoun Falls State Park is one mile north of Abbeville, just off the Savannah River Scenic Highway. With such an abundance of outdoor recreational opportunities, Abbeville County annually attracts hunters, fishermen, and nature lovers of all kinds. LOWRY WARE

Ferguson, Lester W. *Abbeville County: Southern Life-Styles Lost in Time.* Spartanburg, S.C.: Reprint Company, 1993.

Lander, Ernest McPherson. *Tales of Calhoun Falls.* Spartanburg, S.C.: Reprint Company, 1991.

Ware, Lowry. *Old Abbeville: Scenes of the Past of a Town Where Old Time Things Are Not Forgotten.* Columbia, S.C.: SCMAR, 1992.

ACE Basin. The ACE Basin consists of around 350,000 acres in the watershed of the Ashepoo, Combahee, and Edisto Rivers in the South Carolina lowcountry, which drains one-fifth of the state. The ACE Basin encompasses a range of ecosystem types from forested uplands to tidal marsh (salt, brackish, and fresh water). The basin is home for more than 260 permanent and seasonal bird species and seventeen rare or endangered species, including the wood stork and the loggerhead turtle.

History, as much as geography, unites the three rivers. By the 1750s the rivers were lined with plantations dedicated to rice production and using African slaves for the arduous labor required. Most plantations controlled tidal flows by a series of floodgates (rice trunks), dikes, and canals to grow vast amounts of rice. The Civil War and emancipation, along with an increase in both foreign and domestic competition, led to the eventual collapse of rice culture. Through the twentieth century, the ACE Basin experienced almost no industrial development, which kept the landscape largely intact as forest and estuary.

In 1988 Ducks Unlimited, the Nature Conservancy, the U.S. Fish and Wildlife Service, and the South Carolina Department of Natural Resources joined forces to create the ACE Basin Project to preserve the landscape and wildlife habitat. The combined federal, state, and private conservation groups used purchases of public land, conservation easements, and other methods to preserve 135,980 acres of land by 2000. JAMES H. TUTEN

Blagden, Tom. *South Carolina's Wetland Wilderness: The ACE Basin.* Englewood, Colo.: Westcliffe, 1992.

Linder, Suzanne Cameron. *Historical Atlas of the Rice Plantations of the ACE River Basin–1860.* Columbia: South Carolina Department of Archives and History, 1995.

ACE Basin National Wildlife Refuge. Established in 1990, the ACE Basin National Wildlife Refuge (NWR) is part of the federal system of refuges managed by the U.S. Fish and Wildlife Service. The refuge represents the federal role in the larger ACE Basin Project with two units, one on the Combahee River and the other on the Edisto River.

The headquarters for the NWR is located at the Grove, a rice plantation begun in 1825 on the Edisto River. The plantation house dates from 1828 and was listed in the National Register of Historic Places in 1978. The Nature Conservancy purchased the Grove in 1991 and sold it to the U.S. Fish and Wildlife Service the following year.

With a total of nearly twelve thousand acres, the ACE Basin NWR is managed for wildlife with careful attention given to habitat preservation. The estuary is home to a wide variety of birds, fish,

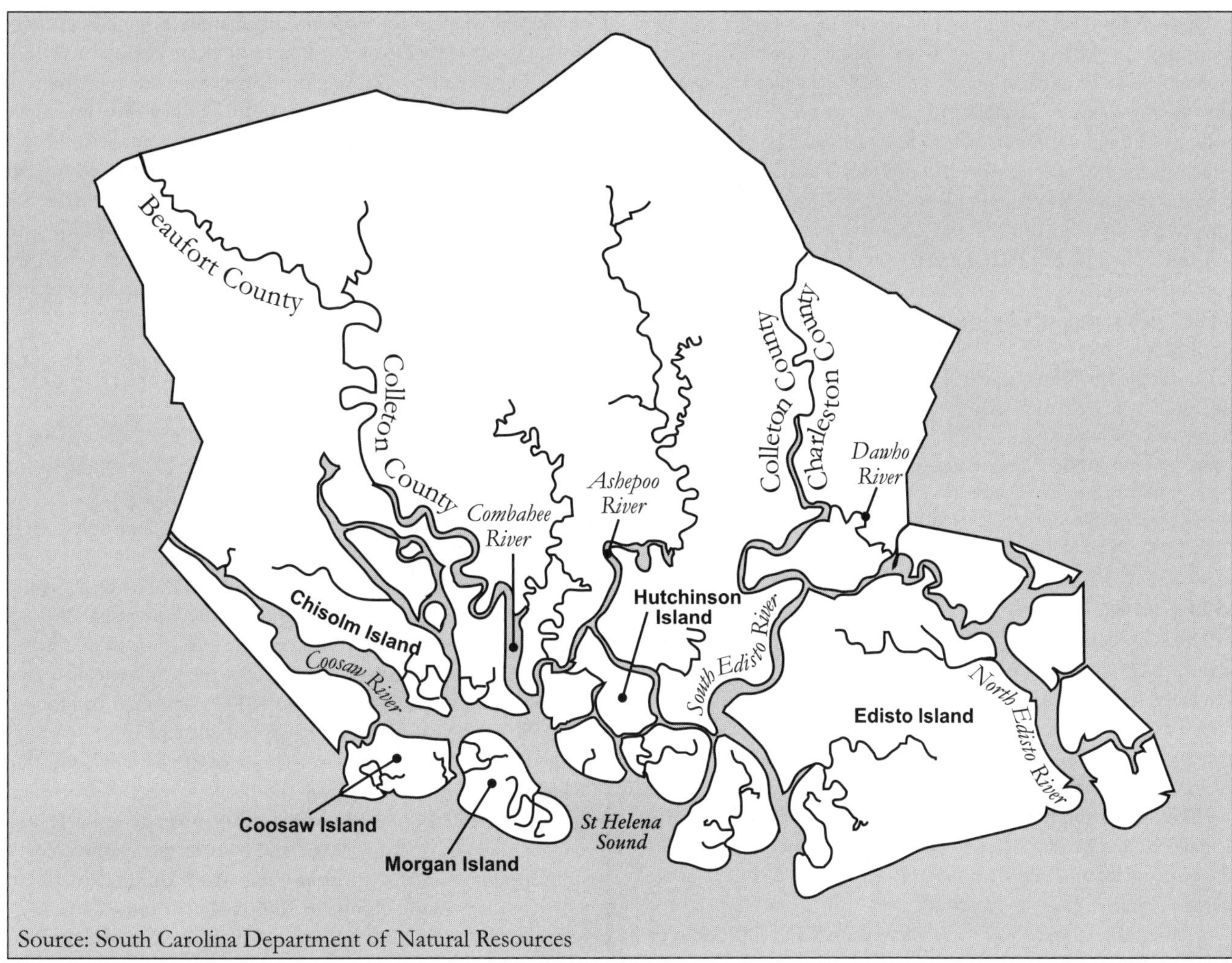

The ACE Basin

and game, including such endangered and threatened species as wood storks, osprey, bald eagles, and shortnose sturgeon. Limited public fishing and hunting for deer and waterfowl are permitted. With the completion of additional purchases, the future size of the refuge may reach eighteen thousand acres.

The refuge contains canals and dikes from the days when the land was home to large rice plantations. Through control of water levels, the former rice fields are used to encourage habitats for waterfowl and other bird species. Additionally, the NWR uses controlled burning as a tool for creating and maintaining habitat for turkey, quail, and songbirds. JAMES H. TUTEN

Blagden, Tom. *South Carolina's Wetland Wilderness: The ACE Basin.* Englewood, Colo.: Westcliffe, 1992.

Linder, Suzanne Cameron. *Historical Atlas of the Rice Plantations of the ACE River Basin–1860.* Columbia: South Carolina Department of Archives and History, 1995.

Adams, Edward Clarkson Leverett (1876–1946). Physician, author. Adams was born in Weston, Richland County, on January 5, 1876, the eldest son of James Ironsides Adams and Caroline Pinckney Leverett. He was educated in the public and private grade schools of Gadsden and Columbia, and later at Clemson College, Maryland Medical College in Baltimore, the Charleston Medical College (where he received his M.D.), the University of Pennsylvania, and Rotunda Hospital in Dublin, Ireland. On June 10, 1910, Adams married Amanda M. Smith. They had two children. Adams served in the United States Army during the Spanish-American War. He volunteered again for active duty during World War I, serving in France as a captain in the Eighty-First ("Wildcat") Division. He returned to Columbia in 1918. After several years of medical practice, Adams retired to devote more of his time to farming on his Bluff Road plantation, to run unsuccessfully for lieutenant governor in 1922, and to write sketches, two books, and a play about the black inhabitants of Richland County.

Adams's books and stories about the African American residents of lower Richland County brought him both regional and national attention as an author who was able to present the black dialect with great precision, and also as a white author who unhesitatingly portrayed the hardships of racial prejudice in the 1920s and 1930s. His first volume, *Congaree Sketches,* was published by the University of North Carolina Press in 1927. Here he introduced the poor blacks of the Congaree swamp and their meticulously rendered dialect that would form the imaginative foundation for the many stories that followed. The first collection was immediately successful. After reading a copy of *Congaree Sketches* brought to him by a Scribner's representative, the editor Maxwell Perkins wrote to Adams directly, and Adams's next volume, *Nigger to Nigger,* appeared under the prestigious Scribner's imprint in 1928. The chairperson of the board of the National Association for the Advancement of Colored People (NAACP), Mary White Ovington, who had earlier remarked on the high quality of Adams's insights into the mind of African Americans in *Congaree Sketches,* also admired *Nigger to Nigger* for its poignant descriptions of the tragic lives of its poor black characters.

With the 1929 publication of *Potee's Gal: A Drama of Negro Life Near the Big Congaree Swamps,* Adams was thrust directly into the spotlight of public opinion when the Stage Society of Columbia adopted it for production with an entirely black cast. The great public outcry against this decision overwhelmed the quality of the play and the objections of Adams and his many friends. After a bitter exchange of letters with their detractors in the local newspapers, the Stage Society's board of governors canceled the two productions that had been scheduled for February 5, 1929. *Potee's Gal* was never produced on the stage.

Adams died at his home in Columbia on November 1, 1946. He was buried in the cemetery at St. John's Episcopal Church in Congaree. JACOB RIVERS

Adams, Edward Clarkson Leverett. *Tales of the Congaree.* Edited by Robert G. O'Meally. Chapel Hill: University of North Carolina Press, 1987.

———. Vertical Biographical File and Papers. South Caroliniana Library, University of South Carolina, Columbia.

Adams, James Hopkins (1812–1861). Governor. Born on March 15, 1812, in Richland District, Adams was the son of Henry Walker Adams, a prominent cotton planter, and Mary Howell Hart Goodwyn. He attended Minervaville Academy in Richland before being sent to Partridge Military Academy in Middleton, Connecticut, in 1826. Graduating from Yale in 1831, Adams returned to South Carolina and took possession of his sizable inheritance, including Live Oak Plantation in lower Richland District. On April 10, 1832, he married Jane Margaret Scott. They had nine children. A successful cotton planter, Adams owned 192 slaves and $80,000 in real estate by 1860.

In 1834 Adams was elected to represent Richland District in the S.C. House of Representatives. He served three more terms in the House (1836–1838, 1840–1841, 1848–1849) and two in the S.C. Senate (1850–1851, 1852–1853). On December 11, 1854, the General Assembly elected Adams governor. Adams assumed office during a lull in sectional hostilities. South Carolina repudiated secession during the crisis over the Compromise of 1850. That same year, the death of John C. Calhoun created a void in South Carolina's political leadership that left factions competing for power. Adams belonged to a faction favoring immediate secession, a move calculated to force southern states to choose between joining South Carolina in creating a southern republic or staying in the Union.

Seeking an issue to unify southerners and accelerate the division of North and South, Governor Adams addressed the General Assembly in 1856 and called for the reopening of the international slave trade. His message appealed to logic, asserting that if the slave trade was wrong then so was the institution of slavery. He also hoped to attract nonslaveholders, asking, "Is it wise, is it safe on the part of those who own slaves, to desire to keep their price up to a point that must forever exclude the laboring white man from owning them?" By importing more Africans, Adams believed that prices would fall and allow more southerners to buy slaves. As a result, support for slavery would expand by increasing the number of persons with an economic stake in the institution. The movement to reopen the slave trade had some support but was opposed by most southerners as too radical.

After leaving office in 1856, Adams was a candidate for the U.S. Senate in 1858, but he lost to the more moderate James Chesnut. In 1860 Richland District selected Adams as a delegate to the Secession Convention, where he advocated immediate secession. After South Carolina seceded on December 20, 1860, Adams was one of three commissioners sent to Washington to negotiate the conveyance of federal property to the state. He later voted against the Confederate Constitution, arguing that it retained the same language as the U.S. Constitution, which made the slave trade illegal and failed to guarantee that all Confederate states would allow slavery within its borders. Despite the protest of Adams and others, the constitution was adopted. Adams died shortly thereafter on July 13, 1861, and was buried in the cemetery of St. John's Episcopal Church, Congaree. MICHAEL S. REYNOLDS

Bailey, N. Louise, Mary L. Morgan, and Carolyn R. Taylor, eds. *Biographical Directory of the South Carolina Senate, 1776–1985.* 3 vols. Columbia: University of South Carolina Press, 1986.

Takaki, Ronald T. *A Pro-slavery Crusade: The Agitation to Reopen the African Slave Trade.* New York: Free Press, 1971.

Adams, Mattie Jean (1873–1947). Educator. Adams was born on September 16, 1873, in Utopia, Newberry County, the daughter of Thomas Hill Adams and Eliza Kelley. In 1896 she entered the junior class at South Carolina College (later the University of South Carolina), after graduating from Leesville College in 1892. She was awarded a bachelor of arts degree in 1898, the first woman to graduate from South Carolina College. In 1913 Adams married Professor Lawson B. Haynes, then president of Leesville College.

Adams established herself as a leader in the field of education. For eighteen years she served as the head of the Department of English at Meridian College in Meridian, Mississippi. From 1900 to 1903 she took leave from Meridian to serve as organizer of the South Carolina Women's Christian Temperance Union. She traveled extensively throughout Europe in 1909 and contributed articles on her travels to the *State* newspaper in Columbia. She also attended Oxford College in Oxford, England. She received a master of arts degree from Columbia University in New York City, and later taught for five years at the Teacher's College in Livingston, Alabama. In 1918 Adams was awarded an honorary doctorate from Meridian College. She died in Hendersonville, North Carolina, on December 26, 1947. MARY BASKIN WATERS

Adger, James (1777–1858). Merchant. Adger was born on November 2, 1777, in Moneynick, county Antrim, in the north of Ireland, the son of the linen manufacturer James Adger and Margaret Crawford. His father died in 1783, and his mother soon after married Robert Rodgers. In late 1793 the family emigrated from Ireland, arriving in New York in January 1794. Adger's mother and stepfather opened a grocery business, while young James learned the carpenter's trade. He did not take to it, however, and subsequently apprenticed in the hardware business under the supervision of John Bailey. In 1802 Adger sailed from New York in charge of a hardware cargo bound for Charleston, South Carolina. Making contact with his brother William, who had emigrated from Ireland and settled in Fairfield District, Adger remained in South Carolina. On September 6, 1806, he married Sarah Elizabeth Ellison of Fairfield District. They had nine children.

Adger became one of the wealthiest and most influential merchants of antebellum Charleston. He entered business as a cotton buyer shortly after his arrival in the city, forming the firm of Bones & Adger in partnership with his kinsman Samuel Bones, and then established the hardware firm of James Adger & Company. In 1818 Adger had the good fortune to make the acquaintance of Alexander

Brown of Baltimore, who, together with his sons, oversaw one of the largest mercantile and merchant banking operations in the United States. Adger became the Charleston agent of Brown, a connection that became the primary foundation of Adger's subsequent fortune. Concentrating his varied business activities on East Bay Street, Adger formed a commission and factorage partnership with James Black to create the firm of Adger & Black and then purchased his own wharf. By 1850 Adger held at least $200,000 in real estate and owned eighteen slaves.

Adger used his position and wealth to good effect in the affairs of Charleston. He represented the city for a term in the S.C. House of Representatives from 1826 to 1828 and served Charleston in a variety of municipal roles, including director of the Office of Discount and Deposit, director of the city tobacco inspection warehouse, and as a longtime member of the Charleston Chamber of Commerce. His primary influence, however, came in the time and money he invested in promoting transportation improvements. In 1828 Adger served on the Chamber of Commerce committee investigating construction of a railroad between Charleston and Hamburg. He was also a delegate to the 1845 Memphis Convention to promote internal improvements in the South. Adger perhaps was best known his success in establishing a packet steamship line between Charleston and New York in 1845–1846. Although other prominent Charleston merchants were among the line's investors, the company was popularly know as the "Adger line." By 1853 company assets were valued at $500,000.

Adger died in New York on September 24, 1858. His body was returned to Charleston and buried in the cemetery of the Second Presbyterian Church. TOM DOWNEY

Adger, John B. *My Life and Times, 1810–1899.* Richmond, Va.: Presbyterian Committee of Publication, 1899.

Greb, Gregory Allen. "Charleston, South Carolina, Merchants, 1815–1860: Urban Leadership in the Antebellum South." Ph.D. diss., University of California at San Diego, 1978.

Moore, Alexander, ed. *Biographical Directory of the South Carolina House of Representatives.* Vol. 5, *1816–1828.* Columbia: South Carolina Department of Archives and History, 1992.

African Americans. The first African Americans to live in what is now South Carolina were slaves in the sixteenth century Spanish settlements of San Miguel de Gualdape and Santa Elena. Slavery was very much an integral part of the Caribbean world, which gave rise to both the Spanish and later English colonization efforts in Carolina. Slavery was a recognized institution under the Fundamental Constitutions of Carolina, and within the first year of permanent English settlement there were enslaved Africans in the colony.

During the first decades of settlement, most enslaved persons were imported from the various English West Indian islands. However, by the turn of the eighteenth century, South Carolina was a major market for the transatlantic slave trade. By the end of the colonial period it is estimated that 80 percent of the Africans brought to South Carolina were imported directly from Africa; the remaining 20 percent came from the West Indies.

The expanding nature of the South Carolina economy led to an increased demand for slave labor. South Carolina planters preferred slaves from the Gold Coast, Senegambia, and the Windward Coast and to a lesser extent from Angola. However, there were occasions when enslaved Africans of any ethnicity were marketable. Modern researchers, combing the state's rich colonial records, have been able to identify some twenty-five separate West African ethnicities among the colony's slave population.

The increased importation of enslaved Africans led to South Carolina's having a black majority by 1708. The black majority increased until by 1740 nearly two-thirds of the colony's population was African American. With an influx of white settlers in the later colonial period and the loss of thousands of slaves during the American Revolution, the demographics changed, and the state's population was 56 percent white by 1790.

South Carolina was the only state to reopen the African slave trade after the Revolution, and tens of thousands of Africans were imported. By 1808, when the external slave trade was closed, it is estimated that some 40 percent of all slaves brought to the United States had entered through the port of Charleston. On the journey to becoming black Carolinians, Africans of many different ethnic backgrounds passed through Sullivan's Island, where there was a slave quarantine station. In this sense it was the African counterpart to Europeans' Ellis Island.

The introduction of short staple cotton and the subsequent first great cotton boom created more demand for slave labor. With the external trade closed, Carolinians began to purchase slaves from other states. Between the importation of slaves and the natural increase of those already in South Carolina, the state found itself in 1820 once again with a black majority. And, as had happened in the eighteenth century, that majority increased. On the eve of the Civil War, the state's population was about 59 percent black. In no other southern state was there such a concentration of persons of color. And the black population was omnipresent. Even in the few areas of the state where there were white majority districts, blacks were a considerable presence. Pickens District had the smallest black population (21.9 percent). Other traditionally "white" districts had sizable black populations, such as Horry (30 percent) and Lexington (40 percent).

During the four decades after the Civil War, the state's African American population continued to hover right around 60 percent. Then, beginning in the 1920s, thousands of black Carolinians left the state because of Jim Crow and a lack of economic opportunity. In 1930 the state had a white majority for the first time in 120 years. There would be another major black out-migration the years after World War II, but by the last decades of the twentieth century more African Americans were moving to South Carolina than were leaving the state. In the 2000 census, some 29.5 percent of the state's population was African American. Only Louisiana (30.8 percent) and Mississippi (35.6 percent) has more black residents as a percentage of the population.

The presence of a large black population throughout South Carolina's 335 years of settled history has had a significant impact on the state's cultural, economic, and political development.

Culturally, as historian Charles Joyner has so ably demonstrated, South Carolinians regardless of race have traditions with European and African origins. As can be seen from the way the state's residents cook and dress to the way they dance and speak, African American folkways have blended with European ones to create the culture of twenty-first century South Carolina.

Economically, for nearly two centuries enslaved African Americans were not only the producers of great wealth—primarily as laborers in rice, indigo, and cotton fields—but were in their persons also capital wealth. In 1775 South Carolina was the wealthiest colony in British North America because of the labors of black Carolinians. By the eve of the Civil War, the state had dropped to the third wealthiest state in the nation, but there was a direct correlation between the wealthiest districts in the state and their black populations. It is estimated in 1860 that human property accounted for roughly one-half of the total wealth of South Carolinians. And some historians calculate that 70 percent of the state's wealth in personal property was in slaves.

With the exception of Reconstruction, the politics of the state were shaped for nearly three hundred years by the response of white Carolinians to the black population. And that response was one more of reaction than action. The passing of slave codes, the taxes on imported slaves, the creation of the Township System, the apportionment of the legislature, the gerrymandering of election districts, the Constitution of 1895, and the enactment of Jim Crow legislation were all reactions to specific concerns that the white minority had about the black majority. That would change with the impact of the Civil Rights Act of 1964 and the Voting Rights Act of 1965 and the effect of the civil rights movement.

Since 1670 there has been a visible African American presence in South Carolina. Regardless of individuals' status, that black presence has had an incalculable impact of the cultural, economic, and political development of the state as seen in the twenty-first century. The African American Monument on the State House grounds, in striking detail, depicts that presence. See plate 38. BERNARD E. POWERS, JR.

Gordon, Asa H. *Sketches of Negro Life and and History in South Carolina.* 2d. ed. Columbia: University of South Carolina Press, 1971.

Joyner, Charles. *Shared Traditions: Southern History and Folk Culture.* Urbana: University of Illinois Press, 1999,

Littlefield, Daniel C. *Rice and Slaves: Ethnicity and the Slave Trade to Colonial South Carolina.* Baton Rouge: Louisiana State University Press, 1981.

Newby, Idus A. *Black Carolinians: A History of Blacks in South Carolina from 1895 to 1968.* Columbia: University of South Carolina Press, 1973.

Tindall, George Brown. *South Carolina Negroes, 1877–1900.* Columbia: University of South Carolina Press, 1952.

Williamson, Joel. *After Slavery: The Negro in South Carolina during Reconstruction, 1861–1877.* Hanover, N.H.: Weslyan University Press, University Press of New England, 1990.

Wood, Peter H. *Black Majority: Negroes in Colonial South Carolina from 1670 through the Stono Rebellion.* New York: Alfred A. Knopf, 1974.

African Americans in the Revolutionary War. African Americans contributed to both the American and British causes during the Revolutionary War as laborers, soldiers, sailors, guides, teamsters, cooks, and spies. While it is impossible to know the exact number, it has been traditionally accepted that as many as five thousand African Americans served in the American forces. Perhaps as many as 80,000 to 100,000 slaves either escaped during the war, were taken by the British, or fled with Loyalists and British soldiers afterward. A few hundred of these served in the British ranks. African Americans joined the American or British armies under many different motives and circumstances. Slaves joined when promised freedom for their service, or were seized by one side or the other, or served as substitutes for their owners. Slaveowners were sometimes paid for the labor their slaves provided, but in other instances slaves were seized as military necessity required. Free blacks joined to enhance their status in the community or for monetary reward. When serving as soldiers, African Americans were usually integrated into the ranks. However, the colonies raised a few segregated regiments such as the First Rhode Island Regiment and the black regiment raised by Governor Lord Dunmore of Virginia for the British.

At the beginning of the war, South Carolina patriots attempted to keep slaves on the plantations by passing a law instituting the death penalty for any slave who joined the British. Meanwhile, two South Carolina delegates to the Continental Congress, Edward Rutledge and Thomas Lynch, worked to have the free African Americans who had joined the ranks of the Continental army discharged and excluded from any future enlistments. But other South Carolinians such as Henry and John Laurens were in favor of African Americans serving and of giving slaves their freedom in exchange for military service. Congress even sent John Laurens on a mission to South Carolina in 1779 in hopes of convincing the state to raise three thousand blacks for segregated battalions to be led by white officers. Under this proposal, Congress would pay plantation owners for the slaves recruited into the battalions. The slaveowners would get up to $1,000 for each able-bodied black male under thirty-five years of age, and at the war's conclusion the slave would receive his freedom and $50. The South Carolina legislature quickly rejected the idea. Later, in 1781, they rejected another request by General Nathanael Greene to raise black troops. However, South Carolina slaves were used as bounty to raise white recruits. In 1781 General Thomas Sumter offered one slave to each white citizen who joined as a private soldier for ten months and as many as three grown and one small slave to those who joined as colonels. Sumter did not have these slaves at the time he made this promise. He was banking on slaves he hoped would be seized from Loyalists during future campaigns. General Andrew Pickens also adopted this recruiting incentive, which became known as "Sumter's law," but Francis Marion rejected it, stating that it was "inhuman."

While most African Americans who served in South Carolina, slave or free, were laborers, cooks, or teamsters in the war, a few were combatants. Their presence in the ranks is only known from incidental comments found in contemporary diaries and correspondence. For instance, when Francis Marion crossed into North Carolina to join General Horatio Gates during the summer of 1780, Otho Williams recorded that Marion's men "did not exceed twenty men and boys, some white, some black, and all mounted, but most of them miserably equipped." Once, the South Carolina legislature rewarded a slave named Antigua for his role as an American spy. While the number of African Americans in the South Carolina lines may have been small, blacks made up a significant portion of the crews on South Carolina's ships during the war. African Americans were common in South Carolina's navy, serving as seamen, pilots, and carpenters.

At the end of the war, as many as 25,000 South Carolina slaves left with the British and Loyalists or escaped into the swamps. One band of three hundred Georgia and South Carolina slaves, who called themselves King of England's Soldiers, fled to the Savannah River swamps and survived until May of 1786, when they were burned out by Georgia and South Carolina militia. STEVEN D. SMITH

Foner, Philip S. *Blacks in the American Revolution.* Westport, Conn.: Greenwood, 1976.

Nalty, Bernard C. *Strength for the Fight: A History of Black Americans in the Military.* New York: Free Press, 1986.

Quarles, Benjamin. *The Negro in the American Revolution.* 1961. Reprint, Chapel Hill: University of North Carolina Press, 1996.

African Methodist Episcopal Church. To escape racial discrimination in Philadelphia's Methodist Church, Richard Allen, a former slave, organized the African Methodist Episcopal (AME) Church there in 1787. It is the oldest African American religious denomination and existed mainly in the North before the Civil War. The denomination's origins in South Carolina date to 1818. In 1817 the attempt of white Methodists in Charleston to control the activities of black church members precipitated a mass exodus of 4,367 from the church. The following year many went on to establish the African Church, which was affiliated with the AME denomination. At this time Charleston's membership was second only to that of Philadelphia, and it was the southernmost branch of the denomination. Suspicious of its northern connections and the autonomy the church represented, white authorities routinely harassed its members. Church leaders' involvement in the 1822 Denmark Vesey slave conspiracy led to destruction of the church and dispersal of its membership.

In 1863 the church was reestablished in South Carolina when the first AME missionaries, the Reverends James Lynch and James Hall, began their operations in and around Port Royal, Edisto, and Beaufort. On May 15, 1865, in Charleston, Bishop Daniel Payne organized the South Carolina Conference, which originally also included North Carolina, Georgia, and Florida. African Methodism grew rapidly and was black Carolinians' second largest denomination at the end of the century. In 1880 with 300,000 primarily southern members, the first bishops for the South were elected. All had important ties to South Carolina. Henry McNeal Turner was from Newberry; Richard Cain was the quintessential preacher-politician in Reconstruction South Carolina; and the Sixth Episcopal District, which included South Carolina, was William Dickerson's first appointment.

African Methodist Episcopal Chapel, Bennettsville. Courtesy, South Carolina Historical Society

African Methodism promoted education, and churches frequently housed secular and Sunday schools. To raise the educational level of ministers, Payne Institute was established in Cokesbury in 1870. Relocating to Columbia in 1880, the school was renamed Allen University and was the first college controlled by African Americans in the state. South Carolinians were also in the forefront of the denomination's missionary efforts. In 1878 the AME Liberian Mission Church headed by the Reverend Santania Flegler departed Charleston with the Liberian Exodus participants. Bishop Henry McNeal Turner's efforts organized the denomination in Sierra Leone and Liberia in 1891 and southern Africa in 1896. In 2004 one-third of the denomination's 3.5 million members were Africans and the church was growing most rapidly in western and southern Africa. South Carolina, which constitutes the Seventh Episcopal District, had the third largest membership of the church's nineteen districts.

Advocating "the Gospel of Freedom," African Methodist ministers have played important roles as secular leaders. Between 1868 and 1876 seven AME ministers were elected to the South Carolina state legislature. Church leaders used their offices to articulate community grievances and to protest against lynching and racial discrimination. In 1948 the Reverend Joseph DeLaine organized black parents against racial discrimination in Clarendon County's public schools. The resulting litigation was one of the cases decided in the U.S. Supreme Court's famous *Brown v. Board of Education* decision. The mission of the church has always been broadly based, and its resources have been deployed to address a range of social problems, including HIV-AIDS, health-care disparities, affordable housing, and foster care. BERNARD E. POWERS, JR.

Angell, Stephen W. *Bishop Henry McNeal Turner and African-American Religion in the South.* Knoxville: University of Tennessee Press, 1992.

Hildebrand, Reginald. *The Times Were Strange and Stirring: Methodist Preachers and the Crisis of Emancipation.* Durham, N.C.: Duke University Press, 1995.

James, Frederick C. *African Methodism in South Carolina: A Bicentennial Focus.* N.p.: Seventh Episcopal District, African Methodist Episcopal Church, 1987.

Tindall, George. *South Carolina Negroes: 1877–1900.* 1952. Reprint, Columbia: University of South Carolina Press, 2003.

African Methodist Episcopal Zion Church. One of the seven largest black denominations, the AME Zion Church traces its beginnings to 1796, when William Miller, Francis Jacobs, and other African Americans began meeting separately from the white-controlled John Street Methodist Episcopal Church in New York City. By 1801 these black Methodists had built their own church and incorporated the local congregation. Soon there were two congregations, Zion and Asbury, who as early as 1820 unsuccessfully sought status as a separate conference within the Methodist Episcopal Church.

In 1821 Zion, Asbury, and four other northern congregations held the first annual conference of the African Methodist Episcopal Zion Church (though the nomenclature "Zion" was not officially added until 1848) and became an independent denomination between 1821 and 1824. Zionites played major roles in the antislavery movement, African missions, and movements for political and civil rights for African Americans. The abolitionist Frederick Douglass began public speaking as a Zion preacher, and Harriet Tubman remained with the church until her death.

The Zion Church expanded in decades during and after the Civil War, with the inclusion of many southern blacks, mainly freed people. Membership increased from less than 5,000 in 1860 to approximately 700,000 by 1916. Believing that seeking racial progress was a crucial component of Christian practice, Zionites participated in Reconstruction era government, resisted disfranchisement and segregation, and promoted foreign missions, education, temperance, women's religious and civil equality, and the twentieth century civil rights movement.

The AME Zion Church supports four colleges and publishes the *Star of Zion* newspaper and the journal the *AME Zion Quarterly Review.* Like other major Methodist churches, it has an episcopal government and abides by theology, doctrines, and practices adapted by Methodism's founder, John Wesley, from the Church of England. Organizationally, conferences composed of clergy and laity govern churches locally (quarterly conference), regionally (annual conferences), and nationally and internationally (general conference). The General Conference, meeting quadrennially, is the highest authoritative body, though the Board of Bishops administers the business of the church between general conferences, and it individually and collectively exercises great power. In South Carolina the AME Zion Church was organizationally established in 1867, had three conferences by 1919, and around 1920 became a separate episcopal district. Though South Carolina has many churches in the Zion denomination, North Carolina and Alabama are areas of greater Zion strength. SANDY DWAYNE MARTIN

Martin, Sandy Dwayne. *For God and Race: The Religious and Political Leadership of AMEZ Bishop James Walker Hood.* Columbia: University of South Carolina Press, 1999.

Walls, William J. *The African Methodist Episcopal Zion Church: Reality of the Black Church.* Charlotte, N.C.: AME Zion Publishing House, 1974.

African Theological Archministry, Inc. (Oyotunji Village). In December 1973 a group of African Americans established an independent Yoruba kingdom at Sheldon, fourteen miles from Beaufort. The Kingdom of Oyotunji African Village is headed by Oba (King) Efuntola Oseijeman Adelabu Adefunmi I. *Oyotunji* means "Oyo again awakes" or "Oyo rises again." Oyo was an ancient city-state kingdom in Yorubaland located in present-day Nigeria, Togo, Benin, and Ghana. Leaving the Baptist church as an adolescent, Oba Adefunmi I (born Walter Eugene King in Detroit) embarked on a quest to recover his African spirituality. After visiting Haiti and Cuba in the 1950s, he incorporated the African Theological Archministry: the Yoruba Temple in Harlem, New York, in 1960.

By 1970 King Adefunmi I had moved with his family and a handful of followers to rural Beaufort County where they established the Kingdom of Oyotunji African Village. The village is patterned after the ancient Yoruba kingdoms of Nigeria in governance and religious practices. King Adefunmi I traveled to Nigeria in 1972 and was initiated into the Ifa priesthood. Ifa is the Yoruba god of fate, and his priests serve as diviners or oracles, consulted on all matters spiritual and mundane. The directors of the village were granted a state charter in 1980 as African Theological Archministry, Inc. The archministry's mission is to remove negative stereotypes of African and African American culture by providing a living laboratory of African traditions and by disseminating historical and cultural information. As of 1995 the Oyotunji village reported fifty-one residents. PRESTON L. MCKEVER-FLOYD

Hunt, Carl M. *Oyotunji Village: The Yoruba Movement in America.* Washington, D.C.: University Press of America, 1979.

Agriculture. For most of its history, agriculture virtually defined South Carolina, and no other single force has so profoundly influenced the state's economy, history, demographics, and politics. For example, absent the state's dependence on slave-based staples such as rice and cotton, South Carolina's fanatical defense of slavery to the point of disunion and war seems less tenable.

From the beginning South Carolina was conceived as an agrarian paradise. The Lords Proprietors intended the colony to fill a niche in the English mercantile system by supplying commodities not produced elsewhere in the empire. At first, however, settlers struggled merely to survive. They raised corn, cattle, and hogs for food while seeking a money crop to put the colony on a paying basis. It was a slow process. Experiments with semitropical plants such as ginger, silk, dates, almonds, and olives were disappointing. Desperate for cash, settlers planted tobacco, the crop of Virginia and Maryland, as a makeshift staple until a more suitable commodity could be found. Thus tobacco became, albeit briefly, South Carolina's first cash crop.

The colony's first significant commercial crop was rice. Small-scale experiments evolved into an established crop culture by the

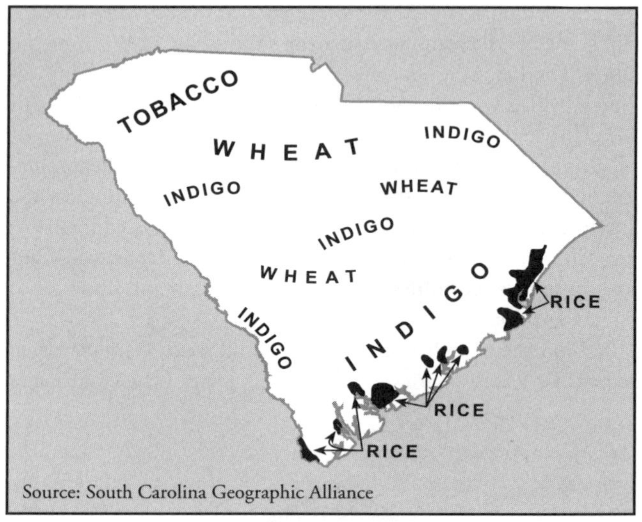

Patterns of colonial agriculture

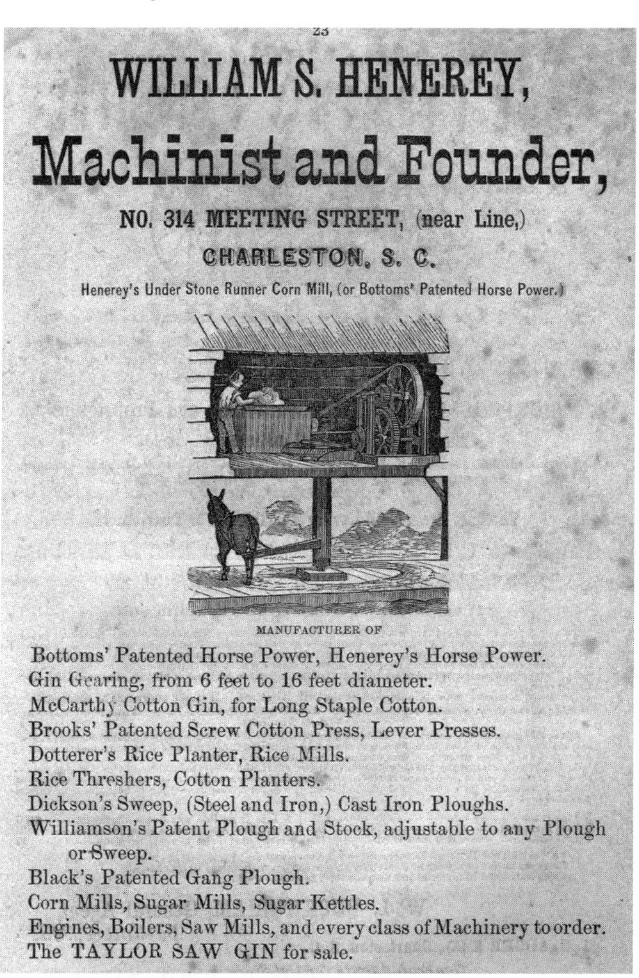

As this nineteenth-century advertisement for South Carolina–made farm machinery indicates, South Carolina's agricultural sector produced a variety of crops. Courtesy, South Carolina Historical Society

1720s. The lowcountry's warm climate and swampy landscape were perfect for growing rice, and an eager market existed as well. Europeans were hungry for Carolina rice, and ships laden with the staple called on London, Hamburg, and Rotterdam. Rice culture required substantial investments of capital and labor, and hundreds of fields were cleared and thousands of enslaved Africans imported to toil in them. Large plantations (some totaling thousands of acres)

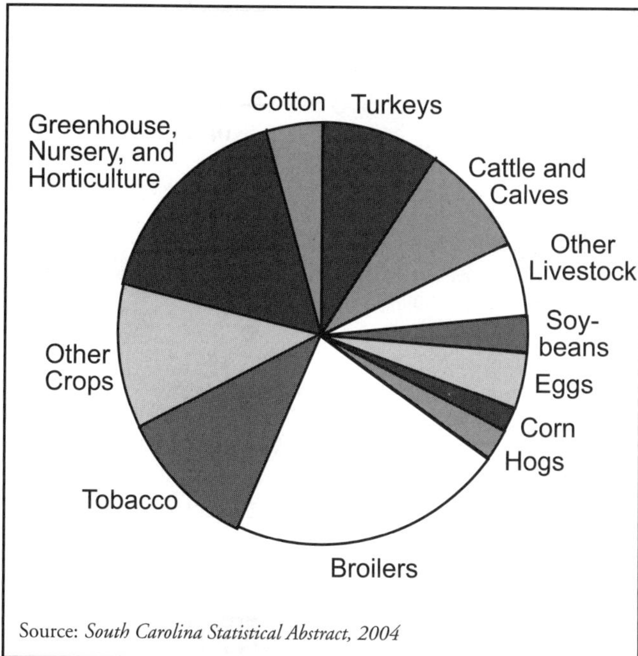

Agricultural income, 2000. At the turn of the 21st century, chickens were the largest cash crop in the state's agricultural sector.

developed along the region's tidewater rivers. Indeed, the expansion of rice and slavery went hand in hand, and by 1740 Africans comprised two-thirds of South Carolina's population. Black majorities were even greater in the heavy rice-producing areas around Georgetown and the ACE Basin. Thus the blend of Northern European and West African influences that became the unique culture of South Carolina began in the rice fields of the lowcountry. Rice (and the bondage that supported it) dominated lowcountry life for 150 years.

In the 1740s indigo became an important staple. Eliza Lucas Pinckney is credited with introducing indigo culture, although experienced French Huguenot settlers doubtless refined the process. The English government encouraged indigo by paying a bounty on the crop. As settlement spread inland, so did indigo. Soon farmers in Colleton, Williamsburg, Camden, and Ninety Six were producing the blue dye. Slavery expanded apace, bringing significant numbers of Africans to the interior for the first time. Independence from Britain ended the subsidy on indigo, and overproduction lowered prices still further. In the 1790s high-grade dye produced in India (another British colony) drove South Carolina indigo from the market. Most producers shifted back to rice or a new commodity: cotton.

At first, only farmers along the coast planted cotton. The Sea Island variety simply did not grow well inland, and the fibers of short-staple (or upland) cotton were difficult to separate from the fuzzy seed. In 1793, however, Eli Whitney's famous "cotton engine" solved the seed extraction problem, and stoked by rising demand, cotton was soon planted in every district in the state. The pace of the cotton boom was remarkable. Between 1793 and 1801 South Carolina's cotton production rose from 94,000 to 20 million pounds, and by 1811 cotton production had passed 40 million pounds.

Cotton was especially important to the backcountry. Although the region's farmers planted a little tobacco and wheat for sale, subsistence farming had been the norm, and backcountry folk mostly grew or bartered to meet their needs. Cotton changed that. The climate and soils of the backcountry were well suited to upland cotton, and the low start-up costs of cotton culture appealed to small farmers. Growers often invested their cotton profits in land and slaves to produce still more cotton. Thus, landless farmers could become yeoman, and yeomen could aspire to planter status. The region became more market oriented as well. Seduced by the lure of cash on the barrelhead, backcountry farmers often forsook food crops for the staple. Thus, within a generation, cotton worked an economic revolution in the South Carolina backcountry. By the 1830s the state's economy was heavily dependent on cotton, and the fortunes of the state rose and fell with the price of the white fiber.

Staple agriculture (the production of cash crops on plantations by slave labor) profoundly influenced South Carolina's worldview and intellectual life as well. Agrarian orthodoxy held that rural life fostered character, respect for the natural world, the dignity of work, devotion to community, family, and God—a way of life in every way superior to the urban North with its anonymous, industrial drudgery. Faced with attacks on slavery in the 1840s and 1850s, the state's best minds countered abolitionist rhetoric with strident defenses of the peculiar institution. According to the brilliant James Henry Hammond, slavery was a positive good that provided society with a needed "mudsill" of common laborers on which higher civilization rested. William Gilmore Simms, the South's leading man of letters, urged fellow southerners to resist the creeping industrial and intellectual hegemony of the North. And Francis W. Pickens declared that "No pursuit is so well calculated to produce stern integrity and devoted patriotism, as agriculture." Their devotion came at a cost. Writing in the 1930s, the historian David Duncan Wallace lamented the antebellum state's "continued glorification of agriculture as morally superior to other industries [that] discouraged the development of other possibilities."

Despite numerous small farms, large-scale rice and cotton plantations dominated South Carolina agriculture in the antebellum decades. For example, the state's mean farm size in 1860 was a substantial 569 acres. By 1860 South Carolina farmers—slave and free, great and small—were producing more than 176 million pounds of cotton and 117 million pounds of rice annually. Sadly, the prosperity of the 1850s only reinforced the notion that protecting slave-based staple agriculture was worth disunion and war.

The Civil War altered South Carolina agriculture in fundamental ways. Most important was the emancipation of slaves and establishment of a free labor force. At first federal authorities imposed a contract system that bound former slaves to employers for a year, after which they were free to leave and work for another. The contract plan was unpopular and soon evolved into some form of tenantry. Laboring families either sharecropped (working for a portion of the crop) or rented acreage for cash or produce. Former slaves entered tenantry expecting it to be a temporary transition to land ownership, but most were disappointed and tenantry became a way of life for the poor of both races for seventy-five years. Lack of capital compounded the problem. Tenants often paid high interest rates for short-term credit, and many slid into perpetual debt. Tenantry also led to a rapid decline in mean farm size. From 569 acres in 1860, the average fell to 143 acres by 1880 and to 65 acres by 1920, a decline approaching ninety percent. The humble wooden tenant house became a common feature on the South Carolina landscape.

Rice never recovered from the Civil War and emancipation. Most freed slaves simply refused to work in the rice swamps, and the peculiar labor demands of rice culture made tenantry impractical. Moreover, new culture areas in Louisiana and Texas undermined the market for Carolina rice. By 1890 the state's rice crop had fallen to one-fourth of prewar levels.

In common with other southern states, South Carolina's cotton culture continued to expand after the Civil War, especially in the Piedmont counties of Anderson, Greenville, Oconee, Pickens, and Spartanburg. By 1880 South Carolina was producing forty-five percent more cotton than in 1860. But demand for the staple did not keep pace with supply, and cotton prices began a long decline. Cotton growers responded to falling prices with increased production that only worsened the problem. By the late 1880s South Carolina farmers were in desperate straits. Between 1886 and 1887 more than one million acres of farmland were sold for taxes. Thousands of dispossessed farmers and tenants simply walked away from cotton fields and into burgeoning textile mills.

The fall of cotton prices sent shock waves through South Carolina, and farmers and merchants began seeking alternatives to a one-crop economy. As a result, several new crop cultures took root in the Palmetto State. In 1887 Barnwell County farmers made profits that "far exceed, per acre, the best cotton crop" by growing watermelons for shipment north. In the Pee Dee, farmers rode the wave of rising demand for cigarette tobaccos by planting bright leaf. With an acre of tobacco worth ten of cotton, the Pee Dee entered a prolonged boom as the countryside prospered and market towns thrived. The arrival of the boll weevil in the early twentieth century compounded the woes of cotton growers and hastened the exit of thousands more from the culture. In the "Ridge" and Piedmont counties, peach trees flourished in former cotton fields and trainloads of fruit rolled north. In St. Matthews, agronomist John Edward Wannamaker sought soybean varieties that would thrive in South Carolina.

World War I raised crop prices to record levels, and the state's farmers breathed easier for a few years. But prices plunged in the 1920s, and farmers responded with self-defeating cycles of overproduction. With the coming of the Great Depression in 1929, many faced foreclosure and ruin, but New Deal farm policies provided immediate relief and addressed long-term problems. The Agricultural Adjustment Act of 1933 (AAA) was especially important. Cotton and tobacco growers benefited most from quota plans that reduced acreage, balanced supply with demand, and raised crop prices. Other programs offered low-cost production credit, conservation funds, and cheap electricity. Truly the New Deal was the most momentous event in South Carolina agriculture since emancipation.

World War II quickened the pace of change. High wartime crop prices helped farmers recover from the Depression and enjoy a rising living standard for the first time in decades. After the war, tractors, implements, and harvesters began replacing tenants on South Carolina farms. Modern fertilizers improved yields with less labor, and cotton acreage declined further as soybeans gained ground. As more rural folk left the land, farms became fewer, larger, and better equipped. The census of 1980 reported an urban majority for the first time with less than two percent of the state's population actively engaged in farming. In the 1980s and 1990s tobacco, the state's leading cash crop, was undermined by health concerns. In the late twentieth century, South Carolina farmers produced a diverse variety of plant and animal crops including grains, fruits, vegetables, poultry, cattle, and hogs as well as some cotton and tobacco. Although increasingly urban and suburban, the Palmetto State has a strong rural tradition, and the quality of rural living attracts greater numbers of South Carolinians every year. Respect for the state's agrarian past endures. ELDRED E. PRINCE, JR.

Clowse, Converse D. *Economic Beginnings in Colonial South Carolina, 1670–1730.* Columbia: University of South Carolina Press, 1971.

Coclanis, Peter A. *The Shadow of a Dream: Economic Life and Death in the South Carolina Lowcountry, 1670–1920.* New York: Oxford University Press, 1989.

Fite, Gilbert C. *Cotton Fields No More: Southern Agriculture, 1865–1980.* Lexington: University Press of Kentucky, 1984.

Ford, Lacy K., Jr. *Origins of Southern Radicalism: The South Carolina Upcountry, 1800–1860.* New York: Oxford University Press, 1988.

Gray, Lewis C. *The History of Agriculture in the Southern United States to 1860.* 2 vols. 1933. Reprint, Gloucester, Mass.: Peter Smith, 1958.

Joyner, Charles W. *Down by the Riverside: A South Carolina Slave Community.* Urbana: University of Illinois Press, 1984.

Kirby, Jack T. *Rural Worlds Lost: The American South, 1920–1960.* Baton Rouge: Louisiana State University Press, 1987.

Kovacik, Charles F., and John J. Winberry. *South Carolina: The Making of a Landscape.* 1987. Reprint, Columbia: University of South Carolina Press, 1989.

Prince, Eldred E., and Robert R. Simpson. *Long Green: The Rise and Fall of Tobacco in South Carolina.* Athens: University of Georgia Press, 2000.

Smith, Alfred G. *Economic Readjustment of an Old Cotton State: South Carolina, 1820–1860.* Columbia: University of South Carolina Press, 1958.

Winberry, John J. "The Reputation of Carolina Indigo." *South Carolina Historical Magazine* 80 (July 1979): 242–50.

Wood, Peter H. *Black Majority: Negroes in Colonial South Carolina from 1670 through the Stono Rebellion.* New York: Knopf, 1974.

Aiken (Aiken County; 2000 pop. 25,337). Incorporated in 1835 and named for railroad president William Aiken, Sr., Aiken owes its existence to the South Carolina Railroad, its personality to its erstwhile "winter colony" of wealthy northern sports enthusiasts, and its economic vitality and relatively cosmopolitan spirit to the U.S. government's massive Savannah River Site nuclear weapons facility.

The railroad tracks that reached Hamburg from Charleston in 1833 passed through sandy farmland, whose elevation of 515 feet soon lured sweltering Charlestonians in the summer and established Aiken's image as a health resort. Local legend says the location of the town was the result of a romance between railroad surveyor Alfred Dexter and Sara Williams, daughter of planter William Williams. "No railroad for me, young man, no girl for you," Williams is said to have insisted. Whether because of this bargain or not, the couple did marry and the train did pass through Williams's property. To pull trains up the steep grade from Horse Creek Valley, a stationary steam engine was placed on a hill just west of the center of town. In 1852 a "cut," or ditch, was dug by slaves though the center of Aiken, lowering the track and eliminating the need for the stationary engine.

A town plan drawn in 1834 by two railroad engineers included wide streets divided by boulevards that distinguished the central city area. By the 1840s its reputation as a healthful locale for tuberculosis sufferers brought more residents and created a small health industry. Later in that decade, William Gregg founded the Graniteville cotton mill five miles west of Aiken. He built his home on Kalmia Hill, between the town and the mill. Other notable early residents included the botanist Henry William Ravenel; College of Charleston president William Peronneau Finley, who also became the town's longtime intendant (mayor); and Dr. E. J. C. Wood, a tireless promoter of local institutions. While the town had its rough element, the presence of Charleston summer refugees and health resort patients from the North gave Aiken society more polish than most inland communities. Its year-round population in 1849 was 683, but the Aiken Hotel received over four hundred requests for winter reservations in 1854. A seminary for boys was opened in

1853 and the town had five churches by 1858, including a Roman Catholic church.

With the outbreak of the Civil War, Camp Butler was established near Aiken, and the Ryan Guards were mustered there in 1861. On February 11, 1865, Confederate cavalry units thwarted Union troopers in a skirmish that probably saved Aiken, as well as Gregg's cotton mill, from the torch (reenactments of the Confederate victory became a popular annual event in the twentieth century). After the war, in 1866, the town council established a committee to promote Aiken in the North. The effort bore fruit, and the Highland Park Hotel was built in 1869 to accommodate winter tourists. In that same year Pennsylvanian Martha Schofield came to Aiken from the Sea Islands to open a school for former slaves. In 1871 Aiken became the seat of newly formed Aiken County. Most county founders were African Americans who held office during Reconstruction. This difficult era ended in 1876, in part due to racial strife near Aiken at Hamburg and Ellenton, as well as the activity of "Red Shirts" in the county.

Aiken's "winter colony" entered its golden era in the early 1890s with the arrival of prominent New York businessman Thomas Hitchcock and his wife, Louise. The Hitchcocks invited friends to join them for the winter to pursue a life of vigorous activity centered around horses and golf. For the next sixty years hundreds of leading northern families, including Whitneys, Vanderbilts, Rutherfurds and Iselins, transformed Aiken with their "cottages" (mansions by local standards) and their passion for golf, foxhunting, and polo and pumped large sums into the economy. One Aiken resident of that era recalled that "we lived on Yankees in the winter and blackberries in the summer." The number of winter colonists dwindled after the mid-twentieth century, but their legacy survived in Aiken's horse industry and the "Triple Crown" races held annually in March, impressive homes such as Joye Cottage and Rye Patch, the venerable Wilcox Inn, and institutions such as Aiken Preparatory School.

Little changed in Aiken until the 1950s, when the cold war spawned the Savannah River Plant, some twelve miles south of the town. Thirty-five thousand construction workers overwhelmed the area, as "trailers" filled virtually every available space. Then, in 1953, came the well-educated Du Pont employees and their families, who transformed the community with their cosmopolitan ideas and drive. The quiet town of some seven thousand residents grew to over forty thousand, including those residing in its suburbs. Schools, churches, businesses, and facilities of all kinds sprang up to accommodate the newcomers, and traffic increased. But Aiken managed to preserve much of its charm, retaining its unpaved streets in the "horsy" section and taking pride in its heritage. The downsizing of the "bomb plant" in the early 1990s slowed Aiken's economy, but predictions of disaster proved premature as city leaders successfully lured new companies to nearby industrial parks, including Kimberly-Clark, Owens Corning, and Bridgestone-Firestone. Another new aspect of the local economy was the retirement industry, which included several "assisted living" facilities. JAMES O. FARMER, JR.

Bebbington, William P. *History of Du Pont at the Savannah River Plant.* Wilmington, Del.: E. I. Du Pont de Nemours, 1990.

Cole, Will. *The Many Faces of Aiken.* Norfolk, Va.: Donning, 1985.

Dillon, Kimberly Ann. "Reconstructing Aiken: Resort Development in Aiken, South Carolina, 1830–1900." Master's thesis, University of South Carolina, 1997.

Farmer, James O., Jr. "A Collision of Cultures: Aiken, South Carolina, Meets the Nuclear Age." *Proceedings of the South Carolina Historical Association* (1995): 40–49.

McClearen, Harber A., and Silas Owen Sheetz. *St. Thaddeus of Aiken: A Church and Its City.* Spartanburg, S.C.: Reprint Company, 1994.

Smith, Harry W. *Life and Sport in Aiken and Those Who Made It.* New York: Derrydale, 1935.

Aiken, David Wyatt (1828–1887). Congressman, agrarian advocate. "D. Wyatt," as he was known, was born in Winnsboro on March 17, 1828, one of nine children of the merchant-planter David Aiken and Nancy Kerr. Aiken was educated at Mount Zion Academy in his hometown, then graduated from South Carolina College in 1849. A marriage to Mattie Gaillard followed on April 27, 1852, and together they had two daughters. Mattie died in 1855, and two years later, on January 27, 1857, Aiken married Virginia Carolina Smith. His second marriage produced eleven children.

Aiken became proprietor of Bellevue Plantation in the early 1850s, precipitating a lifelong commitment to experimentation with farming methods and to agrarian politics. As a result, Aiken became heavily involved in the State Agricultural Society. A life member of the society, Aiken helped to establish the State Fair in Columbia. By the end of the decade, as secession heated up nationwide, Aiken began to voice intermittent support for southern rights. In 1858 he relocated to a new plantation, Coronaca, in Abbeville County, where he helped found the Abbeville Agricultural Society the following year. When the Civil War broke out, Aiken enlisted and rose to the rank of colonel and commander of the Seventh South Carolina Regiment. He was severely wounded at Sharpsburg, a condition that invalided him out of the war and into a post behind the lines, in Macon, Georgia. He was discharged fully in 1864.

A staunch Democrat, from 1864 to 1866 Aiken represented Abbeville District in the S.C. House of Representatives. During Reconstruction, the link he had earlier made between southernism and agrarianism grew stronger. As part owner and writer for the Charleston-based agricultural journal the *Rural Carolinian,* Aiken vocally attacked Republican rule. Democratic—and, therefore, agrarian—ascendancy, he argued, could only occur if farmers threw off the crop-lien system and diversified their output away from cotton. In promotion of these goals, Aiken was active in the National Grange movement. He helped establish many subsidiary organizations in South Carolina in the early 1870s, including the South Carolina State Grange in 1872, of which he was "master" for three years.

In 1877 Aiken entered Congress as a representative of the Third District, a position he held until 1887. Nationally Aiken opposed growth of the federal government at the expense of state authority, notably resisting federal funding of state schools in the 1884 Blair Bill. At the same time, and at variance with fellow Democrats, Aiken promoted a revenue tariff and opposed southern war claims. Throughout the 1880s Aiken became a leading advocate of southern agricultural interests in Congress. In particular he fought for inclusion of the secretary of agriculture in the cabinet, a goal that was eventually met in 1889, after Aiken's death. He died on April 6, 1887, at Cokesbury in Abbeville (later Greenwood) County and was buried in Magnolia Cemetery, Greenwood. The Grange commemorated him as one whose "able pen and eloquent voice were ever used to advocate the rights and interests of farmers." His son Wyatt Aiken would represent South Carolina in Congress from 1903 to 1917. ERIC A. CHEEZUM

Aiken, David Wyatt. Papers. South Caroliniana Library, University of South Carolina, Columbia.

Pritchard, Claudius Hornby, Jr. "Colonel D. Wyatt Aiken, 1828–1887: South Carolina's Militant Agrarian." Master's thesis, Longwood College, 1965.

Aiken, William, Jr. (1806–1887). Governor, congressman. Born in Charleston on January 28, 1806, Aiken was the son of William Aiken, a prominent Charleston merchant and planter, and Henrietta Wyatt. Aiken received his early education from private schools in Charleston and was graduated from South Carolina College in 1825. An extremely wealthy planter, Aiken made a fortune raising cotton and rice and was equally successful in his investments in railroads and other businesses. According to 1850 slave schedules, he possessed 878 slaves in Charleston and Colleton Districts. By 1860 census takers valued his real and personal estates at $290,600 and $72,000, respectively. On February 3, 1831, Aiken married Harriet Lowndes, a union that produced one daughter, Henrietta.

Aiken entered public service in 1838 as a member of the S.C. House of Representatives from St. Philip's and St. Michael's Parishes. Returned to the House by the voters of Charleston in 1840, Aiken was elected to the S.C. Senate in 1842, where he served the next two years. On December 7, 1844, Aiken was elected governor by the General Assembly. As a Unionist, Aiken opposed the radical views of Robert Barnwell Rhett and members of the so-called "Bluffton Movement," which called for secession if Texas was not annexed to the United States as a slave state. Focusing instead on economic development in South Carolina, Governor Aiken placed particular emphasis on railroad expansion throughout the state. In 1845 he called on legislators to convert the state's surplus revenue fund into a revolving fund to supply capital to private railroad companies. Furthermore, Aiken asked the legislature to purchase stock in railroad companies chartered in South Carolina. The General Assembly proved unwilling to support the ambitious plan during Aiken's tenure, but approved a similar plan a year after Aiken left office.

On December 8, 1846, Aiken completed his term and retired to his plantation, but he remained politically active. In 1848 he supported John C. Calhoun's efforts to establish a newspaper in Washington that would represent among other things, "Southern views on the subject of slavery." This was accomplished in 1850 with the short-lived *Southern Press.* That year, Aiken was elected to the U.S. House of Representatives, where he served the Charleston congressional district from 1851 until 1857. In 1856 he was a reluctant candidate for Speaker of the House in a highly contested election. After 133 ballots, Aiken lost to Nathaniel Banks of Massachusetts by a vote of 103 to 100.

Although opposed to both nullification and secession, Aiken gave financial support to the Confederacy during the Civil War. On the defeat of the Confederacy, he was arrested and briefly detained in Washington. Aiken was again elected to the Congress. But on presenting his credentials in February 1867, he was denied his seat by northern members. William Aiken, Jr., died on September 6, 1887, in Flat Rock, North Carolina, and was buried in Magnolia Cemetery in Charleston. MATTHEW A. BYRON

Bailey, N. Louise, Mary L. Morgan, and Carolyn R. Taylor, eds. *Biographical Directory of the South Carolina Senate, 1776–1985.* 3 vols. Columbia: University of South Carolina Press, 1986.

Aiken, William, Sr. (1778–1831). Merchant, planter, banker, railroad developer. A son of James Aiken and Elizabeth Read, William Aiken was born in county Antrim, Northern Ireland, on August 20, 1778. He immigrated to South Carolina with his family in 1789 and settled near the town of Winnsboro in Fairfield County. Before the death of his father in 1798, Aiken was apprenticed to Charleston cotton merchant and factor Samuel Blakely. Aiken matured quickly and often managed the firm when Blakely was away on business. On November 12, 1801, he married Henrietta Wyatt. The marriage produced two sons, one of whom died in childhood.

With support from Blakely, Aiken went into business for himself in 1803 and brought in his brother, David, as an apprentice. Two years later Aiken opened a branch in Winnsboro in order to secure a larger share of the growing inland cotton trade. Utilizing Blakely's international trade connections, Aiken added banking to his accomplishments, later serving as a director of the Planters' and Mechanics' Bank of South Carolina, the Union Insurance Company, and the Charleston branch of the Bank of the United States. Also, he began to purchase rice lands in Colleton District. His son and heir, William Aiken, Jr., would subsequently become one of the largest rice growers in the state. From 1823 to 1830 Aiken represented St. Philip's and St. Michael's Parishes in the S.C. House of Representatives, serving on the committees on accounts, internal improvements, and ways and means.

As one of Charleston's leading businessmen, Aiken was acutely aware of the city's loss of trade to Savannah and other cities. In March 1828 Aiken served on a Chamber of Commerce committee to investigate the feasibility of constructing a railroad from Charleston to the Savannah River near Augusta, Georgia. Accordingly, "a respectable portion of our citizens," wrote planter Elias Horry, "agreed that a railroad would be beneficial to revive the diminishing commerce of the city." Later that year Aiken and others received a charter from the General Assembly authorizing the creation of the South Carolina Canal and Rail Road Company (SCC&RR). Aiken, the railroad's largest investor, was soon chosen as president of the newly chartered company. Under his direction, a route was selected and track began to be laid between Charleston and the new cotton boomtown of Hamburg, across the Savannah River from Augusta. Aiken angered states' rights advocates, however, when he went to Washington, D.C., in an unsuccessful bid to secure a federal subscription to SCC&RR stock. He would not live to see the completion of the railroad. Aiken was thrown from his carriage in Charleston on March 4, 1831, and died from his injuries the following day. He was buried in the Second Presbyterian Churchyard, Charleston, a church he helped to found in 1809. LOUIS P. TOWLES

Derrick, Samuel M. *Centennial History of South Carolina Railroad.* 1930. Reprint, Spartanburg, S.C.: Reprint Company, 1975.

Moore, Alexander, ed. *Biographical Directory of the South Carolina House of Representatives.* Vol. 5, *1816–1828.* Columbia: South Carolina Department of Archives and History, 1992.

Siegling, H. Carter. "The Best Friend of Charleston." *South Carolina History Illustrated* 1 (February 1970): 19–23, 70–71.

Aiken County (1,073 sq. miles; 2000 pop. 142,552). Aiken County was created in 1871 from parts of Barnwell, Edgefield, Lexington, and Orangeburg Counties. Named for William Aiken, first president of the South Carolina Canal and Rail Road Company, it ranks fourth in land area among South Carolina counties. Bounded on the west by the Savannah River, the county lies at the western end of the state's Sandhills region, whose poor soils necessitated the development of alternatives to farming. These nonagricultural alternatives defined much of the county's history.

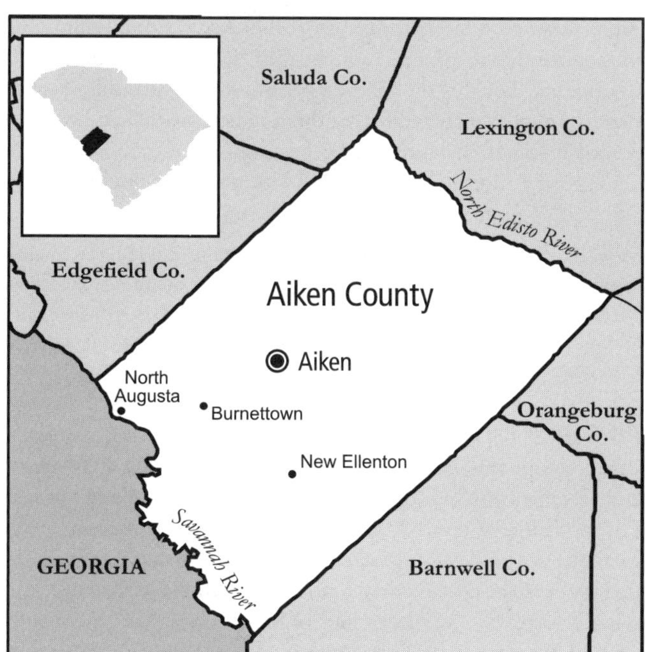

European settlement began in the late 1600s with the arrival of hunters and Indian traders. Early milestones included the building of Fort Moore in 1716 and the establishment of New Windsor township in the 1730s. Edgefield and Winton (later Barnwell) Districts were established in the region in 1785. These districts later claimed the commercial boomtown of Hamburg in 1821 as well as much of the South Carolina Railroad in the 1830s. Aiken, destined to be the seat of Aiken County, was chartered in 1835 and owed its existence to the railroad. Many early residents were refugees from the heat and disease of Charleston summers, and the town gained a reputation as a healthy retreat for sufferers of respiratory ailments. A pivotal event in the area's economic history was the construction of William Gregg's cotton mill at Graniteville in the late 1840s. Other entrepreneurs followed Gregg's example, and by 1900 a string of textile factories occupied the banks of Horse Creek.

The Reconstruction era saw the formation of Aiken County in 1871. The new county quickly became infamous for racial violence and electoral corruption. The large black population of postbellum Hamburg made the town a Republican stronghold and a thorn in the side of militant white Democrats. Tensions culminated during the election campaign of 1876, in which Aiken County witnessed bloody race riots at Hamburg and Ellenton, as well as the birth of the "Red Shirts," whose rough tactics thrilled whites, alarmed blacks, and ultimately defeated the Republicans and ended Reconstruction in the state.

Ironically, this volatile era also saw the arrival of wealthy northern families who found that Aiken County's mild winters and sandy soil made it an ideal winter sports resort. Led by Thomas and Louise Hitchcock of Long Island, New York, and William C. Whitney of Boston, prominent businessmen and their families pursued a vigorous leisure centered around equine sports. Many built large "cottages," and members of this "winter colony" continued their annual visits well into the twentieth century. Their legacy lives on in Aiken's equestrian activities, including "drag" hunts, horse shows, polo, and the "Triple Crown" horse races every March.

The first half of the twentieth century brought little change to the county, with cotton mills remaining the only significant employment option for struggling rural residents. The town of North Augusta, across the river from Augusta, Georgia, emerged at the turn of the century and also catered to winter colonists with its elegant Hampton Terrace Hotel. Peaches, which William Gregg had grown fifty years earlier, became a commercial crop in the "Ridge" area of the northern part of the county with the advent of refrigerated railroad cars.

While county towns became known for leisure and the northern section for its peaches, the Horse Creek Valley gained notoriety for its textile mills and labor militancy. The first major strike among southern textile operatives occurred at Graniteville in 1876. Ten years later the Knights of Labor were active in the valley, and strikes erupted periodically in the first decades of the twentieth century. The inauguration of President Franklin Roosevelt in 1933 sparked a sharp increase in union membership among valley workers, and thousands went on strike that fall for higher wages and better working conditions. When violence broke out, Governor Ibra C. Blackwood called in the National Guard and federal labor officials arrived to mediate the dispute. They urged workers to return to the mills but did not order owners to rehire them. The results were job losses and evictions from company houses for many strikers.

The cold war that followed World War II brought dramatic change. Construction of a billion-dollar nuclear weapons facility, the Savannah River Plant (later Site), in Aiken and Barnwell Counties brought as many as 25,000 jobs to the region, including many science and engineering positions. The sheer number of new arrivals overwhelmed Aiken County's infrastructure, schools, and housing, while cultural differences created tensions between "bombers" and natives. Thus the 1950s were a time of unprecedented adjustment for the county, whose population soared from 53,137 to 81,038 during the decade. By the end of the century, Aiken County reflected the impact of the "bomb plant" with income, education, and nonnative population figures well above state averages. In the 1970s higher education came with the opening of the Aiken campus of the University of South Carolina as well as Aiken Technical College.

Environmental concerns and the end of the cold war in the early 1990s halted nuclear production at the Savannah River Site and reduced the workforce to about twelve thousand. However, new capital investment in the 1980s and 1990s helped offset the loss of SRS jobs. Industrial diversity maintained the county's economic vitality. Many Horse Creek textile mills closed after 1950, but the largest of them, Graniteville, underwent ownership changes and modernized its operations. Other large employers included Kimberly-Clark, Advanced Glassfibers (formerly Owens Corning), and Bridgestone-Firestone. The county's newest industry, "assisted living" facilities, catered to senior citizens who came from across the country to Aiken to retire. While most of the county remained rural, farming employed only a small proportion of its people. Peaches, timber, soybeans, cotton, and livestock were the main commodities. In 1998 the county had 729 farms encompassing 134,000 acres, and its crop and livestock production (not including thoroughbred horses) was valued at $59 million. Entering the twenty-first century, Aiken County's population was concentrated in Aiken and North Augusta and along the corridor linking the two. Other communities included New Ellenton and Jackson abutting the Savannah River Site, and the rural towns Wagener, Salley (home of the "Chittlin' Strut"), and Perry in the eastern part of the county. JAMES O. FARMER, JR.

Cole, Will. *The Many Faces of Aiken.* Norfolk, Va.: Donning, 1985.

Farmer, James O., Jr. "A Collision of Cultures: Aiken, South Carolina, Meets the Nuclear Age." *Proceedings of the South Carolina Historical Association* (1995): 40–49.

Lawrence, Kay. *Heroes, Horses, and High Society.* Columbia: R. L. Bryan, 1971.

Vandervelde, Isabel. *Aiken County: The Only South Carolina County Founded during Reconstruction.* Spartanburg, S.C.: Reprint Company, 1999.

Aiken-Rhett House (Charleston). The Aiken-Rhett House, located in a block-long lot at 48 Elizabeth Street, is one of the most historically significant properties in Charleston. The house and its outbuildings are one of the most complete and best preserved urban domestic complexes of the antebellum era. John Robinson, a wealthy merchant, began construction of the house in the suburb of Wraggborough around 1818. By the early 1830s, the house and lot had become the property of William Aiken, Jr., a congressman, governor, and one of the wealthiest planters in South Carolina. Aiken dramatically altered the property, moving the entrance from Judith Street to Elizabeth Street, adding an eastern wing, enlarging the kitchen and slave quarters, and building a chicken coop, cowshed, and privies. In the 1850s he renovated these structures and added a northwest wing to house his art collection. With the exception of the cowshed, all of these additions and outbuildings have not only survived but also have remained largely unaltered since the 1850s. Following the death of Aiken and his wife, the property was inherited by his daughter and her family, the Rhetts. In 1975 descendants transferred the site to the Charleston Museum, which operated it as a museum and planned to restore the house to its antebellum splendor. Twenty years later, however, the museum sold the site to Historic Charleston Foundation (HCF) for $600,000. The building's unrestored and unaltered condition attracted HCF, which saw in it a unique opportunity to understand and present antebellum urban life and the African American heritage of Charleston to the public. The foundation has no plans to restore or furnish the Aiken-Rhett House complex and instead invites visitors to "marvel at what survives from the ninetieth century rather than search for what is missing." ALEXIA JONES HELSLEY

Poston, Jonathan H. *The Buildings of Charleston: A Guide to the City's Architecture.* Columbia: University of South Carolina Press, 1997.

Weyeneth, Robert R. *Historic Preservation for a Living City: Historic Charleston Foundation, 1947–1997.* Columbia: University of South Carolina Press, 2000.

Aiken Standard (2003 circulation: 13,910 daily and 14,558 Sunday). A daily newspaper published weekday afternoons and weekend mornings in the city of Aiken. The *Aiken Standard* traces its origins to the short-lived *Aiken Press.* The *Aiken Press* ran from 1867 to 1868, with the noted botanist Henry William Ravenel serving as its first editor. Next came the *Aiken Journal* in 1871, which became the *Courier-Journal* in 1874. In 1879 F. B. Henderson bought the newspaper for $1,500 and also purchased the *Aiken Review,* then combined the two into the *Aiken Journal and Review.* In 1904 Alva K. Lorenz and future U.S. senator James F. Byrnes bought the newspaper. In 1934 Ben J. King purchased the *Journal and Review* from Lorenz and combined it with the *Aiken Standard and South Carolina Gazette* (formed in 1930), merging the two newspapers to create the *Aiken Standard and Review.* King listed himself as manager, president, and principal owner. In March 1938 King and his wife, Annie, became sole owners of the publication, which was the only newspaper in Aiken County at the time.

The Aiken area had been a major winter tourist area, but the 1952 arrival of the Savannah River atomic energy plant triggered a boom. The *Standard and Review* became a daily, publishing five mornings a week, and in 1969 it converted to an afternoon newspaper. That same year, the newspaper shortened its name to the *Aiken Standard.* On November 15, 1968, Aiken Communications, Inc., a subsidiary of the Evening Post Publishing Company of Charleston, bought the *Standard and Review,* naming Samuel Cothran publisher and editor. Cothran retired in 1989 and was succeeded by Scott B. Hunter, who began his career as the newspaper's sports editor in 1973. In 2002 Hunter was the publisher and Jeffrey B. Wallace was editor. ROBERT A. PIERCE

McNeely, Patricia G. *The Palmetto Press: The History of South Carolina's Newspapers and the Press Association.* Columbia: South Carolina Press Association, 1998.

Moore, John Hammond, comp. and ed. *South Carolina Newspapers.* Columbia: University of South Carolina Press, 1988.

All Saints Parish. Established on March 16, 1778, All Saints Parish comprised the Waccamaw Neck of what came to be Horry and Georgetown Counties. In 1721 the peninsula became part of Prince George Winyah Parish, but separated from the rest of the parish by the Waccamaw River, it remained isolated and sparsely settled for decades. Because they could only reach the parish church by water, which was "very hazardous in blowing weather," the inhabitants of Waccamaw Neck constructed a chapel of ease on Pawleys Island circa 1736. On May 23, 1767, the Commons House of Assembly created All Saints Parish, granted it two representatives, and the chapel became the new parish church. King George III had recently prohibited the enlargement of colonial legislatures, however, and three years later he disallowed the parish. Shortly after South Carolina declared its independence from Britain, All Saints was reestablished in 1778.

With the introduction of tidal rice culture in the mid-eighteenth century, the Waccamaw River, which had so long been a barrier to the development of the Neck, quickly became its greatest asset. Plantations sprang up along its banks, and by 1810 African slaves made up nearly ninety percent of the parish population. On the eve of the Civil War, per capita wealth for the free residents of All Saints was among the highest in the nation. With 1,092 slaves, Joshua John Ward, a rice planter and warden of All Saints Church, was one of the largest slaveholders in the entire South. With the abolition of the parish system in 1865, All Saints Parish became part of Horry and Georgetown Counties. MATTHEW A. LOCKHART

Bull, Henry DeSaussure. *All Saints Church, Waccamaw, 1739–1968.* 4th ed. Spartanburg, S.C.: Reprint Company, 1994.

Joyner, Charles. *Down by the Riverside: A South Carolina Slave Community.* Urbana: University of Illinois Press, 1984.

Rogers, George C. *The History of Georgetown County, South Carolina.* Columbia: University of South Carolina Press, 1970.

Allan, Glenn (1899–1955). Author, journalist. Born in Charleston on November 15, 1899, Allan was the son of James Allan and Maria Heriot. He grew up in the nearby town of Summerville. He entered the Citadel but in his sophomore year joined the military and was assigned to officers' training camp in Plattsburg, New York, where he was commissioned a second lieutenant in the infantry. He served in various posts, was mustered out in January 1919, and returned to the Citadel, graduating in 1920. He went to work for the H. K. Leiding brokerage and import firm in Charleston, leaving in 1922 to work on a dude ranch in Taos, New Mexico. In his spare time Allan began to write for southwestern newspapers. His first full-time job as a journalist was for the Greenville, South Carolina, *Piedmont* as a sports writer, followed by stints on the *Asheville Citizen* and the *Atlanta Journal.* He gave up journalism for a while to show jumping horses along the eastern seaboard. He and a friend launched *Turf and Tanbark,* a horse magazine that failed.

Allan joined the staff of the *New York Herald Tribune* in 1930 and later was one of the journalists who helped launch the features service of the Associated Press. In 1932 he published his first and only novel, *Old Manoa,* a story of quaint and stereotypical Kentucky characters enmeshed in an improbable plot. He joined the editorial staff of the *New Yorker* in 1936. For years he had been writing free-lance articles on sports and selling short stories to pulp magazines, encouraged by the Charleston writer Octavus Roy Cohen. It was the steady purchase of his works by the *Saturday Evening Post* that prompted him to try fiction writing full-time. He returned to Summerville, living with his mother, summering with her at Pawleys Island. Several of his stories of poor white, quaint, colorful, and ignorant "swampers," some of them showing their comic attempts to survive in a changing South, were collected in a volume of linked tales, *Little Sorrowful* (1946). The book carried an opening essay by Allan's mother and one swamp tale was sold to a film company.

Allan's most popular creation, however, was "Boysi," a comical, stereotypical black servant getting his way with his white employers. He based the character on family servants and wrote the stories, he said, to counter the image of the Negro current in some southern writing. The stories were immensely popular for a time, and a collection of them appeared in 1946 as *Boysi Himself.* Allan's works were light, mildly amusing, and comforting to those who liked to see no change in the status quo. However, they fell quickly out of favor and out of print.

An ardent sportsman and foxhunter, Allan committed suicide on July 23, 1955. He was buried in Summerville's St. Paul's Episcopal Church. HARLAN GREENE

"Glenn Allan, Author, Found Fatally Shot." Charleston *News and Courier,* July 24, 1955, p. A11.

"Glenn Allan Is Buried at Summerville." Charleston *Evening Post,* July 25, 1955, p. A2.

Jones, Katherine M., and Mary Verner Schlaefer. *South Carolina in the Short Story.* Columbia: University of South Carolina Press, 1952.

Tobias, Rowena Wilson. "Summerville Writer Finds South's Present Better Copy than Its Past, Would Keep 'Honest.'" Charleston *News and Courier,* April 7, 1940, p. 3–iii.

Allan, Sarah Campbell (1861–1954). Physician. Allan was born in Charleston on December 7, 1861, one of eight children born to Scottish merchant James Allan and Amy Hobcraft. Allan graduated from the Charleston Female Seminary, a school for young women founded by Henrietta Aiken Kelly when her efforts to have women accepted at the all-male College of Charleston failed. Allan's early life was one of comfort and privilege. At age twenty-nine, she applied for admission to the Medical College of the State of South Carolina and was rejected because she was female. She thought briefly of nursing as an alternative, but her father urged her to pursue her real ambition. After taking a preparatory course for medicine in the recently formed South Carolina College for Women in Columbia, she entered the Women's Medical College of the New York Infirmary for Women and Children in 1891. Following her graduation in 1894, she spent a short period as resident physician at a sanitarium in Baltimore. She returned to Charleston in October 1894 and participated in the first sitting of the South Carolina Medical Board, the only woman to do so. She scored the highest average grade of the fourteen applicants who took the examination and was granted license number 40 by the board in October 1894.

Allan declined an offer of a staff position at Converse College and soon after accepted a position at the South Carolina Hospital for the Insane in Columbia to care for the female patients, a step applauded by the press. She assumed the position on October 1, 1895. Her duties were not confined to patient care. She taught anatomy and physiology to students in a newly instituted nursing program. After more than eleven years of service, she resigned on May 1, 1907, to return to Charleston to care for her father, who died one year later. Although she subsequently accepted occasional requests for consultation on psychiatric patients, she never returned to the regular practice of medicine.

The remaining forty-six years of Allan's life were given over to numerous charitable and civic organizations, as well as the Presbyterian Church. She traveled extensively, read voraciously (in English and French), and was known for her generosity and sense of humor. When asked by a stranger about her earlier years, she sometimes would remark that she had spent eleven years of her life in a mental institution. Allan died at her home on Gadsden Street, Charleston, on February 25, 1954, and was buried in Magnolia Cemetery. W. CURTIS WORTHINGTON

Allan, Sarah C. Biographical file. Waring Historical Library, Medical University of South Carolina, Charleston.

McDermid, Robert M. "Sarah Campbell Allan, M.D. South Carolina's Pioneer Woman Physician: A Biographical Sketch." Unpublished manuscript, Waring Historical Library, Medical University of South Carolina, Charleston.

Worthington, W. Curtis. "Psychiatrist and Humanitarian Sarah Campbell Allan (1861–1954): South Carolina's First Licensed Woman Physician." *Journal of the South Carolina Medical Association* 89 (January 1993): 9–14.

Allen, Gilbert Bruce (b. 1951). Poet, fiction writer, educator. Gilbert Allen was born in Rockville Centre, New York, on New Year's Day, 1951, to Joseph Aloysius Allen and Marie Skocik. He grew up in Long Island and married Barbara Jean Szigeti in 1974. Allen attended Cornell University, completing three degrees there—a bachelor of arts degree in 1972, a master of fine arts in 1974, and a doctorate in 1977. From 1972 to 1975 he was a Ford Foundation fellow. Allen moved to South Carolina in 1977, becoming a professor of English at Furman University.

Allen's first collection of poetry, *In Everything: Poems, 1972–1979,* appeared in 1982 and was followed by three other volumes: *Second Chances* (1991), *Commandments at Eleven* (1994), and *Driving to Distraction* (2003). In addition to poems, he has published articles and short stories. His work includes more than three hundred contributions to magazines such as *American Scholar, Cortland Review, Emrys Journal, Georgia Review, Shenandoah, Pembroke, Image, Southern Humanities Review,* and *College English.* Allen served as assistant editor of the journal *Epoch* from 1972 to 1977 and has edited *Furman Studies.*

In 1991, along with fellow Furman English professor William E. Rogers, Allen became cofounder and coeditor of Ninety-Six Press. Focusing primarily on the works of South Carolina poets, the press has produced twelve books, including *45/96: The Ninety-Six Sampler of South Carolina Poetry.* Allen also continues to compose his own prose pieces.

Allen's poetry combines contemporary philosophical concerns with a format more aligned with earlier poetic styles. As he puts it, his work "tries to document the experience of living in America during the latter half of the twentieth century," combining "both the impulse to believe and the inclination to be skeptical." Along with the theme of family relationships, many common topics in his poetry include parts of nature, particularly cats, trees, and winter. "How anyone gets an idea about anything," Allen says, "is one of the great mysteries." AMY L. WHITE

Allen, Gilbert. "Timber." *Southern Review* 36 (winter 2000): 1–2.

———. "Walking through St. Patrick's, Finding St. Joseph off the Side." *Southern Review* 34 (summer 1998): 405–406.

Allen, William Hervey, Jr. (1889–1949). Poet, novelist. The son of William Hervey Allen, Sr., and Helen Eby Myers, Hervey Allen is known to literary historians as a southern writer, though he was born in Pittsburgh, Pennsylvania, on December 8, 1889, and spent the first thirty years of his life in the North. Young Allen was educated in the public schools of Pittsburgh and received a bachelor of science degree in economics from the University of Pittsburgh in 1915 (a sporting accident had cut short his promising career at the U.S. Naval Academy). While serving in the U.S. Army during World War I, Allen fought in the Meuse-Argonne offensive in France. By the time of the armistice in November 1918, he had risen to the rank of first lieutenant. After a brief period of graduate study at Harvard, Allen was hired as an English instructor at Porter Military Academy in Charleston in 1919.

Allen's move to Charleston coincided with the beginnings of the Poetry Society of South Carolina. Along with John Bennett and Dubose Heyward, Hervey Allen was a driving force behind this organization. In 1922 he and Heyward coauthored *Carolina Chansons: Legends of the Low Country,* a book of local color verse that was enthusiastically received by northern critics, especially by Harriet Monroe, founding editor of *Poetry* magazine. In fact, when Monroe published a special southern issue of *Poetry* in April 1922, Heyward and Allen were chosen as guest editors. In their introduction to this special issue, the two South Carolinians advocated a poetic regionalism that would keep its distance from the main currents of modernism.

In 1922 Heyward moved from the Porter Academy to the High School of Charleston. In 1925 he left South Carolina permanently for a series of jobs in academia and publishing. On June 30, 1927, he married Annette Hyde Andrews of Syracuse, New York. They had three children.

Although Allen spent only six of his sixty years in South Carolina, his association with the Poetry Society came at a crucial time in his development as a writer. His book *Israfel: The Life and Times of Edgar Allan Poe* (1926) traced Poe's complex relationship with Charleston in a manner that had never been previously attempted. Moreover, the regionalist aesthetic he was calling for continued to permeate his own verse.

In 1933 Allen published his long historical novel *Anthony Adverse,* which sold 395,000 copies in its first year. By 1968 sales had passed three million, thus making Allen's book one of the best selling historical novels of all time. Set in early nineteenth-century America and Mexico, this picaresque tale of adventure captivated Depression-era audiences until it was eclipsed by *Gone With the Wind.* Even as he was living far from South Carolina, Allen was using his experience in Charleston in his Civil War novel *Action at Aquila* (1938). Although he could have lived comfortably on his royalties from *Anthony Adverse,* Allen continued writing until shortly before his death of a heart attack on December 28, 1949. He was buried with full military honors at Arlington National Cemetery. MARK WINCHELL

Aiken, David. *Fire in the Cradle: Charleston's Literary Heritage.* Charleston, S.C.: Charleston Press, 1999.

Slavick, William H. *Dubose Heyward.* Boston, Mass.: Twayne, 1981.

Allen Brothers Milling Company. One of Columbia's most celebrated landmarks, the Allen Brothers Milling Company has been recognized by its most enduring icon: a red fluorescent sign advertising its staple product—Adluh Flour—and the likeness of a girl that adorns its products. Nestled within the heart of the Congaree Vista, the family-run milling company in the early twenty-first century remains as a tangible link to the days in which the land between the State House and the Congaree River was associated with light industry and warehouses. As it has for generations, the mill continues to produce cornmeal, mixes, feed, and breeders in addition to what the South Carolina Department of Agriculture has declared "South Carolina's State Flour." Allen Brothers Milling Company has prided itself on the fact that its products are manufactured almost exclusively from yellow corn and wheat from South Carolina and white corn grown in the state and in Tennessee.

B. R. Crooner and family began operating the milling company about 1900. In 1920 the business merged with J. H. Hardin's Columbia Grain and Provision Company. Not long thereafter, the business faced foreclosure and First National Bank assumed the property's operation. The Allen family of Wadesboro, North Carolina, millers since the 1800s, purchased the mill in 1926 and have remained the owners ever since. During World War II, Allen Brothers was one of forty-two mills operating within the state. By 2003 only two remained: Columbia's Adluh Flour Mill and Greenwood Roller Mills in Greenwood.

Much of Allen Brothers' longevity is attributed to the quality of its "table tested" products. For years the company has offered tours of its historical property, which stands as the "third oldest continually operating, electrically powered, soft wheat mill in the United States." JOHN M. SHERRER III

Gordon, Kay. "Adluh: History in the Baking." Columbia *State,* January 26, 1995, pp. D1, D8.

Allen University. Allen University had its origins in Payne Institute, a school established at Cokesbury by the African Methodist Episcopal Church in 1870. The institute, however, became a faltering enterprise, unable to surmount its indebtedness and its unfavorable location in the "quiet village" of Cokesbury. Bishop William F. Dickerson and other clergy decided to move Payne Institute to Columbia, where it became Allen University. The state of South Carolina granted a charter on December 24, 1880, and property was purchased for $6,000.

Within nine years of its charter, Allen had graduated seventy-five persons from the college, law, and normal departments. Though most of the students were South Carolinians, others came from neighboring states and the Caribbean. In 1900 Allen included four buildings on four acres, eight faculty and staff, and 285 students. Five years later, the faculty had increased to seventeen members and enrollment reached 413 students. At the centennial General Conference of African Methodism in 1916, the denomination's Secretary of Education reported that during the preceding quadrennium Allen University's student body ranged between 628 and 667 in the classical, scientific, normal, theological, English, and industrial divisions. The normal and English curricula enrolled more than half of all students. More than sixty students were graduated annually between 1912 and 1916.

Coppin Hall at Allen University was built in 1906–7. Courtesy, South Caroliniana Library

The productive presidency of David Henry Sims, an Oberlin graduate and a future AME Church bishop, developed Allen University into a full-fledged seat of learning. He inaugurated a faculty exchange program with neighboring Benedict College, which allowed students at both campuses to take courses from instructors at the other school. Allen and Benedict also cooperated in a joint summer school. Between 1928 and 1932, students and graduates in the College of Liberal Arts, teacher training, high school, music, and divinity divisions totaled 1,780. Despite these accomplishments, Sims sadly reported in 1932 a deficit of $27,162. As with other educational institutions, the Great Depression seriously harmed Allen's finances.

Well regarded presidents followed Sims, including Knoxville College and Union Theological Seminary alumnus Samuel R. Higgins and David Shannon, another distinguished theologian who had been president of Virginia Union University. Some Allen alumni became leaders in the AME Church, including Bishop Richard Allen Hildebrand and Bishop Vernon R. Byrd. Allen student Melissa Evelyn Thompson Coppin was later graduated from the Women's Medical College in Philadelphia as a doctor of medicine in 1910, and practiced medicine in both Baltimore and Philadelphia. Other distinguished Allen alumni included the minister and civil rights advocate J. A. DeLaine, and the scholars Edward Sweatt and Bettye Collier Thomas.

At the beginning of the twenty-first century, Allen University was still operating under the auspices of the African Methodist Episcopal Church and regularly drawing financial support from the Seventh Episcopal District (South Carolina) and from the denomination. The Reverend Charles E. Young, a former AME Church pastor in West Columbia and Charleston, became president in 2001. That fall, the institution had an enrollment of 1,226 students. DENNIS C. DICKERSON

Ashmore, Nancy Vance. "The Development of the African Methodist Episcopal Church in South Carolina, 1865–1965." Master's thesis, University of South Carolina, 1969.

McMillan, Lewis K. *Negro Higher Education in the State of South Carolina.* [Orangeburg, S.C.], 1952.

Allendale (Allendale County; 2000 pop. 4,052). When trains replaced steamboats, the commercial and social activities of the Buddenville community in southern Barnwell County migrated about five miles farther from the Savannah River to locate beside the railroad in what came to be the town of Allendale. The area around Buddenville boasted prosperous farms, several churches, four stores, and academies teaching music, art, and language. The farmers who transported their produce on the river had wanted a rail connection to Charleston to free them from dependence on cotton buyers in Georgia. Their wish was granted, but the railroad skirted a high ridge and did not run through Buddenville.

After the Charleston and Western Railroad sent the first train through the area in 1872, the new town grew up beside the tracks. Called Allendale after the Allen family, who were prominent residents of the area, the town had a post office constructed eight hundred yards from the railroad depot, and Paul Allen became the first postmaster. Streets and lots were laid out on fifty acres surrounding the depot.

The General Assembly chartered the Town of Allendale on December 20, 1873, and Z. A. Searson became the first mayor. Town planners laid out boulevard-style streets one hundred feet wide with trees and flowers in the medians. A hotel opened in 1873 beside the train depot, and an academy opened within a year. Miss Arnold's Schoolhouse was built in 1875. By the early 1880s, Allendale contained thirty-one stores and more than six hundred inhabitants. African American businesses grew up near the intersection of Main Street and Flat Street. Farmers coming into town tied their wagons on Flat Street, where their horses watered at a trough. A livery sold horses and mules on the lot at Railroad Avenue and Memorial Avenue.

Allendale became the seat of Allendale County with its creation in 1919. As the automobile gained popularity in the twentieth century, tourist-oriented businesses stretched north and south of Allendale on U.S. Highway 301, a main thoroughfare from the Northeast to Florida. Allendale had twenty-six filling stations at one point. National chains, such as Holiday Inn and Howard Johnson, operated motels and restaurants.

Construction of the Savannah River Site after World War II briefly transformed Allendale into a boomtown. But when Interstate 95 opened east of Allendale County, the tourist-oriented economy along U.S. 301 collapsed. Many commercial buildings were abandoned and others deteriorated.

At the turn of the twenty-first century, efforts were made to restore Allendale's streetscape. A grassroots group known as Allendale Green transformed a vacant block into a shady park. The Town of Allendale acquired a hotel building constructed in 1891 beside the railroad. The Allendale County Historical Society beautified the facades along a row of turn-of-the-century storefronts. The Salkehatchie campus of the University of South Carolina renovated the Howard Johnson building as its admissions office. DANIEL MCDONALD JOHNSON

Lawton, Alexania Easterling, and Minnie Reeves Wilson. *Allendale on the Savannah.* Bamberg, S.C.: Bamberg Herald Printers, 1970.

McKissock, Derek. "Allendale Has Seen Many Changes over 125 Years." *Allendale County Citzen Leader,* December 16, 1998, p. A16.

Allendale County (408 sq. miles; 2000 pop. 11,211). Formed in 1919, Allendale is South Carolina's youngest county, yet it contains the oldest known human habitation in the state. Archaeological investigations in Allendale have found evidence of human settlement dating back more than sixteen thousand years. These prehistoric people used "Allendale Chert" in making stone tools.

Europeans began arriving in the area in the 1750s, settling at Matthews Bluff on the Savannah River and Jackson's Branch, a tributary of the Salkehatchie. Other families settled along the headwaters of the Coosawhatchie and its tributaries. In 1759 they organized Coosawhatchie Church, which became Beech Branch Baptist Church. Cattle herding and farming were the mainstays of the pioneer economy.

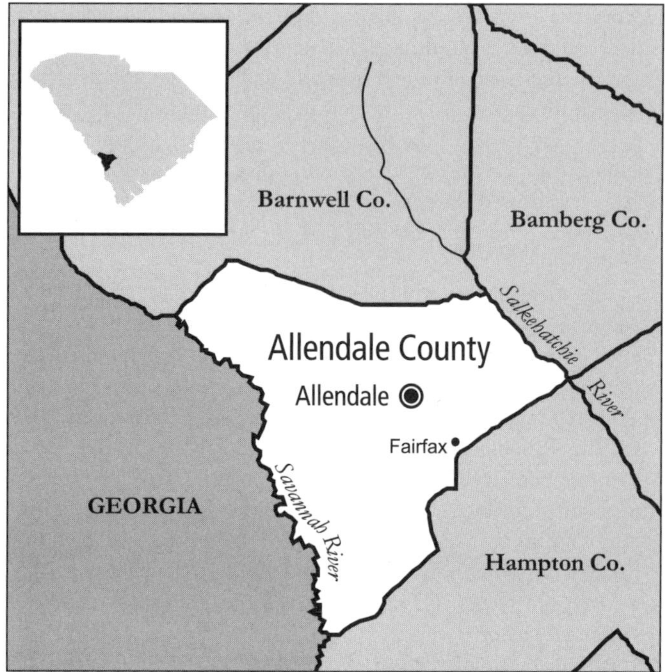

During the Revolutionary War, armies marched up and down the Savannah River and partisan fighters conducted raids. The Pipe Creek Light Horse, a patriot cavalry force consisting of men from what came to be Allendale and Hampton Counties, established a camp at Matthews Bluff. In March 1779, patriots fleeing the disastrous Battle of Brier Creek in Georgia floated on logs or swam across the Savannah River; their commander, General John Ashe, took refuge at Matthews Bluff. In April 1781, the Battle of Wiggins Hill near Burtons Ferry ignited bloody conflict among neighbors.

After the Revolution, the area became more settled, with Baptists, Lutherans, and Methodists each establishing churches in the vicinity. Great Salkehatchie Baptist Church at Ulmer was organized in 1790. St. Nicholas Lutheran Church was founded around 1800. A log building housed Swallow Savannah Methodist Church around 1816. The buildings of Smyrna Baptist Church, organized 1827, and Antioch Christian Church, organized 1833, remained standing at the start of the twenty-first century.

In the antebellum era, Allendale made up the southern third of Barnwell District. With the arrival of cotton and the cotton gin in the 1790s, landowners adopted the plantation system and slaves soon made up the majority of the population. Steamboats, pole boats, and cotton boxes plied the Savannah River during the era, and Allendale was the site of several boat landings. One steamboat line stopped at Matthews Bluff, while a competitor stopped at neighboring Cohens Bluff. Boats also stopped at Johnson's Landing and Little Hell.

During the Civil War, General William T. Sherman's army marched through Allendale County. Union troops spared the Erwinton Plantation house because it was being used as a hospital for malaria sufferers. Brigadier General Hugh Judson Kilpatrick set up headquarters for his Union cavalry at Roselawn. Confederates staged their strongest resistance against Sherman's march to Columbia at Rivers Bridge on the Salkehatchie; the resistance crumbled when Union troops crossed at Bufords Bridge and attacked the Confederates' right flank. In the post–Civil War era, the area continued to rely on an agricultural economy and an African American labor force. As late as 2000, African Americans made up almost seventy-five percent of the population.

Allendale County was formed in 1919 from parts of Barnwell and Hampton Counties because of the inconvenience of traveling to the courthouse in Barnwell or Hampton. The first courthouse was all but destroyed by fire in May 1998. Construction on a new courthouse incorporating the exterior shell of the old began in August 2002.

In the mid-twentieth century, the local economy benefited from travelers along U.S. Highways 301 and 321. Construction of the Savannah River Site, a nuclear weapons production plant, brought more economic opportunity to the area. Robert E. McNair practiced law in Allendale from 1948 until he became governor in 1965. The Salkehatchie Regional Campus of the University of South Carolina opened in Allendale in 1965. However, the opening of Interstate 95 deflated the tourism economy, the end of the cold war led to downsizing at the Savannah River Site, and an agricultural depression drove many farmers out of business. A handful of manufacturers, however, provided some light through the economic gloom, including Scotsman, Clariant, Mohawk, Collum's Lumber, International Apparel, Fairfax Dimension, and Corbett Plywood.

Allendale County entered the twentieth-first century facing a series of economic and social challenges. The county had the lowest per-capita income and the lowest median household income in South Carolina during the final two decades of the twentieth century. More than one third of the individuals and well over one fourth of the families lived in poverty. Half of the families had a female householder with no husband present. In the 1990s, twenty-six percent of births in the county were to teenage mothers. The county also had the highest infant mortality rate and the lowest percentage of high school graduates in the state. In 1999 the South Carolina Board of Education authorized the state to assume management of the Allendale County schools until goals for improvement were met. DANIEL MCDONALD JOHNSON

Lawton, Alexania Easterling, and Minnie Reeves Wilson. *Allendale on the Savannah.* Bamberg, S.C.: Bamberg Herald Printers, 1970.

Allison, Dorothy (b. 1949). Author. Allison was born on April 11, 1949, in Greenville, a self-proclaimed bastard child of an unwed teenage mother who dropped out of seventh grade to work as a waitress. Allison was raised in extreme poverty by her mother and an abusive stepfather, who repeatedly beat and raped her from the time she was five to eleven years old. Though Allison's mother contributed to this scarring childhood by tolerating her husband's violence, she invented Allison's future by keeping a jar of money for her daughter's college education and thus taught her bright daughter that she had a right to excel. Allison was the first in her family to finish high school and went on to Florida Presbyterian College (now Eckerd College) on a National Merit Scholarship. She earned a master's degree in anthropology at the New School for Social Research in New York. In the early 1970s, Allison joined a lesbian-feminist collective and severed all ties to her family until 1981. She credits the women's movement with making possible her writing career, nourished by women friends and lovers who initially helped her overcome a "terrible drive" to burn her journals, stories, and poems.

The Women Who Hate Me (1983), a collection of poetry, published in an expanded version in 1991, focuses on lesbian sexuality and relationships between women. *Trash* (1988) includes stories and poetry with a lesbian-feminist emphasis that were inspired by Allison's working-class, poverty-stricken childhood. "Ours is a culture that hates and fears the poor, queers, and women," she says. "The people I love most are the people society doesn't like."

Allison received mainstream recognition with her first novel, *Bastard Out of Carolina* (1992), which in 1996 was adapted to a film directed by Anjelica Huston. The semi-autobiographical narrative taking place in Allison's hometown explores themes of poverty and choice through the eyes of Bone Boatwright, who draws strength from family stories and, despite beatings and sexual abuse, finds her own voice and identity. Allison takes up the notion of storytelling as survival and weapon in two works of non-fiction, *Skin: Talking about Sex, Class, and Literature* (1994) and *Two or Three Things I Know for Sure* (1995), a lyrical memoir.

Cavedweller (1998), Allison's second novel, follows the character Delia and her attempt to come to terms with her past and its losses. Set in Cayro, Georgia, *Cavedweller* explores the connection between identity and place and continues Allison's desire to record the lives of marginalized southerners. The numerous women who populate the novel meet or live in a world of headstrong Baptists, truck farms, trailers, convenience stores, and beauty parlors. Underneath hides an underworld of caves, mapped or unmapped, in which Delia's daughter Cissy seeks refuge and comfort. Metaphorically representing a journey into the past, the silences of stories, the lesbian body, and more, the caves suggest as well the writer's ambition to uncover the "harder truths" and map paths to redemption.

Allison lives in northern California with her son, Wolf, and her partner, Alix Layman. CLARA JUNCKER

Griffin, Connie. "Going Naked into the World: Recovery and Re/presentation in the Works of Dorothy Allison." *Concerns* 26, no. 3 (1999): 6–20.

Iring, Katrina. "'Writing It Down So That It Would Be Real': Narrative Struggles in Dorothy Allison's *Bastard Out of Carolina*." *College Literature* 25 (spring 1998): 94–107.

Megan, Carolyn E. "Moving toward Truth: An Interview with Dorothy Allison." *Kenyon Review* 16 (fall 1994): 71–83.

Allston, Robert Francis Withers (1801–1864). Legislator, governor, rice planter. Born on April 21, 1801, on Waccamaw Neck in Georgetown District, Allston was the fifth child of Benjamin Allston, Jr., and his wife Charlotte Anne, and was presumably named for two brothers, Robert and Francis Withers, who had assisted Benjamin in a particularly difficult debt transaction in 1800. Until 1809 he resided at Waverly, one of two family plantations on the Pee Dee, but he moved to Georgetown following his father's death in 1809. He attended the free school at Winyah Indigo Society (1809–1812) and John Waldo's classical school (1812–1817).

After four years at the U.S. Military Academy (1817–1821), Allston worked briefly for the Topographical Service. He resigned to return home and assist his mother with the management of the family lands, taking full responsibility for them in 1827. To supplement the family income, in 1823 he secured election by the General Assembly to a four-year term as surveyor-general of South Carolina. In 1828, pressured by friends, he launched his formal political career and won election to the S.C. House of Representatives, where he represented Prince George Winyah Parish from 1828 to 1831. He was subsequently involved in several disputed elections involving the Prince George Winyah S.C. Senate seat for the Twenty-ninth, Thirtieth, and Thirty-first General Assemblies, in large part because of his staunch support of nullification. His political position would best be described in 1838, when he claimed that his views were "based on the principles of Thomas Jefferson, as express'd during the discussion in Virginia in 1798 . . . [and consist of] the belief that a plain, honest, common-sense reading of the Constitution is the only true one and that in legislating for the government of the United States, nothing—absolutely nothing of authority—should be allowed to precedent as such."

The political stress of this period was offset by his marriage without a dowry on April 5, 1832, to Adele Petigru, daughter of William Pettigrew and Louise Gilbert and the sister of Allston's attorney and friend, James L. Petigru. They had at least nine children, five of whom lived to maturity.

After the nullification controversy had passed, Allston was reelected to his Prince George Winyah Senate seat from the Thirty-second (1836–1838) to the Forty-second (1856–1857) General Assemblies. He served on numerous committees and was elected president of the Senate from 1850 to 1856. His political career was capped by his election as governor in December 1856. A lifetime advocate of higher education, serving as a trustee of South Carolina College (1840–1864), Allston called for the transformation of the college into a university and pushed hard for educational reform throughout the state. Following the expiration of his term in December 1858, he served as a Confederate presidential elector (1861) and in a handful of other minor political roles.

Allston spent the last few years of his life trying to save his vast landholdings throughout the Pee Dee region, primarily in Georgetown District. An accomplished planter and agricultural innovator, he had authored several works on rice planting, including the well-regarded *Memoir of the Introduction and Planting of Rice in South-Carolina* (1843) and *Essay on Sea Coast Crops* (1854). In addition to the family plantations at Matanza (name changed to Chicora Wood in 1853) and Waverly, Allston came to control Waties Point and Friendfield (inherited from his aunt in 1840, with Friendfield sold shortly thereafter), Exchange, Nightingale Hall, Waterford, Rose Bank (or Ditchford), Breakwater, Guendalos, Retreat, Holly Hill, and Pipe Down. In addition to these 4,000 acres, Allston owned at least 9,500 acres of pasture and timber lands. In 1863 he added another 1,900 acres with his purchase of Morven plantation in North Carolina. His slaveholdings totaled at least 690 in 1864. Debt and the Civil War greatly reduced the value of his estate. Allston died from pneumonia (with accompanying heart disease) on April 7, 1864, at Chicora Wood. Initially buried at the Prince Frederick, Pee Dee, Chapel, he was later interred in the cemetery at Prince George Winyah Church. ERIC W. PLAAG

Devereux, Anthony Q. *The Life and Times of Robert F. W. Allston.* Georgetown, S.C.: Waccamaw Press, 1976.

Dusinberre, William. *Them Dark Days: Slavery in the American Rice Swamps.* New York: Oxford University Press, 1996.

Easterby, J. H., ed. *The South Carolina Rice Plantation as Revealed in the Papers of Robert F. W. Allston.* 1945. Reprint, Columbia: University of South Carolina Press, 2004.

Allston, Washington (1779–1843). Painter, writer. Allston was born on November 5, 1779, in Georgetown, to William A. Allston, Jr., and Rachel Moore. He descended from an eminent South Carolina family that had settled along the Waccamaw River in the seventeenth century. His father was a colorful figure during the Revolutionary War, serving as a captain under General Francis Marion. The landholdings of the Allston family were extensive and included the property that became Brookgreen Gardens. While still an infant, Allston's father died and his mother married Dr. Henry Collins Flagg of Newport, Rhode Island. Flagg had left Newport to serve as surgeon general of the Army of the South from 1779 to the end of the Revolutionary War.

Attending Mrs. Melescent Calcott's school in Charleston by 1784–1785, Allston's artistic interests blossomed early. Like some of his contemporaries, including Charles Fraser and John Blake White, he was most likely exposed to the work of engraver and painter Thomas Coram and European-trained, neoclassical artist Henry Benbridge, who painted portraits of several family members, including Allston's mother and his half sister, Elizabeth.

In 1787 Allston left Charleston to attend Robert Rogers's school in Newport before matriculating at Harvard University, from which he graduated in 1800. Having declared to his family his intention to pursue an artistic career, Allston made a final visit to Charleston to settle his affairs before traveling abroad to continue his studies. Miniature portrait painter and Newport native Edward Greene Malbone, who had a profound effect on the later career of Charles Fraser, accompanied him.

Even though Allston never returned to South Carolina, most scholars agree that growing up on a well-to-do southern plantation influenced his artistic sensibilities. Throughout his career he paid deference to and acknowledged to his southern origins, particularly his exposure to African American tales and myths. In turn he received the support and patronage of many South Carolinians.

From 1800 to 1818, excepting three years that he spent in Cambridgeport, Massachusetts, Allston was in Europe, where he studied at the Royal Academy with Benjamin West, traveled to Paris with John Vanderlyn, then traveled on to Rome where he came into contact with the innovative group of German classicists, including Joseph Anton Koch and Gottlieb Schick. During this time, Allston revealed his mastery of classical landscape with such works as *Diana and her Nymphs in the Chase* (1805) and *Italian Landscape* (circa 1805–1806), and his interest in literary, particularly Biblical, themes with *The Angel Releasing St. Peter from Prison* (1814–1816) and *Donna Mencia in the Robbers' Cavern* (1815).

Achieving the height of a successful career as a history painter in England, Allston returned to Cambridgeport where he settled for the rest of his life. Facing minimal interest in America for history painting, he spent the remainder of his career producing smaller works such as *Moonlit Landscape* (1819) and his unfinished masterpiece, *Belshazzar's Feast,* which he had begun while living abroad.

Distilling a variety of artistic influences, Allston gave rise to a romantic American vision. He did not limit himself to portraiture, like many of his predecessors, but explored the full scope of visual expression. Not prolific, he left many works unfinished, but his philosophy of art elevated the image of American artists from mere artisans to romantic idealists. After an extended illness, Allston died in Cambridgeport on July 9, 1843. See plate 16. ANGELA D. MACK

Gerdts, William H., and Theodore E. Stebbins. *"A Man of Genius": The Art of Washington Allston (1779–1843).* Boston: Museum of Fine Arts, 1979.

Rice, Noelle Claire. "The Career of Washington Allston." Master's thesis, University of South Carolina, 1996.

Richardson, Edgar Preston. *Washington Allston: A Study of the Romantic Artist in America.* Chicago: University of Chicago Press, 1948.

Wright, Nathalia, ed. *The Correspondence of Washington Allston.* Lexington: University Press of Kentucky, 1993.

Alston, Joseph (ca. 1778–1816). Governor. Scion of one of the great rice planting families of Georgetown District, Alston was born ca. 1778, the son of William "King Billy" Alston and Mary Ashe. Educated by private tutors, Alston attended the College of Charleston from 1793 to 1794. In 1795 he entered the junior class of the College of New Jersey (later Princeton), but withdrew before graduating. Alston studied law under Edward Rutledge, who predicted a brilliant future for his pupil. Admitted to the bar in 1799, Alston practiced only occasionally, devoting his career to the management of his extensive rice plantations in All Saints Parish, comprising 6,287 acres and 204 slaves. On February 2, 1801, Alston married Theodosia Burr, daughter of Vice President Aaron Burr. The couple's only child, Aaron Burr Alston, died at the age of ten on June 30, 1812. A short time later, Theodosia, after departing Georgetown aboard the schooner *Patriot* on December 30, 1812, was lost at sea off the coast of North Carolina.

Although unambitious, Alston entered politics at the insistence of his father-in-law. He was a member of the S.C. House of Representatives from 1802 to 1812, serving as Speaker of the House from 1805 to 1809, the youngest man to hold the office up to that time. Lauded as "a great manager in all political movements," Alston's crucial support of upcountry demands for reapportionment of the legislature led to the adoption of the constitutional amendment of 1808. Also while a House member, he opposed reopening the slave trade, initiated his advocacy of a state penitentiary, and amelioration of the state's draconian penal code. In 1806 Alston became embroiled in the Burr Conspiracy, and while never indicted for support of his father-in-law's grandiose schemes, his reputation suffered thereafter.

On December 10, 1812, Alston was elected governor by a narrow margin after a bitter campaign. As governor, Alston's chief concern was the defense of South Carolina during the War of 1812. His vigorous efforts resulted in the state quickly meeting its quota of five thousand troops, and the construction and garrisoning of forts for coastal defense. His administration also saw the settlement of the state's boundary with North Carolina, the establishment of the Bank of the State of South Carolina, and the raising of a brigade of state troops. Despite these accomplishments, Alston's governorship was one of the most discordant in the history of the state due, in part, to several impolitic actions he took, and the unremitting personal and political animus of E. S. Thomas, editor of the Charleston *City Gazette,* who Alston successfully sued for criminal libel. At the conclusion of his term, Alston served in the S.C. Senate from 1814 to 1815, where he was credited with saving the free school system after the House had voted to abolish it.

Eulogized as a man "Naturally humane and merciful in his disposition," Alston died at Charleston on September 10, 1816, and was buried in the family graveyard at his home plantation, The Oaks. Ironically, like another prominent nineteenth-century political figure, James Chesnut, Alston is primarily remembered as the husband of his legendary wife. PAUL R. BEGLEY

Devereux, Anthony Q. *The Rice Princes: A Rice Epoch Revisited.* Columbia, S.C.: State Company, 1973.

Rogers, George C. *The History of Georgetown County, South Carolina.* Columbia: University of South Carolina Press, 1970.

Wolfe, John Harold. *Jeffersonian Democracy in South Carolina.* Chapel Hill: University of North Carolina Press, 1940.

Alston Wilkes Society. The Methodist minister Eli Alston Wilkes, Jr., founded the Alston Wilkes Society (AWS) in 1962 to help criminal offenders and former offenders, among other groups, regain control of their lives and contribute to society. Although Wilkes died soon after—which was the reason for the honorary renaming—his vocation of rehabilitating adult offenders survives through the hard work of the society's staff and volunteers. In fact,

AWS has reached the status of being the largest nonprofit statewide agency of its kind.

Working closely with corrections agencies at both the state and federal levels, the Alston Wilkes Society serves thousands of people every year. It offers statewide city court mediation, counseling, and employment services for offenders/ex-offenders and the homeless. The society also operates adult halfway houses, veterans' homes, and youth homes. In addition to general services and rehabilitation homes, AWS provides programs such as "Project Take HEART," which is designed to educate homeless persons and offer them skills training in construction and apartment maintenance. These examples are only some of the larger ways that the Alston Wilkes Society has worked for South Carolina and its citizens. Its success demonstrates the positive impact that volunteer agencies can make by offering hope, help, and a second chance to those in need. SUSAN A. KELLEY

Harry, Jennifer L. "Alston Wilkes Society: Rebuilding Lives, Providing Second Chances." *Corrections Today* 64 (August 2002): 14.

Walker, S. Anne. "South Carolina Volunteer Agency Plays Vital Role in Corrections." *Corrections Today* 55 (August 1993): 94–99.

Amethyst. State gemstone. Amethyst is violet or purple-colored quartz. The word amethyst comes from the Greek *amethystos,* meaning "not drunken." This reflects the tradition that ancient Greeks and Romans liked to drink wine from cups studded with the stone, believing that they would not become intoxicated. For centuries it was customary for bishops to wear amethysts in their rings, giving rise to the term "bishop grade" for the finest stones of deep purple. In medieval England, the amethyst was believed to be a protection against disease, and King Edward the Confessor (reigned 1042–1066) is said to have worn the stone for that reason. Amethyst was one of the gems set into the breastplate of ancient Israel's high priest, and it figures in the Book of Revelation (Apocalypse) as one of the precious stones in the foundation of the wall of the Holy City of Jerusalem.

Amethyst became the official South Carolina gemstone by a law signed by Governor Robert McNair on June 24, 1969. The legislators noted that South Carolina is one of the few states "where the gem stone amethyst of good quality is found in the United States" and that "the amethyst is the most prized type of quartz for its wide use and various shades and hue from deep orchid color."

One of the best amethyst finds in the United States occurred in 1965 at the Ellis-Jones Amethyst Mine, near Due West in Abbeville County. This was a fifteen-pound cluster of amethyst crystals of rich purple color. A large group of the Due West crystals was put on display in the Gems and Minerals Section of the National Museum of Natural History in Washington, D.C., and appeared on a postage stamp issued in 1974. DAVID C. R. HEISSER

Lininger, Jay L. "The History of Amethyst at Due West, South Carolina." *Matrix: A Journal of the History of Minerals* 5 (spring 1997): 24–30.

White, John S., and Robert B. Cook. "Amethyst Occurrences of the Eastern United States." *Mineralogical Record* 21 (May–June 1990): 203–13.

Yates, Nancy C. "Amethyst and Granite: The Official Gemstone and Stone of the State of South Carolina." *Sandlapper* 4 (March 1971): 24–27.

Anderson (Anderson County; 2000 pop. 25,514). A new courthouse in the upstate became necessary in December 1826, when Pendleton District was divided into Anderson and Pickens Districts. The General Assembly appointed five commissioners to select a site. They acquired some 150 acres of land near the center of Anderson District for $4.62 an acre. A courthouse was completed in 1828, and a town developed around it. In 1833 the town of Anderson was incorporated. The town grew slowly during its first two decades, with the primary highlight being the founding of Johnson Female University in 1848. However, growth accelerated following the arrival of the Greenville and Columbia Railroad in 1856. Between 1850 and 1860 the number of merchants expanded from sixteen to forty-four.

Near the end of the Civil War, as Union troops marched through the Midlands, a branch of the Confederate treasury was removed from Columbia and located in the building that had housed the Johnson University. For eleven years after the war, Union troops occupied Anderson. The garrison used the Johnson University as headquarters, and the men camped nearby. The first rally held by former Confederate General Wade Hampton in his campaign for governor was held in Anderson on September 2, 1876.

Incorporated as a city in 1882, Anderson became a center of the Piedmont's late nineteenth-century industrial expansion. In 1890 the first of several cotton mills were built on the outskirts of Anderson, and mills soon ringed the city. By 1900 the city had joined Greenville and Spartanburg as the leading textile manufacturing centers in South Carolina.

William C. Whitner led the formation of the Anderson Water, Light and Power Company, building a power plant at High Shoals on Rocky River, four miles from Anderson. A line was run to the town, and power reached Anderson on May 1, 1895. Two years later a larger plant was built at Portman Shoals on the Seneca River, twelve miles from town. Anderson Cotton Mill agreed to use the new source and became the first cotton mill in the South to be powered by long-distance transmitted lines. Electric streetlights and trolley lines soon followed, and a Charleston newspaper dubbed Anderson "The Electric City." Having excess power, power company directors created the Anderson Traction Company in 1904 to operate electric trolleys, running lines to mills at the outskirts of the town and into main residential areas. Looking for still more users, the company built Buena Vista Park, establishing additional trolley lines to handle visitors.

Anderson's prosperity continued into the early twentieth century. A new library and new hospital opened in 1908. In 1910 a successful campaign raised $100,000 to start a college in Anderson. The money was offered to the Baptists, and Anderson College opened in 1912 as a four-year college for women. In 1914 a suburb, North Anderson, was developed, containing two hundred lots that were connected to the city by a trolley line. The suburb merged with Anderson in 1929.

Significant growth continued after World War II as Anderson attracted new, nontextile industries. Although most of this industrial expansion occurred just beyond the city limits, Anderson benefited nevertheless and became a regional retail and commercial center attracting people from both South Carolina and Georgia. A civic center and sports and entertainment center within the city limits garnered attention, as did a new courthouse, completed in 1991. These projects complemented an extensive downtown renovation program marked by the creation of new green space, a resurgence of shops and restaurants, and improved building facades. The 1897 courthouse became a county office building. Entering the twenty-first century, Anderson looked to the future but remembered its past with four historic districts, plus several individual structures listed in the National Register of Historic Places. HURLEY E. BADDERS

Anderson County Tricentennial Committee. *Anderson County Honors the State of South Carolina on Her 300th Birthday: Souvenir Program.* Anderson, S.C.: Anderson County Tricentennial Committee, 1970.
Badders, Hurley E. *Anderson County: A Pictorial History.* Norfolk, Va.: Donning, 1999.
Dickson, Frank. *Journeys into the Past.* Anderson, S.C.: Dickson, 1975.
Watkins, William L. *Anderson County, South Carolina: The Things That Made It Happen.* Anderson, S.C., 1995.

Anderson, Pinkney (1900–1974). Musician. Anderson was born in Laurens on February 12, 1900. Encompassing blues, rags, gospel, ballads, and minstrel tunes, Pink Anderson's music exemplified the southern "songster" tradition. His blues typified the laid-back style popular in the Greenville-Spartanburg area from before World War I. Anderson's eclectic repertoire and engaging personality brought him national attention during the folk music revival of the early 1960s. After moving to Spartanburg as a child, Anderson took up the guitar and played on the streets for change. As a teenager he teamed up with an older, blind musician, Simmie Dooley, from whom he likely learned many of the songs that became staples of his repertoire. Anderson and Dooley recorded together in 1928, cutting four sides for Columbia Records. Anderson would not record again until 1950, but he continued to make his living from music, traveling extensively with medicine shows such as Dr. W. R. Kerr's Indian Remedy Company. Illness sidelined Anderson during the mid-1950s, but his career was rejuvenated after young folk music aficionados sought him out in the early 1960s. He recorded albums for the Prestige/Bluesville label, performed at folk festivals, and appeared in a 1963 documentary, *The Blues.* In the film and on stage he was sometimes joined by his young son, Alvin "Little Pink" Anderson (b. Spartanburg, July 13, 1954), who would go on to perform music in his father's style as an adult. Pink Anderson died in Spartanburg on October 12, 1974. DAVID NELSON

Bastin, Bruce. *Crying for the Carolines.* London: Studio Vista, 1971.
Smith, Michael B. *Carolina Dreams: The Musical Legacy of Upstate South Carolina.* Beverly Hills, Calif.: Marshall Tucker Entertainment, 1997.

Anderson College. Anderson College is a liberal arts college affiliated with the South Carolina Baptist Convention (SCBC). Its roots can be traced to a movement among leading citizens of Anderson to raise funds for the establishment of a women's college. After $100,000 and a thirty-two acre site were secured, the money and land were offered to several denominations with the proviso that they be used to operate a Christian college. The offer was accepted by the SCBC meeting in Laurens in December 1910. Trustees were selected and a charter was granted by the state on February 14, 1911, the date regularly celebrated as Founders Day.

Classes were first offered in the fall of 1912, and bachelor's degrees were offered to women until 1930. In January 1928 Dr. Annie Dove Denmark became president, the first woman to serve as a college president in South Carolina. In the fall of 1930, after a period of financial difficulties, she led the college to change its mission, and it became the first junior college in South Carolina. In 1931 men were admitted as day students only, but over time the college became fully coeducational.

In the 1950s the college again experienced financial difficulty, and the Baptist Convention considered closing it. After an increase in enrollment and financial support, and the receipt of full accreditation in 1959, the convention meeting of 1960 lifted its probation and allowed the college to borrow funds to expand.

Anderson College began offering upper-level undergraduate classes in 1991 and in 1993 again awarded bachelor's degrees. With an enrollment of approximately one thousand students in 2001, the college offered degrees in a range of fields and participated in National Collegiate Athletic Association athletic competition. Its purpose remains "to provide, within a Christian community, a quality liberal arts education for a diverse student body." STUART R. SPRAGUE

Hester, Hubert I. *They That Wait: A History of Anderson College.* Anderson, S.C.: Anderson College, 1969.
King, Joe M. *A History of South Carolina Baptists.* Columbia: General Board of the South Carolina Baptist Convention, 1964.

Anderson County (718 sq. miles; 2000 pop. 165,740). Colonel Robert Anderson was a popular Revolutionary War veteran who served with General Andrew Pickens and who subsequently had three South Carolina places named for him. The first was a briefly prosperous river town named Andersonville, then followed Anderson District and the town of Anderson.

Due to population increases in the South Carolina upstate during the early 1800s, the General Assembly in 1826 divided the large district of Pendleton into two smaller districts: Anderson and Pickens. The town of Pendleton continued for many years as the largest town in Anderson District, larger even than the new courthouse seat. There had been disagreements over just where the new courthouse would be situated, and courts continued to be held in Pendleton for several years.

Antebellum Anderson District was dominated by small farms, which grew grains, raised livestock, and produced increasing amounts of cotton. Plantation agriculture reached Anderson District as well, but not to the degree found in the lower portions of the state. By 1830 twenty-five percent of the district's population was slaves. Transportation improvements brought more substantial change both before and after the Civil War. The Greenville and Columbia Railroad arrived in the mid-1850s, spurring the creation of the new towns of Belton, Honea Path, and Williamston. Later in the century, the towns of Iva and Starr came into being along the line of the Savannah Valley Railroad from Augusta, Georgia.

Industrial development in Anderson County began in earnest in the decades following the Civil War, and gradually replaced agriculture as the foundation of the county economy. Several textile mills commenced operations in the 1870s, although one, the Pendleton Manufacturing Company, had started in 1838. Piedmont, which originated as Garrison Shoals on the Saluda River, opened its first mill in 1876. Downstream on the Saluda River, the first of four mills belonging to the Pelzer Manufacturing Company began in 1881. Over the next few years, cotton mills developed in Anderson, Belton, Honea Path, Iva, and Williamston.

By 1920 Anderson County had nineteen textile mills, trailing only Spartanburg and Greenville. The county also had eight cottonseed oil mills, two fertilizer factories, two machine and foundry companies, and 6,086 automobiles (only Greenville County had more). Despite the industrial boom, "farm to market" roads were improved as well, as there were 8,910 farms in Anderson, the most in the state and nearly 400 more than in second-place Orangeburg County. More than eighty percent of the county remained in farmland, with cotton, corn, oats, and wheat as the primary crops.

Government contracts helped the Anderson County textile industry thrive during World War II. But by the 1990s, foreign competition and decreasing demand had taken its toll on county textile mills, forcing many to cease operation. However, over the same period, diversification helped maintain a healthy manufacturing base. Owens Corning Fiberglass opened a sizable manufacturing facility south of the city of Anderson in 1950, taking advantage of natural gas and ample water supplied to produce its glass-woven products. Industrial growth in Anderson has been among the highest in the nation. Major firms at the start of the twenty-first century included four Milliken and Company plants, two Michelin Tire Corporation plants, Robert Bosch automotive components, BASF Fibers Division, Electrolux Company, several auto-parts-related firms, and a Santee Cooper electric plant. The county also contained twenty-two foreign firms from Canada, Western Europe, and Japan, which were recruited by an energetic county development board that stressed the quality of Anderson County's labor force.

The county's geography altered in the 1960s when the U.S. Army Corps of Engineers completed the Hartwell Dam and Reservoir at a cost $104 million to provide electricity, flood control, and recreation. Located on the Savannah River and its tributaries, the reservoir covers 56,000 acres and has a 960-mile shoreline. The lake brought changes. Land values soared, fine homes were built, and recreation and tourism added millions of dollars to the economy. Lake Hartwell, historic Pendleton, and the Anderson Jockey Lot and Farmers Market became major tourist attractions, thanks in large measure to the access created by the thirty-seven miles of Interstate 85 that cut through the county.

In June 2000 the National Civic League selected Anderson County as one of its ten "All-American" communities. Highlighted projects included the Hanna-Westside Extension Campus, a career center established in Anderson School District Five; the Alliance for a Healthy Future, an $11.5 capital campaign involving six nonprofit agencies; and the Anderson Sports and Entertainment Center, a complex of athletic fields, outdoor theater, and recreation facilities surrounding the Civic Center of Anderson. The county used the theme "Making News, Making Progress." HURLEY E. BADDERS

Anderson County Tricentennial Committee. *Anderson County Honors the State of South Carolina on Her 300th Birthday: Souvenir Program.* Anderson, S.C.: Anderson County Tricentennial Committee, 1970.

Badders, Hurley E. *Anderson County: A Pictorial History.* Norfolk, Va.: Donning, 1999.

Dickson, Frank. *Journeys into the Past.* Anderson, S.C.: Dickson, 1975.

Vandiver, Louise Ayer. *Vandiver's History of Anderson County.* Rev. ed. Anderson, S.C.: R. M. Smith, 1970.

Anderson Independent-Mail (2003 circulation: 38,223 daily and 43,654 Sunday). The *Anderson Independent-Mail,* serving numerous counties in northeastern Georgia and northwestern South Carolina, draws its history from several publications. The first was founded in 1899 as the *Anderson Daily Mail.* The editor and publisher, G. Pierce Browne, also published the *People's Advocate* beginning in 1890. The *Daily Mail* published continuously until merging with the *Anderson Independent* in 1981.

The *Anderson Independent* also figures in the *Independent-Mail's* history. The newspaper was first published in 1924 with Wilton E. Hall serving as editor and publisher. This paper was merged with the *Anderson Daily Tribune* in 1925 to create the *Anderson Independent-Tribune.* Hall purchased the *Daily Mail* in 1930 but continued to publish the two newspapers separately, the *Daily Mail* as an afternoon paper and the *Independent-Tribune* as a morning newspaper. In 1950 the *Independent-Tribune* reverted to the name of *Independent.*

Hall sold these newspapers to Harte-Hanks, Inc., of San Antonio in 1972. In 1981 the two newspapers were formally merged as the *Anderson Independent-Mail.* The newspaper stopped publishing an afternoon edition two years later but continues to publish multiple editions for readers in Georgia and South Carolina. The newspaper became the first in the state to publish daily on the Internet in 1995.

Ownership changed hands again when the F. W. Scripps Company, based in Cincinnati, purchased the newspaper from Harte-Hanks in October 1997. AARON W. MARRS

McNeely, Patricia G. *The Palmetto Press: The History of South Carolina's Newspapers and the Press Association.* Columbia: South Carolina Press Association, 1998.

Anderson Motor Car Company. In 1915 John Gary Anderson, owner of the Rock Hill Buggy Company, realized that the era of horse-drawn transportation was coming to an end. Rock Hill Buggy sales dropped by more than seventy percent that year, and Anderson began converting his buggy factory to the production of automobiles. He traveled to Detroit to see how automobile factories were organized. He also hired Joseph Anglada, an automotive engineer, to design six automobiles that were displayed in the Anderson Motor Company's new showroom in Rock Hill in January 1916. Anderson

During its eight years of operation, the Anderson Motor Car Company proudly advertised that it was the sixth largest automobile plant in the South. Courtesy, Lake County Discovery Museum / Curt Teich Postcard Archives

promised Rock Hill that he would turn the town into the "Detroit of the South."

The first models were a six-passenger touring car and a three-passenger roadster. The base price for the first Anderson model was $1,250. Most of the parts, such as the transmission and engine, came from northern suppliers. Anderson assembled the parts at his factory and, using his experience in the buggy business, constructed the frame and bodies.

At first demand for Anderson's automobiles was brisk. Orders came in from across the nation. Dealerships appeared in Atlanta, Charlotte, Cleveland, Detroit, Boston, and New York City. Anderson even established dealerships in England, China, and Australia. But the demand for automobiles diminished during World War I, and the company survived by building trailers for the federal government. Demand increased after the war, but Anderson's vehicles cost too much for most consumers. Eventually, with increased competition from companies such as Ford and General Motors, Anderson lowered the price of his automobiles and introduced a new model, the Aluminum Light Six, in hopes of boosting sales. The effort failed, and Anderson ceased manufacturing automobiles in 1924. The company's assets were auctioned off in 1926. During its existence, Anderson Motor Car Company built an estimated five to six thousand automobiles, one of which survives in the collections of the South Carolina State Museum. CRAIG S. PASCOE

Anderson, John Gary. *Autobiography: John Gary Anderson 1861–1937.* 2d ed. Spartanburg, S.C.: Reprint Company, 1997.

Pascoe, Craig S. "Manufacturing a New South: The Business Biography of John Gary Anderson." Ph.D. diss., University of Tennessee, 1998.

Andrews (Georgetown County; 2000 pop. 3,068). In 1909 the communities of Harpers and Rosemary merged to create the town of Andrews. Named after Walter Henry Andrews (1873–1935), a Georgetown businessman and a prime mover behind the merger, the town grew rapidly. One year after incorporation, Andrews had a population of 95, and ten years later its population stood at 1,968. The town thrived in the 1920s, due in large part to the Seaboard Airline Railway Company railroad shops and the logging operations of the Atlantic Coast Lumber Company. Andrews quickly acquired a water system and electric plants. Along with its shops and lumber mill, it boasted three tobacco warehouses, a woodworking plant, and a cotton gin.

In 1929 the boom in Andrews quickly went bust when the railroad relocated its repair shops to North Carolina and some seven hundred people left town. While the loss of the railroad workers hurt the town, it was the closing of the lumber mill that plunged Andrews into the depths of the Great Depression. When the Atlantic Coast Lumber Company ceased logging operations in 1932, over fifteen hundred people lost jobs. Additional business closings followed, and the place once known as the fastest growing town for its age in the United States filed for bankruptcy.

The Depression hit both Andrews and Georgetown County hard. Through the assistance of the federal Reconstruction Finance Corporation, the county received relief funds totaling $19,000 in October 1933. The money put 4,200 men to work repairing roads and building bridges for 50¢ a day. By 1936 the wealth of timber around Andrews began to attract new lumber businesses. With the outbreak of World War II, demand for wood products soared and companies such as International Paper, the Andrews Veneer and Lumber Company, the Brooks Veneer Company, and the Santee Pine Company dominated the Andrews economy.

At the end of World War II, citizens created the Andrews Development Board in an attempt to lure new business and create new jobs. Their efforts paid off when Oneita Industries opened a knitting mill in 1958. Over the next several decades, although timber-related jobs remained a significant part of the economy, Andrews became home to textile, steel, and wire manufacturers and chemical companies.

In the 1990s, while the area continued to have high unemployment and underemployment, the town again committed itself to providing new opportunities. In 1993 Andrews joined other communities in the South Carolina Downtown Development Corporation to revitalize the downtown area. In 1996 the town held the first Andrews Gospel Music & Storytelling Festival, which the Southeast Tourism Society included among their "Top Twenty Events in the Southeast." In 2000 plans for a 950-acre industrial park approached fruition and the community gained a new middle school and a new high school. Throughout this period, the people of Andrews faced the challenge of attracting new industries while struggling to maintain a sense of small town community. RICKIE A. GOOD

Andrews Old Town Hall Museum. *History of Andrews.* N.p., 1998.

Rogers, George C. *The History of Georgetown County, South Carolina.* Columbia: University of South Carolina Press, 1970.

Animals. The rich diversity of the fauna of South Carolina has been of interest to naturalists for more than three hundred years. Early accounts were published by the English naturalist James Petiver in 1705, by John Lawson in 1709, and by Mark Catesby, who produced two large illustrated volumes on the natural history of South Carolina in 1731 and 1743. Stephen Elliott, John Bachman, John E. Holbrook, Edmund Ravenel, and Lewis R. Gibbes were prominent investigators of the natural history of the state in the nineteenth century.

Three physiographic areas lie within the boundaries of South Carolina, the Blue Ridge, Piedmont, and coastal plain provinces. Each has its own characteristic habitats, and each contains certain animals that are adapted to those habitats and do not occur in the other two areas. The Blue Ridge province encompasses the mountainous area of the state in Oconee, Pickens, and Greenville Counties and is typified by steep hillsides, rocky cliff faces, and narrow ravines and valleys cut by small waterways. The Piedmont province extends from the foothills of the mountains to the fall line across the middle of the state. A region of rolling hills and elevated plateaus, it is underlain by crystalline rocks that can be seen in the beds of the Saluda and Broad Rivers near their junction on the fall line at Columbia. More than two hundred years of extensive agricultural activities have driven much of the remaining Piedmont wildlife into forested river bottoms. Largest of the three regions, the coastal plain province descends from the Sandhills along the fall line to the Atlantic seashore through a series of terraces of marine sediments laid down from Cretaceous to Pleistocene time. The narrow belt of arid sand hills along the fall line provides a unique habitat favored by certain species. Typically low and flat in its seaward half, the coastal plain is traversed by dark, slow-moving streams and broad river swamps that afford excellent habitat for many animals.

Vertebrates include mammals, birds, reptiles, amphibians, bony fishes, and sharks and rays. Mammals, reptiles, amphibians, and fishes are year-round inhabitants of the state, but some birds are permanent residents and others are seasonal migrants.

Because of the cool, moist conditions in the Blue Ridge province, more salamanders occur there than in the larger but drier Piedmont area. There are numerous types of salamanders in the region, including blackbelly, mountain dusky, seal, seepage, green, blackchin red, mud, Carolina spring, slimy, southern Appalachian, Jordan's, and Blue Ridge two-lined salamanders. Other amphibians of the mountains are the wood frog and the American toad, which also ranges southward into the northwestern Piedmont. The bog turtle, coal skink, northern water snake, northern ringneck snake, and northern copperhead are the only reptiles that do not occur south of the mountains in South Carolina.

Among the fishes occurring in the rocky streams of the mountains are the brook trout, blacknose dace, spotted sucker, and channel catfish. Formerly occurring throughout the state, the black bear is now restricted almost entirely to the mountains. Other mammals of this region are the smoky and pigmy shrews, Keen's bat, swamp rabbit, woodchuck, chipmunk, deer mouse, eastern wood rat, meadow jumping mouse, and the spotted skunk, which also ranges southward to the Sandhills along the Savannah River drainage. Birds of the Blue Ridge region include the blackpoll, black-throated green, and blackburnian warblers; broad-winged hawk; ruffed grouse; common nighthawk; eastern phoebe; common raven; and rose-breasted grosbeak.

Many of the vertebrates found in the Piedmont also occur in the mountains and coastal plain, but some do not range south of the fall line. Among the reptiles the latter group includes the painted turtle, midland water snake, queen snake, and northern black racer. Piedmont amphibians include the red-spotted newt and the northern dusky, northern red, Webster's slimy, white-spotted slimy, four-toed, and Chamberlain's dwarf salamanders; Fowler's toad; and the upland chorus and green frogs. Fishes confined to Piedmont streams are the bluehead chub and the sandbar, yellowfin, and whitefin shiners. Birds that seem to prefer Piedmont habitats include the killdeer, whippoorwill, horned lark, cliff swallow, and Cape May warbler. The white-footed mouse is a Piedmont mammal, and the muskrat occurs there primarily but has been recorded from the eastern counties on the coastal plain.

The coastal plain, with its many streams and heavily wooded swamplands, is home to many more species of vertebrates than the Piedmont. Fishes of this region include the sailfin, ironcolor, and taillight shiners; banded pigmy, banded, mud, and spotted sunfish; flier; longnose gar; bowfin; eastern mudminnow; chain pickerel; pirate perch; tadpole madtom; swampfish; black-spotted topminnow; swamp darter; and striped bass, a marine fish that ascends the larger rivers to spawn and has been introduced into some of the larger lakes of the state.

Seven kinds of aquatic salamanders occur in the coastal plain: the greater, lesser, and dwarf sirens; two-toed amphiuma; dwarf waterdog; and the central and broken-striped newts. Terrestrial forms include the mole, Mabee's, southern dusky, southern red, rusty mud, many-lined, South Carolina slimy, Atlantic Coast slimy, and flatwoods salamanders. Other amphibian inhabitants of the region are the southern and oak toads; green, pine woods, barking, squirrel, and pine barrens tree frogs; upland, Brimley's, southern, and ornate chorus frogs; and the little grass, southern cricket, pig, river, carpenter, bronze, and Carolina gopher frogs.

Reptiles of the coastal plain include the American alligator; the diamondback terrapin of the coastal salt marshes; the chicken and spotted turtles; Florida cooter; southern fence lizard; eastern, island, and mimic glass lizards; banded, redbelly, and brown water snakes; glossy crayfish, black swamp, pine woods, southern hognose, rainbow, and eastern mud snakes; southern black racer; northern and Florida pine snakes; black and yellow rat snakes; eastern coral snake; eastern cottonmouth; copperhead; and the diamondback rattlesnake.

Waterfowl abound in the waterways and marshes of the coastal plain, among them the pied-billed grebe; common loon; double-crested cormorant; anhinga; American and least bitterns; great and snowy egrets; little blue and tricolor herons; black-crowned and yellow-crowned night herons; white ibis; glossy ibis; wood stork; green-winged teal; black duck; northern pintail; northern shoveler; gadwall; canvasback; black scoter; and hooded merganser. Other avian species include the black vulture; swallow-tailed and Mississippi kites; bald eagle; black rail; clapper rail; purple gallinule; semipalmated plover; American avocet; willet; marbled godwit; semipalmated and least sandpipers; laughing gull; Caspian, royal, sandwich, and least terns; black skimmer; ground dove; yellow-bellied sapsucker; red-cockaded and pileated woodpeckers; marsh wren; blue-gray gnatcatcher; black-throated green warbler; prothonotary warbler; painted bunting; Bachman's, seaside, and song sparrows; bobolink; and the boat-tailed grackle. Along the coast, the brown pelican is a familiar sight.

The mammals occurring only on the coastal plain are the yellow and free-tailed bats; marsh rabbit; cotton mouse; and the eastern wood rat. Although most numerous in the mountains, the black bear is still present in small numbers in the large coastal plain river swamps.

Most of the mammals of South Carolina are found throughout the state. These are the opossum; southeastern, short-tailed, and least shrews; eastern and star-nosed moles; eastern pipistrelle; big brown, silver-haired, red, Seminole, hoary, evening, and big-eared bats; eastern cottontail; gray, flying, and fox squirrels; rice rat; eastern harvest mouse; golden mouse; cotton rat; pine vole; gray fox; raccoon; long-tailed weasel; mink; striped skunk; river otter; bobcat; and white-tailed deer. Formerly extirpated by trappers, the beaver has reestablished itself throughout much of the state. Originally occurring only in the mountains, the red fox was introduced into the rest of the state by hunters. The cougar once occurred throughout South Carolina, but its modern-day presence is questionable, and the few that possibly remain are restricted primarily to the river swamps and bottomlands.

Reptiles that occur throughout all or most of the state include the snapping, musk, eastern box, and mud turtles; eastern river cooter; yellowbelly slider; spiny softshell; green anole; northern fence lizard; ground, five-lined, southeastern five-lived, and broadhead skinks; six-lined racerunner; slender glass lizard; eastern garter, eastern ribbon, brown, redbelly, rough earth, smooth earth, southern ringneck, eastern hognose, worm, scarlet, rough green, northern pine, black rat, and southeastern crowned snakes; eastern coachwhip; eastern, mole, and scarlet kingsnakes; copperhead; and Carolina pigmy and timber rattlesnakes. Several amphibians also are found throughout all or most of the state: the eastern tiger, spotted, marbled, southern two-lined, and southern three-lined salamanders; eastern spadefoot and eastern narrowmouth toads; gray tree frog; spring peeper; bullfrog, and southern leopard frog.

Fishes occurring in all or most of the drainages of the state include the American eel, American shad, gizzard shad, redfin pickerel, golden shiner, eastern silvery minnow, spottail shiner, silver redhorse, white catfish, yellow bullhead, brown bullhead, mosquito fish, black crappie, largemouth bass, warmouth, bluegill, and the yellow perch.

More than one hundred species of birds are found throughout the state either as permanent residents or seasonal migrants. Among them are the great blue heron; wood duck; blue-winged teal; ring-necked duck; bufflehead; turkey vulture; osprey; red-shouldered hawk; American kestrel; peregrine falcon; northern bobwhite; American coot; Wilson's plover; upland sandpiper; Hudsonian god-wit; common snipe; American woodcock; herring gull; mourning dove; yellow-billed cuckoo; barn, screech, great horned, and barred owls; chuck-will's-widow; ruby-throated hummingbird; red-headed woodpecker; downy woodpecker; northern flicker; great crested and scissor-tailed flycatchers; purple martin; bank and barn swallows; blue jay; American crow; Carolina chickadee; white-breasted nuthatch; Carolina wren; golden-crowned kinglet; eastern bluebird; wood thrush; American robin; gray catbird; northern mockingbird; brown thrasher; loggerhead shrike; white-eyed vireo; magnolia, hooded, and yellow-throated warblers; common yel-lowthroat; yellow-breasted chat; northern cardinal; blue grosbeak; indigo bunting; rufous-sided towhee; field, savannah, and house sparrows; red-winged blackbird; eastern meadowlark; brown-headed cowbird; orchard oriole; and American goldfinch.

Several hundred species of marine fishes occur in the coastal waters of South Carolina. Although vertebrates are more noticeable because of their relatively larger size, they are vastly outnumbered by the thousands of species of invertebrate animals that inhabit South Carolina and its seacoast environments. Comprising about ninety-five percent of all living species of animals, invertebrates include insects, spiders, mollusks, worms, sponges, bryozoans, cnidarians, and echinoderms. ALBERT E. SANDERS

"An Account of Animals and Shells Sent from Carolina to Mr. James Petiver, F.R.S." *Philosophical Transactions* [of the Royal Society of London] 24 (1704–1705): 1952–60.

Barnes, Robert D. *Invertebrate Zoology.* 3d. ed. Philadelphia: Saunders, 1974.

Catesby, Mark. *The Natural History of Carolina, Florida, and the Bahamas.* 2 vols. London, 1731–1743.

Conant, Roger, and Joseph T. Collins. *A Field Guide to Reptiles and Amphibians: Eastern and Central North America.* 3d ed. Boston: Houghton Mifflin, 1998.

Golley, Frank B. *South Carolina Mammals.* Charleston, S.C.: Charleston Museum, 1966.

Harrison, Julian R., III, and Sheldon I. Guttman. "A New Species of *Eurycea* (Caudata: Plethodontidae) from North and South Carolina." *Southeastern Naturalist* 2, no. 2 (2003): 159–78.

Lawson, John. *A New Voyage to Carolina.* 1709. Reprint, Chapel Hill: University of North Carolina Press, 1967.

Page, Lawrence M., and Brooks M. Burr. *Field Guide to Freshwater Fishes: North America North of Mexico.* Boston: Houghton Mifflin, 1991.

Post, William, and Sidney A. Gauthreaux. *Status and Distribution of South Carolina Birds.* Charleston, S.C.: Charleston Museum, 1989.

Sanders, Albert E., and William D. Anderson, Jr. *Natural History Investigations in South Carolina from Colonial Times to the Present.* Columbia: University of South Carolina Press, 1999.

Zingmark, Richard G, ed. *An Annotated Checklist of the Biota of the Coastal Zone of South Carolina.* Columbia: University of South Carolina Press, 1978.

Ansel, Martin Frederick (1850–1945). Governor. Martin F. Ansel was born in Charleston on December 12, 1850, the son of German immigrants John Ansel and Frederica Bowers. He received his basic education within the common school system in Walhalla, where the family had moved in 1857. He began to read law in 1868 under the auspices of Columbia attorney James H. Whitner. Admitted to the South Carolina Bar in September 1870, Ansel left his native state and established a law practice in Franklin, North Carolina. In 1876 Ansel returned to South Carolina, relocating to Greenville, where he was among the leading attorneys in the upcountry. On February 21, 1878, Ansel married Ophelia Speight. The couple had two daughters. Three years after Ophelia's death in 1895, Ansel married Addie R. Hollingsworth Harris.

Ansel served Greenville County in the S.C. House of Representatives from 1882 until 1887. In 1888 Ansel was elected solicitor of the Eighth Judicial District, an office he held for thirteen years. In 1902 Ansel made an unsuccessful bid for the gubernatorial nomination in the Democratic Party primary. Although losing to Duncan C. Heyward, Ansel's strong showing convinced supporters that he would be successful in a future election. In 1906 Ansel became the nominee for governor in the Democratic primary. He ran unopposed in the November general election and garnered 30,251 votes in that token contest. He was the first person of German ancestry to occupy the governor's chair in South Carolina.

Inaugurated on January 15, 1907, Ansel held a first term that was most memorable for the abolishment of the controversial state liquor dispensary system by the General Assembly. Although a statewide ban on the sale of alcoholic beverages became law, counties were permitted to exercise the local "option" of retaining dispensaries. It was a notable victory for Ansel, who campaigned as a leading advocate of local option and personally favored prohibition. Ansel also pushed legislators to increase financial support to South Carolina's public schools and place secondary schools under direct state supervision. Other developments during Ansel's governorship included the founding of the Confederate Veterans' Home in Columbia and the creation of the South Carolina Office of Public Health. In addition Ansel successfully urged the establishment of the State Department of Insurance. South Carolina voters approved of Ansel's first term performance. In 1908 his reelection was without opposition in both the primary and general elections. By gaining 61,060 votes in the second contest, Ansel had nearly doubled his previous electoral mandate.

After retiring from office in January 1911, Ansel resumed his private legal practice in Greenville. In 1920 he was elected judge of the Greenville County Court, and he remained an influential figure in state politics until his death on August 23, 1945. MILES S. RICHARDS

Wallace, David Duncan. *The History of South Carolina.* 4 vols. New York: American Historical Society, 1934.

Archdale, John (1642–1717). Proprietor, governor. Born in England in 1642, Archdale was a son of London merchant Thomas Archdale and Mary Nevill. Little is known of his early years, although he possessed an estate in Buckinghamshire and was brought into the Quaker movement in the 1670s. In 1673 he married Ann Cary, a widow, and they had four children. Archdale also helped raise her son, Thomas Cary, who later became a governor of North Carolina.

Archdale was introduced to colonial America by his brother-in-law, Fernando Gorges, who held a claim on the proprietorship of Maine. Arriving in New England in 1664, Archdale spent a year overseeing Gorges's interests. In 1681 Archdale purchased a share in the Carolina proprietorship in trust for his son Thomas Archdale. From 1683 to 1686 he presided as governor of North Carolina when Seth Sothel was absent from the province. In August 1694 Archdale was chosen by his fellow proprietors as governor of the Carolinas, and he arrived in Charleston the following year.

Archdale arrived with broad discretion from the proprietors to settle the factionalism that had crippled earlier efforts to govern South Carolina. In the spirit of reconciliation, Archdale met with leaders from both the antiproprietary and proprietary parties, reorganized the council, and treated the Indians with great kindness. However, his refusal to offer concessions on land, taxation, and self-rule created an impasse similar to that experienced by earlier governors. To make headway, he was obliged to exceed his instructions. With England at war with France, Archdale capitalized on local Francophobia and excluded French Huguenots from the Commons House of Assembly. He also simplified land grant procedures, allowing each grant a rent-free period of five years. Furthermore, quitrents prior to 1695 were forgiven and fees could now be paid in produce, rather than hard money. More importantly, laws passed by the Commons House of Assembly and proprietary deputies in Carolina could not be repealed by London without the consent of the assembly, unless it involved a question of royal prerogative or enumerated proprietary rights. These provisions became known as Archdale's Laws, and although never ratified by the proprietors, they essentially remained in effect for two decades. Having pacified the assembly, Archdale succeeded in passing a spate of legislation, including South Carolina's first comprehensive slave law.

Archdale left for England in 1696, appointing his cousin Joseph Blake as deputy governor. The province was quiet, but the matter of control that had divided the colony since the 1680s was not yet settled. Archdale's healing administration proved only a temporary calm in the turbulent politics of the proprietary era. Archdale never returned to Carolina. He sold his proprietary share to Joseph Blake in 1696, possibly because Lord Craven was unhappy with the concessions that Archdale granted the colony. In 1705 Archdale bought a second share, and after three years, he gave it to his daughter. His exact date of death is unknown, but Archdale was buried on July 4, 1717, at High Wycombe Church in Buckinghamshire, England. LOUIS P. TOWLES

Hood, Henry. *The Public Career of John Archdale, 1642–1717.* Greensboro: North Carolina Friends Society, 1976.

McCrady, Edward. *The History of South Carolina under the Proprietary Government, 1670–1719.* New York: Macmillan, 1897.

Sirmans, M. Eugene. *Colonial South Carolina: A Political History, 1663–1763.* Chapel Hill: University of North Carolina Press, 1966.

Weeks, Stephen B. "John Archdale, and Some of His Descendants." *Magazine of American History* 29 (February 1893): 157–62.

Architecture. The architecture of South Carolina historically has been shaped by cultural and geographic diversity, undulating political and economic fortunes, and an overwhelmingly agrarian landscape. English building traditions were the major influence of the colonial era, although African slaves, Huguenot immigrants, and other cultural groups also made important contributions. The subtropical climate and wealth created by plantation agriculture led to the emergence of distinctive forms and, in some cases, exceptionally sophisticated buildings. At the same time, the dominant theme in South Carolina architecture has always been the vernacular: common buildings designed to serve utilitarian purposes and lacking significant stylistic ornamentation. In the decades after the Civil War, the growth of inland towns and cities brought greater variety to the built environment, and increasing integration with the national economy gave prevailing trends in style and design a greater influence on communities statewide. Recent decades have been dominated by suburban sprawl and the architecture of mass retailing, the rise of vacation resorts and retirement communities in the lowcountry, and the persistence of regionally distinctive building traditions.

Cultural diversity was central to the architectural development of early Charleston, where the population included English immigrants, French Protestants, and Barbadians as well as smaller numbers of Scots, Sephardic Jews, and Germans. Commingled in the built environment were building traditions and stylistic preferences that arrived with each of these groups. Enslaved Africans made contributions of indeterminable value by imparting design influences from their own cultural roots and by providing the vast majority of the labor needed for production of building materials and construction. The combined influence of these cultural groups provided the basis for the architecturally distinctive environment that took shape in eighteenth-century Charleston.

The city's traditional Georgian architecture reached full maturity in the rebuilding campaign that followed the devastating fire of 1740. By about 1760 Charleston was among the wealthiest cities in the English colonies and architecturally one of the most sophisticated. Construction of major buildings such as St. Michael's Church (1752–1761), the Statehouse (1753–1760), and the Exchange and Custom House (1767–1771) and a residential building boom signified its rising status. The emergence of the famed Charleston "single house" as a distinct building type occurred during the mid-eighteenth century. Built on a rectangular plan with its narrow side set directly against the street, the single house was a creative response to the scarcity of space in the city, and its side piazzas and room layout attempted to mitigate the oppressive lowcountry heat by allowing summer breezes to circulate through the main living spaces.

Charleston's importance as a center of the building trades increased in the early national period, when the planter-merchant elite enjoyed renewed wealth from exports of rice and Sea Island cotton. The most opulent surviving residences from the early nineteenth century include the Joseph Manigault House (ca. 1803), the Nathaniel Russell House (ca. 1808), the Patrick Duncan House (ca. 1802–1816; used as Ashley Hall school since 1909), and the Aiken-Rhett House (ca. 1818). Construction of public and commercial buildings dominated later decades. The trend began with the Robert Mills–designed Fireproof Building (1822–1827) and gained strength after the economic doldrums of the late 1820s and the nullification crisis passed. The Meeting Street Theatre (1835–1837); Market Hall (1840–1841); and two Greek Revival–style buildings, the Charleston Hotel (1838–1839) and Hibernian Hall (1839–1841), were especially significant.

The architecture of smaller port towns such as Beaufort and Georgetown differed from that in the coastal cities of Charleston and Savannah. With freestanding homes on large lots and loosely ordered business districts, these towns were less urban in character. Georgian, Federal, and Greek Revival influences predominated. Georgetown's best-known landmarks include Prince George Winyah Episcopal Church (1742–1746), the Market Building (1842), and Winyah Indigo Society Hall (1857). Among the highlights of Beaufort's exceptionally rich built environment are the Federal-style John Mark Verdier House (ca. 1786); Marshlands (ca. 1814), a frame house set on an English basement that displays a combination of Federal and West Indian influences; and Greek Revival residences such as the Dr. John A. Johnson House (ca. 1850) and the Edward Means House (ca. 1853). Tabby, a cement made of lime, sand, and oyster shells, was used extensively in Beaufort and the surrounding area in the eighteenth and early nineteenth centuries. Important examples of tabby construction include the Beaufort Arsenal (1795; rebuilt 1852), the Elizabeth Barnwell-Gogh

House (ca. 1780), and the Thomas Fuller House (ca. 1786; also known as the Tabby Manse).

In contrast to the coastal plain, the architecture of the upstate reflected its frontier setting. Even fairly large plantation houses often lacked refinement. Ornamentation, if present at all, was limited to fireplace mantles, door and window surrounds, and entry halls. Most yeoman farmers lived in small, one- or two-room houses of log or frame construction. Saddlebags, double-pen, and hall-and-parlor floor plans were common, and scattered examples of dogtrot houses—typically two rooms built around an open central passageway—could be found in the Midlands, Appalachian foothills, and upper Savannah River Valley. Log construction remained common in the upstate well into the nineteenth century.

The building form most closely identified with upstate plantations is commonly known as the Carolina farmhouse or I-house. Two stories tall with a lateral-gable roof, houses of this type usually have a central hall plan and are two rooms wide and one room deep. The vast majority of those built in South Carolina have exterior end chimneys. The form derives from English antecedents and became common in the tidewater South after the Revolutionary War. Over time, owners often added decorative embellishments and rearward additions. Although far less ubiquitous today than in the nineteenth century, examples of the type are still common on the rolling landscape of the upstate.

The Greek Revival, which appeared in Charleston and Columbia in the 1820s and remained popular until the Civil War, was the dominant style of the late antebellum period. Archetypal domestic examples include Milford (1839) near Pinewood; Magnolia (1855) near Eastover; the Chisolm-Alston House (1834–1836) and the Robert William Roper House (1838–1839) in Charleston; and the Rankin-Harwell House (1857; also known as the Columns) near Mars Bluff. The influence of the Greek Revival also extended to more modest dwellings. Throughout the Pee Dee and in cotton-prosperous upstate counties such as Laurens and Union, countless examples of what became an archetypal form—a raised cottage, one or one-and-a-half stories in height, with a lateral-gable roof and a projecting central portico with columns—demonstrated the popularity of the style. The best-known examples of this type are Bonnie Shade (ca. 1854) in Florence and two houses in Laurens: the Thomas Badgett House (built before 1846) and the Allen Dial House (ca. 1855).

The architecture of slavery was a powerful presence in the South Carolina countryside. Providing shelter for the number of slaves needed to work a large plantation required extensive housing. Rows of slave cabins—often called the "slave street"—stood in the rear or to the side of the planter's residence. The quality and type of slave housing varied greatly. One-room structures of log, earthfast, or frame construction were most prevalent, and saddlebag houses and other double-pen forms with central chimneys were also fairly common. Wattle-and-daub walls, dirt floors, mud-and-stick chimneys, and crowded conditions were the norm. Only on large plantations did owners sometimes provide better quality housing, occasionally with modest decorative features that mirrored the architectural style of the plantation house. For many slaves, living conditions improved only marginally after emancipation, and the housing occupied by white tenants and sharecroppers, although better than that of their black counterparts, still left much to be desired.

The construction of two monumental public buildings, the new state capitol in Columbia and the Custom House in Charleston, drew national attention during the 1850s. Work on the new state capitol began in 1855 under the direction of John R. Niernsee, whose design melded classicism and monumentality within the central block-with-wings form that by then had become virtually standard for state capitol buildings. The Civil War halted construction in 1862. Although hastily fitted with a temporary roof in 1867, the building was not fully completed for another forty years and stood as a grim reminder of the war's costs. Construction of the Custom House began in 1849. The Boston architect Ammi B. Young prepared the original plans, which called for a cruciform building finished in granite with four Roman Corinthian porticos and a Renaissance dome. Edward B. White supervised construction. The project proceeded at a steady pace in the early 1850s before suffering delays and cost overruns, and rising sectional tensions eventually halted construction. In 1859 Congress did not pass an appropriation to continue construction, and, like the new state capitol in Columbia, the Custom House became a symbol of unrealized civic ambitions. The building was finally completed in 1879 without the planned dome and side porticos.

The emergence of upstate towns and cities in the 1880s and 1890s marked a new phase of building that reflected the development of transportation connections and commercial ties to regional and national markets. Railroad depots, trackside warehouses, and main street commercial buildings were central to the economy of the New South and symbolized the prevailing spirit of commerce and progress. Union stations built in major cities served as civic gateways to their communities and often featured flamboyant Romanesque Revival or Italianate styling. Small town depots often displayed Stick-style accents. Commercial buildings featured pressed metal, cast stone, and terra cotta ornamentation. Italianate, Romanesque, and Victorian influences were common.

The growth of the upstate was closely tied to the development of the textile industry. Most of the mills built in antebellum South Carolina were small brick buildings, generally three or four stories tall and large enough to accommodate roughly five thousand spindles. By contrast, the factory buildings needed for the mills of the New South were considerably larger. In 1880 the typical South Carolina mill still had fewer than 6,000 spindles, but by 1910 that number had increased to more than 25,000. South Carolina firms such as Lockwood, Greene and Company, J. E. Sirrine, and W. B. Smith Whaley became leaders in mill design and engineering.

Mill villages were central to the architectural transformation of the upstate. Worker housing was adapted from common vernacular types. Double-pen and gable-wing cottages and duplexes were especially common. Although simple and outfitted with few amenities, mill housing represented an improvement in living conditions for families from rural areas. The layout of early villages tended to be informal, but systematic planning became the norm after about 1880. Grid street patterns remained prevalent until after the turn of the century, when curvilinear streets inspired by contemporary trends in suburban design became fashionable. In the early twentieth century textile firms added landscaping, better-quality housing, and community buildings to make mill village life more appealing. No matter what the layout and amenities, however, a well-defined sense of social and corporate order was evident in the built environment. The mill was the focal point of the community, and buildings with a civic role such as churches, the mill store, and the community center were prominently placed. The large, stylish houses occupied by mill managers and their families held commanding locations. Worker housing occupied the lowest rung of the ladder.

As the textile boom gained strength, the emergence of the southern middle class created unprecedented demand for housing in towns and cities, sparking a wave of residential construction that began in the 1880s and gained strength in later decades. Home buyers favored nationally popular styles and folk housing forms ornamented with Queen Anne and Neoclassical details. New construction initially occurred on the periphery of town centers and spread outward into undeveloped areas. Bungalows and Craftsman-style houses were popular in suburban neighborhoods, and upscale developments also included houses designed in the Neoclassical, Colonial Revival, and Tudor Revival styles.

The expansion of public services in the late nineteenth and early twentieth centuries resulted in the construction of new public and institutional buildings, including courthouses, city halls, post offices, and libraries. Neoclassicism dominated public architecture in the New South. Architects such as William Augustus Edwards, who designed courthouses in nine South Carolina counties, employed monumental classical orders and rusticated stonework to convey a sense of civic authority. James Burwell Urquhart, Charles Coker Wilson, and James J. Baldwin produced Neoclassical designs for public schools and buildings on college and university campuses. Italianate and Romanesque influences were also popular before about 1900. Clemson University, Winthrop College, and Coker College were among the educational institutions that grew significantly during the era.

The architecture of black colleges and universities fit squarely within a similar stylistic idiom. Most of the state's historically black colleges and universities, including Allen, Voorhees, and South Carolina State, trace their beginnings to the 1880s and 1890s. Black architects and builders played a leading role in their design and construction, and students enrolled in mechanical arts classes often provided labor for construction. William Wilson Cooke, a Greenville native who in 1907 became the first African American to serve as a senior architectural designer in the U.S. Supervising Architect's Office, designed Lee Library (1898) and Tingley Memorial Hall (1908) at Claflin College. Miller F. Whittaker designed several buildings at South Carolina State and later served as its president.

In the twentieth century, the combined influence of several factors produced dramatic changes in South Carolina architecture. Federal programs were especially important. During the New Deal, the Works Progress Administration (WPA) erected new schools, post offices, and courthouses in communities statewide, and the Civilian Conservation Corps (CCC) built seventeen state parks with rustic-style architecture and naturalistic landscape features. Defense spending during World War II resulted in the expansion of existing facilities such as Fort Jackson and Parris Island and the creation of Naval Air Station Beaufort and Naval Weapons Station Charleston. The architecture of the cold war arrived in the early 1950s with the construction of the Savannah River Plant, a mammoth facility near Aiken designed to produce fuel for nuclear weapons.

In the decades after World War II, a surge of suburban and exurban development reshaped the architecture and landscape of South Carolina. The postwar housing boom added substantial numbers of new residential units to many communities, especially larger cities such as Columbia and Charleston, and introduced modern house forms such as the ranch and split-level. As residential subdivisions developed along municipal perimeters, retail stores abandoned traditional Main Street locations in favor of suburban shopping centers and strip malls. Adding to urban and suburban growth were changes made possible by the civil rights revolution and the rise of the Sunbelt South. The collapse of Jim Crow and rising wages in southeastern cities opened up the floodgates for an influx of population from other parts of the country that contributed to housing demand and new business development. Starting in the mid-1980s, the proliferation of so-called "big box" retail stores and the acceleration of commercial and residential development fueled the phenomenon known as urban sprawl, which dramatically changed the appearance of communities throughout the state.

Contemporary architectural design reflects the tensions present in South Carolina's changing society. The glass and concrete office towers that dominate the skylines of Columbia and Greenville stand in stark contrast to the spirit of traditionalism that has been the hallmark of southern architecture for more than three centuries. In the lowcountry, the juxtaposition between former rice plantations and the architecture of the modern tourist economy, with its beachfront hotels, waterfront condominiums, and golf-course housing developments, is equally striking. Paradoxes evident in the present-day built environment reflect a deeply rooted tendency to embrace change in the name of "progress" while holding fast to old identities. The result is a rich and varied legacy that encompasses the vernacular and the high style, the rustic and the urbane, the conservative and the avant-garde. DANIEL J. VIVIAN

Bryan, John M. *Creating the South Carolina State House.* Columbia: University of South Carolina Press, 1999.

Lane, Mills. *Architecture of the Old South: South Carolina.* Savannah, Ga.: Beehive, 1984.

Lounsbury, Carl. *From Statehouse to Courthouse: An Architectural History of South Carolina's Colonial Capitol and Charleston County Courthouse.* Columbia: University of South Carolina Press, 2001.

Poston, Jonathan H. *The Buildings of Charleston: A Guide to the City's Architecture.* Columbia: University of South Carolina Press, 1997.

Ravenel, Beatrice St. Julien. *Architects of Charleston.* 1945. Reprint, Columbia: University of South Carolina Press, 1992.

Severens, Kenneth. *Charleston Antebellum Architecture and Civic Destiny.* Knoxville: University of Tennessee Press, 1988.

Wells, John E., and Robert E. Dalton. *The South Carolina Architects, 1885–1935: A Biographical Directory.* Richmond, Va.: New South Architectural Press, 1992.

Art. Throughout the history of South Carolina, art has reflected the tastes and aspirations of its citizenry. Beginning in the 1920s, art has had a significant economic impact by virtue of its role in fostering tourism and later through museums dedicated to art.

The earliest artists in the state came to document native people, flora, and fauna. Jacques Le Moyne de Morgues made watercolors of coastal settlements following a 1564 expedition; these were converted by Theodor deBry into engravings that were widely circulated abroad. Similarly, the purpose of Mark Catesby's work was to disseminate visual and textual information about the bird and plant life of the Southeast. Hand-colored engravings illustrate his *Natural History of Carolina, Florida, and the Bahamas.* Maps and topographical prints, such as W. H. Toms's 1739 *Prospect of Charles Town,* were also used to promote commerce and settlement.

Reflecting the conservative taste of early residents and the influence of the mother country, portraiture was the dominant art form throughout the eighteenth century and well into the next. Charleston was home to many portraitists, beginning with Henrietta Dering Johnston, this country's first professional woman artist and first pastellist. Jeremiah Theus painted the planters and merchants of the pre-Revolutionary era, providing a visual social registry of the period. In addition to patronizing resident artists, individuals commissioned portraits from such itinerants as the stylish Englishman John Wollaston, who came to Charleston in 1765, and Henry Benbridge, who was in Charleston from 1772 to 1784. Miniaturists—artists who painted likenesses in watercolor on ivory mounted in lockets or small leather cases—were popular from the mid-eighteenth century until the 1850s, when their work was largely supplanted by the invention of photography. Edward Green Malbone, whose Charleston portraits are acclaimed as his best, and Charles Fraser were the most renowned miniature portrait painters working in South Carolina.

Early South Carolinians also patronized artists while abroad or in Philadelphia and New York. Members of the Middleton family sat for the highly regarded royal painter Benjamin West. Charleston merchant Miles Brewton had his portrait done by Sir Joshua Reynolds in London, and the planter Ralph Izard and his wife were painted by John Singleton Copley in Rome. Many military figures and statesmen, such as Colonel William Moultrie and William Loughton Smith, had their portraits painted by the prominent artists of the day, Charles Willson Peale and Gilbert Stuart. The city fathers of Charleston commissioned nationally known artists to paint significant historical figures: John Trumbull painted George Washington in 1792; Samuel F. B. Morse did the same for James Monroe in 1819; and George Healy painted a posthumous likeness of John C. Calhoun in 1850. These portraits and others hang in Charleston City Hall. Thomas Sully of Philadelphia, perhaps because of his boyhood connections to Charleston and several sojourns there in the 1840s, was a favorite portraitist among South Carolinians throughout the antebellum period.

In the Midlands, the upstate, and on plantations, portraiture dominated. The demand was often filled by itinerants, and artists such as William Harrison Scarborough, James De Veaux, and William Kennedy Barclay developed long lists of clients across the state. With the exception of small views of lowcountry plantations by Thomas Coram and Charles Fraser, an indigenous landscape tradition did not develop until much later. Several native artists who were disinclined toward portraiture, including Washington Allston and Louis Rémy Mignot, pursued their art outside the confines of their native state. Others sustained themselves by painting portraits, but also developed other specialties. Thomas Wightman emerged as the South's preeminent painter of fruit still lifes, and Fraser diversified his production by rendering "fancy pieces" and landscapes of other locales derived from prints.

With a few exceptions, painting dominated over sculpture in the history of art in South Carolina. Two notable examples of public sculpture in Charleston are the larger-than-life-size 1770 statue of William Pitt, Earl of Chatham, by Joseph Wilton, which at one time stood at the intersection of Broad and Meeting Streets, and the marble statue of John C. Calhoun by Hiram Powers, which graced City Hall until its destruction in the Civil War. In Columbia ambitious pedimental sculptures designed by Henry Kirke Brown for the State House were destroyed when the capital was burned in 1865.

In general the taste of South Carolinians has been consistently conservative. Many aspiring collectors acquired fine furniture and decorative arts while abroad and preferred European paintings—often copies after old masters—over work created locally. Subjects ranged from history and portraiture to genre and religion. Significant collectors of this sort included in Charleston the Middletons, the Manigaults, Ralph Izard, Joseph Allen Smith, and Governor William Aiken; in Columbia, Robert Gibbes and John Preston; and at Redcliffe Plantation, James Henry Hammond.

For the most part art was a private matter, even though in the 1790s the press called for the establishment of an art gallery. In 1821 the South Carolina Academy of Fine Arts was organized. It held annual exhibitions of loaned objects and work by local artists but soon suffered from apathy and lack of financial support. Beginning in 1849 the South Carolina Institute hosted annual fairs where examples of fine and mechanical art were displayed side by side. In Charleston, South Carolina Society Hall and the Apprentice's Library Society were venues for art exhibitions. At the former, in 1857, a career survey of Fraser's work was held featuring 319 objects, and at the latter, the emerging collection of the newly founded (1857) Carolina Art Association was on view when the library's building was consumed by the fire of 1861.

The Civil War and Reconstruction were not conducive to furthering art. Charleston native William Aiken Walker was one of the few artists to make a living during the time, supporting himself with stereotypical paintings of former slaves that he sold at modest prices across the South.

With the advent of the twentieth century, art slowly gained more prominence. The South Carolina West Indian Exposition of 1901–1902 featured local and imported art in several of its exhibition halls. Across the state women assumed leadership roles, in part because a career in art was more genteel than office work and also because of their desire to foster an appreciation for culture and for the past. In Charleston artists along with preservationists and writers brought national attention at a time when the city was seeking economic renewal. Known as the Charleston Renaissance, this grassroots movement reshaped the destiny of the lowcountry by nurturing the nascent tourist industry. Painters and printmakers created picturesque images that became widely circulated through exhibitions, publications, and as souvenirs for tourists. The artists who contributed most to this phenomenon were Alice Ravenel Huger Smith, Elizabeth O'Neill Verner, Anna Heyward Taylor, and Alfred Hutty.

Much of the art created during the period was scenic—literally, in terms of the landscape, which in many areas was being transformed; and more generically in figurative subjects that embraced local color. African American artist Edwin Harleston painted landscapes, but his success lay in portraiture. After studying at the prestigious Boston Museum School, he returned to Charleston where he rendered sensitive portraits of other middle-class African Americans.

At the same time, artists in other locations created art that celebrated the state's attributes. Prints were the preferred medium for many, reflecting the nationwide revival of etching and the emerging interest in lithography. In Sumter, Elizabeth White produced delicately etched landscapes that contrast sharply with the atmospheric and moody etchings of the Kingstree artist James Cooper. Margaret Law of Spartanburg tended to use lithography, perhaps because of its closeness to drawing, and many of her prints were renditions of her drawings or paintings.

In addition to making their own art, many of the women artists were actively involved in art organizations. At the Gibbes Art Gallery, Alice Smith helped to organize exhibitions, while in Greenville, Margaret Moore Walker spearheaded the founding in 1935 of the Fine Arts League, which showcased the work of area artists. Caroline Guignard, a native of Columbia who was active in the local art association, participated with Verner in the Southern States Art League. Founded in Charleston in 1921, the league sought to foster an appreciation for the fine arts throughout the region.

Until midcentury the Gibbes Art Gallery was the state's only art museum. It was the home, too, of the Charleston Sketch Club, a group that held critiques and hosted out-of-town speakers and, beginning in the 1930s, mounted an annual sidewalk sale. Other parts of the state were without permanent facilities for art, although a precocious Arts and Crafts Club was founded in Spartanburg in 1907. Under the leadership of Margaret Law and Josephine Sibley Couper, the group purchased choice works by Robert Henri and Birge Harrison. In Columbia the Art Association hosted displays, lectures, and concerts in private homes.

At the University of South Carolina, Catherine B. Heyward founded an art program in the mid-1920s, and James Cooper was among the first to receive an art certificate in 1925. Female colleges, in general, were more disposed to teaching art. In 1924 August Cook arrived from Philadelphia to teach art at Converse College in Spartanburg and remained as department head for more than four decades. In the mid-1910s, for a period of about five months, Georgia O'Keeffe taught art classes at Columbia College. Although she enjoyed the climate and liked her students, O'Keeffe felt desperately isolated.

Two South Carolinians, Laura Glenn Douglas from Winnsboro and William H. Johnson of Florence, studied in New York and Europe. Douglas ultimately discarded modernism in favor of a more traditional approach, perhaps to gain acceptance in her native state. Johnson, after almost a decade abroad, settled in New York, taught in Harlem, and developed a distinctive vision that embraced modernism and his own African roots.

In the 1930s federally sponsored projects included community art galleries in Greenville and in Columbia, the transformation of the derelict Planters Hotel in Charleston into the Dock Street Theatre, and murals or sculptures for sixteen federal buildings under the auspices of the U.S. Treasury Department's Section of Fine Arts. In South Carolina none of the commissions were awarded to local artists. Why this was the case remains unclear. Many never applied, perhaps due to a deep-seated resistance to government control. Women artists may have felt it was unseemly to seek public commissions. Most were accustomed to working on a small scale that was aesthetically and technically distinct from the scale of mural work.

Photography was also an important aspect of the New Deal. Because of its agrarian character and overwhelming poverty, the South was a favored destination for Farm Security Administration (FSA) photographers, who rarely glorified what they encountered. Walker Evans concentrated on modest farm buildings and churches in disrepair, while Marion Post Wolcott focused her lens on farmers and dockworkers, on poor blacks and poor whites, at work and at leisure. In contrast Doris Ulmann, who was not affiliated with the FSA, used the medium more pictorially. Avoiding harsh realities, Ulmann composed softly focused images of rural blacks in the same romantic way that Charleston artists rendered flower vendors.

In the 1950s another generation of artists stepped forward, more independent of tradition and more expansive than their forebears. Many were instrumental in art education. William Halsey, a native of Charleston, attended school in Boston, spent years working in Mexico, and in the early 1950s toyed with the idea of moving to New York. Instead he returned home and created heavily textured collages and assemblages that reflect his environment. He taught at the Gibbes School with his wife Corrie McCallum, and was artist in residence at the College of Charleston for twenty years.

At the University of South Carolina, the stature of the art department grew in the 1940s with the addition of Augusta Witkowsky, an art historian, and the painters Catharine Rembert and Edmund Yaghjian. They embraced modernist ideas, which they imparted to their students, many of whom were studying under the GI Bill. In 1957 Carl Blair arrived from Kansas to become the mainstay of the art department at Bob Jones University until his retirement more than forty years later. At African American colleges Claflin and South Carolina State, the accomplished artists Arthur Rose and Leo Twiggs established art departments that emphasized foundation courses based on the model of the Bauhaus, which was also the basis of the curriculum at Clemson University. Prior to the establishment of the department of visual studies there in 1967, the painter Robert Hunter and the sculptor John Acorn taught the elements of design to architecture students. In 1970 Clemson began its master of fine arts program, and Jeanet Dreskin of Greenville was its first graduate.

Some artists, such as Merton Simpson and Jasper Johns, left the state to study and work in New York. Simpson studied at New York University and emerged as a preeminent dealer of African art. Johns emerged as a leading figure of the post–Abstract Expressionist era.

Museums and art organizations experienced growth in the 1950s. In Columbia the Columbia Museum of Art was established with Dr. Richard Craft at the helm. The Greenville Art Association purchased a forty-room mansion in 1958. Five years later, in 1963, the Greenville Museum Commission was chartered by the state. In 1952 the Guild of South Carolina Artists began to circulate annual exhibitions of work by members across the state. Another annual event was the Springs Mills Art Contest sponsored by Springs Industries of Lancaster, which featured a salon-style installation of every work submitted and a juried traveling show with cash awards. In 1967 the newly formed South Carolina Arts Commission, with partial funding from the National Endowment for the Arts, allocated funds annually for the formation of the state art collection.

As part of the celebration of South Carolina's tricentennial in 1970, each of the major museums organized an exhibition: Charleston, *Art in South Carolina 1670–1970;* Columbia, *South Carolina Architecture 1670–1970;* and Greenville, *Contemporary Artists of South Carolina.* In his introduction to the contemporary volume, Greenville Museum director Jack Morris, Jr., cited a climate of indifference with few exhibition and sales opportunities, the lack of critical feedback, and the absence of accredited advanced degree programs in art. Of the thirty-nine artists, ten were women and most were teachers. The style of their work ranged from conservative/traditional to experimental abstraction.

The late 1970s and 1980s saw increased art activity on many fronts. College and university departments expanded, recruiting out-of-state artists as faculty members. Art museums expanded their buildings and received accreditation from the American Association of Museums, an affirmation of their growing status and professionalism. The Spoleto USA Festival emerged as a significant venue for the display of national figures, such as Louise Nevelson and Roy Lichtenstein, while Piccolo Festival, its grassroots counterpart, offered opportunities for South Carolina artists. Galleries for the exhibition and sale of art gradually took hold in Charleston and also in Greenville, where the Tempo Hampton III Galleries were established by 1970. Later the Congaree Vista area of Columbia developed commercial venues for art.

Despite the demise of both the Springs Mill annual exhibit and the Guild of South Carolina Artists, the decade of the 1990s was characterized by even more art activity. In addition to the greater quantity of art available, the art created and exhibited was more diverse than ever, with artists of color and self-taught artists gaining recognition in museum exhibitions. The South Carolina State Museum, opened in 1988, asserted a leadership role in this area and collaborated with the Arts Commission to host juried exhibitions triennially. In addition the State Museum, Spoleto Festival, and

Clemson University's Botanical Garden mounted important outdoor public sculpture programs, and public art projects in Rock Hill, Greenville, Columbia, and Camden have brought national and local artists into the context of everyday life. MARTHA R. SEVERENS

Bilodeau, Francis W., and Mrs. Thomas J. Tobias. *Art in South Carolina, 1670–1970.* Columbia: South Carolina Tricentennial Commission, 1970.

McInnis, Maurie D. *In Pursuit of Refinement: Charlestonians Abroad, 1740–1860.* Columbia: University of South Carolina Press, 1999.

Moltke-Hansen, David, ed. *Art in the Lives of South Carolinians.* 2 vols. Charleston, S.C.: Carolina Art Association, 1978.

Morris, Jack A. *Contemporary Artists of South Carolina.* Columbia: South Carolina Tricentennial Commission, 1970.

Rutledge, Anna Wells. *Artists in the Life of Charleston.* Philadelphia: American Philosophical Society, 1949.

Severens, Martha R. *The Charleston Renaissance.* Spartanburg, S.C.: Saraland, 1998.

Ashley River. Mile for mile, the relatively short Ashley River is perhaps unrivaled in the Southeast, if not the nation, for its history, its diversity of habitats, and its location in a major city. Emerging from the Wassamassaw and Cypress Swamps in Berkeley and Dorchester Counties, it flows only about sixty miles before joining the Cooper River in Charleston harbor. Its basin of 232,012 acres encompasses much of the Charleston metropolitan region, which includes Summerville and North Charleston.

Despite its short length, the river transitions through three separate types of riverine ecosystems: a blackwater stream, a freshwater tidal river, and a saltwater tidal river, each producing extensive and different types of wetlands. These diverse ecosystems and their transitional zones generate an abundant variety of plants and animals and represent the natural history of the lower coastal plain of the state. Since first inhabited by Native Americans, this diverse river region has provided people with rich and accessible resources.

The Ashley River played a central role in the history of South Carolina. The colony's first English settlement was established along its banks at Albemarle Point in 1670. Originally named the Kiawah River after the region's Native American inhabitants, the river was renamed in honor of Lord Anthony Ashley Cooper, one of the original Lords Proprietors. A decade later the settlement was relocated to the peninsula downstream, where the Ashley joins the Cooper to form an outstanding harbor, opening into the Atlantic. This juncture enabled Charleston to become a major colonial seaport, even though the Ashley was short and did not connect the seaport with the interior via a navigable waterway. This circumstance helped isolate the lowcountry from the upstate and promoted settlement of the upstate by immigrants from North Carolina and Virginia rather than from Charleston.

Although limited to the coastal area, the Ashley did serve as an important route of regional transportation and commerce. Its navigable terminus was Dorchester, a major trading post settled in 1697 about twenty miles upstream from Charleston. Along the river's length were established prominent plantations, such as Middleton Place, Magnolia, and Drayton Hall. Vessels ranging from canoes to rice barges and schooners connected these places and were manned by Europeans and African Americans, both enslaved and free. During the postbellum era, phosphate was mined extensively from lands on both sides of the Ashley, and docks for barges lined the river. These varied activities left some important archaeological sites. As a result of its historical significance and natural beauty, the Ashley was named a National Historic District in 1994 and a State Scenic River in 1999.

The Ashley River has remained a vital resource for South Carolina. Its presence in metropolitan Charleston, its wealth of historic sites, its diversity of habitats, and its scenic beauty all combine to make the Ashley River region a highly desirable place to live and an unparalleled resource for tourism and outdoor recreation. The irony is that its qualities also make the Ashley highly vulnerable to the negative effects of suburban sprawl, pollution, and heavy boat traffic. Private organizations, public agencies, and citizens are taking steps to protect the Ashley and to find ways to balance conservation and growth. Caught amidst these contending pressures, the future of the Ashley River will indicate much about South Carolina in the years to come. GEORGE MCDANIEL

Shakarjian, Mikel J. *Ashley River Eligibility Study for the South Carolina Scenic Rivers Program.* Columbia: South Carolina Department of Natural Resources, 1998.

Ashley River Road. The Ashley River Road is one of the oldest roads in South Carolina. It began as a Native American trading path, paralleling the Ashley River, and later served the colonists of the original Charleston settlement. The Lords Proprietors authorized the road in 1690. The modern road consists of an approximately fifteen-mile portion of S.C. Highway 61 up to Bacon's Bridge Road (S.C. Highway 165). During the colonial era, numerous plantations lined the route, as did St. Andrew's Episcopal Church (1706). In 1721 a law was passed to protect the shade trees along its route, a forerunner of modern ordinances that protect trees and require buffers.

In the years after the Civil War, Ashley River Road communities, especially those of newly emancipated African Americans, established numerous churches along its routes, including Springfield Baptist, St. Andrew's Episcopal, St. Philip's African Methodist Episcopal, and Ashley River Road Missionary Baptist. Since World War II, suburban development has increasingly moved from Charleston up the Ashley River Road. Of major significance was the prevention by preservationists of an exit off Interstate 526 onto the Ashley River Road. Instead traffic was shifted to a new four-lane highway paralleling the road to the west.

Scenic sections of the eleven-mile segment from Church Creek almost to S.C. Highway 165 are still canopied by forests festooned with Spanish moss. In 1983 the road was placed in the National Register of Historic Places. It was designated a State Scenic Byway in 1998 and a National Scenic Byway in 2000. Historic sites along its route, such as Drayton Hall, Magnolia Gardens, and Middleton Place, attract hundreds of thousands of people each year, making the road one of the most popular historic routes in the state. Increasing suburban sprawl and the pressures of traffic, however, render the future of this unique road uncertain. GEORGE MCDANIEL

Ashmore, Harry Scott (1916–1998). Author, editor, Pulitzer Prize winner. Born in Greenville on July 28, 1916, to William Green Ashmore and Nancy Elizabeth Scott, Harry Ashmore grew up in relative poverty but obtained a general science degree from Clemson College in 1937. He demonstrated exceptional writing skills and pursued a journalism career after serving as editor on his high school and college newspapers.

Ashmore's reputation as a journalist grew at the *Greenville Piedmont* and *Greenville News,* garnering him a Nieman Fellowship in 1941. His editorials at the *Charlotte (N.C.) News* led to a job at the *Arkansas Gazette* in 1947.

One of several southern journalists whose "liberal" views on desegregation and civil rights attracted national attention and local scorn, Ashmore won a Pulitzer Prize for his editorials opposing Arkansas Governor Orval Faubus's attempt to stop the integration of Little Rock's Central High School in 1957. However, Ashmore shunned the "liberal" tag, claiming to be a gradualist—supporting the removal of the "separate but equal" system by degrees.

Ashmore's 1954 book, *The Negro and the Schools,* summarized a massive Ford Foundation research project on the disparate biracial educational system in the South. Chief Justice Earl Warren of the U.S. Supreme Court later told Ashmore the research findings influenced the Court's desegregation implementation decision.

After leaving the *Gazette* in 1959, Ashmore served as editor in chief of *Encyclopaedia Britannica* and joined Robert Maynard Hutchins's Center for the Study of Democratic Institutions in Santa Barbara, California, where he lived until his death. During his career Ashmore wrote ten books, many of which discussed the changing attitudes in the New South. He explained, "All of these books of mine, with all the examining, I'm trying to examine my own attitude. How did I get to this point from where I started? What changed my mind?" Ashmore died in Santa Barbara on January 20, 1998. NATHANIA K. SAWYER

Ashmore, Harry S. *Civil Rights and Wrongs: A Memoir of Race and Politics, 1944–1996.* Rev. ed. Columbia: University of South Carolina Press, 1997.

———. *An Epitaph for Dixie.* New York: Norton, 1958.

Sawyer, Nathania K. "Harry S. Ashmore: On the Way to Everywhere." Master's thesis, University of Arkansas at Little Rock, 2001.

Ashwood Plantation. Located in Lee County, the Ashwood Plantation project was a government-sponsored agricultural community established as a resettlement site for tenant farmers displaced by the Great Depression. In 1934 the Federal Emergency Relief Administration (FERA) acquired 7,000 acres south of Bishopville, including the 2,200-acre Ashwood Plantation of former governor Richard I. Manning. Other parcels ultimately raised the total to about 11,000 acres. A succession of state and federal agencies would oversee the project in the ensuing years, including the federal Resettlement Administration, the South Carolina Rural Resettlement Corporation, and the federal Farm Security Administration (FSA). Project directors planned to settle about two hundred families at Ashwood. After proving their mettle as renters, settlers could purchase small farms on extended credit, receive advice in agronomy and farm management, and eventually become self-sufficient yeomen.

By the late 1930s, the project had built homes for about 160 families, who rented crop land for $3.50 per acre. Woodlands and pasturage were furnished free of charge. Rental allowances were based on the number of draft animals a family owned. A tenant with one horse (or, more commonly, one mule) could rent thirty acres, while a two-horse tenant might rent fifty acres. In addition to housing, the FSA built three schools, an auditorium and gymnasium, a medical facility, a shop, and a community center.

Despite the best intentions, Ashwood was dogged by problems. Many Ashwood residents and administrators lacked farming experience. Others did not demonstrate a satisfactory work ethic. Yet another problem was the size of the farms; low crop prices made the smallest units financially unsustainable. The FSA disbanded the project in 1944 and turned over the property to local administration. The lands were eventually sold and most of the surviving buildings were razed in the 1980s. LAWRENCE J. KENT

Hayes, Jack Irby. *South Carolina and the New Deal.* Columbia: University of South Carolina Press, 2001.

Hiott, William David. "New Deal Resettlement in South Carolina." Master's thesis, University of South Carolina, 1986.

"Rehabilitation Project in Lee County Approved." Columbia *State,* October 19, 1934, p. 2.

Asian religions. In 1965 the United States Congress passed laws that liberalized existing statutes regarding the entry of Asian immigrants. This had significant effect on the religious landscape of South Carolina. By the 1980s the state had become home to emergent communities of Asian migrants—East Indians and especially Cambodians, Vietnamese, and Laotians from Southeast Asia—looking for educational, financial, and professional opportunities. In the beginning, most religious practices centered on home worship. As the communities grew, more effort was given to the construction of temples. In Spartanburg County, Southeast Asian immigrants introduced forms of Theravadan Buddhism and by 2001 had established three temples—one by Laotians, two by Cambodians. These temples provided a location for annual festival events, such as *Visakha* ("Buddha Day") and New Year ceremonies, and for special family ancestral rites. For the ceremonies, the Cambodian communities, which were made up of only lay members, relied on visits from itinerant monk priests from the Northeast.

Among Asian religious traditions, those introduced by Indian immigrants—including Hindu, Jain, and Sikh groups—have probably had greater impact on South Carolina's religious landscape. Prior to the 1960s, the most notable Hindu presence in South Carolina was the Meher Baba Spiritual Center at Myrtle Beach founded in the late 1950s. Interest in the center, however, came largely from persons with no East Indian background. The arrival of Indian families made more evident the importance of ritual and social components of Hindu religious experience. Indians moved into small towns throughout the state, but the majority lived in cities along the corridor of Interstates 85, 26, and 20. By the late 1990s the Indian community from the upstate to the Columbia area had grown to about seven hundred families.

In the 1980s Hindus, who represented the largest group among Indians, founded temples in Greenville (Vedic Center), Spartanburg (Hindu Society), and Columbia (Hindu Temple). The majority came from Gujarat, in northwest India, but in the 1990s increasing numbers arrived from south and central India. They worked in a variety of professions and occupations, from medical to retailing, from hotel management to engineering. Though much of religious life for Hindus revolved around the home, the temples provided space for important ritual and social events. Members sponsored regular *pujas* (prayer services) and *Balvihar* (Sunday school) classes and scheduled throughout the year a variety of annual religious festivals. Probably the most popular festivals among South Carolina Hindus have been *Diwali,* the traditional New Year celebration, and the *Navaratri* (Nine Nights), a special *puja* for the Goddess Durga. These rites facilitated links among members with different regional, ethnic, and devotional backgrounds and became an effective venue for social networking among Hindus throughout South Carolina. Consequently the ecumenical character of temple life has become one of the striking features of Hindu practice in the state.

Among Indian migrants, Jains were among the first East Indians to come to South Carolina. At both the Vedic Center in Greenville, where they were among the founding members, and the Hindu Temple in Columbia, Jain families maintained close relations with area Hindus. The altar of both temples included a *murti* of Mahavira, the founder of Jainism, among the *murti* of other Hindu deities. Throughout the 1990s Jains sponsored workshops on *ahimsa* (nonviolence) and observed festival events, often in conjunction with their Hindu compatriots. Their most important ritual observance happens every spring with celebration of the birth of Mahavira.

The fourth Indian religious group of note in the state has been Sikhism. Most Sikhs live in the Columbia area, where they founded a *Gurdwara* (temple) in 1994. Among major ritual events, the one most widely celebrated among South Carolina Sikhs has been the observance of the birthday of their founder Guru Nanak, which usually takes place in November. SAMUEL I. BRITT

McKever-Floyd, Preston L. "Masks of the Sacred: Religious Pluralism in South Carolina." In *Religion in South Carolina,* edited by Charles H. Lippy. Columbia: University of South Carolina Press, 1993.

Williams, Raymond Brady. "Sacred Threads of Several Textures." In *A Sacred Thread: Modern Transmission of Hindu Traditions in India and Abroad,* edited by Raymond Brady Williams. Chambersburg, Pa.: Anima, 1992.

Asparagus. Asparagus was an important cash crop in South Carolina from the 1910s until the mid-1930s. Commercial asparagus production began in response to the "cotton problem." With cotton prices low and the boll weevil creeping ever closer, farmers in the "Ridge" counties of Aiken, Edgefield, and Saluda began planting asparagus to supplement their dwindling cotton incomes. By 1916 Ridge farmers had organized an Asparagus Growers Association and shipped forty-four railroad carloads of asparagus to northern markets. High food prices during World War I helped to spread asparagus culture. Soon the neighboring counties of Barnwell and Orangeburg were shipping asparagus as well. The most intensive culture area centered around Elko and Williston.

Trimming asparagus for shipment in specially shaped baskets. Courtesy, South Carolina Historical Society

Asparagus continued to gain ground after World War I. By 1923 South Carolina was shipping hundreds of carloads of asparagus yearly and ranked among the top five asparagus-producing states. Asparagus culture required patience, and sometimes growers did not turn a profit until the third year. Although not a quick moneymaker, asparagus offered substantial returns to the patient grower. By the late 1920s some asparagus growers were earning as much as $180 per acre, about four times the value of cotton.

Asparagus culture declined during the Great Depression of the 1930s. Adverse weather and weakening markets undermined the crop in the Palmetto State. Ultimately, South Carolina's market share was absorbed by California and Florida, and peach orchards rose where cotton and asparagus once flourished. BECKY WALTON

Associate Reformed Presbyterian Church. This denomination traces its origin to eighteenth-century controversies in the Church of Scotland. One controversy was over the right of a Presbyterian congregation to call its pastor. Protesters challenged the British law that gave noblemen in certain parts of Scotland the right to select pastors, and when courts ruled in favor of the nobility, some pastors and people withdrew from the Church of Scotland and formed new Presbyterian congregations and denominations. A theological controversy, involving some of the same protestors, challenged the moralism of the Church of Scotland and of the Scottish Enlightenment and emphasized a covenant of grace.

Scots and Scots-Irish immigrants brought this Presbyterian tradition to North America. In 1782 the Associate Reformed Presbyterian Church in the United States was organized in Philadelphia. The Associate Reformed Synod of the South, later called the General Synod, was organized in 1803 and became known as the Associate Reformed Presbyterian Church.

While the denomination has always been small and has never had the theological or cultural influence of the larger Presbyterian denominations, it has had remarkable cultural cohesion and the loyalty of generations of Associate Reformed Presbyterian families. This cohesion and loyalty have been particularly obvious in South Carolina, where Erskine College and Erskine Theological Seminary have served as bearers of the tradition and as institutions that have nurtured deep loyalties. ARPs have been well known in South Carolina for their Sabbatarianism and their insistence on singing only psalms in worship. ERSKINE CLARKE

Burleigh, John H. S. *A History of the Church of Scotland.* New York: Oxford University Press, 1960.

Ware, Lowry Price, and James Wylie Gettys. *The Second Century: A History of the Associate Reformed Presbyterians, 1882–1982.* Greenville, S.C.: Associate Reformed Presbyterian Center, 1983.

Atlantic Beach (Horry County; 2000 pop. 351). A historically black beach community, Atlantic Beach is located fifteen miles north of Myrtle Beach. Atlantic Beach was chartered as a municipality in 1966, and most of its property remains in the hands of African Americans and is known as the "Black Pearl of the Grand Strand."

Atlantic Beach flourished during the 1940s and 1950s as one of the few places on the East Coast where black families could enjoy beach vacations during the era of segregation. The land was largely uninhabited until the early 1930s, when the developer George Tyson purchased two tracts of land to be developed as a beach community for African Americans. In the 1940s Tyson sold the property to the Atlantic Beach Company, a group of ten to twelve black educators, doctors, lawyers, and morticians, mostly from the Carolinas. Atlantic Beach Company divided the town into more than one hundred lots for sale, which African Americans purchased to build nightclubs, restaurants, private homes, hotels, restaurants, and other businesses, many of which no longer exist. Hurricane Hazel in 1954 destroyed many oceanfront homes and hotels, most of which were not rebuilt due to lack of insurance. Integration in the 1960s also hastened the town's decline, as black families by then had more choices for enjoying the Atlantic Ocean. In 1980 the Carolina Knight Riders hosted one of the first motorcycle rallies for blacks and based it in Atlantic Beach. The event continued to be a major attraction for the area into the twenty-first century. BARBARA STOKES

McLean, Chandra. "A Vision of the Future." Myrtle Beach *Sun News,* August 6, 2000, pp. C1, C4.

Moredock, Will. *Banana Republic: A Year in the Heart of Myrtle Beach.* Charleston, S.C.: Frontline, 2004.

Attakulla Kulla (?–ca. 1780). Cherokee leader, diplomat. Born on the Big Island of the French Broad River, Attakulla Kulla's birth year is unknown, but biographers place it between 1700 and 1712. Also known as Little Carpenter, he was an influential leader of the Cherokees in the mid-1700s. As a diplomat, he worked to advance the causes of the Overhill Cherokees of eastern Tennessee, especially in the area of trade problems.

In the spring of 1730, Attakulla Kulla was part of a delegation of Cherokees taken to London to cement a recent allegiance to King George II. Although Attakulla Kulla never forgot this trip, his loyalties to his people superseded those to Britain. Around 1750 he visited the Shawnees of Ohio and the Senecas of New York, two nations allied with the French. He returned with stories that the Carolina government was trying to encourage the Catawbas and Creeks to fight the Cherokees. The arrival of northern tribes plus the circulation of these stories prompted the people of the Lower Towns to acts of violence against the white traders among them. The Carolina government responded with a trade embargo against the Cherokees.

As part of the price of restoring trade, the Carolinians required that Attakulla Kulla be turned over. Before he could be captured, however, Attakulla Kulla left for Williamsburg, Virginia, in June 1751, seeking to bypass the Carolina Indian trade and establish relations with Virginia. South Carolina Governor James Glen moved to circumvent such actions and dispatched a letter to Virginia denouncing Attakulla Kulla as a man of no standing among his people. He further warned that Virginia traders would be seized if they entered the Cherokee country that was within the boundaries of South Carolina.

Attakulla Kulla's mission failed, and in 1753 he made peace with Governor Glen by accepting missions for the colonial government. During his meeting with Glen, Attakulla Kulla justified his past disaffection by noting that the Overhill Cherokees lacked sufficient trade goods and traders. To correct these trade irregularities and eliminate the presence of French Indian allies, Attakulla Kulla requested in 1757 that South Carolina build a chain of forts in the backcountry. The Carolinians responded by constructing Fort Prince George in South Carolina and Fort Loudoun in Tennessee.

In the spring of 1759, officers from Fort Prince George abused several women in the Cherokee village of Keowee, prompting the formation of a war party from the Lower Town Cherokees of western South Carolina that killed twenty-two Carolinians. Governor William Henry Lyttelton responded by placing the Cherokees under a trade embargo so severe that a delegation of chiefs visited Charleston to seek relief. Lyttelton held them as hostages until the Cherokees who had killed the Carolinians turned themselves in for punishment. Attakulla Kulla negotiated a treaty with Lyttelton to allow some chiefs to be released while retaining the others to await exchange. Although more bloodshed followed, one of the Overhill headmen, Old Hopp of Chota, concluded a peace treaty that ended Carolina's Cherokee War.

During the Revolutionary War, Superintendent of Indian Affairs John Stuart contacted Attakulla Kulla hoping to use the Cherokees against the Carolina rebels. Not long after, patriot forces reached out to the Cherokees and invited a delegation including Attakulla Kulla to Williamsburg. The aging chief declined the request for aid stating, "We cannot fight our Father, King George." Before the conclusion of the war, Attakulla Kulla died, either in 1780 or 1781. MICHAEL P. MORRIS

Hatley, M. Thomas. *The Dividing Paths: Cherokees and South Carolinians through the Era of Revolution.* New York: Oxford University Press, 1993.

Kelly, James C. "Notable Persons in Cherokee History: Attakullakulla." *Journal of Cherokee Studies* 3 (winter 1978): 2–34.

Milling, Chapman J. *Red Carolinians.* 1940. Reprint, Columbia: University of South Carolina Press, 1969.

Morris, Michael P. *The Bringing of Wonder: Trade and the Indians of the Southeast, 1700–1783.* Westport, Conn.: Greenwood, 1999.

———. "The High Price of Trade: Anglo-Indian Trade Mistakes and the Fort Loudoun Disaster." *Journal of Cherokee Studies* 17 (1997): 3–15.

Atwater, Harvey LeRoy (1951–1991). Political adviser. Lee Atwater was born on February 27, 1951, in Atlanta, Georgia, the son of Harvey Dillard Atwater, an insurance agent, and Sarah Alma Page. The Atwaters eventually settled in Columbia. A 1969 graduate of A. C. Flora High School in Columbia, Atwater earned his bachelor of arts degree in history four years later from Newberry College. Atwater received a master's degree in mass communications from the University of South Carolina in 1977. In 1978 he married Sally Dunbar of Union. They had three children.

Atwater spent much of his early political career managing campaigns for prominent South Carolinians, including Carroll Campbell in 1974 and 1976, Strom Thurmond in 1978, and Floyd Spence in 1980. In these elections Atwater gained his reputation as a shrewd yet negative campaigner willing to use almost any tactic to get his candidate elected. According to Atwater, "Republicans in the South could not win elections by talking about issues. . . . You had to make the case that the other candidate was a bad guy."

In 1980 Atwater helped manage Ronald Reagan's presidential campaign in South Carolina. After Reagan's victory, Atwater was rewarded with a position in the Reagan administration in the Office of Political Affairs. In 1988 Atwater became a chief political strategist for Vice President George Bush's campaign for president against Massachusetts governor Michael Dukakis. Atwater solidified his controversial reputation by using a racially charged campaign advertisement featuring Willie Horton, a black convicted murderer who escaped from a Massachusetts penitentiary while on a weekend furlough and who subsequently attacked a white couple in their Maryland home. The advertisement linked Horton with Dukakis in the minds of voters, branding him with the negative image of being a Massachusetts liberal who was soft on crime and too indulgent of minorities. The Horton advertisement became a defining moment in the conservative reemergence in American politics. Bush overcame an early deficit in the polls to win the 1988 election by a solid margin, and Atwater became the chairman of the Republican National Committee (RNC).

In 1990 Atwater developed an inoperable brain tumor, forcing him to resign his chairmanship at the RNC. He died on March 29, 1991, in Washington, D.C., and was buried in Greenlawn Cemetery, Columbia. AARON L. HABERMAN

Atwater, Lee, with Todd Brewster. "Lee Atwater's Last Campaign." *Life* 14 (February 1991): 58–67.

Brady, John. *Bad Boy: The Life and Politics of Lee Atwater.* Reading, Mass.: Addison Wesley, 1997.

Carter, Dan T. *From George Wallace to Newt Gingrich: Race and the Conservative Counterrevolution, 1963–1994.* Baton Rouge: Louisiana State University Press, 1996.

Atzjar (ats jaar, achar). A bright ochre mixed pickle, this recipe is one of the world's oldest, and its path to South Carolina was along the international spice and slave trade routes. Originating in Java, where each district has its own version, recipes for *achar* traveled through Asia and India, where the term is generic for both oil and brine pickles; to Madagascar, where pickled mangos were prized; to South Africa, where the Dutch imported Malaysian slaves; up the west coast of Africa, whence came South Carolina rice plantation slaves; and directly to Charleston. Only in the lowcountry does the recipe appear in English-language cookbooks of the time. Harriott Pinckney Horry recorded her "Ats Jaar Pickle" in her South Carolina colonial plantation cookbook about 1770. It contains garlic (rare in English cookery of the period), ginger, cabbage, long pepper, vinegar, mixed fruits and vegetables, and turmeric, which is native to Java and gives the pickle its distinctive color. The dish is typical of the traditional lowcountry kitchen, and it accompanies the area's unique, elaborate rice dishes. Throughout the first half of the twentieth century, Charleston restaurants routinely offered atzjar pickles before meals. The elaborate two-day pickling process was out of favor for many years, but the recipe was revived with the resurgence of interest in regional foodways in the late 1980s. JOHN MARTIN TAYLOR

Hess, Karen. *The Carolina Rice Kitchen: The African Connection.* Columbia: University of South Carolina Press, 1992.
Hooker, Richard J., ed. *A Colonial Plantation Cookbook: The Receipt Book of Harriott Pinckney Horry, 1770.* Columbia: University of South Carolina Press, 1984.
Taylor, John Martin. *Hoppin' John's Lowcountry Cooking: Recipes and Ruminations from Charleston and the Carolina Coastal Plain.* New York: Bantam, 1992.

Audubon, John James (1785–1851). Artist, naturalist, ornithologist. Audubon was born Jean Rabine Fougere in Les Cayes, Santo Domingo (later Haiti), on April 26, 1785, the son of a French sea captain, Jean Audubon, and a servant, Jeanne Rabine. His mother died seven months after his birth, and in 1788 he was brought to his father's native home in Nantes, France. Spending his youth on a nearby country estate, Audubon developed the habit of observing and drawing birds and wildlife in nature, which he would develop into his vocation as an artist-naturalist.

Audubon's father sent him to America in 1803 to manage his plantation, Mill Grove, near Philadelphia. In 1808 he married Lucy Bakewell, and they settled in Kentucky. Audubon continued to hunt, study, and draw birds in Kentucky, Louisiana, Pennsylvania, and Ohio. By 1820 he was supporting himself as a portrait artist and taxidermist when he determined to accomplish his dream of accurately portraying and publishing all the birds of North America. He spent the next decades traveling in America, England, and France to undertake this monumental project, published as *The Birds of America* between 1827 and 1838 and issued by subscription in sets of five prints each. The oversized, four-volume folio comprises 435 hand-colored, aquatint engravings based on Audubon's brilliant, detailed, and realistic watercolors of native birds. The artist continually refined his sketches and innovative techniques to render the birds life-sized in dynamic, fully dimensional poses, a dramatic transformation of the flatter, more static formal traditions of his noted predecessors, Mark Catesby and Alexander Wilson. To accompany the images, he published his *Ornithological Biography* in five volumes between 1830 and 1839, providing written descriptions of all the bird species, as well as numerous essays on nature and culture.

John James Audubon. Courtesy, South Carolina Historical Society

In 1831 Audubon traveled to Charleston to find and paint southern birds for *The Birds of America.* His lowcountry travels took him to Sullivan's Island, Cole Island, and Liberty Hall Plantation northwest of Charleston. Audubon befriended the Lutheran minister and avid naturalist John Bachman, who became a lifelong friend and associate. Bachman helped the artist collect, store, and document new species. During the 1830s, between collecting expeditions to Florida and Labrador, Audubon made Bachman's home the center of his work in America. There he had a studio and space to prepare and draw specimens, and he was assisted by Maria Martin, Bachman's sister-in-law, who painted botanical settings for his paintings. Audubon also sold subscriptions to *The Birds of America* to the Charleston Library Society and South Carolina College.

The original edition of *The Birds of America* established Audubon's reputation as America's leading nature artist, while the wide success of a second, smaller edition provided him with financial security for the first time in his career. In 1841 he purchased Minnie's Land, an estate named for his wife, located on the Hudson River in upper Manhattan, and settled with his family for the last productive years of his life. He made his last American expedition to the upper Missouri River in 1843 to produce work for the his final three-volume work, *The Viviparous Quadrupeds of North America* (1845–1848), coauthored by Bachman and completed by his sons, Victor Gifford and John Woodhouse Audubon. Audubon died on January 27, 1851, in New York City. See plate 7. ROBERTA KEFALOS SOKOLITZ

Ford, Alice. *John James Audubon.* Norman: University of Oklahoma Press, 1964.
Foshay, Ella M. *John James Audubon.* New York: Abrams, 1997.
Sanders, Albert E., Warren Ripley, and William A. Jordan. *Audubon: The Charleston Connection.* Charleston, S.C.: Charleston Museum, 1986.
Shuler, Jay. *Had I the Wings: The Friendship of Bachman and Audubon.* Athens: University of Georgia Press, 1995.

Avery Normal Institute. Founded in 1865, the Avery Normal Institute was the first accredited secondary school for African Americans in Charleston. The school, established by the New York–based American Missionary Association (AMA), was initially named in honor of New York abolitionist Lewis Tappan. Renamed Saxton after Union general Rufus B. Saxton, an assistant commissioner of the Freedmen's Bureau, the school was temporarily located in several buildings confiscated by the federal government. It was staffed with northern white missionaries and members of Charleston's antebellum free black community, such as the Cardozo brothers, Thomas and Francis. Thomas W. Cardozo was the school's first principal (1865–1866), and Francis was the second (1866–1868).

Avery Normal Institute, 1868. Courtesy, Avery Research Center for African American History and Culture

Francis Cardozo campaigned to construct a permanent building. He persuaded the AMA's traveling secretary, E. P. Smith, to seek $10,000 from the estate of the late Reverend Charles Avery of Pittsburgh, Pennsylvania. With additional aid from the Freedmen's Bureau, the new school building, renamed Avery, was finished in 1868. Cardozo expanded the school's mission beyond primary and secondary education to include teacher training. Prohibited from teaching in all but one of Charleston's black public schools, many graduates taught in one-room schoolhouses all over South Carolina, especially in the lowcountry. Graduates excelled as educators. Subsequent principals, such as Morrison A. Holmes, continued the school's tradition of high standards.

Principal Benjamin Cox (1915–1936) and his wife, Jeanette Keeble Cox, revitalized Avery. Cox was the first black principal since Cardozo. In 1917 Avery became a bulwark for the establishment of the city's chapter of the National Association for the Advancement of Colored People (NAACP). Its first president was Edwin Harleston (Avery, 1900), a noted artist. Principals Frank DeCosta (Avery, 1927) and L. Howard Bennett (Avery, 1931) moved the school in a more progressive direction.

Principal John F. Potts presided over Avery's transition to a public school in 1947. Coinciding with the U.S. Supreme Court's decision in *Brown v. Board of Education,* the county school board closed Avery in 1954, citing financial reasons. Avery students and teachers had long been active in the state's civil rights movement and continued to be so even after the school was closed. Avery activists included Septima Clark, J. Andrew Simmons, John McCray, John H. Wrighten, Jr., Arthur J. Clement, Jr., and J. Arthur Brown.

Averyites also became leaders in preserving the lowcountry's African American heritage. In 1978 the Avery Institute of Afro-American History and Culture was established to save and renovate the original Avery school building at 125 Bull Street as a repository of African American history and culture. With Lucille S. Whipper (Avery, 1944) as its first president, the organization joined the College of Charleston to found the Avery Research Center for African American History and Culture. On October 6, 1990, the grand opening of the renovated building took place. EDMUND L. DRAGO

Drago, Edmund L. *Initiative, Paternalism, and Race Relations: Charleston's Avery Normal Institute.* Athens: University of Georgia Press, 1990.

Ayers, Sara Lee Harris Sanders (1919–2002). Native American potter. Ayers was born on August 22, 1919, on the Catawba Indian Reservation near Rock Hill. She was the daughter of David Adams "Toad" Harris, a full-blooded Catawba and former chief, and Dorothy Minerva Price, who was of Irish descent. Sara (sometimes spelled "Sarah") Lee was named for her father's mother. She began selling pottery at the Cherokee Indian Reservation in North Carolina when she was nine. At fourteen Ayers married a Catawba, Kirk Sanders. Since her mother was not a Catawba, Ayers probably learned to make pottery with her mother-in-law Arzada Brown Sanders. By 1939 Ayers's work was so desired that she spent half the year selling her pots in Pennsylvania and the other half working in a Rock Hill textile mill. Kirk Sanders died in 1945, and the following year Ayers married Hazel Ayers, later known as Foxx, a full-blooded Catawba. They had three children. The Ayers family left the reservation in 1962 and moved to West Columbia, where they continued their pottery business until her retirement in the late 1990s.

Catawba women have made pottery for hundreds of years, and archaeologists credit them with sustaining the tribe through this traditional pottery, which is the oldest art form still produced in South Carolina. For Ayers and other master Catawba potters, the turning point in prices paid for their work occurred at a 1973 show at the Columbia Museum of Art. Pieces that had sold for just a few dollars began selling for as much as $125 per piece. These new prices offered economic viability and laid the foundation for the revival of Catawba pottery.

Clay is dug from under six to seven feet of soil from special clay holes in the Catawba River basin near the reservation. Catawba clay is rich in mica and iron oxide. The clay has mottles of orange, gray, tan, black, or gray that are visible in the finished pot. A puttylike pipe clay and a sandy, firmer blue clay are dug, then mixed by hand until it is the consistency for forming. Instead of using a wheel, the potter makes a round pancake to form the base and then builds the sides with coils of clay. The coils are blended together by pinching and pulling and using mussel shells to shape the walls, knives to cut away extra clay, and rubbing rocks to polish. Molds are used to make the Indian heads and pipes. The surface is not glazed, and the pots are fired for the desired surface in a pit. Ayers specialized in forming and decorating pots, and Foxx in making pipes and firing.

Ayers received many awards and honors. Examples of her work are in the collections of the Native American Museum and Heye Foundation in New York City, the Museum of York County (S.C.), the McKissick Museum at the University of South Carolina, the

South Carolina State Museum, and the Mint Museum in Charlotte, North Carolina. The Schiele Museum in Gastonia, North Carolina, has an extensive study collection of her work. Ayers died on November 25, 2002, and was buried in the Church of the Latter-day Saints cemetery on the Catawba reservation. See plate 5. CAROLYN SUNG

Blumer, Thomas. *Catawaba Indian Pottery: The Survival of a Folk Tradition.* Tuscaloosa: University of Alabama Press, 2004.

Obituary. Columbia *State,* November 27, 2002, p. B4.

Ayllón, Lucas Vázquez de (ca. 1480–1526). Colonizer, explorer. The founder of the first Spanish town in the territory of what came to be the United States, Ayllón was born circa 1480 in Toledo, Spain, to Juan Vázquez de Ayllón and Inés de Villalobos. In 1504 Ayllón arrived in the Spanish colony of Hispaniola to serve as a district judge. He became a judge on the Caribbean region's highest appeals court in 1511. Through these positions, Ayllón gained wealth and power. In 1514 he married Ana de Becerra, a member of a prominent Caribbean family. In addition to his service to the royal government, Ayllón owned estates and participated in trade and slaving ventures. On one of these expeditions, in 1521, an Indian called "Francisco de Chicora" was captured. Francisco, who was from the coast of what later became South Carolina, became Ayllón's slave and told the judge fantastic stories about his homeland. Whether or not Ayllón believed all of Francisco's tales, he used them to inspire royal interest in the conquest of the southeastern coast of North America. In June 1523 Charles V granted Ayllón a contract to establish a Spanish presence in the region from thirty-five to thirty-seven degrees north latitude, although the document also listed the names of places to the south, including Francisco de Chicora's land at approximately thirty-three degrees north latitude. The contract named Ayllón governor of the colony and granted him a range of privileges in exchange for funding and carrying out this expedition.

Ayllón's colony did not succeed, but his efforts contributed much to European interest in and knowledge of the southeastern coast of North America. After departing Puerto Plata in July 1526, Ayllón and his expedition of six hundred first landed in the area of Winyah Bay in what would become South Carolina and then traveled south to an unknown location, where they founded the town of San Miguel de Gualdape in September 1526. Most of San Miguel's inhabitants soon perished, including Ayllón, and conflict broke out among the survivors. By mid-November 1526 the town had been abandoned. Despite this failure, the stories Ayllón and his slave, Francisco de Chicora, told about the wonders of this land found their way into the writings of the chronicler Peter Martyr and circulated throughout Europe. Pedro de Quejo's 1525 voyage of exploration that Ayllón sponsored also contributed greatly to the Spaniards' knowledge of this coast. Ayllón's own expedition provided further information about this region. Some of the maps drawn after 1526 display the caption "land of Ayllón" in the area of what became South Carolina and Georgia and describe this land and Ayllón's experiences there. Lucas Vázquez de Ayllón died on St. Luke's Day, October 18, 1526, at San Miguel de Gualdape. He left his widow with large debts from his expedition and five young children to raise. One son, also named Lucas Vázquez de Ayllón, later received his own royal contract to conquer and settle the land that had claimed his father's life. KAREN L. PAAR

Cook, Jeannine, ed. *Columbus and the Land of Ayllón: The Exploration and Settlement of the Southeast.* Valona, Ga.: Lower Altamaha Historical Society—Ayllón, 1992.

Hoffman, Paul E. *A New Andalucia and a Way to the Orient: The American Southeast during the Sixteenth Century.* Baton Rouge: Louisiana State University Press, 1990.

Quinn, David B., ed. *New American World: A Documentary History of North America to 1612.* Vol. 1, *America from Concept to Discovery: Early Exploration of North America.* New York: Arno, 1979.

B

Babcock, Havilah (1898–1964). Educator, writer. Babcock was born on March 6, 1898, in Appomattox, Virginia, the son of Homer Curtis Babcock and Rosa Blanche Moore. He earned an A.B. from Elon College in 1918, then pursued graduate studies at Columbia University, the University of Virginia (A.M., 1923), and the University of South Carolina (Ph.D., 1927). On June 3, 1919, he married Alice Hudson Cheatham. He briefly taught high school English in Virginia before joining the faculty at the College of William and Mary in 1921. In 1926 Babcock came to the University of South Carolina (USC) on a year's sabbatical leave. He found the people, school, and state so hospitable that he stayed thirty-eight years, joining the English department and becoming a fixture at the university.

At USC, Babcock was an institution about whom truths and legends were freely circulated. He might begin a class with "I'll give twenty-five cents to anyone who can spell Houyhnhnm," and reportedly he greeted students with a broadside of snowballs after a rare southern snowfall. His jovial bond with students made his courses the most sought after at the university, causing students to sign up a year in advance for his English 129 course entitled "I Want a Word." In this vocabulary and semantics course, students learned of the charm and power of words as they listened to Babcock reveal their nuances and connotations.

Babcock was equally at home in the field as at the blackboard. He used the outdoors as a canvas to draw a vast array of colorful characters, becoming a master of the hunting-fishing tale. His stories were replete with references to English and American literature. More than one hundred of his stories found their way into print in a variety of newspapers and magazines, including *Field and Stream.* Anthologies of his works include *My Health Is Better in November* (1947), *Tales of Quails 'n' Such* (1951), *I Don't Want to Shoot an Elephant* (1958), and *Jaybirds Go to Hell on Friday, and Other Stories* (1964). His writing traveled the literary spectrum with ease. In his novel *The Education of Pretty Boy* (1960), Babcock wrote of a young boy's gun-shy bird dog because he thought the dog "was too pretty not to be immortal."

Babcock's writings continued their popularity years after his death. A reviewer from the *New York Times* once compared his writing to "a rare old Bourbon you want to make last as long as possible." A counterpart at *Field and Stream* applied a similar metaphor: "Like a good wine," Babcock's stories "grow better with age." Babcock died in Columbia on December 10, 1964, and was buried in Appomattox, Virginia. FRANCIS NEUFFER

Babcock, Havilah. *The Best of Babcock.* New York: Holt, Rinehart, and Winston, 1974.

Neuffer, Claude Henry. "Havilah Babcock: Virginia Carolinian." *Georgia Review* 21 (fall 1967): 297–310.

Babcock, James Woods (1856–1922). Psychiatrist, mental hospital superintendent. Babcock was born on August 12, 1856, in Chester, the son of the physician Sidney E. Babcock and Margaret Woods. After graduating from Phillips Exeter Academy and Harvard College, he received an M.D. from Harvard Medical School in 1886. He interned at the Insane Department of the Massachusetts State Almshouse at Tewkesbury and studied mental diseases in Europe. From 1887 to 1891 he was assistant physician at McLean Hospital for the Insane in Somerville, Massachusetts.

In 1891 Babcock became superintendent of the South Carolina State Lunatic Asylum in Columbia, its first to have been trained in psychiatry. Babcock arrived eager to modernize and improve the institution. The physical plant had deteriorated since the 1860s, and the asylum had become largely custodial in function. With the help of Katherine Guion, a nurse he met at McLean, he established the Training School for Nurses in 1892. He married Guion in 1892; the couple had three children. In 1895 Babcock convinced the General Assembly to change the asylum's name to South Carolina State Hospital for the Insane. But Babcock faced severe obstacles. The General Assembly, perennially hostile to debt and taxes, failed to increase appropriations. The hospital spent less per patient than most other state hospitals did, and its mortality rates were among the highest in the nation. Part of the problem was Babcock's retiring personality, which led him to shun confrontations with legislators over appropriations. He also failed to gain effective control over his own staff, but this was partly because they were appointed by and accountable to the hospital's regents rather than to Babcock.

Babcock's most significant contribution to medicine was his work on pellagra, a deadly niacin-deficiency disease that afflicted many southerners in the early twentieth century. Pellagra, which often produced depression and mania, sent thousands of people to the state hospital, where many of them died. In 1907 Babcock diagnosed several cases of pellagra at the hospital, becoming one of the first American physicians to report its presence in the United States. Between 1910 and 1912 he published several articles on the subject and helped to found the National Association for the Study of Pellagra, serving as its first president from 1910 to 1912.

In 1909 the General Assembly ordered an investigation of conditions at the state hospital. The investigating committee uncovered many examples of overcrowding and substandard facilities, staffing, and care but disagreed as to the extent of Babcock's responsibility and on a solution. In 1913 and 1914 he clashed with Governor Cole Blease over Blease's demand that he fire assistant physician Eleanora B. Saunders. Blease tried to force both of them out, but another legislative investigation in 1914 exonerated them. Nevertheless, Babcock resigned soon after and opened the state's first private mental hospital, Columbia's Waverley Sanitarium, in 1915. He also lectured on psychiatry at the Medical College of South Carolina in Charleston. He died in Columbia on March 3, 1922. PETER MCCANDLESS

Etheridge, Elizabeth. *The Butterfly Caste: A Social History of Pellagra in the South.* Westport, Conn.: Greenwood, 1972.

McCandless, Peter. *Moonlight, Magnolias, and Madness: Insanity in South Carolina from the Colonial Period to the Progressive Era.* Chapel Hill: University of North Carolina Press, 1996.

Bachman, John (1790–1874). Clergyman, naturalist. Bachman was born in Rhinebeck, New York, on February 4, 1790, the son of Jacob Bachman, a farmer, and his wife, Eva (Shop?). Reared on a farm in Rensselaer County, New York, Bachman developed an interest in natural history. After tutoring by a Lutheran minister, he entered a college in Philadelphia, but an attack of tuberculosis forced him to withdraw. He later studied theology in Philadelphia and became a Lutheran pastor in 1813. Another bout with tuberculosis prompted him to seek relief in a warmer climate, and he moved to Charleston, South Carolina, in 1815 to serve as minister of St. John's Lutheran Church. On January 16, 1816, he married Harriet Martin. They had fourteen children, five of whom died in infancy. Following Harriet's death in 1847, Bachman married her sister, Maria Martin, in 1848. Devoted to his ministerial duties, Bachman also led in the formation of the South Carolina Synod and a Lutheran college in Newberry.

Meanwhile, Bachman continued his pursuit of natural history, mainly studying the flora, birds, and mammals of the region. During the 1830s he began to publish articles in scientific journals, a development fostered by a chance meeting with the noted bird artist John James Audubon in Charleston in 1831. A close relationship followed, and each helped the other. Bachman lent considerable assistance to Audubon in his study of birds, and Audubon encouraged Bachman to publish his scientific inquiries. Eventually each of the two Audubon sons married a Bachman daughter, thus strengthening the Bachman-Audubon bond.

Among Bachman's most significant publications were the descriptions of several mammals previously unknown in scientific works, particularly certain squirrels, mice, rabbits, shrews, and moles. During a trip to Europe in 1836, Bachman enhanced his reputation as a mammalogist, and soon thereafter he began a collaborative project with Audubon and his sons on a book describing and illustrating all of the known mammals of North America. Audubon and his son John Woodhouse Audubon did the illustrations, and Bachman wrote the scientific descriptions. First issued serially in thirty parts, the illustrations were published in three bound volumes between 1845 and 1853 as *The Viviparous Quadrupeds of North America.* Three volumes of text appeared successively in 1849, 1851, and 1854, and a single volume combining text and illustrations was published in 1854. In the later volumes, the title was altered to *The Quadrupeds of North America.* In all of his work taken together, Bachman contributed thirty-one descriptions of mammals new to science, including eleven that were coauthored with Audubon. Thus, Bachman became one of America's important pioneering mammalogists.

Actively involved in the affairs of Charleston, Bachman served as president of the Literary and Philosophical Society and the Elliott Society of Natural History. From 1848 to 1853 he was professor of natural history at the College of Charleston. In the meantime, between 1848 and 1855 Bachman also gained notice for his defense of the idea of the unity of all human races. In a long-running debate with the noted Philadelphia craniologist Samuel George Morton, the renowned naturalist Louis Agassiz, and the southern physician Josiah C. Nott, Bachman consistently presented a sound scientific case for all races of humans as members of the same species. Drawing on his keen knowledge of the nature of species, he presented his argument in numerous articles and in *The Doctrine of the Unity of the Human Races, Examined on the Principles of Science,* published in 1850.

Yet Bachman condoned slavery, and he was an unyielding defender of states' rights. He championed the secession of South Carolina from the Union and worked vigorously to support the Confederacy. After the war, Bachman continued as the pastor of St. John's until a stroke in 1871 forced him to curtail his work. He died in Charleston on February 24, 1874, and was buried in the church that he had served for nearly six decades. LESTER D. STEPHENS

Shuler, Jay. *Had I the Wings: The Friendship of Bachman and Audubon.* Athens: University of Georgia Press, 1995.

Stephens, Lester D. *Science, Race, and Religion in the American South: John Bachman and the Charleston Circle of Naturalists, 1815–1895.* Chapel Hill: University of North Carolina Press, 2000.

Bachman's warbler. The history of this small, brightly colored warbler (*Vermivora bachmanii*) is closely tied to South Carolina. The species was discovered by the Reverend John Bachman in 1832 on the Edisto River a few miles north of Jacksonborough. In 1833 John J. Audubon painted a male and named the species after his friend Bachman. The Bachman's warbler is believed to be extinct. The last acceptable report was made in 1958, when John H. Dick photographed a male in Charleston County near the original discovery site.

Based on historical collections, the Bachman's warbler is believed to have once been common and widespread in the Southeast. The warbler inhabited the edges or open interiors of swamps. Most of the few nests that have been found were in thickets of cane and brambles.

Initially the species apparently benefited from the activities of early settlers, both Indians and Europeans, who created suitable openings in the forest. By 1900, however, the species had become rare, perhaps due to extensive destruction of hardwood swamps for agriculture. At the same time, large areas of the warbler's wintering grounds in Cuba were destroyed for agriculture.

No Bachman's warblers have been found on territory since 1961. Through 1978 at least six reports had been made from I'On Swamp, north of Charleston. Despite extensive searches, none of these has been verified. WILLIAM POST

Hamel, Paul B. *Bachman's Warbler: A Species in Peril.* Washington, D.C.: Smithsonian Institution Press, 1986.

———. "Bachman's Warbler (*Vermivora bachmanii*)." In *The Birds of North America,* no. 150. Philadelphia, Pa.: Academy of Natural Sciences, 1995.

Bacot, Ada White (1832–1911). Civil War nurse, diarist. Bacot was born on December 31, 1832, near Society Hill in Darlington District, the eldest of six children born to Peter Samuel Bacot and Anna Jane White. Although educated at St. Mary's Academy in Raleigh, North Carolina, Bacot spent most of her youth in South Carolina at Roseville Plantation, Darlington District. In 1851 she married her second cousin Thomas Wainwright Bacot, Jr., and moved to Arnmore Plantation, near her childhood home. Over the next few years, she dealt with the death of two daughters and her husband.

On January 4, 1861, Bacot volunteered to become a nurse for the Confederacy. Shortly before making her decision she wrote, "[M]any are the misgivings I am forced to acknowledge, but hope is strong, & faith in almight[y] God who has never yet forsaken the oppressed makes me more at ease than I otherwise would be." Frustrated by her inability to secure enough money to travel to Virginia, on October 13 she wrote Robert Woodward Barnwell, head of South Carolina Hospital Aid Association, to volunteer her services. With Barnwell's help, she was finally able to travel to Charlottesville, Virginia, on December 11.

The association had four hospitals in the area, and Bacot served in Monticello Hospital. Like most women working in the hospitals, she found her activities in the wards restricted. Prevailing social attitudes considered it unseemly for respectable women to spend much time with sick and wounded soldiers, whose care was left primarily to male ward attendants and convalescent soldiers. Instead, Bacot supervised the preparation of meals and laundered sheets and clothing. Her only interactions with the men came when she visited them, helped them write letters, and read Scripture to them.

Bacot kept a diary but recorded little about her hospital work. Published many years after her death, the diary provides insight into the social life of a single, young, upper-class southern woman during the Civil War. She wrote a great deal about her social life at the Maupin House, where she boarded with several South Carolina nurses and doctors. Her religious faith and devotion to her state dominated her entries. An Episcopalian, she prayed for guidance and patience and sought to improve herself with meditation and Scripture daily. She described her devotion to South Carolina as "that of an affectionate daughter for a mother, the purest love in the world." For Bacot, nursing was a socially respectable way for a daughter of wealth and privilege to serve God and country.

For unknown reasons, Bacot left nursing and returned to South Carolina at the end of 1863. She married two more times before her death on April 11, 1911. She was buried in the family cemetery at Roseville Plantation. T. JASON SODERSTRUM

Bacot, Ada W. *A Confederate Nurse: The Diary of Ada W. Bacot, 1860–1863.* Edited by Jean V. Berlin. Columbia: University of South Carolina Press, 1994.

Baha'is. The Baha'i faith is one of the world's youngest religions and as of 2004 claims a following of 17,530 in South Carolina, one of the largest concentrations of Baha'is in the United States. The religion was founded by Mírzá Husayn' 'Alí (1817–1892), who later became known as "Bahá'u'lláh" ("The Glory of God."). "Baha'i" is derived from "baha" ("glory and splendor") and is the designation of the adherents to the faith.

The religion grew out of the Babi faith, founded in 1844 by Siyyid 'Alí Muhammad, the "Bab" ("Gate"). Leadership of the Baha'i community passed from Bahá'u'lláh to his eldest son, 'Abdu'l-Baha, and finally to Shoghi Effendi Rabbani, Bahá'u'lláh's eldest grandson. Shoghi Effendi translated his great-grandfather's writings into English, which aided in the global growth of the religion. Some of the religion's principles are the oneness of humankind, the common foundation of all religions, religion and science as integral parts of truth, the equality of men and women, and the elimination of prejudice of all kinds.

Bahá'u'lláh's teachings were brought to South Carolina by the son of a slave, Louis G. Gregory (1874–1951), a native of Charleston and a 1902 graduate of Howard University Law School. Becoming a confirmed believer in the Baha'i faith in 1909, he made his first teaching trip to Charleston and seven other southern cities the following year. Gregory grew to international prominence in the Baha'i faith; thus the eponym of the Louis G. Gregory Baha'i Institute and radio station WLGI in Hemingway. PRESTON L. MCKEVER-FLOYD

Hatcher, William S., and J. Douglas Martin. *The Bahá'í Faith: The Emerging Global Religion.* New ed. Wilmette, Ill.: Baha'i Publishing Trust, 2002.

Morrison, Gayle. *To Move the World: Louis G. Gregory and the Advancement of Racial Unity in America.* Wilmette, Ill.: Baha'i Publishing Trust, 1982.

Baker, Augusta Braxton (1911–1998). Librarian, master storyteller. Baker, the first African American to hold an administrative position in the New York Public Library, was born on April 1, 1911, in Baltimore, Maryland, the daughter of Winfort Braxton and Mabel Gough. Her father was educated at Morgan College and taught mathematics. Keeping with the custom of the times, her mother retired from elementary school teaching following Baker's birth. Baker's mother had a profound influence on and nurtured her love of reading and her overall education. "I was an only child, and I was fair prey, you see, for my mother to teach," Baker noted in a 1989 interview. Baker also cited her grandmother's influence on the development of her literary abilities: "my earliest recollection too . . . was a storytelling grandmother, and that may have been the seed for my later interest in storytelling." Having developed an early love of literature and literacy, Augusta was advanced in elementary school and subsequently graduated from high school at age fifteen. She entered the University of Pittsburgh, where she met and married her first husband, James Baker. The marriage produced one son. The two moved to Albany, New York, where Baker continued her studies at New York State College for Teachers, earning a B.A. in education in 1933 and a B.S. in library science in 1934. The Baker marriage ended in divorce, and on November 23, 1944, Augusta married Gordon Alexander.

During her accomplished career as a children's librarian with the New York Public Library, Baker received the first Dutton-Macrae Award in 1953 for advanced study of library work with children. Her knowledge and capabilities were recognized by the Georgia Teachers and Education Association (GTEA) in 1956 when they requested that she provide consultation toward the advancement of the Librarians' Section of the organization. She later served as consultant to other organizations and programs, including the long-running television series *Sesame Street.* She was an early supporter and contributor to the development of the Coretta Scott King Book Award, which was first presented at the American Library Association Conference in 1970, and in 1974 she was the first African American to receive the Clarence Day Award.

In 1980 Baker joined the University of South Carolina (USC) and became "Storyteller-in-Residence." This position was created for Baker, and her goals were to teach others how to create enthusiasm in children about stories and reading. In 1987 the city of Columbia established a yearly festival in her honor, "A(ugusta) Baker's Dozen: A Celebration of Stories," recognizing the importance of stories and storytelling. Through the joint efforts of the USC College of Library and Information Science and the Richland County Public Library, each celebration features authors, illustrators, storytellers, and a keynote address focusing on Baker's lifelong dedication to the creation and expansion of African American children's literature, the development of literacy skills among children and young adults, and the increased usage of libraries among children and adults. She received honorary doctor of letters degrees from St. John's University in 1978 and from the University of South Carolina in 1986. Augusta Baker retired from USC in 1994 and died in Columbia on February 23, 1998. RHONDA JEFFRIES

Baker, Augusta. "My Years as a Children's Librarian." In *The Black Librarian in America,* edited by E. J. Josey. Metuchen, N.J.: Scarecrow, 1970.

Baldwin, William Plews, III (b. 1944). Novelist. Baldwin was born in McClellanville on October 27, 1944. He is the son of William P. Baldwin, Jr., a wildlife biologist and real-estate broker, and Agnes Leland, a title researcher and historian. He was raised in the lowcountry in Savannah, Georgia, and in Bluffton and Summerville, South Carolina. He graduated from high school in Summerville in 1962. He married Lillian Morrison on August 15, 1965, and they have two sons, Aaron and Malcolm. Baldwin is a would-have-been architect with two degrees from Clemson University, a B.A. in history (1966) and an M.A. in English (1968). After university he returned to McClellanville and has remained in the area, where he has made a living by crabbing, oystering, shrimping, serving as a magistrate, writing screenplays for Hollywood, designing and building houses, and by writing fiction.

Baldwin has said: "I think of myself as a novelist. Whenever I get ahead in life, I write a novel, which is why I stay broke." His first novel, *The Hard to Catch Mercy* (1993), was universally well received, winning the Lillian Smith Award for Fiction and becoming a Book-of-the-Month Club selection. In the oral tradition of the South, the novel is narrated by the fourteen-year-old Willie T. Allson, who in the year 1916 is sent on a mythic journey to gain his manhood. With humor and passion he tells the entertaining and anecdote-filled story of the Allson family and their life in the South Carolina lowcountry. The landscape comes to life, and the characters stand out as highly original and yet convincingly real human beings of that place and time. It is a grotesque, violent, and above all compelling story of initiation and recognition. The boy learns about revenge, death, sex, the importance of the past in the present, the "failures" of his family's collective memory, and the possibility of happiness. All in all, Baldwin's first novel was a splendid entry for him into the ranks of accomplished South Carolina novelists.

The fun Baldwin had with his stereotyping of classic southern fiction in his first novel was continued, and perhaps exaggerated, in his second, *The Fennel Family Papers* (1996). In this novel he satirized a young historian's pathetic attempt to get tenure by securing and publishing the historic papers of an ancient, notorious, and decadent family, the Fennels. The Swiftian tale of the eccentric South Carolina family, who supposedly were keepers of the lighthouse of Dog Tooth Shoal since before the Revolutionary War, is darkly comic. From the story of the naively ambitious academic's research among the violent and mad members of the Fennel family, Baldwin created unforgettable and hilarious satire.

Baldwin has also published four nonfiction books with the photographer Jane Iseley about historic Charleston and the plantations of the lowcountry. He has published two oral history reports featuring Mrs. Emily Whaley (1913–1998), grande dame of Charleston society, and her recollections of her garden, cuisine, recipes, and entertaining. In a similar vein is his oral history report *Heaven Is a Beautiful Place* (2000), based on his conversations with Genevieve C. "Sister" Peterkin (b. 1928), which is a memoir of life at Murrell's Inlet on the South Carolina coast. JAN NORDBY GRETLUND

Abbott, Reginald. "*The Hard to Catch Mercy:* A Review." *Southern Quarterly* 32 (summer 1994): 169–71.

Ball, William Watts (1868–1952). Editor. Ball was born on December 9, 1868, in Laurens County, the son of the attorney Beaufort Ball and Eliza Watts. He attended Adger (preparatory) College at Walhalla and was graduated from South Carolina College in 1887, receiving his LL.D. in 1889. He also attended the summer law school of the University of Virginia. Although he was admitted to the South Carolina Bar in 1890, he never practiced law. On April 21, 1897, he married Fay Witte. The couple had five children.

Ball, the first editor of the *Laurens Advertiser,* was also a reporter for the *Philadelphia Press* and city editor of the *Florida Times Union.* He served as editor of the *State* of Columbia, the Charleston *Evening Post,* the *Greenville News,* and the *News and Courier* of Charleston. During his editorship of the *State,* from 1913 to 1923, he championed the aging ideals of Bourbon followers of General Wade Hampton and targeted such reformers and populists as Coleman Blease. The controversial and nomadic journalist served as the University of South Carolina's first journalism dean from 1923 to 1927, when he moved to Charleston. There, as editor of the *News and Courier* (1927–1951), he relentlessly attacked the Roosevelt administration and the New Deal. He won national recognition for his editorial fight for repeal of Prohibition. In his book, *The State That Forgot* (1932), Ball was an outspoken critic of democracy. At one time he famously declared, "I love liberty . . . I hate equality." His biographer John D. Stark described Ball as a "rigid traditionalist" who epitomized "the sort of aristocratic conservatism so often associated with John Randolph of Roanoke."

Ball received honorary degrees from the University of South Carolina in 1919 and Oglethorpe University in 1937. He retired in January 1951 and died in Charleston on October 14, 1952. He was buried in Magnolia Cemetery. ROBERT A. PIERCE

Ball, William. *The State That Forgot: South Carolina's Surrender to Democracy.* Indianapolis, Ind.: Bobbs-Merrill, 1932.

Holden, Charles J. *In the Great Maelstrom: Conservatives in Post–Civil War South Carolina.* Columbia: University of South Carolina Press, 2002.

Stark, John D. *Damned Upcountryman: William Watts Ball, a Study in American Conservatism.* Durham, N.C.: Duke University Press, 1968.

Bamberg (Bamberg County; 2000 pop. 3,733). Like many South Carolina towns, Bamberg was a product of the railroad. Bamberg began around 1832 with the construction of a water tower by the South Carolina Canal and Rail Road Company. The site became variously known as Seventy-Six, Simmon's Turnout, and Lowery's Turnout. The South Carolina General Assembly incorporated the town in 1855 and named it in honor of William Seaborn Bamberg, who had acquired the site in 1846. He and his brothers, Isaac S. Bamberg and General Francis Marion Bamberg, and others settled the area and began creating the town. Bamberg's first post office opened by 1860. With the creation of Bamberg County in 1897, the town of Bamberg became the county seat.

Located in the coastal plain, Bamberg thrived with the railroad and became the commercial center for surrounding farms and plantations. Among its more notable neighbors was the writer William Gilmore Simms, who lived at his Woodlands Plantation three miles south of town. Another nearby resident was Dr. Francis F. Carroll, who, with his slave Louis Carroll, conducted experiments with the first submarine spar torpedo at Clear Pond, nine miles south of town. In 1865 Union cavalry destroyed the depot and railroad tracks in Bamberg.

After a postwar recovery, Bamberg was prospering again by the 1880s and 1890s. By 1880 the town had a population of 648 and was shipping five thousand bales of cotton annually from its depot. Successful residents built homes on Railroad Avenue and adjacent streets. In 1892 several prominent residents, including General Francis Marion Bamberg, Mayor E. R. Hays, and H. J. Brabham, built the Bamberg Cotton Mill.

Bamberg garnered attention as the site of the Carlisle Fitting School, which was founded by South Carolina Methodists in 1892 and named in honor of James H. Carlisle, president of Wofford College. Until 1932 Carlisle functioned as a preparatory school for Wofford College. The site was leased in 1932 to Colonel James F.

Risher, who revamped the curriculum and renamed the institution Carlisle Military School in 1943. The school closed in 1977.

Entering the twentieth century, Bamberg was the most active cotton market between Augusta and Charleston. The coming of the boll weevil in 1921 ended this era of prosperity. Bamberg's role as a commercial and transportation center waned during the economic depression of the 1920s and 1930s. The town retained some importance as a shipping point for Bamberg County watermelons, as a livestock auction center, and as an overnight stop for tourists traveling to Florida on U.S. Highway 301.

Steady, if unspectacular, growth continued throughout the latter half of the twentieth century. In 1983 the 1880–1930 residential area of the town was listed in the National Register of Historic Places. The town later acquired the railroad berm through its center and created a greenway with a walking trail. In 2001 Bamberg hosted its first Antiques TreasureFest, an annual festival that features antiques and collectibles and a barbecue cook-off. ALEXIA JONES HELSLEY

Brabham, Otis. *The Tale of a Town—Bamberg and Vicinity.* N.p., 1952.

Copeland, D. Graham. "Many Years After: A Bit of History and Some Recollections of Bamberg with Appendix of Data Concerning a Few Bamberg County Families and Their Connections." Unpublished manuscript. February 23, 1940. Caroliniana Library, University of South Carolina, Columbia.

Jones, Virginia Kearse. *Founding and Settlement of Bamberg.* N.p., 1938.

Bamberg County (393 sq. miles; 2000 pop. 16,658). Bamberg County, located in the inner coastal plain in south-central South Carolina, was formed from the southeastern section of Barnwell County in 1897. It is named for Francis Marion Bamberg (1838–1905), the grandson of John Bamberg, who arrived in the area in 1798 and was thought to have originally come from Bavaria before stopping in Pennsylvania during the Revolutionary War period.

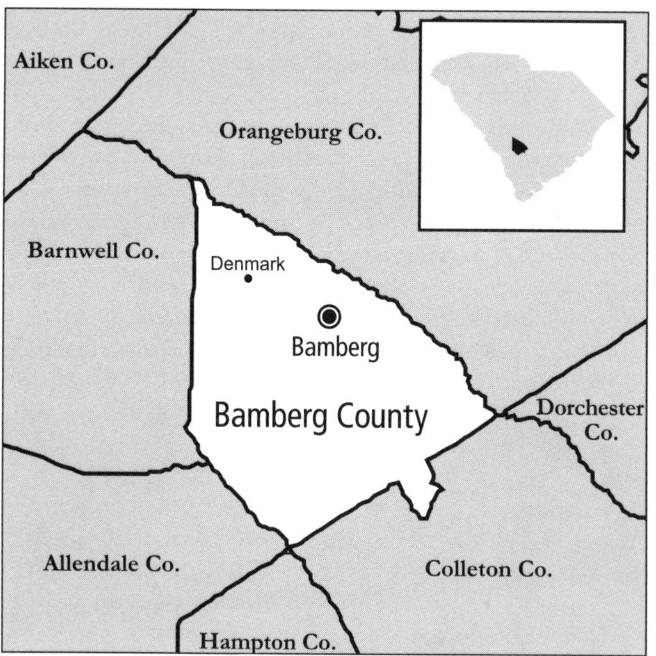

The Bamberg area was originally populated by the Edisto tribe of the Muskhogean Indians. German, Swiss, Scots-Irish, English, and Huguenot settlers began arriving during the mid-eighteenth century. The 136-mile South Carolina Railroad, completed in 1833, passed through the area, and a railroad water tank marked the beginning of the town of Bamberg, which would become the county seat. During the Civil War, the combatants included the Bamberg Guards, commanded by Captain Isaac S. Bamberg. The namesake for the county, Francis M. Bamberg, enlisted as a private and after the war was appointed a general on Governor Wade Hampton's staff. In February 1865 Confederate soldiers lost a skirmish to General William T. Sherman's troops at Rivers Bridge, near a site that became Rivers Bridge State Park.

The first newspaper, the *Chronicle,* was established in 1880. Two years later a bridge was built across the Edisto River to attract trade from Orangeburg County. The site was near a later bridge on U.S. Highway 301. By the 1890s cotton fed the region's economy, aided by such enterprises as the Bamberg Cotton Mill and later the Bamberg Cotton Oil Mill. Carlisle Fitting School, founded in 1892 at Bamberg as a branch of Wofford College, became a prep school for boys. It closed in 1977.

On January 19, 1897, voters approved the creation of Bamberg County. By year's end, a courthouse and county jail had been built at the town of Bamberg. The nearby town of Denmark was another important urban center in the new county.

During World War I twenty Bamberg County citizens were killed, while the influenza epidemic at home claimed several prominent residents. The county produced 35,000 bales of cotton in 1918, but after the boll weevil appeared in 1921, production fell to 4,000 bales. Many farmers turned to dairying and tobacco growing, although tobacco prices also fell. During the Great Depression of the 1930s, thirteen county banks closed and Bamberg was one of twenty-seven South Carolina counties with an unemployment rate of more than thirty percent. In a nationally hailed experiment in 1927 to control mosquito larvae, Howell's Old Mill was sprayed with Paris green. During World War II the county again lost twenty servicemen. A prisoner-of-war camp was located at Rhoad Park in Bamberg.

The economy recovered somewhat after the war. Many residents were employed at the nearby Savannah River atomic energy plant and at related industries. A county hospital was completed at Bamberg in 1952. The location of U.S. Highway 301 through the county, including the town of Bamberg, boosted the economy. A radio station began operations in 1957.

The 1900 census, the county's first, showed 17,296 residents. After an increase in 1920, the county's population has generally declined ever since. The population loss and federally mandated changes in legislative districting in 1974 eroded the rural county's once significant political influence. Court rulings and federal legislation shifted political power toward black voters, who outnumbered whites by a margin of just under two to one by 2000. In 1978 Rufus Grigsby and W. H. Nimmons became the first African Americans elected to Bamberg County Council. The Democrats, with a strong African American base, have maintained predominance in the county, which has never voted for a Republican presidential candidate.

Early in the twenty-first century, despite a declining agricultural economy, Bamberg County remained a heavy producer of corn, soybeans, wheat, cotton, and sorghum. Nonagricultural interests were hurt by the diversion of traffic from U.S. Highway 301 to new interstate routes. The area has sought to capitalize on recreation and tourism opportunities through the South Carolina Heritage Corridor project. The county's publicized sites include Rivers Bridge State Park, Best Friend Rail Trail, the Denmark railroad depot and train museum, Broxton Bridge plantation, a hunting preserve, the author William Gilmore Simms's plantation home, and various fishing spots. The county has an airport with a three-thousand-foot runway. Located in the Denmark area are Voorhees Junior College, a predominantly black Episcopal institution, and Denmark Technical College. Major towns include Bamberg with a 2000 population of 3,733, Denmark with 3,328, and Ehrhardt with 614. ROBERT A. PIERCE

Bamberg County Committee, Inc. *Bamberg County Celebrating South Carolina's Tricentennial, 1670–1970.* [Bamberg, S.C.], 1970.

Lawrence, Margaret Spann. *History of Bamberg County, South Carolina, Commemorating One Hundred Years (1897–1997).* Spartanburg, S.C.: Reprint Company, 2003.

Bank of Charleston / South Carolina National Bank. The Bank of Charleston traces its beginnings to 1818 as the Office of Discount and Deposit, South Carolina's branch of the Second Bank of the United States (BUS). After President Andrew Jackson refused to renew the BUS charter in 1834, South Carolina businessmen moved to create a financial institution able to supply the resources necessary to ensure the state's continued trade with European markets. On December 17, 1834, a group of Charleston investors under the guidance of Henry Gourdin secured a charter for the Bank of Charleston from the General Assembly. The formal organization of the bank took place in November 1835 with James Hamilton, Jr., installed as president. The new bank used the same workforce and building that served the old Office of Discount and Deposit.

As the largest private bank in antebellum South Carolina, the Bank of Charleston soon became regional in interest, opening agencies in the coastal cities of Apalachicola, Florida; Mobile, Alabama; and New Orleans. By 1860 the bank was one of the strongest financial institutions in the Southeast, with a reputation that carried across the Atlantic to the commercial centers of Western Europe.

When South Carolina seceded from the Union in 1860, the Bank of Charleston lent $100,000 to the state to support the new government. It would subsequently lend a total of $1.5 million to the Confederate government. The money was never repaid. The bank's assets of $6 million dwindled during the war, leaving the institution insolvent by the time of the Confederacy's collapse in 1865. Despite this setback, the Bank of Charleston was the only bank in South Carolina to resume business after the Civil War, thanks to timely loans from England arranged by bank president Charles T. Lowndes. The bank reopened its doors in 1870.

The twentieth century brought significant changes to banking. In 1914 the Bank of Charleston joined the new Federal Reserve System as a part of the Richmond district. The rise of suburbs prompted the bank to embrace branch banking in 1922 to capture both individual and small business accounts. The greatest change for the bank came in 1926, when its directors took advantage of the newly passed McFadden Act to consolidate with small banks in Greenville and Columbia to form the South Carolina National Bank (SCNB).

By the time of the Great Depression, SCNB was the largest bank in the state. It suffered badly during the economic downtown. The drastic drop in deposits put the bank at risk for collapse. The Emergency Banking Act of 1933 forced its reorganization under the guidance of federal bank examiners. SCNB subsequently prospered, using advertising for the first time in 1951, and with consumer lending becoming an increasingly important revenue source. In 1968 the bank expanded into automobile loans. It began using automatic teller machines in 1972. Wachovia acquired SCNB, South Carolina's last major independent bank, in 1991. CARYN E. NEUMANN

Clark, W. A. *The History of the Banking Institutions Organized in South Carolina Prior to 1860.* Columbia: Historical Commission of South Carolina, 1922.

Lindley, James G. *South Carolina National: The First 150 Years.* New York: Newcomen Society, 1985.

Rogers, George C., and Ronald E. Bridwell. *The South Carolina National Bank.* Columbia: South Carolina National Bank, 1984.

Stoney, Samuel Gaillard. *The Story of South Carolina's Senior Bank.* Columbia, S.C.: R. L. Bryan, 1955.

Bank of the State of South Carolina. The General Assembly chartered the Bank of the State of South Carolina (BSSC) in December 1812. Easily passing both houses of the legislature, the charter gave the new bank the power to circulate currency and act as the financial agent of the state. The main branch of the BSSC was located in Charleston (the financial center of the state), and the new bank catered to both commercial and agricultural interests, offering planters relatively easy terms of repayment and low rates of interest. The bank was run by a president and twelve directors elected annually by the General Assembly. Stephen Elliott served as the first president.

Elliott expanded the operations of the bank during his tenure, establishing branches in Columbia (1814), Georgetown (1817), and Camden (1822). A fourth branch would be established in the upstate at Abbeville in 1861. The bank proved to be an effective financial arm of the state, absorbing excess tax revenue that significantly expanded its operating capital. The BSSC grew into a powerful, well-funded institution that promoted currency stability. It posted more than $1.4 million in net profits for the state during Elliott's tenure.

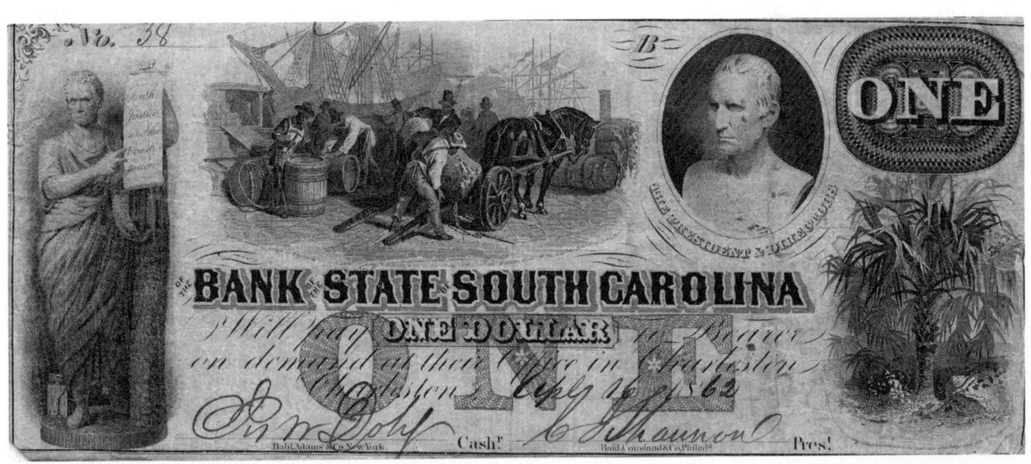

The Bank of the State of South Carolina was authorized to issue its own currency. Courtesy, South Carolina Department of Archives and History

Charles Jones Colcock was elected president of the BSSC in 1830, serving until his death in 1839. Colcock further expanded the BSSC's influence by establishing agencies in important market towns such as Hamburg and in the global financial centers of New York City and Liverpool, England. Rechartered in 1833, the bank briefly suspended specie payments during the Panic of 1837, but the institution weathered the financial crisis relatively well. Following a fire that decimated Charleston in 1838, the legislature authorized the sale of $2 million in bonds to aid Charleston. Proceeds were then deposited with the BSSC, which provided victims of the fire with low interest loans. The plan helped rebuild Charleston and expanded the operating capital of the bank.

Franklin H. Elmore succeeded Colcock as president in 1839. A controversial figure deeply involved in state politics, Elmore would have the most contentious tenure in the history of the bank. Throughout the 1840s opponents of the BSSC, led by Christopher G. Memminger and James H. Hammond, agitated for liquidation of the bank, arguing that the state should not be in the banking business and accusing Elmore and BSSC directors of cronyism and corruption. In particular, Elmore's involvement with the Nesbitt Manufacturing Company caused a stir, with critics charging that Elmore used his influence to provide the Nesbitt Company with loan extensions and readjustments of its debt. The BSSC remained a volatile political topic in the state until Elmore was appointed to the U.S. Senate following the death of Calhoun in 1850.

Elmore's successor, Charles M. Furman, was decidedly less political than his predecessor, and attacks on the bank subsided. Indeed, the bank would enjoy its greatest prosperity during the 1850s. It also helped to underwrite the modernization and expansion of the state's transportation network by serving as the state's agent in the purchase of hundreds of thousands of dollars in railroad stock. By 1860 the bank had working capital of almost $4 million.

During the Civil War, the BSSC wholeheartedly supported the state's war effort and the Confederate government. By 1863, due to staggering inflation, the resources of the bank were valued at $15 million, but more than half of this total was in Confederate securities or currency that became worthless at the end of the war. An attempt to recharter the bank was defeated in 1866. In 1868 the General Assembly ordered that the remaining assets of the bank be turned over to the state. Lawsuits over the proper distribution of assets to the bank's creditors clogged the courts until the 1880s. MICHAEL S. REYNOLDS

Elmore, Franklin Harper. *Defence of the Bank of the State of South Carolina, in a Series of Letters Addressed to the People of South Carolina.* Columbia, S.C.: Palmetto-State Banner Office, [1850?].

Ford, Lacy K., Jr. *Origins of Southern Radicalism: The South Carolina Upcountry, 1800–1860.* New York: Oxford University Press, 1988.

Lesesne, J. Mauldin. *The Bank of the State of South Carolina: A General and Political History.* Columbia: University of South Carolina Press, 1970.

Banks, Anna De Costa (1869–1930). Nurse. Banks was born in Charleston on September 2, 1869. She studied in that city's African American schools. Banks was one of the first students to earn a diploma from the Hampton Institute's Training School for Nurses in Virginia and became a registered nurse in 1893. Banks was employed as head nurse of Hampton's Dixie Hospital for two years.

By 1898 Banks was named the first head nurse at Charleston Hospital and Training School, and she dedicated her life to nursing and seeking more equitable health care for African Americans. Promoted to superintendent of nurses, Banks devoted more than thirty-two years to this hospital and the training of nurses. She also was a visiting public-health nurse for the Ladies Benevolent Society of Charleston for twenty-four years and a collector interacting with black policyholders for the Metropolitan Life Insurance Company.

In 1899 Banks wrote an article for the eighth annual report of the Hampton Training School for Nurses and Dixie Hospital discussing the problems black nurses faced. She stressed the need for funds to create hospitals to offer practical training for black nurses who were denied assignments to rounds in most hospitals because of segregation. Hospital personnel even refused to permit African American nurses to gain experience by attending lectures in wards specifically for black patients. Banks emphasized that black nurses must be trained to prevent whites from securing all of the available nursing positions and that doctors expected and demanded trained nurses instead of "mormers" and "grannies" who informally provided health care. Banks noted that racial violence intensified the need for emergency services and nursing schools for blacks, and she stated that victims of racially motivated assaults had fled to her hospital from throughout South Carolina. Banks sought donations from African American churches and societies and established the Hospital Association to generate funds through membership pledges and fairs. She printed a journal that reported hospital news and goals.

Sometimes discouraged by the overwhelming nature of her work, Banks commented, "Our hospital work is entirely among the poor, ignorant, and superstitious class of colored people of Charleston and its counties," consisting mostly of those "who believe in all kinds of signs and conjuration." Despite the black populace's ignorance and reluctance to consult physicians, Banks believed that they deserved quality health care, asking, "Should we not try to do something to relieve the suffering of these poor people by placing hospitals and medical aid within their reach?" Estimating that only half of her hospital's patients could pay the three-dollar weekly costs, Banks frequently encountered financial obstacles. She was bolstered by some community support, stating, "Many times just as I am about to give up, some kind friend sends us a dollar or fifty cents to keep it going."

Banks died on November 29, 1930, and was believed to be the oldest trained nurse in South Carolina at that time. When McClennan Hospital was relocated closer to the Medical University of South Carolina in 1959, it was renamed McClennan-Banks Hospital to reflect Banks's influence on regional health care. ELIZABETH D. SCHAFER

Hine, Darlene Clark. *Black Women in White: Racial Conflict and Cooperation in the Nursing Profession 1890–1950.* Bloomington: Indiana University Press, 1989.

———, ed. *Black Women in the Nursing Profession: A Documentary History.* New York: Garland, 1985.

Thoms, Adah B. *Pathfinders: A History of the Progress of Colored Graduate Nurses.* 1929. Reprint, New York: Garland, 1985.

Banov, Leon (1888–1971). Physician, public health official. Banov was born in Suwalki, Poland, on July 5, 1888, the son of Alexander Banov and Sonia Danielewicz. He immigrated to South Carolina at the age of eight to join his parents in Charleston. Banov did not attend high school but read at home and held a series of odd jobs. He enjoyed working in a pharmacy, which led him to enroll in the Pharmacy School of the Medical College of South Carolina, where he received the Ph.G. in 1907. Banov's return to the Medical College and lifelong interest in preventive medicine were stimulated by his sister's death from tuberculosis. He received the M.D. in 1917. In 1912 he married Minnie Monash. The couple had three children.

In 1920 an appropriation of $10,000 from the state and a grant from the Rockefeller Foundation helped establish Charleston County's health department. Dr. James A. Hayne, director of the state Board of Health, made Banov the county's first health officer after recalling the extensive overtime Banov worked as a city bacteriologist and food inspector during the World War I influenza pandemic. As county health officer, Banov and his staff—a secretary, a public health nurse, and two sanitary inspectors—instituted routine medical examinations of schoolchildren, enforced existing laws requiring smallpox vaccinations, and advocated inoculation against typhoid. The county's infant mortality rate led the nation, so Banov secured funding from the federal Children's Bureau and the Rockefeller Foundation to establish schools for midwives, well-baby clinics, parenting programs, and a nursing service. Since tuberculosis was especially severe in Charleston during the 1920s, Banov built an eighty-bed sanatorium seven miles outside the city and promoted public awareness of the disease through newspaper articles and radio spots.

Beginning in 1926, Banov served as the public health officer for both the county and the city of Charleston. He combined the two departments in 1936 and remained as director until his retirement in 1962. Despite South Carolina's small public health allocations, Banov attracted the attention of peers throughout the country and both federal and private funding sources because of his efficiency and diligence. When Charleston County was dropped from the birth registration area in the mid-1920s because physicians and midwives failed to submit the required number of records, Banov began sending greeting cards to newborns with enclosed birth records. Parents appreciated the gesture and pressured attendants to report births more accurately so that they could receive copies of the birth certificates. Charleston was among the sites selected for the initial demonstration of the Salk polio vaccine due to Banov's reputation and record keeping. Banov remained steadfast in his commitment to vaccinating large numbers of patients at specialized clinics despite a county doctor's threat to shoot him for curtailing his practice. He also prevailed when the county Medical Society opposed the free clinics he organized to dispense diphtheria toxoid. For Banov, preventive medicine and the health of Charleston's poor and working-class citizens trumped the private practices of individual physicians.

After his retirement, Banov further developed his love of carpentry, gardening to attract birds, painting, and sculpture. He enjoyed good health into his eighties and saw his son Leon, Jr., follow him as a physician. Banov was killed in an auto accident on November 4, 1971, and was buried in the Kahal Kadosh Beth Elohim Cemetery in Charleston. PATRICIA EVRIDGE HILL

Banov, Leon. *As I Recall: The Story of the Charleston County Health Department.* Columbia, S.C.: R. L. Bryan, 1970.

A Quarter of a Century of Public Health in Charleston, South Carolina. Charleston, S.C.: Charleston County Department of Health, [1945?].

Smith, William Atmar. *Leon Banov, M.D., and Public Health in Charleston.* Columbia, S.C.: R. L. Bryan, 1968.

Baptist Educational and Missionary Convention. During the Reconstruction era, Baptist congregations serving African Americans quickly formed throughout rural South Carolina. Because Baptists historically emphasized the autonomy of local congregations and because the churches were widely scattered, there was little impetus to organize them into a separate denomination. Nor were Baptist churches affiliated with African American denominations that had roots in the North, as was the case with Methodist congregations that identified with the African Methodist Episcopal Church or the African Methodist Zion Church.

But growth brought with it a need to coordinate some activities, particularly in religious education in Sunday schools, missionary and evangelism activities, and training for clergy. In 1876 representatives from some of these independent African American Baptist congregations met in Sumter and organized the Colored Baptist Educational, Missionary, and Sunday School Convention to provide leadership. The name was later changed to the Baptist Educational and Missionary Convention, and the body is known popularly as the "Baptist E & M."

To provide more higher educational opportunities for African Americans, the convention founded Morris College in Sumter in 1908. In the early twenty-first century the convention continued to support Morris, as well as Benedict and Friendship colleges. The convention provided training opportunities for local church leaders who work in neighborhood evangelism, Sunday schools, and women's auxiliaries. As with other African American churches and denominations, the convention has also been involved in social causes; from the outset, for example, Baptist E & M offered an insurance program to members.

By 1916 the convention had grown to some 225,000 members. Estimates in 2000 suggested that around 1,500 congregations with an aggregate membership approaching 450,000 had ties to the convention. The convention has its headquarters in Columbia and holds membership in the South Carolina Christian Action Council.
C. N. WILLBORN

Lippy, Charles H., ed. *Religion in South Carolina.* Columbia: University of South Carolina Press, 1993.

Baptists. Baptists are by far the largest religious group in South Carolina, and in many ways they are the most diverse. They are black and white, Asian and Hispanic, rich and poor, educated and uneducated, and liberal and conservative in their politics, their social views, and their theology. Some Baptist congregations are among the largest in the state, with thousands of members, but most churches have fewer than three hundred congregants. Southern Baptists are the largest denominational group, but National Baptists and Independent Baptists are also numerous. Other smaller groups of Baptists, such as Two Seed in the Spirit or Primitive Baptists, come and go.

As different as Baptist groups or even churches within a group may be from each other, almost all Baptists share a commitment to believers' baptism by immersion, the Bible as the primary source of faith, and a congregational church polity. Most could be identified theologically as evangelical Calvinists, but they have traditionally been noncreedal. Although ministers may have a great deal of influence within their own congregations, and some have influence beyond that, Baptists have no formal hierarchy, which in part accounts for their diversity.

Baptists were relatively few during the colonial era, and their membership has always been largely working and middle class, but the denomination has nevertheless had a profound influence on South Carolina and its development. The commitment and zeal of these average folk, who believe that all church members have an obligation to minister, led to tremendous growth in their churches. Based on the group's enthusiasm for counting their baptisms, some have said that "there are more Baptists than people" in the state.

But Baptist influence does not stop with their sheer numbers. Baptist evangelical zeal and commitment to service have profoundly

The First Baptist Church in Charleston is considered the mother church of the Southern Baptist Convention. Photograph by Rick Rhodes

influenced the nature of life and religious practice in South Carolina, which has been integral to the state's identity as part of the Bible Belt. The rugged independence of Baptists undoubtedly influenced the formation of South Carolina's particular brand of politics. This same sense of independence, along with a belief in the all-sufficiency of the Bible, led many Baptists to be far less concerned with having an educated clergy than other groups were. Over the years, despite the existence of respected Baptist educational institutions such as Furman University, these attitudes may have contributed to a lack of emphasis on education in some circles, not only in the pulpits but also in the larger society.

The tensions over issues such as the importance of education and the independence of local congregations were present almost from the beginning and are reflected in the state's two earliest Baptist groups, Regular Baptists and Separate Baptists. Regular Baptists, more than the Separates, were inclined toward educated ministers and organizational structures that extended beyond the local church. Eventually these differences were ingeniously overcome. Under the creative leadership of men such as Richard Furman and William B. Johnson, most Baptists in the state were united, beginning in 1821, in what was in many ways a novel organizational form, the South Carolina Baptist Convention. Its loose institutional structure encouraged cooperation in the support of missions and education while still allowing a great deal of congregational independence.

This same strategy would influence the structure of the regional (now national) body of the Southern Baptist Convention, founded in 1845 after Baptists of the South broke with the Triennial Convention (founded in 1814), a break that was one of many early signs of the coming Civil War. Today the largest percentage of white Baptist churches in the state are affiliated with both the South Carolina Baptist Convention and the Southern Baptist Convention, although membership in one does not necessarily involve membership in the other.

In the nineteenth century, African slaves often attended church with their masters, most of whom were not Baptists. But after the Civil War, freed Christian slaves were attracted to Baptist polity because of the congregational autonomy, the flexibility in worship style, and the absence of ordination requirements. Hence, the number of African American Baptists grew quickly. Eventually many of these churches affiliated with the National Baptist Convention, but many others remained small and independent.

Beginning as early as the 1950s, the same sense of autonomy and freedom that characterized Baptists placed African American Baptist churches and ministers at the forefront of the civil rights movement, not only nationally but also in South Carolina. Integration was eventually achieved, but not usually in the churches. Despite their many similarities, black Baptists and white Baptists have remained largely separate groups, and some white Baptists opposed the civil rights efforts of their African American brothers and sisters.

Just as the Baptist ideal of the priesthood of the believer inspired independence and social action among African American Baptists, so too it inspired Southern Baptist women to move out of their traditional domain to act independently on behalf of missions. In South Carolina, as in most states, the Woman's Missionary Union was a powerful force, raising much money for traditional missions. But sometimes these same forces led to unexpected consequences. The second woman ordained in the Southern Baptist Convention was ordained in Columbia in 1971. This event signaled the changing times ahead.

Baptists have usually been conservative, but contrary to popular opinion, until recently most have not been fundamentalists. Indeed, independent fundamentalist Baptists, such as those associated with Bob Jones University, were the exception rather than the rule until the late twentieth century. Baptists were so much at the center of South Carolina culture that when the first wave of fundamentalism developed at the turn of the twentieth century in the urban Northeast, South Carolina Baptists had no need to acquire the militant exclusivism so much identified with that movement.

With the burst of growth and urbanization associated with the rise of the Sunbelt, along with all of the other upheavals of the 1960s, this began to change. By the 1980s fundamentalists began to gain influence in the South Carolina Baptist Convention, which led to calls for more uniformity in belief and practice, especially on issues such as the ordination of women. Tensions with so-called moderate Baptists increased, and in the 1990s events such as the organization of the more moderate Cooperative Baptist Fellowship and the convention's break with Furman University made it clear that Baptist identity had become polarized. HELEN LEE TURNER

King, Joe M. *A History of South Carolina Baptists.* Columbia: General Board of the South Carolina Baptist Convention, 1964.

Owens, Loulie Latimer. *Saints of Clay: The Shaping of South Carolina Baptists.* Columbia, S.C.: R. L. Bryan, 1971.

Turner, Helen Lee. "The Evangelical Traditions I: Baptists." In *Religion in South Carolina,* edited by Charles H. Lippy. Columbia: University of South Carolina Press, 1993.

Barbados. South Carolina's origins are so closely tied to the British West Indian colony of Barbados that it has been called a "Colony of a Colony." The historian Jack Greene has called Barbados the "culture hearth" of the southeastern, slavery-dominated plantation economy. Surprisingly little is yet known of the origins of South Carolina's early leaders. Although the Barbadian influence has probably been overstated and South Carolina's plantation owners never became absentee landlords to the degree of the West Indian sugar planters, South Carolina did come to more closely resemble the West Indies than did any of the other English mainland colonies.

Initially settled by the English in 1627, Barbados had become an exceedingly wealthy, sugar-dominated economy by the time of

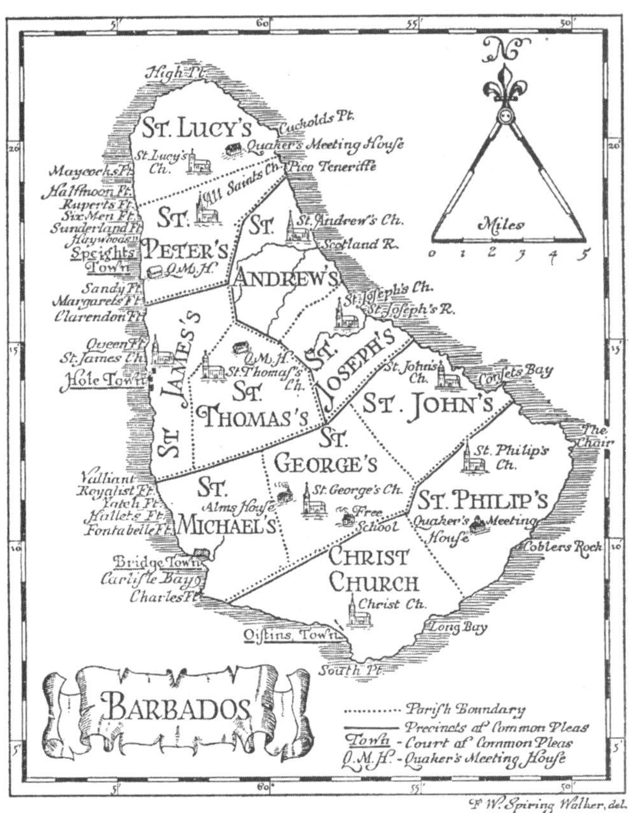

A map of seventeenth-century Barbados; nine of the eleven parish names would later be used in South Carolina. Vincent T. Harlow, *A History of Barbados, 1625–1685*, p. 335

South Carolina's settlement in 1670. Sir John Colleton, who probably led the effort to gain the Carolina charter for eight English noblemen, had become a Barbadian planter after the defeat of the royalist cause in the Puritan Revolution. Anthony Ashley Cooper, later the first earl of Shaftesbury and the leading proprietor in the settling of South Carolina, had also owned a Barbados plantation. First Shaftesbury, who had other strong Caribbean interests, and then the Colleton family provided the leadership for the settlement's owners until almost the end of the seventeenth century.

Initially the Lords Proprietors hoped to populate their colony with settlers from Barbados and other New World colonies rather than from England. A group of "Barbadian Adventurers" sent an exploratory expedition in 1663, obtained concessions from the proprietors, and attempted to establish a settlement at Cape Fear. Although the Barbadian settlement at Cape Fear was abandoned in 1667, the subsequent successful 1669 settling expedition from England picked up some Barbadians on its way to Carolina. Much of the shipping from England in the early years came via Barbados, and substantial numbers of Barbadians, both white and black, immigrated to the Carolina lowcountry.

Barbados has a total of only 166 square miles of land, and by 1670 most of it was tied up in increasingly fewer and larger sugar "factories." South Carolina offered both opportunities for younger sons and smaller farmers and the prospect of provisions to feed the Barbadians. Although the emigration of freemen, indentured servants, and slaves from Barbados was large only in South Carolina's early years (and has been inflated by misidentification of persons only passing through the West Indies on their way to Carolina), the ties between the colonies remained strong. Provisions and barrel staves were among South Carolina's earliest profitable enterprises and remained a substantial portion of exports even after large rice plantations cultivated by slave labor came to dominate the colony after the 1690s. Lowcountry parishes with slave populations of more than eighty percent and appalling mortality rates even shared the names of parishes in Barbados. As late as 1766, the South Carolina Commons House of Assembly appropriated £785 to help those who had lost their homes in the great Bridgetown fire.

Proprietary South Carolina's powerful Goose Creek political faction contained Barbadians. Their efforts to circumvent the proprietors' prohibitions against selling Native Americans into slavery and dealing with pirates plagued the colony's owners for years. Sir John Yeamans, who abandoned the earlier failed Barbadian settlement at Cape Fear and arranged the murder of his paramour's husband so that he could marry her, has been cited by the historian Robert Weir as "in many ways the archetype of the aggressive Barbadians" and "a pirate ashore." While serving as South Carolina's third governor from 1672 to 1674, he infuriated Lord Shaftesbury by making profits selling to Barbados provisions that were desperately needed in Carolina. Proprietary South Carolina had two other Barbadian governors: James Colleton, a brother of the man who then held the Colleton family share in the enterprise; and Robert Gibbes, who bribed his way into the governor's office in 1710.

Rice became as important in South Carolina as sugar was in Barbados, but Carolinians never relied on a single crop to the same degree that their island counterparts did. South Carolina's slave code, modeled on that of Barbados, was the harshest on the continent. Whatever the proportion of Barbadian influence, South Carolina's small white elite faction became exceedingly wealthy. The ties between the two colonies were closer than those between some other parts of the Atlantic world, but by the mid-eighteenth century Charleston had become South Carolina's cultural center.
CHARLES H. LESSER

Campbell, P[eter]. F. *Some Early Barbadian History.* St. Michael, Barbados: by the author, 1993.

Greene, Jack P. "Colonial South Carolina and the Caribbean Connection." *South Carolina Historical Magazine* 88 (October 1987): 192–210.

Lesser, Charles H. *South Carolina Begins: The Records of a Proprietary Colony, 1663–1721.* Columbia: South Carolina Department of Archives and History, 1995.

Barbecue. South Carolina barbecue is slowly cooked, hand-pulled or shredded pork that is flavored with a tangy sauce and usually served with side dishes such as rice, hash, cole slaw, sweet pickles, white bread, and iced tea. Barbecue often is served on festive occasions such as holidays, family reunions, weddings, church and community fund-raisers, football tailgating parties, and political meetings. It varies widely across the state with respect to cooking methods, cuts of pork, sauce type, and side dishes served. Barbecue is often the topic of friendly debate since many South Carolinians have strong preferences for particular types that reflect the cultural character and identity of specific regions or places.

Traditionally the pork is cooked in an open pit fueled by hardwood coals. The pit usually is a rectangular cement block structure of variable length, about three feet high and five to six feet wide, with either iron or steel rods across the narrow width. Openings at floor level allow for refueling and air circulation control. Hot hickory or oak coals are placed at the bottom, and the meat is suspended above the coals on the rods. The pit usually is housed in a shelter-like building with partially screened walls. Many restaurants have

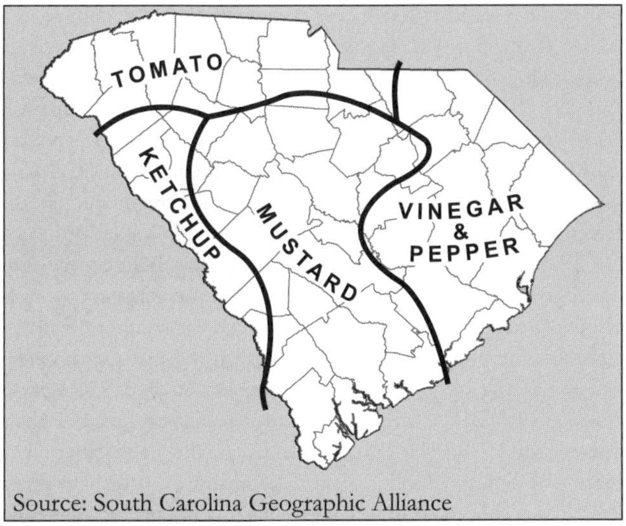

Source: South Carolina Geographic Alliance

South Carolina's four barbeque regions

converted to gas or electric cookers and abandoned the open pit because it is labor intensive and the cost of wood is high. There is an endless variety of portable cookers, and each's design is as much a point of pride as is the barbecue.

The whole hog typically is cooked in the coastal plain regions, while shoulders, hams, or Boston butts are used in the Piedmont. There are at least four basic sauce types. Watery thin and fiery hot pepper and vinegar concoctions dominate the Pee Dee region, while the upstate and Savannah River areas favor peppery tomato or milder ketchup-based sauces. A yellow-mustard-based sauce is favored in the Midlands. As sauce types differ from place to place, their uses also vary. Some use sauce as a baster while the meat is cooked; others douse the meat with sauce after it is cooked; and sometimes the meat is served without sauce, allowing consumer discretion. Sauces often are derived from secret family recipes, and each sauce has a strong regional following.

Some barbecue restaurants serve one or two side dishes, while all-you-can-eat barbecue buffets in the coastal plain regions include a wide assortment of regional specialties. These may include greens such as turnip, mustard, or collard; baked beans, green beans cooked in fatback, or butter beans; peas such as crowder, field, or black-eyed; sweet potatoes; fried okra; and sweet or creamed corn. Barbecued and fried chicken, pork skins, ribs, and banana pudding are other common buffet selections. Regional specialties such as chicken bog and liver hash are served in the Pee Dee, while the northeastern Piedmont is known for its hash barbecue and chicken stew. Many barbecue restaurants post a familiar sign urging patrons not to waste food: "TAKE ALL YOU WANT, BUT EAT ALL YOU TAKE." Most cater to families and rarely serve alcoholic beverages. CHARLES F. KOVACIK

Egerton, John. *Southern Food: At Home, on the Road, in History.* New York: Knopf, 1987.

Elie, Lolis Eric. *Smokestack Lightning: Adventures in the Heart of Barbecue Country.* New York: Farrar, Straus, and Giroux, 1996.

Johnson, Greg, and Vince Staten. *Real Barbecue.* New York: Perennial, 1988.

Wall, Allie Patricia, and Ron L. Layne. *Hog Heaven: A Guide to South Carolina Barbecue.* Lexington, S.C.: Sandlapper Store, 1979.

Barhamville Academy. Founded in 1828, Barhamville Academy was the common name for the South Carolina Female Collegiate Institute, an institution for the higher education of women that was located outside of Columbia. It was founded by Dr. Elias Marks (1790–1886), a physician and educator who served as principal of the Columbia Female Academy from 1817 to 1828. The school was located on property northeast of Columbia that Marks called "Barhamville" to honor his late wife, Jane Barham, a teacher who shared his commitment to the development of women's intellectual abilities.

The school opened in 1828 as the South Carolina Female Institute, but in 1835 it added "Collegiate" to its name, reflecting the institution's provision of a rigorous four-year classical curriculum. Marks was joined in his work by his second wife, Julia Warne, a graduate of Emma Willard's Troy Female Seminary in New York and a former teacher. The school attracted boarding and day students, with a total enrollment of more than 120 students in 1855. The renowned surgeon J. Marion Sims recalled in his memoir that "it was the first and only school of its character in the South." Among its most notable graduates were Ann Pamela Cunningham, who led the efforts to preserve Mount Vernon, and Martha Bulloch Roosevelt, the mother of President Theodore Roosevelt.

Dr. and Mrs. Marks retired from the school in 1861. In 1862 it continued under the leadership of Madame Acelie Togno, who had run a successful girls' school in Charleston, and in 1863 Madame Sophie Sosnowski was in charge. The institution closed after the Civil War. The buildings were destroyed by fire in 1869. A historic marker on Two Notch Road in northeast Columbia marks the school's location. BELINDA F. GERGEL

Cohen, Hennig, ed. *A Barhamville Miscellany.* Columbia: University of South Carolina Press, 1956.

Rembert, Sarah H. "Barhamville: A Columbia Antebellum Girls School." *South Carolina History Illustrated* 1 (February 1970): 44–48.

Barnwell (Barnwell County; 2000 pop. 5,035). Originally located on the old Stage Coach Road from Charleston to Augusta, Barnwell was first called Red Hill. Like Barnwell County, the town was named for John Barnwell of Beaufort. The first county courthouse was built in 1800 on five acres given by Benjamin Odom. Subsequent courthouses were built in 1819, 1830, 1848, 1871, and 1879. With several renovations and additions, the 1879 building continued to serve as the Barnwell County Courthouse into the twenty-first century.

Although important as the district seat of justice, Barnwell grew slowly. By the mid-1820s the village contained just 120 inhabitants. The town was incorporated in December 1829. The line of the South Carolina Canal and Rail Road Company passed some ten miles to the west of Barnwell in the 1830s, and the town's economic importance declined relative to the newer railroad towns such as Blackville and Williston. Barnwell would not gain a railroad until 1880, when a short line connecting the town with Blackville was completed.

Late in the Civil War, in February 1865, Barnwell was occupied by federal troops under the command of General Hugh Judson Kilpatrick. Most businesses and public buildings, except for the churches, were destroyed. As a result, the county courthouse resided for several years in nearby Blackville before returning to Barnwell in 1875. Court was held in the Barnwell Presbyterian Church until a new courthouse was completed in 1879. Despite the carnage wrought by the war, more than a dozen antebellum houses survive in Barnwell, including the office used in the latter half of the 1800s by Dr. Todd, a physician and brother-in-law of Abraham Lincoln.

Perhaps Barnwell's most enduring feature is the 1858 free-standing vertical sundial located in front of the courthouse. It was given to the town by Joseph Duncan Allen, a wealthy planter, politician, and soldier. In 1907 a portion of the five acres given by Benjamin Odom, later containing the Confederate Monument, was named Calhoun Park honoring Clinton Calhoun, longtime mayor of Barnwell.

Barnwell remained a commercial center for county farmers well into the twentieth century. This situation changed in the years following World War II, however, as the town and county began to move from an agricultural to an industrial-based economy. The coming of the Savannah River Plant in the 1950s briefly swelled the town's population to some fifteen thousand during the time of construction. Most of these temporary residents left once the plant was completed in the mid-1950s, but enough remained to more than double the population of Barnwell during the decade, from 2,005 in 1950 to 4,568 by 1960. Aggressive recruitment efforts by local leaders helped attract major industrial plants to Barnwell during the 1950s, including a $10 million woolens plant opened by Amerotron in 1956 (later acquired by Deering-Milliken) and an optical parts and machinery factory built by Shuron Optical Company a few years later.

Barnwell's population peaked at 5,572 in 1980 and stabilized at about 5,000 entering the twenty-first century. Residents enjoy access to a thriving industrial park, airport, library, hospital, strong churches, community theater, museum, and recreational programs. A portion of the 135-acre Lake Edgar Brown lies within the city limits of Barnwell. ELLEN BUSH JENKINS AND POSEY BELCHER

Barnwell County Heritage Book Committee. *Barnwell County Heritage, South Carolina.* Marceline, Mo.: Walsworth, 1994.

Flynn, Jean Martin. *A History of the Barnwell First Baptist Church and Antebellum Barnwell.* Barnwell, S.C.: Barnwell First Baptist Church, 2002.

Barnwell, John (ca. 1671–1724). Soldier. Barnwell was born in Dublin, Ireland, the son of Alderman Matthew Barnwell and Margaret Carberry. Matthew Barnwell was killed in the Siege of Derry in 1690 as a captain in James II's Irish Army, which attempted to restore the last Stuart king to the English throne. The family seat, Archerstown in county Meath, was forfeited as a consequence of these events.

John Barnwell immigrated to South Carolina in 1701. He became a protégé of Governor Nathaniel Johnson and Chief Justice Nicholas Trott. Barnwell was appointed deputy surveyor (1703), clerk of the council (1703), and deputy secretary of the council (1704). As a surveyor, he mapped the newly settled Sea Islands around Port Royal Sound. It was there that he staked his claim to 6,500 acres of land. Barnwell became one of the first British settlers of Port Royal Island and an active trader with the nearby Yamassee Indians.

In 1711 Barnwell was chosen to lead a South Carolina expedition against an uprising of the Tuscarora Indians in eastern North Carolina. With a small army of thirty Carolinians and three hundred Native Americans, Barnwell successfully assaulted the Tuscarora town of Narhantes and burned the Tuscarora villages in eastern North Carolina. Though the campaign met with some criticism in North Carolina because Tuscarora had not been completely dislodged, "Tuscarora Jack" Barnwell nevertheless returned to a hero's welcome in South Carolina.

On April 15, 1715, the Yamassee War erupted suddenly at Pocotaligo, near Beaufort. The initial massacre took the lives of Indian Commissioner Thomas Nairne and most of the British settlers south of the Edisto River. Barnwell and the settlers on Port Royal Island escaped to a British merchant ship at anchor in the Beaufort River. Barnwell led the Port Royal militia in a counterattack that destroyed the principal Yamassee villages south of the Combahee River. The Yamassee warriors retreated to Spanish Florida, from whence they continued to raid the Port Royal area until 1728. During this period Barnwell commanded the "Carolina Scouts," a waterborne militia force that patrolled the inland passage between Charleston and St. Augustine.

In 1719, after the overthrow of the proprietary regime, the provisional government sent Barnwell to London as its agent to convince the Board of Trade to settle and defend the southern frontier. At this time he presented the "Barnwell Plan" of settlement, which called for a ring of royal garrisons from the coast of Georgia to Tennessee, surrounded by royal grants of free land to attract settlers. Returning in 1720 with Francis Nicholson, the first acting royal governor of South Carolina, and a company of British soldiers, Barnwell was able to construct Fort King George on the Altamaha River at Darien, Georgia. This was the first British settlement (1721) in what was later the royal colony of Georgia.

Barnwell died at Port Royal on May 4, 1724. He was survived by his wife Anne Berners and six children whose descendants formed the core of the sea island planter elite and political leadership until the Civil War. LAWRENCE S. ROWLAND

Barnwell, Stephen B. *Story of an American Family.* Marquette, Mich., 1969.

Edgar, Walter B., and N. Louise Bailey, eds. *Biographical Directory of the South Carolina House of Representatives.* Vol. 2, *The Commons House of Assembly, 1692–1775.* Columbia: University of South Carolina Press, 1977.

Rowland, Lawrence S., Alexander Moore, and George C. Rogers. *The History of Beaufort County, South Carolina.* Vol. 1, *1514–1861.* Columbia: University of South Carolina Press, 1996.

Salley, Alexander S. "Barnwell of South Carolina." *South Carolina Historical and Genealogical Magazine* 2 (January 1901): 46–88.

Barnwell, Robert Woodward (1801–1882). Educator, congressman, U.S. senator. Barnwell was born near Beaufort on August 10, 1801, the son of planter and politician Robert Gibbes Barnwell and Elizabeth Hayne Wigg. He received his early education in Beaufort and Charleston and in 1817 entered Harvard, where he was the valedictorian of the class of 1821. Barnwell returned to Charleston to read law in the offices of James Hamilton, Jr., and James L. Petigru. He was admitted to the bar in 1823 and established a law practice in Beaufort District with his cousin Robert Barnwell Rhett.

In 1826 he was elected to the state General Assembly, where he represented Prince William's Parish for a single term in the House of Representatives. The following year, on August 9, 1827, he married his second cousin Eliza Barnwell, with whom he had thirteen children. He ran successfully for Congress in 1828 and served from 1829 to 1833. Barnwell was a prominent nullifier, attending the nullification convention and signing the Ordinance of Nullification. Though he was unopposed for reelection, he retired at the end of his second term.

Barnwell returned to Beaufort to manage his legal practice and planting interests. In late 1835 he replaced the controversial Thomas Cooper as president of South Carolina College. Barnwell succeeded in restoring the college's public credibility, as evidenced by rising enrollment and legislative appropriations for construction projects and book purchases. Blaming ill health, he resigned the presidency in 1841. His relationship with South Carolina College endured, however, and he remained a trustee almost continuously until his death.

After the death of U.S. Senator Franklin H. Elmore, Governor Whitemarsh B. Seabrook appointed Barnwell to the U.S. Senate, where he served from June 4 to December 8, 1850. During his brief term, the Senate considered the legislation making up the Compromise of 1850. Barnwell opposed many of the proposals, including the admission of California as a free state. Although he served as a delegate to the Nashville Convention (1850) and to the Southern Rights Convention (1852), Barnwell was among the leading "cooperationists," considering separate state secession to be "fraught with danger."

With the election of Abraham Lincoln in 1860, Barnwell changed his position and embraced secession. He signed the Ordinance of Secession and was elected one of three commissioners to negotiate with President James Buchanan for the transfer of federal property in South Carolina to state control. He sat in the Provisional Confederate Congress in Montgomery, serving as its temporary chairman in February 1861 and as a member of the committee that drafted the Confederate constitution. Confederate president Jefferson Davis offered Barnwell the position of secretary of state, but he declined. He represented South Carolina in the Confederate Senate for the duration of its existence and was among South Carolina's few consistent supporters of the Davis administration.

His wealth destroyed in the war, Barnwell in late 1865 returned to the reorganized and renamed University of South Carolina to serve as chairman of the faculty, the institution's chief executive. He served until 1873, when, following the takeover of the university's board of trustees by the Radical Republicans, Barnwell was dismissed. He opened a private school for girls in Columbia, but after the university was closed in 1877, Governor Wade Hampton III appointed Barnwell to serve as the institution's librarian, secretary, and treasurer. He held the post until his death in Columbia on November 24, 1882. He was buried in the St. Helena Episcopal Churchyard, Beaufort. HENRY H. LESESNE

Barnwell, John. "Hamlet to Hotspur: Letters of Robert Woodward Barnwell to Robert Barnwell Rhett." *South Carolina Historical Magazine* 77 (October 1976): 236–56.

Hollis, Daniel W. "Robert W. Barnwell." *South Carolina Historical Magazine* 56 (July 1955): 131–37.

———. *University of South Carolina.* 2 vols. Columbia: University of South Carolina Press, 1951, 1956.

Moore, Alexander, ed. *Biographical Directory of the South Carolina House of Representatives.* Vol. 5, *1816–1828.* Columbia: South Carolina Department of Archives and History, 1992.

Barnwell County (548 sq. miles; 2000 pop. 23,478). Barnwell District, now Barnwell County, was created in 1798 from the area formerly known as Winton County. Located at the southwestern edge of South Carolina, the district originally encompassed 1,440 square miles but lost most of its territory to the creation of Aiken County (1871), Bamberg County (1897), and Allendale County (1919). The district was named for John Barnwell of Beaufort in recognition of his military service to South Carolina.

For its first 150 years, the Barnwell economy had an agricultural base. Thick pine forests blanketing the district slowed the expansion of agriculture somewhat, but by 1850 only neighboring Edgefield District produced more cotton than Barnwell. Cotton wealth led to a concomitant rise in the district's slave population. Although whites comprised almost eighty percent of the Barnwell population in 1800, they had become a minority by 1850. The district's wealth of waterways, including the Savannah, Edisto, and Salkehatchie Rivers and their many tributaries, were significant sources of timber and

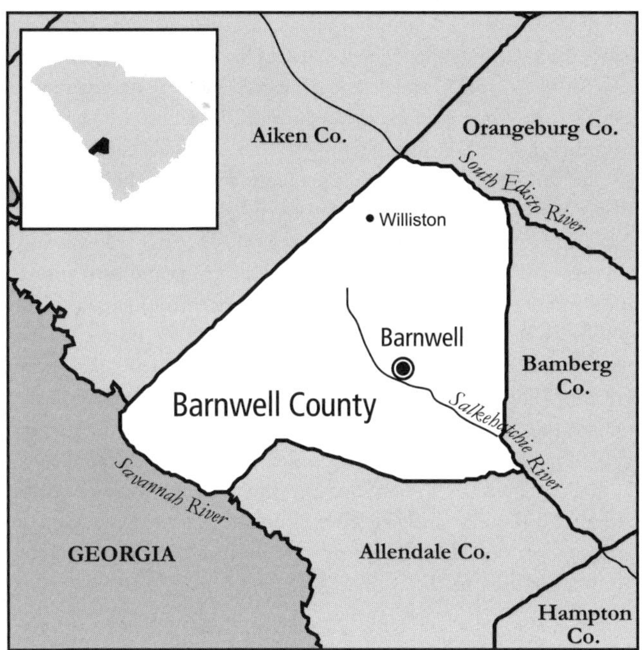

lumber for lowcountry markets. The completion of a railroad from Charleston to Hamburg through Barnwell District in 1833 spurred additional development, transforming quiet villages and turnouts into bustling centers of local trade, including the towns of Williston, Elko, and Blackville.

Federal troops destroyed most of the businesses in Barnwell County in February 1865. After the Civil War, Barnwell farmers continued to produce cotton. But as prices declined, many turned to truck farming, especially asparagus and melons. In 1880 a new railroad connected Blackville and Barnwell. In addition to its agriculture, Barnwell County became known in the twentieth century for its powerful political leaders, which critics dubbed the "Barnwell Ring." Longtime S.C. Senate president Edgar A. Brown and House Speaker Solomon Blatt hailed from Barnwell County, as did Winchester C. Smith, chairman of the Ways and Means Committee, and Governor Emile Harley.

In 1950 the U.S. Government announced plans for the Savannah River Site, a massive nuclear weapons facility that would be located in Aiken and Barnwell Counties. This had a profound effect on Barnwell's geography and economy. The western third of the county was taken by the federal facility, including most of Barnwell's frontage on the Savannah River. Some six thousand people residing within the site's boundaries were forced to relocate, including the entire town of Dunbarton. Many residents moved to other sections of Barnwell County. The influx of construction crews, plant employees, and their families transformed Barnwell.

At the start of the twenty-first century, Barnwell County had seven townships: Barnwell, Blackville, Elko, Hilda, Kline, Snelling, and Williston, with Barnwell being the largest. The county is governed by the Barnwell County Council, comprised of members representing the three school districts and one member at large. Besides three public school districts, the county also has a career center used by each. Higher education opportunities were made available by a branch of Denmark Technical College and the Salkehatchie branch campus of the University of South Carolina in nearby Allendale.

By 2000 manufacturing provided more than one-fourth of the jobs in Barnwell County (less than two percent of the workforce remained employed in agriculture). Industrial parks occupy locations in or near the towns of Barnwell, Blackville, Snelling, and Williston. Major employers included Chem-Nuclear Systems, Dayco Corporation, Milliken and Company, and EFCO, Inc. The Economic Development Commission, created in 1987, vigorously pursued new industries, and Barnwell, Bamberg, and Allendale Counties created the TriCounty Alliance to encourage economic development for the region. Barnwell County Airport in Barnwell accommodates private and corporate planes with two 5,000-foot lighted runways.

Barnwell County offers an abundance of sports and recreational opportunities, including excellent fishing, game hunting, and boating. The 135-acre Lake Edgar Brown located in Barnwell and Barnwell State Park near Blackville offer individual and group recreation. Three golf courses and several walking trails are popular with outdoor enthusiasts. Well-known historic sites in the county include the Church of the Holy Apostles in Barnwell, the 1858 sundial that was given by Joseph Duncan Allen and is situated in front of the courthouse, and Healing Springs near Blackville. The Heritage Corridor Nature Trail dissects Barnwell County, bringing additional visitors to the region. ELLEN BUSH JENKINS AND POSEY BELCHER

Barnwell County Heritage Book Committee. *Barnwell County Heritage, South Carolina.* Marceline, Mo.: Walsworth, 1994.

Downey, Tom. *Planting a Capitalist South: Masters, Merchants, and Manufacturers in the Southern Interior, 1790–1860.* Baton Rouge: Louisiana State University Press, 2005.

Reynolds, Emily Bellinger, and Joan Reynolds Faunt, comps. *The County Officers and Officers of Barnwell County, S.C., 1775–1975: A Record.* Spartanburg, S.C.: Reprint Company, 1976.

Barrett, James Lee (1929–1989). Screenwriter. Once described as "perhaps the most prolific hyphenate (writer-producer) in Hollywood," James Lee Barrett was born on November 19, 1929, in Charlotte, North Carolina, the son of James Hamlin Barrett and Anne Blake. He grew up in Anderson, South Carolina. Following the early death of his mother, he was reared by four schoolteacher aunts and was remembered as an independent and mischievous boy who chafed under the hand of authority. He served as a reporter for his high school newspaper and attained the rank of Eagle Scout in a local Boy Scout troop.

Barrett pursued his education at Anderson College, Furman University, Pennsylvania State University, Columbia University, and the Art Students League in New York. After a stint in the U.S. Marine Corps he moved to New York City, where, failing to place any of the numerous short stories he had written, he began to try his hand at writing material for television. His first breakthrough was the production of his teleplay *Cold Harbor,* and soon after Barrett was writing for the big New York television market: Kraft Theatre, Playhouse 90, and Armstrong Circle Theatre. One of his Kraft teleplays, *Murder of a Sand Flea,* based on a Marine experience, caught the eye of the actor Jack Webb, who brought Barrett to Hollywood to adapt it into a movie. It was released in 1957 as *The D.I.,* and Barrett remained in the film capital for the rest of his life.

During the next thirty years Barrett wrote the scripts for some of Hollywood's most successful film and television productions. Among his most popular films were *The Greatest Story Ever Told, The Green Berets,* and *Smoky and the Bandit.* His screenplay for the comedy *The Cheyenne Social Club* won a Writers Guild of America award in 1970. One of his most enduring works has been the film *Shenandoah,* whose star, James Stewart, became a good friend. Barrett's musical book for the stage version of *Shenandoah* won him a Tony Award.

Barrett's made-for-television films include *Belle Star, Angel City, The Day Christ Died, Mayflower: The Pilgrim Experience, The Law & Charlie Dodge, April Morning, Stagecoach, Poker Alice, Vengeance,* and *The Quick and the Dead.* He created pilots for such productions as *The Doctors Brandon, Big Bad John, The Judge, When the Whistle Blows, Running Hot, The Cowboys, You the Jury,* and *Big Man, Little Lady.* He wrote the seven-hour, three-part miniseries *The Awakening Land* and the holiday special *Stubby Pringle's Christmas.* He developed *In the Heat of the Night* for television and was the originator of the popular series *Our House.* "I've told mostly about people," Barrett remarked near the end of his career. "And that, really, is what makes a good motion picture—the people and how real they are. Always the people."

Barrett was a member of the Academy of Motion Picture Arts and Sciences; the writers' Guild of America, West; the Dramatists' Guild; and the Authors' League of America. In 1998 he was inducted into the South Carolina Academy of Authors. He and his wife, Danish-born Merete Engelstoft Barrett, were the parents of five children. Barrett died of cancer on October 15, 1989, at his home in Templeton, California. THOMAS L. JOHNSON

Barrett, James Lee. Papers. South Caroliniana Library, University of South Carolina, Columbia.

Barrier islands. Barrier islands, which run parallel to the Atlantic and Gulf coasts, are so named because they shield the mainland (as well as inland Sea Islands) from damage caused by sea storms. South Carolina has thirty-five barrier islands, more than any other state except Florida. Among South Carolina's major barrier islands (from north to south) are Waites, Pawleys, Debordieu, North, South, Cedar, Murphy, Dewees, Isle of Palms, Sullivan's, Morris, Folly, Kiawah, Seabrook, Botany, Harbor, Hunting, Fripp, Hilton Head, and Daufuskie. Hilton Head, the state's largest barrier island, actually consists of an erosion remnant island as well as a barrier island; the two are separated by Broad Creek.

Two types of Sea Islands border the South Carolina coast: barrier islands and erosion remnant islands. Located inland from the ocean, erosion remnant islands originally were part of the mainland. When Ice Age glaciers lowered sea levels, streams cut river valleys into the newly dry land. But once the glaciers melted, the ocean level rose and flooded the river valleys. Less is known about the creation of barrier islands, and two theories exist regarding their origin. The first argues that barrier islands began as offshore sandbars, which waves built up with sand deposits. The second theory suggests that they are sand dune ridges remaining from the big glacier meltdown.

Barrier islands tend to possess an elongated shape. In general, the northern end is longer than the southern end, which is constantly affected by erosion. While varying in size and shape, all barrier islands generally share certain characteristics. Each is shaped by ocean surfs, which constantly shift and erode their beaches. Grassy dunes occupy the terrain immediately behind their beaches, while the interior of barrier islands is dominated by maritime forests and wetlands. Most barrier islands possess lee or bay-side salt marshes that face the mainland. Besides protecting the coastlines, barrier islands provide crucial habitats for vital flora and fauna such as algae, sea oats and bitter pancum, sawgrass, crabs, offshore and inshore fish, snakes, deer, raccoons, opossums, sea turtles, and sea fowl. These salt marsh ecosystems also act as filters, purifying runoffs from inland waterways. Unlike the more stable inland Sea Islands, barrier islands—which border the ocean—are dynamic; their terrain is constantly changing. Despite this inherent instability, South

Carolina's barrier islands were heavily developed throughout the latter half of the twentieth century as vacationers made their beaches popular tourist attractions.

The histories of Edingsville Beach and Morris Island perhaps best illustrate the fragile and dynamic nature of barrier islands. Edingsville, off Edisto Island, once supported a bustling summer vacation village, until a hurricane in 1893 swept away much of the island. Since then, the island has remained a sandy bar, supporting primarily only shrubby growth. Morris Island's rapid erosion is attributed to Charleston harbor's jetties. In the late nineteenth century the Morris Island Lighthouse sat 2,700 feet inshore. A century later it stands approximately 2,000 feet offshore. FORD WALPOLE

Ballantine, Todd. *Tideland Treasure.* New ed. Hilton Head, S.C.: Deerfield, 1991.

Lennon, Gered, et al. *Living with the South Carolina Coast.* Durham, N.C.: Duke University Press, 1996.

Murphy, Carolyn H. *Carolina Rocks! The Geology of South Carolina.* Orangeburg, S.C.: Sandlapper, 1995.

Barringer Building (Columbia). Located at 1338 Main Street, the Barringer Building enjoys the distinction of being Columbia's first skyscraper. At twelve stories, the 1903 structure once was such a prominent landmark within the capital city that citizens were known to have remarked, "Augusta, why it's only eighty miles from the skyscraper!" This popularity even prompted the building's likeness to be captured on postcards, particularly in the years immediately following the skyscraper's construction.

Designed by the New York architect James Brite, the Barringer Building initially was home to the National Loan and Exchange Bank, the largest financial institution in South Carolina. However, the property derives its name instead from a later owner, the Barringer Corporation, which operated there from 1953 to 1974.

Architecturally, the Barringer Building draws its inspiration from the Chicago School of design that came into vogue in the 1880s. By that time in America, engineering advancements allowed modern buildings to reach greater heights with the advent of steel girder construction, high-pressure water systems, and electric elevators. Stylistically, the Barringer Building resembles a column. The first and second floors constitute a rusticated base achieved through limestone blocks. Meanwhile, nine stories of red masonry, contrasting sharply with the floors below, are visually analogous to the shaft. The topmost floor represents the column's capital, which juxtaposes sandstone keystones and garlands with a red brick background. Following renovations in the 1960s, this story's most distinctive feature, a copper cornice, thought then to have been a safety hazard, has been missing. The building was listed in the National Register of Historic Places in 1979. JOHN M. SHERRER III

"Columbia's Modern Skyscraper." Columbia *State,* October 18, 1903, p. 23.

Barry, Margaret Catherine Moore (1752–1823). Revolutionary War heroine. "Kate" Barry was born Margaret Catherine Moore in county Antrim, Ireland, the daughter of Charles and Mary Moore. In 1763 her father received a land grant in South Carolina, which eventually became Walnut Grove plantation in Spartanburg County. She married Andrew Barry (ca. 1744–1811), and they lived at Walnut Grove.

During the Revolutionary War, Andrew Barry served as a captain in the militia under Major Henry White and Colonel John Thomas, Jr. Before the engagement in January 1781 that became known as the Battle of Cowpens, General Daniel Morgan sent messages through the countryside to summon the militia to muster and join his army. Kate Barry helped carry the call to arms by riding through the neighborhood. She also served as a scout for the patriot forces. When captured, she refused to reveal the position of her husband's company, and some accounts reported that the British beat her in retaliation.

Kate Barry's ride before the Battle of Cowpens was memorialized in poetry and monuments. Her activities not only helped patriot forces, but also served as anti-British propaganda. Regardless of whether the story of British brutality was true, the story was used as support for the case against the British military in the South. Kate Barry died in 1823 and was buried in the cemetery at Walnut Grove. BRENDA THOMPSON SCHOOLFIELD

Babits, Lawrence E. *A Devil of a Whipping: The Battle of Cowpens.* Chapel Hill: University of North Carolina Press, 1998.

Moss, Bobby Gilmer. *The Patriots at the Cowpens.* Greenville, S.C.: A Press, 1985.

Bartram, John (1699–1777), and **William Bartram** (1739–1823). Naturalists. John Bartram was born in Marple, Pennsylvania, on March 23, 1699, the son of the farmer William Bartram and his wife, Elizabeth Hunt. Beginning around 1727, Bartram became interested in botany, a subject in which he was largely self-taught. Through a London correspondent and fellow Quaker, Peter Collinson, Bartram became a participant in the international world of botanical exchange, sending seeds, bulbs, and cuttings of American plants to Europe and receiving payment or other botanical specimens in exchange. Bartram's skill became recognized in the learned communities of America and Europe. The great Swedish natural historian Carl Linnaeus is said to have referred to Bartram as the finest natural botanist in the world. Bartram contributed specimens to enable Mark Catesby, then in London, to finish his *Natural History of Carolina, Florida and the Bahama Islands* (1731–1748) and exchanged seeds and bulbs with Martha Logan, the owner of a famous Charleston garden.

Bartram's first botanizing trip to South Carolina occurred in 1762, when he explored the interior of the state. It was followed by a longer trip to the southeastern British colonies in 1765, when Bartram was appointed King's Botanist. This appointment shocked the Scottish physician and botanist Alexander Garden, Bartram's Charleston friend, who found it "rather hyperbolical" that Bartram, a collector rather than a learned botanist, should be appointed to such a position. Regardless of Garden's shock, Charleston, with its port facilities and active scientific community, was a logical departing point for Bartram's expedition, and he arrived there in July 1765 on his way to Florida. He also spent some time in Charleston in 1766 on the way back, purchasing equipment and slaves for a rice plantation that his son William Bartram was trying to set up in Florida, a venture which proved a total failure. Bartram's account of his trip, *The Diary of a Journey through the Carolinas, Georgia, and Florida: From July 1, 1765 to April 10, 1766,* not published until 1942, is principally of botanical interest. John Bartram died on September 22, 1777, in Kingsessing, Pennsylvania.

William Bartram was born on April 9, 1739, in Philadelphia, the son of John Bartram and his second wife, Anne Mendenhall. William's keen interest in botany and natural history was manifest early in his life, causing his father to despair of finding a remunerative career for the young man. He was a gifted illustrator and accompanied his father on his trip to the southeastern colonies in 1765.

William Bartram is best known for his narrative of a series of expeditions in southeastern North America from 1772 to 1776,

Travels through North & South Carolina, Georgia, East & West Florida, the Cherokee Country, the Extensive Territories of the Muscogulges, or Creek Confederacy, and the Country of the Choctaws Containing an Account of the Soil and Natural Productions of Those Regions, Together with Observations on the Manners of the Indians (1791). This trip was sponsored by Bartram's patron, the Englishman John Fothergill. Charleston again was the starting point for the expedition. Bartram's friends there included Alexander Garden and Dr. Lionel Chalmers, who furnished Bartram with introductions to prominent persons in the Southeast. Bartram arrived in April 1773, staying in Charleston only a few days before leaving for Savannah. Bartram's travels in South Carolina, unlike his father's, were restricted to the area of Charleston, the coast, and the area of the South Carolina–Georgia border. He returned to Charleston in the fall of 1774 to stay over the winter and again in 1776 before returning to the Philadelphia area, where he spent the rest of his life.

William Bartram's interests were broader than his father's. In addition to botany, his book contains a great deal of information about animal life and both English and Indian societies. He was more sympathetic to the Indians than were most Anglo-American writers of the time. *Travels through North & South Carolina* was more popular in Europe, where it went through several editions and translations, than in the United States, where it was not reprinted until 1928. Its influence was greatest, not among natural historians, but among Romantic poets, most notably Samuel Taylor Coleridge and William Wordsworth. William Bartram, who never married, died on July 22, 1823, at his home near Philadelphia. WILLIAM E. BURNS

Earnest, Ernest. *John and William Bartram: Botanists and Explorers.* Philadelphia: University of Pennsylvania Press, 1940.

Slaughter, Thomas P. *The Natures of John and William Bartram.* New York: Knopf, 1996.

Baruch, Bernard Mannes (1870–1965). Speculator, financier, presidential adviser. Baruch was born in Camden on August 19, 1870, the second son of Dr. Simon Baruch and Isabella Wolfe. Both his parents were Jews, and Baruch's father had immigrated to the United States from Poland in 1855. The Civil War and Reconstruction left Baruch sensitive both to the physical destruction and political chaos of warfare and to the limited opportunities of the New South. The state loomed large in Baruch's identity, however, shaping his politics and outlook and leading him to comment in later years that he was a South Carolinian "at heart."

Seeking greater research opportunities for himself and a better education system for his sons, Simon Baruch relocated his family in 1881 to New York City. There, in autumn 1884, Bernard Baruch entered City College, where he excelled in languages and political economy. Although he entertained the notion of enrolling at West Point, a childhood injury had left him deaf in his left ear and ultimately ruled out a military career. Baruch graduated fifteenth in his class at City College in June 1889.

Baruch began an illustrious career on Wall Street in 1891 as a clerk for the broker Arthur Housman. An astute observer of the market, Baruch made a name for himself with his encyclopedic knowledge of a vast array of topics from railway routes to business law. By 1895 he had become a junior partner with A. A. Housman and Company. After shrewd trading in sugar stocks during the spring and summer of 1897, Baruch had made enough money to purchase a seat on the New York Stock Exchange, and to marry Annie Griffen on October 20, 1897. The marriage produced three children by 1905. Business was fruitful too. Establishing his own brokerage in 1903, Baruch possessed a trading acumen that earned him a fortune, a reputation for risky but successful speculating, and a nickname: "The Lone Wolf of Wall Street." In 1905 he purchased Hobcaw Barony, a 17,000-acre plantation near Georgetown, South Carolina. In the ensuing years, Hobcaw would play host to prominent political, business, and literary figures, including Winston Churchill, George C. Marshall, and Franklin Roosevelt.

Baruch entered public life in 1916. His interest in preparing America for entry into World War I led President Woodrow Wilson to appoint Baruch to the Business Advisory Commission to the Council of National Defense. Other appointments followed before Baruch joined the War Industries Board (WIB) at its formation on August 1, 1917. A close adviser to Wilson on mobilization, Baruch urged greater centralization, gradually accepting that a successful war effort might demand federal intervention in private industry. When mobilization faltered during the winter of 1917–1918, Baruch's advice was heeded. After bureaucratic reorganization, the WIB became the focus of mobilization, with Wilson appointing Baruch its chairman in March 1918.

After World War I, Baruch resigned his position but remained an influential figure in the national Democratic Party. In December 1918 Baruch joined Wilson's peace delegation in Paris as an economic adviser, stridently supporting Wilsonian principled internationalism at home and abroad. With the decline of Wilson as the head of the Democratic Party, Baruch's star also faded. Riven with infighting during the 1920s, the party required Baruch's money more than his wisdom, although the stockbroker occasionally acted as power broker for favored political hopefuls.

Nevertheless, Baruch became an elder statesman of the party. Although he had advised Republican presidents Harding, Coolidge, and Hoover, Democrats still knew the value of his support. Franklin Roosevelt relied on him for advice on policy during the Depression—despite Baruch's occasional criticism of the New Deal—and turned to him to help guide both economic mobilization and demobilization for World War II. Baruch hoped to participate in framing the postwar international order. Although President Harry Truman appointed Baruch in 1946 to the United Nations Atomic Energy Commission, the new president had few attachments to the Wall Street financier, and a rift soon developed between the two men. Baruch spent the 1950s crusading against the inflationary economy, and concerns about the growth of government led him to support Republican candidate Dwight Eisenhower in the 1952 presidential election. During the 1950s and 1960s he remained an American icon but grew increasingly detached from politics.

Reflecting in 1960 on changes he had witnessed in policy making, this Wilsonian reared in the southern tradition of limited government and the Wall Street tradition of laissez-faire could observe: "Today, the old kind of 'do-nothing government' is dead. Government intervention has been made necessary by the growing complexity of society." Baruch died on June 20, 1965, in New York City. ERIC A. CHEEZUM

Baruch, Bernard M. *Baruch: My Own Story.* New York: Henry Holt, 1957.

———. *Baruch: The Public Years.* New York: Holt, Rinehart and Winston, 1960.

Grant, James. *Bernard M. Baruch: The Adventures of a Wall Street Legend.* New York: Simon and Schuster, 1983.

Schwarz, Jordan A. *The Speculator: Bernard M. Baruch in Washington, 1917–1965.* Chapel Hill: University of North Carolina Press, 1981.

Baseball. Union troops introduced baseball to South Carolina during the late stages of the Civil War. The game soon blossomed into a major social and athletic event in many rural and urban communities during Reconstruction. Both Columbia and Charleston formed local teams that played against the northern occupation forces. By the time Wade Hampton III became governor in 1877, the game was firmly established. In a game played the following year in Charleston between the "Carolinas" and the "Palmettoes," attendance was so large that fans disrupted play by crowding onto the field. Spectators' interest also included wagers on their favorite side. By 1886 professionalism had come to South Carolina's game. Charleston's Southern Association team reportedly paid its players as much as $2,000. Its biggest rivals in these early years were Georgia teams. Some Charleston fans even paid 15¢ to follow away games telegraphed, play-by-play, into Hibernian Hall. Amateur and semiprofessional baseball had equally large followings. By 1889 Camden was the site of a "flourishing Base Ball Association owning a park where the best amateur games of the State are played." Two years earlier, a lively game in Greenwood between the "Columbias" and the "Greenvilles" was so competitive that a riot nearly ensued after the Greenville team won, 7 to 6.

The Anderson Cotton Mill baseball team, 1902. Courtesy, Pendleton District Commission

By the end of the nineteenth century, some of the state's most loyal baseball fans were found in South Carolina's mill villages. In the 1870s and 1880s, when the textile industry began taking root in the upstate, mill-sponsored baseball clubs emerged, and they were thriving by the start of the twentieth century. Initially, mill teams consisted of the best players in each local workforce. But as the rivalries between mill towns grew, owners sought better talent and recruited talented players from outside the community, sometimes snatching the best players from rival mills. Mill baseball provided textile communities with both entertainment and a source of pride. One of the earliest mill champions was the Piedmont team led by Champ Osteen. In 1899, after beating most of the local opposition, the Piedmont squad received a challenge from a team from Augusta, Georgia, which they also defeated. Until the twentieth century, mill leagues were informal and focused on local tournaments and other games throughout the summer months. Some of the first organized mill leagues appeared in 1908 with the formation of the South Carolina Mill League and the Greenville Mill League. During the next half-century, regional mill leagues developed throughout the upstate and the Midlands, including teams from Anderson to Gaffney and Graniteville to Winnsboro. Hundreds and sometimes thousands of fans attended local games. Hotly contested matches sometimes led to fights both on and off the field. Perhaps the greatest triumph for any mill town came in 1936, when the Spartanburg American Legion team won the state's first national championship in any sport by defeating a Los Angeles team in a five-game series (some twenty thousand fans attended the fifth and deciding game). Mill leagues continued to thrive into the post–World War II era. But by the early 1950s, automobiles and televisions undermined mill league baseball's following. Attendance dwindled, and by the early 1960s the textile leagues had virtually ceased to exist.

Baseball continued to thrive in other leagues. In August 1875 one of the first recorded intercollegiate games in the state saw an all-black team from the University of South Carolina defeat an all-black team from an Orangeburg college by a score of 41 to 10. By the late nineteenth century the University of South Carolina and Clemson began their long baseball rivalry. Other schools also organized varsity squads around the same time, including Benedict, South Carolina State College, the Citadel, Furman, and Wofford. Competition centered on in-state schools and neighboring ones in North Carolina and Georgia. In 1958 Clemson became the first South Carolina school to reach the College World Series. Since then, competition for honors and star players accelerated at all levels of college baseball as each of the state's schools competed to reach the College World Series. Several college stars have advanced to play professionally.

The minor league system that fed players into the major leagues has given excitement and pleasure to South Carolina fans since the 1900s. One of the most endearing of these has been the South Atlantic League, which began play in 1904. Initially consisting of teams from South Carolina, Georgia, and Florida, franchises have come and gone from Columbia, Charleston, and Greenville during a century of play. Other minor leagues that flourished at one time or another in the state include the Carolina League (Greenville, Spartanburg, and Greenwood) and the Palmetto League, ca. 1934–1951 (Orangeburg, Hartsville, Lake City, Kingstree, Georgetown, Camden, and Sumter).

Until the 1950s these minor and amateur leagues were segregated, allowing only white ball players. Black amateur leagues flourished in many areas of the state, but little documentation of their history remains. The earliest documented black textile league game occurred on September 4, 1895, in Newberry County between Newberry Mills and their counterparts from Anderson. Black textile teams disappeared for the same reasons that their white counterparts did during the 1950s. While Jackie Robinson integrated the major leagues in 1947 and South Carolina native Larry Doby followed three months later as the first African American in the American League, the desegregation of baseball in South Carolina took longer. In 1955 one of the first African Americans to play professionally in the state was Frank Robinson, who starred with the Columbia Reds and later had a Hall of Fame career in the major leagues with the Cincinnati Reds and the Baltimore Orioles.

Youth baseball took the longest to integrate. When the black Cannon Street YMCA team from Charleston fielded an all-star team to compete in the 1955 Little League, white teams in the state refused to play against them. Other teams from the Southeast followed South Carolina's lead, ignoring instructions from Little League headquarters in Williamsport, Pennsylvania, directing that they play. Although the Cannon Street team was declared the winner by default, they could only watch the Little League World Series after being declared ineligible because they had not earned the right on the playing field. Having refused to accept Little League directives to allow black teams, white officials from South Carolina and other southern states formed an independent organization called Little Boys Baseball, Inc. In 1956 a Greenville entry won the league's first World Series. The fledgling league changed its name to Dixie Youth Baseball in 1962 after Little League officials protested that Little Boys Baseball infringed on their trademark. By the middle of the decade Dixie Youth Baseball finally desegregated. FRITZ HAMER

Darby, Cecil, ed. *South Atlantic League Dope Book.* N.p., 1948.

Donehue, J. Douglas. "Baseball in '49." Orangeburg *Times and Democrat,* April 10, 1983, pp. B1, B4.

Moore, John H. *Columbia and Richland County: A South Carolina Community, 1740–1990.* Columbia: University of South Carolina Press, 1993.

———. *South Carolina in the 1880s: A Gazetteer.* Orangeburg, S.C.: Sandlapper, 1989.

Perry, Thomas. *Textile League Baseball: South Carolina's Mill Teams, 1880–1955.* Jefferson, N.C.: McFarland, 1993.

Price, Tom. *A Century of Gamecocks: Memorable Baseball Moments.* Columbia, S.C.: Summerhouse, 1996.

Sapakoff, Gene. "Little League's Civil War." *Sports Illustrated* 83 (October 30, 1995).

Bates, Clayton (1907–1998). Tap dancer. Born in Fountain Inn on October 11, 1907, Clayton "Peg Leg" Bates came from an extremely poor sharecropping family, whose father deserted them when Bates was only three years old. During World War I, Bates took a job in a cottonseed-oil mill. Soon after he began working there, the lights failed and the twelve-year-old accidentally stepped into the open auger conveyer. The equipment chewed up his leg so badly that an amputation was necessary. Since hospitals were segregated, the doctor performed the procedure on the family's kitchen table.

Bates had a desire to dance that persisted despite the loss of his leg. So, fitted with an artificial wooden limb—or "peg"—he adapted tap dancing steps to his own specifications. By age fifteen he was entrenched in a professional career as a tap dancer. He worked his way up from minstrel shows to carnivals, from the African American vaudeville circuit TOBA (Theatre Owners Booking Association) to the white vaudeville circuits. Throughout the 1930s he played top Harlem nightclubs, including the Cotton Club, Connie's Inn, and Club Zanzibar. In the late 1930s he was the opening act for the Ed Sullivan Revue, traveled the Keith and Loews circuits, and appeared to great acclaim on Australia's Tivoli circuit. He performed throughout the 1940s, including dancing in the popular Los Angeles version of Ken Murray's Blackouts. Bates had an active career in television, including twenty-one appearances on the Ed Sullivan Show, the most by a tap dancer. In the 1960s he opened the Peg Leg Bates Country Club in Kerhonkson, New York, which catered to a primarily African American clientele. Bates retired from dancing in 1989 and died at Fountain Inn on December 6, 1998. He was buried in Palentown Cemetery, Ulster County, New York. RUSTY E. FRANK

Frank, Rusty E. *Tap! The Greatest Tap Dance Stars and Their Stories, 1900–1955.* New York: Morrow, 1990.

Obituary. *New York Times.* December 8, 1998, p. B10.

Bates, Lester Lee, Sr. (1904–1988). Mayor of Columbia. Born in the Hell Hole Swamp area of Berkeley County on September 7, 1904, Bates was the son of Alfred G. Bates and Ella Cumbee. He began his elementary schooling with Mormon missionaries, but at age twelve he took a job as a water boy for a logging crew. That year he suffered a near-fatal accident when he fell beneath the wheel of a train. Taken to Charleston for surgery, he remained in treatment for a year. After a brief return to Berkeley County, he went back to Charleston and worked during the day while attending night school at the Salvation Army. During his lengthy recuperation, the young out-of-town patient came to the attention of the congregation of the First Baptist Church of Charleston. One of the church families took him into their home during his recuperation; their daughter, Julia Burk, later became his wife in 1927. The couple had two children.

At age nineteen, Bates became an agent with the Industrial Life and Health Insurance Company (later to become Life of Georgia). In 1931 he became a district manager with Atlantic Coast Life. He founded Capital Life and Health Insurance Company in 1936 and in 1955, the New South Life Insurance Company.

Bates was elected to Columbia City Council in 1944 and served there for eight years. In 1958 he was elected mayor of Columbia. He was reelected without opposition in 1962 and 1966. Columbia experienced a period of rapid growth during the Bates years. One of his first actions as mayor was the appointment of a study group to investigate the improvement of air service for the area. As a result, the Richland-Lexington Airport District began operating the Columbia Metropolitan Airport in 1962. The airport began operations in a newly built facility in 1965. In 1968 Bates enlisted the support of South Carolina's congressional delegation in a successful drive to incorporate the U.S. Army's Fort Jackson into the Columbia city limits, a move that increased the population of the city by twenty thousand people. Also in 1968 the City of Columbia, Richland County, and the University of South Carolina completed construction of the Carolina Coliseum.

For many, the richest legacy of the Bates years is his role in the civil rights movement of the early 1960s. As many cities across the region were facing violent reactions to desegregation, Bates was determined that Columbia would integrate peacefully. To that end, he assembled committees of black and white community leaders, with whom he first met separately, to discuss how best to avoid violence. The committees then merged and orchestrated the peaceful desegregation of Columbia's lunch counters in 1962, two years before the passage of the 1964 Civil Rights Act. This group became the forerunner of the Greater Columbia Community Relations Council.

Columbia was twice awarded the All-America City designation during Bates's tenure as mayor. At the end of his third term in 1970, he was appointed to the South Carolina Insurance Commission and awarded an honorary doctor of laws degree by the University of South Carolina. Bates died in Columbia on February 24, 1988, and was buried in the Eccles United Methodist Churchyard in Moncks Corner. The Greater Columbia Community Relations Council, descended from his original desegregation committees, presented its first Distinguished Service Award to him posthumously in 1994. JULIA ARRANTS

Becker, Paul R. "Lester Bates Helped Bridge Gap for Area." Columbia *State,* January 14, 2000, p. A12.

"City Grew under Bates." *Columbia Record,* February 25, 1988, pp. A1, A13.

"Kress Is a Civil Rights Landmark." Columbia *State,* February 16, 2000, p. B3.

Moore, John Hammond. *Columbia and Richland County: A South Carolina Community, 1740–1990.* Columbia: University of South Carolina Press, 1993.

Sponhour, Michael, and Dawn Hinshaw. "'Secret' Plan Helped Keep the Peace." Columbia *State,* February 1, 1994, pp. A1, A6.

Batesburg-Leesville (Lexington County; 2000 pop. 5,517). Before consolidating in 1993, Batesburg and Leesville were "friendly but separate Twins" that grew up back-to-back in the extreme western section of Lexington County. Located on the "Ridge" separating the Saluda and Edisto River basins, the towns originated on Native American trading paths that became early roads from Augusta to Columbia and from the coast to the upcountry. The crossroads soon sprouted a handful of taverns and stage stops, including one that tradition holds entertained President George Washington during a visit in 1791. In 1869 the Charlotte, Columbia, and Augusta Railroad laid tracks through the villages and established a depot in each. Leesville was incorporated on February 23, 1875, and Batesburg on May 31, 1877.

For more than a century, the economy of Batesburg revolved around cotton. Courtesy, South Carolina Historical Society

Although separated by only a narrow strip of land, the two towns nevertheless developed distinct identities. Batesburg faced west and served as a market and distribution center for Ridge farmers in Edgefield, Aiken, and Saluda Counties. Facing east, Leesville serviced the Sandhills of western Lexington County. The sawmill in Batesburg produced building lumber, while that in Leesville cut railroad crossties. Even the religious makeup of the towns differed: Batesburg was mainly Baptist, while Lutherans predominated in Leesville, although Methodists were well represented in both towns. In the 1880s Leesville became a college town when the Leesville English and Classical Institute opened. Later redesignated Leesville College, the coeducational school was fully accredited to grant both bachelor's and master's degrees before closing in 1910. The progressive institution was the first in the state to teach physical education to girls. When the college closed, many of its faculty and students transferred to Newberry College. While Leesville became a center of education, Batesburg enhanced its commercial and industrial standing. By 1900 Batesburg had thirty-three stores, a bank, and a cotton factory: Middleburg Mills.

The move toward a merger of the towns began in the 1920s with the construction of a consolidated high school. The Batesburg-Leesville Chamber of Commerce was formed in 1946, and in the 1970s Batesburg annexed the land dividing the towns. A difficult economy in the 1980s sparked the final push, as civic and business leaders sought to streamline local government services and strengthen the tax base. In January 1992 voters passed a referendum to consolidate Batesburg and Leesville, and the merger was completed by the end of the following year.

Entering the twenty-first century, Batesburg-Leesville contained three historic districts, two business districts, a central shopping center, and two regionally famous barbecue restaurants (Shealy's and Hite's). Each May, Batesburg-Leesville hosts the South Carolina Poultry Festival, which draws thousands of visitors to the Twin Cities. Many denominations sustain the religious life of the town, while the Ridge Arts Council, the Ridge Chorus, and the Batesburg-Leesville Historical Society support cultural activities. Despite changes, Batesburg-Leesville has preserved enough of its heritage to retain much of its rural character and charm. TOM DOWNEY

Batesburg-Leesville Chamber of Commerce. *Batesburg-Leesville Area History.* Shawnee Mission, Kans.: Inter-Collegiate Press, [1982?].

"Batesburg-Leesville Consolidation Complete." Columbia *State,* December 9, 1993, p. B1.

Battery, The. The Battery designates, jointly and separately, the sea wall and park at the southern tip of the Charleston peninsula. In 1670 the first Carolina colonists noted an expanse of sand and bleached oyster shells at the confluence of the Cooper and Ashley Rivers. Their term "Oyster Point" originally described the peninsula in general, but after Charleston was relocated to the eastern shore of the peninsula in 1680, the terms "Oyster Point" and "White Point" were used to refer specifically to its southernmost tip.

Although it lay outside the walled boundaries of the early city, White Point represented an important defensive site. Broughton's Battery (later called Fort Wilkins) was erected on this site in 1737 and served through the 1780s. In the 1750s an earthwork sea wall was built along the Cooper River to Broughton's Battery and a short distance along the Ashley River. The fort was demolished about 1789, but the sea walls were progressively strengthened. By the time the existing stone and masonry sea wall was completed in 1820, the wall and promenading grounds at the tip of the peninsula were commonly known as "the Battery." The northern and western boundaries of the point were later enclosed, and in 1837 White Point Garden was designated a municipal park.

During the Civil War the park was transformed into two earthwork forts: Battery Ramsay to the east and the King Street Battery to the west. After the war, these fortifications were removed and the area was again configured as a park. Today, White Point Gardens includes several cannons, memorial tablets, and statues that pay tribute to significant events and people in local history. A memorial bandstand erected in 1907 provides a central focus to the grounds. These features, along with the fine views and promenade afforded by the sea walls, have long made the Battery a popular destination for both locals and visitors. NICHOLAS MICHAEL BUTLER

Ripley, Warren. *The Battery, Charleston, South Carolina.* Charleston, S.C.: News and Courier, 1977.

Battery Wagner. Battery Wagner was the principal fortification on Morris Island during the Civil War. It was constructed during the summer of 1862 and named for Lieutenant Colonel Thomas M. Wagner. The powerful earthwork stretched across the island and was designed to keep the enemy from Cummings Point, the closest land to Fort Sumter. In the summer of 1863 it thwarted a Union attack against Charleston.

In the spring of 1863, the Federals planned a joint operation that called for a quick seizure of Morris Island, the erection of breeching batteries on Cummings Point, the bombardment and capture of Fort Sumter, and the removal of harbor obstructions to allow ironclads to enter the harbor and capture Charleston. On July 10, 1863, a combined Federal force commanded by General Quincy A. Gillmore and Rear Admiral John Dahlgren attacked from Folly Island and captured most of Morris Island. At dawn on July 11, 1863, Wagner's garrison of 1,800 men under Colonel Charles

Members of the 54th Massachusetts Regiment posed for the photographer in Battery Wagner after its occupation by Union forces. Courtesy, South Carolina Historical Society

Olmstead stopped a 1,230-man Union brigade. The Federals then constructed siege batteries and on July 18 opened a daylong land and naval bombardment of Battery Wagner. A Union division commanded by General Truman Seymour was drawn up to attack Wagner. It was spearheaded by the Fifty-fourth Massachusetts, a regiment of black soldiers led by Colonel Robert Shaw. Some 1,600 men under General William B. Taliaferro defended Wagner. The attack commenced at dusk, and though part of Wagner was overrun, the Federals were thrown back, suffering 1,515 casualties of the 5,000 men engaged. Among the dead was Colonel Shaw. The Confederates suffered 222 casualties.

The attack showed the ability of earthen fortifications to absorb bombardments and retain their ability to resist attacks. The fine performance of the Fifty-fourth Massachusetts troops sparked an increase in the recruitment of African Americans and demonstrated that they could be used as frontline troops. For his actions in the attack, Sergeant William Carney became the first black soldier to be awarded the Congressional Medal of Honor. The battle also forced the Confederacy to revise its laws that required the reenslavement or execution of captured black troops and instead to accept them as legitimate Union soldiers.

After the failed assaults, the Federals opened siege operations against Wagner. They also began constructing heavy breeching batteries. On August 17, 1863, these batteries, which contained the largest rifled guns ever used in combat in the United States, opened on Fort Sumter. In less than two weeks the masonry fortification was reduced to rubble, but as long as the Confederates held Wagner, the Federals could not capture Sumter. By September 6 the Union siege lines had reached Wagner, and that evening the battery and the rest of Morris Island was evacuated. A subsequent Union amphibious assault against Sumter was defeated, and the campaign ended. The tenacious defense of Battery Wagner had given the Confederates enough time to rework their defensive scheme and thwart the Union attack, temporarily saving Sumter and Charleston from capture. Total casualties for the campaign were 2,318 Federals and 1,022 Confederates. STEPHEN R. WISE

Emilio, Luis F. *A Brave Black Regiment: History of the Fifty-Fourth Regiment of Massachusetts Volunteer Infantry 1863–1865.* New York: Arno, 1969.

Gillmore, Quincy Adams. *Engineer and Artillery Operations against the Defences of Charleston Harbor in 1863.* New York: Nostrand, 1865.

Jervey, Theodore D. "Charleston during the Civil War." In *Annual Report of the American Historical Association for the Year 1913,* vol. 1. Washington, D.C.: Government Printing Office, 1915.

Wise, Stephen R. *Gate of Hell: Campaign for Charleston Harbor, 1863.* Columbia: University of South Carolina Press, 1994.

Beach music. Beach music, as it is known in the South, originated in the coastal Carolinas in the years following World War II. The term referred to African American "race" music (later called rhythm and blues, or R&B) that could be found in South Carolina only on jukeboxes in the beachside jump joints and saloons.

With the notable exception of WLAC, a 50,000-watt radio station in Nashville whose signal blanketed the South, most regional broadcasters refused to play the raw, sexually suggestive songs. WAIM in Anderson proudly advertised that it aired "No Jungle Music." The "race" recordings were mostly sold by mail order.

However, along the coast, the decline of big-band swing prompted young white dancers to seek out alternative music. George Lineberry, one of the young white dancers who worked for a local amusements company in Myrtle Beach until 1948, took it upon himself to install "race" records on jukeboxes in white establishments, including the popular oceanfront pavilion in the heart of the tourist district. Lineberry chose records that he and his friends had discovered on visits to black nightclubs. Because it was mostly heard at the beach, this exciting, hard-to-find new music genre became known to white visitors as beach music. "This was the devil's music—you just didn't listen to it in the average white southern home," said Marion Carter, founder of Ripete Records, a beach music specialty label in Elliott, South Carolina.

In later years a tamer version of the music grew in popularity as it became associated with the popular shag, now the state's official dance. An offshoot, a pop version of the R&B sound often called "bubblegum beach," is distinguished by simplistic lyrics celebrating youthful romance, alcohol highs, and a carefree life at the Carolina beaches. In 2001 beach music (without a firm definition) was designated South Carolina's official state music. FRANK BEACHAM

Beacham and LeGrand. Partners James Douthit Beacham (1891–1956) and Leon LeGrand (ca. 1893–1963) were Greenville's most popular architects during the 1920s, when the city boomed with construction. Beacham, a Greenville native, was educated at Furman University, Clemson College (1909), and Virginia Polytechnic Institute (1911). LeGrand, from Sumter, studied with Rudolph E. Lee at Clemson (1915). Both worked for J. E. Sirrine & Co. after World War I.

Beacham and LeGrand began their partnership in 1920 by designing Greenville's Salvation Army Hospital. In the decade that followed, they were commissioned to design some of the city's most important buildings: the ten-story Chamber of Commerce building; the Ramsay Fine Arts Center at the Greenville Woman's College; the Working Benevolent Society Temple, built as a center for black professionals and small businesses on Broad Street; the County Tuberculosis Hospital; and the Burgiss Shrine Hospital for Crippled Children. The partners also designed downtown stores, warehouses, movie theaters, residences, Augusta Road Elementary School, and the Children of Israel Synagogue. In 1925 they opened a second office in Asheville, North Carolina.

The ability of Beacham and LeGrand to combine southern vernacular designs, especially colonial or Georgian revival styles, with the functional demands of modern buildings made them successful. Their most important Greenville commission was probably the Chamber of Commerce building, which combined elaborate Sullivanesque decorative motifs with practicality—including telephone connections and washbasins in every office. Their practice slowed during the Great Depression and ended in 1942. After World War II they practiced separately. JUDITH T. BAINBRIDGE

"J. D. Beacham, an Architect, Dies Suddenly." *Greenville News,* July 20, 1956, p. 33.

Obituary. *Greenville News,* May 5, 1963, p. D4.

Wells, John E., and Robert E. Dalton. *The South Carolina Architects, 1885–1935: A Biographical Directory.* Richmond, Va.: New South Architectural Press, 1992.

Beacon Drive-In. In 1946 John B. White opened the Beacon Drive-In restaurant on the outskirts of the city of Spartanburg. The name was selected in deference to a proposed beacon that was to shine forth from the rooftop. White, who had begun working at a local drive-in at the age of eleven, was an astute businessman, a showman of sorts. He constructed a helicopter landing pad across the street and erected a series of billboards along highways advertising, for example, "You Are Only 100 Miles from the Famous Beacon Drive-In." If a competitor opened nearby, local lore holds that White would tell his cooks, "Put more meat on the bread, pile more fries and rings on top." When White ran the enterprise, the Beacon served an evangelical role in the community. Easter services were held at sunrise in the asphalt parking lot, and revivals—complete with a gospel band and a throng of worshipers—were staged each Sunday in August. Also popular was a July Fourth "I love America" celebration.

Though White sold the enterprise in 1998, the Beacon continues to do a high volume of business. Among the signature dishes is the "Chili Cheeseburger a Plenty" (a traditional cheeseburger smothered in chili and then topped with a tangle of French fries and onion rings) and the "Pig Dinner" (ten scoops of ice cream atop two bananas, the whole affair smothered in whipped cream).

One colorful figure at the Beacon, J. C. Stroble, was a veteran of more than forty years as a curb-hop and order-taker. "Let's Don't Boogie-Jive. Let's Merchandise!" read a placard that hung above his head. Even after a bout with glaucoma dimmed Stroble's sight, he worked the crowds ably. "Talk!" he would boom as customers approached. "I'm ready for you. Come on with it. Tell me! Tell me!" JOHN T. EDGE

Edge, John T. *Southern Belly: The Ultimate Food Lover's Companion to the South.* Athens, Ga.: Hill Street, 2000.

Rogers, Aida. "Big, Loud, Cheap and Good." *Sandlapper* 7 (spring 1996): 29–31.

Beasley, David Muldrow (b. 1957). Governor. Beasley was born in Lamar on February 26, 1957, the son of Richard and Jacqueline Beasley. He graduated from Lamar High School in 1975 and attended Clemson University from 1976 to 1978. He transferred to the University of South Carolina in 1979 after being elected to the S.C. House of Representatives at the age of twenty-two. He received his undergraduate degree in 1979 and his law degree from the University of South Carolina School of Law in 1983. He married Mary Wood Payne on June 18, 1988. They have three children.

Beasley served in the S.C. House of Representatives from 1979 to 1994. He was originally elected as a Democrat representing Darlington and Marlboro Counties, and his legislative focus was on education. Beasley was chair of the Joint Legislative Committee on Education, chair of the House Education and Public Works Committee, and vice chair of the Joint Legislative Committee on Children. From 1987 to 1988 he was majority leader, and in 1991 he was elected Speaker Pro Tempore.

In the fall of 1991, Beasley switched to the Republican Party because he felt that "the Democratic Party was moving so far to the left" and "that Republican philosophy and Republican policies were more in line with what is good for America over the long term." In 1994 Beasley defeated Tommy Hartnett and Arthur Ravenel to win the Republican Party's nomination for governor. He then defeated Democrat Nick Theodore in November.

In his early years as governor, Beasley was perceived as a rising star within the Republican Party and was selected as chair of the Republican Governors' Association. His conservative political philosophy emphasized that social problems could best be solved by creating wealth through the private sector. During his first three years as governor, more than $16 billion in private-sector capital investments was made in South Carolina. During the same period, property and business taxes were reduced by more than $1 billion. Beasley also supported welfare reform through a welfare-to-work program that gave tax credits to businesses that hired welfare workers. In addition he helped start the Putting Families First Foundation, which brought together churches, local chambers of commerce, and other voluntary organizations to assist welfare families in making the transition from public assistance to self-support.

In 1998 Beasley was defeated in his bid for reelection by Democrat Jim Hodges, who ran on a platform emphasizing education and the creation of a state lottery to provide additional funding for education. Analysts attributed Beasley's defeat to the get-out-the-vote efforts of the Democratic Party, financial contributions made by video poker and prolottery supporters to the Hodges campaign, and Beasley's growing identification with Christian conservatives. Beasley had angered conservative supporters during his term, however, by calling for the removal of the Confederate flag from above the State House dome. In June 1999 he moved to his farm in Society Hill and joined the Bingham Consulting Group, an international business and consulting firm. In 2003 he received the John F. Kennedy Profile in Courage Award for his stand on the Confederate flag. WILLIAM V. MOORE

Hayward, Steven. "Beasley Makes It Finah in Carolina." *Policy Review* 89 (May–June 1998): 9–10.

Beaufort (Beaufort County; 2000 pop. 12,950). Beaufort was chartered on January 17, 1711. It is the second-oldest town in South Carolina and was named for Henry Somerset, the second duke of Beaufort, a proprietor of Carolina from 1700 to 1714. The town was laid out around a fort and blockhouse that had been built in 1706 to guard against Spanish invasion. For thirty years Beaufort was a military outpost of the Carolina colony and the southern frontier of British North America. The Yamassee Indians destroyed the town in 1715, but Beaufort recovered quickly. In 1740 the colonial legislature passed "An Act to Encourage the Better Settling the Town of Beaufort," which enlarged the town to the west and added new streets. In 1748 two additional streets were laid out to the west, marking the limits of Beaufort in the colonial era. Beaufort became the center of the Sea Islands and the seat of Beaufort District in 1769. The regional economy based on rice plantations on the mainland and indigo plantations on the Sea Islands brought an economic boom to Beaufort in the years prior to the Revolutionary War. Beaufort also became a shipbuilding center, utilizing local live oak trees for ship timbers.

Beaufort's historic district has changed little from this turn-of-the-twentieth-century scene. Courtesy, South Carolina Historical Society

During the political disputes leading to the Revolutionary War, the royal governor Lord Montagu called the Commons House of Assembly to meet in Beaufort, not Charleston, in October 1772. For four days Beaufort was the colonial seat of government before the angry legislators forced Montagu to move the assembly back to Charleston. The "Beaufort Assembly" helped inspire the fourth clause of the Declaration of Independence, which included Beaufort resident Thomas Heyward, Jr., among its signers. During the Revolutionary War, the British occupied Beaufort almost continuously from June 1779 to December 1781. Much of the colonial economy was destroyed by warfare and damaged by a population sharply divided between patriots and Loyalists. Beaufort's leading Loyalist was Major Andrew DeVeaux, who fled Beaufort for Florida, outfitted a small private army, and recaptured the Bahama Islands in 1783 for the British. Loyalists who fled to the Bahamas successfully planted cotton seeds and then shipped seeds back to relatives in South Carolina. This precipitated the state's first cotton boom and brought fabulous prosperity to Beaufort.

In the antebellum era, Beaufort became a summer retreat for rich Sea Island cotton planters and even richer mainland rice planters, who maintained a wealthy and cultivated society in the town. Beaufort College, the second-oldest college in South Carolina, was founded in 1795. The Beaufort Arsenal (1798), the Baptist Church of Beaufort (1804), and the Beaufort Library Society (1807) respectively became the leading military, religious, and intellectual institutions of the town. By 1860 Beaufort was one of the wealthiest towns in America and a center of the secession movement, led by Beaufort native Robert Barnwell Rhett, the "Father of Secession" in South Carolina. During the Civil War, Beaufort was the first southern city conquered by Union forces after the U.S. Navy victory in Port Royal Sound on November 7, 1861. Beaufort became the headquarters of the U.S. Army, Department of the South, and most of the buildings were converted into hospitals for Union army wounded. At the end of the war, a National Cemetery was laid out north of Boundary Street as a burial place for Civil War dead.

Beaufort became a leading center of the Reconstruction regime in South Carolina. Beaufort's military governor, Major General Rufus Saxton, directed the U.S. Bureau of Refugees, Freedmen and Abandoned Lands in South Carolina, and Beaufort was the site of the first Freedmen's Bank in the state. A leading political figure of the Reconstruction era was Robert Smalls, a Beaufort native and former slave. Smalls organized the Republican Party in Beaufort in 1866 and served in the state legislature and U.S. Congress for many years between 1868 and 1887. He authored the public school provision of the constitution of 1868 and was the founder of Beaufort School District One, which established the town's first public school in 1868.

From 1870 to 1893 Beaufort prospered as a commercial and industrial center led by transplanted northern or immigrant merchants and capitalists. Cotton, timber, phosphate mining, and shipping all transformed Beaufort from a model of the Old South before the war to a model of the New South after the war. However, a series of natural disasters and economic changes caused a rapid reversal of fortunes. In 1893 a hurricane demolished the town and flooded neighboring Sea Islands. The phosphate industry migrated to Florida shortly thereafter. The last commercial rice crop was produced on the Combahee River in 1914, and the world decline in cotton prices ended Beaufort's historic crop by 1919. In 1907 an accidental fire burned down much of the central business district. These events signaled for Beaufort a long economic decline that hit bottom during the Depression of the 1930s.

During the 1920s the old cotton docks and warehouses along the Bay Street waterfront were converted for use by the new gasoline-powered shrimp trawlers that had moved up from Florida. Some of the old cotton fields were converted to vegetable farming, and many of the old rice fields were converted to hunting preserves. None of these new businesses provided more than a fraction of what the old cotton, phosphate, and timber industries had provided, and therefore Beaufort declined as a commercial center.

During World War II, Beaufort began to revive based on the payroll provided by the U.S. Marine Corps Recruit Depot on Parris Island, established in 1915, and the U.S. Naval Air Station, which opened in 1943. The military's impact on the town's economy increased further with the establishment of a naval hospital at Beaufort in 1949. Since then, Beaufort has grown steadily, supported by the U.S. Marine Corps and a regular stream of tourists. In the twentieth century the evocative, Old South charm of Beaufort attracted not only visitors and retirees but also Hollywood movie producers. *The Great Santini, The Big Chill, Prince of Tides, Forces of Nature,* and the Oscar winner *Forrest Gump* were all filmed in Beaufort, adding to the prospering local economy. LAWRENCE S. ROWLAND

McTeer, J. E. *Beaufort Now and Then.* Beaufort, S.C.: Beaufort Book Company, 1971.

Rowland, Lawrence S., Alexander Moore, and George C. Rogers. *The History of Beaufort County, South Carolina.* Vol. 1, *1514–1861.* Columbia: University of South Carolina Press, 1996.

Beaufort County (587 sq. miles; 2000 pop. 120,937). Beaufort County occupies the southernmost corner of South Carolina. Geographically, Beaufort has generally been defined by the Combahee and Salkehatchie Rivers on the northeast, the Savannah River on the southwest, and the Atlantic Ocean on the southeast. The region was first part of the proprietary county of Granville and later comprised the parishes of St. Helena's (1712), Prince William's (1745), St. Peter's (1746), and St. Luke's (1767). In 1769 the four parishes were combined into the Beaufort Judicial District. The parishes were abolished in 1865 and replaced by Beaufort County in 1868. Ten years later Beaufort was divided almost in half to create

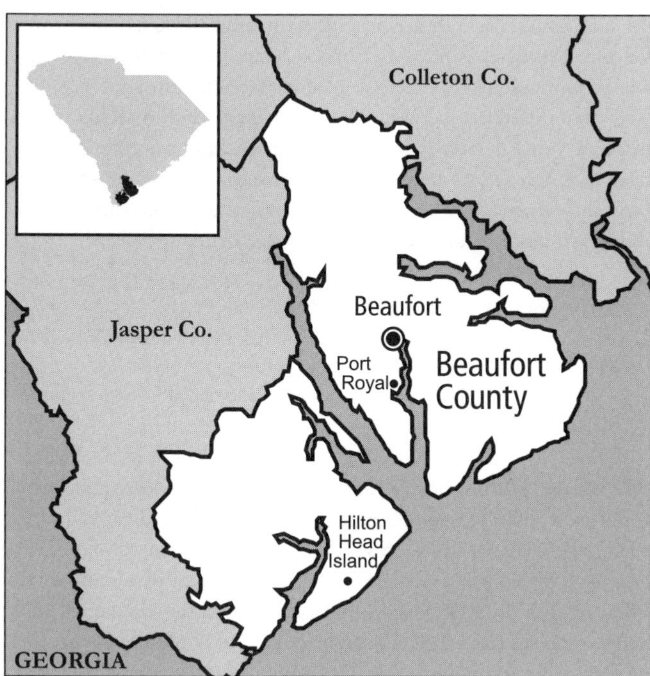

Hampton County, and in 1912 Jasper County was formed from portions of Hampton and Beaufort Counties.

Beaufort has one of the oldest records of European settlement on the North American continent, including the French on Parris Island in 1562, the Spanish at Santa Elena from 1566 to 1587, and the Scots of Stuart Town from 1684 to 1686. In 1670 the first fleet of English colonists arrived at Port Royal from Barbados, Bermuda, and the Bahamas to establish the Carolina colony. Fear of the Spaniards forced the Carolina colonists north to establish Charleston on the Ashley River. Continued military threats from Spanish Florida led the British to establish a fort (1706) and the town of Beaufort (1711) on Port Royal Island. By the early eighteenth century, Beaufort entered the plantation era. Cattle, rice, and indigo formed the foundation of this economy, as did the labor of African slaves. Slave importations between 1730 and 1776 transformed the population of Beaufort. A black majority was achieved by 1730 and remained until 1960.

During the Revolutionary War, Beaufort was divided between Loyalists and patriots. The district was overrun by the British in 1779, recaptured by the Americans in late 1779, and then reconquered and occupied by the British from April 1780 to December 1781. The war left Beaufort damaged and depopulated. Many Loyalists found refuge in the Bahamas and took thousands of their slaves with them. There, they successfully planted "Anguilla seed" cotton and shipped seeds to their relatives in South Carolina. William Elliott II grew the first large crop of Sea Island cotton in South Carolina at his Myrtle Bank plantation on Hilton Head Island in 1790, instigating a cotton boom that lasted until the mid-1820s. Together, cotton and rice brought great wealth to the Sea Islands and made the Beaufort region one of the richest in antebellum America. The boom also expanded the institution of slavery. The years 1800–1810 saw almost a doubling of the Sea Islands slave population, many of whom came from the Congo and Angola regions of Africa. This African influence contributed to the distinctive Gullah culture that survived on the Sea Islands of Beaufort County into the twenty-first century.

Beaufort planters were staunch defenders of slavery and leaders of the secessionist movement. When the Civil War began, Beaufort was the first Confederate city to fall into Union hands. On November 7, 1861, one of the largest U.S. Navy fleets of the nineteenth century steamed into Port Royal Sound, demolished Confederate forts on Hilton Head and Bay Point, and conquered the Sea Islands. Beaufort became the headquarters of the U.S. Army, Department of the South, and the staging base for Union army expeditions up and down the coast. Port Royal Sound became the headquarters for the South Atlantic Blockading Squadron. The Beaufort Sea Islands were also the site of the "Port Royal Experiment," an attempt by northern philanthropists to prepare slaves for freedom. The most lasting result of the experiment was the establishment of free schools for former slaves, including the famous Penn School begun by Laura Towne on St. Helena Island in 1862.

When the Civil War ended, few planters returned to the Sea Islands. The federal government confiscated most of their lands, and the Thirteenth Amendment freed their slaves. Beaufort County contained a large black voting majority and became a Republican stronghold during Reconstruction. The Reconstruction years were also uniquely prosperous for Beaufort County. Phosphate mining, cotton, timber, and the completion of the Port Royal and Augusta Railroad in 1873 provided jobs and opportunity for many county residents. Port Royal harbor experienced its most active maritime era from 1870 to 1900, with lumber and phosphate schooners and deep-draft steamships making Port Royal a regular port-of-call. In 1877 the U.S. Navy established the Port Royal Naval Station, where dozens of warships were stationed.

Beginning in the 1890s, Beaufort County was struck by a series of misfortunes from which it took half a century to recover. In 1893 a hurricane swept the Sea Islands killing as many as two thousand residents and inflicting severe property damage. During the 1890s richer phosphate beds were discovered in Florida and the industry abandoned South Carolina. In 1899 the Port Royal Naval Station moved to Charleston. These events and the decline of world cotton prices caused a long economic downturn for Beaufort County, which brought about the out-migration of Sea Island blacks to northern industrial cities. In 1900 there were 32,137 African Americans in Beaufort County. By 1940 there were only 14,780.

The first half of the twentieth century was a time of hardship in Beaufort, which by then had declined into one of the poorest places in America. Truck farming succeeded in many of these years, but it was a poor replacement for cotton. Commercial fishing was introduced in the 1920s and provided a fair living in good years for a few local families. What kept the county afloat in the lean years was the U.S. Marine Corps, whose recruit depot on Parris Island provided badly needed payrolls to the Beaufort economy. The military presence expanded in 1943 with the establishment of the Naval Air Station, Beaufort (later the U.S. Marine Corps Air Station, Beaufort). Together, these Marine Corps installations remained the largest employers in Beaufort County into the next century.

In 1957 the first bridge to Hilton Head Island was opened and the recreation, retirement, and tourism boom in Beaufort County began. Before 1957 Hilton Head Island was one of the poorest and most isolated communities in a poor county. At the end of the century, Hilton Head Island (incorporated in 1983) had become the richest municipality in South Carolina. Beaufort County had achieved the highest per capita income in the state. With an economy based on tourists, retirees, and the U.S. Marine Corps, Beaufort County was the fastest growing county in South Carolina at the end of the twentieth century. LAWRENCE S. ROWLAND

Danielson, Michael N. *Profits and Politics in Paradise: The Development of Hilton Head Island.* Columbia: University of South Carolina Press, 1995.
Greer, Margaret. *The Sands of Time: A History of Hilton Head Island.* Hilton Head Island, S.C.: SouthArt, 1989.
McLaren, Lynn. *Ebb Tide—Flood Tide: Beaufort County . . . Jewel of the Low County.* Columbia: University of South Carolina Press, 1991.
McTeer, J. E. *Beaufort, Now and Then.* Beaufort, S.C.: Beaufort Book Company, 1971.
Rowland, Lawrence S., Alexander Moore, and George C. Rogers. *The History of Beaufort County, South Carolina.* Vol. 1, *1514–1861.* Columbia: University of South Carolina Press, 1996.

Beaufort Gazette (2003 circulation: 11,440 daily and 10,937 Sunday). A morning newspaper, daily and Sunday, published in the city of Beaufort. The *Beaufort Gazette* was founded in 1897 by the attorney William Elliott, Jr., and Sheriff W. G. Prentiss. Prentiss died in 1898, and the next year Elliott moved to Columbia. W. P. Waterhouse, the new owner of the *Gazette,* located the newspaper at his cotton warehouse. Niels Christensen, Jr., a political ally of Waterhouse and future state senator, bought the *Gazette* in 1903 primarily to espouse his progressive political views. The *Palmetto Post* was merged into the *Gazette* in 1907.

In 1922 Christensen sold the *Gazette* for $10,000 to a group of investors sponsored by the Beaufort Chamber of Commerce. A fire gutted the newspaper offices in 1924. Three years later a group of forty-six investors bought the *Gazette* and named A. S. Morrall president and publisher. In order to cut costs during the Depression, the editor E. O. Wilson dismissed his reporters and advertised that citizens would have to bring the news directly to his office. The newspaper was cut from eight pages to four but managed to survive.

The Evening Post Publishing Company of Charleston, publishers of the two Charleston dailies, bought the *Gazette* in 1963 and named T. Miles Burbage editor and publisher. The newspaper occupied a new plant in March 1973 and began to publish five days a week on April 30. The *Gazette* was sold in 1975 to the News and Observer Publishing Company of Raleigh, North Carolina, which also owned the *Island Packet* of Hilton Head Island. The *Gazette* was converted from an afternoon paper to a morning newspaper in 1990. That same year the newspaper was sold to McClatchy Newspapers of Sacramento, California. A Sunday issue was added in 1991, and a Saturday edition in 1995. ROBERT A. PIERCE

McNeely, Patricia G. *The Palmetto Press: The History of South Carolina's Newspapers and the Press Association.* Columbia: South Carolina Press Association, 1998.

Beaufort National Cemetery. Located in the city of Beaufort on Boundary Street and U.S. Highway 21, the cemetery was authorized by President Abraham Lincoln in a letter dated February 10, 1863. The site was part of a sixty-four-acre tract known as Polly's Grove Plantation. Union general David Hunter purchased the land for $75 at an 1863 tax sale of properties confiscated by the federal government. After the Civil War, the government retained twenty-nine acres for the cemetery and turned the balance over to the town of Beaufort, which established a municipal cemetery on part of the land.

The Beaufort National Cemetery contains the remains of more than 7,500 Civil War soldiers, 4,019 of whom are unknown and 117 of whom are known Confederates; the latter are buried in a separate section. In addition, the cemetery contains the graves of some 7,000 veterans of American wars and one World War II German sailor. The cemetery is still open for veterans and family members. Once well outside town limits, the National Cemetery is now within the city boundaries. In accordance with original plans, headstones fan out 180 degrees in rows, similar to spokes of half of a wagon wheel, with each gravestone angled to face the entrance flagpole. The only difference between the gravestones of U.S. soldiers and those of Confederates is that tops of the former are curved, while those of Confederates are pointed. At the start of the twenty-first century, the cemetery was expanded by twenty acres on adjacent land secured from the South Carolina National Guard. GERHARD SPIELER

Spieler, Gerhard. "Beaufort National Cemetery Was Once 'Polly's Grove.'" *Beaufort Gazette,* May 16, 1989, p. C5.
———. "City Acquired Cemetery from U.S." *Beaufort Gazette,* October 24, 1995, p. A12.
———. "Graves of Confederate Veterans to be Decorated." *Beaufort Gazette,* May 8, 1990, p. C4.

Beauty pageants. South Carolinians frequently boast that South Carolina women are more beautiful than any others. That claim has been bolstered four times: in 1954 Miriam Stevenson of Winnsboro became Miss Universe; in 1957 Marian McKnight of Manning was Miss America; in 1980 Shawn Weatherly of Sumter was named Miss Universe; and in 1993 Kimberly Aiken of Columbia (the first African American Miss South Carolina) became Miss America. National and international titles aside, however, South Carolina has beauty pageants to celebrate almost every possible age, special interest, location, and agricultural product.

Kimberly Aiken, Miss America 1994, was South Carolina's second Miss America. Courtesy of the Miss America Organization

The most famous of these is the Miss South Carolina pageant. The Miss America pageant began in 1921, but for years South Carolina was represented in Atlantic City by contestants from individual cities. The first official Miss South Carolina pageant was held in 1937. The popular success of the Miss America contest and its state franchises led to an upsurge of beauty pageants. Imitations of the Miss America format resulted in Miss South Carolina–World and Miss South Carolina–USA contests by the early 1950s, and local promotional pageants flourished.

Among the more well known of these local contests are the Miss Sun Fun and Miss Bikini Wahine pageants, held during Myrtle Beach's Sun Fun Festival, which attract contestants from across the state and spectators from across the country. Other festival beauty pageants around the state have produced such winners as Miss Bright Leaf Tobacco, the Maid of Cotton, the Peach Queen, the Watermelon Queen, the Collard Queen, and the Iris Princess. The numbers vary, but there are usually between two and three hundred local festivals every year in South Carolina, and most of them have beauty pageants.

During the long years of segregation, beauty pageants were as race-separated as water fountains and waiting rooms were. Left out of the standard beauty contests, African American women created such competitions as Miss Black South Carolina and Miss Black Palmetto. Although the Miss South Carolina pageant had its first black contestant in 1980, some of these black-only beauty pageants continue.

Age is no barrier to being in a beauty pageant. The usual age range for standard pageants is eighteen to twenty-four, but Columbia's Miss Flame pageant, for instance, has categories for contestants as young as four months, and many other pageants have prizes at the "Wee Miss" and "Tiny Tot" levels. In addition to teen categories in many of the other contests, there are numerous pageants especially for teenage girls, such as Miss South Carolina Teen All-American and South Carolina Junior Miss. At the other end of the pageant cycle, competitions include Mrs. South Carolina and Ms. Senior.

Although many thought that beauty pageants would die out in a postfeminist world, this did not happen. Instead, pageants have been touted as being about qualities other than appearance or talent, such as personality, achievement, intellect, and volunteer work. MALIE HEIDER

Broom, Margaret Shea. *The Portrait of Palmetto Perfection.* Easley, S.C.: Martin Printing, 1993.

Burwell, Barbara Peterson, and Polly Peterson Bowles. *Becoming a Beauty Queen.* New York: Prentice Hall, 1987.

Ittner-McManus, Renee. "Cuteness Rules for Little Beauty Queens, Primping Comes before Potty Training." Columbia *State,* September 23, 2000, p. D1.

Owens, Linda. "Miss S.C. Contestants React to Pageant Rule." Columbia *State,* July 7, 1980, p. B1.

Bee, Barnard Elliott (1824–1861). Soldier. Bee was born in Charleston on February 8, 1824, the son of Barnard Elliott Bee and Ann Wragg Fayssoux. Bee's father moved to Texas in 1835, and the family followed in 1839. Bee received an at-large appointment to the U.S. Military Academy in 1841 and graduated thirty-third in his class in 1845. He was appointed a brevet second lieutenant in time to participate in the Mexican-American War. Bee was present with Zachary Taylor's army at Palo Alto and Resaca de la Palma and was then sent on recruiting service. He joined Winfield Scott's army in 1847, was at the siege of Vera Cruz, and was wounded at Cerro Gordo. He received brevet promotions to first lieutenant for Cerro Gordo and captain for Chapultepec. In 1853 South Carolina awarded him a sword of honor for his gallantry during the war.

Bee remained in the army after the war and was stationed at various western posts. He was at Fort Laramie, Dakota Territory, when South Carolina seceded. On March 3, 1861, Bee resigned from the U.S. Army to accept a commission in Confederate service. Bee quickly advanced from major to brigadier general and was in command of the Third Brigade of the Army of the Shenandoah in June 1861. Bee's brigade was the first to reinforce General Pierre G. T. Beauregard at Manassas Junction, Virginia, and he was instrumental in ensuring the Confederate victory on July 21, 1861, by delaying the Union advance. While holding off the Federals, Bee saw the brigade of Thomas J. Jackson standing to the rear and not assisting his command. Bee called out, "There is Jackson standing like a stone wall." Controversy continues over whether he meant the statement as a compliment or a criticism. Nevertheless, Bee is credited with giving "Stonewall" Jackson his nickname. Bee fell mortally wounded during the battle and died the next day, July 22, 1861. He was buried in Pendleton. JACK ALLEN MEYER

Davis, William C., and Julie Hoffman, eds. *The Confederate General.* 4 vols. to date. Harrisburg, Pa.: National Historical Society, 1991– .

Freeman, Douglas Southall. *Lee's Lieutenants: A Study in Command.* 3 vols. New York: Scribner's, 1942–1944.

Warner, Ezra J. *Generals in Gray: Lives of the Confederate Commanders.* Baton Rouge: Louisiana State University Press, 1959.

Beech Island (Aiken County; 2000 pop. 4,843). Named for the beech trees growing in the wetlands of the nearby Savannah River swamp and possibly a dead river island, Beech Island began in the 1680s as Savano Town, an important Indian trading center. In 1716, after several Indian uprisings, the British constructed a fort (later Fort Moore) at Savano Town to protect the upcountry trade and guard the western entrance to South Carolina. The surrounding area became part of New Windsor Township in the 1730s. Offers of free land attracted European Protestants to the new township, including fifty Swiss families brought by John Tobler in 1737. These Swiss settled on the rich farmland along the Savannah River and began Beech Island's agricultural economy.

Agriculture reached its zenith in Beech Island in the years prior to the Civil War. The neighborhood was the site of several large plantations, such as Governor James Henry Hammond's 7,500-acre Silver Bluff Plantation and his smaller, more opulent Redcliffe Plantation. In 1856 Hammond and others organized the Beech Island Farmer's Club for the diffusion of agricultural knowledge. Many large plantation homes were built from the early 1800s until the start of the Civil War. Following the war, sharecroppers did most of the farming. Not until after the Great Depression did agriculture again thrive in Beech Island, with successful farms raising beef and dairy cattle, hogs, corn, wheat, and soybeans.

Farming was the main employment until the early 1950s, when the Urquhart electrical generating station and the Savannah River Site were constructed. A new four-lane highway was built to handle the bumper-to-bumper plant traffic from Beech Island to the "Bomb Plant." By 1966 construction began on the first industrial plant to locate in Beech Island, Kimberly-Clark Corporation, which produced paper products. Another plant, Amoco Foam, a producer of polystyrene food containers, followed in 1974. Both plants are located on farmland originally granted to Beech Island's Swiss settlers by King George II. JACQUELINE PRIOR BARTLEY

Maness, Harold. *Forgotten Outpost: Fort Moore & Savannah Town, 1685–1765.* Pickens, S.C.: BPB Publications, 1986.

Nylund, Rowena. *Redcliffe Plantation State Park, a Visitor's Guide.* Columbia: South Carolina Department of Parks, Recreation and Tourism, 1991.

Beech Island Agricultural Club. The Beech Island Agricultural Club originally convened as the ABC Farmer's Club in 1846. The organization met monthly in a rural Aiken County clubhouse. Meetings were dedicated to education, experimentation, and discussion. Each gathering began with a large meal and the election of a chairman for the next meeting. Members conducted experiments in all phases of agriculture and animal husbandry, attempted various industrial pursuits, and were particularly concerned with slavery. The care and control of slaves eventually dominated club activities, and by 1851 the group merged with a local slave patrol to form the Beech Island Agricultural and Police Society.

Reorganized in 1856 as the Beech Island Farmer's Club, and rededicated to its original mission of scientific agriculture, the organization continued to be based on its 1846 bylaws. The new club had each member attempt, and report on, one farming experiment annually. The club also hosted public barbecues, usually for political purposes. On July 22, 1858, U.S. Senator James Henry Hammond, a founding member of the club, made his controversial "Beech Island Speech," in which he sought to check the growing secessionist impulse by avowing that cooperation with the federal government was the best means to address southern grievances.

The organization survived at the start of the twenty-first century as the Beech Island Agricultural Club. Continuing to meet under the 1846 charter, the club is the oldest continually active agricultural society in South Carolina. The club maintains a tradition of inviting influential guest speakers, including Wade Hampton III, John D. Rockefeller, William Howard Taft, James Byrnes, and Strom Thurmond. A state historical marker commemorating the club stands near the clubhouse on U.S. Highway 278 in Aiken County. ROBERT T. OLIVER

Beech Island Farmer's Club. Records, 1846–1934. Typescript. South Caroliniana Library, University of South Carolina, Columbia.

Cordle, Charles. "Activities of Beech Island Farmers Clubs, 1846–1862." *Georgia Historical Review* 36 (March 1952): 22–31.

Roper, Donna K. "To Promote and Improve Agriculture: A Study of Four Antebellum South Carolina Farmers' Societies." Master's thesis, University of South Carolina, 1989.

Belton (Anderson County; 2000 pop. 4,461). Belton began in the 1850s as the site of a proposed junction of the Greenville and Columbia Railroad and spur line to Anderson planned by the Blue Ridge Railroad. The town was named in honor of Judge John Belton O'Neall, president of the Greenville and Columbia Railroad. Dr. George Brown donated several acres of land for a railroad depot and a school building. The town was incorporated in 1855, and the first intendant (mayor) was Charles C. Chamberlain, a railroad supervisor. Broadway Presbyterian Church, established in the late 1700s about five miles from where Belton was later established, was relocated to the new town to become its first house of worship. Area farmers soon made Belton an important local market, and McGee's Hotel became a popular stop for travelers on the Greenville and Columbia Railroad. An 1860 census taken by the local militia counted a population of 183 whites and 30 slaves.

The Rice family can be credited with much of Belton's growth after the Civil War. Brothers Enoch and Joel Rice started a brick mill in the late 1860s and also operated a traveling gin, which made a seasonal circuit among nearby cotton farms. In 1882 the brothers built the Rice block of buildings on the north side of the town square and the gin was placed there. They later built and operated a cottonseed oil mill and a grist and flour mill.

Belton's first major industry, the Belton Cotton Mill, commenced operations in 1900. Blair Mills and Rice Mills, owned by the Rice family, opened several years later and remained Belton's largest employers into the twenty-first century. Blair Mills started in 1908 and was the first mill in the nation to manufacture terry cloth. In the twentieth century, industrial diversification brought plants operated by Goodman Conveyor, Rockwell Automotive, and Wells Aluminum.

Tennis has been popular in Belton since the late nineteenth century. The town is home to the Palmetto Tennis Championships, drawing several hundred youth annually. The Victorian-styled railroad depot became the home to the S.C. Tennis Hall of Fame, the Ruth Drake Museum, the Belton branch of the Anderson County Library, and a large space for meetings and special events. HURLEY E. BADDERS

Anderson County Tricentennial Committee. *Anderson County Honors the State of South Carolina on Her 300th Birthday: Souvenir Program.* Anderson, S.C.: Anderson County Tricentennial Committee, 1970.

Grubbs, Max Wilton. "A History of the Social, Economic & Political Development of Belton, South Carolina." Master's thesis, Clemson University, 1960.

Herd, E. Don. *Early History of Belton, South Carolina, 1700–1860.* Williamston, S.C.: by the author, 1959.

Sketches of Belton, South Carolina. Belton, S.C.: Belton Times, 1911.

Benbridge, Henry (1743–1812). Artist. An accomplished portrait painter and miniaturist, Henry Benbridge settled in Charleston in 1773 and worked for nearly two decades in the Neo-Classical style. Born on October 20, 1743, in Philadelphia, little is known about his early training. It is likely that he was exposed to a variety of artists working in Philadelphia during the time of his youth, including Benjamin West, William Willams, John Hesselius, and Matthew Pratt.

In 1764 Benbridge traveled abroad to further his studies. Traditionally he has been identified as one of the sitters in Matthew Pratt's *The American School,* suggesting that his first stop was London. By 1765 Benbridge was in Rome sharing quarters with the successful Irish sculptor Christopher Hewetson. Benbridge enrolled in the academy of Pompeo Batoni, a favorite of the British on the grand tour. Probably at the suggestion of Benjamin West, he became acquainted with the work of Anton Raphael Mengs, a leading contemporary artist whom West copied. In 1769, after four years of study, Benbridge left Italy for London, where Benjamin West served as his primary contact. While there, Benbridge attempted to advance his reputation as an artist by exhibiting a full-length portrait of the Corsican hero Pascal Paoli through the Free Society of Artists and portraits of Thomas Coombe and Benjamin Franklin at the Royal Academy.

In 1770 Benbridge returned to Philadelphia, presumably to continue his career as an artist. While few paintings exist from this period, he was elected a member of the American Philosophical Society in 1771. In 1772 he married Esther "Hetty" Sage, who is identified as a miniature portraitist. They had one son, Henry.

In contrast to his time in Philadelphia and London, Benbridge achieved success almost immediately on settling in Charleston. Replacing the rigid colonial portrait style of the aging Jeremiah Theus, Benbridge worked instead in a manner that demonstrated the many different sources and influences he was exposed to in Europe. His study of classical antiquity and grand tour portraiture were the bases for his quick rise. Wealthy planters and those with ties to Philadelphia and London comprised the majority of Benbridge's initial Charleston commissions. Among the earliest were portraits of Middleton family members.

Eventually Benbridge's Revolutionary sentiments became apparent in his choice of subjects. When Charleston fell to British forces in 1780, Benbridge—a patriot—was imprisoned on a ship and exiled to St. Augustine along with other colonial sympathizers. Sent to Philadelphia on his release in 1783, Benbridge was back in Charleston by 1784. Many of his sitters after the Revolutionary War were connected to him through political sentiment or their incarceration in St. Augustine. A series of portraits of Charleston Revolutionary War heroes dates from this postwar period.

Why or when Benbridge left Charleston is unclear. His last known correspondence to his sister, Mrs. Elizabeth Gordon Saltar, is dated 1787 and suggests that he did not want for commissions in the area. He continued to appear in the city directory until 1790. In 1799 the painter Thomas Sully encountered him in Norfolk, Virginia, where he may have been living with his son. Scant paintings are known to exist from this later part of his life. The exact date of his death is unclear, but he was buried in Christ Church Cemetery, Philadelphia, on January 25, 1812. ANGELA D. MACK

Mack, Angela D. "Henry Benbridge: Charleston Portrait Painter." *Magazine Antiques* 158 (November 2000): 726–33.

McInnis, Maurie D. *Henry Benbridge, 1743–1812, Charleston Portrait Painter.* Charleston, S.C.: Carolina Art Association, 2000.

Stewart, Robert G. *Henry Benbridge (1743–1812): American Portrait Painter.* Washington, D.C.: Smithsonian Institution Press, 1971.

Benedict College. A historically black college in Columbia, Benedict College was founded in 1870 on the site of an eighty-acre plantation. Rhode Island native Bathsheba Benedict, serving with the Baptist Home Mission Society, purchased the property with the long-term goal of educating recently emancipated African Americans.

Originally named Benedict Institute, the school began with a class of ten men, one building (a dilapidated former slave master's house), and one teacher, the Reverend Timothy L. Dodge, a college-educated northern minister who would become the school's first president. These first students followed a curriculum of grammar school subjects, Bible study, and theology. Later, additional courses were added to train Benedict's students for work as teachers and ministers.

In 1894 the school was chartered by the General Assembly as a liberal arts college and became Benedict College. During the next three and a half decades, the college continued to be led by white northern clergymen. In 1930, however, the first African American president was appointed. The Reverend John J. Starks, an 1891 graduate of Benedict, began a succession of African American leaders of the college.

Throughout the twentieth century, Benedict College expanded its campus, its curriculum, its student body, and its significance to the Columbia region and beyond. Scholars such as Benjamin Mays and Benjamin Payton helped to bring national attention to Benedict, as did the achievements of its alumni, which included the civil rights activists Septima Clark and Modjeska Simkins. During the 1990s, the section of the campus at the corner of Harden and Taylor Streets in downtown Columbia underwent substantial renovations to all of its historic sites, dormitories, and administration buildings. Also in the 1990s, football returned to Benedict after a twenty-nine-year hiatus. Shortly thereafter, Benedict and South Carolina State University briefly rekindled their football rivalry in the Palmetto Capital City Classic until South Carolina State pulled out in 2004.

By the end of the twentieth century, under the leadership of Dr. David Swinton, Benedict College saw its enrollment grow to nearly three thousand students, making it, in terms of enrollment, one of the largest historically black colleges in the Carolinas and one of the largest private colleges in South Carolina. In 2003 the college broke ground on its multimillion-dollar, sixty-one-acre LeRoy Walker Athletic and Wellness Complex (named after Olympic president emeritus Dr. LeRoy T. Walker, alumnus of the class of 1940). The college planned the complex not only to serve the fitness needs of students and faculty, but also to house the stadium of the Benedict Tigers football team. In 2004 Benedict began developing graduate courses in business and religion to complement its bachelor's degree offerings in twenty-nine areas. STEPHEN CRISWELL

Davis, Marianna W. *The Enduring Dream: History of Benedict College, 1870–1995.* Columbia, S.C.: Benedict College, 1995.

Bennett, John (1865–1956). Author, artist. The son of John Bennett and Eliza Jane McClintick, Bennett was born in Chillicothe, Ohio, on May 17, 1865. Wanting to become an artist, he had to work to support his family instead. In the 1880s he published prose and silhouettes for children in *St. Nicholas Magazine.* The publication serialized his most famous work, *Master Skylark,* which appeared in book form in 1897. A tale of Shakespeare's time, it is considered one of the best American historical novels for children. Its success convinced Bennett to drop out of the New York Art Students League and write another book. In 1898 ill health drove him to Charleston, where he renewed his acquaintance with the Smythe family, whom he had met a few years before at Salt Sulphur Springs, West Virginia. Bennett's second book, *Barnaby Lee,* was published in 1902. Its proceeds enabled him to marry Susan Smythe the same year. Turning his attention to the riches of the area, he wrote *The Treasure of Peyre Gaillard* (1906).

John Bennett. Courtesy, South Carolina Historical Society

During these years Bennett tried to interest publishers in African American spirituals, and he made a close study of Gullah, the language of lowcountry blacks. He also studied black folklore, amassing tales of the disappearing oral tradition. He presented a lecture on this subject in 1908, but the local press castigated him for using blacks as a subject. Dejected, he nearly gave up writing. During World War I he came into contact with the younger DuBose Heyward, as they raised money for Liberty Loans. After the war, when the Pittsburgh native and war veteran Hervey Allen came to town, Heyward and Allen became friends, and both turned to Bennett, who mentored them in weekly "fanging" sessions. Stirred by the new spirit of modern poetry, Allen, Heyward, and Bennett joined with a group of fledgling women poets under Laura Bragg, including Elizabeth von Kolnitz (later Hyer) and Josephine Pinckney. Together they launched the Poetry Society of South Carolina in 1921. Bennett agreed to participate only after being assured that he would be a figurehead. But as the careers of the younger artists took off, Bennett was left to run the organization.

Bennett published one folktale, *Madame Margot,* in 1921 but was not able to complete the collection as *The Doctor to the Dead* until 1946. In the interim he published a collection of his earlier silhouette tales, *The Pigtail of Ah Lee Ben Loo* (1928). Although his work is notable, perhaps his greatest contribution was to individuals and fields of study. He was a pioneer in the study of many African American and other historical topics and was instrumental in the creation and publication of Heyward's landmark novel *Porgy* (1925). As founder and sustainer of the Poetry Society of South Carolina, Bennett was a key player in the revival of literary and cultural life in the city and the state. The father of three, Bennett died on December 28, 1956, and was buried in Magnolia Cemetery. HARLAN GREENE

Greene, Harlan. *Mr. Skylark: John Bennett and the Charleston Renaissance.* Athens: University of Georgia Press, 2001.

Bennett, Thomas, Jr. (1781–1865). Governor. Bennett was born on August 14, 1781, the son of the architect Thomas Bennett and Anna Hayes Warnock. He married Mary Lightbourn Stone on February 19, 1801. The couple eventually had seven children. Beginning as his father's partner, Bennett built a lucrative lumber and rice mill business in Charleston. His rice mills, known as Cannonsborough Mills, included a twenty-two-pestle mill driven by steam power and a fourteen-pestle mill driven by tide power from an eighty-seven-acre pond. A prominent lowcountry entrepreneur, Bennett held business positions that included director of the South Carolina Homespun Company (1808), incorporator of the Planters and Merchants Bank (1810), director of Bank of the State of South Carolina (1811–1814, 1826–1827), and director of the Louisville, Cincinnati and Charleston Railroad (1836–1837). He was also active in the Charleston Chamber of Commerce and held local political offices, including intendant (mayor) of Charleston from 1812 to 1813. Through his second marriage, to Jane Burgess Gordon, on March 5, 1840, Bennett obtained three lowcountry plantations. By 1850 he owned 260 slaves, and ten years later his Charleston estate was valued at $275,800.

Governor Thomas Bennett, Jr. (1781–1863), by William Harrison Scarborough, Oil on canvas. Gibbes Museum of Art / Carolina Art Association

In 1804 Bennett was elected by St. Philip's and St. Michael's Parishes to the South Carolina General Assembly, where he served six terms in the House of Representatives by 1817 and sat as Speaker of the House from 1814 to 1817. Victorious in a special election for the S.C. Senate in 1819, he resigned on December 7, 1820, upon being elected governor. During his tenure (1820–1822), Bennett opposed the slave trade, advocated increased leniency in the criminal and slave codes, and promoted internal improvements. Bennett also presided over the state during the thwarted Denmark Vesey slave insurrection, in the aftermath of which dozens of accused participants were hanged or exiled, including three of Bennett's trusted house slaves.

It was Bennett's response to the Vesey crisis for which he is best remembered. In a message to the General Assembly on November 22, 1822, the governor chastised Charleston authorities for the mass execution of alleged conspirators. Bennett criticized courts for accepting without question testimony that was "the offspring of treachery or revenge," offered by witnesses who were obviously attempting to save their own lives. While Bennett agreed that some type of plot was afoot, he refused to accept the hysterical response of city residents, who, "in a pitch of excitement," turned scattered rumors into a slave conspiracy involving hundreds or even thousands of participants. Part of Bennett's opinion was based on racial stereotypes. He simply doubted the capability of African slaves to mount such an uprising and trusted implicitly in the "habitual respect" slaves held for their masters. Despite such doubts, Bennett nevertheless cooperated with Charleston officials during the crisis. "Thus," the historian Richard Wade surmised, "Charleston stumbled into tragedy."

Bennett supported the Unionists in the nullification crisis of 1832 and briefly represented the city parishes again in the S.C. Senate from 1837 to1839. He died on January 30, 1865, and was buried in Magnolia Cemetery. ERNEST MCPHERSON LANDER, JR.

Bailey, N. Louise, Mary L. Morgan, and Carolyn R. Taylor, eds. *Biographical Directory of the South Carolina Senate, 1776–1985.* 3 vols. Columbia: University of South Carolina Press, 1986.

Lofton, John. *Insurrection in South Carolina: The Turbulent World of Denmark Vesey.* Yellow Springs, Ohio: Antioch, 1964.

Wade, Richard C. "The Vesey Plot: A Reconsideration." *Journal of Southern History* 30 (May 1964): 143–61.

Bennettsville (Marlboro County; 2000 pop. 9,425). Bennettsville was established on December 14, 1819, when the General Assembly moved the Marlboro District courthouse to a more central location. The new district seat was named for the sitting governor, Thomas Bennett. A three-acre square was selected on a bluff above Crooked Creek, on the stage road running between Society Hill, South Carolina, and Fayetteville, North Carolina. By 1824 a Robert Mills–designed courthouse was completed, and a town slowly developed around the square. By 1860 Bennettsville contained about thirty houses, three churches, and two fraternal lodges, with stores, offices, and artisan shops surrounding the town square. The town suffered a disastrous setback on March 6, 1865, when Union forces captured Bennettsville and burned cotton warehouses, barns, and the office of Dr. Alexander McLeod, a signer of the Ordinance of Secession. However, Bennettsville had the only courthouse from the old Cheraws District to survive the torch, which left district and county records intact from 1785.

Prosperity returned in the 1880s with the arrival of the railroad, which greatly benefited county cotton farmers. New businesses and industries followed, including the Bank of Marlboro (1884), the Bennettsville Cotton Exchange (1886), the Marlboro Cotton Oil Company (1889), and the Marlboro Mill Company (1894). Bennettsville's "boom" continued into the 1920s as city streets were paved, electricity arrived, and water and sewer systems were installed. Traffic on U.S. Highways 15 and 401 introduced a flourishing tourist trade along Main Street, which sprouted hotels, tourist homes, cafés, theaters, and motor courts. World War II brought to Bennettsville Palmer Field, an army flight-training base that opened in August 1941. When flight training ended, German prisoners of war were billeted at the airfield, where they supplied labor to local farms.

After the war, the mechanization of Marlboro County agriculture led surplus farm laborers to seek opportunity in Bennettsville, and African Americans soon comprised more than half the city's population and workforce. The migration marked the beginning of Bennettsville's shift from an agricultural economy to a more industrial one. A variety of new industries arrived in the latter half of the twentieth century, including Willamette Industries, Marley Engineered Products, Mohawk Carpet's Oak River Mill, SoPakCo, Powell Manufacturing Company, Bennettsville Printing LLC, Reliance Trading Company, OxBodies Inc., Musashi Inc., and International Cup Corp.

During the 1950s the U.S. Highway 15-401 bypass was built, which became the site for much of Bennettsville's commercial development. Crooked Creek was dammed to create Lake Wallace, an 846-acre recreational lake and waterfowl preserve. Attractive residential developments soon appeared on both sides of the lake. By the 1970s Cottingham Boulevard, the S.C. Highway 9 bypass, served travelers passing through Bennettsville on their way to the Grand Strand. Another addition to the Bennettsville economy came in 1989 with the opening of the Evans Correctional Institution, which housed some twelve hundred state inmates. Noteworthy natives of Bennettsville include former Bank of America chairman Hugh L. McColl, Jr., Children's Defense Fund chair Marian Wright Edelman, and former congressman John L. Napier. WILLIAM LIGHT KINNEY, JR.

Hudson, Joshua Hilary. *Sketches and Reminiscences.* Columbia, S.C.: State Company, 1903.

Kinney, William Light, Jr. *Sherman's March: A Review.* Bennettsville, S.C.: Marlboro Herald-Advocate, 1961.

Marlboro County, South Carolina: A Pictorial History. Bennettsville, S.C.: Marlborough Historical Society, 1996.

McColl, D. D. *Sketches of Old Marlboro.* Columbia, S.C.: State Company, 1916.

Thomas, J. A. W. *A History of Marlboro County, with Traditions and Sketches of Numerous Families.* 1897. Reprint, Baltimore: Regional Publishing, 1971.

Benton, Brook (1931–1988). Musician. Benton was born Benjamin Franklin Peay on September 19, 1931, in Camden. His father was a bricklayer and choir director of a Methodist church. The young Benton delivered milk for a local dairy, sang with his father's choir and the Camden Jubilee Singers, and began writing songs.

Benton moved to New York in 1948 and worked at a variety of odd jobs, performing with several gospel and rhythm-and-blues (R&B) groups and recording "demos" of his and other writers' songs. He and partner Clyde Otis wrote hits for Nat King Cole ("Looking Back") and Clyde McPhatter ("A Lover's Question"), among others. In 1959 Benton recorded "It's Just a Matter of Time," the first of twenty-three Top Forty hits in the next five years and the first of his eighteen million-sellers. "Endlessly," "So Many Ways," "Thank You, Pretty Baby," "Fools Rush In," and "Kiddio" followed within the next eighteen months. A 1960 pairing with the temperamental Dinah Washington was personally difficult, but "Baby (You've Got What It Takes)" and "Rocking Good Way" made the Top Ten. Some of Benton's other hits looked back to his gospel roots ("Shadrack") and cashed in on the folk-music craze ("Frankie and Johnny," "The Boll Weevil Song").

After the "British Invasion" by the Beatles and other groups, however, Mercury Records let Benton's contract lapse. He recorded several unsuccessful albums with different companies—one included "San Francisco (Wear Some Flowers in Your Hair)," "Ode to Billy Joe," and "Stick-to-it-ivity" ("a philosophical saga of Sam and Curly, two dissimilar frogs")—and he covered hits by other artists ranging from Frank Sinatra ("My Way") to Johnny Cash ("I Walk the Line") in genres ranging from country to disco. His only major hit after 1965 was his memorably languid version of "Rainy Night in Georgia" (1970), recorded for Jerry Wexler of Atlantic Records. He remained a popular nightclub and concert performer on the oldies circuit, however, especially in Great Britain.

Benton will be remembered for some of the songs he wrote and for his stylish delivery. Opinions differ about the lush strings that often accompanied him—roughly the R&B equivalent of the "Nashville Sound"—but his rich, gospel-inflected baritone recalled predecessors such as Billy Eckstine and set the stage for the explosion of "soul music" in the 1960s. He died in New York City on April 9, 1988, and was survived by his wife, Mary, and their four children. JOHN SHELTON REED

"Brook Benton: On the Comeback Trail." *Ebony* 33 (May 1978): 164–66, 168.

French, Howard W. "Brook Benton, Singer of Hit Tunes, Known for His Ballads, Dies at 56." *New York Times,* April 10, 1988, p. 36.

Berkeley County (1,098 sq. miles; 2000 pop. 142,651). Created on May 10, 1682, Berkeley was one of South Carolina's first three counties. It was named for two of the Lords Proprietors, Lord John Berkeley and his younger brother, Sir William Berkeley. At that time Charleston served as the county's seat of justice. Over the next two centuries, the boundaries and organization of the Berkeley County area underwent several alterations. From the early eighteenth century until the close of the Civil War, the area was the location of several lowcountry parishes, including St. John's Berkeley, St. James Goose Creek, St. Thomas and St. Denis, and St. Stephen's. With the abolishment of the parish system in 1865, Berkeley became part of Charleston County. In 1882 the General Assembly reestablished Berkeley County. Its area was reduced several times in the following decades, and Berkeley established its modern boundaries by 1921. Mount Pleasant served as the county seat from 1882 until 1895, when Charleston County annexed the town. Moncks Corner was selected as the new Berkeley County seat in an election that same year.

Initially a center of the colony's thriving Indian trade, the Berkeley County region grew to economic prominence as one of the premier agricultural centers of colonial America. English and French Huguenot planters developed a thriving rice and indigo culture

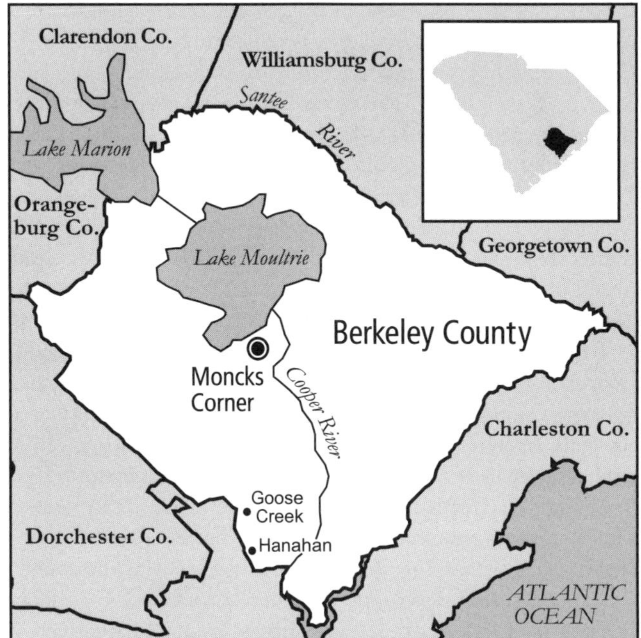

along the Cooper and Santee Rivers. As early as the late 1670s, English colonists from Barbados settled in the Goose Creek area, which became the home base of the politically powerful "Goose Creek Men." Immense rice fortunes were made on some of the richest agricultural land in the American colonies. Cosmopolitan planters such as Ralph Izard traveled the world and attained a level of sophistication seldom matched by the inhabitants of other British colonies. Early plantations included Medway, constructed in 1686 on Back River, which survives as the oldest house in South Carolina. Middleburg Plantation, established around 1699 on the Cooper River's east branch, is considered the state's oldest wooden house.

Several Berkeley planters achieved prominent roles in the push toward independence from Britain. The Revolutionary War produced Berkeley County's most famous native son, Francis Marion, as well as General William Moultrie and the statesman Henry Laurens. But the war wreaked havoc, disrupting the agricultural trade on which the colony had gained prominence. Beginning in 1793, Moultrie introduced cotton cultivation at his North Hampton plantation, heralding a shift from an exclusive reliance on rice, indigo, and naval stores. The accumulation of wealth in Berkeley was directly due to the labor of African American slaves, and African Americans comprised a majority of the region's population for most of its history. In 1790 the Berkeley County area had approximately 103,000 slaves to some 30,000 whites. By 1820 blacks comprised a two-to-one majority, a ratio that continued throughout the remainder of the antebellum era.

Reconstruction plunged Berkeley County into turmoil, as the wealth and opulence of antebellum days vanished. The overwhelming black majority in Berkeley made the area a Republican Party stronghold until the 1880s, helping to elect several African Americans to the state General Assembly and the U.S. House of Representatives. With the return of Democratic rule in South Carolina in 1877, whites quickly worked to dilute the political influence of black voters. In 1882 legislators created the "Black" Seventh District, a meandering congressional district that contained almost twenty-five percent of the state's black voters, including all of Berkeley County. By condensing black voters into a single district, the statewide political influence of Berkeley County's black majority was contained, before being practically eliminated with the disfranchisement of African Americans by the state constitution of 1895.

In the late nineteenth and early twentieth centuries, the Berkeley County economy centered on timbering and farming, the latter built on sharecropping. The system kept many people, both black and white, perpetually in debt, living from crop to crop. Manufacturing was virtually nonexistent. During Prohibition in the 1920s, Berkeley earned a notorious reputation for its underground economy in the illegal manufacture of moonshine whiskey. The county's black majority declined in the twentieth century as a steady stream of African Americans left Berkeley for urban centers of the mid-Atlantic and northeastern states.

Beginning in 1939, an influx of federal dollars into the Santee Cooper hydroelectric project (which submerged a large portion of Berkeley County under the waters of Lake Moultrie) initiated an economic revival. This continued through World War II, as county residents and newcomers flocked to jobs at the Charleston Naval Base and the Charleston Naval Shipyard. The county seat of Moncks Corner grew into a thriving town, but not to the degree of Goose Creek, which emerged in the postwar years as the county's largest municipality. Its growth was spurred by cold-war-era military spending and continued as new arrivals to the Charleston area moved into burgeoning residential subdivisions such as Crowfield Plantation. By 1990 the Berkeley County population had become three-quarters white.

By the end of the twentieth century, Berkeley County had evolved from its agricultural past into a mecca for manufacturing. The Bushy Park industrial corridor, first developed in the mid-1950s along the Cooper River, became home to the manufacturing facilities of such well-known multinational firms as Dupont, Bayer, and Agfa. In the late 1970s an aluminum smelter, Alcoa-Mount Holly, was built between Goose Creek and Moncks Corner. In the mid-1990s the huge Nucor steel mill was constructed in the Cainhoy and Huger communities. In 1995 Berkeley became the first county in South Carolina to secure $1 billion in new capital investment in one year. The 1,044-acre Mount Holly Commerce Park, a public-private venture between Moncks Corner and Goose Creek, was dedicated in October 1999. The Charleston Naval Weapons Station is almost entirely located in Berkeley County, as is the Francis Marion National Forest. WILLARD STRONG

Chamber of Commerce (Moncks Corner, S.C.). *Berkeley County, South Carolina.* N.p., [1955?].

Cross, J. Russell. *Historic Ramblin's through Berkeley.* Columbia, S.C.: R. L. Bryan, 1985.

Orvin, Maxwell Clayton. *Historic Berkeley County, South Carolina, 1671–1900.* Charleston, S.C.: COMPRINT, 1973.

Bernardin, Joseph Louis (1928–1996). Catholic cardinal. Bernardin was born in Columbia on April 2, 1928, the elder child and only son of Joseph Bernardin, a master stonecutter, and Maria Maddalena Simion. His parents had emigrated in 1927 from Tonàdico, in the Italian Province of Trent. His father died when Joseph was four, and his mother worked as a seamstress to support her two children. Bernardin was educated in Columbia's Catholic and public schools. He entered a premedical program at the University of South Carolina, but then decided to study for the priesthood. He attended St. Mary's Seminary, Baltimore, and the Catholic University of America, where he earned a master's degree in education.

Joseph Cardinal Bernardin. Photograph by Brooks, Bethesda, Maryland

Ordained in 1952, Bernardin served at St. Joseph's Church, Charleston, and taught for two years at Bishop England High School. For twelve years he worked in the chancery of the Diocese of Charleston, eventually serving as chancellor, vicar-general, and diocesan administrator. During those years Bernardin shared parochial duties at the Cathedral of St. John the Baptist, saying mass, hearing confessions, and training altar boys. He was a leader in efforts to desegregate South Carolina's Catholic schools.

Bernardin worked closely with Paul J. Hallinan, Bishop of Charleston (1958–1962), a scholarly, pastoral prelate who became Bernardin's mentor. After Hallinan was named Archbishop of Atlanta in 1962, he secured Bernardin's appointment as his auxiliary bishop in 1966. As a result Bernardin became the country's youngest bishop at the time. In 1968 Bernardin was elected general secretary of the National Conference of Catholic Bishops. He was appointed Archbishop of Cincinnati four years later and became Archbishop of Chicago, the country's largest diocese, in 1982. Pope John Paul II elevated him to the College of Cardinals in 1983.

Bernardin was a popular bishop, renowned for administrative skill and respected for his work to benefit children, the elderly, the poor, and the sick. He became a nationally respected spokesperson for American Catholicism. Often mentioned as a possible future pope, he dismissed such speculation as unrealistic. He chaired a committee of American bishops who wrote *The Challenge of Peace,* a 1983 national pastoral letter questioning use of nuclear weapons. An opponent of abortion, he also opposed the death penalty and assisted suicide, and promoted active efforts to alleviate poverty. He spoke out for a "consistent ethic of life," asserting that Catholic tradition "calls for positive legal action to prevent the killing of the unborn and the aged and positive societal action to provide shelter for the homeless and education for the illiterate." Concern about the spread of AIDS led him to speak out for understanding and kind treatment of people with the disease.

Bernardin worked to promote mutual respect and friendship with non-Catholics and to foster dialogue between Christians and Jews. Even as he achieved international status, Bernardin remained attentive to the church and his many friends in South Carolina. His numerous honorary degrees and awards included the Presidential Medal of Freedom in 1996. In 1995 Bernardin was diagnosed with pancreatic cancer. He died in Chicago on November 14, 1996, and was buried in Mount Carmel Cemetery, Chicago. DAVID C. R. HEISSER

Bernardin, Joseph Louis. *Selected Works of Joseph Cardinal Bernardin.* Edited by Alphonse Spilly. 2 vols. Collegeville, Minn.: Liturgical Press, 2000.

Kennedy, Eugene. *Bernardin: Life to the Full.* Chicago: Bonus Books, 1997.

Unsworth, Tim. *I Am Your Brother Joseph: Cardinal Bernardin of Chicago.* New York: Crossroad, 1997.

White, John H. *This Man Bernardin.* Chicago: Loyola Press, 1996.

Bessinger, Maurice (b. 1930). Businessman. Bessinger, born in Orangeburg County on July 14, 1930, is founder of the Piggie Park restaurant chain. He is a restaurant impresario of the old school, a P. T. Barnum of the barbecue world, an evangelical Christian who has all but declared barbecue a sacrament. "All the Old Testament sacrifices were cooked with wood," he told a newspaper reporter in 1996, "and that was ordained by God."

Bessinger has been cooking hams over hickory wood in West Columbia since the early 1950s. The main restaurant is a sprawling complex built, like many drive-ins of an earlier era, in a hub-and-spoke pattern with the dining room at the center and corrugated tin-topped awnings radiating outward. Just inside the door sits a pile of pamphlets and newspaper clippings attesting to Bessinger's barbecue acumen or pleading that nonbelievers heed the Word of God. Other pamphlets tout a peculiar brand of southern heritage and boast titles such as "The Truth about the Confederate Battle Flag."

Like fellow restaurateur Lester Maddox of Georgia, Bessinger once entertained political aspirations. On passage of the Civil Rights Act of 1964, which stipulated that businesses engaged in interstate commerce must desegregate, he took a stand. In July 1964 Bessinger, who at that time owned four Piggie Park restaurants, refused a black minister who attempted to enter one of his restaurants. The case—*Newman v. Piggie Park Enterprises*—went to the U.S. Supreme Court. In 1968 the court handed down a unanimous ruling against Bessinger. Also during the 1960s Bessinger served as president of the National Association for the Advancement of White People. Under his leadership the organization distributed fliers that proclaimed, "You are white because your ancestors believed in segregation." Bessinger attempted to leverage his notoriety in a bid for public office. Unlike Maddox, who was installed as governor of Georgia in 1967, Bessinger failed in his 1974 bid for governor, despite a proven ability to curry press coverage by way of stunts such as parading about Columbia on a white horse named Queen.

The year before his bid for governor, Bessinger underwent a religious conversion. He later erected a mission in the midst of Piggie Park, right beside the pits, where on Wednesdays he led a Bible-study class. "When you have a truly religious conversion," Bessinger told a reporter, "you don't see black and white, you don't see rich and poor." Bessinger's critics argue that he has not mellowed. In July 2000, when the South Carolina legislature removed the Confederate battle flag from the State House dome, Bessinger raised a Confederate battle flag over each of his nine restaurants and reaped a whirlwind of criticism that resulted in the withdrawal of his bottled mustard-based barbecue sauces from grocery chains. JOHN T. EDGE

Bessinger, Maurice. *Defending My Heritage.* West Columbia, S.C.: LMBONE-LEHONE, 2001.

Hicks, Brian. "Politics Spice Barbecue Brothers' Conflicts." *Charleston Post and Courier,* January 14, 2001, pp. A1, A9.

Hitt, Jack. "A Confederacy of Sauces." *New York Times Magazine,* August 26, 2001, pp. 28–31.

Best Friend of Charleston. Commissioned by the South Carolina Canal and Rail Road Company, the *Best Friend of Charleston* was the first locomotive built in the United States for public service. Constructed in New York City at the West Point Foundry to run on the Charleston-Hamburg line, the *Best Friend* was christened by hopeful supporters on its Charleston arrival in October 1830. The locomotive had its formal debut on Christmas Day 1830, pulling passenger cars from Charleston to Dorchester. Its performance exceeded expectations, with one observer writing that passengers "flew on the wings of the wind at the speed of fifteen to twenty miles per hour, annihilating time and space."

In 1831 the *Best Friend* was used to carry mail, freight, and passengers. A second engine, the *West Point,* went into use on the Charleston-Hamburg line in March 1831 but never achieved the same speeds as those of the *Best Friend.* The South Carolina Canal and Rail Road Company used slaves to work on the line, both as laborers and as firemen to regulate the steam engine. At one point the company even considered the use of black engineers to serve under the management of white conductors, although the suggestion seems to have been dropped.

In June 1831 an accident brought an end to the *Best Friend.* A slave fireman closed up a safety valve on the boiler while the locomotive was stopped at a platform. When the *Best Friend* began to move again, a terrible explosion threw the boiler twenty feet into the air, killing the fireman, scalding the engineer, and injuring several workers. The engine was rebuilt and rechristened the *Phoenix.* W. SCOTT POOLE

Derrick, Samuel. *Centennial History of South Carolina Railroad.* 1930. Reprint, Spartanburg, S.C.: Reprint Company, 1975.

Siegling, H. Carter. "The Best Friend of Charleston." *South Carolina History Illustrated* 1 (February 1970): 19–23, 70–71.

Beth Elohim (Charleston). Holy Congregation House of God was founded in Charleston in 1749 as an Orthodox Sephardic congregation by Jewish settlers, mainly from England. The Reverend Moses Cohen was its religious leader, Joseph Tobias its first parnass (president), and Isaac DaCosta its hazan (reader). They worshiped in houses converted into synagogues until 1794, when they dedicated a handsome cupolaed synagogue on Hasell Street. At that time Beth Elohim, with about four hundred members, was the largest Jewish congregation in the United States.

Kahal Kadosh Beth Elohim Synagogue. Painting by Solomon Carvalho. Courtesy, American Jewish Archives, Hebrew Union College, Cincinnati, Ohio

In 1764 the congregation bought the DaCosta family burial ground on Coming Street as a congregational cemetery, now the oldest surviving Jewish cemetery in the South. Members of the congregation organized the Hebrew Benevolent Society (1784) and the Hebrew Orphan Society (1801), both still in existence.

In 1824 forty-eight members of Beth Elohim, led by Isaac Harby and Abraham Moise, whose requests for changes in worship services had been rejected by the *adjunta* (board of trustees), formed the Reform Society of Israelites. This was the first attempt to reform Judaism in the United States; it functioned for nine years.

In 1838 a citywide fire destroyed the 1794 synagogue. Beth Elohim then built and dedicated a Greek-revival-style building in 1841 as its new synagogue, now the second-oldest Jewish synagogue in the United States and the longest in continuous service. With the approval of the Reverend Gustavus Poznanski, the congregation decided to install an organ to provide music during services—a first in American Jewish history—and to reform ritual practices and observances, thus becoming the first Reform congregation in the United States.

This change caused the withdrawal of the Orthodox members, who formed a new congregation, Kahal Kadosh Shearit Israel (Holy Congregation Remnant of Israel). The two congregations shared the Hasell Street synagogue until a civil case found in favor of the reformers. Shearit Israel then built its own synagogue on Wentworth Street (no longer extant).

Impoverished by the Civil War, and with two damaged buildings, the two congregations amalgamated into Beth Elohim. They compromised their religious differences. But as the years passed, the congregation moved solidly into the ranks of Reform Judaism and became a charter member of the Union of American Hebrew Congregations in 1876.

Originally, the 1841 synagogue's interior was arranged according to Sephardic custom, with women occupying the balconies. In 1879 pew seating was introduced, allowing families to sit together in worship, and the balconies were removed after the earthquake of 1886. Women have been voting members of the congregation since 1920 and full participants in all congregational matters. The synagogue, now the oldest surviving Reform synagogue in the world, became a National Historic Landmark in 1980. SOLOMON BREIBART

Breibart, Solomon. "The Synagogues of Kahal Kadosh Beth Elohim." *South Carolina Historical Magazine* 80 (July 1979): 215–35.

Hagy, James William. *This Happy Land: The Jews of Colonial and Antebellum Charleston.* Tuscaloosa: University of Alabama Press, 1993.

Bethune, Mary McLeod (1875–1955). Educator, social activist, government official. The daughter and sister of former slaves, Bethune was born the fifteenth of seventeen siblings, near Mayesville on July 10, 1875. After emancipation, her father and mother, Samuel McLeod and Patsy McIntosh, worked on plantations for wages until they managed to buy land for cotton farming and build a small cabin for their family.

Bethune gained an educational opportunity rare for black children of the time when the Trinity Presbyterian Mission School opened in 1885 about five miles from her home. She attended for three years when she was not needed in the fields, absorbing learning in both industrial and academic subjects. She also learned domestic arts from her mother, whom Bethune later credited with holding the family together and with engineering their successful transition from slavery to self-sustenance.

With a scholarship from a teacher in Colorado, Bethune continued her education at Scotia Seminary for Negro Girls (later Barber-Scotia College) in Concord, North Carolina. As a student there, she

Mary McLeod Bethune, probably at Shanklin School, Beaufort County. Courtesy, South Caroliniana Library, University of South Carolina

particularly honed her public-speaking and singing skills. On graduation in 1894 she entered the Bible Institute for Home and Foreign Missions (later Moody Bible Institute) in Chicago with hopes of preparing for an overseas mission assignment. When she graduated a year later, however, she discovered that the Mission Board did not make overseas appointments to African Americans. Instead, she began the career as an American educator that would bring her national acclaim and provide her a platform for activism in racial equality.

As a teacher at the Haines Institute in Augusta, Georgia, Bethune found a role model and mentor in Lucy Craft Laney, the first African American female to found and manage a major secondary school. Bethune left Haines after one year to teach at Presbyterian-sponsored Kendall Institute in Sumter, where she met Albertus Bethune, a native of nearby Wedgefield, whom she married in May 1898. The couple moved to Savannah, Georgia, where Albertus had found work and where their only child, Albert, was born. By 1899 they moved to Palatka, Florida, where Bethune was urged by the Presbyterian Church to establish a mission school. In 1904, in the resort community of Daytona, she opened the Daytona Normal and Industrial School for Negro Girls.

An expert fund-raiser and eloquent speaker among the wealthy northerners who visited Daytona Beach, Bethune developed her small school into a major institution. By 1910 more than one hundred students attended the all-grades school to study academic, industrial, and religious subjects. In 1911 Bethune founded the McLeod Hospital to provide the first local medical opportunity for African Americans and to train African American health-care professionals. Her school also ran a large farm and various social service outreach missions. The Methodist Episcopal Church affiliated with the growing school in 1923 and merged it with the Cookman Institute, a coeducational Methodist school in Jacksonville. Bethune soon added a junior college; and in 1929 the institution became Bethune-Cookman College, with Bethune serving as its president until 1942.

Bethune's widespread influence on behalf of African Americans began with her presidency of the Florida Federation of Colored Women's Clubs (1917–1924). She later served as president of the Southeastern Association of Colored Women, president of the Florida State Teachers Association, president of the National Association of Colored Women, founder and president of the National Council of Negro Women, member of President Herbert Hoover's Commission on Home Building and Home Ownership, vice president of the National Urban League, and vice president of the National Association for the Advancement of Colored People. With these local and national platforms, her influence ranged from establishing community welfare projects for African Americans to convincing U.S. Army officials to include black women at all levels in the Women's Army Auxiliary Corps (WAAC).

Bethune gained her greatest national renown when President Franklin Roosevelt tapped her as an adviser on New Deal programs and spokesperson to and for African Americans concerning his administration's reform policies. In 1936 he appointed her director of the Office of Negro Affairs in the National Youth Administration, a post she held for eight years and from which she was able to assure that thousands of black youths received a fair share of government-supported college funding, job training, and employment opportunities.

As an educator and civil rights activist, Bethune was recognized with numerous national awards and honorary academic degrees. Among the first of these was an honorary master of science degree from South Carolina State University. She also received an honorary LL.D. from Howard University and honorary doctorate degrees in humanities from Bennett College, West Virginia State College, and Rollins College. Bethune spent most of the last five years of her life in retirement at her home on the Bethune-Cookman College campus. She died of a heart attack on May 18, 1955, and was buried at Bethune-Cookman. KATHERINE REYNOLDS CHADDOCK

Fleming, Sheila Y. *Bethune-Cookman College, 1904–1994: The Answered Prayer to a Dream.* Virginia Beach, Va.: Donning, 1995.

Holt, Rackham. *Mary McLeod Bethune: A Biography.* Garden City, N.Y.: Doubleday, 1964.

McCluskey, Audrey, and Elaine M. Smith, eds. *Mary McLeod Bethune: Building a Better World; Essays and Selected Documents.* Bloomington: Indiana University Press, 1999.

Bettis Academy. Established in Trenton (Edgefield County) in 1881 by the Reverend Alexander Bettis, this school provided former slaves and their children with a basic education of reading and writing as well as skills and trades. A former slave who could neither write nor read, Bettis organized the Mt. Canaan Missionary and Educational Union to raise the $300 used in purchasing the land for the boarding school. While there was an emphasis on teacher education, the school's primary focus was on industrial training. At a time when the state neglected the education of its black citizens, Bettis Academy offered educational opportunities when few professions were open to blacks. Consisting of fourteen buildings, the school was accredited by the state as a junior college in 1933. This course of study allowed graduates to teach in South Carolina's elementary schools or enter four-year colleges as juniors. Beginning in 1940 the school was overseen by interested northerners, such as Clement Biddle and Alice Angell, who obtained a grant from the General Education Board, a philanthropic organization established by John D. Rockefeller in 1903. Funds were used to construct a seven-room home-economics building and to purchase farm equipment and vehicles. Bettis closed in 1952 when South Carolina began improving statewide public education for blacks. In 1998 Bettis Academy and Junior College was listed in the National Register of Historic Places. LOUISE ALLEN

Bettis Academy. Records, 1939–1948. South Caroliniana Library, University of South Carolina, Columbia.

Nicholson, Alfred W. *Brief Sketch of the Life and Labors of Rev. Alexander Bettis; Also an Account of the Founding and Development of the Bettis Academy.* Trenton, S.C.: by the author, 1913.

Big Apple. This dance was born in the mid-1930s in a black nightclub operated by a man named Fat Sam on Park Street in downtown Columbia, in what was once the House of Peace Synagogue. The Big Apple was popularized nationally when it was taken to Manhattan by University of South Carolina students. A combination of the square dance and various jazz routines of the 1920s, the Big Apple caught the attention of white college students who, encouraged by Fat Sam, paid 10¢ to watch dancers from the nightclub balcony. Soon they were repeating the steps at fraternity parties. By the spring of 1937 the Big Apple was attracting more than local attention. In August of that year several student couples performed the dance at New York's Roxy Theatre and then toured cities throughout the Northeast. The Big Apple received such an enthusiastic reception that it became a brief national craze.

According to a 1937 report in *Time,* the routine opened with the dancers in a circle led by a caller, somewhat like the Virginia Reel. The fundamental steps seemed to be the Lindy Hop with bits of the

A couple dancing the "Big Apple" in the Columbia nightclub that gave the dance craze its name. Courtesy, Historic Columbia Foundation

Black Bottom, Suzy-Q, Charleston, Shag, Truckin', and an Indian rain dance thrown in. It all ended on an irreverent note as the group leaned back, arms outstretched to the heavens, and shouted "Praise Allah!"

After about a year the Big Apple dance faded from view and so did the nightclub. The building was moved to its present location adjacent to the Richland County Library and restored to its former elegance in the late 1980s. It is operated by the Historic Columbia Foundation and is rented for various social events. JOHN H. MOORE

"Big Apple." *Time* 30 (September 13, 1937): 37–38.

"Big Apple Is New Dance Craze Sweeping the South." *Life* 3 (August 9, 1937): 22.

Maxey, Russell. "The Big Apple." Columbia *State Magazine,* May 30, 1982, pp. 5–6.

Big Thursday. For more than six decades, the story of the lively football competition between the Gamecocks of South Carolina College (now the University of South Carolina, or USC) and the Tigers of Clemson College (now Clemson University) was the story of "Big Thursday," the culmination of State Fair week. The rivalry started on Thursday, November 12, 1896, at the fairgrounds in Columbia before about 2,000 fans. The contest gained popularity in its early years, but the two schools did not compete for seven years following a riot after the 1902 game. Over the next decade, the Thursday matchup became known as the State Fair Classic. By the 1910s it had become a "combination picnic, fashion parade, political rally and drinking bout" for approximately 4,500 spectators.

Through the 1910s and 1920s the annual competition became bigger and bigger. Enlargements to the small wooden bowl stadium on the fairgrounds did little to relieve overcrowded conditions that led to many scuffles among the approximately 14,000 fans. In 1934 USC completed a new steel-and-concrete stadium on land adjoining the fairgrounds, with seating for more than 17,000 fans. Big Thursday's popularity exploded after World War II. In 1946, after a counterfeit ticket scandal, fans broke down the general admission gate and flooded the field throughout the game. Attendance continued to keep pace as stadium capacity increased to 34,000 by 1949 and to 44,000 by 1957.

Each school developed Big Thursday traditions, including burning the Tiger at USC the night before the game and the burial of the Gamecock at Clemson on the Tuesday before students traveled to Columbia. Schools, businesses, and government offices closed for the state's most colorful sports contest and "the biggest social event of the year." By the late 1950s, however, Clemson was pushing for an end-of-season game played on an alternating home schedule, in part so that Clemson could share the tourist money that surrounded the game. Both schools agreed that 1959 would be the last Big Thursday game, which Clemson won, 27–0. Big Thursday ended with Clemson holding a 33–21–3 advantage. SUSAN GIAIMO HIOTT

Barton, Donald F. *Big Thursday, 1896–1959: Historical Souvenir Program.* Columbia: University of South Carolina, 1959.

Gault, Harper. *Big Thursday in South Carolina: The Story of the Carolina-Clemson Game, 1896–1947.* N.p., 1947.

Griffin, John Chandler. *Carolina vs. Clemson, Clemson vs. Carolina: A Century of Unparalleled Rivalry in College Football.* Columbia, S.C.: Summerhouse, 1998.

Billings, John Shaw (1898–1975). Journalist. Billings was born on May 11, 1898, at Redcliffe Plantation in Beech Island, the eldest son of John Sedgewick Billings and Katherine Hammond. He was the great-grandson of James Henry Hammond, the eminent South Carolina politician of the antebellum era. Although a South Carolina native, Billings resided much of his life in New York City. During his childhood, however, the family made many extended visits to Redcliffe. After graduating in May 1916 from St. Paul's School in Concord, New Hampshire, Billings enrolled at Harvard University.

In January 1917 Billings left college to fight in World War I. Initially he drove both trucks and ambulances for the French military. Following America's entry into the fighting in April 1917, Billings transferred to the U.S. Army Air Corps. At his discharge in January 1919 he held the rank of second lieutenant. On returning to the United States, Billings went back to Harvard.

Although a good student, Billings grew bored with his academic routine. In January 1920 he became involved with a gubernatorial campaign in Connecticut. That autumn he decided not to return to college, dropping out one term short of graduation. In 1921 he became a political reporter for the Brooklyn *Daily Eagle.* Ten months later he was assigned to that newspaper's Washington bureau. In September 1922, during a visit to Redcliffe, Billings met Frederica W. Wade, a Beech Island neighbor. They were married on April 19, 1924, at Beech Island Presbyterian Church.

In 1928 Billings succeeded Henry Cabot Lodge II as the Washington, D.C., correspondent for *Time,* a weekly newsmagazine. Billings relocated to New York City in January 1929 when he became national affairs editor of *Time.* During the next quarter-century he rose steadily within the Time Inc. editorial hierarchy. In November 1933 he was promoted to managing editor of *Time.* Three years later he assumed the managing editorship of *Life,* a new weekly pictorial magazine. The eight years in that position were considered the most noteworthy of his journalistic career. When he retired in May 1954, Billings was the editorial director of all Time Inc. publications. Only Henry R. Luce, the editor in chief, possessed more editorial authority.

In March 1935 Billings's aunt Julia Hammond Richards had died, leaving Redcliffe Plantation without an occupant. Being the most affluent Hammond descendant, Billings agreed to purchase the plantation. During the next several decades he spent a considerable personal fortune renovating the entire property, especially the mansion. On retiring, Billings returned permanently to Redcliffe, spending his last years there.

Following a long illness, Frederica Wade Billings died in 1963. Billings subsequently married, on September 10, 1963, Elise Lake

Chase of Augusta, Georgia. His only child, Frederica Wade Billings, Jr., had died in childhood. In 1973 he bequeathed Redcliffe Plantation to the state of South Carolina. The property was to become a state park after Billings's passing. Throughout much of his life Billings had maintained an extensive daily diary. Increasing frail heath finally forced him to curtail that activity in June 1974. Fourteen months later, on August 25, 1975, Billings died in Augusta, survived by his second wife. He was interred in the Hammond family cemetery at Redcliffe. MILES S. RICHARDS

Billings, John Shaw. Papers. South Caroliniana Library, University of South Carolina, Columbia.

Bleser, Carol, ed. *The Hammonds of Redcliffe.* New York: Oxford University Press, 1981.

Morris, Sylvia Jukes. *Rage for Fame: The Ascent of Clare Boothe Luce.* New York: Random House, 1997.

Swanberg, W. A. *Luce and His Empire.* New York: Scribner's, 1972.

Williams, William Bates. "John Shaw Billings: The Man behind the Editor." Master's thesis, University of South Carolina, 1978.

Bishopville (Lee County; 2000 pop. 3,670). Bishopville, the Lee County seat, traces its origins to prehistoric days, when two Indian trails crossed near the future center of the town. European settlement began in the late eighteenth century when William Singleton purchased a 465-acre tract from a Daniel Carter in 1790. Singleton and his wife, Frances, operated a tavern at the intersection of the two roads, which travelers dubbed Singleton's Cross Roads. William died in 1798, and Frances operated the log cabin tavern until her death in 1820. The following year the Singleton family sold the property to Dr. Jacques Bishop, who operated a general store from 1821 to 1837 under the name of C. C. Campbell and Co. During this time Singleton's Cross Roads was rechristened as Bishopville. The first population count appeared during the vote for nullification (1830), which recorded 106 votes for and 11 votes against. By 1850 the village contained twelve stores. A sawmill appeared in 1880 and inspired construction of the Bishopville and Sumter Railroad. The Seaboard Air Line extended its main line from McBee to Bishopville in 1887, and the town was incorporated the following year.

Education in Bishopville began in 1803 when John Fraser built the first public school in the village. The Bishopville Academy was chartered in 1839 and operated for the next ten years. Despite these promising educational foundations, Bishopville did not establish its first permanent library until 1943.

The first Bishopville newspaper, the *Bishopville Leader,* appeared in the spring of 1902 and was followed the same year by the *Lee County Vindicator.* Within six months the two newspapers merged to form the *Leader and Vindicator.* In 1920 W. J. Strickland bought the newspaper and renamed it the *Lee County Messenger.* The *Lee County Observer* evolved from the *Messenger* in 1982.

Aside from its role as the seat of Lee County government, Bishopville has also served as a business and cultural center throughout its existence. Two blocks of Main Street are listed on the National Register of Historic Places. The Opera House (ca. 1900), which originally served as the county courthouse, was later restored for use as a community cultural events center. In 1994 Bishopville opened the South Carolina Cotton Museum, a center to preserve and present the cotton heritage of the town and Lee County. JANSON L. COX

Gregorie, Anne King. *History of Sumter County, South Carolina.* Sumter, S.C.: Library Board of Sumter County, 1954.

Lee County Bicentennial Commission. *Lee County, South Carolina: A Bicentennial Look at Its Land, People, Heritage & Future.* N.p.: Reeves, 1976.

Lee County Chamber of Commerce. *Lee County, South Carolina: Past and Present.* Dallas, Tex.: Taylor Publishing, 1992.

Black business districts. While African Americans owned businesses in South Carolina since the colonial period, during that time these establishments usually consisted of blacksmith shops, harness shops, and other service industries. These early businesses were owned by free blacks, but they served and operated within both the black communities and the white communities of their respective areas.

Black business districts appeared in South Carolina and other southern states after the public segregation of the races became legal in the 1890s. New laws forced many businesses either to provide separate facilities for black customers or to deny service to African American patrons altogether. Black entrepreneurs stepped in to establish operations in which African Americans could be served with courtesy and dignity. Residential segregation in many cities restricted most of these businesses to African American sections of these towns and cities. This led to the beginning of black business districts.

In the predominantly rural areas of South Carolina, black business districts usually consisted of a few small concerns such as funeral homes, hair-care establishments, tailors, and clothing stores, as well as churches and schools. Cities with sizable black populations contained full-fledged black business districts with a variety of establishments. Such districts were usually centered around a major street where African Americans lived or congregated. Along the vicinity of Spartanburg's "Baptist and Methodist Sides" (named after the respective concentrations of churches in this city's black neighborhoods), some businesses owned and patronized by African Americans included the Hotel Hudson, the John and Nina Littlejohn Hospital, the Eli Chapman Real Estate Company, and Charles Bomar's Grocery Store. Columbia's "Black Downtown" (surrounding Washington Street) included the Victory Savings Bank, Nathaniel Frederick's Law Office, the Blue Ribbon Taxi Company, and the Mutual Grocery Store. Near King and Spring Streets in Charleston, establishments owned and operated by blacks included the Lincoln Theater, the John Dart Library, the Hotel James, and the C. O. Credit Union. By the 1930s Greenville's black business district east of South Main Street also contained members of a small black professional class, which included doctors, dentists, tailors, librarians, funeral directors, and a veterinarian.

After the civil rights movement ended legal segregation in South Carolina's public places, many black businesses declined or disappeared. Many African Americans began to patronize white-owned establishments to which they had previously been denied access. Gentrification and urban-renewal projects also demolished many of the traditionally black business districts. In spite of these developments, African American businesses continued to survive and thrive at the end of the twentieth century. DAMON FORDHAM

Deas-Moore, Vennie. *Columbia, South Carolina.* Charleston, S.C.: Arcadia, 2000.

Huff, Archie Vernon, Jr. *Greenville: The History of the City and County in the South Carolina Piedmont.* Columbia: University of South Carolina Press, 1995.

Meffert, John, Sherman Pyatt, and the Avery Research Center. *Charleston, South Carolina.* Charleston, S.C.: Arcadia, 2000.

Moore, John Hammond. *Columbia and Richland County: A South Carolina Community, 1740–1990.* Columbia: University of South Carolina Press, 1993.

Pruitt, Dwain C. *Things Hidden: An Introduction to the History of Blacks in Spartanburg.* Spartanburg, S.C.: Community Relations Office, 1995.

Black Codes (1865–1866). Among the most significant—and obvious—consequences of the Civil War were the emancipation of slaves and the abolition of slavery. Although the Freedmen's Bureau and the Union army had established some rudimentary labor guidelines for former slaves, the status of former slaves and their civil and economic rights were left largely undetermined at the war's end. In 1865, with little direction forthcoming from Washington and with the South in economic and social chaos, the states of the former Confederacy drew up "Black Codes" to clarify the standing of African Americans.

In South Carolina the provisional governor Benjamin F. Perry realized that the greatest problem facing the state was economic distress, since abolition had destroyed the traditional slave-labor-based agricultural system. Perry commissioned Armistead Burt and David Wardlaw to draw up state regulations designed to define the status of former slaves and stabilize the labor problem. The two lawyers, assisted by Edmund Rhett, presented the state's Black Codes to the legislature in October 1865, and they were adopted in December.

The three main laws—with their extensive articles—that comprised South Carolina's Black Codes addressed three general areas: new rights following abolition, new restrictions following abolition, and more specific decrees directed toward the labor issue. The first law recognized the abolition of slavery and defined "black," since the distinction between whites and African Americans needed to be clearly and carefully drawn. African Americans were now allowed to own property (unless restricted under a different article), enter into contracts, sue in court, and attend school. The code also legalized African American marriages, accepted as de facto in the Old South but technically extralegal.

The second law set forth restrictions that actually curtailed rights enjoyed by free blacks before the Civil War. Included were prohibitions on the sale of goods without an employer's or magistrate's consent, prohibitions on the possession of firearms (a small fowling piece was allowed), and details of the developing legal situation. African Americans could not appear as witnesses in criminal cases, could not serve on juries, and could only swear out *complaints* against white persons before white magistrates. Whites, however, had the authority to *arrest* a "person of color" suspected of a misdemeanor.

The third section of the Black Codes concentrated on the labor question. It imposed a "sunrise to sunset" workday for those in agriculture, along with a strict set of regulations regarding movement, breaks, dining periods, and even conversation. The law not only assumed agriculture as the livelihood of most African Americans but also coerced it; African Americans could choose to be only field hands or hired servants, and any other occupation required a license from a judge. As with other southern states, South Carolina also imposed harsh penalties for vagrants, those who had no permanent abode or no formal employment contract. These persons could be imprisoned, forced to perform public labor, or auctioned to needy employers. With white judges, expensive licenses, and criminal vagrancy, the Black Codes assured a stable and sizable supply of experienced black farm laborers.

As with other southern states, South Carolina misread the political climate and underestimated the North's dedication to transforming the South. Whether viewed as practical solutions or racist abuses, the Black Codes were certainly political mistakes. For many southern whites, the Black Codes represented a reasonable compromise between slavery and free labor. Considering the drastic changes and shocks that southern society had already suffered, some thought it best to move ahead slowly. But Republicans in the North saw it differently. A few "radicals" noted that missing from the Black Codes was any discussion of political rights. More generally, Republicans in and out of government were offended by what the codes did include, which amounted to an attempt to re-create, within the confines of an altered national Constitution, as much of the antebellum South as possible.

After four years of war, Republicans in Congress were not ready to accept a social, economic, and political return to the antebellum years. With the convening of Congress in December 1865, Republicans set out first to overturn the Black Codes; then to sweep away President Andrew Johnson, the South's last defender; and finally to establish a new social, economic, and political order in the South. The Civil Rights Act of 1866, the Military Reconstruction Acts of 1867, and the Fourteenth Amendment all nullified the Black Codes and created a foundation for a New South. Ironically, large parts of these devices would prove as fleeting as the Black Codes, and within a generation northern indifference and racism would allow southern white conservatism once again to redefine the place of African Americans in America. RICHARD ZUCZEK

Carter, Dan T. *When the War Was Over: The Failure of Self-Reconstruction in the South, 1865–1867.* Baton Rouge: Louisiana State University Press, 1985.

Wilson, Theodore Brantner. *The Black Codes of the South.* University: University of Alabama Press, 1965.

Zuczek, Richard. *State of Rebellion: Reconstruction in South Carolina.* Columbia: University of South Carolina Press, 1996.

Black River. The Black River takes its name from its tea-colored waters. The river begins in the Sandhills of Lee County and is joined by Rocky Bluff Swamp near Sumter. The Pocotaligo River flows into the Black between Manning and Kingstree. After traveling over 150 miles in Sumter, Clarendon, Williamsburg, and Georgetown Counties, the Black River becomes part of the Great Pee Dee River near Georgetown.

In Georgetown County, where the river becomes tidal, planters developed rice plantations along its banks, such as Kensington and Weehaw, which lasted from the middle of the eighteenth century to

The Black River. Photograph by Robert Clark. Courtesy, South Carolina Department of Natural Resources

the early twentieth century. Some of these plantations, such as Richmond, also produced indigo before the Revolutionary War. Owners of Black River plantations included elite families of rice planters such as Allston, Kinloch, Middleton, and Cheves.

In some places the Black River is swamplike, while in others it is swift moving with a sandy bottom. With the exception of the town of Kingstree and the final stretch in Georgetown County, the banks of the Black River remain forested and largely undisturbed by development. Since the collapse of the rice culture, South Carolinians have mostly used the Black River basin as a resource for timbering, hunting, and fishing.

In 2001 seventy-five miles of the Black River in Clarendon, Williamsburg, and Georgetown Counties became a State Scenic River. Since then, efforts have been under way to protect the river from development and preserve its natural beauty and value as a wildlife habitat. JAMES H. TUTEN

Linder, Suzanne Cameron, and Marta Leslie Thacker. *Historical Atlas of the Rice Plantations of Georgetown County and the Santee River.* Columbia: South Carolina Department of Archives and History for the Historic Ricefields Association, 2001.

"Black" Seventh District. After the census of 1880, South Carolina won an additional two seats in the U.S. House of Representatives, increasing from five to seven. The need for redistricting was seized upon by the state's Democratic leaders as an opportunity to insure that enfranchised African Americans and the Republican Party were neutralized.

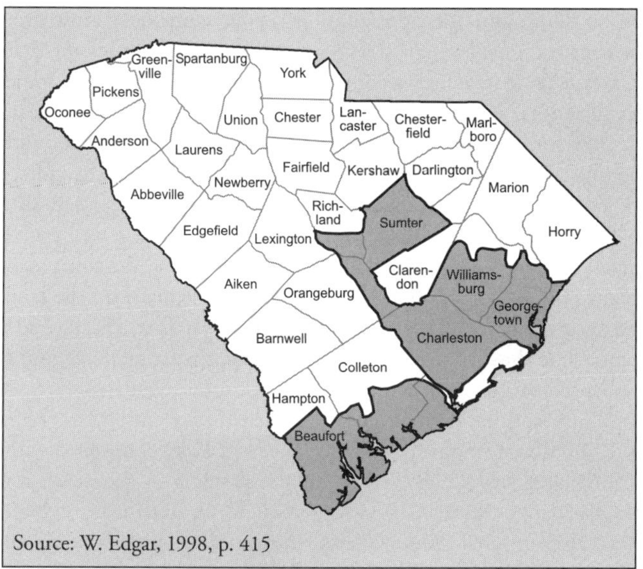

South Carolina's Seventh Congressional District, 1882

Governor Johnson Hagood called a special session for redistricting to begin on June 27, 1882. Reapportionment proceeded on the basis of the "Dibble Plan," named for its author, U.S. Congressman Samuel Dibble of Orangeburg. Dibble's intent was to pack as many African American voters as possible into one district so that Democrats could more easily win the other six. The plan created seven districts, one of which snaked across the state and included portions of nine different counties. The new Seventh District stretched from the Savannah River to Winyah Bay on the coast (excluding the city of Charleston) and from the Atlantic to the Sandhills nearly one hundred miles inland. Although the bill was protested by Republicans, it passed the General Assembly after little debate, and the special session adjourned on July 5.

African American voters possessed a numerical majority in five of the seven new districts, but this majority was overwhelming in the Seventh: of the 38,000 voters, 31,000 were African American. The segregation of black voters into the "Black" Seventh, as it came to be known, had the desired effect. The Democrats did not even field a candidate in that district in 1882, and a white Republican, Edmund Mackey, won the election. In 1886, however, Democrats began to contest the seat. The former slave and Republican George Washington Murray won in 1896 but lost in the following election. He was the last African American to represent South Carolina in Congress for nearly a century. AARON W. MARRS

Blackbeard (?–1718). Pirate. Most commonly known today as Edward Teach, in the Carolinas in the early eighteenth century Blackbeard was called Edward Thatch. Since confusion about his real name has confounded researchers into his background, his birthplace and parentage remain unknown. Contemporaries connected him with Jamaica, London, and Bristol, England. Although he was reputed to have had numerous wives, only two are mentioned in the documents—unnamed women in London and Bath, North Carolina.

Surfacing in Jamaica in mid-1717, Blackbeard in eighteen months carved an extraordinarily successful career as a pirate, creating an indelible image of "the fiercest pirate of them all" and making him a global icon. A tall and domineering figure possessing a volatile and charismatic personality, Blackbeard cultivated a reputation as "a Devil incarnate" that was enhanced by his boarding ships while brandishing numerous weapons and while wreathed in smoke from burning tapers in his beard and hair. Like most pirates of his era, he began as a privateer during Queen Anne's War (1701–1713) under the command of Benjamin Hornigold, who at war's end became a pirate chieftain on New Providence Island, Bahamas.

Blackbeard's first piratical voyage was with Hornigold in summer 1717 to the North American coast from the Carolinas to Delaware Bay. In the fall Blackbeard commanded Stede Bonnet's sloop *Revenge* in another rampage on the same coast, taking eleven prizes. Cruising in the Leeward Islands in November, Blackbeard seized the French slave ship *Concorde,* heavily armed it, and named it *Queen Anne's Revenge.* With *Revenge* and *Queen Anne's Revenge,* Blackbeard swept across the Caribbean.

The pirate captains separated over the winter but reunited by chance in March 1718 off the Central American Spanish Main. Blackbeard now sailed north to the Carolinas with a four-ship flotilla, mounting at least sixty guns, the most powerful maritime force in the hemisphere. Arriving off Charleston, South Carolina, in mid-May, he blockaded the port for a week, seizing prizes and hostages for ransom. This infamous feat "struck a great Terror to the whole Province of Carolina." Plundering eight or nine ships for supplies and specie, Blackbeard held hostages, including Samuel Wragg, a councilman. Under the threat of the hostages being murdered, a reluctant Governor Robert Johnson agreed to a ransom of a valuable chest of medicine.

From Charleston, Blackbeard sailed to isolated North Carolina, where at Beaufort Inlet in June two of his vessels—*Queen Anne's Revenge* and *Adventure*—wrecked. He took the royal pardon from Governor Charles Eden, married in Bath, and scaled down his illegal activities. Blackbeard established a camp at Ocracoke Inlet, the chief entrance to the colony, and appeared virtually to have retired from piracy. Uneasy at having a notorious pirate nearby, however, Virginia governor Alexander Spottswood invaded North Carolina with a naval and land force. Blackbeard was cornered at Ocracoke on November 22, 1718, by Lieutenant Robert Maynard's flotilla and killed. His surviving men were tried, and the condemned pirates were executed in Williamsburg, Virginia. LINDLEY S. BUTLER

Butler, Lindley S. *Pirates, Privateers, and Rebel Raiders of the Carolina Coast.* Chapel Hill: University of North Carolina Press, 2000.

Lee, Robert E. *Blackbeard the Pirate: A Reappraisal of His Life and Times.* Winston-Salem, N.C.: John F. Blair, 1974.

Rankin, Hugh F. *The Golden Age of Piracy.* Williamsburg, Va.: Colonial Williamsburg, 1969.

Blackville (Barnwell County; 2000 pop. 2,973). Incorporated in 1837, Blackville originated as a depository on the South Carolina Railroad in Barnwell District. It was named for Alexander Black, a railroad superintendent, but was briefly renamed Clinton in honor of Revolutionary War hero General James Clinton. However, in 1851 the town name reverted to Blackville after sectional pride led residents to conclude that it was more fitting to honor a southern railroad entrepreneur than a northern general.

Prior to the Civil War, Blackville prospered as a cotton reception point, which stimulated the development of a bustling mercantile community. Although much of Blackville was destroyed by Union forces in February 1865, the town recovered quickly. In the years immediately following the war, Blackville briefly served as the county seat before that returned to the town of Barnwell in the mid-1870s. By the 1880s Blackville contained thirty-three stores, four churches, four schools, several saw and grist mills, and a population of almost one thousand. The town continued to thrive as a cotton market, shipping some four thousand bales of cotton annually.

Devastating fires struck Blackville in 1876 and 1887, but the town survived to maintain its role as a commercial and transportation center for Barnwell County farmers. Truck farming grew during the first half of the twentieth century, and large quantities of cucumbers, watermelons, and asparagus were sent from the town each year. Blackville residents further benefited from the establishment of the Commercial Bank of Blackville in 1917 and the installation of the town's first water system in 1933. By 1940 the population stood at 1,456.

Although agriculture declined in importance throughout the region in the decades following World War II, Blackville experienced population growth over the same period, particularly in its African American community. Between 1950 and 1980 the town's population more than doubled, from 1,295 to 2,840, with African Americans making up over two-thirds of the total. The location of the massive Savannah River Site plant in Barnwell County in the 1950s inspired some of the increase, but most came about from new manufacturing plants. By the 1960s factories operated by the Blackville Manufacturing Company (a maker of ladies' apparel) and the Ducane Heating Corporation employed hundreds of Blackville inhabitants and attracted new residents. Only seven percent of the workforce remained in agriculture by 1980.

The final decades of the twentieth century found Blackville struggling to maintain its position of economic importance within Barnwell County. In 1979 more than one-fifth of Blackville families lived below the poverty line, and the removal of the town's railroad line in the late 1980s further added to difficulties. Like other areas of South Carolina, Blackville turned to recreation and tourism to revitalize the economy. In the 1990s residents cooperated with state agencies in attempts to restore and preserve the town's historic downtown. Blackville was also designated as the site of a regional heritage center on the South Carolina National Heritage Corridor. TOM DOWNEY

Barnwell County Heritage Book Committee. *Barnwell County Heritage, South Carolina.* Marceline, Mo.: Walsworth, 1994.

Crass, David Colin, and Mark J. Brooks, eds. *Cotton and Black Draught: Consumer Behavior on a Postbellum Farm.* [Columbia]: Savannah River Archaeological Research Program and the South Carolina Institute of Archaeology and Anthropology, 1995.

Downey, Tom. *Planting a Capitalist South: Masters, Merchants, and Manufacturers in the Southern Interior, 1790–1860.* Baton Rouge: Louisiana State University Press, 2005.

Maddox, Annette Milliken. *The Long Shadow of the Big Brick: A History of the First Baptist Church, Blackville, South Carolina, 1846–1996.* Blackville, S.C.: First Baptist Church, 1996.

Blackwood, Ibra Charles (1878–1936). Governor. Born in Blackwood, Spartanburg County, on November 21, 1878, Ibra Blackwood was the son of Charles Blackwood and Louvina Burns. After graduating from Wofford College in 1898, Blackwood read law and was admitted to the bar in 1902. That same year he was elected to the General Assembly, where he represented Spartanburg County for a single term in the House. In 1913 Blackwood became director of the South Carolina tax agency. Three years later he was elected solicitor of the Seventh Judicial Circuit. Blackwood made an unsuccessful bid for governor in 1926, losing to John G. Richards. He won four years later by narrowly defeating Olin D. Johnston in the Democratic primary.

In his 1931 inaugural address, Blackwood called for judicial reform. During the previous administration, controversy arose over the constitutionality of a massive $65 million highway measure that increased the state debt without a popular vote. Furthermore, some circuit judges had augmented their "expense money" in violation of the state constitution. Blackwood endorsed a strict interpretation of the constitution and a reduction of political pressures on the judiciary, but more important issues demanded the governor's attention.

Blackwood entered office with the Great Depression well under way in South Carolina. The boll weevil, drought, and the collapse of tenant farming forced thousands of South Carolinians off the land and into towns or out of the state entirely. At first, Blackwood's approach to the dire economic situation was conventional. He urged a balanced budget, which the state constitution mandated even in times of hardship. He reduced the salaries of state employees, who, by 1933, were being paid in scrip. In 1932 Blackwood joined with U.S. Senator James F. Byrnes to endorse Franklin D. Roosevelt for the presidency. Roosevelt's victory brought an avalanche of New Deal assistance to South Carolina, including the Agricultural Adjustment Administration and the Civilian Conservation Corps, which brought relief to thousands of South Carolinians in the form of public works projects. One of the most lasting of these New Deal initiatives was the enormous Santee Cooper electrification project, which was secured through the extensive lobbying efforts of Governor Blackwood and Senator Byrnes.

Perhaps the greatest crisis of Blackwood's administration occurred during the General Textile Strike of September 1934, when half of the state's textile workforce went on strike to protest wage cuts and poor working conditions. When union picket lines went up around the state, Blackwood called out the National Guard and empowered "constables without compensation" to patrol mill villages. Blackwood justified his promanagement stance by claiming that South Carolina was "suffering a ruthless and insolent invasion" by groups engaged in "illegal and destructive enterprises." On

September 6 several of these "constables" fired on striking workers at Honea Path, killing seven and wounding fourteen. It was the worst violence of the strike. Blackwood left office the following year and resumed his law practice in Spartanburg, where he died of a heart attack on February 12, 1936. JOSEPH EDWARD LEE

Hayes, Jack Irby. *South Carolina and the New Deal.* Columbia: University of South Carolina Press, 2001.

Simon, Bryant. *A Fabric of Defeat: The Politics of South Carolina Millhands, 1910–1948.* Chapel Hill: University of North Carolina Press, 1998.

Blair, Frank (1915–1995). Broadcaster, author. Born in Yemassee on May 30, 1915, Blair was the son of the telegrapher Frank S. Blair and Hannah Pinckney. He attended the College of Charleston in 1933. On October 20, 1935, he married Lillian Stoddard. They had eight children. During World War II he served in the U.S. Navy as a flight instructor and transport pilot, attaining the rank of lieutenant.

A deep-voiced newscaster, a mainstay of NBC's "The Today Show" from 1952 to 1975, Blair got his start in broadcasting in October 1935, when he convinced officials at WCSC-Radio in Charleston to let him start a news show. From this $15-a-week job he moved on to Columbia and Greenville stations, then to WOL in Washington, D.C., where he served from 1939 to 1942. After World War II he briefly managed station WSCR-Radio in Scranton, Pennsylvania.

Blair joined NBC-TV in 1950 and moderated "The American Forum of the Air," a debate program. He was named Washington, D.C., correspondent for "The Today Show," which was launched on January 14, 1952, as an experimental morning news program. The innovative enterprise eventually won acclaim with Dave Garroway and Jack Lescoulie as hosts and Blair as newscaster. Blair worked with twenty-five hosts during his twenty-three years on the show. In his autobiography, *Let's Be Frank about It,* Blair described the pressures of the job and his bouts with alcohol. He resigned from the show on March 14, 1975, and retired to Hilton Head Island, South Carolina, but continued recording commercials and syndicated radio programs.

Blair was honored by Georgetown University, where he was a broadcast instructor; Xavier University; the University of Missouri; and the Boy Scouts of America. He received honorary degrees from Nasson College, Le Moyne College, Niagara University, and the Citadel. He died at Hilton Head Island on March 14, 1995. ROBERT A. PIERCE

Blair, Frank. *Let's Be Frank about It.* Garden City, N.J.: Doubleday, 1979.

Blake, Joseph (1663–1700). Governor. Blake was a leader of the Dissenter political faction in South Carolina and a supporter of the Lords Proprietors in their disputes with local political leaders. He was born in England, the son of Benjamin Blake and Elizabeth Wilson. His baptism was recorded at Bridgewater, Somersetshire, on April 26, 1663. Somersetshire was a Dissenter stronghold during the late seventeenth century and the home of the prominent Dissenter families of Morton, Blake, and Axtell. Branches of these families immigrated to Carolina in the 1680s. The date Blake immigrated to Carolina is uncertain, but by 1689 he was active in local politics. Blake's first wife was Deborah Morton, daughter of Governor Joseph Morton, but the date of their marriage is unknown. The couple had no children. Following Deborah's death, Blake in December 1698 wed Elizabeth Axtell Turgis, daughter of Landgrave Daniel Axtell. The couple had two children.

Sometime after his arrival in Carolina, Blake was named a proprietary deputy and member of the Grand Council. When Seth Sothell seized control of the governorship in 1690, he banished Governor Sir James Colleton and ousted Blake from the council. Blake returned to the Grand Council during Philip Ludwell's brief term as governor and remained a member until November 1694, when he succeeded Landgrave Thomas Smith as governor. In that year Blake purchased the proprietary share of Sir John Berkeley and became one of the second generation of Lords Proprietors. Blake's appointment was ratified by the other proprietors, but within a short time a new governor was on the scene. John Archdale, a Quaker by faith and another proprietor, arrived at Charleston and assumed the post in August 1695. In England the proprietors had appointed Archdale in the hope that one of their number governing on the scene would diminish the political rancor that gripped the province. Archdale's brief term was deemed a success. He returned to England in October 1696 and appointed Blake deputy governor, which office he held until his death in 1700.

Factional politics returned with considerable vigor during Blake's administration. Anglican "Goose Creek Men," named for their place of residence, grew increasingly vocal in their opposition to the proprietors in England and their governor in Charleston. Political fighting over the Indian trade and the role of French Huguenots in Carolina society were among the divisive issues. Blake supported Huguenot naturalization and enacted an important statute in March 1697 that expanded the rights of non-English settlers. However, his term was marked by local disputes and conflict with Edward Randolph, British surveyor of the customs, over Blake's abuses of British customs laws and admiralty courts. After the British Parliament enacted the Navigation Act of 1696 to strengthen control over colonial trade, the Board of Trade dispatched Randolph to America to investigate the colonial customs system and make recommendations to improve it. He visited Charleston in November 1698 and remained there for five months, where he administered an oath to Governor Blake and other officials to uphold the Navigation Act. But he soon discovered that Blake was a notorious offender against the act. Randolph accused Blake and his brother-in-law, Joseph Morton, admiralty judge, of fraudulently condemning vessels as contraband and then colluding to purchase at auction ships and cargoes at bargain prices. Randolph also reported that Blake and others took bribes to ignore smuggling and traded with pirates and the Spanish in Florida.

The case of the *Cole and Bean* galley was the most blatant episode. In September 1699 the colonist Edmund Bellinger filed a complaint in admiralty court against the *Cole and Bean,* a small trading vessel, for violation of the Navigation Act. Judge Joseph Morton heard the case. He condemned the vessel and ordered it sold at auction. The London shipowners appealed the verdict to the English Privy Council, and Morton's verdict was reversed in 1701. While in Charleston, Randolph observed the proceedings in that case. He reported to the crown Blake's actions and the proprietors' negligence in enforcing English laws. Randolph's reports led to a sweeping review of charter colonies in America aimed to bring them more directly under crown authority.

Blake's death in office on September 7, 1700, precipitated a power struggle in the council over his successor. Dissenters supported Joseph Morton and the Anglicans opposed him, asserting that Morton was ineligible to be proprietary governor because he held a royal commission as admiralty judge. They then opposed Edmund Bellinger, another Dissenter, because he was vice admiralty judge. The Anglicans' argument prevailed in the council, and James Moore became deputy governor. The succession of Moore, an Anglican and opponent of the proprietors, was a blow to Dissenter control in Carolina and exacerbated conflict both in the province and between colonial leaders and with the Lords Proprietors. ALEXANDER MOORE

Blake Family. Files. South Carolina Historical Society, Charleston.

Moore, John Alexander. "Royalizing South Carolina: The Revolution of 1719 and the Evolution of Early South Carolina Government." Ph.D. diss., University of South Carolina, 1991.

Toppan, Robert Noxon, and Alfred Thomas Scrope Goodrick, eds. *Edward Randolph, Including His Letters and Official Papers from the New England, Middle, and Southern Colonies in America.* 7 vols. 1898. Reprint, New York: Burt Franklin, 1967.

Blake Plateau. The Blake Plateau is a large, relatively shallow (eight hundred to twelve hundred meters) carbonate bank that lies two hundred miles off Charleston on the continental shelf. It runs from near Cape Hatteras in North Carolina, past South Carolina and eastern Florida, to just north of the Bahamas. At the eastern, seaward edge of the plateau, the Blake Bahamas Scarp descends eighteen thousand feet toward the abyssal plain below. This scarp forms the highest geologic structure east of the Rocky Mountains.

The structure of the Blake Plateau clearly illustrates the process of the North American/African separation beginning in the Late Triassic period (208 million years before present) as well as the development of continental shelves generally. It also provides additional evidence through recent sediment and fossil analyses of the events occurring at the Cretaceous/Tertiary boundary that led to the great mass extinctions of many animal and plant species of that time.

The Blake Plateau began to form as the North American plate disengaged from the African plate in the Late Triassic period, forming the Atlantic Ocean. Beginning with rifting that shattered the subsurface, lava flows and down-faulted valleys formed at the edges of the continents and offshore. Later sediments formed a progressively thicker wedge seaward. As rifting continued during the Jurassic period, the carbonate deposits formed in what was then a warm, shallow sea: the early Atlantic Ocean. The weight of the deposits of sediments and of the carbonates bent the crust downward, which allowed more deposition, allowing the carbonates to reach a thickness of more than thirty thousand feet (ten kilometers).

The plateau is of economic interest because of the 1970 and 1996 discoveries of immense deposits of hydrocarbons in the form of methane and methane hydrate that may be developed commercially in the future. Many geologists now believe that this immense carbonate bank may contain huge quantities of usable methane gas. CAROLYN H. MURPHY

Murphy, Carolyn H. *Carolina Rocks! The Geology of South Carolina.* Orangeburg, S.C.: Sandlapper, 1995.

Blanchard, Felix Anthony, Jr. (b. 1924). Football player, Heisman Trophy recipient. "Doc" Blanchard was born in McColl on December 11, 1924, the son of Felix Blanchard and Mary Tatum. When Blanchard was eight years old, his family moved to Bishopville in Lee County. As the son of a physician, townspeople called Blanchard "Little Doc," attaching a nickname that followed him for a lifetime.

Blanchard started playing football as a junior high student in Bishopville, then attended St. Stanislaus Prep School in Bay St. Louis, Mississippi, where he excelled in football. In 1942 he enrolled at the University of North Carolina, where he starred on the school's freshmen football team. On being drafted the following year, he was inducted at Fort Jackson, and he was later accepted for officer candidates school. In 1944 he was appointed to the U.S. Military Academy at West Point, New York.

Standing six feet tall and weighing more than two hundred pounds, Blanchard distinguished himself as a fullback on the West Point football teams from 1944 to 1946. He received the Heisman Trophy as the nation's top collegiate player in 1945, the first junior to gain that recognition, and was named to the All-America teams in 1944, 1945, and 1946. Blanchard also was recipient of the Maxwell Award in 1945 as the nation's top football player and became the first football player to receive the Sullivan Award as the country's most outstanding amateur athlete. Army compiled a 27–0–1 record during his three years with the team, which included two national championships.

At West Point, Blanchard teamed with the halfback Glenn Davis in a devastating offense, in which Blanchard was known as "Mr. Inside" and Davis as "Mr. Outside." Davis was runner-up to Blanchard in the 1945 Heisman voting and won the Heisman Trophy in 1946. Typical of reaction to Blanchard's prowess was a comment by Notre Dame coach Ed McKeever following Army's 59–0 rout of the Fighting Irish in 1944. "I have just seen Superman in the flesh," said McKeever. "He wears number 35 and goes by the name of Blanchard." During his career at West Point, Blanchard compiled 1,908 total yards and scored thirty-eight touchdowns. A linebacker on defense, he also punted and returned kickoffs. On the Army track team, he ran the 100-yard dash in ten seconds and heaved the shot put 54 feet.

Following graduation, Blanchard made the U.S. Air Force his career, flying missions as a fighter pilot in both the Korean and Vietnam Wars. On October 12, 1948, he married Jody King of San Antonio, Texas, who died in 1994. Their marriage produced three children. Blanchard retired with the rank of colonel in 1971 and made his home in San Antonio, Texas.

Blanchard was inducted into the National Football Foundation's College Football Hall of Fame in 1959. The Interstate 20 / U.S. Highway 15 interchange nearby has been named in his honor. A quiet, unassuming individual, Blanchard made little of his athletic accomplishments. He donated his Heisman Trophy to St. Stanislaus Prep School for display, commenting, "I really don't miss seeing it around." DON BARTON

Fimrite, Ron. "Mr. Inside & Mr. Outside." *Sports Illustrated* 69 (November 21, 1988): 76–92.

Newhouse, Dave. *Heismen: After the Glory.* St. Louis, Mo.: Sporting News, 1985.

Spear, Bob. "Bishopville's Favorite Son." Columbia *State,* October 18, 2002, pp. C1, C4.

Blatt, Solomon (1895–1986). Legislator. Blatt was born in Blackville on February 27, 1895, the second son of Nathan and Mollie Blatt. His father, an Orthodox Jew who had emigrated from Russia in 1893, ran a store in Blackville. Blatt attended the University of South Carolina from 1912 to 1917, graduating with a law degree. He was admitted to the bar in June 1917, and in December 1917 he joined the law firm of future governor J. Emile Harley. During World War I, Blatt served in France from 1918 to 1919. On March 18, 1920, he married Ethel Green. They had one son.

Blatt's political career began in 1930, when he ran for a seat in the S.C. House of Representatives from Barnwell County. He was

Solomon Blatt. Courtesy, Modern Political Collections, University of South Carolina

defeated in the run-off primary but was elected without opposition two years later. This marked the beginning of a political career in the House that would span six decades. In 1935 he was elected Speaker Pro Tem. Two years later he was chosen Speaker of the House of Representatives. He held this position from 1937 to 1973 with the exception of the period from 1947 to 1951, when he did not oppose Governor Strom Thurmond's candidate for Speaker, C. Bruce Littlejohn. In 1951 Blatt was reelected Speaker of the House by a vote of 113 to 9. He held the position until stepping down in 1973. He remained in the House of Representatives, however, where members gave him the honorary designation of Speaker Emeritus.

As a political leader, Blatt was a conservative. He defined good government as a mixture of progressive action and judicial restraint, all exerted toward balance, for the right thing in the right amount of time. As a legislator, he was a strong supporter of public education. He supported the establishment of a three percent sales tax for education, the technical education system, and educational television. He advocated efforts by the state to expand the physical facilities of the state's colleges and universities. He also served on the Barnwell District Board of Education from 1927 to 1962 and the University of South Carolina Board of Trustees from 1936 to 1948. He supported the state hospital and resisted efforts to reinstitute Prohibition in the state. He was a strong proponent of industrial development and was supportive of the establishment of the Savannah River Site as well as the development of the state's ports. He felt that industry and government should cooperate in order to achieve development. As such, he was a leader in the passage of the state's right-to-work law in 1954. He also was a proponent of highway improvements. Not only did South Carolina develop many roads in rural areas, the state also developed its interstate highway system more quickly than was the case with most states.

Blatt died on May 14, 1986. At the time of his death he was the longest-serving state legislator in the United States, having served for more than fifty-three years. The man who considered himself "just a darn good country lawyer" was buried next to Holy Apostle Episcopal Church in Barnwell. WILLIAM V. MOORE

Blatt, Solomon. Papers. Modern Political Collections, South Caroliniana Library, University of South Carolina, Columbia.

Cauthen, John. *Speaker Blatt: His Challenges Were Greater.* Columbia, S.C.: R. L. Bryan, 1965.

Renick, Timothy D. "Solomon Blatt: An Explanation into the Conservative Racial Views of a Jewish Politician in the Deep South, 1937–1986, with an Accompanying Guide to the Solomon Blatt Papers." Master's thesis, University of South Carolina, 1989.

Blease, Coleman Livingston (1868–1942). Governor, U.S. senator. Blease was born near Newberry on October 8, 1868, the son of Henry Horatio Blease and Mary Ann Livingston. From 1884 to 1886 Blease attended Newberry College, and he earned a bachelor of laws degree from Georgetown University in 1889. He was admitted to the South Carolina Bar that same year. In 1890 Blease married Lillie B. Summers, who died in 1914. In 1939 he married Caroline Floyd, but the couple separated a year later. Both marriages were childless.

Coleman Livingston Blease. Courtesy, South Caroliniana Library

Blease entered public service in 1890, when he was elected to represent Newberry in the S.C. House of Representatives. Reelected in 1892, he was elevated to the position of Speaker Pro Tempore of the sixtieth General Assembly (1892–1893). Defeated in reelection bids in 1894 and 1896, Blease returned to the House in 1899. He was ambitious for higher office and made unsuccessful runs for the office of lieutenant governor in 1900 and 1902, then won election to the S.C. Senate from Newberry in 1905. Two years later he served as President Pro Tempore of the Senate for the sixty-seventh General Assembly (1907–1908). Blease ran unsuccessfully for governor in 1906 and 1908 but won the office in 1910 and was subsequently reelected in 1912.

Blease's two terms as governor were the high-water mark of perhaps the most polarizing figure in South Carolina political history. His appeal was primarily among a new class of South Carolinians that emerged early in the twentieth century: the white mill worker. Part of Blease's attraction among mill workers was his flamboyant style and his unmatched stump-speaking ability. But he also identified with working-class whites, especially the mill workers, and capitalized on their desire to be treated as equals. Blease understood their fear that they were being marginalized by middle-class society. While critics saw him as nothing more than a demagogue and as lacking any concrete substance, "Coley" became the champion of mill workers who had little use for progressive "do-gooders" or government regulators who intruded in their workplaces and homes. Neither reformer nor innovator, Blease was an obstructionist who blocked legislation that threatened the ability of operatives "to manage their own affairs." Confronting Blease's overwhelming support from mill operatives was his equally solid opposition among middle- and upper-class South Carolinians, who denounced "Bleasism" as a threat to law and order. The controversy surrounding Blease brought supporters and opponents to polls in staggering numbers, with voter participation topping eighty percent in the 1912 gubernatorial campaign.

As governor, Blease emphasized individual freedom for whites and racism. He opposed government regulation, even if its purpose was to benefit the same mill workers to whom he appealed. He denounced an act to limit working hours for mill employees, believing it interfered with parents' control over their children. He vetoed legislation to inspect factories for safety and health considerations, stating that a man ought to be able to work under any conditions he chose. He opposed compulsory education as an attempt to replace parents with "the paid agents of the State in the control of children," and he vetoed four compulsory attendance bills while governor. He was against the medical examination of schoolchildren, asserting that he would pardon any man who killed a doctor who violated his daughter's modesty.

While promoting equality for white mill workers, Blease also appealed to racial bigotry and accused opponents of attempting to reduce white mill workers to the same level as African Americans. He labeled blacks as "baboons" and "apes" and urged that there be no spending of white men's taxes on black schools. As governor, Blease promoted separation of the races on chain gangs and defended lynching, stating, "whenever the Constitution comes between me and the virtue of the white women of the South, I say to hell with the Constitution." He promised that he would pardon any lyncher convicted by a jury. Blease's relationship with the General Assembly was tumultuous, and his numerous vetoes were frequently overridden by the legislature. His language was often coarse and vulgar, forcing state newspapers to delete portions of his speeches from print. One Blease veto message was so inflammatory that state legislators expunged it from the printed journal.

Despite his volatile tenure, there were some accomplishments during his reign as governor. These included the establishment of a state tuberculosis sanitarium, the adoption of the medical college in Charleston as a public institution, the creation of a special tax on hydroelectric companies, the support for better provision for common schools, and the abolition of the penitentiary hosiery mill because of unhealthy conditions.

Blease resigned as governor five days before the end of his term so that he would not have to hand his office over to Richard I. Manning, who was elected on an anti-Blease platform of progressive reform. Blease failed in attempts to return to the governor's chair in 1916 and 1922, and likewise failed in 1914 and 1918 to win election to the U.S. Senate. However, in 1924 he won election to the U.S. Senate with the slogan "Roll up yer sleeves and say what cha' please; the man fer the office is Cole L. Blease." During his one term Blease had no influence in national Democratic circles since he refused to be bound by party caucuses. He did support the nomination of Judge John J. Parker to the U.S. Supreme Court while many other southern senators did not. He voted against reducing federal income taxes, and he contributed to the successful effort to get a third federal judgeship for South Carolina. He was successful in getting the King's Mountain Battlefield bill passed. In 1930 he was defeated in his bid for reelection by James F. Byrnes. Although he still enjoyed a loyal following in South Carolina, Blease never again commanded enough votes to return to the governor's mansion, losing attempts in 1934 and 1938. In 1941 he was elected a member of the State Unemployment Compensation Commission. He died on January 19, 1942, in Columbia and was buried in Newberry. WILLIAM V. MOORE

Burnside, Ronald D. "The Governorship of Coleman Livingston Blease of South Carolina, 1911–1915." Ph.D. diss., Indiana University, 1963.

Carlton, David L. *Mill and Town in South Carolina, 1880–1920.* Baton Rouge: Louisiana State University Press, 1982.

Hollis, Daniel. "Cole Blease and the Senatorial Campaign of 1924." *Proceedings of the South Carolina Historical Association* (1978): 53–68.

Mixon, Kenneth Wayne. "The Senatorial Career of Coleman Livingston Blease, 1925–1931." Master's thesis, University of South Carolina, 1970.

Simon, Bryant. "The Appeal of Cole Blease of South Carolina: Race, Class, and Sex in the New South." *Journal of Southern History* 62 (February 1996): 57–86.

Blenheim ginger ale. Blenheim ginger ale has its origins in the Marlboro County village of Blenheim. During the late 1890s Dr. C. R. May began adding Jamaican ginger to the mineral water gathered from a local artesian spring. At the time, wealthy planters were building summer homes in the area. He prescribed the concoction as a palatable digestive aid. In the early 1900s May joined forces with A. J. Matheson to bottle the nonalcoholic ale. Though the company developed different flavor combinations over the years—including a pineapple-orange soda—the spicy, ginger-flavored soft drink known as Old Number Three has remained the primary product.

Until 1993 Blenheim Bottling Company avoided any attempts at modernization. Each bottle was taken off the production line and hand-shaken to mix the granulated sugar into the ale. That laborious process ended when Alan Schafer, proprietor of the South of the Border entertainment complex located just south of the North Carolina state line, bought out the bottler and built a modern plant. The old plant closed, and production moved to a new home alongside Pedro's Pleasure Palace and other attractions of South of the Border.

Despite a marketing push that began in the late 1990s, Blenheim ginger ale is not widely distributed outside the Carolinas. The spicy ale has, however, developed a cult following among food and wine aficionados. In a February 25, 1998, *New York Times* article, the journalist Bill Grimes described the taste in this way: "The first swallow brings on a four-sneeze fit. The second one clears out the sinuses and leaves the tongue and throat throbbing with prickly heat." JOHN T. EDGE

Craft, Robert L. "Some Like It Hot." *Carolina Lifestyle* 1 (August 1982): 62–67.

Grimes, William. "A Southern Ginger Ale with Sting in Its Tail." *New York Times,* February 25, 1998, p. F5.

White, Forrest. "Hot Stuff: Hale to the Ale in Blenheim Town." *Charleston Post and Courier,* September 22, 1993, pp. D1, D2.

Blockade-running. Throughout the Civil War, government and civilian goods were shipped into the Confederate states on vessels known as blockade-runners. The vessels that carried these supplies through the northern blockade were vital components in a trade that sustained the Confederate armies. Though South Carolina had numerous harbors and inlets, only Charleston had the proper railroad connections and port facilities to sustain an efficient overseas trade. A blockade was established off Charleston on May 28, 1861. Large sailing ships that could carry a profitable cargo were easily captured, so the mainstay of the trade quickly became specialized, steam-propelled blockade-runners that could outrun enemy gunboats and carry 500 to 2,000 bales of cotton.

Though the Confederate government operated blockade-runners, the majority of the vessels were owned and run by private companies that made tremendous profits by importing supplies and exporting cotton. The majority of the war's blockade-running firms were formed at Charleston. Among them were the Palmetto, Chicora, and Charleston Importing and Exporting Companies and the Importing and Exporting Company of South Carolina. The South's largest and most successful blockade-running firm was operated by George A. Trenholm, who oversaw the Charleston-based John Fraser and Company and its Liverpool office, Fraser, Trenholm and Company, which was operated by Charles K. Prioleau.

Trenholm's firms operated some thirty-five blockade-runners; shipped more than 45,000 bales of cotton, or nearly twenty percent of all cotton to leave the South during the war; and imported tons of civilian and military goods. The firm worked closely with the Confederate government and served as the Confederacy's bankers in Europe. The firm made an estimated $20 million.

Charleston served as the Confederacy's main port from November 1861 to July 1863. During this time some thirty-six steam-powered blockade-runners made 125 trips in and out of Charleston, carrying out nearly 30,000 bales of cotton. The majority of the ships operated out of Nassau, although some came from Havana and Bermuda. Primarily private companies used Charleston, while Wilmington, North Carolina, was home to the government's blockade-runners. Most vessels entered Charleston through the main ship channel parallel to Morris Island, while others used the shallower Maffitt's Channel, which ran along Sullivan's Island. The two channels joined off Fort Sumter where an opening was maintained through the harbor's obstructions. In the summer of 1863 a Federal attack on Charleston captured Morris Island, closed the main ship channel, and placed Union warships close to Fort Sumter. The tightened blockade caused blockade-runners to shift their operations to Wilmington.

Blockade-running at Charleston virtually ceased until the late summer of 1864, when companies began running in small steamers using Maffitt's Channel. Among the firms sending vessels to Charleston was the Importing and Exporting Company of South Carolina, which in 1864 had entered into a partnership with the state of South Carolina to carry in goods needed by the state for its soldiers and civilians.

From the fall of 1864 until February 1865, another twenty steamers completed ninety runs in and out of Charleston. The vessels brought in valuable supplies, including hundreds of thousands of shoes and other needed quartermaster goods. One of the vessels using Charleston was the *Syren.* Owned by the Charleston Importing and Exporting Company, she was the war's most successful blockade-runner, making thirty-three trips through the blockade, fifteen of them to Charleston. The last blockade-runner to clear Charleston was the *G. T. Watson,* which escaped on February 17, 1865. The next morning the occupying Union forces captured the *Syren,* which had arrived on the previous day. After the fall of Charleston, the Confederacy prepared Georgetown as a possible port of entry, but no vessels came to the port before its occupation by the Union navy.

Charleston was the second-most-active port in the Confederacy (Wilmington, North Carolina, was first). Supplies were essential to sustaining the war effort, and the government cotton shipped from Charleston was used to finance the South's purchasing operations in Europe. Charleston blockade-running firms made tremendous profits. Although Trenholm and his partners were unable to retain their proceeds due to litigation by the federal government, dividends from other firms paid to such individuals as George W. Williams, an officer and investor in numerous companies, were used to help revive Charleston's postwar shipping trade. STEPHEN R. WISE

Foster, Kevin. "Phantoms, Will of the Wisps and the Dare, or the Search for Speed under Steam: The Design of Blockade Running Steamships." Master's thesis, East Carolina University, 1991.

Nepveux, Ethel Trenholm S. *George A. Trenholm: Financial Genius of the Confederacy.* Anderson, S.C.: Electric Printing Company, 1999.

Wise, Stephen R. *Lifeline of the Confederacy: Blockade Running during the Civil War.* Columbia: University of South Carolina Press, 1988.

Blue, Gilbert (b. 1933). Catawba leader. Chief Gilbert Blue of the Catawba Nation was born on December 5, 1933, on the Catawba Indian Reservation to Guy Larson Blue and Eva George Starnes. Chief Blue joined the U.S. Navy in 1951, serving until 1960. While in the navy, he earned his GED and went on to take some college courses. He married Elizabeth Sharpe in October 1963. They have three children.

The grandson of former chief Samuel Taylor Blue, Gilbert Blue was elected chief of the Catawba Tribe of South Carolina in 1973. Under Chief Blue's leadership, the Catawba successfully pursued their lawsuit against the state of South Carolina for land claims under the Nations Ford Treaty of 1840 and their quest for the reinstatement of status as a federally recognized Indian tribe. The Catawba Indian Tribe of South Carolina Land Claims Settlement Act of 1993, which provided for resolution of both demands, was passed by Congress in 1993, and the final agreement was signed by South Carolina Governor Carroll Campbell on November 29, 1994.

Chief Blue has been active in Native American issues and organizations. He was elected to the board of directors of the Native American Rights Fund (NARF) in 1996 and served as chairman of its board in 2000 and 2001. He is the representative for the Catawba to the National Congress of American Indians (NCAI) and has served on the state board of the U.S. Commission on Civil Rights. He was an original board member of the Rock Hill "No Room for Racism" Committee and has been involved in numerous other civil rights issues. He is an active member of the Church of Jesus Christ of Latter Day Saints, in which he has served in various leadership positions. ANNE M. MCCULLOCH

Newhall, Richard. "Catawbas' Chief Values Traditions." Rock Hill *Evening Herald,* September 26, 1973, pp. 1, 14.

Blue, Samuel Taylor, Jr. (1872–1959). Catawba leader. Samuel Taylor Blue, chief of the Catawba Tribe for three administrations (1931–1938, 1941–1943, and 1956–1958), was born on August 15, 1872, on the Catawba Indian Reservation near Rock Hill. His Indian name was Namé Patki, which means "Big Bear." The son of a white farmer, Samuel Taylor Blue, Sr., and a Catawba woman, Margaret George Brown, Blue spent most of his life on the reservation, where he learned much of the history and culture of his people. He spoke the Catawba language, though not fluently, and was an authority on tribal history. Because of his character and charisma, he was referred to as "Chief" for much of his life. In July 1887, at age fourteen, he married Minnie Hester George, by whom he had three children. After her death he married Hester Louisa Jean Canty on May 8, 1897. He had another twenty children with her. Hester Louisa was reputed to be the last full-blood Catawba. She was a master potter and a fluent speaker of the Catawba language, and she seems to have been well regarded both inside and outside the tribe, as was her husband.

Chief Samuel Blue was the driving force behind the political revival of the Catawba tribe. It was during his second administration that the Catawba finally became a federally recognized tribe and recovered parts of their original reservation. Chief Blue was also a spiritual leader, serving for forty years as president of the Catawba branch of the Mormon Church, to which most tribal members belonged. On a trip to Salt Lake City, he was given the headdress and regalia of the western Sioux. He often wore the regalia for tourists who expected that kind of dress by Indians, even though the traditional attire of the Catawba was quite different. Chief Blue died on April 16, 1959. ANNE M. MCCULLOCH

Brown, Douglas Summers. *The Catawba Indians: The People of the River.* Columbia: University of South Carolina Press, 1966.
Hall, Jerry. "'Big Bear Is Dead': Chief Blue Bids Farewell." Rock Hill *Evening Herald,* April 17, 1959, p. 5.

Blue granite. State stone. Blue granite was designated the state stone by a law approved by Governor Robert McNair on June 24, 1969. Legislators declared that "the blue granite stone of this State has been widely used to beautify all areas of South Carolina." The state is famed for Winnsboro blue granite, which was quarried for many years in Fairfield County. The stone is of light blue color and contains particles of mica, feldspar, and quartz. It is much prized in construction and decoration.

Granite is a coarse-grained igneous stone produced by slow cooling and solidification of molten rock. Winnsboro blue has been used in the construction of churches, houses, gravestones, and fence posts since the early nineteenth century. The Winnsboro Granite Company quarried and shipped the "beautiful blue" for many years, and the stone acquired national renown as "the silk of the trade." It has been used in such structures as New York City's Flat-Iron Building, the old Charleston Post Office, and the great dry dock of the Charleston Naval Shipyard. It was used for the Jean Ribaut Monument at the U.S. Marine Corps Depot at Parris Island and for Charleston's John C. Calhoun Monument. The Fairfield granites won a medal and diploma at the World's Columbian Exposition in 1893.

After Winnsboro blue was no longer quarried in South Carolina, stocks still remained in the state, and the stone was still found in Elberton, Georgia. In 2002 the Willis Dimension Stone Company of Elberton donated Winnsboro blue to Shaw Air Force Base to be used for a monument to firefighters who served at New York City's "Ground Zero" on September 11, 2001. DAVID C. R. HEISSER

Jacobs, Thornwell. *Story of "The Silk of the Trade."* Rion, S.C.: Winnsboro Blue Granite, 1952.
South Carolina. Department of Agriculture, Commerce and Immigration. *The Granite Industry of South Carolina, U.S.A.* Columbia, S.C.: State Company, 1906.
Yates, Nancy C. "Amethyst and Granite: The Official Gemstone and Stone of the State of South Carolina." *Sandlapper* 4 (March 1971): 24–27.

Blue Ridge. The Blue Ridge in South Carolina forms the smallest of the geological provinces. There are commonly two understandings of the Blue Ridge. The first is the geologic Blue Ridge, which is found only in Oconee County, bounded on the west by the Chattooga River and on the east by the Brevard Fault. The second is the geographic Blue Ridge, which includes both the Blue Ridge Mountains and inner Piedmont mountains such as Sassafras, Pinnacle, and Table Rock. The geologic Blue Ridge refers to the rocks of the region and their histories, and the geographic Blue Ridge refers to the shape of the land. The distinction is important because the two areas have different geologic histories; they were formed at different times and contain different rocks.

The size of the geologic Blue Ridge is so small in South Carolina that only by looking at its continuation into Georgia, North Carolina, and Virginia could geologists form reasonable interpretations of its history. The Blue Ridge appears to lie over an eroded mountain system known as the Grenville Range, which once formed the edge of a much smaller North America. As the east coast of North America rifted apart from another plate during the late Precambrian period, extensive sedimentary deposits and volcanics developed on the continental shelf. Then, in the Ordovician period, a collision occurred with what were perhaps a previously detached continental fragment and an island arc that moved toward and eventually welded onto North America. During the millions of years that the collision developed, the rocks of the continental shelf were shoved upward into what must have been a high mountain range. This became the Blue Ridge. During later continental collisions, lastly with the African plate during the Pennsylvanian to Permian time, the remnants of the eroded Blue Ridge were again thrust upward. In the Great Smoky Mountains of North Carolina and Tennessee, there exist "coves," such as Cades Cove, which are areas where overlying, older Blue Ridge rock has eroded to form a "window" onto younger Ordovician sediments that lie underneath. Applying this understanding to the Blue Ridge in South Carolina allows geologists to argue that while the Blue Ridge is related to the rocks of the Piedmont by events in the past, it has a different age, structure, and history than they do. The rocks of the Blue Ridge in South Carolina include gneisses, schists, metagreywackes, pegmatites, and amphibolites that were formed from heat and pressure applied to the original sediments and volcanics of the Precambrian continental shelf rocks.

The Blue Ridge in winter. Photograph by Phillip Jones. Courtesy, South Carolina Department of Natural Resources

The Blue Ridge contains many interesting geologic features that are clearly visible in particular sites. The Blue Ridge is contained primarily within the boundary of the Sumter National Forest, including the town of Mountain Rest. A popular area to visit and explore the geology is the Chattooga River valley, where rocks can be observed along the many hiking trails in the area. Included between the East Fork of the Chattooga River and Georgia is Ellicott Rock, which marks the intersection of South Carolina, North Carolina, and Georgia. In addition, the Chauga River provides large and clear rock exposures in several areas and flows through a scenic ten-mile gorge.

The Brevard Fault is the geologic boundary between the Blue Ridge and the inner Piedmont belt. It is found from Virginia to Alabama. The Brevard Fault ranges in size from one-third of a mile to two miles wide, forming a valley in places. Geologists believe that it forms the root of the Blue Ridge thrust sheet. The movement of the fault crushed the nearby rock, weakening the surrounding rock, which allowed erosion to carry the rock fragments away easily, creating a valley.

The geographic Blue Ridge includes the land area at and above the Blue Ridge Escarpment, including the geologic Blue Ridge Mountains within South Carolina. This area, located in Oconee, Pickens, and Greenville Counties, includes some of the most scenic highlands and mountains in the state and contains South Carolina's highest point, Sassafras Mountain, which stands at 3,554 feet above sea level. The geology of the inner Piedmont, like the Blue Ridge, also involves a collision of what is thought to have been a continental fragment, with a much earlier North America during the Ordovician period. Later collisions between continental plates, namely African and possibly South America, created metamorphic conditions that altered the granites to metagranites, or migmatites. Over millions of years the land was uplifted and highly eroded, and these metagranites rose to the surface. The results of this process include mountains such as Table Rock, Caesars Head, and Sassafras, among many others. CAROLYN H. MURPHY

Able, Gene. *Exploring South Carolina: Wild and Natural Places.* Rock Hill, S.C.: Palmetto Byways, 1995.

Kovacik, Charles F., and John J. Winberry. *South Carolina: The Making of a Landscape.* 1987. Reprint, Columbia: University of South Carolina Press, 1989.

Murphy, Carolyn H. *Carolina Rocks! The Geology of South Carolina.* Orangeburg, S.C.: Sandlapper, 1995.

Blue Ridge Railroad. Chartered in 1852, the Blue Ridge Railroad revived earlier plans to connect Charleston to the Midwest by rail, a scheme first put forth by the failed Louisville, Cincinnati and Charleston Railroad in the 1830s. The proposed route of the Blue Ridge commenced at Anderson, then passed through Pendleton and the new settlement of Walhalla before passing into Rabun County, Georgia, on its way to Knoxville, Tennessee, and points beyond. The new town of Belton would arise at the junction of the Blue Ridge with the Greenville and Columbia Railroad.

Primarily supported by Charleston merchants and built by Irish and German immigrants and local slaves, the Blue Ridge Railroad was intended to return the port city to commercial prominence in the region. Funding was problematic, however, with investors outside of Charleston displaying little interest in the project. Only a massive infusion of state funds in the mid-1850s kept the Blue Ridge Railroad alive, but it was not enough to complete the line. Districts not connected by the route and competing railroad projects bitterly opposed additional funding by the General Assembly, forcing the company to cease construction in 1859 due to financial troubles and mismanagement. The thirty-three-mile line cost almost $2.5 million, with the most costly and famous portion of the route being the uncompleted Stumphouse Mountain Tunnel. The German settlement of Walhalla became the terminus of the unfinished route.

After the Civil War, the idea of finishing the railroad was revived, but financial difficulties quickly overtook the company. In 1868 Governor Robert Scott persuaded the General Assembly to issue bonds to pay for the completion of the route. The attempt was usurped by corrupt legislators of both parties, who worked to have the state sell its interest in the Blue Ridge to private interests at greatly reduced prices. The corruption of the Blue Ridge "ring" became one of the most notorious examples of the fiscal misconduct of the Reconstruction era. Despite the initial postwar interest, the Blue Ridge Railroad added no more track to its antebellum line. In October 1874 the assets of the controversial company were broken up, and the completed portion of the track was eventually incorporated into the Southern Railway System. MATTHEW C. SMITH

Brown, George Dewitt. "A History of the Blue Ridge Railroad, 1852–1874." Master's thesis, University of South Carolina, 1967.

Ford, Lacy K., Jr. *Origins of Southern Radicalism: The South Carolina Upcountry, 1800–1860.* New York: Oxford University Press, 1988.

Haughey, Jim. "Tunnel Hill: An Irish Mining Community in the Western Carolinas." *Proceedings of the South Carolina Historical Association* (2004): 51–62.

Williamson, Joel. *After Slavery: The Negro in South Carolina during Reconstruction, 1861–1877.* Chapel Hill: University of North Carolina Press, 1965.

Blues. A powerful form of secular African American musical and cultural expression, blues developed in the South around the turn of the twentieth century, a product of the large plantations and railroad, mining, and logging camps where black workers congregated. With thickly idiomatic, metaphorically charged lyrics, early blues songs confronted everyday life with humor and resilience but also reflected the oppression and social isolation faced by African Americans during the Jim Crow era. While blues has evolved into an international art form played in a multitude of styles, its musical essence lies in the use of "blue" notes or tones to convey emotion and the role of instrumental accompaniment—usually guitar, piano, or harmonica—to punctuate or "second" the singer.

As blues spread throughout the South in the early decades of the twentieth century, regional styles and traditions developed. In South Carolina, the hotbed was the Greenville-Spartanburg area, where a coterie of talented guitarists contributed to a style that became known as the "Piedmont" or East Coast school of blues. While versatile in its scope, the Piedmont sound is typified by ragtime influences, intricate finger-picked guitar playing, shrill and raucous harmonica blowing, and playful lyrics.

Widely acknowledged by his peers as the most dexterous of the early Greenville-Spartanburg blues musicians, the blind guitarist Willie Walker (1896–1933) left a legacy of only two recorded songs, his 1930 pairing of "South Carolina Rag" and "Betty and Dupree." While he preferred sacred lyrics to secular, one of Walker's Greenville contemporaries, the virtuosic guitarist Rev. "Blind" Gary Davis (1896–1972), played an even larger role in shaping and spreading the East Coast blues style. A mentor to North Carolinian Blind Boy Fuller, one of the most popular bluesmen with African American audiences of the 1930s, Davis later influenced a younger generation of musicians during the folk revival of the early 1960s, among them Bob Dylan. Josh White (1914–1969), yet another gifted guitarist living in Greenville during the 1920s, also became a prominent figure in folk music circles after establishing himself as a blues and gospel recording artist for the African American market in the 1930s.

While Davis and White furthered their musical careers in New York City, other South Carolinians kept the blues tradition alive back home. One of the most accomplished of these artists was the guitarist Pinkney "Pink" Anderson (1900–1974), a songster with a repertoire of blues, rags, gospel, and ballads who traveled widely with medicine shows, recorded albums, and became well known on the folk circuit in the early 1960s. Anderson got his start on the streets of Spartanburg accompanying the blind guitarist Simeon "Simmie" Dooley (1881–1961). Among Anderson's later musical partners were the talented guitarist Charles Henry "Baby" Tate (1910–1972), a Georgia native who moved to Greenville as a child, and Arthur "Peg Leg Sam" Jackson (1911–1977), an inventive harmonica ace and medicine show veteran, hobo, and storyteller who returned regularly from the road to his home in Jonesville.

Of the many African Americans who were born in South Carolina but left the state as children during the large migrations to northern cities, some were notable performers who made careers in various styles of blues. These artists included the vaudeville singer Clara Smith (1895–1935), who was born in Spartanburg and began recording in New York in the 1920s; the classic blues vocalist Bertha "Chippie" Hill (1905–1950), a native of Charleston who moved to New York in her teens; and the influential guitarist Francis "Scrapper" Blackwell (1903–1962), who grew up in Indianapolis after leaving rural South Carolina. Among later expatriates were two Blackville natives: Joseph Benjamin "J. B." Hutto (1926–1983), who made his name as a slide guitarist in Chicago; and Marvin Sease (b. 1946), a popular soul and blues vocalist who based his career in New York after starting off in Charleston-area gospel groups.

During the 1980s and 1990s and into the twenty-first century, South Carolinians of all races continued to enjoy blues performances at nightclubs and festivals. The state's most prominent resident artists included Bishopville guitarist Drink Small (b. 1933), an eclectic stylist of blues, gospel, and soul music; Pomaria vocalist Nappy Brown (b. 1929), a veteran rhythm-and-blues entertainer; and the blind Greenville guitarist Cootie Stark (b. 1927), an Abbeville native who learned from Baby Tate and others in the Piedmont a blues style that once thrived on the street corners of Greenville and Spartanburg. DAVID NELSON

Bastin, Bruce. *Crying for the Carolines.* London: Studio Vista, 1971.

———. *Red River Blues: The Blues Tradition in the Southeast.* Urbana: University of Illinois Press, 1986.

Bluffton (Beaufort County; 2000 pop. 1,275). Bluffton originated as a summer resort for antebellum plantation owners of St. Luke's Parish in Beaufort District. Located on the twenty-foot-high bluffs of the May River and facing the cool, southerly winds, it was an ideal summer refuge for planter families. The town, known first simply as May River and then later as Kirk's Bluff, was officially named Bluffton in 1844. The town's streets were formally laid out in the late 1830s, and Bluffton was incorporated by the General Assembly in 1852.

For more than a century, Bluffton—with its moss-draped oaks and quiet streets—has been a summer retreat. Courtesy, South Carolina Historical Society

Cotton wealth and steamboat service from Savannah led to the construction of a growing number of summer cottages in antebellum Bluffton. Additional construction included several general stores along Calhoun Street, two churches, and a school for the children of planters.

With the capture of Hilton Head Island by Union forces in November 1861, residents evacuated Bluffton, which was subsequently attacked and burned by Union troops in June 1863, destroying more than two-thirds of the homes. The attack may have been retribution for the role played by Blufftonians in the secession movement. The first secession movement in the state was started in 1844 by the planters of St. Luke's Parish and became known as the "Bluffton Movement."

The building of the Coastal Highway (U.S. 17) and bridging of the Savannah River in 1926 ushered in a new phase in Bluffton's history, when its status as a center of local trade gradually diminished following the discontinuation of riverboat service to the town. Bluffton's economy depended mainly on its seafood business and construction of oyster sloops. While Bluffton continued to draw summer residents, its economy declined until the construction of the Talmadge Bridge, which created a shorter route to Savannah, and the construction of a bridge connection to Hilton Head Island. The development of Hilton Head as a major tourist destination in the early 1970s marked a revitalization of Bluffton. Annexations and the spread of Hilton Head's resort and tourism economy led to a seventy-five percent increase in Bluffton's population during the 1990s. ROBERT S. JONES, JR.

A Longer Short History of Bluffton, South Carolina and Its Environs. 2d ed. Hilton Head Island, S.C.: Bluffton Historical Preservation Society, 1988.

Rowland, Lawrence S., Alexander Moore, and George C. Rogers. *The History of Beaufort County, South Carolina.* Vol. 1, *1514–1861.* Columbia: University of South Carolina Press, 1996.

Bluffton Movement (1844). On July 31, 1844, under a large oak tree (the "Secession Oak") in Bluffton, South Carolina, the first organized political movement with the express goal of South Carolina's independent secession from the Union was born. The "Bluffton Movement," as it became known, was a call to secession if the South was not guaranteed its rights to slavery, a lower tariff, and states' rights.

Aggrieved by the Tariff of 1842 and the refusal of Congress to annex Texas, St. Luke's Parish planters formed a committee and called for a meeting of individuals and their local congressman, Robert Barnwell Rhett, to speak about these issues that had plagued the South since the 1820s. Invitations were sent to nearby parishes, prominent men, and area newspapers (including those in Charleston and Savannah). At this dinner and others to follow, Rhett, a longtime nullifier and disunionist, attempted to rally support for a state convention. He hoped such a convention would nullify the Tariff of 1842 or urge South Carolina's immediate secession from the Union. These measures were considered by most, both within and outside of the state, as being extremely radical.

St. Luke's Parish planters (dubbed the "Bluffton Boys") took the lead in agitating for "nullification or secession" throughout the state, drawing additional support from such prominent political figures as James Henry Hammond, William Gilmore Simms, and George McDuffie. Their political ideology began the radical separatist policy that would eventually bring Rhett into national prominence as the chief spokesman for southern secession. In the short term, however, the movement's extreme platform lost momentum quickly. The movement attracted few followers outside of the Beaufort region, due in large measure to John C. Calhoun's opposition to the movement and its goals. Other Blufftonites were appeased by a compromise tariff passed by Congress in 1846 and the annexation of Texas as a slave state. The ideological descendants of the Bluffton Movement, however, would reappear in the secession crisis of the early 1850s and in the eventual withdrawal of South Carolina from the Union in December 1860. ROBERT S. JONES, JR.

Boucher, Chauncey. "The Annexation of Texas and the Bluffton Movement in South Carolina." *Mississippi Valley Historical Review* 6 (June 1919): 3–33.

Faust, Drew Gilpin. *James Henry Hammond and the Old South: A Design for Mastery.* Baton Rouge: Louisiana State University Press, 1982.

Rowland, Lawrence S., Alexander Moore, and George C. Rogers. *The History of Beaufort County, South Carolina.* Vol. 1, *1514–1861.* Columbia: University of South Carolina Press, 1996.

BMW. The German upscale automaker Bayerische Motoren Werke (BMW) originated in 1916 as an aviation-engine manufacturing company. The company expanded to produce motorcycles and automobiles in 1923 and 1929, respectively. In 1994 BMW opened its first complete automobile manufacturing line outside Germany in Greer, South Carolina.

The Z4 on the assembly line at the BMW facility in Greer. Courtesy, BMW

Spartanburg County won a major recruiting battle over BMW's first non-Bavarian factory on June 23, 1992, when the company chose Greer over approximately 250 other localities around the world. BMW's decision was hailed both locally and internationally as the crowning achievement of the South Carolina Piedmont's campaign for international industrial recruitment.

The company came to South Carolina largely because of the state's industrial training program, which secured access to labor trained according to BMW's specific needs and requirements. Additionally, South Carolina's transportation infrastructure with railroads, highways, and deep-water ports provided BMW with quick access to North American and global markets. Also, Spartanburg agreed to buy out previous inhabitants and provide an eight-hundred-acre tract of land that BMW wanted near the airport, adjacent to Interstate 85.

The Greer factory started in 1994 by producing BMW's 318i models but expanded to Z3 roadsters in 1995 and X5 sports activity vehicles in 1999. BMW has continuously expanded its Greer factory both in size and production. By 2001 its capital investment in the region had grown to $1.9 billion. The factory covers 2.3 million square feet and employs more than 4,000 people. The factory's suppliers employ approximately 7,200 workers in the state. MARKO MAUNULA

Board of Public Works. The national trend toward improving waterways and other public facilities led South Carolina to create the Board of Public Works in December 1819. The enabling legislation created a five-person board headed by two paid acting commissioners—originally, Abram Blanding and Thomas Baker. Blanding was responsible for the Department of Roads, Rivers and Canals, and Baker for the Department of Public Buildings. The board replaced the office of the civil and military engineer.

The board hired William Jay, one of its members, to develop stock plans for new courthouses and jails. This interest in conformity was, in part, an attempt to control costs. In 1820 the Board of Public Works hired Robert Mills to replace Jay. Mills revised Jay's plans for buildings under construction and developed plans of his own. Mills denounced the move toward uniformity as not considering local needs and available building materials. He also criticized Jay's designs for their inconvenient layout and lack of fireproof space for record storage.

With an eye to the future, Mills chastised the General Assembly for selecting low bids without regard to the "permanency" of the product. In addition, he advocated a new system of awarding contracts.

In December 1822 the South Carolina General Assembly abolished the board and divided its responsibilities between its former commissioners. Blanding became the superintendent of public works, and Mills became the superintendent of public buildings. The board effected an enviable record for construction, with at least eleven courthouse projects begun or completed during its brief tenure and with several more completed shortly after its abolishment. ALEXIA JONES HELSLEY

Kohn, David, and Bess Glenn. *Internal Improvement in South Carolina, 1817–1828.* Washington, D.C., 1938.
Waddell, Gene, and Rhodri Windsor Liscombe. *Robert Mills's Courthouses and Jails.* Easley, S.C.: Southern Historical Press, 1981.

Bob Jones University. Bob Jones University (BJU) is a private institution founded in 1927 by the evangelist Bob Jones, Sr., at College Point, Florida. Hard hit by the Great Depression, the school relocated to Cleveland, Tennessee, in 1933 and then to its present campus in Greenville, South Carolina, in 1947. Enrollment in some 150 undergraduate and graduate majors has remained around five thousand since the 1980s.

Headed by four generations of Jones family evangelists, the university emerged from the separatist fundamentalist movement and has from its inception been committed to "combating all atheistic, agnostic, pagan and so-called scientific adulterations of the gospel." Wary of any secular standards of education, the university eschews accreditation by external agencies, although it is state-certified to offer degrees from the bachelor's level through the Ph.D.

The fundamentalism informing "the world's most unusual university" (as BJU describes itself) emphasizes biblical literalism, noncooperation with all Protestant denominations, a strident anti-Catholicism, and dissociation from other academic institutions. Maintaining distance from all falsehood is, for separatist fundamentalism, essential to securing the purity of the faith. Hence, Bob Jones, Jr., labeled Protestant evangelist Billy Graham, once a student at the school, as "doing more harm" to Christianity than any other individual because Graham sought interdenominational support for his evangelistic crusades.

While striving for an academic excellence fortified by this sense of spiritual purity, the university has maintained strict codes of conduct governing relations between the sexes and leisure behavior, even when students are off campus. Participation in most secular forms of entertainment is prohibited. Although highly critical of popular culture, BJU has developed strong academic programs in communications media, ranging from music to cinema, and is noted for the high quality of its operatic and theatrical productions. Its museum houses one of the more important collections of religious art in the nation, with particular strengths in medieval and Renaissance religious painting.

The commitment to separatism also extended to contact between the races, even among those who were part of the university community. For its first half-century, the university maintained a policy of strict segregation. BJU did not admit African Americans until 1975 and prohibited interracial dating among students. As a result of BJU's racial policies, the Internal Revenue Service sought to revoke the school's tax-exempt status, an action upheld by the U.S. Supreme Court in 1983. By the close of the twentieth century, rigid segregation had ended, although interracial contact remained regulated.

The university's separatist bent meant that students and faculty for many years eschewed active participation in politics and other aspects of public life. But as the surrounding culture became more religiously and ideologically pluralistic in the twenty-first century, the Jones family and members of the university community became identified with conservative political causes and lent open support to candidates whose views reflected the fundamentalist perspective and social values of the school.

Not denominationally affiliated, BJU anchors a network of independent separatist fundamentalist congregations, many of which have university alumni as pastors. Radio station WMUU has extended the university's influence and further linked together those within BJU's orbit. As well, believing that secular humanism pervades public education, the university has published curriculum materials for fundamentalist-oriented elementary and secondary schools and for use in home schooling. CHARLES H. LIPPY

Dalhouse, Mark Taylor. *An Island in the Lake of Fire: Bob Jones University, Fundamentalism, and the Separatist Movement.* Athens: University of Georgia Press, 1996.

Dollar, George. *A History of Fundamentalism in America.* Greenville, S.C.: Bob Jones University Press, 1973.

Wright, Melton. *Fortress of Faith: The Story of Bob Jones University.* Grand Rapids, Mich.: Eerdmans, 1960.

Bob Jones University Museum and Gallery. In 1965 the collection of the Bob Jones University Museum and Gallery opened to the public on Thanksgiving Day with a display of some forty Old Master paintings. The majority of the collection had been organized and preserved by Dr. Bob Jones, Jr. The museum is a separate foundation that enjoys the tax-exempt status lost by Bob Jones University (BJU) in the 1970s. Its collections contain around four hundred representative works of Flemish, Dutch, German, French, Italian, and Spanish painting from the fourteenth through the nineteenth centuries. Among them are outstanding examples from the brushes of Tintoretto, Titian, Veronese, Botticelli, Preti, Reni, Le Brun, Gerard David, Cranach, Murillo, Ribera, Rubens, and Van Dyck.

Bob Jones University Museum. Courtesy, Bob Jones University Museum and Gallery

BJU Museum and Gallery displays paintings, period furniture, and decorative arts and also houses a collection of Egyptian, Mesopotamian, Roman, and Hebrew antiquities representing thirty-seven centuries of past cultures. In addition, it contains an unusual collection of Russian icons with representative works from the fourteenth through twentieth centuries, beginning with the Novgorod school and progressing through the reign of Nicholas II, the last Russian czar.

As a visual library and valuable resource, BJU Museum and Gallery presents a record of the culture, religion, and history of ages past. More than twenty thousand people visit the collection each year. Thousands of students, families, and adults participate in the gallery's educational and cultural offerings, such as the annual *Living Gallery* presentation, music performances, focus exhibitions, guided tours, and more. SARAH MCCOY

Boineau, Charles Evans, Jr. (1923–2005). Legislator. Boineau was the first Republican to be elected to the South Carolina General Assembly in the twentieth century. He was born on September 27, 1923, in Columbia to Charles E. Boineau and Bessie Tripett. Raised in Camden, he was educated in public schools and attended the Citadel from 1941 to 1943. During World War II he served as a navy fighter pilot in the Pacific.

Returning to Columbia in 1945, Boineau joined the family's trucking company, engaged in local business affairs, and was director of the Columbia Chamber of Commerce from 1956 to 1958. In the 1950s he was active in Richland County politics, and following his involvement in the group South Carolina Democrats for Nixon in 1960, he affiliated with the state's fledgling Republican Party.

In early 1961 a vacancy occurred in the county's S.C. House of Representatives delegation, requiring a special off-year election to fill the unexpired term. Although a Republican had not held a seat in the General Assembly since 1902, local party leaders moved quickly to recruit Boineau as their candidate. He faced Joe Berry, Jr., who gained ballot access by petition but had the official backing of the Richland County Democratic organization. A third candidate, W. R. Hanahan, waged a write-in campaign.

At the outset, Boineau pledged to run his own campaign on national issues. He focused on President John Kennedy's "New Frontier," arguing that the administration's policies were taking the country "down the road to socialism." His effort was largely financed from small contributions, although Spartanburg textile executive Roger Milliken personally funded one-tenth of his expenses. Boineau also relied on a business-oriented political action committee for support.

In the August 8 election, Boineau won handily with fifty-five percent of the vote. He ran strongest in white precincts in Columbia, while Joe Berry, his principal opponent, received disproportionate support from black precincts and in the county's less urbanized areas. In victory, Boineau said that he had "proved that 'Republican' is not a bad word" in South Carolina. The story of his election was reported around the world, and he received hundreds of congratulatory notes and telephone calls from throughout the country. "You did it!" wrote Republican U.S. Senator Barry Goldwater of Arizona. "You will go down in history as the first Republican to crack the solid ranks of the Democrats in South Carolina."

In 1962 Boineau sought reelection, this time running with a full slate of Republican House candidates, but all were defeated. In 1964 he was again a candidate for the S.C. House of Representatives but was again unsuccessful. The same year he was a delegate to the Republican national convention in San Francisco that nominated Barry Goldwater for president.

After his elected service, Boineau and his wife, Elizabeth Boatright Boineau, resided in Columbia. He died in Columbia June 1, 2005, and was buried in the columbarium of Trinity Episcopal Cathedral, Columbia. NEAL D. THIGPEN

Boineau, Charles Evans, Jr. Papers. Modern Political Collections, South Caroliniana Library, University of South Carolina, Columbia.

Kalk, Bruce H. *The Origins of the Southern Strategy: Two-Party Competition in South Carolina, 1950–1972.* Lanham, Md.: Lexington Books, 2001.

Sampson, Gregory B. "The Rise of the 'New' Republican Party in South Carolina, 1948–1974: A Case Study of Political Change in the Deep South." Ph.D. diss., University of North Carolina at Chapel Hill, 1984.

Bolden, Charles Frank, Jr. (b. 1946). Soldier, astronaut. Bolden was born in Columbia on August 19, 1946, the son of Charles Bolden, a high school teacher and football coach, and Ethel M. Bolden, a high school librarian. He graduated from C. A. Johnson High School in 1964. He received a B.S. degree in electrical science from the United States Naval Academy (1968) and an M.S. in systems management from the University of Southern California (1977). Bolden married Alexis "Jackie" Walker of Columbia on June 8, 1968. They have two children.

Charles Bolden. Courtesy, NASA

Bolden became a naval aviator in 1970 and flew more than one hundred combat missions from 1972 to 1973 during the Vietnam War. In 1979 Bolden graduated from the U.S. Naval Test Pilot School. The following year he was selected by the National Aeronautics and Space Administration (NASA) for training, and he became an astronaut in August 1981. Bolden is a veteran of four space flights. In January 1986 he served as part of the crew of the space shuttle *Columbia,* which deployed the SATCOM KU satellite, and performed experiments in astrophysics and materials processing. Four years later, in April 1990, Bolden piloted the space shuttle *Discovery,* whose crew deployed the Hubble Space Telescope.

In March 1992 Bolden commanded the space shuttle *Atlantis.* Among its other accomplishments, the crew operated the Atmospheric Laboratory for Applications and Science Cargo (ATLAS-1), a series of experiments that measured the physical and chemical composition of Earth's atmosphere. Following his third space mission, Bolden was selected to serve as the assistant deputy administrator of NASA at its Washington, D.C., headquarters. He returned to the space shuttle program two years later in February 1994 as commander of the first joint U.S.-Russian space shuttle mission on his second flight aboard the space shuttle *Discovery.* The mission carried the Space Habitation Module-2 and the Wake Shield Facility-01 and conducted joint U.S.-Russian scientific experiments. On completion of his fourth shuttle mission, Bolden had logged more than 680 hours in space.

Bolden left NASA in 1994 to return to operational duty in the U.S. Marine Corps as deputy commandant of midshipmen at the Naval Academy. He subsequently served in a variety of command positions. He served as deputy commander, U.S. Forces, Japan, from 1998 to 2000. In August 2000 he was named commanding general of the Third Marine Aircraft Wing at the Marine Corps Air Station Miramar in San Diego, California. Bolden has received military and NASA decorations, including the Distinguished Flying Cross, and holds honorary doctorates from several institutions, including the University of South Carolina and Winthrop University. MARY S. MILLER

Bond Bill (1929). The 1929 Highway Bond Bill authorized the State Highway Commission to sell bonds to build a system of hard-surfaced roads throughout the state. Beginning with the creation of the State Highway Commission in 1917, state officials had used available gas tax revenue to build roads on a pay-as-you-go basis. This proved to be a slow process, and lowcountry legislators decided to have the state borrow funds to undertake a major road-building campaign. Legislators from the upcountry opposed the concept, as many of their counties had already built roads with local funds. They recognized that as the most populous and most heavily industrialized region of the state, they would bear most of the cost while the lowcountry would reap most of the benefit. However, lowcountry legislators dominated the General Assembly, and they used their power to secure passage.

The 1929 Bond Bill pledged automobile license tag and gas tax revenue to repay the bonds, and as such, the bonds did not count against the state's debt limit. The state supreme court, in an en banc session in which the five justices sat with the fourteen circuit judges, upheld the constitutionality of the act. The circuit judges, who traveled the state's deplorable roads more frequently, outvoted the supreme court justices. By 1932, when the entire state budget was only about $8 million, the Highway Commission had sold nearly $50 million in bonds.

The Bond Bill created a state agency, the Highway Department, which was financially independent of the General Assembly and beyond the control of future governors. The fight over the Bond Bill of 1929 marked another of the occasional struggles between upcountry and lowcountry legislators, and was a precursor to the struggle in 1935, when Governor Olin Johnston called out the National Guard in an unsuccessful bid to wrest control of the Highway Department from its politically powerful leader, Ben Sawyer. The highway building campaign also represented an early state effort to promote industrial development in the lowcountry. R. PHILLIP STONE II

Carlton, David L. "Unbalanced Growth and Industrialization: The Case of South Carolina." In *Developing Dixie: Modernization in a Traditional Society,* edited by Winfred B. Moore, Jr., Joseph F. Tripp, and Lyon G. Tyler, Jr. Westport, Conn.: Greenwood, 1988.

Moore, John Hammond. *The South Carolina Highway Department, 1917–1987.* Columbia: University of South Carolina Press, 1987.

Bonham, James Butler (1807–1836). Soldier. Bonham was born in Edgefield District on February 20, 1807, the son of James Bonham and Sophia Butler Smith. He was expelled from South Carolina College in 1827 for participating in a protest over the quality of the food served at the college boardinghouse. He then studied law and set up practice in Pendleton in 1830. During the nullification crisis of 1832 he commanded an artillery company in Charleston, but by 1834 he was practicing law in Montgomery, Alabama. When the Texas revolution broke out, Bonham went to Mobile and helped raise the Mobile Greys, volunteers for service in Texas. On December 1, 1835, he wrote to Sam Houston offering to serve without pay, land, or rations. He was commissioned a second lieutenant in the Texas cavalry, although he never served in an organized unit. In late December he was practicing law in Brazoria.

Bonham rode with James Bowie into San Antonio de Béxar and the Alamo in early January 1836. About February 16, 1836, Bonham was sent by Lieutenant Colonel William Travis with letters requesting reinforcements. Bonham was unable to convince Colonel James W. Fannin to act, but he did return with a letter written on March 1, 1836, by Major Robert M. "Three-Legged Willie" Williamson promising help and urging Travis to hold out. On March 3 Bonham dashed through the Mexican lines and carried this letter into the Alamo. Williamson's promise raised the spirits of the defenders, but it was too late. On March 6 Santa Anna ordered the final attack, and Bonham, along with six other South Carolinians, died defending the Alamo. The town of Bonham, Texas, was named in his honor. JACK ALLEN MEYER

Groneman, Bill. *Alamo Defenders: A Genealogy, the People and Their Words.* Austin, Tex.: Eakin, 1990.

Nofi, Albert A. *The Alamo and the Texas War of Independence, September 30, 1835 to April 21, 1836: Heroes, Myths, and History.* Conshohocken, Pa.: Combined Books, 1992.

Roberts, Randy, and James S. Olson. *A Line in the Sand: The Alamo in Blood and Memory.* New York: Free Press, 2001.

Bonham, Milledge Luke (1813–1890). Soldier, congressman, governor. Born on December 25, 1813, in Edgefield District near the present town of Saluda, Bonham was the eighth child of James Bonham and Sophie Butler Smith. He attended local academies in Edgefield and entered South Carolina College as a junior in 1833. His studies imbued him with the ardent states' rights position of the college's president at that time, Thomas Cooper. After graduating as valedictorian in 1834, he returned home to manage the family plantations and study law. He volunteered for the Seminole War in 1836 and was a staff officer.

Admitted to the bar in 1837, Bonham gained prominence as an attorney and militia officer. By 1843 Bonham had been elected a major general in the state militia, a position he held until 1852. Between 1840 and 1843 he served in the S.C. House of Representatives from Edgefield District. On November 13, 1845, he married Ann Patience Griffin. They had fourteen children. Appointed a lieutenant colonel in the U.S. Army in 1847, Bonham saw action in Mexico and was wounded on August 20, 1847. Promoted to colonel, he served as an occupational governor until being mustered out on July 25, 1848.

Bonham was elected solicitor of the state's southern circuit in 1848. He held this position until elected to the U.S. House of Representatives in 1857, filling the seat left vacant by the death of his cousin Preston Brooks. An active ally of his southern colleagues in Congress, he supported the admission of Kansas as a slave state and opposed the Morrill Bill, which would have used federal funds to support land-grant colleges in the states. Following South Carolina's secession, Bonham withdrew from Congress on December 21, 1860. Appointed commander in chief of the South Carolina army with the rank of major general on February 23, 1861, he agreed to serve under General P. G. T. Beauregard during the Fort Sumter crisis. On April 23 Bonham received an appointment as brigadier general in the Confederate army and led the first brigade of South Carolina troops to Virginia. Although commended for his actions during the First Battle of Manassas, Bonham resigned his commission in January 1862 over questions of seniority.

Elected to the Confederate Congress in the fall of 1861, Bonham generally opposed the administration of Jefferson Davis. A dark horse candidate for governor, he was elected on December 17, 1862. As governor, Bonham sought to strengthen state laws on conscription, slave impressments, and desertion, taking positions more in support of the Confederate government. The constant military threat against the state during his term compelled regular militia reorganizations and ardent appeals for veteran Confederate troops for coastal defenses.

Bonham left office at the end of 1864 and received a brigadier general commission on February 9, 1865. However, he was unable to take the field before the war ended. He declined to serve in the 1865 constitutional convention but served in the S.C. House of Representatives from October 1865 until December 1866. A member of the Taxpayer's Convention in 1871, Bonham was a strong supporter of Wade Hampton's campaign for governor in 1876. He became South Carolina's first railroad commissioner in 1878 and worked to strengthen the powers of the commission. He died at White Sulphur Springs, Virginia, on August 27, 1890, and was buried in Elmwood Cemetery, Columbia. PATRICK MCCAWLEY

Bonham, Milledge Luke. Papers. South Caroliniana Library, University of South Carolina, Columbia.

Cauthen, Charles E. *South Carolina Goes to War, 1860–1865.* Chapel Hill: University of North Carolina Press, 1950.

Bonnet, Stede (1688–1718). Pirate. Bonnet was christened in Christ Church Parish, Barbados, on July 29, 1688, the son of Edward Bonnet, a planter, and Sarah Whetstone. Establishing his residence in St. Michael's Parish, Bonnet married Mary Allamby on November 21, 1709, and they had three children. A major in the local militia, Bonnet was a member of the island's planter elite until 1717, when he purchased and armed the sloop *Revenge* and left his family to pursue a career as a pirate.

Bonnet sailed north to prey upon the crowded sea-lanes of the North American coastline, plundering ships from Chesapeake Bay to New York and then off Charleston, South Carolina. After refitting at the remote Cape Fear Inlet, Bonnet headed toward the Caribbean, where a clash with a Spanish man-of-war left him wounded and the *Revenge* badly damaged. Bonnet met Blackbeard at New Providence Island, Bahamas, and brought him aboard to command the *Revenge* while Bonnet recuperated. In October, on a foray north to Delaware Bay, the pirates despoiled eleven vessels. After Blackbeard seized the powerfully armed ship that he named *Queen Anne's Revenge,* the pirate captains separated until a chance rendezvous in March 1718 off the central American Spanish Main. Having suffered a recent defeat, Bonnet relinquished his command of *Revenge* and joined Blackbeard aboard *Queen Anne's Revenge.* Augmenting their flotilla with two sloops, Blackbeard and Bonnet returned to the Carolinas, arriving off Charleston in mid-May 1718.

During a weeklong blockade of the important colonial port, numerous vessels were looted and hostages seized and held for a ransom of valuable medicines. The pirates then sailed to refit off the isolated coast of North Carolina, where *Revenge* and a small sloop safely entered Beaufort Inlet but *Queen Anne's Revenge* and *Adventure* wrecked.

Bonnet received a royal pardon from North Carolina governor Charles Eden at Bath, resumed command of *Revenge,* and went to sea with a crew gathered at Beaufort from men marooned by Blackbeard. Bonnet returned to piracy, using aliases and renaming his sloop *Royal James.* Off Virginia and Delaware Bay, he reaped a rich harvest of thirteen prizes in two months. By mid-August, Bonnet had sailed his four-vessel flotilla to his Cape Fear lair for lengthy repairs. Escaped prisoners raised the alarm at Charleston, which had recently suffered another humiliating blockade by the infamous pirate Charles Vane. An aroused Governor Robert Johnson responded with a provincial naval force of the armed sloops *Henry* and *Sea Nymph,* commanded by the capable Colonel William Rhett. Rhett entered the Cape Fear River at dusk on September 26. The next morning a fierce six-hour battle was fought with cannons and small arms, ending with the surrender of Bonnet and his remaining men. Rhett returned to Charleston with thirty-six prisoners, "to the great Joy of the whole Province of Carolina."

While awaiting trial, Bonnet escaped on October 24 and hid on Sullivan's Island until he was recaptured on November 6 by Colonel Rhett and returned to Charleston. Meanwhile, on October 28 Bonnet's crew were tried before Chief Justice Nicholas Trott, and all but three were found guilty. On November 8 most of Bonnet's condemned crew were executed. Bonnet's trial opened on November 10. He was convicted and was hanged on December 10, 1718, at White Point (now the Battery, Charleston). LINDLEY S. BUTLER

Butler, Lindley S. *Pirates, Privateers, and Rebel Raiders of the Carolina Coast.* Chapel Hill: University of North Carolina Press, 2000.

Leland, John G. *Stede Bonnet: "Gentleman Pirate" of the Carolina Coast.* Charleston, S.C.: Charleston Reproductions, 1972.

Rankin, Hugh F. *The Golden Age of Piracy.* Williamsburg, Va.: Colonial Williamsburg, 1969.

Boone, Thomas (ca. 1730–1812). Governor. Of all South Carolina's royal governors, only one, Thomas Boone, could be counted as a "native son." Although born in England in 1730 or 1731 and educated at Eton and Cambridge, Boone had strong hereditary ties to South Carolina. His father, Charles, a London merchant and member of Parliament, was the nephew of Joseph Boone, a leading politician of proprietary South Carolina. His mother, Elizabeth Garth, was a descendant of one of South Carolina's founding families, the Colletons. Boone first traveled to South Carolina in 1752 to claim Boone's Barony, a plantation in St. Bartholomew's Parish that he inherited from his great-uncle Joseph. He returned to England two years later but in 1758 departed again for South Carolina with the idea of settling. He married a South Carolinian, Sarah Ann (Tattnall) Peronneau. The couple had no children.

Through the influence of relatives in Parliament, Boone in late 1759 was appointed governor of New Jersey, where he proved popular and his administration was characterized as "publickly kind and benevolent." Because of his harmonious tenure in New Jersey, as well as his Carolina connections, Boone appeared to be a likely candidate for the Board of Trade's most difficult assignment: the governorship of South Carolina. The colony's Commons House of Assembly frequently clashed with its governors and was rapidly acquiring power at the expense of royal prerogative.

Boone arrived in Charleston in December 1761 to a population satisfied with the appointment of one of their own as governor. However, Boone quickly dashed any hope of a peaceful administration. His instructions from the Board of Trade directed him to obtain a revision of the Election Act of 1721 and thereby check the power of the Commons House of Assembly. When Boone raised the question, the Commons received it coldly. He therefore made the impolitic decision to force the issue and punish the Commons for refusing to grant the sought-after revision. In September 1762 Boone charged that the assemblyman Christopher Gadsden had been elected illegally, and Boone refused to administer the oath of office. When the Commons seated Gadsden anyway, Boone dissolved the assembly. When a new assembly convened in November 1762, it resolved not to conduct any business until the governor apologized and acknowledged the right of the Commons to judge the qualifications of its members. Boone stubbornly refused, and the ensuing gridlock brought government to a virtual standstill. Boone tried to gain allies by doling out warrants for land south of the Altamaha River in Georgia (which South Carolina claimed under its proprietary charter), but the damage was done. England was at war with France and needed the full cooperation of her colonies. Boone gave up his struggle and left South Carolina in May 1764. Two months later the Board of Trade admonished him for acting with "more Zeal than Prudence."

Boone spent the remainder of his life in England. In December 1769 he received an appointment as a commissioner of customs, an office he held until 1805. He died at his home in Kent on September 25, 1812. MATTHEW A. LOCKHART

Greene, Jack P. "The Gadsden Election Controversy and the Revolutionary Movement in South Carolina." *Mississippi Valley Historical Review* 46 (December 1959): 469–92.

Namier, L. B. "Charles Garth and His Connexions." *English Historical Review* 54 (July 1939): 443–70.

Sirmans, M. Eugene. *Colonial South Carolina: A Political History, 1663–1763.* Chapel Hill: University of North Carolina Press, 1966.

Boonesborough Township. Boonesborough was one in the second wave of townships that South Carolina laid out during the mid-eighteenth century to defend her frontier from the Cherokee. Patrick Calhoun, father of John C. Calhoun, surveyed the 20,500-acre township on the headwaters of Long Cane Creek in 1762. The Cherokee Path crossed near the center of the township, and its northwestern corner approached the present-day town of Due West in Abbeville County. Boonesborough lay between the Carolinians and the Lower Cherokee towns. The majority of the settlers were Irish or Scots-Irish, many of whom came in response to the Bounty Act of 1761, which authorized free land and other settlement incentives.

The genesis of Boonesborough Township lay in the 1761 petition of John Pouag, the Reverend John Baxter, John Greg, John Rae, and David Rae for a grant of forty thousand acres to be reserved for the settlement of Irish immigrants. Pouag and Greg were merchants of Charleston and London, respectively, while Baxter had brought settlers from Belfast to Williamsburg Township. Governor Thomas Boone, for whom the township was named, and the Royal Council authorized the petitioners to select sites for two townships. One became Boonesborough (sometimes called Belfast), and the other became Londonborough. At least sixteen immigrants had land surveyed in the township in 1763, and others followed in 1764 and

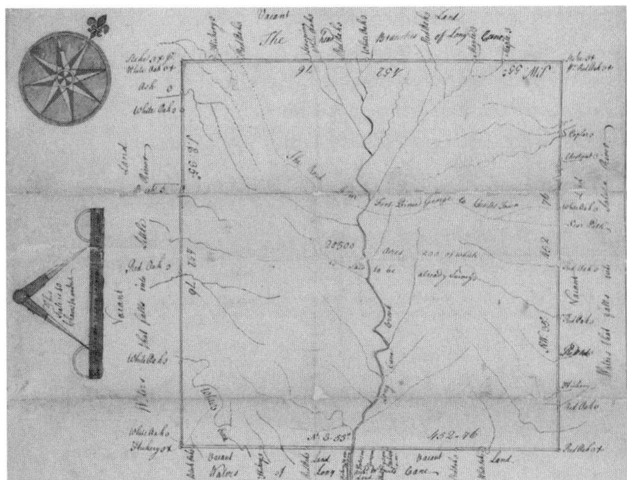

The 1762 plat for Boonesborough Township. Courtesy, South Carolina Department of Archives and History

1765. Surnames for the early settlers included Seawright, Brown, Hawthorn, Baxter, Templeton, Colvill, McCullough, McCracken, Forsith, Paxton, and Dickson. ALEXIA JONES HELSLEY

Meriwether, Robert L. *The Expansion of South Carolina, 1729–1765.* Kingsport, Tenn.: Southern Publishers, 1940.

Bosc, Louis Augustin Guillaume (1759–1828). Naturalist. Born in Paris, France, on January 29, 1759, Bosc was the son of Paul Bosc d'Antic and Marie-Angélique Lamy d'Hangest. His father was a glassmaker and physician who was acquainted with most of the great naturalists of that time. Louis acquired an interest in natural history at an early age and attended the College of Dijon, but little is known of his studies there.

Bosc joined the French postal service in Paris at age eighteen and began to attend natural history lectures at the Garden of the King, where he met prominent French naturalists such as Buffon and Jussieu. Through them he gained a broad view of the natural world, his interests extending from plants to both vertebrate and invertebrate zoology. At the Garden of the King he also became a friend of the botanist-horticulturist André Michaux. Bosc's first scientific paper, published in 1784, was the description of a new genus among the cochineal insects. During the early 1790s he continued to publish notes on insects, mollusks, birds, and plants. He was active in the French Revolution but lost his position with the postal service. Wishing to escape the turmoil of postrevolutionary France, Bosc decided to visit Michaux at the French Garden of the Republic near Charleston, South Carolina, with the hopes of collecting natural history material while awaiting the possibility of appointment to a consular position in the United States.

Bosc and his fourteen-year-old son, Louis, arrived in Charleston in October 1796, but Bosc was shocked to learn that Michaux had gone to France. With no prospect of working with Michaux, Bosc had to fend for himself and set about collecting natural history specimens. He made frequent trips into the woods and swamps near Charleston and sent specimens and descriptions of mammals, birds, reptiles, amphibians, fish, insects, worms, mollusks, and plants to his colleagues at the Muséum d'Histoire Naturelle in Paris. Among his discoveries were four species of frogs (among them the handsome green tree frog, *Hyla cinerea*), three of turtles, and one species of lizard, found during his stay in Charleston. He also collected three new species of fish in Charleston harbor. He was especially interested in invertebrates, and the names of fourteen new species of coelenterates, mollusks, worms, and crabs that he described from South Carolina are still valid today, among them the familiar fiddler crab (*Uca pugilator*) of coastal salt marshes.

Bosc returned to Paris in 1798 and the following year married his cousin Suzanne Bosc. Among his many publications, the most important was a ten-volume work on the natural history of worms, mollusks, and crustaceans (1802). In 1825 he became a professor at the Muséum d'Histoire Naturelle. An accomplished naturalist who devoted himself to science without thought of personal gain, Bosc was an important figure in his time. He died in Paris on July 10, 1828. ALBERT E. SANDERS

Beale, Georgia R. "Bosc and the Exequatur." *Prologue* 10 (fall 1978): 133–51.

Harper, Francis. "Some Works of Bartram, Daudin, Latreille, and Sonnini, and Their Bearing upon North American Herpetological Nomenclature." *American Midland Naturalist* 23 (May 1940): 692–723.

Hellmayr, C. E. "Louis Bosc, Ornitologue Oublié." *Alauda,* 1st ser., 2d year, no. 2 (April 1930): 122–32.

Sanders, Albert E., and William D. Anderson, Jr. *Natural History Investigations in South Carolina from Colonial Times to the Present.* Columbia: University of South Carolina Press, 1999.

Bouchillon, Christopher Allen (1893–1968). Musician. Although largely forgotten today, Chris Bouchillon probably ranks as South Carolina's first notable country music personality. He was the first person to popularize "the talking blues" form of song delivery. Bouchillon was born on August 21, 1893, in Oconee County. In the early twentieth century his family moved to Greenville, where his father, John, found work at the Mountain City Iron Foundry. The elder Bouchillon played the old-time banjo and taught his sons—Charley, Uris, and Chris—the basics of traditional string-band music. In July 1925 the boys went to Atlanta and made four recordings for the Okeh label as the Bouchillon Trio, but only one of these recordings was ever issued.

In November 1926 Chris returned to Atlanta for the first of six sessions for Columbia Records. His initial effort resulted in "Talking Blues" and "Hannah (Won't You Open That Door)," both of which went on to become highly successful and widely copied numbers that sold nearly 100,000 copies. One of his 1927 recordings, "Born in Hard Luck"/"The Medicine Show," also did quite well, racking up sales in excess of 40,000 at a time when anything that sold more than 20,000 copies could be considered a hit. In all, Bouchillon cut thirty masters for Columbia through October 1928, of which twenty-two were released. On one session his wife assisted on vocals, and his brothers perhaps assisted on another. All of his recorded repertoire could be classified as humor-oriented and probably had origins in vaudeville or minstrel shows.

With the onset of the Great Depression, Bouchillon's recording career terminated. He owned and operated a dry cleaning establishment in Greenville, seemingly without knowledge of how influential his early recordings had been. He spent his last years in obscurity in Florida and is believed to have died in West Palm Beach in September 1968. In 1987 Old Homestead Records of Brighton, Michigan, released a vinyl album containing eighteen of his recordings. IVAN M. TRIBE

The Original Talking Blues Man. Brighton, Mich.: Old Homestead, 1987. Sound recording.

Boudo, Louis (ca. 1786–1827), and **Heloise Boudo** (?–ca. 1837). Silversmiths, goldsmiths, jewelers. Louis and Heloise Boudo were among Charleston's best-known and most successful antebellum silversmiths and jewelers. Louis Boudo arrived in Charleston from Santo Domingo about 1809. He established himself as "goldsmith, jeweler and hairworker" in a brief partnership with Nicholas Maurer before opening his own shop on the corner of Church and Queen Streets. There, in addition to representing himself as a jeweler and watchmaker, he advertised the manufacture of silver spoons and other silver work. Boudo's best-known piece is a silver map case made on behalf of the state of South Carolina for General Lafayette during his farewell tour of America in 1825; this case is now in the Metropolitan Museum of Art. Silver work marked "LS. BOUDO" or "BOUDO" in Roman capitals in a scroll or shaped rectangle includes a decanter label held by the Metropolitan Museum of Art; a pap boat owned by the Museum of Early Southern Decorative Arts in Winston-Salem, North Carolina; and other pieces in the Charleston Museum and private collections. Boudo died in Charleston on January 11, 1827.

In 1811 Louis Boudo married Heloise (Louise) Simonet, the daughter of Eugenie Magniant and Stephen Simonet of Charleston. The marriage produced three children. Following Louis's death, Heloise Boudo administered his estate and continued in the "manufactory of gold and silver work" at various addresses on King Street, paying cash for gold and silver and carrying on the jewelry business "in all its branches." Heloise Boudo's silver work was typically marked with "H. BOUDO" in a rectangle accompanied by three pseudohallmarks. She was one of few female silversmiths in nineteenth-century America, and examples of her work are found in the Charleston Museum, Yale University's Garvan Collection, and private collections. Heloise and Louis Boudo's daughter, Erma LeRoy, continued the jewelry business after her mother's death ca. 1837. MARIE H. NELSON

Burton, E. Milton. *South Carolina Silversmiths 1690–1860.* Revised and edited by Warren Ripley. Charleston, S.C.: Charleston Museum, 1991.

Nelson, Marie. "Heloise Boudo, Charleston Silversmith." In *MESDA 1992 Summer Institute Research Report.* Winston-Salem, N.C.: Museum of Early Southern Decorative Arts, 1992.

Bowater. Headquartered in Greenville, Bowater Incorporated is a world leader in the manufacture of newsprint and coated groundwood papers. The company began in England in 1889 as a family-run paper supply business. In 1924 family members incorporated as Bowater Paper Company and commenced paper manufacturing operations. During the ensuing decades, the company went international by establishing plants in Scandinavia, Canada, and the United States. Bowater opened its first U.S. facility in Calhoun, Tennessee, then set its sights on constructing a massive paper and pulp mill at Catawba in York County, South Carolina. The successful recruitment of Bowater was an early high-water mark in South Carolina's campaign to attract foreign manufacturing, but it also underscored the lengths to which state leaders would go to secure industrial development.

In order to bring Bowater to South Carolina, Governor George Bell Timmerman called a special session of the General Assembly in June 1956, during which he urged legislators to amend state laws in order to encourage the English company to locate in the state. Legislators obliged by rewriting the state's foreign ownership laws, which had limited foreigners to holding no more than 500 acres of land. The revised law permitted Bowater, or any foreign corporation, to acquire as many as 500,000 acres. The state's Pollution Control Authority likewise accommodated Bowater by exempting the company from some recently enacted pollution control standards. Although a few critics accused Timmerman and the General Assembly of selling the state's birthright for "a mess of pottage," the overall reaction to Bowater's arrival in South Carolina was overwhelmingly positive. Construction on the Catawba plant began soon after, and the completed facility was dedicated in 1959.

The Catawba mill produces coated paper, uncoated groundwood paper, and pulp, with a total annual production capacity of 982,000 short tons. Catawba's Pulp Mill No. 2 reached a milestone of 2 million tons in 1996. Its Pulp Mill No. 3 is the largest coated groundwood machine in North America. The relationship between Bowater and South Carolina was further strengthened in 1993, when the company moved its North American headquarters to Greenville. RICK D. BOULWARE

Cobb, James C. *The Selling of the South: The Southern Crusade for Industrial Development, 1936–1980.* Baton Rouge: Louisiana State University Press, 1982.

Reader, W. J. *Bowater: A History.* New York: Cambridge University Press, 1981.

Bowles, Crandall Close (b. 1947). Businesswoman. In 1998 Bowles began serving as chair and chief executive officer (CEO) of Springs Industries, whose corporate headquarters are in Fort Mill. Born in Fort Mill on October 16, 1947, she was the first of eight children of H. William Close and Anne Kingsley Springs. A direct descendent of the textile manufacturing pioneers Samuel Elliott White and Leroy Springs, Bowles is the fifth generation to run Springs Industries. As a CEO, Bowles is regularly ranked among the top women executives in the country.

Bowles earned a B.A. in economics from Wellesley College in 1969 and an M.B.A. from Columbia University. Her first employment was in New York, where she worked as a statistician for Morgan Stanley & Co. In 1971 she married Erskine B. Bowles, a North Carolinian she had met at Morgan Stanley. They moved to Charlotte, North Carolina, in 1972, where he built an investment bank and they raised their three children. Erskine Bowles would go on to serve as White House chief of staff during the presidential administration of William Clinton.

Prior to becoming CEO, Crandall Bowles was a financial analyst for Springs Industries and executive vice president and later president of Springs Company, the Close family's investment management arm. According to *Business Week,* "For a decade, she ran the $700 million Close family fortune, and she still leads her mother and seven siblings in overseeing the real estate, insurance, and railroad holdings that complement a controlling stake in . . . Springs." She later received more extensive training by serving posts in corporate planning, textile manufacturing, and bath products for Springs Industries before becoming its president and chief operating officer in 1997. RICK D. BOULWARE

Barker, Robert, Richard S. Dunham, and Nicole Harris. "Just Which One Is the 'Other' Bowles?" *Business Week* 3532 (June 23, 1997): 131–33.

Boyce, James Petigru (1827–1888). Minister, educator. Boyce was born in Charleston on January 11, 1827, to Ker Boyce, a cotton merchant, and Amanda Jane Caroline Johnston. James Petigru Boyce was intellectually gifted and graduated from Brown University in 1847. Soon after his graduation, he experienced a religious conversion and worked as an editor of the *Southern Baptist* in Charleston. He attended Princeton Theological Seminary for two years and then returned to South Carolina in 1851 to become a pastor at the Baptist Church in Columbia.

Boyce soon returned to the academy, accepting a position at Furman University as professor of theology in 1855. On December 20, 1858, he married Lizzie Llewellyn Ficklen of Washington, Georgia. While at Furman, Boyce became interested in the idea of establishing an independent seminary. Southern Baptists had been considering a separate theological institution after their split from northern Baptists in 1845. Boyce gave a speech before the state convention of South Carolina Baptists in 1856, arguing for the necessity of a separate Baptist seminary. In response, the convention proposed to put forth $100,000 toward the endowment of a seminary located in Greenville if the same sum was raised by others.

At the Southern Baptists' Educational Convention held in Louisville in May 1857, the proposal from the South Carolina Baptists was accepted, and Boyce went about the task of securing the money. The institution opened in 1859 as the Southern Baptist Theological Seminary, and Boyce served as its first president.

Like his father and his namesake, James L. Petigru, Boyce opposed secession. He ran for election to what became the Secession Convention of December 1860 as an antisecession candidate, along with Benjamin F. Perry. Boyce was defeated, and in the fall of 1861 he joined a regiment being raised by his friend Charles J. Elford, in which he served as chaplain. The following year Boyce left the seminary and went to the coast with his regiment, but he resigned that May. In October he was elected to the S.C. House of Representatives to represent Greenville District. He lost an election to the Confederate Congress in 1863 but was reelected to the state legislature in 1864 and served until the end of the Civil War. He also served as aide-de-camp to Governor Andrew Magrath, with the rank of lieutenant colonel. Just before the burning of Columbia, Boyce accompanied Magrath to Charlotte, North Carolina.

After the Civil War, Boyce returned to the seminary and attempted to place it on sound financial footing. In 1872 the decision was made to move the seminary to Louisville, Kentucky. That same year Boyce was elected president of the Southern Baptist Convention, a position he held until 1879 and then again in 1888. He continued to teach at the seminary, but his declining health led him to travel in Europe. He died in Pau, France, on December 28, 1888, and was buried at Cave Hill Cemetery in Louisville.

In 1974 the Southern Baptist Theological Seminary named Boyce Bible School, which offered associate of arts degrees, in Boyce's honor. In 1998 the school was renamed Boyce College and began offering bachelor's degrees. AARON W. MARRS

Broadus, John Albert. *Memoir of James Petigru Boyce, D.D., LL.D.: Late President of the Southern Baptist Theological Seminary, Louisville, Ky.* New York: A.C. Armstrong and Son, 1893.

Boyce, Ker (1787–1854). Merchant, bank president. Boyce was born on April 8, 1787, in Newberry District, the son of John Boyce and Elizabeth Miller. Possessed of little formal education, he entered trade as a clerk in a store operated by the merchant John McMorries. He opened his own store in Newberry in 1814, from which he conducted a profitable overland trade with the city of Philadelphia. Around June 1815 he married Nancy Johnston, the daughter of his Newberry business mentor, John Johnston. They had four children. Following Nancy's death in 1823, he married her sister, Amanda Jane Johnston, despite the disapproval of his Presbyterian congregation. His second marriage produced five children before Amanda's death in 1837.

Although prospering as a young upcountry merchant, Boyce left Newberry in 1817 and opened a store on King Street in Charleston in partnership with his brother-in-law, Samuel Johnston. As had Boyce's earlier business ventures, this one soon thrived. The partnership established a factorage and commission house on East Bay around 1825, which, despite the death of Johnston and temporary setbacks, made Boyce a wealthy man and an influential member of Charleston's business community. Wealth begot wealth, as Boyce invested the profits from his East Bay business into a series of other business enterprises, including the Bank of Charleston, the Charleston Hotel, a commercial block on Hayne Street, the Graniteville Manufacturing Company, and several insurance, railroad, and manufacturing enterprises. He served as president of the Bank of Charleston from 1837 to 1841, successfully guiding the institution through the financial turmoil that followed the Panic of 1837. At various times from the 1820s to the 1850s, he sat on the boards of several of the leading business enterprises in the state, including the South Carolina Railroad and the Bank of the State of South Carolina. He was president of the Charleston Chamber of Commerce from 1840 to 1846.

An active participant in state and local politics, Boyce represented Charleston in the S.C. House of Representatives from 1832 to 1839 and in the S.C. Senate from 1840 to 1847. In the General Assembly he was an influential advocate for the state's commercial interests. He also played a key role in providing John C. Calhoun with the backing of many of the city's leading bankers, including James Gadsden and Henry W. Conner. Although Democrats, this financial triumvirate also helped direct the movement to support the Whig candidate for president in 1848, Zachary Taylor.

By the time of his death, Boyce was one of the wealthiest men in South Carolina and the entire South, despite the fact that he owned only a handful of slaves and had no planting interests. An inventory of his estate listed stocks, bonds, and notes totaling almost $1 million and real property worth more than $160,000. Boyce died in Columbia on March 19, 1854. TOM DOWNEY

Bailey, N. Louise, Mary L. Morgan, and Carolyn R. Taylor, eds. *Biographical Directory of the South Carolina Senate, 1776–1985.* 3 vols. Columbia: University of South Carolina Press, 1986.

O'Neall, John Belton. *Annals of Newberry, Historical, Biographical, and Anecdotical.* Charleston, S.C.: S. G. Courtnay, 1859.

Stoney, Samuel Gaillard. *The Story of South Carolina's Senior Bank.* Columbia, S.C.: R. L. Bryan, 1955.

Boyd, Blanche McCrary (b. 1945). Writer, educator. Boyd was born in Charleston on August 31, 1945, the daughter of Charles Fant McCrary and Mildred McDaniel. She attended Duke University, earned her B.A. from Pomona College in 1967, and received a Wallace Stegner Fellowship from Stanford University, where she completed her M.A. in 1971. Boyd joined the faculty at Connecticut College in 1982. In 1988 she was awarded a National Endowment for the Arts Fiction Fellowship. Four years later she received the Lambda Literary Award for her novel *The Revolution of Little Girls,* and in 1993–1994 she received a Guggenheim Fellowship.

Boyd has published four novels: *Nerves* (1973), *Mourning the Death of Magic* (1977), *The Revolution of Little Girls* (1991), and *Terminal Velocity* (1997). The last two are part of a trilogy telling the story of Ellen Burns, a Charleston native who experiences an unsatisfying marriage, experiments with heavy drinking and drugs, and loses herself through various affairs and lifestyle changes. Part three of the trilogy is titled "Children of Nod." While each novel can be read on its own, Boyd explains that they are ultimately meant to be viewed together, "like transparencies that alone show complete images, but reveal a unique perspective when combined."

Boyd's fiction reveals a deep concern with the culture of the South. Much of her work addresses civil rights injustices or gender-identity issues within southern culture. *Mourning* is about three girls raised in the South during the 1950s and 1960s who are disillusioned with racism and class discrimination. Boyd's 1981 collection of essays, *The Redneck Way of Knowledge: Down-Home Tales,* features autobiographical accounts of the South Carolina world she knows well. One critic described Boyd's literary voice as "wild, original, witty, imaginative . . . the direct, buckshot explosion of a lady redneck turned narrator." Boyd is known for capturing both the tumult of a time period and a region's response to such social change.

Boyd's work has won wide recognition. The *Atlanta Journal-Constitution* praised *The Revolution of Little Girls* as "Funny . . . lively and wry, insightful and poignant. [A] psychedelic and unsettling journey into a Southern heart of darkness." A reviewer for *Publishers Weekly* said that Boyd has "established a solid reputation as one of America's most unpredictable literary outlaws." Such attention to the more controversial issues within her writing is balanced with compliments on the craft of her fiction. Her work has also been published in periodicals such as *Esquire, New York Times Magazine, Premiere,* and *Voice Literary Supplement.* Divorced in 1971, Boyd created a life partnership with Leslie Hyman in 1999, and the couple has two children. AMY L. WHITE

Cole, Clarence Bard. "The Revelations of Blanche McCrary Boyd." *Christopher Street* 14 (October 1991): 11.

Gordon, Emily. "Terminal Velocity." *The Nation* 265 (September 1997): 32.

Schuessler, Jennifer. "Blanche McCrary Boyd: Writing Against Gravity." *Publishers Weekly* 244 (June 1997): 64.

Boykin spaniel. The Boykin spaniel was originally bred in South Carolina before the 1920s. This amiable, small, dark brown retriever is a superb hunter and loving family pet. It was bred to provide an ideal dog for hunting fowl in the swamps along the Wateree River, which demanded a sturdy, compact dog built for boat travel and capable of retrieving on land or water. Lemuel Whitaker "Whit" Boykin, a planter and sportsman from the Boykin community near Camden, tested many dogs to answer these needs. With luck and selective breeding, the multipurpose retriever was being bred to type by the 1920s. The precursor of the breed was reportedly a stray spaniel-type dog that befriended Spartanburg banker Alexander L. White around 1905. After the spunky dog showed an aptitude for retrieving, White sent the dog, called "Dumpy," to his friend and hunting partner Whit Boykin. In Boykin's hands this little stray developed into a superb turkey dog and waterfowl retriever. The popularity of the breed grew steadily, and the Boykin's ability in the field and amiable nature brought the dog praise in all forms. The Boykin Spaniel Society was founded, with headquarters in Camden, in 1977 and counted 2,544 human members by 2000. In that same year the official Boykin spaniel registry, begun in 1979, listed 16,285 Boykins in forty-nine states and many foreign countries. On March 26, 1985, Governor Richard Riley signed into law an act making the Boykin spaniel the official South Carolina state dog. MIKE CREEL

A Boykin spaniel in the field. Photograph by Robert Clark. Courtesy, South Carolina Department of Natural Resources

Creel, Mike, and Lynn Kelley. *The Boykin Spaniel: South Carolina's Dog.* Columbia, S.C.: Summerhouse, 1997.

Bragg, Laura (1881–1978). Museum administrator, educator. Born in Northbridge, Massachusetts, on October 9, 1881, Bragg was the daughter of Reverend Lyman Bragg and Sarah Klotz. Deaf by the age of six, Bragg was educated by private tutors but attended public high schools. A member of Simmons College's first graduating class of 1906, she earned a degree in library science. Her first professional positions were in Maine and at the New York City Library.

Laura Bragg. Courtesy, South Carolina Historical Society

Hired by Dr. Paul Rea in 1909 to be the Charleston Museum's librarian, Bragg was soon promoted to curator of books and public instruction. Seeing herself as an educator and social missionary, she used her position to cross both racial and class lines with her educational program, the first in a southern museum. She developed a southern nature study course and created traveling school exhibits to illustrate it. These portable wooden boxes opened to display nature or cultural scenes and included teachers' stories. By 1913 the museum began providing them to the city's private and public schools—both black and white. Recognizing the educational value of Bragg's work, the school board required teachers to take their classes to the museum weekly and to use her curriculum and exhibits. These educational tools became so well known that the museum sent them to black and white schools in Charleston County and across the state. They were also used to train teachers at the state's normal schools.

In October 1920 Bragg was named director of the Charleston Museum and became the first woman in the country to hold such a position at a publicly supported museum. Soon thereafter she opened the museum to black patrons one afternoon a week. She continued the educational focus of the museum and added a children's library and a reading room that lent books. These efforts were the forerunners of the Charleston Free Library, which opened in January 1931. She was both its trustee and its first librarian.

Bragg's other efforts included preserving the state's cultural history, such as Edgefield pottery, and she was instrumental in the purchase and restoration of the Heyward-Washington House. She influenced the development of museums across the Southeast through a field study conducted for the American Association of Museums (AAM). As a result of this work, she was named to the governing board of the AAM and taught museum administration at Columbia University for three years.

Bragg was among the six founders of the Poetry Society of South Carolina and a founder of the Southern States Art League and of the Southern Museum Conference. She was named to the first edition of *Women in America* in 1923, to *Who's Who among North American Authors* in 1925, and to the 1974 edition of the *Standard Biographical Dictionary of Notable Women.*

In 1931 Bragg became the director of the Berkshire Museum in Massachusetts. Her modern-art exhibits and education program garnered national attention in the *New York Times,* the *New Yorker,* and *Art Digest.* Bragg retired to Charleston in 1939, where she lived until her death on May 16, 1978. LOUISE ALLEN

Allen, Louise Anderson. *A Bluestocking in Charleston: The Life and Career of Laura Bragg.* Columbia: University of South Carolina Press, 2001.

Brainerd Institute. A historically black primary, secondary, and normal school located in Chester, Brainerd Institute was one of the first educational institutions for newly freed African Americans following the Civil War. Under the guidance of the Freedmen's Bureau, E. E. Richmond, a white woman from New York City, opened a school in a log cabin on the abandoned Brawley Plantation just outside of Chester. The school soon moved inside city limits, with Richmond and Carolyn I. Kent of New Jersey providing instruction. Typical of Freedmen's Bureau–sponsored schools, the institute offered classes during the day, at night, and on Sunday for both former slaves and poor whites. The school would become atypical in later years, however, by emphasizing a liberal arts education rather than the industrial and agricultural arts stressed at most African American institutions.

With the end of the Freedmen's Bureau, the school found a new sponsor in the Board of Missions of the New York Presbyterian Church. Reverend Samuel Loomis, sent by the board, joined with Richmond and Kent to offer religious and educational instruction. Loomis named the school Brainerd Mission in honor of George Brainerd, a pioneer missionary to Native Americans. The Brainerd school experienced steady growth, teaching an average of 145 pupils per year in grades one through ten. In 1888 it moved to DeGraffenried Place, a ten-acre site in Chester. The institute gained its first black leader, J. D. Martin, in 1928. Brainerd Junior College opened in 1934 to train teachers. Both institutions closed in 1939, citing increased public school opportunities for blacks and financial strains. The actress Phylicia Rashad, daughter of an alumna, purchased the former campus in 1997 and began restoration work on the only surviving building, Kumler Hall. CARYN E. NEUMANN

Purvis, Michelle Dawn Gammon. "The Brainerd Institute: An Example of the Contributions of the Presbyterian Church, U.S.A. to African-American Education." Constance B. Schulz Collection, South Caroliniana Library, University of South Carolina, Columbia.

Branchville (Orangeburg County; 2000 pop. 1,083). Incorporated in 1858, Branchville is known as Orangeburg County's "railroad town" because of its recognition as the oldest railroad junction in the world. The South Carolina Canal and Rail Road Company completed its track to Branchville from Charleston on November 7, 1832. From this place, the railroad would later branch off to serve Columbia. This was not the first time that travelers had to choose a route at Branchville. The spot was also where a trail used by Native Americans split at a massive oak tree, with branches leading to the modern towns of North Augusta and Orangeburg. The first European settlers, led by Andrew Frederick of Prussia, arrived shortly after 1734 at the spot where the trail split.

For more than a century, railroad passenger service was the economic stimulus for Branchville. Every September, Branchville's railroad history comes to the forefront during "Raylrode Daze Festivul," a weekend event that centers around the town's historic railroad depot/museum. Since passenger service was terminated in 1962, the town's economy has been mainly dependent on agriculture. At the beginning of the twenty-first century, Branchville experienced growth in its retail community with the addition of several new businesses. Branchville Wood Products, owned by Cox Industries, was a leading employer of people in the area.

Along with its railroad history, Branchville looks back on a great high school baseball past. For five consecutive years, from 1945 to 1949, the town's Yellow Jackets were South Carolina's Class C baseball champions. In those five years the Branchville teams amassed a record of ninety-five wins and only nine losses. DEAN B. LIVINGSTON

Myers, Frank K. "Branchville Is One of State's Oldest Communities." Orangeburg *Times and Democrat,* July 9, 1961, p. B3.
Ott, John. "New School, Business Seen as Positive Changes." Orangeburg *Times and Democrat,* October 6, 2002, p. 18.

Brandon Mill. Located two miles west of downtown Greenville, the community of Brandon emerged shortly after the construction of Brandon Mill in 1901. Founded by J. Irving Westervelt and initially named Quentin, the original Brandon Mill had 10,000 spindles and 400 looms. Around the factory the company built sixty-six cottages for mill employees. Westervelt soon changed the mill's name to Brandon after a town near Belfast, Ireland, where textiles had long been produced. The mill enjoyed immediate success; between 1908 and 1910 Westervelt constructed another building at a cost of $1.4 million. Westervelt's finances foundered in 1913, however, and he sold the mill to Aug W. Smith of Spartanburg. By 1916 Brandon Mill had 86,000 spindles and assets worth $1.5 million. With Smith as mill president, New York agents Woodward and Baldwin controlled the mill's stock and consolidated the mill with nearby Poinsett Mill, forming the Brandon Corporation in 1928.

Falling cotton prices in the 1920s and the Great Depression of the 1930s ruined the market for textile goods, and Smith struggled to keep Brandon Mill open by lobbying New York investors for help. Only the start of war production in the 1940s saved the mill from bankruptcy.

Brandon Mill continued to manufacture cotton goods for the first few decades of the post–World War II era, until falling demand for domestic textile goods forced the plant's closure in March 1977. After that, the Brandon community nearly vanished before the Greenville County Redevelopment Authority acted to refurbish what had once been "one of the prettiest cotton mill villages in the state." By the mid-1990s Brandon was again a stable neighborhood, with seventy percent of the community's homes occupied and the mill building leased to K&M Fabrics. In 2000 Focus Golf began $500,000 renovations, transforming the old mill into a multipurpose facility. DARREN GREM

Bainbridge, Judith. *Greenville Communities.* Greenville, S.C.: Judith Bainbridge, 1996.

Bratton, John (1831–1898). Soldier, congressman. Bratton was born on March 7, 1831, in Winnsboro, the son of William Bratton (1773–1850) and Isabella Means. He was the grandson of William Bratton (ca. 1742–1815), of Revolutionary War fame. John's father moved to Fairfield County probably in the early 1800s, where he became a prominent and successful doctor in Winnsboro. John Bratton attended Mount Zion Institute, then graduated from South Carolina College in 1850. He enrolled at the Medical College of South Carolina, graduating in 1854. Returning to Fairfield District, he combined a career in medicine with his interest in agriculture. In 1859 Bratton married Elizabeth Porcher DuBose, a member of another prominent Fairfield family. The marriage produced nine children. By 1860 Bratton was an established planter, with real estate valued at $21,000 and seventy-six slaves.

Following the withdrawal of South Carolina from the Union in December 1860, Bratton joined a local volunteer company known as the Fairfield Fencibles and was elected as first lieutenant. In April 1861 the company became part of the Sixth Regiment, South Carolina Volunteers. Following this reorganization, Bratton resigned his commission and reenlisted as a private in June 1861. He advanced through the ranks with remarkable speed, becoming colonel and commanding officer of the Sixth Regiment in April 1862. Bratton was wounded at the Battle of Seven Pines on May 31, 1862, and captured. Exchanged in 1863, he rejoined his old regiment. Following the death of General Micah Jenkins of South Carolina at the Battle of the Wilderness in May 1864, Bratton was promoted to brigadier general, commanding Bratton's Brigade, Field's Division, First Corps, Army of Northern Virginia. Bratton served in this position until the army's surrender at Appomattox on April 9, 1865.

Bratton returned to Fairfield County and entered politics. A conservative Democrat, he served as a delegate to the 1865 South Carolina constitutional convention and represented Fairfield County in the S.C. Senate from 1865 to 1866. A loyal political lieutenant of Wade Hampton, in 1880 Bratton was elected chairman of the state Democratic executive committee and chosen state comptroller general by the General Assembly. He ran for governor in 1882 but failed to win his party's nomination. In the fall of 1884 Bratton was elected to Congress to fill the unexpired term of John H. Evins, who had died in office. Taking his seat in the U.S. House of Representatives on December 8, 1884, Bratton served until March 3, 1885, and did not seek reelection. Still revered by conservative Democrats, Bratton again ran for governor in 1890 but lost to the political insurgent Benjamin Tillman. Bratton then retired from political life. He died in Winnsboro on January 12, 1898, and was buried in the cemetery of the Episcopal Church. SAM THOMAS

Austin, Joseph Luke. *General John Bratton: Sumter to Appomattox in Letters to His Wife.* Sewanee, Tenn.: Proctor's Hall, 2003.

Bailey, N. Louise, Mary L. Morgan, and Carolyn R. Taylor, eds. *Biographical Directory of the South Carolina Senate, 1776–1985.* 3 vols. Columbia: University of South Carolina Press, 1986.

Cooper, William J., Jr. *The Conservative Regime: South Carolina, 1877–1890.* Baltimore, Md.: Johns Hopkins Press, 1968.

Bratton, William (ca. 1742–1815). Soldier, legislator. Bratton was born in county Antrim, Northern Ireland, and immigrated with his family to America not long afterward. Family traditions recorded in the nineteenth century stated that Bratton lived in Pennsylvania, Virginia, and North Carolina before moving to South Carolina in the 1760s. Beginning in 1765, an extended family of Brattons—including John, Robert, Thomas, Hugh, and William Bratton—moved into the area of present-day York County as part of a larger migration of Scots-Irish into the Carolina Piedmont immediately after the French and Indian War. William Bratton probably married his wife, Martha Robinson or Robertson (ca. 1750–1816), about this same time. They had eight children. In 1766 Bratton purchased two hundred acres of land on the South Fork of Fishing Creek. The Brattons' original two-story log house, which probably dates from this same period, still exists as the Colonel William Bratton House at Historic Brattonsville in York County.

During the Revolutionary War, Bratton served as a South Carolina militia commander and rose from the rank of captain at the beginning of the war to colonel by late 1780, when he commanded a regiment in the partisan brigade of General Thomas Sumter. Early on the morning of July 12, 1780, an important battle was fought near Bratton's home on the neighboring plantation of James Williamson; this battle is today known as the Battle of Williamson's Plantation or, locally, as Huck's Defeat. A force of about 133 local militiamen under the command of Bratton, William Hill, John McClure, Edward Lacey and others ambushed and defeated a mixed force of about 120 British Provincials and Loyalist militia under the command of Captain Christian Huck of the British Legion. This battle was the first significant defeat of British forces by South Carolina militia after the surrender of Charleston in May 1780, and it revitalized the patriot cause in the upstate.

Bratton served as a regimental commander in Sumter's Brigade until the end of the Revolution. After the war, he served as a justice of the peace for York County, sheriff of Pinckney District, and a state legislator in both the House of Representatives (1785–1790) and the Senate (1791–1794). He also operated a small store, was a successful planter and businessman, and owned several slaves. William and Martha Bratton were early members of Bethesda Presbyterian Church, one of the oldest churches in the region. Bratton died on February 9, 1815, and was buried in the Bethesda Presbyterian Church cemetery. His children and grandchildren expanded the homesite into a large nineteenth-century plantation, which became known as the village of Brattonsville. MICHAEL C. SCOGGINS

Bailey, N. Louise, and Elizabeth Ivey Cooper, eds. *Biographical Directory of the South Carolina House of Representatives.* Vol. 3, *1775–1790.* Columbia: University of South Carolina Press, 1981.

Moore, Maurice A. *Reminiscences of York.* Edited by Elmer O. Parker. Greenville, S.C.: A Press, 1981.

Brattonsville. Brattonsville is the site of a large eighteenth- and nineteenth-century plantation in southern York County situated on the south fork of Fishing Creek. The settlement began in 1766 as the two-hundred-acre farm of Colonel William Bratton (ca. 1742–1815), but by the early nineteenth century Brattonsville had become one of the largest plantations in the upstate. William Bratton's youngest son, John Simpson Bratton (1789–1843), inherited the bulk of the estate after his father's death, and he constructed the large two-story Georgian plantation home now known as the Homestead. He also operated a post office and store at Brattonsville and converted his parents' old log house into the Brattonsville Female

Academy. His wife, Harriet Rainey Bratton (1795–1843), continued to operate the plantation after her husband's death, remodeling the Homestead and building the two-story Brick House. John Simpson Bratton II (1819–1888) followed in his father's footsteps and became a wealthy cotton planter, and in the early 1850s he built a two-story mansion in the Italianate villa style, originally named Forest Hall but now called Hightower Hall. The Brattons actively supported the Confederacy during the Civil War, and following the conflict the family's fortunes began to decline. The Brattons left the plantation and moved to the nearby town of Yorkville (now York) in the early twentieth century, and Brattonsville was turned over to tenant farmers. In the 1970s the property was acquired by the York County Historical Commission and converted into a historic site, now known as Historic Brattonsville. MICHAEL C. SCOGGINS

Mendenhall, Samuel Brooks. *Tales of York County.* Rock Hill, S.C.: Reynolds and Reynolds, 1989.

Moore, Maurice A. *Reminiscences of York.* Edited by Elmer O. Parker. Greenville, S.C.: A Press, 1981.

Wilkins, Joseph C., Howell C. Hunter, Jr., and Richard F. Carillo. *Historical, Architectural, and Archeological Research at Brattonsville (38YK21), York County, South Carolina.* Columbia: Institute of Archeology and Anthropology, University of South Carolina, 1975.

Brawley, Benjamin Griffith (1882–1939). Educator, author, editor, clergyman. Brawley was born on April 22, 1882, in Columbia to prominent Baptist parents. His father, the Reverend Edward McKnight Brawley, is remembered as the founder of Morris College in Sumter. "My mother [Margaret Saphronia Dickerson] was from Columbia," Brawley wrote in 1925, "and it was in Columbia, almost in the shadow of the State House, that I first sat up and took notice." A gifted and enthusiastic student, he earned degrees from the University of Chicago (A.B., 1906) and Harvard (M.A., 1908). In 1912 Brawley married Hilda Damaris Prowd. The couple had no children. In 1921 he was ordained as a Baptist minister by the Massachusetts Baptist Convention. For two years in the early 1920s he served as pastor of the Messiah Baptist Church of Brockton, Massachusetts.

Between 1902 and 1939 Brawley taught English at various predominantly black colleges in the South and East. He was twice at Atlanta Baptist College (later Morehouse College), from 1902 to 1910 and again from 1912 to 1920. The fellow South Carolinian, educator, and writer Benjamin Mays singled Brawley out as one of the "few able, dedicated teachers who made the Morehouse man believe he was 'somebody.'" From 1923 to 1931 Brawley was on the English faculty at Shaw University in Raleigh, North Carolina. He served as professor of English at Howard University in Washington, D.C., during two separate periods: from 1910 to 1912 and from 1931 until his death.

Brawley developed into a prolific writer, contributing works to such periodicals as *Bookman, Dial, North American Review, Sewanee Review,* and *Reviewer.* But it was in his writing and editing of books about the African American experience that he pioneered. While he was teaching at Morehouse in 1909, a student pleaded with him to write a textbook that would enable black students to learn something of the experiences and accomplishments of their own people. Four years later, in 1913, Macmillan published his book *A Short History of the American Negro.* In the ensuing years Brawley wrote or edited *History of Morehouse College* (1917), *Africa and the War* (1918), *Your Negro Neighbor* (1918), *New Era Declamations* (1918), *The Negro in American Literature in the United States* (1918), *Women of Achievement* (1919), *A Social History of the American Negro* (1921), *A Short History of the English Drama* (1921), *Freshman Year English* (1929), *Dr. Dillard of the Jeanes Fund* (1930), *History of the English Hymn* (1932), *The Negro Genius* (1937), and *The Best Stories of Paul Lawrence Dunbar* (1938). In 1925 Knopf published his college textbook *New Survey of English Literature.* The University of North Carolina Press brought out three of his last five books: *Early Negro American Writers* (1935), *Paul Lawrence Dunbar: Poet of His People* (1936), and *Negro Builders and Heroes* (1937).

By the mid-1930s the federal Works Progress Administration in South Carolina had identified Brawley as one of the state's half-dozen outstanding African Americans. Perhaps his chief significance as a writer lay in his ability to articulate what he referred to as "the Negro problem"—the presence and plight of blacks in America. In a 1922 article in *The Bookman,* Brawley noted "the strange prominence of the Negro throughout the whole course of American history." Brawley insisted on articulating a positive black self-awareness, which was not typical of literature about African Americans at the time. "Literature should be not only history but prophecy," he wrote, "not only the record of our striving but also the mirror of our hopes and dreams." He later expanded his interest beyond the well-being of African American boys and girls alone. "What we want," he declared, "is that EVERY boy and girl shall receive the full promise of American life. No one is so high that he does not need our interest, nor is anyone so low that he should not have his chance."

Brawley died on February 1, 1939, at his home in Washington, D.C. In 1991 he was inducted into the South Carolina Academy of Authors. THOMAS L. JOHNSON

Brawley, Benjamin G. "The Negro in American Literature." *The Bookman* 56 (October 1922): 137–41.

———. Papers. Moorland-Spingarn Research Center, Howard University, Washington, D.C.

Parker, John W. "Benjamin Brawley—Teacher and Scholar." *Phylon* 10 (first quarter 1949): 15–24.

———. "Benjamin Brawley and the American Cultural Tradition." *Phylon* 16 (second quarter 1955): 183–94.

———. "A Bibliography of the Published Writings of Benjamin Griffith Brawley." *North Carolina Historical Review* 34 (April 1957): 165–78.

Brawley, Edward McKnight (1851–1923). Missionary, educator. Brawley was born on March 18, 1851, in Charleston to free African American parents, James and Ann Brawley. In 1861 his parents sent him to Philadelphia to further his education. After three years of grammar school, Brawley attended the Philadelphia Institute for Colored Youth until 1866. On returning to Charleston, Brawley was a shoemaker's apprentice for several years. In September 1870 he became the first full-time theology student at Howard University in Washington, D.C. However, three months later Brawley transferred to Bucknell University in Lewisburg, Pennsylvania, and became that institution's first African American student. With the aid of various white benefactors Brawley was able to pay his tuition. During summer recesses he earned additional income as a Baptist lay preacher. Following graduation in 1875, Brawley was ordained by the council of a white Baptist church in Lewisburg.

The American Baptist Publication Society hired Brawley to perform missionary service among black South Carolinians. Although there were numerous black Baptist congregations statewide, Brawley found no existing state convention. Accordingly, in 1876 he organized the Colored Baptist Educational, Missionary, and Sunday

School Convention. He went on to organize numerous local Sunday school programs throughout the state. A key ally in these endeavors was the Reverend Jacob Legare, pastor of the Morris Street Baptist Church in Charleston. Meanwhile, Brawley raised funds for Benedict College in Columbia, where he also served on the faculty.

Brawley's personal life was disrupted in 1877 with the death of his first wife, Mary Warrick Brawley. In December 1879 he married Margaret Dickerson. The marriage produced four children. The couple's second son, Benjamin Griffith Brawley, became a noted African American educator.

In October 1883 Brawley accepted the presidency of the Alabama Baptist Normal and Theological School and moved to Selma, Alabama. During his tenure the school expanded and became known as Selma University. Due to his wife's failing health, Brawley later relocated to Sumter, South Carolina, to assume a pastorate. While there, he was instrumental in founding Morris College in 1908 and served as its first president. During this period Brawley devoted much effort to promoting missionary activities in Africa, especially in Liberia. He also was editor of the *Baptist Tribune,* a weekly denominational journal, and wrote various monographs, including *Sin and Salvation,* a popular African American evangelism textbook. Throughout his career Brawley was noted widely as an energetic, accomplished public speaker.

Brawley served as pastor of the White Rock Baptist Church in Durham, North Carolina, from 1912 to 1920. During his last three years, Brawley was a professor of Old Testament history at Shaw University in Raleigh, North Carolina. On January 13, 1923, he died in Raleigh following a brief illness. He was interred within the White Rock Baptist Churchyard, Durham, North Carolina. MILES S. RICHARDS

Pegues, Albert W. *Our Baptist Ministers and Schools.* Springfield, Mass.: Willey, 1892.

Tindall, George Brown. *South Carolina Negroes, 1877–1900.* 1952. Reprint, Columbia: University of South Carolina Press, 2003.

Brewton, Miles (1731–1775). Merchant, legislator. Brewton was born on January 29, 1731, in Charleston to Robert Brewton, a prosperous goldsmith, and his second wife, Mary Griffith. His grandfather Miles Brewton had immigrated to South Carolina from Barbados in 1684 and became a goldsmith and militia officer. Since his family's trade was allied to banking, young Miles was well placed for a career in finance and trade. Twice during the 1750s, he traveled to England to finish his education and establish commercial ties. Between 1756 and his death, Brewton conducted business in several partnerships and was part-owner in eight commercial vessels. His partnerships dealt largely with the exportation of domestic produce, but he also made substantial profits in the importation of slaves. On May 19, 1759, Brewton further expanded his fortune and influence by marrying Mary Izard, daughter of Joseph Izard and Ann Bull. The couple had three children. Through his marriage, numerous land grants, and purchases, Brewton accumulated a large quantity of real estate. However, he made his fortune principally as a merchant rather than as a planter, becoming one of the wealthiest men in South Carolina.

In 1769 Brewton constructed a grand house on King Street and decorated it in the latest English taste. Still standing in the early twenty-first century, the structure is considered one of the finest examples of Georgian architecture in America. During a visit to Charleston in 1773, the Bostonian Josiah Quincy, Jr., dined at Brewton's town house with several prominent local figures. He described Brewton as "a gentleman of very large fortune" and marveled at his host's conspicuous wealth. He pronounced the mansion "the grandest hall I ever beheld" and its furnishings "vastly pretty."

In public life, Brewton was active in the Charleston Library Society and was an officer of the South Carolina Society. In his will he left a legacy of £500 sterling to support the South Carolina Society's free primary school and £1,000 sterling to establish a college in South Carolina. He served as a commissioner of several public bodies in Charleston, including the Work House and Markets and the projects to build the Exchange and magazines. In 1773 he was elected vice president of the Charleston Chamber of Commerce. Brewton served in the Commons House of Assembly from 1765 until his death, representing the parishes of St. Philip's, St. John's Colleton, and St. Michael's in succession. In 1773 Lieutenant Governor William Bull recommended him for a seat on the Royal Council, but Brewton's support of antigovernment measures led him to decline the seat. In July 1774 Brewton stood as a conservative South Carolina candidate for the First Continental Congress, but he lost to the more radical Christopher Gadsden. Brewton represented the parishes of St. Philip's and St. Michael's in the First Provincial Congress in 1775 and there was elected to the Council of Safety. Lord William Campbell, the last royal governor of South Carolina, was married to Mary Brewton's first cousin, and on his arrival in Charleston in 1775 he briefly resided at Brewton's King Street mansion. Also in 1775 Brewton was reelected to the Provincial Congress for its second term, but he would not be able to serve in that body. In late August 1775, on a voyage from Charleston to Philadelphia, Brewton and his family were lost at sea. See plate 10. NICHOLAS MICHAEL BUTLER

Edgar, Walter, and N. Louise Bailey, eds. *Biographical Directory of the South Carolina House of Representatives.* Vol. 2, *The Commons House of Assembly, 1692–1775.* Columbia: University of South Carolina Press, 1977.

Quincy, Josiah, Jr. "Journal of Josiah Quincy, Junior, 1773." *Proceedings of the Massachusetts Historical Society* 49 (June 1916): 424–81.

Salley, A. S., Jr. "Col. Miles Brewton and Some of His Descendants." *South Carolina Historical and Genealogical Magazine* 2 (April 1901): 128–52.

Briggs v. Elliott (1954). *Briggs v. Elliott* was one of five cases, collectively entitled *Brown et al. v. Board of Education of Topeka, Shawnee County, KS, et al.,* argued before the United States Supreme Court on December 9–11, 1952, and December 7–9, 1953, by attorneys from the National Association for the Advancement of Colored People (NAACP). The historic decision of *Brown v. Board of Education* rendered the doctrine of "separate but equal" public education unconstitutional and led to the movement to desegregate public schools throughout the United States. Originally a lawsuit filed by twenty African American parents in Clarendon County for equal educational opportunities for their children, *Briggs v. Elliott* was the first case in the twentieth century to challenge the constitutionality of racially segregated schools. The case carries the names of the lead plaintiff, Harry Briggs, who had five children in the school district, and Roderick W. Elliott, chairman of School District 22.

Ironically, the plaintiffs in the case that eventually became the *Briggs* case just wanted the Clarendon County school board to provide a school bus for their children. Some African American children had to ford or row across a stream (when it was flooded) and then walk an additional nine miles in order to attend Scott's Branch School in Summerton. Others had to walk at least five miles one way to attend the school. After a young boy drowned in the newly created Lake Marion reservoir, which separated several African

The men and women who signed the petition that resulted in the case that led to the Brown Decision in 1954. Photograph by Cecil Williams

American communities from the school, in 1948 Reverend Joseph Armstrong DeLaine, a minister of the African Methodist Episcopal Church, urged a local African American farmer, Levi Pearson, to sue for a school bus. The case, *Levi Pearson v. Clarendon County and School District No. 26,* was filed by NAACP attorney Harold Boulware of Columbia. The case was withdrawn, however, when it was discovered that Pearson's residence straddled the county line and that he paid taxes in a different district.

Subsequently, DeLaine and Boulware met with attorneys from the NAACP's national office to request support for another case challenging the school board's refusal to provide African American children with transportation. At first the NAACP's chief legal counsel, Thurgood Marshall, turned down their request. But he changed his mind and decided to support another challenge if DeLaine would obtain twenty petitioners from the Clarendon County community to support a case to equalize all aspects of education for African American children—including facilities, teachers' salaries, books, and supplies—as well as transportation.

Marshall agreed to represent the plaintiffs because their case represented an opportunity for the NAACP to continue its campaign against unequal, segregated education for African Americans in the southern states. The campaign, which began in 1935 under the leadership of the NAACP's first chief legal counsel, Charles Hamilton Houston, had developed as a three-pronged strategy to improve African American education in the South. First, Houston wanted to ensure that African American teachers in the southern states received salaries equal to those of white teachers. Second, he wanted to ensure that the southern states provided transportation for African American students to and from their schools. Third, he wanted to ensure that the southern states provided graduate and professional education and training for African American students. Houston's strategy was based on using the "separate but equal" doctrine established in the 1896 *Plessy v. Ferguson* decision to force the southern states to provide African American students an education that was truly equal to that of white students. It did not challenge the doctrine directly or demand integration. From 1938 to 1948 Houston's successor and former student Thurgood Marshall continued his strategy, but by the latter year he was ready for a full, frontal assault on the constitutionality of segregated schools.

In November 1950 Marshall presented the case of the twenty plaintiffs from Clarendon County to the federal district court in Charleston. During the pretrial hearing he was encouraged by federal judge J. Waties Waring of Charleston not to argue for a "separate but equal" education, or one that would only equalize African American schools in a segregated system. Judge Waring encouraged him instead to present a case arguing for schools for African American children that would truly be equal by asking for an end to segregation in the state's public schools. Taking Waring's advice, in May 1951 Marshall returned to the federal court and presented his case for ending segregation in the state's public schools. He introduced evidence showing how the African American schools in Clarendon County were grossly unequal to those for whites in facilities, teacher-to-student ratios, class sizes, and expenditures per student. The attorneys representing the state of South Carolina sought to defuse this argument by announcing that Governor James F. Byrnes was going to introduce a new sales tax to raise money to improve the state's African American schools. But Marshall also presented testimony from the sociologist Kenneth Clark documenting the harmful effects of segregation on the lives and psyches of African American children in South Carolina. Arguing the case before a three-judge panel, which included Waring and two segregationists, Judges John J. Parker and George Bell Timmerman, Marshall lost the case. Only Judge Waring supported his argument and offered a dissenting opinion against segregated schools in South Carolina.

The *Briggs* case was appealed to the United States Supreme Court, where it became part of the famous *Brown* case. NAACP attorneys Robert Carter and Thurgood Marshall argued the case on behalf of its South Carolina plaintiffs, while former U.S. solicitor general John W. Davis represented the state in its defense of its segregated school system. On May 17, 1954, the Supreme Court ruled in favor of the plaintiffs and declared, unanimously, segregation in public schools unconstitutional.

Despite the case's favorable outcome, its South Carolina plaintiffs suffered tremendous hardships for their decision to pursue justice for their children. Reverend DeLaine was shot at, his house was burned to the ground, and he was eventually forced to flee the state. Harry Briggs, the lead plaintiff, lost his job as a gas station attendant. Levi Pearson, the plaintiff in the first attempt to obtain only a school bus, had his loans called in, and he had to watch his crops for 1948 rot in the fields because he could not rent the machinery to harvest them. Other plaintiffs and supporters of the case were harassed; fired from their jobs as teachers, matrons, and housekeepers; and kicked off the land of white landowners for whom they were sharecropping. Due to the designation of this landmark case as the "*Brown* case" or the "*Brown* decision" in American legal history, the sacrifices of these South Carolinians who filed the first major case to challenge the constitutionally of segregated schools have frequently been overlooked in the nation's history books. W. MARVIN DULANEY

DeLaine, Brumit B., and Ophelia DeLaine Gona. *Briggs v. Elliott: Clarendon County's Quest for Equality; A Brief History.* Pine Brook, N.J.: O. Gona, 2002.

DuBose, Sonny. *The Road to* Brown: *The Leadership of a Soldier of the Cross, Reverend J. A. DeLaine.* Orangeburg, S.C.: Williams, 2002.

Kluger, Richard. *Simple Justice: The History of Brown v. Board of Education and Black America's Struggle for Equality.* New York: Knopf, 1975.

Lochbaum, Julia Magruder. "The Word Made Flesh: The Desegregation Leadership of the Rev. J. A. DeLaine." Ph.D. diss., University of South Carolina, 1993.

Patterson, James T. *Brown v. Board of Education: A Civil Rights Milestone and Its Troubled Legacy.* New York: Oxford University Press, 2001.

Williams, Juan. *Thurgood Marshall: American Revolutionary.* New York: Times Books, 1998.

Bristow, Gwen (1903–1980). Novelist. Gwen Bristow, who would come to be referred to as "Carolina's Best Seller," was born in Marion on September 16, 1903, the daughter of the Baptist minister and hospital superintendent Louis Judson Bristow and Caroline Cornelia Winkler. She made her writing debut in 1916 in Columbia's *State* newspaper as a seventh-grade Taylor School reporter. Although she attended Columbia High School, she graduated at Abbeville, where her father had returned as pastor. After attending Anderson College for a year, she transferred to Judson College in Marion, Alabama, where in 1924 she received her A.B. degree. In 1925, following a year's study at Columbia University's Pulitzer School of Journalism in New York, she became a reporter for the *Times-Picayune* in New Orleans. There she met and married Bruce Manning, a newspaper reporter who eventually became a Hollywood screenwriter and film producer. Together they collaborated on the writing of four mystery novels between 1930 and 1932: *The Invisible Host* (1930), *The Gutenburg Murders* (1931), *Two and Two Make Twenty-Two* (1932), and *The Mardi Gras Murders* (1932).

By the summer of 1934 they had moved to California, where Bristow began to experiment with historical fiction. The result of this was the publication of *Deep Summer* (1937), her first best-seller and the first installment in her Louisiana Plantation Trilogy. The next two in the series soon followed: *The Handsome Road* (1938) and *This Side of Glory* (1940). Her World War II romance novel, *Tomorrow Is Forever,* appeared in 1943 and in 1946 was made into a film starring Orson Welles and Claudette Colbert. The next two novels, *Jubilee Trail* (1950) and *Celia Garth* (1959), became Literary Guild selections. By the time of the publication of the latter book, which is a story of Charleston in the Revolutionary War, sales of Bristow's books had reached nearly three million copies, exclusive of book clubs. *Calico Palace,* her last novel, was published in 1970. Bristow's final book, *Golden Dreams,* came out in 1980 and was a nonfiction account of the gold rush and the founding of California.

Bristow's natural storytelling ability, neatly devised and detailed plots, sharply drawn characters, telling eye for landscape and its detail, use of common sense, gift for dramatic effect, and emotional sincerity were the characteristics of her work that critics and reviewers singled out for praise. Margaret Wallace spoke of her "solid and versatile talent as a novelist." The critic Susan Quinn Berneis claimed that Bristow's greatest skill was reserved for "the unfolding of American history as displayed around the lives of the people who created it." And Eugene Armfield remarked that she belonged "among those Southern novelists who [were] trying to interpret the South and its past in critical terms." Furthermore, her books had universal appeal: various ones were translated into German, French, Italian, Norwegian, Danish, Swedish, Finnish, Czechoslovakian, Dutch, Spanish, and Portuguese.

Bristow died in New Orleans on August 16, 1980. On April 15, 2000, she was inducted into the South Carolina Academy of Authors. THOMAS L. JOHNSON

Bristow, Gwen. Papers. South Caroliniana Library, University of South Carolina, Columbia.

Lowry, Julia B. "Carolina's Gwen Bristow Finds She's Obliged to Write!" Columbia *State Magazine,* November 5, 1950, pp. 6–7.

MacNebb, Betty L. "Gwen Bristow: Carolina's Best Seller." *South Carolina Magazine* 12 (July 1949): 8, 10.

Theriot, Billie J. "Gwen Bristow: A Biography with Criticism of Her Plantation Trilogy." Ph.D. diss., Louisiana State University, 1994.

Brodie, Laura (1908–2004). Herpetologist. Brodie was born in the family home at Rockwood Farm five miles southeast of Leesville on July 7, 1908, the daughter of Furman Edward Brodie and Ida Johnson. At an early age she developed an interest in the living things around the farm, located in the rural western corner of Lexington County. When she was twelve years old, her father scolded her for killing a harmless snake, and the incident awakened her to the fact that all snakes are not venomous. That knowledge sparked an interest in reptiles that led her to roam the woods and fields around the farm in search of the various kinds of snakes and lizards that inhabited the region. Short of stature but full of energy, Brodie had little difficulty in catching the elusive creatures and soon began holding snakes in captivity for observation. In her early teens she set up her "Rockwood Museum" in a small outbuilding near her house. There she kept various natural history items from around the farm and eventually maintained seventeen cages of reptiles and amphibians. Undaunted even by venomous snakes, she collected a deadly eastern coral snake shortly before her fifteenth birthday and added a cottonmouth the following year. But she had few reference books to help her identify all of her specimens, so her mother took Brodie, along with some of her reptiles and amphibians, to Columbia to see Professor Julian D. Corrington, a herpetologist in the biology department at the University of South Carolina. Corrington identified them for her and encouraged the teenager to pursue a career in herpetology (the study of reptiles and amphibians).

While Brodie was at Winthrop College during the late 1920s, her biology professor noticed her interest and called her to the attention of Howard K. Gloyd, a well-known herpetologist. Gloyd helped Brodie get a position at the University of Michigan Museum of Zoology, where there was an excellent program in herpetology under the direction of Alexander G. Ruthven. During her first year there she stayed with Frank N. Blanchard and his wife, and Blanchard taught her many of the procedures used by professional herpetologists. On trips back to her Leesville home she collected many specimens for the University of Michigan collection.

In 1946 Brodie joined the staff of the herpetology department at the Chicago Natural History Museum (now the Field Museum of Natural History), where she assisted the noted herpetologist Karl P. Schmidt and collected specimens for the museum. By that time she had also collected many reptiles and amphibians for other museums as well. But in 1956 she was nearly killed in an auto accident in Chicago, and her lengthy recovery period effectively brought an end to her full-time career in herpetology. She returned to her childhood home near Leesville, where she remained a unique individual and an important contributor to the herpetology collections of some of America's largest museums. ALBERT E. SANDERS

Sanders, Albert E., and William D. Anderson, Jr. *Natural History Investigations in South Carolina from Colonial Times to the Present.* Columbia: University of South Carolina Press, 1999.

Brookgreen Gardens. The Archer M. and Anna Hyatt Huntington Sculpture Garden at Brookgreen rests on thirty acres of display gardens in the middle of some 9,100 acres of the South Carolina lowcountry stretching from the Atlantic Ocean to the Waccamaw River. The site is best known for its beautiful display gardens and its unrivaled American figurative sculpture collection, as well as its commitment to conservation and preservation. It was created in 1931 by the sculptor Anna Hyatt Huntington and her husband, Archer M. Huntington. They opened the nonprofit site to the public the following year. Comprised of four former rice plantations,

Brookgreen was envisioned as a showcase of art and nature, a sanctuary where monumental works of art would be displayed against a tapestry of magnificent live-oak trees and towering pines.

More than 550 pieces of sculpture are displayed in an outdoor setting, grouped with plants carefully selected to set off the smooth, classic lines of marble, bronze, and even gold-leaf figurative sculpture. In addition to works by Anna Hyatt Huntington and several contemporary sculptors, the Brookgreen collection includes pieces by Frederic Remington, Herbert Adams, Augustus Saint-Gaudens, Daniel Chester French, and John Quincy Adams Ward. Ten garden "rooms" are highlighted by ponds, fountains, and sculpture set off by native plants and seasonal flowers. Native animals can be observed along the wildlife trail, and the entire area has been designated a wildlife preserve. The Lowcountry Center on the grounds tells the story of the land through exhibits, plants, sculpture, and excursions.

As of 2001, nearly 200,000 visitors annually enjoyed daily tours, seasonal events, and programs at Brookgreen. The site is accredited by the American Association of Museums and was designated a National Historic Landmark in 1992. MONA PRUFER

Rawls, Walton H., ed. *A Century of American Sculpture: Treasures from the Brookgreen Gardens.* 2d ed. New York: Abbeville, 1988.

Tarbox, Gurdon L. *Brookgreen Gardens: Where Art and Nature Meet, 1931–1991.* New York: Newcomen Society of the United States, 1991.

Brooks, Preston Smith (1819–1857). Congressman. Brooks, the son of Whitfield Brooks and Mary Carroll, was born on August 6, 1819, on the family plantation near the town of Edgefield. He attended Moses Waddel's academy at Willington and went on to South Carolina College, from which he was expelled in 1839 just prior to his graduation. Following the death of his first wife, Caroline H. Means, whom he had married on March 11, 1841, Brooks married her cousin Martha C. Means in 1843. His second marriage produced four children. In 1844 Edgefield District elected him to the General Assembly, where he served a single term. During the Mexican War, Brooks served as captain of the Ninety Six Company of the Palmetto Regiment and then returned to private life as a planter. In 1852 Brooks stood for election to the U.S. House of Representatives as a States' Rights Democrat and was elected to the Thirty-third (1853–1854) and Thirty-fourth (1855–1857) Congresses.

Preston Brooks. Courtesy, South Caroliniana Library

A political moderate, Brooks had a career in Congress that revolved around the issue of slavery in the territories, specifically the political repercussions of the Wilmot Proviso and the Compromise of 1850. Believing sectional compromises on slavery and tariff legislation never worked in the South's favor, he favored a policy of congressional nonintervention regarding both the national economy and slavery in the territories. He welcomed the Kansas-Nebraska Act of 1854 as a sign of the North's willingness to open all the western territories to settlement by southerners. But when northern Democrats insisted that Congress or territorial governments could restrict the legal protection of slavery, Brooks's enthusiasm for the Democratic Party and his hope for the Union began to wane.

Brooks is best known for his assault on U.S. Senator Charles Sumner of Massachusetts in May 1856. Following the eruption of violence on the Kansas frontier, Sumner delivered a speech unusually harsh by the Senate's standards. He assailed South Carolina's role in American history (especially during the Revolutionary War) and even attacked by name Senator Andrew P. Butler (who was a distant cousin of Brooks). With the aged Butler unable to defend himself or his state, the task fell to his nearest relative, Congressman Brooks, whose familiarity with South Carolina's traditions of family honor was surpassed only by his fluency with the *code duello.* After considering his alternatives and waiting for Senator Sumner to apologize publicly, Brooks decided to punish Sumner. On May 22 he entered the Senate chamber after the Senate had adjourned and found Sumner at his desk. Brooks delivered several blows to Sumner's head with a gutta-percha cane, and the senator fell senseless to the floor.

Violence among congressmen and senators was not unknown before the Civil War, but heightened sectional and party tensions propelled the Brooks-Sumner affair to national prominence. To many northerners, the incident highlighted the impetuousness of proslavery advocates. Many southerners appreciated Brooks's courage, and several state legislatures passed resolutions supporting him. The historian William Gienapp considered the affair to be a key factor in the emergence of the Republican Party in the North.

A special House committee recommended Brooks's expulsion, but its report failed to receive the necessary two-thirds vote. Though Brooks denied the House's constitutional jurisdiction over the matter, he resigned in July 1856 and was subsequently reelected to fill his own vacancy. He died suddenly on January 27, 1857, in Washington, D.C., and was interred at Willow Brook Cemetery, Edgefield. CAREY M. ROBERTS

Gienapp, William E. "The Crime against Sumner: The Caning of Charles Sumner and the Rise of the Republican Party." *Civil War History* 25 (September 1979): 218–45.

Mathis, Robert Neil. "Preston Smith Brooks: The Man and His Image." *South Carolina Historical Magazine* 79 (October 1978): 296–310.

Broughton, Thomas (?–1737). Legislator, lieutenant governor. Broughton was among the most controversial figures in the early political history of South Carolina. Little is known about his early life. He was the son of Andrew Broughton and was probably born in England. Around 1683 he married Anne Johnson, the daughter of Nathaniel Johnson, who would serve as governor of South Carolina from 1703 to 1709. The marriage produced at least seven children. By the mid-1690s Broughton had settled in South Carolina, emigrating from the West Indies.

Broughton quickly became involved in the Indian trade and used his connection to Johnson to advance his position. In 1702 Broughton made an unsuccessful attempt to secure a monopoly on the Indian trade from the Commons House of Assembly. Considered by many to be an unscrupulous trader, Broughton was prosecuted in 1708 by the Indian agent Thomas Nairne on charges that Broughton had enslaved friendly Cherokees and misappropriated deerskins that belonged to the province. Governor Johnson came to the aid of his son-in-law, and Broughton was acquitted, while Nairne was arrested for treason based on the dubious testimony of two witnesses. Broughton invested his trade profits in planting ventures. He acquired at least four plantations, including Mulberry on the Cooper River, where he built a massive, Jacobian-style brick mansion dubbed "Mulberry Castle."

Broughton's political career began in 1696, when he was first elected to the Commons House of Assembly. He represented Craven and Berkeley Counties until 1703 and then again from 1716 to 1717, when he served as Speaker. He also served as a deputy to the proprietor John Lord Carteret and was appointed to the Grand Council in 1705. Other influential offices held by Broughton included surveyor general (1707), commissioner of the Indian trade (1719), and collector of the Port of Charleston (1721). In 1725 St. Thomas and St. Denis Parish returned Broughton to the Commons House, where he again served as Speaker until 1727.

Following the death of Governor Edward Tynte in June 1710, Broughton was a leading candidate for the governorship. He lost, however, after Robert Gibbes bribed a councilor and secured the post for himself. Broughton and armed supporters marched on Charleston in protest but withdrew shortly thereafter. Capitalizing again on family connections, Broughton became lieutenant governor of South Carolina in 1731, after being recommended by Governor Robert Johnson, his brother-in-law. Following Johnson's death in May 1735, Broughton assumed the role of acting governor. His brief administration was marked by a renewal of factional tensions in South Carolina, a situation exacerbated by Broughton's inept and arrogant actions in office. He repeatedly angered the Commons by interfering with appropriation bills, which the Commons deemed to be its sole prerogative. His maladministration of Johnson's township system brought the township fund to the brink of insolvency. Broughton also antagonized the younger colony of Georgia by backing South Carolina merchants in their attempt to establish control over the Creek Indian trade, claiming that no colony had the right to interfere with the licensed traders of another (even though the South Carolina traders were operating in Georgia territory). Georgia retaliated by strictly enforcing its own Indian trade laws and by seizing several South Carolina vessels in the Savannah River. The quarrel between the two colonies would not subside until after Broughton's death on November 22, 1737.
NATHAN E. STALVEY

Edgar, Walter, and N. Louise Bailey, eds. *Biographical Directory of the South Carolina House of Representatives.* Vol. 2, *The Commons House of Assembly, 1692–1775.* Columbia: University of South Carolina Press, 1977.

Sirmans, M. Eugene. *Colonial South Carolina: A Political History, 1663–1763.* Chapel Hill: University of North Carolina Press, 1966.

Brown, Edgar Allan (1888–1975). Legislator. Brown was born on July 11, 1888, near Graniteville in Aiken County, the youngest child of Augustus "Gus" Brown and Elizabeth Howard. He attended Graniteville Academy, a school operated by the Graniteville Company, but left school in 1904 just before the beginning of his final year. At the age of sixteen he entered Osborne Business College, and in four months he completed a one-year program in shorthand. He then went to work in Sumter for Witherspoon Brothers, a manufacturer of coffins and caskets. From 1905 to 1906 Brown served as a public reporter in the state. From 1906 to 1908 he was clerk and head stenographer for the law firm of Colonel Daniel Sutherland Henderson in Aiken. In 1909 he was commissioned as

Edgar Brown (right) pictured with State Senator John West at the Carolina Cup in Camden. Courtesy, Modern Political Collections, University of South Carolina

court stenographer of the Second Judicial Circuit in Barnwell, replacing James F. Byrnes, who had been selected solicitor for the circuit. Brown passed the state bar exam in 1910 and became a lawyer. On December 30, 1913, he married Annie Love Sitgreaves, an Aiken schoolteacher. They had one daughter.

Brown was first elected to the S.C. House of Representatives in 1920. He served in the House from 1921 to 1926, serving as Speaker of the House from 1925 to 1926. He was also chair of the state Democratic executive committee from 1922 to 1926. In 1926 he challenged U.S. Senator Ellison D. "Cotton Ed" Smith. This was the first of three unsuccessful attempts by Brown to win a U.S. Senate seat; he lost bids in 1938 and 1954 as well. In 1928 he was elected to the S.C. Senate. He would remain in the S.C. Senate from 1929 until his retirement in 1972, serving as president pro tempore from 1942 to 1972.

When Strom Thurmond ran for governor in 1946, he ran against the Barnwell Ring, which referred to politicians from Barnwell County, including Edgar Brown, who held prominent positions in the General Assembly. In addition to Brown, who held the most powerful position in the Senate, it included Speaker of the House Solomon Blatt, and House Ways and Means chair Winchester Smith. These Barnwell legislators had an inordinate influence in state government, but the "Ring" was more of an election ploy than a description of political decision-making in the state. While Brown and Blatt were the two most powerful legislators in the state, they did not necessarily agree on policy and insisted that there was so such ring.

In September 1954 U.S. Senator Burnet Rhett Maybank died. His death occurred after the Democratic Party's primary but before the general election. The South Carolina Democratic Party's executive committee held a special meeting and decided to select Edgar Brown as the party's candidate rather than hold a special election. In response, Strom Thurmond announced a write-in candidacy for the U.S. Senate, claiming that his campaign was a fight for principle—government by the people instead of government by a small group of committee members. Thurmond's write-in campaign was successful, and he became the first candidate ever elected to Congress by a write-in vote.

Politically, Brown was considered one of the most powerful men in state government through his position as president pro tempore of the Senate and chair of the Senate finance committee. As such, he played an instrumental role in state financial matters. A fiscal conservative, Brown helped to create the South Carolina Budget and Control Board and was credited with keeping the state on a sound financial footing with a triple "A" credit rating. He was a strong proponent of a good road system, especially in rural areas. He was a major supporter of the public school system as well as higher education. While he never attended the institution, he was chair of the Clemson University Board of Trustees and played a significant role in the peaceful integration of Clemson in 1963. He also supported the establishment of the state technical education system and educational television.

Brown retired in 1972, ending a legislative career that spanned fifty years. He died on June 26, 1975, from injuries received in an automobile accident near Barnwell. The "Bishop from Barnwell" was buried in the cemetery next to the Barnwell Methodist Episcopal Church. WILLIAM V. MOORE

Bailey, N. Louise, Mary L. Morgan, and Carolyn R. Taylor, eds. *Biographical Directory of the South Carolina Senate, 1776–1985.* 3 vols. Columbia: University of South Carolina Press, 1986.

Workman, William D. *The Bishop from Barnwell: The Political Life and Times of Senator Edgar A. Brown.* Columbia, S.C.: R. L. Bryan, 1963.

Brown, James (b. 1933). Musician. James Brown was born near Barnwell on May 3, 1933, to Joe and Susie Brown. Brown is likely South Carolina's most famous twentieth-century entertainer. His career began in the 1950s in Augusta, Georgia, and grew into a music empire with a vast catalog of recordings, countless performances, and a global appeal that continued into the twenty-first century. While he was called the "Godfather of Soul," his body of work forms the rhythmic foundations of funk, disco, and hip-hop. He is arguably the most sampled musical artist of all time.

James Brown. Courtesy, Chris McKay / concertshots.com

Brown's early life was bleak, lonely, and chaotic. His parents separated when he was four. Eventually Brown went to live with his two aunts in Augusta, in a house where he was exposed to gambling, prostitution, bootlegging, and violence. In spite of his disadvantaged upbringing, Brown displayed an irrepressible enthusiasm for music, friendship, and the street life of Augusta. His first public performances progressed from his front porch to his school to local talent nights. At age fifteen he was sent to jail for petty theft but was paroled early. He began seriously to consider a career in music, forming the Flames, the first of a series of backing bands that would contribute to the evolution of his trademark sound. Thus began a life of traveling the road and performing. Brown played the Jim Crow South and beyond, gaining a devoted following and building his reputation with a series of singles. His first hit came with the 1956 release of "Please, Please, Please."

Although his band constantly changed members, it enabled Brown to utilize the talents of musicians such as Fred Wesley, Maceo Parker, Clyde Stubblefield, Bootsy Collins, and Vicki Anderson. A consummate entertainer, Brown gave his audiences the total experience of singing, dancing, and showbiz spectacle. His series of appearances recorded as *Live at the Apollo* (1963) are regarded as the peak of his live shows. Brown hit his stride after the 1965 release of "Papa's Got a Brand New Bag." Subsequent songs including "I Got You (I Feel Good)" (1965), "It's a Man's Man's Man's World" (1966), "Cold Sweat" (1967), "Get on the Good Foot" (1972), and "Sex Machine" (1975) are but a sample of his string of hits, which endured for decades in radio, sales, and film popularity.

Brown paradoxically has been at odds with the government and served as an international cultural symbol of the United States. He met with Hubert Humphrey on stay-in-school initiatives in 1966, played for the troops in Vietnam in 1968, and controversially endorsed Richard Nixon in 1972. Long an antidrug advocate, he struggled with his own demons as late as 1988, when a police car chase that began in Augusta ended across the South Carolina border. Brown received a six-year sentence but was released early in 1991.

James Brown continues to make his home in Beech Island, South Carolina. He was inducted into the Rock and Roll Hall of Fame in 1986 and received a Kennedy Center Honor in 2003. He has been married three times and has six children. HEATHER BUGGY

Brown, James, and Bruce Tucker. *James Brown: The Godfather of Soul.* 2d ed. New York: Thunder's Mouth, 1997.

Brown, Lucy Hughes (1863–1911). Physician. Brown was born in April 1863 in North Carolina and was orphaned. She graduated in 1885 from Scotia Seminary in North Carolina. After completing a medical degree at the Women's Medical College of Pennsylvania in Philadelphia in March 1894, she was the first African American woman to receive a professional license from the North Carolina Medical Board. She established a practice at Wilmington, North Carolina, and married Reverend David Brown, who was the minister of a Wilmington Presbyterian church. They had one daughter. Brown's marriage provided community resources and connections that aided her philanthropic efforts to improve conditions for African Americans.

After practicing medicine in North Carolina for two years, Brown moved to Charleston and became the first black female physician to practice in South Carolina. With several other African Americans, she contributed to the establishment of the Cannon Hospital and Training School for Nurses in 1897, which was later renamed McClennan-Banks Hospital. At this hospital Brown headed the department of nursing training. She presented lectures and stressed that practical experience was preferable to textbook knowledge, although she advised students to prepare with a combination of both classroom and practical knowledge. During a two-year program, students spent the first year attending lectures and gaining practical skills in the hospital. The second year was devoted to practical hospital work and assisting cases in the adjacent communities. The first class of nurses benefiting from Brown's guidance graduated in 1898.

As a recipe for their success, Brown urged graduates to embrace "great adaptability, good judgement, the ability to hold one's tongue and a willingness to do work outside the usual line," and to good-naturedly "take for their services what their patients can afford to pay." She frequently disseminated advice through her roles as an editor of the *Hospital Herald* and as secretary of the Cannon Hospital Association.

Brown also worked to advance the condition of African American women outside the Cannon Hospital. She served as a delegate to the National Colored Woman's Congress at the 1895 Atlanta Exposition and assisted in the creating of resolutions addressing southern race relations and demanding safer conditions for women on public transportation. Brown retired in 1904 due to illness and died on June 26, 1911. ELIZABETH D. SCHAFER

Hine, Darlene Clark. *Black Women in White: Racial Conflict and Cooperation in the Nursing Profession, 1890–1950.* Bloomington: Indiana University Press, 1989.

———, ed. *Black Women in the Nursing Profession: A Documentary History.* New York: Garland, 1985.

Martin, Maxine Smith. "Dr. Lucy Hughes Brown (1863–1911): A Pioneer African-American Physician." *Journal of the South Carolina Medical Association* 89 (January 1993): 15–19.

Brown, Morris (1770–1849). Clergyman. Brown, a free mulatto, was born in Charleston on January 8, 1770. He had little or no formal education and, although he learned to read the Bible, depended on others to write letters for him. A deeply religious man, Brown was serving in Charleston as a Methodist lay preacher by the early nineteenth century. He received a license to preach and organized an African congregation in Charleston in the early 1810s. The parish became popular among African Americans, both slave and free, and initially drew fourteen hundred members. Brown benefited from the encouragement of Bishop Francis Asbury, who considered him as one of the most effective "colored missionaries" in the lowcountry. However, after white church officials in Charleston reduced the control that black Methodists heretofore exercised over their church affairs, Brown led most of them from the denomination in 1817 in protest. They formed an African church, and Brown traveled to Philadelphia, where in 1818 he was admitted as an elder in the African Methodist Episcopal (AME) Church. His Charleston church, which had grown to more than three thousand members, affiliated with this northern black denomination.

Among the members of Brown's AME congregation in Charleston was Denmark Vesey. When Vesey's plot to lead a slave uprising was uncovered in 1822, accusations surfaced that sought to connect Brown to the conspiracy. Fearing implication, he fled to Philadelphia, and his church in Charleston was closed. Richard Allen, the founder of the AME Church and its first bishop, gave Brown refuge and made him his assistant. In 1828 Brown was elected as the second bishop of the growing African Methodist Episcopal Church. After Allen's death in 1831, Brown became the church's sole bishop.

Although largely illiterate, Brown promoted education among church members, whom he encouraged to attend schools where available. When his fellow Charlestonian Daniel Payne joined the AME ministry in 1842, Brown encouraged his efforts to improve clerical education. Brown was actively involved in secular reforms. He was a leader in Philadelphia's American Moral Reform Society, an African American organization advocating antislavery, racial integration, and myriad other social reforms. He traveled extensively, expanding the church from its northeastern base westward. By 1840 he added the Ohio Conference along with the Upper Canada and Indiana Conferences to the denomination. His authority also extended southward to the church's missionary station on Haiti. During Brown's bishopric, the denominational membership doubled to more than seventeen thousand.

Brown suffered a serious stroke in 1844 that left him partially paralyzed. He died in Philadelphia on May 9, 1849, and was survived by his wife, Maria, and six children. Morris Brown College in Atlanta and churches in Charleston and Philadelphia are named in his memory. DENNIS C. DICKERSON AND BERNARD E. POWERS, JR.

Handy, James A. *Scraps of African Methodist Episcopal History.* Philadelphia: A.M.E. Book Concern, 1902.

Wikramanayake, Marina. *A World in Shadow: The Free Black in Antebellum South Carolina.* Columbia: University of South Carolina Press, 1973.

Wright, Richard R. *The Bishops of the African Methodist Episcopal Church.* Nashville: A.M.E. Sunday School Union, 1963.

Brown, Thomas (1750–1825). Soldier. Brown was among the most notorious Loyalist commanders in the South during the Revolutionary War. He was born on May 27, 1750, in Whitby, England. Having acquired large tracts of the "Ceded Lands" near Augusta, Georgia, he immigrated to Georgia in the autumn of 1774. Brown promptly established a sizable plantation and became involved in local politics, particularly in expressing his opposition to the revolutionary movement. On August 2, 1775, a committee of the local Sons of Liberty seized and tortured him when Brown refused to renounce allegiance to his king. Making an escape, he fled to the South Carolina backcountry where he joined an active group of Loyalists. He set to work against the commission sent to the interior by the Charleston Council of Safety to gain support for the American effort and assisted in organizing an armed Loyalist force. Brown was among the Tory leaders at a confrontation with a rebel force near Ninety Six in September 1775. After a truce, he went to Charleston to confer with South Carolina's royal governor Lord William Campbell but was arrested by the Council of Safety and ordered to leave Charleston.

Finding refuge in British-held St. Augustine, Florida, Brown was commissioned a lieutenant colonel in June 1776 by East Florida's royal governor Patrick Tonyn and authorized to raise a regiment of mounted rangers. In the early years of the war, the rangers and their Creek and Cherokee allies patrolled the Georgia–South Carolina frontier. By 1779 the British held most of Georgia, which made East Florida's security seem certain. Brown's regiment was deactivated in June and reorganized as the King's Carolina Rangers, a regular provincial corps. That same month he was appointed one of two British superintendents of the Southern Indian Department, thereby putting Creek and Cherokee relations under his control.

At the onset of 1780, Brown established his headquarters at Augusta and directed the activities of Tories and Indians against the patriots. He was wounded in an attack on the town in mid-September 1780 by an American force commanded by Elijah Clarke. After the unsuccessful siege, Brown ordered thirteen prisoners hanged for parole violations. A second siege, led by Colonel Henry Lee of the Continental army and General Andrew Pickens of the South Carolina militia, forced Brown to submit on June 5, 1781. After being exchanged, Brown made his headquarters as Indian superintendent in Savannah, until the evacuation of that city by the British in July 1782, and then in St. Augustine. Following the return of Florida to Spain, he moved to the Bahamas to start life anew. In one of David Ramsey's histories of the war, Brown wrote an impassioned defense of his conduct in reply to charges of cruelty. Brown died on his St. Vincent Island plantation on August 3, 1825. SAMUEL K. FORE

Cashin, Edward J. *The King's Ranger: Thomas Brown and the American Revolution on the Southern Frontier.* Athens: University of Georgia Press, 1989.

Lambert, Robert Stansbury. *South Carolina Loyalists in the American Revolution.* Columbia: University of South Carolina Press, 1987.

Olson, Gary D. "Dr. David Ramsay and Lt. Colonel Thomas Brown: Patriot Historian and Loyalist Critic." *South Carolina Historical Magazine* 77 (October 1976): 257–67.

———. "Loyalists and the American Revolution: Thomas Brown and the South Carolina Backcountry, 1775–1776." *South Carolina Historical Magazine* 68 (October 1967): 201–19; 69 (January 1968): 44–56.

Brown, William Melvin, Jr. (1934–1994). Manufacturer. Born in Charleston on February 19, 1934, Brown was the son of William Melvin Brown, a bricklayer and artisan, and Eva Taylor. Following graduation from Immaculate Conception High School, Brown entered South Carolina State College, where he received a bachelor of science degree in 1955. He served two years in the U.S. Army, then taught biology and coached basketball and football in Charleston County public schools from 1958 to 1963. On June 4, 1960, Brown married Juanita Washington of Charleston. They had one daughter and one son. Brown went on to earn a master's degree from Atlanta University in 1964. Returning to Charleston, Brown went to work for Metropolitan Life Insurance Company, becoming the first black insurance consultant in Charleston. For five of his six years at MetLife, Brown was a million-dollar salesperson.

Brown's experience in developing pension and insurance programs for large businesses convinced him that he could operate his own business. In 1972 he created American Development Corporation (ADCOR), the first minority-owned manufacturing plant in the Southeast. It was financed largely by a $200,000 Small Business Administration loan, which Brown paid back in three years. A federal program guaranteed government contracts for qualified minority entrepreneurs. Overcoming a difficult start, Brown and ADCOR soon began to prosper. Attending evening classes, Brown earned an M.B.A. degree from Webster College in St. Louis in 1974. By the early 1990s ADCOR was realizing revenues of more than $30 million annually and employed 350 men and women. The manufacturing equipment and environmental testing facilities were geared mostly to sophisticated defense contracts. ADCOR produced such items as five-thousand-gallon tankers, ribbon bridge erection boats, hydraulic test systems, ammunition trailers, and electronic vans and was a subcontractor for Patriot missile launchers. When defense spending was cut, ADCOR produced thousands of wheeled mail containers for the U.S. Postal Service. By the time of Brown's death, ADCOR was the largest minority-owned manufacturing company in the United States.

Brown was the first African American named to the Charleston Aviation Authority board, the Palmetto Business Forum, the State Ports Authority Board, and the South Carolina Business Hall of Fame. In 1992 he was appointed to a seven-year term on the South Carolina Public Service Authority (Santee Cooper). He was a member of various other boards including the South Carolina Chamber of Commerce, the Clemson University board of visitors, the Talladega College board of directors, and the South Carolina State Educational Foundation board of directors. In 1991 *Upscale* magazine recognized Brown among the "Annual Power Brokers," which included business executives, entertainers, and religious leaders. He died on June 7, 1994, following an extended illness. He was buried in Live Oak Memorial Gardens, Charleston. ROBERT A. PIERCE

Bartelme, Tony. "Local Civic Leader W. M. Brown Dies." Charleston *Post and Courier,* June 8, 1994, pp. B1, B4.

Lunan, Bert, and Robert A. Pierce. *Legacy of Leadership.* Columbia: South Carolina Business Hall of Fame, 1999.

Brown Fellowship Society. Established on November 1, 1790, by free persons of color in Charleston, the Brown Fellowship Society is one of the earliest institutions founded by free African Americans in South Carolina. It is only one of the myriad organizations that gave structure to the free black community and functioned primarily as a mutual aid association. During its early history, free blacks received minimal benefits from public services and had to provide for their own needs. The organization maintained its own cemetery in downtown Charleston, and if a deceased member left insufficient funds for the care of survivors, the society provided assistance. In the early antebellum years the society established a school, and as but one example of its charitable work, it supported and educated a young orphan named Daniel Payne, who later became a bishop in the AME Church. Membership was originally limited to fifty men drawn from Charleston's free mulatto elite and their descendants. Traditionally these men were artisans, and they sometimes maintained businesses. The treasury of the organization provided a source of capital for enterprising members who speculated in real estate and made other investments. Beginning in the late nineteenth century, some members were college-educated professionals. Affiliation with the society became a marker of aristocratic status within Charleston's black community. The society had its own building and held regular banquets and celebrations. Before the Civil War, meetings of free blacks could arouse white suspicion, so as a precautionary measure, the discussion of politics and religious subjects was banned at meetings. Some of the more prominent surnames on its membership rolls were Holloway, DeReef, Kinloch, Mitchell, Weston, Mushington, and McKinlay. Although the benevolent function of the Brown Fellowship Society was supplanted largely by private insurance and equal access to public services, it continued as a social and burial society into the 1990s. BERNARD E. POWERS, JR.

Drago, Edmund L. *Initiative, Paternalism, and Race Relations: Charleston's Avery Normal Institute.* Athens: University of Georgia Press, 1990.

Fitchett, Horace. "The Free Negro in Charleston, South Carolina." Ph.D. diss., University of Chicago, 1950.

Gatewood, Willard. *Aristocrats of Color: The Black Elite, 1880–1920.* Bloomington: Indiana University Press, 1990.

Harris, Robert L., Jr. "Charleston's Free Afro-American Elite: The Brown Fellowship Society and the Humane Brotherhood." *South Carolina Historical Magazine* 82 (October 1981): 289–310.

Wikramanayake, Marina. *A World in Shadow: The Free Black in Antebellum South Carolina.* Columbia: University of South Carolina Press, 1973.

Bryan, Hugh (1699–1753). Planter, evangelist. Bryan was born in South Carolina, the son of Joseph Bryan and Janet Cochran. His father was a native of England and an earlier settler of the colony's southern frontier. As a youth, Hugh Bryan was captured by Indians during the Yamassee War of 1715, but he was released a year later at St. Augustine in Spanish East Florida. According to later testimony, while a captive Bryan "met with a Bible among the *Indians,*" which sustained him during his ordeal and laid the groundwork for his future spirituality. Returning to South Carolina, Bryan took up residence in St. Bartholomew's Parish and then St. Helena's Parish, where he quickly rose in the local social and economic hierarchy. By the late 1730s Bryan was a leading rice planter, cattle raiser, and slaveholder. His marriage on January 2, 1734, to Catherine Barnwell, the daughter of John "Tuscarora Jack" Barnwell, further advanced his position.

During a severe illness in 1739, Catherine Bryan underwent a conversion to evangelical Christianity. Impressed by his wife's devotion and her subsequent miraculous recovery, Hugh Bryan converted as well. When the English evangelist George Whitefield visited Georgia in 1740, the Bryans traveled to hear him and became enthusiastic followers. Under Whitefield's guidance, Hugh Bryan began to apply his understanding of religious writing to contemporary events. He saw the Stono slave rebellion of 1739, a disastrous fire in Charleston in 1740, droughts, and outbreaks of epidemic disease as signs of God's displeasure with South Carolina. He actively evangelized among his slaves and prophesied that the colony would be destroyed by "African Hosts" unless it repented and turned from its misguided ways. In January 1741 Bryan's warnings were printed in the *South-Carolina Gazette.* This aroused the ire of the residents of Charleston, who arrested Bryan and Whitefield and charged them with libel and contempt "against the King's peace." Both were released after a few days. Whitefield sailed for England, and Bryan returned to St. Helena's Parish, where he continued to evangelize, instruct his slaves in the fundamentals of religion, and call on the people of South Carolina to atone for their sins.

Bryan's activities did not go unnoticed by the Commons House of Assembly, which became increasingly alarmed at reports of the "frequent and great Assemblies of Negroes in the Parish of St. Helena." In February 1742, when Bryan sent the assembly a journal of his predictions that God would use the slave population to punish those who profaned his laws, the Commons House ordered his arrest. Bryan fled and underwent a grave crisis of faith. Witnesses claimed that, like Moses, he attempted to part the waters of a creek and cross that way, and he was nearly drowned. Shortly thereafter, Bryan wrote the Speaker of the House apologizing for "the Dishonour I've done to God, as well as the Disquiet which I may have occasioned to my Country."

Bryan returned to his plantation, where he continued to teach religion to slaves but no longer prophesied about slave rebellions as punishment for the worldliness of South Carolinians. He married Mary Prioleau on October 25, 1744, and died on his plantation on December 31, 1753. He was buried in the cemetery of Stoney Creek Independent Church, a dissenter congregation that he helped to found. NATHAN E. STALVEY

Edgar, Walter, and N. Louise Bailey, eds. *Biographical Directory of the South Carolina House of Representatives.* Vol. 2, *The Commons House of Assembly, 1692–1775.* Columbia: University of South Carolina Press, 1977.

Gallay, Alan. "The Great Awakening in the Deep South: George Whitefield, the Bryan Family, and the Origins of Slaveholders' Paternalism." *Journal of Southern History* 53 (August 1987): 369–94.

Jackson, Harvey H. "Hugh Bryan and the Evangelical Movement in Colonial South Carolina." *William and Mary Quarterly,* 3d ser., 43 (October 1986): 594–614.

Schmidt, Leigh Eric. "'The Grand Prophet,' Hugh Bryan: Early Evangelicalism's Challenge to the Establishment of Slavery in the Colonial South." *South Carolina Historical Magazine* 87 (October 1986): 238–50.

Bull, Stephen (?–1800). Soldier, legislator. Bull was born in South Carolina, the only surviving son of Stephen Bull and Martha Godin. He was descended from one of the first families of colonial South Carolina and was the nephew of Lieutenant Governor William Bull, Jr. Bull inherited Sheldon Plantation in Prince William's Parish. His family's prominence thrust him into political leadership. He represented Prince William's in the Commons House of Assembly from 1757 to 1760 and served as a justice of the peace from 1756 to 1769.

On the eve of the Revolutionary War, Bull was the colonel commanding the Beaufort District militia regiment. Unlike most members of his family, Bull supported the American cause and took up arms against the king. He led his regiment in the occupation of Savannah in 1776, a decisive event in bolstering Georgia patriots and driving Loyalists from Savannah. In 1778 Bull was promoted to brigadier general and led his regiment in the ill-fated American campaign against British East Florida. Command of the American forces was divided between General Robert Howe of the Continental army and Governor John Houston of Georgia. The American army never got past the Loyalist fort at St. Mary's, Georgia.

Bull participated with General William Moultrie in the American victory at Port Royal Island on February 3, 1779. Two months later the lowcountry was overrun by British General Augustine Prevost's invasion from Georgia, and defeat and desertions decimated Bull's regiment. After the fall of Charleston in May 1780, Bull went into self-imposed exile in Virginia and Maryland and offered no more service to the patriot cause.

Politically, Bull was elected from Prince William's Parish to the First and Second Provincial Congresses in 1775 and 1776 and the First and Second General Assemblies of South Carolina from 1776 to 1778. After the war Bull was a member of the S.C. House of Representatives from 1783 to 1790. He was twice elected to the S.C. Senate but declined to serve.

Bull was married first to Elizabeth Woodward, on December 18, 1755, and then to Ann Barnwell, on May 24, 1772. By his second wife he had three daughters: Charlotte, Mary, and Sarah. Bull died in 1800 and was buried at the ancestral seat at Ashley Hall, but he was later interred in Magnolia Cemetery, Charleston. LAWRENCE S. ROWLAND

Bailey, N. Louise, Mary L. Morgan, and Carolyn R. Taylor, eds. *Biographical Directory of the South Carolina Senate.* 3 vols. Columbia: University of South Carolina Press, 1986.

"Bull Family of South Carolina." *South Carolina Historical and Genealogical Magazine* 1 (January 1900): 76–90.

Rowland, Lawrence S., Alexander Moore, and George C. Rogers. *The History of Beaufort County, South Carolina.* Vol. 1, *1514–1861.* Columbia: University of South Carolina Press, 1996.

Bull, William (1683–1755). Planter, lieutenant governor. Bull was born in April 1683 in St. Andrew's Parish, the son of Stephen Bull, one of the original English settlers of South Carolina. His father was a successful planter and Indian trader, and William Bull added to his father's patrimony. Bull had a long political career that began in the proprietary era and continued for thirty-five years after South Carolina became a royal colony in 1720. Under a succession of proprietary governors he held several local commissions: church warden, road and ferry commissioner of St. Andrew's Parish, justice of the peace, and Revenue Act manager in 1716. Bull represented Berkeley and Craven Counties in the Eighth, Tenth, and Fifteenth Assemblies (1706–1708, 1716–1717) and was appointed by the Lords Proprietors to the Grand Council in 1719. As a militia officer he served in the Tuscarora and Yamassee Wars and was a proponent of reform in the colony's Indian trade policies.

Bull was a member of the Grand Council during the Revolution of 1719. Those rebels who ousted the Lords Proprietors considered Bull to be opposed to the revolution but permitted him to remain on the Council. During the 1720s Bull was a valuable member of the government. He served continuously on the Grand Council from 1719 to 1755 and as its president, and he was lieutenant governor from 1738 until his death in 1755. He was commissioner of the Indian Trade in 1721–1722 and revived the trade in the aftermath of the Yamassee War. A skilled surveyor, he assisted General James Oglethorpe in the settlement of Georgia and in selecting the site of Savannah.

As a long-serving, native-born Council member, Bull's attachments to colonial prerogative increased the power of the Commons House of Assembly. During a 1730s controversy over fiscal authority, Bull sided with the Commons House and asserted that body's prerogative to create money bills, an important element of colonial independence. From 1737 until the arrival of Governor James Glen in 1743, Bull was acting governor. During that time he led the provincial forces in suppressing the Stono Rebellion (1739) and assisted James Oglethorpe in Georgia's unsuccessful attack on Spanish St. Augustine (1740). Bull's son William Bull II (1710–1791) was for many years Speaker of the Commons House, and their joint political strength helped shape the province's political culture.

Bull inherited Ashley Hall, a plantation on the Ashley River. In 1704 he built a handsome brick mansion on the site and with his kinfolks, the Draytons and the Middletons, transformed the Ashley River area into a showplace of the planter elite. Bull was also among the early settlers in Prince William's Parish on the colony's southern frontier. His plantation, called Sheldon, was the main source of his economic wealth. Bull was the progenitor of a political dynasty of interconnected families. In addition to their sons Stephen and William, Bull and his wife, Mary Quintyne, were the parents of three daughters. Elizabeth married Thomas Drayton of Magnolia Plantation; Charlotta married Thomas's brother, John Drayton of Drayton Hall; and Henrietta married Henry Middleton of Middleton Place. These Ashley River families have had roles in South Carolina history for three centuries.

William Bull died on March 21, 1755, and was buried in the Prince William's Parish churchyard. The popular name of that church was Sheldon, taken from Bull's nearby plantation. ALEXANDER MOORE

Bull, Kinloch, Jr. *The Oligarchs in Colonial and Revolutionary Charleston: Lieutenant Governor William Bull II and His Family.* Columbia: University of South Carolina Press, 1991.

Edgar, Walter, and N. Louise Bailey, eds. *Biographical Directory of the South Carolina House of Representatives.* Vol. 2, *The Commons House of Assembly, 1692–1775.* Columbia: University of South Carolina Press, 1977.

Meroney, Geraldine M. *Inseparable Loyalty: A Biography of William Bull.* Norcross, Ga.: Harrison, 1991.

Sirmans, M. Eugene. "Masters of Ashley Hall: A Biographical Study of the Bull Family of Colonial South Carolina, 1670–1737." Ph.D. diss., Princeton University, 1959.

Bull, William, II (1710–1791). Lieutenant governor. Bull was born on September 24, 1710, at Ashley Hall Plantation, the son of William Bull (1683–1755) and Mary Quintyne. He was educated in London, England, at Westminster School and received an M.D. degree at Leyden University in the Netherlands. Bull was the first native-born American to earn a doctor of medicine degree. He did not establish a professional medical practice, but rather had a prolific career as a planter-politician.

Bull followed his father into politics when he was elected to the Commons House of Assembly for St. Andrew's Parish (1736). For thirteen years he represented St. John's Berkeley, St. Bartholomew's, and Prince William's Parishes. While a member and occasional Speaker of the House, he collaborated with his father, a member of the Royal Council, to expand colonial authority. In 1749 he joined the Royal Council. Ten years later, in 1759, Bull became president of the Council and lieutenant governor, and he held that post until his political career ended in 1775. During that period he was acting governor on five occasions, for a total of eight years of service. Bull opposed William Henry Lyttelton's Cherokee War policies, and when Lyttelton left the province in 1760, Bull started negotiations to end the war.

Bull's second term as acting governor (1764–1766) coincided with the Stamp Act crisis in the American colonies. He was not a strong supporter of the act but dutifully performed his job as a royal appointee. He clashed with radical members of the Commons House, including his brothers-in-law, Henry Middleton and John Drayton, and suffered the opprobrium of Charleston's Sons of Liberty. Despite difficulties, he was able to steer a course between the opposing factions. He negotiated the reopening of the Port of Charleston and the colonial courts, which had been closed by boycotts and the fear of mob violence if tax stamps were sold. Bull encouraged the expansion of the colony into the backcountry. As lieutenant and acting governor, he took a conciliatory approach to the Regulator movement and supported the creation of new parishes (election districts), schools, and courts in the backcountry.

During the 1770s Bull's political views grew increasingly out of step as South Carolina and other colonies moved toward radical opposition to the crown. The year 1775 was one of crisis in Bull's life and in the independence movement in South Carolina. Henry Middleton was president of the Continental Congress in Philadelphia, and the Provincial Congress of South Carolina began to organize for independence. Its Council of Safety, which included among its members Henry Laurens, William Henry Drayton, and Arthur Middleton, planned to take over the executive duties of a revolutionary government. Lord William Campbell, the last royal governor, arrived at Charleston on June 18, 1775, and took office, but his term lasted only three months. On September 15 he was forced to flee the city for refuge on a British warship in Charleston harbor. The revolution was under way, and Bull's position was an impossible one. He resigned from the Royal Council and retired to his Ashley Hall plantation. In 1777 he refused to take the oath of allegiance to the revolutionary government and was banished from the state. He executed deeds of trust and powers of attorney to his nephew Stephen Bull and other revolutionaries for his properties, then left for England on May 4, 1777.

Charleston was captured by British forces in May 1780, and in February 1781 Bull returned home. He became intendant general on the Board of Police, the body that governed occupied Charleston. He vainly sought clemency for the captured patriot Colonel Isaac Hayne, who was hanged by the British for breaking his parole. Despite his mediating actions, the General Assembly ordered Bull's property confiscated as punishment for his collaboration with the occupiers. His plantations, slaves, and personal property were appraised at £51,554 sterling. When the British evacuated Charleston in December 1782, Bull sailed back to England into a second, permanent exile. Despite his efforts to return to South Carolina after the Revolution, he was unsuccessful. He recovered his properties, and his name was removed, post facto, from the list of banished Loyalists. William Bull died in London on July 4, 1791, and was buried in St. Andrews Holburn Church, London. He was survived by his wife, Hannah Beale, daughter of Othniel Beale, whom he had wed on August 17, 1746. The couple had no children, and his considerable estate was divided among the children of his siblings. ALEXANDER MOORE

Bull, Kinloch, Jr. *The Oligarchs in Colonial and Revolutionary Charleston: Lieutenant Governor William Bull II and His Family.* Columbia: University of South Carolina Press, 1991.

Edgar, Walter, and N. Louise Bailey, eds. *Biographical Directory of the South Carolina House of Representatives.* Vol. 2, *The Commons House of Assembly, 1692–1775.* Columbia: University of South Carolina Press, 1977.

Meroney, Geraldine M. *Inseparable Loyalty: A Biography of William Bull.* Norcross, Ga.: Harrison, 1991.

Sirmans, M. Eugene. "Masters of Ashley Hall: A Biographical Study of the Bull Family of Colonial South Carolina, 1670–1737." Ph.D. diss., Princeton University, 1959.

Burke, Aedanus (1743–1802). Jurist, congressman. Born in Galway, Ireland, on June 16, 1743, Burke received his early education at a Jesuit seminary at St. Omer, France. Few details regarding his early life are known. In 1769 he immigrated to Virginia, where evidence suggests that he read law. After visiting the West Indies, he arrived in South Carolina in 1775 and served in the state militia during the Revolutionary War. In the absence of other interested candidates, he was elected a judge in March 1778 to sit on the Court of Common Pleas and General Sessions. He was captured at the fall of Charleston in 1780 and spent sixteen months in captivity, but he later advocated leniency toward Loyalists in the state.

When the South Carolina courts were reestablished after the Revolution, Burke resumed his seat on the bench. On an expedition to Georgia to purchase land near Savannah, he was elected chief justice of Georgia by the state assembly, but Burke declined the office in order to return to South Carolina.

Around the time of the British evacuation of Charleston in December 1782, Burke began a series of writings under the pseudonym "Cassius." His *Address to the Freemen of South Carolina* attacked the excesses and legitimacy of the Jacksonborough Assembly. He became a leading critic of the Society of the Cincinnati with the publication of *Considerations on the Society or Order of the Cincinnati* (1783), which depicted the society as elitist, hereditary, and repugnant to republican government. In an anonymous tract, *A Few Salutary Hints,* he attacked Great Britain and the British merchants in Charleston, espousing anti-Federalist principles.

Burke sat intermittently in the South Carolina General Assembly from 1779 until 1788. By 1785 he was recognized as a legal scholar and, with Henry Pendleton and John F. Grimké, was appointed to prepare a digest of state laws. In 1788 Burke was a leading opponent of the proposed U.S. Constitution, but on its ratification he pledged his support for the new government.

Burke was elected as an anti-Federalist to the First Congress of the United States, commencing service in New York on March 4, 1789. He served on thirty-three committees and was instrumental in crafting bills that led to the judiciary act and the creation of the Library of Congress, the postal system, and the patent system. His congressional service was marked by an incident with Alexander Hamilton, whom Burke felt had slighted southern soldiers when Hamilton eulogized General Nathanael Greene. The Burke-Hamilton enmity, fueled by Republican-Federalist antagonism, did not subside. A decade later Burke served as second to Aaron Burr in a duel with John B. Church, brother-in-law of Alexander Hamilton.

Burke served one term in Congress and declined to stand for reelection in 1790, when the legislature passed a law prohibiting a state judge from leaving the state. In 1799 he was elected chancellor of the Court of Equity in Charleston and served until his death in Charleston on March 30, 1802. Burke never married. He was interred in the cemetery of the Chapel of Ease of St. Bartholomew's Parish, near Jacksonborough in Colleton County. His portrait hangs in Hibernian Hall in Charleston. JOHN L. NAPIER

Meleney, John C. *The Public Life of Aedanus Burke: Revolutionary Republican in Post-Revolutionary South Carolina.* Columbia: University of South Carolina Press, 1989.

Burnettown (Aiken County; 2000 pop. 2,720). Incorporated in 1941, Burnettown is located in the Horse Creek Valley of Aiken County. In the late 1800s and early 1900s the area was only land with a dirt road running through it. In 1890 Daniel Burnette obtained land on one side of the dirt road. In 1901 he sold a few lots, homes were built, and the property became known as "Mr. Burnette's land." A portion was later traversed by the route of a proposed interurban trolley line between Aiken and Augusta, Georgia. As word spread about the trolley line, people built houses on both sides of the proposed tracks. When the trolley began operation in 1902, people realized that there was no name for this land between the mill villages of Langley and Bath. Passengers boarding or departing the trolley at this point decided to call the site Burnette Town. The trolley was discontinued in 1929, and its tracks were taken up and replaced by a road. Improvements in the surrounding mill towns took place as well. Water lines were laid and a new road was paved, which became S.C. Highway 421. Later a more modern highway was built on the opposite side of Horse Creek; this road became U.S. Highway 1.

In the late 1920s and early 1930s, after the demise of the trolley line, a few enterprising men in the Horse Creek Valley bought cars to taxi mill employees to work. To continue this business, however, it was necessary to have an incorporated town between Aiken and Augusta to license these taxis to pick up passengers on the highway. Like most textile towns, Langley and Bath were owned by the mills and therefore not incorporated. Since it was not a mill town, Burnettown opted to incorporate. On June 5, 1941, a charter was issued to this town of 423 people. George R. Dillon was elected as the first mayor.

To celebrate the town's fiftieth birthday, a street dance was held in 1991. This event evolved into a weeklong annual celebration—the Sassafras Festival—now attended by several thousand people the first week of October.

The 2000 census recorded that Burnettown was the fastest-growing town in South Carolina, with a population that grew from just 493 in 1990 to 2,720 by 2000 (a 452 percent increase). Most of this increase was the result of a series of annexations that took place in the 1990s. With the decline of the textile industry in the late twentieth century, the workforce has become more diverse. Many residents still work in textile plants, but many others work in education or local government, or they commute to the Savannah River Site. Recent improvements include construction of the Fun Valley Sassafras Park and a partnership with the Veterans of Foreign Wars (VFW) to establish Horse Creek/Midland Valley Veterans Park. PATRICIA DIAMOND

Burroughs & Chapin. Burroughs & Chapin Company, Inc., was formed in 1990 when the century-old Burroughs & Collins Company of Conway merged with Myrtle Beach Farms Company. Headquartered in Myrtle Beach and holding tens of thousands of acres throughout Horry County, Burroughs & Chapin is dedicated to coastal economic development and attracting new businesses to Myrtle Beach and the Grand Strand. The firm is the linear descendant of the business partnership formed in 1895 by Franklin

Burroughs and B. G. Collins. In 1912 Simeon B. Chapin, a Chicago financier, joined Burroughs's sons to form Myrtle Beach Farms Company. Pairing Chapin's money and business expertise with the Burroughs brothers' vast land holdings, Myrtle Beach Farms led Horry County through an extended period of robust economic growth and development for Myrtle Beach, the Grand Strand, and Horry County.

The company, however, has not been without controversy. Its development of Grand Strand properties for commercial and residential uses has been criticized for encroachment on crucial coastal habitats. In 1999 the company and four partners purchased 4,600 acres along the Congaree River in Richland County, where they planned to create a mixed commercial/residential development called "Green Diamond." Many groups and individuals opposed the development as environmentally dangerous. After an extensive public relations campaign and an unsuccessful lawsuit against the Federal Emergency Management Agency over the accuracy of a federal flood map of the site, Burroughs & Chapin failed to win approval for the ambitious project. By April 2003 the chairman of the board admitted, "Green Diamond is no longer a possibility." RICK D. BOULWARE

Burroughs, Franklin Gorham (1834–1897). Manufacturer, merchant, land developer. Born on December 28, 1834, in Martin County, North Carolina, Burroughs was the son of Anthony Burroughs and Ethelinda Cobb. Entering into farming at a young age, Burroughs soon became frustrated with the business. In 1857, with a gift of $40 from his mother, Burroughs left North Carolina to work for a cousin in a mercantile and turpentine business at Conway, South Carolina. That same year, on his own initiative, he won contracts to construct a bridge and gallows for the town. The following year he became involved in the short-lived partnership of Singleton and Burroughs.

In July 1861 Burroughs entered the military as a private in the Confederate service. After nine months of coastal defense duty in the Georgetown area, he took part in heavy fighting, including the battles of Chickamauga, Missionary Ridge, Atlanta, and Franklin. In December 1864 he was captured in the Battle of Nashville and imprisoned at Camp Douglas near Chicago. On his way home after the war, he was quartered at Greensboro (North Carolina) Female Institute and was so well cared for there that he later sent four of his five daughters to the institute. On November 15, 1866, he married Adeline Cooper of Conway. They had eleven children, eight surviving infancy.

After his marriage, Burroughs expanded his turpentine and retail businesses. Among his partners were William D. Gurganus, a relative, and Hampton Hart. In 1895 Burroughs and B. G. Collins incorporated a partnership dealing with manufacturing, naval stores, land, and mercantile stores in key Horry County localities. The naval stores business declined after an 1893 hurricane ravaged timberland, but their real estate business thrived. Although he never displayed an interest in politics, Burroughs was recognized as one of Horry County's dominant figures from 1870 to his death in 1897. He lacked formal schooling but believed strongly in education and dominated the local school board. He saw that his daughters received higher education. Burroughs never spent the $40 he brought from North Carolina but passed the original coins down to his eight children.

Although Myrtle Beach was not founded in his lifetime, Burroughs dreamed of a coastal resort midway between New York and Miami. He set in motion the building of a railroad to what is now Myrtle Beach, and his sons completed his plan—a major step toward developing the resort. His widow named Myrtle Beach for the plant that thrived there. The Burroughs heirs, along with Simeon Chapin, built a remarkable business that was to include forestry, farming, shopping centers, theme parks, and golf courses. Burroughs died on February 25, 1897. He was inducted into the South Carolina Business Hall of Fame in 1993. ROBERT A. PIERCE

Bedford, A. Goff. *The Independent Republic: A Survey of Horry County South Carolina History.* 2d ed. Conway, S.C.: Horry County Historical Society, 1989.

Lewis, Catherine H. *Horry County, South Carolina, 1730–1993.* Columbia: University of South Carolina Press, 1998.

Lunan, Bert, and Robert A. Pierce. *Legacy of Leadership.* Columbia: South Carolina Business Hall of Fame, 1999.

Burroughs, Franklin Gorham, Jr. (b. 1942). Essayist, environmentalist, educator. Burroughs was born on March 7, 1942, in Conway to Franklin Gorham Burroughs, Sr., and Geraldine Bryan. In 1964 he earned his B.A. from the University of the South, and then at Harvard University he completed his A.M. in 1965 and his Ph.D. in 1970. In 1968 he began teaching at Bowdoin College in Maine, where he continued until his retirement in the fall of 2000.

Burroughs's work, often compared to that of New England poet Henry David Thoreau, was collected in *Best American Essays* in 1987 and 1989. In 1989 he was awarded the Pushcart Prize for nature essays. His collection *Billy Watson's Croker Sack* appeared in 1991, followed by a paperback edition in 1992. That same year his book *Horry and the Waccamaw* was published, and it was later reprinted in 1998 with the title *The River Home: A Return to the Carolina Low Country.*

The River Home tells the story of Burroughs's canoe trip down the Waccamaw River, focusing on the South Carolina counties of Horry and Georgetown, the same country landscapes that he remembered from childhood. His journey was inspired by his discovery of Nathaniel Holmes Bishop's *The Voyage of the Paper Canoe* (1878), recounting that author's East Coast river voyage. Donald Dederick wrote that Burroughs's story "is not simply a recapitulation of a famous canoe trip, but a well-written tribute to an area and its people, economy, and history." *The River Home* is about the intimate relationship between human beings and the land—about how people's customs and language reflect their environment in complex ways.

In 1999 Burroughs's "Compression Wood" was collected in *Best American Essays.* Part literary analysis and part personal narrative of a trip to South Carolina, the piece once again takes up his familiar theme of the relationship between people and place. Driving north through Pennsylvania after visiting his native Conway, Burroughs thinks about the questions "What do you do?" and "Where do you come from?" Along with philosophical speculation and poetry analysis, the essay accomplishes a sketch of a man called McIver, whom Burroughs has grown up with and who embodies his environmental values. Working with lumber salvaged from Hurricane Hugo wreckage, McIver says, "People who don't work with primary resources don't understand reality. And not understanding reality is a functional definition of insanity."

"Compression Wood" contains astute cultural observation as well: "When you stop for gas in the Virginia tidewater, you hear that something has happened to the language. Tongues seem to have lost their agility. Vowels and consonants thicken and soften; cadences and sentences ooze and eddy and ebb, and you can stand there, half listening to the attendant and half thinking of the silt-laden, leisurely rivers and streams and swamps that wind through this flat country and in fact created it. . . . " The essay's insights reflect much of Burroughs's philosophy: "Where you're from is never simply a matter of geography. It involves intersections of history, economics, family, and so forth, as well as the coordinates of latitude and longitude. Self-location, with or without maps, is ultimately as complicated and incomplete a process as self-knowledge." AMY L. WHITE

Burroughs, Franklin. "Compression Wood." *American Scholar* 67 (spring 1998): 123–37.

Crum, Robert. "Book Reviews—'Billy Watson's Croker Sack' by Franklin Burroughs." *Georgia Review* 45 (winter 1991): 808.

Dederick, Donald H. "Sports & Recreation—'Horry and the Waccamaw' by Franklin Burroughs." *Library Journal* 117 (January 1992): 140.

Ives, Nancy R. "Literature—'Billy Watson's Croker Sack' by Franklin Burroughs." *Library Journal* 116 (January 1991): 104.

Burt, Armistead (1802–1883). Lawyer, congressman. Burt was born in Edgefield District on November 13, 1802, the oldest of nine children of Francis Burt, a Revolutionary War veteran from Virginia, and Katherine Miles of Beaufort District. In 1807 the family moved to Pendleton District, where Burt attended Pendleton Academy before preparing for a career in law. He was admitted to the bar in 1823.

In 1828 Burt married Martha Catherine Calhoun of Abbeville District, the daughter of John C. Calhoun's older brother William. The couple moved to Abbeville, where Burt built his law practice. Burt first knew his wife's famous uncle as a Pendleton neighbor and eventually became his confidant and protégé. He supported Calhoun's opposition to the 1828 "Tariff of Abominations" and was appointed secretary of the 1832 state convention, which passed the Ordinance of Nullification, which declared the federal tariff null and void in South Carolina.

Burt represented Abbeville District in the General Assembly for three terms (1834–1835, 1838–1839, 1840–1841). He was elected to the U.S. House of Representatives in 1842 and took his seat in Congress in March 1843. He sat in Congress for ten years, serving on the Judiciary Committee and as chair of the Military Affairs Committee from 1849 to 1853. Burt was an accepted spokesman in the House for Calhoun's prosouthern policy, particularly preserving states' rights, reducing tariffs, and maintaining the balance between slave and free states as the country expanded into the Western territories. He helped care for Calhoun during his last illness in 1850.

In 1853 Burt left Congress and returned to Abbeville District to supervise Orange Hill, his thriving plantation near the Savannah River. He also participated in local politics, voicing a moderate approach to secession. He urged that South Carolina should act only in cooperation with other southern states. In 1858 Burt moved to the town of Abbeville to focus on his law practice. During the Civil War he supervised enlistments and was custodian for the property and affairs of local soldiers.

In April 1865 Confederate First Lady Varina Howell Davis and her family stayed in the Burt home for twelve days after they fled Richmond. They left Abbeville two days before Jefferson Davis, Secretary of War John C. Breckinridge, and the Confederacy's senior military advisers arrived. On May 2, 1865, at Burt's house, the leaders held their final council of war. On advice from his advisers, Davis agreed that further resistance was impossible and that the Confederate cause was lost.

After the war Burt was selected to draft the state's "Black Codes," which white South Carolinians used to regulate the labor and movements of former slaves. During Reconstruction he continued his Abbeville law practice while participating in the movement to discredit and remove the state's Republican leadership. In 1868 Burt served as president of the first Convention of South Carolina Democratic Clubs and the state Democratic Convention, as well as a delegate to the national Democratic Convention. Burt participated in the Taxpayers' Conventions of 1871 and 1874, preparing reports detailing corruption within state government. He also supported Wade Hampton's 1876 campaign for governor. Burt died in his law office on October 30, 1883. He was buried in Trinity Episcopal Cemetery in Abbeville. SUSAN GIAIMO HIOTT

Burt, Armistead. Papers. Manuscript Department, William R. Perkins Library, Duke University, Durham, North Carolina.

Burts, Robert M. "The Life of Armistead Burt." Master's thesis, Duke University, 1945.

Burton, Edward Milby (1898–1977). Museum director, naturalist, historian. Born in Germantown, Pennsylvania, on June 5, 1898, Burton was the son of Elliot H. Burton and Aline Roussell. When he was two months old the family moved to Charleston, South Carolina, where his father established a highly successful lumber company. Of French parentage, his mother valued the arts and gracious living and had young Milby, as he was called, tutored in French and German. She took him abroad and introduced him to museums, requiring him to look carefully at everything so that he could describe to her the most important items he had seen. Through those experiences he developed an early interest in museum work.

After graduation from Gaud High School, Burton went to work at the Burton Lumber Company. As a young man his avid interest in hunting and fishing grew into an interest in natural history. In 1924 he joined a prominent Charleston insurance firm, and on March 1, 1924, he married Sally Morris Pinckney. He became a member of the board of trustees of the Charleston Museum in 1930 and was instrumental in the acquisition of the Arthur T. Wayne ornithological collection for the museum. In 1932 he was appointed director of the Charleston Museum, a position for which he was well suited. His membership in the Preservation Society, the St. Cecilia Society, and the Carolina Plantation Society opened many doors to funds for the support of museum projects.

Burton set out to enlarge the museum's collection of freshwater fish, collecting in streams throughout the state. By 1934 he had personally added 3,156 specimens to the collection, and those specimens were the basis for Henry Fowler's large monograph on South Carolina fish in 1935. During the late 1930s he secured the historic Joseph Manigault House for the museum, thereby saving it from destruction. At the same time, he was publishing notes reporting new records of fish from South Carolina. His museum career was interrupted by service in the U.S. Navy during World War II, during which he was awarded the Silver Star for courage under fire.

Burton's intense interest in the culture and history of the South Carolina lowcountry resulted in three landmark books: *South Carolina Silversmiths, 1690–1860* (1942); *Charleston Furniture, 1700–1825* (1955); and the critically acclaimed Civil War narrative *The Siege of Charleston, 1861–1865* (1970). He also contributed crucial editorial work on *South Carolina Bird Life* (1949), by Alexander Sprunt and E. Burnham Chamberlain, regarded as one of the best state-bird books. Burton was knowledgeable in many fields, and his academic pursuits led him to membership in the Walpole Society, the American Society of Ichthyologists and Herpetologists, the American Ornithological Union, and the South Carolina Historical Society. He was included in *American Men of Science* and held an honorary doctorate of law degree from the College of Charleston.

A dynamic individual with charm, refinement, and an engaging personality, Burton spent forty years as director of the Charleston Museum, retiring in 1972. He died in Charleston on August 27, 1977, leaving many friends and admirers and an international reputation. He was buried in the cemetery at old St. Andrew's Church. ALBERT E. SANDERS

Byrd, Sam. "E. Milby Burton, Charleston's Best Showman." *South Carolina Magazine* 13 (June 1950): 10, 25.

"Milby Burton, Ex-Director of Museum, Dies." Charleston *News and Courier*, August 29, 1977, pp. A1, A9.

Sanders, Albert E., and William D. Anderson, Jr. *Natural History Investigations in South Carolina from Colonial Times to the Present.* Columbia: University of South Carolina Press, 1999.

Busbee, Cyril B. (1908–2001). Educator. Busbee was born on December 17, 1908, in Wagener, the son of William Judson Busbee and Minnie Toole. He received a bachelor's degree from the University of South Carolina in 1928, followed by a master's degree in 1938. He married Thelma Ecord in 1929, and they had two children, Cyril and Carolyn.

In his early career Busbee was a teacher, coach, and administrator at Homerville, Georgia; Windsor, South Carolina; and Baron DeKalb schools in Westville, South Carolina. In 1943 he moved to Brookland-Cayce schools (which later became Lexington District Two), where he rose to superintendent. He served in the U.S. Navy during World War II in the European theater. After returning to his school district in 1946, he remained as superintendent for twenty-one years. As an administrator, he was considered quite teacher-oriented.

When Dr. Jesse T. Anderson retired as state superintendent of education in 1966, Busbee won election to the position. In the election he surmounted the first serious Republican challenge in a century, beating Dr. Inez C. Eddings with fifty-three percent of the vote. Busbee ran as a moderate conservative and won despite the unpopularity in South Carolina of the national Democratic educational policies of the Johnson administration. Four years later he easily won reelection against Eddings, and he was unopposed in 1974. After three terms as state superintendent, he retired in 1979.

Under federal desegregation guidelines, the state had to create a unitary school system instead of the racially separate systems that had been in place prior to the *Brown v. Board of Education* decision. Federal guidelines quashed tactics such as freedom-of-choice plans that many districts utilized to circumvent or slow desegregation. Busing to achieve a racial balance was emphasized in the new regulations. Busbee's calm, moderate leadership as superintendent proved a great asset during these times. The process for South Carolina was not without some opposition, most notably the Lamar Riots of 1970, but the state fared better than many other southern states did in accepting, however reluctantly, full integration of schools. Busbee received credit for the relatively calm transition. His leadership was instrumental in the shift from the traditional conservative perspective of federal meddling in local educational matters, to political acceptance of federal dollars for education as an advantage to the state. The state enacted a statewide kindergarten program, and the state's free basic textbook program was expanded to include all grade levels. Busbee also oversaw the opening of fifty-six vocational centers for high school students.

After retirement, Busbee worked as a consultant to the president of the University of South Carolina. He also served as a director of C&S National Bank and the Lexington Medical Center. During his retirement he lived in Cayce, where he died on September 6, 2001. He was interred at Southland Memorial Gardens. DAN G. RUFF

Obituary. Columbia *State*, September 7, 2001, p. B4.

Butler, Andrew Pickens (1796–1857). Jurist, U.S. senator. Butler, the son of General William Butler and Behethland Foote Moore—both heroes of the Revolutionary War—was born on November 18, 1796, in Edgefield District. He was schooled first at Moses Waddel's academy at Willington in Abbeville District and then at South Carolina College, from which he was graduated in 1817. On admission to the bar in 1819, Butler set up a law practice in Columbia. Soon after, he returned to Edgefield, where he maintained a lucrative legal practice and operated a plantation at his Stonelands estate. Butler, who owned one thousand acres and sixty-four slaves by 1850, owed much of his wealth and prestige to his distinguished lineage and his family's position among the local elite. Butler's first wife, Susan Anne Simkins, died on May 22, 1830, just months after their marriage. Two years later, in 1832, Butler wed Harriet Hayne. The couple had one child, daughter Eloise, before Harriet's death in 1834. He never married again.

Butler also owed his early prominence and much of his later political influence to his friendship with John C. Calhoun. In 1824 Butler won election to the South Carolina General Assembly, representing Edgefield District in the S.C. House from 1824 to 1831 and in the S.C. Senate from 1832 to 1833. During his Senate tenure he became a staunch Calhoun ally in the nullification controversy, even raising a company of cavalry, the Edgefield Hussars, after President Andrew Jackson threatened to invade the state. His alliance with Calhoun probably forced Butler to appear more radical than he actually was, and it was only after Calhoun's death that Butler's relative moderation became apparent.

In 1833 Butler accepted an appointment as a state judge, serving on the bench until 1846. Contemporaries who described him as pleasing and congenial in person found that he could often be sour, short, and sarcastic on the bench, and opinions of his effectiveness varied from decisive and efficient to bored and disinterested. In 1846 he seemed to welcome the opportunity to fill one of South Carolina's seats in the U.S. Senate, vacated by the resignation of George McDuffie. Partly due to Calhoun's influence, he won that election and was reelected in 1848 and 1854.

Still in Calhoun's shadow, Butler assumed the senior senator's extreme sectional stance during what was a fiery era in American politics. Like Calhoun, he denied that the federal government had any power over slavery in the territories. He opposed the admission of California, which was poised to enter the Union as a free state, and called for a stronger fugitive slave law. On Calhoun's death in 1850, however, Butler subtly changed his position. As sectional controversy reached a crescendo that summer, Butler endorsed the Compromise of 1850. From then on, and even as fire-eaters at home were pushing for secession, his public remarks tended to decry sectional alienation and civil strife.

Despite his inclination toward compromise, Butler remained a staunch advocate of slavery and a critic of abolitionists' agitation. In 1854 Butler supported the Kansas-Nebraska Act, which repealed the Missouri Compromise and instituted popular sovereignty in the

Kansas territory. His support of Kansas-Nebraska and some well-placed barbs about abolitionists soon engaged him in a verbal duel with Senator Charles Sumner of Massachusetts. The two exchanged occasional caustic remarks for two years until, in May 1856, the quarrel blew up into one of the most notorious episodes of political violence in U.S. history.

Indeed, Butler is perhaps best remembered for his role in the affair—even though he was not present for one minute of it. On May 19 and 20, Sumner launched into a speech entitled "The Crime against Kansas." His villain was Butler, who was absent. Butler was "the Don Quixote of slavery," and his mistress in this morality play, "though ugly to others, is always lovely to him; though polluted in the sight of the world, is chaste in his sight . . . the harlot, Slavery." Sumner then compounded the insult by mocking Butler's habit of spitting when he spoke. On May 22, in an incident that some historians view as a critical turning point toward civil war, Butler's cousin Preston S. Brooks avenged his kinsman by caning Sumner on the floor of the Senate. Sumner was incapacitated for three years; Butler, however, defended the act as necessary and honorable. Almost exactly a year later, on May 25, 1857, Butler died at his home in Edgefield. PAUL CHRISTOPHER ANDERSON

Burton, Orville Vernon. *In My Father's House Are Many Mansions: Family and Community in Edgefield, South Carolina.* Chapel Hill: University of North Carolina Press, 1985.

Butler, Andrew P. Papers. South Caroliniana Library, University of South Carolina, Columbia.

Gradin, Harlan Joel. "Losing Control: The Caning of Charles Sumner and the Breakdown of Antebellum Political Culture." Ph.D. diss., University of North Carolina at Chapel Hill, 1991.

Butler, Matthew Calbraith (1836–1909). Soldier, U.S. senator. Born at Eagle's Crag near Greenville on March 8, 1836, Butler was the son of Dr. William Butler and Jane Tweedy Perry. He attended Greenville Male Academy and moved with his family to Fort Gibson, Indian Territory, where his father served as Cherokee Indian agent from 1849 until his death in 1850. In the autumn of 1851, Calbraith, as he was called, arrived in Edgefield District to live with his uncle Andrew P. Butler. Educated at the Edgefield Male Academy, he entered South Carolina College in October 1854 but withdrew in 1856 after participating in the student "guard house riot." Returning to Edgefield, Butler studied law and was admitted to the bar in December 1857. On February 25, 1858, Butler married Maria Simkins Pickens. The couple had eight children. In 1860 Butler was elected from Edgefield to the S.C. House of Representatives.

On June 14, 1861, the Edgefield Hussars, with Butler as captain, were mustered into Confederate service as part of the Hampton Legion. Butler's field commander, Wade Hampton III, deemed him the finest cavalry officer he ever saw. His actions at First Manassas led to his promotion to major on July 21, 1861. In August 1862 Butler became colonel of the Second South Carolina Cavalry. At the Battle of Brandy Station (June 9, 1863) he lost his right foot to an artillery shell, but his contributions in that battle led to his promotion to brigadier general on September 1, 1863. While still on crutches, Butler returned to active duty in early 1864. His conspicuous service in the Virginia theater led to his elevation to major general on December 7, 1864. Butler and his division were ordered to South Carolina on January 19, 1865, in a vain attempt to thwart Sherman's march. Butler surrendered in April 1865 and was soon paroled.

Returning to Edgefield, Butler received a presidential pardon on October 27, 1865, and resumed his legal practice and political activities. Reelected to the General Assembly in 1865, Butler advocated a measure granting civil rights to former slaves and voted against passage of the controversial "Black Codes," to be used by white South Carolinians to regulate former slaves' labor and movements. In 1870 he ran unsuccessfully as a Democrat for lieutenant governor on the fusionist Union Reform Party ticket, and he was a member of the 1871 and 1874 taxpayers conventions. He was a central figure in the Hamburg Massacre of July 1876, although not a participant in its violence. Concluding that reform was impossible in cooperation with state Republicans and that appeals for black support were futile, Butler became a champion of the "straight-out" Democratic movement of 1876, and with Martin W. Gary he orchestrated the "Edgefield Plan" of campaign, which was to restore Democratic rule to South Carolina through fraud, intimidation, and violence. After Butler was elected to the U.S. Senate in December 1876, his victory was unsuccessfully contested by the Republican candidate David T. Corbin. Butler took his seat on November 30, 1877. Reelected in 1882 and 1888, he remained in the Senate until March 3, 1895, and served as chairman of the Committee on Civil Service and Retrenchment (Forty-sixth Congress) and the Committee on Interstate Commerce (Fifty-third Congress). As a senator, Butler supported civil service reform, a strong navy, and the elevation of the agriculture department to cabinet-level status. He also secured nearly $5 million in federal funds for South Carolina harbor and river improvements and public buildings. In 1890 Butler instigated a national debate with his introduction of a bill to provide federal aid to blacks who would emigrate to Africa. Responding to South Carolina's agrarian movement, Butler shifted his position from that of a conservative Democrat to one favoring such Populist measures as the free coinage of silver and a federal income tax.

Defeated for reelection in 1894 by Benjamin R. Tillman, Butler remained in Washington, forming the law firm of Shelley, Butler and Martin. On May 28, 1898, President William McKinley appointed Butler major general of volunteers in the Spanish-American War. As a member of the Cuban Peace Commission, Butler oversaw the evacuation of Spanish troops from the island, and he was honorably discharged on April 15, 1899. Resuming his legal practice, he maintained business interests in New York and Philadelphia and became president of the Hidalgo Pla cer Mining and Milling Company of Mexico in January 1904.

On January 14, 1905, Butler married Nancy Bostic Whitman of Washington, D.C. (Maria Butler had died in 1900.) Handsome, courtly, and possessed of a fiery temperament and a keen eye for the ladies, Butler was characterized by one of his sons as a complete military man and a stern but loving father. An Episcopalian for most of his life, he was received into the Catholic Church on his seventy-third birthday. He died on April 14, 1909, in Columbia and was buried in Edgefield's Willowbrook Cemetery. PAUL R. BEGLEY

Brooks, Ulysses R. *Butler and His Cavalry in the War of Secession, 1861–1865.* Columbia, S.C.: State Company, 1909.

Cooper, William J., Jr. *The Conservative Regime: South Carolina, 1877–1890.* Baltimore: Johns Hopkins Press, 1968.

Martin, Samuel J. *Southern Hero: Matthew Calbraith Butler, Confederate General, Hampton Red Shirt, and U.S. Senator.* Mechanicsburg, Pa.: Stackpole, 2001.

Butler, Pierce (1744–1822). Soldier, planter, statesman. Butler was born on July 11, 1744, in county Carlow, Ireland, the son of Henrietta Percy and Sir Richard Butler, fifth baronet of Cloughgrenan. His parents purchased a commission for Butler in the British army, and he rose through the ranks quickly. In 1766 he attained the rank of major, and in 1768 Butler's regiment (the Twenty-ninth Foot) was transferred to South Carolina. Butler gained entry into Charleston society through his marriage to Mary Middleton on January 10, 1771. When his regiment returned to England in 1773, Butler sold his commission and remained in Charleston.

While proud of his aristocratic heritage, Butler nevertheless supported the patriot cause during the Revolutionary War. Governor John Rutledge appointed Butler as the state's adjutant general in 1779, placing him in charge of organizing, training, and mobilizing the South Carolina militia. Though given the rank of brigadier, Butler preferred his previous title of "major." After the fall of Charleston in May 1780, Butler joined the army of Horatio Gates in North Carolina and remained with the Continental army until the end of the war. Butler returned to South Carolina to find his family exiled, his plantations burned, and some two hundred of his slaves confiscated by the British. Despite these deprivations, he still favored leniency for the state's Loyalists and supported the return of their confiscated property.

Although Butler served in the General Assembly from 1776 to 1789, his most significant political accomplishments came at the national level. In 1787 the legislature elected Butler to both the Confederation Congress and the constitutional convention scheduled to meet later that spring in Philadelphia. In the constitutional debates, Butler generally supported proposals for a strong central government, a single executive, and wealth rather than population as the basis of representation. He also championed South Carolina interests, especially slavery, and vigorously opposed the three-fifths compromise, arguing that slaves represented property wealth and should be counted fully for purposes of representation. "Money is strength," he argued, "and every state ought to have its weight in the national council in proportion to the quantity it possesses." Butler also proposed the measure that would eventually be incorporated into the Constitution as the Fugitive Slave clause. Though not entirely satisfied with the final document, he urged its ratification as an improvement over the ineffective Articles of Confederation.

After the convention, Butler returned to the state legislature, where he upheld the interests of the emerging backcountry. His services were rewarded by his election as South Carolina's first U.S. senator, and he took his seat in New York in June 1789. During his term Butler allied himself with the Federalist Party, supporting the financial program of Alexander Hamilton. Concern for South Carolina interests also was a Butler priority, with one Senate colleague, William Maclay of Pennsylvania, calling him "the most local and partial creature I ever heard open a mouth."

After his reelection to the Senate in 1792, Butler's growing sectional interests sparked a reversal in his political allegiances. Breaking with the Federalists, Butler became a vocal Jeffersonian and was mentioned as a possible vice-presidential choice in 1796. Butler resigned from the Senate on October 25, 1796, but returned in 1802 to fill the unexpired term of John Ewing Colhoun. But Butler soon fell out with the Jeffersonians as well. Believing that the Jeffersonians had strayed too far from their principles, he resigned his Senate seat in 1804. Butler had hoped that the nation had changed its political "diet" by electing Thomas Jefferson in 1800, but he declared that Jefferson's administration was "pork still with only a change of sauce." So deep was his rift with the administration that he even gave refuge to Jefferson's disgraced vice president, Aaron Burr, after Burr killed Alexander Hamilton in their famous duel at Weehawken, New Jersey.

Following his departure from the U.S. Senate, Butler concentrated on his numerous landholdings. Beginning in the 1790s, Butler had acquired large tracts of land, especially in Ninety Six District as well as along the coastal region of Georgia. By 1809 Butler was one of the South's wealthiest planters. His six Georgia plantations produced large crops of rice and cotton through the labor of some 540 slaves. By his death, Butler owned more than 1,000 slaves and his estate was valued at more than $1 million. After his wife's death in 1790, Butler became largely an absentee landlord, residing most of the year in Philadelphia and coming south only once a year to visit his holdings.

Butler came out of retirement briefly in 1816 to become a director of the Second Bank of the United States. Declining health forced him to refuse a second term. After an extended illness, Butler died on February 15, 1822, and was buried in Philadelphia's Christ Church Cemetery. KEVIN M. GANNON

Bell, Malcolm. *Major Butler's Legacy: Five Generations of a Slaveholding Family.* Athens: University of Georgia Press, 1987.

Coghlan, Francis. "Pierce Butler, 1744–1822, First Senator from South Carolina." *South Carolina Historical Magazine* 78 (April 1977): 104–19.

Sikes, Lewright Browning. *The Public Life of Pierce Butler, South Carolina Statesman.* Washington, D.C.: University of America Press, 1979.

Butler, Pierce Mason (1798–1847). Soldier, governor. Pierce Mason Butler was born on April 11, 1798, at Mount Welling Plantation, the family estate in Edgefield District. He was the sixth son of William Butler and Behethland Moore. Butler attended Moses Waddel's academy at Willington and graduated from South Carolina College. Through the influence of his local congressman and Secretary of War John C. Calhoun, Butler gained an army commission as second lieutenant on August 13, 1819. Three years later Butler was promoted to first lieutenant and transferred to the U.S. Seventh Infantry Regiment at Fort Smith, Arkansas Territory. In 1824 he commanded a detachment that built and garrisoned Fort Gibson, Indian Territory (modern-day Oklahoma). The following year Butler, by now a captain, commanded the survey party that mapped the military road between Fort Gibson and Fort Smith. During this period Butler met Miranda Julia Duval, whom he married on May 22, 1826.

On October 1, 1829, Butler resigned his commission and returned to South Carolina. He established residence near Columbia at Dogwood Plantation, a 154-acre plantation worked by twenty-seven slaves. However, Butler never made cotton planting the main source of his livelihood. In 1830 he secured an executive position with the Columbia branch of the Bank of the State of South Carolina, serving as branch president from 1833 until 1836.

In September 1832 the voters of Richland District elected Butler to the state nullification convention. Butler attended as a dedicated nullifier and served on the "Committee of Twenty-One," which drafted the Ordinance of Nullification. He strongly opposed having the state legislature set the date when the ordinance should take effect, believing that moderates would delay implementation for an indefinite period. On November 22 he initiated an unsuccessful effort to fix January 1, 1833, as the initial enforcement date. By April 1833 both South Carolina and the federal government had drawn back from their hard-line positions. With the return to quieter times, Butler retired from public affairs to concentrate on his business concerns.

In 1835 the Seminole Indians in Florida began an armed struggle against the United States. Among the forces called out to suppress them was the South Carolina Mounted Volunteers, commanded by Lieutenant Colonel Butler. However, he spent most of his tour of duty at Tampa Bay as commandant of a munitions depot. In April 1836 he was granted an honorable discharge due to crippling arthritis.

Returning to Columbia, Butler discovered that various state political leaders were seeking to elect him governor. He emphatically stated that he would not actively seek the office but would accept only as a "point of honor." On December 19, 1836, the General Assembly elected Butler to the governorship. In his inaugural address, Butler called on South Carolinians to forget divisive issues and pledged to revitalize the state's militia system.

Two crises confronted Butler during his term as governor. During his first year, the state and nation suffered through the Panic of 1837, which Butler blamed on the banking policies of President Andrew Jackson. In an 1837 message to the legislature, he declared that currency regulation was vital to recovery and voiced his support for rechartering a national bank. In April 1838 the city of Charleston experienced a devastating fire that caused nearly $4 million in damage. Although private sources provided some relief, the amount was insufficient. Butler summoned the legislature into a special session to consider the problem. Legislators responded by passing the Fire Loan Bill, which authorized the state to make up to $2 million in loans to rebuild the city.

After leaving office in December 1838, Butler tried to regain his personal financial solvency. Over the next several years he toured the southwestern states in search of opportunities and made an unsuccessful bid to gain the lucrative federal post of collector of customs in Charleston. In August 1841 President John Tyler appointed Butler federal agent to the Cherokee. He held this position until 1845, when ill health forced his resignation. At the outbreak of the Mexican War in 1846, Butler was appointed colonel and commander of the Palmetto Regiment. On August 20, 1847, while leading his troops against a Mexican position at Churubusco, Butler received a serious leg wound. Despite the injury, he remained with his command. Several minutes later he was killed instantly when a musket ball penetrated his skull. His body was returned to Columbia and buried in the Trinity Episcopal churchyard. In December 1853 Butler's remains were interred within the family cemetery at Saluda. MILES S. RICHARDS

Foreman, Carolyn T. "Pierce Mason Butler." *Chronicles of Oklahoma* 30, no. 1 (1952): 6–28.

Jervey, Theodore D. "The Butlers of South Carolina." *South Carolina Historical and Genealogical Magazine* 4 (October 1903): 296–311.

Richards, Miles S. "Pierce Mason Butler: The South Carolina Years, 1830–1841." *South Carolina Historical Magazine* 87 (January 1986): 14–29.

Butler, Susan Dart (1888–1959). Librarian. Susan Dart Butler was born in Charleston in 1888, the oldest of five children born to John Lewis Dart and Julia Pierre. Her father was born a free person of color in 1854 and was well educated. In 1882 he graduated from Newton Theological Seminary in Massachusetts and was ordained a Baptist minister. Reverend Dart returned to South Carolina in 1886, when he accepted a position at the Morris Street Baptist Church in Charleston.

The primary source of entertainment in the Dart home was reading. Butler's father was an avid reader and maintained an excellent collection of books in his personal library, which his children and young men in his parish were allowed to use. Butler began first grade in 1895 at a private school because the public schools for African Americans were horribly overcrowded. A firm believer in education, the Reverend Dart raised money to construct a six-room building, named Dart Hall, on his own property to accommodate about 150 schoolchildren.

The Darts ensured their children the best education possible. Butler attended Avery Institute in Charleston, Atlanta University in Georgia, and the McDowell Millinery School in Boston. Her mother hoped that Butler would work as a milliner (a maker of women's hats), which she did for about five years. Her father's enthusiasm for books and reading, however, eventually led Butler to librarianship. In 1912 she married Nathaniel Lowe Butler, a native of Boston involved in the real estate business. The couple had one son, Nathaniel.

In 1927 Susan Butler opened a free library and reading room in Dart Hall, using her father's books, folding chairs, and two tables. The reading room was open Mondays, Wednesdays, and Fridays from 5:00 to 8:00 P.M. Dart served as librarian and operated the room with donations and at her own expense until the Charleston Free Library established the Dart Hall Branch in 1931. The Charleston County Free Library and its branches received money from the Rosenwald Fund and the Carnegie Foundation, while the Dart family rented the building to the county for one dollar a year. The Dart Hall Branch opened to the African American public with 3,600 books. The branch was staffed by three librarians including Butler, who became head librarian after one year. During the summer of 1932 she attended the Hampton Institute in Virginia, where she took course work in library science. In 1947 she earned a bachelor's degree in library science from North Carolina College in Durham.

Among the special services offered to promote the Dart Hall Branch were story hour programs for small children, summer reading projects for older children, book discussion groups for adults, bookmobiles, and programs to help local schools. In 1952 Charleston County purchased Dart Hall and developed plans to continue the library branch. Butler retired in May 1957 after twenty-six years as branch librarian. She died two years later. In 1968 the Charleston County Council built the John L. Dart Library, which was dedicated on December 12, 1968. LISA ENNIS

Bolden, Ethel Evangeline Martin. "Susan Dart Butler: Pioneer Librarian." Master's thesis, Atlanta University, 1959.

Byars, Betsy Cromer (b. 1928). Writer. Byars was born in Charlotte, North Carolina, on August 7, 1928, the daughter of George Guy Cromer and Nan Rugheimer. After attending Furman University in Greenville, South Carolina, she graduated in 1950 from Queens College in Charlotte with a bachelor of arts degree in English, although she had begun college as a mathematics major. On June 24, 1950, she married Edward Ford Byars, a professor of engineering and a writer. Byars began her writing career with magazine articles until dedicating herself to children's literature. In 1962 her first book, *Clementine,* was published. It was the first of many books that Byars would create from her personal experiences.

Among her numerous novels, Byars won the most critical acclaim for *The Summer of the Swans* (1970), the story of a young girl named Sara and her experiences with her mentally handicapped brother, Charlie. This book won many honors, including the John

Newbery Medal from the American Library Association. In total, Byars has written more than fifty books, including *The Night Swimmers* (1980), *Wanted . . . Mud Blossom* (1991), and *Keeper of the Doves* (2002). Several have been adapted for television. In her autobiography, *The Moon and I,* published in 1991, Byars used the arrival of a blacksnake she named Moon to reveal her insights on a writer's life along with anecdotes from her childhood.

Byars has three daughters and a son. With her daughters Betsy Duffey and Laurie Myers, she wrote *My Dog, My Hero* (2000). Byars resides in Clemson with her husband. R. F. STALVEY

Byars, Betsy. *The Moon and I.* Englewood Cliffs, N.J.: J. Messner, 1991.

Byrnes, James Francis (1882–1972). Congressman, U.S. senator, U.S. Supreme Court justice, U.S. secretary of state, governor. Byrnes was born in Charleston on May 2, 1882, the son of James Francis Byrnes, an Irish Catholic city clerk, and his Irish Catholic wife, Elizabeth McSweeney. Seven weeks before his birth, Byrnes's father died of tuberculosis, leaving "Jimmy" to be reared by his widowed mother. She had gone briefly to New York to learn dressmaking in order to support him, his sister, an invalid grandmother, an aunt, and a nephew. In his early teens Byrnes left school to work in a Charleston law office to help support the family. His public career began in 1900 when Judge James Aldrich of Aiken appointed him court stenographer for the six-county Second Judicial Circuit. When not traveling to circuit court sessions between Aiken and Beaufort, Byrnes studied law in Judge Aldrich's office, and by 1904 he was licensed to practice law. He began singing "barber shop tenor" in the choir of Aiken's St. Thaddeus Episcopal Church, where Maude Busch, a Converse College student, also sang and attended church. With the blessings of his mother and against the advice of his local parish priest, he married "Miss Maude" on May 2, 1906, and soon after converted to the Episcopal faith. Much to their regret, the marriage was childless.

James F. Byrnes (right) campaigning in Columbia for presidential hopeful Dwight David Eisenhower. Courtesy, South Caroliniana Library

Over his lifetime Byrnes held many public positions, coming closer than any other South Carolinian in the twentieth century to obtaining the national political influence wielded by John C. Calhoun in the nineteenth century. In 1908 Byrnes was elected circuit court solicitor. At that time solicitors spent part of the year in Columbia assisting legislators in bill drafting. Building on political connections from the circuit court and the legislature, he was elected U.S. congressman and served for fourteen years (1911–1925). He was elected the first time by fifty-seven votes in a primary runoff after campaigning as "a live wire" and "a self-made man."

During his time in the U.S. House, he formed close relationships with Democratic leader Champ Clark from Missouri and Illinois Republican "Uncle" Joe Cannon. From them he learned how to manage legislation. Byrnes helped establish the first national highway system, including U.S. Highway 1 through his hometown of Aiken, based on payments to states for roads used by mail carriers or in interstate commerce. For Byrnes, federal aid to the states to offset their costs in maintaining national government responsibilities was consistent with the Constitution. Byrnes worked on House appropriations, especially financing military operations during World War I, and came to know Franklin D. Roosevelt. Byrnes was also instrumental in passage of the Budget and Accounting Act of 1921, which consolidated the power of the House Appropriations Committee and created a director of the budget.

In 1924 Byrnes was defeated in a bid for the U.S. Senate by Cole L. Blease. Some Bleasites exploited anti-Catholic feelings in the upstate by circulating a political ad from a Charleston newspaper in which twenty former altar boys at St. Patrick's Catholic Church had endorsed Byrnes. Byrnes's adamant refusal to join the revived Ku Klux Klan may have also contributed to his defeat. Afterward, Byrnes took up the practice of law with Sam J. Nicholls and Cecil C. Wyche in Spartanburg. He moved from Aiken because he felt awkward charging fees to his neighbors and political supporters.

Byrnes unseated Blease in 1930 and was elected U.S. senator in 1936. Byrnes had maintained his earlier association with Roosevelt, advising him to run for governor of New York in 1924 and supporting his run for the presidency in 1932. As a senator, Byrnes became an influential advocate of President Roosevelt's New Deal programs, helping to write many of the emergency economic laws in "the first 100 days" of Roosevelt's administration. He was instrumental in securing federal funding for the Santee Cooper project. In the 1936 election, Byrnes pointed out that South Carolina had gotten about $24 in federal assistance for each dollar it had paid in federal taxes.

In 1941 Byrnes resigned from the Senate when Roosevelt appointed him associate justice of the U.S. Supreme Court. While a justice, Byrnes was responsible for fifteen or more decisions. *Edwards v. California* was his first. Based on the Commerce Clause, this opinion reversed a state court conviction of a man who brought his wife's unemployed brother into California. At the time, California law forbade knowingly bringing an indigent into the state. In another Byrnes opinion, *Ward v. Texas,* the Supreme Court reversed a state court murder conviction of an uneducated African American due to an extorted confession. The accused man was subsequently acquitted.

Sixteen months after joining the Supreme Court, in October 1942 Byrnes resigned so that President Roosevelt could appoint him director of the Office of Economic Stabilization, which coordinated federal efforts to control the inflationary effects of increased war spending. In May 1943 Byrnes became director of war mobilization, a position with enough powers to earn him the nickname "Assistant President." Like Bernard Baruch, who had served President Woodrow Wilson in a similar capacity during World War I, Byrnes was responsible for unifying the nation's industrial production programs for World War II.

With such a distinguished record, Byrnes was widely rumored to be Roosevelt's nominee for vice president in 1944. His chances failed after he was opposed by Catholic political leaders who characterized him as a deserter to his native church, by northern minorities who feared him as a segregationist, and by organized labor who opposed his anti-labor-union, right-to-work views. In January 1945 Byrnes accompanied Roosevelt to Yalta for the conference with Winston Churchill and Joseph Stalin.

After Roosevelt's death, Byrnes served as U.S. secretary of state under President Harry Truman from July 3, 1945, until January 20, 1947. His activities were central in defining postwar U.S. foreign policy. Along with President Truman, he was one of four representatives at the Potsdam Conference near Berlin in July 1945, and he confronted ongoing issues among the Allies and the Soviets. A September 1946 speech by Byrnes at Stuttgart, West Germany, countered European fears that the United States would return to isolationism and retreat as a world power. Byrnes reassured the German people that the United States would help reestablish their nation on a sound basis and assist in plans for a provisional government. He also restated the United States' commitment to maintain troops in Germany. This had the effect of blunting Soviet claims that only they favored German recovery and self-government. The French and the British were also encouraged to accept the Truman administration's policies for rebuilding postwar Europe, since it was evident that the United States would not sacrifice them for an exclusive American-Soviet friendship.

Byrnes subsequently feuded with Truman over the politics of foreign policy, the appointment of his successor as secretary of state, and a speech at Washington and Lee University in which Byrnes criticized the power of the national government. He returned to Spartanburg but practiced law with a Washington, D.C., firm until spring 1949. Displeased with Truman and the national Democratic Party, Byrnes supported Strom Thurmond's 1948 "Dixiecrat" bid for president. In the process, he ruptured his old friendship with state senator Edgar A. Brown, whom he had known years before in Aiken.

Nevertheless, Byrnes was elected governor in 1950 in a "welcome home" atmosphere. He proposed some reforms, including more funds for the state hospital for the mentally ill. Central, however, was his position on racial segregation and public education. In his inaugural address in 1951, Byrnes proposed a sales tax to provide "substantial equality" in segregated public school facilities. The legislature subsequently passed a three-percent general sales tax to pay for new school buildings, better school bus transportation, and more organized school districts in an effort to upgrade education for African Americans. As an advocate of the "separate but equal" policy, Byrnes remained a segregationist. Critics saw his stance as a lost opportunity for perhaps the only political leader in the region with sufficient national stature, a "modern day Calhoun," to exercise the leadership to end racial segregation. Instead, Byrnes blamed "Negro agitators" and "Washington politicians" and even threatened to abandon the public school system rather than desegregate. His politics became more and more distant from the national Democratic Party. In 1952 he endorsed Dwight D. Eisenhower, the Republican presidential candidate, and invited "Ike" to speak from the State House steps in Columbia. Byrnes supported Eisenhower in 1956 and Richard M. Nixon in the 1960 presidential election.

Byrnes wrote two autobiographies, *Speaking Frankly* (1947) and *All in One Lifetime* (1958). The royalties were donated to the Byrnes Foundation, which granted college scholarships to South Carolina orphans. Byrnes left a series of political legacies in South Carolina, the nation, and the world. His advocacy of highway and New Deal legislation provided numerous material benefits to South Carolinians. His services to President Roosevelt had a major impact on the national economy during World War II. His role as secretary of state was instrumental in defining postwar foreign policy. In the 1950s and 1960s Byrnes's support of Republican presidential candidates was a key factor in the party's revitalization in the South.

After several years of declining health, Byrnes died in his Columbia home on April 9, 1972. He was buried in the Trinity Episcopal Church cemetery. COLE BLEASE GRAHAM, JR

Byrnes, James F. *All in One Lifetime.* New York: Harper, 1958.

———. *Speaking Frankly.* New York: Harper, 1947.

Clements, Kendrick A., ed. *James F. Byrnes and the Origins of the Cold War.* Durham, N.C.: Carolina Academic Press, 1982.

Moore, Winfred B. "James F. Byrnes: The Road to Politics, 1882–1910." *South Carolina Historical Magazine* 84 (April 1983): 72–88.

———. "New South Statesman: The Political Career of James F. Byrnes, 1911–1941." Ph.D. diss., Duke University, 1976.

Robertson, David. *Sly and Able: A Political Biography of James F. Byrnes.* New York: Norton, 1994.

Cabinetmakers. Cabinetmaking, or the production of furniture ranging from the highly decorative to the utilitarian, in South Carolina generally followed logical patterns of immigration, settlement, and consumption. The prevalent styles within any given city or community have reflected a combination of the desires of the patrons and the abilities and training of the artisans.

This library bookcase made in Charleston (circa 1765–1775) is an excellent example of the style and craftsmanship of the city's cabinetmakers. Collection of the Museum of Early Southern Decorative Arts, Winston-Salem, North Carolina

In the earliest period of the state, the epicenter of cabinetmaking was Charleston. Influenced by importation of objects, ideas, and artisans, cabinetmaking followed evolving lines of commerce between England and its wealthiest North American colony. The earliest furniture to survive in Charleston and the lowcountry was the work of Huguenot artisans, who were among the first settlers, working in the Baroque idiom. This style was to remain prevalent until the end of the proprietary period in the 1730s, when an influx of British artisans, combined with a patronage that sought to establish an aristocracy based on that of Great Britain, caused a dramatic shift in taste. Looking to Great Britain, patrons desired and artisans emulated and adapted that which was fashionable in London. This overtly British style was to remain in fashion until the 1760s, when immigrant German-speaking artisans arrived to establish an Anglo-Germanic style that had virtually no parallel in colonial America. After the Revolutionary War, and with the evolution of intercoastal trade, the sources of influence (artisans as well as objects) tended to come from the North, primarily New York, Philadelphia, and Salem, Massachusetts.

The final period of stylistic transition occurred at the end of the eighteenth century with the arrival of skilled artisans from Scotland, many of whom had worked in the North prior to settling in Charleston. Their influence is readily recognizable in the finest Neoclassical cabinetwork in Charleston in the late eighteenth and early nineteenth centuries and was to be disseminated throughout the state during the first quarter of the nineteenth century. Following this period, the cabinetmaking industry in Charleston went into decline as the economy destabilized and less expensive and more fashionable imports began arriving from northern cities, primarily New York. The materials utilized by cabinetmakers in the lowcountry tended to be imported woods, such as mahogany and satinwood, in the primary (visible) areas and indigenous woods in the secondary positions. Utilitarian furniture was made of indigenous woods. After the middle of the eighteenth century, imported woods such as northern white pine arrived from New England and, due to its low price and ease of working, became the secondary wood of choice.

Patterns of migration and settlement in the lowcountry outside of the urban coastal ports such as Charleston and Georgetown generally followed navigable waterways. These settlements contained numerous cabinetmakers who provided a broad range of decorative and utilitarian cabinetwork. With respect to the decorative work, they often adapted and reinterpreted the design and decoration of cabinetwork that was fashionable in the coastal ports, resulting in the establishment of a vernacular style. The materials utilized were much the same as those seen in the port cities since the numerous navigable waterways facilitated their distribution.

Above the fall line, transportation via waterways was difficult, resulting in a differentiation of materials utilized for cabinetwork and the approaches artisans took. With the settlement of the upcountry, there was a convergence of artisans and patrons from varying ethnic backgrounds, and the cabinetwork tended to reflect these ethnicities, particularly among the utilitarian pieces. Once settlements were established and attached to the various lines of commerce that produced wealth, a market arose for the more decorative cabinetwork, both imported and locally made. The more decorative locally made objects were largely composed of indigenous woods such as walnut, cherry, river birch, yellow pine, and poplar in the primary positions and yellow pine, poplar, and oak in the secondary positions. An awareness of the fashionable cabinetwork being produced in the urban coastal areas is readily apparent not only in the style of the work but also in the application of finishes to the various woods. Work composed of yellow pine and poplar in the primary position typically was painted in a vernacular fashion that emulated the color and grain patterns of more expensive imported woods such as mahogany. The cabinetwork utilizing birch in the primary position was almost exclusively finished with a semitransparent tinted finish, unless being used for contrast with a darker wood, to give the work the appearance of the more desirable mahogany. Work utilizing walnut and cherry typically had a transparent finish, which allowed the color and grain of the woods to serve as the primary visual experience.

After the first quarter of the nineteenth century, the expansion of South Carolina's transportation system greatly facilitated the importation of cheaper, more fashionable furniture from the North, resulting in a gradual disappearance of South Carolina cabinetmakers. Well into the nineteenth and early twentieth centuries, however, limited numbers of cabinetmakers continued to work throughout the state, often reinterpreting earlier styles. Surviving works by South Carolina cabinetmakers can be found in the collections of Colonial Williamsburg and the Museum of Early Southern Decorative Arts in Winston-Salem, North Carolina. Other examples exist in various house museums and in private hands. GEORGE C. WILLIAMS

Burton, E. Milby. *Charleston Furniture 1700–1825.* 1955. Reprint, Columbia: University of South Carolina Press, 1997.

Rauschenberg, Bradford L., and John Bivins, Jr. *The Furniture of Charleston 1680–1820.* Vol. 3, *The Cabinetmakers.* Winston-Salem, N.C.: Museum of Early Southern Decorative Arts, 2003.

Caesar (Cesar) (ca. 1682–ca. 1754). Slave, medical practitioner. Caesar was a slave and medical practitioner who gained his freedom in 1750 in exchange for revealing his knowledge of cures for poison and rattlesnake bite. He is widely considered to be the first African American to have his medical findings appear in print. In November 1749 a member of the Commons House of Assembly acquainted other members with "a Negro Man named Caesar belonging to Mr. John Norman of Beach Hill" who had reportedly cured several people "who had been poisoned by Slaves." Caesar informed the representative that he would divulge the secret of his remedy for a "reasonable Reward." Intrigued by the offer, the assembly appointed a committee to investigate Caesar's claims and, if valid, determine his compensation. Several prominent witnesses testified to the efficacy of Caesar's cure, including Dr. William Miles and Henry Middleton. Caesar's master, John Norman, stated that his slave had "done many Services in a physical Way, and in particular had frequently cured the Bite of Rattle Snakes, and [Norman] never knew him to fail in any one Attempt." He added that Caesar was also "very famous in . . . the Cure of Pleurisies." Satisfied of the effectiveness of Caesar's antidote, the Commons House granted the elderly slave (he was believed to have been "aged near sixty-seven Years") his freedom and an annual annuity of £100 currency for the remainder of his life. Norman was granted £500 in compensation.

The May 7–14, 1750, issue of the *South-Carolina Gazette* published Caesar's cures for the benefit of the public. According to the *Gazette,* they never failed:

> The Negro CAESAR's Cure for Poison. Take the roots of *Plantane* and wild *Hoare-hound,* fresh or dried, three ounces, boil them together in two quarts of water to one quart, and strain it; of this decoction let the patient take one third part three mornings fasting successively, from which if he finds any relief, it must be continued, 'till he is perfectly recovered: On the contrary, if he finds no alteration after the third dose, it is a sign that the patient has not been poisoned at all, or that it has been with such poison as *Caesar*'s antidotes will not remedy, so may leave off the decoction.
>
> CAESAR's Cure for the bite of a Rattle-snake. Take of the roots of *Plantane* or *Hoare-hound* (in summer roots and branches together) a sufficient quantity, bruise them in a mortar, and squeeze out the juice, of which give, as soon as possible, one large spoonful; if he is swells, you must force it down his throat: This generally will cure; but if the patient finds no relief in an hour after, you may give another spoonful, which never fails.

Demand for Caesar's cures was so great that the *Gazette* reprinted them the following year in its February 25–March 4, 1751, issue. They subsequently found their way into publications from across North America and even England, including the August 1750 issue of the *Gentleman's Magazine* of London, John Tobler's *South-Carolina and Georgia Almanack* in 1777, *Massachusetts Magazine* in 1792, and in the 1797 edition of Scottish physician William Buchan's classic work of lay medicine, *Domestic Medicine.* The Commons House continued to pay Caesar's annual annuity until April 1754, when the House journal recorded a payment of £70.16.08 to the "Estate of Dr. Caesar, deceased, 8 months and a half annuity." He died sometime before March 5, 1754, when the *Gazette* advertised the sale of his effects at public auction. These effects included "one negro wench, some provisions and household goods." VENNIE DEAS-MOORE

Easterby, J. H., ed. *The Journal of the Commons House of Assembly.* Vol. 9, *March 28, 1749–March 19, 1750.* Columbia: South Carolina Archives Department, 1962.

Klauber, Laurence M. *Rattlesnakes: Their Habits, Life Histories, and Influence on Mankind.* 2d ed. 2 vols. Berkeley: University of California Press, 1997.

Lipscomb, Terry W., ed. *The Journal of the Commons House of Assembly.* Vol. 12, *November 21, 1752–September 6, 1754.* Columbia: University of South Carolina Press, 1983.

Caesars Head State Park. Located in Greenville County near its border with North Carolina, Caesars Head State Park was established in 1979. In 1996 the park became part of the Mountain Bridge Wilderness Area, which also includes Jones Gap State Park and Wildcat Wayside. Formed about 409 million years ago, Caesars Head rises 3,266 feet above sea level on the southern edge of the Blue Ridge Escarpment. It is a granitic gneiss formation protruding above the valley as a prominent monadnock.

The Blue Ridge region receives the greatest precipitation in South Carolina, and the rainfall at Caesars Head averages seventy-nine

Caesar's Head. Photograph by Carl Julian for the WPA. Courtesy, South Caroliniana Library, University of South Carolina, University of South Carolina

inches annually. The streams and rivers formed by the surface water include the Middle Saluda River, Matthews Creek, Coldspring Branch, and Oil Camp Creek. The biodiversity of the park is represented by more than 500 species of plants, 44 species of reptiles and amphibians, 41 species of mammals, 159 species of birds, and 10 species of fish.

The 7,467-acre park once belonged to the Cherokees but was ceded to the state in 1816. By the mid–nineteenth century 500 acres at Caesars Head had been purchased by Colonel Benjamin Hagood, who built a hotel there in 1860. By the 1920s a highway had been constructed. Houses were built and a small summer community developed at Caesars Head.

How this mountain resort got its name is not known. Prominent among the legends are three versions. The first involves a hunting dog named Caesar. This dog jumped off the cliff while in pursuit of his prey, and the distraught owner named the cliff after his dog. A second is concerned with the corruption of the Cherokee word for Indian Chief, *sachem*. The final simply says that the rock resembles the profile of Julius Caesar. DAVID H. REMBERT, JR.

Murphy, Carolyn H. *Carolina Rocks! The Geology of South Carolina.* Orangeburg, S.C.: Sandlapper, 1995.

Cain, Daniel James Cahusac (1817–1888). Physician, medical editor. Born in St. John's Berkeley Parish on November 4, 1817, Cain received his earliest schooling in Charleston. He then attended South Carolina College in Columbia for undergraduate studies before graduating with an M.D. from the Medical College of the State of South Carolina in 1838. Like many other ambitious antebellum American physicians, Cain went to Paris for the continuation of his medical career. Drawn by the opportunities of anatomical and clinical study afforded at the great Parisian medical schools and hospitals, he spent four years as an assistant to some of the leading figures in French clinical medicine.

When he returned to the United States, Cain quickly came to enjoy a prominent position among Charleston's physician elite, occupying significant posts at public and private medical institutions in the city, as well as operating a lucrative private practice. In 1849, as recording secretary for the South Carolina Medical Association, he helped organize the group's annual meeting in Charleston. Catalogs, circulars, and advertisements list Cain as an instructor at the Medical College in 1850, while in 1852 he taught at the Charleston Preparatory Medical Institute. Cain also served as president of the Medical Society of South Carolina in 1861. Another significant landmark in Cain's professional career in Charleston was his joint editorship, with Francis Peyre Porcher, of the *Southern Journal of Medicine and Pharmacy* (later the *Charleston Medical Journal and Review*) from 1850 through 1855. Other highlights in Cain's medical career included his appointment as an attending physician to the city's Marine and Roper Hospitals and his operation, with Dr. Julian John Chisolm, of a private hospital "for the treatment of the diseases of Negroes."

In addition to his editorial duties, Cain was also a prolific medical journalist, contributing articles to almost every volume of the *Charleston Medical Journal and Review* from 1846 to 1860. Perhaps inspired by his graduate training in Paris, some of Cain's submissions to the *Charleston Medical Journal and Review* were composed of detailed clinical observations, such as "Case of Fracture of the Vertebrae" (1850), "A Case of Ulceration and Stricture of the Esophagus" (1848), and "Observations on Pseudo-Apoplexy, with Permanently Slow Pulse" (1849). Cain's other principal medical writings included his contribution to a history of Charleston's 1854 yellow fever epidemic, published in 1856.

Following the Civil War, Cain continued his practice in Charleston, enjoying a reputation as one of the most popular family physicians in the city. In 1869 he moved to Asheville, North Carolina, for health reasons. Toward the end of his life Cain went to live in Aiken with his daughter. He died in Charleston on March 12, 1888, while on a consultation visit to his longtime colleague and personal physician Francis Peyre Porcher. STEPHEN C. KENNY

Waring, Joseph I. *A History of Medicine in South Carolina.* Vol. 2, *1825–1900.* Columbia: South Carolina Medical Association, 1967.

Cain, Richard Harvey (1825–1887). Minister, abolitionist, legislator. Cain was born a free person of color in Greenbriar County, Virginia, on April 12, 1825. He grew to maturity in Ohio, where he attended Wilberforce University. Beginning in the late 1840s, Cain served as an African Methodist Episcopal (AME) minister. By the late 1850s he was an active abolitionist and worked with famous activists such as Frederick Douglass and Martin Delaney. During the Civil War, Cain was pastor of a church in Brooklyn, New York. In May 1865, to his great delight, he was transferred to South Carolina as superintendent of AME missions for the state. Cain was responsible for building Emmanuel AME Church in Charleston, which is considered the state's most historic AME congregation. By 1866 its membership had grown to more than two thousand. Cain approached his responsibilities with considerable zeal, organizing churches throughout the countryside. Contemporaries credited him with much of the church's success in the immediate post–Civil War era.

Cain was also motivated by a deeply held black nationalist ideology and sought every opportunity to give black Carolinians greater control over their lives. In 1866 he bought the *South Carolina Leader* newspaper, becoming perhaps the first African American newspaper editor in South Carolina. After Cain changed its name to the *Missionary Record,* the paper covered religion, literature, and politics, becoming an important voice for black Carolinians.

From his earliest days in South Carolina, Cain was involved in politics. He was an honorary delegate to the November 1865 Colored Peoples Convention in Charleston, which was one of the earliest forums where black Carolinians demanded equal civil and political rights. In 1867 he helped organize the state Republican Party, and he later served as party chairman for Charleston County. As a delegate to the 1868 constitutional convention, Cain was an outspoken advocate of universal male suffrage. He worked hard to promote landownership among the landless. He opposed the convention's call for a debt moratorium, instead believing that planter indebtedness would force sales to the working class. Cain was an architect of the South Carolina Land Commission, designed to help small farmers purchase land, and later served on that commission. Cain also purchased land north of Charleston, which he resold to freedmen. The settlement evolved into the black town of Lincolnville. Cain served in the S.C. Senate from 1868 to 1870 and was twice elected to Congress, serving from 1873 to 1875 and from 1877 to 1879. In state politics he was considered a reformer who frequently railed against corruption within Republican ranks. While he was in Congress, his most public efforts were on behalf of the Civil Rights Act of 1875, the country's first federal public accommodations law.

The demise of Reconstruction in South Carolina took Cain's career in new directions. In 1877 he encouraged some black

Carolinians to seek their fortune in Africa and supported the Liberian Exodus movement. In 1880 he was among the first three men elected bishops in the AME Church from the South, and he was given responsibility for Louisiana and Texas. In Texas he served as founder and president of Paul Quinn College in Waco. Cain moved to Washington, D.C., in 1884 and died there on January 18, 1887. BERNARD E. POWERS, JR.

Bailey, N. Louise, Mary L. Morgan, and Carolyn R. Taylor, eds. *Biographical Directory of the South Carolina Senate, 1776–1985.* 3 vols. Columbia: University of South Carolina Press, 1986.

Foner, Eric. *Freedom's Lawmakers: A Directory of Black Officeholders during Reconstruction.* Rev. ed. Baton Rouge: Louisiana State University Press, 1996.

Holt, Thomas. *Black over White: Negro Political Leadership in South Carolina during Reconstruction.* Urbana: University of Illinois Press, 1977.

Mann, Kenneth E. "Richard Harvey Cain, Congressman, Minister and Champion for Civil Rights." *Negro History Bulletin* 35 (March 1972): 64–66.

Powers, Bernard E., Jr. "'I Go to Set the Captives Free': The Activism of Richard Harvey Cain, Nationalist Churchman and Reconstruction-Era Leader." In *The Southern Elite and Social Change,* edited by Randy Finley and Thomas DeBlack. Fayetteville: University of Arkansas Press, 2002.

Cainhoy Riot (October 16, 1876). The Cainhoy Riot was one of the many deadly frays that erupted during the 1876 gubernatorial campaign. As with other outbreaks of racial violence in 1876, it involved white gun clubs and the African American militia, but Cainhoy ended with a difference: when it was over, more whites lay dead than blacks.

A Republican political meeting was scheduled for October 16 at the Brick House, some thirty miles up the Cooper River from Charleston. With the experience of several serious collisions already behind them, African Americans came prepared, and hundreds of militiamen attended the meeting, though for reasons that remain a mystery, they stored their guns in nearby buildings. They became agitated when Charleston County Democratic gun clubs began to arrive by steamer from the city. Democrats demanded "equal time" to speak, a scuffle ensued, and shots rang out. Soon the African Americans were breaking out their rifles, while the outnumbered whites sent the steamer back to Charleston for reinforcements. They arrived to find the battle over, the combatants dispersed, and seven dead men—six whites and one African American. More than a dozen of both races lay wounded.

The affair at Cainhoy finally prompted federal action. On October 17 President Ulysses S. Grant issued a proclamation ordering all private armed organizations to disband and ordered more U.S. troops into the state. Nearly twelve hundred federal soldiers would be on duty for the 1876 election, a consequence Republican incumbent Daniel H. Chamberlain had hoped for and Democratic challenger Wade Hampton III had warned against. But soldiers were only a temporary, piecemeal fix and could not quell all disturbances or protect all Republicans. In the end, even this small victory undercut the legitimacy of the Republican-controlled state government. RICHARD ZUCZEK

Hennessey, Melinda Meeks. "Racial Violence during Reconstruction: The 1876 Riots in Charleston and Cainhoy." *South Carolina Historical Magazine* 86 (April 1985): 100–112.

Zuczek, Richard. *State of Rebellion: Reconstruction in South Carolina.* Columbia: University of South Carolina Press, 1996.

Calhoun, John Caldwell (1782–1850). Congressman, secretary of war, vice president of the United States, U.S. senator. Calhoun was born in Abbeville District on March 18, 1782, the third son of Patrick Calhoun, an upcountry planter and former legislator, and Martha Caldwell. A prodigy, the young Calhoun lost his father at an early age. His older brothers, William and James, already successful cotton planters and merchants, helped finance his education. Calhoun attended rural upcountry academies before entering Yale at age twenty and graduating in two years. He then attended Litchfield Law School in Connecticut before reading law in Charleston with the distinguished attorney William Henry DeSaussure, a prominent Federalist. Calhoun returned to Abbeville and began the practice of law, which he disliked. He quickly turned his attention to politics, winning election to the S.C. House of Representatives in 1808. During his one term as a state legislator, Calhoun supported a white manhood suffrage amendment to the state constitution (adopted in 1810). In 1810 Calhoun ran successfully for Congress as a Jeffersonian Republican and an aggressive champion of national rights in the international arena, thus beginning a long, distinguished, and controversial career in national politics. Before taking his seat in Congress, Calhoun attended to some personal business, marrying his second cousin Floride Bonneau Colhoun on January 8, 1811. The couple eventually had ten children, of whom seven lived to maturity.

During his career Calhoun evolved from "War Hawk" (a faction of Republican congressmen seeking war against Great Britain) nationalist to independent nullifier to strategist for a unified regional (southern) defense of slavery. His winding political odyssey reflected his evolving analysis of the relationship between the nation and its sections. Calhoun insisted that the success of the republican experiment in self-government depended not only on the proper distribution of power between the states and the federal government but also on maintaining equilibrium between the sections. In the aftermath of the near-disastrous War of 1812, Calhoun championed a strong nationalist program to increase security and foster commerce across the nation. He sought to "bind the republic together" through tariffs to help infant industry, a second national bank to stabilize the nation's troubled finances and sustain commerce, and an ambitious system of federally funded internal improvements designed to promote sectional economic interdependence. During his service as secretary of war during the presidency of James Monroe, Calhoun again pursued an aggressive policy to improve military training, education, and engineering; continue transportation improvements; and reduce national reliance on poorly trained state militias in favor of regular troops. In these efforts, his ambitious plans often attracted opposition from economy-minded members of the Monroe cabinet.

Like other members of the Monroe cabinet, Calhoun used his position to advance his presidential ambitions through persuasion and patronage. The North Carolina congressman Bartlett Yancey enviously noted Calhoun's "talent" for "gaining on strangers" through his power of conversation. At this point in his career, Calhoun drew support chiefly from former Federalists and Republicans with strong nationalist sympathies—people who supported his dream of fostering economic interdependence among sections as a means of strengthening the bonds of union. In the crowded presidential field of 1824, Calhoun's relative youth worked against him, and the entry of the military hero Andrew Jackson, another South Carolina native whose candidacy triggered a wave of popular enthusiasm not previously seen in American politics, doomed his chances. Thus, Calhoun withdrew from the race and sought the vice presidency, which he won easily. As vice president, however, Calhoun quickly broke with new president John Quincy Adams when the Massachusetts native insisted on appointing Speaker of the House Henry Clay as secretary of state. Calhoun believed that Adams's choice of the wily Kentuckian for the key cabinet slot gave credence to Jackson's charge that a "corrupt bargain" between Adams and Clay had denied the presidency to the old "Hero of New Orleans," who had won the popular vote. Calhoun quickly emerged as a key figure in the pro-Jackson opposition to the Adams administration.

Despite his prominence in the emerging Jackson coalition, and his easy reelection as vice president on the Jackson ticket in 1828, Calhoun's youthful nationalism had waned by the late 1820s, falling victim to the emergence of a persistent factional majority favoring protective tariffs. Calhoun, along with many other southerners, judged these tariffs as unfair to the South and harmful to the southern staple economy. The South Carolinian now feared the centrifugal pull of divergent sectional forces less than he did the gradual consolidation of power in the hands of the national government. To stop this steady accretion of federal power, to relieve the slaveholding South from the economic burden of the tariff, and to guard against possible federal interference with slavery at some future date, Calhoun developed the idea of nullification. Nullification, as Calhoun fashioned it, was a constitutional mechanism that allowed an individual state, falling back on its claim to original sovereignty, to suspend operation of a federal law it deemed unconstitutional, unless or until three-fourths of the states decided otherwise.

Inside South Carolina the nullification campaign mobilized the Palmetto electorate as never before, and the canvass for election of delegates to the special convention turned the state into "a great talking and eating machine" as courthouse debates and political barbecues became the order of the day. This campaign generated high levels of voter turnout across the state. But the hotly contested nullification battle, which the nullifiers won with roughly sixty percent of the popular vote, left the state bitterly divided and with armed conflict looming in some districts, forcing Calhoun into the role of peacemaker, which he fulfilled skillfully. Outside of South Carolina, the doctrine of nullification attracted less support than Calhoun and his allies expected. Nullification suffered political defeat when President Jackson discredited the movement politically by equating it with disunion and isolating Calhoun from the southern wing of the emerging Democratic Party.

With the political failure of nullification, Calhoun gradually emerged as the leading strategist of an evolving southern sectionalism. Only a united South, Calhoun repeatedly maintained over the final decade of his life, could protect its rights (especially the right to hold slaves) within the Union. A united South, acting in concert and transcending partisan divisions, Calhoun claimed, could readily defend the region's slaveholding society against threats from a northern majority increasingly hostile toward slavery. Near the end of his life, Calhoun feared that the too-powerful national government would fall into the hands of an antislavery majority. "I am a Southern man and a slaveholder . . . I would rather meet with any extremity upon earth than give up one inch of our equality," Calhoun told the Senate in 1847. His remedy centered on the maintenance of sectional political equilibrium within the Union through the adoption of a constitutional amendment allowing a sectional minority to veto federal legislation. Calhoun failed to unite the South behind his ideas, however, because most southerners thought that slavery was best defended through continued southern influence on national parties. With partisan differences still dividing the South internally, and the controversy over the expansion of slavery in full flower, Calhoun died on March 31, 1850, in Washington from respiratory complications related to tuberculosis. In April he was buried in St. Philip's Churchyard in Charleston.

In life, Calhoun was hardly the brooding and forbidding figure portrayed in later mythology. In 1829, when the Beaufort planter and scholar William Elliott first met Calhoun, he called the vice president "a very eloquent and imposing man in his conversation—and a most subtle politician." Throughout a turbulent political career, Calhoun proved a loving and even indulgent father, who sacrificed financially to advance his sons and who maintained a close and intellectually stimulating relationship with his daughter Anna Maria Calhoun Clemson, who followed politics closely and became an engaging correspondent. He was also a devoted and dutiful husband to a wife who grew more withdrawn and difficult with age. An energetic political correspondent to a large network of friends, allies, and political contacts and an accomplished cotton planter, Calhoun enjoyed time at his Fort Hill plantation in the far upcountry of South Carolina (later the site of Clemson University). But neither Calhoun's family and friends nor his plantation engaged his energies as much as politics did. A man of considerable intellectual gifts, Calhoun maintained a focus on politics throughout his adult life. His political ambition, and particularly his presidential aspirations, drew sharp and frequent criticism from his opponents. But for the most part, people who knew Calhoun well, including some of his most determined opponents in South Carolina, admired his prodigious ability and conceded his capacity for magnanimity and compromise.

Calhoun's chief contribution to American political thought consisted of his thoughtful reconsideration of the republican wisdom received from the founders. The founders had embraced Madison's theory of extended republics to solve the problem of majoritarian tyranny in a democratic republic. Madison argued that the multiplicity of factions included in a large republic, and the geographic distance separating them, would render the formation of a durable and oppressive majority impossible. As plausible as this argument seemed in the 1780s, Calhoun recognized that the rise of partisan politics left it outmoded by the 1840s. Political parties, taking advantage of transportation and communication improvements and using expanding federal patronage aggressively, had easily overcome the barriers of distance and diversity that Madison believed would block the formation of lasting majorities.

In his major speeches and writings of the nullification era and with the posthumous publication of his two systematic political treatises, *A Disquisition on Government* and *A Discourse on the Constitution of the United States,* Calhoun found a check on majority power in giving significant minority interests veto power. He maintained that the appropriate expression of a society's political will came not through the opinion of a numerical majority, but through the consensus that emerged when all of the community's component interests were consulted. Calhoun sought a government by supramajority, a consensus reached by obtaining the common consent of the society's conflicting interests. He called this calculus of consent government by the concurrent majority. In Calhoun's mind, the power of the concurrent majority, when given an adequate instrument of its expression (for example, nullification, sectional veto), could serve as a check on the power of renegade numerical majorities. In an era of democracy, Calhoun sought to check the power of one kind of majority (numerical) with that of another (concurrent).

Rooted in his admitted desire to protect slavery in the American South, Calhoun's theoretical positions were often dismissed by critics as special pleading. The differing interests protected in Calhoun's ideas were sectional, and it was unclear how minority interests within sections would be protected. The consensus and harmony that Calhoun thought government by concurrent majority would produce seemed likely to prove illusory, with stalemate and paralysis their likely surrogates. To Americans enamored by the expansion of democracy (at least for white males) and opportunity (for free Americans) during the so-called Age of Jackson, Calhoun's government by concurrent majority seemed an anachronism, a strangely antimajoritarian project in a fiercely majoritarian age. But if Calhoun's remedy seemed conservative and impractical, his indictment of the excesses of majority rule, and his exposition of a conservative, post-Madisonian republicanism that highlighted the obsolescence of much of the founders' logic, earned him a deserved reputation as one of nineteenth-century America's foremost political thinkers. The problem that Calhoun identified and grappled with throughout his career—the difficulty of protecting the rights of political minorities against the power of elected majorities—remains one of the most vexing dilemmas of modern democracy. For all of his flaws, and the tragedy involved in the employment of his vast talents in defense of racial slavery, Calhoun still stands as second only to James Madison as an original political thinker among practicing politicians in American life. See plate 18. LACY FORD

Bartlett, Irving H. *John C. Calhoun: A Biography.* New York: Norton, 1993.

Ford, Lacy K., Jr. "Inventing the Concurrent Majority: Madison, Calhoun, and the Problem of Majoritarianism in American Political Thought." *Journal of Southern History* 60 (February 1994): 19–58.

———. "Republican Ideology in a Slave Society: The Political Economy of John C. Calhoun." *Journal of Southern History* 54 (August 1988): 405–24.

Meriwether, Robert L., W. Edwin Hemphill, Clyde N. Wilson, et al., eds. *The Papers of John C. Calhoun.* 28 vols. Columbia: University of South Carolina Press, 1959–2003.

Niven, John. *John C. Calhoun and the Price of Union: A Biography.* Baton Rouge: Louisiana State University Press, 1988.

Peterson, Merrill D. *The Great Triumvirate: Webster, Clay, and Calhoun.* New York: Oxford University Press, 1987.

Wilson, Clyde N., ed. *The Essential Calhoun: Selections from Writings, Speeches and Letters.* New Brunswick, N.J.: Transaction, 2000.

Wiltse, Charles M. *John C. Calhoun.* 3 vols. Indianapolis: Bobbs-Merrill, 1944–1951.

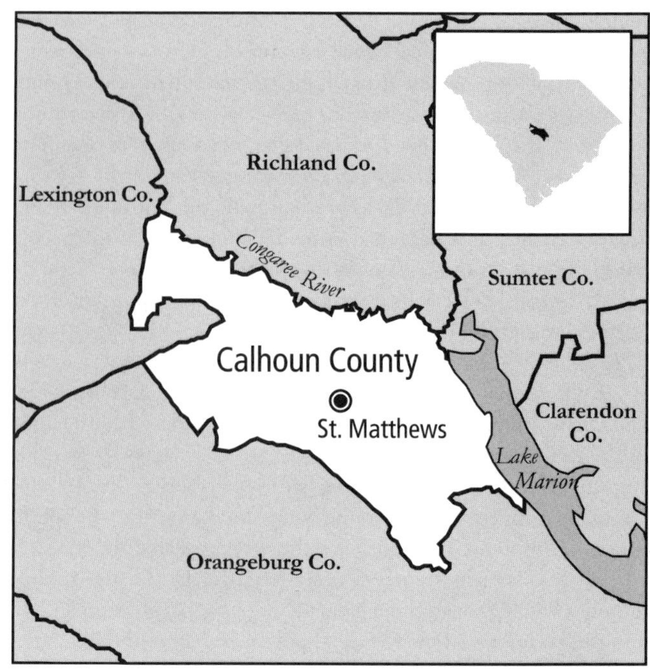

Calhoun County (380 sq. miles; 2000 pop. 15,185). Named in honor of John C. Calhoun, the county was created in 1908 from parts of Orangeburg and Lexington Counties. Located near the center of the state and bound on the north by the Congaree River and on the east by the Santee River and Lake Marion, Calhoun is the fifth-youngest and second-smallest county in South Carolina. Though small in area, its geography is remarkably varied, ranging from red and sand hills, to deep river valleys, and to coastal plains with rich, loamy soils.

The original inhabitants of the area were the Congaree and Santee Indians. A handful of European traders arrived at the start of the eighteenth century. However, substantial settlement did not occur until the 1730s, when Swiss and German immigrants took up residence in the townships of Saxe-Gotha, Orangeburg, and Amelia. In 1768 the latter two townships were organized into St. Matthew's Parish. The region saw considerable activity during the Revolutionary War and contributed several patriot leaders, including Colonel William Thomson, whose command played a vital role in the successful American defense of Sullivan's Island in 1776; Alexander Gillon, commodore of the South Carolina Navy; and the heroines Rebecca Motte and Emily Geiger. Following the war, the Calhoun County region developed a flourishing plantation economy based on cotton and slave labor. In the 1840s a branch of the South Carolina Railroad was built through the area, sparking the growth of the town of Lewisville, which was renamed St. Matthews in 1876 and eventually became the Calhoun County seat. The Union army of General William T. Sherman blazed a destructive trail though the area in 1865, but it recovered in the decades that followed. In 1894 a second railroad, the Manchester and Augusta, arrived and spawned the towns of Creston, Lone Star, and Cameron.

The initial attempt to create Calhoun County came in 1890, but the measure was defeated in the General Assembly. Although a second effort failed in 1896, agitation for a new county continued among local business leaders and farmers, particularly in the vicinity of St. Matthews. In May 1907 they formed the Calhoun County Association to promote their cause. Its first president, the merchant Ed Wimberly, contracted pneumonia while campaigning for the county in a rainstorm and died in June. Inspired by Wimberly's martyrdom, the movement gained momentum under the leadership of Dr. T. H. Dreher and J. E. Wannamaker. In December 1907 a referendum on the new county won an overwhelming public endorsement, 603 to 111. Opponents contested the results, but in January 1908 the state supreme court upheld the election and Calhoun became South Carolina's forty-second county. The cornerstone of the courthouse was laid in St. Matthews on May 29, 1913. The Greek-revival structure was designed by W. A. Edwards and was added to the National Register of Historic Places in 1981. Donations by local citizens covered much of the building costs.

The first decade of Calhoun County's existence was auspicious. By 1920 St. Matthews bustled with 1,780 residents, numerous stores, two banks, a school, cotton gins, a fertilizer factory, an ice factory, and a bottling plant. Creston, Lone Star, and Cameron emerged as important cotton- and timber-shipping points, with

Lone Star also serving as the site of the Calsico Hardwood Lumber plant. The county's prosperity evaporated with the arrival of the boll weevil in the early 1920s. The boll weevil touched off a downward economic spiral in Calhoun County that lasted through the Depression of the 1930s and into the decades beyond. A decline in cotton production was matched with a decline in population. Many farms failed and were sold for taxes, although a handful of farmers survived by diversifying their operations into pecan groves, cattle and hogs, and truck farming. Although the Bank of Cameron was one of the few in the state not to close in 1933, the overall trend remained gloomy. While the county population had been 18,380 in 1920, it had dwindled to 12,206 by 1980. Calhoun was one of the few counties in South Carolina to lose population between 1950 and 1980. While much of the state abandoned cotton in favor of industry after World War II, Calhoun County remained wed to cotton production. Calhoun, Dillon, Marlboro, and Orangeburg Counties harvested over 309,000 acres of cotton in 1945, almost one-third the state total. By 1982 the same counties devoted only 80,830 acres to cotton, but this represented eighty-five percent of South Carolina's harvested cotton acreage.

The first major industry in Calhoun County was Carolina Eastman, a manufacturer of plastic materials and resins, in 1962. By the 1990s the county's low tax rate, proximity to Columbia, and access to Interstate 26 had attracted additional industry, but none as large as Carolina Eastman, which employed more than seven hundred people. Although Calhoun County was recognized as one hundred percent rural by the U.S. Census Bureau as late as 1990, the inroads by industry nevertheless led to significant changes. By the end of the twentieth century, manufacturing funded more than half of Calhoun County's property tax and provided almost half of its employment. Agriculture remained a vital part of the county economy. In 1999 crop and livestock receipts totaled $14,599,000 and Calhoun County ranked third in South Carolina in cotton production.

Despite its small size and relatively brief existence, Calhoun County is not without its share of accomplished residents and institutions. The Pulitzer Prize–winning author Julia Peterkin made her home at Lang Syne Plantation. The county also claimed the state supreme court justice J. G. Stabler and the legendary state legislator L. Marion Gressette, who represented Calhoun County in the S.C. Senate for forty-eight years. Since the 1950s St. Matthews has been home to the Calhoun County Museum and Cultural Center, a recipient of the prestigious Elizabeth O'Neill Verner Governor's Award for outstanding contributions to the arts in South Carolina. DEBBIE ROLAND

Calhoun County Historical Commission. *A Brief History of Calhoun County.* St. Matthews, S.C.: Calhoun County Historical Commission, 1960.

Culler, Daniel Marchant. *Orangeburgh District, 1768–1868: History and Records.* Spartanburg, S.C.: Reprint Company, 1995.

Callen, Maude Daniel (1898–1990). Nurse. Callen was born on November 8, 1898, in Quincy, Florida, one of thirteen children born to Harrison and Amanda Daniel. She was orphaned by age seven and raised by an uncle. She married William Dewer Callen in 1921 and graduated from Florida A&M College the following year. Callen continued her studies at the Georgia Infirmary in Savannah and completed nurse midwife training at the Tuskegee Institute in Alabama. In 1923 Callen, now a registered nurse, arrived in Berkeley County, South Carolina, as a missionary with the Protestant Episcopal Church.

Callen was often the sole health-care provider, teacher, and nutritionist for the remote and dispersed population of a four-hundred-square-mile area. She taught children how to read and write and held vaccination clinics at local schools for smallpox and diphtheria (one of these clinics inoculated fifteen hundred children). Callen also collected and distributed clothing and helped transport the very sick to the few hospitals that would treat African American patients. She developed clinics to help families maintain proper nutrition and held the county's first venereal-disease clinic.

Callen is best remembered for her work as a nurse midwife, delivering more than one thousand babies and providing prenatal and postnatal care to mothers. Recognizing that lay midwives provided the only care for many of the African Americans in rural South Carolina, Callen sought opportunities for educating women in midwifery. Many lay midwives clung to superstition and outdated traditions, such as using potions made from wasp nests or requiring new mothers to leave their hair unbrushed for a month after giving birth. Callen began a lecture series in 1926 and later organized a two-week program to train women on basic medical practices. Once a student completed the program she received a license and a uniform, which gave the women a sense of accomplishment and pride.

Callen worked long, irregular hours. Although some patients came to her, some traveling more than 50 miles, she easily logged over 36,000 miles a year in her own car. During the Depression, Callen worked with only church and community support. In 1935 the Social Security Act established the Division of Maternal and Child Health, which hired Callen as a public health nurse to supervise midwives. As one of the first nurses in Berkeley County to receive training in the delivery and care of premature babies, Callen was an important resource for new midwives.

In the 1940s Dr. Hilla Sheriff joined the Division of Maternal and Child Health. Unlike most doctors, she recognized the importance of lay midwives to the poor and disenfranchised. Callen and Sheriff worked together to train midwives to provide responsible medical care. Sheriff depended on Callen to help educate the illiterate lay midwives. The duo soon secured the Penn Center as a place for their Midwife Training Institute. Midwives returned every four years to renew their licenses.

Callen retired in 1971. Her work and generosity were recognized with an honorary doctorate from Clemson University and induction into the South Carolina Hall of Fame. She died at her home in Pineville on January 25, 1990, and was buried in White Cemetery, near St. Stephen. LISA ENNIS

Hill, Patricia Evridge. "Maude E. Callen." In *Doctors, Nurses, and Medical Practitioners: A Bio-Bibliographical Sourcebook,* edited by Lois N. Magner. Westport, Conn.: Greenwood, 1997.

"Maude Daniel Callen—Nurse and Nationally Recognized Humanitarian—Dies." Moncks Corner *Berkeley Independent,* January 31, 1990, p. B2.

Smith, Eugene W. "Nurse Midwife." *Life* 31 (December 3, 1951): 134–45.

Camden (Kershaw County; 2000 pop. 66,682). Located in the Midlands, Camden boasts more than sixty well-preserved buildings in its historic district that attest to a rich past and to a lifestyle respectful of that heritage. Settlement of Camden evolved from instructions by King George II in 1730 to locate a backcountry township on the Wateree River. Fredericksburg, laid out in 1733 and 1734 on swampland, proved uninhabitable, and immigrants soon dispersed into the surrounding countryside. About 1750 a colony of Irish Quakers settled on scattered plantations and befriended Catawba Indians of the area. In 1758 Joseph Kershaw, the "father of Camden," established a store on Pinetree Creek, a Wateree tributary. Located on the path between Charleston and the Catawba Nation, Kershaw's store was a convenient place to collect and process local produce, especially wheat, before it was forwarded to Charleston. Here the village of Pine Tree Hill developed as a milling and trading center. Within a decade the thriving settlement was renamed in honor of Charles Pratt, Lord Camden, a champion of colonial rights, and a formal plan was drawn up to guide development. In 1791 Camden was the second town in the state to be incorporated by the General Assembly.

During the Revolutionary War, British troops under Lord Cornwallis occupied Camden for nearly a year during their campaign to subdue the backcountry. Among those imprisoned by the British in the Camden jail was the young Andrew Jackson. Two major battles were fought near the town: the Battle of Camden on August 15–16, 1780, which saw a disastrous American defeat; and the Battle of Hobkirk Hill on April 25, 1781, in which the victorious British suffered such heavy casualties that they withdrew from Camden a few weeks later.

The evacuating British destroyed much of the town, including its jail, flour mills, and several private homes. But Camden recovered quickly. A series of fires in following years redirected growth northward from the old town center. Prosperity increased as the area's plantation economy grew, based on cotton and slave labor. Anxiety arose briefly among the white population in July 1816 when an alleged slave insurrection was uncovered. Seventeen slaves were arrested and tried as ringleaders in the conspiracy, five of whom were convicted and executed. Besides free whites and African slaves, a sizable free black community was present among the Camden citizenry by 1830. The prosperous town entertained George Washington in 1791 and the Marquis de Lafayette in 1825. Other arrivals helped the town progress further. The Bank of Camden was organized in 1822, and a branch of the South Carolina Railroad reached Camden in 1848.

The Civil War halted economic prosperity as Camden's leading citizenry embraced the Confederate cause. The town experienced invasion twice in 1865, first by a detachment of General William T. Sherman's men in February, then by troops under General Edward E. Potter in April. Public buildings, the depots, and the Wateree bridge were destroyed, as was much private property. The town was garrisoned by Federal troops for nine months after the close of the war. The first local public school for African American children was begun on a square of town property in 1867. In 1880 northern missionaries established Browning Home, a private school for the children of freedmen. The school became Boylan-Haven-Mather Academy and was open until the mid–twentieth century.

By the end of the nineteenth century, Camden possessed three railroad lines. Two textile factories at the edge of town attracted workers from impoverished farms. A graded public school system was inaugurated in both white and black schools. The Camden Town Council coordinated programs to vaccinate citizens, pave streets, and expand water and light services. In 1913 the Camden Hospital opened, thanks in part to the Wall Street financier and native son Bernard M. Baruch, whose donation to the project was made in memory of his father, a former Camden physician. In 1915 a Carnegie grant made possible a handsome public library building, which later housed the Camden Archives and Museum.

Another northern invasion, this one consisting of wealthy tourists, began in the 1880s when the area's mild winters lured visitors to Camden as a health retreat and then as a tourist resort and a sports mecca. Three grand hotels and numerous smaller establishments catered to affluent guests. Although the hotel era ended with World War II, its effects lingered. Tourists renovated antebellum homes and became seasonal or permanent residents, thereby helping to preserve the distinctive architecture of Camden. Golf and polo were introduced to entertain tourists. Equestrian interest evolved into a multimillion-dollar industry. The Carolina Cup steeplechase, begun in 1930 at the Springdale Race Course, became an annual spring event. The Colonial Cup, an international steeplechase held in the fall, was inaugurated in 1970 on the same course.

Depressed economic conditions in textiles and agriculture in the 1920s and 1930s had a negative effect on much of the Camden populace. The onset of World War II brought many changes. In 1941 a school for pilots opened adjacent to the Camden airport, and both British and American airmen received flight instruction there. The facilities of Southern Aviation School afterward became the home of the Camden Military Academy, a private secondary school, while an updated Woodward Field continued airport operations. After the war, home building expanded and job opportunities increased, especially after 1950 when the opening of a Dupont plant nearby spurred industrialization. Citizens also worked to improve cultural and recreational opportunities. The Camden and Kershaw County Fine Arts Center united the talents of citizens into a variety of cultural activities, while 178 acres of city parks provided year-round recreation. In association with the National Park Service, Historic Camden opened on the site of the original town, re-creating glimpses of colonial life for visitors. Community leaders continued to focus on economic development to build a modern city, while remaining respectful of its past. JOAN A. INABINET

Daniels, John H. *Nothing Could Be Finer.* Camden, S.C.: John Culler, 1996.
Ernst, Joseph A., and H. Roy Merrens. "'Camden's Turrets Pierce the Skies!': The Urban Process in the Southern Colonies during the Eighteenth Century." *William and Mary Quarterly,* 3d ser., 30 (October 1973): 549–74.
Kirkland, Thomas J., and Robert M. Kennedy. *Historic Camden.* 2 vols. 1905. Reprint, Camden, S.C.: Kershaw County Historical Society, 1994.
Montgomery, Rachel. *Camden Heritage: Yesterday and Today.* Columbia, S.C.: R. L. Bryan, 1971.

Camden, Battle of (August 16, 1780). In early April 1780, as British forces tightened their grip around Charleston, the Maryland Division, the Delaware Regiment, and the First Continental Artillery Regiment received orders to march for the Southern Department, where they were expected to serve as the main component of a Charleston relief expedition. With the fall of Charleston on May 12, this element of the Continental army, under the command of Major General Baron Johann de Kalb, became the only significant force in the South. The Continental Congress, however, felt that the crisis deserved a more illustrious savior and appointed Major General Horatio Gates, the hero of the Saratoga campaign, to command the Southern Department. He arrived in de Kalb's camp at Buffalo Ford in North Carolina on July 25.

The new commander resolved to advance on the British outpost at Camden, South Carolina. De Kalb agreed but suggested taking the route via Salisbury and Charlotte through friendly country in order to obtain food and supplies for the army. Gates instead chose a direct march to catch the British garrison by surprise. The "grand army" (as Gates called his force) set out immediately on July 27 on a long and weary march with little to eat. North Carolina and

Virginia militiamen eventually joined the American forces, which added to their logistical difficulties.

In Charleston, the British general Charles, Lord Cornwallis learned of Gates's advance and marched to Camden with a reinforcement of one thousand soldiers, doubling the size of the Camden garrison. On arrival, Cornwallis started north from Camden to intercept the enemy. The two armies bumped into each other six miles north of Camden on the night of August 15 but withdrew to await the morning. Both sides were hemmed into a narrow battlefront by the swamps near Saunder's Creek. This should have worked to the advantage of the Americans, who had numerical superiority, but in positioning his forces Gates made a fatal error. He placed all of his seasoned units on the right and the untrained militia on the left, unsupported by the Continental reserve. When the British attacked the next morning, the redcoats charged into the American left wing and routed the militiamen. Many threw down their muskets and ran without firing a shot. The British infantry wheeled left into the flank of de Kalb's Continentals. Fighting was fierce, but the Maryland and Delaware Regiments were outnumbered and soon succumbed. De Kalb fought bravely until he fell mortally wounded.

Approximately eight hundred Americans were killed or wounded, and another one thousand were taken prisoner. The army that Gates had inherited was destroyed, and he reputedly departed the battlefield with the initial British assault and rode posthaste all the way to Charlotte. The defeat at Camden was one of the worst losses suffered by the Continental army. British and Loyalist morale soared as a consequence, but Cornwallis still had to deal with bands of marauding partisans before moving into North Carolina. By the time Cornwallis had seemingly solidified his control of South Carolina, a reformed American army was organizing in North Carolina. SAMUEL K. FORE

Lumpkin, Henry. *From Savannah to Yorktown: The American Revolution in the South.* Columbia: University of South Carolina Press, 1981.

Nelson, Paul David. *General Horatio Gates: A Biography.* Baton Rouge: Louisiana State University Press, 1976.

Camp, Wofford Benjamin (1894–1986). Agriculturalist, entrepreneur. "Bill" Camp was born on March 14, 1894, near Gaffney in present-day Cherokee County. He was the sixth of eight children born to the middle-class farmer John Clayton Camp and Mary Jane Atkins. Camp grew up immersed in the upland cotton culture. He attended public schools in Gaffney and entered Clemson Agricultural College in 1912. At Clemson, Camp majored in agronomy with special emphasis on cotton breeding, graduating in 1916. On December 14, 1921, he married Georgia Anna App. The marriage produced two sons. Georgia died in 1943, and on January 18, 1956, Camp married Louise Wise. Camp's second marriage produced three children.

After graduation, Camp worked briefly in the South Carolina lowcountry studying Sea Island cotton. In 1917 he joined the United States Department of Agriculture's Cotton Section. Seeking a fabric for aircraft manufacture, the agency sent Camp to California to conduct cotton experiments. With the boll weevil ravaging the South, the agency hoped to foster cotton culture west of the Rocky Mountains. Camp introduced the long-staple Pima variety in California's San Joaquin Valley and as far south as Arizona. Camp's efforts bore fruit, and soon thousands of acres were thriving. Later he recommended another variety, Acala, which was also planted widely. For bringing a promising crop to the state, Camp was hailed as California's "Cotton Man."

In the 1930s Camp went to Washington as a policy maker with the Agricultural Adjustment Administration. Returning to California in 1936, he acquired land near Bakersfield and launched his own farming operation. Camp prospered, amassing a considerable fortune. A generous man, he endowed institutions in California as well as in his native South Carolina. Camp received honorary doctorates from several colleges, including his alma mater, Clemson University, in 1982. He died on August 1, 1986, in Bakersfield, California. ELDRED E. PRINCE, JR.

Briggs, William J., and Henry Cauthen. *The Cotton Man: Notes on the Life and Times of Wofford B. ("Bill") Camp.* Columbia: University of South Carolina Press, 1983.

Camp Croft. This United States Army Training Center, located on 22,000 acres southeast of Spartanburg, was established on December 5, 1940. Named after Major General Edward Croft (1874–1938), a Greenville County native and chief of Army Infantry, Camp Croft was one of several training centers established across the nation as the United States began rebuilding its armed forces prior to Pearl Harbor. At its peak the facility trained an estimated twenty thousand recruits every three months. To establish the base, many people were forced to leave their homes and farms to make way for the new installation. The federal government paid landowners up to $281,000 for appropriating their property. Like most military training centers, Camp Croft provided a much needed boost to the local economy, injecting new jobs and higher wages for people across the social strata. This was especially true during its construction, when nearly twelve thousand workers were employed with a weekly payroll of $400,000. After construction was completed in early 1941, the center employed some three hundred civilians during its service. Conversely, Croft put a severe strain on the housing, recreation, and health facilities of the small upstate community. During the last year and a half of the war, Croft also housed nearly one thousand German prisoners of war, the second-largest number in the state. After the training center was deactivated on July 31, 1945, the land was turned over for various civilian purposes, including residential housing and businesses. Another part was dedicated in 1949 as Croft State Park. FRITZ HAMER

Fields, Elizabeth Arnett. "Post World War II Development of Surplus Military Installations in South Carolina." Master's thesis, University of South Carolina, 1994.

Moore, John H. "Nazi Troopers in South Carolina, 1944–1946." *South Carolina Historical Magazine* 81 (October 1980): 306–15.

Racine, Philip. *Spartanburg County: A Pictorial History.* Virginia Beach, Va.: Donning, 1980.

Camp meetings. These outdoor services of worship held for a week or longer were characterized by the encampment of the participants, often near an established church. The meetings were sometimes accompanied by emotional outbursts and resulted in dramatic conversion experiences. Eventually a brush arbor, wagons, and tents were replaced by a central tabernacle for worship and wooden structures for family groups (still known as "tents"). While only a few camp meetings continue to be held annually in South Carolina, they flourished during the first half of the nineteenth century and are associated with the religious revival known as the Second Great Awakening.

One of the earliest documented camp meetings in the United States was held in Logan County, Kentucky, near the Tennessee line in June 1800. James McGready, a Presbyterian minister, was conducting a quarterly Communion service, and two brothers, John McGee, a Methodist preacher, and William, a Presbyterian minister, joined him. In July the McGees returned to Logan County and held a meeting that thousands attended. Preaching night and day was accompanied by shouts, groans, and muscular contractions known as "the jerks." The Methodist bishop Francis Asbury participated in his first camp meeting in that area in October. Traveling through South Carolina in January 1801, Asbury read accounts of the frontier meetings to listeners, who were stirred by the news.

Camp meetings seem to have entered South Carolina from Mecklenburg County, North Carolina. In March 1802 some 160 wagons brought five thousand people to a meeting south of Charlotte near the state line. In April twelve thousand people attended a gathering near Lancaster, which was followed by a meeting in May in the Waxhaws and another in June at Hanging Rock. Camp meeting fever spread to Spartanburg in July. Week after week there were reports of similar meetings across the state.

At first camp meetings were conducted cooperatively by Presbyterians, Baptists, and Methodists. But the Old School Presbyterians in the South were generally skeptical of the emotional excesses associated with the movement, and Baptists were divided in their support. Richard Furman, pastor of the Charleston Baptist Church, traveled to Lancaster to see a camp meeting for himself. While he approved, most Baptists withdrew, refusing to cooperate with ministers of a different "faith and order." Soon the Methodists had the field to themselves. Between 1802, when the movement began in the state, and 1805 Methodist membership doubled—from 7,443 to 16,089. By the outbreak of the Civil War virtually every Methodist circuit in the state had a camp meeting. Methodists living in towns and cities left their homes and moved to nearby campgrounds for the annual meetings. Camp meetings were not only religious in nature but were also major social events in a predominantly rural culture. Rowdiness and misbehavior were often major concerns of religious leaders.

After the Civil War, the new black Methodist denominations established camp meetings. Out of Indian Field Camp Meeting near St. George developed Shady Grove, both of which remain active. Mount Carmel Camp Meeting near Heath Springs was established by the African Methodist Episcopal Zion Church. Generally, the camp meeting fervor began to wane in the second half of the nineteenth century. Camp meeting structures burned and often were not replaced. Churches in cities and towns began to emulate the urban revivals conducted by Dwight L. Moody in the North. Itinerant southern evangelists copied Moody's pattern.

With the rise of the Holiness movement in the late nineteenth century, some denominations that developed out of Methodism and Pentecostalism adopted camp meetings. The Wesleyan Church has a campground near Greer, and the Church of God conducts a camp meeting near Mauldin. A. V. HUFF, JR.

Betts, Albert D. *History of South Carolina Methodism.* Columbia, S.C.: Advocate Press, 1952.

Boles, John B. *The Great Revival, 1787–1805: The Origins of the Southern Evangelical Mind.* Lexington: University Press of Kentucky, 1972.

Jenkins, James. *Experience, Labors and Sufferings of Rev. James Jenkins of the South Carolina Conference.* 1842. Reprint, Columbia, S.C.: State Commercial Printing Company, 1958.

Camp Sevier. Camp Sevier was a temporary cantonment site in Greenville County created to train federalized National Guard soldiers during World War I. It was named in honor of the Revolutionary War hero John Sevier, a leader of patriot militia at Kings Mountain and later governor of Tennessee. Soldiers from South Carolina began to occupy the site, four miles northeast of the city of Greenville, on July 10, 1917. Construction began a week later, and the formal establishment of the post took place on July 18. During the next two months, various National Guard units from South Carolina, North Carolina, and Tennessee began to arrive at the camp. Before training could begin in earnest, land had to be cleared and facilities constructed. Once all units had reported, soldiers were trained in a range of common infantry skills and in new modes of warfare, such as gas defense and the use of the machine gun. Covering some nineteen hundred acres, the camp provided ample room for artillery instruction as well. This first group of guardsmen was formed into the Thirtieth, or "Old Hickory," Division, which trained at the post until May 1918 and was followed by the Eighty-first and Twentieth Divisions, respectively. In all, an estimated 100,000 men had undergone vital training at Camp Sevier by the spring of 1919. With the signing of the Armistice on November 11, 1918, the post was designated as a demobilization center on December 3 and was closed as a military training facility on April 8, 1919. SAMUEL K. FORE

Doyle, Alex C. *Completion Report of Camp Sevier, Greenville, S.C.* Greenville, S.C., 1919.

Huff, Archie Vernon, Jr. *Greenville: The History of the City and County in the South Carolina Piedmont.* Columbia: University of South Carolina Press, 1995.

Withington, Frances Marshall. "Camp Sevier, 1917–1918." *Proceedings and Papers of the Greenville County Historical Society* 4 (1971): 76–85.

Camp Sorghum. In the wake of a yellow fever epidemic among federal prisoners in Charleston, Confederate authorities transferred thirteen hundred to fourteen hundred Union officers to the South Carolina interior in late 1864 to prevent them from infecting the local populace. They also believed that the prisoners were less likely to be liberated by Sherman if they were moved inland. The first prisoners

Soldiers in training at Camp Sevier. Courtesy, South Caroliniana Library, University of South Carolina

arrived in October 1864 and were interned in a five-acre field near Columbia, on a hill overlooking the west side of the Saluda River (now West Columbia). To supplement the few tents available, many prisoners built makeshift structures by digging holes in the ground and covering them with tree branches. Because their diet consisted of cornmeal and molasses, the Union prisoners began calling their site "Camp Sorghum." Due to poor sanitation and inadequate shelter, disease and malnutrition were rampant. As many as twenty to fifty prisoners died daily. To alleviate the poor conditions, Confederate authorities allowed limited paroles to find food and better sanitation beyond the camp boundaries. Sometimes this was used as a ruse to escape. Other methods of escape included bribing the guards or feigning illness to go to the hospital outside the camp's boundaries. One Confederate official claimed that Sorghum's 373 escapes were due to guards who were "very raw recruits [who] . . . require constant watching and instruction." In December 1864 the camp was closed and the prisoners transferred across the river to Columbia, where they were interned near the South Carolina Lunatic Asylum until Sherman captured Columbia on February 17, 1865. The Union force liberated some of the prisoners, while others were forced north with their Confederate captors until released the following month in North Carolina. FRITZ HAMER

Anderson, George L., ed. *A Petition Regarding the Conditions in C.S.M. Prison at Columbia, S.C.: Addressed to the Confederate Authorities.* Lawrence: University of Kansas Libraries, 1962.

Lord, Francis. "Camp Sorghum." *Sandlapper* 8 (August 1975): 29–33.

Camp Wadsworth. This site in Spartanburg County was one of sixteen chosen nationally as a U.S. Army training camp in the summer of 1917. It included two thousand acres on the western edge of Spartanburg. Because the first division assigned to the upstate camp was from New York, it was named after General James S. Wadsworth, a New York native who served with distinction in the Civil War. Military and civilian work crews constructed about one thousand buildings, including ten storehouses, a hospital unit with sixty-five buildings, and six YMCA structures. The men lived in tents divided up into regiments, eight men to a tent. The first elements of the Twenty-seventh Division arrived in early September, and within a month the camp was occupied by mostly New Yorkers. By late autumn one visitor wrote that Spartanburg seemed full of people from the northern state. As training began in earnest, an artillery range was created further west in the Greenville hills. The influx of arrivals put a strain on the upstate town, creating crowded conditions and housing shortages but plenty of business. School enrollments rose in a matter of weeks by twenty percent. When the Twenty-seventh Division finally left for Europe, the Sixth and then the Ninety-sixth Divisions replaced it. After the usual celebrations following the announcement of the Armistice, plans were soon implemented to deactivate the camp. Local appeals to keep the camp open failed, and it closed on March 25, 1919. FRITZ HAMER

Writer's Program. South Carolina. *A History of Spartanburg County.* 1940. Reprint, Spartanburg, S.C.: Reprint Company, 1976.

Campbell, Carroll Ashmore, Jr. (1940–2005). Legislator, congressman, governor. Campbell was born on July 24, 1940, in Greenville, the son of Carroll Ashmore Campbell and Anne Williams. He was educated at the McCallie School in Chattanooga, Tennessee, and attended the University of South Carolina and American University. On September 5, 1959, he married Iris Rhodes of Greenville. They have two sons.

Carroll A. Campbell, Jr. Courtesy, Modern Political Collections, University of South Carolina

Campbell's political career began when he was elected to the S.C. House of Representatives in 1971. In 1973 he became assistant minority leader. In 1974 he was the Republican Party's nominee for lieutenant governor but was defeated. In 1975 he served as executive assistant to Governor James Edwards. Campbell was elected to the S.C. Senate in 1976, and in 1978 he was elected to the U.S. House of Representatives from the Fourth Congressional District. He served in Congress from 1979 until 1986. In 1979 he was named outstanding freshman congressman. While in Congress he served on the Appropriations Committee and the Ways and Means Committee.

In November 1986 Campbell was elected governor of South Carolina as a Republican, receiving fifty-one percent of the vote. He was reelected for a second term in 1990, receiving more than sixty-nine percent of the vote. He also played major roles in the presidential campaigns of Ronald Reagan and George Bush and served as chairman of the National Governors Association.

During Campbell's two terms as governor, South Carolina experienced Hurricane Hugo, a major recession, and the "Lost Trust" vote-buying scandal in the General Assembly. These events gave him the opportunity to increase the stature and decision-making authority of the governor. Following Hurricane Hugo in 1989, the governor's office became the focus of response and recovery efforts for the state. The office coordinated the federal, state, and private relief efforts in the aftermath of the hurricane. These efforts helped establish the governor as the state's crisis manager.

Campbell's response to the state's recession was to enact a series of budget cuts for some state agencies rather than raise taxes. In 1988 he began sending an executive budget to the state's Budget and Control Board. This body, comprised of the governor, the comptroller general, the state treasurer, the chair of the House Ways and Means Committee, and the chair of the Senate Finance Committee, had historically developed the budget for the state. Campbell's initiative resulted in the budgetary statutes being revised to allow the governor to develop and submit a proposed budget to that body. Campbell used the 1990 "Lost Trust" vote-buying scandal to restructure the state's bureaucracy. In 1991 he created a citizens panel for the purpose of making recommendations on state government reform. From this came a reorganization plan that was passed by the General Assembly in 1993 and which consolidated 145 state agencies. Thirteen of the agencies formed the nucleus of a cabinet that increased the governor's power since the agency heads were subject to gubernatorial appointment and removal and reported directly to the governor. The Campbell administration was also recognized for its success in recruiting industry. During his administration the state experienced unprecedented capital investments, including the recruitment of BMW to Greer and the pharmaceutical company Hoffman-Laroche to Florence.

Campbell was instrumental in the development of the Republican Party in South Carolina. He used his position as governor to assist Republicans in building a viable structure and raising funds. This made it easier for the party to recruit candidates. He also personally recruited candidates to run and persuaded some Democratic legislators to switch parties. In 1994 the Republican Party, for the first time since Reconstruction, constituted a majority of the members of the S.C. House of Representatives. A former executive director of the S.C. Republican Party claimed that Carroll Campbell did more for the Republican Party than any other single individual in the state had done. When Campbell left office in January 1995, he had an approval rating of seventy-two percent.

After leaving office, Campbell became president of the American Life Insurance Council in Washington, D.C. In 1996 he considered running for president, but this was a short-lived venture. That year he was also on Republican Party presidential nominee Bob Dole's short list for vice president but was not chosen. In October 2001 in an open letter to the people of South Carolina, he announced that he had been diagnosed with the early stages of Alzheimer's disease. He died December 7, 2005 and was buried in the cemetery at All Saints Episcopal Church, Pawleys Island. WILLIAM V. MOORE

Bailey, N. Louise, Mary L. Morgan, and Carolyn R. Taylor, eds. *Biographical Directory of the South Carolina Senate, 1776–1985.* 3 vols. Columbia: University of South Carolina Press, 1986.

Graham, Cole Blease, Jr., and William V. Moore. *South Carolina Politics and Government.* Lincoln: University of Nebraska Press, 1994.

Campbell, Lord William (ca. 1730–1778). Governor. A younger son of John Campbell, fourth duke of Argyll, William entered the navy in 1745 and served in India. As captain of the HMS *Nightingale,* in 1763 he put into Charleston, where he met Sarah Izard, a rich heiress, then on the verge of marriage to another. But Campbell prevailed, and they were married on April 17, 1763. Returning to Britain, he successfully ran for Parliament from Argyllshire. In 1766 the Rockingham administration appointed him governor of Nova Scotia, and in June 1773 his family's influence secured his promotion to the governorship of South Carolina.

Campbell arrived in Charleston in June 1775. By then the Revolutionary Provincial Congress and its Council of Safety had usurped royal authority, and Campbell faced impossible obstacles as governor. Rumors that he was bringing arms for British-instigated Indian attacks and slave insurrections complicated his task and eventually led Revolutionary authorities to execute Thomas Jeremiah, a free black harbor pilot who was accused of being a ringleader of the impending uprising. Campbell believed him to be innocent but was powerless to intervene. The governor, however, was able to correspond with Loyalists in the backcountry. His optimistic reports of their strength contributed later to British decisions to attack South Carolina in 1776 and 1780. After Revolutionary leaders discovered Campbell's clandestine activities, he fled from Charleston on September 15, 1775. The departure of South Carolina's last royal governor enabled Revolutionary leaders to claim that George III, like King James II during the Glorious Revolution, had "abdicated the government," and accordingly, "WE OWE NO OBEDIENCE TO HIM."

During the British naval attack on Sullivan's Island in June 1776, Campbell commanded cannons aboard the HMS *Bristol* and received wounds from which he never completely recovered. Two years later he died at Southampton, England, during the first week of September 1778. ROBERT M. WEIR

Olwell, Robert. *Masters, Slaves, and Subjects: The Culture of Power in the South Carolina Low Country, 1740–1790.* Ithaca, N.Y.: Cornell University Press, 1998.

Weir, Robert M. *Colonial South Carolina: A History.* 1983. Reprint, Columbia: University of South Carolina Press, 1997.

Canal Holdings. Based in Conway, Canal Holdings (formerly Canal Industries) has been a cornerstone of the timber industry and its development in the Carolinas since 1937. R. H. "Hutch" Gibson and Edwin Craig Wall, Sr., founded Canal Wood Corporation in September 1937 to supply pulpwood to International Paper Company's Georgetown mill. Their combined $2,000 investment led to the formation of additional forestry and wood-products companies in the Southeast. The company name was changed to Canal Holdings in 2001. As one of the largest privately owned forestry-products companies in the Southeast, Canal produces wood chips, provides timberland management services and real estate development and sales, and handles the transport of wood fiber through North Carolina ports. At one point the business fortune of Wall, who had bought out Gibson, was estimated to be as high as $100 million.

Installed posthumously in the South Carolina Business Hall of Fame in 1986, Wall was a driving force in the economic development of Horry County. He served on the Horry County Development Board and the State Development Board and was a member of the boards of the Conway Chamber of Commerce, Forest Farmers Association, and Conway Hospital. An original member of the Coastal Education Foundation, Wall also promoted education as a member of the Horry County Higher Education Commission and as chairman of the South Carolina Commission on Higher Education. He helped organize Coastal Carolina College (later Coastal Carolina University), and its College of Business Administration bears his name. BARBARA STOKES

Bailey, Isaac J. "Canal Industries Sells Largest Subsidiary to N.C. Group." Myrtle Beach *Sun News,* February 10, 2001, pp. A1, A6.

———. "Smaller Canal Holdings to Sell Offices." Myrtle Beach *Sun News,* December 7, 2001, pp. D1, D3.

Lunan, Bert, and Robert A. Pierce. *Legacy of Leadership.* Columbia: South Carolina Business Hall of Fame, 1999.

Can-Am Days. Can-Am Days is the abbreviated name for the annual Canadian-American Days Festival in the Myrtle Beach area. The Myrtle Beach Area Chamber of Commerce began the festival in 1961 as a means of attracting vacationing Canadian families during their annual winter school break. It started with a simple observation: local businesspeople noticed a large number of automobiles with Ontario license plates during mid-March. They learned that these Canadians were stopping in the Myrtle Beach area on their way to Florida. After making this discovery, business leaders cast about for ways to turn these overnight stops into longer visits.

Each year Can-Am Days features more than sixty events and activities during a nine-day period, including tours, concerts, tournaments, and unique events such as the International Kitefest and the Little Olympics. The events and activities are held to coincide with Ontario's school holiday. Entertainment is the immediate thrust of the festival, but the main effort is to enhance awareness of the Myrtle Beach/Grand Strand name in the minds of potential vacationers. The chamber and its affiliated businesses conduct extensive advertising and promotional campaigns each year, and the success of Can-Am Days has increased Canadian visitation to the Grand Strand throughout the year.

The festival has received scores of awards, ranging from a commendation by the South Carolina General Assembly in 1971 to being named as South Carolina's Top Tourist Attraction in 1972. In 1994 and again in 1997 the festival received the Shining Example Award as the most outstanding festival of the year by the Southeast Tourism Society. ASHBY WARD

Cannon Street Hospital and Training School for Nurses. In 1896 Alonzo G. McClennan called a meeting of the black physicians of Charleston to discuss the establishment of a "Nurse training school for Negro women." Laws concerning segregation prevented African Americans from utilizing the training ward at City Hospital. McClennan and his associates began efforts to create a hospital that was "owned and conducted by the colored people of Charleston." Prominent members of the African American community spearheaded the efforts of churches, benevolent associations, and individuals to raise money to purchase a building and fund the operation. On November 11, 1896, the building at 135 Cannon Street opened as the Hospital and Training School for Nurses, the first medical institution for African Americans in South Carolina.

The founders of the school believed that the professionalization of nurses was key to the successful operation of modern scientific medicine. Students learned lessons about anatomy and physiology, midwifery, hygiene and bandaging, exercise and care of the sick, and the preparation of nutritious food. Besides comforting the patients, nurses were trained to better assist physicians in the detection, treatment, and monitoring of diseases. McClennan was particularly concerned with high infant mortality rates, and he railed against the influence of amateur midwives who seemed to "kill as many babies as they please."

Administrators understood the need to address the mortality rates of African Americans. In 1898 black Charlestonians died at twice the rate of whites. The school attempted to reach out and provide care to all without regard to the patient's ability to pay. By October 1899 a clinic providing free treatment and medicine for children was organized in connection with the hospital. For at least the first eight years the hospital turned no patients away.

Never lavishly financed, the school nevertheless kept its doors open with donations of money and supplies. But by the 1950s the building at 135 Cannon Street could no longer pass health inspections. The Hospital and Training School for Nurses closed its doors on June 1, 1959, and its services were replaced by the new McClennan-Banks Memorial Hospital. DAVID S. BROWN

Downing, L. C. "Early Negro Hospitals." *Journal of the National Medical Association* 33 (1941): 13–18.

Cape Romain National Wildlife Refuge. Cape Romain National Wildlife Refuge was established in 1932 as a wintering ground for migratory waterfowl. Located in Charleston County and stretching for twenty-two miles along the coast between Charleston and the Santee River delta, Cape Romain is a rich natural resource. In its shallow bays, tides combine the life-giving nourishment of the ocean with the nutrient-laden freshwaters of rivers to make one of the most productive environments on earth. Plants and animals from the land, rivers, and ocean are all present at Cape Romain, and all are dependent on the delicate balance of the marshlands.

In support of wildlife's battle for survival, refuge administrators have employed wildlife management techniques that include relocation of threatened loggerhead sea-turtle eggs, a red-wolf breeding program on Bulls Island, and management of artificial ponds for waterfowl, wading birds, and alligators. Cape Romain Refuge is host to 335 bird species, 12 types of amphibians, 24 reptile species, and 36 varieties of mammals.

The refuge is open sunrise to sunset, seven days a week, year-round. The only facilities accessible by automobile are the refuge office, Sewee Visitor Center, and Garris Landing. Bulls Island lies nearly three miles off the mainland and is reached by boat or private ferry. Public-use opportunities include an observation/fishing pier at Garris Landing and Sewee Visitor Center on the mainland. On Bulls Island there are eighteen miles of trails and roads to hike, a seven-mile stretch of beach, picnic tables, a weather shelter, and an observation platform. Saltwater fishing is permitted, and limited hunting is offered. Interpretive exhibits and literature can be found at the Sewee Visitor Center. LARRY DAVIS

Capers, Ellison (1837–1908). Educator, soldier, minister. Capers was born in Charleston on October 14, 1837, to William Capers and Susan McGill. The Capers men were active and prominent as lawyers, soldiers, and religious leaders. William Capers was a well-known Methodist minister and bishop and an instrumental voice in the 1844 sectional split of the church.

Ellison Capers. Courtesy, South Caroliniana Library, University of South Carolina

Much in Ellison Capers's early life mirrored the lives of his ancestors. He attended the South Carolina Military Academy (the Citadel), graduating in 1857. Afterward he read law, though he never practiced, and taught at the academy as a professor of mathematics and rhetoric. The outbreak of the Civil War cut short his teaching career. Partly on the strength of his military education, he was elected major of a regiment of South Carolina volunteers and participated in the bombardment of Fort Sumter. Then began a steady, if unspectacular rise. He helped recruit the Twenty-fourth

South Carolina Infantry and was elected its lieutenant colonel. Stationed along the South Carolina coast, the regiment saw action at Secessionville on June 16, 1862—with Capers personally handling an artillery battery that was tardy coming into action. For this he won high praise as well as personal satisfaction, calling it a "delightful" experience. "I am satisfied that the fire of this battery," he reported, "contributed no little to our success, and am gratified . . . that the general commanding rode to the battery during the close of the engagement and warmly thanked us for our work." The Twenty-fourth South Carolina was transferred to Mississippi in 1863, and it served with the Army of Tennessee until the end of the war. Capers fought in most of the army's major engagements, suffering wounds at Jackson, Chickamauga, and Franklin. Along the way he was promoted to colonel and then, on March 1, 1865, to brigadier general. He was one of only four Citadel graduates to attain the rank of general in the Confederate army.

Life in peacetime South Carolina proved adventurous. From 1866 to 1868, during an interregnum of sorts between the war and the establishment of Republican power in the state, Capers served as secretary of state. Although an active Democrat, Capers found his calling in the Episcopal ministry. From 1867 to 1893 he was minister to parishes in Greenville and Columbia. In 1894 he became bishop of the Diocese of South Carolina. In 1904 he accepted the chancellorship of the University of the South, a position he held until shortly before his death. Because of the ties among Confederate memorial activities, religious instruction, and higher education, these positions also gave Capers a high profile in the Lost Cause movement. Capers was active in the Southern Historical Society, edited the South Carolina volume of Clement A. Evans's *Confederate Military History,* and was chaplain general of the United Confederate Veterans.

Capers married Charlotte Rebecca Palmer on February 24, 1859. Together they had seven children. He died in Columbia on April 22, 1908, and was buried at Trinity Episcopal Church in Columbia. PAUL CHRISTOPHER ANDERSON

Capers, Walter B. *The Soldier Bishop: Ellison Capers.* New York: Neale, 1912.

Wilson, Charles Reagan. *Baptized in Blood: The Religion of the Lost Cause, 1865–1920.* Athens: University of Georgia Press, 1980.

Capers, William (1790–1855). Clergyman. Capers was born on January 26, 1790, in St. Thomas Parish near Charleston, the son of William and Mary Capers. His father, a rice planter, and his maternal grandfather, John Singeltary, were early converts to Methodism in South Carolina. Educated in Georgetown and at Roberts Academy in Stateburg, near his family's summer home, Capers entered South Carolina College in 1805. In 1808 he left college to read law in the office of Judge John S. Richardson. That same year he was converted at a Methodist camp meeting, joined the Methodist Episcopal Church, and was admitted on trial to the South Carolina Conference. On January 13, 1813, Capers married Anna White. The couple had a daughter and a son before Anna's death in December 1815. On October 31, 1816, Capers married Susan McGill of Kershaw District.

Capers became one of the most influential Southern Methodist preachers of his generation. He founded the Asbury Mission to the Creek Indians in Alabama in 1821 and served as its superintendent until 1824. Appointed to Charleston in 1825, he edited the *Wesleyan Journal* until 1827. In 1828, while serving as presiding elder of Charleston District, he traveled to England as American representative to the British Methodist Conference. In 1829 he led

William Capers. Courtesy, South Carolina Historical Society

in the creation of missions to slaves on lowcountry plantations, and in 1833 he published a catechism for the oral instruction of the slaves. From 1837 to 1840 he edited the *Southern Christian Advocate,* established for Methodists in the South by the General Conference of the denomination. As secretary of the Southern Missionary Department of the Methodist Episcopal Church from 1840 to 1844, he extended the mission to slaves to every southern state. In 1844 the eighty missionaries under his supervision cared for more than 22,000 slave members.

In the tumultuous General Conference of 1844, in which the church divided into Northern and Southern branches, Capers was a leading proponent of the Southern cause. In May 1846 he was elected one of the first bishops of the Methodist Episcopal Church, South. Though his episcopal duties took him across the South, he maintained a residence at Box Cottage in Anderson. Capers died there on January 29, 1855, and was buried at the Washington Street Church in Columbia. His son Ellison Capers and his grandson William Tertius Capers became bishops of the Episcopal Church in South Carolina and Texas, respectively. A. V. HUFF, JR.

Mathews, Donald G. *Slavery and Methodism: A Chapter in American Morality, 1780–1845.* Princeton, N.J.: Princeton University Press, 1965.

Reily, Duncan A. "William Capers: An Evaluation of His Life and Thought." Ph.D. diss., Emory University, 1972.

Wightman, William M. *Life of William Capers.* Nashville: Southern Methodist Publishing House, 1858.

Cardozo, Francis Lewis (1836–1903). Clergyman, educator, politician. Cardozo was born in Charleston on January 1, 1836, to Lydia Weston, a free black woman, and Isaac Cardozo, a Jew who served as a weigher in the city's customhouse. He attended schools for free blacks, then worked as a carpenter and shipbuilder before enrolling at the University of Glasgow in Scotland in 1858. He later studied at seminaries in Edinburgh and London and became an ordained Presbyterian minister. In 1864 he returned to the United States and became pastor of the Temple Street Congregational Church in New Haven, Connecticut. That same year he married Catherine Rowena Howell. They had six children. In 1865 Cardozo returned to Charleston as an agent of the American Missionary Association (AMA). On his arrival he replaced his brother, Thomas, as superintendent of the school established by the AMA for African Americans. Cardozo directed the transformation of the school into the Avery Normal Institute, which became an important training ground for black leaders in South Carolina.

Shortly after his return to South Carolina, Cardozo became involved in Reconstruction politics. As a delegate to the 1868 constitutional convention, he served as chair of the education committee and advocated a statewide system of integrated public education. In 1868 he was elected secretary of state, becoming the first African American in the United States elected to statewide office. While in office, Cardozo oversaw and reformed the controversial South Carolina Land Commission, which distributed land to thousands of former slaves. Elected state treasurer in 1872, Cardozo drew praise from both Republican and Democratic newspapers for his honesty and scrupulous management of public funds. In 1874 a handful of legislators attempted to have Cardozo impeached after he refused to cooperate in their corruption schemes, but Cardozo successfully refuted the charges.

Francis L. Cardozo. Courtesy, South Caroliniana Library, University of South Carolina

Cardozo won reelection as state treasurer in 1874 and 1876, but his political career came to an end with the return of the Democrats to power. On April 14, 1877, Governor Wade Hampton III sent Cardozo a letter demanding that he vacate his office. Cardozo relented on May 1. Soon after, he was indicted for corruption as part of a systematic attempt by Democrats to destroy the reputation of the Republican Party and its black leaders. Cardozo was the highest-ranking target of the prosecutions. With his reputation for honesty, he demanded a trial, and in November 1877 he was tried for conspiracy to issue a fraudulent pay certificate. Despite the questionable evidence against him and Cardozo's able defense, a jury of six blacks and six whites convicted Cardozo by an improper majority vote. He spent more than six months in jail before being pardoned in April 1879 by Governor William Simpson after federal election fraud charges against some white Democrats were dismissed.

Cardozo accepted a position in Washington, D.C., with the U.S. Treasury Department in 1878 and relocated to that city permanently after his pardon. In 1884 he left the treasury and began to teach in the public schools of Washington. As principal of the Colored Preparatory High School from 1884 to 1896 (later renamed the M Street High School), he introduced a business curriculum and made the institution the premier African American preparatory school in the nation. Cardozo died in Washington on July 22, 1903. W. LEWIS BURKE

Burke, W. Lewis. "Post-Reconstruction Justice: The Prosecution and Trial of Francis Lewis Cardozo." *South Carolina Law Review* 53 (winter 2002): 361–413.

———. "The Radical Law School: The University of South Carolina School of Law and Its African American Graduates, 1873–1877." In *At Freedom's Door: African American Founding Fathers and Lawyers in Reconstruction South Carolina,* edited by James Lowell Underwood and W. Lewis Burke, Jr. Columbia: University of South Carolina Press, 2000.

———. "Reconstruction, Corruption, and the Redeemers' Prosecution of Francis Lewis Cardozo." *American Nineteenth Century History* 2 (autumn 2001): 67–106.

Hine, William C. "Black Politicians in Reconstruction Charleston, South Carolina: A Collective Study." *Journal of Southern History* 49 (November 1983): 555–84.

Holt, Thomas. *Black over White: Negro Political Leadership in South Carolina during Reconstruction.* Urbana: University of Illinois Press, 1977.

Richardson, Joe. "Francis L. Cardozo: Black Educator during Reconstruction." *Journal of Negro Education* 73 (winter 1979): 73–83.

Sweat, Edward F. "Francis L. Cardozo—Profile of Integrity in Reconstruction Politics." *Journal of Negro History* 46 (October 1961): 217–32.

"Carolina." State song. South Carolina's oldest official song is "Carolina," with words by Henry Timrod (1828–1867) set to music by Anne (Annie) Custis Burgess (1874–1910). The General Assembly adopted it as the official state anthem on February 11, 1911.

Henry Timrod was a Charlestonian who became one of South Carolina's most beloved poets. "Carolina" was one of his most popular patriotic Civil War poems, in which the poet called on the people to rise up and defend their state against the Northern invaders until "all thy fields and fens and meres / Shall bristle like thy palm with spears."

Anne Custis Burgess was born in Mayesville, Sumter County. She earned a degree in music from Converse College and taught music in Summerton, Williamston, and at Winthrop College. She also wrote and published poetry. Her setting of Timrod's "Carolina" received its first public performance in 1905 and was published the following year.

In 1911 the South Carolina Daughters of the American Revolution presented a memorial to the General Assembly asking that "Carolina" be adopted as the official state song and observing that Anne Burgess's composition had been praised by noted American professors of music and other leaders, including Charleston's respected former mayor William Ashmead Courtenay. The opening lines of the song are "Call on thy children of the hill, / Wake swamp and river, coast and rill, / Rouse all thy strength and all thy skill, / Carolina! Carolina!" DAVID C. R. HEISSER

"Carolina—The Hymn of the Palmetto State." Columbia *State,* March 26, 1911, p. 25.

Hladczuk, John, and Sharon Schneider Hladczuk. *State Songs: Anthems and Their Origins.* Lanham, Md.: Scarecrow, 2000.

Wauchope, George. *Writers of South Carolina.* Columbia, S.C.: State Company, 1910.

Carolina. Ship. In 1663 King Charles II of England rewarded eight of his supporters with a grant for a large tract of land in North America. Lying between thirty-one and thirty-six degrees of latitude, the Province of Carolina stretched from the Atlantic to the Pacific Ocean.

In August 1669 the Lords Proprietors' fleet—the *Carolina,* the *Port Royal,* and the *Albemarle*—carrying the first settlers for Carolina was ready to sail. The fleet was commanded by Joseph West, who was later appointed governor of the colony. The *Carolina,* the largest of the three ships, was a two-hundred-ton frigate that carried ninety-three passengers. A typical frigate of the era was a three-masted vessel that was smaller and faster than many ships of the age.

En route to Barbados, the fleet landed in Ireland, where several colonists left the expedition. After forty days the ships reached Barbados, where a storm destroyed the *Albemarle.* After acquiring the sloop *The Three Brothers,* the fleet sailed to Nevis. Abandoning the *Port Royal* there, the *Carolina* and *The Three Brothers* continued to Bermuda. A storm drove *The Three Brothers* toward Virginia. Undeterred, the expedition acquired another sloop in Bermuda and eventually reached South Carolina in April 1670. Settlers on the *Carolina* first explored Port Royal, their intended settlement site, but chose instead to settle up the Ashley River. In May 1670 the settlers sent the *Carolina* to Virginia for supplies and to Barbados for sixty-four additional settlers. Of the three ships that left England to found the new colony, only the *Carolina* had successfully reached what would become South Carolina. ALEXIA JONES HELSLEY

Waring, Joseph I. *The First Voyage and Settlement at Charles Town, 1670–1680.* Columbia: University of South Carolina Press, 1970.

Carolina Art Association. Organized in 1857 by a group of prominent lowcountry planters and factors, the Carolina Art Association of Charleston was officially chartered by the General Assembly on December 21, 1858. Its purpose was the cultivation of the arts and art education. Initial exhibitions and meetings were held on the upper floor of the Apprentices Library on Meeting Street.

The association entered a period of dormancy during and after the Civil War but reemerged by 1878. In 1882, under the presidency of Dr. Gabriel E. Manigault, the association purchased "The Depository" on Chalmers Street and began an art school. Although within two years the school had an enrollment of five hundred students, it closed in 1892 due to a lack of funds. However, the association and the city of Charleston received a gift of $100,000 from the estate of James S. Gibbes (1819–1888), whose will directed that the money be used to acquire a building for "the exhibition of paintings" and the general promotion of the arts. In 1905 the Carolina Art Association moved into a new home: the Gibbes Memorial Art Gallery. In 1932 the association's board of directors hired its first professional director, Robert N. S. Whitelaw.

The association focused on collecting American art with significant connections to Charleston and the lowcountry. From 1937 to 1950 the association partnered with an existing theater group to operate the Dock Street Theatre. Its community role broadened through involvement with the Civil Services Committee, a group organized and sponsored by the association to study the impact of modernization on Charleston. In 1944 the association published an architectural survey of the city, *This Is Charleston,* which spurred the creation of Historic Charleston Foundation. For the state's tricentennial celebration, the Carolina Art Association organized a major exhibition: *Art in South Carolina 1670–1970.* In 1974 the group received accreditation for the Gibbes Museum of Art from the American Association of Museums. Entering the twenty-first century, the association continued in its mission to cultivate the arts and art education in the Charleston area. PAUL FIGUEROA

Mouzon, Harold A. "The Carolina Art Association: Its First Hundred Years." *South Carolina Historical Magazine* 59 (July 1958): 125–38.

Carolina bays. Carolina bays are elliptical, shallow depressions found on unconsolidated sediments of the coastal plain region of eastern North America from Maryland to Florida. Most of these unique geomorphic features occur in North and South Carolina, with Horry and Dillon Counties having the most bays. Of the thousands of bays that once dotted the coastal plain, only about 219 have been preserved, and only 36 of these are in pristine condition. Carolina bays are found both singly and overlapping, but most have their long axes aligned generally in a northwest/southeast direction. They range in size from three acres to thousands of acres. Most of the bays in South Carolina are dry all year round; many fill with water during the rainy season; and some are wet all year round. Many bays contain cypress-tupelo communities, Virginia bays, red maples, sweet gums, and willows, among other tree species. The moss that grew in many of the bays over time created thick deposits of peat that in the past were harvested for garden use.

Lewis Ocean Bay is a typical Carolina bay. Photograph by Phillip Jones. Courtesy, South Carolina Department of Natural Resources

Carolina bays form unique habitats occupied by several endangered animal and plant species, including bobcat, osprey, bear, mock bishop's weed, and rose coreopsis. In the past, rather than treasuring and seeking to preserve the bays, loggers cut their trees, drained them, and then used their rich, organic soils for farming. Many bays continue to be cultivated, but both private owners and government agencies are working to preserve as many as possible.

There are three major theories regarding the formation of Carolina bays, but the definitive explanation has yet to emerge. The most accepted theory proposes that during the Pleistocene epoch prevailing southwest winds blew across water-filled depressions near the coast and, in time, the wind and water sculpted the land into northwest-southeast trending bays. Less accepted is the theory that the bays were formed in inland estuaries or tidal flats sculpted by tidal eddy currents. Least plausible, but most dramatic and enticing, is the theory that meteorites hit the coastal sediments and formed the bays. This theory gained acceptance in the 1930s before earth science had the sophisticated technologies and data analyses that are used today. It is now clear that the meteorite theory is unsupported by any geologic evidence. There are no gravity or magnetic data to support meteorite impact, nor is there any shocked quartz in the sand around the bays. Meteorites generally create round craters, not ovals, and the shape of the Carolina bays is overwhelmingly elliptical. Also, there are no bays found in Piedmont rock, a necessity if a random meteor shower had occurred; they are found only on the coastal plain. Woods Bay State Park near Turbeville and Little Pee Dee State Park near Dillon have been established to preserve the bays and are available for the public to visit. CAROLYN H. MURPHY

Kovacik, Charles F., and John J. Winberry. *South Carolina: The Making of a Landscape.* 1987. Reprint, Columbia: University of South Carolina Press, 1989.

Murphy, Carolyn H. *Carolina Rocks! The Geology of South Carolina.* Orangeburg, S.C.: Sandlapper, 1995.

Carolina Black Corps. During the latter years of the Revolutionary War in South Carolina, British commanders used African American slaves, freemen, and refugees in a variety of military capacities. Although employed primarily as laborers, black Carolinians occasionally were armed by the British and used in combat. In the spring of 1782, the British formed a group of about one hundred black men into a cavalry detachment, which was used for patrol duty but also saw combat. During the final stages of Nathanael Greene's Southern Campaign, he reported that the British had as many as seven hundred black men under arms in South Carolina.

With the evacuation of Charleston pending in late 1782, British commanders pondered the fate of black soldiers under their command. A need for a black pioneer corps on the West Indian island of St. Lucia encouraged British commander Guy Carleton to order that those slaves promised freedom by the British be purchased from their owners and that volunteers from among them be enlisted for service in the West Indies at a pay rate of 8d per day. In December 1782 some 264 African American troops from South Carolina, under the command of Captain William Mackrill, arrived at St. Lucia, where they were organized into the Carolina Corps, or Carolina Black Corps. The unit served on St. Lucia until the end of the war, when it was transferred to the island of Grenada.

With the end of the war, the Carolina Black Corps continued as a provincial unit paid and supplied by the British government. It was the first black regiment to become a permanent part of the West Indian peacetime defense establishment. Although the regiment was used mainly for labor and fatigue duties, at least one company of the Carolina Black Corps was organized as dragoons (cavalry) and used to track maroons and other rebel slaves in the Caribbean. After some fifteen years of service, surviving elements of the Carolina Black Corps were enlisted into the First West India Regiment in 1798. CHARLES W. TOTH

Quarles, Benjamin. *The Negro in the American Revolution.* 1961. Reprint, Chapel Hill: University of North Carolina Press, 1996.

Tyson, George F. "The Carolina Black Corps: Legacy of Revolution (1782–1798)." *Revista/Review Interamericana* 5 (winter 1975/1976): 648–64.

Carolina Cup. The inaugural Carolina Cup was run in 1930 at Ernest Woodward's Springdale Race Course in Camden. A sterling trophy crafted in Ireland in 1704 and dedicated to the great horseman Thomas Hitchcock was secured for the occasion. Three thousand spectators gathered on a cold and damp March 22 for an opening card of three races and to watch Ballast II gallop to victory over a three-mile course of timber fences to win the feature, the Carolina Cup. A replica of the trophy and possession of the original for one year was awarded to the owner and rider Noel Lang.

Destined to become one of the most popular stops on the national steeplechase circuit, the Carolina Cup is among the oldest surviving race meets in America and the largest in terms of faithful fans. Except for three years during World War II, the Carolina Cup has been run annually since 1930. Thoroughbred racehorses are still touted as the feature of the day, but the tradition goes far beyond the superb steeplechasing over fences. Four generations have now gathered at this sporting and social bash, and the date of the Carolina Cup is marked on the calendar long in advance. Crowds have swelled, and a grandstand, College Park, the Rail, and Infield now surround the historic racecourse. Each new year welcomes families and friends, a little politicking, and a lot of socializing amid a sea of fashions and tailgate parties. HOPE COOPER

Trubiano, Ernie. *The Carolina Cup: 50 Years of Steeplechasing and Socializing.* Columbia, S.C.: R. L. Bryan, 1982.

Carolina gold rice. Carolina gold rice is named for the magnificent golden color of the ripe plants in early autumn. However, so wealthy did it make the early planters of the lowcountry, it could also refer to its financial importance. By the early 1720s rice had become the major crop in the colony, with some 6 million pounds shipped to England annually. As early as 1710 British writers were declaring its superiority as the "weightiest, largest, cleanest, and whitest . . . in the Habitable World." Botanists and historians are uncertain of its origins, but the plant flourished in the lowcountry for two hundred years.

By the middle of the nineteenth century, more than 75,000 acres of land were producing rice in the lowcountry, yielding 160 million pounds. By 1860 seventy percent of the 5 million bushels produced in America were being grown in South Carolina. Plantation owners demanded slaves from the West Coast of Africa, where wetland rice farming was common. The West Africans cleared the land, built the elaborate systems of sluices and dikes, planted the grain with the traditional African heel-and-toe technique, flooded the fields at proper intervals, chased destructive birds away, harvested the rice by hand, wove the winnowing or "fanner" basket from bulrushes and sweet grass, and carved the enormous wooden mortars and pestles for hulling. From seed to table, Carolina gold was the domain of the enslaved. South Carolina was renowned for its rice kitchens with elaborate Creole dishes prepared by accomplished African cooks.

After the Civil War, the demise of rice culture in South Carolina was gradual and complete. Rice was introduced into other states, where mechanical equipment that was too heavy for the marshy soil of the lowcountry replaced expensive hand labor. Floods, the silting caused by upstream cotton farming, and a series of destructive hurricanes between 1893 and 1911 put an end to commercial rice production in the state. JOHN MARTIN TAYLOR

Doar, David. *Rice and Rice Planting in the South Carolina Low Country.* 1936. Reprint, Charleston, S.C.: Charleston Museum, 1970.

Hess, Karen. *The Carolina Rice Kitchen: The African Connection.* Columbia: University of South Carolina Press, 1992.

Joyner, Charles W. *Down by the Riverside: A South Carolina Slave Community.* Urbana: University of Illinois Press, 1984.

Littlefield, Daniel C. *Rice and Slaves: Ethnicity and the Slave Trade in Colonial South Carolina.* Baton Rouge: Louisiana State University Press, 1981.

Taylor, John Martin. *Hoppin' John's Lowcountry Cooking: Recipes and Ruminations from Charleston and the Carolina Coastal Plain.* New York: Bantam, 1992.

Carolina I-house. The I-house is a relatively new architectural term. Fred Kniffen first coined it in 1936, when he used it "in the absence of any common term, either folk or architectural," to describe the house type he identified initially in the "I" states of Indiana, Illinois, and Iowa. More a description of a house form or shape than a distinct style, "I-house" was not a term used by eighteenth- and nineteenth-century architects and builders. The distinguishing characteristics are a full two-story height, a one-room depth, and a length of two or more rooms. The I-house conveys a tall, narrow appearance. It is constructed of wood, brick, stone, or log with its entrance on the long side. Kniffen traced the origins of this house form evolving from the English, single room, end-chimney house to full-blown examples in the Middle Atlantic region of Delaware and the Chesapeake by the late seventeenth century. It was carried southward as part of the great mid-eighteenth-century migration along the Appalachian Mountains into the backcountry of the Carolinas. From there it was carried into the Deep South and by way of the Ohio River into the Midwest. The ubiquitous I-house had become the symbol of economic success in the rural landscape of South Carolina's upcountry by the middle of the nineteenth century and remained so well into the early twentieth century.

The early I-house had two rooms on the ground floor. One room, the hall, functioned as the kitchen, workroom, or dining room; the other, the parlor, was used for more formal activities. By the nineteenth century and with increased attention to symmetry, a center hall containing the stairway was present in most floor plans. Examples in Carolina typically have three to five windows across the front on the second story; a chimney on either gable end; a front porch; a back porch, which is often enclosed as a lean-to; and/or a kitchen ell added to the rear. As an occupant's wealth increased, a simpler house form such as a single-story dogtrot could evolve into an I-house with the addition of a second story, conversion of the breezeway into the hall, and covering the whole with weatherboards. Its tall, shallow form with short spans was easy to construct, provided excellent ventilation through the main rooms, and presented an impressive public face to signal the economic status of the owner. The architectural historian Michael Southern has argued that the durability of this form through time may in part be attributed to its adaptability to receive detailing and ornamentation from the various popular styles of the nineteenth century, such as the Federal, Greek-revival, Italianate, and even Gothic styles. While retaining a traditional floor plan, the occupants were able to dress up their homes outwardly to indicate that they were attuned to the latest architectural trends. Thus, the Carolina I-house established itself as the signature house form of the upland part of the state throughout the nineteenth century. JOHN C. LARSON

Foster, Gerald. *American Houses: A Field Guide to the Architecture of the Home.* New York: Houghton Mifflin, 2004.

Glassie, Henry. *Pattern in the Material Folk Culture of the Eastern United States.* Philadelphia: University of Pennsylvania Press, 1968.

Kniffen, Fred. "Folk Housing: Key to Diffusion." In *Common Places: Readings in American Vernacular Architecture,* edited by Dell Upton and John Michael Vlach. Athens: University of Georgia Press, 1986.

Southern, Michael T. "The I-House as a Carrier of Style in Three Counties of the Northeastern Piedmont." In *Carolina Dwelling,* edited by Doug Swaim. Raleigh: North Carolina State University, 1978.

Carolina mantid. State insect. The Carolina mantid (*Stagmomantis carolina*) became the state insect by a law approved by Governor Carroll Campbell on June 1, 1988. The legislators recognized the mantis as "a beneficial insect" found throughout the state and declared it to be "a perfect specimen of living science" for schoolchildren.

The Carolina species is the mantis most commonly found in the United States, ranging from New Jersey, southern New York, and Indiana south to Florida and west to Texas. It is brown or green, and adults measure from two to two and one-quarter inches in length. Like all mantises, the state insect is called a "praying mantis," from the way it holds up its enormous front legs, as if in an attitude of prayer. In fact, the forelegs jerk out to seize prey that the mantis eats. The name "mantis" means "diviner" and was given to the insect by ancient Greeks, who believed that it possessed supernatural powers. The earliest known fossil mantises date from 25 million to 36 million years ago.

The Carolina mantid is a predator that eats virtually any insects it can catch, so it serves as a natural biological control agent. Its prey can include other mantises, and the females are famous for connubial cannibalism, often devouring their male partners after mating. They are harmless to humans. During legislative debate on the bill, Representative Derwood L. Aydlette, Jr., of Charleston humorously proposed designating instead the palmetto bug (cockroach), as a protest against legislative time and expense "involved in having all these little state symbols." DAVID C. R. HEISSER

Gaulden, Sid. "Cockroach Proposal Fails in S.C. House." Charleston *Post and Courier,* April 28, 1988, p. B1.

Prete, Frederick R., et al. *The Praying Mantids.* Baltimore: Johns Hopkins University Press, 1999.

Carolina parakeet. Now extinct, the Carolina parakeet (*Conuropsis carolinensis*) was a dove-sized (about thirty-five centimeters long) bird with a bright green body, yellow head, and orange face. Mark Catesby, an English naturalist living in Charleston, painted the parakeet in 1731, thus providing the first scientific description of the species. The species was abundant in early America, and its range extended to New York, Colorado, and Florida. The Carolina parakeet was well known for its ability to withstand harsh winters, due to the winter availability of its main foods: cockleburs, thistle seeds, and sandspurs.

The parakeets nested in tree hollows, usually in mature bottomland forests composed of cypress or sycamores. Although it is believed that a high fraction of the population did not breed each year, low reproductive rates may have been balanced by longevity. Many captive Carolina parakeets lived ten years, and one was believed to have attained thirty years.

Several theories exist regarding what caused the extinction of the species, including hunting, loss of mature swamp forests, competition with imported honeybees for nest holes, reduced food supply, and disease. Disease has been generally accepted as the main cause. The parrots were highly social and often roosted together, which would explain the rapid spread of a disease. In the 1800s naturalists noted declines in parakeet numbers, and by 1900 it was apparent that the parakeet was rare outside southern Florida. One of the last verified sightings occurred in June 1938 when Warren and Hollie Shokes saw a pair with a young bird in the Santee River swamp of Georgetown County. Thus, South Carolina was the site of both the first sketch and a final sighting of the Carolina parakeet. See plate 7. WILLIAM POST

Forshaw, Joseph M. *Parrots of the World.* 3d ed. Willoughby, Australia: Lansdowne Editions and Weldon, 1989.

McKinley, Daniel. "Historial Review of the Carolina Parakeet in the Carolinas." *Brimleyana* 1 (March 1979): 81–98.

Snyder, Noel F. R., and Keith Russell. "Carolina Parakeet (*Conuropsis carolinensis*)." In *The Birds of North America,* no. 667. Philadelphia: Birds of North America, 2002.

Carolina Sandhills National Wildlife Refuge. Carolina Sandhills National Wildlife Refuge was established in 1939, when the federal government acquired land under the provisions of the Resettlement Act. The 45,348-acre refuge in Chesterfield County is situated along the fall line separating the Atlantic coastal plain and the Piedmont Plateau in what is known as the Sandhills region of South Carolina. Due to its location, the refuge is home to a variety of plants, animals, and habitat types characteristic of both regions. The rolling sandhills and deep sandy soils are remnants of an ancient coastal shoreline of the Atlantic Ocean.

Among the diverse group of fauna and flora that exist in the Carolina Sandhills are several species that are listed as threatened or endangered. These include the pine barrens treefrog, sandhills chub, white wicky, and Well's pixie-moss. Also included in this group is the red-cockaded woodpecker. The refuge supports more than one hundred groups of these cooperative breeders, giving it the largest population of red-cockaded woodpeckers in the National Wildlife Refuge System. This bird requires mature pines, often those averaging seventy-five to ninety-five years old, to create nesting cavities and extensive pine forests to meet its foraging requirements.

Among the many management activities that take place in the refuge, prescribed burning is the most beneficial to wildlife and habitat. This practice reduces wildfire hazards through fuel reduction and maintains and restores the habitat for threatened plant species and many animal species such as turkey, quail, deer, and the red-cockaded woodpecker.

Public-use opportunities include nine miles of paved drive for visitors, three nature trails, two observation towers, a photography blind, and a recreational area. Several ponds and lakes are open to fishing, and limited hunting is permitted for several species. Interpretive displays and literature can be found at the refuge office and the main entrances. GREGORY Z. BOLING

United States. Department of the Interior. Fish and Wildlife Service. *Carolina Sandhills National Wildlife Refuge.* Washington, D.C.: Government Printing Office, 2002.

Carolina wolf spider. State spider. South Carolina became the first state to designate an official spider when the General Assembly chose the Carolina wolf spider in legislation approved by Governor Jim Hodges on July 21, 2000. The accepted scientific name was formerly *Lycosa carolinensis,* but it is now *Hogna carolinensis.* Skyler B. Hutto, a third-grade student at Sheridan Elementary School in Orangeburg, originally suggested to the General Assembly that the spider be so honored.

The Carolina wolf spider is found throughout the continental United States and is most common in the South from Virginia to Texas. It is the largest American wolf spider. The adult male can attain nearly an inch in body length, while the female can be an inch or more. Instead of catching prey in webs, wolf spiders are ground hunters that pounce on insects, kill with venomous bites, then consume their victims. Wolves are colored in mottled browns and grays that provide camouflage among leaves on the forest floor.

The state spider is normally shy of humans but may bite if touched or threatened. While not fatal, its bite can be painful, like a bee sting. The female may dig a burrow five to eight inches deep, and spend some time there. A good mother, she carries her egg sac (a pea-sized silk ball) around in her fangs until the eggs hatch. She then carries her newly hatched spiderlings on her back for a time. When the egg yolk on which the young live is depleted, they begin eyeing each other as prey, then disperse to live on their own. DAVID C. R. HEISSER

Gertsch, Willis J. *American Spiders.* 2d ed. New York: Van Nostrand Reinhold, 1979.

Langley, Lynne. "State Spider a Keen Hunter and Dutiful Parent." Charleston *Post and Courier,* July 16, 2000, p. F10.

Carolina wren. State bird. The Carolina wren (*Thyrothorus ludovicianus*) became South Carolina's official state bird with the signing of an act by Governor Strom Thurmond on April 3, 1948. The act also made it a crime to kill a wren intentionally. It had been recognized unofficially as the state bird since early in the twentieth century, but in 1939 the General Assembly designated the mockingbird (*Mimus polyglottus*) instead. The 1948 act repealed the 1939 designation. The wren was deemed a better choice since it includes "Carolina" in its name, is a permanent resident in every part of South Carolina, and sings practically year-round.

Carolina Wren. Photograph by Phillip Jones. Courtesy, South Carolina Department of Natural Resources

The Carolina wren is a small, energetic bird, five to six inches in length, frequenting human dwellings and gardens, as well as wild habitats. The bird lives mainly in the eastern United States and in Central America. It has chestnut brown upper parts, cinnamon under parts, and a distinctive white stripe over the eye. Its scientific name means "reed-jumping [bird] of Louisiana."

The wren eats mainly insects and spiders. Male and female wrens pair-bond year-round. Nests may be constructed in gardens and porches of houses. The female customarily lays four or five eggs, sometimes raising three broods in a season. The male is a good father and shares in caring for the young. The Carolina wren is not a migratory bird. Although it ranges as far north as southern New York, it is sensitive to cold weather and may perish in hard winters. The Carolina wren is beneficial to South Carolina agriculture on account of the great quantities of insects—including caterpillars—it consumes. DAVID C. R. HEISSER

Haggerty, Thomas M., and Eugene S. Morton. "Carolina Wren." In *The Birds of North America,* no. 188. Philadelphia: Academy of Natural Sciences of Philadelphia, 1995.

Sprunt, Alexander, Jr., and E. Burnham Chamberlain. *South Carolina Bird Life.* Rev. ed. Columbia: University of South Carolina Press, 1970.

Carroll, Richard (1860–1929). Clergyman. Born in Barnwell District (later Bamberg County) on November 2, 1860, Richard Carroll rose from slavery and emerged as one of the most influential African Americans in South Carolina in the early twentieth century. Described as a mulatto by contemporaries, Carroll worked as a house servant for the L. L. Rice family near Denmark, as did his mother.

In his midteens Carroll attended a revival near Denmark conducted by the Reverend A. W. Lamar, the secretary-treasurer of the South Carolina Baptist Convention. The revival led Carroll to a religious conversion, and he later contemplated a career in the ministry. Faced with few professional and educational opportunities in his rural community, Carroll moved to Columbia to attend Benedict Institute. At Benedict and later at Shaw University in Raleigh, North Carolina, he broadened his theological training and honed his oratorical skills.

On entering the ministry, Carroll pastored several churches throughout the state, including the Springfield Baptist Church in Greenville. Subsequently he worked as a traveling evangelist, an agent of the American Baptist Publication Society, and as an itinerant minister and colporteur for the Southern Baptist Home Mission Board. Additionally he served as an officer and life member of the Baptist Educational, Missionary, and Sunday School Convention, the largest association of African American Baptists in South Carolina.

During the Spanish-American War, Carroll served as a military chaplain for the Tenth U.S. Infantry. Following the war he edited a series of newspapers in Columbia, including the short-lived *Christian Soldier* and *The Southern Ploughman,* a semimonthly publication. In 1899 Carroll secured funding from a northern philanthropist and local white benefactors to purchase a 225-acre tract on the outskirts of Columbia to establish an industrial home for African American children.

Throughout Carroll's public career, his sharp intellect and stirring oratory commanded large audiences across the state. While highly critical of blatant acts of white racism, such as the 1905 production of Thomas Dixon's *The Clansman* on a Columbia stage, Carroll devised a conservative and pragmatic posture on issues concerning race relations, segregation, and white supremacy. Modeling his work after Booker T. Washington's Tuskegee Machine, Carroll voiced strong opposition to the social activism of W. E. B. Du Bois's Niagara Movement and underscored the precepts of self-help, economic development, and moral uplift as the best remedy to the "Negro Problem." In published speeches and writings Carroll discouraged political agitation, counseled against black migration to northern cities, and appealed to the paternalist sensibilities of his white supporters. His rhetoric of racial self-help and political conservatism found a receptive audience among white newspapers, particularly William E. Gonzales's *State* in Columbia.

In 1907 in Columbia, Carroll organized the first of a series of annual conferences on race relations that attracted African American leaders from across the country and prominent white South Carolinians. Booker T. Washington spoke at the inaugural meeting and endorsed Carroll's work. Underscoring the importance of economic development in black communities, Carroll subsequently established a black employment bureau in Columbia's African American business district and, like Washington, offered support and counsel to enterprising African Americans seeking to secure jobs and open businesses. The Columbia businessman and civic leader Isaac Samuel Leevy was one of several young people who benefited from Carroll's advice and intervention. Leevy, along with the lawyer and educator Nathaniel J. Frederick and others, assisted Carroll in developing and promoting an annual and highly successful State Colored Fair.

In 1883 Carroll married Mary Magdalene Sims, one of the first college graduates of Benedict. They had four children. After Mary's death, Carroll married Carrie Julia McDaniel in 1914. After suffering a debilitating stroke and retiring from public life, Carroll died in Columbia on October 29, 1929. He was buried in Randolph Cemetery. BOBBY J. DONALDSON

Carroll, Richard. Papers. South Caroliniana Library, University of South Carolina, Columbia.

Carroll, Richard, and T. H. Wiseman. *Thoughts.* Columbia, S.C.: Lewie Printing, [1920].

Moore, John Hammond. *Columbia and Richland County: A South Carolina Community, 1740–1990.* Columbia: University of South Carolina Press, 1993.

Newby, I. A. *Black Carolinians: A History of Blacks in South Carolina from 1895 to 1968.* Columbia: University of South Carolina Press, 1973.

Carson, Jane Caroline Petigru (1820–1892). Painter. Caroline (as she was known) Petigru Carson was born in Charleston on January 4, 1820, the first daughter and second child of the prominent Charleston attorney James Louis Petigru and his wife, Jane Amelia Postell. Educated first at Miss Susan Robertson's school in Charleston and then at Madame Binsse's finishing school in New York, as an adult she added Latin and Italian to her fluent French and improved her amateurish art skills by study at New York's Cooper Union as well as with various European painters in Rome. On December 16, 1841, she married the Cooper River rice planter William Augustus Carson (1800–1856). The marriage produced two sons. In poor health and separated from her alcoholic husband after 1850, Carson frequently sought medical advice in New York, where for long periods she was an active socialite. A committed Unionist, Carson left Charleston forever in June 1861, living in New York until 1872. Supported there largely by her own and her father's northern friends, she supplemented her income from their aid and a meager inheritance from her husband's estate by painting portraits and tinting photographs.

In 1872, after her health improved and her sons were educated, Carson realized her lifelong aspiration to live and paint in Rome, where she joined an active Anglo-American art colony. An accomplished linguist and an avid reader of history and literature whose correspondence and conversation drew intellectuals and diplomats as well as artists into her circle, Carson displayed both the conventional propriety expected of Charleston ladies and the independence required to pursue the unconventional goals that attracted her.

Purchased largely by American and British tourists, many of whom were her friends, Carson's most popular paintings were botanically detailed watercolors of flowers or copies of paintings in churches, palaces, and museums. In 1876 she became the only woman and only American member of the Roman Society of Watercolorists (Societa degli Acquarellisti in Roma). She preferred, however, to paint oil portraits. Carson was not a painter of the first rank, and much of her work appears to have been lost. Portraits of her father are currently owned by the University of South Carolina Law School, the South Carolina Supreme Court, and the South Carolina Historical Society. The Gibbes Museum of Art in Charleston, the Greenville County Museum, and the Morris Museum in Augusta, Georgia, have samples of her paintings and sketches. The most comprehensive holdings of her work, especially of her landscapes, are in the Ashton and LaVonne Phillips collection in Charleston. Some of them are reproduced in *The Roman Years* (2003), a published collection of Carson's letters.

As the American and British art colony and much of the foreign tourist trade shifted from Rome to Florence, Carson's career and social life dwindled. She died in Rome on August 15, 1892, and was buried there in the Protestant (Acattolico) cemetery. JANE H. PEASE AND WILLIAM H. PEASE

Pease, Jane H., and William H. Pease. *A Family of Women: The Carolina Petigrus in Peace and War.* Chapel Hill: University of North Carolina Press, 1999.

Pease, William H., and Jane H. Pease, eds. *The Roman Years of a South Carolina Artist: Caroline Carson's Letters Home, 1872–1892.* Columbia: University of South Carolina Press, 2003.

Casey, Claude (1912–1999). Musician, songwriter. Casey was born in Enoree on September 13, 1912, the son of James Casey and Sallie Griffin. Raised in a musical family, Casey began performing with local string bands in his early teens. In the mid-1920s the Caseys moved to Danville, Virginia, where Claude made his first radio appearance in 1929 on WBTM. Two years later he had his own fifteen-minute program, billing himself as the "Carolina Hobo" and assembling the first aggregation of his most enduring ensemble, the Pine State Playboys. Casey's career struggled through the early

1930s, and he alternated between music and mill work for several years. In 1937 he made his first recordings, cutting six masters for the American Record Corporation in New York, but none was released.

In 1938 Casey and the Pine State Playboys cut eighteen sides for Bluebird in Charlotte, North Carolina, and Rock Hill, South Carolina, which featured Casey on vocals and rhythm guitar, Jimmie Rouse on fiddle, and Willie Coates on piano. Two years later a revamped Playboys lineup recorded ten more tracks for RCA Victor in Atlanta. The Pine State Playboys were essentially a small western swing combo, deeply influenced by the foot-stomping rhythms of Texas performers Bob Wills and Milton Brown. In 1941 Casey was hired by Charlotte radio station WBT, where he became a featured performer both as a solo act and with the station's popular bands, the Briarhoppers and the Tennessee Ramblers. He also appeared in several motion pictures during the 1940s, including *Swing Your Partner* (1943) and *Square Dance Jubilee* (1949). In 1942 Casey married Ruth Derrick. The couple had two sons.

Casey's career continued to prosper after World War II. In the early 1950s his new act, Claude Casey and his Sage Dusters, moved to WGAC in Augusta, Georgia, then to WFBC-TV in Greenville. He made his final recordings in Nashville for MGM in 1953. In the early 1960s Casey retired to Johnston, his wife's hometown, where they founded radio station WJES. In 1987 Old Homestead Records released a collection of Casey's recordings. He died in Johnston on June 24, 1999, and was buried at Sunset Gardens Memorial Park. TOM DOWNEY

Casey, Claude. *Pine State Honky Tonk.* Brighton, Mich.: Old Homestead Records, 1987. Sound recording.

Charlotte Country Music Story. [Raleigh]: North Carolina Arts Council, Folklife Section, 1985.

McCloud, Barry. *Definitive Country: The Ultimate Encyclopedia of Country Music and Its Performers.* New York: Berkley, 1995.

Obituary. Columbia *State,* June 25, 1999, p. B4.

Cash, Wilbur Joseph (1900–1941). Author. A writer and an acerbic commentator on southern life, Cash was born in Gaffney on May 2, 1900. The oldest child of John William Cash and Nannie Lutitia Hamrick, he was named Joseph Wilbur Cash. Disliking his first name, Cash reversed the order and used the initial J. rather than Joseph. His father managed the company store for a local cotton mill. Cash was graduated from Boiling Springs High School in North Carolina in 1917 and enlisted in the Students' Army Training corps—a home-front service during World War I. Following the end of his enlistment, Cash entered Wofford College. After one year at Wofford, Cash attended Valparaiso University in Indiana and then in 1920 enrolled at Wake Forest University in North Carolina. At Wake Forest he wrote for student publications and discovered the writings of H. L. Mencken.

After graduating in 1922, Cash attended law school for a year and then tried teaching—first at Georgetown College in Kentucky and later at Hendersonville School for Boys in North Carolina. Returning to writing, Cash had a brief stint with the Chicago *Post* before joining the *Charlotte (N.C.) News* in 1926. In 1928 ill health forced him to return to Boiling Springs. He edited the short-lived *Cleveland (N.C.) Press* and in 1929 wrote "Jehovah of the Tar Heels," which appeared in Mencken's *American Mercury.* "Jehovah of the Tar Heels" was an exposé of the anti-Catholicism of U.S. Senator Furnifold M. Simmons, an anti–Al Smith Democrat. Later that year his second article, "The Mind of the South," caught the attention of the editors at Alfred A. Knopf. In March 1936 the publisher contracted with Cash to write a history of the South. Finding free-lancing difficult in the dark days of the Depression, Cash returned to the *Charlotte News* in 1935 and stayed there until 1940. While in Charlotte, he married Mary Northrop on Christmas Day 1940.

Cash's masterpiece and only book, *The Mind of the South,* appeared in February 1941 to wide critical praise. An instant classic that has not been out of print since its initial publication, the work sought to dispel myths about the "Old South" by tracing the pervasive influence of racism on southern history and culture. Antebellum ideals remained dominant in the twentieth century South, despite the upheavals of the Civil War, Reconstruction, industrialization, urbanization, and Depression. Indeed, Cash's compelling chronicle of the persistence of an Old South mentality, especially its emphasis on race, individualism, and agriculture, led the author to assert that much of southern history has been a march "from the present toward the past." National publications hailed *The Mind of the South,* and even many southern reviewers found much to admire in Cash's penetrating analysis of the region.

Awarded a prestigious Guggenheim fellowship, Cash traveled with his wife to Mexico, where he planned to write his first novel. In Mexico, Cash's history of psychological instability, alcohol abuse, and ill health caught up with him. Ill with dysentery and in a state of paranoia and depression, Cash fled to another hotel. On July 1, 1941, searchers found him in the Hotel Reforma hanging by his own necktie. Cash's body was cremated and his ashes buried in Sunset Cemetery, Shelby, North Carolina. ALEXIA JONES HELSLEY

Clayton, Bruce. *W. J. Cash: A Life.* Baton Rouge: Louisiana State University Press, 1991.

Morrison, Joseph L. *W. J. Cash: Southern Prophet.* New York: Knopf, 1967.

Cashwell, Gaston Barnabus (1862–1916). Clergyman. Popularly known as the "apostle of Pentecost in the South," Cashwell was instrumental in bringing the Pentecostal message to South Carolina in the opening years of the twentieth century. Cashwell was born on April 5, 1862, in Sampson County, North Carolina, and spent most of his active ministry based in North Carolina. In 1898 he married Helen Lee Lovie. The couple had five children.

Ordained in the Methodist Episcopal Church, South, Cashwell came under the influence of Ambrose Blackman Crumpler, a fellow North Carolinian who left Methodism to help organize the Holiness Association of North Carolina. Cashwell joined the Pentecostal Holiness Church in 1903. He went to Los Angeles in 1906 when he learned of the revivals there, which were led by the African American evangelist William J. Seymour and where persons experienced gifts of the Spirit, such as speaking in tongues.

After receiving the gift of tongues, Cashwell returned to North Carolina, where he led a Pentecostal revival in Dunn. In 1907 he journeyed to Toccoa, just across the Georgia state line from Oconee County, South Carolina, where he led another successful revival. On his way back to North Carolina, he planted Pentecostalism in South Carolina through upstate revivals in Anderson, Iva, and West Union and also in Lake City and Clinton. The Presbyterian pastor Nickels John Holmes, then living in Columbia, attended the revival in West Union and became a confirmed Pentecostal. As a result, he made his Altamont Bible and Missionary Institute, later renamed as the Holmes College of the Bible, a center for Pentecostal activity in the state.

Although Cashwell published a Pentecostal periodical and is credited with introducing Church of God (Cleveland, Tennessee) founder Ambrose J. Tomlinson to Pentecostal thinking, in his later years he distanced himself from the movement and returned to the Methodist Episcopal Church, South. Before his death he turned his attention to social issues, founding a home for reforming prostitutes and also an orphanage in North Carolina. Nonetheless, he is credited with stirring many southern holiness churches, including those in South Carolina, to move into such Pentecostal denominations as the Pentecostal Holiness Church, the Church of God (Cleveland, Tennessee), the Pentecostal Free Will Baptist Church, and the Assemblies of God. Cashwell died on March 4, 1916, in Dunn, North Carolina. NANCY A. HARDESTY

Anderson, Robert Mapes. *Vision of the Disinherited: The Making of American Pentecostalism.* New York: Oxford University Press, 1979.

Synan, Vinson. *The Holiness-Pentecostal Tradition: Charismatic Movements in the Twentieth Century.* 2d ed. Grand Rapids, Mich.: Eerdmans, 1997.

Catawba pottery. Among the Catawba Indians in present-day York County, an unbroken chain of pottery production has helped preserve a cultural identity that was nearly lost after European settlement. Ten thousand strong when settlers first arrived, their population was reduced to less than one hundred by 1849. Traditionally, women made pottery; but when the population declined so severely, *everybody* had to make pottery. This activity helped maintain community traditions and is now one of the purest folk art forms in this country.

Utilizing clay dug near the Catawba River, the Catawbas' methods of production are nearly unchanged since the Woodland (1000 B.C.E.–600 C.E.) and Mississippian (600–1600 C.E.) periods. Impurities are removed from pipe and pan clay, and then pots are handbuilt using traditional coiling techniques. Protruding features, such as handles and legs, are attached by riveting (pushing the attachment through a hole pierced in the pot) rather than by direct application to the surface. This technique creates features that will not break off easily. Once pots are air dried, the surface is scraped even with a piece of bone, antler, or a knife and then burnished to a shine with a smooth river stone. These stones are prized possessions, handed down from mother to daughter through the generations. Decoration, if desired, is then incised into the surface. Firing is often in two stages. A fire is built in a pit and the pots placed near it to heat. Then the warmed pots are placed in the pit to complete the process. Smoke from the burning wood creates distinctive patterns on the surfaces of the pots.

In Rock Hill, South Carolina, Catawba pottery was sold at the gates of Winthrop University from 1895 through the 1920s. It was taken door-to-door, sold and traded for clothing and other goods on the main road through the reservation, and traded with local merchants as recently as the 1960s.

Population declines have not been the only threats to the survival of this pre-Columbian art form. The economic pressures that made production and sale of pottery necessary to the Catawbas' survival also dictated changes. Beginning in the 1920s, merchants in the Cherokee region of western North Carolina became an important market for Catawba pottery. Their buyers were tourists and their concern was money, not the quality of the pots they offered. Under pressures to produce vast quantities of work, the potters' craftsmanship declined. Their clumsy pots became smaller, thick walled, less symmetrical, and poorly fired. By the time the tourist trade ended in the late 1960s, few potters remained active.

The first museum exhibition to focus on Catawba Indian pottery was the York County Children's Nature Museum in 1952. It would be more than twenty years before the native craft would be brought to the public again. An exhibition in 1972, *Catawba Indian Trade Pottery of the Historic Period,* at the Columbia Museum of Art gave these potters the recognition they needed to begin a revival of this purest of South Carolina folk arts. Prices and public interest went up and have continued to do so. New potters continue the tradition, learning from their parents and from the surviving master potters. These contemporary masters strive for the qualities—gracefully curved and well-crafted shapes, delicately decorated, beautifully burnished, properly fired—found in work done before the Cherokee trade period. PAUL E. MATHENY III

Blumer, Thomas J. *Catawba Indian Pottery: The Survival of a Folk Tradition.* Tuscaloosa: University of Alabama Press, 2004.

Blumer, Thomas, and Charles G. Zug. *Catawba Clay: Pottery from the Catawba Nation.* Exhibition catalog. North Carolina Pottery Center, 2000.

Williams, Lesley, and Tom Stanley. *Catawba Pottery: Legacy of Survival.* Exhibition catalog. South Carolina Arts Commission, 1995.

Catawbas. Catawba legend relates that the tribe arrived in South Carolina, near present-day Fort Mill, from the north a few hundred years before European contact. The first recorded contact with these people was by Hernando de Soto in 1540. There is no known origin for the name Catawba, as the members called themselves "Ye Iswa," meaning "the people of the river," but the name was in common usage by the beginning of the eighteenth century. The Catawbas were ferocious warriors feared not only by neighboring tribes but also by Indian nations to the north. For years the Catawbas and the nations of the Iroquois Confederation had traveled back and forth along the Appalachian trails to raid each other's towns. However, when the British arrived, the Catawbas befriended their new neighbors, and a strong trade alliance began. That alliance led the Catawbas to fight alongside the British in the French and Indian War and the Cherokee War. Despite this history of alliance with the British, however, the Catawbas supported the patriot cause during the Revolutionary War. In return for their alliance in the French and Indian War, King George III in the 1763 Treaty of Augusta ceded the Catawba tribe of South Carolina a tract of land "fifteen miles square" comprising approximately 144,000 acres.

European settlers began moving onto the Catawba reservation sometime before the Revolutionary War. One of the first European settlers among the Catawbas was Thomas "Kanawha" Spratt II, who settled on the land near present-day Fort Mill about 1761. Though Spratt got along well with his Catawba neighbors, he soon began selling parcels of land that he had leased from the Catawbas. Within a few years, almost all of the most fertile tracts within the reservation

A Catawba family at the turn of the last century. Courtesy, CCPP Archives, Catawba Cultural Center

had been leased to English colonists. In 1782 the Catawbas petitioned Congress to secure their land so that it would not be "Intruded into by force, nor alienated even with their own consent." Not wanting to deal with the tribe, Congress the following year passed a resolution stating that the British title over the Catawba Nation had passed into the hands of South Carolina. Congress recommended that South Carolina "take such measures for the satisfaction and security of the said tribe as the said legislature shall, in their wisdom, think fit." Thus, the Catawba Nation became the beneficiary of a trust relationship with the state of South Carolina rather than with the United States.

Settlers continued to invade Catawba lands. By the early 1800s virtually all of their remaining land had been leased out. The non-Indian leaseholders worried about the permanence of their leases, so in 1838 Governor Patrick Noble authorized commissioners to enter into negotiations with the Catawbas for the sale of their land. The Catawbas were willing to part with full title if the state provided enough money for land acquisition near the Cherokees in North Carolina. In 1840 the Catawba Nation and the state of South Carolina entered into the Treaty of Nation Ford, which provided that the Catawbas would cede the land granted to them under the Treaty of Augusta in 1763 in return for a tract of land of approximately three hundred acres in North Carolina; if no such tract could be procured to their satisfaction, they were to be given $5,000 by the state. The commissioners further promised that the state would pay the Catawbas $2,500 at or immediately after the time of their removal and $1,500 each year thereafter for the space of nine years.

Unfortunately, in its haste to remove the Catawbas, South Carolina had neglected to secure North Carolina's permission to have the Catawbas moved to the Cherokee reservation. When the permission was belatedly requested, North Carolina refused. Some Catawbas journeyed to the Cherokee reservation and did reside there for a time; however, old tribal jealousies and the stress suffered by the remaining Cherokees as a result of the Trail of Tears tragedy prevented them from making a permanent home with the Cherokees. Eventually most of the Catawbas found themselves back on their former soil but without land or money. The settlement of $2,500 and the annual payment of $1,500 promised them under the 1840 treaty were withheld by the state because the Catawbas had returned to the ceded land. The plight of the Catawbas led the South Carolina Indian agent Joseph White in 1843 to secure for them a tract of 630 acres near the center of the "Old Reservation."

South Carolina and the United States continued to try to rid themselves of the "Catawba problem." Congress appropriated money in 1848 and again in 1854 in an effort to remove the Catawbas west of the Mississippi. Conflict between South Carolina and the tribe over the provisions of the Treaty of Nation Ford continued until 1905, when the Catawbas launched a legal battle to recover their lands.

The Catawba tribe, unlike many eastern bands, was able to maintain its internal cohesiveness and social identity throughout the nineteenth century despite the lack of federal or state protection. In 1911 Charles Davis of the Bureau of Indian Affairs reported that, in his opinion, the four leading factors in maintaining tribal identity were size, tribal organization, religion, and character. The tribe was small at that time, consisting of only ninety-seven individuals recognized by South Carolina as living on or near the Catawba reservation. Since the tribe had not intermarried much with their white neighbors and virtually not at all with their black neighbors, according to one observer, "[t]he large majority are so nearly full blood as to retain the Indian characteristics, and by reason thereof they have retained their tribal life and organization." During the twentieth century there was more intermarriage with non-Indians, which affected the physical characteristics of the tribal members but not their Indian status. Because the Catawba membership rolls have been based on "descendancy" rather than "blood quantum," as found among the western tribes, intermarriage with non-Indians did not affect the legally recognized Indian status of the Catawba children.

Religion also affected internal cohesion. Most members of the Catawba tribe converted to the Mormon religion in the 1880s, and as late as the 1950s the majority of the tribe still affiliated with the Mormon Church. The double minority status of tribal members (race and religion) tended to bind them together against the outside world. In the bipolar racial world of South Carolina during the era of segregation, Catawba Indians felt themselves ostracized, not considering themselves "black" but not being accepted as "white" (South Carolina census takers in the early twentieth century listed Catawba Indians as "black" because they had no category for Indian). As Mormons among a population of Baptists, Methodists, and Episcopalians, the Catawbas were further marginalized. Ironically, it was this isolation and marginalization that helped to insure the tribal identity of the Catawbas. Banned from attending the white schools and refusing to attend the black schools, the Catawbas erected, with the help of the Mormon Church, a school on the reservation, another factor that helped retain their community.

In 1934 the South Carolina General Assembly passed a resolution recommending that the care and maintenance of the Catawba Indians should be transferred to the United States government. However, it was not until 1943 that a Memorandum of Understanding was signed between the tribe, the state, and the U.S. Department of the Interior. South Carolina acquired 3,434 acres of farmland for a federal reservation and conveyed it to the department secretary. The tribe adopted a constitution under the Indian Reorganization Act, and the federal government assumed its trust responsibility over tribal affairs.

Federal recognition of the Catawbas was short-lived. In keeping with the federal government's overall termination philosophy instituted in 1953, both federal and state authorities approached the Catawbas in 1958 with a proposal for termination. The Bureau of Indian Affairs assured the Catawbas that their long-standing land claim against the state of South Carolina based on the Treaty of Augusta and the Treaty of Nation Ford (which still had not been resolved) would be unaffected by the termination. In 1962 the federal trust relationship between the United States and the Catawba tribe was terminated, and the 3,434-acre federal reservation was divided up and distributed to tribal members. South Carolina continued to hold the 640-acre tract from the 1840 treaty in trust for the tribe. At the time of termination there were 631 enrolled tribal members.

The activism of the American Indian Movement (AIM) in the early 1970s served to reignite the determination of the Catawbas—and many other tribes—to reinstitute their land claim. The tribe contacted the Native American Rights Fund (NARF), and in 1976 papers were filed with the Department of the Interior to recover the land recognized under the 1763 Treaty of Augusta. Negotiations were proceeding between the tribe, the state, and the federal government until protests to those negotiations came from non-Indian landowners and nonresident tribal members who wanted to join in the action in hopes of securing land, benefits, or both. Negotiations stalled, and an impasse continued until 1980 when the Catawbas filed suit in federal district court to recover possession of the 1763 treaty reservation.

After a decade in the courts, the Fourth Circuit Court found in 1989 that there was still some standing for the claim. That ruling made it possible for the Catawba tribe to institute land claims, not only against South Carolina but also against an estimated 61,000 landowners. At this point Congressman John Spratt (a descendant of Thomas "Kanawha" Spratt), Governor Carroll Campbell, and Secretary of the Interior Manuel Lujan expressed their interest in a negotiated settlement. Negotiations began again in 1990. In Congress on January 5, 1993, Spratt introduced the Catawba Indian Tribe of South Carolina Land Claims Settlement Act of 1993. Congress passed the act that summer, and the final agreement was signed by Governor Campbell on November 29, 1994, at the Catawba reservation. (The tribe had already voted on February 20, 1993, by a margin of 289 to 42 to accept the settlement.)

The settlement provided that the Catawbas would once again become a federally recognized tribe. An amount of $50 million would be put into trust funds for land acquisition, economic development, education, social services, and elderly assistance. The tribe was given ten years to expand the existing reservation to 3,600 acres. Tribal jurisdiction was recognized over basic governmental powers, including zoning, misdemeanors, business regulation, taxation, and membership, but South Carolina reserved the right to continue to exercise criminal jurisdiction on the reservation.

At the dawn of the twenty-first century, the Catawba Nation continued to be a strong and forceful voice for the rights of Native Americans. The noble heritage of this ancient people is being reinvigorated through cultural awareness, particularly relating to pottery making, and through the education of the children in the traditional language and customs of the people. ANNE M. MCCULLOCH

Brown, Douglas Summers. *The Catawba Indians: The People of the River.* Columbia: University of South Carolina Press, 1966.

Merrell, James H. *The Indians' New World: Catawbas and Their Neighbors from European Contact through the Era of Removal.* Chapel Hill: University of North Carolina Press, 1989.

Wilkins, David, and Anne M. McCulloch. "'Constructing' Nations within States: The Quest for Federal Recognition by the Catawba and Lumbee Tribes." *American Indian Quarterly* 19 (fall 1995): 361–88.

Catesby, Mark (1682–1749). Naturalist, artist. Catesby was born in or near the village of Castle Hedingham, Essex, England, on March 24, 1682, the son of John Catesby and Elizabeth Jekyll. Little is known of his early life, but he probably attended the grammar school in the nearby town of Sudbury. After spending a portion of his young manhood in London, Catesby came to America in 1712 to visit his sister in Virginia. Possessing a keen interest in natural history, he collected plants and made some bird paintings there. Returning to England in 1719 with some plants that proved to be new to science, he realized that he had missed a great opportunity to record some of the flora and fauna of eastern America, most of which had not been described or illustrated. With the financial backing of the physician-naturalist Sir Hans Sloane, the botanist William Sherard, the royal governor of South Carolina Francis Nicholson, and several other patrons, Catesby came to Charleston in 1722 to gather specimens and notes for an illustrated work on the natural history of the Carolina region.

"As I arrived at the beginning of the Summer, I unexpectedly found this Country possessed not only with all the Animals and Vegetables of *Virginia,* but abounding with an even greater variety," he wrote. The following year he journeyed to the "Upper uninhabited Parts of the Country" around Fort Moore on the Savannah River and then took "several Journeys with the *Indians* higher up the Rivers, towards the Mountains," which introduced him to more new plants and "afforded . . . the Diversion of Hunting Buffaloes, Bears, Panthers, and other wild Beasts." Catesby recorded his specimens with notes and sketches. "In designing the Plants I always did them while fresh and just gather'd: and the Animals, particularly the birds, I painted while alive (except a very few) and gave them their Gestures peculiar to every kind of Bird, and . . . adapted the Birds to those Plants on which they fed, or have any relation to."

He left Charleston in 1725 and went on to Florida and to the Bahamas. On his return to England, Catesby began preparing the plates and text for his publication, teaching himself the art of engraving to avoid the high cost of a commercial engraver. His richly illustrated work, *The Natural History of Carolina, Florida, and the Bahama Islands,* appeared in two volumes, the first completed in 1731 and the second in 1743. They contain 220 hand-colored plates illustrating 171 plants and 228 mammals, birds, reptiles, amphibians, fish, and insects. Not a trained artist, Catesby did not figure all of his animal subjects as well as might be desired, but many of his plants are exceptional. His report of the "grinders of an Elephant" found on the Stono River near Charleston was the first published record of fossil remains of the mammoth in South Carolina. The first extensively illustrated work on the natural history of any region of North America, Catesby's volumes were used by Linnaeus for the inclusion of North American flora and fauna in his system of classification of plants and animals.

Catesby's marriage to Elizabeth Rowland in 1747 produced a daughter and a son. He died in London on December 23, 1749. See plate 6. ALBERT E. SANDERS

Allen, Elsa Guerdrum. "The History of American Ornithology before Audubon." *Transactions of the American Philosophical Society* 41 (1951): 387–591.

Catesby, Mark. *The Natural History of Carolina, Florida, and the Bahama Islands.* 2 vols. London, 1731–1743.

Frick, George Frederick, and Raymond Phineas Stearns. *Mark Catesby: The Colonial Audubon.* Urbana: University of Illinois Press, 1961.

Meyers, Amy R. W., and Margaret Beck Pritchard, eds. *Empire's Nature: Mark Catesby's New World Vision.* Chapel Hill: University of North Carolina Press, 1998.

Sanders, Albert E., and William D. Anderson, Jr. *Natural History Investigations in South Carolina from Colonial Times to the Present.* Columbia: University of South Carolina Press, 1999.

Catholics. Catholic interest in Carolina began with Spanish efforts to establish a foothold in the late sixteenth century, but the Spanish left no discernible Catholic presence by the time the English established their colony in the late seventeenth century. Despite the colony's efforts to recruit widely for settlers, the South Carolina Assembly banned Catholic and Irish immigrants in 1716 for fear they would conspire with the Spanish in Florida to attack the colony. A few Catholics came anyway, mostly as indentured servants and in 1756 as Acadian refugees from Nova Scotia. Supposed links between the few Catholics in the colony and the Stono slave rebellion in 1739 and with Loyalism during the Revolutionary War, and more important, the lack of any established Catholic church in the colony, led Catholics to abandon their faith or at least to shy away from any public demonstration of their Catholicism. Still, individual Catholics found fortune in the colony and served the patriot cause.

Organized Catholic life began in 1788 with the arrival of the first stationed priest in Charleston and with the pledge of several Catholic laymen to build a church. In 1789 five Catholics acquired a lot and a run-down building for the church, marking the first public Catholic space in the state. The following year the Catholic population numbered roughly two hundred persons, "mostly poor" and concentrated in or near the city. In 1820 the Catholic Church established the diocese of Charleston, which then encompassed Georgia and both South and North Carolina (Georgia became the separate diocese of Savannah in 1850 and North Carolina the diocese of Raleigh in 1924). Most Catholics, however, lived in or near Charleston, which emerged as the center of Catholic life in the region with its churches, schools, hospitals, and orphanages. Struggles between laity and bishops over control of the appointment and character of priests, church finances, and social issues wracked the church during the early nineteenth century, and the lack of priests to serve the backcountry limited the church's ability to meet the needs of a scattered Catholic population throughout the century.

No problem so vexed Catholicism in South Carolina as did the shortage of priests. The Catholic Church at first relied on foreign-born priests to staff parishes but during the twentieth century turned to American-born priests and religious orders to meet basic needs. Still, the one-priest parish remained the norm for the church in South Carolina. From 1850 to 1960, of all the southern states, South Carolina had the lowest or second-lowest density of Catholics in its total population. Upcountry parishes often shared priests, relying on missions and religious sisters to provide spiritual, educational, and social service needs, thus giving the upcountry church a missionary character it retained throughout the twentieth century. In 1950 only 96 priests and 230 religious sisters served the 17,508 Catholics in the state, spread across forty-two parishes and twenty-six missions. In 2000, 2 bishops, 87 diocesan priests, 34 religious priests, and 29 sisters served a Catholic population numbering 130,255 in eighty-five parishes and thirty missions. Most Catholics were concentrated in Charleston and Columbia, the only places with Catholic infrastructures of high schools, hospitals, and other associations necessary for a full Catholic institutional life. Catholics comprised only three percent of the state's total population in 2000.

A closer examination of the Catholic profile, however, reveals that the Catholic presence and character had changed significantly since the mid-1960s. Vietnamese refugees, Central and South American immigrants, and northern-born migrants made up an increasing percentage of a Catholic population that had grown more than sevenfold in fifty years. Since the late 1960s Vatican II, which emphasized greater lay involvement in religious and administrative functions within the parish, eased somewhat the continued shortage of priests and shifted authority, and worship styles, from ecclesiastical determination to a more local variety.

Historically, Roman Catholics have "fit in" with the dominant South Carolina social and political culture. The Catholic Church emphasized a bricks-and-mortar approach to building and sustaining Catholicism in the diocese, as elsewhere, and foreswore engagement in controversial political and social issues. Bishop John England (1820–1842) acquired national recognition for his proposal to adapt a more "American" and "democratic" model of lay participation in church affairs, without conceding any ecclesiastical authority. Bishop Patrick Lynch (1858–1882) gained favor among southerners for his staunch defense of slavery and his willingness to serve as a Confederate legate to Rome in hopes of gaining recognition for the Confederacy. Such accommodation to southern "principles" ensured Catholics' acceptance. Spasms of nativism and anti-Catholicism occurred, as in the 1880s when Catholic bishops sought state aid for parochial schools, but South Carolina evinced little of the anti-Catholicism that marked southern populism, Ku Kluxism, and cold-war fears of "foreign" subversion elsewhere, especially in Georgia. In South Carolina the Catholic Church moved cautiously regarding racial segregation, establishing the first separate "black parish," St. Peter's in Charleston, in 1867 and practicing de facto segregation in schools and social services into the mid–twentieth century, despite a special ministry to blacks. The diocese quietly desegregated its schools in 1963 to coincide with the desegregation of public schools. Catholic opposition to divorce and abortion also won friends among conservative Protestants in the "culture wars" of the 1980s and after. An upsurge in Catholics coming to the diocese in the 1990s kept the church focused on issues of church building and staffing and, except for ecumenical gatherings, largely out of the public eye. RANDALL M. MILLER

Madden, Richard C. *Catholics in South Carolina: A Record.* Lanham, Md.: University Press of America, 1985.

McNally, Michael J. "A Peculiar Institution: A History of Catholic Parish Life in the Southeast (1850–1980)." In *The American Catholic Parish: A History from 1850 to the Present.* Vol. 1, *The Northeast, Southeast and South Central States,* edited by Jay P. Dolan. Mahwah, N.J.: Paulist Press, 1987.

Miller, Randall M. "Roman Catholicism in South Carolina." In *Religion in South Carolina,* edited by Charles H. Lippy. Columbia: University of South Carolina Press, 1993.

Miller, Randall M., and Jon L. Wakelyn, eds. *Catholics in the Old South: Essays on Church and Culture.* Rev. ed. Macon, Ga.: Mercer University Press, 1999.

Smith, Mark M. "Remembering Mary, Shaping Revolt: Reconsidering the Stono Rebellion." *Journal of Southern History* 67 (August 2001): 513–34.

Cattle ranching. Cow pens, cattle drives, and open range herding—distinctive characteristics typically associated with the American West—were important features of the agricultural landscape during the colonial period in South Carolina. British settlers, especially colonists of Celtic ancestry such as the Welsh and Scots-Irish, brought husbandry traditions to colonial South Carolina. Many enslaved West Africans also had extensive knowledge of cattle raising. Cattle ranching, a lucrative frontier occupation, appeared first in the lowcountry, where black bondsmen became America's first "cowboys." Using the open range system, livestock foraged during the day in the swamps, forests, and pastures. Cattle were usually penned in the evenings and during branding, cattle sales, and butchering. Periodically, large cattle drives occurred, and drovers or "crackers" using cattle whips herded livestock to the ports of Charleston and Savannah. The livestock was then butchered and the beef packed in barrels for shipment to Caribbean plantations and urban centers in the northern colonies.

By the early 1700s beef and pork were leading agricultural exports. As plantation agriculture became established in the lowcountry, cattle ranching shifted to the backcountry beginning in the 1730s. The sandy upper coastal plain soils, ill suited for agriculture, were ideal for cattle. Consequently, the Edisto, Salkehatchie, and Savannah valleys eventually became the principal areas of cattle ranching in colonial South Carolina. Herds of several hundred head of cattle were common. Capital amassed from livestock also encouraged the later development of plantation agriculture among the sons of backcountry cattle raisers. The cattle ranching tradition that germinated in South Carolina and other areas of the southern backcountry subsequently spread to the frontier of the middle South during the early nineteenth century and eventually developed into the large-scale ranching and cowboy culture typical of the West. MARK D. GROOVER AND RICHARD D. BROOKS

Brooks, Richard D., Mark D. Groover, and Samuel C. Smith. *Living on the Edge: The Archaeology of Cattle Raisers in the South Carolina Backcountry.* Columbia: South Carolina Institute of Archaeology and Anthropology, University of South Carolina, 2000.

Groover, Mark D., and Richard D. Brooks. "The Catherine Brown Cowpen and Thomas Howell Site: Material Characteristics of Cattle Raisers in the South Carolina Backcountry." *Southeastern Archaeology* 22 (summer 2003): 92–111.

Jordan, Terry G. *North American Cattle-Ranching Frontiers: Origins, Diffusion, and Differentiation.* Albuquerque: University of New Mexico Press, 1993.

Otto, John S. "Livestock-Raising in Early South Carolina, 1670–1700: Prelude to the Rice Plantation Economy." *Agricultural History* 61 (fall 1987): 13–24.

Cayce (Lexington County; 2000 pop. 12,150). Cayce encompasses approximately fifteen square miles on the Congaree River opposite Columbia. The city is the descendant of the colonial trading village of Granby. In 1817 the Cayce family made the former Fort Granby their private residence, and it eventually came to be known as the Cayce House. During the Civil War, Caroline Rucker Cayce opened the doors of the house to soldiers and travelers making the journey to and from the lowcountry. The coming of the railroads in the nineteenth century gave birth to the modern city of Cayce. The area at that time was known as Cayce Crossing. In 1914 when the town was incorporated, the name Cayce was chosen to honor "Uncle Billy," who owned the general store. That same year the Cayce family built a new home in what was becoming downtown and moved there to be closer to the center of town and the family's general store.

By 1940 Cayce had become predominantly a railroad town. With the jobs and payroll they generated, railroads made a substantial contribution to the city for many years. Both the Southern and the Seaboard Railroads handled passengers and mail. In addition to the railroads, lumberyards, a quarry, and a fertilizer plant were the principal places of employment. During the 1940s and 1950s the city experienced phenomenal growth, sharing in the expansion of the Columbia metropolitan area after World War II. By the 1950s the new McMillan (Blossom Street) Bridge was built to better connect this thriving suburb to the capital city.

During the 1960s and 1970s the center of Cayce's business moved along Knox Abbott Drive. A new City Hall complex was built to accommodate Cayce's growing needs. A modern public safety building was added to house its growing fire department and award-winning police department. Cayce was becoming home to many large and small businesses, with restaurant chains and shopping centers built in ever increasing numbers. The granite quarry and railroads remained major industries along with a large steel mill, a concrete pipe manufacturing plant, distribution centers, and manufacturing facilities. The creation of the Columbia Metropolitan Airport played a part in Cayce's growth. In the late 1980s a group of dedicated citizens built the Cayce Historical Museum. Opened in April 1991, the museum became an important educational and cultural resource. Growth continued into the twenty-first century, and commercial development on both sides of the Congaree continued to drive the expansion of the "City by the River." LEO REDMOND

Scott, Edwin J. *Random Recollections of a Long Life, 1806 to 1876.* 1884. Reprint, Columbia, S.C.: R. L. Bryan, 1969.

Central (Pickens County; 2000 pop. 3,522). The town of Central came into being when the Atlantic and Richmond Air Line (later the Southern Railroad) laid a track through Pickens County in 1873. The location of the future town was midway between Atlanta and Charlotte (about 133 miles each way), and the company chose the site to locate its repair operations. "Central Station" contained shops for railroad workers, and engines were refueled and changed using a turntable. A depot and houses were erected for railroad employees, and stores opened soon after. On March 17, 1875, Central was incorporated as a town, with boundaries extending one-half mile in each direction from the depot. A sizable hotel was constructed in a grove of trees beside the tracks. Its reputation for good food soon spread, and the structure's function extended beyond an eatery. It served as a ticket office and waiting room, as quarters for telegraph operators and dispatchers, and as a sample room where traveling salesmen might display their merchandise.

The thriving little town experienced misfortune in the late 1890s. First, the Southern Railroad moved its repair shops to Greenville, with dire results to Central. "Houses were vacant and business was at a standstill," observed a local writer. Then a fire destroyed a large portion of Main Street.

A measure of prosperity returned in the early 1900s when local businessmen created opportunities for employment at Issaqueena Mill (a textile operation that expanded on the nearby Norris Cotton Mill). Wesleyan College (which became Southern Wesleyan University) began classes in the fall of 1906, and individuals associated with its operation swelled the town's population. This growth came to an abrupt halt during the Depression of the early 1930s. Central's two banks failed, mill stocks fell, and Issaqueena Mill passed into receivership.

Railroads and cotton mills declined in importance throughout the region in the last half of the twentieth century, but Central nevertheless grew in the 1990s, thanks to an expanded road system, new industries, restaurants, a library, recreational facilities, Clemson and Southern Wesleyan student apartments, and new homes. During that decade the Central Heritage Society cooperated with the South Carolina Heritage Corridor in attempts to restore and preserve the town's historic areas. Central History Museum (the former home of the Morgan family) was designated as a site on the state's Heritage Corridor. The old Central High School was listed in the National Register of Historic Places in 1994. Other Central attractions include the Central Community Club (formerly Central Colored School), Freedoms Hill Church, Red Caboose, Old City Hall/Jail, and Collins Ole Towne. G. ANNE SHERIFF

Allen, Mattie May Morgan. *Central: Yesterday and Today.* Taylors, S.C.: Faith Printing, 1973.

Chalmers, Lionel (1715–1777). Physician, scientist. Chalmers was born in Campbelltown, Argyllshire, Scotland, in 1715. He studied medicine at one of the Scottish universities, probably St. Andrews, but did not complete the M.D. degree. Chalmers arrived in Charleston in 1737 and found himself in competition with established practitioners. He apparently found it difficult at first to make a living, but a major smallpox epidemic in 1738 may have helped him to establish a modest practice. His marriage to Martha Logan in 1739 most likely improved his financial situation. Around 1740 he entered into a partnership with Dr. John Lining that endured until 1754.

When Chalmers and Lining became partners, Lining was already recording weather data and conducting metabolic experiments on himself in an attempt to record the effects of meteorological change on the human body. Between 1750 and 1759 Chalmers compiled his own series of meteorological records in Charleston, which he later used along with Lining's in his best-known work, *An Account of the Weather and Diseases in South Carolina* (London, 1776). In 1767 he published *Essay on Fevers,* subsequently republished in London (1768) and in Riga in German (1773).

During the 1750s Chalmers began corresponding with the influential Quaker physician-naturalist Dr. John Fothergill of London. Chalmers addressed his first publication, "Of the Opisthotonos and the Tetanus," to Fothergill; it was published in *Medical Observations and Inquiries* in 1758. Fothergill helped with the editing and publishing details of Chalmers's book on weather and diseases. Chalmers aided Fothergill's interests in natural history by exchanging plant and animal specimens. He also served as Fothergill's agent in disbursing funds raised for the expedition of the Philadelphia naturalist William Bartram through the Carolinas, Georgia, and Florida. In 1756 Chalmers got St. Andrews University to confer on him the M.D. degree. In this he was aided by his friend Robert Whytt, a physician on the faculty of the University of Edinburgh and a graduate of St. Andrews.

Chalmers's writings did not mark a significant development in medicine, but he was highly regarded in his time by British physicians such as Fothergill, Whytt, and William Cullen of Edinburgh University, one of the most influential teachers of medicine in the late eighteenth century. Chalmers died in Charleston on May 8, 1777, after having served as a justice of the peace, port physician, and a member of the Charleston Library Society. PETER MCCANDLESS

Fothergill, John. *Chain of Friendship: Selected Letters of Dr. John Fothergill of London, 1735–1780.* Edited by Betsy C. Corner and Christopher C. Booth. Cambridge: Belknap Press of Harvard University Press, 1971.

Stearns, Raymond P. *Science in the British Colonies of North America.* Urbana: University of Illinois Press, 1970.

Waring, Joseph I. "Lionel Chalmers and William Cullen's Treatment of Fevers." *Journal of the History of Medicine and Allied Sciences* 8 (October 1953): 445–47.

———. "Lionel Chalmers, Medical Author." *Bulletin of the History of Medicine* 33 (July–August 1958): 349–55.

Chamberlain, Daniel Henry (1835–1907). Governor. Chamberlain was born in West Brookfield, Massachusetts, on June 23, 1835, the ninth of ten children born to Eli Chamberlain and Achsah Forbes. He graduated from Worcester High School in 1857 and Yale University in 1862. The following year he left Harvard Law School to serve as an officer with the Fifth Massachusetts Cavalry, a black regiment. He came to South Carolina in 1866 to tend to the affairs of a deceased classmate. On December 16, 1867, he married Alice Ingersoll of Bangor, Maine. They had four children.

Chamberlain entered South Carolina politics in 1868 as a delegate to the state constitutional convention from Berkeley District. From 1868 to 1872 he served as attorney general in Governor Robert K. Scott's administration. He was also a member of the financial board, an agency tainted by corruption involving the state land commission and the sale of Blue Ridge Railroad bonds. Chamberlain vigorously denied benefiting from these scandals and publicly criticized Republican corruption. In 1871 he joined Democrats in organizing a state taxpayers' convention to press for reform and limits to state appropriations. Failing to gain the Republican nomination for governor in 1872, Chamberlain practiced law in Charleston. In 1873 he was elected to the board of trustees of the University of South Carolina as the first black students and faculty joined the institution.

In 1874, with the support of the black leaders Francis L. Cardozo and Robert Brown Elliott, Chamberlain became the Republican

Daniel H. Chamberlain. Courtesy, South Caroliniana Library, University of South Carolina

candidate for governor, and he won the general election that fall. Opposed to Republicans he regarded as corrupt and too radical, Chamberlain cultivated the support of moderate Democrats led by the Charleston newspaper editor Francis W. Dawson. As governor, he vetoed twenty spending and patronage measures he considered reckless. In 1875 he alienated many Republicans when he refused to sign commissions that would have enabled William J. Whipper and Franklin J. Moses, Jr., to serve as circuit court judges.

By 1876 it appeared that Chamberlain's strategy to gain Democratic support for his reelection would pay political dividends as Dawson repeatedly praised the governor in the pages of the Charleston *News and Courier.* But when "straight-out" Democrats murdered several black militia members in the Hamburg Massacre of July 1876, Chamberlain condemned the killings and asked Washington for federal troops to quell the violence. Moderate Democrats deserted Chamberlain and threw their support behind Wade Hampton III. In the violent campaign that ensued, Hampton's supporters threatened and intimidated Republican candidates and black voters. Chamberlain and the black leader Robert Smalls were hooted off the platform by an angry mob at Edgefield during the campaign. Both the Democrats and Republicans claimed victory in the 1876 election, and a prolonged controversy followed. For a time Hampton and Chamberlain each insisted that he was the state's chief executive. But in April 1877 President Rutherford B. Hayes informed Chamberlain that he supported Hampton and subsequently withdrew federal troops from South Carolina.

Chamberlain departed South Carolina and became a successful Wall Street lawyer. Embittered by his experiences as governor, he vilified the Hayes administration for its "treachery" in abandoning black South Carolinians to white Democrats. In 1881 Chamberlain defended the black West Point cadet Johnson C. Whittaker in his highly publicized court-martial case. However, in the years that followed, Chamberlain shifted in his racial attitudes. In a series of articles Chamberlain described his increasing disillusionment with Reconstruction and criticized attempts to secure voting rights and political power for African Americans. From 1883 to 1897 he was a professor of constitutional law at Cornell University. On his retirement he traveled extensively in Europe before settling in Charlottesville, Virginia, where he died of cancer on April 13, 1907. WILLIAM C. HINE

Allen, Walter. *Governor Chamberlain's Administration in South Carolina, a Chapter of Reconstruction in the Southern States.* 1888. Reprint, New York: Negro Universities Press, 1969.

Chamberlain, Daniel H. Governors' Papers. South Carolina Department of Archives and History, Columbia.

Current, Richard Nelson. *Those Terrible Carpetbaggers.* New York: Oxford University Press, 1988.

Green, James. *Personal Recollections of Daniel Henry Chamberlain, Once Governor of South Carolina.* Worcester, Mass.: Davis & Banister, 1908.

Chamberlain, Edward Burnham (1895–1986). Ornithologist, herpetologist, museum curator. Born in Charleston on March 19, 1895, Chamberlain was a son of Norman Allison Chamberlain and Emmie Julia Davis. He grew up in and attended high school in Charleston. On June 18, 1918, he married Margaret McKee Sanders. The couple had two sons.

At an early age, Chamberlain and his twin brother, Rhett, began to spend time at the Charleston Museum, and in 1908 Burnham donated a palm warbler and two nests of the marsh wren to its collections. These were the first of many specimens that Chamberlain would contribute during more than sixty years of careful study of South Carolina natural history. About 1909 the Chamberlain twins met Arthur T. Wayne, the foremost ornithologist in the state, who taught them much about birds and the preparation of bird skins.

In 1916 President Woodrow Wilson sent soldiers under General John J. Pershing to the Mexican border to stop the raids of Pancho Villa. Among Pershing's forces were the Charleston Light Dragoons, with Burnham and Rhett Chamberlain as two of its members. The Chamberlains took advantage of the military posting to explore the semidesert habitat. The Dragoons went overseas during World War I, but Burnham Chamberlain earlier had left the unit to attend Officer's Training Camp. He was appointed second lieutenant in August 1917 and promoted to first lieutenant a year later.

Returning to civilian life, Chamberlain worked for a time with the Standard Oil Company, but his love of natural history was irresistible. In 1924, after a one-year internship at the U.S. National Museum (Smithsonian Institution), he became head of the preparation department at the Charleston Museum. Along with Alexander Sprunt, Jr., a part-time employee of the museum, Chamberlain made a special effort to build the bird-skin collection and also worked to enlarge the collections of amphibians, reptiles, and mammals. Eventually he became a curator with broad duties that included preparation of exhibits, public instruction, and the collection, preparation, and maintenance of specimens. In 1938, supported by a grant from the Carnegie Foundation, Chamberlain visited many major museums in Britain and the European continent to study techniques of exhibiting and methods of preparation.

During World War II and immediately afterward, Chamberlain was saddled with many extra duties, including curatorship of the collections of firearms and edged weapons and maintenance of the building. These additional assignments, along with his regular work as curator of vertebrate zoology, led to serious deterioration of his health. He retired in 1952. Despite the burdens of his position, Chamberlain produced more than sixty scientific publications, mostly on birds but also on amphibians, reptiles, and mammals. His most important contribution was *South Carolina Bird Life,* written with Sprunt. In later years, with his health improved, Chamberlain provided assistance to the museum in various matters, particularly curatorship. He died in Charleston on May 7, 1986, and was buried in Magnolia Cemetery. WILLIAM D. ANDERSON, JR.

Sanders, Albert E., and William D. Anderson, Jr. *Natural History Investigations in South Carolina from Colonial Times to the Present.* Columbia: University of South Carolina Press, 1999.

Sprunt, Alexander, Jr., and E. Burnham Chamberlain. *South Carolina Bird Life.* Rev. ed. Columbia: University of South Carolina Press, 1970.

Chapin, Sarah Flournoy Moore (ca. 1830–1896). Temperance leader, social reformer. Chapin was born in Charleston, the eldest child of George Washington Moore, an itinerant Methodist minister, and Elizabeth Martha Vigneron Simons. She was educated at Cokesbury, Abbeville District, and married Leonard Chapin, a prosperous Charleston businessman, on August 12, 1847. The couple had no children.

Known as Sallie F. Chapin, she became one of South Carolina's most visible nineteenth-century women leaders. Chapin's path to leadership began with home-front activities in Charleston during the Civil War. While her husband served in the Confederate cavalry, Chapin organized and served as president of the Soldiers Relief Society and the Ladies Auxiliary Christian Association. After the war she became an active member of the Charleston Ladies Memorial Association and led the Ladies Christian Association. She authored *Fitz-Hugh St. Clair, the South Carolina Rebel Boy* (1872), a commentary on southern life that went through two published editions.

Widowed in 1879, Chapin attended a temperance convention in 1880 in Ocean Grove, New Jersey, where she reportedly made an impromptu address that galvanized her commitment to the emerging national women's temperance movement. She drew the attention of Frances Willard, the leader of the Women's Christian Temperance Union (WCTU), an organization that soon became the largest and most influential women's group in the nineteenth century. In June 1880 Chapin organized the first local chapter of the WCTU in South Carolina in Charleston. Six months later she presented the Charleston City Council with a petition, which was "thirty yards long bound in silk and signed by 5,000 ladies," to ban the sale of alcohol.

Chapin immediately launched efforts to organize women throughout South Carolina in the temperance cause. By 1882 local chapters had been established in Columbia, Charleston, Greenville, Spartanburg, Blackville, Orangeburg, Union, and Abbeville. She spearheaded the formation of the South Carolina Women's Temperance Union in 1883, and it became the first state chapter of the national organization in the South. Chapin would serve as president of the state WCTU until her death in 1896. At Frances Willard's request, Chapin served as national superintendent of the WCTU's Southern Department, a position she held from 1883 to 1889.

In the 1880s Chapin was the most prominent woman reformer in South Carolina. She visited communities around the state to meet with women and to enlist their active involvement in temperance advocacy. Her activities were widely covered in local newspapers. A powerful lecturer, she drew the attention of women and men, and her lectures became the first exposure to women's public leadership for many of her audiences and followers.

Under Chapin's able leadership the WCTU attracted a substantial following of elite white women, with more than fifteen hundred members in 1891. Chapin and the WCTU advocated Prohibition, a temperance curriculum for schools, establishment of a state-supported industrial training school for young women, and an increase in the legal age of consent from ten to eighteen for young women. She met with mixed success. In 1892 South Carolina citizens approved a Prohibition referendum to ban the sale of alcohol, only to have Governor Benjamin Tillman orchestrate a state monopoly to regulate its sale. A temperance curriculum would be approved by the legislature in 1896. In 1891 the General Assembly, in part due to Chapin's articles and speeches, took over the Winthrop Training School in Columbia and created the Winthrop Normal and Industrial College, a forerunner of Winthrop University. The assembly also raised the age of consent to sixteen in 1896. Chapin was a reluctant supporter of women's suffrage, initially expressing opposition on the grounds of states' rights and her concerns that the suffrage controversy would cloud the cause of temperance.

Chapin's ultimate contribution to South Carolina was her creation of a voluntary association that enabled elite white women to participate in the public life of their communities in the late nineteenth century. She died of cancer on April 19, 1896, and was buried in Magnolia Cemetery in Charleston. BELINDA F. GERGEL

Mims, Florence Adams. *Recorded History of South Carolina Woman's Christian Temperance Union from 1881–1901.* Edgefield, S.C., [1950?].

Willard, Frances E. *Woman and Temperance.* Hartford, Conn.: Park Publishing, 1883.

Chapman, Martha Marshall, II (b. 1949). Musician. Marshall Chapman was born in Spartanburg on January 7, 1949, to James Alfred Chapman and Martha Cloud. Her great-grandfather, also named James Alfred Chapman, founded Inman Mills near Spartanburg in 1902. Chapman's first five years were spent in Enoree. A mill merger in 1954 brought the family to Spartanburg, where Marshall spent the rest of her childhood. She moved to Nashville to attend Vanderbilt University and has lived there most of her adult life. In Nashville, Chapman began her professional career, which by the early twenty-first century would consist of more than 250 original songs and eight full-length record albums. Classified by many as a country-music artist, Chapman and her style nonetheless have been difficult to categorize. Her success in the 1970s was linked to the popularity of "outlaw" country artists—Nashville rejects including Willie Nelson, Waylon Jennings, and Kris Kristofferson. Her songs have been recorded by an eclectic group of performers, including Sawyer Brown, Jimmy Buffett, Joe Cocker, Jessi Colter, Dion, Crystal Gayle, Tompall Glaser, Emmylou Harris, John Hiatt, Ronnie Milsap, Olivia Newton-John, the Earl Scruggs Revue, Irma Thomas, Tanya Tucker, Conway Twitty, and Wynnona, among many others. Her best-known song, "Betty's Bein' Bad," has been certified by Broadcast Music Incorporated as having been performed more than one million times. In 2003 Chapman published *Goodbye, Little Rock and Roller,* an autobiographical account woven around twelve of her songs and including reminiscences of her early days in South Carolina both in and around Spartanburg and at Pawleys Island. JOHN F. JAKUBS

Chapman, Marshall. *Goodbye, Little Rock and Roller.* New York: St. Martin's, 2003.

Charismatics. Charismatics are mainline Christians who speak in tongues and practice such gifts of the Holy Spirit as prophecy and healing. While some Episcopal and Roman Catholic churches in South Carolina sponsor regular charismatic prayer services, a more visible outgrowth of the movement is large independent congregations described as "full-gospel" or "charismatic."

The movement began in the 1960s when Episcopalians in California and Roman Catholics in the Midwest experienced speaking in tongues. Some groups, drawn by New Testament examples, started communities. The Alleluia Community in Augusta, Georgia, did so. About a dozen Catholic charismatic prayer groups met across South Carolina by the mid-1990s.

Among Protestants in the 1980s, St. Giles Presbyterian and Resurrection Lutheran (Missouri Synod) in Charlotte, the independent Resurrection Lutheran Church in Greer, and Savannah's Trinity United Methodist joined the movement. Southern Baptists strongly opposed speaking in tongues, although by 1987 approximately four hundred Southern Baptist churches stressed the "fullness of the Holy Spirit." The movement was reinvigorated in the 1990s by the "Toronto Blessing," a revival characterized by uncontrollable, healing laughter. In South Carolina this was taken up by prayer groups in such churches as St. Francis Episcopal in Greenville.

Independent charismatic congregations have two sources. Some were founded by leaders whose charismatic experiences were not welcomed in their original denominations. Other charismatic congregations have roots in traditional Pentecostal denominations. There the source of disaffection has often been divorce. Pentecostals have traditionally forbidden it, while charismatic congregations usually welcome single and divorced persons.

At Evangel Cathedral in Spartanburg the founding minister was Assembly of God. Staff has included Roman Catholic and Church of the Nazarene clergy. The congregation practices healing, exorcism, prophecy, and other gifts. At the beginning of the twenty-first century the Evangel Fellowship of Ministers and Churches International could claim some seventy similar churches around the state and across the South, with a missionary training center in Walhalla. Mount Zion Christian Fellowship in Greenville grew out of a 1979 Baptist Bible study concerning divine healing. The rapidly growing World Redemption Outreach Center in Greenville attracts a multiracial congregation. NANCY A. HARDESTY

Hocken, P. D. "Charismatic Movement." In *The New International Dictionary of Pentecostal and Charismatic Movements.* Rev. ed. Edited by Stanley M. Burgess. Grand Rapids, Mich.: Zondervan, 2002.

Ranaghan, Kevin, and Dorothy Ranaghan. *Catholic Pentecostals.* Paramus, N.J.: Paulist Press, 1969.

Sherrill, John. *They Speak with Other Tongues.* Rev. ed. Grand Rapids, Mich.: Chosen Books, 2004.

Charlesfort. A mid-sixteenth-century French outpost in Port Royal Sound, Charlesfort was the first French settlement in the present-day United States. During the 1980s archaeologists located its site on Parris Island.

In early 1562 Gaspard Coligny de Châtillon, the admiral of France, dispatched the Norman mariner Jean Ribault to lead two royal ships and 150 men to survey the east coast of North America and locate a site for a future French colony. Landing near modern-day Jacksonville, Florida, Ribault established relations with various native peoples as he took his ships north to Port Royal Sound. Impressed by the apparent potential of this area for a colony, Ribault, before returning to France, left behind more than two dozen volunteers, who constructed a small wooden fort that they named after their king. From here they intended to explore the area while waiting for Ribault to return with supplies and more settlers.

However, civil war in France prevented Ribault from resupplying Charlesfort. Over the next fourteen months mutiny, conflict with the local Indians, and shortages of food threatened the survival of the fort, and the decision was made to abandon the area. Attempting an Atlantic crossing in an open boat, the survivors had been reduced to cannibalism by the time they were rescued by an English ship. A few months later Coligny sponsored a second and larger French colonization attempt, on the St. John's River in Florida, which lasted a year before being captured by Spanish troops. JOHN T. MCGRATH

Hoffman, Paul E. *A New Andalucia and a Way to the Orient: The American Southeast during the Sixteenth Century.* Baton Rouge: Louisiana State University Press, 1990.

Laudonnière, René Goulaine de. *Three Voyages.* Gainesville: University Presses of Florida, 1975.

McGrath, John T. *The French in Early Florida: In the Eye of the Hurricane.* Gainesville: University Press of Florida, 2000.

Charleston (Charleston County; 2000 pop. 96,650). Charleston was the first permanent European settlement in Carolina, its first seat of government, and the most important city in the southern United States well into the nineteenth century. While it thereafter declined in relative size and importance, the city nevertheless continued to act as if it still had a major role to play in the state, the region, and the country; and from time to time it has done just that.

In April 1670 three ships carrying settlers from England and the Caribbean sailed into a harbor of two rivers, soon named the Cooper and the Ashley (after one of the Lords Proprietors financing the colony, Anthony Ashley Cooper). These settlers founded Charles Towne, named for King Charles II of England, at Albemarle Point on the west bank of the Ashley River. Barricaded from local Indians and the Spanish, the town grew steadily and survived a transplanting to Oyster Point at the tip of the peninsula by 1680. Again walls went up, making it the only walled city in British North America.

There was a central gate at what is now the intersection of Broad and Meeting Streets; the city stretched north to what became Cumberland Street, east to the Cooper River, south to later Water Street, and then west to Meeting Street. A "Grand Modell" was drawn up with regular streets, but creeks and marshes (whose bounds reappear when heavy rains cause flooding) impeded settlement. Those residing within the walls were indentured servants, some middle-class English, settlers from the Caribbean, and African slaves.

Although there was the social and cultural mixing common in seaports (the city's architecture would blend English and Caribbean influences into the ubiquitous Charleston single house), an elite presented themselves quite early in the history of Charleston. They would dominate the small middle class, artisans, and the vast masses of poor whites and African Americans well into the twentieth century. This intermingling of high style and sophisticated continental taste with the language and lore of Africa in a lush subtropical setting would create much of the tension and color of the place's politics, history, and culture—as the writer John Bennett would later say of the mix, "A city . . . with Mediterranean manners and Caribbean ways."

By the time the colony passed from the Lords Proprietors to the British crown, Charleston had survived hurricanes and threats from Indians, the nearby Spanish, and pirates. The western walls came down by 1720; it doubled in size from its original eighty acres by 1740. As more and more slaves were funneled through Charleston,

Charleston, 1789. Courtesy, South Carolina Historical Society

the city began its domination of the plantation lowcountry. The wealth of some of its citizens, based on rice, indigo, and then cotton, was four times that of the nearest comparable place. The city showed the results. The first recorded performance of an American opera had occurred in Charleston; the St. Cecilia Society, dedicated to music, was founded in 1762; and there were brilliant theatrical seasons. Artists did portraits of patrons, and sons were sent to England for schooling.

This ostentatious display of wealth fueled fulminations against the city. The many acts of God visited upon Charleston, including fires (1740, 1778), hurricanes, and epidemics of smallpox, cholera, and yellow fever, were punishments on the prideful place, many decreed. Yet despite its sinful reputation, the city has also had a distinguished religious history. It was visited by the Wesleys (Methodism's founders), had the first Catholic church in the Carolinas and Georgia, was home to the South's first Baptist congregation, and by 1800 supported the largest Jewish population in the country. Later the city would see America's first Reform Jewish Society, and Mary Baker Eddy, founder of Christian Science, would live here briefly.

By the time of the Revolutionary War, Charleston, consisting of the parishes of St. Michael's and St. Philip's, was the fourth-largest city in America, and to some, the most handsome. It would have been a great prize had the British attack against it succeeded, but a fleet was repulsed at Fort Moultrie on nearby Sullivan's Island on June 28, 1776. Although there was tension between Loyalists and patriots, there was relative peace until Charleston came under British siege. They approached from the north, overcoming the defenses at what is still called Line Street. The city fell in May 1780 and remained under British rule until December 14, 1782, when a fleet left with 3,700 loyal whites, 5,000 slaves, and spoils that included the bells of St. Michael's Episcopal Church (eventually returned).

In 1783 the city was officially incorporated, becoming Charleston after being known as Charles Towne and Charlestown. The first intendant, or mayor, Richard Hutson, was reelected in 1784 in a vicious battle, beginning the trend for many contentious mayoral elections to come. Most of the sixteen thousand people living on the peninsula were poor and had no political spokesmen.

By the 1790s things were improving. A new orphan house rose; it would bring the city much pride and attention, as many of its inmates, orphaned by the diseases bred of poor sanitation, bad water, and seeping privies, would rise to positions of prominence. The College of Charleston, chartered in 1785, opened its doors. George Washington visited in 1791. The South Carolina Jockey Club began running races at the Washington Race Course, and Race Week would become one of the high points of the social season in the antebellum era. After the slave revolts in St. Domingue, there was a second influx of French speakers, following the Huguenots who had come in the 1680s. The refugees brought with them an increasing fear of black insurrection. By 1800 Charleston had a population of 10,104 blacks—slaves and free—and only 8,820 whites; the black majority would continue.

New buildings were going up first in Federal and later in Greek-revival styles. Ansonborough, north of the city market, had been the first suburb. Harleston Village, the site of an early golf course, sported larger houses that were further apart than the cluttered eighteenth-century buildings on Tradd and Church Streets. This gave the western edge of the city a different feel. The land on the southeastern side of the peninsula, fortified during the War of 1812, led to the development of pleasure gardens in the 1830s and sea walls in the 1840s and 1850s, which came to be known as "the Battery." Charleston had ceased being the capital of South Carolina in 1786, but state offices were still in the city, later to be ensconced in native son Robert Mills's Fireproof Building just north of the "four corners of law"—where St. Michael's Church, City Hall, the courthouse, and the police station (later the U.S. Post Office) met at Broad and Meeting Streets.

In 1822, with trade falling off and the city embarking on a series of improvements, there came a defining (but still not clearly understood) turning point in Charleston's history. In May rumors of a slave rebellion led by Denmark Vesey, a free person of color, reached the white elite. He and thirty-four others were hanged. So closed and questionable were the court proceedings that facts are hard to discern. The local government built an armory in 1825 for defense of the city that later became home to the Citadel. The fear of further rebellions, abolitionism, and restricting slavery in new territories worried Charlestonians. As its editors, writers, and politicians defended slavery and nullification, the city's position as the "capital of Southern Civilization" began to take shape in the popular imagination. The city was home to some nationally important gentlemen scientists and naturalists, following an eighteenth-century tradition.

To link Charleston with the growing west, local politicians began to invest heavily in railroad schemes, keeping the city in debt for generations. In 1833 the longest railroad in the world under one management linked Charleston and Hamburg, siphoning off trade from the Georgia cities of Augusta and Savannah. Although trains now brought goods to town, a significant obstacle was that the ruling elite permitted no steam engines or railroad tracks south of present-day Calhoun Street. Quality of life, a constant Charleston theme, was not to be disrupted, so all rail cargoes had to be unloaded and carted through the city to the docks.

Charleston suffered a major fire in its central business district in 1838. In 1849 the city doubled in size as the neck area was annexed. In 1850 John C. Calhoun died, and the city draped itself in black to bury its states' rights champion. The name of Boundary Street was changed to Calhoun, as in the nullification years Union Street became State Street. Charleston street signs showed the direction in which the South was moving.

The port of Charleston (circa 1938). Courtesy, Calhoun County Museum

The city was the scene of the split Democratic convention in April 1860, as well as the Secession Convention in December that took South Carolina out of the Union. Fort Sumter, in its harbor, was the last toehold of Federal troops in the area. In April 1861, when Southern forces shelled it, it became the site of the beginning of the Civil War. Charleston came under Union shelling in 1863, forcing many to move north of Calhoun Street. The city was abandoned in February 1865, and although the siege had not destroyed many buildings, as much as one-third of the city had been lost in a fire in December 1861. Many of its valuables and records, stored in Columbia, were lost when the capital city burned during Sherman's occupation.

For fifteen months or so Charleston was the virtual capital of North and South Carolina as it served the military headquarters of the occupying Federal forces. Freed slaves poured in and, along with many of the free people of color who had been the elite of their race, stepped forward to take positions of power. But at the end of Reconstruction, the white elite took the reins of power again. Charleston's black citizens were unfairly treated and denied rights, and the city suffered race riots in 1866, 1876, and 1919. Despite occasional racial clashes, however, the city experienced less of the militant and violent racism that erupted in other American cities in the nineteenth and twentieth centuries. Part of this was possibly due to the physical nature of the city. Until gentrification changed living patterns by the middle and late twentieth century, Charleston had been one of the most integrated cities in the country with blacks and whites living next door to each other. Shared sufferings—poverty; an earthquake in 1886 that caused $6 million in damage and eighty-three deaths; hurricanes in 1885, 1893, and 1911, which killed rice production in the lowcountry; and a common inheritance and alienation from the rest of the country—helped seal the fates of blacks and whites together.

There were flurries of economic improvements, but for the most part the city remained impoverished. The 1901–1902 South Carolina Inter-State and West Indian Exposition on the outskirts of town, staged to encourage investment, failed. Governor Benjamin Tillman railed against the aristocrats and pleasure lovers of Charleston as merchants openly flouted the restrictive alcohol and vice laws. The city was out of sync with the rest of the state and the country. Visually, too, it differed. The lack of prosperity for a century had saved its old structures from destruction and modernization. It seemed to be asleep, looking backward to a more glorious time.

World War I began the waking of this sleeping beauty. The navy base located north of the city in 1901 became headquarters of the Sixth Naval District. Thousands of service men and workers moved in. With Europe closed and the Florida land boom in progress, tourists were venturing down the twisted, unpaved streets. In the 1920s Mayor Tom Stoney coined the phrase "America's most historic city," and the city marketed itself as the home of a dance, the Charleston, that may have sprung from its African American citizens. The link was made complete in 1929 when the Cooper River Bridge opened, allowing highway travelers to drive into town. To counter the changes brought by automobiles, the arrival of the wealthy, and the appearance of gas stations where mansions used to be, citizens founded the Society for the Preservation of Old Dwellings in 1920 and later passed the first historic preservation laws in the country. The latter, done in 1931, made the city's 1783 motto *Aedes Mores Juraque Curat* (She guards her buildings and her ways) prophetic.

As old and new collided, the inheritors of the old ways began to deal with change. An artistic movement called the Charleston Renaissance resulted, and for a brief moment writers such as DuBose Heyward, John Bennett, Herbert Ravenel Sass, and Josephine Pinckney and visual artists such as Alfred Hutty, Elizabeth O'Neill Verner, and Alice Ravenel Huger Smith led a southern cultural awakening. Intrigued, the American composer George Gershwin based his opera *Porgy and Bess* on the novel and play *Porgy* by DuBose Heyward. The humble beggar, in his goat cart, has been the vehicle to take the city to audiences all over the world.

When *Porgy and Bess* had its Charleston premiere in 1970, it gave the city the opportunity to integrate socially at cultural functions at the moment when the city (and the state) was celebrating its three hundredth anniversary. Such integration was made possible only after the federal judge J. Waties Waring of Charleston declared that separate facilities were per se unequal, which made him a pariah in his native city. Rivers High School, the first public high school in the state to do so, integrated in 1963. But a tense hospital strike by black workers had the city under martial law in 1969.

Those coming to celebrate the state's birth at Charles Towne Landing, the city's original site, could look across the river to a much-changed place. Marshes south of Tradd Street had been filled in, and suburbs west of the Ashley had been annexed. The military base, the port, and tourism drove the local economy. The international Spoleto Arts Festival began in 1977 and merged tourism, culture, and business, contributing to the city's image and economy. In the 1980s a great battle erupted over the redevelopment of a block of downtown for a hotel convention site. It pitted business interests against preservationists, both of whom said they represented the best interests of the city. There was much fear of financial loss in the 1990s, but the city survived the closing of the navy base.

At the beginning of the twenty-first century, the city was competing with its incorporated neighbors Mount Pleasant and North Charleston to house the *Hunley*, the Confederate submarine lost in its harbor and then recovered, while others fought bitterly for and against the expansion of its container port, the second largest on the East Coast. As the nature of the city changes, its detractors and defenders become more passionate. Called one of America's most livable cities one year, it is noted for its congestion the next. It is not just a downtown but also suburbs, rich and poor, black and white, and immigrant. Like one of its eccentrics whom citizens pride themselves in accommodating, Charleston continues on, confident in its self-proclaimed destiny as one of America's most significant cities. "[A]ll untroubled in her faith," the Confederate poet Henry Timrod had testified earlier, "she waits the triumph or the tomb." See plate 8. HARLAN GREENE

An aerial view of modern urban development along the Ashley River. Photograph by Bill Murtin. Courtesy, City of Charleston

Fraser, Walter J. *Charleston! Charleston! The History of a Southern City.* Columbia: University of South Carolina Press, 1989.

Raven, James. *London Booksellers and American Customers: Transatlantic Literary Community and the Charleston Library Society, 1748–1811.* Columbia: University of South Carolina Press, 2002.

Rosen, Robert. *A Short History of Charleston.* San Francisco: Lexikos, 1982.

Charleston, Siege of (April–May 1780). The siege of Charleston marked the commencement of major British operations in the South during the Revolutionary War. Although they threatened Sullivan's Island in 1776 and secured Georgia in 1779, British efforts against the rebellious southern colonies were limited prior to 1780. General Sir Henry Clinton and Admiral Marriot Arbuthnot led a force from New York in December 1779 to attack Charleston. More than ten thousand British soldiers and sailors eventually served in the campaign. Major General Benjamin Lincoln held Charleston with six thousand men. The British landed on Seabrook Island on February 11–12, 1780, marched across Johns and James Islands, moved up the Ashley River, and crossed at Drayton Hall on March 29.

On April 1, British working parties began the first siege parallel. The American fortifications stretched across Charleston Neck between the Ashley and Cooper Rivers; the focal point was a tabby horn-work, a remnant of which remains in Marion Square. On April 8, British warships forced their way past Fort Moultrie, which gave them control of Charleston harbor. Two days later Clinton and Arbuthnot summoned the garrison, offering them the chance to surrender; General Lincoln responded that "duty and inclination" dictated that he defend the city "to the last extremity." The British commenced bombarding Charleston from their siege-works on April 13, and the two sides exchanged artillery and small arms fire from then until the end of the siege. The besiegers advanced toward Charleston using approach trenches and completed a second parallel on April 17.

Informed by his officers that their fortifications were too weak to hold and provisions were running low, Lincoln called a council of war to discuss their options. Some officers, including Brigadier Generals Lachlan McIntosh and William Moultrie, favored evacuating the army, but civilian officials, led by Lieutenant Governor Christopher Gadsden and Thomas Ferguson of the Privy Council, strongly discouraged the attempt. Ferguson even threatened to turn the civilians of Charleston against them. Ultimately, Lincoln and his officers offered terms of capitulation that would give the British the city and allow the American army to retreat to the backcountry. Clinton and Arbuthnot adamantly refused these proposals.

The British, meanwhile, endeavored to surround Charleston. On April 14 a force under Banastre Tarleton smashed the American cavalry posted near Moncks Corner, giving the British access to the region east of the Cooper. Clinton sent Lord Cornwallis and a detachment of troops over the Cooper to block American escape attempts. When the Americans evacuated Lempriere's Point (Hobcaw) and the Royal Navy captured Fort Moultrie, the British effectively enveloped Charleston. The completion of their third parallel allowed them to hammer the city from even closer distance. The city surrendered to the British on May 12, 1780. General Clinton disallowed the honors of war for the rebel army, meaning

A British plan of the Siege of Charleston, 1780. Courtesy, Private Collection, Columbia, South Carolina

that they filed out of the city with colors cased and with their drummers forbidden to play a British march. The capture of Lincoln's army at Charleston was the worst American defeat of the Revolutionary War. The British victory gave them a foothold from which to begin their conquest of the southern states, an effort that eventually failed. In that sense, the triumph against Charleston was the beginning of the end for the British in America. CARL BORICK

Clinton, Henry. *The American Rebellion: Sir Henry Clinton's Narrative of His Campaigns, 1775–1782, with an Appendix of Original Documents.* Edited by William B. Willcox. New Haven, Conn.: Yale University Press, 1954.

Moultrie, William. *Memoirs of the American Revolution.* 1802. Reprint, New York: New York Times, 1968.

Uhlendorf, Bernhard A., ed. *The Siege of Charleston, with an Account of the Province of South Carolina: Diaries and Letters of Hessian Officers from the von Jungkenn Papers in the William L. Clements Library.* Ann Arbor: University of Michigan Press, 1938.

Ward, Christopher. *The War of the Revolution.* 2 vols. New York: Macmillan, 1952.

Charleston, Siege of (1863–1865). Though a continuous enemy presence off Charleston was maintained by the Federals from May 28, 1861, when the Union navy established its blockade, Charleston did not find itself under constant attack until July 1863. Previously the city had survived the sinking of a "Stone Fleet" (old whaling vessels sunk in the shipping channel as an obstruction in late 1861 and early 1862), a land attack directed against Secessionville in June 1862, and a naval assault against the harbor defenses by nine ironclads on April 7, 1863. The defeat of the separate army and navy attacks resulted in the formation of a combined naval and land assault led by General Quincy A. Gillmore and Rear Admiral John A. Dahlgren. On July 10, 1863, the date that Charleston newspapers declared as the start of the siege, Union troops stormed ashore and captured most of Morris Island, but they were stopped on July 11 and 18 from taking Battery Wagner. Gillmore undertook siege operations, forcing the evacuation of Wagner and Morris Island on September 7, 1863.

During this time bombardments of Fort Sumter and Charleston commenced, and they continued throughout the war. A small boat attack on Fort Sumter, an attempt to capture it by surprise, failed on September 9, 1863. Charleston remained under intermittent bombardment from August 1863 until it was evacuated in February 1865. Though only five individuals would be killed by the cannonade, Charlestonians moved north of Calhoun Street and along the Ashley River. The downtown area became known as the "Shell District." The historic churches, houses, and graveyards were damaged and some destroyed by Union shells. When Jefferson Davis visited Charleston in November 1863, he declared that it was better to leave the city "a heap of ruins" than to surrender.

Throughout the war resourceful and energetic officers such as P. G. T. Beauregard, Roswell Ripley, Robert E. Lee, John C. Pemberton, Samuel Jones, and William Hardee commanded Charleston. They employed every conceivable method of defense including the use of floating mines, ironclad rams, torpedo boats, and a submarine. In October 1863 the Confederate torpedo boat *David* rammed the Union ironclad frigate *New Ironsides.* Early the following year the *H. L. Hunley* carried out the world's first successful submarine attack, sinking the USS *Housatonic* on February 17, 1864.

In February 1864 a Union advance on Johns Island under General Alexander Schimmelfennig failed. Early in July 1864 the city's defenders turned back attacks under General J. P. Hatch against James and Johns Islands. Active operations other than the bombardment of Sumter and Charleston slowed until early 1865 when General William T. Sherman began his march into South Carolina. Once the Confederates realized that Sherman's objective was Columbia, Beauregard, the department commander, ordered the Charleston garrison to the state capital, but contradictory orders from Jefferson Davis delayed the movement. Even so, Charleston could not hold. As the Charlestonian Jacob Schirmer wrote in his diary, "total ruin is staring us in our faces." With its interior connections severed, Federal troops landing at Bulls Bay north of the city, and enemy troops advancing overland from the south, Charleston was finally evacuated on February 17, 1865, ending its 567-day siege. See plate 21. ROBERT N. ROSEN

Burton, E. Milby. *The Siege of Charleston, 1861–1865.* Columbia: University of South Carolina Press, 1970.

Gillmore, Quincy Adams. *Engineer and Artillery Operations against the Defences of Charleston Harbor in 1863.* New York: Nostrand, 1865.

Johnson, John. *The Defense of Charleston Harbor, Including Fort Sumter and the Adjacent Islands, 1863–1865.* 1890. Reprint, Germantown, Tenn.: Guild Bindery Press, 1994.

Rosen, Robert N. *Confederate Charleston: An Illustrated History of the City and the People during the Civil War.* Columbia: University of South Carolina Press, 1994.

Wise, Stephen R. *Gate of Hell: Campaign for Charleston Harbor, 1863.* Columbia: University of South Carolina Press, 1994.

Charleston Air Force Base. In 1941, just prior to the attack on Pearl Harbor, the U.S. Army took over Charleston Municipal

Airport to develop an air base to train B-24 crews. In 1943 the base was reassigned to Air Transport Command to train flight crews for transport aircraft. Following the conclusion of the war the base was deactivated. During the Korean conflict the base was refurbished for $28 million and rededicated in late 1953, becoming a major link in the nation's Military Air Transport Service.

The cold-war base served as host to the 456th Troop Carrier Wing, flying and maintaining C-119 aircraft, known as "Flying Box Cars." It provided support and intelligence data during the Cuban missile crisis and later transported supplies and troops to Vietnam. Charleston Air Force Base planes also provided medical support to troops in Indochina and evacuated the wounded back to the United States. In 1993 it became the first U.S. Air Force base to receive the massive C-17 aircraft, which led to ten years of extensive renovations and modernization, including new facilities and flight simulators along with new housing for personnel. By the 1990s the base's host unit was the 437th Airlift Wing, operating aircraft to provide logistical and troop support to Operation Desert Storm (1990–1991) and the Balkans Crisis (1995–1999). Early in the twenty-first century, the base was providing support to U.S. initiatives in the Middle East, the Balkans, and Afghanistan. During fiscal year 1999, active-duty and reserve personnel numbering 7,595 were stationed at Charleston Air Force Base and providing an estimated annual economic impact to local communities of $439 million. FRITZ HAMER

University of South Carolina Legacy Project. *The Cold War in South Carolina, 1945–1991: An Inventory of Department of Defense Cold War Era Cultural and Historical Resources in the State of South Carolina; Final Report.* Vol. 3, *The Department of the Air Force in South Carolina.* Aberdeen Proving Ground, Md.: Legacy Resource Management Program, United States Department of Defense, 1995.

Charleston County (919 sq. miles; 2000 pop. 309,969). About 1682, in the first blueprint for South Carolina as an English colony, there was no Charleston County. Charles Towne, as the first city of South Carolina was then called, was the hub of Berkeley County. Charleston District appeared in 1769 as one of seven judicial districts formed to administer law in the colony. In its modern configuration, Charleston County is a long sliver of land—mainland and islands—bounded at the north and south by the South Santee and South Edisto Rivers. It has existed only since 1882.

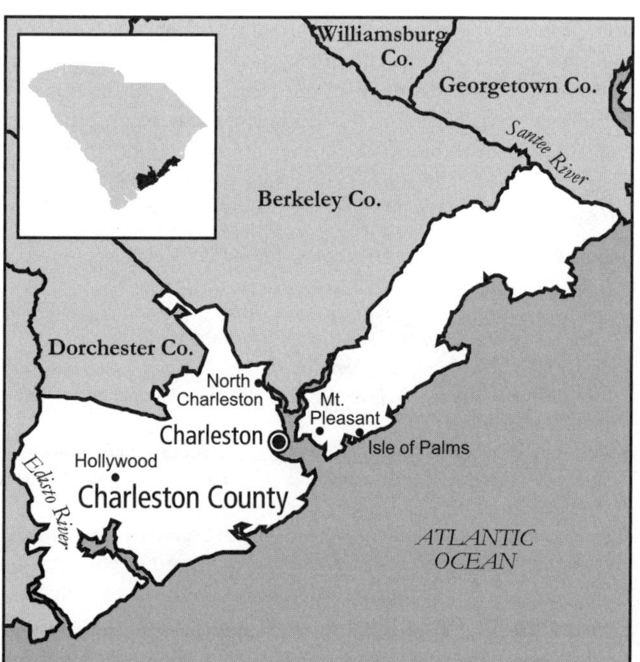

For two centuries before the Civil War, European and African immigrants along the lowlands that constitute modern Charleston County braved attacks from Indians, Spaniards, and Frenchmen and struggled with heat, malaria, and hurricanes to erect town and country bases. These settlers eventually turned the damp, dark soil to the production of specialized crops to be shipped from Charleston, notably rice, indigo, and Sea Island cotton. As fortunes were made by masters in both city and hinterland, they built substantial houses and lifestyles.

The plantation economy was built on a conjunction of rich soil and slave labor, and declined once these circumstances changed. After the Civil War sounded the death knell of slavery, the county struggled to establish a new identity, new economy, and new society. For a brief time former slaves enjoyed civil and political rights. However, due to resourceful and persistent white opposition, early gains were lost. Pressed by poverty as well as social and political inequities, many former slaves emigrated. Farming declined, and those who stuck with it concentrated on foodstuffs trucked to Charleston or more distant urban markets.

After a long era of readjustment, during which some observers proclaimed its demise, Charleston County experienced an economic as well as social and cultural renaissance. Though the fruits were long delayed, seeds of the revival were planted early in the twentieth century. Significant improvements in infrastructure tied the county together just as the automobile came into general use. Charleston County had been divided by its rivers. The Ashley River was crossed by a public bridge in 1921. In 1929 Grace Memorial Bridge tied the city of Charleston and the northern reaches of the county with its span across the Cooper River. It operated as a toll bridge until it was purchased by the county in 1941. Under the leadership of James Cosgrove, the county put down the first piece of concrete paving—less than a mile long—in 1918.

After 1940, with the aid of federally funded road and harbor improvements, the State Ports Authority at Charleston tapped into a growing world economy and repeatedly exceeded records for tons of goods funneling through the city. An additional economic asset, the United States Naval Base and Shipyard, which opened in Charleston's northern suburbs in 1901, grew prodigiously during and after World War II. By the 1980s the base encompassed 20,000 acres and employed 35,000 civilians, mostly newcomers drawn from across the southeastern United States. Subsequently, the area of North Charleston was already a thickly settled community by the time of its incorporation in 1972. In 1953, thanks to cold-war threats and the influence of U.S. Representative Mendel Rivers, the Charleston Air Force Base was dedicated as a major military transport facility. In the civilian realm, Charleston Municipal Airport (present-day Charleston International Airport) was situated within North Charleston's corporate bounds in 1931. It became the busiest airport in the state by the end of the century.

When the naval complex closed in 1996, negative effects were less than had been anticipated. The economy was buoyed by Charleston's booming container-ship business, as well as high-tech industrial development independent of military spending in North Charleston. Additional strength was added by the fields of health care and higher education, especially by the campuses of the Medical University of South Carolina, the College of Charleston, and the Citadel. Meanwhile, attractive beaches and a historical and cultural texture made Kiawah and Seabrook Islands, Isle of Palms, and Charleston major tourist and retirement attractions.

Most of the growth that took place in the last half of the twentieth century occurred outside the city of Charleston. North Charleston boasted a population of 75,000 in 1995, the third largest in the state. Mount Pleasant, one of seven other places in the county that achieved the status of incorporated town, had a population of more than 40,000 in the year 2000. Its annual growth rate of eight percent was so phenomenal that town leaders felt compelled to establish limits on new residential and industrial construction. The trend toward suburbanization was unmistakable: the city of Charleston, encompassing two-thirds of the county's population in 1910, accounted for only one-fourth of a total of 309,969 at the end of the century.

Modern government in Charleston County depended on a delicate balance of county officers (county council, school board, sheriff, and coroner) and city or town administrations, all elected by overlapping constituencies and mutually concerned with quality of life. The public agenda at the new millennium includes problems associated with education, an aging transportation infrastructure, and the costs and benefits of prosperity, especially the impact of unregulated growth and congestion. During the year 2000, in a gesture of solidarity, Charleston County Council, which had a budget of $123.5 million in fiscal year 2000–2001, joined forces with some constituent city and town administrations. Together, these overlapping authorities developed a comprehensive plan to address suburban sprawl and save green space; build additional parks, schools, and new bridges; and construct a regional mass-transit-system monorail. LAYLON WAYNE JORDAN

Coclanis, Peter A. *The Shadow of a Dream: Economic Life and Death in the South Carolina Low Country, 1670–1920.* New York: Oxford University Press, 1989.

Fraser, Walter J. *Charleston! Charleston! The History of a Southern City.* Columbia: University of South Carolina Press, 1989.

Lesesne, Thomas P. *History of Charleston County.* Charleston, S.C.: A. H. Cawston, 1931.

Moore, Jamie W. *The Lowcountry Engineers: Military Missions and Economic Development in the Charleston District.* Charleston, S.C.: U.S. Army Corps of Engineers, 1981.

Charleston hospital workers' strike (1969). In Charleston in 1969 issues of race, class, and gender coalesced in a strike of more than four hundred African American hospital workers, mostly female, against the all-white administrations of the Medical College Hospital (MCH) and Charleston County Hospital (CCH). The strike against MCH lasted one hundred days during spring and summer; the one at CCH went on for an additional three weeks. What had begun as a dispute between employers and employees quickly transformed into a national and international debate over civil rights, unionization of public sector workers, and gender roles.

Long-term factors regarding the crisis included white Charleston's tradition of paternalistic, hegemonic race relations as well as their long-standing opposition to unions. Short-term factors included black nurses' aides being paid less than whites for the same work; being paid (along with licensed practical nurses, orderlies, kitchen and laundry staff, and other "nonprofessional" workers) $1.30 an hour, 30¢ below the minimum wage; and the lack of respect shown by many white hospital workers to their black colleagues, often demonstrated by racist comments in their presence or directed at them. Other aspects of institutional racism at MCH included the lack of black students at the nursing school and the lack of black physicians on staff.

The catalyst for black hospital workers to organize occurred in February 1967. When a white head nurse would not give five "nonprofessional" black workers the customary access to patients' charts, they refused to work—and were fired the next day. The five asked Mary Moultrie, a black nurse's aide, to help them. She talked with Bill Saunders, a factory worker, activist, and community liaison with the local office of the Department of Health, Education, and Welfare (HEW), and Isaiah Bennett, a veteran union organizer. Small groups of workers began meeting weekly at local churches without publicity in fear of reprisals, while HEW investigated the firings. The workers were reinstated, but the meetings continued and attendance slowly increased to several hundred. CCH workers, led by Rosetta Simmons, joined the meetings. During these discussions, workers found that they faced the same discriminatory attitudes and practices throughout the hospital. Faced with an unresponsive administration, workers concluded that they needed a national union to represent them. Bennett suggested Local 1199 of the Retail, Wholesale, and Department Store Workers, which had already organized hospital workers in New York City. When Moultrie and others requested help in September 1968, the union responded, showing interest in organizing southern workers. Soon Local 1199B was chartered in Charleston and Mary Moultrie was elected president.

In February 1969 Local 1199B officially requested formal recognition from MCH. On March 18 MCH president William McCord met with Moultrie and a delegation of workers. But McCord brought an anti-union delegation outnumbering Moultrie's group. Convinced that negotiations in good faith were not possible, Moultrie and her colleagues walked out of the meeting. Other workers joined Moultrie's group, and they briefly took over the president's office in protest. After the workers returned to their jobs, twelve of them were fired. That night Local 1199B voted to go on strike at MCH, demanding recognition of the union, a meaningful grievance procedure, a 30¢ increase in MCH's minimum hourly wage to the federal standard of $1.60—and the rehiring of the fired strikers.

On March 20 the strike began and picket lines formed at MCH, quickly followed by an injunction severely limiting picketing. McCord stated that he would not "turn a 25 million dollar complex over to a bunch of people who don't have a grammar school education." McCord and Governor Robert McNair declared that the state's right-to-work law precluded union recognition of MCH workers. On March 29 CCH workers also went on strike. As arrests for violation of the injunction increased, Dr. Ralph David Abernathy of the Southern Christian Leadership Conference (SCLC) arrived in Charleston on March 31 and spoke to 1,500 strikers and their supporters. SCLC, still recovering from the assassination of its first leader, Dr. Martin Luther King, Jr., in Memphis a year earlier, saw the Charleston strike as a way to work with Local 1199B in a "Union Power, Soul Power" alliance that could give SCLC a badly needed victory. Abernathy also saw involvement as a way of demonstrating his leadership ability as King's successor. The presence of SCLC helped overcome divisions among local black leaders and rallied much of Charleston's black community in support of the strike. On April 25 Abernathy and 101 demonstrators were arrested and Governor McNair ordered 500 National Guardsmen with fixed bayonets to patrol city streets. Three nights later Coretta Scott King told more than 3,000 supporters that her late husband would have been there if he were alive. The next day she led a mass march in the hospital area. On May 1 Governor McNair ordered a curfew in Charleston from 9:00 P.M. to 5:00 A.M. and declared a state of emergency in the city when incidents of rock-throwing and fire-bombing increased as the strike dragged on and frustrations grew. The *New York Times* had already termed the strike "the country's tensest civil rights struggle." On May 2 Abernathy was released from jail on bond, partly to try to defuse the situation.

The continuation of the strike hurt Charleston's economy and reputation. Supporters honored SCLC's call for a boycott of city businesses. In addition, tourists tended to avoid a city with racial strife and a curfew. Convention business shriveled up. Observers estimated that the strike ultimately cost Charleston more than $15 million in lost revenue. Economic pressures intensified political pressure to settle the strike.

On Mother's Day, May 11, more than five thousand marchers heard Abernathy, Moultrie, Walter Reuther of the United Auto Workers, and five congressmen denounce the intransigence of white state officials in strike negotiations. On June 2 the curfew ended, but the arrest of Abernathy on June 20 led to a near-riot and the curfew was reinstated. Leaders of the predominately black International Longshoremen Association speculated about closing the port of Charleston to increase pressure for a fair settlement. Meanwhile, negotiations between Bill Saunders, representing the strikers, and MCH vice president William Huff led to an agreement. The twelve fired workers would be rehired, pay would be raised to the federal level, and a formal grievance procedure and a credit union would be established; but no union recognition or official collective bargaining would be permitted. The workers accepted the compromise, but McCord balked, backed by U.S. Senator Strom Thurmond and Congressman L. Mendel Rivers. However, when an HEW investigation charged MCH with thirty-seven violations of civil rights statutes and threatened to cut off $12 million in federal funds, McCord finally yielded. MCH strikers claimed victory, and CCH workers soon settled their strike on similar terms.

The strike's results were significant at the time. Female MCH and CCH workers believed that their actions had led to "a new relationship of mutual respect and dignity" on the job and to improved race relations in the community. In 1970 Charleston elected its first black state legislator since Reconstruction as well as several black city council members. But Local 1199B in Charleston folded after a year, undercut by its lack of official standing. Twenty-five years after the strike, Mary Moultrie lamented that "a lot of things change, and then you see them gradually regressing." In 1996 the Department of Labor cited the Medical University of South Carolina for four violations of discrimination laws and fourteen other related employment practices. GEORGE W. HOPKINS

Abernathy, Ralph. *And the Walls Came Tumbling Down.* New York: Harper & Row, 1989.

Estes, Steve. "'I Am Somebody': The Charleston Hospital Strike of 1969." *Avery Review* (spring 2000): 8–32.

Fink, Leon. "Union Power, Soul Power: The Story of 1199B and Labor's Search for a Southern Strategy." *Southern Changes* 5 (March/April 1983): 9–20.

Fink, Leon, and Brian Greenberg. *Upheaval in the Quiet Zone: A History of the Hospital Workers' Union, Local 1199.* Urbana: University of Illinois Press, 1989.

Hoffius, Steve. "Charleston Hospital Workers' Strike, 1969." In *Working Lives: The Southern Exposure History of Labor in the South,* edited by Marc S. Miller. New York: Pantheon, 1980.

O'Neill, Steven. "The Struggle for Black Equality Comes to Charleston: The Hospital Strike of 1969." *Proceedings of the South Carolina Historical Association* (1986): 82–91.

Charleston International Airport. The Charleston Airport Corporation formed in 1928 and opened a privately owned airport on August 10, 1929. In 1931 the city of Charleston arranged a $60,000 bond issue to purchase part of the property and further develop the airfield. The Works Progress Administration helped significantly in developing the facilities during the 1930s, and Charleston continued to run the airport until World War II.

In 1942 Charleston Municipal Airport became part of the nation's defense system. The Army Air Corps maintained full control but permitted commercial flying. The army closed the base in 1946 and released its 2,050 acres and $13 million improvements back to the city. During the late 1940s the city got a new passenger terminal partly funded by a $240,000 grant from the Civil Aeronautics Administration. The terminal, the first in the Southeast to be modernized after World War II, opened in 1949.

The Korean War led to reactivation of the airport as a military air base. The city of Charleston and the U.S. Air Force agreed in 1952 on terms of control of the base and signed a new Joint Use Agreement in 1973 that transferred ownership of Charleston Municipal Airport to a newly formed airport authority. In 1979 Charleston County Aviation Airport Authority assumed control of the airport and expanded the civil aviation facilities. A 1,300-acre site adjoining the southern area was purchased from Georgia-Pacific Company for a new terminal complex that was opened in April 1985. The terminal included an international concourse to accommodate operations of the Military Airlift Command. ROBERT A. PIERCE

Charleston ironwork. Elements of decorative iron first appeared on the buildings of Charleston during the middle decades of the eighteenth century. Local blacksmiths advertising in the local newspapers offered "all kinds of scrollwork for grates and staircases." These decorative elements, primarily English in style, closely followed the published patterns of the prominent British architect and furniture designer Robert Adam. Much of Charleston's oldest surviving architectural wrought iron can be linked to an Adam-style communion railing at St. Michael's Church that was fashioned in London and installed in 1772. The lines of several noteworthy eighteenth-century balconies, railings, and window grills seen on prominent homes throughout Charleston were copied from this colonial import.

During the nineteenth century German and Swiss blacksmiths, following patterns provided by local architects, dominated the production of Charleston's wrought-iron decoration. In 1822 Jacob Roh built the large iron gates, which were designed by Abraham P. Reeves, for the entrance of St. John's Lutheran Church. Christopher Werner, the dominant blacksmith in Charleston from the 1830s to the 1870s, created the much-celebrated Sword Gate, which was designed by the architect Charles F. Reichert. Werner was also responsible for the gates and fences that surround the College of Charleston, all of them designed by Edward Brickell White in 1852. During the first half of the nineteenth century Charleston ironwork moved away from English influences to embrace the Greek-revival fashion that came to symbolize democratic principles and thus a new American identity. The gates enclosing the cemetery at St. Michael's Church, created sometime in the early 1840s by I. M. Justi, are the most noteworthy examples of wrought-iron decoration done in this style. The funerary urns seen in the upper portions of Justi's gates are prime examples of Grecian classicism.

During the second half of the nineteenth century, more and more cast-iron elements were used to embellish Charleston's iron gates and fences. These mass-produced elements were created mainly in New York, Philadelphia, and Boston and shipped south to satisfy the new demand for solid, lifelike replicas of flowers, leaves, and branches that were favored during the Victorian period. By the 1870s Charlestonians could boast of their own cast-iron foundries; E. Merker, C. R. Valk, and John F. Riley were prominent local producers. But given the earlier dominance of wrought-iron designs and the survival of so many examples of extraordinary eighteenth-century works, Charleston retained its preference for hand-forged decorative iron created by blacksmiths. The use of cast-iron decoration continued but remained a minor element in the embellishment of houses, churches, banks, and other public buildings.

Julius Ortmann satisfied Charleston's demand for blacksmith-made decorative iron through the 1920s. However, during the Great Depression, when the prospects of all industries were dreary, the demand for the skills of ornamental specialists was especially feeble. During this period general blacksmiths, men who mainly shoed horses and did repair work, occasionally stepped forward to take on the challenge of decorative commissions. Peter Simmons, best known as a farrier and wheelwright, could, when asked, also fashion gates and window grills. His most talented apprentice, Philip Simmons, came of age during this period and was able to find enough clients interested in authentic wrought iron to launch his career chiefly as an ornamental ironworker. Over the past sixty years he has not only created more than two hundred decorative commissions but has also received the highest honors South Carolina can bestow on an artisan. His work can be seen all over Charleston and in several museums, including the South Carolina State Museum and the Smithsonian Institution. JOHN MICHAEL VLACH

Deas, Alston. *The Early Ironwork of Charleston.* Columbia, S.C.: Bostick & Thornley, 1941.

Vlach, John Michael. "'Keeping On Keeping On': African American Craft during the Era of Revivals." In *Revivals! Diverse Traditions, 1920–1940: The History of Twentieth-Century American Craft,* edited by Janet Kardon. New York: Abrams, 1994.

———. "Metalwork in the Carolinas." In *Carolina Folk: The Cradle of a Southern Tradition,* edited by George D. Terry and Lynn Robertson Myers. Columbia: McKissick Museum, University of South Carolina, 1985.

Charleston Library Society. The Charleston Library Society is the third-oldest institutional library in the United States. On December 28, 1748, a group of Charlestonians met to establish a private subscription library to support education and the arts and sciences. The society secured a charter of incorporation in 1755 and established a tradition in which the colony's royal governors were society presidents. This tradition lasted until the Revolutionary War. By 1778 the society's book and periodical collection numbered five thousand volumes. Society members promoted a colonial college in 1770 that eventually became the College of Charleston. Three years later, in 1773, the society started a natural science collection that became the Charleston Museum.

The Charleston fire of 1778 destroyed all but a handful of the society's books. In 1863 the society's librarian sent one-half of the library's collections to Columbia, but they were destroyed there in 1865. In 1874 Charleston's Apprentice Library Society (founded in 1824) and the Library Society merged their resources. When the South Carolina Jockey Club disbanded in 1900, it transferred its property to the Library Society. The society sold the Washington Racecourse and established an endowment that has continued to provide revenue into the twenty-first century. In 1914 the society constructed a new building at 164 King Street. Eighty-two years later, in 1996, the society expanded into a large adjacent building, which houses a children's reading room, audio and video collections, and offices.

Among the collections of the Charleston Library Society are rare books, pamphlets, a manuscript collection, and the society's records. The most significant collection is the society's newspaper files, which contain the world's largest and most complete collection of eighteenth- and nineteenth-century Charleston newspapers. Society members have free access to the collections, including its circulating library, and nonmembers pay a daily research fee. ALEXANDER MOORE

Porcher, Elizabeth L. *The History of the Charleston Library Society.* New York: Elizabethan Press, 1931.

Raven, James. *London Booksellers and American Customers: Transatlantic Literary Community and the Charleston Library Society, 1748–1811.* Columbia: University of South Carolina Press, 2002.

Charleston Mercury. Although begun as a literary journal, the *Charleston Mercury* developed into one of the state's most radical and combative newspapers. In 1821 the New Jersey native and bookseller Edward Morford founded the *Charleston Mercury and Morning Advertiser.* In 1823 it was purchased by Henry Laurens Pinckney, who transformed the newspaper into a partisan organ for John C. Calhoun. That same year it established a "country" or triweekly issue in order to expand circulation. In 1825 the name of the paper was shortened to *Charleston Mercury.* The newspaper became a strong proponent of nullification in March 1830; it was alone among Charleston newspapers in taking this position, and doing so helped solidify its lengthy antebellum rivalry with the more moderate *Charleston Courier.*

Although the newspaper changed hands several times through the 1840s and 1850s, the editorial tone remained aggressive and merciless toward its enemies. This occasionally led to flare-ups outside the pages of the newspaper. The coeditor William R. Taber was killed in an 1856 duel by an angry relative of one of the paper's targets. The Rhett family had been associated with the *Mercury* since the mid-1840s, and the family bought the paper outright in 1857, with Robert Barnwell Rhett, Jr., assuming complete control of the newspaper the following year. The newspaper called loudly for secession. When that was achieved, the paper turned its attention to criticizing the Confederate government. Personal attacks on Jefferson Davis were matched by attacks on the Confederate Congress for not opposing Davis's agenda and for conducting a defensive military strategy. The newspaper also complained that government censorship restricted journalists from completely reporting on the war effort.

Rhett prepared for the war better than most editors did by ordering a new press before the start of hostilities. In part this allowed the *Mercury* to continue publishing when other papers foundered for lack of equipment or resources. The press was moved to Columbia in autumn 1864 but was burned when the city fell. Rhett started the *Mercury* again after the war, but the newspaper failed in November 1868. AARON W. MARRS

Coussons, John Stanford. "Thirty Years with Calhoun, Rhett, and the *Charleston Mercury:* A Chapter in South Carolina Politics." Ph.D. diss., Louisiana State University, 1971.

Davis, William C. *Rhett: The Turbulent Life and Times of a Fire-Eater.* Columbia: University of South Carolina Press, 2001.

Osthaus, Carl R. *Partisans of the Southern Press: Editorial Spokesmen of the Nineteenth Century.* Lexington: University Press of Kentucky, 1994.

Prior, Granville Torrey. "A History of the *Charleston Mercury,* 1822–1852." Ph.D. diss., Harvard University, 1946.

Charleston Museum. Founded in 1773, the Charleston Museum is the oldest municipal museum in the United States. It originated as an auxiliary of the Charleston Library Society dedicated to the collection, preservation, and study of "materials promoting a Natural History" of South Carolina. Charles Cotesworth Pinckney and Thomas Heyward, Jr., were early curators. Botanical and zoological specimens and cultural artifacts have comprised the majority of the museum's collections since its founding. The collections moved often during the eighteenth and nineteenth centuries and were housed in private homes and public buildings. From 1792 until 1815 the museum occupied the upper floor of the Charleston County Courthouse at Meeting and Broad Streets. In 1815 the collections were transferred to the Literary and Philosophical Society of South Carolina. The society obtained a state appropriation of $10,000 and funds from the city of Charleston to expand. Later in the century the museum was in the Medical College of South Carolina on Queen Street. In 1850 the Literary and Philosophical Society transferred the collections to the College of Charleston. The museum secured its first independent home and autonomy in 1907 when it moved to the Thompson Auditorium at the corner of Rutledge Avenue and Calhoun Street. The institution adopted the name Charleston Museum and became an independent municipal institution.

Innovative directors, including Laura Bragg, the first female museum director in the United States, expanded the size and variety of the museum collections, published scientific and archaeological studies, and inaugurated ambitious public education programs. In 1980 the museum moved to a new building at 360 Meeting Street. For the first time since its founding, the museum had a home for its collections, research facilities, and archives in a building designed to be a museum. The Charleston Museum sponsors publications and cultural events in addition to chronicling the natural and cultural history of South Carolina. ALEXANDER MOORE

Allen, Louise Anderson. *A Bluestocking in Charleston: The Life and Career of Laura Bragg.* Columbia: University of South Carolina Press, 2001.

Borowsky, Caroline M. "The Charleston Museum." *Museum News* 41 (1963): 11–21.

Sanders, Albert E., and William D. Anderson, Jr. *Natural History Investigations in South Carolina from Colonial Times to the Present.* Columbia: University of South Carolina Press, 1999.

Charleston Naval Shipyard. Established in 1901 and deactivated 1995, the Charleston Naval Shipyard served as headquarters for the U.S. Navy's Sixth District for most of its history. Variously known as the Charleston Navy Yard, the Charleston Naval Shipyard, and the Charleston Naval Base, the facility traced its origins to a U.S. Navy base located at Parris Island in Beaufort County. Following a lobbying effort by U.S. Senator Ben Tillman, the navy transferred the base in 1901 to a less isolated location on the Cooper River about ten miles north of the port of Charleston. Local leaders hoped that the navy base would provide a much-needed economic stimulus. But it would be nearly two decades before the facility began to realize these expectations. The workforce grew slowly, numbering about 1,200 by the time the United States entered

A 1901 view of the newly opened drydock facilities at the Charleston Naval Yard. Courtesy, South Caroliniana Library, University of South Carolina

World War I in 1917. Once the country was at war, the facility grew dramatically. At its wartime peak 5,000 civilians were employed, with the navy's only clothing factory employing an additional 1,000 women. Furthermore, the yard's training center taught 25,000 navy personnel in various skills and built a one-thousand-bed hospital. Numerous vessels were repaired, and eight submarine chasers and one gunboat were constructed.

With the end of the war in 1918, the yard's workforce was steadily reduced until it numbered just 479 in 1924. Slated for decommissioning in 1922, lobbying efforts by local politicians and U.S. Senator Ellison "Cotton Ed" Smith convinced the navy to keep the facility operating. While the base remained active through the 1920s, it had few duties. Only five small vessels were built, and not many more were repaired. As the Depression began taking hold of the nation in 1930, activity slowed even further. Looking for ways to cut costs, the navy again slated the Charleston facility for closure. But once again Washington's intentions were forestalled when South Carolina's congressional delegation protested.

New Deal spending and lobbying by U.S. Senator James Byrnes helped the Charleston Naval Base secure a $3.2 million contract in 1933 for manufacturing gunboats. This small windfall employed 500 workers and led to an order for the base's first destroyer in 1936. By the eve of Pearl Harbor the once-stagnating facility had become a thriving shipbuilding and repair center for destroyers and other smaller navy craft. The workforce expanded to 10,000. Such accelerated growth caused strains on the city's infrastructure. Housing, transportation, and schools became overburdened.

World War II saw the Charleston Navy Yard reach its highest employment and shipbuilding rate. Women and minorities joined the yard's workforce, which reached an unprecedented total of 26,000 by 1944. Their efforts were crucial in making the facility a center for invasion-craft production, Landing Ship Tanks (LSTs) and Landing Ship Mediums (LSMs). During the war more than 200 vessels of all sorts were built, including 20 destroyers and 140 LSMs. Many more vessels were repaired. The huge influx of workers and their families accelerated the need for housing, transportation, and schools in Charleston. The navy worked with local and federal agencies to improve the situation. Along with new schools and day-care centers, twenty thousand housing units had been built by the last months of the war.

In the last months of the war the Charleston facility began laying off its workforce. By September 1946 employment at the yard had fallen below ten thousand. Before the end of the decade

Washington again proposed closing the lowcountry facility. However, the outbreak of the Korean War in 1950 revived the facility once again. During the cold war the Charleston Naval Shipyard (as it became known) became a center for refitting the navy's nuclear submarine fleet. Until his death in 1970, the lowcountry congressman L. Mendel Rivers was the base's biggest champion, using his political influence on the Armed Services Committee to strengthen and expand the facility. Some of these new installations included a fifth dry dock (1962) to overhaul Polaris submarines and other vessels, a navy missile assembly complex, and a fleet missile training center.

Until the collapse of the Soviet Union, the Charleston Naval Shipyard remained instrumental in the navy's nuclear submarine program. After 1990 the lowcountry facility became less important. Despite efforts by the state's congressional delegation, the base was deactivated in 1995, which dealt a serious, albeit temporary, blow to the Charleston area economy. Buildings and grounds have been turned over to a civilian agency for conversion to various uses. FRITZ HAMER

Hamer, Fritz P. "A Southern City Enters the Twentieth Century: Charleston, Its Navy Yard, and World War II, 1940–1948." Ph.D. diss., University of South Carolina, 1998.

Hopkins, George W. "From Naval Pauper to Naval Power: The Development of Charleston's Metropolitan-Military Complex." In *Martial Metropolis: U.S. Cities in War and Peace,* edited by Roger W. Lotchin. New York: Praeger, 1984.

McNeil, Jim. *Charleston's Navy Yard: A Picture History.* Charleston, S.C.: CokerCraft, 1985.

Moore, John H. "Charleston in World War I: Seeds of Change." *South Carolina Historical Magazine* 86 (January 1985): 39–49.

———. "No Room, No Rice, No Grits: Charleston's Time of Trouble, 1942–1944." *South Atlantic Quarterly* 85 (winter 1986): 23–31.

Charleston Orphan House. Before Independence, St. Philip's Parish cared for Charleston's orphans by placing them with local families. After disestablishment of the Anglican Church, such children became a civic responsibility. In 1790 the city council established the Charleston Orphan House "for the purpose of supporting and educating poor orphan children, and those of poor, distressed and disabled parents who are unable to support and maintain them." It was the first public orphanage in America. Soon the building that would eventually house thousands of children was erected at Boundary (later Calhoun) and St. Philip Streets, accompanied by the notable 1802 chapel designed by the architect Gabriel Manigault.

The Charleston Orphan House in the early twentieth century. Courtesy, South Caroliniana Library, University of South Carolina

Some five thousand children, a minority of whom were full orphans, passed through the institution over the next century and a half. Up to the mid–nineteenth century most residents received a few years of formal education in the Orphan House school and then were apprenticed—boys to local craftsmen, and girls to learn housewifery from mistresses. Other inmates spent a relatively brief part of their youth in the institution before returning to their families, often after their widowed mothers had remarried. Some Orphan House alumni such as Christopher Memminger and Andrew Buist Murray achieved fame, but for the vast majority the Orphan House secured a relatively humane childhood and prepared them to work productively as adults.

The Orphan House was an institution of deep pride to Charlestonians, who made sure that prominent visitors such as Presidents Washington, Monroe, and Taft toured the grounds. But the needs of poor families changed over time, and so did the Orphan House. In 1951 all children in residence moved to the new facility at Oak Grove in North Charleston, which continued into the twenty-first century as the Carolina Youth Development Center. The Orphan House and its chapel—survivors of fire, hurricane, earthquake, and Union naval bombardment—were demolished soon thereafter and replaced by a department store, which eventually closed. JOHN E. MURRAY

Bellows, Barbara L. *Benevolence among Slaveholders: Assisting the Poor in Charleston, 1670–1860.* Baton Rouge: Louisiana State University Press, 1993.

King, Susan L. "The Charleston Orphan House: The First One Hundred Years." *Proceedings of the South Carolina Historical Association* (1998): 106–15.

Murray, John E. "Fates of Orphans: Poor Children in Antebellum Charleston." *Journal of Interdisciplinary History* 33 (spring 2003): 519–45.

Charleston Poorhouse and Hospital. In 1768 the Commons House of Assembly authorized the construction of a "Poor House and Hospital" in Charleston to care for the city's growing population of paupers. Situated on a four-acre lot on Mazyck Street near the Ashley River, the three-story brick structure began admitting the sick and destitute around 1770. The new facility replaced an older poorhouse built in the 1730s, which became the city workhouse. Following the incorporation of Charleston in 1783, the new Poorhouse and Hospital was placed under the control of the city's commissioners of the poor.

Envisioned as an advance in the humane treatment of the sick and uplift of the deserving poor, the Charleston Poorhouse and Hospital was intended to serve as an infirmary for the physically and mentally ill and to provide shelter, food, and reform for the needy. At times the poorhouse also operated as a lockup for sailors and vagrants from Charleston's streets and docks, blurring the already vague distinctions between the institution's multifaceted role as hospital, workhouse, almshouse, and jail. Despite its well-intentioned mission, by the middle of the antebellum period the Charleston Poorhouse and Hospital had devolved into a wretched dumping ground and haven of last resort for the city's victims of poverty, alcoholism, and disease. "Unearthly whoopings and hallooings" emanated at all hours from cells housing "lunatics," while remaining wards, cells, and sickbeds contained a transient population of drunks, vagrants, widows, orphans, and diseased in various stages of recovery or demise. Between 1830 and 1848 some 7,320 men, women, and children (almost all white) resorted to the care of the

Poorhouse and Hospital. In 1856, dismayed by the dreadful reputation of the Poorhouse and Hospital, city commissioners moved the poorhouse to an abandoned factory on Columbus Street, renaming it the Alms House. Medical care for the sick and insane poor was contracted to the trustees of the newly built Roper Hospital, whose physicians were granted use of the poorhouse's hospital wards. The remainder of the building was renovated to serve as a house of correction. BRENDA THOMPSON SCHOOLFIELD

Bellows, Barbara L. *Benevolence among Slaveholders: Assisting the Poor in Charleston, 1670–1860.* Baton Rouge: Louisiana State University Press, 1993.

Klebaner, Benjamin Joseph. "Public Poor Relief in Charleston, 1800–1860." *South Carolina Historical Magazine* 55 (October 1954): 210–20.

McCandless, Peter. *Moonlight, Magnolias, and Madness: Insanity in South Carolina from the Colonial Period to the Progressive Era.* Chapel Hill: University of North Carolina Press, 1996.

Charleston Renaissance (ca. 1915–1940). The Charleston Renaissance was a multifaceted cultural renewal that took place in the years between World Wars I and II. Artists, musicians, writers, historians, and preservationists, individually and in groups, fueled a revival that reshaped the city's destiny. Such organizations as the Charleston Sketch Club and the Charleston Etchers' Club, the Society for the Preservation of Spirituals, the Jenkins Orphanage Band, the Poetry Society of South Carolina, and the Society for the Preservation of Old Dwellings provided opportunities for groups to foster artistic expression deeply rooted in Charleston's past. Many individuals, largely natives, were responsible for shepherding these organizations: Alice Ravenel Huger Smith and Elizabeth O'Neill Verner; Augustine T. Smythe and Herbert Ravenel Sass; DuBose Heyward, John Bennett, Josephine Pinckney, and Julia Peterkin; Susan Pringle Frost, Alston Deas, and Albert Simons.

The Charleston Renaissance benefited from a large number of books, many illustrated with paintings and prints by local artists, as well as documentary photographs. A seminal volume was *The Dwelling Houses of Charleston, South Carolina,* published in 1917 and consisting of house histories by D. E. H. Smith accompanied by picturesque drawings by his daughter, Alice Smith. Ten years later Albert Simons and his partner Samuel Lapham issued the lavishly illustrated volume *The Early Architecture of Charleston.* Both books instilled a sense of pride in Charleston's architectural past and stimulated the historic preservation movement. Spurred by these individuals, Susan Frost, and others active in the preservation society, the municipal government in 1931 passed the nation's first preservation ordinance and established the Board of Architectural Review to oversee all demolitions and changes to structures in the historic district.

That same year the spiritual society issued *The Carolina Low-Country,* a compendium of essays on plantation life, with an emphasis on spirituals. These and the many other books published at this time served to document Charleston's cultural heritage, and because they were accessible and easily transported they served to disseminate the charms of the lowcountry to a broad audience. One story, more than any other, brought national attention to Charleston: the tale of Porgy, by DuBose Heyward. It appeared in 1925, first as a novel, then as a play on Broadway in 1928, and finally in its best known form, as the folk opera *Porgy and Bess* in 1935.

Although an art colony per se never emerged, artists created images that served to attract visitors to the area. Initially, the artwork of Alice Smith, Elizabeth O'Neill Verner, Anna Heyward Taylor, other local aspirants, and Alfred Hutty (a transplanted northerner) emphasized picturesque views that veiled the reality of a city that had seen brighter times. These paintings and prints were exhibited in such places as Chicago, Washington, and Philadelphia, broadening the appreciation for the lowcountry. Because the watercolors were often small-scale and the prints accessibly priced, many tourists purchased them as souvenirs of their visits. Ultimately, other artists were enticed to the area, converting Charleston into a mecca of sorts for painters and printmakers.

The country gradually became Charleston-conscious, and as a result tourists began to come, especially in the spring, to "America's Most Historic City." Tourism was enhanced by improved transportation, not least of which was the opening of the Cooper River Bridge in 1929, which facilitated automobile traffic with the north and provided makers of sweet-grass baskets direct access to passing motorists. Hotels such as the Francis Marion and the Fort Sumter were built in the early 1920s to accommodate the influx of visitors. Azalea festivals, musicals, and house and garden tours were offered as entertainment but also served as fund-raisers. Former plantations, such as Magnolia Gardens and Middleton Place, welcomed tourists to their newly restored gardens. Most of the visitors were northerners, and many of the wealthier ones purchased derelict area plantations, which they restored and transformed into hunting preserves. Among the more notable figures who came to coastal Carolina in the 1930s were Solomon R. Guggenheim, who loaned to the Gibbes Museum of Art his collection of nonobjective painting for its inaugural exhibition; Archer M. and Anna Hyatt Huntington, who acquired various Allston family plantations to form Brookgreen Gardens; and Mr. and Mrs. Benjamin Kittredge, who transformed the old rice fields at Dean Hall plantation into Cypress Gardens.

Through words, melodies, pictures, and even a dance step, the idea of Charleston was broadcast across the nation. Although local residents realized that Charleston was undergoing a dramatic revitalization, the phrase "The Charleston Renaissance" did not get widespread usage until the 1980s, although the word "renaissance" occurred occasionally in newspaper accounts. The designation coalesced in 1985 when the Catfish Row Company sponsored a production of *Porgy and Bess* on the folk opera's fiftieth anniversary and the Gibbes Museum of Art mounted an exhibition, *Charleston in the Era of Porgy and Bess.* MARTHA R. SEVERENS

Hutchisson, James M., and Harlan Greene, eds. *Renaissance in Charleston: Art and Life in the Carolina Low Country, 1900–1940.* Athens: University of Georgia Press, 2003.

Severens, Martha R. *The Charleston Renaissance.* Spartanburg, S.C.: Saraland, 1998.

Worthington, Curtis. *Literary Charleston: A Lowcountry Reader.* Charleston, S.C.: Wyrick, 1996.

Charleston Riot (1876). As the crucial local, state, and national elections of 1876 approached, tensions between the races in South Carolina reached a boiling point. White Democrats sought to reclaim political power lost as a result of the Civil War and Reconstruction. Using violence, intimidation, economic blackmail, and fraud, Democrats attempted to cow blacks into submission to the old order. Five riots occurred in two counties of the state, Aiken and Charleston. In Aiken County the riots were usually white-on-black violence. In Charleston County they tended to be the other way around. Charleston County black Republicans were particularly incensed by Democratic attempts to induce black voters to leave the Republican Party and vote Democratic in 1876. In Charleston angry black Republicans resented the men from their race who changed sides, frequently threatening them with physical violence and often carrying out their threats. Democrats sought to protect their black recruits, thereby setting up confrontations with black Republican activists.

Matters came to a head in September 1876. On September 1 Democrats held a ward meeting, at which several blacks made fiery speeches denouncing the Republican Party. After the meeting, one of the speakers, a black porter named Isaac Rivers, was attacked. On September 6, fresh from their own ward meetings, black Republicans gathered at Archer's Hall to hear speeches made by their Democratic opponents. J. R. Jenkins, a black Democrat, angered the Republicans with a verbal assault that impugned the intelligence of black women who encouraged black men to vote the Republican ticket. A group of black Republicans pursued the white and black Democrats to the Citadel green, where one white man, fearing attack, fired a pistol in the air to frighten the Republicans. Instead, the action drew hundreds of additional black men to the spot, and a riot ensued with the Democrats retreating and asking for protection from federal troops stationed at the Citadel. As the night progressed, more and more black men roamed the city, their anger increasing. A full-scale riot ensued with blacks beating any white men they encountered. "For the next few days, Charleston was in turmoil as blacks continued to attack whites randomly, making it unsafe for whites to venture out on the streets, particularly at night." White opposition to the violence was modest and ineffective. Federal troops did not intervene. One black and one white died in the riot, while six policemen, a handful of blacks, and at least fifty whites were injured.

The activism and aggression against whites displayed by Charleston blacks set that city apart from others in the South during Reconstruction. While southern ports such as New Orleans and Mobile likewise experienced Reconstruction era riots, blacks tended to be the victims rather than the aggressors. Charleston's black community drew on its majority status in the city, as well as a tradition of militancy and violence that dated back to the Stono Rebellion and the Vesey conspiracy, to aggressively protect their newly found freedoms, including the right to vote and to hold political office. They had the numbers, as well as the political and racial consciousness, to do so until the end of Reconstruction in 1877. GLENNON GRAHAM

Hennessey, Melinda Meek. "Racial Violence during Reconstruction: The 1876 Riots in Charleston and Cainhoy." *South Carolina Historical Magazine* 86 (April 1985): 100–112.

Jenkins, Wilbert L. *Seizing the New Day: African Americans in Post–Civil War Charleston.* Bloomington: Indiana University Press, 1998.

Powers, Bernard E. *Black Charlestonians: A Social History, 1822–1885.* Fayetteville: University of Arkansas Press, 1994.

Charleston Riot (1919). This was the earliest major incident in a nationwide outbreak of racial violence that came to be known as the "Red Summer." Race riots bloodied the streets of some two dozen American communities between April and October 1919. The clashes were in large measure due to white fears over a newfound assertiveness demonstrated by the black servicemen returning from World War I, and paralleled the hysterical antiforeign, antiradical "Red Scare" of 1919 and 1920.

According to the May 11, 1919, edition of the Charleston *News and Courier,* trouble began when rumors spread that a black man had shot a white sailor in a local pool hall. White servicemen, accompanied by local whites, raided a shooting gallery and began attacking black passersby. Other African Americans responded with gunfire as several black businesses were destroyed by the rioters. United States Marines were ordered to detain all sailors at the navy yard, and some blacks were disarmed. By the time hostilities ceased that night, three African Americans were dead, seventeen were wounded, and seven white sailors had received severe injuries.

The newly formed Charleston branch of the National Association for the Advancement of Colored People (NAACP) called on the U.S. Navy to punish the sailors and to compensate black businessmen for their losses. They also asked Mayor Tristram Hyde for protection against future mobs, the hiring of black policemen, and the formation of an interracial committee to prevent future riots. Hyde agreed to all of these requests except the hiring of black policemen, thus providing the Charleston NAACP with their first partial victory. DAMON FORDHAM

Drago, Edmund L. *Initiative, Paternalism, and Race Relations: Charleston's Avery Normal Institute.* Athens: University of Georgia Press, 1990.

Waskow, Arthur. *From Race Riot to Sit-In, 1919 and the 1960s: A Study in the Connections between Conflict and Violence.* Garden City, N.Y.: Doubleday, 1966.

Charleston single house. The single house is the building form most closely associated with eighteenth-century Charleston architecture. It first appeared in the early eighteenth century and emerged as a favored residential form after the fire of 1740. The typical single house stands two or more stories in height and is built on a rectangular plan with its narrow end facing the street. Each floor has two rooms with a central stair-hall in between. Piazzas occupy the long wall facing the inside of the lot, and the chimneys are located on the opposite wall, in the rear of the house.

Architectural historians have devoted considerable study to the origins of the single house. The most common explanation holds that the form developed as a response to the hot and humid lowcountry summers and the scarcity of space in the urban environment. The tall, slender profile allowed breezes to circulate freely across the broad piazzas and through the main rooms. The orientation of the house removed it from direct engagement with the public street, secluding the occupants from the life of the city. In the words of the architectural historian Kenneth Severens, "As a freestanding house communicating more with a side garden than with the street, the single house offered a masterful but still vernacular solution to the residential problems of achieving comfort, privacy, and propriety." Gene Waddell, however, has suggested that fire protection was a more important consideration. Observing that the single house became popular after the fire that swept through the waterfront district in 1740, Waddell has argued that its freestanding form and nearly solid rear wall represented a departure from the paired dwellings and row houses of the colonial era and reflected a desire for increased fire protection in a dense urban environment. Another interpretation has been offered by Bernard Herman, who argued that the social and symbolic stature of the single house and the dependencies found in the rear—slave quarters, carriage houses, and outbuildings—effectively made it the urban equivalent of the plantation "big house." The organization of the lot placed formal social spaces nearest the street and utilitarian activities in the rear, while the house offered a vantage point for the occupants to keep watch over their domestic slaves and access in and out of the lot. Viewed in this context, the development of the single house reflected Charleston's role as the gateway between the world of Atlantic mercantilism and the lowcountry plantation landscape.

The single house is widely recognized as one of the most distinctive vernacular forms in the South. Numerous examples remain in the historic core of the city. Among those that illustrate the evolution of the form are the Charles Elliott House at 43 Legare Street (ca. 1759; altered in 1911); 90 and 94 Church Street (ca. 1760–1765); the Robert Pringle House at 70 Tradd Street (ca. 1774); the Simmons-Edwards House at 14 Legare Street (ca. 1800); and the Timothy Ford House at 54 Meeting Street (ca. 1800–1806). DANIEL J. VIVIAN

Herman, Bernard. "The Charleston Single House." In *The Buildings of Charleston: A Guide to the City's Architecture,* by Jonathan H. Poston. Columbia: University of South Carolina Press, 1997.

Severens, Kenneth. *Charleston Antebellum Architecture and Civic Destiny.* Knoxville: University of Tennessee Press, 1988.

Waddell, Gene. "The Charleston Single House . . . An Architectural Survey." *Preservation Progress* 22 (March 1977): 4–8.

Charleston Southern University. Charleston Southern University is a private, liberal arts university affiliated with the South Carolina Baptist Convention. Its roots can be traced to the 1950s, when interest in a Baptist college for the lowcountry became apparent among the churches in that area. Baptist leaders sought support for the effort to build a new college. Action by the South Carolina Baptist Convention in 1958 assured that if sufficient funds could be raised, consideration would be given to founding a college. It was initially proposed as an affiliate of Furman University.

In 1960 a charter for a college was obtained from the secretary of state, and in 1964 the South Carolina Baptist Convention accepted the new Baptist College at Charleston as an institution of the convention. The first students enrolled in January 1965, initially meeting in church facilities and housed in a downtown hotel. In September 1966 a new campus opened north of the city in Charleston County. The first bachelor's degrees were awarded in June 1968. Regional accreditation was received in December 1970. After a change of administration in 1984, an effort was initiated to select a less generic name that reflected both the heritage and the direction of the institution. In November 1990 the name Charleston Southern University was accepted. Its geography, its roots as a Southern Baptist institution, and its emerging role as a university were all reflected in the new name.

Charleston Southern has built on its mission, "promoting academic excellence in a Christian environment," by offering more than thirty undergraduate and graduate degree programs, thirty-five student organizations, and eighteen National Collegiate Athletic Association Division I athletic teams. With a 2001 enrollment of some 2,600 students, the school became South Carolina's second-largest accredited independent university. STUART R. SPRAGUE

King, Joe M. *A History of South Carolina Baptists.* Columbia: General Board of the South Carolina Baptist Convention, 1964.

Charleston Tea Plantation. Charleston Tea Plantation produces the only tea grown in the United States on Wadmalaw Island, thirty miles south of Charleston. The plantation is operated by William Barclay Hall, a third-generation tea-taster, and Mack Fleming, the horticulturist who developed the company's mechanical harvester for Lipton, the original developer of the land. It is planted with more than 125 acres of tea, *Camellia sinensis.* Tea and camellias have celebrated histories in South Carolina. Although Boston's Tea Party is more renowned, Charleston officials also confiscated British tea in the city's harbor. However, rather than destroying it, they hid it in the Old Exchange Building before secretly selling it to sympathizers of independence to fund the Revolutionary War effort. Ornamental camellias first arrived in America at Middleton Plantation near Charleston in 1799 with the French botanist André Michaux. Their popularity spread throughout the Republic, but South Carolina is the only state ever to have produced *Camellia sinensis* commercially.

Dr. Junius Smith first attempted tea cultivation in Greenville in 1848. He was successful at propagating the plants, but the operation ceased after his death in 1853. Dr. Alexis Forster was successful in Georgetown from 1874 to 1879, but his tea plants were similarly abandoned when he died. In 1888 Dr. Charles Shepard established the Pinehurst Tea Plantation in Summerville and gained fame for his oolong tea, which is partially oxidized. Thousands of plants were propagated from Shepard's cuttings and were planted near Rantowles, just south of Charleston, in 1903, but family disputes resulted in the dissolution of that venture in 1907. The present Charleston Tea Plantation was begun in 1963 by Thomas J. Lipton, scion of the tea magnate. Charleston Tea Plantation produces black tea, which is totally oxidized before being dried. In 2003 Bigelow Tea purchased the plantation, with plans to rename the operation Charleston Tea Gardens. Tea, the drink steeped from the leaves, is second in worldwide popularity after water. JOHN MARTIN TAYLOR

Rogers, Aida. "Tastiest Tea in North America: The Charleston Tea Plantation." *Sandlapper* 4 (autumn 1993): 30–34.

Walcott, Susan M. "Tea Production in South Carolina." *Southeastern Geographer* 39 (May 1999): 61–74.

Charter schools. South Carolina law defines a charter school as a "public, nonsectarian, nonreligious, nonhome-based, nonprofit corporation forming a school which operates within a public school district." Charter schools are semi-autonomous public schools that operate under contract with local school boards for a charter of three years. Nationally, the first charter school opened in 1991 in Minnesota. Five years later, in 1996, the South Carolina General Assembly and Governor David Beasley approved the Charter School Act, joining twenty-four other states that had authorized charter schools. State Superintendent of Education Inez Tenenbaum stated that "South Carolina charter schools offer avenues by which parents, teachers, and community members can take risks and create new, innovative and more flexible ways of educating their children within the public school system." In December 1997 the State Department of Education awarded four implementation grants of up to $150,000 each and eighteen planning grants of up to $40,000. Eight charter schools were in operation in South Carolina by the fall of 2001.

Charter schools are intended to improve learning, increase opportunities, encourage innovative teaching methods, establish new forms of accountability, create professional opportunities for teachers, and to generally assist South Carolina in reaching academic excellence. Charter schools are small. Across the nation, the median enrollment is 137 students per school. In South Carolina, per school enrollment ranges from 15 to 200 students with a mean of 70 students. Challenges faced by charter schools include start-up costs, obtaining suitable facilities, creating time for planning, maintaining cash flow, and attracting and maintaining staff and students. In South Carolina and the nation, supporters emphasize the ability of charter schools to stimulate change in the public education system, create a competitive market to force change, and highlight autonomy as a means of facilitating innovative educational models.

Critics argue that charter schools accelerate the "brain drain" effect on traditional schools, siphon off scarce financial support, and erode support for public schools. In 1997 the Beaufort County school board rejected an application for a proposed charter school, fearing that the new school would become "a white enclave in a district split almost evenly between blacks and whites." In 2000 a South Carolina judge ruled the state's charter school law unconstitutional due to its clause that the racial makeup of charter school enrollments cannot differ from that of its host school district by more than ten percent. Without racial quotas, however, many are concerned that charter schools have the potential to resegregate schooling. Such controversies have combined to limit the number of charter schools in South Carolina to just thirteen schools as of 2002, one of the lowest rates in the nation. Supporters, however, contend that charter schools are a response to the erosion of support for public education. In 1999 U.S. Secretary of Education Richard W. Riley, a former governor of South Carolina, declared, "The outpouring of involvement [in charter schools] is a testament to the American ideal of quality education for all, community service, and the power of grass roots efforts to bring about change." AMY DONNELLY

Bowman, Darcia Harris. "Judge Overturns South Carolina's Charter School Law." *Education Week* 19 (May 24, 2000): 25.

Smith, Gina. "Judges to Review Racial Quotas in Charter Schools." Columbia *State,* December 4, 2002, pp. A1, A9.

Sweeney, Nicole. "Charter School Offers Unique Alternative." Columbia *State,* December 15, 2002, pp. D1, D5.

United States. Department of Education. Office of Educational Research and Improvement. Education Resources Information Center. *A Study of Charter Schools.* Washington, D.C.: Government Printing Office, 1997–2000.

Weil, Danny. *Charter Schools: A Reference Handbook.* Santa Barbara, Calif.: ABC-Clio, 2000.

Chattooga River. The Chattooga River begins as springs and rivulets near Cashiers in the North Carolina mountains. It flows a narrow, twisting, mostly southwestwardly route before joining the Tallulah River in Lake Tugaloo. For most of its forty miles, the Chattooga forms the boundary between Georgia and South Carolina. It drops almost a half-mile as the land transitions from the Appalachians to the upper Piedmont. The Chattooga watershed includes approximately 278 square miles.

Native Americans favored hunting grounds near the Chattooga, and at least three Indian trails crossed the river. A small Cherokee settlement called Chattooga town was located near the modern S.C. Highway 28 bridge. The naturalists William Bartram and André Michaux described the flora and fauna of the area in the late eighteenth century. A few scattered white settlements appeared after 1830. By the early 1900s the Chattooga River was used to float logs stripped from the surrounding lands to mills downstream. The 1911 Weeks Law, which authorized the Forest Service to acquire land to form the Nantahala, Sumter, and Chattahoochee National Forests, helped protect the Chattooga's path through the three forests.

Through this protection, the Chattooga has remained one of the few free-flowing streams in the Southeast and has retained its primitive character. On May 10, 1974, Congress designated the Chattooga River a National Wild and Scenic River, the first east of the Mississippi. A protected corridor was created on both sides of the river. Sixty-eight percent of the Chattooga is classified as "wild" and five percent as "scenic." Twenty-seven percent of the river is classified for recreation. Outdoor enthusiasts flock to the Chattooga for its trout fishing, primitive camping, hiking, and floating. It is considered one of the best white-water rivers in the southern Appalachians, with challenging Class III to Class V rapids along the lower section. The river provided the location for the film *Deliverance.* There are five major access points along the river, but some concerns have arisen that increasing recreational use of the river will destroy its wild and scenic character. SUSAN GIAIMO HIOTT

Clay, Butch. *The Chattooga River Sourcebook: A Comprehensive Guide to the River and Its Natural History.* Birmingham, Ala.: Chattooga River Publishing, 1995.

Checker, Chubby (b. 1941). Singer. Chubby Checker was born Ernest Evans on October 3, 1941, in Spring Gully near Andrews, the son of a tobacco farmer. He moved to Philadelphia at age seven and later attended South Philadelphia High School with the future teen idols Fabian and Frankie Avalon. Evans attracted the attention of Dick Clark, host of the national television show *American Bandstand,* in the late 1950s. Clark wanted to send out a Christmas phonograph record to friends, one that consisted of holiday greetings from singers imitating rock and roll stars. Evans was in the studio doing these imitations when Clark's wife Bobbie noticed him and suggested dubbing him "Chubby Checker," a play on the name of the recording star Fats Domino.

After the Christmas record was released commercially as *The Class* in 1959 on the Cameo-Parkway label (partially owned by Clark), in 1960 Checker covered "The Twist," a song written and released previously by Hank Ballard. "The Twist" was associated with a dance that consisted of partners swiveling their hips and arms while standing apart from each other. This dance was unknown outside the African American community, where it had achieved some popularity. Clark noted some of his *American Bandstand* teenagers "twisting" and soon encouraged Cameo-Parkway to exploit this dance with a cover recording of the Ballard song. With television exposure on *American Bandstand* and on the *Ed Sullivan Show,* Checker's recording of "The Twist" became a huge hit and remained the biggest-selling single record of all time well into the 1970s. The associated dance craze crossed over to the mainstream and became an international phenomenon, spawning records of the same genre by many artists in the United States and abroad.

During the early 1960s Checker had thirty more chart hits. Eleven of these reached the top twenty, including a re-release of "The Twist" in 1962 that reached number one and made Checker the only artist to have had the same single song at number one on different releases. Other hits included "The Hucklebuck" (1960), "Pony Time" (1961), "Let's Twist Again" (1961), "The Fly" (1961), "Slow Twistin'" (1962), "Dancin' Party" (1962), "Popeye (The Hitchhiker)" (1962), "Limbo Rock" (1962), "Birdland" (1963), and "Loddy Lo" (1963). Many of these songs introduced new dance styles, and Checker maintains that he was the inventor of "dancing apart to the beat." In 1961 he was awarded a Grammy for Best Rock and Roll Recording ("Let's Twist Again").

As the dance craze era ended, Chubby Checker remade his image several times to match the changes in the music industry, but he did not return to the charts until 1988, with "The Twist (Yo Twist)," accompanied by the rap artists The Fat Boys. Checker has continued to tour and perform, relying on varying combinations of nostalgia and new material. He has repackaged himself as the rapper Chubby C.

Chubby Checker is, to some extent, an American icon. He has sold more than 250 million records and has appeared in at least twelve films and on numerous television shows, always playing himself. JOHN F. JAKUBS

Clark, Dick, and Richard Robinson. *Rock, Roll & Remember.* New York: Crowell, 1976.

Garofalo, Reebee. *Rockin' Out: Popular Music in the USA.* 2d ed. Upper Saddle River, N.J.: Prentice Hall, 2002.

Gillett, Charlie. *The Sound of the City: The Rise of Rock and Roll.* Rev. ed. London: Souvenir Press, 1983.

Chem-Nuclear Systems, L.L.C. Chem-Nuclear began operating a low-level radioactive waste disposal facility in Barnwell County in 1970. In accordance with legislation passed by the South Carolina General Assembly in 2000, the site will be closed on June 30, 2008, to all states other than South Carolina, New Jersey, and Connecticut, which are members of the Atlantic Interstate Low-Level Radioactive Waste Management Compact.

Chem-Nuclear was organized by a group of investors whose residences were overwhelmingly in Washington State. Because South Carolina had important nuclear reactors used to generate electricity, the Savannah River Site, and other activities that created low-level radioactive waste, it was considered a good state in which to locate a low-level radioactive waste disposal facility.

After the 1979 near-meltdown at Three Mile Island, Pennsylvania, and the federal Waste Policy Act of 1980, Chem-Nuclear faced regulatory pressure on the amount of waste it could accept. Between 1980 and 2000 the South Carolina General Assembly adopted several legislative proposals to reduce the volume of waste buried at the Barnwell site. In 2000 Governor James Hodges led the effort to close the site in 2008 to all except the Atlantic Compact members.

In 1982 Chem-Nuclear was acquired by Waste Management, Inc., of Chicago and remained a subsidiary of that corporation until 1998, when it was bought by Duratek, Inc., of Columbia, Maryland. Although Chem-Nuclear has operated other lines of business related to low-level radioactive waste, including trucking, research, nuclear reactor waste management and treatment, and waste reduction, by 2004 its operations were mostly limited to managing the functions at the Barnwell disposal facility. Throughout its history Chem-Nuclear has enjoyed support from the people in Barnwell because of its record of regulatory-environmental compliance and its contributions to the economic, civic, and educational life of Barnwell County. DONALD L. FOWLER

Cheraw (Chesterfield County; 2000 pop. 5,524). Cheraw is located at the head of navigation of the Great Pee Dee River. Before the arrival of European settlers, the Cheraw Indians maintained a village near the site. Decimated by smallpox in the 1730s, the Cheraws abandoned the region, leaving only their name at the small trading village. Europeans began moving into the area during this time. Most were of English descent, and many brought slaves along with their households. Others were Irish, Huguenots, or Scots. In the 1760s the merchants Joseph and Eli Kershaw laid out the present street system and town green. The Kershaws called the town Chatham, but the name never gained wide acceptance. Cheraw or Cheraw Hill continued to be used interchangeably with Chatham. Cheraw became the official name at the town's incorporation in 1820.

Cheraw's position on the Great Pee Dee made it an important point of trade and commerce from its inception. Corn, tobacco, indigo, and rice were grown in the more fertile land. Naval stores and cattle raising, with the related tanning and curing industries, were also major sources of income. Following the creation of St. David's Parish in 1768, the town became the site of the parish church, which was completed in 1774. During the Revolutionary War, Cheraw was part of the British line of defense that included Camden and Ninety Six. The British Seventy-first Highlanders held the town for a time, and General Nathanael Greene of the Continental army had his camp just across the river in the winter of 1780–1781. The war in this region was a true civil war and left the area devastated. Recovery was slow, and real growth did not occur in Cheraw until the advent of steam navigation on the Pee Dee.

Moses Rogers brought the first steamboat, *The Great Pee Dee,* to Cheraw in 1819. In 1823 the first covered bridge was built across the river. These improvements led to rapid growth in Cheraw. The remainder of the lots from Eli Kershaw's estate were auctioned, and over the next decade numerous homes and public buildings were constructed. By 1825 Cheraw was one of South Carolina's chief market towns, with 150 houses and between twelve hundred and thirteen hundred inhabitants. Twenty thousand bales of cotton were shipped from Cheraw annually. A fire destroyed much of the business district in 1835, but the railroad arrived in the 1850s and Cheraw continued as a regional center of business, culture, and religion.

During the Civil War, Cheraw was a haven for refugees and a repository for military stores. In March 1865 the town hosted the Union army of General William T. Sherman for several days. Although the business district was destroyed in an accidental explosion and there was widespread looting, no public buildings or dwellings were burned. The town was destitute after the war, but prosperity began to return by 1900 with the arrival of the timber industry and the expansion of railroads in the county. By 1922 Cheraw had a population of four thousand, two railroad lines, a cotton gin, a knitting mill, oil and lumber mills, machine shops, and brickworks. Cheraw bankers and cotton brokers built imposing colonial-revival residences. New public schools for both blacks and whites were built. Coulter Academy, a private boarding school, served the area's African American students. A drastic drop in cotton prices during the 1920s dealt Cheraw an economic blow, which was exacerbated by the Depression of the 1930s. The completion of U.S. Highway 1 in 1931 helped offset some of the decline, as did New Deal projects that created Cheraw State Park and Sand Hills State Forest.

In 1950 a serious effort was undertaken to recruit industry, and manufacturing plants began relocating to the Cheraw area. In the 1960s continuing recruitment and improvements in education and infrastructure attracted major industries. By the end of the century Cheraw had a healthy mix of textile, metal fabricating, and other manufacturing interests, many of which were owned by international companies. In the 1990s civic improvements including Arrowhead Park, a theater, a new library, and police and fire stations added to the quality of life. Cheraw has taken pride in its trees and in its historic district, 213 acres of which are listed on the National Register of Historic Places. While continuing to recruit new businesses, Cheraw also preserved its antebellum core, tree-lined streets, and town green. SARAH CAIN SPRUILL

Gregg, Alexander. *History of the Old Cheraws.* 1867. Reprint, Greenville, S.C.: Southern Historical Press, 1991.

Holcomb, Brent H. *St. David's Parish, South Carolina: Minutes of the Vestry, 1768–1832, Parish Register, 1819–1924.* Easley, S.C.: Southern Historical Press, 1979.

Johnson, George Lloyd, Jr. *The Frontier in the Colonial South: South Carolina Backcountry, 1736–1800.* Westport, Conn.: Greenwood, 1997.
Nelson, Larry E. "Sherman at Cheraw." *South Carolina Historical Magazine* 100 (October 1999): 328–54.

Cherokee County (393 sq. miles; 2000 pop. 52,537). With its county seat located at Gaffney, its largest town, Cherokee County was created in 1897. The county is named for the Cherokee Indians, who before the Revolutionary War used the area as one of their principal campgrounds. Carved out of Union, Spartanburg, and York Counties, Cherokee County was made possible by the coming of the railroad in 1873 and the simplified requirements to form new counties written into the South Carolina Constitution of 1895. The local secession movement, led by the citizens of the towns of Gaffney and Blacksburg and the townships of Limestone Springs, Draytonville, Gowdeysville, White Springs, and Morgan, won an election in December 1896, and Cherokee County was created by the General Assembly in January 1897.

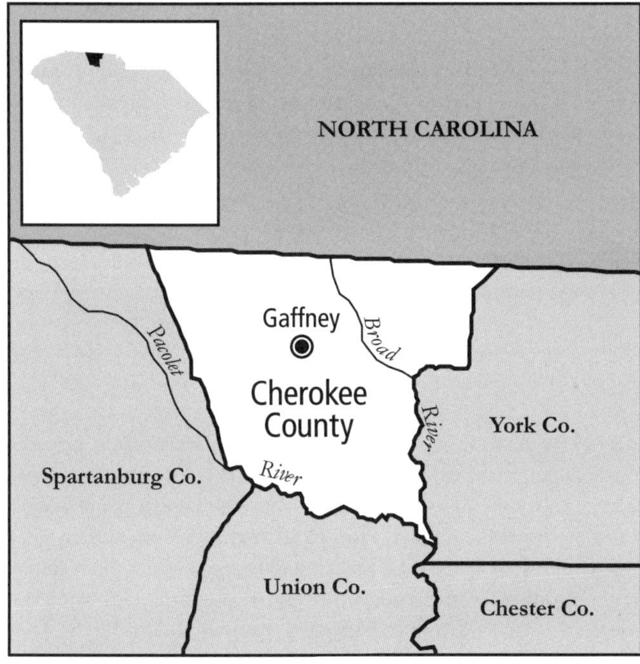

Cherokee's population, 21,359 in 1900, grew slowly and was concentrated in the northern part of the county. Despite an established agricultural economy and a developing textile industry, economic opportunities stagnated. In 1920 Cherokee had 27,570 residents, but the Depression and World War II delayed regional growth, and many sought opportunities elsewhere. By 1940 Cherokee had added only 6,000 people. It was not until 1980 that the population reached 40,983. Additional growth came between 1990 and 2000 as Cherokee added new industries and became a bedroom community for the adjacent counties of York and Spartanburg.

Economically, Cherokee was the heart of the "Old Iron District." The iron industry that had flourished in the 1700s and 1800s was gone by the end of the Civil War. In the 1880s iron production gave way to railroad construction. By 1880 the Atlanta and Charlotte Air Line crossed the county, establishing stations at Blacksburg and Gaffney. A flurry of local construction prepared hotels, restaurants, and shops for expected travelers. Following the railroad and dependent on its transportation facilities were textile mills, such as the Cherokee Falls Manufacturing Company (1882), the Gaffney Manufacturing Company (1892), Limestone Mills (1900), and Hamrick Mills (1907). These concerns, and others like them, were built by men such as J. A. Deal, Rufus P. Roberts, Joseph C. Plonk, L. Baker, Dr. Wylie C. Hamrick, and Adolphus N. Wood, who either lived in the community or moved there. They encouraged local investment in their mills, offered a more favorable wage than agriculture, provided improved living conditions, and furnished employment for thousands. However, many residents, especially those in the southern part of the county, were bound to agriculture and refused to sacrifice their way of life for the confinement of mill life. They continued to produce cotton and mixed grains as they had for nearly a century. Only the decline of cotton prices in the 1880s forced farmers to explore other options. One possibility that became a reality was fruit growing, particularly apples and peaches. These orchard crops had been tried successfully across the upstate and proved compatible with the soil and climate. By 1900 Cherokee had made a start by producing 364 bushels of peaches.

Meanwhile, textiles carried the county into the twentieth century, providing increased employment during the years of World War I and into the 1920s. New mills with modern technology suggested continued prosperity, but oversupply and decreased demand curtailed mill production by the late 1920s. Cherokee Falls and Gaffney Manufacturing survived but changed hands, and W. C. Hamrick's five mills, like the others, retrenched and consolidated. Over the next two decades, Cherokee experienced an extended economic downturn.

The Depression and its aftermath were softened somewhat by the peach. Production doubled from 1,572 bushels in 1910 to 3,302 bushels in 1920. The harvest of 1930 marketed 6,000 bushels, and the crop more than quadrupled by 1940. In 1950 Cherokee was responsible for 70,100 units of the state's total. The county began with 32,079 peach trees in 1900, and by 1940 county orchards contained 150,000 trees. This number doubled ten years later, and by 1982 Cherokee produced ten percent of South Carolina's peaches and shipped nearly 35 million pounds out of state. At the beginning of the twenty-first century, the county was exceeded in production only by Edgefield, Spartanburg, and Saluda, helping to make South Carolina the second-largest peach producer in the United States. Symbolic of the presence of this valuable fruit is the giant peach water tower near Interstate 85 and the annual South Carolina Peach Festival. Begun in 1976 as a one-day celebration, the festival—noted for the largest peach pie and the largest peach milkshake in the world—grew into a ten-day celebration and established new attendance records every year until 1995.

The growth of the interstate system in the 1960s enhanced efforts at diversification. Textiles briefly blossomed anew and trucking, food processing, industrial metalwork, truck and dairy farms, and woodcutting joined a list of new industries that found Cherokee's location attractive. By 2000, 44.3 percent of the population was engaged in manufacturing with 18.2 percent in trade, as opposed to 10.3 percent and 5.1 percent, respectively, in 1900. Agriculture, which had dominated the county at the turn of the century, had declined markedly, except for peaches. Cherokee's citizens by the 1990s were engaged in a building boom, providing services and governmental oversight in addition to traditional roles in the manufacturing, wholesale, and retail professions. Part of the growing world of services are those offered by the county's historical sites and recreational areas. Among the most widely known are Kings Mountain and Cowpens, the sites of two decisive American victories over the British in the Revolutionary War. Also important are the

Adam Goudelock house (1780), the John Nuckles house (1790), the Robert Scruggs house (1787), and the single-room Possum Trott School. The world of Possum Trott, which permitted students in Cherokee to leave school at the age of fourteen to join the workforce, is past. Now the county's growing dependence on higher education is symbolized by institutions such as Limestone College in Gaffney. LOUIS P. TOWLES

Cherokee County. Gaffney, S.C.: Cherokee County Chamber of Commerce, 2000.

Johnson, Elmer Douglas. *A Brief History of Cherokee County, South Carolina.* Gaffney, S.C.: Chamber of Commerce, 1952.

Moss, Bobby G. *The Old Iron District: A Study of the Development of Cherokee County, 1750–1897.* Clinton, S.C.: Jacobs, 1972.

Cherokee Foothills Scenic Highway. The 112-mile Cherokee Foothills Scenic Highway provides a richly attractive alternative to Interstate 85, with which it links at each end—at the Georgia state line in southern Oconee County and in the city of Gaffney in Cherokee County. In between, the highway rises through the foothills of the Blue Ridge Mountains in northern Oconee, Pickens, and Greenville Counties and across the rolling terrain of Spartanburg and Cherokee Counties. Yet, the road also provides a vital transportation route for the growing number of residents, industries, and commercial businesses located in the northernmost parts of the state.

In addition to the scenic vistas of Table Rock, Hogback, Caesars Head, Glassy, Sassafras, and numerous smaller mountains, the Cherokee Foothills Scenic Highway passes many of the region's major waterways. Often called the "freshwater coast," the area includes Lake Keowee, Lake Hartwell, and Lake Jocassee, as well as the Oolenoy, South Saluda, Middle Saluda, North Saluda, South Pacolet, and North Pacolet Rivers. Many roadside waterfalls are accessible from the highway, including Whitewater Falls, Issaqueena Falls, Raven Cliff, Wildcat Creek Falls, and Blythe Shoals Falls.

The Cherokee Foothills Scenic Highway delivers travelers to numerous recreational opportunities. It passes seven state parks: Lake Hartwell, Oconee, Devil's Fork, Keowee-Toxaway, Table Rock, Caesars Head, and Jones Gap. Many summer camps also are reached from the highway. The area is culturally rich as the ancestral home of the Cherokees, who called the mountains "the Great Blue Hills of God." Historic sites such as Cowpens National Battlefield, Oconee Station, Campbell's Covered Bridge, and the Poinsett Bridge document the white settlers in the region.

The Cherokee Foothills route was designated a Scenic Highway in 1976. It became a National Scenic Byway in 1998, making it eligible for federal money for road improvements, scenic pullovers, and special enhancements. SUSAN GIAIMO HIOTT

Morgan, Laura E. "A Visual Analysis, Development Guidelines and Management Plan for the Cherokee Foothills Scenic Highway." Master's thesis, Clemson University, 1994.

"33 Roads Selected for Special Designations." Charleston *Post and Courier,* June 14, 1998, p. B8.

Cherokee Path. The Cherokee Path was one of the most important trade networks of early Carolina, connecting the city of Charleston with the Cherokee Indians of South Carolina, Georgia, North Carolina, and Tennessee. Access to the tribe was originally by way of the Savannah River, over which Charleston merchants conveyed their goods to Savannah Town (Augusta). Here, Native American nations bought and resold these goods, eventually putting them into Cherokee hands either through a trail that led from Savannah Town to Keowee, the first of the Cherokee lower towns, or via the Creek Indians of northern Georgia.

Following the Yamassee War (1715–1718), the trade between the English and Cherokees shifted eastward. Traders moved northward along the Santee River to Fort Congaree and then northwest through Saluda Old Town and Ninety Six to the Dividing Path on the Savannah River. Here, a trail to the west led to Cherokee villages along the Tugaloo River and to the Creeks, but the more traveled northern path alongside the Chattooga and Little Tennessee Rivers accessed the Cherokee lower, middle, and upper settlements, a total of at least sixty villages and upward of eleven thousand inhabitants in 1715.

These towns produced quality deer hides, pelts, baskets, and chestnuts. At first they delivered these goods to neutral trade depots such as Fort Congaree. But increased demand for metal trade goods, red cloth, muskets, ammunition, and powder led to the establishment of trade stations among the lower villages and the middle towns. Fort Prince George was built at Keowee in 1753 to protect the trade.

The Cherokee Path, hundreds of miles long and yet only a trail, was gradually improved. Horses replaced Indian bearers, and inns were opened along the way to accommodate the traders, travelers, settlers, and soldiers who made the trail their own. LOUIS P. TOWLES

Crane, Verner. *The Southern Frontier, 1670–1732.* Durham, N.C.: Duke University Press, 1928.

Hatley, M. Thomas. *The Dividing Paths: Cherokees and South Carolinians through the Era of the Revolution.* New York: Oxford University Press, 1993.

Meriwether, Robert. *The Expansion of South Carolina, 1729–1765.* Kingsport, Tenn.: Southern Publishers, 1940.

Cherokee War (1759–1761). The Cherokee War was partly a local, southeastern phase of the French and Indian War (1754–1763) and partly the result of the Cherokees' long-held resentments against abuses by English colonists. Prior to 1759 the Cherokees were allied with the English against the French and many served as mercenaries on the Virginia frontier. Around 1755 the Cherokee population was between 7,700 and 9,000, including women and children. They lived in the Piedmont and Appalachian valleys of Virginia and the Carolinas and were divided geographically into lower, middle, and upper towns. Tensions along the western frontier produced isolated incidents of violence between the Cherokees and European settlers. The conflict that led to war began in Virginia in late 1758, when settlers attacked and killed several Cherokee warriors returning from battles against the French. The Cherokees retaliated in North Carolina in spring 1759, and the conflict spread southward.

Militia soldiers at Fort Prince George in South Carolina abused local Cherokee women and sparked reprisals in which South Carolina settlers were killed. In Charleston, Governor William Lyttelton met a Cherokee delegation, led by headmen Oconostota and Osteneco. Lyttelton took the headmen and their companions hostage and carried them along with an expeditionary force of nearly thirteen hundred men up to Fort Prince George. There he negotiated a treaty, signed on December 22, 1759, which provided for Cherokee headmen to be kept hostage until several known Cherokee murderers were surrendered. The treaty did not secure peace. On February 1, 1760, warriors attacked a train of refugees near Long Cane Creek. Two weeks later Oconostota, a signer of the Lyttelton treaty and a former Fort Prince George hostage, set an ambush for Lieutenant Richard Cotymore, commander of the fort. Luring Cotymore from the fort, the Cherokees attacked. Cotymore died, and the garrison executed their remaining hostages in revenge. Governor Lyttelton requested British troops to assist the war effort and then returned to England, leaving the colony in the hands of Lieutenant Governor William Bull, Jr.

Colonel Archibald Montgomery and sixteen hundred British soldiers marched into upcountry South Carolina in April and May 1760 to defeat the Cherokees. Montgomery's troops burned Estatoe and other lower towns and relieved the garrison at Fort Prince George. Montgomery returned to Charleston convinced that the frontier had been pacified. However, the tribes of the upper towns continued their warfare and laid siege to Fort Loudoun, near the French Broad River, in present-day Tennessee. On August 8, 1760, the besiegers, led by Oconostota, offered the garrison safe passage to Fort Prince George. But once the troops were outside the fort, the Cherokees attacked, killing its commander, Captain Paul Demere, and twenty-three others (the number of hostages killed at Fort Prince George), and they took many captives. Governor Bull took two courses of action. He negotiated to ransom hostages and prepared another expedition.

In May and June 1761 Colonel James Grant, a Scot who had served with Montgomery, led an expedition of more than 2,400 troops to subdue the middle and upper towns. Grant's troops defeated Cherokee forces and systematically destroyed towns and crops. Fifteen towns and fifteen thousand acres of crops were destroyed, breaking the Cherokees' power to wage war. By July the Cherokees were defeated, and they negotiated a treaty, which was signed in Charleston on September 23, 1761. By these treaty terms, both Cherokees and colonists agreed to exchange captives. Little Carpenter, a pro-English headman, was named emperor of the Cherokees, and all Frenchmen in Cherokee territory were to be expelled. Finally, a dividing line was established that separated the Cherokees from South Carolina lands. In the division, the lower towns lost much of their hunting lands to Carolina settlers. James Adair, an Indian trader and sympathizer, recorded in his *History of the American Indians* (1775) that after the war the Cherokee population had been reduced to 2,300 warriors or about 6,900 in number. ALEXANDER MOORE

Alden, John Richard. *John Stuart and the Southern Colonial Frontier: A Study of Indian Relations, War, Trade, and Land Problems in the Southern Wilderness, 1754–1775.* 1944. Reprint, New York: Gordian, 1966.

Anderson, William L. "Cherokee War (1759–1761)." In *Colonial Wars of North America, 1512–1763,* edited by Alan Gallay. New York: Garland, 1996.

Corkran, David H. *The Cherokee Frontier: Conflict and Survival, 1740–1762.* Norman: University of Oklahoma Press, 1962.

Hatley, M. Thomas. *The Dividing Paths: Cherokees and South Carolinians through the Era of Revolution.* New York: Oxford University Press, 1993.

Oliphant, John. *Peace and War on the Anglo-Cherokee Frontier, 1756–1763.* Baton Rouge: Louisiana State University Press, 2001.

Cherokee War (1776). The Cherokee War of 1776 was an early episode in the Revolutionary War. In the summer of 1775 John Stuart, British superintendent of Indian affairs for the southern district, left his home in Charleston and moved to Florida. From there he worked to preserve the allegiance to Great Britain of the Cherokees and other Native American tribes. Stuart's assistant superintendent, Alexander Cameron, established a base of operations among the Cherokees and directed their actions against the Whigs. Combined with backcountry Loyalists, the Indians would prove a formidable force to be used against the rebels.

The Cherokees were the most powerful tribe in the region and the first to take action. The start of the Cherokee War dates from July 1, 1776, when the Cherokees struck along the western frontier. Isolated farmsteads in Ninety Six and Spartan Districts were overrun and the inhabitants killed. The backcountry militia leaders Andrew Williamson, Francis Salvador, and Andrew Pickens gathered their units and marched against the Cherokees. At Lyndley's Fort on July 15, settlers near the Saluda River were besieged by the Cherokees and Loyalists. The attackers were driven off and several men captured. On examination they were discovered to be white men dressed and painted in Cherokee fashion.

Under directions from Charleston, Williamson and other upcountry militia captains undertook a campaign to destroy Cherokee resistance. Whig militia traveled from town to town destroying buildings and crops and dispersing the populations. By the end of the summer, Cherokee resistance was broken and the British plan to direct Indian allies against the Whigs was defeated.

The summer campaign produced two notable engagements. On August 1, 1776, a combined Loyalist and Cherokee force, led by Alexander Cameron, ambushed Andrew Williamson at Esseneca Ford, also called Seneca Old Town. Williamson's command of 330 faced as many as 1,200 Cherokees and Loyalists, who hid behind palisades. Initially driven back, the Whigs lost one of their leaders, Captain Francis Salvador of Ninety Six. Lieutenant Colonel Leroy Hammond and a troop of horsemen counterattacked and held off the Cherokees long enough for Williamson to regroup. The timely arrival of Andrew Pickens with reinforcements turned the tide of battle. Cameron and his force retreated but were pursued by the Whigs, who burned every Cherokee village and field they discovered.

About two weeks after the Esseneca battle, Williamson was made a colonel of militia and given command of a combined force of Georgians and South Carolinians. His command systematically destroyed the lower towns of the Cherokees. On August 12 Andrew Pickens and twenty-five men were ambushed by the Cherokees at Tamassee, in present-day Oconee County. As the Cherokees emerged from the woods, Pickens ordered his men to form a defensive circle. Hand-to-hand fighting and high casualties on both sides marked the "Ring Fight" as the most desperate of the war. Pickens lost eleven men, and the Cherokees suffered sixty-five killed and fourteen wounded warriors left behind.

By the fall of 1776 the major campaign of the war had concluded. The Cherokees lost as many as two thousand killed and, despite continued British support, could fight no longer. The following spring a Cherokee delegation led by Attakulla Kulla met with officials from North and South Carolina, Georgia, and Virginia at Dewitt's Corner, in Ninety Six District. They signed a treaty on May 20, 1777, that included a cease-fire and a cession of much of the Cherokee lands within present-day Anderson, Oconee, and Pickens Counties. A few Cherokees refused to recognize the treaty. They continued raids along the Carolina-Indian border until the conclusion of the Revolutionary War. ALEXANDER MOORE

Gordon, John W. *South Carolina and the American Revolution: A Battlefield History.* Columbia: University of South Carolina Press, 2003.

Hatley, M. Thomas. *The Dividing Paths: Cherokees and South Carolinians through the Era of Revolution.* New York: Oxford University Press, 1993.

Lumpkin, Henry. *From Savannah to Yorktown: The American Revolution in the South.* Columbia: University of South Carolina Press, 1981.

Cherokees. The Cherokees were one of the largest southeastern Native American nations with which Carolina colonists had contact. Modern descendants are in three federally recognized groups, including the Eastern Band Cherokee of western North Carolina. When combined, the Cherokees constitute one of the largest Indian nations in the United States.

A Cherokee Indian embassy to England, 1730. Courtesy, South Caroliniana Library, University of South Carolina

Cherokee tradition holds that the Creator placed the Cherokees in the southeastern mountains. Archaeological and linguistic evidence indicates that the Cherokees were at one time a people living in and around the Great Lakes region of North America. The Cherokees arrived in the southeastern United States around 1400 C.E., leaving the Great Lakes after conflicts with the Iroquois and Delawares. At the time of European contact, their sphere of influence encompassed most of northwestern South Carolina and stretched north and west to the Ohio River to include most of Kentucky and Tennessee as well as parts of West Virginia, Virginia, North Carolina, Georgia, and Alabama. By the mid–seventeenth century, Cherokee settlements in South Carolina, known as the lower towns, included Seneca, Keowee, Toxaway, and Jocassee.

Stable villages were possible because of the Cherokees' reliance on agriculture, especially corn. Agriculture was the domain of Cherokee women, and women retained important positions in Cherokee decision-making and politics. Men focused their attention on hunting and trade. The Cherokee towns scattered through the Appalachians, although politically autonomous, comprised an extensive trade network thanks in part to numerous rivers navigable by canoes.

European traders moved into Cherokee country soon after they established permanent settlements on the South Carolina coast. There they acted as both businessmen and diplomats, often working for the governors of Carolina. During the Yamassee War, the trader Eleazar Wiggan urged the Cherokees to fight in support of the Charleston settlers. Some Cherokees came to the Carolinians' aid, but others did not feel that the Carolinians fulfilled their treaty obligations. After the Yamassee War, Carolina-Cherokee trade became easier. Although, like most southern tribes, the Cherokees supplied Charleston merchants with deerskins, the finely crafted baskets made by Cherokee women commanded the highest exchange rates.

In the spring of 1730 Sir Alexander Cuming took a small delegation of Cherokees to London to cement a recent allegiance to King George II. Presented at court on June 18, 1730, they were described as being "naked, except an Apron about their middles, and a Horse's Tail hung down behind; their Faces, shoulders &c. were painted and spotted with red, blue, and green etc."

By midcentury the international rivalry among Spain, France, and England was intensifying, and the Cherokees felt the impact of that struggle. When Cherokee leaders notified Governor James Glen in the fall of 1746 that outlying Cherokees near the Mississippi River were being influenced by the French and their Indian allies, Glen recommended that the English build a chain of forts through the territory of their Indian allies. Eventually the Carolina government constructed Fort Prince George and Fort Loudoun, located in modern Pickens, South Carolina, and Loudon, Tennessee, respectively. Fort Prince George became a source of confrontation in 1759, after soldiers at the fort abused Cherokees in the area and Cherokees retaliated against settlers. Tenuous peace came with a Cherokee surrender in 1761, but the Revolutionary War sparked additional border conflict.

During the Revolutionary War, British and patriot agents vied for Cherokee trade and support. Despite overtures from both groups, most Cherokees sided with the British in the Revolution. When colonists settled on Cherokee lands in the Holston River Valley of northeastern Tennessee, Cherokee forces attacked their settlements. As a result, patriot leaders throughout the Southeast called for their destruction. A multicolony army assembled in 1776 to attack Cherokee towns and food stores. At one Cherokee town in South Carolina, the army destroyed six thousand bushels of corn and the South Carolina government paid this army a bounty for Cherokee scalps. This full-scale assault effectively ended Cherokee participation in the Revolutionary War, and in 1777 the Cherokees ceded most of their South Carolina land. The Cherokees acknowledged the United States in the Treaty of Hopewell in 1785, signed near present-day Seneca. On March 22, 1816, the Cherokees ceded their last strip of land in South Carolina. MICHAEL P. MORRIS

Hatley, M. Thomas. *The Dividing Paths: Cherokees and South Carolinians through the Era of Revolution.* New York: Oxford University Press, 1993.

Kelly, James C. "Notable Persons in Cherokee History: Attakulla Kulla." *Journal of Cherokee Studies* 3 (winter 1978): 2–34.

Mails, Thomas E. *The Cherokee People: The Story of the Cherokees from Earliest Origins to Contemporary Times.* Tulsa, Okla.: Council Oak, 1992.

Morris, Michael. *The Bringing of Wonder: Trade and the Indians of the Southeast, 1700–1783.* Westport, Conn.: Greenwood, 1999.

Perdue, Theda, and Michael Green. *The Cherokee Removal: A Brief History with Documents.* Boston: Bedford, 1995.

Chesnut, James, Jr. (1815–1885). U.S. senator, soldier. Born on January 18, 1815, at Camden, Chesnut was the son of James Chesnut, one of South Carolina's wealthiest planters, and Mary Cox. Chesnut attended local schools before entering the College of New Jersey (Princeton) as a sophomore in 1832. He gave the valedictory address at his graduation in 1835. Returning home, Chesnut sought a position as aide to the governor but at his father's insistence read law at the Charleston office of James L. Petigru. He was admitted to the bar in 1837 and began to practice law in Camden. With the death of his older brother in 1839, James became the heir apparent to his father's vast fortune. On April 23, 1840, James married Mary Boykin Miller of Stateburg. The couple had no children.

Chesnut served as representative from Kershaw District in the S.C. House of Representatives from 1840 to 1845 and from 1850 to 1851. He attended the Nashville Convention in 1850, served as a presidential elector in 1856, and was a trustee of South Carolina College between 1853 and 1858. He was elected to the S.C. Senate in 1852, serving as its president from 1856 to 1858. On December 3, 1858, he was elected to fill the U.S. Senate seat vacated by the death of Josiah J. Evans. Chesnut was considered a moderate in

South Carolina politics. He was a strong defender of slavery and states' rights but saw secession as viable only as a last resort and with the complete cooperation of other southern states.

Following the election of Abraham Lincoln, Chesnut resigned his seat on November 10, 1860, the first southern senator to do so. The Senate refused to accept the resignation and later expelled him with other southern senators. Chesnut returned home and became a delegate to the Secession Convention, where he served on the committee that drafted the ordinance. The convention elected Chesnut as a delegate to the Confederate Provisional Congress in January 1861, where he served on the committee writing the Confederate constitution. In the initial crisis at Fort Sumter, Chesnut served as a volunteer aide (with the rank of colonel) to General Pierre G. T. Beauregard and was part of the delegation that demanded the fort's surrender on April 12, 1861. He also served on Beauregard's staff in Virginia at the first Battle of Bull Run on July 21, 1861.

In November, Chesnut failed to win election to the permanent Confederate Congress due to his reluctance to promote himself for the seat. Increasing concerns over the leadership abilities of Governor Francis Pickens led the secession convention to reconvene in December and create an executive council to direct the affairs of the state. On January 7, 1862, Chesnut was elected to the council and became chief of the Military Department, a position that effectively supplanted the governor as the state's commander in chief.

Jefferson Davis commissioned Chesnut as an aide-de-camp with the rank of colonel on April 19, 1862, and asked him to come to Richmond. But Chesnut remained in South Carolina, where through the council he implemented measures to raise troops for the war and increase the readiness of the militia. Chesnut also led the council's efforts to furnish slave labor for building coastal defenses and the production of scarce niter for gunpowder. After the demise of the council on December 18, 1862, Chesnut traveled to Richmond to take his place on Davis's staff. His duties involved advising the Confederate president on military matters, visiting the various departments and reporting on military conditions, and acting as a liaison with the South Carolina government. On April 23, 1864, he was appointed brigadier general and assigned to command the reserve troops in South Carolina, a position he held through the remainder of the war.

His father's death in 1866 left Chesnut with extensive landholdings but even larger debts from which he never recovered. He remained politically active, serving as a delegate to the 1868 Democratic National Convention and participating in the 1871 and 1874 Taxpayers' Conventions. He opposed the policies and corruption of the Reconstruction governments and strongly supported Wade Hampton's 1876 gubernatorial race. Although he had applied for a pardon in 1865, it was not granted until 1878. He died in Camden on February 1, 1885, and was buried at the family cemetery at Knight's Hill. PATRICK MCCAWLEY

Tollison, Marjorie Spelts. "James Chesnut, Jr." Master's thesis, University of South Carolina, 1954.

Muhlenfeld, Elisabeth. *Mary Boykin Chesnut: A Biography.* Baton Rouge: Louisiana State University Press, 1981.

Chesnut, Mary Boykin Miller (1823–1886). Diarist. Chesnut was born on her father's plantation near Stateburg in Sumter District on March 31, 1823. She is recognized as "the preeminent writer of the Confederacy" because of the diary she kept during the Civil War and revised for publication in the early 1880s. No other southern writer of her era possessed the combination of literary cultivation, psychological perception, opportunity to observe closely the upper echelons of the Confederacy, and a willingness to write candidly about people, events, and issues—including slavery. The resulting publication, much revised and more appropriately labeled a memoir, secured her place in southern literary history.

Mary Boykin Chesnut. Courtesy, South Caroliniana Library, University of South Carolina

Chesnut was the eldest child of Stephen Decatur Miller and Mary Boykin. Her father, a leader in the states' rights campaign, was elected governor in 1828 and U.S. senator in 1830. Thus, she grew up in a political environment. She received as good an education as could be provided a southern girl of her day, first at home and then at Madame Talvande's French School for Young Ladies in Charleston, where she acquired all of the intellectual and social equipment needed to flourish in her milieu. Her father's death in 1838 ended her carefree childhood, and she soon accepted a marriage proposal from James Chesnut, Jr., whom she had met in Charleston. They were married on April 23, 1840; she was barely seventeen.

Her new home, Mulberry, the baronial Chesnut plantation just south of Camden, was dominated by her parents-in-law, who would live twenty-five more years. Childless, Mary found little satisfaction and suffered bouts of depression and illness in this unfulfilling setting. She regarded her father-in-law, James Chesnut, Sr., as a tyrant and was appalled at the liberties he took with his female slaves. Although the couple moved to their own house in Camden in 1848, it was not until her husband's election to the U.S. Senate in 1858 that she found a society that suited her gifts and her zest for life. In Washington she flourished as a charming literary lady and valuable asset to her husband, attracting the admiration of several prominent men and arousing her husband's jealousy. Among her intimate friends was Varina Davis, wife of the senator and future Confederate president Jefferson Davis. When the secession of South Carolina ended this idyllic life after only two years, Chesnut quickly became an ardent southern patriot.

Chesnut began keeping a diary in February 1861, confessing regret that she had not done so earlier. James's prominent role in the new Confederacy carried her to the centers of action and allowed her to witness and record her impressions of those dramatic times. She was in Montgomery, Alabama, while the provisional Confederate government was being formed, in Charleston for the bombardment of Fort Sumter, and in Richmond when the new government moved to its permanent capitol. All the while she recorded her perceptive observations of people and events, and the frustrations of a spirited woman in a world of men, many of whom she considered too "discrete, cautious, lazy for the roles they were playing." The couple returned to South Carolina in 1862 as James became chairman of the state's Executive Council. James, urged on by Mary, accepted a post as aide to President Davis in December, and again in Richmond she experienced and wrote about the highs and lows of war. The death of her mother-in-law in 1864 brought them home again to care for his father, now ninety-three and blind.

In early 1865 Union forces ravaged Mulberry and the Chesnuts took refuge in North Carolina and then in Chester, South Carolina. After the war James inherited his father's property but also large debts. A butter-and-egg business provided the little cash they had for some time, but they grew closer as a couple. Since her father-in-law's will left his property to his son and, on James's death (he died in 1885), to his grandsons, Chesnut found security only in the new Camden home built for her in the early 1870s. There she completed the revisions and extensions of her war diary by the mid-1880s. However, before it was published, Mary Chesnut died of a heart attack on November 22, 1886. She was buried next to her husband in Knight's Hill Cemetery in Camden. JAMES O. FARMER, JR.

DeCredico, Mary A. *Mary Boykin Chesnut: A Confederate Woman's Life.* Madison, Wis.: Madison House, 1996.

Muhlenfeld, Elisabeth. *Mary Boykin Chesnut: A Biography.* Baton Rouge: Louisiana State University Press, 1981.

Woodward, C. Vann, ed. *Mary Chesnut's Civil War.* New Haven, Conn.: Yale University Press, 1981.

Woodward, C. Vann, and Elisabeth Muhlenfeld, eds. *The Private Mary Chesnut: The Unpublished Civil War Diaries.* New York: Oxford University Press, 1984.

Chester (Chester County; 2000 pop. 6,476). In 1791 Chesterville (shortened to Chester in the nineteenth century) was surveyed to be the Chester County seat. Both the town and county were named after Chester County, Pennsylvania, where many of the area's first European settlers originated. By the early 1800s the village boasted a courthouse, a jail, and male and female academies. The site was incorporated as a town in 1849 and received a city charter in 1889.

In the antebellum era Chester grew slowly around the property of the Stewart family, and by 1835 it contained at least twelve buildings, including the courthouse and a Baptist church. The arrival of the Charlotte and South Carolina Railroad in 1851 brought prosperity and prominence to Chester and gave local farmers the opportunity to send their crops to markets across the state. In 1852 a new courthouse was constructed and the state legislature chartered the Bank of Chester, which opened for business the next year. During the Civil War, the Chester railroad depot was a stopping point for Confederate wounded returning from battlefields throughout the South.

In 1879 the state allowed Chester County schools to incorporate into the Chester Graded School, making it the second such school in the state when it opened its doors the following year. In 1888 local entrepreneurs organized Chester's first cotton mill, the Chester Manufacturing Company, which commenced operations with one hundred looms and its own dye works. City leaders constructed a second cotton mill in 1900, the Wylie Mill, which was eventually acquired by Springs Industries. As in most of the surrounding county, textile mills remained the dominant industrial employer well into the next century.

During the first decades of the twentieth century, Chester steadily added the trappings of a modern, progressive city. The city already possessed its own modern communications network, the Chester Telephone Company, organized in 1897. Dr. S. W. Pryor established the Magdelene Hospital in 1904. After a fire destroyed the hospital in 1916, it was replaced by the Pryor Hospital. City bond issues in 1920 and 1922 paved most of the streets in Chester and built a new high school, which opened in 1924. In the decades following World War II, both the city and county of Chester worked for economic diversification to reduce reliance on two dominant employers, the textile giants Springs Industries and J. P. Stevens. In the early 1960s city and county leaders established the Chester County Board of Commerce, which attracted new manufacturers, such as Schlegel Corporation and Sun Chemical Corporation. A boost to the morale and economy of Chester came in 1983 when the city became the setting for a CBS television miniseries, "Chiefs," based on Stuart Wood's 1981 best-seller. Film production provided a welcome diversion for Chesterites at a time when declines in agriculture and the textile industry left the local economy in the doldrums. RON CHEPESIUK

Chepesiuk, Ronald. *Chester County: A Pictorial History.* Norfolk, Va.: Donning, 1984.

Chepesiuk, Ronald, Gina Price White, and J. Edward Lee. *Along the Catawba River.* Charleston, S.C.: Arcadia, 1999.

Chester County (581 sq. miles; 2000 pop. 34,068). Named for Chester County, Pennsylvania, Chester was one of seven counties created in 1785 from the old Camden Judicial District. Situated in the rolling hills of South Carolina's eastern Piedmont, Chester is bounded on the east by the Catawba River and on the west by the Broad River. Unlike other counties established at the same time, Chester's dimensions have never been altered, and its distinct rectangular shape is unique among South Carolina counties. The county seat of Chesterville (later Chester) was created in 1791.

Prior to European settlement, the Chester region served as a buffer between the powerful Catawba and Cherokee Indian nations. The land teemed with large game and was used as a hunting ground by both tribes. Around 1750 Scots-Irish immigrants from Pennsylvania and Virginia began arriving. Settlement, however, was slow. Despite agreements reached between the new arrivals and native inhabitants, Chester County was still a dangerous place. For protection, early settlers built two forts, Steel's Fort on Fishing Creek and Taylor's Fort at Lands Ford.

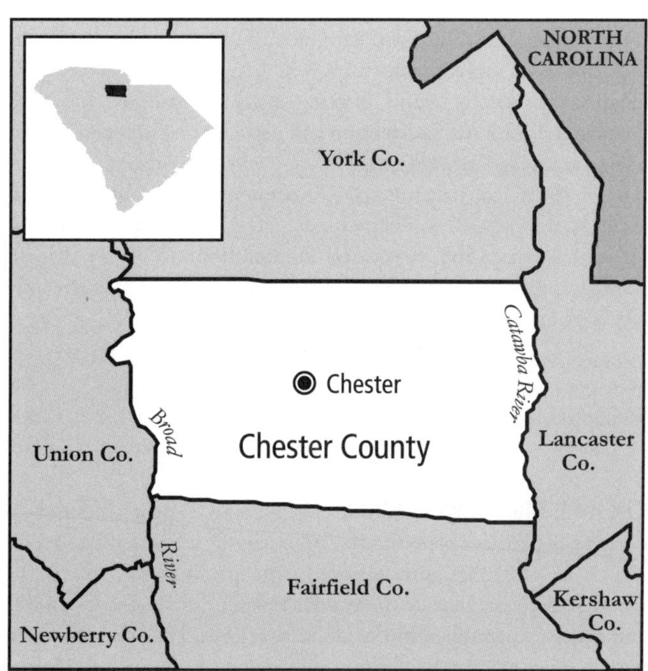

Despite early hardships, the tide of immigration continued until the Revolutionary War, when the citizens of the future county played their role in defeating the British in South Carolina. Battles in the area, such as at Fishdam Ford (November 9, 1780), where patriot forces under Thomas Sumter routed a redcoat detachment, demoralized the British and foreshadowed their major defeat at Cowpens, which marked the turning point in the war of the South.

Redesignated as a district at the start of the nineteenth century, Chester grew at a moderate pace and joined neighboring districts in establishing an agricultural economy based on cotton and slavery. In 1800 the district population stood at 8,158, with 7,021 free and 1,164 slaves. By 1830 the population had more than doubled, with slaves constituting more than two-fifths of the total. But as the slave population grew, the white population stagnated as declining soil productivity and low cotton prices sparked a migration of Chester District farmers to cheap, fresh land in the Southwest. From 1830 to 1860 the white population of Chester grew by only five percent. By 1850 Chester had become a black majority district.

The completion of the Charlotte and South Carolina Railroad in 1852, which was funded in part by wealthy Chester planters and merchants, increased economic activity in the district, but the advent of the Civil War brought the flush times to a halt. The district contributed five companies to the Confederate army, and Chester men saw action on many of the great battlefields of the war. Of the 1,941 men who served, 367 never returned. General William T. Sherman's army passed through the southeastern portion of Chester District in late February 1865 pillaging the countryside but sparing the district courthouse.

Chester County expected to revive its flagging postwar economy in 1873, when the General Assembly chartered the Cheraw and Chester Railroad. However, work did not begin until 1879 and was plagued with financial troubles. The line was never completed. Chester had better success later in the century in joining the textile mill boom spreading across the South. With growing cotton becoming less profitable, Chester business leaders turned to manufacturing as a way to stimulate the county economy. As a result, the textile industry gradually replaced agriculture as the dominant force in the economy. In 1888 operations commenced at the Chester Manufacturing Company, followed four years later by the Catawba Spinning Company. In the early twentieth century Chester County benefited from the construction of hydroelectric power plants on the Catawba River at Rock Hill, Great Falls, and Rocky Mount. The appearance of electric power spawned several more cotton mills, and together the two industries came to dominate the economic life of Chester County.

Chester County, like other cotton-producing counties, did not enjoy the prosperity experienced by other regions in the 1920s. Even before the onset of the Depression of the 1930s, low cotton prices and overproduction by the textile industry had already brought about hard times. However, the onset of World War II marked a return to prosperity, as textile mills worked overtime to fill lucrative defense contracts.

Chester County did not experience any significant economic changes in the years immediately following the war. Springs Mills in Chester, along with J. P. Stevens Mills in Great Falls and Manetta Mills in Lando, continued to be the county's largest employers. But there was little diversification. By the 1960s a movement to encourage the establishment of new businesses took shape in Chester County, spearheaded by the formation of the Chester County Board of Commerce and Development. This new organization gave a boost to the economy by recruiting new industry, including the Schlegel Corporation plant in 1961, Sun Chemical Corporation in 1963, and Roman Chemical Company in 1964. By 1981 sixty-one percent of the Chester County workforce was employed in manufacturing. This increased industrial growth extended into the 1970s, as nineteen more plants were established in the county. Contrasting with this industrial growth, however, was a steady decline in agricultural production, which shifted away from cotton and toward the raising of beef and dairy cattle. While in 1949 twenty thousand acres of cotton were under cultivation, by the early 1970s less than a thousand acres was used for that crop.

In the twentieth century's last two decades, the county continued its efforts to advance economically, but residents still remembered their past with pride. One symbol of the respect for the area's heritage was the movement in the early 1980s to save Chester's historic city hall. Given a $150,000 facelift and a new roof, the building was rededicated on May 14, 1983. The city hall became the center of Chester County as it entered the new millennium. RON CHEPESIUK

Chepesiuk, Ronald. *Chester County: A Pictorial History.* Norfolk, Va.: Donning, 1984.

Chepesiuk, Ronald, Gina Price White, and J. Edward Lee. *Along the Catawba River.* Charleston, S.C.: Arcadia, 1999.

Chesterfield County (799 sq. miles; 2000 pop. 42,768). Chesterfield County was established in 1785 when the state legislature divided the Cheraws Judicial District into three counties. Like other South Carolina counties, Chesterfield may have taken its name from English nobility, in this instance Philip Stanhope, the earl of Chesterfield. The name might also have originated in Chesterfield County, Virginia, from which many early settlers arrived. Prior to the arrival of European settlers, the Cheraw Indians occupied the region. Of Siouan stock, they were decimated by disease and departed in the early eighteenth century, joining the Catawba Confederacy.

The first European colonists lived chiefly near the Great Pee Dee River, their main source of transportation. The first known settlers were forced upriver when the Welsh received a land grant in 1736 that ran along the river to the North Carolina line. However, the

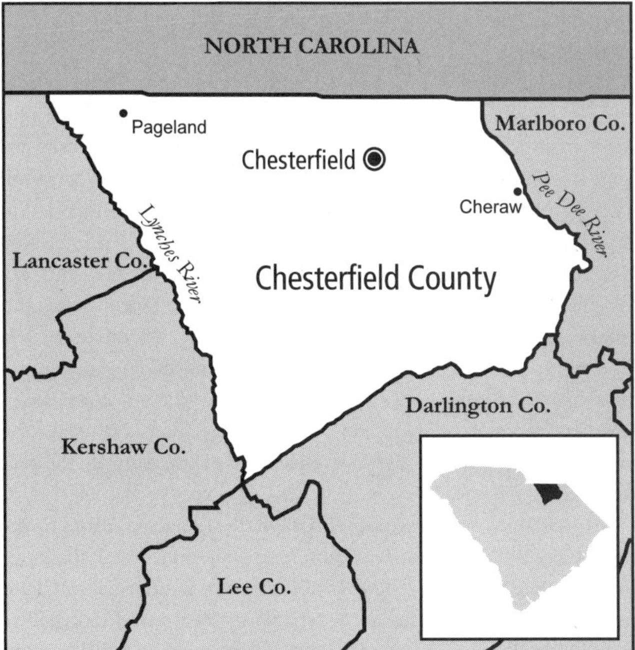

Welsh mainly settled near Society Hill to the south. Most of the earliest settlers in Chesterfield County were English, later joined by Scots, French, and Irish. These immigrants brought with them the county's first African slaves. The earliest settlement was at Cheraw Hill, located at the head of navigation for the Great Pee Dee River. In the western part of the county, the Great Wagon Road brought new settlers from Virginia and the mid-Atlantic colonies. In 1768 St. David's Parish was established to serve both religious and civic needs in the region. The Revolutionary War brought civil war to the upper Pee Dee. Recognized by both sides as a place of strategic importance, Cheraw was occupied by British and American troops at various times. The war devastated the region and resulted in an economic depression that lasted for decades.

Following the creation of Chesterfield County in 1785, a courthouse was constructed near its geographic center, which eventually evolved into the village of Chesterfield. By the early 1800s Cheraw and Mt. Croghan each had a post office. The appearance of steamboats on the Great Pee Dee in 1819 brought rapid prosperity to Chesterfield County in general and to Cheraw in particular. The town was incorporated in 1820 and was one of the state's leading commercial towns during the antebellum era. Vast pine barrens kept the population low in many parts of Chesterfield. Robert Mills's *Atlas* of 1825 showed settlement widely scattered across the county. Because the sand hills did not support intensive agriculture, the slave population was never large. There was some mining, including the Brewer Gold Mine near Jefferson, while along the "Stage and Main Post Road" several taverns sheltered travelers. Overall, the county grew slowly and sporadically during the first half of the nineteenth century.

On November 19, 1860, at Chesterfield Courthouse, one of the first secession meetings in the state was held. At the Secession Convention, John Inglis of Cheraw introduced the resolution calling for South Carolina to secede from the Union. The resulting war brought tumult and numerous refugees to the region. In March 1865 the county was in the path of the Union army under General William T. Sherman. Mt. Croghan and much of Chesterfield, including the Robert Mills–designed courthouse, were burned. Cheraw, which played unwilling host to most of Sherman's army, fared better. Only its business district was destroyed in an accidental explosion.

The Civil War left the county destitute. The timber industry that grew in the Carolinas at the turn of the century extended the railroads from Cheraw out into the county and brought the first real hope of economic recovery. The railroads gave isolated sand-hill farmers their first convenient access to outside markets and aided in the formation of several new towns. When the railroad reached Chesterfield in 1901, the town immediately began to grow. In 1902 the village of Flint Hill was relocated to meet the railroad line and renamed Ruby. In 1904 Adolphus High Page, president of the Cheraw and Lancaster Railroad, extended his line to Blakeney's Crossroads. The crossroads was renamed Pageland and later gained fame for its watermelons. Likewise named for railroad officials, the towns of Patrick and McBee evolved around depots built by the Seaboard Air Line.

At one time one of the poorest and most illiterate counties in the state, Chesterfield made great economic and educational strides in the twentieth century. In the 1930s large tracts of worn-out land were acquired by the state and federal governments and returned to pine forest. Part of this land became Cheraw State Park in 1934 (South Carolina's first state park), while other tracts became Sand Hills State Forest and Carolina Sandhills National Wildlife Refuge.

The county consistently produced excellent fruits, particularly watermelons and peaches, and Chesterfield County remained largely agricultural until the 1960s. In the 1950s and 1960s there was a major push to attract industry. Improvements in education (especially the establishment of Chesterfield Marlboro Technical College), health care, the public library system, and the county's infrastructure made this effort a success. By 2000 the county had a mix of industry, agriculture, and mining operations while maintaining a pleasant rural landscape. Major manufacturing plants included Takata Restraint Systems at Cheraw, A. O. Smith Water Products at McBee, and Conbraco Industries at Pageland.

Cheraw, a state leader in historic preservation, successfully managed to industrialize while maintaining its picturesque antebellum core. Pageland and Chesterfield likewise worked to improve their historic downtowns in the last years of the twentieth century. New uses for the more than 96,000 acres of public land in the county, such as the H. Cooper Black Field Trial Center, began to attract more visitors. County and city officials continued to recruit industry, and the growth of Charlotte, North Carolina, began to have an impact, bringing in new residents and businesses, particularly in the western part of the county. SARAH CAIN SPRUILL

Gregg, Alexander. *History of the Old Cheraws.* 1867. Reprint, Greenville, S.C.: Southern Historical Press, 1991.

Holcomb, Brent H. *St. David's Parish, South Carolina Minutes of the Vestry, 1768–1832, Parish Register, 1819–1924.* Easley, S.C.: Southern Historical Press, 1979.

Johnson, George Lloyd, Jr. *The Frontier in the Colonial South: South Carolina Backcountry, 1736–1800.* Westport, Conn.: Greenwood, 1997.

Nelson, Larry E. "Sherman at Cheraw." *South Carolina Historical Magazine* 100 (October 1999): 328–54.

Cheves, Langdon (1776–1857). Legislator, congressman, bank president. Cheves was born at Bull Town Fort in Abbeville District on September 17, 1776, the son of Alexander and Mary Langdon Cheves. His initial schooling took place at private academies in Abbeville District and Charleston. But much of his education was acquired through intensive personal study. He married Mary Elizabeth Dulles on May 6, 1806. The marriage produced fourteen children, including the noted author and essayist Louisa Cheves McCord.

Cheves read law in Charleston and was admitted to the bar by 1797. Within a decade his law practice was statewide. Although

Langdon Cheves. Courtesy, South Carolina Historical Society

most of his close legal colleagues were Federalists, Cheves remained a Jeffersonian Republican throughout his active political career. He was outspoken in his political convictions to such a degree that opponents referred to him as the "political Jesuit."

In 1802 the voters of Charleston elected Cheves to the S.C. House of Representatives. He held this seat until 1809, when he became state attorney general. In 1810 he was elected to the U.S. House of Representatives, becoming part of a notable quartet of South Carolina lawmakers that included John C. Calhoun, William Lowndes, and David R. Williams. All were active "War Hawks," a faction of Republican congressmen seeking war against Great Britain.

In 1812 Cheves was a key leader in the successful effort to retain Henry Clay of Kentucky as Speaker of the House. In return, Clay rewarded him with the chairmanship of the Ways and Means Committee. As an influential member of the Naval Affairs Committee, Cheves framed many crucial military appropriation measures during the War of 1812. He succeeded Clay as Speaker of the House in January 1814, after Clay was named to the peace commission that would negotiate an end to the war in December 1814.

Cheves declined an offer to join President James Madison's cabinet as secretary of the treasury, and he retired from Congress in 1815. He returned to Charleston, accepting a seat on the S.C. Court of Appeals in 1816 and resuming his lucrative private law practice.

In 1819 President James Monroe appointed Cheves president of the Second National Bank of the United States. Claiming that his predecessor's mismanagement had left that institution "prostrate," Cheves instituted a strict retrenchment program of fewer loans, higher interest rates, and a sharp reduction of bank notes in circulation. His actions enraged many, and may have exacerbated the depression following the Panic of 1819, but the bank regained its financial footing. He resigned from this position in 1822. Monroe subsequently appointed Cheves chief commissioner of war claims as stipulated under the Treaty of Ghent. He remained in this post until all of the outstanding international war claims were adjusted successfully. Throughout these years Cheves resided in Philadelphia and Lancaster, Pennsylvania, where he actively practiced law.

Cheves returned to South Carolina in 1829. His long absence prohibited a direct role in state politics, and he instead quietly became a political power broker. Although he sided with the Unionists during the nullification crisis, Cheves later called for a more vigorous defense of southern rights. In 1850 he was chosen as a delegate to the southern states convention held at Nashville. Responding to the Compromise of 1850, Cheves declared, "The Rubicon is passed—the Union is already dissolved." He urged southerners to "unite and your slave property will be protected." Like a growing number of southern radicals, Cheves came to the conclusion that secession was the only palatable answer to the sectional crisis in America.

During the last two decades of his life Cheves was a successful lawyer and rice planter, dividing his time between his country mansion, the Delta, near Savannah, Georgia, and a summer retreat in Pendleton. He died in Columbia on June 26, 1857, and was buried in Magnolia Cemetery, Charleston. MILES S. RICHARDS

Huff, Archie Vernon. *Langdon Cheves of South Carolina.* Columbia: University of South Carolina Press, 1977.

Perkins, Edward J. "Langdon Cheves and the Panic of 1819: A Reassessment." *Journal of Economic History* 44 (June 1983): 455–61.

Chicken bog. While anecdotal evidence exists that the name chicken bog was related to the "boggy" nature of its home, the Pee Dee, the southern writer James Villas states in his book *Stews, Bogs and Burgoos* that a "bog (unlike a pilau) is any stew that includes wet, soggy rice." In her benchmark work, *The Carolina Rice Kitchen,* Karen Hess is more specific, describing chicken bog as a pilau made in large batches, which would always cause it to end up wet. The culinary historian Damon Lee Fowler defines chicken bog as "a highly localized form of pilau, probably of African provenance, in the U.S. found only in South Carolina." From research in the Pee Dee region for his documentary film *Southern Stews: A Taste of the South,* Stan Woodward concluded that "while fondly cherished as the native stew of the Pee Dee . . . the name chicken bog was never well documented by its users . . . because it was a commonplace high protein meal that fed a lot of people in a poor environment."

Traditionally, the only ingredients are chicken, rice, sausage, and onions, seasoned with salt and plenty of black pepper. The best chicken to use is an older hen, past good egg production, free-range and full of flavor; the second choice is a fat roaster. The chicken is poached, and then its meat is pulled off the bone, not chopped. The fat is removed from the broth, and then the rice, chicken, sausage, and onions all simmer gently together in the broth until the rice is "done."

Whether chicken bog is eaten with a fork or a spoon depends on the cook. Even for a respected Pee Dee "bogmaster," says Woodward, cooking bog in fifty-gallon wash pots is an art. It is "good bog if the rice is plump and moist, holds on to one another real good and sits up above a little gravy in the bottom of the pot and don't cling to the chicken."

Chicken bog is the main attraction at the annual Democratic stump meeting at Galivants Ferry, near the Little Pee Dee River. Traditional accompaniments are snap beans, white rolls, and Pepsi. The same combination is served in Loris, a small town north of Myrtle Beach. Loris residents decided in 1979 to make chicken bog the theme for an annual festival in October, which centers around the "Bog-Off," a cooking competition for the best chicken bog. In 2001 attendance at the festival numbered approximately twenty thousand. MARION B. SULLIVAN

Egerton, John. *Southern Food: At Home, on the Road, in History.* New York: Knopf, 1987.

Hess, Karen. *The Carolina Rice Kitchen: The African Connection.* Columbia: University of South Carolina Press, 1992.

Southern Stews: A Taste of the South. Produced and directed by Stan Woodward. Greenville, S.C.: Woodward Studio, 2002. Videocassette.

Villas, James. *Stews, Bogs and Burgoos.* New York: Morrow, 1997.

Chicora, Francisco de. Indian captive. Born in the early sixteenth century, the man Spaniards baptized as "Francisco" was a native of the present-day South Carolina coast in the area of Winyah Bay. Francisco was a youth or a young man in 1521, when Spanish slave raiders captured him with a group of sixty men and women from a land whose name the Spaniards understood to be "Chicora." The raiders took their captives to Santo Domingo on the island of Hispaniola, where they divided the survivors among the men who had funded the expedition. In this way Francisco became the slave of the judge Lucas Vázquez de Ayllón. Ayllón took Francisco to Spain not long after his capture. During this visit, the sixteenth-century chroniclers Peter Martyr and Gonzalo Fernández de Oviedo heard Francisco's tales about the wealth and marvels of his homeland. Martyr recorded Francisco's account and brought it wide circulation in Europe. Oviedo was more skeptical and later claimed that Francisco had deceived Ayllón in an effort to return home. Ayllón used Francisco's description of Chicora to inspire interest in this region and to gain a royal contract to conquer and settle it in June 1523. Francisco de Chicora accompanied the Ayllón expedition as a translator and guide when it sailed in July 1526. However, soon after Ayllón's ships arrived in the area of Winyah Bay, Francisco fled inland with the expedition's other captive Indians. The Spaniards never saw him again. KAREN L. PAAR

Hoffman, Paul E. *A New Andalucia and a Way to the Orient: The American Southeast during the Sixteenth Century.* Baton Rouge: Louisiana State University Press, 1990.

Quinn, David B., ed. *New American World: A Documentary History of North America to 1612.* Vol. 1, *America from Concept to Discovery: Early Exploration of North America.* New York: Arno, 1979.

Child labor. The transformation of the United States into an industrialized nation brought changes that adversely affected workers. Most new jobs required more machines and fewer skills, which enabled managers to replace expensive skilled labor with those who would be relatively unskilled and paid considerably less. In South Carolina children, some as young as five years of age, were hired in great numbers by the state's burgeoning textile industry, some of whom were used to replace emancipated slaves. The practice by textile mills of hiring entire families helped ensure the availability of child labor.

Young mill operators. Courtesy, South Caroliniana Library, University of South Carolina

Cheap to employ, easily controlled, and with small, nimble fingers, children were well suited to perform the repetitive, minor tasks that the textile industry demanded. A typical child's job was that of spinner. This worker would watch rotating bobbins for breaks in the cotton. When the cotton broke, the child would quickly mend it and then brush the lint from the machine frame. She might tend six or seven rows of bobbins and work ten to twelve hours a day, six days a week. The labor of such children came at a high price. Mill children had a characteristic pallor from working from dawn until dusk, and some had lost fingers, hands, or arms from reaching into the machinery. Others had chronic bronchitis and other lung diseases from working long hours in a humid, lint-filled environment. Additionally, hours spent in the factory were hours that were not spent in school. Labor practices such as these trapped children in a cycle of poverty by interfering with their education and physical development.

At the same time, as more children entered the workforce, new ideas about child development also emerged. Americans began to see childhood as a series of stages, each with specific physical and psychological demands that had to be satisfied for the child to develop into a healthy adult able to fulfill his or her potential. Pressure for child labor laws increased. The first child labor bill introduced in South Carolina came in 1884, when Michael F. Kennedy of Charleston proposed an age limit of ten years. The bill died in the S.C. Senate. Subsequent legislation introduced in 1887 and 1889 likewise failed to be enacted. Governor Miles B. McSweeney declared such reform efforts as dangerous intrusions into what he and others considered a family matter, and he warned that children would be forced out of the mills and into idleness. To supporters of child labor, work kept youngsters out of trouble, gave them early self-reliance, and provided extra money for their families. Many South Carolinians feared that since the state had lured industry through the promise of cheap labor, an end to child labor would check industrial progress by crippling existing mills and preventing others from opening.

By the start of the twentieth century, South Carolina lacked both child labor laws and compulsory education laws. Children made up more than one-fourth of the textile workforce in the state in 1900. The illiteracy rate of mill children under fourteen years of age topped fifty percent, more than three times the statewide average. Reformers displayed photographs of Carolina mill children to illustrate the horrors of child labor. Under such pressure, beginning in 1903 South Carolina instituted reforms designed to influence the supply of child labor, such as minimum ages for employment and compulsory education. The laws were weakly enforced, however, and easy to evade. A Chester factory overseer reported in 1909 that the names of underage workers did not appear in the company books because their pay went to an older brother or sister. In 1915 the state required a signed statement by a parent or guardian that a child was of the legal employment age. By requiring only a signed statement of age instead of a verifiable document, the state permitted abuses by parents desperate for the wages of children. Additionally, any child over the age of twelve with a widowed mother or crippled father was excused from the age limit. Orphans could be employed at any age, and one child is reported to have begun work at the age of five. Domestic and agricultural workers were exempt from the regulations.

Child labor gradually disappeared during the 1920s and 1930s because of changes within the textile industry. Jobs came to require more skills because increased production standards mandated more expert handling. Improved machines involved a greater capital investment, but careless hands could spoil raw material and not get full use of the machinery. During the 1930s more women entered the workforce, and the real income of the working class began to rise. All of these factors combined to lessen the demand for unskilled workers and to reduce the need for families to send children to work. CARYN E. NEUMANN

Carlton, David L. *Mill and Town in South Carolina, 1880–1920.* Baton Rouge: Louisiana State University Press, 1982.

Davidson, Elizabeth H. *Child Labor Legislation in the Southern Textile States.* Chapel Hill: University of North Carolina Press, 1939.

McKelway, Alexander J. *Child Labor in the Carolinas.* New York, 1909.

Childress, Alice (1920–1994). Actress, theater director, playwright, novelist. Childress was born in Charleston on October 12, 1920, to Alonzo Herndon and Florence White. Although she was taken to New York City quite early and raised by her grandmother Eliza Campbell, she maintained a connection to the lowcountry through a network of Charlestonians living in Harlem. She did not finish high school and first worked professionally as an actress in 1940, when she joined the American Negro Theater. She rose to director, a position she held for nearly twelve years. She acted in plays on and off Broadway and later in films. Her first one-act play, *Florence,* was produced in 1949. *Just a Little Simple,* an adaptation of a Langston Hughes work, followed in 1952. *Gold through the Trees,* the first play by a black woman to be staged professionally in the American theater, was produced in 1952. *Trouble in Mind,* about black actors having to play stereotypical black roles created by whites, won an Obie for best Off-Broadway play in 1956, making her the first woman to win that award.

Her work paved the way for later black playwrights such as Lorraine Hansberry. After her first marriage ended, in 1957 she married Nathan Woodward, a future collaborator on many projects. She lectured to colleges and universities in the 1960s. Perhaps her most famous play, *A Wedding Band,* a tale focusing on an interracial love affair in Charleston, circa 1918, premiered at the University of Michigan in 1966. The play was staged by Joseph Papp at the New York Public Shakespeare Theater in 1972 and was televised nationally. It, like many of her other works, enthralled some and angered others, prompting periodic banning. Other dramatic works included *The Young Martin Luther King; When the Rattlesnake Sounds; "Moms,"* about Moms Mabley; *The World on a Hill,* about West Indian life; *Wine in the Wilderness,* about ghetto and middle-class black youths; *Mojo;* and *String,* based on the Guy De Maupassant short story "A Piece of String."

In 1977 Childress published *A Short Walk,* a novel of a woman growing up in Charleston, going into show business, and ending up in New York. Her better-known novels were for young adults and included *A Hero Ain't Nothing But a Sandwich* (1973), a compelling look at a drug-addicted youth with no happy endings inferred; its banning was part of a case taken to the U.S. Supreme Court in 1983. *Rainbow Jordan* (1980), another young-adult novel, centered on a daughter perpetually seeking her mother's love. Childress received many national and international awards for individual works and for lifetime achievement. Considering herself a Charlestonian, she visited the state in 1977 with her husband, with whom she wrote *A Sea Island Song,* a musical and dramatic tribute to the Gullah culture of the Sea Islands. *The Wedding Band* was produced in the state at the time, and "Alice Childress Weeks" were proclaimed in Columbia and Charleston. Her audiences ranged from children, to college and university students, to theatergoers and readers; she brought to all her intelligence and unflinching, but understanding look at people and their problems, regardless of race. She died in Queens, New York, on August 14, 1994. HARLAN GREENE

Brown-Guillory, Elizabeth. *Their Place on the Stage: Black Women Playwrights in America.* New York: Greenwood, 1988.

Salem, Dorothy, ed. *African American Women: A Biographical Dictionary.* New York: Garland, 1993.

Chisolm, Julian John (1830–1903). Physician. Chisolm was born in Charleston on April 16, 1830, the son of Robert Trail Chisolm and Harriet Emily Schutt. He graduated from the Medical College of the State of South Carolina in 1850. He continued his studies in London and Paris for the better part of two years before returning to Charleston to practice in 1852. In 1858 he became professor of surgery at the Medical College. The following year he returned to Europe and observed the treatment of the wounded from the battles of Magenta and Solferino in hospitals in Milan during the Austro-Italian War, a matter that was to be of significance in the Civil War. Soon after his return to his chair at the Medical College, the war began and he served as a medical officer for its duration. His book, *A Manual of Military Surgery,* based in part on his experiences in Italy, was of major importance in the treatment of the wounded. In response to strong demand, additional editions were published in 1861, 1862, and 1864. In addition to this major contribution to the Confederate war effort, Chisolm devised a more efficient inhaler for the administration of chloroform, an anesthetic that was in short supply in the Confederate army.

After the war, Chisolm resumed his chair in surgery, becoming dean of the Medical College in 1867. He also served as president of the Medical Society of South Carolina from 1865 to 1867. Because professional prospects in postwar Charleston were bleak, in 1868 Chisolm moved to Baltimore, where he joined the University of Maryland Medical School and became its dean in 1869.

Chisolm's career in Baltimore was one of unbroken success. On a third trip to Europe in 1871, he emphasized the study of diseases of the eyes and ears and concentrated his practice on those fields on his return. Chisolm belonged to major organizations devoted to his specialty and contributed more than one hundred papers to its literature. The honorary degree of doctor of letters was conferred on him in 1892 by the University of South Carolina. His most famous patient was Helen Keller, whom he referred to Alexander Graham Bell because he felt that she could learn to talk and be educated although she would never see or hear. A devout Presbyterian, Chisolm and other prominent Baltimore citizens in 1877 established the Presbyterian Eye, Ear and Throat Charity Hospital for people with limited means.

Chisolm married twice. On February 3, 1852, he married a cousin, Mary Eddings Chisolm. The marriage produced two children, Julia and Francis Miles. Mary Chisolm died on March 29, 1888. On June 16, 1894, Chisolm married Elizabeth Steele. His second marriage produced a daughter, Katherine.

In September 1894 Chisolm suffered a stroke, from which he never completely recovered. He died in Petersburg, Virginia, on November 1, 1903, and was buried in Greenmount Cemetery, Baltimore. W. CURTIS WORTHINGTON

Memoir in Honor of Julian John Chisolm, M.D., upon the One Hundredth Anniversary of His Birth by the Members of His Family and Former Associates. [Baltimore, 1930].

Sherman, Roger. "Julian John Chisolm, M.D., Confederate Surgeon." *American Surgeon* 52 (January 1986): 1–8.

Waring, James I. *A History of Medicine in South Carolina.* 3 vols. Columbia: South Carolina Medical Association, 1964–1971.

Worthington, W. Curtis. "Confederates, Chloroform and Cataracts: Julian John Chisolm (1830–1903)." *Southern Medical Journal* 79 (June 1986): 748–52.

Chreitzberg, Cema Sitton (1888–1972). Churchwoman. Chreitzberg was born on March 7, 1888, in Autun, Anderson County, the daughter of John and Leila Sitton. Little is known of her childhood. She entered Converse College in 1904 and earned a bachelor's degree in literature in 1908 and a bachelor of music degree in 1910. In 1911 she married Augustus M. Chreitzberg, a Wofford graduate and Spartanburg businessman. The couple settled in Spartanburg and raised three daughters and a son.

Chreitzberg devoted herself to church work. She was an active member of Spartanburg's Bethel Methodist Church, serving as a Sunday school teacher, president of the church women's organization, and a member of several church administrative committees.

She was a founder of the Bethlehem Center, an educational and community center in one of Spartanburg's black communities sponsored by Bethel Methodist Church. A driving force behind the development of the Bethlehem Center, Chreitzberg served as president of the organization's board from the early 1920s until 1953. In its early days the Bethlehem Center provided health and nutrition classes for new mothers, recreational facilities for young people, and classes on many topics. The Bethlehem Center continues to provide a variety of social services for Spartanburg's South Side community.

Chreitzberg was also an avid gardener. She kept a gardening journal throughout her adult life and became locally famous for the elaborate garden she designed at her home. An active member of the local and South Carolina garden clubs, she served as a judge at many horticultural contests and edited a column on gardening in the Spartanburg *Herald.*

Late in life Chreitzberg took over the rearing of two granddaughters after the death of her eldest daughter. In 1958 she noted in a Converse College alumnae reunion questionnaire, "I'm still rearing children and that is a 'man-sized' job." That same year Converse College honored her with its Mary Mildred Sullivan Award for exemplary community service. Chreitzberg died on February 20, 1972, and was buried in Oakwood Cemetery. MELISSA WALKER

Cheatham, Suzanne. "Cema Sitton Chreitzberg." In *The Lives They Lived: A Look at Women in the History of Spartanburg,* edited by Linda Powers Bilanchone. Spartanburg, S.C.: Spartanburg Sesquicentennial Focus on Women Committee, 1981.

Christ Church Parish. Located on the low, sandy strip of land "South-east of Wandoe river" in modern Charleston County, Christ Church was one of the ten original parishes created by the Church Act of 1706. Shortly after Charleston was founded in 1670, settlement spilled across the harbor onto the Wando peninsula. A brisk provisions trade in beef, vegetables, and orchard products soon developed between the small farmers of the area and the city. With the introduction of rice as a staple crop in the early eighteenth century, Christ Church became a parish of planters and slaves. By 1720 African slaves made up nearly eighty-six percent of the parish population, and by 1730 the threat of insurrection in Christ Church had become so great that, as one early rector noted, "the People are forced to come to Church with Guns loaded."

The first church to serve the parish was a small timber structure built in 1707. The congregation quickly outgrew the church and was already in the process of planning a larger one when the building was destroyed by fire in 1725. Construction of a new brick church began immediately and was completed in 1727. Although the edifice was burned by the British in 1782 and its interior demolished by Union troops in 1865, the original walls still stand as part of the present Christ Episcopal Church in modern-day Mount Pleasant. With the abolition of the parish system in 1865, Christ Church Parish became part of Berkeley County. MATTHEW A. LOCKHART

Gregorie, Anne King. *Christ Church, 1706–1959: A Plantation Parish of the South Carolina Establishment.* Charleston, S.C.: Dalcho Historical Society, 1961.

Linder, Suzanne Cameron. *Anglican Churches in Colonial South Carolina: Their History and Architecture.* Charleston, S.C.: Wyrick, 2000.

Christensen, Abbie Mandana Holmes (1852–1938). Folklorist, educator, suffragist. Christensen was born in Westborough, Massachusetts, on January 28, 1852, the eldest daughter of Reuben G. Holmes and Rebecca Winch. In 1864 her abolitionist family moved to Beaufort, South Carolina, where her mother became a teacher in a school for freed people and her father engaged in business and was elected to the 1868 constitutional convention. Christensen taught in a Beaufort County public school from 1870 to 1872. She attended Mount Holyoke Female Seminary in South Hadley, Massachusetts, from 1872 to 1874.

A pioneer in the field of African American folklore, Christensen published her first story, "De Wolf, de Rabbit an' de Tar Baby," in the *Springfield (Mass.) Daily Republican* on June 2, 1874. Her career as a collector of Gullah folklore culminated in her book *Afro-American Folk Lore as Told 'Round Cabin Fires on the Sea Islands of South Carolina* (1892). Returning to Beaufort, she married Niels Christensen, a Danish immigrant and former captain of U.S. Colored Troops, in 1875. Niels Christensen became a successful real estate, hardware, and lumber merchant. The couple had six children.

Abbie Christensen became a woman suffragist in 1891, as a founding member of the South Carolina Equal Rights Association. In 1902 Christensen used the profits from the sale of *Afro-American Folk Lore* to begin the Port Royal Agricultural School, a boarding and day school for African American children, located in the rural Beaufort County area known as Burton. The Tuskegee graduates Joseph and India Shanklin ran the school from 1905 to the 1940s, working closely with Christensen. In Beaufort, Christensen joined several white women's clubs and played a leading role in conservation and urban landscaping efforts spearheaded by the Civic League. In 1917 Christensen became one of the first educators in the nation to found a Montessori School, which she operated in her home in Beaufort. She returned to the cause of woman suffrage, founding the South Carolina Equal Suffrage League in Spartanburg in 1914 together with her daughter Andrea Christensen Patterson and other South Carolina clubwomen. She also received assistance from her son, Niels Christensen, Jr., the publisher and editor of the *Beaufort Gazette* (1903–1921) and a state senator (1905–1924), who introduced an unsuccessful S.C. Senate resolution to ratify the Nineteenth Amendment in 1920.

Abbie Christensen was a progressive force for women's rights, black and white education, racial tolerance, and social welfare in South Carolina from the 1890s until her death. In 1931 she joined the Association of Southern Women for the Prevention of Lynching. At the age of eighty, Christensen entered politics as an elector for Norman Thomas, the American Socialist Party candidate for president in 1932. Christensen died at the home of her daughter Andrea Patterson in Greenville on September 21, 1938. She was buried at Beaufort Baptist Church. MONICA MARIA TETZLAFF

Tetzlaff, Monica Maria. *Cultivating a New South: Abbie Holmes Christensen and the Politics of Race and Gender, 1852–1938.* Columbia: University of South Carolina Press, 2002.

Christian Coalition. The Christian Coalition is a national organization founded in 1989 by Pat Robertson, the founder of the Christian Broadcast Network and host of the television show *The 700 Club.* It serves as a grassroots organization for conservative Christians to be involved in community, social, and political action. The Christian Coalition grew in membership nationally during the 1990s and by its own estimates to nearly two million by 2002. The Christian Coalition during the 1990s became a significant force within the Republican Party with its ability to get several of its key agenda points on the party platform during the Republican national conventions in 1992, 1996, and 2000. The Christian Coalition's support helped the Republican Party achieve its overwhelming victory in the 1994 mid-term elections. The Coalition actively campaigned for the GOP's "Contract with America" and later proposed a "Contract with the American Family," which highlighted the specific interests of conservative Christians.

The South Carolina chapter of the Christian Coalition was founded on July 27, 1992, in Charleston with Roberta Combs of Hanahan, a former treasurer of the South Carolina Republican Party, serving as chair. Combs later replaced Pat Robertson as president of the national Christian Coalition in December 2001. Like the national organization, the South Carolina Christian Coalition has been heavily focused on political activism, stating that members "are driven by the belief that people of faith have a right and a responsibility to be involved in the world around them." In particular the organization has focused on raising the profile of what they term "pro-family" issues. Prior to the national elections in 1992, 1996, and 2000, the organization distributed hundreds of thousands of voter guides regarding these profamily issues, which included abortion, education vouchers, gay rights, the death penalty, pornography, and school prayer.

The South Carolina Christian Coalition had mixed success during the 1990s in gaining leadership positions within the state Republican Party. In 1992 nearly half of the state's delegation to the Republican national convention was made up of conservative Christians with ties to the Christian Coalition. In 2000 the organization had only a few members at the Republican national convention. At the same time, however, many political commentators credited the South Carolina Christian Coalition with helping Texas governor George W. Bush win the South Carolina Republican presidential primary in 2000. The strong support of the Coalition following Bush's controversial decision to speak at the fundamentalist Bob Jones University in Greenville helped provide the difference in Bush's race against Arizona senator John McCain and gave Bush the momentum to capture the Republican nomination and eventually the presidency. AARON L. HABERMAN

Martin, William. *With God on Our Side: The Rise of the Religious Right in America.* New York: Broadway Books, 1996.

Watson, Justin. *The Christian Coalition: Dreams of Restoration, Demands for Recognition.* New York: St. Martin's, 1997.

Christian Methodist Episcopal Church. One of the seven largest African American denominations, the CME Church was originally titled the Colored Methodist Episcopal Church. Organized in Jackson, Tennessee, in 1870, it amicably emerged from the Methodist Episcopal Church, South (MES). When the Civil War began, more than 207,000 blacks were members of the white-controlled MES, but only 70,000 remained in 1870. Many white MES members desired blacks to depart. Likewise, African Americans were unhappy with the prospects of remaining in a church with slavery-era rules of white supremacy intact, but neither did they desire union with the northern-based African Methodist Episcopal or African Methodist Episcopal Zion Churches.

As a condition for the transference of church property to the new organization, the CME agreed with the MES not to permit the use of church facilities for political activities, which would most likely differ profoundly from those of most southern whites. For this reason the CME was often dubbed "the Rebel church," an unfair characterization since individual CME congregations were politically engaged and the denomination has adopted political positions corresponding to other black churches. The church title was changed from "Colored" to "Christian" in 1954.

The CME supports four colleges and the Charles H. Phillips School of Theology of the Interdenominational Theological Seminary, publishes the *Christian Index,* and participates in pan-Methodist and interdenominational ecumenical organizations, such as the National Council of Churches. Notable persons associated with the CME include the bishops William H. Miles and Richard H. Vanderhorst (a South Carolina native), the women's rights advocate Helena B. Cobb, Channing H. Tobias of the National Association for the Advancement of Colored People (NAACP), the historian John Hope Franklin, and the author Alex Haley.

The smallest of the three black Methodist groups, the CME has close to one million members in the United States and abroad, especially in the Caribbean and Africa. Its polity basically mirrors that of other major American Methodist denominations, featuring an episcopal governance with general, annual, and quarterly conferences, and boards focused on various aspects of church life. It also shares Methodist doctrines, theology, and rituals. The publishing house and headquarters are in Memphis, Tennessee. While a national and international body, the CME is strongest in the South, especially Tennessee, Georgia, Mississippi, and Alabama. The South Carolina Annual Conference, established in 1870, is in the Seventh Episcopal District along with the District of Columbia and eight other states along the Atlantic seaboard. SANDY DWAYNE MARTIN

Lakey, Othal Hawthorne. *The History of the CME Church.* Rev. ed. Memphis, Tenn.: CME Publishing House, 1996.

Lincoln, C. Eric, and Lawrence H. Mamiya. *The Black Church in the African American Experience.* Durham: Duke University Press, 1990.

Christian-Jewish Congress of South Carolina. The Christian-Jewish Congress of South Carolina was formed in 1976 as the state's first organization to foster dialogue and cooperation between Christians and Jews. It emerged out of conversations between the South Carolina Christian Action Council and the Jewish Welfare Federations in Columbia, Charleston, and Greenville.

The organization's motto was "conversation, not conversion," and its objectives focused on education and cooperation. It sought to correct misunderstandings between the faith communities, especially forms of anti-Semitism and anti-Judaism that occasionally surfaced in communities across the state. Chapters were established in Columbia, Charleston, and Greenville and met for regular meetings in living rooms or houses of worship. An annual meeting was held in Columbia from 1976 to 1988. Prominent national speakers addressed topics such as the plight of Soviet Jewry, prospects for peace in the Middle East, prayer in the public schools, and black-Jewish relations. The organization was instrumental in cohosting the Eleventh National Workshop on Christian-Jewish Relations, held in Charleston in March 1989. One of the major sessions of the national meeting included a Muslim leader, anticipating the more inclusive interfaith dialogues formed in the years following.

After the demise of the statewide organization in the late 1980s, local Jewish-Christian dialogue groups continued to meet in Charleston, Columbia, and other communities. During the 1990s leaders of interfaith dialogue established more inclusive dialogue groups to reflect the growing religious diversity of South Carolina. CARL D. EVANS

Church Act (1706). Enacted on November 30, 1706, this statute established the Church of England as the official, tax-supported church of South Carolina, a privileged status it would retain for seven decades. During the first decade of the eighteenth century, English Anglicans undertook a bitter campaign to exclude non-Anglicans, or "dissenters," from public office in England. Lord Granville, the senior proprietor of Carolina, played a leading role in the persecutions, which inevitably spilled across the Atlantic to South Carolina. With Granville's backing, South Carolina Anglicans seized control of the Commons House of Assembly from local dissenters in 1704. Two years later the assembly passed the Church Act. According to its provisions, the act allowed dissenters to practice their faiths and participate in politics but they were denied public support for their churches or the right to perform marriages.

The act divided the province into ten parishes and required the allocation of land for Anglican churches, cemeteries, messuages (parsonages), and glebes (agricultural plots belonging to parish churches). Buildings and "suitable outbuildings" were to be erected at public expense where they did not already exist, and Anglican-approved rectors, or ministers, were to be employed by the province. Each parish was to choose seven vestrymen, whose job it was to administer the parish; to record births, deaths, and marriages; and to appoint a clerk and sexton to serve the church. All parishioners were required to conform to the rites of the Church of England via the Book of Common Prayer, while officeholders were compelled to affirm their faith and to take parliamentary oaths of allegiance and supremacy.

From 1716 until the end of the colonial period, parish vestries were the only local government in the province. In 1778, during the Revolutionary War, the General Assembly disestablished the Church of England in South Carolina. LOUIS P. TOWLES

Bolton, S. Charles. *Southern Anglicanism: The Church of England in Colonial South Carolina.* Westport, Conn.: Greenwood, 1982.

Dalcho, Frederick. *An Historical Account of the Protestant Episcopal Church in South-Carolina.* 1820. Reprint, New York: Arno, 1972.

Church of England. Although there were Christians in England before 597, the beginning of the church in England can be dated to the consecration of Augustine as archbishop of Canterbury in November 597. Under Henry VIII (1509–1547) the Church of England separated from the papacy and Roman Catholicism, and under Elizabeth I (1558–1603) the Church of England was defined and established as catholic and reformed.

The first Church of England, or Anglican, house of worship in South Carolina was built in Charleston about 1681, with the Reverend Atkin Williamson serving as its first priest. The church was named St. Philip's but usually was called the English Church.

In the first decades of their colony, the Lords Proprietors followed a policy of religious toleration and encouraged immigrants from a variety of religious backgrounds to settle in South Carolina. However, by the start of the eighteenth century, changes in proprietary membership resulted in moves to establish the Church of England in South Carolina. The new senior proprietor in London, Lord Granville, was a High Tory who supported efforts to exclude non-Anglicans from public life. His efforts in England carried over to South Carolina. As a result, the proprietors began to court their former political enemies, the Goose Creek Men, who were primarily Church of England members. The arrival of Nathaniel Johnson, also a High Tory, as governor in 1703 initiated a series of measures that strengthened the establishment of the Church of England in South Carolina.

In May 1704 the Commons House of Assembly passed a law making the reception of the Holy Eucharist according to the use of the Church of England compulsory for members of the assembly. The law was a blatant attempt to remove non-Anglicans from public office and was disallowed by English authorities. In November 1706 the assembly replaced the previous act with "An Act for the Establishment of Religious Worship in this Province, according to the Church of England; and for the Erecting of Churches for the public Worship of God; and also for the Maintenance of Ministers, and the building convenient Houses for them." Commonly referred to as the Church Act, it made the Church of England the established, or official, church of South Carolina.

The act divided the colony into ten parishes: St. Philip's, Christ Church, St. Thomas, St. John's, St. James Goose Creek, St. Andrew's, St. Denis, St. Paul's, St. Bartholomew's, and St. James Santee. Once established, the Church of England was supported by public monies, with provision made for clergy salaries and the erection of churches and rectories. Parishes were given glebes (farmlands for the support of clergyman), and the 1662 Book of Common Prayer became the official liturgy for the province.

Although the Church of England was established in South Carolina, it was relatively weak, and other denominations were tolerated. Not having a bishop was the primary reason for its weakness. Henry Compton, bishop of London from 1676 until 1713, addressed this problem by naming commissaries to the colonies. While commissaries could not ordain or confirm, they could provide leadership, call conferences of clergy, and discipline errant clergy. In 1707 Bishop Compton appointed the Reverend Gideon Johnston the first commissary to the Carolinas. He arrived in South Carolina in 1708 and became the rector of St. Philip's, Charleston. The second commissary was William Treadwell Bull, who served from 1717 until 1723. The third and most influential commissary in South Carolina was Alexander Garden, who held the office from 1729 until his resignation in 1749.

During the Revolutionary War, the Church of England suffered in all the colonies. In the colonies where the Church of England was established, such as South Carolina, legislation was passed to disestablish it. This happened in South Carolina in 1778. On May 12, 1785, the Church of England in South Carolina organized as the Protestant Episcopal Church in South Carolina. DONALD S. ARMENTROUT

Bolton, S. Charles. *Southern Anglicanism: The Church of England in Colonial South Carolina.* Westport, Conn.: Greenwood, 1982.

Dalcho, Frederick. *An Historical Account of the Protestant Episcopal Church in South-Carolina.* 1820. Reprint, New York: Arno, 1972.

Sirmans, M. Eugene. *Colonial South Carolina: A Political History, 1663–1763.* Chapel Hill: University of North Carolina Press, 1966.

Weir, Robert M. *Colonial South Carolina: A History.* 1983. Reprint, Columbia: University of South Carolina Press, 1997.

Church of the Cross (Bluffton). Sited on a wooded bluff above a curve in the May River, the Episcopal Church of the Cross is a beautiful and serene lowcountry chapel. The congregation of cotton planters who had formed at the small village of Bluffton, near Hilton Head Island, advertised in the *Charleston Courier* in July 1854 for someone to design a church "of wood with brick foundations, and not to exceed the estimated cost of five thousand dollars." They chose the architect Edward Brickell White, who had designed Charleston's Huguenot Church and Grace Episcopal Church and was completing Trinity Church in Columbia. The "handsome cruciform Gothic building capable of holding five-to-six hundred people" was consecrated on July 19, 1857. It was built of cypress with a shingled cypress roof. Entered through an arched door under a trefoil window and flanking shuttered lancet windows, it opened to an interior with exposed pine beams, box pews, a slave gallery, pale pink plaster walls, and rose-tinted glass windows. White successfully adapted high style Gothic-revival motifs to a rural wooden church in a style that has become known as "Carpenter Gothic," but that label does not adequately describe his achievement. The church is a small architectural gem; it was listed in the National Register of Historic Places in 1975. JUDITH T. BAINBRIDGE

Church of the Cross, Bluffton. Courtesy, South Carolina Department of Archives and History

Ravenel, Beatrice St. Julian. *Architects of Charleston.* 1945. Reprint, Columbia: University of South Carolina Press, 1992.

Thomas, Albert Sidney. *A Historical Account of the Protestant Episcopal Church in South Carolina, 1820–1957.* Columbia, S.C.: R. L. Bryan, 1957.

Church of the Nativity (Union). Located in Union, the Church of the Nativity (consecrated in 1859) is a remarkably effective example of the "Ecclesiological" architectural style favored by the Episcopal Church in America and the Anglican Communion throughout the world in the 1840s and 1850s. John D. McCollough, its rector, served as supervising architect for the small upstate church, using plans of St. Anne's, Fredericton, New Brunswick, Canada, obtained from the New York architectural firm of Wills & Dudley. Frank Wills was an English Ecclesiologist architect whose success designing churches in Fredericton had led him to set up a mail-order practice in church designs and interior furnishings in 1848.

Ecclesiologists, strongly influenced by the Oxford movement with its emphasis on sacrament and mystery, insisted on a return to architectural models of the late Middle Ages (a style that they called "Second Point Gothic") for nineteenth-century Anglican churches. Their proposed designs emphasized pointed arches and windows, stone construction, flying buttresses, recessed chancels, and stained glass. The Church of the Nativity, the first stone Episcopal church in the state, had them all and an unusual bellcote as well.

The church, funded primarily by wealthy members of the congregation, cost about $16,000. McCollough carved its bishop's chair, rector's chair, altar rails, lecterns, and pews. When the church was consecrated, *The Southern Episcopalian* (October 1859) called it "an exquisite gem," a judgment reflected by its inclusion in the National Register of Historic Places in 1974. JUDITH T. BAINBRIDGE

Church of the Nativity, Union. Courtesy, South Carolina Department of Archives and History

Bainbridge, Judith T. *"Building the Walls of Jerusalem": John DeWitt McCollough and His Churches.* Spartanburg, S.C.: Reprint Company, 2000.

Pearson, Lennart. "The Church of the Nativity and the Frank Wills Connection." *South Carolina Historical Magazine* 100 (July 1999): 241–54.

Thomas, Albert Sidney. *A Historical Account of the Protestant Episcopal Church in South Carolina, 1820–1957.* Columbia, S.C.: R. L. Bryan, 1957.

Circular Congregational Church (Charleston). Circular Congregational Church, dedicated in 1892, is the fourth house of worship on this site at 150 Meeting Street in Charleston. Its Richardsonian Romanesque style reflects Charleston's tradition of adopting current architectural fashion for ecclesiastical buildings, despite the city's famous conservatism in residential design.

Followers of many creeds populated early Charleston. The city's first congregations, St. Philip's (Church of England) and the Dissenter's Society, were organized in 1681. Builders of the "White Meeting House" that gave Meeting Street its name, the Dissenters included Presbyterians, Huguenots, and Congregationalists. French Protestants soon had their own church and others withdrew to form First (Scots) Presbyterian, but the independent church flourished, dedicating a larger building in 1732.

As the new church became overcrowded, the Dissenters planned a separate building on Archdale Street. The new building (today's Unitarian Church) was completed in 1787, and for thirty years two preachers each gave Sunday sermons at both churches. In 1802 there was again a waiting list for pews, and the church agreed to replace its building on Meeting Street. The third edifice, designed by Robert Mills and completed in 1806, was noted for its circular design.

The great fire of 1861 left only the brick walls of Mills's building standing. For years the church retained its identity while meeting in borrowed spaces, although before 1870 most of the black members separated to form Plymouth Congregational Church. Circular Church's earliest records show African American baptisms as well as white, and black communicants (both slaves and free) were often the majority. Some African Americans remained even after Plymouth was organized.

The 1886 earthquake finally made the ruined walls of Circular Church a safety hazard, and the congregation resolved to rebuild. Designed by the New York firm of Stephenson and Greene, the new church was erected by the Charlestonian Henry Oliver, who faced its walls with brick from the 1806 structure. The church was listed in the National Register of Historic Places in 1973, and the 1806 Parish House was designated a National Historic Landmark the same year. SARAH FICK

Edwards, George N. *A History of the Independent or Congregational Church in Charleston, South Carolina.* Boston: Pilgrim Press, 1947.

Jacoby, Mary Moore, ed. *The Churches of Charleston and the Lowcountry.* Columbia: University of South Carolina Press, 1993.

Citadel, The. The Citadel originated in 1822 as an arsenal and guardhouse to defend white Charlestonians from possible slave uprisings. In 1832, during the nullification crisis, federal troops were withdrawn from the arsenal, known as the State Citadel, to Fort Moultrie and were replaced by local guardsmen. A decade later in 1842, the General Assembly combined the State Citadel with the Arsenal in Columbia to create the South Carolina Military Academy. Like other southern states, South Carolina believed that a military education would instill education, discipline, character, and patriotic devotion in its young men.

Until 1922, the Citadel's Corps of Cadets was housed in this antebellum structure. Courtesy, South Caroliniana Library, University of South Carolina

When South Carolina seceded from the Union in December 1860, Citadel cadets helped shore up defenses around Charleston harbor. One month later they assembled on Morris Island and fired cannon shots at the *Star of the West* as it steamed to supply the Federal garrison at Fort Sumter, forcing the vessel to abort its mission. Citadel alumni claim that these were the first shots fired in the Civil War.

In February 1865 Union soldiers occupied the Citadel, where they remained for fourteen years. Through the efforts of state legislators and members of the Association of Graduates, the War Department withdrew Federal troops quietly and without explanation in the spring of 1879. Alumni and legislators immediately pushed the General Assembly to reopen the school. Led by the former Confederate general Johnson Hagood, supporters argued that the Citadel was still relevant to the needs of the state. However, its new mission was not to defend South Carolina against the federal government, but rather to combine a useful education with the virtues of military discipline, uniting the sons of all South Carolinians, whether rich or poor, into an egalitarian Corps of Cadets. Their arguments prevailed, and the Citadel reopened in October 1882.

Soon after, the barracks were overflowing with "paying cadets," sons of the more prosperous and prominent citizens, and with "beneficiary cadets," boys from poorer families in every county who were selected by competitive examination to receive full scholarships. By 1918 the buildings on Marion Square no longer could accommodate the 350-man Corps of Cadets. That same year the city of Charleston transferred one hundred acres between Hampton Park and the Ashley River for the construction of the "Greater Citadel." Four years later the towering new barracks were filled with cadets and new buildings accommodated classrooms, faculty, and staff.

This expansion did not occur without "growing pains." Hazing of freshmen, known as "rats," had become endemic, and the "detail" system bound them to serve the demands of upperclassmen. These practices invoked the ire of General Charles P. Summerall, who became president of the institution after his retirement in 1931 as army chief of staff. His blistering rebuke of cadet leadership led to the elimination of the "detail system" and a sharp reduction of hazing incidents. Summerall also secured federal and private funds to establish scholarships, construct new buildings, and enhance the professional standing of the faculty. He left a solid foundation for retired general Mark W. Clark, who succeeded Summerall in 1955. Throughout the ten years of his presidency, Clark utilized his World War II fame to increase enrollment, establish an endowment, and upgrade campus facilities. At the same time, he vigorously resisted the admission of African American men, echoing the belief of thousands of Citadel graduates that integration was part of a communist plot to take over America. In 1965, as South Carolina colleges moved toward the integration of their student bodies, Clark announced his retirement. One year later the Citadel admitted its first African American, Charles Foster.

The Citadel created master's degree programs for men and women in 1965. However, in spite of the admission of women to the national service academies, as well as its own graduate programs, the Citadel continued to reject the admission of women into the cadet corps. In 1995 the Fourth U.S. Circuit Court of Appeals ordered the Citadel to admit its first female, Shannon Faulkner. However, after six days on campus in the spotlight of national and international media attention, she left and returned home. In 1996 the U.S. Supreme Court ruled that Virginia Military Institute's all-male policy was unconstitutional, and in June the Citadel Board of Visitors voted unanimously to admit women into the Corps of Cadets. In August four women entered the corps. Two withdrew after they charged upperclassmen with hazing, but two, Nancy Mace and Petra Lovetinska, completed their "knob year" and went on to become the first female cadet graduates of the Citadel. In the fall of 2004 the cadet corps of 1,964 included 120 women and 151 African Americans. W. GARY NICHOLS

Andrew, Rod. *Long Gray Lines: The Southern Military School Tradition, 1839–1915.* Chapel Hill: University of North Carolina Press, 2001.

Baker, Gary R. *Cadets in Gray: The Story of the Cadets of the South Carolina Military Academy and the Cadet Rangers in the Civil War.* Columbia, S.C.: Palmetto Bookworks, 1989.

Bond, Oliver J. *The Story of the Citadel.* 1936. Reprint, Greenville, S.C.: Southern Historical Press, 1989.

MacCaulay, Alexander S., Jr. "Discipline and Rebellion: The Citadel Rebellion of 1898." *South Carolina Historical Magazine* 103 (January 2002): 30–47.

Manegold, Catherine S. *In Glory's Shadow: Shannon Faulkner, the Citadel and a Changing America.* New York: Knopf, 1999.

Nichols, W. Gary. "The General as College President: Charles P. Summerall and Mark W. Clark as Presidents of the Citadel." *South Carolina Historical Magazine* 95 (October 1994): 314–35.

Citizens' Councils. Founded in 1954 in Indianola, Mississippi, Citizens' Councils quickly spread across the South. The organizations promoted membership as a "respectable" way for disgruntled segregationists to protest civil rights activism. The councils distributed prosegregation propaganda and attempted to protect the legality of racial segregation throughout the South. They publicly renounced violence but encouraged organized economic pressure against African Americans and whites who were sympathetic to the black freedom struggle.

South Carolina's first Citizens' Councils appeared in Orangeburg County in August 1955. The first chapters were formed in the city of Orangeburg and the small town of Elloree. They emerged after local civil rights activists circulated petitions demanding the immediate integration of the county's schools in accordance with the 1954 *Brown v. Board of Education* decision of the U.S. Supreme Court.

The establishment of Citizens' Councils spread rapidly through South Carolina. On October 10, 1955, representatives from thirty-eight council chapters met in Columbia and formed the Association of Citizens' Councils of South Carolina (ACCSC). The ACCSC was part of the Citizens' Councils of America, which was based in Mississippi. The council movement peaked in South Carolina in 1956. In January 1956 a Citizens' Council rally in Columbia drew more than four thousand people to hear U.S. Senator James O. Eastland of Mississippi speak at the state capitol. By July 1, 1956, Citizens' Councils in South Carolina claimed forty thousand members and fifty-five councils.

The two crowning achievements of Citizens' Councils in South Carolina were their political activism and a protracted campaign of economic intimidation against African American activists. The councils and other "states' rights" organizations collected enough signatures to place a slate of "independent electors" on the 1956 presidential ballot. They also challenged local officials to prove their allegiance to segregated society by publicly aligning themselves with the councils. Economic intimidation was most apparent in Orangeburg County. There, Citizens' Council members circulated the names of African Americans who had signed the desegregation petitions and targeted civil rights activists for economic retaliation by firing employees, calling in loans, and refusing credit to petition signers and their families. For many civil rights leaders, pressure from Citizens' Councils led to the loss of house, home, and occupation.

The first ACCSC chairman was Micah Jenkins, who also served as chairman of the Charleston Citizens' Council. Jenkins was a Charleston-area nursery owner and Clemson College graduate. The driving force behind the movement in South Carolina, however, was S. Emory Rogers. Rogers had represented the Summerton School Board in *Briggs v. Elliot* and served as the organization's executive secretary. He retired from Citizens' Councils in December 1956, and Jenkins resigned in 1957. Following these departures, ACCSC leadership changed hands numerous times. Without steady leadership, council membership rapidly declined, and the group's influence diminished. By 1958 the Charleston *News and Courier* declared that the organization was on a "siesta." Although ACCSC remained active well into the 1960s, membership never rose above one thousand after 1958. JOHN W. WHITE

Bartley, Numan V. *The Rise of Massive Resistance: Race and Politics in the South during the 1950's.* Baton Rouge: Louisiana State University Press, 1969.
Hine, William C. "Civil Rights and Campus Wrongs: South Carolina State College Students Protest, 1955–1968." *South Carolina Historical Magazine* 97 (October 1996): 310–31.
McMillen, Neil R. *The Citizens' Council: Organized Resistance to the Second Reconstruction, 1954–64.* Urbana: University of Illinois Press, 1971.
Quint, Howard. *Profile in Black and White: A Frank Portrait of South Carolina.* Washington, D.C.: Public Affairs, 1958.

Civil Rights Act (1964). The Civil Rights Act of 1964 was the most comprehensive federal civil rights legislation passed since Reconstruction. Addressing all spheres of public life—social, political, and economic—the act guaranteed all American citizens access to public facilities, accommodations, and schools that received federal money, as well as ensuring their ability to vote in federal elections and to be employed on a nondiscriminatory basis. It also included, among its ten titles, provisions for the creation of the U.S. Civil Rights Commission and the Equal Employment Opportunity Commission. Overall, this comprehensive federal law was designed to challenge and overturn the overt segregation and discrimination that African Americans continued to confront in southern states such as South Carolina.

The civil rights bill was originally proposed under the administration of President John F. Kennedy in 1963, but it was passed after his assassination when Lyndon B. Johnson succeeded him as president. Johnson used his parliamentary skills to secure the bill. In February 1964 it passed the House by an overwhelming vote of 290 to 130. It took another four months, however, to clear the Senate, where the fear was that Senator Strom Thurmond and other southern senators would try to kill it by a filibuster. Thurmond had set a filibuster record (24 hours, 18 minutes) in an attempt to block Senate approval of a previous civil rights bill in 1957. Despite opposition to the bill from southern congressmen such as Thurmond, the Senate voted cloture in June and passed the bill by a vote of 73 to 27. President Johnson signed it into law on July 2, 1964.

The Civil Rights Act of 1964 proved to be important in ending segregation and discrimination in South Carolina's public schools and public accommodations. From the *Brown* decision of 1954 through 1963, white citizens adopted the stance of "massive resistance" to desegregation and fought the efforts of the National Association for the Advancement of Colored People (NAACP) and the federal courts to change the "southern way of life." The state's political leadership, for example, passed laws to outlaw the NAACP and to force its members who held public jobs to resign from the organization or be fired. Nevertheless, prior to the passage of the Civil Rights Act of 1964, the sit-in movement of 1960 as well as other civil rights agitation in the state had made some progress. In 1963 white leadership in several of the state's major cities met with African American leaders and began the process of desegregating schools and opening up public facilities and accommodations to African American citizens. In Charleston, for example, African American and white leaders formed a Community Relations Committee to negotiate the desegregation of downtown hotels and other public accommodations. In addition, the state's two largest universities, Clemson and the University of South Carolina, admitted their first African American students without any violent incidents. Thus, the passage of the act served to encourage and to legitimize the process of desegregation that the state's African American and white leaders had already undertaken. W. MARVIN DULANEY

Franklin, John Hope, and Alfred A. Moss. *From Slavery to Freedom: A History of African Americans.* 8th ed. New York: Knopf, 2000.

Lytle, Clifford M. "The History of the Civil Rights Bill of 1964." *Journal of Negro History* 51 (October 1966): 275–96.

Smyth, William D. "Segregation in Charleston in the 1950s: A Decade of Transition." *South Carolina Historical Magazine* 92 (April 1991): 99–123.

Solomon, W. E. "The Problem of Desegregation in South Carolina." *Journal of Negro Education* 25 (summer 1956): 315–23.

Sproat, John G. "'Firm Flexibility': Perspectives on Desegregation in South Carolina." In *New Perspectives on Race and Slavery in America: Essays in Honor of Kenneth M. Stampp,* edited by Robert H. Abzug and Stephen E. Maizlish. Lexington: University Press of Kentucky, 1986.

Whalen, Charles W., and Barbara Whalen. *The Longest Debate: A Legislative History of the 1964 Civil Rights Act.* Washington, D.C.: Seven Locks, 1985.

Civil rights movement. During Reconstruction, South Carolina experimented briefly with interracial democracy. African American males voted and participated in government on the local, state, and federal level as officeholders and appointed officials. A new state constitution of 1868 expanded civil rights and women's rights, and instituted public education. Reconstruction in South Carolina lasted longer than in any other state, and South Carolina's black Republicans achieved as great a degree of political power as did African Americans elsewhere. These circumstances evaporated, however, following the overthrow of Republican rule in the state elections of 1876. With the reestablishment of conservative white rule, legislators spent the next several decades undermining the gains of Reconstruction. In education, they resegregated the University of South Carolina and drastically cut support for black schools. On the economic front, because so many white and black landless families became sharecroppers and tenants after the Civil War, Democrats repealed laws favorable to tenants and instituted lien laws to favor landowners and merchants. Politicians went beyond custom and wrote employment discrimination into South Carolina law. The textile industry, a major employment opportunity for the landless and the jobless in the postbellum South, developed as a whites-only labor enterprise.

The Democratic Party's white elite also worked to disfranchise black voters in South Carolina, beginning with the notorious Eight Box Law of 1882, which reduced the number of black voters from 58,000 in 1880 to less than 14,000 by 1888. In the 1890s Benjamin Ryan Tillman gained control of the Democratic Party, with a regime that was as racist and as committed to white supremacy as any in the South. Tillman forces avowed their intention to disfranchise African Americans by rewriting the state constitution, which they did in 1895. The following year the State Democratic Executive Committee prohibited all African Americans from voting in the primary, which was, in a one-party system, the only election that mattered. African Americans were effectively disfranchised for the next sixty-five years. As late as 1940 only 3,000 African Americans in South Carolina were registered to vote.

In 1963, black Charlestonians boycotted business that refused to hire African Americans. Courtesy, Avery Research Center for African American History and Culture

During the 1930s and 1940s African Americans such as the journalist John McCray, the National Association for the Advancement of Colored People (NAACP) leader I. DeQuincey Newman, the activist Modjeska Simkins, and others encouraged sustained activism as a means of effecting racial change. Esau Jenkins, a black businessman from Charleston, with help from the NAACP activist and native Charlestonian Septima Clark, the Highlander Folk School founder Myles Horton (white), the beautician Bernice Robinson, and Guy and Candie Carawan (whites who moved to Johns Island) began citizenship schools in the late 1940s and early 1950s to help African Americans obtain the right to vote, learn about legal rights and strategies for civil disobedience, and fight white supremacy. These schools became an effective tool of the civil rights movement, encouraging thousands to take part in demonstrations.

In the 1940s both supporters and opponents of segregation stepped up their efforts to maintain or challenge the racial status quo in South Carolina. During World War II the state did not allow absentee ballots for those in the armed services because they wanted to exclude African American soldiers from voting. In 1944 the South Carolina legislature passed a resolution denouncing any "amalgamation" of the races. It further resolved an affirmation of "White Supremacy as now prevailing in the South" and pledged "lives and our sacred honor to maintain it, whatever the cost, in War and Peace." At the war's end, the brutal beating of the U.S. veteran Isaac Woodard in South Carolina spurred President Harry Truman toward civil rights and influenced Truman's 1948 order to end the segregation of all military facilities. This executive order had an extensive impact in South Carolina, with its numerous facilities.

In 1942 a small group of African American activists organized the South Carolina Negro Citizens Committee to raise money to challenge the white primary. When in 1944 the U.S. Supreme Court overturned the white primary, South Carolina led the way in devising other means to keep African Americans out of the Democratic primary. When the NAACP challenged the "private" primary in federal court, Judge J. Waties Waring of Charleston ruled that because the Democratic primary was the vehicle through which all public officials were chosen, it remained a state action and that excluding some citizens from primary elections violated the Fourteenth and Fifteenth Amendments. The Democratic Party then extended the literacy test required for general elections to the primary. Furthermore, they would allow qualified African Americans to vote only if they swore an oath: to support "the social, religious, and educational separation of the races." In 1948, in *Brown v. Baskin,* Waring overturned that allowance and issued a court order that voting "be opened to all parties irrespective of race, color, creed or condition."

By 1944 a statewide African American protest organization had been organized: the Progressive Democratic Party led by John McCray. This group unsuccessfully challenged the seating of South Carolina's all-white delegation at the 1944 Democratic National

Convention; it also sponsored Osceola McKaine as a candidate for the U.S. Senate against the Democrat Olin Johnston. The Progressive Democrats and the NAACP mounted a registration drive that increased the number of black voters on the rolls to 50,000 by 1946. Despite Ku Klux Klan marches and cross burnings, 35,000 black voters went to the polls in the 1948 primary, the same year that Governor Strom Thurmond headed the "Dixiecrat" Party in protest of the civil rights plank of the Democratic Party. In 1950 African Americans provided the margin of victory for New Dealer Olin Johnston over Strom Thurmond for the Senate.

At this time Governor James F. Byrnes began to move the state toward a sophisticated, "moderate" approach in resisting racial integration. During his campaign for governor, he recommended gerrymandering school districts according to segregated residential patterns. To forestall integration, Byrnes used a significant portion of a new sales tax for the education of African American children, and white leaders throughout the state began equalizing the facilities of white and black schools in an attempt to maintain segregation. Byrnes went so far as to recommend that South Carolina eliminate from its constitution the provision for public schools, which it did. Byrnes also created the so-called segregation committee, chaired by state representative L. Marion Gressette. This special school committee coordinated efforts to maintain the racial status quo. The South Carolina legislature even passed a resolution that gave itself the right to nullify or overrule federal laws. This technique of bending a little to prevent larger changes gave the state another decade of segregation. By 1963 only Mississippi and South Carolina had not even token integration of schools.

Believing that education was a key to freedom, African Americans made separate and unequal education the foremost target of the civil rights movement in South Carolina. In the early 1940s the NAACP brought court cases to equalize teachers' salaries. Black South Carolinians' most dramatic and influential success against institutionalized white racism involved the *Briggs v. Elliot* case against the Summerton School District of Clarendon County. In his ruling on this case, Judge Waring was the first federal judge to render an opinion that segregation was unconstitutional when he dissented in favor of the African American plaintiffs. This case culminated in the *Brown* decision, which eventually outlawed segregated schools. The South Carolina parents who brought this suit, who wanted a decent education for their children, suffered mightily for their efforts, and their leader, the Reverend Joseph Alfred DeLaine, had to flee the state as a fugitive. In 1974, the year the exiled DeLaine passed away, the school district where he started that lawsuit had three thousand black children and one white child attending public schools. In response to integration, the state allowed students to attend schools in any district where the parents owned any amount of property. Most school districts did not integrate until 1971, and in some areas private segregation academies continued to attract white students into the twenty-first century.

South Carolina heralds the moderation of its leadership during the civil rights era, especially when compared to the actions of leaders in other Deep South states. Moderate leaders put accommodation over confrontation and worked within the legal framework. But these same leaders also did all they could to manipulate the government and the legal system to forestall civil rights. Just as the South Carolina attorney general's office had adamantly defended the principles of public school segregation before the U.S. Supreme Court in *Brown v. Board of Education,* the South Carolina congressional delegation resolutely and unanimously opposed every civil rights bill proposed to Congress into the 1960s. Senator Thurmond mounted a record filibuster against the 1957 Civil Rights Bill. South Carolina also led the challenge to the 1965 Voting Rights Act in *South Carolina v. Katzenbach.* In denying that challenge and affirming the constitutionality of the Voting Rights Act, Chief Justice Earl Warren stated that South Carolina's history of white supremacy and racial discrimination at the ballot box justified the intrusive measures provided by the act.

South Carolina whites bitterly opposed federal court decisions on integration. As demands for justice grew in the African American community, white backlash inexorably followed. In 1957, in the Orangeburg County town of Wells, seventeen white men attacked a sixty-year-old black farmhand. The Holly Hill magistrate fined the leader of the white mob $50 for disorderly conduct and charged the farmhand with assault and battery for trying to defend himself. Freedom riders confronted their first problems in South Carolina. In 1961, when the freedom riders first headed south to test compliance with the Supreme Court's 1959 ruling on the integration of interstate transportation facilities, trouble occurred in Rock Hill. There, the seminarian John Lewis (later a congressman from Georgia) entered a "white only" waiting room at the bus terminal, and white youths beat both Lewis and his white traveling companion.

In the 1950s African Americans formed another organization to promote civil rights in South Carolina, the Congress of Racial Equality (CORE). James McCain, the former head of the Black Teacher's Association in South Carolina, organized seven CORE groups throughout the state to work on voter registration. CORE later proved instrumental in the South Carolina sit-in movement. Despite the urging of CORE's national leadership that he enlist as many whites as possible, McCain found that joining an interracial civil rights organization, or even supporting a black voter registration drive, was unthinkable for most white Carolinians. CORE and the NAACP had some rivalry, but the two organizations eventually worked out a tacit division of the state.

At the same time that organizations were working in the educational and political arenas, the civil rights movement developed a third agenda: integration of day-to-day services. The student sit-in movement that began in Greensboro, North Carolina, moved next to South Carolina, where students sat-in at lunch counters in Rock Hill in February 1960. Students in South Carolina engaged in demonstrations for the next three years and went to jail throughout the state. Charleston retained segregated lunch counters as late as June 1963, refusing to change until after it suffered through turbulent rioting.

White Citizens' Councils, most active in those parts of the state where African Americans were the majority, tended to focus their animosity on the NAACP, the catalyst for most African American lawsuits in desegregation cases. Dedicated teachers such as Septima Clark lost their jobs and their retirement benefits when they would not forgo their NAACP membership. Other NAACP members and their relatives were also fired, and in some cases African American leaders had to flee the state to avoid violence and legal prosecution. In 1956 the General Assembly adopted laws making NAACP members ineligible for state employment, requiring investigation of NAACP activity at the traditionally black South Carolina State College, and revising the state's barratry laws for use against NAACP attorneys who fought for civil rights litigation. CORE organizer Frank Robinson was also a target, forced out of his real estate and home-building business when local banks cut off his credit because of his voter-registration activities.

Despite the insistence of some Carolinians on white supremacy, some progress occurred during the 1960s. In January 1963 Harvey Gantt peacefully desegregated Clemson University, and in the fall of that year African American students desegregated the University of South Carolina. By 1965 every public and many private colleges had admitted African American students. Under court order in August 1963, eleven African American children entered previously all-white schools in District 20 in the city of Charleston, the first school district in the state to desegregate. Through freedom-of-choice plans and other stalling mechanisms, it was not until 1971 that most public schools in the state integrated.

Nor was violence from angry whites entirely eliminated. In 1968 in Orangeburg, law enforcement officers shot thirty African American students, killing three. These students from Claflin College and South Carolina State College had been protesting a segregated bowling alley. Two year later, in Lamar, two hundred white men armed with ax handles, chains, and stones stormed three school buses transporting African American students to the high school.

South Carolina whites continued efforts to keep black registration down and sometimes did not count all the votes cast by African Americans. South Carolina had no elected black officials in 1965. Yet, thanks to earlier civil rights activity, thirty-seven percent of eligible African Americans that year were already registered to vote. The passage of two landmark federal laws, the Civil Rights Act of 1964 and the Voting Rights Act of 1965, and the enforcement of the one-person, one-vote rule in redistricting dramatically changed the face of the civil rights movement in South Carolina. The Voting Rights Act eliminated literacy tests and allowed African Americans to register in record numbers. By 1967 black voter registration had climbed to fifty-one percent of the age-eligible population. These voters demanded more progressive leadership and politics. Almost immediately the white-supremacist rhetoric that had been a hallmark of the state's political leaders for more than a century was eliminated. By and large, South Carolina's white officials grudgingly conceded, as in the rest of the South, that the Voting Rights Act made it impossible to prevent African American citizens from registering and casting their ballots.

The increase in black voters should have delivered more influence in local politics and the election of black candidates, but this did not materialize because political power in South Carolina was not responsive to the local electorate. A system of legislative county government, which the Tillman forces had established for disfranchisement in the 1890s, had abolished county and township elections because conservative whites disliked the association between elected local governments and the African American citizenry. The power of legislative delegations over county government remained largely intact from 1895 until 1965, effectively eliminating the opportunity of African Americans to elect local officials of their choice, even in places where they were an overwhelming majority of the population. In December 1965 a federal court ordered the S.C. Senate to redistrict according to the one-person, one-vote principle. Although conservative white legislators attempted to devise redistricting plans to minimize the chances of electing African American legislators, the Voting Rights Act brought enormous change to South Carolina politics. In 1970 James L. Felder and I. S. Leevy Johnson of Columbia and Herbert U. Fielding of Charleston became the first African Americans elected to the General Assembly since the turn of the century. Between 1974 and 1989 there was an increase in the proportion of African Americans elected to county councils, city councils, and school boards. Most of this increase resulted from the change from at-large to single-member district plans brought about by litigation under the Voting Rights Act. As the civil rights movement shifted from protest to politics and litigation, the major changes in civil rights with an enfranchised black electorate have occurred in the legislatures and in the courtroom—not as dramatic as protests and demonstrations, but just as significant.

After the Civil Rights Act of 1964 and the Voting Rights Act of 1965, the protest movement attempted to tackle economic issues. Only enforcement of the Civil Rights Act of 1964 integrated the cotton mills, although most mill villages remained residentially segregated. In 1969 African American hospital workers in Charleston, mostly women, went on strike for one hundred days. The Southern Christian Leadership Conference and Ralph Abernathy supported the strike, and the workers won some concessions. The national news media compared the Charleston strike to the sanitation strike in Memphis, where Martin Luther King, Jr., had been killed the year before.

South Carolina at the start of the twenty-first century was not the South Carolina of turn-of-the-century Jim Crowism or of the civil rights activities of the 1940s, 1950s, and 1960s. Legal barriers that minimized African American participation are disappearing, and many younger blacks and whites do not remember blatant segregation. Because of enforcement of the Voting Rights Act, African Americans today freely register to vote. The NAACP worked successfully to create a "black" congressional district, and in 1992 South Carolinians elected an African American, James Clyburn, to represent them in the U.S. House of Representatives. These gains, however, have come from enforcement of federal laws, not from white leadership within the state. The civil rights movement in South Carolina and the nation also inspired other groups to demand their rights, including people with disabilities, women, and gays and lesbians. ORVILLE VERNON BURTON

Bass, Jack, and Walter DeVries. *The Transformation of Southern Politics: Social Change and Political Consequence since 1945.* 1976. Reprint, Athens: University of Georgia Press, 1995.

Burton, Orville Vernon. "'The Black Squint of the Law': Racism in South Carolina." In *The Meaning of South Carolina History: Essays in Honor of George C. Rogers, Jr.,* edited by David R. Chesnutt and Clyde N. Wilson. Columbia: University of South Carolina Press, 1991.

———. "South Carolina." In *The Quiet Revolution in the South: The Impact of the Voting Rights Act, 1965–1990,* edited by Chandler Davidson and Bernard Grofman. Princeton, N.J.: Princeton University Press, 1994.

Newby, I. A. *Black Carolinians: A History of Blacks in South Carolina from 1895 to 1968.* Columbia: University of South Carolina Press, 1973.

Quint, Howard H. *Profile in Black and White: A Frank Portrait of South Carolina.* Washington, D.C.: Public Affairs, 1958.

Sproat, John G. "'Firm Flexibility': Perspectives on Desegregation in South Carolina." In *New Perspectives on Race and Slavery in America: Essays in Honor of Kenneth M. Stampp,* edited by Robert H. Abzug and Stephen E. Maizlish. Lexington: University Press of Kentucky, 1986.

Civil War (1861–1865). In early 1865, as General William Tecumseh Sherman's armies crossed the Savannah River from Georgia into the Palmetto State, one Federal soldier shouted, "Boys, this is old South Carolina, let's give her hell!" South Carolina had long been a symbol of disunion, secession, and defiance of authority; had been the first southern state to secede; and had been the site of the first shots of the war at Fort Sumter. Her reputation ensured that Union troops would hasten, and northern civilians celebrate, her downfall.

On the morning of April 12, 1861, Charlestonians flocked to the city's rooftops to witness the Confederate bombardment of Fort Sumter and the beginning of the Civil War. *Harper's Weekly,* May 4, 1861. Courtesy, South Caroliniana Library, University of South Carolina

Most white South Carolinians had long believed that their economic prosperity, political interests, and social stability were inextricably tied to the concept of states' rights, the institution of slavery, and the plantation system as it had evolved since the colonial era. For more than thirty years, the fire-eaters among them had defended their society against enemies both real and imagined, convinced that Yankee abolitionists wanted to take their slaves from them and were willing to trample their self-respect, freedom, and liberty in doing so. Their agitation made South Carolina foremost in a movement that advocated secession from the Union and the creation of a separate southern nation. In 1860, with the election of Abraham Lincoln (a "Black Republican") as president, the radicals finally found the justification they had sought for so many years.

South Carolinians soon elected delegates to a secession convention, which first convened in Columbia in mid-December but met for only one day before adjourning amid a smallpox scare and reconvening in Charleston. On December 20, 1860, the delegates voted unanimously to secede, declaring that Lincoln's "opinions and purposes are hostile to slavery" and announcing that South Carolina had "resumed her position among the nations of the world." The convention, hoping to influence like-minded southerners, invited other states to send commissioners to a meeting in Montgomery to discuss the creation of a new nation. It also authorized Governor Francis W. Pickens to appoint an Executive Council to assist him in handling the diplomatic and military affairs of a newly independent republic.

Even before the state seceded, South Carolina had already begun making preparations for a war that most of her citizens believed either would never actually occur or would be of short duration. Militia companies, some of them with lineages dating back to the Revolutionary War, were joined by new units raised in cities, towns, and communities all over the state to accommodate the flood of enthusiastic volunteers.

Pickens and other state authorities viewed the presence of four United States military installations in and around Charleston—Fort Moultrie, Fort Sumter, Castle Pinckney, and the U.S. Arsenal—as an insult to South Carolina's sovereignty and a threat to her safety. Major Robert Anderson, commanding a small garrison of Federal troops at Fort Moultrie, viewed his position on the mainland as untenable and moved his men out to Fort Sumter under the cover of night the week after the state seceded. Tensions escalated as state troops seized the other three installations and waited impatiently for the Federals' next move.

In January 1861, when Federal authorities sent the ship *Star of the West* to resupply Anderson's garrison, batteries on Morris Island, including one manned by cadets from the Citadel, fired on the ship. As she neared Fort Sumter cannon fire from Fort Moultrie forced her to withdraw. Though the episode was technically an act of war, an uneasy peace lasted for the next two months. Pickens and his Executive Council continued preparing for war, but as the Confederate government became well established and its authorities started assuming the responsibility for military and diplomatic affairs, the council had outlived its purpose and was abolished in April.

By that time the fighting had already begun. At the end of March, Abraham Lincoln, who inherited the secession crisis from President James Buchanan, decided to send additional supplies to Fort Sumter in spite of warnings from his advisers that it might mean war. While the supplies were on their way, General P. G. T. Beauregard, the Confederate commander in Charleston, demanded that Anderson surrender the fort. When Anderson refused, Beauregard ordered the batteries surrounding the harbor to open fire. The first shells fell early on the morning of April 12, 1861, and though the outmanned and outgunned Federals responded, the outcome was never in doubt. By the next afternoon Anderson surrendered, completing the first Confederate victory of the war.

As Lincoln called for 75,000 volunteers to put down the rebellion, and as the states of the upper South responded by calling their own secession conventions, South Carolinians continued to flock to the colors. More than 60,000 of them saw Confederate service during the war. Reserve and home guard units had little real impact but were nonetheless a presence in their own communities. Several regular Confederate units were commanded by officers with at least some military experience or education, but many more of them were raised and commanded by men better known for their political careers or family connections than anything else. Many units were first sent to defend Charleston or other points in the lowcountry and remained there for most of the war. Others responded to calls for assistance once it became obvious that Virginia would be the major battlefield in the East, and they began arriving there that spring and summer. Still others organized later in 1861 or early in 1862 spent a few months in their home state before serving for most of the war in other states, primarily in Mississippi, Tennessee, and Georgia. Several men born or raised in South Carolina became general officers, among them Stephen Elliott, Jr., and Johnson Hagood, who served for most of the war in their home state; Richard H. Anderson, Matthew C. Butler, Wade Hampton, Micah Jenkins, Joseph B. Kershaw, and James Longstreet, who served in the Army of Northern Virginia; and Ellison Capers, States Rights Gist, and Arthur M. Manigault, who served in the Army of Tennessee.

The Palmetto State was not a major battleground during the war, though it did see a few major campaigns and several minor engagements. The first significant action in the state occurred in the fall of 1861 when the United States Navy, seeking a port that might serve as a base for its blockade of the southern coast, sent an expedition toward Port Royal and Beaufort. On November 7, 1861, Commander Samuel F. Du Pont's fleet shelled the Confederate defenses guarding Port Royal Sound and quickly forced their garrisons to withdraw. Over the next few weeks Federal troops occupied Beaufort, Port Royal, Hilton Head, and the neighboring Sea Islands. Planters and other whites in the area fled their homes, leaving behind thousands of blacks whose status was somewhere between enslaved and free.

The Port Royal disaster, for which Pickens and his administration were widely criticized by politicians, newspaper editors, and refugees forced to flee their homes, resulted in the creation of a new Executive Council in early 1862. This council assumed much more power than the first one had. It declared martial law in portions of the lowcountry, established quotas for the enlistment of additional troops into Confederate service, required slaveowners to loan their slaves out for long- or short-term tasks considered critical to the war effort, and took food and other supplies to distribute among units defending the state. It operated in spite of widespread grumbling from those who believed that it was infringing on the powers of the legislature and the judiciary and on the civil liberties of individuals. Amid almost constant criticism and controversy, the General Assembly abolished the Executive Council in December 1862.

Hilton Head and Port Royal Sound would serve as a headquarters for Federal land and naval forces for the rest of the war, a staging point from which they would launch numerous combined operations against Charleston and the rest of the coast. Officials of the U.S. Department of the Treasury soon began a project known as the "Port Royal Experiment," by which civil and military authorities took charge of abandoned Sea Island cotton plantations and offered wages for freedmen and freedwomen to work the fields. Northern teachers and missionaries came south to help educate those who were still technically considered "contraband of war." General David Hunter recruited freedmen on the Sea Islands to organize one of the first black regiments in the United States Army, despite having no real authority to do so before the Emancipation Proclamation took effect in the portions of South Carolina under Union occupation on January 1, 1863.

It soon became obvious that the Federals would focus most of their attention on Charleston, which they described as "that viper's nest and breeding place of rebellion." As a result troops were concentrated in and around Charleston and to a lesser extent along the strategically vital Charleston and Savannah Railroad. In the late spring of 1862, the Federals launched an expedition against James Island, the main line of Confederate defenses south of the city. On June 16, 1862, General Henry Benham ordered an ill-advised assault against a well-placed earthwork at Secessionville and was repulsed with heavy losses. The battle stopped the Union advance and buoyed Confederate morale after the losses of Nashville and New Orleans earlier that year.

On the home front civilians adjusted to the changes forced on them by the war. Shortages in food—whether subsistence items or more nonessential ones—depended largely on the locale, with citizens in rural communities generally managing better than those in cities such as Charleston and Columbia, which saw increasingly higher prices in inflationary times. Prices demanded for clothing, household items, and other goods rose steadily as well, affected both by the Union blockade of Charleston and by deficiencies in manufacturing and transportation throughout the South. Some South Carolinians saved or hoarded what they could, while others took advantage of the times to speculate and charge exorbitant prices for poor quality goods. If relatively few South Carolinians were in real distress until the war's final months, all of them felt the pinch of wartime. Families with husbands and fathers in the Confederate armies were hit particularly hard, and soldiers' relief societies and churches tried to help as best they could.

Conscription, in which all men between the ages of eighteen and thirty-five (later forty-five) were drafted for Confederate service, was unpopular at best and unmanageable at worst. State authorities drafted those they could get between the ages of sixteen and sixty-five for the home guard and reserves. By 1863 some men either evaded the draft or deserted once they were enlisted, with individuals and groups hiding out in the mountain districts in the northwestern corner of the state, often called "the Dark Corner."

Charleston and Columbia were the most significant centers of political, economic, military, and social activity throughout the war. Charleston was the headquarters of the Confederate Department of South Carolina and Georgia (later the Department of South Carolina, Georgia, and Florida). Other Confederate offices there included the former U.S. Arsenal, the Charleston Naval Station, a collector of customs, and a district office of the Quartermaster General's Department. Columbia, as the state capital and the geographic center of the state, had its population swelled by a tremendous influx of refugees. Confederate offices there included the Columbia Arsenal, a branch of the Naval Powder Works, a Bureau of Conscription, and a district headquarters of the Nitre and Mining Bureau. By 1862 most Confederate currency was engraved and printed in Charleston or Columbia, then sent to Richmond for distribution. When the Treasury Note Bureau was established in 1864 in Columbia, it took over the entire operation from engraving to distribution, employing young women to sign and cut sheets of currency and bonds.

State and local governments made necessary adjustments as well, implementing policies intended to support the war effort. Milledge L. Bonham succeeded Pickens as governor in December 1862, serving until December 1864. As the war progressed, some politicians expressed opposition not only to Confederate measures such as conscription and impressments, or to the course of the war, but also to Jefferson Davis as president. Newspaper editors such as Robert Barnwell Rhett, Jr., of the *Charleston Mercury* heaped scorn on Davis and his administration at every turn. Andrew G. Magrath succeeded Bonham as governor in December 1864, serving only a few months before the war's end.

Slaves and free blacks alike found that the upheaval of the war and its uncertainties loosened restrictions not only on their daily lives but also on their relationships and interactions with whites at all levels of society. Whites living in the midst of blacks who outnumbered them had long feared slave rebellions. During the war, however, the absence of many slaveowners and their sons in military service meant that overseers and owners' wives ran their plantations and farms and that reports or rumors of dissatisfaction among slaves were commonplace. When state and Confederate authorities impressed slaves from reluctant owners, it became more difficult than ever to keep growing crops and raising livestock at prewar levels.

South Carolina units played significant roles defending the low-country for two and a half years after Secessionville, most notably near Charleston, where they repulsed an attack by a Union ironclad squadron in April 7, 1863. On July 10, 1863, General Quincy Gillmore opened a campaign against Charleston by landing forces on Morris Island in an attempt to gain a foothold from which to operate against Charleston. On July 18 the Federals launched an attack on Battery Wagner, the major Confederate earthwork on Morris Island. The assault, notable as one of the first in which the United States Army employed black troops, was a complete failure and resulted in heavy casualties. Though unsuccessful in capturing Charleston, Gillmore's activities initiated a siege that lasted until February 1865. During this period the Federals carried out two major bombardments from batteries on Morris Island against Fort Sumter and began firing shells into Charleston, which accomplished little other than the destruction of property and the intimidation of civilians. A third and final major bombardment of Fort Sumter occurred the next summer, and a Federal movement from Port Royal against the railroad junction at Gopher Hill (Ridgeland) in conjunction with Sherman's march from Atlanta in late November 1864 resulted in an inconclusive engagement at Honey Hill.

In September 1864 a military prison was established at Florence. As many as twelve thousand Union prisoners, most of them transferred from the prison at Andersonville, Georgia, were held there during the war's final winter. Almost three thousand of them died before Sherman's advance through the state closed the prison in February 1865.

In January 1865 Sherman began shifting his army's right wing through Beaufort to Pocotaligo. Then on February 1 the soldiers at Pocotaligo moved inland while Sherman's left wing crossed the Savannah River and marched through Robertsville and Lawtonville. The only engagement of any consequence before he approached Columbia occurred on February 2 and 3 at Rivers Bridge on the Salkehatchie River. Some eight thousand Federals attempting to cross there were delayed briefly by nine hundred Confederates, who were quickly outflanked and forced to withdraw, clearing the way for Sherman's advance through the state. Though Sherman feinted as if he were headed for Charleston, his force reached the outskirts of Columbia by February 16. Charleston was quietly evacuated the next day, at the same time that the major Confederate force defending the two Carolinas evacuated Columbia.

The 55th Massachusetts led Union forces into Charleston, February 17, 1865. Courtesy, South Carolina Historical Society

In 1867 the nation's first monument honoring fallen Confederates was erected in Cheraw. This particular image was taken May 10, 1900—Confederate Memorial Day. Courtesy, Cheraw Visitors Bureau

In the capital city, Sherman's soldiers ransacked both the existing State House and the new unfinished one, and many of them roamed the streets drinking, frightening citizens, and looting at will. High winds throughout the night of February 17–18 helped spread multiple fires, and about a third of the city burned, although numerous Union officers and men tried to reestablish order and help Columbians save their homes and churches. Sherman continued toward North Carolina, occasionally skirmishing along the way and burning or ransacking portions of Winnsboro, Camden, Chester, and Cheraw during the next two weeks. A limited Federal raid by troops under General Edward E. Potter in April made its way through Georgetown, Manning, Sumter, and Camden and was the last significant military operation in the state during the war.

One of the more painful costs of Confederate defeat was that 18,000 to 21,000 men, or one of every fourteen white South Carolinians, had been killed or mortally wounded or had died from disease. The most significant consequence of Union victory was the emancipation of 400,000 slaves and their subsequent attempt to adjust to their new place in South Carolina society. Whether bitter amid defeat, devastation, and memories of the past or optimistic amid victory, freedom, and expectations for the future, South Carolinians would struggle with the results—and the legacy—of the war for generations to come. J. TRACY POWER

Barrett, John G. *Sherman's March through the Carolinas.* Chapel Hill: University of North Carolina Press, 1956.

Brennan, Patrick. *Secessionville: Assault on Charleston.* Campbell, Calif.: Savas, 1996.

Burton, E. Milby. *The Siege of Charleston, 1861–1865.* Columbia: University of South Carolina Press, 1970.

Cauthen, Charles E. *South Carolina Goes to War, 1860–1865.* Chapel Hill: University of North Carolina Press, 1950.

Davis, William C. *The Cause Lost: Myths and Realities of the Confederacy.* Lawrence: University Press of Kansas, 1996.

Glatthaar, Joseph T. *The March to the Sea and Beyond: Sherman's Troops in the Savannah and Carolinas Campaigns.* New York: New York University Press, 1985.

Hudson, Leonne M. "A Confederate Victory at Grahamville: Fighting at Honey Hill." *South Carolina Historical Magazine* 94 (January 1993): 19–33.

Lucas, Marion Brunson. *Sherman and the Burning of Columbia.* 1976. Reprint, Columbia: University of South Carolina Press, 2000.

Moore, John Hammond. *Southern Homefront, 1861–1865.* Columbia, S.C.: Summerhouse, 1998.

Power, J. Tracy. "'This Indescribably Ugly Salkehatchie': The Battle of Rivers Bridge, 2–3 February 1865." In *Rivers Bridge State Park Visitors Guide,* by Daniel J. Bell and J. Tracy Power. Columbia: South Carolina Department of Parks, Recreation, and Tourism, 1992.

Rose, Willie Lee. *Rehearsal for Reconstruction: The Port Royal Experiment.* 1964. Reprint, Athens: University of Georgia Press, 1999.

Rosen, Robert N. *Confederate Charleston: An Illustrated History of the City and the People during the Civil War.* Columbia: University of South Carolina Press, 1994.

Wise, Stephen R. *Gate of Hell: Campaign for Charleston Harbor, 1863.* Columbia: University of South Carolina Press, 1994.

Civilian Conservation Corps. Franklin Delano Roosevelt's Civilian Conservation Corps (CCC) was a New Deal federal initiative that put millions of unemployed men to work on conservation projects. Initially known as the Emergency Conservation Work program, the CCC represented an unprecedented effort to combine social welfare with conservation on public and private lands. Between 1933 and 1942 South Carolina's CCC camps employed more than 49,000 workers, many between the ages of eighteen and twenty-five. In countless hours of backbreaking and often tedious work, CCC workers fought soil erosion and wildfires, created a state parks system, built roads and trails, erected fire towers, and carried out extensive reforestation projects. Wages sent home by CCC workers helped many families weather the Great Depression.

One of the CCC's most notable accomplishments was its rustic-style architectural legacy. As a national style, rustic architecture developed in resort and park settings during the early twentieth century. It combined naturalistic landscape design and elements of the Shingle, Adirondack Great Camp, Prairie, and Craftsman architectural styles. By relying heavily on local materials such as stone and hand-hewn logs, rustic-style buildings appeared as though they had been constructed by frontier craftsmen using only primitive hand tools in harmony with natural surroundings and local building traditions. CCC rustic landscaping emphasized use of native plant species, curvilinear roads and paths, and the creation of romantic settings that encouraged outdoor recreation and exploration of nature.

In South Carolina, the CCC worked with state and federal agencies, especially the National Park Service and the U.S. Forest Service, to develop seventeen state parks, several fish hatcheries, and national forest recreation areas. All of these sites exemplify rustic design principles. Buildings at Oconee, Table Rock, and Paris Mountain state parks and the Walhalla fish hatchery reflect the surrounding mountain environment and pioneer building traditions. Several cabins, picnic shelters, and a lodge are built of hand-hewn chestnut logs. The Paris Mountain bathhouse, a low-lying stone building, rises out of the ground, fully integrated with the surrounding landscape. On the coast, several CCC buildings that are no longer standing also reflected their surroundings. At Hunting Island, the CCC constructed a picnic shelter out of local palmetto logs and thatch, and the former Myrtle Beach State Park bathhouse featured a massive, plantation-inspired portico. In the central part of the state, many structures at Poinsett State Park incorporated locally quarried coquina rock.

The CCC's most important legacy was the role it played in the transformation of South Carolina's rural landscape. By the 1930s intensive cotton farming and logging had left much of the state's land devastated by deforestation, fires, gullies, and sheet erosion. The CCC began the process of land restoration by building hundreds of miles of terraces and planting more than fifty-six million tree seedlings. The state's extensive forests of today can be traced back to the pioneering conservation efforts and the visionary planning of the CCC. AL HESTER

McClelland, Linda Flint. *Presenting Nature: The Historic Landscape Design of the National Park Service, 1916 to 1942.* Washington, D.C.: National Park Service, 1993.

Merrill, Perry. *Roosevelt's Forest Army: A History of the CCC, 1933–1942.* Montpelier, Vt.: P. H. Merrill, 1981.

National Register of Historic Places. Historic Resources of South Carolina State Parks, Multiple Property Listing. South Carolina Department of Archives and History, Columbia.

National Register of Historic Places. Paris Mountain State Park Historic District, 1998. South Carolina Department of Archives and History, Columbia.

National Register of Historic Places. Table Rock State Park Historic District, 1989. South Carolina Department of Archives and History, Columbia.

Waller, Robert A. "The Civilian Conservation Corps and the Emergence of South Carolina's State Park System, 1933–1942." *South Carolina Historical Magazine* 104 (April 2003): 101–25.

Claflin University. Responding to the urgent need to educate former slaves, northern Methodists established Claflin University in Orangeburg, South Carolina, in 1869. Governor William Claflin of Massachusetts and his father, Lee, provided financial support to start the institution. The Claflin family purchased the former site of the Orangeburg Female Institute. They then merged Baker Biblical Institute in Charleston and the Camden Normal Training School and renamed these institutions Claflin University. The university opened its doors on October 27, 1869, without regard to race, color, creed, religion, or complexion. On December 18, 1869, the school received a charter from the South Carolina General Assembly and became the first historically black college or university in the state. Claflin awarded its first bachelor's degrees in 1882.

A panoramic view of Claflin University, 1884. *Historical and Descriptive View of the State of South Carolina.* Courtesy, South Carolina Historical Society

A decline in funding during the 1890s, however, threatened the school. Annual appropriations from the Missionary Society of the Methodist Church, the Methodist Conference, the Freedmen's Aid Society, the John F. Slater Fund, and the South Carolina General Assembly had enabled the institution to offer both an industrial education and liberal arts degrees. But the General Assembly withdrew support for the school in 1895 and in the following year funded the creation of a nonsectarian school for blacks on land taken from Claflin: the Colored Normal, Industrial, Agricultural and Mechanical College of South Carolina (later South Carolina

State University). Moreover, determining that land grant schools like the one adjacent to Claflin were better-suited to offer industrial education, the Freedmen's Aid Society ended its financial assistance. The Methodist Church altered Claflin's designation from university to college because the school did not meet rigorous academic standards.

By the Great Depression, Claflin had changed its curriculum. The school offered fewer courses in the industrial arts and had established a business department. Black males and white females from Boston made up the majority of the faculty. Enrollment in the grammar department (grades one through eight) declined until, by 1937, only twenty-four students were enrolled.

The racial turmoil of the 1950s and 1960s galvanized Claflin students, and many became involved in the civil rights movement in Orangeburg. They joined dozens of demonstrators at South Carolina State College and led a boycott of white merchants, protested against segregated schools and dining facilities, and later turned their attention to voter registration efforts. Claflin protestors were present when state troopers killed three demonstrators on the South Carolina State campus in 1968.

Enrollment increased during the 1970s, and the school added more majors. After a decline in enrollment during the 1980s, the student population rebounded the following decade. Claflin reinstated its historic designation as a university in 1999 and has maintained its affiliation with the United Methodist Church. In 2004 Claflin graduated 304 students with bachelor's degrees and 17 students from its M.B.A. program, which began in 2002. JACKIE R. BOOKER

Fairley, Charlestine R. "A History of Claflin College, 1869–1987." Ph.D. diss., University of South Carolina, 1990.

Gore, Blinzy L. *On a Hilltop High: The Origin and History of Claflin College to 1984.* Spartanburg, S.C.: Reprint Company, 1994.

Hine, William C. "Civil Rights and Campus Wrongs: South Carolina State College Students Protest, 1955–1968." *South Carolina Historical Magazine* 97 (October 1996): 310–31.

Clarendon County (607 sq. miles; 2000 pop. 32,502). The first Clarendon County was created in 1785 but was combined with Claremont and Salem Counties to form Sumter District in 1800. In 1855 the legislature established Clarendon District from the southern half of Sumter, which became Clarendon County once again following a new state constitution in 1868. The county was named in honor of Edward Hyde, Earl of Clarendon, one of the original eight Lords Proprietors. Located in east-central South Carolina, modern Clarendon County is bordered on three sides by Sumter, Florence, and Williamsburg Counties, while the Santee River, in the form of Lake Marion, forms Clarendon's southern boundary. The county seat is Manning, named for the distinguished Manning family.

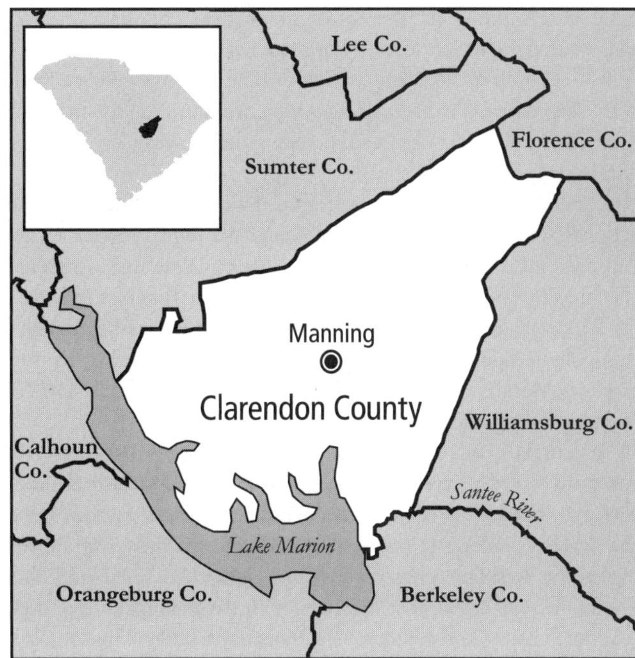

The first Europeans arrived in the mid–eighteenth century and consisted of Scots-Irish Protestants and French Huguenots. During the Revolutionary War the area witnessed several battles. At Nelson's Ferry in August 1780, General Francis Marion freed 150 American prisoners, while killing or capturing twenty-six British. The following February, Marion engaged the enemy at Halfway Swamp and again forced a British retreat. General Thomas Sumter attacked Fort Watson at Wright's Bluff in the same month but was defeated. Soon after, an outnumbered Marion successfully attacked the British at Wyboo Swamp and forced a British surrender at the second battle at Fort Watson, in April 1781.

As was the case with other coastal plain districts, the antebellum Clarendon economy revolved around slavery and cotton. The area's gently sloping hills and loamy soil proved well suited to cotton production and established the economic foundation for two of South Carolina's wealthiest and most influential families, the Richardsons and the Mannings. Five family members from Clarendon served as governor: James Burchell Richardson (1802–1804); Richard Irving Manning (1824–1826); John Peter Richardson II (1840–1842); John Laurence Manning (1852–1854); and John Peter Richardson III (1886–1890). A third member of the Manning family, Richard I. Manning of neighboring Sumter County, served as governor from 1915 to 1919. Altogether, the Richardson-Manning family produced more South Carolina governors than any other.

During the Civil War, Clarendon District supplied three companies to the Confederate cause. Colonel Richard I. Manning recruited and equipped, at his own expense, the Manning Guards in April 1861. That same year Colonel H. L. Benbow took command of Clarendon's largest company, the Sprott Guards. A third collection of volunteers formed what came to be known as Keels' Company. Union forces under the command of General Edward E. Potter marched into Manning on April 8, 1865, and virtually destroyed the town, including the courthouse and jail. In a special edition of the local newspaper, printed and renamed *Banner of Freedom* on April 10, 1865, Potter exhorted town residents to "calmly consider the necessities of their present condition . . . you have been overpowered by numbers and are a conquered people today."

Agriculture continued to dominate the Clarendon economy following the war, with cotton and corn remaining the primary crops until the turn of the century. In the late 1890s R. D. Cothran introduced tobacco and became a vocal proponent for cultivating the crop. In the early twentieth century, Clarendon's economy expanded into agricultural processing as well as farming. By 1927 the county was home to three canneries, two tobacco warehouses, several lumber and planing mills, cotton gins, a fertilizer factory, an oil stove factory, an ice factory, and a printing plant.

In the twentieth century Clarendon County became the starting point for one of the landmark events of the American civil rights movement. In 1950 a group of African American parents from Clarendon County, led by the Reverend Joseph A. DeLaine, filed suit in a federal district court to force South Carolina to provide equal state funding for the education of their children. The legendary civil rights attorney Thurgood Marshall argued the case, known as *Briggs v. Elliot,* in Charleston. The *Briggs* case formed part of the larger *Brown v. Board of Education* decision in 1954, in which the U.S. Supreme Court unanimously struck down racial segregation in the public schools.

Clarendon natives who have found their way into the state and national spotlight include the following: the tennis legend Althea Gibson of Silver, who became the first African American woman to play at Wimbledon and the U.S. Open, and the first to win singles titles in each; the artist Anne Worsham Richardson of Turbeville, nationally recognized for her wildlife drawings; and the horticulturist James Mack Fleming of Alcolu, who co-owns the Charleston Tea Plantation, the only tea farm in the United States.

At century's end, two-fifths of Clarendon County was forest and one-third was dedicated to farming. Traditional agricultural products continued to predominate, including tobacco, cotton, corn, and soybeans. More recent additions include cucumbers and other vegetables. Residents not involved in tilling the soil could find employment in the timber industry or in the manufacture of auto bearings, textiles, and stainless steel transport tankers. The county is rich in natural resources and recreational facilities. Lake Marion, 95 square miles of water and 450 miles of shoreline created in 1942, provides ample opportunity for fishing, golfing, hunting, boating, swimming, camping, and hiking. The area is rated one of the top fishing spots in the nation for crappie, bass, bream, catfish, and striped bass. In 1941 the Santee National Wildlife Refuge was created to maintain the natural habitat of wildlife that was destroyed during construction of the Santee Cooper hydroelectric and navigation projects. Indeed, "Santee-Cooper Country," as it is commonly called, is more widely known for its recreational value than for the electric power that Lake Marion and Lake Moultrie were built to provide. Locals and visitors alike enjoy Woods Bay State Park, a 1,541-acre nature preserve established in 1973. With economic potential, abundant natural resources, and a rich history, Clarendon County entered the twenty-first century full of promise. LAUREN DECKER

Clarendon Cameos. Manning, S.C.: Clarendon County Historical Society, 1976.

Hornsby, Benjamin F. *Stepping Stone to the Supreme Court: Clarendon County, South Carolina.* Columbia: South Carolina Department of Archives and History, 1992.

Orvin, Virginia Kirkland Galluchat. *History of Clarendon County, 1700 to 1961.* N.p., 1961.

Clark, Septima Poinsette (1898–1987). Educator, civil rights activist. Clark was born on May 3, 1898, in Charleston, the second of eight children born to the former slave Peter Poinsette and his freeborn wife, Victoria Anderson. Clark's mother spent part of her early childhood in Haiti, which gave her a unique look at racism in the United States. The gentle and nonviolent composure of Peter Poinsette gave Septima the balance needed to withstand the difficulties she would later face as a human-rights advocate.

Clark attended Avery Institute, completing the teacher training program in 1916. Her parents sacrificed to pay the private school's tuition because of its reputation for academic excellence. The Licentiate of Instruction allowed her to teach at Promise Land School, an overcrowded and underfunded rural school for African Americans on Johns Island (state law prohibited African Americans from teaching in Charleston's public schools). After three years on the island, Clark was well versed in the economic, health, and educational deficiencies facing most southern black communities. In 1919 she took a teaching position at Avery, where she joined the artist Edwin Harleston and former congressman Thomas E. Miller in petitioning the state legislature to permit black employment in Charleston's public schools. Their campaign succeeded the following year, which motivated Clark to further challenge the racial status quo in South Carolina. In May 1920 she married Nerie Clark. Her first child, a daughter, died shortly after birth, but her son, Nerie Jr., was a focal point of her life, especially after her husband's untimely death from kidney failure in 1925.

Septima Poinsette Clark. Courtesy, Avery Research Center for African American History and Culture

A series of moves to Hickory, North Carolina; Dayton, Ohio; and back to Johns Island culminated with Septima Clark accepting a third-grade teaching position in Columbia. Her exposure to professional and civic organizations of the city, some of which were integrated, fortified her resolve to bring change to her state. In both Columbia and Charleston, where she returned in 1947, Clark was an active member of the Methodist Church, the Teachers' Association of South Carolina, the black local affiliate of the Young Women's Christian Association, the Federated Women's Clubs of South Carolina, and the National Association for the Advancement of Colored People (NAACP). Among her fellow activists were the businesswoman Modjeska Monteith Simkins, Booker T. Washington High School principal J. Andrew Simmons, the political organizer John McCray, and NAACP attorney Harold Boulware.

Back in Charleston, Clark acquired a radical reputation for insisting on "choosing her own friends," both black and white, from whom she learned a great deal about the political process. Clark's dismissal from the Charleston County School System in 1956, after she and two other teachers refused to disavow membership in the NAACP, was partially attributed to her public friendship with the controversial Judge J. Waties Waring and his wife. After nearly forty years in the state's schools, Clark was without a job, and she was denied her small but hard-earned pension until 1976, when annual payments were finally reinstated.

In 1953 Clark visited the Highlander Folk School in Monteagle, Tennessee, where she became well versed in the interracial community organizing work of the school. Clark became director of workshops and recruited South Carolinians such as Esau Jenkins, Mary Lee Davis, Herbert Fielding, and her cousin Bernice Robinson. Clark is credited with the creation in 1957 of the "citizenship school" model, which ultimately engaged thousands of ordinary people in literacy and political education throughout the South. The program was adopted by the Southern Christian Leadership Conference and Martin Luther King, Jr. By the early 1960s Clark earned a reputation as "Mother Conscience" to hundreds of youth workers and community organizers.

In 1975 Clark was elected to the Charleston School Board. She received an honorary doctorate of humane letters from the College of Charleston in 1978 and received a Living Legacy Award from President Jimmy Carter in 1979. South Carolina's highest award, the Order of the Palmetto, was given to her in 1982. Septima Poinsette Clark died on Johns Island on December 15, 1987, and was buried at her beloved Old Bethel United Methodist Church. MILLICENT ELLISON BROWN

Brown, Millicent E. "Civil Rights Activism in Charleston, South Carolina, 1940–1970." Ph.D. diss., Florida State University, 1997.

Clark, Septima Poinsette. *Echo in My Soul.* New York: Dutton, 1962.

———. Papers. Robert Scott Small Library, College of Charleston, Charleston.

Gyant, LaVerne, and Deborah F. Atwater. "Septima Clark's Rhetorical and Ethnic Legacy." *Journal of Black Studies* 26 (May 1996): 577–92.

McFadden, Grace Jordan. "Septima P. Clark and the Struggle for Human Rights." In *Women in the Civil Rights Movement,* edited by Vicki Crawford, Jacqueline Ann Rouse, and Barbara Woods. Brooklyn, N.Y.: Carlson, 1990.

Classical music. The first permanent English settlers in South Carolina arrived in 1670, bringing their European musical traditions with them. Psalmody (the singing of psalms in divine worship) was the primary music of the colonists, and by 1700 singing schools provided both musical and devotional training. Although sacred music remained the predominant music of the colonies, the flourishing musical patronage of Charleston, which was the fourth-largest city in British North America by 1742, continued to cultivate the European classical style. As early as 1732 the *South-Carolina Gazette* reported on the second public concert given in the colonies. The St. Cecilia Society, the oldest musical society in the United States, was formed in 1762, providing formal musical instruction and offering concerts until 1822, when it became an exclusive social cotillion.

In the upstate, English, Scots, and Irish settlers brought the secular, oral tradition of the ballad, whose early influence on the development of art music is evidenced by the 1735 production of Colley Cibber's *Flora, or Hob in the Well.* The English Ballad Opera Company presented this first performance of an opera in America in a courtroom above Shepheard's Tavern in Charleston.

By 1800 northeastern singing schools were virtually extinct, although they remained active throughout the rural southern areas well into the nineteenth century. The singing master William Walker, born near Cross Keys in Union County, compiled *Southern Harmony,* which was first published in 1835 in Spartanburg. According to its author, the revolutionary tune book sold more than 600,000 copies and contained hymns, psalms, and anthems published in the popular shape-note tradition designed to assist untrained musicians.

While sacred music was thriving in the rural areas, the refined musical tastes of Charleston's society continued to prefer the European secular tradition. In addition to the active concert life, the dissemination of western art music persisted during the heyday of American piano production during the latter part of the nineteenth century. Because of the great demand for classical and, eventually, popular sheet music, the Seigling Music House (1819–1970) established a retail music store on King Street in Charleston and also operated a music-publishing firm, issuing the works and arrangements of local and European composers. Julian Selby of Columbia was another publisher who issued general and music materials during the 1860s.

After the Civil War, the South's musical activities were slow to resume, but South Carolina's cultural life soon prospered with the construction of music halls such as the Newberry Opera House (1881), the establishment of schools such as the Charleston Conservatory (1884), and the founding of numerous ensembles such as the state's first all-black touring group, the Jenkins Orphanage Band (circa 1895), which played a mixture of ragtime, military, and popular music.

By the twentieth century, classical music was melding with indigenous influences, initiating the shift to a distinctly American musical style and the emergence of native composers such as George Gershwin, who incorporated American idioms into *Porgy and Bess* (1935), the most frequently performed American opera. Set on Cabbage Row (Gershwin called it Catfish Row) in Charleston, the opera includes a mixture of indigenous Gullah spirituals, hymns, and blues, which Gershwin studied during his 1934 visit to Folly Island.

The two most prominent composers native to the state are Lily Strickland (1887–1958) of Anderson and Carlisle Floyd (b. 1926) of Latta. Strickland incorporated spirituals, lullabies, and ethnic folk music into more than four hundred vocal and instrumental compositions, her most famous being "Mah Lindy Lou." Floyd, best known for his opera *Susannah,* has composed several other operas, song cycles, music for piano, and music for orchestra and chorus. Although not native South Carolinians, two other important twentieth-century composers who have impacted musical activity in the state are Ernst Bacon (1898–1990), former dean of and piano professor at Converse College (1938–1945), and Don Gillis (1912–1978), composer in residence and director of the media arts institute at the University of South Carolina from 1973 until his death in 1978.

Musical endeavors continue to prosper in the state's educational institutions as well as in amateur and professional performing groups such as the Charleston Symphony (founded in 1936), the Greenville Symphony (founded in 1948), and the South Carolina Philharmonic (founded in 1963). South Carolina is also home to the internationally renowned Spoleto Festival, which serves as a forum for traditional and contemporary works as well as new and young artists. JENNIFER OTTERVIK

Kingman, Daniel. *American Music: A Panorama.* 2d ed. New York: Schirmer, 1990.

Sadie, Stanley, ed. *New Grove Dictionary of Music and Musicians.* 2d ed. 29 vols. New York: Grove's Dictionaries, 2001.

Simons, Elizabeth Potter. *Music in Charleston from 1732–1919.* Charleston, S.C.: J. J. Furlong, 1927.

Sonneck, Oscar. *Early Concert-Life in America (1731–1800).* 1907. Reprint, New York: Da Capo, 1978.

———. *Early Opera in America.* New York: Schirmer, 1915.

Clays. South Carolina produced the first kaolin mines in the United States. Today it contains some of the most productive clay beds in the United States, second only to neighboring Georgia. The predominant clay region in South Carolina follows the trend of the Sandhills across the upper coastal plain, with major production centered in Aiken County near the towns of Aiken, Bath, and Langley. Smaller mines are in production in several other counties including Clarendon, Fairfield, Kershaw, Richland, and Lexington.

Clay was first mined for pottery production in southern Edgefield District (later Aiken County), which became a center of pottery making in the state. In England the eighteenth-century china manufacturer Josiah Wedgwood wrote of important kaolin deposits in the colonies, including South Carolina. Before the Revolutionary War, small quantities of South Carolina clay were shipped to England and used in Wedgwood's pottery factories. In 1848 Michael Tuomey wrote in his report on the geology of South Carolina that there was "porcelain clay or kaolin" at Hamburg, Aiken, and Graniteville.

Today, South Carolina produces clay not for pottery but for industrial uses, including paper manufacture. Because clay particles are so small, inert, and insoluble, they are used to fill in microscopic holes in paper and then to coat the surface, which gives magazine paper a high gloss. South Carolina kaolin is also used as an additive to rubber and fiberglass. In addition, clays are mined for the manufacture of brick products. For many years South Carolina also produced fuller's earth, a clay that was used as an industrial absorbent.

The clays that formed the deep deposits mined in South Carolina were derived from the weathering and erosion of rocks, many from the high mountains that stood to the north and northwest. These mountains were composed largely of granites, gneisses, schists, and phyllites, all of which contain the minerals feldspar and mica, which over time and with exposure to the elements were altered chemically into clay. Because the quartz in these rocks is stable at the surface and so does not weather quickly, this hard and durable quartz became sand as the rocks disintegrated. Over millions of years streams and rivers carried sand and the fine clay particles to lakes and to the sea, where they were deposited together and differentially, the sand settling nearer the shore and the lighter clay settling further offshore. As the clay settled into the ocean it formed deposits hundreds of feet thick. The ages of the clay mined in South Carolina run from the Cretaceous period to the early and middle Tertiary period. The deposits of Cretaceous clays, called "soft clays," are much smaller than those of the more abundant Tertiary clays and are used primarily to produce brick. The younger Tertiary clays, called "hard clays," are used generally for other industrial purposes.

The clay mines of South Carolina are all open-pit. Commonly, one hundred feet of overburden is removed to get to the clay, which currently runs to no higher than eighty percent purity. Mines use small draglines, power shovels, front-end loaders, and hydraulic backhoes to dig the clay. The collected clay then goes through a refining process called beneficiation, through which the clay is dried, pulverized, air floated, collected, and shipped to destinations largely out of state.

An understanding of the geology of South Carolina's clay deposits, including the ages of the clay beds and the sequence of their depositional history, has been derived partly through the study and interpretation of many types of marine fossils found within them. Signs of many species of both vertebrate and invertebrate animals as well as plants have been found. These have included nannofossils (extremely small marine fossils, usually algae), sharks, rays, barnacles, shells, and burrows. Scientists continue to study the clays of the state both to understand South Carolina's geology further and to identify new sources of the clays that have provided such great economic benefit. CAROLYN H. MURPHY

Murphy, Carolyn H. *Carolina Rocks! The Geology of South Carolina.* Orangeburg, S.C.: Sandlapper, 1995.

Nystrom, Paul G., Jr., and Ralph H. Willoughby, eds. *Geological Investigations Related to the Stratigraphy in the Kaolin Mining District, Aiken County, South Carolina: Carolina Geological Society Fieldtrip Guidebook, October 9–10, 1982.* Columbia: South Carolina Geological Survey, 1982.

Clemson (Pickens County; 2000 pop. 11,939). This small college town began as Town of Calhoun, incorporated on December 24, 1892, and located about a mile from the new campus of Clemson Agricultural College. The Calhoun Land Company (CLC), chartered in 1893, owned six hundred acres situated along the Atlanta and Charlotte Air Line Railway (later Southern Railway), but little existed there except the depot. The CLC placed the first lots for sale on July 4, 1893, claiming that the property "affords a beautiful site for a large town near the Clemson Agricultural College." As the town grew, it provided housing and shopping for the college population, including a grocery store, a blacksmith, a livery stable, a bank, boardinghouses, and drugstores. In 1899 the former Clemson cadet Isaac L. Keller opened a shop he called "Judge Keller's," which operated in town for over one hundred years. The first church was Fort Hill Presbyterian, organized in 1895, which met upstairs in Boggs' Store until its sanctuary was completed the next year. By 1900 Calhoun's population stood at 209.

The train depot proved essential to Clemson's prosperity. Through it passed most of the people and supplies connected with the town and college. Due to confusion caused by the simultaneous existence of post offices named Calhoun, Fort Hill, and Clemson College, plus Calhoun Falls and Fort Mill in other parts of the state, goods were often misdirected and the wrong tickets issued to train passengers. In 1943 a residents' petition resulted in a June 5 vote, after which the name was changed to Town of Clemson by a vote of fifty-six to nine. The Clemson Town Council made it official by its June 11 ordinance. The changeover of the sign at the railroad station on October 1, 1943, sparked a newspaper article covering the big event.

During the 1960s the city of Clemson tripled in area due to an aggressive annexation policy. The population grew nearly six hundred percent between 1960 and 1995. Improved roads and public services, a new Clemson Indoor Recreation Center, and the successful city-university cooperative operation of the Clemson Area Transit system, known as CAT, provided further examples of a dynamic town. As the second half of the twentieth century progressed, more businesses grew up along the main street between campus and the old Calhoun section, which eventually spilled over along U.S. Highway 123 and beyond. The Clemson Area Chamber of Commerce adopted "In Season Every Season" as its slogan, emphasizing that Clemson had more to offer than football games, and that they were always willing to roll out the orange carpet. DONNA K. ROPER

Bryan, Wright. *Clemson: An Informal History of the University, 1889–1979.* Columbia, S.C.: R. L. Bryan, 1979.

Calhoun Land Company Records. Pendleton District Commission, Pendleton.

McMahon, Sean H. *Country Church and College Town: A History of Fort Hill Presbyterian Church, 1895–1995.* Clemson, S.C.: Fort Hill Presbyterian Church, 1994.

Clemson, Thomas Green, IV (1807–1888). Engineer, agriculturalist, college founder. Thomas Green Clemson IV was born in Philadelphia on July 1, 1807, the third of six children of Thomas Green Clemson III, a prosperous merchant, and Elizabeth Baker. He studied at schools in Philadelphia and at the American Literary, Scientific, and Military Academy in Norwich, Vermont. Clemson continued his education in Paris, attending lectures at the Sorbonne Royal College and earning a diploma as assayer from the Royal School of Mines in 1831. He worked as a mining engineer in the United States and abroad, and published numerous scientific articles.

Clemson married John C. Calhoun's favorite daughter, Anna Maria, on November 13, 1838, at Calhoun's Fort Hill plantation near Pendleton. They had four children, two of whom lived to adulthood. In 1844 Calhoun recommended Clemson's appointment as chargé d'affaires to Belgium, the highest-ranking American diplomat to that country, where he served until 1851. Eventually settling in Maryland, Clemson made a name for himself as a leading agricultural chemist. He also promoted his belief in the value of scientific education and helped organize Maryland Agricultural College (later the University of Maryland).

In 1860 Clemson was appointed superintendent of agricultural affairs, a predecessor of the modern secretary of agriculture. Tensions were flaring between the North and the South, however, and Clemson's sympathies lay with his wife's home state. He resigned his federal position in March 1861. Clemson joined the Confederacy in May 1863 and served in the Nitre and Mining Bureau, Trans-Mississippi Department, until June 1865. After parole he joined his family at his mother-in-law's home in Pendleton.

One of Clemson's most passionate postwar goals was to establish a college to provide practical education in agriculture and the sciences, as he believed that there would be "no hope for the South short of widespread scientific education." He continued the cause while serving as vice president and then president of the Pendleton Farmers Society from 1867 to 1869, but he soon became discouraged by the state's poverty and the lack of support. In addition, Clemson was in continually poor health and grieving over the deaths of his two children, seventeen days apart, in 1871. The Clemsons took possession of Calhoun's Fort Hill estate in 1872 and decided to use the property to establish a college. Clemson continued the plan after Anna's death in 1875, meeting with supporters such as Benjamin Tillman, who had been working toward a similar goal. During the 1880s, in drafts of his will and letters to his attorneys, Clemson worked out his plans for a "high seminary of learning," which would provide a course of studies "in theoretic and practical instruction in those sciences and arts which bear directly upon agriculture."

Clemson died on April 6, 1888, and was buried in St. Paul's Episcopal churchyard in Pendleton. He left 814 acres of land and more than $80,000 in assets to the state of South Carolina for the college he envisioned. The state formally accepted the bequest on December 6, 1889, after a lengthy debate and a court battle on behalf of Clemson's only grandchild. Clemson's seven handpicked life trustees and six additional trustees selected by the General Assembly helped bring Clemson Agricultural College (now Clemson University) to its opening day on July 7, 1893. SUSAN GIAIMO HIOTT

Clemson, Thomas Green. Papers. Special Collections, Clemson University Libraries, Clemson.

Holmes, Alester G., and George R. Sherrill. *Thomas Green Clemson: His Life and Work.* Richmond, Va.: Garrett and Massie, 1937.

Lander, Ernest McPherson. *The Calhoun Family and Thomas Green Clemson: The Decline of a Southern Patriarchy.* Columbia: University of South Carolina Press, 1983.

———. "The Founder Thomas Green Clemson, 1807–1888." In *Tradition: A History of the Presidency of Clemson University,* edited by Donald M. McKale. Macon, Ga.: Mercer University Press, 1988.

Clemson Blue Cheese. In 1940 a Clemson College dairy professor wondered if he could cure blue mold cheese in the dark, cool, damp interior of Stumphouse Mountain Tunnel near Walhalla in Oconee County, similar to the way Roquefort cheese is cured in caves in France. His goal also was to use surplus milk from local cows, including Clemson's own herd. After two years of limited production, cheese making was halted due to shortages of supplies and personnel during World War II. It resumed in 1953 after Clemson purchased Stumphouse Mountain Tunnel. That year Clemson's dairy department produced approximately 2,500 pounds of blue cheese. They manufactured the cheese on campus and then took it thirty miles to the tunnel to cure.

Difficulties maintaining sanitary conditions in the tunnel, particularly during warm summer months, as well as its distance from campus limited the tunnel's usefulness. In 1958 the university moved the cheese-making process to air-conditioned cheese rooms in the campus's new food-industry building Newman Hall. Clemson continued to produce its namesake cheese on a limited basis, increasing production to approximately 20,000 pounds annually by 1980 and 43,000 pounds by 2003. Through the years university faculty and students have experimented with ways to improve the production, packaging, and marketing of the cheese, which has been sold on campus, through mail order, and, at times, in limited markets. Clemson Blue Cheese Dressing was introduced in 1998.

Clemson Blue Cheese is an "artisan cheese," produced by hand with no preservatives and using milk specially processed with a high fat content. Each 288-gallon vat makes about 240 pounds of cheese. The cheese is salted, waxed, and then aged for six months before each hoop is scraped and packaged. Although Clemson Blue Cheese has never been a profit-making venture, it has earned excellent reviews from food critics and has been a popular public-relations tool, spreading the Clemson name around the globe. SUSAN GIAIMO HIOTT

Clemson University Department of Food Science and Human Nutrition. "Clemson Blue Cheese." http://www.clemson.edu/foodscience/bluecheese.htm.

Clemson University. Clemson University originated in a heated political contest during the late 1880s. The agrarian reformer Ben Tillman, leader of the politically powerful Farmers' Association, had pushed for the establishment of a separate agricultural college in South Carolina since 1885. The movement had been thwarted by conservatives in state government, who did not want a new state-funded college to compete for funding or prestige with South Carolina College. However, Tillman and his supporters benefited from a propitious turn of events. In 1888 Thomas G. Clemson, son-in-law of John C. Calhoun, died and left his Fort Hill estate in Oconee County and an $80,000 endowment to the state in order to create a separate agricultural college. Tillman and his followers seized on the Clemson will and canvassed the state urging the General Assembly to accept the bequest and its terms. Conservative governor John P. Richardson and trustees of South Carolina College led the opposition, arguing instead that the Clemson bequest be used to strengthen the agricultural program already in place at South Carolina College. After almost a year of bitter public debate, in December 1888 the General Assembly passed the Clemson College bill, which a reluctant Governor Richardson signed the following year.

Besides the Clemson bequest, additional funding came from the federal government through the Hatch Act and Morrill Act, which provided funds in support of agricultural and land grant institutions. Clemson's will created a unique board of thirteen trustees, seven of whom Clemson named as "life" trustees with the power to replace their members, while the remaining six trustees were to be appointed by the General Assembly. The trustees retained full power

Tillman Hall, Clemson University. Courtesy, Clemson University Photograph Collection, Special Collections, Clemson University Libraries

under the original state charter to set all rules, policies, and courses of studies. Through the life trustees majority, the mission of Clemson was to be forever upheld free from legislative influence.

Clemson Agricultural College opened in 1893. As Clemson was a land grant school, the Morrill Act required the inclusion of military instruction. Clemson took this requirement seriously and created a formal corps of cadets, whose members wore uniforms and were subject to strict military discipline. In 1893 the 446 cadets, ranging in age from fifteen to twenty-eight, reported to their barracks and learned the Cadet Rules of Conduct under the guidance of a West Point graduate and fifteen professors. The strict discipline met with periodic challenge from the student body. In 1908 some 306 cadets were expelled for leaving campus without permission as an April Fools' Day prank, an incident that came to be known as the "Pendleton Guards Rebellion." Student walkouts culminated in 1924 when 500 cadets left the campus to protest the military discipline, the lack of a student government, and poor mess hall conditions. College authorities responded by dismissing 23 students and suspending 112 others. The unpopular mess hall officer, Captain J. D. Harcombe, was retained and later memorialized when the Harcombe Food Center and Commons was named in his honor.

With the United States entry into World War I in April 1917, the entire senior class wired President Woodrow Wilson and collectively volunteered for military service. Graduation that year had more diplomas awarded in absentia than in person, and enrollment dropped to 662. The campus was largely turned over to military training, including the creation of the Student Army Training Corps, a training school for enlisted men. The postwar influenza pandemic reached Clemson in 1918 and 1919, resulting in two deaths and the temporary closing of the college. Clemson cadets served in World War II and Korea. In fact, Clemson supplied more officers to the army during the first two years of World War II than did any other institution in the country except Texas A&M.

Following World War II, Clemson's enrollment grew dramatically, reaching 3,756 in the 1947–1948 academic year. But enrollment dropped as Clemson's military discipline and all-male student body became less and less attractive to a new generation of students. By 1955 trustees bowed to change and Clemson College became a civilian, coeducational institution. The previous barracks became dorms, and other rules began to relax as social mores changed. More changes affected student-body diversity when a young black man named Harvey Gantt of Charleston enrolled at Clemson in 1963 as an architecture major. Trustees and local officials worked hard to make sure that integration at Clemson went smoothly and without the embarrassing riots that occurred in Mississippi. The *Saturday Evening Post* declared that Clemson's plan was "the most complete and carefully thought-out one ever drawn up in the United States to meet the threat of racial violence." Much of the change during this era took place during the presidency of Robert Cook Edwards. During his twenty-one-year tenure (1958–1979) Clemson saw its enrollment grow from 3,500 to 11,000, and in 1964 the General Assembly officially authorized Clemson's status as a university.

In addition to academics, Clemson has also been known for its athletic programs, especially its football team. The program started in 1896 under the direction of Walter Riggs, who also introduced the school's mascot, the tiger. In its first season Clemson beat Furman and Wofford but lost to the University of South Carolina (USC). This set up a rivalry unequaled by any other in the state between the Gamecocks of USC and the Tigers of Clemson, who have battled annually almost every year since their initial meeting. In 1934 the athletic program created an alumni giving fund that started with initial pledges of ten dollars a year. The "IPTAY" ("I Pay Ten A Year") program has raised millions of dollars for scholarships and the construction of athletic facilities.

Under the leadership of fourteen presidents since its inception, Clemson's mission continues to focus primarily on agriculture, engineering, and science, although academic offerings have expanded to include degree programs in the arts, humanities, education, and business. Since 1996 Clemson has been organized into five colleges, which offer bachelor's, master's, and doctoral degrees in approximately 135 programs of study. Clemson offers degrees unique in South Carolina in architecture, forestry and agriculture, ceramic engineering, and textile engineering and management. In 2001 the student body of 17,101 included students from all fifty states and more than eighty foreign countries. LINDA HOWE

Andrew, Rod. *Long Gray Lines: The Southern Military School Tradition, 1839–1915.* Chapel Hill: University of North Carolina Press, 2001.

Bast, Kirk K. "'As Different as Heaven and Hell': The Desegregation of Clemson College." *Proceedings of the South Carolina Historical Association* (1994): 38–44.

Bryan, Wright. *Clemson: An Informal History of the University, 1889–1979.* Columbia, S.C.: R. L. Bryan, 1979.

McKale, Donald M., ed. *Tradition: A History of the Presidency of Clemson University.* Macon, Ga.: Mercer University Press, 1988.

Clemson University Cooperative Extension Service. The Cooperative Extension Service was created on May 8, 1914, when President Woodrow Wilson signed the Smith-Lever Act, legislation coauthored by South Carolina congressman Asbury F. Lever. The act ended the rivalry between state agriculture commissioners and land grant colleges over the administration of extension work. In its place, Smith-Lever created a partnership of federal, state, and local governments that worked to improve the quality of rural life by disseminating the latest information to farmers, homemakers, and communities. The South Carolina General Assembly accepted Smith-Lever by a joint resolution approved by the governor on February 12, 1915, which designated the Clemson Agricultural and Mechanical College as the state agency for agricultural extension work. The first efforts in South Carolina actually took place in 1906 with support from the federal government, the General Education Board of the Rockefeller Foundation, and by the state through Clemson. In 1907 Seaman Knapp, head of extension work for the U.S. Department of Agriculture (USDA), came to South Carolina and appointed two district agents and five county agents. W. W. Long, who came to Clemson from the USDA in 1913 to head up extension work, was the first director under the Smith-Lever Act. Along with Edith Parrott, state home demonstration agent, Long built Cooperative Extension Service work around a nucleus of workers appointed during the previous seven years. Agents relied heavily on teaching techniques developed by Knapp, who came to be known as the father of agricultural demonstration work. He believed that a demonstration farm using Cooperative Extension Service recommendations would persuade others to follow the same practices.

Under the same philosophy, the Cooperative Extension Service evolved as the public's information needs changed. By the start of the twenty-first century, efforts focused more on families and youth, while still maintaining a strong agricultural base and its traditional emphasis on economic and community development, environmental issues, food safety, and nutrition. Clemson's Cooperative Extension Service sponsors the 4–H program, which reaches more than 104,000 South Carolina youths through school and community programs, special-interest clubs, and camping. Offices are located in all forty-six counties, staffed by 165 county agents plus support personnel and backed by seventy specialists stationed on the Clemson University campus and at Research and Education Centers at Charleston, Blackville, Florence, and in Richland County. Staff members are trained in disciplines such as agronomy, animal science, entomology, forestry, plant pathology, economics, and food and nutrition. Personnel serve as an unbiased source of information for families, agricultural and forestry producers, and food industry professionals, much of it developed at Clemson's South Carolina Agriculture and Forestry Research System. THOMAS W. LOLLIS

Woodall, Clyde E. *The History of South Carolina Cooperative Extension Service.* Clemson, S.C., 1998.

Clemson University national football championship (1981). On January 1, 1982, the Clemson University Tigers defeated the University of Nebraska Cornhuskers 22 to 15 at the Orange Bowl in Miami, Florida. The following day the United Press International Board of Coaches and the Associated Press national poll of sportswriters and sportscasters voted Clemson the number one team in the nation, thus making official the first national title in any sport for Clemson University and the state of South Carolina.

The Tigers entered the Orange Bowl with eleven consecutive wins. Their opponents that season included Wofford, Tulane, Georgia, Kentucky, Virginia, Duke, North Carolina State, Wake Forest, North Carolina, Maryland, and South Carolina. They were coached by Danny Ford, a native of Gadsden, Alabama, and captain of the University of Alabama "Crimson Tide" in 1969. After serving as an assistant coach at Alabama, Virginia Tech, and Clemson, Ford became the Tigers' head coach in late 1978. Just thirty-three years old in 1981, he was the youngest coach in the history of college football to win a national championship and was voted the Atlantic Coast Conference coach of the year in 1981 by the ACC Sports Writers Association.

The win in Miami earned each team approximately $875,000, at that time the largest payout in Orange Bowl history. The victory, however, was clouded by rumors of irregularities in methods of recruiting players. In March 1982 the National Collegiate Athletic Association (NCAA) began an investigation of the Clemson football program; in November of that year, after finding seventy violations of recruiting and other practices, the NCAA placed the Clemson football program on probation for two years. Shortly thereafter, the Atlantic Coast Conference put Clemson on probation for three years.

In spite of these restrictions, the national championship brought recognition to the team. Of the 1981 roster, eleven players became All-Americans in their careers, thirty-one were drafted into the National Football League, and six became Super Bowl champions. D. S. TAYLOR

Blackman, Sam, Bob Bradley, and Chuck Kriese. *Clemson: Where the Tigers Play.* Champaign, Ill.: Sports Publishing, 1999.

Ellis, Steve, and Kerry Capps. *Roar from the Top, a Cinderella Story: The 1981 National Champion Clemson Tigers.* Clemson, S.C., 1982.

McKale, Donald F., ed. *Tradition: A History of the Presidency of Clemson University.* Macon, Ga.: Mercer University Press, 1988.

Cleveland, Georgia Alden (1851–1914). Writer, activist. Cleveland was born in Laurensville, Georgia, on December 6, 1851, the daughter of Robert M. Cleveland and Fannie Leonard. She spent most of her early years in Bedford County, Tennessee. On November 4, 1871, she married John Bomar Cleveland of Spartanburg, South Carolina. They had seven children. John, a prominent businessman and industrialist, was related to President Grover Cleveland and served as a delegate to the 1884 Democratic National Convention. Both Georgia and her husband were noted for their generosity, charity, and humanity in the Spartanburg community. They played leading roles in the founding of Converse College in 1889, and their daughters attended school there. They lived within walking distance of both Converse and Wofford, and they were actively involved in each campus's activities, frequently entertaining students in their home.

Georgia Alden Cleveland kept a detailed dairy from 1890 to 1914 in which she chronicled life as an upper-class, married, southern white female. Because of the richness of her entries, she left a legacy of South Carolina upcountry history that is useful on several levels: not only does it document local, state, and regional history, but it also serves as a valuable record of Victorian female domesticity and a rare peek into a snippet of southern feminine life, from the mundane to the grand, over the course of twenty-four years.

Cleveland's diary recorded a myriad of social, political, cultural, educational, and religious activities that filled her active life, including membership in the Women's Christian Temperance Movement, Daughters of the American Revolution, and United Daughters of the Confederacy. Furthermore, her entries are all-encompassing, ranging from local, national, and world news events to customary domestic activities such as gardening, housekeeping, sewing, and paying social calls, while noting such meticulous details as weather conditions, temperatures, and lists of crops planted. She also wrote of births, deaths, and sicknesses among relatives and friends. She regularly traveled throughout South Carolina and the Southeast, even making a trip to the Chicago World's Fair in 1893, and her descriptions of these destinations provide historically significant details and insights into that period. But her delight in her children, her strong Episcopal faith, and her charity to others are the prominent features throughout her diary that serve to underscore her strong character as an authentic authoress of South Carolina history and southern womanhood.

Cleveland's last diary entry was January 23, 1914. She died in Baltimore on March 1, 1914, following surgery for stomach cancer. She was buried in the Episcopal Church of the Advent Cemetery in Spartanburg. LAURA BARFIELD

Cleveland, Mrs. John B. [Georgia Alden]. "Diary of Mrs. John B. Cleveland." Typescript. South Caroliniana Library, University of South Carolina, Columbia.
"Mrs. Cleveland's Funeral Today." Spartanburg *Herald,* March 3, 1914, p. 1.

Cleveland School fire (May 17, 1923). Cleveland Public School was situated in Kershaw County, six miles southeast of Camden. This two-story wooden frame edifice was constructed on acreage donated by the Chestnut family. During the evening of May 17, 1923, a sizable crowd was attending the school's graduation ceremonies. After receiving their diplomas, the graduating class members were presenting a short comedy, *Miss Topsy Turvy,* on the stage in the second-floor auditorium. Participants later recalled that more than three hundred persons were in the room, which measured just forty by twenty feet.

The building's primary construction flaw was that no stairway extended to the first-floor hallway. Instead, the sole exit was a narrow doorway leading from a cloakroom toward an exterior wooden stairwell. Furthermore, the stage was located at the opposite end of the auditorium. The play was in progress when several onlookers noticed that smoke was coming from backstage.

A large oil lamp had been attached by wire to the ceiling, quite close to the curtains. Apparently, intense heat from the burner was scorching the wiring wrapped around the hook. This fixture's heavy weight ultimately pulled it downward. After the lamp struck the stage floor, its oil spilled in all directions, igniting an intense fire. Terrified spectators rushed toward the cloakroom, and dozens of persons were trampled to death as they congregated at the doorway. Simultaneously, the crowd's collective weight caused the wooden stairs to collapse. Many victims not hurt during their falls later were injured seriously by falling debris. Others died after being overcome by the thick smoke. Several small children survived by being tossed to onlookers below.

Within an hour the Cleveland School was destroyed totally. Numerous corpses burnt beyond recognition were found amidst the ruins. The official death toll was tabulated at seventy-seven. Approximately twenty-five victims received positive identifications. Because entire families were wiped out, in many cases no survivors could be located to identify the corpses. Unclaimed bodies were interred within a mass grave at the nearby Beulah Methodist Church Cemetery. MILES S. RICHARDS

Moseley, John Oliver. *The Terrible Cleveland Fire: Its Victims and Survivors.* Charleston, S.C.: Southern Printing & Publishing, 1923.

Climate. South Carolina's climate is classified as humid subtropical, which is typical of middle-latitude locations situated on eastern margins of large continents. Rainfall is abundant and distributed fairly evenly throughout the year. There is a seasonal variation in temperatures ranging from hot and humid summers to mild winters with some below-freezing temperatures. Within this general framework, however, climate varies considerably across the state.

Most of the state receives between forty-six and fifty inches of rain annually, but Caesars Head in the Blue Ridge region averages seventy-nine inches. Temperatures generally decrease from the coastal plain to the Blue Ridge, as illustrated by the mean and the mean daily minimum temperatures for Charleston, Columbia, and the Greenville/Spartanburg areas (see table). Summers tend to be hot across the state, but Columbia and the Midlands area tend to have higher July temperatures.

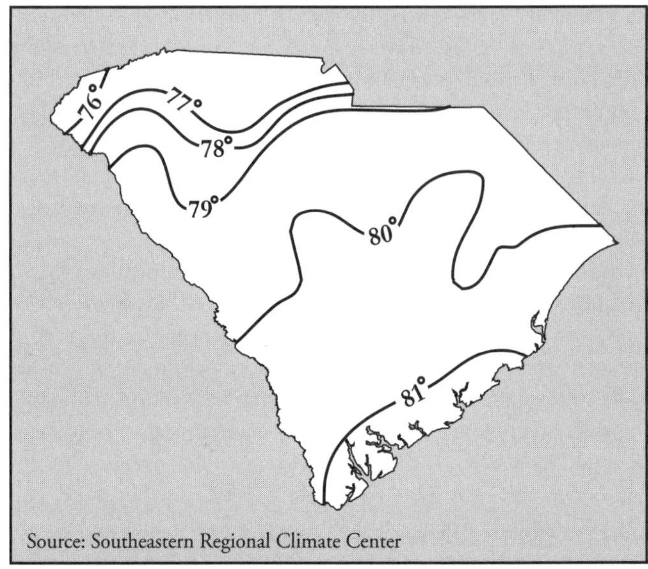

Average temperatures in July

Rainfall provides almost all of the precipitation, but snow, sleet, and hail occasionally do occur. Precipitation is recorded in each month, but there is seasonal variation. Frequent and sometimes violent late afternoon and early evening convectional thunderstorms are characteristic of summer. These storms are generally brief, but rainfall can be heavy with high winds, thunder, and lightning. Frontal precipitation is common during the winter and can include snow or sleet but usually is characterized by heavy cloud cover with drizzle or steady rain that can last for hours. These different rainfall types along with temperature variations represent South Carolina's annual cycle of climatic variation.

Winter normally is typified by the presence of cold, dry continental air masses making December, January, and February the three coldest months. On occasion, two to five times per year, polar air masses can invade the state, bringing very cold temperatures for several days. A typical cold-front scenario begins with warm, moist air; cloudy skies; and southerly winds. As the front approaches, the sky becomes gray with clouds, and precipitation begins first as drizzle and then becomes heavy rain. Temperatures drop as the rain continues. The heavy rain then gives way to drizzle, the sky clears, and northerly winds dominate. Southerly winds often follow, bringing in maritime air from the Caribbean and South Atlantic, and mild temperatures. Coastal temperatures are moderated by the Atlantic Ocean and the warm Gulf Stream, while the higher elevations of the upper Piedmont and Blue Ridge experience colder temperatures. Charleston, for example, has a higher mean daily minimum temperature than either Columbia or the Greenville/Spartanburg area.

Snowfall is rare along the coast—about once every three years—and is more common in the upper Piedmont and Blue Ridge. Except for those in the Blue Ridge region, accumulations usually melt away in a day or two. February is statistically the snow month. The record snowfall occurred in February 1973, with twenty-four inches recorded at Rimini, sixteen inches at Columbia, seven inches at Charleston, and little or no snowfall in the upstate. Even light snowfalls can disrupt traffic, and schools, offices, and businesses often close. Occasional ice storms also create severe road problems and power outages.

Spring is a transition season from low winter temperatures and frontal precipitation to high temperatures and convectional rainfall characteristic of summer. The number of cold fronts diminishes as continental air masses are replaced by warmer maritime tropical air. Similarly, the cloudy and steady rain caused by passing cold fronts is replaced by the puffy cumulus clouds and thunderstorms associated with convectional precipitation during March, April, and May. These changing atmospheric conditions are favorable for the development of tornadoes.

Tornadoes form during all seasons of the year, but about one-third the annual total is recorded in April and May. South Carolina averages about ten tornadoes a year. A series of tornadoes passing through two corridors between Anderson and York Counties and across the Midlands from Aiken to Florence Counties left 77 people dead and 800 injured on April 30, 1924. More recently, 21 people died and 448 were injured when eight or nine separate tornadoes swept through the lower Piedmont from McCormick to Marlboro Counties on March 28, 1984.

Summer's hot and humid weather prevails from June through August, and the heat is relatively unbroken. Contrasting with winter, temperatures are about the same across much of the state except for cooler temperatures at higher elevations of the Blue Ridge region. The single most important factor influencing South Carolina's summer weather is the Bermuda high, an extremely large subtropical high-pressure cell centered over the Atlantic. Its clockwise circulation normally causes a southerly flow of warm and humid maritime tropical air over the state, resulting in high temperatures and the necessary moisture for convectional thunderstorms. These thunderstorms account for about one-third of the annual rainfall, making summer the wettest season of the year.

The Bermuda high, however, sometimes stalls or becomes stationary off the coast, and its stable subsiding air can prevent the normal convection process. This stymies cloud and thunderstorm development, causing hot sunny days and stagnant air conditions. Sometimes these dry conditions last for weeks or even months, causing droughts. July is usually Columbia's wettest month with a mean 5.54 inches of rainfall. But only 0.57 of an inch was recorded in July 1973.

Fall, like spring, is a transitional season. Temperatures slowly become cooler, and the high humidity of summer wanes between September and November. Dry continental air masses become more frequent. Because there is less water vapor in the atmosphere, the state receives only about twenty percent of its annual precipitation in the fall. October and November are statistically the two driest months of the year. Nearly one-half of all fall days are warm and sunny with bright blue skies. Since there is little cloud cover, nights are cool to cold. The rapid cooling of the earth's surface often results in fog during the night and early morning hours.

Hurricanes are most common in early fall and late summer, and September poses the greatest threat. Damage along the coast is caused by the winds, but most death and destruction results from flooding. The deadliest hurricane to date struck Beaufort in August 1893, and an estimated two thousand people died. Hurricane Hazel hit the Myrtle Beach area in October 1954 with a storm surge estimated at seventeen feet, which washed away oceanfront dunes, destroyed fishing piers, and damaged houses. Hurricane Hugo struck Charleston at high tide with a fifteen- to twenty-foot storm surge and raced inland in September 1989. Winds, clocked at 138 mph with gusts of more than 160 mph, and flooding caused twenty-six deaths and left fifty thousand to seventy thousand homeless. Damage was estimated at more than $6 billion. CHARLES F. KOVACIK

Climate Characteristics of Charleston, Columbia, and the Greenville/Spartanburg Area

	Charleston	*Columbia*	*Greenville/ Spartanburg*
Mean Temperature	65.6°F	64.8°F	54.5°F
Mean Daily — Maximum July Temperature	90.1°F	92.4°F	88.7°F
Mean Daily — Minimum January Temperature	37.9°F	33.6°F	30.9°F
Lowest Temperature	6°F 1/1985	1°F 1/1985	-19°F 1/1985
Highest Temperature	105°F 8/1/1999	109°F 6/29/1998	99°F 8/21/1983
Average Yearly Rainfall	51.5 in.	48.3 in.	50.2 in.
Wettest year	1945 74.9 in.	1959 74.5 in.	1979 106.9 in.
Driest year	1931 28.8 in.	1951 29.8 in.	1967 12.1 in.

Source: South Carolina State Climatology Office, Department of Natural Resources, Columbia, S.C., and National Climatic Center, Asheville, N.C.

Kovacik, Charles F., and John J. Winberry. *South Carolina: The Making of a Landscape.* 1987. Reprint, Columbia: University of South Carolina Press, 1989.

Purvis, John C., Wes Tyler, and Scott F. Sidlow. *General Characteristics of South Carolina's Climate.* Columbia: South Carolina State Climatology Office, [1990].

Clinton (Laurens County; 2000 pop. 8,091). Clinton grew up around the intersection of two roads, one connecting Greenville with Columbia and the other Spartanburg with Augusta. In the 1850s the Laurens-to-Newberry railroad began running through this intersection, known as the Five Points or Five Forks, resulting in lots being sold for the development of a town. As the community grew into an important railroad way station, it was named for Henry Clinton Young, an attorney from nearby Laurens. By 1858 Clinton had both Methodist and Presbyterian congregations, as well as a public school. However, when the Presbyterian minister William Plumer Jacobs arrived in Clinton in 1864, he described the village as having a bad reputation for "gander-pulling, gambling and drinking, rowdyism, brawling and other little disorders." In that same year Clinton was incorporated.

Following the Civil War, the future of Clinton appeared bleak. The railroad ceased operation, and Laurens County was plagued with racial violence. However, prospects rose in the 1870s, thanks to the efforts of Dr. Jacobs and the local entrepreneur Mercer Silas Bailey. In 1872 Jacobs became head of the Clinton Library Society, which began holding public lectures. Jacobs worked to organize the Thornwell Orphanage to help children who had lost their parents during the war. By 1874 the main orphanage building, the Home of Peace, had been built. In the 1880s Jacobs established Clinton College, which became Presbyterian College in 1890. The first building, Alumni Hall, was built the following year. Meanwhile, Bailey opened a bank and helped secure a new railroad connection for Clinton: the Georgia, Carolina, and Northern. In 1896 Bailey built the town's first textile mill, the Clinton Mill. It was followed by the Lydia Mill in 1902.

Clinton's growth continued steadily through the early 1900s. In 1920 the State Training School for the Feeble Minded (later renamed Whitten Center), an institution for the mentally handicapped, was established. With the orphanage and the college, it was the third important institution operating in Clinton. By 1930 Clinton's population had reached 5,643. In the decade that followed, the town's water supply and streets were improved and a National Guard Armory was built. The Presbyterian College and Community Library opened in 1942, built with funds provided by the Works Progress Administration. The 1940s and 1950s saw additional industry enter the community and several new schools built.

At the start of the twenty-first century, textiles still played a vital role in the Clinton economy. In addition to Presbyterian College and Whitten Center, other major employers manufactured metal bearings, building products, and printed products. Many retirees relocated to Clinton because of the facilities of the Presbyterian Home and Bailey Manor Retirement Center, as well as the cultural opportunities afforded by Presbyterian College and the county arts council, concert association, and little theater group. WILLIAM COPELAND COOPER

Bolick, Julian Stevenson. *A Laurens County Sketchbook.* Clinton, S.C.: Jacobs, 1973.

The Scrapbook: A Compilation of Historical Facts about Places and Events of Laurens County, South Carolina. N.p.: Laurens County Historical Society and Laurens County Arts Council, 1982.

Clover (York County; 2000 pop. 4,014). Although Clover celebrated its centennial in 1987, the town's history goes back to the mid-1870s, when the Chester and Lenoir Railroad placed a five-thousand-gallon water tank at the site of the future town. According to local legend, water spilling from the tank yielded a patch of clover on the ground, giving the town its earlier name of Clover Patch. One of Clover's earliest boosters was William Beaty Smith, who, along with his sons, constructed some of the first retail establishments in town. The town's first congregation, the Clover Presbyterian Church, was established in 1881, and a post office opened three years later. Clover was chartered by the General Assembly on December 24, 1887, with around one hundred residents, most of them migrants from western York County. Early businesses included a blacksmith shop, general merchandise stores, a grocery, several boardinghouses, a furniture store, and a funeral service. The town was rechartered by the secretary of state on December 9, 1904. In 1890 Smith built the town's first textile mill, the Clover Spinning Mill. Additional mills followed in the early twentieth century: Hawthorne Mill in 1917 and Hampshire Mill in 1923. With this business growth came population expansion, and the population neared three thousand by the 1930s. In 1985 Duke Energy constructed the Catawba Nuclear Power Plant near Clover. Although the railroad line that helped give birth to Clover was abandoned in the early 1980s, textiles and manufacturing have remained important to Clover's economy. In 1999 the junction of Main and Kings Mountain Streets was designated a historic district. AARON W. MARRS

Clyburn, James Enos (b. 1940). Congressman. Clyburn was born in Sumter on July 21, 1940, to Enos and Alameta Clyburn. He attended Mather Academy, a private high school for African Americans in Camden, and earned a B.S. from South Carolina State College in 1962. While attending South Carolina State, he participated in sit-ins to desegregate public facilities in Orangeburg. He met his wife, Emily England, at South Carolina State, and they were married in 1961. They are the parents of three daughters.

Clyburn has had an extensive career in public service. From 1962 to 1971 he lived in Charleston, where he taught school, served as an employment counselor, and directed two youth and community development projects. From 1971 to 1974 he served on the staff of Governor John C. West. In 1974 Governor West appointed him as South Carolina human affairs commissioner. He served for eighteen years under both Democratic and Republican governors.

Clyburn's public career also included several runs for public office. In 1970 he ran unsuccessfully for a seat in the General Assembly. While he was human affairs commissioner, he ran unsuccessfully for the office of secretary of state in 1978 and 1986. In 1992 Clyburn ran for the Sixth District congressional seat, which had been created when the U.S. Justice Department ordered the General Assembly to redraw the state's district lines to create a "majority minority" congressional seat. Clyburn won, becoming South Carolina's first African American congressman since 1897.

Clyburn represents the state's "largest and poorest legislative district," and this has led him to support legislation that addresses issues such as health care, transportation, environmental justice, and education. He is the only South Carolina legislator to receive perfect scores on the Americans for Democratic Action and Children's Defense Fund legislative report cards, two advocacy groups that measure the level of support by lawmakers for liberal and progressive legislation. Clyburn also became a strong advocate for historic preservation and free trade. In 1995 he supported legislation to create the state's Heritage Corridor, and he has been an advocate of more funding to support the state's heritage and historic sites. In 2000 he visited Cuba to explore trade agreements that would end the U.S. embargo against that nation and benefit South Carolina by opening up a new market for the state's farmers.

In 1998 Clyburn was elected chairman of the Congressional Black Caucus (CBC). He was the first southerner to hold the chairmanship of the thirty-eight-member organization, and his election signaled a new direction for African Americans in Congress. As a congressman from the South with a large rural and poor constituency, Clyburn focused his agenda for the CBC on building coalitions with Republicans and other caucuses in Congress to garner support for issues such as economic development and public transportation. This was a shift from the traditional civil rights agenda that had dominated the CBC's agenda for the first twenty-seven years of its existence. In 2004 Clyburn won election to Congress for a seventh term. W. MARVIN DULANEY

Botsch, Carol Sears, et al. *African-Americans and the Palmetto State.* Columbia: South Carolina State Department of Education, 1994.

Derfner, Jeremy. "The New Black Caucus." *American Prospect* 11 (March 27, 2000): 16–19.

Coastal Carolina University. Located in Horry County between Conway and Myrtle Beach, Coastal Carolina University is a public comprehensive liberal arts institution granting bachelor's degrees in forty fields of study and master's degrees in education. Coastal Carolina began in 1954 when concerned citizens met at the Horry County Memorial Library to discuss establishing a local college. At a subsequent meeting the group voted to become a nonprofit organization, Coastal Educational Foundation, Inc. On September 20,

1954, they opened Coastal Carolina Junior College as a branch of the College of Charleston. There were fifty-three students in that first term, taught by part-time faculty after hours in Conway High School. Coastal Carolina Junior College became an independent institution in 1958 when the College of Charleston discontinued the extension program. At that time a voter referendum in Horry County approved funding for the college by a four-to-one margin. Coastal Carolina became a regional campus of the University of South Carolina (USC) in 1960.

In 1961 Coastal Carolina acquired a large tract of land between U.S. Highways 501 and 504 in Horry County, most of which was donated by Burroughs Timber Company and International Paper Company. After a major fund-raising drive, ground was broken for the present campus in 1962. As enrollment grew, the college added a third year to the curriculum in 1973, followed by a fourth year in 1974. The first bachelor's degrees were awarded in 1975. By 1989 enrollment topped four thousand and Coastal Carolina began to consider becoming an independent institution, separate from the University of South Carolina. In June 1992 the USC Board of Trustees endorsed USC president John Palms's recommendation that Coastal become independent. On July 1, 1993, by an act of the legislature, Coastal Carolina University became an independent, state-supported institution. Robert R. Ingle, who was chancellor when the university attained independent status, became the first president.

At the start of the twenty-first century, Coastal Carolina had an enrollment of more than 4,600 students and some 200 full-time faculty. While more than half of the students are South Carolina residents, the remainder come from all over the United States and more than forty countries. The campus consists of some forty buildings on the 260-acre main campus, plus 1,062 acres on Waites Island, a barrier island north of Myrtle Beach used for marine science and wetland biology study. The college also maintains the Center for Marine and Wetland Studies on U.S. Highway 501. Coastal Carolina University is accredited by the Southern Association of Colleges and Schools. The E. Craig Wall, Sr., College of Business Administration is accredited by the International Association for Management Education, and the College of Education is accredited by the National Council for the Accreditation of Teacher Education and by the South Carolina Board of Education. WILLIAM P. MORRIS

Coastal plain. The coastal plain is South Carolina's largest landform region, forming two-thirds of the state and encompassing approximately twenty thousand square miles. It includes the land from the Sandhills to the coast. The coastal plain continues into nearby states and is found from New Jersey to Texas. The eastern coastal plain formed through the erosion of mountain ranges to the north and west—the Blue Ridge, the Piedmont ranges, and the present Appalachian Mountains. In addition, the sea rose and fell many times over millions of years, forming extensive deposits of offshore limestone that is visible today at the surface in many areas of the coastal plain. Other unconsolidated sediments are found on the surface and at depth. These include sands, clays, and silt that eroded from the highlands and settled out onto the ocean floor. These sediments later were exposed as sea levels fell. Over time the sediments were eroded and redeposited repeatedly by rivers and estuaries, thus constructing the complex geomorphology of the coastal plain. In South Carolina the coastal plain is divided into three sections according to elevation and topography: upper, middle, and lower.

The upper coastal plain is that section lying between the Sandhills and the Orangeburg Scarp. The region is composed largely of sands and clays, the oldest formation of which is the Middendorf, which is a one-hundred-million-year-old Cretaceous-period clay that in places underlies the Sandhills and is exposed in eroded locations. A second distinctive feature of the upper coastal plain is the Aiken Plateau, which crosses the center of the state from Aiken to the Orangeburg Scarp west of Sumter. The Congaree and Wateree Rivers cut the plateau such that only small, eroded remnants remain beyond Aiken and Lexington Counties. These remnants, the Richland Red Hills and the High Hills of Santee, form small but interesting and scenic ridges. Also on the Aiken Plateau is Peachtree Rock, a small but fascinating sandstone remnant in Lexington County.

Sandy soil, thick undergrowth, and moss-draped oaks are a familiar sight in the coastal plain. Photograph by Walter Connolly for the Federal Writers' Project. Courtesy, South Caroliniana Library, University of South Carolina

The middle coastal plain begins at the base of the Orangeburg Scarp and continues only a few miles to the Surry Scarp, where the lower coastal plain begins. Six escarpments and seven terraces run from the Orangeburg Scarp to the coast, which represent six ocean limits and seven temporary ocean floors of their day, from the Pliocene to the Holocene epochs. The largest of these escarpments is the Surry Scarp, which is a younger and much smaller escarpment than the Orangeburg, rising only to 130 feet. It formed 85,000 years ago during the last advancement of the ocean during the Pleistocene epoch. The Surry Scarp illustrates the complex erosional history of the area. As it traverses the coastal plain, the Surry Scarp shows evidence of beach ridges, a barrier island shoreline, and portions of a river valley.

The geologic features found in the coastal plain are many. They include floodplains of the large rivers that traverse the area, including the Congaree, Wateree, Pee Dee, and Santee. There are near-pristine river bottomlands and swamps, estuaries, and other wetlands, including those found at Congaree Swamp National Monument, Four-Holes Swamp, and the ACE Basin. Dark coastal plain rivers run gently and clearly from the base of the Sandhills to the coast. The coastal plain is the only region in the state that contains Carolina bays, unique elliptical depressions that dot the region. The coastal plain also contains a unique area of karst topography along the western edge of Lake Marion in Orangeburg County. These caves and sinkholes formed over millions of years as acidic groundwater reacted with the Santee limestone of the area.

The geology of the coastal plain provides the state with important fossil sites. The Santee limestone contains important Eocene-epoch marine fossils found in quarries of Dorchester and Berkeley Counties. Many other formations throughout the coastal plain contain fossils ranging in age from the Cretaceous period to the Holocene epoch. In addition, Pleistocene plant fossils have been recovered from sand and gravel quarries located along the Pee Dee, Wateree, and Pocotaligo Rivers. Of particular interest was the 1987 discovery in Williamsburg County of the first dinosaur fossils ever located in the state.

The coastal plain also includes the Coastal Zone, the land approximately ten miles inland from the coast. The coast is divided into three sections: the Grand Strand, which was created by currents into a welded barrier island terrain; the Santee River Delta, the largest delta on the eastern seaboard; and the Barrier and Sea Island Complex, which runs from the Santee Delta south of Georgetown into Georgia and north Florida. Located on the Georgia Embayment, the Sea Islands formed as sea levels rose and drowned the coastline. The barrier islands formed as sea levels slowed about six thousand years ago. The barrier islands are eroding in some instances and growing in others, but there is generally less sediment in place due in part to the damming of the Santee River and subsequent loss of sediment at the delta. Three examples of large-scale erosion can be seen at Hunting, Bull, and North Islands.

The resources of the coastal plain include limestone, clay, sand, and gravel dug from the many open-pit quarries located across the region. Clay is mined primarily in Aiken County, but deposits are also found in Orangeburg and Dorchester Counties, among others. Sand is quarried extensively in Lexington County and from smaller local quarries in many sites across the region. The coastal plain is the most productive and largest agricultural area in the state. The sandy soils, while not rich in organic matter, with artificial fertilization support tobacco, corn, cotton, soybeans, wheat, and other crops. The coastal plain also supports a large pulp industry with large stands of fast-growing loblolly pine trees.

The beauty of the coastal plain is perhaps its greatest resource, not only because it fuels South Carolina's tourist economy, but also because it reflects the successful preservation of irreplaceable ecosystems. Nearly forty percent of the coastal lands are held in trust, either as preserves or as public parks and other recreational areas. Some of these trust sites include the ACE Basin Preserve, Cape Romain National Wildlife Refuge, Pinckney Island National Wildlife Refuge, Francis Marion National Forest, and many state parks, including those at Edisto Beach, Hunting Island, Huntington Beach, and Myrtle Beach. CAROLYN H. MURPHY

Kovacik, Charles F., and John J. Winberry. *South Carolina: The Making of a Landscape.* 1987. Reprint, Columbia: University of South Carolina Press, 1989.

Murphy, Carolyn H. *Carolina Rocks! The Geology of South Carolina.* Orangeburg, S.C.: Sandlapper, 1995.

Cockfighting. Cockfighting is a blood sport that has existed in South Carolina from colonial times up to the present, despite the fact that it was banned by the General Assembly in 1887 and carries a felony charge for participants and less severe penalties for spectators. Cockfighting remains popular in the state, and the oldest continuously published magazine for cockers (as cockfighters style themselves), *Grit and Steel,* emanates from Gaffney. The University of South Carolina uses the gamecock as its mascot.

In a typical cockfight, long steel spikes are attached to the legs of the cocks. The carefully bred birds are then brought into the pit, where they fight, almost always to the death. Some contests last less than a minute, while others can stretch for hours. Though animal rights activists insist that the sport is sadistic and cruel, cockers view themselves as the custodians of an ancient tradition of courage, competition, and masculine aggression, citing various prominent Americans who engaged in the practice, such as Andrew Jackson and George Washington.

Cockfighting was an import from the British Isles during the colonial period. It coexisted with horseracing, cards, and dice as legitimate arenas for gambling among colonial gentlemen. As such, the practice of cockfighting was closely related to the notion of honor that pervaded South Carolina's gentry class. Men of property could compete openly through their wagers, acting out rituals of power by staking large sums of money. In antebellum South Carolina cockfighting cut across a broader swath of society, and poorer whites and some slaves participated in cockfights. Cockfighting reached the height of its popularity before the Civil War. Twenty-first-century cockfights are, for the most part, more clandestine affairs that occur in rural areas of the state. MATTHEW H. JENNINGS

Herzog, Harold A., Jr. "Cockfighting." In *Encyclopedia of Southern Culture,* edited by Charles Reagan Wilson and William Ferris. Chapel Hill: University of North Carolina Press, 1989.

Wyatt-Brown, Bertram. *Honor and Violence in the Old South.* New York: Oxford University Press, 1986.

Cofitachiqui. Cofitachiqui is the name of a sixteenth- and seventeenth-century Native American chiefdom as well as one of the principal towns of that chiefdom. The towns of Cofitachiqui and neighboring Talimeco were located on a bank of the Wateree River below the fall line near Camden. In 1540 Hernando De Soto visited both towns, and between 1566 and 1568 Juan Pardo led expeditions to the province from the Spanish town of Santa Elena. On arriving at Cofitachiqui, De Soto was met by a young woman the Spanish called the "Lady of Cofitachiqui." According to her, the province had suffered a great pestilence, and she ruled following the death of a male relative. Her realm included the central portion of present-day South Carolina and may have extended to the coast and as far northwest as the Appalachian Mountains. Narratives describe Talimeco with approximately five hundred houses and as the principal town of the province, but it had been abandoned after the epidemic. In this vacant town was a mound surmounted by a large temple covered with woven matting and containing carved wooden statues, the bones of past leaders, and a large number of pearls. At Talimeco the explorers also found Spanish artifacts believed to have come from the ill-fated 1526 colony of Lucas Vázquez de Ayllón. The English explorer Henry Woodward visited Cofitachiqui in 1670, and the last known reference to the town is the name "Cotuchike" on the circa 1685 map drawn by Joel Gascoyne and based on a survey by Maurice Mathews. Scholars differ on the language and ethnic identity of the chiefdom. According to these arguments, the people of the Cofitachiqui spoke either a Muskhogean or a Siouan language. If they spoke Muskhogean, they were likely related to the Creek Indians of Georgia and Alabama, and they probably migrated westward in the late seventeenth century. If, however, they spoke a Siouan language, then the Catawba and related tribes are probably descendants of the chiefdom. CHESTER B. DEPRATTER

Baker, Steven G. "Cofitachique: Fair Province of Carolina." Master's thesis, University of South Carolina, 1974.

DePratter, Chester B. "Cofitachiqui: Ethnohistorical and Archaeological Evidence." In *Studies in South Carolina Archaeology: Essays in Honor of Robert L. Stephenson,* edited by Albert C. Goodyear III and Glen T. Hanson. Columbia: South Carolina Institute of Archaeology and Anthropology, University of South Carolina, 1989.

Duncan, David Ewing. *Hernando de Soto: A Savage Quest in the Americas.* New York: Crown, 1995.

Vega, Garcilaso de la. *The Florida of the Inca.* Translated and edited by John Grier Varner and Jeannette Johnson Varner. Austin: University of Texas Press, 1951.

Waddell, Gene. "Cofitachiqui." *Carologue* 16 (autumn 2000): 8–15.

Coker, Charles Westfield (1879–1931). Businessman, philanthropist, social reformer. The youngest son of James Lide Coker and Susan Stout, Coker was born in Hartsville on July 13, 1879. Growing up in an entrepreneurial family, Charles became involved in various Coker businesses at an early age, including the family mercantile store, J. L. Coker and Company, and the Carolina Fiber Company, which produced pulp paper. When the family organized the Southern Novelty Company in Hartsville in 1899 to manufacture paper cones for the southern textile industry from this pulp paper, Charles became its first treasurer and chief salesman. On October 15, 1903, Coker married Carrie H. Lide. The marriage produced two sons, James Lide III and Charles.

In his father's declining years, Coker increased his management role in the company, and in 1918 he succeeded him as president, a position he held until his death. It was Charles Coker who brought modern industrial and managerial practice to the family-controlled business, which changed its name to Sonoco Products Company in 1923. He established an industrial research and development program, developed a dedicated sales staff, and emphasized long-range planning. The cone industry was difficult and competitive because it required only a limited capital investment and production was relatively easy and inexpensive. This fact forced Coker to be efficient in production and farsighted in technology. Marketing, at which he excelled, was all-important. In such a competitive industry Coker profited not just on the quantity of cones he could sell but also by insuring their quality. A key to success was industrial research to improve the company's equipment and production methods. When rayon came into the textile industry, Sonoco responded successfully by developing a new type of cone to handle rayon spinning. Sonoco was closely tied to the textile industry, a fact that led Coker to seek diversification in product lines as well as overseas markets during the 1920s and 1930s.

Like other family members, Coker found time away from his business interests to fulfill what he felt were equally important civic and social obligations. He served as Hartsville mayor (1907–1908, 1917–1918) and as a state senator from Darlington County (1930). His special interest was in social work and welfare. He served on the state board of public welfare (1920–1928) and led the effort to establish social work councils in each South Carolina county, providing reform in such areas as public health, education, juvenile delinquency, transportation, and prisons. In 1930 President Herbert Hoover appointed Coker to the President's Commission on Housing Relief. His efforts in social reform and industrial development ended abruptly with his death from a heart attack on November 21, 1931. He was buried in the First Baptist churchyard, Hartsville. Coker's sons followed their father into leadership positions at Sonoco. NED L. IRWIN

Bailey, N. Louise, Mary L. Morgan, and Carolyn R. Taylor, eds. *Biographical Directory of the South Carolina Senate, 1776–1985.* 3 vols. Columbia: University of South Carolina Press, 1986.

Coker, Charles W. *The Story of Sonoco Products Company.* New York: Newcomen Society in North America, 1976.

Simpson, George Lee, Jr. *The Cokers of Carolina: A Social Biography of a Family.* Chapel Hill: University of North Carolina Press, 1956.

Coker, David Robert (1870–1938). Businessman, plant breeder, philanthropist. The second son of James Lide Coker and Susan Stout, David Coker was born in Hartsville on November 20, 1870. His father was a successful merchant and owned large agricultural holdings, enterprises in which David became actively involved following his 1891 graduation from the University of South Carolina. Coker married Jessie Ruth Richardson on September 10, 1894. The couple had five children. Following the death of his first wife in 1913, Coker married Margaret May Roper in 1915. His second marriage produced three children.

An illness in 1897 led Coker to withdraw temporarily from management of J. L. Coker and Company, the family store, and to focus on his first experiments with plant breeding. His business experience with farmers at the store made him conscious of the difficult conditions under which postbellum southern farmers survived. He saw a need not only for better seed to provide more productive crops but also for a change in attitude from traditional to more modern methods of farming. This dual focus remained at the forefront of Coker's efforts in plant breeding and the subsequent development of the Coker's Pedigreed Seed Company.

Coker became noted for his development of improved strains of cotton, especially significant in the cotton-raising Pee Dee region where he lived. Through his younger brother William, a botany professor, Coker began an association with Herbert J. Webber of the United States Department of Agriculture, which was to have an important influence in bringing greater scientific method to Coker's experimental work. Coker's Pedigreed Seed Company was formally organized in 1913 to manage these plant-breeding operations, with David Coker as president. The company, which became a major regional seed house, developed improved types of cotton, corn, oats, tobacco, melons, and other crops that helped revitalize and change twentieth-century southern agriculture. Its informative seed catalog became both an important promotional tool for the company and a boon to farmers throughout the South. The company's trademark red heart with the words "Blood Will Tell" emphasized quality seed. From the World War I era until his death, Coker became an agricultural evangelist, promoting diversification, improved farming methods, and his seeds through numerous speeches, articles, and personal visits. To expand the market for short-fiber cotton, he developed relationships with Carolina textile mill owners to successfully test and promote its use, thus expanding the market for the farmers who bought his seed.

Coker had an equally active civic career. He was mayor of Hartsville (1902–1904); newspaper editor; bank president; an original member of the Federal Reserve Bank of Richmond, Va.; chairman of the South Carolina Council of Defense and state food administrator during World War I; and an active leader in the state Democratic Party. He continued the family tradition of philanthropic work, being a trustee and major benefactor of Coker College and of his alma mater. Coker died on November 28, 1938, at his Hartsville residence and was buried in First Baptist churchyard, Hartsville. NED L. IRWIN

Coclanis, Peter A. "Seeds of Reform: David R. Coker, Premium Cotton, and the Campaign to Modernize the Rural South." *South Carolina Historical Magazine* 102 (July 2001): 202–18.

Coker, David R. Papers. South Caroliniana Library, University of South Carolina, Columbia.

Rogers, James A., with Larry E. Nelson. *Mr. D. R.: A Biography of David R. Coker.* Hartsville, S.C.: Coker College Press, 1994.

Simpson, George Lee, Jr. *The Cokers of Carolina: A Social Biography of a Family.* Chapel Hill: University of North Carolina Press, 1956.

Coker, Elizabeth Boatwright (1909–1993). Writer. Once referred to by a friend as "South Carolina's First Lady of Letters," Elizabeth Boatwright Coker was born in Darlington on April 21, 1909, the daughter of Purvis Jenkins Boatwright and Bessie Heard. Her career as a published writer began in 1925 when, as an eleventh-grade student, she won the Poetry Society of South Carolina's Carroll Prize for her poem "Noches." She went on to become editor of the literary magazine at Converse College, where she earned a B.A. in 1929. She later did graduate work at Middlebury College in Vermont. On September 27, 1930, she married James Lide Coker III, who subsequently became president of Sonoco Products Company in Hartsville. The marriage produced two children. Except for summer retreats to Blowing Rock, North Carolina, and periods of schooling and travel, Coker spent the rest of her life in Hartsville.

Elizabeth Boatwright Coker. Courtesy, South Caroliniana Library, University of South Carolina

Between 1950 and 1981 Coker published nine novels in the genre of the historical romance, allowing her to exploit her deep interest in all periods of the southern and South Carolina experience. Her first novel, *Daughter of Strangers* (1950), was a dramatic treatment of racial identity set in New Orleans and the South Carolina lowcountry of the 1830s and 1840s. It remained on the *New York Times* best-seller list for six months and was a selection of the Fiction Book Club. After reading the book, fellow South Carolina writer Chapman Milling claimed that Coker was "a national writer to be reckoned with." Her next novel, *The Day of the Peacock* (1952), was set in a twentieth-century South Carolina mill village and explored the struggle between old wealth and new labor through the lives of those whose existences were tied to "the most modern spinning plant in the new South of today." *India Allan* (1953) shifted in action between South Carolina and Virginia, portraying the lives of South Carolinians caught up in the dramatic events of secession, Civil War, and Reconstruction. Two more novels followed in quick succession, *The Big Drum* (1957) and *La Belle* (1959), the latter a spirited portrait of Marie Boozer, the notorious southern belle who "flirted her way to the top of South Carolina society" before riding away with Sherman's army after the burning of Columbia.

Coker's sixth novel, *Lady Rich* (1963), was distinguished for its Elizabethan English setting. Her 1968 work, *The Bees,* returned to twentieth-century South Carolina for its depiction of a prominent family at odds with itself. *Blood Red Roses* (1977), for which Bantam Books paid a record price for the paperback rights, told the story of Hilton Head Island during the Civil War. *The Grasshopper King* (1981) concerned the doomed Mexican Empire of Maximilian and Carlotta.

In addition to writing novels, Coker reviewed books and published satirical poems in various newspapers, magazines, and anthologies. In 1962 she won the International P.E.N. Short Story Contest of the American Branch of P.E.N. For some four decades she was deeply engaged in other efforts that defined her era's literary and cultural life in South Carolina and the region. She stayed in touch with other writers, encouraged new talent, and appeared as a reader and lecturer in innumerable programs. She taught seminars in colleges and universities and lectured throughout the South. She was inducted into the South Carolina Academy of Authors in 1991, and in 1992 she was selected for membership in the South Carolina Hall of Fame. She died in Hartsville on September 1, 1993, and was buried in Magnolia Cemetery, Charleston. THOMAS L. JOHNSON

Coker, Elizabeth Boatwright. Papers. South Caroliniana Library, University of South Carolina, Columbia.

Coker, James Lide, Jr. (1863–1931). Entrepreneur, engineer, industrialist. Coker was the eldest son of James Lide Coker and Susan Stout. He was born at Society Hill on November 23, 1863, as his father lay seriously wounded in Chattanooga following serious injury in the Battle of Lookout Mountain. The senior Coker survived the war and began to develop various business enterprises in Hartsville and Darlington County. His son took an active part in these businesses as he grew older, including service with the main family enterprise, J. L. Coker and Company, a large mercantile establishment.

Coker's practical aptitude for mechanical things led in 1884 to his attending Stevens Institute of Technology in Hoboken, New Jersey, where he graduated with an engineering degree. In his senior thesis he studied the process of making paper from wood pulp and conceived the idea of substituting the cheap and readily available southern pine for the hardwoods then in general use. On September 10, 1889, Coker married Vivian Gay, daughter of the landscape painter Edward Gay. The couple had three children.

When Coker returned to Hartsville after college, he convinced his father to help finance experiments on his scheme, no one having previously attempted the pulp process with pine timber. Working with the American Sulphite Pulp Company, which held a patent of the sulphite process, Coker built an experimental pulp mill in Hartsville in 1890 and, with his father, formed the Carolina Fiber Company. After much difficulty, Coker proved the process effective and began manufacturing the first wood pulp made from pine. His mill and process had a significant influence on the future development of the southern pulp mill industry. In the years following, Coker expanded the firm as it supplied pulp and paper products throughout the country. A man of remarkable mechanical ability, Coker invented much of the machinery and developed the new processes needed in the southern pulp mill industry. Best known as an inventive engineer, he was less adept as a daily business manager. Here the financial acumen of his father and the hiring of good subordinates proved important for the company's ultimate success.

Heavily involved in the cotton and textile business, the Coker family soon expanded the paper-product line into the production of paper cones and tubes used in the spinning process by textile mills. The Southern Novelty Company was formed in 1899 to produce and supply such products to the textile industry and was an example of the Cokers' ability to develop regional enterprises from local needs. Southern Novelty was located alongside the fiber plant, and the two firms had a symbiotic, as well as familial, relationship; James headed Carolina Fiber, and younger brother Charles eventually led

Southern Novelty (renamed Sonoco in 1923). In 1941 the two separate operating companies combined. James Coker died on December 23, 1931, in Hartsville, where he was also buried. NED L. IRWIN

Simpson, George Lee, Jr. *The Cokers of Carolina: A Social Biography of a Family.* Chapel Hill: University of North Carolina Press, 1956.

Coker, James Lide, Sr. (1837–1918). Businessman, entrepreneur, philanthropist. Son of Caleb Coker and Hannah Lide, Coker was born on January 3, 1837, near Society Hill, where his father was a planter and a merchant. He was educated at the local St. David's Academy, the Citadel, and Harvard. At Harvard he spent 1857 studying with Louis Agassiz and Asa Gray to better prepare himself for managing agricultural property. When his father gave Coker property in Hartsville, he became one of the first in the state to adapt scientific methods to agriculture, an interest his son David R. Coker later expanded into Coker's Pedigreed Seed Company. On March 28, 1860, Coker married Susan Stout, daughter of a Baptist minister. Their marriage produced a remarkable set of sons—James Jr., David, William, and Charles—who became state and regional leaders in business, agriculture, and education.

James L. Coker, Sr. Courtesy, South Caroliniana Library, University of South Carolina

During the Civil War, Coker served in the Ninth (later the Sixth) South Carolina Infantry, reaching the rank of major. Seriously wounded at Lookout Mountain in 1863, he took nearly a year to recover. After a torturous journey home, Coker found the area devastated and began the task of rebuilding his farm and his community. J. L. Coker and Company, a general merchandise store, opened in 1865. The store prospered, serving an extensive cotton-growing region of the state and eventually becoming one of the South's largest stores.

Coker's work with cotton farmers led him into the business of cotton factoring and manufacturing. He founded a cotton mill, a cotton gin, and a cottonseed-oil mill, and with G. A. Norwood he established a cotton firm at Charleston with which he was associated from 1874 to 1881. After this time he focused most of his enterprises in Darlington County, where he established the Darlington National Bank (1884) and the Bank of Hartsville (1903) and built a railroad (1889) to connect his Hartsville businesses to the world. With son James Jr. he organized the Carolina Fiber Company (1889), the first plant to commercially produce wood pulp from pine. His textile interests led him to establish, with son Charles, the Southern Novelty Company (1899) to manufacture the paper cones and tubes needed in yarn mills. Eventually these two firms were merged to form Sonoco, a major international producer of packaging products. The seed company, incorporated in 1913 with his son David, became a renowned southern seed and plant producer. Coker's business activities did much to influence and promote industrial, commercial, and agricultural development in the state.

Along with his varied business concerns, Coker took a strong interest in promoting education. Largely through his efforts and financing, Coker College, originally a liberal arts college for women (later coeducational), was established in Hartsville in 1908. Coker's long and successful career provided a human face to the state's successful transition from the Old South to the New South. At the time of his death on June 25, 1918, Coker was considered the wealthiest citizen of the state and, perhaps, its most versatile postbellum entrepreneur. He was buried in the First Baptist Church Cemetery, Hartsville. NED L. IRWIN

Coker, James Lide. Papers. South Caroliniana Library, University of South Carolina, Columbia.

Recollections of the Major: James Lide Coker, 1837–1918. Hartsville, S.C.: Hartsville Museum, 1997.

Simpson, George Lee, Jr. *The Cokers of Carolina: A Social Biography of a Family.* Chapel Hill: University of North Carolina Press, 1956.

Coker College. Founded in 1908, Coker College is an independent liberal arts college located in Hartsville. Named for Major James Lide Coker, the college is the product of his philanthropic efforts to improve the state's educational opportunities. This work began with the establishment of Welsh Neck High School in 1894. In 1907 the creation of a statewide public high school system alleviated the need for private high schools, and Coker embraced the opportunity to convert the high school into a women's college. Thus, Coker College was born. The burgeoning business enterprises of the Coker family provided funds to support the new institution. Major Coker donated $25,000 for the construction of an administration building in 1909; $150,000 for the college's endowment in 1910; and $65,000 for a one-hundred-bed dormitory in 1914.

At the start of the twentieth century, the college maintained its Christian nondenominational roots. The earliest catalog noted that "no attempt whatsoever to influence pupils in their denominational preferences will be made or tolerated." Major Coker believed that education, rather than religion, was the primary purpose of higher education. In 1944 the college broke its ties to the Baptist Association and reorganized its self-perpetuating board.

After Coker's death in 1918, his heirs ensured his legacy. Successive generations funded construction, including the library (1962), the student center (1971), and a performing arts center (1997). Kalmia Gardens, a thirty-acre nature preserve, was donated to the college in 1965. Perhaps most telling of the family's contributions to the college is that prior to 1969 all college facilities were built without debt.

Despite challenges, Coker College held on to its roots in the liberal arts. In 1929 a $400,000 endowment campaign was wiped away by the stock market crash. Enrollment wavered; the board authorized new course offerings to include business administration and "areas of vocational and professional demand." In the years following World War II, returning veterans enrolled. Officially, the college became coeducational in 1969, and the first men enrolled in 1970. Under a mandate by the Civil Rights Act, the college opened its doors to minorities, and the first African American female enrolled in 1968. The 1960s also witnessed increasing competition from

Winthrop College in Rock Hill. In order to remain competitive, Coker instituted several programs designed to broaden the college's reach and income. The Military Degree Completion Program was instituted in 1970 to assist National Guardsmen and, later, soldiers stationed at Fort Jackson with college course work. The college also agreed to house the Governor's School for Science and Mathematics, thus utilizing college facilities and serving statewide needs.

In 2000 Coker's on-campus enrollment of more than four hundred was drawn by its solid reputation, as noted by *U.S. News & World Report* and *Barron's* college reviews. Such distinctions were gleaned from Coker's "round table" teaching style, as most classes were taught around large tables, thus fostering classroom dialogue. Many classes had fewer than twelve students, and eighty-five percent of the faculty held the highest degrees in their fields. The student population was seventy percent female and approximately twenty percent African American. JULIE ROTHOLZ

Simpson, Robert R. *A Century of Education: Welsh Neck High School and Coker College.* Hartsville, S.C.: Coker College Press, 1994.

Coker's Pedigreed Seed Company. Coker's Pedigreed Seed Company had its origins in the efforts of David R. Coker to develop and market a highly productive variety of upland cotton that yielded fiber of superior quality and length. With the help of university-trained botanists, Coker undertook his experimental work in the early twentieth century. Exploiting the natural variability of cotton and using plant-to-row methods, Coker brought his first variety, "Hartsville No. 5," to market in 1909. The focus was on cotton, but Coker expanded the project to include corn, oats, rye, peas, and sorghum. Managed at first as a division of J. L. Coker and Company, Pedigreed Seed Company was incorporated in 1918 as a separate business with headquarters in Hartsville. The company name officially became Coker's Pedigreed Seed Company in 1923.

Over the years the company maintained a staff of talented plant breeders and became a major supplier of improved seeds for field crops. Tobacco became part of the work in 1927. The company engaged in breeding soybeans as that crop became common in the South. By the mid-1960s the company had seed-breeding operations in several states and Mexico and was supplying the seeds for the majority of acreage devoted to cotton, oats, and flue-cured tobacco in the southeastern United States. The Coker family, which had owned and operated the company from the beginning, sold it in 1978 to KWS Seed Company of Einbeck, Germany. Northrup King Company acquired Coker's Pedigreed Seed Company in 1988 and terminated the operations in Hartsville. LARRY NELSON

Coker Pedigreed Seed Company produced an amazing variety of seeds, including giant Coker 811 Hybrid Corn. Courtesy, Richard E. Gettys

Coclanis, Peter A. "Seeds of Reform: David R. Coker, Premium Cotton, and the Campaign to Modernize the Rural South." *South Carolina Historical Magazine* 102 (July 2001): 202–18.

Rogers, James A., with Larry Nelson. *Mr. D. R.: A Biography of David R. Coker.* Hartsville, S.C.: Coker College Press, 1994.

Simpson, George Lee, Jr. *The Cokers of Carolina: A Social Biography of a Family.* Chapel Hill: University of North Carolina Press, 1956.

Cold war (1945–1991). The cold war was the period of intense ideological and military competition between the United States and the Soviet Union that began after World War II and lasted until the Soviet collapse in 1991. The longest-running single episode of armed confrontation in the American experience, it proved to have wide-ranging impacts on the people, life, and economy of South Carolina. In the 1950s schoolchildren practiced emergency drills, canisters of food and water were stored in public buildings, and radio and television stations announced periodic tests of the civil-defense system. When the cold war turned hot—as it did in the so-called "proxy wars" against the "Soviet surrogates" North Korea and China, 1950–1953, or Vietnam, 1960–1975—South Carolina sent forth to the fight its share of sons and daughters. Because of the cold war, the state gained new population groups and new waves of defense, economic, educational, and transportation activity. The cold war continued the role of federal expenditure that commenced during the New Deal and greatly expanded during World War II. Defense dollars created jobs, attracted new types of workers, and helped accelerate the process of urbanization. Finally, the era saw the end of the segregation by law of blacks and whites that had been the state's legacy since Reconstruction.

The term "cold war" meant that a dangerous, protracted struggle was at hand, one that could reach the brink of war and go beyond it. Against the Soviets, President Harry Truman devised a strategy of containment, an essential element of which was the ability to deter Soviet nuclear attack against the United States. The premise of deterrence was simple: any attack would be met by a devastating American response against the Soviet Union. This was a task in which South Carolina played a direct and vital role. Beginning in the early 1960s, nuclear-powered submarines of the U.S. Navy began plying in and out of Charleston harbor. The largest, designated fleet ballistic submarines, carried nuclear warhead-tipped, submarine-launched ballistic missiles (or SLBMs). The other type, attack submarines, had the mission of seeking out and destroying Soviet submarines before these could launch their own SLBMs against targets in the United States. In South Carolina the only accident or mishap involving dangerous weapons of this sort occurred in 1958. In that year a U.S. Air Force bomber on a training mission accidentally dropped an atomic weapon over a rural area near Florence. The triggering device went off and flattened farm buildings, but the warhead did not detonate. The incident involved no loss of life or casualties.

Cold-war defense spending in South Carolina flowed from decisions made within a framework established by the National Security Act of 1947. Thanks to congressmen such as L. Mendel Rivers, South Carolina would receive, as the cold war progressed, its full share or more of the new military installations and facilities judged essential to national security. Results included the World War II naval air station at Beaufort reopening as a U.S. Marine Corps air station, additional units at Shaw Air Force Base near Sumter, and upgrading and expanding the Marine Corps Recruit Depot at Parris Island and Fort Jackson near Columbia.

South Carolina also played a direct role in the manufacture of materials used in thermonuclear weapons. The Savannah River Site, designed in 1950, came to include nuclear reactors and heavy water and nuclear fuel facilities, as well as a capability for meeting waste-management requirements—meaning that high-level radioactive waste would be stored there.

Another piece of cold-war legislation of great importance to South Carolina was the Interstate Highway Act of 1956. Although a central purpose of this act was to ensure that military forces could move freely about the United States, in South Carolina the Interstate Highway Act proved to have a far broader significance. Tourists now came to South Carolina's beaches and recreational areas in increasing numbers, continuing a trend reaching back to well before World War II. So also did new residents, attracted by the opportunities of working to construct the new bases and installations needed for defense. Other workers were drawn to service-industry opportunities in those areas where the bases and facilities were located. In addition, the military brought new population groups to the state. One group comprised the young men and women in their teens and twenties who had been ordered to the state on active duty. A second group was the retirees who had completed their active service and tended to settle in the coastal areas or near bases where they had served. The areas around Beaufort, Charleston, Columbia, Myrtle Beach, and Sumter thus tended to gain substantial numbers of military retirees. This process began at the outset of the cold war and continued after its end.

These various factors—the defense dollars spent for military construction, the tourists and new residents flowing to beaches or new jobs over improved highway systems, the waves of military retirees—were mirrored in the experiences of other states in which, as in South Carolina, substantial cold-war expenditures occurred. But unlike California and Texas, South Carolina did not gain, for example, the same sorts of highly technical, defense-related industries such as aerospace, communications, or computers. Some manufacture of infantry small arms and even some small warships did occur, but for the most part South Carolina did not win the same levels of federal funding as did other southern states in the areas of research or defense manufacturing.

Key elected officials recognized that the state's educational system might be a factor in attracting—or failing to attract—such industries. In 1960 Governor Ernest F. Hollings led an initiative that resulted in the creation of South Carolina's technical education system. But not until 1983 did South Carolina create the South Carolina Research Authority (SCRA), an effort to assist higher education and research entities in attracting research and development enterprises to the state. This effort lagged behind similar ones in neighboring southern states.

In the Korean War 467 South Carolinians died, and 896 perished in the Vietnam War—substantial losses indeed for a state relatively small in population. The U.S. Army's First Cavalry Division departed in August 1965 from Charleston's army depot for the first large ground battles of that war. Tens of thousands of soldiers and U.S. Marines initially trained at Fort Jackson and Parris Island served in Vietnam. Myrtle Beach– and Shaw-trained U.S. Air Force fighter pilots and U.S. Marine pilots from Beaufort flew their perilous and costly missions in South Vietnam and against Hanoi and Haiphong. Neither they nor the soldiers and Marines on the ground could know at the time that a Charleston-based U.S. Navy communications specialist, John Walker, was selling secrets—in fact, the highest-level United States operational code—to the Soviets, meaning that the Soviets' North Vietnamese allies could receive knowledge of American moves before they were made.

Yet the long cold-war struggle finally came to an end. For the final event of the contest, the Soviet Union, spent by costly arms races and beset by myriad systemic problems, at last dissolved into its component parts. The Charleston naval base and the U.S. Air Force base at Myrtle Beach proved casualties of this victory and closed under the Defense Base Closure and Realignment Act of 1990. South Carolina retained, however, the rest of the bases originally employed in the waging of the cold war. JOHN W. GORDON

Clements, Kendrick A., ed. *James F. Byrnes and the Origins of the Cold War.* Durham, N.C.: Carolina Academic Press, 1982.

Petit, J. Percival. *South Carolina and the Sea.* Vol. 2, *Day by Day toward Five Centuries, 1492–1985 A.D.* Isle of Palms, S.C.: Le Petit Maison, 1986.

Schulman, Bruce J. *From Cotton Belt to Sunbelt: Federal Policy, Economic Development, and the Transformation of the South, 1938–1990.* New York: Oxford University Press, 1991.

University of South Carolina Legacy Project. *The Cold War in South Carolina, 1945–1991: An Inventory of Department of Defense Cold War Era Cultural and Historical Resources in the State of South Carolina: Final Report.* 4 vols. Aberdeen Proving Ground, Md.: Legacy Resource Management Program, United States Department of Defense, 1995.

Wallace, Meghan Wynne. "Selling Armageddon: An Analysis of the Promotion of Cold War Civil Defense in Columbia, South Carolina through the Study of Material Culture." Master's thesis, University of South Carolina, 1999.

Colhoun, John Ewing (ca. 1749–1802). U.S. senator. Born in Virginia, Colhoun was the son of Ezekial Calhoun and Jane Ewing. When still a boy, Colhoun moved with his extended family to Long Canes region of the South Carolina backcountry in what is now Abbeville County. Through marriage and land acquisition, the Calhouns (as most of his family chose to spell the name) gained economic and political clout in the backcountry and soon counted themselves among the region's most prominent families. Colhoun graduated from the College of New Jersey (later Princeton) in 1774, then moved to Charleston to study law. During the Revolutionary War he served as a militia captain and aide-de-camp to General Andrew Pickens. In 1779 Colhoun became a member of the Mount Zion Society, an organization formed two years earlier that established a school at Winnsboro to educate the sons of prominent South Carolinians. Although the school struggled to maintain operations, it helped promote formal education in the backcountry as well as contacts among lowcountry and backcountry elites. Admitted to the bar in 1783, Colhoun opened a practice in Charleston. On October 8, 1786, Colhoun cemented his ties to the lowcountry elite by marrying Floride Bonneau, heiress to an extensive plantation in St. John's Berkeley Parish. The couple eventually had eight children. Discontinuing his legal practice, Colhoun focused on his plantations in the lowcountry and in Ninety Six District, where he controlled thousands of acres. At the time of his death, he owned at least 108 slaves.

Colhoun entered the General Assembly in 1779 and remained a fixture in the S.C. House of Representatives over the next two decades, representing at various times the backcountry districts of Ninety Six and Pendleton as well as the lowcountry parish of St. Stephen's. He was also a backcountry delegate to the state convention that ratified the U.S. Constitution in 1788, although he missed the voting. During the 1790s Colhoun was a key member of Pierce Butler's Republican coalition of backcountry planters, whose guarded conservatism bridged the political gap between the democratic views of staunch backcountry Republicans and the conservative beliefs of lowcountry Federalists.

In December 1800 Colhoun was elected by the General Assembly to the U.S. Senate, narrowly ousting arch-Federalist Jacob Read as part of the electoral "revolution" that placed Thomas Jefferson in the presidency. Taking his seat on March 4, 1801, Colhoun soon broke with the Jefferson administration when he sided with the Federalist opposition in supporting the preservation of an independent federal judiciary. Congressional Republicans had attempted to circumvent the Federalist leanings of the Supreme Court by altering the tenure of members from "during good behavior" to "during the pleasure of the Legislature." Colhoun denounced this attempt to undermine the court's independence as "repugnant to the express letter and spirit of the Constitution." Colhoun's Senate service was cut short by his untimely death on October 26, 1802, in Pendleton District, where he was buried in his family cemetery. JAMES SPADY

Bailey, N. Louise, and Elizabeth Ivey Cooper, eds. *Biographical Directory of the South Carolina House of Representatives.* Vol. 3, *1775–1790.* Columbia: University of South Carolina Press, 1981.

Colhoun, John Ewing. Papers. South Caroliniana Library, University of South Carolina, Columbia.

Klein, Rachel N. *Unification of a Slave State: The Rise of the Planter Class in the South Carolina Backcountry, 1760–1808.* Chapel Hill: University of North Carolina Press, 1990.

College of Charleston. Although plans for a college at Charleston had been discussed throughout the eighteenth century, it was not until March 1785 that the General Assembly passed an act authorizing the creation of a college "in or near the city of Charleston." On public land at Charleston's western edge, rooms were fashioned out of an old military barracks, and instruction began on January 1, 1790.

The school struggled to survive over the next several decades. Classes emphasized moral discipline along with a classical liberal arts education, which included Latin and Greek, literature, rhetoric, and philosophy. The Reverend Robert Smith was the school's first president, clerics dominated the faculty, and daily routines included vespers. Out of sixty students who started in 1790, six earned bachelor's degrees four years later. Because of an insufficiency of advanced students and library, they were the last collegiate graduates for a third of a century. In the early nineteenth century the college functioned as a college preparatory school. College course work resumed in the 1820s, with an enlarged library funded by the city of Charleston, a new main building (now Randolph Hall), and a faculty of laymen. The 1830 enrollment of sixty-two in college classes would not be surpassed until 1904.

A rift among trustees, faculty, and students over discipline and power led to a suspension of operations in 1836. A request of the trustees for the intervention of Charleston mayor Robert Y. Hayne resulted in 1837 in a publicly funded city college, one of the earliest in the nation. City fathers charged the institution to be a source of cultural and economic improvement, "a Popular Institution, intended for the benefit of the great body of the people." Under President William T. Brantley (1838–1844), the precollege part of the curriculum was discarded, the college faculty strengthened by the addition of John Bachman and Lewis R. Gibbes, and student

The cistern and the old main building at the College of Charleston are still as much the focal point of the campus as they were during the 1930s. Photograph by Lincoln Highton for the Works Progress Administration. Courtesy, South Caroliniana Library, University of South Carolina

fees reduced. Ten scholarships were offered on the basis of need. Noticed by William Gilmore Simms in 1857 as a "literary college of excellent local standing," the school had an average annual attendance of fifty in the 1840s and 1850s. The college barely survived the Civil War and its aftermath. Despite dwindling numbers of students, it adhered to a liberal arts base while others restructured their offerings around modern knowledge. City support was meager, and enrollment declined.

President Harrison Randolph's long tenure (1897–1941) effectively established a new college. The specialization of "majors" and many social science and science laboratory courses came forth along with distinctive B.A. and B.S. degrees. Language and mathematics requirements for bachelor's degrees were reduced, but the master of arts added a year of course work to the thesis. Money was raised and dormitories built. New extracurricular activities, student associations, and intercollegiate sports appeared. Enrollments rose steadily and reached 90 in 1908, most of the gain coming from outside Charleston. In the fall of 1918, with most men of college age enlisted in military service in Europe, the trustees admitted the first women, and two years later they proclaimed a free college for white residents. The original group of 10 women grew to 184 in 1935 (forty-four percent of the student body), when, with the encouragement of subsidies from Charleston County Council, theoretical and practical courses in education found a place in the curriculum.

By agreement of city, county, and school officials, the College of Charleston returned to private status in 1949 in order to avoid racial integration. In 1967 political and legal pressures, reinforced by fiscal difficulties, opened the doors to black students. Shaky finances also induced President Theodore S. Stern to negotiate the transfer of the college to the state of South Carolina in 1970.

The acceleration of change continued. Under the able leadership of Stern and his successors, with regular injections of state money and more vigorous private fund-raising, the college grew. The faculty increased from twenty-five to more than four hundred, with new departments added to traditional programs and organized in five undergraduate schools: Arts, Business and Economics, Education, Humanities and Social Sciences, and Sciences and Mathematics. A graduate school, styled University of Charleston, appeared as well, although the core of the curriculum remained in the liberal arts. The physical plant expanded from seven buildings to over a hundred. The student body, increasingly diverse and academically qualified, exceeded twelve thousand when capped in 1999. Entering the twenty-first century, the College of Charleston enjoyed an enhanced academic reputation. LAYLON WAYNE JORDAN

Easterby, J. H. *A History of the College of Charleston.* Charleston, S.C., 1935.

O'Brien, Michael, and David Moltke-Hansen, eds. *Intellectual Life in Antebellum Charleston.* Knoxville: University of Tennessee Press, 1986.

Randolph, Harrison. "The Old Education and the New." *Proceedings of the Association of Colleges and Secondary Schools of the Southern States* (1916): 46–59.

Rogers, George C., Jr. "The College of Charleston and the Year 1785." *South Carolina Historical Magazine* 86 (October 1985): 282–95.

Colleton, James (?–ca. 1706). Governor. Colleton was born in England, the son of the Carolina proprietor Sir John Colleton and Katherine Amy. He was also the younger brother of the proprietor Sir Peter Colleton. In the 1670s James moved to Barbados, where he became a leading landholder. Alarmed by the reputation that South Carolina had earned as a haven for pirates, the Lords Proprietors appointed Colleton governor on August 31, 1686, with instructions to investigate the character of relations between the colony's leaders and the pirates who plagued shipping around the Caribbean.

On his arrival in South Carolina in November 1686, Colleton strictly enforced the antipiracy policy, apparently with some success. It soon became forgotten, though, as Colleton became embroiled in a furor generated by a pair of devastating Spanish raids on South Carolina in August and December of the same year. Outraged at these attacks, in which the invaders destroyed the Scottish settlement at Stuart's Town and pillaged some coastal plantations, the Carolinians decided to attempt a military reprisal against the Spanish in Florida. England and Spain, however, were officially at peace, and Colleton declared martial law in order to prevent the ill-advised adventure against Florida.

Once the clamor for revenge had subsided, the governor convened a parliament in February 1689. Unfortunately for Colleton, this gathering enabled the colony's most powerful faction, the Goose Creek Men, to regain their political advantage. Their agenda also had a personal edge. Its leader, Maurice Mathews, a former client of Sir Peter Colleton, had broken with the Colleton family over the persistent involvement of Mathews and his associates in the Indian slave trade, which formed the foundation of their wealth and political status in the colony. When the parliament convened, the Goose Creek Men suggested to the naive Colleton that he deserved an increase in pay and that he should introduce legislation establishing an excise on imported liquors and use the revenue to augment the governor's salary. When Colleton unwittingly agreed, Mathews and his allies turned on him by voting against the bill "and then cried out against the Governor, who would enslave and ruin the people." In the subsequent political uproar, Colleton was forced to dissolve the parliament. A new one convened in February 1690, but the governor had no better success.

With England now at war with France, the legislative failure to create a military establishment in South Carolina left the colony desperately exposed, particularly after the English colony of St. Christopher's in the Caribbean fell to the French. Faced with this new emergency, Colleton accepted the arguments of Carolina's proprietary allies and declared martial law a second time, a move which his opponents quickly denounced as contemptible.

For a time, though, the dangers posed by the French kept the Goose Creek Men at bay. John Stewart, a supporter of Colleton, defended the governor to the approval of many in the colony. Just as Colleton seemed to have finally secured an upper hand, however, the proprietor Seth Sothell arrived in 1690. Ignoring their previous objections to the Fundamental Constitutions, the Goose Creek Men supported Sothell's successful claim to the governorship as a resident proprietor. This provided a pretext for not only removing Colleton as governor but also permanently barring him from office and banishing him from the colony. Although the proprietors retroactively approved his declaration of martial law, Colleton never returned to South Carolina. He died in Barbados around 1706. L. H. ROPER

Buchanan, J. E. "The Colleton Family and the Early History of South Carolina and Barbados." Ph.D. diss., University of Edinburgh, 1989.

Sirmans, M. Eugene. *Colonial South Carolina: A Political History, 1663–1763.* Chapel Hill: University of North Carolina Press, 1966.

Smith, Henry A. M. "The Colleton Family in South Carolina." *South Carolina Historical and Genealogical Magazine* 1 (October 1900): 325–41.

Colleton, Sir John (1608–1666). Proprietor. Born in England, possibly in Devonshire, Colleton was a son of Peter Colleton, who was the sheriff of Exeter, and Ursula Hull. On November 19, 1634, he married Katherine Amy, daughter of William Amy of Exton, Devonshire. They had at least five children. Colleton was a soldier and a courtier to King Charles I and spent more than £40,000 of his own money to support the king during the English Civil War (1642–1649). Following the trial and execution of Charles I, Colleton and his family fled to the protection of relatives in Barbados. There, Colleton became a counselor, judge, merchant, and planter, with sizable landholdings in three island parishes. During this period he also became interested in exploring and settling North America.

Colleton returned to England in 1659. Settling in London, he joined George Monck and William and John Berkeley, his cousins, and others in returning Charles II (1660–1685) to the throne. Colleton was knighted in 1661 for his service and loyalty to the crown and was appointed to the Council for Foreign Plantations and the Royal African Company.

Until his death, Colleton was the foremost leader of the Lords Proprietors. These included Monck, the two Berkeleys, Edmund Hyde, William Craven, George Carteret, and Anthony Ashley Cooper. They comprised the king's closest advisers and largest creditors, who in 1663 accepted a collective land grant of more than 850,000 square miles between Virginia and Spanish Florida in exchange for what was owed them individually. Under Colleton's direction, the proprietors set out to populate "Carolina" with settlers from existing New World colonies, including New England, Virginia, and the Caribbean islands, especially Barbados. The latter island's booming sugar economy led to overcrowding, and by the 1660s the surplus population began spilling over to neighboring islands. Colleton convinced the other proprietors that these Barbadians were experienced colonists who could afford to pay the expenses of colonization themselves. In return, the proprietors stood to make handsome profits simply by recruiting them to Carolina and renting them land. Colleton's efforts were briefly rewarded by the establishment of a Barbadian settlement on the Cape Fear River in 1665. However, Colleton died the following year, on April 16, 1666, and his Cape Fear venture foundered shortly thereafter. LOUIS P. TOWLES

Powell, William S. *The Proprietors of Carolina.* Raleigh, N.C.: Carolina Charter Tercentenary Commission, 1963.

Sirmans, M. Eugene. *Colonial South Carolina: A Political History, 1663–1763.* Chapel Hill: University of North Carolina Press, 1966.

Colleton County (1,056 sq. miles; 2000 pop. 38,264). First visited by Robert Sandford in 1666 while he was reconnoitering the southeastern seaboard of North America for Lord Anthony Ashley Cooper, Colleton County was one of three original counties organized in the English province of Carolina in 1682. However, Colleton was divided into three parishes by 1730 (St. Bartholomew's, St. Paul's, and St. John's Colleton), which took over most county responsibilities, including oversight of elections. Lying south and west of Charleston between the Stono and Combahee Rivers, the first-manifestation Colleton was somewhat larger than its current counterpart. Colleton County, with roughly its modern functions and boundaries (shorn of St. John's Parish, a fragment of which, the town of Edisto Beach, returned in 1975), dates from 1868, when parishes and judicial districts were abolished. The fifth-largest county in South Carolina, Colleton is bordered by Charleston, Dorchester, Bamberg, Hampton, and Beaufort Counties, and touches the Atlantic Ocean at its southeastern tip.

By 1720 Colleton was the most populous rural district in South Carolina, with 1,240 free inhabitants, mostly English, and 1,778 servants and slaves, mostly African. These early arrivals scattered along navigable waterways among patches of native inhabitants, from whom they had taken or purchased land. The early Colleton environment was rich but dangerous, subject to debilitating diseases, Spanish and French attack, hurricanes, and slave uprisings. Undaunted, the immigrants cleared land; erected houses and fences; herded cattle, pigs, and horses; and grew provisions while experimenting with various cash crops. For the most fortunate and hardy individuals and families, living standards improved and assets, particularly land and slaves, accumulated. Along the swamps and tidal streams of the Combahee, Ashepoo, and Edisto Rivers, planters cultivated rice, which they exported in vast quantities from the nearby port of Charleston. On higher ground they produced a fine grade of indigo. The average wealth for free inhabitants in the region rose to dizzying heights, which helped make South Carolina the wealthiest British colony on the North American mainland.

In the last quarter of the eighteenth century, Colleton was dotted with several villages, including Willtown and Jacksonborough along the coast, and Walterboro, a summer resort lying inland. Jacksonborough was the first county seat. In early 1782, with Charleston occupied by British forces and the patriot General Nathanael Greene headquartered at nearby Round O, the state legislature met at Jacksonborough under the leadership of Governor John Mathews, a Colleton planter.

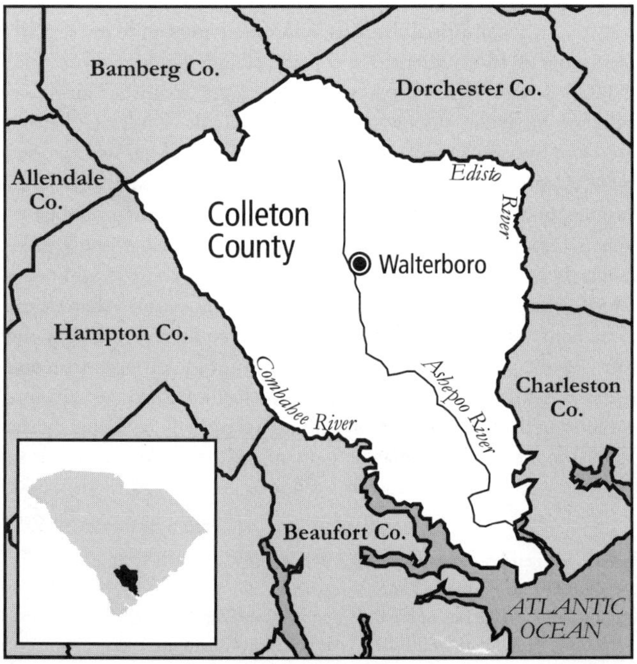

Independence brought significant, but not fundamental, change. The General Assembly created Colleton District in 1800, but the economy ran in old grooves, centered on African slave labor and rice exports, although cotton replaced indigo as the second most important crop. By 1860 the population of Colleton District was more than three-quarters black (the third-highest African American concentration in the state) and free per capita wealth reckoned in 1996 dollars was $63,236, the sixth-highest in South Carolina, which was a wealthy state. As a rule, blacks were slaves whose skills and labor were essential to Colleton's prosperity but who had neither wealth nor power themselves. There were exceptions. Justus Angel and Mistress L. Horry, both African Americans, were free planters, each owning eighty-four slaves. Moreover, visitors who stopped at William Skirving's well-run plantation on the Combahee were amazed to find that Solomon, Skirving's black driver, managed the entire operation himself.

In 1861 the white men of Colleton went to war in defense of slavery and states' rights. After the cause was lost and slaves were freed, white and black people alike faced a difficult transition. Despite a short boom in fertilizer manufacturing and more durable forest industries spearheaded by the timber giant Westvaco, agriculture remained central to the Colleton economy. But the old prosperity eluded farmers of both races. Through the first half of the twentieth century, black and white children went to separate schools. Education was hampered by poor facilities, lack of money and teachers, fluctuating attendance, and an overall emphasis on subsistence over preparation for a better future. Young people, especially blacks, emigrated. By the Depression of the 1930s, Colleton had an unemployment rate of more than thirty percent. Many residents were saved from starvation only by the timely arrival of federal assistance.

At the end of the twentieth century, the rice lands had reverted to freshwater swamps and the Ashepoo had one of the most pristine river environments in the United States. The races were roughly equal in numbers and nearer in condition than they had ever been, with the five-member county council including two African Americans in 2000. Colleton farmers of both races produced corn, soybeans, and wheat on smaller and fewer farms, and all shared the problems of agriculture elsewhere: high productivity, low prices, and fickle weather. But with a four percent increase in urban employment between 1993 and 2000 in towns such as Walterboro (the county seat since 1817), Colleton County won recognition in a national magazine's list of South Carolina's seven top counties for economic growth. Still, in the 1999–2000 school year, fifty-five percent of Colleton County students qualified for lunch subsidies under federal poverty guidelines. LAYLON WAYNE JORDAN

Glover, Beulah. *Narratives of Colleton County, South Carolina.* N.p., 1963.

Jordan, Laylon Wayne, and Elizabeth Stringfellow. *A Place Called St. John's.* Spartanburg, S.C.: Reprint Company, 1998.

Mikell, Isaac Jenkins. *Rumbling of the Chariot Wheels.* Columbia, S.C.: State Company, 1923.

Puckette, Clara C. *Edisto: A Sea Island Principality.* Cleveland, Ohio: Seaforth, 1978.

Colonial agents. The wealth of the eighteenth-century British Empire was founded on commerce and overseas trade, a trade enhanced by its American plantations. Within a few decades of South Carolina's settlement in 1670, the colony developed a flourishing rice culture, owed partly to the agricultural know-how of its African American slaves. In 1704 Parliament named rice an enumerated commodity, meaning that it had to be carried in British ships and landed in British ports. Yet rice's natural markets were in the Iberian Peninsula and northern Europe. Transshipment via a British port could mean loss-making spoilage. South Carolina, like Britain's other American colonies, had no elected representative in Parliament to argue for its interests. The problem for South Carolina then was how to get Parliament to pay attention to its particular concerns. Parliament, too, desired an informed source on its distant settlement.

The answer was a permanent colonial agent, paid for by the colony's Commons House of Assembly. In 1712 South Carolina's legislature passed an act appointing its first permanent agent to remove "the pressure which the Trade of this colony now lies under . . . by a fair and impartial representation of the same to the Parliament of Great Britain." The colonial agent reported regularly to the Commons House on matters of interest to the colony. He could present petitions and propose bills in Parliament favorable to the colony's needs and arrange "expert witnesses" to give supporting evidence before the committees created to consider them. He liaised with the Board of Trade, the agency mainly responsible for overseas commerce. In the early 1760s Lord George Grenville, the British prime minister, consulted him on matters of colonial policy. In time the agent came to represent all the colony's interests, but the leading interest continued to be trade.

Later the agent was joined by an informal network of British and homegrown Carolina merchants whose lobbying tactics brought off such improvements to South Carolina's commerce as direct shipment of rice to ports south of Cape Finisterre, Spain (1730), and to the Canary, Azores, Caribbean, and foreign West Indian Islands (1764). Another success was Parliament's passage in 1748 of a bounty on indigo, South Carolina's second-most-important export crop. During an acute grain shortage in Great Britain in the 1760s, the agent Charles Garth and the Carolina merchants succeeded in gaining a temporary duty exemption on rice imports to Great Britain despite the powerful corn law lobby. In 1766 Garth, with the other colonial agents, promoted repeal of the Stamp Act. Garth argued South Carolina's case in strictly commercial terms, that the colony's trade could not bear the expense. Those were the arguments that Parliament was prepared to hear. After 1770 when colonial arguments became more rights based, Garth and most of the other colonial agents (and their British merchant supporters) sheared away. The loss of the colonial agent meant the loss of the colony's only voice within Parliament, while the breakup of his supporting mercantile networks eliminated an important unofficial source of reciprocal information and negotiation with the mother country, and hurried the Revolution. REBECCA STARR

Namier, Lewis. "Charles Garth, Agent for South Carolina." *English Historical Review* 54 (October 1939): 632–52.

Starr, Rebecca. *A School for Politics: Commercial Lobbying and Political Culture in Early South Carolina.* Baltimore: Johns Hopkins University Press, 1998.

Colonoware. On historic-period sites in South Carolina, archaeologists often find locally made, hand-built, unglazed pottery that was fired in open hearths rather than kilns. Vessels and sherds of this ware may be found on the sites of Indian camps and villages, the city lots of Charleston and other towns, underwater near wharves and ferries, and on small farms and large plantations. This broad class of pottery has been termed colonoware.

Colonoware is most closely associated with Native Americans and African Americans, but associations vary considerably. Although the pottery was a distinctive local creation, it had roots and influences that came from Europe and Africa as well as North America. From the earliest Spanish incursions into the Southeast, Europeans and Africans had contact with Native Americans, and some of these immigrants lived with Native Americans during the sixteenth century. Every aspect of life changed or was threatened with change, and this change included everyday items such as containers.

As English proprietors began establishing their colonies, they brought enslaved African Americans from the West Indies, and to this population they added Native American slaves, especially women and children from the mission villages of Spanish-held Florida. Once rice became the basic crop, planters imported large numbers of enslaved Africans. In the 1700s and early 1800s plantation slaves, especially in the region of Charleston and Berkeley Counties, used large amounts of colonoware. Some of this colonoware was made in free Indian villages and sold or traded to people on the plantations, but most of it appears to have been plantation made. During this period the most common forms were small bowls and jars that were likely to have been used for both cooking and serving medicine as well as food. Some colonoware bowls from this period have centered cross marks similar to the BaKongo cosmogram of Central Africa. Generally, colonoware disappeared in the middle of the nineteenth century; however, this broad class of pottery continued to be made by Native Americans and a few others into the twentieth century. LELAND FERGUSON

Columbia (Richland County; 2000 pop. 116,278). Named for Christopher Columbus and created in 1786 as the nation's first truly planned capital city, Columbia has a unique history indeed. While now the setting for state, county, and municipal governments, it took shape in the wilderness near the geographic center of South Carolina, thus answering the demands of the populous upcountry for an administrative authority more "Centrical" than far-off Charleston.

After considerable legislative bickering, in April 1786 five commissioners (all of whom owned property in the area and had personal stakes in the proceedings) purchased 2,471 acres from ten individuals. This land, two miles square, was subsequently divided into a grid of ten streets to the mile, in theory establishing four hundred city blocks, with eight acres reserved for public buildings. Most exceptional, perhaps, were the proposed thoroughfares. The two principal avenues splitting the would-be metropolis into four equal parts, as well as boundary streets on the perimeter, would be 150 feet wide, and all other streets would be 100 feet in width. The street plan was a marked departure from the narrow pathways found in older communities. In subsequent years a wag said that this scheme was devised to prevent mosquitoes from spreading malaria, the assumption being that they had a very limited flight range. Although town planners often scorned the basic grid pattern as monotonous and uninspired, these broad streets later became the envy of scores of cities and a delight to residents, suburban commuters, and visiting tourists.

Lowcountry politicians were loath to see state government move inland and did whatever they could to impede this transfer of power.

Sale of lots (some of them inexplicably under the waters of the Congaree) went slowly, but in January 1790 the General Assembly was able to hold a brief initial session in the new, if primitive, State House. In May of the following year, George Washington stopped briefly while en route from Augusta to Camden. Although honored at a public dinner in the unfinished capitol, the president did not lavish praise on a community he described as "an uncleared wood, with very few houses in it, and those all wooden ones." The town, he agreed, was laid out on a grand scale. But Washington thought that it should have been located below the falls of the Congaree, thus facilitating the flow of goods and fostering trade.

These casual comments, sagacious indeed, underscored a problem that bedeviled Columbia's pioneer generation: how to take advantage of nearby waterways to stimulate commercial development. Columbia's growth during the first half of the nineteenth century was steady, but hardly spectacular. Aided by turnpikes, canals, and (in time) railroads, it could count some 3,000 residents in 1830 and almost twice that number two decades later. Until 1900 the black-white ratio varied from census to census, with first one race and then the other more numerous. Since that time, however, whites have predominated, although black ranks (except for the 1950s) always have registered an increase, rising to 42,837 in 1990, or about forty-two percent of all city residents. Total population peaked at 113,542 in 1970 before slipping a bit in the succeeding two decades as a result of white flight to expanding suburbs such as Forest Acres, Irmo, and St. Andrews.

As the state capital, as well as the site of its premier institution of higher education (South Carolina College), Columbia was in the midst of the political turmoil leading up to the Civil War. During the conflict the city became a vital center of military, refugee, and home-front activity, pressures that swelled the resident population to some twenty thousand, or about half that of its arch rival Charleston. Although far removed from the fighting for most of the war, Columbia suffered a cruel baptism of fire in February 1865 after the Union army of General William T. Sherman entered the city. In the wake of a chaotic Confederate retreat and Sherman's arrival on February 17, fires broke out across the city and were quickly blown out of control by gusty winds. The following morning one-third of Columbia lay in ruins.

Despite the turmoil of Reconstruction, Columbia ended the nineteenth century on an upbeat note. For the first time in modern history the telephone, electric lights, trolley cars, rail travel, and improvements in education made town life infinitely more attractive than life in the countryside. Some movers and shakers dreamed that Columbia would become a winter resort like Camden or Aiken, but urban growth and industrialization altered such hopes. The city in 1894 became the site of Columbia Mills, the world's first electric-powered textile mill (which later housed the South Carolina State Museum), and eventually grew into a major center of textile manufacturing. By the beginning of the twentieth century, Columbia was also home to several institutions of higher learning. In addition to the University of South Carolina, Allen University, Benedict College, and Columbia Female College (later Columbia College) exerted considerable influence throughout the community.

The opening decades of a new century were nearly as tumultuous as those that South Carolinians had just experienced—war, a disastrous economic depression, and perplexing social trends that tended to undermine and even destroy well-entrenched sectional mores. This was, of course, a Jim Crow world, but several factors softened some features of stern segregation. These included the presence of two thriving black colleges (Allen and Benedict), able leadership in the white business community, and the sound judgment of Richard Carroll, Columbia's "Booker T. Washington," a man whose civil rights work was later carried on by N. J. Frederick, Isaac Leevy, and Modjeska Simkins.

In 1937 Columbia won fleeting fame when university students popularized intricate steps they saw at a black nightspot, the Big Apple Club, which initiated a dance craze that swept the nation. Of more lasting impact was this community's enduring fascination with footlights and greasepaint. The Town Theatre, established in 1919, eventually became one of the nation's oldest community playhouses, and its efforts were later augmented by nearly a dozen regional drama venues where audiences continue to cheer the hero and boo the villain.

Founded in compromise, Columbia usually exerted a moderating influence in both local and state affairs, seeking a "middle" way appropriate for those speaking on behalf of a vague expanse of land known as the Midlands. Forces rural and urban, farm and factory, upland and coastal often have been mitigated somewhat by a conciliatory stance that remained alive and vigorous even at the end of the twentieth century.

Although Columbia embraced city-manager government in 1950, mayors such as Lester Bates, Kirkman Finlay, Jr., and Bob Coble charted a steady course in an era that often required difficult decisions. These included how to deal with the needs of a population becoming less agricultural (2,428 farms in the region in 1940; only 799 in 1964) and urban sprawl that often ignored traditional boundaries. Plans to annex some of these border upstarts in 1959 and 1960 led to a backlash and the immediate incorporation of several bedroom satellites. Temporarily, this thwarted efforts of Columbia boosters to break the 100,000 mark.

The economic surge fueling expansion was rooted in the growth of government payrolls (local, state, and federal) and reflected a proliferation of new and unusual services at all levels, as well as expansion of the University of South Carolina and Fort Jackson (the latter was annexed to the city in 1968, increasing the municipal domain from twenty to one hundred square miles). In 1980, for example, the Columbia–Richland County community had 116,637 workers over the age of sixteen. Of that number, almost one-third were government employees—21,204 state, 8,380 city-county, and 7,168 federal. That same year only about 1,000 individuals were farming.

A *Washington Post* reporter who toured the Columbia area in 1989 found a region rife with serendipity, neither big city nor small town, existing in an attractive, leisurely, uncrowded setting. He was struck by the broad avenues that all but eliminated traffic jams. "Turn your head briefly and you will miss what passes for the evening rush hour." For him, this was a place where "landscape and history come together for the curious traveler." His special joy was "an unexpected cache" of newsreel films he discovered at USC's McKissick Museum. For others, this "special joy" might be historic homes, the award-winning Riverbanks Zoo, exhibits at the State Museum, the strikingly modern Richland County Public Library, or an afternoon spent cheering on the Gamecocks at Williams Brice Stadium.

Columbia continues to be a multifaceted community that defies easy classification. Almost from birth it was home to a college but was clearly not a college town. It built cotton mills and acquired a huge military base, yet became neither a mill town nor a "soldier" town, except perhaps in wartime. Tourists certainly have been welcome; nevertheless, their welfare never took precedence over the needs and concerns of permanent residents. Dreams of becoming a river port went nowhere, but thanks to nearby Lake Murray, Columbia became something of a "lake" city. The newsman Robert A. Pierce saw this general reluctance to be pigeonholed as Columbia's greatest asset. The diversity made South Carolina's capital, in his opinion, "Everyman's city." If nothing else, thanks to its amorphous mix, Columbia, not its satellites with their shopping malls and endless housing tracts, defines the community that observers agree is "the heart of the Midlands." See plate 19. JOHN H. MOORE

A Columbia Reader, 1786–1986. Edited by the Institute for Southern Studies and the South Caroliniana Library. Columbia, S.C.: R. L. Bryan, 1986.

Edgar, Walter B., and Deborah K. Woolley. *Columbia: Portrait of a City.* Norfolk, Va.: Donning, 1986.

Green, Mary Fulton. "A Profile of Columbia in 1850." *South Carolina Historical Magazine* 70 (April 1969): 104–21.

Hennig, Helen Kohn, ed. *Columbia: Capital City of South Carolina, 1786–1936.* Columbia, S.C.: Columbia Sesqui-Centennial Commission, 1936.

Moore, John Hammond. *Columbia and Richland County: A South Carolina Community, 1740–1990.* Columbia: University of South Carolina Press, 1993.

Columbia, burning of (February 17–18, 1865). On the morning of February 16, 1865, General William T. Sherman's Union army, 58,000 strong, stood poised to capture the South Carolina capital. When the Federal force resumed its northward march four days later, one-third of the city lay in ashes, giving rise to one of the Civil War's persistent controversies: Who burned Columbia?

Confused by Sherman's tactics, Confederate general P. G. T. Beauregard scattered his meager forces in an arc stretching from Charleston through Columbia to Augusta, Georgia, resulting in an inadequate defense for all cities. In early February, after concentrating his divided columns along a railroad from Windsor to Midway, Sherman marched virtually unopposed on Columbia.

Columbia was in chaos when Mayor Thomas J. Goodwyn surrendered the city at midmorning on Thursday, February 17. The previous night mobs of straggling soldiers and townspeople had plundered businesses and warehouses abandoned during the failed Confederate evacuation. Stacks of ragged cotton bales, ordered by General Wade Hampton to be rolled out of warehouses with the intention of burning them to keep them out of Union hands, lined the streets. Driven by a strong wind, loose cotton blew over the ground and snagged on buildings and trees, giving the city the appearance of a snowstorm.

Local whites and blacks exacerbated the tumult by offering wine and whiskey to Union troops filing into Columbia. Soldiers steadily dropped out of line, and during the afternoon straggling troops, with alcohol in their hands, accumulated. To allay growing concerns, Union general Oliver O. Howard ordered extensive stocks of alcohol destroyed.

Fires also complicated the evacuation and capture of Columbia. The Congaree River bridge was still smoldering before dawn on February 17 when cotton fires illuminated the city. Hours later the South Carolina Railroad depot exploded and burned, and as their last act, retreating Confederate troops set fire to the Charlotte Railroad depot. Both stations were still burning about 11:00 A.M. when occupying Union troops reported cotton fires on Richardson (now Main) Street near the town hall. About 1:00 P.M. a blaze flared up at the jail, and during the afternoon at least six fires, mostly in cotton stacked in the streets, broke out at downtown locations. Near 8:00 P.M. another fire began in the center of town.

At approximately 5:00 P.M., as drunkenness increased and security deteriorated, Howard ordered in fresh troops to arrest disorderly soldiers. The troops arrived about 8:00 P.M. and found Richardson Street in flames. This last of a series of unexplained fires was the conflagration that burned Columbia. Nourished by wooden buildings with common walls and a strong wind that wafted burning shingles into the air, the fire spread rapidly. Howard, most of the other Union generals, and the local fire companies soon began fighting the fire, but their efforts failed and the flames quickly raged out of control. Sherman arrived on the scene about 11:00 P.M.

As the fire spread, a riot unfolded in the streets of Columbia, during which some Union soldiers engaged in frightful misconduct. Gangs of troops taunted citizens, stole or destroyed property, and plundered burning houses. Other soldiers accosted citizens in the streets and sometimes took their possessions by brute force. Still others engaged in incendiarism, the most notorious of their crimes. Dr. Robert W. Gibbes, an antiquarian and naturalist, left a detailed account of arson when drunken soldiers burned his home. Accounts of Union soldiers fighting fires and protecting people and property also exist.

About 3:00 A.M. the wind and the fire subsided. Simultaneously, a fresh brigade of troops entered Columbia and suppressed the riot. In the process, 2 soldiers were killed and 30 wounded; 370 soldiers and civilians were arrested. That no citizens died during the fire was small consolation. When Columbians looked around the next morning, they saw massive devastation. About one-third of the town had burned, totaling 458 buildings, of which 265 were residences.

Smoke still lingered over the South Carolina capital when the war of words began over "Who burned Columbia?" Hampton proclaimed Sherman a barbarian, and South Carolinians began gathering evidence against the Northern commander and his troops. Testimony gathered over several years pronounced Sherman guilty,

Columbia after the fire of February 17, 1865. Courtesy, South Caroliniana Library, University of South Carolina

though eyewitness accounts of specific acts of violence and incendiarism were few. In 1873 a claims commission investigating the events in Columbia assessed no blame.

Though traumatic for all inhabitants, the tragic events of the burning of Columbia were an accident of war, the fault of no single individual. The event remains a controversial issue in South Carolina history. Former Confederates and their sympathizers held the event as a prime example of Northern depravations and cruelty inflicted on Southerners. Even after more than a century, the burning of Columbia still served occasionally as a rallying point for some white South Carolinians against "Yankees" and the Federal government. MARION B. LUCAS

Lucas, Marion Brunson. *Sherman and the Burning of Columbia.* 1976. Reprint, Columbia: University of South Carolina Press, 2000.

Marszalek, John F. *Sherman: A Soldier's Passion for Order.* New York: Free Press, 1993.

Columbia Army Air Base. Columbia Army Air Base served as a training center for B-25 bomber crews during World War II. Selected in 1940 as one of 250 sites across the nation where federal funds would be used to construct an airfield, it was originally designated Lexington County Airport to be owned and operated by the county. Construction on two runways began in June 1941. As it neared completion in November, six hundred workers were employed in constructing barracks, a hangar, and a control tower to accommodate seven squadrons. After Japan's attack on Pearl Harbor, the U.S. Army Air Force took control.

The declaration of war witnessed a huge expansion. Flyers known as the "Doolittle Raiders" arrived in February 1942 to train for their daring attack on Japan two months later. The air base's main role was to train newly commissioned pilots, bombardiers, and navigators in flying B-25 bombers. Each crew received at least two hundred hours of flying before transferring to a war theater. Practice bombing runs were important exercises for all crews. Several islands in Lake Murray were used as targets, and one was known long after the war as "Bomb Island." By spring 1945 the Columbia base had nearly eight thousand officers and enlisted personnel. With the conflict's conclusion came a rapid demobilization. Between 1946 and 1947 the base was assigned to standby status and used as a reserve training facility, although some commercial flights began to use the base before the war's end. Two years after the Axis surrendered, the U.S. Air Force declared the base surplus and the airfield became home to commercial aviation full time. In 1949 it was renamed Columbia Metropolitan Airport. FRITZ HAMER

Maxey, Russell. *Airports of Columbia: A History in Photographs & Headlines.* Columbia, S.C.: Palmetto Publishing, 1987.

Columbia Canal. Completed in 1824, the Columbia Canal originally extended three miles below the city of Columbia off Laurel Street. It was one of several canals constructed by the state of South Carolina in the 1820s to improve transportation links between the upstate and Charleston. The canal was located on the east bank of the Congaree River, near the junction of the Broad and Saluda Rivers, and cost $206,000 to build. After its completion, it transported an average of thirty thousand bales of cotton each year to Charleston. During early years of operation the canal experienced many problems, especially the fluctuating water levels that periodically restricted navigation. In 1840 the state decided that it would no longer subsidize the canal. The construction of railroads supplanted the need for canals to transport goods.

The Confederate government used the canal during the Civil War to run powder works. After the war the state tried to dispose of the canal, but had little success. While its usefulness as a transportation source declined, the canal had excellent prospects for power generation. A sawmill, a water pumping station, and a gristmill (operated by the neighboring state penitentiary) all used the Columbia Canal as a power source. In 1891 the canal was sold to the Columbia Water Power Company, which built a powerhouse on the canal in 1894 to produce electricity for its new electric textile plant, Columbia Mills. The power plant was rebuilt in 1896, and as of 1998 the Columbia Canal hydroelectric plant still produced fifty thousand megawatt hours of electricity per year. In 1979 the Columbia Canal was listed in the National Register of Historic Places. Four years later the city of Columbia opened Riverfront Park, which included a two-and-one-half-mile walking trail along the canal. LLOYD JOHNSON

Moore, John Hammond. *Columbia and Richland County: A South Carolina Community, 1740–1900.* Columbia: University of South Carolina Press, 1989.

Pierce, Robert A. *SCANA's First 150 Years: Building on Success.* Columbia, S.C.: SCANA, 1996.

Pogue, Nell C. *South Carolina Electric & Gas Company, 1846–1964.* Columbia, S.C.: SCE&G, 1964.

Smith, Fenelon DeVere. "The Economic Development of the Textile Industry in the Columbia, South Carolina, Area, from 1790 through 1916." Ph.D. diss., University of Kentucky, 1952.

Columbia College. Chartered in 1854 by the South Carolina Methodist Conference, Columbia College is the eleventh-oldest women's college in the United States and one of only two women's colleges in South Carolina. Initially opened as Columbia Female College, its first students entered in 1859 in a newly erected facility on Plain Street (now Hampton Street) in Columbia. The faculty was comprised of ten women and six men, under the presidency of Whitefoord Smith, a prominent Methodist minister. The student body numbered 121, and 13 students comprised the first graduating class in June 1860. The college closed after the Civil War and reopened in 1873. In 1882 a group of graduates established the Columbia College Alumnae Association to further the aims of the institution; it was the fifth such organization of women's college graduates in the country.

The college dropped the word "female" from its official name in 1904. In 1905 the institution relocated to a new facility on land donated by the benefactors F. H. Hyatt and John T. Sloan in the Eau Claire neighborhood, north of the city. Although this facility was destroyed by fire in 1909, the college quickly rebuilt. It was accredited by the Southern Association of Schools and Colleges in 1938.

In 1948 the Methodist Conference merged Columbia College and Wofford College under a single administration at Wofford. Alumnae and friends convinced conference leaders to reinstate Columbia College as an autonomous institution in 1950. Under the presidency of R. Wright Spears (1951–1977), the college began a significant building program and enrollment dramatically increased. Fire swept the campus once again in 1964, and alumnae worked closely with President Spears to raise funds for new buildings. Columbia College admitted its first African American students in 1966.

Throughout its history, the college has focused its attention on the higher educational needs of women, and curricular offerings have reflected the social and economic changes impacting women's experiences. Public service has been a key emphasis in the college's

The Columbia College campus as it appeared at the turn of the last century. Courtesy, Columbia College

mission. Among the college's most notable graduates are Wil Lou Gray (class of 1903), champion of adult education and literacy programs in South Carolina; Elizabeth Johnson Patterson (class of 1961), the first woman from South Carolina elected to a full term in the United States Congress; and Karen Johnson Williams (class of 1973), the first woman to serve on the Fourth Circuit of the United States Court of Appeals.

The college curriculum is grounded in the liberal arts tradition. Undergraduate majors are offered in forty-two academic areas, and the college confers bachelor of arts, bachelor of science, bachelor of fine arts, and bachelor of music degrees. The college implemented a coeducational undergraduate evening division in 1999 and provides coeducational graduate programs in education and conflict management.

Columbia College is governed by a board of trustees approved by the South Carolina United Methodist Conference. The board selected its first woman president, Phyllis O. Bonanno, in 1997. Caroline Bagley Whitson was selected in 2001 as Columbia College's seventeenth president. BELINDA F. GERGEL

Israel, Charles, and Elizabeth DuRant. *Columbia College.* Charleston, S.C.: Arcadia, 2001.

Savory, Jerold. *Columbia College: The Arial Era.* Columbia, S.C.: Columbia College, 1979.

Winn, Evelyn Barksdale. "History of Columbia College." Master's thesis, University of South Carolina, 1927.

Columbia Farms. Columbia Farms commenced operations in 1982 with facilities that had earlier been utilized by the Southeastern Poultry Company. Initially the property consisted of a feed mill and a hatchery in Leesville as well as a processing plant in Columbia and a distribution center in Charleston. At that time nearly 250,000 birds were processed each week by 250 workers. During the following months Columbia Farms engaged in aggressive expansion, and in seven years the company increased production to 650,000 chickens per week and added distribution centers in Conway, Greenville, and Florence as well as two in North Carolina. Within ten years the corporation owned a distribution facility in Massachusetts and had acquired a feed company with sites in Lavonia, Georgia, and Greenville, largely to meet the rising needs within the company. By that time the corporation was shipping 1.2 million birds each seven days with a labor force of more than 1,000 workers.

By 1992 Columbia Farms had grown to become the largest poultry processor in the state and one of South Carolina's ten largest privately held companies. In July 1998 the company divested itself of its Massachusetts operation, sold its interest in a joint venture undertaken some time before, and was acquired in total by Nash Johnson and Sons' Farms of Rose Hill, North Carolina. Columbia Farms continued to operate under its corporate trade name. The parent company additionally markets a variety of poultry products under its familiar House of Raeford brand. Columbia Farms actively promotes the export of chickens and chicken parts to customers around the world through its company-created export arm, Agri Trade. Products shipped overseas include dark meat, viscera, and 250,000 pounds of chicken feet each month to Asia. BARRY A. PRICE

Rogers, Aida. "Poultry in Motion." *Sandlapper* 6 (spring 1995): 20–24.

Columbia International University. Founded as an undergraduate college in 1921, Columbia International University has been one of the symbolic centers to which fundamentalists and conservative evangelical Protestants in South Carolina have gravitated. The school traces its roots to the work of Emily Dick, who held Bible classes in homes, sewing classes for women, and programs for children in the mill villages around Columbia beginning in 1913. A former student at Chicago's Moody Bible Institute, Dick voiced the need for a similar school to train laypersons for work in Protestant churches in South Carolina. What was then called Southern Bible Institute opened in Columbia in the fall of 1921. The following year Robert Crawford McQuilkin, a popular Bible conference speaker in South Carolina and elsewhere, became dean. He changed the name to Columbia Bible College when he became president in 1923. At that time the school offered only a two-year course in Bible studies. McQuilkin shaped the school as a fundamentalist institution and thus helped plant fundamentalism in South Carolina.

Under McQuilkin's leadership, the college began to expand its curriculum and degree programs, offering not only a four-year baccalaureate degree but also an M.A. in Bible Education beginning in 1936. Additional professional programs were established in the affiliated Columbia Biblical Seminary and School of Missions. The major focus remained training persons to be pastors, missionaries, youth and children's workers, Bible teachers, and Christian education directors. In 1960 the entire operation moved from downtown Columbia to a four hundred-acre suburban campus.

Renamed Columbia International University in 1994, the institution retains its fundamentalist orientation, still requiring all students to have a major in Bible studies, even if enrolled in one of the sixteen professional programs. In 2002 undergraduate enrollment was around 700, with 25 opting for the distance learning program. An additional 75 students were pursuing degrees in six programs in education and one in counseling offered through the graduate school. Seminary curricula leading to M.A. and M.Div. degrees enrolled around 300, with an additional 125 opting for the distance learning tracks. A doctor of ministry program drew around 50 more. Thus, in 2002 total enrollment hovered around 1,300. NANCY A. HARDESTY

Glass, William R. *Strangers in Zion: Fundamentalists in the South, 1900–1950.* Macon, Ga.: Mercer University Press, 2001.

Mathews, R. Arthur. *Towers Pointing Upward.* Columbia, S.C.: Columbia Bible College, 1973.

McQuilkin, Marguerite. *Always in Triumph: The Life of Robert C. McQuilkin.* Columbia, S.C.: Bible College Bookstore, 1956.

Columbia Metropolitan Airport. The airport, which serves Midlands South Carolina, is located on a small knoll in Lexington County at an elevation of 235 feet. The Lexington County Airport, a landing area, was established at the site about 1940. Prior to World War II, passenger flights in Columbia used Owens Field, which was first served by Eastern Airlines in 1932. During World War II, the

U.S. War Department acquired the Lexington County field and expanded runways, hangars, roads, and buildings. In early 1942 the heralded Doolittle Raiders trained at the base for their carrier-based raid on Tokyo.

After the war, the field reverted to peacetime use and airline operations were moved there from Owens Field. The city of Columbia established a terminal, which burned but was quickly replaced. A new terminal was opened in 1965 and underwent a $50 million renovation in 1997. Since 1962 the Richland-Lexington Airport District has operated the airport. The governing board was the twelve-member Richland-Lexington Airport Commission, which represented a breakthrough in relations between often-hostile Lexington and Richland Counties. Members represent both counties and the city of Columbia. In 2004 the airport had a 108-acre foreign-trade (duty-free) zone and served more than 1.2 million passengers annually. ROBERT A. PIERCE

Maxey, Russell. *Airports of Columbia: A History in Photographs & Headlines.* Columbia, S.C.: Palmetto Publishing, 1987.

Columbia Mills. The first textile mill in the world to be powered exclusively by electricity, the Columbia Mills Company was chartered in 1893 with an initial capitalization of $700,000. An expansion and upgrade of the Columbia Canal in 1891 by the Columbia Water Power Company had significantly improved the power-generation potential of the waterway, making it suitable to power modern, large-scale manufacturing for the first time in its history. To avoid flooding, however, the site of the Columbia Mill was on a bluff, six hundred feet from the canal, which made traditional mechanical power transmission impractical. Instead, company directors (all from the North) opted to use electric motors as the motive power for their factory. Sidney B. Paine, a General Electric salesman, proposed using polyphase alternating current and induction motors. Unlike direct current shunt motors, induction motors provided a reliable current, did not spark, and were well protected against dirt. Such motors would keep the textile machinery moving at a constant speed and, more importantly, would not set the lint-filled building on fire.

Work on the mill began in April 1893, and operations officially commenced in April 1894. Lockwood, Greene and Company designed the plant, and William A. Chapman and Company of Providence, Rhode Island, supervised construction. Two 1,000-horsepower turbines at the end of the Columbia Canal supplied electricity to operate fourteen 65-horsepower electric motors located throughout the mill. The motors were placed on the ceiling, thereby taking no floor space and allowing more room for textile machinery. A mill village for employees, "Aretasville," was built across the river in West Columbia and named for Aretas Blood of New Hampshire, the president of the Columbia Mills Company. The success of the Columbia plant revolutionized textile mills by opening the electric era. The new mill specialized in duck, a durable plain-weave cloth widely used for belting, awnings, and tents, and sailcloth, a heavy duck made to withstand the elements in all kinds of weather. Mount Vernon–Woodberry Cotton Duck Company of Baltimore acquired Columbia Mills in 1899. By 1907 the mill operated more than thirty thousand spindles and had twelve hundred employees. Production continued until 1981, when operations were relocated to a smaller plant. Mount Vernon Mills donated the old building to the state, which transformed it into the South Carolina State Museum in the late 1980s. CARYN E. NEUMANN

Kohn, August. *The Cotton Mills of South Carolina.* 1907. Reprint, Spartanburg, S.C.: Reprint Company, 1975.

Passer, Harold C. *The Electrical Manufacturers, 1875–1900.* Cambridge: Harvard University Press, 1953.

Smith, Fenelon DeVere. "The Economic Development of the Textile Industry in the Columbia, South Carolina, Area, from 1790 through 1916." Ph.D. diss., University of Kentucky, 1952.

Columbia Museum of Art. The Columbia Museum of Art was established in 1950 as an art, history, and science museum and included the Gibbes Planetarium. In 1990 the mission statement was changed to focus entirely on American and European fine, design, and decorative arts from the medieval period to the present. In 1998 the museum was relocated from the Taylor House on Bull Street to a new facility on Main Street.

The museum's collection contains more than seven thousand paintings, works-on-paper, and examples of the decorative arts. Gifts from the Kress Foundation in 1954 and 1963 enhanced the collection with works by such artists as Bernardo Bellotto, Sandro Botticelli, François Boucher, Canaletto, Francesco Guardi, Nicholas Maes, and Tintoretto. Other early gifts included Claude Monet's *The Seine at Giverny* and Frederic Remington's *Bronco Buster.* Between 1998 and 2001 important new acquisitions to the collection included works by Alexander Archipenko, James Brooks, Joseph Cornell, Richard Hamilton, Jasper Johns, Roy Lichtenstein, Sam Maloof, Henry Moore, Robert Motherwell, Gustav Stickley, Mark Tobey, Carrie Mae Weems, and Andy Warhol.

Resources within the museum include an art library, an auditorium with a fully equipped audio-visual booth and onstage dual projection screens, and a teacher resource center. The art library contains a collection of fourteen thousand volumes, exhibition catalogs, art periodicals, selected auction catalogs, auction-sales-result publications, and specialized art dictionaries and encyclopedias. The museum plays an active role in children's art education programs. School programs are curriculum based and include both gallery and studio activities that encourage learning through interaction and response. The museum is accredited by the American Association of Museums. ELLEN WOODOFF

Columbia Theological Seminary. An institution of the Presbyterian Church (USA), the seminary was founded in 1828 in Lexington, Georgia, and was moved to Columbia, South Carolina, where classes began in 1831. Influential citizens of Columbia, wanting "a southern theological seminary," helped purchase the Ainsley Hall mansion to house the seminary.

Following the model of Andover and Princeton theological seminaries, Columbia was a graduate professional institution with a three-year curriculum. The requirement of a college education was intended to ensure that entering students had the philosophical and linguistic background provided by a collegiate education and the general culture and manners taught in the colleges. The curriculum was organized around the study of the Hebrew and Greek scriptures, church history, and systematic and practical theology.

While Columbia attracted a substantial New England presence in the faculty and student body during the antebellum period, the strength of the institution was linked to the South Carolina and Georgia lowcountry. Leading faculty members included George Howe, Charles Colcock Jones, Benjamin Morgan Palmer, John Adger, and James Henley Thornwell. They taught an Old School Calvinism that understood truth to be propositional. Their organic view of society was used in defense of slavery and against the rising tides of bourgeois individualism and the anarchy of the modern world.

The years following the Civil War were marked by financial and intellectual crises. Woodrow Wilson's father, Joseph, and his uncle James Woodrow were members of the faculty during this period. In 1928 Columbia Theological Seminary moved to the outskirts of Atlanta. Socially and theologically it was a move away from the Old South and toward the New South. By the end of the twentieth century, while remaining deeply Presbyterian in its ethos, Columbia was broadly ecumenical in its faculty and students. It had an endowment of more than $170 million and students and scholars from fifteen countries. ERSKINE CLARKE

Clarke, Erskine. *Our Southern Zion: A History of Calvinism in the South Carolina Low Country, 1690–1990.* Tuscaloosa: University of Alabama Press, 1996.

Farmer, James O. *The Metaphysical Confederacy: James Henley Thornwell and the Synthesis of Southern Values.* Macon, Ga.: Mercer University Press, 1986.

LaMotte, Louis C. *Colored Light: The Story of the Influence of Columbia Theological Seminary, 1828–1936.* Richmond, Va.: Presbyterian Committee of Publication, 1937.

Coming, Affra Harleston (ca. 1651–1698). Pioneer of early South Carolina. The Harlestons were a family of some means in seventeenth-century England. However, the family's property had been so ravaged by the English Civil War that two of the family's children, Charles and Affra, left England for South Carolina in 1669. Affra came on the *Carolina* as an indentured servant with a two-year obligation to her sponsor, after which she would receive one hundred acres of land. Affra and a ship's mate on the *Carolina,* John Coming, formed an attachment during the long trip, which included a horrific storm off the Leeward Islands that convinced Affra never to cross the ocean again. When they arrived at Port Royal in February 1670, Coming decided to continue his courtship of Affra while continuing to work as a ship's mate.

Married in 1672 when she was free from indenture, Affra and Coming founded a substantial plantation, Comingtee on the Cooper River; acquired their own servants; and ceded part of their land claim at Oyster Point for the construction of what is now Charleston. Although the Comings never had children of their own, they frequently took in orphaned children from the area and sponsored the immigration of several of Coming's nephews as their heirs. John Coming, having risen in society to the rank of ship's captain and member of the colony's Grand Council, died on August 20, 1694, after accumulating another 740 acres of land.

Affra, who survived her husband by four years, built a house in Charleston at the intersection of Wentworth and Philips Streets and donated seventeen acres to St. Philip's Church in Charleston, beginning the parish's property. Although her brother Charles abandoned his South Carolina claims and moved to Barbados, the siblings prepared the way to the colony for other Harlestons from England and Ireland, and for Coming's Ball half-siblings and their children. Affra Harleston Coming died on December 28, 1698, and is believed to have been buried beside her husband at Comingtee Plantation. MARGARET SANKEY

Middleton, Margaret Simons. *Affra Harleston and Old Charles-Towne in South Carolina.* Columbia, S.C.: R. L. Bryan, 1971.

Commission of Indian Trade. In 1707 the Commons House of Assembly created the Board of Indian Commissioners to regulate the traffic between Indian traders and nations such as the Cherokees, Creeks, and Catawbas. These nine men were to license private traders, who had to pay £8 currency for a license and give a bond worth £100 currency. The law also called for the creation of an Indian agent, who was to spend at least ten months in the Indian lands. The agent was paid £250 annually in exchange for handling any complaints as well as managing the trade. Commissioners had to address problems such as traders who extended excessive credit to Indians in order to force land cessions, with some traders enslaving Indians who could not pay their trade debts. Other traders liberally sold rum in the Indian lands, usually to the detriment of the tribes. The inability of the board to end these abuses led to the disastrous Yamassee War of 1715–1718.

After the war, the South Carolina government assumed a direct monopoly over the Indian trade, forcing the private traders out. A new law created a public corporation of five commissioners under the direction of the Commons House of Assembly. The act replaced the single Indian agent with government traders, called factors, stationed with the major tribes. Factors were to trade only with tribes friendly to Carolina. They were not to extend credit to such tribes and were to maintain detailed information about tribal affairs of their host nations. Theophilus Hastings was the factor to the Cherokees, while William Watis was stationed among three smaller tribes, the Waccamaws, Wawees, and Peedees. Private traders who continued to trade illegally would be fined and have their goods confiscated.

By 1731 rules required each factor to appear in Charleston to renew his one-year license before the secretary of the Indian commission. As before, the factor was limited to one major tribe and forbidden to trade with others. The historian Verner Crane noted that the South Carolina Indian commission system was probably the best among the North American colonies with respect to planning and efficiency. MICHAEL P. MORRIS

Crane, Verner. *The Southern Frontier, 1670–1732.* Durham, N.C.: Duke University Press, 1928.

McDowell, William L., ed. *Journals of the Commissioners of the Indian Trade, September 20, 1710–August 29, 1718.* Columbia: South Carolina Archives Department, 1955.

Morris, Michael P. *The Bringing of Wonder: Trade and the Indians of the Southeast, 1700–1783.* Westport, Conn.: Greenwood, 1999.

Commission on Women. The governor's Commission on Women was established in 1971. Governor John West appointed the first seven commissioners, and in 1972 federal funding provided for an executive director. However, there was no state funding until 1974, when $10,000 was appropriated. The commission's mission was to promote equal opportunity and improve the status of women in the state by identifying problems and recommending ways to eliminate discriminatory practices. The first project, which studied female employment practices in state agencies, showed that women were disproportionately clustered in low-paying jobs. A *Legal Guide for Women* was prepared in 1975, giving information on citizenship, credit and finance, education, employment, health, marriage, divorce, parental rights, social security, and wills and estates. Under the leadership of chairperson Barbara Moxon, a major effort was made to get more South Carolina women appointed to public boards and commissions. The first staff member was hired in 1979, and the commission gained authority to receive and disburse grants and to disseminate materials on the rights, responsibilities, and status of women.

From 1987 to 1999 the work of the commission grew to include Women of Achievement awards and developing a Women's History

Month annual celebration. In 1999 the commission made domestic violence prevention, women's health issues, and expanded female participation in government its new priorities. The commission works closely with the governor's office and was funded out of its budget until 2003, when Governor Mark Sanford vetoed funding for the commission. It remained a small organization and sponsored projects in cooperation with other state agencies. The staff also worked to pass legislation that affects the status and health of women. Major concerns included South Carolina's low rank in the number of elected women officeholders and high rank in number of domestic violence cases. ALICE H. HENDERSON

Commons House of Assembly (1670–1776). The dominant political institution in colonial South Carolina was the Commons House of Assembly (changed simply to "the Assembly" in 1744). It served as the lower house of the provincial legislature and was the only popularly elected branch of government in the colony. The chief theme in the early history of the Commons House was its transformation from an impotent institution to an imperious political body that jealously guarded its immense authority. Under the Fundamental Constitutions, elected representatives of the people sat together with the nobility and Lords Proprietors in a unicameral assembly (called parliaments). They had the power only to ratify or reject the statutes proposed by the Grand Council. Not until 1692 did the proprietors, responding to increasing complaints by the delegates about their lack of power, allow them to sit as a separate house, to initiate legislation, and to approve tax measures.

Over the next half-century the assemblymen, seeking to make the lower house a mirror image of the English House of Commons, usurped enormous political power from the royal governor and council. By the mid-1700s the Assembly had assumed ironclad control over all aspects of government: initiating laws, appointing revenue officers, establishing courts, supervising the Indian trade, selecting the colonial agent in London, auditing and reviewing all accounts of public officers, overseeing elections, and administering all governmental expenditures. However, the Assembly was not content with just dominating provincial affairs. It intentionally retarded the development of local government by refusing to delegate broad taxing powers to local governmental institutions. Instead, the Assembly appointed commissioners to spend the money it granted and to carry out the minutest details of local administration. In short, the Commons House of Assembly reigned supreme in South Carolina.

The Assembly's wide use of commissions and its strict control of the expenditures of local government helped to make it the hardest-working legislative body in the American colonies. Moreover, the election law of 1721 required the Commons House of Assembly to meet at least once every six months, usually in the winter and fall when planters were in Charleston for pleasure or business. With sessions lasting several months, coupled with emergency sessions called by the governor, it was not uncommon for the Assembly to sit eight months of the year. No other colonial assembly endured such long sessions. When in session, the Commons House usually met six days a week for at least six hours a day.

The long legislative sessions of the Commons House, along with the fact that members served without pay, effectively prevented all but the wealthiest and most civic-spirited men from serving in that body. Under the Fundamental Constitutions, however, any twenty-one-year-old man with five hundred acres of land could serve in the Commons House of Assembly. Under the king, aspiring assemblymen had to own at least five hundred acres and ten slaves (twenty after 1745) or £1,000 in chattels. Perhaps half the colony's adult white males met these qualifications for Commons House service. Still, voters, motivated by a negative view of human nature and a desire to control man's irrational side, elected to the Commons House economically independent (that is, very wealthy), virtuous, and able men. This shared common political ideology (often referred to as "country ideology"), combined with the colony's unrivaled economic prosperity, the constant threat of a slave rebellion, possible attack by the French and Spanish, the common economic interests between planters and merchants, and extensive intermarriage among them, encouraged a remarkable degree of political harmony to prevail in the Commons House. The lack of political discord, along with capable members committed to voluntary public service, enabled the assembly to effectively administer provincial affairs to the general satisfaction of its constituents. One glaring exception was the enormous dissatisfaction among the numerous backcountry residents who lacked representation in the Assembly until late in the colonial period. Still, the Commons House of Assembly, with its immense authority, relative independence, and general competence, provided an important legacy that later enabled the revolutionary Provincial Congress and the state General Assembly (the linear heirs of the Commons House) to effectively govern South Carolina during the turbulent decades of the late eighteenth century. KEITH KRAWCZYNSKI

Edgar, Walter, and N. Louise Bailey, eds. *Biographical Directory of the South Carolina House of Representatives.* Vol. 2, *The Commons House of Assembly, 1692–1775.* Columbia: University of South Carolina Press, 1977.

Knepper, David M. "The Political Structure of Colonial South Carolina, 1743–1776." Ph.D. diss., University of Virginia, 1971.

Sirmans, M. Eugene. *Colonial South Carolina: A Political History, 1663–1763.* Chapel Hill: University of North Carolina Press, 1966.

Weir, Robert M. *Colonial South Carolina: A History.* 1983. Reprint, Columbia: University of South Carolina Press, 1997.

Whitney, Edson L. *Government of the Colony of South Carolina.* 1895. Reprint, New York: Negro Universities Press, 1969.

Compromise of 1808. The Compromise of 1808 represented the culmination of efforts by upcountry leaders to secure equitable representation in the General Assembly. South Carolina's constitution of 1778 allotted 64 of 202 seats in the new S.C. House of Representatives to backcountry districts. The increasing population of the backcountry, however, led to calls for a more balanced distribution of seats.

The 1790 constitution placated residents in the upper part of the state by moving the capital from Charleston to Columbia, but otherwise contained little to appease the upcountry. Property qualifications for public office were strengthened, and no allowance was made for a system of reapportionment or apportioning the House according to population. As a result, upcountry politicians began to organize for more effective change. In 1794 the Representative Reform Association was founded in Columbia. The association created committees around the upcountry, and one member, Robert Goodloe Harper, published *An Address to the People of South-Carolina,* arguing that the upcountry's population was woefully underrepresented in the General Assembly. He also hinted that the upcountry would be better off without slavery. Lowcountry opponents seized this last point and contended that backcountry representatives were extremists.

The association undertook a petition drive to compel the General Assembly to consider reapportionment, but reapportionment failed on an almost strictly sectional vote. Upcountry politicians modified their rhetoric and pledged their support for slavery, but it would take a larger shift in the state's political landscape to effect broader change. Lowcountry politics was driven by Federalist concerns, but Federalist influence declined in South Carolina in the late 1790s. Federalists were not able to make political inroads in the upcountry, and Republicans moved to take their places in state government. Economic changes also helped change the mood. Cotton expansion in the upcountry helped wed the interests of the state's sections, and also increased the slave population of the backcountry districts.

Change became possible when prominent lowcountry leaders such as Joseph Alston joined the reapportionment cause. Alston, a wealthy planter representing Christ Church Parish, pushed for reform in 1804 and 1807. In both years he argued that the backcountry was sufficiently supportive of slavery as to render previous concerns moot. Furthermore, he argued that reform would remove a major source of contention in the state. Alston succeeded where Harper and his associates had failed. In 1808 the General Assembly passed a constitutional amendment that apportioned the S.C. House of Representatives according to white population and taxation. Thus, one representative would represent $^{1}/_{62}$ of the state's population and one would represent $^{1}/_{62}$ of taxes collected, yielding the House's 124 members. The Compromise of 1808 also allowed for reapportionment to take place once every ten years. Property qualifications for voting were eliminated in 1810.

The Compromise of 1808 settled the issue of representation of the upcountry and helped to unify the state. Ironically, what began as a movement to protect backcountry interests reached fruition only when economic changes in the upcountry meant that upcountry and lowcountry planters found much on which to agree. The lowcountry may have ceded some political control in the Compromise of 1808, but it did so only after the upcountry was certain to protect slavery. AARON W. MARRS

Ford, Lacy K., Jr. *Origins of Southern Radicalism: The South Carolina Upcountry, 1800–1860.* New York: Oxford University Press, 1988.

Klein, Rachel N. *Unification of a Slave State: The Rise of the Planter Class in the South Carolina Backcountry, 1760–1808.* Chapel Hill: University of North Carolina Press, 1990.

Confederate flag controversy. In February 1962 the General Assembly passed a joint resolution that placed a version of the Confederate Army of Northern Virginia's battle flag atop the dome of the State House. Generating little attention or publicity at the time, the presence of the flag above the Palmetto State's legislative seat would become an enduring public controversy in the 1980s and 1990s. Controversy would linger after the banner's removal from the dome and its placement on a flagstaff behind the monument to South Carolina's Confederate soldiers on the State House grounds in July 2000.

The placing of the Confederate banner in the public and political arena marked a change in the way that white South Carolinians paid tribute to Confederate symbolism. In the years following the Civil War and in the first half of the twentieth century, use of the emblem had primarily belonged to veteran and heritage groups such as the United Daughters of the Confederacy and the Kappa Alpha college fraternity. Following the 1948 "Dixiecrat" campaign, and the use of the flag as a symbol by the presidential candidate and South Carolina governor Strom Thurmond, popular display of the flag increased.

The joint resolution to place the flag on the State House dome occurred in the midst of the celebration of both the Civil War Centennial and the South's continued "massive resistance" against efforts aimed at ending segregation. Many white South Carolinians came to see the flag as a symbol of an earlier southern resistance in the face of outside intrusion, while others simply viewed it as representative of the state's strong connection to its past. Moreover, there was precedent for displaying the battle flag: a flag was first hung in the chamber of the S.C. House of Representatives in 1938 and in the S.C. Senate in 1956.

Several elements fueled the birth of the controversy in the 1980s and 1990s. Black South Carolinians, working through grassroots organizations and with larger national organizations, had found their political voice and could bring pressure on state government to remove what they considered an offensive symbol. Meanwhile, the growth of a new national conservative movement created a strong traditionalist movement among southern whites. New organizations such as the South Carolina Council of Conservative Citizens joined with heritage groups such as the Sons of Confederate Veterans to fight the removal of the flag. Finally, the controversy coincided with rapid economic development that brought to the region an influx of new arrivals with little or no connection to the state's Confederate past. New and old South Carolinians alike worried that the flag controversy would slow the pace of economic expansion.

In 1996, influenced by the concerns of the South Carolina business community, Republican governor David Beasley expressed his support for building an African American history monument on the State House grounds and the placement of the Confederate flag at the monument to Confederate soldiers, a compromise that had been discussed since the 1994 legislative session. Though receiving support from the legislative black caucus and well-known South Carolinians such as Strom Thurmond and Richard Riley, Beasley faced dissension in his own party and severe criticism from Republican attorney general Charlie Condon. Conflict grew as racial incidents plagued South Carolina in 1996, including the opening of a "Klan museum" in Laurens, a rash of church burnings, and the murder of three black teenagers by Klansmen returning from a proflag rally.

The final decision to remove the controversial symbol came in 2000 amidst increasing pressure from the South Carolina Chamber of Commerce and other business groups, as well as a national boycott of South Carolina instituted by the National Association for the Advancement of Colored People (NAACP). In a special ceremony held on July 1, 2000, two cadets from the Citadel, one white and one African American, lowered the flag from the dome and placed it near the Confederate monument on the grounds of the State House. The flags were also removed from the chambers of the S.C. House and Senate. The NAACP vowed to continue its economic boycott, however, with the goal of having the flag removed completely from the State House grounds. W. SCOTT POOLE

Martinez, J. Michael, William D. Richardson, and Ron McNich-Su, eds. *Confederate Symbols in the Contemporary South.* Gainesville: University Press of Florida, 2000.

Prince, K. Michael. *Rally 'round the Flag, Boys!: South Carolina and the Confederate Flag.* Columbia: University of South Carolina Press, 2004.

Confederation of South Carolina Local Historical Societies. On April 4, 1964, representatives of fourteen historical societies met at Batesburg-Leesville and organized the Confederation of South Carolina Local Historical Societies. The Lexington County

Historical Society sponsored the meeting, and Charles E. Lee, then director of the South Carolina Department of Archives and History, advocated its creation. The confederation exists to "strengthen and enrich local cultural, political, and economic institutions through the preservation and study of historical documents, sites, buildings, and artifacts, and to further this purpose through the dissemination and exchange of information and the exercise of cooperative endeavor."

Members of the confederation include historical organizations, foundations, commissions, museums, archives, preservation groups, and patriotic societies. Since 1965 the confederation has sponsored an annual Landmark Conference to spotlight the local history of a particular area of South Carolina. It also offers a broad program of awards and serves as the official nominating body for the South Carolina Hall of Fame.

The confederation honors member organizations with Awards of Merit for publications, public programming, volunteerism, and public relations. The confederation also recognizes the best papers by high school juniors and seniors in South Carolina's National History Day competition and presents the Margaret Watson History Award to the best college or university student paper on a South Carolina history topic. The confederation is the unified voice for local historical societies at the state, regional, and national levels. As of 2004 it had sixty-five member organizations. ALEXIA JONES HELSLEY

Congaree National Park. South Carolina's only national park, Congaree is located on 22,200 acres in the Congaree River floodplain of lower Richland County. Established by Congress as a national monument in 1976 and redesignated a national park in 2003, Congaree protects the last significant stand of old-growth, bottomland hardwood forest remaining in the United States. The Congaree forest, often referred to as the "Redwoods of the East," is the tallest in eastern North America and one of the tallest temperate deciduous forests in the world. It is home to numerous trees of record size, including several state and national champions.

Between 1890 and 1905 the Chicago lumberman Francis Beidler purchased 165,000 acres of choice timberland in South Carolina, including a huge, near-virgin tract on the eastern bank of the Congaree River. His Santee River Cypress Lumber Company started a program of selective cutting on the Congaree tract, but Beidler, a devoted conservationist, permitted only limited logging. Around 1910 he ceased operations along the Congaree altogether. When Francis Beidler II demonstrated a renewed interest in logging the tract in the early 1970s, a local group of "wide-eyed, Earth Day–inspired" environmental advocates led by Dreher High School teacher Jim Elder mounted a public campaign to save the Congaree's primordial ecosystem.

More than two-thirds of the park became a congressionally designated wilderness area in 1988, and in 2001 the park opened a commodious, new visitor center. As put in 1976 by the ecologist Richard H. Pough, an early advocate for publicly protecting the forest, Congaree is "a national park that any state would be proud to have." See plate 1. MATTHEW A. LOCKHART

Congaree Swamp: Greatest Unprotected Forest on the Continent. Columbia, S.C., 1975.

Handel, Steven N., et al. *Research Bibliography of the Congaree Swamp National Monument Area.* Columbia: University of South Carolina, 1979.

Michie, James L. *An Archeological Survey of Congaree Swamp: Cultural Resources Inventory and Assessment of a Bottomland Environment in Central South Carolina.* Columbia: Institute of Archaeology and Anthropology, University of South Carolina, 1980.

Congaree River. At the fall line in Columbia, the Broad and Saluda Rivers form the Congaree River. For a little over a mile the Congaree River rolls over rapids, shoals, and interspersed islands before it enters the coastal plain. As is typical of slowly moving mature streams, it meanders through the coastal plain, changing its course frequently. With its main tributaries Gills Creek, Sandy Run, Cedar Creek, Toms Creek, and the Congaree Creek, it forms one of the major rivers of the Santee River Basin, the largest river basin in South Carolina. If the Congaree River flowed in a straight line, it would be only about thirty miles long. However, because of its sinuous course, part of which forms the boundary between Richland and Calhoun Counties, the river flows southeasterly for about sixty miles and then joins the Wateree River to form the Santee River.

The Congaree River was named for the Siouan-speaking Congaree Indians, who settled below the confluence of the Broad and Saluda Rivers after the Yamassee War. At this intersection Old Fort Congaree was established in 1718 in order to protect the deerskin trade and the inward migration of colonists. In 1740 white settlers began populating the area, and indigo and corn were their principal crops.

The Congaree River contains the Congaree Swamp and the Beidler Tract, which represent the last stands of near-virgin southern hardwood forested swamps. Though limits have been placed on timbering these forests, lumbering along the Congaree River has been a major industry since colonial times. A thirty-seven-mile segment of the river was declared eligible for the South Carolina Scenic Rivers Program in 1976. Because of its strategic location, the Congaree River continues to be important for accessing the interior of the state. MICHELINE BROWN

Beasley, Barry R., et al. *South Carolina Rivers Assessment.* Columbia: South Carolina Water Resources Commission, 1988.

Congaree Swamp: Greatest Unprotected Forest on the Continent. Columbia, S.C., 1975.

Michie, James L. *The Discovery of Old Fort Congaree.* Columbia: Institute of Archaeology and Anthropology, University of South Carolina, [1989?].

Conner, Henry Workman (1797–1861). Merchant, banker. Conner was born on March 4, 1797, in Mecklenburg County, North Carolina, the son of James Conner and Lilly Anna Wilson. His father was a native of Ireland, a Revolutionary War veteran, and a cotton planter. Conner attended a private academy near Charlotte until 1814, when he left home in an attempt to join the army during the War of 1812. When Workman was unsuccessful in the effort, his father sent him to Tennessee to oversee family lands there. For the next three years he managed his father's property in that state and dabbled in land speculation and business ventures before returning to North Carolina.

In 1822 Conner arrived in Charleston, South Carolina, and began the factorage and commission house of Conner & Wilson. The firm pioneered the use of steamships to carry freight and passengers between Charleston and towns in the interior of South Carolina and Georgia. In 1833 Conner formed his own hardware importing business, which was likewise a great success. He also became involved in improving and expanding the city's commercial landscape, becoming a leading investor in the construction of a range of new buildings on Hayne Street, including the magnificent Charleston Hotel.

Conner was among the original directors of the Bank of Charleston when it was organized in 1835. The bank was the largest private financial institution in the state and one of the most influential in the entire South. In 1841 Conner was elected president of the bank, a position he held until 1850. Under his leadership the Bank of Charleston greatly expanded its operations, solidifying relationships with banks in Europe and the North, and opening agencies in major ports and interior towns across the Southeast. By the mid-1840s the Bank of Charleston had business connections with no fewer than 123 financial institutions across the nation, which greatly expanded the presence of the Charleston mercantile community.

In 1850 Conner resigned as president of the Bank of Charleston and became president of the South Carolina Railroad, an office he held until 1853. Other business ventures in Charleston and its environs in which Conner was involved included the establishment of the Charleston Gas Light Company in 1848, the erection of the Moultrie House Hotel on Sullivan's Island, and the formation of the Atlantic Steam Navigation Company to run a line of steamships between Charleston and Liverpool. In 1853 he formed a private bank, Henry W. Conner & Son, with offices in Charleston and New Orleans. By the time of his death, few men had contributed more to the antebellum growth and prosperity of Charleston than Conner.

Conner married Juliana Margaret Courtney on June 7, 1827. They had two sons. Although active in city and state politics, Conner operated mostly behind the scenes. He was a frequent correspondent of John C. Calhoun and, together with Charleston business leaders such as Ker Boyce and James Gadsden, became one of Calhoun's leading allies in the lowcountry. Conner was elected to the Secession Convention of December 1860 and was among those who signed the Ordinance of Secession. He died shortly thereafter, on January 11, 1861, and was buried in the cemetery of St. Michael's Church in Charleston. TOM DOWNEY

"Gallery of Industry and Enterprise: Henry W. Conner, of Charleston." *De Bow's Review* 10 (May 1851): 578–81.

May, John Amasa, and Joan Reynolds Faunt, eds. *South Carolina Secedes.* Columbia: University of South Carolina Press, 1960.

Stoney, Samuel Gaillard. *The Story of South Carolina's Senior Bank.* Columbia, S.C.: R. L. Bryan, 1955.

Conroy, Donald Patrick (b. 1945). Author. Pat Conroy was born on October 26, 1945, in Atlanta, Georgia, the first of seven children born to Donald Conroy and Frances Peek. Despite numerous moves with his U.S. Marine Corps father, Conroy maintained a southern identity. His father was transferred to Beaufort, South Carolina, in 1961. Conroy enrolled in Beaufort High School, where he starred athletically, academically, and personally. With a difficult home life, Conroy flourished under the encouragement of his English teachers, J. Eugene Norris and R. Millen Ellis, and his principal, William E. Dufford. He enrolled at the Citadel and was graduated in 1967. At the Citadel he was captain of the basketball team and selected most valuable player.

After graduation Conroy taught at Beaufort High School, then at the elementary school on Daufuskie Island, a poor, isolated corner of the South Carolina Sea Islands. Fired by school administrators for his unorthodox approach to teaching his nearly illiterate black students, Conroy turned to writing to vent his frustration and earn a living. *The Water Is Wide,* a largely autobiographical novel of his experiences on Daufuskie, was published in 1972 and became a critical and commercial success. Turning to writing full time, Conroy followed with four more novels inspired in large measure by his formative and young-adult years: *The Great Santini* (1976), *Lords of Discipline* (1980), *Prince of Tides* (1986), and *Beach Music* (1995). Each became a national best-seller, and together they established Conroy as one of the nation's most popular writers and appealing storytellers. He has also published two works of nonfiction: *The Boo* (1970; a biography of the Citadel's assistant commandant of cadets) and *My Losing Season* (2002; a memoir of his senior year at the Citadel). His first four novels were made into major motion pictures, with the film version of *The Prince of Tides* earning seven Academy Award nominations, including one for Conroy for best screenplay.

Pat Conroy. © David G. Spielman, 1997, New Orleans

At times critics have censured Conroy's novels for their similarity of characters, themes, and setting. Yet these same traits have attracted legions of loyal readers. A consummate storyteller, Conroy in his novels relates tales of family conflict, fathers and father figures, racism, and coming of age, all against the consistent backdrop of the South Carolina lowcountry. Humor and pathos are frequent bedfellows. Influenced by Thomas Wolfe, Conroy writes deceptively complex sagas with lyrical descriptions of people and places. Steeped in southern history and mores, his stories connect with readers on a variety of levels. With equal parts fiction and autobiography, Conroy writes of growing up in a military family, of coping with the stresses of dysfunctional family life, of the challenges of relationships, and of the ebb and flow of life.

Conroy's work has been recognized with numerous awards and honors, including the National Endowment for the Arts Award for Achievement in Education (1974), the Georgia Governor's Award for Arts (1978), and the Lillian Smith Award for fiction from the Southern Regional Council (1981). Closer to home, Conroy has been elected to the South Carolina Hall of Fame and the South Carolina Academy of Authors, was the first recipient of the Governor's Award in the Humanities for Distinguished Achievement from the South Carolina Humanities Council in 1994, and received the Order of the Palmetto in 2002.

Conroy has been married three times: to Barbara Bolling Jones in 1969; to Lenora Gurevitz in 1981; and to the author Cassandra King in 1995. He has two daughters. Residing on Fripp Island, Conroy continues to pursue his loves—writing, cooking, and living. ALEXIA JONES HELSLEY AND J. EUGENE NORRIS

Burns, Landon C. *Pat Conroy: A Critical Companion.* Westport, Conn.: Greenwood, 1996.

Conservative Party. The term "Conservative Party" has a distinct meaning in southern history in general and in South Carolina history in particular. It refers to the organization that led the overthrow of Republican Reconstruction and dominated southern politics until the agrarian revolt of the 1890s. The men who led these parties have been given different designations, chiefly Bourbons, Redeemers, or Conservatives, more precisely Conservative Democrats.

In South Carolina the dominion of the Conservative Party had a specific beginning and ending: the election of the Confederate hero Wade Hampton III as governor in 1876 and the election of Benjamin R. Tillman as governor in 1890, following a bitter campaign in which Tillman had vilified the Conservatives for being wedded to the past and neglecting the state's real problems. Taking control of their state after almost a decade of Republican rule, South Carolina Conservatives saw themselves as redeeming their home from alien forces. To them, redemption had a single purpose: restoring the South Carolina they believed had been lost in the turbulent years since 1865. The Conservative leadership was made up overwhelmingly of men who had come of age in antebellum South Carolina and who had led their state's forces during the Civil War, a struggle they judged a holy cause that must always be honored. As evangels of restoration, they offered no new programs to a state reeling from a disastrous war and the financial debacle caused initially by the Panic of 1873 and in the 1880s by the long decline in agricultural prices.

Yet, in trying to restore their vision of a former—and in their minds a better—South Carolina, Conservatives put their mark on their state and its subsequent history. They strove for political unity by proclaiming the Democratic Party as the only legitimate political voice. The Republican Party, which according to them stood for conflict and foreign values, must be suppressed. The renewal of South Carolina College controlled by native whites was essential, for that institution was seen as having the vital mission of inculcating the ideals and worthiness of the past in the future leaders of the state.

Although the Conservatives accepted the end of slavery, they rejected any notion of social or political equality for the freed slaves. They were determined that South Carolina would be ruled by whites, though whites remained a minority of the population. But shunning violence for racial control as wrong, impractical, and politically precarious, they turned to legislation. With complex election laws and redistricting they severely restricted black political participation and power.

On the economic front Conservatives followed the antebellum pattern, encouraging industrial development while retaining the belief that agriculture would remain central in the state's economy. But for the grinding agricultural depression of the 1880s they had no prescription. Although the Conservatives led their state for only fourteen years, the South Carolina they constructed—of white supremacy, of the holiness of the Democratic Party, of reverence for the Confederacy—predominated until well into the second half of the twentieth century. WILLIAM J. COOPER, JR.

Cooper, William J., Jr. *The Conservative Regime: South Carolina, 1877–1890.* Baltimore: Johns Hopkins Press, 1968.

Kantrowitz, Stephen. *Ben Tillman and the Reconstruction of White Supremacy.* Chapel Hill: University of North Carolina Press, 2000.

Constitutions. South Carolina's royal charter of 1663 allowed eight Lords Proprietors to develop a code of laws for the colony with the advice and consent of selected settlers. The result was the 1669 Fundamental Constitutions. Although revised several times until abandoned in 1698, the Fundamental Constitutions framed the colony as a social hierarchy, encouraging new settlement based on landownership and a provision for religious freedom. It also inspired the colonial Commons House of Assembly, which became the significant governing body of the colony.

South Carolina adopted its first state constitution in 1776. Since then, it has adopted six more: in 1778, 1790, 1861, 1865, 1868, and 1895. The constitutions of 1790, 1868, and 1895 are especially noteworthy since they were adopted at critical turning points in the state's history: in 1790 after the state entered the federal union; in 1868 during Reconstruction; and in 1895 after general economic distress. The revision and modernization of the 1895 constitution, especially since 1966 in response to federal civil rights policies and state and local reform pressures, caused some to say that there is actually an "eighth" South Carolina constitution.

South Carolina became a free and independent state on March 26, 1776, more than three months before the Declaration of Independence. The state's Provincial Congress adopted a plan of government that was to last until the disputes with Great Britain could be settled. The Provincial Congress dissolved into a General Assembly with a popularly elected lower house, which then elected thirteen of its members to an upper house. It also elected a chief executive, or "president," a vice president, and a chief justice. Political power stayed firmly in legislative hands and with lowcountry legislators. The upcountry area had a large, white population but was permitted to elect only 64 of the 202 members of the General Assembly.

Under the 1778 constitution, "president" was replaced by "governor," who was still elected by the General Assembly. The Anglican Church was disestablished, and the upper house became the popularly elected S.C. Senate. The representation imbalance in the legislature was adjusted so that the upcountry share approached forty percent. In 1786 the General Assembly relocated the capital from Charleston to Columbia, symbolizing increased statewide unity. The following year the General Assembly banned the importation of new slaves. On May 23, 1788, South Carolina ratified the United States Constitution.

With pressure from the upcountry for increased representation and the new atmosphere under the United States Constitution, a new state constitution emerged, this time from a convention of elected delegates. In the 1790 legislative session the General Assembly ratified the third state constitution, and it remained in force until 1861. The constitution of 1790 continued the legislative dominance of lowcountry planters by apportioning representation on the basis of wealth. The legislatively elected governor had no veto power. The key to "aristocratic stability" was political control by white male owners of land and slaves. A S.C. House member had to own five hundred acres of land and ten slaves in his district. One could also qualify as a House member by owning £150 sterling worth of debt-free real estate or, if not a resident of the parish, £500 sterling. Senators had to own twice as much. Voting was limited to white males, each of whom could vote in any district where he owned fifty acres of land or a lot in town, or in his residential district if he paid three shillings sterling tax there. The power of the 1790 legislature was virtually complete over all matters of government in South Carolina. The General Assembly made all of the laws and elected holders of all major offices, including the governor, presidential electors, U.S. senators, and many local officials.

An amendment to the constitution in 1808 gave upcountry white males control of the lower house by a sixteen-vote majority.

Under terms of the Compromise of 1808, each election district would have one senator, except for Charleston with two. Each election district would also have one representative for $^1/_{62}$ of the white population and $^1/_{62}$ of the state's taxable wealth. Despite the changes, the values of the planter elite continued to prevail since plantation agriculture continued to spread into the upcountry. This expansion added to the harmony of political and economic opinion in South Carolina that would eventually support secession.

The Secession Convention first met in Columbia in December 1860 and then moved to Charleston, where it adopted and signed the Ordinance of Secession on December 20. The convention also made some changes in the wording of the 1790 constitution to accommodate withdrawal from the federal Union, but it changed little else. Under the constitution of 1861, the General Assembly continued to elect the governor.

A new state constitution was required for readmission to the Union after the Civil War. President Andrew Johnson appointed a provisional governor, Benjamin F. Perry, to register eligible voters (adult males who had taken an oath of allegiance to the United States) to elect delegates to a state constitutional convention. Each parish and district elected as many delegates as it had members in the lower house. By not counting senators, Perry tried to advance population-based equity at the convention. The new constitution of 1865 was ratified on September 27, 1865, by the convention rather than by popular vote. It perpetuated the values of the pre–Civil War elite and adopted only limited democratic reforms.

The 1865 constitutional convention created closer parity between the upcountry and the lowcountry by replacing parishes with more uniformly defined election districts. Each district was given one senator, except Charleston with two. The S.C. House of Representatives was apportioned on the basis of white population and wealth measured by taxes paid on property based on current values rather than outdated ones.

The 1865 constitution made only limited moves toward democracy. Legislators continued to elect presidential electors, but the governor was now popularly elected to a four-year term and granted veto power. Property qualifications for office holding were abolished, but the civil rights of former slaves were not satisfactorily defined. Qualified blacks were still not eligible to vote. Aggravated by South Carolina's insistence on electing former Confederate heroes to Congress and its passage of "Black Codes" to strictly regulate former slaves, Congress disallowed the 1865 constitution and ordered the creation of a new one.

Under authority of the congressional Reconstruction Acts, a state constitutional convention met in Charleston on January 14, 1868. Under federal military supervision, African American men voted in South Carolina for the first time in the election for delegates, and three-fifths of the total were black. Many whites refused to participate in the ratification election. The new constitution remains the only whole constitution to be submitted directly to the popular electorate for approval. The United States Congress ratified it on April 16, 1868.

The 1868 constitution was revolutionary because it embodied many democratic principles absent from previous constitutions. The new document provided for population alone, rather than wealth or the combination of wealth and population, as the basis for House representation. It also continued popular election of the governor. Additionally, the 1868 constitution abolished debtors' prison, provided for public education, abolished property ownership as a qualification for office holding, granted some rights to women, and created counties.

The popularly elected governor was given a veto that required a two-thirds vote of the General Assembly to override. A two-thirds legislative vote was also required to issue any bonded debt. In 1873 an additional amendment required that two-thirds of the voters confirm an increase in the general obligation debt of the state.

The 1868 constitution's Article X provided for a uniform system of free public schools. Although not implemented until decades later, the constitution mandated that the schools should operate for at least six months each year and that all children had to attend school at least twenty-four months (four academic years) as soon as enough facilities were available. Provisions for the deaf and blind were also ordered. Schools were financed by a poll tax, and an 1878 amendment added a property tax to increase support for public education. Maintenance of the state university was made mandatory, and the creation of a normal school and an agricultural college were also required.

The status of the newly freed slaves was also solidified in the 1868 constitution. Race was abolished as a limit on male suffrage. Disfranchisement could be only for murder, robbery, and dueling. The Black Codes that had flourished under the constitution of 1865 were overturned. There was no provision against interracial marriage, and all the public schools were open to all races.

Stirrings that led to the constitutional convention of 1895 began in the 1880s with agricultural and labor groups. The 1895 constitution was adopted by a convention and not submitted to a popular referendum. Under the new constitutional authority, the Black Codes would reemerge as Jim Crow laws in forms subtle enough to avoid immediate conflict with the Fifteenth Amendment to the U.S. Constitution.

Benjamin R. Tillman had been elected governor in 1890 by appealing to white farmers, a minority of the state's total population. Poor whites and conservative aristocrats also feared the political manipulation of the large African American majority vote by planters, professional men, and business leaders. Under Tillman's leadership, the state steered the narrow course of disfranchising South Carolina's African Americans without disfranchising poor, illiterate whites or stirring the national government to act on the U.S. Constitution's provisions protecting black civil rights. The key to disfranchising African Americans was the new suffrage clause in the 1895 constitution. The provision gave the right to vote to all males who were paying taxes on property assessed at $300 or more and who were able to read and write the state constitution. Even if a black male voter owned enough property, the constitutional literacy tests could be used by local, white voting registrars to disqualify him. Literacy tests could be used to exclude uncooperative poor whites also. The poll tax was not abolished until 1951, and unregulated local voter registration continued until passage of the federal Voting Rights Act in 1965.

The South Carolina tradition of legislative control of local government, as old as colonial times, was also continued. The 1895 constitution made no provision for locally elected county governing bodies. The legislative delegation from each county became the county governing board. A special, "local government" session was reserved for the end of each legislative year to pass a budget, or "supply bill," for each county.

Despite the preoccupation with race, many of the reform-oriented features of the 1868 constitution were retained. Among them were the governor's veto, limited legal rights for women, and the provisions for public education. However, the practical side of the 1895 revisions was that the executive department remained split into many offices, including popularly elected state agency heads. The formal powers of the governor were generally restrained, especially by limits to a two-year term with potential for only one reelection.

As early as the 1920s, the professor David D. Wallace questioned whether the 1895 constitution needed replacement. By the middle of the twentieth century, criticism of the 1895 constitution has become more extensive. For example, by 1966 the constitution contained 330 amendments, most of which dealt with bonded debt limits for local governments, especially school districts. It was not until 1968 that a constitutional amendment to change the bonded debt of a county could be voted on just within the county and not statewide. South Carolina had the ninth-longest constitution in the country in 1960. The constitution was cluttered with decisions just as easily made and changed by statute.

Many citizens and organized groups had recommended constitutional revision, but this was without practical results before the 1960s. A study committee (called the West Committee) was created by the General Assembly in 1966 to evaluate the need for revision. Based on its findings, the committee was additionally charged "to recommend provisions which may be included in a new constitution, to suggest methods to eliminate archaic provisions, and to propose methods to bring about changes."

The Committee to Make a Study of the South Carolina Constitution of 1895 made its report to the General Assembly in July 1969. In the course of its work, the committee focused on each section of the 1895 document, painstakingly reviewed each one, and made a specific evaluation to carry over or delete a section. For a section that was to be carried over, the report recommended any needed revisions. The committee also drafted and made the case for some new sections in the constitution. It proposed seventeen new articles to the General Assembly to be considered through an article-by-article amendment process aligned with the original seventeen articles in the 1895 constitution. The General Assembly also approved the study committee's proposal for appointment of a legislative steering committee of five senators and five representatives to shepherd the individual articles through the legislature to general election referendums.

The plan was to complete the article-by-article revision in committee and submit all seventeen articles at the same time in the 1970 general election. Each proposed article had first to be authorized by a two-thirds vote of the S.C. House and Senate and then approved by a majority of general election voters. The revised article then had to be ratified again by the General Assembly before it was finally included in the constitution. The date of ratification was the effective date for the new amendment.

The hope for complete revision in one general election was not achieved. Five revised articles were approved by voters in 1970 and ratified in 1971. Since then, developments have gone more slowly. Article III regarding the legislative branch has not been revised, but an amendment in 1977 fixed the times and terms of the legislative session. In 1979 a general reserve fund requirement was ratified under this article.

The original 1895 Article X was the constitution's most amended section. The new article restricted the right of the state, its political subdivisions, and school districts to issue bonds and gave the General Assembly power to define limits and additional procedures for incurring general obligation debt. These restrictions limited the use of specific constitutional amendments as means to incur excessive or careless debt. Revised Article X on finance and taxation was ratified on May 4, 1977. It identified categories and formulas for the assessment of property.

Among other revisions, new Article V provided for a unified court system under the supervision of the state Supreme Court. This article was overhauled again after a successful constitutional referendum in 1984 to add a Court of Appeals between the state Supreme Court and the sixteen Judicial Circuit courts. A 1988 amendment established a statewide grand jury to give the state attorney general more flexibility in prosecuting cases, especially drug cases. Experts felt that handling evidence to win indictments would be easier through the statewide grand jury than through a jury with authority limited to a single county.

Revised Article VI clarified and increased the removal powers of the governor by allowing him to suspend any state or local official, except legislators or judges, who was indicted by a grand jury. This article also included the "long ballot," whereby South Carolina elects a secretary of state, an attorney general, a treasurer, a superintendent of education, a comptroller general, a commissioner of agriculture, and an adjutant general to terms coterminous with that of the governor.

Article VIII on local government allowed local governing bodies for counties to replace the General Assembly's tradition of special legislation. The article also required alternate forms of local government. It combined two articles from the 1895 constitution (VII-Counties and VIII-Municipalities).

The article on alcoholic liquors and beverages (Article VIII-A) established the minibottle policy in South Carolina. Historically the state had been plagued with different approaches to regulation of liquor ranging from prohibition to a cumbersome "brown-bag" arrangement. Consensus was difficult because of "wet vs. dry" debates and preferences across the state. By letting the voters decide, the legislature could reach a decision on the problem, define a productive source of tax revenue for public education as well as alcohol programs, and improve the image of the state for tourists and businesspeople.

Article XI, Public Education, required a free public school system and permitted indirect state aid to students. The article created a State Board of Education made up of one member from each of the sixteen judicial circuits elected by the legislative delegation within each circuit and rotated among the counties within. The governor would appoint an additional member to the board.

The need for changes has continued as parts of the constitution have become out-of-date or been challenged, especially as South Carolina's rural traditions have given way to urbanization, industrialization, and tourism. These changes have inevitably led to more fluid social and political attitudes than those existing in the past. The revised and amended state constitution as it stood in the early twenty-first century established the foundations for more independent and effective executive and judicial branches and created a basis for more self-directed local governments. Hence, South Carolina joined other states that have increasingly relied on their state constitutions, rather than immediate legislative action, for directing important public policy decisions. COLE BLEASE GRAHAM, JR.

Green, Fletcher M. *Constitutional Development in the South Atlantic States, 1776–1860: A Study in the Evolution of Democracy.* 1930. Reprint, New York: Da Capo, 1971.

Tarr, G. Alan. *Understanding State Constitutions.* Princeton, N.J.: Princeton University Press, 1998.

Underwood, James L. *The Constitution of South Carolina.* 4 vols. Columbia: University of South Carolina Press, 1986–1994.

Wallace, David D. *The South Carolina Constitution of 1895.* Columbia: University of South Carolina Bureau of Publications, 1927.

Continental Regiments. In the aftermath of the battles at Lexington and Concord, the Continental Congress passed resolutions that created the Continental army in June 1775. Accordingly, a committee addressed the need for maintaining a regular army, and Congress began the task of apportioning quotas to the states. On November 4, 1775, Congress resolved to maintain "at the continental expense" three battalions for the defense of South Carolina. Continental regiments were units authorized for use by the Continental Congress and were distinct from state militia forces.

The First Provincial Congress of South Carolina raised two regiments of infantry to protect the lowcountry against the British and a third to protect the backcountry from potential Indian raids during the summer of 1775. The first two regiments, designated the First and Second State Regiments, were adopted by the Continental Congress as the First and Second South Carolina Regiments on September 20, 1776, retroactively dated November 4, 1775. The third unit, designated as a regiment of mounted riflemen, was also adopted retroactively into the Continental Line on November 12, 1775, and designated the Third South Carolina Regiment of Rangers.

The Second Provincial Congress of South Carolina authorized a fourth regiment, an artillery unit, on November 13, 1775, and two additional infantry regiments in late February 1776. Composed of three Charleston artillery companies, the Fourth South Carolina Regiment (Artillery) was placed on the Continental Establishment on June 18, 1776, and in October two independent artillery companies from Georgetown and Beaufort were added to its ranks. The Fifth and Sixth South Carolina Regiments, deemed Rifle Regiments, were adopted into the Continental Line on March 25, 1776.

Detachments from all South Carolina Continental Regiments participated in campaigns in South Carolina, Georgia, and Florida from the "Snow Campaign" in 1775 to the Siege of Charleston in the spring of 1780. The Second Regiment successfully defended against a naval bombardment while the Third Regiment prevented an amphibious assault on the eastern end of Sullivan's Island on June 28, 1776. Additionally, all six units participated in the disastrous allied siege of Savannah in October 1779. With the exception of the Fifth and Sixth Regiments, which were consolidated with the First and Second Regiments in February 1780, all regiments of the South Carolina Continental Line were part of the American force that surrendered Charleston on May 12, 1780. Prominent members of the South Carolina Continental Line included Christopher Gadsden, William Moultrie, Francis Marion, Richard Richardson, and William Jasper. SAMUEL K. FORE

Regiment Commander(s)

First S.C. Regiment
Col. Christopher Gadsden (June 17, 1775–Sept. 16, 1776)
Col. Charles Pinckney (Sept. 16, 1776–1780)

Second S.C. Regiment
Col. William Moultrie (June 17, 1775–Sept. 16, 1776)
Col. Isaac Motte (Sept. 16, 1776–1780)

Third S.C. Regiment (Mounted Rangers)
Lt. Col. William Thomson (June 17, 1775–1780)

Fourth S.C. Regiment (Artillery)
Lt. Col. Owen Roberts (Sept. 16, 1776–June 20, 1779)
Col. Barnard Beekman (June 20, 1779–1780)

Fifth S.C. Regiment (First S.C. Rifles)
Col. Isaac Huger (Sept. 17, 1776–Jan. 9, 1777)
Lt. Col. Alexander McIntosh (Jan. 1777–1780)

Sixth S.C. Regiment (Second S.C. Rifles)
Lt. Col. Thomas Sumter (Sept. 20, 1776–1780)

Berg, Fred Anderson. *Encyclopedia of Continental Army Units: Battalions, Regiments and Independent Corps.* Harrisburg, Pa.: Stackpole, 1972.

Erd, Darby, and Fitzhugh McMaster. "The First and Second South Carolina Regiments, 1775–1780." *Military Collector & Historian* 29 (summer 1977): 70–73.

———. "The Third South Carolina Regiment (Rangers), 1775–1780." *Military Collector & Historian* 32 (summer 1980): 72–73.

Risley, Clyde A., and Fitzhugh McMaster. "Fourth South Carolina Regiment (Artillery), 1775–1780." *Military Collector & Historian* 31 (fall 1979): 124–25.

Salley, Alexander S., comp. *Records of the Regiments of the South Carolina Line in the Revolutionary War.* Baltimore: Genealogical Publishing, 1977.

Wright, Robert K. *The Continental Army.* Washington, D.C.: U.S. Army Center for Military History, 1984.

Continental shelf. The continental shelf that lies off South Carolina's coast is part of a larger continental shelf that runs from Canada to Mexico. It is formed, in part, by a continuation of the sediments of the coastal plain that are covered by seawater. The continental shelf has been exposed as much as one hundred miles off the present coastline at various times during the geologic history of the state. This was due to ancient sea levels rising and falling many times over millions of years. Today, South Carolina's continental shelf is a passive margin, meaning that it is not colliding with any other land, as it once did millions of years ago. Instead, it is trailing along North America's active western margin that is presently leading the continent toward Asia. Sediments, therefore, have accumulated on South Carolina's continental shelf to a thickness of thousands of feet over the past 225 million years.

Continental shelf sediments include clays, sands, shales, and sandstones that eroded from mountains to the north and northwest. This thick wedge of sediments lies atop older metamorphic and igneous continental Piedmont rocks. The heavy weight of these rocks, as well as the cooling of the crust, bent the shelf, a process that continues as more sediment is added through erosion of the land and deposition. The continental shelf also contains lava sheets, diabase dikes, and other remnants of volcanoes active during the Jurassic period as North America and Africa rifted apart. Limestone banks several thousand feet thick are located farther seaward and have been explored by oil companies, which found natural gas and oil deposits that may be economically useful in the future. CAROLYN H. MURPHY

King, Philip B. *The Evolution of North America.* Rev. ed. Princeton, N.J.: Princeton University Press, 1977.

Murphy, Carolyn H. *Carolina Rocks! The Geology of South Carolina.* Orangeburg, S.C.: Sandlapper, 1995.

Contrabands. Contrabands were slaves who fled to or were taken behind Northern lines during the Civil War prior to the Emancipation Proclamation. Early in the war, the North had no established policy to deal with escaped slaves. Many Union officers returned the slaves as required under the 1850 Fugitive Slave Law. Others believed that returning the slaves was aiding the Confederates.

The Union general Benjamin Franklin Butler claimed to be the first to apply the term "contraband" to escaped slaves in May 1861. Three slaves had escaped to the Union lines in Virginia and stated that they had been made to work on Confederate defenses. When a

Confederate officer demanded their return, Butler refused, remarking that since they were property, as claimed by the Confederacy, and were being used in war against the United States, they were legitimate contraband of war. Butler used the slaves to construct fortifications but also gave them rations and pay. Butler's solution was quickly adopted by other Northern officers. It gained legal standing in August 1861 when the U.S. Congress passed the First Confiscation Act, declaring legal the seizure of all Southern property used to aid the rebellion—including slaves.

Major General David Hunter, in command of the North's Southern Department on Hilton Head, South Carolina, took Butler's idea one step further when on April 13, 1862, he declared slaves behind his lines to be confiscated and free. He organized male contraband slaves into the First South Carolina Volunteer Regiment, outfitting them with blue coats and red pants and using them as guards and laborers. President Abraham Lincoln disallowed Hunter's declaration but remained silent about the First South Carolina Volunteers. In September 1862 Lincoln issued the Emancipation Proclamation, to go into effect on January 1, 1863, asserting that all slaves in the rebellion were "forever free." STEPHEN D. SMITH

Nalty, Bernard C. *Strength for the Fight: A History of Black Americans in the Military.* New York: Free Press, 1986.

Trudeau, Noah Andre. *Like Men of War: Black Troops in the Civil War, 1862–1865.* New York: Little, Brown, 1998.

Converse, Dexter Edgar (1829–1899). Industrialist. Converse was born on April 21, 1829, in Swanton, Vermont, the second child of Orlin Converse and Louise Twichell. After his father died in 1833, Converse went to live with his aunt and uncle in Trois Rivieres, Quebec, where he worked in his uncle's woolen mill until he was twenty-one. In 1850 he went to work in a cotton mill in Cohoes, New York. Converse was in school only a few years, but his real education came in his understanding of how the mill machinery worked and how the business was operated.

In 1854 Converse took this knowledge and went south to the Carolina Piedmont, where the textile industry was beginning to expand. He worked for a few months as the superintendent of a cotton mill in Lincolnton, North Carolina, before moving to the Bivingsville Cotton Factory in Spartanburg District, South Carolina, in February 1855. He soon became the mill's manager and within a year was a member of the firm. With his career established, Converse married his cousin Helen Twichell on September 17, 1856. During the Civil War, Converse was assigned to run the mill rather than serve in the army. After the war, the Bivingsville mill made a quick recovery. When its founder died in 1868, Converse and his brother-in-law, Albert H. Twichell, bought the outstanding stock, and in 1870 they changed the company's name to D. E. Converse and Company. The enterprise prospered even in the economically uncertain 1870s. In 1878 Bivingsville was renamed Glendale.

In 1880 Converse began the first of his two most important ventures. He bought Hurricane Shoals on the Pacolet River, the site of the former South Carolina Iron Works, and organized the Clifton Manufacturing Company. By 1882 Clifton Factory was in operation with 500 employees, 7,000 spindles, and 150 looms. At the end of the decade, Converse opened another mill near the first, Clifton Number Two. During the 1890s the profits from Clifton ranged between twenty-five and thirty percent. On the basis of this success, Converse opened Clifton Number Three in 1896, giving the Clifton complex the capacity to manufacture 150,000 yards of cloth each day.

In addition to establishing one of the most important industrial enterprises in Spartanburg County, Converse contributed to the educational institution in Spartanburg that bears his name. On March 29, 1889, Converse College was established to serve the needs of Spartanburg's young women. Converse was elected president of the Converse College Company, and the college opened in 1890. Converse also helped establish a preparatory school in 1889 affiliated with the college. In February 1891 he moved his family from Glendale to a new mansion on Pine Street in downtown Spartanburg, where he died on October 4, 1899. Originally buried on the Converse College grounds, his remains were later moved to Oakwood Cemetery. BRUCE E. BAKER

Kilber, Lillian Adele. *The History of Converse College, 1889–1971.* Spartanburg, S.C.: Converse College, 1973.

Converse College. Converse College was founded in 1889 by a group of Spartanburg leaders to provide for the education of young middle-class women. The institution was named to honor its founder Dexter Edgar Converse, a local textile-mill owner and one of the town's most respected men. Converse later wrote, "It is my conviction that the well-being of any country depends much upon the culture of her women, and I have done what I could to found a college that would provide for women thorough and liberal education, so that for them the highest motives may become clear purposes and fixed habits of life."

The founders purchased the site of the defunct St. John's College on Main Street in Spartanburg and secured funds for erecting the first building. They appointed Benjamin Franklin Wilson, pastor of the First Presbyterian Church, the first president of the college (1890–1902). The college opened its doors in the fall of 1890, enrolling 117 students. Unlike many southern women's colleges, Converse offered students a course of study roughly equivalent to that offered by male colleges. Until 1898 the college also included a preparatory department.

During the tenure of its second president, Robert Paine Pell (1902–1932), Converse College expanded its physical plant, endowment, and enrollment and increased its academic standards. The college established a School of Music in 1910. Two year later Converse was accepted into the Association of Colleges and Preparatory Schools of the Southern States. Converse's highly respected conservatory-style musical education drew students from all over the United States. The faculty and students of the music school, as well as local alumnae, spearheaded the development of the South Atlantic States Music Festival, an annual event that brought musicians with national and international stature to perform in Spartanburg.

Converse College with the memorial to founder Dexter Edward Converse. Courtesy. South Caroliniana Library, University of South Carolina

The middle of the century brought challenges. Like most southern colleges, Converse struggled with declining enrollment and financial difficulties during the Great Depression, but enrollment began to grow again by the 1935–1936 academic year. With the entrance of the United States into World War II, the college opened its doors to educational programs for soldiers stationed at nearby Camp Croft and to Wofford College juniors and seniors after their classroom buildings became army training facilities.

The late twentieth century brought more changes. The administration focused on building a high-quality faculty, hiring more faculty with Ph.D.s. The college added a Master of Arts in Teaching program in 1962, the first of several coeducational graduate programs Converse would add in the coming years. In 1968 the college admitted its first African American student, and in the ensuing decades its student body grew in ethnic and economic diversity. Converse II, a bachelor's degree program specially tailored for adult women over twenty-five, was established in 1983.

In 2000 the college was listed among the top fifteen regional colleges and universities in the Southeast by *U.S. News and World Report.* Under the leadership of its eighth president, Nancy Oliver Gray, Converse pursued a $75 million capital campaign and an expansion of its physical plant.

Converse has educated thousands of South Carolina and southeastern women who became leaders in their communities, their professions, and the arts. Among the college's most famous alumnae are the novelist Julia Mood Peterkin (A.B., 1897; A.M., 1898); the composer Lily Strickland (1901–1904; honorary D.M., 1924); the novelist Elizabeth Boatwright Coker (A.B., 1929); and the historian Carol Bleser (A.B., 1960). MELISSA WALKER

Gee, Mary Wilson. *Yes, Ma'am, Miss Gee.* Charlotte, N.C.: Heritage House, 1957.

Kibler, Lillian Adele. *The History of Converse College, 1889–1971.* Spartanburg, S.C.: Converse College, 1973.

McCandless, Amy Thompson. *The Past in the Present: Women's Higher Education in the Twentieth-Century American South.* Tuscaloosa: University of Alabama Press, 1999.

Convict leasing. Convict leasing represents a specific type of prison labor that emerged in the post–Civil War South. Typically, leasing was an arrangement by which individuals convicted of felonies were hired out to private companies who worked inmates as they chose beyond the walls of the state prison. Leasing represented the decentralization of state authority and an emphasis on punishment over reform as the guiding principle of incarceration. The adoption of convict leasing set the South apart from the North, where a new reformatory prison ideology was taking hold. However, South Carolina, one of three states that had not built a state penitentiary prior to the Civil War, built one shortly after the war's close. Thus, at a time when most other southern states were moving away from the principle of a centrally run penitentiary system, South Carolina moved to adopt the northern model.

The exact origins of convict leasing in South Carolina remain unclear. Scholars have argued that a February 1872 act provided for the hiring out of convicts from the Columbia Penitentiary to private individuals. However, the details of this act bear no resemblance to legislation passed in other southern states establishing leasing. Prison officials did hire out an unknown but relatively small number of convicts from 1873 to 1874 to private individuals as a means of securing needed money. However, in March 1874, at the urging of black South Carolinians, Republicans passed legislation expressly forbidding the hire of inmates beyond the prison's walls.

Throughout the late nineteenth century African Americans were resolutely opposed to the establishment of convict leasing in South Carolina. Black South Carolinians understood that leasing represented an assault on the creation of a northern-style penitentiary system and an abandonment of the principle of convict rehabilitation. For African Americans, the decentralized nature of the convict lease system evoked memories of gang labor and plantation justice that they associated with slavery. The relative strength of African Americans within the Republican Party during Reconstruction even prevented Republican governor Daniel H. Chamberlain from moving forward with an 1875 proposal to establish the convict lease system.

South Carolina became the only state where the responsibility for the establishment of leasing resided solely with the Democratic Party. Having successfully wrested political power from Republicans in 1876, Democratic politicians moved quickly to enact leasing legislation. In April 1877 Governor Wade Hampton III called for the passage of a bill by which "the labor of the convicts in the penitentiary could be made profitable," and the Democratic-controlled legislature obliged. With the eclipse of Republican and African American political power, the state's first true convict leasing bill became law on June 8, 1877. Over the next few months and years Democrats passed additional measures firmly entrenching leasing as one method of employing South Carolina's felony convicts.

South Carolina made its first contracts for the hire of state inmates in the summer of 1877. Penitentiary officials leased out more than 270 inmates to labor for three separate employers, including 100 convicts sent to work for the Greenwood and Augusta Railroad. During the next twenty years, penitentiary officials continued to hire out convicts. Typically, larger companies hired between 50 and 100 inmates to work on railroads, mine phosphate, or labor as farm hands. While the state sought large lease contracts, all types of arrangements were made, and some contractors hired as few as 10 inmates for seasonal work on smaller farms. The lease proved lucrative to the state for a time, and in the early 1880s prison officials did not ask for any appropriations.

Conditions for convicts working in the lease system varied widely. At times prisoners labored under horrifying circumstances. An 1879 investigation revealed that inmates working at the Greenwood and Augusta Railroad camp in Edgefield County were "infected with scurvy, and with an eruption which was evidently caused by vermin on their persons." Between 1877 and 1879 fifty-one percent of convicts hired by the railroad died. Other operations were so lenient that one citizen wrote to penitentiary officials complaining that inmates hired by J. R. Fowler were allowed "to go to Laurens [and] to other places . . . without regular armed guards."

Convict leasing came to an end in South Carolina in the 1890s. Its origins lay in the economic demands of a war-torn region and in whites' desire to use the state's criminal justice system to control a newly emancipated black population. Changing economic circumstances in the 1890s robbed leasing of its financial appeal, and the emerging architecture of Jim Crow segregation and disfranchisement meant that leasing was no longer needed as a tool of racial subordination. By 1897 South Carolina had abandoned the lease system, choosing instead to work convicts on state-run prison farms or in industrial shops within the walls of the penitentiary. HENRY KAMERLING

Ayers, Edward L. *Vengeance and Justice: Crime and Punishment in the 19th Century American South.* New York: Oxford University Press, 1984.

Kamerling, Henry. "'Too Much Time for the Crime I Done': Race, Ethnicity, and the Politics of Punishment in Illinois and South Carolina, 1865–1900." Ph.D. diss., University of Illinois at Urbana-Champaign, 1998.

Mancini, Matthew J. *One Dies, Get Another: Convict Leasing in the American South, 1866–1928.* Columbia: University of South Carolina Press, 1996.

Conway (Horry County; 2000 pop. 11,788). Conway, originally named Kingston Village, was established on a bluff of the Waccamaw River about 1735. Kingston became the seat of Kingston County, created in 1785 from the northern third of the Georgetown Judicial District. In 1801 the county was granted autonomy by the state legislature and renamed in honor of Peter Horry, a hero of the Revolutionary War. At the same time, the royalist-sounding name of Kingston Village was changed to Conwayborough for Robert Conway, a popular local politician. In 1883 the General Assembly shortened the name to Conway.

As a county seat, Conway benefited from the jobs and trade the courthouse drew to town. But for much of the nineteenth century, Horry was reckoned the poorest county in the state, so this commerce was often meager. For nearly two hundred years Conway's fortunes were linked to the Waccamaw River. Midway between the Waccamaw's source in Columbus County, North Carolina, and its mouth at Georgetown, Conway was well placed to benefit from river traffic. Unlike most South Carolina counties, however, Horry never developed a plantation culture, and only low value-added products such as timber and naval stores passed through Conway.

Conway grew slowly. When Bishop Francis Asbury visited Conway in 1801, he estimated the population at "not more than one hundred persons." A generation later in 1826 Robert Mills reported twenty-five houses and "about one hundred" inhabitants. By 1860 Conway had almost 300 residents. When the town incorporated in 1898 (after 160 years of habitation) the population stood at 705.

The arrival of the railroad and telegraph in 1887 linked Conway to the world. With better transportation and communications came greater opportunity and swifter growth. In the 1890s bright leaf tobacco became Horry's first major cash crop, and the county began a long period of sustained growth. Conway merchants established a tobacco market in 1899. A dependable cash crop revitalized Conway, and the town flourished in the early twentieth century. Between 1900 and 1940 Conway's population quadrupled to 3,011.

After World War II, Horry's beaches began attracting visitors in ever greater numbers, and Conwegians contributed energy and capital to developing the Grand Strand. The thriving sun-belt economy offered varied employment to local residents. By the 1960s many Conway residents were commuting to jobs in Myrtle Beach. This trend continued and intensified in the 1970s and 1980s as agriculture declined.

In the 1960s Coastal Carolina College, established in 1954 as a branch of the University of South Carolina, began to play a significant role in Conway's economy. A new campus was constructed in suburban Conway, and at century's end, Coastal was Conway's largest employer with 546 permanent employees.

Conwegians have sought to preserve their past even as they enjoy the present. Many historically significant residences, churches, and commercial and public buildings are listed on the National Register of Historic Places. Conway's Downtown Historic District, anchored by the 1825 Robert Mills–designed City Hall, is home to many upscale shops and restaurants. ELDRED E. PRINCE, JR.

Bedford, A. Goff. *The Independent Republic: A Historical Survey of Horry County, South Carolina.* 2d ed. Conway, S.C.: Horry County Historical Society, 1989.

Lewis, Catherine H. *Horry County, South Carolina, 1730–1993.* Columbia: University of South Carolina Press, 1998.

Prince, Eldred E., and Robert R. Simpson. *Long Green: The Rise and Fall of Tobacco in South Carolina.* Athens: University of Georgia Press, 2000.

Coogler, John Gordon (1865–1901). Poet. J. Gordon Coogler achieved notoriety in the nineteenth and twentieth centuries as one of South Carolina's, and the South's, most famous and arguably worst poets. He was born on December 3, 1865, in Richland County near the town of Doko (now Blythewood). By the mid-1880s he was living in Columbia and working as a journeyman printer. He printed, at his own expense, his first volume of poetry around this time. He quickly followed it with two more volumes and soon established himself as a poet with appeal to the masses. Through tireless self-promotion, Coogler and his poetry garnered the attention of readers and reviewers from across the nation, who found his work entertaining if not aesthetic. Facetious reviews and parodies of his work found their way into dozens of newspapers and other periodicals. By 1895 Coogler had opened his own printing shop on Lady Street in Columbia, where he advertised "Poems written while you wait." In 1897 Coogler printed a one-volume edition of his complete works, *Purely Original Verse,* which sold more than five thousand copies, mostly to customers from outside the South. By then, according to Columbia's *State* newspaper, he had become "by a freak of fate . . . the most widely celebrated citizen of Columbia." He died in Columbia on September 9, 1901, and was buried in Elmwood Cemetery.

Coogler's verse received tongue-in-cheek praise from literary critics of the day from Atlanta, Washington, D.C., New York, and London. The writer and critic H. L. Mencken secured literary immortality for Coogler in 1916 when he referred to Coogler as "the last bard of Dixie" in his disparaging review of southern literature, "Sahara of the Bozart." Mencken began the review with the Cooglerian couplet "Alas! For the South, her books have grown fewer—She never was given to literature." Gradually the term "Cooglerism" entered the language, meaning a solemn absurdity.

Coogler's poetic couplets preceded the inane greeting-card rhymes of the twentieth century, and as such he was ahead of his time. Coogler died believing the praise to be genuine and had included several of his reviews in his newer editions. He addressed his critics in verse, adding with humility: "You'll never see this head too large for my hat / You may watch it and feel it as oft as you choose / But you'll learn, as millions of people have learned / Of my character and name thro my innocent muse."

Coogler achieved a poetic revival in 1974 with the reprint of *Purely Original Verse* by Claude and Irene Neuffer. Literary critics and national columnists of the day enjoyed the revival as much as Mencken had years earlier. Orders for copies were received from across the country and across the world. The conservative editor Robert Tyrrell began honoring the year's worst book with the J. Gordon Coogler Award. Observing the renewed enthusiasm for the "bard of the Congaree" in the 1980s, the columnist William F. Buckley concluded, "Coogler, tonight, sleeps with the immortals." FRANCIS NEUFFER

Cohen, Henry Hennig. "J. Gordon Coogler and His Purely Original Verse." Master's thesis, University of South Carolina, 1948.

Coogler, J. Gordon. Papers. South Caroliniana Library, University of South Carolina, Columbia.

———. *Purely Original Verse.* 1897. Reprint, Columbia, S.C.: Vogue, 1974.

LaBorde, Rene. "Coogler Revisited." *Southern Partisan* 3 (winter 1983): 31–33, 41.

Cook Mountain. (Richland County). Cook Mountain is a twelve-hundred-acre hill located in eastern Richland County near Eastover. It stands four hundred feet above sea level and has both geological and ecological significance. The mountain is composed of sediments that form the eroded remnants of the Aiken Plateau, which runs from Aiken County through parts of Lexington, Richland, Lee, and Sumter Counties. Remnants of the plateau also include the Richland Red Hills and the High Hills of Santee. Over millions of years the Aiken Plateau was cut and eroded by both the Congaree and Wateree Rivers, leaving Cook Mountain isolated between them as a small monadnock, an isolated hill or mountain exposed by erosion.

The sediments that form Cook Mountain are largely composed of clays, clayey sands, marls, and sands capped by ironstone. Silicified shells are found within the sediments on the mountain, as are "paint pots," pockets of colorful minerals encased in sediment shells. The sediments of the McBean Formation found on Cook Mountain are largely from the Eocene epoch. These sediments and rocks formed as the ocean levels in South Carolina rose and fell, and they are exposed at the surface today because of erosional processes and uplift. Globally, sea levels fell, and locally, the Aiken Plateau rose due to rebound, partially as a result of but long after separation of the North American plate from the African plate early in the Mesozoic era.

Cook Mountain also contains varied ecosystems within close proximity to each other within a small area. It is home to many animal species and plants, including longleaf pine, mixed hardwood forest, and river-bottom hardwoods. CAROLYN H. MURPHY

Gordon, Kay. "Discovering the Connections." *Sandlapper* 12 (spring 2001): 56–57.

Cooke, William Wilson (1871–1949). Architect. Born on December 27, 1871, in Greenville, Cooke was the son of the former slave Wilson Cooke and his wife, Magdalena Walker, a free woman of color before the Civil War. Cooke's father was Greenville's most prominent black citizen. He owned a grocery store and a tannery and served in the South Carolina General Assembly in 1868. W. W. Cooke attended school in Greenville until he was fourteen. He worked as a carpenter's apprentice until 1888, when he entered the Literary and Industrial Department at Claflin College in Orangeburg. Cooke studied architectural drawing and completed the preparatory course in 1893. From 1893 to 1894 he assisted the vocational superintendent. In 1894 he was elected superintendent of industrial arts at Georgia State Industrial College for Colored Youth in Savannah. After three years he returned to Claflin as superintendent of manual training and industrial arts. During the next five years he earned a bachelor of science in technology degree (1902) at Claflin, studied architecture at Massachusetts Institute of Technology and art history at Columbia University, and designed the Slater Training Building, where Claflin's industrial courses were held.

Between 1902 and 1907 Cooke was a practicing architect, employed by the Freedman's Aid Society and Women's Missionary Society of the Methodist Episcopal Church. He worked primarily at Claflin and in Orangeburg, although he designed three buildings at Cookman Institute in Jacksonville, Florida. At Claflin he was the architect for two dormitories, the Soules Home for Girls, and Tingley Memorial Hall. In addition, in 1903 he designed a large residence for the black attorney John Hammond Fordham. Between 1905 and 1907 Cooke had an office in Greenville. He married Anne Miller, a daughter of S.C. State president Thomas Miller. The couple had two children.

In 1907 Cooke took a three-day federal civil service examination in Boston (blacks were not allowed to take the test in Washington, D.C.). He passed and was assigned to the office of the supervising architect at the United States Treasury Department, the first black man to be employed there. His initial appointment was as an architectural draftsman. In 1909 he was transferred to Field Operations, where he supervised the construction of federal courthouses and post offices in Pennsylvania, Ohio, and Illinois. He remained in the position until 1918, when he was promoted and transferred to the War Department as director of vocational guidance and training for Negro labor battalions at Wilberforce University in Ohio.

After the war Cooke practiced architecture in Gary, Indiana. He was the first African American to obtain an Indiana state architect's license (1929). But the Depression ruined his business, and in 1931 he returned to the supervising architect's office as a construction engineer. He retired in 1941 and died on August 25, 1949. He was buried at Fern Oak Cemetery in Griffith, Indiana. JUDITH T. BAINBRIDGE

Fitchett, E. Horace. "The Role of Claflin College in Negro Life in South Carolina." *Journal of Negro Education* 12 (winter 1943): 42–66.

Wells, John E., and Robert E. Dalton. *The South Carolina Architects, 1885–1935: A Biographical Directory.* Richmond, Va.: New South Architectural Press, 1992.

Williams, Barbara Cook. "William Wilson Cooke." In *African American Architects: A Biographical Dictionary, 1865–1945,* edited by Dreck Spurlock Wilson. New York: Routledge, 2004.

Cooper, Anthony Ashley (1621–1683). Lord Proprietor, first earl of Shaftesbury. Anthony Ashley Cooper was born at Wimborne St. Giles in Dorset, England, on July 22, 1621, the son of Sir John Cooper and Anne Ashley. Both families were of the rising landed gentry. Wimborne St. Giles, his grandfather Ashley's estate, became his country seat and over the centuries has remained the home of the earls of Shaftesbury. After a year at Exeter College, Oxford, Ashley Cooper entered the Inns of Court in 1638. His marriage the next year to Margaret Coventry, daughter of the keeper of the great seal for King Charles I, marked the beginning of his political career.

Ashley Cooper was initially a royalist during the English Civil Wars but twice changed sides. King Charles II rewarded his role in the 1660 restoration of the monarchy by making him Baron Ashley of Wimborne St. Giles in 1661. That same year he became chancellor of the Exchequer. In 1663 the king granted the joint proprietorship of Carolina to Lord Ashley and seven other English noblemen.

The Carolina proprietors initially hoped to people their American lands with settlers from other colonies, but attempts failed. In 1669 Lord Ashley rescued the foundering colonial enterprise by persuading the other proprietors to finance a settlement expedition from England. With the aid of John Locke, who was a

Anthony Ashley Cooper. Courtesy, South Carolina Historical Society

member of his household and secretary to the proprietorship, Lord Ashley wrote the Fundamental Constitutions for the colony and oversaw arrangements for the expedition that brought the first permanent English settlers to South Carolina. Lord Ashley was a member of the Royal Society and had a passion for experimenting with fruit trees at Wimborne St. Giles. The proprietors had high hopes for profits from their colonial enterprise, but for Lord Ashley, his "darling" Carolina was also a grand political and agricultural experiment.

During the colony's earliest years, Lord Ashley's political fortunes continued to rise. In 1672 King Charles II made him lord high chancellor, the highest officer in the government, and elevated his rank in the nobility by titling him the first earl of Shaftesbury. Shaftesbury became the leader of the exclusionist party, a faction that sought to prevent the king's Roman Catholic brother James from succeeding to the throne. In 1673 he was dismissed from office. The government came to see efforts to recruit Scots and French Huguenot settlers for Carolina as part of a treasonous plot against the king. Twice Shaftesbury was imprisoned in the Tower of London, but the other proprietors continued to rely on him to manage development in South Carolina. The exclusionists became known as the Whigs by 1680, and Shaftesbury can be credited as the founder of both South Carolina and the Whig Party in England.

Shaftesbury established a plantation and trading post on his twelve-thousand-acre St. Giles Seignory on the Ashley River. As his political fortunes plummeted, he considered moving to Carolina but instead in 1682 went into exile in Amsterdam, where he died on January 21, 1683. CHARLES H. LESSER

Cheves, Langdon, ed. *The Shaftesbury Papers.* 1897. Reprint, Charleston, S.C.: Tempus, 2000.
Haley, K. H. D. *The First Earl of Shaftesbury.* Oxford: Clarendon, 1968.
Lesser, Charles H. *South Carolina Begins: The Records of a Proprietary Colony, 1663–1721.* Columbia: South Carolina Department of Archives and History, 1995.

Cooper, Robert Archer (1874–1953). Governor. Robert A. Cooper was born on June 12, 1874, in Waterloo Township, Laurens County, the son of Henry Addison Cooper and Elizabeth Archer. He graduated from Jones High School in Abbeville, and after reading law he ultimately received an LL.D. from the Polytechnic Institute at San German, Puerto Rico. On admission to the South Carolina Bar in 1898, he established a law practice in Laurens. On March 22, 1899, Cooper married Mamie Machen. Following her death in 1914, Cooper married Dorcas Calmes on November 15, 1917.

In 1900 Laurens County elected Cooper to the S.C. House of Representatives, where he served until 1904. The following year he became solicitor of the Eighth Judicial Circuit. He resigned in 1912 to resume his lucrative private practice. In August 1918, thanks in part to the support of the outgoing governor Richard I. Manning, Cooper defeated several rivals to secure the gubernatorial nomination in the Democratic Party primary. On November 5 he won an uncontested general election, and he was sworn into office on January 21, 1919.

Emulating the progressive policies of his predecessor, Cooper proposed an ambitious reform program, notably statewide compulsory public school attendance. Cooper and his legislative allies enacted measures that guaranteed seven-month public school terms, as well as higher salaries for public educators. He advocated a notable expansion of state public health services. He also successfully pressured the legislature for money to pave South Carolina roadways. To finance road construction projects, Cooper proposed a reevaluation of property taxes throughout the state and rigid enforcement of state tax laws. Despite bitter objections from various legislators, Cooper also secured legislation that limited the work schedule for textile workers to ten hours per day and fifty-five hours per week.

Buoyed by the optimism of a strong wartime economy, South Carolina voters approved of Governor Cooper's ambitious agenda and reelected him in 1920. Unfortunately, Cooper's second term as governor was marked by a serious agricultural depression and postwar economic recession that undercut public support for his progressive programs. Cooper resigned on May 20, 1922, following his appointment to the Federal Farm Loan Board, a post he held for five years. He served also as assistant to the chairman of the Executive Committee of the Democratic National Committee from 1929 to 1932. Two years later President Franklin D. Roosevelt nominated Cooper to be the U.S. district judge for Puerto Rico. After retiring from the bench in 1947, Cooper died on August 7, 1953, and was buried in Greenville. MILES S. RICHARDS

Wallace, David Duncan. *The History of South Carolina.* 4 vols. New York: American Historical Society, 1934.

Cooper, Thomas (1759–1839). Educator, scientist. Thomas Cooper was born on October 22, 1759, in Westminster, England. His father was also named Thomas Cooper; his mother's name is unknown. Little is known about his childhood or family. In 1779 he began studying at Oxford, and although he did not obtain a degree, he went on to work as a lawyer and a chemist. On August 12, 1779, he married Alice Greenwood, with whom he had five children.

Thomas Cooper, oil portrait by Andrew Deveaux. Courtesy South Caroliniana Library, University of South Carolina

A philosophical radical, Cooper was discouraged by England's conservative reaction to the French Revolution. He left the country in 1794 and settled in Pennsylvania. There he worked as a lawyer and a physician and became associated with the Jeffersonian Republican opposition to Federalism. Republican political triumphs eventually lifted him to a state judgeship in 1804. During this time he began to grow more conservative as the result of attacks on the judiciary by radical democrats. He was forced out of office in 1811. After leaving politics, Cooper turned to teaching chemistry and worked at a variety of schools before arriving at South Carolina College (later the University of South Carolina) in 1820. His first wife had died in 1800, and in 1811 he married Elizabeth Pratt Hemming, with whom he had three children.

In South Carolina, Cooper completed his philosophical journey and became an ardent proponent of states' rights. He was appointed the second president of South Carolina College in May 1820 and taught courses in chemistry, mineralogy, and political economy. Cooper also established himself early as an opponent of religious orthodoxy, which led to confrontation with the state's Presbyterians that played across the pages of pamphlets and newspapers.

Whatever political capital Cooper may have lost by arguing against religion he regained among many by his adoption of states' rights and proslavery views. Although he had authored an antislavery pamphlet while living in England, Cooper purchased two slave families on his arrival in South Carolina. Cooper also opposed tariffs that would injure the southern staple economy. In 1824 he wrote his first major pamphlet that espoused states' rights philosophy, and he later became a strong supporter of nullification. Although he was not politically active in the movement, his writings led opponents of nullification to recognize him as the intellectual leader of the nullifiers.

Cooper resigned from the college presidency on November 27, 1833, effective January 1 of the following year. His resignation stemmed in part from legislative pressure from those who disapproved of his anticlerical stance. Cooper remained active nonetheless in his retirement, authoring works on chemistry and law, including the five-volume *Statutes at Large of South Carolina* (1836–1839). He died on May 11, 1839, in Columbia and was buried in that city's Trinity Churchyard. Cooper's legacy at the University of South Carolina was recognized in 1976 when the undergraduate library was reopened as a research library and renamed the Thomas Cooper Library. AARON W. MARRS

Malone, Dumas. *The Public Life of Thomas Cooper, 1783–1839.* 1926. Reprint, Columbia: University of South Carolina Press, 1961.

Cooper River. The Cooper River and its tributaries drain much of the central portion of the lowcountry. The river flows out of Lake Moultrie, which is in turn fed by Lake Marion. The river combines with the Ashley to form Charleston harbor. It borders several cities, including North Charleston, Mount Pleasant, and Charleston. English colonists named both rivers in honor of one of the Lords Proprietors, Lord Anthony Ashley Cooper.

Early colonists established farms and settlements along the Cooper River and at Goose Creek, a tributary. In the 1700s landowners began using slaves to carve out rice plantations along the river. By the Revolution, the Cooper and several of its tributaries were important in Carolina rice culture. Rice became the most important industry in the lowcountry, and the Cooper River boasted some of the finest plantations, including Limerick, Kensington, Medway, and others. Cooper River planters assumed an important place in South Carolina politics and society. However, the industry declined in the late nineteenth century, and the plantations were idle by World War I.

Humans have altered the Cooper River in profound ways. In the 1790s work began on the Santee Canal, which joined the Santee River to the Cooper and allowed barge traffic from the backcountry directly to Charleston. In the 1930s Lake Moultrie on the upper part of the Cooper was completed, inundating some eighteenth- and nineteenth-century plantations. It also had a diversion canal that connected the Santee and Cooper Rivers. This dramatically increased the speed at which water flowed in the Cooper River so that hydroelectric power could be generated. However, it had the unintended consequence of raising silt deposits in Charleston harbor. In 1985 the Army Corps added a rediversion canal that forced some water back into the Santee and alleviated some of these problems.

While the Cooper River served as a convenient source of water travel, it simultaneously hindered north-south travel. For hundreds of years Charlestonians used ferries to cross the river. That changed with the completion of the Cooper River Bridge in 1929. A second, wider bridge was added in 1966. Construction of a third bridge to replace its predecessors was completed in 2005.

With the failure of rice culture in the early twentieth century, the banks of the Cooper River were turned to other purposes. Though many plantations remained intact as country houses, some were subdivided into housing and others became industrial sites. There has been no bigger single developer on the Cooper than the U.S. Navy. At its peak during the cold war, the base, naval shipyard, and submarine station constituted one of the nation's largest naval facilities.

At the beginning of the twenty-first century the Cooper River continued to be an industrial hub for the Charleston area and remained the center of the busy shipping industry through its container-ship specialization. Heavily used for shipping, industry, and for recreation, the Cooper River had unfortunately become one of the most polluted rivers in the state. JAMES H. TUTEN

Ball, Edward. *Slaves in the Family.* New York: Farrar, Straus and Giroux, 1998.

Irving, John Beaufain. *A Day on Cooper River.* 1842. Reprint, Columbia, S.C.: R. L. Bryan, 1969.

Cooper River bridges. In 1927 a group of Charleston businessmen, led by Harry F. Barkerding and Charles R. Allen, formed Cooper River Bridge, Inc., to promote the construction of a span connecting Charleston and Mount Pleasant. Financing for the project was found in Chicago through the Federal Securities Corporation. Initially, the bridge was to cost no more than $3 million; however, by the time the contracts were signed, the figure had grown to $5.7 million. Tolls were to be charged to pay for the enterprise. Ground was broken at the foot of Lee and America Streets on February 7, 1928. Waddell and Hardesty of New York City designed the bridge, and the Foundation Company of New York City performed the construction. The steel used weighed more than 26,562,000 pounds, and the concrete exceeded 52,757 tons.

The modern concrete pylons of the Arthur Ravenel Bridge rise beside the steel trusses of the old Silas Pearman Bridge. Photograph by Michael Mathis. Courtesy, City of Charleston

When opened on August 8, 1929, the Cooper River Bridge was the longest span of its type in the world—2.7 miles long and 20 feet wide. In 1943 it was officially named the John P. Grace Memorial Bridge in honor of the former mayor of Charleston who had fought to have the bridge built. Tolls failed to cover costs, however, and Charleston County purchased the bridge in 1941 for $4,400,000. In 1945 the county sold the bridge to the state for $4,150,000. On February 24, 1946, a boat, *Nicaragua Victory,* crashed into the span, causing extensive damage and killing five people. Tolls were removed in June 1946, allowing vehicles to cross free of charge. By the early 1960s the two-lane roadway was totally inadequate for the growing population. A new three-lane bridge, the Silas N. Pearman, opened in 1966. Thirty years later area leaders began planning for a new, eight-lane, single-span bridge. Ground breaking for this new bridge took place in 2002, and it opened in 2005. SUSAN KING

Annan, Jason, and Pamela Gabriel. *The Great Cooper River Bridge.* Columbia: University of South Carolina Press, 2002.

Cooperationists. Cooperationists eventually emerged as the dominant political faction during South Carolina's secession crisis of 1850–1851. They believed that slavery could ultimately be preserved only through disunion, but they differed with radical secessionists over the feasibility of South Carolina seceding alone. The specter of secession came to a head following the Wilmot Proviso, which sought to exclude slavery from territory acquired from the Mexican War, and the so-called Compromise of 1850, which most South Carolinians saw as a series of southern concessions to northerners.

In South Carolina the secession crisis of 1850–1851 saw the state divide into three political factions. A small coterie of Unionists opposed secession outright. Separate secessionists, however, wanted South Carolina to secede regardless of whether other states joined her, and this faction enjoyed an organizational advantage through the winter and spring of 1850–1851. Cooperationists matched and eventually surpassed the efforts of their radical opponents. By the second half of 1851, the cooperationists were gaining momentum across the state, particularly in Charleston, where in September they held a "Southern Co-operation and Anti-Secession" meeting and rally.

Cooperationists invoked the experience of nullification, when the state was without a single ally in an impending armed confrontation with the federal government. They warned that separate secession would produce abortive violence, dooming future action by a combination of slaveholding states. Cooperationists predicted that even in the absence of force, separate secession would produce economic ruin. It raised the possibility of tariffs in trade with states remaining in the Union and could subject the state to commercial boycotts or a naval blockade. Separate secession would also force South Carolina to incur the expenses of maintaining all the institutions and agencies necessary for a sovereign state. In those circumstances, cooperationists argued, slavery would be less rather than more secure.

Secessionists and cooperationists agreed to make the scheduled October 1851 election for delegates to the now chimerical Southern Congress a referendum on separate secession. The cooperationists triumphed, collecting 58.8 percent of the votes cast and carrying all but one of the state's congressional districts. Their victory postponed South Carolina's secession for almost a decade. JOHN BARNWELL

Barnwell, John. *Love of Order: South Carolina's First Secession Crisis.* Chapel Hill: University of North Carolina Press, 1982.

Ford, Lacy K., Jr. *Origins of Southern Radicalism: The South Carolina Upcountry, 1800–1860.* New York: Oxford University Press, 1988.

Cooperative Baptist Fellowship. Organized in 1992, the Cooperative Baptist Fellowship (CBF) is affiliated with the national body (headquartered in Atlanta, Georgia) by the same name, which was founded a year earlier in response to dissatisfaction with denominational leadership after the fundamentalist takeover of the Southern Baptist Convention in the early 1980s. Of particular concern to the CBF is the maintenance of "distinctive Baptist principles," such as the priesthood of the believer, the separation of church and state, and the autonomy of the local church. The priorities of the CBF include "doing missions in a world without borders" and "affirming diversity, including . . . ethnicity, race, and gender, as a gift from God." These priorities translate into practices not accepted by many Baptists, such as the ordination of women and an emphasis on efforts to cooperate with non-Baptist religious groups. The CBF operates under the direction of its Coordinating Council and, since 1998, a staff coordinator, the first of whom was Marion C. Aldridge of Columbia. The CBF of South Carolina supports a variety of projects, including a partnership with Baptists of Belgium and the Carolina Poverty Initiative, as well as missionaries, but the sharing of resources is their primary concern. Churches may affiliate with both the South Carolina Baptist Convention and the CBF or the CBF alone, and though relatively small, the CBF has drawn money and members from the South Carolina Baptist Convention. Congregations affiliated with the CBF of South Carolina range in size from more than two thousand to fewer than one hundred. HELEN LEE TURNER

Watson, E. C. *A History of the SC/CBF.* Columbia, S.C., 2002.

Coram, Thomas (ca. 1757–1811). Engraver, painter. Born in Bristol, England, Coram was the son of John Coram, a merchant. He immigrated to Charleston, South Carolina, in 1769, where he joined his father and older brother, John, in the mercantile business. During the Revolutionary War, Thomas Coram served briefly in the Continental army as a private, although he apparently accepted British protection after the fall of Charleston in May 1780.

Coram was largely a self-taught artist, although he may have received some instruction from the painter Henry Benbridge. Coram advertised his skills as an engraver as early as 1778 and was designing paper money for South Carolina as early as 1779. By 1781 newspaper notices were identifying him as "Thomas Coram, engraver" and his residence was listed as 28 Queen Street, where he lived with his wife, Ann. The couple had no children. Few examples of Coram's engravings survive, but his own bookplate, a seal for the Charleston Library Society, and several bills of credit created for the state of South Carolina evidence his skill. Three engraved views of the June 1776 Battle of Sullivan's Island taken from original paintings by Coram, examples of which are not known, were published and exhibited in Charleston long after his death.

In 1784 Coram advertised the opening of a drawing school "for the purpose of instructing youth in that useful and pleasing art." One of his most noted pupils was the artist Charles Fraser, who is known to have taken lessons from Coram in 1795. Their friendship may have begun as early as 1793, however, through a shared interest in the theater.

Coram's ability and style as a figure painter are known only through a handful of objects. They include the small head-and-shoulder portrait of Mrs. Thomas Glover, inscribed and dated 1794, and an oversize panel painting of Christ blessing children, which hung in the Charleston Orphan House chapel. His sketchbooks, however, attest to his development as a landscape painter.

The first known professional artist in the South to explore the art of landscape for purely aesthetic purposes, Coram derived his initial style and approach by studying and copying picturesque English books and engravings. He relied heavily on the concepts put forth by the English art theorist William Gilpin, whose publications espoused the concept of "picturesque beauty." In America, Gilpin's volumes served as instruction books on how to paint landscape and were copied widely by both professional and amateur artists. Coram skillfully adapted Gilpin's models to original views of Charleston and its environs.

Coram's earliest known sketchbook, *Sketches Taken from W. Gilpin's Observations on the River Wye and several parts of South Wales,* dated 1791, consists of fifteen oils copied from Gilpin's earliest illustrated volume. The next year Coram produced *Sketchbook from Nature,* which included views of Charleston and the St. James Goose Creek plantation of Charles Glover. Two circa 1800 views portray the house of Thomas Radcliffe and Mulberry Plantation. Coram's sketchbooks and landscapes serve as an essential link between British and American concepts of the picturesque.

Coram died in Charleston on May 2, 1811. He was buried in the cemetery of St. Philip's Church. The Charleston Orphan House was the beneficiary of the bulk of his estate, including his sizable library. The largest collection of Coram's work is in the Gibbes Museum of Art in Charleston. See plate 9. ANGELA D. MACK

Batson, Whaley. "Thomas Coram: Charleston Artist." *Journal of Early Southern Decorative Arts* 1 (November 1975): 35–47.

Heisser, David C. R. "'Warrior Queen of the Ocean': The Story of Charleston and Its Seal." *South Carolina Historical Magazine* 93 (July–October 1992): 167–95.

Kefalos, Roberta. "Poetry of Place: Landscapes of Thomas Coram and Charles Fraser." *American Art Review* 10 (May–June 1998): 122–27.

Middleton, Margaret Simons. "Thomas Coram, Engraver and Painter." *Magazine Antiques* 29 (June 1936): 242–44.

Obituary. Charleston *Times,* May 3, 1811.

Prime, Alfred Coxe. *The Arts and Crafts in Philadelphia, Maryland and South Carolina, 1721–1785.* 2 vols. 1929. Reprint, New York: Da Capo, 1969.

Corcoran, James Andrew (1820–1889). Theologian, educator, editor. Corcoran was born in Charleston on March 30, 1820, the fourth child of John Corcoran, a grocer, and his wife Jane O'Farrell. The Corcorans emigrated from Ireland in 1816 and settled in Charleston, where they operated a small grocery on King Street. John Corcoran died in 1819, and James was born five months later. Jane Corcoran continued to run the grocery and later operated a dry-goods store, raising James and his older brother John alone. She died in 1832, having made arrangements for the boys' care.

Corcoran attended the boys' Classical Academy founded in Charleston by John England, Charleston's first Catholic bishop. England sent him to Rome in 1833 for seminary studies, and he excelled in history, theology, and ancient and modern languages and was noted for his elegant Latin. In 1842 he was ordained and received a doctorate of theology. Returning to Charleston in 1843, he did parish work at St. Mary's Church and St. Finbar's Cathedral, and taught at St. John the Baptist Seminary and the Catholic English and Classical School.

From 1850 to 1861 Corcoran served as editor of the *United States Catholic Miscellany,* the newspaper founded by Bishop England. In its pages he defended Catholicism against its critics. He vigorously defended states' rights and castigated abolitionists, whom he thought were motivated by anti-Catholicism and the nativist Know-Nothing movement. For Corcoran, the right to secede was "an imperative necessity, for the South to put an end to the insults, menaces and aggression from which she had so long suffered." He maintained that his church permitted slavery, that is, the retention in bondage of descendants of those originally enslaved. When South Carolina did secede, Corcoran renamed the paper the *Catholic Miscellany,* expunging "those two obnoxious words" "United States." The paper was destroyed in the great Charleston fire of December 1861. From 1861 to 1868 Corcoran was pastor at Wilmington, North Carolina, and distinguished himself by his work to alleviate suffering of both Catholics and non-Catholics. He served as vicar general of the Diocese of Charleston. Loyal to the Confederacy to the end, he resisted taking the oath of allegiance to the United States.

Corcoran's theological learning and elegant Latin style earned him a national reputation. In 1868 he was chosen by the American bishops as their representative in Rome to participate in preparatory work for the First Vatican Council. There he successfully opposed European proposals to condemn the American principles of freedom of worship and separation of church and state. While believing in papal infallibility, Corcoran thought it inopportune to proclaim it as Catholic dogma. During the Vatican Council he assisted Archbishop Martin John Spalding of Baltimore in preparing a compromise definition of papal authority, one less emphatic than what was ultimately proclaimed.

Returning to America after the Vatican Council, Corcoran became professor of theology, scripture, and Hebrew at St. Charles Borromeo Seminary, Overbrook, Pennsylvania. Under his leadership, its educational program emphasized modern scholarship and student access to a good library. In 1876 he founded the *American Catholic Quarterly Review,* a national journal of Catholic opinion on theology, history, political, and social topics. After a long bout with Bright's disease, Corcoran died in Philadelphia on July 16, 1889. He was buried in the Cathedral of Saints Peter and Paul, Philadelphia. DAVID C. R. HEISSER

Corcoran, James A. *Stock Misrepresentations of Catholic Doctrines.* Cleveland, Ohio: Catholic Universe Press, 1902.

Hennesey, James J. "James A. Corcoran's Mission to Rome, 1868–1869." *Catholic Historical Review* 48 (July 1962): 157–81.

Lofton, Edward Dennis. "Reverend Doctor James A. Corcoran and the 'United States Catholic Miscellany.'" *Records of the American Catholic Historical Society of Philadelphia* 93 (1982): 77–101.

Lowman, Mary Marcian, Sister. "James Andrew Corcoran, Editor, Theologian, Scholar (1820–1889)." Ph.D. diss., St. Louis University, 1958.

McNally, Michael J. "James A. Corcoran and St. Charles Borromeo Seminary-Overbrook, 1871–1907." *American Catholic Studies* 110 (spring–winter 1999): 49–69.

Corn. This versatile grain has played an important role in the diet and economy of South Carolina since prehistory. Indians were growing maize (an ancestor of modern corn) in South Carolina before the first Europeans and Africans came. The newcomers quickly learned to cultivate this vital grain, and corn culture rapidly spread up and down the tidewater rivers of the lowcountry. Settlers took corn with them into the interior. By the mid–eighteenth century, corn was the centerpiece of subsistence agriculture in South Carolina and the foundation of the colonial diet.

South Carolinians, like other rural Americans, ate corn in some form at virtually every meal. Corn was consumed fresh as a vegetable; it was also ground into meal and baked or fried into various breads. As flour, it was used to coat meats, vegetables, and fish for frying. Corn was rendered into syrup and distilled into whiskey. Hominy, a corn derivative, gave the South its most beloved signature dish: grits. Virtually the entire plant entered the food chain. The grain was fed to poultry and the stalks and shucks to cattle and swine. Thus, corn was turned into chicken, beef, pork, eggs, and dairy products. Nothing was wasted: corn worms were plucked from harvested ears and fed to poultry. Farmers also fed corn fodder to draft animals (horses, mules, and oxen). Therefore, as a staple of the diets of man and beast, corn was arguably the most important fuel in preindustrial America.

Although South Carolinians consumed most of their corn, they turned some into cash. As early as the 1680s, barrels of corn were being sold to the West Indies, and corn remained a cash crop through the colonial period, albeit in small amounts. More corn could have been sold, but ready markets were not always available. At best, therefore, a farmer might hope to feed himself and his livestock and clear a few extra dollars per year. Some farmers distilled their corn to decrease bulk and increase value. Corn whiskey enjoyed a lively market as a desirable commodity for sale or barter.

In the nineteenth century, corn became the universal secondary crop. The grain was raised on virtually every farm in the state as farmers paired corn with the prevailing staple. On lowcountry rice plantations, corn grew on the high ground. Inland farmers planted corn in rotation with cotton, and tobacco growers included corn in their crop cycle. All learned to plant beans or peas with corn and thus raise two food crops in a single field.

Corn had cultural as well as economic significance in the Palmetto State. In the agrarian world of antebellum South Carolina, people were considered truly independent only if they controlled their own livelihood and supplied their own sustenance. As the basic food crop, corn was central to this ethos of self-sufficiency. In the 1850s strong demand for cotton tempted many farmers to reduce corn acreage in favor of the staple. To others, however, increasing one's market orientation at the expense of subsistence was a lamentable departure from common sense.

The disruptions of the Civil War and Reconstruction depressed the state's economic output for many years, and not until 1891 did corn production reach prewar levels. In 1900 South Carolina farmers harvested a record 1,740,000 acres of corn. And South Carolina's corn production continued to expand during the twentieth century. Genetically engineered seed, commercial fertilizers, and mechanized cultivation multiplied yields dramatically. Greater yields, especially after 1950, enabled growers to raise more grain from fewer acres. And corn became more of a cash crop. As tractors replaced horses and supermarkets replaced smokehouses, less corn was eaten and more was sold. Production basically responded to prices and rainfall, and South Carolina farmers sold a record 52 million bushels in 1976. But declining prices in the fourth quarter of the twentieth century discouraged corn production. In 2001 the state made only 25 million bushels—the same as in 1915—and corn had fallen to eleventh place in cash value to South Carolina farmers. ELDRED E. PRINCE, JR.

Clowse, Converse D. *Economic Beginnings in Colonial South Carolina, 1670–1730.* Columbia: University of South Carolina Press, 1971.

Ford, Lacy K., Jr. *The Origins of Southern Radicalism: The South Carolina Upcountry, 1800–1860.* New York: Oxford University Press, 1988.

Kovacik, Charles F., and John J. Winberry. *South Carolina: The Making of a Landscape.* 1987. Reprint, Columbia: University of South Carolina Press, 1989.

Cornbread. Cornbread has been the most common daily bread in South Carolina since its founding. Sarah Rutledge included thirty-four variations in *The Carolina Housewife* in 1847. By then, the traditional hoe cake, or johnny cake, or pone—a simple hearth bread of cornmeal and water—had evolved into many elaborate forms. Recipes traveled up and down the eastern seaboard and along the trading routes inland. Corn from Virginia—a white dent corn, which dries well in the field—was preferred. Robert Beverley described the wealthy Virginia planters preferring corn pone to wheat bread as early as 1705. In Savannah, Georgia, just across the river from South Carolina, a letter from 1738 describes the "large, broad, and white" Virginia corn, which would not grow well in the lowcountry.

Corn, like rice, was much less expensive than wheat, and both grains filled breads of all sorts. But cornbread—whether made with cooked grits, coarse meal, or fine corn flour—has maintained its popularity, from the Piedmont to the coast, throughout South Carolina's history, whereas virtually all of the rice breads have disappeared from Carolina tables. Recipes for simple hearth cakes made with ground cereals appear in all cultures where grains are grown. English settlers in the colonies replaced oats with rice or corn. Mary Randolph published two recipes in *The Virginia House-Wife* in 1824, both certainly from the Carolina lowcountry: boiled rice was used in one; "homony"—what Charlestonians call cooked corn grits—"boiled and mixed with rice flour" was used in the other. Just over twenty years later all of Sarah Rutledge's recipes would point to modern forms, with milk or buttermilk, eggs, and leavening added to this classic quick bread that is served alongside pilaus and gumbos, and with salads and greens; only two of them contained sugar. JOHN MARTIN TAYLOR

Beverley, Robert. *The History and Present State of Virginia.* 1705. Reprint, Indianapolis: Bobbs-Merrill, 1971.

Randolph, Mary. *The Virginia House-Wife.* 1824. Reprint, Columbia: University of South Carolina Press, 1984.

Rutledge, Sarah. *The Carolina Housewife.* 1847. Reprint, Columbia: University of South Carolina Press, 1979.

Corrington, Julian Dana (1887–1979). Biologist, educator. Corrington was born in Hot Springs, Arkansas, on December 22, 1887, the son of Joe W. Corrington and his wife, Jesse W. Knox. He graduated from Cornell University (A.B., 1913; Ph.D., 1925). In 1915 he married Veronica Elisabeth Flicke, with whom he had a son and a daughter. Corrington worked as an assistant in zoology and later as museum curator at Cornell, and he served as a second lieutenant in the U.S. Army during World War I.

In 1921 Corrington arrived in Columbia to join the biology faculty at the University of South Carolina (USC). A man with broad zoological interests, Corrington began working on the then little-known herpetology (study of amphibians and reptiles) of the Columbia region, an area of considerable biological importance as a result of its location on the fall line between the Piedmont and the coastal plain. The fauna of that area has a mixture of animals occurring in those two geomorphic provinces, and crosses between subspecies occurring on opposite sides of the fall line are commonly found in the Columbia region. Corrington's studies of the amphibians and reptiles of the environs of Columbia emphasized the ecology of the forms encountered. He built a small, but important, collection of amphibians and reptiles at USC and published two papers based on his research on the local fauna. One of these, "Herpetology of the Columbia, South Carolina, Region" (1929), was a particularly significant contribution, being the first publication in many years to deal in detail with amphibians and reptiles of South Carolina. In addition to his own research, Corrington supervised the preparation of two master's theses on animals of the Columbia area—one on salamanders, the other on frogs and toads. Corrington also published on invertebrates, shark morphology, and birds; was especially interested in microscopy (writing *Adventures with the Microscope* [1934]; *Working with the Microscope* [1941]; and

Exploring with Your Microscope [1957]); and did editorial work for *Nature Magazine, Bios,* and *Natural History.*

Corrington departed Columbia for Syracuse University in 1926 and remained there for four years, subsequently holding positions at Drew University, University of Rochester, and Washington College. He joined the faculty of the University of Miami (Florida) as an assistant professor of zoology in 1944, became a full professor in 1947, and chaired the department from 1953 to 1957. Corrington died in Coral Gables, Florida, on November 29, 1979. WILLIAM D. ANDERSON, JR.

Corrington, Julian D. "Herpetology of the Columbia, South Carolina, Region." *Copeia* 172 (November 15, 1929): 58–83.

Sanders, Albert E., and William D. Anderson, Jr. *Natural History Investigations in South Carolina from Colonial Times to the Present.* Columbia: University of South Carolina Press, 1999.

Cotton. Cotton served as an important staple crop during the antebellum period and continued as the foundation of the state's economy from the postbellum period through World War II. While production steadily declined to a low in the 1980s, the crop made a resurgence by the end of the century. Two basic types of cotton have been grown in South Carolina. The cultivation of Sea Island or long staple cotton was restricted to coastal areas south of Charleston. Upland or short staple cotton was successfully grown in the interior and accounted for the spread of the plantation system through most of the state.

Some claim that the Sea Island variety was the highest quality cotton in the world. It had a long silky fiber or staple (1.5 to 2.5 inches) and could be spun into a thin thread that could be woven into the finest quality cloth and laces. Several types of long staple Sea Island cotton were grown, but the highest quality was grown only on the Sea Islands south of Charleston. It was especially significant on Edisto Island and in the Beaufort area. A substantially longer growing season and somewhat lower rainfall were the factors that limited production to the islands as opposed to the mainland, and Sea Island cotton acreage stabilized by the 1830s. Because its range was limited and the crop was profitable, planters used innovative techniques to increase yield or expand the cultivable area. Salt marsh grass and mud were used as fertilizers, ditches were dug to drain low land, and salt marsh was reclaimed. The Civil War and its aftermath destroyed the Sea Island economic and social structure, and agriculture was neglected. The postbellum period saw some adjustments, but the industry deteriorated and was no longer economically viable by the 1910s. The final blow was the invasion of the boll weevil in the 1910s and 1920s.

Until the early 1960s, the planting, picking, and shipping of cotton remained much as it had for more than 150 years. Courtesy, South Caroliniana Library, University of South Carolina

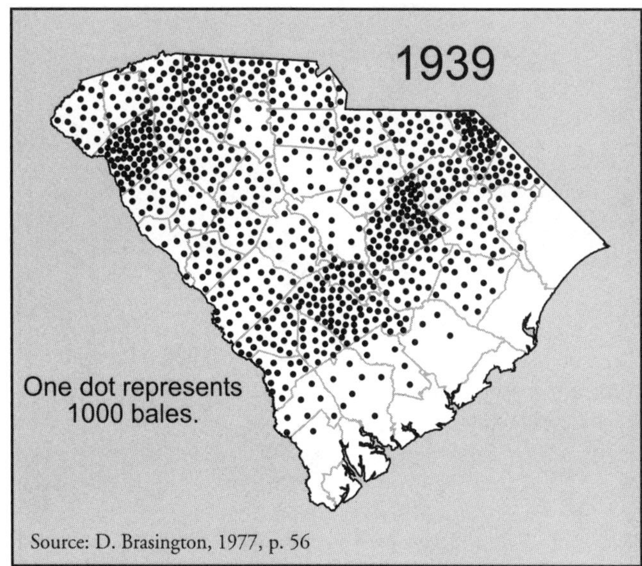

Cotton production, 1939. Prior to World War II, the state's farmers harvested more than one million acres of cotton a year.

Eli Whitney's invention of the cotton gin, demand created by the British textile industry, and an improved transportation system were major factors for the rapid spread of upland or short staple cotton (0.5 to 0.75 inches) into the backcountry during the first decade of the nineteenth century. As late as 1820 South Carolina produced more than one-half the nation's cotton, and it was the major crop in nearly every district of the state except those along the coast. Abbeville, Edgefield, Fairfield, and Laurens Districts were leading producers.

While upland cotton planters knew of various conservation practices, few were practiced. They normally followed a pattern of clearing forest, planting cotton until yields declined, planting corn, abandoning the field, and then clearing new land. The major investment was in labor (slaves), and yield was measured in labor units.

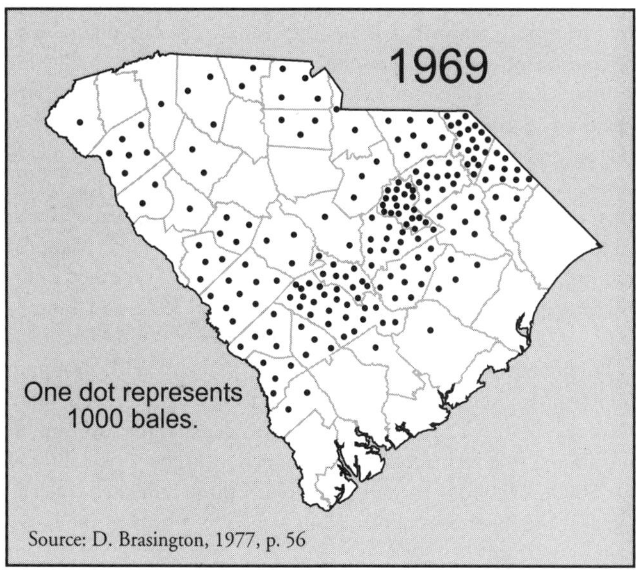

Cotton production, 1969. By the late 1960s, less than 100,000 acres of cotton were harvested annually.

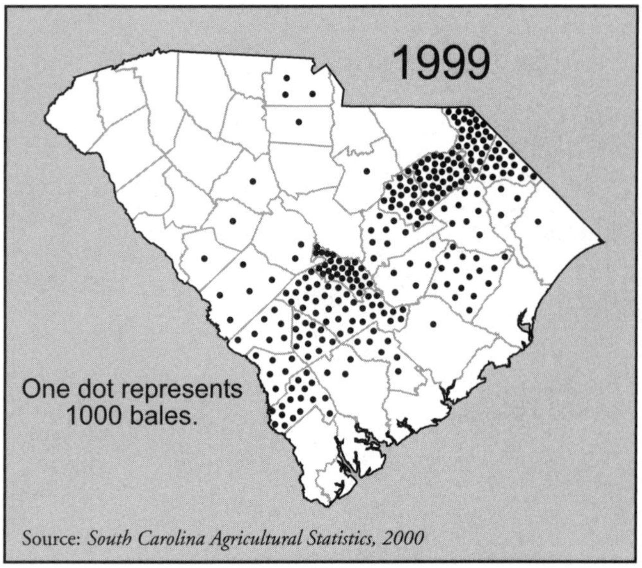

1999

One dot represents 1000 bales.

Source: *South Carolina Agricultural Statistics, 2000*

Cotton production, 1999. At the turn of the twenty-first century, cotton production had risen but was still concentrated in the inner coastal plain.

Land was inexpensive relative to labor cost. When soil nutrients were depleted and the yield per slave unit declined, fresh land was cleared.

Cotton was the basis of the state's agricultural economy at the end of the antebellum period, employing more than eighty percent of the slave labor force. Three-fourths of the crop was produced in the lower Piedmont and inner coastal plain. Even though production continued to increase, South Carolina accounted for less than ten percent of the national crop in 1850, as Georgia, Alabama, and Mississippi became major producers. As the cotton frontier moved west, following available and cheaper land, many South Carolinians made the trek.

Cotton production totaled about 280,000 bales in 1860 but declined to less than 180,000 bales in 1870. By 1911, however, production reached its peak at 1.6 million bales. It was produced on more than forty percent of the state's improved farmland and provided the basis of the state's economy and the tenancy system. The upper Piedmont and inner coastal plain were the chief production areas in the 1920s and 1930s.

After World War II, cotton slowly disappeared from the Piedmont and became concentrated in the inner coastal plain. The Piedmont counties of Anderson, Spartanburg, and Greenville, for example, harvested cotton on more than 150,000 acres in 1945. Less than 12,500 acres were planted in the three counties in 1970 and only about 1,600 acres in 1982. This followed nationwide trends in which the tractor and other machinery, pesticides, herbicides, and additional components of scientific agriculture have favored large farms and cultivation of the most productive land. Marginal land was taken out of production. Land in farms was just over 11 million acres in 1945, only about 5.6 million acres in 1982, and 4.8 million in 2000. The Piedmont accounted for most of this decline.

Production declined dramatically after World War II, dropping to a low of 53,000 bales in 1983. Strong demand, good prices, more effective boll weevil control, and decreased demand for soybeans all contributed to a revival of cotton production in the 1990s. By the year 2000, 379,000 bales were produced. Cotton remained concentrated in the inner coastal plain, but some was grown in the lower Piedmont. CHARLES F. KOVACIK

Aiken, Charles S. *The Cotton Plantation South since the Civil War.* Baltimore: Johns Hopkins University Press, 1998.

Gray, Lewis C. *History of Agriculture in the Southern United States to 1860.* 2 vols. Washington, D.C.: Carnegie Institution, 1933.

Kovacik, Charles F., and Robert E. Mason. "Changes in the South Carolina Sea Island Cotton Industry." *Southeastern Geographer* 25 (November 1985): 77–104.

Council of Safety. Prompted by rumors of British-sponsored slave and Indian attacks and news of the hostilities between British and patriot forces at Lexington and Concord, the Provincial Congress of South Carolina met for an emergency session in early June 1775. Congressional delegates hastened to cope with the rapidly deteriorating situation and began to prepare to defend the state. The congress also called for the election of a new assembly to meet later in the year. For the interim, however, it created a powerful thirteen-member committee to act as the supreme executive power in the province and to be called the Council of Safety. All thirteen members were elected to the council by ballot on the evening of June 14, 1775, including Henry Laurens, who was designated to serve as the council's president. Peter Timothy, the secretary for the Provincial Congress, would serve as secretary.

Regarding public affairs so urgent, the council held its first meeting only two days after its creation. Chief among the business of the council was the command and administration of the provincial military force and issuing paper currency to finance military expenses. Once the threat of a slave revolt in the lowcountry had subsided, the council turned its attention to the backcountry. In addition to the Indian problem, a strong Loyalist presence began to emerge there. In an attempt to convert the disaffected, the council sent one of its most fervent members, William Henry Drayton, and two like-minded clergymen, William Tennent and Oliver Hart, on a mission into the interior of the state. But the results were disappointing. By mid-November fighting had broken out between patriots and Tories, and the council directed military operations through year's end.

When the Provincial Congress met again in November, it elected a new Council of Safety on November 16, 1775. Three new members replaced three members who had resigned, while the rest retained their seats, including Henry Laurens as president. The new council first met on November 30, 1775, and constituted the executive power of the province until the adoption of a permanent government in March 1776. SAMUEL K. FORE

Chesnutt, David R., et al., eds. *Papers of Henry Laurens.* Vol. 10, *Dec. 12, 1774–Jan. 4, 1776.* Columbia: University of South Carolina Press, 1985.

———. *Papers of Henry Laurens.* Vol. 11, *Jan. 5, 1776–Nov. 1, 1777.* Columbia: University of South Carolina Press, 1988.

"Journal of the Council of Safety, for the Province of South Carolina, 1775." In *Collections of the South Carolina Historical Society.* Vol. 2. Charleston: South Carolina Historical Society, 1858.

"Journal of the Second Council of Safety, Appointed by the Provisional Congress, November, 1775." In *Collections of the South Carolina Historical Society.* Vol. 3. Charleston: South Carolina Historical Society, 1859.

Krawczynski, Keith. *William Henry Drayton: South Carolina Revolutionary Patriot.* Baton Rouge: Louisiana State University Press, 2001.

Counties, districts, and parishes. County government in South Carolina represents both the old and the new. It represents the old in the sense that county government can trace its roots to the early colonial period in South Carolina. It represents the new because amendments to the South Carolina constitution passed in 1973 and the Local Government Act of 1975 (also known as the "Home Rule Act") gave county governments "limited" home rule that granted authority to provide services ranging from animal control to zoning.

In 1682 the Lords Proprietors created three counties, Berkeley, Craven, and Colleton; Granville County was added later. The primary functions of these counties were administering justice, granting land, and the election of representatives. The Church Act of 1706 established the Church of England in South Carolina and also created ten parishes to carry out the church's work. These parishes obtained a civil function to join their ecclesiastical one in 1716, when parishes became election districts for the colony. Besides serving as election districts, parishes recorded vital statistics, cared for the poor and orphans, provided doctors, and operated free schools.

New parishes were added throughout the colonial period, although the development of parishes in the backcountry did not keep pace with its rising population. In 1770 there were twenty-four parishes, of which only three were in the backcountry. Demands for better government led to the creation of seven judicial districts in 1769 that incorporated all the settled area of the colony. These districts brought some legal services to the backcountry but did not supply all the benefits of the parishes.

Counties, districts, and parishes all existed in South Carolina after independence from Great Britain. Under the 1778 constitution, the parish and the district were election districts for the General Assembly. This gave the lowcountry, with its numerous small parishes, a distinct advantage. Despite having over half the white population in the state, the backcountry received less than half of the seats in the House of Representatives. Although each district or parish was allotted one senator, Charleston had two parishes,

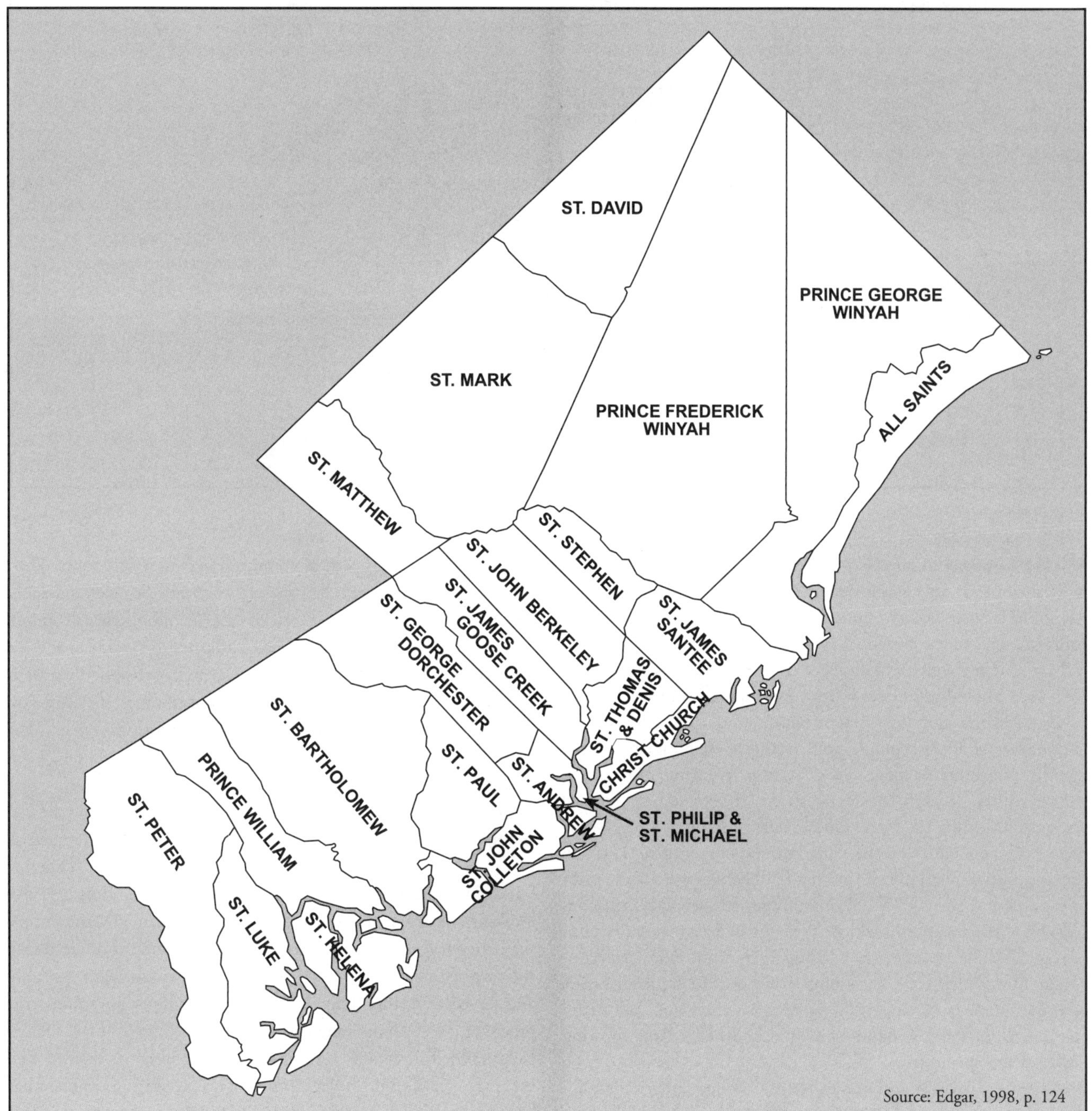

Parishes, 1775

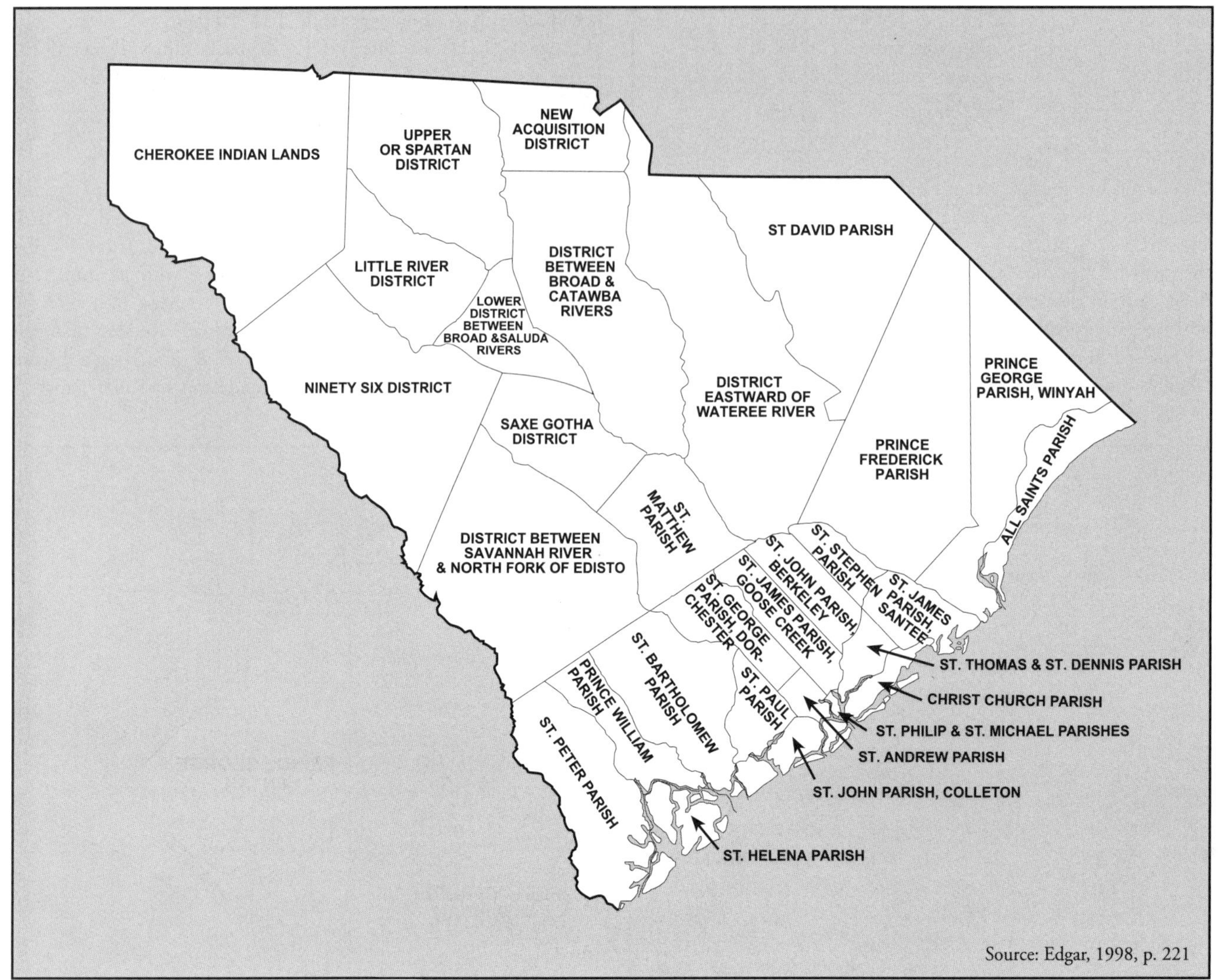

Election Districts ca. 1776

inflating its power. A survey of uniform counties within the seven judicial districts was commissioned in 1783. In 1785 the General Assembly created twenty counties and established a small claims court in each county. Nevertheless, the creation of the new counties did not change the role and duties of district courts. District justices continued to hold sessions at district courthouse towns.

By 1800 this early experiment with counties came to an end. Despite serious efforts, counties were unable to establish clearly their identity and utility as extensions of state government. Most of the counties that existed became districts that assumed judicial responsibilities for their geographic areas. Although roughly the same size, these judicial districts had overlapping jurisdictions and responsibilities. It is noteworthy that few changes were made prior to the end of the Civil War. During this period there was little consistency in the manner in which services that had previously been provided by the counties (for example, education and road construction) were delivered. The Compromise of 1808 settled the issue of apportionment. By apportioning seats based on population and tax collection, the lowcountry finally acknowledged the growing power of the upcountry.

After the Civil War, counties in South Carolina underwent a significant transformation. In 1868 the state constitution abolished the parishes and designated judicial districts formally as counties. It also created a three-man board of commissioners in each county. These boards of commissioners had the power to collect taxes and spend revenue for a limited range of services, including roads, bridges, schools, and public buildings. Their authority to tax and spend was limited to purposes specified by the General Assembly. Because of this limited authority, this view of the responsibilities of county government became known as the "county purpose doctrine." This long-standing doctrine continued until passage of the Local Government Act of 1975.

It was also during this period that Dillon's Rule became the prevailing principle on the roles and responsibilities of county government. Named for Iowa Supreme Court justice John F. Dillon, a leading authority on municipal government, Dillon's Rule held that local governments were solely the creature of state government. As such they had no authority beyond that delegated to them by the state legislature. This became the accepted view in South Carolina and served to further limit the authority of county governments to provide services. Combining the county purpose doctrine and Dillon's Rule resulted in county government being limited to those powers expressly identified by the legislature. Hence, county government had little if any discretion and their very existence relied on the goodwill of the General Assembly.

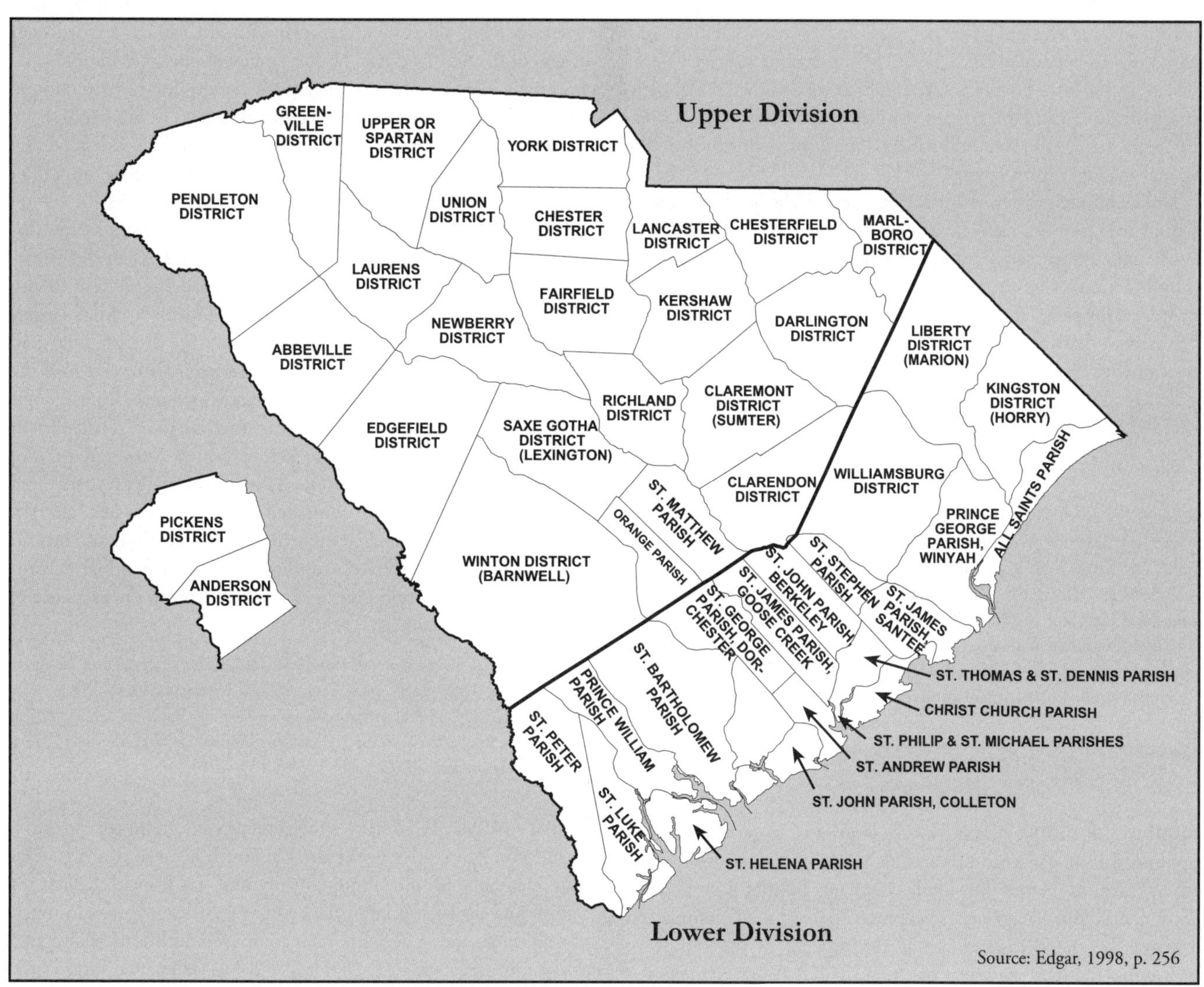

Election Districts, 1790

For a brief period in the late nineteenth century, counties were legislated out of existence. In 1890 the constitutional provisions relating to counties were repealed by the General Assembly. However, the constitution of 1895 re-created counties and specified their duties and powers. In general those duties and responsibilities included the authorization or provision for schools, roads, bridges, and public buildings. Counties continued to have a limited role in local governance, being primarily an extension of state government.

During this period a county's legislative delegation (the state senator and representatives) was the de facto governing authority for county government. The South Carolina General Assembly could pass legislation directed at any single county. It also annually passed the "supply bill," the county's operating budget. The delegation's power was further enhanced because the General Assembly tended to defer to individual county delegations in all matters related to the counties they represented.

Changes to the state constitution in 1973 (ratified as Article VIII) and passage of the Local Government Act of 1975 changed the landscape of county government in South Carolina by expanding and clarifying its duties, responsibilities, and authority. After these changes, the powers of county government were characterized typically as "limited" home rule because the General Assembly still retained the substantial authority to expand or restrict the powers of county government. For example, through the Local Government Fiscal Authority Act of 1997, the General Assembly clearly defined the limits of county government's authority to generate revenue to meet local needs.

In the early twenty-first century counties could best be described as general-purpose governments having general powers and providing a range of local services, such as law enforcement, construction and maintenance of roads and bridges, water and sewer service, collection and disposal of solid waste, land-use planning, public libraries, economic development, recreation, buying and selling property, entering into contracts, eminent domain, assessment of ad valorem property taxes, and establishing uniform service charges.

The 1975 statute authorized four forms of county government. The council form vests all responsibilities for making policy and administering county government in the county council. The council has both executive and legislative power. In the council-supervisor form, a supervisor is elected at large. The supervisor is both the chairman of county council and the chief administrative officer of the county. In the council-administrator form, council hires an administrator who is the chief administrative officer of the county and is responsible for all departments for which the council has control. The council-manager form is similar to the council-administrator form with one major exception. In the council-manager form, the auditor and the treasurer may be appointed by council rather than elected. Once appointed, they report to the county manager. As of November 2004, the bulk of South Carolina's counties had the council-administrator form (thirty-four counties), followed by the council form (six), the council-supervisor form (four), and the council-manager form (two).

Unlike municipalities, created in response to the needs of a group of residents, counties were created as "creatures" of the state. Their power and authority are limited to what is approved by the General Assembly. County governments still provide and support state-level services. However, their powers and responsibilities have also increased so that today in many ways they are similar to municipal governments. As the needs and expectations of the citizens continue to change, county government in South Carolina can be expected to continue to evolve. DENNIS LAMBRIES

A Handbook for South Carolina County Officials. Columbia: South Carolina Association of Counties, 1999.

Hannum, Eleanor. "The Parish in South Carolina, 1706–1868." Master's thesis, University of South Carolina, 1970.

Krane, Dale, Platon N. Rigos, and Melvin B. Hill, Jr. *Home Rule in America A Fifty-State Handbook.* Washington, D.C.: CQ Press, 2001.

Long, John Hamilton, Gordon DenBoer, and Kathryn Ford Thorne. *Atlas of Historical County Boundaries: South Carolina.* New York: Scribner's, 1997.

Stauffer, Michael E. *The Formation of Counties in South Carolina.* Columbia: South Carolina Department of Archives and History, 1994.

Tyer, Charlie B., ed. *South Carolina Government: An Introduction.* Columbia: Institute for Public Service and Policy Research, University of South Carolina, 2002.

Country ideology. Country ideology was a series of ideas expounded in the seventeenth and eighteenth centuries by English writers such as Henry St. John, Viscount Bolinbroke, Thomas Gordon, and John Trenchard. These men opposed the accumulation of power by the British crown at the expense of the House of Commons, the representatives of the people. A fringe element critiquing the existing order, these writers won few adherents in England, yet their work heavily influenced the political culture of colonial America, where colonists perceived themselves on the margins of empire. The effect of country ideology on South Carolina was different and more pervasive than anywhere else in British North America.

At the heart of country ideology was a profound distrust of human nature. Endowed with reason, man deserved the liberty to chart his own destiny, yet he inevitably hurt others in his quest for fulfillment. Government became necessary to protect liberty, but government was composed of imperfect men who could never be trusted to use power selflessly. Furthermore, power tended to accumulate in the hands of a few men and threaten liberty. Thus the representatives of the people should hold the power of the purse and control taxation. As independent men of property and cultivation, representatives acted in the best interests of their constituents and protected them from the expansion of executive authority.

In other colonies country ideology took hold amid factional strife, as public men brandished these ideas against their opponents. In South Carolina, however, country ideology proved an adhesive that united elite leaders. These men shared interests and fears. Amid general prosperity and mutual economic interests, they feared attacks by foreign powers or inland Native American nations and were nervous about the potential rebelliousness of their slave majority. Service in the Commons House of Assembly allowed them to put into practice this ideology, as they struggled against successive governors who, aided by a compliant Royal Council, seemed bent on aggrandizing their power at the expense of liberty. Factional strife potentially played into the governor's hands, for he could build power by playing one faction against another. Representatives in South Carolina, therefore, prided themselves on their independence and never formed permanent alignments, unless they united in resistance to arbitrary power.

This ideology amplified such political controversies as the dispute over Christopher Gadsden's election in 1762, when the assembly defended its prerogatives against executive encroachment. It also lay behind the move toward revolution, as South Carolina's leaders reacted to an outside threat manifested by the British king and Parliament. The influence of country ideology continued into the nineteenth century, when lowcountry and upcountry elites gradually formed common interests and fears that mirrored those of their colonial forebears. Unlike other states, South Carolina did not develop a viable two-party system. Though the state's leaders often disagreed vehemently and competed in hotly contested election campaigns, they disdained permanent parties or factions and instead united against the perceived arbitrary power of a national government that imposed oppressive tariffs and threatened the existence of slavery. GREGORY D. MASSEY

Ford, Lacy K., Jr. *Origins of Southern Radicalism: The South Carolina Upcountry, 1800–1860.* New York: Oxford University Press, 1988.

Weir, Robert M. "'The Harmony We Were Famous For': An Interpretation of Prerevolutionary South Carolina Politics." *William and Mary Quarterly,* 3d ser., 26 (October 1969): 473–501.

Country music. "Country" is the contemporary term for the music of common white folks of the rural South. It evolved over the years from elements of old Protestant hymns, traditional ballads of English and Scottish origins, dance music, African American musical traditions, and material of such composed traditions as designed for the minstrel stage and early-day "Tin-Pan-Alley." Country music as known in modern America began to develop in the early and mid-1920s when it first began to appear on radio stations and phonograph recordings. In addition to rural residents generally, the music seems to have been especially popular among textile workers in the cotton-mill villages. Country song lyrics, with their varying degrees of sadness and sentimentality, touches of rowdiness, reverence, and occasional self-deprecating humor have a way of expressing the thoughts and feelings of ordinary folk in a manner that, while unappealing to the more sophisticated, reaches their souls when other cultural forms do not. Through the years the music has become more complex, more commercial, and more electric, while still managing to retain much of its original character.

Early practitioners of country music in South Carolina included the Bouchillon Trio and Chris Bouchillon, the latter of whom drew much of his music from minstrel traditions and made several recordings for Columbia, most notably "The Talking Blues" in 1926. Early country music featured numerous string bands comprised of fiddle music with rhythm background furnished by guitar, banjo, and sometimes mandolin. Pioneer artists in this field included the Aiken County String Band, who in 1927 cut such tunes as "Carolina Stompdown" and "Harrisburg Itch" for the Okeh label. The duo of Charlie Parker and Mack Woolbright from Union made six sides for Columbia in 1927 that included such sentimental songs as "Grandmother's Old Arm Chair" and the humorous "The Man That Wrote Home Sweet Home Never Was a Married Man." South Carolina–born steel guitarist Jimmie Tarlton, while living in

Columbus, Georgia, recorded many numbers for Columbia beginning in 1927 as half of the duet act of Darby and Tarlton, including the earliest known versions of "Birmingham Jail" and "Columbus Stockade Blues."

While musicians continued to record during the Great Depression, radio programs probably played a more significant role in the dissemination of country-music sounds. Stations of note that broadcast country radio programs in South Carolina included WIS Columbia, WFBC Greenville, and WSPA Spartanburg. Influential stations in neighboring states that had numerous South Carolinians in their listening audience included WBT Charlotte, WPTF Raleigh, WSB Atlanta, and on Saturday nights WSM in Nashville. Among the notable groups heard on these stations were Mainer's Mountaineers, the Dixon Brothers, the Monroe Brothers, Fisher Hendley, Cliff Carlisle, the Blue Sky Boys, Claude Casey's Pine State Playboys, the Briarhoppers, and Byron Parker's Mountaineers (later known as the WIS Hillbillies and finally as the Hired Hands), who made WIS their permanent base after 1937. The banjo-picking comic DeWitt "Snuffy" Jenkins and the fiddler Homer "Pappy" Sherill dominated this group musically. In 1938 the American Record Corporation held recording sessions in Columbia, and in 1938 and 1939 Blue Records conducted similar sessions in Rock Hill, possibly because of disputes with the musicians' union in Charlotte.

In the past half-century country music has continued to be popular in South Carolina, although the state has contributed few performers who have attained national fame. Arthur "Guitar Boogie" Smith of Kershaw County eventually became the dominant figure on the Charlotte scene. One of the major stars of the 1960s, Bill Anderson, spent his early years in the Palmetto State, and two of the more significant figures in bluegrass music, the late vocalist Charlie Moore and the influential banjo picker Don Reno, hailed from the South Carolina Piedmont. The late Carl Story, known as the father of bluegrass gospel music, spent the last quarter-century of his life in Greer, where he did disc-jockey work when not on the road. The gospel pianist and Greenville native Hovie Lister led the Atlanta-based Statesmen Quartet for more than a half-century. Southern gospel groups such as the contemporary Palmetto State Quartet still play a significant role on the sacred-music scene.

Although South Carolina may not have produced as many country stars as neighboring states have, country fans are abundant and many radio stations have adopted country formats. Furthermore, the Myrtle Beach area, as one of the South's major tourist attractions, has increasingly had its share of country music venues. With such theaters and programs as the "Carolina Opry," the Grand Strand is rapidly gaining a name as "Branson East." ABBY GAIL GOODNITE AND IVAN M. TRIBE

Cowpens, Battle of (January 17, 1781). In mid-December 1780 General Daniel Morgan positioned his "Flying Army" on the Pacolet River to threaten the British stronghold of Ninety Six. British general Lord Cornwallis responded by dispatching Lieutenant Colonel Banastre Tarleton to protect Ninety Six and drive Morgan from South Carolina. Learning that Ninety Six was safe, Tarleton moved against Morgan with 1,250 men.

Morgan withdrew and assembled his force on January 16, 1781, at Hannah's Cowpens, a well-known local site situated near the North Carolina border in present-day Cherokee County. When the British reached the battlefield about daybreak on January 17, Morgan, reinforced by militia to about two thousand men, was ready to fight. He deployed more than three hundred North Carolina, South Carolina, and Georgia riflemen skirmishers, which forced Tarleton to deploy. Behind these skirmishers, Colonel Andrew Pickens led one thousand militiamen from the South Carolina upcountry, placing them on the reverse slope and hiding many from British scouts. A third line of Delaware, Maryland, and Virginia Continentals, Virginia State Troops, and militia was to their rear, arranged so as to allow a militia withdrawal without disrupting their ranks. Continental cavalry and militia waited for an opportunity to strike.

British infantry advanced and drove back the skirmishers. Other British infantry deployed and went forward, their flanks covered by dragoons. When the British closed within thirty yards, militia fired at least five battalion volleys. Despite losses, the British charged with bayonets, routing the militia. From this point three separate lines of advance occurred. The British infantry reformed and moved within thirty yards of the Continentals, engaging them in a firefight, and British dragoons advanced on both flanks. On the American left, British dragoons scattered reforming militia. The British, in turn, were repulsed by William Washington's cavalry. On the American right, British Legion dragoons and the Seventy-first Scottish Highlanders advanced, driving off North Carolina skirmishers and then taking position beyond the American right flank. These British dragoons also were repulsed by Washington's cavalry, who charged through them, turned, and charged back.

Outflanked, the American third line commander, John Eager Howard, ordered a right company to turn and oppose the Highlanders. For several reasons the maneuver failed, and a withdrawal commenced with the Highlanders in hot pursuit. One hundred yards upfield, the Americans, who reloaded as they withdrew, turned and fired, so shocking the Highlanders that many collapsed while others ran. They were pursued by American infantry and dragoons who swept the battlefield. Tarleton's infantrymen were virtually all captured, but most British dragoons escaped. Total British casualties were about 800. American casualties were approximately 25 killed and 124 wounded.

The Battle of Cowpens was a turning point in the Revolutionary War. To recapture the prisoners, Cornwallis lightened his army and pursued Morgan and then Greene across North Carolina. This "Race to the Dan" wore out the British. They did win a costly victory at Guilford Courthouse (March 15, 1781), then marched to the coast and on to Virginia, where Cornwallis surrendered to a combined Franco-American army at Yorktown (October 19, 1781). After Guilford Courthouse, Greene returned to South Carolina and defeated British forces in a "War of Posts" during the summer of 1781. Greene's support of partisans, especially Francis Marion and Andrew Pickens, drove the British to the coast by October 1781, effectively ending British domination of interior South Carolina. See plate 11. LAWRENCE E. BABITS

Babits, Lawrence E. *A Devil of a Whipping: The Battle of Cowpens.* Chapel Hill: University of North Carolina Press, 1998.

Fleming, Thomas J. *Cowpens: "Downright Fighting": The Story of Cowpens.* Washington, D.C.: National Park Service, 1988.

Moncure, John. *The Cowpens Staff Ride and Battlefield Tour.* Fort Leavenworth, Kans.: Combat Studies Institute, 1966.

Crafts, William (1787–1826). Legislator, writer, reformer. Crafts was born in Charleston on January 24, 1787, the son of William Crafts and Margaret Tebout. His father, a Boston merchant who moved to Charleston in 1783, achieved considerable wealth. The younger Crafts received a classical education in Charleston and entered Harvard in 1802. He graduated with distinction in 1805, returned to Charleston, and studied law there and at Harvard. He was admitted to the South Carolina Bar in 1809. Crafts achieved no great success or reputation as a lawyer, apparently because he lacked the discipline to attend to the finer details of the law. But he won local prominence as a writer and orator, especially for his speeches on behalf of various reforming causes. In 1807 he joined Stephen Elliott, Thomas Smith Grimké, and others to found the Conversation or Literary Club. Crafts and Hugh Swinton Legaré were the dominant literary figures in the city during the first part of the nineteenth century.

Crafts was elected to the S.C. House of Representatives from St. Philip's and St. Michael's Parishes, serving from 1810 to 1812 and again in 1813, but he failed to achieve one of his cherished goals: election to the U.S. Congress. Crafts's political ambitions were undoubtedly thwarted by his Federalist affiliations and opposition to the War of 1812. Some of his contemporaries blamed an indolent manner and an attachment to unrealistic goals for his failure to achieve greater things. Yet Crafts played a significant role in several reform movements of the early nineteenth century. He helped to expand the rights of Catholics and Jews. In 1813 he gave what many people considered his finest speech in the General Assembly on behalf of a successful fight to prevent the abolition of the new system of free schools. He also supported the campaign to establish the Medical College of South Carolina in Charleston, which opened in 1824.

Crafts was a strong advocate for the education of the hearing- and speech-impaired. Around 1820 his interest in this cause brought him into alliance with key supporters of a state lunatic asylum, men such as Samuel Farrow and James Davis, who had been campaigning for such an institution for several years. In 1821 Crafts was elected to the S.C. Senate, where he would serve for the remainder of his life. Soon after his arrival, he convinced legislators in a moving speech to pass an act authorizing a state lunatic asylum and school for the deaf and dumb. But the funds allotted proved insufficient for both projects. Plans for the school were abandoned, while cost overruns, political squabbling, and delays on the asylum project slowed its opening until 1828.

Crafts, who married his cousin Caroline Homes of Boston in 1823, did not live to see the asylum finished. After a long illness, he died on September 23, 1826, in Lebanon Springs, New York, where he had gone to restore his health. He was buried in the King's Chapel Churchyard in Boston. PETER MCCANDLESS

Bailey, N. Louise, Mary L. Morgan, and Carolyn R. Taylor, eds. *Biographical Directory of the South Carolina Senate, 1776–1985.* 3 vols. Columbia: University of South Carolina Press, 1986.

Crafts, William. *A Selection in Prose and Poetry from the Miscellaneous Writings of William Crafts, to Which Is Prefixed, a Memoir of His Life.* Charleston, S.C.: C. C. Sebring and J. S. Burges, 1828.

McCandless, Peter. *Moonlight, Magnolias, and Madness: Insanity in South Carolina from the Colonial Period to the Progressive Era.* Chapel Hill: University of North Carolina Press, 1996.

Craven, Charles (1682–1754). Governor. Craven was born in England on May 6, 1682. He was a younger son of Sir William Craven, one of the original Lords Proprietors of Carolina, and his wife, Lady Margaret Clapham. Sir William died in 1697, and his eldest son inherited his titles and the proprietary share of Carolina. Charles Craven secured the appointment of deputy governor of Carolina in February 1711 and arrived in the colony in March 1712. He had one of the longest tenures of any proprietary-era governor, and despite political conflict and the outbreak of the Yamassee War in 1715, his was considered one of the most successful terms of office.

Craven worked constructively with a fractious Commons House of Assembly and was able to secure the passage of important legislation. He accomplished this by respecting the privileges and prerogatives of the Commons House instead of quarreling with it over issues of precedent and procedure. In his first message as governor, Craven pledged not to interfere with liberty of conscience, a welcome change from the oppressive Church of England's authority that had been a hallmark of Governor Nathaniel Johnson's term. Among Craven's successes were the reception act of 1712 which established English common and statute law in Carolina, election laws that briefly imposed order on Carolina's chaotic political processes, and legislation to reform Indian trade and to encourage immigration.

Despite his efforts to secure peace with regional Indian tribes, Craven ended up leading the colonists and allied Indian tribes in the first year of the most devastating Indian conflict ever to strike South Carolina. The Yamassee War broke out on April 15, 1715, and for almost a year threatened the survival of the English settlement of Carolina. The Yamassee and other regional tribes, including the Creeks, Catawbas, Shawnee, and others, banded together to drive the Carolinians into the sea. Craven commanded Carolina troops from the outbreak of the war until he departed the colony in April 1716. A fanciful depiction of Craven in battle with the Yamassee appeared in Peter Schenck's encyclopedia, published in the Netherlands in 1716.

Despite his successes as governor and his leadership in the Yamassee War, Craven clashed with the Lords Proprietors. Political enemies in Carolina, Nicholas Trott and Sir William Rhett, reported to the proprietors that Craven had not promoted their interests. In response to Craven's perceived betrayal, the proprietors gave Nicholas Trott extraordinary powers over legislation in the province. A member of the Grand Council and chief justice as well, Trott secured a de facto veto over all legislation. This direct challenge to Craven's authority was one he could not accept. The Commons House supported Craven with resolutions and statements to the proprietors during early 1715, only a month before the outbreak of the Yamassee War. On February 9, 1715, Craven informed the Commons House of his intention to resign and return to England to defend his actions in person. Before he could leave, the Yamassee War broke out and Craven postponed his departure to lead the defense of the province. Political unrest grew in the Commons House in reaction to the proprietors' unwillingness to assist the province during the conflict. On August 24, 1715, the Commons House drafted a petition to King George I, asking that the crown take over the province and extend imperial protection. Craven refused to endorse the petition because it was a direct attack on the proprietors. Despite his refusal, the Commons House sent the petition to England. Craven's loyalty to the proprietors, in the face of their actions against him, was deemed evidence of his character. By April 1716 the war situation was sufficiently stabilized for him to embark for England.

Craven left the province in April 1716 and appointed Robert Daniel to serve during his absence. He never returned to South Carolina. From his arrival in 1712 to his departure in 1716, Craven had sustained a congenial working relationship with the Commons House. The need for cooperation to survive the Yamassee War naturally forced governor and Commons House to put aside political quarrels, but the degree of cooperation had surpassed bare necessity. Political bonds forged among Commons House members revealed that unity of purpose could be achieved in South Carolina. That unity of purpose revealed itself three years later when the province revolted against the Lords Proprietors and established a royal government. Craven died on December 26, 1754, in Berkshire, England. ALEXANDER MOORE

Moore, John Alexander. "Royalizing South Carolina: The Revolution of 1719 and the Evolution of Early South Carolina Government." Ph.D. diss., University of South Carolina, 1991.

Sirmans, M. Eugene. *Colonial South Carolina: A Political History, 1663–1763.* Chapel Hill: University of North Carolina Press, 1966.

Crum, William Demosthenes (1859–1912). Physician, civic leader, political activist. Crum was born on February 9, 1859, the son of Darius Crum, a German American, and Charlotte C. Crum, a free woman of color. He grew up near Orangeburg. In 1875 he graduated from Avery Normal Institute in Charleston, then attended the University of South Carolina and later Howard University, where he earned a medical degree in 1881. Returning to Charleston, he began his practice and later joined the staff of the African American–operated McClennan Hospital and Training School for Nurses. Crum eventually became the hospital's chief administrator and Charleston's most prominent black resident. In 1883 he married Ellen Craft, the daughter of the famous fugitive slave abolitionists William and Ellen Craft of Georgia. Crum also enjoyed close relations with nationally prominent African Americans, such as the Washington, D.C., businessman Whitefield McKinlay and the newspaper editors Harry Smith and T. Thomas Fortune. Crum's most important friendship was with Booker T. Washington, president of Tuskegee Institute in Alabama and sometime political adviser to Republican presidents, who was considered the most influential African American leader in the country. Crum and Washington organized the Negro Department at the 1901–1902 South Carolina Inter-State and West Indian Exposition in Charleston.

Crum was extensively involved in politics, chairing the Charleston County Republican Party for more than two decades and serving as a delegate to party national conventions from 1884 to 1904. During this era of rising disfranchisement, two conflicting trends affected southern Republicanism. African American politicians sought to retain influence through the party machinery and by securing federal patronage. White Republicans, however, tried to strengthen the party by attracting Democrats with jobs and party influence. South Carolina Republicans were deeply divided by this conflict, which worsened because neither President William McKinley nor President Theodore Roosevelt (by 1902) appointed blacks to important positions in the state. Acting on Washington's recommendation, however, Roosevelt nominated Crum as collector of customs for the port of Charleston in late 1902. The action was an attempt to unify the Republican Party in South Carolina, while pacifying African American critics in the state and in the North.

William D. Crum. Courtesy, Avery Research Center for African American History and Culture

Widespread southern opposition to the nomination catapulted Crum into national prominence. Even the *New York Times* and the *New York Herald* criticized the nomination as ill advised. In South Carolina, U.S. Senator Ben Tillman and the editor James C. Hemphill of the Charleston *News and Courier* jointly denounced Crum. Tillman temporarily derailed the nomination, but Roosevelt kept Crum in the position through interim appointments, until his January 1905 confirmation. Stunned by his critics, Roosevelt won praise for his stand among African Americans, for whom Crum's nomination had become a cause célèbre. In 1904 the South Carolina delegation to the Republican national convention was unanimously committed to Roosevelt, and intraparty cooperation prevailed.

Crum continued as collector through Roosevelt's second term but resigned after William Taft became president in 1909. In exchange for his cooperation, Taft appointed Crum as minister to Liberia, a diplomatic post traditionally held by African Americans. He discharged his responsibilities capably during a particularly difficult period in Liberia's history. In the summer of 1912 he contracted an illness and returned to Charleston, where he died on December 7, 1912. BERNARD E. POWERS, JR.

Gatewood, Willard B. "Theodore Roosevelt and Southern Republicans: The Case of South Carolina, 1901–1904." *South Carolina Historical Magazine* 70 (October 1969): 251–66.

———. "William D. Crum: A Negro in Politics." *Journal of Negro History* 53 (October 1968): 301–20.

Padgett, James A. "Ministers to Liberia and Their Diplomacy." *Journal of Negro History* 22 (January 1937): 50–92.

Scheiner, Seth M. "President Theodore Roosevelt and the Negro, 1901–1908." *Journal of Negro History* 47 (July 1962): 169–82.

Culp, Napoleon Brown (b. 1929). Musician. "Nappy" Brown was born Napoleon Brown Culp in Charlotte, North Carolina, on October 12, 1929. A powerful singer and sometimes outrageous performer, Brown became identified as a South Carolina artist after settling in the Columbia area in the late 1960s. He is best known, however, for the popular recordings he made while living in Newark, New Jersey, during the 1950s heyday of rhythm and blues. Brown got his start in gospel music in the 1940s as a member of the Golden Bells, Selah Jubilee Singers, and Heavenly Lights. After turning to rhythm and blues in the mid-1950s, he became a mainstay at Savoy Records, recording the national hits "Don't Be Angry," "Pitter Patter," and "It Don't Hurt No More." Brown's intense, shouting rhythm-and-blues vocal style remained rooted in gospel but was also distinguished by his unusual rolling of consonants. A prison term reportedly sidetracked Brown for much of the 1960s, and he returned to the gospel field in the 1970s, recording an album for Savoy as Napoleon Brown and the Southern Sisters. Drawing on his signature vocal style, uninhibited stage antics, and penchant for licentious lyrics, Brown changed directions once again to become a fixture on the contemporary blues scene during the 1980s and 1990s, cutting albums for various labels including Landslide, Alligator, Black Top, Ichiban, and New Moon. DAVID NELSON

Santelli, Robert. *The Big Book of Blues.* New York: Penguin, 1993.

Cunningham, Ann Pamela (1816–1875). Preservationist. Born on the Rosemont plantation in Laurens District on August 15, 1816, Cunningham was the daughter of the upcountry planter Robert Cunningham and Louisa Byrd of Virginia. As a young girl Cunningham was educated by a governess, and she later attended the South Carolina Female Institute at Barhamville. She distinguished herself with her riding ability and keen intelligence. At age seventeen Cunningham was thrown from her horse, an accident that permanently injured her spine and left her an invalid. She was sent north by her parents in hopes of receiving better medical care.

On returning to South Carolina after a summer visit with her daughter in Philadelphia, Louisa Byrd Cunningham observed the dilapidated state of George Washington's home at Mount Vernon. From her sickbed Ann Pamela Cunningham immediately penned an appeal to the "Ladies of the South!" to raise funds to purchase and renovate Mount Vernon. The *Charleston Mercury* printed the letter, and soon thereafter a meeting to raise funds was held in Laurens County. Women in the North and the South formed "Mount Vernon Associations," and in 1856 the Virginia legislature granted a charter to the Mount Vernon Ladies' Association of the Union, with Ann Pamela Cunningham as its first regent. After much negotiating, John Augustine Washington, Jr., great-grandnephew of George Washington and then owner of Mount Vernon, agreed to sell the property to the organization, contingent on their success in raising $200,000. The money was raised, and in 1860 Washington relinquished the property to the association. Throughout her life Cunningham maintained that Washington's house and grounds must be "preserved with sacred reverence . . . in the state that he left them."

Family obligations and ill health kept Cunningham in South Carolina throughout the duration of the Civil War. She returned to Mount Vernon in 1866, but her declining health and increasing use of laudanum led the board to doubt her ability to preside. In 1872 the Board of Vice-Regents asked Cunningham to "refrain from all interference with the administration of finances and the management of the estate." At its next meeting, Cunningham announced her intent to retire as regent. Unable to attend the Grand Council's meeting of 1874, Cunningham sent a farewell address, which declared, "Ladies, the home of Washington is in your charge. . . . Let one spot in this grand country of ours be saved from 'change'! Upon you rests this duty." Her address has been read at the openings of the annual meetings of the Mount Vernon Ladies' Association every year since 1907. Just as Cunningham envisioned, the Mount Vernon Ladies' Association remains governed by a board of regents comprised solely of women. In one of the most successful historic preservation programs in the country, Mount Vernon is maintained solely by funding from sales and from private donations and is the only historic site in the country that is open to the public 365 days of the year. Cunningham died on May 1, 1875, at Rosemont and was buried at the First Presbyterian Church in Columbia. COURTNEY L. TOLLISON

Ann Pamela Cunningham. Courtesy, South Caroliniana Library, University of South Carolina

Alexander, Edward P. *Museum Masters: Their Museums and Their Influence.* Nashville, Tenn.: American Association for State and Local History, 1983.

King, Grace. *Mount Vernon on the Potomac: History of the Mount Vernon Ladies' Association of the Union.* New York: Macmillan, 1929.

Thane, Elswyth. *Mount Vernon Is Ours: The Story of Its Preservation.* New York: Duell, Sloan, and Pearce, 1966.

Cunningham, Frank Harrison (1880–1928) and Joseph Gilbert Cunningham (1882–1969). Architects. The Cunningham brothers were prolific architects in the upstate from 1907 into the 1950s. Among the hundreds of projects they designed, the Imperial Hotel in Greenville (1911) and Easley High School Auditorium (1909) are listed in the National Register of Historic Places. Their Greenville Memorial Auditorium (1940–1957) was a significant Greenville landmark until its demolition in the late 1990s.

Frank and Joseph Cunningham were born in Greenville (Frank on March 3, 1880, and Joseph on July 19, 1882). Both graduated from Clemson College in 1903 with degrees in textile engineering. While Clemson did not have a program in architecture at the time, Rudolph E. Lee taught engineering drafting and structural design as early as 1902. The Cunninghams worked for a time with the noted textile architect and engineer J. E. Sirrine. By 1909 they were practicing as engineers and architects in Greenville. They worked together until Frank's death on November 26, 1928. Joseph retired about 1960 and died on January 19, 1969.

The Cunninghams designed dozens of residences, commercial buildings, schools, and churches. While most residences and commercial buildings were in Greenville, they designed schools across the state, including in Orangeburg, Pendleton, St. Matthews, Woodruff, Paris, Prosperity, Bush River in Newberry County, Tumbling Shoals, Pickens, Jonesville, and Travelers Rest.

The buildings designed by the Cunninghams were generally utilitarian and lack significant stylistic flourishes. They were among the first to integrate newly available steel construction with traditional brick bearing wall construction, with the Easley High School Auditorium using light steel trusses with massive rivet plates. The Imperial Hotel in Greenville continued the approach and has a steel skeleton frame carrying much of the load of the floors, but the walls are load-bearing masonry, not fully integrated with the skeleton frame. ROBERT W. BAINBRIDGE

Bainbridge, Robert W. "Rudolph E. Lee and Architecture at Clemson." In *Campus Preservation and Clemson Historic Resources.* Clemson, S.C.: Clemson University College of Architecture, Arts and Humanities, Department of Planning and Landscape Architecture, 1995.

Wells, John E., and Robert E. Dalton. *The South Carolina Architects 1885–1935: A Biographical Directory.* Richmond, Va.: New South Architectural Press, 1992.

Cunningham, William (?–1787). Soldier. By the end of the Revolutionary War, the Tory partisan William Cunningham had gained an unenviable reputation in South Carolina and the epithet "Bloody Bill." A cousin of the upcountry Loyalist brothers Robert and Patrick Cunningham, William first appeared in South Carolina in the 1760s. At the outset of the Revolution, Cunningham sided with the patriots and served in the militia force that marched on the frontier post of Fort Charlotte in 1775 and in the Cherokee expedition of 1776. According to legend, Cunningham developed a relentless animosity for all patriots in 1778 after the murder of his invalid brother by backcountry Whigs.

When the British gained control of South Carolina in mid-1780, Cunningham enlisted in the provincial militia forces under the British major Patrick Ferguson. After the evacuation of Ninety Six by the British the following summer, Cunningham mustered a company of some forty men and, from a base camp in the Blue Ridge Mountains, led them on forays into the South Carolina backcountry. Rewarded with a promotion to major, Cunningham filled the ranks of his unit to some three hundred strong and set out in late autumn 1781 on an expedition that would become known as the "Bloody Scout."

Advancing to the upcountry from Charleston, Cunningham's main force overtook and attacked a small party of thirty militia under the command of Captain Sterling Turner at Cloud's Creek on November 17, 1781. Cunningham ordered that no quarter be given after learning that Turner's force was responsible for the death of a Tory captain. After defeating Turner, Cunningham pressed on to attack a small post commanded by Colonel Joseph Hayes on the Little River only two days later. Hayes, with a handful of defenders, offered a stubborn resistance but was eventually forced to surrender. Cunningham apprehended Hayes, who reportedly still possessed a proposal of humane treatment from Cunningham in his hand, and hanged him and his executive officer. When the pole they were using as gallows broke, the Loyalists were said to have hacked Hayes and Williams to death with swords and then to have killed twelve more of the prisoners.

Cunningham began a retreat toward Charleston after learning that elements of militia forces led by Andrew Pickens and Thomas Sumter were converging on him. Retreating into the swamps near Orangeburg, Cunningham managed to elude the patriots and return to Charleston. He continued to lead raids into the South Carolina interior throughout 1782 but fled to the safety of East Florida shortly before the British evacuated Charleston in December. Still, reports of "Bloody Bill" leading incursions continued to circulate, and in 1783 the General Assembly enacted legislation intended to capture him and other "notorious offenders who disturb the peace." Spanish authorities expelled Cunningham from East Florida in 1785, claiming that he was involved in looting along the St. Mary's River. He died in Nassau, Bahamas, on January 18, 1787. SAMUEL K. FORE

Lambert, Robert Stansbury. *South Carolina Loyalists in the American Revolution.* Columbia: University of South Carolina Press, 1987.

Lumpkin, Henry. *From Savannah to Yorktown: The American Revolution in the South.* Columbia: University of South Carolina Press, 1981.

Siebert, Wilbur H. *Loyalists in East Florida, 1774 to 1785: The Most Important Documents Pertaining Thereto, Edited with an Accompanying Narrative.* 2 vols. DeLand: Florida State Historical Society, 1929.

Dabbs, Edith Mitchell (1906–1991). Author, churchwoman, community activist. Edith Dabbs was born in Dalzell (Sumter County) on November 10, 1906, the daughter of Vermelle Wells and John Hampton Mitchell. Growing up in Greenville, she attended Six Mile Academy and Greenville Women's College (later Furman University). She graduated from Coker College in 1927 with a B.A. in English and Latin, and she then taught high school English and French for five years. In 1935 she married her former Coker English professor, the author James McBride Dabbs, whose first wife had died two years before, leaving him with two daughters. Edith and James had three children of their own, and in 1937 they moved back to his family home, Rip Raps Plantation, in Mayesville (Sumter County), where he farmed and wrote and she became engaged in a variety of community activities.

Through the 1940s and 1950s Edith Dabbs was active in the work of the United Church Women (an ecumenical Christian organization that changed its name in 1966 to Church Women United), serving two terms as South Carolina state president from 1951 to 1955, during which time the state council grew from half a dozen white women to ten city councils and an integrated annual gathering of two hundred church people. She would write later that "this was the first statewide integrated organization" in South Carolina except for the South Carolina Council on Human Relations (of which she was a life member of the board of directors). She also served for many years on the United Church Women's national Public Relations Committee. Working in affiliation with the Associated Press, United Press International, and Religious News Service, she initiated weekly religious news-interview programs in several cities and wrote hundreds of scripts for radio and television spots.

In the 1960s Edith Dabbs developed an interest in the historic Penn School on St. Helena Island, precursor to the community action agency Penn Community Services, which James Dabbs headed as chairman of the board of trustees. While she was collecting islander stories in the preparation of her 1970 book *Walking Tall,* she discovered a cache of old photographs and negatives that led her to publish *Face of an Island* (1970). After James Dabbs's death in 1970, Edith's growing interest in the island and its people led to her receiving research grants from the Field Foundation (1972) and the Ford Foundation (1974–1975) and eventually to her publication of *Sea Island Diary: A History of St. Helena Island* (1983).

In 1977 Dabbs received an honorary doctor of humanities degree from Francis Marion College, and in 1978 she received the Valiant Woman Award from Church Women United. She was also named a life member of the board of directors of the Southern Regional Council, an Atlanta-based human rights organization of which James McBride Dabbs had served as president in the 1960s. Edith Dabbs died at Rip Raps Plantation on February 28, 1991, and was buried at Salem Black River Presbyterian Church in Mayesville.
ELIZABETH JACOWAY

Dabbs, Edith M. Interview by Elizabeth Jacoway. Tape recording, October 4, 1975. Southern Oral History Program, Southern Historical Collection, University of North Carolina, Chapel Hill.

———. *Sea Island Diary: A History of St. Helena Island.* Spartanburg, S.C.: Reprint Co., 1983.

Dabbs, James McBride (1896–1970). Writer, teacher, theologian, civil rights leader. Dabbs was perhaps South Carolina's most distinguished resident essayist of the twentieth century. Born on May 8, 1896, in the Salem community of eastern Sumter County, Dabbs was the son of the farmer Eugene Whitefield Dabbs and Alice Maude McBride. After receiving his private education in the one-room rural Salem School, Dabbs went on to graduate from the University of South Carolina (USC) as one of the top students in the class of 1916. Between 1913 and 1916 he filled pages of the college's literary magazine with his poems, short stories, and prose sketches. In 1917 he earned a master's degree in psychology from Clark University in Worcester, Massachusetts, and then served as a field artillery officer in the U.S. Army (1917–1919). On May 11, 1918, Dabbs married Barnwell native Jessie Clyde Armstrong. The marriage produced two daughters.

After teaching in North Carolina from 1919 to 1920, Dabbs returned to USC to teach English. In 1924 he became professor of English at Coker College in Hartsville, where he served as head of the department from 1925 to 1937. He retired in 1942 as a part-time faculty member, commuting from Rip Raps Plantation, his ancestral farm in east Sumter County. Following the death of Jessie Dabbs in 1933, Dabbs married Edith Mitchell on June 11, 1935. They had three children.

Moving to Rip Raps in 1937, Dabbs established a dual pattern of writing and farming that would last the rest of his life. He had begun to establish his reputation as a master of formal and informal essays in the early 1930s, when he began publishing in some of the country's leading journals and rubbing literary shoulders with such writers as Ernest Hemingway, Robert Frost, and Robert Penn Warren. Although Dabbs was not one of the twelve contributors to the famous 1930 volume *I'll Take My Stand,* he addressed early on many of the same themes and issues about which the Southern Agrarians wrote: the distinctiveness of the South, the mixed blessings of industrialization, education, the African American presence and identity, and southern religion. But he "out-Agrarianed" the Agrarians in one respect: he moved back to the farm. The Sumter artist Elizabeth White, his friend, spoke of Dabbs as "a man of letters and of lettuce."

In the 1940s Dabbs began to identify and address the issue of race relations and the inequities experienced by black southerners. At the end of 1946 he wrote a pamphlet entitled *When Justice and Expediency Meet,* in which he stated unequivocally that "both justice and expediency indicate that the Negro should be permitted to vote in the Democratic primary in South Carolina." By April 1947 he had assumed the chairmanship of the South Carolina Division of the Southern Regional Council, and in 1948 he was a delegate to the Charlottesville Declaratory Conference on Civil Rights, which met to approve "a declaration calling for an end to racial segregation and discrimination."

During the 1950s and 1960s Dabbs attended innumerable conferences as a speaker or resource person on matters of racial equity, human relations, and social justice. He wrote frequent letters to newspaper editors expressing his view that racial segregation was variously unjust, tragic, nonsensical, hypocritical, impractical, discourteous, silly, and un-American. From 1958 to 1964 he served as president of the Southern Regional Council, the Atlanta-based interracial organization that focused on bringing about positive social and political change in the South. Martin Luther King, Jr., in his 1963 "Letter from Birmingham Jail," included Dabbs among the half dozen "white brothers in the South [who] have grasped the meaning of this social revolution and committed themselves to it."

Dabbs was also one of the South's principal twentieth-century Christian churchmen and theologians, although he never claimed this distinction for himself. He certainly was the chief lay theologian of his denomination, the Presbyterian Church of the United States. For more than thirty years he contributed essays and articles to such journals as *Christendom,* the *Christian Century,* and *Presbyterian Outlook.* He served for years on his denomination's advisory Committee on Christian Action and Permanent Committee on Christian Relations. As a member of these two committees he drafted one of the Presbyterian Church's most eloquent theological pronouncements on social justice, "Justice, Law, and Order," which was officially adopted by the General Assembly of his church in 1969. He summed up a lifetime of views on Christian faith, practice, and churchmanship in *Haunted by God.* Published posthumously in 1972, the book focused primarily on the religious significance of southern culture. Despite the presence of evil in southern life and culture, "evils almost beyond compare," he insisted that "somehow we've never ceased being haunted by God."

In addition to *Haunted by God,* Dabbs wrote an autobiography, *The Road Home* (1960), and three other books. *The Southern Heritage* (1958), a history of race relations in the South, won the 1959 National Brotherhood Media Award. In *Who Speaks for the South?* (1964) Dabbs analyzed southern character, and the book was hailed as "the most perceptive book about the South and the southern mind and southern history since W. J. Cash's . . . *The Mind of the South* (1941)." In *Civil Rights in Recent Southern Fiction* (1969) Dabbs linked fiction with African Americans in general and with the civil rights movement in particular. Around the themes of tragedy and loneliness are centered most of the others, he observed, and all of them "are tied up with the relation of blacks and whites. This is the core problem of Southern life."

The southern literary critic and historian Fred Hobson has written that James McBride Dabbs was "not only one of the most committed and compassionate interpreters of the South but also one of the most astute. . . . He is a Southerner to be read and heeded, both for what he suggests about the South and what he suggests about himself." Dabbs died at Rip Raps on May 30, 1970, and was buried at Salem Black River Presbyterian "Brick" Church. THOMAS L. JOHNSON

Johnson, Thomas L. *A Day in May.* Hartsville, S.C.: Coker College, 1996.

———. "James McBride Dabbs: A Life Story." Ph.D. diss., University of South Carolina, 1980.

Dacus, Ida Jane (1875–1964). Librarian. Dacus (pronounced "Day-cus") was born on September 9, 1875, in Williamston, Anderson County, the first of four children of John Arving Dacus and Sara Elizabeth Hogg. She attended Williamston Female Academy (later Lander College) before entering Winthrop Normal and Industrial College in Rock Hill in 1896, the year classes began at the college. At Winthrop, Dacus was one of three scholarship girls assigned to care for the school's meager library, which consisted of two hundred books and a study hall. At the end of her junior year she was asked to take over the library full-time. She was appointed at a salary of $20 per month plus board.

In 1901 Dacus took a nationwide competitive exam and won a scholarship to Drexel Institute in Philadelphia to study library science. The following year she received her certificate along with fifteen others and became the first professionally trained librarian in South Carolina and one of the first in the entire South. Dacus returned as head librarian to Winthrop, where she worked until her retirement in 1945. When she began as head librarian, the holdings numbered 5,184 books and 5,000 volumes of government publications. The Carnegie Foundation in 1905 pledged $20,000 to build a college library but in January 1906 increased the sum to $30,000 plus 500 books if the new library would offer library methods and act as a training school. The new library opened the following June.

As librarian, Dacus had the task of approving "everything from basic design to window sashes" and also of carrying out the pledge of supporting library education. In 1907 she inaugurated two classes in library science, the first in reference (required of all freshmen) and a second in elementary library methods for schoolteachers. Her work was so respected that instructors of library methods from around the county began using her courses at their institutions. Library methods courses, a rarity in 1907, had become the norm by the late 1920s. As late as the 1960s Winthrop still offered an undergraduate library science degree.

Dacus was an active professional and regularly attended meetings of the S.C. Teachers' Association, the National Education Association, and the American Library Association. "Miss Ida," as she was known to Winthrop scholars, endeared herself to her students. She shared her love of flowers and growing things, and created "Miss Dacus Garden," which was one of the loveliest spots on the campus.

Dacus retired in 1945 at age seventy. In her retirement she supervised operations of her Williamston home place, a three-hundred-acre cotton farm, and found time for extensive gardening, apron making, and quilt collecting. On May 30, 1959, she was presented with Winthrop College's Mary Mildred Sullivan Medallion, its highest alumna award, for her "outstanding service to mankind." Following a short illness, Dacus died on October 18, 1964, and was buried in the Williamston Cemetery. In 1969 Winthrop dedicated its new library to Dacus. The Dacus Library stands in front of the Winthrop Training School, testifying to the pioneering librarian who devoted her life to furthering education in South Carolina through libraries and library education. CAROLYN SUNG

Dacus, Ida Jane. Clippings File. Dacus Library, Winthrop University, Rock Hill.

Grier, Ralph E., ed. *South Carolina and Her Builders.* Columbia, S.C.: Carolina Biographical Association, 1930.

Obituary. *Anderson Independent,* October 19, 1964, p. 6.

Daise, Ron (b. 1956) and Natalie Daise (b. 1960). Educators, entertainers. Well known for bringing Gullah culture to national and international television audiences, Ron and Natalie Daise have spent the last two decades researching, performing, and publishing information about the dynamic history of lowcountry African Americans. Born in the Cedar Grove community of St. Helena Island on January 29, 1956, Ron Daise grew up singing at home, at school, and in church choirs. After earning a B.A. in mass media arts from Hampton Institute in Virginia, Daise returned home to explore the Gullah culture of his youth. As the first African American reporter for the *Beaufort Gazette,* Daise had the opportunity to talk to many elderly Sea Island residents about the history of the Gullah community. This wealth of information formed the basis for his 1986 book, *Reminiscences of Sea Island Heritage.*

Ron Daise and Natalie Daise, his wife since 1985, have tirelessly performed the program *Sea Island Montage,* a multimedia theater performance that combines photographs, storytelling, song, and dance. Natalie, a native of Rochester, New York, was born on November 11, 1960, into a musical family. In 1994 the Daises launched the children's television program *Gullah Gullah Island,* which aired on the Nick Jr. cable television network through 1997. Several other projects followed, including the music production *Sweet Surprises.* Completed in 2000, *Sweet Surprises* features original love songs written and performed by Ron Daise. In the same year Natalie Daise opened Miss Natalie's Workshop. Located on St. Helena Island, the shop features handcrafted Gullah gifts and arts and crafts workshops. In addition, the Daises have numerous children's books and audio and video productions to their credit. Strong advocates for the importance of recognizing Gullah language and culture, the Daises have ensured that people around the world are familiar with the Gullah history tied to the South Carolina Sea Islands. They reside in Beaufort with their two children. SADDLER TAYLOR

Daise, Ronald. *Little Muddy Waters: A Gullah Folk Tale.* Beaufort, S.C.: G.O.G. Enterprises, 1997.

———. *Reminiscences of Sea Island Heritage.* Orangeburg, S.C.: Sandlapper, 1986.

Dale, Thomas (ca. 1700–1750). Physician, author, entrepreneur. Dale was born in Hoxton, England, into a family of pharmacists. He learned medicine from his father, Francis Dale, and pharmaceutical botany from his uncle, Samuel Dale of Braintree, one of Britain's premier plant men. His medical education was completed in the Netherlands at Leiden, where he earned an M.D. in 1723. Dale attempted to establish a practice in London, specializing in urinary and reproductive tract disorders, but found the city glutted with doctors. He supported himself by translating Latin medical treatises into English for London booksellers. Dale's London career collapsed in 1732 with his marriage to an older woman, Marie, with a lurid reputation.

Dale and his wife abandoned London for South Carolina, arriving in March 1732. He came just as yellow fever began spreading through the city, and his services were put to use immediately. In August, Dale's wife died of the fever. Once more a bachelor, on March 28, 1733, he entered the elite circle of colonial society through a marriage to Mary Brewton, daughter of Colonel Miles Brewton (ca. 1675–1745), a successful goldsmith and powder receiver of the colony, and patriarch of a family rapidly ascending in Charleston society. Advocate General Charles Pinckney brokered the match. Mary Dale died in 1737, and Dale would subsequently marry two more times: in 1738 to Anne Smith (d. 1743) and in 1743 to Hannah Simons (d. 1751). Dale's marriages produced five children.

To the merchants and planters of Charleston, Dale appeared as an embodiment of the virtues of civility: he was learned, witty, and sociable. A regular communicant of the Anglican Church, he was respectably religious. Yet he promoted worldly arts, such as the theater, providing prologues for the first professional theater productions in the city. Having tasted failure in the metropolis, Dale managed his affairs in Charleston to insure his triumph in Carolina. He destroyed the reputation of his rival pharmacist in the colony, James Kilpatrick, in a literary paper war over Kilpatrick's treatment of smallpox. He applied his pharmaceutical knowledge to the manufacture of gin flavoring and became a successful distiller. He undertook special medical services for the colony, treating the queen of the Catawbas. He contributed greatly to the establishment of the colony's first insurance scheme and the formation of the Charleston Library Society. His ability and trustworthiness were such that in 1734 Governor Robert Johnson appointed him a judge, despite Dale's lack of formal legal training. He retained his seat on the bench until his death. He was elected to a term in the Commons House of Assembly in 1749.

Throughout his life Dale regarded himself as a participant in the transatlantic republic of letters. He corresponded with and sent specimens to naturalists in England and the European continent, particularly Johan Frederic Gronovius of Leiden. He knew many of the London booksellers personally, imported quantities of the latest imprints, and served at times as the Carolina agent for major literary projects, such as Bayle's *Encyclopedia.* He supplied essays for the *South-Carolina Gazette* under several pseudonyms. He occasionally sent poems and essays overseas to his friend Thomas Birch, the historian, for publication in metropolitan periodicals. It is for his poems, his writings, and his witty letters to Thomas Birch that Dale is best known today. Dale died in Charleston on September 16, 1750. His son Thomas Simmons Dale later became a significant physician in Britain. DAVID S. SHIELDS

Edgar, Walter, and N. Louise Bailey, eds. *Biographical Directory of the South Carolina House of Representatives.* Vol. 2, *The Commons House of Assembly, 1692–1775.* Columbia: University of South Carolina Press, 1977.

Shields, David S. *Civil Tongues and Polite Letters in British America.* Chapel Hill: University of North Carolina Press, 1997.

Daniel, Beth (b. 1956). Professional golfer. Daniel was born on October 14, 1956, in Charleston, the daughter of Robert and Lucia Daniel. She first drew national attention in 1975 while a student at Furman University (from which she graduated in 1978), winning the United States Women's Amateur golf championship in her first appearance. She repeated that accomplishment in 1977, and in 1976 and 1978 she represented the United States on the Curtis Cup team, which competes against an amateur squad from Great Britain and Ireland.

In 1979 Daniel turned professional and earned her first win on the Ladies Professional Golf Association (LPGA) tour at the Patty Berg Classic. She was named Rookie of the Year. Her four victories the following year brought Player of the Year honors, an award she received again in 1990 and 1994. In 1990 she recorded a career-high seven first-place finishes, including the LPGA Championship. She was recognized by United Press International (UPI) as their female Athlete of the Year and by a resolution from the South Carolina General Assembly. Daniel's victories stretched across four decades, including seventeen wins in the 1980s, fourteen in the 1990s, and one in 2003.

Daniel has received many awards for her golfing prowess, including being selected as only the sixteenth member of the prestigious LPGA Hall of Fame in 1999. In 1995 Daniel was inducted into the South Carolina Golf Hall of Fame, and in 2000 she entered the World Golf Hall of Fame. Daniel represented the United States six times in the Solheim Cup competition against teams of top European golfers. She also earned the Vare Trophy for lowest scoring average three times (1989, 1990, and 1994). NANCY G. ROSOFF

Johnson, Anne Janette. *Great Women in Sports.* Detroit: Visible Ink, 1996.
"L.P.G.A. Hall of Fame Adds Alcott and Daniel." *New York Times,* February 10, 1999, p. D8.

Daniel, Charles Ezra (1895–1964). Businessman, U.S. senator. Daniel was born in Elberton, Georgia, on November 11, 1895, the eldest son of James Fleming Daniel, a millwright, and Leila Mildred Adams. Daniel was to become twentieth-century South Carolina's most successful businessman and one of its most influential political figures.

Daniel moved with his family to Anderson, South Carolina, in 1900. He learned the construction trade while working in his father's millwright operation. In Anderson, Daniel attended school and worked a summer job at Townsend Lumber Company. He earned a scholarship to the Citadel, where he spent two years before the onset of World War I. In 1917 Daniel volunteered for service and went to France as an infantry officer. In 1919 Daniel returned to Anderson and began building mill village houses. He earned a reputation for quality production and gradually worked his way into more complex projects. On November 25, 1924, he married Homozel "Mickey" Mickel.

Daniel pushed ahead even during the Great Depression. Ironically, given his later reputation as a staunch conservative, earnings from New Deal construction projects enabled him to establish his own firm, Daniel Construction Company, in 1934. During World War II, Daniel obtained numerous defense contracts for construction of aluminum plants, shipyards, and air bases throughout the South. Daniel moved to Greenville in 1942 when his firm constructed Donaldson Air Base south of the city. In 1942 Daniel and Roger Milliken built the DeFore Plant in Clemson to produce military tire cord. This single-story, windowless, air-conditioned mill revolutionized textile plant design.

After the war Daniel defined the art of industrial recruiting. Daniel Construction built plants for such firms as Celanese, DuPont, Milliken, Monsanto, J. P. Stevens, and Textron. During his lifetime Daniel's company built 250 manufacturing plants in South Carolina alone. Daniel also moved into paper mill and power plant construction and expanded operations into the Gulf Coast, the Midwest, the Caribbean, and Europe. To further attract industry, Daniel helped establish the State Development Board in 1945. Believing that South Carolina's key industrial advantage was a union-free workforce, Daniel backed the state's 1954 right-to-work law.

In politics, Daniel grew increasingly disillusioned with the national Democratic Party, especially its support for organized labor. A Dixiecrat in 1948, Daniel campaigned openly for Republican presidential candidates from 1952 until his death. In 1954, on the death of U.S. Senator Burnet R. Maybank, Governor James F. Byrnes appointed Daniel to complete Maybank's term. Daniel took office on November 8, 1954, but resigned his seat on December 24 in favor of senator-elect Strom Thurmond, the winner of a celebrated write-in campaign.

Daniel realized early on that South Carolina's racially segregated society was an impediment to progress. He addressed the issue in his "Watermelon Speech" in Hampton on July 1, 1961. Here Daniel suggested that South Carolinians "forsake some of their old ways" to improve opportunities for both blacks and whites.

On June 29, 1964, state and local officials broke ground for the Daniel Building, a twenty-five-story office building in downtown Greenville. Charles Daniel, however, did not live to see its completion. He died of lung cancer in Greenville on September 13, 1964. JAMES A. DUNLAP III

Canup, Claude R., and William D. Workman, Jr. *Charles E. Daniel: His Philosophy and Legacy.* Columbia, S.C.: R. L. Bryan, 1981.
Dunlap, James A., III. "Changing Symbols of Success: Economic Development in Twentieth Century Greenville, South Carolina." Ph.D. diss., University of South Carolina, 1994.
Lunan, Bert, and Robert A. Pierce. *Legacy of Leadership.* Columbia: South Carolina Business Hall of Fame, 1999.

Daniel, William Henry (1841–1915). Farmer, businessman, tobacco pioneer. Born in North Carolina on March 1, 1841, "Buck" Daniel was a teamster in his family's freight business in the Cape Fear region of that state. He joined the Confederate army in 1861, served in Virginia, and ended the war a prisoner in Elmira, New York. After the war Daniel came to South Carolina and settled in Marion County near Nichols. For several years he worked with James Battle in the naval stores business under the name of Battle and Daniel. In 1874 Daniel moved a few miles west to a new station stop—Mullins—on the Wilmington, Columbia, and Augusta Railroad. There Daniel founded a general mercantile business called W. H. Daniel Supply Company.

As prices for cotton and naval stores declined in the 1880s, local farmers were seeking a new cash crop. By the 1890s farmers in nearby Florence and Darlington Counties were successfully growing bright leaf tobacco. In 1894 Daniel raised eight acres of Bright Leaf and shipped his curings to a Danville, Virginia, market. Pleased with his profits, Daniel encouraged Marion County farmers to plant the new staple. To promote tobacco culture, Daniel enlisted experienced leaf growers from North Carolina as "instructors." In 1895 Daniel led a group of investors to build Planter's Warehouse, establishing Mullins as a tobacco market. Mullins soon became the state's leading leaf market, its population tripling within five years. Daniel also led in the founding of the Bank of Mullins, the town's first bank, in 1899. Daniel died in Mullins on October 24, 1915. He was buried in Cederdale Cemetery, Mullins. ELDRED E. PRINCE, JR.

Prince, Eldred E., Jr., and Robert R. Simpson. *Long Green: The Rise and Fall of Tobacco in South Carolina.* Athens: University of Georgia Press, 2000.
Sass, Herbert Ravenel. *The Story of the South Carolina Lowcountry.* West Columbia, S.C.: J. F. Hyer, 1956.

Daniels, David Carlton (b. 1966). Countertenor. A native of Spartanburg, Daniels was born on March 12, 1966, the son of Perry and Phyllis Daniels, two former voice teachers at Converse College. In addition to studying voice with his mother, he took piano and cello lessons. At age eleven Daniels performed the boy-soprano role of Elijah under Robert Shaw at the Brevard Music Center. During his senior year at Spartanburg High School, he won the Music Teachers National Association competition.

After attending Cincinnati's College-Conservatory of Music on scholarship, Daniels (then a tenor) received a master's degree from the University of Michigan, where he studied with George Shirley. Near the end of his graduate program in 1992, Daniels declared himself a countertenor, a voice type most often associated with the castrati of the eighteenth century, although his sound is atypical of the modern countertenor's male falsetto. His breakthrough came in 1994 when he was cast as a mezzo-soprano (Nerone) in Monteverdi's *L'Incoronazione di Poppea* at the Glimmerglass Opera Festival at Cooperstown, New York.

In 1999 Daniels made his Metropolitan Opera debut as Sesto in Handel's *Giulio Cesare.* He has appeared with numerous companies, such as the New York City Opera, the Glimmerglass Opera, the San Francisco Opera, Boston's Lyric Opera and Handel and Haydn Societies, the English National Opera, the Royal Opera, the Glyndebourne Festival, and the Bavarian State Opera. Daniels has also received critical acclaim for his impressive recital repertoire of French song literature from the nineteenth and twentieth centuries, performing in places such as New York, London, Munich, Paris, and Edinburgh.

Daniels was nominated for a Grammy Award in 1999 for his recording of Handel arias. Other notable honors include the 1997 Richard Tucker Award, *Musical America*'s Vocalist of the Year for 1999, and *BBC Music Magazine*'s 2000 Male Singer of the Year. He resides in Silver Spring, Maryland. JENNIFER OTTERVIK

Milnes, Rodney. "People: David Daniels." *Opera* 49 (October 1998): 1154–60.

Waleson, Heidi. "The New Countertenors." *Early Music America* 6 (spring 2000): 18–25, 46.

Dark Corner. Since early in the nineteenth century, extreme northeastern Greenville County, especially the remote, rugged environs of Glassy and Hogback Mountains, has been known as the "Dark Corner." Although opened to settlement following the Revolutionary War, the area remained sparsely populated well into the twentieth century. Its antebellum inhabitants were subsistence farmers who gained a reputation at the county seat for being poor, uneducated, prone to violence, and fiercely independent. They were staunch Unionists during the nullification and secession crises and on the outbreak of civil war were slow to support the Confederacy. "Few Dark Corner men . . . have volunteered," a Greenvillian wrote in August 1861. "It is to be hoped that some light will yet break upon their darkness."

The isolated hills and hollows of Dark Corner were a haven for Confederate deserters during the war and in succeeding decades for countless illicit whiskey distillers. For many cash-strapped mountaineers, the financial rewards from making and marketing untaxed moonshine far outweighed the risks of detection by federal revenue agents. As one Dark Corner native put it, he "could make three gallons of corn whiskey from a bushel of corn and sell it for one or two dollars per gallon when he could only get sixty cents for his corn." The same individual recalled that there were "as many as twenty distilleries in two miles of each other." Some struggling families left Dark Corner early in the twentieth century, seeking employment in Piedmont textile mills.

Improved roads after World War II made Dark Corner more accessible to outsiders. By the 1990s a stream of affluent new residents, principally retirees and commuting professionals from Greenville and Spartanburg, had discovered the spectacular mountain vistas and relatively inexpensive land of one of the most culturally and historically unique sections of South Carolina. MATTHEW A. LOCKHART

Batson, Mann. *The Upper Part of Greenville County, South Carolina.* Taylors, S.C.: Faith Printing, 1993.

Crain, J. Dean. *A Mountain Boy's Life Story.* Greenville, S.C.: Baptist Courier, 1914.

Huff, Archie Vernon, Jr. *Greenville: The History of the City and County in the South Carolina Piedmont.* Columbia: University of South Carolina Press, 1995.

Lawrence, James Walton, Sr. *Hogback Country.* Landrum, S.C.: News Leader, 1982.

Darlington (Darlington County; 2000 pop. 6,720). Darlington, the "Pearl of the Pee Dee," lies on a bluff overlooking Swift Creek. Following the formation of Darlington County in 1785, the rival settlements of Mechanicsville and Cuffey Town vied to become the county seat. As a compromise, according to one account, rival supporters rode on horseback "from their respective communities" toward each other and built the courthouse on the spot where they met, the plantation of John King.

The town grew slowly. In 1806 fire destroyed the courthouse, and a replacement was built in the 1820s. In 1818 residents organized the Darlington Society to build Darlington Academy, later St. John's School. By 1826 Robert Mills described the town as having a "handsome new brick court-house and jail; besides several private houses, and the requisite taverns." The town was incorporated in 1835 and had rail service by 1856. In 1860 the local militia, the Darlington Guards, was the first company in the state to answer the call of Governor Francis W. Pickens for volunteers. In March 1865 Federal troops burned the depot and railroad trestles. By July, Darlington had become the command center for the Military District of Eastern South Carolina.

Another devastating fire in 1866 destroyed the courthouse, jail, and business district. Despite the setback, Darlington began to grow following the Civil War. Between 1871 and 1891 the Darlington Agricultural Society promoted local agriculture by holding a series of annual fairs. On May 7, 1883, residents chartered the Darlington Manufacturing Company, the town's first textile mill. Sold to Deering Milliken & Company in 1900, it operated until 1956, when owners closed the mill after workers voted to unionize. During the 1890s other businesses opened, but the introduction of tobacco brought the biggest change. Darlington blossomed as a tobacco center and became the largest tobacco market in South Carolina.

Darlington also gained notoriety in the 1890s as the site of the so-called "Dispensary War," which reflected the unpopularity of the state dispensary system in the Pee Dee region. In March 1894 a group of dispensary constables intervened in a dispute at the railroad depot, and a gunfight ensued. When the smoke cleared, two Darlingtonians and one constable were dead and several more were wounded. Sensational accounts of the "war" filled state newspapers, and Governor Benjamin Tillman called out the state militia to restore order.

The twentieth century was marked by a construction boom. A new town hall–opera house was built in 1901, new facilities were constructed for St. John's School in 1902, and a new courthouse was completed in 1904. World War I ended Darlington's good times. Agricultural recession, bank failures, the Great Depression, and another major fire in 1930 led to a period of stagnation. During the 1930s the Works Progress Administration constructed a new armory, a new gymnasium, and a new county jail. In 1938 the Individual Drinking Cup Company, later Dixie Cup, opened a plant.

The end of World War II brought a housing boom to the area. In 1950 the prototype of the Darlington Speedway opened on the outskirts of town. The first race, held on Labor Day 1950, inaugurated a new period of NASCAR (National Association for Stock Car Auto Racing)-induced prosperity. Darlington celebrated its 150th anniversary on December 19, 1985, and in 1988 created the City of Darlington Multiple Resource Area to celebrate and preserve its past. ALEXIA JONES HELSLEY

Ervin, Eliza Cowan, and Horace Fraser Rudisill, eds. *Darlingtoniana: A History of People, Places and Events in Darlington County, South Carolina.* Columbia, S.C.: R. L. Bryan, 1964.

Rudisill, Horace Fraser. *Darlington County: A Pictorial History.* Norfolk, Va.: Donning, 1986.

Darlington County (561 sq. miles; 2000 pop. 67,394). Darlington County was created on March 12, 1785, out of the southern third of the colonial-era judicial district of Cheraws. It became Darlington District in 1798, then reverted back to county status in 1868. Darlington lost territory in 1888 with the formation of Florence County and again in 1902 by the creation of Lee County.

For over sixty years after the first settlements at Charleston, the area that is now Darlington County was still unsettled by Europeans. In an effort to induce settlers, the colonial government set aside an immense tract of land along both sides of the Pee Dee River for the exclusive use of Welsh Baptists of Pennsylvania planning to emigrate southward. The Welshmen came and built a civilization out of the wilderness. They founded the Welsh Neck Baptist Church in 1738, near present-day Society Hill, which survived to become the second-oldest Baptist church in South Carolina. The Welsh cultivated money crops of flax, hemp, and indigo. Livestock raising was prevalent, and "Cheraw bacon" became popular in Charleston and other colonial markets. By the late 1700s the strict Welsh Baptist identity was eroded by an influx of new settlers, mostly from North Carolina and lower Virginia. But Darlington District continued to be a stronghold of the Baptist denomination, albeit a diminishing one, virtually to the present day.

In 1774 a petit-jury presentment issued at the Cheraws courthouse at Long Bluff, later Society Hill, became one of the earliest declarations of grievances against the British crown in South Carolina as well as the American colonies. The British court-martial and execution of the patriot Adam Cusack also took place there. This same neighborhood gave rise to the St. David's Society, formed in 1777 to promote education and incorporated the following year. The school that society members founded gained a statewide reputation for excellence and furnished two of the original faculty to the South Carolina College. As a resource for the original school, one of the earliest lending libraries in the state was organized in 1826 at Society Hill and served the entire community until the mid-twentieth century. Coker College in Hartsville is considered by some to be a lineal descendant of old St. David's. Hartsville is also the location of the state-supported Governor's School for Science and Mathematics, which caters to gifted students. A college preparatory school, Trinity Collegiate, and several private schools comprise the excellent educational facilities of the county.

During the Civil War, Darlington County escaped the worst effects of General Sherman's army, being out of the direct line of his march through the state. However, detachments from the main force pillaged the district, destroying several bridges and burning cotton plantations.

As in education, Darlington County was also an industrial pioneer in South Carolina. Governor David R. Williams made a successful attempt at manufacturing in 1812 when he established a water-powered cotton mill on Cedar Creek to produce rough cloth and cotton bagging. For seventy years there was no other industry of consequence. The abundance of cotton spawned two cotton mills, one in Darlington in 1885 and one in Hartsville in 1900. Although the Coker family members were major stockholders in these factories, both were eventually taken into the Milliken chain of mills. Milliken stockholders closed the Darlington Mill in 1956 after its employees voted to unionize, which resulted in two decades of litigation and hearings over the legality of the action. The Hartsville Mill continued operations until 1984, when it was unable to compete with cheaper foreign labor.

In the 1890s a Confederate veteran, Major James Lide Coker, and his son, J. L. Coker, Jr., founded two companies for the purpose of converting southern pine timber into paper products. The two companies merged into the Sonoco Products Company in 1923. The company grew and became a global organization with factories all over the world but retained Hartsville as its world headquarters. Internationally known "Dixie Cup" cups and plates have been produced in Darlington since the 1930s. Darlington County also became known for its steel production, with Nucor of Dovesville leading the field. Increased industrial activity in the county prompted Carolina Power and Light to construct a steam generating plant on Black Creek near Hartsville in 1959. It was converted to nuclear power several years later and greatly facilitated the expansion of the county's industrial base. That base continued to grow through the end of the twentieth century with manufactured products ranging from fiberglass boats to aluminum ladders.

Despite its notable industrial sector, agriculture dominated the way of life in Darlington. As early as 1768 local planters formed a "Planters Club," about which little is known. The Darlington Agricultural Society has met annually since its formation in 1846 and is one of the oldest agricultural societies in the state. Cotton was king until dethroned by flue-cured tobacco early in the twentieth century. By the 1990s tobacco was in serious trouble and production greatly diminished. Although many small farms have disappeared, agriculture remained a vital factor in the local economy at the end of the twentieth century.

The long agricultural tradition in the county gave rise to the development of numerous heritage-wildlife preserves, parks, and gardens. Two are located on Black Creek, one at Hartsville and one at Darlington, with another on the Pee Dee River at Mechanicsville. An extensive botanical garden, Kalmia Gardens, on Black Creek in Hartsville dates back to the early 1930s. Land was acquired at Society Hill for a state park to be centered around the extinct colonial village of Long Bluff.

The sport of racing has been popular in Darlington County since the early days of horse racing on the large plantations. At Darlington a racetrack for horses and motorcycles existed prior to World War I.

Auto racing did not appear in full force until 1950 when the Darlington Raceway was built. The fame of this track has made "Darlington" almost synonymous with auto racing nationwide. It was home of the Southern 500 race every Labor Day weekend until 2004, when the race date was moved to November. Nearby, the Darlington International Dragway hosts two major racing events each year. HORACE FRASER RUDISILL

Ervin, Eliza Cowan, and Horace Fraser Rudisill, eds. *Darlingtoniana: A History of People, Places and Events in Darlington County, South Carolina.* Columbia, S.C.: R. L. Bryan, 1964.

Rudisill, Horace Fraser, comp. *Darlington County: A Pictorial History.* Norfolk, Va.: Donning, 1986.

———. *Historical Tours in Darlington County.* Darlington, S.C.: Darlington County Tricentennial Committee, 1970.

Darlington Raceway. "The Track Too Tough To Tame." "The Lady in Black." These two titles provide some indication of the respect and awe National Association for Stock Car Auto Racing (NASCAR) drivers and fans have for Darlington Raceway, the oldest superspeedway hosting Winston Cup events.

The contractor Harold Brasington completed Darlington Raceway in 1950. Brasington had attended the Indianapolis 500 in 1933 and dreamed of building a similar track in his hometown. Although many people laughed at the notion of building such a facility in rural South Carolina, Brasington persisted, and with financing from local business leaders and the donation of seventy acres of land by J. S. (Sherman) Ramsey, Brasington carved the high-banked, egg-shaped, 1.25-mile facility out of the sandy soil of the South Carolina coastal plain. The track was later redesigned to its current 1.366-mile configuration.

The track hosted its first race, the Southern 500, on Labor Day (September 4) 1950 in conjunction with the fledgling NASCAR Grand National series (which later became Nextel Cup) and its owner-promoter Bill France. The success of that first race at Darlington made the small South Carolina town a fixture on the Winston Cup tour. Since 1960 Darlington has hosted annually two races in NASCAR's top division.

Darlington's unique shape, coarse racing surface, and preferred racing line that runs dangerously close to the racetrack's retaining wall make it one of the most challenging tracks on the circuit. South Carolinian David Pearson, the most successful driver at Darlington with ten Winston Cup victories, once argued, "At Darlington you don't race the other drivers. You race the track." Dale Earnhardt expressed the satisfaction drivers feel when they conquer this track: "there's no victory so sweet, so memorable, as whipping Darlington Raceway."

The track is now owned and operated by the International Speedway Corporation. Darlington Raceway is also home to the Joe Weatherly Stock Car Museum and the National Motorsports Press Association Hall of Fame. DANIEL S. PIERCE

Bledsoe, Jerry. *The World's Number One, Flat-Out, All-Time Great Stock Car Racing Book.* Garden City, N.Y.: Doubleday, 1975.

Chapin, Kim. *Fast as White Lightning: The Story of Stock Car Racing.* Rev. ed. New York: Three Rivers, 1998.

Daufuskie Island. Daufuskie Island, one of the Sea Islands, is near the mouth of the Savannah River at the southern tip of Beaufort County. Eight miles square and inhabited by just 279 residents in 2000, the island is bordered by salt marshes and oyster beds that are affected daily by six- to eight-foot tides. Live oaks, palmettos, magnolias, and pines thrive in the semitropical climate.

The name Daufuskie is attributed to a Creek Indian word meaning "land with a point." Various Native American groups inhabited Daufuskie until the early eighteenth century. In 1714 Colonel Robert Daniell of Charleston received a barony that included the island. The southern tip of Daufuskie, Bloody Point, was named for the blood shed during the Yamassee Indian War. In 1715 the Carolina Scouts attacked a band of Yamassee and Creek Indians who had staged an assault on the island. Yamassees from Spanish Florida continued to raid the area intermittently until 1728.

Daufuskie Island planters raised indigo in the eighteenth century and Sea Island cotton during the antebellum period. After the Civil War, Daufuskie's economy was based on cotton, lumber, and oysters. Most residents worked either as pickers or in the cannery owned by L. P. Maggioni and Company from Beaufort. Men sailed to beds to handpick the oysters. Pollution from the Savannah River caused the failure of the industry by 1959.

Because of the island's geographic isolation (no bridge connects Daufuskie to the mainland), native Daufuskie Islanders have maintained many of their Gullah traditions. Several historic churches, homes, and schools on the island reflect this culture. The author Pat Conroy taught in the two-room Mary Fields School in 1969 and then documented his experiences in his novel *The Water Is Wide.* The isolation of Daufuskie's Gullah culture ended in the early 1980s, however, when developers purchased portions of the island and established high-income residential and resort communities. NATALIE HARVEY HEFTER

Burn, Billie. *An Island Named Daufuskie.* Spartanburg, S.C.: Reprint Company, 1991.

This was the scene at Darlington Raceway as beauty queen, pace car, and late model convertibles take the parade lap of the 1958 Rebel 300 NASCAR stock car race. Courtesy, Darlington Raceway

Rowland, Lawrence S., Alexander Moore, and George C. Rogers. *The History of Beaufort County, South Carolina.* Vol. 1, *1514–1861.* Columbia: University of South Carolina Press, 1996.

Slaughter, Sabra C. "'The Old Ones Die and the Young Ones Leaving': The Effects of Modernization on the Community of Daufuskie Island, South Carolina." Ph.D. diss., University of Michigan, 1985.

Davenport, Guy (b. 1927–2005). Writer, educator, illustrator. Davenport was born in Anderson on November 23, 1927, the son of Guy Mattison Davenport and Marie Fant. He showed a literary inclination from an early age. When he was twelve he created his own "newspaper," *The Franklin Street News,* precociously reporting on "visits, birthdays, the births of kittens and puppies." As a child, Davenport received private tutoring at Anderson College. He went on to study at Duke (B.A., 1948) and Oxford (B.Litt., 1950) on a Rhodes scholarship, where he wrote his thesis on James Joyce's *Ulysses.* He served with the Army Airborne Corps (1950–1952) and began his teaching career at Washington University in St. Louis (1952–1955). In 1952, while conducting research for an article, he formed a lasting acquaintance with the modernist poet Ezra Pound. Subsequently he visited the writer during his imprisonment at St. Elizabeth's Hospital for the Insane. When Davenport completed his Ph.D. at Harvard (1961), Pound was the subject of his dissertation.

Davenport considered himself a teacher foremost and his writings as "an extension of the classroom," the creative component of a searching mind. In 1963 he started teaching at the University of Kentucky, an institution that he has been associated with ever since. He was honored with the Alumni Distinguished Professor citation in 1983, retired in 1991, and became a professor emeritus in 1992.

Davenport was also a prolific writer in multiple genres and an illustrator for his own books and others. He authored more than twenty books, including two poetry collections. He also published book-length translations of classical texts by Sappho, Diogenes, and Heracleitus. Davenport's articles appeared in *Virginia Quarterly Review, Life, New York Times Book Review,* and *National Review,* where he was a contributing editor (1962–1983). His interest in the history of ideas and his broad learning imbued his fiction with its rarefied texture: it was densely allusive, frequently experimental, and classically informed. He described his stories as "lessons in history." Davenport's stories require close reading, appropriate for a man who proclaimed that "[a]rt is always the replacing of indifference by attention."

Representative volumes of Davenport's short stories include *Da Vinci's Bicycle: Ten Stories* (1979) and *Twelve Stories* (1997). *The Geography of the Imagination* (1981) and *Every Force Evolves a Form* (1987) collect sixty of Davenport's highly regarded critical essays, touching on such provocative thinkers as Ludwig Wittgenstein, Charles Olson, and Samuel Beckett. An intellectual jack-of-all-trades, Davenport was a South Carolinian who became an internationally respected man of letters. BRYAN A. GIEMZA

Crane, Joan, and Richard Noble. *Guy Davenport: A Descriptive Bibliography, 1947–1955.* Haverford, Pa.: Green Shade, 1996.

"Guy Davenport." In *Contemporary Authors, New Revision Series.* Vol. 73. Detroit: Gale, 1981.

Reece, Erik Anderson. *A Balance of Quinces: The Paintings and Drawings of Guy Davenport.* New York: New Directions, 1996.

David. The Confederate torpedo boat *David* was a small, steam-driven, surface vessel armed with a pole-mounted explosive charge called a spar torpedo. David Ebaugh built the *David* at Stoney Landing, on the Cooper River, for the Southern Torpedo Company, a consortium of South Carolina businessmen inspired by a bounty placed on the destruction of Union blockaders off Charleston. Completed in 1863, the unusual-looking craft closely resembled a cigar, with a cylindrical center section and conical ends. It measured forty-eight feet six inches in length and five feet in diameter and was powered by a small double-cylinder engine that turned a single propeller. Amidship a large open hatchway contained the steam machinery and cramped space for four crewmen. Attached to the *David*'s bow was a stationary fourteen-foot-long metal pole with an explosive torpedo containing sixty-five pounds of black powder and four pressure-sensitive fuses. The torpedo exploded when driven into the hull of an enemy warship. Heavily ballasted, the *David* floated low in the water with little more visible than its hatch combing and smokestack.

Commanded by naval lieutenant William T. Glassell, the *David* attacked the USS *New Ironsides* off Charleston on October 5, 1863, but failed to sink the much-feared ironclad when the torpedo exploded too near the water's surface. Following modifications, the *David* made several more attacks on Union warships, but all proved abortive. Although the *David* failed to sink an enemy vessel, both sides recognized the weapon's value. The Union navy went to great lengths to protect its blockaders from torpedo attacks, while at Charleston and elsewhere the Confederates commenced numerous other boats of similar design that were generically known as "Davids." The *David*'s final disposition is unknown, but it was likely one of several torpedo boats found in Charleston after the city's fall.
ROBERT HOLCOMBE, JR.

"David C. Ebaugh on the Building of 'The David.'" *South Carolina Historical Magazine* 54 (January 1953): 32–36.

Perry, Milton F. *Infernal Machines: The Story of Confederate Submarine and Mine Warfare.* Baton Rouge: Louisiana State University Press, 1965.

Tomb, James H. "Submarines and Torpedo Boats, C.S.N." *Confederate Veteran* 22 (April 1914): 168–69.

Davie, William Richardson (1756–1820). Soldier, jurist, statesman. Davie was born on June 22, 1756, in Egremont Parish, Cumberlandshire, England, the eldest child of Archibald Davie and Mary Richardson. In 1764 he immigrated with his family to America, where he was raised by his uncle, the Reverend William Richardson, minister of the Waxhaw Presbyterian Church. From his uncle he received his early education, and he was enrolled in Queen's College in Charlotte, North Carolina. He entered the College of New Jersey (Princeton) in 1774 and graduated with first honors in 1776. In 1779 at the Battle of Stono, Davie was severely wounded leading a charge and barely escaped capture. It took nearly a year to recover from the wounds.

The following year, using his considerable inheritance from his uncle, Davie raised and outfitted a troop of his own. Commissioned a major, he led his men in action at the Battle of the Waxhaws (May 29, 1780), Hanging Rock (August 6, 1780), and various places in and around the Waxhaw settlement. At Hanging Rock, Davie was observed by a thirteen-year-old Andrew Jackson, the future seventh president of the United States. For the remainder of his days Jackson would consider Davie to be the beau ideal of a soldier. Davie's small command, which included white settlers and Catawba Indians, was never surprised or dispersed during its existence. His talents soon caught the eye of General Nathanael Greene. He persuaded Davie to become commissary general of the Southern Army in early 1781. In this post he served admirably, being able to feed the army even though the land in both Carolinas had been devastated by war.

After the war ended, Davie settled in Halifax, North Carolina. He married Sarah Jones on April 11, 1782, and they were the parents of six children. Taking an active role in North Carolina politics, he served in the North Carolina House of Commons from 1784 until 1798, when he was elected governor. He favored a lenient policy toward Loyalists and was the leading figure in the establishment of the University of North Carolina in 1789. In 1787 Davie was a delegate to the Constitutional Convention in Philadelphia. A lifelong Federalist, he approved of the Constitution and campaigned vigorously for its passage. In 1799 President John Adams appointed Davie as one of three delegates to negotiate agreements on amity and commerce with France.

Davie returned to South Carolina in late 1805, retiring to his Tivoli plantation in Lancaster District. An active member of the South Carolina Agricultural Society, Davie also assisted in negotiating the boundary dispute between North and South Carolina. In 1812 he was nominated for vice president on the Federalist ticket and was briefly considered for command of the U.S. Army during the War of 1812. His last public office was as a commissioner of the Board of Public Works in South Carolina. Davie died on November 5, 1820, and was buried at Old Waxhaw Presbyterian Church in Lancaster. RHETT A. ADAMS

Robinson, Blackwell. *William R. Davie.* Chapel Hill: University of North Carolina Press, 1957.

Davis, Gary (1896–1972). Musician. Davis was born in Laurens County on April 30, 1896. A highly accomplished and innovative guitarist who influenced numerous blues and folk musicians, Reverend "Blind" Gary Davis honed his style during the 1920s in the rich musical milieu of the Greenville-Spartanburg region. Known foremost for his complex finger-picking style on six- and twelve-string guitars, Davis also possessed a captivating, emotional vocal style that lent added intensity to his religious songs.

After losing his eyesight as a child, Davis was encouraged to take up the guitar by his grandmother. As a teenager he performed at house parties around Laurens, already proficient on banjo and harmonica as well as guitar. During the 1920s he played in a string band in Greenville, refining his musical skills around other talented guitarists including Willie Walker and a young Josh White. Although he learned some of Walker's repertoire, Davis crafted his own style and is considered to be a progenitor rather than a follower of the "Piedmont" blues sound that developed in the Southeast. Davis moved to Durham, North Carolina, in the early 1930s; attended a school for the blind; and was ordained as a Baptist minister in 1933. In Durham he played the tobacco warehouses for change and influenced the guitarist Blind Boy Fuller, with whom he traveled to New York City in 1935 to make his first recordings. Davis settled in New York around 1940 and continued to record during the next thirty years for a variety of labels. Finding a new audience with young, predominantly white fans of folk and blues, he became a major presence on the folk revival circuit during the late 1950s and early 1960s, performing at festivals, coffeehouses and clubs. Davis died in Hammonton, New Jersey, on May 5, 1972. DAVID NELSON

Bastin, Bruce. *Red River Blues: The Blues Tradition in the Southeast.* Urbana: University of Illinois Press, 1995.

Tilling, Robert. *"Oh What a Beautiful City": A Tribute to Rev. Gary Davis (1896–1972).* Jersey, Channel Islands: Paul Mill, 1992.

Davis, James (1774–1838). Physician, planter, legislator. The first physician to the South Carolina State Hospital, Davis was born on December 8, 1774, in Worcester County, Maryland, the son of Solomon Davis and Mary Smock. He moved to Laurens District, South Carolina, in 1784 and trained as a physician under George Ross between 1795 and 1797. On June 27, 1799, Davis married Catherine Ross, the daughter of his mentor. The couple had eight children. About 1800 Davis moved to Union District, where he founded the Union Library Society. From 1804 to 1808 he served as a state senator from Union. Around 1810 he moved to Columbia, where he established a successful medical practice, became a director of the Columbia branch of the Bank of the State of South Carolina, and was active in civic affairs.

Davis's most significant public undertaking was his involvement in the campaign to establish a public lunatic asylum in Columbia. In this quest he was allied with Samuel Farrow and William Crafts, the two men usually credited with the establishment of the institution. Davis was involved in the asylum campaign for several years before the General Assembly voted funds for its construction in 1821. Subsequently he served on the commission that oversaw its construction, a slow, controversial process that involved significant cost overruns. He also sat on the board of trustees that brought it into operation after the construction was finished and served as its first physician between 1828 and 1835. Daniel Trezevant, who succeeded him as physician, claimed that credit for the asylum belonged to Davis as much as to Farrow and Crafts.

During the asylum's first years, Davis wrote many letters and essays in the public press encouraging people to support the institution. The early years of the asylum's existence were difficult, both financially and in terms of securing enough patients, adequate staff, and even basic amenities. At times the asylum was unable to purchase enough clothing, bedding, and food for the patients. Mortality and recovery rates were worse than in the later antebellum period. The recovery rate during Davis's period of tenure, nineteen percent, was much lower than the eighty to ninety percent he and other asylum advocates had predicted. Davis was often ill during his tenure as asylum physician, and for several months in 1833 and 1834 he was unable to attend to his duties. He resigned in January 1835 and died in Fairfield District on August 4, 1838. He was buried in the First Presbyterian Churchyard, Columbia. PETER MCCANDLESS

Bailey, N. Louise, Mary L. Morgan, and Carolyn R. Taylor, eds. *Biographical Directory of the South Carolina Senate, 1776–1985.* 3 vols. Columbia: University of South Carolina Press, 1986.

McCandless, Peter. *Moonlight, Magnolias, and Madness: Insanity in South Carolina from the Colonial Period to the Progressive Era.* Chapel Hill: University of North Carolina Press, 1996.

Obituary. Columbia *Southern Times and State Gazette,* August 17, 1838.

Trezevant, Daniel. *Letters to His Excellency Governor Manning on the Lunatic Asylum.* 1854. Reprint, New York: Arno, 1973.

Dawson, Francis Warrington (1840–1889). Journalist. Born Austin John Reeks in London, England, on May 17, 1840, Dawson was the son of Austin Reeks and Mary Perkins. He changed his name in adulthood. Dawson was educated in London schools. He was first married to Virginia Fourgeaud of Charleston, a Frenchwoman, in 1867. On January 27, 1874, he married Sarah Morgan, daughter of Judge Thomas Gibbes Morgan of Louisiana. They had two children.

Dawson wrote at least four comedies in London. A romanticist and adventurer who espoused the Southern cause in the Civil War, he joined the crew of a Confederate cruiser that sailed from Southampton in 1862 to run the Union blockade. He went on to serve in the Confederate army, engaging in eleven battles and suffering wounds three times before being captured. After the war he worked on the *Richmond Examiner* and *Richmond Dispatch* in Virginia and then went to Charleston, where he was employed by the *Charleston Mercury* in 1866. A year later he joined Bartholomew Rochelot Riordan, whom he had known on the *Examiner,* and they bought a share of the *Charleston News.* In April 1873 they acquired the much older *Charleston Courier* and combined the two papers as the *News and Courier.* Dawson became editor.

The energetic Dawson and the *News and Courier* became known for speed in news gathering, accuracy, and far-flung coverage, with correspondents in Washington, D.C., and Columbia. Dawson often took courageous, if unpopular stands. He favored putting African Americans on the ballot in Charleston municipal elections. In 1876 he supported Republican governor Daniel Chamberlain against Wade Hampton in the gubernatorial race. But after Hampton won the Democratic nomination, the *News and Courier* supported him. Dawson initially backed the Agrarian radical Benjamin "Pitchfork Ben" Tillman but later rejected him as a demagogue, a racist, and an opportunist. Dawson was among the leading New South advocates who promoted building cotton mills and diversifying agriculture, including the introduction of tobacco. A devout Catholic, Dawson headed a crusade against dueling that led Pope Leo XIII to name him a Knight of the Order of St. Gregory the Great in 1888. Dawson also fiercely opposed lynching.

Ironically, this ardent spokesman against violence died of gunshot wounds on March 12, 1889. He had gone to the office of Dr. Thomas B. McDow, whom he accused of making "dishonorable advances" toward the Swiss governess of his children. The physician shot and killed him. McDow was acquitted, however, claiming self-defense. Dawson was buried in St. Lawrence Cemetery. ROBERT A. PIERCE

Clark, E. Culpepper. *Francis Warrington Dawson and the Politics of Restoration: South Carolina, 1874–1889.* University: University of Alabama Press, 1980.

Cooper, William J., Jr. *The Conservative Regime: South Carolina, 1877–1890.* Baltimore: Johns Hopkins Press, 1968.

Jones, Lewis P. "Two Roads Tried—And One Detour." *South Carolina Historical Magazine* 79 (July 1978): 206–18.

Logan, S. Frank. "Francis W. Dawson, 1840–1889: South Carolina Editor." Master's thesis, Duke University, 1947.

De Bow, James Dunwoody Brownson (1820–1867). Editor. De Bow was born in Charleston on July 10, 1820, the son of Garrett De Bow and Mary Bridget Norton. Garret De Bow was a native of New Jersey who prospered as a merchant in New York before he relocated to South Carolina. Young James De Bow attended Cokesbury Institute in Abbeville District before entering the College of Charleston, where he graduated at the head of his class in 1843. He was admitted to the bar the following year.

Not satisfied with his new profession, De Bow began contributing political essays to the Charleston-based *Southern Quarterly Review* and soon became one of its editors. One of his articles, "Oregon and the Oregon Question" in July 1845, was noticed abroad and debated in the French Chamber of Deputies. In the same year De Bow served as secretary at the Southern Commercial Convention held in Memphis, which debated internal improvements for the South.

The discussion of economic issues led De Bow to launch a monthly magazine devoted to business matters in the South. With the support of John C. Calhoun, Joel Poinsett, and others, De Bow left Charleston for the more thriving port of New Orleans, where he published the first issue of the *Commercial Review of the South and Southwest* in January 1846. The title was soon shortened to *De Bow's Review.* Although the magazine initially faced difficulties getting contributors and subscribers, De Bow's editorials soon gave him a reputation as a fervent sectionalist. His articles appeared regularly, representing his outspoken and violent partisanship when debating on matters threatening to divide the nation. He defended slavery against abolitionists and concluded that the North threatened to stifle the southern economy and destroy its social order by limiting the expansion of slavery. He felt that protective tariffs were desirable and believed that regional manufacturing and banking had great potential. Despite his calls for economic diversification in the South, he expected agriculture to remain predominant and encouraged farmers to adopt the latest technology and to pursue innovation in agricultural science.

In addition to publishing his *Review,* De Bow became the head of the new Louisiana Bureau of Statistics and a superintendent of the United States Census under President Franklin Pierce. He issued the seventh census of 1850, and in 1854 the Senate printed his *Statistical View of the United States.* After leaving this post in 1855, he gave public lectures and organized economic curricula in universities. He contributed largely to commercial conventions held in the South before the Civil War, particularly with respect to a southern terminus for a transcontinental railroad, direct trade between the South and Europe, and a canal through Central America.

During the Civil War, the Confederate government made De Bow its chief agent for the purchase and sale of cotton. His rhetoric and desperate support for the Confederacy were crushed with the Union victory. He died on February 27, 1867, while on a trip to Elizabeth, New Jersey. De Bow had married twice. In 1854 he married Caroline Poe, and the couple had two children before Caroline's death in 1858. In 1860 he wed Martha Johns of Nashville, with whom he had four children. TOMOKO YAGYU

Durden, Robert F. "J. B. D. De Bow: Convolutions of a Slavery Expansionist." *Journal of Southern History* 17 (November 1951): 441–61.

McMillen, James Adelbert, ed. *The Works of James D. B. De Bow: A Bibliography of De Bow's Review with a Check List of His Miscellaneous Writings, Including Contributions to Periodicals and a List of References Relating to James D. B. De Bow.* Hattiesburg, Miss.: Book Farm, 1950.

Skipper, Ottis Clark. *J. D. B. De Bow: Magazinist of the Old South.* Athens: University of Georgia Press, 1958.

De Brahm, William Gerard (1718–1799). Military engineer, surveyor, cartographer. De Brahm was born in Koblenz, Germany, on August 20, 1718, the son of Johann Phillip von Brahm, a court musician to the elector of Triers. As a member of the lesser nobility De Brahm received an excellent early education. After a successful career as a military engineer in the Bavarian army, De Brahm married and renounced the Roman Catholic religion. Forced to resign his commission, he was befriended by a Lutheran Church leader who was the only non-English trustee administering the colony of Georgia. De Brahm was placed in charge of a contingent of 156 German-speaking emigrants bound for Ebenezer, a German settlement near Savannah.

On arrival in Georgia in 1751, De Brahm was quickly recognized in both Georgia and South Carolina for his talents as a surveyor and an engineer. In the spring of 1752 De Brahm was selected by Governor James Glen of South Carolina to design and construct a system of fortifications for Charleston. At this time De Brahm dropped the prefix "von" and adopted the more fashionable "De," which he used throughout his remaining life.

De Brahm submitted an artistic "Plan of a Project to Fortifie Charlestown," with an estimated cost of some £294,140 sterling. This was deemed far too expensive, and a greatly simplified plan was undertaken in 1755. While De Brahm was supervising the construction of Charleston's works, in 1755 Governor Glen appointed him South Carolina's interim surveyor general of lands and inspector and controller of quitrents.

In a peace treaty with the Cherokee Indians signed in May 1755, Governor Glen promised to construct a fort deep in the Indian country. De Brahm was charged with the design and construction of the works later named Fort Loudon. Once construction began in what is now eastern Tennessee, De Brahm and the commander of the military force had a serious falling-out. In 1757 De Brahm returned to Georgia, where he worked to improve that colony's fortifications.

On October 20, 1757, De Brahm's fortunes rose with the publication of his cartographic opus, "A Map of South Carolina and a Part of Georgia." The elegant and precedent-setting map brought De Brahm to the attention of Europe. It was employed as evidence by both South Carolina and Georgia in a 1990 U.S. Supreme Court case concerning their boundary in the lower Savannah River. In 1764 De Brahm received a royal commission as surveyor general for the Southern District of North America. In addition, he was appointed as the surveyor general of lands for the new colony of East Florida. De Brahm soon took up residence in St. Augustine, where he engaged in surveys and map preparation for the next six years.

In 1771 De Brahm was ordered to London to answer charges that had grown from a feud with East Florida's royal governor. While there, his book on Florida sailing instructions entered print as *The Atlantic Pilot,* which included the first published map of the Gulf Stream. Exonerated of all charges, De Brahm was given the use of an armed sloop to continue his surveys. He arrived in Charleston in 1775, just in time to experience the outbreak of the Revolutionary War. His vessel was commandeered, and De Brahm, loyal to his king, became a prisoner at large in Charleston. De Brahm remained in Charleston until June 27, 1777, when he was allowed to sail back to England. Unsuccessful at regaining his royal offices, he left London in 1791 to take up residence in Philadelphia. He died on June 6, 1799, and was buried in the Friends burying ground in Germantown, Pennsylvania. LOUIS DE VORSEY

De Brahm, William Gerhard. *The Atlantic Pilot.* Edited by Louis De Vorsey. Gainesville: University Presses of Florida, 1974.

———. *De Brahm's Report of the General Survey in the Southern District of North America.* Edited by Louis De Vorsey. Columbia: University of South Carolina Press, 1971.

De Vorsey, Louis. "De Brahm's East Florida on the Eve of Revolution: The Materials for Its Recreation." In *Eighteenth Century Florida and Its Borderlands,* edited by Samuel Proctor. Gainesville: University Presses of Florida, 1975.

———. "William Gerhard De Brahm 1718–1799." *Geographers Biblio-graphic Studies* 10 (1986): 41–47.

De Kalb, Johann (1721–1780). Soldier. The man who was to be known in America as "Baron de Kalb" was born Johann Kalb to peasant parents in the Bavarian hamlet of Hüttendorf, Germany, on June 19, 1721. He began his military service in 1743 as a lieutenant in a French army regiment under the name of Jean de Kalb. His military career in Europe culminated in 1776, when he was commissioned a brigadier general in the French army. De Kalb subsequently decided to seek his military fortune in America, where he was contracted as a major general in the Continental army. Along with the young Marquis de Lafayette, de Kalb sailed for the colonies in April 1777 and arrived off the coast of Georgetown, South Carolina, in June.

After three years of service with the Continental army, de Kalb received an assignment equivalent with his rank. On April 3, 1780, he was ordered to the relief of Charleston, South Carolina, at the head of the Maryland and Delaware Continental regiments. On July 25, 1780, de Kalb surrendered command to Major General Horatio Gates at Deep River, North Carolina, but remained with the army at the head of his division. Gates chose to directly attack the British garrison at Camden. Three weeks later, on August 16, Gates met Lord Cornwallis six miles north of Camden near Saunder's Creek. Shortly after the action began, the American militia broke and fled in disorder. The Continentals under de Kalb stood firm and were almost annihilated. De Kalb fell with several wounds and died three days later, on August 19, 1780, a prisoner of war. He was buried by his captors with military honors. In 1825 Lafayette, his comrade in arms, laid the cornerstone of a monument to de Kalb in Camden. SAMUEL K. FORE

Kapp, Friedrich. *Life of John Kalb.* New York: Holt, 1884.

Sifton, Paul G., ed. "La Caroline Méridionale: Some French Sources of South Carolina Revolutionary History, with Two Unpublished Letters of Baron de Kalb." *South Carolina Historical Magazine* 66 (April 1965): 102–8.

Zucker, A. E. *General de Kalb, Lafayette's Mentor.* Chapel Hill: University of North Carolina Press, 1966.

De Leon, Edwin (1818–1891). Diplomat, writer. De Leon was born in Charleston on May 4, 1818, to Mardici Heinrich De Leon and Rebecca Lopez-y-Nuñez. His father was a prominent Jewish physician, and his brothers also had notable careers: Thomas Cooper as a journalist and author, and David Camden as surgeon general of the Confederate Medical Department. Edwin De Leon was a prolific writer, respected diplomat, and dedicated propagandist for the South.

Growing up in Columbia, De Leon read widely in his father's extensive library (destroyed in 1865) and attended South Carolina College. Graduating in 1837, he was admitted to the bar in 1840. From 1842 to 1848 he coedited the *Savannah (Ga.) Republican.* He drew the attention of southern Democrats in Congress, who in 1850 invited De Leon to Washington, where he and Ellwood Fisher founded the proslavery *Southern Press.* De Leon was friendly with politicians including Jefferson Davis and Franklin Pierce, and with writers such as James Fenimore Cooper, Henry Wadsworth Longfellow, and Nathaniel Hawthorne, with whom he traveled in Italy. He also spent time with Mormon leader Joseph Smith at Nauvoo, Illinois, and knew William Thackeray, Charles Dickens, and Alfred, Lord Tennyson later in England.

In 1853 President Franklin Pierce appointed De Leon diplomatic agent and consul general to Egypt, a position reaffirmed by Pierce's successor, James Buchanan. De Leon distinguished himself in Turkish-controlled Egypt by his boldness, most notably in protecting Greek inhabitants from a massacre during the Crimean War. Awarded the Cross of His Royal Order of the Saviour by King Otho of Greece, De Leon graciously turned the honor down on grounds that decorations violated the spirit of republicanism.

Hearing news of the outbreak of the Civil War, De Leon immediately resigned his position and returned to the South, where he ran the blockade at New Orleans and made his way to Jefferson Davis's home in Richmond, Virginia. Davis appointed him diplomatic agent for the Confederacy to Europe, and he arrived in England in June 1862. Finding a propaganda apparatus already in place, De Leon moved on to France, where he argued the Southern cause and defended slavery as a benevolent institution in a thirty-two-page pamphlet entitled *La Vérité sur les Etats Confédérés d'Amérique* (*The Truth about the Confederate States of America*). Despite a vigorous effort, he was unable to secure official French support and, having alienated Judah P. Benjamin, Davis's powerful secretary of war, received a letter announcing his dismissal in February 1864.

After the war De Leon returned to America and worked to reestablish the Democratic Party in the South, campaigning for Horatio Seymour for president in 1868 and Horace Greeley in 1872. Living primarily in New York, he also traveled in Europe and the Middle East, helping to establish Egypt's telephone system in 1881. He published widely in newspapers and journals such as the *Southern Quarterly Review* and *Harper's* and wrote several books, including a novel, *Askaros Kossis, the Copt* (1870), and *Thirty Years of My Life on Three Continents* (1890), a memoir. He died on December 1, 1891, in New York City. HUGH DAVIS

Cullop, Charles P. "Edwin De Leon, Jefferson Davis' Propagandist." *Civil War History* 8 (December 1962): 386–400.

De Leon, Edwin. *Thirty Years of My Life on Three Continents.* 2 vols. London: Ward and Downey, 1890.

Sutherland, Daniel E. "Edwin DeLeon and Liberal Republicanism in Georgia: Horace Greeley's Campaign for President in a Southern State." *Historian* 47 (November 1984): 38–57.

De Leon, Thomas Cooper (1839–1914). Author, editor, publisher. De Leon was born in Columbia on May 21, 1839, the youngest of six children of Dr. Mardici Heinrich De Leon, a surgeon and sixty-year resident of the capital, and Rebecca Lopez-y-Nuñez, from an old Charleston family. Educated at Rugby Academy in Washington, D.C.; Portland, Maine; and at Georgetown College (now University), De Leon worked as an audit clerk in the bureau of topographical engineers in Washington, D.C., from 1858 to 1861, when he resigned and joined the Confederate government. During the war he worked as a civil servant in Montgomery and Richmond. After the war he moved to Baltimore, where he edited the *Cosmopolite Magazine* for a year, and then to New York, where he wrote for newspapers and magazines.

In 1868 De Leon relocated to Mobile, Alabama, where he lived until his death. He was the managing editor of the Mobile *Register* until 1877, when he became chief editor. In addition to his active publishing career, De Leon managed a Mobile theater, supervised competitive militia drill teams, and coordinated Mardi Gras activities in Pensacola and Mobile. One fellow newspaperman, Erwin Craighead, described him as "so quick of thought, so well informed, so resourceful and capable, that it was natural for him to take leadership and command."

Despite his ability and accomplishments, however, De Leon had the reputation of being difficult and imperious. He lost his eyesight in 1903 and was thereafter referred to as "The blind laureate of the Lost Cause." Throughout his life he was an indefatigable novelist, playwright, poet, editor, and translator. Among his many works are *South Songs* (editor, 1866); *Hamlet, Ye Dismal Prince* (1870, alleged to be the first American play to run one hundred nights); *The Soldier's Souvenir* (a guide to National Guard units, 1887); *Creole and Puritan* (a novel, 1889), *Society as I Have Found It* (1890); *Four Years in Rebel Capitals* (1890); *Belles, Beaux and Brains of the '60s* (1907); and *Old Vets' Gossip* (1910). His writing is characterized by an easy, graceful familiarity and a puckish wit. A lifelong bachelor, De Leon died on March 14, 1914, and was buried in Mobile's Magnolia Cemetery. JOHN S. SLEDGE

De Leon, Thomas Cooper. *Belles, Beaux and Brains of the '60s.* 1907. Reprint, New York: Arno, 1974.

De Soto's exploration of South Carolina (1540). Hernando De Soto's exploration of present-day South Carolina took place from April to May of 1540, one year into the journey that began in May 1539 at Tampa Bay and ended in September 1543 at the Pánuco River in Mexico. De Soto's travels through South Carolina were part of an expedition that wound its way throughout the interior of the present-day southeastern United States and into Texas. Hernando De Soto organized this expedition in fulfillment of his contract to explore and settle this vast region—then known as "La Florida"—for the king of Spain. But De Soto never proceeded beyond the exploration phase of his contract. Instead, he sought to find native societies in La Florida with the riches he had seen in the conquest of Peru. Rumors not only of gold and silver but also of abundant food shaped the route De Soto and his army of six hundred soldiers, as well as African and Native American slaves, took through the Southeast. In the course of their journey, De Soto and his troops plundered many Indian towns and subjected the inhabitants to cruelties such as rape, torture, and enslavement. De Soto failed to find the wealth he sought, and approximately half of the expedition's members—including its leader—perished during their long march. But De Soto's exploration provided Spain with knowledge of the interior of this vast continent.

De Soto entered the territory of present-day South Carolina in search of the chiefdom of Cofitachiqui, reported to contain great wealth. Indians in present Georgia confirmed the account De Soto had heard but warned him of the great wilderness that lay between them and this powerful chiefdom. Undaunted, De Soto and his troops continued on their way. They crossed the Savannah River into present South Carolina in the area of the Clark Hill Reservoir and then traveled northeast across the Saluda and Broad Rivers. Reports of a wilderness proved true. The expedition was growing desperate for food when a scout found the town of Hymahi, or Aymay, at the confluence of the Wateree and Congaree Rivers. The Spaniards devoured Hymahi's food stores and then traveled north along the Wateree River to a town of the Cofitachiqui chiefdom in the area of present Camden. Cofitachiqui failed to meet De Soto's expectations for wealth or abundance of food, although the chiefdom's leader—whom the Spaniards called the "Lady of Cofitachiqui"—fed them well and gave them freshwater pearls. De Soto's men plundered mortuary houses there for more pearls. The Spaniards also seized corn from the chiefdom's stores at Ilasi, near present Cheraw, before they headed northwest to the North Carolina mountains. They took the leader of Cofitachiqui as their hostage, but she soon fled and returned home with one of the expedition's African slaves as her husband. In the 1560s, well within the memories of some of their inhabitants, Spaniards would return with the Juan Pardo expeditions to some of the towns De Soto visited. KAREN L. PAAR

Clayton, Lawrence A., Vernon James Knight, Jr., and Edward C. Moore. *The De Soto Chronicles: The Expedition of Hernando de Soto to North America in 1539–1543.* 2 vols. Tuscaloosa: University of Alabama Press, 1993.

Hudson, Charles. *Knights of Spain, Warriors of the Sun: Hernando de Soto and the South's Ancient Chiefdoms.* Athens: University of Georgia Press, 1997.

Death penalty. South Carolina is one of thirty-eight states that authorize the death penalty. Murder is the only state crime for which one may be executed. Because of the severity of the penalty, special procedures exist for death penalty trials. For example, death penalty trials are "bifurcated," a term that means a trial is divided into two parts. The first segment is the guilt or innocence phase in which a prosecutor must prove to a jury, beyond a reasonable doubt, that the offender did in fact commit the murder and acted with extreme disregard for human life. If the jury returns a verdict of "guilty," the trial then moves to the penalty phase. Here the prosecutor must show that aggravating circumstances exist that would warrant the most extreme punishment. If the prosecutor can demonstrate that one of these factors was present during the commission of the crime, the jury may opt, but is not required, to impose a sentence of death. Much as in the guilt phase, the defense will use the penalty phase to introduce mitigating circumstances that demonstrate that the crime in question does not satisfy the requirements for death.

Prior to 1912 executions were carried out by individual counties. The method of choice at that time was hanging. On August 6, 1912, the state began executions by electrocution. The original death row and death house were located at the Central Correctional Institution (CCI) in Columbia. The last execution to take place at the CCI site was in 1986. In 1988 the state established a new Capital Punishment Facility located at the Broad River Correctional Institution (BRCI) in Columbia. The first execution occurred there in 1990. Death row was also moved temporarily from CCI to BRCI. By 1997 death row for men was permanently located at Lieber Correctional Institution in Ridgeville. For women it was located at the Camille Griffin Graham Correctional Institution in Columbia. The rationale for not having death row located in the same facility as the death house is that it allows the correctional staff who deal with the inmates on a daily basis on death row to avoid any responsibility in carrying out the death warrant. From 1912 to 1995 the method of execution was death by electrocution. However, in 1995 the state legislature adopted a second method, that of lethal injection. Inmates under a death sentence are allowed to choose the method by which the sentence is carried out. If an inmate does not select a method and was sentenced prior to 1995, then he or she will be executed by electrocution. If the inmate does not select a method and was sentenced after 1995, the default choice is lethal injection.

Between 1912 and 2000 South Carolina put 266 people to death, 203 blacks and 63 whites. Of these, 241 took place prior to 1962, when questions about the constitutionality of the death penalty led to a moratorium on executions until 1985. The youngest person ever executed was fourteen years old; the oldest was sixty-six years old. South Carolina has executed two women: Sue Logue in 1943 and Rosa Stinette in 1947. REID C. TOTH

Allard, John. "Changing of the Guard." Columbia *State,* February 13, 1994, pp. D1, D6–D7.

Christman, Roger E. "'Dear Governor Blackwood have you a little boy? Would you wont him Burned in the Electric Chair?': Juvenile Justice and Executions in South Carolina, 1894–1962." Master's thesis, University of South Carolina, 1998.

Watson, Patricia Seets, and William Shepard McAninch. *Guide to South Carolina Criminal Law and Procedure.* 5th ed. Columbia: University of South Carolina Press, 1997.

"Death Valley." Clemson Memorial Stadium, popularly known as "Death Valley," is the third playing field for Clemson football. Clemson football was initially played on the military parade ground in front of Tillman Hall, known as Bowman Field. Prior to the construction of Memorial Stadium, the Tigers played on Riggs Field, named for former president and football coach Walter Merritt Riggs, who came from Auburn University bringing the tiger mascot and orange uniforms to Clemson. Riggs Field survives as Clemson's soccer field.

Howard's Rock—from Death Valley, California to Death Valley, South Carolina. Courtesy, Sports Information, Athletic Department, Clemson University

Clemson Memorial Stadium opened in 1942. Expanded over the years, the facility is an imposing place to play—so imposing that football coach Lonnie McMillian of Presbyterian College dubbed it "Death Valley" because his teams always got "killed" on the field. Coach Frank Howard began using the term in the 1950s, and it stuck. With a seating capacity of more than eighty thousand, "Death Valley" comes to life each fall as students, alumni, and fans converge in a sea of orange. The pregame tradition of the team running down the hill after rubbing Howard's Rock while the Clemson University Tiger Band plays "Tiger Rag" has been called one of the most exciting twenty-five seconds in college football.

The "Number 1" on the stadium scoreboard signifies the 1981 National Collegiate Athletic Association (NCAA) National Championship under former head coach Danny Ford. Notables in Clemson football lore are recognized in Death Valley's Clemson Ring of Honor, begun in 1994. Adjacent to the west end zone is the IPTAY athletic office, which lists the major bowl game appearances through the years. The trademarked tiger paw is the unmistakable symbol of Death Valley, from the tiger paws on the field and helmets to the tiger paws on the cheeks of fans. Other sights and sounds include the dotting of the *I* in the Tiger Band's formation and the Tiger Roar from the scoreboards. WILLIAM D. HIOTT

Debutante balls. The debutante ball as a rite of passage for young girls probably evolved from a seventeenth-century European custom in which aristocratic families presented their daughters at court to help them find suitable husbands. While a debutante may be presented to South Carolina society at an individual ball, tea dance, or other party given by her parents, the social events that accompany the debutante season across the state usually revolve around the official debutante balls held by organizations created specifically for that purpose.

The grande dame of these ball organizations in South Carolina is Charleston's St. Cecilia Society. Officially organized as a musical society in 1762, St. Cecilia turned to purely social events in 1822, and ever since then its ball has been considered the most exclusive in the state. The second organization appeared in 1889, when a group of Columbia women decided to develop the Assembly Ball as a social event modeled after the St. Cecilia, with the stated purpose of giving "their daughters a dignified background, and a fitting, yet attractive opportunity for them to be presented to society." The Assembly Ball was followed in 1890 by the Cotillion, organized by a group of Columbia men. Although the spread of debutante balls continued slowly for a while—Greenville's first Assembly Ball was held in 1923—as the twentieth century progressed and South Carolina's population grew, so did the number of debutante organizations. Small towns began to have them, and the larger cities added new ones. Some of these societies, such as St. Cecilia, were men's organizations, while other societies were women's organizations; others gave couples equal status. The specific criteria for being invited to join a debutante society were usually shrouded in secrecy, but wealth was not necessarily a determinant. Lineage and ties of friendship were more likely to be important.

Although each ball has particular features that may make it slightly different from every other ball, there is a pattern that is the basis for all the debutante ball variants. Each debutante wears a white gown, is presented by her father or another male relative, and curtseys before the members of society to whom she is being introduced. Then she takes the arm of her escort and participates in a Grand March, at the end of which all the debutantes take a collective bow, and the dancing begins.

The procession of debutantes in South Carolina has stopped only for the Civil War and World War II. Although during the turbulence of the Vietnam era it was often difficult for parents to persuade their daughters that a debut was important, debutante balls not only survived that period but also flourished afterward. A South Carolina newspaper might well describe three or four debutante balls held on the same night between Thanksgiving and January. The debut as a way to find a husband may be an anachronism, but the debutante ball as an excuse to have a good time was still going strong in the early twenty-first century. MALIE HEIDER

Fraser, Walter J. *Charleston! Charleston! The History of a Southern City.* Columbia: University of South Carolina Press, 1989.

Graydon, Nell. *Tales of Columbia.* Columbia, S.C.: R. L. Bryan, 1964.

Hennig, Helen Kohn, ed. *Columbia: Capital City of South Carolina, 1786–1936.* Columbia, S.C.: Columbia Sesqui-Centennial Commission, 1936.

Women's History in South Carolina Collection. Vertical Files. South Caroliniana Library, University of South Carolina, Columbia.

Deerskin trade. Shortly after establishing the colony of South Carolina in 1670, European settlers began trading manufactured goods for deerskins obtained by Native Americans. A leading economic activity during the colonial period, the skin trade provided an initial foothold along the frontier. Drawing Indians into the formative global economy of the period, the peltry trade was also a substantial source of social change that significantly restructured Native American culture.

In the late 1600s and early 1700s the deerskin trade comprised at least half of the colony's export revenue. By the 1740s deerskins were second among leading colonial exports, behind rice, and by the 1760s the peltry trade ranked third in economic value behind rice and indigo. In 1747 deerskins exported from the colony were worth £57,143 sterling, but by 1769 their annual value had declined to £18,422 sterling. Charleston was the economic hub of the skin trade during the colonial period in South Carolina.

Charleston merchants, supplied by factors in England, maintained trade links extending from North Carolina and Virginia along the Atlantic coast, to East Tennessee and Georgia, and as far west as modern Alabama and Mississippi along the Gulf coast. Factors in England provided Indian traders with trade goods that were transported into the South Carolina backcountry along trade paths and the major river systems. The trade goods were in turn used to stock Indian trading posts that were located along major transportation routes. Indian trading posts, such as George Galphin's at Silver Bluff on the Savannah River or Old Fort Congaree near present-day Columbia, were similar to frontier forts. Square or rectangular in shape, trading posts were often palisaded with wooden stockades and contained trade houses and residences.

At trading posts the Catawbas, Cherokees, Creeks, Choctaws, and Chickasaws exchanged dressed deerskins for blankets, firearms, shot, gunpowder, cloth, axes, hoes, and brass kettles. In 1763 a pound of dressed deerskins was worth six shillings. The dressed skins, eventually used to make clothes, were packed in barrels by traders and shipped to England to supply the formative garment industry. The deerskin trade encouraged settlement of the frontier, and yet it also had a deleterious effect on Native American groups. The peltry trade eroded Native American self-sufficiency and during the eighteenth century fostered material dependency on European trade goods. Further, unscrupulous traders advanced substantial credit to many Native American groups, which left them deeply in debt. As compensation for trade debt, Native Americans were eventually forced to cede lands to the colonial government. The Creeks and Cherokees in South Carolina relinquished millions of acres of tribal land in the early 1770s to pay their trade debts. By the third quarter of the eighteenth century, the deerskin trade had diminished in economic importance in South Carolina, although the peltry trade continued to be practiced on the edge of the frontier during the nineteenth century as settlement expanded across western North America. MARK D. GROOVER

Braund, Kathryn E. Holland. *Deerskins and Duffels: The Creek Indian Trade with Anglo-America, 1685–1815.* Lincoln: University of Nebraska Press, 1993.

Dunaway, Wilma A. "The Southern Fur Trade and the Incorporation of Southern Appalachia into the World Economy, 1690–1763." *Review of the Fernand Braudel Center* 17 (spring 1994): 215–42.

Sellers, Leila. *Charleston Business on the Eve of the American Revolution.* Chapel Hill: University of North Carolina Press, 1934.

DeLaine, Joseph Armstrong (1898–1974). Clergyman, civil rights activist. DeLaine was born on July 2, 1898, near Manning, one of thirteen children born to Henry Charles DeLaine and Tisbia Gamble. He was raised primarily in the Manning area but spent some time in the nearby Summerton community while his father pastored the Liberty Hill AME Church. After completing high school in Manning, DeLaine attended Allen University in Columbia, earning tuition money by working as a laborer. Completing his A.B. degree in 1931, DeLaine entered Allen University's Dickerson

Seminary to pursue a bachelor of divinity degree. He preached as opportunities arose and worked for his brothers in various construction trades. Also during 1931 DeLaine was called to pastor Stover's Chapel in Columbia. There he met a dynamic young woman named Mattie Belton. They were married on November 12, 1931, forming a union of shared beliefs, commitments, and activism. The couple had three children.

Joseph Armstrong DeLaine. Photograph by Cecil J. Williams

After graduation and a series of teaching and pastoral positions, DeLaine accepted an appointment from the AME Church as pastor of the Spring Hill Church in Clarendon County. He assumed a teacher's position at Bob Johnson School near Davis Station between Manning and Summerton. Mattie DeLaine became a teacher at the Spring Hill Community School.

During his tenure at Bob Johnson School, the lack of buses and the terrible school facilities began to weigh heavily on DeLaine. He knew that black students were at a tremendous disadvantage in their learning environment. These feelings led to the first case challenging the lack of school buses for African American children, filed on March 16, 1948, in federal court. After the case was dismissed on a technicality, DeLaine, with the encouragement of the National Association for the Advancement of Colored People and its chief legal counsel, Thurgood Marshall, persuaded twenty Clarendon County parents to sign a new lawsuit requesting equal educational facilities. That suit, *Briggs v. Elliott,* challenged the constitutionality of segregation and was heard in arguments before a federal district court in Charleston in May 1951. Not surprisingly, a three-judge panel decided two-to-one against the defendants (Judge J. Waties Waring cast the dissenting vote). However, the case was appealed to the U.S. Supreme Court, where it was one of the five cases constituting the landmark *Brown v. Board of Education* decision on May 17, 1954, which marked the beginning of the end of legal segregation in American public schools and society.

For his actions, DeLaine became the target of a series of hate crimes. He and his wife lost their jobs, and white merchants cut off their credit. The AME Church transferred DeLaine to Lake City early in 1951, and his home in Summerton was destroyed by fire the following October. After a series of night-rider attacks on their Lake City home, DeLaine responded in kind with gunfire on October 10, 1955. After the incident, a warrant for "Assault and Battery with Intent to Kill" was issued against DeLaine. Forced to leave his native state, he later wrote the FBI that he fled South Carolina, "Not to escape justice, but to escape injustice." The warrant remained in effect for the remainder of DeLaine's life and was not dropped until October 10, 2000. Never able to return to South Carolina, DeLaine lived the remainder of his life in New York and North Carolina. He died on August 3, 1974, in Charlotte, North Carolina. SONNY DUBOSE

DeLaine, Joseph A. Papers. South Caroliniana Library, University of South Carolina, Columbia.

DuBose, Sonny. *The Road to Brown: The Leadership of a Soldier of the Cross, Reverend J. A. DeLaine.* Orangeburg, S.C.: Williams, 2002.

Egerton, John. *Speak Now against the Day: The Generation before the Civil Rights Movement in the South.* New York: Knopf, 1994.

Kluger, Richard. *Simple Justice: The History of Brown v. Board of Education and Black America's Struggle for Equality.* New York: Knopf, 1975.

Lochbaum, Julia Magruder. "The Word Made Flesh: The Desegregation Leadership of the Rev. J. A. DeLaine." Ph.D. diss., University of South Carolina, 1993.

Delany, Martin Robinson (1812–1885). Soldier, army officer, Freedmen's Bureau official. Delany was born in Charles Town, Virginia (now West Virginia), on May 6, 1812, the youngest child of Samuel Delany, an enslaved carpenter, and Patti Peace, a free seamstress. In 1822 Martin's mother took him and her other four children to live in Chambersburg, Pennsylvania. Martin's father followed in 1823 after purchasing his freedom. In 1831 Martin moved to Pittsburgh, where he attended night school and studied medicine, which he practiced intermittently thereafter. He attended Harvard Medical School in 1850, but protests from white students limited his attendance to a single term. Delany married Catherine Richards on March 15, 1843. The couple had seven children who survived infancy.

In Pittsburgh, Delany began his efforts to advance the condition of African Americans. Between 1843 and 1847 he developed a black-nationalist perspective in the columns of his weekly newspaper, the *Mystery.* He called for the creation of separate black institutions and advocated black migration beyond the borders of the United States. From December 1847 to June 1849 he coedited the Rochester, New York, *North Star* with Frederick Douglass, although the two men had quite different views concerning the future of African Americans. During the 1850s Delany advocated both black migration and abolition. In 1856 he moved his family to Canada, and in 1859 he traveled to Africa in hope of establishing an African American colony in Nigeria.

As the Civil War began, Delany continued to promote black colonization in Africa. But following the Emancipation Proclamation in 1863, he turned to recruiting black Union troops. In February 1865 he became the first black major in the U.S. Army. Stationed in South Carolina shortly before the war ended, Delany stayed on to become a Freedmen's Bureau official on Hilton Head Island. He began as a fierce advocate of the rights of the former slaves and urged them to become self-sufficient. Yet he refused to challenge the property rights of white landowners and accepted the need for year-long labor contracts for black agricultural workers.

Following the termination of the Freedmen's Bureau in 1868, Delany engaged in South Carolina politics. At first a loyal Republican, he gained appointments in 1870 as the chief agent of the state's Bureau of Agricultural Statistics, in 1873 as U.S. Customs inspector in Charleston, and in 1875 as a judge in that city. But Ku Klux Klan violence, the failure of former slaves to meet his expectations, and corruption within South Carolina's Republican-dominated government led him to imagine that reconciliation with the former slave-owners who controlled the state's Democratic Party might best serve black interests. In 1874 he became a leader in the state's Independent Republican Party, which appealed mainly to white Democrats. In 1876 he angered many black South Carolinians by supporting Democratic gubernatorial nominee Wade Hampton. Thereafter Delany supported a failed scheme to send black colonists to Liberia. He left South Carolina in 1880 and, though in declining health, sought unsuccessfully to go to Africa. Delany died in Wilberforce, Pennsylvania, on January 24, 1885. STANLEY HARROLD

Levine, Robert S. *Martin Delany, Frederick Douglass, and the Politics of Representative Identity.* Chapel Hill: University of North Carolina Press, 1997.

Sterling, Dorothy. *The Making of an Afro-American: Martin Robinson Delany, 1812–1885.* 1971. Reprint, New York: Da Capo, 1996.

Ullman, Victor. *Martin R. Delany: The Beginnings of Black Nationalism.* Boston: Beacon, 1971.

DeLarge, Robert Carlos (1842–1874). Legislator, congressman. DeLarge was born on March 15, 1842, in Aiken, the son of a slave-owning mulatto tailor and his Haitian-born wife. At a time when few African Americans received any schooling, DeLarge attended primary school in North Carolina before returning to South Carolina to attend Wood High School in Charleston. He learned the barbering trade before enlisting in the Confederate navy. DeLarge's reasons for supporting the Confederacy are unknown, but as a free person of color and member of South Carolina's brown elite, he may have viewed Union troops as invaders. Apparently he later regretted his actions since he donated most of his wartime earnings to the Republican Party.

Shortly after the end of the Civil War, DeLarge became an ardent Republican and began to work earnestly for the betterment of African Americans. In 1865 he took office as an agent of the Freedmen's Bureau. A gifted orator noted for his passion, DeLarge used his political skills to help organize the Republican Party in South Carolina. In 1865 he attended the Colored People's Convention meeting at the Zion Church of Charleston, where he chaired the credentials committee. The convention adopted DeLarge's resolution calling for the establishment of a universal public school system. Though he did not favor giving the vote to illiterates of either race, DeLarge signed a petition asking for impartial male suffrage. As a member of the platform committee of the 1867 South Carolina Republican Convention, DeLarge again sought public schools as well as the abolition of capital punishment, universal male suffrage with literacy restrictions, tax reform, assistance to the poor of both races, funds for such internal improvements, and land distribution. Elected to the South Carolina General Assembly in 1867, DeLarge served on the powerful Ways and Means Committee. In 1870 he was appointed to head the South Carolina Land Commission, in which post he supervised the sale of land to freedmen. His brief tenure at the Land Commission was lackluster, however, and did little to lessen the agency's reputation for mismanagement and corruption.

DeLarge capped his political career in 1870 by narrowly beating the white Republican Christopher C. Bowen to serve the Second Congressional District in the U.S. House of Representatives. He took his seat on March 4, 1871. Placed on the Committee on Manufactures, he also urged legislation to protect Republicans from intimidation and to protect African Americans from racial violence. Unfortunately, Bowen weakened DeLarge's effectiveness by contesting the election and thereby consuming much of the young congressman's time. The House Committee on Elections began considering *C. C. Bowen v. R. C. DeLarge* in December 1871 but failed to reach a conclusion until January 1873. At that time they removed DeLarge from office because such irregularities existed in the election as to make the victor impossible to determine. DeLarge did not pursue reelection because his health had already begun to fail. His appointment as a Charleston magistrate in 1873 was his last public office. He died in Charleston on February 14, 1874, of consumption. He was buried in the Brown Fellowship Society Cemetery. CARYN E. NEUMANN

Bleser, Carol K. Rothrock. *The Promised Land: The History of the South Carolina Land Commission, 1869–1890.* Columbia: University of South Carolina Press, 1969.

Foner, Eric. *Freedom's Lawmakers: A Directory of Black Officeholders during Reconstruction.* Rev. ed. Baton Rouge: Louisiana State University Press, 1996.

Middleton, Stephen, ed. *Black Congressmen during Reconstruction: A Documentary Sourcebook.* Westport, Conn.: Praeger, 2002.

DeMint, James Warren (b. 1951). U.S. senator. On November 2, 2004, Jim DeMint won the United States Senate seat that Democrat Ernest Hollings held for nearly forty years. DeMint's victory gave South Carolina two Republican senators for the first time since Reconstruction.

DeMint was born on September 2, 1951, in Greenville, South Carolina, to Tom E. DeMint and Betty DeMint Batson. His mother was a single parent who raised DeMint and his three siblings. DeMint credits her with instilling in him a strong work ethic; he often says that she ran the family home like an army camp. DeMint graduated from Wade Hampton High School in Greenville. He then left South Carolina to attend the University of Tennessee, where in 1973 he earned a bachelor's degree. After graduating, he married his high school sweetheart, Debbie Henderson. They have four children. DeMint later returned to school, completing an M.B.A. from Clemson University in 1981. He is active in the Presbyterian Church of America, serving as a deacon at Mitchell Road Presbyterian Church in Greenville.

Before entering politics, DeMint owned the DeMint Group—an upstate advertising, marketing, and planning firm. In 1992 he became interested in running for office while volunteering for Bob Inglis's first campaign for the U.S. House. Six years later when Congressman Inglis ran for the U.S. Senate, DeMint took the opportunity to run for Inglis's seat.

He won and served as South Carolina's Fourth District congressman from 1999 to 2004. DeMint considers himself a conservative who believes in the principles of limited government, a strong national defense, and traditional family values. In the House he supported tax reform plans including a bill that would eliminate the Internal Revenue Service and replace most federal taxes with a national sales tax. In Congress he introduced legislation to reform Social Security by allowing younger workers to invest part of their payroll taxes in private retirement accounts.

To become a U.S. senator, DeMint first won a crowded Republican primary in 2004, eventually defeating former governor David Beasley in a run-off election. Then in the general election he faced the Democratic candidate and state superintendent of education Inez Tenenbaum. The two battled it out in what the Columbia *State* newspaper described as "one of the nastiest campaigns in recent memory." Both political parties and outside advocacy groups poured millions of dollars into the campaign, and DeMint won with fifty-four percent of the vote. CATHERINE COLLINS REYNOLDS

Democratic Party. Thomas Jefferson's ideological split with Alexander Hamilton found an appreciative audience in post–Revolutionary War South Carolina and provided the beginnings of the Democratic Party in the state. Charles Pinckney emerged as an early leader, sharing Jefferson's belief in strict construction of the Constitution. Pinckney's opposition to the Jay Treaty also found resonance among South Carolinians who wished to be reimbursed for slaves lost to Great Britain during the Revolutionary War. When Federalists nominated Charles Cotesworth Pinckney as their vice-presidential candidate in 1800, Charles Pinckney continued to support the Jeffersonians even though it meant a break with his family. Pinckney, however, picked the winning side: Jefferson won the presidency, and Democratic-Republican John Drayton became governor of South Carolina. Democratic-Republicans and their successors, the Democrats, would hold the governorship continuously until 1865.

After Pinckney brought South Carolina into the Democratic fold, South Carolinians continued to play an important role in the national Democratic Party throughout the antebellum years. Native sons Andrew Jackson and John C. Calhoun took prominent, if occasionally conflicting, roles. The main leader of the party in the state was Calhoun, who was generally able to quell opposition both within the party and from the Whig Party. During this period the party had strongholds not only among wealthy lowcountry planters but also among independent upcountry farmers. Both groups found the party's promise of protection from outside encroachment—and thus the protection of slavery—to be an appealing one.

The national Democratic Party was unable to stay united long enough to prevent civil war, and the party's hold on South Carolina was briefly broken at the war's end. But the election of Wade Hampton III in 1876 once again gave the party a stranglehold on the office of governor for nearly a century. Meaningful political debate could largely take place only *within* the Democratic Party in the years following Reconstruction. The Republican Party was anathema to white South Carolinians, having been the party of Abraham Lincoln and Reconstruction. Although there were vast differences of ideology, style, and sophistication among state Democrats, one overriding, enduring value and purpose held it together: maintaining a segregated party and society and "keeping the Negro population in their place," as well as an intense aversion to the Republican Party.

For decades, stump meetings, such as this one in Walterboro in 1946, were used by the Democrat Party to present its candidates to the people. Courtesy, Modern Political Collections, University of South Carolina

Conflicts within the Democratic Party included elites versus populists, lowcountry versus upstate, mill workers versus mill owners, and conflicts of personality among political leaders. Without question, the dominant, controlling influence in South Carolina politics (and therefore the Democratic Party) was the established, elite, conservative economic and social order. In those few instances in which a true populist emerged and achieved political success, he was soon co-opted or defeated by the established order. There were some nods to democracy, however: the South Carolina Democratic Party was one of the first parties to use the primary as a method of nominating its candidates. The primary was first used in Pickens County in 1876. While ostensibly democratic, the primary became an effective tool for excluding African American participation in politics.

It is difficult to exaggerate the dominance of the Democratic Party in South Carolina during the first fifty years of the twentieth century. In every presidential election except that of 1948, the Democratic candidate received the state's electoral votes. All of its U.S. senators and members of the U.S. House of Representatives were Democrats, save one. Virtually every member of the General Assembly and every local elected official was a Democrat—a *white* Democrat. African Americans were *legally* excluded from participation in the state's only meaningful election, the Democratic primary. This exclusion was successfully challenged in federal court, first in Texas and then in 1947 in the South Carolina case *Elmore v. Rice.* While this decision ended the legal prohibition to African American participation, it did not effectively open the primaries to blacks.

Changes precipitated by World War II affected South Carolina politics radically and irrevocably. When President Harry Truman integrated the armed forces and recommended a comprehensive civil rights program, many white South Carolinians were shocked, even horrified, by these threats to their state's system of racial segregation. As a result, South Carolina gave its electoral votes to Strom Thurmond's Dixiecrats in 1948. With the emergence of an increasingly successful civil rights movement, white South Carolinians believed that the national Democratic Party was becoming hostile to their racial mores. White South Carolinians found other problems with national Democrats who seemed to be more sympathetic to anti–Vietnam War activism and more tolerant of changing gender roles. These changes, combined with a lack of effective organization among state and local Democratic organizations, contributed to the disintegration of the Democratic Party in South Carolina.

Republicans in South Carolina seized on the advocacy of civil right programs by national Democrats and painted a clearly different image of themselves. They also appealed to the state's growing middle class. Republicans tended to be better organized and had a clearer issue orientation than Democrats did. Republicans were consistent in their conservatism on economic matters and their opposition to civil rights initiatives. Democrats responded to these shifting, uncertain circumstances by trying to separate themselves from the positions of their national Democratic cohorts. But they had to do this with great caution and care because African Americans in South Carolina became an increasingly significant portion of the Democratic base. Too much disagreement with the national Democratic Party would alienate black South Carolinians.

In a special election in 1961 a Republican, Charles Boineau, was elected to the South Carolina General Assembly. Even though he was defeated at the next regular election, Boineau's election foreshadowed a major political shift in the state. In 1964, the year in which U.S. Senator Strom Thurmond switched from the Democratic Party to the Republican Party, South Carolina gave its electoral votes to the Republican presidential nominee for the first time in the twentieth century. As of the early twenty-first century, only one time since then has the state voted for the Democratic candidate for president, for Georgian Jimmy Carter in 1976. In 1964 Congressman Albert Watson from the Second Congressional District backed Barry Goldwater for president, switched parties, resigned, ran in a special election, and won. Of the state's six congressional districts, only two (the Fifth and the Sixth) remained in Democratic hands during the last two decades of the twentieth century.

The shift was also felt at the state level. Republicans claimed the governorship in 1974, when James B. Edwards won the general election. Although Democrat Dick Riley recaptured the governor's mansion in 1978, Republicans occupied it for twelve years after Carroll Campbell was first elected in 1986. During these twelve years, Republicans built their party, while Democrats wandered in a proverbial wilderness with little leadership, little money, and hardly any organization. Losses were suffered at all levels. In every election from 1970 to 1994 Democrats suffered a net loss of seats in the General Assembly. These legislative setbacks were matched by comparable defeats at the local level.

Two court-imposed changes affected Democratic elective prospects in South Carolina. First, the doctrine of "one-man, one-vote" caused a substantial shift of legislative power from rural areas to urban areas. Because the urban areas were centers of Republican strength, this shift abetted Republican growth. The second change, single-member districts, was adopted because multimember districts resulted in disproportionately small percentages of African Americans being elected to office. Creating majority black legislative districts had four political effects: more Republicans were elected; more black Democrats were elected; fewer white Democrats were elected; and the total number of Democrats elected declined.

These legal changes reinforced the effects of the social, cultural, and economic changes that occurred in South Carolina since 1947. In that year South Carolina was a solidly Democratic state from top to bottom. By 2000 it had become a majority Republican state, although the margin enjoyed by the Republicans was not nearly so great as was the Democratic advantage in 1947.

Democrats began to show signs of recovery in 1996. While Republican Bob Dole took South Carolina's electoral votes, William Clinton's presidential campaign provided enough cohesion to enable South Carolina Democrats to fight the Republicans to a draw in other races. Building on this base, and taking advantage of Republican miscues, Democratic gubernatorial candidate Jim Hodges won a surprisingly convincing race in 1998. Democrats reelected Senator Ernest F. Hollings and gained five seats in the General Assembly. But in 2002 Hodges lost his race for reelection and Democrats suffered losses in the General Assembly and at the local level; in 2004 Hollings was replaced by Republican James DeMint.

The legacy of the civil rights movement was still evident in voting patterns at the beginning of the twenty-first century. The South Carolina Democratic Party had a single dependable base: the African American community, which constituted approximately twenty-five percent of the total vote in statewide races. Only about twenty-five percent of whites regularly voted for Democrats in statewide races, and most of this vote was scattered throughout the state. Thus, the second half of the twentieth century witnessed a transformation of South Carolina from the reliably Democratic state it had been since the time of Charles Pinckney to an increasingly consistent Republican state. DONALD L. FOWLER

Bass, Jack, and Walter DeVries. *The Transformation of Southern Politics: Social Change and Political Consequence since 1945.* 1976. Reprint, Athens: University of Georgia Press, 1995.

Black, Earl, and Merle Black. *Politics and Society in the South.* Cambridge: Harvard University Press, 1987.

———. *The Rise of Southern Republicans.* Cambridge: Belknap Press of Harvard University Press, 2002.

Ford, Lacy K., Jr. *Origins of Southern Radicalism: The South Carolina Upcountry, 1800–1860.* New York: Oxford University Press, 1988.

Key, V. O., Jr. *Southern Politics in State and Nation.* Rev. ed. Knoxville: University of Tennessee Press, 1984.

Matthews, Marty D. *Forgotten Founder: The Life and Times of Charles Pinckney.* Columbia: University of South Carolina Press, 2004.

Scher, Richard K. *Politics in the New South: Republicanism, Race and Leadership in the Twentieth Century.* 2d ed. Armonk, N.Y.: M. E. Sharpe, 1997.

Denmark (Bamberg County; 2000 pop. 3,328). The community was first established in 1837 as a turnout on the South Carolina Canal and Rail Road Company line. It was named Graham's Turnout for Captain Zachariah G. Graham. The village's first church, the Ghents Branch Baptist Church, was founded in 1834, with First Baptist Church organized ten years later. Cotton, melons, corn, grain, and timber were mainstay products in the area and were carried to markets by the railroad.

On December 22, 1870, the town was incorporated as Grahams and became Denmark on December 23, 1891. The name honored Colonel Isadore Denmark, president of the Southbound Railroad Company. The town of Denmark was in Barnwell County until the formation of Bamberg County in 1897.

After the Civil War, Denmark was a mercantile center for the surrounding agricultural area. The People's Bank became the town's first bank. The Grahams *News* was founded in 1888. Two years later the Grahams Wagon Works factory was established with J. G. W. Guess as president. One of the town's early landmarks was the Denmark Hotel, built in 1893. The coeducational Grahams Collegiate Institute was another civic improvement of note. In 1891 Denmark's population was 2,056.

Denmark became an important office for the American Telephone and Telegraph Company and was a transportation center, boasting three major railroad systems in the late 1800s. Gradually the business district shifted west toward its present location near the railroad junctions. The town's progress ebbed and flowed with the rural agricultural economy, but occasionally a major business, such as a John Deere factory in the 1920s, moved in.

The town's political landscape changed during the twentieth century, as blacks, who heavily outnumbered whites, won the right to vote in the 1960s. Orlando E. White was elected the first black mayor of Denmark in 1989. By the early twenty-first century, all members of the town council and the mayor were black. The town is the home of Voorhees College, a predominantly black institution that was founded in 1897, and Denmark Technical College, which evolved from a trade school established in 1948.

Denmark's population grew during the decades after World War II, reaching 3,321 in 1960, 4,110 in 1970, and 4,434 in 1980. By 2000, however, the population had decreased to 3,328. Denmark's fortunes had begun to wane by 2000, and the town suffered several financial problems.

Denmark's notable sons include the artist Jim Harrison, whose canvases capture the South's rural past and who established a studio and gallery in downtown Denmark. Cleveland Sellers, another native, was a leading civil rights activist who later joined the faculty of the University of South Carolina. Denmark has advertised its wares through the South Carolina Heritage Corridor project and hosts a Dogwood Festival each spring. ROBERT A. PIERCE

Bamburg County Committee, Inc. *Bamberg County Celebrating South Carolina's Tricentennial, 1670–1970.* [Bamberg, S.C.], 1970.

Lawrence, Margaret Spann. *History of Bamberg County, South Carolina, Commemorating One Hundred Years (1897–1977).* Spartanburg, S.C. Reprint Company, 2003.

Morris, Hazel, and Denmark-Olar Middle School Students. *The History of Denmark, South Carolina.* Denmark, S.C., 1989.

Dennis, Rembert Coney (1915–1992). Attorney, legislator. Dennis was born at Pinopolis on August 27, 1915, the second son of Edward James Dennis (1877–1930) and Ella Mae Coney.

Rembert Dennis served almost fifty years (1939–1988) in the General Assembly, forty-six of which were in the state Senate, where he was chairman of the Finance Committee (1972–1988) and president pro tempore (1984–1988). He was the third generation of Dennises to serve Berkeley County in the General Assembly, a succession that included his grandfather Edward James Dennis (1844–1904) and his father and concluded with the retirement of Dennis in 1988. His entry into politics was prompted by two family tragedies in the early 1930s, the assassination of his father in 1930 and the death of his older brother, E. J. Dennis III, from influenza the following year. Until that time Rembert Dennis had ambitions of becoming a dentist or a doctor. He was educated at Furman University, where he was elected student body president twice, played football and track, and graduated in 1936 as an honor student. He received his law degree from the University of South Carolina Law School in 1940, two years after he had been elected by Berkeley County to the state House of Representatives, where he served two terms (1939–1942). He was elected by the same county to the state Senate in 1942 and served continuously from 1943 until his retirement in 1988. On October 3, 1944, Rembert Dennis married Natalie Brown of McCormick. They had six children.

Dennis came to statewide attention in 1954 when—as a member of the State Democratic Party Executive Committee—he offered the motion to make Senator Edgar Brown the party's candidate for the U.S. Senate after the unexpected death of the incumbent Burnet Maybank. This nomination led to the surprise write-in victory in the November general election of Strom Thurmond over Brown. Dennis later rose to prominence as Brown's lieutenant in the Finance Committee, becoming that committee's second vice chairman in 1969 after an unsuccessful bid for election to the S.C. Supreme Court in 1966. At the death of Brown in 1972, Dennis became chairman of the Finance Committee, a position he held for the next sixteen years. In 1984 he succeeded Marion Gressette as president pro tempore of the Senate. In his capacity as chairman of the Finance Committee and ex officio member of the Budget and Control Board, Dennis was a staunch supporter of the state's fiscal conservatism and maintaining its AAA bond rating on Wall Street.

Dennis was also an avid outdoorsman; he was widely known as a marksman and fisherman and was famous for his interest in horses, dogs, and stalking the wild turkey. A descendant of early Berkeley County settlers, he acquired in 1970 the historic Lewisfield Plantation on the Cooper River near Moncks Corner and restored it as his family home. In 1984 and 1985 he was involved in a pair of automobile accidents, from which he suffered serious injury. Declining health forced Dennis to retire from the General Assembly in 1988. He died at Lewisfield on June 20, 1992, and was buried in St. John's Baptist Church Cemetery, Pinopolis. PHILIP G. GROSE, JR.

Bailey, N. Louis, Mary L. Morgan, and Carolyn R. Taylor, eds. *Biographical Directory of the South Carolina Senate, 1776–1985.* 3 vols. Columbia: University of South Carolina Press, 1986.

Bradley, Colleen. "The Last Giant: Senator Rembert C. Dennis of Berkeley County." Master's thesis, University of South Carolina, 1995.

Dennis, Rembert C. Interview, September 19, 1980. South Carolina Department of Archives and History, Columbia.

———. Papers. Modern Political Collections, South Caroliniana Library, University of South Carolina, Columbia.

Dent, Frederick Baily (b. 1922). Textile executive, U.S. secretary of commerce, diplomat. Born in Cape May, New Jersey, on August 17, 1922, and raised in Greenwich, Connecticut, Dent is the son of Magruder Dent and Edith Baily. He married the late Mildred Carrington Harrison on March 11, 1944, and they have five children. Dent attended St. Paul's preparatory school in Concord, New Hampshire, and then earned a bachelor of arts degree in political institutions from Yale University in 1943. He served in the U.S. Navy until 1946, spending time in the Pacific during World War II, then remained in the U.S. Naval Reserves until 1957.

In 1946 Dent joined the textile sales firm Joshua L. Baily & Company of New York, which was founded by his great-grandfather. He moved south, to Spartanburg, in 1947 to learn the manufacturing end of the business and wound up staying at Mayfair Mills in Arcadia, becoming president in 1958. Under his leadership the company expanded from two mills to six—five in South Carolina and one in Georgia—producing goods for the apparel and household industries.

Dent merged his interest in government with his career in industry through his significant involvement on state, national, and international levels. He was president of the South Carolina Textile Manufacturers Association in 1960 and president of the American Textile Manufacturers Institute (ATMI) in 1968, and he earned membership in the prestigious Business Council, made up of leaders in American industry. In addition, he served as chairman of the Spartanburg County Industrial Commission from 1960 to 1965, then served as chairman of its successor, the Spartanburg County Planning and Development Commission, from 1965 to 1972. During his chairmanship the local textile industry received $600 million in government funds. In the 1960s, with the backing of South Carolina senator Strom Thurmond, he traveled overseas, negotiating trade agreements to limit textile exports to the United States.

Dent's involvement in ATMI, as a member of the Commission on an All-Volunteer Army, and as a supporter of President Richard Nixon during his second presidential election gained him the recognition of the Nixon administration. In 1973 Dent was confirmed as Nixon's third secretary of commerce. Dent continued to serve under President Gerald Ford until 1975, when he was named a special representative for trade negotiations with the rank of ambassador in Ford's cabinet. Through his work in Washington, Dent is credited with introducing an energy conservation program for industry, organizing the National Energy Conservation Council, and establishing private-sector trade and economic councils in the Soviet Union and China.

In 1977 Dent returned to Mayfair Mills, where his son Frederick B. "Rick" Dent, Jr., had joined the company. In 1988 Dent was named chairman of the board, with Rick Dent assuming responsibilities as president and CEO. In 2001 the company filed Chapter

11 bankruptcy and closed its plants. However, Dent remained active in the community through the Arts Partnership of Greater Spartanburg, Spartanburg Day School, Spartanburg Technical College, and the Brevard (North Carolina) Music Center. TANYA BORDEAUX HAMM

Dent, Harry Shuler (b. 1930). Political strategist, lay minister. Dent was born in St. Matthews on February 21, 1930, the son of Hampton Dent and Sallie Prickett. An Eagle Scout and high school valedictorian, he graduated in 1951 from Presbyterian College with degrees in history and English. He married Betty Francis on August 16, 1951. They have four children.

Dent served as driver for Governor J. Strom Thurmond in his unsuccessful 1950 campaign for the U.S. Senate against the incumbent Olin D. Johnston. After army duty during the Korean War, Dent worked in Washington as a journalist before joining Thurmond's Senate staff in 1955. Dent soon became his administration assistant (staff director) and political confidant. Enrolling in night school, Dent earned a law degree in 1958 from George Washington University and a master's in law in 1959 from Georgetown Law School. He was a major influence in Thurmond's switch to the Republican Party in 1964 and in shaping what became the Republican "Southern strategy," a racial appeal to the segregationist inclinations of southern whites. As a matter of principle, Dent worked to have the South recognized as an important part of the United States and not taken for granted. He served as state chairman of the Republican Party and had a key role in Richard Nixon's successful presidential campaign in 1968. After the election, Dent joined the White House staff as counsel to the president. He returned to South Carolina in 1973, however, disillusioned by the deepening Watergate scandal.

Dent practiced law for several years while making the transition to a full-time commitment to an interdenominational lay ministry. He received a graduate certificate in Bible and mission in 1982 from Columbia Bible College (now Columbia International University) and spoke in more than one thousand churches. From 1982 to 1985 he served as the first director of the Billy Graham Lay Center in Asheville, North Carolina. He also visited seven countries as part of his lay ministry, concentrating on Romania, which he visited sixteen times. He helped establish a trade agreement between Romania and the United States, and he worked with Providence Hospital in Columbia to develop an exchange program with a hospital in Cluj-Napoca, Romania.

Dent authored five books. *The Prodigal South Returns to Power* (1978) is an inside account of national and southern politics during the 1960s and 1970s. Dent's other writings include *A Layman Looks through the Bible for God's Will* (1983), *Cover-Up: The Watergate in All of Us* (1986), *Right vs. Wrong: Solutions to the American Nightmare* (1992), and *Teaching Jack and Jill Right vs. Wrong in the Homes and Schools* (1996). JACK BASS

DeSaussure, Henry William (1763–1839). Lawyer, jurist, statesman. DeSaussure was born on August 16, 1763, at Pocotaligo, Beaufort District, the son of the merchant Daniel DeSaussure and Mary McPherson. While still in his teens, DeSaussure participated in the defense of Charleston during the Revolutionary War and was taken prisoner by the British in May 1780, but he was later released and exiled to Philadelphia. It was in Philadelphia that DeSaussure entered the career that would define his public life by studying law under Jared Ingersoll. DeSaussure was admitted to the Pennsylvania Bar in 1784. The following year he returned to South Carolina, married Elizabeth Ford, and opened a legal practice with his brother-in-law Timothy Ford.

DeSaussure quickly became a prominent voice in lowcountry politics, aligning himself with the Federalist Party (in which he served as a presidential elector in 1796) and holding civic posts in Charleston throughout his career. He also served as a member of the 1790 convention in Columbia that drafted a new state constitution. Elected to the South Carolina General Assembly in 1791 from St. Philip's and St. Michael's Parishes, he served in that body throughout the 1790s, the only interruption occurring with his appointment as director of the U.S. Mint in 1795 (though he only occupied the post for four months).

In the legislature, DeSaussure quickly became an advocate for lowcountry interests and the legal profession that he represented. He served his profession by participating actively in the 1791 reorganization of South Carolina's circuit court system and defended the political power of the lowcountry by opposing upcountry demands for reapportionment of the state legislature. According to DeSaussure, though the upcountry's population was growing rapidly, there were few from that region with the necessary intellectual refinement to serve in higher political office. DeSaussure and many of his fellow lowcountrymen feared that upcountry growth would overwhelm their interests, especially the protections given to both plantation and slave holdings. Regarding the increasingly egalitarian rhetoric of upcountry leaders and their yeomen constituents with "dread," he warned of the "ultimate effects of a degrading, calumnating democracy."

Reelected to the General Assembly in 1800, DeSaussure was instrumental in the incorporation of South Carolina College (later the University of South Carolina). He saw the institution as a way in which the future leadership of South Carolina could be imbued with the qualities necessary for political leadership. Despite his opposition to earlier reapportionment schemes, by 1800 DeSaussure recognized that the upcountry would soon provide the bulk of South Carolina's leaders. "We of the lower country well knew that the power of the State was thence forward to be in the upper country," he later recalled, "and we desired our future rulers to be educated men." Returning to the General Assembly in 1808, this time from St. Paul's Parish, DeSaussure saw his prophecy realized. The Compromise of 1808 brought legislative reapportionment based on both population and wealth and gave the upcountry an equal voice with coastal parishes in state politics.

Though elected to another term in 1808, DeSaussure resigned his seat in December to become a judge of the South Carolina Court of Equity. He held this office until the court's reorganization in 1824, when he became chancellor of the Court of Appeals in Equity. DeSaussure was an active jurist, writing over half of the court's decisions throughout his tenure. In addition, he compiled and published *Reports of the Court of Chancery and Court of Equity in South Carolina from the Revolution till 1813* (1817–1819), which further enhanced his legal reputation. Politically, DeSaussure retained sympathy for the Federalist viewpoint, even as both the party and its remaining members disappeared from the public sphere. He remained a Unionist during the nullification crisis of the early 1830s, although he vehemently opposed the use of protective tariffs by the federal government and argued that the continuation of such a sectionally motivated policy would guarantee "the separation of the Union which I pray God I may not live to see."

DeSaussure did not live to see the escalation of the sectional crisis, however. Failing health caused him to retire from the bench in

1837, and he succumbed to a prolonged illness on March 26, 1839, while visiting Charleston. DeSaussure was buried in his family churchyard in Columbia. KEVIN M. GANNON

DeSaussure, Henry William. Papers. South Caroliniana Library, University of South Carolina, Columbia.

DeSaussure Family. Papers. South Carolina Historical Society, Charleston.

Harper, William. *Memoir of the Life, Character, and Public Services of the Late Hon. Henry Wm. DeSaussure.* Charleston, S.C.: Riley, 1841.

DeSaussure, William Ford (1792–1870). U.S. senator. DeSaussure was born in Charleston on February 22, 1792, the son of Chancellor Henry William DeSaussure and Eliza Ford. He graduated from Harvard University in 1810. After his admission to the bar in 1813, he practiced law in Columbia. He married Sara Davie, a daughter of North Carolina governor William Richardson Davie. A son, Colonel William Davie DeSaussure, was killed at the Battle of Gettysburg in 1863.

DeSaussure served as intendant (mayor) of Columbia from 1826 to 1828. In 1846 Richland District elected him to the state House of Representatives, where he served until 1850. In 1852 he was chosen to complete the term of Robert Barnwell Rhett in the U.S. Senate and served from May 10, 1852, until March 3, 1853. Although in office less than a year, DeSaussure considered the Senate to be "grand theater, the arena where proud Sovereignties are fighting for their rights." An ardent supporter of southern rights, DeSaussure at one time courted Pennsylvania senator James Cooper to encourage his state to join the secession movement, enticing Pennsylvania with promises of a monopoly on the southern market for coal, iron, and manufactures. DeSaussure remained politically active after leaving the Senate. He represented Richland District at the Secession Convention in 1860 and signed the Ordinance of Secession. In later years he resumed his law practice and remained active in the affairs of South Carolina College (later the University of South Carolina), where he served as a trustee from 1833 to 1865. DeSaussure died in Columbia on March 13, 1870. He was buried in the First Presbyterian Church Cemetery. VERONICA BRUCE MCCONNELL

May, John Amasa, and Joan Reynolds Faunt, eds. *South Carolina Secedes.* Columbia: University of South Carolina Press, 1960.

Deveaux, Andrew, IV (1758–1812). Loyalist. Deveaux was born in Beaufort on April 30, 1758. His father was Andrew Deveaux III, a wealthy planter and cattleman on Port Royal Island, and his mother was Catherine Barnwell, a granddaughter of "Tuscarora Jack" Barnwell. His father was prominent in local politics as a member of the St. Helena's Parish vestry and as commissioner to build the first Beaufort District courthouse in 1769. He was also a well-known Loyalist who was among the delegation of Beaufort men who encouraged Governor Charles Montagu to move the colonial capital from Charleston to Beaufort in 1772.

With the outbreak of the Revolutionary War in 1775, Andrew Deveaux III was subjected to insults and harassment by the local patriot sympathizers. This prompted Andrew Deveaux IV to form a body of Loyalist ruffians, who disrupted patriot meetings in Beaufort whenever possible. This local rivalry continued for several years until the arrival of British troops from Savannah on Port Royal Island in February 1779. Deveaux assisted the British landing and joined the invading army. Deveaux and his Loyalist partisans are believed to have been responsible for burning the Prince William Parish church at Sheldon in April 1779. Deveaux was commissioned as a major in the South Carolina Loyalist militia known as the "Royal Foresters" and served the British army occupying South Carolina for the next three years. He was second in command of the Loyalist garrison at Fort Balfour in Beaufort District in 1781. In 1782 he was among the British occupation garrison in Charleston. He led several daring and successful waterborne raids among the Sea Islands and actually occupied Beaufort for two weeks in March 1782.

When the British evacuated Charleston in December 1782, Deveaux, now a lieutenant colonel, left with them. His father's estates were confiscated, and most of his family became refugees in St. Augustine, Florida. In 1783 Deveaux raised a small army of volunteers from the Carolina Loyalist refugees in Florida and outfitted six small-armed vessels at his own expense. With this little fleet he sailed to Nassau, Bahamas, which was then occupied by seven hundred Spanish soldiers from Cuba. Nassau had been captured from the British in 1782 by a combined American and Spanish fleet. Deveaux successfully blockaded the harbor and by daring maneuvers forced the surrender of superior Spanish forces. By this conquest Deveaux was made de facto governor of the Bahamas from April to September 1783. By the terms of the Treaty of Paris in 1783, the Bahama Islands remained part of the British Empire and southern Loyalists were given large grants of Bahamian lands. The Bahamian Loyalists took over the politics of the colony, populated the islands with their slaves, and began growing a crop later known in America as Sea Island cotton.

Deveaux traveled to London, where he was awarded half-pay as a lieutenant colonel in the British army for his service to the crown. He then moved to New York, where he married a wealthy heiress, Anna Maria Verplanck. They settled at Red Hook, Duchess County, New York. Deveaux died in New York City on July 11, 1812, as a result of injuries sustained in a fall from a balcony. LAWRENCE S. ROWLAND

Rowland, Lawrence S., Alexander Moore, and George C. Rogers. *The History of Beaufort County.* Vol. 1, *1514–1861.* Columbia: University of South Carolina Press, 1996.

Saunders, Gail. *Bahamian Loyalists and Their Slaves.* London: Macmillan, 1983.

———. *Slavery in the Bahamas, 1648–1838.* Nassau: D. G. Saunders, 1985.

Siebert, Wilbur H. *Loyalists in East Florida, 1774 to 1785: The Most Important Documents Pertaining Thereto, Edited with an Accompanying Narrative.* 2 vols. DeLand: Florida State Historical Society, 1929.

Dial, Nathaniel Barksdale (1862–1940). U.S. senator. Dial was born near Laurens on April 24, 1862, to Albert Dial, a prominent local farmer, and Martha Rebecca Barksdale. He attended Laurens County schools, the University of Richmond, and Vanderbilt University. After a year of law school at the University of Virginia, Dial returned to South Carolina in 1883 and established a law practice in Laurens. That same year he married Ruth Mitchell of Batesburg. The couple eventually had six children. After the death of his first wife in 1900, Dial married Josephine Minter of Laurens. They had two children.

Influenced by the New South movement, Dial became an advocate for improving the region's economy by building financial institutions, developing energy sources, and industrialization. Between 1887 and 1897 Dial served three terms as mayor of Laurens and was instrumental in getting streets paved, having bridges and public buildings built, and obtaining electric, water, and telephone services. As an entrepreneur, he helped establish the Enterprise National Bank and the Home Trust Company in Laurens and was involved with the Laurens Cotton Mill and the Ware Shoals Manufacturing Company. To support these operations, Dial secured financing, started a company to manufacture brick needed for construction, and formed the Reedy River Power Company to ensure an adequate electricity supply. In 1910 Dial helped create the Laurens Glass Company after silica deposits were found nearby. During his lifetime Dial was credited with doing more to create industrial development in his corner of the state than any other individual.

In 1912 Dial entered his first statewide political race and challenged Benjamin Ryan Tillman for the U.S. Senate. As Tillman had a strong political base, the relatively unknown Dial was soundly defeated. He was not a good public speaker and scorned the fact that people wanted to be entertained at political rallies. In 1918 Dial again challenged Tillman and former governor Coleman L. Blease for a Senate seat. Tillman suffered a fatal stroke before the campaign began, and Dial effectively attacked Blease for his refusal to support President Woodrow Wilson and U.S. involvement in World War I. Dial's strategy worked, and he defeated Blease in the August Democratic primary.

After he claimed his Senate seat on May 19, 1919, Dial's conservatism prevented him from supporting measures that would have helped relieve the distress of South Carolina farmers. He opposed federal minimum wage and child-labor laws, and his objections to the World War I bonus bill cost him support among veterans. In 1924 Blease, whose popularity had risen, unseated Dial. Two years later Dial again ran for the Senate, challenging the popular incumbent Ellison D. Smith. Despite campaign literature that touted his successful opposition to a "Yankee pension bill" and claims that he saved taxpayers "more than any man in Congress," Dial finished third in the three-way contest.

After the 1926 loss, Dial remained in Washington and practiced law despite setbacks suffered by his South Carolina business interests, especially during the Depression. After years of poor health, Dial died on December 11, 1940, in Washington. He was buried in Laurens. WILLIAM COPELAND COOPER

Slaunwhite, Jerry L. "The Public Career of Nathaniel Barksdale Dial." Ph.D. diss., University of South Carolina, 1978.

Dickey, James (1923–1997). Poet, novelist, educator. Considered in the 1960s to be the chief rival to Robert Lowell as the major poet of the generation, James Dickey spent almost thirty years as resident poet and Carolina Professor of English at the University of South Carolina in Columbia. Dickey was born on February 2, 1923, in Atlanta, Georgia, the son of Eugene Dickey and Maibelle Swift. He graduated from North Fulton High School in 1941. After an unhappy preparatory year at Darlington Academy in Rome, Georgia, he enrolled for the fall semester of 1942 at Clemson College to play football. He performed well only in one game, but his Clemson experience established a basis for a myth of Dickey as sports star. At the end of the football season, he left Clemson to join the U.S. Army Air Corps. He served in the Pacific as a radar observer.

After the war Dickey moved on to Vanderbilt University. He received a bachelor's degree with high honors in 1949 and an M.A. in 1950. He married Maxine Webster Syerson on November 4, 1948. The marriage produced two sons. Dickey taught at Rice University until he was recalled for the war in Korea. After the war he returned to Rice until 1954, when he received a *Sewanee Review* fellowship to spend a year in Europe writing poetry.

On his return, Dickey accepted an instructorship at the University of Florida but resigned in response to verbal flack received from reading a poem in progress, "My Father's Body." After six years as a copywriter and director in advertising firms in New York and Atlanta, he was awarded a Guggenheim Fellowship in 1961. This permitted a return to Europe, where he, like many other southern writers, wrote about the South from a faraway country. He abandoned his moneymaking advertising career to go "barnstorming for poetry." Dickey performed well as poet-in-residence at Reed College (1963–1964), San Fernando Valley State (1965), and the University of Wisconsin (1966), climaxed by his appointment as poetry consultant (1966–1968) at the Library of Congress, where he was successful at setting up readings.

James Dickey. © David G. Speilman-97, New Orleans

In 1968 Dickey was appointed the first Carolina Professor at the University of South Carolina and settled in Columbia, beginning thirty years of distinguished teaching there. Maxine Dickey died on October 27, 1976. Shortly thereafter, on December 30, 1976, Dickey married a student, Deborah Dodson. The couple had one daughter.

Dickey published widely, including books of poetry, novels, essays and criticism, children's books, and a few expensive coffee-table books. Two of the three volumes of literary criticism, *The Suspect in Poetry* (1964) and *Babel to Byzantium: Poets and Poetry Today* (1965), were published during the 1960s. Dickey identified the "suspect" in poetry as a failure to involve the reader. His readings of the Cambridge anthropologists, his discovery of Theodore Roethke, and a friendship with the poet James Wright led to an interest in "country surrealism," a blending of nature and fantasy. Dickey also mastered an empathetic exchange of identity, as with his dog sleeping on his feet, or with a dead soldier whose helmet he donned, or with a flight attendant falling to her death. "The String," a poem from his first book, *Into the Stone* (1960), introduced the theme of the survivor, beginning with Dickey's view of himself as a replacement child for a dead brother. A plenitude of like poems appeared in *Drowning with Others* (1962), *Helmets* (1964), and *Buckdancer's Choice* (1965), which won the National Book Award. A climax came with his novel *Deliverance* (1970), followed by a powerful film version highlighting the naturalism and primitivism of both novel and poetry. His "energized" protagonist or persona "beholds" nature, regains an original relationship, and experiences deliverance from the bonds of civilized life.

Success encouraged Dickey to take greater risks with two big, overly complex novels: one about flying, *Alnilam* (1987); and one about war and killing, *To the White Sea* (1991). Some critics found in Dickey little more than a pretentious "more life school" yearning, while others such as Harold Bloom credited Dickey with a contribution to the American sublime. One thing is clear: the earlier Dickey was largely successful with long lines that advance both the narrative and the lyric. After the summer of *Deliverance,* the lines "loosened," a split line experiment largely failed, and the dramatic became rhetorical. Most of the "good" poems were written in a decade from the 1960s into the 1970s, with the exception of a few good lyrics in *Puella* (1982) and some good narrative moments in *The Eagle's Mile* (1990). Randall Jarrell said that for a poet to be major, lightning had to strike a dozen poems. It struck enough for Dickey to deserve consideration as South Carolina's best resident poet since Henry Timrod.

The final word on Dickey was "decline"—decline from his reputation as a major poet in the 1960s, decline from his status as a brilliant performer to unseemly public behavior, and decline in health. Dickey died in Columbia on January 19, 1997, and was buried in the All Saints Waccamaw graveyard on Pawleys Island. RICHARD CALHOUN

Calhoun, Richard J., and Robert W. Hill. *James Dickey.* Boston: Twayne, 1983.

Dickey, James. *The Whole Motion: Collected Poems, 1945–1992.* Middleton, Conn.: Wesleyan University Press, 1992.

Hart, Henry. *James Dickey: The World as a Lie.* New York: Picador, 2000.

Kirschten, Robert, ed. *"Struggling for Wings": The Art of James Dickey.* Columbia: University of South Carolina Press, 1997.

Dickson, Samuel Henry (1798–1872). Physician, essayist. Dickson was born in Charleston on September 20, 1798, the son of the Scots-Irish immigrants Samuel Dickson and Mary Neilson. He began his higher education at the College of Charleston, entered Yale in 1811, and received the A.B. degree in 1814. He returned to Charleston and studied medicine with Dr. Philip G. Prioleau and entered practice during a yellow fever epidemic in 1817. He received his medical degree from the University of Pennsylvania in 1819 and again returned to Charleston. Yellow fever struck Charleston again in 1819, and Dickson began a steady rise to prominence in the medical community after competently directing the Marine Hospital and a temporary medical facility in Hampstead during the epidemic.

Dickson's stature rests in two quite different intellectual arenas, medicine and literature. He advocated improvements in medical education that were well in advance of his time. Early in his career, he was an influential figure in the chartering of the Medical College of South Carolina (1823). He was elected professor of medicine in the new school and gave the inaugural address for the first entering class in 1824. He retained this position through the reorganization of the original faculty into the Medical College of the State of South Carolina in 1833. He joined the faculty of the New York University Medical College in 1847 but remained for only three years.

Dickson's reputation increased to the point that he was pursued by several medical schools. In 1857 he accepted an appointment to the faculty of the Jefferson Medical College in Philadelphia, where he remained for the rest of his life. Dickson was a frequent contributor to medical journals and wrote several well-received books on medicine, including *A Manual of Pathology and Medicine* and *Essays on Pathology and Therapeutics.*

Dickson was a talented speaker and essayist on nonmedical subjects. His literary interests led him to associate with many of the prominent literary figures of the day, including William Gilmore Simms. Illustrative of these interests were *An Oration Delivered at New Haven before the Phi Beta Kappa Society* (1842) and a nostalgic poem, *I Sigh for the Land of Cyprus and Pine* (1845). He was an honorary member of nine literary or philosophical societies, as well as ten state medical societies. He received the LL.D. degree from New York University in 1853.

Dickson married three times: first in November 1821 to Elizabeth B. Robertson, who died in 1832; in 1834 to his sister-in-law, Irene Robertson, who died in 1842; and to Marie Seabrook Dupre in 1845. Two married daughters, Elizabeth and Sarah, were living in Charleston in 1858. Dickson died in Philadelphia on March 31, 1872. He was buried in Woodlawn Cemetery in West Philadelphia.
W. CURTIS WORTHINGTON

Radbill, Samuel X. "Samuel Henry Dickson: Pioneer Southern Medical Educator." In *Annals of Medical History.* Vol. 4. New York: Paul Hober, 1942.

Waring, Joseph I. *A History of Medicine in South Carolina.* Vol. 2, *1825–1900.* Columbia: South Carolina Medical Association, 1967.

Dillon (Dillon County; 2000 pop. 6,316). In the late 1800s, the need arose in northeastern South Carolina for a north-south rail line to bypass the long loop eastward through Wilmington, North Carolina. To solve the problem, the Florence Railroad Company planned a line from Pee Dee, near Florence, to the North Carolina border, which would also pass through the town of Little Rock in upper Marion County. However, the project seemed doomed when several Little Rock landowners refused to grant rights-of-way. James W. Dillon, a Little Rock merchant, and his son, Thomas, recognized the importance of the railroad to local development. Acting quickly, they obtained options on fifty acres, about five miles east of Little Rock, which they then offered to the railroad on the condition that a depot and a town named Dillon would be located there. The offer was accepted, and construction of the railroad began in 1886. The depot was built in a marshy clearing. Settlers quickly followed, and the fledgling town of Dillon soon took shape. While construction of the railroad was under way, the Little Rock physician John H. David arrived in Dillon and instructed railroad engineers to plot a circle one mile in diameter from the depot. Within this circle wide streets were laid, parallel and perpendicular, forming perfect blocks three hundred feet square. The state legislature approved Dillon's application for a municipal charter on December 22, 1888.

When Dillon County was formed in 1910, it became necessary to construct a courthouse in Dillon, the county seat. James and Thomas Dillon contributed $25,000 toward its construction, as well as half of the full block needed for its location. Work on the impressive two-story, beaux arts structure was completed at a cost of $100,000. In 1999 the courthouse underwent a $1 million renovation. To celebrate the completed project, a special session of the S.C. Supreme Court was held in the beautifully decorated courtroom, with many dignitaries in attendance.

In 1928, thanks to the influence of Dillon County senator Robert S. Rogers and Dr. Wade Stackhouse, a Dillonite who chaired the S.C. Coastal Highway Commission, U.S. Highway 301 was routed through Dillon. This highway became the major overland route between New York and Florida. Located about the midpoint of the route, Dillon became a popular stop-over point, and tourist business flourished. In 1950 Alan Schafer, a prominent businessman from Little Rock, built a small diner on Highway 301 at the North Carolina border. From this modest beginning he developed South of the Border, a giant tourist complex. The nearby community of Dillon enjoyed many benefits from its operation, as well as from Schafer's generosity.

The citizens of Dillon possessed an optimistic outlook for their community as it entered the twenty-first century. Dillon had a new library, plans for a Young Men's Christian Association and community center, a downtown revitalization project, and Salley Huggins-Cook, the city's youngest and first female mayor. W. R. BRADDY

Stokes, Durwood T. *The History of Dillon County, South Carolina.* Columbia: University of South Carolina Press, 1978.

Dillon County (405 sq. miles; 2000 pop. 30,722). Dillon County, known as "The Golden Land," was formed in 1910 from the upper portion of Marion County. Its triangular shape is bound on the east by North Carolina and the Lumber River and on the west by Marlboro County and the Great Pee Dee River. Its southern boundary was painstakingly drawn so that at least five hundred square miles remained in Marion County and at least four hundred miles were included in the new county, as required by the state constitution.

Settlers were slow to come to the area that became Dillon County. It was isolated and occupied by the Sara Indians, who were hostile toward the encroachments of European settlers. Roads were primitive and few. Most early settlers came to the northern part of the territory, near the Little Pee Dee River, which developed into a community named Harleesville, later Little Rock. Upper Marion's first post office opened there in 1807. Although the fertile soil was highly productive, poor transportation made it difficult for residents to market surplus grains and staple crops. As a result, the earliest commercial venture was raising cattle, which were driven overland to supply beef to the lowcountry. As river and road transportation improved, residents of upper Marion intensified their farming efforts. As in much of antebellum South Carolina, cotton became the dominant crop. By 1860 planters and farmers along the upper Little Pee Dee Valley produced 4,564 bales of cotton. Agriculture would dominate the region's economy throughout the nineteenth century.

The county's struggle for political independence began in 1895 with the adoption of a state constitution that eased restrictions on creating new counties. The political leaders of lower Marion did everything they could to prevent the separation. With the population concentrated in lower Marion, political control rested there. But while the rich farmland of upper Marion produced large property taxes, government expenditures for road maintenance and services were kept low. As a result, upper Marion's leaders grew determined to have their own county. The construction of the Florence Railroad Line through upper Marion, with stations at Dillon and Latta, added to the new county movement by improving transportation and shipping facilities, which spurred rapid population growth. Finally, after five elections, three surveys, and fifteen years of political maneuvering, all of the requirements for the creation of the new county were met. In a referendum on December 14, 1909, voters supported a new county by an overwhelming margin, 1,615 to 272. Dillon was selected as the name based on the name of its largest town.

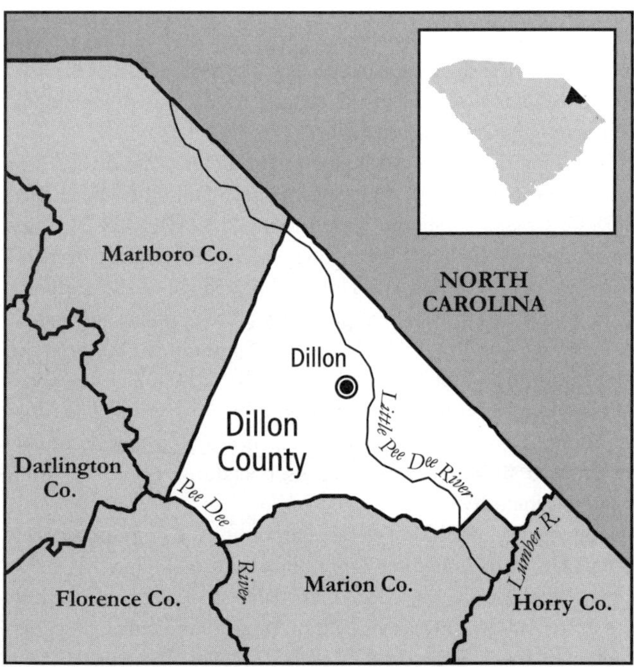

Agriculture continued as the backbone of Dillon County's economy at the start of the twentieth century. A combination of climate, water resources, and fertile terrain created excellent growing conditions. However, following the onslaught of the boll weevil and disastrously low prices during the Depression of the 1930s, cotton gradually fell out of favor, forcing farmers to seek an alternate crop. Tobacco was the answer. Income from the "golden weed" grew dramatically and quickly overtook cotton as the leading money crop. By 1997 Dillon County's tobacco yield had grown to $18.6 million, with cotton a distant second at $5.4 million. During the last half of the twentieth century, farm size and methodology changed dramatically, with machinery replacing manual labor to a large degree. Dillon County farms grew larger in size and fewer in number. In 1950 the county had 3,336 farms, averaging sixty-three acres. By 1997 the number of farms had dropped to 199, while average acreage increased to 458 acres. Mechanized farming forced many families off the land.

As in many South Carolina counties, Dillon's industry had consisted mostly of cotton mills, which became increasingly outdated as the twentieth century progressed. In 1954 Dillon County's industrial base expanded significantly with the arrival of Dixiana Mills, a division of Mohawk Carpets, which created badly needed jobs for displaced farm workers and others. In 1995 Dixiana stunned the county by closing its Dillon plant and moving to Calhoun, Georgia. Fortunately, in 1992 Perdue Farms, Inc., had established in Dillon a chicken processing plant, which helped to replace many of the lost jobs. In 2000 Perdue employed 1,250 workers. In addition, each week local farmers raised 1.25 million chickens from Perdue's hatchery in Dillon. As the new century began, there were twenty-one industries in Dillon County employing approximately 3,500 people. The balance between agriculture and industry worked to maintain a healthy economy.

Besides the county seat of Dillon, the county is home to two other incorporated towns. Latta was established in 1887 as a station for the Florence Railroad. Located seven miles south of Dillon, this community established its cultural and educational leadership long before the county was formed. Hofwyl Academy, built in 1853 near the present town, was widely recognized as the foremost educational facility in upper Marion. It was the forerunner of Latta's public school system, which proved its excellence in many ways over the years. From 1997 to 1999 the SAT scores of Latta students exceeded those of the county's other two districts by more than one hundred points. The Latta Library, built with a tax levy and a $5,000 grant from the Carnegie Foundation, became the county's first library in 1914 and became the nucleus of the Dillon County library system.

Lake View, originally called Ford's Mill, is thirteen miles east of Dillon. It began as a pond and gristmill in 1792, which makes its origin the earliest of the county's three incorporated towns. Lake View proudly claims Page's Mill Pond, with its moss-draped cypress trees, black waters, and carefully preserved gristmill, to be the most picturesque spot in Dillon County. The town also has a reputation for excellence in athletics, with its teams earning eight state championships in football, six in baseball, and one in basketball. In 2001

Josh Cribb of Lake View became the first South Carolina high school pitcher to go an entire season without allowing an earned run. At the end of the twentieth century, life in Dillon County was aptly characterized by its motto: "Quietly Progressive." W. R. BRADDY

Stokes, Durward T. *The History of Dillon County, South Carolina.* Columbia: University of South Carolina Press, 1978.

Dispensary. In 1892 South Carolina adopted the dispensary system, which gave the state a monopoly on the sale of liquor. In the early 1890s South Carolina was poised to adopt statewide prohibition. Governor Benjamin Tillman, however, pressured the legislature to pass instead his proposal for state liquor monopoly legislation. Basing his idea on European models, Tillman portrayed the dispensary as a compromise between the private sale of liquor and prohibition that would promote temperance and clean up politics.

The dispensary law prohibited the manufacture of liquor and provided that only the government could sell liquor. Each county chose to have either a dispensary or prohibition, with all but two counties eventually choosing to establish dispensaries. The state board of control set dispensary policies and also appointed county boards of control, which in turn appointed local dispensers. Dispensers sold liquor at set prices and divided the profits among the state, the municipality, and the county. The law also created a special liquor constabulary.

From beginning to end, the dispensary failed to work as designed. The constables charged with enforcing the law bore the brunt of resistance. In Darlington a riot over attempted implementation of the system led to a revolt of the state militia. Tillman responded by imposing martial law. Moreover, the system lost its temperance trappings and soon turned into a money-making machine. Patronage battles and widespread corruption characterized its operations.

TROOPS GUARDING THE DARLINGTON (S. C.) DISPENSARY.

Governor Tillman called out the militia to protect the dispensary in Darlington after dispensary officials fired on local residents and caused a riot. Courtesy, South Carolina Historical Society

Overwhelmed by these problems, the state dismantled the dispensary system. In 1907 the system was closed, but counties were allowed to continue local dispensaries. Six counties kept the system; their vast business prompted six others to join them by 1913. In the meantime, prohibition was gaining momentum in the South and the nation. In a 1915 referendum the state voted to adopt prohibition and shut down the dispensaries. But following the failure of national prohibition in 1933, many states followed South Carolina's lead and created state liquor monopoly systems. RICHARD F. HAMM

Eubanks, John Evans. *Ben Tillman's Baby: The Dispensary System of South Carolina, 1892–1915.* Augusta, Ga., 1950.

Heath, Frederick M., and Harriet H. Kinard. "Prohibition in South Carolina, 1880–1940: An Overview." *Proceedings of the South Carolina Historical Association* (1980): 118–32.

Hendricks, Ellen Alexander. "The South Carolina Dispensary System." *North Carolina Historical Review* 22 (April 1945): 176–97; (July 1945): 320–49.

Wallace, Rita Foster. "South Carolina State Dispensary, 1893–1907." Master's thesis, University of South Carolina, 1996.

A quart dispensary bottle featuring the palmetto tree. Courtesy, Calhoun County Museum

Dissenters. From the earliest years of European settlement in South Carolina, religious dissenters (non-Anglicans) comprised a significant part of its population and played an important role in its government, economy, and society. The eight Lords Proprietors of Carolina envisioned for their colony a model structure of religious toleration, partly to attract nonconforming settlers. To that end, they guaranteed "full and free Liberty of Conscience" to all settlers and assured dissenters that they would not be taxed for the support of the Anglican Church. This policy attracted Presbyterians and Baptists from England, as well as Huguenots seeking refuge after the revocation of the Edict of Nantes in 1685. Numerous Anglicans from Barbados also came to the colony, settling primarily near Goose Creek. Cognizant of the potentially toxic mixture of these many different religious faiths, the Lords Proprietors tried to make religion politically neutral by prohibiting ministers from sitting in the legislature or holding public office and by allowing dissenters the right to serve in the government. In this noble goal, however, the proprietors failed.

Confrontation between the evenly matched dissenters and Anglicans caused considerable political friction in South Carolina for decades. Throughout the seventeenth century the Goose Creek Men, who controlled local government and who rejected the policy of religious toleration, consistently opposed proprietary policy. The dissenters, grateful for the policy of religious toleration that had given them a place of refuge, supported the proprietors. The proprietors tried repeatedly to break the power of the Goose Creek Men, but their attempts only provoked political disorder. After 1700 the proprietors, seeking a compromise with the Goose Creek Men, reversed their policy on religious toleration and sought to establish the Church of England as the state church of South Carolina. In 1704 the Anglican governor Sir Nathaniel Johnson pushed through the Assembly a Test Act requiring all members to conform to the

The Congregational Church in Charleston was built on the site of the first dissenting meeting house in the city and gave Meeting Street its name. Courtesy, South Carolina Historical Society

Church of England and an Establishment Act making the Church of England "settled and Established" in the colony. The dissenters quickly protested against these two acts to the English Parliament, arguing that they were unprecedented in the colonies, contrary to the Carolina charter, and discriminatory. The House of Lords concurred with the dissenters and disallowed both acts. The Anglican-dominated Assembly responded in 1706 by passing a more moderate Establishment Act that allowed dissenters full political participation. This policy of moderation toward dissenters contributed to relative religious harmony through the remainder of royal rule.

One area of exception to this religious harmony was the backcountry, where the Anglican clergymen failed to make an appeal to the numerous Presbyterian and Baptist dissenters residing in the region. Instead, the Anglican-controlled Assembly fueled sectional and religious tension by refusing to provide the frontier inhabitants with courts, jails, representation, schools, and churches. In the early 1760s dissenters in the region complained to the legislature that they paid taxes to support Anglican churches and ministers in the lowcountry while they had none of either. On the eve of revolution, lowcountry patriot leaders realized that the success of their cause required the support of the backcountry majority. Thus, they promised religious freedom to dissenters in hopes of enticing them to support the local rebellion. The Presbyterian minister and patriot leader William Tennent petitioned the General Assembly in 1777 to disestablish the Anglican Church. In 1778 the Assembly adopted a second state constitution that disestablished the Church of England but still required voters to believe in God and legislators to be Protestants. Only with the 1790 constitution did religious freedom and separation of church and state prevail in South Carolina. KEITH KRAWCZYNSKI

Bolton, S. Charles. *Southern Anglicanism: The Church of England in Colonial South Carolina.* Westport, Conn.: Greenwood, 1982.

Curry, Thomas J. *The First Freedoms: Church and State in America to the Passage of the First Amendment.* New York: Oxford University Press, 1986.

Sirmans, M. Eugene. *Colonial South Carolina: A Political History, 1663–1763.* Chapel Hill: University of North Carolina Press, 1966.

Divorce. On December 20, 1878, the South Carolina legislature repealed the state's short-lived divorce law, intentionally granting South Carolina the unique status of being the only state in the nation to prohibit divorce. For the next seventy-one years South Carolina stood alone and consistently refused to grant divorces to its citizens. While other states had been legalizing divorce since the early nineteenth century, South Carolina steadfastly refused, disapproving of government interference in any "domestic institution."

For a brief period before this hard-core stance was resumed, Reconstruction legislators had enacted the state's first divorce law in 1872. Defending divorce as biblically justified and practically necessary to remedy problems that inevitably arose in the course of human relationships, the Republican-controlled legislature passed a law that allowed divorce on two grounds only, adultery and desertion. From 1872 to 1878 the courts granted 157 divorces. When white Democrats regained control of state government, they diligently attacked much legislation enacted by the Republicans, including the divorce law. Arguing that the law violated the sanctity of family and marriage, Democrats repealed the law in 1878. For the next fifteen years a bill advocating some form of divorce appeared before at least one house of the General Assembly almost every year and failed. At the constitutional convention of 1895 the perennial divorce debate surfaced. Delegate Daniel Henderson argued that the state's relentless stand against divorce offered incentives to those who destroyed homes and winked at the "crime of adultery." Opponents prevailed, however, strengthening their position with a clause in the 1895 constitution that prohibited divorce. One journalist's comment expressed the sentiments of many: "As our State stands today in a distinguished minority of right, her position is an honorable one and should never be changed." Similar prideful assertions accompanied every defense of South Carolina's extreme position against divorce for the next half-century.

Although divorce was forbidden, South Carolinians were not exempt from desertions, bigamy, abusive marriages, adulterous relationships, and illegitimate children. In fact, desertion functioned as a de facto divorce in South Carolina. Defiantly opposing divorce did not restore the state to its antebellum stature, increase personal incomes, or educate its populace, but it could foster self-respect for a state that trailed the nation in most indicators of well-being. Moreover, white South Carolinians, still bitter over Reconstruction, could point to South Carolina's only departure from its historic stance and equate it with an era they despised. While it was only a legal mirage that South Carolina marriages never deteriorated because the state provided no legal mechanism for their dissolution, it was an illusion that mattered to many. With pressure from a changing world in the World War II era, South Carolina amended the state constitution in 1949 and the legislature passed a law allowing divorce on four grounds: adultery, desertion, physical cruelty, and habitual drunkenness. JANET G. HUDSON

Hudson, Janet. "From Constitution to Constitution, 1868–1895: South Carolina's Unique Stance on Divorce." *South Carolina Historical Magazine* 98 (January 1997): 75–96.

Dixie Hummingbirds. Started in 1928 by twelve-year-old James Davis and neighborhood friends Bonnie Gipson, Jr., Fred Owens, and Barney Parks, the gospel quartet—and later quintet—influenced scores of gospel, soul, and rock and roll artists. First called the Sterling High School Quartet, named for the high school the young men attended in their hometown of Greenville, the group made the transition from a cappella harmony singing at the Bethel Church of God to electrified music.

The group was singing professionally in churches and on the radio by the mid-1930s, and Davis wanted to name the group the South Carolina Hummingbirds but determined that that would be too long. The Birds, as their fans affectionately came to call them, drove to New York City to record twelve old-time harmony sides for the Decca label in 1938. That same year, with the addition of the thirteen-year-old singer and Spartanburg native Ira Tucker, the group moved toward a more powerful electric sound that served as a precursor to rock music. The group moved to Philadelphia in 1942, and Tucker worked his way from backing tenor into the group's fiery and flamboyant (for the times and the genre of music) lead singer. By their 1952 recordings on the Peacock label, the Birds were on their way to gospel stardom.

The group is perhaps best known for their re-recording of "Loves Me Like a Rock" with the singer-songwriter Paul Simon in 1973, for which they won a Grammy Award. Artists as prominent as Stevie Wonder credit the Birds as a direct musical influence, drawing on Tucker's audience interaction and his soaring, pleading vocals. William Bobo, who joined the group after Tucker, is considered to be one of the great bass singers in the history of American popular music. One reviewer wrote that the group claimed "almost universal recognition as the greatest Southern quartet of their generation." ALAN RICHARD

Bogdanov, Vladmir, Chris Woodstra, and Stephen Thomas Erlewine, eds. *All Music Guide to the Blues.* San Francisco, Calif.: Backbeat, 2003.

Cooper, Peter. *Hub City Music Makers: One Southern Town's Popular Music Legacy.* Spartanburg, S.C.: Holocene, 1997.

Zolten, J. Jerome. *Great God A' Mighty! The Dixie Hummingbirds: Celebrating the Rise of Soul Gospel Music.* New York: Oxford University Press, 2003.

Dixiecrats. The Dixiecrats were a political party organized in 1948 by disgruntled white southern Democrats dismayed over their region's declining influence within the national Democratic Party. The Dixiecrats, more formally known as the States' Rights Democratic Party, were committed to states' rights and the maintenance of segregation, and opposed to federal intervention in the interest of promoting civil rights. Although the roots of the Dixiecrat revolt lay in the 1930s, the impetus for the Dixiecrat movement included President Harry Truman's civil rights program, introduced in February 1948; the civil rights plank in the national Democratic Party's 1948 presidential platform; and the unprecedented political mobilization by southern blacks in the immediate postwar era. The Dixiecrat movement was strongest in the "black belt," particularly in states with large African American populations. In South Carolina, Dixiecrat strength drew from below the fall line.

When southern conservatives failed to prevent the nomination of Harry Truman at the 1948 Democratic National Convention, some six thousand participants from thirteen southern states converged on Birmingham, Alabama, on July 17, 1948, to hold their own convention. Participants from South Carolina, Alabama, and Mississippi made up the majority of those in attendance. Governor J. Strom Thurmond of South Carolina and Governor Fielding Wright of Mississippi were nominated as the presidential and vice-presidential candidates of the States' Rights Democrats. Their goal was to win the 127 electoral college votes of the southern states. This would prevent either Republican Party nominee Thomas Dewey or Harry Truman from winning the 266 electoral votes necessary for election, thus throwing the contest into the House of Representatives, where the South would hold eleven of the forty-eight votes. In the House election it was believed that southern Democrats would be able to deadlock the election until either party had agreed to drop its own civil rights plank.

The Dixiecrats' platform was limited and negative. They opposed federal anti-lynching and anti-poll-tax legislation and a permanent Fair Employment Practices Commission (which Dixiecrats claimed would impose racial hiring quotas on employers), and were pledged to uphold segregation and white supremacy. The Dixiecrats argued that such legislation infringed on the rights of the states as set forth in the Constitution. Their electoral success depended on their ability to convince the individual states to pledge their Democratic Party electors to the States' Rights candidates.

Governor Strom Thurmond and his wife Jean Crouch Thurmond flew to Houston, Texas, for him to accept the Dixiecrat nomination for the presidency. Courtesy, Clemson. Photograph Collection, Special Collections, Clemson University Libraries

To the surprise of most Americans, Truman was elected president on November 2, 1948. The Dixiecrats received thirty-nine electoral votes, one-fifth of the popular vote in the South, and 98.8 percent of the total Dixiecrat vote was from the South. The Dixiecrats carried Alabama, South Carolina, Mississippi, and Louisiana, where Thurmond and Wright were listed as the Democratic Party nominees.

Although the Dixiecrats have been dismissed as a failed third party, they were essential to southern political change. The Dixiecrat Party broke the solid South's historic allegiance to the national Democratic Party and in doing so inaugurated an unpredictable era in which white southerners grappled with a variety of vehicles designed to thwart racial progress. Although the Dixiecrats as a distinct political entity did not survive past 1948, white southerners used the movement's organizational and intellectual framework to create new political institutions and new alliances in their desperate attempt to stymie racial progress and preserve power. Some Dixiecrats returned to the Democratic Party, while others remained uncomfortable with the party's civil rights position and chose to be political independents in the 1950s. In South Carolina many former Dixiecrats joined "Independents for Eisenhower" in 1952. Many independents eventually joined the Republican Party in the 1960s. The most famous convert was Strom Thurmond, who supported Republican Barry Goldwater in the 1964 presidential election and who ran for reelection to the U.S. Senate as a Republican in 1966. The Dixiecrats ultimately represent a transitional middle ground between the national Democratic Party, political independence, and eventually, for some, the Republican Party. KARI FREDERICKSON

Cohodas, Nadine. *Strom Thurmond and the Politics of Southern Change.* New York: Simon and Schuster, 1993.

Frederickson, Kari. *The Dixiecrat Revolt and the End of the Solid South, 1932–1968.* Chapel Hill: University of North Carolina Press, 2001.

Garson, Robert A. *The Democratic Party and the Politics of Sectionalism, 1941–1948.* Baton Rouge: Louisiana State University Press, 1974.

Dixon, Dorsey (1897–1968), and **Howard Dixon** (1903–1961). Musicians. The Dixon Brothers, popular in the mid-to-late 1930s, composed many original songs on diverse subjects, including the life and labors of textile mill workers. With Dorsey on guitar and Howard leading on steel guitar, their sound was more distinct than the traditional mandolin-guitar or twin guitar duets. Their vocal harmony—albeit somewhat rough—nonetheless had a style uniquely their own.

The Dixon brothers' parents, William McQuillan Dixon and Mary M. Braddock, worked as mill workers in Darlington, where Dorsey Murdock Dixon was born on October 14, 1897, and Howard Briten Dixon was born on June 19, 1903. At age twelve Dorsey began laboring in the mills, as did Howard at age ten. During World War I both worked on the railroad, but they returned to textile work, settling in East Rockingham, North Carolina. The boys played for local dances until the Columbia artist Jimmie Tarlton visited their community and inspired them to greater ambitions. Tarlton's skills on the steel guitar impressed Howard, who started playing that instrument. The Dixons began appearing on radio on WBT Charlotte's "Crazy Barn Dance," and they also appeared on WPTF Raleigh.

The Dixons recorded for two and one-half years for Bluebird, beginning in February 1936, and some of their material was also leased to Montgomery Ward. They cut some fifty-five sides, some of which are exceedingly rare. Most of their songs tended to be either originals or parodies composed by Dorsey. Among their popular numbers of a protest nature were "Sales Tax on the Women" and "How Can a Broke Man Be Happy." Their humorous lyrics included "The Intoxicated Rat" and "She Tickles Me." Songs such as "School House Fire," "Down with the Old Canoe," "Two Little Rosebuds," and "I Didn't Hear Anybody Pray" (also known as "Wreck on the Highway") commemorated local tragedies. Among their many memorable sacred originals were "Wonderful Day" and "Not Turning Backward." Lyrics that concerned life in the textile mills included "Weave Room Blues," "Spinning Room Blues," and "Weaver's Life."

Not only did Dorsey and Howard perform together as the Dixon Brothers, but Dorsey and his wife Beatrice recorded six sacred duets. Howard and a friend, Frank Gerald, recorded eighteen numbers under the name Rambling Duet. Another mill worker named Mutt Evans joined them on a few cuts. Howard Dixon also did some radio work as a band member for Wade Mainer at WWNC Asheville.

Both Dixons ended their performing careers and returned to the Aleo Mills in East Rockingham. Dorsey finally got credit for writing "Wreck on the Highway" after 1946. Howard worked as part of a local quartet called the Reaping Harvesters until suffering a fatal heart attack on March 24, 1961. Soon afterward the folklorists Eugene Earle and Archie Green rediscovered Dorsey and made field recordings of him and his older sister Nancy, released on a Testament album in 1964. Dorsey also made an appearance at the Newport Folk Festival in 1963, and three of his new recordings came out on a Vanguard album. After suffering a heart attack, Dorsey went to Florida and lived with his son, Dorsey Jr. He died there on April 17, 1968, a revered figure among old-time music buffs. The enduring appeal of the Dixons can be demonstrated by the fact that most of their music has been reissued, first on vinyl albums and again on compact disc. ABBY GAIL GOODNITE

Paris, Mike. "The Dixons of South Carolina." *Old Time Music* 10 (autumn 1973): 13–16.

Doby, Lawrence Edward (1923–2003). Baseball player. Larry Doby was the first African American to play baseball in the American League and the second African American to manage a major-league team. He was born in Camden on December 13, 1923, the son of David Doby and Etta Brooks. His father was a horse groomer who spent winters in Camden and summers in Saratoga, New York. Doby spent much of his childhood living with relatives and attended Mather Academy in Camden. In 1938 he moved to Patterson, New Jersey, to live with his mother and became a star athlete at Eastside High School. Doby briefly attended both Long Island University and Virginia Union in 1942 and played his first professional baseball game that year under the alias "Larry Walker" to protect his amateur status. In 1946 Doby married Helyn Curvy, and the couple eventually had five children.

Larry Doby. Courtesy, Lou Brissey of North Augusta, South Carolina

After four seasons with the Newark Eagles of the Negro Leagues, Doby was signed by the Cleveland Indians of the American League on July 5, 1947, only eleven weeks after Jackie Robinson became the first black player in modern major-league baseball. Although he started his career as an infielder, the Indians moved Doby to center field to take advantage of his speed. In his thirteen-year career Doby batted .283, with 253 home runs and 969 runs batted in. A seven-time All-Star from 1949 to 1955, Doby led the American League with thirty-two home runs in both 1952 and 1954, and the major leagues with a .541 slugging average in 1952. After the 1955 season, Doby was traded to the Chicago White Sox, where he played for two years. He returned to the Indians and played briefly with the Detroit Tigers before retiring in 1959.

After 1959 Doby worked as a scout and hitting coach for teams including the Chicago White Sox and the Montreal Expos. He returned as a player briefly in 1962, when he became one of the first Americans to play professionally in Japan. On June 30, 1978, Doby became the manager of the Chicago White Sox, making him the second black manager in the major leagues (Frank Robinson, who played in Columbia in a minor league, was the first). Doby finished the season with the White Sox, posting a record of thirty-seven wins and fifty losses. He was not retained. In the 1980s Doby served as director of community relations for the National Basketball Association's New Jersey Nets and on an advisory commission appointed by baseball commissioner Peter Ueberroth promoting black management in baseball. He received an honorary doctorate from Montclair State College in Montclair, New Jersey. Doby was elected to the South Carolina Athletic Hall of Fame in 1994 and to the National Baseball Hall of Fame in 1998. He died at his home in Montclair, New Jersey, on June 18, 2003. DAN G. RUFF

"Baseball Pioneer, S.C. Native Doby Dies." Columbia *State,* June 19, 2003, pp. A1, A10.

Moore, Joseph Thomas. *Pride against Prejudice: The Biography of Larry Doby.* New York: Greenwood, 1988.

Dock Street Theatre (Charleston). Incorporating the nineteenth-century facade of the Planters' Hotel, the Dock Street Theatre at 135 Meeting Street in Charleston is a fine example of New Deal construction. Whether viewed from Church Street or Queen Street, it illustrates a key tenet of historic preservation: retaining streetscapes.

By 1736 Charleston boasted a theater, one of the earliest in the colonies. Fronting on Queen Street (then called Dock Street), the theater had been lost by the turn of the nineteenth century. In 1809 the proprietor of the Planters' Hotel informed her patrons that she had purchased the "large and commodious house at the corner of Church and Queen" and furnished it "in a genteel manner."

The hotel remained a favorite downtown residence of plantation families until after the Civil War, but in the early 1930s it was vacant and in ruinous condition. When Charleston was admitted to the Federal Emergency Relief Administration's "historical program," this was the building chosen for restoration. In 1935 the city bought the property; FERA provided funding and an architect, Douglas D. Ellington.

Working with the local architects Albert Simons and Samuel Lapham, Ellington designed a new theater behind the brownstone facade. Adjoining support buildings were remodeled while the main site was cleared. Historic brick was reused for exterior walls, and woodwork from the ca. 1806 Radcliffe-King Mansion was installed in reception rooms, but the interior details of the theater were frankly copied from area landmarks.

Despite delays with the transition from FERA to the Works Progress Administration (WPA), the project never lapsed entirely, and Ellington, Simons, and Lapham remained involved until completion. Although most laborers were federal program enrollees, one craftsman, John Smith, "a negro artisan not on the relief rolls," received recognition for his "painstaking and expert work on plaster cornices and medallions."

At the grand opening in November 1937, WPA chief Harry Hopkins joined hundreds of white Charlestonians for a revival of *The Recruiting Officer,* the first play performed at the original Dock Street Theatre. Under the management of the city of Charleston, Dock Street Theatre has expanded its audience to become a fixture in the cultural affairs of the lowcountry. The building was listed in the National Register of Historic Places in 1973. SARAH FICK

"Formal Opening Begins Tonight at Dock St. Theater." Charleson *News and Courier,* November 26, 1937, pp. 1, 2.

Simons, Albert. "Dock St. Theater, Planters Hotel Add to City's Architectural Wealth." Charleson *News and Courier,* November 21, 1937, p. C2.

Stockton, Robert. "Former Planter's Hotel Wins National Acclaim." Charleston *News and Courier,* July 16, 1973, p. B1.

"Dr. Buzzard." The title "Dr. Buzzard" has been claimed by numerous root workers (practitioners of West African–derived folk medicine and magic, commonly referred to as voodoo, hoodoo, or conjuring) along the South Carolina and Georgia coasts. The most well-known, if not the original, Dr. Buzzard was Stephany Robinson, an African American from St. Helena Island who began practicing root work in the early 1900s. He continued attracting clients, both locally and from around the country, until his death in early 1947. According to legend, Robinson's father was a "witch doctor" who had been brought directly to St. Helena from West Africa, despite the antebellum ban on the importation of slaves from Africa. He was said to have wielded enormous spiritual power, which he passed on to his son.

Robinson's specialty was "chewing the root" in court, a practice designed to protect criminal defendants from guilty verdicts or harsh sentences. This practice brought Robinson in conflict with J. E. McTeer, sheriff of Beaufort County from 1926 to 1963. McTeer attempted to charge Robinson with practicing medicine without a license but failed when his primary witness went into convulsions on the witness stand. McTeer's subsequent attempts to convict Robinson failed until, according to McTeer's memoirs, the sheriff began studying root work and promoted the rumor that he himself was a powerful "doctor." When Robinson's son drove his car into a causeway and drowned, Dr. Buzzard called a truce and promised to give up medicine but not "spells." When Robinson died, he passed on his business to his son-in-law, who was known locally as "Buzzy." Other root workers apparently borrowed the name Dr. Buzzard, hoping to cash in on Robinson's notoriety, and a practice that began during his life continued long after his death. STEPHEN CRISWELL

Hyatt, Harry Middleton, ed. *Hoodoo, Conjuration, Witchcraft, Rootwork.* 5 vols. Washington, D.C., 1970–1973.

McTeer, J. E. *Fifty Years as a Low Country Witch Doctor.* Beaufort, S.C.: Beaufort Book Company, 1976.

Pinckney, Roger. *Blue Roots: African-American Folk Magic of the Gullah People.* 2d ed. Orangeburg, S.C.: Sandlapper, 2003.

Donaldson, John Owen (1898–1930). Aviator. Donaldson was born on May 14, 1898, in Fort Yates, North Dakota, where his father, Thomas Quinton Donaldson, served as an army officer. Most of Donaldson's youth was spent in Greenville, his father's hometown. After attending local schools, Donaldson attended Furman College before transferring to Cornell University in New York. Before completing his studies, he joined the Canadian Air Service before the United States entered World War I in 1917. He completed his training overseas at the English School for Air Fighting. His first combat mission occurred in July 1918 north of Amiens, France, with the Number 32 Squadron of the Royal Air Force. During his two months in combat, Donaldson became a highly skilled fighter pilot and one of America's top ten aces of World War I, shooting down nine aircraft and two balloons before he was forced down behind enemy lines on September 1.

After two escape attempts, Donaldson and three other airmen successfully crossed into neutral Holland before the end of the war. For his service, Donaldson was awarded the Distinguished Service Cross by the Prince of Wales, the Belgian Croix de Guerre, and many other citations. Following the Armistice, Donaldson continued his interest in aviation. He took first place in the army's transcontinental air race in October 1919 and competed in many other aviation competitions after resigning his commission in 1920. Two years later he married Harriet McCullough of Atlanta. They had no children. In 1926 Donaldson became president of Newark (N.J.) Air Service, Inc. On September 7, 1930, during a stunt-flying performance at an air show in Philadelphia, Donaldson was killed when his plane crashed. In 1951 Greenville Air Base was renamed Donaldson Air Base in his honor. FRITZ HAMER

Hudson, James J. "Lieutenant John O. Donaldson: World War I Air Ace and Escape Artist." *Air University Review* 37 (January–February 1986): 88–92.

Donaldson Air Base. Early in World War II, the U.S. Army Air Force leased more than two thousand acres of land from the city and county of Greenville to construct what was then known as Greenville Army Air Base, with barracks, hangars, and related buildings to train B-25 crews. Located six miles south of the city, the air base cost an estimated $7.5 million to build and had a monthly payroll of $250,000. Its planes flew throughout the state and the Southeast, with some bombing practice centered on an isolated area below Caesars Head in the northern part of the county. The base was deactivated at the war's conclusion but then was reconstituted in early 1946 to become headquarters for the nation's Troop Carrier Command. Later redesignated Military Air Transport Command, its aircraft flew to all parts of the world to provide supplies and troops in emergencies. Its planes played roles in the 1948 Berlin Airlift and during the crisis in the Belgium Congo more than a decade later. During its peak period in the 1950s, some 2,200 men were stationed at the base. In 1951 the facility was named in honor of Major John O. Donaldson of Greenville, a World War I ace. The base was considered as a possible site for the U.S. Air Force Academy but lost out to Colorado Springs, Colorado. By 1961 the U.S. Air Force deactivated Donaldson, but a few personnel maintained and guarded its facilities until it was closed two years later. The land was returned to the local government and its buildings and equipment sold to them for more than $400,000. Soon afterward the site became the Greenville Municipal Airport and an industrial park. FRITZ HAMER

Huff, Archie Vernon, Jr. *Greenville: The History of the City and County in the South Carolina Piedmont.* Columbia: University of South Carolina Press, 1995.

Todd, Leonard. "Donaldson Center Industrial Air Park." *Proceedings and Papers of the Greenville County Historical Society* 8 (1984–1990): 133–43.

Doolittle Raiders. On April 18, 1942, eighty Americans and sixteen B-25 bombers carried out the first attack on the Japanese Islands following Pearl Harbor. The participants began training for the mission in Columbia. After the surprise Japanese attack on Pearl Harbor, President Franklin Roosevelt directed his military leaders to find a way to strike back. The assignment was given to Colonel Jimmy Doolittle, an aircraft pioneer who was one of the nation's preeminent flyers in the 1930s. He was authorized to select and train sixteen crews to fly land-based B-25s off the deck of an aircraft carrier, a first in aviation history.

In early February most of the crews assembled at Columbia Army Air Base, where they volunteered for the secret mission. After preliminary flight tests, the crews flew to Eglin Air Base in Florida for six weeks of intensive instruction and flight training. On April 1 the Raiders and their planes left the West Coast aboard the carrier *Hornet.* Seventeen days later they flew off the carrier deck to strike Japan. They all reached their targets and then headed to China. While the raid had no strategic value, it nevertheless gave the American nation a tremendous morale boost. Most of the Raiders made it to the mainland but ran out of fuel before they could land, forcing them to bail out or crash with their aircraft. Three died and eight were captured, three of whom were executed. The other five were sentenced to life imprisonment. The rest made it back to friendly lines despite some close encounters with Japanese pursuers.

Two of the Raiders were South Carolina natives. Lieutenant Horace Crouch from Columbia graduated from the Citadel in 1940 and served as navigator aboard Plane Ten. He survived, served the remainder of the war in the Far East, and returned home to continue his military career and later teach. Lieutenant William Farrow from Darlington, a former student of the University of South Carolina, piloted Plane Sixteen. He was captured and executed by the Japanese on October 15, 1942. FRITZ HAMER

Cohen, Stan. *Destination, Tokyo: A Pictorial History of Doolittle's Tokyo Raid, April 18, 1942.* Missoula, Mont.: Pictorial Histories, 1983.

Maxey, Russell. *Airports of Columbia: A History in Photographs & Headlines.* Columbia, S.C.: Palmetto Publishing, 1987.

Schultz, Duane. *The Doolittle Raid.* New York: St. Martin's, 1988.

Dorchester. In 1697 Congregationalists from Massachusetts settled on the north bank of the Ashley River and founded Dorchester as a market village about twenty miles northwest of Charleston. Although it remained small, Dorchester played a significant role in the economy and society of the upper Ashley. Village merchants marketed crops and sold a variety of manufactured goods. Local Anglicans completed the parish church of St. George's Dorchester in the center of the village in 1720. A free school was in operation by 1761. From 1757 to 1760, during the French and Indian War, the colony erected a tabby fort and brick powder magazine in Dorchester. During the Revolutionary War the town served as an outpost first for patriot forces and then for British troops.

Dorchester was gradually abandoned following the Revolutionary War. Loss of population, an unhealthy location, and war-time destruction all contributed to the town's demise. Summerville gradually displaced Dorchester, with most of Dorchester's institutions—even bricks from its buildings—transferred to the newer community nearby. Although the bell tower of the Anglican church and the fort are the only remaining structures from Dorchester, the archaeological record of the town's existence is remarkably well preserved. The South Carolina state parks service has managed the site of Dorchester since 1960. Colonial Dorchester State Historic Site is notable for its rich archaeological resources and historical documentation interpreting the state's colonial and Revolutionary War eras. DANIEL BELL

Bell, Daniel. *Old Dorchester State Park: Visitor's Guide.* Columbia: South Carolina Department of Parks, Recreation and Tourism, 1995.

Sigmon, Daniel Ray. "Dorchester, St. George's Parish, South Carolina: The Rise and Decline of a Colonial Frontier Village." Master's thesis, University of South Carolina, 1992.

Smith, Henry A. M. "The Town of Dorchester, in South Carolina—A Sketch of Its History." *South Carolina Historical and Genealogical Magazine* 6 (April 1905): 62–95.

Dorchester County (575 sq. miles; 2000 pop. 96,413). The lowcountry county of Dorchester was established by the General Assembly in 1897 with territory carved from sections from Colleton and Berkeley Counties. Shaped roughly like a bow tie, Dorchester County is bordered by Colleton, Orangeburg, Berkeley, and Charleston Counties. The county seat, St. George, is in the northwestern part of the county, while the largest town, Summerville, and majority of the county's population are located at the southeastern end. Although Dorchester is among the youngest South Carolina counties, it has a long history. The county takes its name from a colonial town founded on the northern bank of the Ashley River in

1696 by Congregationalists from Dorchester, Massachusetts. Proprietary- and colonial-era planters settled on the upper branches of the Ashley River and the middle reaches of the Edisto River. These rivers and their swamplands have been the defining geographical features of the county since its earliest settlement. During the colonial and antebellum eras the land that became Dorchester was part of St. Paul's, St. Andrew's, St. James Goose Creek, and St. George's Dorchester Parishes.

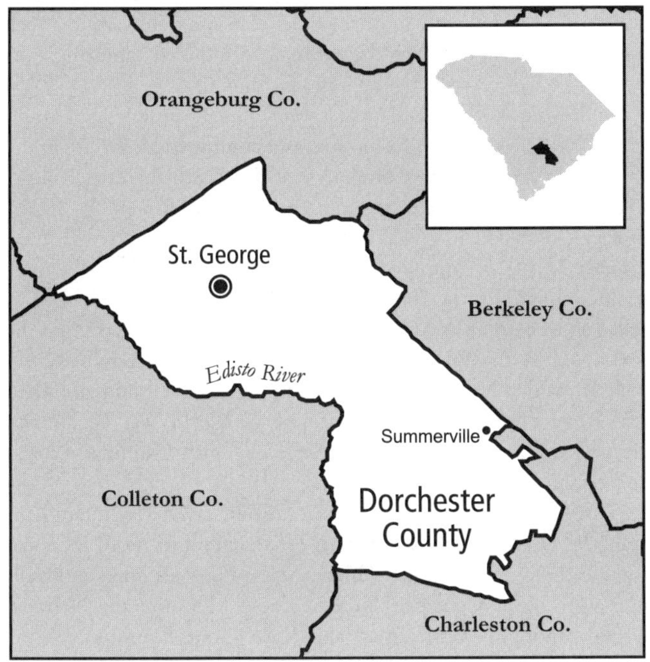

The town of Dorchester was the local market town and also a regional center of worship. St. George's Dorchester Parish church was the Anglican place of worship and a political center. In 1724 the Commons House of Assembly incorporated the Dorchester Free School, which provided for a local school and maintenance of charity scholars (the Free School Board still existed at the start of the twenty-first century). Dorchester was also a center of the Indian trade. In the early years of settlement, the Dorchester-area parishes were the colony's western frontier. The Yamassee War briefly depopulated the region as native inhabitants drove settlers back toward the safety of Charleston. In 1720 the Primus Plot created great alarm among white residents after the planned slave rebellion was discovered. Nineteen years later the Stono Rebellion began in St. Paul's Parish and swept southward toward the Spanish settlements of Florida. In 1757 colonial officials authorized construction of a tabby fort at the town of Dorchester, which subsequently made the region an active theater of combat during the Revolutionary War. William Gilmore Simms wrote a series of Revolutionary War–theme novels set in and near Dorchester that provided insights into the political and social culture of the region during that time.

The Dorchester region became home to expansive rice plantations that provided wealth and prestige to several prominent families. Henry Middleton founded Middleton Place on the Ashley River in 1741, and his extended family created a plantation network that provided great wealth. The Waring, Perry, Blake, Izard, and Pringle families also centered their planting activities in the Four Holes and Great Cypress swamps. During the nineteenth century settlements moved farther inland to take up lands for farming cotton in addition to rice. The village of Summerville superseded Dorchester when the Presbyterian White Meeting House and St. George Dorchester Episcopal Church moved into the town. In 1831 the South Carolina Canal and Rail Road Company built a railway through Summerville, creating an additional stimulus to growth. During the Civil War, the summer retreat was a safe haven for low-country refugees until 1865, when Federal troops pushed inland from their island bases. These troops burned Middleton Place Plantation and other homes on the Ashley River. They then occupied and bivouacked in Summerville after April 1865.

The town of George's Station was incorporated in 1874 as a railroad stop. Fourteen years later, in 1889, the town was renamed St. George, recalling the old parish of St. George's Dorchester. When Dorchester County was incorporated, a hotly contested election named St. George the county seat. Summerville residents protested the election, but a runoff confirmed that the county seat would be in the rural portion of the county, not in its densely populated southern corner.

As it entered the twentieth century, Dorchester remained divided between a rural, sparsely populated upper portion and a lower portion that contained the majority of county residents and close ties to the mixed economy of the coast. African Americans made up the majority of the county's population until 1960. In 1910 the population was 17,891 of which 10,982 were black. The first decades of the twentieth century brought slow but steady growth as the effects of industrialization and New Deal programs of the 1930s helped create an economic base less dependent on agriculture. In 1940 the county population was 19,928 and African Americans accounted for 11,439 of that total.

The modern history of Dorchester County is closely tied to the urbanization of Charleston and North Charleston. As the economy and population of this metropolitan area expanded, Dorchester became a popular residence for those working in greater Charleston. The county saw explosive population growth after 1970 as well as a steady influx of businesses, retirement homes, hospital complexes, and light industry. From a population of 24,383 in 1960, the 1990 population more than tripled to 83,060. How to manage the high rate of growth in population and business investment was a challenge that Dorchester faced at the start of the twenty-first century.

Dorchester County is the home of the Francis Beidler National Forest, one of the few remaining virgin tupelo swamps in the world. Givhans Ferry State Park, built as a Civilian Conservation Corps project, and Old Fort Dorchester State Park are recreational areas. Old Dorchester State Park is the site of the colonial town of Dorchester and contains the largely intact tabby Fort Dorchester. Communities of Native Americans inhabit rural settlements. The Natchez-Kussos, formally unrecognized as a tribe, live in the Four Holes Swamp region, near the town of Dorchester. ALEXANDER MOORE

Walker, Legare. *Dorchester County: A History of its Genesis, of the Lands Constituting Its Area, and of Some of Its Settlements, Institutions, Relics, Events, and Other Matters of an Historical Nature, Especially with Respect to Its Southeastern Part.* 1941. Reprint, Charleston, S.C.: J. W. Parker, 1979.

Dorn, William Jennings Bryan (b. 1916–2005). Congressman. Dorn was born in Greenwood on April 14, 1916, one of ten children born to Thomas Elbert Dorn and Pearl Griffith. His father, an educator and school superintendent, named his son after the famous orator William Jennings Bryan in hopes he would have a political career. Dorn attended public schools in Greenwood and graduated from Greenwood High School. In 1938 he was elected to the South Carolina House of Representatives. Two years later he was elected to the South Carolina Senate, but he resigned shortly thereafter to join the armed forces during World War II. From 1942 to 1945 he served in the U.S. Army Air Force.

Following World War II, Dorn returned to politics. In 1946 he won his first election to the U.S. House of Representatives from the Third District. When he entered Congress at the age of thirty, he was one of the four youngest members. Two years later, however, he made an unsuccessful bid for the U.S. Senate seat held by Burnet Maybank. On December 8, 1948, Dorn married Mildred Johnson, associate editor of *U.S. News and World Report.* The marriage produced five children. In 1950 Dorn was reelected to the congressional seat he had given up to run for the U.S. Senate. He served continuously in that position until 1974, when he ran for governor of South Carolina.

As a congressman, Dorn established a record as a strong supporter of military and defense spending. He was also a champion of veterans and supported numerous legislative acts for their assistance. From 1973 to 1974 he was chair of the Veterans' Affairs Committee. He also served on the Public Works Committee and used his position to support the building of numerous dams in South Carolina. As a representative from the textile section of the state, he was a vocal supporter of restrictions on foreign imports of textiles. Once considered a conservative segregationist, Dorn evolved into a progressive populist. He supported most of Lyndon Johnson's antipoverty program, and in 1965 he was the only Deep South congressman to oppose antibusing legislation. In 1971 he was the only South Carolina House member to vote for funds to establish a Washington memorial for the black educator Mary McLeod Bethune, a South Carolina native.

Dorn unsuccessfully ran for governor twice, in 1974 and in 1978. In 1974 he lost the Democratic primary to newcomer Charles "Pug" Ravenel, but he became the Democratic candidate when Ravenel was declared ineligible by the S.C. Supreme Court. With the Democratic Party bitterly divided, Dorn was defeated by Republican James Edwards in the general election. In 1978 Dorn finished third in the Democratic primary for governor. From 1980 to 1984 he was chair of the South Carolina Democratic Party.

Following his retirement from politics he taught at Lander College and the University of South Carolina at Spartanburg (which became USC-Upstate). He also served as state commander of the American Legion from 1979 to 1980. In 1984 he was named one of the forty most influential persons in South Carolina, and in 1987 his portrait was hung in the State House. WILLIAM V. MOORE

Barron, Robert G. "Challenge and Change: William Jennings Bryan Dorn and the Cold War, 1947–1965." Master's thesis, University of South Carolina, 1994.

Dorn, William Jennings Bryan. Papers. Modern Political Collections, South Caroliniana Library, University of South Carolina, Columbia.

Dorn, William Jennings Bryan, and Scott Derks. *Dorn: Of the People.* Columbia, S.C.: Bruccoli Clark Layman, 1988.

Dozier, James Cordie (1885–1974). Soldier, Medal of Honor recipient. Dozier was born on February 17, 1885, in Galivants Ferry, the son of James Henry Dozier and Julie Marie Best. He moved with his family to Rock Hill and later enrolled at Wofford College in Spartanburg. Dozier began his military career at age nineteen, when he enlisted in the First Infantry Regiment at Rock Hill, which the federal government mobilized into service in 1916 and sent to the Mexican border. By 1917 Dozier had been promoted to first lieutenant and his unit redesignated as the 118th Infantry, Thirtieth Division. During World War I this unit became the U.S. Army's most decorated division. Dozier was one of six of its members to be awarded the Congressional Medal of Honor for "Conspicuous gallantry and intrepidity above and beyond the call of duty" in action near Montbrehain, France, October 8, 1918. In command of two platoons, Dozier was painfully wounded in the shoulder but continued to lead his men. When his command was held up by heavy machine gun fire, he deployed his men in the best cover available and with another soldier continued forward to attack a machine gun nest, killing the entire crew and later capturing Germans who had taken refuge in a nearby dugout.

Following World War I, Dozier wed Tallulah Little of Laurens on June 10, 1920, settled in Columbia, and continued his service in the military by reorganizing Company I of the 118th Infantry. Following the death in office of Adjutant General Robert E. Craig, Dozier—then a major—was appointed to fill the unexpired term on January 22, 1926. Promoted to the rank of brigadier general, Dozier took command of the South Carolina National Guard, which consisted of more than two thousand officers and men. In addition, he was asked by the War Department to take over custody of Camp Jackson, which he maintained as a training site for National Guard and Reserve units until the beginning of World War II. He was elected adjutant general by the people of South Carolina in 1926 and remained in office until retiring in 1959.

During the thirty-three years that Dozier served as adjutant general, the South Carolina National Guard grew to more than ten thousand officers and enlisted men, scores of new armories and facilities were built, Congaree Air Base (now McEntire Air National Guard Station) was acquired, and a new state headquarters was constructed. Under his leadership, the South Carolina National Guard evolved from a small, low-visibility institution—to which an individual was invited to join—to a modern fighting force of citizen soldiers ready to respond to state or national emergencies.

Dozier died on October 24, 1974, at his home in Columbia and was buried in Elmwood Cemetery. Both Fort Jackson and the S.C.

James C. Dozier at the unveiling of his portrait at Fort Jackson. Courtesy, South Caroliniana Library, University of South Carolina

National Guard have named buildings in his honor. ELIZABETH DOZIER STEEDLY

"Former Adjutant General Dozier Dies at Age 89." Columbia *State,* October 25, 1974, pp. A1, A13.

Hunter, Jim. "Columbia Man Reflects on Act Which Led to Medal of Honor." Columbia *State,* October 11, 1962, p. B15.

United States. Department of the Army. Public Information Division. *The Medal of Honor of the United States Army.* Washington, D.C.: Government Printing Office, 1948.

Dozier, Therese Knecht (b. 1952). 1985 National Teacher of the Year. Dozier was born in Vietnam on June 17, 1952, the daughter of a Vietnamese woman and a former German officer who fled Germany at the close of World War II. Lawrence Knecht, a U.S. Army officer stationed in Vietnam, and his wife adopted Dozier and her brother in 1954. They became the first Vietnamese children to be adopted by an American couple, which required a special act of Congress. Dozier graduated valedictorian from Charlotte High School in Punta Gorda, Florida, in 1970. She entered the University of Florida in 1970 and received a B.A. (summa cum laude) in social studies education in 1974. She completed her M.Ed. at the University of Florida in 1976. Dozier began teaching in Gainesville, Florida, at Lincoln Middle School in 1974 and then transferred to Miami Edison Middle School in 1976.

In 1977 Dozier moved to South Carolina and began teaching at Irmo High School. Immensely popular with her students, she was named South Carolina Teacher of the Year in 1985. Later that same year she received the National Teacher of the Year Award from President Ronald Reagan. She took a hiatus from Irmo High School from 1986 to 1989 to teach social studies at the Singapore American School in Singapore. She later served as an instructor and coordinator of Professional Development Schools at the University of South Carolina from 1991 to 1992. She earned her Ed.D. in curriculum and instruction from USC in 1995.

Leaving Irmo High School, Dozier served as senior adviser to U.S. Secretary of Education Richard Riley from 1993 to 2001. In 2001 she accepted the position of national teacher-in-residence and associate professor in the School of Education at Virginia Commonwealth University, Richmond, Virginia. TIMOTHY J. BERGEN, JR.

Miller, Mary Susan. "Teacher of the Year." *Good Housekeeping* 200 (May 1985): 102–6.

Sparks, Dennis. "It All Comes Down to the Teacher: National View of Education Brings the Focus to the Person in Front of the Classroom; Interview with Terry Dozier." *Journal of Staff Development* 21 (fall 2000): 1–4.

Drayton, John (1766–1822). Governor, jurist, author. Born on June 22, 1766, a son of the revolutionary leader William Henry Drayton and Dorothy Golightly, John Drayton received his early education at the Charleston Grammar School. At age ten he accompanied his father to York, Pennsylvania, where William Henry served as a delegate to the Continental Congress. John Drayton attended Nassau Grammar School in New Jersey until the unexpected death of his father in September 1779 forced his return to South Carolina. A year later his mother died of unknown causes, leaving Drayton an orphan. For several years he lived with various relatives and family friends until deciding to study law in the office of Charles Cotesworth Pinckney. In 1788 he was admitted to the Charleston Bar and soon opened a legal practice. Steering him toward the legal profession was his desire to overturn his grandfather John Drayton's last will and testament, which disinherited his father, William Henry. It galled him that his uncle Charles inherited the patriarch's magnificent Georgian plantation home Drayton Hall, which he considered to be his father's and, therefore, his own birthright. Although his suit filed against Charles Drayton in 1793 failed to award him Drayton Hall, John Drayton still received a large financial award, money which allowed him the independence to become active in public affairs.

John Drayton's interest in civic affairs was encouraged at an early age by his father, who John claimed, "Brought him forward by gradual advances for a knowledge of public affairs; fondly hoping, that one day, he might be useful to his country." John's political achievements equaled and perhaps surpassed those of his distinguished father. While still in his twenties and early thirties, John Drayton served as warden of Charleston in 1789, a member of the South Carolina House of Representatives from 1792 to 1798, and lieutenant governor from 1798 to 1800. On the death of Governor Edward Rutledge on January 23, 1800, thirty-three-year-old John Drayton became governor of South Carolina on an interim basis until his election to a full two-year term in December 1800. He devoted most of his energy while governor toward the establishment of South Carolina College in Columbia to advance public learning and to help unify the state. Following his term as governor, he again served as warden of Charleston and was one of its representatives in the Senate until 1808, when he again won election as governor. In 1812 President James Madison appointed him federal judge of the U.S. District Court in South Carolina, a post he held for the remainder of his life.

Although Drayton had a long and illustrious career as a politician and jurist, he is perhaps most remembered for his achievements as a writer and botanist. In 1794 he published his *Letters Written during a Tour through the Northern and Eastern States of America,* a work which lauded the educational system in Massachusetts as superior to that in South Carolina. He used the findings to justify the need for an institution of higher learning in his state. Even more influential was his 1802 publication, *A View of South Carolina, as Respecting Her Natural and Civil Concerns,* a work perhaps inspired by Thomas Jefferson's *Notes on Virginia.* In it, Drayton demonstrated both his extensive knowledge of botany and his skill as an artist. The book was translated into several languages and was favorably reviewed throughout Europe. Indeed, the recognition received from *A View of South Carolina* earned him membership in the Royal Society of Sciences in Germany in 1804. Drayton spent much of the last years of his life compiling and editing his father's papers, which he published in 1821 in two volumes under the title *Memoirs of the American Revolution, from Its Commencement to the Year 1776, Inclusive; As Relating to the State of South Carolina and Occasionally Referring to the States of North Carolina and Georgia.* This compilation, which contains a lengthy biographical sketch of William Henry Drayton, is as much a history of the Revolution in South Carolina as it is a lasting tribute to his father's contributions.

On November 6, 1794, John Drayton married Hester Rose Tidyman, the daughter of Philip Tidyman and Hester Rose. They had seven children before her death in 1816. John Drayton died on November 22, 1822. KEITH KRAWCZYNSKI

Griffin, Dorothy Gail. "The Eighteenth Century Draytons of Drayton Hall." Ph.D. diss., Emory University, 1985.

Krawczynski, Keith. *William Henry Drayton: South Carolina Revolutionary Patriot.* Baton Rouge: Louisiana State University Press, 2001.

Drayton, Percival (1812–1865). Naval officer. Drayton was born on August 25, 1812, in Charleston, the son of William Drayton (1776–1846) and Ann Gadsden. His father served in Congress from 1825 to 1833 and was a leading opponent of nullification in the early 1830s, and he eventually moved his family from Charleston to Philadelphia. Drayton's older brother, Thomas Fenwick Drayton, was a graduate of the U.S. Military Academy. After army service, Thomas returned to South Carolina and became a successful planter and state senator.

At age fifteen, Percival Drayton was appointed midshipman in the U.S. Navy. He entered the service twenty years prior to the founding of the naval academy at Annapolis, and his naval training followed the old pattern inherited from England. Future naval officers began their professional lives not at formal schools but by learning the ropes at sea as midshipmen. He served aboard frigates engaged in protecting U.S. commerce abroad or showing the flag on distant stations. His assignments took him to the Brazilian, Mediterranean, and Pacific squadrons. Eventually he commanded the schooner USS *Enterprise* and served in a variety of vessels, including the *Mississippi,* the navy's third steam-powered warship.

At the outbreak of the Civil War, Drayton held the rank of commander. Of the navy's fifteen hundred officers, one-quarter left to serve with the South. But Drayton did not and chose instead the cause of Union. In November 1861 he commanded a ship in the Port Royal expedition, in which Union forces captured Hilton Head Island, Beaufort, and Parris Island in order to gain a base for operations against Savannah and Charleston. In the battle his brother Thomas, a Confederate brigadier general, commanded the forts whose guns exchanged fire with Drayton's ship.

Drayton's performance won him promotion to captain and command of one of the new Ericsson-designed *Monitor*-class ironclads, the USS *Passaic.* In April 1863 Drayton took part in the attempt to use nine ironclads—the first time armored vessels were employed in anything approaching a fleet action—to fight their way into Charleston harbor. The attack proved unsuccessful, but Drayton was soon named flag captain under Rear Admiral David Farragut. He commanded Farragut's flagship, USS *Hartford,* at the Battle of Mobile Bay in August 1864. It was to Drayton that Farragut shouted the command famously associated with that action: "Damn the torpedoes! Full steam ahead!"

Following the battle, Drayton accompanied Farragut to a triumphal reception in New York. In South Carolina, however, he was regarded quite differently. The General Assembly passed measures formally condemning him to legal banishment and exile. He was not to return in any event. Four months after the war ended, while serving in Washington as chief of the Bureau of Navigation, Drayton died on August 4, 1865, following a brief illness. He had never married. JOHN W. GORDON

Ammen, Daniel. *The Navy in the Civil War.* Vol. 2, *The Atlantic Coast.* 1883. Reprint, Harrisburg, Pa.: Archive Society, 1992.

Canney, Donald L. *Lincoln's Navy: The Ships, Men and Organization, 1861–65.* Annapolis, Md.: Naval Institute Press, 1998.

Halsey, Ashley, Jr. "I Rue the Day I Got into the Ironclad Business." *Civil War Times Illustrated* 4 (April 1965): 28–34.

Mahan, A. T. *The Navy in the Civil War.* Vol. 3, *The Gulf and Inland Waters.* 1883. Reprint, Harrisburg, Pa.: Archive Society, 1992.

Drayton, William Henry (1742–1779). Revolutionary leader, planter. Drayton was born in September 1742 at Drayton Hall in St. Andrew's Parish, the son of John Drayton, a wealthy planter and member of the Provincial Council, and Charlotta Bull, daughter of Lieutenant Governor William Bull. At the age of ten William Henry went to England to complete his education, but he returned home at the behest of his father in 1763 before he could finish his degree at Balliol College, Oxford. A year later Drayton married Dorothy Golightly, one of the wealthiest heiresses in the colony. Their union produced four children, of whom only Mary and John survived childhood.

Financially secure and politically well connected, William Henry sought public office. He won a seat in the South Carolina Royal Assembly in 1765 but lost it in the following election because of indifferent service. Nevertheless, Drayton found himself at the center of political affairs. In July 1769 he wrote a polemic in the *South-Carolina Gazette* opposing the popular extralegal nonimportation association (established in defiance to the recently enacted Townshend Duties) as "*a base, illegal decree*" designed to "*ruin* and *overthrow* our *happy constitution.*" The letter started a caustic five-month public debate with nonimportation leaders that changed few minds and resulted in Drayton's being ostracized politically, socially, and economically in South Carolina. In January 1770 he sailed for England, where he hoped his views would find greater acceptance.

In England, Drayton was introduced at court as a supporter of the crown's prerogative. To further display his loyalty, Drayton published in 1771 *The Letters of Freeman,* a compilation of his newspaper articles on the nonimportation debate. His allegiance earned him a position on the Provincial Council in Charleston. However, Drayton's aspiration for additional posts was frustrated when the Ministry appointed Englishmen to numerous offices that Drayton sought for himself. Increasing his frustration was Parliament's passage in 1774 of the Coercive Acts, measures which convinced Drayton that the "liberty and property of the American [were] at the pleasure of a despotic power." In August of that year Drayton vented his personal and intellectual frustration with the crown and Parliament in *A Letter from Freeman,* a pamphlet addressed to the First Continental Congress in which he outlined American rights and proposed a blueprint for the reform of the British Empire that denied Parliament's jurisdiction over the colonies. Drayton further antagonized crown officers both in London and in Charleston when on his tour of the circuit courts in November 1774 he urged grand jurymen to select "freedom over slavery" and defy British authority. Drayton's *Freeman* essay and judicial charges prompted a disappointed William Bull to suspend his nephew from the Provincial Council in early 1775.

However, Drayton's outspoken views made him one of the most popular Whigs in the colony. He won a seat in the Provincial Congress in January 1775 and soon after sat on all important revolutionary committees. Drayton used his extensive powers to lead raids against the city's royal post office and armories, thereby obtaining both crucial information regarding the intentions of the British Ministry and arms for the patriot forces. During the summer of 1775, Drayton led a five-man commission on a six-week tour of the backcountry to suppress the large number of Loyalists in the region. In the face of great odds, Drayton managed to procure a treaty of neutrality from Loyalist leaders at a conference in the town of Ninety Six.

Whig leaders in Charleston rewarded Drayton for his achievement by electing him president of the Provincial Congress. In this role he encouraged the creation of a navy, raising and training troops and erecting fortifications. Speaking to the Provincial Congress on February 6, 1776, Drayton became the first prominent Carolinian to openly call for the establishment of a new government and separation from Great Britain. The next month that body drafted a constitution replacing the royal charter. Drayton went on to play a leading role in creating the new state constitution adopted in 1778.

In January of that year Drayton also proposed numerous amendments to the recently published Articles of Confederation. Attached to his proposal was an alternative plan of confederation augmenting the power of the individual states and protecting southern interests.

Drayton's essay on America's first federal charter perhaps explains his election to the Continental Congress in 1778. A tireless worker, Drayton served on nearly ninety ad hoc and five standing committees during his seventeen months in Congress. As one of America's most effective polemicists, Drayton focused on opposing British attempts at reconciliation. His last months in Congress, however, were spent in various bitter quarrels in that politically charged body. In his spare time Drayton compiled documents for a history of the Revolution, an undertaking left unfinished when he died of typhus in Philadelphia on September 3, 1779. KEITH KRAWCZYNSKI

Dabney, William M., and Marion Dargan. *William Henry Drayton and the American Revolution.* Albuquerque: University of New Mexico Press, 1962.

Drayton, John. *Memoirs of the American Revolution as Relating to the State of South Carolina.* 2 vols. 1821. Reprint, New York: New York Times, 1969.

Gibbes, Robert W. *Documentary History of the American Revolution.* 3 vols. 1853–1857. Reprint, Spartanburg, S.C.: Reprint Company, 1972.

Krawczynski, Keith. *William Henry Drayton: South Carolina Revolutionary Patriot.* Baton Rouge: Louisiana State University Press, 2001.

Drayton Hall (Charleston County). Established in 1738, Drayton Hall is a historic plantation located between the Ashley River and Ashley River Road, about nine miles from Charleston. At the time of its construction, its two-story, brick main house with raised basement was representative of current English Georgian architecture and was inspired by the designs of the Italian Renaissance architect Andrea Palladio. However, its recessed, two-story portico—the earliest of its kind in America—probably had no English precedent and was directly derived from Palladio's *The Four Books of Architecture,* republished in 1715. Thus, Drayton Hall combined Old World design and eighteenth-century fashion with the tastes of the owner, the abilities of colonial craftspeople—black and white, free and enslaved—and the climate of the lowcountry to create a uniquely American architectural form.

John Drayton (ca. 1715–1779), born on the adjoining Magnolia Plantation, founded Drayton Hall at age twenty-three, and it remained in possession of the Drayton family for seven generations. As the seat of vast plantation holdings in the eighteenth and nineteenth centuries, Drayton Hall was the home of scores of African Americans who lived and worked there as slaves and later as free men, including the Bowens family, whose ancestors probably arrived as slaves from Barbados with the Draytons. In 1974 the National Trust for Historic Preservation, the state of South Carolina, and the Historic Charleston Foundation acquired Drayton Hall from the Drayton family. They chose to preserve the site "as is" rather than restore or reconstruct it to an earlier or specific time period, making its main house one of the oldest unrestored plantation houses in America that is open to the public. GEORGE MCDANIEL

Drayton Hall. Courtesy, South Carolina Department of Archives and History

Drovers. From around 1800 until the 1880s, livestock from Kentucky, Tennessee, Georgia, and North Carolina were driven through Greenville County to the seaport of Charleston, destined for northern markets in Baltimore, Philadelphia, and New York or south to Florida and the West Indies. These drives were made possible by the completion of a road from Greenville County across the mountains and into Knoxville, Tennessee, in the late 1790s. Herds consisted primarily of cattle or hogs but also included sheep, mules, horses, and turkeys.

There were some standardized practices in being a drover. A typical cattle drive consisted of 100 to 120 head of cattle attended by three drovers: one on horseback and two on foot. Drovers became expert whip-crackers, and the term "crackers" may have derived from the long whips they used. Turkeys were driven in flocks of 400 to 600, which roosted in trees at night and were guided during the day by whips with strips of red flannel attached.

Drovers contributed to the prosperity of the districts through which they passed, as taverns, stations, and farms provided feed, pens, and accommodations. Expenses for a drive of 100 cattle from Kentucky were about $1,500. Hogs were driven about eight miles daily. One thousand swine consumed about twenty-four bushels of corn a day, which had to be purchased along the route. There were reported instances of drives consisting of 5,000 head, and some stations boasted of handling more than 150,000 head in a year. Taverns and campsites appeared along the drive route, with some gradually developing into significant settlements, such as the town of Travelers Rest.

The expansion of railroads into the upcountry and across the mountains, coupled with the gradual decline of open-range grazing, led to the demise of the droving trade. It had largely disappeared from South Carolina by the mid-1880s. SALLIE D. CLARKSON

Batson, Mann. *Early Travel and Accommodations along the Roads of the Upper Part of Greenville County, South Carolina and Surrounding Areas.* Travelers Rest, S.C., 1995.

Gray, Lewis C. *History of Agriculture in the Southern United States to 1860.* 2 vols. Washington, D.C.: Carnegie Institution, 1933.

Huff, Archie Vernon, Jr. *Greenville: The History of the City and County in the South Carolina Piedmont.* Columbia: University of South Carolina Press, 1995.

Parr, Elizabeth L. "Kentucky's Overland Trade with the Ante-Bellum South." *Filson Club History Quarterly* 2 (January 1928): 71–81.

DuBose, William Porcher (1836–1918). Professor, theologian. DuBose was born near Winnsboro on April 11, 1836, the son of Theodore DuBose, a plantation owner, and his wife, Jane Porcher. He graduated from the Citadel in 1855 and received his M.A. from the University of Virginia in 1859. He studied for the ordained ministry at the Theological Seminary of the Protestant Episcopal Church in the Diocese of South Carolina at Camden. DuBose served as an adjutant in the Confederate army, and after his ordination as deacon on December 13, 1863, he served as chaplain to Confederate soldiers. He was ordained as a priest on September 9, 1866, and served as rector of Trinity Church, Abbeville, from 1868 to 1871. From 1871 until 1883 he was chaplain at the newly established University of the South at Sewanee, Tennessee, where he helped to establish the School of Theology and was its second dean from 1894 to 1908.

DuBose is recognized as a major theologian in the history of the Episcopal Church. He published seven books, the first of which was *The Soteriology of the New Testament* (1892), which was his New Testament theology. *The Gospel in the Gospels* (1906) was a study in the synoptic gospels (Matthew, Mark, and Luke), and *The Gospel According to St. Paul* (1907) was a study of Romans and Pauline theology. *High Priesthood and Sacrifice* (1908) was a study of Hebrews, and *The Reason of Life* (1911) was a study of the Johannine literature. These five books established DuBose as a major New Testament theologian. In 1896 he published *The Ecumenical Councils,* a study of the first seven ecumenical councils of the church. He discussed his experience and theology in his autobiographical *Turning Points in My Life* (1912).

DuBose was a leading liberal catholic theologian in the Episcopal Church in the late nineteenth and early twentieth centuries. His catholicity was expressed in his concern for the unity of the church and in his commitment to the Bible as the church's book. He insisted that the Bible is both human and divine: its form is human, and its content is divine. His theology was rooted in the first seven ecumenical councils, which defined and described Jesus Christ as fully human, fully divine, in one person. He also expressed his catholicity in centering theology in the life, death, and resurrection of Jesus Christ, and in his understanding of the church and its sacraments as the continuing presence of Jesus Christ. His liberalism was expressed in his commitment to the critical study of scripture; his recognition of the development of doctrine; his unending search for truth wherever it might be found; his understanding of evolution, process, and growth; and in his efforts to reconcile historic Christianity with modern ideas. His work was recognized in England during his lifetime as the writings of a major incarnational theologian. He died in Sewanee, Tennessee, on August 18, 1918. DONALD S. ARMENTROUT

Alexander, Jon, ed. *William Porcher DuBose: Selected Writings.* New York: Paulist Press, 1988.

Armentrout, Donald S., ed. *A DuBose Reader: Selections from the Writings of William Porcher DuBose.* Sewanee, Tenn.: University of the South, 1984.

Slocum, Robert Boak. *The Theology of William Porcher DuBose: Life, Movement, and Being.* Columbia: University of South Carolina Press, 2000.

Dueling. Duels took place in South Carolina from colonial times until 1880, when the General Assembly officially outlawed the practice. The practice of dueling reached its peak between 1800 and 1860. Though it occurred throughout the English colonies and the United States, the practice was concentrated in the South, and South Carolina was the site of a disproportionate number of duels. Some late twentieth-century scholars have linked the practice of dueling to the practice of plantation slavery, since white planters in South Carolina placed themselves at the top of a highly volatile and stratified society, in which honor and dishonor were matters of great public importance. Duels could be fought for any number of breaches in the code of honor that was supposed to inform personal relationships among South Carolina's elite. The code of honor, a body of largely unwritten law understood by most members of the upper class, was a means to protect men's status and manhood from real and perceived threats. One common thread appears to run through nearly all of the duels fought in the South: that of accusing someone else of lying, an accusation also known as "giving the lie." To refuse a duel after being "given the lie" would prove one's cowardice and thereby bring his honor and manhood into question.

Once a gentleman's honor was called into question, a series of formal, highly ritualized steps took place. The rules governing dueling had developed over several centuries but were codified in Ireland in the 1770s in the *code duello.* An American version of the rules was published in Charleston in 1838 by John Lyde Wilson, who had served as governor of South Carolina from 1822 to 1824. The code duello provided that whoever gave the first offense must make the first apology, and that if no apology was forthcoming, a duel could ensue. The code duello also provided details about the proper positioning of the body and other particulars. Wilson's American *Code of Honor,* unlike its Irish cousin, allowed blows to be returned but insisted that a formal duel follow. Once attempts at reconciliation were exhausted, the duelists and their assistants (principals and seconds) agreed to settle their differences on the field of honor, often in the presence of a surgeon, his assistant, and crowds that sometimes reached into the hundreds.

The dueling weapon of choice for a South Carolina gentleman was the pistol. During the colonial period cumbersome and inaccurate matchlocks and flintlocks were used, but the advent of the percussion pistol in the 1820s allowed for greater accuracy, and dueling pistols became elaborately decorated objects of art. Sometimes duelists and their seconds drew up excruciatingly detailed contracts. On the dueling grounds seconds flipped coins to determine which would give the "ready" and which would choose positions. Once all of the details had been worked out, the principals would take their places, and on hearing the signal, each would attempt to shoot the other. Even when large crowds of onlookers gathered, they usually remained silent during the proceedings, accentuating the solemn, genteel tone of the event. Duels did not always end in death; Wilson's rules stipulated that any wound could end a duel unless the wounded party wanted another round. If any serious breach of dueling etiquette occurred, the seconds could shoot the offending principal—or each other in extreme cases.

Many of South Carolina's leading colonial and antebellum men participated in duels as either principals or seconds. Though dueling had its detractors—most notably the clergy, the Society of the Cincinnati, and some newspaper editors—there was no serious social stigma attached to it until the later years of the nineteenth century. Dueling gradually fell out of favor, however, and the practice was eventually outlawed formally after the infamous Cash-Shannon duel of 1880. In July of that year Colonel E. B. C. Cash killed William Shannon in a duel. The Charleson *News and Courier,* edited by the English-born Captain Francis W. Dawson, denounced the duel. Cash, who had barely escaped lynching after the duel, was charged with murder. His first trial resulted in a hung jury and a second jury voted to acquit, but public opinion had shifted against dueling. In 1880 the General Assembly equated dueling with murder and required an oath of those holding public office that they would neither send nor receive challenges while in the service of the public. Though no known formal duels have taken place in South Carolina since the Cash-Shannon duel, violence, often a result of personal or political disputes between white men, continued to be fairly widespread. MATTHEW H. JENNINGS

Cochran, Hamilton. *Noted American Duels and Hostile Encounters.* Philadelphia: Chilton, 1963.

Greenberg, Kenneth S. *Honor & Slavery: Lies, Duels, Noses, Masks, Dressing as a Woman, Gifts, Strangers, Death, Humanitarianism, Slave Rebellions,*

The Proslavery Argument, Baseball, Hunting, and Gambling in the Old South. Princeton, N.J.: Princeton University Press, 1996.

Matthews, Nancy Torrance. "The Duel in Nineteenth Century South Carolina: Custom over Written Law." *Proceedings of the South Carolina Historical Association* (1979): 79–94.

Williams, Jack K. *Dueling in the Old South: Vignettes of Social History.* College Station: Texas A&M University Press, 1980.

Duke's mayonnaise. Duke's mayonnaise is one of the South's favorite condiments, whipped white gold sold in squat glass jars affixed with a simple yellow label. Though now owned by C. F. Sauer Company of Richmond, Virginia, Duke's mayonnaise is still produced in Greenville, the city of its birth.

Eugenia Duke mixed her first batch of mayonnaise in her home on Manly Street sometime in the early years of the twentieth century (1917 is the date most often cited). Duke got her start making sandwiches and selling them to local drugstore soda fountains and corner groceries. She baked her own bread, roasted her own meats, and, most importantly, made a fine mayonnaise. Unlike in the commercial versions that were coming on the market, there was no sugar in Duke's mayonnaise recipe, nor did she whip in egg whites as filler. And thanks to her use of cider vinegar, her product had a pleasing tartness.

During World War I, Duke expanded her business, selling sandwiches to servicemen stationed at nearby Fort Sevier. Soon soldiers were writing her, each asking that a jar or two be shipped to faraway Georgia or Virginia, and Duke was in the mayonnaise-manufacturing business. Her business expanded rapidly. In 1920 she sold the sandwich business to her bookkeeper Alan Hart of Mauldin. In 1923 she opened a mayonnaise-manufacturing plant in Greenville. In 1929 she sold her mayonnaise-manufacturing business along with her prized recipe to the C. F. Sauer Company and moved to California, where she operated a catering business. JOHN T. EDGE

Edge, John T. *Southern Belly: The Ultimate Food Lover's Companion to the South.* Athens, Ga.: Hill Street, 2000.

Sloan, Kathleen Lewis. "Hold the Mayo? Not If It Says 'Duke's.'" *Sandlapper* 2 (December 1991): 108–9.

Thompson, Samantha. "Pass the Mayo." *Greenville News,* June 25, 1995, upstate business sec., pp. 8–10.

Duncan (Spartanburg County; 2000 pop. 2,870). Duncan was chartered by the General Assembly on December 24, 1890, and rechartered by the secretary of state on August 15, 1896. It was named after Leroy Duncan (1836–1881) of Spartanburg County, who owned most of the land in the area. Prior to its charter under that name, the area had been served by post offices known as New Hope (ca. 1811) and Vernonsville (ca. 1854). The main impetus for development in the area came when the Atlanta and Richmond Air-line Railway began operations between Spartanburg and Greenville. In 1874 Leroy Duncan purchased land where the railroad and Gap Creek Road intersected. The area was then alternatively known as Duncan's Crossing or Duncans. By the mid-1880s the population had climbed to about two hundred residents. A telephone exchange was chartered in 1909 with between fifty and seventy-five subscribers. In 1914 the town was served by an electric train line, the Piedmont and Northern, which allowed people to commute to and from Greenville, Spartanburg, and Greer. In the late twentieth century, research and manufacturing provided hundreds of jobs in Duncan. W. R. Grace and Company opened a research center in 1963 to develop flexible packaging materials under the Cryovac name. The opening of the German automobile company BMW's assembly plant at nearby Greer in 1994 brought new opportunities to Duncan as well. AARON W. MARRS

Hughes, Nell, and Frederick Tucker. *Pictorial History of Old Duncan.* Greenville, S.C.: A Press, 1998.

Dunovant, John (1825–1864). Soldier. Dunovant was born on March 5, 1825, in Chester, the son of Dr. John Dunovant and Margaret Sloan Quay. Two of his brothers, Alexander and Robert, would be signers of the Ordinance of Secession. John Dunovant fought in the Mexican War as a sergeant in the famed Palmetto Regiment, and in 1855 he was commissioned in the regular army as captain of the Tenth U.S. Infantry. Accessible details of his army service, like details of his early life, are sketchy. Despite lacking a formal military education, Dunovant had used the Mexican War as a springboard into one of the few professions outside planting that southerners respected.

Dunovant resigned his army commission in early 1861 and was appointed major in the South Carolina volunteers. During the bombardment of Fort Sumter, Dunovant earned plaudits for his handling of his command at Fort Moultrie. He was afterward commissioned colonel of the First South Carolina Regiment, which saw duty, but not much action, in and around Charleston. According to Governor Francis W. Pickens, Dunovant's unit became "the best drilled Regiment in the Service." Dunovant commanded the unit until falling from grace in the summer of 1862.

The most flagrant event in Dunovant's fall was his August 1862 court-martial for drunkenness—a charge that remained tied to his reputation and probably contributed to his death. Dunovant was cashiered, with Confederate president Jefferson Davis's approval. Yet both previous and subsequent events suggest something at work other than concern for military sobriety. Sometime before the court-martial, Dunovant fell out with a superior, General Roswell S. Ripley, over troop dispositions. And soon after being run out of the service, with several officers weighing in on his behalf, Dunovant was returned to duty as colonel of the Fifth South Carolina cavalry.

Duty with this unit gave Dunovant a chance to redeem himself. Transferred with other South Carolina units to the Army of Northern Virginia in the spring of 1864—one historian notes that Dunovant and his men "were garbed in neat, even snazzy uniforms, their officers wearing white cotton gloves"—the Fifth S.C. saw action in some of the grittiest fighting of the war. Dunovant earned high praise for his efforts at places such as Drewry's Bluff, Cold Harbor, and Trevilian Station, proving himself to be more capable in combat than he was in the boredom of South Carolina garrison duty. Davis, who earlier had supported Dunovant's court-martial sentence, elevated him to the temporary rank of brigadier general in August.

Dunovant was killed on October 1, 1864, during a cavalry charge along the Vaughan Road near Petersburg. In previous days he had made several mistakes in both tactics and reconnaissance; those blunders and past smears on his record may have contributed to what was a desperate gamble at best and a reckless decision at worst. Yet some measure of Dunovant's effectiveness as a combat officer can be read into Union reports. Dunovant was shot by Sergeant James T. Clancy of the First New Jersey cavalry. For that shot—which occurred "within ten yards of our line," according to one report, and which had the effect of "confusing the enemy and greatly aiding his repulse," according to another—Clancy was awarded the Congressional Medal of Honor. Dunovant was buried in the family cemetery near Chester, South Carolina. PAUL CHRISTOPHER ANDERSON

Longacre, Edward G. *Lee's Cavalrymen: A History of the Mounted Force of the Army of Northern Virginia, 1861–1865.* Mechanicsburg, Pa.: Stackpole, 2002.

Warner, Ezra J. *Generals in Gray: Lives of the Confederate Commanders.* Baton Rouge: Louisiana State University Press, 1959.

Durban, Pam Rosa (b. 1947). Author. Durban was born Rosa Palmer Durban in Aiken on March 4, 1947, the daughter of Frampton Wyman Durban, a real-estate appraiser, and Maria Hertwig. The writer grew up in Aiken, where her family has lived for generations. In the family tradition she attended a Catholic grade school, St. Mary Help of Christians. She left Aiken to attend the University of North Carolina, Greensboro, where she was graduated in 1969. In the 1970s she wrote as a free-lancer for *Osceola,* a newspaper published by people associated with Clemson University.

Durban worked as a contributing editor for the *Atlanta Gazette* in 1974 and 1975. In Atlanta she taped interviews with women in a textile mill community and published them as *Cabbagetown Families* in 1976. Portions of the book were made into a play called *Cabbagetown: Three Women.* She attended the Writers' Workshop at the University of Iowa, from which she received her M.F.A. in 1979. On June 18, 1983, she married Frank H. Hunter, a photographer. Their son, Wylie, was born in July 1987, and she received a Whiting Writer's Award the same year. She was a founding editor of the magazine *Five Points* and served as its fiction editor from 1996 to 2001.

Durban has taught creative writing at the University of New York at Geneseo (1979–1980), Murray State (1980–1981), Ohio University at Athens (1981–1986), and Georgia State University (1986–2001), where she was awarded an NEA Fellowship in 1998. In 2001 she became Doris Betts Distinguished Professor of Creative Writing at the University of North Carolina at Chapel Hill.

Throughout the early 1980s Durban published short stories in periodicals, and in 1985 she collected seven of them in *All Set about with Fever Trees, and Other Stories.* The well-received stories are mostly set in the South, and the South Carolina roots are evident. In a Faulknerian way, Durban tries new ways of communicating timeless and impressive experiments in storytelling. *The Laughing Place* (1993), her first novel, is a stylistic triumph with its graceful and poetical narrative voice. It is a story about a woman who returns to her hometown in South Carolina to learn about her home, her father's life, and the family secrets. The novel is a major statement on the southern obsession with the past.

On the publication of her second novel, *So Far Back* (2000), Durban said: "I've been influenced by my upbringing in all sorts of ways, and I became especially aware of that when I was writing *So Far Back.* That book deals with what I see as some fundamental South Carolina attitudes, and I realized as I was writing it that I'm very conversant with them all." The novel is about the last descendant of an old Charleston family and her life in the 1990s. Through a diary of an ancestor from the 1830s, she discovers how her life is entangled in the family history. For that outstanding novel Durban was awarded the Lillian Smith Award for Fiction. JAN NORDBY GRETLUND

Reid, Cheryl. "Making Fictions: An Interview with Pam Durban." *Carolina Quarterly* 52 (summer 2000): 61–77.

Dutch Fork. The Dutch Fork lies in a fork between the Broad and Saluda Rivers that includes parts of the modern counties of Newberry, Lexington, and Richland. Although a fertile region, the Dutch Fork was not the site of a colonial township, nor was it a way station on the major Indian trade routes. Consequently, European settlement in the region did not begin until the 1740s.

As the good land in nearby Saxe-Gotha Township was claimed, immigrants looked to the Dutch Fork for their bounty grants. Many of the early settlers were German speakers, although other settlers, such as Samuel Hollenshed from New Jersey, came to the Dutch Fork via the Great Wagon Road. Other population elements included Indian traders and soldiers discharged from their companies at Fort Granby. The preponderance of German-speaking settlers, however, gave the area its name—Dutch Fork for *deutsch Volk* (German people).

During the Revolutionary War, Germans in the Dutch Fork were cool toward the patriot cause, believing that they owed their land (and therefore their loyalty) to George III (who was of German descent). The relative isolation of the area allowed German culture and language to survive into the early twentieth century. The creation of Lake Murray during the 1930s inundated part of the Fork. In the ensuing decades, suburban sprawl from Columbia encroached and converted much of the rural landscape into shopping malls and housing subdivisions. ALEXIA JONES HELSLEY

Able, Gene, ed. *Irmo and the Dutch Fork Legacy: A Centennial Celebration.* Irmo, S.C.: Independent News, 1990.

Meriwether, Robert L. *The Expansion of South Carolina, 1729–1765.* Kingsport, Tenn.: Southern Publishers, 1940.

E

Earle, Joseph Haynsworth (1847–1897). U.S. senator. Earle was born in Greenville on April 30, 1847, the youngest child of Elias Earle and Susan Haynsworth. Orphaned at five, Earle was raised in Sumter District by his maternal aunt and her husband. He left a Sumter academy in 1864 to enlist in the Confederate army. After the Civil War, he attended Furman University from 1866 to 1868 but left without obtaining a degree. On May 19, 1869, he married his cousin Anna M. Earle of Anderson. The couple had nine children. Admitted to the bar in 1870, Earle began a law practice in Anderson. He moved his practice to Sumter in the mid-1870s and then to Greenville in 1891.

In 1878 Earle was elected to the state House of Representatives from Sumter County, serving until 1880. He served in the state Senate from 1882 to 1885 and as attorney general of South Carolina from 1886 to 1890. Conservative Democrats put forth Earle as a candidate for governor in 1890, but his moderate demeanor was no match for the popular bombast of the eventual winner, Benjamin R. Tillman. In 1892, in the spirit of party unity, Earle declined another nomination for governor. An appreciative Tillmanite majority in the legislature rewarded Earle by electing him as a circuit judge in 1894, and he served in that capacity until January 1897.

In 1896 Earle defeated the unpopular John Gary Evans for the Democratic nomination to the U.S. Senate in the state's first direct primary. Earle's victory was an initial step toward healing the extreme factionalism that had dominated South Carolina politics for most of the previous decade. Unfortunately, Earle's tenure as senator lasted only weeks, ending when he died suddenly on May 20, 1897, of Bright's disease (a kidney disorder). He was buried at Christ Church Cemetery in Greenville. MICHAEL ROBERT MOUNTER

Bailey, N. Louise, Mary L. Morgan, and Carolyn R. Taylor, eds. *Biographical Directory of the South Carolina Senate, 1776–1985.* 3 vols. Columbia: University of South Carolina Press, 1986.

Simkins, Francis Butler. *Pitchfork Ben Tillman: South Carolinian.* Baton Rouge: Louisiana State University Press, 1944.

Earle, Willie, lynching of (February 17, 1947). The murder of Willie Earle is believed to be the last racial lynching in South Carolina. On February 16, 1947, Earle, a twenty-five-year-old black man from Greenville, was arrested for the robbery and stabbing of a white Greenville taxi driver, Thomas Watson Brown. The next day a mob of thirty-five men abducted Earle from his cell in the Pickens County Jail and drove him to the outskirts of Greenville, where they lynched him. Earle's body, badly mutilated from stab wounds in the chest and shotgun wounds in the head, was recovered the same day. Thomas Brown, the original stabbing victim, died hours after Earle. According to some contemporaries—including Earle's mother, his neighbors, and the executive secretary of the National Association for the Advancement of Colored People, Walter White—no evidence existed to link Earle to the murder of Brown.

Officials at the state and federal levels were quick to condemn the lynching and to pursue Earle's murderers. South Carolina Governor J. Strom Thurmond immediately denounced mob violence and promised an investigation by state authorities. By the end of February, Federal Bureau of Investigation agents, dispatched to Greenville by U.S. Attorney General Tom C. Clark, had obtained signed statements from twenty-six men who admitted their participation in the lynching. A Greenville County grand jury subsequently indicted thirty-one men—most of whom were taxi drivers—for murder, conspiracy to commit murder, and accessory before and accessory after the fact of murder.

Begun on May 12, 1947, the Greenville lynching trial generated interest within South Carolina and throughout the nation. The simple fact that the trial took place was evidence of a changing racial order, as were the efforts of the presiding judge to make the proceedings as impartial as possible. Still, many white South Carolinians sympathized with the defendants, believing that the lynching was regrettable but probably unavoidable in light of the crime for which Earle was accused. After a trial of ten days, in which the defense declined to present any witnesses or evidence, the jury found the defendants not guilty on all counts. Appalled, the judge refused to thank the jury for their service.

The most significant legacy of the Earle case was to stimulate efforts on behalf of civil rights. According to leaders in the Progressive Democratic Party of South Carolina, the lynching strengthened the resolve of black Carolinians, a development that helped accelerate political activism throughout the state. The Earle case also influenced officials at the federal level, including President Harry S. Truman and members of his President's Committee on Civil Rights. Exposing the limitations of state efforts to prevent mob violence and to promote racial equality, the Earle lynching and the acquittal of the lynch mob played a key role in convincing the Truman administration to take a stronger stand for federal action to defend civil rights. ADAM MACK

Frederickson, Kari. "'The Slowest State' and 'Most Backward Community': Racial Violence in South Carolina and Federal Civil-Rights Legislation, 1946–1948." *South Carolina Historical Magazine* 98 (April 1997): 177–202.

Gravely, Will. "Reliving South Carolina's Last Lynching: The Witness of Tessie Earle Robinson." *South Carolina Review* 29 (spring 1997): 4–17.

West, Rebecca. "Opera in Greenville." *New Yorker* 23 (June 14, 1947): 31–59.

Earley, Charity Edna Adams (1918–2002). Army officer. Earley was born on December 5, 1918, in Kittrell, North Carolina, the oldest of four children born to the Reverend and Mrs. E. A. Adams. Raised in Columbia, Earley attended Waverly School and was valedictorian of her class at Booker T. Washington High School. She received a scholarship to Wilberforce College in Ohio, where she majored in math and physics and graduated in 1938. While there, she was active in the Women's Self-Government Association, National Association for the Advancement of Colored People, Young Women's Christian Association, and Delta Sigma Theta sorority.

Earley returned to Columbia after college and taught junior high school mathematics and general science while working on a master's degree in vocational psychology. In 1942 she joined the Women's Army Auxiliary Corps (later Women's Army Corps or WACs) and entered the first class of African American female officer candidates in July at Fort Des Moines, Iowa. On August 29, 1942, the class was called to receive their commissions alphabetically and Earley (then still Adams) became the first African American female officer in the WACs. She spent the next two years at Fort Des Moines and rose in rank to become the Training Center's control officer in early 1944. In March 1945, shortly after her promotion to major, Earley took command of the 6888th Central Postal Directory Battalion in Birmingham, England. While she was in command of the 6888th, the unit moved to France. At the end of the war she had achieved the rank of lieutenant colonel and was the highest-ranking black female officer in the WACs.

Earley left the army in March 1946 and earned a master's degree in vocational psychology from Ohio State University. In 1949 she married Stanley A. Earley, Jr., a medical student, and they lived in Switzerland while he attended medical school. On returning to the United States, they settled in Dayton, Ohio. Earley raised a son and daughter while maintaining an active career in charity and service organizations such as the United Way, American Red Cross, Young Women's Christian Association, the Urban League, and the United Negro College Fund. She also served as codirector of the Black Leadership Development Program, was a member of the board of directors for Dayton Power and Light, and was a member of the board of trustees of Sinclair Community College. In 1989 her autobiography, *One Woman's Army,* was published.

Earley was inducted into the Ohio Women's Hall of Fame in 1979, was named one of the Smithsonian Institution's 110 most important historical black women, and was inducted into the South Carolina Black Hall of Fame in 1991. The Smithsonian also held a program in her honor at the National Postal Museum in 1996. She received honorary doctorates from Wilberforce University and the University of Dayton. At a salute to African Americans in World War II on February 17, 1995, she introduced the guest of honor, President William Jefferson Clinton. Earley died in Dayton on January 13, 2002. STEVEN D. SMITH

Earley, Charity Adams. *One Woman's Army: A Black Officer Remembers the WAC.* 1989. Reprint, College Station: Texas A&M University Press, 1996.

Obituary. Columbia *State,* January 22, 2002, p. B6.

Earthquake rods. Earthquake rods are long pieces of iron several inches in diameter that are inserted through the walls of buildings to reinforce them. These rods are screwed into turnbuckles or toggles and are secured at the outside ends with large washers and nuts. Repairmen ran these rods through the walls of hundreds of buildings injured by the great Charleston earthquake of 1886 to guard them from further injury. Many of the buildings fitted with this hardware after the earthquake are located in the Charleston region, although buildings as far away as Savannah, Georgia, display them as well.

Often called "earthquake bolts," these iron reinforcement rods commonly were incorporated into buildings in Charleston and elsewhere before the great earthquake. Their initial purpose, however, usually was to safeguard against gales and hurricanes rather than to protect from the rending and wrenching of earthquakes.

Owners who objected to seeing unadorned rod ends on the exteriors of their buildings covered them with stucco or capped them with cast-iron decorations depicting such objects as stars, concentric circles, long rectangular bars, lion heads, butterflies, diamonds, s's, v's, x's, and crosses. While the rod portions of earthquake rods are seldom visible, in some buildings no effort has been made to conceal them, such as in St. Paul's Episcopal Church in Summerville.

Tourists often are fascinated with earthquake rod caps, and they have become a standard decorative element in much of Charleston's architecture. Tour guides point them out, and some hotels and bed and breakfasts that have them advertise the fact in their promotional literature. Some modern buildings, such as the Omni Hotel at Charleston Place, even feature faux earthquake rod caps on their exterior walls. KENNETH E. PETERS

Peters, Kenneth E., and Robert B. Herrmann, comps. and eds. *First-Hand Observations of the Charleston Earthquake of August 31, 1886, and Other Earthquake Materials.* Columbia: South Carolina Geological Survey, 1986.

Earthquakes. Earthquakes (seismic events) have impacted South Carolina for thousands of years. The state's earthquakes have been tectonic; that is, they have resulted from intraplate displacements on the North American plate and not from interplate movements. They generally have caused little serious damage. Exceptions have been the massive Charleston earthquake of 1886 and the Union County earthquake of 1913. Earthquakes in South Carolina historically have been unpredictable and quite varied in their nature.

According to seismologists, South Carolina is one of the most seismically active states east of the Mississippi River, with most activity taking place in the Charleston-Summerville area. All except five or six of the state's northeastern counties have been the source of earthquakes at one time or another. Between February 1698,

Repairing St. Michael's Church, Charleston, following the 1886 earthquake. Courtesy, Calhoun County Museum

when South Carolinians first reported feeling an earthquake, and 2002 South Carolina witnessed about 180 earthquakes that have measured a magnitude 3 or greater on a 10-point scale (or a V on a modified Mercalli Intensity Scale of I to XII). Most seismologists consider such events to be major earthquakes.

Since the late 1600s, South Carolina has had twelve earthquakes with magnitudes of 4.0 to 4.9 and three with magnitudes of 5.0–5.9 (these three, however, were aftershocks to the great 1886 earthquake). Eight originated near Charleston and Summerville. The other seven originated in Union County, Pickens County, Columbia/Lake Murray, McBee, Bowman, Orangeburg, and Lake Jocassee.

Earthquake activity in South Carolina did not capture much attention until the giant Charleston earthquake of August 31, 1886. With a moment magnitude of 7.3 and an intensity of X, the 1886 earthquake remains the largest and most powerful seismic event to occur in the southeastern United States. It was also one of the first major U.S. earthquakes to be systematically and scientifically documented by the U.S. Geological Survey (USGS). The epicenter was south of Summerville at Middleton Plantation along the Ashley River. Its cause was movement at the junction of two intraplate faults—the north-northeast trending Woodstock fault and the northwest trending Ashley River fault. The earthquake hit at 9:51 P.M. Charleston time, and it shook the port city for thirty-five to seventy seconds (an unusually long time for an earthquake). It was followed by almost daily aftershocks for several weeks. Strong aftershocks shook the Charleston-Summerville area on September 2, 3, and 5, and even stronger ones impacted the area on October 22 and November 5. Many seismologists contend that aftershocks to the great earthquake continued at least into 1893. Upward of fifty-three of these aftershocks had magnitudes of 3.3 or more.

The Charleston earthquake was felt across two million square miles, including all of South Carolina, most of the United States east of the Mississippi River, and as far away as Canada, Cuba, and Bermuda. Of the eastern U.S. earthquakes, it was second only to the mammoth New Madrid, Missouri, earthquakes of 1811 and 1812 in the area that it impacted. The earthquake caused extensive damage to buildings not only in Charleston and Summerville, but also in Augusta and Savannah, Georgia. It destroyed two millpond dams in Aiken County and created a three-foot-high wave that inundated rice fields along the Cooper River and affected ships in Charleston's harbor and at sea. It reportedly chased rats out of sewers in New York City, rocked lighthouses along the New York seacoast, and felled chimneys in Kentucky and Ohio. The death toll eventually reached eighty-three in Charleston alone, with additional deaths attributed to the earthquake occurring elsewhere in South Carolina and in other states. The earthquake caused more than $5 million worth of damage in Charleston, whose estimated total assets in buildings in 1886 was about $22.5 million. It was South Carolina's worst natural disaster until Hurricane Hugo in 1989.

The Charleston-Summerville area continues to be by far the most seismically active area in the state. But, as South Carolina's seismic history shows, other areas also can have earthquakes. In the 1980s governments and organizations increasingly worried about threats from future earthquakes. In 1981 concerned South Carolinians formed the S.C. Seismic Safety Consortium (SCSSC) to work with the newly created Southeastern United States Safety Consortium (SEUSSC) in developing comprehensive action plans for earthquake preparedness. However, even with planning, a major earthquake would create major problems for the state's population and infrastructure. In the twentieth century, some rivers and streams in South Carolina were dammed to create hydroelectric, flood control, and recreational facilities or, in the cases of the Monticello Reservoir and Lake Keowee, sources of water cooling for atomic energy plants. Many of the dams were built on or near fault zones. To date, earthquakes have not broken or weakened the dams. In 2001, however, officials with the federal government, noting significant earthquakes in the Columbia region in 1945 and 1964, decided to make a concerted effort to protect area inhabitants against a major earthquake. Concerned about the capacity of the Lake Murray dam to withstand such an earthquake, they mandated the construction of a back-up dam to the existing earthen dam that was constructed in the late 1920s. An earthquake of magnitude 3.3 (intensity IV) in 1975 at Lake Jocassee also has caused speculation about that lake's dam. KENNETH E. PETERS

Dutton, Clarence E. *The Charleston Earthquake of August 31, 1886.* Arlington, Va.: Department of the Interior, Geological Survey, 1979.

Gohn, Gregory S., ed. *Studies Related to the Charleston, South Carolina, Earthquake of 1886: Tectonics and Seismicity.* Geological Survey Professional Paper 1313. Washington, D.C.: Government Printing Office, 1983.

Peters, Kenneth E. "Economic Consequences of the Charleston Earthquake." *Proceedings of the South Carolina Historical Association* (1986): 70–81.

Peters, Kenneth E., and Robert B. Herrmann, comps. and eds. *First-Hand Observations of the Charleston Earthquake of August 31, 1886, and Other Earthquake Materials.* Columbia: South Carolina Geological Survey, 1986.

Talwani, Pradeep. *South Carolina Earthquakes, 1698–1995.* Columbia: South Carolina Seismic Network, 1996.

Visvanathan, T. R. *Earthquakes in South Carolina.* Columbia: South Carolina Geological Survey, 1980.

Easley (Pickens County; 2000 pop. 17,754). As the Atlanta and Charlotte Airline Railroad was being completed through Pickens County in 1873, Robert Elliott Holcombe proposed to railroad authorities that he would build a depot at his own expense if the line went through property he either owned or had an option to buy. His offer was accepted, and Holcombe laid out business and residential lots that sold well. The General Assembly granted the new town a charter of incorporation on January 20, 1874. Holcombe was elected the town's first intendant (mayor). In 1895 the town limits were extended due to growth, and the town of Easley was rechartered under the stipulations of a new uniform charter law.

Many would have thought the new town would be named for Holcombe, who became the first depot agent, but Holcombe asked that it be named for William King Easley, an attorney who was born in Pickens County near the Greenville County line. While Easley maintained his home there, much of his work was in Greenville, where he served as attorney for the rail line.

As with many other towns in South Carolina's upcountry, the railroad and cotton mills brought dramatic growth to Easley. The first mill was begun in 1890 when John M. Geer, a cotton buyer from Piedmont Mills who came often to buy Easley's cotton, told Easley citizens that if they would raise the stock, he would begin a mill. The stock was raised, Easley Cotton Mills was organized, and Geer was elected president and treasurer. Later two mills in nearby Liberty were purchased by the Easley corporation. In 1902 Glenwood Cotton Mills was begun, and Alice Mills followed in 1910.

Diversification of industry developed in more recent times, and Easley has a healthy retail trade. Nontextile firms that have opened in Easley include Danford Fluid Power, manufacturers of pumps and motors; and Perception, Inc., manufacturers of kayaks. Ortec makes chemicals for the textile industry. Textile mills still in operation include Alice, Mayfair, and Hollingsworth Saco-Lowell. They employ in excess of 4,300 people.

Easley is home to more than eighty churches representing sixteen denominations. The Palmetto Baptist Medical Center has 109 beds and seventy-two doctors. Numerous subdivisions, mostly to the east and south of the city, are occupied largely by persons working in the adjoining Greenville County. Growth within the city has been constant, however, with a seventeen percent increase in population during the 1990s. HURLEY E. BADDERS

Browning, Wilt. *Linthead: Growing Up in a Carolina Cotton Mill Village.* Asheboro, N.C.: Down Home Press, 1990.

Easley Mill Memories, 1900–1991. Easley, S.C.: Easley Mill Reunion Committee, 1991.

Pickensville-Easley History. Easley, S.C.: Forest Acres/McKissick Quest Program, 1989.

Eastern tiger swallowtail. State butterfly. The tiger swallowtail (*Papilio glaucus*) became South Carolina's official butterfly by an act signed into law by Governor Carroll Campbell on March 29, 1994. The General Assembly acted especially at the behest of the members of the Garden Club of South Carolina, who selected the butterfly "because it can be seen in deciduous woods, along streams, rivers, and wooded swamps, and in towns and cities throughout South Carolina."

This popular butterfly, easy to recognize by its yellow, tiger-striped wings, is often specified as the eastern tiger swallowtail (*Papilio glaucus glaucus*) to distinguish it from similar western, Canadian, and Mexican subspecies. The eastern subspecies ranges throughout the American South and the eastern United States, north to the Great Lakes, and west to the Great Plains.

The earliest evidence of the butterfly in South Carolina came from the brush of the English naturalist Mark Catesby, who sojourned in the lowcountry in the 1720s. Engravings of Catesby's watercolors of the tiger swallowtail appeared in his *Natural History of Carolina, Florida, and the Bahama Islands* (1732–1743).

Tiger swallowtails appear in South Carolina woods, fields, and gardens in early spring, and there are at least three or four generations every year. The adult has a wingspan from 3S to 6 inches across. Males are yellow with tiger striping, but females have two distinct color morphs: yellow and black. It is believed that females with black wing coloring mimic other black butterflies that are toxic, and this mimicry protects them from predators.

The caterpillar is bright green with two huge yellow eyespots on the head end. These give the larva an almost snakelike appearance, probably to discourage predators. DAVID C. R. HEISSER

Mikula, Rick, and Caludia Mikula. *Garden Butterflies of North America.* Minocqua, Wis.: Willow Creek, 1997.

Opler, Paul A. *A Field Guide to Eastern Butterflies.* Boston: Houghton Mifflin, 1992.

Scott, James A. *The Butterflies of North America.* Stanford, Calif.: Stanford University Press, 1986.

Ebenezer colony. Ebenezer, founded in 1734, was located some twenty-five miles up the Savannah River on the Georgia side. This unique settlement of Lutheran refugees from Salzburg, Austria, was included in the Lutheran Synod of South Carolina until the formation of the Georgia Synod in 1860. Its early inhabitants caught the imagination of many on both sides of the Atlantic because of their courage under persecution, their industry, and their singular piety, which made its impact on the surrounding society. At the time of the Revolutionary War the settlement numbered some two thousand, second only to Savannah in the colony of Georgia.

Two pastors provided both secular and spiritual leadership for the Salzburgers: Johann Martin Bolzius and Israel Christian Gronau. The extensive diaries and correspondence of the dominant partner, Bolzius, provide remarkable insight into the history of the settlement and shed light on nearby German settlements in South Carolina. Ebenezer, blessed with strong pastoral leadership, for a time regularly sent sermons and devotional literature to South Carolina German Lutherans, who were less well organized. Since the Ebenezer colony sustained a rather somber piety, the Salzburgers became increasingly critical of their South Carolina neighbors, who seemed to them more intent on economic gain than a life of discipleship. The exemplary character of the Salzburgers inspired praise from such notable visitors as John Wesley and George Whitefield, the latter characterizing Ebenezer as the biblical land of Goshen in the midst of Egypt. Whitefield was also a benefactor, securing contributions to help support the settlement.

The Revolutionary War led to much plundering of Ebenezer property and caused devastating conflict among the inhabitants. Never regaining its earlier prosperity, the community gradually dissipated. In the last half of the twentieth century the historic Jerusalem Church was restored and nearby a Lutheran retreat center was established. PAUL JERSILD

Jones, George Fenwick. *The Georgia Dutch: From the Rhine and Danube to the Savannah, 1733–1783.* Athens: University of Georgia Press, 1992.

———. *The Salzburger Saga: Religious Exiles and Other Germans along the Savannah.* Athens: University of Georgia Press, 1984.

Strobel, P. A. *The Salzburgers and Their Descendants.* 1855. Reprint, Athens: University of Georgia Press, 1953.

Edelman, Marian Wright (b. 1939). Lawyer, civil rights and children's rights advocate. Edelman was born on June 6, 1939, in Bennettsville, the daughter of the Baptist minister Arthur Jerome Wright and Maggie Leola Bowen. She graduated from Marlboro

Marian Wright Edelman. Courtesy, The Heinz Awards (Jim Harrison, Photographer)

Training High School in 1956; from Spelman College in Atlanta, Georgia, in 1960; and from Yale Law School in 1963.

Edelman became active in civil rights as a student at Spelman College. Following the historic sit-in of four black students at a Woolworth's lunch counter in Greensboro, North Carolina, Edelman and seventy-seven other students were arrested on March 15, 1960, for conducting a sit-in at Atlanta restaurants that served only whites. After graduating from law school, Edelman spent a year, on an Earl Warren Fellowship, at the National Association for the Advancement of Colored People Legal Defense and Educational Fund (LDF), where she learned to litigate a variety of civil-rights-related cases. From 1964 to 1968 she served as director of the LDF office in Jackson, Mississippi, where she became the first black woman to pass the state's bar exam. During her time in Mississippi, Edelman expanded her horizons beyond civil rights to include the issue of children's rights. In 1965 she helped develop the Child Development Group of Mississippi, which ran Head Start programs for the state's poor children after the state refused to accept federal funds. For three years she prodded federal officials who were being pressured to discontinue the funding by Mississippi's powerful and racist U.S. senators James Eastland and John Stennis.

After four years of protracted struggle, Edelman decided to leave Mississippi. The abject poverty and feudal conditions she had observed in Mississippi affected her vision profoundly. In 1968 she took a position in Washington, D.C., as the legal counsel for Martin Luther King, Jr.'s planned "Poor People's Campaign." On July 14, 1968, she married Peter Edelman, a legislative aid to U.S. Senator Robert F. Kennedy. They met in 1967 when her future husband accompanied Kennedy to Mississippi and witnessed its poverty firsthand. Their union was the first interracial marriage in Virginia after the U.S. Supreme Court outlawed the state's miscegenation law in *Loving v. Commonwealth of Virginia.* The couple has three sons: Joshua, Jonah, and Ezra.

Edelman founded the Washington Research Project to develop legal strategies to benefit the poor. She continued as the project's director while also directing the Center for Law and Education at Harvard University, where she had accompanied her husband in 1971. The Washington Research Project ultimately became the Children's Defense Fund (CDF) in 1973. The CDF became one of the nation's strongest and most influential advocates for children in the United States, especially the children of the poor, minorities, and the disabled, and worked to ensure a safe, healthy, and moral start for all children in America. Edelman has served on the boards of trustees at Spelman College and Yale University. She has received numerous awards, including the prestigious MacArthur Foundation Fellowship and the Presidential Medal of Freedom. She has also written five books, one of which, *Lanterns: A Memoir of Mentors,* reveals the formative influence of her South Carolina youth. CARMEN V. HARRIS

Edelman, Marian Wright. *Lanterns: A Memoir of Mentors.* Boston: Beacon, 1999.

———. *The Measure of Our Success: A Letter to My Children and Yours.* Boston: Beacon, 1992.

Edens, J. Drake, Jr. (1925–1982). Republican Party leader. Edens organized the modern Republican Party in South Carolina. He was born on May 13, 1925, in Columbia, the son of J. Drake Edens, Sr., and May Youmans. After serving in the U.S. Marine Corps, in 1946 he married Ferrell McCracken. Edens earned a bachelor's degree from the University of South Carolina in 1949 and until 1955 was vice president of his family's food store chain. Following the company's merger, he became self-employed with numerous business interests.

Edens's initial involvement with the Republican Party occurred during the 1960 presidential campaign. In 1961 he was cochair of the successful campaign of Charles Boineau, the first Republican elected to the General Assembly in the twentieth century. He was also manager of the 1962 U.S. Senate campaign of the journalist William D. Workman, who received a surprising forty-three percent of the vote as a Republican challenger to veteran Democrat Olin D. Johnston.

From 1963 to 1965 Edens was chairman of the state Republican Party. He worked methodically to strengthen and expand the party organization statewide. His party-building activities took him to every corner of South Carolina. He eventually established the foundation for a state party that thereafter posed a serious electoral challenge to the Democrats.

Edens, an early supporter of Barry Goldwater for president, reached a high point at the 1964 Republican National Convention when he rose to announce the state delegation's vote: "I am humbly grateful that we can do this for America. South Carolina casts sixteen votes for Senator Barry Goldwater." With that, Goldwater had the majority needed for the nomination. In autumn 1964, with Edens as his state campaign chairman, Goldwater carried South Carolina for the first Republican victory in a presidential election since 1876. Nationally, however, Goldwater lost in a landslide election to Lyndon B. Johnson.

In 1965 Edens became the state's Republican national committeeman, and in 1965 he was chosen one of the committee's four national vice chairmen. In the space of just five years, he had risen from relative obscurity to become the highest-placed southerner in the national Republican Party.

Edens was a delegate to the national Republican convention twice more, in 1968 and 1976, and remained on the national committee until 1972. By the mid-1970s, however, he had yielded leadership of the state party to relative newcomers to the Republicans.

An avid outdoorsman and conservationist, Edens in 1976 was named to the South Carolina Wildlife Commission and in 1979 was elevated to the chairmanship of the commission by Democratic governor Richard W. Riley. By the early 1980s Edens continued to pursue these interests despite declining health. On July 30, 1982, at the Isle of Palms beach, Edens accidentally drowned while swimming. In death he was remembered as "Mr. Republican" and the "father of the Republican Party in South Carolina." Columbia's *State* newspaper editorialized, "We know of few South Carolinians who were more respected than Mr. Edens." NEAL D. THIGPEN

Edens, J. Drake, Jr. Papers. Modern Political Collections, South Caroliniana Library, University of South Carolina, Columbia.

Sampson, Gregory B. "The Rise of the 'New' Republican Party in South Carolina, 1948–1974: A Case Study of Political Change in the Deep South." Ph.D. diss., University of North Carolina at Chapel Hill, 1984.

Surratt, Clark. "Edens Praised for Service to State." Columbia *State,* July 31, 1982, pp. A1, A7.

Edgefield (Edgefield County; 2000 pop. 4,449). Edgefield was founded as the Edgefield County seat in 1791 because of its central geographic location. Alternately referred to as Edgefield Court House, Edgefield Village, and Edgefield, the town was incorporated in 1830.

From the early to mid–nineteenth century, Edgefield was the political and social center of the district. The *Edgefield Advertiser,* the oldest newspaper in South Carolina to publish continuously under the same nameplate, began operation in 1836. The present-day courthouse was built in 1839 on a high point in the village and followed the design characteristics of the noted South Carolina architect Robert Mills. The town was particularly known in the antebellum period for its great number of accomplished lawyers, many of whom became state political leaders. These included Francis Pickens, Francis Wardlaw, George McDuffie, John C. Sheppard, and James O. Sheppard. However, despite its leading role in politics and its wealth, Edgefield was not a commercial center. Most local cotton dealing and shipping business was conducted at Hamburg or Augusta on the Savannah River.

Edgefield continued to be the district's focus of political activity during Reconstruction. Rallies were held in the courthouse square, as were information sessions for freedmen. The town grew as African Americans established their own social and religious institutions after the Civil War, such as the Macedonia Baptist Church in 1868. Reconstruction leaders and former Edgefield slaves Paris Simkins and Lawrence Cain won seats in the state legislature and led local militia groups. At the same time, pre–Civil War political leaders and former Confederate military officers from Edgefield, such as Martin Gary and Matthew Butler, were some of the most ardent opponents of the Reconstruction government.

Industry did not develop in Edgefield until 1890 when the Edgefield Ginning, Milling, and Fertilizer Company opened. The mill was an important economic resource both in the cotton purchased from local farmers and in the large number of persons it employed. Daniel Augustus Tompkins later purchased the company and built a textile mill next to the oil mill in 1898. The mill and nearby worker housing were located in the Cumberland neighborhood, named for the Cumberland Gap Railroad that ran from Edgefield to Charleston. The mill later was sold to the Kendall Company and remained the town's most important industry through the first half of the twentieth century.

Edgefield suffered through difficult financial times in the second half of the twentieth century when the mill ceased operation. The town's distance from major highways and interstates also hindered its growth, and its population stagnated. While the agricultural and logging industries remained important employers, beginning in the 1990s Edgefield worked to attract new manufacturing development and expand tourism. From these efforts, the town was named as a discovery center location in the South Carolina National Heritage Corridor, and the National Wild Turkey Federation moved its headquarters to Edgefield and opened the Wild Turkey Center and Museum. MARY SHERRER

Burton, Orville Vernon. *In My Father's House Are Many Mansions: Family and Community in Edgefield, South Carolina.* Chapel Hill: University of North Carolina Press, 1985.

Chapman, John A. *History of Edgefield County from the Earliest Settlements to 1897.* 1897. Reprint, Spartanburg, S.C.: Reprint Company, 1980.

Edgefield Advertiser (2003 circulation: estimated 500 weekly). The *Edgefield Advertiser* began publication on February 11, 1836, making it the oldest newspaper in South Carolina to publish continuously under the same nameplate. The newspaper's history, however, stretches back to May 27, 1811, when Thomas M. Davenport began publishing the *Anti-Monarchist and South-Carolina Advertiser* at Edgefield Court House to support President James Madison's plans for stronger national defense. After the War of 1812, Davenport sold the newspaper to Benjamin McNary. McNary changed the name to *South-Carolina Republican* and moved the newspaper to nearby Pottersville, where it was bought in 1824 by John Lofton and Abner Landrum.

Five years later the *Republican* was purchased by Francis Hugh Wardlaw, John Bacon, and Warren Mays. They returned the newspaper to Edgefield Court House, where it was bought in 1836 by Maximillian LaBorde and James Jones. That year the name was changed for the final time, to *Edgefield Advertiser.* Under the leadership of William Francis Durisoe, the newspaper became an ardent advocate of southern rights prior to the Civil War. After the war, the newspaper protested new freedoms given to African Americans and backed Wade Hampton.

The newspaper retained its forthright style throughout the twentieth century. William Walton Mims assumed control of the newspaper in 1937, and the staunchly conservative newspaper was not afraid to take unpopular stands on local issues. Mims retained the editorship through the end of 2002. On January 1, 2003, Suzanne Gile Mims Derrick became the editor and the *Advertiser* reoriented itself as a weekly newspaper devoted to community news and concerns. AARON W. MARRS

Edgefield Advertiser. Sesquicentennial edition. March 5, 1986.

Mims, Eleanor Elizabeth. "The Editors of the Edgefield Advertiser: Oldest Newspaper in South Carolina." Master's thesis, University of South Carolina, 1930.

Edgefield County (502 sq. miles; 2000 pop. 24,595). Edgefield County was created in 1785 from the southern portion of the backcountry judicial district of Ninety Six. It became Edgefield District in 1800, following a reorganization of the county system. Bounded by the Savannah and Saluda Rivers and the districts of Abbeville, Barnwell, Orangeburg, and Lexington, Edgefield originally encompassed 1,702 square miles and was the largest inland district in the state. Legend asserts that the name arose from Edgefield's location on the western "edge" of South Carolina. With its vast area embracing a varied cultural and physical geography, one historian aptly described antebellum Edgefield as "more a region than a county."

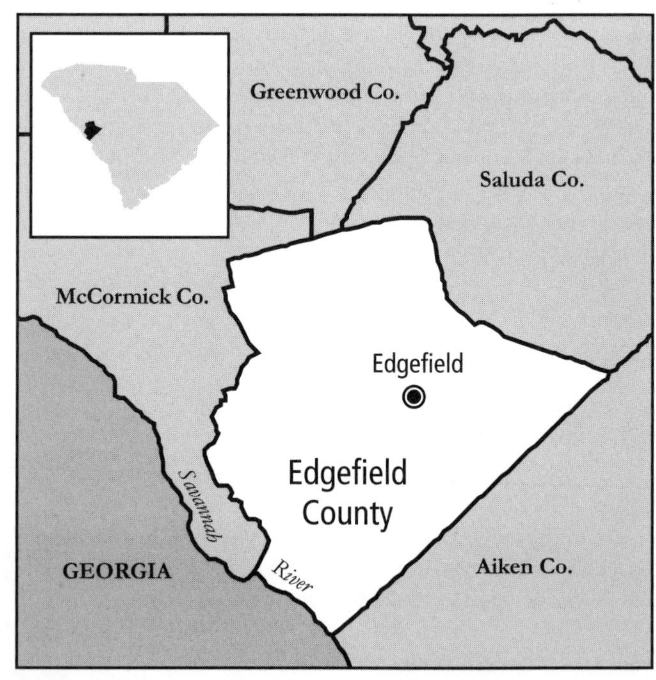

European immigration into the Edgefield area began around 1750. Most new arrivals were Scots-Irish, who migrated to Edgefield from Pennsylvania and Virginia. Smaller numbers of Swiss, French Huguenots, and Germans established settlements at New Windsor, New Bordeaux, and elsewhere. During this same era, European arrivals carried the first African American slaves into Edgefield. Later, coastal planters entered Edgefield to establish plantations, which led to dramatic increases in the slave population.

Agriculture dominated Edgefield's economy throughout its history. Early settlers grew grains and raised impressive numbers of cattle and hogs. Staple crops, particularly tobacco, grew in significance by the 1790s. However, it was cotton that came to define the agricultural economy of the district. Incorporating the newly invented gin and short-staple varieties of cotton plants, Edgefield was at the center of the South's inland cotton boom of the early 1800s. Production expanded throughout the antebellum era. By 1860 Edgefield District led South Carolina in the number of cotton bales produced. The slave population of the district grew accordingly. By 1830 slaves comprised a majority of Edgefield's population. Three decades later Edgefield's total of 24,060 slaves was the largest of any inland district in the state.

Antebellum Edgefield also contained a modest but influential manufacturing sector. The Horse Creek Valley in the southern part of the district was home to the pioneering textile factories of Graniteville and Vaucluse, as well as a paper mill and a porcelain factory. Pottery works utilized the district's clay deposits, particularly at the artisan enclave of Pottersville, just north of Edgefield Court House. Edgefield pottery found a strong regional market, and pieces by slave potters such as "Dave" became highly prized by collectors in the late twentieth century. In addition, Edgefield was the site of a lucrative gold mine operated by William "Billy" Dorn and later purchased by the reaper tycoon Cyrus McCormick.

Besides cotton, Edgefield came to be known for producing political leaders and for its frequently volatile political culture. The county produced ten South Carolina governors, five lieutenant governors, and several national political figures. Antebellum U.S. senators George McDuffie, Andrew P. Butler, and James Henry Hammond were residents of Edgefield, as was Congressman Preston Brooks, who gained national notoriety for caning Charles Sumner of Massachusetts on the floor of the U.S. Senate. The 1876 plan of district representative Martin W. Gary to restore Democratic rule to South Carolina through fraud, intimidation, and violence came to be known as the "Edgefield Plan." Later political leaders included the agrarian radical "Pitchfork Ben" Tillman and long-serving U.S. senator J. Strom Thurmond.

The decades following the Civil War brought significant changes. After its redesignation as a county in 1868, Edgefield gradually saw its area reduced by more than two-thirds, as sections of the county went to create the new counties of Aiken (1871), Saluda (1895), Greenwood (1897), and McCormick (1916). Railroads reached Edgefield during the 1870s and 1880s and spawned the towns of Johnston, Ridge Spring, and Trenton. By the turn of the century, manufacturing, especially textiles, began to play a growing role in the Edgefield economy, although the county remained overwhelmingly rural.

For much of the twentieth century Edgefield saw its economic and political positions within South Carolina dwindle. Between 1920 and 1970 the county's population decreased from 23,928 to 15,692. Declines in agriculture spurred much of this out-migration, as total farm acreage shrank from 224,850 acres in 1920 to just 71,425 acres by 1997. Agriculture remained central to Edgefield, however, but with cotton replaced in importance by the famous peach orchards of the county's "Ridge" section, as well as increases in poultry, cattle, and dairy production. Manufacturing and service-related jobs continued to gain prominence as well. Major textile firms such as the Riegel Textile Corporation (later Mount Vernon Riegel) and Milliken & Company opened substantial mills in Edgefield County after World War II, as did smaller textile companies such as Star Fibers and the Stone Manufacturing Company. Although the addition of manufacturing jobs in the 1980s and 1990s helped Edgefield reverse its population decline, the county still lagged behind much of South Carolina in per capita income. In 1970 more than one-third of Edgefield workers commuted to jobs outside the county. As late as 1980 more than one-fourth of county residents lived below the poverty line.

Edgefield showed signs of revitalizing its economic fortunes by the end of the twentieth century. The county continued to aggressively recruit new businesses, such as Menardi and Concurrent Technologies Corporation, by touting Edgefield's railroad and highway connections and its close proximity to Columbia and Augusta, Georgia. The county also tapped its history and rural image to enhance its appeal to tourists and retirees. Edgefield residents were active participants in developing the South Carolina National Heritage Corridor, while Old Edgefield Pottery, established in 1992, contributed to a renewed interest in Edgefield's pottery tradition. In addition, Edgefield County emerged as a focal point of conservation efforts. The National Wild Turkey Federation built its Wild Turkey Center and museum near the town of Edgefield, and Quail Unlimited and Waterfowl USA are also located in the county. Together these three national organizations worked to promote the conservation and restoration of wildlife in Edgefield and beyond. TOM DOWNEY

Burton, Orville Vernon. *In My Father's House Are Many Mansions: Family and Community in Edgefield, South Carolina.* Chapel Hill: University of North Carolina Press, 1985.

Butterfield, Fox. *All God's Children: The Bosket Family and the American Tradition of Violence.* New York: Knopf, 1995.

Chapman, John A. *History of Edgefield County from the Earliest Settlements to 1897.* 1897. Reprint, Spartanburg, S.C.: Reprint Company, 1980.

Downey, Tom. *Planting a Capitalist South: Masters, Merchants, and Manufacturers in the Southern Interior, 1790–1860.* Baton Rouge: Louisiana State University Press, 2006.

Ford, Lacy K., Jr. "Origins of the Edgefield Tradition: The Late Antebellum Experience and the Roots of Political Insurgency." *South Carolina Historical Magazine* 98 (October 1997): 328–48.

Edgefield pottery. The term "Edgefield pottery" is used to identify alkaline-glazed stoneware first produced in Edgefield District in the 1810s. Edgefield pottery blends the cultural traditions of England, Europe, Asia, and Africa. Many of the potters came from English, Irish, and German backgrounds and contributed their forms and techniques, while African American slaves performed the majority of the labor-intensive tasks. The distinctive glaze (made of wood ash, feldspar, clay, and water) and use of the groundhog kiln were typical of pottery techniques used in the Far East.

By 1817 the Landrum family was the first to produce alkaline-glazed stoneware at Pottersville, thereby capitalizing on the need for low-cost, durable pottery in South Carolina and the surrounding states. Some scholars believe that Dr. Abner Landrum read the letters of Pere d'Entrecolles describing the manufacture of porcelain, while others argue that Richard Champion brought this knowledge from England to Camden, South Carolina. Up until the production

A storage jar made for H. A. Kenrick of Hamburg (circa 1850). Courtesy, McKissick Museum, University of South Carolina

of pottery in Edgefield, utilitarian wares had to be purchased from the northern states or from Europe. In North Carolina the Moravians were producing lead-glazed earthenware, but lead was expensive and poisonous. Earthenware broke more easily than the high-fired, more durable stoneware. Churns, storage jars, pitchers, jugs, plates, and cups were produced in great quantities. At the peak of production in the 1850s, as many as five factories turned out upward of fifty thousand gallons of pottery annually. The stoneware was sold statewide via wagon and railway. Most potters advertised the production of vessels holding up to twenty gallons, at a price of ten cents a gallon.

At the Lewis Miles Factory, an enslaved African American potter named Dave made enormous jars that held as much as forty gallons. Dave, who later took the name David Drake, was a literate slave who signed and dated many of his works and occasionally wrote a poem on the side, such as, "Great & noble jar / hold sheep goat and bear, May 13, 1859."

Slip-glazed wares were produced in order to compete with more decorative ceramics produced in the North and those imported from Europe. At the Phoenix Factory and Colin Rhodes Factory, popular design motifs included bell flowers, loops, and swags created in iron or kaolin slip or written advertisements and pictorial scenes of girls in hoop skirts. Figural vessels and "face jugs" were produced between 1840 and 1880, the majority of which were made by African Americans, possibly for their own use. Major factories included Pottersville Stoneware Manufactory, John Landrum Pottery, Colin Rhodes Factory, Lewis Miles Factory, Miles Mill, Phoenix Factory, B. F. Landrum Factory, Trapp and Chandler, Palmetto Brickworks, Seigler Pottery, Baynham Pottery, Hahn Pottery, South Carolina Pottery Company, and Roundtree-Bodie Pottery.

The Edgefield pottery tradition migrated westward into Georgia, Alabama, Mississippi, Louisiana, and Texas. Inexpensive glass production and the collapse of the plantation system led to the demise of the Edgefield pottery production in the early twentieth century. Many examples of Edgefield pottery survive, however, and have become highly sought after by museums and private collectors. The tradition has attracted a high level of scholarly attention, and the price of individual pieces has reached tens of thousands of dollars. JILL BEUTE KOVERMAN

Baldwin, Cinda K. *Great and Noble Jar: Traditional Stoneware of South Carolina.* Athens: University of Georgia Press, 1993.

Koverman, Jill Beute, ed. *"I Made This Jar . . .": The Life and Works of the Enslaved African-American Potter, Dave.* Columbia: McKissick Museum, University of South Carolina, 1998.

———. *Making Faces: Southern Face Vessels from 1840–1990.* Columbia: McKissick Museum, University of South Carolina, 2001.

Edisto. At the time of English colonization, the Edisto Indians were a tribe living between the Savannah and Edisto Rivers. Originally inhabitants of St. Helena Island, the tribe relocated in the late 1500s to Edisto Island. The English captain William Hilton first contacted this tribe when his ship, *Adventure,* visited St. Helena's Sound in 1663. Hilton observed that the Edistos knew many Spanish words and had regular visits from the Spaniards at St. Augustine. He also made records of the Edisto villages, noting that each contained a round house of about two hundred feet in diameter covered with palmetto leaves.

In 1666 Robert Sandford made contact with the same tribe. Sandford was met by an Edisto chief named Shadoo, who insisted that the group visit his nearby village. Touring the Edisto settlement, the Sandford party described the same round council house as noted by Hilton. The men wrote, "Round the house from each side the throne quite to the Entrance were lower benches filled with the whole rabble of Men and Women and children in the center." Of particular interest to the group was the chief, a woman who extended great hospitality to the group. The cultural exchange went quite well, and the Edisto chief returned with Sandford to spend the night as a guest aboard his ship.

Eventually, Edisto land was acquired by treaty by the Carolina colony between 1670 and 1686, as were the lands of most smaller coastal tribes, such as the St. Helenas, the Ashepoos, and the Stonos. Coastal tribes such as the Edisto could not withstand occasional English slave raids and epidemic diseases. Most tribes lost their identity, and remnants were adopted by tribes further inland. MICHAEL P. MORRIS

Crane, Verner. *The Southern Frontier, 1670–1732.* Durham, N.C.: Duke University Press, 1928.

Josephy, Alvin M. *500 Nations: An Illustrated History of North American Indians.* New York: Knopf, 1994.

Milling, Chapman J. *Red Carolinians.* 1940. Reprint, Columbia: University of South Carolina Press, 1969.

Salley, Alexander S. *Narratives of Early Carolina, 1650–1708.* New York: Scribner's, 1911.

Edisto Island (Charleston County; 2000 pop. 1,558). Located between the mouths of the North and South Edisto Rivers south of Charleston, Edisto Island is a lowcountry Sea Island of approximately sixty-eight square miles. The island is shielded from the Atlantic Ocean by Edisto Beach, a barrier island municipality contained in Colleton County and linked to Edisto Island by a causeway.

Edisto Island derives its name from the Edisto Indians, the island's initial inhabitants (an Indian mound built by the Edistos survives at Edisto Beach State Park). In the mid-1500s Spanish settlers arrived on the island they called "Oristo" and established a Jesuit mission. Englishman Robert Sandford explored Edisto in 1666, and a decade later the "Edistow" deeded the island to the Lords Proprietors. The Spanish raided an English settlement on Edisto in 1686, but Anglo settlers and their African slaves remained and increased in the ensuing decades. Edisto Presbyterian Church was organized in 1710 and Trinity Episcopal Church in 1774. The salinity of the island's wetlands inhibited rice production, but indigo production flourished in the mid–eighteenth century. From the late eighteenth century until the early twentieth century, Edisto Island was a center of Sea Island cotton production, until the boll weevil devastated the crop in the early 1920s. Edisto farmers thereafter produced cabbage, potatoes, cattle, and tomatoes. In 1920 the Dawhoo Bridge connected the isolated island to the mainland. The bridge subsequently was replaced by a high, fixed-span bridge. FORD WALPOLE

Connor, Amy S., and Sheila L. Beardsley. *Edisto Island: A Family Affair.* Dover, N.H.: Arcadia, 1998.

Puckette, Clara C. *Edisto: A Sea Island Principality.* Cleveland: Seaforth, 1978.

Edisto Memorial Gardens. Edisto Gardens were established in the 1920s when azaleas were planted to beautify five acres in the city of Orangeburg. "Memorial" was added to the garden's name in 1950, and a large fountain at the entrance honors the memory of those who gave their lives in World War I, World War II, the Korean War, and in Vietnam. Located on the Edisto River, the gardens feature Horne Wetlands Park, where a boardwalk, boat dock, gazebo, and educational interpretative shelter allow visitors to appreciate the flora and fauna of a free-flowing black-water river surrounded by old tupelo and cypress trees.

The gardens have expanded over the years, growing to include diverse plantings and natural areas covering more than 150 acres. Thousands of roses have been planted since the 1951 establishment of the rose garden, which became an official All-American Rose Selections test garden in 1973. New introductions as well as former award-winning roses are displayed in the gardens, and the annual South Carolina Festival of Roses celebrates their blooming in late April.

The peak spring bloom of azaleas, dogwoods, and crab apples typically occurs from mid-March to mid-April. Rose varieties including grandifloras, climbing, and miniatures bloom from April through November, and a butterfly garden and sensory garden provide spring, summer, and fall interest. Winter in the garden is celebrated with the Children's Garden Christmas light display featuring animated and still displays and lighted cherry trees. Access is free, and the garden is open seven days a week. MARY TAYLOR HAQUE

Edisto River. Rising in the coastal plain, the Edisto is one of the longest free-flowing black-water rivers in North America. The river takes its characteristic hue from the tannic acid created by the decomposition of leaves and branches. The Edisto River is formed by the joining of its north and south forks on the border of Orangeburg and Bamberg Counties and, along its course, provides the natural boundary between Dorchester and Colleton Counties. It divides into two tidewater estuarial channels, forming Edisto Island, before meeting the Atlantic Ocean in St. Helena Sound. The river flows for about 250 unobstructed river miles from its headwaters to the ocean. The Edisto is part of the ACE Basin, a coastal river system that includes the Ashepoo and the Combahee and drains about twenty percent of the state.

Pottery recovered near the Edisto suggests that Native Americans lived by the river over three thousand years ago. When Europeans and Africans first entered the area, they found that it was home to the Kussos, a Native American tribe. The Kussos were joined by a splinter group of Natchez Indians in the early 1700s, and the two formed a single tribe that would eventually take the name Edisto after the river that flowed through their territory. Descendants of both the Kusso-Natchez Indians and African slaves still call the area of the Edisto River Basin their home.

By the late eighteenth century, rice plantations in tidally affected reaches of the Edisto began implementing tidewater rice culture. Thousands of slaves labored to clear fields and build dams, sluices, and gates. The lengthy Edisto was also used to transport upland cotton and timber to the coast in the antebellum years before the railroads superseded rivers as avenues of commerce.

The Edisto River flows through sparsely populated and generally undeveloped forest and cypress-tupelo swamps, and has been nationally recognized for its scenic beauty and ecological value. The unique character of the river has been preserved through ongoing conservation efforts. ROBERT STEVENS

Kovacik, Charles F., and John J. Winberry. *South Carolina: The Making of a Landscape.* 1987. Reprint, Columbia: University of South Carolina Press, 1989.

Marshall, William D., ed. *Assessing Change in the Edisto River Basin: An Ecological Characterization.* Columbia: South Carolina Water Resources Commission, 1993.

Education. For much of the state's history, education was left principally to families. Nonetheless, while historically the state's support of schooling has been hesitant, sporadic, and limited, the last two decades of the twentieth century witnessed growing attention to schools. By the end of the twentieth century, reform of South Carolina public schools had entered the forefront of political debate.

Reflecting the English roots of colonial South Carolina society, early education was centered in the home and church. For formal education wealthy, white families might hire tutors or send their children to private schools in Charleston. Education for crafts was provided through apprenticeships.

The first expressions of public support for "free schools" came in the early eighteenth century. Some individuals had bequeathed money for the purpose of supporting free schools. In 1712 "An Act for Founding and Erecting of a Free School in Charlestown" was passed, actually recognizing a school already established in Charleston under John Douglas, but also providing limited public funds for the support of free schools established in other parishes as well. Masters had to be Anglicans, and instruction was required "in Grammar, and other arts and sciences and useful learning, and also in the principles of the Christian religion."

Free schools were operated for the children of poor whites who could not afford a private school or tutor. Organizations establishing such schools included the South Carolina Society, the Winyaw Indigo Society, the Mt. Zion Society, and the Anglican Society for the Propagation of the Gospel in Foreign Parts. The most long-lived of such schools was a manual training school established in the Abbeville District through a 1797 bequest by John de la Howe.

Educational opportunities for black South Carolinians were extremely limited. While the wives of masters might instruct favorite slaves in Christianity and the reading of the Bible—and occasionally black students received instruction in free schools, most notably at the school of the Reverend Alexander Garden in

Charleston—most whites were skeptical of the value of educating blacks. Beginning in 1740 and continuing throughout the colonial and antebellum periods, the South Carolina legislature passed statutes limiting the teaching of writing and reading to slaves and free blacks. Despite these laws, schools for free blacks supported by religious and fraternal organizations survived in Charleston during the antebellum period.

Throughout the colonial period and beyond, private education remained the norm. Tuition-charging academies were the mainstay of secondary education. Notable schools included the Mt. Bethel Academy in Newberry, Moses Waddel's Willington Academy in Abbeville District, and Madame Ann Mason Talvande's French School for Young Ladies in Charleston. Other private academies sprang up throughout the state, sometimes with limited state support. The curricula of these schools tended to the classics, Greek, Latin, and mathematics but varied according to the gender of the students. One female academy in Columbia, for example, offered a course of study that included belles lettres, French, music, drawing, and plain and ornamental needlework. There were 117 academies in the state by 1840 and more than 200 in 1860. An 1850 act provided support for the establishment of military schools in Anderson, Marion, and Spartanburg.

In 1811 the General Assembly passed a new free school act authorizing the establishment of schools in each district equal to its number of representatives in the legislature. The state subsidized these schools at a meager level, and any white child could attend free, with priority given to orphans or children of the poor. These free schools came to be seen as "pauper schools," a stigma that kept many away. Typically the quality of both the buildings and the instruction was low. In 1860 there were only 1,395 teachers operating 1,270 schools for 18,915 students.

The "common school" movement that swept the North and Midwest during the 1840s and 1850s missed South Carolina. State leaders debated the need for education for the laboring classes, and most seemed to feel that it would make them dissatisfied with their lot. Most estimates suggest that by 1860 only half of the state's white children received any schooling. Charleston was the exception. There, city fathers combined state allocations with a local tax to support schools attractive to all social classes, thus removing the "pauper school" stigma. The scheme included a city high school for girls to which was appended a normal, or teacher-training, school.

The central change to South Carolina society resulting from the Civil War was the abolition of slavery. As federal troops occupied the Sea Islands, and later the entire state, teachers sponsored by northern philanthropic and missionary societies followed, establishing schools for former slaves. Notable among these were the Penn School on St. Helena Island and the Avery Institute in Charleston. Enthusiasm among freedmen for education was high.

The constitution of 1868, shaped by Republicans during Radical Reconstruction, made the legislature responsible for "a uniform system of public schools." Reflective of the concerns of the newly enfranchised freedmen, these schools were to be "open to all the children and the youths of the State, without regard to race and color." Most whites interpreted the attempt to offer free, public education to all as the imposition of a plan for social and racial equality. Schools were quickly segregated, the legislature was slow to provide funds, and mismanagement and fraud undermined the system. By 1877 there were 2,552 schoolhouses in the state, but more than half were made of logs and only twenty-nine of brick. The vast majority were one-room, nongraded schools providing only elementary education and with an average school term of just four months. The limited impact of this system is suggested by high illiteracy rates. In 1880 twenty-two percent of whites and more than seventy-eight percent of blacks in South Carolina were completely illiterate.

The school system remained in poor shape as Reconstruction ended in South Carolina and the political system was reclaimed by conservative Democrats. The dominant philosophy was characterized by extreme fiscal conservatism along with the belief that education remained primarily a private matter and that laboring whites and, especially blacks, needed little schooling. The constitution of 1895, designed to disfranchise blacks, prescribed a dual school system. Nonetheless, there were positive developments. Attention was paid to teacher training, and the Winthrop Training School for Teachers was opened in Columbia in 1887 and then relocated to Rock Hill. In 1901 a systematic course of study was developed by the State Department of Education. In 1907 the General Assembly allowed larger districts to establish high schools. By the early twentieth century, state efforts were supplemented by those of philanthropic organizations, with some efforts being directed specifically at education for blacks, including the Rosenwald Fund (for school buildings), the Slater Fund (for industrial education), and the provision of Jeanes Teachers for rural, black schools.

Despite some progress, underfunding and inequity continued to characterize the state system as a whole. In urban areas reformers focused on improving schools as a basis for economic growth. Columbia built several new schools, and Spartanburg County had perhaps the best-funded system in the state. A compulsory attendance law was passed in 1919, and the State Department of Education began teacher certification in 1920. As mill villages grew, schools were provided with a mix of public and private funds. But in 1920 South Carolina had the lowest expenditure per pupil in the nation. The school year ranged from 180 days in some localities to only 90 in others. White schools received funding at much higher rates than black schools. When Dillon County raised its taxes to provide better schools, the distribution per pupil for whites was twelve times greater than for blacks. By 1927 there were 279 high schools for whites but only 10 for blacks. In an attempt to address some of these inequities, at least for white students, the General Assembly passed the "6–0–1" law in 1924, providing teacher salaries for six months if the local district would pick up the seventh and abide by certain state regulations and minimum standards.

At midcentury South Carolina schools remained in perilous condition. In the face of rising concern over the quality of the schools, the legislature commissioned the George Peabody College for Teachers in Nashville, Tennessee, to survey the schools and make recommendations for their improvement. Published in 1948, the survey revealed a host of problems: 1,680 separate school districts in the state, expenditures per child in the wealthiest districts at more than twice that in the poorest, state spending per pupil and teacher salaries below the national and southern averages, and school completion rates half the national average. These dismal figures hid the discrepancies between spending on white students and that on black students. In Clarendon County, for example, per-pupil expenditure during 1949–1950 was $179 per white child and only $43 per black child.

An attempt by black parents in one Clarendon County district to secure bus transportation for their children led to a lawsuit challenging segregated schools. As *Briggs v. Elliott* worked its way through the federal courts, the white leadership of the state was forced to confront the inadequacies and inequities in South Carolina schools. The legislature approved a $75 million bond issue supported by a three percent sales tax to address school issues and, the white power structure hoped, forestall desegregation. Court-ordered desegregation came as a result of *Brown v. Board of Education* (1954), the decision that also addressed *Briggs v. Elliott,* and although South Carolina was slow to comply, in the fall of 1963 eleven black children were admitted to previously all-white schools in Charleston. By 1970–1971 South Carolina schools were fully desegregated.

In a strange twist of fate, white resistance to desegregation finally brought the kind of attention to the public schools that they had so long needed. While still behind in some areas, since the 1970s South Carolina schools fully participated in the national debates over schooling and the consequent policy experiments that characterized schools throughout the nation. The Education Finance Act of 1977 identified a "defined minimum program" for South Carolina schools and attempted to address financial inequities in the schools. The Basic Skills Assessment Act (1978) and the Educator Improvement Act (1979) reflected the "back to basics" movement in education and teacher competency.

Accountability and assessment are key to understanding education in South Carolina in the last two decades of the twentieth century. Evidence of the shortcomings of the educational system in South Carolina included the fact that in the early 1980s, on the Comprehensive Test of Basic Skills (CTBS), a national standardized test required by South Carolina since 1973, averages in all grades tested were below the national average in all tested subjects. On the Basic Skills Assessment Program (BSAP), required since 1978 in grades one, three, six, eight, and eleven, the disparity in scores made by white students and those of African American students was growing. Repeatedly South Carolina was ranked last on the Scholastic Assessment Test (SAT), a test that predicts college performance. During the 1980s and 1990s the General Assembly passed a series of laws that directed the educational system to become more responsible for the development of schoolchildren.

The South Carolina Education Improvement Act (EIA) in 1984 and the 1989 Target 2000: School Reform for the Next Decade were comprehensive public school reform packages that brought South Carolina into the mainstream of educational reform. Funds were allocated for half-day child-development programs, kindergarten for all five-year-olds, special programs for gifted and talented students, and remedial programs for those children who did not pass the basic skills exam. Higher-order thinking skills were required to be included in the school curricula, as well as discipline-based art, music, dance, and drama. Requirements for graduation increased, and dropout- prevention programs were funded. Schools, teachers, and principals were offered monetary bonuses for good test scores. The EIA represented the largest increase in school funding per child in the country. On the other hand, hundreds of South Carolina teachers (most of them African American) were slated to lose their jobs because they were not meeting the standards set by the EIA, and African American students made up a disproportionate number of those failing the exit exam. By 1989 the state's graduation rate had risen three percent, and although South Carolina continued to rank last in SAT scores, the state's average had the largest increase of any state in six years.

During the 1990s a series of laws addressed specific school issues. The primary purpose of the Early Childhood Development and Academic Assistance Act of 1993 was to place emphasis on early childhood education and remediation in the elementary grades. It promoted developmentally appropriate curricula and parenting/family literacy. The 1994 School-to-Work Transition Act clarified the connection between school and the workplace by abolishing the "general track," which did not prepare students for either technical vocations or college, and requiring that all students be placed in either a "tech prep" or "college prep" curriculum. These curricula were to provide rigorous preparation in marketable occupational and academic skills. The Charter School Act of 1996 was intended to provide an opportunity for flexible, innovative, and substantially deregulated public schools. Competition with these schools was seen as a healthy stimulant for change and improvement.

The South Carolina Education Accountability Act (EAA) of 1998 created a performance-based accountability system by setting grade-level standards, requiring district and school report cards to be published in newspapers beginning in 2001, and creating an oversight committee to monitor and evaluate the implementation of the act. School-readiness tests, grade-level academic standards, and standard-based assessments were required, with academic plans for each child who did not perform at grade level. The Palmetto Achievement Challenge Tests (PACT) were developed in-state as the standards-based assessment tool, replacing the BSAP. The first PACT testing in 1999 indicated that a third of South Carolina's elementary- and middle-school students were not prepared to enter the next grade level. To enable the state to compare its students with others across the country, Terra Nova, a nationally standardized test, replaced the Stanford 8 (used 1990–1994) and the Metropolitan Achievement Test 7 (used 1995–1998). Terra Nova was administered to around thirteen percent of students in grades three, six, and nine for the first time in April 1999.

The end of the century saw two more education acts, the First Steps to School Readiness Act of 1999 and the Parental Involvement in Their Children's Education Act of 2000. First Steps was intended to ensure that children arrived at first grade healthy and ready to learn. Its goals included supporting parents in optimizing their children's development through access to health care, nutrition, and preschool programs. The Parental Involvement Act was intended to heighten parental awareness of the importance of their role in the development and education of their children. Schools were challenged to become more "parent friendly." Both acts reflected the state's awareness and adoption of contemporary educational research and its implications for schooling. While years of neglect cannot be remedied overnight, the state is clearly expending great efforts to foster effective twenty-first-century schools. DEBORAH M. SWITZER AND ROBERT P. GREEN, JR.

Green, Robert P., Jr. "School Reform South Carolina Style: Mid–Twentieth Century to Present." In *The Organization of Public Education in South Carolina,* edited by John H. Walker, Michael D. Richardson, and Thomas I. Parks. Dubuque, Iowa: Kendall/Hunt, 1992.

Jones, Lewis P. "History of Education in South Carolina: Colonial to Mid–Twentieth Century." In *The Organization of Public Education in South Carolina,* edited by John H. Walker, Michael D. Richardson, and Thomas I. Parks. Dubuque, Iowa: Kendall/Hunt, 1992.

Education Accountability Act (1998). The Education Accountability Act (EAA) of 1998 placed South Carolina in the mainstream of education accountability reform. The EAA required the State Board of Education to establish specific standards in math, English/language arts, science, and social studies. These standards were to provide the basis for student assessment in grades three through eight as well as a high school exit exam. The legislation also called for the development of end-of-course exams in certain high school courses. The purpose of these tests was to hold students and schools accountable for learning. Students who scored below the standard were to have educational plans developed for them and, based on further performance, were required to go to summer school, be placed on academic probation, or face retention. Student achievement was also to be used to evaluate each public school. Schools were to be graded annually on their students' absolute performance against the standards and their students' rate of improvement.

Beginning in 2001, school and district "report cards," indicating whether the local schools were rated as excellent, good, average, below average, or unsatisfactory, were sent to parents and published in local newspapers. In anticipation of low-scoring schools and districts, the legislation provided for various intervention strategies, including improvement plans, grants for low-performing schools, and on-site specialists who would help teachers improve student scores. The legislation also called for class-size reduction for unsatisfactory schools. In cases of continued academic failure, the State Board of Education was granted authority to replace school principals, replace district superintendents, or assume management of the district. To recognize high-scoring schools, the legislation established the Palmetto Gold and Silver Awards Program to reward schools for academic achievement. An Education Oversight Committee (EOC), composed of a representative of the governor's office, representatives from the state legislature, educators, and businesspeople, was created to monitor and evaluate implementation of the EAA. ROBERT P. GREEN, JR.

Education Finance Act (1977). School finance reform first emerged as an important issue in South Carolina in the early 1970s, when lawsuits challenging the constitutionality of state school funding systems in California, Texas, and New Jersey received national attention. The Education Finance Act (EFA) was signed by Governor James Edwards on June 10, 1977; first appeared in the state Appropriations Act in 1978; and was phased in over five years.

EFA is a "foundation program," the type of school-funding system used in most states. Conceptually, foundation programs are designed to provide a "fiscal foundation"—a minimum funding level—that will enable schools to deliver a set of core education services. They are also called "equalization grants" because funding assistance from the state is intended to equalize—or compensate for—differences in local property wealth. All school districts are required to fund a portion of the foundation program through local property taxes, but property-poor districts receive more state aid, while property-rich districts receive less.

Despite EFA's goal of funding equalization, disparities in per-pupil spending between rich and poor districts still exist because EFA does not limit how much local tax revenue can be raised beyond the required local contribution. Further, since EFA revenue accounts for only about half of all state assistance to schools, nonequalized revenue from other state funding sources further contributes to spending disparities. Since 1977 some policy reports have recommended changes to EFA to accommodate the increased costs associated with special-education students and an expanding set of "core educational services." DONALD TETREAULT

Education Improvement Act (1984). The Education Improvement Act (EIA) was the culmination of a decade of legislative action to improve South Carolina's public schools. Spurred by the 1983 publication of *A Nation at Risk,* Governor Richard W. Riley energized a coalition of business and political leaders and educators to advocate new programs and to dedicate the first increase in sales tax since the 1950s to support the changes. In the 1970s South Carolina had revised the school finance system and educator preparation and implemented a basic skills testing program. The EIA employed a different approach to school reform. Rather than acting on individual aspects of schooling, the legislation recognized the integrated and comprehensive nature of public education. New programs addressed seven fundamental areas: raising the level of student performance; teaching and testing the basic skills; elevating the teaching profession; improving leadership; implementing quality controls and rewarding productivity; creating partnerships among schools, businesses, and communities; and providing school buildings.

Riley played a critical role in the passage of the act, using the governor's office to focus the state on student achievement. In addition, the development of a grassroots coalition and the recognition that student achievement is dependent on quality teaching were crucial to enacting the legislation.

Although not all EIA programs have survived, the dedicated sales tax has been maintained in a separate revenue fund and continues to be used for increasing the level of South Carolina's student achievement. The EIA has remained a primary vehicle for comprehensive educational reform by stimulating other reform-oriented legislation such as the Target 2000 Act of 1989, the Early Childhood Development and Academic Assistance Act of 1993, and the Education Accountability Act of 1998. JO ANNE ANDERSON

United States. National Commission on Excellence in Education. *A Nation at Risk: The Imperative for Educational Reform; A Report to the Nation and the Secretary of Education, United States Department of Education.* Washington, D.C.: The Commission, 1983.

Edwards, James Burrows (b. 1927). Governor, U.S. secretary of energy, college president. Jim Edwards was the first Republican governor of South Carolina in the twentieth century. He was born on June 24, 1927, in Hawthorne, Florida, to the schoolteachers Ordie Morton Edwards and Bertie Rae Hieronymus. The family moved to Charleston when Edwards was only one year old. After serving in the U.S. Maritime Service from 1944 to 1947, he continued his education and graduated from the College of Charleston in 1950. The following year Edwards married Ann Norris Darlington of Edgefield, and they eventually had two children He earned the D.M.D. degree from the University of Louisville School of Dentistry in 1955 and interned in oral surgery at the University of Pennsylvania Graduate Medical School. On completion of his medical training in 1960, Edwards returned to South Carolina and established an oral-surgery practice in Mount Pleasant.

During the 1960s Edwards became active in the South Carolina Republican Party. Initially attracted to the party by the conservative philosophy of Barry Goldwater, Edwards served as chairman of the Charleston County Republican Party from 1964 to 1969 and gradually assumed statewide influence in the party. In 1971 Edwards lost a special election for Congress, but he won a seat in the S.C. Senate the following year. Colleagues in both parties liked the affable Edwards. Democratic senator Ernest Hollings described Edwards as "an honest fellow who's got his own positions and is not the partisan type."

In 1974 Edwards challenged General William C. Westmoreland in the first modern statewide Republican primary for governor. In the July 16 election, Edwards won an upset victory. While Westmoreland

James B. Edwards. Courtesy, Modern Political Collections, University of South Carolina

carried more counties, Edwards overwhelmingly carried Charleston County, where he gained a strong following from building the local party. In the general election Edwards faced William Jennings Bryan Dorn, who became the Democratic candidate after the state supreme court ruled that the primary winner, Charles "Pug" Ravenel, did not meet the state's residency requirements. In the campaign Edwards assumed the reform mantle and gained many disaffected Democratic and independent votes. In a close contest, Edwards won the governorship by 18,500 votes, carrying 50.5 percent of the total cast. Recalling his highly improbable election, Edwards quipped, "No amount of planning beats darn luck." His election as governor became a landmark in the growth of modern two-party politics in South Carolina.

The Edwards campaign emphasized, "No debts and no deals." He sought to hold the line on state payrolls and curbed welfare fraud by reforming the State Department of Social Services. He pushed successfully for the landmark Education Finance Act and established the South Carolina Energy Research Institute to coordinate energy development. During his term, his friendship with California governor Ronald Reagan drew attention, and Edwards was one of two Republican governors who backed Reagan's challenge to President Gerald Ford in 1976.

As governor, Edwards won praise, and even his detractors admitted that the former oral surgeon had done considerably better than expected. He was an effective but not a dominant governor, limited by the weak institutional powers of office and an overwhelmingly Democratic legislature. Although his political popularity was high, Edwards never sought elective office again and returned to his oral-surgery practice at the end of his term in January 1979.

When Ronald Reagan became president in 1981, he named Edwards secretary of energy. Although ideologically compatible with Reagan, Edwards had little experience in energy matters or Washington politics. Early in his two-year stint in the Department of Energy, Edwards admitted that he did not run the department, but rather, "It ran me." He emphasized the expansion of nuclear energy resources and decontrol of crude oil prices, and he revamped Carter administration programs that featured conservation and development of alternative fuels. He stepped back from the Reagan administration's initial plans to eliminate the Department of Energy but did propose downsizing the department.

Resigning as secretary on November 5, 1982, Edwards returned to South Carolina to become president of the Medical University of South Carolina in Charleston. Under his leadership, MUSC thrived, expanding into new areas of medical research and securing a tenfold increase in research funding. Edwards retired in 1999 to widespread praise for his leadership, thereby capping his remarkable public career. DAN G. RUFF

Bailey, N. Louise, Mary L. Morgan, and Carolyn R. Taylor, eds. *Biographical Directory of the South Carolina Senate, 1776–1985.* 3 vols. Columbia: University of South Carolina Press, 1986.

Shirley, J. Clyde. *Uncommon Victory: 1974 Gubernatorial Campaign of James B. Edwards.* Columbia, S.C.: R. L. Bryan, 1978.

Edwards, William Augustus (1866–1939). Architect. Edwards was born on December 8, 1866, in Darlington to Augustus F. Edwards and Elizabeth S. Hart. He was educated at St. David's Academy in Society Hill and Richmond College and was among the first class at South Carolina College to earn a B.S. in mechanical engineering in 1889. In 1893 Edwards began his architectural career in Roanoke, Virginia, as a draftsman for Charles Coker Wilson, who returned to South Carolina in 1895 with Edwards to open an office in Columbia. Wilson & Edwards thrived, with more than fifty buildings to their credit between 1896 and 1900, in South Carolina, North Carolina, Virginia, Georgia, and Florida. Edwards directed the firm's work in 1899–1900 while Wilson studied abroad.

Dissolving their partnership in 1901, Edwards took Frank C. Walter as a partner by 1902 and maintained a successful practice in Columbia until they relocated to Atlanta in 1908. Among their more important commissions were sixteen standard public-school designs prepared for the State Board of Education as part of a statewide program of public-school construction and adapted in numerous communities across the upstate, including Laurens, Union, Pelzer, Greer, and Walhalla. In addition they designed courthouses in Darlington (1903), Kershaw (1904–1905), Sumter (1905–1906), Abbeville (1907–1908), and Lee (1907–1909) Counties; the Abbeville City Hall and Opera House; the McMaster School of Columbia (1909–1910); and the Withers Training School at Winthrop College in Rock Hill. Walter left the partnership in 1911, but Edwards's Atlanta-based practice continued to flourish with more South Carolina courthouse commissions, including those for Dillon (1911), Calhoun (1913), York (1914), and Jasper (1914–1915) Counties; Darlington's First Baptist Church (1911–1912); Columbia's Union National Bank Building (1912–1914); other buildings at Winthrop College; and several for the South Carolina School for the Deaf and the Blind near Spartanburg.

In 1915 Edwards took as a partner William J. Sayward, a former associate of New York architects McKim, Mead & White, and continued a successful practice, concentrating on collegiate work in South Carolina, Florida, and Georgia. Throughout his long and varied career, Edwards won distinction as both a collegiate designer and a county courthouse architect, having to his credit a number of campuses throughout the Southeast and nine county courthouses in South Carolina between 1903 and 1915. Edwards died in Atlanta on March 30, 1939. ANDREW W. CHANDLER

National Register Nomination Files. "Courthouses in South Carolina Designed by William Augustus Edwards." Thematic Resources, July 1981. South Carolina Department of Archives and History, Columbia.

Wells, John E., and Robert E. Dalton. *The South Carolina Architects, 1885–1935: A Biographical Directory.* Richmond, Va.: New South Architectural Press, 1992.

Withey, Henry F., and Elsie Rathburn Withey. *Biographical Dictionary of American Architects (Deceased).* 1956. Reprint, Los Angeles: Hennessey and Ingalls, 1970.

Eight Box Law (1882). The Eight Box Law of 1882 was an election law designed to ensure white supremacy in South Carolina without violating the Fifteenth Amendment, which barred states from depriving their citizens of the vote on the basis of race. Even after the defeat of Reconstruction, Congress still enforced the amendment on several occasions; one such case in 1880 seated an African American candidate for Congress who had lost a fraudulent election. The genius of the Eight Box Law was to sidestep constitutional issues by making no reference to race; instead, African Americans would be deprived of their votes through discriminatory enforcement.

Largely the work of the attorney and legislator Edward McCrady, the law provided for separate ballot boxes for each of eight types of office, including, for example, state senator, state representative, congressman, governor, lieutenant governor, and other statewide offices. Any ballot cast in an incorrect box was disallowed. In an early draft of the law, the only way to identify the boxes was by labels written on them; thus the system served as an effective literacy test. In the final version, however, election managers were required, "on the demand of the voter," to read the labels to the voter. This provision allowed for discriminatory enforcement: the election manager could read the correct labels to an illiterate white man but read incorrect labels to an illiterate black man. Such action would be a violation of state law, not federal law, and would be difficult to prove in court.

Many southern states during the 1880s and 1890s attempted to disfranchise blacks by deception. South Carolina's system of multiple ballot boxes was a unique innovation. Other provisions of the 1882 law, however, may have contributed at least as much to disfranchisement. In addition to the voting procedure described above, the law also established an extremely restrictive registration process.

The law was dramatically successful in fulfilling its intent: to maintain white supremacy without provoking intervention by the federal government. Whereas in 1880 as many as 58,000 blacks had voted in South Carolina, by 1888 the number was reduced to fewer than 14,000. This drastic reduction was accomplished despite less resort to fraud and violence by whites. The 1895 constitution reduced still further the number of black South Carolinians who managed to vote, but most of the work of disfranchisement had been accomplished by the 1882 law. HYMAN S. RUBIN III

Cooper, William J., Jr. *The Conservative Regime: South Carolina, 1877–1890.* Baltimore: Johns Hopkins Press, 1968.

Tindall, George Brown. *South Carolina Negroes, 1877–1900.* 1952. Reprint, Columbia: University of South Carolina Press, 2003.

Eikerenkoetter, Frederick Joseph, II (b. 1935). Clergyman, educator. Eikerenkoetter was born in Ridgeland on June 1, 1935, the son of Frederick Joseph Eikerenkoetter, Sr., and Rema Matthews. At age fourteen he followed his father into the ministry when he became assistant pastor of the Bible Way Church in Ridgeland. After graduating from high school in 1952, he attended several fundamentalist Bible colleges, received a Th.D. from American Divinity School in New York in 1960, spent two years in the U.S. Air Force chaplain service, and then returned to South Carolina to found the United Church of Jesus Christ for All People. In 1964 he moved his ministry north and established the Miracle Temple in Boston, where he began to call himself "Rev. Ike." In 1966 he transferred his operation to New York City, where he founded, under the aegis of his United Christian Evangelistic Association, what was to become Christ United Church, occupying an elaborate former Loew's theater at 175th and Broadway.

He used radio, direct mail, and a nationwide evangelistic campaign to build a large following, particularly among African Americans. Rev. Ike transformed what had been a conventional healing ministry into a vehicle for instruction in a system of positive thinking he has called Mind Science, the Science of Living, and more recently, Thinkonomics. He presented this system of self-improvement in his book *Rev. Ike's Secrets for Health, Joy and Prosperity—For YOU!,* in sermons, in audio- and videotapes, on radio and television, in *Miracles RIGHT NOW!* magazine, and in courses taught at the United Church Schools, which he serves as founder and chancellor. He is assisted in the pastorate of the United Church by his wife, the Reverend Eula M. Dent Eikerenkoetter, senior copastor; and his son, the Right Reverend Xavier Frederick Eikerenkoetter, bishop coadjutor. WILLIAM MARTIN

Martin, William C. "This Man Says He's the Divine Sweetheart of the Universe." *Esquire* 81 (June 1974): 76–78, 140–44.

Eleanor Clubs. During the early years of World War II, white South Carolinians, like other southerners, passed rumors of "Eleanor Clubs" back and forth. They told each other that African American cooks and laundresses, inspired by the liberal views of first lady Eleanor Roosevelt, were organizing quasi-unions to raise their pay or leave domestic employment altogether. Club members, again according to the rumors, vowed to have "a white woman in every kitchen by Christmas." After that, they would start to press for social equality and finally for the overthrow of white-led government.

By the spring of 1942, the rumors of Eleanor Clubs had become so widespread and alarming that public officials, including Mrs. Roosevelt, called in the Federal Bureau of Investigation (FBI) to see if they were true. South Carolina officials launched their own inquiry. Governor Richard Jeffries wrote each of the state's forty-six sheriffs asking them to search for Eleanor Clubs. A Columbia lawman reported that he discovered an "Eleanor Society" in Cheraw, where at one meeting "cooks and nurses" decided that they "would not work for less than $6 per week." But most people came to the same conclusion as a Dillon police officer, who said that while "there has been talk of the 'Eleanor Roosevelt Society,' after investigating, I find all of this to be just false rumors." The editor of the *Carolina Times,* an African American newspaper, thought he knew the real source of these misleading and hysterical reports. "The 'Eleanor Club' issue," he stated, "is a . . . dastardly attempt to besmirch the name of the devoted helpmate of our war-burdened president, both of whom are doing all they can to make the Negro feel his responsibility to his country by giving him an opportunity to share in the benefits of democracy and render his best service to the nation in one of its darkest hours."

By the time of the D-day invasion in June 1944, the Eleanor Club rumors had evaporated. Few whites, it seems, spoke anymore of sinister plots hatched by the first lady. But that did not mean that the racial tensions and misconceptions that had given rise to these unsubstantiated stories were gone in South Carolina. They just took different forms. BRYANT SIMON

Jeffries, Richard. Papers. South Caroliniana Library, University of South Carolina, Columbia.

Odum, Howard. *Race and Rumors of Race: The American South in the Early Forties.* 1943. Reprint, Baltimore: Johns Hopkins University Press, 1997.

Simon, Bryant. "Fearing Eleanor: Racial Anxieties and Wartime Rumors in the American South, 1940–1945." In *Labor in the Modern South,* edited by Glenn T. Eskew. Athens: University of Georgia Press, 2001.

Election Act (1716). This act ended the tradition, begun in 1692, of holding all elections for the Commons House of Assembly in Charleston. The reform allowed members to be chosen from their own parishes and saved voters the "great expense of time and money" required to travel to the city. It was also designed to help prevent "the bad effects" that had long plagued elections in Charleston, including rioting, beatings, and election fraud. In addition, it reduced the political influence of the city and the two men who controlled it, Nicholas Trott and William Rhett.

The act laid out voting requirements and electoral districts. Each candidate for the Commons House of Assembly was required to reside in the area he was to represent and to be worth £500 currency or possess an equal amount of land. A voter had to be male, white, Christian, twenty-one years of age, at least six months in residency, and worth £30. Voting was managed by the wardens of each Anglican parish church. In the event that a delegate should die or fail to qualify for office between election and the seating of the assembly, the governor and the council could issue writs for another election. Assemblymen vied for thirty seats. The city of Charleston, St. Paul's, and St. Andrew's contained four each, with St. Thomas and St. Denis, St. Bartholomew's, St. Helena's, St. James Goose Creek, and St. John's having three apiece. Christ Church was granted two and St. James Santee one. Sixteen assemblymen comprised a quorum.

Although popular among Carolinians, the 1716 act was disallowed by the Lords Proprietors in an attempt to reestablish their authority in the colony. In 1721 the Commons House passed a slightly modified Election Act that, with minor revisions, established election procedures in South Carolina until the Revolutionary War.

LOUIS P. TOWLES

Cooper, Thomas, and David J. McCord, eds. *The Statutes at Large of South Carolina.* 10 vols. Columbia, S.C.: A. S. Johnston, 1836–1841.

Sirmans, M. Eugene. *Colonial South Carolina: A Political History, 1663–1763.* Chapel Hill: University of North Carolina Press, 1966.

Election of 1876. During most of Reconstruction in South Carolina, the Democratic Party did not field tickets in statewide elections. Because of the state's large African American majority and the freedmen's loyalty to the party of Abraham Lincoln, the Republican Party had a firm grasp on state politics. Democrats could hope to wield influence only by siding with one Republican faction against another. While that strategy produced tangible gains for Democrats, especially in 1874, Democrats in 1876 determined to make a campaign for a "straight-out" Democratic ticket. They nominated for governor Wade Hampton III, South Carolina's highest-ranking Confederate officer, and other leading Confederate officers filled out the ticket. The Democratic strategy of "force without violence" depended on the ability of Democrats to intimidate or coerce Republicans into abstaining, but without provoking federal intervention in the state's affairs.

Democrats sought to deter Republican enthusiasm by riding wherever Republican officials were planning to speak, creating a disturbance, and breaking up or taking over the rally. Usually they demanded equal time to respond to Republican speeches; often they disrupted Republican speakers with loud shouting or the brandishing of guns. While such tactics were unlikely to persuade voters of the superiority of Democratic ideas, they were effective in making the point that the Republican state government could not protect its own leaders, not to mention rank-and-file supporters. On election day in 1876 they appeared at the polls armed and in force, and they attempted to prevent African Americans from voting. In this objective of reducing the Republican vote Democrats were unsuccessful, as the Republican Party achieved its highest vote total of the entire Reconstruction period for incumbent governor Daniel H. Chamberlain.

They were much more successful, however, in piling up new Democratic votes. Hampton's candidacy and the grassroots "Red Shirt" organizations created a fever pitch of excitement among the whites. The straightforward campaign for white supremacy gave the white masses a clear end and a clear means to that end. Rallies were held in every county of the state, often including rituals in which Hampton would come upon a woman dressed as "South Carolina" and raise her up from the dust or liberate her from her chains. There were parades, music, and cheers upon cheers, especially when Hampton spoke. Hampton undoubtedly gained the votes of many whites who had never voted before during Reconstruction. At the same time, his frequent promises to respect the civil rights of blacks won him favor in the North.

It must be remembered, however, that the full voting strength of white South Carolina was still insufficient to win a fair election. According to an 1875 special state census, South Carolina had 74,193 white men over age twenty-one and 110,735 black men over age twenty-one. The Democrats polled 92,261 votes and the Republicans polled 91,127 in 1876. Therefore, either 18,000 African Americans voted for Hampton (as he reportedly believed) or his victory was owed to ballot box stuffing, repeat voting, and illegal voting. All these tactics were admitted by Democratic leaders in their memoirs—Georgians crossed state lines to vote, Red Shirts rode from polling place to polling place voting everywhere they went, Democrats folded multiple "tissue ballots" inside their regular paper ballots. Edgefield County reported two thousand more votes than it had eligible voters.

With fraud so obvious, the Republican-controlled State Board of Canvassers seized the opportunity to grab the election. They declared invalid the votes of both Edgefield and Laurens Counties, which had gone heavily for Hampton despite being solidly Republican in the past. Throwing out those counties gave Republicans control of the state House of Representatives, and that body had the authority to determine the winner of the election for governor. When the General Assembly met, the disputed members from Edgefield and Laurens Counties were excluded, and the House organized along Republican lines. The Democrats walked out in protest and, incorporating the disputed members, declared themselves a quorum. They then returned to the State House, forced their way in, and began to conduct business. For four months South Carolina had two legislatures—each one debating bills and passing laws. The state had two governors as well, with both Hampton and Chamberlain attempting to exercise the powers of that office.

The election had national as well as local significance. Presidential candidates Samuel Tilden and Rutherford Hayes were so tightly deadlocked in electoral votes that South Carolina's votes would determine who became president. On the face of the returns Hayes, a Republican, won; but he had to wait for a national bipartisan election commission to side with him and Democrats to cease their delaying tactics before his election was assured in late February

1877. Once elected, Hayes adopted a "hands-off" policy toward the South. In April of that year Chamberlain, knowing that the federal government would not maintain him in office, resigned. Reconstruction in South Carolina was over. HYMAN S. RUBIN III

Sheppard, William Arthur. *Red Shirts Remembered: Southern Brigadiers of the Reconstruction Period.* Atlanta: Ruralist Press, 1940.

Simkins, Francis B. "The Election of 1876 in South Carolina." *South Atlantic Quarterly* 21 (July 1922): 225–40; (October 1922): 335–51.

Williams, Alfred B. *Hampton and His Red Shirts: South Carolina's Deliverance in 1876.* Charleston, S.C.: Walker, Evans, and Cogswell, 1935.

Zuczek, Richard. *State of Rebellion: Reconstruction in South Carolina.* Columbia: University of South Carolina Press, 1996.

Electrification. During the late nineteenth century, the use of electricity by municipalities and in private residences was a growing phenomenon in South Carolina. New inventions such as light bulbs, telephones, and electric water pumps fueled consumer demand for access to electrical power in rural as well as urban areas.

In 1884 the State House received power from the first electric generating facility in the state. Three years later Columbia converted its streetlights from gas to electricity. This was a trend followed elsewhere: as electricity spread to other towns it was used mostly for street lighting rather than residences. Residential power, however, could turn up in surprising places. Pelzer residents received power at their homes when the mill went electric in 1895; most Columbia residents did not have electricity for several more years. By the turn of the century, South Carolina's cities, towns, and mill villages provided electrical power to their residents with facilities that were either privately owned or paid for with taxes. The lifestyles of rural South Carolinians, by contrast, remained much as they had for centuries.

Progressive politicians soon began to promote legislation that would provide government funding for rural electrification, claiming that private utility companies such as Carolina Power and Light (formed in 1908) and the South Carolina Power Company (formed in 1926) ignored the needs of rural people. The utilities spent a considerable amount of money on the maintenance of poles, wires, and meters. Stringing lines for miles to reach farms cut into their profit margins, so, understandably, they preferred the denser urban markets.

This situation resulted in political efforts in South Carolina and throughout the United States to build government-owned utility companies, which could extend power to the rural population. The creation of the Tennessee Valley Authority (TVA) in 1933 provided for the construction of the first government-owned utility specifically intended for distribution to rural consumers.

In South Carolina a similar project was planned. The Santee Cooper power plant, technically the South Carolina Public Service Authority and known as the "little TVA," was a project championed by Charleston mayor Burnet Maybank and U.S. senator James F. Byrnes. The intent of the project was to provide cheap electrical power generated by the state to rural residents in the lowcountry. Officially authorized in 1934, the S.C. Public Service Authority was immediately sued by various private utility companies that questioned the constitutionality of the project.

Until the lawsuits questioning its right to exist were resolved, the S.C. Public Service Authority was unable to borrow money from the newly created Rural Electrification Administration (REA) in Washington. These low-cost loans available through the federal REA were crucial to the completion of the project, since state funding was impossible in Depression-era South Carolina. Accordingly, the state government created the South Carolina Rural Electrification Administration (SCREA) in March 1935. The following November, SCREA received its first loan of $542,328 for the purpose of providing electrical power to rural residents.

SCREA was created to borrow federal money to build lines in rural areas. It was also the distribution arm of the S.C. Public Service Authority. The grand vision was of a huge electrical power plant providing current to the entire state. The immediate result was a total politicization of the building of the electrical grid in rural South Carolina.

The board of directors of SCREA consisted of the governor, the comptroller general, the state treasurer, and the presidents of the University of South Carolina, the Citadel, Clemson, and Winthrop. There were also two members directly appointed by the governor to two-year terms. The structure of this borrowing agency slowed the pace of rural electrification in South Carolina, and focus on the Santee Cooper project tended to monopolize SCREA's efforts at building distribution lines.

SCREA's attempts to build rural lines were also hindered by the private utility companies. Although they questioned the constitutionality of the Santee Cooper project, which as a generating facility would be in direct competition with them, they did not question the legality of a state-owned distribution system. They merely tried to hamper its construction by building "spite lines," lines hurriedly built in areas that had already been cleared and surveyed at state expense. The spite lines cost SCREA much time and effort because it lost revenue for these lines after expending time and money to prepare for them.

Competition from public utilities, the focus on providing funds for the stalled Santee Cooper project, and political cronyism set the stage for the failure of SCREA. Widespread criticism of the agency eventually became an issue at the national level. In 1939 the REA made the decision to terminate loans to SCREA, effectively ending its attempts at rural electrification in South Carolina.

Instead, the REA began lending its money to electric cooperatives, which were grassroots organizations formed by farmers and county businessmen to facilitate rural line construction. Requirements for membership varied from county to county but were similar: members agreed to pay sign-up fees and promised to use a certain amount of current each month. The Williams Act, passed by the state legislature in 1940, required SCREA to transfer all of its lines to the local cooperatives. In 1939 the state had 1,853 miles of REA-financed lines. By 1941 the number had increased to 7,617 miles of line.

The Santee Cooper project cleared all legal hurdles and construction began in 1938. Material shortages during World War II caused delays in cooperative activity and on the Santee Cooper project during the 1940s, but all of South Carolina's rural areas were wired by the late 1950s. RULINDA PRICE

Brown, D. Clayton. "Modernizing Rural Life: South Carolina's Push for Public Rural Electrification." *South Carolina Historical Magazine* 99 (January 1998): 66–85.

Edgar, Walter B. *History of Santee Cooper, 1934–1984.* Columbia, S.C.: R. L. Bryan, 1984.

Hayes, Jack Irby. *South Carolina and the New Deal.* Columbia: University of South Carolina Press, 2001.

Price, Rulinda. "Rural Electrification in Upstate South Carolina in the Early Twentieth Century: A Study of the Political and Social Factors Affecting the Diffusion of Technology." Master's thesis, Clemson University, 1998.

Elfe, Thomas (ca. 1719–1775). Cabinetmaker. Elfe was most likely born in London and immigrated to Charleston by 1745. He is the individual most often associated with the pre–Revolutionary cabinetmaking industry in Charleston due to the survival of one of his account books covering the period from 1765 until his death in 1775. The book contains information that addresses not only Elfe's business and personal accounts, but also the structure and mechanics of a successful urban colonial cabinet shop.

Elfe's accounts reveal the general structure of his shop, the types of labor and raw materials he utilized, and the extensive list of clients and associated artisans with whom he conducted business. The labor consisted of cabinetmakers, journeymen (day laborers), and slaves. Slaves were often hired out to other artisans, and the charges associated with this practice reveal that many of them were highly skilled artisans in their own right. The inventory of raw materials is helpful in identifying the woods from which Elfe's cabinetwork was composed. His utilization of indigenous woods serves to differentiate his work, as well as that of other Charleston cabinetmakers of the era, from that produced abroad or in other regions of colonial America. The descriptions of various forms within his inventory are helpful in identifying appropriate period terminology and expand the decorative vocabulary that is applicable to pre–Revolutionary War cabinetwork in Charleston and the colonies. Elfe's clients during the ten-year period numbered nearly three hundred, ranging from members of Charleston's elite planter and merchant class to the artisan class, which provided necessary specialized trades such as carving, gilding, and upholstering. One of the most valuable aspects of the account book is its illumination of the extensive and complex network of allied trades that were interdependent on one another for success.

The information contained within the personal accounts, in addition to other public records, demonstrates Elfe's highly diversified interests aside from cabinetmaking. He owned and leased numerous properties within Charleston and in the surrounding environs, loaned money, speculated in real estate, served as a jurist, and was philanthropic with his income. He was also a family man, marrying Mary Hancock in 1748 (she died one year later) and Rachel Prideau in 1755, with whom he had several children. On his death on November 28, 1775, Elfe was described in his obituary as an "honest and industrious man." The evaluation of his estate was £38,243.16.2 sterling, making him the wealthiest cabinetmaker to have practiced in South Carolina before the Revolution. Despite the scale of Elfe's cabinetmaking business, no fully documented example of his work is known to exist. GEORGE C. WILLIAMS

Burton, E. Milby. *Charleston Furniture 1700–1825.* 1955. Reprint, Columbia: University of South Carolina Press, 1997.

———. *Thomas Elfe, Charleston Cabinetmaker.* Charleston, S.C.: Charleston Museum, 1952.

Kolbe, John Christian. "Thomas Elfe, Eighteenth Century Charleston Cabinetmaker." Master's thesis, University of South Carolina, 1980.

Rauschenberg, Bradford L., and John Bivins, Jr. *The Furniture of Charleston 1680–1820.* Vol. 3, *The Cabinetmakers.* Winston-Salem, N.C.: Museum of Early Southern Decorative Arts, 2003.

Ellenton Riot (September 1876). The Ellenton Riot was one of many racial clashes that occurred in the tense atmosphere of the 1876 gubernatorial campaign. The altercation featured many of the classic elements of conflict in South Carolina during Reconstruction, including allegations of African American criminal activity, paramilitary vigilante action by whites, hostility toward the black militia, and the profound inadequacies of the Republican state government.

Trouble began in early September along the Aiken-Barnwell county line, following reports of an assault by African Americans on an elderly white woman. Although the rumors were later proved unfounded, they were perfect grist for the campaign mill in 1876, when South Carolina war hero Wade Hampton III and the Democrats were attempting to unseat Republican carpetbagger Daniel H. Chamberlain. Seemingly trivial incidents proved to conservatives that Republicans and their notions of racial equality only delivered lawlessness and disorder. A warrant was issued for the arrest of the alleged perpetrators, which prompted the local black militia to gather for the protection of the accused. By September 16, white "gun clubs" and "rifle clubs" had mobilized in response, and the area around Ellenton in Aiken County was the setting for a deadly cat-and-mouse game that lasted several days.

White "gun clubs" scoured the region around Ellenton from September 16 through September 19, ostensibly searching for the attackers of the elderly woman. No African Americans were safe, and accounts indicate that field crews, families at home, evening political meetings, and even church gatherings were targets of white assailants. Only the intervention of the U.S. Army ended the killing spree. Fortunately for the hundred-or-so African Americans gathered at Rouse's Bridge on September 19, Captain Thomas Lloyd and units of the Eighteenth Infantry arrived just before hundreds of armed whites. Lloyd negotiated a compromise with the leader of the gun clubs, A. P. Butler, which called on both of the unorganized armies to retire and disband. The human cost was high: at least two whites were dead, with three wounded, while estimates of the death toll among African Americans ranged from thirty to more than one hundred. Among the dead was state legislator Simon Coker, who was shot in the head while praying for mercy.

Despite vitriolic rhetoric on the part of Governor Chamberlain and the Republicans, the only action that followed was an official call for all unauthorized armed associations to disband. Recognizing that state authorities could not curb Democratic restlessness, Chamberlain was hoping to pave the way for federal action; if citizens disobeyed the governor, he could then legally turn to the federal government for further assistance. Unfortunately for Chamberlain and state Republicans, such assistance was sporadic and short-lived, amounting to little more than the shifting of existing troops from trouble spot to trouble spot. No prosecutions followed the Ellenton Riot at the state level (murder) or at the federal level (civil rights violations). As with the Hamburg Riot in July and the Cainhoy Riot the following October, such altercations added fuel to an already heated political campaign and further undercut the legitimacy of the Republican state government. RICHARD ZUCZEK

Allen, Walter. *Governor Chamberlain's Administration in South Carolina, a Chapter of Reconstruction in the Southern States.* 1888. Reprint, New York: Negro Universities Press, 1969.

Smith, Mark M. "'All Is Not Quiet in Our Hellish County': Facts, Fiction, Politics, and Race—The Ellenton Riot of 1876." *South Carolina Historical Magazine* 95 (April 1994): 142–55.

Zuczek, Richard. *State of Rebellion: Reconstruction in South Carolina.* Columbia: University of South Carolina Press, 1996.

Ellerbe, William Haselden (1862–1899). Governor. Ellerbe was born on April 7, 1862, the son of the Marion District planter William Shackelford Ellerbe and Sarah Elizabeth Haselden. Ellerbe began his education at Pine Hill Academy in Marion. He attended Wofford College and Vanderbilt University but, due to poor health, withdrew without taking a degree. Returning to Marion County,

Ellerbe purchased his own plantation and established a lucrative mercantile business in the town of Marion. On June 29, 1887, Ellerbe married Henrietta Rogers. The couple eventually had six children.

Ellerbe entered politics in 1889 when he joined the Farmers Alliance. However, his membership was suspended when it was discovered that he engaged in merchandising. In 1890 Ellerbe became state comptroller general, the youngest man ever elected to statewide office in South Carolina. He was reelected in 1892. Considered to be a more moderate member of Benjamin R. Tillman's "Reform" faction, he was one of four Tillman followers who ran for governor in 1894. Tillman, the outgoing governor, eventually lent his tremendous prestige and support to another candidate, John Gary Evans, a lawyer from Aiken and Tillman's spokesman in the S.C. House of Representatives. Evans won, but many Tillman supporters expressed dismay that leadership within their party had gone to a lawyer rather than to a farmer, Ellerbe.

Ellerbe won the election for governor in 1896 at the age of thirty-four. This election was the first to utilize the new county primary election system established by the state constitution the previous year. At the beginning of his term, South Carolina was in an economic depression due largely to low cotton prices. Conditions improved somewhat during his tenure. During his governorship, racial segregation became more rigid, as railroads operating in South Carolina were required to provide separate coaches for blacks and whites. Positive accomplishments included the organization of four new counties in 1897: Dorchester, Bamberg, Greenwood, and Cherokee. Ellerbe energetically promoted the state's mobilization efforts during the Spanish-American War. He pushed for the establishment of a juvenile reformatory, which became a reality the year after his death. In addition, he received some credit for the lull in partisan discord within state politics during his tenure.

Ellerbe won reelection in 1898, despite a strong challenge from Claudius C. Featherstone, an upcountry lawyer who ran independently as a prohibitionist. The main issue in the contest was the increasingly corrupt and unpopular dispensary system, by which the state had controlled the sale of alcohol since 1892. Fearing defeat and hoping for support from Columbia's newspaper, the *State,* Ellerbe privately informed its editor, Narcisco G. Gonzales, that he intended to soften his insistence on the dispensary plan. After the election, however, Ellerbe tried to backpedal closer to his original stance. Gonzalez then exposed their agreement, publishing part of their correspondence. Ellerbe, however, died of illness on June 2, 1899, and the *State* subsequently declared that it had never doubted Ellerbe's stated intention to relieve factional strife within the state.

ROD ANDREW, JR.

Simkins, Francis Butler. *The Tillman Movement in South Carolina.* Durham, N.C.: Duke University Press, 1926.

Wallace, David Duncan. *The History of South Carolina.* 4 vols. New York: American Historical Society, 1935.

Ellicott Rock (Oconee County). Ellicott Rock is located in the Ellicott Rock Wilderness Area that overlaps parts of South Carolina, Georgia, and North Carolina. Located in extreme northwestern South Carolina in Sumter National Forest, the wilderness area contains 2,859 acres in South Carolina. Ellicott Rock is found within the Blue Ridge terrain, which is made up of rock that formed from Precambrian sediments and volcanics that were later metamorphosed into the hard schists and gneisses of the area. The Blue Ridge was emplaced during the formation of South Carolina in the Ordovician period and then was thrust up and over younger rocks to its present location. The Blue Ridge rocks in South Carolina are found only in Oconee County. Ellicott Rock is a metamorphic gneiss that is characteristic of the Blue Ridge region.

Ellicott Rock is important historically because it marks the boundary between three states. Andrew Ellicott, a surveyor, was commissioned by North Carolina and Georgia to determine the South Carolina/Georgia boundary, which he accomplished in 1811. At the completion of his survey, he cut a mark into the rock on the east bank of the Chattooga River. The rock and the wilderness area are named after his accomplishment. Later his findings were challenged by other surveyors, who altered the boundary in 1813 when they recalculated it and moved the thirty-fifth parallel to ten feet south of Ellicott Rock. They inscribed another rock, which is also visible today, with the inscription "LAT 35A 1813 NC+SC."

CAROLYN H. MURPHY

Frazier, Joey. "In Quest of . . . Ellicott's Infamous Rock." *Sandlapper* 6 (summer 1995): 14–15.

Murphy, Carolyn H. *Carolina Rocks! The Geology of South Carolina.* Orangeburg, S.C.: Sandlapper, 1995.

Elliott, Irene Dillard (1892–1978). Educator, author, community leader. Born in Laurens County on August 7, 1892, Elliott was the youngest of ten children of James Park Dillard and Elizabeth Irene Byrd. She attended Laurens County public schools, Presbyterian College, and George Peabody College in Nashville, Tennessee. In 1912 she received her bachelor's degree from Randolph-Macon Woman's College in Lynchburg, Virginia. Elliott served as principal of the high school in Cross Hill for two years before returning to Randolph-Macon as an instructor of English. After seven years, she assumed the principalship of a small grammar school in Columbia. During this time Elliott pursued her M.A. degree at the University of South Carolina (USC), which she received in 1921. Dissatisfied with her job, she became determined to receive a Ph.D. She began her doctoral studies in English at the University of North Carolina in 1923 and commenced work on a dissertation, which was later published as *A History of Literature in South Carolina* (1950). In 1924 Elliott became the first woman to receive a Ph.D. from the University of North Carolina.

Elliott accepted an invitation to become the first dean of women at the University of South Carolina, an institution that had recently become fully coeducational. Beginning her work in the fall of 1924, she also served as a full professor until 1935, when ill health forced her retirement. During her years as dean, Elliott helped make smooth what might have been a bumpy process of coeducation. Early in her residence in Columbia, she met Charles Bell Elliott, a member of the USC Law School faculty. They were married on July 30, 1931.

Along with her marriage and work at USC, Elliott became involved in many civic, educational, and cultural organizations. Among these were the American Association of University Women, Phi Beta Kappa, and the Daughters of the American Revolution (DAR). The descendant of Revolutionary War heroes, Elliott established the USC chapter of the DAR and served as the South Carolina state organizing secretary.

With veterans flooding American colleges and universities after World War II, Elliott returned to teaching at the University of South Carolina, where she held the rank of associate professor from 1946 to 1964. She was active in organizing Great Books courses and also engaged in genealogical study. Continued interest in Laurens County led to Elliott's coeditorship of *South Carolina's*

Distinguished Women of Laurens County: ". . . Most of Whom Were Redheaded" (1972).

Elliott showed how difficult it was for a woman of limited financial means to attain the education she desired and the circuitous route essential to achieving her dreams of becoming a scholar. She never forgot her good fortune or those who helped her. As a dean and professor, she attempted to grant similar opportunities to the young women who came under her tutelage. As testimony to her teaching skills, each year the University of South Carolina awards the Irene D. Elliott Award for Outstanding Teaching. Elliott died in Columbia on April 5, 1978, and was buried in the First Presbyterian Churchyard. MARIAN ELIZABETH STROBEL

Tolbert, Marguerite, Irene Dillard Elliott, and Wil Lou Gray, eds. *South Carolina's Distinguished Women of Laurens County: ". . . Most of Whom Were Redheaded."* Columbia, S.C.: R. L. Bryan, 1972.

Elliott, Robert Brown (1842–1884). Legislator, congressman. Details of Elliott's early life are uncertain. His modern biographer, Peggy Lamson, believes that he was born on August 11, 1842, in Liverpool, England, of unknown West Indian parents. Contemporary accounts state that he was born in Boston, educated at High Holborn Academy in London, and graduated from Eton College in 1859, although no evidence survives to corroborate these claims. It does seem likely that he did enjoy a substantial degree of formal education, since Elliott was universally acknowledged to be highly literate and learned. In 1867 Elliott moved from Boston to Charleston, South Carolina, where he accepted a position as an associate editor of a black-owned Republican newspaper, the *South Carolina Leader.* Around 1870 he is believed to have married Grace Lee Rollin, a member of a distinguished Charleston free black family. The couple had no children.

In South Carolina, Elliott's education and ability quickly placed him among the most influential African Americans in the state. In 1868 Elliott, Jonathan J. Wright, and William Whipper were the first African Americans admitted to the South Carolina Bar. Elliott soon after turned to politics. He was an adept orator and first entered the political spotlight as a delegate to the 1868 constitutional convention. That same year he was an unsuccessful candidate for lieutenant governor but was elected to the state House of Representatives from Barnwell County. Serving in the House from 1868 to 1870, Elliott chaired the committee on railroads and sat on the committee on privileges and elections. His political skills were apparent to allies and opponents alike, with one conservative newspaper reporter describing Elliott as "the ablest negro in South Carolina." He was chosen state assistant adjutant general in 1869, in which role he was responsible for organizing the militia, but he resigned in December 1870 in protest over Republican Party corruption. Also in 1869 Elliott was elected president of a state labor convention, which sought to improve working conditions among the state's newly emancipated black laborers.

In 1870 Elliott defeated a white candidate for his first of two terms in Congress. The first full-blooded man of color elected to Congress, Elliott took his seat in the U.S. House of Representatives on March 4, 1871. He employed his oratorical skills to condemn the Ku Klux Klan in South Carolina and to champion civil rights for African Americans. He resigned from Congress in 1874 and returned to the South Carolina General Assembly, where he served as Speaker of the House from 1874 to 1876.

Elliott's political career ended following the controversial election of 1876 and the return of the Democratic Party to power in South Carolina. He spent most of his later years as an outspoken, controversial Republican Party leader frustrated at the loss of federal support for black civil rights. Following a series of federal patronage positions in South Carolina and Louisiana, and failed law practices, Elliott died penniless in New Orleans of malarial fever on August 9, 1884. He was buried in that city's St. Louis Cemetery Number 2. MILLICENT ELLISON BROWN

Holt, Thomas C. *Black over White: Negro Political Leadership in South Carolina during Reconstruction.* Urbana: University of Illinois Press, 1977.

Lamson, Peggy. *The Glorious Failure: Black Congressman Robert Brown Elliott and the Reconstruction in South Carolina.* New York: Norton, 1973.

Williamson, Joel. *After Slavery: The Negro in South Carolina during Reconstruction, 1861–1877.* Chapel Hill: University of North Carolina Press, 1965.

Elliott, Stephen (1771–1830). Legislator, banker, botanist. Elliott was born on November 11, 1771, in Beaufort, the youngest son of William Elliott and Mary Barnwell. After the death of both parents, he grew up in the home of his older brother, William. In 1791 he graduated from Yale College, where he was elected to Phi Beta Kappa.

Returning to Beaufort, Elliott quickly assumed an active role in the political and economic affairs of South Carolina. On January 28, 1796, he married Esther Wylly Habersham of Savannah, the daughter of James Habersham. The marriage produced thirteen children. From 1794 to 1800 Elliott represented St. Helena's Parish for three terms in the state House of Representatives. In 1808 parish voters elected him to the state Senate, where he sponsored two important pieces of legislation. In 1811 he was instrumental in the passage of the Free School Act, which created the state's first public-school system. The following year he wrote the act to create the Bank of the State of South Carolina. He resigned his Senate seat in 1812 to become president of the bank, a position he held until his death. Elliott also had sizable plantation interests in South Carolina and Georgia, including Silk Hope and Vallambrosa plantations on the Ogeechee River in Georgia. He grew rice and subsistence crops and experimented with crop rotation. Moving to Charleston in 1812, he subsequently sold his Georgia plantations.

Although a highly respected legislator and banker, Elliott is perhaps best remembered for his activities as a botanist. His initial interest was geology, but a long trip northward in 1808 focused his attention on plants. He learned much from Dr. John Brickell and later named the genus *Brickellia* in his honor. In Lancaster, Pennsylvania, Elliott met Henry Muhlenberg, the premier botanist in America at that time. They maintained an active correspondence, with Muhlenberg urging Elliott to make his research public. He assembled a magnificent library and acquired a small farm at which he planted a wide variety of seeds, roots, and bulbs. In addition to his personal collecting activities, he also persuaded some sixty persons to gather specimens, which he added to his herbarium (later preserved at the Charleston Museum). Between 1816 and 1824 he published *A Sketch of the Botany of South-Carolina and Georgia,* issued in thirteen parts. He soon became an exacting and meticulous botanist, with correspondents across the United States, Canada, and Europe. His other publications included "Observations on the Genus *Glycine,* and Some of Its Kindred Genera" (1818) and "Some Observations on the Culture of the Cherokee or Nondescript Rose as a Hedge Plant," written in 1814 but published posthumously.

In Charleston, Elliott found a variety of additional outlets for his wide-ranging talents. He was president of the Literary and

Philosophical Society of South Carolina (1814–1830), a trustee of South Carolina College (1820–1829), and a trustee of the College of Charleston (1826–1830). He devised a book classification system for the Charleston Library Society. He played an important role in the creation of the Medical College of South Carolina, where he lectured in 1824 as its first professor of natural history and botany. He helped oversee the Orphan House and served on other civic boards. As a commissioner of the South Carolina Canal and Railroad Company, he urged building a transportation network with Charleston as its terminus. In 1828 Elliott and Hugh Swinton Legaré launched the *Southern Review,* a quarterly literary magazine.

When the American Geological Society was formed in 1819, Elliott was one of its vice presidents. He was a member of the Academy of Natural Sciences of Philadelphia, the American Philosophical Society, and the Linnaean Society in Paris, France. He was a fellow of the American Academy of Arts and Sciences and an honorary member of the Lyceum of Natural History of New York. He was honored with the LL.D. from Yale (1819), Harvard (1822), and Columbia (1825). The Medical College of South Carolina bestowed an honorary M.D. in 1825.

Elliott died on March 28, 1830. He was buried at St. Paul's Radcliffeborough in Charleston. GEORGE A. ROGERS

Barnwell, Stephen B. *Story of an American Family.* Marquette, Mich., 1969.

Elliott, Stephen. *A Sketch of the Botany of South-Carolina and Georgia.* 2 vols. 1816–1824. Reprint, New York: Hafner, 1971.

Lesesne, J. Mauldin. *The Bank of the State of South Carolina: A General and Political History.* Columbia: University of South Carolina Press, 1970.

Moultrie, James, Jr. *An Eulogium on Stephen Elliott, M.D. & L.L.D.* Charleston, S.C.: A. E. Miller, 1830.

Rogers, George A. "Stephen Elliott, a Southern Humanist." In *The Humanist in His World,* edited by Barbara W. Bitter and Frederick K. Sanders. Greenwood, S.C.: Attic, 1976.

Elliott, William, III (1788–1863). Author, planter, politician. Elliott was the scion of one of South Carolina's wealthiest and most distinguished families. He was born on April 27, 1788, in Beaufort, descended from the pioneer families of the old Beaufort District, principally the Elliotts and the Barnwells. His father, William Elliott II, was a patriot soldier in the Revolutionary War and pioneer of Sea Island cotton culture in South Carolina. As a consequence, William Elliott III, the eldest son, became one of the wealthiest planters in South Carolina. In 1860 he owned twelve plantations in the lowcountry; a summer home in Flat Rock, North Carolina; and 217 slaves.

Elliott was educated at Beaufort College (1803–1806) and at Harvard College (1806–1808). Elliott withdrew from Harvard due to ill health before his graduation. In 1810 Harvard awarded him an honorary bachelor of arts degree as a consequence of his outstanding academic record. In 1815 he was awarded a master of arts degree from Harvard. In May 1817 Elliott married Anne Hutchinson Smith. The couple had nine children.

Elliott returned to Beaufort to pursue a career in planting, politics, and literature. He was known as one of the South's most progressive and scientific planters. He wrote articles for the *Southern Agriculturist* and was notable for his studies in seed selection and for his promotion of diversification in southern agriculture. He was the perennial president of the Beaufort Agricultural Society, and in 1839 he was vice president of the South Carolina Agricultural Society. In 1855 Elliott represented South Carolina at the Paris Exposition, where he delivered a speech, in French, on Sea Island cotton to the Imperial and Central Agricultural Society. In the heyday of the antebellum plantation economy, Elliott produced some of the world's best long staple cotton, known on the Atlantic market as "Elliott Cream Cotton."

As was common for men of his class, Elliott was also a political leader. He served in the South Carolina House of Representatives from 1814 to 1815 and again from 1826 to 1829. He served in the South Carolina Senate from 1818 to 1821 and again in 1831. He was also intendant (mayor) of Beaufort from 1819 to 1824. Elliott's political career was cut short when he resigned from the Senate and chastised his constituents for their support of nullification. Though always a defender of slavery, Elliott was nevertheless a staunch Unionist, a conviction not shared by the majority of the voters in Beaufort District.

Elliott is best remembered for his literary publications. In addition to his agricultural writings, Elliott was a frequent contributor to the *Southern Quarterly Review.* In 1850 he published a five-act drama, *Fiesco: A Tragedy.* Elliott's most famous and lasting contribution to southern literature is *Carolina Sports by Land and Water,* published in Charleston in 1846. This book was a compilation of his articles on lowcountry hunting and fishing for the Charleston newspapers and was written under the pen names "Venator" and "Piscator." Popular in its day, it has since become a classic of the American outdoor genre and remained in print in the twenty-first century. Elliott died at his home in Flat Rock, North Carolina, on February 3, 1863. LAWRENCE S. ROWLAND

Bailey, N. Louise, Mary L. Morgan, and Carolyn R. Taylor, eds. *Biographical Directory of the South Carolina Senate, 1776–1985.* 3 vols. Columbia: University of South Carolina Press, 1986.

Barnwell, Stephen B. *Story of an American Family.* Marquette, Mich., 1969.

Rowland, Lawrence S., Alexander Moore, and George C. Rogers. *The History of Beaufort County.* Vol. 1, *1514–1861.* Columbia: University of South Carolina Press, 1996.

Scafidel, Beverly. "The Letters of William Elliott." Ph.D. diss., University of South Carolina, 1978.

Elliott Society of Natural History. Founded in Charleston in November 1853, the Elliott Society of Natural History was established for the purpose of promoting the study of natural history, especially in South Carolina. Named after the city's noted botanist Stephen Elliott, the organization represented the maturation of scientific interests in Charleston, which by then was the center of natural history studies in the South.

Encouraged by the renowned naturalist Louis Agassiz, the Charleston Museum curator Francis Simmons Holmes played a key role in establishing the society. Eager to emulate the highly successful natural history society founded in Philadelphia in 1812 and the one established in Boston in 1830, Charleston scientists joined with Holmes in creating the Elliott Society. Unlike its sister organizations in the North, however, the society was hampered by a comparatively small urban population and scarcity of funds. Nevertheless, although its membership never exceeded eighty during the antebellum period and while monthly attendance was usually low, it succeeded admirably and managed to publish one volume of its proceedings and one issue of a journal prior to the Civil War. Especially supportive of the society were the naturalists John McCrady and Lewis R. Gibbes, the latter of whom served as the society's president for most of its existence.

Inactive during the Civil War, the Elliott Society resumed its activities soon afterward. In an attempt to broaden its appeal, the organization changed its name to the Elliott Society of Science and

Arts in 1867. Although it enjoyed brief periods of revival, the society was moribund by 1891, thus ending its notable contributions to the study of natural history in South Carolina. LESTER D. STEPHENS

Stephens, Lester D. *Science, Race, and Religion in the American South: John Bachman and the Charleston Circle of Naturalists, 1815–1895.* Chapel Hill: University of North Carolina Press, 2000.

———. "Scientific Societies in the Old South: The Elliott Society and the New Orleans Academy of Sciences." In *Science and Medicine in the Old South,* edited by R. N. Numbers and T. L. Savitt. Baton Rouge: Louisiana State University Press, 1989.

Ellis, Mary Gordon (1890–1934). Legislator. Ellis was born on April 21, 1890, in Gourdin, Williamsburg County, one of ten children of Alexander McKnight Gordon and Mary Lee Gamble. She graduated from Kingstree High School in 1909 and taught at Sutton's School for a year. Awarded a scholarship to Winthrop Training School (College), she earned her B.A. in 1913. After graduation she taught for three years in Jasper County schools. In 1914 she met and married Junius Gather Ellis, a farmer and turpentine producer. She became the mother of three children. When her children were of school age, she boarded them with relatives in Savannah, where they would receive a better education. This belief in education soon propelled her into Jasper County politics.

Just four years after the ratification of the Nineteenth Amendment, which granted women the right to vote, Ellis was elected superintendent of education of Jasper County, serving from 1924 until 1928. Her school reforms stressed better teacher training, school facilities improvement, additional school supplies, and more texts. She firmly believed that education was for all children, and she provided the segregated black schools with new books instead of hand-me-downs from the white schools. However, her decisions to hire an African American administrator for black schools and to provide bus transportation for black children alienated some white citizens. In 1928 Jasper County House member H. K. Purdy had her fired. Her response was to oppose him in the next election. When Purdy filed to run for the South Carolina Senate, Ellis did as well. She won.

Elected in 1928 and taking her seat in January 1929, "Mary G," as she was called by the all-male state Senate, became the first woman to serve in that body. Elected twice (1929–1930 and 1931–1932), Ellis served on the committees of education, incorporations, military, and charitable institutions, among others. An active senator, she proposed bills, offered amendments, debated issues, and did committee work. In particular, she championed human rights issues, especially those affecting women and African Americans. Although her public career was brief, Ellis's progressive views on educational and racial issues stood out in an era often dominated by white supremacy and segregation. Regarding her own home county, she stated, "No society with 1,000 white adults and 4,000 black adults can survive unless all have equal education opportunities." But her pioneering message was rarely acted on, and those favoring her positions have often been rejected (later efforts in Jasper County to name a public facility after her have all failed). Even attempts to have her portrait hung in the South Carolina State House were refused for decades. Only in 1995 did her picture take its place in the Senate chamber.

Ellis became ill with ovarian cancer and was unable to campaign effectively for reelection in 1932. She was defeated in the Democratic Party primary. She died on September 9, 1934, and was buried in Williamsburg Cemetery in Kingstree. WILLIAM S. BROCKINGTON, JR.

Bailey, N. Louise, Mary L. Morgan, and Carolyn R. Taylor, eds. *Biographical Directory of the South Carolina Senate, 1776–1985.* 3 vols. Columbia: University of South Carolina Press, 1986.

Berman, Pat. "The Road to Equal Rights." Columbia *State,* August 26, 2000, p. D3.

Bodie, Idella. *South Carolina Women.* Orangeburg, S.C.: Sandlapper, 1991.

Ellis, Mary Gordon. Vertical Files Collection. South Caroliniana Library, University of South Carolina, Columbia.

Ellison, Lillian (b. ca. 1923). Professional wrestler. Known to the world as the "Fabulous Moolah," Ellison was born in "Tookiedo," South Carolina, the youngest and only daughter in a family of twelve boys. She spent her childhood on a farm, living life as a rural tomboy and fighting her brothers and anyone else who challenged her. Ellison was eight years old when her mother passed away. She spent her summers picking cotton and dreamed of becoming an aviator. Her father introduced her to professional wrestling on trips to Columbia for Tuesday night matches. She would then practice these moves on her brothers. At one of these matches young Lillian first saw Mildred Burke, the "Women's Champ," and got the idea that she too might one day become a wrestling champion.

"The Fabulous Moolah," pictured here as "Slave Girl Moolah, World's Jr. Heavyweight Champion." Courtesy, Lillian Ellison, "The Fabulous Moolah"

The family moved to Columbia in Ellison's teen years, and the pressure of so many protective brothers drove her to marry at age fourteen. She gave birth to her first and only child, Mary, at age fifteen. Wrestling was in her blood, however, and she soon went on the road to pursue her dreams. She fought her first professional match in 1949 in Boston against June Byers; she lost. Ellison spent years on the road, negotiating with a string of shady promoters and managers who more often than not exploited the wrestlers they represented. After spending several years as the character "Slave Girl Moolah," a valet of sorts for male wrestlers such as the "Elephant Boy," she came into her own as the "Fabulous Moolah." When asked why she wanted to be in the ring, she famously replied, "I want to wrestle for the moolah!" She would maintain this stage persona for the next six decades, holding the Women's Championship belt from 1956 to 1984, only to regain it in 1985 disguised as the "Masked Spider Lady." From her days of backyard brawling with her many brothers, she brought an "anything goes" attitude to the ring, relishing the role of the bad girl who broke the rules by using dirty tricks, blunt objects, hair pulling, kicking, and cheap shots landed after the bell. Sensing that the crowd loved to hate a villain, Ellison pioneered this aspect of wrestling showmanship. Although she fought less often in her later years, she had sporadic victories as late as 1999, when she won the World Wrestling Federation women's title.

Ellison's life as a female professional wrestler was unprecedented. She faced down opponents in the ring and out of it, defying the male-dominated world of wrestling. Female wrestling was illegal in many states as late as the 1970s. Ellison and the legendary promoter Vince McMahon challenged and defeated this ban, enabling Ellison to become the first woman to wrestle legally in Madison Square Garden in 1972 in front of nearly twenty thousand stunned fans. Over the span of her career, wrestling evolved from a marginal traveling sideshow to one of the most popular forms of entertainment in America, in part due to cable television and pay-per-view. Her alliance with the McMahon family enabled her to profit handsomely from the sacrifices of her early career.

In 2003 Ellison was inducted into the Professional Wrestling Hall of Fame. Never one to back down from a fight, she celebrated her eightieth birthday with Vince McMahon, Jr., at a "Rock and Wrestling" bout in Columbia, defeating her opponent. In 2004 Ellison still resided in Columbia, on a street that bears her wrestling sobriquet. HEATHER BUGGY

Ellison, Lillian. *The Fabulous Moolah: First Goddess of the Squared Circle.* New York: HarperCollins, 2002.

Lipsyte, Robert. "They Hate Me but They Love Me." *New York Times,* March 17, 1969, p. 52.

Pincus, Arthur. "19,512 Quiet Fans See Women Wrestle for First Time in State." *New York Times,* July 2, 1972, p. S7.

Ellison, William (ca. 1790–1861). Free black entrepreneur. Originally named April, Ellison was the mulatto offspring of a slave woman and one of the Ellison men who owned her near Winnsboro in Fairfield District. In approximately 1802 he began an exceptional fourteen-year apprenticeship with a local cotton-gin maker. While slaves sometimes acquired skills, they typically remained unskilled all their lives. April's apprenticeship allowed him to learn the craft of gin making, which also required mastering the skills of the blacksmith, machinist, and carpenter along with reading, writing, and arithmetic. As he gained more experience, April visited outlying plantations and did repair work there. During his free time he worked for wages, and by 1816 he had acquired the funds to purchase his freedom. Once free, April relocated to the town of Stateburg in Sumter District. By 1817 he purchased and freed his enslaved wife Matilda and their daughter Eliza Ann. In 1820 April legally changed his name to William. In freedom, the Ellisons had three sons.

The early antebellum decades were auspicious for Ellison, as the expanding "Cotton Kingdom" increased demand for his skills. After purchasing land in Stateburg in the early 1820s, Ellison established a shop and soon manufactured his own brand of cotton gin. While most of his patronage was local, he occasionally shipped the "Ellison Gin" as far west as Mississippi. In addition to gin repair and manufacture, Ellison provided blacksmith and carpentry services. Slaves were essential to Ellison's success. He hired them, trained slave apprentices, and by 1820 had become a slaveowner. Many of the men were trained artisans, but as Ellison acquired nearby farmland, most of his slaves were employed in cotton production. It has been estimated that by the 1850s, the profits from Ellison's plantation exceeded those of his shop. In 1860 he owned nearly nine hundred acres of land and sixty-three slaves, which he conservatively valued at $53,000. His estate exceeded the total wealth of the other 328 free blacks in Sumter District by several times, and he was among the top ten percent of all slaveholders and landholders in the district.

Ellison's ability to avoid offending white racial sensibilities and his demonstrated commitment to planter values through investment in land and slaves afforded him unique opportunities. For example, in 1838 Ellison purchased his family mansion, known as Wisdom Hall, from Stephen Miller, a former congressman and governor of South Carolina. His family worshiped at Holy Cross Episcopal Church, and while other black people were confined to the galleries, the Ellisons sat in their own pew at the rear of the main floor. Ultimately, Ellison could not escape the racial strictures of his society, and even he had to comply with the law requiring free blacks to have white guardians. On the eve of the Civil War, as white suspicion and persecution of free blacks increased, Ellison contemplated emigrating from the South. He died on December 5, 1861. BERNARD E. POWERS, JR.

Johnson, Michael P., and James L. Roark. *Black Masters: A Free Family of Color in the Old South.* New York: Norton, 1984.

———. *No Chariot Let Down: Charleston's Free People of Color on the Eve of the Civil War.* Chapel Hill: University of North Carolina Press, 1984.

Koger, Larry. *Black Slaveowners: Free Black Slave Masters in South Carolina, 1790–1860.* 1985. Reprint, Columbia: University of South Carolina Press, 1995.

Wikramanayake, Marina. *A World in Shadow: The Free Black in Antebellum South Carolina.* Columbia: University of South Carolina Press, 1973.

Elmore, Franklin Harper (1799–1850). Congressman, banker, U.S. senator. Born on October 15, 1799, in Laurens District, Elmore was the son of John Archer Elmore and Sarah Saxon. After receiving his early education in the academies near Laurens, Elmore entered South Carolina College in 1817 and graduated two years later. After graduating, he studied law with Andrew P. Butler at Laurens Court House and was admitted to the bar in 1821. Elmore then moved to Walterboro, the seat of Colleton District, and began his practice. Quickly proving his ability as a lawyer, Elmore was appointed solicitor of the Southern Circuit in 1822 and held the post as the region's criminal prosecutor until 1836. In 1825 the General Assembly elected Elmore as a trustee of South Carolina College, a post to which he was reelected in 1829 and 1833. Elmore married Harriet Chesnut Taylor on May 10, 1827. The couple had twelve children.

In 1836 James H. Hammond resigned from the U.S. House of Representatives and Elmore was elected to fill the vacated seat. He took his seat on December 19 and was subsequently reelected to a full, two-year term in 1837. While in Congress, Elmore voted with the Democrats and was a faithful ally of John C. Calhoun. Among the more contentious national issues of the time was the increase in antislavery agitation by northern abolitionists. In a series of published letters to James G. Birney of the American Anti-slavery Society, Elmore defended slavery, claiming that "the two races cannot exist together upon terms of equality—the extirpation of one and the ruin of the other *would be inevitable.*" Like Calhoun, Elmore was a staunch proponent of railroad expansion and advocate of federal aid to southern railroads.

A year after completing his term in the House in 1839, Elmore was elected president of the Bank of the State of South Carolina (BSSC). During his tenure the bank prospered and proved itself to be a vital institution of economic development in the state. Despite the overall economic success of the BSSC, an increasingly vocal antibank faction developed in South Carolina. The bank's critics charged that Elmore and the bank's directors used the institution's resources to reward friends and further their political agenda, criticism not entirely without foundation. Elmore and Robert Barnwell Rhett led what was called at the time the "Rhett-Elmore clique," a group of lowcountry Calhoun supporters who wielded significant power from the mid-1830s until 1850 and at times alienated other factions in the state.

After Calhoun died in 1850, Elmore was appointed by Governor Whitemarsh Seabrook to fill the vacant seat in the U.S. Senate. Elmore took his seat on April 11 but died in Washington on May 29, 1850, of a recurring illness. Although he held political office for just a few brief years, Franklin Elmore was a behind-the-scenes political force in antebellum South Carolina. He was buried in the churchyard of First Presbyterian in Columbia. MICHAEL S. REYNOLDS

Correspondence between the Hon. F. H. Elmore and James G. Birney. 1838. Reprint, New York: Arno, 1969.

Lesesne, J. Mauldin. *The Bank of the State of South Carolina: A General and Political History.* Columbia: University of South Carolina Press, 1970.

O'Neall, John Belton. *Biographical Sketches of the Bench and Bar of South Carolina.* 2 vols. Charleston, S.C.: S. G. Courtney, 1859.

Elmore v. Rice (1947). One month after the South Carolina General Assembly repealed all statutes related to party primaries in the state in order to maintain its white primary, African American leaders formed the Progressive Democratic Party for the purpose of challenging the white primary system. In 1946 George Elmore, an African American who was eligible to vote in general elections, was denied the right to vote in the Democratic Party primary in Richland County in which party nominees for the U.S. Senate, the U.S. House of Representatives, and state offices were chosen. Citing several provisions of the U.S. Constitution, Elmore claimed that his right to choose members of Congress had been violated because of his race. He also argued that his right to participate on an equal basis in state and federal elections had been denied, since the primaries controlled the choice of elected officials.

The case was heard by U.S. District Judge J. Waties Waring, a native Charlestonian. Waring noted that since 1900 every governor and member of the General Assembly and Congress elected in the general election had been the nominee of the state's Democratic Party, which during the previous twenty-five years was the only party in South Carolina holding statewide primaries. He concluded that the repeal of all statutes and regulations in 1944 made no appreciable difference in the selection process of state officials and that the sole purpose of repealing the statutes and constitutional provisions was to prevent blacks from voting. Waring concluded that the state's Democratic Party was acting for and on behalf of the citizens of South Carolina and that the party's primary election was the only practical place where the voters could make their choices in selecting elected officials at the federal and state levels. He added the cutting comment that it was "time for South Carolina to rejoin the Union. It is time to fall in step with the other states and to adopt the American way of conducting elections."

After the decision in *Elmore v. Rice,* black Columbians waited in line for hours to exercise their right to vote in the 1948 Democratic primary. Courtesy, South Caroliniana Library, University of South Carolina

The response of the state's Democratic Party Executive Committee was to require that everyone who voted in the party's primary would have to take an oath stating that they would support the social, religious, and educational separation of the races. At least six local Democratic county committees, however, ignored the oath and began registering African American voters. In July 1948 Judge Waring's court rejected the oath. Waring's decisions were affirmed by the U.S. Court of Appeals for the Fourth Circuit. The U.S. Supreme Court refused to review the case. Democratic Party chair W. P. Baskin subsequently advised county chairs to enroll all constitutionally qualified electors on July 23, 1948. By the time of the August 1948 primary, some 35,000 African Americans were registered to vote and the white primary in South Carolina ceased to exist. WILLIAM V. MOORE

Lander, Ernest McPherson. *A History of South Carolina, 1865–1960.* 2d ed. Columbia: University of South Carolina Press, 1970.

Underwood, James L. *The Constitution of South Carolina.* Vol. 4, *The Struggle for Political Equality.* Columbia: University of South Carolina Press, 1994.

Yarbrough, Tinsley E. *A Passion for Justice: J. Waties Waring and Civil Rights.* New York: Oxford University Press, 1987.

Emancipation. The experience of slavery's demise varied around the state and followed the progress of the Civil War. Freedom came early and suddenly to Port Royal when on November 7, 1861, Union forces bombarded and occupied the area. Black Carolinians in the vicinity referred to this occasion as the "Day of the Big Gun Shoot," and during the next several weeks Federal troops seized Beaufort, the rest of Hilton Head, St. Helena, Ladys, and other nearby islands. Most planters fled the Federal troops and attempted to persuade or coerce their slaves to accompany them northward toward Charleston or into the interior, away from the path of the invasion. While many relocated with their owners, a substantial number resisted evacuation; some were killed for their refusal. In the early stages of the war freedom could be fleeting, as Confederates sometimes attempted to recapture fugitives from places where Union control was tentative. In August 1863 forty-one slaves, mainly women and children, were recaptured in such a raid on Barnwell Island. Port Royal was more secure, and for the duration of the war, under Federal authority, former slaves cultivated the deserted plantations. Northern missionaries and teachers came to provide them with education and religious instruction. This Port Royal Experiment was the first major site where black Carolinians experienced the fruits of emancipation, and thousands of fugitives were attracted there.

As early as January 1861 slaves were running away from plantations north of Charleston and along the Savannah River, and the appearance of Federal vessels along the coast encouraged further escapes. In spring and summer 1862 hundreds of fugitives from around Georgetown fled to Federal ships probing adjacent waterways. One of the boldest Union forays along the coast was led by the fugitive slave and abolitionist Harriet Tubman, who worked as a nurse and spy for the Federal cause. On June 2, 1863, she guided three gunboats loaded with troops from the Second South Carolina United States Colored Troops up the Combahee River past deadly torpedoes to locations where fugitives were hiding. Over 750 fugitives were rescued that night alone.

Most of South Carolina remained outside the main theater of battle until the final months of the war. The Union army entered the state in February 1865; Charleston, Columbia, and Georgetown fell, and by late May key interior locations were occupied. Although emancipation had been accomplished months earlier in the lowcountry, in the upstate planters often prevented the slaves from learning that they were free. In Spartanburg District it took a direct

The Emancipation Proclamation was first read in South Carolina in Beaufort, January 1, 1863. Courtesy, Avery Research Center for African American History and Culture

order from the Union army in August to compel some planters to inform slaves of their freedom. Whenever Union troops drew near, the slave system fell apart. Slaves sometimes simply disappeared into the Union lines. Whites were caught off guard by such displays of disloyalty and "ingratitude," which were widespread in 1865. Some freed people were more brazen in the display of their liberty. From Camden, Mary Chestnut wrote of maids who "dressed themselves in their mistresses' gowns before the owners' faces and walked off." Freedmen organized paramilitary units for their own protection and to appropriate the planters' homes and movable property. Some even physically punished overseers and other white men deemed especially offensive.

Southern whites feared that emancipation would engulf the region in a blood bath as the former slaves sought vengeance against their owners. That is why in early 1865 leading Pee Dee planters petitioned the Union army, in the name of "common humanity & Christian civilization," for protection against "disorderly & lawless . . . if not savage and barbarous" Negroes with insurrectionary designs. In another case, a planter's daughter wrote, "what I most fear . . . is not the Yankees, but the negroes, cut off from all help . . . what will become of us?" These fears were greatly exacerbated when black troops were present. Near Charleston another fearful white predicted that the future would be "written in blood . . . if the negro troops are not removed and our own negroes made to submit to the civil laws." As shorthand for these apprehensions, whites frequently referred to an impending second Santo Domingo. White Carolinians believed that the celebratory atmosphere and the ready availability of liquor made either July Fourth or the days following Christmas the most likely times for insurrection. Their fears proved unfounded.

Slavery's demise brought numerous celebrations. Thousands of freedmen converged on Camp Saxton, near Beaufort, to hear the reading of the Emancipation Proclamation on January 1, 1863. Unlike certain Union-controlled locations that were exempted from its provisions, none of South Carolina was excluded. In a program of prayers, speeches, and hymns, the pinnacle was reached when freedmen spontaneously began singing "My Country, 'Tis of Thee." In mid-March black Charlestonians organized a massive parade in which the mock corpse of slavery was displayed prominently on a hearse as joyous marchers wound their way through the streets of the city. In the last year of the war, Charleston's Washington Race Course was used as a prison for Union soldiers, and 257 perished from disease and exposure and were buried in unmarked graves there. Recognizing the sacrifice of these soldiers, in April 1865 black churchmen landscaped the burial site, marked the graves, and surrounded the area with a fence; on the archway above the entrance the words "Martyrs of the Race Course" were written. On May 1, black Charlestonians organized a procession and ceremony to consecrate this cemetery. Approximately 2,800 black children led the procession and scattered flowers on the graves as they passed. They were followed by the Patriotic Association of Colored Men and other organizations, black soldiers, and individual black and white citizens. Speeches were given, patriotic songs such as "The Star-Spangled Banner" and "John Brown's Body" were sung, and the site was dedicated by the prayers of black ministers. A reporter from the *New York Tribune* recorded the day's events as "a procession of friends and mourners as South Carolina and the United States never saw before." By celebrating their emancipation and the lives sacrificed to achieve it, black Charlestonians thus established what many believe to have been America's first Decoration Day, eventually called Memorial Day.

Emancipation initiated an unprecedented era of mobility for black Carolinians. Slaveholders described the freed peoples' "aimless wanderings" as evidence of their idleness, but the reality was much different. Of those who deserted their owners, many eventually returned to work on a free-labor basis. Others desired to test their freedom by seeking new employers and occupations. Rural whites tried to thwart this show of initiative. In Edgefield District in 1866, a former Confederate officer organized "Regulators" to threaten and even murder freed people who attempted to leave their former owners. Some freed people migrated to cities seeking safety, to find relatives separated by sale or the exigencies of war, and for the amenities more frequently available there.

Cities witnessed great changes in race relations because blacks and whites experienced a variety of regular contacts and the freedmen vigorously asserted their rights. They ventured boldly into previously interdicted zones such as public parks and conveyances. Urban workers such as Charleston's longshoremen by 1867 organized themselves into associations to demand higher wages. Schools could be most easily and efficiently organized in cities, and freedmen's aid societies assisted in their creation. Prohibited by law from an education before the war, in its aftermath black Carolinians of all ages enthusiastically unraveled the mysteries of reading and writing as symbol and substance of their new freedom. Desiring to take control of their religious lives, black Carolinians left the white churches they attended while enslaved and established new ones. Before the war there were 46,640 blacks attending Southern Methodist churches in the state, but by 1876 only 421 were left as freed people affiliated with the African Methodists and northern Methodists. Black Baptists and Presbyterians joined northern branches of these denominations. The scope of change in cities engendered confidence among urban freed people that alarmed the rural whites who observed them. One incredulous white man from Pendleton who journeyed to the capital concluded: "No Negro is improved by a visit to Columbia . . . & a visit to Charleston is his certain destruction."

Most black Carolinians resided in the countryside, and their major problem was that emancipation occurred without substantial redistribution of land. Therefore, sharecropping developed on Midlands and upstate cotton lands, where tenants typically worked a fifty-acre plot for between one-third and three-quarters of the crop. On rice lands workers were paid wages or rented plots in exchange for working two days each week for the landowners. Women played an especially important role in the transformation of agricultural labor. As emancipation redefined the familial roles of black women, they frequently reduced the amount of labor they were willing to do outside the home. This was especially apparent on Georgetown rice plantations, where from 1866 to 1868 the number of female full hands declined thirty-five percent.

More than a single event, emancipation was a process that only began with physical freedom. The countless decisions black Carolinians made to transform their lives produced an immediate impact during the Civil War. However, the full implications of emancipation for politics, race, and labor relations were not fully apparent in 1865 and dramatically shaped South Carolina's history over the next decade. BERNARD E. POWERS, JR.

Blight, David. *Race and Reunion: The Civil War in American Memory.* Cambridge: Belknap Press of Harvard University Press, 2001.

Roark, James L. *Masters without Slaves: Southern Planters in the Civil War and Reconstruction.* New York: Norton, 1977.

Rose, Willie Lee. *Rehearsal for Reconstruction: The Port Royal Experiment.* 1964. Reprint, Athens: University of Georgia Press, 1999.

Schwalm, Leslie A. *A Hard Fight for We: Women's Transition from Slavery to Freedom in South Carolina.* Urbana: University of Illinois Press, 1997.

Weiner, Marlin F. *Mistresses and Slaves: Plantation Women in South Carolina, 1830–80.* Urbana: University of Illinois Press, 1998.

Williamson, Joel. *After Slavery: The Negro in South Carolina during Reconstruction, 1861–1877.* Chapel Hill: University of North Carolina Press, 1965.

Emancipation Day celebrations. The tradition of marking the end of slavery with Emancipation Day celebrations began in South Carolina on January 1, 1863—the day the Emancipation Proclamation of President Abraham Lincoln declared three million slaves in the Confederate states to be "thenceforward, and forever free." Since then, African Americans in South Carolina have gathered annually on New Year's Day to commemorate the "Day of Jubilee" with food, song, dance, and prayer.

Emancipation Day celebrations in America can be traced back to January 1, 1808, when the United States officially ended its participation in the international slave trade. Other significant events in the fight against slavery (West Indian emancipation, passage of the Thirteenth Amendment, first notification of emancipation in east Texas) provide alternate days (August 1, February 1, June 19, respectively) for Emancipation Day celebrations in other regions of the country. In South Carolina, however, New Year's Day overshadows these counterparts.

From the first Emancipation Day celebration in Port Royal, when thousands of former slaves traveled significant distances to enjoy a day of singing, feasting, and oratory, African Americans in South Carolina have invested the holiday with secular and sacred significance. During the Reconstruction Era, Emancipation Day celebrations were means by which African Americans publicly dramatized their newfound freedom. The occasions varied widely in size, location (from town squares to churches), form (from barbeques to military parades), and tone (from moderate calls for hard work and thrift to fiery sermons and appeals for radical political change).

Preparations for the 1877 Emancipation Day Parade in Charleston. *Leslie's Illustrated Newspaper*, February 3, 1877. Courtesy, South Caroliniana Library, University of South Carolina

Despite opposition from some whites, Emancipation Day celebrations drew large crowds across South Carolina during the decades following the Civil War. While the number of occasions and participants dwindled after Reconstruction, Emancipation Day celebrations remained vital rituals for South Carolina's African American community well into the twentieth century. ETHAN J. KYTLE

Clark, Kathleen. "Celebrating Freedom: Emancipation Day Celebrations and African American Memory in the Early Reconstruction South." In *Where These Memories Grow: History, Memory, and Southern Identity,* edited by W. Fitzhugh Brundage. Chapel Hill: University of North Carolina Press, 2000.

Wiggins, William H., Jr. "'Lift Every Voice': A Study of Afro-American Emancipation Celebrations." In *Discovering Afro-America,* edited by Roger D. Abrahams and John F. Szwed. Leiden, Netherlands: Brill, 1975.

———. *O Freedom! Afro-American Emancipation Celebrations.* Knoxville: University of Tennessee Press, 1987.

Wiggins, William H., Jr., and Douglas DeNatale, eds. *Jubilation! African American Celebrations in the Southeast.* Columbia: McKissick Museum, University of South Carolina, 1993.

England, John (1786–1842). Catholic bishop, educator. England was born in Cork, Ireland, on September 23, 1786, the eldest son of Thomas England, a successful tobacco merchant, and Honora Lordan. He received a good education in Cork's Protestant schools. After initially preparing for a legal career, England decided to study for the priesthood and was ordained in 1808. In Cork he served in various parishes and headed the diocesan schools and seminary. He edited a patriotic secular newspaper and was prominent in the movement for Catholic emancipation and opposition to the British government's attempt to veto bishops' appointments.

In 1820 Pope Pius VII appointed England the first bishop of the Diocese of Charleston, encompassing the states of North Carolina, South Carolina, and Georgia. At England's arrival in Charleston, the diocese had three priests and five thousand Catholics. The Catholic community was disorganized and had experienced years of dissension and schism. England addressed these problems with tact and energy, earning the nickname "Steam Bishop." He traveled repeatedly to all corners of his huge diocese, set up parishes, recruited priests, and established a boys' academy in Charleston and a seminary to train new priests. In 1829 he founded the Sisters of Charity of Our Lady of Mercy. England was one of the first Irish American bishops and became an important leader of the Irish community nationwide.

John England. Courtesy, South Carolina Historical Society

England's modern views on education and free expression and his experience of British persecution of Irish Catholics led him to embrace American democracy and influenced his vision of a free church in a free society. He was the first important American Catholic theoretician of freedom of religion and separation of church and state. In 1822 England founded the first regularly published American Catholic newspaper, the *United States Catholic Miscellany.*

In 1826 England became the first Catholic priest to address Congress. There, he asserted that Catholicism and the Constitution were compatible: "I would not allow to the Pope or to any bishop of our church, outside the Union, the smallest interference with the humblest vote at our most insignificant balloting box." To reconcile traditional Catholicism with American democracy, England established a diocesan constitution. Under these new regulations, parishes elected lay vestries to take care of the church's financial and physical needs. Lay delegates and clergy met in annual conventions to deliberate and pass resolutions for the bishop's approval. This system was successful in promoting Catholic unity and support for the church, but subsequent bishops ignored England's example.

England abhorred slavery but stated that his church permitted retention in servitude of descendants of those originally enslaved. He hoped that American slavery would not continue, but he saw no quick end to it. He worked to improve the condition of blacks. In 1835 he established a Charleston academy for free colored youths, but threats of white mob violence forced its closure.

Affable and sophisticated, England was well received in South Carolina society. He was active in the Charleston Library Society and the Literary and Philosophical Society, serving as a curator of the latter's natural history museum. His health declined during 1841, and he died in Charleston on April 11, 1842. He was buried in the crypt of the Cathedral of St. John the Baptist, Charleston.
DAVID C. R. HEISSER

Carey, Patrick. *An Immigrant Bishop: John England's Adaptation of Irish Catholicism to American Republicanism.* Yonkers, N.Y.: U.S. Catholic Historical Society, 1982.

Guilday, Peter. *The Life and Times of John England.* 2 vols. 1927. Reprint, New York: Arno, 1969.

Kearns, Daniel F. "Bishop John England and the Possibilities of Catholic Republicanism." *South Carolina Historical Magazine* 102 (January 2001): 47–75.

Messmer, Sebastian G., ed. *The Works of Right Reverend John England, First Bishop of Charleston.* 7 vols. Cleveland: Arthur H. Clarke, 1908.

Saunders, R. Frank, and George Rogers. "Bishop John England of Charleston: Catholic Spokesman and Southern Intellectual, 1820–1842." *Journal of the Early Republic* 13 (fall 1993): 301–22.

English. One of the enduring myths of American history is the centuries-old assertion that the thirteen original colonies were "English" colonies. While they were governed by the English, the colonies were not peopled only by individuals of English ancestry. Almost one-half of Virginia's white population has been identified as ethnically English. New York, often cited as having one of the more heterogeneous colonial populations, was some forty-four percent English. For all of the colonies in what would become the United States, on average nearly fifty-eight percent of the European settlers were of English descent.

South Carolina was far below the colonial average and had one of the most diverse populations in British North America. For more than two-thirds of its colonial history (1706–1775), settlers of European extraction were a minority of the population. And within the European minority, no single nationality was a majority. Persons of English descent were the largest European ethnic group, comprising some 36.7 percent of the white population. Except for Pennsylvania, this was the smallest English population (in terms of percentage) in the thirteen colonies. Just as the European population was diverse, so were the origins of the colony's English settlers.

In 1670 a group of about 130 white immigrants arrived in South Carolina. Almost all were from the mother country, but a small number of English men and women were from the English islands in the West Indies. Although there were only a handful of real Barbadians in the first group of 130 settlers in 1670, during the next twenty years a majority of the whites who settled in South Carolina came from Barbados, the prosperous island colony that was often called "Little England." While the settlers who emigrated from the islands to South Carolina were ethnically "English," culturally they were Anglo-Caribbean—an important distinction.

In South Carolina, regardless of the islands from whence they came, they were referred to as "Barbadians." These Anglo-Caribbeans who emigrated from the various English colonies in the West Indies—Barbados, Jamaica, Antigua, Nevis, St. Christopher's, and Grenada—became a powerful presence in the new colony. Quickly rising to prominence, these English settlers who had spent time in the West Indies established the cultural ethos that shaped the development of the colony. The influence of the Barbadians was so pervasive that many historians consider South Carolina to be the colony of Barbados—not of England.

In addition to the Anglo-Caribbeans, settlers from another English colony, Massachusetts Bay, came to South Carolina. In 1695 a group from the town of Dorchester settled on the banks of the

Ashley River some twenty miles above Charleston and founded the town of Dorchester. The surrounding land was poor, and the New Englanders never seemed to adapt to their new environment. After several generations, the congregation of New England Puritans voted to move to Georgia.

The mother country furnished the bulk of the English settlers after 1700. And they, too, were a diverse lot, representing any number of counties from the English Channel to the borderlands with Scotland.

Although the English were the largest white minority in the colony, they were a majority of the white population in the lowcountry—about eighty percent. During the first generation of settlement, the English majority in the lowcountry did not welcome non-English settlers. After some Frenchmen were elected to the Commons House of Assembly, an angry petition reflected the ethnocentricity of the majority: "Shall the Frenchmen, who cannot speak our language, make our laws?" Given such attitudes, it is no wonder that many non-English settlers opted to assimilate themselves into the majority population. But as they did so, they altered the Englishness of the colony's culture.

Given their numbers in comparison to the other eight European ethnicities in South Carolina, it is not surprising that there was a strong English cast to the institutions and society that developed. However, especially in the area of culture, what appeared to be English was not always so. In speech, words and phrases from other ethnic groups crept into general use, and the famed lilting Charleston accent is clearly a result of the impact of West African speech patterns. English architectural and furniture styles were modified for the climate or by artisans from other cultures. For example, one of the best-known pieces of South Carolina–made furniture, the library bookcase in the Heyward-Washington House, appears on the surface to be right out of English design books. On closer examination, however, the detail and construction are unquestionably Germanic.

The various ethnic groups sometimes established self-help or mutual-aid societies that later morphed into social organizations. The impetus behind these groups was an effort to preserve some of their ethnic heritage in the melting pot that was colonial South Carolina. The Scots were the first ethnic group to form such an organization, the St. Andrew's Society. Seven years later the St. George's Society, named for the patron saint of England, was founded for the benefit of Englishmen and their descendants.

During the decade after the French and Indian War, almost every European ethnicity in the colony was represented in the Commons House of Assembly. Yet, whether of Scot, German, French, Welsh, or English descent, almost to a man they demanded that South Carolinians were entitled to the "rights of Englishmen." In fact, the colony's delegation to the First Continental Congress illustrates the dominance of English political thought. Only one delegate, Christopher Gadsden, was really English. Thomas Lynch's forebears were Irish, and those of John and Edward Rutledge were from Northern Ireland. Henry Middleton's ancestors were English but Anglo-Caribbean. The cultural life of the colony reflected the alteration of English models by the diverse elements of the colonial population. However, the reverse was true in the political sphere. By the 1760s the colony's political life and thought were completely English. The significance of England, the mother country, even to those who were not English can be seen in the remark of the proud Huguenot Henry Laurens, who referred to England as "home." WALTER EDGAR

Edgar, Walter. *South Carolina: A History.* Columbia: University of South Carolina Press, 1998.

McDonald, Forrest, and Ellen Shapiro McDonald. "The Ethnic Origins of the American People, 1790." *William and Mary Quarterly,* 3d ser., 37 (April 1980): 179–99.

English, Alexander (b. 1954). Basketball player. English was born on January 5, 1954, in Columbia to James H. English and Johnnie Mae Glasgow.

After a successful start at Dreher High School in Columbia, English opted to play basketball for the University of South Carolina (USC). After he enrolled in 1972, his impact on the program was immediate. English started every game (111) during his four years at USC and never averaged less than the 14.6 points per game he posted his freshman year. By the end of his college career in 1976 he had became the school's career-scoring leader with 1,972 points, making 53.8 percent of his shots during that span. He became the fourth player to have his number (22) retired.

In 1976 English moved to the National Basketball Association as the second-round pick and twenty-third overall of the Milwaukee Bucks, with whom he spent two seasons in a reserve role. He became a free agent in 1978 and signed with the Indiana Pacers. Two years later the Denver Nuggets acquired him in a fateful trade for George McGinnis.

The fluent run-and-shoot style of the coach Doug Moe was tailor-made for English's smooth game. He averaged 21.3 points in his final twenty-four games of that season, a sign of things to come. By the end of his career in Denver in 1990, English had become the most prolific scorer of the 1980s. He won the scoring championship in 1982–1983 with 28.4 points per game, played in eight NBA All-Stars games, and led his team to nine play-off spots. He scored 2,000 or more points in eight straight seasons.

English left the rebuilding Nuggets in 1990, signing as a free agent with the Dallas Mavericks. He averaged 9.7 points in a reserve role and left the NBA as a player at the end of that season, finishing with 25,613 career points, a 21.5 average per game, and a 50.7 field-goal-shooting percent for fifteen seasons. English was the seventh-leading scorer in league history at the time of his retirement from the NBA. Denver retired his jersey (2) in 1992.

English accepted a position as director of player programs for the National Basketball Players Association in New York and oversaw the league's programs on alcohol and drug abuse, HIV/AIDS, and player orientation. He established Flick2, a company that represents players in marketing opportunities, in 1996 and has worked as an analyst for Fox Sports and CNNSI.

Interest in a coaching career led English to become the head coach of the North Charleston Lowgators in the fledgling National Basketball Development League in 2001–2002. The Lowgators posted a 36–20 record and reached the league finals. English accepted a post as director of player development for the Atlanta Hawks before the 2002–2003 season and later became an assistant coach.

English was inducted into the Naismith Basketball Hall of Fame in 1997, his first year of eligibility, and served as a member of its board of directors. English was a member of the USC Board of Trustees from 1999 to 2003. He is a member of the University of South Carolina Athletic Hall of Fame (1988) and the South Carolina Athletic Hall of Fame (1993). W. K. MITCHELL

Enoree River. The Enoree River flows approximately seventy miles from its source in northern Greenville County to its confluence with the Broad River above Columbia. Its basin encompasses more than 730 square miles across South Carolina's Piedmont, the largest part of which is forestlands, with a small percentage characterized as urban. Along the way, the river's route provides borders for parts of Greenville, Spartanburg, Laurens, Union, and Newberry Counties.

Like other Piedmont rivers, the Enoree faces challenges regarding water quality, both from pollution and from sand-mining operations that cause the river to erode its banks heavily and fill its flow with sediment. It is, however, a different river upstream than it is downstream. Soon after the Enoree leaves its source, it edges metropolitan Greenville, where heavy streamside development, including clear-cut logging down to the river's edge, and paved surfaces create rapid runoff filled with pollution, especially petroleum and related products. As it passes by Greenville and through Laurens and Union Counties, the river is rocky and features frequent rapids. Around these shoals the Enoree once supported textile mills, most notably at Pelham, Whitmire, and Enoree.

Past Enoree, as the river widens and the terrain flattens, the Enoree River enters the Sumter National Forest. Here the river is bordered by wide, open floodplains shaded by hardwoods and carpeted with fallen leaves. After hard rains, the river frequently leaves its banks, flowing into the bordering floodplains. Evidence of erosion, in the form of fallen trees along the banks, exists as the river runs through the forest and into the Broad River in Newberry County.

The Enoree River has remained an undiscovered resource for paddlers for many years. However, public and private efforts to create safe access points have permitted a growing number of recreational paddlers to enjoy the river. CAROLINE FOSTER

Foster, Caroline. "River of Muscadines." *South Carolina Wildlife* 51 (March–April 2004): 12–21.

Ensor, Joshua Fulton (1834–1907). Physician. Ensor was born in Butler, Maryland, on December 12, 1834. He received his medical training at the University of Maryland, from which he graduated in 1861. During the Civil War he served with distinction as a surgeon in the Union army. In November 1862 he married Henrietta Kemp. They had two daughters.

After the war, Ensor became active in the Republican Party and moved to South Carolina. In 1870 Governor Robert K. Scott appointed him superintendent of the South Carolina Lunatic Asylum. Contrary to the expectations of many South Carolinians, Ensor proved to be competent, honest, resourceful, and adamant in defense of the needs of the institution and its patients. At times he was one of the harshest critics of the government that appointed him, particularly for its failure to provide adequate appropriations. Ensor was appalled by the condition of the asylum when he assumed his duties, claiming that the buildings were overcrowded, poorly ventilated and heated, and unsanitary. He complained particularly about the facilities allotted to the black patients, calling them a disgrace to the state and his own party. Unable to secure adequate state funds for the changes he envisioned, Ensor borrowed from merchants in Columbia and Philadelphia, using future appropriations and even his own salary as credit. With this money, he secured central heating, indoor plumbing, underground sewers, new furniture and carpeting, new dining and bathing facilities, and many items for the patients' amusement and occupation.

Ensor's tenure at the asylum was politically significant. He publicized the asylum's plight in the state's newspapers, adding to the embarrassment of the Republican government and providing fodder for Democrats, who overthrew the Reconstruction regime after the elections of 1876. Ensor helped lead a Republican reform movement. In 1874 he served as campaign manager for the successful Republican reform candidate for governor, Daniel H. Chamberlain. Although Ensor was subsequently somewhat disappointed with Chamberlain's efforts to aid the asylum, he supported his reelection in 1876. In 1877 Ensor was the first state official to recognize the legitimacy of the new Democratic governor, Wade Hampton, when he appealed to him rather than to Chamberlain for desperately needed aid for the asylum's patients. Although Ensor won the respect of many Democrats, Hampton forced him from the superintendent's office in November 1877.

Ensor resided in South Carolina for the rest of his life but remained a Republican. He subsequently held several federal posts, including chief inspector and surveyor of the Port of Charleston and chief raiding deputy for the Bureau of Internal Revenue. In 1894 he resumed the practice of medicine in Columbia. President William McKinley appointed him postmaster of Columbia in 1897, and he remained in that post until his death in Columbia on August 9, 1907. PETER MCCANDLESS

McCandless, Peter. *Moonlight, Magnolias, and Madness: Insanity in South Carolina from the Colonial Period to the Progressive Era.* Chapel Hill: University of North Carolina Press, 1996.

Obituary. *Journal of the South Carolina Medical Association* 3 (August 1907): 152–53.

Enterprise Railroad. Chartered on March 1, 1870, with a capital of $250,000, this railroad is unique in South Carolina history: with one exception, its initial board of directors consisted entirely of African Americans. Constructed in 1874, the railroad used horse-drawn carriages to carry passengers and freight, connecting wharves and railroad depots throughout the city of Charleston. The company was directed by such prominent African Americans as Richard H. Cain, William R. Jervey, William McKinlay, Joseph H. Rainey, and Robert Smalls. The board reflected the diversity of African American economic leadership after the Civil War, representing a shift away from the antebellum free-black elite. Only McKinlay had been a free-black taxpayer prior to the Civil War. In contrast, Smalls and Jervey were former slaves and held seats in the General Assembly during Reconstruction, and Cain was one of several northern blacks on the board.

Despite its black leadership, the Enterprise Railroad created some tension within Charleston's African American community. Three-quarters of the city's draymen were black, and they feared that the new railroad would diminish their business. Supporters of the railroad argued that jobs would actually be increased since the railroad would ease the passage of freight into and through Charleston. Led by an African American Presbyterian minister, Hezekiah H. Hunter, the draymen protested the railroad to little avail.

The Enterprise Railroad continued to operate into the 1880s, but the role of African Americans in directing its operations had declined by the end of the Reconstruction period. By the close of the 1870s, the direction of the railroad was in the hands of whites. AARON W. MARRS

Powers, Bernard E. *Black Charlestonians: A Social History, 1822–1885.* Fayetteville: University of Arkansas Press, 1994.

Epidemics. An epidemic disease is generally defined as one that affects an unusually high number of individuals within a population or region simultaneously. Epidemic diseases are often contrasted to endemic diseases, those constantly present but which do not necessarily affect large numbers of people. The terms are far from precise, however. Some diseases may be endemic to a particular place but be labeled epidemic when they reach a certain indeterminate level of incidence.

From the 1680s to the early twentieth century, South Carolina, especially the lowcountry, had a deserved reputation as an unhealthy place. Disease killed enormous numbers of Europeans and Africans, virtually annihilated Native Americans, and proved a significant barrier to European immigration. It thus played a major role in shaping the demographic profile of the colony and the state. The biggest contributor to high morbidity (disease) and mortality rates was infectious disease, especially malaria, dysentery, smallpox, and yellow fever. Malaria (known then as ague and fever or as intermittent, remittent, or country fever) and dysentery (bloody flux) were endemic and occasionally epidemic from the first years of European and African settlement until the early twentieth century. Endemic or epidemic, they were perhaps the greatest contributors to morbidity and mortality rates until the late nineteenth century and remained significant problems until the 1940s.

Yet malaria and dysentery received less public attention and aroused less fear than smallpox and yellow fever, which were more clearly epidemic in the traditional definition. Not only were they repulsive diseases that could infect and kill large numbers of people in a short time, but epidemics of smallpox and yellow fever invariably brought stagnation of trade and quarantine of people on ships, in houses, or in pesthouses on Sullivan's Island.

The first major outbreak of smallpox, in 1697–1698, killed between two hundred and three hundred settlers out of a total population of no more than five thousand. Several other smallpox epidemics struck South Carolina between 1711 and 1763, and then the disease virtually disappeared until 1816, perhaps due to widespread inoculation and vaccination. In the later nineteenth century smallpox revived in epidemic form several times, probably because of neglect of vaccination. In 1905 the state passed a compulsory vaccination law. The disease was eradicated from South Carolina by 1930.

The smallpox epidemics of 1738 and 1760 are particularly notable in South Carolina history. The epidemic of 1738, which spread through the colony from a slave ship, the *London Frigate*, infected more than two thousand of the roughly six thousand people in Charleston and killed more than three hundred. It also produced a major controversy over the first known use of inoculation as a preventive measure in South Carolina.

Unlike most smallpox epidemics, which arrived via ships, the epidemic of 1760 most likely came from the upcountry. It was apparently spread throughout the colony by soldiers returning to Charleston in December 1759 from Governor William Lyttleton's expedition against the Cherokees. Precise statistics are impossible, but in Charleston alone about one-half to three-fourths of the population of about eight thousand were infected naturally or by inoculation and perhaps as many as nine hundred died. Mortality was especially high among Africans and French Arcadian refugees.

Smallpox was particularly devastating to South Carolina's Native American populations. It was largely responsible for the decline of South Carolina's Indian population from about ten thousand in 1685 to about three hundred east of the mountains by 1790. In 1697 and 1698 smallpox destroyed the Pemlicos and killed untold numbers of Indian people hundreds of miles inland. The epidemic that struck the backcountry in late 1759 killed almost one-half of the Catawbas. By then this people who had numbered about four thousand in the 1690s could muster only one hundred fighting men. The number of Cherokees dropped by about two-thirds during the eighteenth century, largely due to smallpox.

Yellow fever, named for the jaundiced appearance of its victims, was generally confined to ports, such as Charleston and Beaufort. It was unusual, but not unknown, in rural areas. The disease was usually imported in slave ships from Africa and the Caribbean. Yellow fever seems to have first struck Charleston in a devastating epidemic in 1699 that killed several hundred inhabitants. One observer claimed that the effects were far worse than those from the Great Plague of London (1665), given the comparative smallness of Charleston: "Shops shut up for six weeks, nothing but carrying medicines, digging graves, carting the dead; to the great astonishment of all beholders." Yellow fever visited Charleston with similar results every five to ten years until 1748 and then virtually disappeared until the 1790s. Between 1792 and 1800 yellow fever epidemics struck the city seven times. Epidemics in Charleston were common once again from the 1820s to the 1870s and particularly severe in the 1850s.

The epidemic of 1858, which killed more than eight hundred people in the city, was the worst of the nineteenth century. It also differed from most others in that it seemed to affect the entire spectrum of the population. In most epidemics the victims were said to be children, recent immigrants, and visitors—hence the source of the name "Strangers Fever." The last yellow fever epidemics struck the state in 1876 (Charleston) and 1877 (Port Royal), but fear of the disease continued for decades.

Many other diseases, notably influenza, pneumonia, measles, diphtheria, scarlet fever, polio, typhoid, pellagra, and tuberculosis, have produced major epidemics in the state. Influenza ("flu") has reached epidemic status many times throughout the history of South Carolina. Influenza mortality has usually been small compared to the large numbers infected in epidemics. But a major exception to this occurred in 1918 and 1919, when the worst pandemic (worldwide epidemic) since the fourteenth-century plague infected about ten percent of the state's population (about 150,000–170,000) and killed between 4,000 and 5,000 people.

By the 1950s most of the old epidemic diseases were eliminated or greatly reduced in incidence and virulence by a combination of improvements in diet, housing, and public health with immunization and drugs, notably antibiotics. In South Carolina, as in the developed world generally, acute infectious diseases have largely been replaced by chronic degenerative diseases such as cancer, heart disease, stroke, and chronic obstructive pulmonary disease (emphysema, asthma, and chronic bronchitis). PETER MCCANDLESS

Banov, Leon. *A Quarter Century of Public Health in Charleston, South Carolina.* Charleston, S.C.: Charleston County Department of Health, [1945?].

Duffy, John. *Epidemics in Colonial America.* Baton Rouge: Louisiana State University Press, 1953.

Farley, M. Foster. *An Account of the History of Stranger's Fever in Charleston, 1699–1876.* Washington, D.C.: University Press of America, 1978.

Krebsbach, Suzanne. "The Great Charlestown Smallpox Epidemic of 1760." *South Carolina Historical Magazine* 96 (January 1996): 30–37.

Waring, Joseph I. *A History of Medicine in South Carolina.* 3 vols. Columbia: South Carolina Medical Association, 1964–1971.

Wood, Peter. "The Impact of Smallpox on the Native Population of the 18th Century South." *New York State Journal of Medicine* 87 (January 1987): 30–36.

Episcopalians. In all thirteen American colonies those persons later called Episcopalians were members of the Church of England, sometimes called Anglicans. After the Revolutionary War, the Church of England was disestablished in South Carolina, North Carolina, Georgia, Maryland, and Virginia. On May 12, 1785, the Church of England in South Carolina organized itself as the Protestant Episcopal Church in South Carolina. At the third General Convention at Philadelphia in 1789, the Protestant Episcopal Church in the United States of America (PECUSA) was organized when the constitution and canons of the Protestant Episcopal Church were adopted and the *Book of Common Prayer* (1789) was approved. In 1967 the General Convention approved the alternative name, Episcopal Church in the United States (ECUSA).

The Episcopal Church affirms the historic creeds of the Christian tradition (for example, the Apostles and Nicene creeds) as the basis for doctrine, which is also summarized in the Thirty-nine Articles of faith of the Church of England. Its worship follows liturgical orders set forth in the *Book of Common Prayer.* The liturgy offers some flexibility; a congregation following the more formal orders of service is called "high church," while one following the more simple liturgy is called "low church." The word "Episcopal" comes from the Greek for "bishop," indicating that geographic units (called dioceses) are administered by bishops. A diocesan convention of clergy and lay delegates from each congregation meets annually. Bishops and delegates, both clergy and lay, from all dioceses meet every three years in the General Convention, the body that sets broad policy guidelines and recommended programs for dioceses across the nation.

During the antebellum era, the Episcopal Church in South Carolina was dominated by the state's elite, with its strength concentrated in the lowcountry, especially Charleston, although most large communities in the state had Episcopal congregations. Although most slaves and free blacks belonged to evangelical denominations, by 1860 blacks made up almost half (2,960) of the state's 6,126 Episcopalians. The Protestant Episcopal Church in the Diocese of South Carolina withdrew from the PECUSA on June 20, 1861, and joined the Protestant Episcopal Church in the Confederate States on February 14, 1862. With the collapse of the Confederacy, the Diocese of South Carolina returned to the PECUSA on February 11, 1866.

With the exception of the Civil War years, Episcopalians in South Carolina have been supportive of the national church. At the eleventh General Convention in 1814, a clerical deputy from the Diocese of South Carolina, the Reverend Christopher E. Gadsden, introduced a resolution to establish a general seminary for the whole church. On May 27, 1817, the General Convention adopted resolutions approving the establishment of the General Theological Seminary in New York City, and it opened on May 1, 1819. Because of the developing sectional conflict over slavery, the Diocese of South Carolina opened the Theological Seminary of the Protestant Episcopal Church in the Diocese of South Carolina at Camden on January 18, 1859. It closed on June 30, 1862, reopened in Spartanburg in October 1866, and then permanently suspended operations in 1868.

Episcopalians in South Carolina also have been committed to education. In 1850 they opened the Episcopal Church Home for Children in Charleston, an orphanage. It moved to York in 1910. The Diocese of South Carolina was one of the founding dioceses of the University of the South at Sewanee, Tennessee, in 1857. On December 9, 1867, the Reverend A. Toomer Porter opened the Holy Communion Church Institute in Charleston. In 1886 the name was changed to the Porter Military Academy. In 1897 Elizabeth Evelyn Wright founded a school for blacks in Denmark, South Carolina, which became the Voorhees Industrial School. In 1924 the dioceses of South Carolina and Upper South Carolina took over the operation of the school, which became Voorhees College.

The 1922 General Convention voted to divide the Diocese of South Carolina into the Diocese of South Carolina (bishop in Charleston) and the Diocese of Upper South Carolina (bishop in Columbia). The diocese was divided because it had become too large for one bishop to administer. The new Diocese of Upper South Carolina held its Primary Convention at Trinity Church, Columbia, October 10–11, 1922. On September 20, 1963, the Church of St. Luke and St. Paul, Charleston, became the Cathedral of St. Luke and St. Paul. On January 19, 1977, Trinity Church, Columbia, became Trinity Cathedral. As of January 25, 2001, the Diocese of South Carolina had seventy-six parishes, 26,275 baptized members, and 20,878 confirmed communicants. As of that same date, the Diocese of Upper South Carolina had sixty-two parishes, 26,211 baptized members, and 22,833 confirmed communicants.

DONALD S. ARMENTROUT

Armentrout, Don S., and Robert Boak Slocum, eds. *Documents of Witness: A History of the Episcopal Church, 1782–1985.* New York: Church Hymnal Corporation, 1994.

Prichard, Robert W. *A History of the Episcopal Church.* Rev. ed. Harrisburg, Pa.: Morehouse, 1999.

Thomas, Albert Sidney. *A Historical Account of the Protestant Episcopal Church in South Carolina, 1820–1957.* Columbia, S.C.: R. L. Bryan, 1957.

Erosion. The landscape of South Carolina is highly eroded. The state, and indeed most of eastern North America, was formed by collision with other land that thrust up high mountain ranges. The eroded roots of these mountains are exposed as the Blue Ridge and Piedmont terrains, which form the upper one-third of the state. The coastal plain makes up the lower two-thirds of the state, formed largely from the sedimentary products of the erosion of upstate mountains. This erosion has provided many of the state's valuable mineral and rock products, including clay, granite, sand, and topsoil. In contrast, some human activities adversely affected erosion, which caused a tremendous loss of topsoil during the late nineteenth and early twentieth centuries that still affects the environment today.

Erosion is the natural, geologic process whereby rock and other earth materials are loosened or dissolved from their original positions and redeposited elsewhere. The high mountains that were uplifted as South Carolina formed 505 million to 245 million years ago have almost completely worn down. The rocks of the Blue Ridge and Piedmont are the remnant cores of mountains that are gone. The sands and clays that were produced by the erosion of these mountains were carried downstream. They formed an immense wedge of sediments that begin thinly at the Sandhills in the upper coastal plain and continue thickening seaward until, at the coast and on the lower coastal plain, this wedge is many thousands of feet thick. The sediments continue off the coast and make up huge deposits that overlie Piedmont basement rock on the continental shelf. They are composed of clays, shales, sands, and sandstones and are interlayered with limestones that give evidence for intermittent changes in sea level over time.

South Carolina contains many interesting erosional features, among which are caves. On the western edge of Lake Marion at and near Santee State Park lies the only site of karst topography in the state—caves and sinkholes cut into the limestone on the coastal

More than a century of poor farming practices led to terrible soil erosion in the upcountry. Photograph by the U.S. Forestry Service. Courtesy, South Caroliniana Library, University of South Carolina

plain. Caves form through weathering as acidic water percolates through basic limestone, initiating a chemical reaction that displaces the limestone. At Santee, as the acidic groundwater moved through and hollowed out the limestone in the Santee caves, some of the roofs collapsed to form sinkholes, some retained water to become small ponds, and some remained dry. The caves contain an underground river system that is visible in places through holes in the rock called "chimneys."

Other erosional structures include the Blue Ridge Escarpment and the towering sheer rock faces of Table Rock, Caesars Head, and other prominent monadnocks. These are exposed through the erosional process brought on by the rise and fall of the sea level, uplift of the land through isostatic rebound, and through heating and cooling of the land during and after collision and disengagement. A closer look at the rocks shows erosional features characteristic of granite. Because granites are formed deep underground under tremendous pressure, the minerals that compose them are less stable at the surface. Over time, the granite reacts to the release of pressure by exfoliating, or popping off in large slabs to form its characteristic rounded surfaces.

To the south, the Orangeburg Scarp is a steep grade formed as a wave-cut ridge by the sea. Adjacent to the scarp are the Sandhills, discontinuous ridges of sand and clay that cut the state diagonally from northeast to southwest. The sediments that make up the Sandhills eroded over millions of years from the mountains to the north and northwest. They were carried by streams and rivers downslope, where they were transported further by wind and ocean currents and shaped into huge deposits of sand. In the Piedmont, the consistent elevation of the ridges shows that what was once the rock of high mountains wore away, and then the terrain was again uplifted and dissected anew by the many streams of the region.

Along the coast, storms and high tides are often the cause of erosion. Photograph by Phillip Jones. Courtesy, South Carolina Department of Natural Resources

The erosion of the soils in South Carolina is a chapter in soil management that has had an impact on the entire country. In the nineteenth and twentieth centuries, many of the state's farmers were careless, even cavalier, about soil management. The demand for cotton led South Carolina farmers to plant on the highly sloped land of the upstate with little thought to the ultimate effects on the soil and the long-term health of agriculture. Consequently, it is estimated that nearly forty percent of South Carolina's arable topsoil was lost to erosion. This, in turn, affected the rivers as sediments moved downslope, killing fish and permanently altering the ecology of the rivers. To address the problem of erosion in South Carolina and elsewhere, in 1933 the federal government created the United States Soil Conservation Service to help manage and preserve the soils throughout the country. CAROLYN H. MURPHY

Kovacik, Charles F., and John J. Winberry. *South Carolina: The Making of a Landscape.* 1987. Reprint, Columbia: University of South Carolina Press, 1989.

Murphy, Carolyn H. *Carolina Rocks! The Geology of South Carolina.* Orangeburg, S.C.: Sandlapper, 1995.

Erskine College. In 1836 the General Synod of the Associate Reformed Presbyterian Church organized an academy in Due West. A professor of divinity was added the next year, and the institution was incorporated as Clark and Erskine Seminary. When more faculty were added in 1839, the institution became the first four-year denominational college in South Carolina. About 1843 the name was shortened to Erskine College and the theological seminary became an adjunct of the college. The school took its name from the eighteenth-century Scottish theologian and reformer Ebenezer Erskine. While women began attending the college in 1894, their numbers were significantly increased when the Due West Female College, organized in 1859 by Associate Reformed Presbyterians, merged with Erskine in 1927.

From its founding, the college played an important role in nurturing the social and cultural cohesion of the Associate Reformed Presbyterian Church. Generations of Associate Reformed Presbyterians from across the South sent their children to college in Due West. In addition to its formal curriculum, Erskine taught an ethic of simplicity, frugality, the value of work, social responsibility, and the importance of the life of the mind. A moderate Calvinism that emphasized not only God's sovereignty but also God's grace marked the life of the town, the church, and the college.

In the 1830s leaders in the establishment of Erskine challenged the South Carolina law that made it illegal to teach slaves to read. They insisted that Christian liberty to obey the Word of God and to teach their slaves to read the Bible overrode the rights of slaveowners to protect their property. Their resistance continued into the 1850s.

Following the Civil War, the college struggled to rebuild its endowment, which had been largely wiped out, and its enrollment, which had reached more than one hundred students before the war. The poverty of the region and the isolation of Due West from centers of population made the recovery long and difficult. Nevertheless, Erskine was able to receive accreditation from the Southern Association of Colleges in 1925. Beginning in the 1950s, the college successfully conducted capital fund campaigns that allowed for expansion of the campus and a substantial increase in its endowment. A campaign begun in 1992 raised more than $30 million.

Erskine boasts faculty who have won state and regional awards for excellence in teaching. By the late 1990s the college had an undergraduate enrollment of 575 and a faculty of forty full-time and ten part-time professors, and it had been classified by the Carnegie Foundation as a BAI institution, the foundation's top classification of liberal arts colleges nationally. While Erskine continued to maintain its close ties with the Associate Reformed Presbyterian Church, it was drawing students from more diverse backgrounds. ERSKINE CLARKE

Ware, Lowry. *A Place Called Due West: The Home of Erskine College.* Columbia, S.C.: R. L. Bryan, 1997.

Ware, Lowry Price, and James Wylie Gettys. *The Second Century: A History of the Associate Reformed Presbyterians, 1882–1982.* Greenville, S.C.: Associate Reformed Presbyterian Center, 1983.

Erskine Theological Seminary. Erskine Theological Seminary originated with the 1837 incorporation of Clark and Erskine Seminary in Due West, later shortened to Erskine College. Around 1843 the theological seminary became an adjunct of the college. Erskine Theological Seminary was formally separated from the college in 1858 but continued under the same board of trustees. The institutions were reunited administratively in 1926, with the seminary serving as a professional school of the college.

The formation of the seminary by the Associate Reformed Presbyterian Synod reflected the church's Scottish heritage and insistence on an educated ministry. While the seminary adopted a three-year, postbaccalaureate curriculum after the model of Andover Theological Seminary, its relationship with the college gave it something of the character of a divinity school.

For generations the seminary played an important role in nurturing the cultural and theological cohesion of the Associate Reformed Presbyterian Church with its tight network of families centered in the South Carolina upstate. The seminary taught a moderate Calvinism that emphasized an ethic of simplicity, frugality, and a commitment to the life of the mind. Disruptions in the Southern Presbyterian Church (Presbyterian Church in the United States) in the 1970s brought some of the church's most conservative members to the seminary and challenged the old theological and familial cohesion of the institution and denomination. Since the 1980s the seminary has attracted students from a variety of denominational backgrounds, especially in its doctor of ministry program. ERSKINE CLARKE

Associate Reformed Presbyterian Church. *Sesquicentennial History, Mainly Covering the Period, 1902–1951.* Clinton, S.C.: Jacobs, 1951.

Ware, Lowry Price, and James Wylie Gettys. *The Second Century: A History of the Associate Reformed Presbyterians, 1882–1982.* Greenville, S.C.: Associate Reformed Presbyterian Center, 1983.

Esquerita (ca. 1935–1986). Musician. Born Eskew Reeder, Jr., in Greenville, Esquerita was among the wildest musical acts to grace the formative years of rock and roll. A self-taught pianist, Esquerita performed initially in a local Baptist church, but by his late teens he had become the house rock and roll act at Greenville's Owl Club, performing as "Professor Eskew Reeder." Paul Peek, rhythm guitarist to the recording star Gene Vincent, discovered Esquerita and brought him to the attention of Capitol Records. Esquerita recorded twenty-eight songs for the label in 1958, twelve of which were released the following year as an LP titled *Esquerita!* Sporting a six-inch pompadour, rhinestone sunglasses, and a raucous yet rhythmic piano-playing style, Esquerita produced debut recordings that have been hailed by *All Music Guide* as "some of the most untamed and unabashed sides ever issued by a major label." Although his early recordings stand as classics among rock and roll aficionados, they did not bring Esquerita great success. Dropped by Capitol, he continued to record songs for minor labels throughout the 1960s, including a fledgling Motown label in 1963, most of which were never released. By the end of the decade he was recording under the moniker "The Magnificent Malochi." Little is known of his later activities, although some of his material was reissued in the 1970s and 1980s. He died in poverty in Harlem, New York, on October 23, 1986. TOM DOWNEY

Smith, Michael B. *Carolina Dreams: The Musical Legacy of Upstate South Carolina.* Beverly Hills, Calif.: Marshall Tucker Entertainment, 1997.

Eutaw Springs, Battle of (September 8, 1781). The Battle of Eutaw Springs was the last major engagement in South Carolina between American and British forces during the Revolutionary War. In the bloody encounter, some two thousand Continental and militia soldiers commanded by General Nathanael Greene clashed with 2,300 British regulars and Loyalists under Lieutenant Colonel Alexander Stewart. Although Greene was forced to leave the field, the British were equally mauled and retreated to Charleston, abandoning the South Carolina upcountry. The battle site is located in Orangeburg County near Eutawville, and a portion of the battlefield is a state historic site.

British forces were at Eutaw Springs on September 7, encamped near a sturdy two-story brick home with palisaded garden, when Greene completed the consolidation of his forces at Burdell's plantation about seven miles away. Early the following morning, Greene put his army on the march. Stewart was not aware that the Americans were so close, and he had that morning sent out foragers to collect sweet potatoes. Four miles from Eutaw Springs, the vanguard of the American army ran into the British escort protecting the rooting party. Many of the unarmed foragers were captured. Reacting quickly, Stewart sent forward additional troops to delay the Americans and formed his main army in a single line about two hundred yards west of his Eutaw Springs campgrounds. He anchored his right flank on Eutaw Creek with the brick house, occupied by a covering force, behind the line. Greene used a formation that had seen success at the Battle of Cowpens. The militiamen were placed in the front line, with the battle-hardened Continentals behind them in the second line. Advancing, the Americans pushed back the British skirmishers until they met the main body, at which point there began a bloody back-and-forth duel. Eventually the center of the American line began to buckle under the intense action, and Stewart directed an advance. But his forces became disorderly and Greene saw his opportunity. He ordered the Continentals forward in a bayonet attack that forced the British left flank to fall back and retreat through their campsite. On the verge of a major victory, many of the American troops thought the battle won and left the fighting to loot the British camp. This action cost Greene his victory, for the British right flank had not retreated and those secure in the house began a heavy fire, which threw the Americans into confusion and allowed Stewart to rally his troops for a counterattack. Greene got control of his troops before disaster struck, and behind a covering force they retreated back to Burdell's, leaving the field and two artillery pieces to the British. Losses on both sides were high: the British admitted to 683 killed, wounded, and missing; and the

Americans reported 517. Among the American unit commanders were many notable patriots, including Francis Marion; Otho Williams; William Washington, who was captured; Henry Lee; Andrew Pickens, who was wounded; and Wade Hampton. STEVEN D. SMITH

McCrady, Edward. *The History of South Carolina in the Revolution.* 2 vols. New York: Macmillan, 1901–1902.

Pancake, John S. *This Destructive War: The British Campaign in the Carolinas, 1780–1782.* University: University of Alabama Press, 1985.

Evangel Cathedral (Spartanburg). Evangel Cathedral of Spartanburg, one of the state's megachurches, has its roots in an old-fashioned tent revival in 1928. Participants in the revival founded an Assemblies of God church on Wofford Street. In 1968, when Houston Miles became pastor, membership was 175. A new revival, led by Venita Mack and organized by the Full Gospel Businessmen International (FGBI), took place in the church beginning in July 1971. After two weeks the FGBI pulled out, but the meetings continued for several months under the church's sponsorship. The revival dramatically changed the church. It became a center of the charismatic movement in the Southeast, a position it would maintain for several years. It also left the Assemblies of God to become nondenominational and became racially integrated, one of the first churches in the state to do so.

In 1973 the church moved to a location close to the intersection of Interstates 85 and 26. Continued growth led in 1988 to another move, to a sanctuary with a seating capacity of five thousand. As it has grown, Evangel Cathedral has had an impact worldwide. Informal networking with pastors in the 1970s culminated in the creation of Evangel Fellowship International (EFI), an umbrella organization and fellowship that includes hundreds of churches worldwide and functions effectively like a denominational structure. Although Miles retired from the senior pastorate of Evangel Cathedral in 1999, he continued to lead EFI. In 1999 membership was 2,500. Theologically, the church is evangelical. Its worship style is contemporary, making use of drama and multimedia presentations, and has left its Pentecostal roots behind. D. JONATHAN GRIESER

Evans, Emily Plume (?–1942). Suffragist, clubwoman. Evans was born in Waterbury, Connecticut, the daughter of the wealthy manufacturer, banker, and legislator David S. Plume and his wife, Abbie Richardson. Little is known about her early education. In 1895 South Carolina Governor John Gary Evans met Emily Plume on a visit to New York. They courted for two years. On December 15, 1897, after Evans left the governor's office, Emily Plume married him in Waterbury. The couple settled into a new home in Spartanburg and had one child, Emily Victoria.

Evans was active in activities at Spartanburg's Episcopal Church of the Advent and in the local chapter of the General Federation of Women's Clubs. In 1912 she and Helen G. Howland formed Spartanburg's first women's suffrage organization, the New Era Club. One of the organization's first actions was to wire President-elect Woodrow Wilson with an appeal to support voting rights for women.

Evans was also a founding member of the South Carolina Equal Suffrage League, formed in Spartanburg on May 15, 1915. She was elected vice president and later president of the state organization. Evans served as the South Carolina delegate to the National Women's Suffrage Association convention in Washington in 1915. Once Congress passed a suffrage amendment in 1917, Evans and other members of the South Carolina Equal Suffrage League vigorously lobbied lawmakers to vote for ratification, holding rallies in every congressional district. Ratification failed in the S.C. Senate in 1917, but South Carolina women received the right to vote in 1920 when Tennessee became the thirty-sixth state to ratify the Nineteenth Amendment, making it federal law. (South Carolina did not formally ratify the Nineteenth Amendment until 1969.) Later in 1920 Evans was a founding member of the League of Women Voters of South Carolina.

Evans was also active in efforts to improve working conditions for women and children in the state's textile mills. In 1916 she became chair of the Committee on Social and Industrial Conditions of the South Carolina Federation of Women's Clubs. She lobbied for the eight-hour day, more stringent child labor laws, and enforcement of the state's compulsory education laws. In addition, Evans was a president of Spartanburg's Florence Crittenden Circle, an organization devoted to "the prevention and correction of wayward girls."

At the end of her life, fearing the threat posed by the rise of the Nazi war machine, Evans lobbied South Carolina's congressional delegation to support an alliance between Britain and the United States. She died on April 4, 1942, and was buried in her husband's hometown of Edgefield. MELISSA WALKER

Elhassani, Joyce. "Emily Plume Evans." In *The Lives They Lived: A Look at Women in the History of Spartanburg,* edited by Linda Powers Bilanchone. Spartanburg, S.C.: Spartanburg Sesquicentennial Focus on Women Committee, 1981.

Evans, John Gary (1863–1942). Governor. Evans, a son of the Confederate general Nathan George Evans and Ann Victoria Gary, was born on October 15, 1863, in Cokesbury, Abbeville District, South Carolina. He attended Cokesbury Conference School and then entered Union College in Schenectady, New York, in 1879. Following the death of his uncle and guardian, Martin Witherspoon Gary, in 1881, Evans returned to the South and studied law in Augusta, Georgia. He was admitted to the bar in Georgia and South Carolina in 1885 and began practicing law in Aiken.

Though he was a lawyer rather than a farmer, Evans had strong ties to the "Reform" or "Farmers'" movement of Benjamin R. Tillman. He represented Aiken County in the House of Representatives from 1888 to 1891 and in the state Senate from 1892 to 1894. Known as a brilliant speaker and forceful politician, Evans quickly became a leader within the Tillman faction of the Democratic Party. He favored educational improvements, separate accommodations and schools for African Americans, the repeal of civil rights laws, a new constitution, and the establishment of a state dispensary system to control the sale of alcohol.

Evans was Tillman's choice to succeed him as governor in 1894. He was nominated at the "Reform" Democratic convention, which practically excluded conservative party members from the nominating process. On December 4, 1894, he was inaugurated as governor of South Carolina and became the youngest man ever to hold the office. Evans presided over the 1895 state constitutional convention that virtually disfranchised the state's black citizens, outlawed interracial marriages, and legalized school segregation. The convention also adopted an antilynching measure that he supported. The state was authorized to fine county governments up to$2,000 if a lynching occurred within its jurisdiction and if the county's law-enforcement authorities had been found negligent. Under Evans, the hiring out of state convicts ceased, and instead the state put prisoners to work on public roads. The state's economy was depressed under Evans's tenure due to cotton prices that fell as low as 4¢ per pound, but that was not the main reason for his unpopularity. Conservatives sneered that the procedure by which he was nominated was corrupt, and even many Tillman followers distrusted his motives for being a Tillmanite and opposed his strict enforcement of the unpopular dispensary laws.

In 1896 Evans lost a bid for the U.S. Senate. He moved to Spartanburg after the election and married Emily Mansfield Plume of Connecticut in 1897. He served as a major in the Spanish-American War and for a time as the military governor of Havana. He ran for the U.S. Senate three more times but was never elected. Although he remained active in public life for over two more decades, Evans served in only one other elected post: state representative for Spartanburg from 1923 to 1924. He died on June 26, 1942, in Spartanburg, survived by his wife and their one daughter. He was buried at Willowbrook Cemetery in Edgefield. ROD ANDREW, JR.

Bailey, N. Louise, Mary L. Morgan, and Carolyn R. Taylor, eds. *Biographical Directory of the South Carolina Senate, 1776–1985.* 3 vols. Columbia: University of South Carolina Press, 1986.

Hendrick, Carlanna Lindamood. "John Gary Evans: A Political Biography." Ph.D. diss., University of South Carolina, 1966.

Evans, Josiah James (1786–1858). Jurist, U.S. senator. Born on November 27, 1786, in Marlboro District, Evans was of Welsh descent and the son of Thomas Evans, a prominent Revolutionary War soldier and early South Carolina legislator, and Elizabeth Hodges. He received his early academic training in Fayetteville, North Carolina, and graduated third in his class from South Carolina College in 1808. He then studied law under his brother-in-law and was admitted to the bar on November 28, 1811. On Christmas Day 1813 Evans married Dorothy DeWitt of Society Hill. The marriage produced five children. Evans began accumulating land in Marlboro, Chesterfield, and Darlington Districts and eventually acquired more than 220 slaves.

Evans was elected to the S.C. House of Representatives from Marlboro District in 1812. He was returned to the legislature by Darlington District in 1816 but resigned following his election as solicitor for the Northern Circuit, an office to which he was returned several times without opposition. Simultaneous with his legislative service, Evans served as commissioner and register in equity for the Northern Circuit and as an aide to Governor Joseph Alston. In 1818 Evans was elected as a South Carolina College trustee, a position he held for thirty-four years.

In 1829 Evans was appointed judge of the Court of General Sessions and Common Pleas, serving on that court until 1835 and thereafter on the appellate court until 1852. While a judge, Evans authored a digest of South Carolina statute law published as *Road Law* in 1850, but his claim to legal renown was his involvement as the leading advocate in sustaining the will of Mason Lee. Lee, an eccentric bachelor who owned a large tract of land on the Pee Dee River, directed that the principal part of his property be given to the states of Tennessee and South Carolina, rather than to the Wiggins, his natural heirs at law. The heirs contested the will on the ground that Lee was a mental imbecile. The will further directed, however, that if the heirs should contest the provisions of the will, Lee's executor, state senator Robeson Carloss, should employ the best legal talent in the state to uphold its provisions. Carloss employed Evans as lead counsel. The will was upheld in what became a test for testamentary capacity and legal competency in the state and is one of the most legendary cases cited in South Carolina legal history.

The South Carolina legislature elected Evans to the U.S. Senate in 1852 as a Democrat to succeed Senator William F. DeSaussure. During his six years in the Senate, he chaired both the Committee to Audit and Control the Contingent Expense and the Committee on Revolutionary Claims. Although a supporter of states' rights and strong defender of his native state against the virulent attacks of Massachusetts senator Charles Sumner, Evans did not support disunion.

Evans died on May 6, 1858, in Washington, D.C. A portrait, inscribed by Matthew Brady, hangs at the Darlington County Historical Commission, and Evans Correctional Institution in Bennettsville bears his name. He was interred in a private cemetery at his home in Society Hill. JOHN L. NAPIER

Bailey, N. Louise, ed. *Biographical Directory of the South Carolina House of Representatives.* Vol. 4, *1791–1815.* Columbia: University of South Carolina Press, 1984.

O'Neall, John Belton. *Biographical Sketches of the Bench and Bar of South Carolina.* 2 vols. Charleston, S.C.: S. G. Courtney, 1859.

Thomas, J. A. W. *A History of Marlboro County, with Traditions and Sketches of Numerous Families.* 1897. Reprint, Baltimore: Regional Publishing, 1971.

Evans, Matilda Arabella (1872–1935). Physician. Evans was born in Aiken on May 13, 1872, the daughter of Anderson Evans and Hariett Corley. Determined to obtain an education, Evans secured admission to the Schofield Normal and Industrial School. The founder of the school, Martha Schofield, encouraged Evans to attend classes in Oberlin College's preparatory department from 1887 to 1891. Evans later wrote a biography of her mentor, *Martha Schofield, Pioneer Negro Educator* (1916).

Evans developed an interest in medicine and aspired to become a foreign medical missionary. From 1891 to 1893 she taught at Schofield, saving money to enroll in the Women's Medical College of Pennsylvania at Philadelphia. The sole African American student in her class, Evans graduated in 1897. Aware of the inadequate health care available for South Carolina blacks, she decided to improve medical care and sanitation in her home state, becoming Columbia's first female physician.

Because southern blacks suffered high mortality rates due to insufficient health care and neglect, Evans decided that hospitals were the greatest need. She treated both black and white patients in her home and organized the Columbia Clinic Association. By 1901 Evans had stopped her private practice to establish and serve as superintendent of the Taylor Lane Hospital and Training School for Nurses, Columbia's first black hospital. Patients came from as far away as North Carolina and Georgia, and Evans sometimes drove patients in her wagon to the hospital. She emphasized training of African American nurses. Her clinic assured public access to free health care and education. Patients could see specialists, including a dentist, and receive vaccinations. Evans was particularly concerned about black children, approximately half of whom needed health care. She generously paid for examinations of African American public-school students and convinced schools to employ regular physicals.

Focusing on preventative medicine, Evans established the Negro Health Care Association of South Carolina with the goal of placing a black nurse in each county. Although Evans did not accomplish that objective, she realized the need to deliver medical information services directly to people's homes.

During the Depression, Evans concentrated on providing maternity and infant health care after federal funds for those services ceased. Assisted by black businessmen, in 1932 she opened the

Evans Clinic in Columbia. The state board of health and the Richland County Health Department offered support that enabled the clinic to schedule regular hours. Evans's walk-in clinics and hospital were the first available for many Deep South blacks and alerted them to improved health practices.

Admired for her patient advocacy and humanitarian work to improve living standards, Evans was president of the Palmetto State Medical Society. She also organized and served as president of the Colored Congaree Medical Society. She created a weekly paper, *The Negro Health Journal of South Carolina.* Evans sought financial support for black women to attend medical school, emphasizing that she needed more graduate physicians to staff her hospital. After her sister died, Evans raised her five children. Evans died on November 17, 1935, in Columbia and was buried in that city's Palmetto Cemetery. ELIZABETH D. SCHAFER

Beardsley, Edward H. *A History of Neglect: Health Care for Blacks and Mill Workers in the Twentieth-Century South.* Knoxville: University of Tennessee Press, 1987.

Hine, Darlene Clark. "The Corporeal and Ocular Veil: Dr. Matilda A. Evans (1872–1935) and the Complexity of Southern History." *Journal of Southern History* 70 (February 2004): 3–34.

Sterling, Dorothy, ed. *We Are Your Sisters: Black Women in the Nineteenth Century.* New York: Norton, 1984.

Tindall, George Brown. *South Carolina Negroes, 1877–1900.* 1952. Reprint, Columbia: University of South Carolina Press, 2003.

Everett, Percival (b. 1956). Author, editor, educator. Everett was born at Fort Gordon, Georgia, on December 22, 1956, the son of Percival Leonard, a dentist, and his wife, Dorothy Stinson. He was raised in Columbia, South Carolina, where he graduated from A.C. Flora High School before earning a bachelor's degree from the University of Miami in 1977 and—after two years of postgraduate study at the University of Oregon—a master's degree from Brown University in 1982.

Everett drew on his experiences as a young African American growing up in Columbia in his first novel, *Suder* (1983), which received laudatory reviews across the United States. Though the novel's black protagonist is a professional baseball player in the Pacific Northwest, much of the narrative is given over to memories of his Carolina childhood.

The critical success of *Suder* helped gain Everett the position of professor of English and director of the creative writing program at the University of Kentucky (1985–1989). He then taught at the University of Notre Dame before moving to California in 1992, where he taught first at the University of California at Riverside and then at the University of Southern California. In addition to his writing and teaching, Everett has long served as an editor of the distinguished literary journal *Callaloo,* which publishes critical studies of and original works by black writers from around the world. Despite his long absence from South Carolina, he involved himself in state politics when he unexpectedly spoke out against the presence of the Confederate flag atop the State House while participating in both the Elizabeth O'Neill Verner Awards ceremonies and the Spoleto Festival in 1989.

Though some of his fiction since *Suder,* such as *Walk Me to the Distance* (1985), draws at least partly on southern origins and themes, Everett's creative work has more generally focused on the American West or—as in *Zulus* (1989), set in a postapocalyptic future—more imagined settings. As a black southern writer in exile, Everett might be favorably compared with Oklahoma's Ralph Ellison, with whom he also shares an abiding interest in European and African myth as well as a staunch refusal to limit African American fiction to mere "protest writing." While *Suder,* for example, contains satirical indictments of southern racism, *Erasure* (2002)—favorably reviewed across the United States and abroad—ultimately condemns a publishing industry that favors grim portraits of black ghetto life over stories told by African American authors who try to transcend or ignore racial boundaries. The frustrated writer-protagonist of this novel, a man who has intellectually escaped from confining notions of race but finds he must peddle stereotypical images of black life in order to sell his books, clearly bears a close resemblance to Everett. FARRELL O'GORMAN

Starr, William W. "Artists Make Statements at Spoleto." Columbia *State,* June 4, 1989, p. F1.

———. "Author Everett Prizes Privacy." Columbia *State,* May 29, 1994, p. F1.

———. "Flag Issue Flies Anew." Columbia *State,* May 7, 1989, p. D2.

Exchange Building (Charleston). One of the grandest and most significant public buildings constructed in colonial America, the Exchange and Customs House at 122 East Bay was designed by William Rigby Naylor in 1766 and constructed by Peter and John Adam Horlbeck between 1767 and 1771 on the site of the earlier "Court of Guard" and Half-Moon Battery. The original design included a cellar, a first-floor open arcaded piazza, and a large second-floor assembly room. The roof was hipped with a parapet and lead-coated cupola.

During the colonial era, royal governors were greeted at the east portico, the front of the building facing Charleston harbor. On December 3, 1773, a large gathering of Charlestonians met there to protest British tea taxes. While the British occupied Charleston from 1780 to 1782, many prominent citizens were confined in the cellar as political and military prisoners. After 1783 the Exchange became City Hall and was the site of South Carolina's convention to ratify the federal Constitution in 1788. The building also hosted visits to Charleston by George Washington in 1791 and the Marquis de Lafayette in 1825. Later architectural changes included removal of the west stair wings, enclosure of the arcaded piazza, and stuccoing of the Flemish bond exterior. For much of the nineteenth century it served as a post office.

Threatened by demolition, the Exchange became the property of the Rebecca Motte Chapter of the Daughters of the American

The plans for the west elevation (land side) of the Exchange Building in Charleston. Courtesy, South Carolina Department of Archives and History

Revolution in 1921. It was designated a National Historic Landmark in 1975. Since 1976 the building has been administered by the Old Exchange Building Commission. A renovation undertaken as part of the American bicentennial observance returned the building to use in 1981. The Exchange Building was subsequently operated as a museum dedicated to the preservation and interpretation of the history of the Old Exchange, the city of Charleston, and colonial and antebellum America. JOHN LAURENS

Miller, Ruth, and Ann Taylor Andras. *Witness to History: Charleston's Old Exchange and Provost Dungeon.* Orangeburg, S.C.: Sandlapper, 1986.

Poston, Jonathan H. *The Buildings of Charleston: A Guide to the City's Architecture.* Columbia: University of South Carolina Press, 1997.

Executive Councils (1861–1862). The secession of South Carolina on December 20, 1860, necessitated state assumption of responsibilities formerly carried out by the federal government. To assist the governor, the Secession Convention passed an ordinance on December 27, 1860, establishing the Executive Council, consisting of the governor, the lieutenant governor, and four persons appointed by the governor and confirmed by the convention. Governor Francis W. Pickens appointed David F. Jamison, Andrew G. Magrath, Christopher G. Memminger, and Albert C. Garlington to the council, which met and organized on January 3, 1861. The Executive Council was modeled on the federal cabinet, and administrative duties were divided by function. Magrath assumed the duties of foreign affairs; Jamison, war; Memminger, treasury; and Garlington, interior affairs. Lieutenant Governor William W. Harllee was given responsibility for postal and custom matters. On February 2 Pickens appointed Edward Frost to replace Memminger, who had been elected to the Montgomery Convention.

The council met almost daily through early March. The formation of the Confederate government lessened the need for the council, and on April 8 the convention directed the governor to relieve the members as soon as public necessity allowed. Although the Executive Council no longer met, some members continued their duties through the end of the year. As late as February 1862, Wilmot G. DeSaussure, who had replaced Edward Frost in June 1861, was still actively seeking reimbursement from the Confederate government for funds expended in defending Charleston harbor.

The Union invasion of Port Royal in November 1861 and the Charleston fire the following month led to public questioning of Pickens's leadership. In response, the reconvened Secession Convention on January 7, 1862, created a council to exercise executive power. The new body was composed of the governor, the lieutenant governor, and three members elected by the convention. The convention provided the Executive Council with a broad range of power to conduct affairs related to the war effort, including matters of martial law, impressment, conscription, and war-material production.

James Chesnut, Jr., Attorney General Isaac W. Hayne, and William H. Gist were elected to the council by the convention and exerted considerable influence. Chesnut suggested that the council create several administrative departments. He became chief of the military department, effectively supplanting Governor Pickens as commander in chief. Hayne headed the Department of Justice and Police. Gist and Harllee jointly ran the Department of Treasury and Finance. On March 24 Gist became the chief of the newly created Department of Construction and Manufacturing.

Although effective in marshaling the state's meager resources for a concerted war effort, the Executive Council engendered widespread opposition because of its extralegal nature and concentrated power. Pickens and his supporters felt that the council illegally usurped his constitutional authority, although he actively participated in council proceedings through the fall of 1862. On September 17, 1862, the Secession Convention left the Executive Council's fate in the hands of the legislature. The legislature abolished the Executive Council on December 18, 1862, and invalidated all of its actions except fiscal contracts. PATRICK MCCAWLEY

Cauthen, Charles E. *South Carolina Goes to War, 1860–1865.* Chapel Hill: University of North Carolina Press, 1950.

———, ed. *Journals of the South Carolina Executive Councils of 1861 and 1862.* Columbia: South Carolina Archives Department, 1956.

F

Fairfax (Allendale County; 2000 pop. 3,206). The origins of Fairfax can be traced back to the site of Owen's Store, which was located at the crossing of roads running toward Augusta and Orangeburg; the site is beside the Fairfax Cemetery. The cemetery is the site of Bethlehem Baptist Church, which was organized by 1854, relocated in 1914, and renamed First Baptist Church in 1944. Other white congregations organized a Methodist church in the 1850s and a Lutheran church in 1898. Black congregations organized Nazarene Baptist Church in 1877, Bethel AME about 1878, and St. Phillip Baptist Church in 1891.

The first postmaster was appointed around 1870, with the post office called Sanders. The Port Royal Railroad, an east-west line, began operation through the town in 1873. The train stop was called Campbellton Station. To consolidate Sanders and Campbellton, proposed names were placed in a hat and a child drew "Fairfax." The town received its first charter on December 26, 1893. Fairfax was incorporated in 1896 with W. J. Sanders as mayor. The town was rechartered on May 16, 1898.

When the Florida Central Railroad put in a north-south line, commerce clustered around the junction. F. M. Young built the first brick store and also operated a telephone company, generated electricity, ginned cotton, extracted cotton oil, and made ice. F. M. Young, Jr., whose tasks in the family business included wiring houses for Delco generators, started an electrical contracting business in 1928 that later specialized in large projects such as schools and commercial buildings. W. J. Young was an esteemed physician. His wife, Virginia Durant Young, was a suffragette and author who operated the *Fairfax Enterprise* in the 1890s. The Youngs willed their house and books to the town as a library. The house, circa 1881, is listed in the National Register of Historic Places. Dr. Young also bequeathed the nucleus of the funding for the Allendale County Hospital and required that it be located in Fairfax.

G. S. O'Neal started the Standard Oil Operations in town in 1890. Bell Telephone Company built lines to Fairfax in 1906. By the mid-1900s several manufacturing and processing plants had been established, the Pal Theater opened, and civic organizations were formed. Town Hall was constructed in 1940. Fairfax offered motels, filling stations, restaurants, and bus stops for travelers on U.S. Highways 321 and 278.

The first African American on the Fairfax Town Council, Quillie Devore, served from 1969 to 1990. An African American woman, Olivia Cohen, served as mayor from 1987 to 1995. The Sprint-Fairfax Operation, the first of three high-tech telecommunications facilities, was built in 1986. The Allendale Correctional Institute opened in 1989, and its inmates represented 35.2 percent of Fairfax's population in 2000. Merchants still sell hardware, groceries, fuel, and farm supplies in Fairfax. Highway traffic hums through the crossroads, trains rumble down the north-south and east-west tracks, and technicians route signals through telecommunications networks. DANIEL MCDONALD JOHNSON

Lawton, Alexania Easterling, and Minnie Reeves Wilson. *Allendale on the Savannah.* Bamberg, S.C.: Bamberg Herald Printers, 1970.

Loadholt, Adrienne. *Centennial Celebration, 1893–1993, Town of Fairfax, South Carolina.* Fairfax, S.C.: Town of Fairfax, 1993.

Fairfield County (687 sq. miles; 2000 pop. 23,454). Fairfield County, lying in the lower Piedmont, is a geologically diverse region with topography ranging from level plains to hilly terrain. The county lies primarily between the Broad and Wateree Rivers north of Richland County. Originally part of the 1769 court district of Camden, the area became Fairfield District in 1800 and then Fairfield County in 1868.

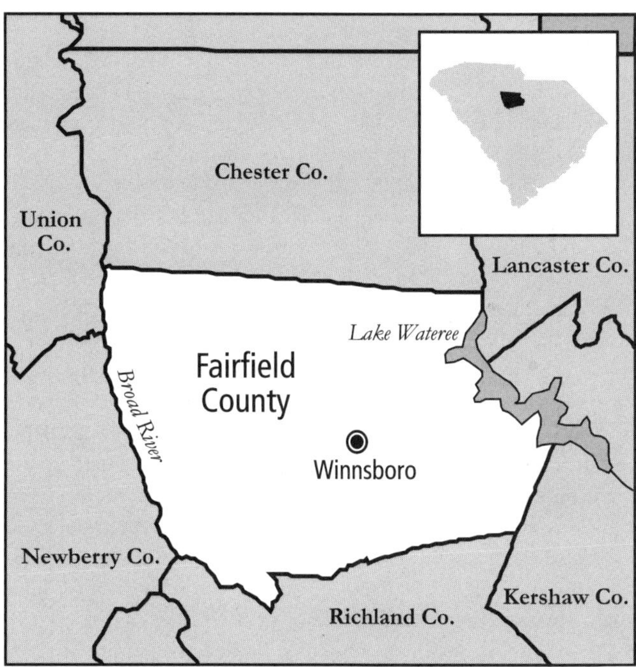

Mississippian mound builders were active in the Fairfield region from 1300 to 1400 C.E. At the time of European settlement, the Catawba and other Native Americans possibly used the area as a hunting preserve. The first Europeans arrived between 1740 and 1770 and settled along the Broad, Wateree, and Little Rivers. In 1740 Thomas Nightingale, an early settler, established a cowpen on Little River near the site of the future county seat of Winnsboro. Some of these early Europeans came overland from Charleston, while others traveled down the Great Wagon Road from Pennsylvania and Virginia. Most settlers engaged in trapping, hunting, and raising livestock.

During the 1760s Fairfield was a center of Regulator activity, as Thomas Woodward and other upcountry South Carolinians sought to curb lawlessness and create a circuit court system. Agitation by the Regulators led to the passage of the Circuit Court Act of 1769 and the creation of Camden District. The Regulator quest for justice carried over into strong sentiments for independence. The Fairfield area produced patriot leaders including General Richard Winn (namesake of the county seat of Winnsboro), Captain Thomas Woodward, Captain James Kincaid, and Major John Pearson.

Fairfield was the site of several important engagements during the Revolutionary War. In 1780 patriots under the command of Colonel William Bratton, Major Richard Winn, and Captain John McClure routed a Tory force at Mobley's meetinghouse, one of the first patriot victories following the British occupation of Charlestown. Other battles fought in Fairfield took place at Rocky Mount, Caldwell's Place, and Dutchman's Creek. The British commander Lord Cornwallis occupied Winnsboro from October 1780 to early January 1781. Tradition holds that the county derived its name from Cornwallis's exclamation "What fair fields!"

Early settlers established Presbyterian, Baptist, Associate Reformed, and interdenominational centers of worship. Many of the Scots-Irish Covenanters who followed the Reverend William Martin to South Carolina are interred in the graveyard of Richmond Covenanter Church. The Reverend Philip Mulkey brought Separate Baptist beliefs to Fairfield. His preaching led to the establishment of several Baptist churches in the backcountry. In 1803 the Associate Reformed (Presbyterian) Synod of South Carolina was organized at the Old Brick Church near Jenkinsville.

In addition to religion, the early settlers were interested in education. In the 1780s the Mount Zion Society, organized in Charleston in 1777, established a school for boys in Winnsboro. Other residents founded the Feasterville Female and Male Academy in 1842. In 1837 Furman Institution moved from Stateburg to Winnsboro.

Following the Revolution, agriculture increased in importance. The production of small grains flourished initially, but with the introduction of the cotton gin Fairfield became a major producer of short-staple cotton. The growth of cotton production led to an increase in the number of slaves. By 1840 Fairfield planters were among the largest cotton producers and slaveowners in the Midlands and contributed heavily to the construction of the Charlotte and South Carolina Railroad through the district in the early 1850s. Despite cotton prosperity, the white population declined in the antebellum period as residents sought fresh lands in the West. By 1850 African slaves comprised two-thirds of the district's population.

The secession movement thrived in cotton-dependent Fairfield, and four prominent residents—including former governor John Hugh Means—signed the Ordinance of Secession. Approximately two thousand Fairfield men enlisted in Confederate service. In February 1865 three columns of Sherman's army crossed Fairfield and destroyed much property, including some buildings in Winnsboro and Ridgeway. Also in February 1865 the Confederate general P. G. T. Beauregard, after evacuating Columbia, briefly used the Century House in Ridgeway as his headquarters.

Following the Civil War, African Americans in Fairfield sought educational opportunities and independent places of worship. Educators founded the Fairfield Institute in 1869. Before merging with Brainerd Institute in Chester, the school had grown to one hundred students. Kelly Miller, professor and dean at Howard University, was a student at the Fairfield Institute. Also, African Americans organized St. Paul's Baptist Church in 1873, and members of the African Methodist Episcopal Church established the Camp Welfare camp meeting by 1876.

The importance of agriculture persisted in post–Civil War Fairfield and only began to wane in the 1950s. Commercial districts developed in Winnsboro during Reconstruction and in Ridgeway in the early twentieth century. The post–Civil War period also brought economic diversification with the Winnsboro Granite Company and systematic granite quarrying, the Rockton and Rion Railroad, textile manufacturing, and timber and pulpwood production. Fairfield Blue Granite, a valuable county resource, is considered the "silk of the trade." Also, Shivar Springs Bottling Company operated from ca. 1900 to ca. 1950, bottling first mineral water and later soft drinks. Fairfield County, home of Sumter National Forest, is one of South Carolina's leading pulpwood producers. In the mid-1900s Parr Shoals on the Broad River was the first nuclear power facility in the Southeast. The acquisition of Mack Trucks in the 1980s was hailed as a boon to the Fairfield economy, but the plant was closed in 2002. Despite subsequent economic setbacks, Fairfield County strives to preserve its historic character and structures through the creation of historic districts, to develop a viable tourist industry, and to provide educational and occupational opportunities for its residents. ALEXIA JONES HELSLEY

Bellardo, Lewis. "A Social and Economic History of Fairfield County, South Carolina, 1865–1871." Ph.D. diss., University of Kentucky, 1979.

Bolick, Julian Stevenson. *A Fairfield Sketchbook.* Clinton, S.C.: Jacobs, 1963.

McMaster, Fitz Hugh. *History of Fairfield County, South Carolina: From "Before the White Man Came" to 1942.* 1946. Reprint, Spartanburg, S.C.: Reprint Company, 1980.

Farmers' Alliance. Organized in Texas in the late 1870s, the National Farmers' Alliance and Industrial Union, along with its segregated counterpart the Colored Farmers' National Alliance, addressed the problems of debt and depressed commodity prices that confronted much of rural America. From Texas, the Alliance spread rapidly across the South and the Great Plains in the 1880s. "Travelling lecturers" established a network of suballiances that educated local farmers on Alliance programs. In particular, Alliance leaders advocated cooperative enterprises, such as bulk purchasing or marketing exchanges, which would bypass merchants and other "middlemen" who siphoned off farmers' income. As it grew, the Alliance gave rise to a defiant agrarian consciousness across the South.

In South Carolina, the Alliance movement "swept over our state like a wave" in the late 1880s, first appearing in the Pee Dee region. The state's first county alliance was organized in Marion County in 1887, followed by a statewide South Carolina Alliance in July 1888 and a Colored Farmers' Alliance in June 1889. By 1890 over one thousand suballiances existed in the state, which claimed over eighty thousand members, black and white.

To provide an alternative to the oppressive crop lien system, the South Carolina Alliance established a state exchange (a central retail market) in Greenville in 1889, which moved to Columbia in 1891. The exchange amassed $225,000 in capital and a $17,000 surplus in 1894. But by operating on a cash-only basis, the benefits of the exchange reached only a limited number of farmers. Less successful commercial ventures included over twenty cooperative enterprises, among them warehouses, stores, publishing companies, and a planned Alliance bank. But Alliance men lacked business expertise and capital, and their commercial ventures seldom succeeded. The Alliance exchange in Columbia closed in 1899.

The Alliance's economic focus soon included political action. The state Alliance organized a successful boycott of jute bagging from 1888 to 1890, forcing a decline in jute prices and demonstrating the potential influence of the organization. By 1890 the Alliance provided a forum for anti-Bourbon politicians as Alliance man Ben Tillman was elected governor, state Alliance president Eli T. Stackhouse was elected to Congress, and almost a third of state legislators were Alliance members. In office, Tillman remained an Alliance member but emphasized his own organization, the Farmers' Association, as the responsible alternative to conservative Democrats. Frustrated with the unwillingness of Tillman and other "Alliance Democrats'" to act on Alliance demands, Alliance leaders began to advocate a third party.

No South Carolina Alliance member was present at the 1892 St. Louis Convention, where the Farmers' Alliance endorsed the People's Party and the language and agenda that came to be known as populism. Tillman abhorred populism's biracial appeal and third-party tactics but needed Alliance support to promote his own ambitions. Campaigning for reelection in 1892, Tillman neutralized the ideological influence of the Alliance and co-opted its organizational strength into his political machine. Once back in office, Tillman subsumed the state Alliance's political identity into his Democratic faction and did little to advance the Alliance's agenda. The Alliance soon collapsed in South Carolina, with the populist presidential ticket receiving just 2,410 votes statewide in 1892. The demise of the Farmers' Alliance reflected the difficulty of establishing a biracial political movement in South Carolina and was a harbinger of the movement's fate throughout the South. ELI A. POLIAKOFF

Church, Joseph. "The Farmers' Alliance and the Populist Movement in South Carolina (1887–1896)." Master's thesis, University of South Carolina, 1953.

Goodwyn, Lawrence. *The Populist Moment: A Short History of the Agrarian Revolt in America.* New York: Oxford University Press, 1978.

Kantrowitz, Stephen. *Ben Tillman and the Reconstruction of White Supremacy.* Chapel Hill: University of North Carolina Press, 2000.

McMath, Robert C., Jr. *Populist Vanguard: A History of the Southern Farmers' Alliance.* Chapel Hill: University of North Carolina Press, 1975.

Farmers' and Exchange Bank (Charleston). Completed in 1854, the Farmers' and Exchange Bank is among the finest examples of the Moorish-revival style in the United States. It was one of several bank buildings designed by the architectural firm of Jones and Lee in the mid-1850s as Charleston's financial district expanded northward up East Bay Street. Whereas Charleston banking institutions had traditionally favored conservatively styled buildings, the directors of the Farmers' and Exchange Bank made a radical departure in introducing the city to the most flamboyant of the nineteenth-century exotic revivals.

The bank was designed by the architect Francis D. Lee, who described it as "Saracenic" in style. The two-story facade is arranged in a three-bay format and clad in mottled New Jersey and Connecticut brownstone. Its exuberant ornamentation includes rounded horseshoe arches and Eastern-inspired decorative motifs. The mass of the cornice is formed by muquarnas, or honeycomb vaulting, a common feature in Islamic architecture. On the interior a paved vestibule leads to the main banking room. This opulent space is twenty-one feet wide and nearly fifty feet in length and features arcaded walls, elaborate plaster ornamentation, and a coffered ceiling and skylight.

In a city known for its traditional architecture, the Farmers' and Exchange Bank is a bold and striking anomaly. The building was designated a National Historic Landmark by the U.S. Department of the Interior in 1973. It remains in private ownership. DANIEL J. VIVIAN

Lane, Mills. *Architecture of the Old South: South Carolina.* Savannah, Ga.: Beehive, 1984.

Poston, Jonathan H. *The Buildings of Charleston: A Guide to the City's Architecture.* Columbia: University of South Carolina Press, 1997.

Severens, Kenneth. *Charleston Antebellum Architecture and Civic Destiny.* Knoxville: University of Tennessee Press, 1988.

Farmers' Association. The Farmers' Association was the vehicle for Benjamin Ryan Tillman's political ambitions in the mid-1880s. Farmers' clubs or agricultural improvement groups already existed across the state; Tillman hoped to unite them in supporting his goals of agricultural, educational, and governmental reform while challenging the ruling conservative wing of the Democratic Party.

Tillman canvassed the state, speaking at local clubs and getting editorials printed and reprinted in newspapers. The response was substantial. In Newberry County hundreds of farmers turned out for the convention of the Jalapa Farmers' Club in March 1886. Other clubs received similar response or were created throughout the spring and summer of 1886. The Farmers' Association held its first statewide meeting in Columbia in April 1886. All of the delegates were white—and Tillman made it clear that the Farmers' Association was for whites only—but some conservative Democrats were present.

Although the association's early rhetoric claimed that it was separate from the Democratic Party, it quickly became a means for Tillman to preempt the party's movements. In Darlington County the same man was vice president of the county Democratic Party convention and the county Farmers' Association convention. Farmers' Association groups often met before local Democratic Party conventions and determined the slates of candidates to be proposed at the party functions. By early 1887 Democratic Party and Farmers' Association groups met at the same time or association representatives simply took control of party proceedings.

The relationship between the two groups did not always work to Tillman's advantage. Conservative Democrats initially held off the Tillman challenge, and at the end of 1887 the Farmers' Association was struggling. Two events helped revitalize the movement. First, the founding of Clemson College in 1888 meant that Tillman could claim he had achieved one of his long-standing goals. Second, the nationwide growth of the Farmers' Alliance movement sparked new enthusiasm for grassroots organizing among South Carolina's farmers. The progressive Farmers' Alliance drew members from the Farmers' Association, and the leadership of the two groups overlapped.

Tillman's work at local organizing paid off in 1890. In January, Farmers' Association president G. W. Shell urged farmers to hold a nominating convention separate from that of the Democratic Party. A convention was held in March, and after some engineering by Tillman's associates, the convention agreed to nominate candidates. Tillman was "nominated" as a candidate for governor despite the fact that his name was not put up to vote.

The "Shell Manifesto" and Tillman's nomination threw into sharp relief the formerly blurry lines separating the Farmers' Alliance, the Farmers' Association, and the Democratic Party when the last two groups did not endorse the March convention. But conservative Democrats were unable to agree on a single candidate to oppose Tillman and found their local organizations overmatched by the Farmers' Association. Tillman's grasp of the nomination in August 1890 proved the effectiveness of his local organization. Although the Farmers' Association had initially claimed distance from politics, in reality it effectively helped propel Tillman to the governorship. AARON W. MARRS

Cooper, William J., Jr. *The Conservative Regime: South Carolina, 1877–1890.* Baltimore: Johns Hopkins Press, 1968.

Kantrowitz, Stephen. *Ben Tillman and the Reconstruction of White Supremacy.* Chapel Hill: University of North Carolina Press, 2000.

Farrow, Samuel (1759–1824). Congressman, legislator, reformer. Born in Virginia in 1759, Farrow was the son of John Farrow and Rosannah Waters. The family moved to South Carolina a few years after his birth, settling near Spartanburg in Ninety Six District. Farrow fought for the patriot cause in the Revolutionary War and achieved the rank of colonel. He had little formal education, but fellow lawyer John Belton O'Neall recalled him as the most dedicated and persistent member of the bar and praised his persuasive ability. After the Revolution, Farrow became a Democratic-Republican. In 1794 or 1795 he married Elizabeth Herndon of Newberry. They had no children. He was elected lieutenant governor in 1810 and a U.S. congressman in 1812. In 1816 Spartanburg District elected Farrow to the South Carolina House of Representatives, where he pursued a goal he had conceived several years before: the creation of a state lunatic asylum.

Initially, Farrow made little progress in this endeavor because of the state's preoccupation with the events leading to the War of 1812. In the postwar years, however, political and economic conditions were more favorable to the asylum initiative. In 1817 the state began to implement an ambitious scheme of public works. The following year the state House of Representatives approved Farrow's motion to appoint a special committee to investigate the condition of the insane in South Carolina. The committee, which Farrow chaired, reported that the state contained numerous lunatics who needed the protection and care an asylum would provide. The legislature, with little dissent, passed several resolutions calling for the construction of an asylum in Columbia. But the act to establish the institution was delayed by the financial panic of 1819, a budget deficit, and legislative opposition to expensive public projects. In 1820 Farrow tried but failed to get an asylum act through the General Assembly. The following year he was not reelected to the House, but his ally William Crafts, Jr., of Charleston secured a seat in the state Senate and succeeded in achieving Farrow's goal. In 1822 Farrow was reelected to the House and appointed to the legislative commission to oversee the asylum's construction. He did not live to see it completed. He died in Columbia on November 18, 1824, and was buried at Head's Ford on the Enoree River in Spartanburg District. The asylum that he had fought so hard to establish did not open until 1828. PETER MCCANDLESS

McCandless, Peter. *Moonlight, Magnolias, and Madness: Insanity in South Carolina from the Colonial Period to the Progressive Era.* Chapel Hill: University of North Carolina Press, 1996.

Moore, Alexander, ed. *Biographical Directory of the South Carolina House of Representatives.* Vol. 5, *1816–1828.* Columbia: South Carolina Department of Archives and History, 1992.

O'Neall, John Belton. *Biographical Sketches of the Bench and Bar of South Carolina.* 2 vols. Charleston, S.C.: S. G. Courtney, 1859.

Trezevant, Daniel. *Letters to His Excellency Governor Manning on the Lunatic Asylum.* 1854. Reprint, New York: Arno, 1973.

Fayssoux, Peter (ca. 1745–1795). Physician. Fayssoux was born and grew up in Charleston, the son of Daniel Fayssoux, a Huguenot émigré, and his wife Frances. In 1766 Fayssoux went to medical school in Edinburgh, where he was a classmate of Benjamin Rush. Returning to South Carolina in 1769, he found the city full of quacks: "It is Sufficient for a man to call himself a Doctor, & he immediately becomes one, & finds fools to employ him," he complained to Rush. On January 29, 1772, Fayssoux married Sarah "Sally" Wilson, who died in 1776. The following year, on March 29, 1777, Fayssoux married Ann Smith Johnston. The marriages produced thirteen children, six of whom died in infancy or early childhood.

Early in the Revolutionary War, Fayssoux attended the sick on James Island and provided advice on extracting salt from seawater. By 1778 he was serving as "senior physician" of the South Carolina branch of the Continental army, having been appointed by Dr. David Oliphant, director of the hospital. Fayssoux was with General William Moultrie at the Battle of Sullivan's Island on June 28, 1776. In 1779, when Moultrie repulsed a British force threatening Beaufort, Fayssoux was given the task of remaining with the sick until Moultrie could supply the necessary carriages to remove them. In 1780 Fayssoux was named physician and surgeon general of the Southern Department. Captured at the fall of Charleston, he was released in order to attend to the sick and wounded in the city. After the Battle of Eutaw Springs on September 8, 1781, the responsibility for the wounded fell to Fayssoux. At the end of the war Fayssoux was treating the sick and wounded in Camden, where he stayed until March 1782.

After the war Fayssoux became a member of the Faculty of Physic in Charleston, which was the first evidence of organized medicine in South Carolina. Along with Alexander Baron and David Ramsay, Fayssoux comprised the organizing committee charged with reporting a plan to improve "the Science of Medicine . . . amongst the Practitioners in this City." He was a founding member and the first president of the Medical Society of South Carolina, which held its first meeting at Fayssoux's home on December 24, 1789. Though he made no literary contributions to medicine, his leadership in the early organization of medicine and his contributions to the Revolution placed him among the major medical figures of his time. His peers described Fayssoux as "possessed of a clear discriminating judgment" and as a skillful practitioner of "the Healing Art."

In 1786 Fayssoux was elected to the General Assembly, where he represented St. John's Berkeley Parish until 1790. He voted against ratification of the federal Constitution in 1788 but afterward accepted the new government amicably. In addition to his medical and political activities, Fayssoux was involved with the Charleston Library Society, the Charleston Museum (as a curator), the Society of the Cincinnati (founding member), and the St. Cecilia Society. He died on February 1, 1795, of apoplectic stroke and was buried in the churchyard of First (Scots) Presbyterian Church, Charleston. JANE MCCUTCHEN BROWN

Davidson, Chalmers G. *Friend of the People: The Life of Dr. Peter Fayssoux of Charleston, South Carolina.* Columbia: Medical Association of South Carolina, 1950.

Waring, Joseph I. *History of Medicine in South Carolina.* Vol. 1, *1670–1825.* Columbia: South Carolina Medical Association, 1964.

Federalist Party. During the 1790s and into the first decade of the nineteenth century, the Federalist Party flourished in South Carolina, holding the lion's share of political power in the state. Based primarily in the lowcountry, Federalism in South Carolina reflected the elitist environment of its leaders. Among the central Federalist figures in South Carolina's were lowcountry planters such as Charles Cotesworth Pinckney, Thomas Pinckney, John Rutledge, Timothy Ford, Ralph Izard, Joseph Alston, and William Loughton Smith. South Carolina Federalists played a significant role in the party nationally as well. Thomas Pinckney was the Federalist candidate for vice president in 1796, while Charles Cotesworth Pinckney stood for the same position in 1800 and was the party's choice for president in the 1804 and 1808 elections.

South Carolina Federalists were early subscribers to the emerging party's ideology. In the first federal Congress, Congressman William Loughton Smith emerged as a major spokesman for Secretary of the Treasury Alexander Hamilton's economic program, which promised security and stability to both national finances and the business classes of the new republic. South Carolina's Federalists shared the probusiness and procommercial attitudes of their colleagues from other states. However, the primacy of slavery within their state's society and economy meant that the defense of commercial interests by South Carolina Federalists took a different tone than that of their counterparts from other regions, at times becoming quite defensive toward perceived attacks on slavery. William Loughton Smith, for example, spoke out against petitions sent to the first Congress by Quaker groups that were critical of the institution, asking of the petitioners, "Why did not they leave that, which they call God's work, to be managed by Himself?"

Despite this type of regional variation, South Carolina Federalism reflected the interests and goals of the Federalists nationwide. In foreign policy, they favored a pro-British stance (reflecting primarily the commercial and mercantile focus of Federalism). Yet, the 1795 Jay Treaty—despite the fact that it was quite favorable to Great Britain—caused a division within South Carolina's Federalist Party, with some Federalists (such as John Rutledge) arguing that the treaty conceded too much to England and thus degraded the honor of the United States. Whatever their views on the Jay Treaty, however, South Carolina's Federalists were uniformly suspicious of France, especially after that nation's revolution, which had begun in 1789 and took a more radical turn by the mid-1790s. The successful slave revolt on St. Domingue (Haiti) that consciously modeled itself on the ideals of the French Revolution confirmed their belief in the dangers inherent in the radical ideology of France. As tensions between the United States and France rose throughout the decade, special envoys were sent to France by President John Adams to attempt a negotiation of the issues between the two nations. Included in this delegation was Charles Cotesworth Pinckney. In what became known as the XYZ Affair, Pinckney responded to the demands of the French ministry for a bribe to smooth negotiations by angrily exclaiming, "No! No! Not a sixpence!"—a phrase that would become a widely reprinted statement of Americans' defiance toward what was seen as bullying by European despots. Despite the surge of popularity for both President Adams and the Federalists during the crisis with France, however, the repressive Alien and Sedition Acts passed in 1798 by the Federalist Congress lent strength to the Republican opposition, a trend felt acutely by South Carolina's Federalists.

National politics were not the only elements threatening the power of Federalism in South Carolina by the end of the 1790s. Party divisions within the state derived much of their strength and focus from the ongoing debate over representation and power between the established parishes of the lowcountry and the burgeoning new districts of the upcountry. The political dimensions of this debate were clear, with the Republican-dominated upcountry districts arguing for an equal share of legislative power with the Federalist-controlled lowcountry. The Compromise of 1808, in which legislative apportionment took into account both wealth and population figures and thus became roughly equal between the two regions, confirmed the eclipse of the state's Federalists in the face of a growing Republican ascendancy. Signs of this eclipse were already evident by this point, however. The Federalist presidential ticket of Adams and Thomas Pinckney did not carry the state in 1796, a significant blow to the Federalists' prestige. The national backlash against the Alien and Sedition Acts added further to the Federalists' decline. By 1804, after the defeat of Charles Cotesworth Pinckney by Republican Thomas Jefferson, Federalism was essentially dead in South Carolina, as it was throughout much of the nation. Yet, during its heyday in South Carolina, Federalism had been the unifying ideology for a powerful planter and commercial elite that had guided the state's affairs during the tumultuous post–Revolutionary War years. KEVIN M. GANNON

Elkins, Stanley, and Eric McKitrick. *The Age of Federalism.* New York: Oxford University Press, 1993.

Kaplanoff, Mark D. "Making the South Solid: Politics and the Structure of Society in South Carolina, 1790–1815." Ph.D. diss., Cambridge University, 1979.

Phillips, Ulrich B. "The South Carolina Federalists." *American Historical Review* 14 (April 1909): 529–43; (July 1909): 731–43.

Rogers, George C. *Evolution of a Federalist: William Loughton Smith of Charleston (1758–1812).* Columbia: University of South Carolina Press, 1962.

Female benevolent societies. Female benevolent societies rose to prominence in South Carolina and the nation in the years between the American Revolution and the Civil War. Voluntary in nature, these societies frequently emerged from existing antebellum reform groups or from soldiers' aid societies of the Civil War. By the 1790s the first female benevolent societies appeared in communities across the nation to augment efforts at poor relief conducted by local governments. Dominated by women from the middle and upper classes of society, female benevolent societies not only helped the poor but also were an outgrowth of the religious fervor of the Second Great Awakening, which sparked a renewed interest in helping the less fortunate.

Among the best-known and most active female benevolent societies in antebellum South Carolina was the Ladies Benevolent Society of Charleston. Formed in 1813 and inspired by the motto "I was sick and you visited me," the society initially provided home health care to the sick and poor of the city in response to the effects of the War of 1812. The leadership was provided by Sarah Hopton Russell and her sister, Mary Christiana Hopton Gregorie, women of means who had the time to dedicate themselves to charity work. Members of the society were well connected, from the upper class, and tended to be Episcopalians. Careful not to become an auxiliary to a men's organization, members of the Ladies Benevolent Society controlled their own finances, as is evident by their charter stating that the treasurer had to be an unmarried woman. Realizing that the poor suffered spiritually as well as materially, some society members formed the Charleston Female Domestic Missionary Society in 1818 to provide religious benevolence in the form of an outreach ministry.

By the 1820s women's associations successfully competed for charitable money with established men's groups, such as the South Carolina Society. Although charity was seen as women's work, men controlled the public policies and most of the institutions themselves. The religious rather than the political aspects of charity opened the door for women to become active participants in society. By 1861 the Ladies Benevolent Society was raising $4,000 annually, and its meetings were held in public spaces traditionally occupied by men, such as the commissioners' conference room of the Charleston Orphan House.

Even before the first shots of the Civil War, women began transforming their female benevolent societies into soldiers' aid societies. In Charleston groups such as the Soldiers' Relief Society and the

Ladies Charleston Volunteer Aid Society began rolling bandages in January 1861. Within months South Carolina's women had formed 150 aid groups. "Wayside hospitals" popped up along railroad lines to care for wounded soldiers being sent home. A woman from Pendleton recalled, "This little hospital was kept up until poverty closed its door, for we had not so much as a pot of cowpeas to send down." After the war many of these societies transformed themselves into Ladies' Memorial Associations that commemorated the Confederate dead.

Nineteenth-century women were able to make charity work their "career," but society deemed their work as an extension of women's roles as wives and mothers. In this way, female benevolent societies and other voluntary associations gave women the opportunity to participate in public life without challenging the social and legal boundaries of the women's private sphere. Female benevolent societies and, later, women's associations compiled valuable skills that would prepare women for a full and active political life, culminating with the winning of woman suffrage in 1920. CATHERINE FITZGERALD

Bellows, Barbara L. *Benevolence among Slaveholders: Assisting the Poor in Charleston, 1670–1860.* Baton Rouge: Louisiana State University Press, 1993.

Johnson, Joan M. "'This Wonderful Dream Nation!': Black and White South Carolina Women and the Creation of the New South, 1898–1930." Ph.D. diss., University of California at Los Angeles, 1997.

Scott, Anne Firor. *Natural Allies: Women's Associations in American History.* Urbana: University of Illinois Press, 1991.

Feme sole traders. Feme sole traders (married women engaged in trade) held a unique legal status in eighteenth- and nineteenth-century South Carolina. The laws and customs of the time prevented married women from undertaking commercial dealings without the consent of their husbands. An important exception to this state of affairs, however, was the granting of feme sole trading status. As a feme sole trader, a married woman became "as if sole" or unmarried in the eyes of the law regarding her economic status.

Statutes regarding feme sole trading in South Carolina first appeared in the early eighteenth century. In 1712, noting the presence of feme sole traders who "do contract debts . . . with design to defraud the persons to whom they are indebted by sheltering and defending themselves from any suit brought against them by reason of their coverture [married status]," the Commons House of Assembly passed an Attachment Act with provisions making a feme sole trader "liable to any suit or action to be brought against her for any debt contracted as a sole trader . . . as if such woman was sole and not under coverture."

In 1734 the assembly revised the Attachment Act to grant feme sole traders the power to sue in their husbands' names and with their husbands' consent. By 1744 the assembly had determined that owing to the absence of husbands or difficulty in obtaining husbands' approval, the method prescribed for feme sole traders to recover debts owed them was "very tedious and almost impracticable." The assembly empowered feme sole traders to sue for debts owed them, naming the husbands for conformity, without the need to obtain his consent.

Because the activities of a feme sole trader could deprive the husband of services that marriage entitled him to, his consent was required, as was his agreement not to meddle in her business dealings. Although registration was not required, more than six hundred deeds or contracts conveying feme sole trader status were registered between 1754 and 1824. It is unknown how many other women operated taverns, inns, or boardinghouses; kept shops; ran bakeries; sold liquor, provisions, dry goods, poultry, livestock, and other farm commodities; and engaged in other suitable female employments with only the tacit consent of their husbands.

Feme sole trader status was frequently granted in legal separations (divorce was prohibited) in lieu of alimony. In cases of extended absence, banishment, or desertion by the husband, feme sole trader status was granted automatically. Court cases do not always provide clear evidence as to whether a woman acted as an agent for her husband or as a sole trader. In 1823 legislation was enacted to "regulate the mode in which married women shall become Sole Traders or Dealers." Women with husbands were thereafter required to give monthly public notice of their intentions to conduct business on their own behalf.

Although South Carolina's feme sole trader statutes (which differed from those of Pennsylvania and Massachusetts) were enacted primarily to protect the traders' creditors, Carolinians recognized that feme sole trading contributed to the growth of commerce, fostered greater financial security for families, and lessened the likelihood that public assistance would be needed in cases of profligacy, insolvency, desertion, or extended absences by husbands. A feme sole trader could provide an alternative or second income for the family and protect property and income from her husband's creditors. Conversely, his resources were immune from her creditors. Primarily an urban and laboring-class phenomenon, feme sole trading was a conscious family strategy employed to prevent or mitigate real and potential financial hardships. MARIE H. NELSON

Parramore, Mary Roberts. "'For Her Sole and Separate Use': Feme Sole Trader Status in Early South Carolina." Master's thesis, University of South Carolina, 1991.

Salmon, Marylynn. *Women and the Law of Property in Early America.* Chapel Hill: University of North Carolina Press, 1986.

Fenwick Hall (Johns Island). Fenwick Hall, earlier known as Headquarters Plantation, stands on Johns Island near the Stono River, presenting its primary facade toward River Road. About 1730 John Fenwick constructed the original section, "a fine example of the symmetry and grace of Georgian design." The regular proportions of its two-story brick facade are accented by strong brick quoins.

In the mid–eighteenth century Fenwick's son, Edward, constructed two-story brick flanking buildings, one a stable for fine racehorses, the other for coaches and carriage horses. These flankers, on line with the residence, lengthened the visual plane of the domestic compound. A half-century later John Gibbes added a perpendicular wing along one end of the house, its ends projecting as polygonal bays in a style made fashionable by the Adam brothers of England. Robert Brown offered the plantation for sale in 1810, two thousand acres with "an exceeding good dwelling house, containing 13 upright rooms, a large kitchen and stable all built of bricks. . . . The grounds around the buildings are elegantly laid out."

After several planters enjoyed Fenwick Hall and profited from its rich land, Daniel J. Townsend purchased the tract in 1840. His family held Fenwick Hall until 1876. By 1930 the property was in deplorable condition, mirroring the decline of many former showplaces after the demise of Sea Island cotton. The Charleston architects Simons and Lapham thoroughly reworked the building for Victor Morawetz of New York, retaining the notable interior detail and adding small side wings. Morawetz also constructed a swimming pool building and improved the grounds with rows of live oaks parallel to the ancient avenue. SARAH FICK

Iseley, N. Jane, William P. Baldwin, and Agnes L. Baldwin. *Plantations of the Low Country: South Carolina 1697–1865.* Greensboro, N.C.: Legacy Publications, 1985.

Shaffer, E. T. H. *Carolina Gardens.* 2d ed. Chapel Hill: University of North Carolina Press, 1939.

Stoney, Samuel G. *Plantations of the South Carolina Low Country.* 5th ed. Charleston, S.C.: Carolina Art Association, 1964.

Ferries. The earliest ferries in South Carolina carried settlers across the Ashley, Cooper, Santee, and other lowcountry waterways. Early ferries, sometimes called "boats" or "galleys," were important for transportation but were frequently poorly constructed, haphazardly manned, and expensive to the everyday traveler. Accordingly, the General Assembly in 1709 passed the first of many laws governing the location, management, and fees associated with ferries. Under the law, the ferry master was to provide for the passage of one man at one pence and a "man and horse from one side of [the river] to the other" at a cost of two pence. Most ferries took the name of an early licensee: Mazyck, Skrine, Garner, Vance, Murry, or Nelson. Others were known only by the location: Strawberry Ferry, Ashley River Ferry, or South Island Ferry. One, across the Black River, was referred to only as the "Potato Ferry."

The first boats were large canoes or flat-bottom scows that were powered by paddles, oars, or poles. Within one hundred years, flatboats capable of holding a wagon or carriage had become commonplace. The heavier load necessitated a pulley/winch system to move the flatboat and cargo against the current, and costs rose accordingly. In 1805 the toll on a team or carriage was $1.00, and a man and horse was 12.5¢. A barrel of freight was 25¢.

Ferry operations in antebellum South Carolina were closely regulated by the General Assembly, which established rates of toll and the duties of ferry operators. Negligent operators or those who attempted to extort higher tolls could be fined or have their ferry licenses taken away. The General Assembly could not, however, regulate nature. Floods, drought, and storms frequently interrupted ferry operations. Still, with bridges difficult to build and expensive, ferries were a vital link in the state's transportation system throughout the eighteenth and much of the nineteenth centuries. Their number increased from several dozen crossings in 1775 to more than one hundred by 1825. As the state's population spread inland in the early nineteenth century, ferries became increasingly prevalent in the backcountry.

The destruction or elimination of all but twenty ferries by 1865 was the beginning of the end for the institution. Steamboats and railroads lessened the need for ferries throughout the nineteenth century, while the arrival of the automobile finished it off in the twentieth century. Formed in 1917, the South Carolina Highway Department utilized taxes on automobiles, automobile dealerships, and gasoline to build the state's first system of modern roads and bridges. With the assistance of federal money, South Carolina acquired thousands of miles of new roads and hundreds of bridges. A few ferries persisted until well into the twentieth century, such as Ashe's Ferry at Van Wyck or Scott's Ferry on the Savannah, but most were replaced by bridges. Places such as Givhans Ferry State Park in Dorchester County and Galivants Ferry in Horry County, however, provide reminders of the prevalence and importance of ferries in the state's transportation history. LOUIS P. TOWLES

Downey, Tom. *Planting a Capitalist South: Masters, Merchants, and Manufacturers in the Southern Interior, 1790–1860.* Baton Rouge: Louisiana State University Press, 2006.

Gilmore, Edward C. "South Carolina River Ferries." *South Carolina History Illustrated* 1 (May 1970): 44–48.

Meriwether, Robert L. *The Expansion of South Carolina, 1729–1765.* Kingsport, Tenn.: Southern Publishers, 1940.

Merrens, H. Roy, ed. *The Colonial South Carolina Scene, 1697–1774: Contemporary Views.* Columbia: University of South Carolina Press, 1977.

Moore, John Hammond. *The South Carolina Highway Department, 1917–1987.* Columbia: University of South Carolina Press, 1987.

Fielding, Herbert Ulysses (b. 1923). Civil rights activist, legislator. Fielding was born in Charleston on July 6, 1923, the son of Julius P. Fielding and Sadie E. Gaillard. He graduated from Avery Normal Institute in Charleston. From 1943 to 1946 he served in the U.S. Army in the American and European theaters. He married Thelma Erenne Stent of Charleston on December 24, 1946. They had three sons. Fielding earned a B.S. from West Virginia State College in 1948.

Fielding, a funeral home director, was a civil rights activist and leader in the African American community in Charleston in the 1950s and 1960s. As early as 1952 he ran for political office in order to encourage blacks to vote and to become politically active. In the early 1960s Fielding was involved in the Charleston Movement, a National Association for the Advancement of Colored People–backed organization formed to oppose discrimination and segregation in public facilities and businesses in Charleston. In June 1963 he was arrested while trying to be served at the Fort Sumter Hotel in Charleston. He was one of four black leaders who met with the city's mayor to end segregation of public facilities and other discriminatory practices in Charleston. He also was a member of a biracial community relations committee formed in 1963 following the sit-ins and mass demonstrations. In 1966 he was the first recipient of the Charleston Business and Professional Men's Association's Man of the Year award.

In 1970 Fielding became one of the first three African Americans elected to the South Carolina General Assembly since 1900. He was reelected in 1972 and served a third term from 1983 to 1984. In 1984 he was elected to the state Senate, where he served until 1992. Fielding was a candidate for the Sixth Congressional District seat in 1992 but was defeated by James Clyburn in the Democratic primary.

Politically, Fielding was a pragmatist who attributed much of his political success to the development of a broad platform that appealed to blacks and whites from all income groups. Within the legislative arena, he was an advocate for changes that had an impact on the African American community. These included the creation of single-member legislative districts, the elimination of the full-slate rule (which required voters to cast as many votes as there were seats to be filled in an election), the creation of a State Human Relations Commission, and funding for sickle-cell anemia testing. In 1975 he received the Legislative Black Caucus Award for his work in the General Assembly.

Fielding did not seek reelection to public office following his 1992 congressional campaign. He continued to be active in community and political affairs in Charleston. WILLIAM V. MOORE

Bailey, N. Louise, Mary L. Morgan, and Carolyn R. Taylor, eds. *Biographical Directory of the South Carolina Senate, 1776–1985.* 3 vols. Columbia: University of South Carolina Press, 1986.

O'Neill, Stephen. "From the Shadows of Slavery: The Civil Rights Years in Charleston." Ph.D. diss., University of Virginia, 1994.

Fields, Mamie Elizabeth Garvin (1888–1987). Educator, community activist. Fields was born on August 13, 1888, in Charleston, the daughter of George Garvin and Rebecca Bellinger. She began attending school at age three at Miss Anna Eliza Izzard's School, which was run by her cousin. She later attended the "public" Shaw school, named for the commander of the Fifty-fourth Massachusetts, Robert Gould Shaw. She attended high school and college at Claflin College, where she received her licentiate of instruction, which made her eligible to teach, and a diploma in domestic science.

Fields wanted to be a missionary, but her parents refused to permit it. She began teaching in the black schools of rural South Carolina in 1908. She taught at several one- and two-teacher schools and served as principal of the Miller Hill school. She married Robert Lucas Fields on April 29, 1914. The marriage produced two children. After Fields married, she moved to Charlotte, North Carolina, where her husband was employed as a bricklayer. The couple moved back to Charleston around the time of World War I, then moved to New York around 1923 after the employment situation for blacks in Charleston deteriorated. The family was back in Charleston by 1926, and Fields returned to full-time teaching. She retired in 1943.

Fields was active in many organizations that focused on improving conditions and opportunities for African Americans. She joined the City Federation of Colored Women's Clubs in 1916 and was inspired by Mary Church Terrell's speech on the "Modern Woman," which emphasized service to the race, the community, and to elevating Negro womanhood. Later, fellow South Carolinian Mary McLeod Bethune offered Fields support and encouragement in club work. She joined the National Association for the Advancement of Colored People and took part in the successful campaign in 1919 to employ only black teachers in black schools. She was also a member of the Charleston Interracial Committee that sought to secure public services for African Americans. Although she cooperated with whites on the committee, she was also part of a restless handful of well-educated black Charlestonians who pushed for improved recreational and educational facilities for the African American community. As a schoolteacher, Fields worked to get her students access to government services and to expose them to the world beyond their rural lives.

After her retirement, Fields remained active. She served two terms as president of the state Federation of Women's Clubs and one term as statistician of the national federation. After her husband died, she worked for two years with the Marion Birnie Wilkinson orphanage for girls. She was instrumental in 1969 in helping to organize Charleston's first public day-care center for the children of working mothers, after several young children died in house fires.

Fields received numerous awards from diverse organizations, including women's groups and black fraternities and sororities. In 1972 she was named the state's Outstanding Older Citizen by the South Carolina Commission on Aging. Fields died on July 30, 1987, at her home in Charleston and was buried in the Reserved Fellowship Association Cemetery. CARMEN V. HARRIS

Fields, Mamie Garvin, with Karen Fields. *Lemon Swamp and Other Places: A Carolina Memoir.* New York: Free Press, 1983.

Simms, Lois. *Profiles of African American Females in the Low Country of South Carolina.* Charleston, S.C.: Avery Research Center, 1992.

Figg, Robert McCormick, Jr. (1901–1991). Lawyer, public servant, legal educator. Figg was one of the most influential South Carolina attorneys of his generation, supporting the development of the state's ports and law school while opposing school desegregation. He was born in Radford, Virginia, on August 29, 1901, to Robert Figg, Sr., and Helen Josephine Cecil. The family moved to Charleston in 1915 so that the elder Figg could assume a position at the Charleston Navy Yard. The younger Figg graduated from Porter Military Academy in 1916 and from the College of Charleston in 1920. After attending law school at Columbia University for two years, Figg returned to Charleston before graduating and was admitted to the bar in 1922. He joined the law firm of Rutledge, Hyde, and Mann, and within two years he had become a partner.

With the backing of Mayor Burnet R. Maybank's political organization, Figg won a seat in the state House of Representatives in 1932. Two years later he was elected solicitor of the Ninth Judicial Circuit. Figg served as solicitor for twelve years and earned a reputation for honesty and efficiency. During that era solicitors drafted legislation for the General Assembly, and one of Figg's most important achievements was drafting the act that created the South Carolina State Ports Authority.

Figg's involvement with the S.C. Ports Authority continued for nearly thirty years. He served as its legal counsel and an adviser to its management. He negotiated the transfer of city, navy, and private property to the Ports Authority, bringing unified control to much of the port. He solicited business for the port from the federal government and from private industry and helped mediate between the often fractious personalities on the Ports Authority's board.

A strong supporter of Strom Thurmond, Figg advised the South Carolina governor in his 1948 presidential bid as well as in his 1950 and 1954 races for the U.S. Senate. He served on the Dixiecrat campaign steering committee and wrote some of Thurmond's speeches. Figg also was involved in the legal defense of the white primary and in the state's defense in the *Briggs v. Elliott* school desegregation case. With the support of Governor James F. Byrnes, Figg framed much of the state's strategy, though other attorneys presented most of the arguments. His opposition to school desegregation most likely cost him an appointment to the federal bench.

From 1959 until 1970 Figg served as dean of the University of South Carolina (USC) Law School, where he helped modernize the school's facilities. Retiring from USC in 1970, he served as president of the South Carolina Bar Association.

Figg married Sallie Alexander Tobias of Charleston in 1927, and they had three children. Sallie Figg died in 1986, and after a period of declining health Robert Figg died in Columbia on January 31, 1991. R. PHILLIP STONE II

Koehler-Shepley, Thomas. "Robert McC. Figg, Jr.: South Carolina's Lawyers' Lawyer." Master's thesis, University of South Carolina, 1994.

Film industry. South Carolina's commercial film industry is almost as old as filmmaking itself. The first documented filmed images of South Carolina were in newsreels taken at the 1902 Charleston Exposition. Motion pictures as novelty and entertainment became popular in the first decade of the twentieth century. The early motion picture industry developed on the East Coast, primarily in New York City. However, lower production costs and a better climate prompted the industry to relocate many productions southward. The first fictional production made in South Carolina was *The Southerners* in 1914. A Civil War film, it highlighted the scenery of the lowcountry and used Citadel cadets in the re-created battle scenes. Working in the South was enticing enough for film companies to create South Carolina's first commercial film studio in Charleston's Princess Theater.

Beaufort, with its historic homes and moss-draped oaks, has been the setting for a number of motion pictures including *Forrest Gump* and *The Prince of Tides*. Courtesy, South Caroliniana Library, University of South Carolina

The leadership of Charleston realized that having motion picture productions in town was good for the economy. In 1916 the Chamber of Commerce established a Department of Publicity to actively recruit production companies. Their efforts were successful, and at least ten productions were filmed as a direct result of their promotion. Activity continued at a rapid pace until World War I, when local interest in film production was diverted elsewhere. Nevertheless, numerous other films were made throughout the 1920s, including *Pied Piper Malone* (1924), which was filmed in Georgetown. After the 1920s the Hollywood studio system reigned and production outside of California was severely limited. However, three pictures of note were filmed in South Carolina because of the need for special on-location shots: *Carolina* (1933) was filmed at the Rankin Plantation (The Columns) near Florence; *A Guy Named Joe* (1944) used the airfields at Sumter and Columbia; and *Reap the Wild Wind* (1942), an Academy Award winner, was the first South Carolina picture filmed in Technicolor. Although Hollywood found it desirable to film in the Palmetto State on an intermittent basis, the state abandoned actively petitioning for their business. One reason was because Hollywood films throughout this period frequently perpetuated the stereotypes of southerners as plantation owners, eccentrics, hicks, or buffoons.

The stagnant economy of the 1970s prompted the state government to revisit the idea of luring productions to South Carolina. The studio system of old had been dying a slow death, stereotypes had softened, and filmmakers routinely filmed on location. Other southern states competed vigorously for their share in millions of production dollars. Not to be left out, Governor John West, through the Arts Commission, launched a campaign to promote film production in South Carolina. Although there was sporadic success throughout the 1970s, by 1980 the efforts reached fruition when the South Carolina Film Office was established. This office worked closely with arts, tourism, and development groups to foster a local support industry and to facilitate motion picture production. Within three years the office was credited with generating a statewide economic impact of almost $30 million. Since the establishment of the Film Office, South Carolina can boast that hundreds of movies, television episodes, and commercials have been made by major and independent producers throughout the state, including such critical and commercial successes as *The Big Chill* (1983), *Daughters of the Dust* (1991), *The Prince of Tides* (1991), *Forrest Gump* (1994), *The Patriot* (2000), *The Legend of Bagger Vance* (2000), *Radio* (2002), and *Cold Mountain* (2003). WHITNEY MILLER

Campbell, Edward. *The Celluloid South.* Knoxville: University of Tennessee Press, 1981.

French, Warren, ed. *The South and Film.* Jackson: University Press of Mississippi, 1981.

Kirby, Jack Temple. *Media-Made Dixie.* Rev. ed. Athens: University of Georgia Press, 1986.

Miller, Whitney. "The History of South Carolina's Film Industry 1902–1990." Master's thesis, University of South Carolina, 1996.

Thompson, Frank. *Lost Films: Important Movies That Disappeared.* Secaucus, N.J.: Carol, 1996.

Finlay, Kirkman, Jr. (1936–1993). Lawyer, mayor of Columbia. Finlay was born in Columbia on August 16, 1936, the son of Kirkman Finlay and Catherine McCarrel. He attended public schools in Columbia and graduated from the University of the South, Sewanee, Tennessee, in 1958, and from Harvard Law School in 1961. After graduation from Harvard, Finlay returned to Columbia to practice law as an associate with the firm of Boyd, Bruton & Lumpkin, ultimately becoming a partner in the firm now known as Haynsworth Sinkler Boyd, P.A. As a lawyer, he specialized in public utilities regulation and corporation law, while maintaining a general practice. On September 10, 1966, he married Mary Fleming Willis. They had two children.

In 1974 Finlay was elected to the Columbia City Council, and in 1978 he was elected mayor, serving until 1986. During his service to the city, Finlay developed civic projects that greatly enhanced the appearance and quality of life in Columbia. His efforts produced the renovation of the fourteen-hundred block of Main Street, with the addition of a multistory office building (the Palmetto Center), a large new hotel, and a parking garage. He convinced officials with Southern Bell and the State Highway Department to abandon plans to build new headquarters in the suburbs and instead to build in downtown Columbia. Under Finlay's tenure, railroads operating in Columbia relocated or eliminated many tracks in order to reduce the number of crossings and facilitate traffic flow. Working with the University of South Carolina (USC) and Richland County, Finlay oversaw the establishment of the Koger Center for the Performing Arts and the transformation of Wheeler Hill, a disadvantaged area near USC, into a desirable residential community. He sponsored a change in the way the Columbia City Council was elected, creating single-member districts that brought to the council its first black members. To revitalize decaying areas of the city, Finlay envisioned a renovation of downtown Columbia and the transformation of Sidney Park from an industrial complex of warehouses and railroad spur tracks into a park surrounded by residential housing. He foresaw and initiated the first steps in the development of the Congaree Vista, another depressed area between Assembly Street and the Congaree River. Finlay was also instrumental in placing the State Museum in the Vista and advocated the removal of the Central Corrections Institution from downtown Columbia.

Finlay served on the vestry and as senior warden of Trinity Episcopal Church and saw its elevation to cathedral status. He also served as vice chancellor of the Episcopal Diocese of Upper South Carolina and as a trustee of the University of the South. In 1985 he received the Elizabeth O'Neill Verner Award for his work in the Congaree Vista, for his efforts in the revitalization of Columbia, and for his role in the creation of the Richland-Lexington Cultural Council. In 1989 he was appointed chairman of the Columbia Development Corporation to oversee the further development of the Congaree Vista. Finlay died in Columbia on June 27, 1993. In April 1994 Sidney Park was renamed Finlay Park in his honor. H. SIMMONS TATE, JR.

Hinshaw, Dawn. "Former Mayor Kirkman Finlay Dies." Columbia *State,* June 28, 1993, pp. A1, A5.

Moore, John Hammond. *Columbia and Richland County: A South Carolina Community, 1740–1990.* Columbia: University of South Carolina Press, 1993.

Finney, Ernest Adolphus, Jr. (b. 1931). Lawyer, jurist, educator. Finney was born in Smithfield, Virginia, on March 23, 1931, to Ernest A. Finney, Sr., and Collen Godwin. His mother died when he was ten days old, and he was raised by his father, an educator. In 1946 his father became dean at Claflin College in Orangeburg, from which Finney graduated in 1952 with an A.B. degree. In 1954 he graduated from South Carolina State University with a Juris Doctor degree. After law school, Finney found it difficult to earn a living from legal work, so he taught in Horry County and waited tables at the Ocean Forest Hotel, where, ironically, Finney attended his first convention of the segregated South Carolina Bar by serving as a waiter. He married Frances Davenport of Newberry in 1955. They had three children.

Ernest Finney, Jr. Courtesy, the Hon. Ernest A. Finney, Jr., Columbia, SC

After five years in Conway, Finney moved his family to Sumter and devoted himself to law practice. He practiced law with Ruben Gray. Working with Matthew J. Perry, Finney gained a reputation as an outstanding defense lawyer and civil rights advocate. Together they defended more than six thousand clients who had been arrested for taking part in freedom rides and demonstrations. One of Finney's most notable defenses was on behalf of nine students in Rock Hill in 1961 who staged one of the first sit-ins in South Carolina. He lost almost every case that went to trial but won all but two on appeal to higher courts. Finney observed, "I have never known abject poverty, but I have known segregation in its worst form. I therefore believe the law is absolutely necessary to protect the rights of all citizens."

In 1963 Finney was appointed chairman of the South Carolina Advisory Commission on Civil Rights. In 1972 he was elected to the South Carolina House of Representatives, one of the first African Americans elected to the General Assembly since the nineteenth century. He served in the state House from 1973 until 1976. Beginning in 1976 he was the first African American to serve as a circuit court judge in South Carolina. He was elected an associate justice of the South Carolina Supreme Court on April 3, 1985. He was elected chief justice on May 11, 1994, making him the first African American chief justice of South Carolina. He assumed office on December 17, 1994, and retired in March 2000. After leaving the bench, he practiced briefly with one son before becoming president of South Carolina State University in the summer of 2002. Finney has received many honors in his career, including honorary doctorates from Claflin College, Coastal Carolina University, the Citadel, Johnson C. Smith University, the College of Charleston, South Carolina State University, and Morris College. He is also a member of the American Law Institute. W. LEWIS BURKE

Richburg, Chris. "NAACP Leader Urges Fighting for Right Cause." Rock Hill *Herald,* June 4, 2000, p. B1.

Finney, Lynn Carol (b. 1957). Poet, writer. Finney was born in Conway on August 26, 1957, the daughter of Ernest A. Finney, Jr., an attorney who became the first African American chief justice of the South Carolina Supreme Court, and Frances Davenport. She took the name "Nikky" during her high school years in Sumter. She attended St. Jude Catholic School until the mid-1960s, when public schools were integrated in the state. With her older brother she was among the first to integrate Central School in Sumter.

Finney left Sumter in 1975 to attend Talladega College in Alabama, where she found her calling as a writer. As a child she had started keeping a journal, and at the age of fifteen she had become interested in the black arts movement. In college she spent her time writing and studying literature, especially that of the African American tradition. During her junior year at Talladega she befriended the poet Nikki Giovanni, who would later play a significant role in her growth as a poet. Finney majored in English in 1979 and won the Whiting Writing Award.

Finney enrolled in the graduate school at Atlanta University to study African American literature but left the program, which did not allow creative writing components in a thesis. Instead she joined Pamoja, a writing collective founded by the writer Toni Cade Bambara. From this workshop came Finney's first book of short poems, *On Wings Made of Gauze,* in 1985.

In 1986 Finney moved to Oakland, California, where she made a living from a series of jobs, from photographer to printer to workshop instructor. In 1993 she began teaching creative writing at the University of Kentucky. There she cofounded The Affrilachian Poets, a collective of African American writers in the Appalachian region.

In 1995 Finney wrote the script for the PBS documentary *For Posterity's Sake: The Story of Morgan and Marvin Smith,* brothers who were photographers in the 1930s. Her second poetry collection, with photographs, *Rice,* was published in Canada in 1995. *Rice* constitutes an important development in American poetry. The poems are set in coastal Carolina, where Carolina gold rice once was a large export crop. Dealing with race, lost values, womanhood, and abuse, the poetry is in plain lyrical words and the imagery is powerfully evocative. Finney emphasizes her ancestry and African lineage, celebrates slaves who rebelled, and delights in the Gullah culture of her home state. PEN American awarded *Rice* the Open Book Award of 1999.

In 1997 Finney became an associate professor at the University of Kentucky and also published a short-story cycle, *Heartwood,* which is about overcoming racial anger, fears, and prejudice in a small community by relying on the soundness of the "heartwood." She published her third book of poetry, *The World Is Round,* in 2003. JAN NORDBY GRETLUND

Dawes, Kwame. "Reading *Rice:* A Local Habitation and a Name." *African American Review* 31 (summer 1997): 269–79.

Finney, Nikky. Foreword to *Good and Bad Hair,* by Bill Gaskins. New Brunswick, N.J.: Rutgers University Press, 1997.

Kraver, Jeraldine. "'Mobile Images': Myth and Resistance in Nikky Finney's Rice." *Southern Literary Journal* 34 (spring 2002): 134–47.

Fire-Baptized Holiness Church. Several different groups have used variations of this name. The initial Fire Baptized Holiness Association was founded in Iowa in 1895 by Benjamin Hardin Irwin. He taught that a Christian could experience salvation, sanctification, and then a "third blessing," a baptism of the Holy Ghost with fire.

Irwin first toured South Carolina in December 1896, preaching in several communities across the state. His first stop was the Piedmont Wesleyan Methodist Meeting House, pastored by Andrew K. Willis. That preaching tour laid the groundwork for the formation of a statewide Fire Baptized Holiness Association. When Irwin called leaders to South Carolina in 1898 to form a national group, he had already founded eight other state associations and two in Canada. Some 140 delegates met in Anderson from July 28 through August 8, 1898, to organize the Fire Baptized Holiness Association (FBHA). The first ruling elder for South Carolina was W. S. Foxworth.

For a time the denomination was headquartered in Olmitz, Iowa, where Irwin published *Live Coals of Fire.* Anderson native Joseph Hillary King was assistant editor. The movement faltered after Irwin in 1900 confessed to "open and gross sin." King became general overseer of the FBHA, and he moved the headquarters and publication in 1902 to Royston, Georgia, a short distance from Anderson where the popular and influential African American FBHA minister William E. Fuller resided.

In 1911 King's branch of the Fire Baptized Holiness Church merged with the Pentecostal Holiness Church at a meeting in Falcon, North Carolina, and took on the Pentecostal Holiness name, signaling its commitment to a Pentecostal identity. Three years earlier, however, African American members of the FBHA had split off from the parent body at the denomination's second national conference held in Anderson in May 1898. Under Fuller's leadership, these churches formed the Colored Fire-Baptized Holiness Church on November 24, 1908. At that time the new group had sixteen ministers, twenty-seven churches, and 925 members and was heavily concentrated in South Carolina and Georgia. To promote educational opportunities for African Americans, the denomination organized the Fuller Normal and Technical Institute in Atlanta in 1912; the school moved to Greenville, South Carolina, in 1923.

In 1922 Fuller's group changed its name to the Fire-Baptized Holiness Church of God, and Fuller received the title of bishop. The denomination took the name Fire-Baptized Holiness Church of God of the Americas in 1926. In 1958, when Fuller died and his son William E. Fuller, Jr., assumed leadership, the denomination's headquarters relocated to Atlanta. Membership figures are uncertain, but estimates for 2000 placed the national total at around 17,500, with the largest clusters still in South Carolina and Georgia. NANCY A. HARDESTY

Fankhauser, Craig Charles. "The Heritage of Faith: An Historical Evaluation of the Holiness Movement in America." Master's thesis, Pittsburg State University, 1983.

Jones, Charles E. *Black Holiness: A Guide to the Study of Black Participation in Wesleyan Perfectionist and Glossolalic Pentecostal Movements.* Metuchen, N.J.: Scarecrow, 1987.

Synan, Vinson. *The Old-Time Power.* Rev. ed. Franklin Springs, Ga.: Advocate Press, 1986.

Fireproof Building (Charleston). Built to serve as the Charleston District Records Office, the Fireproof Building is often called the first building of fireproof construction in the United States. Designed by Robert Mills, it was among the first major projects he undertook after his appointment to the South Carolina Board of Public Works in 1820. Construction began in 1822 and was completed in 1827. Mills used noncombustible materials wherever possible. The structure is built of brick finished in stucco and has a brownstone base. Barrel and groin vaults form the walls and ceilings of the first two stories. The oval stair hall in the center of the building is lit by a cupola and has a cantilevered stone stair that ascends three stories. The window frames and sash are made of iron, and the halls are paved with stone. Stylistically, the Greek-revival building is dominated by two monumental Doric porticos, each with a pediment and four columns resting on an arcaded basement. The completed building differed slightly from Mills's original plans. Construction supervisor John G. Spindle eliminated the belt course and fluted columns specified by Mills, substituted quoins for horizontal channeling, and altered the cornice and third-story window openings. After being occupied by county offices for well over a century, the building was leased to the South Carolina Historical Society in 1955 and became the official headquarters of the organization in 1968. It was designated a National Historic Landmark by the U.S. Department of the Interior in 1973. DANIEL J. VIVIAN

Lane, Mills. *Architecture of the Old South: South Carolina.* Savannah, Ga.: Beehive, 1984.

Poston, Jonathan H. *The Buildings of Charleston: A Guide to the City's Architecture.* Columbia: University of South Carolina Press, 1997.

First South Carolina Regiment. Elements of what became the First South Carolina Infantry Regiment (later designated the Thirty-third United States Colored Troops) were organized in 1862, giving it the distinction of being the first African American United States Army unit in the Civil War.

The driving force behind the establishment of the regiment was Major General David Hunter. A graduate of the United States Military Academy, he was a career officer in the U.S. Army and was also an abolitionist and friend of President Abraham Lincoln. Promoted to major general early in the war, Hunter commanded the Department of the South in May 1862 and issued an order that declared all slaves in South Carolina, Georgia, and Florida free. Soon afterward he began recruiting a military unit composed of black men who lived in the United States–occupied area around Port Royal or who had escaped to Union lines from Confederate-controlled areas of South Carolina and Georgia. After few responded, Hunter ordered that all the able-bodied "negroes" between eighteen and forty-five years of age "capable of bearing arms" be sent to his headquarters. Soon there were enough present to organize a five-hundred-man unit commanded by white officers.

In Washington, President Lincoln was not ready for emancipation or the enlistment of black men into the U.S. Army and required Hunter to rescind the proclamation. However, Lincoln did not directly order that the regiment be disbanded. Hunter hoped that the regiment would eventually be accepted and continued to drill and train the men, who were uniformed in red pants, blue coats, and broad-brimmed hats. But Hunter received no support from the government and in August 1862 disbanded all but one company. Finally the U.S. War Department permitted the organization of black units, and in October the company became Company A, First South Carolina Volunteer Infantry Regiment. Other companies

Members of Company A of the First South Carolina Volunteers, taking the oath of allegiance at Beaufort. Courtesy, Avery Research Center for African American History and Culture

were soon organized, and on January 31, 1863, the First South Carolina was officially mustered into United States service.

The regiment spent most of the war participating in various expeditions, skirmishing, or serving on garrison duty along the coasts of South Carolina, Georgia, and Florida. In February 1864 the unit's designation was changed to the Thirty-third United States Colored Troops. In the summer and fall of 1864 the regiment participated in the operations against Charleston, serving on James, Folly, and Morris Islands and other locations along the South Carolina coast.

With the fall of Charleston in February 1865, the Thirty-third United States Colored Troops served as part of the city's Union garrison. This was followed by service in the District of Savannah, Georgia; at Augusta, Georgia; and then at other locations in the Department of the South until the regiment was mustered out of service in January 1866. RICHARD W. HATCHER III

Dyer, Frederick H. *A Compendium of the War of the Rebellion.* 3 vols. 1908. Reprint, New York: Yoseloff, 1959.

Higginson, Thomas Wentworth. *Army Life in a Black Regiment.* 1870. Reprint, New York: Norton, 1984.

Miller, Edward A., Jr. *Lincoln's Abolitionist General: The Biography of David Hunter.* Columbia: University of South Carolina Press, 1997.

Taylor, Susie King. *A Black Woman's Civil War Memoirs: Reminiscences of My Life in Camp with the 33rd U.S. Colored Troops.* 1902. Reprint, New York: M. Wiener, 1988.

Fish camps. While the term designates a campsite ideal for anglers throughout much of the Palmetto State, "fish camp" for upstate South Carolinians refers to a family-style seafood restaurant serving reasonably priced dinners to a local clientele. Fish camps differ from the calabash restaurants of the coast in that they serve both salt- and freshwater seafood, and from more upscale seafood restaurants in their prices and decor, which frequently consists of uncovered wooden tables, ladder-back chairs, and walls decorated with taxidermic fish. With strong ties to the tradition of community fish fries, the restaurants prepare fish (usually flounder and catfish) deep-fried in a cornmeal-based coating. Menus are augmented with additional offerings such as deviled crab, shrimp, and oysters, and all come with hush puppies, fries, and coleslaw on the side. A few fish camps, such as Old MacDonald's in North Augusta, offer a lowcountry boil or a side of grits, an apparent nod to lowcountry culinary traditions.

Generally, fish camps are located near rivers or lakes, such as the Little River Fish Camp in Saluda and the Lake Wylie Fish Camp in York County. The earliest were established along the Catawba River in South and North Carolina in the 1930s and 1940s and began as sheds where anglers could fry their fresh catches. And while most restaurants purchase their fish from seafood wholesalers and farms, fish camps continue to be found along waterways.

Catering to a loyal, local clientele, many fish camps serve as gathering places, hosting local club meetings and family celebrations and providing many patrons with a regular opportunity to gossip, talk politics, and discuss current events. Politicians have apparently recognized the importance of these restaurants to their constituents and regularly make formal or informal visits. During the 2000 election, the Catawba Fish Camp in Fort Lawn was a key campaign stop for then-candidate George W. Bush, and in 2002 the same fish camp hosted a campaign rally for Democratic governor Jim Hodges. Other popular fish camps include Tall Tales and Wagon Wheel in Cowpens, the Roebuck and Pioneer restaurants of Spartanburg County, Bailey's in Blacksburg, and Wateree in Pageland. STEPHEN CRISWELL

Edge, John T. *Southern Belly: The Ultimate Food Lover's Companion to the South.* Athens, Ga.: Hill Street, 2000.

Fishing, commercial. With extensive estuaries and barrier islands, the coastal areas of South Carolina are an important nursery for fisheries throughout the mid–Atlantic region. Though economically insignificant today when compared to recreational fisheries and tourism, state commercial fisheries are characterized by small-scale individual operators harvesting primarily shrimp, offshore finfish, blue crabs, and oysters.

With the arrival of Europeans, natives created the first commercial fisheries, trading seafood for firearms and clothing. Coastal slaves, after completing their tasks, were frequently allowed to create enterprises including fishing. As early as 1770 the Commons House of Assembly acknowledged, "The business of Fishing is principally carried on by Negroes, Mulattoes, and Mestizoes." Historically, the best-known South Carolina fishery was the "mosquito fleet," immortalized in the famous opera *Porgy and Bess.* The fleet sailed out of Charleston harbor and returned with blackfish, snapper, whiting, and, of course, porgy.

The shrimp industry, centered in Charleston and Beaufort, is the largest South Carolina fishery. In 2002, 3.3 million pounds (heads off) worth $9,029,693 were harvested. Commercial shrimping began in 1925, when a fleet of Florida trawlers moved to Beaufort County. Shrimp were packed with ice in barrels and loaded onto railroad cars destined for New York. During the 1940s Charleston fishermen converted a coastal freight boat, using a block and tackle system to haul shrimp nets out of the water. Harvests expanded until the 1970s but have remained more or less constant since then. The two major shrimp crops are brown shrimp, caught in early summer, and white shrimp, harvested in late summer and throughout the fall. Beginning in the 1990s expanded imports depressed market prices and reduced profits in the industry. The industry peaked in 1995 when 6.9 million pounds (heads off) worth $21,692,665 were harvested. The number of commercial boats declined from a high of 1,016 during fiscal year 1991–1992 to 573 in fiscal year 2002–2003.

The second most important South Carolina fishery is offshore finfish. The offshore industry, fishing for swordfish, mahi-mahi, grouper, snapper, and other deepwater fish, is limited in South Carolina because of the distance between local ports and the Gulf Stream. The industry is concentrated in Murrells Inlet and Charleston. In 2002, 3.1 million pounds worth $5,374,498 dockside were landed in South Carolina. Stock reductions and conservation regulations have decreased landings of some species in recent years.

Like the other fisheries, the blue crab industry in South Carolina has seen better days. The industry grew in the 1930s and 1940s with the advent of canning and pasteurization technology. In Beaufort, Sterling Harris is credited with creating the first crab-picking machine and starting Blue Channel Corporation. Crabmeat and she-crab soup (made with crab roe) became well known as regional delicacies. Crab factories in Port Royal, Beaufort, and McClellanville employed hundreds of pickers to carefully extract the eight to fourteen percent of each crab that is marketable meat. Like the shrimp industry, by the 1990s imported crabmeat had undercut the domestic market. In 2002, 4.4 million pounds of live crabs worth $3,712,428 were harvested. The peak year for blue crabs landed was 1978–1979, at 9.4 million pounds with a value of $1,840,060, and the peak value year was 2001 with 5.4 million pounds worth $5,226,079. The last crab-picking plant closed in 2001. "Basket trade," the sale of live hard-shell blue crabs, still exists. Local crabbers sell to wholesalers, who ship crabs up the coast to Baltimore and New York. Each spring dozens of small-time operators set up "peeler" tanks, harvesting blue crabs when they molt and creating, for a brief time, soft-shell crabs.

In 1893 Maggoni & Company established the first oyster factory in South Carolina on Daufuskie Island. By 1905 sixteen factories operated in the state. Oystering in the state peaked in volume in 1983 when 570,220 bushels worth $1,067,192 were harvested. The greatest value for oysters was in 1981 when 461,401 bushels worth $1,378,227 were landed. The 2002 harvest was 82,510 bushels worth $1,025,346. In Beaufort the last oyster-canning plant in the United States closed in the 1980s. Increased competition from abroad and alternative employment opportunities in the lowcountry contributed to the decline in the industry. In 2003 there was only one full-time fresh-oyster-shucking operation and no canning operation in the state. During the last forty years, numerous mariculture enterprises have come and gone in the state. Catfish, clams, crawfish, and shrimp farming have been attempted, but high labor and land costs (relative to those in Central America and Southeast Asia) and a shorter growing season have contributed to their failure. DAVIS FOLSOM AND DAVID C. SMITH

Leigh, Jack. *Oystering: A Way of Life.* Charleston, S.C.: Carolina Art Association, 1983.

Tibbetts, John H. "The Salty Dogs." *Coastal Heritage* 15 (winter 2000–2001): 3–13.

Fishing Creek, Battle of (August 18, 1780). After the Battle of Camden, Lieutenant Colonel Banastre Tarleton and his British legion pursued the patriot general Thomas Sumter and his troops in the hope of recapturing British prisoners and stores taken by Sumter in a raid just prior to the battle. After an aggressive pursuit, Tarleton's legion neared Sumter's force along the Catawba River in South Carolina. Although Sumter was aware of the British presence across the river, he continued marching up the west bank of the river throughout the morning of August 18, 1780. In the meantime, Tarleton secured boats and sent his command across the river and then continued on a forced march after the enemy.

Sumter, feeling safe in the belief that the British were far enough away on the other side of the river, halted his command to rest at noon at Fishing Creek. The march had been a hard one, under intensely hot and humid conditions and over numerous steep hills, and his men had pushed themselves hard. After posting sentries outside the camp, Sumter allowed his men to stack arms and do as they pleased. Some men napped and some swam in the river, while others lounged around getting drunk.

As Sumter's men relaxed, Tarleton's legion continued their forced march. Many were overcome with the heat, and when they insisted that they could go no further, Tarleton decided to push forward with 160 men, although the enemy force numbered nearly 800. When Tarleton reached the confines of Sumter's camp, he easily subdued the sentries and then swiftly attacked the rebels. His lightning-fast attack made it impossible for the Americans to fight back and left them no choice but to run for their lives. The Americans suffered heavy losses during the fight, including 150 men killed or wounded, 350 captured, and the loss of their British prisoners and plunder and their arms, ammunition wagons, baggage, and other stores. Tarleton's force had just 16 men killed or wounded. Coming on the heels of the humiliating defeat at Camden, the rout of Sumter's force at Fishing Creek marked the low point of the patriot cause in South Carolina. KENDRA DEBANY

Buchanan, John. *The Road to Guilford Courthouse: The American Revolution in the Carolinas.* New York: Wiley, 1997.

Morrill, Dan L. *Southern Campaigns of the American Revolution.* Baltimore: Nautical & Aviation Publishing, 1993.

Russell, David Lee. *The American Revolution in the Southern Colonies.* Jefferson, N.C.: McFarland, 2000.

Fishing, recreational. South Carolina history books have stated for years that the Palmetto State stretches from the "mountains to the sea." As that description implies, the broad range of topography also means a broad range of aquatic habitats, fish, and recreational fishing opportunities. With rivers formed as cold, southern Appalachian mountain streams and warming as they flow through the state toward the Atlantic Ocean, the aquatic habitats and fisheries change dramatically along the way. In addition to the state's rivers, large lakes, small creeks, ponds, bays, marshes, and the Atlantic Ocean all provide for a remarkable variety of places and species for fishing.

Most of the mountain streams in the upcountry of South Carolina, such as the Chattooga, Saluda, and Broad Rivers, originate in the higher elevations of North Carolina. These are cold-water habitats perfect for rainbow, brown, and brook trout. The smaller streams and the headwater tributaries usually contain smaller trout that weigh less than a pound. The larger Chattooga, however, offers not only fish weighing several pounds but also scenic beauty worthy of its designation as a national "wild and scenic" river. Lake Jocassee allows trout to grow to trophy sizes of more than ten pounds because of the abundant threadfin shad population that the trout feed on. This deep, two-tiered fishery allows both cold-water trout and warm-water species such as bass and bluegill to thrive. The S.C. Department of Natural Resources (DNR) supplements the trout populations in the upstate with stockings from their Walhalla Trout Hatchery, and with protective regulations.

As the rivers flow downstream in the state, water temperatures increase and the rivers support warm-water species such as the popular largemouth bass, yellow and white perch, crappie, catfish, and bream, the latter of which usually comprises the many varieties of sunfish. For sport and for table fare, these are all eagerly fished for with tackle ranging from simple cane poles to spin and bait casting rigs to fly outfits.

Large lakes such as Lake Hartwell and Lake Keowee in the upcountry, Lake Greenwood and Lake Murray in the Midlands, and Lake Marion and Lake Moultrie in the lowcountry all provide fishing for the above-named warm-water fish, plus the added bonus of striped bass. Stripers, or rockfish, as they are often called, are the official South Carolina state fish. They are stocked as three- to five-inch fingerling fish by the DNR and can grow to more than forty pounds. This large predatory fish can exist in both freshwater and saltwater, as was found by accident in the early 1940s. A freshwater, riverine population was trapped in Lakes Marion and Moultrie as the Santee and Cooper Rivers were dammed to produce electricity. The DNR began the first striper hatchery program in the country shortly afterward near St. Stephen. The agency has maintained that program to supply fingerlings for fisheries around the state and the country. Striped bass have a large following of fishermen, as the popular largemouth bass does. Most of these fishermen are armed with boats filled with electronic equipment to locate these migratory fish. Striped bass have even fostered an industry of freshwater striper guides on the lakes and are a major component of the tourism industry in the surrounding counties.

As rivers enter the lowcountry, their flow eventually meets the upper tidal waters of the Atlantic Ocean. Fishing for all the freshwater species found further inland is good even in the brackish stretches of slightly saline water where the flows meet and mix. A cast there may result in a hookup with a largemouth bass or with a redfish, flounder, sea trout, sheepshead, or one of the other saltwater species that inhabit the state's inshore estuaries. Below the brackish river stretches, the inshore species of saltwater fish all thrive. Other seasonal, migratory fish such as tarpon and crevalle jack are possible catches in the warmer months.

To add another dimension to fishing along the South Carolina coast, there is also offshore fishing. From just off the beaches out to the artificial reefs there are other species such as black sea bass, Spanish mackerel, bluefish, bonito, king mackerel, grouper, and snapper. To add further to the fishing picture, bull dolphin, sailfish, yellowfin tuna, and marlin roam the Gulf Stream waters more than forty miles out as they move along the Atlantic coast on their seasonal migration patterns. Numerous offshore charter boats, party boats, inshore fishing guides, and commercial piers are available for recreational anglers to fish for these saltwater species. MALCOLM W. LEAPHART, JR.

Flat Nose. "The Lord has something to do with this dog" was the only way Barney Odom could explain the extraordinary powers of his bulldog Flat Nose, whose ability to climb trees brought international attention to Darlington County in the late 1980s. Odom and Flat Nose, residents of the small community of Dovesville, were featured on *The Tonight Show with Johnny Carson* on November 26, 1986, after local and regional media outlets featured Flat Nose's ability to climb pine trees. According to Odom, Flat Nose developed his tree-climbing ability as a puppy despite Odom's efforts to stop him. By the time he was six years old, Flat Nose was owed a kiss by Carson's bandleader Doc Severinsen, who reportedly declared that he would do so to any dog that could climb a tree. After the *Tonight Show* appearance, Flat Nose became an international celebrity, performing at the Super Bowl in 1989, earning a place in the *Guinness Book of World Records,* and appearing on Japanese television commercials. In 1998 the country music band Austin Lounge Lizards immortalized Flat Nose's miraculous aspect in their song "Flatnose, the Tree-Climbing Dog," with lyrics declaring: "He's a miracle dog, climbing dog / Climbing up to Heaven on a log / Precious dog, climbing dog / Flatnose, the tree-climbing dog." Flat Nose made public appearances until mid-1993 and died in Dovesville on December 1, 1993. BENJAMIN T. ZEIGLER

Gatling, Holly. "A Dog's Life: Darlington Man, Flat Nose Are Bark Away from Fame." Columbia *State,* June 1, 1987, pp. B1, B3.

"Death at 14 Ends Flat Nose's Climb to Fame, Fortune." Columbia *State,* December 4, 1993, p. B6.

Florence (Florence County; 2000 pop. 30,248). In the 1850s Florence emerged around the intersection of three railroads: the Wilmington and Manchester, the North Eastern, and the Cheraw and Darlington. William W. Harllee, president of the Wilmington and Manchester, named the town in honor of his daughter, Florence Henning Harllee. On March 9, 1871, the town of Florence was chartered by the state legislature, and the late nineteenth century saw substantial growth. The railroads, consolidated into the Atlantic Coastline Railroad in 1897 (later part of the Amtrak system), constituted the largest taxpayer in the area and helped attract new citizens. A waterworks system (completed in 1903) reduced the danger of fire, an opera house opened to provide entertainment, and newspapers were established. There were Presbyterian, Episcopal, Baptist, Methodist, and Roman Catholic churches, as well as a Jewish congregation and a large number of African American churches. In 1890 the General Assembly incorporated the city of Florence.

The railroad remained the backbone of the economy in Florence, and cotton was gradually replaced by bright leaf tobacco as the major cash crop of the region. The population of 3,395 in 1900 had more than tripled by 1920. Streets were paved, sewers expanded, and Timrod Park established for beauty and recreation. Downtown Florence expanded with the construction of a combination post office and federal court building in 1906 and the seven-story Trust Building in 1919. The Industrial School for Boys was established in Florence in 1906 (later converted to a residential facility for the mental health department), and Clemson College opened its Pee Dee Experimental Station in 1912. In 1923 a bridge over the Pee Dee River brought an increase of automobile traffic into the city, as did the construction of U.S. Highway 301. The citizens were proud of their growing town and noted with enthusiasm the establishment of the Florence Public Library (1903), the McLeod Infirmary (1934), and the Florence Museum (1939). During World War II, Florence was the site of an army air base. In 1958, at the height of the cold war, Florence was nearly the inadvertent target of an atom bomb that was accidentally dropped by a U.S. Air Force bomber. Fortunately, the warhead was not armed, but the explosion of the trigger device injured six people and left a sizable crater near the neighboring town of Mars Bluff.

The railroad yard at Florence. Courtesy, South Caroliniana Library, University of South Carolina

The second half of the twentieth century witnessed further growth and progress. Florence claimed a symphony, a ballet, and the Florence Little Theater, which enjoyed a regional reputation. The city limits expanded and new business emerged to take the place of the declining railroads. The presence of several regionally known dental clinics gave Florence the nickname "Tooth City, U.S.A."; by 1974 some 150,000 persons came to Florence annually for new teeth. DuPont, La-Z-Boy East, Nucor, ESAB Welding and Cutting Products, General Electric Medical Systems, and Roche Carolina were among the major industrial employers, with additional manufacturing firms in the county also contributing to the welfare of the city. The McLeod Regional Medical Center served the eastern part of the state, and the Carolinas Hospital System expanded its range of services. Blue Cross/Blue Shield completed the medical services available in the city.

The progressive reputation of Florence earned it All-American status in 1966, and the population exceeded 25,000 by 1970. During the 1950s and 1960s the Florence *Morning News* advocated the peaceful integration of the public schools and facilities, as the African American population in the city limits reached nearly forty-seven percent. A new civic center provided a home for a professional ice hockey team (the Pee Dee Pride), and Freedom Florence, a softball complex, brought international tournaments to the city. In 1970 Francis Marion College (later University) was established in Florence, supplementing the programs of the Florence-Darlington Technical College. A new city-county complex was built to anchor the downtown skyline, and a large shopping mall went up near the junction of two major tourist arteries, Interstates 20 and 95, which intersected on the western outskirts of Florence. A regional airport also provided service for business and pleasure. By the twenty-first century Florence could take pride in its accomplishments, its growth, and its people. From its origins as a railroad crossroads, Florence had grown into a regional center of business and industry, education, tourism, and health care. CARLANNA H. HENDRICK

King, G. Wayne. *Rise Up So Early: A History of Florence County, South Carolina.* Spartanburg, S.C.: Reprint Company, 1981.

Florence County (800 sq. miles; 2000 pop. 125,761). Created in 1888, Florence County lies between the Great Pee Dee and Lynches Rivers in the eastern part of the state. Before European colonization, the area was inhabited by the Pee Dee (Pedee, Peadea) Indians. European settlement began in the 1730s when the colonial government surveyed Queensborough Township, which attracted Welsh settlers from Wales and Pennsylvania to the area by 1737. Through the remainder of the colonial period, the township attracted a steady stream of immigrants. Many of the colonists in Queensborough were Dissenters rather than members of the state-sanctioned Church of England. The Welsh established the Welch Neck Baptist Church in 1738, and Scots-Irish Presbyterians arrived from Williamsburg Township prior to the Revolutionary War. The population in 1757 was approximately 4,300 Europeans and 500 Africans. Like the majority of colonists in the backcountry, these settlers were farmers who produced cattle, lumber, and indigo.

The settlers in Queensborough Township were heavily involved in both the Regulator movement and the Revolutionary War. During the Regulator period, a large number of colonists favored the vigilante movement. The Mars Bluff area was the scene of a major clash between the government and Regulator forces in 1768. During the Revolutionary War, Francis Marion's partisan group headquartered at Snow's Island, which lies at the confluence of the Lynches and Great Pee Dee Rivers.

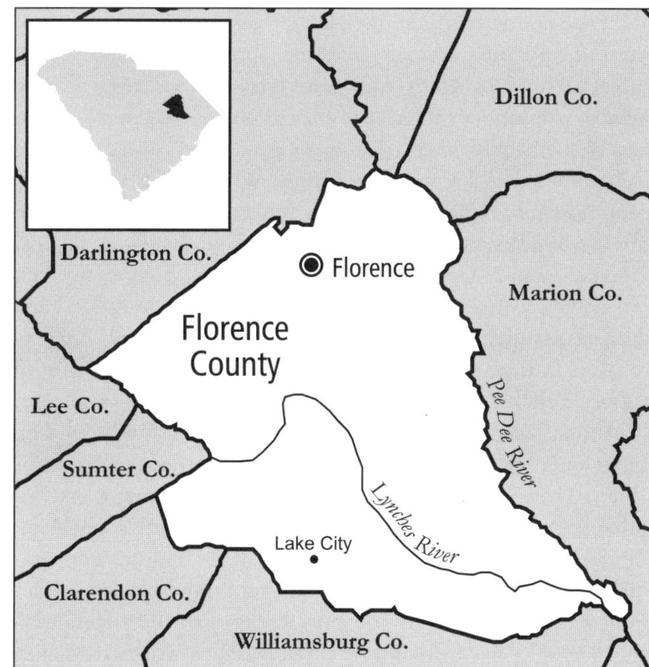

The end of the war brought many changes. In 1785 the legislature split the area in and around Queensborough Township into two counties: Marion and Darlington. Although residents requested that a third county be created between the two, efforts were unsuccessful. The end of the British bounty on indigo left local farmers in search of a new cash crop. They found it in the 1790s with the introduction of the cotton gin. As in the rest of the state, the cultivation of cotton led to a rapid increase in the number of slaves. The 1850 population of Darlington District, which included the future Florence County, contained 10,041 African slaves and 6,747 whites.

By the middle of the nineteenth century, South Carolina worked in earnest to improve transportation links between the interior and the coast. The state chartered several railroad companies, including the Wilmington and Manchester (1846), the Cheraw and Darlington (1849), and the North Eastern Railroad Company (1851). The town of Florence, named after the daughter of Wilmington and Manchester president William W. Harllee, grew up at the intersection of these three railroad lines. The railroads also led to the creation of the town of Timmonsville (1851) and a depot at Grahams (1858), which later became the town of Lake City.

During the Civil War, the Florence area raised two military units, the Pee Dee Light Artillery and the Pee Dee Rifles. These units served in the First South Carolina Regiment. The area was also the site of a volunteer hospital, a prisoner-of-war camp, and a naval yard that produced one gunboat, the CSS *Pee Dee.* At the end of the war, the Florence area was spared the destruction visited upon other South Carolina districts. This and the presence of the railroad helped the area recover swiftly from economic hardship. As early as 1866, several new businesses opened and the North Eastern Railroad built new railroad shops in Florence. The legislature chartered the town of Florence in 1871.

Like the 1780s, the 1880s saw many changes. The Florence "Graded School" system began in 1884. Also in 1884 Frank M. Rogers spearheaded the challenge to "King Cotton's" reign by planting bright leaf tobacco. In addition, the area's rapid growth and strong tax base, coupled with the population's distance from existing courthouses, led to the formation of Florence County from parts of Darlington, Marion, Clarendon, and Williamsburg Counties in 1888.

While cotton remained the mainstay of the county's economy, tobacco cultivation became increasingly profitable. Frank Rogers's successful tobacco crops convinced other farmers to switch to tobacco cultivation, which led to the creation of local tobacco markets in the county. Both tobacco cultivation and tobacco markets grew throughout the twentieth century. While cotton and tobacco continued to be important cash crops throughout the twentieth century, soybeans eventually surpassed both in acres harvested. In 1999 Florence County farmers planted 51,000 acres of soybeans; winter wheat was the second-highest planting at 15,300 acres; and farmers planted 12,500 acres of cotton and 7,730 acres of tobacco. In that year the county ranked fourth in the state in agricultural cash receipts.

Although the county's economy has traditionally been based on agriculture, Florence was home to several industries as early as the 1890s. These included iron- and brickworks, a cottonseed and fertilizer company, a machine manufacturer, and a mattress company. By the 1990s the county contained 139 manufacturing companies that produced plastics, machinery, cars, furniture, fibers, and pharmaceuticals. However, service providers became the largest individual employers, including McLeod Regional Medical Center, Florence School District 1, Blue Cross/Blue Shield of SC/Tricare, and the Carolinas Hospital System.

There are nine cities and towns in Florence County. Florence, the largest with a population of 30,248 in 2000, is the county seat. Lake City, second-largest with a population of 6,748, was the home of astronaut Ronald E. McNair. Other cities include Timmonsville, Johnsonville, Pamplico, Coward, Scranton, Quinby, and Olanta. Higher education in Florence County is provided by Francis Marion University and the Florence-Darlington Technical College. Established in 1970, Francis Marion University sits in the middle of a three-hundred-acre campus and is accredited by the Commission on Colleges of the Southern Association of Colleges and Schools. Florence-Darlington Technical College, established in 1963, offers associate degrees in a variety of fields. Recreation in the county is varied. Lynches River State Park offers nature trails, swimming, and fishing. Woods Bay State Park encompasses several Carolina bays. The county also has numerous golf courses, hunting preserves, and fishing areas. In addition, the county is home to a hockey team, the Florence Little Theater, a symphony orchestra, and several museums. RICKIE A. GOOD

King, G. Wayne. *Rise Up So Early: A History of Florence County, South Carolina.* Spartanburg, S.C.: Reprint Company, 1981.

———. *Some Folks Do: A Pictorial History of Florence County.* Norfolk, Va.: Donning, 1985.

Florence Prison Camp. A backwater for much of the Civil War—a contemporary newspaper described the town as a "name rather than a place"—Florence had an initiation to the conflict that was both deadly and controversial. The fall of Atlanta to General William T. Sherman on September 1 made the prison camps at Andersonville and Millen, Georgia, vulnerable to Federal forces. As a result, in September 1864 Confederate authorities began transferring thousands of Union prisoners from these sites to Florence.

Florence was chosen because of its proximity to three converging railroad lines. Neither the town nor the camp was ready for the sudden rush of Union prisoners—six thousand of whom arrived on September 17. Confederate leaders using slave labor worked quickly on a stockade prison, but it was still incomplete when the first prisoners arrived. Many had been transferred from a temporary facility in Charleston, where smallpox, yellow fever, and scurvy ran rampant. They found conditions no better at Florence. Although Confederate leaders periodically expressed concern about a prisoner mutiny, and particularly about sabotage to rail lines, such fears revealed more about the declining fortunes of the Confederacy than they did about the health and strength of the inmates. The faltering Southern nation simply could not provide basic necessities. Worse, the stockade was built in a swampy bog; six of the prison's twenty-four acres were completely unusable. Nevertheless, twelve thousand Union prisoners were confined there by December. The camp, wrote one observer, was "full of what were once human beings . . . filthy, diseased, famished men, with no hope of relief except by death." At least 2,800 Union prisoners, according to one account, died while in captivity.

Because of these problems and others that plagued the Confederate prison system, the Florence camp was shut down in February 1865. Most of the surviving prisoners were taken to North Carolina, where they were exchanged at various points. PAUL CHRISTOPHER ANDERSON

King, G. Wayne. "Death Camp at Florence." *Civil War Times Illustrated* 12 (January 1974): 35–42.

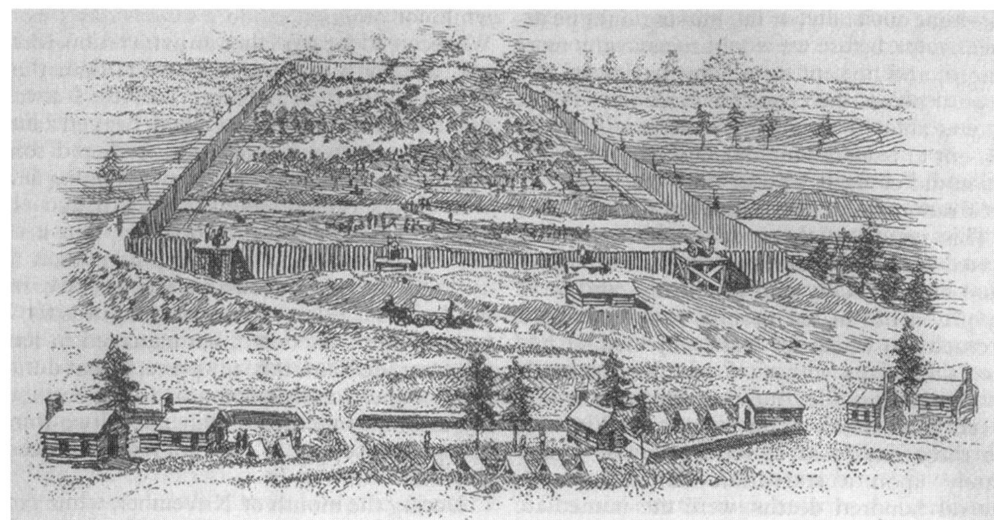

The Confederate Prison at Florence. Courtesy, South Carolina Historical Society

———. *Rise Up So Early: A History of Florence County, South Carolina.* Spartanburg, S.C.: Reprint Company, 1981.

Floyd, Carlisle Sessions (b. 1926). Composer. Born in Latta on June 11, 1926, Floyd is the son of a Methodist minister. He entered Converse College in 1943, studying piano with Ernst Bacon. Floyd followed Bacon to Syracuse University in 1945, eventually earning a B.M. (1946) and an M.M. (1949) in piano and composition. After serving on the music faculty at Florida State University (1947–1976), he was professor of composition at the University of Houston from 1976 until his retirement in 1996. While at FSU, Floyd composed and, in 1955, premiered his opera *Susannah.* Based on the biblical story of Susannah and the Elders but set in 1950s Tennessee, the work won the New York Music Critics' Circle Award in 1956 and was the American operatic entry to the Brussels World's Fair in 1958.

Susannah is the second most frequently performed opera by an American composer, behind George Gershwin's *Porgy and Bess.* A recording on the Virgin Classics label won a Grammy Award in 1994. His opera *Of Mice and Men* (1969), based on the John Steinbeck novel, has had numerous productions by such opera companies as New York City, Utah, San Diego, and Cleveland. His opera *The Passion of Jonathan Wade* (1962, revised 1990) is set in Reconstruction-era Columbia.

In addition to being his own librettist, Floyd has composed more than ten stage works, song cycles, music for orchestra and chorus, and music for piano. He is the recipient of numerous honors and awards, including a Guggenheim Fellowship (1956), an honorary doctorate from Dickinson College (1983), and the National Opera Institute's Award for Service to American Opera (1983). Along with David Gockney, he is codirector of the Houston Opera Studio, a training program for young, aspiring singers and accompanists.
JENNIFER OTTERVIK

Floyd, Carlisle. Papers. South Caroliniana Library, University of South Carolina, Columbia.

Sadie, Stanley, ed. *New Grove Dictionary of Music and Musicians.* 2d ed. 29 vols. New York: Grove's Dictionaries, 2001.

Food. Recipes from the Creole cuisine that evolved in Charleston and the surrounding plantations in the first hundred years of South Carolina's history spread inland. Classic dishes from the lowcountry rice kitchen, such as pilau, okra soup, and rice breads, became popular not only in the upcountry of the state but also up the coast into Maryland and Virginia. Hoppin' John, a bean and rice pilau, became renowned throughout the South, as did fried chicken, collard greens, and cornbread.

By the turn of the eighteenth century, the white population of Charleston and the lowcountry contained a small but influential Huguenot community, with country coastal cooking traditions not unlike those of the English settlers who comprised most of the remaining early Carolinians. In 1730 Germans and Swiss settled in Orangeburg, seventy miles inland, where they grew wheat and cabbage for the lowcountry gentry and raised dairy cattle. Continental European baking and meat cooking and curing skills entered the vernacular. Many of the state's early settlers had first lived in the Caribbean, further adding to the Creole culture. Most important, however, was South Carolina's black majority population. By 1708 Africans and African Americans outnumbered Europeans in the colony. By midcentury the majority outnumbered the minority by two to one. Africans brought with them hunting, fishing, farming, and cooking skills that were well suited to the subtropical environment of the lowcountry.

On any given day for nearly two hundred years, ships filled Charleston harbor. It saw the importation of fresh tropical fruits from Cuba and the Caribbean, spices from around the world, seeds for nearly any herb or vegetable imaginable, the latest cookery books from England, wines from Europe, and cheese from Philadelphia and Boston. The African cooks in the lowcountry most radically influenced the cooking by switching the emphasis from the large roasts of the English and French table to composed one-pot dishes such as pilau and gumbo, with bits of meats strewn in them. Foodstuffs long appreciated in Africa, such as hot peppers, benne (sesame) seeds, okra, tomatoes, and eggplant, entered the colony's kitchens long before the foods were known elsewhere in America and often before they became popular in much of Europe and the British Isles. Coconut cooking in the western world began in Charleston. Native American trading routes to the interior were taken over by the lowcountry gentry, and superior Appalachian corn was ground for use in main dishes and breads.

As cotton farmers moved inland, African American cooks did as well. The diet of the upcountry farmer—often Anglo-Irish who came in large waves of immigration from Virginia and Pennsylvania—was not unlike the diet of his field hands. Plants such as beans that had grown successfully in the lowcountry were bred until they would grow upstate; hundreds of varieties were developed. Pork became the common meat, and hogs roamed the woods to forage. They were penned and slaughtered in the fall and then cured for the winter. After the Civil War, most of the state was poor and stayed poor for a long time. Families exchanged seeds and raised vegetable gardens for their personal use. The long-established traditions of canning and preserving the season's bounty became even more important to the family cook; condiments such as relishes, chutneys, pickles of all sorts, spiced and dried fruits, jams, and syrups came to define the cuisine. Pork chops were served with beans throughout the country, but when those beans were served on rice with a dollop of green tomato or pear relish and the pork was garnished with peach chutney, the meal was not just southern but also Carolinian.

In the middle of the nineteenth century, several artificial means of leavening bread became popular, so that the home cook was freed from the long, hot process of baking yeast bread. Ever quicker versions of cornbread evolved, and biscuits became the bread of choice at the breakfast table. They remain the favored breads in the state. Often the cornbread is deep-fried to make hush puppies. Deep-frying is another cooking technique with strong ties to Africa. In no state is frying more artfully done, from the flash-fried oysters and shrimp on the coast, to the freshwater fish of the Pee Dee and Midlands, to the green tomatoes and okra of the Piedmont. Lard, butter, bacon grease, olive oil, and peanut oil are the preferred cooking fats. Processed foods such as margarine and hydrogenated vegetable oils seldom find favor.

At the heart of the cooking are the foods that grow well in the state, supplemented by wild fish and game. Pork and chicken continue to be the most common meats, and both comprise important industries in the state, along with the saltwater shrimping and crabbing operations. Favored fruits and vegetables include tomatoes, okra, corn, greens, peppers of all kinds, squash, sweet potatoes, dozens of varieties of beans and field peas, cucumbers, scuppernong and muscadine grapes, peaches, strawberries, and melons; peanuts and pecans are widely grown and eaten as well. South Carolina is noted for its sweet tooth; there are legions of pie, cake, cookie, candy, and frozen dessert recipes. Sweetened iced tea is the beverage of choice. JOHN MARTIN TAYLOR

Egerton, John. *Southern Food: At Home, on the Road, in History.* New York: Knopf, 1987.

Hilliard, Sam Bowers. *Hog Meat and Hoecake: Food Supply in the Old South, 1840–1860.* Carbondale: Southern Illinois University Press, 1972.

Kovacik, Charles F. "Eating Out in South Carolina's Cities: The Last Fifty Years." *North American Culture* 4, no. 1 (1988): 53–64.

Taylor, Joe Gray. *Eating, Drinking, and Visiting in the South.* Baton Rouge: Louisiana State University Press, 1982.

Taylor, John Martin. *Hoppin' John's Lowcountry Cooking: Recipes and Ruminations from Charleston and the Carolina Coastal Plain.* New York: Bantam, 1992.

Football. South Carolinians have been playing football since the late nineteenth century. The sport was first played in the Northeast, and in the decades after the Civil War it spread south as cultural ties between the regions were reestablished. College students were the first to play the game, and club teams were formed on campuses across the state. As the sport became more popular, official college teams were organized and intercollegiate play began. The first official game played in the state saw Wofford beat Furman 5–1 (each score counted one point) in Spartanburg on December 14, 1889. The University of South Carolina (USC) played its first game in 1892, losing to Furman 44–0 in Charleston. Four years later Clemson made its football debut, defeating Wofford 14–6 in Greenville; and later the same season USC and Clemson played for the first time, with the Gamecocks winning 12–6.

It was not until after World War I that most state high schools began playing organized football. The economic recovery of the early twentieth century fueled by increased industrialization brought profound cultural changes to the state. Children spent less time in the fields and factories as economic improvements expanded the state's middle class. Teenage boys had more free time, and organized sports such as football became more popular. Stadiums were built for high school teams using local tax dollars, and the boys' exploits on the field became an important point of pride for towns and rural communities. Football increased in popularity in the years after World War II, but due to the segregated structure of the state's school system whites and blacks did not play against each other until after desegregation in 1970. Friday night high school football continues to be an important ritual, with stadiums from Greenville to Charleston filled with thousands of fans rooting for their local teams. John McKissick, head coach at Summerville High School, broke the national record for the most wins by a football coach at any level in 2003 with 510.

College teams were racially segregated until 1970, when Jackie Brown became USC's first African American player. In 1971 Marion Reeves became the first African American to play for Clemson.

Clemson University's 1981 national championship team. Courtesy, Sports Information, Athletic Department, Clemson University

Although the tradition of USC and Clemson playing on "Big Thursday" during the week of the state fair in Columbia ended in 1959, the game continues to draw the largest football crowd in the state each year. Other rivalry games include the Presbyterian College–Newberry College contest for the "Bronze Derby" and the Citadel-Furman rivalry that dates back to 1917. South Carolina State and Benedict College played each other from 1926 to 1966. The schools renewed their rivalry in 1999 and briefly expanded the game to a weeklong festival, the Palmetto Capital City Classic, until South Carolina State pulled out after the 2004 game.

Football at USC and Clemson has become a big business enterprise, with each program having annual budgets that reach into the millions of dollars. Football also brings large sums of money into each school's coffers, paying for many of the less popular sports; most of the revenue comes from ticket sales. USC's Williams Brice Stadium and Clemson's "Death Valley" hold well over eighty thousand fans each and are sold out for the majority of their home games.

There have been significant coaching careers at state colleges. At Clemson, John Heisman, for whom the Heisman Trophy is named, coached the Tigers from 1900 to 1903. Clemson legend Frank Howard coached the Tigers from 1940 to 1969 and holds the record for longest tenure at the school. Danny Ford coached Clemson from 1978 to 1989, with a record of ninety-six wins and twenty-nine losses. The longest tenure at USC was by Rex Enright, who coached the Gamecocks from 1938 to 1942 and from 1946 to 1955. Other USC coaches of national prominence include Paul Dietzel (1966–1974) and Lou Holtz (1999–2004). Furman's W. L. Laval (1915–1927), A. P. McLeod (1932–1942), and Bob King (1958–1972) all coached the Paladins for over ten years. Presbyterian's Walter Johnson (1915–1917, 1919–1940) and Cally Gault (1963–1984) each led the Blue Hose to over one hundred wins. South Carolina State's Willie Jeffries (1973–1978, 1989–2001) is a coaching legend at the Orangeburg school; during his tenure he led the Bulldogs to a record of 122 wins and 72 losses.

The state has produced two national championship teams: Furman, coached by Jimmy Satterfield, defeated Georgia Southern for the 1988 National Collegiate Athletic Association Division I-AA title; and Clemson, under Danny Ford, defeated Nebraska in the Orange Bowl to claim the 1981 NCAA I-A championship. South Carolina colleges have produced scores of All-American players. Two of the best were USC running back George Rogers, who won the Heisman Trophy as the nation's best player in 1980, and Clemson's William "the Refrigerator" Perry, who went on to have an illustrious career with the National Football League's Chicago Bears. DON BARTON

Doyle, Andrew. "Cause Won, Not Lost: Football and Southern Culture, 1892–1983." Ph.D. diss., Emory University, 1998.

———. "Turning the Tide: College Football and Southern Progressivism." *Southern Cultures* 3, no. 3 (1997): 28–51.

Griffin, John Chandler. *Carolina vs. Clemson, Clemson vs. Carolina: A Century of Unparalleled Rivalry in College Football.* Columbia, S.C.: Summerhouse, 1998.

Foothills Trail. South Carolina's first long-distance recreational trail is the Foothills Trail, spanning one hundred miles of backcountry across the upstate. This rugged, often strenuous trail is designated for hiking only and visits some of the most breathtaking places along the North Carolina/South Carolina border. Besides passing through several state parks and the Sumter National Forest, the trail goes around Lake Jocassee and through the Jocassee Gorges Wildlife Management Area.

Natural wonders abound along the Foothills Trail, including waterfalls, bears, deer, grouse, turkeys, trout, salamanders, hemlocks, laurels, rhododendrons, and trilliums. Hikers follow or cross numerous rivers and streams, including the Chattooga, Whitewater, Thompson, Horsepasture, and Middle Saluda. The two cascades of Whitewater Falls are among the highest in the eastern United States. Several mountains add interest as well as weariness to the hiker's task but provide excellent views of the surrounding countryside. Sharp-eyed hikers may also spot petroglyphs or other Native American artifacts.

The Foothills Trail concept came from the Sierra Club and was developed by Duke Power Company; the U.S. Forest Service; the South Carolina Department of Parks, Recreation, and Tourism; and many other organizations and individuals. Trail construction began in 1968, and the nonprofit Foothills Trail Conference was formed in 1974 to manage the trail. Originally, the trail was planned to link Oconee State Park and Table Rock State Park. In the 1980s a "spur" was added to link the trail through the Mountain Bridge State Natural Area to Caesars Head and Jones Gap State Parks. TONY BEBBER

Clark, John, and John Dantzler. *Hiking South Carolina.* Helena, Mont.: Falcon, 1998.

Forest Acres (Richland County; 2000 pop. 10,558). This community, covering nearly five square miles and born amid unique circumstances, is wedged between Columbia and Fort Jackson. On Christmas Day 1934 several residents of historic Quinine Hill took the first steps toward formal organization, primarily because they needed a water system. It became apparent that if they formally incorporated, federal Works Progress Administration funds could be used to fulfill their wishes. So in September 1935 an irregular rectangle of some two square miles parallel to Forest Drive became a city.

The first mayor and leader of the push for incorporated status was John Hughes Cooper, ably assisted by John Henry Hammond. Both had been deeply involved with residential development for nearly twenty years, and Cooper's Forest Land Company was scattering the name "Forest" freely throughout the area: Forest Drive, Forest Lake, and thus Forest Acres.

In 1940 this new entity had 323 residents; a decade later it had 3,240. Original plans were for a quiet, bucolic nirvana. World War II changed this, giving rise to shops and stores serving men and women who flooded into nearby Fort Jackson.

Forest Acres flourished as a bedroom community to Columbia and soon posted one of the highest per capita income levels in the state. It had no police force until 1962 and still relies on Columbia for fire protection. Until 1968 it existed without local property taxes, although county levies were collected and residents each paid a small fee for garbage service. By 2000 the city was governed by a mayor and a four-member council, aided by a staff of seventy, which includes thirty-one police personnel. The city contained two elementary schools, two middle schools, two high schools, and fourteen churches. For reasons not entirely clear, the city seemed to have more than its rightful share of dental offices.

During the years it has spurned merging with Columbia while annexing various neighborhoods, among them the town of Ravenwood. One of these communities, Jackson Heights, is distinguished by streets and avenues bearing college names such as Clemson, Coker, and Converse. Another community along Atascadero Drive flaunts a handful of California names bestowed by a resident who lived and worked on the West Coast during World War II.

Strangely, the dilemma that gave birth to Forest Acres has been largely forgotten. The primary source of water, a spring on Quinine Hill, proved so difficult to maintain that it eventually was abandoned. In 1990 Forest Acres joined the Columbia water system. Nevertheless, that little spring continues to flow quietly, almost secretly, under Forest Drive, at length emptying into Penn Branch behind Richland Mall. As one resident observed, "No one thinks about it anymore." JOHN H. MOORE

Fort Hill (Clemson). The plantation home of John C. Calhoun, Fort Hill was designated a National Historic Landmark in 1960, an honor that was reconfirmed in 1975. Calhoun composed some of his most significant political works at Fort Hill, including his 1828 *South Carolina Exposition and Protest* on constitutional compact theory and the 1831 *Fort Hill Address,* which set forth his theory of nullification.

Calhoun acquired the 1,100-acre plantation in 1825. The core of the main house was erected about 1803 by Dr. James McElhenny, a local Presbyterian pastor, and was called Clergy Hall. Calhoun enlarged it to fourteen rooms and renamed it Fort Hill, named for a fortification built there around 1776. After Calhoun's death in 1850 and the Civil War, the property passed to his son-in-law, Thomas Green Clemson. In his 1888 will, Clemson bequeathed more than 814 acres of the Fort Hill estate to the state of South Carolina for an agricultural college, with a stipulation that the dwelling house "shall never be torn down or altered; but shall be kept in repair with all the articles of furniture and vesture . . . and shall always be open for the inspection of visitors." Since the creation of Clemson University in the 1890s, the school has operated Fort Hill as a house museum as stipulated in Clemson's will.

The Fort Hill complex is comprised of the dwelling house, Calhoun's office, a reconstructed kitchen, and a springhouse. Its architectural style is Greek revival with Federal detailing and with simple, yet elegant interior detailing. Furnishings include a rare Dolphin-style Federal horsehair sofa, a Duncan Phyfe dining table and chairs, and a mahogany sideboard given by Henry Clay and made of wood from the USS *Constitution.* WILLIAM D. HIOTT

Fort Jackson. Established in 1917 as the Sixth National Army Cantonment and named for President Andrew Jackson, this post in Richland County was originally called Camp Jackson. Army engineers selected the site for its sandy soil and year-round temperate climate. Columbia citizens raised money to buy the initial acreage. During World War I, it served primarily as a training ground for new soldiers. Deactivated in 1922, it was transferred in 1925 to the S.C. National Guard. It also hosted recreational facilities and meeting places for civic groups. During the Great Depression, it housed homeless people and Civilian Conservation Corps workers. Reactivated in 1939, Camp Jackson was upgraded to "fort" status in 1940. Most of its surviving wooden buildings—designed to be temporary—were constructed from 1939 to 1941. The reservation meanwhile grew from 23,000 to 53,000 acres. Throughout World War II, the post was again used to train new recruits. It also provided lodging for units awaiting overseas shipment, participating in maneuvers, conducting planning, coordinating draftees, and providing support. Additionally, it served as headquarters for the state's prisoner-of-war camps. In 1949 the Department of Defense announced that Fort Jackson would be closed. Legend holds that President Harry Truman ordered the shutdown to spite Governor Strom Thurmond. Available evidence suggests economics as the major cause.

The Korean War halted the closure. Fort Jackson continued as a training center for new soldiers and mobilized National Guardsmen. Partially because of a rapid influx of black and white draftees in 1950, the fort became one of the first army installations to undergo large-scale desegregation. Although Fort Jackson often stood at the forefront of developments in training, its existence remained tenuous. Local congressmen tried to lower the probability of another base-closing order by lobbying for construction of permanent brick buildings. These efforts began to bear fruit during the 1960s. Unusually close civilian-military ties were cemented in 1968 when the city of Columbia annexed the post. Soldiers receiving training during the 1960s included Cuban expatriates and thousands of young men who went to Vietnam. The post attracted international publicity during the 1967 court-martial of Captain Howard Levy, an antiwar army doctor. The possibility of a shutdown again loomed during the 1970s but was averted through lobbying. In 1977 pioneering experiments with gender-integrated training were conducted there. It was one of the first to implement this change in 1994. The U.S. Army Reserve and National Guard used Fort Jackson to mobilize soldiers for the Persian Gulf War. Defense cutbacks during the 1990s resulted in growth as Fort Jackson gained organizations from installations that closed.

The arrival of the first recruits in 1917 ushered in the installation's site as one of the U.S. Army's most important basic training facilities. Courtesy, South Caroliniana Library, University of South Carolina

By the end of the twentieth century, Fort Jackson was the army's largest training post for new soldiers. Its schools graduated 42,304 people during 2000. Its permanent cadre for that year numbered 4,170, accompanied by 8,745 family members. The fort provided employment for 3,586 civilians and support for retired service members and their families totaling 117,869. Its expenditures added $573.4 million to the local economy. Although it contributed considerably to South Carolina's modernization, its 52,321 acres are largely insulated from development and its forests have become havens for endangered wildlife. ANDREW H. MYERS

Moore, John Hammond. *Columbia and Richland County: A South Carolina Community, 1740–1990.* Columbia: University of South Carolina Press, 1993.

Myers, Andrew H. "Black, White, and Olive Drab: Military-Social Relations during the Civil Rights Movement at Fort Jackson and in Columbia, South Carolina." Ph.D. diss., University of Virginia, 1998.

United States. Army. Army Training Center, Infantry, Fort Jackson, S.C. *50th Anniversary History, 1917–1967, Fort Jackson, South Carolina.* N.p., 1967.

Fort Johnson. Located on Charleston harbor, Fort Johnson was constructed on the northeast point of James Island in 1708. Named after the colony's proprietary governor Nathaniel Johnson, it was apparently built in response to the 1706 French and Spanish attack on Charleston. The original fortification was replaced by a new work in 1759, which was garrisoned under British authority during the colonial period. During the Stamp Act crisis of 1765, Fort Johnson briefly housed revenue stamps and provided protection to British stamp officials. It was occupied by South Carolina troops under the command of Isaac Motte in 1775 and remained in American hands until 1780, when advancing British troops found it destroyed. A third fort was built in 1793, but this was temporally abandoned after a storm breached its sea wall in 1800. Although the fort was frequently reported to be in dilapidated condition, a brick magazine and Martello tower were constructed between 1800 and 1833. The signal shot that commenced the bombardment of Fort Sumter and the beginning of the Civil War was fired from a Fort Johnson mortar battery on April 12, 1861. An amphibious attack conducted on July 3, 1864, by Federal troops stationed on Morris Island was repulsed by the Confederate garrison. On February 17, 1865, Fort Johnson was abandoned during the Confederate evacuation of Charleston. No military construction is documented after 1865. By 1890 the site was an established maritime quarantine station. In 1972 the majority of the Fort Johnson site was dedicated as a marine resources research center under control of the South Carolina Department of Natural Resources. WILLIS J. KEITH

Mustard, Harry S. "On the Building of Fort Johnson." *South Carolina Historical Magazine* 64 (July 1963): 129–35.

Wilcox, Arthur M., and Warren Ripley. *The Civil War at Charleston.* Charleston, S.C.: News and Courier, 1966.

Fort Mill (York County; 2000 pop. 7,587). Although white settlers did not arrive in the area of Fort Mill until the late 1750s, the region was already populated by Native Americans. The Catawbas and Cherokees requested that two forts be built to protect them from their enemies; while Fort Dobbs in North Carolina was completed, no work was ever done on the Fort Mill fort. The planned fort did, however, lend Fort Mill one-half of its name; the other half was supplied by a grist mill on Steele Creek established during the 1770s or 1780s by Isaac Garrison and Theodoric Webb. The post office serving the area had been variously called Pine Hill, White's Store, and Fort Hill. The prior existence of another Fort Hill prompted the name change to Fort Mill in 1830. The town was chartered by the General Assembly on February 12, 1873, and rechartered by the secretary of state on October 11, 1907. The Fort Mill Manufacturing Company was chartered on January 23, 1887, bringing Fort Mill into the textile economy that dominated the upstate. The Fort Mill plant and others in the upstate were combined to form the Springs Cotton Mills in 1931. The mill, which employed twelve hundred people at its peak of operations, was closed in 1983. The area received a boost in population with the arrival of the evangelist minister Jim Bakker's PTL development in 1978. But sustained growth came because Fort Mill was positioned to take advantage of the booming population growth in Charlotte, North Carolina. Fort Mill had become a popular bedroom community by the late 1980s, and industry and residential growth continued to fuel the community through the 1990s. AARON W. MARRS

Bradford, William R., Jr. *Out of the Past: A History of Fort Mill, South Carolina.* N.p., 1997.

Fort Moore. One of the three forts established by the Commons House of Assembly to regulate the Indian trade, Fort Moore was built at the center of a major Indian trade path between the coast and lands far to the west. Completed by 1716 near an old trading center known as Savanna (or Savano) Town, the fort was established to regulate the trade between native groups and colonial traders, whose unscrupulous dealings had led to the Yamassee War (1715–1718), which nearly destroyed the colony. It may have been named for Governor James Moore, an early promoter of Native American trade and advocate of making South Carolina the bulwark of England's southern colonies. Constructed near the banks of the Savannah River (nearly opposite the future settlement of Augusta, Georgia), the fort had four wooden walls with bastions on the corners, a storehouse, and barracks for its garrison. In Fort Moore's early decades, its garrison fluctuated but generally consisted of colonial militia that included a commander, a lieutenant, a sergeant, twenty-four privates, and a few artillery pieces.

For most of its history, Fort Moore served as the province's major Indian trading center for deerskins and other animal hides. In addition it was an important meeting site between colonial authorities and Creek, Choctaw, and Cherokee delegations. Governor James Glenn met a large delegation of Creeks there in his 1746 visit to the upcountry in order to resolve trade disputes. During the late 1740s the fort was rebuilt because its original structure had severely deteriorated. During the first Cherokee War (1759–1761), Fort Moore became a haven for many settlers seeking refuge from bands of Cherokee raiders. Following the defeat of the Cherokees, however, authorities in Charleston chose to abandon Fort Moore since the hide trade had declined significantly and Augusta had long overshadowed it. FRITZ HAMER

Crane, Verner. *The Southern Frontier, 1670–1732.* Durham, N.C.: Duke University Press, 1928.

Easterby, J. H., ed. *The Journal of the Commons House of Assembly.* Vol. 9, *March 28, 1749–March 19, 1750.* Columbia: South Carolina Archives Department, 1962.

Meriwether, Robert L. *The Expansion of South Carolina, 1729–1765.* Kingsport, Tenn.: Southern Publishers, 1940.

Fort Motte. Fort Motte was the plantation home of Rebecca Motte that was fortified by the British during the Revolutionary War. Located on a high prominence overlooking the Congaree River, the fort served as a depot for supply convoys between Charleston, Ninety Six, and Camden. The fort consisted of the Motte house surrounded by a ditch and a parapet. After the capture of Fort Watson, Brigadier General Francis Marion and Lieutenant Colonel Henry Lee moved north on May 6, 1781, and began a siege. In the fort were Lieutenant Donald McPherson with 140 British regulars plus a small detachment of dragoons. A British relief force under the command of Francis Lord Rawdon came within sight on May 11, giving hope to the besieged garrison. However, Marion and Lee, realizing that they had to act quickly, decided to set Mrs. Motte's house on fire. Lee asserted in his *Memoirs* that upon informing Mrs. Motte of their decision she offered the bow and arrows for the task, but William Dobein James, a Marion biographer, dismisses this story, stating that the fire was started by slinging burning rosin onto the roof. Either way, Mrs. Motte's home was set afire and Marion's six-pound cannon kept the British from putting it out. The British were forced to surrender. The fire was extinguished, and that evening Mrs. Motte entertained both the British and American officers. Although only two men died in the battle, several Loyalists were hanged the next day. Marion saved another. STEVEN D. SMITH

James, William Dobein. *A Sketch of the Life of Brig. Gen. Francis Marion.* 1821. Reprint, Marietta, Ga.: Continental Book Company, 1948.

Lee, Henry. *The Revolutionary War Memoirs of General Henry Lee.* 1869. Reprint, New York: Da Capo, 1998.

Rankin, Hugh F. *Francis Marion: The Swamp Fox.* New York: Crowell, 1973.

Fort Moultrie. This was the site of the June 28, 1776, American victory in the Revolutionary War. Fort Moultrie I, the Revolutionary War–era fort, was replaced in 1798 by Fort Moultrie II, which was followed in 1809 by Fort Moultrie III, which served as a military post until 1947.

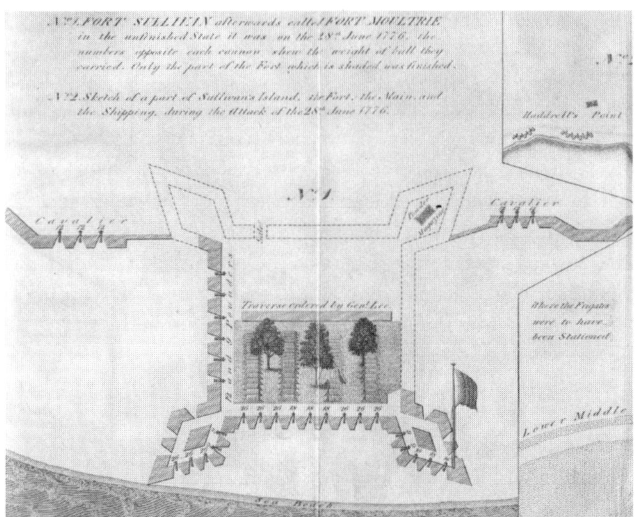

A drawing of the unfinished palmetto-log fort on Sullivan's Island. Courtesy, South Carolina Historical Society

Fort Moultrie I was located on Sullivan's Island at the mouth of Charleston harbor. Construction began in February 1776 on the then-unnamed palmetto log and sand fort. A square fort with corner bastions, its walls were five hundred feet long, more than ten feet high, and sixteen feet apart, with the space between filled with sand. On June 28, 1776, Colonel William Moultrie commanded the half-completed fort, which mounted thirty-one cannons and a garrison of more than four hundred soldiers. In the nine-and-one-half-hour battle, nine British warships with almost three hundred cannons were defeated. After the victory, the fort was completed and named in Moultrie's honor. After the war the fort was not garrisoned and fell into disrepair.

Completed in 1798, the second fort was a five-sided brick, timber, and earthen structure with walls seventeen feet high and sixteen mounted cannons. Built near the site of the 1776 fortification, Fort Moultrie II was almost destroyed by a hurricane in 1804.

The third Fort Moultrie was completed in 1809 on the site of the 1798 fort. It had five fifteen-feet-high brick walls and originally mounted forty cannons. When South Carolina seceded on December 20, 1860, Fort Moultrie III was commanded by Major Robert Anderson, who transferred his command to Fort Sumter on the night of December 26. South Carolina troops moved into Fort Moultrie the next day, and on April 12, 1861, it played a major role in the bombardment of Fort Sumter.

Though heavily damaged by Union bombardments during the Civil War, Fort Moultrie played a key role in the Confederate defense of Charleston harbor. After the war, the fort was repaired but not garrisoned, and by 1887 it was once more in need of major repairs. In 1897 the fort was again garrisoned. After the Spanish-American War in 1898 concrete batteries were built and other improvements were made inside the fort. The army also purchased land on Sullivan's Island to construct more batteries and other structures, establishing the Fort Moultrie Reservation. During World War I as many as three thousand army personnel lived on the reservation. After the war it served as a U.S. Army National Guard and Civilian Conservation Corps training facility.

During World War II the garrison was increased and its defenses improved. While no combat occurred, German U-boats mined the harbor entrance in September 1942. In 1944 an army-navy command post was constructed inside Fort Moultrie to provide a single location to direct the artillery defending the harbor and control the shipping. The Fort Moultrie Reservation was deactivated in 1947 and its buildings sold to private individuals or given to the state of South Carolina. In 1960 Fort Moultrie was transferred by the state to Fort Sumter National Monument, a unit of the National Park Service. RICHARD W. HATCHER III

Stokeley, Jim. *Fort Moultrie: Constant Defender.* Washington, D.C.: United States Department of the Interior, 1985.

Fort Prince George. Fort Prince George was constructed in the fall of 1753 under the supervision of royal governor James Glen. The South Carolina Provincial Assembly considered a fortification amid the lower towns of the Cherokee vital to stabilize conditions on the frontier of the province. The fort lay on the east bank of the Keowee River near the Cherokee village of the same name. It was a one-hundred-foot square ditched fortification, surrounded by palisade-topped earthen walls and with a bastion in each of its corners. The interior sheltered a guardhouse, a storehouse, a kitchen, a magazine, a barracks, and the commandant's residence. Completely rebuilt in 1756, Fort Prince George was garrisoned by a detachment from one of three British Independent Companies.

Since 1758 relations between the Cherokees and the crown had been deteriorating. A peace delegation of Cherokee chiefs was seized in Charleston and then sent to Fort Prince George as hostages. By January 1760 relations between the Cherokees and the crown had become strained to the point of war. Preparations were made inside the stronghold for an attack. On February 16, 1760, the commander of Fort Prince George, Lieutenant Richard Coytmore, was lured outside the walls for a parley and mortally wounded. His outraged men retaliated by executing several hostages confined in the fort. The fortification was besieged sporadically for the next four months, until a relief force under Colonel Archibald Montgomery arrived in June. The fort served as the starting point for the 1762 campaign against the Cherokee middle towns. In 1764 elements of the Sixtieth Regiment of Foot, also known as the Royal American Regiment, assumed garrison duty. Mounting tensions between Great Britain and her North American colonies, however, led to the abandonment of the outpost in 1768.

In the early 1960s Duke Power Company planned construction of a large nuclear power facility in the area of Fort Prince George. In late 1966 assistant state archaeologist John D. Combes began excavating the site until it was flooded by the waters of Lake Keowee in 1968. SAMUEL K. FORE

Hatley, M. Thomas. *The Dividing Paths: Cherokees and South Carolinians through the Era of Revolution.* New York: Oxford University Press, 1993.

McKown, Bryan F. "Fort Prince George and the Cherokee–South Carolina Frontier, 1753–1768." Master's thesis, Clemson University, 1988.

Oliphant, John. *Peace and War on the Anglo-Cherokee Frontier, 1756–1763.* Baton Rouge: Louisiana State University Press, 2001.

Williams, Marshall W. *A Memoir of the Archaeological Excavation of Fort Prince George, Pickens County, South Carolina along with Pertinent Historical Documentation.* Columbia: South Carolina Institute of Archaeology and Anthropology, University of South Carolina, 1998.

Fort San Felipe. Built in 1566, Fort San Felipe was the first fort that Spaniards constructed in the town of Santa Elena on present-day Parris Island, South Carolina. Pedro Menéndez de Avilés, the settlement's founder, placed his fort on the remains of Charlesfort, built by the French in 1562. The choice of the Charlesfort site allowed the Spaniards to raise their structure quickly in an excellent location for the defense of Port Royal Sound. Beyond the site's practical advantages, construction of Fort San Felipe over the French fort had symbolic significance: a fortification bearing the name of the Spanish king Philip II would stand where one named for France's Charles IX had been. Through these and other actions, Spain defied French claims to the Atlantic coast of North America.

The Spaniards constructed Fort San Felipe from sandy soil and other materials of the land. In its early days the fort had a triangular shape with walls made of wood and earth mounded over bundles of sticks piled high. Platforms, or cavaliers, stood at each corner of the fort, and a moat surrounded it. Through repairs and improvements, the structure of Fort San Felipe evolved over time. In 1571 a fire in the munitions house caused the Spaniards to move the fort to another Parris Island location. Fort San Felipe stood at this new site until 1576, when the Guale, Orista, and Escamazu native tribes destroyed it with flaming arrows in an attack on the Santa Elena settlement. KAREN L. PAAR

South, Stanley, and Chester B. DePratter. *Discovery at Santa Elena: Block Excavation, 1993.* Columbia: South Carolina Institute of Archaeology and Anthropology, University of South Carolina, 1996.

Fort Sumter. At 4:30 A.M. on April 12, 1861, the Civil War began when Confederate forces opened fire on the U.S. garrison holding Fort Sumter. The bombardment lasted thirty-four hours, with the formal surrender taking place on April 14.

Named after South Carolina Revolutionary War general Thomas Sumter, Fort Sumter was one of the fortifications built to protect the nation's seacoast after the War of 1812. Construction began in 1829 with the placement of about seventy thousand tons of rock and granite rubble from New England quarries on a shoal located at the harbor's entrance. This two-and-one-half-acre, man-made island served as the foundation on which to build the pentagonal fort. With walls five feet thick and fifty feet high, Fort Sumter was designed to mount 135 heavy cannons and garrison 650 officers and men. The fort was about ninety percent complete when South Carolina seceded on December 20, 1860, and due to the war was never finished.

Two years after the April 1861 bombardment, the next military action against Fort Sumter took place on April 7, 1863. Known as the "Ironclad Attack," this battle lasted two and one-half hours. The fort and other Confederate installations at the harbor's entrance defeated nine Federal gunboats in their attempt to move past the fort and enter Charleston harbor. Three months later, in July, a U.S. Army-Navy force began operations to move onto Morris Island, erect batteries, bombard and capture Fort Sumter, and remove the harbor obstructions so that the navy could enter the harbor and capture Charleston.

Union forces soon controlled Morris Island, except from Battery Wagner to Battery Gregg on Cummings Point. After two failed assaults against Wagner, siege operations were initiated to force the Confederates to give up their hold on the island. This included construction of artillery batteries that mounted the largest rifled guns ever used in combat in the United States.

On August 17, 1863, the first major bombardment of Fort Sumter began with the batteries at ranges from two to two and one-half miles, plus the heavy guns from five Federal warships. In the first seven days more than 5,000 heavy artillery rounds were fired. Outgunned, on August 23 Fort Sumter fired only 6 rounds in its defense, the last ever fired in combat from the fort. With the end of this bombardment on September 2, more than 7,300 rounds had been fired at the fort, giving it the appearance of a mass of ruins.

On the night of September 6, Confederate forces evacuated Morris Island, whereupon Admiral John A. Dahlgren demanded Fort Sumter's surrender. This was rejected, and on the night of September 8 and 9 Dahlgren ordered an amphibious assault against the fort, in which four hundred Union sailors and marines were defeated. The Federals, now in complete control of Morris Island, constructed new batteries up to Cummings Point, and Fort Sumter was shelled at will with tens of thousands of heavy artillery rounds. Though destroyed as an artillery installation, the fort was still a critical front-line position in Charleston's defenses. Using soldiers and slave gangs, Confederate engineers converted the heavily damaged brick fortification into a powerful earthwork.

When Union general William T. Sherman captured Columbia on February 17, 1865, that same evening Confederate forces evacuated Charleston, Fort Sumter, and its other defenses. When U.S. forces entered the fort the next day, they found the interior buildings destroyed and most of its former fifty-foot walls at about half of their original height. During the 587-day siege, more than seven million pounds of artillery projectiles had been fired at the fort.

In the 1870s Sumter was restored to about half of its original height and seventeen cannons were mounted in the fort. Despite this, until the 1890s the fort stood largely neglected, primarily serving as a lighthouse station. However, in 1898, in response to the Spanish-American War, the army constructed Battery Isaac Huger (after South Carolina Revolutionary War general Isaac Huger) across the middle of the fort's parade ground and filled the remaining interior areas with earth to the height of the brick walls. Upon completion in 1899, Battery Isaac Huger mounted two twelve-inch, breech-loading rifled cannons.

The battery was garrisoned during World Wars I and II by the U.S. Coast Artillery Corps. In 1943 its twelve-inch guns were removed and replaced with four ninety-millimeter guns. The fort, considered obsolete by the army after World War II, was closed in 1947, transferred to the National Park Service the following year, and designated Fort Sumter National Monument. See plate 21. RICHARD W. HATCHER III

Burton, E. Milby. *The Siege of Charleston, 1861–1865.* Columbia: University of South Carolina Press, 1970.

Fort Sumter: Anvil of War. Washington, D.C.: Division of Publications, National Park Service, U.S. Department of the Interior, 1984.

Johnson, John. *The Defense of Charleston Harbor, Including Fort Sumter and the Adjacent Islands, 1863–1865.* 1890. Reprint, Germantown, Tenn.: Guild Bindery Press, 1994.

Fort Watson. Fort Watson, named for Colonel John Watson, was one of a series of British supply depots between Charleston and Camden during the Revolutionary War. The fort was located at Wright's Bluff overlooking Scott's Lake and was constructed between late December 1780 and the end of January 1781. Scott's Lake has since been inundated by Lake Marion, and the fort site is protected by the Santee National Wildlife Refuge. The British constructed the formidable stockaded post on top of an ancient Indian mound, surrounding it with three rows of sharpened tree trunks and branches called abatis. On April 15, 1781, the Americans under the command of Francis Marion and Henry Lee invested the fort and began a siege that lasted eight days and ended with its capture. The fort's garrison included seventy-eight regular British soldiers and thirty-six Loyalists under the command of Lieutenant James McKay. With the strong garrison, the abatis, and the cleared land around the fort, Marion and Lee realized that a frontal assault to take the fort would be too costly. At the suggestion of Major Hezekiah Maham, the Americans constructed a log tower near the fort. This allowed riflemen to fire into the fort and protected an assault party that pulled away the abatis, forcing the British to surrender. The fort was destroyed. STEVEN D. SMITH

Ferguson, Leland G. "An Archeological-Historical Analysis of Fort Watson: December 1780–April 1781." In *Research Strategies in Historical Archaeology,* edited by Stanley South. New York: Academic Press, 1977.

James, William Dobein. *A Sketch of the Life of Brig. Gen. Francis Marion.* 1821. Reprint, Marietta, Ga.: Continental Book Company, 1948.

Lee, Henry. *The Revolutionary War Memoirs of General Henry Lee.* 1869. Reprint, New York: Da Capo, 1998.

Rankin, Hugh F. *Francis Marion: The Swamp Fox.* New York: Crowell, 1973.

Forty-Acre Rock (Lancaster County). Forty-Acre Rock harbors one of the most diverse plant habitats in the Piedmont of South Carolina. Actually a fourteen-acre slab of granite (called a monadnock by geologists), the exposed rock was once a magma flow far beneath the earth that cooled and hardened and was revealed only through millennia of erosion. The popular destination is protected under the state's Heritage Trust Program and, with its surrounding area along nearby Flat Creek, offers 1,587 acres of preserve for the benefits of wildlife—both plant and animal—and visitors. The area is registered as a National Natural Landmark.

Nearly a dozen rare, threatened, or endangered species are protected at Forty-Acre Rock, most notably the endangered pool sprite, which flourishes in vernal pools on the rock's surface during early spring months. The tiny pool sprite is one of the most endangered plants in the world and, along with the other plant communities on and around the rock, should be left undisturbed. Lichens, mosses, and some scrubby eastern red cedars also populate the rock face.

Visitors to the rock can enjoy both the expanse of the rock face and the trails winding through distinct habitat types, including a waterfall and cave, additional granite outcroppings, a beaver pond, and upland hardwood and pine forests, where each season brings a different floral display. CAROLINE FOSTER

Foster, Caroline. "Field Trip: Forty-Acre Rock." *South Carolina Wildlife* 45 (March–April 1998): 44–47.

Jerman, Patricia L. *The South Carolina Nature Viewing Guide.* Columbia: South Carolina Department of Natural Resources, 1998.

Fossils. Fossils are any evidence of past life. They may be molds and casts, impressions, tracks, or pollen, to name a few. The study of fossils is the science of paleontology, which is subdivided into many different areas of study. Paleobotanists study fossil plants. Invertebrate and vertebrate paleontologists study fossil animals. Many other lines of study exist, such as paleoclimatology, taphonomy, and paleoecology. Within the confines of South Carolina all of these disciplines, and many others related to the study of paleontology, are useful for understanding the fossil record of the state.

The oldest fossils known from South Carolina are from the early Paleozoic era, from a time period termed the Cambrian period, and are about five hundred million years old. Some species called trilobites have been collected from several sites near Batesburg. Trilobites are the oldest extinct group of aquatic arthropods known and are most closely related to modern-day crustaceans and insects.

The Mesozoic era, "the Age of Reptiles," is present in South Carolina but is limited to only a few sites in the eastern part of the state. Dinosaur remains have been collected from several sites in the Kingstree and Florence areas. Several species of carnivorous dinosaurs and herbivorous duck-billed dinosaurs have been identified, based on teeth and toe bones that are, in some cases, distinctive. Other fossils of this age from the state include mosasaurs, plesiosaurs, ammonites, and a large array of other marine species that lived at the same time. Most of the Mesozoic fossils from the state are from the late Cretaceous period, about seventy to sixty-six million years ago.

The Cenozoic era, sometimes called "the Age of Mammals," encompasses the last sixty-five million years. In terms of fossils, it is the most completely represented period in South Carolina prehistory. Fossils have been collected from all of the major time periods of the era, but some time periods are better understood than others are. The latest time period, the Pleistocene epoch, "the Ice Ages," is the youngest and best studied and understood. This was the time of mammoths, mastodons, giant ground sloths, and bison with horns seven feet from tip to tip, in addition to the many species still alive today, including modern snakes and turtles. Many of South Carolina's clay, sand, and limestone layers, termed "strata," are of marine origin, so many of the fossils from the state represent marine organisms. Some of the earliest North American whales are known from the middle and late Eocene epoch of South Carolina. Archaic mysticete whales, precursors of modern-day baleen whales, are found in the state, along with early toothed whales, or odontocetes. Much of the evolutionary history of whales will be written based on research conducted on fossils collected and studied in South Carolina. Presently more than four hundred species of fossil vertebrates are known from South Carolina, and the list will continue to grow as new site discoveries and study of more fossil materials are undertaken. JAMES KNIGHT

Fountain Inn (Greenville and Laurens Counties; 2000 pop. 6,017). Fountain Inn, formerly a commercial center for southern Greenville County, by the late twentieth century had increasingly become a bedroom community for the burgeoning city of Greenville.

The name Fountain Inn derives from an early nineteenth-century "inn with a fountain" (a gushing spring) on the post road midway between the county seats of Greenville and Laurens. A post office established in 1832 was given the name Fountain Inn. Noah Cannon bought a large tract of land south of the inn following the Civil War and opened a store, but no real center existed until after the 1886 arrival of the Charleston and Western Carolina Railroad, which ran between Laurens and Greenville. Cannon laid out town lots and Fountain Inn was chartered in December of that year.

In 1886 the town had three stores, a school, a Masonic lodge, and a Baptist church. Within three years the Baptists were joined by the Methodists and the Presbyterians to form the usual church triumvirate of upcountry towns. By the early twentieth century the town had grown to over twenty businesses, including two hotels, a cotton gin, a bank, and a pharmacy. Local investors joined the late nineteenth-century textile boom that swept the upstate by opening the Fountain Inn Cotton Mill in 1898. In typical fashion, this led to the establishment of a mill village to provide housing for workers. The village, with its school and churches, was located across the railroad tracks from the rest of the town. Other textile mills followed, but Fountain Inn remained primarily a commercial hub for nearby farmers. Twentieth-century transportation developments reinforced Fountain Inn's prosperity, as the town straddled what emerged as a major north-south highway in the upstate.

The second half of the twentieth century brought a general decline, beginning with the agricultural economy, followed by the textile industry, and compounded by the development of regional shopping malls. However, the rural decline coincided with an increase in the town's population, especially in the number of African Americans. The era also witnessed some loss of community identity as the high school was consolidated, the local paper started serving "The Golden Strip" (Fountain Inn and her neighbors to the north, Simpsonville and Mauldin), and the local beauty queen became "Miss Golden Strip."

By the twenty-first century, some diversification of the industrial base had occurred and the completion of Interstate 385 to Greenville led to considerable residential growth within the city and in the surrounding area. The interstate made it easy for many to work and shop outside the area, and the increased population provided a base for revitalizing the downtown. Nevertheless, Fountain Inn still retained much of its small-town character and charm. JAMES W. BROWN

Coleman, Caroline S., and B. C. Givens, comps. *History of Fountain Inn.* Fountain Inn, S.C.: Tribune-Times, [1965].

Huff, Archie Vernon, Jr. *Greenville: The History of the City and County in the South Carolina Piedmont*. Columbia: University of South Carolina Press, 1995.

Richardson, James M. *History of Greenville County, South Carolina, Narrative and Biographical.* 1930. Reprint, Spartanburg, S.C.: Reprint Company, 1980.

Fox, William Price (b. 1926). Author. Fox was born in Waukegan, Illinois, on April 9, 1926, and grew up in Columbia, South Carolina. After serving as a flight officer aboard B-29s in World War II, Fox returned to Columbia to attend the University of South Carolina, graduating in 1950 with a degree in history. He went to New York City, where he worked as a salesman. During his New York years he attended Caroline Gordon's creative writing classes at the New School, and she encouraged him to shape his short stories for publication.

Fox's first book of short stories, *Southern Fried* (1962), and its continuance, *Southern Fried Plus Six* (1968), are set in Columbia and its environs, where most of Fox's later fiction works are set. Columbia in Fox's writing is the place of moonshine stills, barbecue, drive-ins, baseball games, razor fights, torrid summers, and populist politics. In Fox's work, Columbia is a diverse southern city populated by eccentrics, hustlers, and natural comedians, with a peppering of bullies and petty criminals. Their stories are told with high good humor and liberal doses of biting satire. Fox's first two books of short stories are remarkably popular, having sold more than one million copies.

Fox's novels *Moonshine Light, Moonshine Bright* (1967), *Ruby Red* (1971), *Dixiana Moon* (1981), and *Wild Blue Yonder* (2002) give full range to his talents for character development, depiction of southern humor, and stinging satirical portraits of the flawed among us, notably hypocritical preachers and unctuous con men and politicians.

In addition to writing fiction, Fox is also a journalist of national reputation. He has published articles in *Sports Illustrated, Saturday Evening Post, Harper's, Holiday,* and *Golf Digest,* among others. In the late 1960s he wrote screenplays in Hollywood and New York. His screenplay credits include *Southern Fried* (1967), *Off We Go* (1968), and *Cold Turkey* (1970). In 1969 he wrote a television screenplay, "Fast Nerves," based on his first published short story, for American Playhouse, WNET-TV, New York City.

Fox's writing, both fiction and nonfiction, is characterized by his pervasive conviction that humor is a saving attitude and that traditional southern storytelling is a high art form. Fox's humor writing is also characterized by his uncommon talent for hearing and repeating the southern vernacular language, which carries heavy weight in all of his writing.

Fox's university teaching career started at the University of Iowa, where he taught creative writing at the graduate level for four years (1968–1972). Then he taught article writing at the University of Iowa School of Journalism from 1974 to 1976. In 1976 he joined the faculty of the English department at the University of South Carolina as writer-in-residence. CHARLES ISRAEL

Bruccoli, Matthew J., et al., eds. *Conversations with Writers.* 2 vols. Detroit.: Gale, 1977–1978.

Johnston, Carol. "William Price Fox." In *Dictionary of Literary Biography.* Vol. 2, *American Novelists since World War II.* Edited by Jeffery Helterman and Richard Layman. Detroit: Gale, 1978.

Francis Marion National Forest. Located in the coastal plain of Berkeley and Charleston Counties, the Francis Marion National Forest (FMNF) is composed of more than 250,000 acres of natural area, which was designated a national forest in 1936 by President Franklin Roosevelt. Much of the value of the forest lies in the biodiversity and natural communities found there. The Berkeley/Charleston County area is home to more than fourteen hundred species of plants, or approximately forty-five percent of the total number of plant species found in South Carolina. Among these are fifteen species of insectivorous (bug-eating) plants. The forest contains an exceptional diversity of animal species as well. More than three hundred species of bird have been observed within the forest, including such rarities as swallow-tailed kites and wood storks. The forest is composed of a wide variety of natural habitats, including coastal marshes, maritime forests, swamp forests, hardwood forests, and longleaf pine flat-woods and savannas. Twenty-five large, well-developed Carolina bays are also found within the forest boundaries, providing critical habitats for many rare and unusual species.

The natural areas of the FMNF are home to numerous rare and endangered plant species, including American chaffseed, Canby's dropwort, and pondberry. The large expanses of longleaf pine forests here also provide habitat for the federally endangered red-cockaded woodpecker. This bird, like many other plants and animals found here, is dependant on periodic low-intensity ground fires to keep the pinelands open and prevent invasion by hardwood species. Fire is the most important management tool used in the FMNF.

The FMNF provides miles of hiking trails with nine major trails, including the Swamp Fox trail that crosses most of the natural communities found in the forest. Trails are also provided for equestrian use. Game species abound on the forest and provide ample opportunity for hunting and fishing. Canoe and kayak enthusiasts will find many miles of quiet trails on black-water and tidal areas of Wambaw, Wadboo, Echaw, French Quarter, and Huger Creeks. Four wilderness areas provide more than thirteen thousand acres of unmanaged land for the adventurous explorer. PATRICK MCMILLAN

Francis Marion University. Founded in 1970, Francis Marion University is one of South Carolina's twelve state-supported universities and one of nine comprehensive institutions. In its authorizing legislation in 1969, the name of the institution was Marion State College. However, the name was changed by legislative enactment to Francis Marion College, named for South Carolina's Revolutionary War hero General Francis Marion.

The institution was the product of an effort begun in 1956 to bring higher education to the citizens of the Pee Dee. In 1957 the University of South Carolina opened the Florence Regional Campus, offering two-year programs. Subsequently, the Pee Dee Educational Foundation was chartered to receive and administer funds for a building site and campus construction. In 1968 the Central Pee Dee College District Board was created to provide higher-education opportunities for the citizens of Marion, Dillon, Florence, and Williamsburg Counties. In 1970 Francis Marion College was officially established on a one-hundred-acre site that was donated to the Pee Dee Educational Foundation by the descendants of Joseph Wilds and Sallie Gregg Wallace. What was initially a three-building, two-year regional campus of the University of South Carolina became Francis Marion College, accompanied by plans to build the only comprehensive college campus in the Pee Dee. Since its founding, the campus has expanded to include eighteen buildings on three hundred acres east of Florence.

In 1992 Francis Marion College became Francis Marion University (FMU). The academic program consisted of three schools, ten academic departments, and more than thirty major fields of study. Graduate degrees were offered in business, education, and psychology. FMU's Alumni Association had more than twelve thousand members by the turn of the century, and the university enrolled approximately four thousand students annually.

FMU obtained accreditation by the Commission on Colleges of the Southern Association of Colleges and Schools (SACS) to award bachelor's and master's degrees. Its most popular majors include biology, elementary education, and psychology. It has retained its reputation as an educational resource for the citizens of the Pee Dee region, although it draws almost ten percent of its student body from beyond South Carolina. JULIE ROTHOLZ

Fraser, Charles (1782–1860). Miniature portraitist, painter. One of South Carolina's most distinguished native artists, Charles Fraser achieved national and international recognition as a miniature portraitist during his lifetime. He was born on August 20, 1782, in Charleston, the son of Alexander Fraser and Mary Grimké. Essentially self-taught, Fraser received early encouragement from his boyhood friend and contemporary Thomas Sully, with whom he shared a love of the theater. Fraser's only known formal training was at the age of thirteen with the engraver and painter Thomas Coram, who had opened a drawing school in 1784. Under Coram's supervision, Fraser began several juvenile sketchbooks that include copies after illustrations in travel books by the English artist William Gilpin.

Fraser also enjoyed early friendships with other Charleston artists, including Washington Allston and John Blake White. In 1801 Fraser was introduced to the noted miniature portraitist Edward Greene Malbone, who visited Charleston again in 1802 and 1806 and enjoyed numerous commissions. While a teacher-student relationship remains undocumented, stylistically Fraser's miniature portraits relate closely to those of Malbone. Their friendship is evidenced by Fraser's 1806 visit to Newport, Rhode Island, to see Malbone, and by the fact that Fraser composed the epitaph for Malbone's tomb after his untimely death.

Despite his early interest in art, Fraser was induced to study the law under John Julius Pringle, former attorney general of South Carolina. Admitted to the bar in 1807, Fraser eventually assumed Pringle's practice. In 1818, however, Fraser abandoned the law to pursue a career as an artist. To mark this transition, Fraser initiated an account book, which he maintained with regularity until 1846.

Fraser spent his entire life in his native Charleston painting miniature portraits of his fellow citizens and visiting dignitaries, including the Marquis de Lafayette and John C. Calhoun. He enjoyed a long and acclaimed career and produced an impressive volume of miniature portraits. A detailed system of stippling was the hallmark of his style, and its handling is often a factor in dating his miniatures. He extended his artistic experiences with numerous trips north to locations such as New York, Boston, Hartford, and Philadelphia, where he met the artists John Trumbull, Gilbert Stuart, and Alvin Fisher. During these trips, Fraser produced watercolor sketches of local scenic sights, many of which were published in *Analectic Magazine* as early as 1816. While larger oil paintings are part of his work, Fraser often copied from portraits or engravings. Many of his portrait copies have led to the discovery and identification of the earlier originals.

A community leader, Fraser frequently gave speeches at important events, such as the dedication of Magnolia Cemetery in 1850. He was active in the fledgling South Carolina Academy of Fine Arts and became one of its early directors along with Joel Poinsett, John S. Cogdell, and Samuel F. B. Morse. He served as a trustee of the College of Charleston, his alma mater, from 1817 until 1860. In 1853 he delivered his "Reminiscences of Charleston," which document the major events and cultural changes during his lifetime. In 1857 his patrons and friends honored him with a major retrospective exhibition of his work: 319 miniatures and 139 landscapes, still lifes, and sketches. Fraser died in Charleston on October 5, 1860. The Gibbes Museum of Art in Charleston is the major repository of his work. See plate 15. ANGELA D. MACK

Curtis, Julia. "Redating Sketches from Nature by A. Fraser and C. Fraser." *South Carolina Historical Magazine* 93 (January 1992): 51–62.

O'Neall, John Belton. *Biographical Sketches of the Bench and Bar of South Carolina.* 2 vols. Charleston, S.C.: S. G. Courtney, 1859.

Severens, Martha R., and Charles L. Wyrick, Jr., eds. *Charles Fraser of Charleston.* Charleston, S.C.: Carolina Art Association, 1983.

———, eds. *The Miniature Portrait Collection of the Carolina Art Association.* Charleston, S.C.: Carolina Art Association/Gibbes Art Gallery, 1984.

Sokolitz, Roberta Kefalos. *The Poetry of Place: Landscapes of Thomas Coram and Charles Fraser.* Charleston, S.C.: Carolina Art Association/Gibbes Museum of Art, 1998.

Frazier, Joseph William (b. 1944). Boxer. Joe Frazier was born in Beaufort on January 12, 1944, the youngest of twelve surviving children of Rubin and Dolly Frazier. His parents farmed ten acres and eked out a living largely by working for local white landowners.

Frazier quit school at fourteen and a year later moved to New York to live with relatives, but he found little regular employment. He moved to Philadelphia, where he again lived with relatives and eventually found employment at Cross Brothers, a meat slaughterhouse. By 1961 he had developed a weight problem and went to a Police Athletic League gym.

There Frazier met Duke Dugent, who managed the gym, and the boxing trainer Yancey (Yank) Durham. In less than a year he had lost thirty pounds and gained skill in the ring. Frazier won the Philadelphia

Golden Gloves novice heavyweight championship in 1962, then won three consecutive Middle Atlantic Golden Gloves heavyweight titles from 1962 to 1964.

Frazier married his South Carolina girlfriend Florence Smith in 1963 and continued to work at Cross Brothers and hone his boxing skills. He reached the finals of the 1964 U.S. Olympic Trials against Buster Mathis, to whom he suffered his only amateur loss. Named to the team as an alternate, Frazier got his chance when a hand injury forced Mathis to yield his position on the American team. Frazier defeated Hans Huber of Germany to win the gold medal.

Frazier turned professional after the Olympics and was brought along slowly by Durham for three years. By 1967 he was considered the ranking contender after Muhammad Ali was stripped of the world heavyweight title for resisting the Vietnam draft. Frazier reversed his amateur loss to Buster Mathis with a knockout that won him the New York version of the heavyweight title. After defending that title four times, he won the World Boxing Association (WBA) heavyweight championship by knocking out Jimmy Ellis in 1969.

After a successful defense, Frazier faced Ali, restored to the sport by the courts, in the first of three politically charged bouts. At New York's Madison Square Garden, Frazier won "the Fight of the Century" with a fifteen-round decision on March 8, 1971, to retain his title. He would defend two more times before losing the crown to George Foreman by knockout in January 1973. The year would end with a win over Joe Bugner in England.

Frazier lost his rematch with Ali at Madison Square Garden on January 28, 1974. A third match took place on October 1, 1975, in the Philippines: "The Thrilla in Manila." It was a savage fight, even by the standards of a brutal sport. After fourteen rounds, Frazier's eyes were swollen shut, and his trainer Eddie Futch would not allow him to answer the bell for the final round. A second loss to Foreman in the summer of 1976 prompted Frazier's retirement. Five years later a comeback attempt ended in a draw with Floyd Cummings, and Frazier left the ring for good, closing his career with a 34–4–1 record, including twenty-seven knockouts.

In retirement, Frazier performed as the lead singer of Smokin' Joe and the Knockouts. He also invested in a limousine service and a restaurant. He purchased his former gym in Philadelphia and established an opportunity for aspiring boxers. Frazier was inducted into the South Carolina Athletic Hall of Fame in 1974 and the Boxing Hall of Fame in 1980. W. K. MITCHELL

Frazier, Joe, with Phil Berger. *Smokin' Joe.* New York: Macmillan, 1996.
Kram, Mark. *Ghosts of Manila.* New York: HarperCollins, 2001.

Frederick, Nathaniel Jerome (1877–1938). Lawyer, editor. Frederick was born on November 18, 1877, in Orangeburg County, the son of Benjamin Glenn Frederick and Henrietta Baxter. He earned a B.A. from Claflin College in 1889 and a degree in history and Latin from the University of Wisconsin in 1901. He married Corrine Carroll on September 14, 1904. They had four children. Frederick served as principal of Columbia's Howard School from 1902 until 1918. During this period he also read law. Admitted to the South Carolina Bar in 1913, he opened a law office in Columbia the following year.

Despite the racial barriers that hampered African Americans in the early twentieth century, Frederick became a successful lawyer. Before his death in 1938, he appeared before the South Carolina Supreme Court thirty-three times, more than any African American lawyer up to that time. He won twelve appeals and three of his four criminal cases that appeared before the court. Two of his legal victories drew national attention. In the 1926 case of *State v. Lowman,* Frederick represented three members of the Lowman family, African Americans who had been convicted of murdering the sheriff of Aiken County. Taking the case on appeal, Frederick won a unanimous order for a new trial. At the retrial, Frederick obtained a directed verdict of acquittal of Demond Lowman. The expectation was that a similar result would be obtained the next day for Bertha Lowman and her cousin Clarence. However, Demond was immediately rearrested. On the evening of October 8, 1926, all three Lowmans were dragged from jail and lynched. Despite editorial campaigns and three grand jury investigations, no one was ever brought to trial for the lynching.

The 1929 case of *Ex parte Bess* had a less tragic ending. Ben Bess was a black man who had been convicted of sexually assaulting a white woman. After Bess had served thirteen years of a thirty-year sentence, his alleged victim recanted her testimony. Using the recantation, Frederick obtained a pardon from Governor John G. Richards. After threats of prosecution for perjury, however, the alleged victim withdrew her recantation, whereupon the governor tried to revoke the pardon. Frederick immediately challenged the governor. The state supreme court sat en banc, with all the state circuit court judges, and in a ten-to-eight decision ruled that the governor could not revoke his pardon. Fearing a repeat of the Lowman lynching, Frederick immediately moved Bess out of state.

Frederick was active in other areas of South Carolina's African American community. He was a crusading newspaperman, serving as editor of the *Southern Indicator* and the *Palmetto Leader.* He helped organize the Victory Savings Bank, a black-owned financial institution in Columbia. He was active in the National Association for the Advancement of Colored People and served on its national legal committee. An ardent Republican, Frederick was a delegate to the party's national conventions in 1924, 1928, and 1932. He died in Columbia on September 7, 1938, nearly destitute and was buried in Palmetto Cemetery, Columbia. W. LEWIS BURKE

Caldwell, A. B., ed. *History of the American Negro.* Vol. 3, *South Carolina.* Atlanta: A. B. Caldwell, 1919.
Obituary. Columbia *Palmetto Leader,* September 10, 1938.

Free persons of color. Also known as free blacks, free persons of color occupied an anomalous position in the race-based slave society of antebellum South Carolina. Several factors contributed to their expansion. For personal reasons, especially during the colonial era and early nineteenth century, slaveowners manumitted (freed) slaves by last will and testament. Slaves who accumulated money through trading or by hiring their time were sometimes allowed to purchase their freedom. Meritorious service to society could warrant freedom. An act of 1702 freed slave militiamen who killed or captured an invading enemy. When the slaves Caesar and Sampson invented cures for rattlesnake bite in the 1750s, the legislature emancipated them. Free blacks sometimes descended from Native Americans, while others migrated to South Carolina from other states and foreign countries.

Free blacks never exceeded two percent of the state's antebellum black population, which was consistent with its lower-South neighbors but starkly contrasted with states in the upper South. This disparity occurred because the egalitarianism of the American Revolution and the natural rights doctrine that stimulated manumissions in the upper South were less influential in the lower South. Also, upper-South economic changes facilitated emancipation, while the lower South's emerging Cotton Kingdom increased its dependence on slavery. As early as 1800, almost six percent and sixteen percent of the black populations of Virginia and Maryland respectively were free. The disparities with South Carolina became greater by 1860, when Virginia and Maryland's percentages increased to eleven and forty-nine percent respectively.

Free persons of color were disproportionately female because slaveowners had fewer apprehensions about manumitting women. Also, since miscegenation was legal in South Carolina before the Civil War, white men frequently had sexual relationships with black women, sometimes marrying and emancipating them with their mulatto children. Philippe Stanislaus Noisette, a famous French horticulturist who migrated to Charleston in 1794, had several children by his slave Celestine and went through extraordinary legal means to manumit her and their progeny. In 1860 mulattoes comprised five percent of the state's slave population but seventy-two percent of the free blacks. The term "free persons of color" referred to the mixed ancestry of free blacks in the lower South. Before the Civil War, race was not defined in South Carolina law, leaving race to be determined by reputation and phenotype. Because of this, some free persons of color passed for white.

The state's compelling interest in the slave system led it to regulate private manumissions. A 1722 law required removal of freed slaves unless legislative approval was granted, suggesting that free persons of color were considered unfit for citizenship. An 1800 act required court approval of manumissions in order to prevent elderly or "depraved" slaves from being foisted on society. The antislavery movement, the bitter debate over Missouri's admission as a slave state, and the 1810–1820 expansion of South Carolina's free black population by fifty percent led to a new act in 1820. To curtail free black population growth, the act vested the right of manumission solely in the General Assembly, prohibited immigration of free blacks to the state, and restricted their egress and ingress. The final loopholes were closed by an 1841 act to "Prevent the Emancipation of Slaves." Only two slaves were legally emancipated in the state in 1850, leaving the future expansion of the free black population to depend primarily on natural increase.

Most free blacks resided in the countryside and worked as general laborers or as farm labor. A smaller number were artisans, tenant farmers, or acquired their own land. Reflecting national trends, a disproportionate number resided in cities. In 1860 three percent of the state's slave population resided in Charleston, but one-third of its free blacks lived there. Charleston's economic opportunities attracted free blacks, and by 1850 more than eighty percent of the men worked in skilled or semiskilled occupations as, for example, carpenters, tailors, bricklayers, or wagon drivers. Women frequently worked as domestics or in needlecraft trades. By 1860, 299 Charleston free blacks owned real estate valued at $759,870; half this amount was owned by fourteen percent of all free black property holders. Anthony Weston belonged to this propertied elite and used his millwright skills to accumulate an estate worth $40,000 by 1860. Jehu Jones accumulated a similar estate through real estate speculation and his famous hotel in downtown Charleston. In 1860, 171 free persons of color owned 766 slaves. Frequently these were family members who had been purchased but could not legally be emancipated. Other free blacks held slaves for their labor. In 1860 Daria Thomas, a planter in Union District, used many of his 21 slaves on his cotton farm. Likewise, William Ellison, Sr., of Sumter District used 63 slaves on his plantation and in his cotton gin manufacturing business.

By the early antebellum years, Charleston was the center of a propertied, light-complexioned group of free blacks who enjoyed a well-developed institutional life. The Brown Fellowship Society was established in 1790 for charitable and social purposes, and membership was limited to light-complexioned free blacks. Complexional differences often divided the community, and in 1843 equally elite and "respectable Free Dark Men" established the Humane Brotherhood. Elite free persons of color established private schools, and their children sometimes continued their educations in the North or abroad. William Rollin, a successful entrepreneur, sent his daughter Frances to the renowned Institute for Colored Youth in Philadelphia, while Francis Cardozo attended universities in England and Scotland. Such opportunities were rare but expanded the differences between the elite and most free blacks who experienced material conditions not unlike their enslaved brethren.

All free blacks led somewhat tenuous lives because of their legal disabilities. The presumption was that all blacks were slaves, and free persons of color had to demonstrate on demand that they were legitimately free, making travel to communities where they were unknown dangerous. In 1792 free blacks were subject to a special capitation tax. When accused of crimes, they were tried before slave courts. They could not testify in regular courts for or against whites. Their lives were increasingly circumscribed, especially during times of social instability. New laws following the Denmark Vesey slave conspiracy established fines and enslavement for those leaving the state and attempting to return. Free blacks over age fifteen were also required to have white guardians. As the nation edged toward civil war, the plight of free blacks became more precarious. Reflecting a regional trend, in 1859–1860 South Carolina's legislature considered bills to expel or enslave free blacks. These measures were not passed, but their discussion terrified free persons of color, many of whom fled the state for the North. Most, however, remained until the end to slavery ended their unique social position. BERNARD E. POWERS, JR.

Berlin, Ira. *Slaves without Masters: The Free Negro in the Antebellum South.* New York: Pantheon, 1974.

Burton, Orville Vernon. *In My Father's House Are Many Mansions: Family and Community in Edgefield, South Carolina.* Chapel Hill: University of North Carolina Press, 1985.

Drago, Edmund L. *Initiative, Paternalism, and Race Relations: Charleston's Avery Normal Institute.* Athens: University of Georgia Press, 1990.

Johnson, Michael, and James L. Roark. *Black Masters: A Free Family of Color in the Old South.* New York: Norton, 1984.

Koger, Larry. *Black Slaveowners: Free Black Slave Masters in South Carolina, 1790–1860.* 1985. Reprint, Columbia: University of South Carolina Press, 1995.

Powers, Bernard E. *Black Charlestonians: A Social History, 1822–1885.* Fayetteville: University of Arkansas Press, 1994.

Wikramanayake, Marina. *A World in Shadow: The Free Black in Antebellum South Carolina.* Columbia: University of South Carolina Press, 1973.

Freed, Arthur (1894–1973). Film producer, songwriter. Freed was born in Charleston on September 9, 1894, to Max Freed and Rosa Grossman, both Hungarian immigrants. Freed did not remain in his native city long. The eldest of eight children, he traveled extensively with his family, as required by his father's profession as an art dealer. The family eventually settled in Seattle, where he attended public schools for several years. In 1914 Freed finished Phillips Exeter Academy in New Hampshire, where he began writing poetry. On March 14, 1923, he married Renee Klein, with whom he had a daughter, Barbara.

Freed's love of music and poetry would coalesce to create his success as a lyricist. For two years he performed his original songs for the Marx Brothers' tour. He also gained experience singing for Gus Edwards's celebrated vaudeville show. Even Freed's military service during World War I became a platform for his musical abilities. As an army sergeant, he continued composing and put on shows to entertain the soldiers. His talents received greater recognition after the war, however, when he partnered with Nacio Herb Brown to write songs and produce plays at the Orange Grove Theater in Los Angeles, which the two men jointly purchased. In 1929 the pair was invited to compose songs for Metro Goldwyn Mayer's *Broadway Melody*, which won the Academy Award for best picture. Freed and Brown also wrote "Singin' in the Rain," which appeared in MGM's *Hollywood Revue* (1929).

Freed became best known in his ongoing work with MGM as he helped to fashion and energize the studio's popular musicals. He served as associate producer of *The Wizard of Oz* (1939), shaping its screenplay and casting the unknown Judy Garland as the film's lead. After the movie's tremendous success, he went on to produce films that defined the musical genre, including pictures such as *Meet Me in St. Louis* (1944), *Annie Get Your Gun* (1950), *Singin' in the Rain* (1951), and both *An American in Paris* (1951) and *Gigi* (1958), for which he received Academy Awards. These and other shows emerged to form what is now called the Freed Golden Era in Hollywood. In 1952 Freed received the prestigious Irving G. Thalberg Memorial Award for his exceptional body of work.

During his tenure at MGM, Freed distinguished himself as a shrewd recruiter of talent. He assembled the finest artistic and technical staff, a core group of colleagues referred to as the Freed Unit. Together, they made important cinematic innovations, creating lavish and lively sets, integrating songs more seamlessly with story lines, and filming pictures on location. Freed also achieved a reputation for cultivating musical stars such as Garland and Gene Kelly, who became legendary in the roles in which he cast them.

From 1963 to 1966 Freed served as president of the Motion Picture Academy of Arts and Sciences. In 1968 he won recognition for his service and achievement with an Academy Award. He resigned from MGM in 1970 and died on April 12, 1973, in Hollywood. He was buried in Los Angeles. SANDRA BARRETT MOORE

Fordin, Hugh. *M-G-M's Greatest Musicals: The Arthur Freed Unit.* New York: Da Capo, 1996.

Rimoldi, Oscar A. "Produced by Arthur Freed." *Films in Review* 45 (July–August 1994): 14–22; (September–October 1994): 20–27.

Freedmen's Bureau (1865–1872). The Bureau of Freedmen, Refugees, and Abandoned Lands dispensed poor relief, administered lands abandoned during the Civil War, organized education for freed people, and most importantly, resolved land and labor disputes during the early years of Reconstruction. Created by an act of Congress in March 1865, the bureau grew out of efforts by northern Republicans and reformers to bring the free labor society and culture of the antebellum North to the postemancipation South.

The structure, goals, and accomplishments of the bureau in South Carolina mirrored those in other states. The institution, the first federal social welfare bureaucracy in American history, functioned under the War Department. Under the leadership of Commissioner Oliver Otis Howard in Washington, D.C., each state had an assistant commissioner, with subassistants under him. In South Carolina, General Rufus Saxton opened the state bureau in July 1865. As a prominent Massachusetts attorney and career army officer, Saxton brought the liberal ideas of northern reformers to the state. Additionally, he had headed the Port Royal Experiment with free labor in the Sea Islands during the war. Saxton focused on land distribution and jobs for freed slaves, and he spoke highly of freed people and pursued policies in their interests. This stance brought him into conflict with Commissioner Howard as well as President Andrew Johnson, who revoked General William Tecumseh Sherman's Special Field Order No. 15, through which many freed people in the lowcountry had obtained land.

In January 1866 General Robert K. Scott replaced Saxton as bureau chief in the state and immediately instituted stricter policies on land and labor. Scott came to the position as a typical middle-class northerner, a man who had studied medicine, dabbled in real estate, and tried his hand at merchandising. A political moderate who favored gradual abolition but also supported civil rights for former slaves, Scott enforced a policy of binding labor contracts between freed people and white planters. This system was preferred by Howard as well as planters who were bringing pressure to bear on the bureau. Nonetheless, Scott and his officers sought to balance the interests of former slaves with those of their employers, frequently using Union troops to enforce orders aimed at settling disputes between whites and blacks. Scott resigned the position in July 1867 to enter state politics, one of the few officers in the state to do so. In the following years bureau operations wound down, ending entirely by 1872.

The real work of the bureau in the state was done by its local agents. Usually veterans of the Union army and hailing from the North, these men faced the daunting challenge of adjudicating the frequent and sometimes fundamental disputes between former slaves and former masters. They pursued a variety of policies, a fact that might help explain the widely divergent views of the bureau held by contemporaries and more recent observers. Some agents, such as A. J. Willard in Georgetown, clearly favored the planters. Others, such as the African American Martin R. Delany in the Sea Islands, worked for the benefit of former slaves. Most tried to balance competing interests in the manner pursued by Scott. The Prussian-born émigré Frederick W. Liedtke was typical; for example, he arrested freed people for breach of contract but also strongly sponsored their cases for wages against employers.

Any assessment of the bureau's success or failure must inevitably consider short-term versus long-term consequences as well as possible alternatives. In the short term, if judged by the idealistic goals of its founders, the bureau in South Carolina largely failed. Its educational efforts remained limited, its poor-relief efforts fell vastly short of need, and its aim of bringing peaceful land and labor relations gave way to violence and the descent into formal segregation. In a broader sense, the bureau's mission was limited by the vision of its officers. Firmly entrenched in northern middle-class individualism, their attempts to help former slaves often contradicted freed people's desires for social autonomy and economic self-sufficiency.

Nevertheless, the Freedmen's Bureau did alter the social relations of freedom. Planters did not get all they wanted; physical coercion sanctioned by law did not return. The bureau established the notion of rights for African Americans, even if it took years for those rights to be fully realized. The institution helped provide the limited safety required for black political activism. Perhaps most importantly, by enforcing labor contracts and establishing the beginning of a free labor culture, the bureau nurtured aspirations that would come to fruition many decades later. JAMES D. SCHMIDT

Abbott, Martin. *The Freedmen's Bureau in South Carolina, 1865–1872.* Chapel Hill: University of North Carolina Press, 1967.

Saville, Julie. *The Work of Reconstruction: From Slave to Wage Laborer in South Carolina, 1860–1870.* New York: Cambridge University Press, 1994.

Schmidt, James D. "'A Full-Fledged Government of Men': Freedmen's Bureau Labor Policy in South Carolina, 1865–1868." In *The Freedmen's Bureau and Reconstruction: Reconsiderations,* edited by Paul Cimbala and Randall M. Miller. New York: Fordham University Press, 1999.

Williamson, Joel. *After Slavery: The Negro in South Carolina during Reconstruction, 1861–1877.* Chapel Hill: University of North Carolina Press, 1965.

Freedom Rides (1961–1962). The Freedom Rides were a series of bus trips through the South designed to force compliance with U.S. Supreme Court decisions of 1947 and 1960 banning segregation in interstate bus travel. On May 4, 1961, the Congress of Racial Equality (CORE) launched the first Freedom Ride, sending an interracial group of thirteen on commercial buses from Washington, D.C., to New Orleans, Louisiana. The route included stops in Rock Hill, Winnsboro, and Sumter, South Carolina.

The South Carolina portion of the trip saw the first instance of violent southern opposition. At the Greyhound station in Rock Hill, white youths assaulted three of the Freedom Riders as one African American rider approached the "white" waiting room. Police intervened before any serious injuries occurred and made no arrests. The Freedom Rides passengers next arrived in Winnsboro, where police arrested and subsequently released black riders after they requested service at a lunch counter reserved for whites. No violence or arrests were reported at Sumter, the last stop in South Carolina before the riders entered Georgia. The most serious resistance occurred in Alabama, where whites burned one bus and assaulted riders on both, temporarily interrupting the journey.

The violence in Alabama caught public attention and transformed the Freedom Rides into a national campaign. Throughout the summer of 1961 CORE and other civil rights organizations coordinated additional Freedom Rides, including two well-publicized trips from Washington, D.C., through South Carolina. The first, comprised of ministers and rabbis, stopped briefly in Sumter on the way to Tallahassee, Florida. The second, made up of professionals and representatives from organized labor, stopped overnight in Charleston before continuing on to St. Petersburg, Florida. Police escorted both Freedom Rides for most of the journey; riders in both used the facilities at bus stations in Charleston and Sumter without serious incident.

The later Freedom Rides did not generate the same level of media coverage or public sympathy as CORE's original project. Nevertheless, they constituted part of a larger campaign that forced the federal government to take action against segregated transportation. In September 1961, acting on U.S. Attorney General Robert Kennedy's request, the Interstate Commerce Commission issued an order banning segregation in interstate travel facilities. Additional Freedom Rides tested southern compliance, reporting desegregated travel terminals in most southern communities by the end of 1962. ADAM MACK

Barnes, Catherine A. *Journey from Jim Crow: The Desegregation of Southern Transit.* New York: Columbia University Press, 1983.

Lewis, John. *Walking with the Wind: A Memoir of the Movement.* New York: Simon and Schuster, 1998.

Peck, James. *Freedom Ride.* New York: Simon and Schuster, 1962.

Freeman, Grace Beacham (1916–2002). Poet. Born in Spartanburg on February 18, 1916, Freeman was the daughter of Henry Beacham and Grace Bailey. She attended elementary and high school in the Spartanburg school system and received her undergraduate degree in English, drama, and Latin from Converse College in 1937. In 1993 she received an honorary doctor of letters degree from St. Andrews Presbyterian College.

Freeman taught in the public schools of South Carolina from 1937 through 1942, a period marked by two major events in her life. In 1939 her first adult poetry was published in the *Saturday Evening Post.* On June 11, 1941, she married John Alderman Freeman of Raleigh, North Carolina, whom she had met while visiting relatives in Mars Hill, North Carolina. The Freemans had four children.

In 1952 the family moved to Rock Hill, where John Freeman had accepted a teaching position in the biology department at Winthrop College. From 1954 to 1964 Grace Freeman wrote a column, "At Our House," which was distributed by King Features Syndicate three times a week to newspapers throughout the United States and Canada. In addition to poetry, she wrote plays and radio and television dramas. Her work appeared in literary publications and in the popular press.

Freeman's first collection of poetry, *Children Are Poetry,* was published as a chapbook in 1951. A second chapbook, *Stars and the Land,* was published in 1983. Freeman's first book-length collection, *No Costumes or Masks,* first published in 1975, was honored as the year's Best Book by a South Carolina Poet. A second book, *Midnight to Dawn,* was published in 1981, followed by *Not Set in Stone* in 1986. Later in her life Freeman published poetic tributes to her parents: *This Woman Called Mother* (1992), for which she received the Fortner Writers Forum Award; and *Remembering a Gentle Father* (1996).

From 1973 until 1986 Freeman participated in the South Carolina Arts Commission's Poet-in-the-Schools program. She served as a poetry therapy consultant to the Gastonia, North Carolina, Mental Health Center from 1973 until 1975. Governor Richard Riley appointed Freeman poet laureate of South Carolina in 1985. She held the title for only one year, relinquishing the role shortly before retiring to North Carolina in 1987. She remained active and involved in community affairs until shortly before her death in Asheville, North Carolina, on October 28, 2002, following a brief illness. JULIA ARRANTS

Bigham, Wendy. "Freeman, Former Poet Laureate of South Carolina, Dies at 86." Rock Hill *Herald,* October 30, 2002, pp. B1, B4.

"Distinguished Alumna Award: Dr. Grace Beacham Freeman." *Converse Bulletin* (spring 2002): 24.

Freemasonry. Freemasonry in South Carolina dates to 1735, when Lord Weymouth, Grand Master of the Grand Lodge of England, issued a warrant establishing the office of Provincial Grand Master in the colony of South Carolina. The first Provincial Grand Master was John Hammerton, the receiver general of quitrents in the colony. In 1736 he organized the first Masonic lodge in the colony, Solomon's Lodge number one of Charleston, which became the mother lodge of Freemasonry in South Carolina. Freemasonry continued to spread, eventually covering all areas of the state. By 2003 there were 315 chartered lodges and 47,913 Freemasons under the authority of the Grand Lodge of Ancient Freemasons of South Carolina, which is the descendant of the old Provincial Grand Lodge.

Freemasonry in the state went through a period of disunity after the Revolutionary War. In 1787 a second Grand Lodge was formed in South Carolina, the Grand Lodge of Ancient York Masons, which established many lodges, especially in the backcountry. The original Grand Lodge of Free and Accepted Masons, also known as the Moderns, was not strong enough at this point in time to do much about it. The Moderns had large numbers of Loyalists, and several lodges ceased to exist after many of their members were exiled or chose to leave the colony after the Revolutionary War. The two Grand Lodges argued over jurisdiction until 1817, when they merged to form the Grand Lodge of Ancient Freemasons of South Carolina.

The York and Scottish Rites of Freemasonry have been well received in South Carolina and have deep roots in the state. The origins of the York Rite in South Carolina are not clear, but there is evidence that it existed at the time of the Revolutionary War. The Scottish Rite also dates to the same period, but the Supreme Council of the thirty-third degree (established in Charleston in 1801) is considered the mother council of the world by Scottish Rite Freemasons.

South Carolina's Freemasons have achieved distinction in a variety of fields. Henry Laurens was an active Mason in the colonial period, as was Henry Middleton. Francis Marion and William Richardson Davie both served with distinction in the Revolution. William Gilmore Simms achieved fame as a writer, as did Albert Gallatin Mackey. Prominent Masons of the nineteenth century also included governors John Lyde Wilson, David Johnson, and John Drayton. The twentieth century saw Masons such as Strom Thurmond and James F. Byrnes serve their state and country with distinction. RHETT A. ADAMS

Cornwell, Ross, and Samuel M. Willis. *A History of Freemasonry in South Carolina: The Years 1860–1919.* Charleston: Grand Lodge of Ancient Free Masons of South Carolina, 1979.

Mackey, Albert G. *The History of Freemasonry in South Carolina, 1736–1860, from Its Origin in the Year to the Present Time.* 1861. Reprint, West Columbia, S.C.: Wentworth, 1998.

Freneau, Peter (1757–1813). Editor, legislator. Freneau was born on April 5, 1757, in Monmouth County, New Jersey, the son of Pierre Freneau, a wine merchant and land speculator, and Agnes Watson. He was the younger brother of Philip Freneau, the better-known (and better-remembered) "Poet of the Revolution." Little is known of Peter's early life, but in December 1782 he disembarked at Charleston, South Carolina, where he would spend the remainder of his life. He either arrived with some prominence or attained it soon after, for in 1784 he was appointed deputy secretary of state for South Carolina. He became secretary of state in 1787 and retained the position until 1795. Freneau also operated a variety of business interests, including land speculation and shipping. By the early 1800s he owned shipping vessels, which he engaged for some years in the Madeira trade. Earlier in his shipping career, he had taken part in the sale of at least one slave cargo.

Freneau's primary business and personal interests, however, were in printing. In 1795, in partnership with Seth Paine, he purchased the Charleston *City Gazette and Daily Advertiser.* Three years later the partners established a weekly newspaper, the *Carolina Gazette,* through which they disseminated the ideals and principles of the emerging Republican Party and its guiding light, Vice President Thomas Jefferson. Through his newspaper columns, Freneau became one of the leading Republican organizers in South Carolina, along with U.S. Senator Charles Pinckney. The *Gazette* tirelessly championed Jeffersonian principles and, as his successor noted, "soon obtained a controlling influence in the State." As editor of the state's most influential Republican newspaper, Freneau played a crucial role in securing South Carolina's electoral votes for the party in the bitterly contested election of 1800, which in turn secured the election of Jefferson to the presidency.

In 1806 the voters of St. Philip's and St. Michael's Parishes elected Freneau to the state House of Representatives as part of a broader Republican victory over the long-reigning Federalists of Charleston. Reelected in 1808, he resigned early the following year to accept an appointment from Jefferson as commissioner of loans in South Carolina, possibly a political sinecure from a grateful president for Freneau's efforts on his behalf. He sold his printing and publishing interests in 1810, and his last years were marked by financial reverses. He retained, however, his influential position in the state's Republican ranks, working with Pinckney and other party leaders to secure the election of Langdon Cheves to Congress in 1810. Freneau died in Charleston on November 9, 1813. TOM DOWNEY

Bailey, N. Louise, ed. *Biographical Directory of the South Carolina House of Representatives.* Vol. 4, *1791–1815.* Columbia: University of South Carolina Press, 1984.

Davis, Richard B., and Milledge B. Seigler. "Peter Freneau, Carolina Republican." *Journal of Southern History* 13 (August 1947): 395–405.

Frogmore stew. Perhaps no dish better represents the essential simplicity of lowcountry cuisine than Frogmore stew. Some claim that the one-pot dish originated in the Frogmore community on St. Helena Island, near Beaufort, but the truth is that Frogmore stew (also called Beaufort stew or Louisiana boil) exists throughout the coastal regions of the South. That is its innate beauty—it is like a tidal marsh with infinite variations of creeks, eddies, and bays. There are two main ingredients, fresh shrimp and newly shucked yellow corn, but most anything that is good boiled, such as crabs, redskin potatoes, and even crawfish, can be added. This is a casual meal best eaten with the fingers and served on a picnic table covered with newspaper. Two keys to success with Frogmore stew are to stagger the addition of the ingredients and not to overcook the shrimp. Fill a large steamer pot halfway with water. Add two tablespoons of crab-boil seasoning per gallon of water (or more to taste). Several halved lemons may be added as well. When the seasoned water comes to a boil, add one-inch slices of spicy smoked sausage (¼ pound per person) and boil for five minutes. Add the corn (1½ ears per person, broken into halves or thirds) and boil another five minutes. (Begin timing immediately. Do not wait for it to boil again.) Then add the shrimp (½ pound per person). Cook three minutes, drain, and pile on a table. Serve with lots of paper towels, icy beverages, butter, cocktail sauce, and perhaps tartar sauce. The most important ingredient is the last one: serve Frogmore stew in a Carolina beach house surrounded by friends and family. DAN HUNTLEY

Frost, Susan Pringle (1873–1960). Preservationist, suffragist. Frost was born in Charleston on January 21, 1873, the daughter of Dr. Francis LeJau Frost and Rebecca Brewton Pringle. With ties to several distinguished Charleston families dating back to the eighteenth century, Frost seemed destined to be a lady of leisure following a privileged childhood and two years (1889–1891) at the prominent Saint Mary's Episcopal boarding school in Raleigh, North Carolina. However, with the decline of the Frost and Pringle rice plantations on the Santee River and the failure of her father's fertilizer business, Frost learned basic stenographic skills and entered the workplace: initially as secretary to the architect Bradford Lee Gilbert, designer of the South Carolina Inter-State and West Indian Exposition of 1901–1902; then for sixteen years, until 1918, as court stenographer for the U.S. District Court.

Interest in social concerns and women's issues quickened in this period, and Frost, who never married, became actively involved in women's club work and the women's suffrage movement. As first president of the Charleston Equal Suffrage League, Frost aligned her organization with Alice Paul and the militant wing of the movement, the National Woman's Party, in supporting the federal suffrage amendment and, later, the Equal Rights Amendment. However, Frost's passion was historic preservation and saving Charleston's old houses and architecture from demolition and out-of-state purchasers, a cause that constitutes her greatest legacy.

In 1909 Frost quietly entered Charleston's real estate market, borrowing money to purchase two small properties on Tradd Street, the city's oldest thoroughfare. In short order her crusade became a consuming preservation drive to rehabilitate from slum status the picturesque houses of East Tradd, St. Michael's Alley, and the section of East Bay Street that later became famous as Rainbow Row. In the process, she displaced numerous black Charlestonians from the lower peninsula. Financially overextended, Frost frequently owed key creditors such as Irénée DuPont, a family friend whose loans insured that the three Frost sisters gained sole ownership of their grand birthplace, the Miles Brewton House.

To save another endangered landmark, the Joseph Manigault House, Frost in 1920 founded what became the Preservation Society of Charleston, one of the nation's oldest such groups. She was an early advocate of zoning to preserve old iron- and woodwork, and she championed Charleston's zoning ordinance of 1931, which created the nation's first historic district. She served as zoning monitor on the Board of Adjustment throughout the 1940s. Frost regularly swamped Charleston newspaper editors with letters about preservation goals and needs, and she became celebrated for her public service and quaint eccentricities. Her historic preservation initiatives contributed substantially to the movement that transformed the streets of Charleston and made it a national tourist destination. Frost died in the Miles Brewton House on October 6, 1960, and was buried in Magnolia Cemetery. SIDNEY R. BLAND

Bland, Sidney R. *Preserving Charleston's Past, Shaping Its Future: The Life and Times of Susan Pringle Frost.* 2d ed. Columbia: University of South Carolina Press, 1999.

Hosmer, Charles B. *Preservation Comes of Age: From Williamsburg to the National Trust, 1926–1949.* 2 vols. Charlottesville: University Press of Virginia, 1981.

Fuller, William Edward (1875–1958). Clergyman. Fuller was born in Mountville, Laurens County, on January 29, 1875, the son of the sharecroppers George and Martha Fuller. Orphaned at age four, Fuller was reared by his aunt, Ida Fuller Vance. He was converted in 1892 and joined the New Hope African Methodist Episcopal Church. The following year he received his license to preach. In 1895 Fuller married Martha Wright. They had five children before her death in 1905. His second wife was Emma Clare Wright, whom he married on March 10, 1910. They had seven children. After Emma's death, Fuller married Pauline Birmingham, who was also a pastor.

Fuller believed that he had been sanctified in 1895 after he retreated to a cornfield for a time of intense prayer. After reading about a third blessing, the "baptism of fire," in issues of *The Way of Faith,* edited by J. M. Pike in Columbia, and hearing Benjamin Hardin Irwin preach about this baptism of the Holy Ghost on his preaching tour in South Carolina in 1896, Fuller returned to the same cornfield in 1897 and had another intense religious experience when he received the third blessing.

Around that time Fuller and his family moved to Abbeville. He attended the meeting in Anderson in 1898 when Irwin and Joseph Hillary King organized a new national denomination, the Fire-Baptized Holiness Association. At that time Irwin ordained Fuller, Isaac Gamble from Kingstree, and Uncle Powell Woodbury from Marion as evangelists. Fuller devoted himself to organizing African American congregations for the Fire-Baptized Holiness Association. Within two years he had helped found more than fifty congregations in South Carolina and north Georgia, including churches in Abbeville, Greenwood, Belton, Greenville, Seneca, Greer, Spartanburg, Columbia, and also Atlanta. A dynamic preacher, in 1904 he claimed to have spurred some five hundred conversions. Fuller also served on the denomination's executive committee until 1908.

At a meeting in Greer on November 24, 1908, African American members of the Fire-Baptized Holiness Association formed a separate denomination, first called the Colored Fire-Baptized Holiness Church. Fuller became its first general overseer and then its first bishop in 1922. He also published *The True Witness,* the new denomination's first periodical. He remained the presiding bishop and unquestioned leader of the group, which became the Fire-Baptized Holiness Church of God in 1922 and the Fire-Baptized Holiness Church of God of the Americas in 1926, until his death on January 20, 1958. NANCY A. HARDESTY

Synan, Vinson. *The Holiness-Pentecostal Tradition: Charismatic Movements in the Twentieth Century.* 2d ed. Grand Rapids, Mich.: Eerdmans, 1997.

———. *The Old-Time Power.* Rev. ed. Franklin Springs, Ga.: Advocate Press, 1986.

Fundamental Constitutions of Carolina (1669–1698). Part constitution and part promotional tract, the Fundamental Constitutions of Carolina comprised a much revised document that the Lords Proprietors devised to govern their New World province. In 1663 and 1665 eight supporters of Charles II, the Lords Proprietors of Carolina, secured royal charters to a vast tract of land between 31° and 36° latitude and extending from the Atlantic to the Pacific. Anthony Ashley Cooper, Whig politician and chief proprietor, and his secretary, the future social philosopher John Locke, devised a written constitution for Carolina that featured an elaborate social and governmental structure based on hereditary landownership and, for its time, progressive attitudes toward religious toleration. The guiding principles of the Fundamental Constitutions were that landownership was the bedrock of society and that Carolina's government should be organized to avoid creating a "numerous democracy."

Because the first draft of the Fundamental Constitutions, dated July 21, 1669, is in John Locke's handwriting, scholars have occasionally surmised that he was its author. Early editions of Locke's writings included the Fundamental Constitutions among his works. However, evidence suggests that Ashley Cooper was the chief author of the constitution while Locke acted as his secretary and copyist. The political values of the constitution reflect the influence of the political philosopher James Harrington. In his political utopia in *Oceana* (1656), Harrington described a nation ruled by landed classes and governed by an unalterable written constitution. Locke's *Two Treatises on Civil Government* (1690) and his writings on religious toleration postdate his association with the Lords Proprietors, and their emphasis on social contract and natural law contradict some elements of the Fundamental Constitutions.

The Fundamental Constitutions established a Carolina aristocracy, with the Lords Proprietors at the apex of society, provincial nobles called landgraves and cassiques (or caciques), and freemen. Landless tenants, called leetmen, were the base of the social pyramid described in the constitution. Slavery was authorized and protected. In early versions of the Fundamental Constitutions, the sale and purchase of land were prohibited to preserve the chain of tenancy from the proprietors to the freemen. The written provisions of the constitution were to be unalterable, and upon arriving in Carolina settlers were expected to affirm in writing their allegiance to the proprietors and their support of the Fundamental Constitutions. The province was divided into counties, which were to be the chief units of government. Counties were divided into seigniories, baronies, and precincts, which corresponded to the three classes of society: proprietors, local nobility, and freemen. The amount of land an individual held determined his or her rights and responsibilities in the province.

The highly structured Fundamental Constitutions, with the document's complicated system of government, has been called anachronistic, and the emphasis on landownership and tenancy has been deemed feudalistic. But it also had elements that looked to the future, not the past. The proprietors' insistence on a written constitution as the wellspring of authority and their provisions for considerable religious liberty in the province were innovative. Ultimately, the Fundamental Constitutions was never adopted and was frequently repudiated by Carolinians as impractical and unrealistic. Conflict between the proprietors to implement the constitution and Carolina settlers to determine their own form of government comprehends much of the political history of early Carolina. The structure of government prescribed by the constitution was so complex and required such a large number of settlers of all classes that it never could be established in a small frontier province.

His Excellency JOHN Lord GRANVILLE
Palatine, The Right Hon.ble WILLIAM Lord Craven, The Right Hon.ble John Lord Carteret,
the Right Hon.ble Maurice Ashley Esq.r the Right Hon.ble S.r John Colleton Baronet, and the rest of
of the true and absolute Lords Proprietors of the Proprietors of the Province of Carolina To Laurence
Cromp Esq.r York Herald of Arms Greeting WHEREAS our late Sovereign Lord Charles the Second
King of great Brittaine, France and Ireland and the Dominions thereunto belonging, of his special
Grace and Favour did give and grant unto Edward Earl of Clarendon, George Duke of Albemarl, William
Earl of Craven, John Lord Berkley Anthony Lord Ashley, S.r George Carteret, S.r John Colleton Kn.t and Bar.t
and S.r William Berkeley Kn.t our Predecessors and to their Heires and Successors for ever, together with
the Province of Carolina, Power States, Degrees, both of Titles, Dignities and Honours, there to be Setled
and Sett up as of Men well deserving the same Degrees to bear, and with such Titles to be Honoured and
Adorned, And Whereas by our form of Government It was by our said Predecessors Established and
Constituted, and is by Us and our Heires and Successors for ever to be observed, That there be a certain
Number of Landgraves and Cassiques who may be and are the perpetual and Hereditary Nobles and Peers
of our said Province of Carolina, and to the End that a due Rule and Order of Honor may be Established and
Setled in our Said Province. We therefore the said John Lord Granville Palatine and the rest of the Lord Proprietors of the said Province of Carolina being well Satisfied of the great Integrity, Skill and Ability of you the S.d Laurence
Cromp, Doe hereby make, Constitute and appoint, and hereby have made, constituted and appointed You
the said Laurence Cromp to be President of our Court of Honor and principal Herald of our whole Province
of Carolina, by the Name of Carolina Herald. To hold the same during the Term of Your Natural Life
with such Fees, Perquisites and Proffitts as Shall be approved on and Setled by Us, And as perpetual
Monument of our Favour towards our Landgraves and Cassiques and their Meritt, We do hereby
Authorise, Impower and direct you the said Laurence Cromp Carolina Herald, to devyse, give, Grant
and Assigne to the said Landgraves and Cassiques of our S.d Province upon the Face of the Sun in
its Glory Such Arms and Crests as you Shall think most proper, & upon the Escocheon of the said Arms a
Landgraves & Cassiques Cap of Honor, which said Badges or Distinctions of Honor they are not to make Use till
Assigned by You, And to Invest our Said Landgraves & Cassiques that are already made & to be made, in Robes of
Scarlet Interlaced with Gold, to be by them worn on all great & Solemn Occasions, & also to Invest them with a
Purple Ribbon or Gold Chain, with the Sun in its Glory Pendant at the Same, with this Motto about the
Face of the Said Sun † VIDIT QUE DEUS HANC LUCEM ESSE BONAM, which said Gold Chain and Sun or
Purple Ribbon & Sun, We Injoyne and require them always to appear with. Draughts of all which are depic-
ted in the Margin hereof, & We doe hereby grant & Confirm to the said Landgraves & Cassiques of Our Said Province
and their Heires for Ever all the abovementioned Honorable Distinctions of Nobility. And We do hereby further direct, Grant & Impower You, under Your hand & Seal to devyse, Give, grant and Assign upon the Face of the Sun in its
Glory such Arms & Crests as you Shall think most fitt & proper to all such Inhabitants of our said Province, that
to you shall appear deserving the Same as an Everlasting Monum.t to them & their Posterity of their Rise & Descent
from our S.d Province of Carolina, And We likewise Impower You to hold a Court of Honor & to Cite & Cause to Appear
before You all such Person or Persons, as Shall presume to use any Coat of Arms that they cannot make out their due Right
to, then to deface the Same wheresoever borne or Sett up & make publick Proclamacon thereof, and also we require
that all the Inhabitants aforesaid duely observe the Rules & Orders of your said Court. And you are also hereby
obliged to keep a Register of all Such Arms, Crests or Alterations & Assignm.ts of Arms as Shall by you be granted or
Assigned to any Persons Inhabitants of Our said Province, And You are to preserve & Register the Pedigrees and
Descents of the Severall Familys Inhabitants of Our Said Province, And you are to regulate all Publick & Solemne
Procession & Meetings & all & Singular the premisses abovementioned, We do hereby Impower You by Your Self or Your
Sufficient Deputy or Deputies to performe & Execute, & to doe & perform all & Singular other Matters & things whatsoever
which to your S.d Office shall belong or appertaine Given under Our Hands & the great Seal of Our Province 1 June 1705
Signed by Granville Palatine Craven Granvill for L.d Carteret M: Ashley J Colleton

† Gen: Chap. 1. verse 4.

[Taken] from the Originall in the Custody of Peter Le Neve Esq.r Norroy & now in the Custody of M.r Hodgson of the six Clerks Office, who is one of the Landgraves

The Carolina Herald represents the Chamberlain's Court, one of eight courts described in the Fundamental Constitutions. This court had the responsibility for "all ceremony, precedency, [and] heraldry." Courtesy, South Caroliniana Library, University of South Carolina

To implement the mixed judicial and executive offices described in articles 27 and 28 would have required 134 men, 8 of whom were the proprietors or their deputies, while the remainder, excepting 24 chosen by Commons House members, had to own at least twelve thousand acres. The growth of such a squirearchy would have required decades to achieve.

From 1669 to 1698 the proprietors promulgated four amended versions of their unalterable Fundamental Constitutions, each of which was shorter and granted more political concessions to the Carolinians than its predecessor. The July 21, 1669, version contained 111 articles, but by March 1, 1670, the unaltered text had been renumbered into 120 articles. This 1670 version was published and disseminated as a tool to recruit settlers. Its religious provisions, which permitted settlement by "Heathens, Jews, and other dissenters" and establishment of any church by seven persons with the exception of Catholics, proved a beacon to Baptists, Huguenots, and Congregationalists, who settled in Carolina prior to 1700. The proprietors revised the Fundamental Constitutions twice in 1682 to attract new settlers, publishing them in English, French, and German to appeal to persecuted Protestants throughout Europe. The second 1682 revision was made in response to overtures by Scottish Covenanters interested in leaving Scotland for the New World. Freedom to buy and sell lands was secured, local political bodies secured more authority, and all churches excepting Catholics secured the right to tax their members. In response to these revisions, in 1684 Scottish settlers established Stuart Town on Port Royal Sound. The short-lived settlement was destroyed by the Spanish in 1686. The final version of the Fundamental Constitutions, issued in April 1698, was a pale shadow of its predecessors. It contained only 41 articles and had lost virtually all of its aristocratic provisions. This skeletonlike final version was powerful evidence that by 1698 Carolinians had achieved a good measure of control over their government and would endure little interference from the Lords Proprietors. The 1698 version was debated off and on for several years in the Commons House of Assembly as a bill, not a constitution. Finally, it was tabled in 1706 and never taken up again. Ironically, the rebels who overthrew the Lords Proprietors' government in 1719 used the proprietors' frequent amendment of the constitution as an example of their tyranny and indifference to good government.

Modern scholars identify some positive elements in the Fundamental Constitutions. They consider South Carolina's historic toleration of religious diversity to be a legacy of the constitution. Early settlement by members of persecuted faiths, especially Jews and Huguenots, gave the province a culturally mixed society not found in other southern states. ALEXANDER MOORE

Moore, John Alexander. "Royalizing South Carolina: The Revolution of 1719 and the Evolution of Early South Carolina Government." Ph.D. diss., University of South Carolina, 1991.

Parker, Mattie E. E., ed. *North Carolina Charters and Constitutions, 1578–1698.* Raleigh, N.C.: Carolina Charter Tercentenary Commission, 1963.

Underwood, James L. *The Constitution of South Carolina.* Vol. 3, *Church and State, Morality and Free Expression.* Columbia: University of South Carolina Press, 1992.

Fundamentalists. The designation "fundamentalists" is an umbrella term that takes in many theologically conservative, evangelical Protestants from several denominations and independent congregations. As a movement, fundamentalism emerged in the late nineteenth and early twentieth centuries as a reaction to "modernist" currents that embraced historical-critical methods of studying the Bible and an openness to harmonizing scientific theory and religious faith. In time, fundamentalism came to represent a belief system that stressed a literal interpretation of the Scriptures, acceptance of miracles as historical and scientific facts, the virgin birth of Jesus, his actual physical resurrection, and an anticipated physical second coming of Christ at the end of time.

Fundamentalism gained popular currency nationally after the 1925 Scopes Trial in Dayton, Tennessee, which found a teacher guilty of violating state law prohibiting teaching theories of evolution in the public schools. Images of the South as the "Bible Belt" reinforced popular perception, although for several decades fundamentalism's major inroads were in northern Presbyterian and Baptist denominations.

Fundamentalism only gradually gained a foothold in South Carolina, most likely because most South Carolina Baptists, Methodists, and Presbyterians thought of themselves as theologically orthodox evangelicals who were immune to dangers of modernism. However, in the 1920s some individuals who embraced fundamentalist thinking began to plant their message across denominational lines when they started schools and Bible colleges or spoke at special conferences and meetings in the state.

For example, Columbia Bible Institute (now Columbia International University) president Robert McQuilkin, although a Presbyterian by affiliation, was a committed fundamentalist and also a popular speaker in the late 1920s at annual youth conferences in Clinton, South Carolina, and elsewhere in the South. Bob Jones was a popular evangelist in South Carolina and throughout the South who zealously promoted the fundamentalist perspective long before he moved his college to Greenville in 1947. In some ways the institutions associated with McQuilkin and Jones became symbolic centers of fundamentalism in South Carolina. Graduates from both schools led their congregations into informal networks of churches and individuals committed to preserving strict orthodoxy in matters of belief and personal moral behavior.

For most fundamentalists, society or "the world" was the arena where sin and corruption prevailed, and so long as South Carolina was perceived to nurture a culture that gave more than lip service to orthodoxy, most fundamentalists remained aloof from political engagement. Even within the major Protestant denominations, fundamentalists remained on the sidelines until they believed that orthodoxy was threatened.

For the denominations, that threat came first among Methodists when there were talks of merger among the Methodist Protestant Church, the Methodist Episcopal Church, and the Methodist Episcopal Church, South, that culminated with the formation of the Methodist Church in 1939. Those Methodist bodies that were primarily northern were thought to be infected by modernist thought. No doubt there was also a racial dimension, for the northern bodies also had congregations that were predominantly African American. The (Methodist) Laymen's Association, which opposed reunion, called a meeting in Columbia in 1940 that ultimately led to the founding of the fundamentalist-inclined Southern Methodist Church, a name taken in 1945. Similar currents caused division among South Carolina Presbyterians. Several congregations affiliated with the Presbyterian Church in the United States left that body to help found the Presbyterian Church in America in 1973, more than a decade before the former group was reunited with its northern counterpart.

For the state's largest white Protestant denomination, comprised of churches identified with the Southern Baptist Convention, divisions over fundamentalism began to emerge in the 1970s and 1980s, when more conservative leaders became convinced that agencies affiliated with the denomination, such as Furman University, had been infected by liberal thought and secularism. As fundamentalists gained control of the denominational machinery at both national and state levels, many individual congregations that were loath to split from the denomination formally coalesced into the Cooperative Baptist Fellowship, which was more moderate in its theological posture.

The strength of fundamentalism in South Carolina remains the hundreds of independent congregations, many using the designation of Baptist or some variation of Gospel Fellowship in their names. Among these bodies, the last quarter of the twentieth century witnessed a shift from the earlier posture of remaining strictly separate from social and political involvement. Prompting that shift were the changes that came following the civil rights movement and the integration of public schools and other public facilities. Also vital were convictions that U.S. Supreme Court decisions in the 1960s, affecting such matters as prayer in the public schools, were undermining the religious base of South Carolina common life.

Fundamentalist leaders and churches, for example, rallied around Paul Ellwanger of Anderson in 1980 when he organized an effort, ultimately unsuccessful, to mandate the teaching of creation science in South Carolina public schools. Similar efforts in 1992, this time successful, helped put pressure on the state board of education to require a moment of silent meditation, not a formal prayer, at the start of each school day. Other debates involving schools centered on a curriculum that promoted critical thinking. In all these arenas, fundamentalists tended to become socially engaged in order to assure that orthodox moral values and practice remained foundational to common life in the state. NANCY A. HARDESTY

Glass, William R. *Strangers in Zion: Fundamentalists in the South, 1900–1950.* Macon, Ga.: Mercer University Press, 2001.

Furchgott, Robert Francis (b. 1916). Pharmacologist, Nobel laureate. Furchgott was born in Charleston on June 4, 1916, the second of three sons born to Arthur Furchgott and Pena Sorrentrue. Arthur Furchgott, his father, and his brothers operated Furchgott's Department Store on King Street in Charleston until 1929 when the family moved to Orangeburg and opened a ladies' clothing store. When he was a young boy, Furchgott's first interest was "natural history." He participated in nature study classes and field trips sponsored by the Charleston Museum. After his family moved to Orangeburg, Furchgott became interested in science. He was an avid reader of popular works about scientists and science columns in the *New York Times.*

After graduating from high school in 1933, Furchgott spent his freshman year at the University of South Carolina because he could not afford the tuition at the University of North Carolina. The next year his father moved his business to Goldsboro, North Carolina, and Furchgott enrolled as a sophomore at UNC to major in chemistry. He graduated with a B.S. in 1937 and went on to earn a Ph.D. in biochemistry at Northwestern University in 1940. On November 23, 1941, Furchgott married Lenore Mandelbaum, a New Yorker. They have three daughters.

Furchgott was a research fellow and faculty member at Cornell University College of Medicine from 1940 to 1949 and a faculty member at Washington University School of Medicine in St. Louis from 1949 to 1956. He served as professor and chairman of the Department of Pharmacology at SUNY Downstate Medical Center in Brooklyn from 1956 to 1982 and was later named distinguished professor emeritus. Since 1989 he has been an adjunct professor of pharmacology at the University of Miami School of Medicine and a distinguished university professor at the Medical University of South Carolina.

Furchgott became known for his research in cardiac pharmacology, peripheral adrenergic mechanisms, the theory of drug-receptor mechanisms, and vascular pharmacology and physiology. In the 1950s he developed the helical strip of rabbit thoracic aorta as a model system for studies on drug receptor mechanisms that led to its use in laboratories worldwide. From 1956 to 1978 his research concerned photorelaxation of blood vessels, factors influencing contractility of cardiac muscle, peripheral adrenegic mechanisms, and receptor theory. In 1978 he accidentally discovered that vascular smooth muscle is photosensitive, undergoing reversible relaxation when exposed to ultraviolet light. In 1980 he reported his discovery of the obligatory role of endothelial cells in the relaxation (vasodilation) of arteries by acetylcholine and related muscarinic agonists. Furchgott demonstrated that the relaxation resulted from release of a labile factor (called EDRF endothelium-derived relaxing factor) from the stimulated endothelial cells. In 1986 Furchgott presented evidence that EDRF is nitric oxide (NO) and that the neurotransmitter released by NANC nerves may also be NO. In 1998 Furchgott, Louis J. Ignarro, and Ferid Murad were jointly awarded the Nobel Prize in Physiology or Medicine for their discoveries concerning nitric oxide as a signaling molecule in the cardiovascular system. The discovery that NO is a gas that can act as a signal molecule in the organism has had profound implications for the treatment of cardiovascular conditions and other diseases.

Besides sharing the Nobel Prize, Furchgott was awarded the Albert Lasker Basic Medical Research Award (1996) and numerous other awards. He is the recipient of honorary doctoral degrees (in medicine or science) from eleven universities and is a member of the National Academy of Sciences (1990) and a Fellow of the American Academy of Arts and Sciences (2000). MARY S. MILLER

Furchgott, Robert F. "A Research Trail over Half a Century." *Annual Review of Pharmacology and Toxicology* 35 (1995): 1–27.

Furman, Richard (1755–1825). Minister, educator. Furman was born in Esopus, New York, on October 9, 1755, to Wood Furman and Rachel Brodhead. In 1756 the family moved from New York to Charleston, eventually settling in St. Thomas Parish. Furman was educated at home and mastered both Latin and Greek. His penchant for self-education was recognized when Rhode Island College (later Brown University) awarded him master's (1792) and doctor of divinity degrees (1800).

In 1770 the family moved to the High Hills of Santee, near the fork of the Wateree and Congaree Rivers. Under the influence of a local minister, Joseph Reese, Furman was converted in 1771. Abandoning his Anglican upbringing, Furman embraced the evangelistic Calvinism of Separate Baptists. He was ordained on May 10, 1774, and served as pastor of High Hills Baptist Church (1774–1787) and Charleston Baptist Church (1787–1825). On November 20, 1774, Furman married Elizabeth Haynsworth. They had four children before her death in 1787. Two years later, on May 5, 1789, Furman married Dorothea Burn. His second marriage produced thirteen children.

Furman volunteered to fight during the Revolutionary War, but Governor John Rutledge persuaded him to plead the patriot cause among the Loyalists in western South Carolina instead. Furman's success came to the attention of Lord Cornwallis, who, after capturing Charleston in 1780, apparently offered a £1,000 reward for Furman's capture.

Richard Furman. Courtesy, South Carolina Historical Society

An ardent champion of religious liberty, Furman met with a group of dissenters at High Hills in 1776. Their deliberations helped set the stage for disestablishment of the Church of England in South Carolina two years later. In 1790, as a delegate to the South Carolina constitutional convention, Furman supported extending the right of incorporation to all denominations. Furman's actions generally reflected the era's notion that religious liberty prohibited denominational favoritism but not necessarily church-state interaction (for example, Furman reportedly preached a sermon before Congress in 1814).

Furman greatly influenced the development of the Baptist denomination, although his fellow Baptists sometimes disagreed with his preference for centralized church governance. He was twice elected (1814, 1817) president of the Triennial Baptist Convention, a national organization of Baptists based in Philadelphia. He was also a founder and president of the South Carolina Baptist Convention (1821–1825), the first statewide Baptist organization in America.

Unlike some of his Baptist contemporaries, Furman stressed the importance of an educated ministry. He helped establish an educational fund to train Baptist ministers and also called for a national theological institution; the latter eventually led to the creation of Columbian College (now George Washington University). Other institutions that resulted from his influence were Furman University, the Southern Baptist Theological Seminary, and Mercer University.

Furman initially opposed slavery but reversed his position after he became a slaveowner and came to believe that slavery was economically necessary and morally justified. His "Exposition of the Views of the Baptists Relative to the Coloured Population of the United States" (1822) foreshadowed the intellectual and religious arguments southerners would use for the next four decades to defend slavery. Furman died in Charleston of an intestinal obstruction on August 25, 1825. He was buried in the First Baptist Churchyard, Charleston. A. SCOTT HENDERSON

Rogers, James A. *Richard Furman: Life and Legacy.* Macon, Ga.: Mercer University Press, 1985.

Furman University. On December 3, 1825, the South Carolina Baptist Convention (SCBC) elected a board to organize an institution to train young men for the ministry. The Furman Academy and Theological Institution was established the following year. It officially opened in January 1827 and was named in honor of Richard Furman, a Baptist minister and education pioneer.

Originally located in Edgefield, Furman provided both a "literary" and a theological curriculum. Few students enrolled, however, and the school teetered on insolvency during its first twenty-five years. Furman was closed for a brief period (1834–1837), moved twice (to the High Hills of Santee near Stateburg, 1829–1834; to Fairfield District near Winnsboro, 1837–1850), and had an average enrollment of only ten students.

The reconstructed bell tower from the old Furman campus is a landmark on the strikingly beautiful new campus. Courtesy, Furman University

On December 20, 1850, the state legislature chartered "The Furman University." Classes were held in downtown Greenville until the first building, a two-room wooden cottage, could be erected on a new fifty-acre campus overlooking the Reedy River. The institution was composed of an academic department that offered college-preparatory studies (discontinued in 1916), a collegiate department comprised of six "schools," and a theological department—with graduate studies—that provided justification for Furman's designation as a university. The theological department operated until 1859, when it separated to become the Southern Baptist Theological Seminary, which moved to Louisville, Kentucky, in 1877.

Like most southern institutions, Furman was disrupted by the Civil War. President James C. Furman was a member of the Charleston Secession Convention, and after the Civil War began, most students and several faculty members enlisted in the Confederate forces. The university closed in the fall of 1861 and did not reopen until the winter of 1866, although at the time there was no money even to print a catalog.

Financial problems continued to haunt the school, and near bankruptcy prompted reorganization in 1881. At the turn of the century, Greenville's textile prosperity, along with effective and academically rigorous presidents, brought a surge of northern philanthropy to the school. In December 1924 Furman was accredited by the Southern Association of Colleges. Five days later the president learned that the university had been named one of the collegiate beneficiaries of the Duke Endowment. A watershed in the university's history, this bequest kept Furman alive during the Great Depression. In 1936, with Furman still $170,000 in debt, school officials sought additional funding from the General Education Board of the Rockefeller Foundation to sponsor the Greenville County Council for Community Development. Among other activities, this organization coordinated participation of Furman faculty and students in novel university-community undertakings, including a Citizens Education Center and several teacher-training institutes.

Furman's growth was paralleled by that of the Greenville Woman's College. Initially called the Greenville Baptist Female College, the Woman's College was established in 1854 by the SCBC and governed by Furman's trustees until 1908. The school had high aspirations and inspired teaching but had no endowment. The Woman's College and Furman undertook joint fund-raising campaigns, and their students participated in shared activities. While its extensive music and education programs helped make it the second-largest women's college in the state (Winthrop University was larger), it could not survive the economic chaos of the 1930s, when it gradually became the coordinate women's college of Furman.

In 1950, with highway projects threatening to divide Furman's property and with enrollment at record levels, the university's trustees purchased approximately nine hundred acres for a new campus six miles north of downtown Greenville. Groundbreaking took place in 1953, men moved to the new campus in 1958, and women joined them in 1961. At the urging of Dean Frances Bonner, incoming president Gordon Blackwell, and the rest of the university community, the board of trustees affirmed its support of integration in December 1964, despite protests from the state Baptist Convention. The school was officially integrated a couple of months later. In 1973, after trying to attain one for more than three decades, Furman was awarded a Phi Beta Kappa chapter.

Throughout the twentieth century Furman maintained a balance between intellectual rigor and denominational priorities. This became increasingly difficult in the 1980s with the rise of conservative evangelicals within the SCBC. For that reason, Furman's trustees voted to sever all ties with the SCBC on October 15, 1990; the SCBC officially recognized that break on May 15, 1992. The potential financial consequences of this decision were significant for Furman, but the institution's liberal-arts focus remained unchanged.

Notable Furman graduates include John B. Watson, one of the founders of behavioral psychology; Charles Hard Townes, a Nobel laureate in physics; and Richard Riley, a governor of South Carolina and U.S. secretary of education. A. SCOTT HENDERSON

Bainbridge, Judith T. *Academy and College: The History of the Woman's College of Furman University.* Macon, Ga.: Mercer University Press, 2001.

Reid, Alfred Sandlin. *Furman University: Toward a New Identity, 1925–1975.* Durham, N.C.: Duke University Press, 1976.

Fusionism. A phenomenon of the Reconstruction period, "fusionism" describes the awkward and short-lived political alliance between moderate wings of the South's Democratic and Republican Parties. With newly enfranchised blacks entering the political arena as Republicans, white Democrats (mostly former Confederates) faced a serious challenge to their efforts to regain power. This task was especially difficult in states such as South Carolina, where the black electorate during the 1870s exceeded the white electorate by more than thirty thousand voters. While many South Carolina whites resorted to violent solutions, including the Ku Klux Klan, the state's moderate Democrats pursued more legitimate means, most notably fusionism. Pragmatic in their approach, fusionists acknowledged the numerical reality of Republican domination, yet sought ways to exploit its emerging factional rifts. One of the chief proponents of fusionism in South Carolina was Francis W. Dawson, editor of the Charleson *News and Courier.* Noting the uneasiness of many white Republicans over the growing influence of black leadership, Dawson urged the Democratic Party to vote for these disaffected politicos in the hope of further dividing the opposition. In the process, Dawson and other fusionist Democrats tried to lure a few blacks into their fold with dubious guarantees of civil equality and vague promises of economic opportunity.

Never more than an expedient, fusionism ultimately failed as a viable political alternative. Blacks usually rejected fusionist overtures, rightly seeing them as disingenuous attempts to manipulate their votes. Concomitantly, most whites loathed the idea of cooperating with the Republican Party. To them, fusionism demonstrated weakness and betrayed notions of southern honor and white supremacy by tacitly recognizing blacks to be their political equals. After suffering humiliating defeats in the state elections of 1870, 1872, and 1874, South Carolina Democrats discarded the fusionist strategy in favor of a more aggressive and uncompromising approach. By 1876 white hardliners had supplanted political fusion in most of South Carolina with paramilitary force. Local fusion tickets during the 1880s and early 1890s survived in lowcountry counties such as Beaufort and Georgetown, where white Democrats and black Republicans struck arrangements to share political offices. These remaining attempts at fusion politics, however, would fall victim to the virtual elimination of the black vote in the state constitution of 1895. BEN H. SEVERANCE

Clark, E. Culpepper. *Francis Warrington Dawson and the Politics of Restoration: South Carolina, 1874–1889.* University: University of Alabama Press, 1980.

Perman, Michael. *The Road to Redemption: Southern Politics, 1869–1879.* Chapel Hill: University of North Carolina Press, 1984.

Tindall, George Brown. *South Carolina Negroes, 1877–1900.* 1952. Reprint, Columbia: University of South Carolina Press, 2003.

Zuczek, Richard. *State of Rebellion: Reconstruction in South Carolina.* Columbia: University of South Carolina Press, 1996.

G

Gadsden, Christopher (1724–1805). Patriot, merchant. Gadsden was born in Charleston on February 16, 1724, the son of Elizabeth and Thomas Gadsden, a collector of customs. Gadsden received a classical education in England before completing a four-year apprenticeship to a prominent Philadelphia factor. Between 1745 and 1747 he served as purser aboard the British man-of-war *Aldborough.* With money from his seafaring service and a large inheritance from his parents, who had both died by 1741, Gadsden launched one of the most successful mercantile careers in the province. By 1774 he owned four stores, several merchant vessels, two rice plantations (worked by more than ninety slaves), a residential district called Gadsdenboro in Charleston, and one of the largest wharfs in North America.

Possessing financial independence and a civic spirit, Gadsden pursued public office. In 1757 he began his nearly three decades of service in the Commons House of Assembly. He first revealed himself as a vocal defender of American rights during the Cherokee War by attacking the British colonel James Grant for taking command of local troops above provincial Colonel Thomas Middleton. Gadsden continued to defy British authority as a member of the assembly by opposing the governor and Royal Council in their attempt to infringe on the legislature's right to raise troops, control money bills, and determine the election of its own members. Governor Thomas Boone marked Gadsden a troublemaker in 1762 and used a violation of a minor electoral practice to deny him his seat in the Commons House. The ensuing controversy between the governor and Gadsden swelled the merchant's reputation as a defender of colonial rights and helped transform him into a zealous American patriot.

Gadsden continued to champion American home rule and to oppose Parliamentary supremacy at the Stamp Act Congress in New York in 1765. During the next decade, Gadsden joined with Charleston mechanics (Sons of Liberty) to lead the local "patriot party" against every perceived infringement of America's rights by Parliament. Gadsden's influence and dedication earned him election to the First Continental Congress, where his extremism manifested itself in proposals for Congress to reject all Parliamentary legislation passed since 1763, to attack the British fleet in American waters, and to instruct each colony to prepare for war. Gadsden returned to South Carolina in February 1776 to serve as colonel of the First Regiment and as a member of the Provincial Congress, where he promoted independence and coauthored the South Carolina constitution of 1776. That summer he helped repulse the British navy's attack on Charleston, conduct that earned him a position as brigadier general in the Continental Army. Two years later Gadsden helped secure the disestablishment of the Anglican Church and popular election of senators in the state's 1778 constitution. But the conservative faction dominating the assembly managed to dampen the firebrand's influence in the new government by electing Gadsden to the impotent position of vice president (as the office of lieutenant governor was then known).

While Gadsden's zealous and suspicious personality was ideal for organizing American resistance, it was counterproductive in the post-1776 political structure. In 1777 he impulsively resigned his commission as brigadier general over a petty dispute with General Robert Howe. The following year Gadsden violently upset the masses by favoring leniency toward local Tories. And while serving as lieutenant governor in 1780, Gadsden's irrational temperament cost the United States more than two thousand Continental troops when Charleston fell to the British. Following a ten-month imprisonment in St. Augustine, Gadsden returned to South Carolina to rebuild his many business interests, which suffered considerably during the war. He returned to public service briefly in 1788 to vote for ratification of the United States Constitution and again in 1790 to serve in the state's constitutional convention.

Gadsden married three times. On July 28, 1746, he married Jane Godfrey. The couple had two children. He married Mary Hasell on December 29, 1755. His second marriage produced four children. Following Mary's death in 1768, Gadsden married Ann Wragg on April 14, 1776. They had no children. Gadsden died on August 28, 1805, from head injuries suffered in a fall near his home in Charleston. He was buried in St. Philip's Churchyard.
KEITH KRAWCZYNSKI

Godbold, E. Stanley, Jr., and Robert H. Woody. *Christopher Gadsden and the American Revolution.* Knoxville: University of Tennessee Press, 1982.

McDonough, Daniel J. *Christopher Gadsden and Henry Laurens: The Parallel Lives of Two American Patriots.* Selinsgrove, Pa.: Susquehanna University Press, 2000.

Walsh, Richard. *Charleston's Sons of Liberty: A Study of the Artisans, 1763–1789.* Columbia: University of South Carolina Press, 1959.

———. "Christopher Gadsden: Radical or Conservative Revolutionary?" *South Carolina Historical Magazine* 63 (October 1962): 195–203.

———, ed. *The Writings of Christopher Gadsden, 1746–1805.* Columbia: University of South Carolina Press, 1966.

Gadsden, James (1788–1858). Soldier, railroad president, diplomat. Gadsden was born in Charleston on May 15, 1788, the son of Philip Gadsden and Catherine Edwards. He was also the grandson of Revolutionary War patriot Christopher Gadsden. Gadsden graduated from Yale College in 1806, returned briefly to Charleston, and then decided to join the United States Army. He served as lieutenant of engineers during the War of 1812, and worked throughout the decade on defenses in the Southwest and the Gulf Coast. By 1820 he had risen to the rank of colonel.

Gadsden left the military in 1822, but remained in the service of the government. The following year, he was appointed commissioner in charge of removing the Seminoles from Florida; in this capacity he oversaw the Treaty of Camp Moultrie. The next year he became a member of Florida's territorial Legislative Council, and set up a plantation in Florida. Gadsden County, in northwest Florida, was named for him in 1823. He returned to Charleston in order to marry Susan Gibbes Hort of Charleston on November 6, 1827. The couple had no children. Shortly after his wedding,

Gadsden went back to Florida, where he remained interested in politics for more than a decade. Gadsden hoped to represent Florida in Congress, but was defeated in five separate elections. He returned to Charleston permanently in 1839.

On his return, Gadsden immediately became immersed in the push for internal improvements and expanded southern trade. He became the president of the Louisville, Cincinnati and Charleston Railroad in 1840, an ambitious project to draw the trade of the Midwest to Charleston. This hope was never realized, and Gadsden's presidency oversaw the reincorporation of the Louisville, Cincinnati and Charleston as the South Carolina Rail Road Company (SCRR) in 1843. He remained president of the SCRR until 1850. Gadsden's plans for trade routes to the Midwest and Pacific also found expression with his participation in southern commercial conventions. He was active in commercial conventions in Augusta, Georgia, and Charleston from 1837 to 1839, and served as the chairman of the committee on railroads at the Memphis convention of 1845. Here, he renewed his hope for a rail connection to the Pacific.

Ousted by SCRR shareholders in 1850, Gadsden continued to pursue the transcontinental railroad project, planning a route along the Gila River and determining that the purchase of Mexican territory would expedite matters. It is as the author of the "Gadsden Purchase" that Gadsden secured his place in history. Appointed minister to Mexico by President Franklin Pierce in 1853, Gadsden soon saw an opportunity to acquire land from Santa Anna's Mexico. The result was the purchase, that year, of a strip of land comprising the southern portions of what later became the states of Arizona and New Mexico. With this purchase, Gadsden facilitated the construction of a western railroad, but it would not happen in his lifetime; the Southern Pacific finally connected Los Angeles and New Orleans via Gadsden Purchase land in 1883.

Gadsden's fortunes declined after he bought the land for the United States. Although he remained in Mexico for three years, he accomplished little else of note. His attempts to exert influence in Mexican politics by encouraging democratic revolutionaries prompted the United States government to recall him in 1856. He returned to Charleston and died there on December 26, 1858. AARON W. MARRS

Derrick, Samuel M. *Centennial History of South Carolina Railroad.* 1930. Reprint, Spartanburg, S.C.: Reprint Company, 1975.

Gadsden flag. Consisting of a gray, coiled rattlesnake on a bright yellow background, with the words "DON'T TREAD ON ME" inscribed beneath, the Gadsden flag became a popular symbol of the American Revolution. Dating back to the origins of the French and Indian War, the indigenous rattlesnake had been an important political symbol in the American colonies. In protest to British colonial policy, Benjamin Franklin designed a disconnected serpent with the ominous warning, "Join or Die," as a symbol of unity. Growing in popularity, the rattlesnake later appeared in newspapers and on colonial currency.

Inferential evidence and the weight of tradition attribute the creation of this particular flag to Christopher Gadsden, a delegate from South Carolina to the Continental Congress. Returning to Charleston from Congress, Gadsden presented "an elegant standard" to the South Carolina Provincial Congress on February 9, 1776. This flag was that day ordered preserved in the hall of the South Carolina Provincial Congress. As a member of the Naval Committee of the Continental Congress, Gadsden had also presented the flag to Esek Hopkins, commander-in-chief of the Continental Navy, who used a version of the Gadsden flag as the first navy jack. The rattlesnake and motto were later incorporated into a flag used by the naval forces of South Carolina as fitting symbols of the defensive posture of the disgruntled colonists by 1776. SAMUEL K. FORE

Godbold, E. Stanley, Jr., and Robert H. Woody. *Christopher Gadsden and the American Revolution.* Knoxville: University of Tennessee Press, 1982.

Rankin, Hugh F. "The Naval Flag of the American Revolution." *William and Mary Quarterly,* 3d ser., 11 (July 1954): 339–53.

Richardson, Edward W. *Standards and Colors of the American Revolution.* Philadelphia: University of Pennsylvania Press, 1982.

Gaffney (Cherokee County; 2000 pop. 12,968). Incorporated in 1875, the city of Gaffney was named for Irish immigrant Michael Gaffney. He came to the area in around 1804, bought land, and constructed a house, barns, and a store and tavern. The property, known as Gaffney's Cross Roads or Gaffney's Old Field, became a local gathering place but failed to compete with nearby Limestone Springs, the site of a girl's school and mineral springs patronized by a wealthy clientele. In the early 1870s, Mary Gaffney, Michael's widow, lured the Atlanta and Charlotte Air Line (later the Southern Railway) to her property with the promise of a free right-of-way from the Cross Roads to the Broad River. Seven hundred acres of Gaffney's land was then laid out into town lots. A town government was formed in 1874, and Gaffney was incorporated on March 3, 1875.

Largely because of its proximity to the railroad, the town initially experienced rapid growth. Four hundred citizens in 1880 became 1,631 within ten years, 3,937 by 1900, and 4,767 by 1910. Private schools (1876); a board of health (1881); a newspaper, the *Gaffney Ledger* (1894); the Gaffney School District (1897); a library (1905); hospital (1908); and a board of public works (1909) followed. At the same time, industries such as the Cherokee Falls Manufacturing Company (1882), the Gaffney Manufacturing Company (1892), and the Limestone (1900), Irene (1905), Globe (1905), and Hamrick (1907) mills provided investment and employment opportunities. In 1901 the Merchants and Planters Bank was formed to manage the city's investments.

In 1896 Gaffney, in conjunction with Limestone Springs and Blacksburg, rallied dissent in their respective areas in order to create a separate county. Their effort was endorsed by Governor John Gary Evans, approved by the electorate, and recognized by the General Assembly in January 1897. The result was Cherokee County with Gaffney as its county seat.

Plummeting cotton prices in the 1920s and the Depression of the 1930s slowed the city's growth, as many citizens moved away in search of work because of curtailed mill production. World War II reinvigorated the Gaffney textile mills with war contracts, sparking a renewed population boom in the city as well as its unincorporated mill suburb, East Gaffney. Between 1940 and 1970, the population of Gaffney nearly doubled from 7,636 to 13,253. Growth in the ensuing decades, however, lay in the suburbs. Suburbanites outnumbered city dwellers in 1990 and outstripped them even further in the decade when Cherokee County's eighteen percent growth rate exceeded that of South Carolina as a whole. LOUIS P. TOWLES

Cherokee County. Gaffney, S.C.: Cherokee County Chamber of Commerce, 2000.

Moss, Bobby G. *The Old Iron District: A Study of the Development of Cherokee County: 1750–1897.* Clinton, S.C.: Jacobs, 1972.

150th Anniversary Souvenir Program. Gaffney, S.C.: Gaffney Sesquicentennial, 1954.

Gaillard, David DuBose (1859–1913). Engineer, soldier. David DuBose Gaillard was born on September 4, 1859, in Fulton, Sumter District. His parents were Samuel Isaac Gaillard and Susan Richardson DuBose. Gaillard lived with his parents, grandparents, and sisters in Clarendon until 1872, when he moved to Winnsboro to attend Mount Zion Collegiate Institute. Gaillard entered West Point in 1880 and graduated fifth in his class in 1884. He was commissioned second lieutenant of engineers and would eventually attain the rank of colonel. He and Katherine Ross Davis of Columbia were married in Winnsboro on October 6, 1887. The couple later had one son.

Gaillard's work as an engineer took him around the world: he taught engineering in Willets Point, New York; worked on the international boundary between the United States and Mexico; oversaw the water supply in Washington, D.C.; surveyed the Portland Channel in Alaska; and performed general staff duty in Cuba. His most important work, however, came when he was appointed to work on the Panama Canal.

General George Washington Goethals was made chief engineer of the Panama Canal in 1907, and he selected Gaillard to oversee dredging and excavation. The following year Gaillard took charge of the most challenging section: the "Culebra Cut," which crossed the continental divide. Gaillard worked for years fighting the difficult terrain and constant earth slides. He collapsed on July 26, 1913, and was taken to Johns Hopkins Hospital in Baltimore, where he died on December 5. Culebra Cut was renamed Gaillard Cut in his honor. Gaillard was buried in Arlington National Cemetery in Washington, D.C. AARON W. MARRS

United States. Army. Corps of Engineers. 3d Regiment (Volunteer). *David Du Bose Gaillard.* St. Louis, Mo., 1916.

Gaillard, John (1765–1826). U.S. senator. John Gaillard was born on September 5, 1765, in St. Stephen's Parish, the son of John Gaillard and Judith Peyre. In 1782 his father took British protection and moved his family to England where he enrolled Gaillard in legal studies at London's Middle Temple. Gaillard's ambition, however, lay in areas other than the law. Returning to South Carolina, he married Mary Lord on November 22, 1792. The couple had three children: Edwin, Theodore Samuel, and Anna. Gaillard became a prominent member of lowcountry society and a successful planter with extensive landholdings in St. Stephen's and St. James Santee Parishes. It was in politics, however, that Gaillard achieved his fame, forging a reputation as a statesman respected by members of factions otherwise at odds. Gaillard's political career began in 1794, when he was elected to the South Carolina House of Representatives to represent St. Stephen's Parish. After serving in the Eleventh General Assembly (1794–1795), he became a state senator in 1796, again from St. Stephen's. Reelected several times by his constituents, Gaillard also served as Senate president from 1803 to 1804.

On December 6, 1804, Gaillard resigned his state Senate seat following his election by the General Assembly to complete the remainder of Pierce Butler's term in the U.S. Senate. Taking his seat in the Eighth Congress on January 31, 1805, Gaillard would serve as a U.S. senator until his death in 1826. Politically he was a Democratic-Republican and a supporter of President Thomas Jefferson. He also supported the James Madison administration and joined his South Carolina colleagues in Congress in voting for war with Great Britain in 1812. After the war, Gaillard followed other Carolinians in retreating toward a more states'-rights-oriented position. Along with his fellow senator William Smith, Gaillard opposed measures calling for a protective tariff, the rechartering of the Bank of the United States, and federal aid for internal improvements.

Gaillard's reputation, however, derived not from the stands he took on partisan issues, but from his role as a statesman in the Senate. Gaillard was elected president pro tempore of the Senate (presiding officer in the absence of the vice president—which was often) on ten different occasions during his tenure. Other symbols of his colleagues' respect were also bestowed on him as he was chosen to be one of South Carolina's presidential electors (pledged to Jefferson) in 1804, and was designated by the U.S. Senate as the "teller" (official counter) of the electoral college votes in the 1812 election. Gaillard's reputation and the respect devolved upon him were perhaps aided by the fact that he was never a controversial figure. In a period of often contentious debates in Congress, over issues such as the extension of slavery into the Louisiana Purchase during the Missouri crisis, Gaillard did not enter the fray. Most probably, as the Senate's presiding officer, Gaillard felt that taking sides would be a breach of both decorum and the duties of his office. In an era of controversy, Gaillard was one of the few national political figures that appeared to his colleagues to be above the fray. As described by Senator Thomas Hart Benton, Gaillard preserved order in the Senate "not by authority of rules, but by the graces of deportment . . . There was probably not an instance of disorder or a disagreeable scene in the chamber, during his long continued presidency."

Gaillard's wife died in a drowning accident in May 1799. Taken with illness in early 1826, Gaillard died in Washington, D.C., on February 26 and was buried in the Congressional Cemetery in Washington. KEVIN M. GANNON

Bailey, N. Louise, Mary L. Morgan, and Carolyn R. Taylor, eds. *Biographical Directory of the South Carolina Senate, 1776–1985.* 3 vols. Columbia: University of South Carolina Press, 1986.

Galivants Ferry Stump Meeting. The Galivants Ferry Stump meeting, a Democratic Party tradition since the 1880s, originated during the 1876 gubernatorial candidacy of Wade Hampton, the former general and Confederate hero. The meetings were started in a place called "the Thicket" by Press Daniels, area Democratic club president and executive committeeman. They matured into a tradition under the guidance of the Holliday family. The "stump," which referred to a time when politicians promoted their candidacy by allegedly giving speeches while standing on tree stumps, was moved to a site beside the Holliday family store and continued by four generations of Hollidays, beginning with John W. Holliday. The tradition was carried on by his son, George J. Holliday, who became a state senator; then by his two grandsons, John Monroe Holliday and Joseph W. Holliday; then by his great-grandchildren.

The stump meetings soon drew hundreds who traveled by wagon, buggy, or horseback to hear aspirants to county- and statewide political positions. Over the years, the event assumed a carnival atmosphere, featuring balloons, streamers, chicken bog and barbecue, country and gospel music, and clogging. Politicians such as longtime U.S. Senator Ernest F. "Fritz" Hollings had perfect attendance for decades.

The stumping, which has drawn as many as fifty speakers, has survived the inroads of television and remained a strong Democratic tradition in the twenty-first century. ROBERT A. PIERCE

Thompson, Eldridge. "Where Stumping Is Still the Style." *Sandlapper* 5 (April 1972): 30–32.

Gallagher, Simon Felix (1756–1825). Missionary, educator. Gallagher was born in Ireland (probably Dublin) in 1756. He studied for the Catholic priesthood and was ordained in the Diocese of Dublin. An educated, cultured man, Gallagher described himself as a graduate of the University of Paris and was always referred to as Dr. Gallagher. He immigrated to the United States and, in January 1793, applied to Bishop John Carroll of Baltimore for work as a missionary. Carroll assigned him to be pastor of St. Mary's Church in Charleston, where his name first appeared in the parish register on September 1, 1793. St. Mary's was the first Catholic church in the Carolinas and Georgia, having been organized in 1788.

Charleston Catholics received Gallagher with enthusiasm. Eloquent and personable, he was successful in galvanizing the small community and achieved prominence in Charleston and beyond, earning respect and increased tolerance for Catholics. The congregation had difficulty supporting a pastor, so Gallagher earned income as a member of the faculty at the College of Charleston. Beginning in November 1793, he gave lectures in logic, mathematics, natural philosophy, and astronomy. He was popular with the students and helped to enhance the institution's scholarly reputation. Charleston intellectual Hugh Swinton Legaré called him "the most eminent classical teacher of his day." Gallagher also became a leader in Charleston's Irish community and principal organizer of the Hibernian Society, serving as its first president from 1801 to 1803. For several years he operated the Athenian Academy, a school for Charleston youth. When the General Assembly authorized public schools throughout the state in 1811, Gallagher chaired the Charleston Board of School Supervisors.

Gallagher experienced difficulties with St. Mary's board of trustees, or vestry, which sought to curtail his authority in parish affairs. Stories of a drinking problem triggered a formal complaint by the trustees in 1801, and a demand from Bishop Carroll for his resignation. Gallagher appealed directly to the Vatican, over Carroll's head, declaring that he had been maligned. In 1803 Carroll sent as Gallagher's replacement a French-born priest, who was rejected by most of the congregation. The problem festered for years, eventually causing a schism, partly along Irish-French ethnic lines. The conflict led Carroll's successor, Archbishop Leonard Neale, to place St. Mary's under interdict in 1817, ordering that no sacraments be performed there. The Irish-French split caused public scandal and confusion in the Charleston Catholic community. Gallagher refused to quit, declaring that, "it would be deserting the cause of Religion . . . [if] I should relinquish the sacred ministry."

The Charleston schism was finally resolved by the establishment of the Diocese of Charleston and the arrival of John England as its first bishop in 1820. England reinstated Gallagher as pastor, but the man was past his prime. In 1822 England granted his request for a transfer to a parish in St. Augustine, Florida. For a time Gallagher worked in Havana, Cuba, and later in New Orleans. His last post was a parish in Natchez, Mississippi, where he died on December 13, 1825. DAVID C. R. HEISSER

Buchanan, Scott. "Father Gallagher Eases the Plight of Catholics in Charleston." *New Catholic Miscellany* 32 (September 21, 2000): 7.

Easterby, J. Harold. *A History of the College of Charleston.* Charleston, S.C., 1935.

Guilday, Peter. *The Life and Times of John England.* 2 vols. 1927. Reprint, New York: Arno, 1969.

Madden, Richard C. *Catholics in South Carolina: A Record.* Lanham, Md.: University Press of America, 1985.

Galphin, George (?–1780). Indian trader. Galphin was a native of county Tullamore, Ireland. The son of a linen weaver, he was the eldest of seven children and immigrated to the colony of South Carolina in 1737. By 1745 Galphin was serving as an Indian interpreter for the South Carolina Commons House of Assembly among the powerful Lower Creek Nation in the western region of the colony. As an interpreter, he not only conveyed messages between the Indians and the colonial government, but he also entertained influential Indian leaders on behalf of the colony. Galphin's career as an Indian trader, merchant, land speculator, planter, public servant, and patriot aptly illustrates the level of financial success and influence that some frontier entrepreneurs achieved during the colonial period in South Carolina.

For much of the colonial period, the Indian trade, in which Native Americans bartered deerskins for European goods, was an important formative economic activity. Although many European settlers were involved in the deerskin trade, Galphin and a handful of other traders and merchants were extremely successful in this business and amassed considerable wealth and political influence. By the early 1740s, Galphin had established a trading post at Silver Bluff near New Windsor Township adjacent to the Savannah River (near the modern town of Jackson in Aiken County). Archaeological information indicates the trading post measured approximately 450 by 260 feet and was surrounded by a wooden palisade. The complex contained at least six structures, with a trading area in the south half of the enclosure and a residential area in the north portion of the post. Unlike many traders, Galphin maintained amicable trade relations with the Creek and Cherokee. He was respected by his Native American clients and traveled freely through their territories. At its height, Galphin's trade influence extended south to the Gulf Coast and west to the Mississippi River.

The Indian trade at Silver Bluff began to diminish during the 1760s and the post catered mainly to the settlers that resided in New Windsor Township. By the 1770s, Galphin was devoting much of his time to developing Silver Bluff into a profitable plantation. He continued this activity until the Revolutionary War. During the war, Galphin was a patriot and was instrumental in maintaining neutrality among the Creek and Cherokee. In 1780 Silver Bluff was seized by Loyalists, but it was quickly recaptured by South Carolina militia under the command of Lieutenant Colonel Harry Lee in 1781. Galphin died in December 1780 of unknown causes. When his estate was divided among his heirs, Galphin owned thousands of acres of land in South Carolina and Georgia, sixty-nine slaves, and three residences at Silver Bluff. MARK D. GROOVER

Hamer, Friedrich P. "Indian Traders, Land and Power: Comparative Study of George Galphin on the Southern Frontier and Three Northern Traders." Master's thesis, University of South Carolina, 1976.

Morris, Michael. "George Galphin: Portrait of an Early South Carolina Entrepreneur." *Proceedings of the South Carolina Historical Association* (2002): 29–44.

Scurry, James D., J. Walter Joseph, and Fritz Hamer. *Initial Archaeological Investigations at Silver Bluff Plantation, Aiken County, South Carolina.* Columbia: South Carolina Institute of Archaeology and Anthropology, University of South Carolina, 1980.

Snapp, J. Russell. *John Stuart and the Struggle for Empire on the Southern Frontier.* Baton Rouge: Louisiana State University Press, 1996.

Gander-pulling. Gander-pulling was a blood sport that stressed manly virtues during the colonial and antebellum periods of South Carolina's history. Unlike its more genteel counterparts, such as horse racing, cards, and cockfighting, gander-pulling appears to have been beneath lowcountry men of property, and was likely more popular in frontier areas.

During a typical gander-pull, a live gander was tied upside down by its feet to a tree branch. Farmers then greased the gander's neck, and riders on horseback would pass the tree at a full gallop, attempting to decapitate the bird and thereby win the game. Obviously the gander did not survive the contest, but the riders did not always come away unscathed. Some were unseated in the process, while others lost fingers during the sometimes lengthy and always gruesome spectacle of stretching the neck and finally tearing the gander's head from its body.

Gander-pulls were social gatherings—community festivals of sorts—and in Virginia they often took place on the Monday following Easter. They drew large crowds of spectators, who placed bets on which rider they thought would take the prize. William Gilmore Simms, the famed Charleston novelist and poet, described a gander-pull in his 1852 work *As Good as a Comedy.* Simms's fictional gander-pull (seemingly based on a tournament he had witnessed) takes place in Tennessee, but similar scenes undoubtedly took place in upcountry South Carolina. Simms emphasized the brutal aspects of the sport, as well as its difficulty: "it is only a medium by which his better qualities are employed as agents for his worser nature." Simms also castigates the crowd, whose screams "form no bad echoes to the cries of the goose." There is almost no evidence as to when gander-pulling stopped in South Carolina, but it seems likely that as colonial and antebellum society matured, it moved west with the frontiers of white settlement. MATTHEW H. JENNINGS

Fischer, David Hackett. *Albion's Seed: Four British Folkways in America.* New York: Oxford University Press, 1989.

Simms, William Gilmore. *As Good as a Comedy: Or, the Tennessean's Story.* 1852. Reprint, Columbia: University of South Carolina Press, 1969.

Gantt, Harvey (b. 1943). First African American student at Clemson College (later Clemson University), architect, politician. Gantt was born in Charleston on January 14, 1943, the first of five children born to Christopher C. Gantt and Wilhelmenia Gordon. He attended Charleston's public schools, graduating in 1960 from all-black Burke High School where he played football and sang in the school choir. Inspired by his father, a longtime National Association for the Advancement of Colored People member, Gantt developed a reputation as a leader in the organization's local youth chapter. Articulate yet soft spoken, Gantt assumed much of the responsibility for organizing and motivating peers to participate in protests against segregated public accommodations and local businesses that refused to serve and hire African Americans. Gantt led several protests, notably a sit-in demonstration with twenty-three other teens at the S. H. Kress lunch counter in Charleston in 1960.

Barred because of his race from admission to white-only South Carolina colleges, Gantt attended Iowa State University with the aid of a state stipend, but sued for admission to the architecture program at Clemson College. In January 1963 he became the first African American to attend the school, graduating in 1965. The relative calm of Clemson's desegregation, especially in contrast to the violence that accompanied similar events in Alabama and Mississippi, helped set the stage for peaceful school desegregation throughout South Carolina.

After earning a Master of City Planning degree at the Massachusetts Institute of Technology in 1969, Gantt went on to become a successful architect in Charlotte, North Carolina, and enjoyed a distinguished career in politics. A Democrat, Grant served on the

Harvey Gantt facing reporters on the day he enrolled at Clemson University. Courtesy, Clemson University Photograph Collection, Special Collections, Clemson University Libraries

Charlotte city council (1975–1979), served two terms as mayor pro tem (1981–1983), and two terms as mayor (1983–1987). In 1990 and 1996, he made unsuccessful bids for the U.S. Senate, losing both times to the arch-conservative incumbent, Jesse Helms. Gantt's political appeal was based on his image as being "reasonable," that is, his ability to form broad-based constituencies. Though accused by Helms of being too liberal (Gantt supported abortion rights and affirmative action, and opposed the death penalty), Gantt received strong support from white voters in both races. Gantt married Lucinda "Cindy" Brawley in 1964 and the couple had five children, one of whom died in infancy. MILLICENT ELLISON BROWN

Bast, Kirk K. "'As Different as Heaven and Hell': The Desegregation of Clemson College." *Proceedings of the South Carolina Historical Association* (1994): 38–44.

Haeslly, Lynn. "'We're Becoming the Mayors': An Interview with Sit-In Leader Harvey Gantt, Now Charlotte's Mayor." *Southern Exposure* 14, no. 2 (1986): 44–51.

Gantt, Love Rosa Hirschmann (1876–1935). Physician. Rosa Hirschmann Gantt was born on December 29, 1876, in Camden, the daughter of Solomon Hirschmann and Lena Debrena. Educated in Charleston's public schools, she attended the Medical College of South Carolina (later Medical University of South Carolina) and in 1901 was one of the first two women to graduate from medical school in South Carolina.

After postgraduate work at the Aural and Ophthalmic Institute and New York Ear and Eye Hospital, she received the Certificate of the American Board of Ophthalmic Examiners. She was appointed resident physician at Winthrop College, and a year later became the first woman physician in Spartanburg. Specializing in eye, ear, nose, and throat, she maintained a busy practice for thirty-three years. On March 16, 1905, she married attorney Robert J. Gantt in Spartanburg.

Dr. Gantt was a pioneer in public health, prevention of tuberculosis, medical inspection of schools, and social hygiene. Before establishment of the Spartanburg County Health Department, she created a miniature health service, with herself as doctor. She was the only woman on the draft board during World War I and advanced to a position on the District Advisory Medical Board of Appeals. She served as acting surgeon for the United Public Health Service, a member of the Fosdick Committee of War Camp Community Service, and held a commission from the U.S. Department of Commerce as Medical Examiner of Air Pilots. As president of the Spartanburg branch of the American Medical Association, she served for nine years and in 1932 became president of the American Medical Women's Association. Her efforts contributed to building Spartanburg General Hospital (later Spartanburg Regional Hospital). Gantt received appointments from five South Carolina governors and three U.S. presidents. A widely published author of medical works, she had numerous articles in the *Southern Medical Journal,* many of which received wide recognition in her field.

Gantt was also a leader in Spartanburg's Jewish community. In 1916 she was instrumental in building the first synagogue in Spartanburg, Temple B'nai Israel, and was founder of the Sisterhood of Temple B'nai Israel, known then as the Women's Auxiliary, which raised funds for stained glass windows, pews, and flooring for the children's classrooms. Due to her efforts, the auxiliary provided hospitality for Converse College students, and during World War I offered religious services and entertainment for soldiers at Camp Wadsworth. For the war effort, she organized five hundred women volunteers to work in medical and other services. In 1924 Gantt negotiated with Oakwood Cemetery for a Jewish section, which made Jewish burials possible in Spartanburg for the first time.

In November 1935 Gantt entered Women's Medical College Hospital in Philadelphia, for treatment of a malignant disease. She died two weeks later, on November 16, 1935, and was buried in Spartanburg at Oakwood Cemetery. Her remains were later reburied at Greenlawn Memorial Gardens, Spartanburg. MARSHA POLIAKOFF

Herbert, William Chapman, Jr. *A Brief History of Medicine in the Spartanburg Region and of the Spartanburg County Medical Society 1700–1990.* Spartanburg, S.C.: Reprint Company, 1992.

Poliakoff, Marsha. "Names and Faces of Spartanburg." *Jewish Historical Society of South Carolina* 7 (summer 2002): 9.

Garden, Alexander (ca. 1685–1756). Clergyman. Garden was born in Scotland and educated at Aberdeen University. He became a priest in the Church of England and was rector of Barking Church, near the Tower of London. He came to South Carolina in 1719. Shortly after his arrival he became rector of St. Philip's Church, Charleston, the first Church of England parish in South Carolina. On June 8, 1724, he married Martha Guerard of Charleston. The union produced five children.

Throughout the colonial period, the Church of England did not have bishops in the American colonies. Henry Compton, bishop of London from 1675 until 1713, addressed the problem by naming commissaries to the colonies. The canonical powers of the commissaries were limited. They could not ordain or confirm, but could call meetings of the clergy, discipline the clergy, and enforce morality laws. In general, the bishop of London appointed a commissary in a colony, usually selecting one of the leading local clergy. In 1729 the bishop of London, Edmund Gibson, named Garden the commissary to South Carolina, North Carolina, and the Bahamas. On October 20, 1730, Garden held the first convention of the South Carolina clergy at Charleston. At the meeting the clergy exhibited their letters of ordination and licenses to officiate in the colony.

In 1740 George Whitefield, a Church of England evangelical and itinerant preacher, visited Charleston. He preached in churches of other denominations, violated the rubrics of the *Book of Common Prayer,* and frequently attacked Church of England clergy. Commissary Garden charged him with violating his ordination vows. After a period of controversy between the Whitefield and Garden, Whitefield preached a sermon against Garden based on 2 Timothy 4:14, "Alexander the coppersmith did me much evil; the Lord reward him according to his works." Later Garden suspended Whitefield from the ministry of the Church of England, but that did little to inhibit his work. Garden defended his actions in a pamphlet, *Letters to the Rev. Mr. George Whitefield* (1740).

In addition to his religious duties, Garden also supported the education of people of color in South Carolina. Through his influence and leadership, in 1742 a schoolhouse for African Americans was built in Charleston. Garden purchased, at the expense of the Society for the Propagation of the Gospel, two intelligent black boys and prepared them in this school to teach other black children to read. He wanted slaves to be able "to read the scriptures and understand the nature of Redemption." Garden thought that slaves would receive instruction more readily and willingly from black rather than white teachers. The school in Charleston continued until 1764, and as late as 1819 there were African Americans who had been taught to read by these two boys.

In 1749 Garden resigned as commissary, then resigned the rectorship of St. Philip's in 1753. He was the last commissary to South Carolina. He died at Charleston on September 27, 1756, and was buried in the St. Philip's Churchyard. DON S. ARMENTROUT

Bolton, S. Charles. *Southern Anglicanism: The Church of England in Colonial South Carolina.* Westport, Conn.: Greenwood, 1982.

Hawkins, James Barney. "Alexander Garden: The Commissary in Church and State." Ph.D. diss., Duke University, 1981.

Keen, Quentin Begley. "The Problems of a Commissary: The Reverend Alexander of South Carolina." *Historical Magazine of the Protestant Episcopal Church* 20 (June 1951): 136–55.

Kenney, William Howard, III. "Alexander Garden and George Whitefield: The Significance of Revivalism in South Carolina." *South Carolina Historical Magazine* 71 (January 1970): 1–16.

Pennington, Edgar Legare. "The Reverend Alexander Garden." *Historical Magazine of the Protestant Episcopal Church* 2 (December 1933): 178–94; 3 (March 1934): 48–55; 3(June 1934): 111–19.

Williams, George W., ed. "Letters to the Bishop of London from the Commissaries in South Carolina." *South Carolina Historical Magazine* 78 (April 1977): 120–47; (July 1977): 213–42; (October 1977): 286–317.

Garden, Alexander (1730–1791). Physician, naturalist. Born in January 1730 in the parish of Birse, Scotland, Garden was the son of the parish rector, the Reverend Alexander Garden, and his wife, whose name is not known. Young Alexander attended the parish school in Birse until he was thirteen and then went to the University of Aberdeen to serve as an apprentice to Dr. James Gordon. From Gordon he learned the uses of medicinal plants and years later remembered Gordon as "a very ingenious and skillful physician and botanist, who first initiated me into these studies, and tinctured my mind very early with a relish for them." After serving two years as surgeon's first mate in the Royal Navy, Garden resigned in 1750 to enter the University of Edinburgh with the intention of obtaining a medical degree. He received additional training in medicine and botany, but lacking funds to complete his studies for a degree and concerned that he might have tuberculosis, he left Edinburgh in 1751 to seek a warmer climate. Intrigued by professional opportunities in North America, he accepted a position as an assistant in the medical practice of Dr. William Rose of Charleston and arrived in the city in April 1752.

Fascinated by the vast number of plants that he had never seen, Garden began to collect specimens. He soon became a close friend of Dr. William Bull, another botany enthusiast, who introduced him to the works of Carolus Linnaeus, the great Swedish naturalist whose new system of classification of plants and animals was gaining wide acceptance among naturalists. Garden borrowed Bull's copies of Linnaeus's works and applied his principles of classification to the plants that he collected.

In July 1754 Garden visited the amateur botanist Cadwallader Colden in New York and the noted botanist John Bartram at his garden near Philadelphia. He returned to Charleston determined to further his scientific knowledge and to correspond with men like Linnaeus. That December he and Dr. David Olyphant established a medical practice in the city. In March 1755 Garden began a correspondence with the London naturalist John Ellis that would last until Ellis's death. During the summer of 1755, Garden accompanied a government expedition to Cherokee Indian country in the foothills of the Blue Ridge Mountains in northwestern South Carolina, there discovering the plant commonly known today as silver bell. Shortly after his return, his medical partner moved from the city and Garden was left with the entire practice. On Christmas Day 1755, he and Elizabeth Peronneau were married in St. Philip's Church in Charleston. The union produced two daughters and a son.

By January 1760 Garden had established a correspondence with Linnaeus and begun gathering natural history specimens for Linnaeus's continuing work with the classification of plants and animals. His first shipment was delayed by the smallpox epidemic that raged in Charleston from February until June 1760, during which Garden and his fellow physicians inoculated between 2,400 and 2,800 persons within one two-week period. Garden sent several large shipments of specimens to Linnaeus, consisting primarily of dried fish skins and reptiles preserved in wine. Among them were forty-one new species of fishes, three lizards, thirteen snakes, and one amphibian described for the first time in the twelfth edition of Linnaeus's *Systema naturae.* Those specimens constituted the largest body of material sent to Linnaeus by anyone in North America. They included such familiar fishes as the striped mullet, bluefish, and pompano, and the corn snake, copperhead, eastern king snake, and eastern glass lizard. Garden himself described one new amphibian, *Amphiuma means,* the two-toed amphiuma, an aquatic salamander discovered near Charleston and reported in a letter to John Ellis in 1770.

When the Revolutionary War began in 1775, Garden sympathized with the grievances of the colonists but had no personal reason to desert the British crown. At the end of the war, Garden and other Loyalists were stripped of their property and banished from the country. He sailed for England in December 1782, having lost virtually everything for which he had worked, though he had taken no active part in the war. He and his wife and daughter settled in London, where he died on April 15, 1791. The most important figure in eighteenth-century natural history investigations in South Carolina, Garden is best remembered today for the plant *Gardenia jasminoides,* named for him by John Ellis in 1760. ALBERT E. SANDERS

Berkeley, Edmund, and Dorothy Smith Berkeley. *Dr. Alexander Garden of Charles Town.* Chapel Hill: University of North Carolina Press, 1969.

Sanders, Albert E. "Alexander Garden (1730–1791), Pioneer Naturalist in Colonial America." In *Collection Building in Ichthyology and Herpetology,* edited by Theodore W. Pietsch and William D. Anderson, Jr. Lawrence, Kans.: American Society of Ichthyologists and Herpetologists, 1997.

Smith, J. E. *A Selection of the Correspondence of Linnaeus and Other Naturalists.* 2 vols. 1821. Reprint, New York: Arno, 1978.

Gardens and gardening. Both home and commercial gardening were essential to the survival of colonial settlements in South Carolina. Early commercial growing was limited to fruit and vegetable crops grown near towns, and consisted mostly of small plots surrounded by wattle or split rail "worm" fences. Home gardening included mostly food crops that could be pickled or stored dry, as the winter climate was too warm for root cellars. Few vegetables were eaten raw, and being more fibrous than today's varieties, were usually overcooked. To this day, the term *sallet* or *sallet greens* is applied by some rural South Carolinians to greens grown to be cooked: mustard, turnip, and rape, for example.

This wooden bridge over an old rice field has become an icon of Magnolia Gardens in Charleston County. Courtesy, South Caroliniana Library, University of South Carolina

Colonists from the Caribbean brought tropical food crops that thrived in South Carolina, as well as slaves who knew how to grow and prepare them. Sweet potatoes, okra, southern peas, sweet and hot peppers soon augmented cole crops such as cabbage and collards, and root crops that British settlers knew so well. Indian traders helped to introduce the food crops of Native Americans to colonists, most importantly the "Three Sisters": maize (corn), beans, and squash. The corn was of kinds later known as "field corn" and was grown principally to be dried, stored, and shelled for winter use. Beans were grown mostly to be dried, shelled, and stored, sometimes with hot pepper pods to repel weevils. Squash varieties were mostly hard-shelled, winter-keeper types, not the early maturing "summer squash" that are so popular today. Settlers from France had a long history of eating fresh vegetables, especially salad greens, and they brought seeds with them. However, they had to learn the seasons in the lowcountry before they could grow greens successfully.

Ornamentals came into colonial gardens more slowly than food crops. Curiously, during the period when early plant explorers such as André and François Michaux, John and William Bartram, Mark Catesby, and others were gathering seeds and starts of native American ornamental species to ship to England and the Continent, settlers were slow in introducing the same species into their landscapes. The Michaux garden grew for sale more than 450 varieties of mostly native species. Perhaps native ornamentals caught on slowly because only the landed elite among the settlers had much experience with ornamental crops or the leisure time to grow them. Some of the commoners had grown food crops in the "old country," but others from large towns in England and from Ulster knew little or nothing about cultivating plants of any sort.

Seed production was difficult in the Southeast because of plant diseases and seed-eating insects that infested crops. Therefore even the colonists who had the foresight to bring seeds with them soon had to turn to seed and bulb companies in Europe for supplies. Bulbs reproduced somewhat better than seeds but kinds that could not adapt to the hot, humid summers soon disappeared.

Indigo, rice, and cotton soon produced wealth sufficient to fund the construction of fine homes and gardens, on plantations and in towns. The brick-walled Charleston garden of Henry Laurens, for example, measured 600 by 450 feet. Plantation gardens were much larger, especially those along the Ashley and Cooper Rivers, such as Drayton Hall and Middleton Place. DuBose Heyward described the lowcountry gardens of South Carolina succinctly: "formal gardens blended from their very creation ordered lines with natural beauty, for even the most formal intentions failed to achieve the same results here amid wistful live oaks and Spanish moss, where forests were fragrant with magnolia and jessamine, as in the more sedate landscapes of northern Europe. So the English-planned gardens of Carolina grew and mellowed into gardens unlike any others in the whole world."

Backcountry colonists had less time for ornamentals, and concentrated on basic food crops and spent considerable time clearing land for hay, grain, and vegetables. For many years, upcountry diets consisted mostly of meat from game animals, potatoes ("Irish" potatoes at first), grain, and the occasional dish of "pulse" or "pease" (dried peas or beans). Meanwhile, lowcountry planters brought in plants from all over the world. Charleston was among the first ports of entry for camellias and crape myrtle from Asia, and tropical and semi-tropical ornamentals from the Caribbean. The plant explorer André Michaux and his son François propagated Asian and native American species in their Charleston nursery and sold started plants for town and country gardens. The wealth accumulated by planters allowed them to travel to Europe and bring back inspiration for grand gardens and, sometimes, landscape designers to create them.

The first great boom in home horticulture had to await the coming of accessible education, after which ordinary people could read seed and plant catalogs, seed packets, and later, farm magazines. Until that time, most ornamentals were spread around families and neighbors as "passalong plants" that one could see growing and did not need to read about. Home horticulture began to flourish by the mid–nineteenth century, when great nurseries such as those at Pomaria, South Carolina, and Fruitland in Augusta, Georgia, began to ship easy-to-grow deciduous shrubs and fruit and nut trees. During the first half of the nineteenth century, deciduous flowering shrubs had dominated landscapes, but after the Civil War, the rhododendron species known as "azaleas" and camellias began to bring color to southern landscapes during spring and fall months. The long, essentially green summer hiatus in gardens, seldom broken except by crape myrtles, persisted until the twentieth century when the American garden seed industry opened production on western irrigated lands, making flower and vegetable seeds less expensive and more reliable.

By the 1920s, municipalities began to accumulate enough money to do extensive plantings in parks, but no classical botanical gardens were built in South Carolina until well after World War II. Several gardens have become destinations for tourists from the United States and abroad: Brookgreen Gardens near Pawleys Island, Cypress Gardens at Moncks Corner, Edisto Memorial Gardens at Orangeburg, Kalmia Gardens of Coker College at Hartsville, Magnolia Plantation and Middleton Place near Charleston, Riverbanks Zoo and Botanical Garden at Columbia, the South Carolina Botanical Garden at Clemson University, Blythewood's Singing Oaks Garden, and Swan Lake Iris Gardens at Sumter. Collectively, public gardens have had a huge impact on gardening education through their outreach programs.

Horticultural societies seldom caught on in the South, but garden clubs did. They flourished in nearly every town large enough to support a club. The impact of Master Gardeners on the level of horticultural sophistication in South Carolina became evident beginning in the 1980s, when courses offered to home gardeners allowed them to attain certification level in Master Gardening. Master Gardeners are trained by the Clemson University Extension Service to answer gardening questions and to further their gardening education through community projects.

Home gardening is America's number one hobby, and with its abundant land, good water, and long growing seasons, South Carolina offers one of the best areas in the country for gardening for produce and pleasure. Northerners moving here often feel intimidated by the red clay or sandy coastal soils, and by the seemingly seamless planting seasons, but soon begin enjoying the opportunities they offer for producing year-round color and gourmet food crops. JIM WILSON

Ballard, William Brunson. "Living Historical Horticulture Gardens for South Carolina." Master's thesis, Clemson University, 1971.

Rosenfeld, Lois G. *The Garden Tourist 2001, Southeast: A Guide to Gardens, Garden Tours, Shows and Special Events.* New York: Garden Tourist Press, 2001.

Savage, Henry J., and Elizabeth J. Savage. *André and François-André Michaux.* Charlottesville: University Press of Virginia, 1986.

Shaffer, E. T. H. *Carolina Gardens.* 2d ed. Chapel Hill: University of North Carolina Press, 1939.

Gary, Frank Boyd (1860–1922). U.S. senator, jurist. Gary was born in Cokesbury, Abbeville District, on March 9, 1860, the son of Dr. Franklin Gary and Mary Caroline Blackburn and a nephew of Martin Witherspoon Gary. He was educated at Cokesbury Conference School and Union College at Schenectady, New York. He was admitted to the bar in 1882. On January 6, 1897, he married Marie Lee Evans. They had one son, Frank B. Gary, Jr.

Gary served as a bill clerk in the state legislature for nine years before being elected by Abbeville County to the S.C. House of Representatives in 1890. He remained there until 1900 and served as Speaker of the House from 1896 to 1900. He made an unsuccessful bid for the governorship in 1900. Three years later, Governor Duncan Heyward appointed Gary as special judge to preside over the trial of James Tillman, who was accused of murdering newspaper editor Narciso G. Gonzales. The trial ended in Tillman's acquittal. Gary returned to the S.C. House of Representatives in 1907. In March 1908 he was elected by the General Assembly to fill the U.S. Senate seat left vacant by the death of Asbury Latimer. Taking his predecessor's position on the immigration commission, Gary gave a widely publicized speech on the subject of immigration. He opposed further admission of immigrants from Asia and Eastern Europe, declaring that "it is better that our uncultivated lands shall forever lie fallow, and our water power go unharnessed to the sea, than that we should be overrun by a lot of aliens."

Completing his Senate term on March 3, 1909, Gary briefly returned to private life before being reelected to the S.C. House of Representatives in 1910. In 1912 he was unanimously elected by the General Assembly as a judge of the state's Eighth Judicial Circuit. After a brief illness, Gary died in Charleston on December 7, 1922. He was buried in Long Cane Cemetery, Abbeville. VERONICA BRUCE MCCONNELL

Memorial Exercises Held in Honor of Frank Boyd Gary, Judge of the Eighth Circuit, Before the Supreme Court of South Carolina. [Columbia, S.C., 1923].

Gary, Martin Witherspoon (1831–1881). Soldier, politician. Gary was born in Cokesbury, Abbeville District (later Greenwood County), on March 25, 1831, the son of Thomas Reeder Gary and Mary Ann Porter. He received his early education at Cokesbury Academy and in 1850 enrolled at the South Carolina College, but withdrew in 1852 as a result of his participation in a dispute with trustees and faculty known as "the Biscuit Rebellion." He enrolled at Harvard University, graduating in 1854. Gary returned to South Carolina and read law in the Edgefield office of James P. Carroll. He was admitted to the bar in 1855 and set up practice in Edgefield.

A fervent secessionist, Gary was elected to the S.C. House of Representatives in 1860. After secession he joined Hampton's Legion, beginning his service as an infantry captain. He served until the war's end, participating in every major engagement in which the legion fought. By May 1864 he had attained the rank of brigadier general and took command of a cavalry brigade in the defense of Richmond. At Appomattox he refused to surrender. With some two hundred members of his command, he escaped and joined Jefferson Davis and his cabinet at Greensboro, North Carolina. Gary escorted the party as far as his mother's home in Cokesbury, where he turned over his command and ended his career as a Confederate soldier.

Gary capitalized on the reputation he earned in war. He resumed his law practice in Edgefield, began cotton planting, and undertook a series of business and speculative ventures. With a volatile temper and prone to spasms of profanity, he was known as the "bald eagle of Edgefield." Active in Democratic Party politics, in 1876 he was the most uncompromising and outspoken leader of the "Straight-out" faction of the South Carolina Democratic Party, stressing white supremacy and solidarity while vigorously opposing any cooperation with Republicans or black Carolinians. He backed Wade Hampton for governor in 1876. Gary's plan for the 1876 campaign, frequently known in South Carolina as the "Edgefield plan" after its chief advocate, pitted race against race and advocated the use of electoral fraud, physical intimidation, and even murder to keep blacks and other Republicans from voting. Gary organized rifle clubs of white Democrats (the Red Shirts) to put his plan into action. The statewide violence and disorder that ensued helped tilt the political balance to the Democrats, ensuring the "redemption" of South Carolina after years of Republican rule.

In 1876 and 1878, Edgefield elected Gary to the S.C. Senate. However Gary's ambitions were for higher office. Believing himself chiefly responsible for the Democrat's 1876 victory, he broke with Hampton and other party leaders when he failed to be rewarded with a seat in the U.S. Senate in 1877 and 1879. He was the Hampton machine's most bitter and vocal opponent in the period from 1877 to 1881, protesting payment of the state debt and tax funding for public schools, championing a usury law, and vehemently opposing Hampton's policy of magnanimity toward black Carolinians. Hampton's supporters thwarted Gary's campaign for governor in 1880. His political career over, Gary returned to Edgefield, where he died on April 9, 1881. He was buried near Cokesbury in Tabernacle Cemetery. HENRY H. LESESNE

Bailey, N. Louise, Mary L. Morgan, and Carolyn R. Taylor, eds. *Biographical Directory of the South Carolina Senate, 1776–1985.* 3 vols. Columbia: University of South Carolina Press, 1986.

Cooper, William J., Jr. *The Conservative Regime: South Carolina, 1877–1890.* Baltimore: Johns Hopkins Press, 1968.

Simkins, Francis Butler, and Robert Hilliard Woody. *South Carolina during Reconstruction.* Chapel Hill: University of North Carolina Press, 1932.

Zuczek, Richard. *State of Rebellion: Reconstruction in South Carolina.* Columbia: University of South Carolina Press, 1996.

Gaskins, Donald Henry (1933–1991). Serial killer. Born on March 31, 1933, near the Florence County community of Prospect, Gaskins is considered to be one of South Carolina's most notorious murderers and career criminals. His diminutive height—he was barely five feet tall—and small body frame, gained him the nickname "Pee Wee," a moniker he retained to the end of his life. Gaskins was in legal trouble from an early age. Arrested for viciously beating another youth, Gaskins was incarcerated in a Florence reform school for several years. He returned to the Prospect community when released to live with his grandmother. Gaskins also ran up an extensive police rap sheet, with charges ranging from petty larcenies and auto thefts to aggravated assaults and murders. According to police, Gaskins resided for periods of time near Sumter, Florence, Columbia, Lake City, and North Charleston. While in North Charleston, police uncovered information that eventually implicated Gaskins in a series of murders. Investigations revealed that Gaskins's victims were mostly women, but also a local businessman and an eighteen-month-old child. Several bodies had been buried near Prospect. In all, Gaskins would eventually confess to killing roughly one hundred people, a criminal achievement that biographer Winton Earle called "one of the bloodiest records in the annals of American crime."

Gaskins took on the aura of a folklore character. He was the subject of national news profiles and a CBS Movie of the Week. Initially charged in 1975 in Florence County with five murders, Gaskins was sentenced to death on May 28, 1976. Those convictions were overturned by the South Carolina State Supreme Court in 1976 and remanded to consecutive life sentences. On September 12, 1982, while a prisoner working on death row, Gaskins was charged with murdering inmate Rudolph Tyner, who was awaiting execution for an Horry County murder. On March 24, 1983, Gaskins was convicted of Tyner's murder and sentenced to death. Gaskins was executed in South Carolina's electric chair on September 6, 1991. His remains were cremated and scattered in an undisclosed location. HUGH MUNN

Gaskins, Pee Wee, and Wilton Earle. *Final Truth.* Atlanta: Adept, 1992.

Hall, Frances Swain. *Slaughter in Carolina.* Florence, S.C.: Hummingbird, 1990.

Geddes, John (1777–1828). Governor. Geddes was born in Charleston on Christmas Day 1777, the son of Scots-Irish merchant Henry Geddes. After attending the College of Charleston, he studied law and was admitted to the South Carolina Bar in 1797. On May 30, 1798, Geddes married Harriet Chalmers, a daughter of Charleston artisan Gilbert Chalmers. After Harriet's death in 1803, he married Ann Chalmers on March 28, 1805, who died the following year. The marriages produced at least three children.

Popular and ambitious, Geddes was an ardent Democratic-Republican who gained a political following among the merchants and mechanics of Charleston. He first won office as a city warden in 1799. In 1808 the city parishes of St. Philip's and St. Michael's sent Geddes to the state legislature, where he served in the S.C. House of Representatives until 1815 and was chosen Speaker of the House by the Nineteenth (1810–1812) and Twentieth (1812–1813) General

Assemblies. He won election to the S.C. Senate in 1816 and also served as intendant (mayor) of Charleston from 1817 to 1819.

On December 8, 1818, after four ballots, Geddes was elected governor by the General Assembly, narrowly defeating John Taylor of Richland District. A few months into his term, on April 26, 1819, the city of Charleston was honored with a visit by President James Monroe, who was entertained in grand style for a week by the governor and other dignitaries. Geddes personally covered much of the expense of the celebration, which did considerable injury to his private fortune. Years later, in 1831, the General Assembly appropriated $3,000 to reimburse the governor's heirs. Geddes's term also witnessed the commencement of a statewide internal improvement program, for which the legislature appropriated the unprecedented sum of $1 million in 1818. The governor also followed the bitter debates in Congress over the admission of Missouri as a slave state. Geddes warned the legislature that during the controversy, "principles were advanced, which should put us upon our guard, and the mischievous effects of which, we should counteract by the most efficient measures." State legislators responded by banning free blacks from entering the state, requiring an act of assembly to emancipate slaves, and levying fines and imprisonment on any person caught distributing "inflammatory" writings in the state.

Leaving office in December 1820, Geddes remained an influential figure in Charleston politics. In October 1822, his son, John Geddes, Jr., acquired the Charleston *City Gazette,* which became the organ of the Geddes faction. Narrowly losing an election for the state Senate in 1822, Geddes was elected to another term as intendant the following year. He also maintained his lifelong attachment to the state militia, achieving the rank of brigadier general. On March 4, 1828, Geddes died of a stroke in Charleston. In a melancholy twist of fate, his son John died just hours later. After an elaborate funeral procession through the city, both men were interred in the Second Presbyterian Churchyard. TOM DOWNEY

Bailey, N. Louise, Mary L. Morgan, and Carolyn R. Taylor, eds. *Biographical Directory of the South Carolina Senate, 1776–1985.* 3 vols. Columbia: University of South Carolina Press, 1986.

O'Neall, John Belton. *Biographical Sketches of the Bench and Bar of South Carolina.* 2 vols. Charleston, S.C.: S. G. Courtney, 1859.

Geddings, Eli (ca. 1799–1878). Physician. Geddings was born in Newberry District, reputedly of impoverished parents, and was raised by his stepfather, Major Frederick Gray. As a youth he studied at Abbeville Academy, became a physician's apprentice for two years beginning in 1818, and was licensed in Charleston in 1820. He attended lectures at the University of Pennsylvania in 1821 and 1822, and after a brief practice in Colleton District, he settled in Charleston. He enrolled in the Medical College of South Carolina in 1824 and served as demonstrator in anatomy both before and after becoming the school's first graduate in 1825. He married twice, first to a Mrs. Grey, née Wyatt, with whom he had a daughter and three sons. All three sons became physicians. Geddings and his second wife, Laura Postel, had no children.

After completing his education at hospitals in London and Paris, he returned to Charleston in May 1827 to embark on a career comparable only to James Moultrie in national prestige for a South Carolina medical practitioner in the nineteenth century. Geddings held chairs in a variety of disciplines. After serving as demonstrator of anatomy at the Medical College and conducting his own one-man private school in medicine, he accepted the Chair in Anatomy and Physiology at the University of Maryland in 1831 and held it for six years. Returning to South Carolina, he became Professor of Pathological Anatomy and Medical Jurisprudence at the Medical College in 1837, a post created specifically for him, and he twice held the Chairs of Medicine and Surgery simultaneously.

Geddings was also an active participant in the intellectual life of antebellum Charleston. He was a friend of the author William Gilmore Simms, who dedicated one of his books to Geddings, and was an early subscriber to the works of John James Audubon, whom he also knew.

Geddings made several important contributions to medical literature. While in Baltimore, he founded the *Baltimore Medical and Surgical Journal and Review,* which became the *North American Archives in Medical and Surgical Sciences.* His national reputation attracted offers of professorships in Pennsylvania, New York, Ohio, and Kentucky. Like his contemporary, James Moultrie, Geddings was involved with the educational concerns of the American Medical Association. In 1870 he submitted a report recommending premedical preparation and a nonrepetitive three-year curriculum in medicine. Despite offers from medical schools across the country, Geddings cast his lot with South Carolina and shared in the catastrophe of the Civil War and its aftermath. His library, including the manuscript for a textbook, and his Audubon Folio were destroyed in the burning of Columbia.

With his finances ruined by the war, Geddings was forced to return to active practice at the age of sixty-six. He remained active at the Medical College as professor and consultant until 1873 and continued to serve on an occasional basis until his death in Charleston on October 9, 1878. He was buried in Magnolia Cemetery. W. CURTIS WORTHINGTON

Waring, Joseph I. *A History of Medicine in South Carolina.* Vol. 2, *1825–1900.* Columbia: South Carolina Medical Association, 1967.

Geiger, Emily (ca. 1762–?). Revolutionary War heroine. Geiger was the daughter of John Geiger, a German farmer. Little is known of her early life.

In June 1781 Emily Geiger volunteered to be a courier for General Nathanael Greene, who needed an urgent message delivered to General Thomas Sumter. With the British watching the roads between Greene and Sumter, Geiger argued that a woman could go, since a woman would probably raise less British suspicion than a man. Greene consented and sent her on the mission. Geiger evaded capture the first day, but the British stopped her on the second day. While waiting for the British to bring a woman to search her, she read and memorized Greene's message and then ate it. Finding no incriminating message, the British released her. She found her way to Sumter and delivered the message she had memorized. As a result of her persistence, Sumter's forces met with other patriot forces at British-held Orangeburg to carry out Greene's plan of attack.

After the Revolutionary War, Geiger married a planter named John Threrwitz (or Threewitts). They lived near Granby, South Carolina. Geiger's date of death is unknown. She was buried in Threrwitz Cemetery in Lexington County. BRENDA THOMPSON SCHOOLFIELD

Bodie, Idella. *South Carolina Women.* Orangeburg, S.C.: Sandlapper, 1991.

Harkness, David James. "Heroines of the American Revolution." *University of Tennessee Newsletter* 60 (February 1961): 1–16.

Rhett, Claudine. "Emily Geiger: A Heroine of the Revolution." *American Monthly Magazine* 8 (March 1896): 302–304.

General Assembly. Much of the evolution of the South Carolina General Assembly revolves around attempts by conflicting factions to preserve or gain an advantage in representation. For example, increasingly powerful Carolina-based leaders struggled with proprietary and royal authorities during the colonial era to establish the dominance of the Commons House of Assembly as a basis for political independence (1670–1776). For much of the following century, the burgeoning upcountry struggled against an entrenched low-country elite to increase its representation and influence in the legislature. In the social, economic, and political fallout during the decades after the Civil War, racial conflict dominated as a white minority struggled to maintain control of the General Assembly against the challenges of Reconstruction and the civil rights movement. After 1965, federally mandated redistricting and the creation of single member districts weakened rural delegations in favor of the state's expanding urban and suburban population.

In the earliest years of South Carolina, the Lords Proprietors exercised lawmaking and taxing powers granted them by the king of England to establish a New World colony. The proprietors lived in England, so they selected a governor and, along with major resident landowners, a Grand Council to conduct the affairs of the colony. The proprietors retained veto authority over any Grand Council action. The Grand Council consisted of three groups: representatives of the proprietors, ten colonists chosen by leading landowners to act as a kind of upper legislative house, and a lower or Commons House of Assembly, which consisted of twenty members chosen by the "freemen" of the colony. The Commons House could only discuss proposals from other parts of the Grand Council. After 1682, however, all three groups had to approve any act, thus letting the Commons House exercise legislative initiative. This arrangement stayed intact until the proprietors were overthrown early in the eighteenth century by the general dissatisfaction of the Commons House, which was irked that their legislative initiatives were consistently vetoed by the proprietors.

Reestablished as a royal colony in 1719, a new legislative body was created consisting of two houses. An upper house was designated His Majesty's Council (or Royal Council) and was composed of twelve persons appointed by the king to unlimited terms. The Commons House continued as a lower house, but this time with members elected by the colonists. To qualify as a Commons House member, one had to own five hundred acres and ten slaves or houses and town lots worth £1,000. Only adult white males could serve, and they did not have to be a resident of the parish from which they were elected. To be able to vote for a representative, one had to be a free white male, at least twenty-one years old who professed the Christian religion, a resident for one year, and own a freehold of fifty acres or pay twenty shillings a year in taxes to the colony. The governor was now sent over from England for the term of his service.

The Commons House continued to gain political momentum during the colonial era, especially by insisting on the right to draft bills about money. The colony gradually became an independent place, made rich by self-made men who used the Commons House to promote their interests while protecting themselves against unwanted challenges from the enslaved population or Native Americans.

From 1769 until the start of the Revolutionary War, the Commons House virtually ceased to function as a result of its involvement in the "Wilkes Fund Controversy." John Wilkes attacked King George III in his newspaper and was charged with criminal libel. Wilkes became a symbol of the importance of a free press, of protection from unlawful arrest, and of the right of the people to elect any person "not disqualified" to Parliament. South Carolinians supported Wilkes, and the Commons House in 1769 authorized money to help him pay his debts—an act that was an affront to the king. In the aftermath, the Commons House deadlocked with the Royal Council, and civil government came to a virtual standstill.

The first state constitution in 1776 established a two-house legislative branch. The lower house, with 202 members, was elected by eligible voters from election districts made up of the parishes of the now disestablished Anglican Church. The lower house elected a thirteen-member upper house called the Legislative Council. Both houses elected a president, who served as governor with a veto power, but who could not be reelected. In 1778 a new constitution renamed the president as governor, called the upper house the Senate, and allocated additional lower house seats to the upcountry. Despite having a larger share of the state's free population, the upcountry only received about forty percent of lower house seats. The political center of government remained in Charleston.

In 1788 a state convention met in Charleston to consider ratification of the new U.S. Constitution. The delegates were selected in the same lowcountry-dominated proportions as seats in the General Assembly. The new constitution was ratified by the convention, with most lowcountry delegates supporting it and most upcountry delegates opposing. Upcountry interests immediately pressed for a new convention to deal with representation issues in the state. In the resulting 1790 constitution, counties became the basis for upcountry representation, while parishes remained the representation basis for the lowcountry. Both houses were elected by the people. The lower house was reduced to 124 members, a number which has continued to the present. The vote was still restricted to white males over twenty-one who owned fifty acres or a town lot. House members had to own five hundred acres and ten slaves; senators had to have twice these amounts. The General Assembly not only made laws, but elected the governor, judges, and many local officials.

In the so-called Compromise of 1808, the representation arrangements were changed so that election districts would have one representative for $^{1}/_{62}$ of the state's population and one representative for $^{1}/_{62}$ of its taxable wealth. Each election district would have one senator, except for the city of Charleston which would have two. By recognizing population, the upcountry gained a sixteen vote majority in the lower house and a one vote majority in the Senate. This legislative system continued until the Civil War.

Federally appointed officials temporarily took control of the state after the Civil War. A fresh constitution was devised by whites in 1865, which differed but slightly from the 1790 version. Wealth and population continued as the basis for Senate and House members. Although qualified voters were allowed to elect the governor and presidential electors, the newly emancipated black population was barred from voting. The new General Assembly ratified the Thirteenth Amendment that ended slavery, but refused to ratify the Fourteenth Amendment, which gave civil rights to blacks. In addition the assembly enacted Black Codes that severely limited the rights and privileges of African Americans in the state. In response Congress closed down the state government in 1867 and demanded a new constitution that would recognize the citizenship rights of black South Carolinians.

The constitutional convention in 1868 was composed of seventy-six black and thirty-eight white delegates. Population alone became the basis for representation and the vote was provided for all males, regardless of race. The General Assembly struggled with issues such as funding a system of public education, rebuilding infrastructure, revitalizing the economy, and countering white opposition to Reconstruction. Spurred by the retreat of federal authority in the mid-1870s, white Democrats regained control of the General Assembly in 1876 and a one-party political system gradually emerged as a way to reestablish and ensure white supremacy.

By 1890 South Carolina looked a lot like it would look in 1950. Agriculture had turned into an established sharecropping system dependent on cotton; the building of railroads had created a new "small town" elite; textile mills had begun to migrate south; and Republicans—the hated party of Lincoln—had virtually disappeared from the state's political landscape. Under these conditions, political conservatives—the elites and former Confederate leaders—came to prominence, but did little to relieve the discontent of white farmers who fumed over low prices, high interest and freight rates, and suspicion that the Conservatives were using black voters to stifle legislative responses to their needs.

One leader, Benjamin R. Tillman, was able to articulate the farmers' problems and set events in motion that produced yet another constitutional convention in 1895. The apparatus of government was not changed very much, but the politics were. One purpose was to get around the Fifteenth Amendment to the U.S. Constitution, which gave blacks the right to vote. To counter this, white delegates inserted a clause in the new state constitution that limited the right to vote to adult males who had paid a poll tax six months before the election and who were not guilty of certain crimes. The assumption was that most poor persons, especially blacks, could not pay the tax that early and, even if they did, would not subsequently be able to save a receipt to prove it. Even after passage of the Nineteenth Amendment to the U.S. Constitution in 1920 extended the vote to women, the electorate in South Carolina remained restricted to "acceptable" whites and blacks.

The continuation of counties as election districts gave rise to a "one county-one senator" system of representation in the General Assembly. The county, not population, was the basis for legislative representation. Each county was also apportioned at least one House member. In 1895 there were thirty-five counties. The number grew to forty-six by 1919. State senators dominated the politics and programs of their county through passage of annual "supply bills," by which they controlled their county's budget and most aspects of local government. Since no senator could oppose another's supply bill without risking opposition to his own, legislative approval for a county's schools, roads, courts, law enforcement, or other county purposes really rested in the hands of the senator. House members were dependent on what the senator wanted.

As "emperors of a county-based empire," state senators were extraordinarily powerful political figures well into the twentieth century and the linchpins of the one-party system. Senator Edgar Brown of Barnwell County is perhaps the most potent example of a dominant senator. Speaker of the House Solomon Blatt, also of Barnwell County, advanced rural power in the S.C. House by appointing only one member from each county to a committee, thereby assuring that small counties would outnumber urban counties in most instances. Blatt and Brown were referred to by their critics as the "Barnwell Ring," but more realistically the reference was to a statewide, rural "ring" that excluded growing urban areas from meaningful political power.

The power of rural delegations faced significant changes as national civil rights policies emerged. First the national Voting Rights Act of 1965 extended full voting rights to every individual regardless of race. An expanded electorate gradually demonstrated political success in gaining minority representation in the General Assembly. John Felder, Herbert Fielding, and I. S. Leevy Johnson, elected to the S.C. House in 1970, and I. DeQuincey Newman, elected to the S.C. Senate in 1983, became the first African Americans elected to the General Assembly in the twentieth century.

Next the county delegation system was fundamentally altered by U.S. Supreme Court decisions that mandated population as the basis for representation and prohibited gerrymandering, the arrangement of political district boundaries for the advantage of a particular interest. New districts with equal population per legislator would now have to be drawn after each national census. In 1971 the House first reapportioned in a plan that retained one representative per county. The tactic did not pass federal courts and the House subsequently reapportioned into single member districts on the "one person, one vote" principle. The Senate in 1968 tried a plan of twenty multimember districts through which each senator represented approximately the same number of people. After the 1970 census, forty-six senators were elected from sixteen districts. After 1980, however, the Senate moved to single member districts.

Election districts are adjusted every ten years to reflect changes in population. The redistricting decisions are in the hands of incumbent state legislators, although their decisions are subject to approval by the U.S. Department of Justice and have typically been challenged in federal courts. Since 2001, Republicans have had a majority in both houses and have allocated important committee assignments by party affiliation rather than by years of service. Legislative party caucuses have become more influential in raising campaign money. In addition to the Republicans and Democrats, African American legislators are organized into a separate caucus. The low number of women elected to the General Assembly continues as a topic of political comment by legislative observers. In 2003 only sixteen members of the General Assembly were women, the smallest percentage of female state legislators in the nation.

Contemporary legislators are aided in their work by increased staff support, computer assisted bill management, and the use of individual offices. Annual sessions begin in January and continue until May or June. Many study committees continue throughout the interim. A new General Assembly is convened every two years after November elections in even numbered years. House members are elected for two-year terms and senators are elected for four years. Each must reside in the district from which elected. House members must be a qualified elector at least twenty-one years of age and senators must be twenty-five years old. COLE BLEASE GRAHAM, JR.

Cooper, William J., Jr. *The Conservative Regime: South Carolina, 1877–1890.* Baltimore: Johns Hopkins Press, 1968.

Craven, Wesley F. *The Southern Colonies in the Seventeenth Century, 1607–1689.* Baton Rouge: Louisiana State University Press, 1949.

Edgar, Walter. *South Carolina: A History.* Columbia: University of South Carolina Press, 1998.

Simkins, Francis Butler, and Robert Hilliard Woody. *South Carolina during Reconstruction.* Chapel Hill: University of North Carolina Press, 1932.

Young, Richard D. *A Guide to the General Assembly of South Carolina.* Columbia: Institute of Public Affairs, University of South Carolina, 2000.

General Association of Davidian Seventh-day Adventists. Based in Salem, South Carolina, the organization is an offshoot of the Davidian Seventh-day Adventists, a group which itself broke away from the Seventh-day Adventist Church in the early 1940s. Like other Seventh-day Adventists, the South Carolina–based cluster of congregations believes that followers should worship on the seventh day, or Saturday, rather than Sunday, and that the return of Christ to earth is imminent.

The original Davidian group, which today counts only around fifty congregations headquartered in Missouri, came from the followers of Victor T. Houteff, an immigrant from Bulgaria who was active in Seventh-day Adventist circles in Los Angeles until he was expelled from the church in 1934. He ran afoul of church leaders in his insistence that biblical revelation required the faithful to work more aggressively to reestablish the Davidic monarchy in Israel to anticipate Christ's return. Davidians insist that true believers must be completely separate from the world, which they equate with the evil Babylon of the book of Revelation. Thus, during World War II, Davidians became conscientious objectors. By remaining separate, they hope to keep pure and seal for eternity the 144,000 who will enter heaven after Christ's return.

Houteff's followers splintered into smaller groups after his death in 1955. Houteff's widow, who tried to become their leader, prophesied direct divine intervention in Middle Eastern affairs would occur in 1959. When that prophecy failed, several congregations, including those in South Carolina around Salem, split off.

Well known because of its tragic end is another splinter group, the Branch Davidian Seventh-day Adventists, who gathered around Waco, Texas, and, following David Koresh (who had earlier spent time with the Salem group), confronted federal authorities in 1993. By 2000 the General Association in Salem probably numbered not more than two hundred members. CHARLES H. LIPPY

Adair, Don. *A Davidian Testimony.* Salem, S.C.: Mt. Carmel Center, 1997.

General Textile Strike (September 1934). On September 1, 1934—Labor Day—the United Textile Workers (UTW) launched a nationwide strike. By the end of the first week, almost 500,000 textile workers from Massachusetts to Mississippi had walked off the job. In South Carolina, 43,000 women and men joined the protest, shutting down two-thirds of the state's two hundred textile mills.

The General Textile Strike in South Carolina sprang out of old grievances and fresh hopes. For years mill people worked long hours for low wages in lint-filled factories. Beginning in the 1920s, mill owners, pinched by increased competition, raised workers' machine loads without increasing their pay. Workers called this the "stretch-out," and fought back. Some sabotaged machines. Others moved from mill to mill, hoping to find better conditions. When these individual and family strategies failed, workers joined unions and strikes. In 1929 twelve thousand South Carolina textile workers walked off their jobs in protest against the stretch-out. But hard times continued, and then got worse with the onset of the Great Depression.

Franklin Roosevelt's election in 1932, however, generated hope. Roosevelt promised workers a "new deal" and many believed that better days were just around the corner. On the next to last day of a traditional milestone, the first one hundred days in office, Roosevelt signed the National Industrial Recovery Act (NIRA). Workers marked the event with street dances and parades. As far as they could tell, the NIRA guaranteed higher wages, shorter hours, and the right to join a union. Mill managers read the law differently. Tensions simmered and boiled over with the General Strike, as much a political protest as an industrial rebellion. Workers struck to make their New Deal vision the letter of the law on the shop floor.

During the strike's first few days, factories in South Carolina closed "so rapidly that tabulators almost lost count." Carrying signs that read "Roosevelt Our Greatest Leader" and "We Are Backing Roosevelt 100 Percent," flying squadrons of militant workers fanned the protest's fires. These roving bands of UTW stalwarts vowed to shut down every factory in the state. Sometimes they stood outside of the mills still operating and sang until the workers inside joined the picket line. In a few upcountry towns, the flying squadrons, armed with clubs and bats, invaded the plants, trampling over foremen on their way to cut off the electricity. No one, they said, was to work as long as the strike was on.

South Carolina governor Ibra C. Blackwood declared that the state was being invaded by a wave of "mob rule." Vowing to keep the factories running, Blackwood called out the National Guard and the State Highway Patrol. In Greenville the captain of a "hard-boiled company" armed with tear gas and machine guns, instructed his men "to shoot to kill" if necessary. In other places, the troops arrested members of the flying squadrons and harassed union leaders.

Politics further aggravated the situation. The strike took place during the race for Blackwood's successor. By the time thousands of workers had walked off the job, the field of candidates had been narrowed to two: Olin Johnston and Cole Blease. Both men had strong ties to mill workers. Seeing neither candidate as what the state needed in a moment of crisis, plantation owners, manufacturers, and professionals worried about having to choose either "a communist on the one hand or a man without moral sense on the other."

Everybody's worst fears were realized at the Chiquola Manufacturing Company in Honea Path on September 6, 1934. The General Textile Strike split this Anderson County town down the middle. After three days of fistfights and shouting matches, Honea Path was said to be "near the breaking point." Before the sun came up on the fatal day, a flying squadron rode to town to meet local strike supporters in front of the mill. Inside, lawmen and newly deputized officers readied their defenses. The screech of the morning whistle signaled the battle's start. Striker supporters lurched forward to block the mill gate. Strikebreakers surged to the entrance. One man was smashed over the head with a club and another was jabbed with a picker stick. Suddenly a pistol shot sounded, followed by a flash of furious fire. When the guns fell silent three minutes later, six strikers lay dead and a dozen wounded. Most had been shot in the back, apparently cut down as they fled.

Some predicted that the Honea Path deaths would stifle the strike. But during the next two weeks, picket lines held steady in South Carolina. Still, a crisis loomed for the UTW. From the beginning, relief represented the union's biggest challenge. The UTW had almost no strike funds. Local charities pitched in, but they were not eager to underwrite an industrial rebellion. That left workers dependent on themselves. Throughout the strike, families survived on fatback and corn meal. By the beginning of the strike's third week, even these meager resources started to run low. Desperate for something to eat, a few workers started to trickle back into the mills. Remarkably, however, strike lines bent but didn't break.

Back in Washington, D.C., UTW leaders nonetheless grew hesitant. Unable to provide relief, they feared that hunger would push more strikers back to work. By the middle of September the union men were looking for a face-saving way out of the conflict. On September 20 they got their chance when a Roosevelt-appointed mediation board recommended as a resolution to the strike the establishment of a permanent textile labor mediation board and federal studies to examine the industry's capacity to raise wages and lower workloads. The proposal offered striking workers virtually nothing: no pay hike or union recognition or guarantees that they would have jobs when the strike ended. Still, Roosevelt urged the UTW to accept the agreement, and on September 22 union leader

Francis Gorman, concerned that "force and hunger" were driving millhands across the picket lines, told his members to go back to work, reassuring them that they had won an "overwhelming victory."

"On foot, in truck, and automobiles," a newsman reported on Sunday, September 24, "strikers paraded all night through mill towns and villages singing hymns of joy and celebrating the news that tomorrow the whistles will blow again." But when the mills reopened, many refused to rehire strikers and others took back only UTW members who agreed to sign yellow dog contracts, which forbid union membership. This certainly was not the "overwhelming victory" that Gorman had advertised. For years afterward, some have argued, the defeat hindered the growth of unions in the South. Having been down the path of unionization once and lost, textile workers were weary of the promises of organizers. Eventually official memory of the strike was all but erased from the record. In the 1990s, however, a memorial was erected in Honea Path to honor the men killed in front of the Chiquola plant. BRYANT SIMON

Applebome, Peter. *Dixie Rising.* New York: Times Books, 1996.

Hall, Jacquelyn Dowd, et. al. *Like A Family: The Making of a Southern Cotton Mill World.* Chapel Hill: University of North Carolina Press, 1987.

Irons, Janet. *Testing the New Deal: The General Textile Strike of 1934 in the American South.* Urbana: University of Illinois Press, 2000.

Simon, Bryant. *A Fabric of Defeat: The Politics of South Carolina Millhands, 1910–1948.* Chapel Hill: University of North Carolina Press, 1998.

Geology. The geology of South Carolina begins with plate tectonics. Heat within the earth drives plates together and apart over millions of years. Current ideas in geology propose that such forces began forming South Carolina about 450 million years ago. A smaller North American continent existed at the time. As tectonic plates moved, a continental fragment and a large island arc approached, welding on to what is now eastern North America, shoving up sediments and volcanic rocks from the continental shelf, which formed the Blue Ridge and the inner Piedmont belt. The island arc became the Piedmont of South Carolina, and it extends along much of eastern North America. Overlapping this terrain are the sediments of the coastal plain, both of which continue offshore far out onto the continental shelf.

Geologists have divided South Carolina into a series of belts, from the northwest Blue Ridge, southwest to the inner Piedmont belt, the

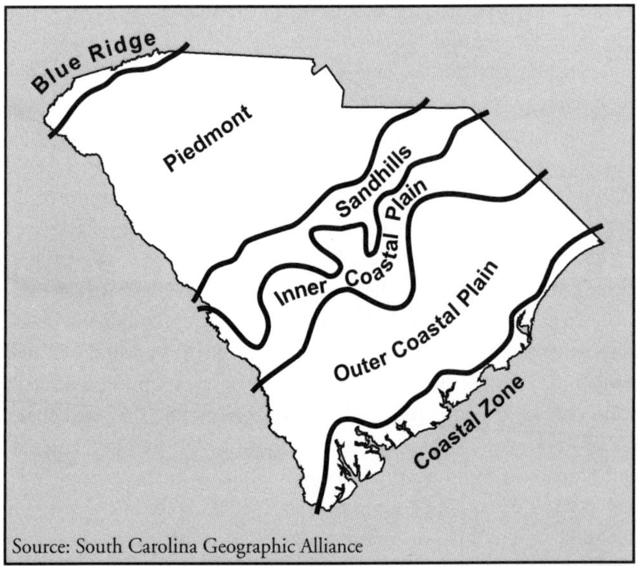

Source: South Carolina Geographic Alliance

The geological landform regions of the state

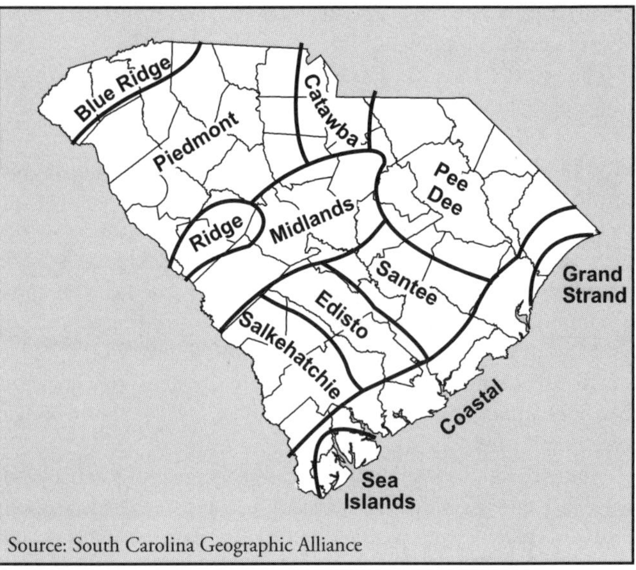

Source: South Carolina Geographic Alliance

The vernacular regions of the state

Kings Mountain belt, the Charlotte belt, the Carolina slate belt, and the Kiokee and Belair belts. While inexact, the belts framework allows distinctions between rocks to be made and categorized.

The Blue Ridge lies over the ancient Grenville Mountains, a Precambrian, eroded mountain system that existed inland from the present eastern coast of North America. As the east coast of North America rifted apart from another plate during the late Precambrian era, extensive sedimentary deposits and volcanics developed on the continental shelf. Then, in the Ordovician period, a collision occurred with what were perhaps a previously detached continental fragment and an island arc that moved toward and eventually welded onto North America. Over the millions of years that the collision developed, the rocks of the continental shelf were shoved upwards into what must have been a very high mountain range, adding both width and height to the continent. This became the Blue Ridge.

During later continental collisions, lastly with the African plate during the Pennsylvanian to Permian time, the remnants of the eroded Blue Ridge were again thrust upwards, moving more than one hundred miles toward the northwest. The rocks of the Blue Ridge in South Carolina include gneisses, schists, metagreywackes, pegmatites, and amphibolites that were formed from heat and pressure applied to the original sediments and volcanics of the Precambrian continental shelf rocks. The metamorphic intensity seen in the Blue Ridge rocks decreases from west to east, implying that its core lies farther to the northwest in North Carolina. In addition, the Blue Ridge also contains some Jurassic diabase dikes emplaced as the North America and African plates separated in the early Mesozoic.

The inner Piedmont belt is thought to be either a disengaged and reattached North American (Laurentian) continental fragment, or a fragment entirely from offshore. It is a highly eroded thrust sheet that contains metamorphic rocks including schists, gneisses, amphibolites, and metagranites. The collision that created the metamorphic belt also heated rock in some places to melting, and so granites formed at depths of more than twelve miles during the Ordovician and Silurian periods. These were later metamorphosed as North America collided further with Europe (Baltica) and Africa in the Devonian and the Pennsylvanian to Permian periods. The geology of the inner Piedmont provides clear and very accessible examples of the geologic story of the formation of the state. The uplifted remnants of the resistant metagranites, schists, and gneisses now stand at the surface as monadnocks, most forming the Blue Ridge Escarpment. These scenic mountains include Table Rock, Caesars Head, Sassafras, Paris, and Pinnacle.

The Kings Mountain belt is a shear zone, the suture between the inner Piedmont belt and the Charlotte and the Carolina slate belts. It is more highly mineralized than the other belts and it has a lower-grade metamorphism, thus the minerals are more stable at the surface, which causes the rocks to be more resistant to weathering. This causes the remnant ridges to stand taller than the surrounding, eroded Piedmont. The rocks of the Kings Mountain belt include metavolvanics, schists, phyllites, quartzites, granites, and marble.

The Charlotte belt is thought to be the core of the island arc that collided with North America in the Ordovician period. It contains more granite and gabbroic plutons than any other belt, which range in age from 735 million to 235 million years old. The Charlotte belt contains highly altered mafic intrusive rocks formed by ocean crust, including gabbro, amphibolite, serpentine, and greenstone-metabasalt. The volcanic island arc created extrusive rocks as well, including ash and tuffs, the eroded remnants of which form many of the rocks seen at the surface today, such as phyllites and schists.

The Carolina slate belt contains the least metamorphosed rocks of all the belts in South Carolina. Island arc sediments formed sands, muds, and ash deposits off its shores, and these in time formed the quartzites, metamudstones, argillites, phyllites, and sericite schists of the slate belt. The slate belt also contains intrusive granites, but most are much shallower and younger than those of the Charlotte belt. They include the granites of Lake Murray, Pageland, Liberty Hill, Winnsboro, and Columbia; and they range in age from 311 million to 286 million years old. In 1982, in metamudstones of the slate belt in Lexington County, new evidence confirmed ideas about the nature of the terrains and the processes that formed South Carolina. Trilobite fossils were discovered in the rocks that were not North American in type. They were from rocks that derived from sediments found in Bohemia, in present-day southern Europe. This could not have been possible except by the rafting of the fragment of land that carried the trilobites onto North America through the movement of the plates.

The Carolina slate belt is also the site of the Crowburg Basin, the only Triassic period redbed in South Carolina. Located just west of Pageland in Chesterfield County, the six-mile-long Crowburg Basin represents the rifting of the North American plate from the African (Gondwana) plate as massive landmass called Pangaea began to break apart early in the Mesozoic era. The crust thinned and faulted downwards all along the eastern North American coast as the plates separated. These Triassic basins then filled with sediments, which today are visible at Crowburg as red fanglomerates. Lava also flowed in much of the state during this period and diabase dikes cut through the rocks, extending for hundreds of miles. These are visible in various road cuts and quarries from the slate belt to the Blue Ridge, and they extend from well offshore on the continental shelf and continue into North Carolina. The Carolina slate belt contains the major South Carolina gold deposits, which produced millions of dollars in gold during the nineteenth and twentieth centuries. The geology of the goldfields is a product of the volcanic nature of the Carolina slate belt and the later movement of minerals as the land was reheated during the orogenies (mountain-building episodes) that formed and transformed the state.

The Kiokee and Belair belts lie at the southwest edge of the Carolina slate belt. They are small in area and are thought to represent a higher-grade metamorphic environment than the slate belt, and may have formed through subduction, when one plate slid beneath another. They are bounded on the north by the Modoc Fault, which runs from Lake Murray to Georgia.

The final and largest section of South Carolina is the coastal plain, which makes up two-thirds of its landmass. The unconsolidated sediments and rocks of this region overlie the hard, crystalline rocks of the Piedmont terrain and they both extend out beyond the coastline as part of the continental shelf. The uppermost section of the coastal plain consists of sands, sandstone, and clays that formed from river-deposited sediments eroded from the Blue Ridge and other high mountains that once stood on the Piedmont. These rocks weathered over time into the clays and sands, which were then reworked by rivers and ocean currents to become back beach ridges and wind-blown dunes of the Miocene and Pliocene epochs. Known today as the Sandhills, the region contains many interesting geologic sites that lie either directly on the sediments, or cut down through and below them to reveal the geologic history of the region. These sites include Peachtree Rock in Lexington County and Sugarloaf Mountain in Chesterfield County. The mineral resources of the upper coastal plain include sand and clay mined in many counties including Lexington and Aiken.

The upper coastal plain becomes the middle coastal plain at the Orangeburg Scarp, the high sea level boundary at the Pliocene epoch. The land then becomes much more level, gently sloping over younger scarps and terraces toward the sea. The sediments that overlie the land on the coastal plain include limestones deposited as the sea levels rose during the Eocene epoch. The Santee limestone is a source of lime and cement and it is the site of the only karst (cave) topography in South Carolina. Eroded by acidic water, the limestone caves still contain active underground rivers, and they contain erosional features including chimneys and sinkholes. The sandy soils of the coastal plain are interrupted by thousands of Carolina bays, elliptical depressions that dot the region. It is thought that the bays were formed as the prevailing southwesterly winds sculpted water-filled depressions that existed near the coast during the Pleistocene epoch.

The lower coastal plain surfaces date from 1.8 million years ago to the present. The coast is divided into three sections: the Grand Strand, the Santee River Delta, and the Barrier and Sea Island Complex. At the Grand Strand the barrier islands have welded onto the shore; at the Santee Delta sediment has been deposited from the immense Santee River system; and the Barrier and Sea Island Complex formed as sea levels rose as glacial ice melted beginning about 15,000 years ago. The Sea Islands are products of sea level rise that drowned river valleys and formed islands cut off from the mainland. The barrier islands attached both to the Sea Islands and directly to the mainland. These islands continue to erode and accumulate at various rates on different islands as their sediment supply changes and as global sea levels rise.

South Carolina geology is currently in a passive, erosional phase. Collision and mountain building have ended for now. The state has developed from processes over a billion years in the making and it has contributed greatly to the field of geology by providing evidence of the universal processes of plate tectonics, a process that gives rise to the dynamic, if slow, transformation of the surface of the earth.

CAROLYN H. MURPHY

Murphy, Carolyn H. *Carolina Rocks! The Geology of South Carolina.* Orangeburg, S.C.: Sandlapper, 1995.

Georgetown (Georgetown County; 2000 pop. 8,950). Located at the confluence of the Sampit River and Winyah Bay, Georgetown was founded by Elisha Screven in 1729 and is the third oldest town in South Carolina. Screven vested control of the town with three trustees in 1735. Two years later, all 224 lots had been sold, though not occupied. The General Assembly governed from 1785 until Georgetown was incorporated in 1805. In 1892 the city was reincorporated under a mayor and council.

In the post–Civil War years, Georgetown's port was a busy place. Courtesy, South Caroliniana Library, University of South Carolina

Georgetown's designation as a port of entry by royal authorities in 1732 greatly improved its prospects. Although rice had been grown in the area since the 1730s, it was indigo that produced the largest fortunes between 1745 and 1775. Port activity in Georgetown thrived and the town briefly supported its own shipbuilding industry to meet demands of area planters. The town matured culturally, as evidenced by the construction of the large brick Anglican Church of Prince George Winyah in 1747 and the stylish town houses built by area planters. During the Revolutionary War, Georgetown was occupied by the British from July 1780 to May 1781. Following their departure, the town served as the main port of supply for the American army of General Nathanael Greene.

After the war, rice replaced indigo as the major cash crop of the district and remained so until the Civil War. But by the 1830s, Georgetown rice planters began taking their business to Charleston. The economic loss to Georgetown was offset somewhat by lumber and turpentine production in the 1850s. And although the town lost part of its commerce to Charleston, Georgetown still supported a variety of businesses, including druggists, dentists, confectioners, jewelers, and carriage-makers. The 1850 census showed Georgetown with 604 whites, 924 slaves, and 100 free persons of color. In the town, slaves performed domestic and menial labor, including working on the docks or in sawmills. Free blacks were often barbers, tailors, carpenters, smiths, and livery stable operators. Jews were also prominent in Georgetown, comprising ten percent of the town's white population as early as 1800. They were well received, becoming members of the Masons, the Library Society, and other social clubs. There have been six Jewish mayors.

During the Civil War, Georgetown was at the mercy of blockading federal ships, which frequently sailed upriver past Georgetown's docks to raid area plantations. Even so, local planters still managed to supply rice to the Confederacy. The torpedo that sank the USS *Harvest Moon* in Winyah Bay in March 1865 was made in the Kaminski building (now the Rice Museum). Federal troops occupied the town in February 1865. During Reconstruction, blacks controlled political life. In 1871 Georgetown native Joseph Hayne Rainey became the first African American to serve in the U.S. Congress (1871 to 1879). After 1876 blacks and whites shared political power under a policy known as "fusion." Fusion worked well in Georgetown until the Constitution of 1895 effectively disfranchised African Americans in South Carolina.

In 1883 Georgetown acquired its first railroad. This, along with renewed shipping activity, helped revive the economy. Most prominent in promoting growth and industry was William Doyle Morgan, who served as mayor from 1892 to 1906. Demand for lumber also added to the general prosperity, and three mills were in operation by 1890. The most important spur to growth came in 1903, when the Atlantic Coast Lumber Company (ACL) built a large mill on the Sampit River. This infusion of northern capital brought jobs and doubled the town's population. In addition to its mill, the ACL built twelve blocks of housing for its workers, ran a company store, and later a hotel. The company quickly became the mainstay of the Georgetown economy. Additional investments in the local economy were made by the U.S. government, which spent $2.5 million for harbor improvements and jetties between 1886 and 1905. Georgetown's turn-of-the-century prosperity seemed to manifest itself everywhere. By 1919 the city had four banks and many Front Street businesses possessed new cast-iron storefronts. Streets were paved, sewer lines laid, electric lights and telephones were installed.

The Georgetown economy suffered terribly with the onset of the Great Depression, particularly from the closing of the ACL in 1932. New Deal public works projects provided some relief. The Lafayette Bridge in 1935 and the paving of U.S. Highway 17 linked Georgetown and the Waccamaw Neck. A Civilian Conservation Corps camp near town was constructed as well as a new high school.

Georgetown expanded in both area and population after 1935. The city annexed former rice plantations to create new subdivisions. The population doubled from six thousand to twelve thousand in the 1950s. In 1935 International Paper (IP) began building the largest pulp and paper plant in the world on the Sampit River, infusing jobs and capital into the economy. IP tapped nearby forests of yellow pine to produce kraft (strong) paper. The company remained the largest employer in the county until the mid-1980s. In 1985 the mill was reconfigured at a cost of $600 million to produce white paper products. In 1968 the State Ports Authority recruited Korf Industries of Germany to Georgetown to build a steel reprocessing plant on the site of the old ACL mill, adjoining the Historic District. Georgetown Steel became the third largest employer in the county.

In the final decades of the twentieth century, the success of the state's coastal area in attracting permanent residents and tourists had profound effects on Georgetown. With the widening of Highway 17 and the building of new bridges over the Waccamaw, the Pee Dee, and the Sampit Rivers, Georgetown's access to the beaches was enhanced. Capitalizing on the boom, the city undertook a downtown revitalization project. Harborwalk, an eleven-hundred-foot boardwalk overlooking the Sampit River, was constructed in 1988 and featured four parks linking it to the business district. A $6 million, five-block streetscape project in the business district was completed in 1993. The influx of people and general prosperity was also reflected in the restoration of colonial and antebellum residences in the Georgetown Historic District. Georgetown continues to maintain its quality of life while progressing into the twenty-first century.
PATRICIA DAVIS DOYLE

Bridwell, Ronald E. *"The Gem of the Atlantic Seaboard."* Georgetown, S.C.: Georgetown Times, 1991.
Georgetown County Library. *A View of Our Past: The Morgan Photographic Collection Depicting Georgetown, South Carolina c. 1890–1915.* Georgetown, S.C.: Georgetown County Library System, 1993.
Rogers, George C. *The History of Georgetown County, South Carolina.* Columbia: University of South Carolina Press, 1970.

Georgetown County (815 sq. miles; 2000 pop. 55,797). Named in honor of King George III of England, Georgetown County lies in the fertile plain surrounding Winyah Bay. Its early wealth lay in the maze of rivers and creeks that traversed the county. Timber and naval stores traveled the Santee, Waccamaw, Pee Dee, and Sampit Rivers to the bay. The marshy coast and low-lying river bottoms produced rice and indigo. Rice grown by a cadre of immensely rich colonial and antebellum planters at one time made Georgetown one of the wealthiest counties in the United States.

Native Americans—the Sampit, Santee, Pee Dee, and Waccamaw, whose names grace the region's rivers—were Georgetown's first inhabitants. Trade with these Native Americans drew the first European settlers. Spaniards under Lucas Vázquez de Ayllón may have reached Georgetown County in the early sixteenth century. A few scholars even tout Georgetown as the site of the ill-fated settlement of San Miguel de Gualdape, the site of the first slave uprising in the North America.

Europeans first acquired land in the area in 1705. The Reverend William Screven settled the future site of the town of Georgetown in 1711. That same year Percival Pawley obtained grants for 2,500 acres on the Pee Dee, Sampit, and Waccamaw Rivers. French, English, and Scottish immigrants settled Georgetown. Trade continued to flourish on Georgetown's myriad waterways. The Brown's Ferry vessel, on display at the Rice Museum in Georgetown, sank between 1730 and 1740. Its surviving cargo of pipes and bottles documents eighteenth-century trade goods.

Three parishes served the eighteenth-century residents of the Georgetown area: Prince George Winyah (1721–1722), Prince Frederick's (1734), and All Saints (1778). The county court act of 1769 named Georgetown as one of seven judicial districts in the colony. In 1785 the South Carolina General Assembly divided Georgetown District into four counties: Winyah, Liberty, Kingston, and Williamsburg. After 1804 Georgetown District approximated the area of Winyah County. With the Constitution of 1868, Georgetown District became Georgetown County.

The movement toward independence found a welcome home in Georgetown, and Thomas Lynch of Hopsewee was one of the signers of the Declaration of Independence. During the Revolutionary War, the Marquis de Lafayette stopped at Benjamin Huger's summer home on June 14, 1777, en route to serve with the Continental forces. General Francis Marion, the "Swamp Fox," defeated a Tory force at Black Mingo Creek on September 14, 1780, and Colonel Peter Horry also prevailed in an encounter with the Tories in 1781. Conversely, a Tory contingent captured Lieutenant Gabriel Marion, nephew of Francis Marion, near White's Bridge in 1780 and killed him.

After the Revolution, the production of indigo waned, but, with technological advances, rice production grew. Starting in 1787, Jonathan Lucas began building water-powered rice mills, then tide-operated rice mills, for leading rice planters. Production expanded and laid the foundation for some of the South's preeminent planting families, including the Alstons, Heriots, Wards, and Westons. In 1840 Georgetown District accounted for almost half of the total rice crop of the United States. In 1850 ninety-one Georgetown planters produced more than 100,000 pounds of rice each. As noted by the historian George Rogers, "Rice was Georgetown's contribution to Western civilization."

The production of labor-intensive crops led to the importation of thousands of African slaves. Many came from the rice-growing Gold Coast of Africa and contributed folk and food ways to the rich cultural mosaic of Georgetown County. In 1860 eighty-five percent of Georgetown County's population of 21,305 were slaves. At least two Georgetown District planters, Joshua John Ward and Plowden Charles Jennet Weston, owned more than one thousand slaves.

With its long coastline, Georgetown feared Federal invasion during the Civil War. In response to this perceived threat, Confederates constructed Battery White on a bluff overlooking Winyah Bay. In November 1862, there were fifty-three men and nine guns at the battery. It was abandoned by February 1865.

With the end of the Civil War, Georgetown faced economic hardship. The rice dikes had been damaged or destroyed, and the planters faced the challenge of negotiating for labor with the recently freed African Americans, who demonstrated little interest in returning to the rice fields. During Reconstruction, with its large black majority, Georgetown County became a Republican Party stronghold. Even after the return of Democratic rule to South Carolina after 1876, African Americans in Georgetown County still held significant political power. They shared control in uneasy cooperation with local whites in a process called "fusion" until 1900, when white control was reestablished.

With the help of the Georgetown Rice Milling Company, the desultory production of rice persisted into the early twentieth century, before succumbing to bankruptcies, outside competition, and a series of devastating hurricanes. Some planters turned to subsistence crops, but most of the former plantations became hunting preserves for wealthy northern sportsmen, including the Hobcaw Barony estate of Bernard Baruch and the Brookgreen estate of Archer Milton and Anna Hyatt Huntington.

The growth of the lumber and pulpwood industry converted thousands of agricultural acres to pine forest. During the first decades of the twentieth century, giant lumbering companies, such as Atlantic Coast Lumber and International Paper, built massive factories near the city of Georgetown and bought up vast tracts of pine lands. Logging railroads, such as the Georgetown and Western, carried timber to the mills. New railroads revived the economy of Georgetown and established the boomtown of Andrews on the Williamsburg County line. This prosperity faltered during the 1930s, and Georgetown County suffered the effects of the Great Depression with particular intensity.

World War II and the expansion of the pulp and paper industry, especially the construction of massive paper mills by International Paper in the 1930s and 1940s, brought about yet another economic revival. Improvements to the port of Georgetown and arrival of Georgetown Steel in the 1960s and 1970s provided a further boost. Finally, improved rail and road access to the county brought thousands of tourists to Georgetown beaches. More sedate than the rambunctious tourist mecca of Myrtle Beach, upscale beach communities such as Murrells Inlet, Litchfield, Pawleys Island, and Debidue Beach have provided a peaceful respite not only for vacationers, but for a spectrum of authors ranging from Julia Peterkin to Mickey Spillane. ALEXIA JONES HELSLEY

Bolick, Julian Stevenson. *Waccamaw Plantations.* Clinton, S.C.: Jacobs, 1946.

Joyner, Charles W. *Down by the Riverside: A South Carolina Slave Community.* Urbana: University of Illinois Press, 1984.

Linder, Suzanne C., and Marta Leslie Thacker. *The Historical Atlas of the Rice Plantations of Georgetown County and the Santee River.* Columbia: South Carolina Department of Archives and History for the Historic Ricefields Association, 2001.

Rogers, George C. *The History of Georgetown County, South Carolina.* Columbia: University of South Carolina Press, 1970.

Georgetown Steel. Founded in 1969, German-owned Georgetown Steel Company was among the earliest foreign-owned companies wooed to South Carolina as part of a campaign to attract foreign investment. A subsidiary of Korf Industries of West Germany, Georgetown Steel provided hundreds of well-paying jobs to the economically depressed city, although pollution from the plant would be a recurring concern throughout its existence. Located in downtown Georgetown, the facility was designed for an annual production of 250,000 tons of reinforcing bars, using powerful electric furnaces. This was the first commercial direct reduction plant ever built. Using temperatures as high as 1500° F, direct reduction produced a high-quality iron free of unwanted impurities, which then became the key ingredient in steel. The Georgetown plant's two electric arc furnaces had a production capacity of 83,333 tons per month, and its rolling mill possessed an annual capacity of 792,000 tons. In 1992 the facility established the world record casting sequence: 24,580 tons in 353 hours and 55 minutes.

By the start of the twenty-first century, rising energy prices, increased costs for raw materials, and weak demand had taken a toll on Georgetown Steel. Owners filed for bankruptcy in October 2003, laying off the plant's 541 employees. RICK D. BOULWARE

Cobb, James C. *The Selling of the South: The Southern Crusade for Industrial Development, 1936–1980.* Baton Rouge: Louisiana State University Press, 1982.

German Friendly Society. Oldest of all German male social organizations in Charleston, the German Friendly Society was founded by Michael Kalteisen (1729–1807), and Daniel Strobel (1734–1806). Meeting in Kalteisen's home on January 15, 1766, sixteen German men constituted themselves as a social and mutual-assistance society to pay sick and death benefits, and allow members to borrow funds at low rates of interest. Almost immediately, German ethnicity was not necessary for membership, nor was the ability to speak German. Constructing its own meetinghouse on Archdale Street in 1801, the society opened a school for boys in 1803, and turned out in October 1814 to help the German Fusiliers build and maintain Charleston's fortifications during the War of 1812. Although not a part of its specified mission, the society established a fund in April 1821 to aid indigent and transient Germans in the city. By the mid-1800s, the society's membership reflected the assimilation of the colonial-period Germans into Charleston society, causing newly immigrating Germans to say they had "lost their Germanness." Other German ethnic societies rose to meet the needs of the new German immigrants, and a pattern emerged of acceptance into the German Friendly Society only after the newcomers had become economically successful. Following the Civil War and the decline in German immigration to Charleston, the society developed into more of a social and charitable organization. In 1942 it changed its name to the Friendly Society of Charleston, but reverted to its original name in 1965. The modern society has a membership limit of two hundred and an eleven-year waiting list to join. MICHAEL EVERETTE BELL

Riley, Helen M. "Michael Kalteisen and the Founding of the German Friendly Society in Charleston." *South Carolina Historical Magazine* 100 (January 1999): 29–48.

Two Hundred and Twenty-Five Years of American History Taken from the Minutes and Other Records of the German Friendly Society of Charleston, South Carolina. Spartanburg, S.C.: Reprint Company, 1999.

Germans. Germans were present in South Carolina at the beginning of settlement. In 1674 German-speaking immigrants settled on James Island, west of the Ashley at Albemarle Point. Populating the townships of Londonborough, New Windsor, Orangeburg, Purrysburg, and Saxe-Gotha, most German-speaking immigrants arriving in the colonial period fell into one of two groups: German-Swiss (Switzers) and Palatines (from upper Bavaria and parts of southwestern Germany). Of these two groups, the German-Swiss tended to be more prosperous, while the Palatines often arrived as redemptioners (indentured servants).

The most prominent contingent of German-speakers was in Charleston, where a vibrant artisan and mercantile community had been established by the decade before the Revolutionary War. Founding St. John's Lutheran Church in 1759 and the German Friendly Society in 1766, they formed a separated ethnic community within the city, generally referred to as Dutchtown. Charleston's Germans were at the forefront of Revolutionary political and military activity. While a large number of the colony's German-speakers sided with the patriots, another sizable contingent, especially among the more recent arrivals in the backcountry, supported the Loyalist cause. In May 1775 Charleston's Germans formed the first German military company in the United States, the German Fusiliers, which distinguished itself at the Battle of Savannah.

Between 1790 and 1830 few Germans came to South Carolina, and German language and culture began to decline in the state. Notable exceptions to this occurred in the so-called Dutch Fork, where language and culture continued into the early twentieth century, and in Charleston, where German organizations formed a strong institutional base for an ethnic community. The few German

Jews who came to Charleston in this period were not invited to join these organizations, nor any of those founded subsequently.

The *Altdeutsch* (colonial-period Germans and their descendants) eventually became more Charlestonian than German. *Altdeutsch* merchants involved themselves in the politics of the city, and two were elected mayor in the early 1840s, Jacob F. Mintzing (1840–1842) and John Schnierle (1842–1845, 1850–1852). This assimilation caused a degree of class division in the late 1830s and early 1840s, when German immigration resumed to the city. The number of new north-German immigrants (*Neudeutsch*) overwhelmed the small institutional base of the *Altdeutsch* community. In order to define their own path to success, a group of emergent *Neudeutsch* leaders created a diversified German-America in the city—one that was based in a blend of *Altdeutsch,* Charleston, and German forms. The organizations they started became the basis for the strong pan-German ethnic community that grew to flower just before the onset of the Civil War. Clearly, the *Neudeutsch* and the *Altdeutsch* had reached an accommodation.

Charleston's German-America was prosperous in the 1850s, with a German grocery or other retail store on almost every corner, its own newspaper (the *Deutsche Zeitung*), a firefighting company, several fraternal and sports organizations, six militia companies, and two Lutheran churches. Several more enterprising immigrants made the trek to develop a German colony at Walhalla in Oconee County, establishing hotels and other businesses, where the wealthy among Charleston's Germans made their summer homes. Few problems were experienced during the anti-immigrant Know-Nothing period, simply because South Carolina's German immigrants adopted the values—states' rights and slavery among them—of their new homeland. During the Civil War, South Carolina's Germans fought and died to preserve those values, resulting in their almost complete assimilation into South Carolina society.

The Civil War effectively ended German immigration to South Carolina, despite the state's efforts to encourage it—in part from a desire to maintain a white voting majority. Separate attempts at promoting German immigration in the 1860s, 1880s, and early twentieth century brought negligible results. Later, both Charleston's and Lexington's German Americans opposed America's entry into World War I. Once war was declared, however, they fully supported the cause. German American influence in South Carolina had waned, however, to the point that the *Deutsche Zeitung* ceased publication in 1917.

Estimated at 15,000 in 1775 and some 30,000 in 1790, Germans had once comprised more than twenty percent of the state's free population. By 1870 their number decreased to 2,754, and by 1920, only 1,079 South Carolinians reported being "German-born." South Carolina's Germans were a diverse lot, and contributed much to the social, political, and cultural history of the state. As they settled, they brought their culture with them, and developed a unique blend of Germanic and South Carolina culture. Exemplified through such diverse manifestations as the state's Lutheran Church, folk art traditions, and the mustard-based barbecue sauce of the Dutch Fork area, South Carolina's Germans found ways to both adjust to their adopted homeland, and maintain their Germanic culture and traditions. See plates 13 and 14. MICHAEL EVERETTE BELL

Bell, Michael Everette. "'Hurrah für dies süsse, dies sonnige Leben': The Anomaly of Charleston, South Carolina's Antebellum German-America." Ph.D. diss., University of South Carolina, 1996.

———. "Regional Identity in the Antebellum South: How German Immigrants Became 'Good' Charlestonians." *South Carolina Historical Magazine* 100 (January 1999): 9–28.

Faust, Albert Bernhard. *The German Element in the United States: With Special Reference to Its Political, Moral, Social, and Educational Influence.* 2 vols. New York: Houghton Mifflin, 1909.

Two Hundred and Twenty-Five Years of American History Taken from the Minutes and Other Records of the German Friendly Society of Charleston, South Carolina. Spartanburg, S.C.: Reprint Company, 1999.

Gibbes, Frances Guignard (1870–1948). Playwright, poet. Gibbes was born in Columbia on October 12, 1870, the daughter of Wade Hampton Gibbes and Jane A. Mason. Inspired by her "urge to write," in 1895 she became the first woman to enroll in South Carolina College (later the University of South Carolina), two years after the General Assembly mandated that women should be allowed to attend the school as special students. She attended classes until 1899 but did not earn a degree.

Gibbes published her first work, *Book of Poems,* in 1902. Her first play, *Jael,* was published in 1922 and won the Town Theatre literary prize that year. *Jael* was followed by *Hilda* (1923), *The Face* (1924), *Up There!* (1932), and *Dawn in Carolina* (1946). Her best-known work was *The Face,* produced in Columbia, New York, Mississippi, and Palm Beach, Florida. Gibbes received numerous awards for her plays. According to a review in the *Times Literary Supplement* (December 13, 1923), she produced works that were "worthy of the Elizabethan tradition of poetic drama."

Gibbes traveled extensively throughout her life. In 1925 she went to France with her husband, Oscar Lovell Keith, Professor of Romance Languages at the University of South Carolina. This excursion, with several university students and Columbia community members, was the first Summer School Abroad Program at the University of South Carolina. Gibbes and Keith had one daughter, Frances Gibbes Keith, born in 1913. Gibbes died on October 4, 1948, and was buried in Elmwood Cemetery, Columbia. MARY BASKIN WATERS

Gibbes, Frances Guignard. Papers. South Caroliniana Library, University of South Carolina, Columbia.

Gibbes, Louis Reeve (1810–1894). Scientist. Gibbes was born in Charleston on August 14, 1810, eldest of the eight children of Lewis Ladson Gibbes and his wife, Maria Henrietta Drayton. Gibbes attended grammar school in Charleston and Philadelphia, then prepared for college at the Pendleton Academy in the South Carolina upcountry, where he excelled in mathematics and the classics. A student of five languages, he showed an early interest in botany, astronomy, and physics. Gibbes entered South Carolina College soon after graduating first in his class from Pendleton Academy in 1827. For a time in 1830 he was the classics teacher and acting principal at Pendleton Academy. Later that year he enrolled in the Medical College of South Carolina, in Charleston.

In 1831 Gibbes left for Columbia to become an instructor in mathematics at his alma mater. There he commenced a study that resulted in the publication in 1835 of *Catalogue of the Phoenogamous Plants of Columbia, S.C., and Its Vicinity,* which listed around 775 species of plants. Gibbes returned to Charleston in 1835 and completed the medical program in March 1836. Soon thereafter, he traveled to Paris to study with several prominent medical professors and naturalists. On returning to Charleston in late 1837, Gibbes accepted appointment as the professor of mathematics at the College of Charleston. Married to Anna Barnwell on September 2, 1848, he was the father of nine children.

During his fifty-four-year career at the College of Charleston, Gibbes taught mathematics, chemistry, physics, and astronomy, and endeared himself to generations of students despite his exacting standards. Although he bore an extremely heavy load as a teacher, Gibbes found time to conduct numerous studies in astronomy, and, from 1848 to 1850, acted as an official celestial observer for the U.S. Coast Survey, using an observatory that he personally constructed. Meanwhile, the energetic scientist published studies of crustacea that earned him a national reputation as the leading authority on the subject in the South.

Over the years, Gibbes also published articles on many other topics, including physics, mineralogy, chemistry, and botany. An avid collector of specimens, he amassed large cabinets of crabs, flora, insects, mollusk shells, and minerals, most of them from South Carolina. Gibbes was devoted to the advancement of science in the South and in his native state in particular, and he played a prominent role in Charleston's Elliott Society of Natural History, before which he presented more papers than any other member. He served as the president of the society for three decades.

A fervent advocate of secession, Gibbes aided the Confederacy in any way he could. As federal troops entered Charleston in February 1865, Gibbes was forced to flee, but he returned to his teaching post immediately after the war ended. Struggling to overcome inadequate resources and to support his family on a meager salary, he continued to teach until 1892. The most versatile of all the scientists in nineteenth-century Charleston, Gibbes received wide acclaim for his studies. He died in Charleston on November 21, 1894, and was buried in Magnolia Cemetery. LESTER D. STEPHENS

Stephens, Lester D. *Science, Race, and Religion in the American South: John Bachman and the Charleston Circle of Naturalists, 1815–1895.* Chapel Hill: University of North Carolina Press, 2000.

Gibbes, Robert (1644–1715). Governor. Robert Gibbes was born in Sandwich, England, on January 9, 1644, the son of Robert Gibbes and Mary Coventry. Both his parents were of the county of Kent gentry, but Gibbes as a young man went out to Barbados with others of his family. He was among the Barbadian "Adventurers" who in 1665 reached agreement with the Lords Proprietors for establishing a settlement in Carolina. The next year both he and his brother, Thomas, were members of the governing assembly at the attempted settlement at Cape Fear, which failed in 1667. By 1672 Gibbes had begun to accumulate large landholdings in South Carolina. Like other Barbadians, he seems to have moved back and forth between the island and mainland colonies for some years. But by 1673, a South Carolina deed referred to Gibbes as "of this Province."

In 1684 Gibbes began his government service in South Carolina with a commission as the colony's sheriff. From 1692 to 1694, he represented Colleton County in the first separate lower house of assembly, a body that later became the Commons House of Assembly. In 1698 Gibbes became the Colleton family's deputy in South Carolina and a member of the Grand Council. Ten years later, he was appointed chief justice of the colony. As one of only three proprietors' deputies in the colony when Governor Edward Tynte died in June 1710, Gibbes proceeded to bribe his way into the governor's office and brought government to a virtual standstill for nearly two years.

Governor Tynte's instructions provided that the other deputies should choose one of their number as interim governor. On a morning soon after Tynte's death, the three deputies (Gibbes, Thomas Broughton, and Fortescue Turberville) chose Broughton, but by afternoon Gibbes had bribed Turberville with the promise of "£100 and three places besides." Turberville changed his vote. Gibbes's misdeed was discovered after Turberville's death in the sickly colony on July 4, 1710, and only Broughton's forbearance prevented civil war between his supporters and those of Gibbes.

Governor Gibbes was able to do little while the colony waited for action by the proprietors. When the Tuscarora Indians rose up against the North Carolinians in 1711, Gibbes sent badly needed Yamassee Indian allies under Colonel John Barnwell to help save the northern colony. But overall, his administration accomplished little. In a 1711 speech to the Commons House, Gibbes expressed alarm at the colony's growing slave majority and proposed harsher penalties for "insolent & mischievous" slaves, legal requirements for masters to provide adequate food and clothing, and the recruitment of white settlers. His administration ended in March 1712 with the arrival of a commission from the proprietors naming Charles Craven governor.

Gibbes married Jane Davis in Barbados on October 24, 1678, and after her death married Mary Davis. His son John Gibbes, one of five children, also served in the Commons House of Assembly, as did two grandsons. Gibbes died in South Carolina on June 24, 1715. CHARLES H. LESSER

Edgar, Walter, and N. Louise Bailey, eds. *Biographical Directory of the South Carolina House of Representatives.* Vol. 2, *The Commons House of Assembly, 1692–1775.* Columbia: University of South Carolina Press, 1977.

Holmes, Henry S. "Robert Gibbes, Governor of South Carolina, and Some of His Descendants." *South Carolina Historical and Genealogical Magazine* 12 (April 1911): 78–105.

Lesser, Charles H. *South Carolina Begins: The Records of a Proprietary Colony, 1663–1721.* Columbia: South Carolina Department of Archives and History, 1995.

Gibbes, Robert Wilson (1809–1866). Naturalist, physician. Gibbes was born in Charleston on July 8, 1809, the son of attorney William Hasell Gibbes and his wife, Mary Wilson. A perceptive student, Gibbes graduated in 1827 from South Carolina College, which soon appointed him as assistant professor of geology and chemistry. During the summers of 1827 and 1828, he studied medicine in Philadelphia and then enrolled in the Medical College of South Carolina where he earned the M.D. degree in 1830. After resigning from the South Carolina College faculty in 1834, Gibbes established a medical practice in Columbia, which he maintained for the rest of his life. Married to Caroline Elizabeth Guignard on December 20, 1827, he was the father of twelve children.

Keenly interested in natural history, Gibbes collected bird specimens, mollusk shells, and minerals. He was especially interested in vertebrate fossils, and it was in the field of paleontology that he made lasting contributions. Among his significant studies was "Description of the Teeth of a new Fossil Animal found in the Green Sand of South Carolina," published in 1845 in the *Proceedings of the Academy of Natural Sciences of Philadelphia.* Gibbes described and named *Dorudon serratus,* a previously unknown primitive whale. During the next six years, he published articles on fossil shark teeth and the extinct mosasaurs (large, lizard-like marine animals). He also contributed to the proceedings of the American Association for the Advancement of Science, one of the many scientific organizations in which he held membership. In 1849 Gibbes published *The Present Earth the Remains of a Former World,* in which he argued that the earth was millions of years older than traditionally believed. He insisted, however, that this fact could be easily reconciled with the biblical story of creation, thus enabling him to account for the ancient age of fossils without questioning the validity of the Scriptures. He published his last scientific paper in 1850.

A man of notable versatility, Gibbes was a patron of the arts and owned an impressive collection of paintings. In 1846 he completed *A Memoir of James De Veaux, of Charleston, S.C.*, a gracefully crafted biography of a talented artist. He also cultivated an interest in the American past, and in 1853 he published *Documentary History of the American Revolution,* which pertained mostly to South Carolina. Throughout most of his career, Gibbes was active in the State Agricultural Society of South Carolina and in the South Carolina Medical Association. He was involved in the cultural and civic affairs of Columbia and served two terms as mayor. In 1852 he acquired the *Daily South Carolinian* and was the editor from 1852 to 1858. During the Civil War, Gibbes served as Surgeon General for South Carolina and otherwise endeavored to improve the medical capacity of the Confederacy. Federal troops destroyed his home and prized collections when they occupied Columbia in February 1865. Gibbes died in Columbia on October 15, 1866. LESTER D. STEPHENS

Jellison, Richard M., and Phillip S. Swartz. "The Scientific Interests of Robert W. Gibbes." *South Carolina Historical Magazine* 66 (April 1965): 77–97.

Sanders, Albert E., and William D. Anderson, Jr. *Natural History Investigations in South Carolina from Colonial Times to the Present.* Columbia: University of South Carolina Press, 1999.

Stephens, Lester D. *Science, Race, and Religion in the American South: John Bachman and the Charleston Circle of Naturalists, 1815–1895.* Chapel Hill: University of North Carolina Press, 2000.

Gibbes Museum of Art. Located on lower Meeting Street in Charleston, the Gibbes Museum of Art is the home of the Carolina Art Association, an organization dedicated to the cultivation of the arts and art education in Charleston since its inception in 1858. The building opened to the public on April 11, 1905, as the James S. Gibbes Memorial Art Gallery. It was named after James Shoolbred Gibbes, whose legacy enabled the association and the city of Charleston to purchase property and erect a building for the display of art and for art instruction. Architect Frank Milburn designed the original two-story edifice in the Beaux Arts style with a notable stained glass dome in the rotunda. In 1976 the association began a building program to remodel and expand the original structure. The enlarged facility of thirty thousand square feet opened to the public in 1978. In 1988 the name of the organization was changed to the Gibbes Museum of Art. It is accredited by the American Association of Museums.

Entering the twenty-first century, the Gibbes Museum housed a collection of more than five hundred paintings, including works by such nationally prominent artists as Benjamin West, Charles Willson Peale, and Gilbert Stuart, and native painters such as William H. Johnson and Edwin Harleston. The museum also maintains a renowned collection of eighteenth- and nineteenth-century miniature portraits and a growing collection of contemporary art. Other noteworthy collections include the Marks Collection of early-twentieth-century photographs, the Read Japanese Print Collection, and the Ballard Collection of European prints and drawings. The museum's archive documents the history of the Carolina Art Association and the artists represented in the collection. Besides mounting permanent and temporary art exhibitions, the museum offers lectures and symposia, family and school programs, and instructional art classes. PAUL FIGUEROA

Mouzon, Harold A. "The Carolina Art Association: Its First Hundred Years." *South Carolina Historical Magazine* 59 (July 1958): 125–38.

Gibbons, Leeza (b. 1957). Television-radio host, producer. Gibbons was born in Hartsville on March 26, 1957, the daughter of Carlos and Jean Gibbons. Raised in Irmo, she attended the University of South Carolina and graduated magna cum laude in 1982 with a degree in journalism.

Gibbons entered broadcast journalism as a host of *PM Magazine* in Dallas and Beaumont, Texas. She also worked as a reporter-anchor in Spartanburg, South Carolina, and was on National Public Radio in Columbia. After cohosting WCBS-TV's *Two on the Town* in New York City, Gibbons entered the national spotlight in 1984 as a reporter-anchor on *Entertainment Tonight,* a nationally syndicated television program. Later Gibbons became executive producer of her own program, *Leeza,* which ran from 1994 to 2000 on NBC. She was nominated for both Outstanding Talk Show and Outstanding Talk Show Host during every year of eligibility. *Leeza* received twenty-seven Daytime Emmy Nominations and won three. Gibbons has been honored with a star on the Hollywood Walk of Fame.

In 1994 Gibbons formed Leeza Gibbons Enterprises (LGE) to develop and produce special projects such as "Assignment E! with Leeza Gibbons" and the Emmy-winning "Teen Files." She also hosted the syndicated radio program *Hollywood Confidential,* which was featured on more than 125 stations.

Gibbons has been particularly active in the fight against Alzheimer's disease, which afflicted her mother, and founded the Leeza Gibbons Memory Foundation. Gibbons received the Congressional Horizon Award for her crusade on children's issues and the University of South Carolina Outstanding Alumnus Award in 1992. She was inducted into the South Carolina Hall of Fame and is a recipient of the Order of the Palmetto.

Gibbons has been married three times. Marriages to John Hicks in 1980 and Christopher Quinten in 1988 each ended in divorce. In 1991 she married actor-architect Stephen Meadows. She has three children. ROBERT A. PIERCE

Gibson, Althea (1927–2003). Tennis champion. Gibson was born in Silver (Clarendon County) on August 25, 1927, the daughter of sharecroppers Daniel and Annie Gibson. The family moved to New York when Althea was three years old. Gibson spent her childhood cutting school and playing sports. She excelled at paddle tennis and caught the attention of Buddy Walker, a Police Athletic League supervisor, who suggested she try regular tennis. Walker took Gibson to practice at the Harlem River Tennis Courts and within days she was beating local male players.

Gibson's success led to membership in New York's most prestigious black tennis club, the Cosmopolitan. Gibson began formal lessons after a year and steadily improved. She won in her first tournament, the all-black American Tennis Association's (ATA) New York State Open Championship. In 1946 Gibson advanced from the ATA's girls' division to the women's division. She lost her first championship match at this level, but two ATA officials, Dr. Hubert Eaton and Dr. Robert Johnson, recognized Gibson's potential and offered to help her with her college education. Gibson, however, had dropped out of high school, so the three struck a deal. During the school year, Gibson would live with Eaton, attend high school, and practice on his private court. During the summers she would live with Johnson and play the ATA circuit.

Gibson dominated the ATA. In 1947 she won the first of ten consecutive ATA national championships. With the help of ATA officials, she finally got her first invitation to an event sponsored by the all-white United States Lawn Tennis Association (USLTA). In 1949 Gibson competed in the Eastern Indoor Championships, reaching the quarterfinals. Gibson did not, however, receive an invitation to play in the outdoor tournaments until another player, Alice Marble, wrote a scathing article against racial discrimination. On August 28, 1950, in Forest Hills, New York, Gibson became the first African American to play in the USLTA championship. Gibson lost in the second round to Wimbledon champion Louise Brough, but her performance ensured her return.

Gibson continued to play nationally and internationally. In 1956 she won sixteen of the eighteen tournaments she entered. That same year she became the first African American to capture a Grand Slam event when she won the French Championship. She went on to win Wimbledon in 1957 and was welcomed home with a ticker tape parade. Ranked as the number one tennis player in 1957, Gibson won her first U.S. championship and was named Female Athlete of the Year by the Associated Press.

In 1958 Gibson remained number one, successfully defending her Wimbledon and U.S. titles and receiving the Associated Press's Female Athlete of the Year award for a second year. Gibson retired from amateur tennis in 1959 and began playing golf in the early 1960s. She broke the color barrier again when, in 1964, she was the first African American to earn a LPGA player's card. In 1971 Gibson began coaching tennis. She coached until 1992 when she retired. After several years of declining health, Gibson died on September 28, 2003, in East Orange, New Jersey. LISA ENNIS

Biracree, Tom. *Althea Gibson.* New York: Chelsea House, 1989.

Gibson, Althea. *I Always Wanted to Be Somebody.* New York: Harper, 1958.

———. *So Much to Live For.* New York: Putnam, 1968.

Woodlum, Janet. *Outstanding Women Athletes: Who They Are and How They Influenced Sports in America.* 2d ed. Phoenix: Oryx, 1998.

Gilbreth, Frank Bunker, Jr. (1911–2001). Writer, newspaper columnist. Gilbreth was born in Plainfield, New Jersey, on March 17, 1911, the fifth child and eldest son of Frank and Lillian Gilbreth, a pair of nationally known engineers and efficiency experts. After attending St. Johns College for a year, Gilbreth went on to the University of Michigan where he was editor of the university's newspaper, the *Michigan Daily.* He graduated in 1933 with a Bachelor of Arts degree. He then worked for the *New York Herald Tribune,* the *Charleston News and Courier, Buenos Aires Herald,* and the Associated Press. During World War II, Gilbreth served in the Pacific as a naval officer and aerial photographer. He left the navy as a lieutenant commander and was awarded a Bronze Star and two Air Medals for his service.

Gilbreth is best known as the coauthor of *Cheaper by the Dozen.* Published in 1949, this book was Gilbreth's collaboration with his older sister, Ernestine Gilbreth Carey, about their childhood as two of twelve children in a house managed like a factory. Translated into thirty languages, *Cheaper by the Dozen,* along with its sequel, *Belles on their Toes,* was a best seller and was made into a successful film. Subsequently, Gilbreth wrote several additional books, including *Innside Nantucket* (1954), about a family-run boarding house, and *Time Out for Happiness* (1971), a biography of his parents.

In 1947 Gilbreth returned to Charleston and joined the staff of the *News and Courier.* For his popular column, "Doing the Charleston," Gilbreth wrote under the pseudonym Ashley Cooper. The column became one of the longest running in American newspaper history. He also assembled a brief dictionary of "Charlestonese," which amusingly discussed the port city's famous drawl. Selections from his column were published in *Ashley Cooper's Doing the Charleston* in 1993. Gilbreth also worked as assistant publisher of the paper and as vice president of Evening Post Publishing Company. The final "Doing the Charleston" ran in 1993, and in 1998 Gilbreth was named to the South Carolina Academy of Authors.

Gilbreth was married to Elizabeth Cauthen from September 9, 1934, until her death in 1954, and to Mary Pringle Manigault from June 4, 1955 until the time of his death. He had a daughter from his first marriage and a son and a daughter from his second. Gilbreth died in Charleston on February 18, 2001, and was buried in Magnolia Cemetery. R. F. STALVEY

Gilbreth, Frank B., Jr. *Ashley Cooper's Doing the Charleston.* Charleston, S.C.: Post and Courier, 1993.

Rowe, Charles R. "Author, Columnist Gilbreth Dies." Charleston *Post and Courier,* February 19, 2001, pp. 1A, 15A.

Gillespie, John Birks (1917–1993). Musician. Dizzy Gillespie was born in Cheraw on October 21, 1917, the son of James Penfield Gillespie, a bricklayer and amateur musician, and Lottie Powe. He began instruction on trumpet and trombone at age twelve and by fifteen was proficient enough to sit in with visiting professional bands. In 1933 he entered the nearby Laurinburg Institute in North Carolina, where he played in the school band. He left two years later without receiving his high school diploma to join his mother in Philadelphia, where she had recently moved.

Leaving Philadelphia for New York in 1937, Gillespie played with sundry groups for two years before joining the popular Cab Calloway Orchestra. Playing with Calloway, he began to display the first elements of a personal style. In his off-hours, Gillespie participated in jam sessions with such forward-looking young players as saxophonist Charlie Parker and pianist Thelonious Monk. Their informal experimentation with advanced harmonies and complex rhythms eventually led to the first modern jazz style, called bebop (or bop), which remains in the twenty-first century the foundation of most jazz performance.

Leaving Calloway in 1941, Gillespie spent short periods with a number of ensembles and began to supply arrangements for the orchestras of Woody Herman and Jimmy Dorsey. While a member of the Benny Carter band, he wrote his famous "A Night in Tunisia." By 1945 he had played with numerous large and small groups, including those of Earl Hines, Billy Eckstine, Coleman Hawkins, Duke Ellington, and John Kirby, and led or co-led small bands of his own.

In 1945 Gillespie and Charlie Parker formed a quintet to perform in the new style at a New York club. Later that year, they participated in some of the first small-group bebop recordings. Those recordings led to Gillespie's reputation as one of the most virtuosic, individualistic, and influential trumpeters in the history of jazz.

A devotee of big bands, Gillespie formed several during his career only to return to the small band format when they failed financially. In 1956 the U.S. Department of State sponsored a big band tour of the Middle East and parts of Europe, followed by a similar state-department-sponsored trip to South America. Between big bands, Gillespie led small ensembles or performed with all-star aggregations such as Jazz at the Philharmonic. As a bandleader, he was among the first to introduce Latin musical elements into modern jazz.

Gillespie performed prolifically throughout the world and received numerous honors. He played for the South Carolina legislature in 1976 and two years later sang a duet with President Jimmy Carter at the White House Jazz Festival. In 1989 President George Bush presented him with the National Medal of Arts. He was inducted into the South Carolina Hall of Fame in 1985. The African American Monument installed on the State House grounds in 2001 contains his likeness. Gillespie died of pancreatic cancer on January 6, 1993. DAVID FRANKLIN

DeVeaux, Scott. *The Birth of Bebop: A Social and Musical History.* Berkeley: University of California Press, 1997.

Gillespie, Dizzy, with Al Fraser. *To Be, Or Not . . . To Bop: Memoirs.* Garden City, N.Y.: Doubleday, 1979.

Owens, Thomas. *Bebop: The Music and Its Players.* New York: Oxford University Press, 1995.

Shipton, Alyn. *Groovin' High: The Life of Dizzy Gillespie.* New York: Oxford University Press, 1999.

Gillisonville Baptist Church (Gillisonville). Situated in Jasper County, on high ground west of the Coosawhatchie River, the pineland village of Gillisonville was settled early in the history of Beaufort District. As with other inland communities, there was little economic activity, and the village remained small. Most houses were occupied only seasonally by planters desiring a healthy summer residence for their families.

From 1790 until 1836, Beaufort District's seat of government was at Coosawhatchie, six miles to the south. Although Coosawhatchie was conveniently located, its proximity to the tidal rice plantations of lower St. Luke's Parish produced a deadly climate. By the mid-1830s the town was decried as "too sickly to occupy," and the courthouse was moved to Gillisonville in 1836. With the coming of the courthouse, the village became a real town. New boardinghouses, taverns, shops, and churches sprang up near the courthouse square, while members of Coosawhatchie Baptist Church, organized in 1832, erected a proud new building just outside town (the exact date of construction is in dispute). The wood-frame edifice is a good example of the Greek Revival "temple" design favored for churches. Four columns support the large, pedimented front-gable end, providing a broad, deep portico. An oversized square tower surmounted by an open belfry dominates the building.

Gillisonsville Baptist Church. Courtesy, South Carolina Department of Archives and History

Most of Gillisonville proper, including the courthouse, was burned by Union troops in January 1865. According to tradition, the Baptist church was undamaged because troops sheltered themselves and their horses there. Although the court was moved to Beaufort during Reconstruction, Gillisonville remained a local trading village. Listed in the National Register of Historic Places in 1971, Gillisonville Baptist Church is still in active use. SARAH FICK

Perry, Grace Fox. *The Moving Finger of Jasper.* [Ridgeland, S.C.: n.p., 1962].

Rowland, Lawrence S., Alexander Moore, and George C. Rogers. *The History of Beaufort County, South Carolina.* Vol. 1, *1514–1861.* Columbia: University of South Carolina Press, 1996.

Gillon, Alexander (1741–1794). Congressman, merchant, naval officer, legislator. Gillon was born in Rotterdam, Holland, on August 13, 1741, the son of Alexander Gillon and Mary Harris. Gillon's fluency in several languages, handsome appearance, and social graces helped him rise quickly in the commercial trade. Gillon first arrived in the American colonies as the master of the brigantine *Surprize,* docking at Philadelphia in December 1764. Within two years, Gillon met Mary Splatt Cripps, widow of William Cripps, and the two were married on July 6, 1766. The union produced one daughter. His wife died in 1787, whereupon Gillon married Ann Purcell on February 10, 1789. This marriage produced three children.

Gillon settled in Charleston in 1766, prospering in commercial ventures, operating a store and merchant vessels. In 1773 he opened the firm of Alexander Gillon & Company with his stepsons, William and John Splatt Cripps. Reorganized under Gillon and William Cripps, the firm operated a store on the bay that sold foodstuffs and wines. The lucrative venture enabled Gillon to retire from the mercantile trade in 1777, at which time he owned a house and lot on East Bay Street, a dock on the Cooper River, another fifteen lots in Charleston, and 5,500 acres of land on the Congaree River.

Gillon first came to public attention when he appeared before the Liberty Tree Committee on January 24, 1770, for violation of the Non-Importation Association boycott. Early in the Revolution, Gillon eagerly attached himself to the patriot cause. He was a member of the Committee of Ninety-Nine (1774), organized the German Fusiliers in 1775 (which he commanded until 1777), and served in the Second Provincial Congress (1775–1776). In 1776 he put his commercial abilities to use supplying munitions to the Continental Congress. In February 1778 Gillon turned down another supply contract with the Continental Congress to accept command of the South Carolina Navy with the rank of commodore. In Amsterdam, in May 1780, Gillon leased the frigate *South Carolina* from the Chevalier Luxembourg of France and set sail from Amsterdam in August 1781. After an ill-fated voyage across the Atlantic, which saw Gillon financially ruined, the *South Carolina* arrived in Philadelphia in May 1782. The *South Carolina* was captured leaving Philadelphia under command of John Joyner in December 1782. The resulting claims against the state arising out of Gillon's brief command of the *South Carolina* were not fully settled until 1856.

After the Revolution, Gillon served in the General Assembly (1783–1791), representing the city districts of St. Philip's and St. Michael's, then the backcountry district of Saxe Gotha. Gillon also became immersed in the conflict between pro-British and anti-British factions in Charleston. He helped found the Marine Anti-Britannic Society and firmly allied himself with Charleston mechanics and the antiaristocratic faction in Charleston politics. In 1784 Gillon lost the election for intendant of Charleston to Richard Hutson, after which he increasingly associated himself with his backcountry supporters and officially moved to his estate, Gillon's Retreat, in Orangeburg District. Reelected to the Tenth General Assembly, Gillon chose instead to serve in Congress (1793–1794) representing the Beaufort-Orangeburg District. He died on October 6, 1794, at Gillon's Retreat and was buried in the plantation cemetery. J. BRYAN COLLARS

Bailey, N. Louise, and Elizabeth Ivey Cooper, eds. *Biographical Directory of the South Carolina House of Representatives.* Vol. 3, *1775–1790.* Columbia: University of South Carolina Press, 1981.

Nadelhaft, Jerome J. *The Disorders of War: The Revolution in South Carolina.* Orono: University of Maine Press, 1981.

Gilman, Caroline Howard (1794–1888). Writer. Born in Boston, Massachusetts, on October 8, 1794, Caroline was the daughter of Samuel Howard, a prosperous shipwright, and Anna Lillie. An orphan by age ten, Caroline was raised in part by an older sister. Her childhood consisted of frequent moves, until the family finally settled in Cambridge. There, a few years later, she met Samuel Gilman, a graduate of the Harvard Divinity School. In 1819 they married and moved immediately to Charleston, South Carolina, where he had been offered a position as minister to a Unitarian congregation. Their marriage produced seven children, with two sons and their youngest daughter dying in infancy.

For Gilman, Charleston was her first permanent home and, even though she retained much affection for the North, she soon came to see herself as a southerner. As hostilities between the two regions increased, Gilman felt compelled to try to reconcile these differences in her writing. From an early age, she had been composing and publishing verse. From 1832 to 1839, as a wife and mother, she turned her attention to publishing and editing a newspaper for young readers and their families called the *Rose-Bud* or *Southern Rose-Bud* and finally, the *Southern Rose.* One of the first publications of its kind, it became hugely popular, especially with women.

In this publication Gilman serialized much of her work, including the novels *Recollections of a Housekeeper* (1834) and *Recollections of a Southern Matron* (1836), both chronicles of domesticity that attempted to show the similarities between households of the North and South, while also stressing the importance of home and hearth. Gilman believed in the power of the family and in women as its moral center. She was convinced that a wife's most important duty was to act with deference in relations with her husband in order to secure domestic tranquility. Gilman counseled women to hold their tongues and, if necessary, to maintain self-control "almost to hypocrisy." She hoped that in attracting both northern and southern readers to her work, she could somehow extend the peace and tranquility of the home to the entire fractious nation. It was a simplistic notion that, like her growing popularity as a writer, would not last beyond the war.

In the mid–nineteenth century Gilman was a well-loved and prolific writer. Between 1835 and 1860, she edited the *Letters of Eliza Wilkinson During the Invasion of Charleston* (1839); produced another novel, *Love's Progress* (1840); published eleven collections of verse, stories, sketches, and "oracles" (used in popular family parlor games); and wrote a tribute to her husband after his death in 1858.

With the firing on Fort Sumter, Gilman surrendered her allegiance to the North and became a strong Southern partisan. In 1862 her home was shelled and she moved to Greenville, where she was active in Confederate volunteer and relief work. On returning to Charleston in 1865, she found most of her possessions and papers either destroyed or stolen.

Gilman spent her last days living with a daughter in Washington, D.C. She published four more books in the 1870s and wrote her last poem at the age of eighty-nine, but she never regained the popularity as a writer that she had enjoyed before the war. She died on September 15, 1888, and was buried beside her husband in the Unitarian cemetery in Charleston. ELLEN CHAMBERLAIN

Beasley, Maurine H. "Caroline H. Gilman." In *Dictionary of Literary Biography.* Vol. 73, *American Magazine Journalists, 1741–1850,* edited by Sam G. Riley. Detroit: Gale, 1988.

Gilman, Samuel Foster (1791–1858). Clergyman. Gilman was born in Gloucester, Massachusetts, on February 16, 1791, the son of merchant Frederick Gilman and his wife, Abigail Hilier Somer. Gilman was schooled privately for Harvard, from which he was graduated in 1811. In 1814 he took a master's degree in theology, also from Harvard. Thereafter, he taught, tutored in mathematics, and prepared for the ministry. In 1819 he married Caroline Howard of Boston. They had seven children.

Reverend Samuel Gilman (1791–1858), by Henry Bounetheau. Watercolor on ivory. Courtesy, Gibbes Museum of Art / Carolina Art Association

In the year of his marriage, Gilman went to Charleston to serve as minister of the Second Independent (or Congregational) Church, which had recently embraced Unitarian views. Under Gilman's leadership, the church expanded and changed its name to the Archdale Street Unitarian Church in 1834. Gilman also helped establish the Charleston Unitarian Book and Tract Society in 1821 and made consistent efforts to spread Unitarian Christianity more widely in the area. Doing so was no easy task in a region generally marked by religious emotionalism and revivalism. Yet Gilman remained staunchly committed to this calling. From his base in Charleston, he promoted additional Unitarian societies, notably in Augusta and Savannah, Georgia, and defended rational religion in print and sermons against attacks by orthodox Calvinist groups.

Gilman's persistence in defending Unitarianism and his growing literary reputation gradually led to his admission into Charleston cultural circles and the acceptance of "Gilman's Church." He and his wife became acknowledged literary figures in Charleston. Gilman's writings appeared in national and regional magazines, such as the *North American Review* and the *Southern Literary Messenger*. His work also appeared in bound volumes, such as his *Memoirs of a New England Village Choir* (1829) and his collected essays, *Contributions to Literature* (1856).

Gilman was somewhat inconsistent in his regional attachments, as seen in his widely separate odes, "Fair Harvard" (1836) and "On the Death of John C. Calhoun" (1850). This dualism usually caused him to prefer national unity and he readily extolled the common heritage of North and South. In response to the nullification crisis, Gilman penned the staunchly nationalistic "Union Ode" (1831) to counter calls for secession and disunion. On the volatile subject of slavery, Gilman maintained a discreet public silence. In private he educated family servants, apparently to prepare them for eventual freedom. When the American Unitarian Association (AUA) intensified its attacks on slavery in the 1850s, Gilman complied with his congregation's wishes to discontinue receiving AUA tracts. Yet he requested that the AUA keep him personally on its mailing lists. Overall Gilman saw his first duty as advancing rational religious understanding, not remaking southern society, and let that duty shape his actions.

Gilman's tireless efforts helped establish Unitarianism as a viable religion in South Carolina and the South, while his religious and secular writings put him at the center of Charleston literary circles. On February 9, 1858, Gilman died suddenly in Kingston, Massachusetts, while on a visit to New England. His body was returned to Charleston and buried in the Archdale Street Church Cemetery. W. CALVIN SMITH

Gibson, George H. "Unitarian Congregations in the Ante-Bellum South." *Proceedings of the Unitarian Historical Society* 12, pt. 2 (1959): 53–78.

Gilman, Samuel. *Contributions to Literature; Descriptive, Critical, Humorous, Biographical, Philosophical, and Poetical.* Boston: Crosby, Nichols, and Company, 1856.

Howe, Daniel Walker. "A Massachusetts Yankee in Senator Calhoun's Court: Samuel Gilman in South Carolina." *New England Quarterly* 44 (June 1971): 197–220.

Macaulay, John A. *Unitarianism in the Antebellum South: The Other Invisible Institution.* Tuscaloosa: University of Alabama Press, 2001.

Girardeau, John LaFayette (1825–1898). Clergyman, educator. Girardeau was born on November 14, 1825, on his family's plantation on James Island, the son of John Bohun Girardeau and Claudia Herne Freer. He attended a school on the island taught by Rawlins Rivers and went to the James Island Presbyterian Church where his parents, grandparents, and numerous relatives were members. Following the death of his mother, he went to the school of the German Friendly Society in Charleston. He entered the College of Charleston at age fourteen and graduated at eighteen. In 1845 he entered Columbia Theological Seminary where he studied under George Howe, Charles Colcock Jones, and Aaron Leland and came under the influence of James Henley Thornwell and Benjamin Morgan Palmer. After his graduation from Columbia in 1848, he served the Wappetaw Independent Presbyterian Church in Christ Church Parish and the Wilton Presbyterian Church at Adams Run on the lower Edisto River. Both of these congregations were composed of wealthy planters and numerous slaves. In 1849 he married Penelope Sarah Hamlin. The couple had ten children.

In 1853 Girardeau was called as pastor to the Anson Street Presbyterian Church, Charleston, a congregation organized for mission to slaves. A powerful preacher who was at home with the Gullah dialect, Girardeau attracted large numbers of African Americans to the congregation. To accommodate the growing crowds, a new church building, Zion Presbyterian, was built on the corner of Calhoun and Meeting Streets primarily with money from the Adger and Smyth families of Charleston. Zion was said to have the largest church sanctuary in the city. A small group of affluent whites belonged to the church, served as officers, and sat in the balcony while the large African American congregation utilized the main floor. Girardeau's work was an experiment in paternalism that drew on the theological and social thought of James H. Thornwell.

During the Civil War, Girardeau served as a chaplain in the Confederate army. He returned to Charleston in 1865 as an advocate for the old order, insisting that southerners must "cling to our identity as a people." He was ousted from the Zion pulpit by northern missionaries, but he later returned at the request of his former black parishioners. His insistence on white leadership for the congregation led to the disaffection of much of the black membership. He resigned in 1875 and accepted a position at Columbia Theological Seminary as Professor of Didactic and Polemic Theology.

At Columbia, Girardeau represented the most conservative elements in the Southern Presbyterian Church. He bitterly opposed his colleague James Woodrow who was advocating a theistic interpretation of evolution. Girardeau wrote several books on theological and liturgical subjects. While he lacked the theological depth and sophistication of his mentors—especially Thornwell—he did have, primarily through the force of his personality and preaching, an influence on his generation of southern white theologians and preachers. He died on June 23, 1898, and was buried in Columbia's Elmwood Cemetery. ERSKINE CLARKE

Blackburn, George, ed. *The Life Work of John L. Girardeau.* Columbia, S.C.: State Company, 1916.

Clarke, Erskine. *Our Southern Zion: A History of Calvinism in the South Carolina Low Country, 1690–1990.* Tuscaloosa: University of Alabama Press, 1996.

Thompson, Ernest Trice. *Presbyterians in the South.* 3 vols. Richmond, Va.: John Knox, 1963–1973.

Gist, States Rights (1831–1864). Lawyer, soldier. Gist was born September 3, 1831, at the family home, Wyoming, in Union District, the ninth of ten children born to Nathaniel Gist and Elizabeth McDaniel. His birth during the nullification crisis prompted his father to give him the unique name.

Schooled at Mount Zion Institute in Winnsboro, Gist was admitted to South Carolina College as a sophomore in 1847. On graduation in 1850 he returned home and began to read law. The following year he entered law school at Harvard University but left the school after one year. In 1853 he was admitted to the South Carolina Bar and established a law office in Unionville. That year Gist joined the state militia, as a captain commanding the Johnson Rifles. The following year, Governor James H. Adams appointed him his aide-de-camp with the rank of lieutenant colonel. In 1856, at age twenty-four, Gist was elected brigadier general, commanding the Ninth Brigade. His cousin, Governor William Henry Gist, appointed him his "Especial Aid-de-Camp" in 1858; in April 1860 General Gist resigned his commission with the Ninth Brigade.

In January 1861 Governor Francis W. Pickens appointed Gist the state's Adjutant and Inspector General. After the bombardment of Fort Sumter in April, Gist went to Virginia and served as a volunteer aide on the staff of Brigadier General Bernard E. Bee. At the Battle of First Manassas, Bee was mortally wounded and Gist was given command of the remnants of the South Carolinian's brigade.

He too was wounded in the battle but recovered and soon returned to the state to resume his duties as Adjutant and Inspector General. On March 20, 1862, Gist resigned and accepted a commission as brigadier general in the Confederate army. He was assigned to the Charleston area, and with the exception of a brief assignment in North Carolina, General Gist served in the defense of the city until May 1863. On May 3 Gist was given command of an infantry brigade and ordered to join a column assembling at Jackson, Mississippi, in response to federal operations against Vicksburg. Just before leaving, he married Jane M. Adams, daughter of former governor Adams, spent two days with his wife, and then headed west. The South Carolinian saw limited action in the Vicksburg campaign. Following the city's surrender, he was ordered to reinforce the Army of Tennessee in northern Georgia.

At the battles of Chickamauga and Chattanooga, and throughout the Atlanta Campaign, Gist proved a reliable and respected commander. Following the evacuation of Atlanta, the Army of Tennessee advanced north and in November entered Tennessee. While leading his brigade in the November 30, 1864, Battle of Franklin, Gist was wounded twice, in the thigh and then in the chest. The second wound proved fatal, and about 8:30 P.M. he died, one of six Confederate generals killed or mortally wounded in the battle. He was buried in a local family cemetery, but in 1866 the remains of States Rights Gist were returned to South Carolina and interred in the Trinity Episcopal Church cemetery in Columbia. RICHARD W. HATCHER III

Cisco, Walter Brian. *States Rights Gist: A South Carolina General of the Civil War.* Shippensburg, Pa.: White Mane, 1991.

Governor William Henry Gist. Portrait by William Harrison Scarborough. Oil on canvas. Courtesy, Greenville County Museum of Art

Gist, William Henry (1807–1874). Governor. Born in Charleston on August 22, 1807, Gist was the son of Francis Fincher Gist and Mary Boyden (Boiden). Following the death of his father in 1819, Gist came into possession of most of the family property, including substantial landholdings in Union District, where he established his home plantation, Rose Hill. Through additional grants and purchases, he added more than 6,700 acres to his original inheritance by 1860. Gist attended South Carolina College but was expelled in 1827 due to his role in the "mess hall rebellion," a student protest against the prohibition of off-campus dining. In 1833 he was indicted as accessory to murder in a confrontation on Union's Main Street, in which his brother-in-law shot and killed man. However, the case was dropped by the circuit court. On May 13, 1828, Gist married Louisa Bowen of Laurens, who died in 1830 eleven days after giving birth to their only child. On October 10, 1832, he married Mary Elizabeth Rice, and their union eventually produced twelve children, although only four lived to adulthood. One of these, William, was killed in the Civil War while leading his regiment at Chattanooga in November 1863.

Gist represented Union District in the state House of Representatives from 1840 to 1843 and in the S.C. Senate from 1844 to 1855. He also acted as lieutenant governor for a period in 1848. An ardent secessionist, Gist was elected governor in 1858. As sectional tensions reached their climax in 1860, Gist did his best to hasten the final push toward secession. His biographer Daniel Bell describes him as "influential" in bringing about disunion, but it is doubtful that his personal leadership was truly essential. By 1860 the movement possessed more momentum than could be attributable to any one man.

In October 1860 he sent his first cousin, States Rights Gist, as his personal emissary to sound out support for secession among the Deep South states. The following month, the governor summoned a special session of the legislature, at which he presented his cousin's favorable reports and asked that a special state convention be called to respond to the election of Abraham Lincoln. Immediately following the completion of his term on December 17, 1860, Gist attended the meeting as a delegate from Union District. Three days later, he placed his signature on the Ordinance of Secession, a document drawn up in the hand of Gist's fellow Union District resident, Benjamin F. Arthur.

During the war Gist sat on the state's governing executive council in 1861. The following year he served as joint head of the Department of Construction and Manufactures. After the war Gist retired to Rose Hill and managed to retain about half of his landholdings. He died on September 30, 1874, and was buried in Union District. ALLAN D. CHARLES

Bell, Daniel J. "Interpretive Booklets for Local Historic Sites: Rose Hill State Park, Union, South Carolina: As A Model." Master's thesis, University of South Carolina, 1983.

Charles, Allan D. *The Narrative History of Union County, South Carolina.* 3d ed. Greenville, S.C.: A Press, 1997.

Gleaves, Richard Howell (1819–1907). Lieutenant governor, jurist, merchant. Gleaves was born July 4, 1819, in Philadelphia, the son of a free black Haitian and an Englishwoman. Educated in Philadelphia and New Orleans, he worked for a time as a trader and steward on the Mississippi River. He lived in Ohio and Pennsylvania from the mid-1840s to the mid-1860s, where he was active in the Prince Hall Masons and helped organize lodges throughout the North. At some point before 1870, he married his wife, Georgianna.

In September 1866 Gleaves moved to Beaufort, South Carolina, where he practiced law and entered into business with Robert Smalls as a merchant and factor. He helped form the South Carolina Union League and was instrumental in the organization of the Republican Party in South Carolina, serving as president of the party's state convention in 1867 and as a state executive committeeman in 1874. During Reconstruction, Gleaves held several state and local offices. From 1870 to 1872, he served as a trial justice, probate judge, and commissioner of elections in Beaufort County. In 1870 he was arrested and charged with election fraud. His first trial resulted in a conviction, but in a second trial he was acquitted. He was elected lieutenant governor of the state in 1872 and reelected in 1874, in which capacity he served as president ex officio of the S.C. Senate. Gleaves also served in the South Carolina state militia as a major and judge advocate in the First Brigade, colonel and aide to the governor, and colonel and judge advocate in the Second Division. He was a trustee of the South Carolina Agricultural College and Mechanics' Institute in 1874 and a warden of Beaufort in 1876.

In 1876 Gleaves ran for reelection on the ticket with incumbent governor Daniel H. Chamberlain. Claiming victory in the general election, Gleaves presided over the first session of the Fifty-Second General Assembly from November 28 to December 22, 1876. When federal authorities recognized Democratic gubernatorial candidate Wade Hampton as governor, however, Gleaves resigned on April 24, 1877. Hampton then appointed him a trial justice for Beaufort on June 9, 1877.

Gleaves left South Carolina in 1877, when a Richland County grand jury indicted him for issuing fraudulent pay certificates to state legislators. He moved to Washington, D.C., where he worked for two years as a clerk in the U.S. Treasury Department before returning to South Carolina as a special inspector of customs for the sixth customs district from 1880 to 1882. After 1882, he moved back to Washington, where he worked as a waiter and steward for the Jefferson Club. Gleaves died in Washington in November 1907.

MICHAEL ROBERT MOUNTER

Bailey, N. Louise, Mary L. Morgan, and Carolyn R. Taylor, eds. *Biographical Directory of the South Carolina Senate, 1776–1985.* 3 vols. Columbia: University of South Carolina Press, 1986.

Foner, Eric. *Freedom's Lawmakers: A Directory of Black Officeholders during Reconstruction.* Rev. ed. Baton Rouge: Louisiana State University Press, 1996.

Glen, James (1701–1777). Governor. Glen was born in Linlithgow, Scotland, sometime in 1701, the eldest son of Alexander Glen and Marion Graham. He studied law at the University of Leiden in the Netherlands and then devoted his career to public service. Following the tradition of his father and two grandfathers, he served on the council of Linlithgow and served as provost (the chief magistrate of a Scottish burgh) from 1724 to 1726 and again from 1730 to 1736. In his quest for imperial office, he secured the support of several influential Scots and was named royal governor of South Carolina in 1738 by prime minister Sir Robert Walpole. Burke's *Peerage* states that Elizabeth Wilson, granddaughter of Sir William Wilson, was the wife of Glen. However, surviving records provide little information about Glen's marriage.

Glen did not arrive in South Carolina until December 1743. The primary reason for his delay in leaving England was inadequate provision for the governor's salary. The Lords of the Treasury finally agreed to provide £800 and left the governor to negotiate housing and other benefits with the South Carolina assembly. This proved difficult as Glen arrived in South Carolina to find "the whole frame of Government unhinged." There was an intense struggle for power in the colony among the governor, the Royal Council, and the Commons House of Assembly, in which the Commons sought to encroach upon royal prerogative at the expense of royal governors.

As governor, Glen remained ever mindful of his royal instructions while attempting to work with both houses of the assembly. He was able to exert influence with his veto and by proroguing the assembly when it proved uncooperative. Glen quickly discovered that many colonial precedents conflicted with imperial orders. The Commons House, for example, selected the public treasurer, issued paper money without required provisions for redemption by a sinking bill, denied the governor's power to make Anglican religious appointments, and ignored English precedents governing elections for the assembly. There were other issues, such as who controlled the commissions for fortifications and the administration of Indian affairs. Selection of agents to represent the colony in England evoked a three-way struggle, but eventually Glen attempted to mediate the more bitter conflict between the two houses of the assembly over this prerogative. When two members of the Commons proposed that the governor sign a tax bill without passage by the council as upper house, he refused the ploy as unconstitutional.

The appointment of the Earl of Halifax as the new president of the Board of Trade in 1748 intensified British supervision of colonial governors and heightened demands for protecting the royal prerogative. This not only made Glen more vulnerable to criticism in England for his conciliatory actions as governor, but also in the colony as the Commons House threatened to complain to imperial officials about his decisions. Yet Glen's position improved in the 1750s. In pragmatic fashion, Glen realigned his political allies by forming connections with the prominent Bull family and other leading planters. He worked more effectively with Lieutenant Governor William Bull, Jr., and provided a fitting climax to cooperation with his eloquent eulogy on the death of William Bull, Sr., in 1755. The marriage of Glen's sister, Margaret, to John Drayton of Drayton Hall in 1752 was also a factor in these new relationships. During his last two years in office, the governor received commendations from the Commons House as its struggle for power turned toward the Council. Glen became a compromiser between the two houses, and he had to defend the right of the council to serve as the upper house of the assembly. Still, imperial officials did not view Glen's handling of the constitutional stalemate in South Carolina with satisfaction, which led to Glen's recall in 1756.

Indian affairs were one of the most critical issues of Glen's administration. He not only visited distant white settlements of the colony more than any other governor, but he was also willing to face frontier hazards to confer directly with Indian leaders. In 1746, for example, Glen met the Cherokees at Saluda near Ninety Six and the Creeks and Chickasaws at Fort Moore on the Savannah River. He arranged land cessions from the Cherokees in 1747, 1753, and 1755. He prevented the Catawbas from taking the traditional blood revenge on the Natchez (Notchees) for murders. In response to a Cherokee request for forts, Glen personally directed the building of Fort Prince George among the lower Cherokees at Keowee in 1753. Glen was en route to build a fort among the upper Cherokees when recalled as governor. However, he was not successful in winning the Choctaws away from French influence due to the failure of the Choctaw revolt of the 1740s.

Governor Glen developed a great love for South Carolina. In 1749 he wrote his *Description of South Carolina,* which was published in 1761. It ranks as the most valuable contemporary account of the colony and compares favorably with any other similar description of American colonies. He vigorously upheld the role of South Carolina against both Virginia and Georgia in Indian affairs, and he objected to Virginia's efforts in seeking Cherokee and Catawba allies for General Edward Braddock's campaign in 1755 against Fort Duquesne. The governor also championed the colony's influence over the Catawbas in contests with North Carolina and advocated a favorable boundary line between the two Carolinas.

Governor Glen's term in South Carolina was the longest of any colonial governor. His administration was marked by success in management of Indian affairs (despite the failure of the Choctaw revolt) and a conscientious effort to uphold the royal prerogative. Having been recalled in 1756, Glen and his wife remained in South Carolina until 1761 and made a modest investment in slaves and a rice plantation near Charleston. On returning to England, Glen arranged for John Drayton to supervise the plantation. He also assisted in the education of Drayton's four sons in England and Scotland. He made loans to Drayton, but the cordial familial relations declined when Drayton did not make regular interest payments on the loan. Glen died on July 18, 1777, and was buried at St. Michael's Church in Linlithgow. W. STITT ROBINSON

Bulloch, Joseph G. B. *A History of the Glen Family of South Carolina and Georgia.* Washington, D.C., 1923.

Robinson, W. Stitt. *James Glen: From Scottish Provost to Royal Governor of South Carolina.* Westport, Conn.: Greenwood, 1996.

Lucile Ellerbe Godbold. Courtesy, Columbia College

Godbold, Lucile Ellerbe (1900–1981). Olympic athlete, educator. More commonly known as "Miss Ludy," Lucile Godbold was born on May 31, 1900, in Marion County. She achieved prominence as one of America's first female Olympic champions and as a pioneer in American women's competitive athletics. Godbold's family moved from Marion County to Estill in Hampton County. A standout athlete at Winthrop College, Godbold broke the United States record in the shot put, the discus throw, and the hop-step-jump (the triple jump) at the college's annual track meet. Winthrop College raised money to send her to qualifying trials in Mamaroneck, New York, where Godbold earned a spot on the track and field team that represented the United States in the First International Track Meet for Women as part of the women's Olympic Games in Paris in 1922. The 1922 women's Olympics were the first of its kind; Olympic events for women were joined with the men's games in 1924. In Paris, Godbold competed in six events and helped the American team place second in the meet. Godbold broke the world's record in the eight pound shot put and secured the gold medal by putting twenty meters and twenty-two centimeters. She also won gold in the hop-step-jump event, placed second in the basketball throw, third in the javelin, and fourth in the three-hundred-meter dash and one-thousand-meter run. An international phenomenon, Godbold received great acclaim on her return to South Carolina. In September of that year, Godbold began her duties as the director of physical education at Columbia College, a private women's college, and remained there for fifty-eight years.

Throughout her life, Godbold earned great recognition, not only for her accomplishments in the Olympic Games, but also for her contributions to Columbia College. Godbold is included in the 1928 edition of *Who's Who in American Sports,* and in the first edition of *Who's Who in American Women,* published in 1957. In 1961 Godbold was the first woman to be elected to the South Carolina Athletic Hall of Fame. In 1972 the town of Estill erected a historical marker in her honor on the fiftieth anniversary of the Paris games. In the same year, the physical education complex at Columbia College was named the Godbold Center in her honor. Despite her athletic accomplishments, Godbold identified herself first and foremost as a teacher, and is remembered for her humility and good humor. On her retirement in 1980, Columbia College awarded her the Columbia College Medallion, the institution's highest honor. She died less than one year later, on April 5, 1981, and is buried in the Lawtonville Cemetery in Estill. Columbia College's annual "Ludy Bowl," a flag football game held every October among the students, continues to commemorate her, as does an endowed scholarship in her name. COURTNEY L. TOLLISON

"American Girls Are Second in Olympics." *New York Times,* August 21, 1922, p. 14.

Rerig, Peter A. "Hometown Girl Makes Gold." *Carologue* 12 (summer 1996): 3.

Spear, Bob. "Step Aside, Boys: Lucile Godbold Made a Name for Herself in Athletics When Men Ruled the Arenas." Columbia *State,* April 4, 1999, p. C1.

Tuttle, Jane P. "Setting the Mark: Lucile Godbold and the First International Track Meet for Women." *South Carolina Historical Magazine* 102 (April 2001): 135–52.

Gold mining. Gold has been mined in South Carolina since the early 1800s. Deposits have generally been concentrated in the lower Piedmont in a geologic zone known as the Carolina slate belt, a band of Precambrian and Cambrian volcanic rock running from Virginia to eastern Alabama. Most early mining operations extracted gold from placer deposits, in which loose gold particles were removed from sand, gravel, or other eroded materials. Lode deposits, in which gold-bearing masses of rock are still in place, required greater outlays of labor and technology to extract and crush the gold-bearing rock, then separate the gold ore from other minerals.

Gold mining began in earnest in South Carolina around 1827. According to legend, Benjamin Haile, a prominent landowner in Lancaster District, was chinking a log cabin with mud from a nearby stream when he noticed flecks of gold. In 1829 Haile made the first shipment of South Carolina gold to the U.S. Mint in Philadelphia. Other gold deposits were discovered shortly thereafter, including the Brewer mine in Chesterfield District, the Ridgeway mine in Fairfield District, and a host of smaller operations in York and Spartanburg Districts. Around 1852, in the western part of Edgefield District (later McCormick County), William Dorn made a gold strike that would make him one of the wealthiest men in the

The Ophir Gold Mine in Union County was one of many that were active in the nineteenth century. Courtesy, South Caroliniana Library, University of South Carolina

upstate. Antebellum production in South Carolina peaked around 1852, however, when just under $127,000 worth of gold was extracted.

Gold mining declined further during the Civil War. General William T. Sherman targeted the Haile mine, which produced pyrites used to make sulphuric acid for the Confederacy. Effective mining was not resumed until the late 1880s, when northern investors began to purchase gold-bearing property and resumed production. The Haile mine was purchased by James Eldredge, a New Yorker who owned the Hobkirk Inn in Camden. Eldredge was then bought out by a New York corporation that began a large-scale twenty-stamp mill operation. Technology was deficient and profits were poor until around 1888, when a German-trained mining engineer, Dr. Adolph Thies, developed a barrel-chlorination process that extracted gold from low-grade sulphite ore. Other advances, such as geological surveys and diamond drilling, further increased production. The Haile mine processed one hundred tons of ore daily in the 1890s and was visited by the foremost mining and metallurgical engineers of the time.

Gold mines in South Carolina were largely dormant from 1900 to 1937. An explosion wrecked the Haile mine in 1908, and it largely ceased operations for the next three decades. But in 1934, the U.S. government increased the price of gold to $35 per ounce, which spurred new mining activity. The Haile mine was rejuvenated in 1937, and became the leading producer of gold in the southeast. World War II brought an end to production, however, when President Franklin Roosevelt ordered the closing of all gold mines. Production in South Carolina all but stopped in the decades following the war, but skyrocketing gold prices in the 1970s and 1980s reinvigorated interest in South Carolina's mines. New extraction techniques added to profitability. The Haile mine reopened in 1981, and by the 1990s gold production had also recommenced at the Brewer, Ridgeway, and Barite Hill (Dorn) sites. South Carolina ranked sixth in the nation in gold production in 1992, but declining profitability and environmental concerns forced most mines to close again by the end of the decade, leaving them to await improvements in technology and location of richer sites that will make resumption of gold mining economically feasible. CANTEY HAILE

McCauley, Camilla K., and J. Robert Butler. *Gold Resources of South Carolina.* Columbia, S.C.: Division of Geology, State Development Board, 1966.
Pardee, Joseph T., and Charles F. Park, Jr. *Gold Deposits of the Southern Piedmont.* Washington, D.C.: Government Printing Office, 1948.
Pittman, Clyde Calhoun. *Death of a Gold Mine.* Great Falls, S.C., 1972.

Goldstein, Joseph Leonard (b. 1940). Scientist, physician, Nobel Laureate. Goldstein was born on April 18, 1940, in Sumter, the only son of Isadore E. Goldstein and Fannie Alpert. Goldstein's research with Michael Brown into cholesterol metabolism and the discovery of low-density LDL receptors brought them joint award of the 1985 Nobel Prize in physiology or medicine.

Goldstein was educated in the public schools of Kingstree, where his parents owned and operated a clothing store. He graduated summa cum laude in 1962 from Washington and Lee University in Lexington, Virginia, with a bachelor of science degree in chemistry. In 1966 he received his medical degree from Southwestern Medical School of the University of Texas Health Science Center in Dallas.

Goldstein and Michael Brown served in the internship and residency program at Massachusetts General Hospital. Together, they discovered the receptor molecule, a structure on cell surfaces that regulates cholesterol levels in blood. They found that the molecule indicates some correlation between blood cholesterol level and heart disease. The National Institutes of Health (NIH), partly because of Goldstein and Brown's work, recommended the lowering of fat in the diet. For their work, the two men received awards from the National Academy of Sciences, the American Chemical Society, the Roche Institute of Molecular Biology, the American Heart Association, and the American Society for Human Genetics.

At the NIH biochemical genetics laboratory, Goldstein studied the molecular biology approach to human disease. He was interested in patients with homozygous familial hypercholesterolemia, a genetically acquired disease that involved a genetic defect causing a metabolic error that results in high blood cholesterol levels and heart attacks. Goldstein then spent two years (1970–1972) as a Special NIH Fellow at the University of Washington at Seattle. There he initiated and completed a population genetic study to determine the frequency of the various hereditary lipid disorders in an unselected population of heart attack survivors.

Goldstein and his colleagues discovered that twenty percent of all heart attack survivors have one of three single-gene-determined types of hereditary hyperlipidemia. One of these disorders was the heterozygous form of familial hypercholesterolemia, which was found to effect one out of every five hundred persons in the general population and one out of every twenty-five heart attack victims. During his fellowship in Seattle, Goldstein became conversant with tissue culture techniques, which proved to be invaluable in his subsequent studies with Brown. Goldstein returned to the University of Texas Health Science Center at Dallas in 1972, where he was named Professor of Medicine and Genetics and Chairman of the Department of Molecular Genetics.

The illuminating research of Goldstein and Brown on the activity of LDL receptors and their function in the management of cholesterol levels has had far-reaching effects. Not only has their work increased understanding of an important aspect of human physiology, but it has also had a practical impact on the prevention and treatment of heart disease. MARSHA POLIAKOFF

Golf. South Carolina is one of the leading golfing states in the nation, in terms of courses, participants, and tournament play. The Grand Strand area alone, anchored by Myrtle Beach, has over one hundred courses, most of which offer vacation packages for tourists. In 2000–2001, the total economic impact of visiting golfers was estimated at $1.5 billion. The state's connection with golf dates back to 1743, when a shipment of 96 golf clubs and 432 golf balls from the port of Leith, Scotland (near Edinburgh), arrived in Charleston. In 1786 the South Carolina Golf Club was established by merchants from Scotland, where the modern game of golf developed.

As of 2004 there were hundreds of courses in South Carolina, 341 of which were members of the South Carolina Golf Association. The SCGA, founded in 1929, sponsored a number of men's, women's, junior, and senior tournaments, including twenty-two designated as major events. The courses on which SCGA-sponsored tournaments are played vary from year to year, and most of the member courses have served as hosts for at least one event.

A number of tournaments of national significance have been played in the Palmetto State. The most prominent is the Heritage tournament of the Professional Golfers Association tour on the Harbour Town course at Hilton Head, begun in 1969. The Ocean Course on Kiawah Island was the site of the 1991 Ryder Cup, in which the United States defeated Europe.

Some of the nation's leading golfing professionals have been either South Carolina natives or have South Carolina connections. Jay Haas, a former Wake Forest University golfer who later made his permanent residence in Greenville, has been one of the most successful players on the PGA tour. He was selected for the United States Ryder Cup teams in 1983, 1995, and 2004, when he became the second oldest player in Ryder Cup history. The state laid claim to the only men's national amateur championship when Chris Patton, a Simpsonville native who played for Clemson University, won the 1989 United States Amateur title.

On the Ladies Professional Golf Association tour, South Carolinians Betsy Rawls and Beth Daniel have been elected to the LPGA Hall of Fame. Rawls, a native of Spartanburg, won fifty-five tour events, including the Women's Open championships in 1951, 1953, 1957, 1959, and 1960, and the LPGA championships in 1959 and 1969. Daniel, a Charleston native who played for Furman University, won the 1990 PGA title among her thirty-two tour victories and was United States Women's Amateur champion in 1976 and 1978. Betsy King, former Furman golfer, won Women's Open championships in 1989 and 1990 and was LPGA champion in 1992. King recorded thirty-four tournament championships on the LPGA tour and is a member of the LPGA Hall of Fame.

College golf is now prominent in South Carolina, with most of the state's institutions producing men's and women's teams. Originally college golf teams were involved mostly in dual meets, but the form is now confined to regional and national tournaments. Among the state's colleges, Clemson and the University of South Carolina have been most prominent in the sport. Clemson has been the only college in South Carolina to win the National Collegiate Athletic Association team championship, having won the 2003 tournament at Norman, Oklahoma. Clemson's Charles Warren, a native of Columbia, won the 1997 NCAA individual championship and later became a regular on the PGA tour. DON BARTON

Fox, William Price. *Golfing in the Carolinas.* Winston-Salem, N.C.: John F. Blair, 1990.

South Carolina. Department of Parks, Recreation and Tourism. *2000–2001 Economic Impact of Golf in South Carolina.* Columbia: South Carolina Department of Parks, Recreation and Tourism, [2002].

Gonzales, Ambrose Elliott (1857–1926). Journalist, businessman. Born on May 29, 1857, in St. Paul's Parish, South Carolina, Gonzales was the son of Cuban general Ambrosio José Gonzales and Harriet Rutledge Elliott. He was raised by his grandmother and aunts in Charleston. Following the Civil War and the death of his mother, Gonzales began learning business as a young man, selling poultry and cutting railroad crossties. He and his younger brother, Narciso, worked as telegraphers at Grahamville, where they fell into favor with Wade Hampton. Gonzales joined his brother at the Charleston *News and Courier* newspaper in 1885, where Narciso had become a leading reporter. Ambrose became the newspaper's general agent, traveling the state telling stories and greeting townspeople. He also developed a following for his corruption-exposing articles and sketches of small towns across the state.

Inspired by the rise of Ben Tillman's hate-mongering but successful campaign for governor in 1890, Ambrose, Narciso, and their younger brother William, founded the *State* newspaper in Columbia as an ardent and outspoken anti-Tillman daily. The first edition appeared on February 18, 1891, with Ambrose holding the titles of publisher, business manager, treasurer, and general manager, all of which he retained until he died. The newspaper was not an

By the 1920s golf had become an important tourist attraction in resort towns such as Camden. Courtesy, South Carolina Historical Society

immediate success, but by the turn of the century was on its way to becoming one of the most influential newspapers in South Carolina. Ambrose's quiet, sober leadership contrasted with Narciso's fiery anti-Tillman editorials, which resulted in his murder at the hands of James H. Tillman, nephew of Governor Tillman, in 1903.

Immediately following the death of his brother, Gonzales reaffirmed to his readers that "The State is pledged anew to the principles for which he gave his life." Under the leadership of Ambrose and his brother William, the *State* staked out its position as South Carolina's leading progressive chronicle of the early twentieth century. William W. Ball, an acting editor of the *State* and later editor of the *News and Courier,* wrote in 1932 that Ambrose Gonzales was "the most important and greatest South Carolinian since Governor Hampton, though South Carolinians do not yet know it." A bachelor, Gonzales died on July 11, 1926, and was buried in Columbia's Elmwood Cemetery. ALAN RICHARD

Jones, Lewis P. *Stormy Petrel: N. G. Gonzales and His State.* Columbia: University of South Carolina Press, 1973.

Latimer, Samuel L., Jr. *The Story of The State, 1891–1969, and the Gonzales Brothers.* Columbia, S.C.: State Printing, 1970.

Pierce, Robert A. *Palmettos and Oaks: A Centennial History of The State, 1891–1991.* Columbia, S.C.: State-Record Company, 1991.

Gonzales, Narciso Gener (1858–1903). Editor. Born on August 5, 1858, in Edingsville on Edisto Island, Narciso G. Gonzales was the son of Ambrosio José Gonzales and Harriet Rutledge Elliott. He was the second of six children. His father had moved to the United States from Cuba in 1848. As a child, Narciso Gonzales was a voracious reader, but his only formal education was a year at St. Timothy's Home School for Boys in Herndon, Virginia. On his return to South Carolina in 1874, he began working as a telegraph operator and became immersed in Democratic Party politics as a supporter of Wade Hampton.

Gonzales's telegraphic skills and his political proclivities led him to become a correspondent for Robert Barnwell Rhett's *Journal of Commerce* in Charleston. He also published a small newspaper of his own in Grahamville, "The Palmetto," which had a run of just two issues. Gonzales's reporting on the Combahee riots of May 1876 beat out Rhett's Charleston rival, the *News and Courier,* and planted the seed for his future in journalism. In 1880 he was invited to join the staff of the *Greenville News* and was soon thereafter hired by the *Charleston News and Courier,* where he worked for several years as a correspondent in Columbia and in Washington, D.C. Gonzales did not conceal his political views and was a vocal opponent of Benjamin R. Tillman's growing popularity in the late 1880s. These confrontations were not limited to the pages of the newspaper. Tillman's nephew, James Tillman, challenged Gonzales to a duel in 1890.

Narciso G. Gonzales. Courtesy, South Caroliniana Library, University of South Carolina

Hoping to give a voice to the conservative wing of the Democratic Party after Ben Tillman's election to the governorship, Gonzales joined with his brother Ambrose to found the State Publishing Company in January 1891, with the financial backing of conservative Democrats. Narciso Gonzales became the editor of the *State,* with its inaugural issue appearing on February 18, 1891. The new paper did not receive a warm welcome from the Tillman administration; the *State*'s reporters were not permitted in the governor's office. Gonzales opposed various causes dear to Tillman throughout the 1890s. He railed against the Dispensary and the constitutional reforms of 1895, and, when Tillman represented South Carolina in the U.S. Senate, he mocked Tillman's mannerisms and deportment.

In addition to berating Tillman and his followers, Gonzales also advanced positive causes. He was a relentless booster of Columbia, economic opportunity, and railroads. He opposed child labor and supported labor unions and public education. Although Gonzales opposed lynching and some Jim Crow legislation, his preferred solution to troubled race relations was the forced emigration of African Americans. When the Spanish-American War broke out in 1898, Gonzales departed for Florida in an attempt to secure a position as guide for American armies. Although unsuccessful in this regard, he still went to Cuba and sent numerous reports back to the *State,* which were published after his death as *In Darkest Cuba.*

Gonzales's feud with the Tillman family ended with his assassination. Gonzales had attacked James Tillman in the press throughout the latter's 1902 gubernatorial campaign. Tillman was not elected, and he shot Gonzales in broad daylight on the corner of Main and Gervais Streets in Columbia on January 15, 1903. Gonzales died four days later and was buried at Elmwood Cemetery. Tillman was acquitted of the crime. A memorial erected in 1905 in Gonzales's honor stands on the corner of Sumter and Senate Streets in Columbia. He was survived by his wife, Lucy Barron, whom he married on November 14, 1901. They had no children. AARON W. MARRS

Hammet, Elizabeth. "Narciso Gener Gonzales." Master's thesis, University of South Carolina, 1930.

Jones, Lewis P. *Stormy Petrel: N. G. Gonzales and His State.* Columbia: University of South Carolina Press, 1973.

Sewell, Michael. "The Gonzales-Tillman Affair: The Public Conflict of a Politician and a Crusading Newspaper Editor." Master's thesis, University of South Carolina, 1967.

Gonzales, William Elliott (1866–1937). Editor. Gonzales was born on April 24, 1866, in Charleston, the son of Ambrosio José Gonzales and his wife, Harriet Rutledge Elliott. Best known as an editor of the *State* newspaper, Gonzales was the youngest of the three Gonzales brothers to run the publication.

The family frequently relocated during William's childhood. By 1869 the Gonzales family had left for Cuba, where his father attempted a career in education. Although initially successful, he failed to retain steady employment. By the time William turned ten years old, his mother had died from yellow fever and his father had deposited his six children with members of his wife's family in Colleton County, South Carolina. During this time, older brother Narciso G. Gonzales became a father figure to young William. Narciso sent William to King's Mountain Military Academy in Yorkville and then to the Citadel in Charleston. Due to a speech impediment,

William quit school in April 1884 with his brother's blessing, and six months later joined Narciso at the *News and Courier* in Charleston. The following year, William began working for the Columbia bureau of the *News and Courier* and moved to the capital city.

While living in Columbia, William met Sara Shiver, the daughter of a wealthy local businessmen. On February 2, 1887, the couple married in a lavish ceremony at Columbia's First Presbyterian Church. Shortly after the marriage, William lost his job with the *News and Courier* as a result of cost cutting by the newspaper. He briefly worked as the secretary to Governor John P. Richardson and participated in several real estate ventures.

By the summer of 1892 Gonzales had joined the staff at the *State* newspaper. He worked as a telegraph editor, proofreader, and headline writer and also wrote features covering topics ranging from criminal trials to travel. By the turn of the century, the *State* had become one of South Carolina's most widely read papers, and William had become news editor. Working under his brother Narciso, William's career in journalism began to take shape. Narciso had served as William's greatest supporter and mentor, and his death at the hands of James Tillman in 1903 severely affected William.

The death of Narciso Gonzales thrust primary responsibility for the newspaper on William's older brother, Ambrose. While his brother ran the paper, William's career flourished. He campaigned enthusiastically for Woodrow Wilson as a Democratic presidential elector. In 1912 William became minister to Cuba, and by 1918 he was named ambassador to Peru. He returned to Columbia, however, following the death of Ambrose Gonzales in 1926. William served as editor, publisher, and president of The State Company, which his family had founded. William Gonzales worked much of his life to ensure the success of the *State* newspaper, striving to maintain its status as a "Columbia Institution." He died in Columbia on October 20, 1937, and was buried in Elmwood Cemetery. KATIE EICHLER

Jones, Lewis P. *Stormy Petrel: N.G. Gonzales and His State.* Columbia: University of South Carolina Press, 1973.

Moore, John Hammond. *Columbia and Richland County: A South Carolina Community, 1740–1990.* Columbia: University of South Carolina Press, 1993.

Goose Creek (Berkeley County; 2000 pop. 29,208). European settlers came to Goose Creek early in the history of the Carolina colony. The unusual name of the waterway may have resulted from its frequent sharp curves that suggested a goose's neck. The rich soil along this Cooper River tributary attracted planters from Barbados, who comprised some of the first settlers. Settlers included Sir John Yeamans and Sir Peter Colleton. The region became the home base of the "Goose Creek Men," the politically and economically powerful faction that consistently challenged the authority of the Lords Proprietors in the colony. While white inhabitants were largely Anglican, many Huguenots were established there after 1700, including the Izard family on the Elms plantation. The Anglican parish of St. James Goose Creek was established in 1706, and the present church was completed in 1719.

By the eighteenth century this prosperous area was famous for its rice production. The prosperity continued throughout the century, and in 1790 the first U.S. census counted a population of 2,787 in St. James Goose Creek Parish, 2,333 of whom were slaves who worked the massive rice plantations. Goose Creek remained a major rice producing region into the nineteenth century, but the Civil War and the end of slavery brought about the demise of the great rice plantations. Hurricanes in the late nineteenth and early twentieth centuries completed the job by destroying rice field dikes.

In the early twentieth century, wealthy northerners bought up land around Goose Creek for hunting preserves and winter homes. The African American population left in large numbers, moving to nearby Charleston or migrating to northern cities. By 1940 the Goose Creek area was a predominantly white community of about five hundred people. Prosperity returned about this time. In November 1941 the United States Ammunition Depot was established near Goose Creek. This facility became the Naval Weapons Annex in 1959. During the same period, industrial development soared in nearby Bushy Park, bringing in even more people.

With growth, the need for an incorporated town became apparent. In 1961 a part of the old Goose Creek area was incorporated into a new town with the same name. In 1978 the Naval Weapons Station was annexed. As a result, the population of Goose Creek underwent a five-fold increase, from 3,656 in 1970 to 17,811 by 1980, making it the largest city in Berkeley County. The continued growth of the Charleston area helped to turn much of Goose Creek into a predominantly white bedroom community. The names of the great plantations that once dominated the area are preserved in the names of housing subdivisions such as Crowfield and Otranto. DAVID E. RISON

Heitzler, Michael J. *Historic Goose Creek, South Carolina, 1670–1980.* Easley, S.C.: Southern Historical Press, 1983.

Stockton, Robert P. *Historic Resources of Berkeley County, South Carolina.* Columbia: South Carolina Department of Archives and History, 1990.

Goose Creek Men. The Goose Creek Men were primarily English Barbadians who immigrated to South Carolina in the seventeenth century seeking land and economic advancement. In order to advance their interests, they formed an opposition faction that for decades exerted considerable influence in Carolina affairs. The shift from tobacco to sugar production in Barbados in the 1640s and 1650s resulted in a dramatic rise in profits and land prices on the island, which greatly reduced opportunities for all but the wealthiest planters. By 1660, servants who had completed their terms of indenture, small and "middling" planters, craftsmen, and younger sons of large planters left Barbados in large numbers. A few returned to England, but most made their way to other Caribbean Islands and the North American colonies. In Carolina, they first settled near the mouth of the Cape Fear River in 1665, then north of Charleston around Goose Creek in 1670. They brought with them proven agricultural and exploration skills, slaves, the parish system, the Anglican Church, and a fierce sense of independence and self-confidence.

The Goose Creek Men were united by common economic interests, such as the trade in Indian slaves and trafficking with pirates. Led by men such as Sir John Yeamans, Maurice Matthews, Robert Daniel, James Moore, James Moore, Jr., and Arthur Middleton, they viewed the Lords Proprietors as political and economic threats to their prosperity and independence. Frequently referred to as the Anti-Proprietary Party, the Goose Creek Men opposed the proprietors at every turn. Gaining control of the Commons House of Assembly, they refused to ratify the Fundamental Constitutions and managed to replace proprietary Governor Joseph West with one of their own, Sir John Yeamans. As a result, proprietary officials, notably Governors West and Joseph Morton, accepted the importance of working with the Goose Creek Men. William, Lord Craven, leader of the proprietors from 1681 to 1697, did not. Throughout the 1680s, the colony was embroiled in bitter factionalism, as

Craven sought to defeat the Goose Creek opposition by strengthening South Carolina's non-Anglican, or dissenter, majority. Craven also tried to intimidate his enemies by removing their leaders from office and denying access to the lucrative Indian trade. In 1686 he sent James Colleton, the brother of proprietor Sir Peter Colleton, to govern South Carolina and rein in the Goose Creek Men once and for all.

Colleton, though experienced, found himself no match for his opponents. They gained his confidence and then led him into a series of political mistakes before deserting him. When he compounded his error by declaring martial law, they undercut his support in the colony with charges of tyranny. Finally they deposed Colleton and in the 1690s established de facto control of the colony through the Commons House of Assembly, which they dominated.

Confrontations between the proprietors and the Goose Creek Men continued, with varying intensity, for another three decades. Proprietary supporters reestablished limited control between 1696 and 1700 before the Goose Creek Men reasserted themselves by championing the establishment of the Church of England. Seven years later, dissenters in the colony, unable to defeat their foes, agreed to cooperate with them. From 1707 to 1719, both sides worked to end proprietary government. The Revolution of 1719, headed by Arthur Middleton, guaranteed the supremacy of the Commons House, a long cherished Goose Creek objective. It was symbolic of the struggle that a Goose Creek man, James Moore, Jr., headed the transitional royal government from 1719 to 1721. LOUIS P. TOWLES

Dunn, Richard S. *Sugar and Slaves: The Rise of the Planter Class in the English West Indies, 1624–1713.* 1972. Reprint, Chapel Hill: University of North Carolina Press, 2000.

Moore, Alexander. "Carolina Whigs: Colleton County Members of the South Carolina Commons House of Assembly, 1692–1720." Master's thesis, University of South Carolina, 1981.

Sirmans, M. Eugene. *Colonial South Carolina: A Political History, 1663–1763.* Chapel Hill: University of North Carolina Press, 1966.

Gospel music. Gospel music as a genre consists of two major categories, white gospel and black gospel. Both styles share similar musical roots that stem from the evangelical religious movements of the 1800s.

Musical practices that led to the development of white gospel originated in the shape-note hymnody of the early nineteenth century, when singing schools were established to teach this technique to settlers in the frontier regions of western and southern states, including South Carolina. In 1835 William "Singin' Billy" Walker of Spartanburg published *Southern Harmony,* an important shape-note songbook that sold more than 600,000 copies during the next twenty-five years. Walker's brother-in-law Benjamin F. White, who was born in Union County, published *The Sacred Harp* in 1844, and this collection also became a cornerstone of the repertory. While the singing school curriculum borrowed from previously established musical traditions, new music that incorporated secular styles and emotional appeal was being composed for the camp meeting revivals that took place at locations such as St. George and Indian Field.

By the 1920s the growing popularity of the music publishing companies (many of which featured shape-note hymnals) and the advent of radio began to bring consistent professionalism to the realm of gospel music. "Southern gospel" was launched with the appearance of the first male gospel quartets; the careers of these groups often began with performances at the intermissions between singing school classes. Although the term "southern gospel" would eventually encompass a variety of styles (country, bluegrass, etc.), the genre at this time was defined by the musical arrangements sold by the Vaughan and Baxter-Stamps publishing companies. Well-known South Carolina quartets from this era included the Hi-Neighbor Quartet from Belton (recorded by Alan Lomax during the 1930s) and the Palmetto State Quartet.

Southern gospel continued to proliferate during the two decades that followed World War II, but the social and political movements of the 1960s and 1970s began to marginalize the constituent audience for this genre. By the 1980s, contemporary Christian music had begun to compete with southern gospel for potential new audiences. In 1988 Charles Waller (who later founded the Southern Gospel Music Association) organized the Grand Ole Gospel Reunion in Greenville. This event brought together old southern gospel groups and served as an inspiration for the video series "Homecoming," which was spearheaded by Bill Gaither. Modern southern gospel in South Carolina is a confluence of past and present musical currents, as heard in the performances of the Red White Family and Bill Wells.

Early black gospel in South Carolina evolved along a similar trajectory that included shape-note hymnody, singing schools, and camp meeting revivals (at locations including Shady Grove and Mount Carmel). Male quartets became prominent in black gospel during the traditional era (from ca. 1930 until ca. 1960), which featured a capella singing and acoustic instruments. Black gospel did not secure a permanent niche on local radio stations until the 1930s, when at least ten different gospel quartets including the Eagle Jubilee Quartet, the Silver Tone Jubilee Quartet, Capitol City Quartet, and the Seven Stars recorded for the Library of Congress from 1936 to 1939. Perhaps the best-known gospel quartet from South Carolina was the Dixie Hummingbirds, one of the most influential groups of the traditional era.

The contemporary gospel era is separated from the traditional era by the addition of multiple lead singers and expanded instrumentation (including electronic instruments). The Brown Brothers of Columbia began singing as an unaccompanied quartet but had added electronic instruments by the 1960s. Louis Johnson of Spartanburg recorded with the Swan Silvertones as an added lead singer; additional recordings that feature two or more leads include those by Charles Brown and Solomon Daniels with the Six Voices of Zion or recordings by the Fabulous Golden Tones of Mullins. Other notable contemporary gospel performers are the Seniors of Harmony from Greenwood and the Spiritualettes.

Black gospel musicians from South Carolina continue to reexamine stylistic practices associated with the traditional era while remaining in sync with cutting-edge musical developments. The Together As One Hymn Choir from Rock Hill revives the earlier styles that provided an early foundation for black gospel. The Gospel Music Workshop of America, the preeminent national organization for black gospel, has several chapters in South Carolina. South Carolina groups such as the Low Country Mass Choir perform songs that reflect the most recent trends in contemporary gospel. WILLARD STRONG

Cusic, Don. *The Sound of Light: A History of Gospel and Christian Music.* Milwaukee: Hal Leonard, 2002.

Goff, James R. *Close Harmony: A History of Southern Gospel.* Chapel Hill: University of North Carolina Press, 2002.

Southern, Eileen. *The Music of Black Americans.* 3d ed. New York: Norton, 1997.

Governors. During the proprietary period (1670–1719), South Carolina governors were appointed by the Lord Proprietors. The next governors were appointed by the British crown from 1719 to 1776. The General Assembly elected governors from 1776 through 1865. From June 30, 1865, through November 29, 1865, the governor was appointed by the president of the United States. Since the end of 1865, governors have been elected by statewide popular vote.

Until late in the twentieth century, gubernatorial candidates were expected to campaign in every county. The opening of tobacco auctions in the Pee Dee always attracted candidates. In this 1946 photograph, gubernatorial hopefuls J. Strom Thurmond and Ransome J. Williams examine tobacco ready for auction. Courtesy, Modern Political Collections, University of South Carolina

Governors appointed by the proprietors worked with a council that was initially composed of separate groups of proprietors' representatives, representatives chosen by local officials, and representatives of the people generally. By 1691 the council was reduced to a two-house legislature that, over time, became dominated by the lower house, the Commons House of Assembly. After 1689 the proprietors appointed a governor for Carolina in Charleston and another for the section "north and east of Cape Fear." Beginning in 1710, a separate governor was continually appointed for North Carolina. An additional governor was appointed in 1682 for a new settlement of Scots, called Stuart's Town, near today's Beaufort until it was destroyed by the Spanish in 1686.

The first governors of South Carolina after American independence held the title "President of State." From adoption of the state's third constitution in 1790 until 1865, governors were elected by the General Assembly to two-year terms. Until 1812 all governors came from Charleston, the economic and political center of the state. The first governor from the upcountry, Andrew Pickens, was elected in 1816. Nevertheless, due to the under representation of the upcountry in the General Assembly, Charleston and the lowcountry remained the center of political, social, and economic power in South Carolina well into the nineteenth century.

Under the 1865 constitution, the governor was popularly elected for the first time. The governor's tenure was for a four-year term, but the term was reduced to two years by the 1868 constitution. An incumbent could run for reelection once. These arrangements remained in place until the 1895 constitution was amended to change the term for the 1926 elections to four years without reelection. The governor could not run for a second four-year term until the constitution was amended prior to the 1982 election.

A governor's power is often measured formally by the occupant's ability to serve more than one term, to propose a budget, to appoint or remove executive branch officers, and to veto legislation. Based on these measures, the governorship in South Carolina has historically been considered weak. The strength of the typical South Carolina governor has more often reflected informal powers such as the governor's personality, ability to persuade legislators, and talent for negotiating compromises.

In recent times, the formal powers of the office have expanded into a stronger executive. The second four-year term is one example. After having shared the power to propose a budget with a budget commission or the State Budget and Control Board since 1920, the modern governor of South Carolina is recognized as the source for the new executive budget proposed for the General Assembly.

Appointment and removal powers have traditionally been limited. For example, a governor could appoint magistrates, but based on a popular local referendum and the advice and consent of the Senate. Intervening boards and commissions, typically filled with legislative appointments, hired many agency directors who operated under direction of the board, not the governor. After the adoption by statute in 1993 of a limited cabinet system of government, eleven cabinet officers may now be removed by the governor and two other cabinet officers may be removed for cause.

An item veto gives the chief executive more institutional strength than a general veto. The item veto has been used by governors for removing special provisos, or "bobtails," from the general appropriations bill. Provisos typically fund a special project as advocated by a local legislator or delegation.

South Carolina's executive branch reflects the "long ballot" by which many officers are defined in the state constitution and elected statewide in addition to the governor. As of 2004, South Carolinians elect a lieutenant governor, secretary of state, attorney general, treasurer, adjutant general, comptroller general, superintendent of education, and commissioner of agriculture. A sweeping report by a citizens' panel, the Governor's Management, Accountability, and Performance Study (MAP) in 2003 proposed the "short ballot" in which only the governor and lieutenant governor would be elected. To further enhance the cabinet-style government, the MAP also recommended that fourteen cabinet departments and clusters should report directly to the governor. A cabinet secretary appointed by the governor and confirmed by the state Senate would lead each cluster.

Whether these recommendations are implemented in whole or in part remains to be seen. What is clear is that the governorship of South Carolina is a dynamic office that has changed frequently, and sometimes dramatically, during the past three hundred years. As the biographies of individual governors show, each has faced common as well as unique challenges, often with mixed results. COLE BLEASE GRAHAM, JR.

Governor	*Term*	*Party*
Proprietary		
William Sayle	1669–1671	
Joseph West	1671–1672, 1674–1682	
John Yeamans	1672–1674	
Joseph Morton	1682–1684, 1685–1686	
Richard Kyrle	1684	
Robert Quary	1685	

Governor	*Term*	*Party*
James Colleton	1686–1690	
Seth Sothell	1690–1692	
Phillip Ludwell	1692–1693	
Thomas Smith	1693–1694	
Joseph Blake	1694–1695, 1697–1700	
John Archdale	1695–1696	
James Moore, Sr.	1700–1703	
Nathaniel Johnson	1703–1709	
Edward Tynte	1709–1710	
Robert Gibbes	1710–1712	
Charles Craven	1712–1717	
Robert Johnson	1717–1719	
James Moore, Jr.	1719–1721	
Royal		
Francis Nicholson	1721–1729	
Robert Johnson	1729–1735	
James Glen	1738–1756	
William H. Lyttelton	1756–1760	
Thomas Boone	1761–1764	
Charles Montagu	1766–1773	
William Campbell	1775	
State		
John Rutledge (President)	1776–1778, 1779–1782	
Rawlins Lowndes (President)	1778–1779	
John Mathews	1782–1783	
Benjamin Guerard	1783–1785	
William Moultrie	1785–1787, 1792–1794	
Thomas Pinckney	1787–1789	
Charles Pinckney	1789–1792, 1796–1798, 1806-1808	
Arnoldus Vanderhorst	1794–1796	Federalist
Edward Rutledge	1798–1800	Federalist
John Drayton	1800–1802, 1808–1810	Dem.-Rep.
James B. Richardson	1802–1804	Dem.-Rep.
Paul Hamilton	1804–1806	Dem.-Rep.
Henry Middleton	1810–1812	Dem.-Rep.
Joseph Alston	1812–1814	Dem.-Rep.
David R. Williams	1814–1816	Dem.-Rep.
Andrew Pickens	1816–1818	Dem.-Rep.
John Geddes	1818–1820	Dem.-Rep.
Thomas Bennett	1820–1822	Dem.-Rep.
John L. Wilson	1822–1824	Dem.-Rep.
Richard I. Manning	1824–1826	Dem.-Rep.
John Taylor	1826–1828	Dem.-Rep.
Stephen D. Miller	1828–1830	Democrat
James Hamilton, Jr.	1830–1832	Democrat
Robert Y. Hayne	1832–1834	Democrat
George McDuffie	1834–1836	Democrat
Pierce M. Butler	1836–1838	Democrat
Patrick Noble	1838–1840	Democrat
Barnabas K. Henagan	1840	Democrat
John P. Richardson	1840–1842	Democrat
James H. Hammond	1842–1844	Democrat

Governor	*Term*	*Party*
William Aiken	1844–1846	Democrat
David Johnson	1846–1848	Democrat
Whitemarsh B. Seabrook	1848–1850	Democrat
John H. Means	1850–1852	Democrat
John L. Manning	1852–1854	Democrat
James H. Adams	1854–1856	Democrat
R. F. W. Allston	1856–1858	Democrat
William H. Gist	1858–1860	Democrat
Francis W. Pickens	1860–1862	Democrat
Milledge L. Bonham	1862–1864	Democrat
Andrew G. Magrath	1864–1865	Democrat
Benjamin F. Perry (provisional)	1865	
James. L. Orr	1865–1868	Conservative
Robert K. Scott	1868–1872	Republican
Franklin J. Moses, Jr.	1872–1874	Republican
Daniel H. Chamberlain	1874–1876	Republican
Wade Hampton III	1876–1879	Democrat
William D. Simpson	1879–1880	Democrat
Thomas B. Jeter	1880	Democrat
Johnson Hagood	1880–1882	Democrat
Hugh S. Thompson	1882–1886	Democrat
John C. Sheppard	1886	Democrat
John P. Richardson	1886–1890	Democrat
Benjamin R. Tillman	1890–1894	Democrat
John G. Evans	1894–1897	Democrat
William H. Ellerbe	1897–1899	Democrat
Miles B. McSweeney	1899–1903	Democrat
Duncan C. Heyward	1903–1907	Democrat
Martin F. Ansel	1907–1911	Democrat
Coleman L. Blease	1911–1915	Democrat
Charles A. Smith	1915	Democrat
Richard I. Manning	1915–1919	Democrat
Robert A. Cooper	1919–1922	Democrat
Wilson G. Harvey	1922–1923	Democrat
Thomas G. McLeod	1923–1927	Democrat
John G. Richards	1927–1931	Democrat
Ibra C. Blackwood	1931–1935	Democrat
Olin D. T. Johnston	1935–1939, 1943–1945	Democrat
Burnet R. Maybank	1939–1941	Democrat
Joseph E. Harley	1941–1942	Democrat
Richard M. Jefferies	1942–1943	Democrat
Ransome J. Williams	1945–1947	Democrat
James Strom Thurmond	1947–1951	Democrat
James F. Byrnes	1951–1955	Democrat
George B. Timmerman	1955–1959	Democrat
Ernest F. Hollings	1959–1963	Democrat
Donald S. Russell	1963–1965	Democrat
Robert E. McNair	1965–1971	Democrat
John C. West	1971–1975	Democrat
James B. Edwards	1975–1979	Republican
Richard W. Riley	1979–1987	Democrat
Carroll A. Campbell, Jr.	1987–1995	Republican
David M. Beasley	1995–1999	Republican
James H. Hodges	1999–2003	Democrat
Mark Sanford	2003–	Republican

Edgar, Walter. *South Carolina: A History.* Columbia: University of South Carolina Press, 1998.

Jones, Lewis P. *South Carolina: One of the Fifty States.* Orangeburg, S.C.: Sandlapper, 1985.

Governor's Mansion (Columbia). Atop one of Columbia's highest points rests the South Carolina Governor's Mansion, seat of the state's executive power and home to its first family. At 16,300 square feet, the two-story stucco building is best described as a grand home that fuses a reverence for the past with modern conveniences.

Until 1869 South Carolina never furnished its executive officer with a residence. Governors used their private homes to serve as the seat of the state's executive office. However, amid the backdrop of a postwar housing shortage, Governor James L. Orr interrupted this tradition. Hoping to secure permanent accommodations for the executive office on a modest budget, Orr proposed to use property already owned by the state. The plan approved by the legislature involved transforming the remnants of the Arsenal Military Academy, which by 1865 lay in ruins save for a few dependencies and "two two-story brick tenement dwelling houses" constructed in 1856 as officers' quarters. Bounded by Richland, Lincoln, Laurel, and Gadsden Streets, the parcel of land and the duplex proved a logical, if not fitting, setting for what would become home to the state's chief executive. Within the year the structure was renovated and Orr's successor, Robert K. Scott, occupied it. However, three successive governors chose to live at their private residences, and it was not until 1879, when William D. Simpson became governor, that the property permanently became the state's official Governor's Mansion.

For the next 125 years the mansion grew to better accommodate the needs of each administration. Rooms were modified, added, or removed. New household conveniences were installed as technology improved. As styles changed, first families purchased new furnishings when possible. The grounds were landscaped. Improvements eventually included purchasing two neighboring antebellum homes—the Lace House in 1968 and the Caldwell-Boyleston Mansion in 1978—to offer more space for state functions and administrative offices. All three buildings became physically and visually connected in 1986 when the 800 block of Richland Street was closed to create the Governor's Green, a plaza featuring a large fountain.

Despite these improvements, by 1999 the former military quarters had been "extended, manipulated, retrofitted, and abused" to the point that a major overhaul was required. Renovation of the building occurred during the next two years with every aspect of the property upgraded including plumbing, wiring, and structural and aesthetic work. New construction added five thousand additional square feet. The building's interior featured a comprehensive selection of South Carolina antiques and fine art. Following its $2.5 million renovation, the Governor's Mansion struck a sympathetic balance of old and new—updated, yet maintaining the historical identity that has made the property a statewide cultural landmark. See plates 24 and 25. JOHN M. SHERRER III

Edwards, Ann D., et al. *The Governor's Mansion of the Palmetto State.* Columbia: State Printing, 1978.

Robertson, Lynn, and John Sherrer. *The Governor's Mansion of South Carolina, 1855–2001.* Columbia, S.C.: Governor's Mansion Foundation, 2002.

Governor's Schools. South Carolina has two Governor's Schools, one emphasizing arts and humanities, another for science and mathematics. The schools offer advanced learning for the gifted and talented in a residential context.

The Governor's School for the Arts and Humanities began at Furman University as a summer honors program in 1981. This school serves as a laboratory for new and emerging concepts in the arts, humanities, and other educational areas. Gifted students can participate in master classes, private studio lessons, individual and ensemble study, seminars, and workshops. In 1999 the school relocated to an eight-acre site near the Reedy River Falls. The campus replicates an Italian village with ambience befitting the arts, located in the heart of Greenville's art community. In addition to a traditional academic curriculum with an interdisciplinary arts and humanities emphasis, art departments include creative writing, dance, music, drama, and visual arts, while the humanities curriculum is an integrating focus for all areas of study.

Governor Carroll Campbell first suggested the establishment of a Governor's School for Science and Mathematics (GSSM). Located in Hartsville, GSSM is a public residential high school for academically gifted and talented juniors and seniors. Among the rare specialized high schools nationally, GSSM's class schedule is more like that of a college than high school. Students are required to do an independent research project. There is a January interim semester for a variety of educational experiences.

Special outreach activities at the two governor's schools include a distance learning program, summer programs, teaching workshops, honors programs, Team Gear Up, and Residential Arts Academies. These programs are available to high school and some middle school students. Graduates of Governor's Schools attend top colleges statewide and nationally with substantial specialized preparation to succeed. DAN G. RUFF

Grace, John Patrick (1874–1940). Politician. Of Irish descent, Grace was born on December 30, 1874, in Charleston, the son of James I. Grace and Elizabeth Daly. On November 27, 1912, he married Ella Barkley Sullivan, but left no heirs. After various employment experiences, Grace was hired by Congressman William Elliott of Beaufort in 1899 to be secretary of his Washington office. Grace graduated from Georgetown University Law School in 1902 and became the law partner of W. Turner Logan in Charleston. A racial progressive for his time, in 1907 Grace defended two black farm laborers charged with breaking the state's peonage law. He not only won an acquittal, but also succeeded in having the federal district court in Charleston rule the peonage law unconstitutional.

Following an unsuccessful run for the U.S. Senate in 1908, Grace ran for mayor of Charleston in 1911. A brash, demagogic campaigner, Grace narrowly won, thanks to strong support in the city's ethnic and working-class wards. During his first term (1911–1915), Grace accelerated park construction, enacted health legislation, improved rail access to Charleston at competitive rates, and tried unsuccessfully to buy the electric company in order to lower rates for consumers.

Associated with the Reform wing of the South Carolina Democratic Party, which was allied with the controversial former governor Cole Blease, Grace was an ardent foe of progressive Governor Richard I. Manning. Manning and Grace clashed over enforcement of state liquor laws in Charleston, which Manning thought too lax. During the heated campaign of 1915, the governor sent militia to police the election, and Grace lost by twenty-eight votes.

Opposed to United States involvement in World War I, Grace edited the *Charleston American* from 1916 to 1917. Pro-German and anti-British, the newspaper attacked President Woodrow Wilson and Governor Manning on the war issue and eventually lost its bulk mail rate. To save the paper, Grace resigned as editor.

In 1919 Grace was again elected mayor of Charleston with one campaign theme—control of the docks. During this administration (1919–1923), Grace bought the decaying wharves from the Terminal Company and waged a tenacious battle to create the Ports Utility Commission—the forerunner of the State Ports Authority—to manage the docks. Also, Grace provided free education at Charleston High School and the College of Charleston and promoted downtown development through the construction of the Fort Sumter and Francis Marion hotels.

In 1923 Thomas P. Stoney defeated Grace in another bitterly contested election. Out of office, Grace still continued his interest in Charleston's development. He made perhaps his greatest contribution to the city with the opening of the Cooper River Bridge in 1929. Grace was president of Cooper River Bridge, Inc., which built the bridge connecting Charleston with Mount Pleasant, Sullivan's Island, and the Isle of Palms. Grace's dream was to make the Isle of Palms a tourist destination that rivaled Miami, Florida. The bridge was a financial failure, however, and Charleston County bought it in 1941 and soon sold it to the state.

Grace died in Charleston on June 25, 1940, and was buried in St. Lawrence Cemetery. In 1943 the Cooper River Bridge was renamed the Grace Memorial Bridge in his honor. ALEXIA JONES HELSLEY AND TERRY LYNN HELSLEY

Annan, Jason, and Pamela Gabriel. *The Great Cooper River Bridge.* Columbia: University of South Carolina Press, 2002.

Boggs, Doyle Willard, Jr. "John Patrick Grace and the Politics of Reform in South Carolina, 1900–1931." Ph.D. diss., University of South Carolina, 1977.

Helsley, Terry Lynn. "'Voices of Dissent': the Antiwar Movement and the State Council of Defense in South Carolina, 1916–1918." Master's thesis, University of South Carolina, 1974.

Rosen, Robert. *A Short History of Charleston.* San Francisco: Lexikos, 1982.

Gragg, Rod (b. 1950). Historian. Gragg was born in Asheville, North Carolina, on May 28, 1950, the son of L. W. ("Skip") Gragg, a small businessman, and Elizabeth Virginia Lunsford. In 1954 the family moved to Conway, South Carolina, where Gragg graduated from Conway High School in 1968. He attended the University of South Carolina where he obtained a bachelor of arts degree in Journalism in 1972 and a Master of Arts degree in American History in 1979. He married Cindy Outlaw of Florence on December 22, 1973, and they have seven children.

Gragg began his writing career in broadcast news at a local radio station while in high school. While attending USC in 1971–1972, he was a member of the capitol press corps, serving as a legislative reporter for AP Sound, a division of the Associated Press. In 1972 he worked as a news editor and reporter for television station WBTW-TV in Florence. From 1974 to 1976, Gragg was news director and early anchor for WWAY-TV, Wilmington, North Carolina, and from 1976 to 1977 he was a news reporter for WBTV in Charlotte, North Carolina. As a newspaper columnist, he wrote for the Myrtle Beach *Sun News* (1980–1986) and the *Charlotte Observer* (1981–1983). Gragg served as executive editor for *Pee Dee Magazine* from 1991 to 1998 and presently serves as a senior editorial consultant for Rudledge Hill Press. In addition, since 1983 he has owned and managed Southern Communications Services, Inc., a marketing and public relations agency serving local, regional, and national clients.

Gragg served as director of public information for Montreat College in North Carolina in 1977–1978 and later as director of public relations at Coastal Carolina University in his hometown (1978–1983). He began teaching history courses on the U.S. military and the American Civil War at Coastal Carolina in the early 1980s and remains an adjunct faculty member in the history department there.

Gragg is the author of thirteen books on American history, including *The Civil War Quiz and Fact Book* (1985); *Confederate Goliath: The Battle of Fort Fisher* (1991), winner of the Fletcher Pratt Award for Civil War History; *The Illustrated Confederate Reader* (1989), winner of the Douglas Southall Freeman Award for History; *Covered with Glory: The 26th North Carolina Infantry at Gettysburg* (2000), winner of the James I. Robertson Award for the Best Civil War Book of the Year; *Commitment to Valor: A Character Portrait of Robert E. Lee* (2001); *From Foxholes and Flight Decks: Letters Home from World War II* (2002); *From Fields of Fire and Glory: Letters of the Civil War* (2002); and *Lewis & Clark: On the Trail of Discovery* (2003). Gragg has earned praise from historians and critics for his books that are rich with history and powerful in their message. Author and historian Clyde N. Wilson wrote about *Covered with Glory,* "A superb story has met a superb writer." LINDA HOLLANDSWORTH

Graham, Lindsey Olin (b. 1955). Lawyer, congressman, U.S. senator. Graham was born in Central on July 9, 1955, the son of Florence James Graham, a restaurant/bar owner, and his wife, Millie. He graduated from the University of South Carolina in 1976 and the University of South Carolina Law School in 1981. From 1982 to 1988 he was on active duty with the Air Force as a staff judge advocate (military attorney). Since then, he has continued his military career in the reserves. Among his duties during the first Gulf War was briefing pilots on the law of armed conflict. Graham left the air force in 1988 and opened a law practice in Oconee County.

Graham served one term in the South Carolina House before being elected to the U.S. House of Representatives during the 1994 "Republican sweep," in which the Republicans seized control of both the Senate and House for the first time in forty years. It was also the first time a Republican had represented South Carolina's Third Congressional District since 1877. In 1994 Graham campaigned on Georgia congressman Newt Gingrich's Contract with America platform, but three years later Graham and a group of conservative Republicans tried unsuccessfully to end Gingrich's tenure as Speaker of the House. Graham came to national prominence in 1998 when he served as a prosecutor in the impeachment trial of President Bill Clinton, convened to determine whether Clinton committed perjury by trying to conceal an affair with a staff intern.

Graham was elected to four terms as U.S. congressman from the Third District. He worked to balance the federal budget, lower taxes, and increase military spending. During the 2000 presidential election, Graham supported U.S. Senator John McCain rather than George W. Bush for the Republican nomination. Graham's support for the somewhat maverick McCain exemplified his occasional willingness to break with the Republican establishment. Graham defeated former judge and College of Charleston president Alex Sanders in 2002 to replace Strom Thurmond in the U.S. Senate. As senator, Graham has supported the agenda of President George W. Bush, voting for the president's tax cut plan and supporting the war in Iraq, although not uncritically. He was an outspoken critic of the way U.S. soldiers treated Iraqi captives in 2004. "When you are the good guys, you've got to act like the good guys," Graham told a television reporter. That same year, Graham showed his willingness to compromise with Democrats when he and Senator Hillary Clinton coauthored a bill to improve benefits for soldiers serving in the National Guard. LYN RIDDLE

Granby. Situated at the head of navigation of the Congaree River, Granby was among the first important trading posts in the South Carolina interior. The town originated as a large Indian village on Congaree Creek. In 1716 colonial officials entered into an agreement with the Cherokee Indians to establish the first inland trading post. With the addition of a fort in 1748, the site became known as Congaree Fort. In 1754 a Swiss immigrant named Friday purchased one hundred acres on the Congaree and established a ferry. The area became known as Granby, where a trading post was built in 1765 by merchants James Chesnut and Joseph Kershaw. This two-story frame building stood for almost two hundred years. Occupied by the British during the Revolutionary War, it was known as Fort Granby and was the site of several skirmishes between British and patriot forces. The wartime heroine Emily Geiger was interrogated by the British during the time they occupied Fort Granby.

After the war, Granby continued to flourish. When Lexington County was established in 1785, Granby was named the seat of government. President George Washington visited Granby on his southern tour in 1791 and recorded a favorable impression of the prosperous town. In 1802 John Drayton described Granby as a settlement of two hundred houses, considerably larger than neighboring Columbia which had between eighty and one hundred houses. But the growth of Columbia eventually eclipsed Granby. Constant flooding forced the removal of the county seat to Lexington in 1820. By 1826 Robert Mills observed that Granby was "nearly deserted." All that remains is the Granby Cemetery, which has gravestones dating to the eighteenth century. LEO REDMOND

Grand Strand. South Carolina's Grand Strand is an uninterrupted strip of sandy beaches that officially stretches along sixty miles of Horry and Georgetown Counties, from the North Carolina / South Carolina border south to Winyah Bay. Unofficially, the Grand Strand has referred to the greater Myrtle Beach area since the early 1920s, following the distribution of a promotional article entitled "Myrtle Beach, South Carolina, America's Finest Strand." Home to approximately 216,000 people, the Grand Strand is an unbroken strip of municipalities and communities strung together by U.S. Highway 17. One of the primary tourist destinations in South Carolina, the Grand Strand hosts more than thirteen million visitors annually. Horry County leads the state in tourism, accounting for more than thirty-eight percent of tourism revenues and forecast to gross approximately $6.6 billion in sales in 2004.

Until the early 1900s the beaches of Horry County were virtually uninhabited due to the county's geographical inaccessibility and poor economy. Indeed, the beach and surrounding marshes were considered worthless for farming, and the lack of natural harbors forestalled any seacoast development. The area that would become Myrtle Beach came into existence because of its rich timber resources, not its pristine beach. Among the timber farmers and companies that worked in the area, Franklin Gorham Burroughs of Conway and Benjamin G. Collins were chief landowners in the county, possessing about 100,000 acres, two-thirds of which were located along the Atlantic coast. By the 1890s, Burroughs realized that geographic obstacles were going to have to be overcome in order to get his company's timber and turpentine to market more efficiently. He also understood that accessibility to visitors would give the beach significant potential as a resort, such as Atlantic City, New Jersey, and Coney Island, New York. The Conway and Seashore Railroad, completed in 1900, immediately began to change the nature of the beach from a timber and agricultural region to a tourist resort. In the twenty-first century, accessibility to the beach and within the area continued to be a challenge, impacting the health of the tourist economy and land development, as well as the quality of life on the Grand Strand.

These magnificent sand dunes at Myrtle Beach were typical of the coastal landscape in the 1930s. Courtesy, South Caroliniana Library, University of South Carolina

From its earliest days, the coast was promoted as a family resort. The first visitors were middle-class and blue-collar families from the Carolinas seeking a summer getaway in their own "backyard." The tourist season originally ran from Easter through Labor Day, but by the 1970s it stretched almost year-round, with attractions to please every age and desire: countless all-you-can-eat seafood restaurants and pancake houses, dozens of miniature golf courses, more than one hundred championship golf courses, eleven campgrounds with a total of seven thousand campsites, amusement parks, arcades, water parks, shopping malls, country-music concert venues, fishing piers, and, of course, the beach. In recent years, Ripley's Aquarium, the Butterfly Pavilion, Planet Hollywood, NASCAR Speed Park, the House of Blues, and Hard Rock Café have joined the Grand Strand entertainment venues. In the 1990s, the Grand Strand added Broadway at the Beach, a 350-acre entertainment and shopping complex, and the Coastal Federal Field stadium, home to baseball's Myrtle Beach Pelicans, a Class A farm team for the Atlanta Braves.

Some visitors came and never left. Retirees have helped make the Myrtle Beach Metropolitan Statistical Area the thirteenth fastest growing area in the nation, according to the 2000 census. Horry County is the number-one choice for retirees relocating to the state. During the 1990s, the county's population of sixty-five years and older grew by fifty percent.

Improvements and additions continued for the Grand Strand into the twenty-first century. Myrtle Beach International Airport underwent a multimillion-dollar expansion, the 1.5-million-square-foot Coastal Grand-Myrtle Beach Mall opened in mid-2004, and construction began on the Grande Dunes Resort, an exclusive mixed-use community covering 2,200 acres of coastal real estate. As the communities of the Grand Strand continued to build and grow, they also actively sought solutions to traffic congestion, environmental and natural resource issues, mounting tax burdens, visual pollution, sprawl, economic diversification, and preservation of the culture that has attracted visitors to the beach for more than one hundred years. BARBARA STOKES

Bedford, A. Goff. *The Independent Republic: A Survey of Horry County South Carolina History.* 2d ed. Conway, S.C.: Horry County Historical Society, 1989.

Lewis, Catherine H. *Horry County, South Carolina, 1730–1993.* Columbia: University of South Carolina Press, 1998.
Rogers, Aïda. "A Grander Strand." *Sandlapper* 13 (summer 2002): 14–19.

Graniteville Company. Chartered by the South Carolina General Assembly in December 1845, the Graniteville Company was one of the earliest and most successful textile manufacturing operations in the South. The guiding light behind its creation was William Gregg, a highly successful Charleston jeweler-turned-manufacturer who became a leading proponent of southern industrialization during the antebellum era. With an initial capitalization of $300,000 raised primarily from the Charleston mercantile community, the company commenced operations in 1849 in a massive granite factory located on the banks of Horse Creek in southern Edgefield District (now Aiken County). After some initial teething, the company quickly proved highly prosperous, producing shirting and sheeting that sold well in markets as far away as Philadelphia and New York. Graniteville was also unusual in that it employed the labor of free white laborers, mostly women and teenaged children, at a time when most southern manufacturers used the labor of black slaves. During the Civil War, Graniteville produced cloth for the Confederate government as well as the civilian market. It was also one of the few southern manufacturing companies to survive the war largely intact, and resumed civilian production shortly after the end to hostilities.

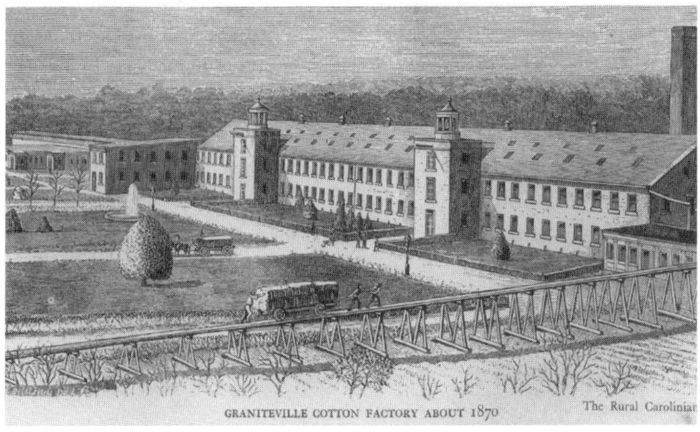

The Graniteville Company was the most successful textile enterprise in nineteenth-century South Carolina. Courtesy, South Carolina Historical Society

The Graniteville Company expanded in the decades following the war, building new factories at neighboring Vaucluse and Warrenville and acquiring two mills (Sibley and Enterprise) in nearby Augusta, Georgia. Declining profits forced the company into receivership briefly in 1915, but it emerged in just seventeen months, thanks to government orders brought about by America's entry into World War I. The 1920s and 1930s were lean years for Graniteville, with increasing competition and the Great Depression taking a toll on company profits. War orders during the 1940s again improved the fortunes of the company, allowing the company to pay off all its debts and embark on a massive postwar modernization plan. In the years following the war, Graniteville Company pioneered the production of permanent-press textiles. Acquired by Avondale Mills, Inc., in 1996, the remaining Graniteville facilities continued to produce high quality denim, cotton, and specialty fabrics. TOM DOWNEY

Gregg-Graniteville Collection. University of South Carolina-Aiken Library, Aiken.
Mitchell, Broadus. *William Gregg: Factory Master of the Old South.* 1928. Reprint, New York: Octagon, 1966.
Special issue on Graniteville. *Textile World* (June 1976).
Wallace, David Duncan. "A Hundred Years of William Gregg and Graniteville." Manuscript. David Duncan Wallace Papers. South Carolina Historical Society, Charleston.

Grave-site decoration. Grave-site decorations in many of South Carolina's African American cemeteries originate from African traditions. West Africans transported to South Carolina as slaves had their own belief system regarding death, burial, and the power of the living and the dead.

West African tradition does not view death in isolation from life or birth, but as complementary to them. The Yoruba believe that death is not the end of life, but a means whereby the earthly existence is transformed to another state of being. In the Akan doctrine, the death of a loved one is only considered a tragedy for the person who adheres to an individualistic philosophy. The Akan recognize that the death of a family member is ripe with opportunities for ancestral intervention. These concepts are key to understanding the ritual of decorating or preparing the grave site.

Care and preparation of the grave site was seen as an obligatory respectful veneration to the dead as well as a precaution for the living. While full of positive possibilities, the recognition of the wrath of an unhappy, vindictive, or unsettled spirit released into the world of the living was always a concern. The grave site was considered to be a base of power activated by substance and ritual.

Shiny or reflective materials like mirrors, silver painted objects, and tin foil were commonly placed on grave sites. The shiny reflective materials may have represented the desire to steer the spirit on a smooth passage over a body of water, or a means for the living to catch a reflective glimpse of the spirit. Medicine bottles, dishes, and eating utensils placed on the graves, sometimes turned upside down and broken to possibly free the spirit and break the chain of death, were probably items used by the deceased during the last stages of illness. Kerosene lanterns and lamps were sometimes placed to light the way of the spirit back home. Messages written in bold, bright colors placed on and around the grave site were considered very potent protective forces. Seashells, very often seen on West African burial sites, were widely utilized on South Carolina's coastal burial sites, and often outlined the grave in a variety of patterns, possibly to confuse malevolent spirits.

African American burial traditions have undergone a tremendous evolution. Modern grave sites, synthesizing African and European practices, utilize more and larger headstones, potted plants, silk flowers, and Styrofoam decorations. But there remains a subtle manifestation of the African heritage in African American burial, mourning, and grave-site practices. DEBORAH WRIGHT

Danquah, J. B. *The Akan Doctrine of God.* 2d. ed. London: Frank Cass, 1968.
Idowu, E. Bolaji. *Olodumare: God in Yoruba Belief.* London: Longmans, 1962.
Jones-Jackson, Patricia. *When Roots Die: Endangered Traditions on the Sea Islands.* Athens: University of Georgia Press, 1987.
Nichols, Elaine, ed. *The Last Miles of the Way: African-American Homegoing Traditions, 1890–Present.* Columbia: South Carolina State Museum, 1989.
Pyatt, Sherman E., and Alan Johns. *A Dictionary and Catalog of African American Folklife of the South.* Westport, Conn.: Greenwood, 1999.
Thompson, Robert F. *Flash of the Spirit: African and Afro-American Art and Philosophy.* New York: Random House, 1983.
Vlach, John M. "Graveyards and Afro-American Art." *Southern Exposure* 5, nos. 2–3 (1977): 161–65.

Gray, Wil Lou (1883–1984). Educator, public servant. Gray was born on August 29, 1883, in Laurens, the middle child and only daughter of William Lafayette Gray, a lawyer, successful merchant-farmer, and state representative from Laurens County, and Sarah Louise Dial, sister of U.S. Senator Nathaniel Barksdale Dial. Her name combining those of her parents, Wil Lou was raised as part of South Carolina's affluent class. The Grays were influential civic leaders, devoted Methodists, conservative Democrats, and contributors to the industrial development of their town. At the age of nine, Gray suffered the loss of her mother from tuberculosis. She lived with relatives until her father remarried and remained in Laurens until her graduation from high school in 1899.

Wil Lou Gray. Courtesy, South Caroliniana Library, University of South Carolina

Gray graduated from Columbia College in 1903 and accepted a teaching position in a one-room, rural schoolhouse in Greenwood County. This experience opened her eyes to the poverty, illiteracy, and public indifference to the problems in her region and inspired Gray to pursue graduate work. At Vanderbilt University in 1905 and Columbia University in 1910, Gray developed a progressive educational philosophy that defined the direction of her career as an educator. At Columbia she studied under William Archibald Dunning and James Harvey Robinson, leading scholars of the day. She was exposed to cutting-edge educational philosophies that promoted the schoolhouse as an agent of democracy, a tenet much evident in Gray's teaching methods. In 1911 she received a master's degree in political science, and she forged a relationship with Columbia that led many scholars over the years to visit South Carolina and observe her work with adult learners.

The combination of Gray's advanced education and her experience as a rural teacher fueled an interest in educational experiments focused on adult learners. Gray's work exposed her to the harsh living conditions and illiteracy of the families in her region and convinced her to do something about "the ignorance of grown people." While serving as supervisor of rural schools in Laurens County, she formed her first adult night school in Youngs Township in 1915. From this humble beginning Gray emerged as a leader in adult education. By 1918 she was a field-worker for the South Carolina Illiteracy Commission and from 1921 to 1946 served as the South Carolina Supervisor of Adult Education. While supervisor, Gray experimented with night schools, summertime lay-by schools (four-week sessions held in August), and adult-oriented educational camps called "opportunity schools." Gray is best known for her opportunity schools, first held in 1921 at the Daughters of the American Revolution camp at Tamassee in Oconee County. Initially open to women only, these summer camps grew to include men and eventually African Americans. Her curriculum included home economics, lessons in etiquette, experiential learning, practical application of skills to everyday experiences, Christianity, and citizenship—legacies of her training and lessons rooted in the values of her class. These summer programs evolved into a year-round boarding school for adults by 1947, when Gray obtained a portion of the Columbia Air Base after World War II. Retiring in 1957, Gray spent the rest of her life volunteering for numerous causes, organizing single-handedly the South Carolina Federation on Aging, a voice for the senior population of the state.

Gray dedicated her life and career to creating opportunities to learn for the disadvantaged people of South Carolina. She transcended race and class barriers by focusing her energy on the eradication of illiteracy through progressive educational programs designed for adults. In a state rife with bigotry and segregation, she "championed equal education for both races without being dismissed as an idle dreamer or revolutionary." She used her influential family and class ties, her church, and the powerful grassroots network of clubwomen and teachers to turn her pioneering work in the field of adult education into reality. She died on March 10, 1984, in Columbia and was buried in City Cemetery, Laurens. Her portrait hangs in the State House as a testament to her years of service to South Carolina. MARY MAC OGDEN MOTLEY

Ayres, DaMaris E. *Let My People Learn: The Biography of Dr. Wil Lou Gray.* Greenwood, S.C.: Attic Press, 1988.

Gray, William S., Wil Lou Gray, and J. W. Tilton. *The Opportunity Schools of South Carolina, An Experimental Study.* New York: American Association for Adult Education, 1932.

Gray, Wil Lou. Papers. South Caroliniana Library, University of South Carolina, Columbia.

Gray, Wil Lou, and Marguerite Tolbert. *A Brief Manual for Adult Teachers in South Carolina.* Columbia, S.C.: State Department of Education, 1944.

Montgomery, Mabel. *South Carolina's Wil Lou Gray.* Columbia, S.C.: Vogue, 1963.

Motley, Mary Mac. "The Making of a Southern Progressive: South Carolina's Wil Lou Gray, 1883–1920." Master's thesis, University of North Carolina at Wilmington, 1997.

Grayson, William John (1788–1863). Politician, planter, poet, essayist. Grayson was born in Beaufort District on November 12, 1788, the son of William John Grayson and Susannah Greene. He spent much of his youth on Parris Island, the inspiration for his later pastoral verse. An avid reader, Grayson attended boarding schools in the North and graduated at the top of his class in 1809 from South Carolina College. He married Sarah Matilda Somarsall of Charleston in 1814 and amassed a fortune as the owner of two Wando River plantations and 170 slaves. Throughout his life he held numerous public offices, serving terms in the S.C. House of Representatives (1813–1815 and 1822–1826); the S.C. Senate (1826–1831); the U.S. House of Representatives (1833–1837); and as Charleston's customs collector (1841–1853).

While editor of the *Beaufort Gazette,* Grayson promoted nullification, winning his Congressional seat in 1832 on the states' rights ticket. He experienced a change of heart after his return to South Carolina and joined the Whig Party, fearful that the South's dependence on cotton would lead to economic disaster. The stridency of Robert Barnwell Rhett and other "fire-eaters" also appears to have chastened Grayson's earlier flirtation with radical political theory. He despaired over the high emotion in American public life and particularly the debates about slavery. As a devoted classicist, Grayson believed that Romanticism's celebration of "human folly and madness" portended cultural decline, a theme he frequented in his late-antebellum essays for *Russell's Magazine.* On the eve of disunion, Grayson's defense of classicism, "What is Poetry?" (1859), articulated his view that in all human endeavor, reason and order must guide behavior and expression.

Grayson is best remembered for his proslavery verse, *The Hireling and the Slave* (1854), a rejoinder (structured in heroic couplets) to Harriet Beecher Stowe's depiction of slavery in *Uncle Tom's Cabin.* Like George Fitzhugh, Grayson found abhorrent the wage labor systems of England and the North, characterizing them as an even greater injustice than slavery. But Grayson was also a Unionist, and vigorously defended the principles of America's founding throughout the sectional crises of the 1850s. In a pamphlet (1850) addressed to Governor Whitemarsh B. Seabrook, Grayson prophesied, "Union is the source of peace, prosperity, and power to the Nation." Secession would herald the victory of abolitionism, the triumph of anarchy. Only the "imprudence" of the southern people and "the rashness" of their leaders, warned Grayson, could make manifest such a catastrophe. For this and his satirical essay, *The Letters of Curtius* (1851), in which he ridiculed the South's material inability to wage war with the federal government, Grayson was removed from the office of customs collector in 1853.

In his *Autobiography,* written during the early years of the Civil War, Grayson mourned the destruction of the United States, whose repair he could not foresee. "I witnessed the death of the great Republic with sorrow. I was born with it and I survive it. It seemed to me an unnatural event for an individual to be longer lived than a powerful State." Grayson also prepared biographies of his friends William Lowndes (the manuscript is believed to have been destroyed in the Charleston fire of 1861), and fellow Unionist James Louis Petigru. His attenuated war diary (May–November 1862) captures the emotional tautness of Charleston during the Union Army's first sustained attempt to capture the city.

Grayson died at his daughter's home in Newberry on October 4, 1863, and was buried in Charleston's Magnolia Cemetery. ELIZABETH ROBESON

Calhoun, Richard J., ed. *Witness to Sorrow: The Antebellum Autobiography of William J. Grayson.* Columbia: University of South Carolina Press, 1990.

Hubbell, Jay B. *The South in American Literature, 1607–1900.* Durham, N.C.: Duke University Press, 1954.

Great Migration. During the 1910s and 1920s, hundreds of thousands of African Americans left the South for the great urban centers of the Northeast and Midwest. Spurred by declining opportunities at home, this internal migration of African Americans in the United States, dubbed the "Great Migration" by historians, significantly altered the racial makeup of the South Carolina population. For most of the state's history prior to the Great Migration, a majority of the population had been African American. During most of the half century prior to the Civil War, black South Carolinians outnumbered whites by a ratio of about three to two. Neither the Civil War nor emancipation significantly changed this ratio, and South Carolina joined Louisiana and Mississippi as the only states in the nation with black majorities. In the early twentieth century, however, about as many African Americans began to leave the state as were born there, while only a comparative few whites left. As a consequence, each subsequent census recorded an increased ratio of whites to blacks. By 1930 the Census Bureau reported that, for the first time since the 1810s, a majority of South Carolinians were white. This out-migration of African Americans continued throughout most of the twentieth century. By 1970, when black Carolinians ceased to flee the state, African Americans made up just under one third of the population of South Carolina, or 790,000 people.

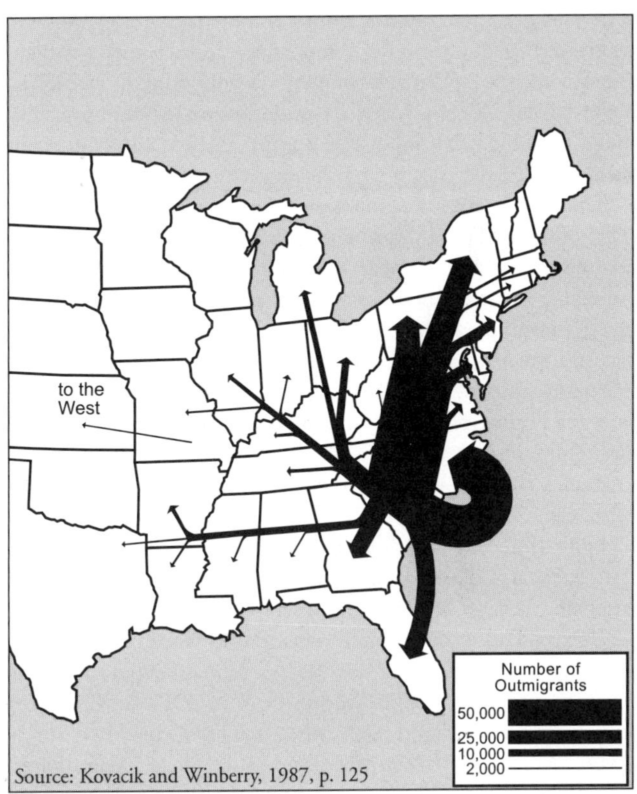

Black out-migration, 1930

Migration had always characterized the lives of black Carolinians, beginning with their forced emigration from Africa in the seventeenth century and through their involuntary dispersal across the South as slaves. During the era of slavery, however, the number of African Americans in South Carolina increased steadily with each census. After 1820 the proportion of blacks to whites remained steady at about three to two. Following the Civil War and emancipation, migration continued, only now blacks chose to migrate. From 1870 through 1900, between 75,000 and 100,000 African Americans left South Carolina each decade, with almost all relocating to other southern states and remaining rural laborers. But the overall racial composition changed little during this time. In 1860 the Census Bureau classified 58.6 percent of South Carolinians as African American; in 1900 it so classified 58.4 percent.

The 1910 census, however, recorded the first significant change in the state's racial balance since the early nineteenth century. Between 1900 and 1910 the percentage of black Carolinians dropped from 58.4 percent to 55.2 percent, even though the total number of African Americans had increased by about 100,000. Equally significant, the direction of migration began to change in 1910, assuming a south-to-north direction. In 1900 only 2.7 percent of the African Americans who had left South Carolina settled in a northern state. In 1940, 75 percent did so. In 1900 about 2,000 black Carolinians had settled in New York; by 1920 the number was 13,000 and reached 41,000 a decade later. By 1940 more than one-third of the black South Carolina migrants settled in New York state. Other northeastern cities likewise saw the number of black South Carolinians in their population increase dramatically during this era. Between 1917 and 1923, almost half of the African Americans leaving South Carolina went to Philadelphia, and by 1930 ten percent of the city's black population had been born in the Palmetto State.

Several forces conspired to create this fundamental shift in the racial demography of South Carolina and the nation. Beginning in the mid-1890s, a series of hurricanes crippled lowcountry rice plantations, which, coupled with competition from other domestic and foreign sources, effectively ended rice cultivation in South Carolina. In addition, by 1920 the boll weevil had reached South Carolina and devastated the cotton crop, leaving tens of thousands of farm laborers with no means of subsistence. At the same time, the 1895 constitution had disenfranchised virtually all black voters and imposed throughout the state a system of racial apartheid that all but denied African Americans access to public education and more lucrative forms of work. Finally, an increase in racial hatred and violence against African Americans likewise encouraged many to leave their native region. These agricultural, political, and social forces were not limited to South Carolina, but characterized the entire lower South in the early twentieth century.

Despite the cold winters and white racial hostility, black South Carolinians looked northward for relief. For many, their initial migration from rural areas took them to small and midsize southern cities such as Charleston and Greenville in South Carolina, or Savannah, Georgia. By 1914, however, opportunities for blacks in the North increased significantly when World War I cut off further European immigration and the North's primary supply of cheap labor. American entry into World War I in 1917 expanded the demand for black labor in the North, a trend that continued during the prosperous 1920s. With the onset of the Great Depression in 1930, migration to the North slowed, but with the outbreak of World War II in 1939, the demand for black labor again expanded as tens of thousands of black South Carolinians fled the state for jobs in the North, especially New York City, Washington, D.C., and Philadelphia. This second wave of black migration continued through the 1960s fueled by postwar prosperity and the civil rights movement. In the 1970s migration from South Carolina slowed in response to improved economic opportunity in the state, desegregation and improvement of public education, and the enforcement of black civil rights, including voting rights and access to public accommodations. Conditions for African Americans improved so much that in the 1980s many African Americans who had left South Carolina returned. Blacks with no South Carolina roots also migrated to the state. According to the 2000 census, African American in-migration to the state exceed out-migration and the proportion of whites to blacks had stabilized at about two to one. WILLIAM B. SCOTT AND PETER M. RUTKOFF

Ballard, Allen B. *One More Day's Journey: The Story of a Family and a People.* New York: McGraw-Hill, 1984.

Devlin, George A. *South Carolina and Black Migration, 1865–1940: In Search of the Promised Land.* New York: Garland, 1989.

Dodd, Don, and Wynelle S. Dodd, eds. *Historical Statistics of the South, 1790–1970.* University: University of Alabama Press, 1973.

Kiser, Clyde Vernon. *Sea Island to City: A Study of St. Helena Islanders in Harlem and Other Urban Centers.* 1932. Reprint, New York: Atheneum, 1969.

Newby, I. A. *Black Carolinians: A History of Blacks in South Carolina from 1895 to 1968.* Columbia: University of South Carolina Press, 1973.

Great Wagon Road. The Great Wagon Road of the eighteenth century, also known as the Great Philadelphia Wagon Road, stretched for almost eight hundred miles from Philadelphia west to Lancaster and York, Pennsylvania, and thence south through Virginia into the Carolina backcountry. The road diverged in South Carolina, with one artery going toward Camden and another toward Ninety Six and the road's southern terminus at Augusta, Georgia. The road originated as an Indian trail, providing a north-south route for hunters and warriors down the Shenandoah Valley and along the foot of the Blue Ridge Mountains. By the 1744 Treaty of Lancaster, natives surrendered their use of this "Warriors' Path" and it developed into the Great Wagon Road, which rapidly saw increased use by German and Scots-Irish immigrants moving south from Pennsylvania into the backcountry. These immigrants developed the famous Conestoga wagon, cleared farmlands, and formed trading posts along the road at places like Salisbury, North Carolina, and Camden, South Carolina. This southern movement of thousands of settlers rapidly populated the Carolina backcountry and gave it a unique Scots-Irish and German flavor. In the closing

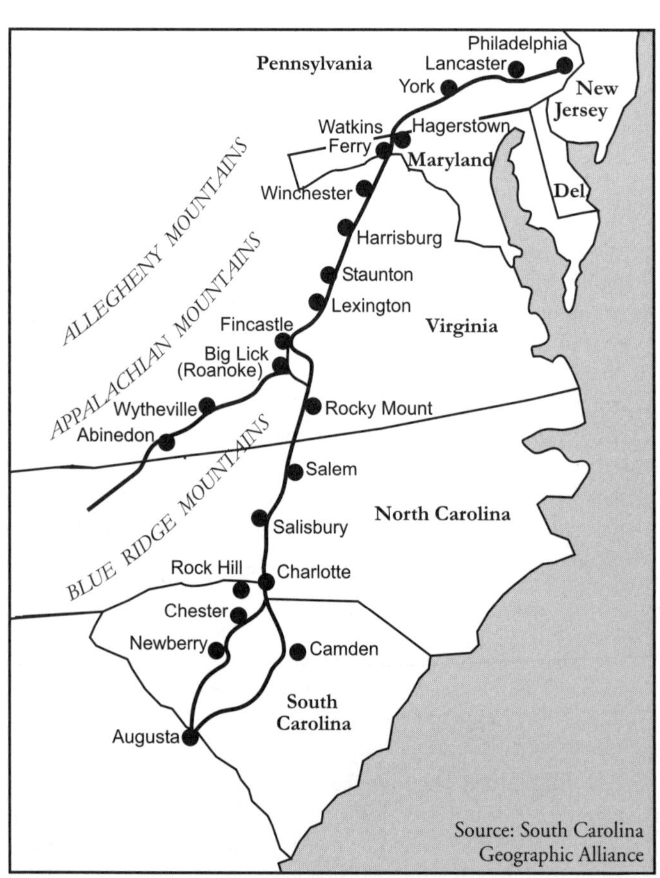

The Great Wagon Road

decades of the colonial era, the Great Wagon Road was among the most heavily traveled in British North America, making it one of the most important frontier movement trails in United States history.

By the mid–nineteenth century, railroads and the migration of the frontier westward decreased the volume of southbound traffic on the road. Decades later, portions of the Interstate and United States Highway systems of the twentieth century traced the route of the Great Wagon Road. W. CALVIN SMITH

Bridenbaugh, Carl. *Myths and Realities, Societies of the Colonial South.* 1952. Reprint, Westport, Conn.: Greenwood, 1981.

Farrant, Don. "The Great Philadelphia Wagon Road." *Heritage Quest* 57 (May/June 1995): 59–60.

Rouse, Parke. *The Great Wagon Road.* 1973. Reprint, Richmond, Va.: Dietz, 1995.

Greeks. Greek immigrants began arriving in South Carolina at the turn of the twentieth century, seeking to escape the economic stagnation of their own country. Their arrival in South Carolina coincided with a burst of development in the state's economy. They quickly found a niche in urban areas as entrepreneurs within the service sector.

Disdaining farm or mill labor, Greeks started out as pushcart merchants. Within a few years of their arrival, they were able to invest in storefront businesses such as confectioneries and restaurants. The Greek-owned restaurant was a common feature on the main street of many Carolina cities and towns. These sandwich shops and lunch counters, usually conspicuous by their quaint names such as the Busy Bee or the Hob Nob Grill, offered new venues where busy New South workers could grab a quick lunch.

Greek entrepreneurs were able to locate their businesses in prime locations in the white business district alongside native white-, Jewish-, and Syrian-owned businesses; they were not segregated into a separate district, as were the state's African American entrepreneurs and professionals.

The success of their businesses was sufficient inducement for Greeks to remain in the state. Their preference for entrepreneurship, the arrival of Greek women, and the consequent growth of families cemented these communities into permanent settlements. Greeks did not reside in ethnic enclaves, and by the 1930s they were well established in middle-class suburban neighborhoods. Their children attended white public schools and the majority graduated from college. Most of the first and second generations followed in the pattern of entrepreneurship or advanced into the professional class.

The formation of permanent settlements resulted in the establishment of Greek Orthodox churches in the state's major cities and towns. The church became the center of Greek cultural and religious life for the immigrants as well as for successive generations. PAULA STATHAKIS

Adallis, D. *History of Columbia, S. C. Greek-American Colony, 1884–1934.* Columbia, S.C.: State Company, [1934].

Boyd, Rosamonde. *The Social Adjustment of the Greeks in Spartanburg, South Carolina.* Spartanburg, S.C.: Williams Printing, [1949?].

Katsos, John. *The Life of John Katsos . . . The Greek Immigrant.* Greenville, S.C.: A Press, 1985.

Stathakis, Paula Maria. "Almost White: Greek and Lebanese-Syrian Immigrants in North and South Carolina, 1900–1940." Ph.D. diss., University of South Carolina, 1996.

Green, Jonathan (b. 1955). Painter, printmaker. Born in rural Gardens Corner in Beaufort County on August 9, 1955, Jonathan Green is the son of Melvin Green and Ruth Johnson. A graduate of Beaufort High School, Green served as a U.S. Air Force illustrator before enrolling as a textile design student at the East Grand Forks Technical Institute in Minnesota. In 1976 he began his formal study of drawing and painting at the Art Institute of Chicago, earning a Bachelor of Fine Arts degree in 1982. He was awarded an honorary Doctor of Fine Arts degree by the University of South Carolina in 1996. While studying in Chicago, Green met his partner and business manager Richard Weedman. Weedman made it possible for Green to pursue independent study abroad to supplement his formal education. While traveling and visiting museums, Green realized that "the best artists are those who paint what they know best. It took a trip to Switzerland and Mexico to return me to Gardens Corner, South Carolina, and begin my body of work 'Gullah life reflections.'"

Best known for depicting the people and landscape of the lowcountry, Green refers to memories of local African American traditions, as well as tales and stories told by members of his extended family and friends. The artist's paintings reflect an authentic historical understanding of lowcountry culture, although he sometimes takes poetic license with his subject matter. Green's lowcountry subjects may or may not be factually realistic, but they communicate a strong sense of conceptual accuracy.

Green's mature style conveys a narrative historicity, simplicity of form, and passionate energy that has been favorably compared with African American masters such as Jacob Lawrence, Elizabeth Catlett, and Romare Bearden but might also be compared with classically modern Europeans such as Gauguin and Matisse. Green's education at the Art Institute of Chicago raised his awareness of traditions in Western and non-Western art that utilize color as a symbolic element—one of the most important stylistic aspects of his work. Green's work also subtly reflects his formal study of textile design and the contemporaneous influence of the Pattern and Decoration movement. Reaching maturity as an artist in the 1980s, he shared in the renewed interest in figurative painting among contemporary collectors and museums.

Coming on the heels of the second of four solo traveling exhibitions, the 1996 publication of *Gullah Images: The Art of Jonathan Green* brought Green's work to a wider and more diverse audience. The artist has been invited to give one-person exhibitions in major museums nationwide and is represented in numerous private and public collections, including those of the Philharmonic Center for the Arts, Naples, Florida; the Morris Museum of Art, Augusta, Georgia; the Norton Museum of Art, West Palm Beach, Florida; the Gibbes Museum of Art, Charleston; and the McKissick Museum of the University of South Carolina, Columbia. Green currently lives and works in Naples, Florida. See plate 32. JAY WILLIAMS

Green, Jonathan. *Gullah Images: The Art of Jonathan Green.* Columbia: University of South Carolina Press, 1996.

Greene, Nathanael (1742–1786). Soldier. Greene was born in Potowomut, Rhode Island, July 27, 1742, the second son of Nathanael Greene and Mary Mott. He was trained in the family iron business. Raised a Quaker, he was read out of meeting after joining the Kentish Guards, a local militia unit. He married Catherine Littlefield around July 20, 1774.

When the Revolutionary War broke out in 1775, Rhode Island troops were formed into a brigade with Greene, a surprise choice, as commander. His appointment was confirmed by the Continental Congress on June 22, 1775, making Greene the youngest general officer in the Continental army. During the siege of Boston, Greene began working with General George Washington, an association that would continue throughout the war. Greene's service with the main ("northern") army included being the first general to command troops not from his own state. His most important contribution was as quartermaster general, successfully reorganizing the main army's supply system. After the defeat of General Horatio Gates at Camden (August 16, 1780), Greene was personally selected by Washington to take charge the southern army. As army commander, Greene never won a battle but did win the war.

Nathanael Greene. Courtesy, South Carolina State Museum

On December 3, 1780, Greene assumed command of the southern army at Charlotte, North Carolina. He soon divided his forces, demonstrating his grasp of both the strategic situation and its logistical requirements. Greene took most of his army to winter at Cheraw, but sent General Daniel Morgan westward in a maneuver that culminated in the Battle of Cowpens (January 17, 1781). After Cowpens, British pursuit of Morgan and Greene turned into the "race to the Dan," eventually resulting in the Battle of Guilford Courthouse (March 15, 1781), which badly damaged Lord Cornwallis's British forces. When Cornwallis marched into Virginia, Greene returned to South Carolina and set about winning back the south.

Greene's strategy in the "War of Posts" was simple but effective. The British could not meet him in open battle unless they consolidated their forces, leaving their garrison posts undefended. While Greene maneuvered to threaten one post, partisan raiders under Francis Marion and Andrew Pickens cooperated by attacking other isolated garrisons. Though he refused to cooperate with Greene, Thomas Sumter's movements also helped keep the British off balance, even as they conflicted with Greene's plans.

Greene's maneuvering brought on the battle at Hobkirk's Hill, April 25, 1781. This American tactical defeat nevertheless forced the British to evacuate Camden. Greene then laid siege to Ninety Six. While Lord Rawdon relieved Ninety Six, he lost key interior garrisons, including Augusta, Georgia, to patriot partisans. Unable to bring Greene to battle, Rawdon evacuated Ninety Six and returned to the coast.

The partisan engagements during the summer of 1781 generally went the American's way. Greene's last major battle occurred when he fought Colonel Alexander Stewart at Eutaw Springs on September 8, 1781. Once again, the British held the field as Greene withdrew with his army intact. The British then retired, occupying a thin coastal zone from Charleston to Savannah that could not supply enough food or forage.

Over the last year of campaigning, Greene aided restoration of civil government by protecting legislative meetings and using his army to restore order in the interior. When the British evacuated Savannah and Charleston, state governments were already in place and operating, providing continuity that went a long way to restoring peace after a brutal civil war. Greene was not a brilliant tactician, but possessed a solid grasp of strategy and logistics. His army provided opposition to the British and a rallying point for Americans. He kept the army in the field because he supplied it, albeit marginally.

Georgia and South Carolina gave Greene plantations in recognition of his service. After the war, Greene lived at Georgia's Mulberry Grove Plantation northwest of Savannah. He died June 19, 1786, and was buried in the cemetery of Christ Episcopal Church in Savannah. His remains were later placed in Savannah's Johnson Square. LAWRENCE E. BABITS

Greene, George W. *Life of Nathanael Greene, Major-General in the Army of the Revolution.* 3 vols. New York: G. P. Putnam and Son, 1867–1871.

Showman, Richard K., and Dennis Conrad, eds. *The Papers of General Nathanael Greene.* 12 vols. to date. Chapel Hill: University of North Carolina Press, 1976– .

Thane, Elswyth. *The Fighting Quaker: Nathanael Greene.* New York: Hawthorne, 1972.

Thayer, Theodore. *Nathanael Greene: Strategist of the American Revolution.* New York: Twayne, 1960.

Greener, Richard Theodore (1844–1922). Teacher, diplomat. Born on January 30, 1844, in Philadelphia, Greener was the son of Richard Wesley Greener and Mary Ann Le Brune. Raised from the age of ten in Boston, Greener attended the Broadway Grammar School in Cambridge, Massachusetts, until he was fourteen, when he dropped out to help support his family. With support from two of his employers, Greener attended the preparatory school at Oberlin College in Ohio from 1862 to 1864 and Phillips Academy in Andover, Massachusetts, from 1864 to 1865. In 1865 Greener was admitted to Harvard University as an experiment in the education of African Americans. In 1870 Greener graduated with honors, earning the distinction of being the first African American to earn a Bachelor of Arts degree from Harvard.

After teaching in Philadelphia and Washington, D.C., Greener accepted the professorship of mental and moral philosophy at the recently integrated University of South Carolina in October 1873, becoming its first black faculty member. In addition to instructing in philosophy, Latin, Greek, and law, Greener taught students in the preparatory school. He gave the university's commencement address in 1874, and served as university librarian for six months in 1875. He earned a law degree from the University of South Carolina in 1876 and was admitted to practice law in the South Carolina Supreme Court. At the request of the Republican Party, Greener spoke at campaign rallies in the Third Congressional District of South Carolina in the 1876 election. On September 24, 1874, he married Genevieve Ida Fleet of Washington, D.C. The couple had seven children, two of whom died in infancy.

When the university was closed in June 1877 by the newly elected Democratic regime, Greener resigned his professorship and moved to Washington, D.C., where he took a position as a clerk in the U.S. Treasury Department. He served as dean of the Howard Law School from 1879 to 1880 and opened a law practice. His most memorable legal case was his defense of Johnson Chesnut Whittaker, a black cadet from South Carolina, who was court-martialed by the U.S. Military Academy in 1881. From 1885 to 1892, Greener served as secretary of the Grant Monument Association and from 1885 to 1890 as a civil service examiner in New York City. In the 1896 presidential election, he served as the head of the "colored men's bureau" of the Republican National Committee in Chicago. In recognition of his service on behalf of the Republican Party, he was appointed as the U.S. commercial agent in Vladivostok, Russia in 1898, a position he held until 1905.

Greener returned to the United States in 1906 and settled in Chicago. He occasionally lectured on his career for the remainder of his life, including on visits to South Carolina in 1906 and 1907. During his 1907 trip to South Carolina, Greener visited Allen University, Benedict College, and South Carolina State College. Although Greener lived in the state for only three and a half years, he considered himself a South Carolinian in exile after 1877. He died in Chicago on May 2, 1922. MICHAEL ROBERT MOUNTER

Mounter, Michael Robert. "Richard Theodore Greener and the African American Individual in a Black and White World." In *At Freedom's Door: African American Founding Fathers and Lawyers in Reconstruction South Carolina,* edited by James Lowell Underwood and W. Lewis Burke. Columbia: University of South Carolina Press, 2000.

Greens. Perhaps nowhere in the United States have greens been so beloved as in the South. South Carolina has a long history of cooking greens—typically collards, turnip greens, and some wild leaf greens.

Greens came to South Carolina from around the world. Collards are widely believed to have arrived here from Africa via the slave route, and turnips, originally eaten more than thirteen hundred years ago, made their way from Asia. England's love of greens is also reflected in our cuisine. Some greens, such as poke salat and dandelion greens grow wild. Others are the tops of a vegetable (beet tops and turnip tops) while others are loose greens (some varieties of turnips that have no root vegetable) or headed greens (cabbage). A complete list of other greens might include collards' cousin kale (also known as cole, colewort, Dutch kool, German kohl and English cole, collarats, and collard-leaves), cabbage sprouts, beet tops, mustard greens, broccoli raab (also called rape and turnip broccoli), and spinach. Cabbage is not commonly included among "greens." Any and all of the above can and are used separately or in conjunction with the traditional collards and turnip greens. Turnip and collard greens are considered better after a frost.

All greens must be washed thoroughly to avoid grittiness. The traditional southern method of cooking collards and turnips is to make a broth with fatback, streak o'lean, ham hocks, or other salted pork or bacon and water (sometimes hot peppers are included). The greens are stripped of tough or yellowed stems and leaves and added to the boiling water. The heat is reduced and the greens left to simmer for up to two hours. They are then cut into smaller pieces, and served hot, sometimes with the pork fried and served as well. Modern cooks frequently substitute chicken broth for the pork. Vinegar with chipped onions, tomato preserves, or hot pepper sauce is frequently kept on the table for seasoning the greens. The pot liquor may be used as a broth or served with the greens in a side dish or bowl.

Greens are highly nutritious; a source of riboflavin, calcium, and iron as well as vitamins A and C. It is thought that the use of salt pork was also important to the diet of southerners in the early days of settlement and following the Civil War, when meat was scarce. When served on New Year's Day, greens are considered a promise of "greenbacks" in the coming year.

New varieties of turnips are now also eaten lightly blanched or, if very tender and young, raw in salads. There are myriad other ways of cooking greens, including blanching and sautéing quickly, or, in the case of spinach, sweated over heat for just a few minutes in the moisture still on the leaves after washing. NATHALIE DUPREE

Betts, Edwin Morris, ed. *Thomas Jefferson's Garden Book, 1766–1824, with Relevant Extracts from His Other Writings.* Philadelphia: American Philosophical Society, 1944.

Randolph, Mary. *The Virginia House-Wife.* 1824. Reprint, Columbia: University of South Carolina Press, 1984.

Sanders, Dori. *Dori Sanders' Country Cooking.* Chapel Hill, N.C.: Algonquin, 1995.

Schneider, Elizabeth. *Vegetables from Amaranth to Zucchini.* New York: Morrow, 2001.

Greenville (Greenville County; 2000 pop. 58,282). The fourth largest city in South Carolina, Greenville traces its origins to 1797 when Lemuel Alston, the largest landowner in Greenville County, laid out the "Greenville C. H. Village of Pleasantburg" on either side of Pearis's wagon road on the east bank of the Reedy River. The county courthouse had been built in the middle of the road in 1795. A few stores, dominated by Jeremiah Cleveland's, opened to serve local farmers, but the lots sold slowly. The delivery of mail, sessions of court, and the arrival of drovers from the north in the fall regulated life in the village.

Life quickened after the War of 1812. When lowcountry planters began to spend the summers in the upcountry, hotels opened and local academies and churches were established. The chief promoter of the village was Vardry McBee, who purchased Alston's 11,028 acres when he moved to Alabama in 1815. McBee opened a store and a pair of mills along the Reedy River. He championed the Greenville and Columbia Railroad, which finally reached the village in 1853. The legislature granted Greenville a municipal charter on December 17, 1831, and the population reached 1,100 by 1843.

In 1851 Furman University opened in temporary quarters on Main Street, and in 1855 the Greenville Baptist Female College (later the Greenville Woman's College) opened on the former site of the Greenville Academies. The Southern Baptist Theological Seminary opened in 1859 but moved to Louisville, Kentucky, in 1877.

Greenville was a Unionist stronghold during the nullification crisis, led by attorney and editor Benjamin F. Perry. However, secessionist sentiment gradually grew in the late 1850s, and Greenville voted to follow the state out of the Union in 1860. Many local residents marched off to war, and lowcountry refugees flooded the town to escape Union occupation of the coast. On May 2, 1865, a detachment of General George Stoneman's Union cavalry, in pursuit of Confederate president Jefferson Davis, raided Greenville and looted a number of homes and businesses. During Reconstruction the Freedmen's Bureau opened an office on Main Street in 1865, and federal troops were stationed in Greenville from 1866 to 1867. Black members of local congregations established separate churches, and a school for African Americans operated with the support of the bureau and northern missionary societies. President Andrew Johnson appointed Benjamin Perry provisional governor in 1865.

Economic changes after 1865 transformed Greenville into a leading cotton market and a center for the growing textile industry. The area's textile industry had antebellum roots, and by 1882 Greenville County had several mills. With new rail connections and an influx of northern capital in the 1890s, Greenville truly caught "mill fever." New factories and mill villages sprang up in and around the city. By 1920 Greenville County had the largest number of spindles in the state, and the city of Greenville was well on its way to becoming the self-proclaimed "Textile Capital of the World."

Other economic and social developments appeared. The first national bank in South Carolina, the National Bank of Greenville, opened in Greenville in 1872, and cotton and fertilizer warehouses operated in the West End area of the city. The coming of the telegraph (1871), the telephone (1882), and paved streets (1883) transformed the town, as did a water system (1888), gas, and electric lights. A city school system began in 1885. By 1900 the population had grown to 11,857. In 1915 the first Southern Textile Exposition opened in Greenville, beginning a tradition of textile machinery shows which continued throughout the twentieth century. Black businesses were common after the Civil War, and whites and blacks lived adjacent to one another. But the South Carolina Constitution of 1895 instituted the era of legal segregation, and in 1912 the city council adopted a segregation ordinance and separate districts for whites and blacks developed.

The location of Camp Wetherill in Greenville in 1898 strengthened the local economy, as did the opening of Camp Sevier during World War I. Duke's Mayonnaise was a direct outgrowth of Mrs. H. C. Duke's sandwich business supplying Camp Sevier; and the Balentine Packing Company opened to supply meat to training camps statewide. In the 1920s economic growth continued. On Main Street, the Poinsett Hotel, the Chamber of Commerce Building, and the Woodside Building (once the tallest building in the state) changed the landscape. Bony H. Peace controlled the local news media, purchasing the *Greenville News* in 1919, the *Piedmont* in 1927, and establishing WFBC Radio in 1933. A municipal airport opened in 1928, and regular airline service began in 1930.

A financial downturn began with the failure of the Bank of Commerce in 1926. In 1929 textile mills curtailed their operations. During the Great Depression of the 1930s, local relief agencies were overwhelmed, and in 1932 Greenville voters supported Franklin D. Roosevelt by a large majority. New Deal agencies opened local offices, and the economy began to improve. Greenville was swept up by World War II. In 1942 the Greenville Army Air Base (later Donaldson Air Force Base) was located near the city. Charles E. Daniel, president of Daniel Construction of Anderson and one of the major contractors for the air base, moved his headquarters to the city. New Deal agencies closed, and textile mills began to operate around the clock.

After 1945 textiles at first continued to expand, but Daniel and others began to plan for a diversified economy. One local product, Texize Household Cleaner, developed a national market, and in the 1950s two radio stations merged with the News-Piedmont Company into Multimedia, Inc., which expanded nationally. In the 1960s, Donaldson Air Force Base was transformed into an industrial park. To meet the demands of the new economy, South Carolina opened the state's first technical education center in Greenville in 1962. Charles Daniel and Roger Milliken of Spartanburg spearheaded the creation of the Greenville-Spartanburg International Airport the same year.

The city annexed suburbs and in 1950 employed its first city manager. Suburban shopping malls, such as McAllister Square, drew retail business from downtown, and Daniel challenged the city to revitalize Main Street. Just prior to his death, he broke ground for the Daniel Building in 1964. A civic center, renamed Heritage Green, provided sites for the county library, the Greenville Little Theatre, and the Greenville County Museum of Art. Under the leadership of Mayor Max Heller (1971–1979) there was greater development downtown. Education was transformed in 1951 with the creation of a single School District of Greenville County. Bob Jones University opened in Greenville in 1947, and Furman University purchased a new campus north of the city in 1950.

Race relations took a violent turn in 1947 with the lynching of a black man, Willie Earle, by a group of white taxicab drivers. The subsequent trial brought international attention. As the civil rights movement developed nationally, local leaders like Daniel were determined that integration in Greenville would be peaceful. On January 1, 1960, the National Association for the Advancement of Colored People staged a march, and a few months later young African Americans began to test local laws at the library and lunch counters. The chamber of commerce appointed a biracial committee to plan strategy and integration began to take place. Finally, under a court order, the county schools desegregated peacefully in February 1970. Jesse Jackson, a native son, became a national figure in the civil rights movement. In 1973 Mayor Heller honored him at a public banquet.

Redevelopment of the central city continued, and in 1990 the Peace Center for the Performing Arts opened on the banks of the Reedy River. Both the city and county became involved in planning development along the river. Despite the decline of the textile industry in the 1980s, the Greenville economy continued to flourish. The city's location along the "mega-growth corridor" between Atlanta, Georgia, and Charlotte, North Carolina, its interstate highway connections, and its business-friendly environment made the area attractive to outside investment. International firms such as Michelin and Hitachi comprised much of Greenville's manufacturing base by the 1990s. Despite the economic boom, Greenville's population remained stagnant, with population increases instead appearing in surrounding bedroom communities such as Mauldin, Simpsonville, and Fountain Inn. See plate 39. A. V. HUFF, JR.

Ehrenhalt, Alan. *The United States of Ambition: Politicians, Power and the Pursuit of Office.* New York: Times Books, 1991.

Huff, Archie Vernon, Jr. *Greenville: The History of the City and County in the South Carolina Piedmont.* Columbia: University of South Carolina Press, 1995.

Sloan, Cliff, and Bob Hall. "It's Good to be Home in Greenville." *Southern Exposure* 7 (spring 1979): 82–93.

Zimmerman, Samuel L. *Negroes in Greenville, 1970: An Exploratory Approach.* Greenville, S.C.: Tricentennial Association, 1970.

Greenville and Columbia Railroad. The Greenville and Columbia Railroad was the first railroad to enter the South Carolina upcountry. Its numerous spurs testified to the widespread demand for railroads in the booming era of cotton production. The road was chartered in 1845 to connect Greenville and Columbia. Originally slated to go through Laurens, agitation from residents in Anderson and Abbeville Districts forced the directors to consider a longer route along the west side of the Saluda River. Residents of each district bought up stock in an effort to secure enough votes for their preferred route, and Anderson and Abbeville carried the day. When the road was completed in 1853, the circuitous 160-mile route included spurs to those two towns. Final construction costs topped $2 million.

The success of the Anderson and Abbeville spurs inspired the creation of other short routes that extended the reach of the Greenville and Columbia in the upstate. In 1854 the Laurens Railroad completed a thirty-two mile line from Laurens to Newberry. The Spartanburg and Union Railroad, completed in 1859, connected those two cities with the Greenville and Columbia at Alston. Finally, the ambitious Blue Ridge Railroad was proposed to depart from Anderson and eventually reach to the Ohio Valley, a prospect that roused the interest of Charleston investors. Few others were interested in the road, however, and the massive expense of blasting through Stumphouse Mountain hampered progress on the proposed line. The project, bearing hopes of reviving Charleston's economic fortunes, had made it only from Anderson to Walhalla when the Civil War began.

The railroad's property in Columbia suffered extensive damage during the Civil War, and flooding in 1866 destroyed forty miles of its track. The railroad reopened later that year, but it was quickly beset with financial difficulties. It went bankrupt in 1872 and fell into receivership in 1878. Two years later the road was purchased by the Richmond Terminal Company. By 1893, after a series of purchases and mergers, the Greenville and Columbia had become part of the Southern Railway system. AARON W. MARRS

Ford, Lacy K., Jr. *Origins of Southern Radicalism: The South Carolina Upcountry, 1800–1860.* New York: Oxford University Press, 1988.

Huff, Archie Vernon, Jr. *Greenville: The History of the City and County in the South Carolina Piedmont.* Columbia: University of South Carolina Press, 1995.

Greenville County (790 sq. miles; 2000 pop. 379,616). Greenville County was created in 1786 out of Cherokee land ceded to the state by the Treaty of DeWitt's Corner in 1777. Originally part of Ninety Six District, the land between the Saluda River and the Indian Boundary Line of 1767 was administratively divided between Spartanburg and Laurens Counties until 1786, when Greenville County was formed. There were a few illegal settlers on Cherokee land in the 1760s, but after the Revolutionary War, state commissioners began to survey and sell parcels of land. Many of the settlers were Scots-Irish or English from Spartanburg and Laurens. More numerous were veterans who applied for state bounty lands. By 1790 blacks—mostly slaves—accounted for over nine percent of the population. Soon the county boasted its own store and a Presbyterian, a Methodist, and two Baptist churches, although the majority of the population was Presbyterian until the Civil War. In 1788 Greenville delegates supported the federal Constitution, unlike most of the backcountry.

The antebellum economy was agricultural, based initially on wheat and corn and a few mills and foundries. The opening of a wagon road across the mountains to Asheville and Knoxville in 1797 brought a brisk droving trade and numerous taverns to the area. The village of Greenville was laid out the same year and became the mercantile center of the district. The early nineteenth century brought the Second Great Awakening and the camp meeting movement, the emergence of state militia musters as social and political gatherings, and the creation of a strong Democratic-Republican Party. After the War of 1812, Rhode Island textile entrepreneurs built a series of mills on local rivers, while westward expansion took many Greenvillians as far west as Texas in search of fresh land. The largest landowner, Vardry McBee, led efforts to build the Greenville and Columbia Railroad, which was completed in 1853. Summer migration of lowcountry planters brought an infusion of culture, including the creation of male and female academies.

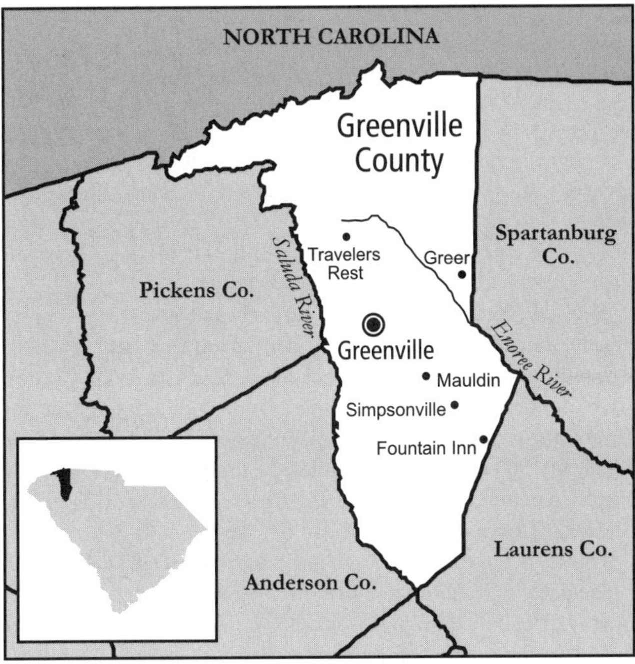

Slavery was another element of lowcountry society that made inroads into antebellum Greenville District. But compared to the rest of the state, its presence was relatively weak. By 1860 only one third of the district population was black. The comparatively low influence of slavery also affected Greenville politically, as the district was strongly Unionist until 1860. It opposed nullification in the 1830s, led by editor and attorney Benjamin F. Perry. However, Perry's leadership was repudiated when Greenville joined the state in its rush to leave the Union in 1860. Though a state arsenal operated in Greenville and three volunteer companies joined the Confederate forces, there were large numbers of deserters and dissatisfaction with the Confederacy. Many lowcountry planters took refuge in Greenville for much of the war.

The end of the Civil War brought major changes: freedom for former slaves, the rapid development of textiles, and the expansion of cotton planting. In the late nineteenth and early twentieth centuries, dozens of textile factories sprang up in Greenville County. Small farmers and sharecroppers migrated to mill villages and the county found itself at the center of a booming textile industry. Black county residents did not benefit from the textile bonanza, but many did become farmers or tradesmen. The completion of the Southern Railway in 1893 and the Atlantic Coast Line in the following decade linked the economy with the nation, although many in the Dark Corner (northern Greenville County) and in Possum Kingdom (southern Greenville County) remained isolated.

In the twentieth century, World War I and the creation of a U.S. Army training facility, Camp Sevier, brought greater contact with the wider world. The economic downturn of the 1920s and 1930s led the county to embrace the New Deal, though the failure of the General Strike of 1934 stifled unionization efforts among county textile workers. Mill owners, led by Thomas F. Parker, attempted to create strong community-based programs in their mill villages. Best known was the Monaghan YMCA, led by L. Peter Hollis. In 1922 the mill executives created the Parker School District, with Hollis as superintendent. It became a showcase for progressive education.

World War II had a major impact, sending large numbers overseas and quickening the textile economy with war contracts. After 1945 agriculture declined and a generation of business leaders, led by construction magnate Charles E. Daniel, began to court diversified industry to replace declining textiles. Donaldson Air Base, built by Daniel during World War II, was transformed into an industrial park in the 1960s. The first technical education center in the state opened in Greenville in 1962 to train workers for the new economy. That same year the Greenville-Spartanburg International Airport opened, thanks to the efforts of Daniel and textile mogul Roger Milliken of Spartanburg. The new interstate highway system crisscrossed the county, spurring development and placing Greenville County in the forefront of the state's economy.

Racial desegregation did not come easily, but after witnessing the violence that broke out in other southern states, local leaders worked to insure that such scenes were not repeated in Greenville County. After a protest march led by the National Association for the Advancement of Colored People on January 1, 1960, barriers began to fall. In 1964 a federal court ordered a limited freedom of choice plan in schools, and in January 1970 the entire school district of Greenville County was integrated.

Politics began to change from one-party Democratic domination to one-party Republican domination. There was strong support for Governor Strom Thurmond's third-party bid for president in 1948, and increasing support for Republican presidential candidates thereafter. Between 1976 and 1980, county Republicans divided between economic conservatives and religious conservatives centered at Bob Jones University, which moved to Greenville in 1947.

Other changes resulted from the "one person-one vote" decision of the U.S. Supreme Court in 1964, which reapportioned legislative representation from counties to election districts of equal population. In the state legislature, rural counties lost their base of power, and metropolitan counties like Greenville gained influence. As the most populous South Carolina county, Greenville became a state leader politically as well as economically. The S.C. House of Representatives elected two Greenville speakers, Rex Carter and David Wilkins, while J. Verne Smith of Greer became a power in the S.C. Senate. Greenville Democrat Richard W. Riley was elected governor in 1978, succeeded by Greenville Republican Carroll A. Campbell in 1988. A. V. HUFF, JR.

Huff, Archie Vernon, Jr. *Greenville: The History of the City and County in the South Carolina Piedmont.* Columbia: University of South Carolina Press, 1995.

Richardson, James M. *History of Greenville County, South Carolina, Narrative and Biographical.* 1930. Reprint, Spartanburg, S.C.: Reprint Company, 1980.

Greenville County Museum of Art. Located on Heritage Green in downtown Greenville, the Greenville County Museum of Art (GCMA) collects and exhibits American art. In 1963 the South Carolina General Assembly established the Greenville County Museum Commission. Ownership of the former Gassaway Mansion, property of the Greenville Art Association since 1958, was transferred to the new museum. In 1974 GCMA moved into its modernist building, designed by Craig, Gaulden & Davis, accommodating almost ninety thousand square feet for spacious exhibition galleries, a museum shop, art storage, a 190-seat auditorium, and classrooms for studio instruction.

Operational funding is derived in part from Greenville County tax millage, and a seven-member museum commission provides oversight. The Museum Association, Inc., with its board of twenty-five individuals, raises funds from the private sector through memberships, an annual antiques show, and other solicitations.

The museum is nationally known for three collection strengths: the Southern Collection, a survey of American art using southern-related examples; *Andrew Wyeth: The Greenville Collection;* and a collection of contemporary art unrivaled in the state. The museum boasts individual works by such twentieth-century masters as George Bellows, Georgia O'Keeffe, Josef Albers, and Philip Guston. The collection includes forty works by Jasper Johns, sixty-eight by Stephen Scott Young, and twenty-six by Andrew Wyeth. A strong and varied exhibition program complements the museum's collection. In 1973 the American Association of Museums accredited GCMA and renewed accreditation in 1986 and 1998. MARTHA R. SEVERENS

Hysinger, Paula Casteel. "History of the Greenville County Museum of Art." In *Greenville County Museum of Art: The Southern Collection.* Greenville, S.C.: Greenville County Museum of Art, 1995.

Greenville News (2003 circulation: 87,622 daily and 116,884 Sunday). The *Greenville News* is a daily newspaper published in the city of Greenville. The Greenville News-Piedmont Company has been the primary print source of news and advertising in northwest South Carolina for most of the twentieth century. The *Greenville Daily News* began in 1874 under the ownership of A. M. Speights, who supported Wade Hampton's bid for governor in 1876. During the 1890s, under the editorship of Alfred B. Williams, the *News* became a leading anti-Tillman newspaper in the upstate. In 1919, with a circulation of less than five thousand, the *Greenville News* was purchased by Bony Hampton Peace, the newspaper's former business manager. Within ten years, Peace had transformed the *Greenville News* into South Carolina's leading newspaper in circulation and advertising. Peace also acquired the *Piedmont,* Greenville's afternoon daily, in 1927 and ran the two newspapers under a single corporate parent. Under the leadership of his son, Roger Craft Peace, the newspapers continued to flourish. In 1968 the Greenville News-Piedmont Company merged with Southeastern Broadcasting Company to form Multimedia, Inc. With its headquarters in Greenville, Multimedia amassed newspaper and broadcast properties throughout the Southeast, plus a television production company and cable television interests.

For much of the twentieth century, the Greenville News-Piedmont Company defended the state's established social, political, and economic order. But as the twenty-first century approached, new management moved the newspaper in a different direction. While remaining fiscally conservative, the newspaper began to address the racial, social, and political inequity that had characterized the state's early history. The *News* distinguished itself in the 1990s with coverage of misappropriation of funds by University of South Carolina president James Holderman, the "Lost Trust" vote-buying scandal in the General Assembly, and stewardship of nuclear weapons facilities in the state. By the turn of the twenty-first century, the *Greenville*

News had a daily circulation of almost 100,000 and 120,000 on Sunday. But the *Piedmont,* once the state's largest afternoon newspaper, followed the trend of its afternoon peers, and closed in 1995. JAMES T. HAMMOND

Huff, Archie Vernon, Jr. *Greenville: The History of the City and County in the South Carolina Piedmont.* Columbia: University of South Carolina Press, 1995.

McNeely, Patricia G. *The Palmetto Press: The History of South Carolina's Newspapers and the Press Association.* Columbia: South Carolina Press Association, 1998.

Greenville Presbyterian Theological Seminary. A transdenominational Reformed seminary organized in 1987, Greenville Presbyterian Theological Seminary understands itself to stand in the theological tradition of South Carolinian James Henley Thornwell and emphasizes a strict adherence to the seventeenth-century Westminster Confession of Faith and Catechisms. It claims commitment to the "Authority of Scripture," "Doctrinal Integrity," "The Use of the Original Languages," "The Preservation of Our Christian Heritage," "Christ-Centered Preaching," and a "Classical Curriculum." While the seminary also emphasizes its accountability to the church, it is not owned and operated by a denomination or judicatory of a denomination. It seeks its accreditation from ecclesiastical bodies rather than accrediting agencies for higher education and the Association of Theological Schools.

The seminary offers six degrees ranging from the Bachelor of Divinity to the Doctor of Theology. In the fall of 2001, it had approximately eighty students and eight regular faculty members. Because the seminary believes "that the Bible prohibits women from teaching or exercising authority over men in the Church," only men are admitted to programs leading to ordination. In its commitments and faculty, the seminary reflects a close connection to Westminster Theological Seminary in Pennsylvania, organized in 1929 as a result of the fundamentalist-modernist controversy in the Presbyterian Church in the United States of America.

A "Propaedeutic" or introductory year with an emphasis on philosophy, logic, and rhetoric is required for men entering programs leading to ordination. ERSKINE CLARKE

Greenville Woman's College. Chartered in 1854 by the South Carolina Baptist Convention, the Greenville Baptist Female College, located a mile from Furman University, opened in 1855 on the former site of the Greenville Academies. Furman trustees controlled the college until 1908 when it became an independent South Carolina Baptist college.

The Greenville Female College (the "Baptist" was dropped in the 1870s) included primary and preparatory departments. Established without endowment, it was rented to presidents until 1894. The college awarded the Bachelor of Arts degree beginning in 1893; after 1918 it added bachelor's degrees in science and music, its strongest department. It was the second largest college for women in the state (next to Winthrop College), with a peak enrollment of 701 in 1920. Sixty percent of its graduates became teachers.

During his nineteen-year (1911–1930) presidency, David Ramsay changed the Female College's name to Greenville Woman's College, doubled enrollment, income, and faculty, instituted rigorous admissions standards, tripled the size of the library and built one of the most impressive fine arts facilities in the South. He could not, however, raise the $500,000 endowment required for accreditation. With budget deficits and intense economic pressures, the college could not survive the Depression. He resigned in 1930. Trustees then agreed to coordinate with Furman University. Between 1931 and 1937 the schools gradually merged, and Greenville Woman's College became Furman University's women's college. Its buildings were demolished after 1961, when women joined men on Furman's new campus. JUDITH T. BAINBRIDGE

Bainbridge, Judith T. *Academy and College: The History of the Woman's College of Furman University.* Macon, Ga.: Mercer University Press, 2001.

Greenville-Spartanburg International Airport. The Greenville-Spartanburg International Airport was the vision of upstate businessmen Charles Daniel of Greenville and Roger Milliken of Spartanburg. Believing a modern airport was necessary for the economic development of the upcountry, in the late 1950s Daniel and Milliken formed a committee to study the project and develop a design plan. On March 25, 1959, the General Assembly combined the counties of Greenville and Spartanburg into a single airport district. Construction of a joint facility began immediately and opened on October 15, 1962.

Located on Interstate 85 in Spartanburg County, the airport lies midway between the two cities. In September 1989, a $40 million terminal expansion increased the number of gates from eight to thirteen. An addition was joined to the original building at an atrial fountain, over which hang handmade stainless steel geese in flight. The world's largest airport mural, 160 feet wide by 12 feet high, runs along the restaurant wall. Entitled "Crafted with Pride in the USA," it was created by Carl Tait. Across from the mural sits the only airside courtyard in the United States. Besides holly hedges, crape myrtles, magnolias, and blooming flowers, the garden is graced with two fountains and six original bronze sculptures by Dennis Smith entitled "Like Petals Unfolding."

Expansions in 1995 and 1999 extended the runway to more than eleven thousand feet. Two federal inspection stations were added to attract international passengers and cargoes. At the start of the twenty-first century, Greenville-Spartanburg International Airport handled more than eighty daily departures and 1.5 million passengers annually. MARILYN M. NELSON

Special section on Greenville-Spartanburg International Airport. *Greenville News,* September 24, 1989.

Huff, Archie Vernon, Jr. *Greenville: The History of the City and County in the South Carolina Piedmont.* Columbia: University of South Carolina Press, 1995.

Greenwood (Greenwood County; 2000 pop. 22,071). In 1823 John McGehee built a summerhouse midway between Abbeville and Cambridge to escape what was regarded as the unhealthy vapors of Cambridge. His wife, Charlotte, called their home Green Wood. A village named Woodville developed nearby, with a post office established in 1837. Its designation was changed to Greenwood in 1850. Construction of the Greenville and Columbia Railroad in 1852 shifted the village business center a half mile to the northwest, where stores and warehouses grew up around the depot. The town was incorporated in 1857.

After the Civil War, Greenwood slowly gained population and new businesses. It became a bustling railroad town, with passenger and freight trains steaming through a village served by three railroads by 1890. The Greenwood economy, based on agriculture and transportation, was altered dramatically in 1890 when William L. Durst opened the Greenwood Cotton Mill. The town emerged as a

"The world's widest main street" in Greenwood. Courtesy, South Caroliniana Library, University of South Carolina

center of textile manufacturing under the leadership of James C. Self, John P. Abney, and F. E. Grier.

Greenwood experienced significant growth in the last decade of the nineteenth century, particularly after the town became the seat of Greenwood County in 1897. Attorneys and businessmen erected handsome houses on streets radiating from the new courthouse square. Local investors, known as "The Syndicate," developed an impressive block of granite buildings to house new businesses. In 1898 entrepreneur Joel Bailey relocated his house and in its place built the Oregon Hotel to serve railroad travelers. Baptists and Presbyterians constructed sanctuaries on adjacent blocks of Main Street.

In 1898 Greenwood developed a municipal electric power and water plant, providing residents with an adequate water supply and access to electricity. Two years earlier, five local businessmen, led by George A. Barksdale, formed the Greenwood Telephone Company and commenced operations in 1898 with forty-two subscribers. To enlarge educational opportunities for young women, state senator Creswell A. C. Waller and other promoters persuaded Methodist clergyman Samuel Lander to relocate his college to Greenwood. Lander College opened on its new campus in 1903 and has been a state college since 1973.

A 1944 tornado slashed through the south side of town, destroying the hospital. Textile magnate James Self replaced it in 1951 with a modern medical facility, Self Memorial Hospital, to serve the lower Piedmont region.

In the closing decades of the twentieth century, Greenwood's evolution continued. A Federal Highway Administration grant removed the railroad tracks from the center of town, while a local project renovated the storefronts on the square. Retail businesses, originally concentrated around the train depots, were displaced by bank buildings and professional offices. The shopping patterns shifted to the outskirts of town, to strip shopping centers along a bypass road and the highway to Abbeville. MARVIN L. CANN

Bowen, Ann Herd. *Greenwood County: A History.* Greenwood, S.C.: The Museum, 1992.

Watson, Margaret J. *Greenwood County Sketches: Old Roads and Early Families.* Greenwood, S.C.: Attic Press, 1970.

Greenwood County (456 sq. miles; 2000 pop. 66,271). Located in the lower Piedmont southwest of the Saluda River, Greenwood County was created in 1897. Its boundaries were carved out of Abbeville and Edgefield Counties. Following a contentious struggle against interests in Abbeville, residents approved the formation of Greenwood County, named for the town selected as the county seat, by a margin of 1,019 to 84. Thus Greenwood joined four other new counties, all established in 1897 to strengthen the rural base of Ben Tillman's political machine.

The new county possessed a rich heritage. In the colonial era, about 1750, Robert Goudy built a store and plantation on the Cherokee Path near Ninety Six. Goudy's establishment became an assembly area and supply depot for British military operations against Cherokee villages during the French and Indian War. After 1769, when the province enlarged its judicial system, Ninety Six became the courthouse town for a huge backcountry district of the same name. Greenwood County also includes the sites of two significant Revolutionary War battles near Ninety Six. From November 19–21, 1775, patriots commanded by Andrew Williamson successfully defended their "rustic fortification" made of "old fence rails joined to a barn," and held off a Loyalist army in the first land battle of the war south of New England. Several years later, in 1781, General Nathanael Greene led Continental and militia units in a lengthy but unsuccessful siege of a British outpost at Ninety Six.

Greenwood escaped most of the ravages of the Civil War. While no armies plundered its towns and farms, many men entered Confederate service and no resident was spared the war's economic dislocations. The Reconstruction era brought several positive changes with the establishment of two new educational institutions for local freedmen, the Brewer Normal and Industrial School (1872) and the Payne Institute (1870), the latter of which relocated to Columbia in 1880 and became Allen University.

Railroads played a vital part in the county's transformation from an agricultural to an industrial economy. The first line through the future Greenwood County, completed in 1852, was the Greenville and Columbia Railroad. Four other lines served the county by 1929 and several towns (Bradley, Hodges, Troy, and Verdery) sprang up along the tracks.

As a "New South" emerged from the region's drive for industrial development, William L. Durst founded the Greenwood Cotton Mill and it began production in 1890. Plagued by inefficient equipment and limited capital, the venture nearly failed in the early 1900s. Only the selection of James Cuthbert Self as president and a generous contract with the Draper Corporation of Massachusetts for new machinery saved the struggling company. By 1935 Self had purchased all the company's stock and made Greenwood Mills a privately held corporation. Several other successful textile mills were launched before 1930, including Grendel Mill (chartered 1896), Ninety Six Cotton Mill (chartered 1902), and Panola Mill (chartered 1910). John Pope Abney acquired the Grendel Mill in 1917 and marked the beginning of Abney Mills, a textile chain that included twenty-seven factories in three states before the corporation was dismantled in the 1970s. On the northern border of the county, future U.S. Senator Nathaniel Dial attempted to develop Ware Shoals Manufacturing Company, expecting to drive its looms with hydroelectric power generated from the Saluda River. When Dial encountered financial difficulties in 1905, he persuaded a New York businessman, Benjamin Riegel, to invest. Riegel moved to South Carolina where he developed Riegel Mill and its model industrial village of Ware Shoals.

The Great Depression reshaped both the economy and the landscape of the county. Agricultural production and the number of farms declined. Textile companies struggled to survive and fought efforts to unionize employees. The most significant New Deal project was the construction of Buzzards' Roost Dam on the Saluda River to impound Lake Greenwood and generate electricity with a county-owned power plant. Completed in 1940, the dam provided jobs and cheap power, while Lake Greenwood created recreational facilities and an abundant supply of water for new industry.

Faced with disappointing growth in the decade after World War II, the chamber of commerce launched a campaign to attract more diverse industry. The initial success came in 1959 when Chemstrand Corporation (later Solutia) built a multimillion-dollar nylon plant on Lake Greenwood. The county's industrial payroll grew as other major companies (Westinghouse, Kemet, Velux America) chose Greenwood for manufacturing facilities. The most dramatic economic advance came in 1988 when Fuji Photo Film located its North American headquarters in Greenwood County. Its factories produced offset printing film, videotape, photography film, and QuickSnap cameras.

Greenwood County is home to two institutions of higher education, Lander University and Piedmont Technical College. The Greenwood Genetic Center is an internationally acclaimed medical research facility and Self Memorial Hospital, established after a devastating 1944 tornado, serves regional health care needs.

Residents of Greenwood County who achieved national recognition include Francis Salvador (ca. 1747–1776), the first Jewish member of the South Carolina legislature and the first in America to die in the Revolutionary War. The Reverend Samuel Lander, founder of Lander University, was an early champion of higher education for women. Two young boys who lived in the county when it was formed became national figures by midcentury: Louis Booker Wright, author and editor of works on colonial America and Elizabethan England, was director of the Folger Shakespeare Library in Washington, D.C.; Benjamin Elijah Mays won national praise as an influential civil rights leader and president of Morehouse College in Atlanta, Georgia. MARVIN L. CANN

Bowen, Ann Herd. *Greenwood County: A History.* Greenwood, S.C.: The Museum, 1992.

Watson, Margaret J. *Greenwood County Sketches: Old Roads and Early Families.* Greenwood, S.C.: Attic Press, 1970.

Wright, Louis Booker. *Barefoot in Arcadia: Memories of a More Innocent Era.* Columbia: University of South Carolina Press, 1974.

Greer (Greenville County; 2000 pop. 16,843). Situated midway between Greenville and Spartanburg, the city of Greer originated along the line of the Richmond and Danville Air Line Railway. In 1873 the railroad instituted a flag stop on the property of Manning Greer, and the site came to be known in turns as Greer's Depot, Greer's Station, and simply Greer's (or Greers). An act incorporating the town of Greer's was approved by the General Assembly in 1876. Although the "s" would be dropped informally in the ensuing years, the city did not officially become Greer until 1976.

Greer's business district at the turn of the twentieth century. Courtesy, South Caroliniana Library, University of South Carolina

The new town quickly established a prosperous business environment, claiming fourteen stores by the early 1880s. Four cotton mills were in operation by 1908. The principal business district along Trade Street sprouted a number of impressive multistory business edifices named for the city's leading business families, including the Bennett, Bailey, and Marchant buildings. Many of these were listed in the National Register of Historic Places in 1997. By the start of the 1920s, Greer had a population of almost 2,300. By the late 1920s, the growing town was home to three banks, two newspapers, and a public library. Sixteen passenger trains passed daily along the lines of the Southern Railway and the electric Piedmont and Northern Railway. Town markets sold some nine thousand bales of cotton and a considerable amount of peaches annually.

Like the rest of the upstate, Greer suffered through hard times during the Depression of the 1930s. Some relief was afforded by the establishment of a Civilian Conservation Corps camp near the town in 1934, which provided food, lodging, and employment for two hundred men. That same year, however, "flying squadrons" of the United Textile Workers visited Greer during the General Textile Strike and briefly forced the town's four mills to close.

Greer more than shared in the general economic prosperity of the Greenville-Spartanburg area in the latter decades of the twentieth century. In 1992 German automaker BMW selected the town to be the site of its first complete automobile manufacturing facility outside of Germany. The plant opened in November 1994 and was hailed as the crowning achievement of South Carolina's ongoing efforts to recruit foreign manufacturers. Due in large measure to the arrival of the BMW facility, Greer became one of the fastest growing cities in the state during the 1990s, with a population increase of sixty-three percent during the decade. In 2001 a partnership of public and private interests began implementing its ambitious "Partnership for Tomorrow" plan, which sought to further enhance economic development and revitalize the city center. ROSE MARIE COOPER

Campbell, M. C., comp. *Greer Community Annual, January 1927.* Greer, S.C., 1927.

Cooper, Nancy Vance Ashmore. *Greenville: Woven from the Past.* Sun Valley, Calif.: American Historical Press, 2000.

Kinard, Joe Dew. *A Strong Tower: The Centennial History of the First Baptist Church of Greer, South Carolina, 1880–1980.* Columbia, S.C.: R. L. Bryan, 1980.

Richardson, James M. *History of Greenville County, South Carolina: Narrative and Biographical.* 1930. Reprint, Spartanburg, S.C.: Reprint Company, 1980.

Greer, Bernard Eugene (b. 1948). Writer. Ben Greer was born on December 4, 1948, in Spartanburg, the son of Bernard Eugene Greer, a television newsman, and Margaret Philips. Greer came to the University of South Carolina just as James Dickey and George Garrett were establishing its creative writing program. Greer studied with both of them while working as a prison guard at Columbia's notorious Central Correctional Institution. After graduating with a bachelor of arts degree in 1971, Greer was accepted into the prestigious creative writing program at Hollins College, where he studied poetry and fiction with R. H. W. Dillard and William Jay Smith. After earning his master of arts degree from the Hollins program in 1973, Greer left the South and academia and moved to Maine where he worked on a fishing boat. During this first long Maine winter he began to forge his experiences as a prison guard into his first novel, *Slammer.*

Slammer was published in 1975 and was a critical and popular success. It was hailed for its gritty authenticity, and Greer was praised as a writer "with amazing economy of means" and great promise for the future. In his novel, Greer created a prison that contained hopelessness and terror but also courage and compassion.

Greer's second novel, *Halloween* (1978), demonstrated both his versatility and his desire to recreate himself. Avoiding the temptation to capitalize on *Slammer* with another work about political or social issues, Greer merged the southern gothic family novel with a thriller and created a tale of a psychotic killer and disintegrating family. Taking place during one Halloween night in a southern coastal city, this novel manages to balance the immediate horror of the serial killer with a family that drains the life out of its members. *Halloween* was a commercial success, but some critics missed the gritty reality of *Slammer* and found the new novel stagy and unrealistic. Others saw it as a noble risk, which was not always successful.

In 1979 Greer returned to the University of South Carolina as a faculty member in the English Department's creative writing program. Greer's third novel, *Time Loves a Hero* (1986), brought a young southern writer to a New England island to encounter a wealthy northeastern family. Highly anticipated, this novel represented another radical change of genres. *Loss of Heaven* (1988) was Greer's exploration of a traditional southern family facing the political and social changes of the 1960s. With locales ranging from a Trappist monastery to the jungles of Southeast Asia, and characters like Lyndon Johnson, faded French colonial bureaucrats, southern grandmothers, and civil rights marchers, *Loss of Heaven* was compelling, if perhaps overly ambitious.

In the 1990s Greer became involved with journalistic and political writing as well as other nonfiction projects. Greer's refusal to be typed into one style or genre may have kept him from having the kind of audience that always knows what to expect, but has allowed him to continue to explore and experiment. THORNE COMPTON

Garrett, George. "Ben Greer." In *Dictionary of Literary Biography.* Vol. 6, *American Novelists since World War II, Second Series.* Edited by James E. Kibler. Detriot: Gale, 1980.

Gregg, Maxcy (1814–1862). Soldier. Born in Columbia on August 1, 1814, Gregg was the son of Colonel James Gregg and Cornelia Maxcy. His scholarly interests included botany, ornithology, and astronomy, and he was co-valedictorian of his class when he graduated from South Carolina College in 1836. He read law under his father and was admitted to the bar in 1839. In 1847 he was appointed major in Milledge L. Bonham's regiment of volunteers for the Mexican War, but this unit failed to reach Mexico in time to participate in any major battles. He was a member of the Southern Rights Convention of 1852, and in the late 1850s he advocated reopening the African slave trade. He was a delegate from the Richland District to the 1860 Secession Convention and assisted in writing the Ordinance of Secession. Soon after, the convention authorized the formation of the First Regiment of South Carolina Volunteers for six months' service and Gregg was placed in command. Part of this unit was under fire during the bombardment of Fort Sumter, but it took no casualties.

Gregg's regiment was sent to Richmond and then to Manassas, but its enlistment period expired in early July 1861, just before the Battle of First Manassas (July 21, 1861). Gregg and other officers recruited another "First Regiment," which he commanded in eastern Virginia until he was promoted in December 1861 to brigadier general. His brigade, consisting of three South Carolina regiments, served initially on the South Carolina coast and then was sent to Virginia, where his old regiment and Orr's Regiment of Rifles were added. The brigade was heavily involved in the Seven Days' battles around Richmond, suffering heavy casualties at Gaines Mill (June 27, 1862) and at Frazier's Farm (June 30, 1862). Gregg's brigade fought in Stonewall Jackson's corps at the Second Battle of Manassas (August 29–30, 1862), and at Ox Hill (September 2, 1862) in pursuit of Pope's army. In the Maryland campaign, Gregg's brigade participated in the capture of Harper's Ferry (September 15, 1862) and then made a forced march to Sharpsburg, arriving in the middle of that battle to take a place in the right center of the line, where it joined the fighting that afternoon. After two months of recuperation near Winchester, the brigade participated in the Battle of Fredericksburg (December 13, 1862), where Gregg was mortally wounded while leading his men from a reserve position to close a gap in the Confederate battle line. He died two days later on

December 15, 1862. Robert E. Lee wrote to South Carolina Governor Francis Pickens: "The death of such a man is a costly sacrifice, for it is to men of his high integrity and commanding intellect that the country must look to give character to its councils, that she may be respected and honored by all nations." His remains were returned from Virginia and buried in the cemetery of the First Presbyterian Church, Columbia. DEWITT BOYD STONE, JR.

Caldwell, J. F. J. *The History of a Brigade of South Carolinians Known first as "Gregg's" and Subsequently as "McGowan's Brigade."* Philadelphia: King & Baird, 1866.

Freeman, Douglas Southall. *Lee's Lieutenants: A Study in Command.* 3 vols. New York: Scribner's, 1942–1944.

Krick, Robert K. "Maxcy Gregg: Political Extremist and Confederate General." *Civil War History* 19 (winter 1973): 293–313.

Gregg, William (1800–1867). Manufacturer, industrial promoter. Gregg was born on February 2, 1800, in Monongalia County, Virginia (now West Virginia), the son of William Gregg and Elizabeth Webb. At the age of ten, he was placed with his uncle, Jacob Gregg, a watchmaker and producer of spinning machinery. They moved to Georgia, where the uncle built a textile mill that prospered for several years before failing in the years immediately after the end of the War of 1812, when cheaper European-made goods inundated American markets. Gregg was then apprenticed to a watchmaker and spent the next few years in Kentucky and Virginia. By the mid-1820s, he had set up shop in Columbia, South Carolina, where he built a successful business importing and producing fancy goods, silver, watches, and military paraphernalia. He married Marina Jones of Edgefield District in April 1829. They had four children.

Poor health and the acquisition of a substantial fortune from his business led Gregg to retire in 1837. That same year, he became an investor in the Vaucluse mill in Edgefield District, a struggling textile factory on the verge of bankruptcy. Gregg took over management of the mill, and within a year production at Vaucluse doubled and the mill showed a profit of $5,000. Flush with new profits and renewed health, Gregg relocated to Charleston. He established a new business with two Connecticut partners, Nathaniel and Hezekiah Hayden. Their firm, Hayden, Gregg & Co., became the leading importer and supplier of fancy goods and jewelry in the city, and transformed Gregg into a wealthy and influential member of the Charleston business community.

Around 1844 Gregg toured the leading textile manufacturing centers of the Northeast. Returning to Charleston, he wrote a series of articles that appeared in the *Charleston Courier,* calling on the South to invest in manufacturing and end its reliance on staple agriculture. Later published in pamphlet form, Gregg's *Essays on Domestic Industry* found wide circulation and placed Gregg among the South's leading industrial advocates. Putting his industrial gospel into practice, Gregg and several partners secured a charter from the South Carolina General Assembly in December 1845 to establish the Graniteville Manufacturing Company, with an initial capitalization of $300,000. Erected on the banks of Horse Creek in Edgefield District, the Graniteville factory commenced operations in 1849 and quickly became one of the most successful textile factories in the entire South.

Gregg's industrial writings continued to be published during the 1850s and 1860s in such influential journals as *De Bow's Review* and *Hunt's Merchants' Magazine.* He was elected to the General Assembly from Edgefield District in 1856, but lost a bid for the state Senate two years later. As a member of the Secession Convention in December 1860, he signed the Ordinance of Secession. His Graniteville mill produced cotton cloth for the Confederacy throughout the Civil War. In September 1867, the dam at Graniteville broke and Gregg added his efforts to others standing in waist-deep water to repair the damage. He took ill as a result and died several days later on September 13, 1867. He was buried in Magnolia Cemetery, Charleston. TOM DOWNEY

Downey, Tom. *Planting a Capitalist South: Masters, Merchants, and Manufacturers in the Southern Interior, 1790–1860.* Baton Rouge: Louisiana State University Press, 2005.

Martin, Thomas P., ed. "The Advent of William Gregg and the Graniteville Company." *Journal of Southern History* 11 (August 1945): 389–423.

Mitchell, Broadus. *William Gregg: Factory Master of the Old South.* 1928. Reprint, New York: Octagon, 1966.

Gregorie, Anne King (1887–1960). Historian, teacher, author, editor. Gregorie was born in Savannah, Georgia, on May 20, 1887, the daughter of South Carolina natives Ferdinand Gregorie and Anne Palmer Porcher. Her father was managing plantations in Georgia, but in 1893 returned with his family to Oakland, his father-in-law's plantation near Mount Pleasant. Gregorie lived at Oakland for the next sixteen years, absorbing the area's history, folklore, and myths. She attended the local public school, Victory Point Academy, and obtained a scholarship to Winthrop College, which she entered as a sophomore in 1903. Gregorie graduated in 1906 with a Bachelor of Arts degree and a lifetime license to teach in the state's public schools. After a year of postgraduate study, she embarked on an eleven-year teaching career that took her to schools in Lynchburg, Chester, and, finally, Christ Church Parish. When her mother died in 1918, Gregorie resigned her teaching position, taking over housekeeping for her father and serving his business, F. Gregorie and Sons, as treasurer. This hiatus lasted until 1923, but the five years rekindled her interest in local history.

Anne King Gregorie. Courtesy, South Carolina Historical Society

In 1925 Gregorie embarked on the process of becoming a professional historian. She entered the University of South Carolina and earned a master's degree a year later. That fall she entered the University of Wisconsin as a full-time graduate student, but returned to the University of South Carolina in January 1927. She taught freshman history courses, took courses herself, and completed her dissertation, a biography of Thomas Sumter. Gregorie graduated in 1929, the first woman to receive a doctorate from the Department of History of the University of South Carolina.

Gregorie spent the next four years teaching at Arkansas College and Alabama College while readying *Thomas Sumter* for publication in 1931. Reviews of *Thomas Sumter* stressed the diligence and research that made the book not just a biography, but also a social study of South Carolina's Revolutionary and early-statehood periods. When the Depression ended Gregorie's teaching career in 1933, she returned to Mount Pleasant and wrote twenty-one entries for the *Dictionary of American Biography.* Economically independent through judicious investments of savings and monies earned for her writings, Gregorie began working for the Civil Works Administration, repairing and transcribing historical records. In 1936 she became the director of the South Carolina Historical Records Survey, a Works Projects Administration agency that inventoried records in courthouses, capitols, and churches nationwide. When the project was suspended in 1941, Gregorie had compiled forty-six county records inventories and published fourteen. Completing the work by drafting the first disaster preparedness plan for cultural institutions and records in South Carolina, she turned in earnest to historical writing and editing.

Gregorie's major work for the American Historical Association, *Records of the South Carolina Court of Chancery, 1671–1779,* was published in 1950. Four years later *The History of Sumter County* earned an award of merit from the American Association for State and Local History. Gregorie served as editor of the *South Carolina Historical Magazine* from 1948 until 1958. Lastly, Gregorie fulfilled her life's dream by completing *Christ Church Parish, 1706–1959,* which was published posthumously in 1961. As a historian, Gregorie demonstrated the validity of good local history and the importance of local records. Her heritage and training enabled her to present South Carolina's history with intimacy and insight enriched with anecdotes and tradition. She died on December 4, 1960, and was buried in the Christ Episcopal Churchyard, Mount Pleasant. ROBERTA V. H. COPP

Copp, Roberta V. H. "Of Her Time, Before Her Time: Anne King Gregorie, South Carolina's Singular Historian." *South Carolina Historical Magazine* 91 (October 1990): 231–46.

Surles, Flora Belle. *Anne King Gregorie.* Columbia, S.C.: R. L. Bryan, 1968.

Gressette, Lawrence Marion (1902–1984). Legislator. L. Marion Gressette was born near St. Matthews on February 11, 1902, to John Thomas Gressette and Rosa Emily Wannamaker. He graduated from St. Matthews High School and received a law degree from the University of South Carolina in 1924. Gressette married Florence Beach Howell of Florence on August 18, 1927. Lawrence Marion Gressette, Jr., was born to the couple in 1932.

Gressette served state government as a legislator for more than a half century. He represented Calhoun County for three terms in the state House of Representatives from 1925 to 1932. He later served twenty-three terms in the South Carolina Senate from 1937 to 1984, representing Calhoun County until 1966, then Districts Nineteen, Eleven, and Thirteen after reapportionment. While in the state Senate, Gressette was a longtime member of a number of influential committees, including Judiciary (1937–1984; chairman, 1953–1984), Education (1939–1984; chairman, 1951–1956), Natural Resources(1941–1953; chairman, 1945–1950), Rural Electrification (1942–1975), and many others. He served as president pro tempore of the S.C. Senate from 1972 to 1984. His powers of oratory and persuasion, as well as his silver hair, led colleagues to dub him the "Gray Fox."

Gressette earned special notoriety for his role in the debate over school desegregation. From 1951 to 1966, Gressette chaired a special legislative committee that led legal efforts to avoid desegregation

Marion Gressette. Courtesy, Modern Political Collections, University of South Carolina

in South Carolina. His influence on this committee was so strong that it came to be called the "Gressette Committee." In addition, as chairman of the Senate Judiciary Committee, he worked to preserve the status quo by rejecting many new bills before they reached the state Senate floor. His reputation for such action led some to call his committee "Gressette's Graveyard." Finally, as a protector of state sovereignty against the federal government, Gressette successfully prevented ratification of the federal equal rights amendment by South Carolina in 1978. Commenting on his staunch conservatism, a reporter from the *Charlotte Observer* once described Gressette as "the 20th century embodiment of the conservative lawyer-planter class who ruled South Carolina before the Civil War."

The onset of the civil rights movement and the inevitability of integration, however, forced Gressette to soften his hard-line views. For example, when Clemson College faced integration in 1963, he urged acceptance by his colleagues by saying, "We may have lost the battle but not the war. But this war cannot be won by violence or inflammatory speeches. I have preached peace and good order for too long to change my thinking." Similarly, at the 1970 state Democratic convention, Gressette experienced integration firsthand as he sat with an integrated delegation from Calhoun County. Following reapportionment, Gressette actively campaigned in his heavily black state Senate district. After part of Orangeburg County was added to his district, he became a legislative patron of South Carolina State College, the state's leading traditionally black institution of higher learning,

Gressette received much recognition for his contributions to South Carolina as his life neared the end. He was named Legislator of the Year by the *Greenville News* in 1974. He also received honorary doctorates from the University of South Carolina in 1977, Clemson University in 1980, and the Citadel in 1981. Gressette died in of heart failure on March 1, 1984, and was buried in the West End Cemetery in St. Matthews. FREEMAN BELSER

Bailey, N. Louise, Mary L. Morgan, and Carolyn R. Taylor, eds. *Biographical Directory of the South Carolina Senate, 1776–1985.* 3 vols. Columbia: University of South Carolina Press, 1986.

Gressette Committee (1951–1966). In 1951 the South Carolina General Assembly created the South Carolina School Committee at the request of state senator L. Marion Gressette of Calhoun County.

Following the filing of the *Briggs v. Elliot* case, which challenged the "separate but equal" policy in South Carolina's public schools, the General Assembly created the committee to prepare for, and hopefully thwart, the possibility of federally mandated desegregation. The committee consisted of five members from each house of the General Assembly, five at-large members selected by the governor, with Gressette (for whom the committee came to be known) as chairman.

The Gressette Committee remained dormant until 1954, when the Supreme Court ruled in *Brown v. Board of Education* that segregation was unconstitutional. Gressette made the committee's position on desegregation clear when he declared, "We shall recommend to the Governor and General Assembly continued resistance by every lawful means." All proposals regarding school segregation passed through the committee. The Gressette Committee fought to maintain public school segregation through the use of legislative proposals and legal stall tactics, such as abolishing the compulsory attendance law, denying state aid to schools forced by court order to integrate, and eliminating the automatic rehiring of public school teachers.

Though the committee opposed desegregation and slowed its pace in South Carolina, it advocated nonviolent resistance to change and actually became a vehicle for accommodation by stopping many proposed segregation laws from being debated in the General Assembly. Looking back on the work of the committee, Gressette declared "the committee's real accomplishment was in preventing violence such as occurred in some other southern states." In 1966, on receiving heavy criticism from legislators over legal expenditures and on the conclusion of most legal questions regarding segregation, Gressette called for an end to the committee and the legislature complied. JEREMY RICHARDS

Sproat, John G. "'Firm Flexibility': Perspectives on Desegregation in South Carolina." In *New Perspectives on Race and Slavery in America: Essays in Honor of Kenneth M. Stampp,* edited by Robert H. Abzug and Stephen E. Maizlish. Lexington: University Press of Kentucky, 1986.

Grice Marine Biological Laboratory. Established in 1955 by the College of Charleston as the Fort Johnson Marine Biological Laboratory, its name was changed in November 1965 to George D. Grice Marine Biological Laboratory in honor of the man then president of the college. The laboratory, on James Island about six miles by road from downtown Charleston, is on a portion of the site of old Fort Johnson, close to the end of a peninsula that juts into Charleston Harbor. State and federal laboratories involved in studies of estuarine and marine environments are also located at Fort Johnson.

Laboratory activities include both research and teaching. The college's biology faculty has taught most courses offered, but other local scientists have participated in instruction, most importantly in directing research of many students pursuing the master's degree. Laboratory and office space for resident faculty and facilities for research in many areas of biology are available. Student (both undergraduate and graduate) and faculty research has included studies in cell biology, molecular biology, ecology, fisheries biology, ichthyology, invertebrate zoology, oceanography, physiology, and systematics.

The library at Fort Johnson, jointly operated by the College of Charleston, South Carolina Department of Natural Resources, and National Oceanic and Atmospheric Administration, has significant holdings in marine sciences. Additionally, the laboratory's zoological collections, composed largely of fishes but with an appreciable representation of invertebrates, are utilized in research and teaching and are frequently consulted by investigators from other institutions. WILLIAM D. ANDERSON, JR.

Chamberlain, N. A. "Fort Johnson Marine Biological Laboratory, College of Charleston." *American Zoologist* 3 (August 1963): 274–75.

Sanders, Albert E., and William D. Anderson, Jr. *Natural History Investigations in South Carolina from Colonial Times to the Present.* Columbia: University of South Carolina Press, 1999.

Gridley, Mary Putnam (1850–1939). Civic leader, businesswoman. Gridley was born on September 7, 1850, in Hillston, Massachusetts, the daughter of George Putnam and Mary Jane Shearson. She was educated in the public schools of Boston and graduated from Boston High. She finished Boston Normal School in 1871 and taught for three years in Peabody, Massachusetts. In the 1870s she moved with her family to Greenville, South Carolina, where her father became active in the development of cotton mills.

In 1876 Mary Putnam married Isaac A. Gridley, who died two years later. The couple had no children. Soon after her husband's death, Gridley went to work for her father, who purchased Batesville Mill, a cotton factory, in 1879. Working as her father's assistant and as mill bookkeeper, Gridley mastered the daily operations of management and administration. Following her father's death in 1890, she assumed the position of mill president, the first woman mill president in South Carolina. In this capacity Gridley signed her name "M. P. Gridley," as she believed many questioned women's abilities to lead business enterprises. Gridley remained at the helm of the mill for twenty-two years, until it was sold in 1912.

In 1889 Gridley and Frances Perry Beattie formed the Thursday Club, a literary and study club for elite Greenville women. One of the earliest women's clubs in the south and the first in the state, the Thursday Club signaled the onset of the women's club movement in early-twentieth-century South Carolina. The club provided an opportunity for its members to consider and discuss literature and current events. Beattie served as the club's first president, and Gridley as vice-president. Soon after the club's organization, however, Beattie resigned and Gridley assumed the presidency, a position she held for the next forty years.

Under Gridley's presidency the Thursday Club in 1898 became one of the charter members of the South Carolina Federation of Women's Clubs (SCFWC), an organization that quickly developed an agenda to address a wide range of cultural, educational, and social issues. Gridley assumed a key role in the development of the women's club movement in Greenville and organized a Woman's Bureau to coordinate their various activities. Throughout her life she maintained an active involvement in the SCFWC.

In 1915 Gridley helped spearhead the organization of the Hopewell Tuberculosis Association to provide health services for Greenville's tuberculosis patients. She headed the association's board, and, under her leadership, the group opened a model tuberculosis camp and clinic at the Greenville City Hospital. She advocated and secured support for a comprehensive tuberculosis sanitarium, which opened in 1930 on Piney Mountain.

Gridley's civic activities encompassed a range of interests. She supported women's suffrage and was a leader in the Greenville Equal Suffrage Club. She assumed a critical role in the establishment of the Neblett Free Library in 1897, the first public library in Greenville. Gridley became an advocate for the establishment of public playgrounds for Greenville's youth and was credited with opening and securing staff for six city playgrounds.

In her roles as clubwoman, civic leader and business executive, Gridley represented the emergence of new interests in South Carolina women and their desire to participate in discourse and decision making on public issues. She died in Greenville on December 19, 1939, and was buried in Christ Church cemetery. BELINDA F. GERGEL

Barton, Eleanor Keese. "First Woman's Club in This State Organized by Mrs. M. P. Gridley." *Greenville Piedmont,* April 3, 1931, p. 14.

Chapman, Judson. "Mrs. M. P. Gridley." *Greenville Piedmont,* July 12 1935, pp. 1, 4.

Huff, Archie Vernon, Jr. *Greenville: The History of the City and County in the South Carolina Piedmont.* Columbia: University of South Carolina Press, 1995.

Lesley, Wanda. "Greenvillian Was Ahead of Her Time." *Greenville News-Piedmont,* February 9, 1975, p. 4B.

Pettigrew, Loulie Latimer. *The Thursday Club, Greenville, South Carolina, 1889–1989.* Greenville, S.C.: Graphics Now, 1988.

Grimké, Archibald Henry (1849–1930). Activist, scholar. Grimké was born on August 17, 1849, at Cane Acre plantation outside Charleston, one of three sons of Henry Grimké, a planter and lawyer, and Nancy Weston, a slave in the Grimké family. He was also the nephew of Henry's abolitionist sisters, Sarah and Angelina Grimké. After Henry's death in 1852, his mother took Grimké and his brothers, Francis and John, to Charleston, where, though legally enslaved, they lived a quasi-free existence. With the coming of the Civil War, however, Henry's white son Montague sought to reassert control over them, forcing the brothers into household slavery. In 1862 Grimké ran away, going into hiding for the duration of the war.

After the war, Grimké and his brothers were enrolled in a school for former slaves, where they caught the eye of its principal, the former abolitionist Frances Pillsbury. She arranged for Grimké and his brother Francis to attend Lincoln University in Pennsylvania, which they entered in 1867. In 1868 an article on Lincoln came to the attention of their aunt, Angelina Grimké Weld. The article singled out the Grimké brothers as outstanding students, and Angelina, recognizing the name, sought them out, acknowledged their kinship, and became their patron. With the assistance of her husband, Theodore Dwight Weld, and her sister Sarah, Angelina helped them to complete their work at Lincoln. Grimké received a master's degree in 1872 and continued his education at Harvard Law School.

Following his graduation from Harvard in 1874, Grimké established himself in Boston. He returned to South Carolina only once in his adult life, in 1906. On April 19, 1879, he married Sarah Stanley, daughter of an abolitionist Episcopal priest. The marriage was to dissolve in 1883, but not before the birth of a daughter, Angelina Weld Grimké, who later gained prominence as a poet and writer. Entering politics in 1883 as the editor of a Republican Party newspaper, Grimké soon after broke with the Republicans and became a highly visible activist in Boston's Democratic Party by the end of the decade. He was ultimately rewarded for his loyalty by being named by President Grover Cleveland as the American consul to the Dominican Republic (1894–1899).

On his return to the United States, Grimké settled in Washington, D.C. From 1903 to 1919, he served as president of the American Negro Academy, the leading intellectual organization for African Americans. He also became entangled in the bitter competition between partisans of Booker T. Washington and W. E. B. Du Bois, acknowledging the significance of Washington's achievements, but opposing Washington's more conciliatory approaches to race relations. After 1913 he devoted himself to the National Association for the Advancement of Colored People (NAACP), serving until 1923 on its national board. Through 1924 he also served as president of the District of Columbia branch, becoming a key figure in the NAACP's efforts to oppose racial discrimination at the federal level. Grimké died in Washington on February 25, 1930, and was buried in Harmony Cemetery, Washington, D.C. DICKSON D. BRUCE, JR.

Bruce, Dickson D., Jr. *Archibald Grimké: Portrait of a Black Independent.* Baton Rouge: Louisiana State University Press, 1993.

Meier, August. *Negro Thought in America, 1880–1915: Racial Ideologies in the Age of Booker T. Washington.* Ann Arbor: University of Michigan Press, 1963.

Grimké, John Faucheraud (1752–1819). Legislator, jurist. Grimké was born in Charleston on December 16, 1752, the son of merchant John Paul Grimké and his wife, Mary Faucheraud. After receiving his bachelor of arts degree from Trinity College, Cambridge, in 1774, Grimké returned to Charleston. His marriage to Mary Smith on October 12, 1784, produced fourteen children, including noted abolitionists Angelina and Sarah Grimké.

His judicial prominence stemmed from early political and military involvement. As a student in England in 1774, Grimké joined twenty-eight other Americans in protesting the Boston Port Bill. Shortly after returning to Charleston in September 1775, Grimké organized an artillery unit for service in the Revolutionary War. Rising to the rank of lieutenant colonel by 1779, he was captured at the fall of Charleston. He was later imprisoned by the British for allegedly violating his parole, but escaped to join General Nathanael Greene's army, where he served the remainder of the war.

In 1782 Grimké began the first of five terms representing the city parishes of St. Philip's and St. Michael's in the General Assembly, including a term as Speaker of the House from 1785 to 1786. Soon after the war, the legislature revived state law courts and named Grimké an associate justice of the Court of Common Pleas and General Sessions in March 1783. Many upstate citizens loyal to Britain during the war feared the nascent judiciary would extract revenge and lack impartiality. At his first grand jury charge in Camden in November 1783, Grimké sought to calm those concerns by declaring "We are all Americans" and that "our passions" were the only enemy of legal justice. Soon after his appointment, the legislature created county courts to hear minor cases, where laymen versed in local custom presided. To provide courtroom standards, Grimké published *The South Carolina Justice of Peace* in 1784 as a guide for officers of the new judiciary. In 1790 Grimké published the first updated digest of state laws in fifty years, *The Public Laws of the State of South Carolina.* Listing relevant and applicable laws in the period between the Revolutionary War and ratification of the Constitution, his digest provided a groundwork for judicial uniformity and the professionalization of legal study in South Carolina.

Grimké also resisted outside intimidation of the young state judiciary. In 1785 he encountered hostile debtors on his circuit in Camden. Grimké dismissed the "Camden Court House Riot" as an "illegal measure" and maintained the legitimacy of the court. As a delegate to the state constitutional convention in May 1790, Grimké introduced the provisions separating the judiciary from the legislature and requiring a two-thirds vote for judicial impeachment. In 1811 he took advantage of this proviso to defeat impeachment charges brought against him by political opponents.

During his thirty-six years on the bench, Grimké helped establish fundamental principles of South Carolina jurisprudence by advocating professionalization of legal study, uniformity of law, and judicial independence. After an extended illness, Grimké died in Long Branch, New Jersey, on August 9, 1819. ELI A. POLIAKOFF

King, Stephen Earl. "The Honorable John Faucheraud Grimké of South Carolina." Master's thesis, University of South Carolina, 1993.

Grimké, Sarah Moore (1792–1873), and **Angelina Emily Grimké** (1805–1879). Abolitionists. Sarah Moore Grimké, born on November 26, 1792, and her sister Angelina Emily Grimké, born on February 20, 1805, were the daughters of jurist and cotton planter John Faucheraud Grimké and Mary Smith. With familial ties to many of the lowcountry elite, the Grimké family was among the upper echelon of antebellum Charleston society. However, Sarah and Angelina rejected a privileged lifestyle rooted in a slave economy and became nationally known abolitionists no longer welcome in South Carolina. They first became involved in the public sphere through charity work in Charleston. Their mother was the superintendent of the Ladies Benevolent Society in the late 1820s, and both sisters were members. Serving on the society's visiting committees, they entered the homes of the poor white and free black women of the city. They later described the conditions in which the poor lived in speeches and letters. Sarah also worked as a Sunday school teacher for blacks at St. Philip's Episcopal Church. In this capacity, she questioned why African Americans could not be taught to read the Bible instead of relying on oral instruction. Both sisters began to challenge the contradictions between the teachings of Christian faith and the laws and practices of slaveholding society.

Sarah began spending time in Philadelphia with Quaker friends while Angelina befriended a Charleston minister from the North in 1823. Angelina soon embraced egalitarianism and attended the intimate Quaker services available in Charleston, leading to quarrels with her other siblings and suspicion from the community. In November 1829, Angelina left Charleston for Philadelphia as Sarah had done years earlier. The sisters found acceptance in the North. They joined the American Antislavery Society in 1835 and became the first female antislavery agents, speaking out against racial prejudice and using their firsthand experiences in South Carolina as examples. State and local governments in the South responded to the published letters and speeches of abolitionists by banning all antislavery messages through censorship of local newspapers and incoming mail. In Charleston a mob broke into the post office in July 1835 and burned the antislavery literature. Following the Charleston riot, Angelina wrote a letter to abolitionist William Lloyd Garrison that declared emancipation a cause worth dying for, which Garrison published in his antislavery newspaper, *The Liberator.* Other newspapers reprinted the letter, bringing the Grimké sisters notoriety, and they became pariahs no longer welcome in their native state. After a speaking tour throughout New England, Angelina became the first American woman to speak to a legislative body when she addressed a committee of the Massachusetts legislature in February 1838 asking for a stronger stance against slavery. She proclaimed herself a "repentant slaveholder" and said, "I stand before you as a southerner, exiled from the land of my birth by the sound of the lash and the piteous cry of the slave." Angelina believed, "It is sinful in any human being to resign his or her conscience and free agency to any society or individual." Thus, she rejected not only slavery but also society's restrictions on women.

Sarah and Angelina had cut themselves off from their family and community in the South, but they were not alone in the North. Their intimate circle of friends, which included Harriet Beecher Stowe, was supplemented by new family members. On May 14, 1838, Angelina married Theodore Weld, minister, abolitionist, and temperance speaker. They had two sons and a daughter. Her role as mother did not lessen Angelina's commitment to abolition and, later, women's rights. After emancipation, the Grimké sisters discovered that they had nephews living in the North who were the sons of their younger brother Henry and a slave mistress. The Charleston Grimkés had refused to acknowledge their biracial relatives, but Sarah and Angelina cultivated a friendly relationship with them—a relationship that further distanced them from Charleston's white society. The Grimké sisters remained public figures, supporting women's suffrage until their deaths. Sarah died on December 23, 1873, and Angelina on October 26, 1879. KELLY OBERNUEFEMANN

Birney, Catherine H. *The Grimké Sisters: Sarah and Angelina Grimké, The First American Women Advocates of Abolition and Women's Rights.* 1885. Reprint, New York: Haskell House, 1970.

Lerner, Gerda. *Grimké Sisters from South Carolina: Pioneers for Women's Rights and Abolition.* Rev. ed. Chapel Hill: University of North Carolina Press, 2004.

Grits. Grits is (or are) the coarse-to-fine ground product of a milling process whereby the hull of the dried corn kernel is popped open and the fleshy part is milled into tiny particles. Mill stones carved with grooves radiating outward from the center were set by the miller to grind the dried corn into course, medium, and fine grits as well as corn meal. The two oldest continuously operating water-powered mills in South Carolina were the Ellerbe Mill near Rembert in Sumter County, (1835–1985) and the Hagood Mill above Pickens (1828–1960 and restored and reactivated in the late twentieth century). At the Ellerbe Mill, the miller ground the corn between two milled stone wheels. In order to custom grind the customer's corn to the fineness or coarseness desired, the miller "set the stone" on top using a system of wooden pegs. The vibration of the active mill sent the ground grits particles onto a system of screen mesh, moving them down a path that sifted them through various grades of screen into buckets of meal, then fine, medium, course grits, and the bran for animal feed. As payment, the miller received ten percent of the product milled.

In modern times, grits are mass-produced using steel roller mills. The grits are of a single grind, de-germinated, and otherwise processed for long shelf life. Old-timers claim that the heat from the fast-turning roller mills partially parch the grits. This, they say, accounts for the difference in taste between the stone ground water mill grits and the commercial products today.

Grits, like rice, is a base for other foods and flavorings. "The taste of grits depends on what you put with it," say most South Carolina grits eaters. Favorite complements in South Carolina are red eye gravy, "matus" (tomato) gravy, and shrimp-and-grits in the lowcountry; sausage with sawmill gravy all over the state; and country ham, country fried steak and onion gravy, fried fish and quail as favorite "grits and . . ." dishes. Grits casseroles and soufflés and other exotic forms of grits are popular for more formal dinners and now appear in restaurants featuring popular "New South" cuisine. But the grits purist in the Palmetto State simply adds salt and butter.

Hominy is the Native American word for dried corn and is the name for what we came to call grits. It resulted from pounding what English recipe books called "Indian corn" using wooden mortar and pestle technology. Research has shown that the first flour mills erected by the European settlers in Virginia converted mill stones from grinding grain into flour to grinding corn into hominy "grits," corn meal, and domesticated animal feed. Grits and corn meal displaced flour as the dominate grain-based cooking product in the South. Grist mills proliferated throughout the South and became as much of a mainstay for towns and communities as was the general store.

The World Grits Festival held annually in St. George sees the town swell with thousands of visitors who come to see grits eating contests, recipe contests, and other "grits events." The Martha White Company—a sponsor of the event—reports that more grits are sold per capita in Dorchester County than anywhere else in the world. STAN WOODWARD

Its Grits. Produced and directed by Stan Woodward. 44 min. Woodward Studio, 1980. Videocassette.

Warren, Tim. "True Grits." *Smithsonian* 30 (October 1999): 80–88.

Grosvenor, Vertamae (b. 1938). Writer, culinary anthropologist. Grosvenor was born to Frank and Clara Smart on April 4, 1938, in Fairfax, Allendale County. When she was ten, her family moved from the South Carolina lowcountry, where Grosvenor spoke Gullah, to Philadelphia. By that time, she had developed an interest in food and cooking. After high school, Grosvenor went to Paris and traveled throughout Europe. She has been married twice and has two daughters.

A woman with varied interests, Grosvenor is best known as a writer and culinary anthropologist. During her travels abroad, she became interested in the African diaspora and how African foods and recipes traveled and changed as a result of it. Her first book, *Vibration Cooking; or, The Travel Notes of a Geechee Girl,* was published in 1970. It is a unique combination of recipes, reminiscences, and stories from family and friends. It shows Grosvenor's strong devotion to these people as well as her growing interest in Afro-Atlantic foodways and culinary history. This interest has been further developed in *Vertamae Cooks in the Americas' Family Kitchen* (1996) and *Vertamae Cooks Again* (1999), and in her cooking series, *Seasonings,* for public radio and *Americas' Family Kitchen* on the Public Broadcasting Service (PBS).

Grosvenor's other interests have led her in several directions. She has written for such varied publications as *Ebony,* the *New York Times,* the *Village Voice, Essence, Life,* and the *Washington Post.* In 1972 she published a history of black servitude in the United States. and England, *Thursdays and Every Other Sunday Off: A Domestic Rap.* She has also been an editor for *Elan Magazine* and served on the Literary Task Force for the South Carolina Arts Commission. She has lectured throughout the Americas, catered celebrity affairs, and been a guest on many television shows. She has acted on Broadway and in the movies *Daughters of the Dust* and *Beloved.* She is perhaps best known, however, as a regular contributor to National Public Radio (where she has been a commentator on *All Things Considered*) and PBS.

Throughout her career, Grosvenor has continued her loving explorations of lowcountry culture. She was a writer in residence for the Penn Center on St. Helena Island and worked on the *National Geographic Explorer* documentary, "Gullah." She won an Emmy for "Growing Up Gullah," a story for the Washington, D.C., program, *Capitol Edition.* She has combined her love of theater and cooking in the folk opera, *Nyam,* which is Gullah for "eat." KATHY A. CAMPBELL

Grosvenor, Vertamae. *Vibration Cooking; or, The Travel Notes of a Geechee Girl.* Garden City, N.Y.: Doubleday, 1970.

Guerard, Benjamin (?–1788). Governor. Benjamin Guerard, the son of John Guerard and Elizabeth Hill, was baptized in Charleston at St. Philip's Church on May 23, 1740. The exact date of his birth is unknown. Both his father and grandfather were wealthy Charleston merchants, planters, and public servants. As such, Guerard enjoyed a privileged upbringing and went to England in 1756 to study law at Lincoln's Inn. He was admitted to the South Carolina Bar on January 9, 1761, and set out to follow in the footsteps of his forebears. On November 30, 1766, Guerard married Sarah Middleton. Their marriage was childless.

Guerard represented St. Michael's Parish in the Commons House of Assembly from 1765 to 1768, but spent most of the late 1760s and early 1770s in litigation involving him as the executor of the vast estates of his father and Middleton in-laws. During the Revolutionary War, Guerard lent over £20,000 to the state and served in the militia. After Charleston fell to the British in May 1780, Guerard and other prominent Carolinians were held captive on the prison ship *Pack Horse.* While a prisoner, Guerard attempted to raise funds for the relief of his fellow captives and offered his estate to the British as security. Since the estate had been confiscated, the gesture was rejected by the British but was not soon forgotten by those Guerard had tried to help.

Although he maintained a town house in Charleston, by 1778 Guerard listed St. Helena's Parish as his legal residence and the remainder of his public career was associated with this place. Between 1779 and 1786, Guerard represented the parish four times in the General Assembly: three times in the state House of Representatives and once in the state Senate. In early 1783, Guerard was elected governor by the General Assembly, many members of which were ex-prisoners of war. As governor, Guerard pledged to lead South Carolina "from the Calamities of the uncommonly cruel War" into the "Return of the Blessings of Peace." The task he faced was daunting. South Carolina was deeply in debt and its population, stewing in old war animosities and class antagonism, was badly divided. The governor sought to suppress outlaws plaguing the backcountry and to provide "some small relief" for Charleston's poor. He also led the move to incorporate Charleston in 1783. But while taking a conciliatory stand on most issues, other actions made Guerard some powerful enemies. In an address to the General Assembly on February 2, 1784, he attacked the influential Society of the Cincinnati as aristocratic and undemocratic because membership was based on descent through the eldest line from Continental army officers. A year later, the Pinckney-Middleton-Rutledge political faction saw to the election General William Moultrie, president of the South Carolina Society of the Cincinnati, as Guerard's successor in the governor's chair.

On April 7, 1786, the widower Guerard married Marianne Kennan and retired to Fountainbleu, his 1,474-acre plantation on Goose Creek. Their marriage was also childless. Guerard died on December 21, 1788. MATTHEW A. LOCKHART

Bailey, N. Louise, Mary L. Morgan, and Carolyn R. Taylor, eds. *Biographical Directory of the South Carolina Senate, 1776–1985.* 3 vols. Columbia: University of South Carolina Press, 1986.

Nadelhaft, Jerome J. *The Disorders of War: The Revolution in South Carolina.* Orono: University of Maine Press, 1981.

Guignard, Jane Bruce (1876–1963). Physician. Guignard was born in Aiken County on October 30, 1876, the daughter of John Gabriel Guignard and Jane Bruce Salley. She spent her childhood at the family home, Evergreen, where her parents struggled to make a living from planting. The family moved near Columbia in 1895, and the move provided Jane Guignard with the opportunity to receive formal academic training. She attended the College for Women in Columbia and later received teacher training at the Peabody Teachers College in Nashville, Tennessee. Following her graduation in 1896, Guignard tutored students at home before teaching in Columbia city schools from 1897 to 1900.

After her mother's death in 1900, Guignard's father and brothers decided "Bruce should have her chance at medicine after all." With their financial backing, Guignard entered the Women's Medical College in Philadelphia in 1900. She graduated in 1904. After completing a year as an intern at the Women's Hospital, she returned to Columbia to practice medicine as one of the city's first female physicians. In a small, rented house and office at 1313 Lady Street, Guignard's practice grew "little by little." She served as the attending physician at the College for Women and Columbia College, and between 1905 and 1908 she served as second assistant to Dr. Le Grande Guerry, chief surgeon at Columbia Hospital. Around 1910 Guignard moved into a larger home and practice at 1416 Hampton Street and purchased her first car to assist her with house calls to patients.

Obstetrics and pediatrics became the cornerstone of Guignard's fifty-year medical career. "My first Columbia baby-case was a Negro child at the east end of my own street," she recalled. "The father came for me and carried my bag, I remember, then carried it home again when the baby had arrived. I walked both ways." After witnessing the "shockingly unsanitary and inconvenient surroundings" that accompanied the delivery of poor babies, Guignard established a small nursing home of her own in the 1920s. Supervised by Mrs. Charles Davis, and located near Guignard's Hampton Street office, the home operated as a successful maternity hospital until Davis's health failed in the 1930s and the venture was given up. Thereafter, Guignard became an instrumental force in the development of adequate obstetrical facilities at Columbia Hospital. She also established a training program for black midwives. During her career, she delivered more than one thousand babies in Richland County.

Guignard devoted much of her career to obstetrics, but her general practice also earned her a reputation as a doctor of the people. She looked to a patient's environment, working conditions, emotional state, and medical and family history as important factors in health care. Her marriage of professional expertise with personal history earned her the respect of her patients and colleagues. In recognition of her service to Richland County, a portrait of Guignard was presented to Columbia Hospital in September 1940.

Guignard died of leukemia on January 11, 1963, and was buried in the graveyard of the Trinity Episcopal Church. She bequeathed Still Hopes to the Episcopal dioceses of South Carolina to establish a home for senior citizens. GISELLE ROBERTS

Curry, Jane Guignard. "Jane Bruce Guignard, M.D.: 1876–1963." *Journal of the South Carolina Medical Association* 89 (January 1993): 31–34.

Meriwether, Margaret Babcock. "Columbia's Dr. Guignard." Columbia *State Magazine,* May 25, 1952, pp. 4–5.

Guignard Brick Works. James Sanders Guignard (1780–1856), grandson of a French immigrant to Charleston, began making brick along the Congaree River near Columbia in 1803, first for personal use, then for commercial purposes under the name Guignard Brick Works. Brick from the Guignard plant were used in many of Columbia's historic buildings, including the Confederate Printing Plant at the corner of Gervais and Huger Streets.

During the Civil War, the brick plant fell into disuse. In 1886 Gabriel Alexander Guignard, great-grandson of James Sanders Guignard, moved to the Columbia area from his parents' home near Springfield to revive the brick operation. He mined clay extensively from alluvial deposits along the west bank of the Congaree River southward to the Cayce granite quarry and eventually to the vicinity of Congaree Creek. He installed a private rail line to bring the clay to the plant, which was then located south of the Gervais Street–Meeting Street bridge.

After Gabriel Alexander Guignard's death in 1926, the brick operation was managed by his brother Christopher Gadsden Guignard and sister Susan Richardson Guignard. In 1956 the Guignard family sold a substantial interest in the company to a group of local investors.

In 1974 Guignard Brick Works was sold to the Merry Brothers Company of Augusta, Georgia, which continued to use the Guignard name. At the time of Merry Brothers' acquisition, the operation was moved from the banks of the river to a new plant near U.S. Highway 1 and Interstate 20 east of Lexington, as clay was no longer readily available at the riverfront site, and the equipment there was outdated. Eventually the Merry Brothers Company itself was sold, and the Lexington operation became a part of Boral Brick. The site of the old plant on the west bank of the Congaree River became an apartment complex, though the bee-hive firing kilns still stood. JAMES GUIGNARD

Gullah. The term "Gullah," or "Geechee," describes a unique group of African Americans descended from enslaved Africans who settled in the Sea Islands and lowcountry of South Carolina, Georgia, Florida, and North Carolina. Most of these slaves were brought to the area to cultivate rice since they hailed from the Rice Coast of West Africa, a region that stretches from modern Senegal to southern Liberia. Some ethnic groups, including the Mende, Kissi/Geessi, Susu, and Baga, cultivated rice well before European-African contact. The origin of the term "Gullah" (for residents of the South Carolina lowcountry) is uncertain. Some believe the term derives from "Angola"; alternatively, it could refer to the Gola people of Liberia and Sierra Leone. The term "Geechee" (for residents of the Georgia lowcountry) may come from the Ogeechee River or may refer to the Kissi/Geessi people of Sierra Leone, Guinea, and Liberia. The Gullah/Geechee people of the South Carolina and Georgia lowcountry continue to manifest unique African cultural attributes that have survived for more than three centuries.

Most enslaved Africans in lowcountry South Carolina landed in the region at Sullivan's Island outside Charleston. During the slave trade, Africans from different societies passed through this place and melded together to form a new African American people. They spoke different languages found between Senegambia and Angola, such as Mende, Vai, Kissi, Fula, Gala, Kikongo, Baga, Temne, and Mandinka. Thus, the process of combining different African peoples and languages in the lowcountry ultimately led to the emergence of Gullah or Geechee as a common language. Many words and phrases such as *oonuh* (you), *day clean* (dawn), *how oonuh de do?* (how are you?), and *ooman* (woman), remain in use among Gullah/Geechee speakers.

Until the end of the twentieth century, many looked at Gullah/Geechee as broken English, characteristic of those incapable of speaking standard English. In the 1940s, African American scholar Lorenzo D. Turner undertook a linguistic study to find out the origin and composition of the Gullah/Geechee language. He discovered the presence of many words and syntax of West African language origins in Gullah, especially in languages still spoken along the Rice Coast of West Africa. Linguists have also suggested that some West Africans who were transported to the lowcountry already spoke a creole language that became the ancestor of the Gullah/Geechee language. A strong linguistic similarity exists between Gullah and some creole languages in West Africa, such as Krio, spoken in Freetown, Sierra Leone. Turner's research and other factors, including a growing popular and scholarly interest in the Gullah people and their culture and the visit of Joseph Momoh (president of Sierra Leone) to Gullah country in 1988, have changed the negative image of the Gullah language.

Apart from the development of this unique language, numerous unique African cultural survivals also developed among the Gullah people. The rice culture that developed in the lowcountry was similar to that of the Grain/Rice Coast of West Africa. Many African ethnic groups from the Grain Coast were known for their expertise in rice cultivation long before the initial European contact, and South Carolina's wealth and fame in the eighteenth century owed much to the rice plantations of the lowcountry using African technological know-how and slave labor. Among these experts in rice cultivation were the Baga, Susu, Mende, Kissi, Vai, and their neighbors. Both West Africans from the Grain Coast and Gullah/Geechee people show a common dependency on rice as a dietary staple. Gullah foodways are similar to those of many West Africans, whose diet includes rice, greens, different kinds of beans, corn bread, sweet potatoes, banana cake, and ginger drinks. Gullah people and their African ancestors used rice in most of their ceremonies and rituals.

Gullah/Geechee people developed other unique cultural attributes that still connect them to their ancestral homeland, such as the folk art of sewing coiled grass into baskets and fans, which were generally used in rice harvest, rice storage, and for separating the rice seeds from the husks. Some of the finer baskets (such as *suuku blaie,* a Krio term for a specific kind of basket) were used for storing expensive jewelry. Gullah people are generally Christians, but the Geechee people of Sapelo Island, Georgia, have adopted some Islamic practices in their Baptist teachings, including the belief that God resides in the East, requiring believers to face the east during prayer. The Gullah/Geechee people also added many African rituals of worship, such as the ring shout and the offering of sacrifice. The belief in magic, conjuring, and mysticism played a significant role in Gullah religious practices.

The Gullah/Geechee people of the lowcountry have also developed a rich tradition in folklore. African and slave culture is mainly based on oral tradition. The history of the Gullah people is primarily derived from oral retellings by ancestors, elders, and oral historians. Stories and folklore using animals, such as Brer Rabbit or animal tricksters, representing human characters and behavior play significant roles in Gullah culture. Ron and Natalie Daise, Cornelia Bailey, Queen Quet, Jonathan Green, Philip Simmons, and others contributed to the rich tradition of Gullah/Geechee people especially in the areas of folklore, story telling, literature, and visual arts. Many Gullahs in the past adopted or continued to use African names and naming systems such as Monday, Tamba, Kadiatu, Samba, and Gallah.

Unfortunately the Gullah people, land, culture, and existence are under threat from modern developers. Motivated by profits derived from tourism, real estate developers have built resorts and are eagerly expanding beaches in the Sea Islands. A critical problem facing the Gullah/Geechee people will be mapping out a plan for the coexistence of their culture and coastal development. Federal legislation introduced by U.S. Congressman James Clyburn in 2004 called for the preservation of the Gullah/Geechee culture. The act also called for the creation of a Gullah/Gechee Cultural Heritage Corridor Commission to assist governments in managing the land and waters. Such developments can help protect this important aspect of South Carolina's cultural landscape. M. ALPHA BAH

Daise, Ronald. *Reminiscences of a Sea Island Heritage.* Orangeburg, S.C.: Sandlapper, 1986.

Geraty, Virginia Mixson. *Bittle en' t'ing: Gullah Cooking with Maum Chrish'.* Orangeburg, S.C.: Sandlapper, 1992.

Goodwine, Marquetta L., and the Clarity Press Gullah Project. *The Legacy of Ibo Landing: Gullah Roots of African American Culture.* Atlanta: Clarity, 1998.

Jones-Jackson, Patricia. *When Roots Die: Endangered Traditions on the Sea Islands.* Athens: University of Georgia Press, 1987.

Joyner, Charles W. *Down by the Riverside: A South Carolina Slave Community.* Urbana: University of Illinois Press, 1984.

Littlefield, Daniel C. *Rice and Slaves: Ethnicity and the Slave Trade in Colonial South Carolina.* Baton Rouge: Louisiana State University Press, 1981.

Pollitzer, William. *The Gullah People and Their African Heritage.* Athens: University of Georgia Press, 1999.

Wood, Peter H. *Black Majority: Negroes in Colonial South Carolina from 1670 through the Stono Rebellion.* New York: Knopf, 1974.

H. L. Hunley. On the night of February 17, 1864, the Confederate submarine *H. L. Hunley* attacked and sank the USS *Housatonic* about four miles off Sullivan's Island. This was the first successful sinking of an enemy ship in warfare by a submersible in the history of the world.

Constructed in Mobile, Alabama, the vessel was named for Horace L. Hunley, one of its investors and owners. The iron vessel was forty feet long, five feet tall, and four feet wide. Ballast tanks located in the bow (front) and stern (rear) filled with water to submerge the submarine; to resurface, a pump forced the water out. It was originally designed to pull a "torpedo" (mine) behind, dive under a ship, and have the torpedo explode on contact.

The crew was composed of eight members. A captain at the bow served as the navigator and operated the dive planes, rudder, and pump. The remaining seven crew members, in the vessel's midsection, operated a hand crank connected to the propeller. This method of propulsion could move the submarine through the water as fast as four knots. A bellows, between the captain and crew, was connected to a snorkel and pumped fresh air into the submarine.

In July 1863 the siege of Charleston began when U.S. forces moved onto Morris Island. Confederate general P. G. T. Beauregard had the *H. L. Hunley* brought to Charleston to operate against the U.S. Navy blockading squadron. Once there, it was discovered that the towed torpedo was neither practical nor safe, and it was instead placed on a seventeen-foot-long iron spar. By the time of her final attack, the *Hunley*'s spar was located at the bottom of the bow. There is also evidence that the ninety-pound explosive was designed to be rammed against a wooden hull where barbs fixed it to the vessel and it detached from the spar. The submarine would move back and a lanyard (rope) running from to the submarine to the torpedo would detonate the explosive.

The crew, unfamiliar with the harbor, did not immediately attack the Union ships. Because of the delay, Confederate military authorities confiscated the *H. L. Hunley.* On August 29, 1863, it sank due to human error and five crew members drowned. The vessel was recovered and Hunley regained control of the submarine. During a diving drill in Charleston Harbor on October 15, 1863, it failed to surface and all eight crew members, including Hunley, drowned.

Recovered again, the submarine was moved to a location behind Sullivan's Island at Breach Inlet. Lieutenant George E. Dixon, who had trained on the submarine, assumed command, recruited a new crew, and trained for a mission against the blockading squadron. Influenced by the loss of thirteen crew members in the two accidental sinkings, Beauregard ordered the vessel to operate only on the surface. On the night of February 17, 1864, the submarine attacked and sank the USS *Housatonic.* However, the *H. L. Hunley* was also lost. Discovered in 1995, the submarine was recovered on August 8, 2000, and underwent a multimillion-dollar conservation effort. RICHARD W. HATCHER III

Ragan, Mark K. *The Hunley: Submarines, Sacrifice, & Success in the Civil War.* Rev. ed. Charleston, S.C.: Narwhal, 1999.

Hagler (?–1763). Catawba chief. King Hagler (Haigler, Arataswa) is the best known of the Catawba chieftains. Nothing is known of his early life. He rose to power in 1750 or early 1751 after the previous chief, Young Warrior, and the other headmen of the tribe were ambushed by a group of northern Indians, probably of the Iroquois Confederation. Hagler had been hunting and was not with the group when they were killed. His first official act came in 1751, involving a peace delegation organized by Governor James Glen of South Carolina and Governor Dewitt Clinton of New York to treat with the Iroquois Confederation at Albany, New York. Hagler was accompanied on this journey by William Bull II and five headmen of the Catawba tribe. The Catawba and the Iroquois had been implacable enemies for hundreds of years, leading to much bloodshed between them, despite the great distance separating their lands. After signing the peace treaty, Hagler returned home to discover that a band of "northern Indians" had attacked members of the Catawba tribe. Two more peace envoys were required (1752 and 1761) before peace was finally established between the ancient enemies.

The Catawba under King Hagler supported the British in the French and Indian War by sending a contingent of soldiers to fight with Colonel George Washington in the winter of 1756 and the spring of 1757. A smaller contingent of Catawba returned to Virginia to fight with General John Forbes in 1758. While there they contracted smallpox. On their returning home, the disease quickly spread through the Catawba, killing half their population. King Hagler was not in the village at the time of the outbreak and again escaped death.

The single most important event of King Hagler's reign was the Treaty of Pine Tree Hill, which he negotiated in July 1760. It provided for a reservation fifteen miles square (144,000 acres) on the border of North and South Carolina. The reservation borders were later fixed by the Treaty of Augusta, which was signed on November 5, 1763, shortly after Hagler's death.

Although Hagler is commonly known in history as King Hagler, the title of "King" was not a traditional Indian title. Rather, it was bestowed on him by Governor James Glen sometime in the early 1750s. This was a common custom of colonial governors when dealing with Indian nations. Simultaneously, Governor Arthur Dobbs of North Carolina gave the title to James Bullen, a brave Catawba warrior during the French and Indian War. However, Bullen died before he could successfully challenge Hagler for leadership of the tribe.

On August 30, 1763, Hagler was returning with a servant from visiting the Waxhaws. He was ambushed on the road to Catawba Old Town on Twelve Mile Creek by seven Shawnees, who shot him six times and then scalped him. ANNE M. MCCULLOCH

Brown, Douglas Summers. *The Catawba Indians: The People of the River.* Columbia: University of South Carolina Press, 1966.

Merrell, James H. *The Indians' New World: Catawbas and Their Neighbors from European Contact through the Era of Removal.* Chapel Hill: University of North Carolina Press, 1989.

Milling, Chapman J. Red Carolinians. 1940. Reprint, Columbia: University of South Carolina Press, 1969.

Hagood, Johnson (1829–1898). Soldier, governor. Born in Barnwell District on February 21, 1829, Hagood was the son of Dr. James O'Hear Hagood and Indiana Margaretta Allen. Educated at Richmond Academy in Augusta, Georgia, he entered the Citadel in 1844, graduating with distinction in 1847. Admitted to the bar in 1850, he was appointed deputy adjutant general of militia for South Carolina in 1851 by Governor John H. Means, and served as commissioner in equity for Barnwell District from 1851 to 1861. On November 21, 1854, Hagood married Eloise Brevard Butler, the daughter of U.S. Senator Andrew P. Butler. They had two children.

On January 27, 1861, at the onset of the Civil War, Hagood was elected colonel of the First South Carolina Regiment of Volunteers. Calm and steadfast under fire, he saw action in South Carolina, Virginia, and North Carolina, from the reduction of Fort Sumter in April 1861 to the Battle of Bentonville in March 1865. His gallantry at the Battle of Secessionville led to his promotion as brigadier general on July 21, 1862. Additionally he was placed in charge of the Second and Seventh Military Districts encompassing South Carolina, Georgia, and Florida on July 19, 1862, and February 20, 1864, respectively.

After the war Hagood returned to his plantations in Barnwell and Edgefield Counties. An advocate of scientific agriculture, he championed diversified farming and was a noted breeder of thoroughbred horses. He served as president of the State Agricultural and Mechanical Society (1869–1873) and was an incorporator in 1870 of the Columbia Oil Company. Politically he represented Barnwell in the Forty-seventh General Assembly (1865–1866), ran unsuccessfully for Congress as a Democrat in 1868, and was a member of the 1871 and 1874 Taxpayers' Conventions. Initially a cooperationist with reform Republicans, he was elected state comptroller general in 1876 on the "straight-out" Democratic ticket, although he deplored the violence of the campaign. During the Ellenton Riots of September 1876, he commanded a posse commissioned to make arrests and quell the violence. As comptroller-general, he masterminded the crucial voluntary tax funding of the Hampton administration during the period of dual governments and was reelected in 1878. Overcoming a challenge by Democratic insurgent Martin W. Gary, Hagood was elected governor in 1880. Choosing to serve only one term, his administration enacted legislation that created a stronger railroad commission, reopened the Citadel, and expanded the coverage of artificial limbs for Confederate veterans. Also during his term, white Democrats solidified their control of state government by passing the Eight Box election law and by creating the "Black" Seventh District to contain African American voting power.

Personally reserved and a gifted organizer, politically Hagood was criticized as being overcalculating. Devoted to the Citadel, he served as chairman of the Board of Visitors (1878–1898), and president of the Association of Graduates (1877–1898). Hagood died on January 4, 1898, at his Sherwood plantation and was buried in Barnwell's Holy Apostles Episcopal churchyard. As a mark of respect, the entire corps of cadets, officers, and faculty of the Citadel attended his funeral. PAUL R. BEGLEY

Cooper, William J., Jr. *The Conservative Regime: South Carolina, 1877–1890.* Baltimore: Johns Hopkins Press, 1968.

Hagood, Johnson. *Memoirs of the War of Secession.* Edited by Ulysses R. Brooks. Columbia, S.C.: State Company, 1910.

Hallelujah Singers, The. Hallelujah Singers are a nationally recognized performance troupe offering unique cultural programming by preserving, performing, and celebrating the rich heritage of Sea Island Gullah culture. Organized as a vocal ensemble by Marlena Smalls in 1990 and based in Beaufort, the group promotes Gullah culture through song, story, dance, and dramatic performance.

The Hallelujah Singers present many of the unique customs and rituals that are an integral part of Gullah life. Drawing on extensive research, including interviews with seniors in the community, Smalls and the group have developed programs that combine storytelling and Gullah music—a music form steeped in a rich African American spiritual tradition. They have three professional recordings: *Gullah: Songs of Hope, Faith, and Freedom* (1997); *Joy: A Gullah Christmas* (1998); and *Gullah: Carry Me Home* (1999). The Hallelujah Singers also travel extensively throughout the United States, presenting their "Fa Da Chillun'" outreach program to students and adults. Movie audiences became familiar with the group from their appearance in the motion picture *Forrest Gump,* with Marlena Smalls appearing in the role of "Bubba's Mama." The Hallelujah Singers have also appeared in several national media outlets and continue to broaden their audience base.

Marlena Smalls and the Hallelujah Singers have been recognized for their commitment to the presentation and advocacy of Gullah culture. As a part of its bicentennial celebration, the Library of Congress designated the Hallelujah Singers a "Local Legacy of South Carolina." Other awards include the Jean Laney Harris Folk Heritage Award, the Alpha Kappa Community Service Award, and selection as the South Carolina Ambassadors of the Year for 1998. SADDLER TAYLOR

Halsey, William Melton (1915–1999). Artist. Born in Charleston on March 13, 1915, Halsey was the son of Ashley Halsey and Eleanor Loeb. His father was a partner in the Halsey Lumber Company. Educated in Charleston schools, in 1928 Halsey became a youthful protégé of the Charleston Renaissance artist Elizabeth O'Neill Verner. He attended the University of South Carolina for two years before going to the Boston Museum School (1935–1939), where he studied anatomy and fresco painting. On June 5, 1939, he married Sumter native and fellow artist Corrie McCallum. The couple had three children. In 1939 and 1940 he spent eighteen months in Mexico on a Paige Fellowship from the Museum School. Returning to the Southeast he taught for a short period in Charleston before moving to Savannah to direct the art school at the Telfair Academy. He settled in Charleston permanently in 1945 and supported himself by teaching, first at the Gibbes Art Gallery and then independently. From 1972 until his retirement in 1984 he was artist in residence at the College of Charleston, where the William Halsey Gallery at the Simons Center for the Arts is named in his honor.

Halsey traveled extensively, funded by friends and supporters who were rewarded with a work of art in return for their modest subventions. The Yucatán peninsula in Mexico was one of his favorite destinations, but he also went to Greece, Spain, and Morocco. In 1971, with McCallum, he published *A Travel Sketchbook,* an annotated selection of their drawings, and in 1976 he issued *Maya Journal.* Halsey's early work gained critical attention in several New York exhibitions. Unlike his predecessors who emphasized charm and sunlight in their portrayals of Charleston, Halsey reveled in the decay, colors, and textures offered by the old city. It was precisely these qualities that inspired the nonrepresentational work that dominated his mature output. Instead of painting conventionally in oil on canvas, he elected to use Masonite, which provided a firm backing for his frequent reworkings of the surface. The firmness of the support was advantageous when he added collage elements, such as old paint rags, torn and stained bits of his own clothing, and African textiles given to him by his friend Merton Simpson, a dealer in African art. About 1964 Halsey began to translate his collages into three-dimensional sculptures, largely totemlike assemblages, made from scraps of wood and later metal. Late in his career he worked with oil pastels on paper in a bright range of colors enlivened by expressionist gestures.

A prolific artist, Halsey was active in arts organizations in the state, such as the Guild of South Carolina Artists, and his work was regularly included in a broad range of exhibitions across the Southeast. The Greenville County Museum of Art organized two major exhibitions: in 1972 a retrospective of his work and in 1999 a posthumous exhibition. Halsey is represented in the collections of the Gibbes Museum of Art, the South Carolina State Museum, the Columbia Museum of Art, the Greenville County Museum of Art, and the College of Charleston. Halsey died on February 14, 1999, in Charleston. See plate 30. MARTHA R. SEVERENS

Morris, Jack A., Jr. *William M. Halsey: Retrospective.* Greenville, S.C.: Greenville County Museum of Art, 1972.

Severens, Martha R. *William Halsey.* Greenville, S.C.: Greenville County Museum of Art, 1999.

Hamburg. Founded in 1821 and located on the Savannah River in lower Edgefield District (now Aiken County), the town of Hamburg was one of South Carolina's primary interior markets during much of the antebellum era. It was founded by Henry Shultz, a brash and ambitious German immigrant who had previously made and lost a fortune in the neighboring city of Augusta, Georgia. Angered at the treatment received from the "aristocrats of Augusta," Shultz built his new town opposite the Georgia city in order to secure the trade of the upper Savannah River for South Carolina. The South Carolina General Assembly assisted Shultz in his trade war with a $50,000 loan and by exempting Hamburg town lots from taxation. The new town grew rapidly during the 1820s and acquired even greater promise during the 1830s, when it became the western terminus of the South Carolina Canal and Rail Road Company's line to Charleston and the site of the Bank of Hamburg in 1835. But Hamburg's once bright outlook quickly faded in the ensuing years. Ruinous floods inundated the town several times during the 1840s and 1850s. The opening of the Augusta Canal in the late 1840s siphoned off much of the river traffic of the upper Savannah. Most devastating, the railroad extended its line across the river and into Augusta, taking much of Hamburg's cotton trade with it. By the late 1850s Hamburg's once thriving merchant population began to quit the city. Whites abandoned Hamburg in the years after the Civil War, leaving Hamburg to become a haven for emancipated slaves and a Republican Party bastion during Reconstruction. The town gained infamy in 1876 as the site of the Hamburg Massacre, in which an uncertain number of blacks died at the hands of a Red Shirt mob. After the restoration of the Democratic Party to power in 1876, the General Assembly repealed Hamburg's charter and the town gradually faded out of existence. The site reemerged at the end of the nineteenth century as the city of North Augusta. TOM DOWNEY

Cordle, Charles G. "Henry Shultz and the Founding of Hamburg, South Carolina." In *Studies in Georgia History and Government,* edited by James C. Bonner and Lucien E. Roberts. Athens: University of Georgia Press, 1940.

Downey, Tom. *Planting a Capitalist South: Masters, Merchants, and Manufacturers in the Southern Interior, 1790–1860.* Baton Rouge: Louisiana State University Press, 2006.

Taylor, Rosser H. "Hamburg: An Experiment in Town Promotion." *North Carolina Historical Review* 11 (January 1934): 20–38.

Hamburg Massacre (July 8, 1876). The Hamburg Massacre, a bloody racial clash in a small town in Aiken County, was a turning point in the gubernatorial campaign of 1876. The massacre put into perspective numerous features of post–Civil War South Carolina, including the tensions between—and the growing militancy of—local whites and African Americans, the depth of conservative white hostility, and the precarious existence of Governor Daniel H. Chamberlain's Republican state government.

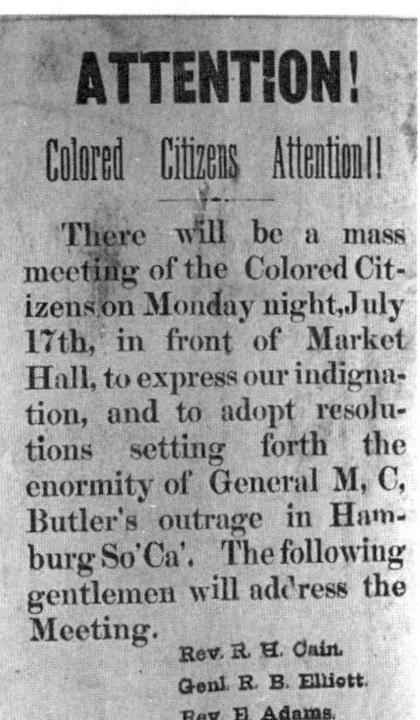

A poster calling for a meeting of black Charlestonians to protest the Hamburg Massacre. Courtesy, South Carolina Historical Society

Hamburg, a largely African American village near the Savannah River, lay astride the route from Augusta, Georgia, to Aiken and Edgefield Counties in South Carolina. On July 4, 1876, two whites, Henry Getsen and Thomas Butler, were apparently stopped and heckled by an African American militia unit who refused to allow passage through town. The antagonism between whites and black militia units was deeply entrenched. The militia, formed by the state's Republican administration to protect the African American community, was unacceptable to many whites. To them, an armed, nearly all-black force in the service of (in their eyes) an illegitimate state government brought animosity rather than security. In July 1876, with elections for the state government only months away, tensions were especially high. The militia commander in Hamburg, a former slave and Union army veteran named Doc Adams, eventually allowed the travelers to pass, but the damage had been done. Angry and offended, Getsen and Butler headed to Edgefield, where they secured the legal services of Matthew C. Butler, a local attorney and Confederate war hero.

Butler (no relation to Thomas) filed suit with Hamburg's trial justice, another former slave and veteran, Prince Rivers. The suit charged the militia, and Adams in particular, with blocking a public highway. Butler demanded that the militia be disbanded and that the arms be surrendered to him. Adams countersued, claiming the travelers had interfered with an official militia drill. A hearing was set for the morning of July 8, but Justice Rivers began to panic when Butler arrived, escorted by scores of armed whites from local gun clubs. Attempting to broker a deal, Rivers offered to ship the militia weapons back to the state armory, but Butler rejected the offer. Fearing a collision, Rivers warned the militia to lay low, and somewhere between eighty and one hundred members subsequently barricaded themselves in a nearby brick warehouse.

This action by the militia, followed closely by the disappearance of the trial justice, may have convinced whites that the African Americans were considering some sort of offensive action. Or, seeing the militia concentrated, rougher types might have seized the opportunity to push for punitive action. Whatever the motivation, by midafternoon the whites, whose numbers had grown to more than two hundred, surrounded the warehouse. Dispute remains over who fired the first shot, but by late afternoon the battle was in full fury, with whites firing at the building while African Americans inside returned fire. Men on both sides were wounded, but the first man killed was white, a young man who was shooting alongside his father.

As dusk set in, an old cannon arrived from Augusta, which quickly rendered the cover of the building useless. After a few rounds from the cannon, militiamen started darting out holes and windows and running toward the neighboring woods. At least one African American was killed as he exited the warehouse, and some thirty or forty were captured by whites. From this group six were selected, marched a fair distance away, and executed. The remainder, already disarmed, were released; several accounts indicate that whites fired on them also, as they fled into the safety of the woods.

The effects of the massacre spread and galvanized the South Carolina Democratic Party, while at the same time it drove a wedge between Republicans at the state and federal levels. White Democrats had been divided over the 1876 gubernatorial campaign, with some arguing for an alliance with Republican Governor Daniel Chamberlain as the safest means of achieving victory. The Hamburg Massacre and its aftermath silenced such talk and catapulted to prominence the "straight-out" strategy, which supported former Confederate general Wade Hampton for governor. Following Hamburg, Governor Chamberlain had condemned whites as the aggressors, pleaded for federal troops to help keep the peace (and then denied doing so), and supported a massive roundup of suspects (nearly one hundred whites were arrested). The federal government turned an all but deaf ear, and President Ulysses S. Grant even displayed annoyance at the governor's inability to maintain order. Hamburg demonstrated Chamberlain's bias and weakness—no prosecutions, in fact, ever occurred—and the federal government's growing indifference. Over the summer and fall numerous confrontations took place, with gun clubs, saber clubs, military parades, and spontaneous (and not-so-spontaneous) riots becoming a central feature of the Democratic campaign. The hard-driving Democratic campaign based on intimidation and force would bring Hampton into the statehouse. RICHARD ZUCZEK

Allen, Walter. *Governor Chamberlain's Administration in South Carolina, A Chapter of Reconstruction in the Southern States.* 1888. Reprint, New York: Negro Universities Press, 1969.

Zuczek, Richard. *State of Rebellion: Reconstruction in South Carolina.* Columbia: University of South Carolina Press, 1996.

Hamilton, James, Jr. (1786–1857). Congressman, governor. Hamilton was born near Charleston on May 8, 1786, to James Hamilton, Sr., a rice planter, and Elizabeth Lynch. He was educated at Newport, Rhode Island, and Dedham, Massachusetts, before returning to Charleston to read law under the tutelage of Daniel Huger and William Drayton. Admitted to the bar in 1810, Hamilton began practice in Drayton's office and later became a partner of James L. Petigru. Volunteering for service in the War of 1812, Hamilton eventually rose to the rank of major. On November 15, 1813, he married the lowcountry heiress Elizabeth Heyward, gaining three plantations and two hundred slaves. The couple had eleven children.

In a state known for its flamboyant politicians, Hamilton was among the most colorful individuals to sit in the governor's chair. As a member of South Carolina's lowcountry aristocracy, Hamilton epitomized the chivalrous manner and deportment of planter society. A famous duelist, he successfully fought fourteen duels, always wounding but never killing his opponents. His prowess on the field of honor made Hamilton a much sought after second. Among the men he seconded were George McDuffie, Oliver Perry, Stephen Decatur, and John Randolph of Roanoke in his celebrated duel with Henry Clay. Hamilton was also one of Charleston's most aggressive and reckless entrepreneurs, whose planting activities and land speculations were combined with extensive investments in numerous business, banking, and mercantile ventures.

Hamilton's political career began in 1819, when he was elected to represent St. Philip's and St. Michael's Parishes in the South Carolina House of Representatives. Twice reelected, Hamilton resigned from the state legislature in December 1822 to fill a vacancy in the U.S. House of Representatives created by the resignation of William Lowndes. In that same year, Hamilton served as intendant (mayor) of Charleston, where he oversaw the response to Denmark Vesey's slave conspiracy. As were most South Carolinians in the early and mid-1820s, Hamilton was a strong nationalist and ardent supporter of Andrew Jackson. He carried these views with him to Washington and, after the election of 1824, led the House opposition to the administration of John Quincy Adams. Hamilton continued to represent Charleston and the lowcountry in Congress until 1829, when he declined reelection and returned to South Carolina.

The passage of the Tariff of 1828 and his gradual conversion to states' rights principles soon soured Hamilton on both an active federal government and Andrew Jackson. In a speech delivered at Walterboro on October 21, 1828, Hamilton publicly renounced his earlier nationalism and called for "a *nullification* by the State" of the despised tariff. Claiming precedent for such action in the Kentucky and Virginia Resolutions of Thomas Jefferson and James Madison, the speech at Walterboro launched the nullification movement in South Carolina and placed Hamilton at its forefront. On December 9, 1830, the legislature elected Hamilton governor and he assumed leadership of the States' Rights and Free Trade Party, which he organized into local associations to popularize free trade ideas. While governor, Hamilton also presided over the 1832 Nullification Convention, which voted to nullify the tariff within South Carolina's borders. After leaving office on December 10, 1832, Hamilton was made a brigadier general of the state militia by the new governor, Robert Hayne. In this role Hamilton prepared the state to defy federal authority with arms if necessary.

After the nullification crisis subsided, Hamilton turned his attention to his far-flung business pursuits, most of which soured in the Panic of 1837 and left him deeply indebted. Hamilton also became interested in the affairs of the newly independent Republic of Texas. He loaned the republic money and in 1838 was appointed loan commissioner for Texas by President Mirabeau Lamar. His duties carried him to Europe where he negotiated several commercial treaties and won recognition of the Republic of Texas from Great Britain and the Netherlands. Relieved of his post in 1842, Hamilton spent much of the remainder of his life shuttling between Texas, South Carolina, and Washington, D.C., trying to gain repayment of the money he loaned to Texas.

On November 15, 1857, Hamilton was en route to Texas, traveling on the steamer *Opelousas,* when it was struck by another ship just off Avery Island, Louisiana. Within half an hour the *Opelousas* had sunk. A gentleman to the end, Hamilton gave his life jacket to a woman and child and helped them into a lifeboat. Seconds later a wave swept Hamilton from the deck of the sinking ship and he drowned. SEAN R. BUSICK

Freehling, William W. *Prelude to Civil War: The Nullification Controversy in South Carolina, 1816–1836.* New York: Harper & Row, 1965.

Kell, Carl Lewis. "A Rhetorical History of James Hamilton, Jr.: The Nullification Era in South Carolina, 1816–1834." Ph.D. diss., University of Kansas, 1971.

Tinkler, Robert. *James Hamilton of South Carolina.* Baton Rouge: Louisiana State University Press, 2004.

Hamilton, Paul (1762–1816). Governor, secretary of the navy. Hamilton was born in St. Paul's Parish on October 16, 1762, the son of Archibald Hamilton and Rebecca Branford. He received instruction from a private tutor in Charleston until 1778, when he left the city to join a local militia company. During the Revolutionary War, Hamilton served in militia units commanded by Francis Marion and William Harden. He participated in several significant actions, including the siege of Savannah (1779), the Battle of Camden (1780), and the capture of Fort Balfour (1781). After the war Hamilton took up planting rice and indigo in St. Paul's and St. Bartholomew's Parishes. By 1788 he owned at least thirty-eight slaves and 1,602 acres of land. On October 10, 1782, he married Mary Wilkinson, and the couple eventually had at least six children.

Well positioned by his military service and family connections, Hamilton turned to politics in the postwar years. He served one term in the General Assembly as a representative from St. Paul's Parish from 1787 to 1789. As a delegate to the South Carolina ratification convention in 1788, Hamilton voted in favor of the federal Constitution. He then represented St. Bartholomew's Parish for three terms in the state Senate during the 1790s, during which time he became a Democratic-Republican in contrast to the Federalist leanings of many of his lowcountry contemporaries. He was an elector for Thomas Jefferson in the 1800 presidential election. While serving as state comptroller of finance, Hamilton was elected governor of South Carolina by the General Assembly on December 10, 1804. During his two-year tenure he advocated military preparedness through improvements to state militia laws and coastal defenses. He also called for a revision of the penal code, requesting that the state's "old sanguinary provincial system" be replaced with a penitentiary system that would provide inmates "time for reflection and amendment." He also urged the General Assembly to ban the Atlantic slave trade, which had been reopened in 1803. Legislators resisted Hamilton's request, however, and the trade remained open until Congress closed it permanently in 1808.

In 1809 President James Madison selected Hamilton to be his secretary of the navy as part of an effort to achieve regional balance in his cabinet appointments. Hamilton proved an inexperienced but competent naval administrator. He advocated fiscal restraint and general military preparedness, including the enlargement of the seventeen-ship U.S. Navy. His one lasting success was in securing congressional support for the creation of a system of naval hospitals in 1811. When war broke out with Britain in 1812, Hamilton, fearing the tiny U.S. Navy would be destroyed, advised Madison to order all vessels to port. He was overruled and Madison implemented a plan to harass British merchant ships. At a presidential ball to celebrate the surrender of HMS *Macedonia,* Hamilton appeared so drunk that Madison requested his resignation. Hamilton subsequently resigned on December 31, 1812. He died at Beaufort on June 30, 1816, and was buried at a private cemetery in Beaufort District. JAMES SPADY

Bailey, N. Louise, Mary L. Morgan, and Carolyn R. Taylor, eds. *Biographical Directory of the South Carolina Senate, 1776–1985.* 3 vols. Columbia: University of South Carolina Press, 1986.

Hammett, Henry Pinckney (1822–1891). Industrialist. Hammett was born on December 31, 1822, in Greenville County, the son of Jesse Hammett and Nancy Davis. After a childhood on his father's farm, Hammett went at the age of eighteen to Augusta, Georgia, where he trained as a clerk in the cotton firm of Matthews & Company. He returned to Greenville to teach school and then worked in a country store near Batesville. In 1848 Hammett married Deborah Jane Bates, the daughter of the textile mill owner William Bates. The couple had six children.

Soon after his marriage, Hammett took charge of cotton purchasing for the Batesville Cotton Mill and became a partner in the firm by the mid-1850s. In 1862 the company purchased land at Garrison Shoals on the Saluda River with the goal of relocating and modernizing the cotton mill. The following year, however, a Charleston company bought the Batesville mill. Hammett purchased the Garrison Shoals property and moved to Greenville, where he became county tax assessor. For the next few years, Hammett served in the public arena, representing Greenville County in the General Assembly from 1865 to 1866. He also served as president of the Greenville and Columbia Railroad from 1866 to 1870.

In the early 1870s Hammett headed a group of area business leaders interested in building a cotton mill on the Garrison Shoals property. On April 30, 1873, subscribers met at Greenville to organize the Piedmont Manufacturing Company. Hammett was elected president of the new firm, which would incorporate a year later with $200,000 in capital stock. Hammett was one of the first postwar mill presidents in South Carolina to adopt the large-scale New England model of factory production. The first mill at Piedmont began operations in March 1876 with 5,000 spindles and 112 looms. Under Hammett's leadership a second mill was added in 1878, then a third in 1890. By 1892 the Piedmont Manufacturing Company operated 47,000 spindles and 1,300 looms with a mill village population of three thousand. China represented an important market for the company's cloth sheeting. Hammett also bought the insolvent Camperdown Mills Company in 1885, which he reorganized as the Camperdown Cotton Mills.

In addition to factory work, Hammett presided over a substantial mill village community including a schoolhouse, town hall, church, and hotel. As did most mill executives, Hammett opposed any unionization efforts. When the Knights of Labor began to organize at Piedmont in 1886, he ordered the mill superintendent to fire any worker who joined the union. He also joined other mill presidents in resisting child labor legislation in 1890. However, Hammett's skillful management expanded economic opportunities for some in the upcountry and served as a model for subsequent mill ventures. He died in Greenville on May 8, 1891. BRUCE W. EELMAN

Carlton, David L. *Mill and Town in South Carolina, 1880–1920.* Baton Rouge: Louisiana State University Press, 1982.

Huff, Archie Vernon, Jr. *Greenville: The History of the City and the County in the South Carolina Piedmont.* Columbia: University of South Carolina Press, 1995.

Hammond, James Henry (1807–1864). Congressman, governor, U.S. senator. Son of the New England emigrant Elisha Hammond and Catherine Fox Spann of Edgefield, Hammond was born on November 15, 1807, in Newberry District. Schooled at home by his father, he entered South Carolina College, a breeding ground for the state's political leaders, at the age of sixteen. While his academic record was not distinguished, Hammond became president of the famous Euphradian Society where he honed his debating skills. After graduating in 1826 he taught school briefly and studied law with William Harper and William Campbell Preston among others. He was admitted to the bar in December 1828.

James Henry Hammond. Courtesy, South Caroliniana Library, University of South Carolina

Hammond came of age politically during the nullification crisis. As were his former teachers, he was an early convert to the idea of a state veto of federal laws. In January 1830 he assumed the helm of the Columbia *Southern Times* and his partisan editorials brought him to the attention of the state's nullifying elite led by John C. Calhoun. They also involved him in a controversy with Unionist congressman James Blair. A duel between the two men was barely averted. In a another incident, after exchanging a series of heated editorials, Hammond got involved in a public brawl with C. F. Daniels, the Unionist editor of the *Camden Journal.*

Hammond's attempts to gain social respectability complemented his political ambitions. His marriage to the lowcountry heiress Catherine Fitzsimons on June 23, 1831, resulted in the acquisition of a large plantation, Silver Bluff, in Barnwell District. The couple eventually had eight children. As an owner of over a hundred slaves, he rapidly ascended to the pinnacle of South Carolina society. For the next few years he devoted himself to a vigorous struggle of wills with his recalcitrant slaves. Engrossed in his plantation, Hammond lost election to the state convention that nullified the federal tariff laws of 1828 and 1832. After President Andrew Jackson responded with a proclamation against nullification, Governor Robert Y. Hayne appointed Hammond as one of his aides de camp and he set about raising two regiments with great zeal. Back in the political limelight, Hammond was elected to Congress in October 1834.

As a congressman, Hammond joined the charmed circle of planter-politicians that composed the state's leadership. During nullification he had loudly questioned the value of a Union that threatened slavery. In Congress he emerged as one of the staunchest advocates for the nonreception of abolitionist petitions during the Gag Rule controversy and gave a memorable speech that celebrated slavery and the hierarchical organization of southern society. In 1836 he suddenly withdrew from politics because of ill health and embarked on an extended tour of Europe.

On his return to South Carolina, Hammond started angling for the governorship. Calhoun's political machine led by Franklin H. Elmore and Robert Barnwell Rhett supported the candidacy of the former Unionist John P. Richardson to effect a reconciliation between nullifiers and Unionists. Hammond suffered a resounding defeat in the gubernatorial election of 1840 but two years later, in December 1842, he was elected governor with the support of the Rhett-Elmore clique. His term was marked by two incidents: the expulsion of Samuel Hoar, a Massachusetts emissary sent to negotiate the imprisonment of black sailors, and the Rhett-led Bluffton movement. Hammond supported the movement, which was nipped in the bud by Calhoun, who worked to unite competing factions in South Carolina behind his presidential bid.

Political failure and personal indiscretions dogged Hammond at this time. His brother-in-law, Wade Hampton II, broke off relations with him when he discovered Hammond's indiscretions with his daughters. Hammond, along with his oldest son, also sexually exploited two of his female slaves, mother and daughter. This led to a public estrangement from his wife. Personal isolation forced him into a life of semiretirement from politics for the next decade.

At home Hammond immersed himself in the life of the mind. One of the founders of the state's agricultural society, he was a vocal advocate of economic diversification and scientific agriculture. Hammond's letters on slavery to the English abolitionist Thomas Clarkson became proslavery classics and were reprinted in *The Proslavery Argument* (1852) and *Cotton Is King* (1860). He is best remembered for his famous "Cotton is King" speech delivered in the U.S. Senate in 1858 during the Kansas debates. Arguing that all societies needed a "mud sill" class to perform the drudgery of labor, he pointed out that democracy threatened not only slavery but also all property and capital.

A staunch defender of slavery, Hammond however was skeptical of the wisdom of slavery expansion. During the Wilmot Proviso controversy and the first secession crisis, he was severely critical of Calhoun's efforts to "agitate in SoCa" and the South. He participated in the Nashville Convention but refused to attend the second meeting after the Compromise of 1850. On Calhoun's death he lost his bid for the vacant senate seat to Rhett, who was committed to single-state secession. Hammond, who now sympathized with southern cooperationists, touted a plan that would keep the state in the Union but sever all its ties to the federal government. In 1857 the legislature elected him to the U.S. Senate because of his relative independence from the two warring factions, the secessionists and the National Democrats, ending his hiatus from state politics.

As senator, Hammond alienated secessionists by arguing that the South could dominate the Union through the Democratic Party. Until the very eve of disunion, Hammond hoped for the defeat of the Republican Party. After Lincoln's election, he resigned from the Senate and supported secession and the establishment of the Confederacy. During the Civil War, he, as were other southern planters, was critical of Jefferson Davis and chafed under Confederate impressment policies. However, he remained committed to the idea of a southern nation and died on November 13, 1864, his body wracked by mercury poisoning, his spirit destroyed by the imminent southern defeat. MANISHA SINHA

Bleser, Carol, ed. *Secret and Sacred: The Diaries of James Henry Hammond, A Southern Slaveholder.* New York: Oxford University Press, 1988.

Faust, Drew Gilpin. *James Henry Hammond and the Old South: A Design for Mastery.* Baton Rouge: Louisiana State University Press, 1982.

Hammond, James Henry. Papers. Library of Congress, Washington, D.C.

———. Papers. South Caroliniana Library, University of South Carolina, Columbia.

Merritt, Elizabeth. *James Henry Hammond, 1807–1864.* Baltimore: Johns Hopkins Press, 1923.

Wilson, Clyde N., ed. *Selections from the Letters and Speeches of the Hon. James H. Hammond, of South Carolina.* Spartanburg, S.C.: Reprint Company, 1978.

Hammond, LeRoy (1728–1790). Planter, entrepreneur, soldier. Hammond was born on February 18, 1728, in Richmond County, Virginia, the son of John Hammond and Katherine Dobyns. In 1765 he moved to Augusta, Georgia, where he soon became a merchant and also operated a ferry across the Savannah River. Before leaving Virginia, he married Mary Ann Taylor, with whom he produced one son. Prior to the Revolutionary War, he purchased six hundred acres of land on the South Carolina side of the Savannah River and lived there by 1771. Operating a store, Hammond also cultivated tobacco and later became a tobacco inspector for the area. By around 1770, the firm of LeRoy Hammond & Company had received more than £10,000 from the colonial government to purchase land and build courthouses and jails in the upcountry.

As war with Britain drew near, Hammond volunteered his services to the patriots. One of his first duties was to aid William Henry Drayton and William Tennant in their 1775 tour of the upcountry to win support among its residents for independence. The following year he served as one of Andrew Williamson's captains in the Cherokee War of 1776. Hammond distinguished himself by rallying his mounted ranger unit after it was ambushed near Seneca Town. The unit was initially stopped and on the verge of running from the field. Hammond dashed forward to rally his men and force the enemy to retreat. While some Loyalists and Cherokees were captured, the main leaders escaped. Two years later, in 1778, Hammond was appointed a commissioner to conciliate the Indian nations and to negotiate a peace with the Upper and Lower Creeks. He served in several skirmishes and battles of the war, including the Battle of Stono (June 20, 1779), the siege of Ninety Six (May 22–June 17, 1781) and the Battle of Eutaw Springs (September 8, 1781). By the summer of 1781 Hammond was serving under General Nathanael Greene, who assigned Hammond's regiment to defend patriot areas against Loyalist incursions.

During and after his military service, Hammond represented Ninety Six District as a representative in the First (1775) and Second (1776) Provincial Congresses, and then in the new General Assembly. In 1776 he resigned from the state House on his election to the Legislative Council. After the war he returned to represent his district in the Third (1779–1780) through the Seventh (1787–1788) General Assemblies. Hammond also served in local offices including justice of the peace for Ninety Six District (1774) and for Edgefield District (1785), road commissioner (1778, 1784), and commissioner for inspection and exportation of tobacco at Snow Hill (1785). At his death, Hammond owned fifty-four slaves, an inspection warehouse at Falmouth in Edgefield District, and two lots in Springfield. He died between May 14, 1790, when his will was written, and July 1790, when it was proved. FRITZ HAMER

Bailey, N. Louise, Mary L. Morgan, and Carolyn R. Taylor, eds. *Biographical Directory of the South Carolina Senate, 1776–1985.* 3 vols. Columbia: University of South Carolina Press, 1986.

Hampton (Hampton County; 2000 pop. 2,837). The town of Hampton came into being with the formation of Hampton County in 1878 and is located near the center of the county. On October 12, 1878, Governor Wade Hampton laid the cornerstone for the courthouse, a two-story brick structure styled after the courthouses of Robert Mills. In 1925 the building was remodeled and enlarged, with the double curved stair leading to the second floor portico removed. The first post office was established in 1872 at a nearby railroad stop called Hoover's, which was about a mile away from the courthouse. When the office moved nearer to the courthouse, it was renamed Hampton Court House, then later shortened to Hampton. The town was chartered on December 23, 1879.

A newspaper, the *Hampton County Guardian,* was founded in 1879 by Miles B. McSweeney, who later served as governor of South Carolina. The earliest churches in Hampton were Hoover's Methodist Episcopal, South (later Hampton United Methodist); Bethlehem Baptist; a Baptist Church at Hoover's that moved nearer "town" and became First Baptist; and Huspah Baptist, which moved into the vacated church at Hoover's. A school for African American children was held at Huspah. In 1896 the site was the forerunner location of what became Voorhees College. A school for white children was built about 1878 near the courthouse.

By the early 1920s Hampton was well laid out with a broad, tree-lined main street, Lee Avenue, spanning the three blocks from the courthouse to the Charleston & Western Carolina railroad depot. The town of eight hundred residents boasted twenty businesses, two hotels, an automobile and tractor agency, two physicians, two banks, and a two-story brick school for white children. Hampton Colored School was built in the late 1920s. In 1931 portions of S.C. Highway 28 in the county were paved, which connected Hampton with Orangeburg and points north, as well as to what became U.S. Highway 17. In 1939 the first Hampton County Watermelon Festival was held. It is the oldest continuous festival in South Carolina.

Near Hoover's in 1933, the American Legion built a "Hut," while the National Guard built an armory there in the early 1940s. Hoover's also became home to Hampton's first modern industry, Plywoods-Plastics, and to schools, housing developments, and the West End business district. In 1955 Westinghouse relocated a Pennsylvania factory to the Plywoods-Plastics site, which at its peak employed 1,100 workers. International Paper bought the facility in 1995.

In the latter twentieth century, Hampton continued to advance toward the economic and social mainstream. The population increased and Hampton became an increasingly prosperous commercial and industrial center. A labor union emerged at Westinghouse in the 1950s. First the black, then the white high schools of Brunson, Hampton, and Varnville consolidated. Later all district schools were integrated. Parks, playgrounds, baseball and softball fields, tennis courts, and a soccer complex provided recreation. A 1940s art deco movie house became a performing arts theater, while an 1892 bank was transformed into the Hampton Museum and Visitors' Center. A town hall, police department, fire department, and public works facility were built, yet the town last raised taxes in 1973. ROSE-MARIE ELTZROTH WILLIAMS

Hampton County Historical Society. *Both Sides of the Swamp: Hampton County.* Rev. ed. Hampton, S.C.: Hampton County Historical Society, 1997.

Hampton, Harry (1897–1980). Writer, conservationist. Hampton was born in Columbia on July 8, 1897, to Frank Hampton and Gertrude Gonzales. He was educated at Porter Military Academy in Charleston, then Randolph Macon Academy in Front Royal, Virginia. He attended the University of South Carolina, where he studied English, history, and foreign language, graduating in 1919. In 1930 he married Mary Rebecca DeLoache. The two had a daughter, Harriott. Mary died in 1970 in a car accident, and Hampton married Elizabeth Heyward McCutcheon two years later.

Soon after graduation from college, Hampton took a job as writer for the *State* newspaper. He was most interested in writing about sports, and in 1930 he began writing the "Woods and Waters" column about outdoor sports. "Woods and Waters" was essentially a crusade for the state's natural lands. In the column and in public speaking engagements around the state, Hampton promoted sportsmanship and wise use of the state's natural resources. His enthusiastic writing style and conservation ethic gained him a following among the state's outdoorsmen and conservationists, and his work had a far-reaching influence on the public's concept of game and fish. His leadership was instrumental in the creation of the Wildlife and Marine Resources Department and the organization of the South Carolina Game and Fish Association, forerunner of the South Carolina Wildlife Federation. One of Hampton's greatest successes was his role in saving the Congaree Swamp, now Congaree Swamp National Park, for which he actively lobbied the General Assembly and anyone else who would listen. For a lifetime of work on behalf of the state's natural resources, Hampton has been called the father of South Carolina's conservation movement.

Harry Hampton. Courtesy, Harriott H. Faucette. Columbia, SC

Hampton published two books: the autobiographical *Woods and Waters and Some Asides,* and a book of poetry, *Random Rhymes,* both published by the State Printing Company. Hampton died in Columbia on November 16, 1980, and was buried at Trinity Cathedral. His legacy, along with his body of work, is the Harry Hampton Memorial Wildlife Fund, a charitable organization that supports outdoor conservation and education programs through the state Department of Natural Resources, including the Palmetto Sportsmen's Classic. CAROLINE FOSTER

Coleman, Nancy. "He Speaks for the Wilderness." *South Carolina Wildlife* 27 (January–February 1980): 14–18.

"Harry Hampton, Conservationist, Journalist, Dies." Columbia *State,* November 17, 1980, p. A1.

Hampton, Wade, I (1754–1835). Planter, soldier, politician. Hampton was born on May 3, 1754, in Virginia, the youngest son of Anthony Hampton and Elizabeth Preston. The family soon after migrated to North Carolina. In the early 1770s several of the Hampton brothers relocated to Ninety Six District, South Carolina, and by April 1774, Wade, along with his parents and other relatives, had moved to the Tyger River valley in present-day Spartanburg County. The brothers were involved in mercantile ventures and trade with the Cherokee Indians in the years before the Revolutionary War. Wade's parents and other family members were killed by an Indian raiding party in late June 1776.

From the beginning of the Revolutionary War, Hampton supported the patriot cause. From 1777 until early 1780 he was an officer and paymaster in the Sixth Continental Regiment. After the fall of Charleston, Hampton signed an oath of allegiance to the British, but used his position as a storekeeper in the Congarees to spy on the British garrison at Granby. Early in 1781 Hampton joined Thomas Sumter as commander of one of the regiments of state troops and took part in the battles at Quinby Bridge (July 17, 1781), Eutaw Springs (September 8, 1781), and Dorchester (December 1, 1781).

Hampton was elected to the General Assembly in 1779, serving several more terms in the 1780s and 1790s. He was also twice elected to the U.S. House of Representatives (1795–1797; 1803–1805) and held other positions of responsibility, including trustee of the South Carolina College (1801–1809). With war again pending with Great Britain in the early 1800s, Hampton again volunteered for military service. He was commissioned as a colonel in the U.S. Army on October 10, 1808. Subsequently promoted to brigadier general (1809) and major general (1813), Hampton served until April 6, 1814, when he resigned after a failed effort to capture Montreal—in conjunction with James Wilkinson—had brought stinging criticism of both men.

Hampton's most lasting fame came from his success as a planter. In 1783 he acquired property on the Congaree River in Richland District, directing much of his time and financial resources to the improvement of his plantations and the more efficient production of his crops. Between 1783 and 1815 he added to his Richland holdings and constantly improved his property, establishing his immensely profitable cotton plantation, Woodlands. In 1799 he produced some six hundred bags of cotton worth an estimated $90,000. During the first decade of the nineteenth century, his Richland District lands produced on average fifteen hundred bales of cotton each year. In 1811 he purchased land in Louisiana that he developed into one of the most productive sugar plantations on the Mississippi. In 1827 sugar and molasses sales from his Louisiana plantations brought him $100,000 annually, making him that state's largest sugar producer. Noted by *Niles' Weekly Register* in 1823 as "probably the richest planter in the South," Hampton had become a national symbol of the wealthy southern slaveowner. He may have owned as many as nine hundred slaves by 1820 in South Carolina and Louisiana.

Hampton married three times. His first wife, Martha Epps Goodwyn, died in May 1784 after only a year of marriage and left no children. Harriet Flud, who married Hampton in August 1786, left two sons at her death in 1794. He married his third wife, Mary Cantey (Harriet Flud's stepsister), in 1801. The third marriage produced six children. Wade Hampton died February 4, 1835, and was buried in Trinity Churchyard, Columbia. RONALD E. BRIDWELL

Bailey, N. Louise, and Elizabeth Ivey Cooper, eds. *Biographical Directory of the South Carolina House of Representatives.* Vol. 3, *1775–1790.* Columbia: University of South Carolina Press, 1981.

Bridwell, Ronald E. "The South's Wealthiest Planter: Wade Hampton I of South Carolina, 1754–1835." Ph.D. diss., University of South Carolina, 1980.

Cauthen, Charles E., ed. *Family Letters of the Three Wade Hamptons, 1782–1901.* Columbia: University of South Carolina Press, 1953.

Meynard, Virginia G. *The Venturers: The Hampton, Harrison, and Earle Families of Virginia, South Carolina, and Texas.* Easley, S.C.: Southern Historical Press, 1981.

Hampton, Wade, II (1791–1858). Planter, soldier, legislator. Hampton was born on April 21, 1791, at Woodlands Plantation, Richland County, the eldest son of Colonel (later General) Wade Hampton I and his second wife, Harriet Flud. As Hampton's father was a Revolutionary War hero, congressman, and one of the wealthiest planters in the South, the son soon took his place among the highest ranks of the planter aristocracy. He was educated at Moses Waddel's Willington Academy and later studied at South Carolina College between 1807 and 1809. Though academically gifted, he left college and accepted a commission as a second lieutenant in the First Light Dragoons in the U.S. Army in 1813, serving under his father's command on the Canadian front against the British in the War of 1812. He was discharged in June 1814 after his father's resignation, but he subsequently served on General Andrew Jackson's staff in January 1815, distinguishing himself in preparing American defenses against the British assault on New Orleans.

After the war Hampton helped manage his father's vast estates in Louisiana, as well as the Millwood-Woodlands complex near Columbia. He became known as an avid hunter, outdoorsman, breeder of thoroughbred horses, and horse racing enthusiast. On March 6, 1817, he married Ann Fitzsimons, daughter of a wealthy Charleston merchant, and settled at Millwood. The couple had eight children. In 1820 he accepted an appointment as deputy inspector general of the South Carolina Militia, became a leader of the Agricultural Society, and was a trustee of South Carolina College from 1826 to 1857. He won election to the South Carolina Senate in 1825. He served two terms and never again sought or held elective office. He played an important role behind the scenes in state politics, however. He was known to favor nullification, but opposed disunion. Especially between 1849 and 1852, he worked vigorously behind the scenes to thwart those who hoped to take South Carolina out of the Union. After 1843 he was an effective and implacable political opponent of his brother-in-law and former friend, Governor James Henry Hammond, whom Hampton discovered had behaved dishonorably toward his teenage daughters.

A tradition states that when Hampton's father died in 1835, the son destroyed the will, which would have left the bulk of the estate to him. It is clear that no will was extant, and his father's lands and slaves were divided between himself, his stepmother, and his half-sisters. He took possession of most of the family holdings in South Carolina and divided his time between them and his own "Walnut Ridge" tract of 2,529 acres in Mississippi, which he had purchased more than a decade earlier. He purchased eight thousand acres in Texas and, with his sons Wade III and Christopher, bought 2,300 acres in Cashiers Valley, North Carolina. He also invested heavily in railroads.

Hampton died suddenly, probably of a stroke, on his Mississippi plantation on February 9, 1858, and was buried at Trinity Church in Columbia. He left vast landholdings but also large debts to his three sons and four unmarried daughters. ROD ANDREW, JR.

Bridwell, Ronald E. "The South's Wealthiest Planter: Wade Hampton I of South Carolina, 1754–1835." Ph.D. diss., University of South Carolina, 1980.

Faust, Drew Gilpin. *James Henry Hammond and the Old South: A Design for Mastery.* Baton Rouge: Louisiana State University Press, 1982.

Meynard, Virginia G. *The Venturers: The Hampton, Harrison, and Earle Families of Virginia, South Carolina, and Texas.* Easley, S.C.: Southern Historical Press, 1981.

Hampton, Wade, III (1818–1902). Planter, soldier, governor, U.S. senator. Hampton was born in Charleston on March 28, 1818, the eldest son of Wade Hampton II and Ann Fitzsimons. A scion of one of the South's wealthiest families, Hampton was educated in private academies at Rice Creek and Columbia before attending South Carolina College, where he was graduated in 1836. A quintessential planter-aristocrat, Hampton may have been the richest planter in the South at the end of the antebellum era, with properties in South Carolina and Mississippi producing annual incomes of as much as $200,000. On October 10, 1838, Hampton wed Margaret Frances Preston, with the marriage eventually producing five children. His first wife died in 1852 and Hampton married Mary Singleton McDuffie on January 27, 1858. Four children were born to this second union.

From 1852 until 1861 Hampton represented Richland District, first in the S.C. House of Representatives and then in the state Senate. As a legislator, Hampton promoted economic development in his district, sponsoring several measures for railroads and manufacturing companies. He also played an active role in support of the state asylum and the construction of a new capitol. He generally avoided debates over secession, which he believed to be an unnecessarily drastic means of protecting southern interests. In 1859 he also spoke out against efforts to reopen the Atlantic slave trade, arguing that the attempt was "fraught with more danger to the South than any other that has been proposed" and characterizing the slave trade as "that odious traffic."

Once secession became fact, Hampton threw himself wholeheartedly behind the Confederate cause. At his own expense Hampton organized the Hampton Legion, a regiment consisting of six companies of infantry, four of cavalry, and one battery of artillery. He was commissioned its colonel in June 1861, and the legion soon after played an important part in the first Battle of Manassas (July 21, 1861). Hampton commanded an infantry brigade in the Peninsula Campaign (April–June 1862) and was wounded in the Battle of Seven Pines (May 31, 1862). He returned to command a cavalry brigade under General J. E. B. Stuart. Hampton proved to be a superb leader of cavalry, who was at his best in leading raids behind the enemy lines, sometimes with great drama. In 1864 Hampton led

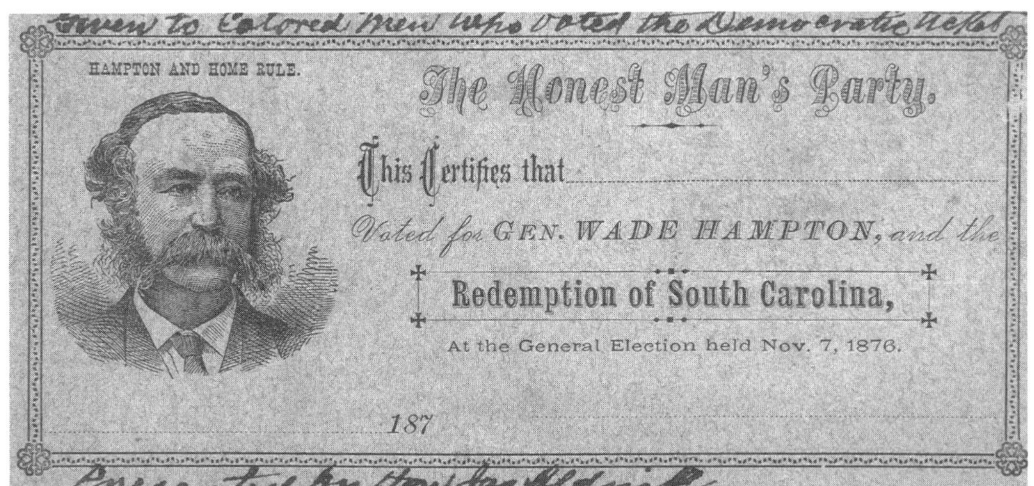

Given to Colored Men who Voted the Democratic ticket

HAMPTON AND HOME RULE.

The Honest Man's Party.

This Certifies that ....

Voted for GEN. WADE HAMPTON, and the

Redemption of South Carolina,

At the General Election held Nov. 7, 1876.

.... 187 ....

Presented by Hon Jas Aldrich

An election "receipt," featuring the image of Wade Hampton. It was given to black Carolinians who voted for Hampton in 1876. Courtesy, South Carolina Historical Society

The reverse of the election "receipt." Courtesy, South Carolina Historical Society

the so-called Beefsteak Raid, capturing 2,468 cattle from the Union army. In August 1864 Hampton became the commander of the cavalry of the Army of Northern Virginia. In that capacity Hampton played an important role in the defense of Richmond in the last months of the war. In January 1865 General Robert E. Lee sent him to defend South Carolina against Sherman's army, but the assignment proved hopeless. By war's end Hampton was one of only three Confederates without West Point training to achieve the rank of lieutenant general.

Hampton returned to Columbia to find his fine homes and estates in ruins. Reconciling himself to defeat and disqualified from holding office due to his Confederate service, he worked to recoup his fortunes, especially by trying to revive his Mississippi plantations. These efforts were to no avail and he ultimately declared bankruptcy in 1868. However, as his former wealth dwindled, Hampton's political prestige grew enormously. His reputation enhanced by his military record, Hampton became politically active in opposing the postwar Republican regime in South Carolina. Pardoned in 1872, Hampton reentered a state political arena awash in violence against the radical government, instigated largely by white Democrats who decried both Republican corruption and the political influence of recently freed African Americans. Amid intensifying attempts to redeem South Carolina for its traditional white leadership, the so-called Bourbons, Hampton emerged as the Democratic leader. By temperament a moderate, Hampton called for an end to the extreme violence initiated by Democratic rifle clubs, fearing that such excesses would only invite further federal intervention in the state. He briefly considered cooperating with the reform elements in the Republican Party. But by 1876 state Democrats decided to run a "straight-out" Democratic slate and convinced Hampton to be their candidate for governor.

The campaign of 1876 was bitter and a hard-fought, with both sides engaging in intimidation and frequent violence. Some Hampton supporters organized themselves into armed units and dressed in red shirts. The Red Shirts were particularly effective in intimidating Republican leaders and their supporters, especially black voters. While Hampton could not curb all the excesses committed by his supporters, he continued to urge moderation and actively courted black voters, winning significant support among African Americans in a close election. To demonstrate Democratic strength without the use of violence, Hampton led a march across the state, drawing large and enthusiastic crowds at each stop. The election results were hotly contested, resulting in the existence of two governors and two legislatures, with Republicans dependent on federal troops to enforce their position. Publicly Hampton continued to call for an end to the political violence and urged Daniel Chamberlain to resign the governor's chair. Behind the scenes Hampton negotiated with federal authorities for the removal federal troops. Finally, in April 1877, President Rutherford B. Hayes withdrew the soldiers and Hampton took office on April 11, effectively bringing Reconstruction in the state to an end. In the eyes of white South Carolinians, Hampton was more than a victorious political candidate. He was their savior.

Hampton's administration was characterized by honesty, fiscal conservatism, and attempts at cooperation across racial and party lines. As governor he supported black suffrage and appointed several African Americans and some Republicans to public office. Economically he advocated fiscal responsibility and urged the funding of the state's debts. Such actions created rifts within his own party, but Hampton's personal prestige overwhelmed all rivals. In 1878 Hampton was returned to the governor's chair without opposition and then elected by the state legislature to the U.S. Senate. Taking office in early 1879, Hampton served in the Senate until 1891. His senatorial policies were generally conservative and Democratic, although he sometimes voted with the opposition. He supported the gold standard and opposed his party by supporting the seating of Republican William Pitt Kellogg from Louisiana. In his last days in office he opposed the Force Bill sponsored by Senator Henry Cabot Lodge, whereby the federal government could again intervene in state elections to protect the interests of black citizens.

As a senator, Hampton exercised less and less influence in South Carolina politics. Forces led first by Martin Gary and later Benjamin Tillman gained influence by advocating redistribution of power to the upstate and to farmers, the political exclusion of African Americans, and the establishment of an agricultural college. Hampton viewed this opposition as a threat to Democratic Party unity, but he had little interest in or understanding of Tillman's growing attraction among white voters. In 1890 Tillman became governor and ousted the Bourbons that Hampton had led to victory in 1876. Once in office Tillman orchestrated Hampton's removal from the Senate by backing John L. M. Irby, who defeated Hampton's bid for reelection.

Leaving his Senate seat in March 1891, Hampton served for a time as commissioner of U.S. Railroads, but his political influence had come to an end. He was financially destitute, and his livelihood depended on holding office and on the generosity of friends and admirers. Supporters canvassed the state for funds to provide him a house in Columbia after his last home burned in 1899. Hampton died in Columbia on April 11, 1902, and was buried in Trinity Episcopal Churchyard, a revered symbol of the best of the old South Carolina. ROBERT K. ACKERMAN

Cooper, William J., Jr. *The Conservative Regime: South Carolina, 1877–1890.* Baltimore: Johns Hopkins Press, 1968.

Jarrell, Hampton M. *Wade Hampton and the Negro: The Road Not Taken.* Columbia: University of South Carolina Press, 1949.

Meynard, Virginia G. *The Venturers: The Hampton, Harrison, and Earle Families of Virginia, South Carolina, and Texas.* Easley, S.C.: Southern Historical Press, 1981.

Wellman, Manly Wade. *Giant in Gray: A Biography of Wade Hampton of South Carolina.* New York: Scribner, 1949.

Zuczek, Richard. *State of Rebellion: Reconstruction in South Carolina.* Columbia: University of South Carolina Press, 1996.

Hampton County (560 sq. miles; 2000 pop. 21,386). Hampton County was created in 1878 from the northern half of Beaufort County. Hampton later lost territory to the creation of Jasper County in 1912, and Allendale County in 1919. The county was named for Wade Hampton III, Confederate general, governor, and U.S. senator. Hampton is the county seat.

After the Beaufort County seat was moved in 1868 from Gillisonville, in the center of the county, to Beaufort, thirty miles southeast, some citizens attempted to secede. They lived north of the Charleston and Savannah Railroad (which bisected Beaufort County), and their petitions cited the great distance to court and the ill effects on their health of the salt marsh surrounding the town of Beaufort. Palmetto, Washington, and Coosawhatchie were suggested as names for the new county. The legislature approved the division after Governor Hampton took office. "Moderate" African Americans supported the new county, believing they could be represented better through a coalition with white Democrats than by the Republicans of Beaufort. Thomas E. Miller, a founder and the first president of South Carolina State University, worked to secure the secession and took credit for naming the county. However, no African Americans were elected officers of the new county.

Hampton County bordered one railroad and was traversed by a second, the Port Royal and Augusta Railroad completed in 1873. This line lay on a sandy ridge east of the Coosawhatchie River Swamp separating the eastern and western portions of the region. (Locally, people and places are identified by their "side of the Swamp," a designation that is as much philosophical as geographical). William H. Mauldin's logging railroad was chartered in 1891

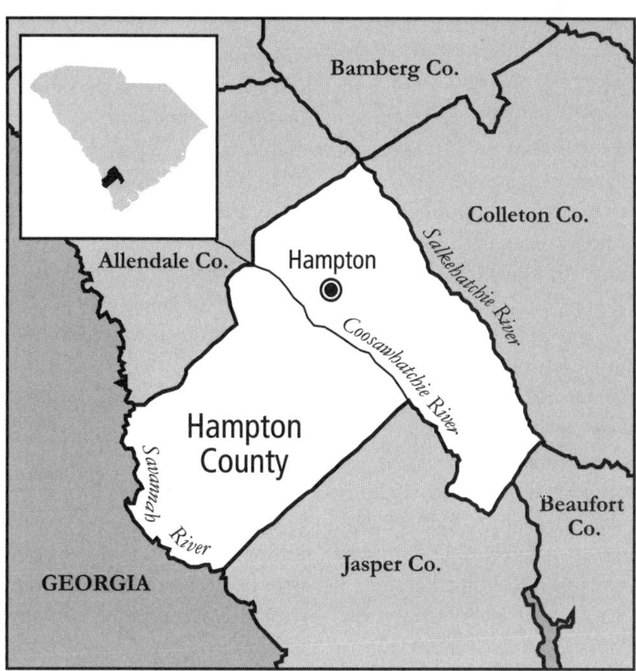

as the Hampton and Branchville Railroad, connecting the Port Royal–Augusta line to the Charleston-Columbia line. The main lines of the Seaboard (1891) and Southern (1900) railroads later served the western part of the county. Villages quickly grew up around the depots, with Brunson the first among them to be incorporated in 1874.

Railroads were important to the timber industry, a mainstay of the lowcountry economy. Turpentine distilleries appeared, and sawmills punctuated the railroads every few miles, their tram roads (logging railroads) running into the swamps of the slow-moving rivers. Smaller operations came and went throughout the early years, but three large sawmills contributed greatly to the county's economy during the agricultural depression of the 1920s: Hamilton Ridge Lumber Company in Estill (1912–1928); the Big Salkehatchie Cypress Company in Varnville (1915–1929); and Lightsey Brothers Lumber Company in Miley (1910–1957). Of the period from 1926 until 1929, one former Varnville sawmill worker said, "I made $1.75 a day when you couldn't make but fifty cents a day doing anything else. You couldn't tote $5.00 worth of groceries. Had to pay somebody to take 'em home for you in a wagon." The best trees cut, the Estill and Varnville mills sold out when lumber prices dropped. When synthetic alternatives became available, the turpentine industry also departed after exhausting the local piney woods tracts.

Railroads were important to farmers, too, delivering fertilizer and taking their cotton to market. Until the boll weevil came to the county in 1919, few farmers had diversified their crops, but sweet potatoes and other truck farm produce soon became important commodities. During the Great Depression of the 1930s, the wealthier or more progressive farmers held on to their land, but those too heavily mortgaged were displaced, along with many tenant farmers and sharecroppers. By the end of the decade, agricultural production, including cotton, was back up. Corn and other feed grains, watermelons, and peanuts became profitable, as did livestock and truck crops.

The turpentine industry reappeared; in 1940 Estill had a thriving operation. Sawmills returned in the 1940s and 1950s to cut second growth timber first cut thirty years earlier. Further, the out-migration of farm labor resulted in much arable land being planted in pine trees, a less labor-intensive crop and a renewable resource. In the early 1940s a Michigan-based wood products industry, Plywoods-Plastics Corporation, located in Hampton. It, and its successor companies Westinghouse and International Paper, became the area's largest employer.

World War II brought defense contracts to Plywoods-Plastics, adding women to the work force. It also brought enlistment and war prisoners. One hundred men of the county's Battery D of the South Carolina National Guard went on active duty in January 1941. The unit was stationed in England and North Africa before joining in the invasion of Sicily in 1943. Back home, from 1943 until 1946, German prisoners of war were imprisoned in Hampton, in one of twelve such camps in South Carolina. The prisoners worked on local farms and in industries.

Diversification improved the economy in the second half of the twentieth century. Most Hampton County industries manufactured plastics or forest-related products, but they also processed soybeans and corn, and ginned cotton. Yemassee became a distribution center for goods manufactured elsewhere and Estill acquired a Federal Correctional Institution. One of the county's four industrial parks gained foreign trade zone status, taking advantage of its proximity to Interstate 95. Soybeans and cotton accounted for most farm acreage, with watermelons as a specialty crop.

An increased emphasis on health and lifelong learning also characterized this period. A nursing home in Estill and a mental health center and regional medical center in Varnville augmented the County Health Center begun in a log structure built by the Works Progress Administration in the 1930s. In the early 1950s twenty school districts were consolidated into two, one on each side of the Coosawhatchie Swamp, and schools have since been built as needed. A private school, Patrick Henry Academy, was organized in Estill in 1965. The Technical College of the Lowcountry maintains a campus in Varnville, and the University of South Carolina—Salkehatchie serves students at its Allendale and Walterboro campuses with continuing education, undergraduate, and graduate courses. The Hampton County Historical Museum, established in 1979, collected local history artifacts and genealogy.

The swamps and rivers, woods and fields offered their bounty to natives, newcomers, and visitors. After the Civil War and into the early twentieth century, northern capitalists bought large tracts of land and established game preserves. Belmont Plantation is now the Webb Wildlife Center, owned by the S.C. Department of Natural Resources. The proportion of all land in farms decreased from two-thirds to less than half between 1950 and 1980, and much of what was lost became pine forests owned by paper companies. They, as well as individual landowners, lease hunting rights to private clubs and to the state for game management areas, and Lake George Warren State Park offers nature-based recreation. ROSE-MARIE ELTZROTH WILLIAMS

Hampton County Historical Society. *Both Sides of the Swamp: Hampton County.* Rev. ed. Hampton, S.C.: Hampton County Historical Society, 1997.

Williams, Rose-Marie Eltzroth. *Railroads and Sawmills, Varnville, S.C., 1872–1997: The Making of a Low Country Town in the New South.* Varnville, S.C.: Varnville Community Council, 1998.

Hampton Plantation (Charleston County). This eighteenth-century house in northern Charleston County was the centerpiece of a large rice plantation and home to members of the Horry, Pinckney, and Rutledge families. Though a construction date has not been conclusively determined, the Horry family, early Huguenot settlers of the Santee Delta area, may have built the house between 1730 and 1759. When first constructed, Hampton was a relatively simple timber-framed farmhouse, but before the end of the eighteenth century it had grown into an impressive Georgian-style mansion. Possibly around 1761 Colonel Daniel Horry undertook an extensive building campaign that included the addition of two large wings, several upstairs rooms, and a ballroom. Sometime prior to 1791 Horry's wife, Harriott Pinckney, supervised the construction of a massive Adamesque portico, one of the earliest of its type in American domestic architecture. By 1804 a traveler to the region described it as a "seat of wealth, splendor, and aristocracy" in the tradition of "cultivated English taste." Hampton Plantation was home to two notable South Carolinians: the pioneering indigo planter Eliza Lucas Pinckney and the poet laureate Archibald Rutledge.

The impressive architectural display of Hampton's mansion was financed with profits created by the intensive cultivation of rice, the lowcountry's basis of wealth. However, the plantation was not just a residence for socially prominent families. It was also a community made up of hundreds of enslaved African Americans, which included field workers and domestic slaves as well as artisans such as blacksmiths, wheelwrights, carpenters, and masons.

Hampton Plantation was designated a National Historic Landmark in 1970. Since 1971 the South Carolina State Park Service has

Hampton Plantation. Courtesy, South Carolina Department of Archives and History

managed the site as a historic house museum. In addition to the house, the plantation also includes a surviving kitchen building, archaeological sites, remnants of rice fields, and extensive twentieth-century gardens. AL HESTER

Smith, Shelley Elizabeth. "The Plantations of Colonial South Carolina: Transmission and Transformation in Provincial Culture." Ph.D. diss., Columbia University, 1999.

South Carolina. Division of State Parks. *A Master Plan for Hampton Plantation State Park.* Columbia: South Carolina Division of State Parks, 1979.

Stoney, Samuel G. *Plantations of the South Carolina Low Country.* 5th ed. Charleston, S.C.: Carolina Art Association, 1964.

Hampton-Preston Mansion (Columbia). Constructed in 1818 for the Columbia merchant Ainsley Hall, this three-story Federal-era townhouse became better known for its subsequent owners. In 1823 the planter Wade Hampton I purchased the property for his third wife. The estate soon became a mecca for the social and political elite. As the Hampton family's wealth increased, so too did the grandeur of their urban estate. The home boasted extensive gardens, featuring both foreign and domestic plants, and a greenhouse for experimental horticulture. Following Hampton's death in 1835, the property was inherited by his wife and children, one of whom, Caroline, married John Smith Preston of Virginia. For the next thirty years, the fame of the residence grew as it hosted such individuals as Presidents Millard Fillmore and Franklin Pierce and Senator Daniel Webster.

During the Union occupation of Columbia in 1865, General John Logan established his headquarters in the house. The property was saved from destruction when Ursuline nuns petitioned General William T. Sherman for its use as a makeshift convent. Depleted finances forced the Prestons to sell the property in 1873, beginning a spate of various occupants that included Reconstruction governor Franklin Moses, and once again, the Ursuline Convent of the Immaculate Conception. From 1890 until 1930 the estate was home to two women's schools, the College for Women (1890–1915) and Chicora College (1915–1930). For the next thirty-five years the property experienced multiple changes in ownership and use, particularly after 1947 when it was subdivided for development. In 1969 the mansion was restored in celebration of the state's tricentennial and debuted one year later as Columbia's third historic house museum. Since 1972 the mansion has been chiefly operated by the Historic Columbia Foundation. JOHN M. SHERRER III

Mary Cantey Hampton in the parlor of the Hampton-Preston Mansion (circa 1863). Courtesy, Historic Columbia Foundation

Sherrer, John M, III. "A Comprehensive History of the Hampton-Preston Mansion in Columbia, South Carolina." Master's thesis, University of South Carolina, 1998.

Hamrick, Wiley Cicero (1860–1931). Industrialist, businessman, politician. W. C. Hamrick was born on June 30, 1860, in Cleveland County, North Carolina, the sixth son of Cameron Street Hamrick and Almira Bridges. Between 1877 and 1882 Hamrick attended Boiling Springs Academy, studied medicine, and completed his medical degree at the College of Physicians and Surgeons in Baltimore. Returning to North Carolina, he began his medical practice and opened a pharmacy in Grover. Finding medicine too strenuous, in 1885 he moved to Shelby and opened a drugstore. On October 15, 1885, he married a young seminary student, Paola I. Turner. They had six children.

After serving in the North Carolina House of Representatives, in 1889 Hamrick moved his family to Clifton, South Carolina, where he opened a mercantile store patronized by employees of the Clifton Manufacturing Company. "Thrown in daily contact with the textile laboring class," Hamrick believed this experience gave him "deep insight into their thoughts and ways." In January 1895 Hamrick accepted a position with the Gaffney Manufacturing Company and moved his family to Gaffney where, in 1897, he opened the Cherokee Drug Company. In Gaffney, Hamrick was a leader in the successful effort to form the new county of Cherokee from adjoining counties and to make Gaffney its county seat.

Early in 1900 Hamrick and other leading citizens of Gaffney organized a cotton manufacturing enterprise, the Limestone Mills. Elected secretary and treasurer, Hamrick oversaw construction and brought the new facility into profitable production. In 1907 a second enterprise, the Hamrick Mill, was organized and Hamrick was again placed in charge. Three additional mills were added to the Hamrick Group, including the Broad River Mill in 1912, the Musgrove Mill in 1920, and the Alma Mill in 1922. Hamrick served as executive officer of the Hamrick Group until his death. He also served in the South Carolina Senate in 1910 and from 1927 to 1934. He was a trustee of Limestone College from 1899 to 1935, serving as chairman from 1921 to 1935.

Hamrick's 1931 autobiography, *Life Values in the New South,* examined problems faced by southern textile manufacturers, their worldview, and their values during the early twentieth century. Hamrick advised textile manufacturers to "capitalize only to the minimum," incurring as little debt as possible, and stressed the importance of a continuous return for investors. Hamrick advocated the paternalistic mill village for housing and caring for mill workers and avoiding unionization. He saw the mill village as an improvement in the lives of most workers who had arrived in Gaffney from the rural countryside. He advised a mix of skilled and unskilled laborers and encouraged managers to use the most advanced technology available. Hamrick died on October 21, 1935, and was buried in Oakland Cemetery in Gaffney. PAMELA C. EDWARDS

Bailey, N. Louise, Mary L. Morgan, and Carolyn R. Taylor, eds. *Biographical Directory of the South Carolina Senate, 1776–1985.* 3 vols. Columbia: University of South Carolina Press, 1986.

Hamrick, Wiley Cicero. *Life Values in the New South.* Charlotte, N.C.: Observer Printing House, 1931.

Hanahan (Berkeley and Charleston Counties; 2000 pop. 12,937). Hanahan is an incorporated city of about twelve square miles in the lower part of Berkeley County, with a small portion in Charleston County. The city is primarily a bedroom community to the city of Charleston. In the eighteenth and nineteenth centuries the land that became Hanahan was prime rice-growing acreage fronting the waters of Goose Creek. By World War I the locality was known as Saxon, the name of a local railroad stop. In 1917 the U.S. Post Office notified the community that it had to change its name to avoid confusion with the post office at Saxon, North Carolina.

The redesignated South Carolina locale was named after James Ross Hanahan. A successful businessman and industrialist, Hanahan was instrumental in having the city of Charleston purchase and operate a publicly owned waterworks system on land in the community. Access to the plant was hampered when Charleston County refused to pave the road to the site because it was only used by waterworks employees, while Berkeley County would not pave it because it was in Charleston County. Serving as the first chairman of the public utility, Hanahan worked through these differences and a road to the facility was paved. In recognition of his service, the station at Saxon was renamed in his honor. The town was incorporated in 1973, with a government consisting of a mayor, a six-member city council, and a full-time town administrator.

Hanahan's attributes included its accessibility to Interstate 26 and its location as the site of the Goose Creek Reservoir, which was built in the 1930s and later became a one-hundred-acre park. The city also contains the main water plant of the Charleston Public Works Commission.

Hanahan's growth in the second half of the twentieth century mirrored that of the Charleston metropolitan area. Between 1970 and 1980 the population of Hanahan soared from 8,376 to 13,224. The closing of the Charleston Naval Base in the early 1990s temporarily halted Hanahan's growth. However, the loss of defense related jobs was partly offset by the presence of nearby industrial employers such as Bayer Corporation (textile dyes), Alumax (aluminum), and Georgia-Pacific Corporation (wood products). RUTH W. CUPP

Berkeley-Charleston-Dorchester Regional Planning Council. *Comprehensive Development Plan, 1975, City of Hanahan, South Carolina.* Charleston, S.C.: The Council, 1975.

"One Suburb Has Growing Pains; the Other, Fears of Shrinking." Columbia *State,* February 8, 1994, p. B3.

Hancock, Gordon Blaine (1884–1970). Educator. Hancock was born on June 23, 1884, in Ninety Six to Robert Hancock and Anne Mark. His father was a well-known Baptist pastor, and his mother was a teacher in Greenwood County.

After completing his initial education at a common school in Ninety Six by 1902, Hancock became a teacher. Two years later he enrolled at Benedict College in Columbia. On receiving a bachelor of arts degree in 1911 he was ordained a Baptist minister. His first active pastorate was at Bethlehem Baptist Church in Newberry. During that same year he married Florence Marie Dickson, a former Benedict classmate. The couple had no children.

In 1912 Hancock became the principal of Seneca Institute, a private coeducational school for African Americans in Oconee County. Stressing vocational education, this facility was modeled closely after Booker T. Washington's Tuskegee Institute in Alabama. Although Hancock shared Washington's basic educational philosophy of self-improvement, he also believed that black southerners should engage in militant action to secure their voting rights. Consequently he angered many influential white South Carolinians. During a speaking tour in Greenville County in 1917, Hancock was threatened by the Ku Klux Klan. Fearing for his personal safety, Hancock resigned his post at Seneca Institute and left the state permanently.

Hancock went north, attending Colgate University in Hamilton, New York, and earning a bachelor of divinity degree in 1920. He subsequently enrolled at Harvard University, majoring in sociology. On obtaining a master of arts degree in 1921, he commenced doctoral studies. Before completing his degree requirements, however, in September 1921 Hancock accepted a professorship at Virginia Union University in Richmond, Virginia. He remained at this institution throughout his academic career, until forced into retirement in 1952. For many years he chaired the Department of History and Sociology. Besides teaching, Hancock was pastor at Moore Street Baptist Church from the late 1920s until 1963.

By 1930 Hancock had become closely associated with W. E. B. Du Bois, the editor of *Crisis,* the official journal of the National Association for the Advancement of Colored People. He periodically wrote articles for *Crisis,* as well as various other major black periodicals. In later years, however, the two men became estranged due to Du Bois's close affiliation with the American Communist Party. A more enduring friendship existed between Hancock and P. B. Young, Sr., the owner-editor of the Norfolk *Journal & Guide,* a black newspaper with a national circulation. Hancock wrote a long-standing weekly column, "Between the Lines," for Young's journal. And he prepared a comparable column with the Associated Negro Press (ANP), which ran nationally for three decades in 114 African American papers.

In October 1942 Hancock was instrumental in convening a conference of black Southern leaders in Durham, North Carolina. He was a primary contributor to the Durham Manifesto, a document that called for African Americans to reject the racial status quo in the South and to secure their right to vote.

Hancock died on July 24, 1970, at his home in Richmond. He was buried at Roselawn Memorial Gardens in Richmond. MILES S. RICHARDS

Gavins, Raymond. *The Perils and Prospects of Southern Black Leadership: Gordon Blaine Hancock, 1884–1970.* Durham, N.C.: Duke University Press, 1977.

Hanging Rock, Battle of (August 6, 1780). After the capitulation of Charleston in May 1780, the British moved quickly to gain a foothold in the South Carolina backcountry. Hanging Rock, so named for a large boulder perched on a knob, was one of several outposts situated to protect the main British base at Camden. The stronghold was nothing more than an open field encampment protected by a makeshift earthen berm. Major William Richardson Davie led a successful partisan raid on the outpost on July 30, 1780.

Colonel Thomas Sumter planned to follow up with a full assault on Hanging Rock for the morning of August 6. In avoiding an enemy sentry, the patriots' line of march took them too far right for a frontal attack. However, they struck a concentrated blow on the vulnerable British left, where the surprised North Carolinian Volunteers fell back in disorder. Pressing the attack, Sumter's men pushed through to the center of the line. At the height of the battle, the Prince of Wales' American Regiment rallied and regrouped, unperceived under the protection of the woods, and poured a deadly fire on the Americans. The Americans returned the fire so effectively that the Loyalist regiment was almost obliterated. This action allowed the detachment of the British Legion on the British right to form a hollow square defense. Moreover, many partisan soldiers stopped fighting to loot the British camp. Sumter learned of the approach of forty dragoons from Rocky Mount and ordered a withdrawal with minimal losses, leaving behind not quite two hundred British killed and wounded. The Battle of Hanging Rock, though not a complete victory, was a significant setback for British forces in the backcountry. SAMUEL K. FORE

Davie, William R. *The Revolutionary War Sketches of William R. Davie.* Edited by Blackwell P. Robinson. Raleigh: North Carolina Department of Cultural Resources, Division of Archives and History, 1976.

Edgar, Walter. *Partisans and Redcoats: The Southern Conflict That Turned the Tide of the American Revolution.* New York: Morrow, 2001.

Lumpkin, Henry. *From Savannah to Yorktown: The American Revolution in the South.* Columbia: University of South Carolina Press, 1981.

Hanover House (Pickens County). Built ca. 1716 by the Huguenot planter Paul de St. Julien in St. John's Berkeley Parish, Hanover House is notable for its Gallic-influenced design. The one-and-one-half-story house is distinguished by two substantial exterior end chimneys, a gambrel roof with a nearly flat upper section, and cypress framing and woodwork. The ground-floor interior walls are of batten board finish to simulate paneling, and the ceiling of the upper-story rooms is made of reversed shiplap paneling for waterproofing. An inscription at the top of one of the chimneys reads, "Peu a Peu"—a reference to the traditional French expression "The bird builds his nest little by little." St. Julien named his plantation after the ruling house of England to show his appreciation for the support and assistance it gave to Huguenot refugees following the revocation of the Edict of Nantes in 1685.

In the late 1930s Hanover was documented by Thomas T. Waterman, a pioneering historian of early southern architecture, as part of the federal Historic American Buildings Survey program. The site of the house and those of about twenty other early plantations were within the bounds of the area to be flooded by the Santee-Cooper hydroelectric project. Waterman found Hanover to be the most architecturally significant structure among the threatened buildings and recommended that it be moved and preserved. It was dismantled and relocated to the to the campus of Clemson University in 1941 and subsequently restored by the Spartanburg Committee of the National Society of the Colonial Dames. It is maintained as a house museum and is open to the public. DANIEL J. VIVIAN

Stoney, Samuel G. *Plantations of the South Carolina Low Country.* 5th ed. Charleston, S.C.: Carolina Art Association, 1964.

Waterman, Thomas T. "A Survey of the Early Buildings in the Region of the Proposed Santee and Pinopolis Reservoirs in South Carolina." Manuscript, 1939. South Caroliniana Library, University of South Carolina, Columbia.

Happyville. Happyville was a short-lived agricultural colony settled in 1905 near Montmorenci in Aiken County by Jewish emigrants from Russia. The venture was encouraged by the state's new immigration bureau, headed by E. J. Watson, a Columbia newspaperman who was secretary of the city's chamber of commerce. Concerned that the South had not benefited from the massive influx of emigrants from Europe, Watson set out to attract industrious newcomers to spark the state's depressed economy.

Watson's campaign was seconded by Jewish leaders in New York, who saw an opportunity to help Jews escape persecution in Russia and to disperse Jewish immigrants around the country. A brochure published in Yiddish and German by the South Carolina Department of Agriculture, Commerce, and Immigration described the state as "the Garden Country of America," ideal for the "Homeseeker, Farmer, Mechanic, Orchardist, Dairyman, Stockraiser, Businessman, Manufacturer, Healthseeker, [and] Tourist."

Opening an office in New York City, Watson courted Charles Weintraub, who had been a piano polisher in Russia before coming to New York, and Weintraub's business associate Morris Latterman. Weintraub and Latterman purchased a 2,200-acre tract known as the Sheffield Phelps Plantation, seven miles from Aiken, along with livestock, farm implements, and several buildings. By January 1906 some ten families and fifteen indivduals had taken up residence.

Most of what is known about the colony comes from an essay by the historian Arnold Shankman, who concluded that the majority of colonists were "free thinkers" and socialists, city dwellers unfamiliar with farming. Shankman's portrayal of the colony has been challenged by the researcher Lawrence M. Ginsberg. Although some contemporary news releases stated that the colonists "have named their location 'Happyville,'" Ginsburg found no single instance in which the colonists themselves used the term. Ginsburg argued that Watson, a man of driving energy and shrewd advertising sense, had himself dubbed the colony "Happyville."

On one point all are agreed: the colony's first year was a disaster. A late frost and heavy rains ruined crops. The rain also washed away a dam the settlers had built to run a grist mill, a saw mill, and a cotton gin. The second year they fared better, their optimism fueled by plans to construct a depot in nearby Montmorenci and a school for immigrant children. The small Jewish community of Aiken welcomed the colonists, though the South Carolinians must have puzzled over the Russians' inexperience with farming and their intellectual and socialist proclivities.

Financial miscalculations, internal dissension, and another harsh winter undermined the prospects for success at Happyville. In May 1908 the residents auctioned off some of their equipment and livestock, and in July they sold their land. By then virtually all the settlers had left Aiken, most returning to New York or New Jersey, some remaining in the South in nonagricultural jobs. DALE ROSENGARTEN

Ginsburg, Lawrence M. "Deconstructing a Frivolous Misnomer along with an Enduring Array of Compounded Historical Innaccuracies." Unpublished typescript, 2005. Special Collections, College of Charleston Library, Charleston.

Shankman, Arnold. "Happyville, the Forgotten Colony." *American Jewish Archives* 30 (April 1978): 3–19.

Harbison State Forest. Harbison State Forest is a 2,177-acre site located in northwest Richland County entirely within the corporate limits of Columbia. The site was acquired in 1945 from the Harbison Agricultural and Industrial Institute, an institution operated by the Board of Missions for Freedmen of the Presbyterian Church,

U.S.A., to educate young African Americans. Located in Irmo, the school was named in honor of Samuel P. Harbison (1840–1905), a wealthy Pennsylvania brick manufacturer and Presbyterian philanthropist. In addition to its educational activities, the Harbison school also owned some 3,600 acres of adjacent land, on which it operated a "Farm Home Community" project. The land was divided into one-acre town lots and twenty-five-acre parcels and sold to "Presbyterian settlers" in the hope of establishing a strong black and Presbyterian community in the area. The experiment fell short of expectations, however, and some 2,100 acres of the land was sold to the South Carolina Forestry Commission in 1945 for $21,000.

For the first thirty years of its ownership, the forestry commission practiced nonintensive forest management limited to periodic improvement harvests or insect salvage. Beginning in the 1980s grants were obtained to begin developing the property as an educational forest. Volunteer groups provided enthusiastic assistance in building and maintaining hiking and bicycle trails.

Because Harbison's mission is primarily one of education, forest management is practiced in small-scale demonstration areas throughout the property. Harvesting, planting, natural regeneration, insect and disease treatment, and prescribed burning are among the practices conducted on the state forest. Artifacts of South Carolina forest history are on display in and around Harbison headquarters. Among the exhibits are a working sawmill, a fire tower, a steam-powered log skidder, and a display of tools from the turpentine industry. SOUTH CAROLINA FORESTRY COMMISSION

Parker, Inez Moore. *The Rise and Decline of the Program of Education for Black Presbyterians of the United Presbyterian Church, U. S. A., 1865–1970.* San Antonio, Tex.: Trinity University Press, 1977.

Harby, Isaac (1788–1828). Journalist, playwright, educator, religious reformer. Harby was born on November 9, 1788, in Charleston, the son of Solomon Harby, an auctioneer, and Rebecca Moses. A talented student, he excelled in classical and literary studies. Entering the College of Charleston in 1805, Harby left without graduating to take up an apprenticeship in the law office of Langdon Cheves. Uninspired by his legal studies, Harby left Cheves's office and opened a private academy, which came to be known simply as "Harby's Academy." Although he made many attempts to support himself and his large family through his literary pursuits, his academy remained the most reliable source of income throughout his career. In 1810 he married Rachael Mordecai of Savannah. The marriage produced nine children, three of whom died in infancy.

Harby lived all but the last six months of his life in Charleston. According to Abraham Moïse, a close friend and biographer, Harby's journalistic career began with the publication of a short-lived literary magazine, the *Quiver* (1807), which was probably the first literary journal published by a Jew in the United States. In 1814 Harby purchased the *Charleston Gazette and Mercantile Advertiser,* which he renamed the *Southern Patriot and Commercial Advertiser.* He owned and edited the publication until 1817. He edited the Charleston *City Gazette* from 1821 to 1823, and was a frequent contributor to the *Charleston Mercury* and other journalistic enterprises.

Harby wrote at least three plays: *Alexander Severus* (ca. 1808), *The Gordian Knot* (1810), and *Alberti* (1819), the last two of which have survived. A respected dramatic critic, Harby's numerous essays reflected his conviction that theater should possess a moral purpose. He also dabbled in politics. Despite an unsuccessful run for the General Assembly in 1822, Harby remained politically active and wielded a significant degree of political influence in his community. In 1824 two Charleston newspapers published a series of his essays on "The Presidency," which supported the candidacy of Andrew Jackson and the democratic policies of republicanism.

Harby's most lasting contribution to South Carolina and the nation, however, came about from his role in the establishment of the Reformed Society of Israelites in 1825—the first organized expression of Jewish religious reform in North America. Harby became the society's most prominent spokesman. In 1825 he published his widely circulated *Discourse before the Reformed Society of Israelites,* which remains a compelling statement of the society's original goals and aspirations. Harby served as the group's president in 1827 and, with the assistance of David N. Carvalho and Abraham Moïse, compiled the society's prayer book.

In an attempt to further his literary career, Harby moved to New York in mid-1828, where he contributed to the *New York Evening Post* and the *New York Mirror,* a leading literary journal. He died of typhoid fever in New York on December 14, 1828, and was buried in Congregation Shearith Israel's cemetery on Manhattan. GARY PHILLIP ZOLA

Moïse, Abraham, and Henry L. Pinckney. *A Selection from the Miscellaneous Writings of the Late Isaac Harby.* Charleston, S.C.: J. S. Burges, 1829.
Moïse, Lucius C. *Biography of Isaac Harby.* Columbia, S.C.: R. L. Bryan, 1931.
Zola, Gary Phillip. *Isaac Harby of Charleston, 1788–1828: Jewish Reformer and Intellectual.* Tuscaloosa: University of Alabama Press, 1994.

Harden, William (1743–1785). Soldier. Harden was born on November 8, 1743, in Prince William's Parish, the son of William Harden and Mary Eberson. A landed planter, he entered military service in the militia of colonial Granville County, rising to the rank of captain by the outbreak of the Revolutionary War. He was elected captain of the Beaufort Volunteer Artillery Company on June 17, 1775, which was later incorporated into the Fourth South Carolina Regiment of the Continental Line in January 1776. Harden was appointed to command Fort Lyttelton near Beaufort, a post he held until April 1777. In the spring of 1779 he was promoted to the rank of colonel, commanding the Regiment of Upper Granville County.

Harden was captured in the fall of Charleston in May 1780 and paroled to his plantation near Beaufort. He chose to ignore his parole and after a few months began to actively recruit a partisan force in the Combahee River region. Harden joined the forces assembling under Francis Marion in late 1780 and returned shortly thereafter to harass the enemy in the districts south of Charleston. In April 1781 Harden's force captured and paroled a Loyalist captain and twenty-five men at a muster field at Four Holes. The following evening a detachment of Harden's regiment forced the surrender of a Loyalist post at Red Hill. Continuing their march, Harden's force suffered a setback at the hands of Colonel Thomas Fenwick at Saltketcher Bridge. After a few days' rest, Harden pressed forward toward Fort Balfour, the only major British fortification between Charleston and the Savannah River. Colonel Fenwick, the fort's commander, was captured outside the fort. After a few hours of negotiation, Harden forced the surrender of the fort without a shot being fired.

Harden's command was not without criticism, however. Governor John Rutledge complained to General Nathanael Greene that Harden, although a "very worthy brave Man," was no disciplinarian, allowing his men to "do as they please." Rutledge later appointed John Barnwell to be brigadier general of the newly created southern militia brigade and Harden, feeling slighted, resigned his commission in November 1781. Although his leadership was not of the same caliber as Marion or Thomas Sumter, Harden nonetheless played an important role in reclaiming South Carolina from British control.

Harden was elected a senator for Prince William's Parish and was present at the Jacksonborough Assembly in January 1782. He married twice, first to Sarah Reid, then to Sarah Cussings. The marriages produced at least four children. Harden held other political offices in Beaufort District before his death on November 28, 1785, in Prince William's Parish. SAMUEL K. FORE

Brown, Tarleton. *Memoirs of Tarleton Brown: A Captain in the Revolutionary Army, Written by Himself.* Edited by Terry W. Lipscomb. Barnwell, S.C.: Barnwell County Museum and Historical Board, 1999.

Daso, Dik A. "Colonel William Harden: The Unsung Partisan Commander." *Proceedings of the South Carolina Historical Association* (1995): 95–111.

Rowland, Lawrence S., Alexander Moore, and George C. Rogers. *The History of Beaufort County, South Carolina.* Vol. 1, *1514–1861.* Columbia: University of South Carolina Press, 1996.

Harleston, Edwin Augustus (1882–1931). Artist, civil rights leader, businessman. "Teddy" Harleston was born in Charleston on March 14, 1882, to the shipper-turned-mortician Edwin Gailliard Harleston and Louisa Moultrie. Harleston won a scholarship to the Avery Normal Institute and graduated valedictorian of his class in 1900. He graduated from Atlanta University in 1904 and, though accepted to Harvard, enrolled in the School of Fine Arts in Boston the next year. He studied in Boston from 1906 to 1912. He graduated from the Renourd Training School for Embalmers in 1917.

Harleston was a founding member of the Charleston chapter of the National Association for the Advancement of Colored People (NAACP) in 1917 and served as its first president. In 1919 he organized a campaign and petition drive to allow black teachers to teach in the black public schools in Charleston. The effort resulted in a change of state law. That same year Harleston attended the NAACP convention in Cleveland, Ohio, as a branch delegate.

On September 15, 1920, Harleston married Elise Forrest in Brooklyn, New York, where she attended photography school. They made their home in Charleston and shared an art studio. The Harlestons adopted their niece Gussie after her mother succumbed to tuberculosis in 1920.

The subject of much of Harleston's early artwork was family, friends, and daily life. "The Charleston Shrimp Man," "The Honey Man," and "The Old Servant" featured images that evoked the rich African American cultural heritage of the lowcountry. Many of Harleston's compositions during World War I illustrated the role of African Americans in the war effort, demonstrating their patriotism, sacrifice, and participation on the war front. His drawing "A Colored Grand Army Man," after a photo taken by Elise, won first place in the NAACP's Spingarn Competition.

By the 1920s Harleston had established a solid reputation as a portrait artist. His strong portraits featured prominent businessmen, civic leaders, and their families—most of whom were African American. His commissioned portraits included Edward Twitchell Ware (president of Atlanta University) and the daughter of W. E. B. Du Bois. On the recommendation of Du Bois, he was commissioned to create an official portrait of the prominent industrialist and philanthropist Pierre Samuel duPont. His noted portraits of South Carolina congressman Thomas Miller and of Aaron Douglas, a premier artist of the "New Negro" movement of the 1920s, are in the collections of the Charleston Museum. Harleston went to Nashville in 1930 at the invitation of Douglas and assisted him in painting murals in the new library at Fisk University.

Harleston died in Charleston on May 10, 1931, and was buried in the Harleston plot of the Unity and Friendship Cemetery. See plate 27. JANE M. ALDRICH

Edwin A. Harleston: Painter of an Era, 1882–1931. Detroit: Your Heritage House, 1983.

McDaniel, Maurine Akua. "Edwin Augustus Harleston, Portrait Painter, 1882–1931." Ph.D. diss., Emory University, 1994.

Harper, Robert Goodloe (1765–1825). Congressman, U.S. senator. Harper was born near Fredericksburg, Virginia, in January 1765, the only son of the cabinetmaker Jesse Harper and his wife, Diana Goodloe. Harper was raised in Granville County, North Carolina, and at the age of fifteen joined a cavalry unit under General Nathanael Greene to resist the invasion of Lord Cornwallis. Following the Revolution, Harper worked as a surveyor in Kentucky, but he continued to aspire to a military career. With the financial support of his father and a small loan from Richard Dobbs Spaight, Harper graduated from the College of New Jersey (now Princeton University) in 1785.

Harper moved to Charleston, South Carolina, following graduation. After being admitted to the bar in 1786, he practiced law at Ninety Six. He returned to Charleston in 1789 where western land speculating consumed most of his time. Thanks to his participation in the reapportionment movement, Harper's political career began in 1794 through a confusing turn of events. In October he was elected to both the General Assembly and the Fourth Congress. However, in November he won a special election to the Third Congress to replace Alexander Gillon, who had died in office. Harper's congressional career representing South Carolina continued until 1801.

After a brief flirtation with pro-French republicanism in the early 1790s, and contrary to what his critics often claimed, Harper remained a dedicated Federalist throughout the remainder of the decade, a position endorsed by his constituents in Ninety Six. He supported western expansion, unlike some New England Federalists. He defended the Jay Treaty with an eloquent address that went through fifteen printings, resisted attempts in the House to expand its role in foreign policy, and worked to strengthen executive autonomy. Although associated with the moderate John Adams wing of the Federalist Party, Harper was steadfastly pro-British, especially after the XYZ affair unleashed a torrent of anti-French sentiment. He led the move to enhance the country's military capability and defended the alien and sedition laws of 1798, which he justified on the existence of a national common law implied by the Constitution.

After retiring from politics in 1801, Harper moved to Baltimore, Maryland, where he had been a de facto resident since 1799. On May 7, 1801, he married Catherine Carroll, daughter of the eminent Charles Carroll of Carrollton. Most of the family wealth remained in Catherine's name, and despite a successful law practice, Harper owed considerable debts throughout the rest of his life.

Harper's oratorical skills attracted numerous influential clients to his law practice, whose cases took Harper before state and federal courts, including the U.S. Supreme Court. Judges John Pickering and Samuel Chase both employed him during their impeachment trials. Harper opposed the War of 1812, but was made a general of the Maryland soldiers who defended Baltimore. Briefly returning to politics, Harper served in the Maryland state senate and in the U.S. Senate. He stood as the Federalist vice-presidential candidate in 1816. A charter member of the American Colonization Society,

Harper helped choose Africa as the location of the colony and proposed the names Liberia and Monrovia later used for the colony and its capital. Harper considered reentering politics, but died suddenly on January 14, 1825. He was interred at Greenmount Cemetery, Baltimore. CAREY M. ROBERTS

Cox, Joseph W. *Champion of Southern Federalism: Robert Goodloe Harper of South Carolina.* Port Washington, N.Y.: Kennikat, 1972.

Papenfuse, Eric Robert. *The Evils of Necessity: Robert Goodloe Harper and the Moral Dilemma of Slavery.* Philadelphia: American Philosophical Society, 1997.

Harper, William (1790–1847). Jurist, U.S. senator. Born on January 17, 1790, on the West Indian island of Antigua, Harper was the son of the Reverend John Harper, a Methodist missionary, and Henrietta Hawes. Brought in 1791 to Charleston, where his father preached at Trinity Church, William grew up in a religious environment. His family later moved to Columbia, where William received his early education in the public schools. He then attended Mount Bethel Academy in Newberry District and Jefferson Monticello Seminary in Fairfield District. In 1805 he became the first student to enroll in South Carolina College, where he graduated in 1808.

Harper first studied medicine in Charleston and later read law under John Joel Chappell in Columbia. After his admission to the bar in 1813, Harper became Chappell's partner and quickly won acclaim among his peers for his legal ability. In December 1813 Harper was elected to the board of trustees of South Carolina College. Three years later, Harper was elected to the General Assembly from Richland District. On July 4, 1816, he married Ann Catherine Coalter. They had two children.

From 1818 until 1823 Harper lived in Missouri, where he had followed his father-in-law, David Coalter. In Missouri, Harper was elected chancellor and, in 1821, was a member of the Missouri Constitutional Convention. Financial concerns and the death of his father-in-law led Harper to return to South Carolina, where he was elected reporter for the South Carolina State Supreme Court in December 1823. During this period he also argued some significant cases. In 1826 Governor Richard I. Manning appointed him to the United States Senate to fill the vacancy caused by the death of Senator John Gaillard. Harper served in the Senate from March 8 until November 29, 1826. He did not seek election in the succeeding session.

In 1827 Harper moved to Charleston, where he again engaged in a successful law practice. The following year the parishes of St. Michael's and St. Philip's elected him to the state House of Representatives, where he was elected Speaker. Within a month, however, Harper was elected chancellor. Resigning the speakership, he moved to Columbia. In 1830 he was elected to the Court of Appeals where he served until 1835.

In 1832 Harper was a delegate to the convention that nullified the tariff. He quickly established himself as a leading figures in the nullification debate. The historian William W. Freehling called Harper "the most skillful dialectician in the nullification movement next to Calhoun." He was a member of the working subcommittee recommending a course of action to the convention, and became the principal author of the Ordinance of Nullification. He also became a forceful voice in the defense of slavery, which he most effectively put forward in his 1837 speech, "Memoir on Slavery."

With the abolishment of the Court of Appeals in 1835, Harper was again elected chancellor, serving in that position until his death in Fairfield District on October 10, 1847. He was interred in the Means Family Burial Ground in Fairfield County. JOHN L. NAPIER

Freehling, William W. *Prelude to Civil War: The Nullification Controversy in South Carolina, 1816–1836.* New York: Harper & Row, 1965.

Moore, Alexander, ed. *Biographical Directory of the South Carolina House of Representatives.* Vol. 5, *1816–1828.* Columbia: South Carolina Department of Archives and History, 1992.

O'Neall, John Belton. *Biographical Sketches of the Bench and Bar of South Carolina.* 2 vols. Charleston, S.C.: S. G. Courtney, 1859.

Harrington, Anna Short (ca. 1897–1955). Portrayer of "Aunt Jemima." Harrington was born near Cheraw, one of ten children born to Daniel and Lelia Short on the plantation of Frank Brooks Pegues. When she was nine, her family moved to Richmond County, North Carolina, where they raised wheat and made their own flour. The Short family worked in Richmond County for approximately fourteen years chopping cotton, hoeing, plowing, cleaning ditch banks, and cooking. As the children came of age, they all left home and went their separate ways.

Anna Short married Weldon Harrington, whose family was from Richmond County. They sharecropped on land near Rockingham, North Carolina. Harrington worked the fields and raised her five children. Weldon Harrington left the family some time in the 1920s. Stories differ as to why he left, but granddaughter Elizabeth Hunter stated that he killed a white landowner then escaped from prison and fled north. Having tremendously difficulty raising her family alone, Anna Harrington journeyed north in 1932 with a well-to-do white family who lived in Nedrow, New York, south of Syracuse. She lived with the family as a cook. Weldon Harrington subsequently found his family living in Syracuse and stayed with them during the late 1930s and early 1940s. As a runaway convict who feared capture, he eventually left Syracuse for Maine, where he died a few years later.

Sometime between 1933 and 1935, Anna Harrington took a job at Syracuse University, where she cooked for several campus fraternities. Ironically, the favorite meal of the students was pancakes. News of Harrington's cooking skills soon spread throughout the state and she was featured in media interviews. Her popularity eventually resulted in her discovery by the Quaker Oats Company, which hired Harrington to travel nationwide portraying "Aunt Jemima" and ultimately made her a national celebrity. Chauffeured or flown by jet around the country, Harrington served Aunt Jemima–brand pancake mix at store openings and other public events, living a lifestyle that eluded most blacks and whites. By the time of her death, the former sharecropper owned two homes and lived in an area occupied by the black elite of Syracuse.

Harrington died in Syracuse in 1955 at age fifty-eight from complications stemming from diabetes. She was buried in Syracuse's Morningside Cemetery. MARILYN KERN-FOXWORTH

Golphin, Vincent F. A. "Anna Harrington Was Proud to Play Role of Aunt Jemima." Santa Ana (Calif.) *Orange County Register,* November 16, 1995, p. El.

Harris, Emily Jane Liles (1827–1899). Diarist, farmer. Born on June 6, 1827, in Spartanburg, Harris was the daughter of Amos Liles and Sarah Daniels. When she was thirteen her parents moved to the Fair Forest area where they settled on a farm with their slaves. Amos Liles sent Emily to the Spartanburg Female Seminary, where she came under the tutelage of Phoebe Paine, a schoolteacher from Windham, Maine. Through Paine's instruction, Emily developed the skill of writing with both elegance and emotion. On April 3, 1846, Emily Liles married David Golightly Harris, the only son of a prominent Spartanburg District surveyor, farmer, and real estate investor. The marriage produced seven children.

By the outbreak of the Civil War in 1861, David and Emily Harris lived near Fair Forest, partially on land inherited from their families. From 1855 to 1870 David kept a journal in which he conscientiously described the life of a small upcountry farmer and slaveholder. When David reluctantly joined the state militia in late 1862, Emily maintained the journal in her husband's absence. Her entries tell much about the struggles endured by Southern farm women in the midst of war. Harris faced numerous challenges, not always with the best of humor. She wrote in 1863: "I shall never get used to being left as the head of affairs at home. The burden is very heavy . . . I am not an independent woman or ever shall be." Despite her modesty and lack of self-confidence, Harris supervised her slaves, butchered hogs, planted her garden, cooked molasses, sheared sheep, and oversaw the planting and harvesting of hay, corn, cotton, and sugarcane. She paid taxes, spun wool, and made sure that winter ice was preserved. She worried constantly about bad weather, the illnesses of her children, and the safety and comfort of her husband. At times isolated and at other times in need of privacy, Emily suffered from frequent bouts of depression, which worsened as the fortunes of the Confederacy waned and living conditions became harsher. "I expect no more rest this side [of] the grave," she wrote. "The wants of the family are never satisfied and their wants weigh heavily on me."

Well-educated, sensitive, and industrious, Harris was representative of the countless farm wives who kept the Confederacy fed while their husbands and sons fought far from home. Gifted with her pen, she gave voice to the arduous lives of her countrywomen and the challenges posed by slaveholding as the institution of slavery neared its end. Far from the idealized "plantation mistress," Harris was a perceptive witness to the impact of war on the home front.

Relieved in 1865 by her husband's return from the war, Emily Harris faced further challenges during Reconstruction. Much of the family wealth disappeared with the emancipation of their slaves, and some land was leased or sold to pay heavy taxes. David Harris died in 1875. Emily survived him and lived with her children until her death in Spartanburg on March 26, 1899. She was buried in the family cemetery in Spartanburg County. MARIAN ELIZABETH STROBEL

Racine, Philip N. "Emily Liles Harris: A Piedmont Farmer during the Civil War." *South Atlantic Quarterly* 79 (autumn 1980): 386–97.

———, ed. *Piedmont Farmer: The Journals of David Golightly Harris, 1855–1870.* Knoxville: University of Tennessee Press, 1990.

Harris, Georgia (1905–1997). Catawba potter. Harris was born on July 29, 1905, on the Catawba reservation near Rock Hill, the daughter of Chief James Harris and his wife, Margaret. Her maternal grandparents were Martha Jane Harris and Absalom "Epp" Harris. Both were potters of some genius. Martha Jane was one of the most talented potters of the nineteenth century, noted for her large vessels, while Epp Harris was a brilliant pipe maker. Georgia Harris grew up watching these talented family members at work in clay, and she began making pottery seriously around the age of ten.

Harris was educated on the reservation at the Catawba Indian School and at the Cherokee Boarding School. When she reached her full strength as a potter, much of the pottery produced by the Catawba was being sold in the mountains of North Carolina. She was immediately offended by the low prices of from 10¢ to 25¢ offered for each vessel. Shunning rank-and-file merchants, Harris sought out dealers who appreciated her art. After the division of tribal assets under the Termination Program (1961), she saw a chance to develop her mind further. Harris obtained a grant to take training as a licensed practical nurse and studied in Lancaster. When she obtained her license and began working in hospitals around Rock Hill, Harris retired from making pottery.

In 1973 Steve Baker convinced Harris to build pots for a show and sale he was curating for the Columbia Museum of Art. Baker's proposal sparked her interest. He insisted that Catawba pottery prices were not fair and should be raised. Recalling the insulting prices offered by the North Carolina merchants, Harris agreed and raised her prices to a high of $125. This was an unthinkable move at the time. Nevertheless, the Columbia Museum of Art show was a great success and Harris sold all her vessels. As a result, she returned to pottery making as a means to supplement her retirement income. Her home was immediately sought out by pottery collectors, anthropologists, historians, archaeologists, journalists, and folklorists.

In 1977, at the Spoleto Festival in Charleston, a titled European bought one of Harris's Indian head pots for the unheard of price of $350. This sale made the handful of Catawba potters sit up and take notice. Over the next few years, the number of active potters approached fifty, largely due to the efforts of Georgia Harris. Everyone admired her pottery-making skills and her confidence in the value of her work. Harris demonstrated pottery in numerous schools and museums, including the Mint Museum of Charlotte, North Carolina; the Schiele Museum in Gastonia, North Carolina; and the Renwick Gallery at the Smithsonian in Washington, D.C. Over the years she taught pottery making to a large number of Catawba. She was a primary instructor in the innovative class of 1976, the first effort the Catawba made to teach pottery making in a formal classroom. She also taught master potters Nola Harris Campbell and Earl Robbins.

By the time Harris retired a second time from pottery making in 1994, the number of active potters approached seventy-five persons. She died in Dallas, Georgia, on January 30, 1997. Later that same year, Harris became the first posthumous recipient of the Nation's Folk Heritage Award from the National Endowment for the Arts. THOMAS J. BLUMER

Blumer, Thomas J. *Catawba Indian Pottery: The Survival of a Folk Tradition.* Tuscaloosa: University of Alabama Press, 2004.

Byers, Dawn. "Georgia Harris, Noted Catawba Potter, Dies." Rock Hill *Herald*, February 1, 1997, pp. A1, A6.

Hart, Oliver (1723–1795). Clergyman. Oliver Hart was born in Warminster, Pennsylvania, on July 5, 1723. He was one of the most influential religious, social, and political leaders of the pre–Revolutionary War South. He began his adult life as a carpenter, though he was also licensed to preach by the Philadelphia Association (Baptist) in 1746. In 1749, after receiving a request from the Charleston Baptist Church for help in locating a pastor, the association encouraged Hart to answer the call and ordained him to the ministry. The Charleston church accepted Hart's unannounced arrival as a sign from God and installed him as minister in 1750, despite his meager education. He would hold that position for thirty years, leading the church in the Regular Baptist tradition. The church's trust was well placed. After educating himself, Hart became a leader not only to his congregation but to Baptists in the entire region. His Regular Baptist heritage inspired him to recruit worthy young men, including Richard Furman, to enter the ministry and to challenge the

Charleston Association and the Charleston Religious Society to raise the funds needed for the education of these ministerial prospects.

Even more significant is Hart's influence on denominational organization. In 1749, before Hart left Pennsylvania, he was one of the twenty-nine signers of a document adopted by the Philadelphia Association on the place and authority of an association in Baptist life. The association, as an organizational form, advocates a single denominational structure to support missions and ministry in a geographical area, as opposed to the society form of organization, which creates multiple organizations for the support of a variety of ministries. Hart brought associational organization to South Carolina, and Baptists in the state would in turn advocate it for the Southern Baptist Convention.

Hart also become a champion of liberty, equality, and cooperation among Christians. He encouraged ministers to preach to Native Americans (thereby recognizing their humanity), and he opposed slavery. He wrote in 1754, "Oh that all Bigotry was rooted out of the earth." In 1775 Hart's involvement in the Revolutionary cause, especially in the recruitment of support for the patriots, both in Charleston and in the backcountry, forced him to flee for a time with his family to the Euhaw tribal lands. By 1777, with the support of Baptist leaders in Virginia, Hart became an activist for religious liberty in South Carolina. In 1780 he was driven once again to the Euhaws by the British advance. From there he went to Hopewell, New Jersey, where he served as pastor until his death. Hart never returned to Charleston, though Richard Furman who succeeded him in the pulpit at Charleston expressed a willingness to step down in deference to his leadership at any time.

Hart was married twice, first to Sarah Brees in 1747, who was the mother of four children who survived infancy (Eleanor, Oliver, John, Mary Baker). His second marriage in 1774 was to Anne Sealey Grimball, who gave him one son, William Rogers. Hart died in Hopewell, New Jersey, on December 31, 1795, and was buried in the Southampton Old School Baptist Cemetery in Southampton, Pennsylvania. HELEN LEE TURNER

Hart, Oliver. Papers. Baptist Historical Collection, Furman University, Greenville.

Owens, Loulie Latimer. *Oliver Hart, 1723–1795: A Biography.* Greenville, S.C.: South Carolina Baptist Historical Society, 1966.

Hartsville (Darlington County; 2000 pop. 7,556). Hartsville owes its existence to Captain Thomas Hart of Society Hill, who purchased much of the original town site in 1817. Kalmia Gardens, a thirty-acre garden near modern Hartsville, is the site of Hart's 1820 plantation house. The community grew slowly until after the Civil War. Hart built a road to Society Hill in 1825 and the community acquired a post office in 1838. In 1850 his son, John L. Hart, settled in the area, donated land for the Hartsville Baptist Church, and established several businesses. To promote the development of scientific agriculture, local planters organized the Hartsville Farmers' Club in 1859.

Though visited by Union troops in 1865, Hartsville escaped the destruction that accompanied visits to other Pee Dee towns. In the postwar years, Hartsville continued its reliance on cotton. In 1880 the town had a population of only fifty. But Hartsville blossomed between 1880 and 1920, primarily due to the efforts of James Lide Coker. After returning from the Civil War in 1865, Coker opened a general store that became J. L. Coker and Company. Coker channeled store profits into other enterprises, securing a railroad connection for Hartsville, then establishing Carolina Fiber Company to process pulpwood. The railroad and Coker's business acumen transformed Hartsville from a quiet farming village into a bustling town, which the General Assembly incorporated in 1891.

Between 1890 and 1910 Hartsville acquired a newspaper, a high school, a bank, a telephone company, and numerous other businesses to become, according to the *Hartsville Messenger,* "the industrial beehive of the Pee Dee." In 1899 James L. Coker, Jr., founded the Southern Novelty Company to manufacture cardboard cones for the textile mills. As the textile industry flourished from 1900 to 1920, so did the Southern Novelty Company, which became Sonoco in 1924. By 1930 Hartsville's population had topped five thousand.

By 1893 the Baptist Church, with Coker's support, had established the Welsh Neck High School, a private institution. With the advent of a public high school, the trustees of Welsh Neck converted their school into Coker College.

With its railroad connections, Hartsville also became the leading cotton market in the Pee Dee, surpassing the county seat of Darlington. David R. Coker, another son of James Lide Coker, developed a long-staple, high-yield cotton that he marketed as "Coker's Pedigreed Seed," then created Coker's Pedigreed Seed Company. Coker Experimental Farms, the site of David Coker's agricultural experiments, was named a National Historic Landmark in 1964.

The Coker family's commitment to Hartsville helped the town weather the boll weevil, recessions, and the Great Depression. During the administration of President Franklin D. Roosevelt, several federal projects were built, including the Hartsville Post Office, the Hartsville Community Center, and Lawton Park and Pavilion. Sonoco's success gave Hartsville a fairly stable economy through the 1930s and beyond.

In addition to Coker College, Hartsville is home to the Governor's School for Science and Mathematics. Founded in 1988, the Governor's School is a public residential magnet school for academically gifted high school juniors and seniors. The Allstate Foundation recognized Hartsville for its efforts to revitalize downtown and named it an All-America City in 1996. Coker College and Sonoco continue to define the character of Hartsville. ALEXIA JONES HELSLEY

Coker, Charles W. *The Story of Sonoco Products Company.* New York: Newcomen Society in North America, 1976.

Wiggins, A. L. M. "Hartsville's Most Creative Years, 1889–1904." Unpublished manuscript, 1966. South Caroliniana Library, University of South Carolina, Columbia.

Hash. Hearty meals have been cooked in large, cast-iron pots since the Middle Ages. Variations are endless and limited only to the imagination of the maker and palate of the consumer. In South Carolina, hash takes the place of honor held by Brunswick Stew in nearby Georgia, Virginia, and North Carolina. Usually served over rice, hash is more than a mere accompaniment to barbecue and maintains an important role as a congregational food. Hash is a community-based tradition, cooked in big pots for large numbers of people. Recipes are far from consistent, with variations built around techniques that spring from rural folklife.

As did other southern stews, hash developed out of a need to turn leftovers, scraps, and whatever one could find into a palatable one-pot dish. While hash variations are countless, three loosely defined geographic regions can be identified. Lowcountry hash can consist of hogsheads and organ meats such as pork liver, cooked down in a stock favoring vinegar and ketchup. Vegetables can include onions, corn, and diced potatoes. Hash from the Midlands typically consists of leaner pork cuts combined with onions, cooked in a mustard-based stock. Finally, upstate hash is largely beef-based with onions, butter, and no dominant ketchup, vinegar, or mustard base. These regions are largely historical and today the most enduring regional difference rests in the sauce or stock.

Recipes perpetuated by hash masters are a source of immense personal and local pride and makers go to great lengths to retain the uniqueness of their hash recipes and cooking techniques. While many rural fire departments, agricultural clubs, and other civic organizations cook hash for community fund-raisers, the most prolific producers are locally owned barbecue restaurants, many of which developed from family "shade tree" cooking traditions. While hash might have been born out of necessity, this one-pot treasure has long since made the transition to a "comfort food." SADDLER TAYLOR

Carolina Hash. Produced and directed by Stan Woodward. Greenville, S.C.: Woodward Studio Limited, 2001. Videocassette.

Taylor, Saddler. "South Carolina Hash: By the Light of the Moon." *North Carolina Folklore Journal* 48 (fall/winter 2001): 80–87.

Haskell, Alexander Cheves (1839–1910). Soldier, legislator, businessman. Born on September 22, 1839, at his family's summer retreat, the Cabins, near Abbeville, Haskell was one of eleven children born to Charles Thomson Haskell and Sophia Cheves. He studied under private tutors and later attended a private school in Charleston before matriculating to the University of South Carolina in 1856, graduating second in his class in 1860.

Haskell enlisted with South Carolina forces at the beginning of the Civil War and soon became a regimental adjutant. He served with the Army of Northern Virginia for most of the war. By March 1864 he had attained the rank of colonel and taken command of the Seventh South Carolina Cavalry. He was wounded four times. The fourth wound, in October 1864, resulted in the loss of his left eye, but he rejoined his regiment in time for Robert E. Lee's last campaign and the surrender at Appomattox.

During Reconstruction, Haskell practiced several professions and played an important role in state politics. He taught school and practiced law in Abbeville from 1865 to 1867, while also serving in the state House of Representatives. He was elected a district court judge in 1867 but resigned his judgeship the same year to accept a law professorship at South Carolina College. In 1868 he resigned his professorship, as required, to serve as a presidential elector in the national election. He then opened a law office in Columbia.

In 1876 Haskell chaired the Democratic Party's State Executive Committee and helped organize the aggressive Red Shirt campaign that brought a narrow victory for Wade Hampton in the race for governor. With the election results disputed, Haskell became the emissary to President Ulysses Grant to press the claims of the Hampton administration. He later became an associate justice on the state supreme court, where he served from 1877 to 1880.

By 1890 Ben Tillman and his supporters had taken control of the Democratic Party and secured for Tillman the Democratic nomination for governor. Haskell bolted the party and ran against Tillman as an Independent, or "straight-out" Democrat. He appealed to black voters, but promised them little. Even many conservatives reluctantly backed Tillman, the mainline Democrat, rather than risk dividing the party and jeopardizing white rule. Haskell lost decisively, 59,159 to 14,828. He later helped organize the *State* newspaper in Columbia, which consistently opposed Tillman and his allies.

Haskell was a prominent business leader in the state for several decades. In the 1870s and 1880s he served as president of the Charlotte, Columbia and Augusta Railroad. He became the first president of the Loan and Exchange Bank of Columbia in 1886 and was a leading banker in the state until his death. He married twice. On September 10, 1861, he wed Rebecca "Decca" Singleton, but she died in June 1862 just days after giving birth to a daughter. On November 23, 1870, Haskell married Alice V. Alexander, with whom he had ten children. Haskell died on April 13, 1910, in Columbia and was buried in Elmwood Cemetery. ROD ANDREW, JR.

Daly, Louise Haskell. *Alexander Cheves Haskell: The Portrait of a Man.* 1934. Reprint, Wilmington, N.C.: Broadfoot, 1989.

Garlington, J. C. *Men of the Time: Sketches of Living Notables.* 1902. Reprint, Spartanburg, S.C.: Reprint Company, 1972.

Hatcher Gardens. The Hatcher Gardens provide an idyllic natural retreat in a suburban neighborhood southwest of downtown Spartanburg. Developed by Harold Hatcher (b. 1907) and his wife beginning in 1969, the horticultural complex has expanded from a single lot to almost ten acres. It includes more than ten thousand trees, plants, and shrubs.

Historically a cotton field carved by an eroded ravine, the site had become an overgrown thicket choked with deep ditches, briars, and trash. Hatcher, an ardent naturalist committed to reclaiming and improving green spaces, chose the unattractive site to put his ideas into practice. During the next twenty-five years, he purchased additional land, filled gullies, and built dams and ponds to conserve water and prevent erosion. Tall pines eventually created a tree canopy that gradually changed the ecology of the site. By 1990 a formerly dry streambed was again flowing naturally.

In the shade of the new canopy, Hatcher planted hundreds of azaleas and one of the largest collections of hostas in the state. Near the entry on Reidville Road there are annuals, a butterfly garden, a water garden, and gazebo.

In 1987 Hatcher donated the garden and some endowment resources to the Spartanburg County Foundation. The garden is managed by the Garden Clubs of Spartanburg, a nonprofit organization supported by more than twenty-five garden clubs in the area. ROBERT W. BAINBRIDGE

Hembree, Michael. *The Seasons of Harold Hatcher.* Spartanburg, S.C.: Hub City Writers Project, 2000.

Hawks, Esther Hill (1833–1906). Teacher, physician. Hawks was born in Hooksett, New Hampshire, on August 4, 1833, the fifth child of Parmenas Hill and Jane Kimball. After attending public schools in her home state, she worked as a teacher and was committed to women's rights and abolition. On October 5, 1854, she married John Milton Hawks, a doctor who shared her reformist views. They traveled to Florida where Hawks taught black children in a small school. She began reading her husband's medical books and in 1855 enrolled in the New England Female Medical College, graduating in 1857 into a profession that was still the domain of men. When war broke out in 1861, she applied for a position as a physician or nurse with the Union army but was repeatedly refused. Dorothea Dix, superintendent of army nurses, proclaimed Hawks too young and attractive to nurse.

Undaunted, Hawks volunteered in Washington hospitals until she was offered a teaching position with the Freedmen's Aid Society in 1862. In that capacity she arrived on the Sea Islands of South Carolina where her husband was serving as a physician. She stated, "I was born to be a missionary," and zealously embraced her new role, teaching classes of hundreds of students. In early 1863 she began working as a teacher with the First South Carolina Volunteers, a regiment of black soldiers recruited from the Union-controlled lowcountry. In April 1863 she joined her husband at the newly established hospital for people of color in Beaufort where she both nursed and taught her patients, who included the wounded of the Fifty-fourth Massachusetts Infantry after their assault on Fort Wagner. Away from the prying eyes of Washington, she utilized her medical skills and supervised the hospital during her husband's frequent absences, which could last as long as three weeks. Hawks doubted she would have been allowed such authority "if my brother had not been hospital steward—or if the patients had been white men." She continued to work in the hospitals and freedmen's schools of South Carolina and Florida throughout the remainder of the war.

In March 1865, after Charleston fell to Federal forces, she joined her husband in the city. Almost immediately, she organized the Colonel Shaw Orphan House for black children on East Bay Street and began supervising the six hundred students of the city's Normal School. After the war Hawks and her husband left South Carolina for Florida where she continued her work as both a teacher and physician. Finally, in September 1870, she returned to the North to practice medicine in Lynn, Massachusetts, where she was active in various charity organizations and served as an officer of the Woman's Rights or Suffrage Club. Although she had been denied an official position as a surgeon, her work during the war was not forgotten. In 1899 the New Hampshire Association of Military Surgeons elected Hawks an honorary member. After a brief illness, she died at her home in Lynn on May 6, 1906. KELLY OBERNUEFEMANN

Hawks, Esther Hill. *A Woman Doctor's Civil War: Esther Hill Hawks' Diary.* Edited by Gerald Schwartz. Columbia: University of South Carolina Press, 1984.

Hayne, Henry E. (1840–?). Legislator, secretary of state. Hayne was born on December 30, 1840, in Charleston, the son of a white father, James Hayne, and his free black wife, Mary. He was the nephew of Robert Y. Hayne, a former U.S. senator and governor of South Carolina. Henry Hayne was educated in Charleston and worked in the city as a tailor. With the outbreak of the Civil War, he volunteered for the Confederate army, but with the intention of escaping to Union lines. In July 1862 he crossed through enemy lines and joined Union forces, enlisting at Beaufort in the Thirty-third Regiment of United States Colored Troops (First South Carolina Volunteers), commanded by Thomas Wentworth Higginson. Enlisting as a private, Hayne was promoted to commissary sergeant in 1863.

Following his discharge in early 1866, Hayne moved to Marion County. In 1868 the Freedmen's Bureau hired him as principal of Madison Colored School, and he later served as a subcommissioner for the South Carolina Land Commission from 1869 to 1871. He served on the Republican state executive committee in 1867 and represented Marion County in the 1868 state constitutional convention. He was chairman of the Marion County Republican Party in 1870 and vice president of the state Union League. He represented Marion County in the state Senate from 1868 to 1872, and as South Carolina's secretary of state from 1872 to 1877. As secretary of state, he took charge of the land commission and was credited for bringing honest and efficient leadership to what had previously been a notoriously mismanaged program.

In 1873 Hayne enrolled in the medical school at the University of South Carolina. Though he left before earning his degree, Hayne was the first black student in the school's history and inaugurated the institution's first attempt at integration, which lasted until 1877. The Republican Party renominated him for secretary of state in 1876. He also served as a member of the state board of canvassers, which certified a Republican victory in the hotly contested election of 1876. The state supreme court, however, found the board to be in contempt, and jailed its members for a time. On May 3, 1877, under intense pressure, Hayne gave up his position as secretary of state to the Democratic candidate, Robert Moorman Sims.

Little is known about Hayne's personal life. He reportedly married on April 29, 1874, but the name of his wife was not given. Sometime before August 1877, Hayne left South Carolina. In January 1885 he was living in Cook County, Illinois with his wife Anna M. His later whereabouts are unknown. MICHAEL ROBERT MOUNTER

Bailey, N. Louise, Mary L. Morgan, and Carolyn R. Taylor, eds. *Biographical Directory of the South Carolina Senate, 1776–1985.* 3 vols. Columbia: University of South Carolina Press, 1986.

Foner, Eric. *Freedom's Lawmakers: A Directory of Black Officeholders during Reconstruction.* Rev. ed. Baton Rouge: Louisiana State University Press, 1996.

Hayne, Isaac (1745–1781). Legislator, soldier. Hayne was born in Colleton County on September 23, 1745, the son of Isaac Hayne and Sarah Williamson. After his father's death in 1751, Hayne inherited Hayne Hall, a nine-hundred-acre plantation in St. Bartholomew's Parish. He expanded his property holdings to include two more plantations, Sycamore and Pearhill; land in the backcountry and in Georgia; town lots in Charleston and Beaufort; and an interest in an ironworks in York District. On July 18, 1765, Hayne married Elizabeth Hutson. They had seven children. He represented St. Bartholomew's Parish in the Commons House of Assembly from 1770 to 1771, and in the state Senate from 1779 to 1780.

The Revolutionary War interrupted Hayne's life as a wealthy planter. At the onset of hostilities, he was a captain in the Colleton County Regiment, but he later resigned his commission after failing to be named colonel of the regiment. Reenlisting as a private, he continued to serve until the fall of Charleston in May 1780. Paroled, he returned to Hayne Hall to sit out the remainder of the war. When the British demanded that all paroled militia return to Charleston and take an oath of allegiance, Hayne reluctantly complied after being threatened with imprisonment. The British then demanded that Hayne take up arms against the patriots. Offended by what he considered a breach of his parole agreement, Hayne refused the British demand and instead rejoined the American forces.

Commissioned a colonel and given command of a regiment, Hayne quickly returned to action. In a daring raid just miles from Charleston, he captured General Andrew Williamson, an American patriot who had later joined the British. The British reacted quickly, however, and a force commanded by Colonel Nisbet Balfour soon overtook the Americans. Hayne was captured and imprisoned in the Exchange Building in Charleston while he awaited trial. The British commander, Lord Rawdon, decided to make an example of Hayne in an attempt to discourage others from joining the patriot cause. For taking up arms after acknowledging himself a subject of the crown, Hayne was charged with treason and hanged on August 4, 1781.

A hue and cry arose over Hayne's execution, with threats of retaliation by the patriots. Commander of the Southern Department, General Nathanael Greene, asked George Washington and Congress for guidance, both of whom urged caution. Following the surrender of the British army of Lord Cornwallis at Yorktown in October 1781, the South Carolina delegation to Congress made an unsuccessful motion to have the British general executed in retaliation for Hayne. Despite the calls for revenge, no British officer suffered Hayne's fate. But comments regarding Hayne's execution would be recorded in the ensuing years by individuals as significant as Benjamin Franklin and Thomas Paine. In 1782 the Duke of Richmond and the British House of Lords unsuccessfully attempted to censure Lord Rawdon. South Carolina author William Gilmore Simms included a character modeled after Hayne in his 1835 novel *The Partisan.*

Hayne was buried in Jacksonborough in the Hayne family cemetery. A monument erected in his memory called Hayne "a noble martyr in behalf of liberty." DAVID K. BOWDEN

Bailey, N. Louise, Mary L. Morgan, and Carolyn R. Taylor, eds. *Biographical Directory of the South Carolina Senate, 1776–1985.* 3 vols. Columbia: University of South Carolina Press, 1986.

Bowden, David K. *The Execution of Isaac Hayne.* Lexington, S.C.: Sandlapper Store, 1977.

Hayne, Paul Hamilton (1830–1886). Poet, editor, essayist. Hayne was born as the only child of a prominent Charleston family on January 1, 1830, and named for his father, a navy lieutenant who died when Hayne was only one year old. He was brought up by his mother, Emily McElhenney, the daughter of a Presbyterian minister, and his uncle, U.S. Senator Robert Young Hayne. The uncle died in 1839 after having decisively influenced his nephew, who wrote an admiring sketch of Robert Hayne in 1878.

Paul Hamilton Hayne. Courtesy, South Carolina Historical Society

Hayne graduated from the College of Charleston (1850), studied law under James Louis Petigru, and was admitted to the bar, but found the legal profession disagreeable. Already in 1845 Hayne had published poems in the *Charleston Courier* under the pseudonym "Alphaeus," and in 1848 he contributed to the *Southern Literary Messenger.* He became the manager of the short-lived *Southern Literary Gazette,* a weekly, and wrote for several journals including *Graham's Magazine.*

On May 20, 1852, Hayne married Mary Middleton Michel, the daughter of a Charleston physician. They had one son. Before the war he published three volumes of poetry, which were representative of the literary taste of the time: *Poems* (1855), with the ambitious poem "The Temptation of Venus"; *Sonnets, and Other Poems* (1857); and *Avolio: A Legend of the Island of Cos* (1860), the title poem of which is an involved narrative effort. His poems were from the start devoted to the universal. The best early work is in the versatile sonnets where the Elizabethan heritage is obvious. And in April of the following year, at the urging of William Gilmore Simms and Henry Timrod, Hayne became the editor of *Russell's Magazine,* which he made a successful periodical. It was the last important literary magazine founded in the South before the war.

Hayne supported South Carolina's withdrawal from the Union. In the fall of 1851 he wrote for the unsuccessful secession organ the *Palmetto Flag.* He wrote poetry in support of the Confederacy, especially in 1862, mostly on the themes of family, native land, and death. Some poems are rousing, such as his "Vicksburg: A Ballad," "Charleston," "Beyond the Potomac," and "My Mother Land." He served as an aide-de-camp to Governor Francis Pickens, but his health put a stop to this after only four months. After the war he was ruined and his Charleston home and library burned, so in 1866 he moved to a small plot of barren pineland and a cabin at Groveton near Augusta, Georgia. It was here at Copse Hill in his reduced circumstances that he wrote some of his best poetry, such as "South Carolina to the States of the North," protesting the exploitation of the South during Reconstruction.

During the last decades of his life Hayne published additional volumes of poetry: *Legends and Lyrics* (1872); *The Mountain of the Lovers: with Poems of Nature and Tradition* (1875) with "Aspects of the Pines"; and *Poems: Complete Edition* (1882) with the lyrical poems "The Mocking-Bird" and "A Dream of the South Winds." In these poems Hayne became a subtle interpreter of nature in her southern aspects.

Hayne lived by selling his poems or essays, mainly to northern journals, such as *Appleton's Journal* and *Lippincott's Magazine.* He was an eclectic critic who judged by personal taste rather than aesthetic standard. Hayne rejected Walt Whitman's free verse and ideas, but recognized the genius of Edgar Allen Poe at an early date. He edited *The Poems of Henry Timrod* (1873) and added "A Memoir"; in youth they were classmates at Christopher Cotes's school in Charleston and had remained friends.

Hayne corresponded with the best writers in the nation and in Europe and was, as one of few in the post-Reconstruction South, respected in academia as a refined poet and cultured man of letters. In this sense Hayne was a vital link between the culture of the antebellum and postbellum South. The year before his death he wrote a reminiscing essay for *The Southern Bivouac* (Louisville) on "Ante-Bellum Charleston," which offers an account of a golden time in the intellectual and cultural life. He died at Copse Hill on July 6, 1886, and was buried in Magnolia Cemetery in Augusta, Georgia. JAN NORDBY GRETLUND

Hubbell, Jay B. *The South in American Literature, 1607–1900.* Durham, N.C.: Duke University Press, 1954.

Moore, Rayburn S. *Paul Hamilton Hayne.* New York: Twayne, 1972.

Parks, Edd Winfield. *Ante-Bellum Southern Literary Critics.* Athens: University of Georgia Press, 1962.

Hayne, Robert Young (1791–1839). U.S. senator, governor. Hayne was born on November 10, 1791, in St. Paul's Parish, Colleton District, to William Hayne and Elizabeth Peronneau. One of fourteen children, Hayne attended private school in Charleston but was unable to attend college because of his family's poor financial situation. He studied law under Langdon Cheves, was admitted to the bar before turning twenty-one, and immediately began a lucrative practice. Marriages to two daughters of prominent Charleston families, Frances Henrietta Pinckney in 1813 and Rebecca Brewton Alston in 1820, greatly enhanced his wealth and social status.

Hayne served as a lieutenant in the Charleston Cadet Infantry during the War of 1812 and was later promoted to captain of the Charleston Riflemen. He was also appointed a quartermaster general of South Carolina in December 1814. Elected to the South Carolina House of Representatives in 1814, Hayne became Speaker in 1818. In December of that year, he was appointed South Carolina's attorney general, serving until 1822. That year the legislature elected Hayne to the U.S. Senate over William Smith, a political rival of John C. Calhoun. During his first years in the Senate, Hayne supported a nationalist agenda. But as did other South Carolina politicians, he became an advocate for states' rights in the late 1820s. Hayne believed that tariffs would lead to the domination of the North over the South, and of the federal government over the state governments. He emerged as one of the most eloquent tariff opponents in Congress.

Robert Y. Hayne. Courtesy, South Carolina Historical Society

The climax of Hayne's senatorial career came after his reelection in 1828. In December 1829 Senator Samuel Foot of Connecticut introduced a measure to restrict the sale of public western lands. Hayne supported Senator Thomas Hart Benton of Missouri, contending that Foot's proposal would restrict access to cheap western land and thereby create a dependent labor source for eastern manufacturers. Furthermore, restricted land sales would inflate prices and provide unnecessary revenue for the federal government, encouraging corruption and consolidation.

Senator Daniel Webster of Massachusetts countered that Hayne's fear of consolidation and Benton's belief in eastern malice toward the West were unfounded. Thus began an oratorical contest that forever linked Hayne and Webster. For two weeks in early 1830, the two senators clashed over western lands, slavery, the Constitution, and nullification. The Webster-Hayne debate concluded with Webster's ringing endorsement of "Liberty and Union, now and forever, one and inseparable." In contrast, Hayne espoused the radical states' rights doctrine of nullification, believing that a state could prevent a federal law from being enforced within its borders. According to Hayne, the South would never allow "any interference, whatever, in their domestic concerns." If the federal government ever attempted to do so, the southern states would consider themselves as "driven from the Union."

In 1832, as the tariff crisis grew, Hayne turned his Senate seat over to John C. Calhoun, nullification's architect, and was rewarded with the governor's chair of South Carolina. When Congress passed another tariff in 1832, Hayne advocated a state nullification convention, then presided over the body which voided the tariff in South Carolina. In response to President Andrew Jackson's "Proclamation to the People of South Carolina" and the Force Bill, Hayne called for ten thousand troops to defend the state from the federal government. However, when Henry Clay offered a compromise for ending the crisis, Hayne supported rescinding the nullification ordinance and served over the body which did so. After the Compromise of 1833 had been effected, Hayne finished his term working to reconcile nullification factions within South Carolina.

While serving as mayor of Charleston from 1835 to 1837, Hayne became interested in railroads as a means to expand trade and commerce in the port city. He proposed extending the existing railroad between Charleston and Hamburg through the Blue Ridge Mountains and into the Old Northwest, opening the states of Kentucky and Ohio as markets for the port of Charleston. Hayne gained support and the states of Tennessee, South Carolina, North Carolina, and Kentucky granted charters for the railroad. The Louisville, Cincinnati and Charleston Railroad Company was formed in 1836, and Hayne served as its first president. Despite a national depression and a loss of enthusiasm, he continued to push his plan, although his dream of a transmontane railroad never reached fruition. Attending a stockholders' meeting in Asheville, North Carolina, Hayne contracted a fever and died there on September 24, 1839. His body was returned to Charleston and interred in St. Michael's Churchyard. TRENTON HIZER

Freehling, William W. *Prelude to Civil War: The Nullification Controversy in South Carolina, 1816–1836.* New York: Harper & Row, 1965.

Hayne, Paul Hamilton. *Lives of Robert Young Hayne and Hugh Swinton Legare.* Charleston, S.C.: Walker, Evans, and Cogswell, 1878.

Jervey, Theodore. *Robert Y. Hayne and His Times.* 1909. Reprint, New York: Da Capo, 1970.

Haynsworth, Clement Furman, Jr. (1912–1989). Attorney, jurist. Haynsworth was born in Greenville on October 30, 1912, to Clement F. Haynsworth and Elsie Hall. He rose in South Carolina legal circles to become a federal appeals court judge, but he is best remembered nationally for his 1969 rejection by the U. S. Senate for a seat on the United States Supreme Court.

One of his ancestors had founded Furman University, and four generations of his family had been lawyers. Haynsworth grew up in Greenville and graduated summa cum laude from Furman in 1933. On his graduation from Harvard Law School in 1936, he joined the family's Greenville law practice. He served as a naval intelligence officer during World War II and was stationed in Charleston and San Diego. After the war he focused his attention on his law practice, where he had become a senior partner.

Haynsworth's family had strong social and business connections throughout South Carolina, having been involved in the textile industry for generations. While never a candidate for public office, he had friends who were active in politics. Though a Democrat, he supported Dwight D. Eisenhower's presidential campaigns, and his close associate, Greenville construction executive Charles E. Daniel, began working to get him named to a federal appellate judgeship. Daniel, a former interim U.S. senator and an Eisenhower Democrat, persuaded both South Carolina senators to support Haynsworth's nomination, though both of them had other candidates in mind. In 1957 Haynsworth became the youngest judge on the Fourth Circuit Court of Appeals.

As a member of the appeals court, Haynsworth was a hardworking jurist. However, the U.S. Supreme Court overturned his court's rulings on several civil rights and labor cases. He became the chief judge of the appeals court in 1964 and earned a reputation as a capable administrator.

When U.S. Supreme Court Justice Abe Fortas resigned from the high court following charges of ethical improprieties, President Richard Nixon nominated Haynsworth to the Supreme Court. Civil rights and labor groups immediately attacked the nomination, pointing to his earlier rulings on the Fourth Circuit. Senator Strom Thurmond worked to secure Haynsworth's confirmation, however, and the Senate Judiciary Committee recommended confirmation by a vote of ten to seven. But allegations that Haynsworth, as a judge, had ruled on a labor relations case where he had an indirect interest, and in another where he bought stock in a company after ruling in its favor raised questions of judicial impropriety. These allegations were enough to sink his nomination, and the Senate rejected him by a vote of fifty-five to forty-five. Haynsworth returned to the Fourth Circuit, serving there until 1981, when he assumed senior judge status.

Haynsworth was married to Dorothy Merry Barkley on November 25, 1946. They had no children, though Mrs. Haynsworth had two sons from a previous marriage. As a senior judge, Haynsworth continued to hear cases until his death on November 22, 1989. He was buried in Greenville's Springwood Cemetery. R. PHILLIP STONE II

Cohodas, Nadine. *Strom Thurmond and the Politics of Southern Change.* New York: Simon and Schuster, 1993.

Frank, John Paul. *Clement Haynsworth, the Senate, and the Supreme Court.* Charlottesville: University Press of Virginia, 1991.

Heath Charter (1629–1663). King Charles I of England granted a proprietary charter on October 30, 1629, to his attorney general Sir Robert Heath. The colony, named "Carolana" in honor of the king, included the territory between 31° and 36° north latitude and west to the edge of the continent. This vast region stretched from Albemarle Sound, North Carolina, to the northern boundary of Florida and west to the Pacific Ocean. As proprietor, Heath was expected to settle and develop his domain with the same broad governing authority as the Bishop of Durham, feudal ruler of the County Palatine of Durham in England. The charter also authorized the proprietor to make laws with "the counsel, assent, and approbation of the Freeholders . . . or the Major part of them."

Heath initially sought settlers from the numerous Huguenots who had taken refuge in England during religious conflicts in France. He soon lost interest when several of these projects failed, and he thereafter restricted his colonists to communicants of the Church of England. A Puritan merchant of Huguenot ancestry, Samuel Vassall, sponsored a coastal exploration to locate settlement sites, but the colonists that followed in 1633 were stranded in Virginia. By 1638 Heath had assigned his proprietary rights to Henry Frederick Howard, Lord Maltravers, who established the County of Norfolk in Carolana but was no more successful than Heath in settling the region. The Heath Charter is important because it was the model for the successful 1663 Carolina Charter, and it was the first colonial charter that included the area of modern South Carolina. LINDLEY S. BUTLER

Kopperman, Paul E. "Profile of Failure: The Carolana Project, 1629–1640." *North Carolina Historical Review* 59 (January 1982): 1–23.

Parker, Mattie E. E., ed. *North Carolina Charters and Constitutions, 1578–1698.* Raleigh, N.C.: Carolina Charter Tercentenary Commission, 1963.

Powell, William S. "Carolana and the Incomparable Roanoke: Explorations and Attempted Settlements, 1620–1663." *North Carolina Historical Review* 51 (January 1974): 1–21.

Hebrew Orphan Society of Charleston. The Hebrew Orphan Society of Charleston is the oldest incorporated Jewish charitable organization in the United States in continuous existence. It was organized by twenty-three members of Congregation Beth Elohim in 1801 and chartered by the General Assembly of South Carolina in 1802, "for the purpose of relieving widows, educating, clothing, and maintaining orphans and children of indigent parents." David Lopez was its first president.

From 1833 to 1931 the society owned a building at Broad Street and Courthouse Square and maintained it as a meeting place, but rented rooms for income. On occasion a Hebrew school was held here, but it was never used as an orphanage, for the society placed and supported their charges in private homes and usually contracted with local private schools for their education.

In 1951 the society joined with Charleston Hebrew Benevolent Society and the Charleston Jewish Federation to create the Charleston Jewish Social Services, which handles the casework formerly done by the Hebrew Orphan Society. The society has also broadened its charity program by using its general fund for contributions to local professional agencies that minister to needy cases regardless of race, religion, or nationality.

The income of the society is derived mostly from bequests and investments. The society also administers the Zipporah M. Solomons Fund to provide nursing care and the N. Edgar Miles M.D. Scholarship Fund for college students.

Membership in the society is by invitation and is limited to thirty-six men and women chosen in recognition of their worthwhile endeavors for the community. SOLOMON BREIBART

Tobias, Thomas J. *The Hebrew Orphan Society of Charleston.* Charleston, S.C.: Hebrew Orphan Society of Charleston, 1957.

Heller, Max (b. 1919). Civic leader, mayor of Greenville. Heller was born on May 28, 1919, in Vienna, Austria, the son of Israel and Leah Heller. Israel Heller, a native of Poland and a veteran of World War I, operated a sales business with his wife. After graduating from gymnasium (high school), Max Heller was apprenticed to a novelty store owner, rising to the position of buyer, and attended business school part time.

On March 11, 1938, Austria was invaded by the Nazis, the elder Hellers lost their business, and Max lost his job. He convinced his parents the family must leave Europe. He wrote to Mary Mills in Greenville, whom he had met in August 1937, and she secured a job for him from Shepard Salzman, president of Piedmont Shirt Company. In August 1938 Max and his sister Paula arrived, followed by their parents. Trude Schonthal, Max's fiancée, left Vienna in 1939 and eventually came to Greenville with her mother by way of Belgium. Her father escaped from a concentration camp in France and joined the family. Max and Trude Heller married in 1942 and have three children.

Heller began work at Piedmont Shirt Company as a stock clerk and eventually became vice president and general manager. In 1946 he established the Williamston Shirt Company, which he sold in 1948. He subsequently formed the Maxton Shirt Company, which he sold in 1962 but continued to work for until 1967.

Meanwhile Heller became active in community affairs. A member of Congregation Beth Israel, he served as president of the congregation. He became concerned about youthful offenders and urban housing for the poor. In 1968 he was elected to the Greenville City Council, and in 1971 he was elected mayor, serving from 1971 to 1979. He championed the desegregation of city hall and membership of municipal commissions, and the building of community centers. To provide more economical public transportation, he led the creation of the Greenville Transit Authority.

Pressed to run for reelection in 1975, Heller agreed if the business community would support and match federal funding for the redevelopment of downtown. The city received one of the first Urban Development Action grants ($7.4 million) and revenue sharing funds ($1.5 million). The convention center in the Hyatt Regency Hotel was named for Heller.

A candidate for Congress in 1978, Heller won the Democratic primary, but lost the general election to Republican Carroll Campbell. Anti-Semitic and nativist overtones characterized the campaign. In 1979 Governor Richard Riley appointed Heller chairman of the State Development Board. In five years Heller oversaw the creation of 67,000 jobs and the South Carolina Research Authority, and the recruitment of diversified companies such as Michelin North America, Union Camp, and Digital Computer. Under his leadership the annual recruitment of industry hit the $1 billion mark.

Back in Greenville, Heller continued to be involved in a host of civic improvement efforts, such as the creation of the Alliance for Quality Education to aid public school improvement. In 2002 Furman University honored the Hellers by naming its endowed community volunteer program the Max and Trude Heller Collegiate Education Service Corps. A. V. HUFF, JR.

Huff, Archie Vernon, Jr. *Greenville: The History of the City and County in the South Carolina Piedmont.* Columbia: University of South Carolina Press, 1995.

Little, Lloyd. "Providing Visionary Guidance for the Upstate." *Greenville News,* December 13, 1992, upstate business section, pp. 1, 6–7.

Hembel, Caroline Etheredge (1918–2001). Pioneer aviator. Hembel was born in Saluda on November 12, 1918, the daughter of Rodney Hammond Etheredge, a farmer and lawyer, and Ora Padget, a housewife, on the family plantation. Enthralled by Amelia Earhart's exploits, Hembel decided to be a pilot at a time when female pilots were a novelty. She attended Furman University from 1937 to 1939 and then the University of South Carolina, where she graduated in 1941. After entering the fledgling Civilian Pilot Training Program in 1939, she became the first female trainee in the Southeast to receive her pilot's license. By 1941 she had obtained her commercial pilot's license, completed the instructor's course, and was an officer of the Ninety Nines (the international women pilots organization). Hembel was assigned to train Navy V-5 aviation cadets at Owens Field in Columbia. On February 14, 1942 she married fellow instructor Les Hembel, a future South Carolina Aviation Hall of Fame inductee. In 1943 she became a WASP (Women's Auxiliary Service Pilots member). In 1945 the Hembels settled in Saluda, raised three children, and pursued an aviation-centered lifestyle. Caroline Hembel competed in several All-Women Transcontinental Air Races during the 1940s. In 1962 she helped her husband establish South Carolina Helicopters, a Saluda firm that became one of America's largest helicopter training schools and has trained pilots from all over the world. Caroline helped to promote the Amelia Earhart postage stamp in 1963, the year she retired from flying. In 1995 the South Carolina Aviation Association named her South Carolina Aviator of the Year and inducted her into the South Carolina Aviation Hall of Fame, making the Hembels the first wife and husband inductees. Caroline Hembel died of congestive heart failure on January 22, 2001, at her Saluda home and was buried in the Red Bank Baptist Church cemetery. ROBERT L. JANISKEE

"Pioneer Aviator Leaves Legacy." Saluda *Standard-Sentinel,* February 1, 2001, p. 1.

Hemphill, James Calvin (1889–1970). Architect. Hemphill was born in Abbeville, the son of state senator Robert Reid Hemphill and Eugenia Cornelia Taylor. He attended the College of Charleston for two years before relocating to Boston. He resumed his studies in architecture at Harvard University Summer School and the Boston Architectural Club. Following his education, he worked for a year in Thomas A. Edison's West Orange, New Jersey, laboratory, then as a draftsman for both Warren & Smith of Boston, and Lockwood, Greene & Company of Boston and Greenville, South Carolina. Returning to Abbeville by 1915, he practiced there briefly before establishing an office in Greenwood in 1916 with J. Ernest Summer of Jacksonville, Florida. Together for only two years, Summer & Hemphill produced plans for, among others, Greenwood's Carnegie Library (1916–1917) and Main Street Methodist Church (1917), the latter in association with Henry D. Harrall of Bennettsville. Most notable though was their five-story Exchange Bank of Newberry (1917).

After service in World War I, Hemphill resumed practice alone until about 1933, when the Great Depression halted all building projects. Among his most notable projects during this period were the Negro Hospital at Brewer Normal Institute in Greenwood, in association with Holmes & Von Schmid of Montclair, New Jersey, and New York City (1923); the Newberry County Hospital (1924–1925); and five Greenwood schools, including the extensive Greenwood High School (1925) in association with Wilson, Berryman & Kennedy of Columbia (1925 and 1929). From 1934 to 1936 Hemphill was headquartered in Columbia, where he supervised several New Deal projects, among them the Historic American Buildings Survey (HABS), in which he produced measured drawings of Robert Mills's Ainsley Hall House. He practiced privately in Columbia from 1936 to 1943, when World War II brought him back into government service, first at Parris Island and later in Washington, D.C. After the war he reestablished his Greenwood practice, and in 1947 he brought his son, James C. Hemphill, Jr., into the firm as an associate.

Other notable designs by Hemphill in Greenwood were his Church of the Resurrection (1932), the Greenwood County Courthouse (1947), the YMCA Building (1948), Self Memorial Hospital (1949–1950), the Greenwood Post Office (1949), and the Greenwood Public Library (1957). From 1917 to 1962 Hemphill developed the Connie Maxwell Children's Home's campus at Greenwood and designed several buildings at the John De La Howe School near McCormick (1965–1969). In addition, he was particularly noted for his many residential designs in Greenwood, Columbia, and throughout South Carolina.

Hemphill served as president of the South Carolina Chapter of the American Institute of Architects in 1946 and was honored by that body in 1966 with its Distinguished Service Award. His career had spanned more than fifty-five years when he died in Greenwood in 1970. ANDREW W. CHANDLER

Wells, John E., and Robert E. Dalton. *The South Carolina Architects, 1885–1935: A Biographical Directory.* Richmond, Va.: New South Architectural Press, 1992.

Wilson, Charles, Samuel Lapham, and Walter F. Petty. *Architectural Practice in South Carolina.* Charleston, S.C., 1963.

Hemphill, Robert Witherspoon, Sr. (1915–1983). Congressman, jurist. Hemphill was born in Chester on May 10, 1915, the son of John McClure Hemphill and Helen Witherspoon. He graduated from Chester High School in 1932, the University of South Carolina in 1936, and received a law degree from that institution two years later. Before World War II, Hemphill practiced law in the family firm.

Shortly after Pearl Harbor, Hemphill enlisted in the army air corps and commenced training as a B-24 bomber pilot in Texas. He went on to complete flight training and served as a pilot until the end of the war, advancing to the rank of major. He married Isabelle Anderson of Asherton, Texas, on June 20, 1942. The marriage produced three children.

Hemphill returned to Chester after the war and immersed himself in his small-town law practice and politics. In late 1946 he won a seat in the South Carolina House of Representatives, served one term, and returned to the family law firm of Hemphill and Hemphill. By 1950 his love of the courtroom persuaded him to seek the office of solicitor of the Sixth South Carolina Judicial Circuit. He served as solicitor from 1951 to 1956, when he was elected to succeed the retiring Congressman James P. Richards.

As a freshman member of Congress, Hemphill clashed with Richards over the issues of foreign aid and America's role in international affairs. In a 1957 speech before the Lancaster Rotary Club, Richards labeled Hemphill a "southern isolationist." The two congressmen, however, quickly, made their peace and Hemphill easily won reelection to Congress in 1958, 1960, and 1962. In Congress, Hemphill formed a friendship with Senator John F. Kennedy of Massachusetts, who spoke at Hemphill's alma mater in 1958. Two years later, Congressman Hemphill endorsed Kennedy for the presidency and campaigned for him.

In late 1963 President Kennedy decided to appoint Hemphill to the federal bench, United States Fourth Judicial Court. The appointment papers, however, were still on his desk when the president was assassinated that November in Dallas. The new chief executive, Lyndon Johnson, endorsed the nomination, and in January 1964 the U.S. Senate approved Hemphill as a federal judge.

For nearly twenty years Judge Hemphill drove from his Chester home to conduct federal court in cities such as Columbia and Greenville. In 1981 Judge Hemphill took senior status and held court, as needed, around the country. He continued to make his home in Chester and teach Sunday school until his death on December 25, 1983. He was buried in the Hopewell Associate Reformed Presbyterian Church Cemetery in Chester. JOSEPH EDWARD LEE

Collins, Ann P. *A Goodly Heritage: History of Chester County, South Carolina.* Columbia, S.C.: R. L. Bryan, 1986.

Hemphill, Robert Witherspoon. Papers. Modern Political Collections, South Caroliniana Library, University of South Carolina, Columbia.

Herald (2003 circulation: 31,238 daily and 33,340 Sunday). The *Herald* publishes every day including Sunday and serves Rock Hill and the surrounding community. Several post–Civil War–era newspapers contributed to the founding of the *Herald.* Most notably, the *Hampton Herald,* named in honor of Wade Hampton III, was formed in 1876. This newspaper was purchased in 1877 by James Morrow Ivy, who gave the newspaper the name *Rock Hill Herald.* The newspaper was a booster of local causes, including the successful effort to move Winthrop Normal and Industrial School (later Winthrop University) to Rock Hill.

In 1911 the newspaper was published every evening except Sundays and took the name *Evening Herald.* By 1947 the newspaper's circulation had increased to 7,500. The newspaper continued to increase its circulation, to 24,000 by 1980, and in 1985 the newspaper was sold to the News and Observer Company of Raleigh, North Carolina. That same year the name reverted back to *Herald.* Shortly thereafter the newspaper added a Sunday edition, and on August 1, 1988, the newspaper began publishing in the morning every day.

In 1990 the News and Observer Company sold the *Herald* to McClatchy Newspapers of Sacramento, California. Three years later, Orage Quarles III became the publisher of the *Herald.* He was the first African American publisher of a daily newspaper in South Carolina, and he served until 1996. He was followed by Jayne Speizer, the *Herald*'s first female publisher. AARON W. MARRS

McNeely, Patricia G. *The Palmetto Press: The History of South Carolina's Newspapers and the Press Association.* Columbia: South Carolina Press Association, 1998.

Herald-Journal (2003 circulation: 49,372 daily and 57,727 Sunday). The Spartanburg *Herald-Journal* can be traced to the *Spartan,* a weekly newspaper founded by attorney T. O. P. Vernon and first published on December 22, 1843. State legislator J. W. Tucker bought half the business in 1851 and then sold to the Trimmier brothers, who hired Vernon back as the associate editor. They changed the newspaper's name to the *Carolina Spartan* in 1860. A paper shortage stopped publication for two weeks during 1863 and between May 1, 1865, and February 1866, when portions of the state were occupied by Union troops. Another Spartanburg newspaper, the *Orphan's Friend,* published by the children of the Carolina Orphan Home, began in 1873 as a weekly. It changed its name to the *Spartanburg Herald* by 1875 and became a daily in 1890. The Journal Publishing Company bought the *Carolina Spartan* in 1900, which became the *Spartanburg Journal* and published six days a week.

Ambrose Gonzales, founder and publisher of the *State* in Columbia, bought the indebted *Herald* in 1905 and hired Charles O. Hearon of Virginia as the editor. Hearon became influential in the state, campaigning for open city council meetings, a state highway system, and industrial development. After learning that the competing *Journal* might become a political organ of controversial Governor Cole Blease, Gonzales reportedly gave $7,000 toward its purchase. The *Herald* bought its competitor in 1914, and the *Journal* became Spartanburg's afternoon newspaper. Hearon and W. W. Holland bought both newspapers from the Gonzales family in 1924. Later purchased in 1947 by Charles E. Marsh of Texas, the newspapers were subsequently bequeathed to a private foundation. They merged to become the *Herald-Journal* on October 1, 1982. The New York Times Newspaper Group bought the *Herald-Journal* in 1985 and on-line service began in 1995. ALAN RICHARD

McNeeley, Patricia G. *The Palmetto Press: The History of South Carolina's Newspapers and the Press Association.* Columbia: South Carolina Press Association, 1998.

Heyward, James (1764–1796), and **Nathaniel Heyward** (1766–1851). Rice planters. Born respectively on April 13, 1764, and January 18, 1766, James and Nathaniel Heyward were the sons of Daniel Heyward and Jane Elizabeth Gignilliat. The brothers were raised at Old House Plantation on the Combahee River, an estuary of Port Royal Sound. When their father died in 1777, both James and Nathaniel inherited small plantations. Soon after the Revolutionary

War, both young men went to Europe for eighteen months of cultural enrichment.

James and Nathaniel returned to the lowcountry and began experimenting with new methods of rice cultivation. James spent much of his life in England and Philadelphia, as a factor for Heyward products. He wed Susan Cole in England on October 4, 1794, and died at Old House plantation on October 4, 1796. He left his plantations (Copenhagen and Hamburg) to his wife who passed them down to Nathaniel when she died.

Nathaniel married Henrietta Manigault on February 27, 1788. Using her $50,000 dowry, Heyward acquired land and other assets, eventually becoming the wealthiest rice planter in South Carolina. Through inheritance and purchase, Nathaniel owned or managed 35,000 acres and as many as two thousand slaves in Charleston, Colleton, and Beaufort Districts. His rice plantations included Ashley and Marshland Farms on the Charleston Neck; Silk Hope, Club House and Pompion Hill along the Cooper River; Blanford, Clay Hall, and Williams Island in the Beaufort District; and Old House, The Bluff, Fife, Amsterdam, Rotterdam, Lewisburg, Savannah, Rose Hill, Pleasant Hill, Middlehouse, Pines, Myrtle Grove, Copenhagen, Hamburg, and Antwerp in Colleton District. Other holdings included a cotton plantation, forest lands, livestock, nine houses in Charleston, plus diverse bonds and securities. By the time of his death at the Bluff Plantation on April 10, 1851, Nathaniel possessed a net worth estimated at just over $2 million, making him by some estimates the wealthiest man in antebellum South Carolina.

The Heyward brothers' success can be attributed to the perfection of rice cultivation in the coastal savannas and swamps of South Carolina. The method, highly labor intensive, utilized a system of earthen levees and ditches to create rice fields and reservoirs of fresh river water for irrigation. An array of wooden irrigation trunks, fitted on either end with floodgates, separated the fields from the river and utilized tidal pressure to either hold the fresh water in the fields or allow its continual circulation. While rice was grown profitably on inland swamp plantations, the tidal irrigation techniques employed by the Heywards increased production considerably. Planters growing rice on inland swamps could produce between six hundred and one thousand pounds of rice per acre. By the 1790s tidal swamp plantations yielded as much as fifteen hundred pounds per acre.

Tidal irrigation techniques changed the social and geographic character of the lowcountry in South Carolina and Georgia. Increased production boosted profits, but the new techniques were expensive to implement and extremely labor intensive. Land prices near coastal rivers rose considerably and the slave labor needed to profitably grow rice demanded an enormous capital investment. The result was that a handful of planters reaped a fabulous financial reward that was out of the reach of poorer whites in the region.
ROBERT T. OLIVER

Chaplin, Joyce E. *An Anxious Pursuit: Agricultural Innovation and Modernity in the Lower South, 1730–1815.* Chapel Hill: University of North Carolina Press, 1993.

Dusinberre, William. *Them Dark Days: Slavery in the American Rice Swamps.* New York: Oxford University Press, 1996.

Heyward, Duncan Clinch. *Seed from Madagascar.* 1937. Reprint, Columbia: University of South Carolina Press, 1993.

Heyward, DuBose (1885–1940). Author. Heyward was born in Charleston on August 31, 1885, the son of Edwin Watkins Heyward and Jane Screven DuBose. Both parents were dispossessed aristocrats from the upstate who had come to Charleston to better their opportunities. Joining the once powerful families in Charleston that had been reduced to genteel poverty by the Civil War, "Ned" Heyward eked out a living in a rice mill then died in a tragic industrial accident when DuBose was not quite three. Thrown on her own resources, Janie, as she was called, took in sewing, ran a boardinghouse on Sullivan's Island, and wrote down Gullah folktales she had heard as a little girl and performed them for local arts groups. This immersion in the Gullah world worked its way into Heyward's imagination as he was growing up, but his hopes for a career in the world of art were forestalled repeatedly by a series of illnesses—the most devastating of which was polio—which left him weakened and directionless.

DuBose Heyward (center) with George and Ira Gershwin. Courtesy, South Carolina Historical Society

Without a college education, he took the only honorable route open to him, as a Heyward, and went into the insurance business with a partner. The agency was successful, and once Heyward solidified his financial base, he gave more time to his first love, poetry writing. In 1920, with John Bennett and Hervey Allen, he founded the Poetry Society of South Carolina, an organization that initiated the great southern literary renaissance of the early twentieth century. Having met such literary luminaries as Carl Sandburg and Amy Lowell, Heyward gained entry to the New Hampshire artists' retreat, the MacDowell Colony, where he met his future wife, Dorothy Hartzell Kuhns, a playwright. Shortly after their wedding in New York on September 22, 1923, she convinced him to throw over the insurance business for full-time writing. At her instigation, and calling on the encyclopedic knowledge about Gullah culture possessed by his mentor, John Bennett, Heyward threw caution aside and wrote *Porgy* (1925), a novel about African American life in Charleston. Revolutionary for its time, the book changed literary depictions of blacks in the United States forever, because in it a white southerner presented African Americans in an honest and realistic way, as opposed to the stereotyped portrayals found in minstrelsy and antebellum narratives. Heyward was mildly ostracized from some quarters of Charleston society for the book, but he took his licks with characteristic grace and self-deprecating humor. Anyway, he was by then enthralled with the New York literary world, who lionized him for his courage in writing *Porgy.* The artists of the Harlem Renaissance feted him, and with Dorothy's considerable assistance in stagecraft, brought a nonmusical version of the *Porgy* to the theater, in the process creating important dramatic roles for African American actors and raising public awareness of their talents. The play forever ended the vaudevillian character of most African American stage works at the time and catapulted Heyward on a trajectory that was to take him up to the highest literary levels.

If to many Charlestonians *Porgy* presented an unorthodox stand on race relations, then *Mamba's Daughters* (1929) must have seemed the work of a lunatic. In it, a white man carried the suitcase of a black girl (albeit in New York), who goes on to perform to a packed house in a hybrid native opera that enfranchises both its black and its white audience. How accurate Heyward's prophecy turned out to be, for six short years later the innovative opera *Porgy and Bess* made its debut. Heyward had a large role in the composition and production of the opera: he authored the lyrics (alone or with Ira Gershwin) to half its songs; he collaborated with George Gershwin on the script and wrote the libretto (the sung dialogue) by himself; and he assisted with rehearsals and all manner of production details. When it opened, however, *Porgy and Bess* was in relative terms a critical and financial failure. Heyward beat a hasty retreat away from New York and back to Charleston. His works since *Mamba* had taken a decided turn toward more overt social criticism of the South, but he also spent his remaining years fostering local playwriting talent as resident dramatist of the Dock Street Theatre, newly restored in 1937. Charleston welcomed him home, but largely as a prodigal son. *Porgy and Bess,* the work that brought him—and his city—unprecedented fame was not performed in Charleston until the South Carolina Tricentennial in June 1970. Heyward died on June 16, 1940, in North Carolina and was buried in the St. Philip's Churchyard, Charleston. JAMES M. HUTCHISSON

Durham, Frank. *DuBose Heyward: The Man Who Wrote "Porgy."* Columbia: University of South Carolina Press, 1954.

Greene, Harlan. "Charleston Childhood: The First Years of DuBose Heyward." *South Carolina Historical Magazine* 83 (April 1982): 154–67.

Hutchisson, James M. *DuBose Heyward: A Charleston Gentleman and the World of Porgy and Bess.* Jackson: University Press of Mississippi, 2000.

Slavick, William. *DuBose Heyward.* Boston: Twayne, 1981.

Heyward, Duncan Clinch (1864–1943). Governor. Heyward was born in Richland District on June 24, 1864, the son of Edward Barnwell Heyward and Catherine Clinch. An orphan by 1871, Heyward resided with his grandparents at their Colleton County rice plantation. He received his basic schooling in Charleston and at Cheltenham Academy in Pennsylvania. For three years (1882–1885), Heyward attended Washington and Lee University in Lexington, Virginia, but did not graduate. On February 11, 1886, he married Mary Elizabeth Campbell. They had four children. As did his illustrious forebears, Heyward earned his primary livelihood as a lowcounty rice planter.

Until 1902 Heyward had refrained from playing a prominent role in South Carolina politics. Unassociated with any particular political faction, Heyward was a good "compromise" candidate for governor. In August 1902 he won the Democratic nomination and was elected in November. He was reelected in 1904.

Entering office on January 20, 1903, Heyward optimistically believed that South Carolina "can look to the future with every degree of confidence and encouragement." Espousing a progressive agenda that foreshadowed the administration of Governor Richard I. Manning, Heyward touted reforms to advance the "general welfare" of his state. Education was his top priority, particularly the encouragement of white children to take advantage of educational opportunities. Heyward's administration helped secure funding for rural schools, increase pay for white teachers, and gradually extended the school term. However, he failed to convince the General Assembly to make school attendance compulsory.

Despite some success in education, most of Heyward's progressive agenda was frustrated by state legislators. His efforts to place the state on a sound fiscal grounding failed to halt deficit spending by the General Assembly or secure an equalization of property tax assessments. Although Heyward signed the Marshall Child Labor Bill, the new law was so watered down by legislators that one newspaper called it "the mildest and most conservative measure that could be arranged and still called a child labor law." And, as were his predecessors, Heyward was bedeviled by the state's dispensary liquor laws. While critical of its administration, Heyward nevertheless believed the system, if properly regulated "will be one of the best solutions to the liquor question." However, in 1904, he signed the Brice Law, which gave individual counties the option to hold referendums on whether to retain or abolish local dispensaries. By 1906 lax enforcement of the dispensary laws led Heyward to denounce the system as "a cloud which throws a shadow over the State."

Heyward left office on January 15, 1907, and never ran for another elective position. He initially concentrated on improving rice production on his Colleton County plantation. But following the demise of coastal rice culture after 1911, Heyward pursued business ventures in Columbia. In 1913 President Woodrow Wilson appointed him to be the collector of federal internal revenue taxes for South Carolina. In 1937 Heyward published *Seed from Madagascar,* a classic study of South Carolina rice culture. He died in Columbia on January 23, 1943. MILES S. RICHARDS

Spigner, Margaret Ola. "The Public Life of D. C. Heyward, 1903–1907." Master's thesis, University of South Carolina, 1951.

Heyward, Thomas, Jr. (1746–1809). Planter, legislator, jurist, signer of the Declaration of Independence. Heyward (designated "Jr." to distinguish him from others of that name in his family), the eldest son of Daniel Heyward and Maria Miles, was born on July 28, 1746, at his father's Old House plantation in St. Helena's Parish. After receiving a classical education, he was sent to London to study law at the Middle Temple in 1765. Returning to South Carolina in 1771, Heyward was admitted to the Charleston Bar on January 22, 1771, and was practicing law in Charleston when elected to represent St. Helena's Parish in the Commons House of Assembly.

Heyward took an active role in opposition to British rule and served on the Committee of Ninety-Nine in 1774, which called for the formation of the First Provincial Congress the following year. He

Thomas Heyward, Jr. Courtesy, South Carolina Historical Society

was additionally one of the thirteen members appointed to the Council of Safety and was reelected to the Second Provincial Congress in late 1775, which resolved itself into the First General Assembly in 1776. The Second Provincial Congress reappointed Heyward to the Council of Safety. Early in 1776 he was chosen to replace the resigning Christopher Gadsden in the Second Continental Congress. That summer Thomas Heyward, Jr., was one of four South Carolinians who signed the Declaration of Independence in Philadelphia.

Sitting in Congress for two years, Heyward returned to South Carolina in 1778 and was appointed a circuit judge in 1779, a position he held for ten years. In that capacity he upheld the confiscation and amercement of Loyalist property after the Revolutionary War. Heyward's political responsibilities did not prevent his military duty. As a captain in the Charleston Artillery Company, he was wounded in the successful defense at Port Royal Island in February 1779. Captured at the head of his battery at the fall of Charleston, Heyward was paroled, but was later recalled and imprisoned at St. Augustine, Florida. Exchanged and sent to Philadelphia, he returned to South Carolina and was elected to the Fourth General Assembly in 1782. Heyward was also a supporter of the federal Constitution and a member of the state convention which ratified it in 1788, and he was a member of the subsequent state constitutional convention.

In 1790 Heyward retired from active public life in order to devote himself to his family and agricultural pursuits at his White Hall Plantation in St. Luke's Parish. He had been a founder and the first president of the Agricultural Society of South Carolina and continued to work with the society until his death. He married twice. On April 20, 1773, he married Elizabeth Mathewes, who died in 1782. On May 4, 1786, Heyward married Elizabeth Savage. Together the marriages produced eight children. Thomas Heyward, Jr., died on April 22, 1809, and was buried in the family cemetery on Old House Plantation in St. Luke's Parish. SAMUEL K. FORE

Edgar, Walter, and N. Louise Bailey, eds. *Biographical Directory of the South Carolina House of Representatives.* Vol. 2, *The Commons House of Assembly, 1692–1775.* Columbia: University of South Carolina Press, 1977.

Hemphill, William E., ed. *Extracts from the Journals of the Provincial Congresses of South Carolina, 1775–1776.* Columbia: South Carolina Archives Department, 1960.

Salley, Alexander S. *Delegates to the Continental Congress from South Carolina, 1774–1789, with Sketches of the Four Who Signed the Declaration of Independence.* Columbia, S.C.: State Company, 1927.

Heyward-Washington House (Charleston). Owned by the Charleston Museum and open to the public, the Heyward-Washington House at 87 Church Street, Charleston, was built in 1772 by the rice planter Thomas Heyward, Jr., who later became a signer of the Declaration of Independence. President George Washington stayed in the house during his visit to Charleston in 1791. The three-story brick double house features four rooms plus a central hall on the first floor. The second floor features a drawing room and a smaller withdrawing room in front and two chambers in the rear; additional chambers are found on the third floor. In the 1880s the Fuseler family converted the property to a bakery, radically altering the first floor of the house to include a storefront. It was saved from destruction by the Charleston Museum and the Society for the Preservation of Old Dwellings in 1929. Architectural research aided restoration of the first floor, while a study of Charleston gardens led to the creation of a period parterre (an ornamental garden with paths between the beds) in the rear lot. The house museum is furnished with period furniture and appointments, including Charleston-made furniture.

Thomas Heyward sold the property in 1794. Archaeology and documents reveal a long history of occupation, both before and after Heyward. A wooden house and outbuildings built in 1730 by the gunsmith John Milner burned in the Charleston fire of 1740. Milner and his son continued the smithing business with the aid of eleven slaves. In 1749 John Milner, Jr., built a brick single house and outbuildings. Thomas Heyward razed the single house but kept Milner's kitchen and stable.

Excavations by the Charleston Museum revealed the houses, activities, and artifacts of the Milners, the Heywards, the antebellum owners, and the enslaved African American occupants. The house was designated a National Historic Landmark in 1970. MARTHA A. ZIERDEN AND RONALD W. ANTHONY

Herold, Elaine B. *Preliminary Report on the Research at the Heyward-Washington House.* Charleston, S.C.: Charleston Museum, 1978.

Poston, Jonathan H. *The Buildings of Charleston: A Guide to the City's Architecture.* Columbia: University of South Carolina Press, 1997.

Zierden, Martha. *Archaeological Testing and Mitigation at the Stable Building, Heyward-Washington House.* Charleston, S.C.: Charleston Museum, 1993.

Zierden, Martha, and Elizabeth Reitz. "Eighteenth-Century Charleston: Aftermath of the Siege of St. Augustine." *El Escribano: The St. Augustine Journal of History* (2002): 113–32.

Hibernian Hall (Charleston). Designed by Philadelphia architect Thomas U. Walter, Hibernian Hall is among the most significant examples of the Greek Revival in Charleston. In the early 1830s the Hibernian Society, a social and charitable organization founded in 1801 to provide aid to Irish immigrants and their families, began making plans to build a meeting hall. After acquiring property on Meeting Street nearly opposite the Fireproof Building, the society held a national competition for the architectural plans. The design submitted by Walter, who later oversaw the enlargement of the U.S. Capitol in Washington, D.C., was ultimately chosen. Construction began in the spring of 1839 and was completed in January 1841.

Walter modeled his design for the building on the Ionic temple on the Ilissus in Athens. The hexastyle portico was originally executed in the Ionic order, but after collapsing in the 1886 earthquake it was awkwardly rebuilt with reproportioned columns and a Corinthian pediment with an Italianate window. Set above the entrance in relief is a gilded Irish harp. The side elevations feature Tuscan pilasters. In contrast to the restrained exterior styling, the interior is an elegant, dramatic space. An extraordinary rotunda with columnar balconies rises three stories to a coffered dome with oculus. The building is surrounded by a wrought-iron fence and cast-iron gas lamps. In addition to hosting countless Hibernian society functions, including the annual St. Patrick's Day banquet, the hall has been used for other major social events, most notably the January Ball of the St. Cecilia Society, Charleston's oldest and most exclusive social function. The U.S. Department of the Interior designated the building a National Historic Landmark in 1973. DANIEL J. VIVIAN

Poston, Jonathan H. *The Buildings of Charleston: A Guide to the City's Architecture.* Columbia: University of South Carolina Press, 1997.

Severens, Kenneth. *Charleston Antebellum Architecture and Civic Destiny.* Knoxville: University of Tennessee Press, 1988.

High Hills of Santee. An eroded upland remnant of an ancient seashore, the High Hills of Santee rise on the eastern side of the upper Santee River and run north through Sumter and Lee Counties paralleling the Wateree River. Nearly twenty-five miles long and five miles wide at their widest point, this chain of hills is situated conspicuously between the level expanse of the coastal plain to the east and the swampy lowland of the Wateree River valley to the west. At their greatest elevation, the High Hills are three hundred feet above the level of the Wateree and offer panoramic vistas more typical of the Piedmont and mountain regions of the state. English naturalist John Lawson, one of the earliest Europeans to explore the High Hills, described them in 1701 as "the most amazing Prospect I had seen since I had been in Carolina."

Eighteenth-century medical theory attributed the fevers and "agues" that ravaged lowcountry South Carolina during the "sickly season" to standing water and the miasmatic vapors supposed to emanate from it. Any environmental conditions that differed from the wet areas of the lowcountry were perceived as healthful. Despite proximity to the Wateree Swamp, the altitude of the High Hills was believed to purify the air and springs. Originally settled by immigrants from Virginia around 1750, by the time of the Revolutionary War the High Hills of Santee were relatively populous and had gained a reputation as a pleasant, salubrious place to spend the summer.

In the early nineteenth century, some seasonal visitors to the High Hills became permanent residents, establishing cotton plantations and erecting grand country seats in place of quaint summer cottages. Although much of the High Hills remained pastoral at the turn of the twenty-first century, certain areas, especially around Stateburg, were becoming increasingly suburbanized. MATTHEW A. LOCKHART

Brewster, Lawrence Fay. *Summer Migrations and Resorts of South Carolina Low-Country Planters.* Durham, N.C.: Duke University Press, 1947.

Gregorie, Anne King. *History of Sumter County, South Carolina.* Sumter, S.C.: Library Board of Sumter County, 1954.

Parler, Josie Platt. *The Past Blows By: On the Road to Poinsett Park.* Sumter, S.C.: Knight Brothers, 1939.

Highway 17. Also known as the Ocean Highway, U.S. Highway 17 enters South Carolina at the North Carolina border near Little River, then hugs the coast for almost two hundred miles before exiting the state at Savannah, Georgia. It is the linear descendent of the King's Highway, a colonial-era post road that connected the American colonies by 1750. Traces of the colonial highway can still be found. In 1931, when Highway 17 was being expanded from New York to Miami, developer John T. Woodside paid to have the highway routed around his hunting preserve, which protected a vestige of the original road. The land was later occupied by the Meher Spiritual Center in Myrtle Beach.

In modern times, Highway 17 has been instrumental in bringing tourists to Myrtle Beach and the Grand Strand, especially during the first half of the twentieth century, when Myrtle Beach was not connected to other major interstate or intrastate highways. General Holmes Springs was largely responsible for opening up the roads to the resort. The first straightening and paving of the King's Highway in South Carolina began in 1927, when bridges were built to cross the main inlets. In 1929 it was completed from the North Carolina state line, south along the coast to Georgetown. The modern route extends to Interstate 95 near Beaufort, closely following the route that Native Americans, early settlers, and even President George Washington traveled many years ago. BARBARA STOKES

Floyd, Blanche W. *Tales Along the Grand Strand of South Carolina.* Winston-Salem, N.C.: Bandit, 1996.

Willcox, Henry Trezevant. *Musings of a Hermit.* 4th ed. Murrells Inlet, S.C.: The Hermitage, 1973.

Highway 301. Construction of this major U.S. highway in South Carolina began in 1932 during the Great Depression, when the federal government began taking over the maintenance and construction of many state roads. The route began at Baltimore, Maryland, and ended at Sarasota, Florida, crossing through many towns in eastern South Carolina, including Dillon, Latta, Florence, Manning, Olanta, Sumerton, Bamberg, and Allendale. From the North Carolina border to the Savannah River, Highway 301 covers a distance of approximately 180 miles.

The Cozy Court near Allendale was typical of the many small "mom and pop" motels that served travelers on Highway 301 between the end of World War II and the opening of I-95. Courtesy, the collection of Samuel Bennett, Allendale, S.C.

The highway's many nicknames are an indication that it was popular among tourists throughout the second quarter of the twentieth century. These names included: "Tobacco Trail," "Highway of Southern Hospitality," "Tourist Highway," "Shortest Route from Maine to Florida," and "The Washington-Florida Short Route." This road was popular among tourists because it avoided some of the larger cities, had no toll bridges or ferries, and was paved its entire length.

During the 1950s this highway was a major U.S. north-south route, well known to travelers in the eastern United States. Even the popular television show *I Love Lucy,* featured an episode where Lucille Ball traveled in an automobile with a woman who always traveled Highway 301 to Florida. This highway created a demand for restaurants and motels in South Carolina. Some popular motels included the Lewis Motel in Olanta, the Santee Motor Company in Manning, the Holiday in Florence, and the Cotton Patch Motel in Bamberg.

The building of Interstate 95 in the late 1950s and 1960s, which ran almost parallel to U.S. 301, caused the tourist traffic to decline on the older highway. Businesses on U.S. 301, particularly the motel operators, had difficulty in maintaining their customer base. Several rebuilt near the interstate, while others operated at a much slower pace. LLOYD JOHNSON

Moore, John Hammond. *The South Carolina Highway Department, 1917–1987.* Columbia: University of South Carolina Press, 1987.

Hill, Daniel Harvey (1821–1889). Soldier. Born in York District on July 12, 1821, Hill was the son of Solomon Hill and Nancy Cabeen. His father died when he was four, and he was raised in an atmosphere of farm work and Presbyterian piety. He attended West Point, ranking twenty-eighth of fifty-six cadets graduating in 1842. During the Mexican War he served in a series of important battles and received a gold sword from the South Carolina legislature for his bravery. During this period Hill wrote a series of unsigned magazine articles criticizing the War Department. On November 2, 1848, Hill married Isabella Morrison of Lincoln County, North Carolina. The couple had nine children.

Shortly after his marriage, Hill resigned from the army to teach mathematics at Washington College in Virginia and then at Davidson College in North Carolina. In 1859 he took command of the new North Carolina Military Institute near Charlotte. When the Civil War began he was appointed colonel of the First Regiment of North Carolina Volunteers. On June 10, 1861, Hill led his men skillfully to victory at Big Bethel Church in the first land battle of the war. He was serving under Colonel John B. Magruder, for whom he had little regard, but who allowed Hill to control the fighting. Promoted to brigadier general, Hill was sent to command at Leesburg, where he criticized his cavalry commander, J. E. B. Stuart, creating a mutual dislike between them.

In 1862 Hill was promoted to major general and placed under General James Longstreet during the Peninsular Campaign, where Hill participated in the various battles of the Seven Days' campaign and showed great personal bravery under fire. At South Mountain (September 14, 1864) an important order addressed to him fell into federal hands, but he was probably not at fault. His division lost more than sixty percent of its strength at Sharpsburg (September 17, 1862), and Hill had three horses shot from under him. The severe winter and his frail nature caused his reassignment to administrative duties in North Carolina and Virginia, where he had ample time to write more complaining letters to various high officials.

In mid-1863 Hill was breveted to lieutenant general and sent to command a corps in Braxton Bragg's Army of Tennessee. At Chickamauga (September 19–20, 1863) he again proved his skill and bravery, but after the partial victory he and many of his compatriots suggested Bragg's removal from command. Jefferson Davis personally intervened in support of Bragg, who then relieved Hill from duty. Davis allowed Hill's rank to lapse back to major general and thereafter refused to clear Hill's reputation. Hill later become a "volunteer aide" to General P. G. T. Beauregard at Petersburg, where he effectively led troops in several engagements. After the war Hill edited a magazine and a newspaper in Charlotte. He then served as president of Arkansas Industrial University (later the University of Arkansas) and president of Georgia Military and Agricultural College. Hill died of cancer in Charlotte, North Carolina, on September 24, 1889, and was buried in the Davidson College Cemetery. DEWITT BOYD STONE, JR.

Bridges, Leonard Hal. *Lee's Maverick General.* New York: McGraw-Hill, 1961.

Freeman, Douglas Southall. *Lee's Lieutenants: A Study in Command.* 3 vols. New York: Scribner's, 1942–1944.

Robertson, James I. "'Old Rawhide': A Military Biography of Daniel Harvey Hill, C.S.A." Master's thesis, Emory University, 1956.

Hillsborough Township. Located on the upper Savannah River in present-day McCormick County, Hillsborough Township was named after Wills Hill, viscount of Hillsborough and president of the British Board of Trade. The settlement originated with a memoir that the Reverend Jean-Louis Gibert addressed to the board of trade in 1763 regarding a project to settle a group of Huguenots in North America. His plan coincided with the desire of the South Carolina government to strengthen the colony's western frontier in the wake of the Cherokee War. In 1764 Gibert's colonization scheme was approved and he received a 28,000-acre grant. About three hundred Huguenots, along with a few Swiss and Germans, settled Hillsborough Township in 1764–1765, 1768, and 1773. The last group, which was originally bound for Nova Scotia, arrived in Charleston under the leadership of Jean-Louis Dumesnil de St. Pierre, a Huguenot gentleman from Normandy. Plans were made for the building of a town that consisted of nearly two hundred lots of one-half acre each, along with a glebe, churchyard, fort, and mill. The town was named New Bordeaux in reference to the port through which most Hillsborough settlers left France. The colonists also planted a 175-acre vineyard, which was to be parceled out in four-acre lots. In addition to raising subsistence crops, the Huguenots attempted to produce silk and cultivate wine but met with little success. Although about twenty frame houses were built in New Bordeaux by the mid-1760s, the town site was largely abandoned before 1770 as the French dispersed throughout the area and mixed with German, English, and Irish settlers. Jean-Louis Gibert died of mushroom poisoning in 1773. Carolina Huguenot surnames from Hillsborough include Gibert, Moragne, Guillebeau, Boutiton, and Gervais. BERTRAND VAN RUYMBEKE

Gibert, Anne C. *Pierre Gibert, Esq., the Devoted Huguenot: A History of the French Settlement of New Bordeaux, South Carolina.* N.p., 1976.

Hirsch, Arthur Henry. *The Huguenots of Colonial South Carolina.* 1928. Reprint, Columbia: University of South Carolina Press, 1999.

Lewis, Kenneth E. *The Guillebeau House: An Eighteenth Century Huguenot Structure in McCormick County, South Carolina.* Columbia: Institute of Archeology and Anthropology, University of South Carolina, 1979.

Meriwether, Robert L. *The Expansion of South Carolina, 1729–1765.* Kingsport, Tenn.: Southern Publishers, 1940.

Hilton Head Island (Beaufort County; 2000 pop. 33,862). Located in the southeast corner of the state, Hilton Head Island is the largest of the islands that flank South Carolina's Atlantic coast. Its natural beauty led to the transformation of Hilton Head from an isolated backwater to a world-famous resort and recreational community during the second half of the twentieth century.

Native Americans lived on Hilton Head for more than two millennia before the arrival of Europeans in Port Royal Sound in the sixteenth century. Harsh conditions and hostile Indians defeated early French and Spanish efforts to colonize islands north of Hilton Head. In 1663 an English explorer, Captain William Hilton, sighted the headland of a "Countrey very pleasant and delightful" and named the island for himself. The first white settler on Hilton Head was Colonel John Barnwell, who came in 1717 to claim a one-thousand-acre land grant from the Lords Proprietors. Others followed and established a plantation economy based on slavery that lasted until the Civil War.

Despite losses inflicted by British attacks during the Revolutionary War and the War of 1812, the island flourished following the introduction of Sea Island cotton in 1790. Planters grew rich, consolidated their land- and slaveholdings, and built fine houses in nearby Beaufort as well as in Charleston and Savannah. The plantation era came to an abrupt end in November 1861 when twelve thousand Union troops captured the island. Hilton Head became a base for the blockade of Charleston and Savannah, as well as for forays inland by the Union army. An estimated fifty thousand sailors, soldiers, officials, merchants, camp followers, smugglers, and black marketers crowded into the raw settlement, including thousands of former slaves from nearby plantations.

Following the war, much of Hilton Head Island reverted to nature. Few landowners returned, and none was able to restore holdings or prosperity. By the end of the nineteenth century, the only land under cultivation was farmed by African Americans on small plots on the northwestern corner of the island. Much of the rest of the island, now covered by magnificent forests, was acquired by wealthy outsiders for use as hunting preserves. Two-thirds of Hilton Head wound up in the hands of two New York financiers, Alfred L. Loomis and Landon K. Thorne. In 1950 Hilton Head had just over one thousand residents, ninety percent of whom were black. The island was isolated from the rest of the state. There was no bridge or ferry service, no electricity, and no telephones.

At this juncture, Hilton Head Island was "rediscovered," this time by timber interests from Hinesville, Georgia. Led by Joseph B. Fraser and Fred C. Hack, the Georgians created the Hilton Head Company, purchased the Loomis-Thorne holdings, and harvested millions of feet of lumber between 1950 and 1952. The Hilton Head Company then turned to selling lots along the beach for vacation cottages. State backing was secured for a ferry, and then for the creation of an agency to build a toll bridge, which opened in 1956. Differences over how the Hilton Head Company should develop its land caused Fraser to withdraw from the firm in return for a sizable parcel on the southern end of the island.

Underlying the breakup was the desire of Joseph Fraser's son, Charles, to create a new kind of resort community, one featuring sensitivity to nature and architectural harmony. Charles E. Fraser organized the Sea Pines Company to develop the family's land, pieced together financing from textile and insurance interests, and set to work to turn his dream into reality. The result was Sea Pines Plantation, an oasis of taste and beauty amidst the hodgepodge of seashore development that characterized much of the Atlantic coast in the 1960s. Sea Pines attracted affluent retirees, second-home buyers, and vacationers; its golf and tennis facilities and their televised tournaments drew national attention; and its architectural controls, gated entry, and mingling of residences and golf courses became prototypes for other developments on Hilton Head, then elsewhere in the state, the South, and into the Caribbean.

With the blossoming of Sea Pines came rapid growth. The Hilton Head Company followed Fraser's lead, as did other developers who encircled the island with gated residential and resort communities. Resort hotels sprang up along the beachfront outside Sea Pines, along with restaurants, stores, banks, and movie theaters. With retirees and vacationers came developers, realtors, architects, lawyers, shopkeepers, doctors, and others who made their livelihood on the booming island. The island's economy survived a serious slump in the wake of the oil crunch in the 1970s and the 1986 bankruptcy of the Hilton Head Company. Annual gross sales doubled between 1975 and 1981, and more than doubled to almost $700 million by 1990. Population grew rapidly, from 2,546 in 1970, to 11,336 in 1980, to 23,694 in 1990, and another fifty percent during the 1990s. Growth reduced the proportion of African Americans, from more than ninety percent in 1950 to less than nine percent half a century later. While growth brought connections to the mainland, better schools and health care, public utilities, and expanding economic opportunities, most blacks remained on the bottom of the economic ladder. Many lived in substandard housing with inadequate water and waste disposal, most worked in lower-paying service jobs, and large numbers were forced to commute long distances because they were priced and zoned out of Hilton Head's housing market.

Growth issues have figured prominently in the modern history of Hilton Head Island. Dissatisfaction over the failure of Beaufort County to control growth on Hilton Head led to a long campaign for political independence, which culminated in the incorporation of the Town of Hilton Head Island in 1983. After incorporation, political conflict between retirees and residents centered on growth issues, involving local elections, referendums on no-growth proposals, and road construction. African Americans opposed incorporation and stricter planning and zoning controls, fearful that affluent whites would limit the ability of blacks to develop or sell their land. Paradoxically, these struggles over growth occurred in a place with the strictest land-use, building, and aesthetic requirements of any community in the state.

Modern Hilton Head Island boasts the state's highest per capita income, excellent schools, superior health care, and fine hotels, restaurants, and shops. Its prosperity has spilled over to much of southern Beaufort County, in the form of resort and retirement communities, housing developments, shopping malls, and thousands of jobs in construction and services. MICHAEL N. DANIELSON

Carse, Robert. *Department of the South: Hilton Head Island in the Civil War.* 1961. Reprint, Hilton Head Island, S.C.: Impressions Printing, 1987.

Danielson, Michael N. *Profits and Politics in Paradise: The Development of Hilton Head Island.* Columbia: University of South Carolina Press, 1995.

Grant, Moses Alexander. *Looking Back: Reminiscences of a Black Family Heritage on Hilton Head Island.* Orangeburg, S.C.: Williams Associates, 1988.

Greer, Margaret. *The Sands of Time: A History of Hilton Head Island.* Rev. ed. Hilton Head Island, S.C.: SouthArt, 1994.

Harvey, Natalie Ann. "The History of Hilton Head Island, South Carolina." Master's thesis, University of South Carolina, 2000.

Hines, John Elbridge (1910–1997). Clergyman, civil rights advocate. Hines is the only South Carolina native to serve as presiding bishop of the Episcopal Church, the denomination's top leadership position. He was born in Seneca on October 3, 1910. Hines received his bachelor of arts degree from the University of the South in 1930, and his bachelor of divinity degree from the Virginia Theological Seminary in 1933. He was ordained deacon on August 31, 1933, and priest on October 28, 1934. Hines was assistant rector of St. Michael and St. George Church, St. Louis, Missouri, from 1933 to 1935; rector of Holy Trinity Church, Hannibal, Missouri, from 1935 to 1937; rector of St. Paul's Church, Augusta, Georgia, from 1937 until 1941; and was rector of Christ Church, Houston, Texas, from 1941 to 1945. On October 18, 1945, Hines was consecrated bishop coadjutor of Texas. He became the fourth bishop of Texas on November 1, 1955, and served until December 31, 1964. He was one of the founders of the Episcopal Theological Seminary of the Southwest at Austin, which opened in 1951. He was elected the twenty-second presiding bishop of the Episcopal Church by the 1964 General Convention and served from January 1, 1965, until May 31, 1974. Just fifty-four when elected, Hines was the youngest presiding bishop in the history of the church.

Hines was committed to racial and social justice and led the Episcopal Church into an era of social activism in the 1960s. He was supportive of ordaining women bishops, priests, and deacons, although that did not happen during his tenure as presiding bishop. Convinced that the church must engage realities of the world around it, the onset of urban rioting in Los Angeles in 1965 spurred Hines to personal involvement. He toured sections of the

Bedford-Stuyvesant neighborhood in Brooklyn where rioting had occurred. He also made trips to troubled black neighborhoods in Newark and Detroit, questioning leaders there as to how church resources might best be used. Armed with this information and his own convictions, Hines stepped into the pulpit at the sixty-seventh General Convention at Seattle in September 1967 and preached a sermon calling the Episcopal Church to social justice. This sermon became the genesis of the General Convention Special Program (GCSP). In response to Hines's sermon and leadership, the 1967 General Convention adopted a $9 million fund and set up the GCSP. It was given top priority for the church's use of personnel, time, and money from 1968 to 1970. Some grants were made to organizations outside the Episcopal Church, some of which were perceived by some Episcopalians as supporters of violence. By 1969 some Episcopal clergy and laity were calling for the end of the GCSP, and the 1973 General Convention ended it. A successor program, the Commission on Community Action and Human Development, continued the principles of the GCSP, albeit on a smaller scale.

Hines was also a leader in the ecumenical movement and supported the National Council of the Churches of Christ in the United States and the Consultation on Church Union (COCU). He died in Austin, Texas, on July 19, 1997. DONALD S. ARMENTROUT

Kesselus, Kenneth. *John E. Hines: Granite on Fire.* Austin, Tex.: Episcopal Theological Seminary of the Southwest, 1995.

Hinton, James Miles (1891–1970). Clergyman, businessman, civil rights leader. Hinton was born on October 28, 1891, in Gates County, North Carolina, to parents who died when was three years old. He was reared by an aunt in New York City, where he attended the Bible Teacher's Training School and worked as a postal clerk. During World War I, Hinton was drafted into the U.S. Army and earned the rank of lieutenant. After the war he began a successful business career with the black-owned Pilgrim Health and Life Insurance Company based in Augusta, Georgia. In 1939 he established a home in Columbia, South Carolina. On his arrival he rapidly earned a reputation as a businessman, minister, and leading civil rights figure.

Hinton's move to Columbia proved a key factor in shaping the future course of the black struggle for racial equality across the Palmetto State. Elected to serve as the president of an ailing National Association for the Advancement of Colored People (NAACP) branch in Columbia shortly after his arrival in 1939, Hinton embraced the role of outspoken civil rights activist only reluctantly. As president of the Columbia branch, Hinton opposed the creation of the South Carolina NAACP State Conference of Branches in the fall of 1939. But as the demands for forceful civil rights leadership grew, Hinton assumed the duties of state conference president, holding the position from 1941 through 1958. During his tenure as state conference president, Hinton led the exponential expansion of the NAACP in South Carolina, taking the struggle for black civil rights into the cities, towns, cotton fields, and rural county churches of South Carolina. "I have never in my life heard anybody speak like he could speak," explained one NAACP official. "When he got through speaking [the people] were ready to go, to do whatever was necessary" to secure their rights. The fights to win equal salaries for black teachers and to vote in the all-white Democratic Party primary were waged and achieved under his leadership. Perhaps more than any single leader in South Carolina, Hinton was also responsible for turning the tide against the Jim Crow doctrine of "separate but equal." Historians credit him with inspiring Clarendon County residents to sue for equal educational opportunities, leading to a suit included in the U.S. Supreme Court's landmark 1954 decision, *Brown v. Board of Education.* Certainly, Hinton had begun demanding that NAACP members take a forceful stand against the doctrine of, in his words, "SEPARATE but NEVER EQUAL," by the fall of 1947. As a forceful advocate of racial equality, Hinton placed his own life and business career on the line. In April 1949 he was abducted in Augusta, beaten, and left facedown in the countryside for daring to champion the cause of racial equality. In January 1956, at the height of the white backlash to *Brown,* Hinton's Columbia home was struck by gunfire.

Hinton remained active in civic matters throughout his life. He also pastored the Second Calvary Baptist Church in Columbia and retired as vice president and agency director of Pilgrim Health and Life in 1965. He died in Augusta, Georgia, on November 21, 1970, and was buried in Palmetto Cemetery in Columbia. PETER F. LAU

Kluger, Richard. *Simple Justice: The History of Brown v. Board of Education and Black America's Struggle for Equality.* New York: Knopf, 1975.

Lau, Peter F. "Freedom Road Territory: The Politics of Civil Rights Struggle in South Carolina during the Jim Crow Era." Ph.D. diss., Rutgers, The State University of New Jersey, 2002.

Hipp, Francis Moffett (1911–1995). Insurance executive. Born in Newberry on March 3, 1911, Hipp was the son of William Frank Hipp and Eunice Jane Halfacre. He attended the Citadel from 1929 to 1931 then transferred to Furman University, where he earned a bachelor of arts degree in 1933. On November 10, 1935, Hipp married Mary Matilda Looper. The marriage produced four children. Following Mary's death in 1962, Hipp married Shirley A. Mattoon on May 11, 1964.

Hipp joined his father's company, Liberty Life Insurance, in 1933, serving first in the investment area, then in marketing. The Greenville-based company also owned radio stations WIS in Columbia and WCSC in Charleston, which later became television stations. Frank Hipp died suddenly in 1943 and the directors elected Francis to succeed him as president and chairman of the board. An energetic leader, Hipp expanded the company into the Southeast through its own agents, and across the nation through financial institutions. In 1950 the Broadcasting Company of the South was formed as the parent company of Liberty's broadcasting entities, and in 1953 Liberty Life's first television station, WIS-TV in Columbia, signed on the air. In 1965, after purchase of WSFA-TV in Montgomery, Alabama, and WTOL-TV in Toledo, Ohio, the Broadcasting Company of the South was renamed Cosmos Broadcasting Corporation to reflect its expanded operations.

In 1967 the Liberty Corporation was formed, with Liberty Life, Cosmos Broadcasting, and Surety Investments merged into it. Headquartered in Greenville, Liberty Corporation was listed on the New York Stock Exchange two years later. In 1979 Hipp relinquished his posts of president and chief executive officer to his son, William Hayne Hipp, but retained the title of board chairman. At his death in 1995 Hipp was the longest-serving chairman of a listed company in the history of the New York Stock Exchange. Liberty had become a diversified holding company with more than $3 billion in assets and revenues of more than $800 million. Liberty Insurance Services, the company's newest subsidiary, was the largest third-party administrator in the life insurance industry. Cosmos Broadcasting owned and operated eleven network-affiliated television stations, a cable advertising sales subsidiary, and a video production company.

As chairman of the State Development Board from 1959 to 1963, Hipp was credited with major successes in recruiting industry to South Carolina. He was a mentor to several South Carolina business leaders and was singled out for his ability to build consensus from differing views. Hipp and the South Carolina textile industrialist H. William Close helped create the University of South Carolina Business Partnership Foundation, and the College of Business Administration's twin buildings were named in their honor. Hipp was chairman of the South Carolina Foundation of Independent Colleges, and he became the recipient of honorary degrees from several South Carolina colleges and universities. In 1980 the South Carolina Chamber of Commerce named Hipp South Carolina Businessman of the Year and in 1985 he was inducted into the South Carolina Business Hall of Fame. He died in Greenville on July 24, 1995, and was buried in Springwood Cemetery. ROBERT A. PIERCE

Lunan, Bert, and Robert A. Pierce. *Legacy of Leadership.* Columbia: South Carolina Business Hall of Fame, 1999.

Hispanics. Hispanics are among South Carolina's oldest and most recent immigrant groups. Long before English settlers founded colonies in the Massachusetts Bay, Spanish explorers laid claim to territory in what is now the United States from the Atlantic to the Pacific. From bases of operation in the Caribbean and Mexico, Spanish emissaries established presidios and missions to protect Spain's northern colonial frontier. In 1526 Spaniard Lucas Vásquez de Ayllón established the first European settlement in present-day South Carolina (and the United States), San Miguel de Gualdape. A variety of difficulties led to its abandonment by 1527, but a second Spanish settlement near present-day Beaufort, Santa Elena, served as the capital of "La Florida," the name given to Spain's holdings in the Southeast, from 1566 to 1576. After Spanish settlers abandoned the Santa Elena site in 1587, Franciscan friars from missions along the coast continued to visit Indian communities in the area. Spain lost its claims to most of present-day South Carolina in the 1670 Treaty of Madrid with Great Britain.

The terms "Hispanic" and "Latino" apply to a broad category of U.S. residents that include persons of Latin American and/or Spanish ancestry. Tremendous diversity exists within these groups in terms of national origin, socioeconomic class, educational attainment, and other characteristics. While a sizable Spanish-speaking population has resided in the United States throughout its history, the volume of Hispanic immigration in the late twentieth century resulted in this group becoming this country's largest minority population by the year 2000.

Following national trends, South Carolina experienced a rise in its Hispanic population beginning in the second half of the twentieth century. New residents of Cuban and Puerto Rican origin arrived beginning in the 1960s, largely due to military and industrial employment. Colombians, most employed in the textile industry, immigrated to the upstate in the 1970s, and beginning in the 1990s large numbers of Mexican and Central American immigrants arrived. Because of these and other factors (as well as factors in Latin America such as deteriorating economic and political conditions), South Carolina was among eight states with the fastest-growing Hispanic population in the 1990s. Census data reports that their numbers more than tripled in that decade to 95,076, or 2.4 percent of the total state population. Analysts agree, however, that Hispanics across the nation are largely undercounted in the census process. The census of 2000 revealed that the majority (fifty-six percent) of Hispanic residents of South Carolina were of Mexican origin, followed by Central and South Americans. Thirteen percent were Puerto Rican, and three percent were of Cuban origin.

The impact of this new population group is seen through changes in popular culture, supermarket and restaurant offerings, bilingual signage, the emergence of Spanish-language media, and in public education. It is also evident in their economic contribution, particularly in labor-intensive, low-wage industries. Further, the purchasing power of Hispanics in South Carolina in 2002 was estimated at more than $2.2 billion. A commission appointed by South Carolina governor Jim Hodges in 2000 recommended that the state government make sweeping changes, particularly in the area of social services, to keep pace with the growing Hispanic population. South Carolina, as did many states that saw tremendous growth in Latino residents, scrambled to accommodate its new residents. ELAINE C. LACY

Humphreys, Jeffrey. "The Multicultural Economy 2002: Buying Power in the New Century." *Georgia Business and Economic Conditions* 62, no. 2 (2002): 1–27.

South Carolina. Commission for Minority Affairs. Hispanic/Latino Ad Hoc Committee. *Findings from the Hispanic/Latino Ad Hoc Committee.* Columbia: South Carolina Commission for Minority Affairs, 2001.

Historic Charleston Foundation. Historic Charleston Foundation (HCF) sprang from the activities of the Carolina Art Association. In 1941 the association began a survey of historic buildings in Charleston, published in 1944 as *This Is Charleston.* In April 1947 HCF was incorporated as a separate organization to preserve buildings still lived in by their owners, instead of as museums.

To raise money, HCF sponsored its first Festival of Houses—a tour of historic homes—in 1948. Fund-raising efforts allowed the group to save numerous important buildings, including the Heyward-Washington House, Nathaniel Russell House, and Bennett Rice Mill. In 1958 HCF was the first preservation group in the country to establish a revolving fund for the purchase and restoration of historic properties; the fund was replenished when the buildings were sold to new occupants. Although HCF received national attention for its use of this method to improve the Ansonborough neighborhood, the project also displaced predominantly lower-class African American residents to make room for more upscale white owners.

In the closing decades of the twentieth century, HCF sought new ways to preserve the city's history without such social effects. The building crafts program, piloted in 1987, provided job training in traditional building crafts for inner-city youth. In the wake of Hurricane Hugo, HCF undertook a fund-raising campaign to help low-income and uninsured property owners sustain the costs of the damage. The Neighborhood Impact Initiative, under way in the 1990s, brought the goals of the revolving fund and building rehabilitation to lower-class neighborhoods and employed the skills of the building crafts program graduates. AARON W. MARRS

Stoney, Samuel G. *This Is Charleston: A Survey of the Architectural Heritage of a Unique American City.* Rev. ed. Charleston, S.C.: Carolina Art Association, 1976.

Weyeneth, Robert R. *Historic Preservation for a Living City: Historic Charleston Foundation, 1947–1997.* Columbia: University of South Carolina Press, 2000.

Historic preservation. Few other states can rival the Palmetto State's devotion to history as measured by the preservation and interpretation of the places and buildings associated with its past.

Antebellum South Carolinians, proud that their state had been the scene of hundreds of battles and smaller actions during the Revolution, observed the anniversaries of victories at Fort Moultrie, Kings Mountain, and Cowpens and erected monuments on those and other battlefields, urging citizens to honor and emulate their patriot ancestors.

In many ways the origins of the historic preservation movement in America can be traced to the determination of one South Carolina woman who believed that Mount Vernon should be a national shrine. In 1853, after the federal government and the Commonwealth of Virginia had both declined to buy the house and plantation for $200,000, rumors circulated that the property might be sold to a group of investors intending to build a hotel. Ann Pamela Cunningham of Laurens District, who had recently seen Mount Vernon and was astonished at its poor condition, wrote a letter addressed to "The Ladies of the South," asking them, "Can you be still with closed souls and purses, while the world cries 'Shame upon America' . . . ? Never! forbid it, shades of the dead . . . !" Cunningham and several friends founded the Mount Vernon Ladies' Association of the Union, gathering momentum first in the South and then across the nation. Within five years the association raised enough money to acquire the house and plantation from John A. Washington, begin renovations, and open the house to the public.

Cabbage Row, or "Catfish Row," on Church Street, Charleston, before it was restored. Courtesy, South Carolina Historical Society

In the first seventy-five years after the Civil War, many white southerners looked more toward the past than toward the future, even if their version of the past was more mythic, perhaps, than historical. Many white South Carolinians looked back to the colonial, Revolutionary, and antebellum years when the state enjoyed immense wealth, social status, and political influence, and none longed for past glories more than Charlestonians, remembering the days when the "Holy City" had been one of the great cities of the South. Though hundreds of Charleston's buildings, some of them predating the Revolution, served as tangible links to that past, there was no significant effort to preserve, maintain, and interpret them until just after World War I.

As new residents began moving to the city, and as automobiles began bringing large numbers of tourists, the real estate developer Susan Pringle Frost worked tirelessly to promote the appreciation of Charleston's architectural heritage and, as she described later, "to preserve her old-world beauty." Alarmed at the proposed demolition of the Joseph Manigault House, Frost and her cousin Nell Pringle founded the Society for the Preservation of Old Dwellings (SPOD), later renamed the Preservation Society of Charleston. The Charleston Museum eventually acquired both the Joseph Manigault House and the Heyward-Washington House, opening them to the public as house museums in the 1930s. Opposing a growing trend in which owners discarded or sold mantels and other essential architectural elements such as bricks, moldings, and ironwork, the society encouraged the preservation of such details in place. Frost soon began purchasing historic houses, renovating them, and renting or putting them back on the market. At first focusing her efforts along the Battery, she later expanded her vision to include most of the peninsula. The SPOD was determined to preserve neighborhoods and streetscapes instead of simply preserving and operating the grandest homes as house museums. In 1931 the SPOD helped draft a zoning ordinance creating the Charleston Old and Historic District, the first historic district in the United States. This district became a model soon followed by cities and towns across the country. Ten years later the society sponsored the first citywide architectural survey in America, an inventory of almost twelve hundred buildings on the lower peninsula with a rating system ranging from "worthy of mention" to "nationally significant." In 1944 more than half the buildings surveyed were included in *This Is Charleston,* a book described as a "vital catalog of the townscape of Charleston" and featuring a text by the architectural historian Samuel G. Stoney. As increased tourism, the growth of urban and rural development, and the preservation of the more recent past became issues of even greater significance after World War II, the Historic Charleston Foundation was founded in 1947. An independent nonprofit organization, it was devoted not only to the preservation and interpretation of historic resources but also to the integration of those resources into city planning efforts. Frances R. Edmunds, who began working for the foundation as its tour director and then served as its executive director for many years, became a national leader in the historic preservation movement. Another major figure in Charleston's modern era has been Mayor Joseph P. Riley, Jr., whose longtime tenure and advocacy of preservation, downtown revitalization, adaptive reuse, and their associated cultural and economic benefits has balanced the growth of a vibrant city with the determination to retain those qualities that make it special.

Other South Carolina cities have enjoyed many successes and endured many frustrations in attempting to identify, document, and preserve their own built environments, from individual buildings to historic districts. As in Charleston, early efforts often focused on saving a particular building, such as the Burt-Stark House in Abbeville, the John Mark Verdier House in Beaufort, the Robert Mills House in Columbia, the Octagon House in Laurens, or the Opera House in Newberry. Later efforts have included residential and commercial districts of varying ages, characters, and sizes, as well as city- or countywide architectural surveys, the adoption of local preservation ordinances, and the integration of preservation into city and county planning.

South Carolina continues to play a leading role in historic preservation through the work of countless local and state government agencies, nonprofit organizations, and individuals. The State Historic Preservation Office (SHPO), part of the South Carolina Department of Archives and History in Columbia, administers the federal historic preservation program in the state. The architects, architectural historians, archaeologists, historians, and historic preservationists on the SHPO staff oversee the National Register of

Historic Places, the statewide survey of historic resources, federal and state grant and tax incentive programs, certified local government programs, the review of projects affecting historic resources as provided for in the National Historic Preservation Act, and the state's historical marker program. The Palmetto Trust for Historic Preservation, a nonprofit statewide organization focusing on advocacy, education, and the funding of preservation projects, was established in 1990. J. TRACY POWER

Bland, Sidney R. *Preserving Charleston's Past, Shaping Its Future: The Life and Times of Susan Pringle Frost.* 2d ed. Columbia: University of South Carolina Press, 1999.

Hosmer, Charles B. *Presence of the Past: A History of the Preservation Movement in the United States before Williamsburg.* New York: Putnam, 1965.

———. *Preservation Comes of Age: From Williamsburg to the National Trust, 1926–1949.* 2 vols. Charlottesville: University Press of Virginia, 1981.

Murtagh, William J. *Keeping Time: The History and Theory of Preservation in America.* Pittstown, N.J.: Main Street Press, 1988.

Weyeneth, Robert R. *Historic Preservation for a Living City: Historic Charleston Foundation, 1947–1997.* Columbia: University of South Carolina Press, 2000.

Hoagland, Jimmie Lee (b. 1939). Journalist. A two-time Pulitzer Prize winner, Jim Hoagland was born on January 22, 1940, in Rock Hill, the son of Lee Roy Hoagland, Jr., and Edith Irene Sullivan. He attended public schools there before entering the University of South Carolina, where he was graduated cum laude in 1961 with a degree in journalism. He worked briefly as a sports writer for the *State* and the *Columbia Record* before winning a scholarship to study French at Aix-en-Provence in southern France. After serving two years with the United States Air Force in Europe, Hoagland worked as copy editor on the international edition of the *New York Times* in Paris from 1964 to 1966.

Hoagland joined the *Washington Post* in 1966 as a metro reporter. But it is in international reporting and commentary that Hoagland has made his mark. He was assigned to Nairobi in 1969 as the *Post*'s correspondent in Africa. For nearly two years he covered colonial wars, the revolution in Rhodesia (now Zimbabwe), and apartheid in South Africa. Hoagland's reporting on apartheid was the basis for his first Pulitzer—for international reporting—in 1971 and also for his book *South Africa: Civilizations in Conflict* (1972). Hoagland became the *Post*'s Middle East correspondent in 1972, covering the Arab world, Israel, and Iran. He moved to Paris in 1976 to cover France, Italy, and Spain. In 1978 he became diplomatic correspondent on the *Post*'s national staff in Washington and in 1979 foreign news editor. Hoagland's second Pulitzer Prize—for distinguished commentary—was awarded in 1991. As associate editor / senior foreign correspondent for the *Post,* he continues his twice-weekly commentary on international affairs. In 2002 he was awarded the Cernobbio-Europa Prize by the European press for his commentary on the aftermath of the September 11, 2001, terrorist attacks on New York City.

"My strength as a foreign correspondent," Hoagland once said, "was that I conveyed a sense of place, a sense of adventure." He lives in Washington, D.C., with his wife, Jane Stanton Hitchcock. TOM MCLEAN

Hobkirk Hill, Battle of (April 25, 1781). Following the Battle of Guilford Courthouse in North Carolina, Major General Nathanael Greene chose not to follow Lord Cornwallis and reentered South Carolina in April of 1781. His plan was to force a British withdrawal from their interior outposts to Charleston. On April 19 his army of some 1,200 Continentals and 250 militia took up a position on Hobkirk Hill, a mile and a half north of Camden.

Francis Lord Rawdon, who commanded the British outpost at Camden, chose to attack the encroaching Americans on April 25. He approached Greene's camp through thick woods and on a narrow front in hope of achieving a surprise. Rawdon's leading forces struck the American picket line at about eleven o'clock in the morning, and the American pickets fought well enough to give Greene time to muster and deploy his forces. Assessing the situation, Greene noted the narrow front of the British column and proposed to launch a double envelopment. But Rawdon quickly brought up his second line and extended his flanks to counter the maneuver. More critically for Greene, the veteran First Maryland Regiment fell into disorder and its commander, Colonel John Gunby, ordered an abrupt withdrawal to reform his unit. The move affected the other units and the American advance faltered, forcing Greene to order a general retreat.

The Americans fell back three miles to the old Camden battlefield and the British were left in possession of the hill. They did not stay there. Rawdon withdrew into his fortification at Camden. Indeed, despite five hundred British reinforcements that arrived two weeks later, Rawdon abandoned his exposed position and began a slow retreat toward Charleston on May 10. Though in itself indecisive, the Battle of Hobkirk Hill marked the beginning of the British withdrawal from the interior of South Carolina. SAMUEL K. FORE

Conrad, Dennis M., and Richard K. Shannon, eds. *The Papers of General Nathanael Greene.* Vol. 8, *30 March–10 July 1781.* Chapel Hill: University of North Carolina Press, 1995.

Kirkland, Thomas J., and Robert M. Kennedy. *Historic Camden.* 2 vols. 1905. Reprint, Camden, S.C.: Kershaw County Historical Society, 1994.

Lumpkin, Henry. *From Savannah to Yorktown: The American Revolution in the South.* Columbia: University of South Carolina Press, 1981.

Hockey. The traditionally Canadian sport of hockey had a minimal presence in South Carolina until the 1990s. Requiring cold weather for ice or expensive indoor ice rinks, the sport attracted little interest. This changed during the 1990s when interest in hockey saw unprecedented growth in the state, sparked by the migration of many northerners to the state and the development of roller hockey. Following close on the heels of this rising interest was the appearance of the state's first professional minor league hockey team, the South Carolina Stingrays. The Stingrays, who play in North Charleston, joined the East Coast Hockey League (ECHL) in 1993 and garnered many fans in the lowcountry. Other ECHL teams soon followed: the Pee Dee Pride in 1997 (renamed the Florence Pride in 2003), the Greenville Grrrowl in 1998, and the Columbia Inferno in 2001. The growth of the ECHL in South Carolina prompted Governor Jim Hodges to declare July 27, 2002, "East Coast Hockey League Day." Additionally, South Carolina, and the South in general, has seen a corresponding rise in the number of people playing hockey. According to USA Hockey, hockey's governing body, the number of players in the Southeastern District (which includes twelve states and the District of Columbia) grew from 4,462 in 1990–1991 to 28,662 in 2001–2002, of which 1,292 were in South Carolina. Beginning as a northern transplant with few southern devotees, hockey has gained a substantial following in South Carolina. BENJAMIN PETERSEN

Gillespie, Bob. "Hockey (Ice and All) Comes to Charleston." Columbia *State,* July 23, 1993, p. C1.

Hodges, James Hovis (b. 1956). Governor. Jim Hodges was born on November 19, 1956, in Lancaster, the son of George and Betty Hodges. He graduated from Lancaster High School in 1975. He attended Davidson College but graduated from the University of South Carolina with a business degree in 1979. While at the university he earned Phi Beta Kappa honors. He received a law degree from the University of South Carolina School of Law in 1982 and returned to Lancaster to practice. On December 2, 1986, Hodges was elected to the South Carolina House of Representatives. He chaired the Judiciary Committee from 1992 to 1994 and served as the S.C. House Democratic Leader after the Republican takeover in 1994. On December 5, 1987, he married Rachel Gardner of Hartsville. They have two sons.

When he began his quest for the governorship in 1998, Hodges was a political unknown, given little chance of unseating Republican David Beasley. Conventional political wisdom held that an incumbent governor in a state which epitomizes "traditional" political culture was virtually guaranteed a second term, unless that incumbent made some major political mistakes. Beasley did exactly that. Halfway through his term, he stated that his reading of the Bible had persuaded him that the Confederate flag should be removed from the top of the State House. Flag supporters, especially white males, the core Republican constituency, were enraged. As the controversy heated up in the election year, Beasley tried to reverse himself, which only served to further alienate his supporters. The governor also called for eliminating video poker, an industry that had begun to flourish in South Carolina. His opposition resulted in a flood of both money and manpower into the Hodges campaign. Beasley also opposed a state lottery, a stance which Jim Hodges skillfully turned into an education measure, appealing to strong public support for improving the state's low ranking on national test scores.

Hodges soundly defeated Beasley with more than fifty-three percent of the vote, winning thirty-five of forty-six counties. His election was heralded as a major triumph for the Democratic Party in a region where victories in statewide elections were increasingly rare.

Education was the centerpiece of Hodges's term as governor. He oversaw the implementation of the education lottery and created a preschool initiative, First Steps, designed to prepare more children for first grade. He won passage of a $1.1 billion school construction initiative and championed increased teacher pay and more parental involvement in the schools. Hodges also initiated the state's first sales tax holiday and the South Carolina SilverCard, which offered prescription drug coverage for the state's senior citizens. He gained national attention in 2002 with his stance against the federal government's shipment of nuclear waste into the state, vowing to lie down in front of the trucks, if necessary, to prevent the shipments from entering South Carolina.

A slowing economy, declining state revenues, and tax cuts by the Republican-controlled General Assembly severely limited Hodges's role as an "activist" governor. He was defeated in 2002 when he sought reelection against Mark Sanford, a well-spoken, politically savvy, three-term Republican congressman from Charleston. After his defeat, Hodges took charge of Hodges Consulting Group, a subsidiary of the law firm Kennedy Covington Lobdell and Hickman, based in Columbia. RONALD ROMINE

Edsall, Thomas B. "South Carolina Incumbent in Unexpected Tussle." *Washington Post,* September 30, 1998, p. A4.

Hoechst. Höchst Aktiengesellschaft, a German chemical company from Frankfurt am Main, was established 1951. In 1965 Hoechst came to Spartanburg in a joint venture with American Hercules company. The venture was created to provide polyester fiber for local textile producers. Soon Hoechst acquired the entire operation. By the early 1970s the factory, with its two thousand workers, had become one of the area's biggest employers. Additionally, the presence of this German company with its German and American staff had turned into a international curiosity.

The company chose to come to Spartanburg County because of its location. According to the calculations of one Hoechst executive, roughly eighty percent of U.S. textile mills were within a 250-mile radius of Spartanburg. Over the years, Hoechst's Spartanburg factory expanded and improved its polyester-based manufacturing line to include large-scale plastic recycling operations and polyester resin production. In 1987, as a result of Hoechst's acquisition of Celanese Corporation, the corporation's North American operations were renamed Hoechst Celanese Corporation. In 1998 Hoechst sold the Spartanburg plant to a U.S.-Mexican joint venture named KoSa. MARKO MAUNULA

"European Business People Like Carolina—And It's Mutual." *U.S. News and World Report* 72 (June 26, 1972): 62–63.

Vogl, Frank. "The Spartanburg Example: How an Old Southern Town Became 'Euroville.'" *Europe: Magazine of the European Community* 213 (May–June 1979): 26–29.

Hogs. Pork has been important to the diet and economy of South Carolina since colonial times. Hogs were probably introduced to South Carolina in the sixteenth century by Spanish explorers. Indians acquired some of these animals, and English settlers purchased swine from the natives when they arrived at Charleston in 1670. Other animals were imported from Barbados, Virginia, and Bermuda. Settlers soon recognized the region's favorable conditions for swine husbandry. Farmers allowed their stock to "range" or forage in local forests, subsisting on natural provender until collected at harvest time. In 1682 an observer noted "many thousand head" of swine were thriving around Charleston. More, in fact, than were needed to feed the colony. As early as the 1680s, South Carolinians were selling pork to other English colonies.

Settlers took hogs with them into the backcountry, and pork in its many forms became a cornerstone of the diet. Hog killing was an important ritual of rural life that endured well into the twentieth century. Animals were slaughtered in cold weather and the meat preserved by salting and smoking. Fresh pork was often barbecued, roasted slowly over hot coals. As the cotton boom swept South Carolina in the early nineteenth century, many farmers abandoned food crops for the white fiber. Pork production fell sharply in the 1850s, dropping by more than 100,000 head during the decade.

After the Civil War, acreage of field crops continued to increase, and stricter fencing laws confined animals to their owner's property. The end of open-range husbandry enabled selective breeding and better veterinary care to improve livestock. South Carolina's hog population settled at around 500,000 in the 1870s and remained stable, with minor fluctuations, for many years.

By the late twentieth century, hog farming had become a highly specialized and capital-intensive enterprise. However, large-scale swine production has unpleasant social and environmental consequences and has encountered opposition in host communities. Meanwhile, the economic importance of pork has steadily declined in South Carolina. Since 1981 hogs have fallen from fifth to eleventh place in value to the state's agricultural economy. Compounding the woes of hog farmers, prices tend to follow a cycle ranging from boom to bust. Since the 1930s government has intervened to stabilize hog prices with varying degrees of success. The crash of hog prices in the late 1990s—prices fell from 60¢ to 15¢ a pound—was catastrophic for many South Carolina producers. At century's end, South Carolina's hog population fell below 250,000 head, the smallest since record keeping began in 1867. ELDRED E. PRINCE, JR.

Fite, Gilbert C. *American Farmers: The New Minority.* Bloomington: Indiana University Press, 1981.

———. *Cotton Fields No More: Southern Agriculture, 1865–1980.* Lexington: University Press of Kentucky, 1984.

Ford, Lacy K., Jr. *Origins of Southern Radicalism: The South Carolina Upcountry, 1800–1860.* New York: Oxford University Press, 1988.

Gray, Lewis C. *History of Agriculture in the Southern United States to 1860.* 2 vols. Washington, D.C.: Carnegie Institution, 1933.

Kirby, Jack Temple. *Rural Worlds Lost: The American South, 1920–1960.* Baton Rouge: Louisiana State University Press, 1987.

Kovacik, Charles F., and John J. Winberry. *South Carolina: The Making of a Landscape.* 1987. Reprint, Columbia: University of South Carolina Press, 1989.

Holbrook, John Edwards (1794–1871). Physician, naturalist. Holbrook was born in Beaufort on December 30, 1794, the son of Silas Holbrook, a schoolteacher, and Mary Edwards. Reared in North Wrentham (later incorporated into Norfolk), Massachusetts, Holbrook attended Day's Academy. He graduated from Brown University in 1815 and enrolled in the medical program of the University of Pennsylvania. Sometime after receiving a medical degree in 1818, Holbrook attended medical lectures at the University of Edinburgh and then in Paris, where he made friends with several prominent naturalists. He returned to the United States in 1822 and soon thereafter established a medical practice in Charleston. In 1824 he became the professor of anatomy at the Medical College of South Carolina and, a decade later, at the newly established Medical College of the State of South Carolina, where he remained until his retirement in 1860. Held in high esteem by his students, Holbrook continued to treat private patients. On May 3, 1827, he married Harriott Pinckney Rutledge. The couple had no children.

Especially interested in comparative anatomy, Holbrook developed a desire to study reptiles and amphibians, and by the mid-1820s he had begun a book describing all of the known snakes, lizards, turtles, frogs, and toads in the United States. This effort resulted in *North American Herpetology,* first published in four volumes between 1836 and 1840 and later revised and expanded into five volumes in 1842. The first comprehensive work on the reptiles and amphibians of North America, mainly those inhabiting the country east of the Mississippi River, it contained beautiful illustrations, mostly done from live specimens. Providing twenty-five taxa, or scientific descriptions, new to science, *North American Herpetology* quickly gained international notice, and its influence endures.

Soon after publishing that volume, Holbrook turned to fishes and in 1847 published the first part of his *Southern Ichthyology; or A Description of the Fishes Inhabiting the Waters of South Carolina, Georgia and Florida.* A second part of this appeared in 1848. Realizing that he must narrow the scope of his work, Holbrook decided to restrict his study to South Carolina. Between 1855 and 1857 he published parts of a volume titled *Ichthyology of South Carolina,* but a fire destroyed the plates before many copies of a bound volume were printed. Holbrook then had new and improved plates produced, and a new edition appeared in 1860. Meanwhile Holbrook had published three journal articles on fishes. Altogether, he established ten new taxa of fishes, which, along with his descriptions of reptiles and amphibians, made Holbrook one of the greatest of the pioneering American naturalists. The National Academy of Sciences elected him to membership in 1868.

Although he was raised in the Northeast and had close relatives living in New England, Holbrook actively supported the South during the Civil War and even served for a time as a field surgeon for the Confederacy. He died at the home of a relative in Norfolk, Massachusetts, on September 8, 1871. LESTER D. STEPHENS

Anderson, William D., Jr. "John Edwards Holbrook's Senckenberg Plates and the Fishes They Portray." *Archives of Natural History* 30 (2003): 1–12.

Anderson, William D., Jr., and Lester D. Stephens. "John Edwards Holbrook (1794–1871) and His *Southern Ichthyology* (1847–1848)." *Archives of Natural History* 29 (2002): 317–32.

Stephens, Lester D. "John Edwards Holbrook (1794–1871) and Lewis Reeve Gibbes (1810–1894): Exemplary Naturalists in the Old South." In *Collection Building in Ichthyology and Herpetology,* edited by Theodore W. Pietsch and William D. Anderson, Jr. Lawrence, Kans.: American Society of Ichthyologists and Herpetologists, 1997.

———. *Science, Race, and Religion in the American South: John Bachman and the Charleston Circle of Naturalists, 1815–1895.* Chapel Hill: University of North Carolina Press, 2000.

Holiness movement. Denominations such as the Wesleyan Church, the Church of the Nazarene, the Salvation Army, and the Christian and Missionary Alliance, all of which have congregations in South Carolina, owe their genesis to a movement in the nineteenth century that emphasized sanctification or the experience of personal holiness as a "second work of grace" in addition to salvation.

The theological roots of sanctification or holiness in these denominations lie in the eighteenth-century teachings of John Wesley, the founder of Methodism. Wesley taught that attaining "perfect love" or holiness, while generally a lifelong process, should be a common spiritual goal. This teaching was modified and popularized by Phoebe Palmer, who believed one could experience sanctification as a distinct experience by committing one's life wholly to Christ. Palmer was a widely read author and celebrated speaker at camp meetings and similar gatherings across the Northeast and overseas in the years right after the Civil War.

Some of those drawn to holiness teaching believed that existing denominations, especially those identified with Methodism, had abandoned this emphasis on holiness. They therefore began to form new denominations that not only promoted holiness theology but also strict codes of personal conduct thought appropriate to those who had experienced holiness.

Holiness spread to South Carolina's second largest Protestant denomination, the Methodist Episcopal Church, South (MECS), in the 1870s and 1880s, although denominational leaders opposed the teaching. In 1894 at the denomination's General Conference in Atlanta, the bishops of the MECS denounced preachers who promoted holiness theology; two years later the South Carolina Annual Conference followed their lead, barring evangelists who taught Holiness from preaching in Methodist churches in the state.

Although some Holiness preachers in South Carolina resigned from the Methodist ministry, most remained in the denomination. Outspoken advocates of Holiness with Methodist ties of some sort included Robert C. Oliver, founder of the Oliver Gospel Mission in Columbia; Obadiah Dugan, founder of the Star Gospel Mission in Charleston; and W. P. B. Kinard, founder of the Epworth Camp Meeting in Greenwood. Some South Carolinians severed ties with the parent Methodist denomination for one of the newer Holiness bodies. S. J. Cowan, for example, became a founding elder in the South Carolina Conference of the Wesleyan Methodist Church in 1893.

In the 1890s some Holiness proponents moved in more radical theological directions, advocating divine healing and premillennial dispensationalism, the idea that history was in the final dispensation before the physical second coming of Christ. Others fused Holiness teaching with Pentecostal notions. Benjamin Hardin Irwin, a Methodist from Iowa who preached throughout the upstate in 1896, promoted a third blessing, baptism of the Holy Ghost and fire, in addition to salvation (the first blessing) and sanctification or holiness (the second blessing).

William E. Fuller, based in Anderson, originally identified with the African Methodist Episcopal Church, but moved first toward Holiness and then more toward Pentecostalism as a founder with Irwin of the Fire-Baptized Holiness Church and later as a leader of the (Colored) Fire-Baptized Holiness Church. The Columbia Methodist John M. Pike, longtime editor of *The Way of Faith,* also moved from a Holiness to a Pentecostal focus after learning of the Pentecostal revivals that broke out in Los Angeles in 1906.

Many South Carolina Holiness churches followed suit, gradually embracing Pentecostal teaching and coalescing into denominations such as the Pentecostal Holiness Church, the Church of God (Cleveland, Tennessee), the Church of God in Christ, and the Assemblies of God.

Yet another strain of Holiness teaching has had a lasting influence on South Carolina's religious culture. Rooted more in the Calvinist Reformed heritage and initially centered in Keswick, England, this expression of Holiness emphasized entire consecration as a way gradually to conquer sin in this life and thus become holy. Wesleyan Holiness tended to see sanctification as more of an instantaneous experience of the eradication of sin from one's life. Nickels John Holmes, founder of the Holmes College of the Bible, blended a Keswick understanding of Holiness with Pentecostal ideas in his own teaching and approach. NANCY A. HARDESTY

Dieter, Melvin E. *The Holiness Revival of the Nineteenth Century.* Metuchen, N.J.: Scarecrow, 1980.

Hardesty, Nancy A. "The Holiness and Pentecostal Movements." In *Religion in South Carolina,* edited by Charles H. Lippy. Columbia: University of South Carolina Press, 1993.

Synan, Vinson. *The Holiness-Pentecostal Tradition: Charismatic Movements in the Twentieth Century.* 2d ed. Grand Rapids, Mich.: Eerdmans, 1997.

Turley, Briane K. *A Wheel within a Wheel: Southern Methodism and the Georgia Holiness Association.* Macon, Ga.: Mercer University Press, 1999.

Holland, Edwin Clifford (ca. 1794–1824). Lawyer, poet, editor. Born in Charleston, Holland was the son of John Holland and Jane Marshall. He became a noted lawyer and essayist, serving late in his life as editor of the Charleston *Times.*

In 1813 Holland published his own collection of poetry, *Odes, Naval Songs, and Other Occasional Poems.* Influenced by the British Romantics' trend of sea poetry, Holland's writing often praised the U.S. Navy and emphasized patriotic themes. In "The Pillar of Glory" he celebrates the United States' stand against Britain in the War of 1812: "Already the storm of contention has hurl'd / From the grasp of Old England the trident of war / The beams of our stars have illumined the world / Unfurl'd our standard beats proud in the air / Wild glares the eagle's eye / Swift as he cuts the sky / Marking the wake where our heroes advance."

In 1818 Holland published a poetic drama entitled *The Corsair: A Melo-Drama, in Four Acts.* The work is a conscious imitation of Lord Byron, the Romantic poet Holland most admired. The preface explains that his inspiration was Byron's poem "The Corsair." "I never read a line, or recalled an image of this magnificent production," wrote Holland, "without feelings of indescribable admiration." He likewise credited the South Carolina landscape for his poetic fervor: "There is a kind of *southern aspect* in our fortunes, absolutely necessary for the perfection of literary plans." *The Corsair* was performed at the Charleston Theatre in 1818.

Holland's most enduring literary work was published anonymously. In response to growing turmoil over the issue of slavery, in 1822 he produced a pamphlet titled *A Refutation of the Calumnies Circulated Against the Southern and Western States, Respecting the Institution and Existence of Slavery Among Them.* Two subtitles further explain Holland's purpose: *To Which Is Added, A Minute and Particular Account of the Actual State and Condition of Their Negro Population; Together with Historical Notices of All the Insurrections That Have Taken Place Since the Settlement of the Country.* A slaveholder, Holland included both his own testimony as well as letters from many of his lawyer friends defending the humane treatment of South Carolina's slaves. He argued that slave life is significantly better than that of the English poor and warned against slave insurrections: "A few hours would decide the conflict, and the *utter extermination* of the black race would be the inevitable consequence." Lamenting the existence of free blacks as "the greatest and most deplorable evil with which we are unhappily afflicted," Holland concluded with the harsh warning, "Let it never be forgotten, that our NEGROES are truly the *Jacobins* of the country . . . the *common enemy of civilized society,* and the barbarians who would, IF THEY COULD, become the DESTROYERS *of our race.*" Holland's work stands both as a historic record of slave insurrections and as a startling document of an educated citizen's honest, but obviously racist, beliefs. He died of yellow fever in Charleston on September 11, 1824, at age thirty. AMY L. WHITE

[Holland, Edwin C.] *A Refutation of the Calumnies Circulated Against the Southern and Western States, Respecting the Institution and Existence of Slavery Among Them.* 1822. Reprint, New York: Negro Universities Press, 1969.

Kettell, Samuel. *Specimens of American Poetry, with Critical and Biographical Notices.* 3 vols. 1829. Reprint, New York: Benjamin Blom, 1967.

Hollings, Ernest Frederick (b. 1922). Governor, U.S. senator. "Fritz" Hollings was born in Charleston on New Year's Day 1922 to the salesman Adolph G. Hollings and Wilhelmine Meyer. He received his bachelor of arts degree from the Citadel in 1942 and entered the U.S. Army, serving in World War II in North Africa and France. On his return from the war in 1945, Hollings entered the University of South Carolina School of Law. On March 30, 1946, he married Martha Patricia Salley. They had five children, two of whom died young. Hollings received his bachelor of laws degree in 1947 and joined the Charleston law firm of Meyer, Goldberg, and Hollings.

In 1948 Hollings ran successfully for the South Carolina House. Representing Charleston County from 1949 to 1954, he became a protégé of Speaker Sol Blatt. Hollings authored a major antilynching bill in 1951 and led in passing the three-percent sales tax adopted that year to finance school needs. He served as Speaker pro tempore from 1951 to 1954. Elected lieutenant governor in 1954, Hollings was particularly active in Governor George Bell Timmerman's administration, working to promote industrial development and economic diversification. The following year Hollings was appointed to the Hoover Commission on Organization of the U.S. Executive Branch.

In 1958 Hollings was elected governor on a multifaceted platform that focused on balancing the state budget, bringing new industry to South Carolina, improving public education, and promoting technical education. Inaugurated in January 1959, Hollings's administration represented a major transitional period in state government. He maximized the authority of the office of governor and used that power to work with the General Assembly in developing the state's resources and programs. His legacy included the establishment of the state's technical education system and educational television network. While helping prepare a skilled labor pool attractive to business, the technical education system also improved employment opportunities generally. The sweeping changes in the state's educational system included significant increases in teacher salaries to bring them closer to the regional average. The State Development Board was expanded and given a leadership role in attracting new business and diversifying the state's economy.

Ernest F. Hollings. Courtesy, Modern Political Collections, University of South Carolina

As it became clear that federal courts would mandate that South Carolina end segregation in its schools, Hollings, who formerly had supported segregation, worked to ensure that integration would occur without the bloodshed and hostility that characterized this transition in other southern states. In his final address to the General Assembly on January 9, 1963, Hollings urged the state to accept integration peacefully. He called on the legislature to exhibit courage and "make clear South Carolina's choice, a government of laws rather than a government of men." Harvey Gantt, a black student, was admitted to Clemson University before the month was out and the University of South Carolina was integrated peacefully in the fall. Don Fowler, a political scientist and former chairman of the national Democratic Party, described Hollings the governor as, "The leader who best exemplified the creativity and leadership that transformed the South to a new era of progress and prosperity. While many have improved and added to the programs that he created, we still work with the basic institutional arrangements he created and we still benefit from them."

In 1962 Hollings unsuccessfully challenged South Carolina's aging but popular senior U.S. senator Olin D. Johnston, in the Democratic primary. When Johnston died in 1965, Donald S. Russell stepped down as governor and was appointed to the Senate by his successor, Robert McNair. In November 1966 Hollings defeated Russell in the special election to fill the remainder of Johnston's unexpired term. Entering the U.S. Senate in January 1967, Hollings became an acknowledged authority on the budget, telecommunications, the environment and oceans, defense, trade, and space. Hollings authored the Coastal Zone Management Act (1972), coauthored the Gramm-Rudman-Hollings Deficit Reduction Act (1985), and led in the creation of the WIC Program (supplemental food program for Women, Infants, and Children) and passage of the Telecommunications Act (1996). His U.S. Senate appointments included the committees on Commerce, Science and Transportation, Appropriations, and Budget. A noted fiscal conservative, Hollings nevertheless enjoyed great success in securing federal dollars for South Carolina projects and was a leading advocate of the textile industry.

His book, *The Case Against Hunger* (1970) was a product of his "Hunger Tours" of 1969, which highlighted the severe problems of the South Carolina poor. Hollings wrote, "I hope by this book to make you believe that hunger exists in this land, that hunger poses dangers to our nation, and that hunger is costing this country far more in dollars than the most elaborate array of feeding programs." The statement reflected his propensity to take the long view on budget issues and spend and sacrifice now in order to improve the lot of the citizenry and save money in the long run, balancing humanity with fiscal conservatism. An immediate product of the Hunger Tours was the inclusion of South Carolina in a national pilot program distributing food stamps.

In 1983 Hollings mounted a campaign for the Democratic presidential nomination. His fresh voice and strong agenda won favor with the media, but failed to excite voters. He withdrew from the crowded field in March 1984.

Divorced from his first wife in 1970, Hollings married Rita "Peatsy" Liddy on August 21, 1971. Mrs. Hollings quickly became an active and skillful advocate for her husband's legislative objectives and political aspirations. During Hollings's 1984 presidential campaign, a Virginia newspaper said of her, "More than any other candidate's wife, she is ready and able to speak up on issues." Reelected to a sixth and final term as U.S. senator in 1998, Hollings continued to state that "performance is better than promise." This was more than a campaign motto; it was his calling card and the reason for his success in politics and government. HERBERT J. HARTSOOK

Hancock, John. "Ernest F. Hollings: Democratic Senator from South Carolina." In *Citizens Look at Congress,* edited by the Ralph Nader Congress Project. Washington, D.C.: Grossman, 1972.

Hollings, Ernest F. *The Case Against Hunger: A Demand for a National Policy.* New York: Cowles, 1970.

———. Oral History. Modern Political Collections, South Caroliniana Library, University of South Carolina.

———. Papers. Modern Political Collections, South Caroliniana Library, University of South Carolina.

Hollis, Lawrence Peter (1883–1978). Educator, social worker. Hollis was born on a cotton farm in Chester County on November 29, 1883, the son of Peter Hollis, a farmer, and Juliet Gaston. He graduated from South Carolina College in 1905, and on June 5, 1907, he married Emma Clyde. The couple had four children. From 1923 to 1951 Hollis served as superintendent of the Parker School, considered one of the more innovative progressive schools in the United States.

In 1911, while employed with the Young Men's Christian Association, Hollis became director of welfare activities for the Monaghan Mill and Parker Cotton Mills in Greenville County. In this role he organized mill communities to create a school district of elementary and secondary schools. "Dr. Pete," as he was affectionately called, merged his belief in progressive education with the vocational needs of the community. The Parker School, called a "Mill-Town Miracle" in a 1941 issue of *Reader's Digest,* served as a model for progressive, community schools, while the Parker District established basic health, aesthetic, vocational, general education, leisure, and environmental programs for both students and adults. Hollis is widely recognized for bringing the sport of basketball to South Carolina, organizing the first troop of Boy Scouts in the state, developing an adult education "People's College" for mill community residents, and creating an annual "Singing Christmas Tree" holiday event.

A charismatic individual who never removed himself from the textile community, Hollis inspired countless anecdotes depicting self-effacing humor, his inspirational traits as educator, and his fundamental "faith in the common man." Mary Ariail and Nancy Smith in *Weaver of Dreams* recorded his educational beliefs as merging family and school: "The school should be the center of a community, and from its doors should flow ideas, love of learning, improvement of home life, readiness for jobs, friendship and love." Hollis represented a familylike presence as he offered advice to Parker students and parents on topics ranging from vocational opportunities to home furnishings. He worked to balance the wishes of employers, who sought a stable, educated, satisfied labor force, with the hopes of an illiterate, poverty-stricken, itinerant community that saw education as an opportunity for advancement. In doing so, Hollis may be questioned for his paternalism and "malefic generosity," a common criticism of progressive education, where the motives of the educator may be seen as self-serving. Under Hollis's direction, the Parker School embraced the objectives of welfare capitalism as they produced a loyal and productive workforce.

With school consolidation in 1951 in an effort to "equalize" education and justify "separate but equal" school systems, Hollis retired as the Parker District merged with over eighty other districts to form the Greenville County School District. His retirement prompted many accolades, including Greenville's Man of the Year, the Retired Educator of South Carolina award, and inclusion in *Look* magazine's one hundred outstanding educators. Hollis died in Greenville on December 13, 1978, and was buried in Springwood Cemetery. CRAIG KRIDEL

Ariail, Mary G., and Nancy J. Smith. *Weaver of Dreams: "A History of the Parker District."* Columbia, S.C.: R. L. Bryan, 1977.

Tippett, James S. *Schools for a Growing Democracy.* Boston: Ginn, 1936.

Hollywood (Charleston County; 2000 pop. 3,946). The automobile bumper sticker declares, "We're the Real Hollywood." In fact, no tourist would confuse this crossroads village on the western edge of Charleston County with California's Tinseltown. However, the declaration does suggest the balance of suburban hustle and pastoral survivals that animated Hollywood, South Carolina, just past its fiftieth birthday.

The town of Hollywood had its origins in the New South era. In the 1880s Charles W. Geraty, scion of an established family of Yonges Island, began a new farming venture on newly purchased land five miles west of the Stono River. Within a short time his business enterprises included a store and a bank within a natural grove of holly trees. Planted in the middle of a farming district, the village grew up along the tracks of the Atlantic Coast Line Railroad and, later, along two-lane S.C. Highway 162. Truck farming was the economic base down to the 1960s, when formidable competition from places such as Florida caused a sharp decline. In that interval, the principal town businesses included a railroad depot, two warehouses, and a facility to provide ice for the storage of potatoes, tomatoes, and cabbage in transit to markets as far away as New York City.

At its incorporation in 1949, Hollywood counted five hundred residents scattered along a one-mile strip of road where S.C. Highway 162 crossed S.C. Highway 165. As truck farming faded and the population dipped to four hundred a decade or two later, town leaders actively sought industrial development, almost landing a helicopter plant of Sikorsky Aircraft in 1969. When that effort failed, Hollywood evolved into a bedroom community, with its small town center providing services to a growing local population.

A gradual accretion of new residents from Charleston and the surrounding county, combined with an aggressive annexation policy, spurred growth after 1980. By 2000 town limits extended sixteen miles along Highway 162, encompassing thirty-three square miles of old plantations, new housing, and a population in the thousands. While some residents still farmed or worked in town, more people commuted by automobile to jobs in Charleston or North Charleston, fifteen or twenty miles away. And some, newcomers and natives alike, enjoyed the leisure pursuits of rural retirement, including hunting and fishing in adjoining wetlands.

In 2000 the population showed a black majority of nearly seventy percent. Racial harmony was apparent after an unsettled period in the 1960s. However, there were signs of cultural cleavage. The mayor, Herbert Gadson, first elected in 1979, was black, as were other members of the city council. Their progrowth agenda, popular among black residents concerned with job creation, was not always popular with a predominantly white minority that viewed such efforts as a threat to the district's rural character. Income levels, though increasing, lagged behind the surrounding area. Ninety-five percent of the students in public schools were black, while white children usually attended private academies.

The completion of a modern sewerage system was the source of local pride. However, some houses still used wood for heating, public garbage collection was not available, and police protection came from Charleston County. LAYLON WAYNE JORDAN

Fick, Sarah. *Charleston County Historical and Architectural Survey.* Charleston, S.C.: Preservation Consultants, 1992.

Lesesne, Thomas P. *History of Charleston County.* Charleston, S.C.: A. H. Cawston, 1931.

Holman, Clarence Hugh (1914–1981). Educator, author. Holman was born in Cross Anchor on February 24, 1914, the son of David Marion Holman and Jessie Pearl Davis. Following early schooling in Gaffney and Clinton, he entered Presbyterian College, where he majored in chemistry and graduated magna cum laude in 1936. He remained at Presbyterian to serve as publicity director until 1939, concurrently earning a bachelor of arts degree in English (1939). He served as Presbyterian's director of radio from 1939 to 1942, writing more than two hundred fifteen-minute plays on southern history as well as teaching radio production and writing. He married Verna Virginia McLeod of Ocala, Florida, on September 1, 1938. Two children were born to their union.

During World War II, Holman held numerous part-time posts: publicity director for the South Carolina Council for National Defense (1942–1944); instructor in physics and academic coordinator, 2199th AAF Base Unit, in Clinton (1942–1945); editor for Jacobs Press: Regional Books in Clinton (1942–1944); and instructor in English at Presbyterian (1942–1944). He served as academic dean at Presbyterian in 1945 and 1946.

The gifted Holman had also begun writing detective novels. The first, *Death Like Thunder,* was published in 1942. Five others followed in rapid succession, the last being *Small Town Murder,* published in 1951 under the pseudonym "Clarence Hunt." Holman did not, however, envision such work to be the center of his professional life. In 1946 he began graduate study in English at the University of North Carolina, earning his doctorate three years later. His dissertation was on "William Gilmore Simms's Theory and Practice of Historical Fiction." Duly impressed with Holman's record as teacher and scholar, the English department at the University of North Carolina invited him to remain as assistant professor.

Holman's ascension through the ranks and to the highest positions in the university was meteoric. He served as chairman of the English department from 1957 to 1962 and was named Kenan Professor of English in 1959. He also held a series of influential administrative positions, including assistant dean (1954–1955) and acting dean (1956–1959) of Arts and Sciences. He was dean of the Graduate School from 1963 to 1966, provost from 1966 to 1968, and special assistant to the chancellor from 1972 to 1978.

Holman enjoyed a lofty position among scholars of American literature. Embracing his southern roots and a sense of the tragic, he gave a major part of his scholarly effort to southern writing. He wrote, cowrote, or edited some twenty-six books of nonfiction and seventy professional articles. He was instrumental in bringing Louis D. Rubin, Jr., to Chapel Hill in 1969, and together they transformed the study of southern letters. They founded the *Southern Literary Journal* and coedited it for two decades. Best known for his writing on Thomas Wolfe and his several revisions of *A Handbook to Literature,* Holman wrote graceful essays on a wide range of authors and was a skilled editor.

Holman's many honors culminated in his appointment as Fellow of the American Academy of Arts and Sciences (1980). South Carolina took pride in the career of this native son. In 1963 Presbyterian College awarded him an honorary doctor of letters degree; in 1969 Clemson University awarded him the doctor of humanities degree to celebrate his dedication as a classroom teacher. Holman died in Chapel Hill on October 13, 1981, and was buried in Chapel Hill Memorial Cemetery. JOSEPH M. FLORA

Holmes, Francis Simmons (1815–1882). Paleontologist, museum curator. Holmes was born in Charleston on December 9, 1815, fourth of seven children of the planter John Holmes and Anna Glover. Educated in Charleston schools until he withdrew at age fourteen, Holmes served for a time as a clerk and later ran a dry goods business. On March 21, 1837, he married Elizabeth S. Toomer, with whom he had seven children. Holmes moved to St. Andrew's Parish in 1838 to operate a large plantation. A skilled farmer, he won a prize for his experiments in agriculture, and in 1842 he published *The Southern Farmer and Market Gardener,* which became a highly successful book. For Holmes, however, interest in farming eventually gave way to his fascination with fossils, especially marine invertebrates, and by 1845 he had amassed a huge collection that gained attention from many naturalists. Holmes also began to publish articles and thereby enhanced his reputation as a naturalist.

In 1844 Holmes met Michael Tuomey, who was then conducting a geological survey of South Carolina, and they soon began to collaborate on a book on fossils. Three years later, the College of Charleston set aside a room for display of many of Holmes's fossils, and these were viewed by the prominent naturalist Louis Agassiz when he visited Charleston. Impressed with the collection, Agassiz touted the work of Holmes, and in 1850, after resolving to establish a natural history museum, the College of Charleston trustees appointed Holmes as the curator.

Assuming the collections of the original museum, and its name as well, the Charleston Museum opened in 1852. Under the leadership of Holmes, the institution soon became the best natural history museum in the South and among the best in the nation at the time. Meanwhile, Holmes played the central role in forming the Elliott Society of Natural History, and he worked with Tuomey to produce *Pleiocene Fossils of South Carolina.* Published in 1857, the volume received considerable praise, and is now a classic work. Tuomey died during the same year, but Holmes continued to work on a second volume, which was published in 1860 as *Post-Pleiocene Fossils of South Carolina.* By the outbreak of the Civil War, Holmes had done much to promote scientific work in South Carolina, earning a national reputation for his activities.

Devoted to the South, Holmes supported secession. During the Civil War, he served first as a director of wayside hospitals in his area and later as superintendent of a nitre works. He resumed direction of the museum after the war but quit in 1868 when college trustees were forced to reduce his salary. Afterwards he played a major role in developing the phosphate industry in South Carolina, publishing *Phosphate Rocks of South Carolina and the "Great Carolina Marl Bed"* in 1870. Following the death of his wife during the war, Holmes married Sarah Hazzard, and fathered six more children. In 1871 he purchased a plantation near Goose Creek but maintained a home in Charleston, where he died on October 19, 1882. LESTER D. STEPHENS

Stephens, Lester D. *Ancient Animals and Other Wondrous Things: The Story of Francis Simmons Holmes, Paleontologist and Curator of the Charleston Museum.* Charleston, S.C.: Charleston Museum, 1988.

———. *Science, Race, and Religion in the American South: John Bachman and the Charleston Circle of Naturalists, 1815–1895.* Chapel Hill: University of North Carolina Press, 2000.

Holmes, Nickels John (1847–1919). Clergyman, educator. A pastor and educator, Holmes was born near Spartanburg on September 9, 1847, the second child of Zelotes Lee Holmes, who had pastored several Presbyterian churches in Laurens County and organized the First Presbyterian Church in Spartanburg. His mother, Catherine Nickels, was the daughter of a Laurens County physician and farmer. In 1859 Zelotes Holmes became a professor at Laurensville Female College. Nickels Holmes joined the Presbyterian Church, U.S., in Clinton in 1863. The following year, as his older sister Olive was dying, she declared to Nickels that "You are to preach the gospel."

Instead, Nickels joined the Confederate army, serving as a prison camp guard in Florence. Between 1866 and 1869 he attended the University of Edinburgh. On his return, he farmed, taught school, and practiced law for several years. On February 29, 1876, he married Lucy Elizabeth Simpson, daughter of the future South Carolina governor W. D. Simpson. Contemplating a new career in politics when he filed to run for county solicitor, Holmes instead felt called to preach and was licensed as a Presbyterian minister. He served churches in Clifton, Fountain Inn, Rock Bridge (near Clinton), Tucapau, and Roebuck in Spartanburg County.

In the summer of 1891 Holmes and his wife attended the annual Bible conference conducted by prominent evangelist Dwight L.

Moody in Northfield, Massachusetts, after reading Moody's *The Secret of Power.* Lucy Holmes experienced the baptism of the Holy Spirit at Northfield and began her own ministry after their return to South Carolina. In 1892 Holmes organized the Second Presbyterian Church in Greenville, serving there until 1895. After he experienced entire sanctification or holiness on July 7, 1895, he became an itinerant evangelist, preaching sanctification and divine healing. He soon withdrew from the Presbyterian Church.

Holmes organized the Brewerton Independent Presbyterian Church in Greenville as a base for his ministry; it later became Tabernacle Pentecostal Church and then Holmes Memorial Church. In 1893 a summer Bible study Holmes led at a family cottage on Paris Mountain led to his forming a school that in time became known as Holmes Bible College.

Holmes began to ponder Pentecostal experience when he read about hundreds receiving the gifts of the spirit at a revival in Los Angeles in 1906, and he began to identify himself as a Pentecostal after attending a revival meeting in West Union in 1907 at the urging of one of the students at his school. He reported that on April 22, 1907, he had experienced the baptism of the Holy Spirit and first spoke in tongues.

From then on, Holmes's revivals, including meetings in Laurens and Clinton as well as in Falcon, North Carolina, carried the Pentecostal message. He quickly became a recognized leader of the Pentecostal movement in South Carolina, and when the Alabama Pentecostal Association expanded into the Southern Pentecostal Association in 1908, Holmes was elected its president.

In 1915 the Tabernacle Church where Holmes was pastor became part of the Pentecostal Holiness Church, although Holmes and his school remained independent. He was serving both as pastor and as president of the school when he died on December 17, 1919. NANCY A. HARDESTY

Holmes, Nickels J. and Lucy S. Holmes. *Life Sketches and Sermons.* Royston, Ga.: Press of the Pentecostal Holiness Church, 1920.

Morgan, David. "N. J. Holmes and the Origins of Pentecostalism." *South Carolina Historical Magazine* 84 (July 1983): 136–51.

Holmes Bible College. The roots of what is popularly called "the oldest Pentecostal school in the world" lie in a Bible study program for young men conducted for several weeks in the summer of 1893 by the Presbyterian pastor Nickels John Holmes at a family cottage on Paris Mountain, outside Greenville. In 1898 Holmes and his wife, Lucy Simpson Holmes, purchased the Altamont Hotel on Paris Mountain for $5,000 and converted it into the Altamont Bible and Missionary Institute.

In January 1901 Holmes moved the operation to Atlanta, where it remained until October 1903 as the Bible and Missionary Institute of Atlanta. He then relocated the enterprise to Columbia, where it used the Oliver Gospel Mission building until June 1905, when the school returned to Paris Mountain. In 1915 Holmes purchased land in Greenville at the corner of Buncombe Street and Briggs Avenue, where the school remains. It received its formal South Carolina charter on January 9, 1911.

While the school was in Columbia, it came under the sway of Pentecostalism. In the winter of 1904–1905 a continuing prayer revival spread through the student body. Then in the fall of 1905 a female student began to speak in tongues during a Bible class. Although Holmes, as leader of the school, remained cautious, he and others eagerly read the reports of Pentecostal outpourings in Los Angeles in 1906 in the popular periodical, *The Way of Faith,* published in Columbia. The next year, Lida Purkey (or Purkie), a student at the school, attended the revival conducted in West Union by Pentecostal advocate Gaston B. Cashwell and persuaded Holmes to attend continuing meetings in West Union, at which Miss Pinkie Blake was leading services as well as both speaking and singing in tongues. Blake came to Columbia to Holmes's school in April 1907, where she found some apprehension about the validity of Pentecostal experience. By June, however, Holmes and the entire student body testified to receiving the gift of tongues. The school has remained oriented to Pentecostalism ever since.

On March 29, 1916, after the return to Greenville, the school took the name Holmes Bible and Missionary Institute. For many years it operated on the "faith principle" whereby students did not pay set fees but whatever they could afford. However, by 2002 the school had instituted modest charges for tuition, room, and board, while not refusing admission to those unable to pay.

Paul F. Beacham (1888–1978), an Oconee County native, succeeded Holmes both as president of the school and as pastor of Homes Memorial Church when Holmes died in 1919. In 1942 the school became Holmes Bible College of Theology and Missions; in 1958, Holmes Theological Seminary; in 1979, Holmes College of the Bible; and in 1998, Holmes Bible College. In 2002, with Richard Waters as president, this bastion of South Carolina Pentecostalism enrolled around one hundred students in programs leading to bachelor's degrees in Bible, theology, and Christian ministry.

Highway construction has encroached on the land housing the Holmes campus; the school has purchased forty acres on Old Buncombe and Duncan Chapel Roads in Greenville with an eye to relocation. NANCY A. HARDESTY

Holmes, Nickels J., and Lucy S. Holmes. *Life Sketches and Sermons.* Royston, Ga.: Press of the Pentecostal Holiness Church, 1920.

Home schooling. Between the mid-1970s and 2002 the number of home-schooled children in the United States grew from approximately fifteen thousand to more than one million. The number of home-schooled students in South Carolina also increased rapidly during this time, from a handful to as many as ten thousand as parents sought alternate academic, religious, philosophical, and social environments in which to educate their children. The majority of home-schooled children in South Carolina are from white, middle-class, evangelical Protestant families, although African American and Hispanic families are choosing to home school in increasing numbers.

Parents home school their children for a variety of practical and personal reasons. Home schooling employs a tutorial method of instruction that is effective, allowing parents to tailor the curriculum to meet the individual learning style, interests, and educational goals of each child. Home-schooled students consistently score well above average on standardized tests. In South Carolina the South Carolina Association of Independent Home Schools (SCAIHS) reported that in 2001 the average SAT score for its students was 1067 compared to the state average of 974. Other parents home school their children because they object to what they perceive is being taught (or not taught) in public and private schools. Inspired by fundamentalist Christianity and a conservative political and social outlook, these parents home school to avoid what they see as secular and non-Christian values espoused in contemporary schools.

Prior to 1984 the home-schooling movement in South Carolina was small, unorganized, and largely unnoticed. But by 1988 the number of home-schooling families had grown dramatically. After being subjected to intensive grassroots activism, the South Carolina

General Assembly passed the first modern piece of home-schooling legislation in 1988, which required local school boards to approve home-schooling programs. The law also required teaching parents without a four-year degree to pass an Education Entrance Examination (EEE) in order to home school. The EEE requirement antagonized home-schooling advocates and ushered in a new round of litigation. In 1990 the South Carolina Association of Independent Home Schools (SCAIHS) was incorporated as a private approval organization for home-school families, negating the need for parents to gain approval from local school districts. The following year the South Carolina Supreme Court struck down the EEE as a requirement for home-schooling parents, which opened the door for SCAIHS to seek a legislative remedy for home-schooling parents. In 1992 the General Assembly enacted legislation that allowed home-schooling parents to join SCAIHS in lieu of being approved by local school districts. In 1996 the General Assembly passed a third law, allowing other associations to approve home-schooling families if specified guidelines were followed. JAMES C. CARPER AND ZAN PETERS TYLER

Carper, James C. "Pluralism to Establishment to Dissent: The Religious and Educational Context of Home Schooling." *Peabody Journal of Education* 75, nos. 1–2 (2000): 8–19.

Tyler, Zan Peters, and James C. Carper. "From Confrontation to Accommodation: Home Schooling in South Carolina." *Peabody Journal of Education* 75, nos. 1–2 (2000): 32–48.

Van Galen, Jane, and Mary Anne Pitman, eds. *Home Schooling: Political, Historical, and Pedagogical Perspectives.* Norwood, N.J.: Ablex, 1991.

Honea Path (Anderson County; 2000 pop. 3,504). A water stop on the Greenville and Columbia Railroad in the 1850s developed into a town whose name origin is uncertain. Honea Path may be misnamed for William Honey, an early landowner and trader, or it may be double-named by Cherokee Indians, with "Honea" being an Indian name for "path" according to folklore. When the town was chartered in 1885, it was referred to as Honey Path in three different places, and early wills and deeds also bear the Honey Path name. However, in 1917 the town was incorporated under the name Honea Path and it has gone by that name ever since.

Located on the Anderson-Abbeville county line, Honea Path became a cotton mill town. Chiquola Manufacturing Company commenced operations in 1903 and has remained the economic mainstay. The mill's early employees included future U.S. senator Olin D. Johnston, who went to work as a sweeper in the mill at age eleven. In 1934 Honea Path was the site of one of the most infamous events in American labor history. Chiquola mill hands joined the general strike that swept the upstate that summer, which badly divided the community. On the morning of September 6, later dubbed "Bloody Thursday," strikers and their supporters gathered to prevent strikebreakers from entering the mill. Fighting broke out, and gunfire erupted. In less than five minutes, six strikers were dead and more than a dozen lay wounded. Under military guard, the Chiquola Mill reopened the following Monday. On Memorial Day 1995, a small granite monument was erected in a Honea Path park to commemorate the tragic event.

As the town entered the twenty-first century, the Chiquola Mill continued as Honea Path's largest employer. However, the town had diversified its economy somewhat. Plants opened nearby that produced synthetic fibers, linens, ladies sportswear, shipping containers, and medical equipment. Among the town's claims to fame is its Carnegie Library, built in 1908. Honea Path is the smallest town in the nation with a Carnegie Library, which remains in use as a branch of the Anderson County Library. HURLEY E. BADDERS

Second Edition of Honea Path Milestones. Honea Path, S.C., 1992.

Simon, Bryant. *A Fabric of Defeat: The Politics of South Carolina Millhands, 1910–1948.* Chapel Hill: University of North Carolina Press, 1998.

Honey Hill, Battle of (November 30, 1864). The Battle of Honey Hill was the first in a series of engagements fought at the headwaters of the Broad River along the Charleston and Savannah Railroad in November and December 1864. Federal forces at Port Royal initiated the campaign in the fall of 1864 to support the movement of General William Tecumseh Sherman's army against Savannah. On November 29, 1864, a six-thousand-man division under General John P. Hatch, including a brigade of marines and sailors, was transported up the Broad River and disembarked at Boyd's Landing for an attack against the railroad junction at Gopher Hill. One half of Hatch's command was made up of black regiments. Bad weather, faulty maps, and poor guides delayed the Federals for an entire day. This allowed the Confederates to mass some fourteen hundred Georgia militia and State Line troops under General Gustavus W. Smith and five hundred South Carolina cavalry and artillerymen under Colonel Charles J. Colcock astride the road to Gopher Hill in fixed fortifications at a spot known as Honey Hill.

On November 30, the Federals were repulsed in numerous attempts to force their way through the Confederate lines. With the arrival of Confederate reinforcements the Northerners pulled back to Boyd's Landing. The battle resulted in 746 Union casualties and, though unreported, the Confederates suffered at least one hundred casualties. A week later Hatch shifted his command to Gregorie's Neck and struck at the railroad near Tulifinny Crossroads. Again the Confederates, now under the command of General Sam Jones, stopped the Union advance short of the railroad. The Federals then made preparations to attack Pocotaligo, but by then Sherman's army had reached the sea, and on December 20, 1864, the Confederates evacuated Savannah. By mid-January elements of Sherman's army linked up with Hatch's division and the Confederates abandoned the railroad line and retreated across the Combahee and Salkehatchie Rivers. STEPHEN R. WISE

Cozzens, Peter. "Smokescreen at Honey Hill." *Civil War Times Illustrated* 38 (February 2000): 32–38.

Emilio, Luis F. *A Brave Black Regiment: History of the Fifty-Fourth Regiment of Massachusetts Volunteer Infantry 1863–1865.* New York: Arno, 1969.

Hudson, Leonne M. "A Confederate Victory at Grahamville: Fighting at Honey Hill." *South Carolina Historical Magazine* 94 (January 1993): 19–33.

Hookworm. Long before hookworm was identified as a parasitic disease, its mostly white victims were a common presence in the South. Pale and listless, with vacant stares and winged shoulder blades, these "lazy" southerners, a staple of northern literature, seemed dismal proof of the human and economic collapse of a once-proud cotton South. But in the early 1900s Washington zoologist Charles W. Stiles exploded the shiftless-southerners thesis and showed that their traits had a biological basis: infestation by a worm, *Necator americanis,* which was native to Africa and had migrated west with the slaves. Nurtured in the South's damp and sandy soil, it caused severe anemia, stunted growth, and often mental retardation in victims. What made *Necator* most threatening, however, was its soaring infection rate (in parts of South Carolina it ranged up to thirty-five per cent).

The starting point of infection was the lack of sanitary privies in most of the rural and mill village South. Thus, human waste containing *Necator* eggs was scattered on bare ground. Within two days the eggs hatched out larvae, which migrated up stems of plants to lie in wait for a returning host. It was then a simple matter—facilitated by southerners' lack of shoes—for larvae to transfer to the host's feet or ankles. They then pierced the skin and traveled to the small intestine. These larvae matured into adult worms, which "hooked" onto tissue and began a blood-feeding that could continue for years. Meanwhile they produced new eggs, which entered the stool to restart the cycle.

When Stiles first reported those findings, the northern press made much of this new southern disease (one paper announcing the discovery of a germ of laziness). Initially southern leaders angrily rejected the findings and resisted calls for health reform, some claiming that northern do-gooders were only trying to profit in the sale of shoes. One Yankee philanthropist, however, was determined to push reform despite resistance. In 1909 John D. Rockefeller and his advisers created the Rockefeller Sanitary Commission for Elimination of Hookworm Disease, which would send experts to some thirty-nine counties in nine states (including South Carolina) with a mission to convince leaders to take steps against this serious malady.

Then in 1911 the commission, wanting swifter progress, shifted from education to treatment, adopting an approach that had worked in Mississippi: the traveling dispensary. Taking the doctor to the people proved hugely successful, partly because treatment (thymol) was free and sure—if potentially dangerous—but mostly because the dispensary had all the flavor of the camp meeting. Going to the dispensary for thymol was similar to going to the revival for religion. Even picnics on the ground were included.

By 1915 when the commission stopped work, 750,000 southerners had received dispensary chemotherapy and hookworm was on the run, aided by the privy-building work of new county health departments. Between 1910 and 1914 infection rates fell sharply everywhere, including South Carolina, which saw a two-thirds drop. After 1915 hookworm still existed, but by the 1940s, thanks to New Deal health spending and the heightened demand for citizen sanitation that accompanied World War II, it was little more than a medical curiousity. ED BEARDSLEY

Beardsley, Edward H. *A History of Neglect: Health Care for Blacks and Mill Workers in the Twentieth-Century South.* Knoxville: University of Tennessee Press, 1987.

Ettling, John. *The Germ of Laziness: Rockefeller Philanthropy and Public Health in the New South.* Cambridge: Harvard University Press, 1981.

Farmer, Henry. "The Hookworm Eradication Program in the South, 1909–1925." Ph.D. diss., University of Georgia, 1970.

United States. Congress. Senate. *Report on Condition of Women and Child Wage-Earners in the United States.* Vol. 17, *Hookworm Disease Among Cotton-Mill Operatives.* 61st Cong., 2d sess., 1910. S. Doc. 645.

Hootie and the Blowfish. Founded in 1986, Hootie and the Blowfish emerged as the most popular rock band on the University of South Carolina college scene in the late 1980s and early 1990s. Consisting of lead singer and rhythm guitarist Darius Rucker (b. 1966 in Charleston), lead guitarist Mark Bryan (b. 1967 in Silver Spring, Maryland), drummer Jim Sonefeld (b. 1964 in Lansing, Michigan), and bassist Dean Felber (b. 1967 in Bethesda, Maryland), the band suddenly grew into a national phenomenon with the release of their major label debut, *Cracked Rear View,* in 1994 on Atlantic Records. The album's sales started slowly but exploded in 1995 following the release of the popular radio hits "Hold My Hand," "Let Her Cry," and "Only Want to Be with You." The album became one of the best-selling recordings in popular music history, selling more than fifteen million copies in the United States by 2002.

Marked by Rucker's soulful singing, and the group's chiming acoustic guitar and sing-along lyrics, "Hootie" (as the band came to be known) fell to earth as quickly as it soared. After winning two Grammy Awards for the first record, the band's second album, *Fairweather Johnson* (1996), reached the number one spot on all music charts, as did its predecessor, but sold only about three million copies. They followed up with *Musical Chairs* (1998) and *Scattered, Smothered, and Covered* (2000), which each garnered respectable reviews if not impressive sales figures. Nevertheless the band continued to make music, releasing *Hootie and the Blowfish* in 2003 and a "best of" record in 2004 while touring and making national TV appearances.

Hootie and the Blowfish appeared live in concert on national television, broadcast from the Horseshoe of the University of South Carolina (1996). Photograph by Jonathan Bové. Courtesy, University Publications, University of South Carolina

In 1996 the group performed a live, nationally televised concert on the Horseshoe at the University of South Carolina campus. That same year the band also helped Columbia obtain the annual Farm Aid concert, starring country singer Willie Nelson and others. The band played for President Bill Clinton's second inaugural ball in Washington. Known for their friendly personalities, the band still sometimes hangs out at the same Five Points bars where they played some of their first concerts, sipping beer and greeting fans. ALAN RICHARD

Bogdanov, Vladimir, Chris Woodstra, and Stephen Thomas Erlewine, eds. *All Music Guide: The Definitive Guide to Popular Music.* 4th ed. San Francisco: Backbeat Books / All Media Guide, 2001.

Hoover Scare (1887). The 1880s were a period of rapid industrial growth and increasing distress for farmers in upstate South Carolina. The events inspired by the activities of the labor organizer Hiram F. Hover (whose surname was commonly misspelled as "Hoover" in contemporary sources) illustrate the responses some factory workers and agricultural laborers made to their difficult circumstances and the response of powerful members of South Carolina society.

Raised in the Shaker community of Mount Lebanon, New York, Hover was employed in the garment trades and traveled the country as a dress cutter. Arriving in Knoxville, Tennessee, in late 1885, he joined the Knights of Labor, the nation's largest labor union. By the following summer, he had settled with his wife in Hickory, North Carolina, but internal disputes led to his departure from the Knights. By January 1887 Hover formed his own organization, the Co-operative Workers of America (CWA), in order both to achieve major reforms in labor laws and to establish cooperative stores. In February 1887 he set out for South Carolina to organize local branches of the CWA. Hover first spoke in Spartanburg, where he addressed an interracial crowd of several hundred people. By March he had moved on to Greenville and Walhalla. The authorities in Walhalla charged Hover with vagrancy but allowed him to flee the state to Georgia, where he continued his organizing activities. On May 19, 1887, a mob of white landowners in Warrenton, Georgia, shot Hover while he was speaking in an African American church. Severely wounded, Hover returned to Hickory and later moved to New York, returning briefly to Atlanta and Greenville in 1889 in a failed attempt to resuscitate the CWA.

Other organizers recruited by Hover created "Hoover clubs," or local branches of the CWA, in the city of Greenville and in the rural area where Greenville, Spartanburg, and Laurens Counties meet. Most of the leaders and members of these CWA branches were landless African American laborers, and the primary goal of the branches was to establish cooperative stores so that members could avoid the entangling web of credit that perpetuated the sharecropping system. Wary of attracting the attention of white landowners, they held their meetings secretly, usually at night in African American churches. By late June, rumors of the existence of these "Hoover clubs" were circulating among whites in Laurens County, who feared a massive uprising by black farmers and laborers in the area. Whites in Laurens County convinced the adjutant general to send arms for a cavalry patrol that they had formed to defend against the anticipated uprising. The fear spread to southern Greenville County, and white landowners formed a vigilance committee. On June 29, 1887, they rounded up the leaders of the CWA branches and held an inquisition at Fairview Presbyterian Church. They ordered the African Americans to abandon the CWA, which they did. The organization's Greenville membership saw this disruption and quietly left the CWA as well. A group in Spartanburg seems to have persisted, however, and it opened a cooperative store in September 1887, though it is unclear how long it operated. The "Hoover Scare," as the newspapers dubbed it, provides an example of collective action by African Americans, and the difficulties they confronted, in the period between Reconstruction and disfranchisement in 1895. BRUCE E. BAKER

Baker, Bruce E. "The 'Hoover Scare' in South Carolina, 1887: An Attempt to Organize Black Farm Labor." *Labor History* 40 (August 1999): 261–82.

Hoppin' John. Hoppin' John is a pilaf made with beans and rice. The recipe came directly to America from West Africa and is typical of the one-pot cooking of the South Carolina lowcountry. As the recipe moved inland, it became the traditional dish for good luck on New Year's Day throughout the South. The first written appearance of the recipe in English was in Sarah Rutledge's *The Carolina Housewife, or House and Home, by a Lady of Charleston,* published anonymously in 1847. Though most often made with black-eyed peas, the original Charleston version called for "One pound of bacon, one pint of red peas, one pint of rice." Red peas are cowpeas, or dried field peas, which are, as are black-eyed peas, more akin to beans. Neither botanists nor linguists are in agreement on the origins of the dish or its ingredients. Likewise, none of several popular studies that attempt to explain the origin of the name of the dish are convincing. The culinary scholar Karen Hess believes that both recipe and name are derived from Hindi, Persian, and Malay words that mean, simply, "cooked rice and beans." Whatever its origins, the dish, originally made with pigeon peas in West Africa, arrived in Charleston and became a favorite of the rice-plantation owners as well as the enslaved. When Sarah Rutledge, who was the daughter of Edward Rutledge, a signer of the Declaration of Independence, and niece of Arthur Middleton, another signer, included the recipe in her collection, it was well established along the eastern seaboard as a classic Charleston dish. JOHN MARTIN TAYLOR

Hess, Karen. *The Carolina Rice Kitchen: The African Connection.* Columbia: University of South Carolina Press, 1992.

Rutledge, Sarah. *The Carolina Housewife.* 1847. Reprint, Columbia: University of South Carolina Press, 1979.

Hopsewee Plantation (Georgetown County). Hopsewee Plantation is best known as the birthplace and boyhood home of Thomas Lynch, Jr. (1749–1779), a signer of the Declaration of Independence. It is located about thirteen miles south of Georgetown at the point where U.S. Highway 17 crosses the north branch of the Santee River. This was also the site of the main colonial thoroughfare running north and south, the "King's Highway."

In 1704 John Bell took out a warrant to survey five hundred acres at a place called "Hobsheewee." Bell chose to settle farther up the North Santee, however, and either sold his warrant or allowed it to lapse. Colonel Thomas Lynch (1675–1738) formed Hopsewee Plantation from a five-hundred-acre grant purchased from John Abraham Motte and a three-hundred-acre grant originally claimed by George Montgomery. Lynch also secured a grant for an island in the Santee River Delta of fourteen hundred acres between Push and Go Creek and Six Mile Creek. The Hopsewee rice fields were on the island. In the 1740s Thomas Lynch, Sr. (ca. 1727–1776), built the house that still stands at Hopsewee. It is a two-and-one-half-story black cypress structure of mortise and tenon construction, set on a brick and tabby foundation. Its double-tiered piazza displays the influence of West Indian architecture in the eighteenth-century lowcountry.

Robert Hume purchased the plantation from Lynch in 1762 for £5,000. His descendants held Hopsewee until 1945. In 1969 Mr. and Mrs. James Maynard acquired the Hopsewee house, renovated the building, and opened it to the public in 1970. Hopsewee was listed in the National Register of Historic Places in 1971 and was designated a National Historic Landmark in 1972. It has remained in private hands but is still open to the public. SUZANNE LINDER

Lachicotte, Alberta Morel. *Georgetown Rice Plantations.* 1955. Reprint, Georgetown, S.C.: Georgetown County Historical Society, 1993.

Linder, Suzanne Cameron, and Marta Leslie Thacker. *Historical Atlas of the Rice Plantations of Georgetown County and the Santee River.* Columbia: South Carolina Department of Archives and History for the Historic Ricefields Association, 2001.

Horry, Peter (ca. 1743–1815). Planter, solider, legislator. Horry was born on March 12, 1743 or 1744, in Prince George Winyah Parish, the son of the Huguenot rice planter John Horry. Educated at the Indigo Society's free school in Georgetown, Peter Horry later served a harsh apprenticeship with a local merchant. By the late 1760s Horry had established a mercantile partnership in Georgetown, which he gave up on inheriting 475 acres from his father. Eventually Horry owned plantations on Winyah Bay and the Santee River as well as land in Ninety Six District and a house in Columbia (later called the Horry-Guignard House). At his death he owned as many as 116 slaves.

Horry's military service began during the Revolutionary War when he was commissioned a captain on June 12, 1775. He served with Francis Marion in the Second South Carolina, which distinguished itself at the Battle of Sullivan's Island in June 1776. After the battle Horry was promoted to major and, in 1779, to lieutenant colonel in the Continental army. In January 1780 he took command of the Fifth South Carolina, with the rank of colonel in the state militia. When the Fifth and other undermanned regiments were merged, Horry's services were not needed and he was released from active duty. At home when Charleston fell in May 1780, Horry went to North Carolina and joined General Johann de Kalb's staff as an observer. In the summer of 1780 he returned to South Carolina and served as one of Marion's most valuable and trusted officers. Late in the war, when Marion attended the legislature at Jacksonborough, he left Horry in command of his brigade. In the meantime, General Nathanael Greene had created two battalions of light cavalry, one commanded by Horry and the other by Hezekiah Maham. Since their new commissions as lieutenant colonels bore the same date, a feud developed between the two men, one result of which was the defeat of Marion's brigade in late February 1782 at Wambaw Bridge. After the two regiments were consolidated under Maham, Horry was appointed commandant at Georgetown, a port vital to Greene's army.

After the war Horry remained in the military service of the state. In 1792 he was given command of the Sixth militia brigade. In 1798 the brigade mobilized to face a rumored invasion by French forces and again in 1802 against a potential slave revolt. He retired from the militia in 1806. A member of the Society of the Cincinnati, Horry collected a sizable archive of war documents and letters. He gave them to Mason Locke "Parson" Weems, fresh from his popular, but contrived, biography of George Washington. Weems took so many liberties in writing the *Life of Marion* (1809) that Horry disassociated himself from the work. Horry also kept a journal from 1812 until shortly before his death, parts of which were published in the 1930s and 1940s in the *South Carolina Historical and Genealogical Magazine.*

Horry represented Prince George Winyah Parish in the state House of Representatives in 1782 and from 1792 to 1794. He sat in the state Senate for the same parish from 1785 to 1787. In 1801, when the legislature established new judicial districts, the state honored his war-time service by creating Horry District.

Horry married Margaret Magdalen Guignard on February 9, 1793, a union that produced no children. He died in Columbia on February 28, 1815, and was buried at Trinity Church, Columbia.
ROY TALBERT, JR.

Bailey, N. Louise, Mary L. Morgan, and Carolyn R. Taylor, eds. *Biographical Directory of the South Carolina Senate, 1776–1985.* 3 vols. Columbia: University of South Carolina Press, 1986.

Salley, Alexander S., ed. "The Journal of General Peter Horry." *South Carolina Historical and Genealogical Magazine* 38–48 (April 1937–April 1947).

———. "Horry's Notes to Weems's *Life of Marion.*" *South Carolina Historical and Genealogical Magazine* 61 (July 1960): 119–22.

Horry County (1,134 sq. miles; 2000 pop. 196,629). Horry is the largest and easternmost of South Carolina's forty-six counties, forming a wedge between North Carolina and the Atlantic Ocean. In 1785 the Georgetown Judicial District was subdivided into four counties, one of which, Kingston County, became Horry District in 1801. In its modern form, the Little Pee Dee River separates Horry County from Dillon, Marion, and Georgetown Counties on the west and south. The county was named for Peter Horry, an officer in the Revolutionary War.

Native Americans (Pee Dees, Chicoras, Socastees, and Waccamaws) inhabited the area long before the first Europeans and Africans came. Some dwelt along the coast, others made their homes along streams that later bore their names. Contact with the newcomers proved catastrophic for the natives. Those not driven out by force often succumbed to unfamiliar diseases to which they lacked immunity. By 1800 hardly a trace of their ancient cultures remained.

It is likely that Spaniards probed Horry's coastline as early as the 1530s, but more than two centuries passed before European and African newcomers gained a foothold in what became Horry County. In the 1670s English settlers began to cluster around South Carolina's harbors and adjacent rivers. In 1735, as part of Governor Robert Johnson's plan to settle the interior, Kingston Township was laid out in the northeastern part of the colony, along the north bank of the Waccamaw River. Slowly pioneer families began entering Horry. Most of them drifted down from North Carolina and Virginia, while a few came up the Waccamaw River from Georgetown. While some brought slaves with them, most were "poor white Protestants" who expected to earn their daily bread by the sweat of their own brows.

Several factors impelled Horry's development in a different direction from other South Carolina counties. In the first place, geography isolated Horry. The Atlantic Ocean on the east and the Pee Dee Swamp on the west and south made communication with other South Carolinians difficult. Ironically, Horry's northern border was mostly dry, level ground, facilitating contact with North Carolina. Tar Heel influences were subtle but persistent, and in many ways Horry came to resemble neighboring North Carolina counties. By the 1840s Horry's political and social isolation gave rise to its nickname, the Independent Republic of Horry.

Horry's economic development was also distinctive. Except for a few miles along the lower Waccamaw River, Horry was too far inland for the tidewater rice culture that dominated the lowcountry. Likewise, the Horry landscape was unsuited to large-scale cotton production. Thus the plantation economy common to other counties never evolved. For example, in 1860 two-thirds of Horry's farms were valued at less than $600 while small farms in neighboring Georgetown County comprised only one-quarter of the total. Horry became a refuge of yeomen farmers subsisting on their modest holdings and bartering with neighbors. The census of 1860 reckoned Horry the poorest county in South Carolina.

Demographics reflected the economy. Few Horry farmers owned slaves, and only the mountain district of Pickens had a greater white majority. Lack of commitment to slavery influenced Horry's politics as well. In 1860 many Horryites opposed secession but closed ranks with their state and region after Fort Sumter. Horry men mustered into the Tenth South Carolina Volunteers and saw service in Mississippi, Tennessee, and Georgia. Defeat and emancipation had less impact on Horry than other counties. Accustomed to doing their own work, most Horry folk simply resumed their lives of toil.

In 1887 a branch of the Wilmington, Columbia, and Augusta Railroad (and its attendant telegraph line) linked Horry County to the outside world. Better transportation and communication opened markets for Horry's forest products, and timber, tar, and turpentine became important exports for several years. Horry farmers felled, tapped, and scraped pine trees for a few extra dollars per year.

In the 1890s Horry embraced bright leaf tobacco as a cash crop. By 1903 thousands of acres of leaf were growing and tobacco markets were thriving in Conway and Loris. Tobacco put Horry's subsistence/barter economy on a cash basis, and Horry farmers marched into the twentieth century in step with world markets. By the 1920s Horry was South Carolina's top tobacco-producing county. Predictably Horry's fortunes rose and fell with tobacco's, booming with high leaf prices and languishing with low ones. The Great Depression of the 1930s caused fewer hardships in Horry than many other places. Horry folk typically lived on their own land and raised their own food, and thus felt less change in their living standard. The federal production control/price support system established for bright leaf in the 1930s protected the income of tobacco growers and stabilized Horry's economy.

Horry County prospered after World War II. A profitable cash crop coupled with the developing resort economy along the coast ushered in an era of sustained growth. In the 1950s Horry's beaches began attracting increasing numbers of tourists, and Myrtle Beach became the centerpiece of Horry's thirty-mile-long Grand Strand. In the 1970s and 1980s capital investment and population flowed into Horry as resort hotels and condominiums rose along the coast and forests were felled for golf courses. Horry's good climate and abundant land helped to transform the county into a world-class golf destination.

By the 1980s Horry had evolved into two distinct cultures: a cosmopolitan, sun-belt economy along the coast and a traditional, agrarian society inland. As tobacco farming declined in the 1980s, many rural folk found service jobs, transforming Horry towns such as Loris and Aynor into bedroom communities. Along with Horry's population growth came greater diversity as significant numbers of Hispanics and Asians joined the workforce in the 1990s. In the late twentieth century, Horry became one of South Carolina's most prosperous counties. But rapid growth strained local infrastructure, and Horry County entered the twenty-first century struggling to meet the demand for expanding services. ELDRED E. PRINCE, JR.

Gragg, Rod. *The Illustrated History of Horry County.* Myrtle Beach, S.C.: Southern Communications, 1994.

Lewis, Catherine H. *Horry County, South Carolina, 1730–1993.* Columbia: University of South Carolina Press, 1998.

Prince, Eldred E., and Robert R. Simpson. *Long Green: The Rise and Fall of Tobacco in South Carolina.* Athens: University of Georgia Press, 2000.

Horse racing. "The Sport of Kings" emerged in South Carolina as soon as colonists gained firm footing and began amassing property and wealth enough to emulate the lifestyles of England and the Caribbean. Before 1754 most horse stock in the colony was for general use. They were small, fleet, strong, and descended from horses brought to Florida by the Spanish and known as the Chicasaw breed.

Charleston was the seat of racing in these early years. The first record of any public running appeared in the *South-Carolina Gazette* in February 1734, announcing a race on Charleston Neck for a prize of a saddle and bridle. The same year, the city formed its first jockey club. In 1735 "The York Course" was set out, followed by "The Newmarket Course," which hosted its first race in 1760. By then, rules of racing were established and prizes of silver or gold were awarded. Many of the early jockeys were slaves.

Interest in improving the breed was intense in the years before and after the Revolution. Horsemen from Charleston and inland river settlements began a campaign of importing fine stallions and mares from England and Virginia. Organized racing took place at Charleston, Edisto, Jacksonborough, Pocotaligo, and Strawberry Ferry. The Hamptons, Singletons, Richardsons, and others were among the inland families dedicated to enlarging the sport beyond Charleston.

Horse racing in Aiken has been popular for more than a century. Courtesy, South Caroliniana Library, University of South Carolina

Recovery following the Revolution brought a huge following to racing. Racing continued in Charleston at the new Washington Course, which coincided with a gala social season of fetes, balls, and dinners. Not to be outdone, the elegant setting and refined audience attending the racing scene at Pinewood claimed to rival that of the British course at Goodwood. St. Matthews, Pendleton, Greenville, Barnwell, Newberry, Laurensville, Deadfall, Beaufort, Georgetown, Camden, and Orangeburg all held races during the antebellum era, and some even had registered jockey clubs.

There is scant information on many of these old tracks with the exception of Charleston, whose past is best recorded. The Camden Jockey Club presided over three racecourses during its existence, while the Columbia Jockey Club oversaw events at the Congaree Course. Fans reveled in these glory days of South Carolina horse racing, but the Civil War brought racing in South Carolina to an end, with most properties sold and stables disbanded. Even the South Carolina Jockey Club dissolved and gave its remaining relics to the Charleston Library.

In spite of the hardships, the lure of the sport brought a revival at the turn of the century. Camden and Aiken made a pointed effort to entice moneyed sportsmen. Having little money but a wealth of land and historic homes, residents partnered with well-heeled northern visitors to create golf, shooting, and equestrian venues. In addition to the new racing centers built during the 1930s, an active South Carolina Turf Club held a circuit during World War II in Newberry, Eutawville, Summerville, St. Matthews, St. Johns, Colleton, Williamsburg, Elloree, and Camden.

In Camden, Ernest Woodward and Harry Kirkover built Springdale Race Course and created the Carolina Cup Race Meet for steeplechasers in 1930. Marion duPont Scott built Wrenfield, a flat track, in 1936 and hosted a few days of trials during the 1950s. She later added the Colonial Cup to the venue at Springdale, which she purchased in 1954. The Carolina Cup and the Colonial Cup continue as significant stops on the steeplechase circuit.

In Aiken steeplechasing began in 1930, followed by harness racing in 1936, and flat racing in 1942. All these events continue as Aiken's Triple Crown in the spring. Aiken also hosts a fall steeplechase meet. The Elloree Trials began in 1962 and are still held. Horse racing returned to Charleston with the creation of the Charleston Steeplechase at Stono Ferry. Even with the absence of legal wagering, a day at the races continues to provide a favorite social and sporting occasion. HOPE COOPER

Hotaling, Edward. *The Great Black Jockeys: The Lives and Times of the Men Who Dominated America's First National Sport.* Rocklin, Calif.: Forum, 1999.

Irving, John Beaufain. *The South Carolina Jockey Club.* 1857. Reprint, Spartanburg, S.C.: Reprint Company, 1975.

Horseshoe (Columbia). Deriving its name from the U-shape orientation of its nineteenth- and early twentieth-century buildings massed around a central green space, the Horseshoe constitutes the historic heart of the University of South Carolina's Columbia campus and features the capital city's greatest concentration of historic buildings. Situated in a west-to-east fashion, the Horseshoe is bounded by Sumter Street to the west, Gibbes Green to the east, and Works Progress Administration–era dormitories to its north and south. No longer home to university professors, the Horseshoe's buildings continue to serve as dormitories, classrooms, and administrative offices.

The Horseshoe's construction began in 1803. The "college grounds," as it was then known, derived its design from a competition in which Charlestonian Robert Mills submitted plans for buildings that drew their inspiration from styles associated with colleges in the Northeast. While Mills's initial designs did not come to fruition, his later concepts were adopted in the construction that followed.

The first structures erected were "South Building" in 1805, later named Rutledge College, and "North Building" in 1809, which became DeSaussure College. Shortly thereafter, a home for the college's president was erected on these buildings' eastern flanks (replaced in 1940 by McKissick Library). Further construction followed. The President's House (1810) and McCutcheon House (1813) both originally served as faculty residences. Another faculty residence, Lieber College (1836), and several student residence halls—Elliott (1837), Pinckney (1837), Harper (1847), and Legare (1847) Colleges—were built to accommodate increasing enrollments. A Mills-designed project was realized in 1840 on the completion of South Caroliniana Library, the nation's oldest freestanding college library.

With its masonry and stucco three- and four-story buildings, the Horseshoe's architectural feel is that of a neoclassical historic district. Stylistically compatible 1930s-era buildings serve as buffers from modern style 1960s and 1970s structures on campus. The Horseshoe was listed in the National Register of Historic Places in 1970. JOHN M. SHERRER III

Bryan, John Morrill. *An Architectural History of the South Carolina College, 1801–1855.* Columbia: University of South Carolina Press, 1976.

Clark, Robert C. *University of South Carolina: A Portrait.* Columbia: University of South Carolina Press, 2001.

Green, Edwin L. *History of the Buildings of the University of South Carolina.* Columbia, S.C.: R. L. Bryan, 1909.

Morris, Philip. "A Walk through History on Campus." *Southern Living* 18 (September 1983): 82–87.

Howard, Frank James (1909–1996). Football coach. Howard was born in Barlow Bend, Alabama, on March 25, 1909. He graduated from Murphy High School in Mobile and earned a scholarship from the *Birmingham News* in 1927 to attend the University of Alabama, where he became a member of the varsity football squad. On graduation in 1931 Howard accepted a position as assistant football coach at Clemson University under head coach Jess Neely. When Neely departed for Rice University in 1940, Howard was chosen as his replacement. As head coach, Howard directed the Clemson football program for the next thirty seasons (1940–1969), achieving a level of success that would not be surpassed at the school until the 1980s. Howard's teams compiled a 165–118–12 record, earned eight conference championships (two Southern, six Atlantic Coast), and appeared in six postseason bowl games, including the Sugar Bowl (1959) and two trips to the Orange Bowl (1951, 1957).

Howard brought attention to the Clemson football program as much with his personality as with victories. Howard's Alabama drawl, rotund shape, and constant tobacco chewing defined his country bumpkin image. On the after-dinner speaking circuit, Howard entertained listeners with colorful stories and wry one-liners. He also gave sportswriters fodder for their columns by carrying on mock feuds with his rival coaches in the southeast, especially Paul Dietzel at the University of South Carolina and D. C. "Peahead" Walker of Wake Forest.

Howard established several traditions that have become a part of the spectacle and pageantry associated with a Clemson football

Frank Howard. Courtesy, Clemson University Photograph Collection, Special Collections, Clemson University Libraries

game. The team's traditional entrance into the stadium by running down a hill at the east end zone began simply as the most convenient route to the field from nearby Fike Field House, where the team dressed. Later Clemson teams, who had the benefit of dressing rooms at the west end of the stadium, continued the tradition by boarding buses and riding back to the east end zone just before kickoff in order to make their ceremonial entrance into the stadium greeted by cheers and the school fight song, "Tiger Rag." Howard also established the tradition of the players rubbing "Howard's Rock" (mounted on a pedestal at the top of the hill) for luck as they entered the stadium. The rock, from Death Valley in California, was given to Howard by a friend after the Clemson Memorial Stadium earned the nickname "Death Valley," especially for opponents such as Presbyterian College and the University of Virginia which Clemson defeated with regularity. Howard never lost to Virginia, referring to them as the "white meat" on the annual football schedule.

Howard married Anna Tribble in 1933 and they had two children. He died on January 26, 1996, and was buried at Cemetery Hill, alongside many former Clemson presidents and faculty. Howard's final resting place on Cemetery Hill overlooks Memorial Stadium and the football field that bears his name. BRADLEY S. SAULS

Blackman, Sam, Bob Bradley, and Chuck Kriese. *Clemson: Where the Tigers Play.* Champaign, Ill.: Sports Publishing, 1999.

Bradley, Bob. *Death Valley Days: The Glory of Clemson Football.* Atlanta: Longstreet, 1991.

McLaurin, Jim. "Friends Hail the King of Clemson." Columbia *State,* January 27, 1996, pp. A1, A5.

Sahadi, Lou. *The Clemson Tigers from 1896 to Glory.* New York: Morrow, 1983.

Hub City Writers Project. A literary arts co-op founded in Spartanburg County in 1995 and modeled after the Depression-era Federal Writers Project, the Hub City Writers Project marshaled the talents of writers across South Carolina and beyond to create a series of books characterized by a strong sense of place. Founded at a coffee shop on Morgan Square in Spartanburg, the nonprofit organization was shepherded in its early years by the Wofford College poet John Lane, the journalists Betsy Teter and Gary Henderson, and the graphic designer / photographer Mark Olencki. From its beginning, Hub City's emphasis was place-based literature that encouraged readers to form a deeper connection with their home territory.

Hub City published in a variety of genres, including fiction, personal essay, poetry, nonfiction, biography, humor, nature writing, children's literature, and history. With its first title, *Hub City Anthology,* the fledgling press asked local authors to write about living in Spartanburg. Strong initial book sales led to a hefty base of charitable donors in the Spartanburg area, allowing Hub City to spread beyond the hometown borders. A 1998 title, *New Southern Harmonies: Four Emerging Fiction Writers,* featured stories by Rosa Shand, George Singleton, Scott Gould, and Deno Trakas, and was named best book of short fiction in North America by *Independent Publisher* magazine. In 2001, in a partnership with the South Carolina Arts Commission, Hub City published *Inheritance: Selections from the South Carolina Fiction Project.* Edited by Janette Turner Hospital, the writer in residence at the University of South Carolina, the collection featured thirty of the more than two hundred winning stories in the long-running state literary contest.

The success of the press led to national media attention, including articles in the *New York Times, Utne Reader,* and *Orion Afield,* and the spin-off of similar efforts in other parts of the country. Among other communities that used the Hub City model to create place-based literature were Beaufort, South Carolina; Flagstaff, Arizona; Fidalgo Island, Washington; and Charlotte, North Carolina.

Hub City's impact was particularly felt in Spartanburg, where the organization enlisted writers to chronicle the community's deep musical roots, vanishing peach farming culture, and complex cotton mill history, then hosted community-wide celebrations for each book's release. In 2000 funding from the National Endowment for the Arts spurred a multidisciplined environmental arts initiative focusing on a damaged local waterway, Lawson's Fork Creek. That same year thousands of residents attended a four-day, book-related festival. These projects and others spurred community activism and broad appreciation for local history and culture.

Hub City writers, who numbered more than 120 by 2003, annually made dozens of visits to schools, colleges, and clubs to encourage reading and creative writing. The organization offered scholarships to prestigious writing workshops to winners of an annual creative writing contest. Hub City sponsored community readings by national literary figures, including Barry Lopez and Janisse Ray, and in 2001 began offering its own regional writing workshop at Wofford College. In 2002 Hub City received the Governor's Elizabeth O'Neill Verner Award for outstanding contribution to the arts in South Carolina. BETSY TETER

Huck, Christian (?–1780). Soldier. Christian Huck, a Loyalist captain of dragoons under Banastre Tarleton, gained notoriety in South Carolina during the Revolutionary War for his vicious acts and excessive use of profanity. A Philadelphia lawyer, Huck was known for his intense hatred of all patriots, especially Scots-Irish Presbyterians, whom he considered the most sympathetic to the rebels. After joining the ranks of the British in New York, he commanded British outposts around Camden, South Carolina, and participated in other actions involving Tarleton's Legion.

In June 1780 Huck and a portion of his command were sent from Rocky Mount toward the vicinity of Fishing Creek to disperse the rebels in that area. Along the way Huck recruited three hundred Loyalists and burned the houses and plantations of known patriots who lived in the Catawba Valley of upper South Carolina. At Fishing Creek, Huck turned his force toward the local church in hopes of capturing Presbyterian pastor and patriot John Simpson. Not finding Simpson, the Tories burned his home to the ground. Huck's command continued its rampage in the New Acquisition District (York County) by destroying White's Mills on Fishing Creek and William Hill's Iron Works, a strategic source of cannon and ordnance for the patriots.

While Huck was wreaking havoc throughout the countryside, five hundred loosely organized patriots set out to find and destroy Huck. One patriot, John McClure, had his home destroyed by Huck, and his family was treated savagely and held as prisoners. One of his daughters managed to elude the captors and brought word to the American camp about the outrages that had occurred. With advance warning of the approach of the Tories and the knowledge of their whereabouts, the patriots went searching for Huck.

Before dawn on July 12, 1780, a force of 250 patriots commanded by Colonel William Bratton tracked Huck down at Williamson's Plantation, located a little more than fifty miles northeast of Camden in the New Acquisition District. Huck had camped his men on poor ground and failed to put out patrols or pickets. Although he had posted sentries on the road in front of the plantation house, they did not hear the approach of the rebels. As a result the Tories, many of whom were still asleep, were taken completely by surprise and easily defeated. When he tried to escape on horse bareback, Huck was shot in the neck and fell from his horse. The wound proved mortal, and Huck died later that day. The majority of his command were either captured or killed.

"Huck's Defeat"—as the battle at Williamson's Plantation came to be known—proved to the patriots that they could measure up to British regulars and that Tarleton's feared legion was not as imposing as they had once thought. After Huck's defeat the patriot ranks swelled with new recruits. KENDRA DEBANY

Buchanan, John. *The Road to Guilford Courthouse: The American Revolution in the Carolinas.* New York: Wiley, 1997.

Edgar, Walter. *Partisans and Redcoats: The Southern Conflict That Turned the Tide of the American Revolution.* New York: Morrow, 2001.

Morrill, Dan L. *Southern Campaigns of the American Revolution.* Baltimore: Nautical & Aviation Publishing, 1993.

Russell, David Lee. *The American Revolution in the Southern Colonies.* Jefferson, N.C.: McFarland, 2000.

Huger, Daniel Elliott (1779–1854). Jurist, U.S. senator. Born on January 28, 1779, on Limerick Plantation near Charleston, Huger was the only son of Daniel Huger, a member of the First United States Congress from South Carolina, and Sabina Elliott. The younger Huger graduated from the College of New Jersey (now Princeton University) in 1798. On November 26, 1800, he married Isabella Izard Middleton, daughter of Arthur Middleton, a signer of the Declaration of Independence. The marriage produced ten children.

Huger was admitted to the Charleston Bar in 1811. He practiced law and from 1803 until 1819 represented St. Andrew's Parish in the state House of Representatives, where he gained a reputation as one of its ablest and most respected members. Of Huger, John Belton O'Neall wrote that when he spoke, "all was silent, and his counsels generally prevailed." During this time he also attended to large landholdings throughout the state.

As a legislator, Huger vigorously espoused the doctrine of representative democracy over the doctrine of instruction by constituents. As a Federalist, he refused to follow his party's opposition to the War of 1812. In 1814 he was commissioned by the state as a brigadier general, but the war ended before his brigade was called up.

On December 11, 1819, Huger was elected judge of the Court of General Sessions and Common Pleas where he served until 1830, when he resigned to participate more actively in the nullification debate. He was again elected to the state House of Representatives, this time from the parishes of St. Philip's and St. Michael's. A Unionist delegate to the state nullification convention, Huger strongly opposed the Ordinance of Nullification in 1832 and 1833. After being defeated in that debate, Huger temporarily retired from politics to tend to his business interests, which included landholdings in Richland, Sumter, and Charleston Districts and approximately two hundred slaves. In 1838 he returned to politics as a state senator for St. Philip's and St. Michael's Parishes, serving for four years.

Following John C. Calhoun's resignation from the United States Senate in 1843 to serve as secretary of state in the cabinet of President John Tyler, Huger was elected by the legislature to take Calhoun's place as a states' rights Democrat. He served from March 4, 1843, until March 3, 1845, when he resigned to return the U.S. Senate seat to Calhoun.

In April 1852, as a delegate for St. Philip's and St. Michael's Parishes, Huger attended South Carolina's states' rights convention in Columbia, where he again urged moderation in the continuing debate over sectional interests. He held numerous other offices and memberships in professional and social organizations and was a trustee for both the College of Charleston and South Carolina College. Huger died on August 21, 1854, on Sullivan's Island, and was interred in Magnolia Cemetery, Charleston. JOHN L. NAPIER

Bailey, N. Louise, ed. *Biographical Directory of the South Carolina House of Representatives.* Vol. 4, *1791–1815.* Columbia: University of South Carolina Press, 1984.

O'Neall, John Belton. *Biographical Sketches of the Bench and Bar of South Carolina.* 2 vols. Charleston, S.C.: S. G. Courtney, 1859.

Huger, Isaac (1743–1797). Soldier. Huger was born on March 19, 1743, at Limerick Plantation on the Cooper River, the second son of Daniel Huger, a Huguenot merchant and planter, and Mary Cordes. The wealth of his family afforded Huger, along with his brothers, an education in Europe. Huger began his military career by serving as an officer in Colonel Thomas Middleton's Provincial South Carolina Regiment during the expedition against the Cherokees in the spring of 1761. On March 23, 1762, Huger married Elizabeth Chalmers. The couple had eight children.

While serving as a representative for the parishes of St. Philip's and St. Michael's in the First Provincial Congress, Huger was appointed a lieutenant colonel in the South Carolina militia and later commissioned a lieutenant colonel in the First South Carolina Regiment on June 17, 1775. He was promoted to colonel on September 16, 1776, and appointed commander of the Fifth South Carolina Regiment. On January 9, 1779, he was promoted to the rank of brigadier general in the Continental army.

Huger fought and was wounded at the Battle of Stono Ferry on June 20, 1779, and commanded the South Carolina and Georgia militia during the siege of Savannah on October 9, 1779. During the siege of Charleston in the spring of 1780, he was placed in command of the light horse and militia outside the city. A surprise attack by Lieutenant Colonel Banastre Tarleton's forces routed and dispersed Huger's troops at Moncks Corner on the morning of April 14, 1780. Illness kept Huger from capture with the surrender of Charleston, and he later rejoined the southern army under Major General Horatio Gates in North Carolina.

Huger was present when Major General Nathanael Greene took command of the Southern Department in Charlotte later in

December. Greene detached his light forces to the western parts of South Carolina and moved his regulars to a camp in the Cheraws, with Huger as his second in command. After the brilliant American victory at Cowpens, Huger was entrusted by Greene to lead the command posted in the Cheraws to rejoin the detached light forces in North Carolina. At the Battle of Guilford Courthouse on March 15, 1781, he commanded a brigade of Virginia Continental regiments and was slightly wounded in action. Commanding the same brigade at the Battle of Hobkirk Hill on April 25, Huger initially stood his ground after the unanticipated withdrawal of the right wing of the American line. With the retreat of the British from the interior to Charleston, Huger was reunited with his family and returned to his home, ending his military service.

Huger represented St. George's Dorchester Parish in the Jacksonborough Assembly in January 1782 and served in the legislature until his election as sheriff of Charleston District in 1785. Familial ties led to his appointment as the first federal marshal for South Carolina in 1789, a position which he held for five years. He died in Charleston on October 6, 1797. SAMUEL K. FORE

Edgar, Walter, and N. Louise Bailey, eds. *Biographical Directory of the South Carolina House of Representatives.* Vol. 2, *The Commons House of Assembly, 1692–1775.* Columbia: University of South Carolina Press, 1977.

Johnson, William. *Sketches of the Life and Correspondence of Nathanael Greene.* 2 vols. 1822. Reprint, New York: Da Capo, 1973.

Moultrie, William. *Memoirs of the American Revolution.* 1802. Reprint, New York: New York Times, 1968.

Huguenot Church (Charleston). Located at 140 Church Street, the French Protestant (Huguenot) Church was the first Gothic Revival ecclesiastical building erected in Charleston, representing a shift away from the conservative styling that had traditionally characterized the city's religious buildings. Construction began in 1844 and was completed the following year. It was designed by Edward B. White and is built of brick finished in stucco. The overall composition lacks the intricate stone sculptural details characteristic of the Gothic architecture of medieval Europe, but blends harmoniously with the color palette and visual textures of Charleston's built environment. The gable form is ornamented with buttresses topped with cast-iron pinnacles, lancet windows, and a crenellated parapet. On the interior, the entry vestibule is separated from the nave by an ingeniously designed screen of sliding wood panels set in pointed arch frames. The vaulted plaster ceiling is embellished with rosette bosses. Liturgical tablets and marble memorial plaques dedicated to Huguenot families line the walls.

Huguenot Church. Courtesy, South Carolina Department of Archives and History

The church was damaged in 1864 during the siege of Charleston and nearly destroyed during the 1886 earthquake. Following a restoration, it became a shrine to all Huguenot settlers of the New World and received only limited use for most of the twentieth century. Descendants of the original members returned to the church in the early 1980s, rehabilitated the building, and instituted a regular schedule of weekly services and programs. The building was designated a National Historic Landmark by the U.S. Department of the Interior in 1973. DANIEL J. VIVIAN

Lane, Mills. *Architecture of the Old South: South Carolina.* Savannah, Ga.: Beehive, 1984.

Poston, Jonathan H. *The Buildings of Charleston: A Guide to the City's Architecture.* Columbia: University of South Carolina Press, 1997.

Severens, Kenneth. *Charleston Antebellum Architecture and Civic Destiny.* Knoxville: University of Tennessee Press, 1988.

Huguenots. Huguenots are French Calvinists. The origins of the term "Huguenot" is uncertain, but historians believe it comes from the Swiss-German word *Eidgenossen,* meaning "confederates," in reference to the Genevan rebellion against the Duke of Savoy in the sixteenth century. The French Reformed church was formally founded in 1559 with the underground meeting of the first national synod in Paris. In the 1560s the Huguenot church reached a peak in terms of the number of congregations and followers (nearly two million) and political and economic influence. However, the Wars of Religion (1562–1598) put an end to this phenomenal growth and permanently weakened the Huguenot church. It was during this tumultuous period of French history that Huguenot privateer and explorer Jean Ribaut led a small group to Parris Island, South Carolina, where they founded the short-lived settlement of Charlesfort (1562–1563). The Edict of Nantes (1598) restored peace to the kingdom and guaranteed the Huguenots religious and civil rights while reaffirming the preeminence of Catholicism.

Throughout the seventeenth century, the Huguenot church went through a period of decline and became increasingly peripheral to France's economic, political, and religious life. This marginalization accelerated in the 1670s and 1680s, when Louis XIV (1643–1715) made religious reunification one of his priorities. At first Huguenots were locally challenged in court about the legitimacy of their churches and banned from certain guilds. Daytime funerals and psalm singing outside the church were outlawed. Violence soon followed legal harassment when, starting in Poitou in 1681, provincial governors were authorized to use military force to obtain conversions. These campaigns, called *dragonnades,* ravaged major Protestant provinces and Huguenots converted by the thousands. Believing that the Huguenot church had become an empty shell, Louis XIV revoked the Edict of Nantes in October 1685, thereby outlawing Calvinism in France. The Huguenots, who by then numbered nearly 800,000, faced a painful choice. They could remain in France and convert to Catholicism(or resist royal policy at the risk of being imprisoned, sent to a convent [women], or the galleys); or flee the kingdom. The majority, about 600,000, chose to recant their faith in the hope of practicing their Calvinism in secret, and a significant number, between 160,000 and 200,000, fled France. A small minority, less than 10,000, refused to recant or leave and were imprisoned, executed, or committed to life sentence in the galleys or to the convents.

The Huguenot migration to South Carolina is part of a larger diaspora, traditionally known as *le Refuge,* which stretches from the late 1670s to the early 1710s. An overwhelming majority of Huguenot refugees opted to settle in France's Protestant neighboring countries, where French Reformed churches had been founded by Huguenot and Walloon (Belgian Calvinist) refugees in the late 1500s. About 60,000 Huguenots emigrated to the Netherlands, 50,000 to England (5,000 of whom eventually moved to Ireland), 40,000 settled in the German States, principally in the Rhineland and Prussia, and about 25,000 relocated in the Swiss Cantons. While the decision to flee was conditioned by a multiplicity of factors, such as age, education, financial resources, and the availability of familial networks, the choice of a destination was often dictated by geographic proximity, and in some cases, influenced by promotional literature. A small number of Huguenots chose to settle overseas. About 2,500 relocated in British North America; New York (800), Virginia (700), South Carolina (500), and New England (300), and a few, about 300, in Dutch South Africa. In the eighteenth century additional groups of Huguenots and Swiss Calvinists settled in South Carolina where they founded the Purrysburg (1732) and Hillsborough (1764) townships, the latter sometimes referred to as New Bordeaux.

The Lords Proprietors originally intended to draw Huguenots to South Carolina to develop silk, wine, and olive oil production, while peopling their colony without weakening the mother country. Between 1679 and 1686 the proprietors had six French promotional pamphlets published in cities, such as London, The Hague, and Geneva, where large numbers of refugees congregated. These tracts presented an Edenic portrait of South Carolina in emphasizing its fertile soil, bountiful rivers, healthy climate, and balanced political system. Huguenots were attracted to Carolina primarily by the promise of cheap land, commercial opportunities, and religious freedom. Except for the arrival of a small group in 1680, the majority of Huguenots settled in the colony between 1684 and 1688, while a handful of refugees came from other colonies, in British North America and the British Caribbean, in the early 1700s. Most refugees were merchants and artisans from France's western provinces, such as Aunis, Saintonge, Poitou, Normandy, and Brittany; and coastal cities, such as La Rochelle, Dieppe, and Le Havre. While a few of them settled in Goose Creek and in the parish of St. John's Berkeley, the Huguenots who came during the proprietary period founded three communities in the lowcountry before 1690. The most important was that of Charleston, where a congregation was founded in 1680 and a church was built in 1687. Huguenots also settled up the Cooper River in Orange Quarter. The third settlement, French Santee, was located south of the Santee River in present-day Georgetown County.

Beyond individual and local resistance, the Huguenot experience in South Carolina was characterized by a rapid and complete integration into Anglo-American society. In 1706 both the Orange Quarter and Santee churches became Anglican parishes under the respective names of St. Denis and St. James Santee, while Charleston Huguenots gradually drifted toward St. Philip's. By the 1730s and 1740s most second-generation Huguenots had virtually abandoned the use of the French language and many, especially among the most affluent, had intermarried with families of British origin.

In 1885 the Charleston-based Huguenot Society of South Carolina was founded to preserve the state's Huguenot memory through the publication of its journal, *Transactions;* the erection of markers wherever Huguenots settled in the state; and the sponsoring of commemorative events. With the Charleston Huguenot Church (1845), the Middleburg Plantation (1697), and the Hanover House (ca. 1716), South Carolina possesses a remarkable Huguenot architectural heritage and with historical figures such as Francis Marion, Gabriel Manigault, and Henry and John Laurens, a true Huguenot pantheon. BERTRAND VAN RUYMBEKE

Baird, Charles W. *History of the Huguenot Emigration to America.* 2 vols. New York: Dodd, Mead, 1885.

Benedict, Philip. *The Huguenot Population of France, 1600–1685: The Demographic Fate and Customs of a Religious Minority.* Philadelphia: American Philosophical Society, 1991.

Butler, Jon. *The Huguenots in America: A Refugee People in New World Society.* Cambridge: Harvard University Press, 1983.

Friedlander, Amy E. "Carolina Huguenots: A Study in Cultural Pluralism in the Low Country, 1679–1768." Ph.D. diss., Emory University, 1979.

Hirsch, Arthur Henry. *The Huguenots of Colonial South Carolina.* 1928. Reprint, Columbia: University of South Carolina Press, 1999.

Van Ruymbeke, Bertrand. "The Huguenots of Proprietary South Carolina: Patterns of Migration and Integration." In *Money, Trade, and Power, The Evolution of South Carolina Plantation Society,* edited by Jack P. Greene, Rosemary Brana-Shute, and Randy J. Sparks. Columbia: University of South Carolina Press, 2001.

Van Ruymbeke, Bertrand, and Randy J. Sparks, eds. *Memory and Identity: The Huguenots in France and the Atlantic Diaspora.* Columbia: University of South Carolina Press, 2003.

Hume, Sophia Wigington (ca. 1702–1774). Minister, writer. Sophia Hume was born to a wealthy Charleston couple, Henry Wigington and Susanna Bayley. Though her maternal grandmother, Mary Fisher, was a well-known Quaker minister, Hume was raised in the Anglican faith of her father and did not embrace Quakerism until midlife. She lived as a typical young Charleston belle, displaying her fine clothes and jewelry at balls, the theater, and other social functions. On June 15, 1721, she married the Charleston attorney Robert Hume. The marriage produced two children before Robert's death in 1737.

Around 1740 Hume, now a widow and extremely ill, reexamined her Anglican faith as well as her life of luxury. She embraced a life of simplicity, moved to London, and joined the Society of Friends. Hume returned to Charleston in late 1747, convinced of the need to warn her neighbors and others of their erring ways. She spent the rest of her life inspiring others through her religious writings and dedication to the Quaker faith. Hume spoke at public meetings and helped revitalize a small Quaker community in Charleston. However, her call to exchange luxury for simplicity fell largely on deaf ears in the port city. In 1748 she traveled to Philadelphia, where she published *An Exhortation to the Inhabitants of the Province of South-Carolina* (1748), in which she defended her theological views and her conversion. To broaden the appeal of her message, Hume used biblical as well as Quaker and non-Quaker religious writers as her sources. She returned to London, where for the next twenty years she continued to write and gain stature in the English Quaker community.

She visited Charleston again in 1767 in an attempt to reinvigorate the moribund Quaker community but achieved little before ill health forced her return to London the following year.

Hume wrote several religious treatises: *An Epistle to the Inhabitants of South Carolina* (1754), *A Caution to Such as Observe Days and Times* (ca. 1763), *A Short Appeal to Men and Women of Reason* (1765), *Extracts from Divers Ancient Testimonies* (1766), *The Justly Celebrated Mrs. Sophia Hume's Advice and Warning to Labourers* (1769). Her writings augmented her preaching, as she continually struggled to reconcile traditional gender expectations with her own career and public visibility. She died in London on January 26, 1774, and was buried in Friends' Burial Ground near Bunhill Field.
KAY J. BLALOCK

Hume, Sophia. *An Exhortation to the Inhabitants of the Province of South-Carolina, to Bring Their Deeds to the Light of Christ, in Their Own Consciences.* Philadelphia: William Bradford, [1748].

———. Papers. Department of Records, Philadelphia Yearly Meeting, Philadelphia.

Humphreys, Josephine (b. 1945). Novelist. Born in Charleston on February 2, 1945, Humphreys is the daughter of William Wirt Humphreys, a corporate board director, and Martha Lynch. She attended schools in Charleston and enrolled at Duke University, where the author Reynolds Price served as her mentor. After receiving her bachelor of arts degree in English in 1967, she went on to Yale University, where she earned a master of arts degree the following year. On November 30, 1968, she married the attorney Thomas A. Hutcheson. She studied at the University of Texas at Austin from 1968 to 1970, returning to Charleston to teach at Baptist College (now Charleston Southern University) from 1970 to 1977. She has two sons, Allen and William.

Josephine Humphreys. © David G. Spielman-97, New Orleans

Drawing praise for its finely honed language and strong characters, Humphreys's first novel, *Dreams of Sleep* (1984) won the Ernest Hemingway Prize for a first book of fiction. The story concerns Alice Reese and her husband Will (a Charleston gynecologist), who have two daughters. When Alice learns that Will is having an affair with his receptionist, she hires Iris Moon as a babysitter to allow herself time away from home. Iris, a teenager from a troubled home but mature beyond her years, idealizes the Reese family and becomes an unlikely catalyst in saving the marriage.

Humphreys's second novel, *Rich in Love* (1987), also depicts a family in crisis and a precocious teenager, in this case the lively narrator Lucille Odom, who Humphreys acknowledged to be modeled after Iris Moon. Lucille's mother abandons her and her father, her pregnant sister Rae returns home to Charleston unhappily married, and Lucille breaks up with her boyfriend. Out of these troubled relationships comes some resolution in Lucille's increased independence and her realization that she is "rich in love." The 1992 film adaptation of the novel starred Katherine Erbe, Albert Finney, and Jill Clayburgh.

Although Humphreys makes no attempt to capture the exact geography of Charleston, her first two novels bring the city to life, touching on its beauty, traditions, and troubled past as it clashes with the new developments on its fringes. Her third novel, *The Fireman's Fair* (1991), also takes the Charleston environs as its setting. Here Humphreys writes from the point of view of bachelor Rob Wyatt, who at age thirty-five decides to quit his law practice. He then meets Billie Poe, a refugee from a bad marriage and also a breath of fresh air for Rob. Billie, as does Iris in *Dreams of Sleep*, has a maturity that belies her age.

In 1994 Humphreys collaborated with the pseudonymous Ruthie Bolton on *Gal: A True Story*, an account of Ruthie's deeply troubled childhood and near miraculous escape into a stable life in Charleston. *Nowhere Else on Earth* (2000), as does Humphreys's previous work, concerns a family in crisis, but in this case the threat derives from racial violence, and the setting is fictitious Scuffletown, North Carolina, at the end of the Civil War. The narrator, Rhoda Strong, is another of the author's memorable and enduring women.
KEN AUTREY

Magee, Rosemary M. "Continuity and Separation: An Interview with Josephine Humphreys." *Southern Review* 27 (autumn 1991): 792–802.

Hunter, Jane Edna Harris (1882–1971). Nurse, social worker. Hunter was born on Woodburn Farm Plantation, near Pendleton, on December 13, 1882, the second of four children of the sharecroppers Edward Harris and Harriet Milner. Briefly educated in a one-room schoolhouse and at a Baptist church school, Hunter moved in with an aunt in 1893 on her father's death. The change in family circumstances eventually meant that Hunter had to enter the workforce. Initially employed as a domestic with a family in Aiken in exchange for room and board, Hunter was treated so badly that neighbors complained. A family in Anderson proved more kind, and one of the daughters taught Hunter to write her name and to read nursery rhymes. In 1896 two African American Presbyterian missionaries who ran a school in Abbeville arranged for Hunter to work her way through Ferguson Academy (now Ferguson-Williams College). She graduated in 1900. About the same time, at the urging of her mother, she married a man forty years her senior, Edward Hunter. The marriage lasted only fifteen months and produced no children.

With her husband's blessing, Hunter moved to Charleston to work in the home of Benjamin Rutledge. In this city she encountered Ella Hunt, an African American Ladies Auxiliary worker. Hunt encouraged the younger woman to pursue a career in nursing and helped Hunter gain admittance in 1902 to the Cannon Street Hospital and Training School for Nurses in Charleston. Her experience in the slums of the city imbued Hunter with a powerful desire to help her fellow blacks escape such deplorable conditions. To gain additional nursing skills, Hunter transferred to the Dixie Hospital and Training School at Hampton Institute in Hampton, Virginia, in 1904.

With her nursing degree in hand, Hunter moved to Cleveland, Ohio, in 1905 because the city purportedly offered good employment opportunities for blacks. Reality did not match rumor and Hunter paid her bills through cleaning jobs while continually attempting to secure private duty nursing positions. Her difficulties, as a southern African American woman attempting to adjust to northern urban life, prompted Hunter to open the Phillis Wheatley Home in 1913, named for the African American slave poet. A strong supporter of Booker T. Washington and his philosophy of industrial education, Hunter housed young black women in the Phillis Wheatley Home and trained them in various professions. The home became the largest independent residence facility for African American women in the United States, but it was not without controversy. Hunter's policy of directing the settlement house's employment bureau to steer black women into domestic service led to allegations that she was contributing to the second-class status accorded blacks. In her 1940 autobiography *A Nickel and a Prayer,* Hunter emphasized that she opposed assimilation and preferred a separate but equal existence for whites and blacks. Forced to retire in 1946, Hunter's final years were marred by mental incapacity. She died in Cleveland on January 19, 1971. CARYN E. NEUMANN

Hunter, Jane Edna. *A Nickel and a Prayer.* Cleveland: Elli Kani, 1940.

Jones, Adrienne Lash. *Jane Edna Hunter: A Case Study of Black Leadership, 1910–1950.* Brooklyn, N.Y.: Carlson, 1990.

Hunter, John (?–1802). Congressman, U.S. senator. Little is known about Hunter's early life. His date of birth and parents are unknown. He engaged in preparatory studies before pursuing agriculture interests near the present-day town of Newberry. He owned considerable real estate, including 640 acres on Twenty Three Mile and Eighteen Mile Creeks in Pendleton District as well as landholdings in other locations. In 1785 Hunter won election to the General Assembly from the Little River District (modern Laurens County) and served until 1790. In 1788 he sat as a delegate from Little River at the state convention to ratify the U.S. Constitution, which he supported. He attended the state constitutional convention in 1790 and served on the committee of privileges. The following year Hunter was elected as the first representative to the General Assembly from the newly created Laurens County. In 1793 he was elected to Congress by the voters of Ninety Six District. After losing a U.S. Senate bid in 1794, Hunter was subsequently chosen by the General Assembly to complete the unexpired term of U.S. Senator Pierce Butler. Taking his seat on January 27, 1797, Hunter served in the U.S. Senate until November 26, 1798, when he resigned and returned to his agriculture pursuits. He served as a presidential elector for the George Washington–John Adams ticket in 1792 and for the Thomas Jefferson–Aaron Burr ticket in 1800. Hunter died in December 1802 and was buried in the Presbyterian Church cemetery at Little River, Newberry County. He was survived by his wife, Sarah, and nine children. VERONICA BRUCE MCCONNELL

Bailey, N. Louise, and Elizabeth Ivey Cooper, eds. *Biographical Directory of the South Carolina House of Representatives.* Vol. 3, *1775–1790.* Columbia: University of South Carolina Press, 1981.

Hunter-Gault, Charlayne (b. 1942). Journalist, civil rights activist. Charlayne Hunter-Gault was born on February 27, 1942, in Due West, the daughter of Charles and Althea Hunter. Raised in Covington, Georgia, then Atlanta, Hunter-Gault attended Wayne State University in Detroit, Michigan, before a judge allowed her and a male classmate to desegregate the University of Georgia. In 1963 she became the first African American woman to graduate from the school. It was the first of many firsts for one of the nation's groundbreaking minority journalists. After a fellowship, she joined WRC-TV in Washington, D.C., as a reporter and news anchor. She worked as the "Talk of the Town" reporter for the *New Yorker* magazine from 1963 to 1968. She joined the reporting staff of the *New York Times* in 1968, creating the newspaper's Harlem bureau and convincing the newspaper's editor to use the term "black" instead of "Negro." She joined public television's "The MacNeil/Lehrer Report" in 1978 as a correspondent, winning many national awards for her reporting on "Apartheid's People," a special series on the struggle for civil rights in South Africa. Later she worked for National Public Radio as the chief African correspondent, and joined CNN in 1999 as the news network's Johannesburg bureau chief. Her 1992 book, *In My Place,* is a memoir of her growing up in the South and recounts her experiences at the University of Georgia. She married twice, first to Walter Stovall in 1963, then to Ron Gault in 1971. The marriages produced a daughter and a son, respectively. She lives in Johannesburg, South Africa. ALAN RICHARD

Hunter-Gault, Charlayne. *In My Place.* New York: Farrar Straus Giroux, 1992.

Hunting. Hunting has long been an important component of the Palmetto State's culture. Indians hunted a wide assortment of game from as early as 13,000 B.C.E. until well after English colonization. They pursued deer, mountain lions, raccoon, rabbit, bear, and other animals for meat and skins, while taking birds for food and feathers. Colonists, too, depended on game for survival. Much of the eighteenth-century trade between Indians and colonists, as well as between the colony and England, was based on animal skins. By the time of the Revolutionary War, however, Carolinians increasingly saw hunting as sport. They also recognized the detrimental effects of unrestricted hunting, and enacted laws to restrict night hunting and to establish seasons for different game animals.

At the turn of the twentieth century, wealthy northern sportsmen discovered the superb hunting grounds of the Carolina lowcountry. Courtesy, South Caroliniana Library, University of South Carolina

Antebellum hunters continued to take game for sport, for food, to protect livestock and crops, and to fulfill their cultural traditions. Planters emulated the English gentry through their choice of game (pursuing deer but not opossum, for example) and by style (hunting on horseback and using firearms). They involved their slaves as hunt masters, dog handlers, and assistants. In some cases slaves hunted for themselves and their families with permission; in others they hunted in secret. Poorer whites hunted for similar reasons if not always for the same game or in the same style as planters. Many yeoman and planters disdained the "pothunters" who hunted for a living and paid little heed to laws and seasons. Efforts to toughen state laws on hunting and increase enforcement met with little success until after the Civil War.

Hunting traditions persisted into the twentieth century despite many changes in the economic and social order of South Carolina. Some planters held on to their plantations primarily for hunting purposes even after abandoning agriculture and taking up residence in the cities. Wealthy northerners purchased plantations in the lowcountry in the 1920s as preserves to hunt deer, quail, and waterfowl. Working-class whites and blacks created formal and informal hunting clubs especially to pool resources and rent hunting land. Clubs tended to be segregated by race and class and, until recently, usually excluded women.

During the twentieth century the state took a more direct and scientific role in developing rules and regulations for hunting. Since 1994 wildlife research, policy development, and law enforcement have been under the auspices of the Department of Natural Resources (SCDNR). Paralleling the growth of the state infrastructure for research and enforcement has been the rise of nongovernmental organizations interested in the preservation of hunting traditions and wildlife. Prominent examples include Ducks Unlimited and the National Wild Turkey Federation, based in Edgefield. Competitive hunting in the form of field trials is now popular as seen at the Grand American, the nation's largest raccoon-hunting field trial, held annually in Orangeburg.

The supply and distribution of game around the state varied historically, affected by geography, land-use patterns, and changes in agricultural practice. In the middle of the twentieth century, mechanized agriculture reduced habitat for quail, which appear in smaller numbers in the state today. Conversely, the decline in the overall importance of agriculture led hunters and landowners to manage land to encourage wildlife by planting food plots and altering tree-harvesting and control-burning practices.

Hunting remains one of the state's most important forms of outdoor recreation, incorporating new technologies into traditional practices. Hunters have access to warmer, lighter camouflage clothing, synthetic calls for deer and fowl, CB radios, satellite-based navigation, and all-terrain vehicles. While some hunters have embraced the development of better weapons such as high-powered rifles with light-gathering scopes, others feel these advanced weapons take the challenge out of the hunt, and instead use so-called primitive weapons such as compound bows.

Hunting is a big business in the state, combining the impact of expenditures on arms, clothing, fuel, dogs, new technologies, land leases, and licenses. In 1996 SCDNR reported receipts from hunting licenses purchased by South Carolinians totaled more than $4 million. A further indication of South Carolina's continued attractiveness to out-of-state hunters is the more than $2.5 million that visiting sportsmen paid for licenses that year.

One result of the important role of hunting in South Carolina's culture has been the development of a body of literature and art. Though never a permanent resident of the state, John James Audubon collaborated with Carolinians such as Maria Martin Bachman on his famous *Birds of America* during the 1830s. The pioneering work on hunting and fishing in the state is William Elliott's *Carolina Sports by Land and Water,* first printed in 1846. In the twentieth century Archibald Rutledge, first poet laureate of South Carolina, continued the tradition of the planter-sportsman established by Elliot through his popular books *Plantation Game Trails* (1921) and *Home by the River* (1941). More recently, Havilah Babcock penned several memoirs of the sporting life, including *My Health Is Better in November* (1947) and *Tales of Quails'n Such* (1951). JAMES H. TUTEN

Babcock, Havilah. *My Health Is Better in November: Thirty-five Stories of Hunting and Fishing in the South.* 1947. Reprint, Columbia: University of South Carolina Press, 1985.

Elliot, William. *William Elliot's Carolina Sports by Land and Water.* 1846. Reprint. Columbia: University of South Carolina Press, 1994.

Marks, Stuart A. *Southern Hunting in Black and White: Nature, History, and Rituals in a Carolina Community.* Princeton, N.J.: Princeton University Press, 1991.

Proctor, Nicholas. *Bathed in Blood: Hunting and Mastery in the Old South.* Charlottesville: University Press of Virginia, 2002.

Hurricanes. The term "hurricane" comes from the West Indian word "huracan," which means "big wind" and is used to describe severe tropical cyclones in the Atlantic Ocean, Gulf of Mexico, Caribbean Sea, and the eastern Pacific Ocean. In the western Pacific, hurricanes are known as typhoons. The development of a hurricane requires an area of low pressure in a region of favorable atmospheric and oceanic conditions. Ocean temperatures must be near or greater than 80° F and wind speeds at mid- and upper-levels of the atmosphere must be light. At the center of the hurricane is the eye, a region of calm winds and subsiding air immediately surrounded by the most violent winds and precipitation called the eye wall. The counterclockwise rotation of cyclones in the Northern Hemisphere creates spiraling rain bands that span outward from the center. The outer rain bands of a hurricane, which can extend over an area three hundred to five hundred miles in width, contain the highest wind and heaviest precipitation away from the eye wall.

In 1989 the eye of Hurricane Hugo crossed the coast near McClellanville, where it tossed these shrimp boats around like so many toys. Photograph by Bill Scroggins. Courtesy, Myrtle Beach *Sun-News*

As the Northern Hemisphere summer approaches, more direct sunlight and longer daylight hours allow tropical oceans to warm sufficiently to support hurricane development. For that reason hurricane season runs from June 1 to November 30 each year in the Atlantic Ocean, Gulf of Mexico, and Caribbean Sea. During this time South Carolina is susceptible to land-falling tropical cyclones ranging in strength from tropical depressions (sustained winds less than 39 mph) to tropical storms (winds of 39 to 73 mph) and hurricanes (winds of 74 mph or higher). Hurricanes are classified into five categories using the Saffir-Simpson scale based on maximum sustained winds, minimum central pressure, storm surge, and damage. Between 1900 and 2004, fifteen hurricanes hit South Carolina directly, making the average landfall once every seven years. Three of the fifteen hurricanes have reached major hurricane status of category 3, 4, or 5 on the Saffir-Simpson scale. The average for any

The Tip-Top Inn, a Pawley's Island landmark, was a victim of Hugo's 135-mph winds and twenty-foot storm surge. Photograph by Bill Scroggins. Courtesy, Myrtle Beach *Sun-News*

tropical storm or hurricane landfall in South Carolina is once every four to five years. Storms that make landfall along the Gulf of Mexico, Georgia, and North Carolina coastline often impact South Carolina as well. The primary threats from hurricanes in South Carolina include storm surge, high winds, rainfall-induced flooding, and tornadoes.

The storm surge develops as high winds pile up water ahead of hurricanes and low pressure near the center causes the sea level to rise. On September 22, 1989, Hurricane Hugo made landfall near Sullivan's Island with a storm surge of twenty feet in Bulls Bay. Storm surge reports of ten to fourteen feet were reported along the entire coastline from Folly Beach to Myrtle Beach. The maximum sustained winds just before landfall in Hugo were estimated at 140 mph. The damage from Hugo was catastrophic with an estimated $10 billion damage from the Caribbean to the U.S. mainland. In South Carolina hurricane force winds were reported inland as far north as York County. Shaw Air Force Base in Sumter experienced winds of 66 mph with gusts to 108 mph. Thousands of acres in the Francis Marion and Sumter National Forest were destroyed.

Thirty years earlier Hurricane Gracie hit Beaufort on September 29, 1959, with 125 mph winds and gusts to 150 mph. The storm surge associated with Gracie was less severe than with Hugo since the hurricane made landfall within an hour of low tide. Rainfall amounts with Gracie totaled three to eight inches in South Carolina and flooding of streams and rivers occurred well inland along the Appalachian Mountains. The main threat from Hurricane Gracie was the high winds and potential for tornadoes. Damage in South Carolina reached an estimated $14 million, with more than half the amount in Charleston County alone. The preliminary report from the Hurricane Warning Center in Miami (now the National Hurricane Center) described the damage as "the worst from a hurricane in the history of Beaufort, South Carolina." Ten deaths were attributed to the storm in South Carolina, primarily due to downed trees and power lines and automobile accidents.

With a forward speed of more than 30 mph and winds more than 130 mph, Hurricane Hazel moved inland near Little River at the border between North and South Carolina on October 15, 1954. Wind gusts were observed to reach 106 mph at Myrtle Beach where more than 170 miles of piers and beachfront property from the Grand Strand northward to near Wilmington, North Carolina, were destroyed. A seventeen-foot storm surge was responsible for $61 million in beach damages, with another $100 million reported inland due to flooding and high winds. Twenty people drowned due to rainfall-induced flooding across the Carolinas as ten to twelve inches of rain fell in the mountainous terrain.

Perhaps the most remarkable storm in South Carolina's hurricane history occurred prior to 1900. Termed the "Great Storm of 1893," the late-August hurricane made landfall along the southern coast with little or no warning. A tremendous storm surge and high winds were responsible for more than two thousand deaths.

In 2004 South Carolina experienced one of the busiest tropical seasons on record with six storms affecting the state throughout the summer. Hurricane Charley became the first direct landfall from a hurricane in fifteen years as the storm made landfall near Cape Romain as a category 1 storm. South Carolina had not experienced a direct hurricane landfall since Hurricane Hugo in September 1989. Less than a month later, Hurricane Gaston, also a category 1 storm, moved inland over the same area. For only the second time since 1900, two hurricanes made landfall in South Carolina during a single Atlantic Basin hurricane season. The last time was in 1959 when Hurricane Cindy preceded the ravaging effects of Hurricane Gracie.

Since Hugo in 1989, the coastal population of South Carolina has increased by nearly 150,000 citizens and the tourist population during the summer months has increased significantly. Storm surge remains the leading potential killer in tropical cyclones along the coast, while inland rain-induced flooding with tropical storms is the most underrated killer with the most observed casualties. In 1999 Hurricane Floyd made landfall in North Carolina but generated floods of one-hundred-year and five-hundred-year proportions in northeastern South Carolina along the Pee Dee, Waccamaw, and Lumber Rivers. See plate 36. SOUTH CAROLINA STATE CLIMATOLOGY OFFICE

Saffir-Simpson Hurricane Scale

Category	*Central Pressure* (millibars)	(inches)	*Winds (m.p.h.)*	*Surge (feet)*	*Examples in S.C.*
1	>980	>29.94	74–95	4–9	"Bob (1985), Cindy (1959)"
2	965–979	28.50–	96–110	6–8	unnamed (1947)
3	945–964	27.91–	111–130	9–12	Gracie (1959)
4	920–944	27.17–	131–155	13–18	Hugo (1989)
5	<920	<27.17	>155	>18	none reported

Marscher, Bill, and Fran Marscher. *The Great Sea Island Storm of 1893.* Macon, Ga.: Mercer University Press, 2004.

Mercantini, Jonathan. "The Great Carolina Hurricane of 1752." *South Carolina Historical Magazine* 103 (October 2002): 351–65.

Purvis, John J., Wes Tyler, and Scott F. Sidlow. *Hurricanes Affecting South Carolina.* Columbia: South Carolina State Climatology Office, 1986.

Hutty, Alfred Heber (1877–1954). Artist. Hutty was born in Grand Haven, Michigan, on September 16, 1877. He grew up in Kansas and at age fifteen won a scholarship to the St. Louis School of Fine Arts. He supported himself by working in a stained glass studio in St. Louis until 1907. He then moved east to attend the summer school of the Art Students League in Woodstock, New York, where the tonalist landscape painter Birge Harrison became his mentor. Hutty obtained a position with the Tiffany Glass Studios, working on commission while living in Woodstock.

In 1919, in pursuit of a warmer place to spend winters, Hutty discovered Charleston, and until three years before his death, he alternated residences between Woodstock in the summer and Charleston in the winter. From 1920 until 1924 he served as the first director of the School of the Carolina Art Association at the Gibbes

Jenkins Band, by Alfred Hutty. Drypoint on paper. Courtesy, Gibbes Museum of Art / Carolina Art Association

Art Gallery. In 1923 he became one of the founding members of the Charleston Etchers' Club. His oil paintings of Charleston streetscapes and lowcountry gardens are impressionistic, a stylistic approach ideally suited to the floral splendor of spring foliage. However, he earned greater fame for his etchings and drypoints. In 1929 the noted art connoisseur and collector Duncan Phillips wrote a small monograph on Hutty. The volume was the second in a series on American etchers and reflects the burgeoning national interest in prints. Phillips discussed Hutty's considerable talent with rendering trees of all kinds, and equated some of his Charleston prints to the work of DuBose Heyward. As a seasonal resident of Charleston from the 1920s through the 1940s, Hutty is closely identified with the Charleston Renaissance.

Unlike the other leading figures—Alice Ravenel Huger Smith, Elizabeth O'Neill Verner, and Anna Heyward Taylor—Hutty was not a native South Carolinian, and he was the only man making art full-time. He aggressively marketed his work, mounting annual exhibitions at the newly opened Fort Sumter Hotel, hoping to appeal to the growing number of tourists. Unlike his female counterparts, Hutty rarely idealized the city and its residents, choosing instead to show the decay and decrepitude that lay around him. His proficiency with drypoint—an enhancement of the etching technique, which created rich, inky lines—complemented his rendering of live oaks draped with Spanish moss, dilapidated old buildings, and animated African Americans. Hutty maintained his press in the old kitchen house of his property at 46 Tradd Street, and from time to time he took on students. He was also active in the local theater group, the Footlight Players. The Gibbes Museum of Art owns the largest public collection of his work, the gift of his widow. His estate and archive, including plates and many trial proofs of his etchings, belong to Carolina Fine Paintings and Prints, Charleston. Other repositories of his work include the Columbia Museum of Art, the Greenville County Museum of Art, the Library of Congress, and the Boston Public Library. Hutty died on June 17, 1954, in Woodstock. MARTHA R. SEVERENS

Phillips, Duncan. *American Etchers.* Vol. 2, *Alfred Hutty.* New York: T. Spencer Hutson, 1929.

Saunders, Boyd, and Ann McAden. *Alfred Hutty and the Charleston Renaissance.* Orangeburg, S.C.: Sandlapper, 1990.

Hyer, Helen von Kolnitz (1896–1983). Poet, writer. Hyer was born on December 30, 1896, in Charleston, to George von Kolnitz and Sarah Holmes. She attended Simmons College from 1917 to 1918 and married Edward Hyer in 1921. The couple had four daughters. From childhood she had a love of poetry and memorized poems from a book of nineteenth-century English verse, reciting them to visitors at her grandparents' home in Mount Pleasant. At Ashley Hall in Charleston, one of her poems was selected as the school song. Hyer won youth poetry prizes as well. Her first poem appeared in *Romance* when she was seventeen; she then was published several times in *Adventure Magazine.*

Hyer joined the Poetry Society of South Carolina in 1920. Although younger than most group members, she impressed her peers. "What really burnt them up was our first poetry contest," Hyer recalled. "I won it; they didn't think a young girl should win." Her first poetry collection, *Santee Songs,* was published in 1923. That volume was followed by *Wine Dark Sea* (1930), *The Wimp and the Woodle, and Other Stories* (1935), *Danger Never Sleeps* (1970), and *What the Wind Forgets a Woman's Heart Remembers* (1975). During her more than fifty years of writing poetry, Hyer's work also appeared in magazines such as *Poet Lore, Argosy,* and the *Christian Science Monitor.*

In 1974 Hyer became South Carolina's second poet laureate—a fitting honor for a poet whose work reflected a deep love for her state. Frequent topics of Hyer's verse include Confederate heroes, South Carolina history, and southern romance. Tennyson and his theme of Camelot was one of her poetic inspirations; Hyer often recreated that magical myth in the familiar world of Carolina's lowcountry. Her attention to the outdoor sounds of South Carolina earned recognition as well. The lyrics of her poem "Santee Lullaby" were used by composer Jim Clemens in his choral arrangement "The Tidelands of Georgetown." Hyer's words became part of the first movement, "River Lullaby," premiered by Georgetown's Indigo Choral Society in 2003.

Hyer's more serious compositions were balanced with playful poems. In 1968 a limerick of hers won the Poetry Society's prize: "A lady who lived just to borrow, / Moved next to us, much to our sorrow. / We fulfilled all her wishes, / Now she has all our dishes— / To our sorrow, we'll borrow, tomorrow." Another playful poem, "Portrait of Two Ancient Ladies," jests: "Her waist is small, her shoes are tight, / She wears black silk and diamond broaches, / Her parlor's full of Hepplewhite / Her kitchen's full of roaches."

Hyer cared about spreading a love of poetry in South Carolina, particularly among the state's young people. She fulfilled her role of poet laureate well, traveling and giving poetry readings, allowing many to hear the musical rhythms of her verse firsthand. She died in Beaufort on November 14, 1983, and was buried in Charleston's Magnolia Cemetery. AMY L. WHITE

Allen, Paul Edward. "Helen von Kolnitz Hyer: South Carolina Poet Laureate." *South Carolina Review* 9 (November 1976): 115–18.

Starr, William. "At 81, Helen Hyer Hops around the State Talking about Poetry." Columbia *State,* May 7, 1978, pp. E1, E2.

Immigration. Immigration and immigrants have long been a facet of life in South Carolina. From the first settlement of the colony of Carolina in 1670 to the present day, foreign migrants have added their own distinctive cultural traits to the area. Immigration was of course a key issue for the colony's original proprietors. They could only make a profit if they could attract settlers. In 1670 the colony offered land for rent for a penny an acre for five years. While Carolina did receive migrants from other colonies and the British Isles, its most important early influx came from the British sugar islands in the Caribbean, particularly Barbados. The Barbadian families gave the burgeoning colony a Caribbean influence which remained important up to the Civil War.

The religious tolerance established in the Fundamental Constitutions of Carolina attracted other immigrants. Numbers of Calvinist Huguenots who fled France after Louis XIV's repeal of the Edict of Nantes in 1685 found new homes in the southern part of Carolina. The first Jewish migrants, mostly of Sephardic origin, were also pleased with the tolerant atmosphere and organized their first congregation in 1749. By 1800 Ashkenazi Jews from Germany and eastern Europe were also settling in the state, and in 1854 some of these newer arrivals formed a separate Polish congregation in Charleston. Many Germans and Swiss French also came to South Carolina in the eighteenth century, recruited by colony-appointed immigration agents. In the 1730s, for example, French and German Swiss settlers founded Purrysburg and Orangeburg respectively. Other French and German settlers also came in the 1760s, settling primarily in the Midlands and upcountry. The colony also supported the introduction of Welsh settlers from Pennsylvania to the Pee Dee area in 1739.

The Mike Petros family operated a popular soda fountain in Mullins. The family traced its origins to early twentieth-century Greek immigrants. Courtesy, South Carolina Tobacco Museum, Mullins

The other major immigrant influence in the colony's interior came from the Scots-Irish. Migrating from Virginia and North Carolina as well as coming directly to South Carolina from Ireland, they found cheap land in the upcountry. These migrants brought their dissenting Presbyterianism with them and became involved in politics. Some of their offspring, such as John C. Calhoun and Andrew Jackson, both of whom had parents born in the north of Ireland, would be prominent on the national stage. While just as much subjects of the British Crown as the English- and Carolina-born settlers, they were seen as foreigners. Their frontier lifestyle shocked the sensibilities of Englishmen such as Anglican clergyman Charles Woodmason. Their strong support for the American Revolution, however, gave them a chance to define what it was to be an American in South Carolina. Indeed, other white ethnic minorities also used the Revolution to solidify their presence in South Carolina society. In the 1790s the political turbulence in Europe brought numbers of political refugees to South Carolina. Republican radicals from France and Ireland were a large element of this group, but the largest was those fleeing the slave revolution of the French colony of St. Domingue (Haiti). These French-speaking refugees and their slaves made a major impact, particularly in Charleston. Many Charlestonians feared that the St. Domingue slaves harbored some of the radical ideas of the "black Jacobins." Ultimately, though, the refugees who were white were accepted and absorbed into the host society. Thus, despite these various immigrations, white South Carolina had by the early nineteenth century achieved a certain homogeneity. Whether of English, Huguenot, Barbadian, Scots-Irish, or German stock, one was a Protestant, fairly prosperous, and believed in white supremacy. The Catholics and the Jews, while somewhat different, were accepted into, as Charleston politician Christopher Memminger put it, "the peerage of white men."

The state of South Carolina did not face its first foreign immigration "problem" until the 1840s and 1850s. The major issue with these new immigrants was that many were poor. Large numbers of Germans (Catholic, Protestant, and Jewish), fleeing political persecution, and Irish, fleeing both political and economic troubles, settled primarily in the state's towns. The Germans had more skills than the Irish and usually worked as artisans or in merchandising. They also organized their own units for the Confederate army. After the Civil War the Germans exerted some political power in the state, electing John A. Wagener as mayor of Charleston in 1871. Although lower on the economic scale, the Irish also made a political impact, particularly in Charleston. Their votes often proved to be the decisive margin in local elections. Their political import was recognized when Irish American and Catholic lawyer Michael Patrick Connor was nominated by the Redeemer Democrats to run for Congress from Charleston in 1876. Although he lost in a disputed and often violent election, he won the seat in the 1878. The Civil War and Reconstruction period, therefore, sealed the immigrants' place in South Carolina. They had fought for the state in the Civil War and ultimately against "Radical" rule, and with their native neighbors they would celebrate the Lost Cause with gusto.

Ironically, however, just as the new white immigrants were finding their place, immigration to the state declined. Charleston, for example, was, thanks to European immigration, majority white in 1860 but majority black by 1870. These racial demographics scared many South Carolina leaders. The post–Civil War period saw an increase in official interest in immigration. Not since colonial times had South Carolina had such a major government effort to attract foreign immigrants. The impetus for these efforts was the desire to replace black labor. Many planters became disillusioned when their former slaves refused to work under conditions of virtual peonage. Even more disturbing to them was the black embrace of the hated Republican Party. After the war, the state appointed a Commissioner of Immigration, the aforementioned John A. Wagener of Charleston, whose task was to attract northern European immigrants. He published a forty-eight-page pamphlet entitled *South Carolina: A Home for the Industrious Immigrant* which touted the benefits of coming to the state. In Barnwell County, one landowner offered to give fifty acres to immigrant families who would improve the land. This immigration effort, however, proved unsuccessful, as only a few hundred immigrants took up the chance to come to South Carolina.

The General Assembly revived immigration efforts in 1881 when it established a Bureau of Immigration. The bureau advertised for European migrants in New York City, organized cheap rates of transportation, and hired a translator to work with the immigrants when they arrived in Columbia. At the cost of about $10,000, the bureau managed to bring in about eight hundred people. Many of the new arrivals, however, did not stay in the state.

The final major effort to bring European immigrants was pushed by Benjamin Tillman in the first decade of the twentieth century. In a quest to solve the "race problem" he hoped that northern Europeans would take over from blacks in the fields of South Carolina. Tillman made numerous speeches advocating this policy and even experimented by renting some of his own land to white immigrants. Also, between 1904 and 1908, some of South Carolina's textile mill owners tried to attract skilled foreign labor. The Cotton Manufacturers Association provided funds to pay for immigrant fares. With this money, the State Department of Agriculture, Commerce, and Immigration sought to recruit immigrants directly from Europe.

A few hundred came, including groups of Germans, Austrians, and French who arrived in Charleston on board the *Wittekind.* As in the previous efforts, however, the state failed in its avowed task. First, Tillman insisted on northern Europeans and openly condemned attempts to recruit southern European, especially Italian, immigrants. While some Italians, Greeks, and Lebanese settled in the state, they were few in number. More Jews came, too, and turned one of Charleston's shopping districts into "Little Jerusalem"; but, again, their numbers were only in the hundreds. Second, these hundreds who did arrive had no real desire to live as tenant farmers in a poor state. They either moved to town and opened stores or left the state altogether. The final death knell came when the federal government disallowed the state from prepaying immigrants' passage to the United States.

In the 1920s federal laws establishing a quota system further hindered foreign immigration. Those foreigners who did enter the United States after 1924 were simply not attracted to South Carolina, its economy, or its politics. In 1940 the foreign-born population of South Carolina stood at 4,915, which was over 5,000 less than it had been in 1860. (Meanwhile, the total population had more than doubled.) The state's white population was thus even more homogenous than it had been on the eve of the Civil War.

It was not until 1970 that the foreign-born population in South Carolina seemed to climb again. A new burst in high-tech industrialization and the spread of air-conditioning brought some immigrants back. The opening of the BMW plant in Greer brought the German population in South Carolina to over seven thousand in 2000. The construction and tourism boom also brought in immigrants. According to the 2000 census, there were over 45,000 immigrants from Central and South America living in South Carolina, making them the largest foreign-born population in the state. The fact that many people from these areas work here temporarily, "illegally," or both, means that this statistic is probably an underestimate. Whatever the true number, it seems certain that, for the first time in over a century, immigration and integrating immigrants have become major issues in the Palmetto State. DAVID T. GLEESON

Dunn, Richard S. "The English Sugar Islands and the Founding of South Carolina." *South Carolina Historical Magazine* 72 (April 1971): 81–93.

Gleeson, David. *The Irish in the South, 1815–1877.* Chapel Hill: University of North Carolina Press, 2001.

Rogers, George C., Jr. "Who Is a South Carolinian?" *South Carolina Historical Magazine* 89 (January 1988): 3–12.

Rosengarten, Theodore, and Dale Rosengarten, eds. *A Portion of the People: Three Hundred Years of Southern Jewish Life.* Columbia: University of South Carolina Press, 2002.

Stathakis, Paula Maria. "Almost White: Greek and Lebanese-Syrian Immigrants in North and South Carolina, 1900–1940." Ph.D. diss., University of South Carolina, 1996.

Strickland, Jeffery G. "Ethnicity and Race in the Urban South: German Immigrants and African Americans in Charleston, South Carolina, during Reconstruction." Ph.D. diss., Florida State University, 2003.

Synnott, Marcia G. "Replacing 'Sambo': Could White Immigrants Solve the Labor Problem in the Carolinas?" *Proceedings of the South Carolina Historical Association* (1982): 77–89.

Independent Baptists. Although all Baptists are independent and congregational in their polity, this group of Baptists is fiercely so, arguing that no ecclesiastical authority is higher than the local church. Most are associated with the fundamentalist-modernist controversy that began in the first half of the nineteenth century and, for that reason, they affirm the classic fundamentals of biblical inerrancy, the belief in Jesus' virgin birth, his substitutionary atonement, his bodily resurrection, and his premillennial return. These Baptists have a highly exclusivist view of human salvation and for this reason emphasize personal conversion, evangelism, and revivalism. Many of them identify with the Landmark Baptist movement, arguing that Baptists are not really Protestant but rather that they can be traced to the early church.

Before the 1950s the Independent Baptist movement in South Carolina was centered around Bible colleges, especially Columbia Bible College (founded as the Southern Bible Institute in 1921 and modeled on the Moody Bible Institute) and Bob Jones University (1927), both of which were less rooted in the state or even in the South than in the North, where the early twentieth-century fundamentalist movement actually had its beginning. Independent Baptists remained a decided minority among Baptists of South Carolina until at least the 1950s, when fundamentalism began to grow among Baptists affiliated with the Southern Baptist Convention. By the late 1980s, Southern Baptists had grown conservative enough that some formerly Independent Baptists began to affiliate with the denomination and thus the South Carolina Baptist Convention. HELEN LEE TURNER

Glass, William R. *Strangers in Zion: Fundamentalists in the South, 1900–1950.* Macon, Ga.: Mercer University Press, 2001.

Leonard, Bill J. "Independent Baptist: From Sectarian Minority to 'Moral Majority.'" *Church History* 56 (December 1987): 504–17.

Index-Journal (2003 circulation: 14,084 daily and 15,456 Sunday). A daily newspaper published in Greenwood, the *Index-Journal* was founded in 1919 with the merger of two earlier papers, the Greenwood *Evening Index* and the *Greenwood Daily Journal*. It now serves the Lakelands area, including Greenwood, Abbeville, McCormick, and Saluda Counties. The *Index-Journal* is one of the last family-owned daily newspapers in the state.

The *Greenwood Journal* began in 1894 while its rival the *Index* commenced three years later in 1897. The *Greenwood Journal* became the *Greenwood Daily Journal* in 1911. After an initial career as a lawyer, Harry Legare Watson (1876–1956) of Phoenix, South Carolina, merged the two papers in 1919 and continued as owner and editor for the rest of his life. Often working from Sunnyside, his residence on Taggart Avenue in Greenwood, Watson composed daily editorials and became well known as a community leader.

After Watson's death, the *Index-Journal* passed to three of its executives: circulation manager Frank Mundy, advertising manager Bill Wilson, and editor Ed Chaffin. The three agreed that the survivors would have the opportunity to purchase the shares of any partner who died. Under this agreement, control of the paper first devolved to Chaffin and Mundy and then to Mundy alone. Mundy's widow Eleanor Mundy took over the paper in 1982 and left it to her daughter Judith Mundy Burns in 1998. Burns remained owner and CEO as of 2003 and an outspoken advocate of community journalism. HARRY L. WATSON II

Indian Affairs Commission. The first Indian Affairs Commission was established by the Lords Proprietors in 1680 "to hear and determine differences between the Christians and the Indians." The expectation was that the commission would help to promote peace between the two peoples. However, after two years the proprietors revoked the commission because it seemed that the commissioners were using their powers to oppress and exploit the Indians rather than protect them from slavery.

By 1710 the commission was again operating, though the colonial governor wielded most of the power over Indian affairs at this time. Records of the commission for the years 1710–1718 and 1750–1757 have been found and published. Although the "Indian Books" of the 1720s, 1730s, and 1740s have been lost, it is fair to say the commission did continue during those decades.

After the Revolutionary War, control over Indian affairs passed to the United States government, though not always willingly or completely. Whereas the Cherokees, because of their population size and their multistate presence, were treated with respect by the new national government, the smaller nations were left to be wards of the states. South Carolina, as did many states, had an agent to report to the General Assembly and the governor on the condition of the Native Americans. Nevertheless, throughout the nineteenth and much of the twentieth century, South Carolina practiced a policy of benign neglect toward its Native American nations. The result was that many of the nations lost their identity by assimilating into the larger European and African populations around them. A few, most notably the Catawbas, managed to maintain a sense of tribal identity throughout the centuries.

In the 1970s, Native Americans, following the lead of other minorities, began demanding their political rights, including self-determination and tribal political sovereignty. The tribes of South Carolina also sought political recognition. In 1993 the Catawbas again became a federally recognized tribe, but the Edisto, the Pee Dee, the Chicora-Waccamaw, and the Santee peoples remained subject to the laws of the State of South Carolina.

In 1999, 2001, and again in 2003, bills were introduced into the South Carolina General Assembly to establish an Indian Affairs Commission, but the bills died in committee. An unofficial South Carolina Indian Affairs Commission was established as a nonprofit organization in November 2000. It is made up of representatives from the following tribes and Indian groups: the American Indian Center of South Carolina, the Beaver Creek Band of Pee Dee Indians, the Catawba Indian Nation, the Chicora Indian Tribe of South Carolina, Inc., the Chaloklowa Chickasaw, the Piedmont American Indian Association (Lower Eastern Cherokee Nation), the Pee Dee Indian Association, the Santee Indian Organization, and the Waccamaw Indian People. The Edisto Indian Organization is also recognized. ANNE M. MCCULLOCH

McDowell, William L., Jr., ed. *Documents Relating to Indian Affairs.* Vol. 2, *1754–1765.* Columbia: University of South Carolina Press, 1970.

Milling, Chapman J. *Red Carolinians.* 1940. Reprint, Columbia: University of South Carolina Press, 1969.

Indian mounds. Dotting South Carolina's streams and rivers are vestiges of her prehistoric past. These mounds offer fragmentary evidence of the cultures that thrived before the Europeans arrived. Five of South Carolina's Indian mounds are listed in the National Register of Historic Places: Adamson Mounds (Kershaw County), Blair Mound (Fairfield County), Lawton Mounds (Allendale County), McCollum Mound (Chester County), and Santee Mound (Clarendon County).

At least sixteen Woodland mounds and nineteen Mississippian mounds have been identified in South Carolina that are at least fifty percent intact. Another eleven known sites have been destroyed or are underwater. Woodland period mounds are located primarily along coastal rivers, while Mississippian mounds are found along inland rivers near the fall line. Beaufort County has the largest concentration of mounds, followed by counties located in the Midlands. Similar mounds are found in Georgia and North Carolina.

The Adamson Mound, Kershaw County. Photograph by Chris Judge. Courtesy, South Carolina Department of Natural Resources

In the late prehistoric period and early contact period, some of South Carolina's mound builders were part of vast Mississippian chiefdoms. South Appalachian Mississippian ceramics indicate that a similar culture embraced South Carolina, Georgia, and neighboring areas. These mounds, built between C.E. 1200 and 1500, were ceremonial, cultural, or administrative in nature and at times were associated with villages and burials. Some of them were also associated with the Pee Dee, Lamar, or Irene culture that flourished ca. C.E. 1400–1700.

Historical evidence suggests that as many as 150 mounds were present in South Carolina at the time of European contact. In 1540 Hernando de Soto encountered the mound dwellers of Cofitachiqui on the Wateree River. The accounts of his journey are important documentary sources for understanding the mound dwellers. During the Revolutionary War, the British recognized the strategic potential of the mounds. They built Fort Watson on the Santee Mound, which patriot forces captured in 1780. Erosion and looting threaten the survival of South Carolina's Indian mounds. ALEXIA JONES HELSLEY

Frierson, John L. "South Carolina Prehistoric Earthen Indian Mounds." Master's thesis, University of South Carolina, 2000.

Holleman, Joey. "Prehistoric Native American Culture of the Southeast: The Moundbuilders." Columbia *State,* November 22, 2001, pp. D1, D4.

Indian trade. The trade between the colony of South Carolina and neighboring Indian tribes officially began in 1674 when the proprietors directed Dr. Henry Woodward, an early inhabitant, to establish peaceful relations and regular trade with either the Cussitaws or the Westos. That fall Woodward elected to return with a visiting group of Westoes to their village on the Savannah River. The visit opened a lucrative trade in skins and slaves provided by the tribe and English trade goods provided by the colonists.

Other early Indian trade partners included the Yamassees, who traded deerskins and later Indian slaves for such things as guns, cloth, rum, hoes, and mirrors. Over time, the trade goods most requested by Indians were guns, ammunition, hatchets, vermilion (red) paint, calico cloth, knives, and hats. Typical Indian traders were often Scots, Scots-Irish, or Irish, who got their start in the business by sending to Britain for trade items, paid for either by cash or on credit. Once shipped, the traders loaded the goods onto packhorses and then headed into Indian country in search of customers.

Indians hunted in the fall and winter, often skinning their animals at hunting lodges. Their exchange with the fur traders took place the following spring at their home villages. Here, Carolina fur traders awaited them to receive payment on trade items sold to Indians the previous year on credit. Current purchases from the traders were made on credit to be paid for with the next season's hunt. Then the backcountry trader left Indian country for Charleston, where his own creditor awaited payment on the trade goods.

While the trade brought items desirable to Carolina tribes, there were also deleterious effects. Indians became dependent on the gun and, if unable to purchase enough in skins, found themselves without the means to hunt for pelts or defend themselves against other armed tribes seeking slaves. Native peoples also allowed certain craft skills to atrophy, such as the ability to fashion stone cookware or hunt with stone weapons, if English trade such as iron pots and firearms goods could provide superior substitutes.

Due to the gun, Indians were able to overhunt their animals. Tribes such as the Yamassees turned to war to obtain slaves from other Indian tribes, and thus intertribal conflicts increased. Perhaps most damaging to native culture was the rum trade. Greedy traders often intercepted warriors on their way back to their village with the year's hunt. The fur traders offered a few friendly drinks to these men, and, once intoxicated, the trappers were easy targets for the traders, who would leave them empty-handed and subject to abuse when they returned to the village with nothing to pay their regular trader.

Although damaging to native culture, the trade was prosperous for Carolina. From 1699 to 1715, Carolina exported on average 54,000 deerskins annually. The greatest single year during that period for trade was 1707 when 121,355 skins were exported.

While lucrative, the Indian trade was also a contentious issue. In 1698 the Commons House of Assembly debated the Indian trade and found it to be "a grievance to settlement and prejudicall to the safety theroff." Some participants in the discussion wanted the trade thrown open to all interested parties, who would then be strictly regulated. Others wanted the trade held in a monopoly. Finally the issue arose of who would regulate the trade—the Commons House of Assembly or the Proprietary Council.

By 1707 the Commons House had taken steps to regulate the trade when it created the Commission of Indian Trade. The act creating the agency outlawed the sale of liquor to Indians and the enslavement of Indians for debt. It required all traders to be licensed at a fee of £8 and to give a bond of £100 to obey trade guidelines. The act created the position of Indian agent, who was to travel through the homelands of major tribes handling any trade-related problems. Thomas Nairne was the first agent. He found it difficult to regulate the trade, and most sources acknowledge that many traders cheated and abused friendly tribes.

No tribe better illustrates the dangers of such conditions than the Yamassees. Plagued by excessive debt, they became angry with their traders. They also resented the Carolinians for allowing settlers to trickle into their lands. The Yamassees resolved to eliminate their trade debt (estimated to be worth at least two years' labor by every adult male Yamassee) with a major strike against the Carolina colony. They attacked the colony's southern frontier on Good Friday, April 15, 1715, and attempted to kill their traders, creditors, and most Euro-Americans in their area, including Nairne. Charleston became a refugee city until the Carolinians managed to divide the tribes and turn them against each other, using the Lower Cherokees to side with them against the Creeks. The damage to the deerskin trade was heavy. Shipments of deerskins did not reach their 1715 levels again until 1722.

Since the Yamassee War was a direct result of the problems of an unregulated trade, the Carolina government assumed a direct monopoly over the Indian trade in 1716, replacing private Indian traders with new government agents, called factors, who were strictly charged to obey stringent new trade guidelines. The new government factors were to monitor tribal activity, manage the trade, and act as diplomats enforcing laws. Larger tribes received one factor plus up to two assistants, and smaller tribes often shared one official.

By 1730 the Carolina Indian trade in skins entered a golden age of prosperity. In 1748 the colony exported 160,000 skins worth some £300,000. Gradually other products displaced the fur trade in both profit and prominence. Rice became an enumerated product with a guaranteed market, as did naval stores such as pitch and tar. Where the Yamassee War disrupted the fur trade, the timber-related industry was unaffected. Government bounties on naval stores alone in 1710 brought Carolina £60,000 sterling or $6 million. While the Indian trade brought the colony its first wealth, it could not keep pace with changing economic needs. MICHAEL P. MORRIS

Crane, Verner. *The Southern Frontier 1670–1732.* Durham, N.C.: Duke University Press, 1928.

Edgar, Walter. *South Carolina: A History.* Columbia: University of South Carolina Press, 1998.

Hudson, Charles. *The Southeastern Indians.* Knoxville: University of Tennessee Press, 1976.

Morris, Michael P. *The Bringing of Wonder: Trade and the Indians of the Southeast, 1700–1783.* Westport, Conn.: Greenwood, 1999.

Rothrock, Mary U. "Carolina Traders among the Overhill Cherokees, 1690–1760." *East Tennessee Historical Society's Publications* 1 (1929): 3–18.

Indigo. Indigo, a plant that produces a blue dye, was an important part of South Carolina's eighteenth-century economy. It was grown commercially from 1747 to 1800 and was second only to rice in export value. Carolina indigo was the fifth most valuable commodity exported by Britain's mainland colonies and was England's primary source of blue dye in the late-colonial era.

South Carolina experimented with indigo production as early as the 1670s but could not compete with superior dyes produced in the West Indies. Cultivating and processing the plant was complex, and planters found other commodities more reliable and easier to produce. Indigo was reintroduced in the 1740s during King George's War (1739–1748), which disrupted the established rice trade by inflating insurance and shipping charges and also cut off Britain's supply of indigo from the French West Indies. In South Carolina, Eliza Lucas Pinckney and Andrew Deveaux experimented with cultivation in the 1730s and 1740s. Pinckney's husband, Charles, printed articles in the *Charleston Gazette* promoting indigo. In London colonial agent James Crokatt persuaded Parliament in 1749 to subsidize Carolina indigo production by placing a bounty of six pence per pound on the dye.

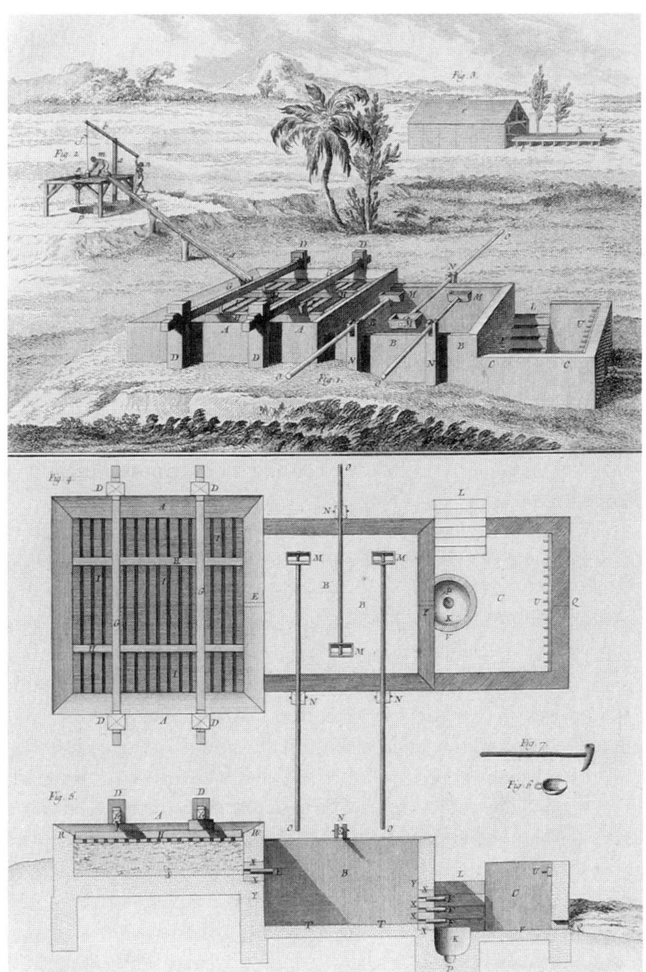

The extraction of dyestuff from indigo required a series of three vats, such as those shown in this drawing. From Beauvais de Raseau, *L 'Arte de l'indigotier* (1770). Courtesy, South Caroliniana Library, University of South Carolina

In addition to economic motives, indigo production also succeeded because it fit within the existing agricultural economy. The crop could be grown on land not suited for rice and tended by slaves, so planters and farmers already committed to plantation agriculture did not have to reconfigure their land and labor. In 1747, 138,300 pounds of dye, worth £16,803 sterling, were exported to England. The amount and value of indigo exports increased in subsequent years, peaking in 1775 with a total of 1,122,200 pounds, valued at £242,395 sterling. England received almost all Carolina indigo exports, although by the 1760s a small percentage was being shipped to northern colonies.

Two varieties of indigo were native to Carolina, *Indigofera Carolinians* and *Indigofera Lespotsepala,* but neither produced a reputable dye. Planters preferred either *Indigofera Tinctoria* or "Guatemala" indigo, a hearty variety that grew well in a range of soil types, or *Indigofera Anil* or "French" indigo, a more delicate variety best suited for rich black soil. Prices paid for the dye varied with quality. In general dye from French or Spanish colonies sold for more than Carolina indigo, whose reputation for quality was less favorable. The cycle of planting, processing, and marketing indigo began in March, when the fields were prepared for sowing. Planting began in early April, with a first harvest in July and often a second harvest in August or September. After cutting, the plant was carried to the processing site, a work area generally shaded by a thatched roof. Specialized equipment included three graduated vats set next to each other, in which the plants would be converted to dye. The conversion involved soaking the plants in the first vat, beating the indigo-soaked water in the second vat until thickened grains formed, then draining away that water into the third vat. The thickened mud that settled to the bottom of the second vat was the indigo paste, which was dried, cut into squares, packed in barrels, and shipped to market during the winter months. Slaves were responsible for most of South Carolina's indigo production. Field slaves planted, weeded, and harvested the crop, and skilled "indigo slaves" worked to convert the plant to dye. Slaves who understood the art of processing the dye had greater value, as an entire year's product depended on the talents of the indigo maker.

Carolina indigo was grown in a variety of locations and in a number of ways. In the parishes south of Charleston, most indigo planters grew the weed in combination with rice, as a "second staple." Planters growing indigo closer to the city were split, with roughly half growing rice and indigo and half growing only indigo. North of Charleston, most planters focused solely on indigo. By the 1760s production expanded from the lowcountry to the interior. Indigo was especially important in Williamsburg Township, where the soil was ideal and the crop was an important part of the local economy. By the 1770s, some indigo was also produced in Orangeburg and Fredericksburg Townships.

The Revolutionary War disrupted production, although the Continental army used Carolina indigo to dye some of its uniforms. Production appeared to recover after the war, as 907,258 pounds of dye were exported in 1787. But indigo exports declined sharply in the 1790s. No longer part of the British Empire, South Carolina indigo growers lost their bounty and market as England turned to India to supply its indigo demand. Carolina planters soon after turned their attention to cotton, another crop that fit neatly into the plantation economy. Indigo was produced and used locally throughout the nineteenth century, but by 1802 it was no longer listed among Carolina's exports. VIRGINIA JELATIS

Chaplin, Joyce E. *An Anxious Pursuit: Agricultural Innovation and Modernity in the Lower South, 1730–1815.* Chapel Hill: University of North Carolina Press, 1993.

Coon, David L. "Eliza Lucas Pinckney and the Reintroduction of Indigo Culture in South Carolina." *Journal of Southern History* 42 (February 1976): 61–76.

Jelatis, Virginia. "Tangled Up in Blue: Indigo Culture and Economy in South Carolina, 1747–1800." Ph.D. diss., University of Minnesota, 1999.

Sharrer, G. Terry. "The Indigo Bonanza in South Carolina, 1740–1790." *Technology and Culture* 12 (July 1971): 447–55.

———. "Indigo in Carolina, 1671–1796." *South Carolina Historical Magazine* 72 (April 1971): 94–103.

Winberry, John J. "Reputation of South Carolina Indigo." *South Carolina Historical Magazine* 80 (July 1979): 242–50.

Industrialization. Industry in early South Carolina was limited and tied closely to the agrarian nature of the colony. Since the lowcountry was settled largely by English planters and their slaves from Barbados, the primary economic focus was on developing a staple crop. By the mid–eighteenth century, indigo and rice were the dominant cash crops. Rice held the most potential for economic success, but the crop required labor-intensive hand milling by slaves. The growing dominance of rice cultivation in the lowcountry led planters to search for more efficient and cost-effective ways to mill the staple for commercial transport. By the Revolutionary era, planters had developed rice-milling factories that utilized water power to drive pestles. Steam power further accelerated the milling process. Aside from this technological innovation, however, the lowcountry witnessed little industrial change through the early nineteenth century.

This turn of the twentieth-century illustration shows old and new industrial technology side by side in Greenville. Courtesy, South Carolina Historical Society

Much of South Carolina's pre–Civil War industrialization was centered in the upcountry. A smaller planter population and more favorable geography contributed to the region's factory development. In the late colonial period, settlers of the backcountry districts including Spartanburg, York, Greenville, and Pendleton discovered important mineral wealth, especially gold and iron. Although small-scale gold mining operations were under way by the time of the Revolution, iron production held the most potential for industrial success. The combination of significant iron veins and river systems to power factories led to the construction of the first iron foundry in Spartanburg in 1773. By the 1850s, the upcountry had eight furnaces employing mostly slave labor to produce about four thousand tons of commercial iron per year. However, the iron industry soon declined due to competition from anthracite regions in Pennsylvania, rising labor costs, and poor transportation routes.

The textile industry was the most significant early industry to take root in the upcountry and Piedmont regions of South Carolina. Some New England manufacturers saw potential for factory operations

International Paper's modern plant and the beautifully restored Kensington Mansion in rural Richland County. Courtesy, International Paper

along the backcountry rivers and set up a handful of small mills there after 1814. Most of the antebellum textile mills remained small, employing mostly white women and children from the surrounding countryside. The exception to this was William Gregg's Graniteville factory, an industrial community based on the mill village of Lowell, Massachusetts.

Prior to the Civil War, industry in South Carolina struggled due to limited financial support, underdeveloped commercial routes, and the institution of slavery. Lowcountry planters dominated the state legislature and rarely supported state funding of industries that were generally located in the upcountry. Since the state lacked a significant railroad infrastructure until the eve of the Civil War, transportation costs were high and markets for industrial products remained local. Finally, slavery itself restricted the home market for industrial products since slaves would not be significant consumers.

During the Civil War, the iron and textile industries operated to capacity, supplying war materials such as ammunition and uniforms. Although much of the machinery was worn-out by war's end due to overuse, the factories largely escaped destruction. As a result, many factory owners and managers were able to recover quickly from the Confederacy's defeat and find new opportunities in a changed economy.

Northern investment, the end of slavery, and an increasing shift to cotton by small farmers all ensured that textile factories became the dominant industry for the remainder of the nineteenth century and well into the twentieth century. Key to the expansion of this industry was rail lines, which drastically reduced transportation costs and fostered town growth. By the early twentieth century, South Carolina was the second largest cotton-textile-producing state, and mill villages dotted the landscape of the Piedmont and upcountry.

Although boosters championed the textile industry for bringing progress and jobs to South Carolina, the factories introduced some of the ambiguous effects of industrialization as well. Mill owners employed white labor, often women and children, to work sixty or more hours per week. Company towns controlled much of the workers' lives and wages remained low compared to factory workers in the North. No significant labor conflict occurred, however, until the Great Depression when management's increased demands on workers led to the General Textile Strike of 1934—up to that point the largest strike in American labor history.

At the same time that the Great Depression brought hardship for mill owners and workers, it also contributed to a critical advance in South Carolina's industrial future. As part of President Franklin D. Roosevelt's New Deal recovery program, the state General Assembly created the South Carolina Public Service Authority in 1934. Tasked with building dams along the Santee and Cooper Rivers for hydroelectric power, the South Carolina Public Service Authority became known as the Santee Cooper project. By 1942 Santee Cooper had constructed a hydroelectric plant at Pinopolis which would be essential in powering new industries both during and after World War II.

World War II revived the struggling textile industry. War-time production demands led many mills to operate continuously using three shifts. Workers at the Charleston Navy Yard produced destroyers and naval weaponry. Employment at the yard skyrocketed from 6,000 in 1941 to 28,000 in 1943. The demand for workers at defense industries, combined with the loss of men to the armed forces, left farmers seriously shorthanded.

Following the war, South Carolina launched an aggressive effort to foster more rapid industrialization. In 1951 the state attracted the DuPont Corporation's Savannah River nuclear weapons facility to Barnwell. The State Development Board was created in 1954 with the specific job of recruiting new industries to the state. The state assembly also created the State Ports Authority to update the Port of Charleston's facilities to accommodate commercial trade. In a move to attract English paper manufacturer Bowater Incorporated, Governor George Bell Timmerman called a special session of the General Assembly in 1956 to amend the state's alien-ownership law so that non-Americans could own up to 500,000 acres of land. In 1959 Bowater completed its paper- and pulp-producing plant in Catawba, representing one of the largest capital investments in South Carolina during the 1950s. Recruitment of multinational industries continued to accelerate in the 1960s. At the urging of Governor Ernest Hollings, the legislature set up a new industrial training program aimed at recruiting companies to an already trained workforce. By the end of that decade, South Carolina was drawing forty percent of its annual industrial investments from overseas.

While many in the state championed the new industries for bringing jobs and a healthier economy, some questioned the costs of such aggressive recruitment. Environmentalists criticized the state Pollution Control Authority's willingness to relax standards to accommodate factories. Labor unions were especially critical of South Carolina's hostility to unionization. In 1954 the South Carolina General Assembly passed a right-to-work law that prevented most unionization efforts and therefore kept wages lower than other regions of the country. The state's resistance to union activity continued through the 1960s and 1970s.

In the 1970s, most new industries were concentrated in the South Carolina upcountry. By 1973 Spartanburg was home to twenty-four foreign corporations employing four thousand workers. In the middle of the decade, Michelin built two plants and later located its American headquarters in Greenville. So many foreign industries were located along the Interstate 85 corridor between Spartanburg and Greenville that locals called it the "autobahn." At the same time, competition from developing countries was bringing South Carolina's textile era to a close.

Industrial expansion continued through the 1980s and 1990s. In 1993 Bowater moved its North American headquarters to Greenville. A year later, BMW opened its first complete automobile manufacturing plant outside Germany in Greer. By the turn of the twenty-first century, manufacturing accounted for just over twenty percent of South Carolina's gross state product. BRUCE W. EELMAN

Carlton, David L. *Mill and Town in South Carolina, 1880–1920.* Baton Rouge: Louisiana State University Press, 1982.

Chaplin, Joyce E. *An Anxious Pursuit: Agricultural Innovation and Modernity in the Lower South, 1730–1815.* Chapel Hill: University of North Carolina Press, 1993.

Cobb, James C. *The Selling of the South: The Southern Crusade for Industrial Development, 1936–1980.* Baton Rouge: Louisiana State University Press, 1982.

Lander, Ernest McPherson, Jr. *The Textile Industry in Antebellum South Carolina.* Baton Rouge: Louisiana State University Press, 1969.

Influenza pandemic of 1918. The influenza pandemic of 1918 infected approximately one-fourth of the population of the United States and killed an estimated 675,000. Globally, roughly 500 million people were infected, with a death toll estimated at between 20 million and 50 million. Influenza mortality rates in 1918 accounted for ten times the number of civilians and twice as many military personnel worldwide who died on all fronts during World War I.

South Carolina did not escape the pandemic. By October 15, approximately 50,000 cases had been reported within the state. By the time the epidemic receded, some 14,250 South Carolinians had died from complications associated with the influenza. The pandemic first struck during the spring of 1918 in the form of a mild flu. By autumn, the full brunt of the influenza arrived. Ninety-nine percent of deaths associated with influenza are caused by complications from pneumonia. In 1918 the mortality rate for influenzal pneumonia was sixty to seventy percent. From October 22 to December 31, 1917, thirty-nine cases of influenza were reported at Camp Jackson in Columbia, with no fatalities. In comparison, by November 30, 1918, officials recorded 8,255 cases of influenza within the camp, with 412 fatalities.

Influenza patients quickly overwhelmed the state's meager medical system. On September 31, the Surgeon General's Office in Washington authorized Dr. F. Simpson to take charge of South Carolina's efforts to control the epidemic and appropriated funds to establish emergency hospitals and employ as many health officers as needed. Columbia had just 150 hospital beds in 1918, forcing the conversion of three buildings at the University of South Carolina into emergency hospitals to receive influenza victims. Charleston was at significant risk from the flu due to its constant influx of military personnel. In response, Charleston's Board of Health banned assemblies of more than five people and ordered all stores to close by sundown. The Citadel was also closed on September 30. From October 5 to November 6, the city health department counted 5,643 cases of influenza and pneumonia within the city limits, as well as 229 influenza-related deaths. In the upstate mill town of Clinton, approximately 600 people were affected, from a population of roughly 3,600. Influenza first appeared in Greenville on October 4 with an infection rate of 1,000 per day over the following four days. In Spartanburg, influenza first struck on September 20. Eleven days later, Spartanburg's Board of Health closed all public gathering places.

Fortunately, by the middle of December, cases of influenza were quickly disappearing, and mortality rates fell back to normal by the beginning of 1919. The pandemic forced South Carolina, and the rest of the country, to reevaluate its public health organizations and better equip them for future public health crises. The pandemic, despite its horrific consequences, helped guide South Carolina toward a future of improved sanitation, increased public health care, and social awareness. LISA J. DIMITRIADIS

Charles, Allan D. "The Influenza Pandemic of 1918–1919: Columbia and South Carolina's Response." *Journal of the South Carolina Medical Association* 73 (August 1977): 367–70.

Crosby, Alfred W. *America's Forgotten Pandemic: The Influenza of 1918.* New York: Cambridge University Press, 1989.

Year Book, 1918, City of Charleston, South Carolina. Charleston, [1919].

Inman Mills. Inman Mills began in 1902 when James A. Chapman opened a four-hundred-loom and fifteen-thousand-spindle plant in the town of Inman in Spartanburg County. The mill made high quality greige, cloth that comes straight from the loom and is gray, rough, and full of blemishes. By 1909 the plant had doubled in capacity, and a four-story addition was added in 1920.

The company's success prompted further expansion. Chapman acquired Riverdale Mills in Enoree in 1934 and merged it with Inman in 1954. Having outgrown the original plant, the mill replaced it with the newly built Saybrook Plant in 1959 in Inman. The Ramey Plant, a 1959 improvement, and the Mountain Shoals Plant, a 1990 addition, were both constructed in Enoree.

Inman Mills uses air-jet and rapier weaving with open-end and air-jet spinning to produce high quality blended greige goods, woven cotton, poly/cotton, and polyester. Inman's major products include oxford (a soft, porous fabric), pique (a medium- to heavy-weight cotton cloth with raised cords), poplin (a tightly woven, high-count cotton), dobby (a heavy cotton with woven geometric figures), and sateen (a satinlike cotton). The fabrics are used in draperies, upholstery, home furnishings, pocketing, and apparel as well as for industrial and institutional purposes. In 2004 the company operated three plants, one at Inman and two at Enoree, which provided jobs to 534 employees. CARYN E. NEUMANN

Jackson, Bobby Dean. "Textiles in the South Carolina Piedmont: A Case Study of the Inman Mills, 1900–1967." Master's thesis, Auburn University, 1968.

Innocenti and Webel. Innocenti and Webel, a landscape architectural firm based on Long Island, New York, is best known for its work on corporate and college campuses in the upstate and midlands of South Carolina. Its early projects were quite different, however. Umberto Innocenti and Richard K. Webel first came to South Carolina to design residential landscapes on lowcountry hunting plantations. The men formed a partnership in 1931 when their employer, Ferruccio Vitale, closed his practice. His clients came to the new firm, and Innocenti and Webel became prominent among the wealthy residents of Long Island, New York.

One of their first major clients, Landon K. Thorne, along with his brother-in-law, Alfred L. Loomis, bought most of Hilton Head Island in the early 1930s, with the intention of alternating their summer playgrounds with a winter hunting estate in the South. They commissioned Innocenti and Webel's design services for both. On their southern plantations as on their northern estates, the new country gentry wanted colonial-revival houses and fine landscapes that gave the appearance of age. Innocenti and Webel provided a strongly architectural garden that related to the house and provided a view from which the owners and their guests could take in the breadth and variety of the property. Webel worked in the Long Island studio, while Innocenti directed the field crews who installed trees, winter-flowering shrubs and bushes, brick walls, ornamental gates, sandy walks, and "classical touches" such as weathered urns and statuettes. Because his partner and office were away in New York, South Carolinians considered the firm's work to be Innocenti's alone.

In the 1930s, Innocenti planted ever larger trees and ornamentals on lowcountry hunting plantations. He completed country seats at Bonnie Doone for Alfred H. Caspary; Mackay Point for George D. Widener, chairman of the U.S. Jockey Club; and Nelson Doubleday's Bonny Hall. In Georgetown County, Innocenti and Webel's country estates included Wedgefield for financier Robert Goelet, Friendfield for Radcliffe Cheston, and Bellefield on Bernard Baruch's Hobcaw Barony.

During the 1940s, the firm's emphasis shifted to corporate projects. In 1952 came Innocenti and Webel's first large-scale work in South Carolina, Furman University's new campus in Greenville. They organized the thousand-acre agricultural tract into broad curves with axial streets and boulevards, planting hundreds of closely spaced trees to transform open fields into sheltered grounds. For decades their plan has allowed Furman to expand by constructing infill buildings within a mature landscape. At the Milliken Company's headquarters, begun outside Spartanburg in 1958, rows and groves of trees line roads and loom over parking areas, courts, and entries, emphasizing the geometric order of the new buildings while making the industrial campus truly a park. As at Furman, the Milliken complex has expanded within its own mature landscape.

From these signature projects, the firm continued to work in South Carolina even after the death of Innocenti (1968) and the retirement of Webel, whose son Richard C. Webel took over as managing partner. Important late-twentieth-century projects include Greenville-Spartanburg Airport, Fluor-Daniel Engineering Center (Greenville), BMW's North American Assembly Plant (Greer), and expansion of the University of South Carolina's main campus in Columbia. SARAH FICK

Graydon, Nell S. *South Carolina Gardens.* Beaufort, S.C.: Beaufort Book Company, 1973.

Hilderbrand, Gary, ed. *Making a Landscape of Continuity: The Practice of Innocenti and Webel.* Cambridge: Harvard University Graduate School of Design, 1997.

Internal improvements campaign (1820s). The availability of waterways made them the primary transportation arteries for South Carolina's settlers. As early as the 1710s, the Commons House of Assembly was enacting legislation to facilitate water traffic. The great geographic barrier to river traffic between the South Carolina upcountry and the coastal ports was the fall line. By 1800 interest in inland navigation spawned during the Revolution had produced the Santee Canal.

The years that followed the War of 1812 saw South Carolina's greatest experiment with a statewide, state-funded, and state-operated system of internal improvements. In 1816 Governor David R. Williams proposed a coordinated plan of improvements. In 1817 his successor, Governor Andrew Pickens, recommended using the state's budget surplus to fund the program. In response, the General Assembly authorized a state civil and military engineer to survey the navigational needs of South Carolina's rivers and to begin work on improving the Broad and Saluda Rivers. Enhanced navigation on these rivers was crucial to the economic development of Columbia, the new capital.

In 1818 engineer John Wilson requested $1 million to fund a massive effort to improve upcountry navigation. Under the leadership of Joel R. Poinsett, the General Assembly funded the request and charged Wilson with improving rivers, building canals, and constructing roads as needed. This appropriation, four times the state's annual budget, reflected a major commitment to fund an extensive transportation network in South Carolina.

In 1819 the General Assembly created the Board of Public Works, with five legislatively elected commissioners to oversee this ambitious enterprise. The board's responsibilities included surveying and building a road from Charleston through Columbia to the North Carolina border, making the Pee Dee, Santee, Wateree, Catawba, Broad, Saluda, Keowee, Edisto, Black, Combahee, and Salkehatchie Rivers navigable, and constructing canals as needed. The board created two offices: a "department of roads, rivers, and canals"; and a "department of public buildings."

The department of roads, rivers, and canals planned eight canals and the State Road that would link Charleston with western North Carolina. Of the eight canals, four—Wateree, Rocky Mount, Landsford, and Fishing Creek—were on the Catawba and Wateree Rivers to improve access to Camden. Two of the canals, the Columbia Canal on the Congaree River and Lockhart Canal on the Broad River, funneled traffic to Columbia. The Saluda and Dreher Canals on the Saluda River were designed to improve transportation to Abbeville and Laurens. All of the canals were built, but only the Columbia Canal was successful. Given the highly politicized nature of the board, especially after a severe recession that followed in the wake of the Panic of 1819, many canals followed less desirable routes and ran well over budget. As a result, revenues generated were rarely sufficient to maintain and operate the canal system. By 1838 six of the eight were no longer in use.

Competition with cotton producers for available slave labor and the dearth of skilled labor in South Carolina increased labor costs. Bonuses and above average wages lured stonecutters, brick masons, and engineers from the Northeast. Cost overruns and lagging completion dates prompted public criticism. In 1822 John Belton O'Neall of Newberry introduced legislation to abolish the board, condemning the project as wasteful and calling the internal improvement fever a "mania" or "folly." William J. Grayson blamed pork-barrel politics for blinding legislators to the deficiencies of the program. Despite the criticism, the General Assembly appointed a superintendent to centralize oversight of public projects and appropriated additional funds to complete those already under construction.

According to the 1827 report of Abraham Blanding, the superintendent of public works, the twenty-five miles of canals cost an average of $50,000 per mile to construct. The committee declared that the canals had opened two thousand miles of river navigation. In reality, the canals suffered from poor construction, inadequate maintenance, and low water flow. By 1828 the balloon had burst. Facing a faltering economy and deep public dissatisfaction, the General Assembly passed the last of the public improvement-era expenditures.

Canal usage dwindled, and in 1840 South Carolina even abandoned the successful Columbia Canal. The railroad, the next great transportation transformation, was at hand. By 1853 the canals were footnotes in South Carolina's history. A later age tapped their potential for power production.

The State Road between Charleston and Columbia was completed in 1829. While the route was unsuccessful as a toll road, usage exceeded expectations once the tolls were removed. The State Road not only connected Charleston and Columbia, but also facilitated the growth of summer colonies in the South Carolina upcountry and the mountains of western North Carolina. ALEXIA JONES HELSLEY

Easterby, J. H., ed. *Transportation in the Ante-Bellum Period.* Columbia: Historical Commission of South Carolina, 1951.

Epting, Carl L. "Inland Navigation in South Carolina and Traffic on the Columbia Canal." *Proceedings of the South Carolina Historical Association* (1936): 18–28.

Hollis, Daniel W. "Costly Delusion: Inland Navigation in the South Carolina Piedmont." *Proceedings of the South Carolina Historical Association* (1968): 29–43.

Kohn, David, and Bess Glenn. *Internal Improvement in South Carolina, 1817–1828.* Washington, D.C., 1938.

Interurbans. More complex than street railways yet smaller than interstate railroads, interurbans occupied a brief position in South Carolina's transportation history. Powered by electricity rather than steam, interurbans facilitated commuter traffic in South Carolina's upcountry and nationally until the coming of the automobile. Running trains by electric power in this country did not receive serious consideration until the end of the nineteenth century. Frank Sprague developed a method of mounting the electric motor in a way that would not subject it to undue shocks. He demonstrated it in 1888 in Virginia, and the invention was an immediate success. The electric-powered railway was clearly technologically superior to previous means of transportation, the horse-drawn streetcar and the cable car. In 1890 seventy percent of American street railways were powered by animals; by 1902 only three percent of street railways were *not* powered by electricity. By 1895 people had begun to recognize the utility of electric railways for traffic between cities.

An advertisement for the Piedmont and Northern Railway. Courtesy, South Carolina Historical Society

Few of these lines operated in the South, but one of the most significant lines in the country was South Carolina's Piedmont and Northern. Developed between 1910 and 1916, eighty-nine miles of track connected Spartanburg, Greenville, and Greenwood, with a spur to Anderson. In addition to the more successful Piedmont and Northern, South Carolina had two other interurban lines. The Augusta-Aiken Railway ran for twenty-six miles between those two cities. The road was operated by the Georgia-Carolina Power Company and opened for business on September 8, 1902, under the name of the Augusta and Columbia Railway Company. Its name changed to Augusta-Aiken after 1911, and the line was abandoned in 1929. The other line was in the lowcountry: the Charleston-Isle of Palms Traction Company, which began operation in August 1898. A ferry took passengers from Charleston to Mount Pleasant, where they boarded the train for a ten-mile ride to the Isle of Palms. The road was originally operated by the Charleston Consolidated Railway, Gas, and Electric Company. The railway entered receivership in 1924 and was abandoned the following year.

Although the Piedmont and Northern remained in operation until 1969, the decline of the Augusta-Aiken and Charleston-Isle of Palms Traction Company mirrored national events. The automobile became affordable and popular in the 1910s, and trucks began to eat away at freight business done by interurban lines. By the 1920s it was clear that automobiles were not a passing fad, and interurbans were abandoned across the country. The Great Depression made a revival of the interurban unlikely, and this once-popular transportation option passed from the landscape. AARON W. MARRS

Fetters, Thomas T., and Peter W. Swanson, Jr. *Piedmont and Northern: The Great Electric System of the South.* San Marino, Calif.: Golden West, 1974.
Hilton, George W., and John F. Due. *The Electric Interurban Railways in America.* Stanford, Calif.: Stanford University Press, 1960.

Intracoastal Waterway. From the earliest times, South Carolina's coastal creeks, rivers, and bays have been used for commerce and communication, providing a transportation route far safer than plying the open ocean. Native Americans in dugout canoes were replaced by white settlers and black slaves using larger craft propelled by oars, poles, paddles, and sails. The advent of steam navigation in the early nineteenth century enhanced the value of inland waterways, and increased efforts were made even before the Civil War to dig "cuts" to connect natural watercourses.

In 1808, amid a heated congressional debate over the constitutionality of using federal funds for internal improvements, Secretary of the Treasury Albert Gallatin offered a report of the country's transportation needs. One of his recommendations called for the building of canals to connect the natural waterways of the Atlantic seaboard to form a continuous route protected from the ocean. While state and local interests began working on local canal projects as early as the 1790s, Gallatin's vision of a continuous waterway was not attained until 1909, when Congress authorized the first surveys of the Intracoastal Waterway. Shortly thereafter, the U.S. Army Corps of Engineers began to make systematic improvements to connect coastal waterways. Congress consolidated these projects in 1917, completing them with the opening of the Atlantic Intracoastal Waterway (AIWW) in 1936.

The 740-mile-long channel of the AIWW runs from Norfolk, Virginia, to Fernandina Beach, Florida, with shallower extensions running south to Key West and north to Boston. The South Carolina portion of the waterway extends for 203 miles and is dredged to an average depth of between nine and eleven feet. While recreational users of the Intracoastal Waterway abound, the route also carries a substantial amount of commercial cargo traffic. In 2000 intracoastal waters in the South Carolina section carried 378,000 tons of cargo, which accounted for twelve percent of the total cargo carried by the entire AIWW. Approximately seventy percent of this cargo was petroleum or pulp and paper products. ALLAN D. CHARLES

Federal Writers' Project. *The Intracoastal Waterway, Norfolk to Key West.* Washington, D.C.: Government Printing Office, 1937.
Parkman, Aubrey. *History of the Waterways of the Atlantic Coast of the United States.* Washington, D.C.: National Waterways Study, U.S. Army Engineer Water Resources Support Center, Institute for Water Resources, 1983.

Iodine. The chemical element iodine derives its name from the violet color of its gaseous form. A rare element (sixty-second in global abundance), it occurs naturally as a trace chemical in certain soils, rocks, seawater, plants, and animals. In humans, it is largely found in the thyroid gland, which secretes iodine-bearing hormones responsible for regulating metabolism. A deficiency of iodine causes an unsightly swelling of the neck and jaw known as a goiter.

In the late 1920s the South Carolina Natural Resources Commission began a public relations campaign to advertise the high iodine levels found in fruits and vegetables grown in the state. Even South Carolina milk was promoted as containing extraordinarily high levels of iodine. Promotional tracts sought to expand the national market for South Carolina produce by warning midwestern and west coast residents of the consequences of iodine deficiency in the young, including enlarged thyroids, mental and physical birth defects, and even sterility. The campaign placed the motto "Iodine" on South Carolina automobile license plates in 1930 and then expanded the phrase in subsequent years to "The Iodine State" and "The Iodine Products State." Columbia radio station WIS took its call letters to promote the "Wonderful Iodine State." Even lowcountry moonshiners around Hell Hole Swamp jumped on the iodine bandwagon, advertising their brand of liquid corn with the slogan "Not a Goiter in a Gallon."

Despite the promotional gimmicks, South Carolina agriculture saw little benefit from the iodine campaign. With the advent of iodized salt in the 1940s, Americans had a convenient dietary supplement and demand for foods high in iodine content declined. ROBERT T. OLIVER

South Carolina. Natural Resources Commission. *South Carolina Iodine: Facts and Figures Showing What It Is and What It Means in Fruits, Vegetables, Sea Food and Milk.* Columbia: South Carolina Natural Resources Commission, 1931.
———. *South Carolina, Her Resources and Inviting Opportunities: The New Era of Iodine.* Columbia: South Carolina Natural Resources Commission, 1932.

Ioor, William (1780–1850). Playwright, physician. Ioor was born on January 4, 1780, in St. George's Dorchester Parish, the son of John Ioor and Elizabeth Bradwell. Descendants of French Huguenots who fled to Holland, Ioor's family was prominent, his grandfather having received a land grant on the Ashley River in Berkeley County from King George III. The author of two dramas, Ioor is South Carolina's first native playwright.

Ioor received a medical degree from the University of Pennsylvania in Philadelphia before the age of twenty and returned to Dorchester to become a practicing physician and farmer. He married Ann Mathewes on December 23, 1802, and the couple had nine children. Also active in politics, he represented St. George Dorchester Parish in the General Assembly from 1800–1801 and 1802–1804. In 1805 Ioor's first play, *Independence; or, Which Do You Like Best, the Peer or the Farmer?* was performed in Charleston. Adapted from a Scottish novel, *The Independent* by Andrew McDonald, Ioor's play is set in England and involves the attempts of a dissipated nobleman and his slippery lawyer to acquire through dubious means the land of an independent yeoman farmer. While the novel primarily concerns the evils of infidelity, Ioor emphasizes the freedom, dignity, and virtue of the small farmer, as well as "the pure pleasure of country life." *Independence* is notable for being an early example of the idealization of the debt-free yeoman farmer, a key tenet of Jeffersonian republicanism.

Ioor's second play, *The Battle of Eutaw Springs,* was the first dramatization of a Revolutionary War battle set in the South and prefigures the literary glorification of that conflict by later South Carolina writers, especially during the 1820s. Composed in 1806 and performed in Charleston in 1807 and 1808, the play was revived in Richmond in 1811 and Philadelphia in 1813. Though somewhat embellished, *The Battle of Eutaw Springs,* which features Nathanael Greene and Francis Marion among other historical figures, is a reasonably accurate account of the encounter that led to the evacuation of the British from Charleston. Strongly anti-British in sentiment, the play was intended to strengthen American resolve in the face of the tensions that eventually resulted in the War of 1812—hence its revival. William Gilmore Simms, who met Ioor on a deer hunt around 1830 and described him as a "cheery, humorous, old gentleman," recognized that the play's success was "due rather to its patriotism than to his literary execution."

Sometime after his plays were produced, Ioor moved to Savannah, Georgia, where he practiced medicine for about fifteen years before moving back to South Carolina, to Greenville District near Pelzer. According to family oral tradition, his habit of freely making loans, many of which were not repaid, led to reduced circumstances and necessitated his move to the country. He died at home on July 30, 1850, and was buried next to his wife in the Springwood Cemetery in Greenville. HUGH DAVIS

Bailey, N. Louise, ed. *Biographical Directory of the South Carolina House of Representatives.* Vol. 4, *1791–1815.* Columbia: University of South Carolina Press, 1984.

Watson, Charles S. *Antebellum Charleston Dramatists.* University: University of Alabama Press, 1976.

IPTAY. IPTAY is a major fund-raising organization to support students and the athletic program at Clemson University. In August 1934 alumnus Rupert H. Fike, a medical doctor in Atlanta, enlisted the help of other alumni to found IPTAY, an acronym for "I Pay Ten A Year." The immediate goal of the organization was to "to provide annual financial support to the athletic department at Clemson and to assist in every way possible to regain for Clemson the high athletic standing which rightfully belongs to her." As founded, IPTAY was a secret order whose members took an oath of secrecy. In 1954 the organization was restructured under the leadership of Robert C. Edwards, who later served as president of Clemson from 1958 to 1979. In spite of a recommendation from a team of consultants that would have destroyed IPTAY, Edwards defended it to the board of trustees and its right to raise money for the athletic program. To further improve efficiency, the organization was restructured to include a board of directors elected from six districts within the state. During the next two decades, the mission and membership of IPTAY grew dramatically. In 1981 the membership topped twenty thousand. A variety of fund-raising campaigns, aided by an official publication, *The Orange and White,* allowed the organization to fund numerous projects: more than two hundred scholarships for athletes; the construction in 1991 of Vickery Hall, a facility built specifically for student athletes; and the IPTAY Academic Scholarship Endowment, which was created to help meet the need for more academic scholarships for nonathletes. In 2000, for the first time in its history, IPTAY's annual fund-raising total exceeded $10 million. In 2003 membership stood at 24,000 distributed throughout the United States and Europe. D. S. TAYLOR

Gault, Harper S., ed. *IPTAY 50: The First Fifty Years.* Columbia, S.C.: R. L. Bryan, 1984.

Irby, John Laurens Manning (1854–1900). U.S. senator. Irby was born in Laurens on September 10, 1854, one of seven children born to the planter and politician James Henderson Irby and Henrietta Earle. After a year at Princeton College in New Jersey, Irby transferred to the University of Virginia, but he left in 1873 without taking a degree. He returned to Laurens to read law and was admitted to the bar in 1876. That same year, he married Nannie MacFarland of Cheraw. The couple had seven children.

Although first active in the state Democratic Party in the election of 1876, Irby did not run for legislative office until 1886, when he was elected to the state House of Representatives from Laurens County. Returned in 1888 and 1890, Irby was unanimously elected Speaker of the House in 1890. During this time, Irby and others persuaded Benjamin Tillman to come out of his self-imposed retirement and lead the reform movement initiated by the Farmers' Alliance as a challenge to conservative control of the Democratic Party. Irby quickly established himself as one of Tillman's most trusted lieutenants. At the Farmers' Alliance convention in March 1890, Irby nominated Tillman for governor and used his considerable political skills to ensure Tillman's nomination at the state Democratic convention in August. As a reward for his loyal service, Irby was elected to the U.S. Senate in December 1890, defeating the revered Wade Hampton and signaling the end of Bourbon rule in South Carolina. Serving in the Senate from 1891 to 1897, Irby failed to establish a noteworthy record. He supported removing the United States from the gold standard and favored increased regulation of banking interests. However, his attendance was sporadic due in large part to his position as chairman of the state Democratic Executive Committee, which necessitated frequent travel to South Carolina. In addition, he disappointed Tillmanites by his failure to wield influence in the distribution of federal patronage in South Carolina, with President Grover Cleveland deferring to Irby's conservative colleague, Senator Mathew C. Butler.

In 1895 Irby led the Laurens County delegation to the state constitutional convention. There, he clashed with Tillman on several issues, most notably Tillman's demand that literacy tests and property ownership be made requirements of voter eligibility. Irby opposed the plan, believing it would disenfranchise too many poor whites who supported the reform Democrats. The conflict left Irby and Tillman permanently estranged. In the summer of 1896, rumors circulated that Irby had accepted whiskey rebates and illegally profited from the sale of state bonds. The story likely originated with Irby's political enemies, who were well aware of his excessive use of alcohol and frequent displays of unruly behavior. Discredited and out of Tillman's favor, Irby did not seek reelection to the Senate in 1896. When his successor, Joseph H. Earle, died only months into his term in 1897, Irby made an unsuccessful bid for the office that summer.

After his defeat, Irby returned to Laurens to practice law. He died on December 9, 1900, and was buried in City Cemetery, Laurens. MICHAEL ROBERT MOUNTER

Slaunwhite, Jerry L. "John L. M. Irby: The Creation of a Crisis." Master's thesis, University of South Carolina, 1973.

Irish. The Irish connection with South Carolina began with the foundation of the Carolina colony. The first surveyor of the colony, Florence O'Sullivan, was an Irishman. As the colony grew in prosperity in the late seventeenth and early eighteenth centuries, Irish families such as the Rutledges, Lynches, and Barnwells gained prominence and formed the first Irish societies in the colony. In the backcountry an increasing presence of Scots-Irish began to dominate that area from the mid–eighteenth century onward. Among these migrants were the parents of Andrew Jackson and the father of John C. Calhoun. In 1841 Calhoun, in his subscription to the Irish

Emigrant Society, unequivocally stated, "I have ever taken pride in my Irish descent." These Scots-Irish were major participants in the Regulator movement and were in the vanguard of the patriotic cause in the Revolutionary War. Prominent lowcountry Irish on the patriot side included the first-generation Carolinian brothers Edward and John Rutledge, signers of the Declaration of Independence and the United States Constitution respectively, and the Irish-born Pierce Butler, who also signed the Constitution and became the first United States senator from South Carolina.

After independence, Irish migration to Carolina continued, and increasingly Catholics were among the numbers. The majority of the petitioners seeking to incorporate St. Mary's Catholic Church in Charleston in 1791 were Irish. An influx of political refugees from Ireland during the late 1790s led to the formation of the Charleston Hibernian Society on St. Patrick's Day 1799. Although predominantly Protestant in membership, the society acknowledged its transatlantic antecedents in the Society of United Irishmen, which had attempted to unite all Irish (Catholics and Protestants) by electing Father Simon Felix Gallagher as its first president.

In the nineteenth century, Catholics dominated the Irish migration into South Carolina, especially between 1845 and 1855 when more than one million left Ireland for North America fleeing the Great Famine. Most of the Irish who came to South Carolina during this period came not directly from Ireland but from other states, and they usually settled in Charleston. The 1860 census counted 4,996 native-born Irish in South Carolina, the high point of the nineteenth century. Nearly two-thirds of them (3,263) lived in Charleston, primarily as poor unskilled and semiskilled workers. Living predominantly along the Cooper River and on the Neck, the Irish lived in rough housing and were susceptible to epidemics. Alcohol abuse, crime, and premature mortality were constant realities. Nevertheless the Irish made a major impact on the city. Along with laboring, they were dominant in the police force and operated all kinds of merchandising ventures. The Catholic diocese, erected in 1820, created two new parishes in the city to cater to the growing Irish flock. The Irish were also active in local politics. Although they often challenged the racial mores of the city by conducting illicit trade with slaves, they did not challenge slavery itself. As strong Democrats, they supported the institution, and the more prosperous Irish showed no hesitation in purchasing human chattel.

There was also a sizable Irish presence in Columbia. The other Irish settlements in the antebellum state were centered around major public works projects. For example, a large Irish community grew at Tunnel Hill near Walhalla in the 1850s to construct a railroad tunnel through Stumphouse Mountain. Other Irish were scattered throughout the state, although they were more likely to be found in the towns.

The Irish in South Carolina continued to keep an interest in Irish affairs throughout the nineteenth and into the twentieth centuries. Every prominent Irish national movement had a South Carolina branch, and future Irish president Eamon De Valera recognized this tradition when he visited Charleston and Columbia in 1920 to speak to supporters of the Irish War of Independence. Along with their nationalist organizations the Irish also retained their ethnicity by supporting the Catholic Church. The first bishop, John England of county Cork, who presided over Catholicism in the Carolinas and Georgia from 1820 until 1842, played the major role in making Catholicism more acceptable in the state. Protégé successors such as the county Monaghan-born Bishop Patrick N. Lynch of Cheraw continued his work of making Catholicism compatible with Carolina values. Among those assisting Lynch in this task were the mostly Irish Sisters of Charity of Our Lady of Mercy, founded by England in 1829, whose works of charity gained even more respect for the new Irish and their faith.

By 1861 the new Irish migrants had become an integrated if not yet an assimilated part of South Carolina society. In secession and civil war, the majority of the Irish supported their adopted state. Irish units from Charleston and Columbia served with distinction. Bishop Lynch became Confederate commissioner to the Vatican. The southern defeat, particularly the destruction in Charleston and Columbia, had a harsh impact on Irish Carolinians. New migrants stopped coming to the state and the Irish-born population never again reached its 1860 level. After 1865 the Irish story in South Carolina became an increasingly Irish-American one. Opponents of Radical Reconstruction, the Irish felt rewarded when Michael Patrick O'Connor of Charleston was elected to Congress in 1878. In that city they remained a vital force in local politics, helping elect one of their own, John Patrick Grace, mayor in 1911 and again in 1919. One of South Carolina's most important politicians, James F. Byrnes, was an altar boy at St. Patrick's Catholic Church in the heart of Irish Charleston before becoming an Episcopalian, United States senator, secretary of state, and governor. The Irish-American tradition in South Carolina politics has been ably continued by leaders such as Governor Richard Riley of Greenville and Mayor Joseph P. Riley, Jr., of Charleston.

By the turn of the twentieth century, the "Irish" had indeed become assimilated into South Carolina, but they continued to show an interest in their ethnic roots. Buoyed in some part by an influx of Irish Americans from other states, there has been a renaissance of interest in Irish heritage among South Carolinians. In 1979 Irish Charlestonians founded the South Carolina Irish Historical Society. In 2003 the Ancient Order of Hibernians had divisions in Myrtle Beach, Charleston, Columbia, and Greenville. The Hibernian Society of Charleston's celebration of St. Patrick's Day remains in the twenty-first century an important city event and, reflecting its ecumenical heritage, the society alternates Catholic and Protestant presidents. DAVID T. GLEESON

Gleeson, David. *The Irish in the South, 1815–1877.* Chapel Hill: University of North Carolina Press, 2001.

Haughey, Jim. "Tunnel Hill: An Irish Mining Community in the Western Carolinas." *Proceedings of the South Carolina Historical Association* (2004): 51–62.

Joyce, Dee Dee. "White, Worker, Irish, and Confederate: Irish Workers' Constructed Identity in Late Antebellum Charleston, South Carolina." Ph.D. diss., State University of New York at Binghamton, 2002.

Leyburn, James G. *The Scotch-Irish: A Social History.* Chapel Hill: University of North Carolina Press, 1962.

Madden, Richard. *Catholics in South Carolina: A Record.* Lanham, Md.: University Press of America, 1985.

Mitchell, Arthur. *The History of the Hibernian Society of Charleston, South Carolina, 1799–1981.* N.p., 1981.

Silver, Christopher. "A New Look at Old South Urbanization: The Irish Worker in Charleston, South Carolina, 1840–1860." In *South Atlantic Urban Studies,* Vol. 3, edited by Samuel M. Hines, et al. Columbia: University of South Carolina Press, 1979.

Irmo (Lexington and Richland Counties; 2000 pop. 11,039). Incorporated on Christmas Eve 1890 and extending one-half mile in all directions from a new railroad depot, Irmo got its name from the surnames of two officers of the fledgling Columbia, Newberry, and Laurens Railroad: C. J. Iredell and H. C. Mosely. The CN & L, locally dubbed the "Crooked, Noisy, and Late," selected this spot as a refueling station for steam locomotives. This facility spawned a few stores that, for over fifty years, served as a town hall, election headquarters, and community center. Finally, in January 1988, a municipal building was dedicated: the Mathias-Lown House, a picturesque Victorian cottage located at the corner of Woodrow Street and Columbia Avenue.

During its first century, this lower Dutch Fork crossroads straddling the Lexington-Richland County line experienced substantial change. The Lake Murray Dam project of the late 1920s brought more than four thousand workmen, creating an unexpected economic boom. It also transformed the region into a recreational mecca for fisherman, water sports enthusiasts, and others mesmerized by the beauty of an enormous, man-made lake covering nearly eighty square miles. Four decades later, the emergence of an interstate highway network sparked suburban growth that saw Irmo's population rise from 408 to 3,957 in the 1970s and nearly triple during the ensuing decades.

Governed by a mayor and four-member council, with the assistance of a town administrator, Irmo has well-staffed police and fire departments and an active chamber of commerce. The community is home to five elementary, two middle, and two high schools, as well as the Harbison Campus of Midlands Technical College. Major regional employers include Fort Jackson, Allied-Signal, Michelin, and Phillips Components. Scores of residents also commute each day to jobs in the greater Columbia area.

Throughout the year residents and visitors enjoy a dozen special events, pageants, and celebrations honoring beauty queens, golf, football, the great outdoors, and—of course—okra. The famed "Okra Strut," held during the last weekend in September, attracts up to eighty thousand spectators and is recognized as one of the top festivals in the Southeast. Inaugurated by the Irmo–Lake Murray Women's Club in the early 1970s as part of a campaign to raise funds for a branch library, it has grown into a much-anticipated event complete with a parade, street dance, music, arts and crafts, food, an okra-eating contest, and a visit from the Green Giant—the Okra Man. And how did the "Strut" get its name? Credit apparently goes to Columbia radioman Gene McKay, who spun a fanciful tale concerning "the ancient Irmese." They were, he vowed, a band of short folk who each season produced a remarkable and much admired okra crop.

Close by Irmo is Harbison Regional Shopping Center, one of the largest concentrations of shops, restaurants, and specialty stores in the state. Located along Harbison Boulevard where it intersects Interstate 26, this actually is a collection of several malls, including Columbiana Centre, which sparked a turf war between Richland and Lexington Counties over tax revenues in the late 1980s. JOHN H. MOORE

Iron industry. Iron making in South Carolina began toward the end of the colonial period. Production was first reported in 1773, when Colonel William Wofford built an ironworks near the present location of Spartanburg. These early establishments were destroyed by the British during the American Revolution, but the industry revived after the war, and several furnaces were in operation by the end of the century. As late as 1808, iron making was reported to be one of the few domestic manufactures carried on for sale in the backcountry region of the state. The iron belt extended across what were the four northwestern districts of York, Spartanburg, Greenville, and Pendleton. Major iron operations included Hill's Iron Works in York District, South Carolina Manufacturing Company in Spartanburg District, and Nesbitt Manufacturing Company and King's Mountain Iron Company on the upper Broad River.

Poor transportation facilities made the industry of greater importance locally, with farm implements forged from the backcountry domestic pig and bar iron in the earlier period. By the mid-1820s, larger manufacturing companies expanding their market to the lowcountry, the exhaustion of local ore supplies, and the Panic of 1819 combined to force the closing of several operations in the iron belt. The center of production relocated to the banks of the Broad River, near the Spartanburg-York boundary. In capital investment, the industry peaked around 1840, and iron production in the late 1840s exceeded four thousand tons a year. By the mid-1850s, eight furnaces were operating in the upper Piedmont, four of which were in Spartanburg.

This fireback was made during the Revolution at the Æra Iron Furnace in York County. Courtesy, Collection of the Museum of Early Southern Decorative Arts, Winston-Salem, North Carolina

From 1795 to 1856, there were no substantial changes in the size or basic principles of operating furnaces. Manufacturers relied on water to power blast furnaces, until droughts in the 1840s forced the purchase of steam engines. Yet, until the Civil War, steam was used primarily as an auxiliary force. Larger operations relied on African American labor, with local or northern whites hired for skilled work and managerial positions.

In the decade before the Civil War, the rapid increase of anthracite furnaces in the North began to drive more expensive charcoal iron from the market. Without railroads in the backcountry until the 1850s, and with increased competition from urban foundries, local iron producers struggled to maintain their market. By then, South Carolina iron was suffering from a depletion of timber resources and a reputation for inferior quality. Eventually, the railroads made available a better and cheaper iron from the North.

In the late nineteenth century, southern iron became unsuitable for conversion into steel by the then dominant Bessemer process, and many of the iron enterprises experienced shifts from southern to northern control. Further, the industry suffered from the pricing system known as "Pittsburgh plus" and the subsequent basing point system until the mid–twentieth century. Many smaller plants have turned to electric arc furnaces for steel making, and the Georgetown Steel Company of South Carolina was the first in the nation to use Direct Reduced Iron in this type of furnace. But the southern steel industry faces competition from abroad and difficulties in maintaining productivity, as represented by the closing of Georgetown Steel in 2003. TOMOKO YAGYU

Chapman, Herman Hollis. *The Iron and Steel Industries of the South.* University: University of Alabama Press, 1953.

Clowse, Converse D. *Economic Beginnings in Colonial South Carolina, 1670–1730.* Columbia: University of South Carolina Press, 1971.

Hoover, Calvin B. *Economic Resources and Policies of the South.* New York: Macmillan, 1951.

Lander, Ernest M., Jr. "The Iron Industry in Ante-Bellum South Carolina." *Journal of Southern History* 20 (August 1954): 337–55.

Moss, Bobby G. *The Old Iron District: A Study of the Development of Cherokee County, 1750–1897.* Clinton, S.C.: Jacobs, 1972.

Irvin, Willis (1890–1950). Architect. A native of Washington, Georgia, Irvin studied architecture at the Georgia Institute of Technology and worked as a draftsman in Atlanta and Savannah before establishing an independent practice in Augusta about 1920. He was a leading designer of upscale residences in the lowcountry of South Carolina and Georgia from the late 1910s through the 1940s.

Irvin was best known for his residential designs. He catered to affluent clients, including many wealthy northerners who bought former plantations for use as winter homes. His goal, he explained in a 1937 promotional catalog, was to create "residential work in that style characteristic of the Old South." In reality, his designs represented a mythical conception of the southern plantation that was grander and more lavish than anything in the "Old South." Monumental porticos, an extensive vocabulary of classical ornamentation, and sumptuous interiors were the hallmarks of his work. Irvin was a consummate stylist of the colonial revival, and he displayed his versatility by also working in the Spanish revival, Tudor revival, and neoclassical styles.

Irvin's work in South Carolina included public schools, churches, commercial buildings, and numerous private homes. His largest residential commissions included houses for James L. Coker III in Hartsville (1931); A. H. Caspary in Ritter (1931); and William Zeigler (ca. 1928), Richard Howe (ca. 1931), and Mrs. Gustavo L. F. G. di Rosa (ca. 1931) in Aiken. He received particular acclaim for designing two elegant residences for *Chicago Tribune* publisher Robert R. McCormick, one in Aiken, the other in Wheaton, Illinois. His commercial buildings included two hotels in Aiken, the Highland Park (1922) and the Henderson (1929).

Irvin died in Aiken on August 8, 1950. His daughter, Helen Stuart Irvin Dowling, who began working with him in the 1940s, carried on the practice after his death. DANIEL J. VIVIAN

Irvin, Willis. *Selections from the Work of Willis Irvin, Architect, Augusta, Georgia.* New York: Architectural Catalog Company, 1937.

Wells, John E., and Robert E. Dalton. *The South Carolina Architects, 1885–1935: A Biographical Directory.* Richmond, Va.: New South Architectural Press, 1992.

"Willis Irvin, Sr., Architect of Aiken, Dies." Columbia *State,* Aug. 9, 1950, p. A-11.

Island Packet (2003 circulation: 18,094 daily and 19,355 Sunday). The *Island Packet* is a morning newspaper, daily and Sunday, published weekday mornings with offices in Bluffton and Hilton Head Island and printed in Beaufort. In 1970 Ralph Hilton, a retired U.S. Foreign Service officer, and two others invested in a newspaper for the upscale community of Hilton Head Island. The first issue was published on July 9, 1970. Hilton became the editor and Thomas Wamsley served as president and business manager. The weekly began with a circulation of three hundred. Volunteers, mostly retired newsmen, were mainstays of the *Packet.* In March 1973 the *Packet* was sold to the News and Observer Publishing Company of Raleigh, North Carolina. The newspaper became a twice-weekly publication the following October.

In 1983 the *Packet* converted from tabloid to broadsheet size, published three times a week, and began home delivery. It became a five-day-a-week daily in 1985 and added a Sunday newspaper in 1987. In January 1990 McClatchy Newspapers of Sacramento, California, purchased the newspaper. The *Packet* added a Saturday issue five years later, and in 1997 began an on-line edition. The *Packet* bills itself as politically independent but has been aggressively proenvironment and has fought to prevent pollution of pristine sites nearby. ROBERT A. PIERCE

McNeely, Patricia G. *The Palmetto Press: The History of South Carolina's Newspapers and the Press Association.* Columbia: South Carolina Press Association, 1998.

Isle of Palms (Charleston County; 2000 pop. 4,583). For all but the last hundred years, Isle of Palms, the longest in a chain of islands between Charleston and Bulls Bay, was uninhabited. However, its palmetto jungles abounded in game and coastal aborigines used it as a larder. Its first recorded name was Hunting Island.

Until well into the twentieth century, visitors could see that the natural landscape gave the island its name. Courtesy, South Caroliniana Library, University of South Carolina

Pirates who prowled the Carolina coast called the deserted sand dunes "Long Island." In June 1776, 2,500 British soldiers camped along its beaches while waiting for the fleet that would rescue them after their failed attack on the rebels at Charleston. Decades later, with Charleston under Union blockade during the Civil War, its waters knew the constant pounding of opposing naval forces. From Breach Inlet on the island's southern end, in February 1864, the first submarine in history to sink an enemy vessel, the *H. L. Hunley,* was sent out against the doomed USS *Housatonic.*

In 1898 Long Island became Isle of Palms and began its modern transformation. Joseph S. Lawrence, a Charleston physician with money and an idea to make more, formed a company to construct a seaside resort with a boardwalk, amusement park, bathhouse, and dance pavilion to be connected to the city of Charleston by ferryboats and electric railways. Completed in 1899, the enterprise was an instant success. Thousands of Charlestonians enjoyed the carousel and cotton candy in the inaugural week. Visitors continued to arrive through World War I and into the 1920s, when new highways and bridges and automobiles replaced ferry and trolley. In the 1930s and 1940s, a succession of owners, including Charleston attorney J. C. Long, expanded development on Isle of Palms with roadway improvements and residential subdivisions. As they anticipated, the island became a summer resort for visitors as well as a bedroom community for Charleston. In 1972 after the year-round residents had attained the status of an incorporated town, the Sea Pines Company of Hilton Head Island developed land on the northern end to fashion Wild Dunes, an exclusive residential and tourist address built around a world-class golf and tennis club.

By the start of the twenty-first century, the Town of Isle of Palms had a budget of $4 million. New costs were paid by property owners and through accommodations taxes levied on the tourists, whose arrival at certain times each year swelled the population three- or fourfold. Though the wilderness had vanished, careful development left some of the natural environment of woods and marshes intact. The beach itself, a long stretch of firm, white sand, endured crowded humanity with a buoyant grace. LAYLON WAYNE JORDAN

Clarke, Philip G. *Isle of Palms.* Paducah, Ky.: Image Graphics, 1998.

Miles, Suzannah Smith. *Time and Tides on the Long Island.* Mount Pleasant, S.C.: Historic Views, 1994.

Petit, James Percival. *Freedom's Four Square Miles.* Columbia, S.C.: R. L. Bryan, 1964.

Item (2003 circulation: 21,471 daily and 21,099 Sunday). A morning newspaper, daily and Sunday, published in the city of Sumter, the *Item* has been published by five generations of the Osteen family since its founding in 1894. The *Item,* which lists itself as independent politically, serves a three-county area: Sumter, Clarendon, and Lee. Its antecedent, the *Watchman and Southron,* was created by Noah Graham Osteen (1843–1936) and the Reverend C. C. Brown in 1881 by merging the *Sumter Watchman* and the *True Southron.* This newspaper was absorbed in 1931 into the *Sumter Daily Item,* which had been created by Noah Osteen's son, Hubert Graham Osteen, in 1894.

The Osteen family continued its connection with the *Daily Item* throughout the remainder of the century. Hubert Duvall Osteen was editor and publisher of the *Daily Item* from 1946 until 1972. His son, Hubert D. Osteen, Jr., who joined the *Daily Item* in 1963, became editor in 1972 and publisher in 1984. He retained both titles into the twenty-first century and was president and chairman of the family-owned corporation, the Osteen Publishing Company. N. G. Osteen, Hubert Graham Osteen, and Hubert Duvall Osteen were each named to the South Carolina Press Association Hall of Fame.

In August 1987 the paper shortened its name to the *Item* and added a Sunday newspaper in August 1987. The *Item* became a morning newspaper on April 1, 2002. As a major voice in the community, the *Item* led campaigns to head off closing of nearby Shaw Air Force Base, which for years has been a major economic force in the community. ROBERT A. PIERCE

McNeely, Patricia G. *The Palmetto Press: The History of South Carolina's Newspapers and the Press Association.* Columbia: South Carolina Press Association, 1998.

Izard, Ralph (1742–1804). Diplomat, congressman, legislator, U.S. senator. Izard was born on January 23, 1742, the son of planter Henry Izard and Margaret Johnson, daughter of South Carolina governor Robert Johnson. At the age of twelve, Izard traveled to England, where he first attended Hackney School and later matriculated at Christ College, Cambridge University, in 1761. Returning to South Carolina in December 1764, Izard inherited extensive property in three lowcountry parishes. He established his home plantation at the Elms, St. James Goose Creek Parish, and built up a beautifully landscaped estate that eventually comprised 2,353 acres. While traveling in New York, Izard met Alice DeLancey, whom he wed on May 1, 1767. The marriage produced fourteen children, seven of whom reached maturity.

In his early years, Izard preferred the life of a cultivated gentleman and did not pursue politics. The Izards moved to London in 1771 and planned to reside in England permanently and live off the income of their South Carolina estates. But the political break between Britain and the American colonies forced the family to move to Paris in 1776.

Izard's presence in Europe made him available for diplomatic service. In May 1777 the Continental Congress elected him commissioner to Tuscany. Because the grand duke of Florence refused to allow representatives of the rebellious colonies into Italy, Izard never made it to Tuscany. He spent the next two years in Paris corresponding with Tuscan officials and becoming entangled in the disputes that divided the official American commissioners in France. Izard developed a particular antipathy toward Benjamin Franklin, which would endure throughout his public career. Frustrated over his status as a diplomat in waiting, Izard resigned in March 1779. Shortly thereafter, Congress recalled him in June 1779 because of his fractured relationship with Franklin and allegations of financial misconduct. On his arrival in Philadelphia in August 1780, Izard explained to Congress the difficulties under which he had operated. Congress responded by exonerating him. Before returning to South Carolina, Izard visited General George Washington's headquarters and successfully lobbied for the appointment of Nathanael Greene as commander of the Continental army in the Southern Department.

In January 1782 the South Carolina legislature elected Izard to the Continental Congress, where he served until September 1783. Izard supported Congress's attempt to raise revenue through a duty on imports. The Revolutionary War's impact on his personal life affected his public positions. He corresponded with New York political leaders to secure lenient treatment of his mother-in-law, who was a suspected Loyalist. He also strongly insisted that the British abide by the article in the peace treaty that prohibited them from removing American property, particularly slaves. Izard estimated that the British confiscated 170 of his own slaves.

With the war's end, Izard set out to rebuild his damaged property in South Carolina. He succeeded in recouping his losses and by 1790 owned 602 slaves, becoming one of the wealthiest planters of his day. He also speculated in nonagricultural endeavors. Earlier than most of his contemporaries, Izard envisioned canals as a means of developing the South Carolina backcountry and cementing that region's political ties to the lowcountry. He helped establish the Santee Canal Company in 1786, on one end of which he planned to build "Izardtown" on lands he owned on the Santee River.

Around this time Izard also acquired two politically prominent sons-in-laws, Gabriel Manigault and William Loughton Smith. Together they formed the Izard-Manigault-Smith, or Goose Creek, faction and played a major role in South Carolina politics for more than a decade. Elected to the state House of Representatives five times between 1782 and 1789, Izard emerged as a "planter-boss of the lowcountry." In December 1786 he exerted his political influence to prevent the election of Thomas Tudor Tucker to the state legislature, resulting in a duel in which Izard shot his opponent in the left thigh. In 1788 Izard helped ensure his son-in-law William Smith's election to the U.S. House of Representatives by authoring *Another Elector for Charleston District,* a broadside that labeled Smith's opponent, David Ramsay, as antislavery and inimical to South Carolina's economic interests.

Izard soon joined his son-in-law in Congress. In January 1789 the South Carolina legislature elected Izard to the U.S. Senate. In the First Congress, he united with other Carolina congressmen in lobbying for federal assumption of state debts, a policy that relieved South Carolina of a crippling financial burden imposed by the war. He opposed passage of the Bill of Rights and strongly objected to the reception of Quaker antislavery petitions. Concerned over rising antislavery sentiment in the North and Europe, he predicted, "The time is at no very great distance when the property in negroes will be rendered of no value." Izard generally supported the Washington administration, though he firmly opposed any executive encroachment on the Senate's prerogatives. His aristocratic and haughty bearing earned him criticism from many contemporaries. Izard served as president pro tempore of the Third Congress from May 1794 to February 1795. At the conclusion of his term, he retired to South Carolina to manage his plantations. In 1797, Izard suffered a stroke that left him an invalid. He died in Charleston on May 30, 1804, and was buried in the St. James Goose Creek Churchyard. GREGORY D. MASSEY

Bowling, Kenneth R., and Helen E. Veit, eds. *The Diary of William Maclay and Other Notes on Senate Debates.* Baltimore: Johns Hopkins University Press, 1988.

Rogers, George C. *Evolution of a Federalist: William Loughton Smith of Charleston (1758–1812).* Columbia: University of South Carolina Press, 1962.

Smith, Paul H., ed. *Letters of Delegates to Congress, 1774–1789.* Vols. 18–20. Washington, D.C.: Library of Congress, 1991–1993.

Plate 1. Congaree Swamp National Park, located on 22,000 acres in lower Richland County, protects the last significant stand of old-growth bottomland hardwood forest in the United States. Courtesy, South Carolina Department of Natural Resources

Plate 2. Rocky Shoals Spider Lily (*Hymenocallis coronaria*) is a rare species found in the Catawaba River near Landsford Canal State Park and the confluence of the Broad and Saluda rivers in Columbia. Photograph by Ted Borg. Courtesy, South Carolina Department of Natural Resources

Plate 3. Jeremiah Theus was a Swiss immigrant who settled in Charleston. He painted this portrait of Mrs. Algernon Wilson in 1756. Collection of the Museum of Early Southern Decorative Arts, Winston-Salem, N.C.

Plate 4. Henrietta Dering Johnston was America's first professional woman artist. Among her noted subjects was Colonel William Rhett, the man who vanquished the pirates off the Carolina coast. Henrietta Dering Johnston, *Colonel William Rhett.* Courtesy, Gibbes Museum of Art / Carolina Art Association

Plate 5 (top left). This traditional Catawba pottery "jar with face handles" was created by Sara Ayers, an internationally-renowned Catawba artist. Courtesy, South Carolina State Museum

Plate 6 (left). As late as the 1760s, there were reports of bison in the South Carolina piedmont. Mark Catesby, *Natural History of Carolina, Florida, and the Bahama Islands* (1731–1743). Courtesy, South Caroliniana Library, University of South Carolina

Plate 7. The Carolina parakeet could once be found in every part of the state. The last one was sighted in Georgetown County in 1938. John James Audubon, "Carolina Parret" from *The Birds of America* (1827–1838). Courtesy, Rare Books and Special Collections, Thomas Cooper Library, University of South Carolina

Plate 8. On the eve of the American Revolution, Charleston was the wealthiest city in British North America. *A View of Charles Town,* by Thomas Leitch, 1774. Collection of the Museum of Early Southern Decorative Arts, Winston-Salem, N.C.

Plate 9. Mulberry Plantation on the Cooper River (1715) with its slave quarters in the foreground. Recent archaeological evidence indicates that the slave quarters may have been West African in design with thatched roofs. Thomas Coram, *A View of Mulberry Plantation.* Courtesy, Gibbes Museum of Art / Carolina Art Association

Plate 10. The Miles Brewton House on King Street in Charleston is considered to be one of the finest colonial homes in the United States. Photograph by Rick Rhodes, Charleston, S.C.

Plate 11. At the Battle of Cowpens, American lieutenant colonel William Washington and British lieutenant colonel Banastre Tarleton came face to face as the battle was drawing to a close. William Tylee Ranney, *Washington and Tarleton Duel*. Photograph by Sam Holland. From the Collection of the State of South Carolina

Plate 12. In the years after the American Revolution, Francis Marion became a national folk hero. This painting depicts Marion and some of his men crossing the Pee Dee River. William Tylee Ranney, *Marion Crossing the Pedee.* Courtesy, Greenville County Museum of Art

Plate 13. This 1787 Fraktur (illuminated baptismal certificate in German Gothic script) of Maria Margareta House indicates the survival of Germanic traditions in the Carolina upcountry. Ehre Vater, artist. Courtesy, Museum of Early Southern Decorative Arts, Winston-Salem, N.C.

Plate 14. This nineteenth-century "Harvest Sun" or "Star Variation" quilt from Lexington County is another indication of the survival of Germanic folk art traditions. Courtesy, McKissick Museum, University of South Carolina

Ruins of Sheldon Church burnt by the British 1781

Remains of the Church in Prince Williams parish Burnt 1781 by the British

Plate 15. Charles Fraser captured in watercolor many lowcountry landmarks. Prince William Parish Church, often called Sheldon Church, was burned first by the British during the American Revolution. Charles Fraser, *Ruins of Sheldon Church in Prince William Parish.* Courtesy, Gibbes Museum of Art / Carolina Art Association

Plate 16. Washington Allston spent many years abroad, studying art in England and on the Continent. He painted *Coastal Scene on the Mediterranean* about 1810. Courtesy, Columbia Museum of Art

Plate 17. The campus of the South Carolina College in the 1830s. Courtesy, South Caroliniana Library, University of South Carolina

Plate 18. John C. Calhoun was painted by many artists in his lifetime. This 1845 portrait is one of the better likenesses of the famed statesman. George Peter Alexander Healey, *Portrait of John C. Calhoun.* Courtesy, Greenville County Museum of Art

Plate 19. A view of Columbia in 1856. The scene is from Sidney Park (rebuilt in the twentieth century as Finlay Park) looking southeast toward the center of town. The artist, A. Grinevald, used artistic license by including a completed new State House featuring a classical spire. Courtesy, South Caroliniana Library, University of South Carolina

Plate 20. William Harrison Scarborough was known primarily for his portraits of noted antebellum South Carolinians. However, he did paint several landscapes, including this one in 1860 of the Reedy River Falls. William Harrison Scarborough, *Falls of the Reedy River, Greenville, South Carolina.* Courtesy, Greenville County Museum of Art

Plate 21. During late 1863 federal forces launched several unsuccessful attacks on Fort Sumter. John Ross Key, *Bombardment of Fort Sumter, Siege of Charleston Harbor, 1863.* Courtesy, Greenville County Museum of Art

Plate 22. The Secession Banner that hung in Institute Hall, Charleston, during the South Carolina Secession Convention. Courtesy, South Carolina Historical Society

Plate 23 (left). The Palmetto Monument was erected in honor of the 441 members of the Palmetto Regiment who perished in the Mexican War. Courtesy, Clerk's Office, South Carolina House of Representatives

Plate 24. In 1908 the State of South Carolina commissioned the Gorham Company to create a complete silver service for the battleship *South Carolina*—one of two predreadnaught ships in the U.S. Navy. The silver is on loan from the National Society of the Daughters of the American Revolution in South Carolina to the Governor's Mansion. Photograph by Robert Clark

Plate 25. The State Dining Room (2001) reflects the care with which the Governor's Mansion was restored (1999–2001). Photograph by Robert Clark

Plate 26. Anna Heyward Taylor, one of the leading artists of the Charleston Renaissance, is best known for her color wood-block prints such as *Sea Turtle, No. 1.* Courtesy, Gibbes Museum of Art / Carolina Art Association

Plate 28 (below). Alice Huger Ravenel Smith, another of the artists of the Charleston Renaissance, used watercolors to capture the haunting beauty of the lowcountry. *The Threshing Floor with a Winnowing-House,* from the series A Carolina Rice Plantation of the Fifties. Courtesy, Gibbes Museum of Art / Carolina Art Association

Plate 27. Edwin Harleston, a native Charlestonian, painted scenes of African American life as well as portraits of prominent black Americans such as *Portrait of Aaron Douglas.* Courtesy, Gibbes Museum of Art / Carolina Art Association

Plate 29. Elizabeth O'Neill Verner's career began in the 1920s and continued into the 1960s. Her portrayals of Charleston's picturesque charms became quite popular. *The Aristocrat.* Courtesy, Greenville County Museum of Art

Plate 30. William Halsey portrayed his native Charleston in a vivid, nonrepresentational manner. *Night Houses.* Courtesy, Greenville County Museum of Art

Plate 31. The Works Progress Administration commissioned a number of murals for federally funded buildings in the state. This mural, by Abraham Lishensky, was originally located in the Woodruff Post Office. Courtesy, South Carolina State Museum

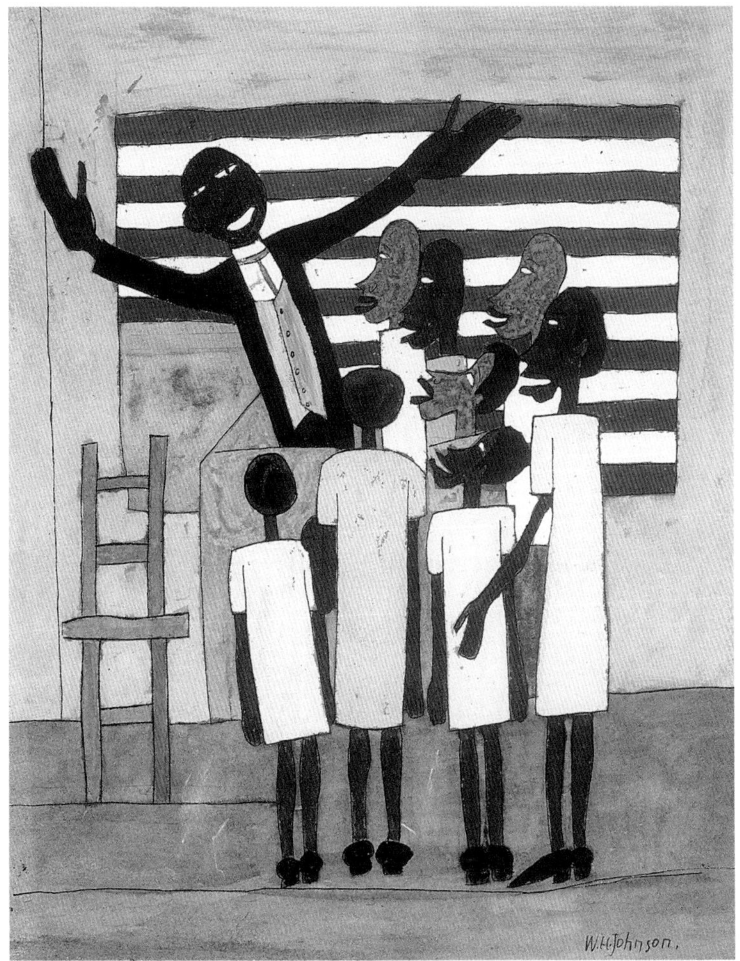

Plate 33. William H. Johnson of Florence became one of the country's most important African American artists of the twentieth century. *Lift Up Thy Voice and Sing* comes from a later period in his career when he turned to his heritage for inspiration. Courtesy, Greenville County Museum of Art

Plate 32. Beaufort County native Jonathan Green is celebrated for his vivid portrayals of the people and the landscapes of the lowcountry. *The Silver Slipper Club* by Jonathan Green, 1990. Oil on canvas, 99" × 67". Private collection. Photograph by Tim Stamm. Courtesy, Jonathan Green Studios, Inc.

Plate 34. Jasper Johns, a pivotal figure in twentieth-century American art, began his famed paintings of flags and targets in the mid-1950s. *Flags 1,* screenprint from thirty-one screens. Courtesy, Greenville County Museum of Art. © Jasper Johns / Licensed by VAGA, New York, N.Y.

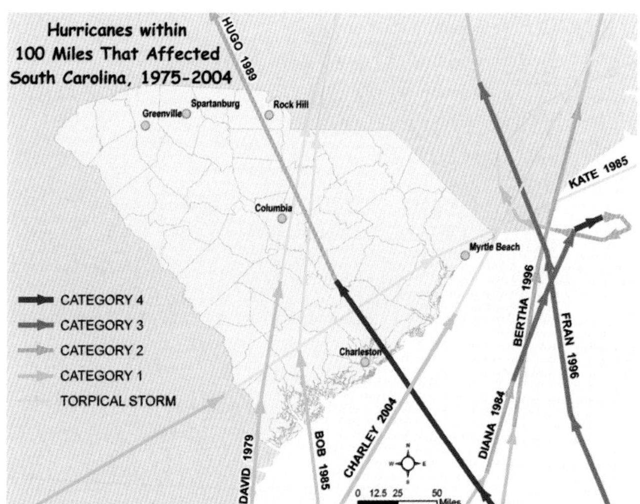

Plate 36. Between 1975 and 1996, some seven hurricanes had an impact on the state. Courtesy, Department of Geography Hazards Research Lab, University of South Carolina

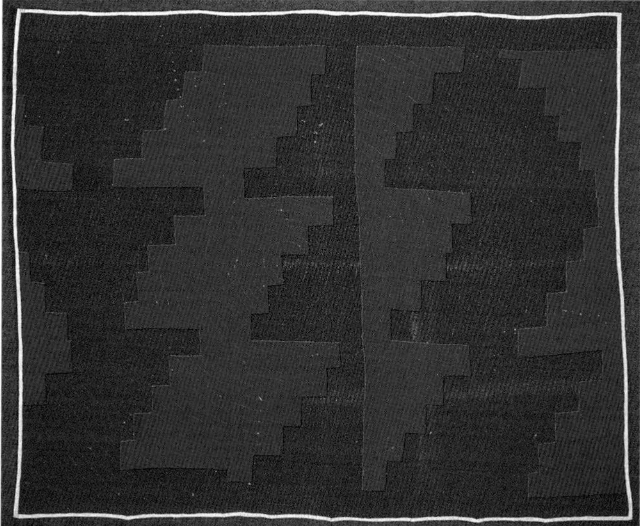

Plate 35. Carrie Grate Coachman of Plantersville made this traditional-design African American "geometric" pieced quilt about 1946. Courtesy, McKissick Museum, University of South Carolina

Plate 37. The Honorable Matthew J. Perry, senior judge of the United States Circuit Court for South Carolina. Portrait by Larry Francis Lebby, American artist (1950–)

Plate 38. When the African American Monument was dedicated in 2001, it was the only memorial of its type on any state house grounds in the nation. The monument, created by Ed Dwight, traces more than three centuries of African American history in the state. Photograph by Sam Holland

Plate 39. A view of the Greenville skyline. Photograph by John R. Brooker

Plate 40. The South Carolina State House. Photograph by Hunter Clarkson

J

Jackson, Andrew (1767–1845). Soldier, U.S. senator, president of the United States. Jackson was born in the Waxhaw settlement of Lancaster District on March 15, 1767, the son of Andrew Jackson and Elizabeth Hutchinson. He is the only South Carolinian to serve as president of the United States. Fatherless at birth, Jackson was raised by his mother in the home of relatives and attended local schools. He lost his mother and older brothers during the Revolution to illnesses. His activities against Tories led to his capture by the British in April 1781. During his capture, an officer demanded that young Jackson clean his boots. Jackson's refusal was rewarded with a sword slash that left scars on his head and hand.

Andrew Jackson, Courtesy, South Caroliniana Library, University of South Carolina

In 1784 Jackson moved to Salisbury, North Carolina, to study law, passing the bar in 1787. He then moved west into what would become Tennessee. Settling in Nashville, he quickly gained notice as a prosecutor and attorney. He fell in love with the married, but separated, Rachel Donelson Robards. The murky circumstances over her divorce, with charges of adultery, and the subsequent marriage to Jackson on January 18, 1794, would haunt Jackson during his presidential campaigns.

His wife's prominent family and his own political associations fueled Jackson's rise in politics. He served at Tennessee's constitutional convention in 1796 and as the state's first U.S. Representative. He served one year in the U.S. Senate before winning election to the Tennessee Superior Court. In 1802 he won a bitter election for the prominent position of major general in the militia.

During the War of 1812, Jackson defeated the Creek Indians at Horseshoe Bend in 1814, which led to a commission as major general in the U.S. Army. Ordered to New Orleans, he gathered a mixed force of irregulars to block a British attempt to seize the city. His stunning victory over British regulars made him a national icon. His popularity increased when he invaded Spanish Florida in 1818 and hanged two British subjects accused of agitating Indians along the Alabama-Georgia border. President James Monroe, Secretary of War John C. Calhoun, and the cabinet came close to disavowing Jackson's actions before a treaty purchasing Florida from Spain ended the crisis.

His tremendous popularity made Jackson a presidential contender. Following a short term as territorial governor of Florida, he returned to Tennessee. Nominated for president in 1822 with little initial support, Jackson reluctantly accepted his election by the Tennessee legislature to the U.S. Senate in 1823. Once in Washington, Jackson spoke out against the rampant corruption and intrigue he found there. In the 1824 presidential election, he received the most popular votes, but failed to gather an Electoral College majority. The U.S. House of Representatives, with the support of Speaker Henry Clay, awarded the presidency to John Quincy Adams, who subsequently appointed Clay as Secretary of State. Jackson fumed at this "corrupt bargain" and considered it a deliberate repudiation of the will of the people.

Jackson resigned his Senate seat and returned to Tennessee in 1825. A coalition of antiadministration foes began to form around him and his call for reform. An early and uneasy alliance was made with Calhoun, and Jackson agreed to finance a newspaper run by a Calhoun supporter, Duff Green. Soon, New York's Martin Van Buren and other prominent politicians added their organizational support to Jackson's candidacy, forming the basis of the modern Democratic Party. A vicious campaign ensued in 1828 fueled by rumors regarding his marriage, but Jackson with Calhoun as his vice presidential candidate swept to an overwhelming victory. Jackson advocated limited government, payment of the national debt, removal of the Indians beyond the Mississippi, and rotation of public officials; he opposed the monopolistic power of the Second Bank of the United States.

The Jackson administration had a troubled start when Peggy O'Neal Eaton, the wife of his secretary of war, was ostracized by Washington society under the lead of Calhoun's wife, Floride. Concurrently, Calhoun's "Exposition and Protest" against the Tariffs of 1824 and 1828 was published, advocating the right of nullification. Although a supporter of states' rights, Jackson was an ardent nationalist and viewed nullification as the first step towards disunion and a repudiation of majority rule. In reply to Calhoun and the growing nullification sentiment, Jackson, at the 1830 annual Jefferson Dinner declared, "Our Union: It must be preserved."

Jackson soon discovered that Calhoun, as secretary of war, had advocated Jackson's arrest and punishment over his invasion of Florida, furthering the split between the two men. Many saw the intrigue of Van Buren behind the schism as a bid to supplant Calhoun as Jackson's successor. The final break occurred when Jackson arranged for a new newspaper to advocate the administration's policies. An attempted reconciliation imploded when Calhoun published his correspondence over the Florida affair. Jackson subsequently purged his cabinet, an action never previously taken. Van Buren assumed Calhoun's spot on the 1832 ticket, cementing his role as Jackson's successor.

The Tariff of 1832 renewed nullification sentiment in South Carolina, despite a drop in duties. In November a South Carolina convention nullified the tariff acts and prohibited the collection of custom duties within the state. On December 10, 1832, Jackson issued a proclamation declaring the actions "incompatible with the existence of the Union . . . and destructive of the great object for which it was formed" and asked for authorization to use force. The president's nationalistic position galvanized support throughout the nation. A compromise tariff and the Wilkins Act, or Force Bill, were signed into law days before Jackson's second inauguration, ending the crisis as well as the political effectiveness of the nullification threat.

Jackson's popularity among the masses, his strong personality and leadership, and his underappreciated political skills redefined and strengthened the presidency during his two terms. His stand against nullification forced southerners to seek other, more drastic means of redress when slavery became the main sectional issue. Jackson's political opponents coalesced into the Whig Party and firmly established the two-party political system. His command of the Democratic Party led to Van Buren's election as president in 1836. Leaving office in 1837, Jackson retired to his home, the Hermitage, outside of Nashville. He died on June 8, 1845, and was buried in his garden. PATRICK MCCAWLEY

Burstein, Andrew. *The Passions of Andrew Jackson.* New York: Knopf, 2003.

Remini, Robert V. *Andrew Jackson.* 3 vols. New York: Harper & Row, 1977–1984.

Wyatt-Brown, Bertram. *The Shaping of Southern Culture: Honor, Grace, and War, 1760s–1880s.* Chapel Hill: University of North Carolina Press, 2001.

Jackson, Jesse Louis (b. 1941). Minister, civil and human rights activist. Jackson was born in Greenville on October 8, 1941, to Helen Burns, a beautician, and Noah Louis Robinson, who was married at the time to another woman and lived next door. His mother later married Charles Henry Jackson, a Greenville postal maintenance worker who became Jesse's stepfather.

Jackson grew up in the segregated South. He graduated from Sterling High, Greenville's all-black school, in 1959. A star athlete and honor student, he was awarded a football scholarship to the University of Illinois, but left after his freshman year. The following year, Jackson transferred to North Carolina A&T State University in Greensboro, where he became a star quarterback. There he became involved in civil rights activities. He helped lead a successful demonstration to end discrimination in downtown stores and was later elected president of the newly formed North Carolina Intercollegiate Council of Human Rights. In his senior year, he was elected student-body president and named southeastern director of the Congress of Racial Equality (CORE). While he was at A&T, Jesse began dating Jacqueline Lavinia Brown, whom he married in 1964. They have five children and live in Chicago.

In 1963 Jackson graduated with a bachelor's degree in sociology. He then attended Chicago Theological Seminary, but dropped out after two years to be involved full-time in the civil rights struggle. He eventually earned a master's degree in theology.

During the 1965 voting rights march in Selma, Alabama, Dr. Martin Luther King, Jr., offered Jackson a position with the Southern Christian Leadership Conference (SCLC). Working with King also helped Jesse decide to become a preacher. In 1968 he was ordained a Baptist minister.

Jackson's breakthrough came in 1967 when King put him in charge of Operation Breadbasket in Chicago. Jackson successfully organized black Chicagoans to boycott bakeries, milk companies, and grocery stores "having heavy minority patronage" to secure better service and more jobs. Afterwards he was directed to expand the project into a national program.

After King's assassination in 1968, a power struggle within SCLC ended with Jackson's resignation and his launching PUSH (People United to Save Humanity, later renamed to Serve Humanity). Several prominent African Americans, including Roberta Flack, Aretha Franklin, Carl Stokes, and Richard Hatcher, were on hand when the new organization was announced in December 1971. The organization had similar goals as Operation Breadbasket: to increase minority employment and business ownership. PUSH later included an educational initiative; Jackson traveled to dozens of schools every year. He encouraged students to stay in school, study harder, and to pledge not to use drugs long before other leaders addressed drug problems. It was during this time he also started using the popular call and response ritual, "I am somebody," in an effort to inspire those who might feel unimportant. Another motivational phase Jack son coined was "keep hope alive." Although he was not the first, Jackson would popularize the term *African American* in redefining the nation's largest minority group.

Under Jackson's leadership, PUSH successfully negotiated and sometimes boycotted businesses in an effort to increase minority employment and opportunities. Jackson's universal call for social justice helped generate awareness on behalf of minorities, women, labor issues, environmental issues, voting rights, and the poor. He became a tireless crusader of political inclusion, culminating with his most ambitious endeavor, his candidacy for the U.S. presidency.

In 1984 Jackson formed the National Rainbow Coalition of "left outs." His energy and charismatic style created a groundswell of excitement as he sought the Democratic Party's presidential nomination in 1984 and 1988. Despite some primary victories, he did not get his party's endorsement. The coalition especially energized Hispanic, Middle Eastern, and African American voters, whose support of other Democratic candidates between 1984 and 1992 had contributed to the party's success.

While Jackson's status grew at home he also began enjoying international respect. This allowed Jackson to negotiate the release of prisoners and hostages in Syria, Cuba, Iraq, Kuwait, Yugoslavia, and Sierra Leone. During the 1990s, he served as President Bill Clinton's special envoy to Africa.

Despite his numerous accomplishments, Jackson has not been without controversy. He has been criticized for verbal misfires, embellishments, and grandstanding, and accused of benefiting personally as a civil rights leader. One of his lowest points in an otherwise phenomenal career came in early 2001, when he acknowledged having a child from an extramarital affair.

Regardless of the negative baggage, entering the twenty-first century Jesse Jackson remained an influential voice for economic equity and human rights. DONALD WEST

Colton, Elizabeth O. *The Jackson Phenomenon: The Man, The Power, The Message.* New York: Doubleday, 1989.

Hertzke, Allen D. *Echoes of Discontent: Jesse Jackson, Pat Robertson, and the Resurgence of Populism.* Washington, D.C.: CQ Press, 1992.
Jackson, Jesse, Roger D. Hatch, and Frank E. Watkins. *Straight from the Heart.* Philadelphia: Fortress, 1987.
Reynolds, Barbara A. *Jesse Jackson, The Man, The Movement, The Myth.* Chicago: Nelson-Hall, 1975.

Jackson, Joseph Jefferson Wofford (1888–1951). Baseball player. "Shoeless Joe" Jackson was born on July 16, 1888, in Pickens County, the son of George and Martha Jackson. His father has been described variously as a tenant farmer, sharecropper, or a sawmill worker. In 1891 or 1892, George Jackson moved his family to Pelzer, then to the Brandon Mill near Greenville to work in textile mills. Jackson began working in the mill helping his father when he was six or seven years old, never attending school and never learning to read or write. At the age of thirteen, he began to work in the mill full time, and shortly after he started playing with the mill baseball team, earning $2.50 a game. He started as a pitcher, then played catcher before settling in as outfielder, a position he would play for the rest of his career. Between 1901 and 1907, he played for various South Carolina mill teams as well as the semiprofessional Greenville Near Leaguers. In 1908 he signed his first professional contract, with the Carolina Spinners in the Class D South Atlantic League. That same year, on July 19, he married Katherine Wynn.

"Shoeless" Joe Jackson, painting by Arthur K. Miller. Courtesy, Arthur K. Miller

It was with the Spinners that Jackson acquired the nickname "Shoeless Joe." Breaking in a new pair of cleats one game, he developed painful blisters on his feet that forced him to play the next game without his shoes. Tagging up at third base after hitting a triple, an opposing fan vented his frustration by shouting "You shoeless bastard, you." Although Jackson played only a single game without his shoes, the nickname stuck.

Connie Mack of the Philadelphia Athletics purchased Jackson's contract during the 1908 season. Jackson played in Philadelphia in parts of the 1908 and 1909 seasons before being traded to the Cleveland Naps (later the Indians) in 1910. In 1911, his first full season in the major leagues, he batted .408. The next two seasons he batted .395 and .373, but lost out all three seasons to Ty Cobb for the batting title. In 1915 Jackson was traded to the Chicago White Sox, leading the team to a World Series title in 1917 and a pennant in 1919.

Jackson is frequently regarded among the greatest natural hitters of all time. He was one of the game's first modern power hitters, always taking a full swing with his hands together and consistently hitting for power. His approach had a strong influence on Babe Ruth and other younger players. His lifetime batting average of .356 is the third highest in baseball history. He was also an excellent fielder with a powerful arm, and his glove was popularly referred to as "the place where triples go to die."

Jackson was barred from organized baseball for his participation in a scheme to throw the World Series in 1919. He was later acquitted of all charges in a jury trial in 1921. Some writers have reexamined the transcripts of the 1921 trial and Jackson's 1924 civil trial and concluded that Jackson was innocent. Jackson played baseball for many different semipro and industrial leagues throughout the 1920s and early 1930s. Returning to South Carolina, he operated a successful dry cleaning business and ran a liquor store for many years in Greenville. He died December 5, 1951, and was buried at Woodlawn Memorial Park in Greenville. DOUG SOUTHARD

Asinof, Eliot. *Eight Men Out.* New York: Ace, 1963.
Fleitz, David L. *Shoeless: The Life and Times of Joe Jackson.* Jefferson, N.C.: McFarland, 2001.
Gropman, Donald. *Say It Ain't So, Joe!: The True Story of Shoeless Joe Jackson.* 2d ed. Secaucus, N.J.: Carol, 1999.

Jackson, Mary (b. 1945). Artist, basket maker. Born in Mount Pleasant on February 15, 1945, the daughter of Joseph and Evelyina Foreman, Jackson grew up in an African American community of basketmakers and learned the craft as a child from her mother. She started creating baskets seriously in the mid-1970s, and soon mastered a variety of shapes and types, including the rice-winnowing tray called the "fanner," grain storage baskets, and flower, market, and sewing baskets for domestic use. Her solo exhibition at the Gibbes Museum of Art in 1984 introduced her to the public. Since then her career has grown dramatically, with representation in major crafts shows, and in the public collections of the Smithsonian Institution, Philadelphia and American Craft Museums, Museum of African American History in Detroit, Boston's Museum of Fine Arts, and U.S. embassies abroad.

Jackson makes her baskets traditionally, from long coils of sweetgrass, pine needles, and bulrush, bound and woven with strong, flexible strips from the palmetto tree. Her innovation has been to create baskets of original design. "From the family I learned all the traditional pieces and styles, and then I just started doing my own designs. I wanted to make something that no one had ever made before. The forms would be different—very simple, yet elegant." This was accomplished in examples such as the "Cobra," a variation of a market basket, and her daring, abstracted interpretation of a fruit basket in the series she calls "Untitled," consisting of a narrow, disk-like base and sweeping handle.

Attentive to formal and decorative qualities in her baskets, Jackson employs the soft, natural color and textures of her materials, creating a subtle interplay of light and dark concentric bands, or dynamic overall patterns. She has control over the building of forms in perfect balance, tension, and symmetry that gives her work a natural solidity and grace. ROBERTA KEFALOS SOKOLITZ

Jacksonborough Assembly (January–February 1782). After a two-year hiatus caused by war, the General Assembly met at Jacksonborough, a small town on the Edisto River about thirty miles from British-occupied Charleston.

The Jacksonborough Assembly's most important work was its decision to confiscate Loyalist estates. This volatile issue became more heated when John Laurens, chair of the committee that determined which individuals would face confiscation, proposed that slaves from confiscated estates be enlisted in the Continental army. His proposal won few adherents, though an opponent noted that legislators fought a "hard Battle on the Subject of arming the Blacks." The final confiscation act reserved some slaves as bounties for whites who enlisted in the state's Continental line and employed other slaves in public service.

Although several prominent legislators, including Aedanus Burke and Christopher Gadsden, opposed punitive legislation, they were a distinct minority. One observer estimated that 700 persons were considered for confiscation, but the legislation passed on February 26 was less sweeping. The confiscation act divided 237 persons into six categories, which included nonresident British citizens, individuals who congratulated the British after their victories, men who joined the Loyalist militia or held British commissions, and "inveterate enemies" of the state. These individuals forfeited their property and were banished from the state. A separate amercement act compelled 47 individuals who accepted British protection to pay a fine worth twelve percent of their estates.

The confiscation legislation proved controversial, and some contemporaries asserted that the assembly was motivated by revenge and greed. After the British departed South Carolina, tempers cooled and subsequent sessions of the General Assembly heard petitions of Loyalists who desired relief. By 1787 almost two-thirds of the individuals facing confiscation and banishment had received reduced penalties and permission to reside in the state. In the short term, the Jacksonborough Assembly satisfied popular clamors for retribution against Loyalists and perhaps prevented vigilante justice. GREGORY D. MASSEY

Lambert, Robert Stansbury. *South Carolina Loyalists in the American Revolution.* Columbia: University of South Carolina Press, 1987.

Salley, Alexander S., ed. *Journal of the House of Representatives of South Carolina. January 8, 1782–February 26, 1782.* Columbia: State Company, 1916.

Weir, Robert M. *"The Last of American Freeman": Studies in the Political Culture of the Colonial and Revolutionary South.* Macon, Ga.: Mercer University Press, 1986.

Jakes, John (b. 1932). Novelist. Jakes was born on March 31, 1932, in Chicago, Illinois, the son of John Adrian Jakes and Bertha Retz. Jakes is a nationally known, best-selling novelist and historian. He and his wife, Rachel Ann Payne Jakes, live most of the year on Hilton Head Island. As an eighteen-year old freshman at Northwestern University, Jakes sold his first short story for $25 and has been a commercial writer ever since. On June 15, 1951, he married Rachel Ann Payne. The marriage produced four children.

Jakes received his Bachelor of Arts degree from DePauw University in 1953 and a master of arts degree in American literature from the Ohio State University in 1954. He worked for several pharmaceutical and advertising companies during the 1950s and 1960s. All the while he was producing two hundred short stories while writing at night. In 1973 he began writing the *Kent Family Chronicles* that eventually ran to eight volumes depicting American history in the age of the Revolution through the eyes of one fictional family. All eight volumes were national best sellers. Between 1982 and 1987, Jakes published his Civil War trilogy, *North and South, Love and War,* and *Heaven and Hell* that featured the fictional South Carolina family of Orrie (Horry) Main. Sixty million copies of these eleven novels are currently in print.

More recent novels have included *California Gold, Homeland,* and *American Dreams.* In 2002 Jakes published *Charleston,* his first full-length historical novel based on the history of his adopted state. The novel chronicles the history of the city, and through it, the history of the state and the old South, from the seventeenth century through the Civil War.

John Jakes. © David G. Spielman-97, New Orleans

Jakes holds honorary degrees from five universities, including his alma mater, Ohio State University. He has been a research fellow of the Department of History at the University of South Carolina and is only the tenth living inductee of the South Carolina Academy of Authors. Two of his novels, *North and South* (1982) and *Homeland* (1993), were nominated for the Pulitzer Prize.

Jakes has been a lifelong devotee of local theater as an actor, director, and scriptwriter of dramas and musicals. He was an early and regular benefactor of the Self Family Arts Center on Hilton Head Island. He is also an expert on the life and works of Charles Dickens. His stage adaptation of *A Christmas Carol* has been produced on Hilton Head and on stages in Alabama, Ohio, and Florida. He wrote a musical adaptation of *Great Expectations,* which has been produced on Hilton Head and in Connecticut. LAWRENCE S. ROWLAND

Jamerson, James (1936–1983). Musician. Jamerson was born on January 29, 1936, in Charleston, the son of James and Elizabeth Jamerson. He demonstrated an aptitude for music at an early age, playing piano by age ten, studying trombone in elementary school, and soaking in jazz, gospel, and blues music from local radio stations.

By 1954 Jamerson had moved to Detroit, where his mother had gone the previous year in search of employment. Enrolling in

Detroit's Northwestern High School, he took up a new instrument: the upright bass. He began playing with local jazz and blues bands, quickly establishing himself as one of the hottest bassists in the Motor City. He was soon in demand by most of Detroit's recording labels. He then came to the attention of a songwriter and producer named Berry Gordy, the talented and ambitious owner of the fledgling Motown label. Jamerson began session work for Gordy around 1959. By the early 1960s, Jamerson had become "Motown's premier groovemaster." As a cornerstone of Motown's renowned studio band, the "Funk Brothers," Jamerson's skill and style on the bass became legendary. He played on almost every Motown record during its 1963–1968 heyday, providing the groove for such immortal records as "Bernadette," "Ain't To Proud To Beg," "I Heard It Through The Grapevine," "You Can't Hurry Love," and Marvin Gaye's classic album *What's Going On.* By some accounts, Jamerson played on more number one records than any musician in the history of rock and roll.

Despite his indisputable genius, Jamerson's increasingly erratic behavior and drinking problems had lowered his standing with Motown by the 1970s. He moved to Los Angeles in 1973 and for a time enjoyed a full schedule of session work, touring, and recording. Alcohol and emotional problems, however, gradually eroded demand for his declining talents. Jamerson died in Los Angeles on August 2, 1983. He was inducted into the Rock and Roll Hall of Fame in 2000. TOM DOWNEY

Miller, Michael. "From the Bottom to the Top, S.C. Bass Player Invented the Foundation of Motown Sound." Columbia *State,* April 22, 2003, pp. D1, D3.

Slutsky, Allan. *Standing in the Shadows of Motown: The Life and Music of Legendary Bassist James Jamerson.* Milwaukee, Wis.: Hal Leonard, 1991.

James, John (1732–1791). Soldier, legislator. John James, son of William James and Elizabeth Witherspoon, was born in Ireland on April 12, 1732. The family migrated to Prince Frederick's Parish, South Carolina, shortly after his birth and James grew to be a prominent planter with large landholdings. Before the Revolutionary War, James owned at least 2,114 acres, including 354 acres on the Black River, 950 acres on the Waccamaw River, 710 acres along the Little Pee Dee River and Lynches Creek, and 100 acres near Indiantown in Williamsburg County. He married Jean Dobein on January 18, 1753. They had five children.

James gained his first military experience as a captain in the provincial militia during the Cherokee War (1759–1761). In 1775 and 1776 he participated in the Second Provincial Congress and the First General Assembly, representing Prince Frederick's Parish. At the outbreak of the Revolutionary War, he was elected a captain in the state militia and served in the defense of Charleston under General William Moultrie, commanding a force of 120 men at a skirmish at Tulifinny Bridge in 1779. Fortunately for James, he was not among those who surrendered when the British captured Charleston in May 1780, having been ordered by Governor John Rutledge to raise a militia unit in the Williamsburg Township region.

William Dobein James, John James's second son, relates the story that after the fall of Charleston, the British demanded loyalty oaths from paroled Americans. James was chosen by the local inhabitants to meet with British authorities in Georgetown to ask if the oaths included the obligation to take up arms against their neighbors still in rebellion. Meeting with a British officer in Georgetown, James was told that not only their loyalty but also their service for the king was demanded. The unarmed James, believing he was being threatened, retreated from the meeting brandishing a chair in front of him. Once clear of the officer, he returned to Williamsburg to report the event. The news of this incident, and that of General Horatio Gates arriving in North Carolina to take charge of a new American army, induced the Williamsburg patriots to return to arms against the British. Once again, James was elected to lead them.

James turned his militia force over to Francis Marion in August 1781 at Witherspoon's Ferry on Lynches Creek. James served under Marion as a major and took part in several skirmishes against the British, including the Battle of Eutaw Springs (September 8, 1781). Shortly after the battle, he was elected to the state legislature and served in the Fourth General Assembly (1782). After the Revolution, he worked to restore his properties, which were heavily damaged during the war, and was again elected to public service, representing Prince Frederick's Parish in the Sixth General Assembly (1785–1786). James died on January 29, 1791, and was buried at Indiantown Presbyterian Church. STEVEN D. SMITH

Bailey, N. Louise, and Elizabeth Ivey Cooper, eds. *Biographical Directory of the South Carolina House of Representatives.* Vol. 3, *1775–1790.* Columbia: University of South Carolina Press, 1981.

Blanchard, Amos. *American Military Biography: Containing the Lives and Characters of the Officers of the Revolution, Who were Most Distinguished in Achieving our National Independence.* New York: Edward J. Swords, 1830.

James, William Dobein. *A Sketch of the Life of Brig. Gen. Francis Marion.* 1821. Reprint, Marietta, Ga.: Continental Book Company, 1948.

Jamestown. Jamestown was the first Huguenot settlement on the Santee River in what became Berkeley County, across the river from the Georgetown/Williamsburg county line. Huguenots settled the Santee region soon after 1672 when the Lords Proprietors resolved to create a colony, or square, of twelve thousand acres at Jamestown. Similar tracts were simultaneously authorized at Charleston and Oyster Point.

The first French missionary in Carolina, the Reverend Pierre Robert, settled on the Santee in what would later become St. James Santee Parish in 1686. The first church of St. James Santee was built of wood with brick foundations before the village was laid out. By 1699 the church had 111 members, and was the largest church outside Charleston. The town was laid out from 1705 to 1706, with thirty-six lots centered on the church and cemetery located in a common area along the river. As with most early settlements, there were few permanent residents. The owners of outlying plantations built town houses in Jamestown in order to attend church and enjoy social interaction.

By 1714 the population had spread down the Santee River and a new Chapel of Ease was authorized at Echaw. Because Jamestown was so close to the river, it was subject to frequent and severe flooding. The community was abandoned in the mid-1700s, and no visible traces remain. The chapel at Echaw was replaced by a brick structure in 1748. In 1754 this new chapel was designated as the parish church of St. James Santee, and the church at Jamestown was abandoned. Anglican minister Charles Woodmason reported in 1765 that the church at Jamestown "fell to decay some Years ago, and has not been since rebuilt." The modern community of Jamestown was established in the twentieth century on high ground well away from the Santee River, near the site of the original town. ROBERT W. BAINBRIDGE

Dalcho, Frederick. *An Historical Account of the Protestant Episcopal Church in South-Carolina.* 1820. Reprint, New York: Arno, 1972.

Hirsch, Arthur Henry. *The Huguenots of Colonial South Carolina.* 1928. Reprint, Columbia: University of South Carolina Press, 1999.

Woodmason, Charles. *The Carolina Backcountry on the Eve of the Revolution: The Journal and Other Writings of Charles Woodmason, Anglican Itinerant.* Edited by Richard J. Hooker. Chapel Hill: University of North Carolina Press, 1953.

Jasper, William (?–1779). Soldier. Little is known of Jasper's origins. Traditionally he has been identified as Irish, but others have argued that he was of German ancestry.

William Jasper. Courtesy, South Carolina Historical Society

On July 7, 1775, in Halifax District, Georgia, William Jasper enlisted in the elite grenadier company of the Second South Carolina Continental Regiment. On June 28, 1776, as a sergeant, he won lasting fame during the British attack on Sullivan's Island, near Charleston. When an enemy shot brought down the fort's flag, Jasper restored the banner while under enemy fire. In 1779 he led dangerous guerrilla raids against British pickets and patrols. At least once, he passed through enemy lines by posing as a deserter. During the Franco-American attack on the British lines around Savannah on October 9, 1779, Jasper received a mortal wound while rescuing one of his regiment's flags. He had placed another flag on a British entrenchment, which is now preserved in the Smithsonian Institution. Jasper left a widow and at least two children, although apparently no descendants are living today.

Jasper became a national hero as a character in the historical novel by Mason L. Weems, *The Life of Gen. Francis Marion* (1809). Weems based this work loosely on a manuscript by Peter Horry. Although Horry dismissed Weems's book, he and other Revolutionary War veterans confirmed Jasper's great personal courage. Eight counties (including Jasper County, South Carolina), numerous towns, and thousands of Americans were named for the man described as "the Brave Sergt. Jasper." ROBERT S. DAVIS

Gamble, Thomas. "The Story of Sergeant William Jasper, Hero of the Revolution: 1775 to 1779." Scrapbook. Georgia Department of Archives and History, Morrow, Georgia.

Jones, George Fenwick. "Sergeant Johann Wilhelm Jasper." *Georgia Historical Quarterly* 65 (spring 1981): 7–15.

Jasper County (656 sq. miles; 2000 pop. 20,678). Jasper County was formed by an act of the legislature on January 30, 1912, from parts of Beaufort and Hampton Counties, an area which contained much of the old lowcountry parishes of St. Peter's and St. Luke's. The southernmost county in the state, Jasper is bound by the Savannah River on the southwest, Hampton County on the north, and Beaufort County on the east. Initially inhabitants wished to name the new county Heyward, in honor of Thomas Heyward, Jr., a signer of the Declaration of Independence who resided in the area. But the effort failed, and the name Jasper was assigned, honoring Revolutionary War hero Sergeant William Jasper. Ridgeland is the county seat.

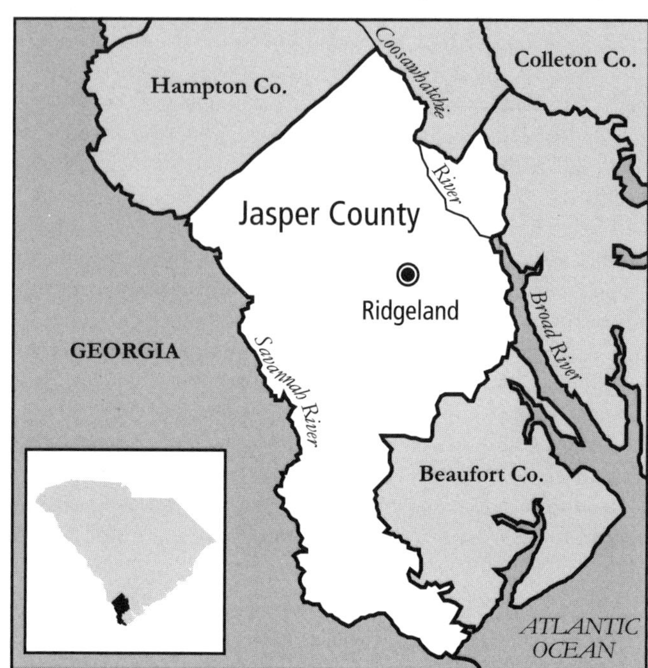

English and Scots settlers arrived in the region in the late 1600s, where they withstood Spanish attacks and the Yamassee War of 1715 to prevail and lay the foundation for future settlement. In the 1730s, an expedition of Swiss Protestants, led by Jean Pierre Purry, settled on a land grant on the Savannah River (about two miles northwest of the modern town of Hardeeville), which was dubbed Purrysburg. The unhealthy and inconvenient location failed to divert trade away from Charleston or Savannah, however, and the population migrated to other parts of South Carolina and Georgia. Descendants of earlier Scots settlers returned to the area in the mid-1700s, where they established the Euhaw Baptist Church, the first church in the county and one of the earliest Baptist churches in the South. Although Purrysburg was the only eighteenth-century town of note in the Jasper vicinity, future towns traced their origins to the colonial era as well, including Robertville, Coosawhatchie, and Grahamville.

By the 1750s, rice and indigo became the cash crop of choice among the residents of St. Peter's Parish. Although indigo disappeared after the Revolutionary War, rice remained the foundation of the area's agricultural wealth through the nineteenth century. By the end of the antebellum era, St. Peter's Parish was the second most productive rice-growing region of South Carolina. None of this could have happened without the importation of thousands of African slaves, who quickly became a large majority. Old church records indicate that slaves may have outnumbered whites in the region by as much as ten to one before the Civil War.

The future county was the site of considerable military action during the Civil War. Union forces arrived in Beaufort District in November 1861. Over the next several years, they made several unsuccessful incursions into the Jasper region in an effort to cut the railroad line between Charleston and Savannah. In one of the largest of these attempts, in November 1864, a force of 1,400 South Carolina and Georgia Confederates defeated a Union force of about 5,500 in the battle at Honey Hill (about two miles east of Grahamville). In February 1865 the army of William T. Sherman crossed the Savannah River into Jasper County and destroyed entire towns and villages, leaving intact only a few scattered outbuildings, two or three churches, and the former home of Thomas Heyward, Jr.

Soon after the war, the Jasper area was again "invaded" by northerners, this time in the form of industrialists buying up lands as investments and for recreation. Beginning in the 1870s, large private hunting preserves, such as the Pineland Club and Okeetee Club, were organized to provide sport and recreation to well-heeled northern members. By the early twentieth century, timber firms such as the Export Lumber Company of Boston and the Argent Lumber Company had acquired large tracts in the Jasper County region. Much of modern Jasper County remained in the hands of timber interests and affluent northern families, although wealthy southerners recently repurchased a good portion. By the end of the twentieth century, many out-of-state hunt clubs leased these lands for the long deer season and excellent hunting throughout the county, which continued to boost the Jasper economy.

Although not located in Jasper County, the development of Hilton Head Island provided employment opportunities for county residents. Sea Island resort development eventually spilled into the county and new arrivals, including many Hispanics, moved in to take advantage of these new jobs. Interstate 95, which opened in the 1970s, also proved to be a boon to the Jasper economy, with businesses springing up near highway interchanges at Hardeeville, Ridgeland, Coosawhatchie, and Pocataligo. New industries came, as did a third wave of northern "invaders" looking for the ideal place to retire. As a result of this late-twentieth-century growth, land values in parts of Jasper County skyrocketed, with owners of waterfront property finding themselves atop gold mines. During the same period, Jasper lost two railroads and all of its sawmills. Most farm acreage was devoted to pulpwood. However, the overall standard of living increased and Jasper boosters believed their county was truly on the move.

Notable residents have included Daniel Heyward, an eighteenth-century entrepreneur; his son Thomas Heyward, Jr., signer of the Declaration of Independence; General Henry Martyn Robert, author of *Robert's Rules of Order;* Mary Ellis, the first female elected to the South Carolina Senate; Air Force General Jacob Edward Smart, the second South Carolina native to achieve four stars; and Air Force General Lloyd Newton, the first African American from South Carolina to receive his fourth star and a former member of the Air Force's Thunderbirds flying team. WOFFORD MALPHRUS

Harvey, Bruce G. *An Architectural and Historical Survey of Jasper County, South Carolina.* Atlanta: Brockington and Associates, 1996.

Malphrus, Wofford E. *A History of Euhaw Baptist Church, 1686–1995.* N.p., 1995.

Perry, Grace Fox. *The Moving Finger of Jasper.* [Ridgeland, S.C.: n.p., 1962].

Rowland, Lawrence S. "'Alone on the River:' The Rise and Fall of the Savannah River Rice Plantations of St. Peter's Parish, South Carolina." *South Carolina Historical Magazine* 88 (April 1987): 121–50.

Trinkley, Michael, and Debi Hacker. *Preliminary Archaeological and Historical Investigations at Old House Plantation, Jasper County, South Carolina.* Columbia, S.C.: Chicora Foundation, 1996.

Jazz. South Carolina has been home to an impressive number of nationally prominent jazz figures as well as the site of many high-caliber jazz activities, including major festivals, comprehensive jazz education programs, and even an award-winning radio show.

Although Cheraw native and bebop pioneer Dizzy Gillespie, a major influence on modern jazz trumpeters, is the best-known and most historically significant jazz musician to have come from the state, many other important performers were either born or spent their formative years in South Carolina, some being alumni of the world-famous youth bands of Charleston's Jenkins Orphanage. Among the earliest South Carolinians to make names for themselves outside the state were tuba player Pete Briggs, who recorded with Louis Armstrong in 1927; trumpeter Jabbo Smith, regarded by many in the 1920s as a serious rival to Armstrong himself; preeminent alto saxophonist Willie Smith; and popular trumpeters Peanuts Holland and Gus Aitken. The Duke Ellington Orchestra included South Carolinians such as trumpeters Bubber Miley, Cat Anderson, and Taft Jordan; clarinetist and saxophonist Jimmy Hamilton; and drummer Rufus Jones. South Carolinians who performed with Count Basie include his longtime guitarist Freddie Green, trumpeter Pete Minger, and saxophonist John C. Williams. Charleston's Fud Livingston became an important arranger for many swing bands. Players who rose to prominence in modern times include saxophonists Lucky Thompson, Odean Pope, Houston Person, Bob Belden, and Chris Potter; guitarist James Blood immigration; drummer Alphonse Mouton; and trombonist Ron Westray.

Two major jazz festivals have brought scores of famous musicians to the state. Since 1980 the annual Spoleto Festival USA in Charleston has presented dozens of top stars, including such luminaries as the Count Basie and Duke Ellington orchestras, Stan Getz, Gerry Mulligan, Sarah Vaughan, Chick Corea, Sonny Rollins, Wayne Shorter, George Shearing, Dianne Reeves, and many more. And for ten years, starting in 1987, Columbia's Main Street Jazz annually imported performers of a similar quality.

Educational institutions, arts presenters, and other organizations bring leading performers to the state on a regular basis. The Hilton Head Jazz Society, founded in 1986, imports name musicians to raise funds for its jazz scholarship program and present master classes at the local schools. The group also holds monthly concerts featuring regional artists.

In the late 1950s, one of the first collegiate jazz bands on the east coast was organized at Newberry College. Shortly afterwards the Newberry College High School Jazz Festival was founded to allow student jazz bands to perform for ratings and comments by nationally known clinicians. Later, after the formation of the South Carolina unit of the National Association of Jazz Educators (now the International Association for Jazz Education) to promote jazz education in the state, the Newberry festival, in conjunction with that organization, introduced the South Carolina All-State High School Jazz Ensemble, whose members are selected by audition from throughout the state.

At the start of the twenty-first century, many of the state's secondary and postsecondary educational institutions provided some form of jazz in their curricula. Offerings included ensembles, classroom courses, clinics conducted by professional artists, and even full majors in jazz. The University of South Carolina at Columbia offered curricula leading to both bachelor's and master's degrees in jazz studies. The South Carolina Jazz Hall of Fame, founded at South Carolina State College in the late 1970s, honors outstanding students, professionals, and support personnel. In 1985 Dizzy Gillespie became its first professional inductee.

The citizens of South Carolina have regular access to high quality jazz through the offerings of South Carolina Educational Television (SCETV) and the South Carolina Educational Radio Network

(SCERN). The latter not only brings the music to citizens throughout the state in the form of locally produced and nationally syndicated programs, but has for more than two decades produced the nationally distributed, Peabody Award–winning "Marian McPartland's Piano Jazz," a weekly program featuring the highly regarded pianist and her guests. In the year 2000, the network's Rock Hill station began to broadcast jazz exclusively and continuously. DAVID FRANKLIN

Chilton, John. *A Jazz Nursery: The Story of the Jenkins' Orphanage Bands of Charleston, South Carolina.* London: Bloomsbury Book Shop, 1980.

Feather, Leonard, and Ira Gitler. *The Biographical Encyclopedia of Jazz.* New York: Oxford University Press, 1999.

Kernfeld, Barry, ed. *The New Grove Dictionary of Jazz.* 2d ed. 3 vols. New York: Grove's, 2001.

Jeanes Teachers. In the early 1900s, most African American children in South Carolina only attended school through the fourth grade for a few months each year in poorly maintained and equipped schools. Most African American teachers had little education. In 1907 Anna T. Jeanes, a wealthy Philadelphia Quaker, donated $1 million to set up the Negro Rural School Fund to provide educational opportunities for black children in the rural South. At the insistence of Jeanes, Booker T. Washington joined a group of mostly white men on the board. As a result, the focus of the program was industrial education at first. The program began with the hiring of the first Jeanes Teacher in Virginia in 1908. The Jeanes Supervisors, mostly African American women, helped teachers in rural schools. Many received training at traditionally black colleges in the South. By 1914 there were 118 Jeanes Teachers or Supervisors working across the South. By 1928, there were 324.

Julia Berry was employed as South Carolina's first Jeanes Industrial Teacher in 1909 in Sumter County. Although ten other Jeanes Teachers began working in the state in 1909, the program grew slowly. Until a State Director of Negro Education was appointed in 1918, no one had the specific responsibility of presenting the program to local communities. The Jeanes Fund initially paid the teachers' salaries, but in order for the program to expand, the state and its counties would have to contribute.

In 1936 the South Carolina Superintendent of Education reported that schools employing Jeanes Teachers were noticeably superior to those that did not. As the state and its counties became convinced of the value of the Jeanes program, they began to assume more of the costs. By the late 1940s, the Southern Education Association, which merged with the Jeanes program and several other educational funds in the 1930s, was covering about eight percent of the cost in South Carolina; the state and its counties were paying the balance.

Jeanes Teachers encouraged self-sufficiency. They taught students and their families to sew, bake, and do carpentry. Jeanes Teachers made home visits to urge children to attend school regularly, interacted with the community, emphasized the need for better health care, and taught families about sanitation. In 1918 the state's fifteen Jeanes Teachers became involved in organizing almost three hundred Homemakers' Clubs with more than 4,600 members as part of the war effort. Over time the emphasis of the Jeanes program shifted from a community focus to an educational focus. Jeanes Teachers sponsored reading workshops, in-service programs for teachers, art exhibits for children, and taught children how to cooperate with each other. They established libraries and helped to raise money for new facilities and schoolbooks.

The end of school segregation in the 1960s led to the demise of the Jeanes Teachers program. Having black Jeanes teachers supervising white teachers in newly integrated school systems was difficult. New federal grants provided funds to meet educational needs. Nevertheless, for more than sixty years, Jeanes Teachers had helped to provide better educational opportunities for African American children in South Carolina. CAROL SEARS BOTSCH

Brawley, Benjamin. *Doctor Dillard of the Jeanes Fund.* Freeport, N.Y.: Books for Libraries, 1971.

Brewton, John E. "The Status of Supervision of Schools for Negroes in the Southeastern States." *Journal of Negro Education* 8 (April 1939): 164–69.

Jones, Lance G. E. *The Jeanes Teacher in the United States 1908–1933.* Chapel Hill: University of North Carolina Press, 1937.

Woodfaulk, Courtney Sanabria. "The Jeanes Teachers of South Carolina: The Emergence, Existence, and Significance of Their Work." Ph.D. diss., University of South Carolina, 1992.

Jefferies, Richard Manning (1888–1964). Attorney, legislator, governor. Jefferies was born at Star Farm, Union County (later Cherokee County) on February 27, 1888, the youngest of eleven children born to John Randolph Jefferies and Mary Henrietta Allen. After graduating from the University of South Carolina in 1910, he moved to Ridgeland, where he read law. While in Ridgeland, he was the superintendent of the elementary school and assisted in the formation of Jasper County. After his marriage to Annie Keith Savage on July 26, 1911, and his admission to the bar in December 1912, Jefferies moved to Walterboro. He served Colleton County as master in equity, and in 1918 was elected probate judge. In 1926 he was elected to his first term in the state Senate. Over the next thirty-two years, he won seven more terms.

In the S.C. Senate, Jefferies quickly attained power and influence. He became part of the loose coalition of fiscally conservative lowcountry legislators known as the "Barnwell Ring." He rose to become state Senate president pro tempore and chairman of the powerful Finance Committee in 1941. However, he would not remain long in either of these positions. When Governor Burnet R. Maybank was elected to the U.S. Senate in November 1941 and Lieutenant Governor Joseph E. Harley died the next February, Jefferies succeeded to the governorship on March 2, 1942.

In his eleven months as governor, Jefferies guided the state through economic and racial upheavals during World War II. He worked to earn federal military contracts for the state and encouraged industrial development. He appointed the Preparedness for Peace Commission in the fall of 1942, charging it with planning a transition from a war-time to a peace-time economy. This proved to be a farsighted decision, for the commission recommended creating the modern State Development Board and proposed other reforms in state government. Jefferies did not seek a term as governor in his own right. Instead he ran for and won his old state Senate seat from Colleton County, which had remained vacant. Having lost his seniority when he became governor, he did not resume any of his leadership posts.

Jefferies was closely involved with the growth of Santee Cooper, the South Carolina Public Service Authority. He was the principal author of the 1934 act creating the authority, and he served as its general counsel until becoming governor. After leaving that office, he became the general manager of the authority. Under his leadership, Santee Cooper became one of the leading supporters of economic development in the lowcountry, providing cheap power to new industry and rural electric cooperatives.

Jefferies was not reelected to his Senate seat in 1958, but remained at the helm of Santee Cooper until his death on April 20,

1964. He left a daughter and a son, who married the daughter of his longtime legislative ally, state Senator Edgar Brown of Barnwell. R. PHILLIP STONE II

Bailey, N. Louise, Mary L. Morgan, and Carolyn R. Taylor, eds. *Biographical Directory of the South Carolina Senate, 1776–1985.* 3 vols. Columbia: University of South Carolina Press, 1986.

Edgar, Walter B. *History of Santee Cooper, 1934–1984.* Columbia, S.C.: R. L. Bryan, 1984.

Jefferies, Richard Manning. Papers. South Caroliniana Library, University of South Carolina, Columbia.

"South Carolina Loses former Governor and State Senator." *South Carolina Magazine* 28 (July 1964): 5–9.

Jenkins, Daniel Joseph (ca. 1862–1937). Businessman, clergyman, community leader. Jenkins was born at Beaufort Bridge in Barnwell District to slave parents. Little is known of his childhood and early life. Those close to him were told that he had been forced off the plantation where he had been born and had moved to Arkansas as a young man. Returning to South Carolina, he met and married Lena James in September 1881. They had eleven children. After his first wife died, he married Eloise C. Harleston, the sister of the artist and civil rights leader Edwin A. Harleston. His second marriage produced one child. Jenkins opened a store in Ladson, Berkeley County, before arriving in Charleston around 1885, where he started a successful lumber business. A minister and orator, he eventually became a pastor of New Tabernacle Fourth Baptist Church in 1892.

As racial lines hardened in South Carolina, black activists addressed the problems of African Americans through religious and secular organizations. The post-Reconstruction period witnessed the rise of black leaders who admonished African Americans to exercise greater race pride, solidarity, self-help, frugality, and to accumulate wealth through business enterprises. The efforts of the Reverend Daniel Jenkins reflected the drive and concerns of many black ministers and professionals. Jenkins, the first dark-complexioned former slave and non-Charlestonian to become a major community leader in the seaport city, criticized Charleston's traditional black leadership for its elitism and color exclusiveness.

Jenkins's greatest contribution to Charleston, however, was the founding of the Jenkins Orphanage. While delivering a lumber order, Jenkins came upon four African American children in a train boxcar, hungry, abandoned, and poorly clothed. He took the children home and, on the following Sunday, he received a donation for the orphans from the New Tabernacle congregation. The church also agreed to form a society to address the plight of other destitute or wayward youth. The Orphan Aid Society was granted a state charter on July 21, 1892.

Jenkins devoted the rest of his life to helping children in need. Many different initiatives were incorporated to finance the orphanage, including the creation of the Jenkins Orphanage Band in 1895. The band became wildly popular and world famous for its music and showmanship. Jenkins also established vocational programs to teach trades to children. A donation of one hundred acres in Ladson later made it possible for the orphanage to teach farming and grow its own food. A printing press was purchased on which apprentices learned the business and the orphanage published its own weekly newspaper, the *Charleston Messenger.*

The antagonism that had once existed between the black elite and Jenkins was gradually reconciled. He effectively cultivated support for his endeavors among the city's black and white leaders. A building next to the city's jail housed the orphanage in its early years before it eventually relocated to North Charleston. At the time of Jenkins's death on July 30, 1937, five thousand children had passed through his orphanage or lived on the farm facilities. In 1985 a portrait of Jenkins was hung in the Charleston City Council chambers, the first such honor bestowed on an African American. DONALD WEST

Chilton, John. *A Jazz Nursery: The Story of the Jenkins' Orphanage Bands of Charleston, South Carolina.* London: Bloomsbury Book Shop, 1980.

Drago, Edmund L. *Initiative, Paternalism, and Race Relations: Charleston's Avery Normal Institute.* Athens: University of Georgia Press, 1990.

Jenkins Orphanage Collection. Avery Research Center for African American History and Culture, College of Charleston, Charleston.

Jenkins, DeWitt (1908–1990). Musician. Born on October 27, 1908, in Harris, North Carolina, DeWitt "Snuffy" Jenkins is known for his long musical partnership with Homer "Pappy" Sherrill and for being a major influence on such better-known banjo players as Earl Scruggs, Don Reno, and Ralph Stanley. Jenkins learned his three-finger technique from local banjo stylists Rex Brooks and Smith Hammett and adopted that style about 1927 when he and his brother Verl began to enter fiddle contests. About 1934 they added two guitar pickers and became the Jenkins String Band on radio station WBT in Charlotte.

In 1937 Jenkins joined J. E. Mainer's Mountaineers at WSPA Spartanburg and that April moved to WIS Columbia. Jenkins recorded with Mainer on Bluebird and was heard prominently on their rendition of "Kiss Me Cindy." After Mainer left the group, announcer Byron Parker took over and they became the WIS Hillbillies on radio and Byron Parker's Mountaineers on record. Homer Sherrill took over the fiddle chores in October 1939. Jenkins and Sherrill would continue to perform as a team until Jenkins's death. In 1946 they had a session with DeLuxe in addition to the sixteen sides they cut for Bluebird in 1940. After Parker died in 1948, the group took the name Hired Hands. When WIS-TV went on the air, they added television to their list of achievements while also playing personal appearances throughout the Carolinas and parts of Georgia, Tennessee, and Virginia. Jenkins became almost as well known for his comedy routines—with washboard and baggy-pants gags—as for his banjo work.

Jenkins's work as a bluegrass banjo pioneer became better known after Mike Seeger placed four of his numbers on the Folkways album *American Banjo Scruggs Style.* In 1962 the Hired Hands recorded an album for Folk-Lyric and two more for Rounder in the 1970s. The growing popularity of bluegrass festivals allowed them to display their skills to a wider audience outside of the Carolinas. Declining health took its toll on the aging picker and he played banjo on only two cuts on the final Hired Hands album for Old Homestead in 1989. Jenkins died from colon cancer on April 30, 1990. ABBY GAIL GOODNITE

Ahrens, Pat J. *A History of the Musical Careers of DeWitt "Snuffy" Jenkins, Banjoist, and Homer "Pappy" Sherrill, Fiddler.* Columbia, S.C., 1970.

"DeWitt 'Snuffy' Jenkins." *Bluegrass Unlimited* 24 (June 1990): 5.

Jenkins, Edmund Thornton (1894–1926). Composer. Jenkins was born April 9, 1894, in Charleston, the son of the Reverend Daniel Jenkins and Lena James. He attended the Avery Normal Institute in Charleston and studied at Atlanta Baptist College (now Morehouse College) from 1908 to 1914. He studied music privately in Charleston with teachers associated with his father's Jenkins Orphanage Bands, and continued his classical music studies in Atlanta. In 1914 the Jenkins Orphanage Band visited England to play at the Anglo-American

Exposition, with Edmund as assistant conductor. He remained in London and enrolled at the Royal Academy of Music (1914–1921). There he won almost every prize or scholarship for which he was eligible, and became a subprofessor of clarinet from 1918 to 1921.

Jenkins was one of the first American composers of orchestral jazz. Ironically, because of racial attitudes in America, he lived most of his brief life as an expatriate, although America, particularly Charleston, remained his source of musical inspiration. In London Jenkins associated with a number of politically active Afro-British and African professionals, confirming his pride in his race. He explored his musical roots in his music: his first major premiere was an orchestral piece, *Folk Rhapsody (On American Folk Tunes)* presented at Wigmore Hall in London on December 7, 1919. The piece featured Negro spirituals, but the main theme was a sprightly and rhythmic folk tune, "Brer Rabbit What Do You Do Dere?" that he had first heard as a boy in Charleston.

Jenkins took advantage of the growing popularity of jazz in London and played clarinet in dance orchestras to support himself while he continued his classical music studies. In 1920 and 1921 he recorded dance numbers with various jazz groups. Around 1922 he relocated to Paris and toured with theatrical productions and dance orchestras on the Continent. He continued writing music on American themes, including a cabaret piece, *Charleston Revue,* set in his hometown, and *Afram* (1924), an operetta dealing with the abduction of an African prince into slavery.

In 1923 Jenkins spent ten months in the United States attempting to raise money for an all-black orchestra and a conservatory for African American students. The projects failed, and Jenkins was unable to support himself in the style he had achieved overseas. He returned to Paris bitterly disillusioned with the racial attitudes of the American music establishment.

In 1925 Jenkins founded his own publishing company, Anglo-Continental-American Music Press. In July his orchestral composition *American Folk Rhapsody: Charlestonia* was performed at the Kursaal in Ostende, Belgium. This folk rhapsody is also based on the "Brer Rabbit" tune, combining classical orchestration with jazz inflections. In 1926 his fame grew in America when his *African War Dance* (1925), another orchestral piece (now lost), won the Holstein Prize.

Jenkins died in a Paris hospital on September 12, 1926, possibly from appendicitis complicated by tuberculosis. His music remained unknown until seventy years after his death, when the Charleston Symphony performed the American premiere of *Charlestonia* on October 4, 1996. SUZANNE FLANDREAU

Green, Jeffrey. P. *Edmund Thornton Jenkins: The Life and Times of an American Black Composer, 1894–1926.* Westport, Conn.: Greenwood, 1982.

Jenkins, Esau (1910–1972). Civil rights activist. Born on July 3, 1910, on Johns Island, Jenkins was the only child of Peter Jenkins and Eva Campbell. He was forced to end his formal education in the fourth grade to help supplement the family's income. At age seventeen, he married Janie Jones. Of their thirteen children, seven survived, all of whom earned college degrees.

When Jenkins saw the injustices that affected black children on Johns Island, he bused his children and others to public schools in Charleston. In 1945 he purchased a bus to bring children to the city. He later transported adults to their jobs. During the daily commutes, Jenkins stressed to the adults the importance of voting and taught them to recite passages from the state constitution (a requirement to vote in South Carolina during that time).

In 1948 Jenkins founded the Progressive Club to educate Sea Island residents. At the suggestion of Septima Clark, Jenkins attended a workshop at the Highlander Folk School in Monteagle, Tennessee, in August 1954. Later that year, he invited Highlander staff, including founder Myles Horton, to visit Johns Island. Jenkins, Bernice Robinson, and Septima Clark collaborated with Highlander to establish a "Citizenship School" on Johns Island. The school was designed to teach adult African Americans to read so that they could register to vote. The first school was a success and the schools soon spread to the other Sea Islands. The success of the first schools in the Sea Islands led Highlander to create others across the South, where tens of thousands of African Americans learned to read and became registered to vote.

After the creation of the Citizenship Schools, Jenkins continued to work on issues of civil rights and social justice: he organized the Citizens Committee of Charleston in 1959, he helped organize the first Head Start center in Charleston, and he pressed Charleston's sanitation department and bus system to hire their first black drivers. In addition to his civic work, Jenkins owned a fruit store, the Hot Spot Record Shop, and the J & P Motel & Café.

Shortly before his death, Jenkins was appointed to the state advisory committee for the U.S. Commission on Civil Rights. Jenkins died on October 30, 1972, and was buried at Wesley United Methodist Church on Johns Island. In June 2003, Jenkins was inducted into the South Carolina Black Hall of Fame. HERB FRAZIER

Carawan, Guy, and Candie Carawan. *Ain't You Got a Right to the Tree of Life? The People of Johns Island, South Carolina—Their Faces, Their Words, and Their Songs.* Rev. ed. Athens: University of Georgia Press, 1989.

Horton, Aimee Isgrig. *The Highlander Folk School: A History of Its Major Programs, 1932–1961.* Brooklyn, N.Y.: Carlson, 1989.

Jenkins, Esau. Papers. Avery Research Center for African American History and Culture, College of Charleston, Charleston.

Jenkins Orphanage Bands. Just before the start of the twentieth century, brass bands comprising African American children from Charleston's Jenkins Orphanage began to travel throughout the eastern United States and as far away as Canada and Europe. They performed rhythmically spirited "ragged" versions of marches, rags, dance tunes, and popular songs of the day. The bands received international acclaim and served as training ground for several of the top jazz musicians of the first half of the century.

Jenkins Orphanage Band. Courtesy, South Carolina Historical Society

The Reverend Daniel J. Jenkins founded the private orphanage in 1892. Around 1895 Jenkins organized a band as a means of soliciting funds for the institution. Beginning with local street corner performances, the young musicians eventually toured the eastern United States and visited England, France, Germany, and Italy. By the time of their return from their first trip abroad, newspaper accounts of their experiences had afforded them an international reputation. They subsequently participated in the St. Louis World's Fair of 1904, the inaugural parades of Presidents Theodore Roosevelt and William Howard Taft, and London's Anglo-American Exposition in 1914. In 1927 a Jenkins Orphanage band appeared in the New York stage production of DuBose Heyward's *Porgy*.

As many as five Jenkins Orphanage bands were on tour during the summers of the 1920s. By the 1950s, however, so few children required the services of the orphanage that it could support only one band. And by the 1980s, the Jenkins Orphanage bands had ceased to exist.

Although the Jenkins groups were not improvising jazz ensembles, but rather brass bands that performed written music in a somewhat jazz-like manner, many members went on to successful careers as jazz musicians. A few, such as trumpeters Augustine "Gus" Aitken, Cladys "Jabbo" Smith, William "Cat" Anderson, and Herbert "Peanuts" Holland and drummer Rufus Jones, became well-known stars. DAVID FRANKLIN

Chilton, John. *A Jazz Nursery: The Story of the Jenkins' Orphanage Bands of Charleston, South Carolina.* London: Bloomsbury Book Shop, 1980.

Jeremiah, Thomas (?–1775). Free black harbor pilot, alleged insurrectionary. Thomas Jeremiah, or "Jerry," was a free person of color who earned a living by navigating ships through the treacherous waters of Charleston harbor. Little is known about his life. It appears that he obtained his freedom sometime in the mid-to-late eighteenth century. In addition to his skills as a harbor pilot, Jeremiah worked as a firefighter and ran the fish market in Charleston's wharf district. Eventually he would become a slaveowner himself, acquiring an estate valued at somewhere between £700 to £1,000 sterling. Earning the respect of his own community as well as a number of prominent white allies, the pilot undoubtedly blurred and transcended the boundaries of race that were becoming ever more sharply drawn during the course of his lifetime. Yet the same skills which initially brought him success and notoriety would ultimately make him a target for suspicion.

Jeremiah's paradoxical relationship to the power structure is perhaps best illustrated by an incident that occurred in 1771. On July 17, he was convicted of assaulting a white ship captain by the name of Thomas Langen—a bold action for a black man living in the pre-Revolutionary South—and was sentenced to an hour in the pillory and ten lashes with a whip. In view of his public deeds, however, Lieutenant Governor William Bull granted him a pardon. Four years later, when open conflict broke out between Great Britain and her North American colonies, Jeremiah would not be so lucky.

In June 1775, he became the foremost suspect in an alleged plot by the British to use the majority of the Carolina populace—enslaved blacks—against the patriot rebels. As a man who had long worked with battleships and fire, Jeremiah appeared to be the most plausible and potentially dangerous link between black Carolinians and the British. Embroiled in a cause célèbre between the last royal governor of South Carolina, Lord William Campbell, and patriot leader Henry Laurens, Thomas Jeremiah was adjudged guilty by patriot authorities and sentenced to die under the Negro Act of 1740.

On August 18, 1775, at twelve o'clock noon, Jeremiah was brought before the gallows in Charleston. Before the noose could be tightened around his neck, he proclaimed his innocence and told his accusers that "God's judgment would one day overtake them for shedding his innocent blood." While the rest of spectacle is difficult to piece together, Jeremiah reportedly met "death like a man and a Christian." After he was asphyxiated, his remains were set on fire—both a reminder and a warning. "Surely," one contemporary concluded, "there is no murder so cruel and dangerous as that committed under the appearance of law and justice." Although we may never know whether he was "guilty" or "innocent," Jeremiah's ordeal illustrated the three-way struggle for power between blacks, Whigs, and Tories that was taking place throughout the lower South on the eve of the Revolutionary War. WILLIAM RYAN

Ryan, William R. "'Under the Color of Law': The Ordeal of Thomas Jeremiah, a Free Black Man, and the Struggle for Power in Revolutionary South Carolina." In *George Washington's South,* edited by Tamara Harvey and Greg O'Brien. Gainesville: University Press of Florida, 2004.

Wood, Peter H. "'Liberty is Sweet': African-American Freedom Struggles in the Years before White Independence." In *Beyond the American Revolution: Explorations in the History of American Radicalism,* edited by Alfred F. Young. DeKalb: Northern Illinois University Press, 1993.

———. "'Taking Care of Business' in Revolutionary South Carolina: Republicanism and the Slave Society." In *The Southern Experience in the American Revolution,* edited by Jeffrey J. Crow and Larry E. Tise. Chapel Hill: University of North Carolina Press, 1978.

Jews. Jews arrived in the British colony of Carolina with the first wave of European settlement. A new outpost in the mercantile traffic of the Atlantic basin, Carolina offered economic opportunities, as well as risks, and a degree of religious tolerance remarkable for the time. The colony's Fundamental Constitutions of 1669 granted freedom of worship to "Jews, Heathens, and other Dissenters from the purity of the Christian Religion." Although the colonial assembly never endorsed the provision, British Charleston became known as a place where people of all faiths—except Catholics—could do business and practice their religion without interference. In 1696 Jews in Charleston allied with French Huguenots to safeguard their rights to trade and the next year to secure citizenship.

Most of Carolina's first Jewish settlers traced their roots to Spain or Portugal. Expelled during the Inquisition at the end of the fifteenth century, the Sephardim (from the Hebrew word for Spain) dispersed around the globe and established themselves in capitals and port cities in northern Europe, the Mediterranean, and the West

Temple Sinai, Sumter, was an indication of the town's thriving Jewish community. Courtesy, South Carolina Historical Society

Indies. In 1749 Charleston's Jewish community chartered Kahal Kadosh Beth Elohim—one of the first five Jewish congregations in America. Like her sister synagogues in New York, Newport, Savannah, and Philadelphia, Beth Elohim was Sephardic in ritual and practice. Charleston's congregation remained so for two generations after the Revolutionary War, though by then the majority of South Carolina Jews were Ashkenazic, hailing from central or eastern Europe.

Following the Revolutionary War, South Carolina's Jewish population surged. When Columbia became the state capital in 1786, seven Jewish men from Charleston were among the first to buy town lots. Jews in Georgetown, Beaufort, and Camden belonged to the business and civic elites. By 1800 Charleston was home to the largest, wealthiest, and most cultured Jewish community in North America—upwards of five hundred individuals, or one-fifth of all Jews in the nation.

Carolina's Jews pursued the same material goals and status symbols as their white neighbors. Those who could afford it owned slaves. The affluent lived in finely furnished houses and traveled abroad. Many Ashkenazim adopted traditional Sephardic practices and assumed an aristocratic view of themselves as "earliest to arrive."

Charleston's highly acculturated Jewish community produced the first movement to reform Judaism in America. In 1824 a group of young, mostly American-born Jews petitioned the governing body of Kahal Kadosh Beth Elohim for shorter services, a sermon preached on the Sabbath, and prayers in English. Rebuffed in their efforts, the dissidents drafted a constitution and established the Reformed Society of Israelites. For eight years the reformers worshiped separately, then returned to the traditional congregation. In 1840 the reform faction prevailed. With the blessing of Beth Elohim's popular minister, Gustavus Poznanski, a proposal to install an organ in the synagogue was adopted by a narrow margin. The traditionalists seceded and formed Shearit Israel (Remnant of Israel), with its own burying ground adjacent to Beth Elohim's Coming Street cemetery. A brick wall separated the dead of the two congregations.

While schism in Beth Elohim divided traditionalists and reformers, a new group of immigrants introduced another brand of orthodoxy to Charleston. People of modest means—peddlers, artisans, metalworkers, bakers—these newcomers from eastern Europe gave the city's Jewish population a more foreign appearance than before. As early as 1852, a *minyan,* or prayer group, began meeting under the leadership of Rabbi Hirsch Zvi Levine, recently arrived from Poland. In 1855 they formally organized as Berith Shalome (now Brith Sholom) or "Covenant of Peace"—the first Ashkenazic congregation in South Carolina and one of the first in the South.

Southern Jews rallied to the Confederate cause during the Civil War. Thousands of Jewish men served in the Southern armies, while Jewish women, in accord with their gentile sisters, threw themselves into the war effort, sewing uniforms, knitting socks, rolling bandages, preparing boxes of clothes and provisions, and working in hospitals to care for the sick and wounded.

After the war, during the period known as Reconstruction, some South Carolinians of Jewish descent supported the Radical Republicans' drive to build a new society (including the notorious "scalawag" governor, Franklin J. Moses, Jr.), but most backed the Redeemers' crusade to restore white rule. Jewish women such as Octavia Harby Moses were prominent in memorializing the "Lost Cause." In the shared experience of defeat, Jewish Confederates demonstrated their fierce sense of belonging to their state and region.

East European migration to America beginning in the 1880s brought about a dramatic increase in the nation's Jewish population. Charleston's Jewish community, which had maintained itself for decades at around seven hundred, doubled between 1905 and 1912. The neighborhood where the "greenhorns" settled was called Little Jerusalem. Immigrant men commonly started out as peddlers, then established small businesses. At one time some forty stores on upper King Street were closed on Saturday, in observance of the Jewish Sabbath. The men held prayer services above stores. The women kept kosher homes. They trained their African American help to make potato kugel and gefilte fish, and they learned, in turn, to fix fried chicken and okra gumbo.

By World War I, Jewish communities in the Midlands and upcountry had grown large enough to support synagogues. Meanwhile, certain country clubs, fraternities, and sororities barred Jews, who responded by forming their own social groups and athletic teams modeled on the ones that kept them out. These organizations helped unify Jews around an ethnic identity without regard to place of birth, date of arrival in America, or degree of observance.

The revival of the Ku Klux Klan with an anti-Semitic agenda disturbed southern Jews' sense of well-being. In the heyday of Jim Crow, however, the primary targets of discrimination were blacks. Jews generally found themselves on the safe side of the racial divide. They demonstrated their loyalty to country and region in patriotic parades and party politics. When the United States entered World War II, Jewish southerners joined in the mobilization to fight the Japanese and Nazi foes.

As a result of the Holocaust in Europe, America's place in world Jewry changed dramatically. By 1945 more than half of all Jewish people were living in the United States. In many ways, South Carolina was a microcosm of the nation. The class of Jewish merchants had begat a generation of lawyers, doctors, accountants, and college teachers, who shifted the Jewish economic niche away from retail business. With the rest of the white American mainstream, urban Jews abandoned the old neighborhoods and moved to the suburbs—a migration that coincided with the first stirrings of the civil rights movement and the rise of Conservative Judaism.

By the end of the twentieth century, Jewish populations in most small towns across the South had dwindled, while suburban and resort congregations continued to grow. South Carolina mirrors the nation in the trend toward more traditional observance that characterizes all divisions of Judaism. The Addlestone Hebrew Academy in Charleston and Lubovitcher habads in Myrtle Beach and Columbia teach Hebrew and religious studies in day schools to an increasingly diverse student population, that includes newcomers from other parts of America, and from Russia and the Middle East as well. DALE ROSENGARTEN

Elzas, Barnett A. *The Jews of South Carolina from the Earliest Times to the Present Day.* 1905. Reprint, Spartanburg, S.C.: Reprint Company, 1972.

Gergel, Belinda, and Richard Gergel. *In Pursuit of the Tree of Life: A History of the Early Jews of Columbia and the Tree of Life Congregation.* Columbia, S.C.: Tree of Life, 1996.

Greenspoon, Leonard J. "Judaism in South Carolina." In *Religion in South Carolina,* edited by Charles H. Lippy. Columbia: University of South Carolina Press, 1993.

Hagy, James William. *This Happy Land: The Jews of Colonial and Antebellum Charleston.* Tuscaloosa: University of Alabama Press, 1993.

Jewish Heritage Collection. Special Collections, College of Charleston Library, Charleston.

Reznikoff, Charles. *The Jews of Charleston: A History of an American Jewish Community.* Philadelphia: Jewish Publication Society of America, 1950.

Rosen, Robert N. *The Jewish Confederates.* Columbia: University of South Carolina Press, 2000.

Rosengarten, Theodore, and Dale Rosengarten, eds. *A Portion of the People: Three Hundred Years of Southern Jewish Life.* Columbia: University of South Carolina Press, 2002.

Joggling boards. Simple in design, a joggling board consists of one plank, or seat, supported by stands at each end. The plank length varies, sometimes extending as long as sixteen feet. Variations include joggling boards that have stands with curved bottoms resembling the rockers on a rocking chair. This allows the user to "joggle" both up and down and sway from side to side. Made with just about any type of wood, fir and cypress are two of the more common varieties. Lauded for their ability to ease arthritic pain and other forms of bodily discomfort, joggling boards have also remained popular with romantic couples, mothers trying to soothe a fitful infant, and children intent on enjoying hours of play.

The joggling board is a tradition with a long history in South Carolina. While the origin of the joggling board has fallen into the murkiness of local legend, they were quite common on the coast by the 1880s. One of the more enduring creation stories involves the Kinloch and Huger families of Acton Plantation in Sumter County. In 1803, after the family patriarch was widowed, a sister moved to the plantation to care for the household. She suffered from severe rheumatism and the "first" joggling board was designed and built for her relief. The popularity of the joggling board spread quickly and, while they have generally been concentrated along the coast, they were also used in other parts of the state. Like the rocking chair, the joggling board has long been a fixture on porches in Pawleys Island, Georgetown, Charleston, and throughout the lowcountry. SADDLER TAYLOR

Smith, Charles F. "On Southernisms." *Transactions of the American Philological Association* 14 (1883): 42–56.

John D. Hollingsworth on Wheels. John D. Hollingsworth on Wheels, Greenville-based manufacturer of steel and flexible wire clothings for cards and other machines for spinning preparation, was founded in 1894. Pinckney C. Hollingsworth of Greenville started the Hollingsworth Company to repair textile machinery. He carried a lathe and grinder by mule to cotton mills in the Carolinas. His son, John D. Hollingsworth, continued the business, which he called J. D. Hollingsworth by Himself. He bought a two-year-old Signal truck in 1919 to haul his equipment, then a few years later he built a large garage-workshop behind his house. Hollingsworth took his son, John D., Jr., along on business trips, and soon the company's name was changed to J. D. Hollingsworth & Son on Wheels.

After the elder Hollingsworth died in 1942, John D., Jr. expanded the company into a major machinery manufacturer with clients worldwide. Revenues grew from $72,000 in 1942 to $11 million in 1963. Until shortly before his death at 83 in 2000, he worked at the plant almost daily.

Hollingsworth left his estate, valued at about $300 million, to the Hollingsworth Foundation with the provision that the profits go to various nonprofits such as Furman University and the Young Men's Christian Association of Greenville. In 2004 the foundation owned the Greenville headquarters with 450 employees as well as Verdae Properties, a real estate company that held thousands of acres of undeveloped land across South Carolina. LYN RIDDLE

John de la Howe School. Located in McCormick, the John de la Howe School originated on land bequeathed by John de la Howe, a wealthy physician who died in 1797. His will left $6,000 dollars in cash and personal property and nearly three thousand acres of land called Lethe Farm in Abbeville District to create a school for the practical education of rural boys and girls. Apathy and mismanagement among the first trustees, however, delayed the implementation of Howe's plan for decades. The school opened as Lethe Agricultural Seminary in January 1832 with twenty-four students. During the antebellum period, students spent equal time in studies and manual labor. Entry ages were set at twelve for boys and ten for girls. The school, though not totally self-sufficient, taught every aspect of farming common in the state.

Following the Civil War and Reconstruction, the Lethe school suffered financial setbacks, which forced its closure from 1882 to 1894. Declining enrollments caused a second closing from 1911 to 1913, which prompted a reorganization, converting the school to a state agency. In 1918 the General Assembly renamed it the "John de la Howe Industrial School" and appointed a managing board of directors. To expand statewide services, the school was relocated to the town of McCormick and larger buildings constructed. The school became one of the first recipients of grants from the Duke Endowment. It began accepting disturbed and disabled children in 1969, and integrated without fanfare shortly thereafter. The administration of superintendent John C. Shiflet (1979–1999) shifted the education focus from college preparatory classes to both college and vocational programs.

The John de la Howe School continues as a state-funded group child-care facility that houses both residential and wilderness programs for approximately 150 school-age children per year who come from families in crisis and are placed for nine to twelve months. Students live in family-like settings in cottages, eat in the central cafeteria, and attend classes at the school until they reach eleventh grade, when they are transported to the nearby high school. Funding is received from the Duke Endowment, the state of South Carolina, student tuition, and fund-raising activities. The 135 acres of land surrounding the school, called the Museum Tract (designated a National Natural Landmark in 1976), contains the largest shortleaf pine stand in the world and is the only virgin forest of its kind remaining in South Carolina. LINDA HOWE

Historical Sketch of the John de la Howe School. Anderson, S.C.: Anderson Printing, 1939.

Still Caring, Still Dreaming: The First Two Hundred Years at John de la Howe School. McCormick, S.C.: John de la Howe School, 1996.

Johns, Jasper (b. 1930). Artist. Johns was born in Augusta, Georgia, on May 15, 1930, probably because its hospital was the closest one to Allendale, South Carolina, where his parents were living. His father, William Jasper Johns, was a farmer and former lawyer who divorced his mother, Jean Riley, by the time the artist was three years old. Johns spent his childhood with various family members in Allendale, Columbia, Batesburg, and Sumter, where he graduated from high school in 1947. He attended the University of South Carolina from September 1947 until December 1948, when he moved to New York. In May 1951 he was inducted into the United States Army and was stationed at Fort Jackson until he was sent to Japan during the Korean War. Upon his discharge he moved to Manhattan and resided there until the mid-1990s, with regular sojourns spent at Edisto Beach, South Carolina (1961–1966), Saint Martin, French West Indies (1969–), and Stony Point, Long Island (1974–1991).

In 1954 Johns destroyed all of his previous work and began two of his signature series: the flag and the target. Four years later his career had clearly been launched: the prestigious Leo Castelli Gallery began to handle his art, the Museum of Modern Art acquired several of his works, and he represented the United States at the Venice Biennale. Johns is a pivotal figure of twentieth-century American art, occupying a critical position that mediates Abstract Expressionism, Pop Art, and Minimalism. Like the latter, he is interested in art materials; he is proficient in a variety of media, including drawing and lithography, oil and encaustic painting, and collage and assemblage. Using commonplace subjects—such as the American flag, numbers, or a beer can—he discharges a fundamental tenet of his art: "Take an object. / Do something to it. / Do something else to it."

Jasper Johns, "Target," 1973 lithograph on paper. Courtesy, Columbia Museum of Art © Jasper Johns / Licensed by VAGA, New York, NY

Johns's career falls into three broad periods: early work characterized by great detachment, abstract work from the early 1960s and 1970s that often emphasizes patterns, and imagery from the 1980s that is more personal and based on early recollections. For example, he incorporated symbols relating to his step-grandmother in several paintings emblematic of his childhood, and in 1992 he employed a floor plan of his grandfather's house in Allendale. Four years later the Museum of Modern Art organized *Jasper Johns: A Retrospective,* which attempted to identify his sources, present his biography and achievements, and assess his place in modern art. In the accompanying catalogue, curator Kirk Varnedoe acknowledged Johns's influential role: "Johns's presence can be felt at or near the origin point of virtually every generative idea of importance in avant-garde painting and sculpture in America for four decades." See plate 34. MARTHA R. SEVERENS

Crichton, Michael. *Jasper Johns.* New York: Abrams, 1977.

Johns, Jasper. *Jasper Johns: Writings, Sketchbooks Notes, Interviews.* Edited by Kirk Varnedoe. New York: Museum of Modern Art, 1996.

Varnedoe, Kirk. *Jasper Johns: A Retrospective.* New York: Museum of Modern Art, 1996.

Johns Island Presbyterian Church. The Johns Island Presbyterian Church is one of the oldest Presbyterian congregations in South Carolina. Scots minister Archibald Stobo founded the congregation in 1710 and the Charles Towne Presbytery in 1722. The building is a fine example of wood churches of the Federal period.

The congregation erected the first church around 1719. It was thirty-eight feet long and thirty-five feet wide, with cypress siding and shingles and a plaster ceiling with a six-foot ornamental sunflower at the center. The church was remodeled in 1792, and Moses Waddell preached at the church in 1793 and 1796.

The present church was built in 1822–1823 under the leadership of Pastor Elipha White. It bears many similarities to Episcopal churches, including clear glass windows with semicircular windows above. Distinctive Presbyterian features include the double entry doors and small rectangular windows at the upper level to light the slave gallery. The risers of the side steps are made of Italian marble. Although the original nine-foot-high pulpit has been lowered, the church still retains high-sided box pews.

The old church survived until it was pulled down in the early 1840s. The new church survived the Civil War and the earthquake of 1886. A later Sunday School addition at the back of the church obscures the simplicity of the meetinghouse form. The congregation has met continuously since the first church was built. ROBERT W. BAINBRIDGE

Isely, N. Jane, William P. Baldwin, and Agnes L. Baldwin. *Plantations of the Low Country: South Carolina 1697–1865.* Greensboro, N.C.: Legacy Publications, 1985.

Jacoby, Mary Moore, ed. *The Churches of Charleston and the Lowcountry.* Columbia: University of South Carolina Press, 1993.

Johnson, David (1782–1855). Jurist, governor. David Johnson was born on October 3, 1782, in Louisa County, Virginia, the son of the Reverend Christopher Johnson, a Baptist Minister, and Elizabeth Dabney. The family immigrated to South Carolina in 1789, where they settled on the Broad River in Chester District. Johnson was educated in the local old field schools, the classical grammar school of the Reverend Joseph Alexander at York, and received private tutoring in mathematics and surveying. Johnson's legal studies began in 1799 under Abraham Nott. After admission to the bar in December 1803, Johnson entered a four-year partnership with Nott at Union, later taking over the practice. Johnson married Barbara Asbury Herndon on June 2, 1807. The couple had eleven children, only four of whom survived their parents.

Johnson's public service in the judiciary began on February 16, 1805, with his appointment as commissioner in equity for the western circuit, a position he held for two years. Elected to the state House of Representatives in 1810, Johnson resigned the seat upon his election as solicitor of the middle circuit on December 4, 1811. In December 1815 Johnson was elected circuit judge, and in 1824 he was elevated to the Court of Appeals, serving as presiding judge from 1830 to 1835. On June 2, 1834, Johnson, with Judge John Belton O'Neall concurring, rendered his most famous decision. A staunch Unionist during the nullification crisis, Johnson ruled as unconstitutional the militia test oath, a part of the Force Bill that implemented the nullification ordinance. Infuriated over the decision, the nullifier majority legislature abolished the court in December 1835. Johnson was then transferred to the Court of Equity and the Court of Appeals in Equity, serving as presiding judge of the latter court from circa 1838 to 1846.

Johnson was unanimously elected governor on December 8, 1846. His governorship was dominated by the Mexican War and the efforts required in raising troops for and provisioning the Palmetto Regiment. An ally of John C. Calhoun, Johnson only supported a defensive war, privately opposing the annexation of any lands south of the Rio Grande. Along with Calhoun, he believed that volunteers were unfit for service in Mexico. In November 1847 Johnson urged the legislature to provide assistance for Palmetto Regiment widows and orphans, which was done with a grant of $5,000. As governor, Johnson also called for the establishment of a permanent executive office, and, believing that pardons usurped the judicial process, granted only one during his entire term. Although adhering to the right of secession, Johnson opposed separate state action on the part of South Carolina.

Johnson attributed his stature as a jurist as based on "a well founded knowledge of the general principles of law, and a sound discretionary judgment in their application with the honest purpose of attaining the truth." He died at Limestone Springs on January 7, 1855, and was buried in the Presbyterian Cemetery at Union. "His mind was like his person," wrote Governor John L. Manning, "grand in every way." PAUL R. BEGLEY

Bailey, N. Louise, ed. *Biographical Directory of the South Carolina House of Representatives.* Vol. 4, *1791–1815.* Columbia: University of South Carolina Press, 1984.

O'Neall, John Belton. *Biographical Sketches of the Bench and Bar of South Carolina.* 2 vols. Charleston, S.C.: S. G. Courtney, 1859.

Scott, Florence Johnson. "Appendix–Letters and Papers of Governor David Johnson and Family, 1810–1855." *Proceedings of the South Carolina Historical Association* (1939): 1–47.

Johnson, Harriet Catherine Frazier (1889–1972). Legislator, state 4–H Club leader. Johnson was born in Pelzer on December 3, 1889, the daughter of Steven Frazier and Susan Rowland. She grew up in Walhalla and after completing high school and a summer session, she taught school. She saved money for college until she could afford to attend in 1913, graduating from Winthrop College in 1917 with a bachelor of arts degree. She was hired by Spartanburg County as a home extension agent, beginning a twenty-five year career with the extension service. On December 11, 1917, she married Richard Hughes Johnson. He died in November 1918 while serving in the army in France during World War I. From 1922 to 1944, Johnson served as head of the state 4–H girls' clubs, headquartered at Winthrop College. She continued her education at Teachers College, Columbia University, earning a bachelor of science degree in 1927 and a master's degree in 1930. She resigned her position in October 1944 to devote her time to civic and church work.

In February 1945 Johnson became the first woman elected to the South Carolina House of Representatives, winning a special election to fill the seat vacated by York County representative Henry Mills, who had resigned to become sergeant-at-arms for the State House. On January 27, 1945, the South Carolina White House Conference met in Columbia and urged women to run for office. Johnson later said that she ran for the General Assembly at the urging of friends and members of the groups that sponsored this meeting, including the American Association of University Women and the Federation of Business and Professional Women in South Carolina. She had a woman campaign manager. After a campaign of less than a week, Johnson defeated her three male opponents by only five votes. Because the S.C. House rules required that members be addressed as "Mr.," the Speaker referred to the Rules Committee a request to change the rules and allow her to be addressed as "Mrs."

During her brief tenure, she served on five committees and focused much of her energy on education programs, especially programs for African American children. She authored a bill to provide schoolbooks for children in York County with a $1 annual rental fee. The bill was so popular that the General Assembly amended it to apply to all high schools in South Carolina. She also authored a bill to establish an industrial school for African American girls. Johnson saw her role as representing her entire constituency rather than as an advocate for women. In this respect she was typical of women legislators of her day. In 1946 she sponsored a resolution to Congress opposing the Equal Rights Amendment.

Johnson served only one term in the legislature. Subsequently she was a Methodist missionary for three years, teaching home economics to women in India. She later served as director of recreation and religious activities for the South Carolina Opportunity School in West Columbia. In 1951 the *Progressive Farmer* magazine named her Woman of the Year for her service in rural progress in South Carolina. Johnson retired to Spartanburg and died there in a nursing home on January 27, 1972. She was buried in Greenlawn Memorial Gardens. CAROL SEARS BOTSCH

Ellis, M. Carolyn, and Joanne V. Hawks. "Ladies in the Gentlemen's Club: South Carolina Women Legislators, 1928–1984." *Proceedings of the South Carolina Historical Association* (1986): 17–32.

Johnson, Isaac Samuel Leevy (b. 1942). Attorney, legislator. Johnson was born in Columbia on May 16, 1942, the son of O. J. Johnson and Ruby Leevy. His maternal grandfather, Isaac S. Leevy, Jr., was a well-known African American undertaker in Columbia and prominent political activist. After graduating in 1960 from C. A. Johnson High School in Columbia, Johnson enrolled at the University of Minnesota, seeking to become a licensed mortician. Two years later he had completed all requirements for an associate of mortuary science (A.M.S.) degree. Johnson returned to Columbia and initially worked for his family's undertaking business.

He resumed his education at Benedict College in Columbia and gained a bachelor of science degree in 1965. Although not the initial African American student to be admitted to the University of South Carolina Law School, Johnson became the first to complete its entire law curriculum while enrolled at the university. His various peers had transferred in 1965 after the closing of the law school at the South Carolina State College in Orangeburg. Johnson received his doctor of law degree in 1968. That same year, on July 6, he married Doris Wright of Columbia. The marriage produced two children.

While his relatives traditionally were well-known Republicans, in 1970 Johnson ran as a Democrat in a successful bid for the South Carolina House of Representatives. He was among the first three African Americans to serve in the General Assembly since the turn of the century. He was defeated for reelection in 1972, but regained his seat two years later. Throughout his tenure, Johnson represented District No. 74 in Richland County. He was a founding member of the South Carolina Legislative Black Caucus. In 1980 Johnson chose not to seek reelection for another term.

As a full partner within the Columbia law firm of Johnson, Toal & Battiste, Johnson gained a reputation as being among the best trial lawyers in South Carolina. He also became the first African American attorney to sit in the House of Delegates, the governing board of the South Carolina Bar Association. In June 1985, he was elected the South Carolina Bar's first black president.

Throughout his career Johnson remained active with various other endeavors. He has been a long-standing member of the board of trustees at Benedict College. Johnson also was active in the South Carolina Conference of the National Association for the Advancement of

Colored People; the National Urban League; and the Columbia Luncheon Club, the first known interracial civic club in South Carolina. Johnson has been president of NUANCE Corporation, a firm that founded WOIC in Columbia, the state's first radio station wholly owned by African Americans. He was inducted into the South Carolina Black Hall of Fame in 1993. MILES S. RICHARDS

Johnson, I. S. Leevy. African American History in South Carolina Vertical Files. South Caroliniana Library, University of South Carolina, Columbia.

Johnson, John Carroll (1882–1967). Architect. J. Carroll Johnson was born on November 9, 1882, in Kristianstad, Sweden, to Peter Pare Johnson and Carolena Samuelson. He immigrated with his family to the United States in 1885 and settled in Chicago, where in 1906 he received a bachelor of science degree in architecture from Armour Institute of Technology. He apprenticed there with Jenney, Mundie & Jensen from 1900 until 1906, when he joined Wood, Donn & Deming of Washington, D.C. He earned a postgraduate degree in architecture from the University of Pennsylvania in 1908, and completed his education in France and Italy in 1909.

In 1910 Johnson accepted a position with Wilson, Sompayrac & Urquhart of Columbia, but by late 1912 had formed a partnership with James B. Urquhart, with whom he designed, among others, Columbia High School (1915), Ridgewood Country Club clubhouse (1916), and Camden's First National Bank (1917). In 1917 Johnson began an independent practice that continued until the Depression and produced such designs as the State Industrial School for Girls (1918), First Presbyterian Church of Kershaw (1920), and three schools in Lancaster (1922). He also designed several buildings on the University of South Carolina campus, including Sloan College (1927), the South Caroliniana Library wing additions (1927–1928), Melton Observatory (1928), and Wardlaw College (1930–1931). In 1938 he associated with Jesse W. Wessinger and, before dissolving that partnership in 1942, designed the Lexington County Courthouse (1939–1940), Sims Dormitory at the University of South Carolina (1939), and the First Baptist Church of West Columbia (1942).

In 1944 Johnson became the University of South Carolina's resident architect, a position he held through 1956 that involved planning campus expansion and designing, among others, Petigru College (1949, in association with Simons & Lapham of Charleston), LeConte College (1952), Osborne Administration Building (1951–1952), and the conversion and renovation of the President's House (1952). Apart from this work, Johnson was perhaps best known for his more than 120 residential designs that included the Benjamin F. Taylor House (1910–1912), the Boyne-Pressley-Spigner House (1915), and two houses for Dr. Robert E. Seibels in Columbia (1927, 1933); the John T. Stevens House in Kershaw (1918); and houses for James L. Coker, Jr. (1923–1924) and J. B. Gilbert (1929) in Hartsville. He was elected a member of the American Institute of Architects in 1916, but later resigned from the South Carolina chapter. Johnson died in Columbia on May 4, 1967, and was buried in Elmwood Cemetery. ANDREW W. CHANDLER

Chandler, Andrew Watson. "'Dialogue With The Past'—J. Carroll Johnson, Architect, and the University of South Carolina, 1912–1956." Master's thesis, University of South Carolina, 1993.

"John C. Johnson, 84, Architect, Dies." Columbia *State*, May 5, 1967, p. A7.

Wells, John E., and Robert E. Dalton. *The South Carolina Architects, 1885–1935: A Biographical Directory.* Richmond, Va.: New South Architectural Press, 1992.

Johnson, Sir Nathaniel (1644–1712). Governor. Born in Durham County, England, Nathaniel Johnson was the son of William Johnson and Margaret Sherwood. He was also the father of Robert Johnson, governor of South Carolina (1717–1719, 1730–1735). Nathaniel became a merchant in the Baltic trade out of Newcastle, representing that city in Parliament. His political views and his service as translator at the sensational murder trial of Count Konigsmark brought him the governorship of the Leeward Islands in 1686. He became a cassique of South Carolina that same year.

As a friend of the government, Johnson's career became embroiled in the hothouse politics of late-seventeenth-century England and his actions rarely escaped suspicions of ulterior motives. In 1689, when William and Mary came to the English throne, Johnson resigned his post and moved to his Carolina plantation, Silk Hope. Some Leeward Island planters, though, claimed that he had conspired with the governor of Martinique to betray the English colony to the French on behalf of James II, the recently deposed English king.

In Carolina, Maurice Mathews recruited Johnson for the Goose Creek Men, persuading Johnson through blackmail over the Martinique scandal and the Konigsmark trial, as well as their common dislike of the Colleton family. Johnson used his position in the Commons House of Assembly to support attacks against Governor James Colleton and the overthrow of his administration by Seth Sothell in 1690. In the meantime, Silk Hope became the scene of experiments in silk production. Although these attempts failed, Johnson later became one of the first lowcountry planters to successfully cultivate rice, the crop that came to be synonymous with South Carolina.

In 1701 Sir Nathaniel swore obedience to Queen Anne, which enabled him to hold governmental office, while John, Lord Granville, became palatine of South Carolina. Granville belonged to the "High Tory" party that advocated a policy of limiting the political rights of dissenters from the Church of England. His attitude enabled the Goose Creek Men to attack their dissenting enemies who had been attracted to South Carolina by the proprietary policy of religious toleration. Granville's appointment of Johnson as governor in June 1702 set the stage for this change in proprietary policy. Johnson assumed office in March 1703.

Under Johnson's auspices, the colony passed two acts in 1704, popularly known as the Exclusion Act and the Church Act. The first permitted only communicants of the Church of England to hold office or serve in the Commons House of Assembly, while the second established the Church of England in South Carolina, set out parishes to institute church authority, and appointed a board of lay overseers with the power to investigate and resolve religious disputes. The acts plunged South Carolina into turmoil. Johnson's opponents took their case to London where they fired a barrage of pamphlets that warned of threats to English liberty and prosperity presented by the new South Carolina government. They also petitioned the House of Lords and the Privy Council to overturn the laws. With Granville's enemies controlling the House of Lords, that body threw the legislation out and the crown directed the proprietors to disallow the acts, calling them "arbitrary oppressions." Undaunted, Johnson and his allies enacted a less rigid Establishment

Act in 1706, which formed the basis of South Carolina's ecclesiastical and local government until 1778.

Johnson also generated outrage through his handling of the Indian trade. The governor's opponents objected to the continued lack of regulation of this trade, as well as the tendency of Johnson and his friends to derive the most benefit from it. Over Johnson's opposition, in 1707 the Commons House passed South Carolina's first act for regulating the Indian trade. However, when Thomas Nairne, the newly appointed Indian agent and vocal opponent of Johnson, attempted to enforce the new regulations, Johnson had him arrested and charged with treason. Nairne eventually gained his liberty, but meaningful regulation of the Indian trade was subsequently doomed.

Even though Johnson led South Carolina's successful defense against a combined French and Spanish invasion force in 1706, the death of Granville that same year increased the influence of Johnson's opponents. In 1709 the proprietors named Edward Tynte to replace Johnson with instructions to restore order to the colony's politics and to bring the Indian trade under control. Meanwhile, Johnson had contracted dysentery. Upon Tynte's arrival in Charleston, Johnson retired to his plantation, where he died in 1712.
L. H. ROPER

Sirmans, M. Eugene. *Colonial South Carolina: A Political History, 1663–1763.* Chapel Hill: University of North Carolina Press, 1966.

Webber, Mabel L. "Sir Nathaniel Johnson and His Son Robert, Governors of South Carolina." *South Carolina Historical and Genealogical Magazine* 38 (October 1937): 109–15.

Johnson, Robert (ca. 1676–1735). Governor. Born in England, Johnson was the son of Sir Nathaniel Johnson and Joanna Overton. Young Johnson spent part of his youth in the Leeward Islands, where his father served as governor from 1686 to 1689. The elder Johnson acquired large landholdings in South Carolina and moved there to develop his property and later served as governor of the province from 1703 until 1709. Due in part to his father's success, Robert was asked by the Lords Proprietors to become governor in 1717.

Like many proprietary governors, Robert Johnson struggled to balance proprietary demands with political realities in South Carolina. In his opening gubernatorial address, Johnson chided those who had shown "disrespectful behaviour" by appealing to England against the Lords Proprietors. In his first year in office, Johnson lobbied the Commons House of Assembly in support of a proprietary plan to raise land prices. When the assembly balked, Johnson countered by blocking an appointment for the position of powder receiver. He eventually acquiesced but rebuked the assemblymen for not submitting to the Lords Proprietors as their "masters."

By the summer of 1718, Johnson began to find common ground with provincials and other elected representatives. He sympathized with provincial concerns that the proprietors neglected the colony. This was most evident in the proprietors' inattention to pirate attacks on the coast. From the time Johnson arrived as governor, sea bandits had periodically taken advantage of Charleston's well-known vulnerability. With no assistance forthcoming from the proprietors, Johnson took matters into his own hands. In late 1718, Johnson personally led a fleet of vessels against two pirate ships blockading Charleston harbor. By the time the offensive ended, notorious buccaneers such as Stede Bonnet and Richard Worley and over forty of their crew were captured and hanged in Charleston. This resolve virtually ended the pirate menace and went far in endearing Johnson to the Carolinians.

The lack of proprietary protection, however, drove local leaders further toward revolt. Johnson had the unenviable task of trying to squelch growing rebellion against the Lords Proprietors, even though he was principally in agreement with the malcontents. In 1718 Johnson resisted proprietary orders to dissolve the assembly. But in July 1719, he complied with their demands and called for new elections. The new assembly, however, was no more in favor of the status quo than its predecessor. In December they refused to recognize the newly formed council and asked Johnson to support the revolution by being the first royal governor of the colony. Citing "my honor as being Intrusted by their Lordships," Johnson refused the offer and was replaced by James Moore, Jr.

Back in England by 1724, Johnson spent much time in London seeking a commission for a royal governorship. In 1727 the Carolina proprietors expressed their intention to sell the colony. Johnson, who enjoyed the confidence of both the proprietors and the English government, was a logical choice to negotiate the transaction. In December 1729, largely due to his successful role in this negotiation, the Privy Council approved his appointment as royal governor of South Carolina.

As royal governor Johnson left an indelible mark on South Carolina history. In addition to his role in the development of Georgia as a buffer to Spanish Florida, Johnson implemented his visionary township system of settlement in South Carolina. Approved by royal officials in 1730, Johnson claimed his township plan would enhance colonial defenses against Indian attacks and stabilize the local economy by encouraging poor European Protestants to settle in the Carolina interior. Also, Johnson argued, the ten proposed townships would provide a much-needed racial balance in light of the growing slave population. "Nothing is so much wanted in Carolina," he said, "as white Inhabitants." With support from British officials and the assembly, Johnson's township system was by all standards a resounding success. By 1735 nine townships had been surveyed and hundreds of Irish, Swiss, German, and Welsh settlers had immigrated into six of them.

Possibly Johnson's greatest overall contribution was his success in restoring social and political harmony during a volatile period in South Carolina's history. Economic setbacks and political infighting reached a fevered pitch by 1728, as local leaders and factions clashed over their differing views of how best to solve their problems. By the next year, government entered a near state of anarchy. The assembly stopped meeting, taxes went uncollected, and courts were at a standstill. Although much of the tension had subsided by the time Johnson assumed his office in 1730, his leadership maintained a delicate consensus that kept the colony from repeating its tumultuous plight. In cases where the colony's welfare would be compromised by a strict interpretation of his instructions, Johnson often opted for the spirit over the letter. For example, in November 1731, he used funds earmarked for township development to reduce colonial debts. The act was clearly outside the confines of his authority, but it greatly reduced the public debt without resorting to tax increases that might have crippled the economy. He was also adept at finding common ground between the council and assembly. During his tenure as royal governor Johnson clashed only twice with the assembly, and in neither case was his overall esteem and effectiveness with that body lessened.

The ability to bring opposing factions together both by his visionary agenda of land reform and his willingness to compromise for the greater good made Johnson, as the historian Eugene Sirmans wrote, "the most remarkable politician in the colonial history of

South Carolina." On his death in Charleston on May 3, 1735, the *South-Carolina Gazette* noted that "the Interest of the Province lay principally at his Heart." The people of South Carolina knew him simply as the "good Governor Robert Johnson." SAMUEL C. SMITH

Sherman, Richard P. *Robert Johnson: Proprietary & Royal Governor of South Carolina.* Columbia: University of South Carolina Press, 1966.

Sirmans, M. Eugene. *Colonial South Carolina: A Political History, 1663–1763.* Chapel Hill: University of North Carolina Press, 1966.

Webber, Mabel L. "Sir Nathaniel Johnson and His Son Robert, Governors of South Carolina." *South Carolina Historical and Genealogical Magazine* 38 (October 1937): 109–15.

Johnson, William, Jr. (1771–1834). U.S. Supreme Court justice. Born in Charleston on December 27, 1771, Johnson was the second son of blacksmith William Johnson and Sarah Nightingale. Graduated first in his class from the College of New Jersey (Princeton) in 1790, Johnson went on to read law under leading Charleston attorney Charles Cotesworth Pinckney, qualifying for the bar in January 1793. The following year, on March 16, Johnson married Sarah C. Bennett, sister of future governor Thomas Bennett. The couple had eight children, only two of whom survived to adulthood, and also adopted a pair of orphaned siblings.

William Johnson. Courtesy, South Caroliniana Library, University of South Carolina

In October 1794 Johnson won election to the state House of Representatives from the city parishes of St. Philip's and St. Michael's. He remained a member until December 1799, serving as Speaker during his third and final term. A lowcountry Democratic-Republican, Johnson opposed both the Jay Treaty and reapportionment but supported judicial reform. His legislative career came to an early end as a result of his appointment to the South Carolina Court of General Sessions and Common Pleas.

On March 22, 1804, Johnson became the first Democratic-Republican to be appointed to the U.S. Supreme Court. Recommended to President Thomas Jefferson for his loyalty and nerve as much as his ability and character, Johnson proved to be an independent jurist. Frequently at odds with his fellow justices, Johnson wrote nearly half of the dissents filed during his three decades on the high bench and almost two-thirds of the concurrences. His opinions rankled both Federalists, who resented his resistance to an expansive interpretation of federal judicial authority, and Democratic-Republicans, who disliked his approbation of broad construction of congressional powers. Committed to national integrity but sympathetic to states' rights, Johnson sought to encourage cooperation between the federal and state governments by defining their relationship in terms of concurrent powers rather than exclusive spheres. In the end, he believed, all government must serve the welfare of the individual. "State rights, or United States' rights are nothing, except as they contribute to the safety and happiness of the people."

During the last dozen years of his life, Johnson fell out of step with popular opinion in South Carolina, as controversy over slavery and protective tariffs inspired increasing radicalism on behalf of states' rights. In 1822 Johnson's criticism of procedural irregularities in the trial of Denmark Vesey and others accused of conspiring to organize a mass slave rebellion alienated panic-stricken Charlestonians, who valued self-preservation more than strict justice. The following year, when Johnson struck down as unconstitutional the Negro Seaman's Acts, state laws intended to help prevent slave insurrections, the press pummeled him, and the state ignored his ruling. In 1830 Johnson's denunciation of nullification made him a laughingstock among nullifiers, who derided his charge of a conspiracy against the Union. It also made him a pariah among Unionists, who disowned his praise for the universally despised "Tariff of Abominations." Two years later, when Johnson refused to allow the constitutionality of the tariff to be put to a Charleston jury, nullifiers accused him of judicial tyranny.

Respected for his legal expertise, Johnson was vilified for the vehemence of his convictions as well as their substance. He died in Brooklyn, New York, on August 4, 1834. ROBERT F. KARACHUK

Morgan, Donald G. *Justice William Johnson, the First Dissenter: The Career and Constitutional Philosophy of a Jeffersonian Judge.* Columbia: University of South Carolina Press, 1954.

Johnson, William Bullein (1782–1862). Clergyman, educator. The son of Joseph Johnson and Mary Bullein, William Bullein Johnson was born on Johns Island on June 13, 1782. Johnson received little formal education, but studied law until his life was changed due to a conversion experience at a religious revival in Beaufort in 1804. Brown University later conferred an honorary master of arts degree on Johnson in 1814. In 1803 Johnson married Henrietta Hornby and the couple had eight children who lived to maturity.

The Baptist church in Beaufort licensed Johnson to preach in January of 1805, and the next year he was called to become pastor of the Eutaw Baptist Church. In 1809 Johnson moved to Columbia and was instrumental in founding the town's First Baptist Church, dedicating the church building in 1811. From 1811 until 1815 he served as pastor of the First Baptist Church in Savannah, Georgia. In 1814 Johnson served as a member of the constitutional committee of the Triennial Convention, the first nationwide organization among Baptists, held in Philadelphia to coordinate mission activities. In 1821 Johnson helped to found the South Carolina Baptist Convention. He wrote a strongly argued address to the denomination and traveled widely speaking in support of the new state organization. He served as the state convention's vice-president from 1821 to 1825 and as president from 1825 to 1852.

In 1822 Johnson became principal of the Greenville Female Academy, holding that position until 1830. While in Greenville, Johnson helped to found the First Baptist Church and served as the congregation's first pastor. In 1830 Johnson was appointed pastor of the Edgefield Baptist Church. He held that position (except for the year 1845) until 1852 and also served as principal of the Edgefield Female Academy. Along with his support of female education, Johnson also used his influence in favor of a better educated Baptist clergy. He raised money for the support of Furman Academy and Theological Institute (now Furman University). Johnson Female Seminary (later Johnson Female University), founded in 1848 in Anderson, was named in his honor.

Johnson served as president of the national Triennial Convention from 1841 to 1844, using his office to foster cooperation between the northern and southern constituencies. Eventually he came to see sectional differences, mainly regarding the morality of slavery, as irreconcilable.

When the sectional split in the Baptist denomination came in 1845, Johnson immediately began work on the constitutional committee for the Southern Baptist Convention (SBC) and served as the new organization's first president from 1845 to 1851. The long-term success of the SBC can be attributed in part to Johnson's adaptation of the organizational plan developed for the South Carolina Baptist Convention. It was a centralized organization, which, unlike the Triennial Convention's "society plan," allowed the SBC to control all benevolent enterprises through elected boards. Johnson described the plan as a "judicious concentration," which still honored the autonomy of the individual church and the Baptist "aversion for all things but the Bible."

After struggling with poor health for many years, Johnson died in Greenville on October 2, 1862. He was buried in the churchyard of First Baptist Church in Anderson. HELEN LEE TURNER

Clayton, J. Glenwood. "William Bullein Johnson and the Formation of the Southern Baptist Convention." *Viewpoints: Georgia Baptist History* 15 (1996): 21–27.

Johnson, William Bullein. *The Gospel Developed through the Government and Order of the Churches of Jesus Christ.* Richmond, Va.: H. K. Ellyson, 1846.

Legendre, Raymond John. "William Bullein Johnson: Pastor, Educator, and Missions Promoter." Ph.D. diss., New Orleans Baptist Theological Seminary, 1995.

Woodson, Hortense. *Giant in the Land: A Biography of William Bullein Johnson.* Nashville.: Broadman, 1950.

Johnson, William Henry (1901–1970). Painter. Born in Florence on March 18, 1901, to Henry Johnson who worked as a fireman for the Atlantic Coast Line Railroad, and Alice Smoot, a cook and domestic, Johnson emerged as one of the most important African American artists of the twentieth century. Johnson's uncle and namesake, Willie Smoot, was a Pullman porter who encouraged his nephew's move to Harlem about 1918. Prior to that time, young Johnson had displayed a talent for drawing and was an avid student and copyist of newspaper cartoons.

Once in New York, Johnson took odd jobs before enrolling in 1921 at the National Academy of Design, where fees were modest and tuition was free. His teachers included Charles Hinton and Charles Curran for drawing and still life, and Charles Webster Hawthorne, who impressed on his students the importance of color. Johnson spent three summers, 1924 to 1926, at Hawthorne's Cape Cod Summer School. When Johnson did not win a coveted traveling scholarship, Hawthorne financed a study trip abroad, calculating that his protégé would face less discrimination in France. Johnson painted for a while in Paris, and in 1928 settled in Cagnes-sur-Mer, in southern France, where he fell under the spell of Chaim Soutine, an expressionistic painter popular at the time.

In late 1929, Johnson returned to the United States for six months, spending time in New York and making a visit to Florence. He was awarded a gold medal by the Harmon Foundation, a philanthropic organization that recognized the achievements of African Americans in literature, music, art, business, and education. In 1930 Johnson married Holcha Krake, a Danish weaver he had met in France, and settled in Kerteminde, Denmark. They traveled extensively; in 1932 they went to Tunisia, and in 1935 to Oslo, Norway, where he met Edvard Munch. In late 1938, under the threat of Nazism, Johnson and Krake left Scandinavia for New York. Under the auspices of the Works Progress Administration, Johnson taught in Harlem, and became actively involved with other African Americans. At this time his work changed dramatically from highly charged and heavily textured oil paintings in the manner of European expressionists to flatter compositions, often in gouache, that reflect his African roots and the rhythms of the Jazz Age. His subject matter shifted as well, toward the African American experience: farming in rural South Carolina, Harlem street life, Negro spirituals, and blacks in the military. Figurative work featured portraits of family and friends and a series devoted to African American heroes.

Because of World War II and several unfortunate occurrences (a studio fire and various illnesses), Johnson and his wife did not prosper. After Krake's death from cancer in 1944, Johnson's mental and physical health deteriorated, and in 1947 he was admitted to the Central Islip State Hospital where he stayed until his death on April 13, 1970, from pancreatitis. His paintings were initially warehoused under the auspices of the Harmon Foundation, but when the foundation closed in 1967, more than 1,150 works were transferred to the National Collection of the Fine Arts (the Smithsonian American Art Museum). Additional examples of his work can be found at the Columbia Museum of Art, Gibbes Museum of Art, Greenville County Museum of Art, and Florence Museum. See plate 33. MARTHA R. SEVERENS

Breeskin, Adelyn D. *William H. Johnson, 1901–1970.* Washington, D.C.: Smithsonian Institution, 1971.

Powell, Richard J. *Homecoming: The Art and Life of William H. Johnson.* Washington, D.C.: Smithsonian Institution, 1991.

Turner, Steve, and Victoria Dailey. *William H. Johnson: Truth be Told.* Los Angeles: Seven Arts, 1998.

Johnson, William Woodward (b. 1931). Banker. Born in North Augusta on February 16, 1931, Johnson is the son of Dewey H. Johnson and Mabel Woodward. He attended Greenwood High School and in 1953 graduated from the University of South Carolina, where, as a football back, he received the Jacobs Blocking Trophy. He married Pierrine Baker of Greenwood on July 26, 1951, and they have four daughters.

Better known by his nickname "Hootie," Johnson moved to Greenwood in 1943 when his father, an executive with Citizens and Southern National Bank, bought controlling interest of the Bank of Greenwood. The younger Johnson worked part-time for his father in high school and joined the bank full-time in 1953 as assistant cashier. In 1961 his father died and Johnson and his brother, Wellsman, took over the bank. In 1965 Johnson became South Carolina's youngest bank president. In 1969 the bank was renamed Bankers Trust of South Carolina. In 1974 the company moved into the twenty-story Bankers Trust Tower, which was Columbia's tallest building at the time.

Bankers Trust merged with North Carolina National Bank in 1986 and the institution eventually became part of NationsBank, then Bank of America. Johnson rose to chairman of the executive committee of Bank of America and was a director of the corporation.

Johnson served in the state House of Representatives from 1957 to 1958 and was cochairman of a committee to develop a plan for desegregation of South Carolina colleges and universities. He called this work, much of it behind the scenes, "probably the most rewarding of any public service I've ever done." Johnson also served on the Columbia Community Relations Council and was a member of the Columbia Urban League and National Urban League boards.

He also was chairman of the South Carolina Research Authority and a member of the State Development Board.

In 1998 Johnson became chairman of Augusta National Golf Club, which hosts the Masters golf tournament, and was credited with overseeing sweeping changes in the event. He also garnered national media attention from his adamant defense of the club's males-only membership policy.

Institutions such as the University of South Carolina, the Medical University of South Carolina, Lander University, Converse College, Benedict College, Clemson University, B'nai B'rith, and the South Carolina Business Hall of Fame have honored Johnson. After fifty years in banking, Johnson retired in 2001. ROBERT A. PIERCE

Lunan, Bert, and Robert A. Pierce. *Legacy of Leadership*. Columbia: South Carolina Business Hall of Fame, 1999.

Johnston, Henrietta de Beaulieu Dering (ca. 1674–1729). Portrait painter. The date and place of Johnston's birth are unknown; possibly near Rennes in northern France. Her parents were Francis and Susanna de Beaulieu, Huguenots, and with them she immigrated to London in 1687. In 1694 she married Robert Dering (1669–ca. 1702), the fifth son of Sir Edward Dering. They settled in Ireland, where Dering died, leaving her a widow with two daughters, one of whom, Mary, later became a lady-in-waiting for the daughters of George II. Henrietta Dering painted pastel portraits, mostly of members of her husband's extended family, which included such noted individuals as the Earl of Barrymore and Sir John Percival (later the Earl of Egmont).

Where and from whom she learned to render portraits is unknown. They resemble in pose and format the work of Sir Godfrey Kneller, a popular English portraitist of the day. She worked exclusively in pastel on paper, a medium that had not yet gained widespread acceptance. Typically, she signed and dated the wooden backings of her portraits; for example, the reverse of her portrait of Philip Percival bears the following inscription: "Henrietta Dering Fecit / Dublin Anno 1704." In 1705 she married the Reverend Gideon Johnston (1668–1716), a graduate of Trinity College, Dublin, who was the vicar at Castlemore.

Appointed bishop's commissary in South Carolina by the bishop of London in April 1708, Johnston and his wife arrived in Charleston. The Reverend Johnston became the rector of St. Philip's Episcopal Church and repeatedly wrote to the Society of the Propagation of the Gospel in Foreign Parts requesting payment of his salary, which was often delayed. In one letter he states: "were it not for the Assistance my wife gives me by drawing of Pictures . . . I shou'd not have been able to live," indicating that Henrietta Johnston was compensated for her portraits, making her the first professional woman artist in America. As in Ireland, her sitters were drawn from her circle of associates, including numerous Huguenots (the Prioleaus, Bacots, DuBoses) and members of her husband's congregation, such as Colonel William Rhett. In contrast to the deep earth tones and sophistication of her Irish pastels, the ones crafted in Charleston are lighter, simpler, and smaller, indicative of the preciousness of her materials, all of which had to be imported. In America her female subjects usually wore delicate chemises, while the male sitters were dressed in street clothes or, occasionally, armor. Each sitter's posture is erect, with the head turned slightly toward the viewer. Typically, large oval eyes dominate the subject's face. About forty portraits are extant. Pastels by Henrietta Dering Johnston are in private collections in Ireland, and in American museums, including: Gibbes Museum of Art, Museum of Early Southern Decorative Arts, Metropolitan Museum of Art, and Greenville County Museum of Art. She died on March 9, 1729, in Charleston and was buried in St. Philip's Churchyard. See plate 4. MARTHA R. SEVERENS

Alexander, Forsyth, ed. *Henrietta Johnston: Who greatly helped . . . by drawing pictures.* Winston-Salem, N.C.: Museum of Early Southern Decorative Arts, 1991.

Middleton, Margaret Simons. *Henrietta Johnston of Charles Town, South Carolina: America's First Pastellist.* Columbia: University of South Carolina Press, 1966.

Severens, Martha R. "Who was Henrietta Johnston?" *Magazine Antiques* 148 (November 1995): 704–709.

Johnston, Olin DeWitt Talmadge (1896–1965). Governor, U.S. senator. Olin Johnston was born on November 18, 1896, on the outskirts of Honea Path, an upcountry mill town, and raised in the countryside by tenant farming parents Ed and Leila Johnston. Like many of their generation, the family left the farm for the factory. This change shaped Johnston for the rest of his life. He would always see himself as a "mill boy," and mill hands, by far the state's largest group of white workers, would always see him as one of them. Johnston was fourteen years old when he heard Cole Blease on the stump "raising Cain." He said he knew then he would be governor of South Carolina. Elected twice to the governor's office and four times to the U.S. Senate, Johnston became one of the most durable figures in twentieth-century South Carolina politics.

When Johnston was eleven, he left the mill school and started to work in the factory. He still managed to earn a high school diploma, attending classes at Spartanburg's Textile Industrial Institute during the day and tending looms at night. After graduation in 1915, he continued to work even after he enrolled at Wofford College. Halfway through his sophomore year, in 1917, Johnston left school for the U.S. Army, seeing action in Europe with the famed 42nd "Rainbow" Division. He returned home a decorated veteran and went right back to school and right back to work. He completed his degree at Wofford in 1921 then moved to Columbia to attend the University of South Carolina.

In 1922, while still a student, Johnston was elected by Anderson County to the state House of Representatives. Two years later, as he wrapped up his first term in the General Assembly, Johnston completed the requirements for his master of arts and law degrees from the University of South Carolina. That same year, on December 28, 1924, he married Gladys Elizabeth Atkinson. Over the next four decades, Gladys became Olin's most trusted advisor and mother of their three children.

The Johnstons moved to Spartanburg, where Olin opened a law practice. He made his living defending workers against evictions and trying to win them fair compensation for injuries suffered on the job. In 1926 and 1928, he was again elected to the state House, this time from Spartanburg. During these two terms, Johnston earned a reputation as an active lawmaker, a friend of the working man, and a fierce opponent of what he called "ring rule."

In 1930 Johnston ran for governor. Some thought the six-foot four-inch lawyer, with jet-black hair and a booming voice was too inexperienced. Promising to end "the economic slavery of the masses," Johnston surprised everyone, winning the largest number of votes in the first primary. But Ibra C. Blackwood defeated him by

Governor and Mrs. Olin D. Johnston with President Franklin D. Roosevelt in the Governor's Mansion, 1938. Courtesy, South Caroliniana Library, University of South Carolina

the slimmest of margins in the run-off. Over the next four years, Johnston prepared for another run for governor. During this time, the nation's political mood shifted sharply. In 1932 Franklin Roosevelt was elected president and soon after launched the New Deal. Johnston jumped on the New Deal bandwagon and stayed there.

Defeating his one-time hero Cole Blease, Johnston was elected governor in 1934. "This marks the end of ring rule," Johnston declared at his January 1935 inauguration. Over the next four years, he led a modest reform movement in the state, starting an ambitious rural electrification program, spearheading the passage of the state's first workers' compensation act and several other pro-labor measures, and establishing the state's first department of labor. But the military takeover of the highway department in the fall of 1935 overshadowed his accomplishments. After a string of bitter disputes with the road bureau, in which Johnston charged the department with exercising "an undue influence among the people," the governor ordered national guardsmen armed with machine guns to seize the agency. Eventually an uneasy compromise was reached, but for the rest of his career, opponents would refer to him as "Machine Gun Olin."

Following a term in the governor's office, Johnston set his sights on the U.S. Senate. In 1938, he took on another political legend, "Cotton Ed" Smith. Throughout the stormy contest, Johnston campaigned as a "100 percent New Dealer," while Smith pledged to uphold states' rights and white supremacy. Despite Roosevelt's endorsement, Johnston lost the race. Three years later, Johnston failed in a second bid for the Senate. Yet in 1942, he was again elected governor. Part way through his term, Johnston confronted a serious challenge to the whites-only Democratic Party rule in the state. In 1944 the U.S. Supreme Court outlawed the white primary. In response, Johnston called a special session of the legislature where lawmakers, following his lead, erased every mention of the white primary from the state constitution. These actions made the Democratic Party a private club; a private club, Johnston wrongly hoped, free from government oversight.

Campaigning now as a stalwart defender of white supremacy, Johnston again ran for the U.S. Senate in 1944. This time he defeated the aging Smith. Johnston would be reelected to the Senate three more times. During his lengthy Washington tenure, he served on the Agriculture and Forestry, District of Columbia, and Judiciary Committees. In 1950 he was elected chair of the patronage-rich Post Office and Civil Service Committee. Using his access to government funds, he made sure towns across South Carolina had new post offices. Eventually he earned the nickname "Mr. Civil Service" because of his tireless devotion to federal employees. While in the Senate, Johnston remained a staunch racial conservative. Like nearly every southern Democrat of his generation, he opposed any and all federal efforts to weaken segregation. Yet on economic issues, he continued to vote like a New Deal liberal, backing trade unions, the extension of rural electrification, the introduction of the school lunch program, and the strengthening of the Social Security system.

When Olin Johnston died on April 18, 1965, at the age of sixty-eight, thousands of ardent supporters came to pay tribute to him. A long line of white women and men, some "with lint in their hair," filed past his casket. They came to honor a legislator and a chief executive whom, they believed, remained throughout his life a true friend of the white working man. He was buried in the Barbers Creek Baptist Church Cemetery, Honea Path. BRYANT SIMON

Faggart, Luther B. "Defending the Faith: The 1950 U.S. Senate Race in South Carolina." Master's thesis, University of South Carolina, 1992.

Huss, John E. *Senator for the South: A Biography of Olin D. Johnston.* Garden City, N.Y.: Doubleday, 1961.

Johnston, Olin D. Papers. Modern Political Collections, South Caroliniana Library, University of South Carolina, Columbia.

Miller, Anthony Barry. "Palmetto Politician: The Early Political Career of Olin D. Johnston, 1896–1945." Ph.D. diss., University of North Carolina at Chapel Hill, 1976.

Simon, Bryant. *A Fabric of Defeat: The Politics of South Carolina Millhands, 1910–1948.* Chapel Hill: University of North Carolina Press, 1998.

Swager, Karen Klein. "Between a Rock and a Hard Place: Olin D. Johnston's Political Position in the South Carolina 1962 Senatorial Race." Master's thesis, University of South Carolina, 1998.

Jones, Jehu (ca. 1769–1833). Free black entrepreneur. Jones belonged to Christopher Rogers, a tailor. Under Rogers, he learned the tailoring trade, becoming proficient his in his own right. When Rogers manumitted him in 1798 for £100 sterling, Jones set up his own business. Jones succeeded and expanded the business with his oldest son, also named Jehu.

In 1802 Jones broadened his entrepreneurial efforts by investing in real estate in Charleston and on Sullivan's Island. His endeavors evidently flourished, for in 1807 he began to buy slaves to assist him in his business ventures. Two years later, he purchased from William Johnson a lot and house on Broad Street behind St. Michael's Church. In 1815 Jones bought the adjoining property at 33 Broad Street, known as the Burrows-Hall House, with adjacent outbuildings for $13,000. The following year he sold the Johnson House to St. Michael's Church. Jones then left the occupation of "tailoring" to his son, Jehu, Jr., and turned his efforts to inn-keeping, a venture in which he had already achieved some success. Jones and his wife Abigail turned 33 Broad Street into a popular hotel, catering to travelers on extended visits, such as the portrait artist Samuel F. B. Morse. Elite white society patronized the establishment and praised it highly for its comfort and fine food. Jones also became prominent in the Charleston's free black social circles and was a member of the prestigious Brown Fellowship Society.

The Denmark Vesey conspiracy of 1822 induced the General Assembly to pass acts to control free blacks more closely. One act, passed in 1822, required all free males "of color" over the age of fifteen to have a white guardian. An 1823 act barred the return of any free black who left the state. Abigail Jones, who had taken her children and grandchildren to New York for a visit prior to the Vesey rebellion, could not return. Through his guardian, Governor John Lide Wilson, Jehu petitioned the assembly for a leave of absence in 1823 to visit his family and then return to South Carolina. The matter was referred to a special committee, and the request granted. In 1827 Jones again petitioned the assembly to visit his family in St. Augustine, but whether he actually did make either visit is uncertain. Local legend relates that he left Charleston disguised as a woman and was seen walking the streets of New York. Abigail never returned to South Carolina, remaining in New York as an innkeeper and predeceasing Jones.

Jones died in 1833, leaving an estate estimated at $40,000 to his three sons and Abigail's daughter, Ann Deas. The inventory of the estate lists furniture and slaves, but not his real estate holdings. Ann, executrix of the will, returned to Charleston and obtained a pardon from the governor for entering the state without permission. She and Eliza A. Johnson bought "Jones Establishment" from the estate, and by 1834 were again open for business. Ann ran "Jones Establishment" until 1847, when it was sold. ROBERTA V. H. COPP

Johnson, Michael P., and James L Roark. *Black Masters: A Free Family of Color in the Old South.* New York: Norton, 1984.

Koger, Larry. *Black Slaveowners: Free Black Slave Masters in South Carolina, 1790–1860.* 1985. Reprint, Columbia: University of South Carolina Press, 1995.

Taylor, Rosser H. *Ante-bellum South Carolina: A Social and Cultural History.* Chapel Hill: University of North Carolina Press, 1942.

Wikramanayake, Marina. *A World in Shadow: The Free Black in Antebellum South Carolina.* Columbia: University of South Carolina Press, 1973.

Jones and Lee. Edward Culliatt Jones (1822–1902) and Francis D. Lee (1826–1885) were a leading force in South Carolina architecture in the 1850s. During a brief but successful partnership, Jones and Lee designed buildings throughout the state and worked extensively in Charleston. With Edward B. White, they were largely responsible for the emergence of romanticism in South Carolina architecture.

Jones and Lee were both native Charlestonians. Jones was born on July 21, 1822, and worked as an apprentice to builder James Curtis before entering architectural practice in 1848. He married Martha J. Small on February 17, 1857. Lee was born in 1826 to William Lee and Elizabeth Markley. Lee graduated from the College of Charleston in 1846, and began working in Jones's office three years later. In 1852 the pair formed a partnership, which took the form of a loosely structured collaboration and lasted until 1857. They worked together on some commissions but handled others independently. Stylistically, the influence of romanticism unified their work, but each architect retained distinctly different design specialties. Jones was known for his Italianate designs, while Lee achieved distinction for his use of the Moorish and Gothic revival styles.

Jones had built a strong practice by the time he and Lee became partners. His early work in Charleston included the Greek revival Trinity Methodist Church (1848–1850) at 275 Meeting Street, Roper Hospital (1850; demolished), and the Italianate Colonel A. S. Ashe House (ca. 1853). The Church of the Holy Cross (1850) at Stateburg and the main building at Wofford College in Spartanburg (1851–1854) were among his first commissions outside of Charleston. After parting with Lee, Jones would continue working throughout the state. His major projects of the late 1850s included Walker Hall (1857–59) at the South Carolina School for the Deaf and Blind near Spartanburg.

Most of the projects that Jones and Lee undertook as partners were in Charleston. They designed the State Bank of South Carolina (1853) and the neighboring Walker, Evans and Cogswell Building (1853–1854), and also remodeled the Charleston Orphan House (1853–1854) and the Planters' and Mechanics' Bank (1853; destroyed). The South Carolina Institute Hall (1854; demolished) was an especially prestigious commission for the firm. Lee received recognition for designing two Moorish-revival structures, the Farmers and Exchange Bank at 141 East Bay Street (1853–1854) and the Fish Market (1856; destroyed). Jones and Lee also designed county jails in Walterboro (1855–1856) and Orangeburg (1857–1860), the Chester County Courthouse (ca. 1855), and the main building at Furman College (1852–1854; demolished).

After dissolving their partnership, Jones and Lee followed remarkably similar paths. Both remained in Charleston and continued to practice architecture, then served in the Confederate army during the Civil War, and later went west. Jones settled in Memphis, Tennessee, where he supervised construction of the Second Presbyterian Church (1891–1892) and also designed the Church of the Holy Trinity in Vicksburg, Mississippi (1870–1894). He died in Memphis on February 12, 1902. Lee moved to St. Louis, Missouri, in 1868 and became a member of the firm of Lee and Annan, which carried out a number of major projects in the 1870s and 1880s. Lee died at Big Stone Lake, Minnesota, on August 26, 1885 and was buried at Bellefontaine Cemetary in St. Louis. DANIEL J. VIVIAN

Lane, Mills. *Architecture of the Old South: South Carolina.* Rev. ed. Savannah, Ga.: Beehive, 1997.

Poston, Jonathan H. *The Buildings of Charleston: A Guide to the City's Architecture.* Columbia: University of South Carolina Press, 1997.

Ravenel, Beatrice St. Julien. *Architects of Charleston.* 1945. Reprint, Columbia: University of South Carolina Press, 1992.

Severens, Kenneth. *Charleston Antebellum Architecture and Civic Destiny.* Knoxville: University of Tennessee Press, 1988.

Jordan, Robert (b. 1948). Writer. Jordan (pseudonym of James Oliver Rigney, Jr.) was born in Charleston on October 17, 1948, the son of James Oliver Rigney and Eva May Grooms. He began reading at an early age, counting Mark Twain and Jules Verne as favorites. In 1968 Jordan joined the United States Army, serving two tours in Vietnam. In 1970 he entered the Citadel, where he graduated in 1974 with a Bachelor of Science degree in physics. Jordan worked as a nuclear engineer until 1978, when he began writing full-time. He wrote his first book, *The Fallon Blood* (1980), under the pseudonym Reagan O'Neal, as well as two sequels, *The Fallon Pride* (1981) and *The Fallon Legacy* (1982). He then produced *The Cheyenne Raiders* (1982), under the name Jackson O'Reilly.

In 1982, adopting the pseudonym Robert Jordan, he published *Conan the Invincible,* the first of seven installments he would add to the highly popular "Conan" fantasy series, based on the creation of 1930s author Robert E. Howard. Dormant for decades, "Conan" enjoyed a revival in the 1960s, long after Howard's death, and a number of authors stepped in to continue the saga. Jordan's additions to the series are among its most popular, with one critic describing his installments as "vigorous, lusty, and full of excellent scene setting."

Jordan's most famous literary accomplishment, the "Wheel of Time" series, debuted in 1990 with the publication of *The Eye of the World.* "Wheel of Time" features the ongoing adventures of Rand, a hero on an epic quest to unite the inhabitants of his world against the evil Dark One. A 1993 review in *New Statesman and Society* complimented Jordan on creating "an entirely convincing and compelling alternative world." Installments of the "Wheel of Time" have appeared on bestsellers lists and have been published in twenty languages. The eleventh book in the series, a prequel entitled *New Spring*, was published in 2004.

On March 28, 1981, Jordan married Harriet McDougal, with whom he has a son. He lives in Charleston. R. F. STALVEY

Thompson, Bill. "Local Author's Fantasy Fiction as Loved as Tolkien's." Charleston *Post and Courier*, February 9, 2003, p. E1.

Joseph Manigault House (Charleston). Located at 350 Meeting Street, this antebellum mansion became an early success story for Charleston's preservation movement when it was saved from destruction in the early 1920s. The Manigault House was designed by gentleman architect Gabriel Manigault for his brother Joseph and built circa 1803. A fine example of a neo-classical urban residence, it stands three stories high, has a hipped slate roof, and is built of brick laid in Flemish bond. A curvilinear bay with an entrance and a Palladian window is centered on the north side; on the south side, facing the garden, is a broad, double-tiered piazza. A small curvilinear bay on the east side is balanced by a semicircular double-tiered piazza on the west. The main rooms feature richly decorated mantles, moldings, and door and window frames. The ceiling of the stair hall is embellished with large plaster medallion ornaments. At the south end of the property is a garden temple with a bellcast roof. A kitchen, stable, and other dependencies originally occupied the northeast corner of the lot; these have long since been destroyed.

By 1920 the house had become a tenement and was threatened with demolition. Susan Pringle Frost founded the Society for the Preservation of Old Dwellings largely to save the Manigault House. It was purchased by the group in May 1920, but the cost of ownership proved financially burdensome. It was sold to a private owner in 1922, and the property and house were eventually donated to the Charleston Museum in the 1930s. The Manigault House was subsequently restored and operates as a museum. It was designated a National Historic Landmark by the U.S. Department of the Interior in 1973. DANIEL J. VIVIAN

Joseph Manigault House. Courtesy, South Carolina Department of Archives and History

Poston, Jonathan H. *The Buildings of Charleston: A Guide to the City's Architecture.* Columbia: University of South Carolina Press, 1997.

Weyeneth, Robert R. *Historic Preservation for a Living City: Historic Charleston Foundation, 1947–1997.* Columbia: University of South Carolina Press, 2000.

Judicial system. The purpose of any state judicial system is to resolve civil disputes among residents and to determine the guilt or innocence of persons accused of crimes and infractions. Article V of the state constitution provides for a uniform system of justice throughout the state.

Although the contemporary courts in South Carolina are more or less "uniform," this is a recent occurrence. Judicial systems developed in a haphazard fashion over the centuries. As new forms of disputes arose—such as traffic violations, domestic disturbances, and massive amounts of civil litigation—new courts were created to meet specialized needs. Predictably, this process led to a state judicial system that was fragmented and lacked consistency. At least six types of trial courts existed by the early 1970s, yet no single judicial district contained all of the types represented. Moreover, the lines of appeal varied. Cases appealed from municipal courts could, in some counties, be taken to the county courts, while in other counties these cases were reviewed by circuit courts. Meanwhile, county courts in one county might have jurisdiction over civil suits of $5,000 or less, while these courts in other counties could hear cases exceeding $11,000 in value. This chaotic situation was finally resolved during a reform movement that occurred between 1975 and 1990. Grounded in recommendations from the American Bar Association, the state constitution was revised to eliminate most of the specialized courts and to provide greater consistency in procedure and jurisdiction.

Following a model that is present in every state, the South Carolina judicial system is now structured hierarchically. The two highest courts are both appellate bodies, meaning that they almost exclusively adjudicate cases that have been referred to them from lower courts. Appellate courts do not establish facts, as do trial courts. Instead, they apply the facts that have been established at lower levels to the relevant laws or policies, and/or they ascertain whether appropriate procedures were followed in the courts below.

The highest court in the state is the South Carolina Supreme Court, which consists of one chief justice and four associate justices. These are selected by the General Assembly to ten-year terms. As the final level of appeal within South Carolina, the state supreme court exercises two types of jurisdiction, mandatory and discretionary. Cases that the court *must* hear (mandatory) arrive by *writ of appeal* from lower trial courts and include such topics as the death penalty, public utility rates, public bond disputes, and election law violations. A far larger amount of the court's time is devoted to discretionary appeals—cases that arrive by *writ of certiorari* and which may *or may not* be decided, depending on the preferences of the justices. In an average year the court will review about three thousand cases and issue about 250 full opinions. Additionally the state supreme court exercises broad administrative powers over the other courts in the state. With the assistance of the Office of the South Carolina Court Administrator, the court prepares the judicial system budget, allocates resources, and assigns lower court judges on the basis of workloads. The S.C. Supreme Court is also responsible for admitting persons to practice law in the state and for disciplining lawyers and judges who commit ethical misconduct.

The other appellate court is the South Carolina Court of Appeals. This entity was established in 1983 to take some of the workload off the state supreme court. It consists of a chief judge and eight associate judges who are elected to staggered six-year terms by the General Assembly. The court usually decides cases in panels of three judges each, but it may meet collectively (*en banc*) to adjudicate extremely important matters. Since its creation, the S.C. Court of Appeals has become the appellate court workhorse in the state. It reviews about 2,500 cases each year, and issues full opinions in about one-third of those disputes. Virtually any matter may be appealed to the court from the trial courts, including many procedural questions concerning the selection of jurors, the impartiality of judges, and the competence of legal counsel provided to indigent defendants.

The remaining courts in the state are all *trial* courts. The most important are the circuit courts, which are the trial courts of general jurisdiction. They hear all civil cases exceeding $7,500 in value, and criminal cases in which the possible penalties are greater than $1,000 or thirty days in jail. Consequently, anyone accused of a serious crime, or suing another person for a significant amount of damages, will appear before a circuit court judge. Most proceedings in circuit courts are decided by juries. Circuit courts are divided into two divisions, General Sessions for criminal cases, and the Court of Common Pleas for civil litigation. South Carolina is divided into sixteen judicial circuits consisting of between two and four counties. Circuit court judges are elected by the General Assembly to six-year terms. Each circuit has one or more resident judges, and the remaining judges are subject to rotation among the other circuits depending on workload demands.

Two types of specialized courts complement the work of the circuit judges. The family court system consists of fifty-two judges who are elected by the General Assembly to six-year terms. There is one family court per judicial circuit. These are the sole forum for cases pertaining to marriage, divorce, separation, child custody, visitation, termination of parental rights, alimony, and name changes. They also have jurisdiction over juveniles who are charged with crimes, except for most traffic and hunting offenses. Probate courts, in contrast, are organized differently. Instead of being arranged by circuit and elected by the General Assembly, probate judges are popularly elected within each county to four-year terms. Thus, there are forty-six probate judges (equal to the number of counties), as well as a number of associate probate judges who are appointed in populous counties to help with the case burden. These courts resolve all cases involving wills, estates, and trusts. Probate judges also supervise the estates of incapacitated individuals and rule on involuntary commitments of citizens to various forms of supervision (alcohol dependency, mental incapacity).

The final two judicial bodies in South Carolina are called *limited jurisdiction* courts due to the relatively insignificant nature of the cases they resolve. Magistrate courts exercise jurisdiction over criminal offenses involving penalties or fines not exceeding $1,000 or imprisonment of thirty days or less. Their civil jurisdiction extends to cases involving up to $7,500. As the most numerous courts in the state, there are more than three hundred magistrates. Magistrates are appointed by the governor on the advice and consent of the state Senate and they need not be attorneys. Magistrates collectively resolve nearly one million cases per year, about fifty percent of which relate to traffic offenses and twenty-five percent civil disputes. Much of their business is resolved simply by bond forfeitures, in that citizens charged with minor offenses (traffic infractions, leash law violations) often pay their fines without appearing in court. Because they play such important roles in the judicial system—hearing so many disputes, and also holding pretrial and preliminary hearings in cases involving individuals charged with serious offenses—magistrates have increasingly been required to obtain specialized training. Recent changes in state law have also added educational qualifications. By 2005, persons lacking a college degree will be ineligible for an appointment as magistrate.

A comparable judicial organization exists in the approximately two hundred locations in which municipal courts have been created by the local governing bodies. Judges in these courts have *no* civil jurisdiction, and are solely intended to hear violations of state statutes and municipal ordinances subject to a fine not exceeding $1,000 or imprisonment not exceeding thirty days. STEVEN W. HAYS

Carbon, Susan, Larry Berkson, and Judy Rosenbaum. "Court Reform in the Twentieth Century: A Critique of the Court Unification Controversy." *Emory Law Journal* 27 (summer 1978): 559–607.

Judson, Mary Camilla (1828–1920). Educator. Mary Judson was born in Clinton, Connecticut, on June 27, 1828, the daughter of Charles Judson and Abi Sherman. When she was fourteen, her father sent her to a private school opened by a recent Yale graduate, where she studied Latin, rhetoric, and sciences. In 1845 her family moved to New Haven. There Judson continued studying under private tutors and in the Yale library. She developed a good command of French, read extensively in English literature, studied art, learned Greek and higher mathematics. The fact that she was not allowed to enroll at Yale because she was a woman awakened a fervent feminist consciousness: "though colleges for women had not yet been dreamed of, occasionally it would be borne in upon some woman's consciousness that she had, not only a soul, but a brain, and that its development was her God-given right as truly as it was her brother's."

In 1857 Judson moved to Greenville, South Carolina, where her brother, Charles, taught at Furman University. She served as Lady Principal of the Johnson Female University in Anderson from 1857 to 1859 and then taught art at the Greenville Baptist Female College. During the Civil War, she taught English and French at the Blythewood Academy near Columbia. In January 1865, when federal troops were nearing Columbia, she returned to the Female College, which Charles Judson then headed. There she introduced "the calisthenics," to encourage young women to exercise. Mount Holyoke College in Massachusetts had pioneered the exercises in 1862. Mary Judson's innovation was probably the first at a southern women's college.

In 1868 Judson returned north to teach at private schools in New York and Pennsylvania. In 1874 Charles Judson invited his sister to return to the struggling Female College, where she became Lady Principal in 1878. She brought with her fifteen years of teaching experience, a rigorous reading background, and a faith in the ability of young women to learn and excel, as well as what one graduate called "the wonderful rigor and stern morality and forceful personality of New England." She breathed into her students "the will to do and dare for intellectual freedom." A discreet feminist, she supported women's suffrage.

Judson taught nearly every subject in the college curriculum, including English, French, art, astronomy, botany, and elocution (a subject she introduced). She started the first club for women in Greenville, the Judson Literary Society, where girls wrote papers, debated topics, and began the college library with society dues of twenty-five cents a year. Her annual calisthenics exercises were graduation highlights. She ignored preachers who considered the rhythmic movements dancing, as well as men who believed that women should not speak in public. In 1901, when the Female College launched a campaign for its third building, an auditorium, she contributed $3,000 towards its total cost of $15,000.

Judson was Lady Principal until 1912, but even after she retired from teaching at 83, she continued to live at the college until her death on December 29, 1920. JUDITH T. BAINBRIDGE

Bainbridge, Judith T. *Academy and College: The History of the Woman's College of Furman University.* Macon, Ga.: Mercer University Press, 2001.

Just, Ernest Everett (1883–1941). Marine biologist. Just was born in Charleston on August 14, 1883, the son of carpenter Charles Frazier Just and Mary Matthews Cooper. His early education was in a small, segregated school operated by his mother on James Island, the Frederick Deming, Jr. Industrial School. At age twelve, Just enrolled in the teacher training program at the Colored Normal, Industrial, Agricultural and Mechanical College of South Carolina in Orangeburg. Graduating in 1899, Just left South Carolina to attend the Kimball Union Academy in Meriden, New Hampshire. With diligence, and aided by scholarships, Just enrolled at Dartmouth College, from which he graduated magna cum laude in 1907. As an African American, Just had little opportunity to pursue a career in science. Instead he joined the faculty of Howard University in Washington, D.C., where he taught English, biology, and zoology. On June 26, 1912, he married Ethel Highwarden, a fellow Howard faculty member. The couple had three children and later divorced.

Despite his teaching and administrative commitments, Just found time to pursue scientific research. In 1909 he was invited to the prestigious Marine Biological Laboratory at Woods Hole, Massachusetts, where he served as a research assistant. After several summers of study and a year's leave of absence from Howard, Just earned a doctorate in zoology from the University of Chicago in 1916. By this time, he had already established himself as an authority on fertilization, publishing his first paper in 1912 and receiving the National Association for the Advancement of Colored People's first Springarn Medal in recognition of his scientific work and "service to his race." There followed, for the remainder of his life, international recognition of his work and publications—especially in Europe—together with frustration and bitterness, because no scientific appointments were made available to him. Of his situation, Just once observed, "You see, I have a profession, but no position." Nevertheless, between 1919 and 1928, he published no fewer than thirty-five scientific articles, primarily on fertilization.

In 1928 Just received a sizable grant from the Julius Rosenwald Fund, which allowed him to pursue research in Europe. Over the next decade, he made at least ten trips to Europe, undertaking research at such prestigious institutions as the Stazione Zoologica in Italy, the Kaiser-Wilhelm Institut für Biologie in Germany, and the Station Biologique in France. On August 11, 1939, he married his German assistant, Maid Hedwig Schnetzler. They had one daughter. That same year, Just published *Biology of the Cell Surface,* a synthesis of much of his life's work, and *Basic Methods for Experiments on Eggs of Marine Animals,* a book of experimental advice.

Just died of pancreatic cancer in Washington, D.C., on October 27, 1941. The distinguished psychiatrist Ben Karpman wrote of his friend's passing: "Professor Just's life was the struggle of a soul in pain. Optimism and frustration struggled within him, and optimism lost." CHARLES E. WYNES

Manning, Kenneth R. *Black Apollo of Science: The Life of Ernest Everett Just.* New York: Oxford University Press, 1983.

Wynes, Charles E. "Ernest Everett Just: Marine Biologist, Man Extraordinaire." *Southern Studies* 33 (spring 1984): 60–70.

Kalmia Gardens. Named for the spectacular display of *Kalmia latifolia* (mountain laurel) growing on a dramatic bluff carved by Black Creek in Darlington County, Kalmia Gardens opened to the public in 1935.

At the top of the sixty-foot-high bluff is a one-room-deep farmhouse built by Thomas Hart around 1820. The house overlooks the floodplain of Black Creek and is surrounded by residential-scale gardens including many exotic ornamentals planted by the garden's founder, May Roper Coker, the wife of David Robert Coker. When the Coker family acquired the land in 1932, "Miss May," an avid gardener, began transforming what had become a dump site. She planted exotic plants including camellias, wisteria, tea-olives, and azaleas and created trails down the bluff into what was then known as "Laurel Land." Miss May gave Kalmia Gardens to Coker College in 1965 as a memorial to her late husband, the founder of the Coker Pedigreed Seed Company.

A wooden boardwalk allows visitors to wander down the steep bluff, over Black Creek, and through the cypress swamp. The changes in terrain create varied habitats that support a diversity of plants and animals. The gardens are frequented by students and visitors of all ages who come to study, celebrate, walk, volunteer, and enjoy the great variety of plants and outdoor spaces found in this beautiful garden along the silent and swift-flowing Black Creek. MARY TAYLOR HAQUE

Kellogg, Clara Louise (1842–1916). Opera singer. Kellogg was born on July 12, 1842, in Sumter, the daughter of George Kellogg and Jane Elizabeth Crosby. Her uncle was the notable American physician and botanist Albert Kellogg. Shortly after her birth, the Kellogg family moved to Connecticut. Because both of her parents were gifted musically, Clara was exposed to music early in her childhood. By adolescence Clara was regarded as being skilled, especially as a singer.

In 1857 the Kellogg family moved to New York. After completing her general education at Ashland Seminary and Musical Institute at Catskill, New York, she commenced intensive vocal training in New York City. In 1861 she made her debut at the Academy of Music as Gilda in Giuseppe Verdi's opera *Rigoletto.* The outbreak of the Civil War forced a cancellation of her first major national tour. Within two years, however, she had gained further acclaim as Marguerite, the heroine of Charles Gounod's *Faust.* Although strongly identified with that particular role, Kellogg would perform the majority of the lyric and dramatic soprano roles in the opera literature. By the height of her career, she had sung more than forty roles.

Kellogg made her European debut in 1867 at Covent Garden in London. During the next decade she toured extensively throughout Europe and North America, becoming one of the first American operatic singers to gain an international reputation. By 1873 she had formed her own touring company, the Clara Kellogg English Opera Company, which advertised itself with the slogan "opera for the people." Kellogg sought to familiarize American audiences with the European opera repertoire. Consequently, her company's performances were sung in English, rather than Italian, German, or French. The troupe disbanded in 1876 after enjoying only moderate success.

In 1887 Kellogg married Carl Strakosch, a well-known New York musical impresario. The couple had no children of their own but did adopt a child. They resided at Kellogg's estate, Elpstone, in New Hartford, Connecticut. Following her marriage, Kellogg stopped touring, and she had ceased performing in public by 1890. She became a respected teacher to a series of gifted younger vocalists, frequently providing financial assistance to numerous struggling musical artists. In 1913 she published an autobiography, *Memoirs of an American Prima Donna.* Following a lengthy illness, Kellogg died at Elpstone on May 13, 1916. MILES S. RICHARDS

Kellogg, Clara Louise. *Memoirs of an American Prima Donna.* New York: G. P. Putnam's Sons, 1913.

Kelsey and Guild. During the first decade of the twentieth century, the Boston-based landscape architecture firm Kelsey and Guild served as consultant to civic improvement groups in Columbia and Greenville and prepared citywide plans for both communities. Although the proposals made by the firm were too ambitious to receive serious consideration, Kelsey and Guild's work set an important precedent for municipal planning in South Carolina.

In January 1904 the textile entrepreneur Thomas Fleming Parker brought Harlan P. Kelsey to Greenville to design the grounds of his Monaghan Mill. At Parker's urging, Kelsey also spoke with business and municipal leaders in Greenville, informing them of the benefits of civic beautification. Kelsey lectured on the same subject in Columbia at a public gathering arranged by Parker's cousin and fellow mill executive Lewis Wardlaw Parker. In promoting the ideals of the nationally popular City Beautiful movement, Kelsey inspired the formation of civic improvement organizations in each city. Citizens in Columbia organized the Civic Improvement League in February 1904, and less than two months later their counterparts in Greenville established the Municipal League.

Each organization hired Kelsey and his partner, Irvin T. Guild, to produce a citywide beautification and improvement plan. In 1905 Kelsey and Guild submitted *The Improvement of Columbia, South Carolina* to the Civic Improvement League, and in 1907 the Municipal League received a similar document entitled *Beautifying and Improving Greenville, South Carolina.* The recommendations contained in each report were similar. Kelsey and Guild proposed that public parks, tree-lined boulevards, and a "civic center"—a grouping of public buildings set amid a landscaped plaza—be created in each city. City Beautiful supporters enthusiastically received their recommendations, but limited public funding prevented municipal officials from implementing more than a few small projects. The Kelsey and Guild plans were significant for introducing the concept of a comprehensive approach to community planning, which influenced municipal policy in communities throughout South Carolina in later decades. DANIEL J. VIVIAN

Kelsey and Guild. *Beautifying and Improving Greenville, South Carolina.* Boston: Kelsey and Guild, 1907.

———. *The Improvement of Columbia, South Carolina.* Harrisburg, Pa.: Mt. Pleasant Press, 1905.

Thacker, Marta Leslie. "Working for the City Beautiful: Civic Improvement in Three South Carolina Communities." Master's thesis, University of South Carolina, 1999.

Kensington Plantation. (Richland County). In the early 1850s, Greek revival remained the favored style for the plantation houses of the South Carolina elite. Matthew Richard Singleton broke with the prevailing fashion when he decided to transform his Lower Richland County plantation house into an elegant Italianate mansion. Singleton, scion of a planter family with extensive landholdings along the Wateree River, moved to Headquarters Plantation in 1844 after returning from a tour of duty in Europe as a military attaché. He immediately began making improvements to the house and grounds. Influenced by his travels in Europe, Singleton renamed the plantation "Kensington" and hired the Charleston architect Edward C. Jones to renovate the main house, which in its original form was probably a small, plain, upcountry farmhouse. By the time the project reached completion in 1854, Jones had created a Renaissance-inspired residence that recalled the country villas of northern Italy.

Kensington Plantation. Courtesy, South Carolina Department of Archives and History

Kensington is a frame house set on a raised basement. The domed central section is flanked by two gabled wings with arched colonnades and fronted by a porte cochere with Corinthian pilasters. The interior centerpiece is the main hall, which rises two and one-half stories to a skylight at the top of the dome and has a second-story balcony. Flanking the hall are two parlors. A short passageway lined with six niches for statuary leads to a long dining room with a coffered, barrel-vaulted ceiling. The formal first-floor rooms feature elaborate plaster ornamentation, and the house originally had a brilliant polychrome color scheme.

In 1981 Kensington Plantation was acquired by the Union Camp Corporation. The main house, unoccupied since about 1940, stood in disrepair. Following consultation with the South Carolina Department of Archives and History and local interest groups, Union Camp undertook a full-scale restoration and established a partnership with the Scarborough-Hamer Foundation to provide interpretive tours for visitors. Kensington is operated as a historic house museum and is open to the public. DANIEL J. VIVIAN

Edgar, Walter B. *A Training Guide for Kensington.* Eastover, S.C.: Union Camp Corporation, 1985.

Lane, Mills. *Architecture of the Old South: South Carolina.* Savannah, Ga.: Beehive, 1984.

Kershaw, Joseph (ca. 1727–1791). Merchant. Kershaw was born in Yorkshire, England, the eldest son of Joseph Kershaw. Little is known about his early years. Around the mid-1750s he and two brothers, Ely and William, immigrated to South Carolina. Joseph became a clerk for the Charleston merchant James Laurens, the elder brother of Henry Laurens. In 1758, however, Kershaw struck out for the colony's interior, establishing a store northwest of Charleston near the Wateree River at Pine Tree Hill. There, acting as an agent for the Charleston firm of Ancrum, Lance, & Loocock, Kershaw laid the foundations for his future success. On October 20, 1762, he married Sarah Mathis. The couple had eight children.

In 1763 Kershaw formed a partnership with his brother Ely, John Chesnut, William Ancrum, and Aaron Loocock. Centered in Charleston, the partnership used Kershaw to provide a base of operations to expand its trade into the interior. Although the partnership experienced mixed success, Kershaw's own mercantile operations made him the leading commercial, and subsequently political, figure in the Wateree River region. His business operations expanded to include a large flour and grist mill, indigo works, a warehouse, a brewery, and a distillery. He and his partners also acquired grants for several thousands of acres of land across the colony. In 1769 Kershaw played a lead role in convincing his Pine Tree Hill neighbors to lay out a series of streets and lots, which became the town of Camden.

Kershaw was elected to the Commons House of Assembly in 1769, in which he was a member of the committee that drew up the Circuit Court Act, which established several new judicial districts in the interior. He was returned to three more assemblies before the start of the Revolutionary War and then was elected to the First (1775) and Second (1775–1776) Provincial Congresses and the first five General Assemblies (1776–1784). As a legislator and militia officer, Kershaw worked to secure interior settlers and Catawba Indians to the patriot cause. A major and later a colonel in the state militia, Kershaw saw action at Purrysburg and Stono River and was captured at the Battle of Camden (August 1780). He was imprisoned at British Honduras and then Bermuda, where he nevertheless was able to mortgage his Carolina lands to secure needed supplies for American forces (the vessel carrying the cargo was unfortunately captured). He was eventually exchanged and returned to South Carolina.

Kershaw spent the last years of his life trying to rebuild his wartorn business enterprises in Camden. He died on December 28, 1791, and was buried in the town's Episcopal cemetery. That year Kershaw County was named in his honor. TOM DOWNEY

Bailey, N. Louise, Mary L. Morgan, and Carolyn R. Taylor, eds. *Biographical Directory of the South Carolina Senate, 1776–1985.* 3 vols. Columbia: University of South Carolina Press, 1986.

Ernst, Joseph A., and H. Roy Merrens. "'Camden's Turrets Pierce the Skies!': The Urban Process in the Southern Colonies during the Eighteenth Century." *William and Mary Quarterly,* 3d ser., 30 (October 1973): 549–74.

Kirkland, Thomas J., and Robert M. Kennedy. *Historic Camden.* 2 vols. 1905. Reprint, Camden, S.C.: Kershaw County Historical Society, 1994.

Kershaw, Joseph Brevard (1822–1894). Soldier, jurist. Kershaw was born on January 5, 1822, in Camden, the son of John Kershaw and Harriet Dubose. After a childhood education in private academies, Kershaw studied law and was admitted to the bar in 1843. On November 6, 1844, he married Lucretia Douglas. The marriage produced ten children. During the Mexican War, Kershaw served as a lieutenant in South Carolina's Palmetto Regiment, but he took ill in June 1847 and returned to South Carolina. He returned to his law practice in Camden and became involved in politics. He represented Kershaw District in the state House of Representatives from 1852 to 1855 and as a delegate to the Secession Convention of December 1860, where he signed the Ordinance of Secession.

Just prior to the outbreak of the Civil War, on April 9, 1861, Kershaw was made colonel of the Second South Carolina Regiment. Its first engagement was at Fort Sumter (April 12, 1861), where the regiment manned the Morris Island fortifications. Shortly thereafter the regiment was sent to Virginia and played an active role in the Confederate victory at First Manassas (July 21, 1861). In January 1862 Kershaw was given command of a brigade, and the following month he was promoted to brigadier general. Admired for his coolness in battle and his decision-making ability, Kershaw led his brigade to action at the Seven Days' battles (June 25–July 1, 1862), Antietam (September 17, 1862), Fredericksburg (December 13, 1862), and during the Chancellorsville campaign in the spring of 1863. Kershaw was also actively involved in the Battle of Gettysburg (July 1–3, 1863). Later that fall he participated in the Knoxville campaign. Returning to Virginia, Kershaw was promoted to major general in May 1864 and given command of the First Division, First Corps of the Army of Northern Virginia. His division saw action in every major Virginia engagement throughout the remainder of the war, including the Wilderness (May 5–6, 1864), Spotsylvania (May 8–12, 1864), and the siege of Petersburg and final defense of Richmond. He was captured just days before the surrender at Appomattox and remained a prisoner until his release in July 1865.

After the war, Kershaw returned to South Carolina, resumed his law practice, and reentered political life. He served in the S.C. Senate from 1865 to 1866, where he was chosen president pro tempore in December 1865. He lost a reelection bid in 1868 and a bid for Congress in 1874. With the return of the Democrats to power in 1876, the General Assembly made Kershaw a circuit court judge in 1877, a position he held until failing health forced him to resign in 1893. In his later years he contributed accounts of his war service for the multivolume *Battles and Leaders of the Civil War* (1887–1888) and briefly oversaw efforts to collect the records of Confederate veterans in South Carolina. He died on April 12, 1894, and was buried in Quaker Cemetery, Camden. KENDRA DEBANY

Bailey, N. Louise, Mary L. Morgan, and Carolyn R. Taylor, eds. *Biographical Directory of the South Carolina Senate, 1776–1985.* 3 vols. Columbia: University of South Carolina Press, 1986.

Freeman, Douglas Southall. *Lee's Lieutenants: A Study in Command.* 3 vols. New York: Scribner's, 1942–1944.

Tagg, Larry. *The Generals of Gettysburg: The Leaders of America's Greatest Battle.* Campbell, Calif.: Savas, 1998.

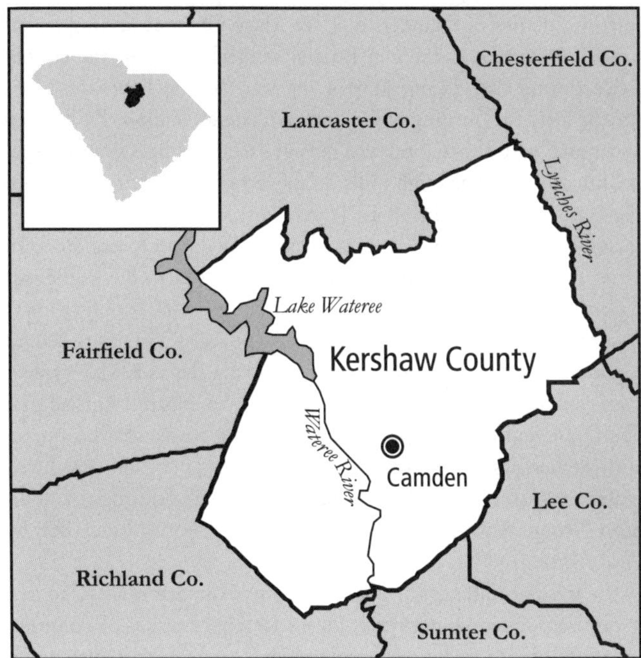

Kershaw County (726 sq. miles; 2000 pop. 52,647). Kershaw County was created in 1791 from portions of Claremont, Fairfield, Lancaster, and Richland Counties. Like other South Carolina counties, Kershaw was designated a "district" from 1800 until 1868, when a new state constitution restored the "county" designation. The first courthouse for Camden District was built in 1771 at Camden, which later became the Kershaw County judicial seat. The county's name honors the Revolutionary War patriot Joseph Kershaw of Camden.

Intersected by the fall line and two rivers, the Lynches and the Wateree, the geography of Kershaw County influenced its settlement and character. The Piedmont soils of the hilly northwest contrast with the meandering river floodplains in the southeastern section and the sandhills terrain predominant in the other areas. European explorers and early immigrants followed waterways and ancient Native American footpaths to enter the region. Some of the state's oldest prehistoric sites are in Kershaw County, including mounds, rock shelters, and Paleo-Indian artifacts. Early visitors to the massive Native American settlement of Cofitachiqui, with its temple mound capital at Mulberry, were Hernando de Soto in 1540, Captain Juan Pardo in 1566 and 1568, and the Englishman Henry Woodward in 1670. Later visitors encountered the Wateree and Catawba Nations. The county seal honors King Haiglar, an eighteenth-century Catawba chieftain who befriended early settlers.

European settlement occurred in several areas. The township of Fredericksburg, part of Governor Robert Johnson's township plan of the 1730s, was not inhabited because of its location in a floodplain. Instead, English settlers and Irish Quakers took up lands on both sides of the Wateree River in the early 1750s, near the head of navigation. Near this central location, the backcountry's most important colonial milling and trading center flourished at Pine Tree Hill (renamed Camden in 1768). Scots-Irish settlers from Pennsylvania also established homesteads along waterways in upper Kershaw County. During the Revolutionary War, the British seized Camden and fortified it as their headquarters in the hotly contested backcountry campaign. Eight battles or skirmishes were fought within the modern county boundary, the largest of which was the American defeat at the Battle of Camden (August 16, 1780).

When hostilities ended, the area recovered quickly. With the advent of the cotton gin, a flourishing economy developed based on plantation agriculture. Demand for virgin soil to maintain cotton profits, however, encouraged planters and farmers to migrate to the southwest in the 1820s. Dependence on African slave labor increased rapidly in the early nineteenth century. By 1850 slaves outnumbered free inhabitants in Kershaw District by more than two to one.

Support for the Confederacy was strong at the outbreak of the Civil War. Camden was the birthplace of six generals who served the Confederate cause. Within the first year of the war, eighty percent of white males over age eighteen had volunteered for service. The wartime diaries of Camden resident Mary Chesnut are important historical sources of the era. Federal soldiers occupied the county twice during the closing year of the war. In late February 1865, shortly after the burning of Columbia, General William T. Sherman encamped with thirty thousand men at Liberty Hill, a wealthy antebellum village in the High Hills. In the last organized incursion into the state, General Edward E. Potter and a force of 2,500 troops, including African Americans, engaged Confederate forces on April 19 at Boykin's Mill, where the last Federal officer to die in the war was killed.

Impoverishment, displacement, and political instability led to migration in and out of the county following the war. Many freedmen sought improved opportunities in the North. Agricultural operations shifted from plantations to smaller farms, sharecropping, and the lien system. Postwar racial and political tensions produced violent excesses, including several duels and the murder of Solomon George Washington Dill, a senator-elect shot in June 1868 by local whites.

In the late nineteenth and early twentieth centuries, Camden became a popular winter resort for wealthy northerners. A common sporting interest in horses among visitors and residents promoted the equine industry, which gave a distinctive character to the county that survived into the modern era. The expansion of railroads in the late nineteenth century improved transportation and helped attract tourists, business, and industry. Several small towns emerged from railroad stops, including Bethune, Cassatt, Lugoff, Blaney (later Elgin), and Westville.

Industrialization proceeded slowly. The first textile mill began in 1838 but burned just before the Civil War. Another mill did not operate until 1890, followed by a third in 1900. Completion of the Wateree Dam in 1919 gave Kershaw a boost by providing electricity and flood control to a county that had sometimes been temporarily divided by the unpredictable river. The dam also created Lake Wateree, which evolved into a popular recreational and residential area. Although some farming families abandoned the land for textile employment, agriculture dominated the lives of most Kershaw residents into the Great Depression of the 1930s.

Industrialization increased significantly in 1950 when E. I. duPont de Nemours began manufacturing orlon (an acrylic fiber) in Lugoff. By century's end, the largest sector of the workforce, thirty percent, was employed in manufacturing, followed by twenty percent in wholesale and retail sectors. DuPont remained the county's largest employer, followed by Standard Corporation, BBA-Nonwovens, Dana Corporation, and Archimica, Inc. Four of these five manufacturers were located in the West Wateree section.

Formerly segregated public schools were racially integrated into a unitary educational system by 1970. Support for public schools remained strong in the county, with less than five percent of the student population attending private schools at the end of the twentieth century.

After more than 250 years of settlement, Kershaw County entered the twenty-first century as one of the state's fastest-growing counties. Interstate 20 whisks workers in and out of the county to jobs in nearby Columbia and elsewhere. Planted timber replaced abandoned farm fields. The threat of pollution to the Wateree River raised environmental concerns. Despite these changes, Kershaw County remained focused on the goal of maintaining the best aspects of its past while meeting the challenges of the present and the future. JOAN A. INABINET

Inabinet, L. Glen, and Joan A. Inabinet, eds. *Kershaw County Legacy: A Commemorative History.* Camden, S.C.: Kershaw County Bicentennial Commission, 1976.

———. *Legacy II: Kershaw County History and Heritage.* Camden, S.C.: Kershaw County Historical Society, 1983.

Kershaw County Historical Society. *A Guide to Selected Historical Sites in Kershaw County/District, South Carolina.* Camden, S.C.: Kershaw County Historical Society, 1992.

Kirkland, Thomas J., and Robert M. Kennedy. *Historic Camden.* 2 vols. 1905. Reprint, Camden, S.C.: Kershaw County Historical Society, 1994.

Keyserling, Harriet (b. 1922). Legislator. Keyserling was born in New York City on April 4, 1922, the only daughter of Isador Hirschfeld, a prominent periodontist, and Pauline Steinberg. She married Herbert Keyserling on June 24, 1944, while he was a young physician in the navy during World War II, and they moved to his hometown of Beaufort, South Carolina, in 1946. They have two daughters and two sons.

The story of Keyserling's transition from a transplanted New York liberal Jewish housewife to an eight-term member of the South Carolina legislature—where beginning at age fifty-four she left a mark battling for the public interest—is told in her much-acclaimed 1998 memoir, *Against the Tide.* Beginning as a shy woman who lacked self-confidence, Keyserling moved from volunteer leader to political activist, first as a member of Beaufort County Council and then winning election to the South Carolina House of Representatives in 1976. "Caring passionately was another change wrought in me by eighteen years in politics," Keyserling wrote. "As my ego gradually built up, it allowed me to feel passionate about causes and people. In my other life I would not let myself feel so strongly about politics or anything else, because I didn't see myself as able to do anything about them. . . . But when I finally found myself in a position of knowing I could make a difference, the passion came bubbling up, like adrenalin during stress. Which is fortunate, because without the intensity and drive created by passion, I could not have won any of those battles and I would not have challenged others, even when I knew they were wrong and I was right."

Keyserling led successful efforts to improve state funding for the arts, became a major critic of state policy on nuclear waste storage, and provided an influential voice on broad policy issues involving energy. She joined with a small group of fellow progressives, the self-named "Crazy Caucus," that throughout the 1980s fought for "the public interest against special interests."

As a legislator, Keyserling worked closely with black Democrats on progressive legislation, especially Governor Richard W. Riley's Education Improvement Act. She writes forthrightly about racial tensions that developed within the Democratic Party after black Democrats joined with Republicans on reapportionment following the 1990 census to create a maximum number of black majority legislative districts. Packing black voters into those districts jeopardized progressive white Democrats such as Keyserling. Some ran again and lost. She was among others who chose to retire, and Republicans soon gained control of the state House of Representatives. Her son Billy succeeded her in the legislature and served two terms, the second as an independent.

Keyserling remained active in state and local issues, returning to family life in Beaufort as a new woman. "I like the fact that I can openly disagree with others and not worry that I may discomfort them or that they might not like me if I challenge them," she says. "I like my new freedom to speak my mind. I feel released from my old shackles of insecurity and timidity." JACK BASS

Keyserling, Harriet. *Against the Tide: A Woman's Political Struggle.* Columbia: University of South Carolina Press, 1998.

Keyserling, Leon Hirsch (1908–1987). Economist, lawyer, presidential adviser. The South Carolina–born son of Jewish immigrants, Leon Keyserling made his mark as an economist and architect of the New Deal of the 1930s. He was born on January 22, 1908, in Beaufort, the first child of William Keyserling and Jennie Hyman. Keyserling's father had come to the United States from Lithuania in 1888 and established himself with the MacDonald, Wilkins and Company cotton gin and wholesale warehouse in Beaufort. Leon spent his early years on St. Helena Island, east of Beaufort, reading books with his mother and developing his gifts of quick comprehension and remarkable memory. In 1917 Leon moved with his parents and three siblings to town, where in the tenth grade he won an award for an essay entitled "A Bigger, Better, and More Beautiful Beaufort." A framed copy hung in his office and, after his retirement, at his home.

At age sixteen, Keyserling left Beaufort and enrolled in Columbia University in New York. He graduated from Columbia with a B.A. in economics in 1928 and from Harvard University Law School in 1931, then returned to Columbia to teach economics. In 1933 he became chief legislative aide to New York senator Robert F. Wagner, and during the next four years he helped design major New Deal economic and employment programs. He was the principal draftsman of a $3 billion public works bill, the wage and hour provisions of the National Industrial Recovery Act (1933), the National Housing Act (1934–1935), the National Labor Relations Act (1935), and portions of the Social Security Act (1935).

During these years Keyserling also worked with the Senate Committee on Banking and Currency and wrote national platforms for the Democratic Party in 1936, 1940, and 1944. He helped to create the U.S. Housing Authority, and as the agency's acting administrator and general counsel oversaw construction of millions of residences for war workers. His 1944 essay on postwar employment has been cited as the basis for the historic Employment Act of 1946, which created the Council of Economic Advisors (CEA) and firmly established a federal government role in the expansion and stability of the national economy.

Keyserling served on President Harry Truman's CEA from 1946 to 1953 and became its chairman in 1950. His interest in public policy continued after his retirement from government in 1953. He founded the Conference on Economic Progress, a private, nonprofit organization that published works criticizing the economic policies of Dwight Eisenhower and John F. Kennedy. During the 1970s he drafted legislation establishing the Department of Housing and Urban Development and the Full Employment and Growth Act (1978).

On October 4, 1940, Keyserling married Mary Dublin, a professor of economics at Sarah Lawrence College. They had no children. Mary Dublin Keyserling went on to become an influential economist and social activist in her own right, serving as head of the Women's Bureau of the Labor Department under President Lyndon B. Johnson. Leon Keyserling died on August 9, 1987, in Washington, D.C. DALE ROSENGARTEN

Brazelton, W. Robert. *Designing US Economic Policy: An Analytical Biography of Leon H. Keyserling.* New York: Palgrave, 2001.
Keyserling Family Papers and Leon Keyserling Papers. Special Collections, College of Charleston Library, Charleston.
Keyserling, Leon. Papers. Lauinger Library, Special Collections Division, Georgetown University, Washington, D.C.
———. Papers and Oral History Interviews. Truman Presidential Museum and Library, Independence, Mo.
———. *Progress or Poverty: The U.S. at the Crossroads.* Washington, D.C.: Conference on Economic Progress, 1964.

Kiawah Island (Charleston County; 2000 pop. 1,163). Kiawah is a small barrier island situated south of Charleston between the mouths of the Stono and North Edisto Rivers. It is named for the Kiawah Indians, who lived in the vicinity at the time of European contact. In 1699 the Lords Proprietors deeded the island to George Rayner. Twenty years later the island became the property of the planter John Stanyarne, who cleared land for indigo production and built a sizable house that came to be known as the Vanderhorst mansion. In 1772 the island was inherited by Stanyarne's two granddaughters, Mary Gibbes and Elizabeth Raven Vanderhorst, wife of Arnoldus Vanderhorst. Kiawah would remain in the possession of the Vanderhorst family for the next 180 years. Indigo gave way to cotton planting on Kiawah by the start of the nineteenth century and remained the primary economic activity on the island into the twentieth century. A series of hurricanes and the arrival of the boll weevil decimated Sea Island cotton by 1918, however, and Kiawah's cotton fields reverted to woodlands. In 1952 C. C. Royal Lumber Company purchased the island from the Vanderhorst family for $125,000. Shortly thereafter, Royal constructed a bridge that connected Kiawah to Johns Island. In 1974 Royal's heirs sold the island for $17,385,000 to Kiawah Island Company, Inc., a subsidiary of Kuwait Investment Corporation, which developed an upscale resort and residential community. In 1988 the town of Kiawah Island was incorporated. A world-famous resort, Kiawah boasts expansive beaches, as well as superb tennis and golf facilities. FORD WALPOLE

Leland, John G. *A History of Kiawah Island.* Kiawah Island, S.C.: Kiawah Island Company, 1977.
Town of Kiawah Island 10th Anniversary Celebration. Kiawah Island, S.C.: Town of Kiawah Island, 1998.

Kilgo, James Patrick (1941–2002). Essayist, novelist. Born on June 27, 1941, in Florence County, Kilgo was the son of John Simpson Kilgo and Caroline Lawton. He grew up in Darlington, attending St. John's Grammar and High School from first grade through graduation. He received his undergraduate degree from Wofford College in 1963 and then attended graduate school at Tulane University, earning his M.A. in 1965 and the Ph.D. in 1972. While working at Lake Junaluska, North Carolina, during the summer of 1961, Kilgo met Jane Guillory, a coworker from Memphis, Tennessee. They were married on August 27, 1963. The marriage produced three children.

While writing his doctoral dissertation, Kilgo moved to Athens, Georgia, to accept a teaching position in the English department at the University of Georgia. On completion of the dissertation, he was offered a position on the English faculty at Georgia, where he played a pivotal role in the development of the university's creative writing program. He remained at Georgia until his retirement in 1999, when he devoted himself full-time to writing.

Kilgo's writing grew out of observations recorded in his private journals, from which developed his personal narrative style. Much of his early work consisted of reflections on the outdoor life and his hunting experiences. When he was in his late thirties, he was asked to write a series of outdoor columns for the *Athens Observer,* a fledgling weekly newspaper. The resulting columns formed the foundation for what would be Kilgo's first book of essays, *Deep Enough for*

Ivorybills (1988). A second book of essays, *Inheritance of Horses,* followed in 1994.

Kilgo's novel, *Daughter of My People* (1998), a fictionalized retelling of a story retrieved from the hidden lore of his own family, was a finalist for the Lillian Smith Award for fiction and the Stephen Crane Award for first novel, and it was the winner of the Townsend Prize, awarded by Georgia Perimeter College and the *Chattahoochee Review. The Hand-Carved Crèche and Other Christmas Stories* (1999) is a collection of Christmas stories and memories gleaned from the author's Darlington childhood and the traditions that shaped it. In addition, Kilgo's essays have been included in numerous publications, including the *Georgia Review, Gettysburg Review,* and *Sewanee Review.*

"You can't write unless you have a story to tell," said Kilgo. He stressed that it must be the writer's story, not necessarily a lived story, but one that engages the writer's passion. He died of cancer on December 8, 2002, in Athens, Georgia. JULIA ARRANTS

Obituary. Columbia *State,* December 12, 2002, p. B4.

Kilpatrick (Kirkpatrick), James (ca. 1696–1770). Physician, medical writer, poet. Kilpatrick (sometimes spelled "Killpatrick") was born near Carrickfergus, Ireland, into a family of merchants. He attended the University of Edinburgh from 1708 to 1709 but did not take a degree. He returned to Ireland and gained some training in medicine but failed to prosper. Immigrating to Charleston around 1717, Kilpatrick practiced medicine and set up a pharmacy where he produced and sold drugs. In 1727 he married Elizabeth Hepworth, daughter of the secretary of the colony. Harboring ambitions to become a major poet, between 1717 and 1738 he wrote a five-canto narrative poem called *The Sea Piece,* which celebrated the mercantilist policies of the eighteenth-century British Empire.

It was Kilpatrick's medical work, however, that won him widespread recognition. During the Charleston smallpox epidemic of 1738, after one of his children died of the disease, he became one of the foremost champions of the controversial new practice of inoculation. Kilpatrick wrote several articles for the *South-Carolina Gazette* defending inoculation against its opponents, who included the editor of the newspaper. From these articles he compiled *An Essay on Inoculation Occasioned by the Smallpox Being Brought into South Carolina in the Year 1738,* which he published in London in 1743. During the epidemic he came into conflict with another prominent Charleston physician and writer, Thomas Dale, over treatment of fever in smallpox. The two men exchanged bitter pamphlets defending their views before the controversy died away, apparently without resolution. The feud spilled over into politics. During early disputes between South Carolina and Georgia, Kilpatrick, whose outlook was imperial, supported the Georgians, while his rival Dale championed South Carolina.

In 1742 Kilpatrick left Charleston for London, changed his name to Kirkpatrick, and attained an M.D. degree. He was once credited with having revived inoculation in Britain after it had fallen into disuse. But it is now believed that his role in this development was less significant. Nevertheless, his *Essay on Inoculation* and his *Analysis of Inoculation* (1754), which was translated into German, French, and Dutch, brought him widespread recognition. He also achieved financial success as an inoculator of British aristocrats, the French royal family, and some wealthy Carolinians. He died in England in 1770. PETER MCCANDLESS

Kirkpatrick, James. *The Analysis of Inoculation.* London: J. Millan, 1754.

———. *An Essay on Inoculation Occasioned by the Smallpox Being Brought into South Carolina in the Year 1738.* London: J. Huggonsohn, 1743.

Shields, David S. "Dr. James Kirkpatrick, American Laureate of Mercantilism." In *The Meaning of South Carolina History: Essays in Honor of George C. Rogers, Jr.,* edited by David R. Chesnutt and Clyde N. Wilson. Columbia: University of South Carolina Press, 1991.

Waring, Joseph I. "James Killpatrick and Smallpox Inoculation in Charlestown." *Annals of Medical History* 10 (1938): 301–8.

King, Joseph Hillery (1869–1946). Clergyman. Born on August 11, 1869, in Anderson County, one of eleven children of poor sharecroppers, King moved with his family to Franklin County, Georgia, in 1883. On his sixteenth birthday he experienced salvation in a Holiness camp meeting near Carnesville, Georgia, under the preaching of the Holiness advocate Reverend William Asbury Dodge. On August 17, 1885, he joined the Methodist Episcopal Church, South (MECS). On October 23, 1885, he experienced sanctification under the ministry of the Reverend A. J. Jarrell, president of the North Georgia Holiness Association. Sensing a call to ministry, he applied in May 1886 to the MECS for an exhorter's license but was denied. He felt there was prejudice against his Holiness views.

After serving a short term in the U.S. Army, King married Willie Irene King in 1890, but the marriage soon ended in divorce because she was not interested in being a minister's wife. In 1891 he was licensed by the northern Methodist Episcopal Church. He served several circuits, including Lookout Mountain near Chattanooga. While there, he completed a three-year course at the U. S. Grant University School of Theology. He also became acquainted with the Iowa preacher Benjamin Hardin Irwin, who taught a "third work of grace," baptism with fire. King was holding revivals in Horry County, South Carolina, in the summer of 1898. He traveled to Anderson in August when Irwin and others formed the national Fire-Baptized Holiness Association. Irwin then sent King to plant churches in eastern Ontario, Canada. In 1900 Irwin called him to the church's headquarters in Iowa to assist in the editing of *Live Coals of Fire.* When Irwin resigned in disgrace soon after, King became overseer of the national church. In 1902 he moved the headquarters to Royston, Georgia.

Although King was initially skeptical about G. B. Cashwell's reports of the Azusa Street revival, he and most of his denomination accepted the Pentecostal message. White members of the Fire Baptized Pentecostal Church merged in 1911 with Cashwell's Pentecostal Holiness Church, taking the latter name. King did not initially head the new body, but in 1917 he was elected general superintendent, a post he held for most of the rest of his life. After his first wife's death in 1920, he married Blanche Leon, a teacher at the church's Franklin Springs (Georgia) Institute. They had four children. King was named bishop in 1937 and died in Anderson County on April 23, 1946. NANCY A. HARDESTY

Synan, Vinson. *The Old-Time Power.* Rev. ed. Franklin Springs, Ga.: Advocate Press, 1986.

King, Mabel (1932–1999). Actress, singer, television personality. King was born in Charleston on December 25, 1932. She had a starring role in Melvin Van Peeble's Broadway hit musical *Don't Play Us Cheap,* in which two imps are sent by the Devil to break up a party in Harlem. She was a talented entertainer whose most memorable role was as the oversized, all-powerful "Mama" in the 1976–1979 ABC sitcom *What's Happening!!* The main comedic events of the show centered on her role as the loving mother to a teenage son,

Roger (Ernest Thomas); his friends Rerun (Fred Berry) and Dwayne (Haywood Nelson); and a precocious daughter, Dee (Danielle Spencer). The series, loosely based on the motion picture *Cooley High,* was one of several all-black-cast programs that succeeded during the 1970s.

King played the part of Evilene, the Wicked Witch of the West, in the Broadway production of *The Wiz.* Her stellar performance earned King a Tony nomination in 1975 for best actress. She reprised her role in a 1978 film version of the musical and subsequently had roles in the films *The Jerk* (1979), *Scrooged* (1988), *Dead Men Don't Die* (1990), and *Tales from the Darkside 6* (1992).

King's career stalled as her health failed. She ultimately lost both her legs to diabetes, a stroke damaged her left hand, and a fall from a wheelchair knocked out her upper teeth. She lived at the Motion Picture and Television Hospital in Woodland Hills, California, for nine years before leaving the facility in August 1999. When asked about the trials and tribulations she had endured, she was quoted in the *Los Angeles Times* in 1995 as saying, "Sure enough, I've been through a lot, but so what? I thank God for my life." She died in Woodland Hills on November 9, 1999. MARILYN KERN-FOXWORTH

King, Susan Dupont Petigru (1824–1875). Author. King was born on October 23, 1824, in Charleston, the fourth child of the lawyer James Louis Petigru and Jane Amelia Postell. "Sue" received a finishing-school education at Madame Talvande's School in Charleston and at Madame Guillon's in Philadelphia. While decidedly intelligent and talented, in personality she was also independent minded and fun loving—and reportedly quick tempered, rebellious, flirtatious, and indiscreet. At the age of eighteen, on March 30, 1843, she married a young local lawyer, Henry Campbell King. A thinly disguised account of their unhappy marriage is presented in "A Marriage of Persuasion," a story in her third book, *Sylvia's World: Crimes Which the Law Does Not Reach.* The marriage produced one child, Adele, before Henry King was fatally wounded at the Battle of Secessionville in 1862.

Susan Petigru King's first book, *Busy Moments in the Life of an Idle Woman,* which contained four short stories and a novella, was published to critical acclaim in late 1853. She followed with *Lily* in 1855 and *Sylvia's World* in 1859. *Gerald Gray's Wife,* completed in 1863 and published the next year, was an extensive and incisive critique of marriage as a joyless liaison of entrapment and an endless struggle of competing wills. Her last known published work, "My Debuts," appeared in *Harper's Magazine* in 1868. In her writing, Susan Petigru King perceived herself to be an American William Makepeace Thackeray. She wrote realistically and satirically about the manners and mores—the sexual politics and unhappy unions—of the Charleston and lowcountry plantation elite in the divorceless South Carolina that she knew well. A contemporary critic in 1870 observed that "Mrs. King despises foolish sentimentalism, and shows up human vice in all of her books. . . . All of her characters are true to nature." The historians Jane and William Pease argue that "King's novels are differentiated by their critical perspective on women's position, their exploration of themes of failure and frustration, and their focus on the drawing room and ballroom rather than the kitchen and nursery."

After the war, King tried unsuccessfully to support herself as a writer, and by 1867 she was working in Washington, D.C., as a government clerk. On August 17, 1870, she married the Republican boss of Charleston County, Congressman Christopher Columbus Bowen. A native Rhode Islander eight years her junior, Bowen was an unsavory but wily character who was turned out of Congress in 1872. The couple returned to Charleston, where Bowen served a term as county sheriff. Largely shunned by family members and polite society alike, King became lonely and unhappy. She died of typhoid pneumonia in Charleston on December 11, 1875, and was buried in the churchyard of St. Michael's Episcopal Church. THOMAS L. JOHNSON

Helsley, Alexia Jones. "Henry Campbell and Susan Petigru King." *Proceedings of the South Carolina Historical Association* (2001): 11–18.

Pease, Jane H., and William H. Pease. *A Family of Women: The Carolina Petigrus in Peace and War.* Chapel Hill: University of North Carolina Press, 1999.

Scafidel, J. R. "Susan Petigru King: An Early South Carolina Realist." In *South Carolina Women Writers: Proceedings of the Reynolds Conference, University of South Carolina, October 24–25, 1975,* edited by James B. Meriwether. Spartanburg, S.C.: Reprint Company, 1979.

King's Highway. The King's Highway, sometimes called the King's High Road, was a post road that stretched from Savannah, Georgia, to St. George's Fort on the Kennebec River in Maine, linking all colonies together after 1750. In time of war it was used to move militia, supplies, and British soldiers from one colony to another. The intercolonial road originated as a series of Native American trails, which were joined together and gradually enlarged to support animal, wagon, and stagecoach traffic. The segments were built at different times by the individual colonies during the seventeenth and eighteenth centuries. Even at its best, the condition of the route was seldom good. Narrow roads, ruts, mud, obstructions, and poorly maintained bridges and ferries were just a few of the inconveniences to be expected. The section between Wilmington and Charleston was judged by some travelers to be "the most tedious and disagreeable of any on the Continent."

The South Carolina section of the King's Highway, built between 1739 and 1750, crossed the North Carolina line just above Little River on its way to Georgetown. It then skirted the Santee delta before passing through Jerveyville (McClellanville) to reach Charleston. The route to Savannah likewise followed the higher ground away from the coast in order to avoid the Edisto, Combahee, and Broad River basins and did not pass an important settlement until it stopped at Purrysburg on the Savannah River. While individuals could travel on foot or by horse, wagon, or carriage, the easiest and most economical mode was by post stagecoach. The driver was responsible for repairs and for fresh horses, accommodations, and food, usually to be found at inns every seven to ten miles along the way. In the twentieth century much of this road became utilized as U.S. Highway 17. LOUIS P. TOWLES

Leland, Jack. "The King's Highway Is Romantic Trail into Lowcountry Past." Charleston *News and Courier,* February 6, 1955, p. A8.

Teal, Harvey S., and Robert J. Stets. *South Carolina Postal History and Illustrated Catalog of Postmarks, 1760–1860.* Lake Oswego, Ore.: Raven, 1989.

Kings Mountain, Battle of (October 7, 1780). On September 12, 1780, the British major Patrick Ferguson sent a message to patriots in the countryside along the border between North Carolina and South Carolina, ordering them to cease opposition or suffer the consequences. Fueled with anti-British sentiment, patriots ignored the ultimatum and gathered in force at Sycamore Shoals along the Watauga River in North Carolina.

Battle of Kings Mountain, depicting the patriot forces surrounding the enemy on the mountain top. Courtesy, South Caroliniana Library, University of South Carolina

Learning that the rebels were gathering in large numbers, Lord Cornwallis sent Ferguson to deal with them and to recruit additional Tories for their cause. When Ferguson and his command reached Gilberton, North Carolina, they learned that the enemy was advancing from the north. Ferguson, fearing that the rebels would outnumber him, marched his command south. He soon realized, however, that the rebels, many of whom were mounted, were outpacing him.

Instead of returning to British lines at Charlotte, as he had originally planned, Ferguson decided to make a stand against the rebels at Kings Mountain in South Carolina, a dominant point in a chain of low mountains that straddled the border with North Carolina. After a sixteen-mile march, Ferguson sent his men up Kings Mountain. Although the British force reached the mountain well in advance of the rebels, they neglected to build breastworks or redoubts. This allowed the American force to sneak their way up the pine-covered slope, moving from tree to tree and picking off Ferguson's men with accurate rifle fire. Once they reached the summit, they were able to fire at the Tories without the obstruction of woods.

Ferguson's command, however, was forced to fight in the open and was armed with less accurate smoothbore muskets. They also had the disadvantage of having to fire downhill, which made them overshoot their targets. The Tories relied on the use of volley fire and massed bayonet charges, which were ill suited for the terrain. Although the Tories were successful in pushing the rebels down the hill in three successive bayonet charges, the rebels regrouped after each attack and finally gained the advantage. Ferguson was killed in the battle, and almost his entire command of more than one thousand men was killed, wounded, or captured.

The American victory provided a much-needed tonic to the patriot cause in the South. Because of the defeat, Cornwallis was forced to delay his movement into North Carolina for a year. The battle also caused the Loyalists in the area to think twice about joining the British and swayed neutrals to join the patriots in their fight for independence. Perhaps most significant was the hope that Kings Mountain gave to the patriots, who were still recovering from their humiliating defeats at Camden and Fishing Creek. KENDRA DEBANY

Buchanan, John. *The Road to Guilford Courthouse: The American Revolution in the Carolinas.* New York: Wiley, 1997.

Lumpkin, Henry. *From Savannah to Yorktown: The American Revolution in the South.* Columbia: University of South Carolina Press, 1981.

Messick, Hank. *King's Mountain: The Epic of the Blue Ridge "Mountain Men" in the American Revolution.* Boston: Little, Brown, 1976.

Middlekauf, Robert F. *The Glorious Cause: The American Revolution, 1763–1789.* 2d ed. New York: Oxford University Press, 2005.

Kingstree (Williamsburg County; 2000 pop. 3,496). The seat of Williamsburg County, Kingstree was founded at the site of a large white pine tree on the east bank of Black River, where an early explorer chopped an arrow, marking it as the "King's Tree." This became the center of Williamsburg Township, one of the townships proposed in the 1730s by Governor Robert Johnson to promote interior settlement and protect the coastal settlers. Forty Scots-Irish settled the township in 1732 and formed Williamsburg Presbyterian Church in 1736. Two years later the church obtained a site for a meetinghouse, which became the township's largest building until the Revolutionary War. The site was resurveyed in 1788, when only five buildings, all smaller than twenty by twenty feet, stood in the town of Williamsburg, which later became Kingstree.

With the establishment of Williamsburg District in 1804, Kingstree became the district seat of justice. The first court was held in 1806, and in 1810 Kingstree got a post office. In 1823 the South Carolina architect Robert Mills designed "a handsome brick courthouse" for the district. Kingstree grew slowly during the early antebellum period. Although the village contained a handful of stores, most of the trade of Williamsburg District was conducted in Georgetown or Charleston. Kingstree's swampy location made malaria endemic, which hindered its early development. The town received a boost, however, with the arrival of the Northeastern Railway from Charleston in 1856.

The village of Kingstree was incorporated in 1866. The draining of bordering marshlands in 1885 greatly reduced the mosquito population and encouraged town development. In 1885 R. C. Logan, who had founded the county's first newspaper, the *Kingstree Star,* in 1856, established the *County Record.* The courthouse was enlarged in 1901 and a sturdy fence erected to provide a park and keep horses and cattle from the square. The Bank of Kingstree opened on September 1, 1901, with a capital stock of $15,000. In 1910 a waterworks and sewage system was installed. Several miles of road were paved with asphalt in 1922.

The first two tobacco sales warehouses were operating in Kingstree by 1909, and Kingstree soon became a major tobacco market. After World War II, tobacco production increased until the 1980s, when production went into a period of steady decline. Several industries, including textile and garment companies, moved in and helped revive the economy. One of the state's largest cotton-ginning operations was located in Kingstree at this time.

After slow initial growth, Kingstree had a population of 2,842 people in 1890, increasing to 3,621 by 1950. One showplace located among Kingstree's many live oaks is Thorntree, home of James Witherspoon (1700–1768). As part of a restoration project, the 1749 structure was moved into the city for police and fire protection. The geneticist Joseph L. Goldstein, the 1985 Nobel laureate in medicine, grew up in Kingstree. ROBERT A. PIERCE

Boddie, William Willis. *History of Williamsburg.* 1923. Reprint, Spartanburg, S.C.: Reprint Company, 1980.

Kirkland, Joseph Lane (1922–1999). Labor leader. Lane Kirkland was born on March 12, 1922, in Camden, to the cotton buyer Randolph Withers Kirkland and Louise Richardson. The family had deep roots in the state. Kirkland's great-great grandfather Thomas Jefferson Withers was a signer of the Ordinance of Secession and the uncle and legal guardian of Mary Boykin Chesnut, author of *Diary from Dixie.* Withers's son-in-law, William Lenox Kirkland, died from wounds suffered at the Battle of Hawes Shop in Virginia in 1864. His son, Thomas Jefferson Kirkland, served as a South Carolina state senator from 1894 to 1896.

Lane Kirkland. Courtesy, George Meany Memorial Archives/RG95–007.6/2 1

Lane Kirkland grew up in Newberry and attended Newberry College for a year. He entered the U.S. Merchant Marine Academy in 1940 and, after graduation in 1942, served as a chief mate on vessels transporting cargo to battlefronts. On June 10, 1944, he married Edith Draper Hollyday. The couple had five daughters before divorcing in 1972. After the war Kirkland enrolled in Georgetown University's School of Foreign Service. In 1948 American Federation of Labor (AFL) president William Green, who was conducting a seminar at the school, informed Kirkland that there was a job opening in the research department of the AFL. After receiving his degree, Kirkland joined the AFL, focusing his attention on pension and Social Security issues. In 1958 he become the director of research for the International Union of Operating Engineers, but he returned to the American Federation of Labor–Congress of Industrial Organizations (AFL-CIO) in 1960 to serve as executive assistant to President George Meany. Kirkland became secretary-treasurer of the organization in 1969. When Meany retired, Kirkland was elected president of the AFL-CIO on November 19, 1979.

Kirkland's first priority as the new head of organized labor was to unite with unions not in the AFL-CIO. During the course of his presidency he achieved reaffiliation with the AFL-CIO of the International Brotherhood of Teamsters, the United Auto Workers, the United Mine Workers, and the International Longshore and Warehouse Union. In addition, both the Brotherhood of Locomotive Engineers and the Writers Guild of America, East joined the federation for the first time. Long an opponent of state-dominated totalitarian unions of both the left and the right, Kirkland turned his attention to providing financial, material, and moral support to the Polish Solidarity movement that emerged from the Gdansk shipyard strike of August 1980. Over the next decade the American trade union movement played a significant role in overcoming Communist rule in Poland and elsewhere in Eastern Europe.

Although challenged in his last years in office by those in the labor movement concerned with declining membership, Kirkland throughout his sixteen-year leadership oversaw increased participation by African Americans, women, and other groups previously neglected within various unions and within the AFL-CIO. In 1994 Kirkland received the Medal of Freedom, this nation's highest civilian award. He retired as AFL-CIO president in 1995 and died in Washington, D.C., on August 14, 1999, survived by his second wife, Irena Neumann, whom he had married on January 19, 1973. ROBERT D. REYNOLDS, JR.

Kirkland, Lane. Papers. George Meany Memorial Archives, Silver Spring, Maryland.

———. Papers. South Caroliniana Library, University of South Carolina, Columbia.

Sawyer, Kathy. "Lane Kirkland: Made in America and Proud to Wear the Union Label." *Washington Post,* July 15, 1984, pp. K1, K4.

Kirkland, Richard Rowland (1843–1863). Soldier. Born in Flat Rock Township near Camden in August 1843, Kirkland was the second-youngest of seven children born to John A. Kirkland and Mary Vaughn. In April 1861 Kirkland enlisted as a private in the Camden Volunteers, which later became part of the Second South Carolina Volunteer Infantry. Attached to the Army of Northern Virginia, Kirkland and his regiment saw extensive action in Virginia. He was promoted to sergeant in the summer of 1862.

Kirkland was immortalized at the Battle of Fredericksburg in December 1862. In the aftermath of a failed Union assault on Marye's Heights, he witnessed hundreds of wounded and dying Union soldiers begging for water. Touched by their cries, Kirkland went to his brigade commander, Joseph B. Kershaw, and declared, "General, I can't stand this." Convincing Kershaw to allow him to aid the Union wounded, Kirkland gathered up a dozen or more canteens and went out onto the battlefield to comfort and assist his fallen enemies. Union soldiers assumed that Kirkland was plundering their dead. When they realized that the Confederate sergeant was aiding the Union wounded, all shooting ceased. Kirkland was cheered as a hero and a humanitarian by both sides.

Promoted to lieutenant after the Battle of Gettysburg, Kirkland was killed in action at Horseshoe Ridge on the second day of the Battle of Chickamauga, September 20, 1863. His remains were interred at the family cemetery on White Oak Creek in Kershaw District. Published accounts of Kirkland's act of heroism circulated in the years after the war, and he was gradually immortalized as the

"Angel of Marye's Heights." He was reburied in 1909 at the Quaker Cemetery in Camden. In 1965 a bronze statue was dedicated in his honor at the Fredericksburg battlefield. EUGENE ALVAREZ

Carroll, Les. *The Angel of Marye's Heights: Sergeant Richard Kirkland's Extraordinary Deed at Fredericksburg.* Columbia, S.C.: Palmetto Bookworks, 1994.

Kershaw, General J. B. "Richard Kirkland, the Humane Hero of Fredericksburg." *Southern Historical Society Papers* 8 (April 1880): 186–88.

Trantham, William D. "Wonderful Story of Richard R. Kirkland." *Confederate Veteran* 16 (March 1908): 105.

Kitt, Eartha (b. 1927). Actress, singer. Kitt was born on January 17, 1927, in St. Matthews, the daughter of John and Anna Mae Kitt. Her black mother was just fourteen years old, and Kitt claimed never to know the identity of her white father nor her own birthday (a group of Benedict College students uncovered her birth certificate in 1997). When Kitt was four years old, her mother's boyfriend forced Anna Mae Kitt to abandon her daughter. Eartha Kitt was abused by the family she went to live with and taunted by her peers for her light skin color. But she and her younger half-sister, Pearl, survived until Eartha was moved to Harlem at age eight to live with her aunt Mamie, who also turned out to be abusive. A teacher spotted Kitt's talent, however, and helped her earn admission to Metropolitan High School (later the New York School of Performing Arts).

Eartha Kitt. Courtesy, Library of Congress, Prints and Photographs Division, Carl Van Vechten Collection, LC-USZ62–128088 DLC

Kitt ran away from home at age sixteen to join the all-black Kathleen Dunham dance troupe, which toured South America and Europe. She left the dancers and turned her sultry voice to cabaret singing in 1949, singing in Paris and then in major European and American cities. The feisty Kitt, projecting the image of a "sex kitten," first drew critical acclaim on the stage in Paris in *Dr. Faustus,* a 1951 adaptation of *Faust* by Orson Welles, who called her "the most exciting woman alive." Later she starred in movies and recorded such teasing pop song hits as "C'est Si Bon" and "I Want to Be Evil."

Ever conscious of racial discrimination, Kitt overcame barriers of prejudice, sometimes militantly, and championed unpopular causes for the downtrodden. In a highly publicized incident in January 1968, she spoke out against the Vietnam War at a White House luncheon sponsored by Lady Bird Johnson. The outburst angered President Lyndon Johnson and triggered a Central Intelligence Agency report that labeled her a "sadistic nymphomaniac." Her career suffered badly in America for several years, but she was popular abroad and regained her fans when she returned to America in 1978.

Kitt's stage credits included *Dr. Faustus* (1951), *New Faces of 1952, Mrs. Patterson* (1954), *Shinbone Alley* (1957), *Timbuktu* (1978), and *Blues in the Night* (1985). Among her films were *New Faces* (1953), *Accused* (1957), *St. Louis Blues* (1957), *Anna Lucasta* (1958), *Mark of the Hawk* (1958), *Saint of Devil's Island* (1961), *Synanon* (1965), *Up the Chastity Belt* (1971), and two French movies. Kitt also made numerous television appearances, including playing the role of Catwoman in the *Batman* television series.

Kitt is known for the seductive, purring style she employed in such albums as *In Person at the Plaza* and *My Way, a Musical Tribute to the Rev. Dr. Martin Luther King, Jr.,* both in 1987. She taught herself to sing in ten languages, including Turkish and Hebrew. She was named Woman of the Year in 1968 by the National Association of Negro Musicians and remains one of the few performers to earn nominations for Tony, Grammy, and Oscar awards.

Kitt authored *Thursday's Child* (1956), *Alone with Me* (1976), *I'm Still Here* (1990), and *Confessions of a Sex Kitten* (1991). She married the real estate mogul William McDonald on June 6, 1960. They divorced in 1965. She has one daughter, Kitt McDonald. After more than fifty years of entertaining, she continued to sing, act, dance, and write into the twenty-first century. ROBERT A. PIERCE

Kitt, Eartha. *Confessions of a Sex Kitten.* New York: Barricade, 1991.

Knights of Labor. Although the Knights of Labor was the first labor organization in America that was truly national in scope, its presence in South Carolina was always tenuous at best. Initially organized in 1869, the Knights of Labor remained a secret society until 1882, when it began to gain members across the country due in part to a flexible organizational structure. Members were organized into Local Assemblies that often consisted of members of the same trade in a particular location but could include members with several different occupations. Unlike earlier trade unions, the Knights attempted to organize men and women, skilled craftsmen and unskilled laborers, and members of all racial and ethnic groups (except the Chinese).

The first two Local Assemblies in South Carolina were made up of telegraph operators in Charleston and Columbia. They organized in 1882 and 1883, respectively, as part of an unsuccessful nationwide strike against Western Union. Further organization of the Knights of Labor in South Carolina lagged until 1885, when the Knights made a nationwide challenge to the railroads controlled by the financier Jay Gould and won. Their success drew in new members from across the county. In South Carolina at least twenty-four Local Assemblies formed in 1886 in the new textile mill towns that were springing up across the upstate as well as in the older mill district of the Horse Creek Valley between Aiken and Augusta.

Despite the rapid increase in membership, developments at both the national and local levels worked against the Knights. In the Great Southwest Strike of 1886, the Knights again attempted to challenge the control of railroad owners, but in this case they lost badly. The Haymarket Affair in May 1886, when anarchists in Chicago were alleged to have thrown a bomb that killed a policeman, created a nationwide backlash against the labor movement and radicals of all kinds. In the Horse Creek Valley of South Carolina and neighboring Augusta, Georgia, the Knights of Labor found themselves in a bitter conflict with mill owners over wages. The Knights of Labor headquarters could offer little assistance and did not approve of striking in the first place, preferring to arbitrate labor disputes. The strike collapsed in November 1886, and by the end of 1887 nearly all of the Local Assemblies in textile mill towns in South Carolina had evaporated.

An even greater blow came when the Knights of Labor held their annual General Assembly in Richmond, Virginia, in 1886. There, the organization's national policies of nondiscrimination came into conflict with southern prejudices and the mores of segregation. The Knights' insistence on racial equality within their organization soured many whites on organized labor. After 1886 some new Local Assemblies were formed, but rather than representing industrial workers, they were primarily composed of tenant farmers and farm laborers. The farmers who owned the land were more likely to support the farmers' movement led by Ben Tillman and the Farmers' Alliance. Although a few Local Assemblies continued to operate in South Carolina, especially in Charleston, they were never a significant factor after the 1886 defeats. BRUCE E. BAKER

Garlock, Jonathan. *Guide to the Local Assemblies of the Knights of Labor.* Westport, Conn.: Greenwood, 1982.

McLaurin, Melton Alonzo. *The Knights of Labor in the South.* Westport, Conn.: Greenwood, 1978.

Ware, Norman. *The Labor Movement in the United States, 1860–1895: A Study in Democracy.* 1929. Reprint, Gloucester, Mass.: Peter Smith, 1959.

Ku Klux Klan. The Ku Klux Klan was a paramilitary organization formed during Reconstruction to oppose the Republican Party and restore white supremacy in the South. Originally founded by former Confederate general Nathan Bedford Forrest in Tennessee in 1866, it spread to every southern state, including South Carolina, by 1868. Most authorities believe that these organizations were independent of each other, but within South Carolina the Klan clearly showed deference to the leading white Democrats. The Klan, or "Ku-Klux" as it was then called, engaged in a variety of violent actions, such as punishing alleged criminals or settling personal scores, but the vast majority of Klan actions were calculated to weaken the Republican Party by intimidating party leaders. Klansmen often whipped and sometimes killed people they regarded as Republican leaders. Victims of such attacks, or "outrages" in the parlance of the time, were almost always Republicans and were usually African Americans. The Klan was particularly strong in the predominantly white upcountry counties, and York County especially experienced a "reign of terror" in the late 1860s.

The Klan was shrouded in secrecy. Klansmen conducting outrages often went in disguise, the most famous of which consisted of

This Thomas Nast cartoon depicts various acts of violence by the KKK against freedmen and women in the South. Courtesy, South Carolina Historical Society

white robes and white conical hoods. Others blackened their faces; still others did not disguise themselves, but rather operated outside their home neighborhoods so as not to be recognized. The suggestion that the white robes evoked superstitious fears in blacks seems to have little empirical justification; if African Americans feared Klansmen, it was not for supernatural reasons. Klansmen were often former Confederate troops, well armed and well trained in combat, and almost always on horseback. Furthermore, they had a well-deserved reputation for ruthlessness.

A typical attack might begin with a late-night raid on the home of a local Republican activist. The worst cases left victims disabled or dead; in other cases only threats were used. Most often the victim would be taken from his house and tortured, often by whipping, and ordered to renounce the Republican Party. Klansmen sometimes confiscated items such as guns or Republican electoral ballots, and they occasionally stole money. There were cases in which wives or children were beaten as well. The most frequent targets, however, were politically active men. Klansmen often justified their actions to the victim, telling him of some wrong he had done; usually the victim's offense was a transgression against white supremacy. When the victim was white, he was often berated for advocating racial equality; when black, for thinking himself the equal of a white man.

Republicans defended themselves as circumstances permitted. Those who were wealthy or who enjoyed high official positions might arrange to have armed guards protect their homes. Humbler Republicans, on hearing that they were being targeted, might choose to sleep in the woods for a time. Residence in Columbia generally protected state legislators, but at least three (the native white Republicans Solomon Dill, James Martin, and Joseph Crews) were gunned down on highways traveling to or from the capital, and another (Benjamin Franklin Randolph, a mulatto from Ohio) was killed in broad daylight while boarding a train.

Democratic leaders frequently denied both the existence of the Klan and the reality of alleged outrages. When presented with indisputable evidence that attacks had occurred, they typically blamed "a few lawless men" for the violence, denying that there was any widespread conspiracy. Tradition holds that the Klan was populated by poor whites. It is more likely, however, that all strata of society were represented and that leadership in the Klan was provided by members of the gentry. Some known leaders included J. Rufus Bratton and James Avery of York and J. Banks Lyle of Spartanburg; other prominent Democrats, such as David Wyatt Aiken, were accused or even indicted for Klan-related violence. Furthermore, even if they or their sons were not members, many white leaders of the state openly sympathized with those being prosecuted on Ku-Klux charges. Wade Hampton III, Armistead Burt, and other leading citizens used their money and influence to provide the best attorneys possible for alleged Klansmen.

In 1871 and 1872 the administration of President Ulysses S. Grant made a large-scale effort to break the Klan, making an example of South Carolina. Declaring a state of rebellion, the president suspended the writ of habeas corpus in the counties of Spartanburg, Union, York, Chester, Laurens, Newberry, Fairfield, Lancaster, and Chesterfield. Federal prosecutors came south to indict hundreds of accused offenders. The size of the task overwhelmed the justice system, and few Klansmen were convicted. Historians debate the efficacy of the administration's actions. The Klan as an organization ceased to exist, and many of its leaders fled the state. Nevertheless, political violence continued and eventually toppled the Reconstruction regime.

Another organization called the Ku Klux Klan was founded in 1915 after the success of the film *Birth of a Nation,* which glorified the Reconstruction Klan. This later Klan added an animus toward Jews and Catholics to the original motivation of preserving white supremacy. The twentieth-century Klan grew to include as many as three million members before it disbanded in the 1940s. Klan groups appeared again during the desegregation crisis of the 1960s and have occasionally been heard from since. The twentieth-century Klan existed in South Carolina but was not as prominent or politically powerful as in other states. HYMAN S. RUBIN III

Chalmers, David M. *Hooded Americanism: The First Century of the Ku Klux Klan, 1865–1965.* Garden City, N.Y.: Doubleday, 1965.

Trelease, Allen. *White Terror: The Ku Klux Klan Conspiracy and Southern Reconstruction.* New York: Harper and Row, 1971.

West, Jerry L. *The Reconstruction Ku Klux Klan in York County, South Carolina, 1865–1877.* Jefferson, N.C.: McFarland, 2002.

Williams, Lou Falkner. *The Great South Carolina Ku Klux Klan Trials, 1871–1872.* Athens: University of Georgia Press, 1996.

Zuczek, Richard. *State of Rebellion: Reconstruction in South Carolina.* Columbia: University of South Carolina Press, 1996.

Kyrle, Sir Richard (?–1684). Governor. Born in Ireland, Kyrle was the son of James Kyrle and Ann Waller. He was knighted and received a landgraveship in Carolina, which entitled him to twelve thousand acres in the fledgling province. The Lords Proprietors commissioned Kyrle governor of Carolina on April 29, 1684. A few documents in the proprietary-era public records attest that he received petitions and made some provincial appointments prior to his departure for Charleston. Kyrle landed in the province sometime after July 28 but died on August 30 or 31, 1684, slightly more than a month after his arrival. His will is dated August 18, 1684, and was proved September 19, 1684. He was survived by his wife Dame Margaret (or Mary) Kyrle, who perished early the next month, leaving as orphans a minor son, Robert; five daughters, Mary, Elizabeth, Katherine, Penelope, and Barbara; and another son, William, probably from a previous marriage, who was executor of Margaret Kyrle's estate. Prior to Kyrle's appointment, the governorships of Carolina had been in the hands of rival political factions living in the province. Historians speculate that the proprietors appointed Kyrle to alleviate some of the political chaos that plagued their province in the late 1670s and 1680s. However, Kyrle's death soon after his arrival did little to alleviate the political battles. Kyrle was succeeded in the governorship by Robert Quary. ALEXANDER MOORE

Lesser, Charles H. *South Carolina Begins: The Records of a Proprietary Colony, 1663–1721.* Columbia: South Carolina Department of Archives and History, 1995.

L

Lady of Cofitachiqui. The leader of a powerful chiefdom, the "Lady" of Cofitachiqui encountered Hernando de Soto and his conquistadors in 1540 as they passed through her territory (probably near the modern town of Camden). Narratives by the Spanish, including Garcilaso de la Vega, portray the encounter as a chivalrous and romantic one, in which the Lady formed a pact of friendship and peace with de Soto by offering him a magnificent strand of pearls from around her neck and graciously supplying provisions. It is more likely that de Soto demanded and received them after attempting to capture the Lady's mother by force in the guise of a friendly visit. Despite the fact that the region had been hit with a pestilence, the natives complied, giving de Soto corn and a large quantity of freshwater pearls. After ascertaining that the region had no gold, only pearls, de Soto and his men, accompanied by the Lady as a hostage, journeyed to the borders of her realm, the village of Xuala, near the Cataloochee River in modern North Carolina, where she and her attendants escaped. The Spanish were fascinated by the young woman ruler, and their later accounts compared her arrival in canoes to Cleopatra's by barge, although their actual treatment of the Lady of Cofitachiqui was far from chivalrous or romantic. MARGARET SANKEY

Galloway, Patricia, ed. *The Hernando de Soto Expedition: History, Historiography and "Discovery" in the Southeast.* Lincoln: University of Nebraska Press, 1997.

King, Grace. *De Soto and His Men in the Land of Florida.* New York: Macmillan, 1898.

Lafaye and Lafaye. Founded by George Eugene Lafaye (1878–1939), the firm of Lafaye and Lafaye was one of the state's most respected and successful architectural practices from the 1910s to the 1970s. Lafaye was educated at Jesuit College before training as a draftsman in several New Orleans firms. He moved to Columbia, South Carolina, in 1900 as chief draftsman for W. B. Smith Whaley & Company. When Whaley left Columbia in 1903, Lafaye entered into partnership with former Whaley associate Gadsden E. Shand to practice under the name Shand and Lafaye until 1907, when he established his own office. Shand and Lafaye designed the Carolina National Bank, the Colonia Hotel, the Ottaray Hotel in Greenville, the Clarendon County Courthouse, the Peoples Bank of Rock Hill, Columbia College's campus, Columbia's Young Men's Christian Association, and the Highland Park Hotel in Aiken.

In 1913 George Lafaye hired his younger brother, Robert Stoddard Lafaye (1892–1972), as a draftsman, but a tour of duty with the U.S. Army during World War I interrupted the association. Returning to Columbia in 1919, Robert Lafaye was made partner the following year. Some of Lafaye and Lafaye's more important pre–World War II commissions were St. John's (Shandon) Episcopal Church, Shandon Presbyterian Church, Township Auditorium, the Columbia Hotel, the U.S. Federal Courthouse in Aiken, the Farm Credit Administration Office Building, the Hartsville Community Center and Market, Providence Hospital, McLeod Infirmary in Florence, the James L. Tapp Department Store, the War Memorial Building, and the Wade Hampton State Office Building.

The firm operated under the name Lafaye and Lafaye until 1937–1938, when Herndon M. Fair and George E. Lafaye, Jr., were made partners. After George Lafaye's death in 1939, Robert Lafaye led the firm until his own death in 1972. The firm continued as Lafaye, Lafaye and Fair until 1946, when longtime chief draftsman Walter F. Petty became an associate. The firm's name changed to Lafaye, Fair, Lafaye and Associates in 1949.

From the 1910s through the 1970s the firm did much of its most important work for state institutions, including the University of South Carolina, Clemson University, South Carolina State College, the South Carolina School for the Deaf and Blind near Spartanburg, the State Training School (Whitten Village) at Clinton, and the South Carolina State Hospital. Important later commissions included the South Carolina National Bank, the Marion Street High-Rise Apartments, and the Episcopal Church's Finlay House Apartments. The firm also received hundreds of residential commissions throughout South Carolina over the years.

Many of the firm's members were active in the state chapter of the American Institute of Architects (AIA). George Lafaye, Herndon Fair, and Walter Petty each served as chapter president, while Robert Lafaye served as vice president throughout World War II. George Lafaye was also an original member of the State Board of Architectural Examiners. Walter Petty served as the board's secretary, was named a fellow in the AIA in 1968, served on state and national boards and committees for historic preservation, and authored the fiftieth-anniversary history of the state's AIA chapter in 1963. ANDREW W. CHANDLER

Lafaye and Lafaye. Papers. South Caroliniana Library, University of South Carolina, Columbia.

Lafaye and Lafaye. *Representative Work: Lafaye and Lafaye, Architects, Columbia, S.C.* Norfolk, Va.: George S. Myers, n.d.

Wells, John E., and Robert E. Dalton. *The South Carolina Architects, 1885–1935: A Biographical Directory.* Richmond, Va.: New South Architectural Press, 1992.

Withey, Henry F., and Elsie Rathburn Withey. *Biographical Dictionary of American Architects (Deceased).* 1956. Reprint, Los Angeles: Hennessey and Ingalls, 1970.

Laing School. Laing School in Mount Pleasant had been called by different names since its establishment in an abandoned church in 1866. Cornelia Hancock, a Civil War nurse and Quaker from New Jersey, is credited with founding the school and served as its first principal. The school was named for Henry M. Laing, treasurer of both the Friends Association for the Aid and Elevation of the Freedmen of Philadelphia and the Pennsylvania Abolition Society, each of which supported the school financially. Its mission was to educate former slaves and inspire them to strive for high ideals and good citizenship and to make worthwhile contributions to society.

The school began with fifty pupils in the remains of the Mount Pleasant Presbyterian Church. In October 1867 it moved to a brick mansion provided by the Freedmen's Bureau. In 1868 the bureau built a two-story school building on the corner of King Street and Royall Avenue, on land donated by the town of Mount Pleasant. Enrollment at the coeducational school soon grew to more than two hundred. Known as the Laing Industrial School, the institution grew and offered seven years of schooling along with courses in sewing, cooking, cobbling, and manual training. An earthquake destroyed the school in 1886, but it was rebuilt on the same site. In 1894 the Pennsylvania Abolition Society became trustee of the school, which it deeded to Charleston County in 1940. It became part of the public school system in 1938 and was the first accredited school for African Americans in South Carolina. The building was condemned and closed in 1953, but a new school, Laing High School, opened that same year on U.S. Highway 17 north of Mount Pleasant.

Since 1974 the institution has operated as Laing Middle School. A South Carolina Highway Marker, which was erected by the Laing High School Alumni Association, stands at the site of the original Laing School. DOROTHY FLUDD RICHARDSON

Bacon, Margaret Hope. *The Quiet Rebels: The Story of Quakers in America.* New York: Basic, 1969.

Munro, Abby D. Papers. South Caroliniana Library, University of South Carolina, Columbia.

One Hundredth Anniversary: Laing High School 1866–1966. Mount Pleasant, S.C.: Laing High School Teachers and Students, 1966.

Lake City (Florence County; 2000 pop. 6,478). Lake City is the second-largest community in Florence County. The site was originally part of Williamsburg Township, which was occupied by Scots-Irish immigrants in the 1730s. By the 1750s people began to settle around the intersection of two major roads, one running from Kingstree to Cheraw and the other from Georgetown to Camden. The first settlement was known as Graham's Crossroads, named for the landowner Aaron F. Graham. In 1856 the North Eastern Railroad began construction on its main line through the area, and in 1874 the town of Graham was incorporated around one of the railroad's new depots. The post office serving the area was known as Lynches Lake Post Office, but since there was a post office with the same name elsewhere in South Carolina, the town changed its name to Lake City on Christmas Eve 1883.

By 1893 the Lake City population had grown to three hundred and the town flourished as the largest strawberry market in the state, shipping between five and seven thousand bushels to the northern markets annually. The railroad also opened other opportunities in truck farming, and the Lake City bean market grew to be one of the largest in the nation. By the 1890s tobacco had emerged as the major crop. The Lake City Warehouse Company built the town's first tobacco warehouse in 1898, and Lake City had three more by the 1920s. Despite the collapse of the strawberry market, truck farming remained strong. Lake City was the fourth-largest truck market in the United States as late as 1941 and in the same year led the world in the production of stringless beans. But the bean market faded abruptly after World War II.

In 1912 Lake City voters considered and rejected the creation of a new county, to be called Rutledge, and the town was annexed to Florence County. From a population of 1,942 in 1930, the town grew steadily through the mid–twentieth century and came to boast a museum, a hospital, a branch of the county library, and a variety of small businesses. By 1960 the population had reached 6,059. Manufacturing entered the picture when the Coleman Company, maker of camping equipment, opened a large plant in Lake City in 1984. The Nan Ya Plastic Corporation became the largest business in the county, employing more than 950 persons. Built in 1990, the plant manufactures resin chips used to make plastic bottles and polyester yarns. Lake City is the longtime host of the Tobacco Festival, a highlight of the fall market season. Battery B, Fourth Battalion, 178th Field Artillery of the South Carolina Army National Guard has been an important part of the community since 1917. Lake City takes special pride in honoring its favorite son, Dr. Ronald E. McNair, a NASA astronaut who was among those killed in the 1986 explosion of the space shuttle *Challenger.* CARLANNA H. HENDRICK

Carter, Margaret L. *History of Lake City, South Carolina.* New York: Carlton, 1976.

King, G. Wayne. *Rise Up So Early: A History of Florence County, South Carolina.* Spartanburg, S.C.: Reprint Company, 1981.

Lakes. All of the large lakes in South Carolina were created during the twentieth century when energy companies built dams on nearly all of the major river systems to produce hydroelectric power. Lake Wateree was the first of the state's large lakes, formed when the Duke Power Company built a hydroelectric dam on the Wateree River in 1919. It is located in northern Kershaw and eastern Fairfield Counties and covers 13,700 acres. Lake Marion, formed after a dam was built on the Santee River in 1942, is the largest lake in the state, encompassing 110,000 acres. Other lakes formed on the Santee River tributaries include Wylie (1925), Murray (1930), Greenwood (1940), and Moultrie (1942). Lakes on the Savannah River system include Strom Thurmond (1954), Hartwell (1963), Keowee (1971), Jocassee (1974), and Russell (1984).

The lakes are managed by the energy companies that operate the dams and the South Carolina Department of Natural Resources. County sheriff departments are in charge of law enforcement on the waterways. The lakes are popular recreational areas during the warm months, and a large number of vacation homes and, increasingly, permanent homes dot their coastlines. The lakes are popular places to swim, boat, and fish. A variety of fish can be found in the state's lakes, including several types of bass, especially largemouth and striped; catfish; crappie; bream; and many others.

The formation of these lakes had a profound impact on the geography of the state. The hundreds of thousands of acres now under water were once inhabited; many small towns, crossroads, and communities have been wiped off the map. Lexington Water Power Company moved around five thousand people, six churches, and two schools in 1930 when Lake Murray was formed in the Midlands. MICHAEL S. REYNOLDS

Kovacik, Charles F., and John J. Winberry. *South Carolina: The Making of a Landscape.* 1987. Reprint, Columbia: University of South Carolina Press, 1989.

Lamar Riots (March 3, 1970). The Lamar Riots, the most violent act against court-ordered school desegregation in South Carolina, occurred when a mob of angry white parents armed with ax handles, bricks, and chains overturned two school buses that had delivered black students to Lamar elementary and high schools in Darlington County.

In January 1970 the U.S. Fourth Circuit Court of Appeals had ordered the Darlington County schools to immediately increase integration among students and teachers. The court had struck down the county's 1965 "freedom of choice" plan that allowed

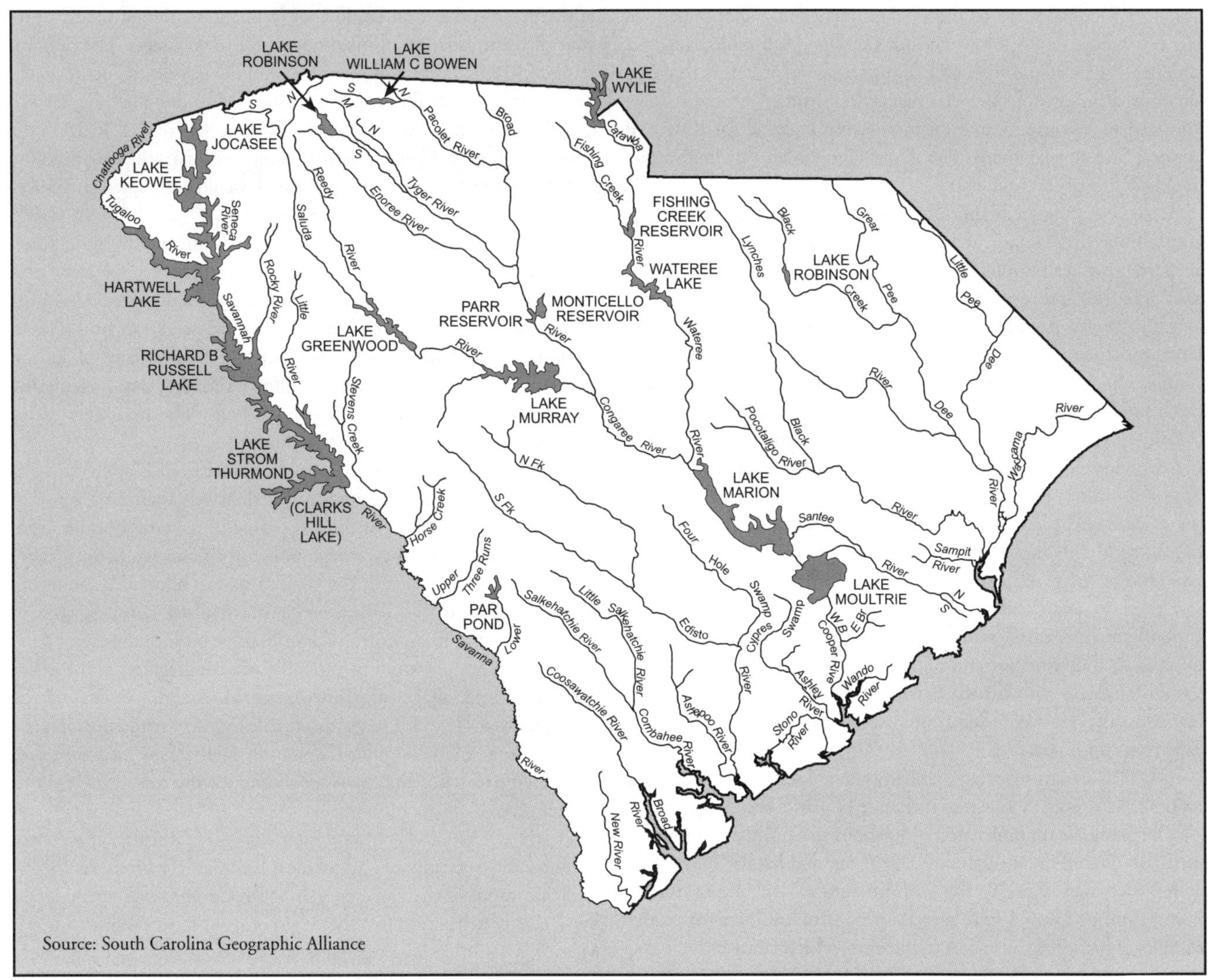

Lakes and rivers of South Carolina

whites and blacks to attend schools of their choice. But in Lamar, a rural community of 1,350 people, one elementary school had nine black students and a high school had ten black students. On the other side of town Spaulding elementary and high schools had no white students. The court ordered that integration take place no later than February 18, 1970. White parents said that the court should wait until the following school year to put the order into effect. They were further enraged by the county's school attendance zones. Allegedly, lines were drawn to keep the children of prominent white residents out of black schools.

The building contractor and restaurant owner Jeryl Best led the white opposition, Citizen for Freedom of Choice, which pushed for a boycott to close the schools. They hoped that if low attendance closed the schools the county would have no choice but to reopen them under the freedom-of-choice plan. Black parents were urged to keep their children out of the schools unless the federal courts promised protection.

On March 3 about 150 to 200 men and women clashed with about 150 South Carolina highway patrolmen and agents with the South Carolina Law Enforcement Division (SLED). Demonstrators and police received minor injuries, and flying glass cut some students when the mob smashed the bus windows. One rioter fired a gunshot during the thirty-five-minute fight. Police responded by firing tear gas into the crowd. Of the forty men charged after the riot, three were sentenced to jail.

Two days after the riot, Vice President Spiro T. Agnew said that the "violence was aimed unbelievably . . . at children who are innocent participants in the court-ordered desegregation of a Southern school district." He promised that those responsible "will be brought to the bar of justice." The violence at Lamar was the first major test of the Nixon administration's policy in handling segregationist violence against southern blacks. But some argued that the White House did not do enough at Lamar, either during or after the riot. U.S. marshals looked on as highway patrolmen and SLED agents fought the mob. The day after the riot, National Guardsmen were at the school to keep the peace. HERB FRAZIER

Bass, Jack. "White Violence in Lamar." *New Republic* 162 (March 28, 1970): 10–12.

McIlwain, William F. "On the Overturning of Two School Buses in Lamar, S.C." *Esquire* 75 (January 1971): 98–103, 162–64.

Lamboll, Elizabeth (ca. 1725–1770). Botanist. Lamboll was born around 1725, probably in Charleston. Historians believe that she was the daughter of Richard Pitts, a local silversmith. She married Thomas Lamboll in November 1743. He was thirty years her senior, and she was his third wife. The couple had one daughter.

Lamboll contributed to the establishment and advancement of scientific gardening in colonial South Carolina. As a skilled amateur gardener, she created one of Charleston's earliest gardens, composed primarily of indigenous flowers, vegetables, shrubs, and trees. Lamboll lived in a house located on the northwest corner of King and Lamboll Streets near the Ashley River. Her garden was landscaped directly south of the residence.

Actively sharing seeds and roots with local gardening enthusiasts, Lamboll may have taught the nursery owner Martha Daniel Logan her gardening techniques. Lamboll showed people useful applications of berries and roots obtained from plants growing in their gardens. Lamboll's friendship with the Philadelphia naturalist John Bartram helped him become the premier botanist in the American colonies. She alerted him to previously unknown plant species, which he described and documented for botanical publications.

While Lamboll enthusiastically pursued gardening, her husband corresponded with Bartram, telling him about the plants she was gathering to ship to him and explaining her cultivation methods. In a letter dated February 16, 1761, Thomas Lamboll revealed how his wife diligently managed her gardens. He outlined the steps she followed to prepare plant beds with mold and to raise or flatten ground as needed to assure adequate moisture for vegetation. Elizabeth Lamboll carefully saved rainwater for her plants and exposed it to sunlight so that cold water would not shock plants. She covered her garden beds with leaves in winter. While planting, Lamboll cleaned roots, removed insects, and used her fingers to dig holes to place roots and seeds.

In 1760 Bartram reported that Lamboll had sent him "two noble cargoes" that initiated a regular exchange of plants such as the magnolia tripetala, or umbrella tree, indigenous to South Carolina. On April 30, 1761, Thomas Lamboll sent Bartram a list of "Flowers & Herbs" that his wife "is fond of procuring," including tulips, aniseed, and peonies. A year later Thomas Lamboll inventoried the contents of his wife's shipments to Bartram, which consisted of oaks, roses, lilies, honeysuckle, asters, and holly.

Accompanied by his son William, Bartram visited the Lambolls' garden in August 1765 when he was named His Majesty's botanist and en route to Florida. When William Bartram remained in Florida to grow indigo, Lamboll gathered and sent him supplies. During their friendship, Lamboll filled barrels full of oranges as gifts for John Bartram. She extended her courteous treatment to Bartram's wife, as indicated by Thomas Lamboll in a letter about harvesting pomegranates in which he stated, "Mrs. Lamboll chose to send Mrs. Bartram a Bisket Cagg full (say 51) of the best she could Pick."

Lamboll died in Charleston in October 1770. Her daughter, Mary Lamboll Thomas, continued to ship plants to William Bartram as her mother had sent specimens to his father. ELIZABETH D. SCHAFER

Cothran, James R. *Gardens of Historic Charleston.* Columbia: University of South Carolina Press, 1995.

Pinckney, Elise. *Thomas and Elizabeth Lamboll: Early Charleston Gardeners.* Charleston, S.C.: Charleston Museum, 1969.

Lancaster (Lancaster County; 2000 pop. 8,177). Originally called Barnetsville, Lancaster was established as the seat of government for Lancaster County. Prior to 1791 court sessions were held near Hanging Rock, but they were moved after Kershaw County was created from the southern part of Lancaster. Since Hanging Rock was no longer at the center of the reconfigured Lancaster County, the new site was chosen. The citizens of Lancaster petitioned the General Assembly in 1801 to incorporate the village, but no action was taken because the local landowner William McKenna sued to prevent the expropriation of his property for town streets. The case was settled in 1824 in favor of the town, and the legislature incorporated Lancaster in 1830. The architect Robert Mills designed the jail and courthouse (completed in 1823 and 1828 respectively). In 1835 the Lancaster Presbyterian Church became the first religious building constructed in the town, and the noted theologian James H. Thornwell was the congregation's first minister.

The region's antebellum economy was dominated by agriculture, and Lancaster served as the district's central market for farm produce, especially cotton. Most Lancaster residents were Unionists during the 1840s and 1850s but supported secession in 1860. In February 1865 Union cavalrymen under the command of Judson Kilpatrick occupied the town of Lancaster for five days, setting fire to the courthouse, jail, and other buildings. The fires were extinguished before much damage was done.

Sharecropping replaced slave labor on area farms after the Civil War, and cotton was cultivated more extensively than ever. By 1920 more than three-fourths of the crop value in the county came from cotton, with a similar percentage of county farms worked by propertyless tenants. Poverty in the rural areas was alleviated somewhat by the opening of the Lancaster Cotton Mill by Leroy Springs in 1896, the first of many cotton factories to be built in the area. Many local farmers sought work in the mills and congregated in the unincorporated mill villages of Midway and Brookland, just beyond the Lancaster town limits. The cotton textile industry gradually replaced agriculture as the economic foundation of the Lancaster area and continued to anchor the town's economy for the rest of the twentieth century.

Between 1940 and 1970 the population of Lancaster more than doubled and educational and medical facilities improved. In 1959 a branch campus of the University of South Carolina was opened, and by 1970 construction of the eight-story Elliott White Springs Memorial Hospital was complete. In the last half of the twentieth century, Lancaster's economy diversified beyond its reliance on Springs Mills. In particular, a nearby Duracell battery plant employed one thousand people and produced one billion alkaline batteries annually. Other town and county residents made the forty-mile commute to jobs in Charlotte, North Carolina. From 1990 to 2000 the city's population dropped slightly from 8,914 to 8,177 while the county's increased by 6,835 people. The 2000 census showed that African Americans made up almost half of the city's population, which also included a small but growing number of Hispanics. MICHAEL S. REYNOLDS

Beaty, Ernest A., and Carl W. McMurray. *Lancaster County: Economic and Social.* Columbia: University of South Carolina, 1923.

Floyd, Viola C., comp. *Historical Notes from Lancaster County, South Carolina.* Lancaster, S.C.: Lancaster County Historical Commission, 1977.

Pettus, Louise. *The Waxhaws.* Rock Hill, S.C.: Regal Graphics, 1993.

Pettus, Louise, and Martha Bishop. *Lancaster County: A Pictorial History.* Norfolk, Va.: Donning, 1984.

Lancaster County (549 sq. miles; 2000 pop. 61,351). Lying in the north-central portion of South Carolina between the Catawba and Lynches Rivers, Lancaster County was created in 1785 from the northeastern part of the Camden Judicial District. The county was named for Lancaster, Pennsylvania, from which many early settlers originated. Prior to white settlement, the Lancaster area was home to at least two Indian nations, the Catawbas and the Waxhaws. Europeans arrived in the early 1750s and settled in the northern part of the county in a region known as the Waxhaws. Most were Scots-Irish immigrants following the Great Wagon Road south from Pennsylvania and Virginia. These early settlers were mostly small farmers, growing wheat and other grains and maintaining livestock. The Lancaster area was the site of Revolutionary War battles and skirmishes, including the Buford Massacre (May 29, 1780) and the Battle of Hanging Rock (August 6, 1780). The first county courts were held at the home of James Ingram near Hanging Rock. However, after Kershaw County was created in 1791 from the southern half of Lancaster, the seat of government was moved to Barnetsville, closer to the new geographic center of the county. The town's name was changed to Lancasterville and later shortened to Lancaster.

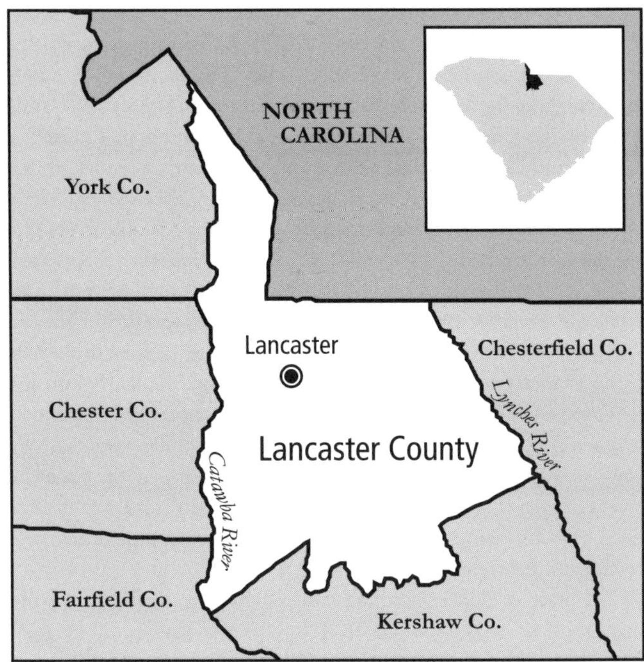

With the arrival of the gin, short-staple cotton was grown extensively in Lancaster, which increased the demand of planters and farmers for slave labor. In 1800 slaves comprised only one-sixth of Lancaster's population. By 1860 almost one-half were slaves. While there were a few large planters, most white residents were small farmers who lived a modest lifestyle raising corn, cotton, and assorted livestock. A degree of economic diversity was supplied by a mine opened by Benjamin Haile after gold was discovered on his plantation in 1827. Most Lancaster citizens opposed nullification in 1832, but they embraced secession after the election of Abraham Lincoln in 1860. By 1863 eighty-eight percent of the district's white males of military age were fighting for the Confederacy.

After the Civil War, sharecropping dominated Lancaster County, locking many white and black farmers in a cycle of debt and poverty. By 1880 more than half of the county's farms were rented for either shares or fixed money. Poverty was especially acute for the former slaves. In 1900 forty-two percent of white farmers owned their farms, compared to just over five percent of black farmers. Both the social life and economy of the county changed dramatically in 1896 when Leroy Springs opened the Lancaster Cotton Mill in the town of Lancaster. The factory was the first major industry in the county, and many poor whites began leaving the countryside to work in the mills. In 1880 just forty-three people worked in manufacturing. By 1900 manufacturing employed 472 people. Cotton mills gradually replaced agriculture in economic importance and dominated the local economy for much of the twentieth century.

The first railroad, built in 1883, connected the town of Lancaster with Chester. By the early 1900s the Southern Railway and the Seaboard Air Line controlled most of the track through the county. The town of Kershaw in southeastern Lancaster County was incorporated in 1888, a year after the community was established as a depot for the Southern Railway. In 1914 Springs built the Kershaw Cotton Mill, providing a vital boost. Heath Springs in the southern section of the county was incorporated in 1890.

Presbyterian, Baptist, and Methodist churches have predominated since the antebellum period. After emancipation, African Americans formed African Methodist Episcopal (AME) and Baptist congregations. One of the oldest is Mt. Carmel AME Zion Church, established in 1866 by the former slave Isom Clinton, who became a bishop in the AME church. Each September, Mt. Carmel hosts one of the largest revival meetings in the state.

Between 1900 and 1960 Lancaster County's population increased from 24,311 to 39,352. Growth occurred only in the white population as the African American population in the county declined from 12,110 to 10,613. During the second half of the twentieth century, cotton textile mills continued to be the economic foundation of Lancaster County. In 1973 Springs Mills employed forty percent of the workforce. However, the area's reliance on Springs lessened somewhat in later decades as new corporations established plants. The paper manufacturer Bowater opened a plant in neighboring York County that employed some Lancaster County residents. About one thousand employees worked for the Duracell factory, producing almost one billion AA alkaline batteries annually. Near Kershaw a state prison opened in 1996 and employed five hundred people and held twelve hundred inmates.

The county saw improvements in educational, medical, and recreational facilities after World War II. A regional campus of the University of South Carolina opened in Lancaster in 1959, and the Elliott White Springs Memorial Hospital opened in 1970. Since 1952 Andrew Jackson State Park has provided camping facilities and hiking trails as well as a fishing pond and a museum. Other areas for outdoor recreation include the Forty Acre Rock / Flat Creek Natural Area. Racing fans patronize the Lancaster Speedway, known as "the fastest half-mile dirt track in the Southeast." As transportation links improved, many Lancaster residents took advantage of their proximity to Charlotte, North Carolina, and commuted to work and shop there. While Lancaster County continued to court new industry, the rapid growth of the Charlotte area presented both opportunities for economic development and problems associated with urban sprawl in communities such as Indian Land and Van Wyck in the northern part of the county. MICHAEL S. REYNOLDS

Beaty, Ernest A., and Carl W. McMurray. *Lancaster County: Economic and Social.* Columbia: University of South Carolina, 1923.

Floyd, Viola C., comp. *Historical Notes from Lancaster County, South Carolina.* Lancaster, S.C.: Lancaster County Historical Commission, 1977.

Pettus, Louise. *The Waxhaws.* Rock Hill, S.C.: Regal Graphics, 1993.

Pettus, Louise, and Martha Bishop. *Lancaster County: A Pictorial History.* Norfolk, Va.: Donning, 1984.

Lancaster Courthouse and Jail. As part of the internal improvements campaign carried out by the South Carolina Board of Public Works in the 1820s, Robert Mills designed at least fourteen courthouses and fourteen jails throughout the state. The Lancaster County courthouse and jail are among the best surviving examples of his work from this period. Set on a raised basement, the two-story brick courthouse is characterized by Palladian symmetry and features a pedimented portico with modified Tuscan columns. A double flight of steps leads to an entrance with a semicircular fanlight set in a molded pediment. The vaulted ground story has solid brick walls no less than two feet thick; those on the second story measure eighteen inches. The courtroom, located on the second floor, is finished with wainscoting and reeded woodwork. The courthouse has remained in use since its construction. Its elegant styling makes it one of the most refined examples of Mills's early public buildings.

Lancaster County Courthouse. Courtesy, South Carolina Department of Archives and History

The jail, located one block from the courthouse, is a two-story stuccoed masonry building with few exterior features. Its design incorporates several innovations advocated by Mills. Barred cells are situated in the center of the prison rooms to facilitate circulation, which Mills believed necessary for inmates' health. Prisoners were also arranged according to their crimes: debtors on the first floor and others above. The austere exterior of the building features stone quoins and belt courses and recessed arches on the ground floor. County officials decided to discontinue use of the building as a jail after a cell-block fire caused the deaths of eleven inmates in December 1979. Today it is an office building. The courthouse and jail were designated as National Historic Landmarks by the U.S. Department of the Interior in 1973. DANIEL J. VIVIAN

Land granting. The granting of land was of immense importance in establishing and shaping South Carolina. In 1663 King Charles II granted the territory of Carolina to the Lords Proprietors, who were supposed to extend the empire westward at a minimum of expense to the crown and to become wealthy as landlords, regranting the land to the settlers. The crown gave the proprietors semifeudal powers appropriate for a colony so remote that the crown would relinquish direct control. The proprietors intended to govern their colony much like a medieval fiefdom, complete with a titled and landed nobility, the titles of which were "landgrave" and "cassique." The intent was to establish a stable and orderly society. The proprietors did not establish a feudal province but rather one of large plantations, which were worked by white indentured servants and African slaves. There were no more titles granted after the proprietors lost control in 1719.

The granting of large estates to titled aristocrats was important in setting a tone for the colony, but the granting of lands by "headrights" to the commoners was much more important. Headrights, an early version of homesteads, were the means of granting land according to the grantees' ability to cultivate the land. The number of acres in a headright grant was determined by the size of the grantee's family, including servants. Hence, the larger the family, the larger the grant. Fifty acres became the normal headright. An indentured servant typically brought two headrights, one for the owner who paid for passage and another for the servant upon achieving freedom. An African slave, being perpetual, earned one headright, and that for the owner.

The proprietors and the royal government granted the land to encourage immigration, to reward beneficial services, to encourage investments in the colony, and to secure revenue. The headrights, while encouraging immigration, also encouraged the acquisition of large numbers of slaves. The colonial leaders, fearful of the increasing number of slaves, sought to entice more "poor white European" immigrants, especially to get them settled in townships arrayed as a protective barrier along the colony's border. To encourage these military enlistments, the colonial government made grants of lands ceded by the Cherokees as bounties. Colonial land grants normally entailed an obligation to pay the grantor quitrents, a feudal vestige that served as revenue and an indication of allegiance.

Land granting involved a series of steps since there was never a central office in charge of the process. During the proprietary period, a settler would petition the governor in council for land, and either the governor or the council could issue a warrant for survey. The surveyor general would then survey the land and return a plat to the secretary of the province, who then wrote the land grant for the approval of the governor or council. This process was suspended in 1719, and land granting began again in 1731 under royal control. Royal surveyors undertook the work formerly done by the surveyor general. Intending to revise the policy, the Board of Trade greatly restricted land grants in 1772 but was unable to complete the policy changes before the Revolutionary War.

The state of South Carolina continued to grant land after the Revolution by passing an act in 1784. Vacant land could be purchased from the state for $10 per hundred acres. The fee was dropped in 1791, and this measure, along with the repeal of the limits to the amount of land that could be granted, fueled land speculation in the state. Consequently the state granted many large tracts of land in the 1780s and 1790s. The process was abetted by decentralizing land granting: the state surveyor general possessed the authority to appoint numerous deputies in the backcountry to assist in surveying the lands. Land granting continued in South Carolina until the Civil War, albeit at a slower pace as the amount of public land was declining. The office of surveyor general was abolished in 1868, and the practice of land granting virtually died out by 1878. ROBERT K. ACKERMAN

Ackerman, Robert K. *South Carolina Colonial Land Policies.* Columbia: University of South Carolina Press, 1977.

Weir, Robert M. *Colonial South Carolina: A History.* 1983. Reprint, Columbia: University of South Carolina Press, 1997.

Lander University. Founded in 1872 by the Reverend Samuel Lander as a private academy for women, by 1973 Lander University had become a regional public institution offering bachelor and graduate degrees.

When the Methodist church in Williamston requested a pastor who could supplement his meager salary by teaching, the bishop dispatched Samuel Lander, already a pioneer in women's education. In lieu of a salary, the church rented an abandoned hotel building, where Lander established the Williamston Female College. The curriculum included primary and secondary instruction as well as collegiate courses in mathematics, natural science, Latin, and belles lettres. An ornamental department taught "Embroidery and other fancy accomplishments." Within a decade the academy enrolled 138 pupils. Lander designed a unique "one study plan" at Williamston whereby students concentrated on a single academic subject for five weeks each term.

On January 14, 1903, Lander agreed to relocate his school to Greenwood, believing that the new county seat and railroad hub might generate increased enrollment and win the long-sought financial support of the Methodist conference. Local boosters donated land and pledged $25,000 to construct a college building.

Lander died on July 14, 1904, only weeks before the school, soon to bear his name, opened in an imposing new building in Greenwood. The board of trustees quickly selected Lander's son-in-law, the Reverend John O. Willson, as president. Willson persuaded the Methodist conference to assume control of the college, a step that brought limited financial support from the church. The college enjoyed modest success during the early years in Greenwood. Enrollment gradually climbed to about four hundred students, and a revised curriculum included teacher preparation. Men were admitted to classes beginning in 1943.

Institutional debt and a limited endowment weakened the college through the Depression and after. Early attempts to gain accreditation by the Southern Association of Colleges and Schools failed largely because of Lander's fiscal instability. In 1947 South Carolina Methodists concluded that with three senior colleges the church's commitment to higher education was overextended. A conference report found Lander College "decidedly deficient" in its physical plant, library resources, faculty, and endowment; it recommended that the church withdraw support from the unaccredited Greenwood school. Faced with the prospect that the college would close, a committee of local businessmen convinced the church to donate the school to Greenwood County under the condition that the property be used solely for educational purposes and that the school gain accreditation within ten years. A public corporation, the Lander Foundation, was chartered on March 17, 1948, to operate the college. The county council approved occasional appropriations to the college until 1951, when county voters approved a four-mill property tax to give the institution a more dependable financial base.

The Lander Foundation appointed Boyce M. Grier, a former public school superintendent, to head the county-owned college. Grier led the college from 1948 to 1966, a critical period when its survival was often in jeopardy. Grier supervised construction of new student apartments and secured financing for a student center. He launched a nursing program with the support of the Self Foundation and quietly managed the challenge of racial integration. His most significant achievement was to win full accreditation from the Southern Association of Colleges and Schools by 1952.

Despite some success, the future of the small college that remained heavily dependent on local government funding was not promising. The administration, trustees, and local political leaders began exploring avenues for securing support from the state legislature. Initial inquiries received encouragement in 1968 from a report submitted to Governor Robert McNair by Moody's Investment Services. The "Moody Report" recommended expansion of higher education to serve geographical areas of the state that historically had limited access to education beyond the high school level.

Greenwood County legislators promoted Lander's interests in the General Assembly. The legislature reacted to the Moody Report by altering the status of three existing institutions—the College of Charleston, Francis Marion College, and Lander College—to create three senior state colleges. On June 14, 1972, Governor John West signed an act transferring Lander College to state control effective July 1, 1973.

Since 1973, under the successive presidencies of Larry A. Jackson, William C. Moran, and Daniel W. Ball, Lander University has constructed a modern campus, increased enrollment to nearly three thousand students, and expanded the undergraduate and graduate degree programs. Although its students come from most states and many foreign countries, as its central mission Lander University continues to serve the South Carolina Piedmont. MARVIN L. CANN

Bowen, Ann Herd. *Greenwood County: A History.* Greenwood, S.C.: The Museum, 1992.

Rogers, James A., and Delores J. Miller. *Quantum Leap: A Story of Three Colleges.* Columbia, S.C.: R. L. Bryan, 1988.

Landgraves and cassiques. "Landgrave" and "cassique" were titles given to the local nobility created by the Lords Proprietors in their plans for the settlement of Carolina. By their 1663 charter from King Charles II, the eight proprietors were endowed with virtually vice regal authority, considered appropriate for the governing of a remote extension of the empire. Their authority included granting titles to a provincial nobility, who would be vassals of the proprietors. Landgraves were to rank just below the Lords Proprietors, while cassiques were to rank below landgraves and constitute the lowest order of Carolina nobility. Landgrave was a German title, while cassique was based on *cacique,* a Spanish term for "Indian chief."

According to the Fundamental Constitutions, Carolina was to be divided into counties of 480,000 acres each. In turn, each county would be divided into forty square tracts of 12,000 acres each. In each county eight tracts, called seigniories, were reserved for the Lords Proprietors (each of whom received one seigniory). An additional eight tracts, called baronies, were to be reserved for one landgrave (who received four baronies) and two cassiques (who received two baronies apiece). On their baronies, landgraves and cassiques would be granted the authority to conduct manorial courts and to have their estates worked by "leetmen" (indentured servants). The manorial courts were the means by which the landgraves and cassiques were to maintain order on their estates. Leetmen were to be voluntarily bound to an estate, similar to medieval serfs. But there is no record of there having been any manorial courts or leetmen in South Carolina. Rather, landgraves and cassiques became owners of large tracts of land, worked at first by white indentured servants and then overwhelmingly by African slaves.

At least twenty-six landgraves and thirteen cassiques were created by the Lords Proprietors, with rights to land totaling 1,364,000 acres. The vast majority of this land went unclaimed, however, with less than 200,000 acres actually granted. The last landgrave was created in 1718; the last cassique in 1715. Some baronies survived the proprietary era and were handed down through the descendants of South Carolina's landgraves and cassiques. In 1686 the proprietors commissioned Nathaniel Johnson as a cassique. He acquired considerable lands along the Cooper River, and he served as governor in the early 1700s. The proprietors elevated him to landgrave in 1703. He received the estate known as the Seewee Barony, which passed to his son Robert, who also served as governor. The Johnson descendants conveyed the barony to Gabriel Manigault, whose family retained possession until 1870. The landgrave Edmund Bellinger

Patent by the Lords Proprietors to Edmond Andros, creating him a landgrave in South Carolina. Courtesy, South Carolina Department of Archives and History

obtained Tomotely Barony in what became Beaufort County. The Izard family owned the bulk of the barony until the Civil War.

While South Carolina never became the feudal society that the proprietors envisioned, it did become a colony of large, staple-producing plantations, which were owned by people who resembled the English country gentry. Landgraves and cassiques were part of the aristocratic ideal that characterized this colony and state, and their grants (and their titles) became part of the culture of the Carolina lowcountry. ROBERT K. ACKERMAN

Ackerman, Robert K. *South Carolina Colonial Land Policies.* Columbia: University of South Carolina Press, 1977.

Sirmans, M. Eugene. *Colonial South Carolina: A Political History, 1663–1763.* Chapel Hill: University of North Carolina Press, 1966.

Smith, Henry A. M. "The Baronies of South Carolina." *South Carolina Historical and Genealogical Magazine* (January 1914): 3–17.

———. "The Baronies of South Carolina, Quenby and the Eastern Branch of Cooper River." *South Carolina Historical and Genealogical Magazine* (January 1917): 3–36.

———. "The Baronies of South Carolina, the Seewee Barony." *South Carolina Historical and Genealogical Magazine* (July 1911): 109–17.

Weir, Robert M. *Colonial South Carolina: A History.* 1983. Reprint, Columbia: University of South Carolina Press, 1997.

Landsford Canal. Landsford Canal is in eastern Chester County near the Catawba River. In 1820 work commenced on the canal, which was designed by Robert Mills and built under the supervision of the Scots engineer Robert Leckie as part of a comprehensive plan of internal improvements undertaken by the state to connect fall line market towns with the upstate. Four canals were built on the Catawba and Wateree Rivers in an attempt to open navigation between Camden and the North Carolina border. Built to bypass shoals at "Land's Ford" on the Catawba River, the Landsford Canal was constructed by local slaves and skilled white labor recruited from the North.

Completed in 1823, Landsford Canal was twelve feet wide, ten feet deep, and two miles long. Five locks raised and lowered barges through the thirty-two-foot fall of the river. Three bridges crossed the canal, and six storm culverts carried streams underneath it. The total expense of construction was estimated at $122,900. Despite the cost and admirable engineering, the Landsford Canal was not a success. A lock located on a poor foundation collapsed in 1824, which necessitated a lengthy and costly repair. Almost no tolls were collected. By 1836 all of the Catawba-Wateree canals were in poor condition, and all traffic through them apparently ceased by the end of the decade. The sturdy granite locks of the Landsford Canal survived, however, to be listed in the National Register of Historic Places in 1969. The site later became the centerpiece of the Landsford Canal State Park. See plate 2. RHETT A. ADAMS

Collins, Ann P. *A Goodly Heritage: History of Chester County, South Carolina.* Columbia, S.C.: R. L. Bryan, 1986.

Hollis, Daniel W. "Costly Delusion: Inland Navigation in the South Carolina Piedmont." *Proceedings of the South Carolina Historical Association* (1968): 29–43.

Kohn, David, and Bess Glenn. *Internal Improvement in South Carolina, 1817–1828.* Washington, D.C., 1938.

Language. South Carolina has been multilingual since 1526 when the Spanish explorer Lucas Vásquez de Allyón attempted the first European settlement in the land called "Chicora," perhaps near present-day Georgetown. From that first contact until statehood in

1776, more than fifty languages of Europe, Africa, and North America were spoken in its towns and villages.

Four major language families, which included numerous languages and dialects, were represented in the speech of indigenous peoples at the time of their early contact with Europeans and Africans. Between the coast and present-day Rock Hill, a common language or dialect of the Muskogean language family was spoken in the 1500s. Indian life on the coastal plain was so disrupted by the Spanish, French, and English incursions, however, that by the 1700s villages only ten or twenty miles apart could no longer understand each other. Catawbas from the north had moved into the state, and their language (related to the Siouan family) was used in the northeastern area around Rock Hill, site of their present-day reservation. Cherokee, belonging to the Iroquoian language family, was spoken in the northwest and was separated from Catawba by a wide boundary formed by the Broad and Catawba Rivers. The Muskogean languages along the coast, also spoken by the Creeks throughout Georgia and Alabama, disappeared from South Carolina around the mid-1700s, leaving traces only in place names such as Waccamaw, Winyah, Sewee, Wando, Kiawah, Stono, Edisto, and Combahee. Latecomers speaking Algonquian languages came down from the mountains to the north and settled for brief time periods along the Savannah and Saluda Rivers that still bear their names. The native languages that lasted longest were Cherokee and Catawba, which were spoken in the upcountry until well into the nineteenth century. The last native speaker of Catawba died early in the twentieth century, while Cherokee is still spoken in the mountains of western North Carolina, as well as among some Cherokees living in Oklahoma. Many Cherokees became literate in their own language, using a syllabary devised by Sequoya in the early 1800s.

European settlers in South Carolina were speakers of six languages belonging to the Indo-European language family: Spanish, French, German, English, Welsh, and Scots. French-speaking Huguenots arrived early, after the Edict of Nantes was revoked in 1685. In the ten years that followed, more than fifteen hundred of these Protestants entered the Carolina colony, founding five churches in Charleston and outlying areas. Huguenots became Anglicans when preachers of their own faith became difficult to obtain, hastening their transition to English by the mid-1700s. Smaller French-speaking groups settled in frontier areas of the colony. Individual Spanish-speaking Jews entered the colony as early as 1697, with a large group settling in Charleston in the mid-1700s. Descendants of Sephardic Jews expelled from Spain and Portugal during the Catholic Inquisition of 1492, most had previously lived in London or the West Indies and used a variety of Spanish (Ladino) as their home language. Their synagogue in Charleston became one of the largest in the colonies, with a congregation of one hundred families by 1800. Another group of German Protestants experiencing persecution in Europe came in small groups beginning in 1732, settling on what was then the outskirts of the colony: Purrysburg, Orangeburg, Saxe-Gotha, and New Windsor. Additional German speakers came to South Carolina from northern colonies via the Great Wagon Road, and by 1752 they numbered some three thousand. A large group settled in lower Dutch Fork in the middle of the state, between the Broad and Saluda Rivers, a place name that is an Anglicized version of *deutsch* (German).

Settlers from the British Isles made up the bulk of the European settlers, with English speakers in the majority. Immigrants from England were in the minority but constituted the elite of the colony. Some of them were younger sons of English gentry, half of whom came from the exhausted lands of the Caribbean colony of Barbados. They spoke a prestige dialect centered around London, were literate, and were active in the colonial government. The *South-Carolina Gazette,* a weekly newspaper that began publication in Charleston in 1732, was distributed widely throughout the colony and lent cohesion to this elite group. A small group of Welsh speakers came down the Great Wagon Road from Philadelphia into the Pee Dee area of South Carolina in 1736 to settle what is still known as Welsh Neck. Their Welsh Neck Baptist Church mothered some thirty-eight more, bringing contact with non-Welsh speakers who hastened the shift to English. Scots and Scots-Irish settlers constituted the majority of Europeans by the latter part of the 1700s. Lowland Scots were often bilingual in Lowland Scots and a dialect of English that the aristocratic English considered "uncouth." The Scots-Irish from Ulster had lived in Ireland for several generations and spoke a distinctive dialect of English. They were often able to read the Bible in English, using a translation authorized in 1611 during the reign of the Protestant King James VI of Scotland, who had become James I of England. After the Act of Union in 1707 between the two countries, immigrants of Scots heritage could enter the colony on equal terms with the English. Attracted by the colony's offer of land free from rent for ten years, more than four thousand came directly from northern Ireland and Scotland or down the Great Wagon Road from other colonies, doubling the European population in South Carolina between 1763 and 1775 and settling mostly in the upcountry. With their arrival, English became the dominant language in European households during the colonial era. English was not, however, the language spoken by most Carolinians.

Up until the Yamassee War of 1715, Indian languages were the most frequently spoken, but by 1730 the majority of people in South Carolina spoke African languages or an African-English creole language called Gullah or Geechee. At the beginning of the colonial era Africans numbered only a few hundred, but by 1775 their numbers had increased to 107,300. Europeans numbered only 71,300 by that date, and Indians had dwindled from 10,000 to 500.

Africans were brought to Carolina in bondage, and any children born to them were also considered property. Concentrated along coastal rice and indigo plantations, Africans sometimes outnumbered Europeans by a ratio of nine to one. Sullivan's Island, where new slaves were quarantined before auction, has been called the "Ellis Island of black Americans." In the latter half of the colonial era, they spoke more than twenty different languages of the large African language family of Niger-Kordofanian. Their homelands were West Africa between present-day Senegal and southern Nigeria and the Angola-Congo region further to the south. The earliest Africans to arrive in the colony with the planters from Barbados probably had learned English as a second language, and those who came during the first fifty years of the colony would also have had opportunity to become bilingual in English. After the 1720s, however, newcomers had little contact with English speakers, and Gullah developed as a common language among Africans. Its grammatical structure was formed from a combination of abstract selections chosen from the early African languages (probably Senegambia and the Gold Coast) spoken in the colony and through principles of language universals, while its vocabulary was primarily English with some African words used for personal names, numbers, and days of the week. Its pronunciation and intonation patterns reflect those of the original African languages. Later arrivals from Africa, many of whom came from the Angola-Congo region that may be the source of the name Gullah as well as many personal names, came until well into the nineteenth century. Gullah is a unique language created in the coastal regions of South Carolina and Georgia for mutual communication between peoples who shared no other common one. European children on large plantations often learned it as a second language from their caretakers and playmates in the slave quarters.

By the late twentieth century, the primary language of South Carolina was English. Gullah had become a language used in the home and in private community exchanges; many outsiders do not realize that it is still spoken. The structural influence of this creole language can be seen in African American varieties of English through the state, as well as the nation, in such features as absence of copulas or the *be*-verbs (*You better throw that [tea] out because it too weak*), absence of *-s* for third-person singular verbs (*He work in the stable right now*), absence of possessive *-s* before nouns (*We go in our cousin car*), and consonant cluster reduction before vowels (*bes' apple*).

By the early twenty-first century preschool children and the elderly who often cared for them continued to speak South Carolina's unique creole language in coastal African American homes. Commonly heard creole constructions in the verb phrase were a preverbal *duh* for habitual action (*She duh hit me* = She's always hitting me); a preverbal *fuh* for obligation (*I fuh clean the house* = I have to clean the house); a preverbal *done* for completed action (*Teria dog done get hit* = Teria's dog got hit); and *been* for simple past (*And then a big bruise been right there*). In a noun phrase, *ee* and *um* can be used as the third-personal pronoun in subject and object positions respectively (*Ee hard?* [referring to a football] versus *And the snake was dead; we throw rock on um* [referring to the snake]); *ee* can also be used to indicate possession (*So that been on her floor, in ee house*); and *yuna* is sometimes used for the second-personal plural pronoun (*Ee say, "This how yuna talk?"* = He said, "Is this how you all talk?").

The English of older Carolinians of European descent reflects original differences between the archaic Scots English introduced by the Scots-Irish farmers of the upcountry and the prestige English used in southeastern England near London, spoken by the plantation owners of the lowcountry. The lifelong association of the landed gentry with the African slaves also influenced their speech. None of the original African languages used *-r* in word-final position, and the prestige dialect surrounding London was an *-r*-less one. By contrast, the English spoken by the Scots-Irish was *-r*-ful. This presence or absence of *-r* after vowels that are followed by a consonant has long been one of the most noticeable differences between upcountry and lowcountry speech. Two former governors displayed this distinction into the twentieth century: Richard W. Riley of Greenville used *r*-ful speech, while Ernest F. Hollings of Charleston referred to the Board of Education as the *Bode* of Education. The small farmers of the Pee Dee region pronounced their *r*'s more like the upcountry residents did. With World War II, many upcountry and Pee Dee residents moved to the Charleston area for work in defense-related industries, and younger speakers in the urban coastal areas began to use more *r*-ful speech.

The Scots-Irish have also left their mark on grammar. Older speakers in the Piedmont and in the Pee Dee use *hit* for the third-person pronoun (*Hit looked all right*), double modals (*I might can cut the grass this evening*), old verb forms (*He holp me with tobacco last year*), and an *a-* prefix on active verbs (*That man jumped up a-running*). Both black and rural white speakers use an unconjugated *be*-verb that probably has different sources, with black speakers restricting it to habitual or repetitive meaning (*She usually be home in the evening*) and white speakers using it for a wider range (*I be done told you about that*).

Distinctive words from many different sources include *spider* for a frying pan, *loft* for an attic room, *granny* for a midwife, *passed* for died, *plunder* for junk, *cornpone* in the Piedmont and *cornbread* in Charleston, *pinders* and *goobers* for peanuts (both of African origin, along with *okra* and *yam*), *biddie* for a young chicken, and *pole cat* for skunk. The common greeting is *Hey,* rather than *Hi* or *Hello.* Relatives are *kinfolks,* and a young child *favors* someone in the family (rather than looks like them).

As a core dialect area in the lower South, South Carolina contains older speech patterns that spread out to the west and south with the opening up of new plantation areas. It shares with other southerners a pronunciation of *I* without an upward glide, so that *buy* almost rhymes with *baa* (*I like white rice* can be a test sentence for most southerners). The vowels *e* and *I* collapse before a nasal (*pen* and *pin* sound the same, forcing speakers to specify a *safety pin* or a *writing pen*). Still other vowel distinctions are kept in the South, while they have been lost elsewhere in the country (*Mary, merry, Marry,* and *Murray* are distinctly different words, as are *cot/caught* and *hawk/hock*).

In the late twentieth century, non-English speakers once again began arriving in South Carolina, but they represented only a small portion of the overwhelmingly English-speaking population. At the 2000 census they numbered almost 200,000, representing five percent of a total population of just over 4 million. Most of these new residents spoke Spanish, French, or German in the home, but more than half of them used English in public. Smaller groups of new residents spoke Tagalog, Greek, Indic, Italian, Chinese, Korean, or Japanese. Within a generation, children in these immigrant families would sound like their classmates in the public schools. However, like South Carolinians before them, they might also have been speaking an ancestral language in the home. PATRICIA CAUSEY NICHOLS

Carver, Craig M. *American Regional Dialects: A Word Geography.* Ann Arbor: University of Michigan Press, 1987.

Dickson, R. J. *Ulster Emigration to Colonial America, 1718–1775.* London: Routledge and Kegan Paul, 1966.

Elzas, Barnett A. *The Jews of South Carolina from the Earliest Times to the Present Day.* 1905. Reprint, Spartanburg, S.C.: Reprint Company, 1972.

Hartmann, Edward George. *Americans from Wales.* Boston: Christopher Publishing House, 1967.

Hirsch, Arthur Henry. *The Huguenots of Colonial South Carolina.* 1928. Reprint, Columbia: University of South Carolina Press, 1999.

Montgomery, Michael, ed. *The Crucible of Carolina: Essays in the Development of Gullah Language and Culture.* Athens: University of Georgia Press, 1994.

Pollitzer, William. *The Gullah People and Their African Heritage.* Athens: University of Georgia Press, 1999.

Turner, Lorenzo Dow. *Africanisms in the Gullah Dialect.* 1949. Reprint, Columbia: University of South Carolina Press, 2002.

Voight, Gilbert P. *The German and German-Swiss Element in South Carolina, 1732–1752.* Columbia: University of South Carolina, 1922.

Wolfram, Walt, and Natalie Schilling-Estes. *American English: Dialects and Variation.* Malden, Mass.: Blackwell, 1998.

Wolfram, Walt, and Erik R. Thomas. *The Development of African American English.* Malden, Mass.: Blackwell, 2002.

Lathan, Robert (1881–1937). Editor, writer, Pulitzer Prize winner. Lathan was born in York County on May 5, 1881, the son of the Reverend Robert Lathan, a Presbyterian minister and educator, and Frances Eleanor Barron. Lathan received his bachelor of arts from

Erskine College and then taught English and journalism from 1898 until 1899. In 1900 Lathan joined the editorial staff of the *State* newspaper in Columbia, where he remained for three years. From 1903 to 1906 he worked as an official court reporter and studied law. After moving to Charleston, in 1906 he became state news editor and city editor of the *News and Courier.* In 1910 he became editor with the *News and Courier,* a position he held until 1927.

The political nature of Lathan's writing underwent substantial growth during this period, which was best represented in his editorial entitled "The Plight of the South," which appeared in the *News and Courier* on November 5, 1924. Something of a culmination of his political philosophy, "Plight of the South" focused on the South's lack of influence and leadership at the national level. "What political leaders has it who possess weight or authority beyond their own States? What constructive policies are its people ready to fight for with the brains and zeal that made them a power in the old days?" The essay offered no solution to the South's "plight" but rather presented its situation in bold terms in the hope that answers might soon be found. "Who is to speak for the South? How many of her citizens are prepared to help formulate her replies?" A highly respected and widely read piece of contemporary journalism, "Plight of the South" earned Lathan and the *News and Courier* the Pulitzer Prize for editorial writing in 1925.

An ardent Democrat, Lathan was also an active affiliate in many professional associations, including the Carnegie Endowment for International Peace and the advisory board to the University of South Carolina School of Journalism. In addition he served as president of the South Carolina Press Association (1925–1926) and was a life member of the Poetry Society of South Carolina. The Carnegie Endowment provided Lathan with opportunities to travel among several western and eastern European locations, where he learned the economic and political histories that surfaced in his later writing.

Lathan closely monitored both the S.C. and the U.S. Supreme Courts. He was concerned about all matters agricultural, as was most pronounced in a July 1926 address before the National Press Association calling for the "radical revision" of the South's agricultural system, in which he stated his belief that "every farmer (should be) a landowner." In the formative years of the Great Depression, Lathan wrote numerous editorials on farm foreclosures and described the rise in joblessness as a unique consequence of "Republican misrule."

Lathan also wrote on the traditional southern themes of states' rights and taxation, which he deemed as continual punishment from the North upon the South. He viewed state government as the "people's government" and was an ardent opponent of American entry into the League of Nations. He spent his last years as editor for the *Asheville (N.C.) Citizen.* He died in Asheville on September 26, 1937. He was survived by his wife, Bessie Early of Darlington, whom he had married in 1904. They had no children. Lathan was buried in Grove Hill Cemetery in Darlington. KRISTIN M. HARKEY

Brennan, Elizabeth A., and Elizabeth C. Clarage, eds. *Who's Who of Pulitzer Prize Winners.* Phoenix: Oryx, 1999.

Lathan, Robert. Papers. South Carolina Historical Society, Charleston.

———. Papers. South Caroliniana Library, University of South Carolina, Columbia.

Sloan, William David, and Laird B. Anderson, eds. *Pulitzer Prize Editorials: America's Best Editorial Writing, 1917–1993.* 2d ed. Ames: Iowa State University Press, 1994.

Latimer, Asbury Churchwell (1851–1908). Congressman, U.S. senator. Latimer was born near Lowndesville, Abbeville District, on July 31, 1851, the son of the farmer Clement T. Latimer and Frances Beulah Young. Latimer had little formal education, although he briefly attended a local common school. After the death of his father in 1876, Latimer took over the management of the family farm. In 1877 he married Sarah Alice Brown. They had five children.

In 1880 Latimer moved to Belton, where he engaged in various business ventures in addition to maintaining his farming interest. In 1890 he became active in the Farmers' Alliance and was selected chairman of the Anderson County Democratic executive committee. In the same year Latimer declined to run for lieutenant governor on the Democratic Party ticket with gubernatorial candidate Benjamin Tillman. Two years later Latimer was elected to the U.S. House of Representatives, where he served for ten years. In 1903 Latimer won election to the U.S. Senate, defeating five other Democratic nominees including former governor John Gary Evans. Despite his lack of formal education, Latimer quickly won the support and confidence of his fellow senators for his hard work and straightforward manner. As Senator Tillman said, Latimer achieved "signal success as a public man."

Active on several Senate committees, Latimer supported the idea that the government was "in a practical working sense, the servant of the American people." Latimer helped draft the 1906 Pure Food and Drug Act, the landmark progressive legislation to improve government inspection of food and medicine. He earned his nickname of "Good Roads" Latimer after securing—against great opposition—a favorable report on the need for federal assistance to improve rural public roads. Latimer hoped to create a model system of transportation to help farmers haul products to market. He believed that the lack of proper roads hindered southern progress and that the "construction and improvement of common roads over which necessaries of life and raw material must pass" would "sustain life and prosperity." Latimer also realized that states could not carry the costs of improving roads without federal support. He justified federal road funding on the grounds that it would benefit national defense and the U.S. Postal Service.

Latimer also supported free delivery of mail to improve rural lives. He used his Senate seat to uplift his agricultural constituency. In his work with the Immigration Commission, Latimer spent time in Europe studying land productivity, roads, wage scales, and costs of living. He intended to compare his findings to conditions in the United States, but on February 20, 1908, Latimer died suddenly of peritonitis following a surgical operation. The Senate dedicated a memorial address in Latimer's honor, which was published in 1909. He was buried in Belton Cemetery, Belton, South Carolina. VERONICA BRUCE MCCONNELL

"Senator Latimer Is Dead." Columbia *State,* February 21, 1908, pp. 1, 3.

Latter-day Saints. Latter-day Saints, often referred to as Mormons, are members of the Church of Jesus Christ of Latter-day Saints. The church's longest-held and basic tenants confirm that they are firm adherents of Jesus Christ, as their name implies. They believe that the church organized by Christ in ancient times was restored in April 1830 by a modern-day prophet, Joseph Smith (1805–1844), to whom had been revealed sacred gold plates that Smith translated and published as the *Book of Mormon.* Smith attracted followers who established settlements in Ohio, Missouri, and Illinois. Latter-day Saints garnered considerable hostility from nonmembers, who took offense at Smith's criticism of established Christian churches, the communalistic organization of early Mormon settlements, and Smith's practice and defense of polygamy (although the latter practice was abandoned and denounced by the church in later years).

The Latter-day Saints have had a continual presence in South Carolina since 1831. Among the earliest members in the state was Emmanual Masters Murphy, who was converted in Tennessee before moving to South Carolina and settling in Union District. When the missionary Lysander M. Davis arrived in the state in 1839, he found that Murphy had a small group of close friends prepared for baptism. Other initial missions to South Carolina proved less successful. The missionary Abraham O. Smoot preached in Charleston for two weeks in April 1842 but left without attracting a single convert.

The church enjoyed more substantial success in the years following the Civil War. In 1875 the Southern States Mission was organized and covered most of the Deep South, including South Carolina. The South Carolina Conference was established in 1882, with local units in Kings Mountain (1882), Gaffney (1883), and Society Hill (1890s) and later in Columbia, Charleston, and Fairfield. In the mid-1880s the church was likewise established among the Catawba Indians at Society Hill. John Black, a non–Latter-day Saint plantation owner near the Catawba reservation, provided a refuge from local mobs for early members and friends, including Native Americans. An estimated ninety-seven percent of the Catawba tribe joined the church, some of whom also moved west. One of their chiefs, Samuel Blue, visited Salt Lake City and spoke at the church's annual general conference in April 1950.

Some of the most severe hostility toward Latter-day Saints in the South was experienced in South Carolina. In 1903 the missionary A. H. Olpin was beaten senseless by a mob and was committed to an insane asylum before being allowed to return to Utah. When mission president Ephraim H. Nye visited Olpin in Columbia and saw the severity of his wounds, he had a heart attack; he died the following day.

Near the turn of the century, the church's policy of gathering new converts to the west was modified, allowing the church to grow numerically in the South. In 1930 there were 3,500 members in South Carolina. In 1947 the first stake, a dioceselike geographical unit, was organized in Columbia. This organization was the second such creation in the Deep South. By 1980 there were 17,000 Saints in South Carolina, and by the end of 2002 that number had increased to nearly 30,000 members living in fifty-six local units. Congregations now serve Greenville, Charleston, Gaffney, Hartsville, Ridgeway, Sumter, Society Hill, Winnsboro, Darlington, and Columbia.

In October 1999 the Columbia Temple, the church's most sacred edifice in the state, was dedicated in Hopkins. By the start of the twenty-first century, increased cooperation between Latter-day Saints and other Christian groups, such as the "Putting Families First" campaign, increased the acceptance for Latter-day Saints in South Carolina. DAVID F. BOONE

Anderson, Ted S. "The Southern States Mission and the Administration of Ben E. Rich, 1898–1908." Master's thesis, Brigham Young University, 1976.

Berrett, LaMar C. "History of the Southern States Mission, 1831–1861." Master's thesis, Brigham Young University, 1960.

Jenson, Andrew. *Encyclopedic History of the Church of Jesus Christ of Latter-day Saints.* Salt Lake City, Utah: Deseret News Publishing, 1941.

Lee, Jerry D. "A Study of the Influence of the Mormon Church on the Catawba Indians of South Carolina: 1882–1975." Master's thesis, Brigham Young University, 1976.

Laurens (Laurens County; 2000 pop. 9,916). Originally called Laurensville, the town became the county seat shortly after Laurens County was established in 1785. A plat by Robert Creswell in 1800 shows the courthouse square surrounded by lots that evolved into the town's commercial center. By the 1820s Laurens contained thirty-five houses, 250 inhabitants, and an 1815 courthouse. Businesses included eight shops advertising ready-made clothing. Future U.S. president Andrew Johnson came to Laurens from North Carolina in 1824 and opened a tailor shop. He met and courted a local woman, Sarah Word, whose mother refused to sanction their marriage because he was a tailor. Stung by the rebuff, Johnson left Laurens after less than two years. By 1840 Laurens had more than a dozen stores and eighty-one registered whiskey distilleries. Its commercial importance was established by its location on the State Road between Charleston and western North Carolina. In 1854 the town saw its economic position enhanced with the completion of the Laurens Railroad, which connected Laurens with the Greenville and Columbia Railroad at Newberry.

There was no military action in the area during the Civil War, although some Charleston refugees relocated to Laurens to escape war dangers in the lowcountry. During Reconstruction, friction between newly enfranchised African Americans and whites culminated in the Laurens Riot of 1870. Because of the racial violence, several upstate counties (including Laurens) were placed under martial law. Laurens began to prosper again in the 1880s. Two new railroads linked the town with Augusta, Greenville, Spartanburg, and Columbia. An 1888 business directory referred to Laurens as the "Atlanta of South Carolina" because of its railroad connections. Between 1880 and 1920 many commercial buildings and churches were built, the Laurens and Watts textile mills went into operation, several banks were established (including the Palmetto Bank), and Laurens Glass began manufacturing bottles. The courthouse square remained the commercial center until the 1960s, when new shopping centers were built on the outskirts of Laurens. During the 1920s and 1930s residents from the country would come to town on Saturday and stores often remained opened until 11:00 P.M.

Following World War II, the economy slowly diversified. At the start of the twenty-first century, textiles played a much smaller role and the glass plant was no longer in operation. Several distribution centers, including Wal-Mart, became major employers, as did companies that manufactured ceramics, pipe fabrication, and metal bearings. Laurens also developed an aggressive downtown revitalization program. West Main Street, a part of the town's historic district, contained many beautiful old homes representing a variety of architectural styles. Major historic attractions include the Episcopal Church of the Epiphany (ca. 1845), the oldest church building in use in the city; James Dunklin House Museum (ca. 1812); Bethel AME Church (ca. 1907); Laurens County Courthouse (ca. 1837–1838, enlarged in 1858 and 1911); Octagon House (ca. 1859); and the Villa (ca. 1859–1861) at Martha Franks Baptist Retirement Center. WILLIAM COPELAND COOPER

Bolick, Julian Stevenson. *A Laurens County Sketchbook.* Clinton, S.C.: Jacobs, 1973.

The Scrapbook: A Compilation of Historical Facts about Places and Events of Laurens County, South Carolina. N.p.: Laurens County Historical Society and Laurens County Arts Council, 1982.

Laurens, Henry (1724–1792). Merchant, planter, statesman, diplomat. Laurens was born on February 24, 1724, in Charleston, the eldest son of John Laurens, a saddler, and Esther Grasset. Both the

Laurens and Grasset families fled France as Huguenot refugees in the 1680s, with John and Esther settling in Charleston about 1715. Henry Laurens provided no details but described his education as "the best . . . which [Charleston] afforded." Following a three-year clerkship in the London countinghouse of James Crokatt, Laurens returned to Charleston in 1747 and formed a commercial partnership with George Austin. Austin & Laurens expanded in 1759 to become Austin, Laurens & (George) Appleby and continued until 1762, when the partnership was dissolved by mutual consent. Laurens subsequently traded on his own. As a merchant, he exported Carolina products (rice, indigo, deerskins, and naval stores) to Britain, Europe, and the West Indies. His vessels returned with wine, textiles, rum, sugar, and slaves. During the early 1760s Laurens's interests expanded to include rice and indigo planting. He owned four South Carolina plantations (Mepkin, Wambaw, Wrights Savannah, and Mount Tacitus), two Georgia plantations (Broughton Island and New Hope), tracts of undeveloped land in both colonies, and town lots in Charleston. The earnings from his mercantile and planting interests made Laurens one of the wealthiest men in America.

Henry Laurens. Courtesy, South Caroliniana Library, University of South Carolina

Laurens entered public service at an early age, holding local and church offices in Charleston as early as 1751. He first sat in the Commons House of Assembly in 1757, representing St. Philip's Parish. He would be reelected to the colonial or state assemblies seventeen times during his lifetime. He served as a lieutenant in the militia in 1757 and as a lieutenant colonel in the provincial regiment during the Cherokee Expedition of 1761. He refused appointment to the Royal Council in 1764.

During the early stages of the Anglo-American conflict, Laurens gained prominence as a political moderate. On October 23, 1765, at the height of the Stamp Act crisis, a mob invaded his home in search of stamped papers. This incident ended without injury but traumatized his wife and increased the conservative merchant-planter's concern for the rights of individuals threatened by the violence and enthusiasm of the revolution. Between 1767 and 1769 royal officials in South Carolina seized his schooners *Wambaw* and *Broughton Island Packet* and the ship *Ann* for alleged customs violations. In response Laurens wrote pamphlets explaining his position and castigating the customs and vice-admiralty officials. He also challenged a customs officer to a duel. This aggressive behavior was not uncommon for Laurens, who sought vindication with dueling pistols on at least five occasions during his lifetime.

Laurens's life took a new direction in May 1770 after the death of his wife, Eleanor Ball. Married to Laurens since June 25, 1750, Eleanor had given birth to twelve or thirteen children. Laurens now made the education of his five surviving children, especially his three sons, his foremost life's work. He suspended direct supervision of his planting and commercial interests and sailed to England in September 1771. From there he traveled to the Continent, where he found suitable schools for his two older sons in Geneva, Switzerland. During the time he spent in England, Laurens and several other South Carolinians in London signed petitions to Parliament and the king seeking redress of American grievances.

The South Carolina to which Laurens returned in 1774 had moved beyond peaceful petition to revolution. Within weeks of his landing, St. Philip's Parish elected him to the First Provincial Congress. In June 1775 he became president of the Provincial Congress and the Council of Safety and consequently the state's chief executive during the establishment of the provincial regiments and the transition from royal to independent status. He contributed to South Carolina's first constitution and served as vice president in the first state government formed in March 1776. He remained an active and moderating force in South Carolina's revolutionary movement from 1775 until he left to serve in the Continental Congress in June 1777.

Laurens has been frequently cited by historians as one of the few citizens in the lower South who expressed opposition to slavery in America as early as the 1770s. In an oft-quoted passage from his correspondence, he wrote (after receiving a copy of the Declaration of Independence), "I abhor slavery," despite participating in the slave trade early in his career, owning 298 slaves as late as 1790, and the fact that there is little evidence that he offered freedom to more than a few of his servants. Laurens understood the harm that slavery posed, to both races, and anticipated that it would end in a bloody conflict. His opposition to slavery, however, had little impact on the institution in South Carolina.

Arriving at Philadelphia in July 1777, Laurens quickly established himself as an active and respected member of the Continental Congress. In November 1777 he succeeded John Hancock as president during one of the most trying times in American history. He took the chair at York, Pennsylvania, where Congress met after Philadelphia had fallen to the British the previous September. During his tenure the Continental army spent its winter encampment at Valley Forge and turmoil in Congress and among Continental officers threatened General George Washington's command. Laurens resigned as president in December 1778 but continued to represent South Carolina in Congress until late 1779. In October that year Congress selected him to travel to Holland and secure a loan and an alliance with the Dutch.

Shortly after departing on his Dutch mission, Laurens, his vessel, and most of his papers were taken by a British warship in September 1780. Charged with high treason, he was a prisoner in the Tower of London from October 1780 through December 1781. After obtaining his parole and subsequent freedom, Laurens learned that he had been named to the American commission to negotiate peace with Britain. The fifteen months spent in confinement ruined his health, however, and permitted him to play only a minor role. Along with Benjamin Franklin, John Adams, and John Jay, Laurens signed the preliminary peace treaty in Paris in November 1782. Traveling to England to regain his health, Laurens did not attend the signing of the definitive treaty in Paris in September 1783.

Laurens returned to South Carolina in January 1785 and withdrew from public affairs. Elected as a delegate to both the 1787 Philadelphia constitutional convention and the 1790 South Carolina constitutional convention, he declined to serve in both. The one minor exception occurred in 1788 when he supported the federal Constitution as a delegate to the South Carolina ratification convention. He spent his declining years successfully rebuilding his war-ravaged estate. He died on December 8, 1792, at his Mepkin plantation on the Cooper River. As stipulated in his will, he chose to have his remains cremated before burial. His ashes were interred at Mepkin. C. JAMES TAYLOR

Clark, Peggy J. "Henry Laurens's Role in the Anglo-American Peace Negotiations." Master's thesis, University of South Carolina, 1991.

Frech, Laura Page. "The Career of Henry Laurens in the Continental Congress, 1777–1779." Ph.D. diss., University of North Carolina at Chapel Hill, 1972.

Hamer, Philip M., et al., eds. *The Papers of Henry Laurens.* 16 vols. Columbia: University of South Carolina Press, 1968–2003.

McDonough, Daniel J. *Christopher Gadsden and Henry Laurens: The Parallel Lives of Two American Patriots.* Selinsgrove, Pa.: Susquehanna University Press, 2000.

Moore, Warner Oland. "Henry Laurens: A Charleston Merchant in the Eighteenth Century, 1747–1771." Ph.D. diss., University of Alabama, 1974.

Wallace, David Duncan. *The Life of Henry Laurens.* New York: Putnam, 1915.

Laurens, John (1754–1782). Soldier, diplomat. Laurens was born in Charleston on October 28, 1754, the son of the prominent merchant and planter Henry Laurens and his wife, Eleanor Ball. After studying under tutors in Charleston, Laurens traveled to London in 1771 for further schooling. He first enrolled in Richard Clarke's school for Carolina boys before moving to Geneva, Switzerland, in May 1772. Laurens lived in Geneva, a city noted for its republicanism and excellence in education, until August 1774, when he returned to London to study law in the Middle Temple at the Inns of Court.

In December 1776 Laurens sailed to Charleston to enlist in the American War of Independence. He left behind in England his pregnant wife, Martha Manning, whom he had secretly married earlier in the year. The following summer he traveled to Philadelphia with his father, who had been elected to the Continental Congress. Laurens joined General George Washington's staff and became the best friend of fellow aide Alexander Hamilton. In the forefront at the battles of Brandywine, Germantown, and Monmouth, Laurens won a reputation for reckless bravery.

After the British shifted military operations to the South, Laurens proposed that South Carolina arm slaves and grant them freedom in return for their military service. In March 1779 Congress approved his idea and commissioned him lieutenant colonel. Elected to the South Carolina House of Representatives, Laurens introduced his black-regiment plan in 1779 and 1780 and met overwhelming defeat each time. His belief that blacks shared a similar nature with whites and could aspire to freedom in a republican society would set Laurens apart from all other prominent South Carolinians in the Revolutionary War period.

At the same time, Laurens continued his military service. When the British threatened Charleston in May 1779, he opposed Governor John Rutledge's offer to surrender the city on the condition that the state be allowed to remain neutral for the duration of the war. That fall Laurens commanded an infantry column in the failed assault on Savannah. After being captured when Charleston surrendered in May 1780, he was exchanged in November.

In December 1780 Congress appointed Laurens special minister to France. He arrived in France in March 1781. In a whirlwind two-month mission he obtained a loan from the Netherlands, military supplies, and French assurances that their navy would operate in American waters that year. Laurens finished his diplomatic duties in time to join Washington at Yorktown, where the timely arrival of the French fleet secured a decisive American victory. Laurens represented the American army in negotiating the British surrender.

Laurens returned to South Carolina and made a final attempt to secure approval of his plan for a black regiment. At Jacksonborough in early 1782, the House again decisively rejected his proposal, though the debate was heated. Laurens served under General Nathanael Greene and spent his final months operating a spy network that gathered intelligence of British activities in Charleston. On August 27, 1782, he was killed in a skirmish on the Combahee River. GREGORY D. MASSEY

Massey, Gregory D. *John Laurens and the American Revolution.* Columbia: University of South Carolina Press, 2000.

Laurens County (715 sq. miles; 2000 pop. 69,567). Located in the Piedmont, Laurens is a county of forests and gently rolling hills. The Enoree River separates Laurens from Spartanburg and Union Counties on the northeast. Newberry County borders on the southeast and Greenville County on the northwest, while the Saluda River and Lake Greenwood separate it from Abbeville and Greenwood Counties on the southwest.

The first known European in the area was John Duncan, a native of Aberdeen, Scotland, who came from Pennsylvania in 1753 and settled near the modern Newberry-Laurens county line. He also brought the first African American slave and the first horse-drawn wagon. Duncan's settlement grew. By the mid-1760s a church was established that became Duncan's Creek Presbyterian Church, the oldest in Laurens County.

Four important Revolutionary War battles took place in Laurens County. On July 15, 1776, patriot forces defeated a combined

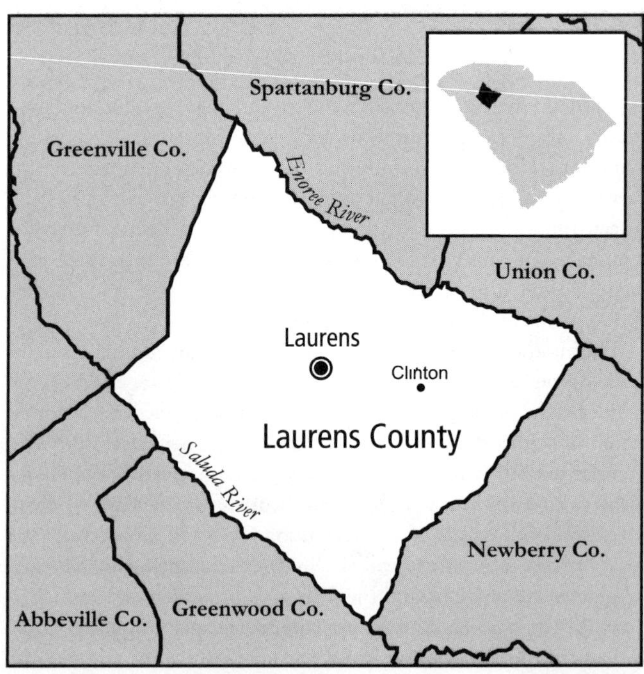

Indian and Tory attack on Lyndley's Fort near Rabun Creek. At the Battle of Musgrove's Mill, a force of rebels attacked British and Tory forces on August 18, 1780, and achieved a decisive victory at the end of a two-day battle. On December 29, 1780, a Tory detachment was defeated at Hammond's Store near present-day Clinton. Near the end of the war, at Hayes Station (eight miles southwest of Clinton), Captain "Bloody Bill" Cunningham attacked a contingent of rebels and killed fourteen.

After the war, Ninety Six District became the chief governmental unit of the backcountry. In 1785 Laurens County, named for the statesman Henry Laurens of Charleston, was one of six counties carved from the district. To select a site for the county seat, a delegation met at the distillery of John Rodgers, near the present Laurens courthouse square. Tradition has it that the men, after imbibing freely, climbed the hill to a level area and chose the spot for the courthouse. More likely, however, the site was selected for its proximity to water and because five important roads connecting the upcountry converged at the point. A wooden courthouse, also used as a church and a schoolhouse, was constructed shortly afterward. An improved courthouse was built between 1837 and 1838 and enlarged in 1857 and 1911.

After the Revolution, the upcountry saw immigrants arrive from Pennsylvania seeking cheap land. By 1800 the population of Laurens County stood at 12,809, of which almost eighty-five percent were white. However, as cotton production expanded, the number of slaves increased. The district produced almost sixteen thousand bales of cotton in 1850. Ten years later the county population reached 23,858, more than half of which were slaves. Villages sprang up and briefly thrived during this period at Cross Hill, Waterloo, Princeton, Gray Court, Owings, Ora, and Mountville. However, they gradually dwindled. Laurens and Clinton became the dominant towns. Antebellum Laurens County was the home of Ann Pamela Cunningham, whose 1853 letter to the *Charleston Mercury* raised awareness about the deplorable condition of George Washington's home at Mount Vernon, Virginia. Cunningham's actions sparked the movement to restore this national historic site.

No military action occurred in Laurens County during the Civil War, although many native sons served in the conflict. In April and May 1865 Union troops passed through the county in pursuit of Confederate president Jefferson Davis, who spent two days and a night in Laurens County during his flight from Richmond. During Reconstruction white residents of Laurens County resented the enfranchisement of newly freed blacks, most of whom supported the despised Republican Party. Whites responded by organizing Democratic clubs that attempted to influence elections through intimidation and violence. As a result of Ku Klux Klan activity across the lower Piedmont and the Laurens Riot of 1870, Laurens and eight other South Carolina counties were placed under martial law in 1871. When Reconstruction ended following the 1876 election of Wade Hampton as governor, Laurens native William Dunlap Simpson became lieutenant governor, and he later served as governor and chief justice of the state supreme court.

Cotton remained the main crop in the decades following the Civil War, with sharecropping replacing slave labor. Like most upcountry counties, Laurens sought to revive its economy by spinning cotton rather than simply growing it. By the turn of the century, textile manufacturing had become an important part of the economy. Laurens Cotton Mill was established in 1895, and Mercer Silas Bailey built a mill in Clinton in 1896. The Lydia, Watts, and Joanna mills also began operations. Company-built villages appeared around these new textile mills to provide housing for employees. Mill villages remained an important economic and social feature of Laurens County until well after World War II. New railroads arrived in the late nineteenth century, including the Charleston and Western Carolina Railroad; the Columbia, Newberry, and Laurens Railroad; and the Georgia, Carolina, and Northern Railroad.

Education expanded in Laurens County during the late nineteenth century. Pratt Suber became the first county superintendent of education in 1874, and Clinton College (later Presbyterian College) was established in 1880. Privately sponsored libraries appeared, eventually evolving into a county library in 1929.

During the first half of the twentieth century, Laurens County experienced steady growth but remained predominantly rural. From a population of 37,382 in 1900, the county grew to 46,974 in 1950 and to 69,567 by 2000. The same period saw a significant change in racial composition, with the African American portion of the population declining from three-fifths in 1900 to just under one-third by 1950. With the exception of a large glass bottle manufacturing plant in the town of Laurens, textiles and agriculture dominated the county economy until World War II.

The decades following the war brought changes. Small rural schools consolidated, and all schools were desegregated. Economic diversification made the county less dependent on textile manufacturing. Michelin, Milliken, and Wal-Mart established large warehouse distribution centers in the county near Laurens and Clinton. New manufacturers included CeramTec, Torrington, Avery Dennison, and Norbord. Several automobile-parts suppliers established facilities in northern Laurens County at Fountain Inn to supply BMW's upstate assembly facility. Retirement centers were built by three church denominations. Because of its location near the rapidly expanding Greenville-Spartanburg metropolitan area, Laurens County stood poised to enjoy continued economic and population growth into the twenty-first century. WILLIAM COPELAND COOPER

Bolick, Julian Stevenson. *A Laurens County Sketchbook.* Clinton, S.C.: Jacobs, 1973.

The Scrapbook: A Compilation of Historical Facts about Places and Events of Laurens County, South Carolina. N.p.: Laurens County Historical Society and Laurens County Arts Council, 1982.

Laurens Glass. When deposits of the mineral silica, important for glassmaking, were found a few miles north of Laurens, a group of local businessmen organized Laurens Glass Works in 1910. Nathaniel B. Dial, who later became a U.S. senator, was among the organizers and was its first president. The local silica was never mined, however, because shipping it from the eastern part of South Carolina proved more cost-efficient.

Laurens Glass struggled during its early years. Skilled glassblowers had to be brought in from Ohio and Pennsylvania. When the company was reorganized in 1913, Nathaniel Dial's nephew Albert was named president and served until 1928. Shortly after this reorganization, Laurens Glass obtained the first license in the United States to manufacture Coca-Cola bottles. The company remained one of the few suppliers of Coke bottles until after World War II. By the mid-1940s the automated Laurens Glass had more than four hundred employees.

Between 1959 and 1968 Laurens Glass expanded, opening plants in Henderson, North Carolina, and Ruston, Louisiana. As the soft drink industry switched to nonglass containers, the company's main product became food jars. In 1968 the company merged with the Indian Head Corporation of Delaware, which moved its glass container headquarters to Laurens in the mid-1970s. Additional mergers further affected company operations, with subsequent corporate owners deeming the Laurens facility no longer cost-effective for modern manufacturing. In 1996 the Laurens Glass plant closed, putting four hundred people out of work. WILLIAM COPELAND COOPER

Biondo, Steve. "Era of Laurens Glass Comes to Close." *Laurens County Advertiser*, June 21, 1996, pp. 1, 16.

The Scrapbook: A Compilation of Historical Facts about Places and Events of Laurens County, South Carolina. N.p.: Laurens County Historical Society and Laurens County Arts Council, 1982.

Lebby, Nathaniel H. (1816–1880). Inventor. Lebby was born in Charleston on August 22, 1816, the son of William Lebby and Frances Scott. He conceived of the mechanism for the world's first hydraulic suction dredge, which became the standard method of modern dredging. The device was first employed in the dredge boat *General Moultrie* in the late 1850s to deepen a new channel through the Charleston harbor bar.

Although it provided the city with an active and prosperous port for almost two centuries, Charleston's harbor had a serious drawback at its mouth—a shifting barrier of sand and debris that lay between one and three miles offshore. As ships got larger, they drew increasingly deeper drafts, which made the problem of the bar more acute with each passing decade. By 1852 the U.S. Coast Survey found that shoaling in the main channel through the bar had reduced its depth to less than eleven feet at low tide, down from an estimated thirteen feet in 1780. As a result federal, state, and local officials began looking for ways to deepen the channel.

By this time Lebby was employed by the South Carolina Railroad. In 1852 he had been awarded a patent for a "water raising apparatus," a steam-driven pump that found frequent employment on rice plantations to flood and drain fields. When in operation, his pumps discharged sizable amounts of mud, sand, and even rocks. Lebby believed that a similar pump would pass through dredged material as well. His working model for a dredge that used a pump to suck up materials through a pipe impressed Captain George Cullum of the U.S. Corps of Engineers, who had assumed charge of public works in the harbor in 1855. Lebby's machine was housed in a New York–built dredge boat, which, christened the *General Moultrie,* went into service in early 1857. The results were spectacular. By June 1858 Lebby's suction pump had been used to remove some 145,000 cubic yards of material, an unprecedented dredging achievement.

Patent and mechanical drawings for the dredging apparatus do not survive, but Captain Cullum recorded a description of Lebby's apparatus in 1857: "a large centrifugal pump six feet in diameter, revolving on a vertical axis, to which an iron 19″ (diameter) suction hose is attached, its lower, or bell-shaped, end resting on the bottom of the channel. The pump is placed in the center of a powerful propeller under the deck in the hold of the vessel and is powered by a steam engine, which is supplied by steam from the propeller boiler."

Lebby received three additional patents after the Civil War: one in 1867 and one in 1869, each for a "Centrifugal Pump"; and a third in 1870 for an "ore washing machine." He never married. Lebby died of consumption in Charleston on February 11, 1880, and was buried at Magnolia Cemetery there. MARY S. MILLER

Bonds, John B. "Opening the Bar: First Dredging at Charleston, 1853–1859." *South Carolina Historical Magazine* 98 (July 1997): 230–50.

Comfort, Jan. "South Carolina Inventors and Inventions, 1790–1873." *South Carolina Magazine of Ancestral Research* 25 (summer 1997): 123–36.

LeConte, John (1818–1891). Scientist, educator. LeConte was born in Liberty County, Georgia, on December 4, 1818, the eldest surviving son of the planter and naturalist Louis LeConte and Ann Quarterman. Reared on a large plantation, LeConte received most of his early education at home. He graduated from the University of Georgia in 1838 and enrolled in the College of Physicians and Surgeons in New York the next year. Soon after receiving the M.D. degree in 1841, he established a medical practice in Savannah, Georgia. Married to Eleanor Josephine Graham in 1841, he had three children.

John LeConte. Courtesy, South Caroliniana Library, University of South Carolina

During his years in Savannah, LeConte wrote several scholarly articles, and in 1846 the University of Georgia appointed him as professor of natural philosophy (chemistry and physics). While there, he published an admirable study of the formation of extruding ice columns in frozen soil. Following disputes with university administrators in 1855, LeConte resigned and returned to the College of Physicians and Surgeons as a lecturer. A year later he moved to Columbia, South Carolina, to become professor of natural philosophy at South Carolina College. During his tenure in Columbia, LeConte continued his scientific inquiries, including a notable paper on the effects of musical sounds on a gas-jet flame, published in 1858. At the request of the secretary of the Smithsonian Institution, LeConte and his brother Joseph, by then also on the South Carolina College faculty, began to develop a table of the "Constants of Nature," and they drafted the manuscript of a textbook in college chemistry.

As the secession movement gained momentum in South Carolina, LeConte expressed opposition, but when the crisis worsened, he changed his position. Heir to a large portion of his late father's plantation, including sixty slaves, LeConte readily consented to aid the Confederacy. During the Civil War he supervised the Nitre and Mining Bureau operations in upper South Carolina. As Union troops neared Columbia early in 1865, LeConte and his brother were charged with responsibility for removing the Nitre and Mining Bureau equipment, but Federal troops intercepted and plundered their wagon train. When he returned to Columbia, LeConte found his family safe and his home intact, but he soon learned that his manuscripts and other papers had been destroyed in the fire that devastated a considerable portion of Columbia.

Discouraged by his losses and displeased with the state of affairs in South Carolina during the ensuing months, LeConte sought employment elsewhere. In 1869 he became professor of physics at the newly established University of California, where he successfully performed his duties for two decades, including service as acting president in 1869 and as president from 1875 to 1881. Although less productive in scholarly writing during his years in California, he published several important scientific articles. LeConte was elected to the National Academy of Sciences in 1878. He died in his home in Berkeley, California, on April 29, 1891. LESTER D. STEPHENS

Lupold, John. "From Physician to Physicist: The Scientific Career of John LeConte, 1818–1891." Ph.D. diss., University of South Carolina, 1970.

Stephens, Lester D. *Joseph LeConte: Gentle Prophet of Evolution.* Baton Rouge: Louisiana State University Press, 1982.

LeConte, Joseph (1823–1901). Geologist, educator. LeConte was born in Liberty County, Georgia, on February 26, 1823, son of the planter and naturalist Louis LeConte and Ann Quarterman. After receiving most of his early education on his father's large plantation, LeConte entered the University of Georgia in 1838 and graduated in 1841. He spent considerable time studying the natural history of his region. In 1844 he enrolled in the College of Physicians and Surgeons in New York, and he received the M.D. degree in 1845. On January 14, 1847, LeConte married Caroline Elizabeth Nisbet, with whom he eventually had five children. Soon after his wedding, LeConte established a medical practice in Macon, Georgia.

Joseph LeConte. Courtesy, South Carolina Historical Society

Continuing to pursue his interest in natural history, LeConte decided in 1850 that he would study with the esteemed scientist Louis Agassiz at the Lawrence Scientific School of Harvard College. On completing the program in 1851, he became professor of chemistry and natural history at Oglethorpe College in Milledgeville, Georgia. A year later he joined the faculty of his alma mater as professor of geology and natural history. Like his brother John, who had been on the University of Georgia faculty since 1846, he found himself at odds with the president of the institution. Following his brother, who resigned in 1855, Joseph left in December 1856 for South Carolina College, where he served as professor of natural history.

Pleased with his situation in Columbia, LeConte endeared himself to his students, took an active part in the cultural affairs of the city, and published articles on topics in geology, religion, art, and education. His career was interrupted in 1861, however, when the Civil War began. Although he owned around sixty slaves and a large plantation inherited from his father, LeConte initially opposed secession. He offered his ardent support of the Confederacy, however, and served it by first helping to manufacture medicines and later by serving in the Nitre and Mining Bureau. As the war drew to a close, LeConte experienced harrowing encounters with Federal forces, and he recorded these in a journal that was published posthumously as *'Ware Sherman* in 1937.

After the war, LeConte busied himself with his teaching duties and with his writings, the most significant of which was a series of articles that became the basis for *Sight: An Exposition of the Principles of Monocular and Binocular Vision.* Published in 1881, it was the first full treatment of the subject in America. LeConte also continued to work on a book that appeared in 1873 as *Religion and Science.* In that work he endeavored to show that no significant conflicts exist between the two fields, and he indicated his emerging view of the validity of the theory of evolution. Meanwhile, in 1869, his concern over political conditions in South Carolina led him to follow his brother John to the University of California. During his tenure of three decades there, LeConte published scores of articles on many subjects, especially geology and the theory of evolution. He also published other books, the most influential of which were *Elements of Geology* and *Evolution and Its Relation to Religious Thought.* The former, published in 1877 and revised four times thereafter, became a widely used college textbook. The latter, published in 1888 and revised in 1891, solidified LeConte's position as a leading advocate of harmonizing Christian beliefs with the theory of evolution.

Immensely popular as a teacher and a founding member of the Sierra Club, LeConte was elected to the National Academy of Sciences in 1875. He served as president of the American Association for the Advancement of Science in 1891 and of the Geological Society of America in 1896. LeConte completed his autobiography shortly before his death on July 6, 1901, while on a camping trip in Yosemite. LESTER D. STEPHENS

Armes, W. D., ed. *The Autobiography of Joseph LeConte.* New York: D. Appleton, 1903.

Stephens, Lester D. *Joseph LeConte: Gentle Prophet of Evolution.* Baton Rouge: Louisiana State University Press, 1982.

Lee, Robert Greene (1886–1978). Clergyman. Lee was born on November 11, 1886, in York County, the son of David Ayers and Sarah Bennett. He was baptized (1898) and ordained (1910) in the Fort Mill Baptist Church. He graduated from Furman University in 1913 and married Bula Gentry that same year. The couple had one daughter and one son.

After serving several smaller pastorates in South Carolina, in 1922 Lee went to the First Baptist Church of New Orleans, where he stayed until 1925. He returned briefly to Charleston to serve the Citadel Square congregation, but in 1927 he went to Memphis, Tennessee, to become pastor of the Bellevue Baptist Church, and he remained there until he retired in 1960. Tennessee was at that time more fertile ground than South Carolina for the brand of fundamentalist Baptist theology for which Lee became famous. His fiery preaching style was well suited to the premillennialist message of his widely known sermon entitled "Payday Someday," which he is said to have preached more than twelve hundred times. He produced numerous sermon collections and was an internationally recognized religious figure. He served three terms (1948–1951) as president of the Southern Baptist Convention. His inspirational message caused many to look for an immanent apocalypse, and that expectation fostered the growth of the fundamentalist movement within the Southern Baptist Convention. Thus, Lee's ideas would eventually return home to South Carolina in the form of the fundamentalist movement that controlled the South Carolina Baptist Convention by the 1990s. Lee died in Memphis on July 20, 1978. His famous sermon, "Payday Someday," is still widely distributed. HELEN LEE TURNER

English, E. Schuyler. *Robert G. Lee, a Chosen Vessel.* Grand Rapids, Mich.: Zondervan, 1949.

Lee, Rudolph Edward (1876–1959). Architect, educator. For more than fifty years Rudolph E. Lee was virtually synonymous with the teaching and practice of architecture at Clemson College. He was born on March 12, 1876, in Anderson, the son of Thomas and Louise Lee. He completed two years at the South Carolina Military Academy (the Citadel) before transferring to Clemson in 1893. Lee received a B.S. in engineering with the college's first graduating class in 1896. By 1898 he was instructor in drawing in the engineering department at Clemson. After postgraduate work at Cornell and the University of Pennsylvania, he was promoted to associate professor and placed at the head of the Drawing and Designing Division. He married Mary Louise Eggleston, and his only child, a daughter, was born in 1902.

In 1907, in association with W. M. Riggs, Lee took on his first design project at Clemson, an expansion of one of the college barracks. Four years later Lee was elected the official architect of Clemson College. In 1912 he became a full professor and was placed in charge of the first course in architectural engineering. In 1913 Lee received his first prestigious commission: designing a new Young Men's Christian Association for Clemson (later renamed Holtzendorf Hall). The work remains his most complete and successful architectural design. While its exterior has a traditional Italian Renaissance style, many interior details were daringly contemporary, including a curved, cantilevered balcony and open steel pipe railings.

In 1915 Lee involved himself in a statewide campaign for better schools and school safety. His activities led to his appointment to the State Board of Architectural Examiners, a position he held for more than thirty years. He served as chairman of the board from 1933 to 1948.

In 1925 Lee renovated Sikes Hall to serve as the college library, designed the Sloan Store in downtown Clemson, and remodeled Holy Trinity Church. Between 1927 and 1939 Lee designed Riggs Hall (1927–1928), the Fike Field House (1929–1932), the new barracks (1935–1936), Long Hall (1936–1937), and the J. E. Sirrine Textile Building (1936–1937). These buildings represent Lee's mature style, with symmetry in plan and details including multicolored brick, limestone banding and sills, wide eaves with brackets and concealed gutters, and orange tile hip roofs. Just below the eaves Lee created elaborate mosaics that are a distinctive hallmark of his work. The five buildings define the character of Clemson and have been consciously emulated in several new building projects.

In the 1930s Lee also built the architecture program at Clemson. He had received the first master of architecture degree in 1928 and was referred to as the head of the Department of Architecture in 1935. He established a strong relationship with the state chapter of the American Institute of Architects, which led to the formation of the Clemson Architectural Foundation in 1940.

Lee retired in 1948. In 1955 he was made an emeritus member of the American Institute of Architects. The gallery in the School of Architecture was named for him just a few days before his death on October 23, 1959. He was buried in Christ Church Cemetery, Greenville. In 1966 the entire new architecture building was named for Lee. ROBERT W. BAINBRIDGE

Bainbridge, Robert W. "Rudolph E. Lee and Architecture at Clemson." In *Campus Preservation and Clemson Historic Resources.* Clemson, S.C.: Clemson University College of Architecture, Arts and Humanities, Department of Planning and Landscape Architecture, 1995.

Bryan, Wright. *Clemson: An Informal History of the University, 1889–1979.* Columbia, S.C.: R. L. Bryan, 1979.

Wells, John E., and Robert E. Dalton. *The South Carolina Architects, 1885–1935: A Biographical Directory.* Richmond, Va.: New South Architectural Press, 1992.

Lee, Samuel J. (1844–1895). Legislator, lawyer. Lee was born on November 27, 1844, on the plantation of Samuel J. McGowan in Abbeville District. His mother was a free black woman. Lee asserted that his father was a Samuel J. Lee of Charleston, but no such person appears in any census records, and some historians have opined that McGowan was his father. At age sixteen, Lee accompanied McGowan in the Civil War, and he said that he was wounded at Second Manassas in 1862 and again near Hanover Junction in 1864. McGowan was a Confederate general and later a South Carolina Supreme Court justice. While there is no official record of Lee's service in the Confederate army, he was photographed with McGowan's regiment armed and in uniform.

After the war, Lee farmed in Abbeville and soon entered politics. He served on the Edgefield County commission in 1868. That same year he was elected to the General Assembly, where he represented Edgefield County from 1868 to 1871 and Aiken County from 1872 to 1874. In 1872 Lee became the first African American elected Speaker of the South Carolina House of Representatives. Two years later he left the legislature and ran unsuccessfully for attorney general. Lee left a trail of scandal in the wake of his political career. He had served as counsel to the legislative committee conducting the investigation that led to the state treasurer Francis Cardozo's impeachment trial in 1874. In 1875 Lee was convicted of issuing fraudulent checks as an Aiken County commissioner. In 1877 he was indicted on numerous counts of public corruption, but in exchange for his testimony against Francis Cardozo, he was granted immunity from prosecution. Lee was again charged with public corruption in Aiken County in 1879, but the charges were dropped.

After relocating to Charleston, Lee began to practice law and went on to become one of the state's most successful black lawyers. Lee was a member of the South Carolina Bar beginning in 1872, and his connections with McGowan and his cooperation with the white establishment in post-Reconstruction South Carolina may have contributed to his legal success. While Lee was a man of little education, he was known for his oratory and legal acumen. He had an unprecedented twenty-seven appearances before the state supreme court, winning nine. While not a political leader after Reconstruction, Lee was active in Republican Party politics and spoke frequently at party functions. He was appointed a general in the state "colored" militia in 1891 and served until his death in Charleston on April 1, 1895. Upon learning of his death, the U.S. Circuit Court adjourned. Six thousand people attended his funeral. He was buried, with military honors, in Friendly Union Cemetery, Charleston. W. LEWIS BURKE

Oldfield, John. "The African American Bar in South Carolina, 1877–1915." In *At Freedom's Door: African American Founding Fathers and Lawyers in Reconstruction South Carolina,* edited by James Lowell Underwood and W. Lewis Burke, Jr. Columbia: University of South Carolina Press, 2000.

Vandervelde, Isabel. *Biography of Samuel Jones Lee.* Aiken, S.C.: Art Studio Press, 1997.

Lee, Stephen Dill (1833–1908). Soldier. Lee was born in Charleston on September 22, 1833, the son of Dr. Thomas Lee, a physician, and Caroline Allison. His family was distantly related to the Lees of Virginia. In 1835 the family moved to Abbeville District. In 1850 Lee received an appointment to the U.S. Military Academy at West Point, where he graduated seventeenth of forty-six in the class of 1854. After seven years of service in artillery and staff positions, he resigned in February 1861 to enter Confederate service. As a member of General P. G. T. Beauregard's staff, he was sent to seek the surrender of Fort Sumter both before and after the bombardment. Lee was then elected captain of the artillery battery of the Hampton Legion, but the late delivery of its cannon prevented the battery from traveling with the legion to First Manassas. In autumn the legion added additional artillery and Lee was promoted to major. Throughout the spring and summer of 1862, he received additional promotions for his leadership and artillery skills during the Peninsular campaign, the Seven Days' campaign, Second Manassas, and Sharpsburg.

Promoted to brigadier general, Lee was sent west to command artillery as the Confederacy attempted to stop the Federals from seizing control of the Mississippi River. He gained a decisive victory over General William T. Sherman at Chickasaw Bayou (December 29, 1862), led an infantry brigade at Champion's Hill (May 16, 1862), and participated in the defense of Vicksburg, where he was captured on July 4, 1863. After being exchanged he was promoted to major general and placed in command of all cavalry in Mississippi and Tennessee. In July 1864 Lee was promoted to lieutenant general and given Hood's Corps in the Army of Tennessee, then defending Atlanta. His corps fought at Ezra Church (July 28, 1864), then lost heavily at Jonesboro (August 31, 1864) as Atlanta began to fall. In the subsequent Nashville campaign, Lee suffered a leg wound in December 1864. During his recuperation in Columbus, Mississippi, he married Regina Lilly Harrison of that city on February 8, 1865. The couple would have one child. After recovering from his wound, Lee returned to duty in the final battles in North Carolina.

After the war Lee returned to Mississippi, where he farmed and dabbled in the insurance business. In 1878 he was elected to the Mississippi Senate, and two years later he became the first president of the Mississippi Agricultural and Mechanical College (later Mississippi State University). In 1890 he entered the race for governor but withdrew at the request of his board of trustees. That same year he refused an offer to become president of Clemson College in his home state of South Carolina. He served for ten years as president of the Mississippi Historical Society, and from that position he assisted in creating the Mississippi Department of Archives and History, chairing its board of trustees for six years. In 1889 he was involved in the founding of the United Confederate Veterans organization, and in 1895 he helped to organize the Vicksburg National Military Park Association and served as its first president. Lee died in Vicksburg on May 28, 1908, and was buried in Friendship Cemetery, Columbus, Mississippi. DEWITT BOYD STONE, JR.

Freeman, Douglas Southall. *Lee's Lieutenants: A Study in Command.* 3 vols. New York: Scribner's, 1942–1944.

Hattaway, Herman. *General Stephen D. Lee.* Jackson: University Press of Mississippi, 1976.

Lipscomb, Dabney. "General Stephen D. Lee: His Life, Character, and Services." *Publications of the Mississippi Historical Society* 10 (1909): 13–33.

Lee County (410 sq. miles; 2000 pop. 20,119). By an act of the General Assembly in 1897, Lee County was created from portions of Sumter, Darlington, and Kershaw Counties and named in honor of General Robert E. Lee. The movement to create a new county came from the northeast section of Sumter County in a region known as Old Salem, whose residents generally supported the political machine of Benjamin R. Tillman. To meet the constitutional size requirement, additional land had to be taken from other counties. Neighboring Darlington County contested the legality of the act, and the state supreme court subsequently annulled it on the grounds that the commissioners of elections had not certified the election. After waiting the required four years for a new election, the majority of area citizens voted in favor of the new county on February 25, 1902. Again the election was contested, and it was not until December 15, 1902, that the supreme court ruled that all requirements had been met and that Bishopville would be the county seat. Residents of the new county celebrated with speeches and by firing a Civil War cannon that had been brought up from the bank of Lynches River. Although natural boundaries were mentioned in the act, the old roads and lines surveyed in 1898 were used to form the new county. In 1914 a small area of land was restored to Sumter County. Another section was returned to Kershaw County in 1921. Since then the boundaries have remained the same.

The first court convened in the Bishopville Opera House on March 2, 1903. The Atlanta architects Edwards and Walters designed a new county courthouse, which the contractor Nicholas Itner completed in 1909. Four years later the people of Lee County

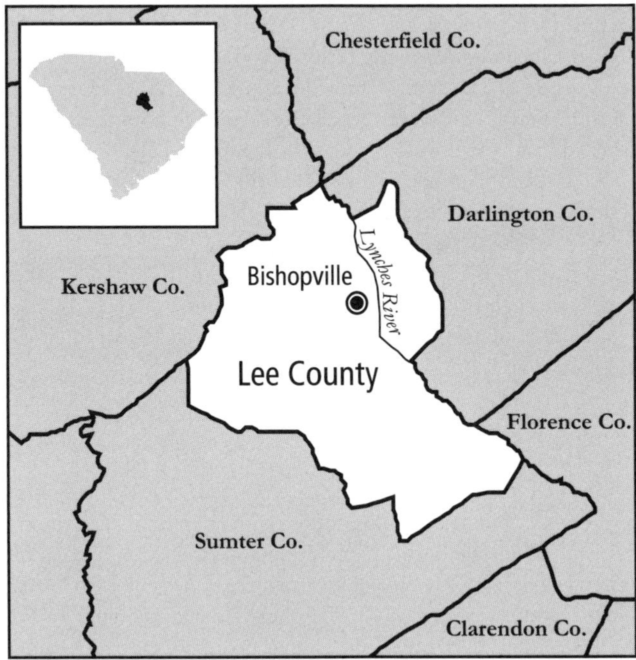

erected a granite monument in front of the courthouse to honor the Confederates who died in the war. Adding to the courthouse memorials, the Lynches River cannon was mounted on a concrete pedestal. County government took a council-administrator form, with a council comprised of seven members elected in a general election and representing specific districts.

Throughout its existence Lee County has been an agricultural community and sometimes is referred to as the "Garden Spot of the Carolinas." Cotton has been the leading crop, and Lee County was the state's largest producer of the staple at the end of the twentieth century. In the early 1900s the county was a major horse and mule market. During the Depression of the 1930s, the federal government purchased 12,500 acres in Lee County to relocate displaced farmers. Named Ashwood, the settlement grew to over twelve hundred residents before poor harvests and a withdrawal of government support forced the abandonment of the project in 1944. With the diversification of farming after World War II, county farmers began to work more than one crop. Soybeans, peanuts, and corn enjoyed increased production, with wheat and cattle gaining in importance as well. Many farmers began to plant small quantities of tobacco. After decades of decline, the horse industry enjoyed renewed growth, while poultry (chickens, turkeys, and quail) claimed a growing share of Lee County's agricultural production.

Many Lee County natives achieved both statewide and national recognition. Mary McLeod Bethune, born in 1875 near Mayesville, became a nationally recognized African American educator and leader. Ellison D. Smith grew up on his family's plantation, Tanglewood, near Lynchburg. First elected to the U.S. Senate in 1908, "Cotton Ed" Smith became a colorful and controversial figure who championed agricultural interests in the South. Corporal James Davison Heriot was posthumously awarded the Congressional Medal of Honor "for conspicuous gallantry and intrepidity above and beyond the call of duty" in the fighting at Vauz Andigny, France, on October 11, 1918. Pearl Fryar's Topiary Garden is a carefully sculpted work created by the skill and artistry of a self-taught topiary sculptor. Fryar appeared on national television and in several international publications for his interesting insights and stories that complement his garden.

Lee County abounds with community events and institutions to commemorate its past and present. The county is the site of the Annual Lynchburg Magnolia Festival, as well as the Lynches River Festival held at Lee State Natural Area in May. Every October the Cotton Festival in Bishopville celebrates the county's cotton heritage, while a weekend-long festival of the life and achievements of Mary McLeod Bethune is held annually at the Mary McLeod Bethune Memorial Park. Cotton is also the unifying theme of the South Carolina Cotton Trail, which starts in Bishopville and winds through Lee and four other counties. A driving tour takes visitors through historic towns that cotton built, as well as through two centuries of mansions, scientific breakthroughs, beautiful fields, and natural areas.

Industry grew in importance in the latter decades of the twentieth century. Two industrial parks were located near the Interstate 20 exits. The county government gained a probusiness reputation and coordinated its efforts at regional economic development with neighboring counties. Leading industrial employers in the county came to include the textile giant Burlington Industries and South Atlantic Canning. Other major employers included the Lee Correctional Institute, located south of Bishopville and operated by the South Carolina Department of Corrections; and the Lee County Landfill administered by Allied Waste Industries, whose operations increased rail traffic through Bishopville and necessitated a major upgrading of the roadbed and track. JANSON L. COX

Gregorie, Anne King. *History of Sumter County, South Carolina.* Sumter, S.C.: Library Board of Sumter County, 1954.

Lee County Bicentennial Commission. *Lee County, South Carolina: A Bicentennial Look at Its Land, People, Heritage & Future.* N.p.: Reeves, 1976.

Lee County Chamber of Commerce. *Lee County, South Carolina: Past and Present.* Dallas, Tex.: Taylor Publishing, 1992.

Leevy, Carroll Moton (b. 1920). Physician, educator. Leevy was born on October 13, 1920, in Columbia to Isaac Leevy and Mary Kirkland. His parents pursued various business ventures, notably a funeral home and ambulance service. While working at the mortuary, the younger Leevy discerned that many African Americans' deaths were due to inadequate health care, as well as poor medical facilities. In May 1937 he graduated with honors from Booker T. Washington High School in Columbia.

Leevy subsequently enrolled in premedical studies at Fisk University in Nashville, Tennessee. Although gaining various academic scholarships, he also performed clerical duties with the National Youth Administration (NYA), a federal New Deal agency. While an undergraduate, Leevy was inducted into Phi Beta Kappa. By 1941 he had graduated summa cum laude from Fisk.

Barred by his race from receiving advanced medical training in South Carolina, Leevy was admitted to the University of Michigan Medical School. In 1942 he was appointed by President Franklin D. Roosevelt to the NYA's National Advisory Committee. This special panel was created to document education inadequacies and improper health care due to race prejudice within NYA facilities. Leevy also enrolled in the U.S. Army Specialized Training Program. Along with a monthly stipend, Leevy gained valuable clinical experience. During his years at the University of Michigan, he gained a reputation as a skilled diagnostician. Consequently he decided to specialize in medical research.

On gaining his M.D. in 1944, Leevy fulfilled his residency requirement at the Jersey City Medical Center in Newark, New Jersey, where he observed that his white colleagues frequently interacted poorly with African American patients. Meanwhile he conducted notable research with changes in fluid metabolism during heart and liver failures, publishing his findings in the *Journal of the American Medical Association.* He further investigated the relationship between diabetes and chronic alcoholism.

Leevy served two stints with the U.S. Navy, achieving the rank of lieutenant commander. From 1954 to 1956 he was stationed at the St. Albans Naval Hospital in Virginia, continuing his extensive research into liver diseases (hepatology). Leevy's work expanded medical knowledge into the basic functions of the liver, as well as its primary disorders. He joined the medical faculty of the New Jersey Medical School (now the University of Medicine and Dentistry of New Jersey) in 1957 and served as chair of the medical department from 1975 to 1991. In 1984 Leevy was named director of the Sammy Davis Jr. National Liver Center, and in 1990 he became director of the New Jersey Medical School Liver Center.

On February 4, 1956, Leevy married Ruth Barboza, a research chemist at the Harvard Medical School, where Leevy had held a research fellowship. They have two children.

Throughout his career Leevy has enjoyed an international reputation as a hepatologist. He has written six books on liver disease and numerous articles for scholarly medical journals, holds two patents, and has shared his extensive knowledge with thousands of medical students as a teacher. He has been the recipient of numerous academic and professional honors. MILES S. RICHARDS

Kessler, James H., et al., eds. *Distinguished African American Scientists of the 20th Century.* Phoenix: Oryx, 1996.

Leevy, Isaac Samuel (1876–1968). Businessman, political activist. Leevy was born on May 3, 1876, in Antioch, Kershaw County. He graduated from Mather Academy in Camden and Hampton Institute in Virginia. After teaching school for a year in Lancaster, South Carolina, he moved to Columbia in 1907. Two years later, on June 23, 1910, he married Mary E. Kirkland, a fellow Kershaw County resident. The couple had four children.

In Columbia, Leevy opened a tailoring shop in 1907, and within three years this business blossomed into the Leevy Department Store, which he ran until 1930. Over the course of his career, Leevy was a founder and president of Victory Savings Bank and directed various business enterprises, including commercial hog farming, furniture sales, an auto repair shop, a beauty salon, a real estate company, and a service station. As the first African American–owned gas station in Columbia, Leevy's station was an important stop for black travelers who were barred from white facilities during the Jim Crow era. His most enduring business was Leevy's Funeral Home.

As a strong proponent of minority education in a state that underfunded segregated black schools, Leevy pushed for the creation of Waverly Elementary School, Leevy Graded School (now Carver Elementary), and Booker T. Washington High School in Columbia. In higher education Leevy helped to found the graduate school at South Carolina State College and served as a trustee of Claflin College.

Leevy faced his toughest challenges in politics. As a black Republican in a state then dominated by white Democrats, he ran unsuccessfully for the General Assembly twice and four times for Congress (in 1916, 1918, 1946, and 1954). In the 1940s Leevy battled the all-white South Carolina Democratic primary. "We are asking for the opportunity to exercise political rights as guaranteed by the United States Constitution," Leevy asserted in 1944. "We are asking for representation in the corporation to which we pay taxes. . . . [We] want a share in the government. All we ask is for a man's chance."

A staunch civil rights advocate, Leevy helped found the Columbia branch of the National Association for the Advancement of Colored People (NAACP) and served on the board of directors for the Southern Christian Leadership Council (SCLC), directed by Martin Luther King, Jr. After half a century of Republican activism, Leevy became a Democrat in 1964. Passage of the Voting Rights Act the next year ushered in a new era of biracial politics in South Carolina that enabled Leevy's grandson, I. S. Leevy Johnson, to become one of the first African American state legislators since Reconstruction.

Leevy died on December 9, 1968, and was buried in Lincoln Cemetery, Columbia. Though he did not live to see his grandson enter the General Assembly in 1970, the election was a fitting testimonial to Leevy's quest for minority political representation in South Carolina. STEVE ESTES

Newby, I. A. *Black Carolinians: A History of Blacks in South Carolina from 1895 to 1968.* Columbia: University of South Carolina Press, 1973.

Legal education. South Carolina has had a practicing bar since the 1690s. While the identities of the first lawyers are somewhat obscure, it is presumed that they were educated in England. Although never adopted, the Fundamental Constitutions prohibited anyone from representing another person in court for a fee, but lawyers were certainly practicing by 1699 and the profession soon grew.

Until 1868 the legal profession in South Carolina was divided between lawyers who practiced in the law courts and solicitors who practiced in the court of chancery. In the simplest terms, law courts heard those cases deriving from the common law (criminal cases, jury trials, actions for recovery of money or personal property), while the chancery courts were presided over by chancellors (judges) who heard matters for which equitable relief could be granted (such as foreclosure of a mortgage) or for an injunction to prevent some threatened action. This law and equity division was similar to the British system, except that South Carolina's legal profession was not divided into barristers and solicitors. In the English system, solicitors prepared the cases (briefed them) and barristers argued or tried the cases in both the law and the equity courts. In South Carolina, the attorneys-at-law prepared and argued their cases in the law courts and the solicitors prepared and argued their cases in the equity courts. Many attorneys were also licensed as solicitors, but since there were separate education requirements, not all attorneys and solicitors practiced in both courts.

A high percentage of members of the colonial bar of South Carolina were educated at the Inns of Court in London and consequently were barristers. While the Charleston Bar was dominated by those educated at the Inns, clearly some legal practitioners were reading law and were admitted by examination of the courts under a court rule adopted in 1712. Even on the eve of the Revolution, twenty-four of thirty-four lawyers in Charleston had been educated at the Inns. The pressure for a highly educated bar started early. In 1721 the Commons House of Assembly decried the poor quality of solicitors and lawyers. In 1722 the chancery court ruled that for admission as a solicitor one had to have been a member of one of the four law colleges in London for five years and attended eight sessions of commons. It is clear, however, that these rules were not strictly applied. For example, the court of chancery admitted individuals who had read law and apparently not studied at the Inns or colleges in England.

After the Revolution, in 1785 the South Carolina General Assembly passed legislation allowing anyone who had resided in the state for four years to be admitted as an attorney-at-law upon examination by the judges of the court of common pleas. This made reading of the law the primary means of education for lawyers since the ties to England and its formal system for education of lawyers had been severed. In 1796 legislation strengthened the standards by requiring three years of reading the law by college graduates or four years for nongraduates for admission. In 1801 those who had read law out of state could be admitted. Reading law would remain the only means for admission as a lawyer or a solicitor until after the Civil War.

Reading law meant just that. The student was required to apprentice under a licensed member of the profession and was expected to read law under the tutelage of the lawyer or solicitor. The chief reading was *Blackstone's Commentaries,* which was one of the most cited sources by the South Carolina courts. However, by 1842 the Law Court of Appeals recommended the reading of ten treatises and twenty-seven statutes and required that students be tested on these materials by the court upon application for admission. Leading members of the bar, such as U.S. Supreme Court Justice William Johnson and U.S. Senator John C. Calhoun, read law. Unlike most lawyers, however, Calhoun also studied law at one of the few law schools in the country, Gould and Reeves in Litchfield, Connecticut.

Formal legal education was slow in coming. An attempt in 1823 to establish a professorship in law at South Carolina College failed in the General Assembly, and a private venture by some members of the Charleston bar, the Forensic Club, ceased after only two lectures in 1826. Formal legal education became available for the first time in 1866. The University of South Carolina (USC) established a law school, appointing Alexander Cheves Haskell as professor. The law school had a turbulent first decade, but it graduated thirty-nine students, including the first eleven black graduates of a public law school in the United States. The university and the law school were closed after the overthrow of the Reconstruction state government in 1877 and then reopened on an all-white basis in 1884. African Americans responded by opening law schools at Claflin College and Allen University. Claflin's law school operated only a short time, but Allen kept its law school open until 1905. The University of South Carolina School of Law has operated continuously since 1884 but was not desegregated again until 1964. While the USC law school admitted its first woman in 1898, it did not have its first female graduate until after 1918, when the South Carolina Bar admitted its first woman, Miss James Perry, a law graduate of the University of California.

The University of South Carolina dominated legal education in the state. In 1886 its graduates were granted admission to the bar without taking an examination, a practice known as the "diploma privilege." In 1910 the faculty expanded from one to three, and the curriculum for the first time included statutory law in addition to common law. In 1922 the school increased its faculty size again, strengthened its entrance requirements, and expanded its curriculum from two years to three years. The school was finally accredited by the American Association of Law Schools in 1924.

Accreditation pressures doomed the only competition USC faced in the 1920s. Furman University operated a law school for eleven years before closing it in 1932 for financial reasons. It had forty-two graduates. South Carolina State University (then the Colored Normal, Industrial, Agricultural, and Mechanical College of South Carolina) opened a law school in 1947 in response to a lawsuit that tried to force the desegregation of the USC School of Law. It operated until 1966 and had fifty-one graduates, including two of the most accomplished lawyers in the state's history, Chief Justice Ernest Finney and U.S. District Court Judge Matthew J. Perry.

Following national trends, on March 1, 1958, the S.C. Supreme Court prohibited reading law and required that all candidates for admission to the bar must be law school graduates. The University of South Carolina law school graduates lost their diploma privilege in 1951, a year after South Carolina State had produced its first graduates. Law school graduation and passage of the state bar examination have been the norm for admission since the 1950s.

Law school education has continued to evolve. The three-year curriculum still covers common law, constitutional law, legal history, and code courses and also includes new and innovative courses such as technology law, health law, environmental law, and a wide range of skills and clinical courses. As of 2004 USC was again not alone in providing legal education in the state. That year a new law school, the Charleston School of Law, opened in Charleston as a private, proprietary law school. W. LEWIS BURKE

Hollis, Daniel Walker. *University of South Carolina.* 2 vols. Columbia: University of South Carolina Press, 1951–1956.

Rogers, George C. *Generations of Lawyers: A History of the South Carolina Bar.* Columbia: South Carolina Bar Foundation, 1992.

Underwood, James Lowell, and W. Lewis Burke, Jr., eds. *At Freedom's Door: African American Founding Fathers and Lawyers in Reconstruction South Carolina.* Columbia: University of South Carolina Press, 2000.

Legaré, Hugh Swinton (1797–1843). Legislator, U.S. attorney general, writer, intellectual. Legaré was born in Charleston on January 2, 1797, of Scots and Huguenot ancestry, the son of Solomon Legaré and Mary Splatt Swinton. A childhood illness left him with stunted limbs. As a boy he studied under the great schoolmaster Moses Waddel at Willington Academy before entering the new South Carolina College as a sophomore in 1811 at the age of fourteen. He was valedictorian of the class of 1814. From 1818 to 1820 he studied abroad—French and Italian in Paris, and jurisprudence in Edinburgh.

Legaré enjoyed successful public and private careers. He studied law in Charleston, served in the General Assembly (1820–1822, 1824–1830), managed a plantation on Johns Island, and served as attorney general of South Carolina from 1830 to 1832. His services, however, were not limited to his native state. In 1832 Legaré was appointed chargé d'affaires in Belgium, and he was elected to Congress in 1836 as a Union Democrat. He was appointed U.S. attorney general in 1841 in John Tyler's cabinet. On Daniel Webster's resignation in 1843, Legaré became secretary of state ad interim, but he would die within three months. He was an effective attorney general who was for states' rights but against nullification.

With Stephen Elliott, Legaré founded the *Southern Review* (1828–1832), which became the model for all subsequent Charleston magazines and was popularly known as Legaré's magazine. He supplied much of its content. At the time of his death Legaré had enough manuscripts for a two-volume edition of his works, which were edited by his sister, Mary Legaré, and published posthumously in 1845. Neither Legaré's works nor his magazine seem quite deserving of the extravagant praise they received during his lifetime. His best-known *Southern Review* essay, "On Classical Learning" (February 1828), made the case for the classics as a staple of the education of the southern gentleman and professional man. His literary taste was for the classics and eighteenth-century neoclassicism; he shared the doubts about the romantics that prevailed among Charleston critics well into the century. He believed that Greek and Latin should be studied from the eighth year through the sixteenth.

The *Southern Review* exemplified the conservatism of southern professional men, especially in Charleston, beginning with issues such as states' rights and high tariffs and extending to agrarianism and slavery. But there were two issues that divided conservatives, unionism and nullification, the latter opposed by Legaré.

As literary critics, Charleston conservatives such as Legaré were slower in accepting romantic theory and practice than were those in New York and Boston, although Legaré did express occasional praise for Lord Byron, Walter Scott, and William Cullen Bryant. South Carolina had a tradition-based society to which Legaré was a leading contributor. A lifelong bachelor, Legaré died in Boston on June 20, 1843. He was buried in Magnolia Cemetery, Charleston. RICHARD CALHOUN

Legaré, Hugh Swinton. *Writings of Hugh Swinton Legaré.* 2 vols. Edited by Mary Swinton Legaré Bullen. 1845–1846. Reprint, New York: Da Capo, 1970.

O'Brien, Michael A. *A Character of Hugh Legaré.* Knoxville: University of Tennessee Press, 1985.

Rhea, Linda. *Hugh Swinton Legaré: A Charleston Intellectual.* Chapel Hill: University of North Carolina Press, 1934.

Legaré, James Mathewes (1823–1859). Writer, painter, inventor. Born on November 26, 1823, in Charleston, Legaré was the son of John D. Legaré, an agricultural editor, and Mary Doughty Mathewes. Although the family name was a prominent one, his particular branch was neither prosperous nor well connected. Legaré graduated from the College of Charleston in 1842 and spent sixteen months studying languages and literature at St. Mary's College in Baltimore, Maryland. During this period he became interested in composing verse and painting oil landscapes. One of his more significant poetic efforts was an elegy, "On the Death of a Kinsman," written in 1843 after learning of the untimely death of Hugh Swinton Legaré, a distant cousin. At least two of his paintings, *Fisherman's Cottage* and *Kids in the Cornfield,* survive and hang in Charleston.

While still in Baltimore, Legaré showed his satiric side by concocting an impressive-sounding but phony family genealogy and passing it off as real. When the hoax was revealed, his aristocratic relatives were outraged. The controversy attracted widespread attention and was reported in newspapers as far away as Boston. It may or may not have prompted Harriet Beecher Stowe, who knew of the family, to take their surname, pronounced "luh-gree," for that of her lowborn villain in *Uncle Tom's Cabin* (1852).

Legaré returned to Charleston in mid-1843 and began studying law in the office of James L. Petigru. However, his interests lay not in law but rather in art and literature. He continued his painting and won praise for his work at local art exhibitions. He also began publishing poems in various literary magazines. By 1845 Legaré had accumulated enough verse to fill a slender book but could find no willing publisher. Nor could Legaré find relief from tuberculosis, which was gradually eroding his health. In 1846 his father moved the family to Aiken, where the dry air was more suitable to Legaré's convalescence.

Having abandoned his legal studies, Legaré sought to make a living writing verse for magazines. In 1848, still unable to find a publisher for his proposed book of verse, he paid William Ticknor and Company in Boston to print five hundred copies and distribute them to various booksellers around the country. He called his little book *Orta-Undis, and Other Poems,* and it was his first and only published volume. The poems, written in the classical lyric mode, celebrate love and nature. His most memorable poems, "To a Lily," "The Reaper," and "Haw-Blossoms," demonstrate his ability to capture unique details of nature with an arresting turn of phrase. Although his book received favorable reviews, the public ignored it. For a while Legaré turned to producing popular fiction, which earned him some income but little acclaim.

On March 20, 1850, Legaré married Anne C. Andrews of Augusta, Georgia, and the two settled in a cottage on his father's property in Aiken. A childless couple, they doted on each other. By this time Legaré had lost interest in writing and had turned his attention to experimenting with mechanical inventions. He received two U.S. patents, one for "plastic-cotton" and one for an improved ivory-frame composition for frame makers. Legaré died in Aiken on May 30, 1859, and was buried there in the cemetery of the St. Thaddeus Episcopal Church. ELLEN CHAMBERLAIN

Hubbell, Jay B. *The South in American Literature, 1607–1900.* Durham, N.C.: Duke University Press, 1954.

Wilkinson, C. P. Seabrook. "James Mathewes Legaré." In *Dictionary of Literary Biography.* Vol. 248, *Antebellum Writers in the South, Second Series,* edited by Kent Ljungquist. Detroit: Gale, 2001.

Leigh, Sir Egerton (ca. 1732–1781). Lawyer, jurist, councillor. In 1753, at about the age of twenty, Egerton Leigh immigrated to South Carolina with his father, Peter Leigh (who left his position as high bailiff of Westminster under charges of improper conduct to succeed Charles Pinckney as the colony's chief justice). With his father's political connections and a dearth of educated men in the colony, Leigh quickly procured some of the most lucrative and treasured offices in the colony—clerk of the court of common pleas, surveyor general, judge of the vice-admiralty court, judge of the court of chancery, and attorney general—within eight years after arriving in the province. Leigh also served as a justice of the peace, vestryman of St. Philip's, and assemblyman until his appointment to the Royal Council in 1759. Income from some of these offices, along with a lucrative law practice and marriage to the heiress Martha Bremar on January 15, 1756, made Leigh one of the wealthiest men in South Carolina and vaulted him into membership in the local elite. Through ability, hard work, and an "unblemished reputation," Leigh cultivated a promising career and demonstrated himself as one of the most able crown servants in South Carolina prior to the Revolutionary War.

But Leigh's meteoric rise was followed by an even quicker downfall. Openly admitting that "I am a downright *Placeman* . . . and that I owe more to the Royal Favor, than any merit I possess can justly claim," Leigh gave earnest and unquestioned support to the British government's colonial policies. To that end, he was the only member of the Charleston Bar to oppose reopening the courts during the Stamp Act crisis without the offensive stamped paper, an action which endeared him to the crown but severely damaged his local reputation and law practice. While serving as judge of the vice-admiralty court, Leigh aggressively enforced imperial trade regulations in four highly publicized court cases; in doing so, he offended several wealthy merchants, including his friend Henry Laurens, with whom he became involved in an acerbic public imbroglio that further damaged Leigh's already-declining reputation. Desperate to regain respect in Carolina society, Leigh sailed for England in 1771 in hopes of obtaining a peerage. His pleadings with the king's advisers earned him a baronetcy but not a peerage. Whatever added esteem Leigh received with this royal benefaction he quickly destroyed in 1772 by entering into a scandalous affair with his wife's young sister, who became pregnant.

In 1773 Leigh further alienated himself from the local elite by using his authority as president of the Royal Council to convince the other councillors, nearly all foreign-born placemen, not to approve a much-needed tax bill until the Commons House rescinded the £1,500 given to the English polemicist and crown critic John Wilkes in 1769. When fellow councillors William Henry Drayton and his father, John, objected vehemently in the local press to the council's stonewalling on this important legislation, Leigh ordered the printer Thomas Powell arrested. In response the younger Drayton repeatedly called Leigh a "damn fool" in the council; later Edward Rutledge, Powell's attorney, denounced Leigh unmercifully in open court. Leigh publicly defended his conduct, but this only reinforced his reputation as an arrogant and obsequious placeman who put loyalty to the crown before the colony's welfare. A pariah in Carolina society, Leigh left for England, where he made an unsuccessful attempt to gain a post in one of the northern provinces. After the conquest of Charleston in 1780, Leigh returned to South Carolina, where he became a member of the military commandant's advisory board, the board of police, and an intendant (mayor) of the capital. He recommended to the ministry that it order civil government restored to the conquered province and that, because of his vast political experience there, it appoint him governor. The ministry did neither. Leigh died in Charleston shortly thereafter, on September 15, 1781, from an unknown illness. KEITH KRAWCZYNSKI

Bellot, H. Hale. "The Leighs in South Carolina." *Transactions of the Royal Historical Society,* 5th ser., 6 (1956): 161–87.

Calhoon, Robert M., and Robert M. Weir. "The Scandalous History of Sir Egerton Leigh." *William and Mary Quarterly,* 3d ser., 26 (January 1969): 47–74.

Edgar, Walter, and N. Louise Bailey, eds. *Biographical Directory of the South Carolina House of Representatives.* Vol. 2, *The Commons House of Assembly, 1692–1775.* Columbia: University of South Carolina Press, 1977.

Greene, Jack P., ed. *The Nature of Colony Constitutions: Two Pamphlets on the Wilkes Fund Controversy in South Carolina.* Columbia: University of South Carolina Press, 1970.

LeJau, Francis (ca. 1665–1717). Clergyman, educator. LeJau was born about 1665 in Angiers, France, of Huguenot parents. When the Edict of Nantes (the ruling that gave the Huguenots some freedom to exercise their religion) was revoked by King Louis XIV in 1685, LeJau fled France and French Protestantism for England and Anglicanism. He received his M.A. (1693), B.D. (1696), and D.D. (1700) from Trinity College, Dublin. Sometime before 1700 LeJau was a canon at St. Paul's Cathedral, London. In 1700 he left England for Antigua, in the West Indies, to be a missionary. In 1705 the Society for the Propagation of the Gospel (SPG) accepted LeJau as a missionary. He left the following year for South Carolina, where he was the first rector to serve the St. James Goose Creek Anglican parish. Next to the commissary (the representative of the bishop of London), LeJau became the most influential Anglican clergyman in South Carolina. When Commissary Gideon Johnson was absent in England or elsewhere, LeJau served St. Philip's Church, Charleston, a leading Anglican church in the South. He acted as deputy to the commissary.

LeJau became known for his work among African and Indian slaves. His interest in the unfortunate began when he was in Antigua and had two thousand slaves under his care. At Goose Creek he ran a school in his home and taught slaves to read. On Sundays he held special church services for Africans and Indians, encouraging slaves to maintain family ties and family fidelity. He also taught and prepared slaves for baptism and communion, actions which frequently provoked opposition from his white parishioners and the slaves' owners.

LeJau worked for the more humane treatment of slaves. He denounced the law that permitted the physical mutilation of runaway slaves and carried on a veritable crusade again brutality, immorality, and profaneness. In spite of his kindness, LeJau did not attempt to abolish slavery. A slaveowner himself, he accepted the institution and justified it on scriptural grounds. He required slaves at their baptism to publicly swear that they did not desire baptism out of some design to get free, but only for the salvation of their souls.

On July 31, 1717, Lejau was appointed rector of St. Philip's Church. At the same time he became the commissary of the bishop of London to South Carolina. Unfortunately, before he could assume these positions, LeJau died in Charleston on September 10, 1717. He was buried at the foot of the altar at Goose Creek Church. DONALD S. ARMENTROUT

Bolton, S. C. "South Carolina and the Reverend Doctor Francis LeJau: Southern Society and the Conscience of an Anglican Missionary." *Historical Magazine of the Protestant Episcopal Church* 40 (March 1971): 63–79.

Hirsch, Arthur Henry. "Reverend Francis LeJau, First Rector of St. James Church, Goose Creek." *Transactions of the Huguenot Society of South Carolina* 34 (1929): 25–43.

LeJau, Francis. *The Carolina Chronicle of Dr. Francis LeJau, 1706–1717.* Edited by Frank J. Klingberg. Berkeley: University of California Press, 1956.

Matteson, Robert S. "Francis LeJau in Ireland." *South Carolina Historical Magazine* 78 (April 1977): 83–91.

Pennington, Edgar Legare. "The Reverend Francis LeJau's Work among Indian and Negro Slaves." *Journal of Southern History* 1 (November 1935): 442–58.

Lesbians and gays. Until the U.S. Supreme Court decision in *Lawrence v. Texas* in June 2003, gays and lesbians in South Carolina legally did not enjoy the same rights as their heterosexual counterparts in society. While the 2003 ruling decriminalized homosexual acts between consenting adults, it did not signal the end of discrimination against homosexuals. Open discrimination against gays and lesbians has been evident in the Palmetto State almost from its founding. When the colonial government adopted English Common Law in 1712, it prohibited sodomy, saying "That if any man lieth with mankind as he lieth with a woman, they both shall suffer death." The General Assembly refined the statute in 1814, writing, "[The] detestable and abominable vice of buggery [sodomy] . . . be from henceforth adjudged felony . . . and that the offender's being hereof convicted by verdict, confession, or outlawry [unlawful flight to avoid prosecution], shall suffer such pains of death and losses and penalties of their goods." Fear of death and the stigma attached to being homosexual, without doubt, led many to hide their sexual identities, making their histories difficult to trace. A few early records, however, do exist to shed light on the plights of homosexuals.

In August 1810 newly elected South Carolina congressman John C. Calhoun wrote to his soon-to-be mother-in-law, Floride Bonneau Colhoun, about a common acquaintance, Wentworth Boisseau. Calhoun was "shocked beyond measure" to learn that his friend Boisseau had engaged in homosexual activity. Calhoun wrote to his mother-in-law: "A whole life of virtue could not restore his character. It is the first instance of that crime ever heard of in this part of the world. I cannot conceive how he contracted the odious habit, except, while a sailor to the West Indies." Though records do not exist to confirm Boisseau's fate, Calhoun's letter suggests that Boisseau was effectively exiled from this state and left to live "a life of contrition, to make his peace with heaven."

Sixteen years after Calhoun wrote to his mother-in-law about Boisseau, another written exchange provided a record of homosexuality in South Carolina. In May 1826 a young Thomas Jefferson Withers, who would become a noted defender of states' rights and a judge on the state court of appeals, wrote to his friend James H. Hammond, who would serve as governor of South Carolina and also as a U.S. senator, about his pleasures of sharing a bed with Hammond. In language that left little to the imagination, Withers urged Hammond to experiment further with homosexual activity. In his September 1826 response to Withers, the nineteen-year-old Hammond did not deny his dalliances with Withers. However, Hammond did exhibit more reservations about their behavior. Hammond expressed concern for what he saw as Withers's wantonness and encouraged his friend to consider marriage and heterosexual family life.

South Carolina, in 1869, was the last state to remove capital punishment for sodomy. Even the rescission of the death penalty did little to encourage gays and lesbians to live openly. In 1895 South Carolina adopted a constitutional amendment barring those convicted of sodomy from voting. (This was repealed in 1970.) While gay and lesbian communities began to coalesce in larger United States cities, such communities did not begin to form in South Carolina until the latter part of the twentieth century. There were individual exceptions to the typical closetedness of most homosexuals. Laura Towne and Ellen Murray, the first principals of the Penn School, founded in 1862 to educate freed African American slaves, were companions for forty years. Laura Bragg, who in 1909 became the first female director of the Charleston Museum, had a longtime relationship with Belle Heyward, which has been documented in their correspondence.

Though South Carolinians might occasionally have tolerated open examples of "Boston marriages," most South Carolinians simply preferred to ignore the existence of their gay and lesbian fellow citizens. Not until the mid- to late 1980s, when the AIDS crisis began to affect the state, were all citizens forced to deal with the issue. In 1989 the General Assembly introduced a bill that would allow the quarantining of people who carried HIV. Members of ACT-UP, a national anti-AIDS activist group, joined South Carolina and Atlanta activists to protest the General Assembly's action, and the bill did not pass.

Throughout most of the twentieth century, homosexuality remained a punishable felony in the state. At the time that the U.S. Supreme Court decriminalized sodomy in 2003, buggery, as it was referred to in the South Carolina code, was punishable by five years in prison or a fine. At the same time, laws banned the recognition of same-sex marriage and offered no legally recognized alternatives, and they did not address discrimination based on sexual orientation.

In spite of what gay and lesbian community members view as discrimination in the South Carolina legal code, they actively participate in political and social groups, including the Alliance for Full Acceptance, the South Carolina Equality Coalition, the South Carolina Gay and Lesbian Pride Movement, the South Carolina Gay and Lesbian Business Guild, and others. ROBERT L. ELLIS, JR.

Duberman, Martin. "'Writhing Bedfellows' in Antebellum South Carolina: Historical Interpretation and the Politics of Evidence." In *Hidden from History: Reclaiming the Gay and Lesbian Past,* edited by Martin Duberman, Martha Vicinus, and George Chauncey. New York: New American Library, 1989.

Sears, James T., and Louise A. Allen. "Museums, Friends, and Lovers in the New South: Laura's Web, 1909–1931." *Journal of Homosexuality* 40, no. 1 (2000): 105–44.

Towne, Laura. *Letters and Diary of Laura M. Towne.* Edited by Rupert Sargent Holland. 1912. Reprint, New York: Negro Universities Press, 1969.

Lettered olive. State shell. The lettered olive (*Oliva sayana*) was declared the official state shell in legislation approved by Governor Richard Riley on May 8, 1984. In the act, legislators described the South Carolina coast as "one of the most widely promoted areas . . . for recreation and tourism" and noted that shelling along the state's beaches had become "increasingly popular among residents as well as with the tourist trade."

The lettered olive is prolific on the South Carolina coast. Dr. Edmund Ravenel, a Charleston physician who attained international renown as a pioneer conchologist, first recognized the lettered olive in 1834. He assembled a famous collection of mollusks from the waters and wetlands of the Charleston area and published the catalog of this collection in 1834. That work contained descriptions of several new mollusks, including the lettered olive.

Oliva sayana is a predatory snail that lives in sandy environments from the intertidal zone down to twenty feet. It spends most of its time burrowing through the sand in search of prey. The shells are two to two and one-half inches in length and are colored grayish tan with brownish-purple zigzag bands. Their supposed resemblance to ancient Egyptian hieroglyphs gave rise to the name "lettered."

Lettered olive. Photograph by Phillip Jones. Courtesy, South Carolina Department of Natural Resources

The shell, much prized by collectors, is highly polished because the mollusk's mantle, or shell building tissue, is large and envelops the entire shell while the creature is burrowing, protecting it from corrosive sand. Lettered olives are sometimes seen on the surface of the sand at night, and it is believed that they can flap their mantle lobes and swim through the shallow water, increasing their predatory range. DAVID C. R. HEISSER

Abbott, R. Tucker. *American Seashells.* 2d ed. New York: Van Nostrand Reinhold, 1974.

Sanders, Albert E., and William D. Anderson, Jr. *Natural History Investigations in South Carolina from Colonial Times to the Present.* Columbia: University of South Carolina Press, 1999.

Stephens, Lester D. *Science, Race, and Religion in the American South: John Bachman and the Charleston Circle of Naturalists, 1815–1895.* Chapel Hill: University of North Carolina Press, 2000.

Lever, Asbury Francis (1875–1940). Congressman. Lever was born near Spring Hill, Lexington County, on January 5, 1875, the son of Asbury Francis Washington Lever, a successful farmer, and Mary Elvira Derrick. After graduating from Newberry College with honors in 1895, Lever taught school for two years before moving to Washington to work for Congressman J. William Stokes. Lever was graduated from Georgetown University Law School in 1899 and was admitted to the South Carolina Bar that same year. In 1911 he married Lucile Scurry Butler, and they eventually had two children. From 1896 to 1900 Lever served as a delegate to state Democratic Party conventions, and in 1900 he was elected to the South Carolina House of Representatives. Following the death of Congressman Stokes in July 1901, Lever was elected to the U.S. House of Representatives to fill the vacancy. He was subsequently reelected to the next eight Congresses.

Lever rose to become chairman of the powerful House Agriculture Committee. He authored or sponsored several important pieces of law that made him a major figure in pre–New Deal federal agricultural policy and earned him the title "grandfather of American agricultural legislation." Lever gained the respect and admiration of

President Woodrow Wilson for his loyalty and service and was noted among his colleagues in Congress for his skill in handling bills in committee and on the House floor.

In particular, Lever worked to foster a cooperative relationship between state and federal governments. The Cooperative Agricultural Extension Act (1914) directed federal money toward educational opportunities for farmers in the form of grants to agricultural colleges, which were then matched by state, county, and local funds. Coauthored by Georgia senator Hoke Smith and better known as the Smith-Lever Act, the act established the Cooperative Extension Service to disseminate agricultural research information and became a cornerstone of the land-grant university system. The Cotton Futures Act (1914) regulated cotton exchanges and set government standards for price grading that removed the most egregious abuses and speculation. The Federal Warehouse Act (1916) improved agricultural storage facilities by allowing the Department of Agriculture to license bonded warehouses in the states and issue warehouse receipts to farmers as collateral for loans. With this act, Lever sought to instill good relations among bankers, businessmen, and farmers, who would jointly own and operate the warehouses. The Farm Loan Act (1916) created twelve federal land banks and the Farm Credit Administration, which reduced the cost of farm loans, stabilized mortgages, and lowered agriculture-related interest rates.

Lever achieved his greatest success during World War I when he successfully pushed the Food and Fuel Control Act (also called the Lever Food Act) through Congress in 1917. The act gave President Wilson authority to create the Food Administration and the Fuel Administration, which received broad authority to regulate producers and distributors so that vital commodities could be allocated to where they were needed for the war effort. Lever wrote a friend in 1917, "I am laboring under the most tremendous strain I have ever experienced. The president tells me that the legislation which has been placed in my hands must win or lose the war." Although opposed by many of his fellow southerners, who believed that the bill would give unconstitutional power to the president and discriminate against farmers, Lever nevertheless saw the measure through to final enactment. In the words of one congressman, Lever "demonstrated rare courage born of real patriotism in reporting a bill which gives broad powers to the Federal Government." Upon the bill's passage, Lever received a standing ovation.

After an abbreviated run for the U.S. Senate in 1918, Lever resigned from the House on August 1, 1919. He worked as a field representative of the Farm Loan Board and in 1933 became director of public relations with the Farm Credit Administration, Southeast Region. In 1930 Lever sought the Democratic nomination for governor but was sidelined by pneumonia early in the campaign. In his later years, as during his congressional tenure, Lever worked to improve the quality of life for rural Americans and hoped that all South Carolinians would play an important role in the creation of a state "rich in all the things that make for a worthwhile and enduring civilization." Lever died on April 28, 1940, of coronary thrombosis at his home, Seven Oaks, in Lexington County and was buried at Clemson College. VERONICA BRUCE MCCONNELL

"Funeral Rites for A. F. Lever Held Tomorrow." Columbia *State,* April 29, 1940, pp. 1, 5.

Lever, Asbury F. Papers. Clemson University Library Special Collections, Clemson.

Lewisohn, Ludwig (1883–1955). Novelist, critic, activist. Born on May 30, 1883, in Berlin, Germany, Lewisohn immigrated to America in 1890 with his assimilated Jewish parents, Jacques Lewisohn and Minna Eloesser. The family stayed with relatives in St. Matthews, South Carolina, for two years before moving on to Charleston, where the young Lewisohn's stellar performance in high school and at the College of Charleston, from which he graduated with a B.A. and M.A. in 1901, sustained the family. He was brilliant but did not fit in, either intellectually or socially. His Semitic looks stamped him as an outsider and denied him access to a fraternity, even though he considered himself Methodist. Charleston gentlemen helped pay for his schooling at Columbia University. The practice of denying professorships in English to Jews so dismayed him that he took no degree. In 1906 he married Mary Arnold Child Crocker, twenty years his senior.

Lewisohn's first novel, *The Broken Snare,* was published in 1908. Trumpeted by the naturalist writer Theodore Dreiser, it was condemned in Charleston for the author's advocacy of "free love." In 1910 he taught German at the University of Wisconsin, and he then taught at Ohio State University from 1911 to 1917. His promoting and translating of German literature at the outbreak of World War I stymied his advancement, which frustrated him greatly. From 1919 to 1924 he was drama critic for the *Nation,* and in 1922 his first important book, *Upstream,* a veiled autobiography in which he grappled with the issues of Puritanism, xenophobia, and the American dream, appeared. Although the term was not in vogue then, his book was a call for pluralism. This landmark work made Lewisohn a champion to intellectuals and immigrants.

In 1924, unable to get a divorce from Crocker, Lewisohn moved to Europe with the singer Thelma Spear. His novel *The Case of Mr. Crump,* set partially in Charleston and based on his disastrous marriage, was published in Paris in 1926. Hailed by Sigmund Freud and Thomas Mann, it is one of the finest naturalistic novels produced by an American in the 1920s. Lewisohn began to investigate his Jewish heritage and write novels and nonfiction regarding it. He was one of the first to see the looming horrors of Hitler. He became an elegant polemicist and propagandist for the Zionist cause, but his fiction suffered, and there was embarrassment to the cause from his personal entanglements. The tabloid press followed his nonmarried life with Spear, their breakup, the histrionic displays of his first wife, and then two subsequent marriages. Only with the death of Crocker and the relaxing of obscenity laws could an unexpurgated edition of *The Case of Mr. Crump* appear in the United States in 1947. By that time much of his critical work—on drama, American life, and literature—was being forgotten, although he had published more than a dozen works on these topics.

In 1948 Lewisohn became a founding member of the Brandeis University faculty. He died in Miami on December 31, 1955. By then Lewisohn, who had been praised and vilified in his lifetime, merited almost no notice and had nearly been forgotten. His great works include some of his literary criticism, *The Case of Mr. Crump, Upstream,* and *The Island Within,* one of his Jewish-themed novels that helped open up the field to the many American Jewish novelists who followed him. HARLAN GREENE

Lainoff, Seymour. *Ludwig Lewisohn.* Boston: Twayne, 1982.

Melnick, Ralph. *The Life and Work of Ludwig Lewisohn.* 2 vols. Detroit: Wayne State University Press, 1998.

Lexington (Lexington County; 2000 pop. 9,793). Lexington, named for the Revolutionary War battle in Massachusetts, was founded in 1820 to replace Granby (now Cayce) as the Lexington District seat. Two acres were purchased from Barbara Drafts Corley in the center of the district on a high sandy ridge, which was deemed healthier than low-lying, flood-prone Granby. Construction of a courthouse and jail soon followed, but the town remained little more than a village for most of its early existence. In the mid-1820s the architect Robert Mills counted just fifteen houses and eighty residents. The town was called Lexington Court House until 1900.

Early settlers were of German and Swiss stock, who became tradesmen, farmers, and artisans known for their industrious habits and Lutheran faith. The first newspapers appeared in 1853, the *Lexington Telegraph* and the *Lexington Flag.* Incorporation came in 1861. At the time the town boasted two churches, a Lutheran seminary (which later moved to nearby Columbia), the private Lexington Academy, a carriage factory, a saw- and gristmill, blacksmiths, two newspapers, a tannery, and a livestock yard. Still too small to be a significant trade center, Lexington instead served as a retail market for manufactured goods from nearby Columbia.

The scorched-earth policy of General William T. Sherman during the Civil War included Lexington, which was all but destroyed by Union troops in February 1865. Especially detrimental was the burning of the Lexington courthouse records.

Small farms with varied crops and a developing lumber industry aided in the postbellum recovery, as did the completion of the Columbia and Augusta Railroad. The *Lexington Dispatch* began in 1871 and merged with the *Lexington County Chronicle* in 2001. The opening of the Lexington Textile Mill in 1890 brought some 150 manufacturing jobs to the area, but the commerce of Lexington remained in the shadow of Columbia to the east and the twin towns of Leesville and Batesburg to the west. In 1894 and 1918 disastrous fires gutted Main Street. The brick buildings that replaced those lost in the fires survive to form the core of the town's historic downtown.

The tiny courthouse town sprang to life in the final decades of the twentieth century, thanks to the sprawling population of the Columbia metropolitan area. Growing from a population of just 969 in 1970 to almost 10,000 in 2000, Lexington became one of the fastest-growing towns in South Carolina. This growth was encouraged by the town's excellent school system, easy access to major highways, and its proximity to Lake Murray, which experienced phenomenal residential development during the 1990s. ELSIE RAST STUART

Scott, Edwin J. *Random Recollections of a Long Life, 1806 to 1876.* 1884. Reprint, Columbia, S.C.: R. L. Bryan, 1969.

Lexington County (699 sq. miles; 2000 pop. 216,014). Straddling the fall line between the Sandhills and the Piedmont, Lexington County is located in the center of the state, bounded by Richland, Calhoun, Orangeburg, Saluda, and Newberry Counties. The county and its county seat were named for the Revolutionary War battle at Lexington, Massachusetts. Lexington County was created from the northern portion of the Orangeburg Judicial District in 1785. It was reorganized as Lexington District in 1804 and Lexington County in 1868. Portions of the county were lost to the creation of Aiken (1871) and Calhoun (1908) Counties and to twentieth-century annexations by Richland County.

The first European settlers arrived around 1718, when the British established a post (later called Granby) near the source of the Congaree River. In 1735 German-Swiss immigrants petitioned to establish a township in the area. Settling west of the confluence of the Saluda and Broad Rivers, more Germans soon followed. The area was originally named Saxe-Gotha in recognition of the German and Swiss descent of its first inhabitants. The term "Dutch Fork," a name for the area between the Saluda and Broad Rivers, came from a corruption of the German word *deutsch,* again denoting the ethnic origin of the early residents. These initial settlers established small farms and were admired for their thrifty and industrious habits. Some residents in the early twenty-first century still held land-grant titles from the king of England.

Although land in the northern part of Lexington District was fertile and well settled, most district soil was sandy and covered in pine forests. This made much of lower Lexington poorly suited for agriculture. As a result, the base of plantation agriculture and slavery established in Lexington was not as firm as that in the rest of the state, especially in comparison with the surrounding middle districts. In 1850 only sixty-eight of eleven hundred families in Lexington owned more than twenty slaves. By 1860 per capita wealth was less than half that of neighboring districts, and Lexington was one of the few districts in antebellum South Carolina in which blacks remained a minority of the population. The relatively modest agricultural opportunities in Lexington were partially offset by timber production, and dozens of sawmills cut high-quality pine and rafted it down the Congaree and Edisto Rivers. No fewer than seventy-three sawmills were operating in the district by 1860. Along the Congaree River brick manufacturing near Granby and the Saluda Factory, an antebellum textile mill operated with slave labor, also contributed to the local economy.

Lexington did not escape the Union army of General William T. Sherman in the closing days of the Civil War. Sherman's forces swept through the district in February 1865, destroying houses and buildings and carrying off large quantities of food, livestock, and household furnishings. An estimated one-quarter of the white male population between the ages of sixteen and sixty was either killed or wounded in the war.

As it was in most of South Carolina, recovery from the effects of the Civil War in Lexington was slow. Small farms would dominate the county's economy until the mid-1950s, but the completion of the Columbia and Augusta Railroad in 1868 helped spur the development of new towns such as Batesburg, Leesville, Summit, and Gilbert. The extension of rail lines in the 1890s from Columbia north toward Newberry and south toward Orangeburg led to the incorporation of additional towns, including Irmo, Ballentine, and Chapin in the Dutch Fork region and Swansea in the southern part of the county. A few small textile mills were also in operation by the early twentieth century.

Entering the twentieth century, Lexington County farmers were still the backbone of the economy. County truck farmers found a handy outlet for their produce at the curbside market in Columbia and could boast with good reason that "Lexington County feeds Columbia." Cotton, corn, and oats were the primary crops, although Lexington was also the state's leading producer of wheat until the late 1920s and a major producer of peaches and other truck crops.

Significant changes began to affect Lexington County as the twentieth century progressed. The completion of the Saluda River Dam in 1930 created Lake Murray, which inundated fifty thousand acres of Lexington County but also created five hundred miles of shoreline. The dam brought cheap hydroelectric power to the county, while the abundance of lakefront property brought new recreation opportunities and skyrocketing real estate values toward the end of the century. Industrial development began to exert a greater influence in the decades following World War II. Mineral resources were tapped to expand brick manufacturing and for the production of glass, kaolin, and road-building materials. Foreign-owned corporations began to make substantial investments in Lexington, particularly from Western Europe and Asia. By the end of the century, major industrial employers included Michelin Tire Corporation of France, Pirelli of Italy, Philips Components of the Netherlands, and TCM Manufacturing of Japan. Despite the increase in industrial activity, agriculture still exerted a strong influence, although row crops gradually took a backseat to livestock production. In 2001 Lexington led all other South Carolina counties in the value of their agricultural output ($107,462,000), primarily due to extensive production of poultry, eggs, and cattle. The county celebrates its rural heritage with annual festivals dedicated to the virtues of poultry, peaches, peanuts, collards, fishing, and okra.

The rapid expansion of the Columbia metropolitan area in the final decades of the twentieth century made Lexington one of the fastest-growing counties in the state. The county's population more than tripled between 1960 and 2000, with most of the growth taking place in the Columbia suburbs of West Columbia, Cayce, and Irmo. The completion of Interstates 20 and 26 in the 1950s helped accelerate this trend, as did Lexington's reputation for fine schools and low taxes. Incoming white middle-class suburbanites joined rural whites to make Lexington County a bastion of conservative politics and of the Republican Party in South Carolina. Notable Lexington County natives and residents include Governor George Bell Timmerman, Jr., and Congressmen Asbury Francis Lever and Floyd Spence. Entering the twenty-first century with one of South Carolina's highest per capita incomes and lowest rates of unemployment, Lexington County seemed set to continue on its prosperous trajectory. ELSIE RAST STUART

Bayne, Coy. *Lake Murray: Legend and Leisure.* 3d ed. Sunset, S.C.: Bayne, 1999.

Rowell, P. E. *Lexington County and Its Towns.* [Lexington, S.C.: Dispatch-Job Press, 1891].

Liberian exodus. The return of the Democratic Party to power in South Carolina in 1876, and the campaign of violence that accompanied it, raised anxiety among African Americans in the state and interest in the possibility of emigration. Similar feelings toward emigration could be found across the South, where blacks endured political weakness, restrictions on their civil rights, and difficulty in finding gainful employment. In many southern states, particularly the lower Mississippi Valley, the frustration of blacks with their poor condition caused some to migrate to the western United States during the exodus of 1879. In South Carolina, interest in emigration became focused on the African nation of Liberia, which was more accessible from the East Coast and because the American Colonization Society had already transported a small number of blacks there in the years immediately following the Civil War, albeit with mixed results.

Black leaders in South Carolina, including Richard Harvey Cain, Harrison Bouey, George Curtis, and the Reverend B. F. Porter, responded to the interest in black emigration by incorporating the Liberian Exodus Joint Stock Steamship Company in the spring of 1877, naming Porter as its president. The American Colonization Society, which did not have enough funds to transport the swelling numbers of black emigrants, welcomed the formation of the Charleston-based company and lent it moral support and advice. In January 1878 hundreds of potential emigrants from all over South Carolina converged on Charleston, despite the opposition of white employers who feared losing cheap labor. The company lacked the necessary funds for a Liberian voyage, but Porter bowed to pressure from hundreds of prospective passengers and hastily acquired a vessel, a clipper ship named the *Azor.* Christened on March 21, 1878, the *Azor* set sail from Charleston a month later carrying 206 emigrants from South Carolina to Liberia. After a forty-two-day passage during which emigrants endured delays, deaths, and unforeseen expenses in Sierra Leone, they arrived in Liberia short of money and supplies. News of the disastrous crossing discouraged hundreds of black South Carolinians who were waiting in Charleston for passage to Liberia. The cost of the *Azor*'s first voyage wiped out the company's capital. The company planned a commercial voyage to Liberia in February 1879 to raise funds, but the ship never sailed. The *Azor* was sold at auction in November 1879.

Some of the *Azor* emigrants returned to South Carolina disappointed, but others enjoyed success in Liberia. In 1880 one of them reported that 173 of the *Azor* emigrants were still in Liberia, with perhaps others in the interior of Africa. Neither the demise of the Liberian Exodus Joint Stock Steamship Company or the opposition of white employers persuaded black South Carolinians to give up the idea of emigrating from the state to Liberia. For at least a few years after the collapse of the company, prospective emigrants sought the help of the American Colonization Society. By the early 1890s reports appeared claiming that several of the leading political and business figures in Liberia had come from South Carolina, including C. L. Parsons, chief justice of the Liberian Supreme Court; Clement Irons, who constructed the first steamship in Liberia in 1888; and the Reverend David Frazier, a member of the Liberian Senate. MICHAEL ROBERT MOUNTER

Painter, Nell Irvin. *Exodusters: Black Migration to Kansas after Reconstruction.* New York: Knopf, 1977.

Tindall, George Brown. *South Carolina Negroes, 1877–1900.* 1952. Reprint, Columbia: University of South Carolina Press, 2003.

Liberty (Pickens County; 2000 pop. 3,009). In the 1870s the Atlanta and Charlotte Air Line Railroad was built through rural Pickens County and spawned several small towns. Local landowner Catherine Templeton deeded a right-of-way to the railroad, and by 1874 local residents had constructed the first depot at what was then called Liberty Station. In the *Pickens Sentinel* of September 9, 1875, the widow Templeton advertised part of her property to be divided into lots and sold. These lots became the business section of the town of Liberty, which was incorporated on March 2, 1876. The town name was often thought to have originated as a corruption of "Salubrity," a local farm and spring that gave the name to a post office in 1839. However, antebellum land records mention a Liberty Spring and a church in the area that became the town of Liberty. The Liberty Post Office was created in 1873 and coexisted for nearly three years with Salubrity, the two being about a mile apart. Salubrity Post Office was discontinued in early 1876.

Businesses in Liberty's first year included four stores, a hotel, a steam sawmill, two blacksmith shops, and an academy. The Brown House offered room and board for teachers, railroad men, traveling preachers, and business travelers beginning in 1893. Other early establishments included a millinery shop and dressmakers in the 1880s, a cotton-seed-oil mill in 1895, a livery stable and new depot in 1896, and a wagon factory in 1897. By 1900 the population of Liberty had reached 368. The first decade of the twentieth century saw two banks and a drugstore open, as well as textile mills. The Woodside Liberty Plant began in 1901, and a second plant, originally the Calumet Mill, was built in 1905.

State funds supported teachers at Liberty School as early as 1837, and two "colored schools" were on record in 1870. Early Liberty churches included the Presbyterians' 1883 structure and the African Methodist Episcopal congregation's Robinson Chapel in 1886.

Business openings in town reflected the changing lives of a rural population. Year by year establishments included more services and products for daily life, such as service stations, dry cleaners, and more grocery stores in the 1920s; the first bus station in the 1930s; and several beauty shops, a car dealership, and a library in the 1940s. The increasing complexity of modern life was reflected in the addition of such businesses as Liberty's first income tax service and first trailer park in the 1950s and a child care center in the 1960s. The relocation of Ohio Gear to Liberty in 1964 added employment opportunities. A town official in 1986 characterized Liberty as a "bedroom town" to the nearby city of Greenville, but one offering diversity to its residents. DONNA K. ROPER

Woodson, Julia Jean, and Anne G. Sheriff. *Liberty, South Carolina: One Hundred Years, 1876–1976.* Greenville, S.C.: A Press, 1992.

Lieber, Francis (1798–1872). Educator, political scientist. Lieber was born in Berlin in the Kingdom of Prussia on March 18, 1798. His father, Friedrich Wilhelm Lieber, was an iron dealer. As a young man, Lieber was arrested for his involvement in nationalist movements and spent four months in prison. Authorities prohibited him from entering Prussian universities, but he nevertheless earned a doctor of philosophy degree from Jena in 1820. He went to Halle University in 1824 and then traveled to London in 1826. In 1827 he arrived in America, becoming director of a Boston gymnasium. His writing flourished, and he became a newspaper correspondent and edited the *Encyclopaedia Americana* (13 volumes, 1829–1833). The encyclopedia brought Lieber widespread renown and the opportunity to meet nationally prominent scholars and leaders, including President Andrew Jackson. On September 21, 1829, he married Matilda Oppenheimer; they had four children.

His reputation firmly established, Lieber became interested in a permanent academic position. With the reorganization of South Carolina College in 1835, Lieber was elected professor of history and political economy. He came to South Carolina primarily to provide for his family but also seeking to use the position as a springboard to a more desirable post at Harvard. Throughout his twenty-year tenure at South Carolina College, he longed to return north and solicited the assistance of friends and acquaintances to rescue him from his southern "exile." Although he privately considered slavery to be "a nasty, dirty, selfish institution," Lieber deferred to his surroundings and maintained a discreet silence in public and even acquired a few slaves of his own. However, his nationalist leanings did garner considerable public animosity, and his arguments in favor of strong national government found few adherents among the ardently states' rights student body. Nevertheless, he was acclaimed as an excellent teacher, and his national reputation as a scholar brought considerable prestige to the college.

Francis Lieber. Courtesy, South Caroliniana Library, University of South Carolina

From 1849 to 1851 Lieber served as acting president of South Carolina College during the illness of President William C. Preston. Lieber hoped for a permanent appointment as president, but theology professor James H. Thornwell was appointed instead in 1851. Following Thornwell's retirement in 1854, Lieber again actively sought the position in a controversial contest that garnered considerable public attention. Lieber lost the presidency this time to mathematics professor Charles F. McCay, a newcomer to the college who had the support of Thornwell and his followers. Deeply disappointed, Lieber blamed his defeat on "Bitter Calvinism," his Unionist views, and suspicion that he was an abolitionist. He resigned from the faculty in December 1855 and left South Carolina the following year. One of Lieber's colleagues called him "a star of the first magnitude . . . one of the brightest and most illustrious on the rolls of the faculty."

In 1857 Lieber went to New York City and accepted a position as chair of political science at Columbia College (now Columbia University). He continued to advise statesmen, writing a monograph that was used in training for field armies during the Civil War. He transferred to Columbia's law school in 1867, teaching constitutional history and public law and specializing in international law. Three year later he was selected as an umpire of the U.S. and Mexican Claims Commission, established to settle claims arising from the Mexican War. Lieber died in New York City on October 2, 1872. DAN G. RUFF

Freidel, Frank B. *Francis Lieber: Nineteenth Century Liberal.* Baton Rouge: Louisiana State University Press, 1947.

Harley, Lewis R. *Francis Lieber: His Life and Political Philosophy.* New York: AMS, 1970.

Hollis, Daniel Walker. *University of South Carolina.* 2 vols. Columbia: University of South Carolina Press, 1951–1956.

Lieber, Oscar Montgomery (1830–1862). Geologist. Lieber was born on September 8, 1830, in Boston, Massachusetts, the eldest son of the distinguished political scientist Francis Lieber and Matilda Oppenheimer. His father joined the faculty of South Carolina College in 1835, and the family moved to Columbia.

In 1839 Lieber traveled to Germany, where he stayed with relatives in Hamburg and attended private schools for six years before returning to Columbia. In 1846, at age sixteen, Lieber assisted Michael Tuomey on the South Carolina geological survey, and he credited Tuomey with fostering his interest in geology as a profession. Lieber returned to Germany the following year and studied at universities in Berlin and Göttingen and at the School of Mines in Freiburg. Returning to the United States in 1850, Lieber served a short time as assistant to the state geologist of Mississippi and Alabama. With the assistance of his father, Lieber published an analytical guidebook, *The Assayer's Guide* (1852), which went through numerous editions. Unable to obtain academic employment that he felt suited his German scientific training, Lieber accepted a position as assistant to Michael Tuomey working on a geological survey of Alabama from 1854 to 1855.

Lieber severed his association with Tuomey over perceived charges of plagiarism and turned his attention toward promoting (using the pen name "Metallicus") a new survey of South Carolina. Renewed interest in mining and internal improvements prompted the General Assembly in December 1855 to issue a resolution authorizing a four-year study and electing Lieber "Geological, Mineralogical and Agricultural Surveyor" of the state. Four annual reports were published between 1857 and 1860 before appropriations were discontinued by the legislature. These reports, each titled *Report on the Survey of South Carolina,* were marked by his German scientific style of writing on theoretical applications of geologic studies and detailed mine examinations. Lieber focused his investigations on mining areas in the upstate. However, the state-sponsored survey failed to meet the legislative intent in relation to internal improvements as the mining industry of upstate South Carolina remained moribund. Lieber's reports were unique among antebellum state geological surveys and represent a style not favored by other American geologists of the period.

As detailed by the historian James O. Breeden, Lieber struggled to meet his father's expectations academically, professionally, and by 1860 politically. Lieber proved his independence by siding with the Confederacy while his brothers and father served the Union. Soon after receiving his commission as a private, Lieber was mortally wounded during the Confederate retreat at the Battle of Williamsburg, Virginia, and he died on May 27, 1862. He was buried in Richmond. LEWIS S. DEAN

Breeden, James O. "Oscar Lieber: Southern Scientist, Southern Patriot." *Civil War History* 36 (September 1990): 226–49.

Millbrooke, Anne. "South Carolina State Geological Surveys of the Nineteenth Century." In *The Geological Sciences in the Antebellum South,* edited by James X. Corgan. University: University of Alabama Press, 1982.

Tuomey, Michael. *The Papers of Michael Tuomey.* Edited by Lewis S. Dean. Spartanburg, S.C.: Reprint Company, 2001.

Lighthouses. South Carolina's 180-mile coastline is replete with bays, inlets, and harbors. To assist shipping and aid navigation, lighthouses and beacons have dotted the South Carolina coast for centuries. The earliest warning lights were probably bonfires lit to aid ships entering the harbor at Charleston. South Carolina's first lighthouse, built in 1767, stood on Middle Bay Island (now a part of Morris Island) in the Charleston harbor.

When the federal government assumed responsibility for all lighthouses in 1789, South Carolina had only one—the Morris Island lighthouse. That year Paul Trapier donated land for a lighthouse on North Island at the mouth of Winyah Bay. The Georgetown lighthouse was completed and lit in 1801. Both the Morris Island and Georgetown lighthouses were rebuilt during the antebellum period, and lighthouses were added on Lighthouse Island (Raccoon Key) at Cape Romain in 1827 and 1857 and on Hunting Island in Beaufort County in 1859.

The Morris Island Lighthouse at the turn of the twentieth century. Courtesy, South Carolina Historical Society

By 1860 four lighthouses—Morris Island, Cape Romain, Georgetown, and Hunting Island—and beacons at Charleston, Morris Island, Sullivan's Island, Fort Sumter, Castle Pinckney, and Battery guarded the South Carolina coast. Upon secession, South Carolina seized the lighthouses. Confederate forces dismantled the lights and sometimes destroyed the lighthouses to prevent their use by Union forces.

Heightened lighthouse activity followed the Civil War. A new lighthouse was built on Morris Island around 1876, the Cape Romain and Georgetown lighthouses were repaired, the Hunting Island light was rebuilt in 1875, and range lights were erected on Daufuskie (Haig's Point and Bloody Point) and Hilton Head Islands. Aligning with the range lights enabled vessels to successfully follow river channels. The Hunting Island light, an important nautical landmark between Savannah and Charleston, warned ships away from the coast.

A story from a hurricane in 1898 illustrates the human side of lighthouse keeping. Adam Fripp, keeper of the Leamington Rear Range Light on Hilton Head, died of a heart attack as the winds extinguished the light. His daughter relit the light, kept it burning through the storm, and then died from the effort a few weeks later.

In the twentieth century the United States Lighthouse Service / United States Coast Guard first automated and later abandoned most of South Carolina's lighthouses. A major exception was the construction of the Sullivan's Island light station (the new Charleston Lighthouse) in 1962. The Georgetown Light is the only one of South Carolina's nineteenth-century lights in active use. The Haig Point (Daufuskie Rear Range) Light, although deactivated, aids private navigation in Calibogue Sound.

The romantic lure of lighthouses has produced two facsimile lights on the South Carolina coast: the Governor's Light built on Little River in 1985; and the Harbor Town Lighthouse built in 1970 at the Sea Pines Plantation on Hilton Head Island. The new and the abandoned lighthouses still stand as landmarks for mariners navigating the South Carolina coast. ALEXIA JONES HELSLEY

Roberts, Bruce. *Southern Lighthouses: Chesapeake Bay to the Gulf of Mexico.* Chester, Conn.: Globe Pequot, 1989.

Limestone College. Limestone College in Gaffney is an independent four-year liberal arts institution offering bachelor of arts and bachelor of science degrees. The school traces its beginnings to 1845, when Thomas Curtis, a Baptist minister from England, established the Limestone Springs Female High School in a former resort hotel near the crossroads community of Gaffney's Tavern. The school's remote location and Curtis's death in 1859 severely hampered efforts to keep the institution alive. The Civil War and Reconstruction curtailed activities, and Curtis's son William was forced to sell the school at auction in 1871. The Limestone Springs property changed hands several times until the late 1870s, when local civic leaders secured a grant from the New York industrialist Peter Cooper. In 1881 they opened the Cooper-Limestone Institute for Young Ladies.

The school underwent its most dramatic transformation in the late 1890s. Investments from several textile men, including John H. Montgomery, created the present institution, Limestone College, in 1898. Improvements included a new main building, Curtis Hall, named in honor of the founder. Lee Davis Lodge, a scholar of wide-ranging interests, was the new president. He oversaw the 1904 construction of the Winnie Davis Hall of History, named for the daughter of Jefferson Davis. In the 1920s the local businessmen James A. Carroll and Wylie Cicero Hamrick directed efforts to enlarge the physical plant. By 1925 the college completed a gymnasium, a science hall, and a building for music and fine arts. During the next forty years, Limestone school developed a solid academic reputation and completed two more buildings, the nine-hundred-seat Fullerton Auditorium (1964) and the A. J. Eastwood Library (1966). The school was racially integrated in 1967.

Faced with a decline in enrollment, Limestone went coeducational in 1970. The school instituted intercollegiate athletics in 1973, and Limestone's athletics program gained national prominence. In 1984 the men's golf team won the National Association of Intercollegiate Athletics (NAIA) National Championship. In 1987 the school hired Gaylord Perry, a former major league pitcher, to initiate its baseball program. Most significant was the Limestone College men's lacrosse team. The team became a national powerhouse, winning the National Collegiate Athletic Association (NCAA) Division II National Championship in 2000 and 2002.

Since the 1990s, Limestone College has centered its efforts on recruiting, fund-raising, and development. The school renovated several campus buildings and initiated a statewide evening program with major sites in Columbia and Charleston. Limestone was also among the first to offer courses via the Internet and eventually established a self-contained, degree-offering "Virtual Campus" program with students located worldwide. JAMES A. DUNLAP III

The Centennial of Limestone College. Gaffney, S.C.: Limestone College, 1945.

Hopper, C. G., Jr., and Bobby G. Moss. *Toward the Light: Photography and Limestone College.* Gaffney, S.C.: Limestone College, 1998.

McMillan, Montague. *Limestone College, a History: 1845–1970.* Gaffney, S.C.: Limestone College, 1970.

Taylor, Walter Carroll. *History of Limestone College.* Gaffney, S.C.: Limestone College, 1937.

Lincoln, Benjamin (1733–1810). Soldier. Lincoln was born in Hingham, Massachusetts, on January 24, 1733, the sixth child of Colonel Benjamin Lincoln and Elizabeth Thaxter. Lincoln rose to prominence in the Seven Years' War, where he gained extensive experience in military planning and organization. A strong supporter of revolutionary activities in Massachusetts, that colony appointed him a major general of militia in February 1776. He served in the campaign around New York in the summer and fall of 1776 and earned Washington's admiration and respect. Acting on Washington's recommendation, the Continental Congress appointed him a major general in the Continental army on February 14, 1777. Later that year he helped Horatio Gates defeat General John Burgoyne's British army in the Saratoga campaign.

Impressed with his abilities, the Continental Congress chose Lincoln to replace Major General Robert Howe as commander of the Southern Department in September 1778. Lincoln arrived in Charleston to take command in December. The British captured Savannah in late December 1778 and in the ensuing months reestablished some control over Georgia. Lincoln's desire to drive the British from Georgia exposed South Carolina to attack and brought the wrath of South Carolinians upon him. In late April 1779 he marched the bulk of his army up the Savannah River and crossed to Augusta, intending to force the British from the Georgia backcountry. General Augustine Prevost, meanwhile, crossed the Savannah and marched his army to Charleston. Lincoln returned to the state, but not before Prevost's troops threatened Charleston and ravaged farms and plantations throughout the lowcountry. Shortly after Prevost's troops withdrew toward Georgia, Lincoln complained to General William Moultrie, "it appears . . . that I have lost the confidence of the people." Lincoln wished to resign from command of the Southern Department, but Moultrie and Governor John Rutledge convinced him to remain. He led American forces in the disastrous Franco-American effort against Savannah in October 1779.

Lincoln had the misfortune to preside over the single worst defeat of American forces during the Revolutionary War, the loss of Charleston. Probably influenced by his experience in the spring campaign of 1779, Lincoln elected to hold Charleston against a strong army and fleet under General Sir Henry Clinton and Admiral Marriot Arbuthnot. Although several officers recommended evacuation, Lincoln decided to keep his army within his works. The Americans staved off the British for six weeks, but Clinton's force eventually applied overwhelming pressure and the city capitulated on May 12, 1780. Governor Rutledge criticized Lincoln for giving up the town, but other South Carolinians praised his conduct. The historian David Ramsay thought that "great praise" was due Lincoln for "baffling, for three months, the greatly superior force of Sir Henry Clinton and Admiral Arbuthnot." Exchanged in November 1780, Lincoln served as second in command to Washington during the Yorktown campaign, accepting the sword of Cornwallis's second in command at the surrender of Yorktown. He later served as head of the newly created War Department and in various positions in Massachusetts government after the war. Lincoln died in Hingham, Massachusetts, on May 9, 1810. CARL BORICK

Mattern, David B. *Benjamin Lincoln and the American Revolution.* Columbia: University of South Carolina Press, 1995.

Moultrie, William. *Memoirs of the American Revolution.* 1802. Reprint, New York: New York Times, 1968.

Ramsay, David. *History of the Revolution in South Carolina, from a British Province to an Independent State.* 2 vols. Trenton, N.J.: Isaac Collins, 1785.

Lindo, Moses (?–1774). Indigo promoter, entrepreneur. Lindo was a major force in turning South Carolina's fledgling indigo trade into the region's second leading agricultural industry in the middle years of the eighteenth century. From field to market he promoted the planting, cultivation, processing, and merchandising of the deep blue dye made from the leaves of the indigo plant.

Born to a family of Sephardic Jews in London, Lindo became an authority on dyes at the Royal Exchange, the city's center of commerce. Impressed by the fine grade of indigo imported from South Carolina, Lindo sailed to Charleston in 1756. There, he secured the position of surveyor and inspector general of indigo and made a small fortune buying and selling indigo and other commodities coveted by Europeans, particularly coffee from the West Indies. Shortly after arriving in America, he bought a ship, which he named *Lindo Packet,* and placed an ad in the city's weekly newspaper offering to pay cash for "a Plantation of 500 acres, with 60 or 70 Negroes." There is no record that a deal was ever consummated, but it is known that Lindo engaged in the slave trade. He imported at least one shipload of slaves from Barbados, and he also owned slaves. In a letter published in the Royal Society's *Philosophical Transactions* for 1763, Lindo announced the invention of "a superior crimson dye" derived from pokeberries. He also claimed to have used a concoction of pokeberries, tobacco, and Roman vitriol to cure yaws, an infectious skin disease common in the crowded slave quarters.

After ten years, Lindo quit his post as indigo surveyor and was appointed appraiser of all dyes and drugs produced in North America. From the time of his arrival in South Carolina until his death in April 1774, indigo production increased fivefold, to more than one million pounds annually. He did not die wealthy, however, as over the years adverse judgments in a string of lawsuits apparently consumed his earnings. TED ROSENGARTEN

Elzas, Barnett A. *The Jews of South Carolina, from the Earliest Times to the Present Day.* 1905. Reprint, Spartanburg, S.C.: Reprint Company, 1972.

Hagy, James William. *This Happy Land: The Jews of Colonial and Antebellum Charleston.* Tuscaloosa: University of Alabama Press, 1993.

Lining, John (1708–1760). Physician, scientist. Lining was born in April 1708 in Lanarkshire, Scotland, the son of Thomas Lining, a minister, and Anne Hamilton. He studied medicine in Scotland and probably at Leyden University in the Netherlands. He immigrated to Charleston in 1728, and by the early 1730s he was advertising the sale of medicinal waters and drugs in the *South-Carolina Gazette.* He served as physician to the poor of St. Philip's Parish and as port physician for the enforcement of quarantine. He built a successful medical practice and entered into partnership with Lionel Chalmers around 1740. In 1750 he married Sarah Hill, an heiress with several valuable parcels of property. They had no children. He abandoned the practice of medicine in 1754 after he was attacked by "gout" and turned to raising indigo and experimenting with electricity. Lining was a justice of the court of general sessions and the court of common pleas, president of the Charleston Library Society, a founder of the St. Andrews's Society, and a Mason.

Lining's scientific pursuits began as early as 1737, when he began making careful meteorological observations using a barometer, a thermometer, and a hygroscope. He continued keeping these records for fifteen years and published some of his results in the *Philosophical Transactions of the Royal Society* of London in 1748 and 1753. These observations, which also appeared in Governor James Glen's *Description of South Carolina* (1761), are reputed to be the earliest published meteorological records from America.

In 1740 Lining started making metabolic, or what he called "statical," experiments on himself, keeping a careful record of his intake of food and output of excretions. He hoped to establish a connection between the effects of weather conditions on bodily functions and disease, particularly the fevers that struck the colony regularly at specific times of the year. Although unable to demonstrate a connection, he sent his observations to the Royal Society, and they were published in the society's *Transactions* in 1742–1743 and 1744–1745. Lionel Chalmers later included them in his *Account of the Weather and Diseases of South Carolina* (1776). Lining was also an avid botanist who collected and sent many plant specimens to Charles Alston and Robert Whytt of Edinburgh University. In a paper published in Edinburgh in 1754, Lining described the benefits and toxicity of the Indian pinkroot as a vermifuge (worm remover or destroyer).

Lining's most significant work on medicine was "A Description of the American Yellow Fever," published in Edinburgh in 1756. This essay is often referred to as the first North American account of yellow fever, but it was preceded by John Moultrie, Jr.'s 1749 Edinburgh dissertation on the disease. Lining presented a clear, detailed clinical description of the disease's symptoms, course, and prognosis. He argued that it was contagious and that it was imported from outside, usually from the West Indies. But he also noted the important, if apparently contradictory, fact that country residents infected while in town did not transmit it to their families. He concluded correctly that one attack of yellow fever conferred future immunity, but incorrectly that Africans were naturally immune to it. Lining died in Charleston on September 21, 1760. PETER MCCANDLESS

Lining, John. "A Description of the American Yellow Fever." *Essays and Observations, Physical and Literary* [Edinburgh] 2 (1756): 370–95.

Riley, James C. *The Eighteenth-Century Campaign to Avoid Disease.* New York: St. Martin's, 1987.

Stearns, Raymond P. *Science in the British Colonies of America.* Urbana: University of Illinois Press, 1970.

Waring, Joseph I. *A History of Medicine in South Carolina.* Vol. 1, *1670–1825.* Columbia: South Carolina Medical Association, 1964.

"Lintheads." A disparaging nickname for cotton mill workers, of unknown origin, "lintheads" is sometimes equated with the term "white trash." It likely came into common usage early in the twentieth century, when the growing number of cotton mills and mill workers began to alter the landscape of South Carolina life. As their ranks grew from 2,000 in 1880 to more than 71,000 by 1930, mill workers became an obvious social presence as well as a political force in South Carolina. Many found this new population threatening, especially after mill workers became the backbone of support for the controversial governor and U.S. senator Cole Blease.

"Linthead" had both a literal and a figurative meaning. A veritable snowstorm of cotton lint in the mills covered workers from head to toe. The term also differentiated mill workers from farmers and townspeople, the other major components of the white population.

Lintheads were disparaged as illiterates and as failed farmers who had become low paid, minimally skilled operatives or machine-tenders, a relatively new occupational category in South Carolina. Benjamin R. Tillman dismissed mill workers as "that damn factory class." They went to the factory because they had no other realistic alternatives; they went there to feed their families and, they hoped, to improve their lot and that of their children.

Cotton mill workers, who played a critical role in the modernization of the South Carolina economy, made the "linthead" epithet a badge of honor. When the former mill operative Olin D. Johnston occupied the governor's office in the 1930s, a poet wrote: "Hats off to the governor / Of the Palmetto State! / They may call him linthead / But I think he's great." Students at Olympia High School in Columbia used to sing "The Linthead Fight Song": "We are a bunch of lintheads, / Lintheads are we. / Born in a factory, / We don't care about spinning around the universe, / Of all the other lintheads, we are the best, / We come from OHS, the halo of all the rest."

TOM TERRILL

Byars, Alvin. *Lintheads.* Cayce, S.C., 1983.

Carlton, David L. *Mill and Town in South Carolina, 1880–1920.* Baton Rouge: Louisiana State University Press, 1982.

Simon, Bryant. *A Fabric of Defeat: The Politics of South Carolina Millhands, 1910–1948.* Chapel Hill: University of North Carolina Press, 1998.

Lister, Hovie Franklin (1926–2001). Musician. For more than half a century Hovie Lister was leader and pianist for the Statesmen Quartet, one of the best-known and most significant exponents of southern gospel music. Born in Greenville on September 17, 1926, Lister learned to play piano at age nine and accompanied his father and uncles in the Lister Brothers Quartet in area churches and on local radio. After completing high school and a course at the Stamps-Baxter School of Music he went to Atlanta, where he became accompanist for the Rangers Quartet, the LeFevre Trio, and the Homeland Harmony Quartet before organizing the Statesmen in 1948. He took the name for this foursome from *The Stateman,* the newspaper organ for the Talmadges, then prominent in Georgia politics. Other significant members of the group have included Doyle Ott, Ed Weatherington, Jake Hess, Denver Crumpler, James Vaughn Hill, and Roland "Rosie" Rozelle.

Over the years the Statesmen Quartet made personal appearances throughout the United States. They recorded extensively for Capital, Skylite, and especially RCA Victor, with whom they were under contract for some eighteen years. The Statesmen also appeared on the soundtracks of two motion pictures, *A Man Called Peter* (1953) and *God Is My Partner* (1957). The Statesmen were guests on many major television network programs and on syndicated programs. For a time Lister merged the Statesmen into an all-star gospel act known as the Masters V, which included him, J. D. Sumner, James Blackwood, Jake Hess, and Roland Rozelle.

A man of versatile interests, Lister became an ordained Southern Baptist minister and was pastor of a church for some years. As a promoter of some renown, he organized the Waycross, Georgia, Sundown to Sunup Gospel Sing, which has raised more than $250,000 for the Shrine Hospitals for Crippled Children. He and his wife Ethel reared two children, remained active with the Statesmen, and resided near Decatur, Georgia, until his death on December 29, 2001, from a rare form of lymph cancer. His musical legacy has probably been described best by the Atlanta journalist Furman Bisher, who called Lister the man "who put rhythm in religion."

IVAN M. TRIBE

Literacy. Illiteracy is a problem that has bedeviled South Carolina for generations. While literacy rates among free white males during the colonial era are estimated to have been quite high, the situation did not persist into the nineteenth century. Historically, dismal support for public education in the state helped spawn a legacy of appalling rates of illiteracy. By 1880 more than three-quarters of the black population and almost one-quarter of the white population were completely illiterate. These rates enabled Ben Tillman and his followers to use literacy qualifications in the 1890s to effectively disenfranchise African American voters. During that same decade, forty-five percent of the state's population over the age of ten could neither read nor write. Illiteracy levels declined somewhat in the early twentieth century, but rates were still high enough at the start of World War II to render thousands of eligible black and white males unfit for military service. In 1948 the state superintendent of education estimated that in South Carolina sixty-two percent of blacks and eighteen percent of whites remained totally or functionally illiterate. Great improvements were made in the ensuing decades, however, and at the start of the twenty-first century South Carolinians were better educated and more literate than at any other time in their history. Nevertheless, factors persisted that placed the state's literacy rates near the bottom in the United States.

Literacy development is both cultural and individual, and it involves a complex set of interrelated variables, including individual experiences, acquisition of skills, and social and economic conditions. Like learning in general, literacy is not acquired by studying or following a sequence of rules. The National Literacy Act of 1991 and the National Assessment of Adult Literacy in 2002 broadly define literacy as an adult's ability to use printed and written information to function in society, to achieve one's goals, and to develop one's knowledge and potential. The National Adult Literacy Survey (NALS) measures literacy by looking at three scales: prose literacy, document literacy, and quantitative literacy. Each scale reflects real-life literacy tasks—for example, finding information in texts, such as newspapers articles; completing forms, such as a Social Security card application; and interpreting charts and graphs, such as a table of employee benefits. The NALS reported in 1998 that twenty-five percent of South Carolina's population was at level 1 on the NALS literacy continuum (level 1 being the lowest of levels 1 through 5). Furthermore fifteen counties in South Carolina had seventy-five percent of the respective populations rated above level 1 literacy, while twelve counties had populations with thirty-seven percent or more rated at level 1 literacy. Level 1 skills include performances such as signing one's name, identifying a country in a short article, locating the expiration date on a driver's license, and totaling a bank deposit entry. It is important to emphasize that level 1 ratings do not equate with illiteracy; rather, they indicate adults who "do not have the full range of economic, social, and personal options open to Americans with higher levels of literacy skills." In school achievement tests, a high percentage of elementary- and middle-grade students performed below standard. Drop-out rates continued to be an issue.

A complex issue such as illiteracy has required a broad range of solutions. South Carolina has enacted a variety of legislation to improve reading, early reading experiences, and family literacy instruction. The 1984 Education Improvement Act (EIA) introduced programs to foster superior performance, improve poor performance, and enhance student achievement. Since 1984 other reform legislation has included the Target 2000 School Reform for the Next Decade Act (1989), the Early Childhood Development and Academic Assistance Act (1993), the School-to-Work Transition Act (1994), and the Education Accountability Act (1998). In an effort to improve literacy in South Carolina, the State Department of Education in partnership with Governor Jim Hodges created the Governor's Institute of Reading. In June 1999 Governor Hodges signed into law the "First Steps to School Readiness" initiative, which listed early-childhood and family literacy as primary goals. In December 1999 the first South Carolina Reading Summit brought literacy educators from all levels—elementary, college, and state department—together to explore how best to meet the literacy needs of children and teachers in South Carolina. In June 2002 the South Carolina Reads initiative set a three-dimensional approach to combat illiteracy: work with teachers to develop a knowledge base in literacy; work with the Early Childhood Office at the State Department of Education to implement an early literacy intervention program; and develop a model to facilitate family literacy. Initiatives such as these held the promise of "creating a culture of literacy in South Carolina." AMY DONNELLY

National Institute for Literacy. *Literacy and Adult Education in the 104th Congress: A Legislative Guide.* Washington, D.C.: National Institute for Literacy, 1995.

———. *The State of Literacy in America: Estimates at the Local, State, and National Levels.* Washington, D.C.: National Institute for Literacy, 1998.

United Nations Educational, Scientific, and Cultural Organization. Division of Statistics on Education. *Compendium of Statistics on Illiteracy.* Paris: UNESCO, 1990.

United States. Department of Education. Office of Educational Research and Improvement. National Center for Educational Statistics. *The NAEP 1998 Writing State Report for South Carolina.* Washington, D.C.: Government Printing Office, 1999.

Literary and Philosophical Society. Established in 1813 in Charleston, the Literary and Philosophical Society of South Carolina was founded mainly to promote scientific interests in the state, including the collection and display of natural history specimens, but it also aimed to foster literary studies and preserve cultural artifacts. The society soon began to receive donations of specimens and artifacts, acquired the holdings of the museum founded by the Charleston Library Society in 1773, and purchased a large private collection. The Charleston banker and noted botanist Stephen Elliott was elected president of the society in 1814 and served until his death in 1830.

By 1819 the organization was prospering and had 138 members. Although not admitted to membership, women regularly attended society meetings. The extant addresses presented before the society indicate a high level of quality. A brief period of decline ensued after the death of Elliott, but the society was revived in 1831 and flourished during the next seven years. Charleston's noted mammalogist John Bachman played a major role in the organization's affairs during that period.

Languishing again by 1839, the society was revived in 1842 as the Literary and Conversation Club. Although attendance thereafter was generally small, the organization continued to consider important topics, such as the nature of the various human races. In 1850 the club's valuable but much-neglected collections, which had already been transferred to the Medical College of the State of South Carolina, became the property of the newly formed Charleston Museum. Thereafter the organization declined, and it was moribund by 1860. LESTER D. STEPHENS

Sanders, Albert E., and William D. Anderson, Jr. *Natural History Investigations in South Carolina, from Colonial Times to the Present.* Columbia: University of South Carolina Press, 1999.

Stephens, Lester D. "The Literary and Philosophical Society of South Carolina: A Forum for Intellectual Progress in Antebellum Charleston." *South Carolina Historical Magazine* 104 (July 2003): 154–75.

———. *Science, Race, and Religion in the American South: John Bachman and the Charleston Circle of Naturalists, 1815–1895.* Chapel Hill: University of North Carolina Press, 2000.

Little Mountain (Newberry County). Little Mountain is a monadnock, an isolated, eroded ridge of bedrock that lies above the general level of the surrounding area. The rocks immediately surrounding Little Mountain eroded faster than the hard rock of which it is made, leaving Little Mountain as a prominent ridge on the landscape. Situated sixteen miles southeast of the town of Newberry, near the town of Little Mountain, it is 2.9 miles long and a half-mile wide, rising from between 630 to 825 feet above sea level. It is the highest point of land between Greenville and Charleston.

Little Mountain lies in the Carolina slate belt and is especially interesting geologically because it is highly mineralized. It is a complex erosional remnant made up largely of mica schists and kyanite quartzite. It is thought to have formed in the early Paleozoic era as part of an island arc offshore from North America. Its rocks formed from eroded material from volcanic flows, ash, and tuffs that later were deposited to form river and beach sands and muds. These were then heated and compressed over time to become the quartzites and other metamorphic rocks that developed about 450 million years ago.

The major metamorphic rock types found in Little Mountain are muscovite mica and chlorite schists, phyllites, muscovite quartzites, and quartzites containing the minerals kyanite and hematite. Among other unusual minerals found at Little Mountain are pyrophyllite, gold, silver, rutile, ilmenite, lazulite, and pseudomorphs of limonite after pyrite. The Little Mountain area also shows evidence of faulting that is thought to have helped to develop some of its interesting mineralization. CAROLYN H. MURPHY

McKenzie, John C., and John F. McCauley. *Geology and Kyanite Resources of Little Mountain, South Carolina.* Columbia, S.C.: Division of Geology, State Development Board, 1968.

Murphy, Carolyn H. *Carolina Rocks! The Geology of South Carolina.* Orangeburg, S.C.: Sandlapper, 1995.

Littlejohn, Cameron Bruce (b. 1913). Attorney, legislator, jurist. Littlejohn was born on July 22, 1913, in Pacolet, the youngest of eight children born to Cameron and Lady Sarah Littlejohn. He entered Wofford College in 1930, where he spent three years before transferring to the University of South Carolina School of Law, receiving the LL.B. degree in 1936. Littlejohn was admitted to the practice of law in the same year. Shortly after opening his practice in Spartanburg, he announced plans to run for the General Assembly. Elected in 1936, he served three terms from 1937 until 1943.

Littlejohn resigned his seat in the House in the summer of 1943 to enter the U.S. Army, and he served until 1946. After the Japanese surrender in August 1945, he was sent to the Philippines, where he helped prosecute Japanese war criminals. Upon his return home, Littlejohn regained his seat in the House of Representatives, and a year later he successfully ran for Speaker of the House, a race that he won by seventeen votes over Thomas H. Pope, Jr. Littlejohn was reelected as Speaker in 1949.

Littlejohn's second term was brief. In February 1949, less than a month after his reelection as Speaker, the General Assembly elected him to the resident judgeship of the Seventh Judicial Circuit, a position he assumed in December 1949. It marked the beginning of a thirty-nine-year judicial career that would see him rise to the position of chief justice of the South Carolina Supreme Court. Littlejohn was serving his seventeenth year as circuit court judge when a vacancy occurred on the supreme court with the death of Chief Justice Claude A. Taylor in January 1966. Littlejohn declared his candidacy for the vacant associate justice position, but so did three other powerful South Carolina political figures: Judge Julius B. (Bubba) Ness, state senator Rembert Dennis, and former governor George Bell Timmerman. There ensued a vigorous contest among the four candidates, in which none could obtain the required majority vote in weekly ballots that extended through the entire 1966 session of the General Assembly.

The election was settled when the legislature reconvened in 1967 with an unusually large number of freshmen senators and House members. Dennis and Timmerman dropped out, and Littlejohn defeated Ness by forty-one votes, bolstered by the support he received from forty-seven freshmen. During his service as associate justice, Littlejohn advocated judicial reform, worked to strengthen admission standards for new attorneys and judges to practice law in the state, and expressed concern about sentencing disparities among judges.

With the retirement of Chief Justice Woodrow Lewis in 1984, Littlejohn ran for and was elected to that position. Although he would serve just sixteen months as chief justice until his retirement, he left a notable impact on the state's court system, particularly in settling the long-standing fight between the legislative and judicial branches over rule-making authority. Under the compromise reached during Littlejohn's tenure, the legislature was granted veto power over court rules with a three-fifths majority of the General Assembly.

Prior to and after his retirement, Littlejohn pursued a writing career and produced three books—*Laugh with the Judge* (1974), *Littlejohn's Half-Century on the Bench and Bar* (1987), and *Littlejohn's Political Memoirs* (1989). For years he also contributed a regular column to the State Bar Association's newsletter, several of which were published in national journals. PHILIIP G. GROSE, JR.

Littlejohn, C. Bruce. Papers. Modern Political Collections, South Caroliniana Library, University of South Carolina, Columbia.

Littlejohn, Nina (1879–1963). Hospital administrator. Littlejohn was born on February 28, 1879, at Wheat Hill in Cherokee County. Her parents, Emanuel and Alice Littlejohn, were landowning farmers. In addition to planting crops on their vast acreage, the Littlejohns raised horses and bees. Nina married Worth Littlejohn, who lived at Near Tickety Creek. The couple moved to Spartanburg, where they built a house at 218 North Dean Street. Worth Littlejohn was a barber, and his Magnolia Street shop catered only to a white clientele. The Littlejohns had one child, a daughter.

Aware that African Americans did not have access to suitable medical care, Littlejohn created the John-Nina Hospital in 1913. This hospital was the first medical facility established specifically for African American patients in Spartanburg, and the only one licensed in Spartanburg County. A member of the Spartanburg Area Chamber of Commerce, Littlejohn had political influence regarding civic programs beneficial for the hospital's improvement. Her husband also utilized his business contacts to secure financial and community support for the hospital. Littlejohn arranged for the two-story medical structure to be constructed next to her house. Between 1913 and 1932 the John-Nina Hospital provided medical services for the area's African American population. Patients were housed in two wards, holding a total of twenty people, and eight rooms, with a maximum occupancy of sixteen. An operating room was fitted with the most state-of-the-art surgical equipment and supplies available at that time. A backyard garden produced fresh vegetables crucial for the nutritious meals that aided patients' healing and recovery.

Aspiring to serve patients and manage staff professionally, Littlejohn took business classes at Claflin College in Orangeburg to improve her administration of the John-Nina Hospital. By 1932 Littlejohn's hospital was absorbed by the Spartanburg General Hospital, which opened an annex for blacks. Although some denounced her support of this segregated wing, Littlejohn was not deterred and persisted in her work to improve community conditions. She wanted to set an example of independence, capability, and fortitude for Spartanburg residents, especially African Americans.

After her husband died, Littlejohn married a Mr. Hunter. She was widowed a second time prior to dying on February 28, 1963, in Spartanburg. She was buried in that city's Lincoln Memorial Gardens. ELIZABETH D. SCHAFER

Lizard Man. In midsummer 1988 the teenager Chris Davis spotted the Lizard Man. The monster was seven feet tall with green, scaly skin, red eyes, and three toes on each foot. Then he slipped away, as lizards do. Deputy Chester Lighty, who patrolled Scape Ore Swamp, four miles south of Bishopville in Lee County, heard talk of the Lizard Man for the next three weeks. Two men described the creature chasing them away from a spring when they attempted to dip water. Tom and Mary Waye drove into the swamp, and the Lizard Man nearly chewed up their car before they escaped. By August 14 the Lizard Man was a national celebrity, having been described on the CBS Evening News on television. More than two hundred calls a day came from as far away as New Zealand and Germany. Governor Carroll Campbell said that nobody had put a handle on what it was or where it came from. A California researcher explained that South Carolina was dealing with a "skunk ape," more commonly known as "Bigfoot." Columbia Radio Station WCOS offered a $1 million reward for the capture of the Lizard Man, but as Governor Campbell said, "This is a very elusive sort of fellow." NANCY RHYNE

"The Legend of the Lizard Man." *Time* 132 (August 15, 1988): 21.

Local government. Local government in South Carolina consists of general-purpose governments and special-purpose governments. Counties and municipalities comprise the general-purpose governments. Special-purpose governments in South Carolina include school districts and special-purpose districts.

Municipalities and counties are political subdivisions of the state. The state constitution and statutes specify the basic governance structure and the general powers, duties, and authorities of counties and municipalities. The most notable piece of legislation defining their structure and authority is the Local Government Act of 1975. Each county in South Carolina operates under one of four forms of government: council, council-supervisor, council-administrator, or council-manager. Municipalities have three options: the council (weak mayor), mayor-council (strong mayor), or council-manager form. The major difference between these forms of local government is where administrative/executive authority lies. In other words, the authority resides either with the council or with an elected official, such as the mayor or county supervisor, or with an appointed manager or administrator.

The constitution and state statutes grant counties and municipalities the authority to exercise broad "police powers." These powers allow them to legislate for the purpose of regulating public health, safety, welfare, morals, and abatements of nuisances, so long as such regulations do not contradict the constitutional and statutory rights of citizens and general state law. The constitution and state statutes also grant counties and municipalities significant and broad latitude and authority to provide services based on the needs and expectations of their citizens. The majority of governmental services that affect the day-to-day lives of citizens are provided by general-purpose local governments—for example, fire and police protection, emergency medical services, infrastructure (water, sewer, drainage, streets, and sidewalks, for instance), parks and recreation, and cultural activities. The notable exception is public education, which is provided at the local government level by the school districts. County and municipal governments in South Carolina employ in excess of thirty thousand citizens to deliver these services.

The ability of counties and municipalities to respond effectively to these demands for services is tempered by the fact that the General Assembly has not extended true "fiscal" home rule to them. This means that counties and municipalities cannot impose taxes that they are not specifically authorized to levy by general state law. This was most recently affirmed by the Fiscal Authority Act (1997), in which the General Assembly stated that a "local governmental body may not impose a new tax after December 31, 1996, unless specifically authorized by the General Assembly." The General Assembly also defined the sources of revenue available to counties and municipalities.

Special-purpose districts usually supply one or a few services that general governments could not or would not provide. They possess significant administrative and fiscal independence from the general-purpose local governments and are separate legal entities. Special-purpose districts were created before implementation of "home rule" by special acts of the General Assembly and were created to respond to demands for services that the counties could not constitutionally or statutorily provide. The Local Government Act prohibits the creation of single-county districts. The services provided by special-purpose districts vary greatly but include, for example, water and sewer services, flood control, recreation, fire services, airports, and zoos. Special-purpose districts are governed by boards and commissions, some elected and some appointed. Special-purpose districts typically are funded through fees and charges for the services they provide, but many do have taxing powers granted in the legislation creating them.

School districts are also special-purpose districts. The eighty-five school districts in South Carolina have the responsibility for providing K–12 public education. The number of students varies greatly from district to district, ranging from more than 57,000 students to less than 500. Each of the school districts has a school board that makes local decisions. The large majority of these school boards are elected, although some are appointed. However, many of the decisions governing the operation of public schools are made by either the legislature or the South Carolina Department of Education. The federal government also mandates certain actions and programs as a condition of receiving federal dollars. Schools are funded primarily through a mix of state and local funding. Some targeted federal dollars also are added to the mix. The fiscal authority of school boards to set the budget varies from total independence to significant limitations imposed on the district in its enabling legislation. JON B. PIERCE

Tyer, Charlie B., ed. *South Carolina Government: An Introduction.* Columbia: Institute for Public Service and Policy Research, University of South Carolina, 2002.

Tyer, Charlie B., and Cole Blease Graham, Jr., eds. *Local Government in South Carolina.* 2 vols. Columbia: Bureau of Governmental Research and Service, University of South Carolina, 1984.

Local Government Act (1975). The Local Government Act of 1975, otherwise known as the Home Rule Act of 1975, was passed by the South Carolina General Assembly to implement the revised Article VIII of the state constitution adopted in 1973 and dealing with local government. As amended, Article VIII conferred home rule on all South Carolina cities and counties and directed the General Assembly to establish standardized forms of city and county government. The 1975 act did this.

Home rule began as a national movement in the late 1800s. It challenged an established doctrine known as Dillon's Rule, which stated that local governments have only those powers specifically delegated to them by the state and are creatures of the state. Dillon's Rule spread from state to state and was even affirmed by the U.S. Supreme Court in 1903 and 1923. It was the controlling principle in South Carolina law as well until the state supreme court case *Williams v. Town of Hilton Head* (1993), in which the court ruled that the principle was invalidated by Article VIII of the constitution.

Prior to home rule in South Carolina, the General Assembly exercised nearly total control over local governments. Legislative delegations made local policy as well as state policy. Counties, for example, typically had their annual budgets passed by their state legislative delegations in Columbia. Cities required special acts of the assembly to allow them to annex territory or provide a new service to their citizens. In short, the legislature engaged in what might be termed "micromanagement" of local government.

Home rule came later to South Carolina than it did to many other states. In the 1960s the decisions of the U.S. Supreme Court in *Baker v. Carr, Wesberry v. Sanders,* and *Reynolds v. Sims* brought about the "one-man, one-vote" requirement for state legislatures, which resulted in the redrawing of legislative and electoral district lines. This, together with urbanization and the growing complexity of state government, led to a movement to give local governments more autonomy and restrict micromanagement by the General Assembly. Reapportionment resulted in a shift of power in the 1970s from rural legislators to urban- and suburban-elected legislators, who were more sympathetic to the home-rule argument.

The 1975 Home Rule Act provided for three forms of city government: weak-mayor, strong-mayor, and council-manager; and four forms of county government: council, council-supervisor, council-administrator, and council-manager. The powers and duties of each of the forms are uniform across the state, but individual cities and counties have discretion over what services they provide. It is notable that in South Carolina home rule applies only to cities and counties. Special-purpose governments and school districts were not given home rule by the 1975 act or Article VIII.

Counties are generally regarded as the primary beneficiaries of home rule in South Carolina since they were subject to a restrictive interpretation of their powers prior to Article VIII and the 1975 act. They now share the same powers as cities and have become "urban service" providers in many parts of South Carolina where large cities are not present.

The Home Rule Act did not, however, explicitly give counties and cities the authority to decide what to tax. Consequently, in the 1993 case of *Williams v. Town of Hilton Head,* the state supreme court interpreted the law as granting that authority. The decision touched off a dispute with the General Assembly, which worked to reassert its prerogative as the final authority regarding local government powers. In 1997 the assembly passed the Fiscal Authority Act, which restricted the fiscal autonomy of cities and counties. Legislators have also resisted any expansion of the rights of cities to annex new territory easily. CHARLIE B. TYER

Easterwood, R. Michael. *The Development and Reorganization of Municipal Government in South Carolina.* Columbia: Bureau of Governmental Research and Service, University of South Carolina, 1984.

Tyer, Charlie B., ed. *South Carolina Government: An Introduction.* Columbia: Institute for Public Service and Policy Research, University of South Carolina, 2002.

Lockwood Greene. Lockwood Greene, the oldest continuously operating professional services firm in the United States, is an international engineering and construction organization based in Spartanburg. The company traces its history to 1832, when David Whitman, a self-taught "mill doctor," began advising New England textile mills about designs for new factories. After Whitman's death in 1858, Amos Lockwood, a mechanical engineer, acquired the Lewiston, Maine, consulting business. He moved the company to Providence, Rhode Island, in 1871 and incorporated A. D. Lockwood & Co.

The company's first major engineering project in South Carolina was designing Piedmont Manufacturing Company on the Saluda River, completed in 1876. Piedmont Mill, the first postbellum cotton mill in the state, became the prototype for mill construction in the South and helped begin the southern textile boom. During the next eleven years, its success led to other important South Carolina commissions at Vaucluse, Glendale, Charleston, Pacolet, and Pelzer. In 1882 Lockwood reorganized the rapidly growing company to include a partner, Stephen Greene, a university-trained textile engineer. Lockwood Greene & Co. provided a full range of services, including design, construction supervision, equipment ordering, and installation scheduling.

After Lockwood's sudden death in 1884, Greene expanded and diversified the company. Between 1882 and 1901, in addition to designing Georgia Institute of Technology, Lockwood Greene & Co. worked on forty percent of all new southern mills and had thirty-nine projects in South Carolina. Among the most innovative of these projects were the 1893 Columbia Mill, the world's first totally electric mill, and the 1895 conversion of Pelzer Mill No. 4 to electricity by transmitting power from the Saluda River four miles away. Business in the state was so active that by 1899 the company had briefly opened its first branch office, in Greenville.

Greene died in 1901, and his son, a twenty-two-year-old engineer, inherited the business. Edwin Greene expanded the company into mill management and ownership, and in 1915 he created Greelock Holding Company with three divisions, including Lockwood Greene & Co., Engineers. By 1928 the textile depression had nearly ruined the company; engineering was its only profitable division. Greelock was liquidated, but twenty-one new partners purchased the Lockwood Greene name and engineering business and continued operating despite intense financial pressures during the Great Depression. They did so by diversifying. Among the firm's major contracts in the 1920s and 1930s were the Atlantic City Auditorium (the home of the Miss America pageant), military installations, highway engineering, and newspaper plants. After World War II the company grew rapidly, with international contracts in Mexico and India, but it also continued to work on major South Carolina projects, including Spartanburg General Hospital, Spartanburg Auditorium, and facilities at Clemson College, the Citadel, Wofford College, and the University of South Carolina. In 1973 the company headquarters moved to Spartanburg.

With revenues in the hundreds of millions of dollars, Lockwood Greene became a tempting takeover target. In 1981 Philipp Holtzmann AG purchased eighty percent of Lockwood Greene's stock; in 1999 the company was integrated into J. A. Jones Inc. In 2003 it was acquired by CH2M Hill, a Denver engineering firm. JUDITH T. BAINBRIDGE

Lincoln, Samuel B. *Lockwood Greene: The History of an Engineering Business, 1832–1958.* Brattleboro, Vt.: Stephen Greene Press, 1960.

The Lockwood Greene Story: One Hundred Years of Engineering Progress. Spartanburg, S.C.: Lockwood Greene, 1986.

Wells, John E., and Robert E. Dalton. *The South Carolina Architects, 1885–1935: A Biographical Directory.* Richmond, Va.: New South Architectural Press, 1992.

Logan, Martha Daniell (1704–1779). Horticulturist. Logan was born on December 29, 1704, in Charleston, the daughter of the landgrave Robert Daniell and Martha Wainwright. Logan's father owned 48,000 acres and was appointed to two terms as the colony's lieutenant governor. Receiving a traditional girl's education, Logan was most influenced by her father's nursery business and learned how to cultivate plants.

When her father died in 1718, thirteen-year-old Logan inherited his vast Wando River property, probably including his nursery. She married George Logan, Jr., in 1719. The couple had eight children. Perhaps due to financial setbacks, Logan tutored and boarded students at her Wando River house. She placed advertisements describing her services in the *South-Carolina Gazette,* and a 1749 advertisement featured Logan's house and properties for sale. In the early 1750s Logan's family moved to town, and she secured employment at a Charleston boarding school. Her husband died in 1764.

Gardening preoccupied Logan's life. Her acquaintance with Elizabeth Lamboll enhanced her awareness of effective methods to cultivate indigenous plants. Sources are unclear whether Logan studied with Lamboll or appropriated her techniques from observation. Other Charleston gardeners gave Logan seeds and roots, although she was disappointed when Dr. Alexander Garden, a gifted gardener, ignored her requests for specimens of unusual plants from his garden.

Because gardening, especially landscaping with rare plants, had become a favored pastime among wealthy Charlestonians, Logan realized that amateur gardeners needed advice. She published the "Gardener's Kalendar," which became a standard text for colonial South Carolina gardeners, and contributed a gardening guide for John Tobler's *South Carolina Almanack* (1752).

Logan exchanged seeds with other botanical enthusiasts, including the naturalist John Bartram. He visited her garden in 1760, initiating a correspondence and trade of specimens. They used a silk bag to send seeds and lists of available plants, along with lists of plants that each desired from the other's geographical area. Logan shipped and received tubs of cuttings and roots on ships traveling between Charleston and Philadelphia, where Bartram lived. Bartram praised her in a letter to a London friend and wrote, "Mrs. Logan's garden is her delight."

As a professional horticulturist, Logan sold roots, cuttings, and seeds at her nursery. She advertised her plants and related products in the *South-Carolina Gazette.* A 1753 advertisement told customers that Logan had "A parcel of very good seed, flower roots, and fruit stones to be sold on the Green near Trott's Point." She offered plant products "just imported from London" and "flouring [*sic*] shrubs and box edging beds." Logan died in Charleston on June 28, 1779, and was buried in St. Philip's Churchyard. ELIZABETH D. SCHAFER

Bodie, Idella. *South Carolina Women.* Orangeburg, S.C.: Sandlapper, 1991.
Hollingsworth, Buckner. *Her Garden Was Her Delight.* New York: Macmillan, 1962.
Prior, Mary B., ed. "Letters of Martha Logan to John Bartram, 1760–1763." *South Carolina Historical Magazine* 59 (January 1958): 38–46.

Loggerhead turtle. State reptile. The loggerhead turtle (*Caretta caretta*), a threatened species, was named the state reptile in an act signed by Governor Carroll Campbell on June 1, 1988. Recognizing the loggerhead as "an important part of the marine ecosystem" and that South Carolina's coastline provides "some of the most pristine nesting areas" for the turtle on the East Coast, the General Assembly declared that the state's responsibility is "to preserve and protect our wildlife and natural resources."

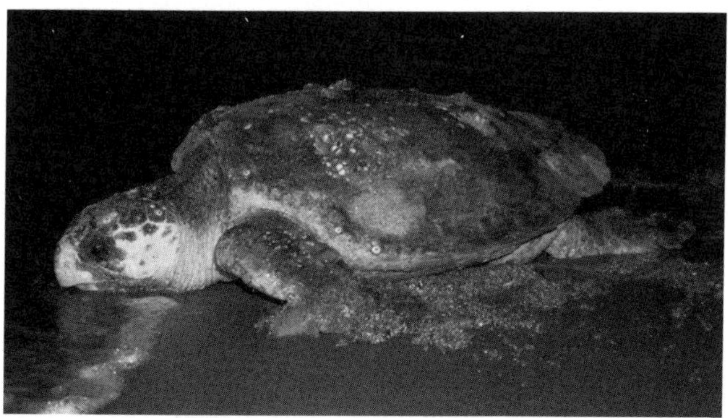

Loggerhead turtle. Photograph by Phillip Jones. Courtesy, South Carolina Department of Natural Resources

The loggerhead is one of the world's eight living species of sea turtles and evolved some sixty-five million to seventy million years ago. At birth, hatchlings are about two inches long. Adults can weigh from 200 to 350 pounds, and their carapace, or upper shell, measures from thirty-three to forty inches in length. The animal is yellow and reddish brown and has a distinctive large head—the source of its name—with powerful jaws enabling it to crush clams, crustaceans, and other food. Its great size and hard shell protect the adult turtle from most predators.

Adult loggerheads in the western Atlantic range from Newfoundland to Argentina, but they nest in the temperate zones. Breeding occurs in the ocean, and females lay their eggs between May and September. South Carolina beaches are favorite nesting grounds. The female comes ashore at night, lays from eighty to two hundred eggs in her nest, then returns to sea. Eggs and hatchlings are prey to many predators, from ants and crabs to dogs, raccoons, birds, and fish in the sea. Hatchlings must head directly to the ocean, and it is estimated that only one in ten thousand loggerhead eggs makes it to maturity. Dangers to the baby turtles include artificial lights on land, for they may head toward those, instead of seaward, and fall victim to predators. It is believed that it requires twelve to thirty years for loggerheads to reach maturity.

Adult loggerheads are imperiled by collisions with boats and, especially, by being trapped in commercial fishing and shrimping trawl nets, in which they drown if they cannot escape. South Carolinians have been active in working to protect nests and hatchlings, and communities have enacted restrictions on coastal lighting during nesting season. State legislation requires turtle excluder devices (TEDs) on trawl nets in order to protect the species. DAVID C. R. HEISSER

Gordon, Kay. "New Life for the Loggerheads." *Sandlapper* 2 (midyear 1991): 76–77.
National Research Council. Committee on Sea Turtle Conservation. *Decline of the Sea Turtles: Causes and Prevention.* Washington, D.C.: National Academy Press, 1990.
Ripple, Jeff. *Sea Turtles.* Stillwater, Minn.: Voyageur, 1996.

Londonborough Township. At times referred to as Belfast and Londonderry, the 22,000-acre Londonborough Township was laid out on Hard Labour Creek in 1762. Originally designed to provide a buffer between the Cherokees and lowcountry plantations, it was primarily populated by poor Palatine Protestants, previously living in England, who had been recruited by Johann Heinrich Christian von Stümpel, a "too hopeful immigration agent." Sponsored by a group of London philanthropists, granted land, and provisioned by the colonial government, these Germans began to arrive in Charleston in December 1764, with the first group of settlers departing for the township in early January 1765. Subsequent groups followed in the spring and early summer, and by autumn 1765 some 250 Germans were settled in and around the township's boundaries.

Despite direct assistance from the colony's government, the township never prospered. Lieutenant Governor William Bull suggested growing hemp and sent several bushels of seed to the Germans, but no significant hemp cultivation developed. Reports described Londonborough Township as "desperately poor" and "their children having 'grown up like savages.'" Mindful of their debt to their benefactors, many of the Germans immigrants sided with the British in the Revolutionary War and apparently left the area at its conclusion. By the time of the 1790 census, most of the original families were no longer listed, and the entire community disappeared in the first decades of the nineteenth century. A historical marker on S.C. State Road 48 in Greenwood County marks the site of settlement. MICHAEL EVERETTE BELL

Bittinger, Lucy Forney. *The Germans in Colonial Times.* Philadelphia: J. B. Lippincott, 1901.
Meriwether, Robert L. *The Expansion of South Carolina, 1729–1765.* Kingsport, Tenn.: Southern Publishers, 1940.
Selig, Robert A. "Emigration, Fraud, Humanitarianism, and the Founding of Londonderry, South Carolina, 1763–1765." *Eighteenth-Century Studies* 23 (fall 1989): 1–23.

Long, William Williams (1861–1934). Agriculturalist. Long was born in Warrenton, North Carolina, on July 4, 1861, the son of Nicholas M. Long and Sallie Hawkins. Orphaned as a young boy, Long was reared by his grandfather Samuel A. Williams. After attending the University of North Carolina from 1880 to 1881, Long returned to Warren County to farm. He served in the North Carolina legislature from 1890 to 1893, then joined the U.S. Department of Agriculture's Bureau of Plant Industry. In 1898 Long married Mary Petit of Lafayette, Indiana. They had no children.

Seaman A. Knapp, head of extension work for the Department of Agriculture, invited Long to join the Farmers Cooperative Demonstration Work as field agent for the South Atlantic states. Long held the position until 1913, when Clemson College asked him to reorganize the Extension Service in South Carolina. He stayed on as director when in 1915 the General Assembly named

Clemson as the Extension Service agent under provisions of the Smith-Lever Act of 1914. Long served as director for the remainder of his life. His longtime friend Clarence Poe, editor of *The Progressive Farmer,* praised Long for his high character, integrity, and interest in "the whole range of country life needs." Through the Extension Service, Long helped improve crop production, the livestock industry, commodity marketing, rural cooperation, and the social life of rural South Carolina. Long insisted that his county agents remain above reproach, and he demanded no less of himself. In 1930 he turned down an offer of an eight-week, expense-paid trip to Chile from a fertilizer concern, explaining that "a public official . . . must be, like Caesar's wife, above suspicion." Long died from a stroke on November 13, 1934, and is buried in Cemetery Hill, Clemson. Long Agricultural Hall on the Clemson campus and W. W. Long 4–H Leadership Center in Aiken County bear his name. THOMAS W. LOLLIS

"Dr. W. W. Long of Clemson College Dies Following Stroke." *Anderson Independent,* November 14, 1934, p. 12.

Longshoremen's Protective Union Association. Chartered in 1869, the Longshoremen Protective Union Association (LPUA) established the legacy of a strong union presence, comprised almost exclusively of African Americans, along Charleston's docks. Their longevity, influence, and success mark Charleston longshoremen as perhaps the most prominent exception to South Carolina's long tradition of anti-unionism.

Before the Civil War the task of loading port cargo was relegated to slave labor. After the war dockworkers found themselves in competition with rural freedmen who made their way to Charleston. The flood of labor depressed wages among port workers. Perhaps emboldened by the role played by African Americans in South Carolina's Reconstruction politics, Charleston's LPUA obtained its charter from the General Assembly on March 19, 1869.

A series of unprecedented strikes solidified the LPUA's control over dockside labor. In January 1868 and September 1869 shipping lines raised wages following union work stoppages, and in 1873 Charleston's Democratic mayor convinced a shipping line to accede to union demands. LPUA leadership soon forced shippers to agree to a closed shop and convinced stevedores to join the union. The union's influence extended beyond Reconstruction; in 1898 the LPUA pressured a shipper into removing imported nonunion workers from Charleston. At the turn of the century longshoring wages in Charleston were double that of Savannah, Georgia, or Wilmington, North Carolina. Ironically, the LPUA was successful in large part due to racial attitudes among potential white strikebreakers. Whites perceived longshoring labor, long the province of Charleston's African Americans, as socially demeaning; other blacks refused to cross the picket lines. Shippers were largely unable to find suitable replacement workers.

From its inception, the LPUA was influential in both Republican and Democratic politics. Local Republicans counseled the union during various strikes, and in 1869 the LPUA successfully conducted a strike to protest a member's dismissal for Republican Party involvement. That year state Republicans called a statewide labor convention in Charleston that included the Speaker of the House and the secretary of state. The LPUA's Democratic influence was exerted through C. H. Simonton, an influential white representative from Charleston, who led legislative efforts to charter the LPUA in 1869, and to recharter it in 1880.

Beyond politics, the LPUA was a respected part of the Charleston community. The association's July 4, 1875, parade was viewed as "exceedingly creditable." Later that year the *News and Courier* hailed the union as "the most powerful organization of the colored laboring class in South Carolina." LPUA action steeled the resolve of other Charleston unions, inspiring a failed 1873 citywide strike that affected nearly all area phosphate, rice, and saw mills.

Hurricanes, an earthquake, port neglect, and poor rail connections damaged the Port of Charleston's viability in the late nineteenth century, and the LPUA lacked adequate work. The union's charter was not renewed in 1900. However, organized Charleston longshoremen resurfaced in 1936 when George German chartered International Longshoremen's Association Local 1422. By the close of the twentieth century, ILA Local 1422 held one of the largest private pension funds in the state, was measured among the most efficient port labor forces in the world, and for a South Carolina labor union, enjoyed unusually broad support among local politicians and business leaders. ELI A. POLIAKOFF

Poliakoff, Eli A. "Charleston's Longshoremen: Organized Labor in the Anti-Union Palmetto State." *South Carolina Historical Magazine* 103 (July 2002): 247–64.

Powers, Bernard E. *Black Charlestonians: A Social History, 1822–1885.* Fayetteville: University of Arkansas Press, 1994.

Longstreet, Augustus Baldwin (1790–1870). Educator, author, clergyman, jurist. Longstreet was born in Augusta, Georgia, on September 22, 1790, the son of William Longstreet and Hannah Randolph. In 1808 he attended Moses Waddel's School in Willington, South Carolina, and boarded with the family of John C. Calhoun. In 1811 Longstreet followed in Calhoun's footsteps, enrolling at Yale College in the junior class and graduating in 1813. He attended the law school in Litchfield, Connecticut, operated by Tapping Reeve and James Gould.

In 1815 Longstreet returned to Georgia, was admitted to the bar, and begin to ride the circuit as an attorney. On March 3, 1817, he married Eliza Frances Park. They had eight children, only two of whom survived to adulthood. In 1821 Longstreet was elected to the Georgia legislature, and the following year he was elected superior court judge of Omalgee District. In 1824 he was a candidate for Congress, but he withdrew after the death of his son.

In the wake of the family tragedy, Longstreet became deeply religious, joined the Methodist Episcopal Church in 1827, and in 1838 was accepted into the ministry. Meanwhile, he returned to the practice of law in Augusta and became a plantation owner. However, he was unsuccessful at planting and sold his land and slaves. He also edited the *States Rights Sentinel* and in 1830 began writing a series of literary sketches of rural life in Georgia, which he published in 1835 as *Georgia Scenes: Characters, Incidents, Etc., in the First Half Century of the Republic.* They were extremely popular and were regularly republished throughout the century. Longstreet's work became known as one of the best examples of southern backwoods humor.

In 1839 Longstreet became president of Emory College in Oxford, Georgia. Becoming well known as a southern apologist, in 1847 he published *A Voice from the South,* a series of strongly worded proslavery letters. In 1849 he became president of Centenary College in Jackson, Louisiana, but he left that post after one year to become president of the University of Mississippi. In 1856, after a bitter dispute with the Know-Nothing Party, he retired from public life.

On November 29, 1856, Longstreet was elected president of South Carolina College with the support of trustees James L. Petigru,

Chancellor Francis H. Wardlaw, and Judge David L. Wardlaw, all fellow students of Waddel's Academy. The new president was not a strong teacher, preferring telling tall tales in his parlor to delivering learned lectures. But he was a strict disciplinarian, and trustees hoped that he would solve disciplinary problems at the college. In 1858 when students protested to demand that Calhoun's birthday become a holiday, Longstreet suspended half the student body. He was also a passionate defender of states' rights and became extremely popular in South Carolina, though he had second thoughts about secession in *Shall South Carolina Begin the War?* He resigned in May 1860, effective a year later. But since civil war had broken out by that time, he agreed to remain until the fall of 1861.

Longstreet returned to Oxford, Mississippi, to be near his daughter, the wife of Lucius Q. C. Lamar, later U.S. senator and Supreme Court justice. He died on July 9, 1870, and was buried in St. Peter's Cemetery, Oxford. A. V. HUFF, JR.

Hollis, Daniel Walker. *University of South Carolina.* Vol. 1, *South Carolina College.* Columbia: University of South Carolina Press, 1951.

Stewart, E. Kate. "Augustus Baldwin Longstreet." In *Dictionary of Literary Biography.* Vol. 248, *Antebellum Writers in the South, Second Series,* edited by Kent Ljungquist. Detroit: Gale, 2001.

Wade, John Donald. *Augustus Baldwin Longstreet: A Study of the Development of Culture in the South.* 1924. Reprint, Athens: University of Georgia Press, 1969.

Longstreet, James Peter (1821–1904). Soldier. Longstreet was born on January 8, 1821, in Edgefield District, the son of James Longstreet and Mary Anne Dent. He spent his formative years in Georgia and Alabama. He entered the U.S. Military Academy at West Point in 1838 and graduated in 1842 near the bottom of his class. His service record after graduation, especially during the Mexican War, was highly commendable, and by 1858 he had achieved the rank of major. On March 8, 1848, he married Maria Garland of Virginia. The marriage produced ten children. Following Maria's death in 1889, Longstreet married Helen Dortch on September 8, 1897.

In June 1861 Longstreet resigned his U.S. Army commission and joined the Confederate army. Entering service as a brigadier general, he distinguished himself as a superb military tactician in several major battles, including First Manassas (July 21, 1861), after which he was promoted to major general. His service in the Army of Northern Virginia included participation in the Peninsular campaign of 1862 and Second Manassas (August 29–30, 1862), where his tactical skill played a key role in the Confederate victory. When Robert E. Lee took charge of the army in June 1862, he made Longstreet his second in command. He became Lee's closest confidant and military adviser, and was made a lieutenant general in October 1862. Longstreet's command fought with distinction at the battles at Sharpsburg (September 17, 1862) and Fredericksburg (December 11–15, 1862). Longstreet's opposition to Pickett's Charge and accusations of foot-dragging on the second and third days of the Battle of Gettysburg (July 1–3, 1863) garnered criticism, largely unjustified, from many postwar historians. Detached for service in the west after Gettysburg, he scored an impressive tactical victory at Chickamauga (September 18–20, 1863), but his 1863–1864 siege of Knoxville, Tennessee, was unsuccessful, and he subsequently rejoined the Army of Northern Virginia. He served brilliantly at the Battle of the Wilderness (May 5–6, 1864), where he sustained a serious wound from friendly fire. He rejoined the army later that year and served until Lee's surrender at Appomattox Courthouse in April 1865.

After the war Longstreet settled in New Orleans and alienated many postwar southerners by joining the Republican Party. After Lee's death in 1870, some of his former subordinates launched a concerted effort to deify their former commander, blaming Longstreet in speeches and writings for the Confederate failure at Gettysburg. He defended his actions in his memoirs, *From Manassas to Appomattox* (1896), which criticized the actions at Gettysburg of Lee and the flamboyant cavalry leader J. E. B. Stuart. Longstreet's political decisions, coupled with his criticism of Lee, effectively eclipsed his standing among surviving Civil War icons. However, this social ostracism did not preclude a life of public service for Longstreet, and he obtained a series of federal posts in the United States and abroad. In 1886 he arrived, uninvited, on horseback and in his Confederate uniform at a meeting of Civil War veterans in Atlanta, where he was embraced by former Confederate president Jefferson Davis. But the gesture did little to rescue his reputation among his fellow southerners. He died on January 2, 1904, in Gainesville, Georgia, where he was buried. WILLIAM SHAUN ALEXANDER

Piston, William Garrett. *Lee's Tarnished Lieutenant: James Longstreet and His Place in Southern History.* Athens: University of Georgia Press, 1987.

Tucker, Glenn. *Lee and Longstreet at Gettysburg.* Indianapolis: Bobbs-Merrill, 1968.

Wert, Jeffrey D. *General James Longstreet: The Confederacy's Most Controversial Soldier.* New York: Simon & Schuster, 1993.

Lords Proprietors of Carolina. King Charles II granted the land that became North and South Carolina to eight English noblemen in 1663. Before the government of King George II bought out the last owners in 1729, nearly fifty individuals owned or claimed to own these eight shares. South Carolina owes its formative beginnings to these shareholders and their joint colonial enterprise.

Most of the eight original proprietors had remained staunch supporters of the Stuart monarchy after the execution of King Charles I in 1649, and others changed sides to become key figures in the restoration of his son in 1660. The original proprietors gained both elevated rank in the English nobility and colonial property as rewards for this service. The titles of the eight initial owners reflect their rise: Edward Hyde, first earl of Clarendon; George Monck, first duke of Albemarle; William Craven, first earl of Craven; Anthony Ashley Cooper, first earl of Shaftesbury; John Berkeley, first baron Berkeley of Stratton, and his brother Sir William Berkeley, governor of Virginia; Sir George Carteret; and Sir John Colleton. No documentary evidence survives for the organization of the joint enterprise, but it is likely that it was suggested by Sir John Colleton, who ran its affairs in the early years until his death in 1667. A second charter in 1665 extinguished lingering claims from an earlier grant to Sir Robert Heath and extended the grant's boundaries.

Settlement attempts by New Englanders and Barbadians failed, but the foundering colonial enterprise was rescued by Anthony Ashley Cooper in 1669. Ashley Cooper, who had not yet become the first earl of Shaftesbury, persuaded the other proprietors to fund an expedition from England that established the first permanent English settlement in South Carolina in 1670. None of the original proprietors ever set foot in their colony. Two of them, the earl of Clarendon and Sir William Berkeley, failed to contribute their shares to the financing of the joint enterprise. Sir Peter Colleton, who inherited his father's share, and the five other active shareholders added the joint proprietorship of the Bahamas to their holdings

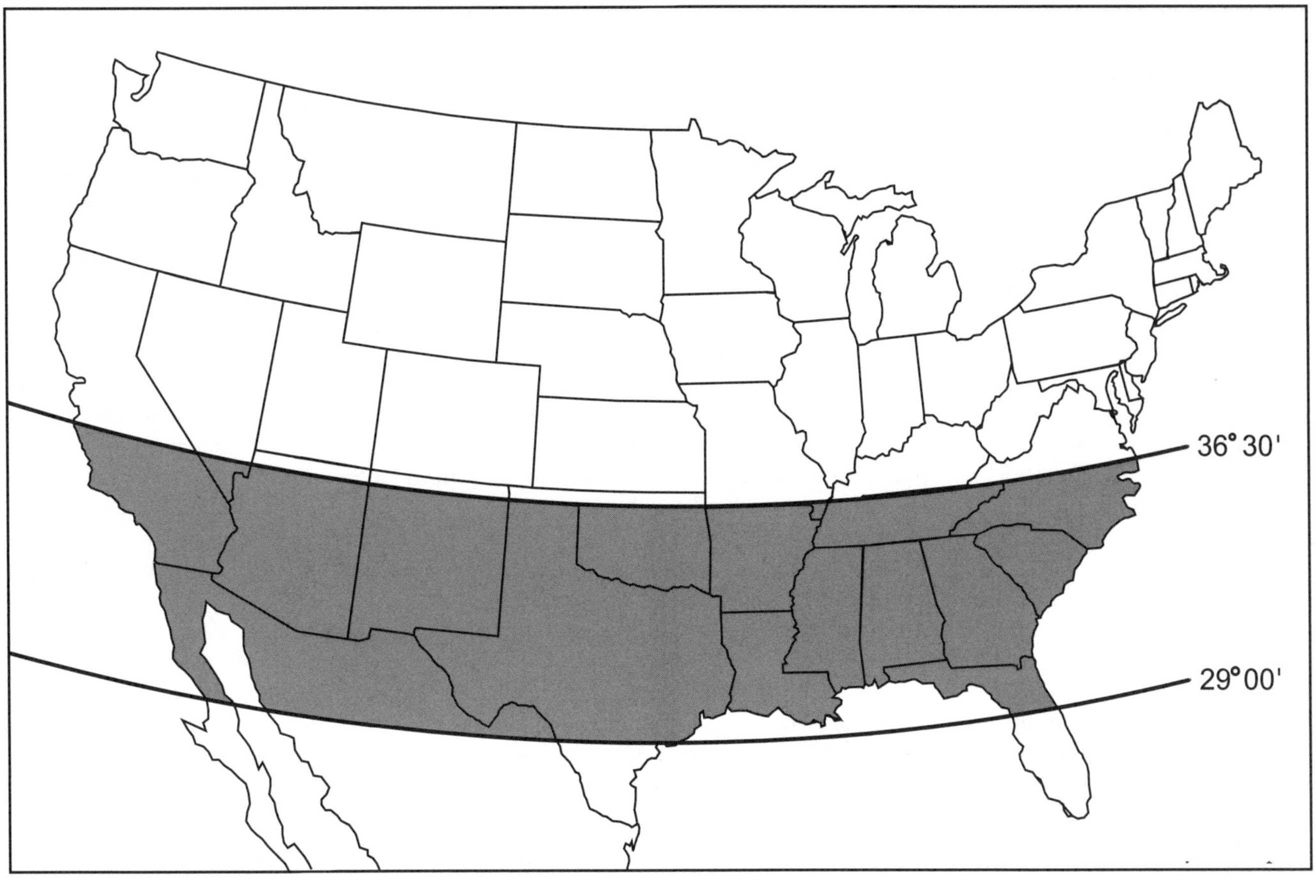

36° 30'

29°00'

The boundaries of the original Carolina grant of 1665

Factional politics under the Lords Proprietors sometimes led to armed confrontations on election day. Courtesy, South Caroliniana Library, University of South Carolina

in the same year that South Carolina was founded. A 1672 agreement to give the Albemarle region, which had been previously settled from neighboring Virginia, to Sir William Berkeley in exchange for his share in the proprietorship fell through. Protracted disputes over the ownership of his share and the Clarendon share necessitated an act of Parliament to assure clear title when the proprietorship was surrendered to the crown in 1729.

Ashley Cooper with assistance from John Locke, who served as secretary to the proprietorship from 1668 to 1675, wrote the Fundamental Constitutions as part of the preparations for the 1669 expedition. That document's elaborate provisions provided a governing structure for the proprietorship as well as the colonial settlements. The group was to be headed by a palatine, whose substantial powers in naming governors and vetoing laws sometimes had a major impact in South Carolina in later years. The title "palatine" had its origins in the feudal powers of the prince/bishops of Durham, powers granted to the shareholders in their charters. The first three palatines, George Monck, John Berkeley, and Sir George Carteret, were more like figureheads during the years from 1669 to 1682 when the earl of Shaftesbury took the lead in managing their affairs and the fledgling South Carolina settlement.

English noblemen supported their opulent lifestyles from the rents from their landed estates, and the proprietors expected to profit handsomely from their vast new American holdings. They were quickly disappointed when in the early years the often-stubborn colonists did not repay the expenses of setting up the colony. Collection of quitrents on land granted to colonists was a continual problem. Dreams of wealth from gold and silver or the production of wine, silk, and olive oil proved all too elusive for the colony's successive proprietary owners. Shares in the joint enterprise were bought and sold over the years, but none of the proprietors reaped much profit from their colonial investment.

Only the Colleton, Carteret, and Craven shares remained in the hands of the families of their original owners in 1729. Later generations of the Colleton family were resident South Carolinians at Fair Lawn Seignory on the upper Cooper River. John Carteret, earl of Granville, the great-great-grandson of the original owner, did not join the other seven shareholders in selling out to the crown and received the Granville District along North Carolina's northern border as his eighth share in the colonial property.

John Archdale, who also served as one of South Carolina's most effective proprietary governors, bought two different shares over the years. Because he was a Quaker, he placed the first in his son's name, and he was subsequently disappointed when that son sold it when he came of age. In contrast to Archdale's positive influence, another purchaser, Seth Sothel, brought disruption and discord when he briefly claimed the governor's office in South Carolina in 1690.

Proprietary efforts to control South Carolina's development were slightly more successful than their hoped-for profits. South Carolinians early on asserted an irritating independence. Attempts by royal officials to void the charter began as early as the 1680s in moves to tighten control over England's colonies. From the South Carolinians' point of view, the proprietors' vetoes of their laws, their failure to adequately support the colony's security, their cessation of further land grants at the same time that they reserved fifteen large tracts for proprietor's baronies, and other grievances had "unhinged the frame of government." In December 1719 the South Carolinians revolted against the proprietary regime and asked the crown to take direct control of the colony. A provisional royal governor arrived in 1721, and negotiations led to the 1729 surrender of the proprietors' ownership of Carolina to the British government. CHARLES H. LESSER

Lesser, Charles H. *South Carolina Begins: The Records of a Proprietary Colony, 1663–1721.* Columbia: South Carolina Department of Archives and History, 1995.

Powell, William S. *The Proprietors of Carolina.* Raleigh, N.C.: Carolina Charter Tercentenary Commission, 1963.

Lott, Robert Bretley (b. 1958). Author, educator. Bret Lott was born in Los Angeles, California, on October 8, 1958, the son of Wilman Sequoia Lott and Barbara Joan Holmes. He married Melanie Kai Swank on June 28, 1980, and they have two sons. Lott's education includes a B.A. from California State University–Long Beach (1981) and an M.F.A. from the University of Massachusetts–Amherst (1984). He has held the position of writer-in-residence at the College of Charleston since 1986 and is a full professor at that institution. Lott is also a faculty member of the Vermont College M.F.A. program. Prior to his tenure at the College of Charleston, he taught English at the Ohio State University and the University of Massachusetts–Amherst.

Publications by Lott include the novels *The Man Who Owned Vermont* (1987), *A Stranger's House* (1988), *Jewel* (1991), *Reed's Beach* (1993), *The Hunt Club* (1998), and *The Song I Knew by Heart* (2004). His short-story collections include *A Dream of Old Leaves* (1989), *How To Get Home* (1996), and *An Evening on the Cusp of the Apocalypse* (2005). Other publications include the memoir *Fathers, Sons and Brothers* (1997) and the essay collection *Before We Get Started: On Writing* (2004). Lott began publishing short stories in 1983, and his fiction and essays have appeared in dozens of literary journals and other publications, including *The Prentice Hall Reader* and *The Best Essays from a Quarter-Century of the Pushcart Prize* (2002).

The primary focus of Lott's writing lies within the homes and hearts of middle-class America, average people leading average lives, seeking happiness and struggling against despair. *Jewel,* his most acclaimed novel, has been translated into half-a-dozen languages. As an Oprah Book Club selection, it was reissued in 1999, along with all his earlier publications. Lott was a student of James Baldwin, though Raymond Carver is his greatest literary influence. Other influences include John Gardner (who taught Carver) and Richard Ford.

Lott directed the Charleston Writers' Conference from 1989 to 1994. Since 2001 he has edited the prestigious literary journal *Crazyhorse,* a publication of the College of Charleston. He has also influenced American letters as a judge for prominent literary competitions and as a panelist for the NEA Fellowships in Creative Writing. Lott has been a Bread Loaf Fellow in Fiction and a recipient of the South Carolina Arts Commission Fellowship in Literature. He won the PEN/NEA Syndicated Fiction Project Award in 1985, 1991, and 1993.

When asked what he considers his most significant contribution to South Carolina letters, Lott replied without hesitation, "My life as a teacher." Though he was reared in California, Lott considers himself a southerner, noting that "My family is from East Texas and Mississippi—I grew up drinking sweet tea and eating fried pork chops. My sensibilities as a person are southern—I just don't have the accent." ELLEN MALPHRUS

Cornett, Sheryl. "A Conversation with Bret Lott." *Image: A Journal of the Arts and Religion* 37 (winter 2002–2003): 47–59.

Newell, C. E. "Lott, Bret." In *Contemporary Southern Writers.* Detroit: St. James, 1999.

Louisville, Cincinnati and Charleston Rail Road Company. This railroad represented the most ambitious dreams of the antebellum Charleston business community: a transportation connection to the markets of the Midwest that would return their city to national prominence. Agitation for such a route began early; an 1832 proposal to survey a route from Columbia to Knoxville failed when North Carolina and Tennessee refused to put forth any money. In 1835 a committee of citizens headed by Robert Y. Hayne proposed surveying a route to Cincinnati, Ohio; that same year the group convinced the South Carolina General Assembly to spend $10,000 to cover the surveys. The company was chartered on December 19, 1835, to connect Charleston and Cincinnati. Louisville was added two months later to appease a Kentucky legislature reluctant to support any project that would benefit only Cincinnati. In 1837 the company purchased stock in the South Carolina Canal and Rail Road Company in an effort to secure a source of revenue. That same year the company began constructing a sixty-mile line from Branchville to Columbia—the only track it ever built. Its charter was later amended by the General Assembly to grant banking privileges in an effort to finance the project. The company in turn organized the South Western Rail Road Bank, but efforts to secure a charter for the bank in the other states along the route proved fruitless.

Despite initial fanfare, the Louisville, Cincinnati and Charleston Rail Road soon foundered because of the inability of the various states to agree on the level of necessary financial commitment, the difficult economic climate following the Panic of 1837, competition from neighboring projects, and the death in 1839 of Hayne, the project's most vigorous supporter. Consolidation with the South

Carolina Canal and Rail Road was considered as early as 1840, and in 1843 the two companies were joined to form the South Carolina Rail Road Company. While Charlestonians would still dream of western trade, the search for a single route connecting their city and the Ohio Valley was effectively over. AARON W. MARRS

Derrick, Samuel M. *Centennial History of South Carolina Railroad.* 1930. Reprint, Spartanburg, S.C.: Reprint Company, 1975.

Phillips, Ulrich Bonnell. *History of Transportation in the Eastern Cotton Belt to 1860.* 1908. Reprint, New York: Octagon, 1968.

Lovers of Meher Baba. Merwan Sheriar Irani, known as Meher Baba, was born in Poona, India, on February 25, 1894, of Persian parents. In 1913, while still in college, he met Hazrat Babajan, an old Muslim woman and one of the five "perfect masters" of the age. Babajan gave him God-realization and made him aware of his high spiritual destiny. Later Merwan met Upasni Maharaj, Hindu perfect master, who for seven years shared gnosis, or divine knowledge, with Merwan. Having attained spiritual perfection, in 1921 he drew together his first close disciples and began his spiritual mission. These disciples gave him the name "Meher Baba" ("Compassionate Father"), and without regard for differences of castes and creeds, he gave them training in moral discipline, love for God, spiritual understanding, and selfless service. His disciples, called "lovers," viewed him as the avatar, or manifestation of God, for this age. Meher Baba traveled to the West six times, first in 1931, when he contacted his early Western disciples, among whom were Princess Norina Matchabelli and Elizabeth Chapin Patterson. His last visit to America was in 1958, when he stayed at a spiritual center in Myrtle Beach that he had opened in 1952 and called "My home in the West." Land for the center was donated by Elizabeth Patterson, daughter of Simeon Chapin, a prominent businessman and developer of Myrtle Beach. The center remained vital and was directed by Kitty Davy, Baba's oldest Western disciple, until her death in December 1991 at one hundred years old. PRESTON L. MCKEVER-FLOYD

Baba, Meher. *Discourses.* 7th ed. Myrtle Beach, S.C.: Sheriar Press, 1987.

Davy, Kitty. *Love Alone Prevails.* Myrtle Beach, S.C.: Sheriar Press, 1981.

Lowcountry baskets. For as long as people of African descent have lived in Carolina, they have made baskets. The early history of the lowcountry coiled grass basket parallels the rise of rice cultivation on the southeastern coast of North America. The skills associated with growing rice and processing the grain were familiar to Africans, especially people from the upper Guinea coast, where Europeans saw rice under cultivation as early as 1446, and people from the inland delta of the Niger River, where rice has been grown for two thousand years. One particular basket—a wide winnowing tray called a "fanner," common to both Senegambia and South Carolina—was essential in separating the grain from its chaff.

Like the grasslands and marshes of western and central Africa, the coastal wetlands of Georgia and South Carolina provide grasses and plant fiber appropriate for making coiled baskets. On lowcountry plantations, enslaved Africans used bulrush most often as the foundation material. To wrap and stitch the rows of the baskets together, people who lived on the Sea Islands fashioned strips from the stems of saw palmettos, while sewers on the mainland used white oak splints.

Following the Civil War, men continued to make agricultural baskets on family farms carved out of the old plantations, while women made household forms such as sewing and storage baskets, carrying trays, and "missionary bags," said to be modeled on bags carried by the Quaker missionaries. With rice production in decline, household baskets came to dominate, and women became more conspicuous in the craft. The shift from "work baskets" to "show baskets" also meant a change in materials from bulrush to sweetgrass and from saw palmetto to cabbage palm.

The sweetgrass revolution at the turn of the twentieth century began in the vicinity of Boone Hall Plantation near the village of Mount Pleasant, across the Cooper River from Charleston. There, around 1916, a young merchant named Clarence W. Legerton contacted Sam Coakley, an elder in the black community, and arranged to come every other Saturday to Coakley's house to buy baskets in quantity to sell retail in his King Street shop and wholesale to department stores in New York and other northern cities.

In 1938 basket maker Viola Jefferson posed by her stand outside Charleston. Note the sign in the background to "STOP AND BUY BASKETS MADE BY C[O]L[ORE]D PEOPLE." Photograph by Bluford Muir. Courtesy, U.S. Forestry Service

Basket production increased dramatically. With the paving of coastal Highway 17 and the opening of the Cooper River Bridge in 1929, basket makers found a way to reach their primary market directly. They began selling baskets on the roadside, displaying them on chairs or overturned crates. As the tourist trade quickened, sewers responded with new basket shapes displayed on an innovative marketing device—the basket stand.

Since the 1970s, suburban and resort development has drastically diminished the local supply of sweetgrass. The highway that once assured the survival of the tradition threatens to run the basket stands off the road. In spite of these dangers, lowcountry basketry continued to thrive into the twenty-first century. To compensate for the sweetgrass shortage, sewers reintroduced bulrush. Baskets became bigger and bolder. As symbols of a distinct African American culture, lowcountry baskets have much significance and meaning. Yet they remain what they have always been: coiled grass vessels that are useful for countless purposes. DALE ROSENGARTEN

Davis, Gerald L. "Afro-American Coil Basketry in Charleston County, South Carolina." In *American Folklife,* edited by Don Yoder. Austin: University of Texas Press, 1976.

Day, Gregory. "Afro-Carolinian Art: Towards the History of a Southern Expressive Tradition." *Contemporary Art / Southeast* 1 (January/February 1978): 10–21.

Day, Virginia Kay. "'My Family Is Me': Women's Kin Networks and Social Power in a Black Sea Island Community." Ph.D. diss., Rutgers University, 1983.

Derby, Doris Adelaide. "Black Women Basket Makers: A Study of Domestic Economy in Charleston County, South Carolina." Ph.D. diss., University of Illinois, 1980.

Rosengarten, Dale. "'Bulrush Is Silver, Sweetgrass Is Gold': The Enduring Art of Sea Grass Basketry." *Folklife Annual 88–89,* edited by James Hardin and Alan Jabbour. Washington, D.C.: American Folklife Center, Library of Congress, 1989.

———. *Row upon Row: Sea Grass Baskets of the South Carolina Lowcountry.* Columbia: McKissick Museum, University of South Carolina, 1986.

———. "Social Origins of the African-American Lowcountry Basket." Ph.D diss., Harvard University, 1997.

Vlach, John Michael. *The Afro-American Tradition in Decorative Arts.* 1978. Reprint, Athens: University of Georgia Press, 1990.

Lowman lynchings. In the early hours of Friday, October 8, 1926, Bertha, twenty-seven years old; Demon, twenty-one; and Clarence Lowman, fourteen (a brother and sister and their first cousin, respectively), were taken from their cells in the Aiken County jail, herded into several "fully loaded" vehicles, and driven to a pine thicket on the outskirts of Aiken, where, according to one account, one thousand persons and several hundred cars waited. The Lowmans were ordered out and shot down by a fusillade of bullets. Demon and Clarence died immediately, but Bertha did not. Charlton Wright, editor of the *Columbia Record,* conjured the grisly image of the woman "clinging to her wretched life, squirming and dragging herself like a broken worm through the bushes, until killed by a merciful bullet through her head." "The negroes," reported the *Aiken Standard,* "were not swung up. Their bodies fell where they stood." According to the coroner, Clarence died from a gunshot blast under the chin, Demon from a .38 revolver shot to the breast, and Bertha from a .38 revolver shot through the left ear. Eyewitnesses said that Aiken County sheriff Nollie Robinson administered the deathblow to Bertha.

Prisoners quartered in the Aiken County jail that night later swore that the Lowmans were forcibly taken from their cells by Sheriff Robinson, his deputy Arthur D. Sheppard, the jailer Rupert Taylor, state constable J. Percy Hart, and local traffic officer John B. Salley. Robinson and Taylor claimed to have been overpowered and knocked unconscious in the jail by a mob that cut the town's electrical line. The darkness, they said, rendered their ability to make identifications impossible.

Eighteen months before, on April 25, 1925, then Aiken County sheriff Henry Hampton Howard, accompanied by his deputies Robinson, Sheppard, and Robert E. McElhaney, had raided the Lowman household near Monetta in search of illegal liquor. Howard and Annie Lowman, the mother of Bertha and Demon, were killed in the incident. No whiskey was found, and no one witnessed Howard's death, but Sam Lowman, the patriarch (who was not home at the time), received a two-year sentence of hard labor for prohibition violation, while Clarence and Demon were sentenced to death, and Bertha to life imprisonment. N. J. Frederick of Columbia, one of a few practicing black attorneys in South Carolina at that time, appealed the sentences of Clarence, Demon, and Bertha to the S.C. Supreme Court and won a retrial. On October 7, 1926, at the close of a third day of testimony, presiding judge Samuel T. Lanham of Spartanburg directed a verdict of not guilty for Demon Lowman. It was widely suspected that Bertha and Clarence might be acquitted the following day.

The news of the Lowmans' deaths stirred a firestorm of state and national outrage. Walter White, assistant secretary of the National Association for the Advancement of Colored People, went to Aiken posing as a New York newspaper reporter. There he gathered startling information from two white residents of the Horse Creek Valley, home to Howard, Robinson, and Sheppard, that implicated the officers as Klansmen and the lynching (and possibly the 1925 liquor raid) as an act of Ku Klux Klan retribution. White convinced Herbert Bayard Swope, editor of the influential *New York World,* to send his own investigative journalist to Aiken to ferret out the details. On November 5, 1926, Oliver H. P. Garrett began filing a long series of sensational front-page accounts that portrayed Aiken County—home to an anomalous population of cotton mill workers, winter colonists such as the Vanderbilts and Whitneys, and a black majority population of agricultural laborers—as a corrupt community managed with a heavy dose of Klan brutality.

In spite of Garrett's revelations, South Carolina governor Thomas G. McLeod and his successor, John G. Richards, chose not to remove Sheriff Robinson from his post, nor to call a special grand jury to hear the state's corroborative evidence. The recalcitrance of Aiken's white citizens was starkly manifest in the county grand jury's refusals to indict anyone for the murders. The Lowmans, the jury insisted, met their deaths "at the hands of parties unknown." ELIZABETH ROBESON

Johnson, James Weldon. "Three Achievements and Their Significance." *Crisis* 34 (September 1927): 222–23.

White, Walter. "I Investigate Lynchings." *American Mercury* 16 (January 1929): 77–84.

Lowndes, Rawlins (1721–1800). Jurist, governor. Lowndes was born in 1721 on St. Kitts in the West Indies, the son of Charles Lowndes and Ruth Rawlins. In 1730 the family migrated to South Carolina, where Lowndes's extravagant father fell into financial ruin and committed suicide in May 1736. His youngest sons, Charles and Rawlins, became wards of South Carolina's provost marshal Robert Hall. Under Hall's tutelage, Rawlins Lowndes learned the intricacies of South Carolina's legal system. In 1745 Lowndes followed his mentor's footsteps and became provost marshal, the chief law enforcement officer of the colony.

On August, 15, 1748, Lowndes married Amarinthia Elliott, whose dowry brought him a plantation on Stono River in St. Paul's Parish. He now qualified for a seat in the Commons House of Assembly and was elected in 1749. After Amarinthia died in childbirth in January 1750, Lowndes acquired Horseshoe Plantation in St. Bartholomew's Parish and thereafter represented that parish in the assembly for most of the following twenty-five years. He was married two more times: to Mary Cartwright on December 23, 1751 (she died in 1770); and to Sarah Jones from January 1773 until his death. These unions produced seven and three children respectively.

Overburdened by his public and private duties, Lowndes experienced declining health, and he resigned as provost marshal in June 1754. He sailed to England to recover his health, returning to South Carolina in December 1755. After his arrival Lowndes rose to prominence in the Commons House of Assembly and held several important committee assignments. In September 1763 the assembly elected Lowndes to the Speaker's chair, where he defended the assembly's prerogatives against encroachments from royal governors, the upper house, and the ministry in England. A political moderate, Lowndes apparently was not daring enough for his colleagues, who replaced him with Peter Manigault in October 1765.

In February 1766 Lowndes was appointed assistant judge, a position he held for six years, and he took legal positions that won him praise. He argued that South Carolina's courts should be opened, despite the Stamp Act's provision that legal documents bear the required stamps. In 1773 Lowndes ruled that the upper house, or Royal Council, composed of placemen who served at the pleasure of the crown, was not equivalent to the British House of Lords. This argument struck a devastating political blow against the Royal Council's prestige and marked the high point of Lowndes's public career.

In October 1772 Lowndes was again elected Speaker of the Commons House of Assembly, and he retained that post until the dissolution of royal government in 1775. A reluctant revolutionary, Lowndes hoped for an accommodation between the colonies and Britain and reportedly reacted to Thomas Paine's *Common Sense* with a stream of profanities. Nevertheless, he held important posts in the early years of the Revolutionary War, serving in the Provincial Congress and on the Council of Safety. When John Rutledge resigned as president (governor) of South Carolina in March 1778 to protest the proposed state constitution, the legislature elected Lowndes.

Lowndes's brief tenure as president proved frustrating. Perhaps influenced by his long service in the legislative branch, he was reluctant to use the powers of his office. Preferring to keep South Carolina's supplies and militia for state use only, Lowndes did not fully cooperate with Continental army generals Robert Howe and Benjamin Lincoln in their efforts to defend the lower South from British attacks. Lowndes retired to private life in February 1779 and thereafter played no major role in the Revolution.

Lowndes suffered extensive property losses during the British occupation of South Carolina. In late 1780 he petitioned to be restored to the rights of a British subject. Though the South Carolina state legislature did not confiscate Lowndes's property because of this decision, he was stripped of his full citizenship until the summer of 1783.

Lowndes's last major public act occurred while he was representing the city parishes in the S.C. House from 1787 to 1790. In 1788 he argued against ratification of the federal constitution and predicted that the South, as a minority section reliant on slavery, would be at the mercy of northern commercial interests. He was elected to his final public office in 1788, serving one term as intendant (mayor) of Charleston. In his final decade, Lowndes recouped the financial losses he had incurred during the Revolution. After a brief illness, he died in Charleston on August 24, 1800, and was buried in St. Philip's Churchyard. GREGORY D. MASSEY

Vipperman, Carl J. *The Rise of Rawlins Lowndes, 1721–1800.* Columbia: University of South Carolina Press, 1978.

Lowndes, William Jones (1782–1822). Congressman. Lowndes was born at Horseshoe Plantation in St. Bartholomew's Parish on February 11, 1782, the son of Rawlins Lowndes and Sarah Jones. Although christened William Jones, he never used his middle name. A severe childhood bout with rheumatic fever left him with an enfeebled body but did nothing to dull his exceptional mind. Educated at private academies in England and Charleston, Lowndes was a model student and outstanding orator. He studied law in the office of Henry William DeSaussure and Timothy Ford and was accepted to the bar in 1804, but he practiced for less than a year before quitting the legal profession. On September 10, 1802, Lowndes married Elizabeth Brewton Pinckney, the daughter of former governor Thomas Pinckney. The marriage produced three children.

In 1804 Lowndes was elected to the General Assembly, representing St. Philip's and St. Michael's Parishes in the House of Representatives until 1808. He quickly became a respected and important member of the assembly, where he supported bills to establish public schools and to prohibit slave importations. He also authored the so-called Compromise of 1808, an amendment to the state constitution that provided the upcountry with more equitable representation in the General Assembly. He was an unsuccessful candidate for the state Senate in 1808.

Although a Democratic-Republican in his political views, Lowndes nevertheless was a strong critic of Thomas Jefferson's handling of the deteriorating relationship between the United States and Britain and France. In 1810 Lowndes was elected to the U.S. House of Representatives, where he became a leading member of the "War Hawks," a faction of young congressmen who strongly favored a military resolution of the nation's dispute with Britain. Working with fellow congressmen Henry Clay, John C. Calhoun, and others, Lowndes pushed to strengthen the nation's defenses and ardently supported America's entry into war in 1812. A gifted legislator and persuasive speaker, Lowndes rapidly established himself as one of the most influential members of Congress. He sat on important committees, serving at different times as chairman of the committees on naval affairs, ways and means, coinage, and foreign affairs. A nationalist, he helped author legislation creating the Second Bank of the United States and supported the enactment of protective tariffs in 1816. In 1817 Lowndes introduced a plan to pay off the national debt, which led to the elimination of the debt by 1835. In his final important public work, Lowndes and Clay led the successful effort in the House to pass the Missouri Compromise of 1820, which admitted Missouri as a slave state but recognized the right of Congress to limit slavery in the territories.

Lowndes's talent and influence in national affairs did not go unrecognized by his contemporaries. He declined two offers to become secretary of war and also turned down diplomatic appointments to Russia, Turkey, and France. Nominated for Speaker of the House in 1820, he lost the election by a single vote. In December 1821 the South Carolina General Assembly nominated Lowndes for the presidency. Sensible of the honor but also embarrassed by the damage the nomination had done to the candidacy of his close friend Calhoun, Lowndes tactfully responded that he did not believe that the presidency was "an office to be either solicited or declined."

During this time, however, Lowndes's health began to deteriorate. He resigned his seat in Congress in May 1822 and sought a change of climate to improve his condition. After spending several months in the North, he sailed for London with his wife and daughter in October. Lowndes died en route on October 27, 1822, and was buried as sea. NATHAN E. STALVEY

Ravenel, Harriott Horry. *Life and Times of William Lowndes of South Carolina, 1782–1822.* Boston: Houghton, Mifflin, 1901.

Vipperman, Carl J. *William Lowndes and the Transition of Southern Politics, 1782–1822.* Chapel Hill: University of North Carolina Press, 1989.

Loyalists. Historians have correctly labeled the American Revolution as the nation's first civil war. No greater example of this internecine struggle can be found than in South Carolina, where the Revolution degenerated into a bitter-brothers war that was fought with little compassion or restraint. A leading factor contributing to this inner conflict was the relatively large number of inhabitants who professed a continuing allegiance to the king of Great Britain. The precise extent of Loyalist strength in South Carolina will never be known because many people switched allegiances as circumstances dictated during the protracted war.

Complicating the task of measuring Loyalist sentiment is the difficulty in defining loyalism. The most conspicuous expression of loyalism was the bearing of arms against patriot forces. At least five thousand South Carolinians took up arms against the Whig government during the Revolution. Thousands more Loyalist-leaning Americans helped to cripple the American cause in South Carolina by spying for the British, supplying them with provisions, attacking stores and supplies belonging to Whig authorities, and other acts of resistance.

Perhaps twenty-five percent of white South Carolinians either actively opposed the movement for independence or supported British authority against the state government during the war. But a far greater number of people resisted the Whig government in subtle but no less debilitating ways, either by refusing to pay their wartime taxes and sell their supplies to the army or by deserting the army as soon as they could and avoiding conscription. Whig leaders saw little distinction between the more ardent Loyalists and the Loyalist-neutrals, those who simply refused to help the patriots unless forced to do so. The Provincial Congress in June 1775 urged all citizens to sign an "Association" as proof of their allegiance to the Whig government and branded any person refusing obedience to its authority as "an enemy to the liberties of America" and subject to patriot vengeance.

Nearly equally troublesome as determining the number of Loyalists in South Carolina is explaining their continued allegiance to the king of Great Britain. Most Loyalists, like the rebels, opposed Parliament's claims to tax America. Unlike the rebels, however, Loyalists doubted that Parliament intended to undermine the colonists' rights as Englishmen. They also thought that separation was illegal and feared that it would lead to a civil war in America.

Other Loyalists sided with the British for more self-serving reasons, particularly crown-appointed officials and former British officers and enlisted men who owed their jobs to the empire and major city merchants who depended on British trade. Loyalists were disproportionately represented among non-English ethnic minorities. In addition, many backcountry settlers opposed the Whig government because of influential local men who cast their lot with Britain, and because their long-standing struggle with the coastal aristocracy for schools, roads, courts, and political representation made them unsympathetic to the patriots' cries of ministerial abuse.

One common element among Loyalists in South Carolina is that nearly all immigrated to the province after 1765; only about one in six was native born. As recent arrivals, they were unlikely to support a movement that was defying the authority from which they had obtained their lands. In short, Loyalists came from every sector of society, with approximately forty-five percent comprised of small farmers; thirty percent of merchants, artisans, and shopkeepers; fifteen percent of large farmers and planters; and ten percent of crown officials and professionals.

Loyalist strength in South Carolina varied according to region. It was weakest in the lowcountry, where the king's friends were greatly outnumbered and where Loyalist leaders failed to organize among themselves and to cultivate public opinion by offering a reasonable alternative to rebellion. Their passive disapproval of Whig measures allowed the patriot party to carry out its revolutionary program there with remarkably little intimidation and violence. However, Whig leaders faced much stronger resistance in the backcountry, where a large party of Loyalists, led by influential men of high intelligence and determination, formed themselves into military units and openly defied Whig measures. To counter resistance there, patriot leaders in Charleston penned and distributed throughout the interior pamphlets explaining the American cause and appointed scores of local leaders to prominent positions in the Whig government and military. Still, large areas of resistance remained in the backcountry.

To confront this serious threat, the Council of Safety in July 1775 appointed William Henry Drayton and William Tennent, both active leaders of the radical faction in the Provincial Congress, as emissaries to the backcountry. Using one-sided arguments, economic coercion, and military threats, Drayton and Tennent convinced some Loyalist leaders in the region to sign a neutrality pact at the village of Ninety Six on September 16. However, other Loyalist leaders, such as Thomas Fletchall, Moses Kirkland, and Robert Cunningham, were upset with Drayton's Machiavellian tactics and raised a large force of king's men (approximately four thousand) to seize Whig munitions in the region and attack their small military outpost at Ninety Six. In response, the Provincial Congress ordered Colonel Richard Richardson to raise an army to crush the backcountry dissidents. In December 1775 Richardson's forces engaged and defeated the Loyalist army at the Great Cane Break near the Cherokee Indian line. This defeat marked the end of Loyalist resistance in the interior until British occupation in 1780.

Despite this defeat at the Great Cane Break, the Loyalist uprising in 1775 had an important effect on British military strategy by convincing English politicians and generals that Loyalists were numerous and pugnacious in the southern backcountry. Thus, when British military efforts faltered in the northern colonies by early 1778, British leaders created a new "southern strategy" to seize key southern ports and, with the aid of Loyalist militiamen, move back toward the north, pacifying one region after another.

The southern strategy succeeded in its earliest stages. The British quickly captured Savannah in December 1778 and occupied Charleston in May 1780 after a lengthy siege. Several hundred South Carolinians, mostly lowcountry merchants, shopkeepers, and artisans interested in maintaining their business operations, signed the oath of allegiance proffered by the British. However, when British forces moved into the interior to liberate and organize the loyal population, they discovered that the king's friends were not so numerous or as steadfast as they had expected. British officers in South Carolina managed to muster only 2,500 men into eighteen poorly supplied militia regiments. Moreover, excesses committed by the British military and their Loyalist allies in their attempt to conquer the backcountry drove many of the uncommitted into the Whig camp and ignited a virulent and bloody civil war that involved people of all ages and both sexes.

Despite the acrimonious and personal nature of fighting in South Carolina during the last years of the conflict, the victorious Whig government treated the defeated Loyalists with relative leniency. However, approximately 4,200 white Loyalists from the state decided that they could not live under a government independent from the king and emigrated from South Carolina to the British Caribbean, East Florida, England, and Canada. Their property, along with that of Loyalists remaining behind, was subject to confiscation by the General Assembly. At their meeting at Jacksonborough in January–February 1782, legislators considered placing as many as seven hundred people on a "confiscation list." The legislature was quickly flooded with petitions for relief from the confiscation law. The assembly, realizing that it was impractical to punish such a large number of Loyalists, most of whom were natives or long-standing residents of the state who found themselves vulnerable after the fall of Charleston, followed a policy of moderation. In most cases, the assembly removed petitioners from the confiscation list and, instead, fined them twelve percent of the value of their property. Although a few people were upset with the legislature's lenient policy toward the former Loyalists, this policy generally helped to restore the state to a relative degree of harmony by eroding much of the bitterness engendered by the protracted war. KEITH KRAWCZYNSKI

Barnwell, Robert W., Jr. "Loyalism in South Carolina, 1765–1785." Ph.D. diss., Duke University, 1941.

Brown, Wallace. *The King's Friends: The Composition and Motives of the American Loyalist Claimants.* Providence, R.I.: Brown University Press, 1965.

Coker, Kathryn Roe. "The Artisan Loyalists of Charleston, South Carolina." In *Loyalists and Community in North America,* edited by Robert M. Calhoon, Timothy M. Barnes, and George A. Rawlyk. Westport, Conn.: Greenwood, 1994.

Lambert, Robert Stansbury. *South Carolina Loyalists in the American Revolution.* Columbia: University of South Carolina Press, 1987.

Singer, Charles. *South Carolina in the Confederation.* 1941. Reprint, Philadelphia: Porcupine, 1976.

Lucas, Jonathan (ca. 1754–1821). Millwright. Lucas was born in Cumberland, England, the son of John Lucas and Ann Noble. His mother's family owned mills in the town of Whitehaven, which undoubtedly served as the source of Lucas's skill as a millwright. Little is known of his early life in England. He married Mary Cooke on May 22, 1774. They had five children before Mary died sometime between 1783 and 1786. He then married Ann Ashburn of Whitehaven.

Lucas immigrated to South Carolina around 1786, which proved a fortuitous time and place for the arrival of a talented young millwright. Lowcountry rice planters had greatly increased the production of their rice fields by employing tidal rice cultivation. But the process of rice milling or "pounding"—removing the outer husk from the rice grains—had failed to evolve in a like manner. Most rice was still pounded by hand with wooden mortars and pestles or by crude pecker or cog mills powered by animals. Neither of these methods kept pace with the rapidly expanding production of tidal rice fields. Planters could sell unhusked or "rough" rice, but for a considerably lower price than cleaned rice.

Soon after his arrival in South Carolina, Lucas was put to work by a Santee River rice planter to improve the output of his plantation's rice mill. Lucas experimented with wind and water as power sources, and within a short time his efforts bore fruit. His new pounding mill design was powered by an undershot waterwheel fed by a mill pond. It was first employed at Peach Island Plantation on the North Santee River in 1787. Lucas continued to improve his design, building his first tide-powered mill in 1791. Two years later at Henry Laurens's Mepkin plantation he built a tide-powered mill, complete with rolling screens, elevators, and packers. The highly automated mill needed just three workers to operate and could pack as many as twenty 600-pound barrels of clean rice on a single tide.

With the assistance of his son Jonathan Jr., Lucas constructed his rice mills throughout the lowcountry, providing a means for South Carolina planters to clean their ever-growing output of rice. He purchased his own plantation on Shem Creek near Charleston, where he also established his own rice- and saw-milling operation. Lucas later purchased land in Charleston and built the city's first toll rice mill. In 1817 Lucas built the first steam-powered rice mill in the United States. Jonathan Lucas, Jr., also had a successful career as a millwright, patenting an improved rice-cleaning machine in 1808 that found great favor in the rice-receiving ports of England and western Europe. His son Jonathan Lucas III built South Carolina's largest antebellum rice mill, West Point Mills, on the Ashley River in 1839. Jonathan Lucas died on April 1, 1821, and was buried in St. Paul's Cemetery, Charleston. TOM DOWNEY

Lander, Ernest M., Jr. "Charleston: Manufacturing Center of the Old South." *Journal of Southern History* 26 (August 1960): 330–51.

Lucas Family. Papers. South Carolina Historical Society, Charleston.

Lucas v. South Carolina Coastal Council (1992). *Lucas v. South Carolina Coastal Council* was a high-profile property-rights case. The case pitted the state of South Carolina's right to regulate the use of property for the "public good" versus the right of individuals to use their property as they see fit or to be justly compensated for the loss of the use of the property.

In 1986 David Lucas bought two residential lots on Isle of Palms. His intention was to build single-family houses on the lots such as were built on the immediately adjoining parcels of land. At the time of purchase, Lucas's lots were not subject to the state's coastal zone building-permit requirements. However, in 1988 the state legislature enacted the Beachfront Management Act. This act directed the Coastal Council to establish a baseline along the shoreline. The building of occupied structures seaward of the baseline was prohibited. The act provided no exceptions. The effect of this action on Lucas was that he was not able to erect any permanent habitable structures on his parcels.

Lucas promptly brought suit in the S.C. Court of Common Pleas of Charleston County, arguing that the Beachfront Management Act's construction prohibition constituted a taking of his property without just compensation. The court of common pleas ruled in Lucas's favor and awarded him damages. The Coastal Council appealed the decision, and the South Carolina Supreme Court ruled in favor of the Coastal Council. Lucas sought redress from the United States Supreme Court, which accepted the case for review. In its decision, handed down on June 29, 1992, the Supreme Court ruled that the state's action in barring the erection of permanent structures rendered Lucas's property useless and therefore that compensation under the "taking clause" should be made. JON B. PIERCE

Cody, Thomas, and Dwight Merriam. "The Supreme Court Takes on 'Takings': *Lucas v. South Carolina Coastal Council.*" *Planning Commissioners Journal* 8 (January/February 1993): 8–9.

Lucas v. South Carolina Coastal Council, 505 U.S. 1003 (1992).

Ludvigson, Susan (b. 1942). Poet. Born in Rice Lake, Wisconsin, on February 13, 1942, Ludvigson is the daughter of the entrepreneur Howard C. Ludvigson and Mabel Helgeland. In 1961 she married David Bartels with whom she had one son. Ludvigson entered the University of Wisconsin–River Falls, from which she earned a B.A., with honors, in English and psychology in 1965. For seven years she taught school in River Falls and in Ann Arbor, Michigan. She received an M.A. in English at the University of North Carolina at Charlotte in 1973 and then studied for two years with James Dickey at the University of South Carolina. She and Bartels divorced in 1974, and she married the novelist Scott Ely in October 1988. Both taught at Winthrop University in Rock Hill, spending part of each year in southern France. Since 1979 Ludvigson's work has earned many awards, including Guggenheim and Fulbright Fellowships.

In a 1986 interview, Ludvigson recalled that she first wrote poems while in her teens. As an adult she became committed to poetry under the influence of colleagues and friends. Her first volume, *Step Carefully in Night Grass,* appeared in 1974. Her second,

Northern Lights (1981), shows greater maturity and began her connection with Louisiana State University Press, which published the six collections that followed. Much of the material depicts memories in which horses, parents, and childhood anxieties are prominent. The middle section, based on nineteenth-century news articles, portrays thirteen troubled Wisconsin women.

In *The Swimmer* (1984), Ludvigson's third collection, poems such as "Trying to Come to Terms" (written in terza rima) express grief following the deaths of three friends. Through this collection, water in its various forms—snow, rain, lakes—becomes symbolic, sometimes suggesting grief, as in "A Day of Snow," sometimes freedom and renewal, as in the title poem. Several poems based on paintings anticipate the visual-arts influence prominent in her later work.

The Beautiful Noon of No Shadow (1986) draws on themes established in earlier collections, such as the power of dreams, and the elemental force of light and dark, of water and sky. "Waiting for Your Life" and "The Will to Believe" (an extended elegy for her father) are longer and more ambitious than previous poems.

Her fifth book, *To Find the Gold* (1990), begins with "The Gold She Finds," a widely praised, nineteen-part poem containing an imaginative reconstruction of the life of the sculptor Camille Claudel and her passionate but troubled relationship with Auguste Rodin. Other poems, such as "This Beginning" and "Paris Aubade," are autobiographical, often touching on life in France.

Everything Winged Must Be Dreaming (1993) contains long poems on marriage and extended relationships. Several, such as "Happiness: The Forbidden Subject," refer to her own marital contentment. As the title suggests, *Trinity* (1996) shows a greater concern with religious themes.

Sweet Confluence (2000) consists of selected poems from previous volumes, as well as twenty new poems, including "Where We Have Come," a kind of elegy for her mother. This volume demonstrates the versatility of form and subject and the maturity that earned Ludvigson her place as a prominent American poet. KEN AUTREY

Swanson, Gayle R., and William B. Thesing. *Conversations with South Carolina Poets.* Winston-Salem, N.C.: John F. Blair, 1986.

Whitehead, Gwendolyn. "Susan Ludvigson." In *Dictionary of Literary Biography.* Vol. 120, *American Poets since World War II, Third Series,* edited by R. S. Gwynn. Detroit: Gale, 1992.

Ludwell, Philip (1638–1723). Governor. Ludwell was born in 1638 in England, the son of Thomas Ludwell and Jane Cottington. By 1663 he had traveled to Virginia, where his cousin William Berkeley was governor. Ludwell utilized this connection and those by marriage with the Bernard, Burwell, and Culpeper families to become a judge (1676), colonial secretary (1676–1677), a member of the Grand Council (1675–1687, 1691–1695), and Speaker of the House of Burgesses (1695–1700). He sided with Berkeley against Nathaniel Bacon, served with distinction during the rebellion, and led the popular, or Assembly, party after Berkeley's death. In 1689 he journeyed to England to defend the prerogatives of the House of Burgesses against the crown.

While there, he accepted the governorship of North Carolina from the Lords Proprietors, but he spent less than six out of forty-eight months (1690–1694) in residence, appearing only when summoned. He reorganized the North Carolina council; appointed Thomas Jarvis, a popular and able councilman, as his deputy; and instituted long-sought and popular quitrent reform.

In November 1691 the proprietors appointed Ludwell governor of all Carolina and sent him to Charleston to reestablish order. His predecessor, Seth Sothel, had overthrown Governor James Colleton with the support of the Goose Creek Men, the colony's antiproprietary faction. Sothel challenged Ludwell's attempts to displace him, while the Goose Creek faction defended the right of the Commons House of Assembly to legislate without permission of the council. They were willing to compromise, but they demanded land and quitrent reform, guarantees for the colony's French immigrants, protection from arbitrary justice and fees, and pardons for themselves as prerequisites.

Ludwell's supporters, the proprietary party, were equally contentious. They openly quarreled with the governor, refused to pay his salary, complained to London that he was taking bribes, and charged that he was falling under the control of the Goose Creek Men. The pirate trade continued to flourish during Ludwell's tenure, but the governor did attempt to curb the illegal Indian slave trade by ordering all traders to remain in Charleston and organizing a conference with Indian leaders to address their grievances.

Despite his limited success in reining in the Indian trade, Ludwell failed to build a base of support within the colony with either the proprietary or antiproprietary faction. With faltering support in both Charleston and London, Ludwell's attempted reforms were denigrated in Carolina and vetoed by the proprietors. In mid-May 1693, little more than a year after his arrival, he departed the city, leaving Thomas Smith as his deputy. Ludwell resumed his seat on the Virginia Council, prior to being named as Speaker of the House. In 1707 he transferred control of his extensive landholdings to his son, Philip, and moved to England, where he died in 1723. LOUIS P. TOWLES

McCrady, Edward. *The History of South Carolina under the Proprietary Government, 1670–1719.* New York: Macmillan, 1897.

Sirmans, M. Eugene. *Colonial South Carolina: A Political History, 1663–1763.* Chapel Hill: University of North Carolina Press, 1966.

Lumpkin, Grace (ca. 1896–1980). Writer, social activist. Lumpkin was born in Milledgeville, Georgia, the ninth of eleven children born to William Wallace Lumpkin and Annette Caroline Morris. Her year of birth is uncertain, but cemetery records suggest that she was born on March 3, 1896. Like many prominent southern families, the Lumpkins suffered a reversal of fortune after the Civil War. William, a Confederate army veteran and devout proponent of the "Lost Cause," moved his family to Columbia around 1900, installing them as parishioners at Trinity Episcopal Church. In 1910 the Lumpkins moved to a farm in Richland County. William Lumpkin died shortly afterward, leaving his large family to fend for itself.

Grace Lumpkin earned a teacher's certificate from Brenau College (1911) and then held various jobs in the Carolinas and in France as a teacher, home demonstration agent, and social worker. At home she conducted night classes for adult farm and mill workers and attended meetings of the nascent interracial cooperation movement. She harbored a desire to write, and in 1925 she moved to New York City, where she took a job with *The World Tomorrow,* a pacifist Quaker publication. Her coverage of the Communist-led textile strikes in Passaic, New Jersey, in 1926 struck a militant chord. Almost immediately Lumpkin went to work for a Soviet-affiliated trading company and joined a chapter of the John Reed Club for leftist writers. Her first published piece, "White Man, a Story," appeared in the September 1927 issue of *New Masses.* Five years later Lumpkin published her first novel, *To Make My Bread,* the material for which she had gathered as a witness to the Gastonia, North

Carolina, textile strikes of 1929. The book, winner of the 1932 Maxim Gorky Prize, chronicles the farm-to-factory transformation of the McClure family; it has been excerpted, anthologized, republished in England, and adapted for the New York stage by Alfred Bein as *Let Freedom Ring*.

Lumpkin's second novel, *A Sign for Cain* (1935), appeared during a frenetic period of speech-making and investigative work in the South on behalf of the Communist Party (which she never officially joined). Her personal life was similarly complicated. She lived with (and perhaps married) Michael Intrator, a labor organizer who had been expelled from the Communist Party in 1929, and another, married couple, Whittaker Chambers and Esther Chemitz, who became Communist spies. Lumpkin and Intrator broke up in the late 1930s, allegedly after an abortion that left her distraught. She subsequently took refuge with an ardently anti-Communist organization run by an Episcopal priest in New York, the Moral Re-Armament Movement.

In 1948 Whittaker Chambers, now an editor at *Time,* accused former State Department official Alger Hiss of spying for the Russians. Investigators interviewed Lumpkin, hoping that she might discredit Chambers's testimony. Instead, she took up her former housemate's defense in a New England speaking tour, lauding Chambers's role in her own renunciation of Communism. She testified before Senator Joseph McCarthy's Permanent Subcommittee on Investigations in 1953, telling the panel that she had written "the fundamental philosophy of communism" into *A Sign for Cain* after party functionaries threatened to "break" her literary career.

Lumpkin's final novel, *Full Circle,* which appeared in 1962, is a fictionalized account of her peculiar ideological and spiritual life journey, which she delineated as her Communist and "return to God" phases. She died in Columbia on March 23, 1980. Though her grave is unmarked, Lumpkin is buried in her family's plot at Elmwood Cemetery in Columbia. ELIZABETH ROBESON

Hall, Jacquelyn Dowd. "Women Writers, the 'Southern Front,' and the Dialectical Imagination." *Journal of Southern History* 69 (February 2003): 3–38.

Lumpkin, Grace. Papers. South Caroliniana Library, University of South Carolina, Columbia.

———. *To Make My Bread.* 1932. Reprint, Urbana: University of Illinois Press, 1995.

Lunz, George Robert, Jr. (1909–1969). Museum curator, marine biologist. Lunz was born in Charleston on February 27, 1909, the son of George Robert Lunz and Mary Whilden Lofton. He graduated from Charleston High School and earned a B.S. (1930) and an M.S. (1932) from the College of Charleston. He received an honorary doctor of science from Clemson College in 1956. On September 2, 1934, he married Elsie Melchers. They had one daughter.

Lunz joined the staff of the Charleston Museum in 1933 and worked primarily on invertebrates and published papers, mainly on crustaceans. In July 1945 the board of trustees of the Charleston Museum agreed to a proposal by trustee H. Jermain Slocum to develop a laboratory for research on the cultivation of oysters, with Lunz serving as director and Slocum providing land and funding. The facility, eventually named Bears Bluff Laboratories, was located in Charleston County on Wadmalaw Island, southwest of the city. In January 1946 the laboratory at Bears Bluff was chartered by the state with its own board of trustees. For a time Lunz wore two hats—one at the museum, the other at Bears Bluff. That situation did not continue, and Lunz eventually left the museum to devote all of his time to Bears Bluff. Working long hours with limited resources, he developed a laboratory where both staff and visiting investigators contributed significantly to the understanding of the estuarine and marine environments of the state. Recognition of his expertise led to his becoming director of the Division of Commercial Fisheries of the South Carolina Wildlife Resources Department, a position he held from 1959 until his death.

Among the activities at Bears Bluff were pond culture of oysters and shrimp, fisheries management, studies of pollution biology, and investigations on the biology of species of fishes. Fifty-two *Contributions from Bears Bluff Laboratories,* documenting some of that work, appeared from June 1947 to December 1969, and Lunz published other papers on the estuarine and marine resources of South Carolina. Bears Bluff was used not only in research by resident scientists and visiting investigators, including scientists from other countries, but also from time to time in the education of undergraduate and graduate students. Lunz's greatest contribution was his founding of the first facility in South Carolina dedicated to the study of wetland, estuarine, and marine environments. His pioneering work in oyster and shrimp culture, his appreciation of the importance of marshlands both to the marine environment and to the human species, and his efforts to awaken the public to the need of protecting wetlands from dredging, filling, draining, and pollution were major contributions. On December 17, 1969, Lunz died of cancer at Charleston's Roper Hospital. He was buried in Magnolia Cemetery. WILLIAM D. ANDERSON, JR.

Lunz, Elsie M. *Contribution Concerning Bears Bluff Laboratories, Wadmalaw Island, S.C., 1945–1969.* N.p., 1970.

Sanders, Albert E., and William D. Anderson, Jr. *Natural History Investigations in South Carolina from Colonial Times to the Present.* Columbia: University of South Carolina Press, 1999.

Lutheran Theological Southern Seminary. One of eight seminaries of the Evangelical Lutheran Church in America, Lutheran Theological Southern Seminary (LTSS) was established by Lutherans of German origin in 1830 and is the nation's second-oldest Lutheran seminary in continuous existence. In Columbia since 1911, the seminary previously occupied several sites in South Carolina and from 1872 to 1884 was located in Salem, Virginia. In meeting its mission "to prepare men and women for the public ministries of the church," the seminary offers three graduate degrees in theology: the master of divinity degree (three academic years and one year of internship) for those preparing for the ordained ministry; the master of arts in religion degree (two academic years) for those preparing for some other professional work in the church or for further graduate study; and the master of sacred theology degree for pastors and other professionals engaged in Christian ministry. In cooperation with the Lutheran Seminary in Philadelphia, a doctor of ministry degree is also offered.

With a student body of approximately 170, LTSS employs fifteen faculty, which includes a director of a program in Atlanta designed for African American students. The seminary requires a January term that involves off-campus cross-cultural experiences and also maintains a cooperative relationship with Lutheran seminaries in Gettysburg and Philadelphia. Although approximately eighty percent of the student body is Lutheran, the seminary also carries an ecumenical flavor, with ten to fifteen other denominations represented. The majority of students come from the Southeast and return to serve churches in that region, but roughly fifteen percent come from other states. PAUL JERSILD

Anderson, H. George, and Robert M. Calhoon, eds. *"A Truly Efficient School of Theology": The Lutheran Theological Southern Seminary in Historical Context, 1830–1980.* Columbia, S.C.: Lutheran Theological Southern Seminary, 1981.

Voigt, Gilbert P. *Lutheran Theological Southern Seminary.* Columbia, S.C.: LTSS Board of Trustees, 1955.

Lutherans. While Lutherans are the third-largest Protestant denomination in the United States, their numbers have never been large in the South. In South Carolina, Lutherans make up less than two percent of the population, with highest concentrations in Newberry and Lexington Counties. Among Protestants, Lutherans typically give greater weight to the historic ("catholic") tradition going back to the ancient church and conduct a liturgy of worship that stands in continuity with that tradition. Their founder, the sixteenth-century German reformer Martin Luther, has profoundly influenced their theology with a strong emphasis on the unmerited love and grace of God. Most Lutherans in South Carolina are affiliated with the Evangelical Lutheran Church in America (ELCA), which contains 165 congregations and 62,000 members.

Early Lutherans in South Carolina were invariably of German descent. The first were a part of the Purrysburg settlement of mainly French Swiss immigrants in the 1730s along the Savannah River. They came in larger numbers from the German Palatinate in 1735, mostly as indentured servants who settled in the Orangeburg area and on lowcountry plantations. In the 1740s there was an influx of German Lutherans into Saxe-Gotha Township, which also attracted significant numbers of Germans from the northern colonies. Lutheran immigration increased considerably in the 1750s, with many settling in Saxe-Gotha and the nearby Dutch Fork. These communities, unlike the Ebenezer colony on the Georgia side of the Savannah River, were not intentionally Lutheran and did not include the spiritual direction of clergy. The first pastor called to minister specifically to South Carolina Lutherans was Johannes Georg Friedrichs from Hanover, Germany, who came in 1755 to serve St. John's congregation in Charleston and subsequently St. Matthew's in Amelia Township.

Efforts to organize began with an ecumenical Union of Churches in 1788, involving nine Lutheran and six Reformed churches, but it expired by 1796. South Carolina Lutherans then joined with Lutheran churches in North Carolina in 1803 as part of the North Carolina Synod. Among factors that stimulated the need for a corporate Lutheran presence was the growing influence of revivalism throughout the South, a phenomenon that most Lutherans did not find appealing in light of their theology and practice. There was also the need for taking a united stand on appropriate practices concerning the slave population. In 1809 it was decided that slaves of Christian masters were eligible for baptism, and five years later a resolution was passed to admit "negroes" to the sacrament of Holy Communion and "make room for them in our Churches." These measures were not intended to challenge the institution of slavery, however, which most Lutherans in the South found morally and theologically acceptable.

Difficulties in traveling long distances, together with a desire to avoid a divisive theological controversy that had erupted among North Carolina congregations, led South Carolina Lutherans to amicably withdraw and form their own synod in 1824. At the synod's beginning there were ten Lutheran ministers and twenty-two congregations. Its first president was Pastor John Bachman of St. John's, Charleston, a theologian-naturalist of unusual talent and competence who maintained a dominant presence for the next four decades in South Carolina Lutheranism. He was the primary force in establishing the first Lutheran seminary in the South (1830) and in affiliating the synod with the national expression of Lutheranism at the time, the General Synod, being elected president of that body in 1835. In the midst of a growing conservatism in Lutheran churches during the mid–nineteenth century, which led to Lutherans keeping their distance from ecumenical involvements and emphasizing their own exclusive version of Christian truths, Bachman's theological openness and gentle nature were powerful examples that helped the synod avoid the divisions that often afflicted others.

The Civil War created a rupture that Lutherans could not avoid, and South Carolina Lutherans played a prominent role in the establishment of the General Synod of the Confederate States of America in 1863. Most Lutherans in the state supported secession and the war effort, with several of their clergy serving as both chaplains and soldiers. In the Reconstruction years the South Carolina Synod became part of the United Synod of the South, which continued until 1917, when synods of the North and the South finally reunited. The twentieth century saw Lutherans increasingly shed their European language and culture, assimilating with mainstream society. Lutheran (ELCA) institutions in South Carolina include Lutheran Theological Southern Seminary in Columbia, Newberry College in Newberry, Lutheran Homes of South Carolina, Inc. (facilities engaged in senior care), and Lutheran Family Services.

PAUL JERSILD

Anderson, H. George. *Lutheranism in the Southeastern States, 1860–1886: A Social History.* The Hague: Mouton, 1969.

Havens, Mary. "The Liturgical Traditions: Lutherans." In *Religion in South Carolina,* edited by Charles H. Lippy. Columbia: University of South Carolina Press, 1993.

Lutheran Church in America, South Carolina Synod. *A History of the Lutheran Church in South Carolina.* Columbia, S.C.: R. L. Bryan, 1971.

———. *A History of the Lutheran Church in South Carolina, 1971–1987.* Columbia, S.C.: R. L. Bryan, 1988.

Lyles, Bissett, Carlisle & Wolff. Founded in 1946 by William Gordon Lyles (1913–1981) and known widely as LBC&W, the firm developed into the premier architectural, engineering, and planning concern in South Carolina and the Southeast by the late 1950s and remained so well into the 1970s. Lyles, born in Whitmire, earned a B.S. in architecture from Clemson College in 1934 and worked for several years with Wessinger & Stork, a prominent local firm. In 1938 Lyles formed a partnership with Bob Stork, his brother-in-law. The designs of Stork & Lyles included Edmunds High School in Sumter, Mount Tabor Lutheran Church in West Columbia, and Grier Hall at Erskine College.

Lyles's military service during World War II with the chief engineer's staff and his design and construction achievements during the war effort set the stage for the establishment of LBC&W. In November 1945 Lyles began assembling the principals of his post-war firm: Thomas J. Bissett of Tampa, Florida; William A. Carlisle of Spartanburg; and Louis M. Wolff of Allendale—all Clemson architectural graduates, World War II veterans, and former associates of Lyles during the war. The firm was established in 1946 as William G. Lyles, Bissett, Carlisle & Wolff, Architects, but was incorporated in 1948 as Lyles, Bissett, Carlisle & Wolff, Architects and Engineers.

LBC&W quickly made a name for itself in the Southeast in post-war, federally assisted housing. During its early years LBC&W designed and built more than 500,000 housing units, including high-rise apartment buildings such as the Cornell Arms and Clair Towers in Columbia, the Darlington Apartments and Howell House in Atlanta, the Sergeant Jasper and Darlington Apartments in Charleston, Calhoun Towers in Greenville, and Clemson House at Clemson. The firm also received commissions from Charleston's Sixth Naval District Engineers, several military installations, Columbia's V.A. Office Building, and sixteen state school districts. College and university work included Clemson's Johnstone Hall and the University of South Carolina's (USC) Russell House and Thomas Cooper Library.

Some of the firm's more notable commissions during the 1960s and 1970s included USC's South Building and Tower, the Humanities Center, the Carolina Coliseum, the Department of Education's Rutledge Building, Columbia's main post office, Clemson's Cooper Library, several buildings for Benedict College, Columbia's C&S National Bank Building and Bankers Trust tower, Charleston's Federal Building and V.A. and naval hospitals, Fort Jackson's Moncrief Memorial Hospital, Richland Memorial Hospital, several buildings for the Medical University of South Carolina, and at least six other high-rise apartment buildings. In 1971 the U.S. Army brought the firm design contracts at Forts Hood, Sill, Campbell, Gordon, Polk, Bragg, and Belvoir. The Edgar Brown Senate Office Building and State House complex and Columbia's First National Bank building are among the firm's later designs.

At its peak in the 1960s, LBC&W employed more than 350 architects, engineers, planners, and support staff located in Maryland; Washington, D.C.; Richmond, Virginia; Greensboro, North Carolina; and Columbia, Spartanburg, and Florence, South Carolina. It was the largest firm of its type in the Southeast and among the nation's twenty-five largest firms. The firm received honors from all quarters for design excellence, community service, and professionalism, including the election of all four of its principals to the College of Fellows of the American Institute of Architects.

LBC&W's merger with Combustion Engineering Company in 1972 strengthened the firm but brought about closure of the Columbia office. Lyles's retirement as the firm's president in 1974, T. J. Bissett's retirement in 1975, and the nationwide economic recession all led to the firm's dissolution by the late 1970s. ANDREW W. CHANDLER

Gordon, Lynn A. "LBC&W: From the Attic to the High-Rise and Beyond." *Sandlapper* 7 (July 1974): 12–14.

Petty, Walter F., Charles Coker Wilson, and Samuel Lapham. *Architectural Practice in South Carolina, 1913–1963.* Columbia, S.C.: State Printing, 1963.

Lyman (Spartanburg County; 2000 pop. 2,659). Lyman's early history stemmed from the economic activity of the Groce family of Greenville. Augustus Belton Groce operated a general merchandise store in the area during the 1870s. The area was known as Groce or Groce's Stop until the arrival of Pacific Mills. In 1923 Pacific Mills announced that it intended to build a textile plant in Groce at a cost of between $7 million and $8.5 million, the largest investment in Spartanburg County up until that time. Pacific Mills not only constructed the mill but also built a model town: 375 houses, a community center, and a twelve-room school. Churches and a National Guard armory were added later. The town was renamed Lyman in honor of Arthur T. Lyman, president of Pacific Mills president from 1900 to 1915, and was incorporated with that name in 1954. At its peak the Lyman plant employed 3,600 workers, more than any other single business site in Spartanburg County. In addition to labor, Lyman residents also enjoyed some recreation, and the town boasted the first lighted baseball field in Spartanburg County.

Lyman became a battleground mill during the General Strike of 1934. Because the mill was neither strongly pro- nor anti-union, it served as a crucial site for both sides of the labor dispute. After the strike began in September, the National Guard was called out and occupied the town. The state's action effectively squelched union activity. There was only one brief strike in the 1940s, and the Congress Industrial Organizations's Operation Dixie also failed to organize the plant. Manufacturing continues to be crucial to Lyman's economy, with corporations such as SEW-Eurodrive exporting products around the globe. AARON W. MARRS

Foster, Vernon, ed. *Spartanburg: Facts, Reminiscences, Folklore.* Spartanburg, S.C.: Reprint Company, 1998.

Lynch, Kenneth Merrill, Sr. (1887–1974). Physician, educator. Lynch was born in Hamilton County, Texas, on November 27, 1887, the son of William Warner Lynch and Martha Miller. After graduating from the University of Texas with an M.D. in 1910, he obtained a residency in pathology at the Philadelphia General Hospital. There he initiated routine microscopic examinations and uncovered an undiagnosed cancer of the lung, beginning a lifelong research interest. In 1913 Lynch moved to South Carolina and became the first professor of pathology at the Medical College of the State of South Carolina and the first full-time pathologist in the state. In January 1914 Lynch married Juanita Kirk from Amarillo, Texas, with whom he would have two children. He later married Lyall Wannamaker of Orangeburg, South Carolina, with whom he also had two children. After service in World War I and a five-year private practice in Dallas, Texas, Lynch returned to South Carolina and the faculty of the Medical College.

Lynch is credited with discovering the first treatment for *Granuloma inguinale,* a venereal disease characterized by ulcerations of the skin of the external genitals. Lynch's exhibit on the subject was awarded a gold medal by the American Medical Association in 1921. In 1930 he published *Protozoan Parasitism of the Alimentary Tract,* which was based on his research related to the in vitro culturing of a parasite flagellate, *Trichomonas hominis.* For this research he was awarded the research medal of the Southern Medical Association (1921), honorable mention in the exhibits of the American Medical Association (1923), and an honorary LL.D. degree from the University of South Carolina (1930). Lynch was a pioneer in the field of industrial dust diseases; he reported the first recorded case of cancer of the lung associated with asbestosis (1935) and published the first full description of kaolinosis (1954), a chronic fibrous reaction in the lungs caused by inhaling kaolin dust. In 1934 he was selected the American editor of the fifteenth edition of *Green's Manual of Pathology.*

In 1943 Lynch became dean of the Medical College of the State of South Carolina. He had the board of trustees change his title to president in 1949. As president of the Medical College, Lynch initiated the concept of a medical center for South Carolina. His expansion program of 1944 called for advancement of medical education, construction of a clinic and hospital, enlargement of the clinical teaching staff, and opportunities for postgraduate work and research—all of which were ultimately achieved. Overcoming opposition from the Medical Society of South Carolina, Lynch oversaw construction of the Medical College Hospital, which was completed in 1955. Lynch's leadership was not limited to the Medical College. He also held numerous positions in local, state, and national professional organizations related to medicine, including the pathology specialty. Lynch retired in 1960 and died November 29, 1974. He was buried in Sunnyside Cemetery, Orangeburg. JANE MCCUTCHEN BROWN

Biographical file. Waring Historical Library, Medical University of South Carolina, Charleston.

Waring, Joseph I. *A History of Medicine in South Carolina.* Vol. 3, *1900–1970.* Columbia: South Carolina Medical Association, 1971.

Worthington, W. Curtis, H. Rawling Pratt-Thomas, and Warren A. Sawyer. *A Family Album: Men Who Made the Medical Center.* Spartanburg, S.C.: Reprint Company, 1991.

Lynch, Patrick Neison (1817–1882). Clergyman, diplomat. Lynch was born in Clones, county Monaghan, Ireland, on March 10, 1817, the eldest son of Conlaw Peter Lynch and his wife, Eleanor MacMahon Neison. The family immigrated to South Carolina in 1819, settling in Cheraw. Conlaw Lynch was a successful builder and businessman, and the Lynches became the leading Catholic family in Cheraw. As a boy Patrick Lynch manifested high intelligence and an interest in becoming a priest, and Bishop John England educated him in his boys' academy and seminary in Charleston, then sent him to Rome to complete his studies. Lynch was ordained in 1840, received a doctorate of theology, and returned to Charleston. There he served as rector of St. Mary's Church and the boys' Classical Academy and edited *The United States Catholic Miscellany.* He was administrator of the Diocese of Charleston in 1855 and was consecrated its third bishop in 1858. When the Civil War broke out, Lynch supported the Confederacy. He and his priests and nuns labored to aid impoverished families and cared for sick and wounded servicemen and prisoners of war. In December 1861 the great Charleston fire destroyed the bishop's residence, his cathedral, and Catholic homes and institutions.

In 1864 Lynch journeyed to Rome as Confederate commissioner to the States of the Church (the Holy See), seeking papal recognition of the Confederacy and to turn European opinion in the South's favor. Despite his efforts, the Vatican never recognized the Confederacy. While in Europe, Lynch published a pamphlet defending slavery as a workable, benign institution. He was the legal owner of about ninety-five slaves, most or all of them diocesan property. Lynch received a presidential pardon before returning to Charleston in late1865. War devastated his diocese, and he lamented, "There are ruins on every side of me. . . . But I trust in God things will come straight." He spent the remainder of his life engaged in raising money to rebuild and to aid his impoverished people. For black Catholics, he founded St. Peter's Church in Charleston and other institutions. Lynch attended the First Vatican Council (1869–1870) and wrote articles about it for *Catholic World.*

Bishop Lynch was also prominent in Charleston's intellectual life. He was an avid member of the Charleston Library Society. He wrote and helped raise funds for the *Southern Quarterly Review,* edited by his friend William Gilmore Simms, and was among the Charlestonians who started *Russell's Magazine.* An enthusiastic proponent of modern science, which he believed to be perfectly compatible with Christian faith, Lynch belonged to the Elliott Natural History Society and was an early member of the American Association for the Advancement of Science. He was especially interested in geology and was one of a committee of scientists who oversaw the drilling and operation of Charleston's artesian wells. He frequently lectured and published on scientific topics, such as the 1874 transit of Venus and the Galileo case.

Following a long illness Bishop Lynch died in Charleston on February 26, 1882. He was buried in the crypt of the Cathedral of St. John the Baptist, Charleston. DAVID C. R. HEISSER

Buchanan, Scott. "Bishop Lynch and the Catholic Church Face the Civil War." *New Catholic Miscellany* 27 (June 22, 1995): 8–10.

Heisser, David C. R. "Bishop Lynch's Civil War Pamphlet on Slavery." *Catholic Historical Review* 84 (October 1998): 681–96.

———. "Bishop Lynch's People: Slaveholding by a South Carolina Prelate." *South Carolina Historical Magazine* 102 (July 2001): 82–106.

Lynch, Thomas, Jr. (1749–1779). Signer of the Declaration of Independence. Born on August 5, 1749, in Prince George Winyah Parish, Lynch was the only son of Thomas Lynch, Sr. (ca. 1727–1776), and Elizabeth Allston. He attended the Indigo Society School in Georgetown and then traveled to England to pursue his education. There, he enrolled at Eton and then Caius College, Cambridge. Lynch also read law at the Middle Temple in London.

After his return to South Carolina in 1772, Lynch abandoned law to become a planter at Peach Tree Plantation in St. James Santee Parish. On May 14, 1772, he married Elizabeth Shubrick, daughter of Thomas Shubrick and Sarah Motte. At his father's urging, Lynch soon thereafter entered public life. He served in the First and Second Provincial Congresses of South Carolina (1774–1776), on the constitutional committee of South Carolina (1776), and in the first General Assembly (1776). In June 1775 Lynch received a commission as captain in the First South Carolina Regiment. While recruiting in North Carolina in July 1775, Lynch contracted a fever that left him in poor health for the remainder of his brief life. With his company he served at Fort Johnson from September 1775 until his election to the Second Continental Congress in March 1776.

Lynch's father had been elected to the First Continental Congress in 1774 but suffered a stroke in early 1776 that left him unable to perform his public duties. The younger Lynch joined his father in Philadelphia and presented his credentials to Congress on April 24. Only twenty-six years old and the second-youngest member of Congress, Thomas Lynch, Jr., was the fifty-second signer of the Declaration of Independence. His father was too ill to sign. Thomas Jr.'s own poor health precluded his continued service in the Congress. Together, father and son left Philadelphia in December 1776 to return to South Carolina, but the senior Lynch died during the trip.

In ill health, Thomas Lynch, Jr., retired to his plantation. He represented St. James Santee Parish in the second (1776–1778) General Assembly. He was reelected in 1779, but his declining health prevented him from completing his full term. On December 17, 1779, in an attempt to regain his health, Lynch and his wife set sail for the south of France. Their ship was lost at sea en route to the West Indies. ALEXIA JONES HELSLEY

Bailey, N. Louise, and Elizabeth Ivey Cooper, eds. *Biographical Directory of the South Carolina House of Representatives.* Vol. 3, *1775–1790.* Columbia: University of South Carolina Press, 1981.

Horne, Paul A., Jr. "Forgotten Leaders: South Carolina's Delegation to the Continental Congress, 1774–1789." Ph.D. diss., University of South Carolina, 1988.

Lynch, Thomas, Sr. (ca. 1727–1776). Legislator, delegate to Continental Congress. Lynch was born in St. James Santee Parish, the son of Thomas Lynch and Sabina Vanderhorst. His father became a wealthy rice planter with several plantations along the Santee River. Lynch's first marriage, in 1745 to Elizabeth Allston, produced three children. On March 6, 1755, Lynch married Hannah Motte, daughter of Jacob Motte and Elizabeth Martin. His second marriage produced one daughter.

A prominent planter, Lynch was active in public affairs. He was the first president of the Winyah Indigo Society (1755–1757) and represented Prince Frederick Parish (1752–1754, 1757–1760), St. James Santee Parish (1754–1757), and Prince George Winyah Parish (1760–1775) in the Commons House of Assembly. Visiting Charleston in early 1773, the Massachusetts lawyer and patriot Josiah Quincy described Lynch in the Commons House as "a man of sense, and a patriot."

From an early date, Lynch opposed efforts by the British to encroach upon colonial autonomy. He was a delegate to the Stamp Act Congress of 1765 in New York and was a member of the Non-Importation Association (1769), serving on its General Committee. As one of South Carolina's best-known and most ardent patriots, Lynch became a great favorite of the Charleston Sons of Liberty. In 1774 Lynch was elected a delegate to the First Continental Congress (1774–1775) in Philadelphia, and he was reelected to the Second Continental Congress (1776). In Congress, Lynch played an active role in the proceedings and earned the respect of his fellow delegates for his "plain, sensible" manner. Silas Deane, a delegate from Connecticut, recorded that Lynch "wears his hair strait, his clothes in the plainest order, and is highly esteemed." Lynch was also elected by St. James Santee Parish to the Second Provincial Congress (1775–1776) and the first South Carolina General Assembly (1776), although he did not participate in either assembly.

While attending Congress in early 1776, Lynch suffered a stroke that left him paralyzed and unable to participate in legislative affairs. In 1776 the South Carolina Provincial Congress elected his son Thomas Lynch, Jr., as a delegate to the Continental Congress in order to assist his father. Although still a delegate, the senior Lynch's declining health prevented him from signing the Declaration of Independence, leaving a gap between the signatures of Edward Rutledge and Thomas Heyward, Jr. However, Thomas Jr. was among the signers.

In December 1776 Lynch left Philadelphia with his son to return to South Carolina. En route, he suffered a second stroke and died in Annapolis, Maryland, where he was buried in St. Anne's Churchyard. ALEXIA JONES HELSLEY

Edgar, Walter, and N. Louise Bailey, eds. *Biographical Directory of the South Carolina House of Representatives.* Vol. 2, *The Commons House of Assembly, 1692–1775.* Columbia: University of South Carolina Press, 1977.

Horne, Paul A., Jr. "Forgotten Leaders: South Carolina's Delegation to the Continental Congress, 1774–1789." Ph.D. diss., University of South Carolina, 1988.

Weir, Robert M. *Colonial South Carolina: A History.* 1983. Reprint, Columbia: University of South Carolina Press, 1997.

Lynches River. Originating at the confluence of two nameless streams in North Carolina, the Lynches River crosses the state line in the Piedmont and flows nearly its entire 175-mile length through South Carolina. From a relatively straight path in the pine forests it becomes a slower, braided waterway as it meanders through wetlands fed by the various tributaries. At the end of its course it is joined by the waters of the Great Sparrow Swamp and then empties into the Pee Dee River. Along the way the Lynches marks parts of the boundaries of Chesterfield, Lancaster, Kershaw, Florence, Lee, Sumter, and Darlington Counties.

After Europeans entered the region in the 1670s, the population of Catawba, Waxhaw, and Pee Dee natives declined. Queensborough Township, one of the original nine townships established in the state in 1759, was located between the Lynches and Pee Dee Rivers. In 1781 Thomas Sumter and his men were attacked outside of Bishopville by British troops but evaded them by traversing the Lynches River over Ratcliff's Bridge, burning the structure behind them to aid their escape. In the late 1700s the Lynches attracted entrepreneurs who set up saw mills, harvested the long leaf pine, and shipped the lumber downstream to Georgetown. In the early nineteenth century counties along the Lynches began producing impressive amounts of cotton, and steamboats carried the bales downriver until the coming of railroads.

In 1880 the river was the site of the last duel ever fought in South Carolina. Ellerbe Cash killed William Shannon near the bridge crossing at U.S. Highway 15, which prompted the South Carolina General Assembly to outlaw dueling.

By the end of the twentieth century the river was primarily used for recreational purposes and was known for its natural beauty, diverse wildlife, and good fishing. In 1994 a fifty-four-mile segment of the river was designated as a State Scenic River, the longest stretch of scenic river in South Carolina. ROBERT STEVENS

Blagden, Tom. *The Rivers of South Carolina.* Englewood, Colo.: Westcliffe, 1999.

King, G. Wayne. *Rise Up So Early: A History of Florence County, South Carolina.* Spartanburg, S.C.: Reprint Company, 1981.

Kovacik, Charles F., and John J. Winberry. *South Carolina: The Making of a Landscape.* 1987. Reprint, Columbia: University of South Carolina Press, 1989.

Lynches River Advisory Council. *Lynches Scenic River Management Plan.* Columbia: South Carolina Department of Natural Resources, 1997.

Lynching. The origin of the word "lynching" has several explanations. The most common account has it derived from Charles Lynch, a justice of the peace in Virginia, who excessively punished Loyalists during the Revolutionary War. Thus, extreme punishment became known as "Lynch Law." Another explanation, from the *Oxford English Dictionary,* suggests that the term derives from Lynches Creek, South Carolina. By 1768 Lynches Creek was known as a meeting site for the Regulators, a group of vigilantes who used violence against their opponents. These early definitions of lynching refer to forms of frontier vigilantism. After the Civil War and Reconstruction, lynching took on a new, racial connotation and was primarily carried out by whites against African Americans. This racial violence gave white southerners a way to express and reaffirm their white southern identity. It also deterred African Americans from attempting to assert the equality granted to them under the Thirteenth Amendment of the U.S. Constitution.

Lynching became so widespread that the years 1882 to 1930 have been termed the "lynching era." The National Association for the Advancement of Colored People (NAACP) defined lynching during this period as murder committed extralegally by three or more persons who claim to be serving justice. Between 1882 and 1930 the number of lynching victims in the South totaled 2,805. South Carolina, with 156, had the second-fewest lynching victims. Mississippi, with 538 victims, had the most.

The justifications for mob violence had little regional variation across the South as they shared the common intention of disenfranchising blacks. During this era, drawing on scientific racism, white southerners created and articulated an image of African American males as black, beastly rapists whose animal-like sexuality threatened white women's purity. White men claimed that lynching was a way to protect themselves and, more importantly, their women from black aggression. Racial violence offered white southerners a chance to "redeem" southern society, restoring it to its pre-Reconstruction state. South Carolina governor Benjamin Tillman represented these beliefs about African Americans and southern white male responsibilities. In

1892 Tillman spoke of his own willingness to lead a lynch mob against any black man who had been accused of raping a white woman.

Antilynching advocates, such as Ida B. Wells and Jesse Ames of the Association of Southern Women for the Prevention of Lynching, revealed that contrary to white claims, the majority of lynch victims were not accused of raping white women. In actuality, only nineteen percent of black victims in the South were accused of rape. Victims were lynched for a wide range of behavior, including such illegalities as murder, theft, arson, and assault, as well as for such disrespectful actions as trying to vote, being disruptive, and frightening a white woman.

South Carolina was the site of one of the largest lynchings. On December 28, 1889, in Barnwell County eight African American men were accused of murdering a local merchant. A mob broke them out of jail, tied them to trees, and then shot them. In 1926 Aiken was the site of the Lowman family lynching. A sheriff and his deputies, all members of the Ku Klux Klan, arrived to arrest one of the Lowman sons. Upon hearing that the boy was gone, the sheriff attacked his sister. The resulting scuffle ended with mother Lowman shot by the sheriff, who in turn was killed by a stray bullet. The remaining Lowmans were arrested and tried. When one brother was acquitted, a Klan-led mob stormed the jail, dragged them out, and shot them.

The last lynching in South Carolina occurred on February 17, 1947, when a white mob murdered Willie Earle, a young black man who had been arrested for murdering a white taxicab driver. Although those responsible were acquitted, Earle's murder marked a turning point for lynching in South Carolina. State and federal law enforcement agents conducted an intensive investigation of the crime that resulted in several arrests and a vigorous prosecution of the accused.

The Earle murder was the culmination of a decline in lynching that occurred during the 1930s and 1940s, which reflected a larger social change. The "Great Migration" of African Americans to northern cities in the 1930s changed labor dynamics in the South. Lynchings, which previously were a form of punishment for interpersonal violence, became a form of social repression, targeted not at criminals but at successful African Americans. By the 1940s the social dynamics that had allowed whites to lynch without fear of repercussions were effectively gone, and so gradually the lynching era came to an end. KRISTINA ANNE DUROCHER

Finnegan, Terrence R. "'At the Hands of Parties Unknown': Lynching in Mississippi and South Carolina, 1881–1940." Ph.D. diss., University of Illinois at Urbana-Champaign, 1993.

Royster, Jacqueline Jones, ed. *Southern Horrors and Other Writings: The Anti-Lynching Campaign of Ida B. Wells, 1892–1900.* Boston: Bedford, 1996.

Tolnay, Stewart E., and E. M. Beck. *A Festival of Violence: An Analysis of Southern Lynchings, 1882–1930.* Urbana: University of Illinois Press, 1995.

Lyttelton, William Henry (1724–1808). Governor. Lyttelton was born on December 24, 1724, in the London parish of St. Martin's-in-the-Fields, the sixth son of Sir Thomas Lyttelton and Christian Temple, daughter of Sir Richard Temple. He attended Eton College and St. Mary Hall, Oxford. In 1748 he attended Middle Temple at the Inns of Court, and later in life he received an honorary doctor of civil law degree from Oxford. Lyttelton married twice. He wed his first wife, Mary MacCartney, in 1761. She died in 1765, and nine years later he married Caroline Bristowe. Each marriage produced a son. Through education and family connections Lyttelton secured preferment in colonial and diplomatic posts and was raised to the Irish and then the British peerage.

Lyttelton began his career as a colonial administrator when he was appointed governor of South Carolina in 1755. Traveling to his post, Lyttelton was captured at sea by French warships and held briefly as a prisoner of war. He arrived at Charleston on June 1, 1756, and held office until he left the colony on April 4, 1760. Lyttelton's tenure was marked by frontier warfare with the Cherokee Indians and by political and constitutional conflicts with the colonial Commons House of Assembly. The French and Indian War (1756–1763) was the American phase of the European Seven Years' War that pitted Britain against France. In America the war was a contest for control of the continent and was fought by European regulars, colonial militias, and rival Native American allies. In South Carolina the Cherokee War of 1759–1761 was a localized campaign in this continental struggle for hegemony.

In 1759 Cherokee Indians in the northwestern corner of the colony murdered several British traders and upcountry settlers. Governor Lyttelton refused to meet a delegation of Cherokee headmen who traveled to Charleston seeking peace. Instead, he led a military expedition into the upcountry as a show of force and brought the delegation with him as hostages. At Fort Prince George he negotiated a treaty with the Cherokees to hand over for trial the murderers of the British settlers and provided that hostages be held as surety that the murderers would be handed over. Other provisions called for the unhindered return of English traders to their posts, the execution of any emissaries the French might send to the Cherokees, and the jurisdiction of the South Carolina government in future disputes between Cherokees and South Carolinians. Despite the treaty, warfare broke out in early 1760, but by that time Lyttelton had received appointment to become governor of Jamaica, although he could not start that post until 1762. He left for England in April 1760, and the war was prosecuted by British colonels Archibald Montgomery and James Grant and by Lieutenant Governor William Bull, Jr.

During his tenure a group of French Acadians sought to settle in South Carolina. Exiled from their homes in Nova Scotia by British policies, they dispersed throughout the mainland colonies. Anti-French sentiment made them unwelcome, and few remained in South Carolina and Georgia. Most moved on and settled in Louisiana. Lyttelton and his assembly continued a long-standing dispute over provincial finances. However, in July 1756 the assembly authorized a budget and some of the dissension subsided.

Lyttelton had a long career as a royal governor, an ambassador, and a member of Parliament after he left South Carolina. He was governor of Jamaica from 1762 to 1766 and British ambassador to Portugal until 1771. After his diplomatic service, he returned to England and was a member of Parliament, representing Bewdley until 1790. Raised to the Irish peerage as Baron Westcote of Ballymore in 1776, he was also named Baron Lyttelton of Frankley in 1794. In his later years Lyttelton wrote "An Historical Account of the Constitution of Jamaica," which was published in a 1792 edition of Jamaican statutes and reprinted in Bryan Edwards's *History, Civil and Commercial, of the British Colonies in the West Indies* (1794). Lyttelton died in Stourbridge, Worcestershire, England, on September 14, 1808. ALEXANDER MOORE

Alden, John Richard. *John Stuart and the Southern Colonial Frontier: A Study of Indian Relations, War, Trade, and Land Problems in the Southern Wilderness, 1754–1775.* 1944. Reprint, New York: Gordian, 1966.

Attig, Clarence John. "William Henry Lyttelton: A Study in Colonial Administration." Ph.D. diss., University of Nebraska, 1958.

Corkran, David H. *The Cherokee Frontier, Conflict and Survival, 1740–1762.* Norman: University of Oklahoma Press, 1962.

Lyttelton, William Henry. Papers. William L. Clements Library, University of Michigan, Ann Arbor.

Mabry, George Lawrence, Jr. (1917–1990). Soldier, Medal of Honor recipient. Mabry was born on September 14, 1917, on his family's farm in Stateburg. He graduated from Hillcrest High School. At first he did not want to attend college, so his father employed him as a farmwork supervisor for a year. This experience changed his mind about school, and he entered Presbyterian College on a baseball scholarship.

Major George Mabry receives the Medal of Honor from President Harry S. Truman. Courtesy, the Mabry Family

Graduating in 1940 with a B.A., Mabry entered the U.S. Army in July as a second lieutenant assigned to the Fourth Division at Fort Benning, Georgia. In 1941 Mabry married Eulena Myers; they eventually had three children. Mabry served in the Fourth Division throughout the war. His first action under enemy fire was at Normandy on June 6, 1944, when he led his company in the first wave onto Utah Beach. During his first combat experience Mabry spearheaded a path through a minefield, captured or killed ten enemy soldiers, and directed a tank assault on enemy machine gun emplacements to open a path to the inland causeways. Soon after, he was one of the first from the seaborne invasion force to link up with troops of the U.S. 101st Airborne Division, who dropped behind enemy lines earlier that morning. By the time he had fought his way across France he had earned promotion to battalion commander. In the fall of 1944 Mabry and his division took part in the bloody campaign to take the Huertgen Forest in western Germany. During this grueling operation of many weeks American forces made little progress at heavy cost.

On November 20, 1944, Mabry earned the Congressional Medal of Honor, the highest award for bravery in the U.S. military. Under heavy enemy fire he prepared a path through a minefield, disconnected a booby-trapped concertina obstacle, and led a successful assault against three enemy bunkers. Despite his achievements, Mabry later wrote a report critical of the American high command in the Huertgen campaign. He bluntly stated that U.S. leaders needlessly committed exhausted troops against enemy defenses without adequate intelligence or support.

After World War II, Mabry chose to make a career of the army. A lieutenant colonel by the end of the war, Mabry steadily earned promotions and retired in 1975 as a major general. He attended the Command and General Staff College (1949–1950), served in Korea, and had assignments in Europe, Central America, and the United States. During the first half of 1957 he commanded the Third Training Regiment at Fort Jackson. He had two tours in Vietnam, the first in 1966 to head a team to evaluate U.S. Army combat operations, the results of which were later published in nine volumes known as the ARCOV report. His last tour was as a chief of staff to the general in charge of all U.S. Army combat units in Indochina (1969–1970). He was the second-most-decorated American serviceman of World War II. Mabry made his home in Columbia after his retirement, where he died on July 13, 1990. FRITZ HAMER

Astor, Gerald. *The Greatest War: Americans in Combat, 1941–1945.* Novato, Calif.: Presidio, 1999.

Howarth, David. "D-Day Part Four: Utah Beach." *Saturday Evening Post,* April 4, 1959, pp. 42–43, 153–54, 157–58.

Osteen, Hubert D., Jr. "George Mabry: The Legacy of One Soldier Will Never Die." Sumter *Item,* July 15, 1990, p. A9.

MacDowell, Rosalie Anderson (b. 1958). Actress, model. "Andie" MacDowell was born in Gaffney on April 21, 1958, the youngest of four daughters born to Marion and Paula MacDowell. Her parents divorced when she was six. As a child, MacDowell longed to be an actress but spent much of her teen years taking care of her mother, who suffered from alcoholism. MacDowell has reflected about her difficult childhood in Gaffney: "Becoming independent is what made it possible to leave a small town and go to the big city in the first place."

MacDowell attended Winthrop College for two years before boldly walking into New York's Elite Model Management with only minimal modeling experience. She became a successful model in Paris and New York. While continuing to represent L'Oreal cosmetics, MacDowell pursued her dream of becoming an actress. Unfortunately, in her first film role as Lady Jane in *Greystoke: The Legend of Tarzan, Lord of the Apes* (1984), the director dubbed her distinctive southern voice with the voice of actress Glenn Close. Overcoming the humiliating setback, MacDowell would go on to receive a Los Angeles Film Critics Award, a Golden Globe nomination, and other honors for portraying a repressed southern housewife in *sex, lies and videotape* (1989). She received a second Golden Globe nomination for playing a shy horticulturist in the romantic comedy *Green Card* (1990) and continued to gain recognition in popular films including *St. Elmo's Fire* (1985), *Groundhog Day* (1993), and *Four Weddings and a Funeral* (1994), for which she received her third Golden Globe nomination.

Preferring a quiet life and her role as a mother to the glamour and pace of Hollywood, MacDowell lived on a Montana ranch and later moved to Asheville, North Carolina. She married the model and musician Paul Qualley in 1986 and had three children before divorcing in 1999. In 2001 MacDowell married the businessman Rhett D. Hartzog, a former schoolmate from Gaffney. SUSAN GIAIMO HIOTT

Mace of the House of Representatives. The Mace is a symbol of the authority of the South Carolina House of Representatives. The scepterlike object rests in a rack at the front of the Speaker's podium whenever the House is in session and is sometimes carried in processions. The Mace has been used by South Carolina legislative bodies, with some interruptions, since it was made for the Commons House of Assembly in 1756. It was crafted in London by Magdalen Feline (d. 1796). She was a master goldsmith who specialized in large pieces, such as bowls and candlesticks, and had her establishment in Covent Garden. Four other Feline maces are preserved in England.

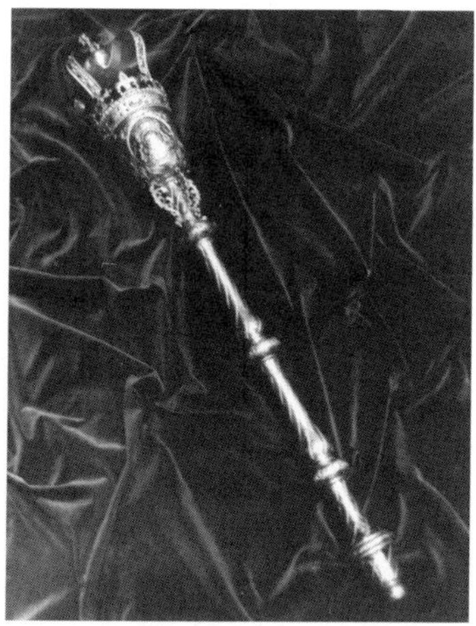

Mace of the South Carolina House of Representatives. Courtesy, The Clerk's Office, South Carolina House of Representatives

South Carolina's Mace is approximately forty-eight inches long, weighs almost eleven pounds, and is fashioned of silver burnished with gold. It is topped by a symbolic royal crown. Around the cylindrical mace-head below the crown are four circular decorative panels: the pictures from the colonial great seal of King George II (with the king receiving a curtsy from a lady personifying the province, and the royal coat of arms) and allegories of commerce and agriculture. After the Revolutionary War, the Mace became the property of the House of Representatives.

Since the Middle Ages ceremonial maces as emblems of authority have been carried before high government, university, and church officials. The ceremonial mace is descended from medieval weapons of war and from kingly scepters. South Carolina's is the oldest mace in continuous use by any American state legislature. DAVID C. R. HEISSER

Heisser, David C. R. "Scepters of Academe: College and University Maces of the Palmetto State." *Carologue* 10 (winter 1994): 11–13, 24.

Heisser, David C. R., and Sandra K. McKinney. *South Carolina's Mace and Its Heritage.* Columbia: South Carolina House of Representatives, 1991.

Salley, Alexander S. *The Mace of the House of Representatives of the State of South Carolina.* Columbia, S.C.: State Company, 1917.

Mackey, Edmund William McGregor (1846–1884). Legislator, congressman. Mackey was one of the state's controversial Republican politicians during Reconstruction and thereafter. Born on March 8, 1846, in Charleston, he received a classical education, but the outbreak of the Civil War prevented his entering college. He was admitted to the practice of law in 1868. In 1874 Mackey married Vicky Sumter, who was part African American. The couple had two sons.

Mackey first entered Republican politics with his election to the state constitutional convention of 1867. Between 1868 and 1875 he held a series of elective offices including county sheriff, Charleston alderman, and member of the state House of Representatives from Charleston County. He also was editor of the *Charleston Republican,* which enabled him to increase his influence in the Republican Party. In 1874 he was a candidate for the U.S. House of Representatives in the state's Second District, and he served for sixteen months until the seat was declared vacant.

Following the disputed election of 1876, the state had competing Speakers of the House of Representatives presiding simultaneously. Mackey is seated on the left with the gavel. Courtesy, South Carolina Historical Society

In October 1876 Mackey was again elected to the General Assembly. However, election returns from several counties were in dispute, with both Republicans and Democrats claiming victory in the gubernatorial and presidential contests and in certain state legislative races. Each side accused the other of fraud. Out of this confused situation emerged two separate State House organizations, one that elected Mackey as the Republican Speaker and one that elected William H. Wallace as the Democratic Speaker. The two competing bodies became known as the "Mackey House" and the "Wallace House." For days they occupied the same chamber, sought to conduct business, and tried to ignore one another. Subsequently, the state supreme court ruled that Wallace, not Mackey, was the "legal speaker of the lawfully constituted House of Representatives." In April 1877 the legally recognized "Wallace House" successfully reduced the Republican contingent in the General Assembly through forced resignations, expulsions, and declaring invalid the election of Republican members from Charleston County, including Mackey.

In 1878 Mackey again sought election to Congress from the Second District and again was unsuccessful. Two years later, in 1880, he made still another try. This time, after challenging the seating of the incumbent Democrat and with the contest still pending, his opponent died and Mackey was awarded the office. In 1882, running in the newly drawn Seventh District that had a black majority, he was easily reelected.

As a native and a Republican who seemed continually to be seeking elective office, Mackey came to be regarded by many in the state as little more than a scalawag opportunist. He was, however, seriously involved in trying to maintain and even strengthen the Republican organization. To that end, he was twice a delegate to Republican National Conventions and from 1880 to 1884 served as chairman of the state party committee.

About halfway through his second term in Congress, on January 27, 1884, Mackey died unexpectedly in Washington, D.C. He was buried in that city's Glenwood Cemetery. NEAL D. THIGPEN

Obituary. *New York Times,* January 29, 1884, p. 5.
Simkins, Francis Butler, and Robert Hilliard Woody. *South Carolina during Reconstruction.* Chapel Hill: University of North Carolina Press, 1932.

Magnolia Cemetery (Charleston). Overlooking the Cooper River north of Charleston, Magnolia Cemetery was established in 1850. An excellent example of the rural cemeteries then popular in mid-nineteenth-century America, it followed the example of such cemeteries as Mount Auburn near Boston, Laurel Hill near Philadelphia, and Green-Wood near New York City.

View in Magnolia Cemetery, Charleston. Courtesy, South Caroliniana Library, University of South Carolina

Magnolia Cemetery, described at its dedication as a "spot most precious to the musing hour," was designed by the Charleston architect Edward C. Jones. It features family plots surrounded by stone coping or cast-iron fences; winding streets and paths with cast-iron benches; ornamental trees and shrubs such as magnolias, live oaks, cedars, and hollies; a small lake; and a vista of the marsh and the nearby river. Gravestones include marble or granite tablets, ledgers, box-tombs, tomb-tables, obelisks, and pedestal-tombs, as well as several prominent mausoleums.

Among the most striking monuments are the Elbert P. Jones Monument (1853), designed by the architect Francis D. Lee; the Vanderhorst Mausoleum (1856), an elaborate Egyptian-revival structure; the Colonel William Washington Monument (1858), designed by the architect Edward Brickell White and sculpted by William T. White and featuring a fluted column with a rattlesnake coiled around it; and the Defenders of Charleston Monument (1882), the focal point of the Confederate section. The cemetery also features many fine examples of work by the White brothers of Charleston—William, Edwin, and Robert—perhaps the most prolific and accomplished stonecutters of nineteenth-century South Carolina. Their stones, often cut from imported Italian marble, are notable for their distinctive lettering and remarkably detailed carving.

Some of the prominent South Carolinians buried here include the antebellum industrialist William Gregg, the U.S. senator and secessionist Robert Barnwell Rhett, the author and poet William Gilmore Simms, the merchant and secretary of the Confederate States Treasury George Alfred Trenholm, and Confederate generals James Conner, Micah Jenkins, Arthur M. Manigault, and Roswell S. Ripley. Captain Horace L. Hunley and the second and third crews of the Confederate submarine *H. L. Hunley* are also interred in Magnolia Cemetery. J. TRACY POWER

Fraser, Charles. *Address Delivered on the Dedication of Magnolia Cemetery, on the 19th November 1850.* Charleston, S.C.: Walker and James, 1850.
Magnolia Cemetery: The Proceedings at the Dedication of the Grounds, to Which Are Appended the Rules, Regulations and Charter of the Company; with a List of Officers and Members of the Board. Charleston, S.C.: Walker and James, 1851.
Phillips, Ted Ashton. "City of the Silent." Typescript, 1995. South Caroliniana Library, University of South Carolina, Columbia.
Simms, William Gilmore. *The City of the Silent: A Poem, by W. Gilmore Simms, Delivered at the Consecration of Magnolia Cemetery, November 19, 1850.* Charleston, S.C.: Walker and James, 1850.
Stuart, Benjamin R. *Magnolia Cemetery: An Interpretation of Some of Its Monuments and Inscriptions.* Charleston, S.C.: Kahrs and Welch, 1896.

Magrath, Andrew Gordon (1813–1893). Jurist, governor. Magrath was born in Charleston on February 8, 1813, the son of the Irish merchant John Magrath and Maria Gordon. After his graduation from South Carolina College in 1831, Magrath briefly attended Harvard Law School, but he acquired most of his legal training in Charleston under the tutelage of James L. Petigru. He was admitted to the bar in 1835. From 1838 to 1841 Magrath represented the city parishes of St. Philip's and St. Michael's in the state House of Representatives. On March 8, 1843, he married Emma D. Mikell of Charleston. The couple had five children. Around 1865 Magrath was married again, this time to Mary Eliza McCord of Columbia. They had no children.

Andrew G. Magrath. Courtesy, South Caroliniana Library, University of South Carolina

In 1856 Magrath was appointed a federal judge to the District Court of South Carolina, which brought him national attention and controversy. His tenure coincided with increasingly strident calls from some southern nationalists to reopen the African slave trade. Although opposed to the trade personally, Magrath nevertheless handed slave-trade proponents a signal victory in 1860. In a decision associated with the cases surrounding the *Echo* and the *Wanderer,* ships seized for illegally transporting African slaves, Magrath stated that the 1820 federal statute on piracy did not apply to the slave trade. "The African slave trade," he declared, "is not piracy." In rejecting the piracy statute, which carried the death penalty, Magrath's decision took some of the teeth out of federal slave-trade laws and was hailed by proslavery and states' rights advocates. Immediately following the 1860 election of Abraham Lincoln, Magrath resigned his judgeship. On November 7 he told a crowded Charleston courtroom that the "department of Government, which I believe has best maintained its integrity and preserved its purity, has been suspended." Admirers later claimed that Magrath's resignation was "the first overt act and irrevocable step" toward secession.

A cooperationist earlier in his career, Magrath supported secession by 1860, feeling "an assurance of what will be the action of the State." He sat in the state's Secession Convention and briefly served as the South Carolina secretary of state. In 1862 he was appointed as a Confederate district judge. His decisions generally opposed the concentration of authority by the Confederate government in Richmond. In December 1864 Magrath was elected governor of South Carolina, the last one chosen by the state legislature. During his brief tenure Magrath was affiliated with other southern governors who criticized the administration of President Jefferson Davis. By 1865 Magrath had become disenchanted with the "moral atrophy" of the southern people. "It is not an unwillingness to oppose the enemy, but a chilling apprehension of the futility of doing so, which affects the people," he wrote at the time. Following the collapse of the Confederacy, Magrath was arrested on May 25, 1865, and imprisoned at Fort Pulaski, Georgia. Released in December, Magrath returned to Charleston and rebuilt his lucrative law practice. He died in Charleston on April 9, 1893, and was buried in Magnolia Cemetery. PAUL CHRISTOPHER ANDERSON

Brooks, Ulysses R. *South Carolina Bench and Bar.* Columbia, S.C.: State Company, 1908.

Magrath, Andrew G. *The Slave Trade Not Declared Piracy by the Act of 1820: The United States versus William C. Corrie; Presentment for Piracy.* Columbia, S.C.: S. G. Courtenay, 1860.

Obituary. Charleston *News and Courier,* April 10, 1893, pp. 1, 2.

Sinha, Manisha. *The Counterrevolution of Slavery: Politics and Ideology in Antebellum South Carolina.* Chapel Hill: University of North Carolina Press, 2000.

Maham, Hezekiah (1739–1789). Soldier, legislator. Born on June 26, 1739, Hezekiah Maham achieved the status of a successful planter in St. Stephen's Parish by 1772. He represented that parish in the Second Provincial Congress at the onset of the Revolutionary War, but it would be through his military service that he would gain distinction. While the details of his early service remain unclear, in records Maham first appears at the head of a volunteer company of militia early in 1776 and is later promoted to the rank of major in a state regiment of light dragoons in 1779. After the fall of Charleston in May 1780, Maham joined Francis Marion's partisan corps and served as a principal commander of cavalry in Marion's brigade.

In the spring of 1781, Marion's partisan band joined with the Continentals of Henry Lee's Legion and marched on Fort Watson, a key British post between Charleston and the backcountry. The garrison was strategically located at the top of an ancient Indian mound, making a conventional assault suicidal. Major Maham suggested that a log tower be assembled with a platform high enough to allow riflemen to fire into the fort. The structure was completed on the morning of April 23, and an American assault party, protected by suppressing rifle fire from the tower, forced the garrison commander to surrender. Though not a new idea to siege warfare, the Maham Tower (as it would come to be known) was effective and would be used by patriot forces at the sieges of Augusta and Ninety Six later in the year.

On June 21, 1781, Maham was promoted to the rank of lieutenant colonel and appointed to command a battalion of light dragoons, which would come to be known as Maham's Legion. The appointment of Peter Horry to raise a similar corps eventually led to a quarrel between the two officers over rank. Nonetheless, Maham led his unit in a crucial assault at the Battle of Quinby Bridge on July 17, 1781. Later, in mid-November, Maham led a raid on a British hospital at Fairlawn Plantation that yielded some one hundred prisoners. In March 1782 the two cavalry units of Horry and Maham were combined under Maham's command. However, he took ill shortly afterward and withdrew to his plantation, where he was promptly captured and paroled by Tories.

Known for his temper, Maham once forced a deputy sheriff to eat and swallow a summons the latter was trying to serve on him. Elected to several terms in the South Carolina General Assembly during and after the Revolution, both as a representative and a senator, Maham also held sundry offices for the parish of St. Stephen's. He married twice. His first wife was Anne Guerin; his second was Mary Palmer. The marriages produced two daughters. Maham died on his plantation sometime between April 4, 1789, when he wrote his will, and June 1, 1789. SAMUEL K. FORE

Lumpkin, Henry. *From Savannah to Yorktown: The American Revolution in the South.* Columbia: University of South Carolina Press, 1981.

Rankin, Hugh F. *Francis Marion: The Swamp Fox.* New York: Crowell, 1973.

Stevens, Michael E. "Wealth, Influence or Powerful Connections: Aedanus Burke and the Case of Hezekiah Maham." *South Carolina Historical Magazine* 81 (April 1980): 163–68.

Weller, Jac. "Irregular but Effective: Partizan Weapons Tactics in the American Revolution, Southern Theatre." *Military Affairs* 21 (autumn 1957): 118–31.

Malaria. Malaria was arguably the most significant disease in the history of South Carolina from the colonial period until the early twentieth century. It attracted less public discussion than yellow fever and smallpox, but its impact in terms of morbidity and mortality was much greater. Whereas yellow fever and smallpox tended to erupt in spectacular but short-lived epidemics, malaria quietly and steadily eroded the lives and energy of a large part of the population. The most common symptoms of malaria are fever, chills, and aches. In classic cases spikes in the fever come at regular intervals. Depending on the severity and type of case, malaria may produce vomiting, severe headaches, jaundice, hemorrhaging, blood clots, an enlarged spleen, and renal failure. Before the late nineteenth century malaria was referred to by various names, including ague and fever, intermittent fever, and remittent fever. From the late colonial period, many South Carolinians called it "country fever" to distinguish it from yellow fever, which was largely confined to Charleston and other ports.

Malaria is a parasitic infection caused by protozoa known as *plasmodia* and transmitted by anopheline mosquitoes. Two types of malaria dominated in South Carolina. Both are highly debilitating diseases that produce lethargy and vulnerability to other infections. *Plasmodium vivax,* which probably came with European settlers in the 1670s, is the less virulent of the two forms. The introduction of the more deadly *Plasmodium falciparum* came with the importation of large numbers of African slaves in the 1680s and after. Many West Africans were immune to *vivax,* and some had acquired or inherited resistance to *falciparum.* The observations of planters and physicians of black resistance to malaria helped give rise to the proslavery argument that blacks were peculiarly adapted to labor in the southern climate. Nevertheless, many blacks suffered severely from *falciparum,* as they still do in parts of Africa.

By the early eighteenth century malaria was endemic in the lowcountry. It continued to plague the region throughout the eighteenth and nineteenth centuries, and was a major contributor to the region's high mortality rates and reputation for unhealthiness. It was particularly dangerous to infants, young children, and pregnant women. The severity of malaria was the result not only of the lowcountry's semitropical climate and marshy topography but also of its plantation economy, particularly the cultivation of rice and indigo, which provided ideal breeding conditions for the anophelines. From the late colonial period, the threat of malaria transformed many of the planting families of the lowcountry into seasonal migrants. They fled the plantations during the summer and early autumn for locations perceived to be less dangerous: the North, Charleston, the pinelands, the upcountry, and the seashore.

During the nineteenth century malaria became a major health problem in much of the state, especially in newly cleared and undrained lands and along river valleys. It reached epidemic status on several occasions during the Civil War and after. In the early twentieth century coastal South Carolina was one of the most persistent hyperendemic pockets of the disease in the country. In the 1930s parasite rates as high as fifty percent were not uncommon among schoolchildren in rural areas, with the highest rates in the coastal counties. In the early 1940s the construction of Santee Cooper hydroelectric dams produced one of the last epidemics of malaria. In the rush to complete the project in the face of war, the upper reservoir (Lake Marion) was not completely cleared of trees. They impeded flow and provided excellent breeding grounds for anophelines. In 1944 thirty-nine percent of people living on the north shore of the lake tested positive for malaria. By the early 1950s, however, the disease had virtually disappeared from the state for reasons that are still not entirely understood, but improvements in mosquito control (especially the development of the pesticide DDT), drainage, housing, and nutrition probably all played a part. PETER MCCANDLESS

Childs, St. Julien Ravenel. *Malaria and Colonization in the Carolina Low Country, 1526–1696.* Baltimore: Johns Hopkins Press, 1940.

Dubisch, Jill. "Low Country Fevers: Cultural Adaptations to Malaria in Antebellum South Carolina." *Social Science and Medicine* 21, no. 6 (1985): 641–47.

Humphreys, Margaret. *Malaria: Poverty, Race, and Public Health in the United States.* Baltimore: Johns Hopkins University Press, 2001.

Kovacik, Charles. "Health Conditions and Town Growth in Colonial and Antebellum South Carolina." *Social Science and Medicine* 12 (1978): 131–36.

Merrens, H. Roy, and George D. Terry. "Dying in Paradise: Malaria, Mortality, and the Perceptual Environment in Colonial South Carolina." *Journal of Southern History* 50 (November 1984): 533–50.

Young, Martin D. "A Short History of Malaria in South Carolina." *Bulletin of the South Carolina Academy of Science* 13 (1951): 12–18.

Manchester State Forest. Located in Sumter County, this 26,000-acre property was acquired in the 1930s by the Federal Resettlement Administration as part of its program to relocate families from worn-out farms to more productive land. From 1935 to 1939 the site was operated as the Poinsett Project. The South Carolina Forestry Commission assumed operation in 1939, changing the name to Poinsett State Forest. The name was finally established as Manchester State Forest in 1949.

Manchester was operated under a fifty-year lease from the federal government. During the early years the Civilian Conservation Corps and the Works Progress Administration were active partners in developing the property. Manchester's mission, as expressed in the lease agreement, was similar to that of Sand Hills: develop as a demonstration conservation area, utilizing the principles of multiple-use management. The Forestry Commission obtained title to the forest property in 1955.

Early on, Manchester posed a significant challenge to managers. Much of the property was infertile, cut-over, and subject to destructive wildfires. About seventy-five percent of the land was considered too poor to produce any kind of crop except trees. Reforestation was a primary concern, but early records show that game management and recreation have been prominent parts of Manchester's management since 1939.

Manchester State Forest includes several historical sites, including Bellfield, the home of Richard I. Manning, governor of South Carolina from 1915 to 1919. Except for salaries of forest workers, Manchester is completely self-supporting. SOUTH CAROLINA FORESTRY COMMISSION

Manigault, Gabriel (1704–1781). Merchant, legislator. Manigault was born on April 21, 1704, in Charleston, the son of Pierre Manigault and Judith Giton. His parents were refugees who fled France after the revocation of the Edict of Nantes. Throughout his life he remained a member of the French Protestant Church in Charleston, but he also owned a pew and worshiped at St. Philip's Church. He married Ann Ashby on April 29, 1730. The marriage produced one son, Peter, who would become a leading figure in the Commons House of Assembly.

Manigault rose from modest origins to become the leading merchant and private banker of colonial South Carolina. He operated retail shops on Tradd Street selling imported wine, fabrics, and dry goods. He also owned several trading vessels, in which he exported rice, naval stores, and other domestic products. Lacking family and business ties with Britain, he traded principally with the West Indies, Philadelphia, and New York. Known to disapprove of the slave trade, Manigault was reluctant to lend money to slave dealers. On a few occasions, however, he did finance the importation of slave cargoes, and at his death he owned nearly three hundred slaves. In his business dealings and personal affairs, he was known as an honest, fair, and benevolent man. He eschewed business partnerships, preferring to conduct business by himself. In addition to trade, Manigault acquired extensive real estate holdings in Charleston and the surrounding area, including Mount Pleasant plantation (from which the present city takes its name) and Silk Hope plantation, where he experimented with silk cultivation and wine production. By the time he retired from business life in 1767, he had amassed a large fortune.

Manigault was an active member and officer of the Charleston Library Society, and for many years he housed that society's collection and its librarian in one of his tenements. He was also a valued member of the South Carolina Society, to which he left a legacy of £5,000 sterling to fund that society's primary school. During his civic career Manigault acted as a commissioner of public bodies, representing such matters as free schools, streets, markets, bills of credit, ferries, and the Indian trade. Between 1733 and 1754 he served in the Commons House of Assembly, representing first the parish of

St. Philip's and later St. Thomas and St. Denis Parish. He held the office of public treasurer of the province from 1735 until 1743, and the accuracy of his accounts contributed to the stability of South Carolina during these difficult years. Manigault was twice recommended by Lieutenant Governor William Bull to a place on the Royal Council, but he declined both offers. His sentiments were with the mechanics of Charleston, who would eventually argue for separation from the British crown.

Although Manigault sought to tread a conservative path in the movement toward American independence, he was also South Carolina's principal Revolutionary War financier. Between 1776 and 1779 he lent the nascent state government a total of £652,500 (South Carolina currency), a sum far greater than was lent by any other individual. After the capitulation of Charleston to the British army in May 1780, Manigault spent his last days on his plantation in Goose Creek. He died on June 5, 1781, and was buried in St. Philip's Parish. NICHOLAS MICHAEL BUTLER

Crouse, Maurice A. "Gabriel Manigault: Charleston Merchant." *South Carolina Historical Magazine* 68 (October 1967): 220–31.

Edgar, Walter, and N. Louise Bailey, eds. *Biographical Directory of the South Carolina House of Representatives.* Vol. 2, *The Commons House of Assembly, 1692–1775.* Columbia: University of South Carolina Press, 1977.

Manigault Family. Papers. South Carolina Historical Society, Charleston.

Manigault, Gabriel (1758–1809). Architect. Manigault was Charleston's leading "gentleman architect" of the early national period. Born on March 17, 1758, he was the son of Peter Manigault and Elizabeth Wragg. While studying law in London in the 1770s, Manigault became familiar with the work of the Scottish architect Robert Adam, the dominant figure in English architecture during the late eighteenth century. He returned to Charleston in 1780 familiar with Adam's brand of neoclassicism, which drew on sources from ancient Rome to the cinquecento.

Manigault returned to Charleston in order to protect his family's property. Although he participated in the defense of Charleston, he took the oath of allegiance to the king several months after the city fell. After the war he turned his attention to rice planting on the nearly 25,000 acres he had inherited. The wealth afforded him the opportunity to pursue architecture.

Manigault brought to Charleston an architectural conception that bridged the Anglo-Palladianism of the mid–eighteenth century and the emergence of the Greek revival in the 1820s. He is generally credited with designing the Branch Bank of the United States (1800–1804), an elegant building dominated by a two-story hall across the facade. As a gentleman architect, Manigault provided the plans but left carpenters Edward Magrath and Joseph Nicholson and mason Andrew Gordon to supervise construction. In 1818 the building became the Charleston City Hall. Manigault produced a more fully realized example of Adamesque classicism in his design for the South Carolina Society Hall (1803–1804), which juxtaposes a subdued exterior with a more elaborate interior. Built on a T-plan with two stories over a service basement, the building features a second-story ballroom with a colonnaded neoclassical canopy. Another important example of Manigault's work was the Orphan House Chapel (1807), a two-story roughcast brick structure with a pediment supported by four engaged columns on the facade.

Manigault excelled as an architect of domestic buildings. About 1803 he designed a house for his brother Joseph at the corner of Meeting and John Streets. Standing three stories tall over a high basement, the house is built of brick and has the character of an urban villa. The exterior is distinguished not by ornament but by full-height curvilinear bays on the north and east elevations and a semicircular double-tiered piazza on the west. The interior plan incorporates a graceful sequence of interconnected entertaining rooms embellished with Adamesque detailing. As with the South Carolina Society Hall, the plain exterior provides no hint of the sumptuous interior decor. The formal entrance hall, dining room, and drawing room feature elaborately carved mantles and moldings, and a large plaster medallion ornaments the ceiling of the stairway.

Manigault also found time for extensive public service. He represented St. James Goose Creek Parish in the South Carolina House of Representatives from 1785 to 1793. Manigault was also a trustee for the College of Charleston and a charter member of the South Carolina Jockey Club. Manigault married Margaret Izard on May 1, 1785. They had ten children, three of whom died in infancy. In 1805 Manigault moved to Philadelphia, and he died there on November 4, 1809. DANIEL J. VIVIAN

Lane, Mills. *Architecture of the Old South: South Carolina.* Savannah, Ga.: Beehive, 1984.

Poston, Jonathan H. *The Buildings of Charleston: A Guide to the City's Architecture.* Columbia: University of South Carolina Press, 1997.

Ravenel, Beatrice St. Julien. *Architects of Charleston.* 1945. Reprint, Columbia: University of South Carolina Press, 1992.

Severens, Kenneth. *Charleston Antebellum Architecture and Civic Destiny.* Knoxville: University of Tennessee Press, 1988.

Manigault, Judith Giton (ca. 1665–1711). Immigrant, matriarch. Manigault was born Judith Giton in La Voulte, Languedoc, France, a stronghold of southern French Protestantism. In 1685 the repeal of the Edict of Nantes by Louis XIV drove many Huguenots (including Judith, two brothers, and her mother) to flee France through Holland to England. From London they boarded a ship headed for the colony of Carolina, where they hoped to live as Protestants, without the threat of forced conversion.

Most of what is known about Manigault comes from a letter she wrote from South Carolina to her brother in Europe. Written around 1688, the letter reveals the sufferings Manigault endured as a refugee and also the hardships faced by some of the earliest immigrants to South Carolina. En route, Judith's mother died of "spotted fever." Midway through their voyage, their ship was seized by authorities at Bermuda, forcing Manigault and her brother Louis to indenture themselves for eight months in exchange for passage to Carolina. Her letter records that once she and her surviving family arrived in Carolina, they "suffered all sorts of evils." Manigault wrote, "I was in this country a full six months, without tasting bread . . . and whilst I worked the ground, like a slave." It took several years before she was able to obtain bread "when I wanted it." The letter became a valuable record of the harshness of life in early South Carolina, and David Ramsay printed an extended portion of the document in his 1808 *History of South Carolina* (although the part of the letter that mentioned her indentured servitude was left out at the request of Manigault's descendants).

Sometime before 1695 Judith married a weaver and fellow Huguenot, Noe Royer. Royer died around 1698, and the following year Judith married Pierre Manigault, another Huguenot refugee. The Manigaults ran a boardinghouse in Charleston and began to build a distillery and cooperage, laying the foundation for an enormous fortune in trade and local commerce run from their warehouse and mercantile businesses. Judith Manigault died in 1711, leaving behind a son, Gabriel, and a daughter, Judith. When Pierre Manigault died in 1729, he had established the family as wealthy and powerful within the colony and had positioned his son to become one of the most influential men in South Carolina. MARGARET SANKEY

Crouse, Maurice A. "The Manigault Family of South Carolina, 1685–1783." Ph.D. diss., Northwestern University, 1964.

Simmons, Slann Legare Clement. "Early Manigault Records." *Transactions of the Huguenot Society of South Carolina* 59 (1954): 24–42.

Manigault, Peter (1731–1773). Lawyer, legislator, planter. Manigault was born on October 10, 1731, in Charleston, the only child of the wealthy merchant Gabriel Manigault and Anne Ashby. He was educated at a classical school in Charleston and served as a law apprentice under Thomas Corbett. From 1750 to 1754 he studied law in London at the Inner Temple. In 1754 Manigault returned to Charleston and established a law office. On June 8, 1755, he married Elizabeth Wragg, with whom he would have seven children, only four of whom survived infancy.

Although Manigault did not actively practice law, his legal training enabled him to pursue a political career, collect debts owed to London merchants, and manage the South Carolina business and plantation interests of absentee landowners. In 1755 Manigault was elected to the Commons House of Assembly, a position he held until he resigned in 1772. During the Stamp Act protests in 1765, he was elected Speaker of the Commons House of Assembly, and he was reelected as Speaker for seven consecutive years. One of the greatest achievements of the Commons House of Assembly during this time was the establishment of the circuit court system throughout the state in 1769.

In order to qualify to be seated in the Commons House of Assembly, one was required to "own a settled plantation of five hundred acres and ten slaves or other property to the value of one thousand pounds." To meet these requirements, Manigault's father deeded him 2,476.5 acres at Port Royal. In 1757 Manigault began acquiring tracts of adjoining land for working plantations. Because of his large land and slave holdings, he became one of the wealthiest men in eighteenth-century British North America. His first plantation collection combined tracts on Goose Creek from the estates of Godin and Wilson and comprised almost 1,300 acres. The Godin property was renamed Steepbrook Plantation and became Manigault's country home. Both of these plantations were managed as one with an overseer supervising eighty-two slaves in the growing of rice, indigo, corn, peas, and potatoes and raising sheep, oxen, cattle, horses, and poultry. A second group of rice plantations on the Santee River, Mount Ann or Manigault's Ferry and Gab Mount or Gaymount, consisted of 2,316 acres employing 110 slaves and included a private ferry across the Santee River. The third major working plantation, Mount Harriet, was created at the confluence of the Congaree and Wateree Rivers. He also owned numerous, smaller tracts of land. According to his 1774 probate inventory, Manigault left an estate valued at £32,737.8 sterling.

In 1772 Manigault resigned from the Commons House of Assembly due to his and his wife's health problems. After his wife died in February 1773, he returned to England to try to regain his health, which was declining. Manigault died in England on November 12, 1773, and his body was returned to Charleston for burial in the family vault of the Huguenot Church. MICHELINE BROWN

Crouse, Maurice A. "The Manigault Family of South Carolina, 1685–1783." Ph.D. diss., Northwestern University, 1964.

———, ed. "Letterbook of Peter Manigault." *South Carolina Historical Magazine* 70 (April 1969): 79–96; (July 1969): 177–95.

Edgar, Walter, and N. Louise Bailey, eds. *Biographical Directory of the South Carolina House of Representatives.* Vol. 2, *The Commons House of Assembly, 1692–1775.* Columbia: University of South Carolina Press, 1977.

Jones, Alice Hanson. *Wealth of a Nation to Be: The American Colonies of the Eve of the Revolution.* New York: Columbia University Press, 1980.

Mann, James Robert (b. 1920). Congressman. Mann was born in Greenville on April 27, 1920, the son of Alfred Clio Mann and Nina Mae Griffin. His father was an attorney and mayor of Greenville. Mann attended the Greenville city schools and graduated with an A.B. degree from the Citadel in 1941. He entered the U.S. Army as a second lieutenant on July 24, 1941, and served forty-six months overseas during World War II. He rose to the rank of lieutenant colonel before his discharge on March 1, 1946. He married Virginia Thomason Brunson of Charleston on January 15, 1945. They have two children.

After World War II, Mann entered the University of South Carolina Law School, where he edited the *South Carolina Law Review* and was elected to Phi Beta Kappa. He graduated magna cum laude in 1947 and began to practice law with the firm of Mann, Arnold, and Mann in Greenville. He was elected to the state House of Representatives in 1948 and served two terms (1949–1952). In 1953 he was appointed solicitor of the Thirteenth Judicial Circuit. He was elected to two terms, serving from 1953 to 1963, when he returned to the practice of law. He served as president of the Greenville Chamber of Commerce (1965).

Mann was elected to the U.S. Congress in 1968 and served from 1969 to 1979. His most notable service was as a member of the Judiciary Committee during the impeachment of Richard Nixon. He crafted portions of the first and second Articles of Impeachment so as to make them acceptable to both Republicans and southern colleagues. On July 27, 1974, the committee voted (twenty-seven to eleven) in favor of impeachment.

In 1975, with the support of U.S. Senator Strom Thurmond, President Gerald Ford was prepared to nominate Mann to the U.S. Court of Military Appeals. Mann declined the appointment, however, citing the lack of opportunity for service offered by the position. Leaving Congress in January 1979, Mann resumed his law practice in Greenville. A. V. HUFF, JR.

Mann, James R. Papers. Modern Political Collections, South Caroliniana Library, University of South Carolina, Columbia.

Manning (Clarendon County; 2000 pop. 4,025). Manning was established in 1855 to provide a central location for a courthouse in the newly created Clarendon District. It was named after a family that produced three South Carolina governors. The city is bordered on three sides by swamps and is near the junction of the Pocotaligo River and Ox Swamp, an area made famous in the Revolutionary War by General Francis Marion, the "Swamp Fox." During the Civil War, General Edward E. Potter raided Manning on April 8, 1865. Just before his arrival, one of Potter's officers was shot and killed in the streets of town by a Confederate scout, which explains why some feel that Manning was treated more harshly than other towns in the area.

Following the war, Manning and the surrounding countryside returned to their economic mainstay—agriculture—and the town prospered. In the early twentieth century Manning possessed a tobacco market, a cannery, lumber mills, and cotton gins. By the 1920s the city added three banks, a private preparatory school, and a hotel. Manning became known as a place "matchless for beauty and hospitality." The writer and broadcaster Walter Winchell, traveling through the area in 1939, wrote that Brooks Street in Manning was the "most beautiful street between Maine and Miami." The city's natural beauty was enhanced by surviving antebellum homes on wide streets lined with stately oaks. The Old Manning Library, built in 1908, with its unusual octagon-shaped interior and its high domed skylight is the only building in the city listed on the National Register of Historic Places. A bronze statue of "Amelia Bedelia," the children's character created by Manning author Peggy Parish, invites the community into the Harvin-Clarendon County Public Library next door.

Although agriculture remained the economic foundation of Manning throughout the twentieth century, its economy nevertheless underwent changes. At one time Manning's biggest industry was its tobacco market, but slumping prices forced the closer of that market in 1931. The city aggressively pursued industrial development in the decades after World War II. By the end of the century, Manning boasted a fifteen-acre industrial park with plants producing auto bearings, textiles, timber, and stainless-steel transport tankers. The city offered tax incentives and other advantages, including comparatively low wages and excellent transportation, to attract companies.

At the start of the twenty-first century, a mayor and six-member city council governed city affairs. Five full-time and thirty-two volunteer firemen and fourteen police officers met safety concerns. Manning echoed the sentiments of former mayor John G. Dinkins, whose comments in a 1940 radio address still rang true to many modern residents: "The Town and County both hold many attractions for new settlers, and investors. It is a good place to visit, and a better place to live." LAUREN DECKER

Clarendon Cameos. Manning, S.C.: Clarendon County Historical Society, 1976.

Orvin, Virginia Kirkland Galluchat. *History of Clarendon County, 1700 to 1961.* N.p., 1961.

Manning, John Laurence (1816–1889). Governor. Manning was born to Richard I. Manning and Elizabeth Peyre Richardson on January 29, 1816, at Hickory Hill, Clarendon District. After engaging a private tutor, Manning attended Hatfield Academy in Camden before proceeding to the College of New Jersey (Princeton University) in 1833. However, after the death of his father in 1836, Manning returned home and enrolled at South Carolina College; he graduated from that institution in 1837. On April 11, 1838, he married Susan Frances Hampton. They had three children. After the death of his first wife in 1845, Manning wed Sally Bland Clark in April 1848, and they eventually had four children.

Manning was born to both privilege and political connections. His father was governor of South Carolina from 1824 to 1826. John Manning became one of the wealthiest men in the South. By 1860 he possessed an estate valued at $2 million, which included plantations in South Carolina and Louisiana and at least 648 slaves. His status, as well as his captivating personal manner, ensured that Manning frequented elite circles. "He is always the handsomest man alive," Mary Boykin Chesnut remarked in her famous diary, "and he can be very agreeable. That is, when he pleases. He does not always please." His high social standing colored his political outlook. When he was asked once why he hated republics, Manning replied, "Because the mob rules republics."

In 1842 Manning was elected by the voters of Clarendon District to the S.C. House of Representatives. He was returned to the House in 1844 and then was elected to the state Senate in 1846. He was serving in the Senate when he was unanimously elected governor on December 9, 1852. Taking office after the secession crisis of 1851, Manning declared that South Carolina was currently "free from cabal and faction." However, the sectional tensions that sparked the crisis had not evaporated. A cooperationist, Manning nevertheless announced in his inaugural address that in a contest between federal and state authority it was "both my inclination and my duty as a States Rights Republican . . . to sustain the constitution and the laws of this commonwealth." But in general, Manning's term coincided with what he called "a brief period of repose" in the sectional crisis.

While governor, Manning supported internal improvements and presided over the renovation of the State House. His primary emphasis was on higher education. Manning viewed collegiate institutions not just as places of learning but also as academies especially designed for young men of "refinement, intelligence, and property" and bulwarks of conservative leadership. This view also influenced his decidedly lukewarm conception of free schools. "I have no hesitation in expressing the opinion that more benefit has arisen from the few thousand dollars expended annually on [colleges] for ten years past," he once remarked, "than has been accrued to the state from the application of the free school appropriations for thirty years previous."

Manning had a particular fondness for South Carolina College, his alma mater and a place he equated with conservative instruction and order. One of his first official acts was the suppression of the so-called "Great Biscuit Rebellion," a revolt of the students at South Carolina College over compulsory room and board fees. Manning, who served as a trustee of the institution from 1841 to 1854 and again from 1865 to 1869, endowed the school's first private scholarship in 1846. He encouraged others to follow his example and asked the legislature during his tenure to continue its "favor and protection" of the institution.

Manning attended the state's Secession Convention, signed the Ordinance of Secession, and sat in the state Senate for the duration of the Civil War. During the war he briefly served on the staff of General P. G. T. Beauregard. Manning also represented Clarendon District in the state Senate from 1861 until November 4, 1865, when he resigned upon his election to the U.S. Senate. However, Congress refused to seat him, and Manning subsequently resigned in December 1866. Except for a brief return to the state Senate in 1878, Manning retired from public service for the remainder of his life. He died in Camden on October 29, 1889, and was buried in Trinity Churchyard, Columbia. PAUL CHRISTOPHER ANDERSON

Bailey, N. Louise, Mary L. Morgan, and Carolyn R. Taylor, eds. *Biographical Directory of the South Carolina Senate, 1776–1985.* 3 vols. Columbia: University of South Carolina Press, 1986.

Chesnut-Miller-Manning Papers. Clemson University Library Special Collections, Clemson.

Manning, John Laurence. Papers. South Caroliniana Library, University of South Carolina, Columbia.

Manning, Richard Irvine (1789–1836). Governor, congressman. Manning was born on May 1, 1789, in the portion of the Camden judicial district that became Claremont County. He was the son of Laurence Manning, South Carolina's first adjutant general, and Susannah Richardson, daughter of Revolutionary War general Richard Richardson. In 1814 Manning married his cousin Elizabeth Peyre Richardson. The marriage produced nine children, including future governor John Laurence Manning and Richard Irvine Manning II, whose own son would serve as governor from 1915 to 1919.

Manning attended Mount Bethel Academy in Newberry District and graduated from South Carolina College in 1811. He served as a captain in defense of Charleston during the War of 1812. Following the war he became a planter in Clarendon District, owning fifty slaves by the time of his death.

In 1822 Manning entered politics by securing election to the state House of Representatives from Clarendon. He served until December 1824, when he resigned his seat following his election as governor. As governor, Manning accompanied the marquis de Lafayette on his March 1825 journey from Columbia to Charleston during his tour of the United States. Although a nationalist, Governor Manning saw the General Assembly begin to take stands against the Bank of the United States and internal improvements. As a result of the Tariff of 1824, legislators formally adopted a nullification stance, despite Manning's opposition.

In 1826 Manning made an unsuccessful bid for a seat in Congress as a Union Party candidate. In 1830 he was defeated by James Hamilton, Jr., in the contest for governor. Manning returned to the General Assembly, however, representing Clarendon District in the state Senate from 1830 to 1833. A staunch opponent of nullification, he voted against the Ordinance of Nullification as one of the few Unionist delegates to the 1832 Nullification Convention. He also served as a vice president at the 1832 Union Convention, which protested against nullification.

In 1834 Manning won a special election to fill a seat in the U.S. House of Representatives left vacant by the death of James Blair. Manning took his seat in December 1834 and secured reelection to Congress the following year. Early in 1836 he spoke in favor of the gag resolution on slavery presented by his House colleague Henry L. Pinckney, which sought to diminish the volatile issue of antislavery petitions presented to Congress. Manning died suddenly while in Philadelphia on May 1, 1836. He was interred in the cemetery of Trinity Church in Columbia. ERIC W. PLAAG

Bailey, N. Louise, Mary L. Morgan, and Carolyn R. Taylor, eds. *Biographical Directory of the South Carolina Senate, 1776–1985.* 3 vols. Columbia: University of South Carolina Press, 1986.

Governor Richard I. Manning with a flag denoting that he had five sons in uniform during World War I. Courtesy, South Carolina State Museum

Manning, Richard Irvine, III (1859–1931). Governor. Manning was born at Holmesley Plantation in Sumter County on August 15, 1859, the son of Richard Irvine Manning II and Elizabeth Allen Sinkler. A member of one of South Carolina's wealthiest and most politically prominent families, Manning was educated at Kenmore Preparatory School in Amherst, Virginia, and the University of Virginia, where he studied law but left after his sophomore year. Returning to Sumter, Manning became a successful planter and businessman. On February 10, 1881, he married Leila Bernard Meredith. The couple eventually had thirteen children.

In 1892 Manning won election from Sumter County to the South Carolina House of Representatives, where he served from 1892 until 1896. He represented Sumter in the state Senate from 1899 to 1906. In 1906 Manning made an unsuccessful run for governor. Campaigning for the office again in 1914, Manning defeated John G. Richards, and he was reelected in 1916, triumphing over the controversial Cole Blease.

Manning's two terms as governor were among the most progressive in South Carolina history. Although descended from privilege, Manning maintained a philosophy that government must act to further the welfare of its citizens and that the privileged had an obligation to assist those less fortunate. Explaining his platform in 1916, Manning told legislators, "We are progressive Democrats and we must have the courage to do justly to each and every class of our citizens, even if it requires legislation hitherto untried by us." His success was due in part to his ability to work closely with state legislators. Following the example of President Woodrow Wilson, Manning addressed the General Assembly in person. He secured the legislature's cooperation by presenting convincing arguments based on the merits of his proposals.

Manning envisioned an expanded government role in confronting the problems facing South Carolina. He advocated greater state involvement in education and in enhancing the economic welfare of its citizens. Manning believed that state government should take over functions not effectively done by local governments and pushed to reform South Carolina's outmoded tax structure in order to provide revenue to pay for these services.

Improvements in the education system became a hallmark of Manning's administration. In 1915 Manning signed a local government option act for compulsory school attendance, the first act of its kind in South Carolina. The state funded teaching training courses, increased teachers' salaries by twenty percent, created a state bureau of teacher certification, and doubled its financial support for education. Manning also secured additional funding to improve the quality of teacher training at the state-supported black college at Orangeburg.

Under Manning's leadership, the state passed a child labor law raising the minimum age for employment from twelve to fourteen. Manning reorganized and modernized the state hospital for the mentally ill, and in order to attract a nationally recognized expert to head the hospital, he supplemented the administrator's salary from his private funds. Other notable accomplishments during his two terms as governor included the establishment of a school for mentally handicapped children, the opening of a state tuberculosis hospital, the creation of an industrial school for delinquent white females, the separation of the State Reformatory for Negro Boys from penitentiary control, the creation of the state highway commission, the reinstatement and reorganization of the South Carolina National Guard, and the introduction of the secret ballot for all elections.

To finance the increased role of the state, Manning created the State Tax Commission. This agency became the major financial and supervisory body of the state's revenue. It started the move to equalize property valuations and made the income tax one of the major sources of revenue for South Carolina by effectively enforcing its income tax laws.

After leaving office, Manning returned to Sumter and devoted himself to his business interests and public service. He was appointed a director of the New York Life Insurance Company and was named president of the Bank of Mayesville in 1921. Manning served as president of the South Carolina Cotton Growers Association and in 1930 was appointed a trustee for the Carnegie Foundation for International Peace. Manning suffered a stroke in May 1931 and died of pneumonia on September 11, 1931, in Columbia. A devout Episcopalian, he was buried at Trinity Churchyard in Columbia. WILLIAM V. MOORE

Burts, Robert Milton. *Richard Irvine Manning and the Progressive Movement in South Carolina.* Columbia: University of South Carolina Press, 1974.

Manning, Richard Irvine. Papers. South Caroliniana Library, University of South Carolina, Columbia.

Manufactured housing. Known also as mobile homes or house trailers, manufactured housing units are built in a factory, transported to sites, and installed. In 2000 one in every six single-family housing starts nationally were manufactured homes, compared to just two percent in 1950. Eight percent of the U.S. population resided in this unsubsidized form of affordable housing, which had roughly half the construction cost of site-built housing. Almost two-thirds of new units were located on private property, with the remainder in land-lease communities. Sixty-five percent of the 273,000 new manufactured housing units in 2000 were located in the South, with 12,300 located in South Carolina.

With almost one of every five households residing in manufactured homes, South Carolina led the nation with the largest percentage of its citizens living in manufactured housing. The 2000 census found 355,499 South Carolinians living in manufactured housing, an increase of about seventeen percent since 1990. Seventy percent were owner occupied, compared to eighty-three percent of single-family housing. Sixty-two percent of households were married, with seventy percent having two to four occupants. Approximately fifteen percent graduated from college, and twenty-six percent had some college education. Roughly nine of ten households used their homes as their primary residences, with seven percent used as second homes.

The primary attraction of manufactured housing was cost. Construction savings were achieved due to mass-production techniques, large-quantity purchase of materials, and the hiring of nonunionized labor. Manufactured housing has been criticized for negatively affecting neighborhood property values and for not appreciating in value. As a result of a 1976 federal Housing and Urban Development code, however, overall quality of manufactured housing has steadily increased, and several national studies have documented that manufactured homes appreciate in value, although not as much as site-built homes. Many manufactured-housing communities followed design regulations similar to conventional subdivisions; some manufacturers had housing prototypes that included steeper roof pitches and two levels. About seventy percent of new units were multisectional and might include such amenities as vaulted ceilings, attached garages, fireplaces, whirlpool tubs, or Sheetrock walls. In South Carolina, manufactured housing was taxed as real property, with assessors using an array of valuation criteria for assessment purposes.

In the early twenty-first century the future of manufactured housing nationally and in South Carolina was bright. Whereas loans for these types of housing were historically difficult to obtain because they were treated more like vehicle loans, federally insured and conventional long-term mortgage programs similar to those for single-family, site-built housing became available. Counties and municipalities were developing standards that encouraged quality manufactured housing and subdivisions, including regulations for minimum unit size, exterior materials, roof pitch, and other zoning and land-development standards. J. TERRENCE FARRIS

"Manufactured Housing Now." *Urban Land* (January 1996): 4–48.

Sanders, Welford. *Manufactured Housing: Regulation, Design Innovations, and Development Options.* Chicago: American Planning Association, 1998.

Van Vliet, Willem, ed. *The Encyclopedia of Housing.* Thousand Oaks, Calif.: Sage, 1998.

Marine Anti-Britannic Society. The Marine Anti-Britannic Society was founded in 1783 at Charleston. The society was created to oppose the easing of restrictions on British merchants and the liberties granted by the General Assembly to returning Loyalists. Prominent members included Alexander Gillon, Dr. John Budd, James Fallon, William Logan, John Ash, John E. Poyas, Jr., and John and Peter Horlbeck.

Led by Gillon, the society fueled anti-British sentiment and unrest during the summer of 1783 and was closely associated with civil disturbances that wracked Charleston in 1783 and 1784. The society was influential in uniting native merchants, mechanics, and artisans in opposition to the oligarchy that controlled the city. In an effort to quell the unrest, the General Assembly incorporated the city of Charleston in August 1783. The act shifted the society's ire from Tories to the assembly and the new city incorporation. Society members felt that they were "menaced by aristocrats who would return essentially to the old order and rob them of the fruit of their labors and suffering in the 'grand old cause.'"

The Marine Anti-Britannic Society faded from prominence after Gillon lost a bitterly contested election for intendant (mayor) of Charleston in 1784. The society's agitation had a lasting effect, however, in that the prewar oligarchy was no longer able to dominate the politics of Charleston as it once had. The organization changed its name to the South Carolina Marine Society and was incorporated by the General Assembly in 1809 to aid impoverished seaman and their families. J. BRYAN COLLARS

Nadelhaft, Jerome J. *The Disorders of War: The Revolution in South Carolina.* Orono: University of Maine Press, 1981.

Walsh, Richard. *Charleston's Sons of Liberty: A Study of the Artisans, 1763–1789.* Columbia: University of South Carolina Press, 1959.

Marine Hospital (Charleston). An act in 1749 to provide a "public hospital for all sick sailors and other transient persons" began the organized care that led to the joint effort by the city of Charleston and the federal government to build the Marine Hospital. In 1830 Congress finally appropriated funds to hire the architect Robert

Mills to design a hospital building. After various changes in the proposed location and construction, building began on the Marine Hospital about 1831 and was completed in 1833. The city began its operation in 1834, using federal funds for maintenance. Charleston's earliest Gothic-revival-style building, the hospital on Franklin Street faced west, with double piazzas for the use of the patients. There were eight wards: three on the first floor for surgical cases and five on the second floor, one for venereal cases and four for medical cases.

At the outbreak of the Civil War the hospital was placed under the direction of the surgeon Alexander N. Talley, medical director of the Confederate forces in South Carolina, but sick seamen still retained the privilege of admission. After a short time the direction of the hospital returned to the municipal authorities, who operated it until the end of the war. Damage from the Union bombardment was so extensive that federal authorities decided the building should be abandoned as a hospital.

From 1866 to 1870 a free school for black children was conducted in the building by the Episcopal Church, staffed by fifteen white Charleston women. In 1895 the Marine Hospital building was occupied by the Jenkins Orphanage, founded for black children in 1891 by the Reverend Daniel J. Jenkins, a black Baptist minister. In 1939 the Housing Authority of Charleston remodeled it as its administrative offices. The two rear wings, weakened by fires, were demolished during the renovation. JANE MCCUTCHEN BROWN

Waring, Joseph I. *A History of Medicine in South Carolina.* 3 vols. Columbia: South Carolina Medical Association, 1964–1971.

———. "The Marine Hospitals of Charleston." *Bulletin of the History of Medicine* 10 (December 1941): 651–65.

Marion (Marion County; 2000 pop. 7,042). Travelers from Charlotte, North Carolina, call Marion "that pretty little town we go through on the way to the beach." One reason for its attractiveness is the tree-shaded public square in the center of town. In 1798 Thomas Godbold, son of the pioneer settler John Godbold, exchanged four acres of land "for the public good" for a dollar and then sold lots surrounding the square. Initially the square was not a beauty spot but the "hitching post" where farmers tied their teams and peddlers hawked their wares. In the 1880s Mrs. C. A. Woods organized the Civic Improvement League, which converted the area into a park.

Originally named Gilesborough in honor of local war hero Colonel Hugh Giles, by 1826 the town was being called Marion after General Francis Marion and the surrounding district. The name became official in 1847 when the town was incorporated. In the 1820s Robert Mills described Marion as containing "about 30 houses, and one hundred inhabitants; a handsome new courthouse, built of brick, a jail, and academy." The town developed in an orderly fashion. Larger homes and churches were built, the Masonic Lodge was erected in 1823, a weekly newspaper was established in 1846, and the Wilmington and Manchester Railroad arrived in 1854. The Great Pee Dee River prevented Sherman's army from visiting Marion in March 1865. Spared the destruction suffered by other towns during the Civil War, Marion was described by a correspondent of the *Nation* in 1865 as "a very pretty little village full of trees and gardens and light, elegant houses."

Marion prospered in the decades following the war and Reconstruction. From 1870 to 1910 the population grew from 2,490 to 6,354. Agriculture remained important to the Marion economy, but the town also turned to industry. By the mid-1930s a lumber mill, a veneer and brick plant, an oil mill, and ironworks operated on the outskirts of town. Many buildings from this era survived into the twenty-first century, situated along streets lined with ancient oaks draped in Spanish moss. The Marion Academy (1886) became the Marion County Museum in 1981. Since 1983 the restored Town Hall and Opera House (1892) has been shared with the Chamber of Commerce. The Carnegie library building (1906) provided a permanent home for a public library organized in 1898, the first tax-supported library in the state. The Marion Historic District was listed in the National Register of Historic Places in 1973. The district was enlarged in 1978 to include more than eighty properties of architectural significance.

An agricultural economy became increasingly diversified after World War II, with local factories producing textiles, clothing, machinery, and luxury yachts. Marion accepted social change as well, although more slowly at times than many other cities did. Town leaders, including African American officials and law enforcement personnel, and a biracial population worked together to encourage commercial development, improve educational facilities, and establish progressive leadership. They also provided numerous municipal services, including city beautification and recreational opportunities, to ensure that Marionites were able to maintain a pleasing, small-town lifestyle as their legacy. THELMA CHILES CLARK

Sellers, W. W. *A History of Marion County, South Carolina.* Columbia, S.C.: R. L. Bryan, 1902.

Marion, Francis (ca. 1732–1795). Soldier. Marion, of Huguenot descent, was born in St. John's Berkeley Parish, the youngest of six children born to Gabriel Marion and Esther Cordes. A planter, Marion in 1773 built his home, Pond Bluff, about four miles south of Eutaw Springs, a site now beneath the waters of Lake Marion. He commenced his military career in the parish militia in 1756 and joined the campaigns against the Cherokees (1759–1761), rising to the rank of first lieutenant. Having served in local offices, he was elected in 1775 to the First Provincial Congress. Commissioned a captain in the state's Second Regiment in June, he participated in the capture of Fort Johnson in September. As a major, Marion distinguished himself at the Battle of Sullivan's Island (June 1776), after which he was commissioned a lieutenant colonel in the Continental army. Marion commanded the Second Regiment at the disastrous Franco-American attack on Savannah in autumn 1779. Away on sick leave due to an accident, he eluded capture when Charleston fell to the British in May 1780. Escaping to North Carolina, he and a small party linked up with Horatio Gates's army preparing for an invasion of South Carolina. Detailed to destroy enemy communication lines, Marion was not present for Gates's defeat at Camden in August.

With a militia commission as brigadier general, Marion organized a partisan force in the Pee Dee region. Between August and December 1780, in an otherwise dismal period for America, Marion gained national recognition for his actions at Great Savannah (August 20), Blue Savannah (September 4), Black Mingo (September 29), Tearcoat Swamp (October 26), Georgetown (November 15), and Halfway Swamp (December 12–13). While some counts place the number of "Marion's Men" at more than two thousand, his band generally consisted of considerably fewer than that and included Continentals. Marion's nickname, the "Swamp Fox," reportedly came from the infamous British officer Banastre Tarleton, who, unable to snare Marion, called him a "damned old fox" and swore that "the devil himself could not catch him."

Marion's small-scale hit-and-run tactics disrupted supply lines, intercepted communications, and hampered the enemy considerably. In December 1780 he established a camp on Snow's Island between the Pee Dee and Lynches Rivers and Clark's Creek. Conditions improved by the spring of 1781, when Marion became a vital part of General Nathanael Greene's combined operations in South Carolina. In 1781 Marion's troops participated in the battles at Fort Watson (April 23), Fort Motte (May 12), Quinby Bridge (July 17), Parker's Ferry (August 13), and Eutaw Springs (September 8). His numerous command problems included Greene's distrust of the militia, his need for Marion's essential horses, an ongoing conflict over rank and command with General Thomas Sumter, and a feud between his subordinates Peter Horry and Hezekiah Maham. This latter feud came to a head while Marion was serving as a senator in the General Assembly at Jacksonborough and resulted in a defeat at the hands of the British at Wambaw Bridge in February 1782. Returning to command, Marion's brigade saw its last engagement at Wadboo Creek in the summer of 1782. Throughout the war, which in South Carolina was a brutally vicious civil conflict, Marion was said to be "humain and Mercifull" but was also known as a severe disciplinarian. Although small in stature, with knees and ankles "badly formed," Marion inspired great loyalty in his ill-clothed, ill-fed, and ill-equipped band.

After the war a penniless Marion, whose plantation had been ruined, was awarded a gold medal, a full Continental colonelcy, and command of Fort Johnson in Charleston harbor. He served in the S.C. Senate in 1783–1786, 1791, and 1792–1794 and was elected to the 1790 state constitutional convention. He continued as a brigadier general in the militia until his retirement in 1794. His finances improved when he married his cousin Mary Esther Videau on April 20, 1786. The union produced no children, but in less than a decade Marion's fortune grew dramatically. Near the end of his life he owned upward of eighteen hundred acres and seventy-three slaves. He died at Pond Bluff on February 27, 1795, and was buried in the family plot at Belle Isle in St. Stephen's Parish. His tomb escaped flooding by the Santee-Cooper project and serves today as a humble monument to the Swamp Fox. His comrade Peter Horry attempted to write a history of Marion's brigade, but it was hopelessly mangled by Mason Locke "Parson" Weems, the first of many to take enormous liberties with Marion's legend. See plate 12. ROY TALBERT, JR.

Bass, Robert. *Swamp Fox: The Life and Campaigns of General Francis Marion.* New York: Holt, 1959.

Rankin, Hugh F. *Francis Marion: The Swamp Fox.* New York: Crowell, 1973.

Simms, William Gilmore. *The Life of Francis Marion.* 1844. Reprint, Freeport, N.Y.: Books for Libraries, 1971.

Marion, Martin Whiteford (b. 1917). Baseball player. Marion was born in Richburg (Chester County) on December 1, 1917, and grew up in the Atlanta, Georgia, area. He is the son of John and Virginia Marion and a collateral descendant of Francis Marion, the "Swamp Fox" of the Revolutionary War. He married Mary Dallas in 1937 and has four daughters. He spent one year at the Georgia Institute of Technology in 1935 and then played briefly for Chattanooga in the Southern League. He then signed a four-year contract with the St. Louis Cardinals that paid $5,000 in its final year; both the size and the length of the contract were unheard of for a minor-league player at the time. He played with Huntington, West Virginia, in 1936 and then for Rochester, New York, in the International League from 1937 to 1939.

Marion made his debut with the Cardinals on April 16, 1940, and was their regular shortstop from 1940 to 1950. He was known as "the Octopus" due to his extremely long arms, and he also went by the nickname "Slats" because he was six feet two inches tall and weighed 170 pounds. He was a seven-time All Star and was voted Most Valuable Player and Player of the Year in 1944. He won four pennants and three World Championships in his ten years with the St. Louis Cardinals. Marion played in 1,572 games, collected 1,448 hits, and was a lifetime .263 hitter with 36 home runs and 624 RBI. Although he did not hit for power or for a high average, he developed a reputation as a clutch hitter. He was also considered the best fielding shortstop of his generation.

A back injury kept Marion from playing in the 1951 season, but he served as manager of the Cardinals that year. He then moved over to the St. Louis Browns and served as their player-manager in 1952 and 1953. Named manager of the Chicago White Sox in the final weeks of the 1954 season, Marion piloted them until the end of the 1956 season. He had a 356–372 record as a manager with three third-place finishes in five full seasons. He purchased the St. Louis Cardinals AAA franchise in Houston in the Texas League in 1960 and ran it for several years. Marion also managed the St. Louis Stadium Club business for many years. DOUG SOUTHARD

Moffi, Larry. *This Side of Cooperstown: An Oral History of Major League Baseball in the 1950s.* Iowa City: University of Iowa Press, 1996.

Marion County (489 sq. miles; 2000 pop. 35,466). Marion County was named to honor General Francis Marion, the Revolutionary War hero whose camp was hidden deep in its swamps. Designated Queensboro Township in 1733, the area became part of Prince Frederick's Parish the following year. In 1785 the northwestern part of the Georgetown Judicial District became Liberty County, which was renamed and reorganized as Marion District in 1800. Much of the southwestern portion of Marion County was ceded to Florence County in 1888, while the northern half of Marion's territory went to the newly formed Dillon County in 1910.

Located in northeastern South Carolina, Marion County is shaped like a knobby sweet potato, with its skinny southern end approximately fifteen miles from the Atlantic Ocean. Horry County lies to the east, Williamsburg and Georgetown Counties to the west. Two rivers, the Great Pee Dee and the Little Pee Dee, flow the length of the county. They merge at its southernmost tip, cross part of Georgetown County, and empty into Winyah Bay. The land is generally level to gently undulant, and the soil is predominantly sandy loam, well suited to agriculture. Food crops, indigo, livestock raising (primarily hogs), timber, and turpentine were the most important products until the introduction of the cotton gin in the 1790s. The availability of slave labor, a more efficient means of removing seed, and a ready market established cotton as the chief money crop for almost a century.

European settlers began moving up the Pee Dee after receiving land grants in 1735 and 1736. This first settlement was named Britton's Neck for Joseph Britton, one of the pioneers. In 1798 the state legislature appointed a commission to choose a site and supervise construction of a courthouse and a jail. A small wooden court building constructed in 1800 soon proved inadequate. The second courthouse, a brick one probably designed by Robert Mills, was built in 1823. That structure was torn down in 1853. The present courthouse was built from a design by Peter H. Hammarskold.

The town of Marion developed around the courthouse. After 1854, when the Wilmington and Manchester Railroad reached the

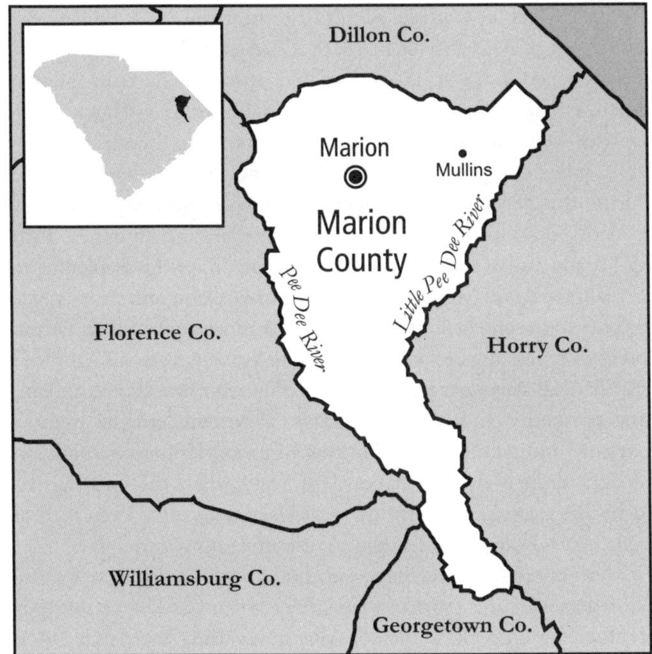

county, new villages appeared. A few miles east of the county seat, the Mullins Railway Station, named for Colonel William Sydney Mullins, became the nucleus for the town of Mullins. Nichols began when Harmon Floyd's land around the depot was sold off as town lots. The town, at first called Floydsville, was later renamed to honor Avoritte Nichols, a prominent resident. Even the tiny hamlet of Pee Dee boasted a hotel near its depot.

The Civil War halted all progress except that related to the war effort. At the Confederate Navy Yard near Pee Dee a wooden gunboat was built and named the CSS *Peedee.* However, this vessel never experienced combat. Federal troops controlled the area upon its completion, and the boat was burned in March 1865 to prevent its falling into enemy hands. Marion County suffered no physical damage from the war. The Great Pee Dee River was at flood stage, and Sherman's troops were unable to cross into the county. It did, however, suffer during Reconstruction. More than thirty years elapsed before it returned to its prewar economic status. The 1880 census reveals that the value of farm property in South Carolina was only half the 1860 assessment. The chaos of the early postwar period gradually evolved into a workable arrangement between the landowners and the free blacks as they first tried wages for farmwork and later sharecropping. By the 1890s many farmers were renting small parcels to black farmers for cash or cotton.

Cotton prices began to decline in the mid-1870s, and the trend continued through the 1890s, intensifying the poverty of county farmers. In the meantime cotton profits from earlier years financed mercantile endeavors and many fine homes showing Victorian influence. The introduction of bright leaf tobacco as a money crop in the last decade of the century brought growers a ray of hope. As tobacco production increased, warehouses were built. Mullins eventually became the largest market in the state. Planters' Warehouse opened in 1895, followed by the Old Brick and Dixon warehouses.

Overproduction of tobacco soon led to unacceptably low prices, a problem that was solved by federal intervention, which limited acreage and established price controls. The mid-1940s found the prosperous larger farms increasing in size as mechanical equipment became available. Many small operators sold their holdings and sought nonfarm employment.

Two early industries in the county were forestry-oriented: Camp Manufacturing Company and the American Box Company. Marion Cotton Oil Company depended on cotton for its ginning and seed-crushing operations. A small cotton mill in Marion presaged the development of the textile industry.

Following World War II the agricultural economy gave way to one that was also industrial and service-oriented, though this change came later than in many other regions of the state. Textile plants led the way, including Heritage Sportswear, Ray-Tex, Hanes L'Eggs, and Blumenthal Mills in Marion and Anvil Mills in Mullins. Other manufacturers arrived as well: American Voting Machines (later ArvinMeritor), Marvel Lighting, and So-Pak-Co (producers of ready-to-eat meals for the U.S. Army) in Mullins; and Rockwell International (wooden shuttles for cotton mills), Russell Stover Candy, and Beneteau USA (sailboats) in Marion. Workers also found employment at Blue Brick in Pee Dee and Pilliod of Carolina (furniture) in Nichols.

Two South Carolina governors were born in Marion County. William H. Ellerbe of Sellers served as governor from 1897 until his death in June 1899, while Mullins native Ransome J. Williams occupied the office from 1945 until 1947. Each section of the county has its own interesting history. Other communities that add their dimensions to the Marion picture are Zion, Gapway, Rains, Centenary, and Gresham.

By the early twentieth-first century a biracial council of seven elected members governed the county. The public schools were integrated, and the old school buildings had been improved or replaced. A technical education facility taught skills to students and prospective employees. A modern medical center served the entire county. The county library system replaced three town libraries. An Arts Council formed in 1996 provided art exhibits and musical and theatrical events with local and outside participation. The County Development Board actively sought new businesses and industry to provide better employment opportunities. Marion County, rich in history and endowed with abundant natural resources, celebrated its bicentennial in 1998 and looked toward future years with courage and confidence. THELMA CHILES CLARK

Prince, Eldred E., and Robert R. Simpson. *Long Green: The Rise and Fall of Tobacco in South Carolina.* Athens: University of Georgia Press, 2000.

Sellers, W. W. *A History of Marion County, South Carolina.* Columbia, S.C.: R. L. Bryan, 1902.

Market Hall (Charleston). Completed in 1841, Market Hall was one of several monumental buildings that arose along Meeting Street in Charleston during the 1830s and early 1840s. Located at 188 Meeting Street, Market Hall occupies a narrow lot between North and South Market Streets that had been used as the public market since the late eighteenth century. It was designed in the form of a Roman temple by Edward Brickell White, the most successful Charleston architect of the late antebellum period. The two-story building is set on a rusticated base and is built of brick covered with a brownstone stucco. The second story is scored in an ashlar pattern. A double flight of brownstone steps leads to a pedimented portico supported by four Doric columns. The elaborate entablature includes bucrania, ram skulls, and triglyphs. The moldings of the column capitals and bases extend along the side and rear elevations. Behind the building, sheds stretch toward the river, which provided space for merchants selling meats, produce, seafood, and other goods in earlier years. The United Daughters of the Confederacy have met in the building since 1899 and in the early twenty-first century used it for their Confederate Museum. Market Hall sustained damage during Hurricane Hugo in 1989 and underwent a $3.5 million restoration that was completed in 2002. The building was designated a National Historic Landmark by the U.S. Department of the Interior in 1973. DANIEL J. VIVIAN

Lane, Mills. *Architecture of the Old South: South Carolina.* Savannah, Ga.: Beehive, 1984.

Poston, Jonathan H. *The Buildings of Charleston: A Guide to the City's Architecture.* Columbia: University of South Carolina Press, 1997.

Severens, Kenneth. *Charleston Antebellum Architecture and Civic Destiny.* Knoxville: University of Tennessee Press, 1988.

Marlboro County (480 sq. miles; 2000 pop. 28,818). Marlboro County was formed on March 12, 1785, and named for John Churchill, first duke of Marlborough. Retaining the same general dimensions throughout its existence, Marlboro County is bounded by the Great Pee Dee River on the west, North Carolina on the north and northeast, and Dillon County on the southeast. The Cheraw Indians occupied the region before European settlers arrived. During the 1730s the British government encouraged settlement along the Pee Dee by enticing Welsh families from Pennsylvania with land grants, tools, and seeds. The area became known as the Welsh Neck. Here, the first Baptist church in the backcountry, Welsh Neck Baptist Church, was established in 1738. English, Scots-Irish, and French settlers arrived soon thereafter. By 1777 the St. David's Society added an academy to the Welsh Neck community.

During the Revolutionary War inhabitants divided among patriots and Tories. Several wartime events took place. At Pegues Place plantation near the North Carolina border, a cartel for a prisoner exchange was signed on May 3, 1781. Near the modern town of Wallace, General Nathanael Greene established his "Camp of Repose," where he assumed command of the Continental army in the South in December 1780. Colonel Abel Kolb's tomb commemorating his murder by Tories is situated in Marlboro, as is the site of the Battle of Hunt's Bluff, where patriots captured a barge filled with ill British troops en route to Georgetown. Another skirmish occurred near Cashua Baptist Church in April 1781.

Marlboro County's first courthouse stood at Gardner's Bluff on the Pee Dee but later moved slightly inland to the northern bank of Crooked Creek at Carlisle. A third site near the creek became the county seat of Bennettsville in 1819. A Robert Mills–designed courthouse opened in 1824. It was replaced in 1852 by a twin-towered structure that survived occupation by Union troops in March 1865. Baptists from the Welsh Neck Church came to Bennettsville in 1832, followed by Methodists in 1834 and Presbyterians in 1855. During this period male and female academies were organized and opened. Additional communities developed around churches, principal roads, and at the county's popular mineral springs at Blenheim.

Planters found Marlboro's loamy soils excellent, and many made fortunes in the antebellum era. In the early nineteenth century cotton and corn replaced grain and indigo as the primary agricultural products. African slaves were responsible for much of Marlboro's agricultural prosperity, and their descendants contributed to the county's economy and culture throughout its history. Marlboro's reputation for agriculture went international in 1889 when the local farmer Zachariah J. Drake set a world's record by producing 255 bushels of shelled corn from a single acre of Marlboro County farmland.

Marlboro sent more than one thousand men to fight for the Confederacy, and a third of them never returned. The county was occupied by General William T. Sherman's army in March 1865, after it crossed the Pee Dee en route to North Carolina. Plantations throughout the county were ravaged by the invading army, as was the town of Bennettsville, where Union general Francis P. Blair made his headquarters at the Jennings-Brown House. Although several town buildings were burned, Marlboro's courthouse was spared, giving Marlboro complete records since 1785.

Like the rest of South Carolina, Marlboro County struggled through the Reconstruction era, although the productivity of county farmlands helped ease the transition from slave labor to sharecropping. Prosperity returned in the 1880s when D. D. McColl brought the first railroad to Marlboro and opened its first bank, the Bank of Marlboro, in 1884. He soon thereafter brought cotton mills to the towns of McColl and Bennettsville. Despite the changes, cotton remained king in Marlboro, and railroads transported harvests to markets and mills far beyond county borders. Urban areas prospered as well, with impressive homes and brick stores and offices appearing in new railroad towns such as Blenheim (incorporated in 1883), McColl (incorporated in 1890), and Dunbar (incorporated in 1894). In Bennettsville a new courthouse opened in 1885, with extensive additions made in the 1950s by the local architect Henry D. Harrall.

The twentieth century brought additions to the landscape and the economy. William White Palmer of Bennettsville, a World War I aerial ace, provided the name for a U.S. Army Air Corps flight-training facility that opened near his hometown just prior to World War II, Palmer Field. Here, cadets arrived from across the nation to train, and some of them married local girls and settled in Marlboro after the war. The base later housed hundreds of German prisoners of war, who assisted local farmers in tending and harvesting crops. Years later Palmer Field became home to Powell Manufacturing Company, a producer of agricultural machinery, tobacco harvesting, and bulk-curing equipment.

Beginning in the late 1940s Marlboro County pursued industrial development to provide jobs for farm laborers idled by increased mechanization of farms. An impressive group of nationally and internationally known firms established plants throughout the county, including Rockwell Automation, Mohasco, Delta Woodside, OxBodies, SoPakCo, Musashi Seimitsu, Reliance Trading, Bennettsville Printing and Folia, Marley, Palmetto Brick, and four

Willamette Industries installations. State government added to county payrolls in 1989 when it opened a medium-to-maximum-security prison, Evans Correctional Institution (named for a Marlboro native, U.S. Senator Josiah Evans). During the 1950s Crooked Creek near Bennettsville was dammed, creating Lake Wallace, a 846-acre recreational lake and wildlife preserve that also served as Bennettsville's water reservoir. Handsome residential subdivisions developed along its shores.

As Marlboro entered the twenty-first century, the county worked to continue its economic expansion while maintaining its heritage. County officials sought to increase Marlboro's ties to the outside world by supporting efforts to widen S.C. Highway 38 and develop a proposed interstate highway from Detroit to the Grand Strand. The South Carolina Cotton Trail, the county's historic buildings, and its historic records attract numerous visitors and genealogists. Improvements to the county-owned Great Pee Dee River Railroad and Avent Airport pointed to Marlboro's pursuit of a promising future, while the county treasures its rich past. WILLIAM LIGHT KINNEY, JR.

Hudson, Joshua Hilary. *Sketches and Reminiscences.* Columbia, S.C.: State Company, 1903.

Kinney, William Light, Jr. *Sherman's March: A Review.* Bennettsville, S.C.: Marlboro Herald-Advocate, 1961.

Marlboro County, South Carolina: A Pictorial History. Bennettsville, S.C.: Marlborough Historical Society, 1996.

McColl, D. D. *Sketches of Old Marlboro.* Columbia, S.C.: State Company, 1916.

Rudisill, Horace Fraser. *Minutes of Saint David's Society, 1777–1835.* Florence, S.C.: The Society, 1986.

Thomas, J. A. W. *A History of Marlboro County, with Traditions and Sketches of Numerous Families.* 1897. Reprint, Baltimore: Regional Publishing, 1971.

Maroons. The history of maroons, or "bands of fugitive slaves living independently from society," in the West Indies and Latin America has been well documented. Maroon activities and slave uprisings were the most militant form of black resistance to slavery, although historians have paid little attention to the history of maroons in the United States. The historian Herbert Aptheker found evidence that at least fifty such communities existed in the country between 1672 and 1864, especially among the sparsely settled mountain, forest, or swampy regions of South Carolina, North Carolina, Virginia, Louisiana, Florida, Georgia, Mississippi, and Alabama. In South Carolina maroon communities were located in areas near rivers, such as the Savannah and the Congaree, and also in lowcountry parishes such as St. John's, St. James Goose Creek, St. George's Dorchester, and Christ Church. Maroons settled in the unpopulated backcountry in the eighteenth century after being forced to migrate from Virginia and North Carolina due to European settlement. By the late 1750s and early 1760s the backcountry was populated by newly arrived European planters and native-born maroons of African, Native American, and European descent who created their own distinctive culture.

The typical South Carolina maroon was a young man who had run away alone. Between 1732 and 1752, however, thirty percent ran away in groups rather than individually. The composition of the maroon groups was both African and Creole in nature, although Creole maroons tended to run away more on their own. Twenty-five percent of runaway groups that were advertised in colonial South Carolina newspapers were comprised of Africans who shared some commonalities, such as regional origins or ethnicity. African runaways in South Carolina generally absconded in groups of two or three, although bands of six to eight were also common. Most maroons were men, but women and children were also present in settlements, often escaping with familial groups.

A fluid relationship existed between maroon communities and Native Americans. In colonial South Carolina black men and Native American women at times ran away together. Frontier Native Americans sometimes provided shelter for runaways. There is evidence that maroons who fled to Spanish Florida banded with Native Americans there in a fight for freedom. On the other hand, some free Native Americans captured runaways for rewards. As early as 1733 South Carolina paid £20 for a live maroon and £10 for the scalp of a dead maroon. Evidence suggests that Catawba and Notchee Indians worked with militia in annihilating some maroon settlements.

Maroon activities varied by community, but many found it difficult to erect homes, care for families, and work the land without supplies. Maroons often traveled to more populated areas such as Charleston for food, clothing, and other goods. Some bartered with free blacks or plantation slaves, while others stole from their former masters or other whites. More violent occurrences, such as bands of maroons attacking and robbing white travelers or plundering houses and plantations, often provoked bloody reprisals. In June 1711, for example, South Carolina inhabitants were in such "great fear and terror" that the government was compelled to raid a maroon settlement. This cycle was repeated over and over, with maroon threats and planter retaliation occurring at times throughout the colonial period and even during the Revolutionary War.

After the war, many maroons who had fought alongside the British in hopes of gaining their freedom were attacked and defeated by state militia. In October 1786 a party of white militiamen clashed with a large maroon community living on an island in the Savannah River, many of whom had served with the British during the war and who called themselves "the King of England's Soldiers." The attack resulted in the death and injury of many maroons and the abandonment of the settlement. If caught, maroon leaders were frequently beheaded, and those who escaped fled even further into the interior. Maroons continued to exist, however, and to fight for their freedom. Incidents such as those in Ashepoo in 1816, Williamsburg County in 1819, Georgetown in 1820, and Jacksonborough in 1822 all produced the same results. Maroons and militiaman fought, with the latter winning each time. Even so, maroons continued to exist. These activities continued even during the Civil War, when a maroon community attacked near Marion in June 1861 demonstrated the existence of maroons up until emancipation. CATHERINE FITZGERALD

Aptheker, Herbert. "Additional Data on American Maroons." *Journal of Negro History* 32 (October 1947): 452–60.

———. "Maroons within the Present Limits of the United States." *Journal of Negro History* 24 (April 1939): 167–84.

Berlin, Ira. *Many Thousands Gone: The First Two Centuries of Slavery in North America.* Cambridge: Belknap Press of Harvard University Press, 1998.

Franklin, John Hope, and Loren Schweninger. *Runaway Slaves: Rebels on the Plantation.* New York: Oxford University Press, 1999.

Johnson, Michael P. "Runaway Slaves and the Slave Communities in South Carolina, 1799 to 1830." *William and Mary Quarterly,* 3d ser., 38 (July 1981): 418–41.

Morgan, Philip D. *Slave Counterpoint: Black Culture in the Eighteenth-Century Chesapeake and Lowcountry.* Chapel Hill: University of North Carolina Press, 1998.

Olwell, Robert. *Masters, Slaves, and Subjects: The Culture of Power in the South Carolina Low Country, 1740–1790.* Ithaca, N.Y.: Cornell University Press, 1998.

Price, Richard, ed. *Maroon Societies: Rebel Slave Communities in the Americas.* 3d ed. Baltimore: Johns Hopkins University Press, 1996.

Marshall Tucker Band. Formed in 1971, the Marshall Tucker Band (MTB) laced its rock and roll with doses of country, blues, and jazz, selling millions of albums in the 1970s and 1980s and influencing acts such as Waylon Jennings, Hank Williams, Jr., Charlie Daniels, and Kid Rock. Named for a blind South Carolinian who tuned pianos, the group kept Spartanburg as a home base, a fact that allowed the upstate town to share the band's limelight. The original MTB included lead guitarist and chief songwriter Toy Caldwell, bass player Tommy Caldwell, lead singer Doug Gray, drummer Paul Riddle, rhythm guitarist George McCorkle, and flutist/saxophone player Jerry Eubanks. Signed to Capricorn Records, MTB released its self-titled debut album in 1973. That album contained a Toy Caldwell composition called "Can't You See," a song that would later be covered by Hank Williams, Jr., Waylon Jennings, and others. The band's most successful album was *Searchin' for a Rainbow* (1975), which included the McCorkle-penned "Fire on the Mountain," a song whose lyrics are displayed at Nashville's Country Music Hall of Fame. Other notable MTB songs include "Take the Highway," "Long Hard Ride," and the Top-Twenty single "Heard It in a Love Song." Each of the band's six albums with Capricorn sold at least 100,000 copies, with two selling more than one million. A late 1970s shift to Warner Brothers Records proved less fruitful.

Tommy Caldwell died in 1980 from injuries sustained in an automobile accident. Former Toy Factory bassist Franklin Wilkie then joined the band, which soon added keyboardist Ronnie Godfrey. Toy Caldwell, McCorkle, and Riddle left the group in 1984, with Caldwell going on to record a solo album in 1992. Caldwell passed away after a heart attack in 1993 at age forty-five. Gray and Eubanks carried on the MTB name, utilizing various supporting musicians, until Eubanks departed in 1996 and left Gray as MTB's only remaining original member. PETER COOPER

Brant, Marley. *Southern Rockers: The Roots and Legacy of Southern Rock.* New York: Billboard, 1999.

Cooper, Peter. *Hub City Music Makers: One Southern Town's Popular Music Legacy.* Spartanburg, S.C.: Holocene, 1997.

Smith, Michael B. *Carolina Dreams: The Musical Legacy of Upstate South Carolina.* Beverly Hills, Calif.: Marshall Tucker Entertainment, 1997.

Marshlands (Beaufort). Located on Federal Street in Beaufort's National Historic Landmark District, Marshlands was completed in 1814 by James Robert Verdier, a physician noted for his successful treatment of yellow fever. Listed individually as a National Historic Landmark in 1975, it is recognized for both its architectural and its historical distinctions. Before twentieth-century modification, the original structure exemplified a popular house type often designated as the Beaufort style.

A raised two-story central block is organized about a central hall that projects north to create a stair tower. Single-story wings enclosed by shed roofs formerly flanked the stair hall on the right and left. The two wings project east and west to create a T-shaped plan. A single-story porch raised on brick, arcaded arches wraps around the house on three sides. The principal facade, on the south, is topped by a pediment masking hipped roof construction enclosing the central block. Entrance is through this south porch. The interior is rich in Federal detailing, with Adamesque mantels, reeded woodwork, interior fanlights, and a graceful spiraling staircase illuminated by a Palladian window.

In an attempt to determine the origins of Beaufort's early domestic buildings, architectural historians have labeled Marshlands as Barbadian or West Indian. Others have described its T-shaped, raised plan and porches wrapping three sides as a pure expression of the Beaufort style. However, there is evidence of similar Federal period structures in rural North Carolina. Whatever the architectural roots of the score of similar buildings found throughout Beaufort's historic district, two factors contributed to the popularity of this style. First, the formula was adaptable, allowing for variation in size, material, style, and cost. Second, the T-shaped houses maximized cross-ventilation without sacrificing architectural distinction.

During the Civil War, Marshlands served as headquarters of the U.S. Sanitary Commission. In her 1939 novel *A Sea Island Lady*, Francis Griswold imagined the house as the home of its heroine. For most of the twentieth century and at the beginning of the twenty-first century, the house was in the family of William Brantley Harvey, Jr., lieutenant governor of South Carolina from 1975 to 1978. MAXINE LUTZ

Historic Resources of the Lowcountry: A Regional Survey of Beaufort County, S.C., Colleton County, S.C., Hampton County, S.C., Jasper County, S.C. 2d ed. Yemassee, S.C.: Lowcountry Council of Governments, 1990.

Schneider, David B., ed. *A Guide to Historic Beaufort.* 9th ed. Beaufort, S.C.: Historic Beaufort Foundation, 1999.

Martin, Dexter Charles (1897–1982). Aviation pioneer. Martin was born on January 2, 1897, in Santa Ana, California, to Jesse Martin and Belle Southwell. The exploits of Glenn Martin, who built gliders in Santa Ana, inspired Martin's interest in flying. He learned to fly from barnstormers in 1919 and received his first pilot license in 1924. According to Martin, he became an aviator "because I didn't have any better sense." Martin married Guynelle Eison on December 15, 1938, and the couple had four children.

In 1927 Martin joined Norman Langley barnstorming as a flying circus. With Langley he performed in North and South Carolina. Martin also delivered movie film to theaters and in 1928 joined Anderson Airways, flying for Mabel Cody's Air Circus. In 1929 that relationship ended when he flew his plane into a mountain, although he survived.

In 1931 Martin sold airplanes in North Carolina, but he returned to Greenville and worked for the passage of the 1935 act creating a South Carolina aeronautics commission. He became the first executive director of the State Aeronautics Commission and served in that capacity until 1950. Initially, Martin focused the commission's efforts on Works Progress Administration airport construction. During World War II the commission developed Lexington County Airport (later the Columbia Metropolitan Airport) to house the Doolittle Raiders' training program. Martin and the South Carolina Aeronautics Commission also cooperated with the U.S. Department of Defense to identify sites for military airports in South Carolina, which resulted in the development of McEntire, Myrtle Beach, and Shaw air bases, among others.

When the Civil Air Patrol was created in November 1941, Martin, given the rank of major, became the first wing commander for South Carolina. Following the Japanese attack on Pearl Harbor, Martin organized a coastal patrol to escort ships leaving South Carolina ports. Martin also led South Carolina to become a pioneer in civilian flight instruction. He developed a training program at Columbia's Owens Field in 1939 and established the Palmetto School of Aeronautics in Columbia to train airplane mechanics.

In his varied aviation career Martin flew across the country in 1927, served as governor-elect Olin D. Johnston's pilot in 1934, and was a member (1938–1972) and president (1940–1945) of the National Association of State Aviation Officers (NASAO). While a member of the NASAO, he chaired a national committee to develop legislative protocols for state and federal control of aviation. Martin left aviation in 1963, and the Aviation Pioneers Hall of Fame inducted him in 1976. Martin died on December 12, 1982, in Columbia. ALEXIA JONES HELSLEY

Maxey, Russell. *Airports of Columbia: A History in Photographs & Headlines.* Columbia, S.C.: Palmetto Publishing, 1987.

Martin, Maria (1796–1863). Artist, naturalist. Martin was born in Charleston on July 6, 1796, the youngest daughter of John Jacob Martin and Rebecca Solars. While no records of her formal schooling have been discovered, it is known that she was well read in literature, French, and German and possessed an interest in music, art, and natural science. By 1827 she and her mother had moved into the home of her brother-in-law, the Lutheran minister and naturalist John Bachman, and her ailing sister Harriet. Martin helped to raise and educate her sister's fourteen children and manage the household.

A devoted and pioneering American naturalist, Bachman encouraged Martin's early interest in natural science and botany. The focus of both of their lives changed when the artist and ornithologist John James Audubon arrived in Charleston in 1831 and began a lifelong friendship and association with them, forged by the later marriage of Audubon's sons to two of Bachman's daughters.

Martin had already rendered sophisticated botanical sketches. Recognizing her talent, Audubon introduced her to his painting techniques, materials, and methods of posing birds, which she absorbed enthusiastically. The following year he began asking her to prepare botanical backgrounds for his work *The Birds of America.* Drawing specimens from Bachman's extensive garden at her own home and from the gardens of such noted Charleston horticulturists as Philippe Noissette and Joel Poinsett, she contributed numerous native plant illustrations and related studies for plates in volumes 2 and 4, such as the rare franklinia for Bachman's warbler and the azaleas and butterflies accompanying Swainson's warbler. In intensive, collaborative work during the 1830s, Audubon commonly painted the birds, and Martin would finish the composition with detailed natural settings or simple habitats. At times he requested that she portray specific botanical elements, such as insects or branches, which were incorporated into the original bird paintings at the London printer by his son Victor.

In response to Audubon's and Bachman's need for fine botanical drawings, Martin made an intensive study of insects, copying both text and illustrations of Thomas Say's *American Entomology* (1824–1828). This copy and related sketches are in the Charleston Museum's collection, while several other examples of Martin's art are at the New-York Historical Society. Audubon acknowledged her work and talent several times in his *Ornithological Biography* (1830–1839) and named a bird species, *Picus martinae* (Maria's Woodpecker), in her honor. In the mid-1830s she produced several sketches for John Holbrook's *North American Herpetology* (1836–1842), although only the image of the black racer snake was attributed to her. Her collaborations with these influential naturalists have made her one of the most important American natural-history artists of the nineteenth century.

Martin often assisted Bachman in his published writings on natural science and religion, and during the production of Audubon's *Viviparous Quadrupeds of North America* (1845–1853), she worked as an editor of the text. Two years after her sister's death, she married Bachman on December 28, 1848. With occasional travel, they remained in their home surrounded by family until 1862, when they left Charleston and took refuge in Columbia. Martin died there on December 27, 1863, and was buried in the Ebenezer Church cemetery. ROBERTA KEFALOS SOKOLITZ

Arnold, Lois Barber. *Four Lives in Science: Women's Education in the Nineteenth Century.* New York: Schocken, 1984.

Bonta, Marcia Myers. *Women in the Field: America's Pioneering Women Naturalists.* College Station: Texas A&M University Press, 1991.

Coffin, Annie Roulhac. "Audubon's Friend—Maria Martin." *New-York Historical Society Quarterly* 49 (January 1965): 29–51.

———. "Maria Martin (1796–1863)." *Art Quarterly* 23 (autumn 1960): 281–300.

Shuler, Jay. *Had I the Wings: The Friendship of Bachman and Audubon.* Athens: University of Georgia Press, 1995.

Valesko, Angela D. "Maria Martin Bachman: Nineteenth Century American Artist-Naturalist." Master's thesis, Kent State University, 2000.

Marvin, Robert E. (1920–2001). Landscape architect. Marvin was born in Colleton County on February 10, 1920, the son of W. R. Marvin and Alta E. Marvin. The grandson of a rice planter, he was raised on the 15,000-acre Bonnie Doone Plantation, where his father was overseer. As a child, Marvin explored the lowcountry marshlands and forests, developing an appreciation for the land and the natural environment. After observing the work of the New York landscape architects Innocenti and Webel on the plantation gardens, Marvin pursued a degree in horticulture at Clemson College. Following graduation in 1941, he served as a captain in the U.S. Army during World War II. He returned to study landscape architecture in the graduate program at the University of Georgia (both of his alma maters would later honor him with distinguished alumni awards). He married Anna Lou Carrington in 1947, and they had two children.

In 1947 Marvin established a private practice in landscape architecture in the town of Walterboro, the county seat of his native Colleton County but far from urbanized areas where most landscape architects tended to congregate. Early in his career he developed a guiding philosophy, "to create and design an environment in which each individual can grow and develop to be a full human being as God intended him to be." Despite the scarcity of work for a landscape architect in Walterboro, Marvin, supported by Anna Lou, set his standards high, determining that he would not be involved in a project without control over "everything outside the walls of the building." Sensitivity to the natural environment was essential to his work. "We need to knock the walls down and let nature in again," he stated. "[M]an needs to get out of his box that technology has created. He needs to wrap his arms around nature."

Because he structured his practice to be responsive to the natural environment of his native Southeast, Marvin focused his energy on regional projects. Some of his notable projects within South Carolina include Harbor Town at Sea Pines Plantation, Hilton Head Island (1969); Henry C. Chambers Park, Beaufort (1976); and the Governor's Mansion and Finlay Park in Columbia.

Marvin was noted for his sensitive design responses to the fragile lowcountry natural environment in which he worked. Uncompromising in his approach to his work, he influenced the next generation of landscape architects profoundly. Marvin was honored with numerous national, regional, and local awards, including induction into the Fellows of the American Society of Landscape Architects, the South Carolina Order of the Palmetto, and the South Carolina Hall of Fame. Records of his professional work and awards have been selected for inclusion in the South Caroliniana Library. Marvin was one of the first landscape architects in South Carolina, and his career spanned six decades. He died on June 25, 2001, and was buried in Live Oak Cemetery in Walterboro. SARAH GEORGIA HARRISON

Thompson, J. William. "Southern Savior." *Landscape Architecture* 87 (June 1997): 74–79, 93–97.

Mason Lee's will. One of South Carolina's most famous legal disputes derived from a celebrated eccentric, Mason Lee (ca. 1775–ca. 1823), and the legal proceedings surrounding the probate of his will. Lee lived in Marlboro District and devised his property to the states of Tennessee and South Carolina in order to defeat inheritance by any of his relations. He directed that proceeds from his large estate be disposed of so that no part of it would be inherited by any of his relations "while wood grows or water runs." Lee authorized his executors to defend his will with the best legal defense that money could buy "again, again, and again."

Originally from North Carolina, Lee, at age thirty, was allegedly struck by lightning that may have first caused his idiosyncrasies. He then moved to Georgia, where he was charged with murder, and he afterward located as a fugitive to Marlboro District, South Carolina. While in Marlboro, Lee accumulated great wealth, but his eccentricities became more pronounced. He slept in a hollow gum log and wore no buttons on his clothes. He believed that all women were witches and that his relatives were in his teeth and used supernatural powers to bewitch. He cut off the quarters of his shoes and drilled holes in his hat to drive the devil from his feet and head.

After Lee's death an intense legal battle ensued among the elite of the South Carolina Bar to settle the estate. To contest the will, the heirs at law employed James R. Ervin, Abram Blanding, and William Harper, three of the state's most prominent lawyers. Lee's executor, Robertson Carloss, engaged Josiah J. Evans and William Campbell Preston, both future U.S. senators, to argue for the will. The state court of appeals affirmed, holding that eccentricity, however great, is not the same as insanity and thus is insufficient to invalidate a will.

Subsequently, the state of Tennessee sold all its interest in the Lee estate to the estate of Robert B. Campbell, a member of Congress from South Carolina. The state of South Carolina through legislation gave its share to Lee's heirs at law. By this time, however, there was little left in the estate since the proceeds had been dissipated by legal fees and the second executor's excesses. The hollow log in which Lee slept is in the Marlborough Historical Society Museum in Bennettsville. JOHN L. NAPIER

Heirs at Law of Mason Lee v. Ex. of Mason Lee, 15 S.C.L. (4 McCord) 183 (1830).

McColl, D. D. *Sketches of Old Marlboro.* Columbia, S.C.: State Company, 1916.

Thomas, J. A. W. *A History of Marlboro County, with Traditions and Sketches of Numerous Families.* 1897. Reprint, Baltimore: Regional Publishing, 1971.

Mather Academy. Mather Academy was the vision of Sarah Babcock Mather. She went to Camden in 1867 and opened a school for African American children. The overcrowded school was financed with her money, and Mather sought to establish a larger institution. She purchased twenty-seven acres near Camden to build a school but soon returned to Massachusetts. The school Mather envisioned was founded twenty years later by the New England Southern Conference (NESC) of the Women's Home Missionary Society of the Methodist Church. As corresponding secretary of the NESC, Mather was able to enlist help in building the school. The conference provided funds for one building, and Fanny O. Browning of Connecticut provided $2,000 for a second structure. In 1887 the Browning Home and Mather Academy opened.

The campus of Mather Academy, Camden. Courtesy, South Caroliniana Library, University of South Carolina

The school grew slowly in the 1890s. The curriculum expanded to include high-school-level science, mathematics, and language courses. Boys were admitted in 1890, and enrollment passed two hundred by 1900, which included thirty-seven girls boarding at the Browning Home, where they were trained as homemakers. By the early 1900s additional buildings had been constructed and a normal-school curriculum added. Enrollment reached almost four hundred students by 1920. In 1934 Mather Academy became an "A" class high school (one of only four in South Carolina) and a member of the Southern Association of Secondary Schools and Colleges. Mather's most noteworthy alumnus, U.S. Representative James Clyburn, was in the 1957 graduating class.

Mather merged in 1959 with the struggling Boylan-Haven School of Jacksonville, Florida, and became Boylan-Haven-Mather Academy. The school remained in Camden, but amid declining enrollment and shrinking dollars it fell into disrepair. Boylan-Haven-Mather Academy graduated its last class in 1983, and its buildings were demolished in 1993. LINDA MEGGETT BROWN

Boylan-Haven-Mather Academy, 1887–1983: 96 Years of Excellence in Camden, South Carolina. [Camden, S.C.], 1983.

Mathews, John (1744–1802). Governor. Mathews was born in Charleston in 1744, the only son of John Mathews and Sarah Gibbes. In 1764 he began the study of law at the Middle Temple in London. Shortly thereafter he returned to South Carolina, where he clerked for Charles Pinckney before his admission to the bar in 1766. Later that year he married Mary Wragg. They had one son.

Mathews entered public service in 1767, when St. Helena's Parish elected him to the Commons House of Assembly. St. John's Colleton Parish returned Mathews in 1772, but he did not become a legislative mainstay until elected to the First and Second Provincial Congresses in 1775 by St. George's Dorchester Parish. Between 1776 and 1790 Mathews served in the first eight General Assemblies, representing at different times St. George's Dorchester Parish and the Charleston parishes of St. Philip's and St. Michael's. Mathews was chosen the first Speaker of the House of Representatives under the constitution of 1778 but left the position after being elected a delegate to the Continental Congress. He was reelected to additional terms in 1779 and 1780.

As a delegate, Mathews served on several important committees, including as chairman of the Committee at Headquarters, which worked closely with General George Washington to supply and organize the army. Mathews was instrumental in securing the appointment of Nathanael Greene as commander of the Southern Department of the Continental army in December 1780. He also thwarted efforts to sacrifice South Carolina and Georgia to gain independence for the other colonies.

Mathews left Congress in December 1781 and returned home. He attended the legislative session at Jacksonborough, where he was elected governor on January 29, 1782. Mathews faced several serious problems: the state was economically devastated; the Continental army in South Carolina was in disrepair; and the British controlled Charleston. Furthermore, the legislature sought to confiscate Loyalist property, a move with which Mathews disagreed. He started the work of reconstructing South Carolina with a census of the state, necessary for future taxation. To augment white troops available for combat, he favored raising a noncombat corps of African laborers, but the measure was rejected by the General Assembly. Finally, on December 14, 1782, Mathews presided over the reoccupation of Charleston by American forces, ending the British threat to South Carolina.

Mathews was succeeded as governor by Benjamin Guerard on February 4, 1783. Mathews's one year in office was the shortest full term of any South Carolina governor. He remained active in the legislature during the 1780s, and in 1784 he was elected as chancellor of the court of chancery. He served on that court and the court of law and equity until 1797. He served as a trustee of the College of Charleston and helped found the St. George's Club, which encouraged the breeding of good horses. In 1799, following the death of his first wife, he married Sarah Rutledge, sister of John and Edward Rutledge. Mathews died in Charleston on October 26, 1802. PAUL A. HORNE, JR.

Horne, Paul A., Jr. "Forgotten Leaders: South Carolina's Delegation to the Continental Congress, 1774–1789." Ph.D. diss., University of South Carolina, 1988.

———. "The Governorship of John Mathews, 1782–1783." Master's thesis, University of South Carolina, 1982.

Nadelhaft, Jerome J. *The Disorders of War: The Revolution in South Carolina.* Orono: University of Maine Press, 1981.

Mauldin (Greenville County; 2000 pop. 15,224). In 1784 former Cherokee land in Greenville County was first made available to white settlers. The earliest to enter the Mauldin area was Benjamin Griffith, who received a grant of one hundred acres in 1784. In 1853 Griffith's great-grandson sold part of the family lands to Willis William Butler, and the local community became Butler's Crossroads. Until the post–Civil War era, the settlement was a poor farming community, whose primary economic asset was its location on the stage road between Laurens and Greenville. Good fortune arrived in 1886, when the Greenville and Laurens Railroad was constructed through the community. On December 24, 1890, Butler's Crossroads was chartered as the town of Mauldin, named in honor of Lieutenant Governor William L. Mauldin, president of the railroad. No town officials were elected until 1910, when Mauldin was finally authorized to choose a mayor and a town council.

During the early twentieth century Mauldin thrived as an agricultural community, with local cotton shipped to outside markets from its train depot. In the 1920s the boll weevil arrived and prosperity departed. A bright spot in this gloomy economic picture came in 1925, when the Greenville to Laurens road through Mauldin was paved; the road eventually evolved into U.S. Highway 276. Unfortunately, even the construction of electric lines by Duke Power in 1929 failed to lift Mauldin from its economic doldrums. By the 1930s abandoned farms and general unemployment made it difficult for citizens to maintain even their town government. In 1932 the town council petitioned the state to revoke its charter. The charter was not actually repealed but merely became inactive. By 1940 most stores were vacant and the train depot closed.

World War II improved conditions. Many families attached to the Greenville Army Air Base moved into the Mauldin area. In 1951 the Mauldin-Simpsonville–Fountain Inn Water District was formed, followed in 1953 by construction of a water line from Greenville through Mauldin to Fountain Inn. The pipeline brought the area its first adequate water supply and stimulated economic growth. A newspaper editorial predicted that the line would make the area a "golden strip" primed for development. The prophecy was fulfilled. Business and industry were attracted to the "golden strip," and Mauldin, the town that almost died, underwent a period of rapid growth.

Discovering that its charter had merely been inactive since 1932, Mauldin revived its town council. In 1957 elections for a mayor and a council were held for the first time in twenty-five years. As nearby Greenville attracted industries in the 1960s and 1970s, many new arrivals preferred to live in residential areas around Mauldin. In 1969 Mauldin was rechartered as a city. Five subdivisions were annexed in 1972. The construction of Interstate 385 contributed to further growth, and Mauldin's median household income became the highest in Greenville County. By 2000 Mauldin was one of the fastest-growing cities in South Carolina, experiencing a tenfold increase in population since 1960. JEFFREY R. WILLIS

Hart, Mildred C. "Mauldin." *Proceedings and Papers of the Greenville County Historical Society* 8 (1984–1990): 43–66.

Huff, Archie Vernon, Jr. *Greenville: The History of the City and County in the South Carolina Piedmont.* Columbia: University of South Carolina Press, 1995.

Walker, Mae, et al. *Mauldin's Legacy and Its People.* Clinton, S.C.: Inter-Collegiate Press, 1984.

Maverick, Samuel Augustus (1803–1870). Lawyer, land speculator. Maverick was born in Pendleton District (now Oconee County) on July 23, 1803, the son of the Charleston businessman Samuel Maverick and Elizabeth Anderson. After graduating from Yale University in 1825, Maverick studied law with the Virginia jurist Henry St. George Tucker and opened a law office in Pendleton. He moved to Georgia in 1833 and then to Alabama, overseeing family lands. Bored with plantation life and unsuited to overseeing slaves, Maverick moved to Texas in pursuit of cheap land, inspired both by his grandfather's success as a land speculator and by his father's entrepreneurial ethic. Arriving in 1835 at the height of the Texas revolution, Maverick joined the Texan forces, but he quickly returned on family business to Alabama, where he married Mary Ann Adams on August 4, 1836. The next year the couple took their firstborn, Samuel Maverick, Jr., and several slaves to Texas, settling in San Antonio. Maverick took a law license and began purchasing land in western Texas, relocating several times but returning to San Antonio for good in 1847.

Maverick's most lasting legacy is the application of his name as a term for unbranded cattle, which was inspired by his unbranded herd on Matagorda Peninsula. Legend has it that he refused to brand his calves because he thought that allowed him to claim all unbranded calves on the range. In reality Maverick was an indifferent cattleman who simply did not bother to brand his small herd and was out of the cattle business entirely by the mid-1850s. He also lent his name to Maverick County in western Texas, where he held more than 300,000 acres at his death. Maverick died on September 2, 1870, and was buried in San Antonio's City Cemetery Number One. BRIAN NANCE

Green, Rena Maverick, ed. *Samuel Maverick, Texan: A Collection of Letters, Journals, and Memoirs.* San Antonio, Tex.: Privately printed, 1952.

Marks, Paula Mitchell. *Turn Your Eyes toward Texas: Pioneers Sam and Mary Maverick.* College Station: Texas A&M University Press, 1989.

Maverick Family. Papers. Barker Texas History Center, University of Texas, Austin.

Maxcy, Jonathan (1768–1820). College president, minister. Maxcy was born in Attleboro, Massachusetts, on September 2, 1768, the eldest son of Levi Maxcy and Ruth Newell. Prepared at Wrentham Academy, he graduated with highest honors in 1787 from Rhode Island College (later Brown University). Baptized in 1789, Maxcy studied for the ministry and was licensed to preach the following year. Jonathan Trumbull painted his portrait (1793) as "preacher of the First Baptist Society of Providence," a position he assumed on September 8, 1791. Maxcy married Susannah Hopkins, daughter of Commodore Esek Hopkins of Providence, on August 22, 1791. Six of their ten children survived infancy. He was elected president pro tempore of Rhode Island College on September 7, 1792, and the youthful Maxcy formally became the school's second president in 1797. Harvard College awarded him the doctor of sacred theology in 1801.

From 1802 to 1804 Maxcy served as the third president of Union College in Schenectady, New York. In 1804, drawn to a warmer climate by chronic health problems, he accepted the $2,500-a-year offer to become the first president of South Carolina College in Columbia. The college opened in January 1805 with nine students and two professors. Maxcy, professor of belles lettres, criticism, and metaphysics, also served on the board of trustees. In 1810 the trustees required the president to submit semiannual reports on the courses offered and student progress, and in 1813 they insisted that juniors and seniors study theology.

The constant problem of disciplining intoxicated and unruly students seriously threatened Maxcy's position from 1813 to 1815 and undoubtedly undermined his health. The faculty tried to gain control over students by imposing suspensions, but the trustees seldom mandated expulsions. When Maxcy's chapel speeches failed to tame students, the trustees' investigating committee charged him, on April 21, 1813, with "many and great derelictions of duty." Experiencing what he described as "the most painful occurrence of my life," Maxcy defended himself (April 24, 1813), but the trustees required the faculty to submit weekly reports to their standing committee. On February 8, 1814, the town militia had to subdue a student rebellion against the disciplinarian professor George Blackburn. The trustees expelled student ringleaders and forced Blackburn to resign. In November 1815 Maxcy's ill health resulted in a trustee resolution for his dismissal, but he successfully defended his presidency. During that time faculty raised academic standards and the college expanded to seven buildings.

Of the three colleges that he presided over, Maxcy made his greatest impact on South Carolina College. Recognized as a teacher more than a scholar, Maxcy emphasized, in *Principles of Rhetorick and Criticism* (1817), "how 'rhetoric' was to contribute to the general collegiate curriculum." Deeply committed to the principle of religious toleration, Maxcy believed that neither civil harmony nor salvation required doctrinal consensus. He died on June 4, 1820, and was buried in the cemetery of the First Presbyterian Church, Columbia. The Maxcy Monument, an obelisk designed by Robert Mills, was dedicated on campus on December 15, 1827, by the student Clariosophic Society, of which Maxcy was a founder and the first honorary member. MARCIA G. SYNNOTT

Hollis, Daniel Walker. *University of South Carolina.* 2 vols. Columbia: University of South Carolina Press, 1951–1956.

Maxcy, Jonathan. Papers. South Caroliniana Library, University of South Carolina, Columbia.

Scott, Patrick Greig. "Jonathan Maxcy and the Aims of Early Nineteenth-Century Rhetorical Teaching." *College English* 4 (January 1983): 21–30.

Maybank, Burnet Rhett (1899–1954). Mayor of Charleston, governor, U.S. senator. Born in Charleston on March 7, 1899, Maybank was the son of Joseph Maybank, a physician, and Harriett Rhett. He attended Porter Military Academy and earned an A.B. degree from the College of Charleston in 1919. He became a successful Charleston cotton broker after learning the business in the office of his uncle, John Frampton Maybank. In November 1923 Maybank married Elizabeth de Rousset Myers. They had three children. After her death in 1947, he married Mary Randolph Piezer on December 10, 1948. The second marriage produced no children.

Burnet R. Maybank. Courtesy, South Caroliniana Library, University of South Carolina

In 1931, in the depths of the Depression, a steering committee of prominent Charleston businessmen asked Maybank, then a city alderman, to run for mayor. Supporters believed him capable of ending the bitter factionalism in city politics and installing an administration equipped to deal with Charleston's worsening financial crisis. Overcoming opposition from the political machine of former mayor John P. Grace, Maybank won in a landslide victory and served as mayor from 1931 to 1938. He also became a protégé of U.S. Senator James F. Byrnes and was active in New Deal efforts to combat the economic crisis of the 1930s.

As mayor, Maybank revamped the city budget and retired much of the accumulated debt. He took advantage of New Deal programs to provide work relief for the unemployed and to improve his community. With federal grants, Maybank repaired public buildings, constructed a gymnasium at the College of Charleston, restored Dock Street Theatre, and added a municipal yacht basin, public swimming pools, a garbage incinerator, and low-income housing. Maybank also chaired the South Carolina Public Service Authority, a public corporation that built the largest New Deal undertaking in the state: the Santee Cooper hydroelectric project.

Maybank's involvement with Santee Cooper enhanced his political standing, and he ran successfully for governor in 1938. Overcoming competition from seven opponents in the Democratic primary, Maybank defeated Wyndham M. Manning in a controversial run-off election, in which a huge majority in Charleston County tipped the election in Maybank's favor. Serving from 1938 to 1941, Maybank found his tenure as governor a frustrating interlude between his service as mayor and his career in the U.S. Senate. In a political system dominated by the legislature, Maybank accomplished little from the governor's chair. Calls to restrict the governor's pardoning power, to create a state police force, to establish a merit system for state employment, and to limit the financial independence of the state highway commission were ignored or defeated by the General Assembly. Maybank gained public approval, if not legislative success, by portraying himself as a populist defender of the public interest against the "Barnwell Ring" of legislative leaders Edgar Brown and Solomon Blatt.

When Byrnes resigned from the U.S. Senate to serve on the U.S. Supreme Court, Maybank defeated former governor Olin D. Johnston in a special election to fill the vacancy. Maybank entered the Senate on November 5, 1941, where he exercised a quiet but potent influence in national affairs. He gained the chairmanship of the Senate Banking Committee and helped shape the post–World War II economy. He championed the development of federal housing policy, provided a solid vote for defense appropriations in the early cold-war era, and supported Democratic presidents on most issues except the repeal of the Taft-Hartley law.

After his reelection in 1942 and again in 1948, Maybank had no opposition in the primary election of 1954 and planned on returning to Washington after the legislative recess. However, while vacationing at his home in Flat Rock, North Carolina, Maybank died of a heart attack on September 1, 1954. He was buried in Magnolia Cemetery. MARVIN L. CANN

Cann, Marvin L. "Burnet Rhett Maybank and the New Deal in South Carolina, 1931–1941." Ph.D. diss., University of North Carolina at Chapel Hill, 1967.

———. "The End of a Political Myth: The South Carolina Gubernatorial Campaign of 1938." *South Carolina Historical Magazine* 72 (July 1971): 139–49.

Mays, Benjamin Elijah (1894–1984). Civil rights activist, writer, college president. Mays was born on August 1, 1894, in rural South Carolina near Rambo in Edgefield County (now Epworth in Greenwood County). He was the youngest of eight children born to Hezekiah Mays and Louvenia Carter, former slaves turned tenant farmers. Growing up in the rural South at a time when African Americans were disfranchised by law, Mays experienced a climate of hate where lynchings and race riots were common. In fact, Mays's first memory was the 1898 Phoenix Riot, in which his cousin was murdered by whites.

Early in life Mays developed an "insatiable desire" for education, but racial inequality and prejudice had severely handicapped his educational career. Struggling against his limited educational background, his family's poverty, and his father's insistence that he remain on the farm, Mays enrolled at the high school of the black South Carolina State College. Four years later, in 1916, Mays graduated at the top of his class and became engaged to fellow student Ellen Harvin.

Benjamin Mays. Courtesy, Avery Research Center for African American History and Culture

Mays looked to continue his education at a northern college. Rejected because of his race from his top choice, Holderness School in New Hampshire, Mays enrolled at Bates College in Lewiston, Maine, where he graduated with honors in 1920. Following graduation, Mays briefly returned home to South Carolina to marry Harvin, who had been teaching home economics at Morris College in Sumter. The couple moved to Chicago, where Mays enrolled at the University of Chicago to study divinity. After three semesters at Chicago and as a result of a personal invitation from John Hope, president of Morehouse, Mays took a teaching position at Morehouse College in Atlanta, Georgia, where he taught algebra and mathematics from 1921 through 1924 and served for a year as acting dean. During his tenure at Morehouse, Mays, who was ordained in 1921, served as the pastor of the Shiloh Baptist Church, which allowed him to grow in his spiritual faith and deal with the loss of his wife Ellen, who died in 1923.

Following the death of his wife, Mays left Morehouse to continue his graduate work at the University of Chicago, where he earned an M.A. in 1925. Although he considered pursuing his Ph.D., Mays instead returned to South Carolina State to teach English. There he met Sadie Gray, who became his second wife in 1926. After marrying, the couple moved to Florida to work with the National Urban League to improve housing, employment, and health conditions of African Americans. A few years later, in 1928, expecting to be fired for challenging segregation, they resigned from their jobs and moved to Atlanta, where Benjamin took a position with the national Young Men's Christian Association (YMCA) and worked to integrate that organization in the North and the South. In 1930 Mays left the YMCA to conduct a study of black churches with fellow minister Joseph W. Nicholson. The study, which focused on 609 urban congregations and 185 rural congregations, was published in 1933 as *The Negro's Church*. In 1931 Mays returned to the University of Chicago School of Religion to finish his Ph.D., which he received in 1935. In 1934, as Mays was finishing his Ph.D., he accepted appointment as dean of the School of Religion at Howard University in Washington, D.C. In this position Mays traveled overseas to visit world leaders, such as Mahatma Gandhi of India.

After six years at Howard, in 1940 Mays accepted an offer to become president of Morehouse College in Atlanta. For the next twenty-seven years Mays worked tirelessly at Morehouse, collecting $15 million in donations, overseeing the construction of eighteen buildings, and conducting well-attended Tuesday morning chapel talks with students. Mays unrelentingly preached engagement, responsibility, and stewardship to his Morehouse students. His inspiring leadership made Morehouse one of the most prestigious black universities in America, which graduated a disproportionately high number of future Ph.D.'s, college presidents, and civil rights leaders. Several of his gifted students, including Julian Bond and Maynard Jackson, went on to become leaders of the national civil rights movement of the 1950s and 1960s, leading one writer to describe Mays as "Schoolmaster of the Movement." One student whom Mays particularly impressed was Martin Luther King, Jr., who often stayed late with Mays to discuss theology. King and Mays became lifelong friends. In 1968 Mays delivered the eulogy at King's funeral.

In 1967 Mays retired as president of Morehouse College and took the position of chairman of the school board in Atlanta, where he worked to correct racial inequalities in the school system. In 1970 Mays finished his autobiography, *Born to Rebel,* which has stood as an invaluable contribution to the study of American race relations. The life of Benjamin E. Mays has been celebrated and respected. He was awarded forty-nine honorary degrees and was inducted into the South Carolina Hall of Fame in 1984. He died on March 28, 1984, in Atlanta. ORVILLE VERNON BURTON AND MATTHEW CHENEY

Bennett, Lerone, Jr. "Benjamin Elijah Mays: The Last of the Great Schoolmasters." *Ebony* 33 (December 1977): 72–80.

Carter, Lawrence E., ed. *Walking Integrity: Benjamin Elijah Mays, Mentor to Martin Luther King Jr.* Macon, Ga.: Mercer University Press, 1998.

Jones, Edward A. *A Candle in the Dark: A History of Morehouse College.* Valley Forge, Pa.: Judson, 1967.

Mays, Benjamin E. *Born to Rebel: An Autobiography.* 1971. Reprint, Athens: University of Georgia Press, 1987.

———. Papers. Moorland-Spingarn Research Center, Howard University, Washington, D.C.

Rovaris, Dereck J. *Mays and Morehouse: How Benjamin E. Mays Developed Morehouse College, 1940–1967.* Silver Spring, Md.: Beckam House, 1995.

McBee, Vardry (1775–1864). Industrialist. McBee was born on June 19, 1775, near Thicketty Creek in Spartanburg County, the tenth child of Vardry McBee and Hannah Echols. Since his father's wealth had been destroyed during the Revolutionary War, McBee received only one year of formal schooling before he had to go to work at the limestone quarry his father once owned. In 1794 McBee moved to Lincolnton, North Carolina, to become an apprentice to his brother-in-law, Joseph Morris, a saddler and innkeeper. After a few years in Lincolnton, McBee traveled, spending time working as a clerk for a Charleston merchant, living with his parents on the Kentucky frontier, and working as a saddler in Sumner County, Tennessee. By 1802 McBee had moved back to Lincolnton to work as a saddler and a dry-goods merchant. On August 16, 1804, McBee married Jane Alexander. The couple had nine children. He slowly accumulated considerable wealth, which enabled him to purchase a plantation and become known as one of the area's most progressive farmers.

Although McBee's name is synonymous with the early development of Greenville, he did not become involved with that town until 1815 and did not live there until he was more than sixty years old. In 1815 he purchased from Lemuel Alston approximately eleven thousand acres comprising most of what is now downtown Greenville. By the early 1830s McBee had established several industrial ventures around Greenville: a brick flour mill at the upper falls of the Reedy River, two gold mines in the northern part of the county, and a complex seven miles below Greenville at what is now Conestee that included a flour mill, a sawmill, a paper mill, a cotton factory, and a woolen factory. He also had mercantile stores in both Greenville and Spartanburg.

Along with his interest in manufacturing and merchandising, McBee became one of the strongest promoters of railroads for the upstate in the 1830s. He was a major force behind the Lousiville, Cincinnati and Charleston Railroad Company, which proposed to link the Midwest to the South. The Panic of 1837 and the opposition of John C. Calhoun doomed this project, but McBee turned his efforts toward establishing a railroad from Columbia to Greenville, which finally reached fruition in 1853. By 1860 McBee was the largest landholder in Greenville District, owning more than $360,000 worth of property, including fifty-six slaves. As the nation approached civil war in the 1850s, McBee remained a strong Unionist.

In addition to his business ventures, McBee played important roles in establishing several institutions that have been central to Greenville's identity. In 1820 he donated land for the Greenville Academy, one of the town's first schools. Although not a particularly religious man, McBee donated land for Christ Episcopal Church, Greenville Baptist Church, Greenville Methodist Church, and First Presbyterian Church. McBee also provided financial support to Furman University when it was established in 1850. McBee died on January 23, 1864, and was buried at Christ Episcopal Church in Greenville. BRUCE E. BAKER

Huff, Archie Vernon, Jr. *Greenville: The History of the City and the County in the South Carolina Piedmont.* Columbia: University of South Carolina Press, 1995.

Lander, Ernest McPherson, Jr. *The Textile Industry in Antebellum South Carolina.* Baton Rouge: Louisiana State University Press, 1969.

Smith, Roy McBee. *Vardry McBee, 1775–1864: Man of Reason in an Age of Extremes.* 2d ed. Spartanburg, S.C.: Laurel Heritage, 1997.

McBee Chapel (Conestee). Located seven miles south of Greenville, McBee Chapel is one of three extant brick octagonal churches in the United States. Probably designed by Vardry McBee, who believed that octagonal form was the most efficient design, and built in 1841 by his millwright John Adams, it was originally served by Methodist circuit riders, and it remains an active Methodist congregation. Constructed for textile mill workers at McBee's nearby Reedy River Factory (ca. 1825), it seated 155 people—large enough to hold most of his employees and their families, who were, according to tradition, required to attend services.

Above a three-foot band of whitewashed stone, the brick walls rise to the eaves of a tapered octagonal roof topped by a louvered turret or cupola, which holds the church bell. Windows ten feet high and with small panes of stained glass are set in five walls; double wooden doors are set in one of the octagonal sides. An original slave balcony has been removed. The church sexton can open the doors with an unusual key that resembles a folding knife.

In 1977 McBee Chapel was listed in the National Register of Historic Places. There have been few modifications except the addition of electricity since it was built, and it still lacks plumbing (outhouses serve as privies). In 1991 its congregation celebrated McBee Chapel's 150th anniversary by repairing, refurbishing, and repainting the building. JUDITH T. BAINBRIDGE

Huff, Archie Vernon, Jr. *Greenville: The History of the City and County in the South Carolina Piedmont.* Columbia: University of South Carolina Press, 1995.

Smith, Roy McBee. *Vardry McBee, 1775–1864: Man of Reason in an Age of Extremes.* 2d ed. Spartanburg, S.C.: Laurel Heritage, 1997.

McCall, James (1741–1781). Soldier. McCall was born on August 11, 1741, on Canacocheque Creek in Pennsylvania. He moved southward with his family in his youth, settling first in western Virginia and, after being driven out by Indians, later in Mecklenburg District, North Carolina. A young James McCall appeared in the ranks of a militia company with his father in 1766 and became active during the North Carolina Regulator insurrection. In the early 1770s he moved to the Long Cane District of South Carolina to settle among his Calhoun relatives.

At the onset of the Revolutionary War, McCall was selected as commander of one of three companies of patriot militia formed in the Long Cane area. He commanded his company in the stand against the Loyalists at Ninety Six in November 1775 and was selected the following summer to command a detachment in a covert mission to capture a party of Tories in the Cherokee country. Advancing carefully, McCall's expedition was ambushed by a larger force of Indians. He and six companions were held captive, but McCall alone managed to escape several weeks later.

As the militia gained more structure in the backcountry, McCall was promoted to major of the Upper Ninety Six District Regiment, commanded by his friend and neighbor Andrew Pickens, and he later participated in the decisive battle at Kettle Creek on February 14, 1779. After the fall of Charleston in May 1780, McCall refused to accept parole and retreated into Georgia to continue operations against the crown with Elijah Clark. Undoubtedly he was one of the more active field commanders in South Carolina, as he participated in the actions at Musgrove's Mill, Augusta, King's Mountain, Fish Dam Ford, Blackstock's Plantation, and Long Cane Creek in the turbulent latter half of 1780.

With Andrew Pickens back in command in late December 1780, McCall was appointed to raise a regiment of dragoons and promoted to the rank of lieutenant colonel. The patriot militia of Ninety Six moved to join Brigadier General Daniel Morgan's camp on the Pacolet River in late December 1780, and McCall's new command was immediately attached to the reduced ranks of Lieutenant Colonel William Washington's corps of light horse to pursue a marauding band of Tories. Washington and McCall caught up with the Tories at Hammond's Old Store and inflicted many casualties on the fleeing band. McCall's regiment formed the reserve under Washington and fought well in the signal victory over Tarleton's forces at Cowpens on January 17, 1781. Retreating into North Carolina before Lord Cornwallis's advance, McCall's contingent operated as an important shielding force for the main Continental army. He returned to South Carolina in early March. While coordinating an offensive on the British outpost at Ninety Six, he died from the effects of a wound and smallpox in April 1781. SAMUEL K. FORE

Lumpkin, Henry. *From Savannah to Yorktown: The American Revolution in the South.* Columbia: University of South Carolina Press, 1981.

McCall, Hugh. *History of Georgia: Containing Brief Sketches of the Most Remarkable Events, Up to the Present Day.* 2 vols. Savannah, Ga.: Seymour & Williams, 1811–1816.

Waring, Alice Noble. *The Fighting Elder: Andrew Pickens (1739–1817).* Columbia: University of South Carolina Press, 1962.

McClennan, Alonzo Clifton (1855–1912). Physician, hospital administrator. Born in Columbia on May 1, 1855, McClennan was orphaned and raised by his uncle Edward Thompson. He attended Benedict Institute and served state senator Richard Cain as a page for three years. When Cain was elected to the U.S. House of Representatives, McClennan parlayed his association with the congressman into an appointment to the U.S. Naval Academy in 1873.

Initially, McClennan was optimistic about his experience as only the second African American admitted to the academy. His light skin, blond hair, and blue eyes did not long protect his racial identity. Previously affable fellow classmen became cold, distant, and vindictive when he was discovered to have African blood. A series of incidents convinced McClennan to leave Annapolis in "disgust at caste prejudice" during his first year. He accepted admission to the Wesleyan Academy in Wilbraham, Massachusetts.

McClennan's stay was brief as he returned home to attend the University of South Carolina in 1875. The return of Democratic control of politics in South Carolina forced McClennan to leave school yet again in 1876. In 1877 he entered Howard University, where he graduated with honors from the school of pharmacy and medicine in 1880. He opened his medical practice in Augusta, Georgia, where he married Ida Veronica Ridley in 1883. In 1884 McClennan relocated to Charleston, South Carolina, where he established the city's first African American drugstore, the People's Pharmacy, in 1892.

In the fall of 1896 McClennan organized a meeting of African American physicians to discuss the establishment of a "nurse training school for Negro women." Jim Crow legislation prevented the training of African Americans at Roper Hospital, and McClennan realized the need for a teaching hospital that could serve the community. He mobilized black and white Charlestonians, and in 1897 the Hospital and Training School for Nurses opened at 135 Cannon Street.

McClennan served as director and surgeon-in-charge. He earned a reputation for running his hospital with an iron hand. He believed that "strict discipline" gave donors confidence in the management and the institution. McClennan's draconian policies were largely checked by his identification, dedication, and personal support of the school. From 1898 to 1900 McClennan edited the *Hospital Herald,* a journal designed to assist in the professional training of nurses and the promotion of domestic and public hygiene. He believed that Charleston's medical community would benefit from having a vehicle through which the physicians and nurses could correspond and exchange observations.

McClennan was a vocal leader in the African American community. He was keenly aware of the importance of African Americans patronizing African American businesses. He lamented that preachers and editorials were necessary to impress upon people to do what "they know to be their plain duty." He told black Charlestonians, "We cannot hope to amount to much as a people, especially in business and the professions, unless we have a sufficient interest in our own young men who depend upon us to give the encouragement and support." McClennan died in Charleston on October 4, 1912. DAVID S. BROWN

Gatewood, William B., Jr. "Alonzo Clifton McClennan: Black Midshipman from South Carolina, 1873–1874." *South Carolina Historical Magazine* 89 (January 1988): 24–39.

Savitt, Todd L. "Walking the Color Line: Alonzo McClennan, the *Hospital Herald,* and Segregated Medicine in Turn-of-the-Twentieth-Century Charleston, South Carolina." *South Carolina Historical Magazine* 104 (October 2003): 228–57.

McColl (Marlboro County; 2000 pop. 2,498). McColl is Marlboro County's second-largest town, located in the eastern part of the county near the North Carolina border. In 1884 local landowners T. B. Gibson and John F. McLaurin attracted the South Carolina and Pacific Railway by offering to build a depot and subscribing to stock in the company. Stores, residences, and warehouses appeared in quick succession, as did Methodist, Baptist, and Presbyterian churches. The community that developed around the depot was eventually named after Duncan Donald McColl, a banker and entrepreneur from nearby Bennettsville and president of the South Carolina and Pacific Railway. Many years later the original rail line was acquired by Marlboro County and operated as the Pee Dee River Railway.

While McColl became a transportation, ginning, and marketing center for eastern Marlboro County farmers, the establishment of McColl Manufacturing Company in 1892 supplied additional growth. By 1896 this mill processed fifty bales of Marlboro County cotton daily and employed three hundred workers, who lived in cottages erected on mill land. More mills followed. Established next were Marie Mill in 1898 and Iceman Mill in 1901, making McColl the county's most industrialized town in the state. In 1903 these mills combined with Bennettsville Manufacturing Company to form Marlboro Cotton Mills. During this period of growth McColl attracted storekeepers, cotton merchants, physicians, druggists, theaters, grocers, barbers, and hotels. Many Main Street buildings constructed during this era survived into the next century. However, with the decline of the textile industry, McColl's mills became used principally as warehouses.

Education in McColl began with the creation of the McColl Academy in the mid-1880s. In 1904 the school relocated to the site of the new McColl Graded School. In 1999 McColl Elementary / Middle School opened a modern facility on the site of the original school building. Several former residents of McColl went on to achieve national acclaim, including Jim Tatum (National Collegiate Athletic Association football coach of the year at the University of Maryland); the 1945 Heisman Trophy winner, Felix A. "Doc" Blanchard; and the professional baseball player Chester Martin. Other McColl natives include White House Chief Steward, the author Preston Bruce, and the contractor Sherwood Liles, whose Tidewater Construction Corporation built the Chesapeake Bay Bridge Tunnel Complex. Entering the twenty-first century, McColl possessed an excellent school, vibrant churches, active civic and literary clubs, and a resurgence of business activity with new retail and service establishments along U.S. Highways 15 and 401. WILLIAM LIGHT KINNEY, JR.

Kendall, Jerry T. *Bennettsville Cotton Mill.* Spartanburg, S.C.: Reprint Company, 1998.

Marlboro County, South Carolina: A Pictorial History. Bennettsville, S.C.: Marlborough Historical Society, 1996.

Rogers, John B. *History of the McColl First Baptist Church, 1772–1972.* Columbia, S.C.: State Printing, 1972.

Thomas, J. A. W. *A History of Marlboro County, with Traditions and Sketches of Numerous Families.* 1897. Reprint, Baltimore: Regional Publishing, 1971.

McColl, Hugh Leon, Jr. (b. 1935). Bank executive. McColl was born in Bennettsville on June 18, 1935, to Hugh L. McColl and Frances Pratt Carroll. McColl earned a B.S. degree in business administration from the University of North Carolina in 1957. He served two years in the United States Marine Corps, attaining the rank of first lieutenant. On October 31, 1959, McColl married Jane Bratton Spratt of York. They have three children.

Banking is a family tradition for McColl. His great-grandfather organized Marlboro County's first bank, and his grandfather was its president. McColl's father, who became president at age twenty-five, liquidated the bank in 1939 and paid off all depositors. McColl's brothers also became bankers, and he married a banker's daughter.

When McColl returned to Bennettsville in 1959, he became a trainee with the American Commercial Bank in Charlotte, which, after a merger with Greensboro's Security National Bank, became North Carolina National Bank (NCNB). He became an officer with NCNB in 1961 and thirteen years later was promoted to president. In 1981 he was named vice chairman and chief operating officer of NCNB Corporation, the bank's holding company, and in March 1982 he was elected president. McColl was named chairman of the board and chief executive officer in September 1983. During the 1980s NCNB expanded from a North Carolina institution with 172 offices to a seven-state operation with 826 full-service offices and more than 28,000 employees.

In July 1991 McColl signed an agreement with C&S/Sovran creating NationsBank, which was then the country's third-largest bank, with $119 billion in assets, two thousand branches, and 59,000 employees. In 1998 NationsBank and BankAmerica of San Francisco merged, resulting in Bank of America with headquarters in Charlotte. At the turn of the century, Bank of America had more than $614 billion in assets and five thousand banking centers in twenty-two states, and it employed 180,000 associates. McColl was chairman and chief executive officer until he retired in 2001.

McColl, known for his tough management style and outspoken nature, was also an active supporter of Charlotte's development. He was the first chairman of the Charlotte Uptown Development Corporation, which coordinated business interests to finance major redevelopment of the central city. Buildings at Queens College and the University of North Carolina attest to his support of the institutions. He was elected to the South Carolina Business Hall of Fame in 1990. After retirement from Bank of America, McColl organized an investment banking company, McColl Partners LLC, of which he became chairman. ROBERT A. PIERCE

Lunan, Bert, and Robert A. Pierce. *Legacy of Leadership.* Columbia: South Carolina Business Hall of Fame, 1999.

McCollough, John DeWitt (1822–1902). Minister, architect. McCollough was born at Society Hill on December 8, 1822, the only child of John Lane McCollough and Sarah DeWitt. Educated at St. David's Academy and South Carolina College, where he earned both B.A. and M.A. degrees in 1840, McCollough then became a Society Hill farmer. In June 1842 he married Harriet Bell Hart. He returned to Columbia in 1847 to prepare for the Episcopal ministry with the Reverend Peter Shand, rector of Trinity, Columbia.

In January 1848 McCullough moved his family to Glenn Springs in Spartanburg District, where he continued his theological studies, designed a small wooden church for the resort village, and carved its interior furnishings. The diocesan magazine called it "a happy specimen of simple Gothic," with a "proper" (deeply recessed) chancel and tower.

In July 1850 Bishop C. E. Gadsden consecrated Calvary, Glenn Springs; ordained McCollough; and appointed him rector of the Church of the Advent in Spartanburg. After designing a temporary chapel for his tiny new congregation and starting missionary activity in Union, Yorkville, and Anderson, he began supervising construction for a permanent Spartanburg church and opened St. John's Episcopal School for boys.

A craftsman without formal training, McCollough was nevertheless aware of the new ideas that were transforming Episcopal church architecture. "Ecclesiologists," influenced by the high-church Oxford movement in England, emphasized the relationship between theology and architecture, believing that new churches should mirror fourteenth-century English Gothic design. Recessed chancels, dark interiors, stained glass, pointed arches, battlements, and cross-topped spires replaced Georgian simplicity. These concepts were disseminated to American churchmen through the journal of the New York Ecclesiology Society. A series of articles on "proper" church architecture in the *Gospel Messenger,* the diocesan magazine, disseminated these ideas to South Carolina.

In the decade before the Civil War, McCollough designed or was supervising architect for seven ecclesiological churches: Christ Church, Greenville (1854); St. Stephen's, Ridgeway (1854); Nativity, Union (1859); Christ Church, Mars Bluff (1859); St. Mark's, Chester (1860); Grace, Anderson (1860); and Advent, Spartanburg (begun 1852, consecrated 1864).

But McCollough's Spartanburg school failed, and he was bankrupt. He moved in 1857 to Winnsboro and later to Union. In 1859 he returned to Spartanburg and Advent, serving as chaplain with Holcombe's Legion during the Civil War. During Reconstruction, desperately poor South Carolinians could no longer build expensive churches. In the postbellum years McCollough provided far simpler designs for churches at Rock Hill, Gaffney, Lancaster, Blacksburg, Willington, Greenwood, Clemson, and Saluda in North Carolina.

In 1874 McCollough resigned as Spartanburg rector, but he continued missionary activity, starting congregations in Gaffney, Blacksburg, Walhalla, and Seneca and serving at Glenn Springs, Union, and Chester. He moved to Walhalla in 1890 to become rector of St. John's, which he may have designed. He certainly was the architect for the second Calvary, Glenn Springs, and with his son, Edward, designed St. Andrews, Greenville, which was completed posthumously. McCollough died on January 23, 1902. He was buried at the Church of the Advent in Spartanburg. JUDITH T. BAINBRIDGE

Bainbridge, Judith T. *"Building the Walls of Jerusalem": John DeWitt McCollough and His Churches.* Spartanburg, S.C.: Reprint Company, 2000.

McCord, Louisa Susanna Cheves (1810–1879). Essayist, poet. Born in Charleston on December 3, 1810, Louisa McCord was the daughter of the South Carolina lawyer Langdon Cheves and Mary Dulles. Her father's career as state attorney general, congressman, and president of the Bank of the United States took the family from Charleston and Columbia to Washington, D.C., and Pennsylvania. As a result, McCord grew up among the political and social elite of the young nation, exposed to both slave and free labor and rural and urban environments. Although her formal education consisted solely of Philadelphia boarding schools, her later writings suggest the veracity of the family legend that her father allowed McCord to study with her brothers as they prepared for college.

Louisa Cheves McCord. Courtesy, Georgia Historical Society

After the death of her mother in 1836, McCord became the de facto mistress of her father's household. By this time Langdon Cheves had returned to South Carolina and purchased or inherited several rice and cotton plantations. McCord had inherited fifty slaves from her grandmother Sophia Dulles in 1830. Just before her wedding to the Columbia lawyer David James McCord on May 20, 1840, Louisa's father presented her with the cotton plantation Lang Syne, located in Orangeburg District. This plantation remained in her name throughout her fifteen-year marriage to David McCord, and she would pass the property on to her son-in-law Augustus Smythe upon his marriage to her daughter Louisa in 1865.

The years between the birth of her third child and the death of her husband (1845–1854) proved most prolific for Louisa McCord's writing. Ensconced in the intellectual and political world of Columbia, where her family lived between the South Carolina College and the State House, McCord published the essays in which she synthesized contemporary thought on the defense of slavery, women's subordination, and political economy. She believed that African Americans constituted a natural working class and that slavery acted as a means of maintaining social order. White women, while intellectually equal to white men, were forced to subordinate themselves within a social hierarchy due to their physical inferiority to white men, whom she believed possessed both the intellect and the physical prowess required to maintain a peaceful society. She warned that abolitionists and the emerging woman's rights movement exposed the nation to unrestrained violence from the working classes, specifically to the threat of slave rebellion. She also wrote on political economy, in support of free markets, and translated the French economist Frederic Bastiat's *Sophisme Economique.* Published under the initials "LSM," her essays appeared in important southern journals such as *De Bow's Review* and *Southern Quarterly Review,* and they were well received and praised by her male contemporaries and were reflective of the dominant opinions of South Carolina's elite classes in the decades preceding the Civil War.

Less renowned are McCord's poetry and drama. Her poetry, written in her twenties, suggests an intellectually ambitious young woman struggling to accept her place in the social order that she described in her essays. Her play, *Caius Gracchus* (1851), is the dramatic culmination of those ideas in the depiction of a stoic mother sacrificing her personal happiness and children for the greater good of republicanism. Little did she guess as she wrote the play that she would find herself in an almost identical position ten years later.

During the Civil War, McCord cast herself as a mother of the Confederacy. McCord became matron of the Confederate hospital set up on the grounds of South Carolina College, and she donated crops, livestock, and uniforms to South Carolina troops. Her greatest sacrifice to the war, however, was her only son, Langdon Cheves McCord, who died as a result of head injuries received at the Second Battle of Manassas in 1862. She, her daughters, her daughter-in-law, her sisters-in-law, and her granddaughter witnessed the Union invasion of South Carolina, during which General Oliver O. Howard occupied her home. His temporary residence possibly saved the house from destruction in the 1865 Columbia fire and placed McCord in a position to negotiate on behalf of the white women remaining in the city. Throughout the ordeal, women of her class, including her friend Mary Chesnut, noted her strength and resilience with awe and admiration.

Although she became the head of the South Carolina Monument Association after the war, the conflict's losses and changes so depressed McCord that she went into a self-imposed exile from South Carolina during the years 1870–1874. When she returned to South Carolina, moving into the Charleston residence of her daughter Louisa McCord Smythe, she began preparations for a biography of her father. A serious stomach ailment identified as "stomach gout" interrupted this work. McCord died on November 23, 1879, and was buried in Magnolia Cemetery. LEIGH FOUGHT

Fought, Leigh. *Southern Womanhood and Slavery: A Biography of Louisa S. McCord, 1810–1879.* Columbia: University of Missouri Press, 2003.

Fox-Genovese, Elizabeth. *Within the Plantation Household: Black and White Women of the Old South.* Chapel Hill: University of North Carolina Press, 1988.

Lounsbury, Richard, ed. *Louisa S. McCord: Political and Social Essays.* Charlottesville: University Press of Virginia, 1995.

———, ed. *Louisa S. McCord: Poems, Drama, Biography, Letters.* Charlottesville: University Press of Virginia, 1996.

McCormick County (360 sq. miles; 2000 pop. 9,958). Named in honor of Cyrus Hall McCormick, inventor of the mechanical reaper, McCormick County was formed in 1916 from portions of Greenwood, Abbeville, and Edgefield Counties. Lying geographically in the forested lower Piedmont of South Carolina and bordering Lake Thurmond and the Savannah River, McCormick is South Carolina's smallest and second-youngest county.

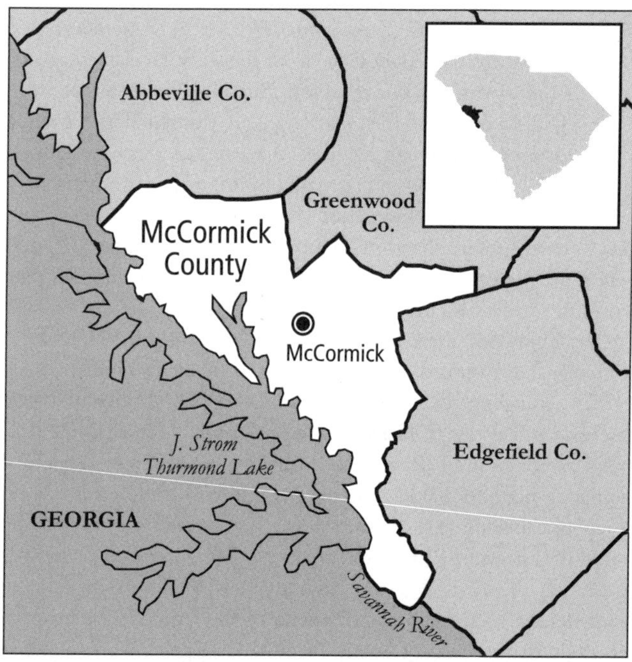

Native Americans, principally of the Cherokee Nation, used the area for hunting grounds prior to European immigration. This practice was disturbed in the 1750s by the arrival of Scots-Irish migrants, led by Patrick Calhoun, who settled at Long Cane Creek in 1756. In the 1760s Huguenots and German Palatines followed, establishing settlements at New Bordeaux and Londonborough, where they experimented with silk, wine, and hemp production. At Willington Academy, established in 1801, Dr. Moses Waddel educated a future generation of South Carolina statesmen, including John C. Calhoun, George McDuffie, and Patrick Noble. After the Revolutionary War a cotton economy, using African American slave labor, began to develop, and by the 1860s it had grown to be the region's dominant institution and source of income. Prominent planters from the area included Dr. John de la Howe, whose estate became a manual training school bearing his name, and the Unionist sympathizer James Louis Petigru.

Gold was first taken from the area between 1847 and 1852 by a local planter named William "Fool Billy" Dorn. As legend has it, Dorn's foxhounds unearthed a gold vein while hunting close to the site of the present-day town. Using slave labor to work his mine, Dorn reputedly extracted between $900,000 and $2 million in profits within ten years. During the Civil War it was claimed that Dorn outfitted an entire regiment of Confederate soldiers. With slave labor no longer available following the South's defeat, the output of Dorn's mine diminished greatly. In the 1980s McCormick County made a serious attempt to capitalize on its history of gold mining. Local history and industrial archaeology, evidenced in the remains of old pits and tunnels scattered around the town of McCormick, were celebrated and explored in the town's Gold Rush festival.

The settlement that developed near mines was known initially as Dorn's Gold Mines and later as Dorn Mine Post Office. In 1871 Cyrus McCormick bought the mines for $20,000 and spent the remainder of his life trying to realize a profit, despite extensive capital outlays for new mining equipment. However, McCormick did give the town an orderly shape and the area a new economic prosperity that ultimately led to a new county. First, McCormick ordered that forty acres be surveyed and laid out in squares, auctioning the thirty-by-one-hundred-foot lots and donating property for churches, a school, and a cemetery. Next, he brought the area into the railway age by purchasing stock in the Augusta and Knoxville Railroad to encourage a rail spur to his mines, which subsequently created thriving railroad stops such as Modoc, Meriwether, Mt. Carmel, and Parksville. In 1882 the Dorn's Gold Mines settlement was incorporated as the town of McCormick, which became the first village in the state to be incorporated as "dry," prohibiting the open sale of liquor for a century. However, prohibition never managed to drain the demand for liquor, and tipplers in the county continued the tradition of supplying their needs and the needs of others by building ingenious, but nevertheless illicit, stills.

The first effort to form the county of McCormick came at the 1895 constitutional convention. By the early 1900s, encouraged by a flourishing agricultural economy, "new county" committee leaders promoted their campaign to the electorate through a new weekly newspaper, the *McCormick Messenger.* By 1916 they had overcome all opposition. However, prosperity in the new county was relatively short-lived. The diminishing importance of mining and the double blow of the boll weevil and the Great Depression devastated the McCormick County economy by the 1930s. Federal projects addressed the county's worst problems, including massive population loss and soil erosion. The Civilian Conservation Corps planted 48,000 acres of pine trees that formed the nucleus of the Long Cane Division of the Sumter National Forest. Community-building programs, such as the Works Progress Administration–built town hall in McCormick, provided jobs for unemployed residents. To solve flooding in Augusta, Georgia, the U.S. Army Corps of Engineers built Clarks Hill (later Lake Thurmond) Dam in the 1940s, providing hydroelectric power and water-based recreation. With the pines came the timber-processing industry, and following World War II textile mills appeared. These remained major employers throughout the remainder of the century.

Two new communities added two thousand residents to McCormick County's population in the 1990s. The state housed more than eleven hundred inmates at the McCormick Correctional Institute (MCI), a maximum-security penal facility, while upward of eight hundred retirees moved to the recreational and retirement community of Savannah Lakes Village on the shores of Lake Thurmond. Although slow to join the South's historic preservation movement, county politicians and planners fully embraced the idea of heritage tourism in the 1980s as an important source of future revenue and employment, especially as more traditional economic activities rapidly disappeared from the county. These developments included the formation of the McCormick Arts Council, the county's participation in South Carolina Heritage Corridor projects, the refurbishment of the town of McCormick's Main Street and the Dorn Mill and Cotton Gin (later the Dorn Mill Center for History and Art), and plans to revive the town of Willington.

In the late 1990s McCormick continued to be designated one hundred percent rural by the U.S. Census Bureau and boasted the greatest proportion of forestland in the state, totaling over ninety percent of all available acreage. The proximity to over seventy thousand acres of lake and river gave rise to the promotion of the county as South Carolina's "Freshwater Coast" and the development of recreational tourism. Recreational and heritage tourism, textiles, and the timber industry comprised McCormick's economic foundation at the end of the twentieth century. STEPHEN C. KENNY

Edmonds, Bobby F. *The Making of McCormick County.* McCormick, S.C.: Cedar Hill, 1999.

Fortenberry, Ken H. *Kill the Messenger: One Man's Fight against Bigotry and Greed.* Atlanta: Peachtree, 1989.

McCottry, Catherine Mae McKee (b. 1921). Physician. McCottry was born on February 3, 1921, in Charlotte, North Carolina. Her parents were John McKee and Violet Miller. McCottry attended Barber Scotia Junior College at Concord, North Carolina, before enrolling at Johnson C. Smith University in Charlotte. She later became that school's first alumna to earn a medical degree. After completing a biology bachelor's degree in 1941, McCottry was accepted at the Howard University School of Medicine in Washington, D.C. Dr. Charles Drew, who developed blood banks, was one of her professors and influenced her surgical skills.

McCottry graduated in 1945 and trained in several residencies, specializing in obstetrics and gynecology at New York's Harlem Hospital, Charlotte's Good Samaritan Hospital, and Chicago's Providence Hospital. In 1946 McCottry began practicing medicine in her hometown and was the first black woman physician there. She received her professional license in 1950. She married Turner McDonald McCottry, a Charleston native and graduate of Meharry Medical College in Nashville, Tennessee. They had two children.

Moving to Charleston in 1952, McCottry joined her husband, who established a general practice with obstetrics and gynecology services. He became chief of staff at the McClennan-Banks Memorial Hospital. The couple were Charleston's first African American team of physicians, and she was the city's first black woman to practice gynecology and obstetrics. Catherine McCottry became noted for her direct patient care services and was a leader in the drive to integrate hospitals in Charleston in the 1960s. She retired from practicing medicine in the early 1970s but continued her medical service in other forums. Her husband died in 1996.

Throughout her career McCottry emphasized public health education, especially for sickle-cell anemia, which affects primarily blacks. She served as chairperson for the health committee of the African American sorority Alpha Kappa Alpha. Many of her educational initiatives addressed young women. McCottry implemented prenatal-care counseling programs for pregnant teenagers. She lectured about prevention, symptoms, and treatments for the American Cancer Society. McCottry also taught young adults about hypertension and stress reduction.

McCottry received numerous awards and accolades for her volunteer and professional work. National politicians including President Bill Clinton, Senators Ernest Hollings and Strom Thurmond, and Congressman James Clyburn wrote commendation letters accompanying the Women Who Make a Difference Award. In 2000 Charleston mayor Joseph P. Riley proclaimed that May 23 was Dr. Catherine McCottry Day. McCottry also was featured in that year's BellSouth Corporation's African American History Calendar. ELIZABETH D. SCHAFER

McCrady, Edward, Jr. (1833–1903). Lawyer, soldier, legislator, historian. McCrady was born on April 8, 1833, in Charleston, the second son of Edward McCrady and Louisa Rebecca Lane. In 1853 he received his degree from the College of Charleston and began to read law in his father's office. Admitted to the bar in 1855, McCrady energetically pursued his career. On February 24, 1863, McCrady married Mary Fraser Davie.

Edward McCrady. Courtesy, South Carolina Historical Society

Following South Carolina's secession in December 1860, McCrady enlisted in Confederate service as a captain. Promoted to lieutenant colonel, McCrady was seriously wounded at Second Manassas (August 29–30, 1862) but returned to active duty to fight at Fredericksburg (December 1862). Injured in 1863, he left combat duty and assumed command of an instructional camp at Madison, Florida, in 1864. After the Civil War, McCrady served as major general in the South Carolina militia and worked with the Survivors' Association to collect records of South Carolina's involvement in the war.

During Reconstruction, McCrady enhanced his legal career by trying bank and railroad cases. He actively campaigned for the election of Wade Hampton III for governor in 1876. McCrady also played a prominent role in the post-Reconstruction disenfranchisement of African Americans, writing the infamous Eight Box Law of 1882. A political conservative, McCrady espoused limiting political participation by blacks and poor whites, leaving the levers of government firmly in the hands of a white elite. Elected to the S.C. House of Representatives, he represented Charleston County from 1880 to 1890.

McCrady wrote political pamphlets before publishing his first historical article, "Education in South Carolina prior to and during the Revolution," in 1883. This initial voyage into historical waters set the tone for future McCrady contributions: unabashed loyalty to South Carolina. In 1889 the editors of the American Commonwealth

Series asked him to write the South Carolina volume. Although he never wrote for the series, this request was the catalyst for McCrady's thirteen-year odyssey into the history of South Carolina. Given his lack of historical education and his continued pursuit of his legal profession, McCrady's four-volume history of South Carolina from 1670 to 1783 is remarkable. The first volume, *The History of South Carolina under the Proprietary Government, 1670–1719,* appeared in 1897. Though largely a chronicle of political events lacking archival documentation and heavily dependant on the work of the historian William J. Rivers, the volume was favorably received. His second volume, *The History of South Carolina under the Royal Government, 1719–76,* was published in 1899 and relied on previous works by David Ramsay and Alexander Hewatt, but in its writing McCrady also consulted colonial newspapers and other printed materials.

McCrady's last two volumes focused on the Revolutionary War in South Carolina. They were *The History of South Carolina in the Revolution, 1775–80* (1901) and *The History of South Carolina in the Revolution, 1780–83* (1902). McCrady treated the Loyalists in South Carolina fairly, but his work reflected his lowcountry bias. Although he preferred shortcuts to detailed research and ignored South Carolina's rich archival holdings, McCrady nevertheless gave the state a readable history of its formative years.

The South Carolina Historical Society elected McCrady president in 1899, and in 1902 the American Historical Association named him second vice president. He died in Charleston on November 1, 1903, and was buried in the cemetery of St. Philip's Church. ALEXIA JONES HELSLEY

Holden, Charles J. *In the Great Maelstrom: Conservatives in Post–Civil War South Carolina.* Columbia: University of South Carolina Press, 2002.

———. "'The Public Business Is Ours': Edward McCrady, Jr. and Conservative Thought in Post Civil War South Carolina, 1865–1890." *South Carolina Historical Magazine* 100 (April 1999): 124–42.

Obituary. Charleston *News and Courier,* November 2, 1903, p. 3.

McCrady, John (1831–1881). Naturalist. McCrady was born in Charleston on October 15, 1831, the third of fourteen children of the attorney Edward McCrady and Louisa Rebecca Lane. After receiving his basic education in Charleston, McCrady attended the College of Charleston from 1846 to 1850. A superior student, he was strongly influenced by the Charleston lectures of Louis Agassiz and, at various times between 1852 and 1855, attended the Lawrence Scientific School of Harvard College to study with that renowned naturalist. On September 1, 1859, he married Sarah Dismukes. The couple had six children.

Although he published some descriptions of fossil echinoderms and presented papers on other topics, McCrady was mainly interested in hydrozoans and jellyfish. In fact, his lengthy monograph "Gymnopthalmata of Charleston Harbor," which was presented before Charleston's Elliott Society of Natural History in 1857 and later published in the first volume of the proceedings of that society, earned him an enduring place as a pioneer in hydrozoan zoology. Of McCrady's taxa (scientific descriptions), two families, five genera, and thirteen species are valid today. McCrady's detailed and clear descriptions and his excellent illustrations are especially notable. Widely recognized in his field, McCrady's name is affixed to several species described by later zoologists.

While his scientific studies, most of which he presented before the Elliott Society, were acknowledged by his Charleston peers, McCrady gained wider recognition during the late 1850s as a proponent of a science of racial differences. Though later refuted as unscientific, his publications won acclaim among defenders of slavery. Rejecting the sound scientific arguments of his fellow Charlestonian and noted mammalogist John Bachman that all humans constitute a single species, McCrady followed his teacher Agassiz in maintaining that the nonwhite races were separate and inferior creations. McCrady's essays, published in Charleston's *Russell's Magazine* and elsewhere, represented the efforts of an able naturalist to articulate a cultural position in scientific terms.

A passionate champion of secession, McCrady served as an officer in the army of the Confederacy. Devastated by the failure of the movement, he suffered severe depression and eventually resigned the faculty post he had held at the College of Charleston since 1855. Recognizing him as a brilliant student of science, however, Agassiz persuaded McCrady in 1873 to accept a position at Harvard's prestigious Museum of Comparative Zoology. Agassiz died a few months later, and McCrady became professor of zoology at Harvard. Frequently ill and troubled by his perception that Yankee supporters and liberal religious views prevailed at Harvard, McCrady resigned in 1877 and joined the faculty of the University of the South in Sewanee, Tennessee. He devoted much of his time to formulating what he called a law of development and to criticizing Charles Darwin's theory of evolution.

After another illness, McCrady died in Nashville, Tennessee, on October 16, 1881. His body was returned to Sewanee for burial. Although he believed that he had been largely forgotten, McCrady left a lasting legacy through his contributions to science. LESTER D. STEPHENS

Stephens, Lester D. *Science, Race, and Religion in the American South: John Bachman and the Charleston Circle of Naturalists, 1815–1895.* Chapel Hill: University of North Carolina Press, 2000.

Stephens, Lester D., and Dale R. Calder. "John McCrady of South Carolina: Pioneer Student of North American Hydrozoa." *Archives of Natural History* 19 (1992): 39–54.

McCray, Carrie Allen (b. 1913). Poet, author. McCray was born in Lynchburg, Virginia, on October 4, 1913, the ninth of ten children born to the lawyer William Patterson Allen and his wife, Mary Rice Hayes, a teacher. When she was seven, McCray's parents moved the family to Montclair, New Jersey. Growing up in Montclair, McCray was conscious of racial tension, including a threatened cross burning. She also enjoyed a strongly supportive family environment established by her parents, who were active members of their community and deeply committed to cultural and civic involvement. As a youngster, McCray was accustomed to the presence of guests in her home, including the poet Langston Hughes and the author James Weldon Johnson. After high school McCray attended Talladega College in Alabama, earning a B.A. degree in 1935. She received a master's degree in social work from New York University in 1955. In 1940 she married Winfield Scott Young. The couple had one son before the marriage ended in divorce in 1945. Her second marriage, to the South Carolina civil rights leader John H. McCray in 1964, lasted until his death in 1987. She has made her home in Columbia since 1986.

Although she spent the bulk of her adult life thinking of herself as a teacher and social worker, McCray was aware that she loved to write. She wrote, in fact, throughout the years of her higher education and her two marriages and child rearing. She did not start to think of herself as a professional writer until she reached the age of seventy-three, at roughly the same time she took up residence in Columbia. Though best known as a poet, McCray is also the author of a personal memoir, *Freedom's Child: The Life of a Confederate*

Carrie Allen McCray. Courtesy, Carrie Allen McCray

General's Black Daughter (1998), which details her discovery that her mother was the child of a Confederate general and his black servant. The book stands as an important contribution to the art of memoir in America as well as to the American tradition of facing social injustice in literature as well as in life.

McCray's published works include "Ajos Means Goodbye," a story published in *Beyond the Angry Black* (1966); "The Black Woman and Family Roles," an article included in *The Black Woman* (1980); and the poetry chapbook *Piece of Time* (1993). Her poetry has been published in magazines and journals including *Ms. Magazine, River Styx, Point,* and *The Squaw Review.* Her work has been anthologized in *Moving beyond Words* (1994) and *The Crimson Edge: Older Women Writing* (1996). PHEBE DAVIDSON

McCray, John Henry (1910–1987). Journalist, civil rights activist. Born in Youngstown, Florida, on August 25, 1910, McCray was the eldest of seven children born to Donald Carlos McCray and Rachel Rebecca Montgomery. At age six, McCray moved with his family to the all-black community of Lincolnville, near Charleston. He attended graded school in Ladson, graduated head of his class from Lincolnville Graded School, and was valedictorian of the class of 1931 at Avery Institute in Charleston. In 1935 McCray earned a chemistry degree from Talladega College in Talladega, Alabama.

Before he began a distinguished career of journalistic and social activism, McCray worked for the North Carolina Mutual Life Insurance Co., the nation's oldest and largest black-owned life insurance company. A love of writing and a sense of social responsibility drew McCray into journalism. He first served as city editor of the *Charleston Messenger* from 1935 to 1938. In 1939 he started his own newspaper, the *Charleston Lighthouse,* which was later named the *Carolina Lighthouse* to reflect McCray's desire to publish a paper with statewide influence. Two years later McCray took over the *People's Informer,* a newspaper printed in Sumter by the Reverend E. A. Parker. Setting up operations in Columbia, McCray published the first edition of the *Lighthouse and Informer* on December 7, 1941.

With its motto of "Shedding Light for a Growing Race," the *Lighthouse and Informer* fearlessly took on South Carolina's white power structure. Unlike most black newspapers of its day, the *Lighthouse and Informer* gave its readers political commentary, society news, entertainment, and sports. But most of all, it carried news about black people from around the United States and the world. Before ceasing publication in 1954, the *Lighthouse and Informer* had become the state's largest and most politically charged black weekly.

McCray's aggressive style often placed him at odds with white society. In October 1949 McCray reported that an alleged rape of a white woman by a black man was in fact consensual sex. A white reporter, independently of McCray, made the same accusation. Both men were subsequently charged with criminal libel. While the white reporter was never brought to trial, McCray was convicted and served two months on a chain gang. While McCray served his time, his newspaper continued to publish, and he even penned a column critical of the judge who sentenced him. After the *Lighthouse and Informer* closed in 1954, McCray edited regional editions of some of America's most prominent black newspapers, including the *Afro-American Newspapers* (1954–1960), the *Pittsburgh Courier* (1960–1962), the *Chicago Defender* (1962–1963), and the *Atlanta Daily World* (February–September 1964).

McCray's influence was felt beyond the newsroom in breaking new political ground for black South Carolinians. As cofounder in 1944 of the Progressive Democratic Party (PDP), the first black Democratic Party in the South, McCray joined those who protested the national Democratic Party's tolerance of unfair treatment of black South Carolinians. He chaired the Progressive Democratic delegations that challenged the seating of delegates to the Democratic National Conventions in 1944, 1948, and 1956.

McCray ended his full-time journalism career in September 1964 when he joined the staff at Talladega College, where he served in a series of posts, including director of public relations. That same year he married Carrie Allen, who had met McCray when they were students at Talladega. All the while McCray continued to write, providing columns for the *Charleston Chronicle,* a weekly newspaper, and *View South,* a monthly magazine in Orangeburg. Allen University in Columbia and Coastal Baptist Institute awarded McCray honorary doctorate degrees. In 1998 he was posthumously inducted into the University of South Carolina College of Journalism and Mass Communication's Diamond Circle, which honors extraordinary contributions to the profession. McCray died on September 15, 1987, in Sylacauga, Alabama. He was buried in Oak Hill Cemetery, Talladega. HERB FRAZIER

Daniel, Pete. *Lost Revolutions: The South in the 1950s.* Chapel Hill: University of North Carolina Press, 2000.

Egerton, John. *Speak Now against the Day: The Generation before the Civil Rights Movement in the South.* New York: Knopf, 1994.

Greenberg, Jack. *Crusaders in the Courts.* New York: BasicBooks, 1994.

McDuffie, George (1790–1851). Congressman, governor, U.S. senator. The son of John and Jane McDuffie, George McDuffie was probably born on August 10, 1790, in Columbia County, Georgia. His family was poor, and he received little formal education in his early years. By age twelve he was clerk in a country store. Soon thereafter he moved to Augusta, Georgia, to clerk for James Calhoun, an older brother of John C. Calhoun. Impressed with McDuffie's intelligence, Calhoun sent him to live with his brother William. McDuffie attended Moses Waddel's school for a year, then entered South Carolina College in the junior class. After graduating in 1813, McDuffie was admitted to the bar and began practicing law in Pendleton. In 1815 he became the law partner of Congressman Eldred Simkins in Edgefield. On May 27, 1829, McDuffie married Mary Rebecca Singleton. They had one daughter before Mary died on September 14, 1830.

In 1818 McDuffie was elected to the S.C. House of Representatives, where he represented Edgefield District for a single term. When Simkins retired from Congress in 1821, McDuffie was elected to succeed his law partner. He entered Congress as a nationalist and supporter of John C. Calhoun. He soon found himself entangled in the political feud between Calhoun and William H. Crawford of Georgia. During the 1821–1822 congressional term, McDuffie engaged William Cumming, a Crawford supporter, in a bitter newspaper battle. McDuffie and Cumming met on the dueling field three times, and twice McDuffie was severely wounded. Despite the fact that he survived, McDuffie's wounds lingered and contributed to the physical and mental decline of his later years.

As a devout nationalist during his first years in Congress, McDuffie considered states' rights to be political heresy. But he changed his position during the 1820s after Congress passed a series of tariffs that he thought harmed South Carolina and unfairly benefited the North. In a widely circulated 1830 speech before Congress, McDuffie asserted that consumers, not producers, bore the brunt of the tariff, which cost southern planters the equivalent of forty out of every one hundred bales of cotton they produced. The "forty-bale" theory, though dubious economics, nevertheless gained wide acceptance among southern planters, who blamed the tariff for low cotton prices.

McDuffie gained national attention during the nullification crisis. He believed nullification to be a legitimate extraconstitutional measure with secession as its logical conclusion. His fiery speeches in support of nullification, and their appeal among South Carolina voters, may have forced Calhoun to realize that his state and many of its politicians were more radical on the issue than he was. According to the historian William Freehling, McDuffie's inflamed oratory, including a description of the Union as a "foul monster," made him "a living embodiment of the wrath of the nullifiers" to many Americans. He actively participated in the 1832 nullification convention, writing the convention's address to the other states of the Union. Curiously, although a fierce proponent of states' rights, McDuffie supported rechartering the Second Bank of the United States, which other states' rights advocates viewed as another federal usurpation of power.

McDuffie resigned from Congress in 1834 to become governor of South Carolina. During his term South Carolina passed laws severely restricting the legal rights of free blacks in the state. Any free black returning to South Carolina was to be sold back into slavery. South Carolina port officials were to arrest any African Americans serving aboard vessels docked in port. No slaves who had been north of the Mason-Dixon line could be imported into South Carolina, and severe penalties would be enacted on any person who assisted slaves in avoiding state law.

McDuffie's political influence declined after his term as governor. A powerful and provocative speaker during times of crisis, he seemed to lack the cool-headed nature to be politically effective at other times. Elected to the U.S. Senate in 1842, he advocated the subtreasury plan proposed by Democrats and supported the annexation of Texas but opposed that of Oregon, believing that no government could rule people three thousand miles away.

Resigning from the Senate in 1846, McDuffie returned to private life in South Carolina. After his retirement, he became deeply depressed and ultimately became insane. McDuffie died on March 11, 1851, in Sumter District. He was buried in the Singleton family cemetery in Wedgefield. TRENTON HIZER

Fletcher, Ralph Henry. "George McDuffie: Orator and Politician." Master's thesis, University of South Carolina, 1986.

Freehling, William W. *Prelude to Civil War: The Nullification Controversy in South Carolina, 1816–1836.* New York: Harper & Row, 1965.

Green, Edwin L. *George McDuffie.* Columbia, S.C.: State Company, 1936.

McEntire Air National Guard Station. McEntire Air National Guard Station is a 2,400-acre airbase in Richland County near Eastover. It is the home of the South Carolina Air National Guard. The airfield, originally called the Congaree Army Airport, was activated on January 31, 1943. Since World War II it has undergone numerous renovations and name changes as military aviation has evolved. In 1944 the field was transferred to the U.S. Navy and became the Marine Corps Auxiliary Air Facility. The Marines used the base as a fighter pilot training facility until November 1945. On December 9, 1946, the base became the home of the South Carolina Air National Guard and was renamed Congaree Air Base. The base was transferred to the South Carolina Air National Guard on November 8, 1955. In 1960 the air installation was briefly renamed the Congaree Air National Guard Base, but on October 16, 1961, its name was changed to McEntire Air National Guard Base to honor Brigadier General Barnie B. McEntire, the South Carolina Air National Guard's first commander, who had been killed in an air accident in May 1961. During takeoff from Olmstead Air Force Base, the engine on his F-104 Starfighter failed. McEntire managed to guide his jet away from a heavily occupied area of Harrisburg, Pennsylvania, before crashing the fighter on an island in the Susquehanna River. The base was renamed McEntire Air National Guard Station on October 1, 1995. STEVEN D. SMITH

Allen, Carroll L., Jr. *History of the South Carolina Air National Guard and McEntire Air National Guard Station.* Eastover, S.C.: History Office, 169th Fighter Wing, McEntire Air National Guard Station, 1998.

McGowan, Clelia Peronneau (1865–1956). Civic leader. McGowan was born in Columbia on January 30, 1865, the daughter of William R. Mathewes and Eliza Peronneau. Her family was from Charleston, and they returned there after living for several years after the Civil War at their summer home in Habersham County, Georgia. McGowan attended Miss Kelly's School and then studied for a year in Sweden with Rosalie Roos, a pioneer in the women's rights movement in that country. In 1885 she married William C. McGowan of Abbeville. They had three children before his death in 1898. After her husband's death, McGowan moved back to Charleston and became increasingly active in civic affairs. She was the president of the League of Women Voters in Charleston, and shortly after ratification of the Nineteenth Amendment, Governor Robert A. Cooper appointed McGowan to the State Board of Education, making her the first woman appointed to public office in South Carolina.

McGowan's commitment to education was reflected in her other activities in public life. She became involved with the Commission on Interracial Cooperation in 1922 and served as chair of the commission's South Carolina chapter through much of the 1920s and 1930s. In this capacity she led efforts to improve schools for African Americans around the state. She also worked to make library facilities available to all South Carolinians. In 1923 McGowan ran for alderwoman of Ward One of Charleston City Council on the platform "A free library for Charleston." She was elected and served one term in Mayor Thomas P. Stoney's administration as one of the first two women elected to Charleston City Council. On the council

McGowan chaired the Committee on Public Charities and was on several other committees devoted to improving health, welfare, and education in Charleston. Long after her term as alderwoman, she continued to serve on the city Housing Authority.

The most lasting monument to McGowan's civic leadership is the Charleston County Library, which grew out of her work with the Commission on Interracial Cooperation. McGowan envisioned a system of libraries in large towns and county seats and small, traveling libraries to serve rural areas. She helped to secure funding for a library in Charleston from the Rosenwald Fund and the Carnegie Corporation. The library was incorporated in 1930 and opened to the public on January 1, 1931. McGowan served on the library board of directors for twenty-six years. She published a volume of poetry, *Plantation Memories, and Other Poems* (1923), and was a charter member of the Poetry Society of South Carolina. At the age of ninety, McGowan retired from her many public commitments. She died in Charleston on August 13, 1956. BRUCE E. BAKER

Allen, Louise Anderson. "Clelia McGowan's Journey: From the Fires of War to a Life of Social Activism." *South Carolina Historical Magazine* 104 (April 2003): 82–100.

McGowan, Clelia P. *Plantation Memories, and Other Poems.* Philadelphia: John C. Winston, 1923.

"Mrs. Clelia P. McGowan, Former Councilwoman, Dies," Charleston *Evening Post,* August 14, 1956, p. A2.

Verner, Betty. "Charleston Woman First to Hold Office in State." Charleston *News and Courier,* February 25, 1931, p. B10.

Waring, Thomas R. "Traveler's Saga Published." Charleston *News and Courier / Evening Post,* July 4, 1982, p. E2.

McGuire, Frank Joseph (1913–1994). Basketball coach. McGuire was born on November 8, 1913, in New York City, the thirteenth child of Robert and Anne McGuire. He grew up in an Irish-Catholic section of Greenwich Village and was educated in Catholic schools, eventually graduating from St. Francis Xavier High School, where he was a stand-out athlete. After high school he attended St. John's University and played for four years on the baseball and basketball teams, graduating in 1937. After graduation, McGuire was hired by his high school alma mater to teach and coach. His tenure at the school was interrupted by service as a naval officer during World War II. McGuire married Patricia Johnson in April 1940. The couple eventually had three children. Patricia died of cancer in 1967, and McGuire married Jane Henderson on June 3, 1972.

McGuire's first college job was at St. John's University, where he coached basketball from 1947 to 1952. During this time he took the Redmen to four postseason tournaments and was named National Collegiate Athletic Association (NCAA) coach of the year his last season at the school. The University of North Carolina hired McGuire to rebuild its basketball program in 1953, and he stayed at UNC until 1961. In 1957 UNC won NCAA championship with a 32–0 record, and McGuire was again named coach of the year.

Professional basketball came knocking on McGuire's door and he answered, leaving the Tarheels for the job as head coach of the National Basketball Association's Philadelphia Warriors in 1961. He coached the NBA team led center Wilt Chamberlain to the semifinals of the NBA championship before losing to the Boston Celtics. The Warriors franchise was sold at the end of the season, and the team moved to California without their one-season coach.

When the University of South Carolina hired McGuire to be the head basketball coach in 1964, no one dreamed that he would change the face of basketball in the Palmetto State forever. His teams started playing in the old 3,200-seat field house, but part of the deal

Frank McGuire. Courtesy, University of South Carolina Athletic Department

that brought McGuire to Columbia ensured that a new coliseum would be built. In four years the team moved into the 12,401-seat Carolina Coliseum, one of the finest facilities in the South and soon to be known as "the house that Frank built." McGuire's most successful teams at USC played in the early 1970s and featured star players such as John Roche, Bobby Cremins, John Ribock, Tom Owens, and Tom Riker. The 1970–1971 and 1971–1972 teams had perfect home records in the tough Atlantic Coast Conference (11–0 and 13–0). In his twelve seasons in the Carolina Coliseum, McGuire's home record was 137 wins and 28 losses. McGuire retired in 1980 with an overall record of 283 wins and 142 losses. In 1977 the Frank McGuire Arena in the Carolina Coliseum was named in his honor.

McGuire remained in Columbia after his retirement. In 1992 he suffered a debilitating stroke, and he died two years later on October 11, 1994. McGuire was buried at the cemetery of St. Peter's Catholic Church in Columbia. RHETT JACKSON AND PARKER EVATT

Barton, Donald F., and Bob Fulton. *Frank McGuire: The Life and Times of a Basketball Legend.* Columbia, S.C.: Summerhouse, 1995.

McKaine, Osceola Enoch (1892–1955). Civil rights activist. McKaine was born in Sumter on December 18, 1892, the eldest son of Selena McKaine Abraham. After his graduation from Lincoln Graded School in 1908, he took employment on a merchant freighter bound for the West Indies. In 1914 McKaine enlisted in the U.S. Army, seeing service in the Philippines, Mexico, and as a supply officer in France during World War I. Following his discharge in

1919, McKaine resided in New York City and served as national field secretary of the League for Democracy (LFD), a black veterans' organization that sought to secure civil rights legislation. He also served as editor for the LFD's journal, the New York *Commoner.* With the LFD's demise in the early 1920s, he quit the *Commoner* and emigrated from New York to Europe.

McKaine settled in Ghent, Belgium, where he and a partner established a popular supper club known as Mac's Place. Following the German occupation of Belgium in May 1940, McKaine returned to the United States. After his arrival in Sumter in December, word of his return spread among African American circles in South Carolina. He became a popular lecturer and wrote articles for leading black journals, including the Columbia *Palmetto Leader.*

In 1941 the Palmetto State Teachers' Association commissioned McKaine to conduct a survey of the salary disparities between white teachers and black teachers. He was instrumental in devising the "Teachers' Defense Fund," which collected money to finance the subsequent equal pay litigation. McKaine also was deeply involved in consultations with Thurgood Marshall, the chief national legal counsel for the National Association for the Advancement of Colored People. The initial salary-equity lawsuit was won by the black teachers of Charleston in February 1944. This was the first civil rights victory by black South Carolinians in six decades.

Meanwhile, McKaine became associate editor of the *Lighthouse and Informer,* an important black newspaper edited by John H. McCray. Early in 1944 this paper called for the creation of a black political organization to challenge the control of state politics by white Democrats. This new grouping became the Progressive Democratic Party (PDP). On May 24, 1944, McKaine was the keynote speaker at the PDP's initial state convention in Columbia. Moreover, he was among eighteen delegates who unsuccessfully challenged the regular state party contingent at the Democratic National Convention that July in Chicago. In August 1944 the PDP ran McKaine for the U.S. Senate against Governor Olin D. Johnston. McKaine was the first black South Carolinian to run for statewide office since Reconstruction. While he was officially accorded only 3,214 votes, election observers believed that McKaine received a much higher tally.

During his last two years in the United States, McKaine continued to work with the PDP, as well as the *Lighthouse and Informer.* In January 1945 he began service on the Adult Advisory Board for the Southern Negro Youth Congress (SNYC). Later that year he became the first black field agent of the Southern Conference of Human Welfare (SCHW), an interracial civil rights organization operating in the South. He traveled extensively throughout the South promoting SCHW's activities, especially voter registration campaigns. His last major civil rights activity was planning the SNYC's youth legislature for October 1946 in Columbia.

In December 1946 McKaine sailed for Europe to resume managing his cabaret, but the club never regained its prewar success. He died in Brussels on November 17, 1955, and was buried in Walker Cemetery, Sumter. MILES S. RICHARDS

Reed, Linda. *Simple Decency & Common Sense: The Southern Conference Movement, 1938–1963.* Bloomington: University of Indiana Press, 1991.

Richards, Miles S. "The Eminent Lieutenant McKaine." *Carologue* 7 (autumn 1991): 6–7, 14–17.

———. "Osceola E. McKaine and the Struggle for Black Civil Rights: 1917–1946." Ph.D. diss., University of South Carolina, 1994.

McKinney, Nina Mae (ca. 1912–1967). Actress, dancer. McKinney was born Nannie Mayme McKinney in Lancaster. Her parents moved to New York City and left McKinney with her great aunt, Carrie Sanders, who worked as a maid and cook for Colonel Leroy Springs of Springs Industries. When McKinney was twelve, her parents sent for her and she went to live in New York. Four years later she began her entertainment career. Sixteen, sexy, and extraordinarily good-looking, she performed as a chorus girl in Lew Leslie's *Blackbirds* revue in 1928 and was subsequently spotted in the production.

In 1929 McKinney achieved national notoriety by appearing as "Chick," the leading lady in one of Hollywood's first all-black motion pictures, *Hallelujah.* It was the first talking picture produced by King Vidor for Metro-Goldwyn-Mayer (MGM). The film revolved around a country fellow who momentarily fell under the charms of McKinney. Some claimed that McKinney, as "Chick," originated the stereotypical roles of the "Black Temptress" and became the first tragic mulatto in talking pictures, the first light-skinned leading lady, and the first recognized black actress of the silver screen. Most reviewers, including those working for black newspapers, gave favorable critiques to the production. Even W. E. B. Du Bois, known for his frequently scathing commentary, wrote, "beautifully staged under severe limitations . . . a sense of real life without the exaggerated farce and horseplay . . . marks *Hallelujah* as epoch-making." Some maligned the production, however, as "reeking with prejudice" and filled with "*insulting niggerisms.*" Fortunately, almost everyone seemed to like Nina Mae McKinney. On the strength of her performance, she signed a five-year contract with MGM. But working in an industry that had no lead roles for African American women, McKinney found that her time at MGM was generally unrewarding.

In 1929 McKinney toured Europe as a cabaret performer, singing in major nightclubs in Paris and London. Dubbed the "Black Garbo" by Richard Watts, Jr., in the *New York Post,* she was embraced by European audiences. She later starred with Paul Robeson in the play *Congo Road* and the English film *Sanders of the River* (1935). She appeared in several independent films, including *Pie Pie Blackbirds* with Eubie Blake, and then returned to Europe in 1932. By the 1930s McKinney was a guest on network radio programs, but her movie career had stalled. She had been cast in small parts in only two movies, *Safe in Hell* (1931) and *Reckless* (1935). Due to discrimination in the industry, McKinney, like other black actors, did not gain steady film work. When her contract with MGM ended, so did her Hollywood career.

In 1940 McKinney returned to the United States and married the musician Jimmy Monroe. She toured the country with her own band and landed roles in some all-black films. Her last starring film role was in *Pinky,* which was released in 1949 and involved the story of an interracial relationship. McKinney died in New York City on May 3, 1967. She was inducted into the Black Filmmakers Hall of Fame in 1978. MARILYN KERN-FOXWORTH

Bogle, Donald. *Brown Sugar.* New York: Da Capo, 1980.

———. *Toms, Coons, Mulattoes, Mammies, and Bucks: An Interpretive History of Blacks in American Film.* 4th ed. New York: Continuum, 2001.

Pettus, Louise. "Lancaster's Celebrated Film Star." *Sandlapper* 7 (spring 1996): 62–63.

McKissick, James Rion (1884–1944). Journalist, educator, university president. McKissick was born in Union on October 13, 1884, the son of Isaac Going McKissick and Sarah Foster. He graduated from South Carolina College in 1905 and attended Harvard

Law School before turning to a career in journalism. At the *Richmond (Va.) Times-Dispatch,* McKissick rose from reporter to chief editorial writer. In 1914 he returned to South Carolina, where he was admitted to the bar and practiced law until joining the *Greenville News* in 1916 as editor. In 1919 McKissick became editor of another leading newspaper, the *Greenville Piedmont.*

McKissick was elected to the University of South Carolina's board of trustees in 1924 and then joined the faculty in 1927 as dean of the School of Journalism. He married Caroline Virginia Dick that same year. During his tenure as dean, he earned a master of arts in journalism from the University of Wisconsin. Although he did not have a doctorate, McKissick excelled as a teacher and mentor to his students, who affectionately dubbed him "the Colonel." In 1936 McKissick became one of the few Carolina alumni to become the university's president. He was devoted to the university, writing in 1942, "I would rather be president of the University than hold any other position in this state and country. . . . If I could live my life over, I would give much more of it to Carolina."

McKissick led the university through the tumultuous times of the Great Depression and World War II. With help through the New Deal, McKissick presided over the construction of a new library and five dormitories, as well as a general refurbishment of the campus. During World War II, McKissick guided the university into the war effort, establishing civilian pilot and laboratory technician training programs, adjusting the curriculum to include defense-oriented science and engineering courses, and establishing the nation's first Red Cross nurse's aide course.

McKissick's greatest accomplishments may have come in public relations for the university. He declared that the institution had long been the target of "unjustifiable criticism" and discrimination in state appropriations because of a century-long "whispering campaign" against the university by its enemies. As a result of his successful efforts to dispel the insinuations that Carolina was an immoral and elitist institution, the university made great gains in popularity.

McKissick died suddenly of a heart attack on September 3, 1944. "The Colonel" was such a respected and beloved figure to students and faculty that they petitioned the university's board of trustees to allow McKissick to be buried on campus, the only person ever to receive such an honor. After the funeral service during which his body lay in state in the new library, students laid McKissick to rest in front of the South Caroliniana Library, which he had helped to establish through the donation of his own personal collection of more than five thousand books, manuscripts, and papers. Several months after his death, the new university library was named for McKissick. ELIZABETH CASSIDY WEST

"M'Kissick Rites to Be Tomorrow." *Columbia Record,* September 4, 1944, pp. 1, 2.

Lesesne, Henry H. *A History of the University of South Carolina, 1940–2000.* Columbia: University of South Carolina Press, 2001.

McKissick family. The McKissick family has been an important force in the textile industry in the upstate since the early twentieth century. Anthony Foster McKissick (1869–1938) was born on June 10, 1869, in Union, the son of Isaac Going McKissick, a lawyer and state legislator, and Sarah Foster. He graduated from South Carolina College in 1889 and earned a master's degree in mechanical engineering at Cornell University in 1895. On December 17, 1891, McKissick married Margaret Adger Smyth (1870–1948), daughter of the textile pioneer Ellison Adger Smyth. From 1891 to 1898 McKissick taught electrical engineering and physics at the Alabama Polytechnic Institute, where he did some of the earliest research in the South on X-rays and the transmission of electric power and its application to farming.

McKissick's career in textiles began in 1899, when he began working as an engineer for the Pelzer Manufacturing Company, where his father-in-law served as president. In 1902 McKissick became president of Grendel Cotton Mills in Greenwood. He joined Ninety Six Cotton Mill as a vice president a few years later and became president of that mill in 1908. McKissick sold his interests in these mills by 1918, temporarily retired from the textile business, and moved from Greenwood to Greenville County. While in Greenville, he served in the S.C. House of Representatives from 1923 to 1926. In 1923, in partnership with his only son, Ellison, Foster McKissick bought Alice Mill in Easley, making substantial improvements to that property. They renamed it the Alice Manufacturing Company. In 1928 Alice Manufacturing Company built another mill between Easley and Pickens. Anthony Foster McKissick retired, again, later that year. He died in Greenville on April 8, 1938.

Ellison Smyth McKissick (1892–1966) was born on September 14, 1892, in Greenville. He attended Woodberry Forest School and Alabama Polytechnic Institute, graduating in June 1915 with a B.S. in civil engineering. He went to work for his father at Grendel, but in 1917 Ellison joined the army and served in World War I, where he was promoted to captain. Returning to Greenville, McKissick went to work for J. E. Sirrine and Company, one of the state's leading textile engineering and design firms. He married Jean Reamsbottom on September 1, 1920, and they had four children. He retired in 1953 and died in Greenville on January 30, 1966.

Ellison Smyth "Bubby" McKissick, Jr. (1928–1998), was born on July 29, 1928, in Greenville, the youngest of his parents' four children. He graduated from Greenville High School and attended Clemson University and Presbyterian College. After completing a tour of duty with the U.S. Marine Corps during the Korean War, McKissick became treasurer of Alice Manufacturing Company in 1953 and was made president two years later. He married Noel Caroline Parker of Greenville on February 19, 1955. They had three children. McKissick oversaw the expansion of the company in the 1950s, including the construction of new mills in Pickens County. He became a national spokesman for the textile industry, serving as president of the American Textile Manufacturers Institute. He retired in 1988, turning over the presidency of Alice Manufacturing Company to his son, Ellison Smyth McKissick III. Ellison Smyth McKissick, Jr., died in Greenville on June 27, 1998. BRUCE E. BAKER

Graydon, Nell S., Augustus T. Graydon, and Margaret McKissick Davis, eds. *The McKissicks of South Carolina: The Stories of a Piedmont Family and Related Lines.* Columbia, S.C., 1965.

Lunan, Bert, and Robert A. Pierce. *Legacy of Leadership.* Columbia: South Carolina Business Hall of Fame, 1999.

McLaurin, John Lowndes (1860–1934). Congressman, U.S. senator. McLaurin was born in Marlboro County on May 9, 1860, the oldest son of Philip Bethea McLaurin and Tommie Jane Weatherly. Both parents came from prosperous antebellum planter families prominent in the Pee Dee. McLaurin was graduated from Carolina Military Institute in Charlotte, North Carolina, in 1880. From 1880 to 1882 he attended law school at the University of Virginia. He was admitted to the South Carolina Bar in 1882 and opened a law office in Bennettsville. On February 19, 1883, McLaurin married

Lenora J. Breeden, the daughter of Thomas J. Breeden, a prosperous Marlboro farmer. Their marriage produced six children.

From 1883 to 1892 McLaurin practiced law with former judge John P. Townsend. In 1885 McLaurin met Benjamin Ryan Tillman when the South Carolina Agricultural and Mechanical Society convened in Bennettsville. During the next five years McLaurin became a supporter of Tillman's Farmers' Association. In 1890, benefiting from Tillman's popularity, McLaurin was elected to the S.C. House of Representatives from Marlboro County. The following year McLaurin was elected attorney general, and he focused on prosecuting cases against the phosphate industry and railroad regulation. In November 1892, with Tillman's endorsement, McLaurin was elected to the U.S. House of Representatives.

As a member of the House from 1892 to 1897, McLaurin increased his influence in state and national politics. On the national scene he was a strong advocate of free silver, frequently using his oratorical talents throughout the nation. In state political circles he was a leading Tillmanite. However, in 1894 McLaurin campaigned against the South Carolina dispensary system and supported William H. Ellerbe for governor over Tillman's handpicked successor, John Gary Evans. In 1895 McLaurin opposed Tillman's plan to convene a constitutional convention. By early 1896 the two men seemed to have set aside their differences, evidenced by McLaurin's spirited defense of Tillman from a verbal attack by Richmond Pearson, a Republican representative from North Carolina.

When U.S. Senator Joseph Earle died in May 1897, Governor William H. Ellerbe appointed McLaurin to the seat. In a special election in August, McLaurin easily defeated two other candidates for the remaining five years of the term. Over the next few years McLaurin began to espouse his program of "Commercial Democracy," which called for the expansion of the protective tariff to cover raw materials produced in the South and advocated the development of the textile industry in the state. McLaurin's final break with Tillman and the Democrats came when he cast the deciding vote that ratified the Treaty of Paris in 1899, which ended the Spanish-American War. Tillman opposed provisions in the treaty that permitted the United States to annex former Spanish colonies, including the Philippines. Over the next two years McLaurin voted with the Republicans on several issues, including subsidizing the shipping industry, the gold standard, and territorial expansion by the United States. The ill feeling between McLaurin and Tillman reached a climax on February 22, 1902. In a speech on the Senate floor, Tillman accused McLaurin of selling his vote on the Treaty of Paris for patronage in South Carolina. McLaurin called the accusation "a willful, deliberate, and malicious lie." Tillman immediately sprang across two desks and landed a blow to McLaurin's forehead. McLaurin responded by hitting Tillman in the nose. After a brief struggle, the two men were separated by nearby senators. The Senate subsequently censured both men, but the fight effectively ended McLaurin's U.S. Senate career as Tillman used his influence to insure that McLaurin could not run for reelection.

After a brief stint practicing law in New York City, McLaurin returned to Marlboro County in 1905 and became an advocate for the cotton farmers, championing the establishment of a cotton warehouse system. A year after his election to the state Senate in 1913, McLaurin successfully guided the Cotton Warehouse Act through the legislature. This act established a state warehouse system to remove surplus cotton from glutted markets in order to boost prices. He was subsequently elected the first warehouse commissioner. Resigning in 1917, McLaurin made an unsuccessful bid for governor in 1918 before returning to Marlboro County to concentrate on his agricultural and business pursuits. He died of a heart attack on July 29, 1934, and was buried in McCall Cemetery, Bennettsville. RODGER E. STROUP

Stroup, Rodger E. "John L. McLaurin: A Political Biography." Ph.D. diss., University of South Carolina, 1980.

McLeod, Thomas Gordon (1868–1932). Governor. McLeod was born in Lynchburg, Sumter County (later Lee County), on December 17, 1868, the son of William James McLeod, a merchant and planter, and Amanda Rogers. After attending public schools in Sumter County, McLeod entered Wofford College in Spartanburg, graduating in 1892 with a B.A. degree. After participating in a summer legal course at the University of Virginia, he returned to South Carolina and read law in the Sumter law offices of Purdy and Reynolds. McLeod was admitted to the South Carolina Bar in 1896 but returned to Lynchburg to manage his father's mercantile business. On December 31, 1902, he married Elizabeth Jane Alford. They had four children. In 1903 McLeod moved his family to Bishopville and established a law practice.

Governor Thomas G. McLeod (left) with evangelist Billy Sunday at the Governor's Mansion. Courtesy, South Caroliniana Library, University of South Carolina

In November 1900 the voters of Sumter County elected McLeod to the state House of Representatives. Two years later he advanced to the upper House as the first elected state senator from the newly created Lee County. He served as lieutenant governor of South Carolina during Governor Martin F. Ansel's two terms in office (1907–1911). In 1910 McLeod lost a bid for governor to Cole Blease, and he lost an election for the U.S. House of Representatives in 1918. In August 1922 McLeod became the Democratic candidate for governor, and he won the office in the November election. He was reelected two years later.

Inaugurated on January 16, 1923, McLeod took office amid a prolonged statewide agricultural depression. Despite the economic crisis, McLeod advocated increased legislative spending on public education. As governor, he signed the 6-0-1 Law, which guaranteed all children in South Carolina at least six months of schooling annually. To relieve the property tax burden of hard-pressed farmers, McLeod advocated luxury taxes as an alternative source of revenue. He also supported attempts to frame a more equitable property tax structure. In 1925 McLeod called a statewide convention to investigate tax reform measures. A "Committee of Seventeen" made extensive recommendations to the legislature the following year, but no serious action was taken. McLeod enjoyed partial success in convincing the General Assembly to appropriate funds to expand and improve the state's road system. During his second term he called for the reorganization of various state agencies to improve government efficiency and endorsed a constitutional amendment to limit the governor to a single four-year term.

With the completion of his second term in January 1927, McLeod resumed his law practice and pursued business and agricultural interests in Lee County and Columbia. He died in Columbia on December 11, 1932, and was buried in the Bishopville Methodist Churchyard. MILES S. RICHARDS

Bailey, N. Louise, Mary L. Morgan, and Carolyn R. Taylor, eds. *Biographical Directory of the South Carolina Senate, 1776–1985.* 3 vols. Columbia: University of South Carolina Press, 1986.

McLeod, Thomas Gordon, and Elizabeth Alford McLeod. Papers. South Caroliniana Library, University of South Carolina, Columbia.

McMillan, Claude Richelieu (1899–1961). Engineer. Born in Mullins on November 8, 1899, McMillan was the son of Malcolm L. McMillan and Mary Alice Keith. He earned a degree in civil engineering from the University of South Carolina in 1922. On January 27, 1923, he joined the South Carolina Highway Department. He married Mary King on December 5, 1923, and they had three children.

Over the years the Highway Department promoted the able engineer and administrator from junior engineer to district engineer, and in January 1941 he was named state highway engineer. As state engineer, McMillan advocated the change from concrete- to bituminous-surfaced highways.

On July 17, 1947, the State Highway Commission dismissed J. Stanley Williamson and named McMillan chief highway commissioner effective July 18. This appointment climaxed months of rivalry between McMillan and his predecessor. A court challenge ensued, and the South Carolina Supreme Court ruled that the Highway Commission could not dismiss a chief commissioner during his elected term "without due cause." Williamson returned with reduced responsibilities, but McMillan held the actual power with the title of "executive secretary." Williamson resigned in September 1948.

McMillan's tenure as chief highway commissioner was one of unparalleled growth. He created a division to oversee license examinations and the Highway Patrol; survived a struggle with Governor Strom Thurmond over converting the patrol into a state police organization; and created a public affairs office. In 1950 he successfully lobbied for a one-cent increase in the state gas tax to fund construction and maintenance of South Carolina's burgeoning highway system. In January 1952 he had signs erected at South Carolina's borders that read "Welcome to South Carolina. See the Best State on the Best Roads."

In addition, McMillan worked to convince the General Assembly that work on a statewide highway system was never complete and that paving farm-to-market (secondary) roads led to increased highway fatalities. To McMillan, the key to safe roadways was the construction of controlled-access highways with frontage roads.

On February 16, 1956, his pioneering vision became a reality when the South Carolina General Assembly approved construction of limited-access highways with adjacent frontage roads. Four months later the U.S. Congress authorized $32.5 billion for road construction and launched the era of the interstate highway.

Active in his profession, McMillan was president of the South Carolina Society of Engineers and of the prestigious American Association of State Highway Officials. In 1957 Clemson University honored him with an honorary doctor of engineering degree.

The pinnacle of McMillan's fourteen-year career was when the U.S. Congress authorized $98 million over three years for South Carolina's interstates. To McMillan, the interstate system was "the greatest public works construction program the world has ever known." He awarded South Carolina's first interstate contract in 1956. After a long illness, McMillan died in Columbia on February 12, 1961, and was buried in Elmwood Cemetery. ALEXIA JONES HELSLEY

Moore, John Hammond. *The South Carolina Highway Department, 1917–1987.* Columbia: University of South Carolina Press, 1987.

McNair, Robert Evander (b. 1923). Attorney, legislator, governor. McNair was born on December 14, 1923, at Cades in Williamsburg County, the only child of Daniel Evander McNair and Claudia Crawford. He was raised at the family home in Berkeley County and graduated from Macedonia High School. During World War II, McNair enlisted in the U.S. Navy, attained the rank of lieutenant (jg), and served twenty-two months in the Pacific theater. He was awarded the Bronze Star Medal for his actions in rescuing thirty-five personnel from a destroyed Liberty Boat. McNair married Josephine Robinson of Allendale in San Francisco on May 30, 1944, only days prior to his being shipped overseas. The marriage produced four children.

Robert Evander McNair as lieutenant governor (circa 1962). Photograph by James G. Wilson. Courtesy, *Greenville News*

After military service, McNair returned to the University of South Carolina, where he earned the A.B. degree in 1947 and the LL.B. in 1948. He entered law practice in Moncks Corner and ran for political office for the first time, losing in a 1948 race for the House of Representatives. It would be the only loss of his political career. The McNairs moved to Allendale, where he set up law practice and ran again for public office. He won the state House seat from Allendale County in 1950 and launched a successful political career that would gain him statewide and national attention over the next two decades.

McNair entered the House of Representatives in 1951 and quickly attained positions. He became chairman of the House Committee on Labor, Commerce, and Industry in his second term and shepherded through the state's right-to-work law that limited the power of labor unions and strengthened the state's industrial recruitment efforts. Two years later, in 1955, McNair became chairman of the powerful House Judiciary Committee, a position he held until he ran for lieutenant governor in 1962. McNair won that contest, defeating Oconee County senator Marshall J. Parker.

McNair became governor on April 22, 1965, upon the resignation of incumbent governor Donald S. Russell, who stepped down to fill the U.S. Senate seat vacated by the death of Olin D. Johnston. McNair was elected to a full term on November 8, 1966, with significant support from newly enfranchised black voters, defeating Republican Joseph O. Rogers of Manning.

The McNair administration coincided with major civil rights initiatives and significant public protests and demonstrations in the last half of the 1960s. In 1967 a classroom boycott at South Carolina State College resulted in the replacement of the college's president, changing of student roles and procedures, and significant new funding for the institution. The following year, on February 8, protests at a segregated bowling alley in Orangeburg resulted in the killing of three demonstrators and the wounding of thirty-two others on the S.C. State campus. At the Medical College Hospital in Charleston, a 113-day strike from March to June 1969 protested wages and working conditions among low-income black workers and sought to gain state recognition for their union local. The governor also faced two weeks of protests against the Vietnam War at the University of South Carolina in the spring of 1970 by students seeking to close the institution in the wake of the shooting deaths of four students at Kent State University in Ohio.

Except for the tragedy at Orangeburg in February 1968, McNair saw the state peacefully through the stormy times without yielding on major policy issues. Settlement of the Charleston strike without union recognition in 1969 and keeping USC open in 1970 without serious injury to students were foremost among many public demonstrations in the state in which his moderate leadership was credited with minimizing violence.

McNair also guided the state peacefully through the first year of total desegregation of the public school system in 1970. He counseled South Carolinians at the time, "We have run out of courts and we have run out of time. We will comply with the court rulings." McNair made the first appointments of black citizens to state boards and commissions and desegregated his own executive staff in the Governor's Office.

McNair's support for public education was also evident in several initiatives. He championed compulsory school attendance as part of a comprehensive package of economic and educational proposals. He was successful in initiating public kindergartens, as well as developing programs designed to smooth the desegregation process. McNair pursued the recruitment of new industries and jobs, and he began the program of soliciting overseas investments, a strategy that blossomed under subsequent governors. It was also at his recommendation that the Department of Parks, Recreation, and Tourism was created in 1967, triggering the state's long and successful development of tourism as a multibillion-dollar industry.

After leaving office in January 1971, McNair established the McNair Law Firm in Columbia, which grew to become one of the major firms in the South. He did not seek or serve in public office again after 1971. PHILIP G. GROSE, JR.

Bass, Jack, and Jack Nelson. *The Orangeburg Massacre.* 2d ed. Macon, Ga.: Mercer University Press, 1996.

McNair, Robert E. Papers. Modern Political Collections, South Caroliniana Library, University of South Carolina, Columbia.

McNair, Ronald Erwin (1950–1986). Astronaut. McNair was born on October 21, 1950, in Lake City, the second of three sons born to Carl McNair, an auto mechanic, and his wife, Pearl Montgomery. Reared in a rural, segregated southern community, McNair

Ronald McNair. Courtesy, NASA

developed an interest in science and space travel at the age of seven when the first *Sputnik* satellite went into orbit. At age nine he challenged his segregated world when he tried to check out books from the Lake City Library and won the privilege of borrowing books.

McNair graduated from Carver High School in 1967 as class valedictorian, having become a serious student fascinated by science at a time when NASA's Apollo missions began to carry human passengers on 500,000-mile flights to the moon and back. He enrolled at North Carolina Agricultural and Technical State University, initially as a music major. But when his aptitude for science was recognized, he was persuaded to concentrate on physics. He graduated magna cum laude from North Carolina A&T with a B.S. in physics in 1971. A Ford Foundation scholarship permitted McNair to attend the Massachusetts Institute of Technology (MIT), where he received his doctorate in physics in 1976. On June 27, 1976, McNair married Cheryl Moore from Jamaica, New York. They had two children.

While at MIT, McNair specialized in quantum electronics and molecular spectroscopy, conducting significant work in the development of laser technology. In 1975 he studied laser physics at the École D'ete Theorique de Physique at Les Houches, France. The following year McNair became a staff physicist at Hughes Research Laboratory in Malibu, California, where he continued his laser research. His work attracted the attention of NASA, and in 1978 McNair was selected as an astronaut candidate. He moved with his family to Houston, Texas. After evaluation and training, McNair qualified as a mission specialist astronaut.

The second African American in space, McNair made his first flight in February 1984 aboard the space shuttle *Challenger.* His assignments included operating a remote sensory camera and a new fifty-foot remote manipulator arm designed to remove damaged satellites in space. He monitored space gases, tested solar cells, and was the first person to play a saxophone in orbit.

McNair was slated to undertake his second shuttle mission in January 1986. His scientific duties were to have included deployment of a telescopic camera to study Haley's Comet. Tragically, the space shuttle *Challenger* exploded shortly after its launch at the Kennedy

Space Center, Florida, on January 28, 1986, killing McNair and his six fellow crew members. McNair was buried in Rest Lawn Cemetery in Lake City. MARY S. MILLER

Kessler, James H., et al., eds. *Distinguished African American Scientists of the 20th Century.* Phoenix: Oryx, 1996.

McGuire, Stephen. "Ronald E. McNair." *Physics Today* 39 (April 1986): 72–73.

McSweeney, Miles Benjamin (1855–1909). Governor. McSweeney was born in Charleston on April 18, 1855, the eldest son of Miles and Mary McSweeney. Following his father's sudden death from yellow fever in 1859, McSweeney helped to support the family by earning money as a newsboy. Later he worked in a Charleston bookstore and became interested in the printing trade. While serving as an apprentice printer, McSweeney completed his basic education by attending night school. He was awarded a scholarship from the Charleston Typographical Union to attend Washington and Lee University in Lexington, Virginia. However, insufficient funds forced him to terminate his studies before he had completed his first term.

Returning to South Carolina, McSweeney relocated in 1877 to Ninety Six, where he published the *Ninety Six Guardian* in partnership with Milledge Bonham. McSweeney later moved to Hampton and started the *Hampton County Guardian* in 1879. He became an active member of the South Carolina Press Association, serving as president from 1885 to 1892. While primarily a journalist, he also pursued a variety of business interests. On July 12, 1886, McSweeney married Mattie Miles Porcher of Hampton. They had six children.

McSweeney became an influential member of the Democratic Party in Hampton County, serving as chairman of the county's Democratic committee from 1884 until 1894. In 1894 he was chosen to represent Hampton County in the state House of Representatives. Two years later McSweeney was elected lieutenant governor, to which office he was returned in 1898. Following the death of Governor William H. Ellerbe, McSweeney was elevated to the governorship on June 3, 1899. The following year McSweeney was elected to a full two-year term after overcoming a considerable challenge from the prohibitionist candidate James A. Hoyt. Much of the credit for McSweeney's victory could be traced to the support he received from U.S. Senator Benjamin R. Tillman.

McSweeney's tenure as governor was generally disappointing. He presided over the opening of the South Carolina Inter-state and West Indian Exposition in Charleston, which failed in its design to revive the city's status as a major Atlantic port. McSweeney also failed to convince the General Assembly to increase funding for public education. His defense of the state liquor dispensary system drew the ire of both prohibitionists and progressive Democrats. Finally, just days before the end of his term, McSweeney's lieutenant governor, James Tillman, shot and killed the newspaper editor Narciso G. Gonzales in front of the State House in Columbia.

Constitutionally ineligible to serve another term, McSweeney left office on January 20, 1903, and returned to private life in Hampton. Although he remained active in the Democratic Party, he never held another public office. After a brief illness, McSweeney died on September 29, 1909, at Mount Hope Sanitarium in Baltimore, Maryland. He was buried in Hampton. MILES S. RICHARDS

Bailey, N. Louise, Mary L. Morgan, and Carolyn R. Taylor, eds. *Biographical Directory of the South Carolina Senate, 1776–1985.* 3 vols. Columbia: University of South Carolina Press, 1986.

"Ex-Gov. M'Sweeney Dies in Hospital." Columbia *State,* September 30, 1909, p. 1.

McTyeire, Holland Nimmons (1824–1889). Clergyman. McTyeire was born on July 28, 1824, near Barnwell, the son of John McTyeire and Elizabeth Amanda Nimmons. Family members were prosperous farmers and devout Methodists. Educated at Cokesbury Conference Institute for one year before the family moved to Alabama in 1838, young McTyeire underwent a profound conversion experience and felt called to the ministry. He attended Collinsworth Institute in Talbotton, Georgia, before enrolling at Randolph-Macon College in Virginia in 1841.

Before McTyeire graduated in 1844, the Methodist Episcopal Church had agreed to separate into two sectional denominations over the slavery issue. McTyeire taught at Randolph-Macon for one year, was admitted on trial into the Virginia Conference in 1845, and was appointed to serve the church in Williamsburg. He was admitted into full connection in 1848 and ordained an elder the following year. Subsequently he served churches in Alabama, Mississippi, and Louisiana. He married Amelia Townsend in Mobile, Alabama, on November 9, 1847. They had eight children.

In 1851 McTyeire was one of the founders of the *New Orleans Christian Advocate,* a church newspaper for the southwestern region, and in 1858 he became editor of the *Christian Advocate* in Nashville, the foremost publication of the denomination. He remained in that position, increasingly championing the Southern cause until Nashville was occupied by the Union army in 1862. After the Civil War he became a leader in reorganizing the denomination, calling for the 1866 meeting of the General Conference. At that meeting he was elected a bishop, and he increasingly became the chief spokesman for the Methodist Episcopal Church, South.

McTyeire was a leader in establishing Central University, later Vanderbilt, in Nashville in 1873, and he secured a $1 million gift from Cornelius Vanderbilt, a distant relation. Conditions of the gift included making McTyeire permanent chair of the board of trust, with veto power over its actions. He was designated the sole custodian of the Vanderbilt gift.

McTyeire was the author of books, including *Duties of Christian Masters* (1859), in which he supported slavery but urged compassionate treatment of slaves within the law. He became the chief authority on the denomination's government, publishing *A Catechism on Church Government* (1869) and *A Manual of Discipline of the Methodist Episcopal Church, South* (1870). His most noteworthy book was *A History of Methodism* (1884), written to commemorate the centennial of American Methodism. While it covered primarily the period prior to the division of the church in 1844, it was widely recognized as a fair and evenhanded treatment. McTyeire died at his home on the Vanderbilt campus on February 15, 1889, and was buried on the campus. A. V. HUFF, JR.

Tigert, John James. *Bishop Holland Nimmons McTyeire, Ecclesiastical and Educational Architect.* Nashville, Tenn.: Vanderbilt University Press, 1955.

Means, John Hugh (1812–1862). Governor. Born on August 18, 1812, in Fairfield District, Means was the son of Boston native Thomas Means and Sarah Milling. Means studied at Mount Zion College in Winnsboro and was graduated from South Carolina College in 1832. On January 24, 1833, he married Sarah Rebecca Stark. The couple had two children. Means became a successful planter in Fairfield District. Reaching maturity in the heady days of nullification, Means became a convert to the gospel of states' rights at an early age. Active in the South Carolina militia, he achieved the rank of brigadier general. After serving a single term in the state House of Representatives from 1844 to 1845, Means established himself as one of the leading fire-eaters in the South Carolina upcountry and vocal advocate of secession, a position put forth as a delegate to the Nashville Convention in 1850.

In the campaigns for the state legislature in the fall of 1850, radicals won control of both houses of the General Assembly and elected Means governor on December 13. In his 1851 message to the assembly, Means baldly declared that "the Federal government, which was instituted for our protection and welfare . . . has directed all its energies to the destruction of that very institution upon which our very vitality depends." The Means administration set about to prepare South Carolina for the possibility of secession and conflict with the federal government. He urged that the state's military establishment be strengthened, and the legislature appropriated $350,000 for the purpose of arming the state and placing South Carolina in a defensive position. In addition, brigade encampments for the state militia were reestablished, and Means organized state forces into ten infantry and five cavalry brigades.

Other actions by Means sought to encourage economic development. In 1852, thanks in part to a strong endorsement from the governor, the politically controversial Bank of the State of South Carolina had its charter extended through 1871. Means also supported the allocation of state funds for railroad development, declaring, "the State cannot spend too much money in the construction of Railroads, providing they are judiciously located, and economically built." However, by the close of his term in 1852, calls for immediate secession had died down, and the fire-eater Means was succeeded as governor by the more moderate John L. Manning.

Means retired to private life but reemerged in December 1860 to sign the Ordinance of Secession. When the Civil War broke out in 1861, Means helped organize an infantry unit and was made colonel of the Seventeenth South Carolina Regiment. During the Second Battle of Manassas (August 29–30, 1862), Means was mortally wounded by a shell fragment. He died on September 1 and was buried in the Means family cemetery in Fairfield District. MATTHEW A. BYRON

Medal of Honor recipients. Approved by the United States Congress in 1862, the Medal of Honor is America's highest award for military valor. Thirty native South Carolinians have been awarded the medal for "conspicuous gallantry and intrepidity" above that of their comrades in arms. On rare occasions the Medal of Honor has been awarded for individual exploits taking place in peacetime. Among them is Shipfitter First Class George Huber Wheeler of Charleston, who received the award for extraordinary heroism during a fire at Coquimbo, Chile, on January 20, 1909.

The first South Carolinian to receive the award during military action was Ernest A. Garlington of Newberry, who earned the honor for "distinguished gallantry" against the Sioux Indians at the Battle of Wounded Knee on December 29, 1890. Early in the following century, naval surgeon Middleton Stuart Elliott of Beaufort and Commander William A. Moffett of Charleston each received the decoration during hostilities against Mexican forces at Vera Cruz in April 1914.

Eight South Carolinians were awarded the medal during World War I, including three who made the supreme sacrifice. Six recipients were members of the 118th Infantry, which received more Medals of Honor than any other regiment in the American Expeditionary Forces. Among them was Providence native Corporal James D. Heriot of the Thirtieth Division. Heriot made a lone thirty-yard dash against a German machine gun nest and forced the team to surrender, only to fall himself later that day. In 1991 the sisters of Corporal Freddie Stowers of Anderson County were presented a posthumous award for his extraordinary courage while attempting to destroy a machine gun that had pinned down his men during World War I. Stowers was the only African American from the war awarded the medal.

While serving in Nicaragua between the world wars, Marine Corporal Donald L. Truesdale of Lugoff saved the lives of the members of his patrol by shielding them from the shock of an errant grenade on April 24, 1932. During World War II five South Carolinians were awarded the medal for courage and self-sacrifice. Marine Sergeant Robert A. Owens of Greenville made a charge against a well-placed Japanese gun that was wreaking havoc on American landing operations in the Solomon Islands on November 1, 1943. His sacrifice silenced the gun and paved the way for a successful invasion.

During fighting in the Korean War, three of the four South Carolina recipients were presented the honor posthumously. The fourth, Marine Staff Sergeant Robert Sidney Kennemore of Greenville, miraculously survived the blast of a grenade on which he had thrown himself to protect his platoon. Seven native South Carolinians were awarded the Medal of Honor during American involvement in Vietnam. The last Medal of Honor action of the Vietnam War occurred on Halloween night 1972, when Greenville native Petty Officer First Class Michael Edwin Thornton saved the life of his team leader Lieutenant Thomas Norris. Thornton's is the rare case of one Medal of Honor recipient receiving the award for saving the life of another recipient. SAMUEL K. FORE

Medal of Honor Recipients

*Name (*posthumous award)*	*Place of Birth*	*Branch*	*Date of Action*
Garlington, Ernest A.	Newberry	Army	December 29, 1890
Wheeler, George Huber	Charleston	Navy	20-Jan-09
Kennedy, John T.	Hendersonville	Army	4-Jul-09
Elliott, Middleton Stuart	Beaufort	Navy	April 21 & 22, 1914
Moffett, William A.	Charleston	Navy	April 21 & 22, 1914
Sullivan, Daniel A. J.	Charleston	Navy	21-May-18
Stowers, Freddie*	Anderson Co.	Army	28-Sep-18
Dozier, James C.	Galivants Ferry	Army	8-Oct-18
Foster, Gary Evans	Spartanburg	Army	8-Oct-18
Hall, Thomas Lee*	Fort Mill	Army	8-Oct-18
Hilton, Richmond Hobson	Westville	Army	11-Oct-18
Heriot, James D.*	Providence	Army	12-Oct-18
Villepigue, John C.	Camden	Army	15-Oct-18
Truesdale, Donald Leroy	Lugoff	USMC	24-Apr-32
Owens, Robert Allen*	Greenville	USMC	1-Nov-43
Smith, Furman L.*	Six Mile	Army	31-May-44
Mabry, George L., Jr.	Sumter	Army	20-Nov-44
McWhorter, William A.*	Liberty	Army	5-Dec-44
Atkins, Thomas E.	Campobello	Army	10-Mar-45
Kennemore, Robert S.	Greenville	USMC	November 27 & 28, 1950
Knight, Noah O.*	Chesterfield Co.	Army	November 23 & 24, 1951

Medal of Honor Recipients (continued)

*Name (*posthumous award)*	*Place of Birth*	*Branch*	*Date of Action*
Watkins, Lewis G.*	Seneca	USMC	7-Oct-52
Barker, Charles H.*	Pickens Co.	Army	4-Jun-53
Williams, Charles Q.	Charleston	Army	June 9 & 10, 1965
Williams, James E.	Rock Hill	Navy	31-Oct-66
Anderson, Webster	Winnsboro	Army	15-Oct-67
Hooper, Joe R.	Piedmont	Army	21-Feb-68
Johnson, Ralph H.*	Charleston	USMC	5-Mar-68
Howe, James D.*	Six Mile	USMC	6-May-70
Thornton, Michael Edwin	Greenville	Navy	31-Oct-72

Above and Beyond: A History of the Medal of Honor from the Civil War to Vietnam. Boston: Boston Publishing, 1985.

South Carolina. Medal of Honor Committee. *South Carolina's Recipients of the Medal of Honor: Second Report to the General Assembly.* Columbia, S.C.: The Committee, 1974.

Medical Society of South Carolina. The fourth-oldest medical society in the United States, the Medical Society of South Carolina was founded in 1789 to "improve the Science of Medicine, promoting liberality in the Profession, and Harmony amongst the Practitioners." Though Charleston physicians predominated, membership was open "to any gentleman of merit in the medical profession." Peter Fayssoux served as the organization's first president.

The society quickly acquired a leading role in medical and public health issues. In 1790 the organization planned a dispensary for the relief of the sick and indigent, which evolved into the Shirras Dispensary and served the Charleston community until merging with Roper Hospital in 1921. The society established a medical library in 1791, which helped physicians stay abreast of current literature. In 1801 the Charleston City Council requested that the society form a board of health, and the society appointed officers and a port physician to serve in this capacity. From 1805 to 1815 the society operated a botanic garden to promote "the study of that valuable branch of Science." In 1817 the General Assembly entrusted the society to serve as an examining committee to license physicians and apothecaries, though a license was not required until 1895.

The Medical College of South Carolina was founded by the society in December 1823, with society members constituting six of the original seven faculty members. The school become a state institution in 1913 and the Medical University of South Carolina in 1969. The society opened Roper Hospital in Charleston in 1856. Although management of the facility passed to CareAlliance Health Services in 1998, the society continued its interest in the hospital as a founding member of the CareAlliance corporation.

The Medical Society of South Carolina provided leadership in the founding of the American Medical Association (1847), the South Carolina Medical Association (1848), and the Charleston County Medical Society (1951). In the early twenty-first century the Medical Society of South Carolina remained an active organization, whose interests and activities continued to respond to ongoing evolution of the medical profession. JANE MCCUTCHEN BROWN

Jervey, Louis P., and W. Curtis Worthington, Jr. *The Medical Society of South Carolina: The First Two Hundred Years.* Charleston: Medical Society of South Carolina, 1990.

Medical Society of South Carolina. Minutes (1789–1986). Waring Historical Library, Medical University of South Carolina, Charleston.

Medical University of South Carolina. At the request of the Medical Society of South Carolina, the General Assembly established the Medical College of South Carolina in December 1823. The school opened the following November. The faculty of six physicians offered two courses of lectures leading to the M.D. degree. From 1824 until 1913 the school received no state funding. Students purchased tickets to lectures and paid laboratory fees. The faculty maintained private practices in addition to their teaching duties. From 1823 to 1861 the school rose to national prominence. A building was constructed in 1826 on the corner of Queen and Franklin Streets adjacent to the Marine Hospital and City Hospital. Roper Hospital, built in the 1850s, was also next to the Medical College building. These facilities served as teaching hospitals for the college.

In 1832 the first town/gown discord occurred when the faculty and the Medical Society disagreed on management of the school. The faculty resigned as a body and applied to the General Assembly for a charter for the Medical College of the State of South Carolina. The factions reconciled in 1839, and the faculty moved back into the society building, but the school retained the newer name of the Medical College of the State of South Carolina. The school closed during the Civil War, and afterward the faculty struggled with little money or other resources. There was also competition from a new medical school established in 1866 at South Carolina College in Columbia. To keep the Medical College going, the faculty abolished fees and made it a free school underwritten by the faculty and trustees.

A pharmacy program began in 1881, with the first students admitted in 1882. It lasted just two years but was reactivated as the School of Pharmacy in 1894. A nursing program began as the School of Nursing of City Hospital in 1883, with the first students accepted in 1884. Roper Hospital oversaw the School of Nursing from 1904 until 1919, when it was merged with the Medical College. The faculty voted to admit women medical students in 1895. They were first accepted in 1897 and graduated in 1901.

In 1913 Dean Robert Wilson, head of the Medical College from 1908 to 1943, campaigned for state ownership of the Medical College, whereby the state would assume some financial responsibility for the institution. This followed the 1910 publication of the "Flexner Report," which was highly critical of the Medical College despite its students' high pass rates on state board examinations. State ownership was attained in 1914. The school moved to a new building, built with funds raised by the Charleston community, on a new campus at Calhoun and Lucas Streets across from Roper Hospital.

An allied health program in medical technology began in the late 1920s, and the first full-time faculty was hired in 1937. Kenneth M. Lynch led the school from 1943 to 1960. The School of Graduate Studies began in 1949, and in 1952 the name changed back to Medical College of South Carolina. A second town/gown flap occurred when Lynch decided that the school should have its own teaching hospital. This was a national trend, but Lynch's proposal was not well received by the Medical Society of South Carolina, which opposed separating the college from its dependence on Roper Hospital. The Medical College Hospital opened in September 1955. A School of Dental Medicine was approved by the General Assembly in 1953, but with no funding. The first students were not accepted until 1967 and graduated in 1971. The School of Allied Health Sciences was created in 1966, consolidating a group of programs. In 1969 the college combined all the school programs into six colleges to become the Medical University of South Carolina (MUSC).

The seventeen-year leadership of James B. Edwards, former governor and former U.S. secretary of energy, saw major growth in endowment and research programs. A third town/gown dispute occurred in the 1990s concerning the proposed management of the teaching hospital by Columbia/HCA (Hospital Corporation of America) Health Care Corporation, a for-profit corporation. By 2000 MUSC had a budget of more than $950 million and six colleges. The institution was widely acknowledged as a major academic health care center, maintaining its commitment to health sciences education, research, and patient care. JANE MCCUTCHEN BROWN

Archives of the Medical University of South Carolina, Charleston.
Medical Society of South Carolina. Minutes (1789–1986). Waring Historical Library, Medical University of South Carolina, Charleston.
Waring, Joseph I. *A History of Medicine in South Carolina.* 3 vols. Columbia: South Carolina Medical Association, 1964–1971.
Worthington, W. Curtis, H. Rawling Pratt-Thomas, and Warren A. Sawyer. *A Family Album: Men Who Made the Medical Center.* Spartanburg, S.C.: Reprint Company, 1991.

Medicine. The first physician in South Carolina of European ancestry appears to have been Henry Woodward, a ship's surgeon in the party that landed in 1666 to assess Carolina for the Lords Proprietors and King Charles II. Although the subsequent colonists had among them "doctors" of unknown abilities, they understood the need for "seasoning" (which probably meant acquisition of malaria), and they sometimes marveled at the cures wrought by Native American medicine men. Early on there were outbreaks of malaria (1684), smallpox (1697), yellow fever (1699), and dysentery (1715). Smallpox, imported from Europe, decimated the Native Americans. The slave trade accounted, at least in part, for later epidemics of smallpox and yellow fever and the endemic occurrence of filariasis—a parasitic infection that persisted in the Charleston area until the 1920s. In 1707 the first quarantine station or "pest house" was built on Sullivan's Island, where newly imported slaves were kept prior to their sale in Charleston and elsewhere.

During the eighteenth century, some South Carolina physicians achieved prominence mainly as naturalists. John Lining, who has been called the first American physiologist on the basis of metabolic observations on himself, excelled in botany and meteorology. Lionel Chalmers published in two volumes *An Account of the Weather and Diseases of South Carolina* (1776) and also an *Essay on Fevers* (1767). Alexander Garden was honored by Linnaeus not only in the naming of the cape jasmine (gardenia) but also in the naming of various fish and reptiles. Lining, Chalmers, and Garden were all born in Scotland, which during the early eighteenth century was the most important center of medical education as a result of the Scottish Enlightenment. William Bull II, by graduating at Leyden in 1734, became the first native-born American to receive his medical degree from another country. Later, John Moultrie, Jr., became the first native-born American to receive a medical degree from Edinburgh, where his dissertation on yellow fever was apparently the first systematic account of that disease to emanate from North America. The first attempt at a hospital in South Carolina consisted of a brick building dedicated in 1738 by the vestry of St. Philip's Parish, Charleston.

The Revolutionary War found the colony's physicians, like others, to be divided in their loyalties. Some, including Garden, returned to England. Noteworthy patriots included David Ramsay, Peter Olyphant, and Peter Fayssoux. Olyphant, Fayssoux, and others were among those captured when Charleston fell on May 12, 1780; they bitterly protested the treatment of prisoners by the British. Olyphant later became director of American hospitals to the army commanded by Nathanael Greene and later deputy director of the hospital of the Southern Army. Fayssoux became surgeon general to the Southern Department and chief physician for the Continental Hospital (that is, the Medical Department).

After the war, in 1789, Fayssoux hosted a meeting of Charleston physicians that led to the formation of the Medical Society of South Carolina. Incorporated "to improve the Science of Medicine, promoting liberality in the Profession, and Harmony amongst the Practitioners," the Medical Society was meant to be a statewide organization but in reality represented mainly the Charleston area. Early functions included a fee bill (1792) and a code of ethics (1810) that included a prohibition of dueling by its members on account of a "professional quarrel."

To celebrate the turn of the nineteenth century, Ramsay presented a *Review of the Improvements, Progress and State of Medicine in the XVIII Century* (1801), an early American medical history. Ramsay also started a medical journal (*Charleston Medical Register*), which did not survive beyond its first issue. More South Carolinians began to obtain medical degrees, now usually from the University of Pennsylvania rather than from Europe. Influenced by Benjamin Rush of Philadelphia, the new graduates promoted the use of bloodletting, which was further enhanced in South Carolina by three local translations of the work of the French physician François-Joseph Victor Broussais. South Carolinians who continued the physician-naturalist tradition of the previous century included John Lewis Edward Whitridge Shecut, whose *Flora Carolinensis* (1806) was the best account of botany in the state up to that time; Edmund Ravenel, an authority on conchology; John Edwards Holbrook, an expert on herpetology and ichthyology; Robert Wilson Gibbes, nationally known for his work on fossils; and Henry William Ravenel, who made major contributions to mycology.

The early nineteenth century gave rise to systematic attempts to improve medicine in South Carolina. In 1817 the General Assembly created two examining boards for physicians, apothecaries, and midwives, one of which was to be in Charleston and the other in Columbia. In 1821 Dr. Thomas Cooper, president of South Carolina College, proposed a medical school that would be divided between Columbia and Charleston. In 1822 the Medical Society of South Carolina endorsed Charleston as the sole site, leading to the opening two years later of the Medical College of South Carolina, which reorganized as the Medical College of the State of South Carolina in 1832. In 1827 the South Carolina Lunatic Asylum in Columbia opened its doors to receive patients. The sixth hospital of its kind in the United States and designed by Robert Mills, the institution reflected progressive concepts in the treatment of mental disease. In 1834 a Marine Hospital, also designed in part by Mills, opened in Charleston to replace earlier efforts to care for sick and disabled seamen. Small, private hospitals for slaves were built in Charleston, including a small surgical infirmary opened by the medical school that could be considered the state's first hospital devoted entirely to teaching. In 1856 Roper Hospital, the first community hospital of any size in South Carolina, opened with a daily charge of about 25¢.

These advances met a public need since, as one visitor wrote, "Carolina passes for the most unhealthy province of the United States." Yellow fever struck Charleston, as it did other large ports on the Atlantic seaboard, with increasing frequency and severity as the city grew subsequent to the Revolution. Malaria was responsible for the "sickly season" extending from May until late October or until the first killing frost, which caused lowcountry planters to leave their plantations for areas that were relatively free of the disease. Asiatic cholera appeared episodically. Attempts to regulate medicine through licensing were unsuccessful because, in the context of Jacksonian democracy, alternative practices (such as the botanic cures put forth by the Thomsonians) prevailed. At the eve of the Civil War, there were fewer than one thousand physicians in the state and only four hospitals of any size: three in Charleston and the State Lunatic Asylum in Columbia.

Among the antebellum South Carolina physicians who achieved national prominence were Josiah Clark Nott of Columbia and James Marion Sims of Lancaster District. Nott and Sims both practiced briefly in South Carolina, made their marks as innovative surgeons in Alabama, and enjoyed later success in New York City. Nott proposed in 1848 that yellow fever was of "animalcular origin" and possibly caused by an insect. Sims's cure of vesicovaginal fistula removed the stumbling block to progress in operative gynecology. Theodore Gaillard Thomas, another native South Carolinian, continued Sims's work in New York. Francis Peyre Porcher of Charleston anticipated the germ theory, publishing an article in 1861 on "Illustrations of Disease with the Microscope: Clinical Investigations." When the American Medical Association (AMA) was formed in 1847, James Moultrie, Jr., of Charleston was made vice president, and he served as president in 1850. Moultrie was largely responsible for the organization of the South Carolina Medical Association (1848), of which he served as first president.

South Carolina physicians contributed substantially to the Confederate cause during the Civil War. Julian John Chisolm of Charleston wrote the Confederacy's definitive surgical manual and designed a chloroform inhaler for administering anesthesia. Francis Peyre Porcher published a botanical manual on *Resources of the Southern Fields and Forests,* which allowed soldiers and physicians to improvise when medicine was unavailable. Samuel Preston Moore of Charleston was surgeon general of the Confederate army. Benjamin Walter Taylor of Columbia served as medical director of the Cavalry Corps, the second-highest-ranking medical position in the Southern armies.

After the war tuberculosis became increasingly common in South Carolina, especially among blacks as many freedmen migrated to the towns and cities. Available data suggest that overall mortality rates were roughly similar for blacks and whites before the Civil War; thereafter, mortality rates for blacks became substantially greater. Physicians, like others, struggled during the Reconstruction era, and medical organizations were relatively inactive. In 1865 Charleston established a full-time health department, believed to be the first in the United States. Thomas Grange Simons was instrumental in establishing national quarantine regulations and also a sewage disposal system in Charleston. Legislative acts created the State Board of Health in 1878 and the State Examining Board for physicians in 1894. Memorial Hospital ("City Hospital") was completed in Charleston in 1888, and in 1893 Columbia Hospital opened with twenty-five beds. By 1900 South Carolina had eleven hundred physicians, most of whom were educated at the Medical College in Charleston. A medical school was established at the University of South Carolina in 1867, but although it lasted until 1876, it never recovered from the resignation of the faculty when a black student was admitted. Reorganization of the AMA in 1901 placed emphasis on county medical societies, which expanded and proliferated in South Carolina. In 1905 the *Journal of the South Carolina Medical Association* was begun, with Dr. Robert Wilson (1867–1946) of Charleston as editor.

By the beginning of the twentieth century, yellow fever had ceased its visitations, but South Carolinians were increasingly afflicted with tuberculosis and were still tormented by smallpox, malaria, hookworm, typhoid, typhus, and diphtheria. In 1907 pellagra, previously thought not to occur in the United States, was recognized in South Carolina. James Woods Babcock of Columbia spearheaded a national movement to eradicate the disease. In 1917 Joseph Goldberger of the United States Public Health Service came to South Carolina, where he supervised many of the experiments that established dietary deficiency as the cause of the disease. The occurrence of pellagra and the prevalence of diseases such as typhoid and hookworm underscored the limited access of the rural poor, blacks, and mill workers to public health measures and to adequate medical care.

Blacks and women were underrepresented in the medical profession of South Carolina, as elsewhere. The census of 1890 counted only thirty black physicians in the state. Blacks found it difficult to obtain medical education and more difficult to obtain hospital positions. In 1896 the Palmetto Medical, Dental, and Pharmaceutical Association was founded for African American professionals largely through the efforts of Charles Catlett Johnson, Sr., of Aiken. Other founding members included James Richelieu Levy of Florence, Lawrence A. Earl of Anderson, and Alonzo Clifton McClennan of Charleston. Sarah Campbell Allan of Charleston was the first woman in South Carolina to be duly qualified and licensed by the State Board of Medical Examiners. Lucy Hughes Brown of Charleston seems to have been the first licensed African American woman physician. The first female graduates of the Medical College in Charleston were Love Rosa Hirschmann (later Gantt) and Emilie Melanie Viett (later Rundlett) of the class of 1901. Hilla Sheriff became known as the "first lady of public health" for her pioneering efforts in the upstate.

The Flexner Report of 1910 rendered a scathing analysis of the Medical College in Charleston, threatening its existence, as it did numerous other schools throughout the United States. In 1913 Dean Robert Wilson convinced the state to assume responsibility for the college with an annual appropriation of $10,000. The school later matured with the addition of full-time faculty members under the leadership of Kenneth Merrill Lynch, and in 1955 a five-hundred-bed teaching hospital was added.

Science-based medicine flourished in South Carolina, as elsewhere, during the twentieth century, and some South Carolinians made significant contributions to the medicine of their eras. Among these were James Woods Babcock, a pioneering alienist (psychiatrist); George H. Bunch of Columbia, first president of the South Carolina Surgical Society; J. Heyward Gibbes of Columbia, an outstanding internist; LeGrand Guerry of Columbia, a surgeon with special expertise in acute appendicitis; J. Decherd Guess of Greenville, a nationally recognized obstetrician and gynecologist; James Adams Hayne, who presided over the State Health Department for thirty-three years and whose son, Theodore Brevard Hayne, was the last student of yellow fever to die of that disease while studying it; Edward F. Parker of Charleston, an innovative otolaryngologist; D. Lesesne Smith of Spartanburg, who helped make the annual Southern Pediatric Seminar a nationally recognized model for continuing medical education; William Weston, Sr., of Columbia, arguably the second full-time pediatrician in the Southeast and an expert on nutritional diseases; and Charles Frederick Williams, who succeeded Babcock as superintendent of the South Carolina State Hospital.

Between 1929 and 1932 Theodore McCann Davis of Greenville developed and perfected transurethral resection of the prostate, which became a standard operation throughout the world. In 1940 Austin Tally Moore of Columbia initiated the era of artificial joints when he implanted the world's first metal hip joint in a patient who had suffered a pathologic fracture of the femur due to a tumor. Between 1942 and his untimely death from the disease he sought to cure, Horace Gilbert Smithy, Jr., of the Medical College of South Carolina in Charleston pioneered aortic and mitral valvulotomies, pivotal events in the evolution of open heart surgery.

The closing decades of the twentieth century bore witness to improvements in South Carolina, as elsewhere in the United States, in health-care delivery systems, hospital-based medicine, public health, and the perceived physician shortage. By 1970, however, there were only 77 physicians per 100,000 persons in South Carolina, and the rural population remained poorly served. This physician shortage led to the founding of the University of South Carolina School of Medicine in Columbia, which opened in 1977. As of 2002, there were 8,872 practicing physicians in South Carolina, or 221 per 100,000 persons, with the state's two medical schools graduating about 200 new physicians each year. The South Carolina Medical Association remains robust, and in 2000–2001 a South Carolina physician, Dr. Randolph D. Smoak, Jr., of Orangeburg, served as president of the American Medical Association.
CHARLES S. BRYAN

South Carolina Medical Association. *A Brief History of the South Carolina Medical Association.* Charleston, S.C., 1948.

Waring, Joseph I. *A History of Medicine in South Carolina.* 3 vols. Columbia: South Carolina Medical Association, 1964–1971.

Woods, Barbara A., and Tracy D. Tisdale-Clawson. *A Golden Century of Black Medicine: An Historical Overview of the Palmetto Medical, Dental, and Pharmaceutical Association, 1896–1996.* Orangeburg: South Carolina State University, 1996.

Worthington, W. Curtis, H. Rawling Pratt-Thomas, and Warren A. Sawyer. *A Family Album: Men Who Made the Medical Center.* Spartanburg, S.C.: Reprint Company, 1991.

Memminger, Christopher Gustavus (1803–1888). Lawyer, politician. Memminger was born on January 9, 1803, in Nayhingen, Württemberg, Germany, to Christopher Godfrey Memminger, an army quartermaster, and Eberhardina Elisabeth Kohler. Following his father's death, Memminger's family immigrated to Charleston, where his mother soon passed away. He was left in the Charleston Orphan House at age four and seven years later was adopted by future governor Thomas Bennett. Educated at South Carolina College, Memminger graduated second in his class in 1819. He began practicing law in 1824, the same year he became a naturalized citizen. Memminger had an active interest in education and helped expand the mission of Charleston's public schools beyond serving only paupers. He and his first wife, Mary Wilkinson, married on October 25, 1832, and had eight children.

Although Memminger would reach the height of his political career as a member of the Confederate cabinet, he was slow to convert to the secessionist cause. He opposed nullification in a satirical pamphlet, *The Book of Nullification* (1832). He was elected to the South Carolina House of Representatives four years later and served almost continuously to the outbreak of the Civil War, chairing the Ways and Means Committee. He opposed separate state secession in 1850 and was a Unionist delegate to the southern rights convention in 1852. Only after John Brown's raid did Memminger believe that separation was necessary. He served as a special commissioner to Virginia in January 1860 to encourage that state to secede, and by the end of the year he was vigorously promoting South Carolina's secession.

Christopher Gustavus Memminger (1803–1888), by Charles Fraser. Watercolor on ivory. Courtesy, Gibbes Museum of Art / Carolina Art Association

Memminger's skills were put to immediate use for the Confederacy, as he chaired the committee to draft the Confederacy's provisional constitution. Jefferson Davis tapped him to be secretary of the treasury in 1861, a position in which Memminger would have enormous difficulties, some of which were beyond his control. His plan to raise money through tariffs was hampered by the Union blockade, and the Confederate congress was reluctant to institute taxation when other sources of income proved useless. Other difficulties were self-imposed. Believing that the war would be short, he did not bother early to plan for the long term; his ideological rigidity prevented him from suggesting that the government sell cotton to pay bills (he feared that this would damage private farmers); and he was considered a heavy-handed administrator and was little liked by military officers desperate for funds. With inflation spiraling out of control, he resigned on June 15, 1864, and moved to his summer home in Flat Rock, North Carolina, where he remained until the end of the war.

Pardoned in 1867, Memminger returned to Charleston to resume his law practice. Although he served one more term in the General Assembly, he never again became active in politics. Instead, he renewed his prewar interest in education, retiring from Charleston's school board in 1885 after more than three decades of service to the city. In 1868 Memminger helped found the Etiwan Phosphate Company, which pioneered the phosphate industry in the state. He also served as president of the Spartanburg and Asheville Railroad. Memminger's wife died in 1878, and he married her sister, Sarah A. Wilkinson. Memminger died on March 7, 1888, in Charleston, and was buried at his country home in Flat Rock, North Carolina.
AARON W. MARRS

Ball, Douglas B. *Financial Failure and Confederate Defeat.* Urbana: University of Illinois Press, 1991.

Capers, Henry D. *The Life and Times of C. G. Memminger.* Richmond, Va.: Everett Waddey, 1893.

Memminger School. Founded in 1858, the State Normal School at Charleston owed its existence to a reform movement that simultaneously erected a modern public school system for the white children of the city, the first in South Carolina. The school was begun by Christopher G. Memminger, a state legislator and chairman of the Charleston school board. Patterned after schools in the northern states, the mission of the Memminger School (as it was called after 1876) was to train female teachers for the state at large as a department of a new city high school for girls (the Charleston High School was then reserved for boys only). The first principal was Frederick A. Sawyer, a native of Boston and future U.S. senator for South Carolina.

Memminger got initial support from state funds and drew students from outside the city. However, the school came to rely primarily on local gifts and taxes. Admission depended on entrance tests and was usually free. The curriculum included courses in education theory and practice, teaching advanced studies in the humanities, mathematics, and science. Eventually, Memminger expanded its scope, providing departments of instruction in domestic science and business. After years of declining enrollments variously attributed to the admission of women to the College of Charleston and wider opportunities for women in the private economy, the flagship Normal Department was discontinued in 1932. By then the school had educated thousands of teachers, business and professional women, and housewives.

In 1933 Memminger was reorganized as a comprehensive high school for white girls, offering classical, general, and prevocational courses. In subsequent decades, as secondary schools of Charleston were integrated by gender and race, Memminger emerged as the name of an elementary school. LAYLON WAYNE JORDAN

Jordan, Laylon Wayne. "Education for Community: C. G. Memminger and the Origination of Common Schools in Antebellum Charleston." *South Carolina Historical Magazine* 83 (April 1982): 99–115.

Memminger Normal School Papers. Archives and Records, Charleston County Schools, North Charleston.

Taylor, Mary. *A History of the Memminger Normal School.* Charleston, S.C.: Walker, Evans, and Cogswell, 1941.

Mennonites. The Mennonites of South Carolina are a Protestant group descended from the Anabaptists of the Reformation. The Anabaptists differed from other Protestants in that they insisted on a conscious choice to join the church (adult baptism), a disciplined church in which members were responsible to each other, and a sharing church in which material needs were met by fellow members. They rejected the union of church and state and the validity of oaths and self-defense, including military service. Because Protestant Reformers such as Martin Luther and John Calvin feared that these distinctive beliefs would undermine the social fabric of Europe and threaten chaos, they and the Catholics persecuted the Anabaptists, executing about four thousand martyrs.

The Amish, from whom about half of the Mennonites in South Carolina were descended, sprang from an internal dispute within the Mennonite Church at the end of the seventeenth century concerning church discipline and relations with those outside the faith. The Amish took the stricter approach, demanding strong church discipline, including excommunication and shunning of disobedient members.

Mennonites began migrating to South Carolina in the late 1960s. By 2003 there were twelve Mennonite churches in South Carolina, concentrated primarily in Abbeville, Aiken, Barnwell, and Oconee Counties. Membership in the state totaled more than seven hundred. Fair Play Church and Foothills Fellowship, both in Oconee County, were established to minister to at-risk juveniles in a camp setting. The other churches were founded to provide Mennonite witnesses in the areas or to provide rural settings for those in old Mennonite communities that were being crowded out by urban development. STEPHEN M. RUSSELL, JR.

Dyck, Cornelius J., and Dennis D. Martin, eds. *The Mennonite Encyclopedia.* 5 vols. Hillsboro, Kans.: Mennonite Bretheren Publishing House, 1955–1990.

Yoder, Elmer S. *The Beachy Amish Mennonite Fellowship Churches.* Hartville, Ohio: Diakonia Ministries, 1987.

Mepkin Abbey (Berkeley County). Located on the Cooper River, Mepkin Abbey has a diverse history. In its early life the property served as the seven-thousand-acre rice plantation and family home of the eighteenth-century statesman Henry Laurens. Surviving traces of the plantation include a family cemetery and a large oak avenue. In 1936 the noted publisher Henry Luce, who established both *Time* and *Life* magazines, purchased the property. While living at Mepkin, Luce and his wife, Claire Booth, hired the architect Edward Durell Stone to construct several buildings on the site, including a forester's lodge, a laundry building, a pump house, and a farm manager's house, made mostly of brick. Stone received his training at Harvard University and the Massachusetts Institute of Technology and spent his early career designing houses in the international style. The buildings at Mepkin reflect his modernist sensibility. The Luces also hired the landscape architect Loutrel Briggs, designer of many important gardens in South Carolina, to create a formal composition of camellias and azaleas overlooking the Cooper River. In 1949 the property was donated to a religious community in keeping with Mrs. Luce's wishes. By the 1960s the property had become a monastery that housed the Trappist monks of the Cistercian Order. The monks of Mepkin Abbey began operating an egg farm, which was still functioning in the early twenty-first century, with several buildings on the property associated with that function. The site also includes an austere Cistercian church in the shape of a cross. In its transition from a rice plantation to a monastery and egg farm, Mepkin Abbey reflects an unusual blending of tradition, modern aesthetics, and spiritual transcendence, making it one of the most unique places in South Carolina. LINDSEY GERTZ

Wilkes, Paul. *Beyond the Walls: Monastic Wisdom for Everyday Life.* New York: Doubleday, 1999.

Mermaid controversy. Popular culture and pre-Darwinian natural history collided in January 1843 when Phineas T. Barnum's notorious "Feejee Mermaid" made its way to South Carolina after several months of controversy and acclaim in New York City. The three-foot "mermaid" (actually a gruesome forgery cobbled together from a monkey torso and the bottom half of a fish) was exhibited at Charleston's Masonic Hall from January 17 to January 21. A ventriloquist and an orangutan were among the other curiosities.

Shortly after the mermaid's arrival, the city's rival newspapers, the *Mercury* and the *Courier,* lined up on opposite sides of a heated and complex debate about the exhibit's authenticity, the authority of expertise, and the relationship between commercial entertainment and scientific knowledge. Beyond its popular appeal, the mermaid touched on disputes among natural historians over the fertility of "hybrid" creatures, the existence of intermediate species in the "great chain of being," and the unity of humankind. The Reverend John Bachman, a Lutheran minister and naturalist, led the antimermaid assault in the *Mercury,* writing under the pseudonym "No Humbug" to denounce the exhibit as a "vice manufacture . . . palmed on our community as a great natural curiosity." Alanson Taylor, Barnum's uncle and manager of the exhibit, replied with a letter of his own suggesting that "No Humbug" could not possibly be a legitimate scientist or a physician, and that his mermaid was too fragile for dissection anyway. Taylor earned the support of the *Courier,* whose editors dismissed Bachman and his supporters as unqualified skeptics who discounted the mermaid without having seen it. Bachman continued to ridicule both the exhibit and the gullibility of the Charleston public. The controversy pitched back and forth, and Taylor was forced to spirit the Feejee Mermaid away before it could be destroyed by angry visitors. DAVID HOOGLAND NOON

Bachman, John. *The Doctrine of the Unity of the Human Race Examined on the Principles of Science.* Charleston, S.C.: C. Canning, 1850.

Bondeson, Jan. *The Feejee Mermaid and Other Essays in Natural and Unnatural History.* Ithaca, N.Y.: Cornell University Press, 1999.

Harris, Neil. *Humbug: The Art of P. T. Barnum.* Boston: Little, Brown, 1973.

Kohlstedt, Sally Gregory. "Entrepreneurs and Intellectuals: Natural History in Early American Museums." In *Mermaids, Mummies, and Mastodons: The Emergence of the American Museum,* edited by William T. Alderson. Washington, D.C.: American Association of Museums, 1992.

Methodist Episcopal Church, South. The debate over slavery at the General Conference of the Methodist Episcopal Church in 1844 resulted in the division of the denomination into northern and southern branches. The critical issue was Georgia bishop James O. Andrew's ownership of slaves, inherited from his wife. By Georgia law he could not free the slaves, and Bishop Andrew offered to retire. The southern delegates refused to support his request, and a Plan of Separation was adopted, allowing the southern annual conference to withdraw and create the Methodist Episcopal Church, South. In 1845 a convention of delegates from conferences in the slaveholding states met in Louisville, Kentucky, and formally created the successor denomination. The following year the first General Conference in Petersburg, Virginia, elected William Capers to the episcopacy, the first South Carolina native to become a Methodist bishop.

The bitterness of division and civil war did not permit serious discussion of unification until the early twentieth century. In 1924 the General Conference of the Methodist Episcopal Church, South, approved a plan of union, but it was defeated by the annual conferences (including South Carolina). In another effort in 1938 South Carolinians supported unification, despite fears of northern domination and racial equality. The following year the Methodist Episcopal Church, South, the Methodist Episcopal Church, and the Methodist Protestant Church (which had split over lay representation in 1830) reunited as the Methodist Church. A. V. HUFF, JR.

Betts, Albert D. *History of South Carolina Methodism.* Columbia, S.C.: Advocate Press, 1952.

Huff, A. V., Jr. "The Evangelical Traditions II: Methodists." In *Religion in South Carolina,* edited by Charles H. Lippy. Columbia: University of South Carolina Press, 1993.

Methodists. John Wesley, the founder of the Methodist movement, visited South Carolina three times from 1736 to 1737 while he was chaplain to the Georgia colony. He published his first hymnbook in Charleston and saw there the horrors of slavery, against which he devoted a lifelong crusade. Wesley's successor in Georgia and fellow Oxford Methodist George Whitefield brought the Great Awakening to the province on a dozen visits between 1738 and 1770.

The first effort to organize Methodism in South Carolina came in 1773 when Joseph Pilmore, one of Wesley's early assistants in America, traveled through the lowcountry to Charleston and Savannah. But the onset of the Revolutionary War curtailed any immediate mission activity.

Once the war was over, a flood of settlers, some of them Methodists, moved into the Pee Dee and the backcountry. In 1784 James Foster, a lay preacher from Virginia, organized class meetings along the Broad, Enoree, and Reedy Rivers. When the Methodist Episcopal Church in America was organized in Baltimore in December 1784, Bishop Francis Asbury received a request to send a preacher to South Carolina. Asbury responded by traveling to the area in early 1785. He organized churches in Georgetown and Charleston, and at the annual conference in April he appointed three preachers to circuits primarily in South Carolina.

Methodism was not warmly received among the planter and merchant elite classes in the lowcountry. Methodist preaching emphasized equality before God and denounced the sins of the wealthy. Women joined the movement in large numbers, and slaves and free blacks flocked to Methodist services. By 1815 there were 4,075 Methodists in Charleston—282 white and 3,793 black.

It was the Second Great Awakening that insured the future of Methodism in the state as a major religious force. In October 1801, while Bishop Asbury was in Greenville District, he received word of the camp meetings in Kentucky and Tennessee. In April 1802 twelve thousand people gathered for the first camp meeting in the state near Lancaster. Others followed quickly, and between 1802 and 1805 membership more than doubled because of camp meeting conversions.

With the expansion of cotton production, Methodists improved their economic status, and their opposition to slavery declined. In 1804 Asbury edited a separate edition of the church *Discipline* for South Carolina omitting the rule against slaveholding. In the area of education, Mount Bethel, the first Methodist academy, opened near Newberry in 1795, followed by Tabernacle, then by Cokesbury Conference School. In 1854 Wofford College for men was established in Spartanburg, and Columbia Female College opened in 1859.

Slavery remained a dilemma for the Methodists, and in 1829 William Capers, a minister and slaveholder, founded missions to slaves on the plantations. At the same time, antislavery agitation began to grow in the North and eventually led to the division of the denomination in 1844. When the state seceded from the union in 1860, Methodists supported the Confederacy.

After the Civil War, missionaries of the Methodist Episcopal Church created a South Carolina Conference for black members and in 1869 established Claflin College (now University) in Orangeburg. Other black Methodists joined the African Methodist Episcopal Church and the African Methodist Episcopal Church, Zion. White Methodist leaders assisted in the formation of the Colored (later Christian) Methodist Episcopal Church.

By the late nineteenth century, Baptists had surpassed Methodists numerically. Camp meetings lost their vigor and gave way to more sedate revival meetings, while women organized missionary societies and joined the Women's Christian Temperance Union. The conference opened Epworth Orphanage in Columbia to serve disadvantaged children. A few ministers, such as Robert C. Oliver, joined the burgeoning Holiness movement.

As the textile industry grew in the New South, Methodist mill owners organized churches in the expanding mill villages. Layman L. P. Hollis of Greenville became a leader in welfare work through the Young Men's Christian Association and the public schools, and the Reverend David E. Camak established the Textile Industrial Institute (now Spartanburg Methodist College) to educate mill workers.

Progressive reform supported the spread of the social gospel. Methodists joined the growing national temperance movement and campaigned for prohibition in the state. They were among the leaders of the Federated Forces, an interdenominational temperance group, and its successor, the South Carolina Christian Action

Council. Wil Lou Gray of Laurens led a state crusade for adult literacy. Some ministers attended the new seminaries, first at Vanderbilt, later at Emory and Duke Universities. There were a few efforts to improve race relations, but white supremacy remained the prevailing orthodoxy. Internal power struggles among the white ministers led to the creation of the Upper South Carolina Conference in 1914. The two conferences reunited in 1948.

When southern and northern Methodists voted to reunite in the Methodist Church in 1939, blacks and whites in the state were placed in racially separate jurisdictions. Nevertheless, a vocal minority of whites withdrew to form the Southern Methodist Church. But the winds of change were blowing stronger. In 1954, in response to *Brown v. Board of Education,* the white conference adopted a tepid resolution applauding "the fine spirit" of interracial understanding in South Carolina, while black ministers, such as I. DeQuincey Newman, joined the civil rights movement. Efforts to merge the white and black conferences began in 1966 under a mandate from the denomination, which merged with the Evangelical United Brethren to form the United Methodist Church in 1968. After lengthy negotiations, the two conferences united in 1972. Nationally, conversations began with the historically black Methodist churches, but there was no progress toward merger.

Race was not the only issue confronting Methodists. In 1964 white conservatives shifted their attention to attacking the National Council of Churches. There were sharp debates over the war in Vietnam. In the 1980s and 1990s the church supported removing the Confederate flag from the dome of the state capitol and opposed a state lottery. Women entered the ministry in larger numbers, and a few churches refused to accept them. Conservative evangelicalism made inroads among clergy and laity. There was continuing concern about church growth, but membership increased only slightly. A. V. HUFF, JR.

Huff, A. V., Jr. "The Evangelical Traditions II: Methodists." In *Religion in South Carolina,* edited by Charles H. Lippy. Columbia: University of South Carolina Press, 1993.

———. "A History of South Carolina United Methodism." In *United Methodist Ministers in South Carolina,* edited by Morgan David Arant and Nancy McCracken Arant. Columbia: South Carolina Conference of the United Methodist Church, 1984.

Mexican War (1846–1848). The roots of the Mexican War can be traced to westward expansion following the War of 1812. Many Americans, including many South Carolinians migrating west in search of cheap land, settled in northern Mexico where liberal land grants of as much as four thousand acres were available. These settlers established an agrarian economy based on slavery. The 1836 revolt that led to the de facto independence of Texas set the stage for future conflict with Mexico. Texas statehood, supported by most South Carolinians, became mired in sectional controversy and was rejected in June 1844. However, in the 1844 presidential campaign James K. Polk ran on a platform of "recovering" lost territories, including Texas. Polk won, but before he was inaugurated, the outgoing president, John Tyler, engineered a proposal for Texas statehood, which was accepted by Texas on July 4, 1845.

To "protect" our newest state, President Polk sent Zachary Taylor and nearly half the U.S. Army into Texas, raising tensions when he ordered Taylor into territory claimed by Mexico along the Rio Grande. Hostilities began on April 25, 1846, when Mexican forces ambushed a patrol led by Captain Seth B. Thornton. Polk quickly sought a declaration of war and money and men to reinforce Taylor. In South Carolina public opinion on the war was mixed. John C. Calhoun fervently opposed the war, believing it posed a grave danger to southern political power, but he was placed in a difficult position by the coupling of the war declaration with provisions for supporting Taylor's army. In the end he abstained from voting on the bill. The editor of the *Charleston Mercury* was highly critical of Polk and defended Calhoun's position. Many other South Carolina newspapers criticized the administration's position as well. On the other hand, the *Abbeville Banner* and the *Greenville Mountaineer* advocated stern measures, including invasion of Mexico. Taylor's victories in northern Mexico muted the opposition. War fever swept the state.

When South Carolina was asked to provide a volunteer regiment, state adjutant general James W. Cantey ignored the fact that the regiment was for the reserve when he issued his guidelines on May 29. His optimistic deadline of June 10 was not met, and it was not until June 29 that ten companies were accepted for service. The news from Secretary of War William Marcy in July that the Palmettos were not needed was devastating. In August 1846 the Wilmot Proviso, a failed attempt by Pennsylvania congressman David Wilmot to prohibit slavery in any territory acquired from Mexico, caused little reaction in South Carolina, and there was increasing public support for the war. Even the editor of the *Mercury,* while fulminating against northern warmongers, opposed withdrawing Taylor's army from northern Mexico.

That autumn the administration's optimistic view of the war collided with Mexico's intransigence, and on November 16 South Carolina was asked to provide a regiment for immediate service. Because the term of service had changed from one year to the duration of the war, the Palmetto Regiment had to be reformed, and many refused to volunteer under the new provisions. In Greenville, for example, where two companies had been formed in June, only forty-two men volunteered and a company could not be formed. War fever had died down in the upstate and on the coast, and except for a company from Charleston, the Palmetto Regiment was raised exclusively in the Midlands.

As the Palmetto Regiment marched to war in 1847, the Wilmot Proviso was being roundly condemned in the South Carolina press. Calhoun, for example, feared that such abolitionist pressure would exacerbate sectional rivalry in the near future. Many agreed. Despite this debate, South Carolinians eagerly anticipated news of the war. Some in the Palmetto Regiment corresponded with their hometown newspapers, and their reports of the battles created intense interest in South Carolina. People wanted to know what "our boys" were doing. When peace came in February 1848 there was a clamor for the return of the volunteers. The surviving Palmetto Regiment finally arrived at Mobile, Alabama, in late June 1848. There they were mustered out and left to find their own way home. The return of the Palmettos generated great excitement in South Carolina. Columbia and Charleston got into a heated debate over which city would "officially" welcome the regiment home. In the end there was a grand celebration in Columbia on July 26 and an equally grand one in Charleston two days later. However, by the end of the year the war with Mexico was all but forgotten. JACK ALLEN MEYER

Johannsen, Robert Walter. *To the Halls of the Montezumas: The Mexican War in the American Imagination.* New York: Oxford University Press, 1985.

Lander, Ernest McPherson, Jr. *Reluctant Imperialists: Calhoun, the South Carolinians, and the Mexican War.* Baton Rouge: Louisiana State University Press, 1980.

Meyer, Jack Allen. *South Carolina in the Mexican War: A History of the Palmetto Regiment of Volunteers, 1846–1917.* Columbia: South Carolina Department of Archives and History, 1996.

Michaux, André (1746–1802), and **François-André Michaux** (1770–1855). Botanists. André Michaux was born on March 7, 1746, at Satory, France, son of the farmer André Michaux and Marie-Charlotte Barbet. Interested in plants from an early age, Michaux in 1785 was commissioned as royal botanist with the mission of finding useful plants for France in America. Originally landing in New York, he arrived in Charleston on September 21, 1786. The city became his base of operations as he ranged over North America as far south as Florida and as far north as Hudson Bay.

The Carolina mountains were among his favorite areas for botanizing. South Carolina plants first described or collected by Michaux include the Oconee bell, the big leaf magnolia, native cane, blue-eyed grass, and the Carolina willow. In all, Michaux was the authority for 188 species native to the Carolinas. In 1790 Michaux was trapped in Charleston by the French Revolution and the freezing of his funding. However, he bore no grudge against the French Republic, becoming a strong supporter of the revolution. A member of the Agricultural Society of South Carolina, Michaux also worked to acclimate foreign plants, mostly Asian, in America. Notable examples include the camellia, the mimosa from Persia, the gingko tree from China, and the crape myrtle from India. Michaux's 111-acre botanical garden near Charleston became a popular visiting spot for city residents. Returning to France in 1796, Michaux wrote the first systematic botanical description of eastern North America, *Flora Boreali-Americana* (1803). Based on Michaux's personal observations, it includes descriptions of many South Carolina plants. Michaux died on Madagascar in November 1802 while accompanying a French expedition to the South Seas.

François-André Michaux was born on August 16, 1770, the son of André Michaux and Cécile Claye. As a young man, François accompanied his father on many of his early explorations. As an adult, he returned to Charleston, arriving on October 9, 1801, in the midst of a yellow fever epidemic. He caught the disease but survived. While in Charleston, Michaux arranged the liquidation of his father's botanical garden, sending plants and seeds back to France and transferring the land and remaining plants to the Agricultural Society of South Carolina, of which he, like his father, was a member. A book about his American travels, *Travels to the West of the Allegheny Mountains* (1804), contains observations on South Carolina. After returning to France, Michaux visited Charleston again while engaged in a project from 1806 to 1808 to find North American trees with useful lumber that could be acclimated in France. After his return to France, Michaux was a principal supplier of scientific books and journals to America until the 1820s, when failing health forced him out of Paris. Charlestonians who received scientific works from Michaux included the Pinckney family, the Library Society of Charleston, the South Carolina Medical Society, and the botanist Stephen Elliott. Michaux died on October 23, 1855, at his home in Vaureal, France, and was buried on its grounds. WILLIAM E. BURNS

Rembert, David H., Jr. "Carolina's French Connection." *South Carolina Wildlife* 41 (March–April 1994): 46–49.

Savage, Henry, Jr., and Elizabeth J. Savage. *André and François-André Michaux.* Charlottesville: University Press of Virginia, 1986.

Michelin. This company is a French tire manufacturing giant whose roots extend to the 1860s. Michelin has approximately 128,000 workers and eighty production facilities on five continents, including a substantial business presence in South Carolina.

Michelin came to South Carolina in the mid-1970s as a part of its massive campaign to expand its North American market share. As the American demand for the Michelin-developed radial tires grew, the company expanded rapidly. Michelin opened its Greenville tire factory in March 1975, followed by a factory for semifinished materials in Anderson later the same year. Laurens testing center opened in 1977, and a truck tire factory in Spartanburg opened one year later. Initial estimates of Michelin's investments in the state were in the hundreds of millions of dollars.

Michelin and South Carolina made a successful match. The company was not secretive about its conservative character and dislike of unions, and in South Carolina, Michelin found a base that suited its corporate values and business objectives. While its corporate culture was in line with South Carolina traditions, local workers welcomed Michelin's high wages and impressive benefits. Over the years the company expanded its operations in the state. In 1985 it even moved its U.S. headquarters from New York to Greenville. MARKO MAUNULA

Scott-Stokes, Henry. "Michelin Quietly Bets a Billion." *New York Times,* January 29, 1978, sec. 3, pp. 1, 7.

Middleton, Arthur (1742–1787). Legislator, signer of the Declaration of Independence. Middleton was born on June 26, 1742, at Middleton Place on the Ashley River in St. Andrew's Parish. He was the son of Henry Middleton and Mary Williams. At age twelve, he was sent to England to complete his education, attending Hackney Academy, Westminster School, and St. John's College (Cambridge) before entering the Middle Temple in London for legal training in 1757. He returned to South Carolina in December 1763. On August 19, 1764, Middleton married the wealthy heiress Mary Izard, daughter of Walter Izard, Jr. The marriage produced nine children.

Possessing financial independence and a civic spirit, Middleton pursued public office. In October 1765 he won a seat in the Commons House of Assembly, where he represented St. Helena's Parish until May 1768. That year he and his wife left for Europe to spend the next three years traveling throughout the Continent studying literature and the fine arts. When Middleton returned to South Carolina in 1771, he avoided political service to oversee his expanding lowcountry rice plantations and his stable of thoroughbreds. However, as the Anglo-American conflict reached the critical stage in 1775, his strong devotion to American rights motivated him to serve in the assembly and on many revolutionary committees.

Middleton soon emerged as a leader within the extreme faction of the local "patriot party" by organizing and leading raids on the royal armories, raising money for the American cause, planning for the defense of Charleston, encouraging attacks against vocal Loyalists, and proposing the confiscation of property belonging to those who had fled the province. Middleton's enthusiasm earned him a position on the panel drafting South Carolina's first constitution in February 1776 and election as a delegate to the Continental Congress in Philadelphia. There, Middleton, fearful of a British attack on his home state, reluctantly signed the Declaration of Independence. During the next two years Middleton helped frame the Articles of Confederation and desperately tried to get greater military assistance from Congress for the lower South. His failure in this latter goal and the counterproductive dissension in the national assembly encouraged Middleton to return to South Carolina, where he felt he could better serve the American cause.

In March 1778 the General Assembly elected Middleton governor under the state's new constitution. However, Middleton refused the honor, partly because he objected to the democratic trends of the

1778 charter and partly because he hoped for some reconciliation with Great Britain given the lack of concern demonstrated by Congress for southern military needs. Still, Middleton provided valuable assistance in the General Assembly until the siege of Charleston in 1780, when he joined the state militia to help defend the capital. When the city fell to the British on May 12, Middleton was captured and sent to St. Augustine as a prisoner of war. In July 1781 he was exchanged and returned to Philadelphia as a delegate to the Continental Congress, where he promoted South Carolina's commercial interests and pushed for the execution of British general Lord Cornwallis.

After his return to South Carolina in 1783, Middleton devoted his energies to repairing his war-ravaged estate. He returned to the General Assembly in 1785 as a representative from St. George's Dorchester Parish and also served as a trustee of the College of Charleston. Middleton died from an unknown fever on January 1, 1787, and was buried in the family mausoleum at Middleton Place. KEITH KRAWCZYNSKI

Edgar, Walter, and N. Louise Bailey, eds. *Biographical Directory of the South Carolina House of Representatives.* Vol. 2, *The Commons House of Assembly, 1692–1775.* Columbia: University of South Carolina Press, 1977.

Horne, Paul A., Jr. "Forgotten Leaders: South Carolina's Delegation to the Continental Congress, 1774–1789." Ph.D. diss., University of South Carolina, 1988.

Lane, George W. "The Middletons of Eighteenth-Century South Carolina: A Colonial Dynasty, 1678–1787." Ph.D. diss., Emory University, 1990.

Middleton, Henry (1717–1784). Planter, politician, president of Continental Congress. The son of Arthur Middleton and Sarah Amory, Middleton was born at The Oaks, his father's plantation in St. James Goose Creek Parish. Upon his father's death in 1737, Middleton inherited property in South Carolina, England, and Barbados. Judicious investments and marriages increased his landholdings to nearly twenty plantations totaling fifty thousand acres and about eight hundred slaves. In 1741 Middleton married Mary Williams. The union produced twelve children. Mary also brought him an estate on the Ashley River, which became known as Middleton Place. In 1762, a year after Mary's death, Middleton married Mary Henrietta Bull, daughter of William Bull, Sr., the colony's lieutenant governor. In January 1776, four years after Mary's death, Middleton married Lady Mary Mackenzie, daughter of the third earl of Cromartie. The last two marriages produced no children but brought Middleton connections to the royal government and British aristocracy, and perhaps explain his conflicted political stances during the revolutionary period.

In the 1740s and 1750s Middleton served intermittently in the Commons House of Assembly, where he represented St. George's Dorchester Parish. He presided as Speaker of the assembly in 1747 and again from 1754 to 1755. In 1755 he was appointed to the Royal Council. Middleton's position on the council entailed a balancing act. Dissenting against the majority, he voted to open the port of Charleston during the Stamp Act crisis of 1765. In 1769, on the other hand, he joined the rest of the council in opposing the assembly's gift to support John Wilkes. In September 1770 he resigned from the Royal Council, and he thereafter was aligned with the revolutionary movement.

His most important contribution to the Revolution began in July 1774, when he was elected to the First Continental Congress. On October 22 Middleton replaced Peyton Randolph of Virginia as president and presided over Congress until it adjourned on October 26. While president, he signed a "Declaration of Rights and Grievances" that was presented to King George III. Reelected in January 1775, Middleton served in the Second Continental Congress from May to November 1775. During this session Congress organized the Continental army and approved an invasion of Canada, moves that foreshadowed the final break with Great Britain. Perhaps it was no coincidence that Middleton, who preferred to moderate any steps toward independence, refused further service in Congress. Resigning on February 16, 1776, Middleton gave way to his son Arthur, a far more outspoken and radical delegate. Thus it was Arthur, and not his father, who would affix his signature to the Declaration of Independence.

Back in South Carolina, Middleton served in the First and Second Provincial Congresses (1775–1776) and sat on the Council of Safety. Between 1776 and 1778 he served on the Legislative Council (the predecessor of the state Senate) and was twice elected to the state House of Representatives from the city parishes of St. Philip's and St. Michael's. Under the state's 1778 constitution, he was elected to the Senate. When the British captured Charleston in 1780, Middleton took the protection of the crown. Despite this action, he incurred no penalty after the war, probably because his contemporaries remembered his political service and his generosity in lending more than £100,000 to the state. Middleton died in Charleston on June 13, 1784. He was buried in the chancel of the St. James Goose Creek Parish church. GREGORY D. MASSEY

Cheves, Langdon. "Middleton of South Carolina." *South Carolina Historical and Genealogical Magazine* 1 (July 1900): 228–62.

Edgar, Walter, and N. Louise Bailey. *Biographical Directory of the South Carolina House of Representatives.* Vol. 2, *The Commons House of Assembly, 1692–1775.* Columbia: University of South Carolina Press, 1977.

McCrady, Edward. *The History of South Carolina in the Revolution, 1775–1780.* New York: Macmillan, 1901.

Middleton, Henry (1770–1846). Legislator, governor, congressman, diplomat. Born in London on September 28, 1770, Middleton was the son of Arthur Middleton, a prominent lowcountry planter and patriot, and Mary Izard. His early life was shaped by the Revolutionary War. Middleton was in Philadelphia when his father signed the Declaration of Independence. Later in the war Middleton saw his father imprisoned by the British and sent to St. Augustine, Florida. Although well tutored at home, Middleton regretted that the Revolution and his father's premature death in 1787 prevented him from attending a university. His uncles Charles Cotesworth Pinckney and Edward Rutledge sent him north in 1790 to obtain "a thorough Knowledge of . . . his own Country." He then went abroad for several years. In England on November 13, 1794, Middleton married Mary Helen Hering, a daughter of a British army officer. The couple had fourteen children, four of whom died in infancy.

On returning to the United States in 1799, Middleton took up management of his family's properties, including three rice plantations on the Combahee River. Around the same time he began a long career in South Carolina politics when elected in 1802 to the state House of Representatives from the parishes of St. Philip's and St. Michael's. Reelected three times, he served in the General Assembly from 1802 until 1809. In addition to serving on the influential Ways and Means Committee, Middleton was appointed to committees dealing with important issues such as incorporation of the state bank, curtailing the slave trade, and legislative reapportionment to reflect the growing upcountry population (which he supported).

By 1808 Middleton, in contrast to various friends and relatives among the lowcountry planters, was aligned with the Democratic-Republicans. Personally popular and politically middle-of-the-road, he was elected to the state Senate in the fall of 1810 and then was chosen governor on December 10. As governor, he pressed successfully for passage of the long-discussed law establishing free public schools. Anticipating war with England, Middleton supported President James Madison and urgently recommended strengthening South Carolina's militia and defenses.

Elected to the U.S. House of Representatives, Middleton represented Charleston District in the Fourteenth and Fifteenth Congresses (1815–1819). Following the War of 1812, Middleton favored efforts to make the United States economically independent. He supported federal appropriations for internal improvements, the tariff of 1816, and the Bank of the United States. In his second term Middleton chaired the House committee investigating the illicit slave trade that was being carried on via Amelia Island. His committee report endorsed the Monroe administration's controversial actions in suppressing the "horde of foreign freebooters" on the island and termed the slave trade "repugnant to justice and humanity." It impressed Secretary of State John Quincy Adams and probably helped to identify Middleton to both Adams and President James Monroe as an ally in South Carolina. During his tour of the South in 1819, Monroe honored Middleton by spending the night at his Ashley River plantation, Middleton Place.

After Adams and Calhoun suggested Middleton for a diplomatic post, Monroe appointed him minister to Russia in early 1820. Because he was knowledgeable about national affairs, already familiar with Europe, and fluent in French, Middleton was exceptionally well prepared for such a post. The Middletons left for Russia in the summer of 1820. Middleton proved an adroit and able diplomat. His first task was to represent American interests during Czar Alexander I's arbitration of the dispute over slaves removed by the British at the end of the War of 1812. In part because of Middleton's presentation of the arguments, the award was in favor of the United States. His forceful protests and well-prepared arguments also helped persuade Russia to withdraw her claim to the Pacific northwest coast below the 54°40′ parallel, thus protecting American fishing and trading rights.

Upon his return home in 1830, Middleton was appalled by the danger posed to the Union by the "baneful doctrine of nullification." Becoming a leader of the Unionists, he reminded South Carolinians of "the high privilege of self-government" and emphasized the necessity of abiding by the decision of the majority. Although he agreed that existing tariff rates were "excessively high," he nevertheless believed that protective tariffs were constitutional. He was one of the few Unionist delegates to the nullification convention in November 1832, and he was a vice president of the Union convention in December 1832, where he adamantly opposed the proposed test oath.

During his later years Middleton, a major slaveholder, was obligated to manage the rice plantations that provided the family's income. A devoted, though sometimes difficult, father and husband, he seemed happiest during the summers he spent with his family in Newport, Rhode Island. Middleton died in Charleston on June 14, 1846, and was buried at Middleton Place. ELIZA COPE HARRISON

Bailey, N. Louise, Mary L. Morgan, and Carolyn R. Taylor, eds. *Biographical Directory of the South Carolina Senate, 1776–1985.* 3 vols. Columbia: University of South Carolina Press, 1986.

Bergquist, Harold E., Jr. "Henry Middleton and the Arbitrament of the Anglo-American Slave Controversy by Tsar Alexander I." *South Carolina Historical Magazine* 82 (January 1981): 20–31.

———. "Russian-American Relations, 1820–1830: The Diplomacy of Henry Middleton, American Minister at St. Petersburg." Ph.D. diss., Boston University, 1970.

Harrison, Eliza Cope, ed. *Best Companions: Letters of Eliza Middleton Fisher and Her Mother, Mary Hering Middleton, from Charleston, Philadelphia, and Newport, 1839–1846.* Columbia: University of South Carolina Press, 2001.

Middleton Place (Dorchester County). Middleton Place is an Ashley River plantation located on Highway 61 (Ashley River Road) just outside Charleston. It was established on land originally granted in 1675 but probably not settled until it passed to John Williams in the early eighteenth century. Henry Middleton (1717–1784) acquired the property through his marriage to Williams's daughter Mary in 1741. Middleton added to the original acreage and began the elegant gardens that have made Middleton Place internationally famous. As the birthplace of Henry Middleton's son Arthur (1742–1787), a signer of the Declaration of Independence, Middleton Place was listed in the National Register of Historic Places and declared a National Historic Landmark in 1971.

An aerial view of Middleton Place featuring the house and gardens with the twin butterfly-shaped lakes. Courtesy, South Carolina Department of Archives and History

The gardens, thought to be the oldest surviving formal landscaped gardens in the United States, are renowned for their collection of *Camellia japonicas,* introduced about 1786 by the French Royal botanist André Michaux. In 1990 the United Nations International Committee on Monuments and Sites named Middleton Place one of six United States gardens having international importance. Burned by Union soldiers in 1865, Middleton Place continued in the Middleton family until 1984, when ownership was vested in the nonprofit Middleton Place Foundation.

Middleton Place includes a museum housed in what was originally the south flank of the former three-building main residence; a plantation chapel built in 1850 above the eighteenth-century springhouse; a rice mill built in 1851; and an 1870s African American freedman's house in the reconstructed stable-yards complex. It is open for public visiting every day of the year except Christmas. BARBARA DOYLE

Mignot, Louis Rémy (1831–1870). Painter. Mignot was born in Charleston on February 3, 1831, into a French-Catholic family. At the age of seventeen he enrolled at the Academy of Fine Arts at The

Hague, where he remained for five years. He became a student of Andreas Schelfhout, a highly regarded Dutch landscape painter. In 1854 he returned to the United States and became actively involved in the New York art world. In the manner of the Hudson River school painters, he went on sketching forays in the Catskill Mountains. He specialized in landscape painting and on several occasions provided the backgrounds to ambitious figure groups, as in *Washington and Lafayette at Mount Vernon,* a collaboration with Thomas P. Rossiter in the collection of the Metropolitan Museum of Art. Mignot's landscapes were exhibited at the prestigious Century Association and the National Academy of Design, where he was elected to the status of associate academician in 1858.

Mignot was one of the first tenants of the Tenth Street Studio Building, the earliest American facility designed specifically for artists. One of his fellow tenants was Frederic Edwin Church, a leading exponent of the second generation of Hudson River school painters. In 1857 Church and Mignot made an expedition to Central and South America, traveling to Guayaquil and Quito, Ecuador; trekking along the "Avenue of Volcanoes"; and taking in such Andean landmarks as Cotopaxi, Cayambe, and Chimborazo. From sketches obtained on this expedition Mignot developed some of his most acclaimed canvases.

On January 11, 1860, Mignot married Zairah Harries of Baltimore. The couple had one son. During the Civil War, Mignot remained in New York until 1862, when he departed for England.

Because his career was relatively short and his works scattered, Mignot has suffered from comparison to his better-known friend Church. While the scholar Katherine Manthorne maintains that "Mignot was arguably the most accomplished southern-born painter of his generation," she also recognizes a fundamental dilemma, namely, "the degree to which he should be classified as a southern artist." Mignot never seems to have painted scenes of his native region. However, during his lifetime critics saluted Mignot's singular ability at rendering humid atmosphere, which they viewed as a direct result of his youth in South Carolina. This was the judgment of the noted art connoisseur Henry Tuckerman, who wrote in 1867, "Quite diverse from the exactitude and vivid forest tints of our Eastern painters, are the southern effects so remarkably rendered by Louis R. Mignot, whose nativity, temperament, and taste combine to make him the efficient delineator of tropical atmosphere and vegetation."

Major paintings by Mignot are in the collections of Greenville County Museum of Art, North Carolina Museum of Art, Detroit Institute of Arts, Brooklyn Museum of Art, and Bowdoin College Museum of Art. On September 22, 1870, Mignot died of smallpox in Brighton, England, and was buried at Brighton Cemetery, Woodvale. MARTHA R. SEVERENS

Manthorne, Katherine E., and John W. Coffey. *The Landscapes of Louis Rémy Mignot: A Southern Painter Abroad.* Washington, D.C.: Smithsonian Institution Press, 1996.

Migrant labor. Migrant labor in South Carolina involves farmwork done by individuals whose principal employment is seasonal agriculture and who travel and live in temporary housing. South Carolina lies on the easternmost of three traditional streams of migrant farmworkers who harvest much of the nation's crops each year. As of the early twenty-first century, from early summer through fall, about fourteen thousand migrant workers could be found in all parts of South Carolina but in greatest concentrations in the lowcountry and in Clarendon and Sumter Counties (vegetables), the Ridge area and Spartanburg County (peaches), and the Pee Dee (tobacco).

From 1980 to 2000 major changes occurred in migrant farm labor in South Carolina. The traditional mix of African American and white workers in the eastern stream and in South Carolina was replaced by a large preponderance of Latinos, mostly Mexicans. In 2001 ninety percent of the clients seen at clinics operated by the S.C. Migrant Health program were Latinos. That same year it was estimated that in South Carolina as well as nationally, approximately half of farmworkers were undocumented immigrants, up from just seven percent in 1989. Large numbers of workers from Mexico who came here as migrant workers "settled in" and established permanent residency. They engaged in farmwork during the harvest period and did manual or factory labor—mostly food processing—during the rest of year, joining a large number of rural white and African American South Carolinians as "seasonal farm workers." In the early twenty-first century South Carolina growers, following national trends, were beginning to participate more heavily (an estimated nine percent of workers in 2002) in the H2A or "guestworker" program, a federal program that imported Mexican nationals who returned home after the harvest season. While the program offered certain wage and other living benefits to workers, many farmworker advocates were opposed to the guestworker program because workers were not allowed to engage in collective bargaining and might not leave the employ of the contracting grower. South Carolina's laws protecting the health and legal rights of migrant and seasonal farmworkers were among the weakest in the nation. Farmworker labor unions, active even in neighboring states such as North Carolina, were not active in South Carolina. DAVID P. HILL

South Carolina. Migrant Farm Workers Commission. *South Carolina Migrant Services.* Columbia: South Carolina Migrant Farm Workers Commission, 1998.

Milburn, Frank Pierce (1868–1926). Architect. Milburn was one of the New South's most successful and prolific architects. He worked throughout the Southeast and designed more than 250 major buildings, primarily railroad stations and public, institutional, and commercial structures. Milburn based his practice in Columbia in 1900 and designed more than fifty significant buildings in South Carolina.

Milburn was born in Bowling Green, Kentucky, on December 12, 1868, the son of the builder and contractor Thomas T. Milburn and Rebecca Anne Sutphin. He studied at Arkansas University and Arkansas Industrial University and began practicing architecture in Louisville, Kentucky, in 1884. In 1890 Milburn married Leonora Lyttle. The couple had two children. That same year Milburn moved to Kenova, West Virginia, and he then relocated his practice again in 1893 to Winston, North Carolina, after winning the commission for the Forsyth County Courthouse. By 1896 Milburn was in Charlotte, North Carolina, where he designed and supervised construction of the Mecklenburg County Courthouse.

In 1899 Milburn received the commission to complete the South Carolina State House and moved to Columbia. By adding a neoclassical dome and porticos to the building, he placed the finishing touches on a project that had dragged on for half a century. The accomplishment, however, was overshadowed by a legislative investigation of the work conducted under his direction. State authorities took Milburn and the contractor to court on charges of fraud and other wrongdoing. The case ended in a mistrial and did not seriously damage Milburn's reputation.

Over the next several years Milburn worked extensively in South Carolina. He designed courthouses in Anderson and Greenville and city halls in Columbia and Darlington. Although already established as a leading designer of major railroad stations, Milburn became the official architect for the Southern Railway Company in 1902. His designs for that company in South Carolina included stations in Columbia, Summerville, Sumter, Spartanburg, Union, Charleston, and Greenville. Other notable projects included the South Carolina Dispensary Building in Columbia, Alumni Hall at Wofford College, and John Thomson Memorial Auditorium and James S. Gibbes Art Gallery in Charleston.

Milburn moved his practice to Washington, D.C., in 1902 and formed a partnership with the architect Michael Heister. The firm had no difficulty obtaining commissions for commercial and federal projects. By the early 1920s Milburn and Heister had designed buildings for the U.S. Department of Labor, the Department of Commerce, and the American Federation of Labor.

Milburn's designs were stylistically eclectic and generally derivative. He favored the neoclassical style, and beaux arts and Romanesque influences were evident in much of his work. After Heister joined the firm, he became the principal designer, leaving Milburn to concentrate on the business side.

With their services in demand elsewhere, Milburn and Heister discontinued work in South Carolina about 1907. In addition to their practice in Washington, the firm remained active in North Carolina and maintained a branch office in Durham that was managed by Milburn's son, Thomas Yancey Milburn, after about 1920. Milburn died in Asheville, North Carolina, on September 21, 1926. DANIEL J. VIVIAN

Wodehouse, Lawrence. "Frank Pierce Milburn (1868–1926), a Major Southern Architect." *North Carolina Historical Review* 50 (July 1973): 289–303.

Miles, William Porcher (1822–1899). Educator, congressman. Miles was born in Walterboro on July 4, 1822, the second son of James Saunders Miles and Sarah B. Warley. He attended the Wellington School and was graduated from the College of Charleston in 1842. He returned to the college as a professor of mathematics in 1843.

In 1855 Miles left the College of Charleston to enter politics. That year he won the election for mayor of Charleston. In this position he reformed and modernized the police department, ending the corruption that had plagued the city. During this period Miles began to develop his idealism and strict interpretation of the Constitution. He had for some time been concerned about the rights of southern states and their freedom to govern themselves without interference. Although Miles did not own slaves, he considered it a right under the Constitution for others to own them. Determined to reach a wider audience, he entered the race for the U.S. House of Representatives and won a seat in 1857. However, Miles had a hard time reconciling his oath as a member of Congress with his views concerning the rights of the state of South Carolina. Following the adoption of the Ordinance of Secession in December 1860, Miles and the entire South Carolina delegation withdrew from Congress.

After secession, Miles was selected as a representative in the provisional and regular Confederate congress. He was also appointed chair of the Military Affairs Committee of the Confederate House of Representatives and served as an aide-de-camp to General P. G. T. Beauregard. In March 1861 Miles proposed a new flag for Confederate troops. His design was accepted, and the new Confederate battle flag was adopted that fall.

In the years following the war Miles did not retreat from his belief that secession was proper, but he never returned to politics. In 1863 he had married Bettie Beirne, the daughter of a wealthy Virginia planter. Following the war he retired to manage the family plantation, Oak Ridge, in Nelson County, Virginia.

After federal troops withdrew from South Carolina in 1877, and after extended debate and several false starts, South Carolina College reopened as South Carolina College of Agriculture and Mechanics. In 1880 the college trustee Charles H. Simonton offered Miles the presidency of the newly reorganized institution. Miles accepted and began his duties in Columbia that fall. In 1882 his father-in-law suffered a stroke. Miles resigned his presidency and went to Louisiana to manage thirteen sugar plantations belonging to the Beirne family. He prospered there with his wife and son until his death on May 11, 1899. He was buried near the Beirne family in Union Cemetery, Union, West Virginia. DAVID H. REMBERT, JR.

Channing, Steven A. *Crisis of Fear: Secession in South Carolina.* New York: Simon and Schuster, 1970.

Hollis, Daniel Walker. *University of South Carolina.* Vol. 2, *College to University.* Columbia: University of South Carolina Press, 1956.

Paine, Sidney Bettis. "William Porcher Miles: The Congressional Years, 1857–1860." Master's thesis, University of South Carolina, 1962.

Walther, Eric H. *The Fire-Eaters.* Baton Rouge: Louisiana State University Press, 1992.

Miles Brewton House (Charleston). The wealthy merchant and slave trader Miles Brewton began construction of this elegant Palladian-inspired residence at 27 King Street in the mid-1760s. It was completed ca. 1769. With its garden and well-preserved outbuildings, it constitutes the centerpiece of what is widely considered to be the finest Georgian town-house complex in America. The contractor Richard Moncrieff oversaw construction of the house. The elaborate interior carving was done by the carpenter Ezra Waite, with the assistance of the master carvers John Lord and Thomas Woodin.

The Brewton House is a two-story, double-pile structure set on a raised basement. The facade features a two-tiered portico with Ionic and Tuscan columns and an oval window set in the pediment. A dual stair with white marble steps leads to the entrance, which is crowned by an elliptical fanlight. The interior features extraordinary craftsmanship, including fully paneled rooms, elaborate carved ornamentation, mahogany doors, and marble mantles. The hall is paved with Purbeck stone imported from Dorset, England, and the mahogany stair is lit by a Venetian window. The second-floor drawing room has a seventeen-foot cove ceiling and a marble mantle. The grounds include a formal garden and a row of outbuildings along the northern edge of the property. The first group of structures, situated nearest the street, was built ca. 1769 and includes a kitchen, a laundry, and a carriage house. Behind the kitchen a cistern and an arcade with stables and storerooms leads to a two-story brick structure built ca. 1820. Extending west from this building is another arcade that leads to an eighteenth-century structure, which is believed to have served as a dairy, privy, or garden folly. Between the house and the outbuildings is a paved courtyard.

The Brewton House is a masterwork of early American architecture and reflects the sophisticated tastes of Charleston's merchants on the eve of the Revolution. It was designated a National Historic Landmark by the U.S. Department of the Interior in 1960. See plate 10. DANIEL J. VIVIAN

Lane, Mills. *Architecture of the Old South: South Carolina.* Savannah, Ga.: Beehive, 1984.

Poston, Jonathan H. *The Buildings of Charleston: A Guide to the City's Architecture.* Columbia: University of South Carolina Press, 1997.

Military education. Military education has long been popular in the American South, and South Carolina has been a leader for this type of instruction. Since the antebellum period, southerners have regarded military education as an excellent way to instill self-discipline, integrity, patriotism, moral virtue, and a sense of civic duty in youths, particularly young men.

Private military academies began appearing in the South in the 1820s, though information about them is sketchy. Richland Academy, for example, opened near Rice Springs Creek in 1827, though it survived only a few years. After the founding of the Virginia Military Institute in 1839, South Carolina and then every other slave state founded state-supported military schools or provided state support for military education programs. The South Carolina Military Academy was founded in 1842 and consisted of the Arsenal Academy in Columbia and the Citadel in Charleston. In 1845 the Arsenal became a preparatory academy for new cadets before they matriculated as upperclassmen to the Citadel. During the 1850s Citadel graduates founded several private military academies, including King's Mountain Military School, Patrick Military Institute, Yorkville Military Academy, Aiken Military Academy, and academies in North Carolina and Georgia.

Supporters of the military system argued that it represented a more democratic, egalitarian way to run a college. In military schools, authority within the corps of cadets depended on class rank and academic standing, not socioeconomic status. Seniority and grades translated into military rank within the corps. Since all students wore uniforms, there were no distinctions in dress between planters' sons and upcountry plowboys. At the Arsenal and the Citadel, poorer cadets who passed competitive examinations paid no tuition, and these "beneficiary" cadets made up about one-half of the Citadel's student body. Additionally, politicians and educators argued that military school graduates could help train and improve the state militia in case of conflict with the federal government or slave revolts. Most importantly, many South Carolinians, including parents, believed that military training was vital for instilling character and discipline in the state's rowdy youth.

On January 9, 1861, Citadel cadets on Morris Island fired artillery shells at a vessel attempting to reinforce Federal troops at Fort Sumter. During the Civil War, state authorities often called the Arsenal and Citadel cadets to active duty. The cadets saw action in December 1864 during the Battle of Tulifinny, suffering eight casualties. They continued in active service until the end of the war.

Union forces burned the Arsenal in 1865 and began a military occupation of the Citadel that lasted until 1879. Citadel alumni, however, founded new private military academies in the state and managed to reopen the Citadel in 1882. The southern military school tradition received another boost after the Civil War as the former Confederate states took advantage of the Morrill Land Grant Act of 1862. This law provided significant federal support to state colleges that focused on "scientific agriculture" and the "mechanic arts," but specified that those schools must also include some instruction in military tactics. Every white, southern land-grant school exceeded that requirement by operating as a full-fledged military school along the lines of Virginia Military Institute (VMI) and the Citadel. When Clemson Agricultural College opened in 1893, for example, it immediately instituted the military system. The land-grant institution now known as South Carolina State University established a strong military program for the state's black youth after the school was reorganized in 1896.

The Citadel, Clemson, and South Carolina State provided hundreds of trained young men to serve in the nation's military forces in the world wars, the Korean War, and Vietnam. These institutions all were proud of their contributions to national defense but continued to regard military training primarily as a way to maintain discipline and instill character, not train for war.

In the twentieth century the southern military school tradition weakened somewhat but remained a recognized part of southern culture. In South Carolina, South Carolina State began moving away from the military requirement by the 1920s, and Clemson disbanded its corps of cadets in 1955. Both schools, however, continued to maintain strong Reserve Officer Training Corps (ROTC) detachments on campus. The Citadel is one of a handful of surviving state-supported military schools. It adapted to changing times by obeying a court order in 1995 to allow women in its corps of cadets. The number of female cadets has increased steadily ever since. Meanwhile, Camden Military Academy thrives as a private military preparatory school. At the turn of the twenty-first century, military education remained an established feature in the South Carolina landscape. ROD ANDREW, JR.

Andrew, Rod. *Long Gray Lines: The Southern Military School Tradition, 1839–1915.* Chapel Hill: University of North Carolina Press, 2001.

Baker, Gary R. *Cadets in Gray: The Story of the Cadets of the South Carolina Military Academy and the Cadet Rangers in the Civil War.* Columbia, S.C.: Palmetto Bookworks, 1989.

Bond, Oliver J. *The Story of the Citadel.* 1936. Reprint, Greenville, S.C.: Southern Historical Press, 1989.

Militia. When the colonists set foot in South Carolina in 1670, they brought with them the traditional English concept of a militia, the idea that every citizen had a duty to assist in the defense of the community. This tradition, dating back to the Anglo-Saxon *fyrd,* was formalized by Henry II in the *Assize of Arms* of 1181 and refined by successive English kings. It established the militia as the primary land defense of England and, by extension, the main defense of her colonies. In 1671 the Grand Council of colonial South Carolina passed a militia ordinance requiring all men aged sixteen to sixty to serve in the militia and to provide their own weapons. The Revolutionary War, fought to a large degree by local Whig and Tory militiamen in South Carolina, ended the colony's governance ties with the mother country but did not end the militia tradition.

During the Confederation government (1781–1789), the national army was minuscule and each state was responsible for its own defense. To bring some uniformity to the system, the Congress of the newly established United States passed what is usually called the Militia Act of 1792. This act required all able-bodied free white male citizens aged eighteen to forty-five to enroll in the militia company nearest their place of residence and to provide themselves, at their own expense, with arms and ammunition. In 1808 this requirement was eased somewhat when the federal government agreed to provide the states with some weapons from federal stocks.

Throughout the first half of the nineteenth century the militias were the backbone of the country's defense. There was, however, a problem for a country bent on expansion. A militia could not be required to serve outside its state. Thus, during the Second Seminole War (1835–1842), South Carolina had to depend on volunteers to serve in Florida when the federal government asked for assistance. The same was true in the Mexican War (1846–1848), which was fought primarily by volunteer units, including the Palmetto Regiment from South Carolina. Therefore, in South Carolina the militia served primarily as a source of manpower for slave patrols that kept order and enforced the restrictions on slave activity. Militia musters also served as focal points for social and political meetings on state and local affairs.

As sectional tensions grew in the 1850s, South Carolina began to improve its militia for possible action in a regional conflict. As a consequence of John Brown's raid on Harper's Ferry in 1859, the state authorized $100,000 for military contingencies. A large portion of militia was called for duty at Charleston during the secession crisis. After the firing on Fort Sumter, militiamen, both individually and as units, joined state regiments that were taken into Confederate service. They were replaced in the militia by older men and men who were exempt from Confederate service. These militia units were called at various times to defend Charleston, guard the coast, and resist Sherman's march through the state.

After the Civil War, the Reconstruction government replaced the antebellum militia with new, segregated companies. Despite occasional confrontations between black militiamen and former Confederate soldiers, the new militia units were never used to challenge the Ku Klux Klan or the Red Shirts, who were frequently better organized and better armed. Once Reconstruction ended, black companies were disbanded and most of the white units were merged into a new force that resurrected the prewar militia organization.

Since the Mexican War, most military thinkers had come to the conclusion that the militia system had to be "modernized" and that volunteer companies were to be preferred over what was by this time an unwilling militia. The Spanish-American War (1898) brought calls for modernization to a head. The National Guard, as the organized state militias were called by this time, proved woefully inadequate during that short war, and Secretary of War Elihu Root began to lobby for a National Reserve under the control of the federal government. The states reacted swiftly to this threat to their control over their own militias, and under intense political pressure from the states, Congress stopped short of establishing a National Reserve, deleting this provision from the Dick Act of 1902. However, the Dick Act did start the National Guard on the road to becoming a federal force by establishing standards that the states were required to meet in order to receive federal funding. The National Defense Act of 1916 completed the process, requiring all members of the National Guard to swear a dual oath, to both the state and the federal government.

Except as permitted by the federal government, the states were not allowed to establish any other military force, reinforcing federal control over the militias. With the entire National Guard federalized by 1917, there was a need for local defense, and the states were given the authority to establish local defense forces. South Carolina adjutant general William Moore issued General Order 162 on December 22, 1917, establishing the Reserve Militia, which consisted of one regiment and an additional battalion. The last unit of this force was disbanded in August 1920. Federal authorization for home defense units expired with the end of World War I.

The situation in early 1941 was strikingly similar to that in 1917. President Franklin D. Roosevelt began ordering National Guard units into federal service on September 16, 1940. Shortly thereafter, the National Defense Act of 1916 was amended to allow the establishment of state defense forces. The act establishing the South Carolina Defense Force was signed into law by Governor Burnet R. Maybank on March 21, 1941. The South Carolina Defense Force, renamed the South Carolina State Guard in 1944, numbered more than six thousand men in the spring of 1942. Members patrolled beaches, guarded sensitive facilities, and provided manpower for search and rescue and recovery from natural disasters until deactivated in August 1947.

With the end of World War II, authorization for state defense forces was again withdrawn. The cold war changed that policy, and in 1954 the federal government authorized state defense forces on a permanent basis, returning to the historic concept of the militia as the defender of the state. The South Carolina State Guard was reactivated by the General Assembly in 1981 and became one of the three components of the Military Department, along with the National Guard (the largest component) and the Emergency Preparedness Division. In 2001 the South Carolina State Guard numbered more than 1,050 men and women assigned to three brigades throughout the state, providing a force multiplier for the National Guard and a secondary defense force for the governor in times of emergency. JACK ALLEN MEYER

Callan, John F., comp. *The Military Laws of the United States.* Baltimore: John Murphy, 1858.

Flynn, Jean Martin. *The Militia in Antebellum South Carolina Society.* Spartanburg, S.C.: Reprint Company, 1991.

Mahon, John K. *History of the Militia and the National Guard.* New York: Macmillan, 1983.

Mill schools. Textile mill entrepreneurs remade the South Carolina landscape in the late nineteenth century. They surrounded their mills with villages and provided schools to educate the children of mill workers and to demonstrate to the public their concern for the community's well-being.

Early mill schools provided elementary education for children of varying academic levels and ages. Pacolet Mills was incorporated in Spartanburg County in 1882. Its school was in operation by 1885 with around eighty to one hundred students. In 1900 the Pacolet mill school had an enrollment of 369 but only three teachers. High student-teacher ratios were common throughout the state: in 1900 the Graniteville mill school had 57.2 pupils per teacher, Tucapau had 75 pupils per teacher, and Glendale had 125 students served by a single teacher. Although schools outside of mill villages also suffered from a lack of teachers, their ratios rarely ranged above 50 students per teacher.

The mill school was a reflection of the individual community and was run with little interference from the state until the advent of the Progressive Era. Prior to South Carolina's compulsory attendance law, children as young as nine went to work in the cotton mills, depending on personal preference or family financial circumstances. In South Carolina the Progressives focused their attention on public education as a vehicle to eliminate what they saw as the "mill problem." Progressives argued that mill schools did little to eradicate the mores of the farm and mountain hollow that they believed were detrimental to South Carolina's future well-being. South Carolina Progressives, led by Governor Richard I. Manning, attempted to set work age limits and require school attendance of those children excluded by law from the workplace. Both proposals met with resistance from the textile operatives, but by 1919 South Carolina had both child labor and compulsory school attendance laws.

In the area of education, the most audacious example of South Carolina's Progressive movement was the creation of a high school in Greenville. By 1922 there were fourteen mill schools in an industrial district that lay in a contiguous arc along the western side of the city. Students wishing to continue their education beyond the eighth grade had to travel to town and pay tuition to attend Greenville High School. Few mill families could afford this option. In 1923 the state legislature created the Parker District, named for Thomas F. Parker, owner of Monaghan Mill and a keen proponent of education in South Carolina's textile community. The centerpiece of the district was Parker High School. Lawrence Peter Hollis, welfare director at Monaghan Mill, was named district superintendent. With this new system, cotton mill owners transferred operation of their mill schools to the state. This led to central control with standardized policy and curriculum. Parker High School thrived under Hollis's leadership and attained nationwide attention in Progressive education circles. The Parker District operated independently until the consolidation of all Greenville County schools in 1951.

Parker High School was part of a broader trend that saw the state increase its control over education. When Buffalo Mill school burned in 1925, it was replaced by a new public school complete with electric lights and indoor plumbing. The passage of the 6-0-1 law in 1924 helped solidify the role of the state in financing public education. The 1950s saw the mill village passing from existence, and South Carolina's mill schools, by then absorbed into modern rationalized school districts across the state, also faded from the scene. JAMES A. DUNLAP III

Burts, Robert Milton. *Richard Irvine Manning and the Progressive Movement in South Carolina.* Columbia: University of South Carolina Press, 1974.

Carlton, David L. *Mill and Town in South Carolina, 1880–1920.* Baton Rouge: Louisiana State University Press, 1982.

Dunlap, James A., III. "Changing Symbols of Success: Economic Development in Twentieth Century Greenville, South Carolina." Ph.D. diss., University of South Carolina, 1994.

Kohn, August. *The Cotton Mills of South Carolina.* 1907. Reprint, Spartanburg, S.C.: Reprint Company, 1975.

Mill villages. The establishment of the Pelzer Manufacturing Company's mill on the Saluda River in Anderson County in the early 1880s marked the beginning of the Piedmont mill village boom. Early textile entrepreneurs built not only factories but frequently also entire villages, such as Piedmont in Greenville County, Clifton and Pacolet in Spartanburg County, and Graniteville and Langley in Aiken County. To ensure a steady supply of labor, employment contracts were signed with whole families, rather than with individuals, and the mill villages were central to this effort to retain employees. Quality housing and other amenities were crucial to attract and retain workers to the often isolated location of early mills. When mill villages were at their peak in the early 1900s, it has been estimated that as much as one-sixth of South Carolina's white population lived and worked in them.

Villages often followed a simple pattern, with workers housed in rows of identical single-family houses or, in some cases, duplexes, while higher-ranking managers lived in larger houses closer to the mills in the community centers. Black employees were housed in separate alleys, often on the other side of the mills from their white counterparts. In addition to housing, mills usually built churches and schools, and they sometimes provided electric lights and other amenities. Many mills retained company stores that sold on credit, and workers were sometimes paid in credits redeemable only at the company stores. Mills provided structured recreation as well, with baseball and softball teams providing a sense of community to boost employee morale.

A panoramic view of Clifton Mill Village, Spartanburg County, 1884. *Historical and Descriptive Review of the State of South Carolina.* Courtesy, South Carolina Historical Society.

Despite the often paternalistic approach to the operation of the villages, many mill villages gained a reputation for crime, disorder, drunkenness, and other vices. Mill workers were often derisively referred to as "lintheads." Mill owners worked to counter this reputation through intensive public relations campaigns. Pelzer and other mill villages prohibited saloons, imposed curfews, and even banned dogs in an effort to appear cleaner and more desirable.

As technology made it possible for mills to locate farther from water power sites and closer to an existing labor supply, the isolated mill villages soon gave way to enclaves established nearer to major towns. But the practice of providing housing, churches, company stores, and recreational facilities continued, as a means of maintaining control over the lives of an increasingly mobile workforce. Such plans, though often couched in the humanitarian language of paternalism, were aimed at forestalling any attraction workers might have toward organizing unions or engaging in other political activities. Thus, mill villages such as Drayton, Berea, Olympia, and many others formed virtually adjacent to, yet socially and politically separate from, Spartanburg, Greenville, and Columbia. Attempting to assuage fears that rural people recruited as mill workers might disturb town life, mill owners began promoting the mills as a positive good that could bring culture, education, and religion to the uncultured, uneducated, and unchurched rural folk. Meanwhile, politicians in smaller towns such as Clinton, Abbeville, and Newberry struggled to compete for the opportunity to build mills, regarding such investment as a virtual guarantee of prosperity much as their antebellum counterparts regarded raising cotton. The town of Clinton, home to Presbyterian College, saw its leading citizen W. P. Jacobs assert that the successful opening of the mill there was proof of God's favor and the town's righteousness.

In an effort to curb costs and preserve profits during the declining economic conditions of the 1920s, mill superintendents tried to get more work out of fewer workers, resulting in a phenomenon workers called the "stretch-out." Conditions deteriorated as mill owners opted to discontinue funding community improvements, and housing and other facilities were allowed to deteriorate. The stretch-out and a series of bitter strikes undermined workers' acceptance of existing conditions and exposed the shortcomings of the highly publicized paternalism of mill owners.

The mill villages were dismantled for many reasons, beginning in the 1920s. The automobile became more affordable, making it easier

Organized sports teams for girls and boys were an important part of mill life. This is a photograph of the girls team from Piedmont Mill (circa 1950). Courtesy, Pendleton District Commission

for workers to commute and easier for them to change jobs if working conditions deteriorated. Tougher child labor laws undermined the custom of hiring entire families to work, making it less cost-efficient for companies to provide housing. Intense competition forced mill owners to reexamine their costs, and often the amenities of the mill villages were allowed to decline. Additionally, during the 1920s many small mills were bought out by larger competitors who seldom had much stake in community life unless it affected the bottom line measurably. Many mill owners, contemplating the increasing mobility of the workforce, concluded that workers would be more likely to remain in the community if they invested in it as homeowners, and they began the process of selling the houses off, with their current occupants sometimes given first option to purchase at a slight discount from market value. Still, the companies remained in charge of the process. In many cases workers with a reputation for complaining or working to unionize were told that they would not be offered the chance to buy, and most white mill neighborhoods remained all-white until federal intervention in the 1960s. As the villages were sold off and institutions supported by the mills declined, the sense of community evident in neighborhood stores, parks, schools, churches, and mill league baseball declined, leaving behind only the physical artifacts of the mill village: rows of identical houses surrounding, in many cases, a silent and empty mill building. STEPHEN WALLACE TAYLOR

Carlton, David L. *Mill and Town in South Carolina, 1880–1920.* Baton Rouge: Louisiana State University Press, 1982.

Hall, Jacquelyn Dowd, et al. *Like a Family: The Making of a Southern Cotton Mill World.* Chapel Hill: University of North Carolina Press, 1987.

Herring, Harriet. *Passing of the Mill Village: Revolution in a Southern Institution.* Chapel Hill: University of North Carolina Press, 1949.

Hodges, James A. *New Deal Labor Policy and the Southern Cotton Textile Industry, 1933–1941.* Knoxville: University of Tennessee Press, 1986.

Moore, Toby. "Dismantling the South's Cotton Mill Village System." In *The Second Wave: Southern Industrialization from the 1940s to the 1970s,* edited by Philip Scranton. Athens: University of Georgia Press, 2001.

Simon, Bryant. *A Fabric of Defeat: The Politics of South Carolina Millhands, 1910–1948.* Chapel Hill: University of North Carolina Press, 1998.

Miller, Kelly, Jr. (1863–1939). Educator, writer. Miller was born on July 18 or 23, 1863, in Winnsboro to Kelly Miller, Sr., a free black man, and Elizabeth Roberts, a slave. His father was a Confederate army veteran. Miller's initial education was at a grammar school in Winnsboro. His considerable skill in mathematics drew the attention of Willard Richardson, a northern missionary. By 1878 Miller was attending Fairfield Institute, also in Winnsboro. Two years later he was awarded a scholarship to the preparatory department of Howard University in Washington, D.C.

After graduating from Howard in 1886, Miller studied sciences and mathematics with Captain Edgar Frisly, a British mathematician at the U.S. Naval Observatory. Through Frisly's influence, Miller became the first African American to attend Johns Hopkins University in Baltimore, but financial considerations forced him to withdraw during his junior year. In 1890 he was appointed to a mathematics professorship at Howard University. He remained there throughout his professional career. He received his M.A. (1901) and LL.D. (1903) from Howard. On July 17, 1894, he married Annie May Butler of Baltimore. Their marriage produced five children.

Early in his career Miller was a professor of both mathematics and sociology. But he eventually chose to concentrate primarily on sociology, believing it to be an effective means to study race relations in America. In 1907 Miller was appointed dean of Howard's College of Arts and Sciences. He remained an active teacher and administrator until his retirement in 1934. His influence on Howard University in the early twentieth century was such that the school was known to many as "Kelly Miller's University."

From his leadership at Howard and through his prolific writings, Miller became a national figure in the debate on race in America. Deemed by most to be a moderate and a harmonizer, he pursued a middle course between the accommodationist views of Booker T. Washington and the more radical stance of W. E. B. Du Bois. Miller agreed with Washington's contention that agriculture was vital to southern blacks. And he did not oppose Washington's emphasis on industrial education. Miller also supported Washington's call for African American clergymen to promote higher education. But, like Du Bois, Miller felt that a liberal arts curriculum was vital for students drawn from the growing urban black population and was absolutely necessary for the creation and expansion of a black professional class of physicians, lawyers, and teachers. By 1912 Miller was actively assisting Du Bois with editing *Crisis,* the official journal of the National Association for the Advancement of Colored People (NAACP). They became estranged in the 1930s, however, when Du Bois became closely associated with the American Communist Party. In contrast, Miller was an outspoken critic of Marxist ideology.

Throughout his career as an educator and spokesman for African Americans, Miller was a prolific author. He wrote numerous articles and pamphlets, many of which were open letters challenging the racial views of public figures. In 1913 he began his own journal, *Kelly Miller's Monographic Magazine.* His 1917 pamphlet *The Disgrace of Democracy: An Open Letter to President Woodrow Wilson* sold more than 250,000 copies. His major monographs were *Race Adjustment* (1908), *Out of the House of Bondage* (1914), and *The Everlasting Stain* (1924).

Miller died at his Washington, D.C., home on December 29, 1939. He was buried in Lincoln Memorial Cemetery in Washington, D.C. MILES S. RICHARDS

Eisenberg, Bernard. "Kelly Miller: The Negro Leader as a Marginal Man." *Journal of Negro History* 45 (July 1960): 182–97.

Meier, August. "The Racial and Educational Philosophy of Kelly Miller, 1895–1915." *Journal of Negro Education* 29 (spring 1960): 121–27.

Wright, W. D. "The Thought and Leadership of Kelly Miller." *Phylon* 39 (June 1978): 180–92.

Miller, Stephen Decatur (1787–1838). Congressman, governor, U.S. senator. Miller was born in the Waxhaws, Lancaster District, on May 8, 1787, the son of William Miller, a farmer, and Margaret White. After being schooled in the classics by a private tutor, he entered South Carolina College and graduated in 1808. Miller studied law in the office of John S. Richardson in Sumter and was admitted to the bar in 1811. Miller settled in Stateburg and married Elizabeth Dick of Sumter in 1814, with whom he had three children, two of whom died in infancy.

Miller's public service began in 1816, when he was elected to Congress to fill the vacancy caused by the resignation of William Mayrant. He was reelected the following year, but his wife's illness prevented his running for an additional term. Miller left Washington in 1819 and resumed his law practice. Two years after the death of his first wife in 1819, Miller married Mary Boykin. Among their four children was the famous diarist Mary Boykin Miller, who married James Chesnut, Jr.

From 1822 to 1828 Miller was a member of the South Carolina Senate and an early leader in the movement toward nullification. In 1824 he offered resolutions that set forth the states'-rights strict constructionist argument and declared federal internal improvement schemes and protective tariffs unconstitutional. The Senate passed the "Miller Resolutions," but they were tabled by the House. The next year, however, William Smith recalled the resolutions, which were passed by both the House and Senate and became the platform of the States' Rights and Free Trade Party in South Carolina. Between 1828 and 1830 Miller served as governor. Through his widely reprinted, rousing speeches he helped popularize nullification.

After completing his term as governor, Miller successfully challenged his onetime ally William Smith for a seat in the U.S. Senate. He told audiences during the campaign that "the ballot box, the jury box, and the cartridge box" are the only three ways to reform oppressive federal legislation. As senator, Miller was a strict-constructionist and defender of the compact theory of Union. He opposed the recharter of the Second Bank of the United States, Henry Clay's 1832 Land Bill, and the Tariff of 1832. Upon passage of the 1832 tariff, Miller joined with the rest of the South Carolina delegation in an "Address to the People of South Carolina." The address rejected the tariff and said that relief from federal power would have to come from the people of the state acting in their sovereign capacity. A delegate to both the 1832 and 1833 nullification conventions, Miller voted for nullification in 1832 and against the test oath in 1833.

Miller resigned from the Senate on March 2, 1833, citing poor health, and retired to land he had purchased in Mississippi. On March 8, 1838, Miller died in Raymond, Mississippi, where he was buried. SEAN R. BUSICK

Freehling, William W. *Prelude to Civil War: The Nullification Controversy in South Carolina, 1816–1836.* New York: Harper & Row, 1965.

Kirkland, Thomas J., and Robert M. Kennedy. *Historic Camden.* Vol. 2, *Nineteenth Century.* 1905. Reprint, Camden, S.C.: Kershaw County Historical Society, 1994.

Miller, Thomas Ezekiel (1849–1938). Political leader, college president. Miller was born on June 17, 1849, in Ferrebeeville in Beaufort District, the son of Richard Miller and Mary Ferrebee. Miller regarded himself as a black man, but his fair complexion led to persistent speculation and controversy about his racial identity. There were allegations that he was white, the son of an unmarried white couple who was raised by black parents.

Thomas E. Miller. Courtesy, South Carolina State University Historical Collection

In the early 1850s Miller moved with his parents to Charleston, where he attended schools organized for free black youngsters. After the Civil War he accompanied Union soldiers to Long Island, New York, and enrolled at Hudson school. He graduated from Lincoln University in Pennsylvania in 1872. He returned to South Carolina and briefly attended the law program at South Carolina College (now the University of South Carolina). He also read law and was admitted to the bar in 1875. He subsequently practiced law in Beaufort, where he had been elected to the county school commission in 1872.

A loyal Republican and politically ambitious, Miller was elected to the state House of Representatives in 1874 and served until 1880. Elected to the state Senate in 1880, he resigned after two years. In 1886 he lost an election to the U.S. House, but in 1888 he defeated William Elliott after a prolonged election controversy. He lost to Elliott in 1890 in another disputed election when the South Carolina Supreme Court ruled that while Miller's ballots had been printed on the required white paper, it was "white paper of a distinctly yellow tinge." He then lost in 1892 to George W. Murray when Murray—a black man—made an issue of Miller's light complexion.

Miller was reelected to the S.C. House in 1894 and was then elected to represent Beaufort in the 1895 constitutional convention. The convention's presiding officer, U.S. Senator Benjamin R. Tillman, was determined to eliminate black men from the political system. Miller eloquently but unsuccessfully fought the effort as he pleaded "for justice to a people whose rights are about to be taken away with one fell swoop." The new constitution included an elaborate set of voter registration qualifications that effectively disfranchised the state's black majority. Miller and the other five black delegates refused to sign the completed constitution.

However, during the convention's deliberations Miller succeeded in enlisting Tillman's support for a provision in the new constitution authorizing the creation of a separate land-grant college for African Americans. Since 1872 the state's land-grant funds had been allocated to the State A&M College, which was under the control of Claflin University, a private Methodist institution in Orangeburg. In 1896 Miller guided legislation through the General Assembly creating the Colored Normal, Industrial, Agricultural and Mechanical College of South Carolina (now South Carolina State University). Shortly thereafter Miller resigned from the House and was named the president of the new institution in Orangeburg.

Miller skillfully administered the college during its first fifteen years. Its primary mission was to train black youngsters in agriculture and the trades. In 1897 he explained, "The work of our college is along the industrial line. We are making educated and worthy school teachers, educated and reliable mechanics, educated, reliable and frugal farmers." In 1910 Miller publicly opposed Coleman Blease's candidacy for governor. But Blease won and promptly demanded and received Miller's resignation.

Miller devoted the remaining twenty-seven years of his life to a variety of community causes. Settling in Charleston, he served on an all-black subcommittee devoted to generating support for World War I. He successfully led a controversial campaign in 1919 to eliminate white teachers from the black public schools in Charleston. Miller moved to Philadelphia in 1923 but returned to Charleston in 1934. He had married Anna M. Hume about 1874, and they were the parents of nine children, seven of which survived until adulthood. Thomas Miller died on April 8, 1938. His legacy was inscribed on his tombstone in the Brotherly Association Cemetery in Charleston: "I served God and all the people, loving the white man not less, but the Negro needed me most." WILLIAM C. HINE

Hine, William C. "Thomas E. Miller and the Early Years of South Carolina State University." *Carologue* 12 (winter 1996): 8–12.

Newby, I. A. *Black Carolinians: A History of Blacks in South Carolina from 1895 to 1968.* Columbia: University of South Carolina Press, 1973.

Tindall, George Brown. *South Carolina Negroes 1877–1900.* 1952. Reprint, Columbia: University of South Carolina Press, 2003.

Milliken, Roger (b. 1915). Businessman, political activist. During his long career, Roger Milliken has built his family's textile business into a burgeoning textile corporation known for its innovative management, technological prowess, and clamlike secretiveness. Milliken has also played a major role in South Carolina's transition to Republican dominance, supporting conservative issues and candidates around the state and the nation.

Milliken was born on October 24, 1915, in New York, the son of Gerrish Milliken and Agnes Gayley. By the time of Roger's birth, the textile company his grandfather Seth had started in 1865 in Portland, Maine, Deering Milliken Company, had grown into a multistate business, including operations in South Carolina. In 1939, two years after graduating from Yale with a degree in French history, Roger joined the family company. He married Justine Van Rensselaer Hooper on June 5, 1948, and they eventually had five children.

In June 1947 Gerrish Milliken died, leaving Roger in charge of the company. Roger Milliken soon moved to Spartanburg and also started to concentrate the company's operations in the South Carolina Piedmont. A man of endless energy, Milliken turned Deering Milliken into one of the biggest and most successful textile corporations in the United States. Industry analysts have widely complimented Deering Milliken's (in 1976 renamed Milliken & Company) effective use of the latest technological and managerial advances. In a business often known for its conservative management style and technological foot-dragging, Milliken & Company's research and development and managerial methods have rewarded the company with the reputation as perhaps the most innovative and dynamic textile corporation in America. Milliken is particularly known for his pioneering work in inventory management.

Milliken has willingly discussed his company's quality management with outsiders, but otherwise he protects both his personal and his company's privacy with a hermitlike determination. The company's ownership remains in the hands of Milliken and his relatives, enabling Milliken to maintain a powerful control over all company-related information, including the size and scope of its operations. Common estimates of Milliken& Company's annual sales have amounted to between $2 billion and $3 billion. According to *Forbes,* Milliken's personal wealth climbed to $1 billion in 1987, and in the succeeding fifteen years the estimates of his wealth ranged between $580 million and $1.4 billion, making Milliken the richest man in South Carolina by a comfortable margin.

In addition to his business career, Milliken has taken an active role in the conservative politics of Spartanburg, South Carolina, and the nation. Soon after relocating in South Carolina, Milliken participated in building the Republican Party in the state, offering the party his energy, leadership, and deep pockets. From 1956 to 1984 he served as a South Carolina delegate to the Republican National Convention. In addition to helping the GOP in South Carolina, he promoted conservative causes and individuals around the nation. In the early 1960s Milliken was one of the king-makers behind Barry Goldwater's presidential campaigns. However, Milliken's benevolence has not been limited to political causes. He has been an active and civic-minded citizen of Spartanburg, supporting local pro bono issues and institutions with his advice and sizable checks.

Milliken's convictions and support for conservative causes run deep and wide. In 1956 he closed down a factory in Darlington after its workers voted to unionize. After a twenty-four-year legal dispute, the courts ordered Milliken to pay $5 million as back pay to the workers affected by the closing. Upset over Xerox company's sponsorship of a 1967 civil rights documentary with allegedly liberal bias, Milliken ordered all Xerox copiers removed from his company's facilities. In 1954 Milliken provided the largest individual contribution—$20,000—to William F. Buckley to get his magazine *National Review* started. Milliken was one of the early contributors to the Heritage Foundation, a conservative, Washington, D.C.–based think tank. Milliken's convictions run so deep that he is known to have ignored possible business opportunities with both Chinese communists and the U.S. Department of Defense.

Milliken has consistently supported candidates who share his conservative values and promise to protect American textile industries from foreign competition. Since the 1980s this protectionist stance has put Milliken occasionally at odds with some of the Republican political leadership and led to his increased support of third-party movements and antiglobalization activists such as Pat Buchanan, Ross Perot, and even Ralph Nader. Milliken was a powerful force in the fights against the North American Free Trade Agreement (NAFTA) and General Agreement on Tariffs and Trade (GATT) tariff reductions. However, he has also expanded his company's operations abroad and has run his factories with foreign machinery since the 1960s. Milliken's decision to invite foreign textile machinery companies to locate in Spartanburg in the early 1960s was one of the key decisions leading to the rapid internationalization of the Piedmont's industrial landscape. MARKO MAUNULA

Davenport, Jim. "In S.C., There's Roger and US." Columbia *State,* March 2, 1992, business sec., pp. 6–7, 16.

"How Roger Milliken Runs Textiles' Premier Performer." *Business Week* (January 19, 1981): 62–65, 68, 73.

Lizza, Ryan. "Silent Partner." *New Republic* 222 (January 10, 2000): 22–25.

Lunan, Bert, and Robert A. Pierce. *Legacy of Leadership.* Columbia: South Carolina Business Hall of Fame, 1999.

Monk, John. "The Last Textile Giant." Columbia *State,* October 7, 2001, pp. D1, D4–D5.

Milliken & Company. In 1865 Seth Milliken and his business partner William Deering became jobbers of dry goods and woolen textiles in Portland, Maine. The company was a success, but Deering left the partnership four years later and moved to Chicago.

However, the company's name remained Deering Milliken until 1976, when it was changed to Milliken & Company.

After only three years in Portland, Seth Milliken moved Deering Milliken's headquarters to New York City. The company expanded rapidly in both size and scope. Deering Milliken came to South Carolina in 1884, when it built a plant in Pacolet. By the time of his death in 1920, Seth Milliken had bought interest in forty-two South Carolina textile mills.

With Seth's son Gerrish leading the company, Deering Milliken in the 1920s was largely acting as a selling agent for southern textile mills. As the Great Depression arrived, Gerrish expanded the company by buying out heavily indebted or bankrupt mills, many of which were deeply indebted to Deering Milliken. Gerrish's acquisitions also included Mercantile Stores Company, a sizable player in national retail markets.

The next change in leadership took place in 1947, when Gerrish died and left his son Roger in charge of the company. Roger Milliken further expanded Deering Milliken's operations in South Carolina, and in 1954 he moved his family to Spartanburg, closer to the center of the company's operations. The young CEO worked successfully to consolidate its possessions, bringing many separately incorporated mills into a single corporation and thus improving the company's logistics and management.

Through the company's Spartanburg-based Milliken Research Corporation, Milliken & Company has become internationally known as a technologically innovative textile company. This research and development center has produced more than fifteen hundred patents. Milliken has also gained praise for its logistically advanced management, especially in inventory control. By the start of the twenty-first century, Milliken& Company's production line stretched from automotive fabrics to carpets, napery items, and fabrics for various types of apparel. Milliken also produced chemicals used in dyes, packaging, plastics, and consumer products.

Milliken & Company has been tight-lipped about its operations and, especially, sales figures. Its ownership is shared between family members and close confidants, thus enabling the company to control the information flow effectively. Milliken & Company's sixty-five South Carolina factories, combined with additional operations in five states and twelve foreign countries, make it in many estimates the biggest textile company in the United States and one of the largest privately owned companies in the world. MARKO MAUNULA

Davenport, Jim. "In S.C., There's Roger and US." Columbia *State,* March 2, 1992, business sec., pp. 6–7, 16.

"How Roger Milliken Runs Textiles' Premier Performer." *Business Week* (January 19, 1981): 62–65, 68, 73.

Lunan, Bert, and Robert A. Pierce. *Legacy of Leadership.* Columbia: South Carolina Business Hall of Fame, 1999.

Mills, Robert (1781–1855). Architect, engineer, author. Mills was born on August 12, 1781, in Charleston, the son of William Mills, a successful Scots immigrant tailor, and Ann Taylor, descendant of the first landgrave of the Carolinas. Little is known about his early education, which took place in Charleston possibly under the tutelage of his older brother, Thomas, or at the College of Charleston. During his formative years in South Carolina, Mills was beguiled by the state's topography and proud of its cultivated, yet revolutionary heritage; but he was anxious for its improvement. The source of his interest in architecture is speculative but reflects his admiration of the quality of building in Charleston, especially in the Palladian taste. In 1800 Mills moved to Washington, D.C., to study under the tutelage of James Hoban, designer of the White House. Mills would subsequently study architecture with Thomas Jefferson (who gave Mills access to his extensive collection of architectural books) and with Benjamin Henry Latrobe, the foremost practitioner of architecture and engineering in the young republic. Not without difficulty Latrobe trained Mills to understand the integral relationships between facade plan and volume and between structure, context, and symbolism. Latrobe also imparted surveying techniques, basic engineering principles, and most usefully, masonry (brick) vault construction.

Mills defined both his personal and public ambition in an 1808 letter to Jefferson, in which he declared his desire to pursue "the honour and benefit of my country." His architectural design and engineering projects would reform architecture through the application of new construction techniques with the rationalist thought espoused by Jefferson. Mills conceived not only a technically modern built environment, but also a progressive nation structured around expanded commerce and communication. He primarily fabricated this order from a blend of colonial Georgian and rational antiquarian styles.

The patronage of Latrobe helped launch Mills's career in Philadelphia and enabled him to marry Eliza Barnwell Smith on October 15, 1808. She came from a landed family in upstate Virginia (now West Virginia). They would have six children. At Philadelphia he worked for religious and professional groups such as the Sansom Street Baptist congregation and Washington Benevolent Society. For the Baptist Church (1811), Mills further simplified and classicized his earlier design for the Congregational Church he had already built in Charleston (1804–1806). The scheme would reappear in his equally inventive reconfiguring of central plan space for the Monumental Church in Richmond (1812–1814) and Baptist Church in Baltimore (1816–1818). Mills's other major Philadelphia work was Washington Hall (1813–1816), for which he again appropriated the Palladian and neoclassical motifs of recessed columnar porticoes and windows to create an effective, if modest, urban monumentality. Other successful commissions from this period include a Presbyterian church in Augusta, Georgia (1807); Burlington County Jail, New Jersey (1808); and refurbishing the Old State House (Independence Hall), Philadelphia (1809). Relocating to Baltimore in 1814, Mills won a commission to design that city's Washington Monument (1814, 1816–1842), which devolved into a narrative of funding cuts and compromise. The completed monument, scaled back but still impressive, incorporated a single column topped with a statue and supported by a simple plinth.

Mills also participated in the modern organization of architectural work and social affairs. He joined efforts to promote professional standards and higher education as well as novel applications of classical styles to contemporary usage. He drafted a manual on architecture intended for builders and amateurs. An advocate of internal improvements, Mills's enthusiasm initially focused on canals but later evolved into railroad proposals, including a scheme for a transcontinental railroad in the early 1850s.

In 1820 he returned to his native South Carolina to accept appointment as acting commissioner of the Board of Public Works to superintend a program of construction across the state. He thereafter was engaged as superintendent of public buildings (1823) and then was hired on a commission basis for the remainder of his residence in the state. His first major commission was the Bethesda Presbyterian Church in Camden (1820–1821), but his time in South Carolina would be best remembered for a series of public buildings. Using standard designs, Mills completed twelve jails, sixteen courthouses, and the County Record Building (Fireproof Building) in Charleston (1821–1827). In the Fireproof Building he adeptly updated colonial Palladian external and internal organization, rendering them more durable through the use of masonry-vaulted construction. Those components were repeated on diminished scale in the main courthouse type, which was distinguished by a raised portico, supported on a secondary arcaded entrance, and flanked by curving staircases. The arrangement was aggrandized in his design for the South Carolina Lunatic Asylum in Columbia (1822) and in the nearby Ainsley Hall House (1823–1825). While resident in Columbia, Mills published a comprehensive plan for a statewide transportation network, *Internal Improvement of South Carolina* (1822), an *Atlas of South Carolina* (1825), and his encyclopedic *Statistics of South Carolina* (1826), a comprehensive overview of the state's history, economy, topography, natural resources, and potential for future development.

In 1830 Mills won a commission to renovate the federal House of Representatives and relocated to the nation's capital. Beginning in 1831, he received a series of official appointments, most notably for designing customhouses for the U.S. Treasury. In 1836 President Andrew Jackson (a fellow South Carolinian) confirmed Mills as architect of the new multistory office complexes for the Treasury (1836–1842) and the Patent Office (1839–1842). In these works Mills intensified the classic revivalism of Latrobe and the sophisticated planning and construction method of his earlier public buildings to create two edifices that established the enduring pattern of federal government architecture. He also raised the standard and sophistication of federal building programs, including the reduction of cost overrun. These major federal commissions gave him the advantage in the Washington Monument competition (1846) and a series of commissions for other public structures, including the Washington Jail (1839–1841), further improvements to the Capitol (especially 1844 and 1850), the General Post Office (1839–1842), and the Winder Building (1847). For the Washington Monument, Mills imagined a spectacular peripheral colonnaded museum of American culture containing a spiral roadway to a viewing platform encircling the massive masonry obelisk. As was the case with his Baltimore monument, however, financial concerns greatly reduced the scale of Mills's original conception. After much difficulty and expenditure, only the obelisk was erected on the Mall (1848–1854, 1880–1884). Financial security and steady employment continued to prove elusive in his later years, however, and he failed to win commissions for the Mall (1841), the Smithsonian Institution (1841), the War and Navy Department (1843–1844), and the Capitol Extension (1850 and 1853). Apart from some financial success with the reprinting of his *Guide to the Capitol of the United States* (1834), he had the consolation of completing a major addition to Jefferson's Rotunda at the University of Virginia at Charlottesville (1851–1852).

Mills justly claimed to originate an architectural profession in the United States but was overtaken by aesthetic and political change, particularly the development of architectural scholarship and structural science. He died in Washington, D.C., on March 3, 1855, and was buried in Congressional Cemetery. RHODRI WINDSOR LISCOMBE

Bryan, John M., ed. *Robert Mills: America's First Architect.* New York: Princeton Architectural Press, 2001.

———. *Robert Mills, Architect.* Washington, D.C.: American Institute of Architects Press, 1989.

Liscombe, Rhodri Windsor. *Altogether American: Robert Mills, Architect and Engineer.* New York: Oxford University Press, 1994.

———. *The Church Architecture of Robert Mills.* Easley, S.C.: Southern Historical Press, 1985.

Waddell, Gene. "Robert Mills's Fireproof Building." *South Carolina Historical Magazine* 80 (April 1979): 105–35.

Waddell, Gene, and Rhodri Windsor Liscombe. *Robert Mills's Courthouses and Jails.* Easley, S.C.: Southern Historical Press, 1981.

Minibottles. The minibottle became part of the South Carolina social scene on March 28, 1973. This change in drinking habits was preceded by statewide rejection of the sale of liquor by the drink in 1966, dissatisfaction with brown bagging (patrons transporting bottles wrapped in paper bags into clubs and restaurants), and recognition of both the potential benefits of increased tourism and the widespread illegal consumption in metropolitan areas.

During the 1972 session, the General Assembly wrestled with a proposal permitting some restaurants, hotels, motels, and private clubs to dispense liquor in bottles of between 1.6 and 2 ounces. Those in favor, including Governor John West, stressed that this would assure quality (the minibottle would be opened in the presence of the purchaser), reduce public drunkenness (since brown baggers would not feel obligated to finish their bottles before departing), and provide considerable tax revenue. Those opposed warned of increased crime and rampant alcoholism.

In November 1972 the electorate backed a constitutional amendment that ended brown bagging by a vote of 143,083 to 103,219. Had the minibottle era been a success? Tourism certainly increased, and chamber-of-commerce folk quickly praised the minibottle as "a more civilized approach" to the traditional cocktail hour than brown bagging. However, drinks became much more expensive, and only Class A restaurants (at least forty-seat capacity) and true nonprofit clubs were supposed to stock minibottles—rules that were not always strictly observed.

By the close of the first decade, some five thousand hotels, motels, clubs, and restaurants were dispensing minis. Revenue was impressive, but not as great as had been predicted. There was reportedly less public drunkenness, and alcohol consumption did not seem to be increasing at an unreasonable rate. But minibottles earned the opposition of some groups, including the hospital industry, chambers of commerce, Mothers Against Drunk Driving, and others. In 2004 nearly sixty percent of South Carolina voters approved a referendum to remove the minibottle requirement from the state constitution. JOHN H. MOORE

George, Mark. "The Impact of the Minibottle." Columbia *State,* September 4, 1977, p. B1.

Slade, David. "Early Returns against Minibottles." Charleston *Post and Courier,* November 3, 2004, pp. A15, A21.

Moise, Edwin Warren (1832–1902). Lawyer, soldier, adjutant general. The descendant of a Sephardic Jewish family from Alsace and the French Caribbean, Moise was born on May 21, 1832, in Charleston, the son of Abraham Moise and Caroline Moses. He was a member of Kahal Kadosh Beth Elohim, Charleston's oldest synagogue, and was educated in local schools. As a young adult, Moise was employed as a clerk. On September 20, 1854, he married Esther Lyon of Petersburg, Virginia. The following year Moise went to work for his uncle Raphael J. Moses, a successful attorney and plantation owner in Columbus, Georgia. Moise ran his uncle's flour mill, kept his books, and read the law.

Moise opposed secession and publicly argued against it. Nevertheless, when the Civil War came he volunteered for Confederate service. In May 1862 he organized a cavalry company in Columbus. Called the Moise Rangers, it was one of only a few companies named for Jewish Confederates. Moise was named captain of the Rangers that became Company A of Claiborne's Seventh Confederate Cavalry. The Seventh served in the southeastern corner of Virginia and in North Carolina. Moise saw a great deal of action in late 1864 and early 1865, including foraging expeditions, the defense of Petersburg during the Bermuda Hundred campaign, the "Great Beefsteak Raid" under General Wade Hampton, and the Battle of Bentonville. He surrendered with Hampton at Greensboro, North Carolina.

After the war, Moise returned to Sumter. He went into law, politics, farming, and journalism. During Reconstruction, Moise was a conservative Democrat and a bitter opponent of the Reconstruction government. In 1876 he enthusiastically supported Wade Hampton, his former commander, for governor and ran for adjutant general on Hampton's ticket, winning that race. Moise was also a commander of the Red Shirts, an armed volunteer organization that supported Hampton.

After being elected adjutant general, Moise commanded the militia in an evenhanded manner. Like Hampton, Moise was a moderate on racial issues. He invited black South Carolinians to join the militia. He served two terms as adjutant general, from 1876 to 1880. An opponent of Benjamin R. Tillman, Moise was defeated in an 1892 race for Congress.

In 1902, at the memorial service for Hampton in Sumter, Moise gave the oration. He died on December 12, 1902, and was buried in Sumter. ROBERT N. ROSEN

Moise, Harold. *The Moise Family of South Carolina.* Columbia, S.C.: R. L. Bryan, 1961.

Rosen, Robert N. *The Jewish Confederates.* Columbia: University of South Carolina Press, 2000.

Moïse, Penina (1797–1880). Educator, poet, hymn writer, activist. Moïse was born on April 23, 1797, in Charleston, the youngest daughter of Abraham and Sarah Moïse. Her father was a trader who came to South Carolina after fleeing the Santo Domingo slave insurrection in 1791. He died when Penina was twelve, forcing her to leave school to take care of her ailing mother.

Despite ending her formal education at the age of twelve, Moïse continued to engage in intellectual efforts. From a young age she found solace in writing poetry. In 1819 Moïse published her first poem. Thereafter the prolific poet submitted her verse to the *Charleston Courier,* the *Boston Daily Times,* the *New Orleans Commercial Times,* the *Washington Union, Godey's Ladies Book,* the *Home Journal of New York Occident,* and the *American Jewish Advocate.* In 1833 Moïse published a volume of secular poems titled *Fancy's Sketch Book.* Demonstrating a cosmopolitan worldview, Moïse addressed the issues of anti-Semitism, politics, and history and also included personal insights on society. Her poems contained romantic, sentimental, and classical themes, as well as emotional and nondenominational religious topics.

An observant Jew, Moïse was an active member in Charleston's Kahal Kadosh Beth Elohim synagogue. In 1841 her brother Abraham and another prominent Jewish Charlestonian, Isaac Harby, spearheaded the effort to alter the synagogue service to a reformed service. Her brother and Harby commissioned Moïse to write the new hymnal. Consequently, Moïse composed the vast majority of the hymns included in the first American Reform Jewish hymnal. Dedicated to the celebration of Judaism and desiring to encourage communal and individual fidelity to Judaism, the poet divided the hymnal into nine sections. Separately and collectively the hymns were designed to promote a continued faith in and a tolerance for Judaism in the midst of a highly evangelical Protestant South. Moïse was also a superintendent of Charleston's first Jewish school.

During the Civil War, Moïse avidly supported the South in her writing and educational efforts. Residing in Sumter during the war, Moïse returned to Charleston at the end of the war blind and ill. She was cared for by her sister and her niece. Continuing with her devotion to education and Judaism, Moïse, her sister, and her niece established a Sunday school in their home for Charleston's younger students. Curricula included classical and religious education. Moïse never married. She died on September 13, 1880, and is buried in the Coming Street Cemetery in Charleston. JENNIFER A. STOLLMAN

Hagy, James. *This Happy Land: The Jews of Colonial and Antebellum Charleston.* Tuscaloosa: University of Alabama Press, 1993.

Moïse, Penina. *Secular and Religious Works of Penina Moise with a Brief Sketch of Her Life.* Charleston, S.C.: Nicholas G. Duffy, 1911.

Reznikoff, Charles. *The Jews of Charleston: A History of an American Jewish Community.* Philadelphia: Jewish Publication Society of America, 1950.

Molloy, Robert (1906–1977). Novelist, editor, critic. Son of R. William Molloy and Edyth Estelle Johnson, Robert Molloy was born on January 9, 1906, in Charleston, the place he would always remember and summon up vividly in his writing. Living first on Tradd Street and then near Colonial Lake, the boy was the next to youngest of five siblings in a comfortably middle-class Catholic family. His first artistic passion was for the piano, and later in life he would be an accomplished musician. At about the age of twelve, following financial reverses, he moved with his family first to Philadelphia and then to New York City. Molloy never spent any significant time in Charleston after that.

A good student, with a flair for languages (many of which he would teach himself later in life), Molloy had his plans for college dashed with his father's death. He supported himself with numerous jobs and married Marion Knapp Jones on June 29, 1929. They would have two sons, Brian and Thomas, both professional musicians. A job as a publisher's reader led him into writing book reviews; translating (with Madeleine Boyd) two of Lucien Pemjean's works from the French (*Captain D'Artagnan* and *When D'Artagnan Was Young*); and translating Spanish-speaking authors, including Romulo Gallegos (*Dona Barbara,* 1931), Luis Spota, and Victor Alba. He also authored articles on European literature for the first edition of the *Columbia Encyclopedia* and contributed to the *Encyclopedia Americana* and *British Authors of the Nineteenth Century.*

By 1936 Molloy was working as book reviewer and copy editor for the New York *Sun.* In that capacity he befriended the British novelist William McFee. Molloy eventually became literary editor of the *Sun* from 1943 to 1945, and interested in writing, he took a course under the gifted writing instructor Sylvia Chatfield Bates. He first wrote short stories, seeing them published over the years in such magazines as *Good Housekeeping, Woman's Home Companion, Colliers,* and others. Bates suggested he try novel writing, and he dedicated his first, *Pride's Way* (1945), to her. In this engaging social comedy of a large Charleston Catholic family, Molloy summoned up the city of his youth, viewing his characters and his native city with affection, humor, and gentle irony. It was the May 1945 Literary Guild selection, a play version was staged in Charleston, and two novels in the same vein followed: *Pound Foolish* (1950) and *A Multitude of Sins* (1953). Two other works featured Charleston exclusively: the nonfiction *Charleston: A Gracious Heritage* (1947) and *An*

Afternoon in March (1958), a fictional retelling of the 1888 Thomas McDow murder of *News and Courier* editor Francis W. Dawson. Molloy's New York City novels include *Uneasy Spring* (1946); *The Best of Intentions* (1949); *The Reunion* (1959), partially set in Charleston; and *The Other Side of the Hill* (1962). The latter two reflect a mature, sophisticated, and urbane worldview, reflective of Molloy. He died in Paramus, New Jersey, on January 27, 1977. HARLAN GREENE

Greene, Karen. "Writer Draws on Charleston Childhood." Charleston *News and Courier*, April 9, 1975, p. B2.

Jones, Katherine M., and Mary Verner Schlaefer. *South Carolina in the Short Story*. Columbia: University of South Carolina Press, 1952.

"Robert Molloy, Writer Is Dead." Charleston *News and Courier*, February 6, 1977, p. A17.

Yoken, Melvin B., ed. *The Letters (1971–1977) of Robert Molloy*. Lewiston, N.Y.: Edwin Mellen, 1989.

Moncks Corner (Berkeley County; 2000 pop. 5,952). The village of Moncks Corner in St. John's Berkeley Parish derived its name from Thomas Monck, who in 1735 purchased one thousand acres in the parish and established Mitton Plantation. Monck's plantation was located at a fork where the Charleston Road intersected with the Cherokee Path. The left branch led to the Congaree River, while the right went toward the Santee River and the Georgetown area. The site was also near Stoney Landing, the head of navigation on the Cooper River thirty-five miles from Charleston. A small commercial community grew up around the plantation. The Swiss immigrant Simeon Theus is credited with opening the first store at the crossroads around 1738. Among others who established stores was John Dawson, Thomas Monck's son-in-law. Old Moncks Corner was "more of a trading post than a town." Planters brought their goods for sale and then returned home.

The crossroads became a point of strategic importance during the siege of Charleston. In April 1780 Banastre Tarleton gained his first notable victory at Moncks Corner, surprising and routing an American force commanded by Isaac Huger and severing Charleston's final link to the backcountry. After the war, the opening of the State Road between Charleston and Columbia and the completion of the Santee Canal caused the village to decline and almost vanish. In 1856 the Northeastern Railroad constructed a new station about a mile away from the old settlement. The railroad station was called Moncks Corner and expanded to include the old property of Thomas Monck.

The railroad gradually revitalized Moncks Corner. The town was incorporated in 1885. Ten years later Moncks Corner became the seat of Berkeley County, succeeding Mount Pleasant, and the first term of court was held in October. The first school was opened in 1913 and the first bank in 1918. The development of the Santee Cooper rural electric project from 1939 to 1941 led to more growth. Between 1930 and 1940 the population of Moncks Corner almost doubled, from 623 to 1,165. Santee Cooper moved its main office to Moncks Corner in 1945, while its creation of Lakes Marion and Moultrie made the town attractive to fishermen and boaters.

In the final two decades of the twentieth century, Moncks Corner benefited from the rapid growth of Berkeley County. During the 1990s the town's annual budget grew from $1 million to $2.2 million. New businesses moved to town, and Moncks Corner recaptured part of its eighteenth-century past by once again becoming a commercial center. DAVID E. RISON

Cross, J. Russell. *Historic Ramblin's through Berkeley*. Columbia, S.C.: R. L. Bryan, 1985.

Stockton, Robert P. *Historic Resources of Berkeley County, South Carolina*. Columbia: South Carolina Department of Archives and History, 1990.

Montagu, Lord Charles Greville (1741–1784). Governor. Born on May 29, 1741, the second son of Robert Montagu, third duke of Manchester, Charles attended Christ Church College, Oxford. He represented Huntingdonshire in the British House of Commons from 1762 to 1765 and in the latter year married Elizabeth Balmer of the same shire. Appointed governor of South Carolina by the Rockingham administration, Montagu arrived in Charleston in June 1766. Granting clemency to several convicted outlaws signaled his good intentions but contributed to the Regulator movement, in which backcountry men inflicted summary justice on wrongdoers. Touring the area in 1769, Montagu informed himself sufficiently to sign the act establishing circuit courts, acquire upcountry acreage for himself, and eventually pardon the Regulators. In July 1769, shortly after South Carolina had joined the nonimportation movement against the Townshend duties, he sailed for England.

His farewell was cordial, but he quickly squandered local goodwill after his return to Charleston in September 1771. Montagu soon convinced several Carolinians that "it was not impossible for a Man to be too great a Fool to make a good Governor." Lacking quarters in town, Montagu commuted from Fort Johnson by boat, while a local satirist ridiculed him for the cannon salutes that heralded his passing. More sympathetic men from Beaufort, he later claimed, offered to build him a house if he moved the capital there, and Montagu visited the area in the spring of 1772.

Meanwhile, he confronted more serious problems in Charleston. One involved a customs collector who successfully defied the governor's orders; the other was an impending conflict with the Commons House of Assembly. In December 1769, while he had been in England, the Commons House had sent £1,500 sterling to London for the use of the opposition politician John Wilkes. Colonial authorities countered with an instruction requiring all future tax bills to include specified restrictions on the use of the funds. But the Commons House had long considered the control of taxation to be its most fundamental right. Accordingly, the Commons House refused to accept the instruction, deadlock ensued, and no tax act passed the legislature for the last six years of the colonial period.

Montagu's subsequent actions made matters worse. Hoping to resolve his political and personal problems in a single stroke, he ignored contrary advice and called the assembly to meet at Beaufort instead of Charleston in October 1772. Leaders of the Commons House from Charleston, he assumed, would be late in arriving; Beaufort members would cooperate in the hope of permanently obtaining the capital; and passage of a tax bill acceptable to the ministry would be the result. But a belated cautionary note from London advised him to be conciliatory, so he met the assembly at Beaufort and sent it back to Charleston before it could proceed to business. "No Measure of any Governor," the *South-Carolina Gazette* reported, "was ever more freely and generally condemned." After the legislature censured him, he dissolved it and called new elections. Reelected members then promptly chose the same Speaker, and Montagu again abruptly dissolved them. Having lost control of the situation, he precipitously sailed for England in March 1773 and soon thereafter resigned the governorship.

Montagu faced problems well beyond his control, but his own blunders increased them exponentially. In particular, moving the meeting of the legislature to Beaufort alienated local leaders, and it—with a similar measure in Massachusetts—would appear in the Declaration of Independence as part of the evidence against King George III, whose representatives had "called together legislative bodies at places unusual, uncomfortable, and distant from the depository of their Public Records, for the sole Purpose of fatiguing them into compliance with his measures."

Montagu's later career presents a puzzle. After returning to England, he made an unsuccessful run for Parliament in 1774. After the Revolutionary War began, an apocryphal story suggests that Montagu offered his services to the American agent in Paris, Benjamin Franklin. The tale is implausible, but not impossible. Still, Montagu became a captain in the Eighty-eighth British Regiment of Foot on December 12, 1780. Sent to British-occupied Charleston, he recruited nearly five hundred American prisoners of war for service against the French and Spanish in the Caribbean. Though his old friend General William Moultrie refused to defect, Montagu's success was sufficient to prompt a repeat performance, and he soon filled a second battalion with prisoners from New York. But the war was almost over, and in November 1783 his regiment was ordered disbanded. Most of his men settled in Nova Scotia, where Montagu died on February 3, 1784. He was buried in St. Paul Churchyard, Halifax. ROBERT M. WEIR

Davis, Robert Scott, Jr. "Lord Montagu's Mission to South Carolina in 1781: American POWs for the King's Service in Jamaica." *South Carolina Historical Magazine* 84 (April 1983): 89–109.

Greene, Jack P. "Bridge to Revolution: The Wilkes Fund Controversy in South Carolina, 1769–1775." *Journal of Southern History* 29 (February 1963): 19–52.

Watson, Alan D. "The Beaufort Removal and the Revolutionary Impulse in South Carolina." *South Carolina Historical Magazine* 84 (July 1983): 121–35.

Weir, Robert M. *Colonial South Carolina: A History.* 1983. Reprint, Columbia: University of South Carolina Press, 1997.

Montgomery, John Henry (1833–1902). Manufacturer, merchant. Montgomery was born on a farm in Hobbysville, Spartanburg County, on December 8, 1833, the eldest son of Benjamin Montgomery and Harriet Moss. In the early 1850s Montgomery worked as a store clerk and then a partner with his brother-in-law in a mercantile business. In 1857 he married Susan A. Holcombe. The union produced eight children. Shortly after marrying, Montgomery entered a general merchandising business with his father-in-law and acquired an interest in a local tannery. He served in the South Carolina Volunteers during the Civil War and attained the rank of captain. Following the war, Montgomery continued to engage in farming and mercantile activities. His successful experimentation with commercial fertilizers led to association with the Baltimore firm of John Merriman, for whom Montgomery became a salesman. In 1874 Montgomery moved to Spartanburg, where he joined the mercantile firm of Walker, Fleming and Company, which was the largest cotton buyer in the county.

In 1881 Montgomery and Walker, Fleming and Company purchased Trough Shoals along the Pacolet River in Spartanburg County as the site for a new textile operation. A year later the Pacolet Manufacturing Company organized with an initial capital stock of $103,000. Montgomery was chosen president and treasurer of the company, and the first mill became operational in 1884. Under Montgomery's guidance, the Pacolet Manufacturing Company expanded to a second mill in 1888 and a third in 1894. By 1895 the company operated more than fifty thousand spindles and maintained a capital stock of $700,000. Montgomery's success was due in part to his skill at attracting northern capital. He brought to Spartanburg Seth M. Milliken of the New York selling house of Deering, Milliken and Company. Montgomery also relied on connections to New England entrepreneurs for his second major mill project, Spartan Mills. Organized in 1888, Spartan Mills merged with Whitfield Mills of Newburyport, Massachusetts, the next year in an arrangement that brought all of Whitfield's machinery to Spartanburg. Montgomery also briefly experimented with the use of black labor in textiles following the 1899 purchase of Charleston Mills. Renamed Vesta Mills, the factory operated only until 1901, when it closed due largely to high competition for both black and white labor in Charleston.

Montgomery played an important role in the development of upcountry mill villages with the construction of company housing, schools, and shops. In November 1885 the Spartanburg *Carolina Spartan* stated that the Pacolet Manufacturing Company served as a "monument of practical utility." Although these mills did offer new opportunities, Montgomery was not always able to provide enough teachers for the schools, and like most mill managers of the period, he resisted unionization efforts.

By 1900 the upcountry mills under Montgomery's presidency were consuming cotton at such a high rate that they had to look further south for enough supply of raw cotton. Two years later Montgomery opened two mills in Georgia, one in Gainesville and the other in New Holland. John Montgomery died on October 31, 1902, shortly after falling from a scaffold at the Gainesville site. He was buried in Oakwood Cemetery, Spartanburg. BRUCE W. EELMAN

Carlton, David L. *Mill and Town in South Carolina, 1880–1920.* Baton Rouge: Louisiana State University Press, 1982.

Obituary. *Spartanburg Journal,* November 1, 1902, p. 1.

Stokes, Allen H. "John H. Montgomery: A Pioneer Southern Industrialist." Master's thesis, University of South Carolina, 1967.

Teter, Betsy Wakefield, ed. *Textile Town: Spartanburg County, South Carolina.* Spartanburg, S.C.: Hub City Writers Project, 2002.

Moore, Andrew Charles (1866–1928). Biologist, educator, church leader. Born on December 27, 1866, at his family home, Fredonia, near Moore in Spartanburg District, Moore was the son of Thomas John Moore and Mary Elizabeth Anderson. He attended the Reidville Male Academy and entered South Carolina College in 1883, earning an A.B. (with honors) in 1887. He married Vivian May of Hale County, Alabama, on September 20, 1900. After serving eleven years as a public school administrator in South Carolina and Alabama, Moore began graduate studies at the University of Chicago in 1898. He was appointed assistant professor of biology, geology, and mineralogy at South Carolina College in 1900 and was promoted to full professor in 1903. Three years later, when South Carolina College became the University of South Carolina, Moore became head of the newly created Department of Biology, a position he held until his death in 1928. He served for some years as dean of the university and on two occasions as acting president. From 1902 until his death, Moore was a member (chairman after 1906) of Columbia's Board of School Commissioners. In 1909 Wofford College awarded him an LL.D.

Moore completed most of the work for his doctorate at the University of Chicago but did not finish his dissertation, part of which was published in the *Botanical Gazette.* While at Chicago, Moore studied the development of the embryo sac of the plant *Lilium philadelphicum* but never published his results. A prepared slide bearing a label in Moore's handwriting, which states "Lilium Philadel . . . 1st meiosis 2nd meiosis ACM Feb '99," indicates a use of the term "meiosis" well before its historically recognized origin and publication. Moore never used "meiosis" in a publication; consequently, his important contribution to the vocabulary of biology was overlooked until its true authorship was pointed out in 1984.

The South Caroliniana Library in Columbia has an unpublished manuscript on the evolution/creationism controversy written by Moore. Apparently written in 1923, about two years before the Scopes Trial in Dayton, Tennessee, and near the peak of the antievolution movement that erupted after World War I, Moore's analytical examination of assertions made by antievolutionists has remained relevant long after his death. Moore read his manuscript "Evolution Once More" before the Kosmos Club, a town-and-gown organization in Columbia, of which he was a charter member and president in 1905–1906. In his treatise Moore exhibited a modern point of view and a mind open to the discoveries of science, which was perhaps surprising when considering his long years of service as an elder in the Presbyterian Church in both Birmingham and Columbia.

The herbarium in the Department of Biological Sciences at the University of South Carolina, initially developed by Moore, and a residence hall and garden on the campus of the university bear Moore's name, as does an elementary school in Columbia. Moore died on September 17, 1928, and was buried in the cemetery of the old Nazareth Church near Spartanburg. WILLIAM D. ANDERSON, JR.

Anderson, William D., Jr. "Andrew C. Moore's 'Evolution Once More': The Evolution-Creationism Controversy from an Early 1920s Perspective." *Bulletin* [Alabama Museum of Natural History] 22 (November 30, 2002): iii–iv, 1–35.

Herr, J. M., Jr. "A Brief Sketch of the Life and Botanical Work of A. C. Moore." *American Journal of Botany* 71 (May 1984, part 2): 106–7.

Hollis, Daniel Walker. *University of South Carolina.* 2 vols. Columbia: University of South Carolina Press, 1951–1956.

Moore, Andrew C. "The Mitoses in the Spore Mother-Cell of *Pallavicinia.*" *Botanical Gazette* 36 (October–November 1903): 384–88.

———. Papers. South Caroliniana Library, University of South Carolina, Columbia.

———. "Sporogenesis in *Pallavicinia.*" *Botanical Gazette* 40 (August 1905): 81–96.

Sanders, Albert E., and William D. Anderson, Jr. *Natural History Investigations in South Carolina from Colonial Times to the Present.* Columbia: University of South Carolina Press, 1999.

Moore, Charles Benjamin (1935–1979). Singer. Charlie Moore possessed one of the great lead-singing voices in bluegrass music, but he never fully received the attention he deserved. With Bill Napier, he turned out nine quality albums on King Records, then cut some sixteen additional solo projects on various labels. Unfortunately, health problems took his life early at the age of forty-four.

Born in Piedmont on February 13, 1935, Moore drew influences from the country radio performers who broadcast from the South Carolina upstate. He developed a smooth vocal style more akin to that of Red Smiley and Clyde Moody than to the mountain-styled bluegrass singers. During the mid-1950s Moore worked on radio and television programs in the western Carolinas, and he made his first single recording for Starday in 1958.

Moore performed with Bill Napier—formerly of the Stanley Brothers—as the Dixie Partners from 1960 until 1967. Napier was adept on banjo, lead guitar, and mandolin, while Charlie handled the singing. In December 1962 they cut the first of nine albums totaling some 108 numbers for King Records. Their best-known number, "Truck Driver's Queen," was covered by other artists. The pair worked on television in Spartanburg and Panama City, Florida, and at various times their band included such well-known musicians as Jimmy Williams, Curly Lambert, Henry Dockery, and Chubby Anthony, although critics sometimes charged their entourage as "somewhat lacking in depth."

After the Moore-Napier relationship dissolved, Charlie did some deejay work before starting a new version of the Dixie Partners in 1970. He first recorded an album for the small Country Jubilee label, followed by two albums for Vetco and one each for Wango, Leather, and Starday (never released). In 1973 he began a string of albums for Old Homestead, the fourth of which, titled *The Fiddler,* contained what became his signature song, "Legend of the Rebel Soldier," which subsequently was included on *The Smithsonian Collection of Classic Country Music.*

Moore suffered recurring health problems, many related to cirrhosis of the liver. In late November 1979, while traveling to Maryland for a show date, he became severely ill. Band members took him to the Johns Hopkins Medical Center, where he slipped into a coma. He died on December 24, 1979. Many of his recordings have been transferred to compact disc. ABBY GAIL GOODNITE

Brumley, Charles. "Charles Benjamin Moore." *Bluegrass Unlimited* 14 (February 1980): 5.

Kuykendall, Pete. "Charlie Moore." *Bluegrass Unlimited* 7 (January 1973): 5–9.

Moore, Darla Dee (b. 1953). Businesswoman, philanthropist. Moore is president of Rainwater, Inc., one of the largest private investment firms in America. She is also the founder of the Palmetto Institute, a private policy research group in South Carolina. She was born on August 1, 1953, in Lake City, the daughter of Eugene T. Moore, a retired teacher, and Lorraine Linsenbardt. Moore earned a B.A. in political science from the University of South Carolina in 1975 and an M.B.A. from George Washington University in 1981. After graduate school, she joined the management training program at Chemical Bank in New York City. There, Moore desperately wanted to make her mark in leveraged buyouts, the hot business trend of the 1980s and male-dominated at the time, but she was never able to penetrate that inner circle. Instead, Moore was more willingly accepted in the Chemical Bank's bankruptcy division, where she specialized in Chapter 11s and made millions for the bank during the late 1980s.

In 1991 Moore married the billionaire Richard Rainwater, and in 1994 she joined his firm, Rainwater, Inc., where she tripled his net worth, estimated at $2 billion in June 2001 by *Fortune.* Known for her swift moves and decisiveness, Moore has been credited for the decision to remove two powerful corporate chieftains: the notorious corporate raider T. Boone Pickens of Mesa (oil and gas) and CEO Rick Scott of Columbia/HCA (health care). She was called "The Toughest Babe in Business" by *Fortune* in 1997, the first time in its seventy-year history that the magazine had profiled a woman for a cover story. A year later she was named to *Fortune's* list of the top fifty most powerful women in American business (she ranked nineteenth).

Moore has also been involved with philanthropic projects over the years, most notably in education. In 1998 she donated $70 million to the University of South Carolina, and the university in response renamed its business school in her honor. More recently, in 2002 Moore and her husband donated $10 million to Clemson University's

Eugene T. Moore School of Education, named for Darla's father, a 1949 Clemson alumnus. RICK D. BOULWARE

Sellers, Patricia. "Don't Mess with Darla." *Fortune* 136 (September 8, 1997): 62–72.

———. "The 50 Most Powerful Women in American Business." *Fortune* 140 (October 25, 1999): 76–98.

Moore, James, Jr. (ca. 1682–1724). Governor. South Carolina's first native-born governor, Moore was the eldest son of former governor James Moore, Sr., and Margaret Berringer. Even though the elder Moore left extensive debts, the intermarriage of his children with other rising Carolina families positioned them to play influential roles in the colony's future. After receiving a portion of his inheritance in 1704, James Jr. established himself as a prosperous planter and represented Berkeley and Craven Counties in the Commons House of Assembly from 1706 to 1708. He married Elizabeth Beresford (date of marriage unknown), and the couple eventually had six children.

Like his father before him, Moore possessed skill in Indian affairs. In 1707 the assembly commissioned him a captain of militia and dispatched him to pursue a band of Savannah River Indians who had robbed Virginia traders. In March 1713 Colonel Moore and John Barnwell led a mixed expedition of whites and Indians into North Carolina against the Tuscarora Indians, who had attacked the province without warning. In a decisive battle, Moore's force crippled the Tuscaroras' ability to make war and enabled North Carolina to survive their onslaught. Two years later the Yamassee Indians and their allies caught South Carolina off guard, and Moore, now a lieutenant general of the colonial militia, contributed significantly to eventual victory in the Yamassee War (1715–1718). While Governor James Craven led forces against the Yamassees, Moore and his younger brother, Maurice, negotiated with the Cherokees. The two men convinced the Indian nation to enter the war on the side of the colonists and arranged to settle outstanding trade disputes. While refusing to accept a post as one of five Indian trade commissioners in 1716, Moore allowed himself to be named sole commissioner eight years later.

In December 1719 the proprietary government of South Carolina was overthrown in the bloodless revolution of 1719. As a recognized war hero and longtime leader in the antiproprietary party, Moore was chosen as provisional governor until England could assume control of the colony. Moore and the assembly quickly set about reconstituting South Carolina's government. They created a "privy council," selected new judges and government officials, and reformed legislative procedures. In May 1721 Moore confronted an attempt by former governor Robert Johnson and others to retake the colony on behalf of the proprietors. The effort was quickly thwarted, and Moore shortly thereafter delivered the government safely into the hands of the first royal governor, Francis Nicholson. Moore returned to the Commons House, where he served as Speaker from 1721 until his death on March 3, 1724. LOUIS P. TOWLES

Crane, Verner. *The Southern Frontier, 1670–1732.* Durham, N.C.: Duke University Press, 1928.

Edgar, Walter, and N. Louise Bailey, eds. *Biographical Directory of the South Carolina House of Representatives.* Vol. 2, *The Commons House of Assembly, 1692–1775.* Columbia: University of South Carolina Press, 1977.

Webber, Mabel L. "The First Governor Moore and His Children." *South Carolina Historical and Genealogical Magazine* 37 (January 1936): 1–23.

Moore, James, Sr. (ca. 1650–1706). Governor. Born around 1650, Moore married Lady Margaret Berringer, stepdaughter of Sir John Yeamans. Their ten children included James Moore, Jr., governor of South Carolina from 1719 to 1721. Moore arrived in South Carolina from Barbados around 1675 and became a leading Indian trader and lieutenant of Maurice Mathews, a leader of the colony's leading political faction, the Goose Creek Men.

As a member of the Grand Council in 1677, Moore helped direct South Carolina's efforts in the Westo War of 1680, which resulted in the Goose Creek faction gaining control over the Indian trade and the annihilation of the Westo Indians. During the 1680s Moore led the protest in parliament against a revision of the Fundamental Constitutions. To the shock of the Lords Proprietors and many colonists, the Goose Creek Men declared that the proprietors could not amend the original 1669 version without advising their colonists beforehand. Moore also led the opposition to paying quitrents in specie, although the proprietors promptly switched to accepting rents paid in merchantable commodities. Colonial objections stemmed not from antiproprietary principle (especially since the amount concerned was small), but from a recognition that the revenue collected went to pay the costs of the provincial government, which from 1683 to 1690 was controlled by Moore's opponents. By 1690 Moore had become the acknowledged leader of the Goose Creek faction in South Carolina. In that same year Moore supported the replacement of Governor James Colleton with the proprietor Seth Sothell, whose arrival from North Carolina gave the Goose Creek Men the opportunity to seize power and drive Colleton out of the colony.

From 1695 to 1700 South Carolina politics remained relatively quiet. However, the death of Governor Joseph Blake in 1700 provided an opportunity for Moore and the Goose Creek Men to stage a coup against their enemies. Joseph Morton, Jr., the senior landgrave in the province and a Moore opponent, should have succeeded to the governorship. But Moore objected to his elevation, arguing that Morton could not hold commissions from the proprietors and the crown simultaneously (Morton was a judge of the vice-admiralty court). Moore's argument persuaded the Grand Council, which rejected Morton and backed Moore as governor on a temporary basis. The Lords Proprietors, who now courted the Goose Creek Men in the name of colonial harmony and a desire to establish the Church of England in South Carolina, supported the elevation of Moore (an Anglican) over Morton (a Dissenter). This new alliance between the proprietors and their longtime adversaries signaled the demise of the Dissenter faction as the proprietary party in South Carolina politics.

With England and Spain now at war, Moore used his new position to direct an attack on St. Augustine in Spanish Florida. In September 1702 Moore led an assault that captured and sacked the town but failed to take the fort. When a Spanish relief fleet arrived from Havana, the Carolinians withdrew. In addition, between 1703 to 1704 Moore led a series of devastating raids on Spanish missions in Florida, in which hundreds of captured Indians were sold into slavery. On a personal level, Moore remained active in the Indian trade, using his position to extend his involvement. As governor, he spoke of reforming the trade, but these words came to nothing when his attention became focused on his contest with the Spanish over who would control the Indian trade in the American Southeast. Moore stepped down to the Grand Council when the proprietors appointed Sir Nathaniel Johnson as governor in 1703. In late 1706 Moore died of yellow fever in Charleston. L. H. ROPER

Read, M. Alston. "Notes on Some Colonial Governors of South Carolina and Their Families." *South Carolina Historical and Genealogical Magazine* 11 (April 1910): 107–22.

Sirmans, M. Eugene. *Colonial South Carolina: A Political History, 1663–1763.* Chapel Hill: University of North Carolina Press, 1966.

Webber, Mabel L. "The First Governor Moore and His Children." *South Carolina Historical and Genealogical Magazine* 37 (January 1936): 1–23.

Moore, Samuel Preston (1813–1889). Surgeon general of the Confederacy. Born in Charleston on September 16, 1813, Moore was the sixth of nine children born to Stephen West Moore and Eleanor Screven Gilbert. Following his graduation from the Medical College of South Carolina, Moore was commissioned an assistant surgeon in the U.S. Army in 1835. He spent the next twenty-five years at a variety of western and southern military posts. During the Mexican War, Moore's administration of the American General Hospital at Carmago impressed a young Jefferson Davis, the future president of the Confederacy. By 1860 Moore was serving as medical purveyor at New Orleans.

In 1861 Moore resigned from the U.S. Army and sought a commission in the Confederate military. Jefferson Davis selected Moore as acting surgeon general of the Confederacy. Moore faced the daunting task of creating Southern medical services from scratch. Known as a stern disciplinarian, he was able to field a medical corps of approximately three thousand officers. This was a major feat considering that only twenty-four officers had served in the U.S. Medical Corps and only twenty-seven of his physicians had surgical experience. One of the more imaginative ways Moore achieved this was to establish a scholarship program so that young Southerners could attend Richmond Medical College. Not only did he have to recruit personnel, he also had to create a system of laboratories to supply medical units. He supplied Confederate women with poppy seeds to cultivate so that the South had a homegrown supply of painkillers. Similarly, he purchased four distilleries to provide six hundred gallons of medical alcohol each day and promoted the appropriation of Union stocks. When a lack of Southern manufacturing facilities led to a shortage of medical equipment, Moore located and acquired instruments from retired or deceased doctors.

Moore promoted research throughout the war. He ordered the surgeon Joseph Jones to search out the causes of unusual infections and diseases affecting soldiers. In 1863 he organized the Association of Army and Navy Surgeons of the Confederate States to gather and disseminate information. This group would outlast the war and merge with the Association of Military Surgeons of the United States in 1914. He also instituted a monthly professional periodical, *The Confederate States Medical and Surgical Journal,* to better educate those under his command.

Moore oversaw each hospital in the South through personal and military correspondence and established large general hospitals, such as Chimborazo in Richmond. His greatest accomplishment might have been the vaccination of the entire Southern army against smallpox in only six weeks, a controversial decision in 1862. In 1913 the *Southern Medical Journal* stated, "Looking back upon what he achieved, at what he created absolutely out of nothing, the marvel grows until it impresses one today as an impossibility."

After taking the oath of amnesty in Richmond on June 22, 1865, Moore retired from the medical practice and focused on managing his financial holdings. He died in Richmond on May 31, 1889, after a violent coughing attack. He was buried in Hollywood Cemetery, Richmond. T. JASON SODERSTRUM

Brooks, Stewart. *Civil War Medicine.* Springfield, Ill.: Charles C. Thomas, 1966.

Cunningham, H. H. *Doctors in Gray: The Confederate Medical Service.* Baton Rouge: Louisiana State University Press, 1958.

Farr, Warr Dahlgren. "Samuel Preston Moore: Confederate Surgeon General." *Civil War History* 41 (March 1995): 41–56.

Moragné, Mary Elizabeth (ca. 1815–1903). Author, diarist. Born in Abbeville District, Mary Moragné was the eldest of eleven children of Isaac Moragné, a planter, and Margaret Blanton Caine. Moragné grew up on her father's small plantation, Oakwood, near New Bordeaux. Her formal education consisted of attending neighborhood schools and local female academies. She was an avid reader and began writing at an early age. She was a keen observer of both the social and the natural worlds around her and recorded these observations in a journal that she began keeping in 1834.

In the fall of 1838 Moragné entered a fiction-writing contest sponsored by the *Augusta Mirror* literary magazine. Her entry, a short historical romance entitled *The British Partizan,* was awarded first prize. The novel was based on the life of her maternal grandfather's uncle, a British sympathizer during the Revolutionary War. Published in the *Mirror* in installments from December 15, 1838, through January 26, 1839, it was immediately popular. Within a month after its appearance, the *Mirror*'s editor William Tappan Thompson published the novel in book format. He became an early, enthusiastic supporter of Moragné and from 1838 through 1842 printed everything she submitted, including her second short novel, *The Rencontre* (1841), as well as several excerpts from her journal and some of her poems.

Moragné's work was well received by her contemporaries. A favorable review appeared in the *Knickerbocker* in May 1839, recommending *The British Partizan* to its readership. Thompson continued to heap praise on her, admiring her style of composition over all other contributors to the *Mirror.* The writer and editor William Gilmore Simms recommended Moragné for inclusion in Evert and George Duyckinck's anthology of American literature, although in the end she was not mentioned there.

In the fall of 1842 Moragné married William Hervey Davis, a Presbyterian minister and pastor of the nearby Willington Presbyterian Church. Together they had nine children. At the time of her marriage, Moragné began to question the propriety of writing romantic fiction, and much to the consternation of her publishers and some family members, she gave it up. She did, however, continue to produce poetry and articles of a religious nature. In 1888 she published a book of her collected poems, *Lays from the Sunny Lands.* She also wrote two textbooks, one on biblical history and the other on science, but was unable to get either work published.

Moragné is best remembered, however, not for her early fiction or poems, but for her unpublished journals covering the years 1834–1842, 1863, 1867, and 1899–1903. They provide readers with careful descriptions and observations of family and community life in the rural South. Their focus is on neither the gentry nor the uneducated, but on the lives of the common folk of the Carolina upcountry—what they thought, how they managed, what they did for entertainment, and the role religion and family played in their lives. In 1951 Moragné's early journals were published by her great-granddaughter Delle Mullen Craven under the title *The Neglected Thread: A Journal from the Calhoun Community, 1836–1842.*

Moragné died in 1903 in Talladega, Alabama. She is buried there in Oak Hill Cemetery. ELLEN CHAMBERLAIN

Craven, Delle Mullen. "The Unpublished Diaries of Mary Moragné Davis." In *South Carolina Women Writers: Proceedings of the Reynolds Conference,*

University of South Carolina, October 24–25, 1975, edited by James B. Meriwether. Spartanburg, S.C.: Reprint Company, 1979.

Endres, Karen A. "Mary Moragné's *The British Partizan.*" In *South Carolina Women Writers: Proceedings of the Reynolds Conference, University of South Carolina, October 24–25, 1975,* edited by James B. Meriwether. Spartanburg, S.C.: Reprint Company, 1979.

Moragné, Mary E. *The Neglected Thread: A Journal from the Calhoun Community, 1836–1842.* Edited by Delle Mullen Craven. Columbia: University of South Carolina Press, 1951.

Mordecai, Moses Cohen (1804–1888). Merchant, shipowner, legislator, civic leader. M. C. Mordecai was Charleston's most prominent Jewish citizen in the decades before the Civil War. Born on February 19, 1804, in Charleston, he was the son of David Mordecai and Reinah Cohen. Although he possessed little formal education, Mordecai became a leading business and civic figure in antebellum Charleston. His firm, Mordecai & Company, was among the city's most prominent importers and shipowners, conducting an extensive trade in fruit, sugar, coffee, and tobacco from the West Indies. He later operated a steamship line between Charleston and Havana, Cuba. His influence and leadership carried into a wide variety of political and civic activities as well. He represented Charleston in the General Assembly in the state House (1844–1845) and state Senate (1854–1857); was a director of the Southwestern Railroad Bank (1840–1852), the Charleston Gas Light Company (1848–1856), the South Carolina Insurance Company (1849–1857), and the Farmers' and Exchange Bank of Charleston (1854–1859); and sat on numerous additional boards and committees. At various times he was vice president of the Charleston Ancient Artillery Society (1830–1847), a member of the Charleston Board of Health (1833–1836), captain of the Marion Artillery (1834), a member of the Committee on Civic Improvements (1837), warden of police (1837), commissioner of markets (1837), a delegate to the Augusta commercial convention (1838), and commissioner of pilotage (1842–1850).

Mordecai lived in a mansion on Meeting Street near St. Michael's Church with his wife, Isabel Lyons, whom he had married on February 20, 1828. They had eight children. Active in the affairs of Beth Elohim Synagogue, Mordecai favored the installation of an organ in the building's new sanctuary, thus siding with the reform faction of the congregation. He served as president of Beth Elohim from 1857 to 1861.

Together with Ker Boyce and B. C. Pressley, in 1851 Mordecai helped launch the *Southern Standard* (later the *Charleston Standard*), a Unionist newspaper that rejected separate state secession and promoted cooperation in political affairs among the southern states. Once South Carolina seceded from the Union, however, Mordecai supported the Confederate cause. His steamer, the *Isabel,* transferred U.S. Army Major Robert Anderson and his command from Fort Sumter to the Union fleet following the opening bombardment of the Civil War. Named for Mordecai's wife, the *Isabel* became a famous blockade-runner during the war.

In February 1865 the Columbia City Council appointed Mordecai "food administrator" to furnish sustenance to its starving citizens. Later that year he and twenty other community leaders were authorized to discuss South Carolina's return to the Union with President Andrew Johnson. Broken by the war, Mordecai moved to Baltimore, where he reestablished Mordecai & Company and operated a steamship line between Baltimore and Charleston. Although he lived the remainder of his years in Maryland, Mordecai nevertheless remained a benefactor to his native state. In 1870 he arranged for his company to bring home the bodies of eighty-four South Carolinians killed at the Battle of Gettysburg, at no cost to their families. Blind for the last eighteen years of his life, Mordecai died in Baltimore on December 30, 1888. DALE ROSENGARTEN

Bailey, N. Louise, Mary L. Morgan, and Carolyn R. Taylor, eds. *Biographical Directory of the South Carolina Senate, 1776–1985.* 3 vols. Columbia: University of South Carolina Press, 1986.

Hagy, James William. *This Happy Land: The Jews of Colonial and Antebellum Charleston.* Tuscaloosa: University of Alabama Press, 1993.

Rosengarten, Theodore, and Dale Rosengarten, eds. *A Portion of the People: Three Hundred Years of Southern Jewish Life.* Columbia: University of South Carolina Press, 2002.

Tobias, Thomas J. Papers. Special Collections, College of Charleston Library, Charleston.

Morning News (2003 circulation: 32,776 daily and 35,504 Sunday). A morning newspaper published daily and Sunday in the city of Florence, the *Morning News* was established as a daily in 1922. The paper's roots can be traced to the *Farmers' Friend,* founded in 1887 by the editor and publisher J. W. Hammond. Following a series of mergers and renamings, the newspaper became a weekly published by the *Florence Daily Times,* which had been established in 1894. The *Daily Times* merged in 1925 with the *Morning News Review,* and in 1929 the newspaper became the *Morning News.*

The publisher's son, Jack O'Dowd, became editor in 1951 for a short-lived stay. A moderate on racial issues, he endorsed the U.S. Supreme Court's desegregation decision, angering Klansmen and other conservatives. Forced to flee the state, he was later employed by the *Chicago Sun-Times.* James A. Rogers, a former employee, returned in 1956 as editor and became a strong progressive spokesman. After J. M. O'Dowd died in 1970, the newspaper was run by a committee and then by the board of directors, including surviving family members, for several years before being sold to Thomson Newspapers in 1981. In October 1995 the newspaper moved to a new facility on Dargan Street. The next year the publisher Thomas Marschel and the editor Frank Sayles added the words "Voice of the Pee Dee" to the newspaper's name to underscore its regional scope. On August 1, 2000, the *Morning News* was sold to Media General, Inc. ROBERT A. PIERCE

McNeely, Patricia G. *The Palmetto Press: The History of South Carolina's Newspapers and the Press Association.* Columbia: South Carolina Press Association, 1998.

Morris College. Morris College is a private, historically black college located in Sumter and founded in 1908 by the Baptist Educational and Missionary Convention of South Carolina. The college was named in honor of the Reverend Frank Morris, a pioneer of the Rocky River Association of Anderson County, a regional group affiliated with the Baptist E & M Convention. The convention had supported Benedict College in Columbia but by 1905 decided to build a college that would be owned and operated by African American Baptists and so withdrew from Benedict. In 1907 the convention accepted twelve acres on North Main Street in Sumter and entered a construction agreement. By 1911 Morris College was operating in two buildings.

The college's first president, Dr. Edward M. Brawley, declared that the college stood for three things, "loyalty to Christ at all times . . . sound scholarship, and devotion to the Negro race." Morris initially offered a curriculum for grammar school, a normal college for training teachers, a theology course, music, dressmaking, truck farming, and domestic science. Morris graduated its first students in

1911. The college organized a college curriculum the next year and awarded its first bachelor's degree in 1915.

During the presidency of Dr. John Jacob Starks (1912–1930), Morris College strengthened both its grammar and college curricula and expanded its campus to include forty acres and six brick buildings. Enrollment reached 1,230 students by 1920. In 1930 Morris entered an arrangement with Benedict College whereby Benedict transferred its high school courses and students to Morris, with Morris dropping its last two college years and changing to junior-college status. The unpopular agreement was ended in 1933 and the junior and senior college years restored.

Morris expanded its liberal arts curriculum in the 1930s and commenced intercollegiate athletic competition in 1932. The high school program was discontinued in 1942. Despite frequent financial problems, the school nevertheless continued to expand. The presidency of Dr. Odell Reubens (1948–1970) oversaw the implementation of education initiatives, including the establishment of a remedial program for incoming freshmen to offset the deficiencies in public school education available to most African Americans. In 1961 enrollment was 898 and the college charter removed the word "Negro," opening the college to all ethnic groups. Eight years later Morris was rated a "Corresponding College" by the Southern Association of Colleges and Schools (SACS).

After Reubens's death in 1970, Morris College had several difficult years before entering an age of growth and accomplishment under the administration of Dr. Luns Richardson (1974–1998). Richardson erased the college's deficit, and its endowment reached $2.8 million by the time of his retirement. In 1978 Morris achieved accreditation by the Commission on Colleges of the SACS. Two years later it completed the $1.3 million Richardson-Johnson Learning Resource Center, a capital expense twice as large as any previous project. Enrollment reached 971 students in 1997, and the number of programs climbed from nine to some twenty majors in six academic divisions. Trustees dissolved the School of Religion in 1996 and replaced it with a program in Christian education. The Morris College motto is "Enter to Learn; Depart to Serve." LINDA MEGGETT BROWN

Vereen-Gordon, Mary, and Janet S. Clayton. *Morris College: A Noble Journey.* Virginia Beach, Va.: Hallmark, 1999.

Morton, Joseph, Sr. (ca. 1630–1688). Governor. Born around 1630 in Wells, Somerset, England, Morton married Elinor Blake(?), with whom he had four children. A prominent Dissenter, Morton traveled to South Carolina as part of the migration of a relatively substantial number of English Dissenters to the colony. He was made governor and landgrave in 1682. The arrival of these English settlers, in conjunction with that of Huguenots and a planned Scottish settlement at Port Royal, gave rise to the belief, both in the colony and among the proprietors, that an orderly colonization and government might finally be established in South Carolina. To further this effort, the proprietors, in response to Scottish initiatives, revised the Fundamental Constitutions to encourage migration of Dissenters to the colony.

Unfortunately, these expectations—and Governor Morton—ran afoul of the Goose Creek Men, who regarded the prospect of substantial numbers of new European arrivals as a threat to their control of the South Carolina political scene and the Indian trade. To counter the actions of the proprietors, the Goose Creek Men objected to the 1682 Fundamental Constitutions on the grounds that both the proprietors and the colonists had ratified the original 1669 version at the time of the colony's founding. Thus, they contended, the proprietors could not change the document without the consent of the South Carolina parliament. The Fundamental Constitutions, the argument continued, had to be unalterable. Otherwise, the colony would be subject to every proprietary whim.

Morton, to the amazement of the proprietors, proved unable to counter this argument. The Fundamental Constitutions remained dormant while plots in Britain against the government delayed migration plans. Morton tried to compel the Commons House of Assembly (which was controlled by the Goose Creek Men) to ratify the document, but twelve members refused. When Morton tried to exclude them from their places, the legislators objected to his highhandedness and reiterated the Goose Creek argument that the 1669 Fundamental Constitutions were unalterable without their consent. The resulting stalemate forced the dissolution of the Carolina parliament and left the constitutions unratified.

Morton further lost favor with the proprietors when he failed to stamp out the Indian slave trade or to chill the warm welcome that pirates had come to find in Carolina. The proprietors replaced Morton with Sir Richard Kyrle in June 1684. Kyrle, though, died shortly after arriving in the province. Morton, as the senior landgrave in the province, then returned to the governor's office on an interim basis from 1685 until 1686.

During this time the vanguard of a promising Scottish colony settled at Stuart's Town near Port Royal. The leader of this group, Lord Cardross, entertained hopes, briefly successful, of trading with neighboring Indians as well as building mines in the west. Morton and other prominent Carolinians welcomed the newcomers. But Cardross's intentions ran contrary to the interests of the Goose Creek Men, who grew alarmed at the success of the Scots in attracting their Indian trading partners to Stuart's Town, especially the Yamassees. This faction retaliated with a warrant for Cardross's arrest on charges of harassing an English trader and renewed their objections to the Fundamental Constitutions. Then, on August 17, 1686, the Spanish sacked Stuart's Town and plundered the coastal plantations of Morton and his supporter Paul Grimball, carrying slaves and property back to St. Augustine. They returned to finish the job in December. An indignant Morton joined the call of the Goose Creek faction in preparing a revenge attack on Florida in November 1687. Only the declaration of martial law by the new governor, James Colleton, prevented the planned reprisal that would have disrupted the shaky peace then existing between Spain and England.

The collapse of this planned assault seems to have marked the end of Morton's public life. Colleton came to the colony with instructions to attack piracy and also to investigate the suspicion that Morton tolerated trade with pirates. The former governor, though, seems to have avoided any punishment, or perhaps his age or infirmity stopped the inquiry. Morton apparently died around January 1688, and his will was probated in November of the same year. His son Joseph Morton, Jr., became a vocal leader of the Dissenters in South Carolina politics in the early eighteenth century. L. H. ROPER

Salley, A. S., Jr. "Governor Joseph Morton and Some of His Descendants." *South Carolina Historical and Genealogical Magazine* 5 (April 1904): 108–16.

Sirmans, M. Eugene. *Colonial South Carolina: A Political History, 1663–1763.* Chapel Hill: University of North Carolina Press, 1966.

Valley, Seabrook Wilkinson. "The Parentage of Governor Morton." *South Carolina Historical Magazine* 74 (July 1973): 164–69.

Moses, Franklin J., Jr. (ca. 1840–1906). Governor. Moses was the son of Franklin J. Moses, a prominent Jewish jurist from Sumter District, and his wife, Jane McLelland. After briefly attending South Carolina College in 1855, Moses withdrew and commenced the study of law. On December 20, 1859, he married Emma Buford Richardson, with whom he had at least one child. An enthusiastic secessionist, Moses served as secretary to Governor Francis W. Pickens and claimed to have raised the Confederate and Palmetto flags over Fort Sumter after its surrender in April 1861. He was drafted into the Confederate army, where he served as an enrollment officer. As editor of the *Sumter News* after the war, Moses supported President Andrew Johnson's Reconstruction policies, which restored many antebellum white leaders to power. He was admitted to the South Carolina Bar in 1868.

This cartoon from *Harper's Weekly* lampooned Moses and the corruption of his administration. Courtesy, South Carolina Historical Society

That same year Moses executed an abrupt political about-face and joined the Republican Party. He served in the 1868 constitutional convention and was elected to the General Assembly. Despite an African American majority in the state House of Representatives, Moses was chosen Speaker over the black leader Robert Brown Elliott. He served as Speaker until 1872.

While serving in the legislature, Moses was appointed adjutant, inspector general, and quartermaster of the state militia by Governor Robert K. Scott. He subsequently arranged to purchase obsolete muskets and have them converted to rifles to arm the virtually all-black militia. In return, Moses secured a "payment" of $10,000 from the state for negotiating the transaction. As Speaker, Moses regularly accepted bribes to expedite the passage of legislation. In 1872 Governor Scott allegedly canceled repayment of a loan he had made to Moses in return for the Speaker's assistance in derailing a resolution to impeach the chief executive.

In 1872, in spite of his notorious reputation for corruption, the Republican state convention nominated Moses for governor. About one-third of the Republican delegates bolted from the convention and instead supported the former Freedmen's Bureau official Reuben Tomlinson. But with no Democratic candidate in the field, Moses easily won the election. Moses was arguably the most corrupt governor in South Carolina history. He sold hundreds of pardons and regularly diverted public money to personal use. He purchased the palatial Hampton-Preston mansion in Columbia. In the words of the Charleston *News and Courier,* he was a "profligate debauchee."

Moses was not renominated for governor in 1874. The General Assembly instead elected him to serve on the state circuit court. However, Governor Daniel H. Chamberlain refused to issue the necessary commission. The last three decades of Moses's life were marked by dissolution, decline, and crime. He filed for bankruptcy in 1875 and was divorced from his wife three years later. He eventually left South Carolina and lived in several northern cities. Addicted to drugs, he supported himself with assorted jobs as journalist and periodically resorted to crime. He served time in several jails. Moses died in poverty in Winthrop, Massachusetts, on December 11, 1906. WILLIAM C. HINE

Current, Richard Nelson. *Those Terrible Carpetbaggers.* New York: Oxford University Press, 1988.

Moses, Franklin, Jr. Governors' Papers. South Carolina Department of Archives and History, Columbia.

Moses, Ottolengui Aaron (1846–1906). Chemist, geologist, inventor. Moses was born in Charleston on February 7, 1846, the son of Aaron I. Moses and Judith Ottolengui. He earned his Ph.D. at the University of Leipzig, Germany. Moses was married to Flora Moses of New York. They had one son, who died in infancy.

Moses and his brother, A. J. Moses, engaged in phosphate mining from 1868 to 1870 at the Massot Farm in Berkeley County. He then served as state inspector of phosphates (1872–1874) and geologist of South Carolina, and was the author of a report, *The Phosphate Deposits of South Carolina,* published by the U.S. Geological Survey in 1882. Moses also received two patents for his own inventions in the 1860s. His first was for washing, screening, and drying phosphate rock, and the second patent was for a blowpipe.

In his capacity as state inspector, Moses performed scientific analyses of shipments of guano and other commercial fertilizers. He also developed a uniform statement of the chemical contents that explained in simple words the composition of a fertilizer that farmers could understand. Moses then assigned market prices to the percentages of phosphate of lime, decomposed lime, and ammonia that represented the cash value at the factory of the contents of fertilizers purchased.

Moses was the founder of the Hebrew Technical Institute in New York City, an institution for free education of poor boys, and served as its director for several years. He was associated with the Montefiore Home, the Hebrew Orphan Asylum, and other charities. He died in New York City on January 3, 1906. MARY S. MILLER

Obituary. *New York Times,* January 6, 1906, p. 9.

Motte, Rebecca Brewton (1737–1815). Revolutionary War heroine. Motte was born on June 15, 1737, at the Santee River plantation of her parents, Robert Brewton and Mary Loughton. She was the sister of Miles Brewton, a leading Charleston merchant. On June 28, 1758, she married Jacob Motte, Jr. (1729–1780), son of the public treasurer of South Carolina, Jacob Motte, Sr. The couple had seven children, but only three daughters survived to adulthood.

The Mottes actively supported the patriot cause. They supplied food for the soldiers and their animals from their plantation, Mount Joseph, in St. Matthew's Parish, near the junction of the Congaree and Wateree Rivers and McCord's Ferry. This advantageous location, however, overlooked a key British supply route. British troops under the command of an officer named McPherson took the Motte house and renamed it Fort Motte. They then dug a trench and built

Rebecca Motte and Francis Marion, May 1781. Cecil Hartley, *The Life of Francis Marion.* Courtesy, South Caroliniana Library, University of South Carolina

a dirt wall to protect the house from patriot attack. The British moved Motte and her household to an outbuilding.

In May 1781 patriot commanders Francis Marion and Henry Lee decided that they would have to burn the house to get the British outpost to surrender. Rebecca Motte gave her consent to the plan and even provided the arrows used to set fire to the roof. The British surrendered after the roof caught fire, and then troops from both sides put out the fire to save the house. Motte reportedly fed all the officers, British and patriot, following the battle.

Motte was connected by the marriages of her daughters to some of the most prominent families in South Carolina, including the Pinckneys, Middletons, and Alstons. Motte died on January 10, 1815, and was buried in the cemetery of St. Philip's Church, Charleston. BRENDA THOMPSON SCHOOLFIELD

Bodie, Idella. *South Carolina Women.* Orangeburg, S.C.: Sandlapper, 1991.

Garden, Alexander. *Anecdotes of the Revolutionary War.* 1822. Reprint, Spartanburg, S.C.: Reprint Company, 1972.

Harkness, David James. "Heroines of the American Revolution." *University of Tennessee Newsletter* 60 (February 1961): 1–16.

Helsley, Alexia Jones. *South Carolinians in the War for American Independence.* Columbia: South Carolina Department of Archives and History, 2000.

Tablet to Mrs. Rebecca Motte, Erected by Rebecca Motte Chapter of the Daughters of the American Revolution, Ceremony of Unveiling at St. Philip's Church, Charleston, S.C., May 9th, 1903. Charleston, S.C.: Dagett, 1903.

Moultrie, James, Jr. (1793–1869). Physician, medical educator. Moultrie was born in Charleston on March 7, 1793, the son of James Moultrie, Sr., and Catherine Judith Lennox. The son, grandson, and great-grandson of physicians, Moultrie received his early education in England. When war between the United States and Great Britain appeared imminent, he returned to South Carolina to finish his studies. After graduating from South Carolina College and studying medicine with two preceptors (medical tutors) in Charleston, he entered the University of Pennsylvania and received his medical degree in 1812. He served as a civilian physician with a South Carolina artillery battalion during the War of 1812 and soon afterward began his practice in Charleston, succeeding his father as port physician. On November 12, 1818, he married Sarah Louise Shrewsbury. They had no children.

Moultrie devoted the rest of his life to medical practice, medical education, organized medicine, and the community, becoming the most prominent South Carolinian in the medical profession during the nineteenth century. He joined the Medical Society of South Carolina, a local Charleston organization, in 1812 and served as its president from 1820 to 1821. He entered the national medical scene in 1818 to work with representatives of other states on developing a pharmacopoeia (a book describing drugs and their uses). In 1847 he was sent by the Medical Society to represent South Carolina in the organizing of the American Medical Association (AMA) and was elected vice president. He became president of the AMA at a meeting in Charleston in 1850. He also helped organize the South Carolina Medical Association in 1848 and was elected its first president.

In 1827 Moultrie made a significant contribution to a circular on the need to improve medical education, which the Medical Society distributed to medical schools across the county. In 1836 Moultrie made a formal presentation of his views on medical education to several influential organizations, including the state legislature and the South Carolina Society for the Advancement of Learning. Moultrie's views on the study of medicine were far in advance of their time. He felt that American medical schools were behind those in Europe and advocated premedical preparation, a medical course of eight months for four successive years, special training for medical teachers, and a full-time salaried faculty. These standards did not gain full acceptance and implementation until the twentieth century.

Moultrie played a role in the establishment of the Medical College of South Carolina, which opened in 1824, but he declined the professorship in anatomy when the legislature failed to offer financial support. In 1833, after a reorganization of the Medical College, he accepted the professorship in physiology.

Moultrie's interests carried beyond medicine. He was a musician and had a strong attachment to fine arts and literature. In addition to his medical associations, he was a member of the Elliott Natural History Society and the South Carolina Historical Society. He accumulated a large and diverse library that was destroyed during the Federal occupation of Charleston in 1865. He died in Charleston on May 29, 1869, and was buried in Magnolia Cemetery. W. CURTIS WORTHINGTON

Davis, N. S. *History of the American Medical Association from its Organization up to January, 1855.* Philadelphia: Lippincott, Grambo, 1855.

Waring, Joseph Ioor. *A History of Medicine in South Carolina.* Vol. 2, *1825–1900.* Columbia: South Carolina Medical Association, 1967.

Moultrie, John (ca. 1699–1771). Physician. Moultrie was born in Culross, Fifeshire, Scotland, a member of the family of Moultrie lairds (landowners) of Roscobie near Dunfermline. He apparently studied medicine at the University of Edinburgh, but it is not clear whether he received the M.D. degree. He spent some time as a surgeon in the British navy before coming in 1728 to Charleston, where he combined his medical practice with planting interests. That same year he married Lucretia Cooper. The couple had five sons. Lucretia died in 1747, and on July 6, 1748, Moultrie married Elizabeth Mathews. His second marriage produced one son.

Moultrie soon established a successful practice. He served as physician to St. Philip's Parish hospital (part of the city's poorhouse) and as a quarantine officer for the province. He was also president of the Faculty of Physic, a body established in May 1755 to advance the professional standing, interests, and income of Charleston's medical men. In particular, and much to the consternation of many local residents, the faculty hoped to increase their fees and secure more prompt payment of them. The announcement of the creation of this body in the *South-Carolina Gazette* was followed by several letters and poems to the newspaper that ridiculed the doctors as greedy and incompetent. The subsequent history and duration of the Faculty of Physic is obscure.

Over time Moultrie's practice increasingly emphasized male midwifery, and he may have focused on it exclusively in his later years. In the eighteenth century, first in Britain and then in its colonies, medical men began to encroach on the traditional female preserve of midwifery. This development was spurred by increased knowledge of the use of forceps delivery taught by men such as William Smellie and William Hunter in Britain and William Shippen (a pupil of Hunter) in America. Moultrie was apparently one of the first American physicians to specialize in obstetrics, along with James Lloyd of Boston. Moultrie seems to have been a popular and highly sought after physician, especially among expectant women. He was also active in the life of the Charleston community. He was president of the St. Andrew's Society, a member of the Charleston Library Society, a justice of the peace, and vestryman of both St. Philip's and St. Michael's Churches. He also served in the Commons House of Assembly from 1760 to 1761. He died in Charleston on December 10, 1771. PETER MCCANDLESS

Edgar, Walter, and N. Louise Bailey, eds. *Biographical Directory of the South Carolina House of Representatives.* Vol. 2, *The Commons House of Assembly, 1692–1775.* Columbia: University of South Carolina Press, 1977.

Leavitt, Judith Walzer. *Brought to Bed: Childbearing in America, 1750 to 1950.* New York: Oxford University Press, 1986.

"Letters from a Colonial Student of Medicine in Edinburgh to His Parents in South Carolina, 1746–1749." *University of Edinburgh Journal* 4 (1930–1931): 270–74.

Waring, Joseph I. *A History of Medicine in South Carolina.* 3 vols. Columbia: South Carolina Medical Association, 1964–1971.

Moultrie, John, Jr. (1729–1798). Physician, planter, political leader. Moultrie was born in Charleston on January 18, 1729, the son of the Scottish-born physician John Moultrie and Lucretia Cooper. He began training as a physician under his father and in 1746 traveled to the University of Edinburgh in Scotland, from which he received his M.D. in 1749. He was the first native-born American to graduate in medicine from Edinburgh, which was then emerging as the leading medical school in the western world.

Moultrie's Latin dissertation on yellow fever, *De Febre Maligna Biliosa Americae* (On the American Malignant Bilious Fever), is notable as one of the earliest clinical descriptions of the disease to come from North America. The work was based on careful observations of the Charleston epidemic of 1745, made while he was assisting his father as an apprentice, and his own experience with a mild attack of the disease. The underlying causes of yellow fever, he claimed, were excessive heat, miasma (putrid air) from the swamps and poorly drained areas, and heavy consumption of spiritous liquors. He noted that the epidemic subsided as the weather cooled; that it was especially common among the poor, those who worked in the sun, sailors, heavy drinkers, and strangers; and that it was rare among those from the West Indies, the wealthy, young children, the temperate, African Americans, and Native Americans. Moultrie's dissertation was not a major contribution to medical knowledge, but its precise clinical descriptions attracted a great deal of attention. It was translated into German and French and published in numerous editions into the nineteenth century.

Moultrie returned to Charleston after receiving his medical degree and seems to have practiced medicine for some years. His marriage on April 28, 1753, to Dorothy Dry Morton, a wealthy heiress, freed him from the financial necessity of medical practice and may have spurred his political career. They had two children, both of whom died in infancy. Dorothy died in 1757. On January 5, 1762, Moultrie eloped with Eleanor Austin, the daughter of George Austin, a wealthy merchant and Royal Navy captain who initially opposed the marriage. Moultrie's second marriage produced six children.

Moultrie's political life began when the governor appointed him a justice of the peace in 1756. During the French and Indian War, he joined the militia and rose to the rank of major. In 1761 he served under Lieutenant Colonel James Grant, a British regular, during an expedition against the Cherokees. In the same year he was elected to the colonial assembly. In 1764 Grant, now governor of East Florida (newly acquired from Spain), appointed Moultrie to his council. Moultrie moved to Florida and soon became the council president. In 1771 Grant named him lieutenant governor. Moultrie prospered as a planter in Florida and amassed a large amount of land and numerous slaves. During the Revolutionary War he remained loyal to the crown. When Great Britain returned control of Florida to Spain in 1783, Moultrie lost his position and fortune and moved to England, where he died on March 19, 1798. He was buried in Shiffnal Churchyard, Shropshire. PETER MCCANDLESS

Edgar, Walter, and N. Louise Bailey, eds. *Biographical Directory of the South Carolina House of Representatives.* Vol. 2, *The Commons House of Assembly, 1692–1775.* Columbia: University of South Carolina Press, 1977.

Townshend, Eleanor. "John Moultrie, Junior, M.D. 1727–1798." *Annals of Medical History,* 3d ser, 2 (1940): 98–109.

Waring, Joseph I. *A History of Medicine in South Carolina.* 3 vols. Columbia: South Carolina Medical Association, 1964–1971.

———. "John Moultrie, Jr. M.D., Lieutenant Governor of East Florida, His Thesis on Yellow Fever." *Journal of the Florida Medical Association* 54 (1967): 772–77.

Moultrie, William (1730–1805). Soldier, governor. Moultrie was born in Charleston on November 23, 1730, the son of physician John Moultrie and Lucretia Cooper. He married Damaris Elizabeth de St. Julien on December 10, 1749, and acquired a large plantation in St. John's Berkeley Parish, where he resided. Three children were born to this union, one dying in infancy. Moultrie later married Hannah Motte Lynch, the widow of Thomas Lynch, in October 1779. They had no children.

In 1752, at the age of twenty-one, Moultrie won election to the Commons House of Assembly from St. John's Berkeley Parish. Over the next four decades Moultrie was a fixture in South Carolina government, representing various lowcountry parishes in royal, revolutionary, and state assemblies almost continually until his retirement from public office in 1794. Equally active in the military, Moultrie served in campaigns against the Cherokees in 1759

General William Moultrie (1739–1805), by Rembrandt Peale. Oil on canvas. Courtesy, Gibbes Museum of Art / Carolina Art Association

and 1760–1761, and attained the rank of colonel of militia by 1774. When the Revolutionary War began the following year, the Second Provincial Congress elected Moultrie as colonel of the Second South Carolina Regiment of Foot. He also designed what has been called the first American battle flag: an indigo blue field with a white crescent in the upper left corner and possibly the word "Liberty" stitched in the center.

Moultrie achieved national fame on June 28, 1776, when he successfully defended Fort Sullivan against a British attack and saved Charleston from capture. Other units contributed to the defense, but it was the famous palmetto-log and sand fort and Moultrie's command of four hundred men and thirty cannons that became forever associated with the victory. Moultrie became an instant hero, thanked by Congress, and the fort was renamed Fort Moultrie in his honor. Soon thereafter, when his regiment became part of the Continental Line, Moultrie was promoted to brigadier general. Moultrie enjoyed further success later in the war. In February 1779, at the Battle of Port Royal Island, Moultrie dislodged the British from the Beaufort region. The following May he saved Charleston again by skillfully delaying a British advance up the coast from Savannah. However, when the British returned to South Carolina the following year, another successful defense of Charleston proved impossible. Serving as second in command to General Benjamin Lincoln, Moultrie vigorously opposed the city's surrender. After Charleston fell in May 1780, Moultrie was imprisoned at Haddrell's Point and later was sent to Philadelphia, where he was exchanged in early 1782. Returning to active duty, Moultrie held the rank of major general at the end of the war.

Resuming a role in politics, Moultrie returned to the General Assembly in 1783. Two years later, on May 10, 1785, he was elected governor. He served until 1787, during which time his legislative and military experience helped greatly in dealing with difficult postwar issues: establishing the state's credit, reorganizing the militia, improving internal navigation, managing the exodus of banished Tories, creating a county court system, and relocating the state capital from Charleston to Columbia. After additional service in the state Senate, Moultrie began a second tenure in the governor's chair in 1792. It proved to be a tumultuous term. Alexander Moultrie, his half brother and longtime state attorney general, was impeached for financial misconduct in 1792. The governor drew fire for his public support of the French Revolution and its emissary in Charleston, Edmond Genêt, who had attempted to license privateers and recruit volunteers to retake Louisiana from Spain for France. Criticism from state legislators and the Washington administration ended Genêt's efforts and forced Moultrie to issue a proclamation forbidding South Carolinians from enlisting in such expeditions.

Leaving office in 1794, Moultrie retired to his plantation in St. John's Berkeley Parish. Aside from political and military service, Moultrie was actively involved in various organizations. He participated in the South Carolina Society and the St. Andrew's Society for nearly fifty years. He helped found the South Carolina Jockey Club in 1758 and the Washington Race Course in Charleston in 1792. In addition, Moultrie served as president of the state Society of the Cincinnati from its inception in 1783 until his death. In 1802 Moultrie published his *Memoirs of the American Revolution,* which remains a classic source on the war. He died in Charleston on September 27, 1805. ROY TALBERT, JR.

Bailey, N. Louise, Mary L. Morgan, and Carolyn R. Taylor, eds. *Biographical Directory of the South Carolina Senate, 1776–1985.* 3 vols. Columbia: University of South Carolina Press, 1986.

Klein, Rachel N. *Unification of a Slave State: The Rise of the Planter Class in the South Carolina Backcountry, 1760–1808.* Chapel Hill: University of North Carolina Press, 1990.

Moultrie, William. *Memoirs of the American Revolution.* 1802. Reprint, New York: New York Times, 1968.

Nadelhaft, Jerome J. *The Disorders of War: The Revolution in South Carolina.* Orono: University of Maine Press, 1981.

Moultrie flag. In January 1776 the South Carolina Council of Safety delivered twenty-three yards of blue cloth to Colonel William Moultrie, commander of the Second South Carolina Regiment. It is not known if this cloth was used to make the unit's colors, but in the colonel's memoirs he wrote: "it was thought necessary to have a flag for the purpose of signals: (as there was no national or state flag at the time) I was desired by the council of safety to have one made, upon which, as the state troops were clothed in blue, and the fort was garrisoned by the first and second regiments, who wore a silver crescent on the front of their caps; I had a large blue flag made with a crescent in the dexter corner, to be uniform with the troops: This was the first American flag which was displayed in South-Carolina."

Ordered to Sullivan's Island, the Second South Carolina was the principal command in the island's half-completed palmetto log and sand fort, and the regiment's colors served as the garrison's flag. During the June 28, 1776, attack by a British fleet, the flagstaff was cut down by artillery. Sergeant William Jasper retrieved the colors, tied them to a staff, and planted them back on the ramparts. The British were defeated, providing the patriot cause its first major victory in the Revolutionary War. In January 1861, after the state's secession from the Union, the legislature drew on the symbolism of the Second South Carolina's colors and the fort's palmetto logs to adopt the official flag of South Carolina. RICHARD W. HATCHER III

Moultrie, William. *Memoirs of the American Revolution.* 1802. Reprint, New York: New York Times, 1968.

Wates, Wylma A. *A Flag Worthy of Your State and People: The History of the South Carolina State Flag.* 2d ed. Columbia: South Carolina Department of Archives and History, 1990.

Mount Dearborn Armory. Situated on an island in the Catawba River in Chester County, Mount Dearborn was initially conceived and selected by President George Washington to be one of the nation's three national arsenal-armories. Years later Congress proposed that a regional military academy be opened there as well. As the new republic planned its defense in the 1790s, this site was planned to store ammunition and make weapons for the South. It was selected along with Harpers Ferry, Virginia, and Springfield, Massachusetts, for their regions.

In 1802, at the urging of Thomas Sumter, Secretary of War Henry Dearborn purchased 523 acres near the village of Rocky Mount. The secretary, for whom the site was named, employed Eli Whitney to consult with the state engineer, Christian Senf, on the best location to build on the new federal land. Part of the plan included the construction of a canal that would be a source of waterpower. Legal disputes with the Catawba Navigation Company prevented the completion of the waterway. By early 1804 construction began on the magazine and arsenal, but the armory was never constructed.

By 1807 the army refocused its defensive priorities on Charleston, and construction at Dearborn slowed. Despite the delays, by 1809 the main buildings were largely completed while construction continued on the barracks and other structures. At this time Mount

Dearborn became a recruiting center for one of the nation's new regiments, as the United States prepared for a possible war with Britain. Not long after its formation, most of the unit was transferred to bolster Charleston's defenses. A small detachment of soldiers remained as caretakers, but it is unclear whether they remained through the War of 1812. For a brief period in early 1816, Congress proposed Mount Dearborn as the site for one of three regional military academies. Eventually lawmakers decided just to provide more funds to West Point in New York. By 1825 the site was reported abandoned, and the land officially returned to the state four years later. FRITZ HAMER

Collins, Ann P. *A Goodly Heritage: History of Chester County, South Carolina.* Columbia, S.C.: R. L. Bryan, 1986.

Wade, Arthur P. "Mount Dearborn: The National Armory at Rocky Mount, South Carolina, 1802–1829." *South Carolina Historical Magazine* 81 (July 1980) 207–31; (October 1980): 316–41.

Mount Pleasant (Charleston County; 2000 pop. 47,609). Mount Pleasant was a small village until the 1970s, when it began a dramatic expansion to become the sixth-largest municipality in South Carolina. Lying on the north side of Charleston harbor, Mount Pleasant occupies what was formerly Christ Church Parish. James Hibben laid out the village in 1803 on the site of the former Mount Pleasant plantation of Jacob Motte. In 1837 the villages of Mount Pleasant and Greenwich were combined and incorporated as the town of Mount Pleasant. The municipal limits later expanded with the annexations of Hilliardsville in 1858 and Lucasville and Hibben's Ferry Tract in 1872.

In the eighteenth century the beachfront locale was a popular haven for Christ Church elites, including Charles Pinckney. Although many colonial residents were rice planters, shipbuilding was also an important component of the early Mount Pleasant economy. With the decline of rice cultivation in the parish in the early nineteenth century, agriculture dwindled in importance to Mount Pleasant, although the town remained a retreat for wealthy planters and merchants. After the Civil War, white and black farmers turned to truck farming. Large planters established commercial farms worked by black wage laborers, while tenants and small landowners grew produce to supplement farm incomes. Commercial fishing and small-scale manufacturing also gained importance in the late nineteenth century. By 1883 Mount Pleasant had a population of 783, four miles of shell-paved streets, nine stores, a sawmill, and a brick and tile factory. In that same year Mount Pleasant became the Berkeley County seat, but it was annexed back to Charleston County in 1895.

Mount Pleasant stagnated in the early twentieth century. Area farmers struggled against competition and a lack of modern transportation links, while a hurricane in 1911 destroyed farmlands and fishing facilities. The situation improved somewhat with the expansion of the Georgetown Highway (U.S. Route 17) and the opening of the Grace Memorial Bridge across the Cooper River in 1929. Black residents near Mount Pleasant tapped into the roadside tourist trade by selling sea grass "show baskets" to passing motorists.

Growth remained modest until 1970. The expansion of the port of Charleston, the growth of lowcountry tourism, the construction of a second Cooper River bridge, and the advent of new highways contributed to a tremendous expansion in population. Between 1970 and 1990 the Mount Pleasant population soared from 6,155 to 30,108. By 1990 seventy-two percent of the Mount Pleasant workforce held "white collar" jobs, which helped give the town one of the highest per capita incomes among South Carolina communities. The profile of town residents became increasingly white, professional, and conservative. Indeed, South Carolina's first Republican governor since Reconstruction, James B. Edwards, hailed from Mount Pleasant. However, Mount Pleasant's rapid growth also sparked concerns over suburban sprawl and strip development. By employing subdivision covenants, development restrictions, and downtown revitalization projects, town leaders worked to balance the human scale and charm of the "Old Village" while providing the services and efficiency of a modern urban hub. AMY THOMPSON MCCANDLESS

Gregorie, Anne King. *Christ Church, 1706–1959: A Plantation Parish of the South Carolina Establishment.* Charleston, S.C.: Dalcho Historical Society, 1961.

McIver, Petrona Royall. *History of Mount Pleasant, South Carolina.* 2d ed. Mount Pleasant, S.C.: Christ Church Parish Preservation Society, 1994.

Mount Zion College. Established in 1777 by an elite group of South Carolina politicians and businessmen who called themselves the Mount Sion (as it was then spelled) Society, the institution started in a small log building as an all-grades public school in Winnsboro. The school, originally called Mt. Sion Institute, closed in 1780, when British troops occupied Winnsboro. It reopened in 1784 with the Reverend Thomas McCaule, a graduate of the College of New Jersey (later Princeton University) and Presbyterian minister, as its principal. In 1785, in its first official action to promote the growth of higher education, the South Carolina legislature officially chartered the school as Mt. Zion College, one of three colleges it chartered on the same day. The others were at Cambridge (later Ninety Six) and Charleston, the latter eventually becoming the College of Charleston.

The all-male Mt. Zion College, which included a great deal of elementary and preparatory learning for youths of all ages, was housed in a more substantial brick building by 1789 and flourished throughout the antebellum period as a strictly disciplined, academically challenging academy whose graduates were well prepared for admission to South Carolina College and other regional institutions. James W. Hudson, principal from 1832 to 1858, was credited with insisting on the noted teachers and high-quality students for which the school became known. Later principals would include well-known South Carolina educators such as William Rivers (1862–1864), R. Means Davis (1877–1882), Patterson Wardlaw (1883–1885), and Leonard T. Baker (1902–1906).

Although the Civil War interrupted operations and the main building succumbed to fire in 1867, the school eventually reestablished itself in a new brick building as Mt. Zion Collegiate Institute, the first graded public school in South Carolina outside Charleston. It continued operation throughout the first half of the twentieth century, eventually becoming a public high school. In 1953 the Mt. Zion Society relinquished its title to the school lands, and the school became part of a consolidated county school system. The 183rd and final commencement exercises for graduates of Mt. Zion Institute (formerly College and Collegiate Institute) were held in 1960 for sixty-seven graduates. KATHERINE REYNOLDS CHADDOCK

LaMotte, Louis C. *Colored Light: The Story of the Influence of Columbia Theological Seminary, 1828–1936.* Richmond, Va.: Presbyterian Committee of Publication, 1937.

McMaster, Fitz Hugh. *History of Fairfield County, South Carolina: From "Before the White Man Came" to 1942.* 1946. Reprint, Spartanburg, S.C.: Reprint Company, 1980.

Thomason, John Furman. *The Foundations of the Public Schools of South Carolina.* Columbia, S.C.: State Company, 1925.

Moving Star Hall (Johns Island). Located in the South Carolina lowcountry, Moving Star Hall provides an example of an antebellum "praise house" that served the slave community, and later the freed people, as a center of social and cultural life. "The Hall," as the people of Johns Island referred to it, featured intense, all-night "prayings" in an expressive and egalitarian worship style. John Smalls, a longtime member of the Hall, told interviewers in the 1960s, "We don't charge nothing to come in Moving Star Hall . . . whether you are white, whether you are dark like myself, or different color, come in. . . . If you want to speak . . . you got the opportunity—we give it to you."

Following emancipation, the Hall served as the headquarters of the Moving Star Society, a fraternal order whose services included both a burial and a "tend the sick" society. Representing the ability of slaves and freed people to create cultural institutions under the most oppressive of conditions, Moving Star Hall continued to serve the people of Johns Island as a place of worship and a community center into the 1960s.

As of 2001, Moving Star Hall provided a place of worship for an African American Pentecostal Church. This new congregation had not broken completely with older practices of worship at the Hall, as evidenced by the intermingling of modern gospel music and elements of the "ring shout" tradition in their worship. The folkways of the people of Johns Island were also kept alive by the Moving Star Hall Singers, who have shared the music of the Hall, stories of lowcountry life, and African folktales at the Charleston Spoleto Festival and the national festival of Afro-American Arts in Atlanta. W. SCOTT POOLE

Carawan, Guy, and Candie Carawan. *Ain't You Got a Right to the Tree of Life? The People of Johns Island, South Carolina—Their Faces, Their Words, and Their Songs.* Rev. ed. Athens: University of Georgia Press, 1989.

Cooper, Nancy Ashmore. "Where Everybody Is Somebody: African American Churches in South Carolina." In *Religion in South Carolina,* edited by Charles H. Lippy. Columbia: University of South Carolina Press, 1993.

Moxon, Barbara Wischan (b. 1921). Political activist. Moxon, the daughter of Ernst Wischan and Helen Leggett, was born on May 2, 1921, in Philadelphia. She received B.A. and M.S. degrees from the University of Pennsylvania, where she served as president of the student government from 1942 until 1943. She married Dr. Robert K. Moxon in 1944 and traveled with their three children for nineteen years in his assignments with the U.S. Navy.

In 1963 the Moxons moved to Columbia, South Carolina, where Barbara became active in the League of Women Voters, serving as state president for three terms (1971–1977). She was appointed and reappointed by governors to the South Carolina Commission on Women from 1974 to 1985 and served as the commission's chairperson. In this position she promoted the statewide project of Women's History Week. From 1977 to 1979 Moxon was also chairperson of ERA South Carolina and led the ultimately unsuccessful attempt to get the South Carolina legislature to ratify the equal rights amendment to the U.S. Constitution. She was active in the American Association of University Women (AAUW) and as state legislative chairperson brought together fifteen public interest groups to support a comprehensive health and sexuality education bill. She headed a new organization called Advocates for Comprehensive Health Education (ACHE), which brought together more than fifty organizations to support legislation strengthening state programs on nutrition, accident prevention, substance abuse, disease prevention, and sexuality education. The latter area was the most controversial, but the legislation passed in 1988 despite vigorous opposition.

When statistics showed that South Carolina was near the bottom of the national list for percentage of female board members, Moxon received a grant from the national AAUW in 1988 to begin a project to get more women appointed to public boards and commissions. She organized and served as chairperson for the Advocates for Women on Boards and Commissions, which developed extensive publicity on the need for more women appointees and provided aid and encouragement to potential female members. Partly as a result of these efforts, women were appointed to the State Board of Education, the Department of Health and Environmental Control Board, the ETV Commission, and the Boards of Trustees of the University of South Carolina, Clemson University, and other state colleges. Her other activities included serving with Planned Parenthood, Common Cause, South Carolina Coalition for Choice, South Carolina Christian Action Council, and the Governor's Task Force on Election Reform. She received both state and national recognition for her varied leadership roles. ALICE H. HENDERSON

Mulberry Plantation (Berkeley County). Built for the planter, Indian trader, and political leader Thomas Broughton, Mulberry is one of the most distinctive eighteenth-century houses in America. Set on a bluff overlooking the west branch of the Cooper River about three miles south of Moncks Corner, the house is stylistically unique and has variously been described as having Jacobean, French, and Anglo-Dutch baroque origins. Its design blends seventeenth-century forms with the formality of eighteenth-century Georgian architecture in a unified composition. The date of construction has generally been accepted as 1714, although evidence suggests that the house may have been finished by 1711. The two-story brick structure is laid in English bond with a molded brick water table. Its overall form has the squat profile typical of early Huguenot-influenced plantation houses in the lowcountry. The square main block has a steeply pitched gambrel roof with jerkinhead (clipped and inward-sloping) gables. Attached at the corners are four one-story brick pavilions with bell-shaped roofs. The floor plan is asymmetrical, with the stair hall set in the rear. The first-floor interior was remodeled with a new staircase and Adamesque cornices and mantles about 1800. The second-story rooms retain their original woodwork.

Mulberry Plantation. Courtesy, South Carolina Department of Archives and History

In 1916 Mulberry was restored under the oversight of the architect Charles Brenden, an Englishman who practiced in New York, and in the 1920s the landscape architect Loutrel Briggs redesigned the grounds. The house was designated a National Historic Landmark by the U.S. Department of the Interior in 1960. Mulberry remains in private ownership. Historic Charleston Foundation holds protective easements on the house and surrounding acreage. See plate 9. DANIEL J. VIVIAN

Lane, Mills. *Architecture of the Old South: South Carolina.* Savannah, Ga.: Beehive, 1984.

Mules. A mule is a hybrid animal that results from breeding a male donkey with a female horse. Although mules have gender (males are called "horse mules" and females "mare mules"), they are sterile and cannot reproduce. For centuries mules have been prized for their intelligence and capacity for work. Farmers typically preferred mules to horses because mules usually lived longer, learned faster, and were better tempered than horses.

Mules were fixtures of rural life in South Carolina for two hundred years. Cotton and tobacco growers alike used mules, and the hearty animals plowed, harrowed, and hauled crops to market in every county in the state. The timber, naval stores, and phosphate industries employed mules as well. Among rural folk, ownership of mules placed landless farmers in a position to negotiate more favorable tenancy arrangements with landlords. An active market in mules existed throughout the year, and any serviceable mule was worth hard cash. Thus, mules were commonly pledged as collateral against loans and advances from banks and merchants.

South Carolina's mule population peaked in the 1920s at around 210,000. As nearly all were imported from Missouri or Texas, the mule trade drained millions of dollars annually from South Carolina farmers. The state's commissioner of agriculture prudently encouraged farmers to raise their own mules, but few heeded his advice.

By the 1940s tractors and trucks were replacing mules on South Carolina farms. The pace of change quickened after World War II, and by the early 1950s mules were the exception rather than the rule. Here and there a beloved animal lived out his days in semiretirement tilling a vegetable garden as plowmen relied more and more on diesel power. BECKY WALTON

Ellenberg, George B. "African Americans, Mules, and the Southern Mindscape, 1850–1950." *Agricultural History* 72 (spring 1988): 381–98.
Kirby, Jack Temple. *Rural Worlds Lost: The American South, 1920–1960.* Baton Rouge: Louisiana State University Press, 1987.
Prince, Eldred E., and Robert R. Simpson. *Long Green: The Rise and Fall of Tobacco in South Carolina.* Athens: University of Georgia Press, 2000.

Mullins (Marion County; 2000 pop. 5,029). The railway depot in the center of downtown Mullins has been associated with the town since its inception. Mullins did not exist when the Wilmington and Manchester Railroad arrived in 1854, but the town grew up around the railway station. The town was named for William Sydney Mullins, who moved into Marion County from North Carolina in the early 1800s after earning a law degree at the University of North Carolina. As a member of the state House of Representatives in 1852, Colonel Mullins helped plan the railroad and determined that its route would cross Marion County. The station was called Mullins Depot to honor him. The popular legislator later served as president of the Wilmington and Manchester Railroad.

Attracted by the commercial activity around the station, a few residents built houses nearby. These first homes were scattered, with no indication of forming an orderly town. Slow initial growth increased rapidly once the fledgling town began to develop. In 1878 only seventy-five residents and three stores occupied Mullins. Twelve years later the population figure had jumped to 282. Within a few more years other stores opened and, of more significance to the establishment of a community, two churches and a school, Mullins Academy, had been built.

In 1891 Dr. C. T. Ford planted an experimental tobacco plot to determine if quality tobacco could be grown in the area. Others followed his lead, receiving good prices for their yield at the Virginia markets. Production of this new agricultural staple expanded with remarkable speed. The first tobacco sales building in Mullins, Planter's Warehouse, was completed in 1894, and the first auction sale was held that same year. Additional warehouses followed. Throughout the twentieth century Mullins remained the largest tobacco market in the state.

The town's development kept pace with the growth of its profitable money crop. Attractive homes appeared, new schools and churches opened, and a weekly newspaper, the *Enterprise,* commenced publication. Several industries were attracted to the area. Mullins Hospital was built in the 1920s through the influence of Dr. Lon McMillan. The Mullins Civic League established a small public library in the early 1900s, and in 1941 the Mullins Library opened in an attractive building on North Main Street. On January 2, 1945, Governor Ransome J. Williams, a local resident, was inaugurated on the steps of the building. John L. McMillan had a long, distinguished career as a congressman from the area. Other Mullins men who held state offices were O. Frank Thornton, secretary of state, and Bill Harrelson, secretary of agriculture.

Tobacco remained the economic and cultural center of Mullins at the beginning of the twenty-first century. The South Carolina Tobacco Museum, located in the old depot, attracted thousands of annual visitors. Tobacco also took center stage in Mullins each September, when the town held its annual Golden Leaf Festival. THELMA CHILES CLARK

Sellers, W. W. *A History of Marion County, South Carolina.* Columbia, S.C.: R. L. Bryan, 1902.

Mullis, Kary Banks (b. 1944). Scientist. Born in Lenoir, North Carolina, on December 28, 1944, Mullis is the son of Cecil Banks Mullis and Bernice Alberta Barker. When he was five years old, Mullis and his family moved to Columbia, South Carolina, where his father worked as a furniture salesman and his mother, after a separation, sold real estate. He attended public schools and graduated from Dreher High School in 1962. He earned a B.S. in chemistry from Georgia Institute of Technology in 1966 and obtained his Ph.D. in biochemistry from the University of California at Berkeley in 1973. He then pursued postdoctoral studies at the University of Kansas Medical School and the University of California at San Francisco. While an undergraduate, he married his first wife, Richards, and had a daughter. Several years later he married his second wife, Cynthia Gibson, and they had two sons. In 1998 Mullis married his third wife, Nancy Cosgrove, and shortly thereafter the couple moved to Newport Beach, California.

Mullis's impact on the world of biotechnology has been described as no less than revolutionary. While employed at the Cetus Corporation in Emeryville, California, he conceived and developed the idea of PCR, polymerase chain reaction, in 1983. This technique amplifies DNA, enabling scientists to make a virtually unlimited number of copies of a single DNA molecule in a short time. The process of PCR found multiple applications in medicine, genetics, and forensics and was the technology behind the highly popular book and movie *Jurassic Park,* in which DNA from dinosaurs was cloned and used to re-create the extinct giant reptiles. Considered by many scientists to be one of the greatest advancements in molecular biology, Mullis's work on PCR garnered him (along with Michael Smith of the University of British Columbia) a share of the Nobel Prize in chemistry in 1993 in recognition of his milestone discovery.

Despite the fame that PCR brought to Mullis, he later focused his attention elsewhere. According to Mullis, he became "tired of PCR" and turned to other areas of science and technology. As a member of the Group for the Reappraisal of the HIV-AIDS Hypothesis, a five-hundred-member protest organization pushing for a reexamination of the cause of AIDS, he became embroiled in controversy concerning the nature of the AIDS virus and the causes of AIDS. Additionally he consulted and lectured around the world on topics ranging from cosmology, mysticism, mathematics, virology, and artificial intelligence. In 1998 he published a book, *Dancing Naked in the Mind Field.* Mullis maintained close ties to his South Carolina roots despite living on the opposite coast. He received an honorary doctorate from the University of South Carolina in 1994, and he co-owns an oil-recycling company in Charleston. JASON S. OVERBY

Mullis, Kary B. *Dancing Naked in the Mind Field.* New York: Pantheon, 1998.

Murray, George Washington (1853–1926). Congressman. Murray was born a slave near Rembert, Sumter District, on September 22, 1853. Although left an orphan in early childhood, he managed to acquire a basic education in Sumter County's public school system after 1865. He attended the University of South Carolina from 1874 to 1876, when that institution was under Republican control. For nearly fifteen years he taught school in Sumter County.

During the last two decades of the nineteenth century, Murray acquired an influential role in Republican affairs. He was the longtime chairman of the Sumter County Republican Party. He came to be known as the "Republican Black Eagle" and served as a delegate to several Republican National Conventions. By the late 1880s Murray was a traveling lecturer for the Colored Farmers Alliance, the African American auxiliary of the all-white Farmers Alliance. From 1890 to 1892 Murray was inspector of customs of the port of Charleston, a position to which he was appointed by President Benjamin Harrison.

In 1892 Murray successfully ran for Congress in the Seventh Congressional District. Serving in the House of Representatives from 1893 to 1897, he was often a legislative maverick. Although a Republican, Murray frequently voted with the agrarian Populist bloc on such issues as the unlimited coinage of silver. He was also outspoken in denouncing the steady rise of racism throughout the United States. In 1895 he undertook an energetic campaign across South Carolina speaking against the black disenfranchisement movement being led by state Democrats. Defeated for reelection in 1898, Murray was the last African American to represent South Carolina in Congress for nearly a century.

After 1900 Murray's primary activities were farming and land speculation. He purchased more than nine thousand acres of farmland in South Carolina, primarily in Sumter County. He divided this extensive acreage into smaller tracts, where black tenant farmers grew cotton. By 1902 he had two hundred families farming on these properties, which he called his "savings bank." In 1903 two of Murray's tenants claimed that he had forged their names on lease agreements. In April 1905 the Sumter County General Sessions Court convicted him of forgery and sentenced Murray to three years at hard labor. His attorneys filed several appeals, but the South Carolina Supreme Court upheld the original sentence in October 1905.

Murray refused to surrender to state authorities and departed with his family from Sumter on a train bound for Chicago. Once established in Illinois, Murray began a successful career selling life insurance and real estate. He became active within Republican politics in Illinois and was a key black lieutenant of Chicago mayor William "Big Bill" Thompson. Despite a standing arrest warrant, Murray made several discreet visits back to South Carolina. In January 1915 he was finally granted a full pardon by Governor Coleman L. Blease, a Democrat noted for being an extreme white supremacist. But Murray never resided again in his native state. He died in Chicago on April 21, 1926, and was buried in Lincoln Cemetery. MILES S. RICHARDS

"Ex-Congressman Geo. W. Murray, Answers 'The Last Roll Call.'" Columbia *Palmetto Leader,* May 8, 1926, pp. 1, 8.

Gaboury, William J. "George Washington Murray and the Fight for Political Democracy in South Carolina." *Journal of Negro History* 62 (July 1977): 258–69.

Tindall, George Brown. *South Carolina Negroes, 1877–1900.* 1952. Reprint, Columbia: University of South Carolina Press, 2003.

Murrells Inlet (Georgetown County; 2000 pop. 5,519). Located twenty-two miles up the Waccamaw Neck from Georgetown, Murrells Inlet first appeared on maps from the early 1800s as either Murray's Inlet or Morrall's, the latter after John Morrall, who purchased 610 acres on the inlet in 1731. By the mid-1800s rice plantations were operating all along the Waccamaw Neck. A handful of planters owned personal "swaths" of the inlet, each having his own "creek boy," a slave whose job was working the inlet for oysters, clams, crabs, shrimp, and fish. During the Civil War, Murrells Inlet became a small port for Confederate forces, and blockade-runners stopped there for supplies such as salt, produced by seawater evaporation in large pans along the shore.

By the close of the nineteenth century, people from inland South Carolina towns, particularly Marion, began to establish a summer colony along the inlet creekfront. The area remained, for the most part, a farming community. While local people caught fish and gathered shellfish for their own tables, the only seafood products that could be shipped from the future "Seafood Capital" were salted mullet, clams, and diamondback terrapin.

If the inlet's seafood could not be shipped out, then people would have to go there to get it; and throughout the twentieth century they did just that. At first they came to down-home, hole-in-the-table oyster roasts and fried shore dinners put on by Murrells Inlet's "founding families": the Morse, Nance, Vereen, Oliver, Chandler, and Lee families. The food was fried and the atmosphere friendly, and the area's popularity grew. A growing fleet of charter and party boats arose, with inlet captains taking visiting anglers offshore. During World War II, captains ran boats for the Crash Boat Station, recovering the bodies of flyers lost in aerial gunnery practice over the area.

After the war, prosperity made Murrells Inlet more accessible, and local seafood restaurants benefited from their close proximity to Myrtle Beach. The salad days lasted until September 1989, when

Hurricane Hugo gave the creekfront a new look overnight. As it had before, the community rebounded. Despite a sixty-six percent increase in local population during the 1990s, commercial development, and economic competition, the community held on to its history and heritage—and to its reputation as a great place to visit, a great place to eat, and a great place to live. C. E. SMITH

Gasque, Pratt. *Rum Gully Tales from Tuck'em Inn: Stories of Murrells Inlet and the Waccamaw Country.* Orangeburg, S.C.: Sandlapper, 1990.

Peterkin, Genevieve. *Heaven Is a Beautiful Place: A Memoir of the South Carolina Coast.* Columbia: University of South Carolina Press, 2000.

Rogers, George C. *History of Georgetown County, South Carolina.* Columbia: University of South Carolina Press, 1970.

Museum of Education. Founded in 1977 by its first curator, Dr. William W. Savage, the Museum of Education was established as a repository for archives, references, and artifacts related to the culture of educational life in South Carolina. It later expanded to house selected archival collections related to education throughout the United States and to include lecture series, catalog publication, oral history recording projects, and researcher services. The museum is funded by the College of Education, University of South Carolina, and is housed with the college in Wardlaw Hall on the main campus in Columbia. Its facilities include a closed archival area, a research area, an exhibition area, and a reference room. The museum is staffed by a director, who is a faculty member in the College of Education, and by student assistants. It is open to the public during the university semesters and at other times upon request.

Most prominent among the archival collections of the museum is a school textbook collection of approximately seven thousand volumes, primarily those used by South Carolina students, dating back to 1789. The higher education catalog and yearbook collection includes academic catalogs and student yearbooks from more than fifty postsecondary schools in South Carolina, starting in the nineteenth century. Noteworthy among the national collections is the John B. Hawley postcard collection, approximately twenty thousand postcards depicting scenes at more than fifteen hundred institutions of higher education. Other special collections include biographical files of South Carolina educators, extinct schools files, photographic files of school and college buildings, and publications of state and school district offices. The professional papers of noteworthy educators include those of former Sarah Lawrence College president Harold Taylor, Black Mountain College founder and former rector John Andrew Rice, and former Columbia College president John Andrew Rice, Sr. KATHERINE REYNOLDS CHADDOCK

Musgrove, Mary (ca. 1700–1765). Mediator between the Creeks and the English. Musgrove was born Coosaponakeesa around 1700 in Coweta, Creek Nation (central Georgia), the daughter of a Lower Creek woman and Edward Griffin, a Charleston trader, and niece of Brims, chief of Coweta. When she was seven years old, her father took her to Pon Pon, South Carolina, to be baptized and educated. She returned to the Creek Nation after the Yamassee War and married Johnny Musgrove, the son of a planter/trader and a Creek woman. Mary and Johnny returned to Pon Pon, had three sons, and built a thriving trade business. In 1732, at the invitation of the Yamacraw leader Tomochichi, the Musgroves moved to Yamacraw (near the future city of Savannah).

In 1733 Georgia founder James Oglethorpe arrived at Yamacraw Bluff to establish an English colony. Musgrove acted as mediator for talks between Tomochichi and Oglethorpe, becoming the latter's interpreter and consultant on Indian affairs. Mary's husband died in 1735. Since all her sons had died too, she stood, as a woman, to lose her extensive property holdings. In 1737 Musgrove married Jacob Matthews, her former indentured servant. She retained her property as a result, making her the wealthiest woman in Georgia as well as the most powerful.

Jacob Matthews died in 1742. Oglethorpe returned to England in 1743, after giving Musgrove the diamond ring from his hand, £200 sterling, and the promise of more money for her services. The following year Musgrove married Thomas Bosomworth, newly appointed rector of the Savannah church.

In 1738, at a public ceremony attended by Oglethorpe, Creek leaders had given Musgrove three hundred prime coastal acres. The gift cemented her relationship with the Creeks but threatened the English, who feared her allegiance with the Creeks. Musgrove spent the next two decades seeking legal recognition of this land, while still negotiating with the Creeks on behalf of the English. By 1749 Musgrove had not only failed to gain title to her land but had been publicly humiliated by Savannah officials who had ignored her pronouncement that she was sovereign queen of the Creeks. To regain her status, Musgrove spent time in Creek Town and planned a trip to London to secure her land. But in May 1752 Musgrove and Bosomworth were asked by Governor James Glen of South Carolina to halt a war between the Creeks and the Cherokees that threatened the colony's welfare and trade.

To quell the Indian war, Glen invited Cherokee leaders to Charleston to discuss peace. On their departure, a group of Lower Creek warriors, led by an Upper Creek chieftain named Acorn Whistler, killed four Cherokee delegates. The ambush jeopardized Glen's reputation with the Cherokees, who would not be pacified until some of the Creek warriors had been killed. Mary Musgrove, in need of money and eager for Glen's support, was the only person the governor could find willing to make such a difficult demand of the Creeks.

Musgrove traveled to the Creek Nation, discussed the situation with the Lower Creek leaders, and persuaded Acorn Whistler's clansman to murder him. She then traveled to the Upper Creek Towns to explain why Acorn Whistler's death was a necessary act of justice. By December 1752 Musgrove secured peace between the Creeks and the Cherokees. The South Carolina legislature failed to pay Musgrove the money Glen had promised but did award her two pieces of land in Colleton County. Glen also pledged that he would urge Georgia legislators to recognize her Georgia land claims.

Colonists in South Carolina and Georgia remained dependent on Musgrove's aid in the years that followed. Her petitions fell on deaf ears until 1757, when Georgia governor Henry Ellis, fearing Creek attack and impressed by Musgrove's negotiating skills, agreed to a compromise drawn up by Bosomworth. Musgrove abandoned most of her claims in exchange for St. Catherines Island and several thousand pounds. Musgrove and Bosomworth retired to St. Catherines in 1759 and remained there for the rest of her life. She likely died in the summer of 1765, for by the following autumn Bosomworth had remarried and made preparations to sell St. Catherines. MICHELE GILLESPIE

Fisher, Doris. "Mary Musgrove: Creek Englishwoman." Ph.D. diss., Emory University, 1990.

Gillespie, Michele. "The Politics of Sex and Race: Mary Musgrove and the Georgia Trustees." In *The Devil's Lane: Sex and Race in the Early South,* edited by Catherine Clinton and Michele Gillespie. New York: Oxford University Press, 1997.

Green, Michael D. "Mary Musgrove: Creating a New World." In *Sifters: Native American Women's Lives,* edited by Theda Perdue. New York: Oxford University Press, 2001.

Muslims. Islamic roots in South Carolina date to the time of slavery, although there are no direct lines in religious practice from then. About twenty percent of the African slaves were from the Senegal-Gambia region, an area pervaded by Islam. Some of the most desirable slaves were Muslim (followers of Islam), some of whom retained their faith even after being taken to Carolina. Lowcountry planters substituted rations of beef for pork for Muslim slaves. Observations of men facing east to pray five times a day were noted by contemporaries.

Muslims maintain the five Pillars of Islam and surrender to Allah. A Muslim believer recognizes that there is no god but Allah, with Muhammad as his messenger. Muslims pray five times a day in the direction of Mecca, give alms to the less fortunate, and make pilgrimages to Mecca at least once in their lifetimes. Muslims also fast, especially during the month of Ramadan.

Arguments over the nature of the Qur'an, and the legitimate line of succession after Muhammad's death, led in part to a split between Sunnis and Shi'ites. Unlike the majority, Shi'ites maintained that the first true caliph and imam, or divinely appointed leader, was Ali, cousin and son-in-law of Muhammad. By contrast, Sunnis accepted leadership and authority from outside the family. Most practitioners in South Carolina are Sunni. *Sunna* means "tradition" and refers to distinctive extra-Qur'anic verbal and practical expressions of Islam that emerged in the seventh and eighth centuries, gaining general acceptance throughout non-Shi'ite Islam.

In the 1960s American perceptions of Islam were altered by the growth of an African American version of the tradition. Known as the Nation of Islam, this movement was in large measure the product of the black experience in America and combined notions of black separatism and supremacy with certain Islamic teachings. Malcolm X became a significant leader in the movement. When he and other leaders discovered orthodox Islam, much of the black Islamic movement moved into greater conformity with orthodox Islam.

Since the 1965 revision of immigration laws, increased numbers of Muslims from the Sunni and Shi'ite lands of Africa and the Middle East have come to America. Although some white Americans have converted through intermarriage, immigration has given Islam a significant and enduring presence in North America. In the 1990s Muslims in America numbered five million, and more than six hundred mosques and centers were established across the United States.

In South Carolina there were active Islamic Centers throughout the state by the start of the twenty-first century, with those in Columbia, York, and Greenville among the largest. In 2000 there were more than five thousand Muslims in the state, and the number continued to grow. Numerous converts to the faith came from within the population of the state's Department of Corrections. One of twenty inmates practices Islam. Several of the state's mosques provide education to preschool- and elementary-school-age children. Education classes for adults and children orient believers to the essentials of Islam, how to pray properly, the history of Islam, and how to read the Qur'an in Arabic. Social implications of the faith are also discussed. There is a strong tendency to reconnect modern believers with the African roots of the early slaves in order to commemorate the sacrifices and contributions of Muslims in the state.
RANDY L. AKERS

Joyner, Charles W. *Down by the Riverside: A South Carolina Slave Community.* Urbana: University of Illinois Press, 1984.

Kerr, Robert McNab, IV. "Island in the United States: A Case Study of Muslim Space in South Carolina." Master's thesis, University of South Carolina, 1998.

Pluralism Project of the Committee on the Study of Religion, Harvard University. http://www.pluralism.org/affiliates/stulting/index.php.

Myrtle Beach (Horry County; 2000 pop. 22,759). The centerpiece of South Carolina's Grand Strand, Myrtle Beach is an international resort and ranks among the state's fastest-growing and most economically significant cities. Until the twentieth century the area was thinly settled by small farmers. The region's central asset was the timber and naval stores of its abundant forests. In the 1880s the Burroughs & Collins Company of Conway began acquiring land for its modest timber value, gradually accumulating about seventy thousand acres.

The area's first settlement was a logging camp. In about 1900 Burroughs & Collins built a railroad from Conway to the coast to extract the timber. The terminus, called New Town, was considered part of the Socastee community. In 1901 the company built a small hotel, the Seaside Inn (two dollars per day including meals) and a general store and began selling oceanfront lots for twenty-five dollars each. The settlement was renamed Myrtle Beach after the wax myrtle, a shrub common to the region. Myrtle Beach soon became popular with Horry County folk, who came by rail for a day, a week, or a season.

In 1912 Simeon B. Chapin, a northern entrepreneur, bought a half-interest in the Burroughs & Collins Company's Myrtle Beach venture. Chapin contributed cash, and the company invested its landholdings. The partnership was named Myrtle Beach Farms, later Burroughs & Chapin, and it has played a central role in the evolution of Myrtle Beach.

In the 1920s the Woodside family of Greenville purchased a large tract, intending to develop Myrtle Beach into an exclusive resort. Their Ocean Forest Hotel and Pine Lakes golf course were completed just in time for the Great Depression. The Woodsides defaulted, and the property reverted to Myrtle Beach Farms. In the late 1930s development was refocused on attracting middle-class visitors as new bridges made the area more accessible by automobile.

During World War II, the U.S. Army Air Corps established a base south of town, and German prisoners of war were housed in the area. After the war, the air base was enlarged and became part of the U.S. Air Force Tactical Air Command. Myrtle Beach Air Force Base contributed substantially to the local economy until its closure in 1993.

In the late 1940s Myrtle Beach began a period of sustained growth as fun-seeking Americans discovered the South Carolina resort. Hurricane Hazel temporarily stalled the postwar boom in 1954, but the lower land prices that resulted created an opportunity to combine small holdings into commercial-sized parcels. Soon, national hotel and restaurant chains acquired properties in Myrtle Beach. Besides its traditional role as a family-oriented beach resort, Myrtle Beach became a golf mecca in the 1970s. Good weather and good golf drew a significant retirement population. Beginning in the 1980s, shopping and entertainment complexes added a year-round dimension to the economy. By 2000 Myrtle Beach poured a torrent of revenue into state coffers, but the need for roads and public services lagged far behind. The natural environment was another casualty of rapid expansion. ELDRED E. PRINCE, JR.

Lewis, Catherine H. *Horry County, South Carolina, 1730–1993.* Columbia: University of South Carolina Press, 1998.

Myrtle Beach Air Force Base. Myrtle Beach AFB originated as a municipal airport. The U.S. Army transformed it into a training base during World War II. It later became a fighter base for the U.S. Air Force Tactical Air Command until its final deactivation in 1993. Soon after the Japanese attack on Pearl Harbor, the U.S. Army Air Force appropriated a civilian airfield at Myrtle Beach to train pilots and their crews in bombing and gunnery, using a range created on the base. During the latter part of the war, a German prisoner-of-war camp was established on the base that interned more than six hundred POWs, who were put to work primarily in the local forest products industry. In 1948 the army deactivated the base and it was returned to the town.

As the cold war intensified in the 1950s, the U.S. Air Force reacquired the land and buildings of the former World War II base and reactivated it in 1956. Myrtle Beach AFB became part of Tactical Air Command, with F-100 Super Saber fighters and an estimated 3,500 military and civilian personnel. During the following two decades, aircraft from Myrtle Beach AFB saw extensive action in Indochina and other theaters.

Early in the 1970s the Myrtle Beach installations were renovated to receive A-10 "Warthog" ground attack aircraft. During the middle of the same decade, civilian planes began using the same field to bring tourists to the Grand Strand. A decade later the air force constructed an A-10 simulator facility on the base. By the late 1980s the facility had 3,600 active-duty military and five hundred civilian personnel. As a result of cuts to military spending brought on by the end of the cold war, Myrtle Beach AFB was closed in 1993. FRITZ HAMER

Cragg, Dan. *Guide to Military Installations.* 2d ed. Harrisburg, Pa.: Stackpole, 1988.
Lewis, Catherine H. *Horry County, South Carolina, 1730–1993.* Columbia: University of South Carolina Press, 1998.
Moore, John H. "Nazi Troopers in South Carolina, 1944–1946." *South Carolina Historical Magazine* 81 (October 1980): 306–15.

Myrtle Beach Pavilion. Located at 812 North Ocean Boulevard in the heart of Myrtle Beach, the Myrtle Beach Pavilion Amusement Park's eleven acres of roller coasters, thrill rides, go-cart tracks, water rides, attractions, arcades, shops, and games have been a tradition for the seaside visitors for generations. Also located at the park is the Attic, Myrtle Beach's only club for those under the age of twenty-one, where a beachside stage is the backdrop for free concerts and dances sponsored by the Myrtle Beach Pavilion.

The original pavilion was a wooden structure that adjoined the Seaside Inn, Myrtle Beach's first hotel, built in 1901. It was used principally for dances during the summer season. Owned and operated by Myrtle Beach Farms Company (later Burroughs & Chapin Company), this structure was replaced in 1923 with "an immense new pavilion," according to the June 19, 1924, *Horry Herald,* with a restaurant, concession stands, and amusements on the lower floor and a dance floor above.

The pavilion burned in 1944, and the current concrete pavilion and amusement park rides reopened in 1949 just north of the old pavilion's location. Myrtle Beach Farms made major renovations to the park in 1978, added a new Ferris wheel in 1987, and built a $5 million roller coaster in 2000. One of the notable features of the Myrtle Beach Pavilion is the hand-carved 1912 Herschell-Spillman carousel, which runs to the music of a ca. 1920 German-made Wurlitzer band organ. BARBARA STOKES

Rhyne, Nancy. *Touring the Coastal South Carolina Backroads.* Winston-Salem, N.C.: John F. Blair, 1992.

N

Nairne, Thomas (d. 1715). Indian agent. Details of Nairne's early life are unknown. He had arrived in South Carolina from Scotland by 1695. In that same year Nairne married Elizabeth E. Quintyne, a widow. The marriage brought Nairne four stepchildren and produced a son named Thomas, born in 1698.

Nairne obtained land grants on St. Helena Island from the Lords Proprietors, eventually amassing some 3,600 acres. By the early 1700s Nairne led Indian raids against Spanish Florida both to weaken the Spanish and to obtain slaves from among their Indian allies. In 1707 he entered the Commons House of Assembly as a representative of Colleton County where he headed a group politically opposed to Governor Nathaniel Johnson. As a legislator, Nairne was part of the assembly that drafted new laws to change the Indian trade, specifically reducing the governor's role and his income derived from it.

In 1707 the Commons House created the Board of Indian Commissioners to regulate the trade. The act created the office of Indian agent, who was to spend at least ten months of the year among tribes to supervise traders and resolve problems. Nairne was Carolina's first official Indian agent, employed at an annual salary of £250. As agent, Nairne traveled across the Southeast and conducted missions to southern tribes such as the Tallapoosas and Chickasaws. He also worked to keep unlicensed traders from participating in the Indian trade, which caused him considerable trouble after he arrested the governor's son-in-law, Thomas Broughton, on charges that he was enslaving friendly Indians and stealing deerskins. Nairne's opposition to Governor Johnson led to Nairne's arrest in June 1708 on charges of treason. Nairne claimed that Governor Johnson had falsely accused him to be rid of a political opponent and to allow the governor to regain his ascendancy over the Indian trade. Nairne was released in November 1708 but lost his office as Indian agent. He sailed for England to defend his actions before the Lords Proprietors, who exonerated him. Upon his return to South Carolina, Nairne was reelected to the Commons House of Assembly in 1711.

In December 1712 Nairne again became South Carolina's Indian agent. His second tenure coincided with rising unrest among neighboring Indian nations, especially the Yamassees, who had been abused by Indian traders and feared the expansion of white settlement into Indian territory. In early 1715 there were rumors in Charleston that the Yamassees would attack to resolve their trade problems. Nairne met two Charleston officials at the Yamassee town of Pocotaligo to negotiate with the tribe. On Good Friday, April 15, hostilities erupted as the Yamassees attacked white settlements along South Carolina's southern frontier, beginning the Yamassee War. Nairne was captured and tortured to death by burning wood splinters into his skin for several days. MICHAEL P. MORRIS

Edgar, Walter, and N. Louise Bailey, eds. *Biographical Directory of the South Carolina House of Representatives.* Vol. 2, *The Commons House of Assembly, 1692–1775.* Columbia: University of South Carolina Press, 1977.

Milling, Chapman J. 1940. Reprint, *Red Carolinians.* Columbia: University of South Carolina Press, 1969.

Moore, Alexander, ed. *Nairne's Muskhogean Journals: The 1708 Expedition to the Mississippi River.* Jackson: University of Mississippi Press, 1988.

Morris, Michael P. *The Bringing of Wonder: Trade and the Southeastern Indians, 1700–1783.* Westport, Conn.: Greenwood, 1999.

Nance, Milligan Maceo, Jr. (1925–2001). University president. Nance was born in Columbia on March 26, 1925, the son of M. Maceo Nance and Louella Stewart. He graduated from Booker T. Washington High School and entered South Carolina State College on a band scholarship in 1942. He enlisted in the U.S. Navy in 1943 and served as a petty officer third-class aboard YP105, a patrol boat engaged in testing mines and torpedoes along the Atlantic coast.

M. Maceo Nance, Jr. Courtesy, South Carolina State University Historical Collection

Nance returned to South Carolina State in 1946 and worked as a campus custodian before his graduation in 1949 with a B.A. in social studies. In 1950 he married Julie E. Washington, a 1947 graduate of South Carolina State. They had two children. After graduation Nance was employed by South Carolina State as a supply clerk for the Reserve Officers' Training Corps (ROTC) program. He steadily advanced through the administrative ranks over the next two decades. He was manager of the bookstore and in 1954 became the director of the student union. In 1953 he earned an M.S. in business from New York University. He was named assistant business manager of South Carolina State in 1957 and was promoted to vice president for business and finance in 1967. When President Benner C. Turner was forced to retire in 1967 after lengthy student protests and a boycott of classes that spring, the newly integrated board of trustees named Nance interim president. Nance's informal, open, and cooperative demeanor was a refreshing and sharp contrast to the seventeen years of autocratic leadership under Turner.

The forty-two-year-old Nance was almost immediately thrust into the most serious and tragic civil rights episode in twentieth-century South Carolina. Persistent vestiges of segregation and discrimination in Orangeburg centering on the whites-only All Star Bowling Lanes provoked student demonstrations and confrontations in which people were injured and property damaged in early February 1968. On February 7 Nance appealed for calm and insisted that students remain on the campus. The following day state highway patrolmen shot into a crowd of agitated and angry students who had gathered on the front of the campus. Three young men were killed and twenty-seven wounded in what came to be known as the Orangeburg Massacre. Nance worked diligently with students, faculty, and local leaders following the tragedy to restore a semblance of harmony to a community deeply divided by racial animosity. In June 1968 the college board of trustees demonstrated confidence in his leadership and named him president.

During Nance's nineteen-year tenure the college experienced dramatic growth and progress. Twenty new degree programs were established, ranging from agribusiness to nursing. However, the program in agriculture was terminated, and the campus farm was transformed into Hillcrest Recreation Center. There were major capital additions including dormitories, classrooms, a theater, a health and physical education complex named for the three young men slain in the massacre, an FM radio station, and the I. P. Stanback Museum and Planetarium. Nance was also a key figure in the formation of the Mid-Eastern Athletic Conference in 1970.

Nance was fair, honest, and politically savvy. He worked closely with South Carolina Senate leader L. Marion Gressette. He was engaging and gregarious, but he could be blunt and would readily tell people—from students and faculty to legislators—what they often preferred not to hear. Nance died March 23, 2001, and was buried at Belleville Memorial Gardens, Orangeburg. WILLIAM C. HINE

Bass, Jack, and Jack Nelson. *The Orangeburg Massacre.* 2d ed. Macon, Ga.: Mercer University Press, 1996.

Hine, William C. "South Carolina State College: A Legacy of Education and Public Service." *Agricultural History* 65 (spring 1991): 149–67.

Potts, John F. *A History of South Carolina State College.* Orangeburg: South Carolina State College, 1978.

Nathaniel Russell House (Charleston). Located at 51 Meeting Street, the Nathaniel Russell House is one of America's finest examples of neoclassical domestic architecture. Completed in 1808, it was built for Nathaniel Russell (1738–1820), a merchant who arrived in Charleston at the age of twenty-seven and quickly amassed a substantial fortune. The architect is unknown. Evidence indicates that the builder relied on architectural pattern books for elements of the design.

Unlike most of Charleston's early urban dwellings, the house is set back from the street about thirty feet and has a front garden entrance. It is built of brick, stands three stories tall, and has a low, hipped roof surmounted by a paneled balustrade. A full-height polygonal bay projects from the south elevation. Tall second-story windows set in recessed arches open to a wrought-iron balcony that wraps around the house, overlooking the garden. The lintels, sills, keystones, and impost stripes are white marble, presumably from a source in New England. Masterful Adamsesque styling is evident throughout the interior. A freestanding elliptical stair with a mahogany handrail rises elegantly from the first to the third story. All of the cornices, chair rails, mantels, and window and door frames are embellished with cast plaster or carved wood ornament. The large, gracefully proportioned rooms and superbly executed decorative work make this one of Charleston's most stunning interiors.

After Russell's death in 1820, the house remained in the family until it was sold to Governor R. F. W. Allston in 1857. It survived the Civil War intact and had several owners before Historic Charleston Foundation purchased it in 1955. Today it is operated as a house museum. The U.S. Department of the Interior designated the Russell House a National Historic Landmark in 1974. DANIEL J. VIVIAN

Lane, Mills. *Architecture of the Old South: South Carolina.* Savannah, Ga.: Beehive, 1984.

Poston, Jonathan H. *The Buildings of Charleston: A Guide to the City's Architecture.* Columbia: University of South Carolina Press, 1997.

National Association for the Advancement of Colored People. The National Association for the Advancement of Colored People (NAACP) was formally founded in 1910 by a group of progressive white northerners and prominent African American leaders, most notable of whom was the Harvard University–trained intellectual, W. E. B. Du Bois. Formed as Jim Crow segregation tightened its grip on life in the South and as racial violence extended its reach into northern cities such as Springfield, Illinois, the NAACP dedicated itself to securing and defending the constitutional rights of African Americans. The organization's first branches in South Carolina were chartered in Charleston and Columbia in 1917. In the years that followed, the NAACP battled to destroy Jim Crow and led the fight for black voting rights, equality, and respect in the Palmetto State. Since its inception, the South Carolina NAACP has been a leader of the African American struggle for civil rights in the South and the United States.

During World War I, black South Carolinians led efforts by the NAACP's national office to expand the organization's presence across the South. In addition to the branches in Columbia and Charleston, the organization took root in Aiken, Anderson, Darlington, Florence, Orangeburg, and Beaufort. The NAACP quickly proved a formidable advocate for African American rights and interests. From battles for better schools, to jobs in the Charleston Navy Yard, to efforts to register black voters, the organization captured the imagination and loyalty of black South Carolinians from all walks of life: male and female, urban and rural, professionals and everyday folk. By 1929 four additional communities chartered NAACP branches (a branch required a minimum of fifty members) and nine others attempted to do so. But a growing white backlash, deteriorating economic conditions, black out-migration, and, at times, ineffectual local leadership prevented the organization from establishing a stronger presence in South Carolina. The early advances made by the organization had eroded substantially by the opening years of the 1930s, with the organization barely maintaining a foothold in the two cities that chartered its first branches.

Between 1943 and 1955 the NAACP in South Carolina experienced a resurgence that firmly established the organization as the leading advocate of African American civil rights and a force for democratic reform in post–World War II America. The organization's resurgence began in the late 1930s, when an unlettered plumber from Cheraw, Levi G. Byrd, began efforts to organize a State Conference of NAACP branches. Despite resistance from members of the Columbia NAACP, Byrd managed to convince twenty-nine representatives from branches in Charleston, Cheraw, Columbia, Florence, Georgetown, Greenville, and Sumter to meet on the campus of Columbia's Benedict College on November 10, 1939, to create a State Conference to coordinate the NAACP's activities on a statewide scale. For the first years of the state organization, members of the Cheraw branch held the key leadership roles, but

Columbians assumed the primary leadership positions by 1943. For more than a decade the Reverend James M. Hinton served as president of the State Conference and Modjeska Montieth Simkins served as the organization's secretary. Byrd served as the organization's treasurer into the 1970s. With the assistance of South Carolina notables such as Osceola E. McKaine, Septima Poinsette Clark, John H. McCray, Harold Boulware (the organization's chief legal counsel), and Eugene A. R. Montgomery, who in 1948 became the State Conference's first full-time and paid executive secretary, Hinton and Simkins led the charge for civil rights and equality into the 1950s.

The NAACP State Conference won a series of important legal victories that struck blows against Jim Crow and charted a path toward the democratization of the state's political system. It secured the equalization of salaries for black and white public schoolteachers in Charleston and Columbia by 1946. The organization's efforts to integrate the University of South Carolina's law school led to the creation of a law school for African Americans at South Carolina State College, which trained prominent attorneys including the civil rights lawyer and future federal court judge Matthew Perry. In conjunction with the Progressive Democratic Party (PDP), the NAACP hastened the passing of the all-white Democratic primary through two major federal court decisions, *Elmore v. Rice* (1947) and *Brown v. Baskin* (1948). But the NAACP in South Carolina is perhaps best known for its participation in the landmark U.S. Supreme Court ruling *Brown v. Board of Education* (1954), which declared segregation in public school education unconstitutional.

Since the mid-1940s the Reverend Joseph A. DeLaine had led efforts to equalize public school facilities in rural Clarendon County. The efforts of DeLaine and other heroic members of Clarendon's black community converged in 1947 with the efforts of the NAACP State Conference and national office to put an end to the injustices of Jim Crow. The result of their combined labors was *Briggs v. Elliott,* one of five cases, and the only one from the Deep South, included in the *Brown* ruling. Although white resistance to the NAACP and efforts to achieve the integration of schools and other public facilities in South Carolina proved formidable in the years following *Brown,* the NAACP survived to remain a champion of African American rights.

During the NAACP's heyday in South Carolina, roughly 1943 to 1955, the number of branches in the state expanded from fifteen to eighty-four and membership topped the ten thousand mark. The organization achieved a presence in the state's urban centers, backwoods, cotton fields, and rural churches. Massive white resistance to the implementation of *Brown,* however, cut the number of branches by more than fifty, and individual membership in the organization plummeted. The General Assembly adopted extreme measures in spring 1956 to curtail the organization's influence, including the prohibition of NAACP members from employment in local, county, and state government.

Partly an effect of massive resistance, younger members of the 1960s civil rights generation often viewed the NAACP as a conservative force in an era of rapid and dramatic change. Yet the NAACP in South Carolina had laid the crucial groundwork for those changes and adapted remarkably well to the revolutionary fervor of the 1960s. Under the leadership of the Reverend I. DeQuincey Newman, the State Conference supported direct action protests as well as legal efforts to integrate the state's schools and public facilities. In Charleston and Rock Hill, respective NAACP stalwarts J. Arthur Brown and the Reverend C. A. Ivory pioneered direct action campaigns, and NAACP College and Youth branches led sit-ins across the state.

The 1960s did not, however, mark an end to the African American struggle for civil rights, equality, and respect in South Carolina. Issues such as access to health care, employment, and the ballot box and the removal of the Confederate battle flag from the State House grounds in Columbia occupied the front lines of the NAACP's ongoing campaign for racial justice as it entered the twenty-first century.

PETER F. LAU

Aba-Mecha, Barbara W. "South Carolina Conference of NAACP: Origin and Major Accomplishments, 1939–1954." *Proceedings of the South Carolina Historical Association* (1981): 1–21.

Baker, R. Scott. "Ambiguous Legacies: The NAACP's Legal Campaign Against Segregation in Charleston, South Carolina, 1935–1975." Ph.D. diss., Columbia University, 1993.

Hoffman, Edwin D. "The Genesis of the Modern Movement for Equal Rights in South Carolina, 1930–1939." *Journal of Negro History* 44 (October 1959): 346–69.

Lau, Peter F. "Freedom Road Territory: The Politics of Civil Rights Struggle in South Carolina during the Jim Crow Era." Ph.D. diss., Rutgers, The State University of New Jersey, 2002.

Newby, I. A. *Black Carolinians: A History of Blacks in South Carolina from 1895 to 1968.* Columbia: University of South Carolina Press, 1973.

National Baptists. The term "National Baptists" refers collectively to the three largest African American Baptist denominations in the United States and in South Carolina. These bodies include the National Baptist Convention of the U.S.A. (1895), the National Baptist Convention of America (1915), and the Progressive National Baptist Convention (1961). All are historically intertwined, with the latter two emerging from the first because of internal controversies. Membership figures are estimates only, but in 2000 the National Baptist Convention of the U.S.A. numbered around 7 million adherents, while the National Baptist Convention of America counted approximately 3.5 million members. In 1995 the Progressive National Baptist Convention numbered around 2.5 million.

National Baptists, with other African American denominations, have been associated with the Palmetto State from their earliest days. During the Great Awakening of the mid–eighteenth century and the steady growth of an evangelical presence in the South that followed, African Americans were drawn to both Baptist and Methodist styles, with their emphasis on religious experience and more emotional expression of spiritual fervor. By the middle of the eighteenth century, long before separate denominations existed, an independent African American Baptist congregation formed on the Silver Bluff plantation in South Carolina, near Augusta, Georgia.

The surge toward racially separate congregations came during the Reconstruction period, with most in South Carolina identifying with either the Methodists or the Baptists. The number of African American Baptist churches in the state multiplied significantly through the efforts of the Freedmen's Bureau and institutions such as Benedict College, which was founded in 1870 to train African American men for the ministry.

Historically, Baptists have encouraged the independence of local congregations, with denominations serving more to coordinate shared activities in areas such as missions and education than to control local church programs. But by 1895 efforts under way nationally to bring together African American Baptist congregations led to the organization of the National Baptist Convention of the U.S.A. Most South Carolina African American Baptist churches are affiliated with this group, although there are some loose ties to the bodies that broke away from the National Baptist Convention of the U.S.A. All of them, however, are more connected to each other than the African American congregations affiliated with the Baptist Educational and Missionary Convention of South Carolina, organized in 1876.

Within South Carolina, in 2000 National Baptists had approximately 500,000 adherents in some fifteen hundred churches. Some South Carolinians, such as Dr. Willie Givens, Jr., and Dr. Arabella Rich, have held executive offices at the national level. All three National Baptist bodies hold membership in the National Council of Churches. C. N. WILLBORN

Hill, Samuel S., ed. *Encyclopedia of Religion in the South.* Macon, Ga.: Mercer University Press, 1984.

Pelt, Owen D., and Ralph Lee Smith. *The Story of the National Baptists.* New York: Vantage Books, 1960.

National Beta Club. The National Beta Club was founded January 8, 1934, at Landrum High School by Dr. John West Harris, faculty member at Wofford College. Reared on a farm and aware of the privations of his day, Harris worked to develop youth for effective leadership and achievement. His high standards and goals were fashioned after Phi Beta Kappa and the Kiwanis and Rotary clubs. He knew achievers made A and B grades, and subsequently chose *Beta* (or B) for the organization's name. He asked principals and superintendents for permission to present his plan to local literary societies and sponsors.

The Landrum High School Literary Society (fifteen members) and sponsor Helen Prince were the first to apply for membership. Before the school year ended, eight other literary societies had become Beta Clubs. By the end of the following year there were seventy-five chapters in four states.

National dues are paid by members, and an endowed foundation supports the organization and its programs. The Student Loan Program assisted fifteen hundred worthy students before it became a Scholarship Program, supported by many national corporations and philanthropists.

Annual Assemblies are held for members and sponsors at the state level, and delegates are elected to an International Convention. Each member receives a membership pin and a certificate, subscription to the Beta Club *Journal,* subscription to Beta Web network, a membership card, and a diploma seal for graduating seniors. Junior Beta Clubs began in junior high schools in 1961.

As of 2005 the National Beta Club, headquartered in Spartanburg, had more than 417,000 members in the United States, the Bahamas, Germany, Guam, Puerto Rico, Russia, and the Virgin Islands. Among the nearly five million former members are Erika Dunlap, Miss America 2004; NFL quarterback Jake Delhomme; former president Bill Clinton; the television journalist Diane Sawyer; and Millard Fuller, the founder of Habitat for Humanity. JAMES WALTON LAWRENCE, SR.

National Dropout Prevention Center. Founded in 1986 at Clemson University, the National Dropout Prevention Center serves as a clearinghouse on dropout prevention related issues, maintains a database (FOCUS) of model programs, and publishes materials on effective dropout prevention strategies. The center was created under the direction of Ester Ferguson, a South Carolina native serving as chair of the New York City National Dropout Prevention Fund. Ferguson came to Clemson to discuss the development of a national center to study dropout prevention. After talks with administrators, Clemson's College of Education was selected to house and develop the center. Initial funding was provided by the state legislature, the governor's office, the Appalachian Regional Commission, General Foods Corporation, and Clemson University.

Offering institutional or individual membership, the center sponsors research projects with school districts, states, and other educational entities and is involved in improving programs and services for at-risk individuals and families. It conducts third-party evaluations promoting accountability, provides leadership in demonstration projects, and develops research-based curriculum tools. Another feature of the center is providing opportunities for professional development. The annual National Dropout Prevention Network Conference, America's At-Risk Youth National FORUM, and other topic-specific institutes are hosted by the center. It publishes the *Journal of At-Risk Issues* and other dropout prevention reports to disseminate up-to-date information about the critical issues of K–12 youth and families in at-risk situations. TONY W. CAWTHON

National Guard. The National Guard in South Carolina evolved out of the nineteenth-century organized militia, which was controlled by the governor and unavailable to supplement federal military forces. The organized militia was renamed the South Carolina National Guard in 1905, the same year the first state-owned armory was built in Columbia. The Dick Act of 1903 started the state militias on the road to federalization by requiring all states to conform to federal standards within two years or lose federal funding. The National Defense Act of 1916, which required a dual oath to the state and federal governments from all National Guardsmen, completed the conversion of state militias into a national reserve. The conversion came just in time for South Carolinians to participate in the campaign on the Mexican border in 1916 and in World War I. Unfortunately, the National Defense Act of 1916 did not require the federal government to maintain the integrity of National Guard units. As a result, most guardsmen found themselves used as replacements, with large numbers of Palmetto guardsmen serving in the 321st Infantry, the 118th Infantry, and the 37th Regiment, a black regiment.

South Carolinians served valiantly in France, and six received the Medal of Honor, including Lieutenant James C. Dozier (who later served as state adjutant general. The South Carolina National Guard was again federalized in World War II. The first units were mobilized on September 16, 1940, and the entire force was mobilized by mid-February 1941. The South Carolina Defense Force, composed of unpaid volunteers, was activated in its place. Two South Carolina units served in the European theater, the 118th Infantry and 178th Field Artillery. Following World War II, the National Guard was reorganized, and in 1946 it gained an air arm, the Air National Guard. While some units and individuals were called up for the Korean War and the 1961 Berlin crisis, the National Guard's role was primarily that of responding to civil disturbances, such as the demonstrations on the University of South Carolina's campus in 1970, or providing manpower when natural disasters struck, such as Hurricane Hugo in 1989.

The South Carolina National Guard integrated in November 1964, but it remained an all-male organization until May 1973 when the first two female members joined the 132d Medical Company at Darlington. Following the Vietnam War, the United States put increasing emphasis on the integration of regular and National Guard forces as a means of maintaining readiness while reducing the size of the active duty military. The increased role of the National

Guard resulted in South Carolina receiving modern, sophisticated equipment and aircraft and a higher level of training. South Carolina National Guard units were deployed during Desert Shield / Desert Storm, in Bosnia, in the Afghanistan campaign, and in Iraq. They also participated in international assistance programs in places such as Honduras and Albania. Following the terrorist attacks on September 11, 2001, homeland defense became a major factor in National Guard training and planning, along with preparing for a major military action, a civil disturbance, or another devastating hurricane. JACK ALLEN MEYER

Cooper, Jerry. *The Rise of the National Guard: The Evolution of the American Militia, 1865–1920.* Lincoln: University of Nebraska Press, 1997.

Mahon, John K. *History of the Militia and the National Guard.* New York: Macmillan, 1983.

Rhodes, Gwen R. *South Carolina Army National Guard.* Dallas, Tex.: Taylor Publishing, 1988.

National Resource Center for the First-Year Experience and Students in Transition. Chartered in 1986, the National Resource Center for the First-Year Experience and Students in Transition at the University of South Carolina is an outgrowth and extension of the University 101 first-year seminar. The course began at USC in 1972 with 239 freshman volunteers and was made an official course two years later. President Thomas Jones used a portion of a Ford Foundation grant to improve undergraduate teaching to support the development of the University 101 program.

The original course focused on three main areas: the meaning of higher education, students' roles at the university, and the university's resources and support services. The program was initially led by J. Manning Hiers. John N. Gardner led the program from 1974 until his retirement in 1999. By the 1974–1975 academic year, University 101 was enrolling almost thirteen hundred freshmen in more than sixty sections of the course. In addition to the course, the program also included an extensive instructor training program. Research conducted at USC and across the country has found that University 101 courses can contribute significantly to student retention from their freshman to sophomore years.

By the 1980s USC was recognized as a national leader in the University 101 movement. USC began sponsoring conferences in 1982 to bring together representatives from institutions across the country to discuss these programs. The National Resource Center for the First-Year Experience and Students in Transition was a further outgrowth of this leadership and coordinates national and international conferences as well as publications including a monograph series and the *Journal of The First-Year Experience and Students in Transition.* JOHN WESLEY LOWERY

Lesesne, Henry H. *A History of the University of South Carolina, 1940–2000.* Columbia: University of South Carolina Press, 2001.

Upcraft, M. Lee, John N. Gardner, and Associates. *The Freshman Year Experience: Helping Students Survive and Succeed in College.* San Francisco: Jossey-Bass, 1989.

Naval stores. For centuries, the resinous products of pine trees—tar, pitch, rosin, and turpentine—were used to preserve and maintain wooden sailing vessels and cordage. As the world's leading maritime power, Great Britain had a vital strategic interest in naval stores. The Royal Navy and British shipping interests had long recognized the potential of their American colonies—especially the Carolinas—to produce naval stores but preferred Scandinavian products to Carolinian, judging the latter "too green." The remoteness from English markets discouraged the Carolina industry as well.

The Great Northern War (1700–1721) changed that. With the entire Baltic at war, Scandinavian products were unavailable to British shipping, and wartime demand drove prices of naval stores to record highs. To encourage a dependable supply of these strategic commodities, Parliament voted an impressive subsidy on American naval stores. Responding to government largesse, South Carolinians were soon reaping handsome profits from the humble yellow pine. By 1720 exports of naval stores had risen to more than forty thousand barrels per annum.

Gathering and processing the raw material was hard work. Workers cut gashes on tree trunks and attached wooden boxes to collect the sap. Later they scraped the wounds and dipped the sap into buckets. Ten thousand trees—about one hundred acres—were considered "a crop" for one man to attend. At a nearby turpentine camp, the "dip" and "scrape" were distilled into turpentine spirits. This method eventually killed the tree. In another method, highly resinous pine stumps and deadfall—called lightwood—were gathered from the forest. Several thousand pounds were slowly burned in an earthen kiln. The highly flammable resin flowed out and was barreled as tar. Boiling reduced the tar to pitch.

By the mid-1720s peace had returned to northern Europe and Parliament suspended the subsidy. The naval stores boom was over, but the industry persisted at a lower level. Naval stores were well suited to South Carolina not only because pine trees covered the state's coastal plain, but also because labor demands were compatible with rice and cotton, and an otherwise idle workforce could be employed in winter. Consumer products such as camphene—a blend of turpentine and alcohol used in lamps—helped to stabilize the industry. Moreover, naval stores were in great demand during the golden age of sail, roughly 1840 to 1880. The federal blockade of southern ports during the Civil War brought the industry to a virtual standstill, but heightened demand during the Franco-Prussian War (1870–1871) helped the industry recover. By 1880 the state was producing about one-third of the South's naval stores, much of them from coastal counties such as Horry and Georgetown.

By the 1890s, however, the naval stores industry was declining in the Palmetto State. Advancements in naval architecture eroded demand for wood and cordage preservatives as shipbuilding evolved from timber to iron and from sail to steam. At the same time, petroleum products were replacing naval stores in industrial applications. For example, kerosene replaced camphene as a lighting source. Moreover, two centuries of exploitation had denuded the state's great pine forests, and the industry left for Georgia, Florida, and Alabama. By the early twentieth century the South Carolina naval stores industry had run its course. The naval stores business has been succeeded by lumber and forest industries, which remain a vital part of South Carolina economy. TOMOKO YAGYU

Clowse, Converse D. *Economic Beginnings in Colonial South Carolina, 1670–1730.* Columbia: University of South Carolina Press, 1971.

Hoover, Calvin B. *Economic Resources and Policies of the South.* New York: Macmillan, 1951.

Joyner, Charles W. "The Far Side of the Forest: Timber and Naval Stores in the Waccamaw Region." *Independent Republic Quarterly* 18 (fall 1984): 13–17.

Perry, Percival. "The Naval-Stores Industry in the Old South, 1790–1860." *Journal of Southern History* 34 (November 1968): 509–26.

Williams, Justin. "English Mercantilism and Carolina Naval Stores, 1705–1776." *Journal of Southern History* 1 (May 1935): 169–85.

Negro Seaman Acts. While the mobility of free blacks was generally restricted before the Civil War, the Negro Seaman Acts were laws uniquely aimed at a specific occupational group. During the antebellum era they proliferated along the southern coastal states. South Carolina was the first to pass such a law and did so in the fearful months following discovery of the Denmark Vesey slave conspiracy in 1822 when Vesey, a free man, sought assistance from foreign free blacks. The goal of the legislation was to forestall potentially dangerous contact between nonresident free blacks and slaves. By its provisions, free black sailors on board ships from outside South Carolina were incarcerated in local jails for the duration of the vessel's visit. Ship captains were responsible for paying the costs incurred. If a captain refused or left without him, the jailed black sailor could be sold as a slave.

The laws contributed to rising antebellum sectional tensions. When challenged by northern ship captains, South Carolina courts upheld the law's constitutionality. However, in 1823 the U.S. Circuit Court ruled the laws unconstitutional and the U.S. attorney general concurred. When Congressman John Quincy Adams had operation of the acts investigated in 1842, South Carolina representatives denounced the inquiry as threatening states' rights and imperiling the Union. In 1844 a Massachusetts agent, dispatched to gather information for further litigation, was denounced by the state legislature, and the threat of Charleston mobs forced him to flee the state. Diplomatic incidents were provoked by these laws and British consuls frequently protested incarceration of black British sailors. Nevertheless, American secretaries of state were impotent in the face of South Carolina's determination to exercise what it considered legitimate police power over its domestic population. BERNARD E. POWERS, JR.

Hamer, Philip M. "Great Britain, the United States, and the Negro Seamen Acts, 1822–1848." *Journal of Southern History* 1 (February 1935): 3–28.

Starobin, Robert S., ed. *Denmark Vesey: The Slave Conspiracy of 1822.* Englewood Cliffs, N.J.: Prentice Hall, 1970.

Wilson, Carol. *Freedom at Risk: The Kidnapping of Free Blacks in America, 1780–1865.* Lexington: University Press of Kentucky, 1994.

Nelson, Annie Greene (1902–1993). Writer, playwright. The first African American South Carolina woman to publish a novel, Nelson was born in Darlington County on December 5, 1902. She was the eldest of fourteen children born to Sylvester and Nancy Greene and received education at a school on the Parrots' Plantation. Nelson overcame an impoverished childhood and later attended Benedict College and earned a degree in both education and nursing from Voorhees College in 1923. At age eighty, she took courses in drama at the University of South Carolina. She taught school in Darlington and Richland Counties and worked as a nurse for several Columbia area hospitals for almost twenty years.

Nelson's public writing career began in 1925 when her poem "What Do You Think of Mother" was published in the *Palmetto Leader* newspaper. She later wrote three novels: *After the Storm* (1942), *The Dawn Appears* (1944), and *Don't Walk on My Dreams* (1961). All three were reprinted in 1976. *To Paw with Love* is an autobiographical account of her own upbringing. Nelson wrote two plays as well: *Weary Fireside Blues,* produced off-Broadway, and *The Parrots' Plantation.* In the early 1990s, just prior to her death, she worked on her manuscript *Eighty, So What?* using the optimistic tone for which her writing was known.

Set in the South Carolina environment she grew up in, Nelson's writing typically recounts what life was like for ordinary African Americans of her community. *After the Storm* is about the people of

Annie Green Nelson. Courtesy, Gary Dickey

the Pee Dee region and shows the home lives and customs of black people and their fight for dignity in the midst of deep poverty. Her first novel's success led to *The Dawn Appears,* which, Nelson said, was "affectionately dedicated to the Pee Dee section of South Carolina." This second novel focuses more specifically on the dynamics of white landlords and black workers on a southern plantation. In her 1961 book, *Don't Walk on My Dreams,* Nelson again combines her own experience with that of others within her community whom she knew or had heard about.

Late in her life, Nelson was still an active author, frequently traveling around the state to give book readings. She received the Lucy Hampton Bostick Award, an annual recognition given by Friends of the Richland County Public Library. She was also honored with the P. Scott Kennedy Award for her contributions to African American theater. What Nelson said about one of her novels perhaps explains her writing in general: "If a person is going to write, it must be a compulsion. A book, a story is something that must be written so people can feel it, see it as it unfolds. The plantation life was one of my most favorite subjects—the faith, the struggle, the perseverance. They never gave up—the strict morals—the hard work. That is why I wrote *After the Storm.*" Nelson died in Columbia on December 23, 1993. AMY L. WHITE

Potts, James. "'Letters to Paw' and African American 'Ecriture': The Autobiography of Annie Greene Nelson." *South Carolina Review* 33 (fall 2000): 63–74.

New Deal. The New Deal was a collection of federal programs enacted between 1933 and 1939 to solve the problems created by the Great Depression. In South Carolina the New Deal brought three R's: recovery for farmers, bankers, textile mill owners, and small businessmen; relief for the unemployed and destitute; and reform in labor-management relations, banking, sale of securities, and retirement. In the process the New Deal radically increased the role of the federal government in the state's economy by creating permanent acreage allotment programs, agricultural credit, compulsory minimum wage / maximum hours requirements, protection for laborers who sought to unionize, Social Security benefits, a public welfare system, the Federal Deposit Insurance Corporation to protect depositors, the Federal Housing Administration to expand housing opportunities, and the Rural Electrification Administration to electrify the countryside.

Even before the stock market crash in October 1929, South Carolina had suffered several years of economic downturn. Cotton began to decline as early as 1920, a victim of overproduction and the boll weevil. In the next five years, the average value of farmland dropped from $65 to $43 per acre. During the 1920s farmers abandoned one-sixth of South Carolina's farms. The collapse of the cotton economy brought down forty-nine percent of the state's banks. In the mid-1920s the state's textile economy joined farming in economic depression. In 1929 shares of stock in the state's 230 textile mills sold for one-half their 1923 price. The onset of the Great Depression made wretched conditions even worse. By 1931 cotton was selling for 6¢ per pound, actually below the cost of production, and the cash value of South Carolina's farm commodities had dropped by half since 1929. In 1932 rural poverty was so severe that taxes were delinquent on almost half the state's farms. There was no market for the securities of textile mills, and average annual textile wages plummeted from $719 in 1929 to $495 in 1932. Not surprisingly, by 1933 one-fourth of the state's population was eligible for public relief.

The New Deal attacked these problems through a host of innovative programs and the creation of a myriad of new federal agencies. Managed on the floor of the U.S. House of Representatives by Congressman Hampton P. Fulmer of Orangeburg, the Agricultural Adjustment Act created the Agricultural Adjustment Administration (AAA), which raised farm prices in South Carolina by reducing surpluses through a permanent acreage-reduction program. In midsummer 1933 farmers in the Palmetto State plowed under 425,000 of their 1,770,000 acres of cotton. In subsequent springs they planted only their allotment. Farmers were paid for acres destroyed or not planted. They also enjoyed higher prices because of the reduction in supply. Similarly, the state's 23,000 tobacco farmers in the Pee Dee reduced their acreage by thirty percent and enjoyed an increase in price per pound from 11.14¢ in 1932 to 21.60¢ in 1934. The reduction in acreage of both crops reduced the need for tenants and thus hastened migration from the countryside to cities and towns. At the same time, the Rural Electrification Administration (REA), set up in 1935, made farm life more tolerable by encouraging rural electrification. The percentage of farms in South Carolina with electricity increased from two in 1934 to almost fifteen by 1940.

Meanwhile the National Industrial Recovery Act of 1933 created both the National Recovery Administration (NRA) and the Public Works Administration (PWA) to bring about business recovery, which in South Carolina meant textiles. Under the NRA, each industry drew up a Code of Fair Competition to allow firms within the industry to raise prices by cutting back production. NRA Code Number 1, the textile code, which was partly written by textile magnate Thomas Marchant of Greenville, required the 230 mills in South Carolina to reduce production from the customary 105 hours a week to 80 hours a week. At the same time, the code forced mills to eliminate child labor, pay a minimum wage of $12 a week, employ each worker for no more than 40 hours a week, and allow workers the right to unionize.

Flaws in the code and its ineffective enforcement led to a host of strikes culminating in the General Textile Strike of 1934, which involved half of South Carolina's eighty thousand workers. The strike ended on management's terms, and its failure had a chilling effect on unionization in South Carolina for years thereafter. Despite the protection of the New Deal's National Labor Relations Act of 1935, which punished mill owners for discharging workers because of union activity, union organizers in South Carolina enjoyed little success in their attempts to unionize the cotton industry in the late 1930s. By 1980 only 6.7 percent of the state's labor force was unionized, the second smallest percentage in the nation. Workers at least could thank the New Deal for the Fair Labor Standards Act of 1938, which set a permanent minimum wage and maximum workweek.

Aiding the NRA in effecting business recovery was the Public Works Administration (PWA), which stimulated purchases in construction and related industries such as steel, cement, and lumber. In South Carolina the PWA was synonymous with the construction of public housing at University Terrace, Gonzales Gardens, and Calhoun Court in Columbia and Cooper River Court, Meeting Street Manor, and Anson Borough Homes in Charleston, eighty-seven schools and ten city halls and courthouses across the state, and massive hydroelectric projects at Buzzard Roost in Greenwood County and Santee Cooper in the lowcountry. Both hydroelectric projects helped mightily in the effort to electrify rural areas, expand recreational opportunities, eradicate malaria, and attract industry to the state. Both also required massive amounts of labor at a time when jobs were scarce.

More important in helping the unemployed were the various relief agencies. The Federal Emergency Relief Act of 1933 appropriated $500 million to be channeled through the forty-eight state relief administrations to alleviate unemployment and human misery. The South Carolina Emergency Relief Administration (SCERA) spent its allotment on both direct relief for unemployables and work relief for those able to work. The latter earned SCERA dollars, and later Civil Works Administration (CWA) dollars, through work at jobs in sewing rooms, libraries, swamp drainage, local infrastructure construction, literacy training, reconstruction of Charleston's Dock Street Theater, and the construction of highways, bridges, and schools.

In 1935 the Roosevelt administration created the Works Progress Administration (WPA) to take over work relief, while insisting that the states assume responsibility for their unemployables. The state of South Carolina, aided by federal grants under Social Security, created the South Carolina Department of Public Welfare to look after the needy. Meanwhile, the WPA undertook the most massive work-relief effort in the state's history. Indeed, for several years the WPA was the state's largest employer. Its fruits included the construction or improvement of 1,138 bridges, 11,699 culverts, 10,000 miles of highways, 2,179 schools, and 1,267 noneducational buildings such as courthouses and jails. Less visible but also valuable were the 2.1 million garments made for the poor in WPA sewing rooms, literacy efforts that all but wiped out illiteracy in the educable population, the publication of the nationally known *South Carolina: A Guide to the Palmetto State* (1941), and music classes and concerts for more than twenty percent of the state's citizens.

The most popular of all New Deal programs in the Palmetto State was the Civilian Conservation Corps (CCC). This program put unemployed young males between the ages of seventeen and twenty-five years into South Carolina's thirty CCC camps to do conservation work, which by 1939 included thinning almost fifty thousand acres of forests, devoting more than 115,000 man-days to planting trees, and spending almost 120,000 hours fighting forest fires. The young men also constructed more than 5,400 miles of fire breaks, almost 1,500 miles of truck trails, and the state's first fourteen state parks. In 1938 alone, an estimated one-fourth of the state's citizens enjoyed the new state parks. By 1939 almost 32,000 South Carolinians had served in the CCC.

Also by 1939, other less visible but equally valuable New Deal agencies had improved conditions in the Palmetto State. The National Youth Administration (NYA) paid $1.1 million in wages to almost twenty thousand high school and college students who could not have remained in school without the jobs provided by the NYA. The Home Owners Loan Corporation (HOLC), which purchased mortgages from lenders and then renegotiated more favorable terms with the borrowers, saved ten percent of the state's nonfarm homes from foreclosure. The Federal Housing Administration (FHA), which insured more than twelve thousand loans totaling almost $15 million, made credit available to home buyers when none existed in the private sector. The presence of Federal Deposit Insurance Corporation (FDIC) insurance so restored popular confidence in banking that bank failures in South Carolina dropped from an average of twenty-five per year between 1921 and 1933 to just two banks in the five years between 1934 and 1939.

Results of the New Deal in South Carolina were mixed. It did not challenge racial segregation, which existed in every New Deal program. Neither did the New Deal dismantle the state's conservative political culture, local power structure, legislative supremacy, or prevailing notions of class, gender, and race. On the other hand, the New Deal restored confidence in democracy, capitalism, and progress. It kept farmers, mill owners, bankers, and mill workers out of bankruptcy long enough for them to prosper during and after World War II. The programs in work relief and public works were responsible for the state's first public housing, two massive hydroelectric complexes, and thousands of miles of highways, bridges, sewage systems, and water systems. The program in industrial recovery and reform brought permanent shorter hours, higher wages, better working conditions, and labor's right to organize. The program for agricultural recovery brought permanent price supports, acreage reduction, agricultural credit, soil conservation, and rural electrification. The New Deal launched the national careers of politicians such as Olin D. Johnston and Burnet Maybank and furthered the career of James F. Byrnes, who helped author or served as Senate floor manager for at least eight major pieces of New Deal legislation. The state's current system of alcoholic beverage control began with the New Deal. Also starting during the New Deal was African American activism, which culminated in the civil rights movement in the decades following World War II. Truly, the New Deal was a watershed in the state's history. See plate 31. JACK IRBY HAYES

Cann, Marvin L. "Burnet Rhett Maybank and the New Deal in South Carolina, 1931–1941." Ph.D. diss., University of North Carolina, 1967.

Hayes, Jack Irby. *South Carolina and the New Deal.* Columbia: University of South Carolina Press, 2001.

Hiott, William D. "New Deal Resettlement in South Carolina." Master's thesis, University of South Carolina, 1986.

Lesesne, Henry H. "Opposition to the New Deal in South Carolina, 1933–1936." Master's thesis, University of South Carolina, 1995.

Prince, Eldred E., and Robert R. Simpson. *Long Green: The Rise and Fall of Tobacco in South Carolina.* Athens: University of Georgia Press, 2000.

New Ellenton (Aiken County; 2000 pop. 2,250). Initially dubbed North Ellenton by the press prior to its incorporation, New Ellenton was an offspring of the cold war in South Carolina and considered by many locals to have been "the first victim of the H-bomb." Incorporated in 1952, New Ellenton was the reincarnation of the town of Ellenton. This predecessor community originated around 1870 as a depot on the Port Royal Railroad. According to legend, the town was named for Mary Ellen Dunbar, a local girl who had apparently enchanted the railroad's president, Stephen Millett. Residing in the Dunbar family's home while surveying the route, Millett named the depot site "Ellen's Town," which was subsequently shortened to Ellenton.

First enumerated in 1880 with a population of just 94, Ellenton enjoyed steady growth through 1950, when the population stood at 746. Ellenton's quiet existence came to an abrupt end, however, following the announcement by the Atomic Energy Commission in November 1950 of plans for the massive Savannah River Site nuclear weapons facility in Barnwell and Aiken counties. Ellenton was the largest community uprooted by the forced relocation of some six thousand residents from the plant site. "New" Ellenton began as a two hundred acre development. Between the new town and the main entrance of the bomb plant, a large part of the plant's 38,500 workers lived in trailer parks during peak construction in 1952. The last resident left Ellenton on April 1, 1952 and New Ellenton was incorporated on April 26.

New Ellenton grew rapidly and sprouted numerous businesses that competed to serve the expanding community. However, once the initial building frenzy at the Savannah River Site was completed and routine operations began, the trailer parks and construction workers disappeared. By 1960 New Ellenton counted 2,309 residents and its population peaked at 2,628 in 1980. Between 1970 and 1990 business declined as the nearby cities of Aiken and Augusta grew and attracted much of New Ellenton's retail trade. This contributed to an eleven percent decline in the town's population between 1990 and 2000. RICHARD D. BROOKS

Browder, Tonya A., and Richard D. Brooks. *Memories of Home: Reminiscences of Ellenton.* Columbia: South Carolina Institute of Archaeology and Anthropology, 1996.

Cassels, Louise. *The Unexpected Exodus.* Aiken, S.C.: Sand Hill Press, 1971.

O'Berry, Lucius Sidney. *Ellenton, SC: My Life . . . Its Death.* Edited by Richard D. Brooks and Tonya A. Browder. Columbia: South Carolina Institute of Archaeology and Anthropology, 1999.

New Era Club. Founded in Spartanburg in 1912, the New Era Club lasted only a short time but was significant as the nucleus of South Carolina's first statewide women's suffrage organization. Earlier suffrage efforts accomplished little, and white southerners generally considered the movement to be a threat to southern culture and a challenge to idealized notions of female behavior. Many white southerners also associated women's suffrage with feminism and abolitionism, which made the movement even more of an anathema. But by the turn of the twentieth century, as prosuffrage actions increased across the country, South Carolina women rallied again, this time successfully.

White and middle-class in its makeup, the New Era Club began disguised as a study group. Thirty Spartanburg women founded the club, they said, "to stimulate interest in civic affairs and to advance the industrial, legal and educational rights of women and children." They met twice monthly to discuss education, public health, and domestic interests. But they also sponsored a section in the Spartanburg *Herald* featuring prosuffrage articles by Anna Howard Shaw, president of the National American Women Suffrage Association (NAWSA), and Hannah Hemphill Coleman, president of the South Carolina Federation of Women's Clubs. In January 1914 the New Era Club publicly declared its true purpose as a suffrage group by joining NAWSA. Soon after, Charleston and Columbia had suffrage clubs. In May 1914 all three clubs, totaling more than four hundred members, united as the South Carolina Equal Suffrage League. By 1915 there were twenty-five branches across the state. Although it failed to convince the General Assembly to ratify the Nineteenth Amendment, the league nevertheless contributed its voice to the national ratification movement that succeeded in 1920. JANE S. GABIN

Herndon, Eliza. "Woman Suffrage in South Carolina: 1872–1920." Master's thesis, University of South Carolina, 1953.

Taylor, Antoinette Elizabeth. "South Carolina and the Enfranchisement of Women: The Later Years." *South Carolina Historical Magazine* 80 (October 1979): 298–310.

"New Southern Cooking." "New Southern Cooking" is a culinary trend that developed during the final three decades of the twentieth century in the American South, and it continued to evolve in the early twenty-first century. For the first time since the South became impoverished in the aftermath of the Civil War, a new affluence provided the climate to experiment with new foods or prepare traditional fare in new ways. An example is grits, a breakfast food cooked for centuries with water, being cooked instead with liquid substitutes such as milk, cream, or broth and served as a delicious part of any meal.

When Jimmy Carter of Georgia was elected president in 1976, southern cuisine came to the forefront. Peanuts, tomatoes, pimentos, hot and sweet multicolored peppers, grits, pecans, rice, greens, corn, chicken, pork, pepper jelly, turnips, shrimp, grouper, flounder, catfish, and other standbys of rural life were combined with newly available foods such as zucchini and Cornish hens. Fresh herbs, widely used in antebellum plantation cooking, reappeared, along with other antebellum foods. There was a move away from frying to techniques considered more healthy and easier for the busy cook. The result keeps and enhances the flavors and mood of traditional southern cooking—less formal, family oriented, flavorful—and yet encompasses the new.

Southern Living Magazine, community cookbooks, and local newspaper food editors such as Lillian Marshall of the *Louisville Courier-Journal* and Anne Byrne of the *Atlanta Journal-Constitution* used recipes from locals and professionals that reflected both the changing foods available in the South and the new uses of traditional southern ingredients. The result set a direction for a broadly rich cuisine that is considered unique in America, documented in Nathalie Dupree's 1986 book *New Southern Cooking,* which coined the term. South Carolina ETV joined in airing the fifty-two-part weekly public television series of the same name, and the concept of "New Southern Cooking" became accepted and expanded by chefs and home cooks in South Carolina.

Lowcountry cuisine in the late twentieth and early twenty-first centuries has added new dimensions to southern cuisine and continues to amplify "New Southern Cooking" in an unprecedented way. R. W. Apple, Jr., writing in the *New York Times,* credited Louis Osteen as the leader of the South Carolina restaurateurs practicing "New Southern Cooking." Other creative chefs of that era included Philip Bardin in Edisto and Donald Barickman and Frank Lee, now in Charleston. Cookbooks and articles using the term have now been published. NATHALIE DUPREE

Barickman, Donald. *Magnolias Southern Cuisine.* Charleston, S.C.: Wyrick & Company, 1995.

Byrn, Anne. *Cooking in the New South: A Modern Approach to Traditional Southern Fare.* Atlanta: Peachtree Publishers, 1994.

Dupree, Nathalie. *New Southern Cooking.* New York: Knopf, 1986.

Osteen, Louis. *Louis Osteen's Carolina Cuisine.* Chapel Hill, N.C.: Algonquin, 1999.

Taylor, John. *The New Southern Cook.* New York: Bantam, 1995.

New Windsor Township. Established in the 1730s as part of Governor Robert Johnson's broader plan to settle the South Carolina interior, New Windsor Township lay along the Savannah River in what is now Aiken County. Its boundaries ran from the mouth of Town Creek to a point seven miles above Fort Moore. Savannah Town was a trading depot on the eastern side of the Savannah across from Augusta, Georgia.

In 1734 Sebastian Zouberbuhler of Appenzell, Switzerland, landed in South Carolina to find a home for Protestant immigrants. In July 1735 he contracted with the Royal Council to transport Swiss settlers for New Windsor Township. The colony promised to survey the land without fees and to provide other necessities.

In August 1736 some 192 persons representing approximately fifty families agreed to follow the Reverend Bartholomew Zouberbuhler (Sebastian's father) and Johannes Tobler (former governor of Appenzell) to Carolina. They arrived at Charleston in February 1737.

Surveyors laid out the town of New Windsor with Fort Moore as its northwestern corner. Most of the early surveys for the Swiss lay between that area and Silver Bluff, ten miles away. Good agricultural land was scarce in the township, which therefore linked the township's economic viability to the Indian trade. By 1748 two groups of Chickasaws, invited by the Royal Council as a defensive buffer, were living near New Windsor.

New Windsor was among the least populous of the 1730s townships and by 1756 had an estimated population of only three hundred. Its reputation for an unhealthy climate and poor land further slowed its development. By the start of the Revolutionary War, only a few farms and a handful of original settlers remained. Many moved across the Savannah River to settle in Augusta and other parts of Georgia. ALEXIA JONES HELSLEY

Crass, David Colin, et al. *Excavations at New Windsor Township, South Carolina.* Columbia: South Carolina Institute of Archaeology and Anthropology, University of South Carolina, 1997.

Maness, Harold S. *Forgotten Outpost: Fort Moore & Savannah Town, 1685–1765.* Pickens, S.C.: BPB Publications, 1986.

Meriwether, Robert L. *The Expansion of South Carolina, 1729–1765.* Kingsport, Tenn.: Southern Publishers, 1940.

Newberry (Newberry County; 2000 pop. 10,580). Newberry is the county seat of Newberry County. In 1785 the General Assembly created the county from the Ninety Six Judicial District. In 1789 the county accepted John Coate's donation of two acres as a courthouse site. The first brick courthouse was built between 1799 and 1801 and torn down in 1850. Jacob Graves designed a replacement courthouse that was first used in 1853. After the Civil War, Osborne Wells repaired the old courthouse and added a symbolic frieze to the entablature of the front gable. The design shows an uprooted palmetto tree (the government of the state of South Carolina) clasped in the beak of an eagle (the United States of America).

Although the most important district town, Newberry remained quite small through most of the antebellum era. In 1826 Robert Mills counted between twenty and thirty dwellings and stores that carried on "considerable business" during court sessions. By 1840 the population stood at just three hundred, and Columbia was the principal market for most district planters. The 1850s, however, marked the start of considerable growth. The influential Bank of the State of

Old Newberry County Court House (1852); the bas-relief in the pediment was added in 1879 and reflects local white sentiment about Reconstruction. Photograph by Suzanne Cameron Linder. Courtesy, Suzanne Cameron Linder

South Carolina established an agency in Newberry in 1851, and the Bank of Newberry was chartered the following year. Town merchants invested in the Greenville and Columbia Railroad, which was completed in 1853 and whose line ran through Newberry. Newberry College was chartered in 1856 and opened in 1859. Between 1850 and 1870 the population almost quadrupled, from 509 to 1,891.

Newberry's prosperity continued throughout the nineteenth century and into the twentieth. In 1873 the *Newberry Herald* claimed that the town was the second largest cotton market in South Carolina, shipping some 24,000 bales annually. That same year the General Assembly approved the incorporation of the Newberry Cotton Mill, which commenced operations in 1884. Two railroads received charters as well, the Newberry and Chester (1873) and the Newberry and Augusta (1874). An opera house opened in 1882, a symbol of the town's prosperity. In 1910 Newberry boasted, among other commercial establishments, two hotels, seven furniture stores, five hardware stores, and four banks. Two new cotton mills, the Mollohon Mill and Oakland Mill, commenced operations respectively in 1902 and 1912.

The 1920s and 1930s brought hard times to Newberry. The arrival of the boll weevil decimated area cotton farms, and town merchants suffered accordingly. Two banks failed, and a third was forced to merge. Workers in Newberry's cotton mills, protesting against the hated "stretch-out," carried out bitter strikes in 1934 and 1936 that divided residents for years.

Following World War II, there was a return to prosperity. Newberry's first radio station, WKDK, went on the air in 1946. New, locally owned businesses included orchid growers Carter and Holmes and Senn Trucking Company. The opening of Interstate 26 and new industries swelled Newberry's population by 12.7 percent between 1960 and 1970. The 1980s brought two natural disasters: a killer tornado on March 28, 1984, and a flood on August 18, 1986.

The renovation of the Newberry Opera House as a performing arts center, completed in 1999, sparked a renaissance of downtown Newberry. Newberry celebrates its past with its historic districts; its diversified economy and revived cultural base suggest a bright future. ALEXIA JONES HELSLEY

Carwile, John B. *Reminiscences of Newberry.* 1890. Reprint, Columbia, S.C.: R. L. Bryan, 1970.

O'Neall, John Belton, and John A. Chapman. *The Annals of Newberry.* 1892. Reprint, Baltimore: Genealogical Publishing, 1974.

Pope, Thomas H. *The History of Newberry County, South Carolina.* 2 vols. Columbia: University of South Carolina Press, 1973–1992.

Newberry College. One of twenty-eight liberal arts colleges of the Evangelical Lutheran Church in America (ELCA), Newberry College was chartered in December 1856 by the South Carolina Lutheran Synod. Under the leadership of the Reverend John Bachman as chairman of the board of trustees, a building was erected in the town of Newberry, a president and several faculty secured, and classes begun in 1859. Almost immediately came the devastating impact of the Civil War, which resulted in the closing of the college. Its buildings were utilized in 1865 as a Confederate hospital and then occupied by federal troops, who inflicted much damage.

The college was removed to Walhalla in 1868 but returned to Newberry in 1877, using rented quarters at first. By its fiftieth anniversary in 1906 four buildings were in use, with two more soon under construction, and enrollment stood at 211 students. The modern campus consists of sixty acres with twenty-four buildings and athletic facilities. Originally an all-male school, in 1930 Newberry merged with Summerland College, a "Lutheran Female College" near Leesville. The merger introduced women resident students to Newberry as well as several women faculty.

The college maintains close relations with the Lutheran Church, relating to four synods of the ELCA: South Carolina, Southeastern, Florida-Bahamas, and Caribbean. Its mission statement asserts, "As a Lutheran college, Newberry College recognizes the value of academic freedom, intellectual dialogue, and diversity of viewpoint. The Lutheran tradition also celebrates the concept of vocation, leading students to prepare for meaningful life experiences, occupations, and service to the world as well as to the church." Accreditation by the Southern Association of Colleges and Secondary Schools occurred in 1936. Enrollment grew to 403 students in 1941, but World War II created severe problems with a loss in enrollment and serious financial difficulties. The college gradually overcame these challenges after the war. Under President A. D. G. Wiles, the 1960s saw significant campus development and enrollment grew to more than eight hundred. Though consistent in their financial support of the college, the four supporting synods have contributed a decreasing percentage of the college's annual budget, and like other church colleges, Newberry has been compelled to depend on its own development efforts that reach well beyond its Lutheran constituency.

The college confers four degrees (bachelor of arts, bachelor of music, bachelor of music education, and bachelor of science) and offers thirty-six majors and thirty-one minors. Several programs are conducted in cooperation with Clemson University, Medical University of South Carolina, Duke University, and Palmetto Baptist Medical Center. Other academic features include independent study, an honors program, internships, and the Center for Service Learning and Community Action, which promotes the value of community service as part of a liberal education. PAUL JERSILD

Bedenbaugh, J. Benjamin. *A Centennial History of Newberry College: 1856–1956.* Newberry, S.C., 1956.

Lutheran Church in America, South Carolina Synod. *A History of the Lutheran Church in South Carolina.* Columbia, S.C.: R. L. Bryan Company, 1971.

Newberry County (631 sq. miles; 2000 pop. 36,108). Newberry County lies between the Broad and Saluda Rivers in the lower Piedmont. The origin of its name is uncertain. Some believe it was the name of an early settler, although no such name exists in surviving records. County historian Judge John Belton O'Neall suggested that the earliest settlers considered the area "as pretty as a new berry."

Nomadic Shawnee Indians lived on the Saluda River in the seventeenth century. Europeans from northern colonies arrived around 1744, with the first inhabitants settling by 1749. German and Swiss immigrants occupied the area between the Broad and Saluda Rivers, later called the Dutch Fork (*deutsch volk,* or German folk), which included the eastern portion of Newberry. By 1749 Dutch Fork had a population of 423. Abundant waterways attracted additional immigrants, and settlement expanded along the Enoree and Little Rivers. Although residents served on both sides of the Revolutionary War, Newberry's overall experience was limited compared to other regions of the state. The region was the site of several skirmishes, the most notable of which was a defeat of British major Patrick Ferguson and a Tory detachment near Whitmire.

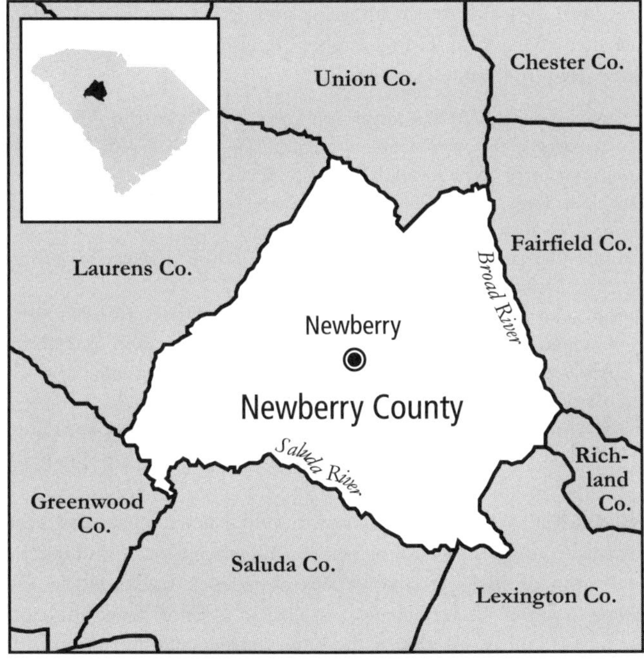

Newberry County was formed in 1785 when the General Assembly divided Ninety Six District into six counties. In 1789 John Coate gave two acres for public buildings and a plan was drawn for a county seat. A decade later, Newberry Court House was a small village with postal service, a courthouse, a jail, residences, and a few taverns and small stores. Reorganized as a district in 1800, Newberry's population stood at 12,906, including some 3,000 slaves.

Although Newberry remained overwhelmingly rural throughout the nineteenth century, several nodes of settlement evolved into villages and towns. Whitmire's first settler, John Duncan, arrived from Pennsylvania in 1752. Thomas Chappell came in 1756 and soon after established a Saluda River ferry and what became the town of Chappells. The Prosperity Meeting House gave its name to the postbellum town of Prosperity, which originated as the village of Frog Level. The town of Peak near the Broad River was named for Greenville and Columbia Railroad superintendent H. T. Peak. Pomaria, originally known as Countsville, was renamed in 1840 after the famous horticultural nursery operated by William Summer.

Like much of the state, Newberry experienced destruction during the Civil War. Homes, businesses, and a portion of the fledgling Newberry College campus were destroyed or damaged by Union troops late in the war. The county experienced economic hardship during Reconstruction, with poor whites and newly freed slaves relegated to sharecropping. Widespread tenancy and an over-reliance on cotton depressed Newberry's agricultural sector for the remainder of the century.

The Newberry Cotton Mill was the largest in the state when it began operating in 1884. Additional mills followed, including Mollohon (1902) and Oakland (1912) in Newberry, and Glen-Lowry (1902) in Whitmire. Textile manufacturing remained the county's primary industrial employer for most of the twentieth century. After World War II, pulpwood became an important factor in the county economy, as did a revitalized agricultural sector. Cotton gave way to dairy and poultry production. Textile plants continued to appear as well, including those opened by the Prosperity Manufacturing Company (1947) and Old School Manufacturing (1958) in Prosperity.

After peaking in 1930 at 34,681, Newberry County's population experienced a progressive decline that did not reverse until 1980. Part of this decline was due to the departure of African Americans, thousands of whom left South Carolina for better opportunities in the North. The Newberry County Development Board was chartered in 1957 to promote industrial development. Economic diversification efforts continued into the 1960s, spurred by the completion of Interstate 26. New manufacturers included Shakespeare Co. in 1965, Owens-Illinois, Inc. in 1966, and Louis Rich Co. in 1966. By the 1990s major products in the county's economy included fiberglass, automobile wheel covers, eggs, poultry feed, and hosiery.

Education in the county went through rapid changes in the late twentieth century. Among the last wave of counties in the state to integrate, Newberry schools achieved racial integration in 1970. Two-party competition arrived with the election of Republican Eugene C. Griffith of Newberry to the state senate in 1966. However, Democrats continued to dominate most local elections through the end of the century. In presidential elections and many statewide elections, Newberry County is a bellwether county, often voting for the winner in the now two-party competitive state. Notable Newberrians of the twentieth century included Governor and U.S. Senator Coleman Blease, state Speaker of the House Thomas H. Pope, Jr., and state Comptroller General James Lander.

Throughout the last half of the twentieth century, Newberry County achieved modest growth. Like most of the state, agriculture declined in importance, as did the increasingly volatile textile industry. By 1990 manufacturing was still the predominant employment sector despite substantial gains in the service sector. The county no longer experienced out-migration. The city of Newberry retained its rural, small town character while building an industrial park to position itself for economic development. In 1999 the town completed a multimillion-dollar renovation of the Newberry Opera House. The facility once again became a performing arts center attracting nationally renowned musicians, providing cultural and artistic offerings, and revitalizing downtown development. DAN G. RUFF

Farley, M. Foster. *Newberry County in the American Revolution.* Newberry, S.C.: Newberry County Bicentennial Commission, 1975.

Newberry County Historical Society. *Bicentennial History of Newberry County.* Dallas, Tex.: Taylor Publishing, 1989.

O'Neall, John Belton, and John A. Chapman. *The Annals of Newberry.* 1892. Reprint, Baltimore: Genealogical Publishing, 1974.

Pope, Thomas H. *The History of Newberry County, South Carolina.* 2 vols. Columbia: University of South Carolina Press, 1973–1992.

Newman, Isaiah DeQuincey (1911–1985). Clergyman, civil rights leader. Born in Darlington County on April 17, 1911, Newman was the son of the Reverend Melton C. Newman and Charlotte Elizabeth Morris. He attended Williamsburg County public schools and Claflin College and was ordained in the United Methodist Church (UMC) in 1931. Three years later he received his bachelor of arts degree from Clark College in Atlanta, then earned his divinity degree from Gammon Theological Seminary in Atlanta in 1937. While serving as a student pastor in Georgia, Newman met Anne Pauline Hinton of Covington, Georgia. They married on April 27, 1937, and later had one child, Emily Morris DeQuincey.

Throughout his varied and distinguished career, Newman thought of himself primarily as a minister, and it was in this role that he made his most significant contributions to South Carolina. For some forty years, he served UMC churches in Georgia and South Carolina and held key positions with the UMC's South Carolina Conference and its General Conference. As a member of the UMC Merger Committee in the 1970s, he played a major role in bringing an end to segregated congregations.

Early in his ministry, Newman identified the struggle for racial equality as a matter of the spirit, as well as a social and political concern, and he developed a preaching style that linked morality with practicality, especially in reference to race relations. Vernon Jordan, a protégé who later became a national civil rights leader, remarked that he always listened carefully whenever Newman prayed, because he "always felt that when I. D. Newman was praying, God was listening. He seemed to have a direct line." Newman noted that every aspect of his career was simply an "extension of ministry."

In 1943 Newman assumed a key position in the emerging civil rights movement when he helped organize the Orangeburg branch of the National Association for the Advancement of Colored People (NAACP). Thereafter he contributed to the NAACP in a variety of capacities, including service as South Carolina field director from 1960 to 1969, the most critical period in the civil rights struggle. Newman was a gentle, self-effacing man, patient and slow to anger, who preferred diplomacy over confrontation. A tenacious advocate for simple justice in race relations, he also believed in nonviolent protest as the most effective means for achieving the goal. His quiet dignity and appeals to reason won him the confidence, and ultimately the support, of key white political and economic leaders. In effect Newman served both as chief strategist for the protest movement and as chief negotiator at the conference table, becoming the "unofficial liaison" between African Americans and the white power structure. Alone among the Deep South states, South Carolina dismantled its structure of legalized segregation with a minimum of violence, in large measure because of his leadership and dedication to peaceful change.

Inevitably Newman became an important player in the state's changing political fortunes. In the 1940s he participated peripherally in founding the Progressive Democratic Party, an effort to change the racial policies of the regular Democratic Party. Although Newman had long been a staunch Republican, by 1958 he concluded that the state Republican Party no longer had a place for him and other African Americans, and he switched his allegiance to the Democrats. Moving quickly into his new party's inner circles, he became a trusted confidant of such state leaders as U.S. Senator Ernest Hollings and Governors Robert McNair and John West, as well as a delegate to several Democratic national conventions.

Extending his personal ministry into the lives of ordinary people, Newman worked to improve the condition of blacks and whites in rural South Carolina. Housing, medical care, the environment, aging, vocational education, and social services in general were among the concerns for which both state and private agencies sought his counsel. In recognition of his contributions, the National Institute on Social Work in Rural Areas in 1982 named him "Rural Citizen of the Year." Honorary degrees from state colleges and universities further acknowledged his achievements, and the University of South Carolina established an endowed professorship in social work in his honor.

On October 25, 1983, Newman became the first African American since 1887 to serve in the state senate. His election and the cordial reception he received from his fellow senators, all of them white, testified symbolically to the extraordinary influence he exerted on South Carolina's social and political development in the twentieth century. Newman served with distinction on several senate committees until ill health forced him to resign his seat on July 31, 1985. He died in Columbia on October 21, 1985, and was buried in Greenlawn Memorial Gardens. JOHN G. SPROAT

Bailey, N. Louise, Mary L. Morgan, and Carolyn R. Taylor, eds. *Biographical Directory of the South Carolina Senate, 1776–1985.* 3 vols. Columbia: University of South Carolina Press, 1986.

Bass, Jack. *Porgy Comes Home: South Carolina . . . After 300 Years.* Columbia, S.C.: R. L. Bryan, 1972.

Grose, Philip G., Jr. "Activist Spirit Still Burns in Rev. Newman." *Columbia State,* October 4, 1981, pp. B1, B13.

Sproat, John G. "'Firm Flexibility': Perspectives on Desegregation in South Carolina." In *New Perspectives on Race and Slavery in America: Essays in Honor of Kenneth M. Stampp,* edited by Robert H. Abzug and Stephen E. Maizlish. Lexington: University Press of Kentucky, 1986.

Stucker, Jan Collins. "Did You Know I. D. Newman Kept You Safe during Desegregation?" *Columbia State Magazine,* March 25, 1984, pp. 8–11.

Newspapers. More than sixteen hundred newspapers have been established in South Carolina since 1732, when Eleazer Phillips, Jr., of Boston printed the colony's first newspaper in Charleston, the *South-Carolina Weekly Journal.* He died in a yellow fever epidemic on July 10, 1732. At almost the same time that Phillips began the *Journal,* Benjamin Franklin's first South Carolina partner, Thomas Whitmarsh, printed the first issue of the *South-Carolina Gazette* on January 8, 1732. Although Whitmarsh died of yellow fever the following year, his newspaper survived to become South Carolina's best-known and most enduring eighteenth-century newspaper. It was restarted February 2, 1734, by Franklin's second partner, Lewis Timothy. The son of a French Protestant refugee, Timothy worked for Franklin in Philadelphia as the first professional librarian in the colonies before moving to South Carolina.

Timothy and his wife, Elizabeth, published the *South-Carolina Gazette* for four years before he died in December 1738. His widow took over the newspaper and became the first female publisher in America. Their son, Peter Timothy, was perhaps the most widely known southern journalist of the eighteenth century, but he printed his last edition of the *Gazette* on July 9, 1780. Shortly thereafter, the British arrested Timothy and several other leading Charlestonians and shipped them to St. Augustine, Florida. Two Loyalist newspapers were published in Charleston during the British occupation, the *Royal South-Carolina Gazette* and the *Royal Gazette.* Both ceased publication by the time the British departed in late 1782.

Under the direction of John Miller of London, the *South Carolina State Gazette and Daily Advertiser* became the first daily newspaper in the state and the third daily in the country in 1784. The state's oldest daily newspaper, the Charleston *Post and Courier,* traces its origins to the establishment of the *Charleston Courier* in 1803. In the period leading up to the Civil War, editors argued openly and sometimes violently about states' rights and preserving the Union, with the *Charleston Mercury* serving as the most influential states' rights organ in the state as well as the South. Nullificationist Turner Bynum, editor of the *Southern Sentinel* in Greenville, was killed in a duel in 1832 by the Unionist editor of the *Greenville Mountaineer,* Benjamin F. Perry. Perry went on to become provisional governor in 1865. Besides Perry, ten other editors or publishers have served as governor of South Carolina.

Publishing a newspaper in South Carolina has often been dangerous. While serving as editor of the *Southern Times* in 1830, a young James Henry Hammond narrowly avoided a duel after his scathing editorials raised the ire of upcountry congressman James Blair. Francis Warrington Dawson, editor of the Charleston *News and Courier,* wrote dozens of editorials denouncing dueling and violence and was challenged to hundreds of duels before being killed in his neighbor's house in 1889 defending the honor of his Swiss governess. A political campaign waged by Narciso G. Gonzales, who founded the *State* in Columbia on February 18, 1891, ended tragically in 1903 when James H. Tillman assassinated the unarmed editor in front of the State House. Defendants in both cases were acquitted of murder, and a juror in the Tillman trial remarked, "Who ever heard of a jury anywhere convicting anyone of killing a newspaper man?"

In 1893 the *State* became the first newspaper in the Carolinas to install Linotype machines, which replaced handset type. By the early 1970s photocomposition and computers made the one-ton machines obsolete, although Carl Kilgus of the *Bamberg Advertizer-Herald* operated a Linotype until 1998. Newspapers entered the Internet age in 1995 when the *Anderson Independent-Mail* launched the first Internet newspaper in South Carolina. Within five years all seventeen daily newspapers and twenty-one of the state's seventy nondaily newspapers were publishing web editions. Only two, the *Aiken Standard* and the *Union Daily Times,* were still afternoon newspapers.

Newspapers once owned by old South Carolina families, such as the Peaces of Greenville, the Gonzales-Hamptons of Columbia, the Simmses of Orangeburg, the Halls of Anderson, and the Patricks of Rock Hill, were sold during the twentieth century to newspaper groups such as Knight-Ridder, The New York Times, Gannett, Media General, Howard, Scripps Howard, and McClatchy. Some are still owned by third- and fourth-generation families, such as the Osteens of Sumter, the Mundys of Greenwood, the Manigaults of Charleston, the Burches of Greer, the Kenneys of Bennettsville, the Wests of Abbeville, and the DeCamp-Sossamons of Gaffney. The combined circulation of South Carolina's newspapers at the beginning of the twenty-first century was 990,740, with a readership of approximately 2.4 million. PATRICIA G. MCNEELY

Cohen, Hennig. *The South Carolina Gazette, 1732–1775.* Columbia: University of South Carolina Press, 1953.

McNeely, Patricia G. *The Palmetto Press: The History of South Carolina's Newspapers and the Press Association.* Columbia: South Carolina Press Association, 1998.

Moore, John Hammond, comp. and ed. *South Carolina Newspapers.* Columbia: University of South Carolina Press, 1988.

Pierce, Robert A. *Palmettos and Oaks: A Centennial History of The State, 1891–1991.* Columbia: State-Record Company, 1991.

Sass, Herbert Ravenel. *Outspoken: 150 Years of the News and Courier.* Columbia: University of South Carolina Press, 1953.

Nicholson, Francis (1655–1728). Governor. Nicholson was born on November 12, 1655, near Richmond, Yorkshire, England. His parentage is uncertain. His mother's identity is unknown, but many believed that he was the illegitimate son of Charles Paulet, Duke of Bolton. Paulet never acknowledged his paternity but assisted young Nicholson through his influence and patronage. Before he made his career as a colonial administrator, Nicholson was a soldier, serving at Tangiers, where he was aide-de-camp to the deputy governor of the short-lived British colony there. In 1686 Nicholson was in Massachusetts with Governor Edmund Andros, where he and Andros tried to organize the Dominion of New England, in the face of colonial opposition. Nicholson was named lieutenant governor of New York in 1688 and became lieutenant governor of Virginia a year later. Unsuccessful in securing the governorship of Virginia, he then took the post as lieutenant governor of Maryland in 1692, serving until 1698. In that year Nicholson was named governor and captain general of Virginia, a post he held for seven years. Nicholson lost his post in 1705 and returned to England. There he worked with the Board of Trade on economic and defense issues, and in 1709, during Queen Anne's War, he commanded colonial troops in an invasion of Canada. The expedition failed, but in 1710 he led an expedition that recaptured Nova Scotia from the French. Two years later Nicholson returned to colonial government when he was named governor of Nova Scotia. He held that post from 1712 to 1714.

In 1720 Nicholson became the first royally appointed governor of South Carolina. In December 1719 the new royal colony had overthrown the government of the Lords Proprietors and petitioned to be brought under the umbrella of royal administration. Arriving at Charleston in May 1721, Nicholson found that the revolutionaries had created a hybrid government, mostly established on traditional British imperial policies but occasionally laced with proprietary-era practices. One of his tasks, as he saw it, was to bring the new royal colony into conformity with imperial policies. He naturally clashed with colonial leaders who had accomplished the revolution. His strong support for the established Church of England alienated colonial Dissenters, and he championed local landowners in their conflict with Charleston merchants over issues such as paper currency, debt relief, and imperial defense. As was the case with his previous colonial appointments, Nicholson's tenure in South Carolina was contentious, but he was successful in preserving the viability of the colony.

The Lords Proprietors retained their charter to the lands of Carolina and tried many expedients to recover political control of their revolted colony. They attacked Nicholson's administration, asserting that the governor was a customs racketeer and active in illegal trade with Spanish Florida. Nicholson left Charleston in May 1725 to confront his accusers in London. In addition to defending his actions in person, Nicholson published *A Vindication of Francis Nicholson* (1724) to answer the charges against him. Despite his intention to return to South Carolina, Nicholson never reclaimed his post. He died in London on March 5, 1728, and was buried in the churchyard of St. George Parish, Hanover Square. ALEXANDER MOORE

McCully, Bruce T. "From the North Riding to Morocco: The Early Years of Governor Francis Nicholson, 1655–1686." *William and Mary Quarterly*, 3d ser., 19 (October 1962): 534–56.

———. "Governor Francis Nicholson, Patron *Par Excellence* of Religion and Learning in Colonial America." *William and Mary Quarterly*, 3d ser., 39 (April 1982): 310–33.

Moore, John Alexander. "Royalizing Carolina: The Revolution of 1719 and the Evolution of Early South Carolina Government." Ph.D. diss., University of South Carolina, 1991.

Nicholson, Francis. Papers. Colonial Williamsburg Foundation, Williamsburg, Virginia.

Webb, Stephen S. "The Strange Career of Francis Nicholson." *William and Mary Quarterly*, 3d ser., 23 (October 1966): 513–48.

Nielsen, Barbara Stock (b. 1942). State superintendent of education. Nielsen was born in Cincinnati, Ohio, on December 2, 1942, the daughter of Marvin and Adele Stock. She married Dr. Dennis J. Nielsen and had two daughters. She earned an Ed.D. from the University of Louisville in 1983 and served as a teacher, curriculum specialist, and administrator in the Jefferson County / Louisville City Public Schools from 1964 to 1980. From 1984 to 1989 she was a curriculum specialist and director of business-community partnerships in the Beaufort County Schools.

In 1990 Nielsen was elected the South Carolina superintendent of education on the Republican ticket, the first woman to hold that position and the second woman in the state to be elected as a constitutional officer. She was reelected by a wide margin in 1994 but chose not to run for a third term in 1998. She was appointed a Senior Fellow at the Clemson University Strom Thurmond Institute in 1999 and made her home in Hilton Head. During her years as superintendent, she was the chief executive officer for the State Department of Education with more than seven hundred employees and a budget of more than $2 billion serving more than twelve hundred schools in the state. Her goals were to make South Carolina a leader in educational reform and to encourage excellence for all students.

Nielsen's accomplishments included the development of curriculum frameworks for all subjects and grades and new performance-based assessments for statewide tests. She oversaw the introduction of computer technology and access to the Internet in all schools, the implementation of full-day kindergarten for all children, the introduction of prekindergarten for at-risk three- and four-year-old children, and the targeting of additional financial and professional assistance to low-performing school districts. In administrative areas, Nielsen reorganized the Department of Education to reduce the levels of management. Other contributions were in the fields of community outreach, improving teachers' professional skills, establishing tax-supported charter schools, improving math and science skills, and developing a model National School to Work program.

Nielsen tried to give more authority to local schools by reducing state regulations and paperwork. She frequently pointed to progress and achievements in the schools while recognizing that the state faced serious educational challenges. During her eight years as superintendent, South Carolina received several national honors for rate of improvement in such areas as technology, arts education, the eight National Education Goals, teacher quality, and financial accountability for school expenditures. In announcing her decision not to run for reelection in 1998, she stated, "We have fundamentally overhauled the system at the state level, and the pieces are now in place. The next frontier is at the local level, and I can help more by working from outside the system rather than inside." Nielsen considered herself an agent of change. Supporters and critics agreed that she worked vigorously to accomplish her goals, some of which remained controversial throughout her terms of office, and that she helped bring national recognition to the state for playing a leadership role in several areas of educational reform. ALICE H. HENDERSON

Niernsee, John Rudolph (1823–1885) and Francis McHenry Niernsee (1849–1899). Architects. John Niernsee was the principal architect responsible for the design and construction of the South Carolina State House and had a significant influence on architectural practice in the state during the second half of the nineteenth century. His son Frank followed in his father's footsteps by finishing the interior of the State House and operating a successful architectural practice in Columbia during the 1880s and 1890s.

John Niernsee was born in Vienna, Austria, in 1823 and immigrated to the United States in 1838. The following year he was hired by Benjamin H. Latrobe, Jr., as a draftsman and engineer with the Baltimore and Ohio Railroad. In 1848 he established a partnership with James Crawford Neilson, another B&O engineer, and in the following decade the architectural firm of Niernsee and Neilson became the largest and most successful in Baltimore. During the same era, Niernsee developed a reputation for serving as a consultant to troubled building projects. After portions of the interior of James Renwick's Smithsonian Castle collapsed in February 1850, Niernsee was one of three architects called in to inspect the damage and recommend repairs.

Niernsee became architect of the new state capitol in Columbia in April 1855. He had initially been summoned to Columbia during the summer of 1854 to inspect the failed foundations built under the direction of Peter H. Hammarskold, and he had served as a consulting architect during George E. Walker's short-lived supervision of the project. Once Niernsee took charge, construction proceeded swiftly. He was far more capable than either of his predecessors and demonstrated considerable skill in administering contracts, overseeing the quarrying of stone from sites along the Congaree River, and managing a labor force that numbered close to five hundred men at its peak in 1860. The arrival of the Civil War halted work on the State House, and Niernsee became engaged in the war effort by serving as a military engineer. After the war he returned to Baltimore and resumed private practice. When the legislature refocused its attention on completing the State House in the early 1880s, Niernsee headed to South Carolina once again and was reappointed architect on January 2, 1885. By then his health was failing, and he had barely finished preparing plans for the project when he died on June 7, 1885. He was buried in St. Peter's churchyard in Columbia.

Frank Niernsee was born in Baltimore in 1849 and spent much of his childhood in antebellum Columbia, where he watched his father supervise the construction of the State House. He studied engineering at the University of Virginia and began practicing architecture with his father in 1878. The first major commission handled by Niernsee & Son was an opera house in Lynchburg, Virginia, from 1878 to 1879. Frank Niernsee moved to Columbia in 1882 and worked in partnership with the engineer Ashbury Gamewell LaMotte from 1893 to 1896. Completing the interior of the State House was his most important achievement. After John Niernsee's death in 1885, state authorities hired his former partner, J. Crawford Neilson, to finish the building, but under his supervision the project was plagued by a litany of small problems. Neilson managed to finish the legislative halls before he was replaced by Frank Niernsee in 1888. Niernsee installed fireproof floors throughout the building and completed the lobby, legislative library, committee rooms, and offices. By 1890 the interior was finished, although it would be another decade before the legislature decided to add porticos and a dome to the exterior.

In addition to his work at the State House, Frank Niernsee had an active practice in Columbia. His designs in the city included St. Paul's Lutheran Church and Ladson Presbyterian Church, and he also supervised the construction of a new municipal waterworks plant in the early 1890s. Niernsee's work elsewhere in South Carolina included a jail and sheriff's residence in Sumter (1892), Maxwell Asylum in Greenwood (1894), school buildings in Sumter (1891) and Camden (1893), and Oakhurst, a stylish residence in Newberry built for Bud Cate Matthews (1894). Niernsee died in Columbia on May 28, 1899, and was buried in Trinity Episcopal Churchyard. DANIEL J. VIVIAN

Bryan, John M. *Creating the South Carolina State House.* Columbia: University of South Carolina Press, 1999.

Wells, John E., and Robert E. Dalton. *The South Carolina Architects, 1885–1935: A Biographical Directory.* Richmond, Va.: New South Architectural Press, 1992.

Ninety Six, Battles of (1775, 1781). Situated in the South Carolina backcountry at the crossroads of important trade routes, Ninety Six was a newly established courthouse town on the eve of the Revolutionary War. The question of independence deeply divided the inhabitants of the district. For many colonists, land grants and protection from Indian incursions created strong devotion toward Great Britain. Others thought that the crown had shirked promises of better government to backcountry settlers and favored independence. With mounting tensions and the absence of British authority, conflict began in the South Carolina backcountry as a civil war.

On July 12, 1775, patriot forces seized nearby Fort Charlotte on the Savannah River. Returning to Ninety Six with captured ammunition, the triumphant party was met by a group of Loyalists who had been informed by a defector from the patriot ranks. The affair ended without bloodshed, and the gunpowder was returned to the fort. Fighting was narrowly averted again a few weeks later when Tory forces gathered and threatened. Whig political leader William Henry Drayton and Major Andrew Williamson countered with a show of force, and the standoff ended with both sides agreeing to a truce on September 16. Weeks later a force of eighteen hundred Loyalists attacked one-third that number of patriots under Williamson, who gathered Whig forces in a hastily erected stockade near Ninety Six on November 18, 1775. The two groups had been jockeying for control of a supply of gunpowder and lead sent to the Cherokees by the colonial government. After three days of fighting with few casualties, the two sides agreed to a brief truce. Although neither side admitted defeat, Loyalist forces failed to recover the ammunition and withdrew. A month later, a substantial patriot force mounted an expedition, the so-called "Snow Campaign," to crush organized Loyalist opposition.

The following year saw an increase in attacks on settlements in Ninety Six District by hostile Cherokees. In late July 1776 Williamson, now a brigadier general, mounted a punitive expedition into the Cherokee Nation, which ended in October. The village of Ninety Six experienced a period of relative peace for the next few years. Although Loyalists remained in the region, the courthouse village retained Whig rule. Crown forces, however, shifted their strategic focus from the northern to the southern colonies with the capture of Savannah in December 1778. Charleston fell in May 1780. Lieutenant Colonel Nisbet Balfour was quickly dispatched up the Cherokee Path to deal with any patriot militia still under arms in the upcountry. Arriving at Ninety Six in late June, he found that rebel leaders had surrendered the fort and munitions to royal authority a few days earlier. By the end of the year, the British had strengthened the old fort's defenses and established Ninety Six as a depot and meeting ground for Tories.

Losses at King's Mountain, Cowpens, and other engagements set the British on less than sure footing in South Carolina by February 1781. After the Battle of Guilford Court House in North Carolina in mid-March, the British commander in the South, Lord Cornwallis, retired to the North Carolina coast with his battered army. Instead of pursuing, the American commander, Major General Nathanael Greene, set out to reduce the chain of posts in occupied South Carolina. Royal forces soon surrendered or abandoned many positions in the northern and central parts of the state, and Greene turned his attention to the western garrison at Ninety Six. American forces arrived in late May. With his chief engineer, Colonel Thaddeus Kosciuszko, Greene surveyed the fortifications and decided to lay siege to the Star Fort, then under the command of New York Loyalist Colonel John Harris Cruger.

For twenty-eight days the small American army steadily dug siege lines and defended them against frequent sallies by the fort's defenders. Other means were tried as well. But on June 17 word of a British relief column reached the besieged village. Greene reluctantly ordered an assault the next day, and for nearly an hour his soldiers bravely tried to breach the fort's defenses without success. When Cruger's men counterattacked successfully, the American commander ordered a retreat. The American army withdrew from Ninety Six two days before British reinforcements arrived. Afterward British commanders deemed the post untenable and abandoned their position within the week. The departing British Army demolished the fortifications and set fire to the few buildings still standing. The civil war would linger in the region for many months, but the withdrawal marked the end of a British presence at Ninety Six. SAMUEL K. FORE

Bass, Robert D. *Ninety Six: The Struggle for the South Carolina Back Country.* Lexington, S.C.: Sandlapper Store, 1978.

Cann, Marvin L. "Prelude to War: The First Battle of Ninety-Six, November 19–21, 1775." *South Carolina Historical Magazine* 76 (October 1975): 197–214.

———. "War in the Backcountry: The Siege of Ninety Six, May 22–June 19, 1781." *South Carolina Historical Magazine* 72 (January 1971): 1–14.

Greene, Jerome A. *Ninety Six: A Historical Narrative.* Denver, Colo.: U.S. Department of the Interior, 1978.

Noble, Patrick (ca. 1787–1840). Governor. A native of Abbeville District, Noble was the son of Alexander Noble and Catherine Calhoun. Throughout his formative years, Noble enjoyed an enviable education, first studying under the tutelage of Dr. Moses Waddel and later graduating from the College of New Jersey (Princeton) in 1806. Returning to South Carolina, Noble studied law in Charleston under the supervision of Langdon Cheves and later in the office of John C. Calhoun at Abbeville Court House. Admitted to the bar in 1809, he briefly practiced in partnership with Calhoun before establishing his own lucrative law office in Abbeville District. On September 5, 1816, Noble married Elizabeth Bonneau Pickens, a union that produced seven children.

In 1814 Abbeville District elected Noble to the S.C. House of Representatives. Reelected to the next four sessions, Noble also served as Speaker of the House from 1818 to 1823. In 1824 Noble declined another term and made an unsuccessful bid for the U.S. Senate. Returning to his law practice, Noble took a hiatus from public life until 1830, when he was chosen lieutenant governor. Abbeville returned Noble to the House in 1832, where he again occupied the Speaker's chair from 1833 to 1835. In 1836 Noble was elected to the S.C. Senate, where his parliamentary experience led to his immediate selection as president of the senate. Reelected two years later, Noble resigned his seat upon his election as governor of South Carolina on December 8, 1838.

An ardent proponent of states' rights, Noble advocated public resistance to the expansion of federal power, which he deemed "highly dangerous, and subversive of our excellent frame of Government." In particular, Noble opposed the national tariff and called on southerners to insist that duties be laid for revenue, not for the protection of northern industry, and only for an amount required by "the economical wants of the Government." He further warned of the growing abolitionist movement in the northern states and urged the legislature to "invigorate" the state militia and prepare South Carolinians "to defend their firesides . . . against the unholy machinations of those who would drench our fields in blood, and sweep our land with the besom of destruction."

Noble had the misfortune of occupying the office of governor in the aftermath of the Panic of 1837, which ruined countless cotton planters and left the South Carolina economy in shambles. Like many Carolinians, Noble placed the burden of blame on state banks, all of which suspended specie payment during the crisis. Noble took the suspensions as a sign that "adherent vices" existed in the banking system and he called on legislators to "probe the evil to the bottom" and thereby "bring back these moneyed corporations, to a healthy performance of their functions." But Noble would not live to complete his term. After a brief illness, he died on April 7, 1840, and was succeeded by Lieutenant Governor Barnabas K. Henagan. Noble was buried in his family cemetery at Oak Hill Plantation, Abbeville District. TOM DOWNEY

Bailey, N. Louise, Mary L. Morgan, and Carolyn R. Taylor, eds. *Biographical Directory of the South Carolina Senate, 1776–1985.* 3 vols. Columbia: University of South Carolina Press, 1986.

North Augusta (Aiken County; 2000 pop. 17,574). North Augusta lies on the Savannah River opposite Augusta, Georgia. Incorporated on April 11, 1906, the city grew on the site of the antebellum town of Hamburg. Following that town's demise after the Civil War, new families settled in the area, including the Butlers, Hahns, and Mealings. By 1880 they had formed the North Augusta Land Company and constructed a new bridge across the Savannah River. James U. Jackson and the North Augusta Land Company built the Thirteenth Street Bridge in 1891. The company donated land for the first school in 1898. By 1903 residents were seeking to incorporate the town.

In the late nineteenth and early twentieth centuries, North Augusta was a popular winter retreat for well-to-do northerners. Excellent rail connections, a mild climate, and its proximity to the large winter colony at Aiken combined to make the town a well-patronized winter destination for tourists from Boston, New York, Philadelphia, and Chicago. Between 1903 and 1916 the famous Hampton Terrace Hotel greeted many notable guests including John D. Rockefeller and president-elect William Howard Taft. Fire destroyed the hotel on December 31, 1916.

Recent archaeology has shed light on North Augusta's historic pottery industry. In the 1990s surveys of the riverbank near the site of Hamburg revealed stoneware shards, traces of kilns, a clay mill, and other evidence of several active potteries. Potters and kaolin exporters came to the North Augusta area as early as 1735. By 1899 at least three potteries operated in Schultz Township (North Augusta). The Edgefield tradition of alkaline glazed pottery persisted in the North Augusta area until 1908. In 1929 a severe flood damaged the works of the potter Mark Baynham, who sued the state, alleging that the construction of highways in the Hamburg–North Augusta area contributed to the destruction of his pottery.

The cold war and the atomic bomb transformed North Augusta in the 1950s. On November 28, 1950, the Atomic Energy Commission announced the construction of the Savannah River Plant, to be located just south of the town. The plant produced rapid growth and development in North Augusta. Population more than tripled, from 3,659 in 1950 to more than 14,000 by 1956. In 1951 the area of North Augusta increased from 722 acres to 5,139 acres. By 2000 an additional 11,500 acres had been annexed, bringing the city's total land area to almost eighteen square miles.

North Augusta celebrated its fiftieth anniversary in 1956. In 1969 North Augusta boasted a median family income seventy-one percent higher than the state as a whole. In 1994 the Savannah River Site and the Graniteville Company were North Augusta's top employers. Environmental concerns, the end of the cold war, and an aging facility led to production cutbacks and employee layoffs at the Savannah River Site in the 1990s. The city has a council form of government and annually hosts cultural events at Creighton Living History and Riverview Parks. ALEXIA JONES HELSLEY

"Golden Memories Panorama": A Historical Spectacle Commemorating the 50th Anniversary of the Founding of North Augusta. North Augusta, S.C., 1956.

Newell, Mark M., and Nick Nichols. *The River Front Potters of North Augusta: Preliminary Report.* Augusta: Georgia Archaeological Institute, 1998.

Vandervelde, Isabel. *Aiken County: The Only South Carolina County Founded during Reconstruction.* Spartanburg, S.C.: Reprint Company, 1999.

North Charleston (Charleston County; 2000 pop. 79,641). A 1997 information guide called North Charleston the "Hub of the Lowcountry." The claim is both apt and ironic. The city once called the "North Area" by residents of Charleston has been much affected by its proximity to the more mature "city by the sea." The irony is that the former service area and suburb, incorporated as recently as 1972 with even its name subordinated to Charleston, was the third largest city in South Carolina in 2000 and the economic and geographic center of the state's largest metropolitan area.

Early settlements of Europeans and Africans in the area that became North Charleston grew rice and indigo for export. However, the shift to tidal rice planting and the loss of the English market for indigo effectively ended production of these staples in the area by 1800. In the first half of the nineteenth century, the vicinity was Charleston's unincorporated economic appendage, through which ran the State Road and, after 1830, the South Carolina Railroad. The corridor was home to a variety of industrial works and a small resident population of native whites, immigrants, and free blacks who worked in them. Later in the century, the area developed fertilizer mines and processing plants that lined the waterfronts of the Ashley and Cooper Rivers.

Little changed until well into the twentieth century. A United States naval base and shipyard relocated to the north area of Charleston from Beaufort in 1901. After three decades of slow growth, the base mushroomed into a giant facility during World War II. From 1938 to 1943 the civilian workforce ballooned from 1,632 to 26,500 people. North Charleston grew with the navy yard. Land was drained and cleared for new residential subdivisions. When Macalloy Steel and other military-based manufacturers moved in as well, the sky glowed from industrial furnaces.

The naval base and Macalloy closed in the post-cold-war 1990s. But North Charleston was saved from obsolescence by the same force that influenced its earlier history: convenient access to Charleston. North Charleston also experienced its own maturation as a community, particularly through the political consolidation that accompanied its incorporation in 1972 under the leadership of its first mayor, John Bourne, and the steady growth of a broad-based industrial and service economy. Charleston International Airport was built in 1931 in what is now the city limits of North Charleston. The continued existence of Charleston Air Force Base, established in the 1940s, has kept the military presence alive in North Charleston. The state's largest retail shopping district developed serendipitously along its Rivers Avenue, the old State Road. At the millennium, North Charleston boasted two colleges, a regional hospital, and the primary regional coliseum and convention center. At the same time, the city began to temper its growth-oriented boosterism with efforts to create a more healthful and attractive environment. LAYLON WAYNE JORDAN

Fick, Sarah. *City of North Charleston: Historical and Architectural Survey.* Charleston, S.C.: Preservation Consultants, 1995.

Fraser, Walter J. *Charleston! Charleston! The History of a Southern City.* Columbia: University of South Carolina Press, 1989.

North Greenville College. North Greenville College traces its roots to the founding of North Greenville High School in 1892. A committee appointed by the North Greenville Baptist Association met that year and settled on a location in Tigerville, began building, and chose a principal. The initial assets were ten acres of land and $2,500. Classes began on January 16, 1893. In 1904 it was chartered as a state high school. It became a part of a system of Mountain Mission Schools supported by the Home Mission Board of the Southern Baptist Convention in 1905 and remained in that relationship until 1929. In 1915 it was renamed North Greenville Baptist Academy.

College-level work was first offered at North Greenville Junior College in 1934. The first junior college degrees were awarded in spring 1936. As resources were shifted to the college, the work of the academy (high school) diminished. The last year in which work in all four levels of the academy was offered was 1940.

The college continued as an institution supported by the North Greenville Baptist Association until 1949, when control was transferred to the General Board of the South Carolina Baptist Convention. In the years following, enrollment increased and facilities expanded, leading to full accreditation in 1958.

In 1992 North Greenville College added bachelor's programs, and the first bachelor's degree was awarded in 1993. With a 2001 enrollment of approximately twelve hundred students, the college continues to award bachelor's degrees in a variety of fields and participates in intercollegiate athletics as a part of the National Collegiate Athletic Association. Its mission has consistently been "to provide a quality educational experience in the context of a genuine Christian commitment." STUART R. SPRAGUE

Flynn, Jean Martin. *A History of North Greenville Junior College.* Tigerville, S.C.: North Greenville Junior College, 1953.

Howard, Henry Jacob. *From These Roots: The Story of North Greenville Junior College 1892–1967.* Tigerville, S.C.: North Greenville Junior College, 1967.

Johnson, Charles D. *Higher Education of Southern Baptists: An Institutional History 1826–1954.* Waco, Tex.: Baylor University Press, 1955.

King, Joe M. *A History of South Carolina Baptists.* Columbia: General Board of the South Carolina Baptist Convention, 1964.

North Myrtle Beach (Horry County; 2000 pop. 10,974). North Myrtle Beach anchors the northern end of South Carolina's Grand Strand. Native Americans sojourned here, and prehistoric shell deposits attest to the area's long-standing popularity as a seasonal resort. Europeans and Africans began settling the region as early as the 1740s. A few families (notably Bellamys, Bessants, Nixons, and Vereens) acquired tracts encompassing much of the area. In time, large holdings were subdivided by sale and inheritance. The plantation culture common farther down the coast never developed here, but the region's dense, old growth forests provided abundant timber and naval stores. Thus, subsistence farming supplemented by fishing and logging became a way of life for generations.

Roberts Pavilion at Ocean Drive (now a part of North Myrtle Beach) was typical of similar structures all along the coast before the tourism boom of the 1960s. Courtesy, South Caroliniana Library

Throughout the nineteenth and early twentieth centuries, farmers from western Horry County came by covered wagon to fish and enjoy the beach. They camped behind the dunes, cooked their catch over open fires, and salted barrels of spots and mullets to take home. It was at once work and recreation for these hearty folk.

With the automobile came paved roads and bridges that linked Horry County to the rest of South Carolina. Locals quickly adapted accommodations to the increasing numbers of tourists. By the 1940s communities were evolving along the north strand. Simple frame houses, some built on stilts, rose along the oceanfront. In 1950 Futch Beach was joined to the Nixon family's Cherry Grove property by filling an inlet that separated them. The new entity was renamed Cherry Grove Beach.

A large tract to the south was developed in 1948 by Charles T. Tilghman, Jr., of Marion County. Tilghman Beach benefited from restrictive covenants and sound planning, becoming an upscale residential enclave. Farther south, Ocean Drive Beach and Crescent Beach were developed by investors from Florence. A pavilion and amusement park drew crowds to play and dance the shag. Windy Hill Beach was developed by Conway investors after World War II. Because Jim Crow laws denied accommodations to blacks and deed restrictions prohibited land sales to "persons of African descent," an all-black resort, Atlantic Beach, was developed by black entrepreneurs.

On October 15, 1954, Hurricane Hazel struck. Many homes and businesses vanished, and others were made uninhabitable. Beach communities were paralyzed by the destruction. Daunted by the prospect of rebuilding, many elected to sell their property at bargain prices. Thus, larger parcels became available for hotel sites and other commercial enterprises. By removing older dwellings and expediting land consolidation, Hurricane Hazel actually accelerated development.

The beach boomed in the 1960s. Summer tourism increased, and new golf courses expanded "beach season" into spring and fall. In 1968 Cherry Grove, Ocean Drive Beach, Crescent Beach, and Windy Hill consolidated into North Myrtle Beach. Atlantic Beach declined the invitation to join. In the 1970s multistory condominiums and hotels began replacing single-family housing on the oceanfront. On the marsh at Cherry Grove, numerous "channels" were dug, draining and filling wetlands for more development. By the early twenty-first century the rapid increase in housing units had strained local resources and infrastructure to the limit. ELDRED E. PRINCE, JR.

Lewis, Catherine H. *Horry County, South Carolina, 1730–1993.* Columbia: University of South Carolina Press, 1998.

Nuclear power. Nuclear power was first used to generate electricity in South Carolina at a small, 17 megawatt (MW = 1,000,000 watts) experimental prototype by South Carolina Electric and Gas (SCE&G) and partners at Parr from 1963 to 1967. Inspired by this and by the Atoms for Peace program of the federal government, in 1967 the General Assembly passed the Atomic Energy and Radiation Control Act (Act No. 223). A primary goal of the act was to attract new, high technology industry (nuclear and otherwise), with the legislation designating responsibility for promoting and developing "atomic energy resources" in South Carolina to the State Development Board. This led to the creation of nuclear-powered electrical generation plants and the creation of the Barnwell Low Level Radioactive Disposal site. The state had earlier experienced the benefits of a similar effort in the early 1950s with the creation of the Savannah River Site (SRS), which produced tritium and plutonium for nuclear weapons and also provided a repository for high-level radioactive waste.

Seven nuclear reactors, with a combined capacity of 6,525 MW, were in operation in South Carolina by 1986; the first one was generating electricity in 1970. By the start of the twenty-first century, more than half (52.2 percent) of the electricity generated in the state was created by nuclear fission, as compared to about 20 percent for the United States as a whole. Few other states can claim such a strong nuclear profile. In terms of the percentage of electricity needs generated with nuclear power, South Carolina is second only to Vermont. In terms of overall nuclear capacity, South Carolina trails only Pennsylvania and Illinois.

Replacing this nuclear production of electricity with coal-fired production would have required more than 22 million metric tons of coal. One gram of plutonium or uranium contains the energy of two tons of coal or one ton of oil. If uranium were replaced with coal, 277,000 tons of sulfur dioxide, 139,000 tons of nitrogen oxides, and 11,740,000 metric tons of carbon dioxide would have been released into the South Carolina atmosphere in 2000 alone.

All of the commercial nuclear reactors in South Carolina are pressurized water reactors. This means that the primary reactor coolant is maintained at a pressure that is high enough to prevent boiling in the reactor core. The core consists of roughly one hundred fuel modules, each of which is made up of a few hundred fuel rods. Inside each sealed fuel rod are cylindrical fuel pellets that contain uranium oxide in a ceramic matrix. The primary coolant carries the heat produced by fission of the uranium atoms to steam generators, where a separate, secondary water circuit is heated to produce steam. This steam is piped outside the primary containment room to turbine generators to produce electricity. As a result of this and the use of cooling water (a third water circuit), the steam is condensed into liquid water and returned to the steam generators. All of this resides inside a secondary containment barrier. These multiple barriers keep nearly all radiation from being released to the environment.

Some low-level radioactive waste (LLRW) is generated in the process of monitoring and maintaining the reactor plant and is buried in the Barnwell LLRW repository. The expended fuel modules are stored on site at the reactor plants, pending the opening of a federal high-level radioactive waste facility under Yucca Mountain, Nevada. South Carolinians are exposed to natural radioactivity that far exceeds what is released by these plants. Medical exposures are even higher. Nevertheless, nuclear power has been, and remains, a controversial subject in South Carolina and elsewhere. Critics cite environmental and safety concerns, especially regarding the storage of radioactive waste in South Carolina and in the wake of highly publicized accidents at nuclear power plants at Three Mile Island in Pennsylvania and at Chernobyl in the Soviet Union. JAMES R. FRYSINGER

Nuclear Reactor Sites in South Carolina, 2001

Site	*Location*	*Operator*	*Electrical Power (MW)*	*Startup Date*	*License Expiration Date*
Robinson 2	Hartsville	CP&L	769	1970	2010
Oconee 1	Seneca	Duke	866	1973	2013
Oconee 2	Seneca	Duke	866	1974	2013
Oconee 3	Seneca	Duke	866	1974	2014
Summer	Jenkinsville	SCE&G	900	1984	2022
Catawba 1	Clover	Duke	1,129	1985	2024
Catawba 2	Clover	Duke	1,129	1986	2026

CP&L = Carolina Power and Light
Duke = Duke Energy
SCE&G = South Carolina Electric and Gas

South Carolina Nuclear Waste Task Force. *Report of the South Carolina Nuclear Waste Task Force.* Vol. 1, *Report of the Task Force, December 15, 1999.* Columbia: South Carolina Nuclear Waste Task Force, 1999.

Nullification. During the nullification crisis of 1828 to 1834, South Carolina planter politicians formulated a new brand of slavery-based politics that would culminate in the formation of the southern confederacy. The crisis, which began as a dispute over federal tariff laws, became intertwined with the politics of slavery and sectionalism. Led by John C. Calhoun, a majority of South Carolina slaveholders claimed that a state had the right to nullify or veto federal laws and secede from the Union. Nullification and secession, according to Calhoun, were the reserved rights of the states and therefore constitutional. Calhoun's constitutional theories and the overtly proslavery discourse of the nullifiers laid the political and ideological foundation for southern nationalism.

The passage of the federal tariff law of 1828 signaled the rise of the nullification controversy in South Carolina. In his famous South Carolina Exposition, which was voted down by the General Assembly, Calhoun claimed that federal import duties were actually a tax on the nation's main exporters, southern planters. Unlike free traders, who opposed the tariff or protective duties in the interest of all consumers, nullifiers claimed that the tariff hurt the South in particular. And they linked their opposition to the tariff to a proslavery position by arguing that northerners intended to interfere with the institution of slavery by impoverishing the South. Calhoun argued that nullification or state interposition would establish a constitutional precedent that would safeguard the interests of the slaveholding minority in a democratic republic. His theory of nullification innovatively combined the antidemocratic sensibility of the Federalists with the states' rights legacy of the Jeffersonians. Calhoun's justification of nullification and secession as constitutional rights of the state also went beyond traditional states' rights doctrine as they were based on an unprecedented notion of absolute state sovereignty. Most old states' righters, including James Madison, condemned nullification as an extraconstitutional and unrepublican theory as it was not mentioned in the U.S. Constitution and because it subverted the cardinal principle of republican government, majority rule.

Calhoun's lieutenants in South Carolina, James Hamilton, Robert Hayne, and George McDuffie, formed the States Rights and Free Trade Party to implement nullification after Calhoun's break with President Andrew Jackson became final. Most of the Calhounites had been nationalists in state politics prior to the tariff controversy. Like Calhoun, their politics somersaulted from one of qualified nationalism to unqualified sectionalism. Older states' rights leaders such as William Smith, John Taylor, and David Rogerson Williams helped to form the opposition Union Party, which also contained Jacksonian Democrats such as Joel Poinsett and Benjamin Perry, and staunch unionists such as James L. Petigru. While the nullifiers gained many adherents in the state's large black belt that encompassed the lowcountry and the lower Piedmont, the base of the Union Party lay in the nonplantation northwestern districts of the state. In order to call a state convention to nullify the federal tariff laws of 1828 and 1832, nullifiers launched a campaign that emphasized sectionalism, the defense of slavery, and opposition to majority rule. Unionists on the other hand appealed to loyalty to the Union and the American experiment in republican government. They also criticized the undemocratic stranglehold of the lowcountry elite on state government. The nullifiers gained the upper hand as they had the support of a majority of the slaveholding planter class that dominated the state's government. Unionists lost the closely contested state legislature elections of 1832. The nullifiers' victory allowed them to dominate the malapportioned General Assembly. Having gained a two-thirds majority in the legislature, nullifiers proceeded to call a convention and enact an ordinance of nullification and oaths of allegiance to the state in order to implement nullification in defiance of federal law.

Upon nullification, however, South Carolina found itself politically isolated in the nation. Even most southern states refused to follow her lead. In a proclamation against nullification, President Jackson endorsed the vision of a perpetual and democratic Union and challenged the constitutionality of nullification and secession, creating an important precedent for Lincoln. Like his proto-Whig rivals Daniel Webster and Henry Clay, Jackson condemned nullification as disunionist. The president also secured the passage of the Wilkins Act, which gave him powers to implement federal tariff laws in South Carolina. Most southern states remained loyal to the party of Jackson, but some prominent members of the slaveholding chivalry—especially in Georgia and Virginia—sympathized with the nullifiers and were wary of Jackson's new nationalism. In the end Calhoun cooperated with Clay to secure the passage of the compromise tariff law of 1833 in Congress.

The state convention rescinded its ordinance of nullification but issued another ordinance nullifying the Wilkins Act, which nullifiers referred to as the Force Bill. The controversy continued in the state, however, as Unionists opposed the new oaths of allegiance enacted by nullifiers. Unionist argued that "test oaths" were unrepublican, as they would stymie freedom of opinion and political dissent in the state. The state court of appeals also declared the oaths unconstitutional, leading some nullifiers to advocate the abolition of the court, which they succeeded in doing in 1835. A compromise reached between leading nullifiers and Unionists, stating that an oath of allegiance to the state was consistent with the loyalty to the U.S. Constitution, finally brought the crisis to an end in South Carolina in 1834. The aftermath of nullification proved fatal to the Unionists, and Calhoun's political machine in South Carolina dominated state politics until his death.

Nullification crystallized South Carolina's early ideological commitment to slavery and southern nationalism. The politics of slavery and separatism inaugurated by nullifiers checked democratic reform and prevented the growth of a two-party system in the state, making South Carolina exceptional even in the context of southern politics. The Carolina doctrine presented an alternative to Jacksonian democracy and party system in the South and finally triumphed when most of the southern states seceded from the Union in 1860–1861. MANISHA SINHA

Bancroft, Frederic. *Calhoun and the South Carolina Nullification Movement.* Baltimore: Johns Hopkins Press, 1928.

Boucher, Chauncey Samuel. *The Nullification Controversy in South Carolina.* Chicago: University of Chicago Press, 1916.

Ellis, Richard E. *The Union at Risk: Jacksonian Democracy, States' Rights and the Nullification Crisis.* New York: Oxford University Press, 1987.

Ford, Lacy K., Jr. *Origins of Southern Radicalism: The South Carolina Upcountry, 1800–1860.* New York: Oxford University Press, 1988.

Freehling, William W. *Prelude to Civil War: The Nullification Controversy in South Carolina, 1816–1836.* New York: Harper & Row, 1965.

Houston, David Franklin. *A Critical Study of Nullification in South Carolina.* New York: Longmans, Green, 1896.

Sinha, Manisha. *The Counterrevolution of Slavery: Politics and Ideology in Antebellum South Carolina.* Chapel Hill: University of North Carolina Press, 2000.

O

Ocean Forest Hotel. Myrtle Beach's magnificent Ocean Forest Hotel opened formally on Friday evening, February 21, 1930. The hotel, standing twenty-nine feet above sea level, with a ten-story wedding-cake tower flanked by two five-story wings, was South Carolina's Statue of Liberty. Together with its gardens, pools, and stables, the hotel occupied thirteen acres. Amenities such as marble stairways, Czechoslovakian crystal chandeliers, Grecian columns, faucets that dispensed salt water to the 202 ventilated bathrooms, oriental rugs in the marble-floored lobby, the grand ballroom, and dining room all attested to the Ocean Forest's inclusion among an exclusive list of world-class hotels. High standards of etiquette were the rule. Gentlemen never entered the dining room without wearing tuxedos. Ladies wore evening gowns. By the 1940s and 1950s patrons altered their lifestyles, and the Ocean Forest Hotel changed with the times. "Resort attire" was accepted, and in the late 1940s Governor Strom Thurmond played volleyball in his swim trunks.

Ocean Forest Hotel. Courtesy, South Caroliniana Library

During the 1960s the owners of the hotel declined to make much-needed improvements. The Ocean Forest showed signs of neglect. The hotel closed its doors in June 1974. On Friday the thirteenth of September 1974, explosives were placed around the hotel. The ten-story building that had taken a year and a half to build was reduced to a pile of rubble in six seconds.

The author Mickey Spillane said, "The Ocean Forest Hotel was a beautiful piece of architecture, and for down here it was actually superb." Thurmond recalled the hotel's "wonderful hospitality, and I consider the visits I made there some of the happiest and most enjoyable trips I have taken." NANCY RHYNE

Gragg, Rod. *The Illustrated History of Horry County.* Myrtle Beach: Southern Communications, 1994.

Lewis, Catherine H. *Horry County, South Carolina, 1730–1993.* Columbia: University of South Carolina Press, 1998.

Monk, John. "Landmark Crumbles to Memory." Myrtle Beach *Sun-News,* September 14, 1974, pp. 1–2.

Oconee bell. The Oconee bell (*Shortia galacifolia*) is a small, evergreen species related to Galax, with white flowers produced in March. It was discovered by French botanist André Michaux in 1787 in the mountains of South Carolina along the Keowee River near the present Jocassee Dam. He never described the plant, and a dried specimen sat in his collection in Paris until Asa Gray of Harvard University saw it in 1839. Gray and others spent nearly forty years trying to find this plant of unknown genus and species in the wild. Unfortunately Gray did not have access to Michaux's journal and thought the discovery location was in the high mountains of North Carolina. He visited Grandfather Mountain (a known collecting site of Michaux) in 1841 but did not find the plant. In 1842 Gray described the plant as *Shortia galacifolia* in honor of Charles Short, a Kentucky botanist, who had never seen the plant.

Oconee Bells. Photograph by Robert Clark. Courtesy, South Carolina Department of Natural Resources

During the next thirty-five years the species remained unknown in the wild, until a seventeen-year-old boy, George M. Hyams, collected it in McDowell County, North Carolina. Oconee bells immediately gained fame and have maintained their popularity ever since. Numerous scientific papers, popular magazine articles, books, and even a song have been dedicated to this plant. Today the Oconee bell is considered a rare plant. Approximately sixty percent of the known populations were destroyed by the construction of Lake Jocassee and Lake Keowee. It currently grows along stream banks and hillsides in Oconee, Pickens, and Greenville Counties in South Carolina and is also known from small populations in North Carolina and northeast Georgia. More populations of Oconee bells are found in South Carolina than in any other state. PATRICK MCMILLAN

Donn, B. Allen, and Steven M. Jones. "Geographical Distribution of *Shortia galacifolia* in Oconee and Pickens Counties, South Carolina." *Journal of the Elisha Mitchell Scientific Society* 95 (spring 1979): 32–41.

Jenkins, Charles F. "Asa Gray and His Quest for *Shortia galacifolia.*" *Arnoldia* 51, no. 4 (1991): 4–11.

Troyer, James R. "The Hyams Family, Father and Sons, Contributors to North Carolina Botany." *Journal of the Elisha Mitchell Scientific Society* 117 (winter 2001): 240–48.

Oconee County (625 sq. miles; 2000 pop. 66,215). Oconee County is the only county in South Carolina bordering on two states—Georgia and North Carolina. Located in the northwest corner of South Carolina at the foot of the Blue Ridge Mountains, the region was home to Cherokee Indians until the Revolutionary War, when they were driven from all except the northernmost section. When the area became a part of South Carolina after the Revolution, it was placed first in Ninety Six District, then Pendleton District, and later Pickens District. Oconee County was created on January 29, 1868, from the western half of Pickens County. The name Oconee derives from the Cherokees and has several interpretations, the most popular being "water eyes of the hills," in reference to the area's many waterfalls and streams.

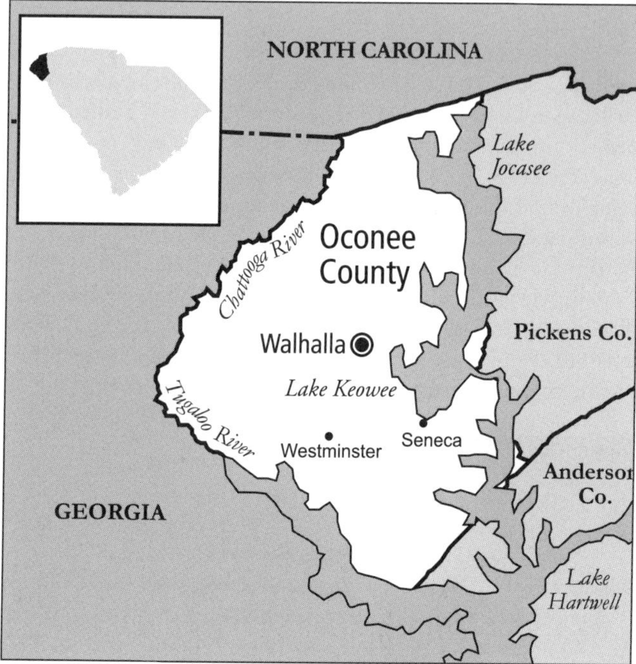

Although a relatively new county, Oconee is nevertheless rich in history. Oconee Station was built in 1792 as one in a series of militia blockhouses along the South Carolina frontier. The site and the adjoining William Richards house (ca. 1802) are maintained as part of Oconee Station State Park. The Old Pickens Presbyterian Church, built in 1827, is listed in the National Register of Historic Places, as is the Oconee Station complex. In the antebellum period, the area was dominated by small farms that produced primarily grains and livestock, although some cotton was produced. In 1850 a group of German settlers led by John Wagener founded the town of Walhalla, which became the county seat in 1868.

Railroads reached this remote part of the state in the 1850s. In an attempt to connect South Carolina with Tennessee and the West by railroad, the Blue Ridge Railroad Company began a line from Anderson that neared Walhalla before the company failed. The Civil War brought an end to the endeavor, leaving the uncompleted Stumphouse Tunnel and two smaller tunnels as lasting reminders of the company's grand vision.

Oconee grew steadily in the late nineteenth century. The Atlanta and Richmond Airline Railroad (later part of the Southern Railway) arrived in Oconee in the 1870s. The town of Seneca, chartered in 1874, was built at the spot where the northern and southern section of the road were joined. The town of Westminster was also established on the railroad in 1874, and was chartered by the General Assembly the following year. Industrial development followed these transportation improvements. Oconee joined many Piedmont counties in becoming home to a number of textile mills. In 1893 the Courtenay Manufacturing Company was established, including its mill village of Newry. Other mills followed, including Seneca's Lonsdale Manufacturing Company in 1901. Employment opportunities attracted rural dwellers to the mills, and agriculture gradually declined in importance. In 1970 there were 4,700 people employed in Oconee County's nine textile mills.

Foreign competition weakened the textile industry during the last decades of the twentieth century, which led the county to look to its natural and scenic resources to supplement its economy. The Chattooga River, which provided the scenery for the film version of James Dickey's novel *Deliverance,* borders Oconee County and forms part of the dividing line between South Carolina and Georgia. The Andrew Pickens Division of the Sumter National Forest comprises 79,000 acres in the county. The Long Creek area is noted for its apples, and the South Carolina Apple Festival has been held every autumn in Westminster since 1972. The Walhalla Fish Hatchery, also in the national forest, raises almost one million trout per year.

In the 1960s Duke Power Company began a power-generating project that resulted in the creation of Lake Jocassee in 1973, just above Lake Keowee. The two lakes were developed as a part of the Keowee-Toxaway complex. Included in the complex are the Oconee Nuclear Station and the Keowee, Jocassee, and Bad Creek hydroelectric stations. The company's World of Energy at Lake Keowee features exhibits showing how electricity is generated.

Recreation has become a major asset to the county. In addition to the Sumter National Forest, there are four state parks (Oconee, Lake Hartwell, Keowee-Toxaway, and Devil's Fork) and several county parks. Hunting is popular in the National Forest. The Chattooga and Chauga Rivers provide rafting, kayaking, and fishing opportunities. Hiking and horseback riding are popular pastimes, as is boating on county lakes. There are eighteen waterfalls in the county, by far the most in the state. The most prominent is the Lower Whitewater Falls. A chain of six waterfalls along the North and South Carolina border is the highest series of falls in eastern North America. The upper falls are in North Carolina, but the impressive lower falls in South Carolina drop two hundred feet and are on the Whitewater River, which spills into Lake Jocassee.

Retirement communitites developed soon after the creation of Oconee County's lakes. The upscale Keowee Key has had a major impact on Lake Keowee, and communities such as Chickasaw Point and Carolina Landing were built on Lake Hartwell. HURLEY E. BADDERS

Aheron, Piper Peters. *Oconee County.* Charleston, S.C.: Arcadia, 1998.

Doyle, Mary Cherry. *Historic Oconee in South Carolina.* 1935. Reprint, Pendleton, S.C.: Old Pendleton District Historical Commission, 1967.

Oconee County Heritage Book Committee. *The Heritage of Oconee County, 1868–1995.* Seneca, S.C.: Blue Ridge Arts Council, 1995.

Octagon House (Laurens). Zelotes Lee Holmes, a Presbyterian clergyman who taught at the Laurens Female College, began constructing an octagonal classroom building and residence in 1858. Granite slabs five feet long, twenty-one inches wide, and eighteen inches deep supported walls of stone and concretelike mortar that ranged from twelve to eighteen inches thick. It was one of the first concrete buildings constructed in the South. The exterior is stucco scored to resemble stone. Holmes supervised its construction by his slaves and with the help of his children. It was completed by the end of 1859.

The Octagon House is centered around a two-story atrium, thirty-five feet high, with a skylight and ventilation ports that drew hot air out of the building. Sleeping rooms on either side of the atrium have separate stairs, which allowed male and female boarding students to communicate with each other from balconies but prevented their physical contact. Sixteen chimneys animate the complex roof structure of the main octagonal building, its four projecting corner rooms, and four porches.

The plan resembles an example in Samuel Sloan's *The Model Architect,* published in 1852. Similar buildings were publicized nationally by Orson Squire Fowler, who published *A Home for All, or the Gravel Wall and Octagon Mode of Building* in 1854.

Holmes's descendants occupied the house until it was sold in 1919 for $8,000. Electricity and indoor bathrooms were added about 1900, and in the 1940s the building was remodeled into four apartments. Listed in the National Register of Historic Places in 1973, the house was rehabilitated as an Arts Center about 1976 but again fell into disrepair by the early 1990s. About 1997 the structure was refurbished by DeWayne Anderson of Winston-Salem for use as a multifamily residential complex. The Octagon House is located at 619 East Main Street in Laurens. ROBERT W. BAINBRIDGE

Lane, Mills. *Architecture of the Old South: South Carolina.* Savannah, Ga.: Beehive, 1997.

Okra. Also known as lady's fingers, gombo, gumbs, quingombo, okro, ochro, bamia, and quiabo, okra is considered by southerners to be a delicacy, in spite of its slippery quality. The poet James Dickey once told an interviewer, "If God had made anything better He'd have kept it for Himself."

Okra (*Abelmoschus esculentus* and *Hibiscus esculentus*), a ribbed vegetable resembling the shape of a manicured lady's finger, arrived in South Carolina at the end of the seventeenth century via the slave trade from Africa. It is doubtful that slaves were able to bring seeds over themselves. Rather, it is believed that ship captains transported the seeds and the African slaves devised the means for growing and cooking it.

The seed pod of a beautiful hibiscus and a member of the mallow family (as is cotton), okra likely originated in Ethiopia, moving from there to North Africa, the Middle East, Brazil, and India. Okra is an African word (*nkruma* in one Ghanaian language) and appears to have been used in South Carolina the way that the word "gumbo" (from the Angolan word *ngombo*) is used in Louisiana. Best picked when small and tender, when under an inch it can be eaten raw or cooked with its cap on. Larger than that, the cap should be sliced off high enough that the inner seeds do not spill out, then the pod sliced. Because of a tendency to mold, it is best used within a day or two of picking. Predominantly green, there are a variety of colors and shapes. Some have a fuzzy, unpleasant coating that can—and should—be removed by rubbing before washing. It is frequently seen pickled, but can be steamed, boiled, braised, and sautéed. Its mucilaginous quality is used to advantage when sliced and used to thicken stews (called gumbos in Louisiana and okra stews in South Carolina). NATHALIE DUPREE

Randolph, Mary. *The Virginia House-Wife.* 1824. Reprint, Columbia: University of South Carolina Press, 1984.

Rutledge, Sarah. *The Carolina Housewife.* 1847. Reprint, Columbia: University of South Carolina Press, 1979.

Schneider, Elizabeth. *Uncommon Fruits & Vegetables: A Commonsense Guide.* New York: Harper & Row, 1986.

Old Brick Church (Fairfield County). Ebenezer Associate Reformed Presbyterian Church, known commonly as the "Old Brick Church," is one of only a handful of eighteenth-century ecclesiastical buildings remaining in the Midlands. Built in 1788, the plain brick-masonry building stands at a site along the Little River about twelve miles from Winnsboro. It replaced an earlier log church erected soon after Presbyterians from Scotland and Ireland began settling in the area in the 1770s. The interior is austere and features long, straight-backed wooden pews, a dais-style pulpit, and a slave gallery. The church and an adjoining cemetery are surrounded by a granite wall that the congregation erected in 1852.

Old Brick Church. Courtesy, South Carolina Department of Archives and History

On May 9, 1803, the church was the site of a gathering of ministers and church elders that resulted in the formation of the Associate Reformed Synod of the Carolinas. Today it is revered as the "mother church" of the A.R.P. faith. Under the ministry of the Reverend James Rogers, the congregation grew until the Civil War. It became dormant in the postbellum era and eventually disappeared from the rolls of the Presbytery before being reorganized by the Reverend A. G. Kirkpatrick in the early 1890s. The congregation began holding its regular meetings at a new building in the 1920s but continued to gather at the Old Brick Church for special services, a tradition that continues.

Listed in the National Register of Historic Places in 1971, the church is perhaps best known for an inscription left on an interior wall by a Union soldier during the late stages of the Civil War. While in pursuit of retreating Confederate forces, Union troops removed portions of the floor and joists to rebuild a bridge over the Little River. One soldier was so troubled by the undertaking that he penciled an apology on an interior wall: "Citizens of this community—please excuse us for defacing your house of worship so much. It was absolutely necessary to effect a crossing over the creek. A Yankee." DANIEL J. VIVIAN

Bigham, John. "The Old Brick Church." *Sandlapper* 7 (August 1974): 49–50.

Ebenezer Associate Reformed Presbyterian Church (Old Brick Church), National Register of Historic Places nomination, State Historic Preservation Office, South Carolina Department of Archives and History, Columbia.

Old Iron District. In the vicinity of the Broad River near the northern border of South Carolina, there are significant deposits of magnetite and specular oxide iron ore, as well as some lesser belts of hematite. Early colonists took advantage of these resources and began to produce iron before the Revolutionary War. Two ironworks were well established in the area by the end of the eighteenth century. This early industry expanded steadily during the antebellum years, with much of the capital for the enterprise coming from affluent planters anxious to enter the manufacturing field. By midcentury a total of eight furnaces had been constructed. Confederate demands for iron caused a notable increase in production during the Civil War, but the end of the conflict marked the beginning of the end for many of the foundries. One of the main reasons for the decline was that anthracite furnaces operating in other parts of the nation produced iron at a lower cost than the charcoal iron produced in the region. By the end of the nineteenth century, the industry had disappeared from the state. About the same time a new county—Cherokee County—was formed from parts of Spartanburg, Union, and York Counties on February 25, 1897. Centered in the middle of the once prosperous iron industry in South Carolina, it is sometimes known as the Old Iron District. SAMUEL K. FORE

Lander, Ernest M., Jr. "The Iron Industry in Ante-Bellum South Carolina." *Journal of Southern History* 20 (August 1954): 337–55.

Moss, Bobby G. *The Old Iron District: A Study of the Development of Cherokee County, 1750–1897.* Clinton, S.C.: Jacobs, 1972.

Oliphant, Mary Chevillette Simms (1891–1988). Historian. Oliphant was born in Barnwell County on January 6, 1891, the daughter of William Gilmore Simms, Jr., and Emma Gertrude Hartzog. Her grandfather was the novelist William Gilmore Simms. In 1911 she enrolled at the College for Women in Columbia, and some of Oliphant's earliest published writing appeared in the *Palmetto,* the student literary magazine. By the time she finished college in 1916 with a bachelor's degree in liberal arts and piano, her skills as a writer were strong enough that the state superintendent of education asked her to update her grandfather's 1860 history of South Carolina for use as a textbook. Oliphant's updated version of the Simms history was adopted in 1917 and revised every five years until 1932, when Oliphant wrote an entirely new South Carolina history textbook. *The Simms History of South Carolina* went through nine editions and was used by South Carolina junior high school students until 1985. In 1927 she wrote *The South Carolina Reader* to accompany her 1917 history. In 1947 Oliphant and her daughter, Mary Simms Oliphant, coauthored a South Carolina reader to introduce third-grade students to their state. Entitled *Gateway to South Carolina,* it was later retitled *South Carolina: From the Mountains to the Sea.*

Mary C. Simms Oliphant. Courtesy, South Caroliniana Library

Mary C. Simms married Albert Drane Oliphant on March 1, 1917. The couple moved to Greenville in 1920, where Oliphant became active in promoting local history. In 1928 she was a member of the Upper Carolina Society and the Historical Records Committee, a forerunner of the Greenville Historical Society. After her husband's death in 1935, Oliphant continued to write despite a bustling household that included her own three children, two of her sisters and their children, and various other relatives.

Oliphant's most ambitious project, and the one for which she is most widely known, began in 1937 when Dr. Benjamin E. Geer, president of Furman University, persuaded her to write a biography of her grandfather, William Gilmore Simms. As she began research, Oliphant realized that it would be necessary to collect, edit, and publish Simms's letters before a proper biography could be written. The University of South Carolina Press published six volumes of Simms correspondence between 1952 and 1982. In 1969 Oliphant collaborated with Donald Davidson to coedit William Gilmore Simms's *Voltmeier, of the Mountain Men,* the first volume in the Centennial Edition of his writings. In the 1940s Oliphant undertook a project only slightly less ambitious than editing the Simms correspondence: creating a bibliography of the work of the prolific state historian Alexander S. Salley. In 1949 Oliphant published *The Works of A. S. Salley: A Descriptive Bibliography.* From 1956 to 1958 Oliphant served as director of the South Carolina State Public Library Association.

Oliphant died on July 27, 1988, in Greenville. She was buried in the cemetary of the Church of the Holy Apostles in Barnwell. BRUCE E. BAKER

Atkinson, Alyce P. "Mary Simms Oliphant: A Fascination with History." *Greenville Piedmont,* July 10, 1981, p. B1.

Bodie, Idella. *South Carolina Women.* Orangeburg, S.C.: Sandlapper, 1991.

Oliver, Robert Campbell (1833–1891). Clergyman. A Methodist minister and gospel mission founder, Oliver was born June 9, 1833, in Edgefield District. He was admitted to the South Carolina Conference of the Methodist Episcopal Church, South, in 1863, in time becoming a recognized leader of the Holiness movement as it spread through South Carolina Methodist circles.

In 1871 Oliver was appointed special agent by the Methodist Episcopal Church, South, to start an orphanage. After raising $15,000 he purchased the campus of the Spartanburg Female College for the orphanage, becoming the first superintendent of the Carolina Orphan Home. Funding was a challenge, however, and the orphanage closed in 1874.

Oliver is best known for a rescue mission he later founded in Columbia to serve as a refuge for homeless and troubled men. He purchased a lot at the corner of Assembly and Taylor streets in Columbia in 1888, for what became the Oliver Rescue Mission. The following year a gospel tabernacle was constructed.

By then Oliver had come under the influence of the Holiness movement. In 1890 he announced his plan to launch a Holiness periodical, *Way of Faith,* with the subtitle *and Neglected Themes.* The prospectus promoting it proclaimed that articles would emphasize "Justification, Entire Sanctification and Divine Healing," as well as tithing and Prohibition. The editorial office was in Columbia, with the Reverend L. R. Pickett of Texas serving as editor, while Oliver was both assistant editor and superintendent of the mission.

At Oliver's death in 1891, the mission property was deeded to a group of trustees to continue the work. J. M. Pike took over leadership of the mission and editorial responsibilities for the *Way of Faith.* The periodical and the mission underwent independent, but related developments after Oliver's death. The *Way of Faith* relocated to Louisville in 1931 when it merged with the *Pentecostal Herald.* The mission continued its humanitarian work, offering a soup kitchen and housing for men. Under the leadership of the Reverend Eli Alston Wilkes, Jr., resident superintendent from 1959 to 1963, it inaugurated a program to serve recently released prisoners that in time became its own organization, the Alston Wilkes Society. Meals on Wheels in Columbia also had its start at the Oliver Gospel Mission.

Oliver was married to (Mary) Frances Thompson, a well-to-do Charleston native whose financial means may have helped the gospel mission get under way. There is no record of children. Oliver died on August 2, 1891, near Cherokee Springs in Spartanburg County. He was buried in Oakwood Cemetery, Spartanburg County. NANCY A. HARDESTY

Betts, Albert D. *History of South Carolina Methodism.* Columbia, S.C.: Advocate Press, 1952.

Olympia Cotton Mill. Olympia Cotton Mill was one of four mills designed and built in Columbia between 1895 and 1904 by the industrialist W. B. Smith Whaley. Construction began in summer 1899, and by 1900 the mill was in operation. Unlike other cotton mills in Columbia that used steam or hydroelectric power, Olympia had its own coal-fired electrical plant that supplied electricity to Olympia and Whaley's three other mills, as well as the Columbia Street Railway Power Company.

In addition to this innovation, Olympia was notable for its sheer scale. The main building was approximately 150 feet by 550 feet and housed just over 100,000 spindles, almost as many as Columbia's other five mills combined. In 1907 Olympia's weave rooms held 2,250 looms. During the first years of the twentieth century, Olympia was frequently lauded as "the world's largest cotton mill under one roof." Olympia was not merely the biggest mill in Columbia; in many ways it was also the best to work for. Partly in order to forestall unionization of the workforce, Whaley provided living conditions better than most mills of the time. The houses in the mill village were good, Olympia School was founded in 1901, and the mill started the first kindergarten and the first playground in the Columbia area.

The financial base of the mill was not so positive, however. Whaley was forced to sell his four mills to Lewis W. Parker in 1911, and the four were renamed Hampton Mills. Parker Cotton Mills Company hit hard times in 1914 and sold Hampton Mills to Pacific Mills of Lawrence, Massachusetts, in 1916. In 1954 Burlington Industries purchased the entire Pacific Mills chain and operated Olympia for another forty years. Olympia survived the wave of mill closings in the 1980s, but a Christmas Eve fire in 1995 seriously damaged the mill. Olympia Mill announced its closing a few months later on June 28, 1996. BRUCE E. BAKER

Byars, Alvin W. *Olympia Pacific: The Way It Was, 1895–1970.* West Columbia, S.C.: Professional Printers, 1981.

Hughes, Bill. "Olympia-Granby Plant to Close." Columbia *State,* June 29, 1996, p. A1.

Power, J. Tracy. "'The Brightest of the Lot': W. B. Smith Whaley and the Rise of the South Carolina Textile Industry, 1893–1903." *South Carolina Historical Magazine* 93 (April 1992): 126–38.

Omar Ibn Said (ca. 1770–1859). Slave, Muslim. A Pullo (plural: Fulbe) from Futa Toro in the Senegambia region of West Africa, Omar was taken into slavery in the late eighteenth century and forced across the Atlantic to the Americas. Records of his life in America indicate that he lived in North and South Carolina.

Omar's ancestors received Islam in the eleventh century. The Fulbe not only championed the religion of Islam but also built the Islamic kingdoms of Futa Toro and Futa Jalon in what became Senegal and Guinea, respectively, and carried out jihad activities in West Africa during the eighteenth century. Omar was taken into slavery during a series of wars in the region.

Having lost his father at the age of five, Omar was raised by his uncle. During his stay with his uncle, he came in contact with some Muslim clerics and became a pious Muslim. It is reported that he prayed five times a day and tried to fulfill all the other four major requirements of Islam, including a pilgrimage to Mecca on foot. He was also married and had a son before his capture.

Omar was one of many African Muslims who were captured and taken to the Americas but whom have not been adequately studied. Unfortunately, there are no details on his capture; many Muslim Fulbe believe that you do not retell the story of difficult times if you want Allah (God) to give you blessings for that suffering.

Omar's American saga unfolded while he was enslaved in Charleston, South Carolina. He arrived in Charleston in 1807 after a voyage of six weeks and was immediately sold to a Mr. Johnson, who proved to be a brutal master and prevented him from performing his daily Islamic prayers. In response, Omar ran away. He spent a month traveling to North Carolina, reaching Fayetteville, where he was arrested while performing his prayers in a church. Omar's imprisonment generated tremendous curiosity because of his ability to read and write. He used the charcoal in his jail cell to write Muslim prayers and appeals in Arabic to the authorities not to return him to Charleston. His former owner was finally paid off by Jim Owen, who took him to his Milton plantation. Omar was happy with his new master to the point that he accepted conversion to Christianity. He remained with Owen until the late antebellum period, serving Owen in many capacities including, in his last position, as a butler at the plantation of his master's brother, Governor John Owen. Despite his conversion to Christianity, "Uncle Moreau" (as Omar was popularly known), who was familiar with both the Holy Bible and the Qur'an, continued to live as a Muslim.

The story of Omar's conversion remains controversial. Many scholars doubt his willingness to convert to Christianity and his sincerity in doing so. Nonetheless, his love and dedication to the Owen brothers, who were both religious, contributed to Omar's acceptance of Christianity. Omar, like numerous other enslaved West African Muslims, retained Islam or some major aspects of the religion while in the New World. Omar Ibn Said died in Fayetteville in 1859 at the age of eighty-nine and was buried at Owen Hill Plantation. M. ALPHA BAH

Austin, Allan. *African Muslims in Antebellum America: Transatlantic Stories and Spiritual Struggles.* New York: Routledge, 1997.

Callcott, George. "Omar Ibn Seid, A Slave Who Wrote an Autobiography in Arabic." *Journal of Negro History* 39 (January 1954): 58–63.

Diouf, Sylviane. *Servants of Allah: African Muslims Enslaved in the Americas.* New York: New York University Press, 1998.

O'Neall, John Belton (1793–1863). Jurist, author, social reformer, entrepreneur. O'Neall, the son of Hugh O'Neall and Anne Kelly, was born April 10, 1793, near Bobo's Mill, Newberry County. Educated first at the Newberry Academy, in 1811 he entered the junior class at South Carolina College, where he served as Clariosophic Society president and graduated second in his class the following year. After teaching for six months in Newberry, O'Neall commenced the study of law with John Caldwell, his brother-in-law, and was admitted to the Columbia Bar in 1814.

O'Neall joined the state militia in 1813, serving as an artillery officer and judge advocate in Colonel Starling Tucker's regiment during the War of 1812. Three years later O'Neall was appointed aide-de-camp to General Andrew Pickens. By 1827 O'Neall had risen to the rank of major general of the Third Division.

First elected to the General Assembly from Newberry District in 1816, O'Neall served one term. He failed to win a second term in 1818 because he had voted to increase the salary of state judges. On June 25, 1818, O'Neall married Helen Pope, daughter of Sampson Pope and Sarah Strother of Newberry. The couple had six

John Belton O'Neall. Courtesy, South Carolina Historical Society

daughters, all of whom predeceased their parents. O'Neall returned to the House of Representatives in 1822, 1824, and 1826, serving as Speaker from 1824 to 1828. While a member of the House, he served on the committee of grievances, inland navigation, internal improvements, judiciary, and roads, bridges and ferries. His support for a $10,000 relief bill for the heirs of Thomas Jefferson caused his defeat in the 1828 November elections, and his retirement from the House.

The General Assembly elected O'Neall as an associate state judge in 1828. After two years of riding the circuit, he was elected to the court of appeals, serving with William Harper and David Johnson until 1835. That year, in two appeals cases, O'Neall and Johnson declared that the state's oath of allegiance established during the nullification crisis was unconstitutional. This decision displeased the General Assembly, so they abolished the court of appeals. However, as a staunch Unionist, O'Neall remained true to his convictions, then and for the next twenty-five years. He was named justice of appeals at law, a position he held until 1850. From 1850 to 1859 O'Neall served as president of the court of appeals at law, followed by four years as chief justice of the state. As a jurist, he authored legal treatises and state law digests. *Negro Law of the Carolinas* (1848), an attempt to guarantee legal protection for slaves while regularizing judicial administration between slaves and free, was one of his most important. A prolific historian as well, O'Neall's most significant endeavors were *Biographical Sketches of the Bench and Bar of South Carolina* (1859) and *The Annals of Newberry* (1859).

Although born a Quaker, O'Neall became a Baptist and a leading Baptist layman. He served as president of the Newberry Bible Society and State Baptist Convention, and as a member of the Furman Institution's Board of Trustees. Throughout his life O'Neall participated in educational institutions, serving as a trustee of Newberry Academy, Erskine College, and South Carolina College. He actively championed female education by writing articles and giving speeches, serving as a trustee of Johnson Female Academy as well as introducing and supporting the State Baptist Convention's resolution that established Furman Female College.

In 1832, to save a friend, O'Neall gave up alcohol and six months later stopped using tobacco. He became an ardent supporter of the temperance movement, joining first the Head's Springs Temperance Society in Newberry and serving multiple years as president. Later he led the South Carolina Temperance Society for twenty-two years. After joining the state's Sons of Temperance in 1849, he was elected president in 1850 and two years later president of the national organization. O'Neall campaigned for temperance by writing and speaking as well. His column, "The Drunkard's Looking Glass," appeared in the *South-Carolina Temperance Advocate* regularly.

A successful planter and businessman, by 1860 O'Neall owned two plantations valued at $60,000 and eighty-three slaves worth $160,000. For more than twenty years as president of the Newberry District Agricultural Society, he encouraged diversification of crops and sponsored annual meetings that attracted many farmers from all over the state. As a businessman, O'Neall was instrumental in founding the Greenville and Columbia Railroad, serving as its president and director for nine years. Additionally, he was a director of the Bank of Newberry and incorporator of the Southern Mutual Life Insurance Company.

A versatile man of strong convictions, O'Neall worked tirelessly to better his profession, his district, his church, and his county. He died December 27, 1863, and was buried in Rosemont Cemetery, Newberry County. ROBERTA V. H. COPP

Moore, Alexander, ed. *Biographical Directory of the South Carolina House of Representatives.* Vol. 5, *1816–1828.* Columbia: South Carolina Department of Archives and History, 1992.

O'Neall, John Belton. *Biographical Sketches of the Bench and Bar of South Carolina.* 2 vols. Charleston, S.C.: S. G. Courtney, 1859.

Pope, Thomas H. *The History of Newberry County, South Carolina.* 2 vols. Columbia: University of South Carolina Press, 1973–1992.

Opera houses. In the period between 1880 and 1920, opera houses flourished in communities across South Carolina. Beginning in the 1880s, as the state recovered from the Civil War, opera houses provided live entertainment for citizens who were able to afford leisure activities. By 1915 there were opera houses in Columbia, Sumter, Greenville, Florence, Newberry, Darlington, Laurens, Marion, Abbeville, and Bishopville, among other communities.

Especially in the larger towns, opera houses were imposing, architecturally distinctive buildings with elaborate interiors. Newberry's three-story brick opera house, featuring a bell tower, was constructed in 1882. Sumter's 1893 opera house was a three-story, Richardson Romanesque stone structure with a one-hundred–foot clock tower. Columbia's second opera house, built in 1900, was three stories with two towers. It had a large stage, concealed overhead machinery for curtains and scenery, an orchestra pit, spectator boxes, and two galleries. In smaller communities, opera houses were more modest and often located on the second floor of multi-purpose buildings. For example, the opera house in Laurens was situated above the city hall, and Marion's opera house was on the second floor of a building that housed the courtroom, jail, and fire department on the first floor.

"Road shows" that traveled the country provided dramatic productions, musical comedies, operas, minstrel shows, and other live entertainment. Columbia's opera house booked Broadway hits and stars such as Sarah Bernhardt, Ethel Barrymore, Lillian Russell, and Nat Goodwin. Even in a smaller community such as Abbeville, special trains brought theater patrons from nearby towns to see traveling shows such as the *Klansman, Yankee Drummer,* the Ziegfield Follies, or an escape artist. The Marion Opera House featured traveling theatrical companies as well as local talent.

By the 1930s the new sound movies had eclipsed live entertainment, and some of the opera houses converted to motion picture theaters. By 1941 *South Carolina: A Guide to the Palmetto State* reported, "Most of the old opera houses in the State have now been pre-empted for movie theatres." In the decades after 1930 most of the opera houses in the state were demolished. A few survived,

Still in use today as a contemporary performance venue, the Newberry Opera House was constructed in 1881. Courtesy, South Caroliniana Library, University of South Carolina

however, and in the last decades of the twentieth century several of them were restored, including the Abbeville Opera House, the Sumter Opera House, the Marion Opera House, and the Newberry Opera House. MARY W. EDMONDS

National Register of Historic Places files. State Historic Preservation Office, South Carolina Department of Archives and History, Columbia.

Operation Lost Trust. Operation Lost Trust was arguably South Carolina's largest and longest-running political scandal. Including the investigation, trials, and retrials, the Operation Lost Trust saga extended from 1989 to 1999. The key player in the FBI's investigation into legislative corruption was Ron Cobb, a lobbyist and former member of the S.C. House of Representatives. He was arrested in April 1989 for trying to buy a kilo of cocaine in a deal orchestrated by the FBI for the purpose of securing his involvement as the front man in the Lost Trust investigation. He told members of the General Assembly that he represented the Alpha Group that was seeking support for a bill legalizing dog- and horse-track betting in South Carolina. Cobb recruited Representatives Robert A. Kohn and Luther Taylor to help in securing legislative votes by paying members money in exchange for their support and votes. The transactions were captured on surveillance tapes.

The federal investigation resulted in the conviction of seventeen members of the South Carolina General Assembly, seven lobbyists, and three others for bribery, extortion, or drug use. All but five of the twenty-seven convictions were the result of guilty pleas. In 1991 and 1992 five legislators were granted new trials because of legal errors. U.S. District Judge Falcon Hawkins then dismissed the charges against the five for alleged misconduct by the federal prosecution team led by U.S. Attorney Bart Daniel. Judge Hawkins's ruling was overturned in November 1998 by the Fourth U.S. Circuit Court of Appeals, which reinstated the criminal charges. During the period between 1991 and 1998 two of the five legislators died after long illnesses. The three remaining defendants were retried in 1999, and all three were convicted. JON B. PIERCE

Green, Richard, Jr. "Retrials to Begin in Ongoing Lost Trust Saga." Charleston *Post and Courier,* May 23, 1999, pp. A1, A14.

Kropf, Schuyler. "Blanding Faces Final Retrial in Lost Trust." Charleston *Post and Courier,* August 15, 1999, p. B2.

———. "Cobb Finds Some Good in His Lost Trust Role." Charleston *Post and Courier,* August 23, 1999, pp. A1, A9.

Opportunity Schools. The first Opportunity School in South Carolina was organized under the direction of the State Department of Education as an experiment in adult education. Dr. Wil Lou Gray, the state supervisor of adult education, created a boarding school for young people who could not attend public school or who had not gone further than the fifth grade. The school opened August 2, 1921, at the Tamassee DAR (Daughters of American Revolution) School in Oconee County. Its primary purpose was to offer undereducated young white women the opportunity to secure intensive instruction during a summer residential experience. Some seventeen women registered as boarders at Tamassee and received instruction from one paid teacher and several volunteers from Winthrop College and the surrounding community.

Opportunity Schools were patterned after Cora Wilson Stewart's Moonlight Schools in Kentucky and named after Emily Griffith's Opportunity School in Denver, Colorado. Inspired in part by the Danish "folk school" concept, the South Carolina Opportunity Schools were based on the premise that a central place was needed where students could learn in an environment free from the pressures of grades, academic standing, degrees, and exams. Residential adult education meant living together, taking meals together, and sharing responsibilities and experiences. The initial goal was to acculturate unschooled, rural mill workers into modern society, especially in the realm of citizenship. Schools offered instruction in reading, writing, arithmetic, spelling, health habits, civics, good manners, domestic science (including hygiene), and arts and crafts work. The virtues of faith in God and country were instilled through the curricular focus on middle-class concepts of culture, including religion, morals, manners, etiquette, and citizenship. For example, students read *Bible Story Reader* and *Country Life Reader* and memorized the Twenty-third Psalm.

The Tamassee experiment led to further efforts to provide evening classes and short-term schools for two or more hours a day during slack periods of agricultural and mill employment. On November 1, 1921, Gray met in Lancaster with the Board of Education of the Upper South Carolina Methodist Conference and outlined a plan that called for one or two colleges to open during August to teach the "three Rs," supplemented by courses in citizenship and, for women, courses in domestic arts. Clemson, Anderson, Erskine, and Lander colleges donated their campuses for one-month sessions, and enrollment continued to increase.

In 1931 the Opportunity School became coeducational for the first time at Clemson College. Five years later the Opportunity School for Negroes opened at Voorhees Industrial School in Denmark. In 1947 the General Assembly appropriated $65,000 to be used for year-round adult schooling. That same year a site on the Columbia Army Air Base became the permanent home of the Opportunity School. Programs expanded in the late 1960s to include undereducated military veterans and clients from Vocational Rehabilitation, CETA / Job Corps, Department of Social Services, dropouts, truants from Juvenile Justice, the National Guard, and state school systems. At the start of the twenty-first century, the Opportunity School continued as an alternative educational source aimed at reaching out to teenagers or young adults who had not completed high school, while meeting the educational needs of the state. SUSAN L. SCHRAMM

Ayres, DaMaris E. *Let My People Learn: The Biography of Dr. Wil Lou Gray.* Greenwood, S.C.: Attic Press, 1988.

Carlton, David L. *Mill and Town in South Carolina, 1880–1920.* Baton Rouge: Louisiana State University Press, 1982.

Gray, William S., Wil Lou Gray, and J. W. Tilton. *The Opportunity Schools of South Carolina, An Experimental Study* New York: American Association for Adult Education, 1932.

Orangeburg (Orangeburg County; 2000 pop. 12,765). Orangeburg is the county seat of one of South Carolina's richest agricultural regions. The town originated with the arrival of 220 German-Swiss immigrants in 1735, who settled along the North Edisto River. These "Switzers" became prosperous farmers, growing wheat, rice, and indigo and shipping timber downriver to Charleston. The first Lutheran congregation in the state was established at Orangeburg; it converted to the Anglican faith in 1750 under the leadership of the Reverend John Giessendanner. Prior to the Revolutionary War, Orangeburg was described as "neatly laid out," but vulnerable to Indian attack, for which several "block houses," or forts, were constructed. In 1768 the colonial government designated Orangeburg as the seat of the Orangeburg judicial district.

Orangeburg played a strategic role during the Revolutionary War, and the town changed hands several times between 1781 and 1782. Generals Thomas Sumter, Francis Marion, and Nathanael Greene all camped or skirmished at Orangeburg, while Governor John Rutledge established his office temporarily at the Donald Bruce House in 1780.

Robert Mills counted just 152 residents (black and white) in Orangeburg during the mid-1820s. But by 1831 the village had grown enough to warrant incorporation by the General Assembly. The railroad reached Orangeburg in August 1840, providing a valuable link between the area's burgeoning plantation economy and the port of Charleston. Antebellum Orangeburg was a nullification and secession stronghold. The proslavery writers George Frederick Holmes and William Gilmore Simms lived nearby, and native son David Flavel Jamison, who helped found the Citadel, presided over the South Carolina Secession Convention. The Union army of General William T. Sherman arrived in February 1865, camping at Orangeburg's Caw Caw Swamp en route to Columbia. Union horses were stabled in the First Baptist Church, and blocks of buildings were set on fire, including the courthouse and railroad depot.

The drama of Reconstruction and the New South played out in microcosm in Orangeburg. Spurred by the resistance of white planters to their new status as free laborers, three black delegates from Orangeburg attended the Colored Peoples Convention in Charleston in November 1865 to petition Congress and the General Assembly for redress against the repressive Black Codes, an action that precipitated Radical Reconstruction. After the withdrawal of federal troops from South Carolina in 1877, Samuel Dibble of Orangeburg devised South Carolina's gerrymandered congressional districts (1882) to dilute the strength of the state's black majority. By the mid-1890s the local newspaper reported that "many colored folks" were leaving the area for Georgia and points west. Despite the exodus, the establishment of Claflin College (1869) and South Carolina State Agricultural and Mechanical College (1896) made Orangeburg a haven for black intellectuals and political activists, and the center of African American education in South Carolina. The *People's Recorder,* a black newspaper, relocated from Columbia to Orangeburg in 1903; a progressive black women's club movement took root in 1911 under the leadership of Mrs. Robert Shaw Wilkinson; a National Association for the Advancement of Colored People (NAACP) chapter of seventy-eight members was established in 1919; and the luminaries Langston Hughes, Mary Bethune McLeod, and George Schuyler visited and lectured at the State College campus.

During the Great Depression the city's banks failed and relief rolls swelled. The New Deal and World War II broke some of Orangeburg's cultural isolation, bringing bureaucrats to administer extensive Works Progress Administration and Civilian Conservation Corps projects; thousands of soldiers, including British and French, received flight training at the Hawthorne School of Aeronautics. In the wake of the 1954 U.S. Supreme Court decision in *Brown v. Board of Education,* fifty-seven black residents petitioned the Orangeburg school board to end segregation locally. The white Citizens Council, under the leadership of W. T. C. Bates, retaliated by firing petitioners from their jobs and boycotting black-owned businesses. Throughout the 1950s and 1960s counterboycotts, sit-ins, and picketing by the students of Claflin and South Carolina State led to mass arrests and investigations, culminating in the Orangeburg Massacre on February 8, 1968. In the midst of this turmoil, Dr. T. E. Wannamaker of Orangeburg helped found the South Carolina Independent School Association and two segregated academies, Wade Hampton and Willington, where the Confederate flag flew and a majority of the town's white students were enrolled. Wannamaker's brother, W. W. Jr., played a key role in the reinvention of the state's Republican Party during the 1950s and 1960s, laying the groundwork for an exodus of white Democrats in the decades that followed.

Agriculture is still predominant, but the local economy has diversified to include international manufacturing concerns. The chamber of commerce has successfully marketed the Edisto Memorial Gardens and its Festival of Roses as an annual springtime destination, drawing thousands of visitors to a resplendent display of roses along the banks of the Edisto River. In spite of its economic advances, Orangeburg in the early twenty-first century remained a community polarized by race. ELIZABETH ROBESON

Ackerman, Hugo S. *A Brief History of Orangeburg.* Columbia, S.C.: Home Federal Savings and Loan Association, [1970?].

Bass, Jack, and Jack Nelson. *The Orangeburg Massacre.* 2d ed. Macon, Ga.: Mercer University Press, 1996.

Culler, Daniel Marchant. *Orangeburgh District, 1768–1868: History and Records.* Spartanburg, S.C.: Reprint Company, 1995.

Salley, Alexander S. *The History of Orangeburg County, South Carolina from Its First Settlement to the Close of the Revolutionary War.* 1898. Reprint, Baltimore: Regional Publishing, 1969.

Orangeburg County (1,106 sq. miles; 2000 pop. 91,582). Created by the Circuit Court Act of 1769, Orangeburg District initially stretched south from Edgefield and Newberry to Beaufort, and between the Congaree and Savannah Rivers. European settlement began in 1735, when some two hundred German Lutherans migrated from Switzerland and established a village on the north fork of the Edisto River, which they named "Orangeburgh" in honor of William IV, Prince of Orange. Over the next three decades these German-Swiss were joined by English, Scots-Irish, and French settlers, as well as a small number of African slaves. These new arrivals suffered through the violent disruptions of the Cherokee War and Regulator movement in the 1760s. The Revolutionary War bitterly divided the district population, with many Orangeburg Germans siding with the British. Opposing military forces swept back and forth across Orangeburg District in a series of clashes in 1781, which included the botched American victory on September 5 at Eutaw Springs.

In the ensuing decades, the boundaries of Orangeburg District shrank while its plantation economy expanded. Portions of Orangeburg went to create the counties of Barnwell (1800), Lexington (1804), Aiken (1871), Bamberg (1897), and Calhoun (1908). The district's economy grew rapidly in the nineteenth century as cotton and slavery profoundly altered society and culture. In 1790 the district had 12,412 white people, 5,931 slaves, and 170 free people of color. By 1860 the white population had declined to 8,108 while the number of slaves nearly tripled to 16,583, and the free black population was 205. In 1860 there were 1,069 slaveowners in the district, thirty-three of which held over 100 slaves. Orangeburg's farms and plantations produced sixteen thousand bales of cotton in 1860, as well as sizable quantities of corn, wheat, oats, rice, sweet potatoes, and wool. In addition, the district contained two carriage factories and several lumber mills, especially along the timber-rich Edisto River. Orangeburg District was also a prominent link in the state's transportation system. The Congaree, Santee, and Edisto Rivers were important navigable waterways, while the State Road between Charleston and Columbia ran through St. Matthews, Cameron, and Holly Hill. In 1833 part of the South Carolina Canal and Rail Road Company's railroad crossed the southern part of Orangeburg. With the construction of a branch line to Columbia, the world's first railroad junction was created at Branchville in 1840.

Religion loomed larger in the lives of most antebellum residents than did public education. There were seventy-one Protestant congregations including forty Methodist, twenty-one Baptist, six Lutheran, three Episcopalian, and one Presbyterian. The Methodists periodically licensed black men to preach. However, there were no public schools in the district during the antebellum era, nor was there a newspaper until the *Edisto Clarion* began publication in 1854. The commitment to cotton and slavery inspired a fierce defense of states' rights. With the firing on Fort Sumter, white men from Orangeburg rallied to the Confederate cause. The Edisto Rifles served with the First South Carolina Regiment and absorbed terrible losses before the conflict ended. In early 1865 General William T. Sherman's Union army cut a path of destruction through the district. With emancipation, former slaves formed schools, churches, and small businesses. During Reconstruction, at least twelve African Americans represented the county in the General Assembly. Marshall Jones, a Democrat who served from 1886 to 1887, was the last black legislator from Orangeburg until the election of Earl Middleton and John Matthews in 1974.

At the turn of the century, cotton remained the economic mainstay. In 1900 the county produced 65,000 bales of cotton on 118,000 acres of land, and in 1918 Orangeburg was the nation's second ranking county in cotton production. However, shared attachment to cotton production did not create unity among blacks and whites. Dissatisfied black cotton pickers struck unsuccessfully for higher wages in 1891. Violence against African Americans was common. Seven black people were lynched between 1897 and 1914, including one woman. The Ku Klux Klan terrorized residents during the 1920s.

Railroad service expanded during the early twentieth century. The Atlantic Coast Line and the Seaboard Airline Railway provided much of the freight and passenger service in Orangeburg. Short line railroads provided service to smaller towns, such as the B&B Railroad that ran from Bowman to Branchville and the Creston-Four Holes Railway that served Elloree, Milligan, Vance, Eutawville, and Holly Hill. The boll weevil and the Great Depression forced the decline of Orangeburg's devotion to cotton. Corn, soybeans, poultry, hogs, and dairy farming gradually claimed many former cotton fields. Many residents, especially African Americans, abandoned the land and migrated to towns or moved north. The Depression brought extreme privation. Only three of the county's banks survived the decade. New Deal programs alleviated some of the misery by bringing sidewalks to Elloree; schools to Canaan, North, and Vance; and a Tri-County hospital to Orangeburg. World War II saw the construction of an air base at North and a pilot training facility near Orangeburg that prepared more than four thousand American and sixteen hundred French aviators. Tourism increased after the war, and U.S. Highway 301 became the principal route between New York and Florida until the completion of Interstate 95 in 1977.

Education underwent difficult advances in the latter half of the twentieth century. Though black parents in Elloree and Orangeburg had petitioned for integration as early as 1955, schools were not effectively desegregated until the 1971–1972 school year. In the meantime several all-white private academies had been created. By the 1990s there was a unified school system with three consolidated districts. Though agriculture remained vital to the county's economy (the value of Orangeburg's agricultural production ranked second among South Carolina counties in 1999), industry assumed an increasingly larger role. By the end of the century, Orangeburg County manufacturers produced chemicals, bearings, wire and cable, diesel pistons, brake pads, lawn mowers, and wood products.

Industrial growth was helped by the founding of the Orangeburg-Calhoun Technical Education Center in 1969. WILLIAM C. HINE

Ackerman, Hugo S. *A Brief History of Orangeburg.* Columbia, S.C.: Home Federal Savings and Loan Association, [1970?].

Culler, Daniel Marchant. *Orangeburgh District 1768–1868: History and Records.* Spartanburg, S.C.: Reprint Company, 1995.

Reflections in Time. Orangeburg, S.C.: Times and Democrat, 1999.

Salley, Alexander S. *The History of Orangeburg County, South Carolina from Its First Settlement to the Close of the Revolutionary War.* 1898. Reprint, Baltimore: Regional Publishing, 1969.

Orangeburg Massacre (February 8, 1968). On the night of February 8, 1968, police gunfire left three young black men dying and twenty-seven wounded on the campus of South Carolina State College in Orangeburg. Exactly thirty-three years later, Governor Jim Hodges addressed an overflow crowd there in the Martin Luther King, Jr. Auditorium, referring directly to the "Orangeburg Massacre"—an identifying term for the event that had been controversial—and called what happened "a great tragedy for our state."

The audience that day included eight men in their fifties—including a clergyman, a college professor, and a retired army lieutenant colonel—who had been shot that fateful night. For the first time they were included in the annual memorial service to the three students who died—Samuel Hammond, Delano Middleton, and Henry Smith. Their deaths, more than two years before the gunfire by Ohio National Guardsmen that killed four on the campus of Kent State University, marked the first such tragedy on any American college campus.

The shooting occurred after three nights of escalating racial tension over efforts by South Carolina State students and others to desegregate the All Star Bowling Lanes. On Monday night, January 29, 1968, six black students entered the bowling alley. As planned, one of the college's two white students had preceded them and was bowling when they entered. When the others asked for bowling lanes, they were told the bowling alley was private. Pointing to the white student, they asked how the bowling alley could be private when a schoolmate was bowling and he was not a member. The white student was ordered to stop bowling, and the students were told to leave. A week later, more than a dozen students returned to the bowling alley. This time bowling alley operator Harry Floyd called the police. The police chief and city administrator evaluated the situation, determined it was explosive, and ordered the alley to close for the night.

The next night at the bowling alley, some students voluntarily had themselves arrested in order to contest trespass charges. As volunteers were escorted to patrol cars, another student told hundreds attending a movie about the arrests. Students poured out of the auditorium and headed downtown. Highway patrolmen carrying riot batons joined local police in front of the bowling alley. One officer reported that he swung his baton and hit someone after a caustic liquid was thrown in his face. Other officers quickly joined in. By evening's end, a policeman and ten students received hospital treatment for injuries, and others were treated at the campus infirmary.

Students returning to campus vented their anger on white-owned businesses, throwing bricks, rocks, and sticks of firewood. In the wake of major urban riots the previous year across America, the state responded as though it were a major civil disorder. Total insurance claims for damages that night, however, amounted to less than $5,000.

On Wednesday, Governor Robert E. McNair called in 250 National Guardsmen and additional highway patrolmen. The day began with city officials meeting with students and staff in the campus auditorium. Students hooted when officials were unable to answer specific grievances. Official attention soon focused on twenty-three-year-old Cleveland Sellers, who had returned to his native South Carolina as third-ranking officer in the Student Nonviolent Coordinating Committee (SNCC) after several years on the front lines of civil rights struggle in Alabama and Mississippi. Frustrated students that night pelted passing cars, and police blockaded the highway. Rumors of "black power" threats spread, merchants armed themselves, and tension continued to mount. Sellers told a reporter Thursday afternoon, "Everyone is looking for a scapegoat."

The shooting occurred at 10:38 that night, after students lit a bonfire and a patrolman advancing to protect firemen was knocked down by a thrown object that bloodied his face. About five minutes later, as taunting students who had retreated into the campus interior headed back toward the bonfire, a patrolman fired a carbine into the air, intended as warning shots. Instead, it triggered a fusillade of police gunfire. The Associated Press misreported the episode as "a heavy exchange of gunfire," but evidence later revealed that while some objects were thrown at police, there was no exchange of gunfire. The students were unarmed. Of sixty-six patrolmen on the scene, nine later told Federal Bureau of Investigation agents they had fired at the students after hearing shots. Some fired more than once. Eight fired riot guns, short-barrel shotguns designed to disperse a crowd or mob, not to maim or kill. The ammunition issued for the riot guns was lethal buckshot, shells used by deer hunters that contain nine to twelve pellets as large as .38 caliber pistol slugs. A ninth patrolman said he fired his service revolver six times as "a spontaneous reaction to the situation," and at least one city policeman fired a shotgun. The gunfire lasted at least eight to ten seconds. No National Guardsmen fired weapons.

When the fire truck arrived to put out the bonfire, Sellers left a room on the campus to see what was happening. He was shot in the armpit. After being identified at the hospital by the sheriff's only black deputy, he was taken to the courthouse, charged with a variety of crimes, and speedily taken to the state penitentiary in Columbia.

At a noon press conference the next day in Columbia, Governor McNair called it "one of the saddest days in the history of South Carolina" and expressed concern that the state's "reputation for racial harmony has been blemished." Three years later, in his final address to the legislature, McNair referred to what happened at Orangeburg as "a scar on our state's conscience."

In the months that followed the shooting, after a grand jury refused to indict the nine patrolmen, U.S. Attorney General Ramsey Clark tried the patrolmen on criminal charges. A jury took less than two hours to acquit the patrolmen on grounds of self-defense. In an interview years later, one of those defendants, Joseph Howard "Red" Lanier, Jr., after serving as Highway Patrol commander, expressed remorse about what had happened and acknowledged that the patrolmen had been "poorly trained."

Meanwhile Sellers was convicted in 1970 of "riot" for his actions at the bowling alley on Tuesday and served seven months in minimum security. He went on to earn a doctorate from the University of North Carolina at Greensboro to go with a master's degree from Harvard he received before going to prison. He later returned to South Carolina, and in 1993 the University of South Carolina hired Sellers as director for its program in African American studies. JACK BASS

Bass, Jack "The Trial of Cleveland Sellers." *New South* (fall 1970): 18–22.

Bass, Jack, and Jack Nelson. *The Orangeburg Massacre.* 2d ed. Macon, Ga.: Mercer University Press, 1996.

Salley, Alexander S. *The History of Orangeburg County, South Carolina from Its First Settlement to the Close of the Revolutionary War.* 1898. Reprint, Baltimore: Regional Publishing, 1969.

Orangeburg Scarp. The Orangeburg Scarp is a wave-cut, steep incline that forms the boundary between the upper and middle coastal plains. This escarpment cuts diagonally across South Carolina, passing near or through parts of Bennettsville, Hartsville, Sumter, Columbia, Orangeburg, and Allendale. As the scarp traverses the state, it reaches heights ranging from 180 to 215 feet above sea level.

The Orangeburg Scarp represents the limit of the ocean during the middle Pliocene epoch. As Earth's climate changed over time, and as the processes of plate tectonics produced more or less lava on Earth's surface, sea levels rose and fell repeatedly over millions of years. This resulted in worldwide sea level changes, the evidences of which are various escarpments visible along the edges of continents. The Orangeburg Scarp is a large, dramatic example that runs from North Carolina to Florida.

The Orangeburg Scarp can be seen in many places across the state. It is easily seen near the city of Orangeburg as it forms a steep grade down to the much flatter terrain of the lower coastal plain. It is also found along the Congaree and Wateree River valleys. In Columbia many important sites lie on the Orangeburg Scarp, including the State House and much of the campus of the University of South Carolina. During the late Pliocene sea levels fell dramatically, and as the sea levels fell, much smaller escarpments formed over the coastal plain, named the Parler, Surry, Dorchester, Summerville, and Bethera Scarps. The current escarpment forming in South Carolina is called the Cainhoy Scarp, found at the coast. CAROLYN H. MURPHY

Murphy, Carolyn H. *Carolina Rocks! The Geology of South Carolina.* Orangeburg, S.C.: Sandlapper, 1995.

Orangeburgh Township. Originally entitled "Edisto," but renamed by its German-speaking Swiss inhabitants to honor William IV, Prince of Orange-Nassau, the 48,000-acre Orangeburgh Township was situated on the North Fork of the Edisto River. A few English-speaking non-German settlers were present in the area from the early 1730s, but active settlement began in 1735, when the first organized immigration of 220 German-Swiss settlers arrived. These were not indentured servants, but were provisioned by the colonial government, granted land, and exempted from taxes for ten years. More German-Swiss immigrants joined them there in subsequent years, so that by the mid-1750s, 45,000 acres had been granted in tracts of 200 acres or less and the township was home to some 800 people. Shepherded by its Lutheran pastor John Ulrich Giessendanner and the Anglican priest John Giessendanner, the German village soon developed into a tightly knit, small farming community and transportation center. Orangeburgh's farmers grew hemp, indigo, and rice and produced enough wheat to help South Carolina reduce its dependence on imported flour from Philadelphia. A few merchants with Charleston connections established businesses there in the 1750s, and a circuit court was established at the village of Orangeburgh in 1769, whereupon the land was resurveyed and a town laid out. By the eve of the Revolutionary War, Orangeburgh Township had been incorporated into St. Matthew's Parish (along with Amelia Township) and was a prosperous German community. MICHAEL EVERETTE BELL

Meriwether, Robert Lee. *The Expansion of South Carolina, 1729–1765.* Kingsport, Tenn.: Southern Publishers, 1940.

Oratory. In the antebellum era and well into the twentieth century, oratory flourished in South Carolina as the expression and reflection of the values of the white male population. Orators described and defended those values in ways that were appreciated by their audiences; they were respected and at times revered as folk heroes. Throughout the South, oratory was the focus of southern life for rural and small-town audiences who had few other entertainments and little connection to the larger world. The impact of oratory was evident, from frequent joint debates held in most political campaigns, to Sunday sermonizing and summer camp meeting revivals, to courtroom lawyers arguing before their juries and large audiences of spectators, to ceremonial occasions such as the Fourth of July. In sum, oratory was a prime means of public education in the issues of the day, religious instruction, and public commemoration. South Carolinians practiced it as well as any other southerners, and better than most.

The love and practice of oratory did not emerge full-grown in antebellum South Carolina. South Carolina College, where training and experience in public speaking was a central focus of higher education, was a hothouse for developing orators. Within a year of the 1805 opening of the college, the first literary and debating club, the Philomathic Society, was organized. Less than a year later it was split into two nearly identical fraternal groups, the Clariosophic and the Euphradian societies. Over the next half-century, virtually every student at South Carolina College belonged to one or the other of these societies, where they heard and presented many a declamation or original oration and debated timely political, social, religious, and historical questions. Students understood, as did most educated southerners, that the supreme skill for a leader was oratory. An early historian of the college called the societies "the nursery of eloquence" and asserted that they provided a strong career start for "many of the distinguished men of Carolina."

One of those distinguished men of Carolina was William C. Preston, called by some South Carolina's Cicero. Preston was considered the "most finished orator of the Southern school." But Preston was only one among many stars in the South Carolina oratorical gallery. In a region that held eloquence in the highest regard, the Palmetto State set the standard for the rest of the South. Probably no other southern state had as many outstanding well-known speakers in the antebellum years. Preston, Hugh Swinton Legaré, John C. Calhoun, James H. Hammond, James Hamilton, Dr. Thomas Cooper, Robert Y. Hayne, William Harper, and George McDuffie held their large and appreciative audiences enthralled by their rhetoric. The large issues of states' rights, nullification, slavery, and impending war provided more than enough impetus for their oratory.

The tradition continued long after the Civil War, focusing primarily on political stump speaking and ceremonial oratory; it was the era of the "southern demagogue" and the "Lost Cause." After Wade Hampton's oratorical recollections of the Civil War helped to "redeem" South Carolina from Reconstruction, Benjamin "Pitchfork Ben" Tillman, Coleman Blease, and Ellison "Cotton Ed" Smith held forth on the hustings, defending the small farmer and upholding white supremacy and racial separation. Their oratory, based on fear tactics and emotion rather than reasoning and valid evidence, exploited the poor whites' ability to vote, their deplorable economic conditions, and their long-standing fear of their black neighbors who were just below them on the economic ladder. Attacking scapegoats such as Wall Street, corporations, railroads, Jews, immigrants, and especially blacks, their language was violent and unrestrained, but they spoke for the little guys in the state who, up to that point, had felt they had no spokesmen.

Another prime venue for oratory in postbellum years, extending well into the twentieth century, was the ubiquitous ceremonial address proclaiming the "Lost Cause." Delivered at countless Confederate veterans' reunions, monument dedications, and Confederate Decoration Day ceremonies throughout South Carolina and the South, this oratorical genre created, glorified, and sustained a mythology of the Old South, the Civil War, and Reconstruction that remained alive long after the last veteran and commemorative orator were in their graves. Remnants of this oratory were still being heard in debates across the state over the placing of the Confederate flag on the State House grounds at the end of the twentieth century.

While radio, television, mass entertainment, and the Internet have made oratory mostly obsolete as a form of education and entertainment, it does continue in perhaps the only, certainly the leading, example of the old tradition of "stump" speaking left in America: the Galivants Ferry Stump Meeting. This popular political event is held every two years on the first or second Monday in May and is highly important in the tradition of South Carolina politics. Begun by Wade Hampton in 1876, this affair has continued unabated and in the early twenty-first century still drew as many as five thousand South Carolinians. W. STUART TOWNS

Braden, Waldo W., ed. *Oratory in the Old South.* Baton Rouge: Louisiana State University Press, 1970.

Logue, Cal M., and Howard Dorgan, eds. *The Oratory of Southern Demagogues.* Baton Rouge: Louisiana State University Press, 1981.

Towns, W. Stuart. *Oratory and Rhetoric in the Nineteenth-Century South: A Rhetoric of Defense.* Westport, Conn.: Praeger, 1998.

———. *Public Address in the Twentieth-Century South: The Evolution of a Region.* Westport, Conn.: Praeger, 1999.

Order of the Palmetto, Order of the Silver Crescent. The Order of the Palmetto was instituted by Governor John C. West in 1971. The honor is awarded by the governor to an individual "in grateful recognition of your contributions and friendship to the State of South Carolina and her people." The honoree receives a certificate signed by the governor and bearing an impression of the state seal. The certificate, designed by the Department of Parks, Recreation and Tourism, features a background image of a palmetto. The award is thought to have been modeled on the Commonwealth of Kentucky's practice of awarding the title of "Colonel" to its honorees.

Concerned that the great numbers of awards might lessen its value, Governor Jim Hodges appointed a screening committee to review nominations and make recommendations for the Order of the Palmetto and other gubernatorial awards. Originally the award bestowed on the recipient the honorary title of "Palmetto Gentleman" or "Palmetto Lady," without any actual attendant rights or privileges. In December 2001 Hodges adopted a new format for the certificate of award, on the recommendation of the screening committee. This omitted the titles "Palmetto Lady (or Gentleman)" in order "to eliminate the distinction between male and female recipients of the award." As of October 2004 over 3,500 Order of the Palmetto Awards have been made.

The Order of the Silver Crescent was initiated by Governor David Beasley in 1997 as a companion award to the Order of the Palmetto and was intended to honor the achievements of South Carolinians aged eighteen or younger. In May 1999 Governor Hodges determined that the Silver Crescent would be awarded to persons of any age for exemplary community contributions and achievements. Each honoree received a certificate decorated with a large crescent moon, signed by the governor, and bearing the governor's seal of office. DAVID C. R. HEISSER

"State Recognition: Order of the Palmetto." Columbia *State,* July 7, 1971, p. B13.

Organized labor. Organized labor in South Carolina has antebellum, perhaps colonial, roots. As early as 1742 white shipwrights in Charleston officially protested allegedly unfair competition from slave labor. Charleston workingmen (1768), mechanics (1794), clerks (1825), and carpenters (1826) organized for patriotic, charitable, or social purposes but apparently not for economic purposes. Charleston typographers formed the first union in South Carolina in 1834 and affiliated with the National Typographical Workers Union, the first national union in the United States. The typographers also introduced South Carolina to union-initiated strikes, in 1852 against the *Charleston Evening News* and the *Charleston Courier* and again in 1860 and 1861, probably over wages. Interestingly, the typographical local was initially reluctant to secede from its national union in 1861. Three years later workers at the Graniteville Manufacturing Company in Edgefield District staged the first known protest by industrial workers in the state.

Emancipation and Reconstruction opened new opportunities for organized labor. Black longshoremen unionized in 1867, beginning the longest living union in the state. The longshoremen aggressively defended their interests during Reconstruction. In 1873 workers in area lumber mills and phosphate mines joined a strike that the longshoremen initiated. The long depression of the 1870s and the fall of Republican state government undermined such strike threats. The depression did not, however, preclude a short, violent strike at Graniteville in 1874.

The economic revival of the 1880s provided a more congenial atmosphere for unionizing. As was true elsewhere in the United States, organized labor was generally more successful in urban areas and among skilled workers. Craft unions expanded their numbers, and a more inclusive unionism found expression in the Knights of Labor, whose growth surged in 1886 into a nation-wide phenomenon. The Knights had a transitory following in Charleston, Columbia, Darlington, Fishing Creek, and the Horse Creek Valley. The Knights took the unusual step of attempting to unionize blacks and whites, usually in segregated locals in the white supremacist South. These attempts involved considerable risk: a Knight organizer who worked in South Carolina and Georgia was lynched in Georgia. One spin-off of the Knights was the short-lived United Labor Party, which ran a candidate in the 1887 mayoral race in Charleston. Columbia's first Labor Day parade, a large, two-day celebration in 1891, indicated that craft unions had greater staying powers than the Knights did.

When the devastating 1890s depression ended, unionization efforts resumed among craft workers and even among some industrial workers. South Carolina's rapidly expanding cotton-manufacturing industry briefly (1900–1902) attracted organizing efforts by the National Union of Textile Workers and its successor, the United Textile Workers. That union had locals in Abbeville, Anderson, Bath, Greenville, the Horse Creek Valley, Rock Hill, Westminster, and

Columbia. The last local, which had one thousand members, was at one time the largest textile local in the world. The local led Columbia's Labor Day Parade in 1900. A year later the local wilted after it was defeated in a major strike against the Granby and Olympia mills in Columbia. The radical Industrial Workers of the World (or "Wobblies") even made an ephemeral if showy appearance in the state. The Wobblies had a local at Fishing Creek in 1914. They probably startled Greenville residents when more than seven hundred of them marched under the Red Flag in the upcountry town, a center of the emerging New South.

Craft unions had deeper roots in the state. The official program of the 1908 Labor Day celebration in Columbia listed twenty-one different craft unions, from barbers, bookbinders, and carpenters, to glassblowers, loom fixers, machinists, painters, tailors, typographers, and weavers. Several merchants placed special advertisements for union members in the program. One boasted that all of his clerks were union members. In 1917 craft unions in the state created the South Carolina Federation of Labor, an affiliate of the American Federation of Labor.

The booming economy of World War I provided unprecedented opportunities for unionization. The ranks of organized labor soared among craft and industrial workers. As elsewhere, this growth declined when the economy slumped drastically after the war ended. The United Textile Workers were particularly damaged by production and wage cuts in textiles in the immediate postwar years. To make matters worse, textiles, the state's largest industry, generally experienced a long-term slump during most of the 1920s, which deepened with the Great Depression of the 1930s.

Cotton manufacturers responded by reducing their workforces and by the "stretch-out"—steep increases in workloads without increases in pay. Desperate and angry, mill hands struck back. In 1929 they engaged in a series of strikes, most notably at Ware Shoals, the site of the only union-led of these strikes. These actions led to a legislative hearing and a report from the South Carolina General Assembly that criticized management. Some in the legislature even proposed legal limits on the number of machines assigned to a worker.

President Franklin Roosevelt and his New Deal offered a very different approach to labor relations than what had prevailed before. Encouraged by the collective bargaining provisions of the National Industrial Recovery Act (1933) and a sympathetic president in the White House, mill hands eagerly joined the United Textile Workers in 1933 and 1934. Greenville textile workers conducted a major, largely unsuccessful strike in 1933, almost a year before the great General Textile Strike. In early September 1934 tens of thousands of South Carolina's textile workers left their looms, some eagerly joining "flying squadrons" of strikers who traveled from mill to mill to call out workers and close plants. Violence and intimidation took place, for which both the strikers and their opponents were to blame. Deaths also occurred, the worst at Honea Path in Anderson County where seven striking workers died. Management, supported by local and state authorities, crushed the strike. Governor Ibra Blackwood weighed in heavily on the side of management and against the strike.

Workers returned to mills where the stretch-out continued and where employers, who abided by the National Industrial Recovery Act only when it suited them, refused to recognize the union or to bargain collectively. However, some employers may have modified some of the labor practices that workers grieved. Many workers were not allowed to return to the mills: companies blacklisted them for life, often colluding with each other in industrywide blackballing.

The defeat of the 1934 strike, one of the largest in American history, may have harmed subsequent efforts to unionize the state's textile workers. Some locals struggled on after the strike and served as the seeds for modest successes at unionizing textiles in the late 1930s and during World War II. On the eve of that war, textiles in South Carolina, as in the rest of the South, remained far less unionized than other major American industries. Thus, unions in South Carolina had a small foundation to build on when World War II presented an extraordinary opportunity for expanding the ranks of unions. Despite the modest foundation of organized labor, the number of unionized workers in South Carolina rose from approximately five thousand in 1938 to almost forty thousand in 1948. Although organized labor's ranks had grown by eight hundred percent in one decade, only a little over nine percent of nonfarm workers in the state were in unions.

Unionized workers in Charleston created a lasting legacy in modern American history. The fourteen hundred black and white employees at an American Tobacco Company plant that produced cigars unionized during World War II. Angered by their poor pay, miserable working conditions, and arbitrary supervisors, workers staged two sit-down strikes at the plant in 1945, then launched a six-month strike from October 1945 to March 1946. Black women were the prime force in the strike, but white workers readily joined in as the rigid racial barriers that prevailed in the plant collapsed on the picket line. Black women on the line sang "We Shall Overcome," which later became an anthem of the civil rights movement.

After the war, organized labor mounted "Operation Dixie" to expand its weak base in the South, especially in the textile South. This major but inept organizing effort ended quietly in 1951 with few successes. More than ineptitude accounted for the defeat of "Operation Dixie." Employers and business groups mounted a broad offensive against organized labor in order to slow its expansion and to reverse its growth. Textile manufacturers were prominent figures in this broad attack, which had considerable success. Business had substantial political support for its anti-union efforts, support that had been growing since the late 1930s.

The voting record of South Carolina's congressional delegation reflected that growth. In 1935 the delegation had voted solidly for the National Labor Relations Act (or Wagner Act). Three years later the delegation split over the Fair Labor Standards Act (maximum hours, minimum wages), even though it did not cover farm or domestic labor. Opponents alleged, among other things, that the legislation was an attempt by northern employers and unions to use government power to force wages up in the South. They feared that higher wages would make the South less desirable for investors that the South wanted and needed urgently to attract. Most of the delegation thereafter joined efforts to limit the Wagner Act. Most, for instance, voted for the National Labor Relations Act of 1947 (or Taft-Hartley Act). Senator Olin D. Johnston was a notable exception on this vote. Taft-Hartley provided that states could pass "right to work" laws that said that employees had the right to work, even in unionized work places, without joining a union. Non-unionized employees may, however, enjoy the wages and benefits a union has obtained from an employer without paying union dues. South Carolina passed a "right to work" law in 1954. South Carolina officials and business leaders stressed that South Carolina is a "right to work state," a state where unions are not welcome. The South Carolina

Chamber of Commerce has been particularly vocal and active in opposing unions and unionization.

Organized labor reached its peak numerically in the mid-1950s. An element of this was the 1955 organizing victory of the Communications Workers of America at Southern Bell. Generally, however, organized labor has been on the defensive. One of its most memorable, or notorious, defeats occurred in 1956 at Darlington, where Deering, Milliken and Company (now Milliken Company) closed a plant rather than negotiate with workers who had elected to have union representation. The legality of the company's actions was a matter of heated controversy. But the company prevailed in what was part of a statewide trend: marginalizing organized labor in South Carolina in the workplace and in public life. A major theme of the state's economic development efforts since World War II has been to emphasize South Carolina's lower labor costs, a result in part of its largely non-union workforce.

Organized labor had a prominent place in the headlines in 1968. Charleston hospital workers struck to protest their low wages and poor working conditions. The strike developed a coalition of support that combined the civil rights movement and unions. Eventually the hospitals addressed worker grievances but refused to negotiate a contract with a hospital workers union. The hospital strike was also credited with igniting significant growth of participation by blacks in the life and politics of Charleston.

Unionization, however, suffered another defeat in the state when, subsequent to the Charleston strike, the state officially adopted a policy of prohibiting public employees from unionizing and of prohibiting public officials from negotiating with public employee unions. However, some associations of public employees, such as the South Carolina Education Association, have been considered to be quasi-unions. By the early years of the twenty-first century, several local governments had breached the barriers against unions and have, at least informally, negotiated with unionized public employees. Unionized public employees have also engaged in lobbying and in pressure group activities on behalf of their interests. Firefighters are the most unionized local public employees in the state. Local 61, founded in 1918, is the oldest firefighter local in the state. The local was reorganized in 1996. South Carolina policy about unions and public employees does not apply to federal employees in the state, some of whom are unionized, such as postal workers.

Organized labor has attracted much less attention since the Charleston hospital strike, a reflection of the small numbers of organized workers in the state. In 1982 there were almost 68,000 unionized employees in the state, or about 5.8 percent of South Carolina nonfarm workers. Twenty years later the number of unionized employees in the state remained about the same, 73,000; the percentage of unionized salaried and workers was 4.9 percent. South Carolina and North Carolina have the lowest unionization rates in the United States.

Still the South Carolina AFL-CIO remains a presence in the state. The United Auto Workers successfully fought state efforts to break the union's contract with Mack Truck when the company opened a new production facility in Winnsboro in 1987. Unionizing efforts continue, and the AFL-CIO actively lobbies for the interests of its members and often for the interests of all employees in the state. The South Carolina AFL-CIO also has the distinction of being one of the few state AFL-CIOs that has a female president.

TOM TERRILL

Brooks, Robert R. R. "The United Textile Workers of America." Ph.D. diss., Yale University, 1935.

Fink, Leon, and Brian Greenberg. *Upheaval in the Quiet Zone: A History of Hospital Workers' Union, Local 1199.* Urbana: University of Illinois Press, 1989.

Fones-Wolf, Elizabeth A. *Selling Free Enterprise: The Business Assault on Labor and Liberalism, 1945–1960.* Urbana: University of Illinois Press, 1994.

Griffith, Barbara S. *The Crisis of American Labor: Operation Dixie and the Defeat of the CIO.* Philadelphia: Temple University Press, 1988.

Irons, Janet. *Testing the New Deal: The General Textile Strike of 1934 in the American South.* Urbana: University of Illinois Press, 2000.

McLaurin, Melton Alonzo. *The Knights of Labor in the South.* Westport, Conn.: Greenwood, 1978.

———. *Paternalism and Protest: Southern Cotton Mill Workers and Organized Labor, 1875–1905.* Westport, Conn.: Greenwood, 1971.

Mitchell, George Sinclair. *Textile Unionism and the South.* Chapel Hill: University of North Carolina Press, 1931.

Poliakoff, Eli. "Charleston's Longshoremen: Organized Labor in the Anti-Labor Palmetto State." *South Carolina Historical Magazine* 103 (July 2002): 247–64.

Simon, Bryant. *A Fabric of Defeat: The Politics of South Carolina Millhands, 1910–1948.* Chapel Hill: University of North Carolina Press, 1998.

Skelton, Billy Ray. "Industrialization and Unionization in North Carolina and South Carolina." Ph.D. diss., Duke University, 1964.

Snowden, Yates. "Notes of Labor Organizations in South Carolina, 1742–1861." In *Bulletin of the University of South Carolina,* no. 38, pt. 4. Columbia: University Press, 1914.

Terrill, Tom. "Murder in Graniteville." In *Toward a New South? Studies in Post–Civil War Southern Communities,* edited by Orville Vernon Burton and Robert C. McMath, Jr. Westport, Conn.: Greenwood, 1982.

Orr, James Lawrence (1822–1873). Congressman, governor. Born at Craytonville, Pendleton District, on May 12, 1822, Orr was the son of Christopher Orr and Martha McCann. Young "Larry," as he was known, attended schools at Anderson, where his family had moved in 1830. In 1839 Orr entered the University of Virginia and studied for two years. Returning to Anderson, he was admitted to the bar in 1843. On November 16, 1843, Orr married Mary Jane Marshall. The couple had seven children.

Orr's public career began in 1843 as editor of the *Anderson Gazette.* He served in the General Assembly (1844–1847), where he championed upcountry interests, supported the popular election of presidential electors, and advocated reform of the free school system. He denounced the secessionist "Bluffton Movement" and the inequitable parish system of legislative apportionment. Elected to the U.S. Congress as a States' Rights Democrat, Orr served five terms from 1849 to 1859. By sentiment a Unionist, Orr nonetheless was an adherent of states' rights and the right of secession. Determining that southern interests would best be protected within a strong Democratic Party, he led the National Democrats in South Carolina from 1852 to 1860 and was responsible for the state sending a delegation to the 1856 Democratic national convention, the first time South Carolina had been represented in such a body. An opponent of the Know-Nothing movement, and initially a supporter of Stephen A. Douglas, Orr's national stature was confirmed with his election on December 7, 1857, as Speaker of the House of Representatives (Thirty-fifth Congress), only the second South

Carolinian to hold that office. With the rupture of the Democratic Party and the election of Abraham Lincoln, Orr supported secession as the South's only recourse. He was a delegate to the Secession Convention, served on the committee to draft the ordinance, and was one of three commissioners sent to Washington to negotiate surrender of the Charleston forts.

Orr's Confederate years were his least gratifying and productive. He raised the First Infantry Regiment Rifles, known as Orr's Rifles, and served as its colonel. In December 1861 Orr was elected to the Confederate Senate where he served until the fall of the Confederacy. A bitter critic of the Jefferson Davis administration, Orr advocated individual and states' rights over the national interest. By 1864, believing defeat inevitable, he supported a negotiated peace.

Orr immediately entered into Reconstruction politics. In 1865 he was a commissioner to negotiate with President Andrew Johnson for the establishment of a provisional government in South Carolina. That same year Orr served as a delegate to the state constitutional convention, where he was recognized as the "chief agent in the formation of the new Constitution." Petitioned by convention members to run for governor, Orr became the first popularly elected chief executive in the state's history. Inaugurated November 29, 1865, he and his administration saw the establishment of a state penitentiary, the provision of artificial limbs for Confederate amputees, the reopening of South Carolina College and other schools, the rebuilding of the state's governmental infrastructure, and passage of the controversial "Black Codes," which Orr felt was unwise. An advocate of limited black suffrage and conciliation toward the North, Orr nevertheless opposed ratification of the Fourteenth Amendment to the U.S. Constitution. He was removed from office by military order on June 30, 1868, to make way for newly elected Governor Robert K. Scott. From 1868 to 1872 Orr served as judge of the eighth judicial circuit. His rulings were marked by leniency to debtors, and he granted the first judicial divorces in the history of the state. In August 1870, concluding that opposition to the Radicals was counterproductive, Orr joined the Republican Party in the hope of effecting reforms. As a delegate to the 1872 Republican national convention, he praised President Ulysses Grant's Ku Klux Klan policy in South Carolina. As reward for his support and as a gesture of reconciliation with the South, Grant nominated Orr as minister to Russia. He was unanimously confirmed on December 11, 1872.

Tall and portly, with a cordial and jovial personality, Orr was lauded by admirers as an astute political pragmatist, while condemned by critics as a self-serving opportunist who abandoned principles to advance his career. But despite his postwar conversion to the Republican Party, his accomplishments and reputation allowed Orr to retain the respect, if not the affection, of his fellow white South Carolinians. Orr arrived in St. Petersburg, Russia, in March 1873 but contracted pneumonia and died on May 5, 1873. He was buried in Anderson's First Presbyterian churchyard. PAUL R. BEGLEY

Breese, Donald H. "James L. Orr, Calhoun, and the Cooperationist Tradition in South Carolina." *South Carolina Historical Magazine* 80 (October 1979): 273–85.

Leemhuis, Roger P. *James L. Orr and the Sectional Conflict.* Washington, D.C.: University Press of America, 1979.

White, Laura. "The National Democrats in South Carolina, 1852 to 1860." *South Atlantic Quarterly* 28 (October 1929): 370–89.

Ottolengui, Rodrigues (1861–1937). Orthodontist, lepidopterist, editor, novelist. Ottolengui was born in Charleston on March 15, 1861, the second of three children born to Daniel Ottolengui, a newspaperman, and Helen Rosalie Rodriguez, an author. His grandfather Benjamin Adolph Rodrigues was a pioneer dentist who played an important part in establishing dentistry in South Carolina.

Ottolengui attended the College of Charleston but moved to New York City in 1877 to serve an apprenticeship under Dr. J. Albert Kimball. He obtained a master of dental surgery degree from the Regents of the State of New York in 1885. Ottolengui then practiced dentistry in the office of Dr. William A. Atkinson, "dean" of the dental profession. He served another apprenticeship with Dr. Norman Kingsley, who tutored him in cleft palate. As Kingsley's protégé, Ottolengui became interested in orthodontics and began writing articles on "regulating" teeth in 1892. He made substantial contributions to pulp canal therapy and cleft palate restoration, and was one of the first dentists to use X rays.

Ottolengui was the author of a dental text, *Methods of Filling Teeth;* a chapter on malocclusion in *Fones's Textbook for Dental Hygienists;* and a collection of dental writings published under the title *Table Talks on Dentistry.* He was a dental editor for almost forty years, starting in 1896 with *Items of Interest,* a periodical (later *Dental Items of Interest*). Ottolengui enlarged it into a journal and inaugurated a department of orthodontics, which he illustrated with drawings of classical figures from mythology. Ottolengui also published the proceedings of the American Society of Orthodontists from 1901 to 1920 until it was taken over by the *International Journal of Orthodontia.*

An avid reader of detective stories, Ottolengui was a pioneer in forensic dentistry and authored at least five mystery novels. Ellery Queen dubbed Ottolengui "one of the most neglected authors in the entire history of the detective story." His first mystery, *An Artist in Crime* (1893), was also published in England, France, Poland, and Germany. Ottolengui's next book, *A Conflict of Evidence* (1893), was followed by *A Modern Wizard* (1894), which was brought to the attention of the Pasteur Institute because of the possibility advanced in the story that some forms of insanity were traceable to microorganisms. He also wrote *The Crime of the Century* (1896) and *Final Proof: Or the Value of Evidence* (1898).

Ottolengui was a charter member of the New York Entomological Society. His interest in the family of noctuid moths, the plusiide (plusias), led him to become an authority in the United States on this group. In 1913 he wrote a monograph on every North American species of plusias, describing fourteen new species and illustrating them with his own photographs. The American Museum of Natural History allotted his collection special space and labeled it "The Ottolengui Collection."

Ottolengui was awarded several honorary doctorates. He was a widower, his wife, May Hall Ottolengui, having died on July 10, 1936. Ottolengui died of a heart ailment and a stroke after a long illness in New York City on July 11, 1937. MARY S. MILLER

"Dr. Ottolengui, 76, Dentist 50 Years." *New York Times,* July 13, 1937, p. 19.

"Dr. Rodrigues Ottolengui, Editor from 1896 to 1937." *Dental Items of Interest* 75 (October 1953): 816–22.

Wahl, Norman. "Vignette Rodrigues Ottolengui, MDS, DDS, LLD, FACD." *American Journal of Orthodontics and Dentofacial Orthopedics* (March 2000): 365–66.

Owens Field. Owens Field, or Columbia Owens Downtown Airport, was the brainchild of Columbia mayor Dr. L. B. Owens. Dedicated on April 25, 1930, the airport was built in the Congaree River floodplain and paved by the federal Works Progress Administration. The first commercial airport in the Midlands, Owens Field is located in the Rosewood area three miles from the center of Columbia. Eastern Airlines began passenger service in 1932, and Delta Airlines followed in 1934.

Through the years Owens Field has offered general aviation services including aircraft repair, sales, service, and flight instruction. Hawthorne Flying Service and Dixie Aviation received a five-year contact to operate Owens Field in 1946. In 1964 Midlands Aviation began operating the facility.

During the 1970s the future of Owens Field was in doubt as neighboring homeowners lobbied for its closure. Richland County, valuing the convenience for business and government officials, approved funds to renovate the airport. Renovations to the field in 1982–83 added a new 4,600-foot runway, hangars, navigational aids, and lighting. A new terminal opened in 1984. To reflect these changes, the airport was renamed Columbia Owens Downtown Airport. By 1989 there were 118 aircraft based at Owens. In 2004 Richland County began work on a major upgrade, to include a new terminal and new hangars. ALEXIA JONES HELSLEY

Maxey, Russell. *Airports of Columbia: A History in Photographs & Headlines.* Columbia, S.C.: Palmetto Publishing, 1987.

P

Pacific Mills. Pacific Mills began in Lawrence, Massachusetts, in 1850. After steady success, the company found that it could not weave enough cloth to keep its printing machines and bleaching kiers, or tubs, busy. To get more cloth, Pacific expanded into the South in 1915 by buying four of the sixteen mills of the financially distressed and South Carolina–based Parker Mills.

The new mills, collectively called Columbia Pacific Mills, consisted of Olympia, Granby, Richland, and Capital City Mills in Columbia. Mill villages containing 650 houses came with the purchase. In 1923 Pacific bought 750 acres of land eleven miles from Spartanburg to open Lyman Pacific Mills and another company town. The Columbia operations produced gray cloth that was shipped to Lyman or Lawrence for printing, dyeing, bleaching, and finishing. The Olympia mill had the distinction of having the largest spinning room in the world in the 1920s, with 100,320 spindles. Such massive operations made Pacific into the world's largest manufacturer of percale, a medium-weight, plain-woven printed cotton commonly used in bedsheets.

During World War II, Pacific's South Carolina mills turned out more than 350 million yards of fabric for the war effort. This cotton cloth made millions of uniforms, shirts, shorts, sheets, mattress covers, raincoats, and camouflage items. In 1954 Burlington Industries bought the entire Pacific Mills chain but retained the label because Columbia had established a reputation for high-quality bedsheets, pillow cases, and towels. M. Lowenstein & Sons bought the mills in 1955, however, and removed the Pacific name. The new owners closed the Capital City and Richland mills in 1975 and 1981, respectively. Springs Industries acquired Lowenstein in 1985 and continued to operate the Olympia and Granby mills until 1996, when the aging plants were closed. CARYN E. NEUMANN

Byars, Alvin W. *Olympia Pacific: The Way It Was, 1895–1970.* West Columbia, S.C.: Professional Printers, 1981.

Monk, Fred. "Mills Interwoven with City's History." Columbia *State,* June 29, 1996, p. A10.

Pacolet (Spartanburg County; 2000 pop. 2,690). A cluster of towns in Spartanburg County have held the Pacolet name: Pacolet, Central Pacolet, Pacolet Mills, and Pacolet Park. Prior to the Revolutionary War, the area around Pacolet was known as Grindal Shoals. The area was open for settlement after colonial governor James Glen made an agreement with the Cherokees in 1753. Some people believe that "Pacolet" is a Cherokee word meaning "fast-running horse," while others hold that the word comes from the last name of an early French settler. The area was known as Buzzard's Roost in the early nineteenth century because of the large amount of cockfighting in the area. A railroad station opened in 1859 with the name Pacolet Station.

In 1881 the textile manufacturing pioneer John H. Montgomery and his associates purchased 350 acres on the Pacolet River at Trough Shoals. The General Assembly incorporated the Pacolet Manufacturing Company the following year, and by 1884 a three-story, 10,000-spindle mill was in full operation. Two more mills were built, and by 1895 the three mills at Pacolet had a combined capacity of 53,424 spindles and 1,864 looms, making it the largest textile manufacturing complex in Spartanburg County. Pacolet was chartered by the secretary of state on May 6, 1896. Disaster struck the community on June 6, 1903, when the Pacolet River flooded and destroyed Pacolet Mills 1 and 2 and severely damaged Mill 3. Pacolet and Clifton Mills sustained the most damage in the flood, with total losses estimated at $3.5 million. Although the Pacolet mills were unionized during the General Strike of 1934, the strike was ineffective and union workers were generally fired by the mills.

The Montgomery family continued to operate the Pacolet mills until 1947, when they were sold to Roger Milliken. In 1967 they were consolidated into Deering Milliken, which ceased operations at Pacolet in 1983 and dismantled the mill buildings, a hotel, and some of the ornate houses that lined Victor Park. Unlike many upcountry mill villages, however, the town of Pacolet survived, thanks in part to well-built and maintained mill housing that kept its value and a municipal government that continued to provide services to town residents even after the mills had gone. "Pacolet endured," observed the local historian Betsy Teter, "though much of its history existed only in photographs." AARON W. MARRS

Leonard, Michael. *Our Heritage: A Community History of Spartanburg County, S.C.* Spartanburg, S.C.: Band & White, 1986.

Stokes, Allen H. "John H. Montgomery: A Pioneer Southern Industrialist." Master's thesis, University of South Carolina, 1967.

Teter, Betsy Wakefield, ed. *Textile Town: Spartanburg County, South Carolina.* Spartanburg, S.C.: Hub City Writers Project, 2002.

Waldrep, George Calvin. *Southern Workers and the Search for Community: Spartanburg County, South Carolina.* Urbana: University of Illinois Press, 2000.

Pageland (Chesterfield County; 2000 pop. 2,521). Pageland is situated on a sand ridge immediately adjacent to the clay hills of the Piedmont. These soil types made farming possible, though arduous. From the early years, mineral production was also important. Pageland was primarily settled by English, German, Welsh, and Scots-Irish from Pennsylvania, Virginia, or surrounding South Carolina counties. Reece Shelby seems to have been the first to receive a state land grant in the Pageland area in 1788. Around the same time, Irish native John Blakeney came to the region and built a trading post by 1815. For most of the nineteenth century the settlement was known as Blakeney's Crossroads or Old Store Township. In 1857 the place was sufficiently important to obtain a post office.

During Reconstruction tax sales placed a great deal of property on the auction block, and much of it was purchased by a man named Fox for New England speculators. After backlash to the blatant land grab, Fox disappeared and most of what became Pageland was purchased by Messrs. McGregor, Maynard, Godfrey, and Sowell.

Real growth occurred here after the coming of the railroad from Cheraw. In 1904 the Chesterfield and Lancaster Railroad reached Old Store, which contained only a handful of dwellings and stores. Realizing what the railroad would mean, residents renamed the community Pageland in honor of Adolphus High "Captain Dolly" Page, president of the railroad. Page's father-in-law, a civil engineer, laid out lots in the village. In 1907 the Chesterfield Land and Development Company auctioned these lots at a public sale.

Pageland received its charter in January 1908, with a population of 157. By 1910 there were drug, furniture, clothing, and general stores. There was also the Pageland Buggy and Wagon Company, and the Pageland Manufacturing Company made furniture and building materials. A livery stable, a hotel, and a school were built that year. The following year Pageland boasted a newspaper, a second hotel, and a bank, and the population had increased to around 800. Like many boom towns, Pageland acquired a reputation as a rather rough place, leading to the enactment of a curfew in 1912.

In 1920, although the principal agricultural product remained cotton, melons and peaches were gaining in importance. Pageland billed itself the "Watermelon Capital of the World" and became well known for these melons. In 1951 Pageland began a Watermelon Festival in July that attracted thousands of visitors annually.

By the 1980s years of out-migration from the farms caused growth in the area to stagnate. Downtown appeared to be dying. In 1987 the town committed to the state's Small Towns Program, which substantially improved the appearance of the business district. With the arrival of a Wal-Mart distribution center and the explosive growth of nearby Charlotte, Pageland saw major changes in the 1990s with new businesses, restaurants, and major road improvements. SARAH CAIN SPRUILL

Gregg, Alexander. *History of the Old Cheraws.* 1867. Reprint, Greenville, S.C.: Southern Historical Press, 1982.

Smith, Beth Laney. *The Voices of Pageland.* Charlotte, N.C.: Laney-Smith, 1997.

Palmer, Benjamin Morgan (1818–1902). Presbyterian clergyman, educator. Palmer was born in Charleston on January 25, 1818, the son of Edward Palmer, a teacher, and Sarah Bunce. Both parents had New England ancestry. In 1821 Edward Palmer entered Andover Theological Seminary in Massachusetts to prepare for the Presbyterian ministry. His family remained in Charleston until 1823, when they joined him for the last two years of his theological training. The family returned in 1824 to the South Carolina lowcountry, where Edward Palmer served churches until 1874.

Benjamin Palmer entered Amherst College at fourteen and became friends with New Englanders including Henry Ward Beecher. He was said to be at the top of his class when, during his second year, he was expelled for refusing to divulge the secrets of a literary society. Palmer graduated with first honors from the University of Georgia in 1838 and entered Columbia Theological Seminary. Following his graduation in 1841, he accepted a call to the First Presbyterian Church of Savannah. That same year, on October 7, he married Augusta McConnell, the stepdaughter of Professor George Howe of Columbia Theological Seminary. Through her mother, Augusta was related to one of Georgia's largest slaveholding families.

In 1843 Palmer accepted a call to the First Presbyterian Church of Columbia, which he served for the next eleven years. In Columbia he was part of a circle of Presbyterian intellectuals that included James Henley Thornwell, Joseph LeConte, and Louisa Cheves McCord. With George Howe and Thornwell, he in 1847 established the *Southern Presbyterian Review,* perhaps the most influential and certainly the most scholarly religious journal published in the South at the time. In 1854 he accepted a call to Columbia Theological Seminary as professor of ecclesiastical history and polity. Two years later he became pastor of the First Presbyterian Church, New Orleans.

While Palmer was associated with conservative theological and political circles that had strong Unionist sympathies, he became a vigorous supporter of secession and the southern cause after the election of Abraham Lincoln. His Thanksgiving Day sermon in 1860 propelled him to national prominence with his defense of the rights of secession and slavery. "We defend the cause of God and religion," he told his New Orleans congregation, while he insisted that the "abolition spirit is undeniably atheistic." Admirers had the sermon reprinted frequently and widely circulated. In 1861 he became the first moderator of the Presbyterian Church in the Confederate States of America. During the war he traveled throughout the South preaching and speaking and providing important ideological support to the Confederate cause. When New Orleans fell to Union forces, Palmer returned to Columbia and filled his old pulpit and briefly, after Thornwell's death, a professorship at the seminary. The fire following Sherman's entrance into Columbia destroyed much of Palmer's library and many of his personal papers.

After the war, Palmer returned to New Orleans, where he was a highly regarded pastor who ministered with great compassion to the victims of yellow fever epidemics. He was a founder of the weekly *Southwestern Presbyterian* and was influential in establishing Southwestern Presbyterian University, now Rhodes College, in Memphis. Palmer died on May 28, 1902, following a street accident in New Orleans and was buried in that city's Metarie Cemetery. ERSKINE CLARKE

Johnson, Thomas Cary. *The Life and Letters of Benjamin Morgan Palmer.* Richmond, Va.: Presbyterian Committee of Publication, 1906.

Thompson, Ernest Trice. *Presbyterians in the South.* 3 vols. Richmond, Va.: John Knox, 1963–1973.

Palmer Field. A pilot training airfield and German prisoner-of-war camp located near Bennettsville from 1941 to 1945, Palmer Field was named in honor of Captain William W. Palmer, a Bennettsville resident who earned a Distinguished Service Cross in World War I serving with Eddie Rickenbacker's Ninety-fourth Pursuit Squadron. Built in the summer of 1941 on the site of several abandoned cotton fields, the airfield included barracks, a ground school, and administration buildings. The U.S. Army contracted with the Georgia Air Service to operate the flight school. In October 1941 the first cadets began training with a civilian staff of sixteen flight instructors, which grew to fifty-nine by the end of the following month along with some two hundred support personnel. Palmer Field was a primary training facility, the first of three stages toward earning a pilot's commission. Each class trained on Stearman PT-17s for nine weeks before moving on to the next stage at another field. The first graduating class had its ceremony disrupted on December 7, 1941, because of the Japanese attack on Pearl Harbor that same day. An estimated two thousand trainees came through Palmer from 1941 until early 1944. Late the same year Palmer Field became a prisoner-of-war camp for an estimated 244 Germans who were employed on local farms and forestry enterprises. By the middle of 1945 the camp was deactivated. Later the site served as a drive-in movie theater and then a chicken farm before Powell Manufacturing purchased it for manufacturing tobacco-growing equipment in the early 1960s. FRITZ HAMER

Moore, John H. "Nazi Troopers in South Carolina, 1944–1946." *South Carolina Historical Magazine* 81 (October 1980): 306–15.

Palmetto. State tree. South Carolina's state tree is the *Sabal palmetto,* so designated by a legislative act approved by Governor Burnet R. Maybank on March 17, 1939. The palmetto has appeared on the state seal since the Revolutionary War and on the state flag since 1861. The word "palmetto" comes from the Spanish *palmito* ("little palm"), and the origin of *Sabal* is uncertain.

For centuries the Palmetto has been a state symbol. In his poem "Carolina," Henry Timrod wrote of the state's "proud armorial trees." Photograph by Michael Foster. Courtesy, South Carolina Department of Natural Resources

The palmetto is a branchless palm with long, fanlike evergreen leaves that spread atop a thick stem, or trunk. Botanists do not consider it a true tree since it lacks a solid wood trunk. The palmetto's range is the coastal area from North Carolina to Florida and the Florida Panhandle. It can grow as high as sixty-five feet, and mature South Carolina natives average thirty- to forty-feet tall.

The popular name "cabbage palmetto" comes from the terminal bud, or heart, of the stem. This can be eaten raw or cooked, and its taste resembles that of cabbage. Removal of the heart kills the tree. In the past some native Americans and European colonists also ate the ripe black berries, and these are still a favorite of birds.

Palmetto is a wind-adapted species, and its soft trunk and strong root system allow it to bend with high winds without breaking or being uprooted. Spongy palmetto logs were used in the construction of the Sullivan's Island fort (later called Fort Moultrie) that absorbed British navy cannonballs, without shattering, in the battle of June 28, 1776—giving South Carolina troops the victory that is commemorated on the state seal and flag. The *Sabal palmetto* is also the state tree of Florida and appears on Florida's seal and flag. DAVID C. R. HEISSER

Heisser, David C. R. *The State Seal of South Carolina: A Short History.* Columbia: South Carolina Department of Archives and History, 1992.

Laurie, Pete. "Palmetto Pride." *South Carolina Wildlife* 35 (July–August 1988): 16–23.

Porcher, Richard D., and Douglas A. Rayner. *A Guide to the Wildflowers of South Carolina.* Columbia: University of South Carolina Press, 2001.

Shumake, Janice. "In Praise of the Palmetto." Charleston *Post and Courier,* July 21, 2002, pp. D1, D4.

Palmetto Armory. The Palmetto Armory was a short-lived effort to establish a weapons-manufacturing capability in South Carolina during the secession crisis of 1849–1852. Northern attempts to block the spread of slavery into the newly acquired southwestern territories led many South Carolinians to consider secession. In 1850, following Governor Whitemarsh B. Seabrook's recommendation, the General Assembly created a Board of Ordnance and appropriated $350,000 for weapons and munitions. A consortium of William Glaze, Benjamin Flagg, and James Boatwright received a contract in 1851 to produce muskets, rifles, pistols, cavalry sabers, and artillery sabers, all of which were to be of the current federal pattern and were to be manufactured wholly within the state.

The Palmetto Armory obtained some equipment through Flagg's contacts with northern manufacturers, particularly Asa Waters. But, although Glaze and his company were supposed to manufacture all weapons in South Carolina, there is convincing evidence that most of the components for the firearms and all of the edged weapons were produced elsewhere and merely assembled in South Carolina. Production ceased in May 1853 when the contract was terminated by the state for lack of funds. By this time Glaze had delivered 6,020 muskets, 1,000 rifles, 1,000 dragoon pistols, 2,000 cavalry sabers, and 526 artillery sabers. With no further contracts forthcoming, Glaze converted the Palmetto Armory into the Palmetto Iron Works. Although he attempted to obtain contracts for weapons at the beginning of the Civil War, Glaze was unsuccessful and produced only a few artillery projectiles. JACK ALLEN MEYER

Meyer, Jack Allen. *William Glaze and the Palmetto Armory.* 2d ed. Columbia: South Carolina State Museum, 1994.

Palmetto bug. Three hundred million years ago, during the Carboniferous period, cockroaches (or palmetto bugs) and their insect relatives (crickets, grasshoppers, dragonflies, cicadas, and mayflies) made their appearance on earth. It took another 150 million years, and the development of flowers, before butterflies, moths, bees, wasps, and true flies appeared. While thousands of species have become extinct, the cockroach thrives. It is truly an ancient survivor and is well adapted to its current circumstance.

The American cockroach or palmetto bug is the largest of the cockroaches to infest our homes and is well known by citizens of the South Carolina coastal plain. The smokey-brown roach is closely related to the American cockroach, and they are often lumped together by pest-control specialists as the palmetto bug. They differ from the German cockroach, another of the cockroach pests, in size and habitat. The palmetto bug may grow to one and a half inches in length and has reddish-brown wings. Both males and females have fully developed wings and can run fast and fly. They live in moist, warm areas and are usually found in basements, under decks, in ivy outside the home, in mulch, and in tool sheds and garages. They love city sewer systems. The palmetto bug survives for a single year, and during that time the female produces approximately 150 offspring.

The German cockroach is smaller, less than an inch in length, and is light brown with two dark stripes traversing the length of the body. Like palmetto bugs, they eat food of all kinds. However, they prefer produce departments in grocery stores and may actually ride home with you from the market in shopping bags. They tend to hide in kitchen cabinets and under washing machines and refrigerators, and they are rarely seen in daylight.

There are several myths concerning the origin of the term "palmetto bug." One is that the insect drew its name from its home in the stubs of palm fronds left on the trunks of palmetto trees. Another is that proper South Carolinians did not have common cockroaches in their homes, but rather a more genteel insect they dubbed the "palmetto bug." With the advent of electricity, homeowners found that with a flick of a switch in the kitchen, they might see dozens of roaches heading for a hiding place. Rural women sometimes jokingly referred to the vain attempt to stomp the intruders as the "bug dance." Whether native or immigrant, the palmetto bug is very much a part of South Carolina from the mountains to the sea. DAVID H. REMBERT, JR.

Bennett, Gary W., et al. *Truman's Scientific Guide to Pest Control Operations.* 6th ed. West Layfayette, Ind.: Purdue University, 2003.

Farb, Peter, et al. *The Insects.* Rev. ed. Alexandria, Va.: Time-Life, 1980.

Palmetto Building (Columbia). When completed in 1913 at a cost of $300,000, the Palmetto Building in Columbia was the tallest building in the Carolinas and one of the most stylish skyscrapers in the South. Its sleek, vertical form represented the cutting edge of architectural design and added a sense of metropolitan sophistication to the skyline of South Carolina's capital city. In a reference to the celebrated skyscraper that had been finished earlier the same year in New York City, the *Columbia Record* described the Palmetto Building as the "'Woolworth' Building of South Carolina." Standing at the corner of Main and Washington Streets directly opposite Columbia's first skyscraper, the National Loan and Exchange Bank Building (1903), the Palmetto Building towered over the central business district and immediately became one of the city's most prestigious business addresses.

Designed by the New York architect Julius Harder for the Palmetto National Bank, the Palmetto Building is fifteen stories tall and is built of steel-frame construction on a U-shaped plan. The limestone base and glazed terra cotta facades feature Gothic-revival styling, foliated pilasters and entablatures, and a specially designed palmetto tree motif. The building culminates in a crown comprised of banded Gothic arches, a handsome copper cornice, and a stone parapet. The elaborately decorated ground-floor banking room features a mosaic tile floor with a palmetto tree inlay. In its form and ornamentation, the Palmetto Building reflects the strong beaux arts influence that was common among skyscraper designs of the era, and it continues to stand among Columbia's most recognizable landmarks. The building was listed in the National Register of Historic Places in 1980. DANIEL J. VIVIAN

"Architect Harder Describes Palmetto Building," *Columbia Record,* December 21, 1913.

Palmetto Medical, Dental, and Pharmaceutical Association. Throughout the nineteenth century African American physicians in South Carolina faced hostility from the white community, received the worst patients, were barred from hospitals and clinics, and lacked access to many medications and supplies. In 1896 Dr. C. C. Johnson of Aiken organized black physicians to promote their interests and insure that concerted actions were taken to solve their problems. Unable to join the racially segregated American Medical Association, five South Carolina physicians organized the Palmetto State Medical Association in 1896 as a vehicle to improve health care for African Americans and to graduate more medically trained professionals.

The association faced some hurdles. It was hard to find meeting places and lodging. Speakers did not want to come to the racially segregated South. Early meetings focused on the advancement of medical science and efforts to lower black mortality rates. In 1936 the first annual clinic offering free medical treatment was held in connection with the annual meeting.

In the 1940s efforts of the association shifted toward preserving the organization and toward the larger issue of desegregation. In 1941 Dr. L. W. Long called for more training and state-sponsored scholarships for African American medical students. He also voiced the need for black practitioners to be hired by tax-supported institutions, as well as for African American representation on the board of the S.C. Department of Health. The group had changed its name to the Palmetto Medical, Dental, and Pharmaceutical Association by 1950, and it spent the 1950s, 1960s, and 1970s raising monies to educate talented African Americans. In the 1960s members of the association aggressively worked to promote the integration of society. By 1967 the Palmetto Medical, Dental, and Pharmaceutical Association (PMDPA) hoped to take advantage of current events that "twisted and molded the dominating power structure."

Activism continued in the post-civil-rights era as the PMDPA established the Palmetto Political Action Committee. This nonpartisan and voluntary organization provided support for candidates, maintained close liaison with public service organizations, and provided information to members about legislative activities. At the centennial meeting of the PMDPA in 1996, the theme of the gathering echoed, on a larger scale, the goals of the founders as the members continued their efforts to prepare African American youths to carry on "democratic ideals, culture, traditions, and leadership in the free world." DAVID S. BROWN

Palmetto Pigeon Plant. While serving as an infantry captain during World War I, the Sumter attorney Wendell M. Levi set up the Pigeon Section of the U.S. Army Signal Corps, having had experience raising homing pigeons as a hobby. Harold Moïse, an air force pilot and a graduate civil engineer with building expertise, shared Levi's interest in pigeons. In 1923 the two men founded the Palmetto Pigeon Plant on thirteen acres of farmland in Sumter County and recruited state senator Davis Moïse to be vice president of the firm.

Palmetto's original breeding stock came from the pigeons Levi raised for the army. The plant gradually expanded to become America's largest squab producer and the sole supplier of pigeons for use in medical and dietary research. Squabs—young pigeons that have not yet flown—are considered haute cuisine in many parts of the world. Farm-raised or wild, pigeons were common fare in Carolina until fifty years ago. Besides squabs, the Sumter plant also raised and processed poussins (young chickens) and quail, and bought partridges, rabbits, and additional squabs from growers around the state.

Palmetto Pigeon Plant was operated by Levi and Moïse family members until 1990, when Anthony Barwick, a Pineville native and recent graduate in poultry science at Clemson University, became manager. In 1997 Barwick purchased the Moïse family stock and became president and CEO of the company. Wendell M. Levi, Jr., served as secretary-treasurer.

A $4 million business with sixty employees in 2002, Palmetto Pigeon reached a level of production its founders could not have imagined. The plant's 20,000 pairs of pigeons produced an average of 7,000 squabs a week. Also, 230,000 poussins and 80,000 black chickens were shipped yearly to brokers in New Orleans, New York, Houston, Dallas, Chicago, Denver, Los Angeles, and San Francisco and distributed to restaurants, retailers, retail groceries, airlines, and cruise ships. By the early twenty-first century consumers worldwide could buy Palmetto poussins and squabs through the prestigious distributor D'Artagnan. DALE ROSENGARTEN

Levi, Wendell Mitchell. *Making Pigeons Pay: A Manual of Practical Information on the Management, Selection, Breeding, Feeding, and Marketing of Pigeons.* 1946. Reprint, Sumter, S.C.: Levi Publishing, 1968.

———. Papers. Special Collections, College of Charleston Library, Charleston, South Carolina.

———. *The Pigeon.* 1941. Reprint, Sumter, S.C.: Levi Publishing, 1992.

Sullivan, Marion. "A Cook's Tour: Preserving the Flavors of the Lowcountry." *Charleston* 16 (September–October 2002): 106–10.

Palmetto Regiment. The Palmetto Regiment, South Carolina's contribution to the Mexican War (1846–1848), was formed on June 29, 1846, with Pierce Mason Butler elected as colonel. Initially the War Department informed the Palmettos that they were not needed. Finally, on November 16, a South Carolina regiment was requested for immediate service. Since the term of enlistment was changed from one year to the duration of the war, the regiment had to be rebuilt. This proved difficult but was finally accomplished, and the regiment reported to Camp Magnolia, near Charleston. On December 27–28 the Palmettos departed for Mobile, Alabama. From Mobile they sailed to Lobos Island and, after intensive training, landed on March 8, 1847, below Vera Cruz, helping to establish the siege lines there.

"Palmetto Regiment Quickstep," written to honor the valor of the Palmetto Regiment in the Mexican War. Courtesy, South Carolina Historical Society

After a debilitating expedition to Alvarado (March 30–April 6) the Palmettos marched through Jalapa to Puebla, where the army remained until departing for the Valley of Mexico on August 7. The Palmettos were involved in two battles on August 20: Contreras, against token opposition; and Churubusco, where Colonel Butler was killed in heavy fighting. The Palmettos lost eleven killed and 126 wounded. After a brief armistice, the army resumed the offensive on September 12, attacking Chapultepec and Mexico City. At the Garita de Bélen, the Palmettos were the first regiment to enter Mexico City. On May 29, 1848, after months of garrison duty, the Palmetto Regiment left for home, arriving at Mobile over the period June 24–29. They were mustered out there and left to find their own way home. Of 1,048 men enrolled, 441 did not return. See plate 23. JACK ALLEN MEYER

Lander, Ernest McPherson, Jr. *Reluctant Imperialists: Calhoun, the South Carolinians, and the Mexican War.* Baton Rouge: Louisiana State University Press, 1980.

Meyer, Jack Allen. *South Carolina in the Mexican War: A History of the Palmetto Regiment of Volunteers, 1846–1917.* Columbia: South Carolina Department of Archives and History, 1996.

Palmetto Trail. The Palmetto Trail is South Carolina's first cross-state recreational trail. It is designed as an easy to moderate hiking and mountain-biking trail. When complete, the more than four-hundred-mile mountains-to the-sea trail will link Oconee State Park, near Walhalla, with the Intracoastal Waterway at Buck Hall Recreation Area, near Awendaw. Enthusiasts may choose to hike or bike the entire trail or accomplish one or two "passages" at a time.

Along the Palmetto Trail users visit South Carolina's forests, parks, historic sites, wildlife refuges, the State House, a military base, and a variety of private and corporate lands. Highlights of the trail include open vistas of the Intracoastal Waterway, Lake Moultrie, the Wateree River, and landscapes ranging from rolling farmlands to mountaintops. There are waterfalls, boardwalks, historic sites, small towns, and barbeque restaurants. Hikers and bikers may see ospreys, eagles, deer, turkeys, alligators, and a variety of warblers, herons, snakes, turtles, butterflies, dragonflies, trees, and wildflowers.

The vision for the Palmetto Trail began in 1994 through the efforts of the nonprofit Palmetto Conservation Foundation, working with the South Carolina Department of Parks, Recreation, and Tourism. The trail is supported by the General Assembly, numerous public and private landowners and land managers, and corporate and private contributions. Trail construction has been aided by the many land managers, the AmeriCorps National Civilian Community Corps, the South Carolina National Guard, Santee Cooper, Boy Scouts of America, and many volunteer groups and individuals. TONY BEBBER

Lambert, Yon, Jim Schmid, and Oliver Buckles. *The Palmetto Trail Lowcountry Guide.* Columbia, S.C.: Palmetto Conservation Foundation, 2000.

Paper and pulpwood industry. From the first century C.E. until the first decades of the nineteenth century, papermaking technology remained virtually unchanged. Discovered in China, the process began by reducing rags, cotton, and linen to a fine pulp by vigorous beating while suspended in water. A measure of the solution was then brought up on a frame of bronze wire mesh, piece by piece, and drained of excess liquid. In successive steps, more water was extracted by pressing sheets and alternating layers of felt together several times until the individual sheets were finally dry. This technology was later imported to America and was in use until well after the Revolutionary War. It was also the process first utilized for papermaking in the Palmetto State.

The first mention of a paper mill in South Carolina is found in the correspondence of Benjamin Waring of Columbia in 1806, when he wrote, "I suppose you have heard of my erecting a Paper-mill." By 1809 the Waring enterprise was making and shipping printing papers and a lower-grade wrapping paper to various customers, at least partly through the firm of Waring and Hayne in Charleston. The fate of Waring's mill is unclear, but by the 1820s paper was being manufactured in the Columbia area and parts of the upstate. The firm of White and Bicknell was operating a paper plant in Columbia in 1832, by then the only such enterprise in the state, but that year it was destroyed by fire. Other attempts at paper manufacturing during the nineteenth century were uneven, with the best-known example being the Bath paper mill near Graniteville in Edgefield District, which manufactured paper for the Confederacy.

By 1893 James Lide Coker of Hartsville had organized the first company in the state to make wood pulp for paper production on a commercial scale. Soon a paper mill that created paper cones for the miles of yarn produced by the state's textile industry was in operation. Named the Southern Novelty Company, it later became Sonoco.

The dawn of the twentieth century witnessed the birth of the modern paper industry in the South. Advances in rendering wood fiber into usable pulp on a commercially profitable scale, as well as dwindling supplies of suitable wood in the North, sparked the creation of new paper plants in the South. A new technology, the sulphite process, was developed in 1910, making kraft paper (a strong paper or paperboard made from wood pulp) a viable component of total paper production. Kraft paper would be a specialty of these newer southern mills, used most notably for brown paper bags and corrugated boxes. From 1900 to 1939 the output of paper contributed by southern mills increased from one percent to twenty-one percent of the nationwide production. Inexpensive labor, transportation improvements, a shift to electric and steam power, and improvements in the utilization of southern forest products all contributed to the rise of paper as a southern industry. By the mid-1930s, with the arrival in Charleston County of the West Virginia Pulp and Paper Company (later Westvaco) and of International Paper Company in Georgetown County, the industry had assumed a place of importance in the South Carolina economy. Together these massive facilities (Georgetown had the largest paper mill in the world for years) brought more than $6 million in wages to the state during the worse years of the Great Depression. In addition, wood products from South Carolina were being exported to paper and pulp mills in Tennessee, Georgia, and North Carolina.

In 1958 the English paper manufacturer Bowater Corporation commenced production at a new plant in York County, which by 2000 was a leading producer of newsprint and coated and uncoated groundwood papers. In 1984 Union Camp did likewise in Eastover, producing fine white uncoated and unbleached paper. By 2000 the Georgetown mill of International Paper was producing envelope stock; heavyweight Bristol for tags, file folders, and index cards; and pulp for personal needs and other market segments. Westvaco produced paperboard, unbleached kraft paper, food and drink cartons, corrugated cartons, and material for core laminates. Other pulp and paper manufacturers in 2000 included Georgia-Pacific in York and Orangeburg Counties, Smurfit-Stone Container Corporation in Florence, and Willamette Industries in Marlboro County.

Coinciding with the rise of pulp and paper in the state, forest management and utilization improved. By the mid 1950s more than half of the tree farms of the nation were found in the South, including 140 in South Carolina. Besides producing paper and pulp, the industries have encouraged a range of related wood-based manufacturing, including box plants, plywood, lumber, and wood-chip facilities. BARRY A. PRICE

Daniels, Jonathan. *The Forest Is the Future.* New York: International Paper Company, 1957.

Lander, Ernest McPherson, Jr. "Paper Manufacturing in South Carolina before the Civil War." *North Carolina Historical Review* 29 (April 1952): 220–27.

Ohanian, Nancy Kane. *The American Pulp and Paper Industry, 1900–1940.* Westport, Conn.: Greenwood, 1993.

Stevenson, Louis T. *The Background and Economics of American Papermaking.* New York: Harper and Brothers, 1947.

Pardo, Juan. Spanish soldier, explorer. Juan Pardo was born in Cuenca, Spain, in the first half of the sixteenth century. He traveled to Spanish Florida in the fleet of General Sancho de Archiniega in 1566 as the captain of one of the six military companies sent to reinforce the colony founded by Governor Pedro Menéndez de Avilés in 1565. Captain Pardo's company was the only one from the Archiniega expedition posted to the Spanish town of Santa Elena, which was located on present-day Parris Island, South Carolina. When Pardo arrived at Santa Elena with 250 men in July 1566, a mutiny had greatly reduced the number of Spanish troops there. Supplies were also short, however, so when Governor Menéndez visited Santa Elena in August 1566, he ordered Pardo to take some of his men to find an overland route between Santa Elena and the silver mines of Zacatecas, Mexico. Menéndez instructed Pardo to make peace with the Indians he met on his way, secure their obedience to the Spanish king, and offer them instruction in the Catholic faith. An inability to calculate longitude accurately led these men to severely underestimate the actual distance between Zacatecas and the Atlantic coast.

Pardo never reached the mines of Mexico, but his two expeditions—the last major Spanish military explorations of the interior of the Southeast—provide a valuable window to the peoples of these lands in the mid–sixteenth century. Pardo first departed from Santa Elena on December 1, 1566, with 125 men and headed northwest through the interior of South Carolina and into western North Carolina. He returned to Santa Elena on March 7, 1567, after receiving a summons to respond to an anticipated French attack. Pardo set out on his second expedition from Santa Elena on September 1, 1567, and followed basically the same route, although this journey took him into eastern Tennessee. He visited several of the towns that Hernando De Soto had passed through more than twenty-five years before. Pardo's notary recorded a high degree of compliance with the orders the captain had given on the first expedition, including having the Indians grow corn and construct buildings for the Spaniards. On his return from the second expedition, Pardo collected as much corn as he could and distributed his men among six forts in an attempt to strengthen the Spanish presence inland and force the Indian population to support the soldiers. Two of these forts were in present-day South Carolina—Fort Santo Tomás at Cofitachiqui, or Canos, near Camden and Fort Nuestra Señora at the native town of Orista on the coast. Within months of Pardo's return to Santa Elena on March 2, 1568, Indians had destroyed the inland forts.

Pardo served as the lieutenant governor at Santa Elena until around April 1569. He departed the Florida colony for Spain during the summer of 1569, and further details about his life and death are unknown. KAREN L. PAAR

Hudson, Charles. *The Juan Pardo Expeditions: Exploration of the Carolinas and Tennessee, 1566–1568.* Washington, D.C.: Smithsonian Institution Press, 1990.

Parish, Margaret Cecile (1927–1988). Author. "Peggy" Parish was born in Manning on July 14, 1927, the daughter of Herman Stanley Parish and Cecile Rogers. She attended Manning public schools and graduated from the University of South Carolina with a degree in English in 1948. Parish also completed graduate work at Peabody College of Vanderbilt University in 1950. She lived briefly in Oklahoma and Kentucky before moving to New York to teach reading and to serve as director of second and third grades at the Dalton School in New York City. While teaching at Dalton, Parish began writing books for children. Her first book, *My Golden Book of Manners,* was published by Golden Pleasure Books in 1962. A second book, *Let's Be Indians,* published in 1963, remained a popular children's book for decades.

International fame for Parish, however, followed the creation and publication of *Amelia Bedelia* in 1964. The title character is a maid who interprets everything literally, leading her to use real sponges to make a sponge cake and to "dress" a turkey in stylish clothes, much to the delight of children all over the world. *Thank You, Amelia Bedelia* (1965) and *Amelia Bedelia and the Surprise Show* (1967) followed. Ultimately, Parish wrote a series of eleven books about Amelia Bedelia and her comic antics, as well as more than thirty other children's books. Her books have sold more than seven million copies and have been translated into many different languages.

In 1972 Parish returned to her hometown, where she continued her writing until her untimely death in 1988. She won a Palmetto State Award, a Garden State Children's Book Award, and a School Library Journal award for *Dinosaur Time* in 1977. Parish also received the Milner Award from the city of Atlanta in 1984 and the Keystone State Children's Book Award from the state of Pennsylvania in 1986 for *Teach Us, Amelia Bedelia.* In addition to continuing her writing after returning to Manning, Parish became the children's book reviewer for the "Carolina Today" television show on WIS-TV in Columbia. She also participated in teacher workshops and taught creative writing techniques to elementary-school children. In 1988, to celebrate Amelia Bedelia's twenty-fifth birthday, the publishers Harper and Row and Greenwillow and Avon sponsored celebrations across the nation, encouraging students to send thousands of cards and letters to special mailboxes installed in libraries and bookstores. In August 1988 Parish published *Amelia's Family Album.* Three months later, on November 19, 1988, she died of a ruptured abdominal aneurysm in a Manning hospital. A bronze statue of Amelia Bedelia, commissioned by the citizens of Manning in 1999, stands in front of the Clarendon County Library. BARBARA OWENS GOGGANS

Obituary. Columbia *State,* November 20, 1988, p. D6.

Park Seed Company. Founded in 1868 by George Watt Park, Park Seed Company is an example of true American ingenuity. It started when Park, then fifteen years old, gathered seeds from his mother's Pennsylvania garden and sold them to his neighbors. From this beginning, Park started *Park's Floral Magazine,* which eventually had a circulation of more than 1 million and the Park catalog, which grew to more than 5 million in circulation.

Mary Barratt, whose family lived in what is now South Greenwood, was a county home-demonstration agent who wrote Park asking for some free seeds. He replied that he could not give away his seed, but he could give free advice. Thus began a two-year correspondence that ended with Park's coming to South Carolina, where he married Barratt in 1918.

Today Park Seed Company uses not just catalogs, but also the Internet to bring annual flowers, vegetables, perennial plants, bulbs, and gardening supplies to American gardeners. The company is known for being first with new varieties and for having one of the most extensive listings of flowers and vegetables of any retail gardening company in the United States. In 1975 Park extended its product line by purchasing Wayside Gardens, a nursery catalog that sells shrubs, trees, hardy perennials, and bulbs. This made Park seed the largest family-owned retail gardening company in the country.

The Park Gardens, located north of Greenwood on Highway 254, are the largest trial grounds in the Southeast. Though open to the public year round, they are at their peak in June and July, with thousands of flowers, hundreds of vegetables, and scores of container plants. KAREN PARK JENNINGS

Parker School. The Parker School in Greenville County was one of the more innovative progressive schools in the United States during the 1930s and 1940s. Described in 1941 as a "mill town miracle" by *Reader's Digest,* the Parker School embodied basic tenets of community education and progressive education. Lawrence P. Hollis organized the school to reflect Greenville mill owner Thomas Parker's utopian vision of work, school, and society. Mill village elementary schools in the west-side textile area of Greenville first constituted the Parker District in 1923; Parker High School opened one year later. In 1951 the Parker School District consolidated with other districts to form the Greenville Public School District. In 1985 the Parker High School building was closed and converted to a middle school.

Attending to the "needs of the child," the Parker School established health, aesthetic, vocational, general education, leisure, and environmental programs for both students and adults. The school's elementary course of study emphasized learning units and the "project method," an instructional method focused on students' activities rather than on the printed book and recitation. The secondary-school program connected traditional subjects with a focus on "centers of interest." A nationally recognized materials bureau collected documents used for student/teacher-developed resource units. School activities took students into the surrounding community and throughout the state. While recognized throughout the United States for its innovative school practices, the Parker School embraced the objectives of welfare capitalism; its focus on "vocation as textile training" rather than "vocation as general culture" actually served to exclude the Parker School from a progressive education tradition. CRAIG KRIDEL

Ariail, Mary G., and Nancy J. Smith. *Weaver of Dreams: A History of the Parker District.* Columbia, S.C.: R. L. Bryan, 1977.

Tippett, James. *Schools for a Growing Democracy.* Boston: Ginn, 1936.

Parker's Ferry, Battle of (August 30, 1781). During the summer of 1781, Tories roved the countryside surrounding Charleston. Patriot colonel William Harden commanded a dwindling militia force south of the Edisto River and requested assistance from Brigadier General Francis Marion to counter this threat. Arriving at the village of Round "O" on August 22, Marion set out to gather intelligence. He learned that a force of one hundred Tories under Colonel William "Bloody Bill" Cunningham was assembling on the banks of the Pon Pon River (present-day Edisto River) to join a larger body of British and Hessian regulars and Loyalist militiamen. Marion quickly prepared an ambush to prevent the juncture.

On August 30 the patriot force took position in the thick woods of a swamp about forty yards from the road and within a mile of Parker's Ferry. A few light horsemen were sent forward as decoys. As the British force approached in the late afternoon, a Tory sentry noticed a white cockade—the mark of Marion's men—in a soldier's cap in the woodline. Musket fire was exchanged, and the horsemen charged, forcing the Tories back toward the ferry. From a distance, British lieutenant colonel DeBorck watched the engagement and ordered Major Thomas Fraser to charge with his dragoons. Fraser's men galloped blindly into the trap. As the British cavalrymen came abreast of the American position, they received several volleys of fire. Low on ammunition, Marion withdrew when a column of enemy infantrymen arrived on the scene. British losses were estimated at about twenty-five killed and eighty wounded, with minimal harm to Marion's force. This small but effective engagement checked the British cavalry and put a stop to the marauding of the Tories so that they never posed a threat in the region again. SAMUEL K. FORE

Daso, Dik A. "Colonel William Harden: The Unsung Partisan Commander." *Proceedings of the South Carolina Historical Association* (1995): 95–111.

James, William Dobein. *A Sketch of the Life of Brig. Gen. Francis Marion.* 1821. Reprint, Marietta, Ga.: Continental Book Company, 1948.
Lumpkin, Henry. *From Savannah to Yorktown: The American Revolution in the South.* Columbia: University of South Carolina Press, 1981.

Parris Island. Parris Island is in coastal Beaufort County and is approximately four miles long and three miles wide. The famous Marine Corps Recruit training base is surrounded by Port Royal harbor and the Beaufort and Broad Rivers, and includes Archer's, Ballast, and Ribbon Creeks. Parris Island is a protected sea and animal wildlife refuge that lists structures on the Register of National Historic Sites. Another recruit depot is in San Diego, California, but Parris Island is older and trains all female Marine recruits.

The French built and then abandoned Charlesfort on Parris Island in 1562. The Spanish subsequently occupied the island and built Santa Elena. The English crown first granted the island to Robert Daniel in 1698. It was later purchased by Edward Archer, who in 1715 sold it to Colonel Alexander Parris, whose name for the island survived.

The Parris Island vicinity fell to Union forces during the Civil War in November 1861. During Reconstruction and after, the spacious Port Royal harbor welcomed all types of ships, and a Port Royal (Parris Island) Naval Station was formally dedicated on June 26, 1891. A hurricane and tidal wave inundated the island on August 28, 1893, and it was reported that several thousand persons died along the South Carolina coast.

Between 1909 and 1911 a Parris Island Marine Officers' School was founded, and a temporary recruit training program was short-lived. Parris Island in 1911 was designated the U.S. Naval Disciplinary Barracks, Port Royal, a military prison site. Yet, as World War I neared, U.S. Marines warranted a unified and larger facility to replace its recruit training at Norfolk, Virginia, and at other naval bases in the United States.

The Port Royal Naval Station was transferred to the Marine Corps on October 25, 1915, and was renamed Marine Barracks, Port Royal. However, the Port Royal mailing address resulted in confusion between the base and the nearby town of Port Royal. The Marines accepted the designation Marine Barracks, Paris (spelled with one *r*) Island. In 1919 the Marine Corps clarified that the colonel's name was spelled with two *r*'s, and the correct spelling, Parris, was adopted.

The island base expanded from 1915 to 1917, and especially when the United States entered World War I. Parris Island trained approximately 46,000 World War I recruits. The base was connected to the mainland during the 1920s via the construction of an earthen causeway and a bridge spanning Archer's Creek. The Great Depression threatened Parris Island's closing during the 1930s, when recruit training was significantly curtailed. The Naval Disciplinary Barracks closed in 1933, but a Page Field aviation facility became operational in 1934. A devastating 1940 hurricane severely damaged Parris Island but inadvertently contributed to the growth and modernization of the base on the eve of World War II.

In January 1918 some two thousand Marines on the parade ground at Parris Island formed the Marine Corps emblem for a World War I photographer. Courtesy, South Caroliniana Library, University of South Carolina

Parris Island from 1941 to 1945 trained 240,509 World War II recruits. The tremendous base expansion greatly altered the Beaufort vicinity, more so than during the previous war. In 1946 the base was designated as the Marine Corps Recruit Depot, Parris Island, South Carolina, as the demands of war-time training were greatly reduced. Yet, the respite was brief. The Korean War (1950–1953) revitalized the base, which saw the largest number of recruits in training on the island at any one time. In 1952 there were 21,540 recruits.

During the mid and late 1950s Parris Island entered a modernization period that introduced permanent brick recruit barracks and more beautification of the base. Scores of old buildings were razed or removed from the post. Parris Island received international attention when a training accident resulted in the deaths of six recruits, who drowned in Ribbon Creek, on April 8, 1956. The ensuing investigation resulted in significant changes to the recruit training program.

An impressive off-base Broad River Bridge was dedicated in 1958. It and one other span reduced the distance from Parris Island to Savannah, Georgia, by half. The bridges facilitated remarkable growth in the South Carolina lowcountry and on Hilton Head. More modernization and base expansion ensued during and after the Vietnam War.

Parris Island was designated as Marine Corps Recruit Depot / Eastern Recruiting Region, Parris Island, South Carolina, in 1983. Visitors to the base were welcome to attend recruit graduations and to visit the Parris Island Museum and designated location of Charlesfort. Parris Island has been the subject of numerous motion pictures, documentaries, and books. EUGENE ALVAREZ

Alvarez, Eugene. *Parris Island.* Charleston, S.C.: Arcadia, 2002.

Particular Baptists. Thought to be the first group of English Baptists to practice baptism by immersion around 1640, Particular Baptists held to the 1689 London Confession of Faith and earlier related documents. Calvinist in theology, they influenced significantly the Regular Baptist movement in South Carolina beginning in the late seventeenth century. In contrast to English General Baptists, however, Particular Baptists believed in a predestined atonement for a "particular" or limited number of elect and "perseverance of the saints," that is, the belief that once one is saved, one is always saved. Like most Baptists, Particulars practiced believer's baptism, while insisting, unlike in the General tradition, that only the elect would experience conversion. Both groups affirmed religious liberty, but unlike the General Baptists, Particulars insisted that each congregation was complete and independent. In colonial South Carolina, the influence of both English Baptist traditions was felt, and at times it was divisive. The congregation at Stono, founded about 1728 as a branch of the Particular Baptist Church at Charleston, underwent a schism around 1735. Fights ensued over property, but in the end the Particular tradition dominated there and elsewhere, at least in most historical interpretations. As with other Calvinists in the New World, under the influence of eighteenth-century Great Awakening revivals, the Calvinism of Particular Baptists was modified enough for them to say that in God's predetermination of redemption, the salvation of all was sought. By the time of the Revolutionary War, most Baptists had grown away from their English background and had assumed their own identities. HELEN LEE TURNER

King, Joe M. *A History of South Carolina Baptists.* Columbia: General Board of the South Carolina Baptist Convention, 1964.
McBeth, H. Leon. *The Baptist Heritage.* Nashville, Tenn.: Broadman, 1987.

Partisans. After the fall of Charleston in May 1780, bands of partisans, or irregular soldiers, sprang up to fight royal control of South Carolina during the Revolutionary War. Subsequently, many backcountry militiamen surrendered and were paroled to their homes instead of serving as prisoners of war. Some refused, however, and fled across the Savannah River to join rebel forces in Georgia. In the meantime, crown forces established garrisons in key parts in the interior of the state, all the while committing depredations against the conquered, including the massacre at the Waxhaws. Moreover, British commander Sir Henry Clinton revoked the paroles of rebel militiamen and required them to join Loyalist militias or be considered fugitives.

In an attempt to preserve state government, Governor John Rutledge fled Charleston in April, and he later moved into North Carolina as the British army advanced inland. With the perception of no real civil authority, many chose to oppose the British and Tories on their own "by force of arms," using organizations loosely based on the state's militia system. In the New Acquisition District (in the Catawba River Valley), patriots began almost immediately to organize and equip themselves for a campaign. In the first days of June 1780, Whig commanders John McClure and William Bratton struck successful blows against Tory forces gathering at Alexander's Old Field and Mobley's Meeting House.

Over the next few months partisan forces, under such commanders as Thomas Sumter and Francis Marion, began to make significant gains against occupying forces. These irregular forces sometimes met the enemy in open battle and other times made hit-and-run raids on vital supply and communication lines. By year's end, Lord Cornwallis, the British commander in the South, was hindered in his intended advance into North Carolina. Practically all of Cornwallis's resources were engaged in pursuing partisan forces in portions of South Carolina. When General Nathanael Greene took command of the Continental army in late 1780, he wisely sought to incorporate partisan forces into his strategic plan for the following year. A prime example of this was his detaching Henry Lee's Legion to Brigadier General Francis Marion's command for the siege of Fort Motte in May 1781.

Several factors have been attributed to partisans' successes. Chief among them was their mobility as they were by and large inseparable from their horses. Although serious fighting was done dismounted, they were able to ride swiftly into and out of conflict and harass the enemy whenever and wherever possible. Some of them were trained, experienced soldiers, and the partisans were primarily residents of the South Carolina backcountry and were accustomed to hunting and defending themselves against Native Americans. Therefore, the frontiersmen were well trained with the weapons and tactics required for unconventional warfare. The partisans also had their particular problems. Oftentimes leaders, such as Sumter, refused to follow directives from General Greene. With little or no financial backing, partisans were plagued with reduced turnouts and desertions. Despite these difficulties, the partisans played a key role in derailing Clinton's southern strategy and in driving the British from South Carolina. SAMUEL K. FORE

Edgar, Walter. *Partisans and Redcoats: The Southern Conflict That Turned the Tide of the American Revolution.* New York: Morrow, 2001.
Ferguson, Clyde R. "Functions of the Partisan Militia in the South during the American Revolution: An Interpretation." In *The Revolutionary War in the South—Power, Conflict, and Leadership: Essays in Honor of John Richard Alden,* edited by W. Robert Higgins. Durham, N.C.: Duke University Press, 1979.
Weigley, Russell F. *The Partisan War: The South Carolina Campaign of 1780–1782.* Columbia: South Carolina Tricentennial Commission, 1970.

Patent medicines. Like other English colonies, colonial South Carolina dosed itself primarily with patented remedies imported from Great Britain. Home-manufactured remedies occasionally made an appearance as well—for example, the nostrum advertised by the "Dutch Ladies" in Charleston in 1743, which claimed to be a "Choice Cure for the Flux, Fevers, Worms, bad Stomach [and] Pains in the Head." Other imported medicines, such as British Oil and Dalby's Carminative, were pirated by Charleston manufacturers and produced well into the twentieth century.

Nationalism spurred by the Revolution increased the number of American-made nostrums, although few originated in South Carolina or the South. During the Civil War, Confederate nationalism prompted the Charleston druggists Van Schaack and Grierson to advertise "SOUTHERN PREPARATIONS!" and listed ten patent medicines produced within Confederate boundaries, ranging from the "Cherokee Remedy" to "McLean's Volcanic Oil Liniment."

South Carolinians became great patent-medicine users after the war, but the market was dominated by northern-produced goods. A Columbia editor complained in 1866 that the southern press sold cut-rate advertising to Yankee "patent blood-suckers." Before 1865 ended, a Charleston druggist resumed shipping southern botanicals for packaged remedies made in Massachusetts. Countless southern barns were painted with ads for northern nostrums. Patent medicines were made in the South, but most developed only regional or local markets. When pellagra was identified at the beginning of the twentieth century, Spartanburg contributed Pellagracide and Ez-X-Ba to the sure-cure category. The latter was made by Ezxba W. Dedmond, an uneducated field hand who claimed that its secret had been imparted to him by God. An African American from Orangeburg, William F. Edwards, concocted Dy-O-Fe, promoted mainly to blacks as a virtual panacea.

Notices of judgment for cases settled under the Food and Drugs Act of 1906 during its early decades reveal more instances of nostrums shipped into South Carolina. Regulators in Charleston seized products made in Georgia, North Carolina, and Maryland. A 1929 case, however, dealt with Owen's Oil, made in Union and promoted with extravagant curative claims for numerous severe ailments. Seized in Charleston, the case came to trial and no claimant appeared, so the court ordered that the nostrum be destroyed. Another patent medicine, Dr. Neuffer's Lung Tonic, marketed by the Abbeville physician G. A. Neuffer during World War I, promised to combat influenza and prevent consumption. Neuffer's tonic flourished until banned by the Food and Drug Administration in 1975. JAMES HARVEY YOUNG

Neuffer, Irene. "The Passing of Dr. Neuffer's Lung Tonic." *Sandlapper* 8 (November 1975): 19–21.
Young, James Harvey. "Patent Medicines: An Element in Southern Distinctiveness?" In *Disease and Distinctiveness in the American South,* edited by

Todd L. Savitt and James Harvey Young. Knoxville: University of Tennessee Press, 1988.

———. "Self-Dosage." In *Encyclopedia of Southern Culture,* edited by Charles Reagan Wilson and William Ferris. Chapel Hill: University of North Carolina Press, 1989.

Patterson, Gladys Elizabeth Johnston (b. 1939). Legislator, congresswoman. Born in Columbia on November 18, 1939, "Liz" Patterson is the third child of Olin Dewitt Johnston and Gladys Atkinson. Her father served both as governor of South Carolina and as a U.S. senator. She received a public school elementary education in Kensington, Maryland, and graduated from Spartanburg High School in 1957. After receiving her B.A. degree from Columbia College in 1961, Patterson did graduate work in political science at the University of South Carolina. After completing her formal education, Patterson served as a public affairs officer with the Peace Corps (1962–1964), with VISTA (1965–1966) in Washington, D.C., and as an administrator with the Head Start program in Columbia (1966–1968). She married the attorney Dwight Fleming Patterson of Spartanburg on April 15, 1967. The marriage produced three children.

Often active in community and Democratic Party politics, Patterson worked as a staff assistant for Congressman James Mann in 1969 and 1970. In 1975 she was elected to the Spartanburg County Council to fill an unexpired term, serving until 1976. Patterson was later elected to the South Carolina Senate, where she served from 1979 to 1986. In office, Patterson advocated fiscal responsibility and carefully scrutinized budgets to eliminate what she deemed to be unnecessary spending. She also favored improved health care and educational services. While in the state Senate, Patterson served as a member of the Governor's Task Force on Hunger and Nutrition.

In 1986 Patterson ran for the U.S. Congress. In the predominantly Republican Fourth District, she defeated Republican candidate William Workman III, the mayor of Greenville. She served in Congress for three terms (1987–1993). Known as a conservative Democrat, Patterson continued to promote budget reform. She also served on committees dealing with banking, veterans' affairs, hunger, and international competitiveness. In addition, she was a member and later chair of the bipartisan Congressional Textile Caucus, a group dedicated to promoting the textile industry, traditionally a major source of jobs in upstate South Carolina.

Patterson lost her reelection bid in 1992 to conservative Republican Bob Inglis of Greenville. During the campaign, Inglis highlighted his dedication to term limits and his opposition to political action committees, which had provided a large portion of Patterson's campaign contributions. The Christian Coalition, which opposed her, also figured in Patterson's defeat. After the election, in discussing her loss, Patterson stated about her constituents, "I thought they would realize how hard I'd worked for them." She added, "I know these people. . . . They know me. I can't believe they would question my life, my God, my religion."

Not yet ready to abandon her political career, Patterson sought the office of lieutenant governor in 1994. She won a contested Democratic primary but lost in the general election to Republican Bob Peeler. Having already begun work as director of continuing education at Converse College, she remained in that post after her election defeat. In her life, Patterson has exemplified the improved public options available to southern women of her generation. MARIAN ELIZABETH STROBEL

Bailey, N. Louise, Mary L. Morgan, and Carolyn R. Taylor, eds. *Biographical Directory of the South Carolina Senate, 1776–1985.* 3 vols. Columbia: University of South Carolina Press, 1986.

Patterson, Elizabeth Johnston. Papers. Modern Political Collections, South Caroliniana Library, University of South Carolina, Columbia.

Rosenfeld, Megan. "Anatomy of a Defeat." *Washington Post,* November 12, 1992, pp. D1, D8.

Patterson, John James (1830–1912). U.S. senator. Patterson was born in Waterloo, Pennsylvania, on August 8, 1830. He graduated from Jefferson College in 1848, after which he went into the newspaper business. He edited the Juniata *Sentinel* in 1852 and then became an owner and editor of the Harrisburg *Telegraph,* the "home organ" of Simon Cameron, one of the state's most powerful Republicans. Patterson was elected to the Pennsylvania House of Representatives in 1854 and served one term. He served in the Civil War as a captain in a volunteer infantry unit. In 1862 he sought election to Congress but was defeated. From 1863 to 1869 he was a banker in Pennsylvania.

In 1869 Patterson moved to Columbia, South Carolina, where he was involved in banking and railroad development. In that connection he was accused of bribing legislators to pass laws favorable to his interests, but no action was taken. In 1872 Patterson was a candidate for the U.S. Senate from South Carolina. It was alleged that his only qualification was money with which to bribe legislators. On the day of the election, the Republican Columbia *Daily Union* warned that "the people will regard his election as a direct bargain and sale." He won the election but was immediately arrested for bribery based on the statements of two legislators who claimed that they had been paid to vote for him. He was never tried, although newspaper reports accused him of using as much as $50,000 to secure his election. From that time forward, Patterson carried the nickname "Honest John"—honest because if he promised a bribe, he always paid it. While many of the allegations against Patterson are questionable, some legislators who voted for him later complained that they had not received promised bribes, with one quoting Patterson as saying that "the damned election had cost him more than it was worth."

Serving in the Senate from 1873 to 1879, Patterson advocated stronger federal enforcement of Reconstruction measures and increased federal appropriations for the South. In the disputed election of 1876, Patterson supported the Republican claimants to election, unlike South Carolina's other Republican senator, the conservative Thomas J. Robertson. Patterson argued in Washington for federal support for South Carolina Republicans, but to no avail. In 1877, after Democrats had retaken control of the state, Patterson and other leading Republicans were indicted on bribery and corruption charges. However, the administration of Wade Hampton III abandoned its investigations after federal officials agreed to drop charges of election fraud against South Carolina Democrats. Although cleared, Patterson was not a candidate for reelection in 1878.

After leaving the Senate, Patterson remained in Washington until 1886, when he returned to Pennsylvania and engaged in business. He died of pneumonia in Mifflintown, Pennsylvania, on September 28, 1912, and was buried in the Westminster Presbyterian churchyard. HYMAN S. RUBIN III

Current, Richard Nelson. *Those Terrible Carpetbaggers.* New York: Oxford University Press, 1988.

Reynolds, John S. *Reconstruction in South Carolina, 1865–1877.* 1905. Reprint, New York: Negro Universities Press, 1969.

Seip, Terry. *The South Returns to Congress: Men, Economic Measures, and Intersectional Relationships, 1868–1879.* Baton Rouge: Louisiana State University Press, 1983.

Paul, Marian Baxter (1897–1980). Public health official. Marian Baxter Paul gave thirty years of public service to South Carolina as the supervisor of Negro Home Demonstration Work, which provided instruction to thousands of rural black households in food preparation and production, hygiene, and sanitation. Her tenure was the longest of any supervisor with that organization—from 1931 until 1959. She was born on April 4, 1897, in Georgetown County, the daughter of Jonathan and Harriet Baxter. She married R. Hopton Paul, a Columbia tailor. They had no children. Nothing is known about her formative education. She attended Hampton University before graduating with a degree in home economics from Pennsylvania State College. After returning home, she worked as a Jeanes rural teacher supervisor in Georgetown County. She later taught at Booker T. Washington High School in Columbia until she became state agent for Negro Home Demonstration Work. In South Carolina, as well as other southern and border states, the extension service was racially segregated.

In 1931 there were only eight counties that employed Negro Home Demonstration agents. Many of these women lacked college degrees. It was directly through the efforts of Marian Paul that the staff employed thirty-five agents and six assistant agents by 1957. Paul recruited agents mostly from South Carolina State College, giving many college-educated African American women employment opportunities outside school teaching. Paul taught her agents to carry out demonstration programs effectively. She encouraged them to respond to local needs and to encourage community involvement in the planning of their programs and also through clubs and county extension councils. These activities gave black South Carolinians practical experience in organization and leadership that would become vital during the civil rights era.

One of the singular accomplishments of Paul's career was her idea to build a modern home in a rural community to offer blacks an opportunity to learn that they could afford modestly priced, yet comfortable homes. She played a key role in securing a grant from the General Education Board for the home's construction. The house was erected in the Jeremiah Community of Williamsburg County. Negro Home Demonstration agents from around the state brought clients to "vacation" in the house and to learn skills ranging from home design to homemaking.

Paul's work ranged far afield. State government agencies routinely used her as a conduit to provide services to blacks in need. She worked with federal agencies during the New Deal era to help rural blacks gain access to a variety of relief and recovery services. During World War II she actively worked with the United Service Organization (USO) and with war bond drives. She was one of two black members of the executive board of the South Carolina Human Relations Council. In her annual reports, Paul commented on the politics of her time and pointed out the unjust treatment of African Americans in South Carolina. Her service to her race placed her in the vanguard of the state's black leadership. Paul died on June 27, 1980, and was buried in Palmetto Cemetery, Columbia. CARMEN V. HARRIS

Harris, Carmen V. "Grace under Pressure: The Black Home Extension Service in South Carolina, 1919–1966." In *Rethinking Home Economics: Women and the History of a Profession,* edited by Sarah Stage and Virginia Vincenti. Ithaca, N.Y.: Cornell University Press, 1997.

Pawleys Island (Georgetown County; 2000 pop. 138). Situated on the Waccamaw Neck in Georgetown County, Pawleys Island is one of the oldest summer resorts on the east coast. In the eighteenth century rice planters, their families, and slaves stayed in cottages of cypress and pine near the saltwater to escape malaria. By 1822 cottages appeared on the island, and by 1858 eleven stood on this four-mile-long, one-quarter-mile-wide stretch of sand.

The decline of rice caused a rise in timber harvesting, and Atlantic Coast Lumber Company bought land on the neck. In 1901 the company ran a railroad from the river to the beach, bought or built houses, and created an employee retreat. Others opened homes to paying guests. Beginning in 1905, northerners bought river plantations as winter retreats.

Pawleys Island. Photograph by Larry Early. Courtesy, Larry Early, Raleigh, N.C.

In the early twentieth century U.S. Highway 17, connecting New York to Miami, passed through the community. The Hammock Shop opened on the highway by 1939, as did restaurants and stores. Marlow's Store sold items ranging from caviar to flip-flops. Area residents once earned a living farming, fishing, logging, or commuting to the paper mill or to motels. In 1954 Hurricane Hazel destroyed many houses on the island, yet spurred an interest in the resort. In the 1980s plantations were developed as golf communities and many visitors made the island their permanent home. In 1985 the town of Pawleys Island incorporated. Hurricane Hugo in 1989 brought major challenges to homeowners and businesses on the Waccamaw Neck.

Pawleys retains an "arrogantly shabby" uniqueness. Creek docks, porches, and lookouts define its skyline. A mixed culture of natives and newcomers and of affluence and poverty, Pawleys has strong traditions. The spirit of the "Gray Man," a local legend, is said to appear to warn islanders of impending storms in this barefoot paradise. LEE G. BROCKINGTON

Bolick, Julian. *The Return of the Gray Man.* Clinton, S.C.: Jacobs, 1961.
Chase, Eugene B., and Lee G. Brockington. *Pawleys Island: Stories from the Porch.* Pawleys Island, S.C.: Pawleys Island Civic Association, 2003.
Chase, Eugene B., Katherine H. Richardson, et al. *Pawleys Island Historically Speaking.* Pawleys Island, S.C.: Pawleys Island Civic Association, 1994.
Linder, Suzanne Cameron, and Marta Leslie Thacker. *Historical Atlas of the Rice Plantations of Georgetown County and the Santee River.* Columbia: South Carolina Department of Archives and History for the Historic Ricefields Association, 2001.

Payne, Daniel Alexander (1811–1893). Educator, clergyman. Payne was born free in Charleston on February 24, 1811, to London and Martha Payne but was orphaned as a child. He was trained early in Methodist traditions at Cumberland Methodist Church. He served apprenticeships in carpentry and tailoring and was formally educated in one of Charleston's free black private schools. Payne chose to pursue a life of belles lettres, opening his own school in 1829. He mainly taught free black students, but his student body of approximately sixty pupils also included some slaves, who were instructed clandestinely. Payne's career as an educator in Charleston was short-lived, however. White Carolinians, apprehensive about the abolitionist movement, were further alarmed by the advanced subjects that free blacks such as Payne were teaching. In 1834 a new state law prohibited both slave literacy and schools maintained by free blacks.

Unable to continue as a South Carolina educator, Payne sought the advice of friends and white minsters such as John Bachman, the well-known Lutheran pastor and naturalist. After receiving letters of introduction from these men to their northern friends, in 1835 Payne left South Carolina to enroll at Gettysburg Theological Seminary in Pennsylvania. In 1837 he received his ordination as a Lutheran minister, becoming the second African American to do so (the first being Jehu Jones, Jr., also a Charlestonian). Unable to find a Lutheran appointment, Payne eventually moved to Philadelphia, where contact with the African Methodist Episcopal (AME) Church led him to join its ministry in 1842. During the remaining antebellum years he filled appointments in Philadelphia, Washington, D.C., and Baltimore. In 1848 he was appointed the first historiographer of the church and wrote its first official history. In 1852 Payne was elected bishop and was the first with formal theological training.

Payne was the perennial educator. While in Philadelphia he established a school, a Sunday school, and a literary society. As a minister and bishop, through his efforts to improve clerical preparation, Payne became the architect of the formally educated AME ministry. He argued that better-educated clergymen were more efficient and better able to elevate the race. Nevertheless, his efforts frequently caused contentious debate. Even so, with the assistance and encouragement of Bishop Morris Brown (another Charlestonian), the 1844 General Conference adopted recommendations of Payne's committee on education, requiring a formal curriculum for future ministers. His crowning achievement as a churchman and educator occurred in 1863, when he persuaded the church to purchase Wilberforce University in Ohio. This was the first college in the country controlled by African Americans, and Payne served as its president until 1876.

In 1863 Bishop Payne dispatched the first AME missionaries into the lower South, where they focused their initial efforts among the freedmen near Beaufort, South Carolina. In May 1865 Bishop Payne returned to South Carolina to preside over the establishment of the South Carolina Conference of the AME Church. One of his greatest post–Civil War challenges was to assist in supplying enough trained clergymen for a church that was rapidly expanding. In his later ministry he continued promoting educational opportunities for African Americans.

Payne married twice. In 1847 he married Julia Ferris, who died a year later in childbirth. He married Eliza J. Clark in 1853. Payne died on November 29, 1893, in Wilberforce, Ohio. He was buried in Laurel Cemetery, Baltimore. BERNARD E. POWERS, JR.

Coan, Josephus R. *Daniel Alexander Payne.* Philadelphia: A.M.E. Book Concern, 1935.

Dickerson, Dennis C. *Religion, Race, and Region: Research Notes on A.M.E. Church History.* Nashville, Tenn.: A.M.E.C. Sunday School Union, 1995.

Killian, Charles D. "Bishop Daniel A. Payne: An Apostle of Wesley." *Methodist History* 24 (1986): 107–19.

Payne, Daniel A. *Recollections of Seventy Years.* 1888. Reprint, New York: Arno, 1969.

Stange, Douglas C. "A Note on Daniel A. Payne." *Negro History Bulletin* 28 (October 1964): 9–10.

Peace, Roger Craft (1899–1968). Journalist, businessman, U.S. senator. Peace was born on May 19, 1899, in Greenville. He was the son of Bony Hampton Peace and Laura Estelle Chandler. Bony Peace was the business manager for the *Greenville News,* and Roger began working as a reporter for that newspaper in 1914. Although his college career was briefly interrupted by service in World War I, he graduated from Furman University in 1919. The next year he married Etca Tindal Walker. They had two children.

Bony Peace bought the *Greenville News* in 1919, and Roger joined the permanent staff as sports editor. By 1924 he was in his father's old position of business manager. The Peace family continued to acquire more media outlets in the upstate. In 1927 they purchased their Greenville rival, the *Greenville Piedmont,* an afternoon paper. The company was known as the Greenville News-Piedmont Company, and Peace became the publisher and president of the company when his father died in 1934. Around the same time, the company started Greenville's first radio station, WFBC. The company also gave Greenville its first television station, WFBC-TV, in 1953. In 1954 the company expanded its operations into other states when it purchased newspapers in Asheville, North Carolina. In 1967 the broadcasting and publishing interests were merged to form Multimedia, Inc., with Peace as chairman. Building on its holdings in South Carolina and North Carolina, Multimedia expanded operations into Georgia, Alabama, and Tennessee.

In addition to overseeing the media company, Peace devoted much of his life to public service. When James F. Byrnes was appointed to the United States Supreme Court in 1941, Governor Burnet R. Maybank appointed Peace to fill Byrnes's seat in the United States Senate for a four-month interim period. During World War II, Peace chaired South Carolina's Preparedness for Peace Commission, which developed plans for the state's economy after the war. He was a member of the State Research Planning and Development Board from 1945 to 1955. Peace also aided his local community by serving as president of the Greater Greenville Chamber of Commerce and as a trustee of Furman University.

In 1957 Peace was awarded an honorary doctorate from the University of South Carolina. Posthumous honors included induction into the South Carolina Press Association Hall of Fame in 1981 and induction into the South Carolina Business Hall of Fame in 1991. Greenville's Peace Center for the Performing Arts, completed in 1990, was built thanks to a generous gift from the Peace family.

Peace died on August 21, 1968, at his home in Greenville. He was preceded in death by his first wife, who died on June 21, 1965, and his second wife, Amy Newgren, whom he married on April 9, 1966, and who died on September 19, 1967. Peace was buried in Springwood Cemetery. AARON W. MARRS

Lunan, Bert, and Robert A. Pierce. *Legacy of Leadership.* Columbia: South Carolina Business Hall of Fame, 1999.

"Roger Peace, News Media Builder, Dies." *Greenville News,* August 22, 1968, p. 1.

Peaches. State fruit. The peach (*Prunus persica,* Rosaceae) is a temperate-zone stone fruit that is grown widely around the world. Peaches originated in China, where they have been cultivated for thousands of years. From China, peaches migrated to ancient Persia and then to Europe. In the 1600s the Spaniards introduced peaches to North America. By the early 1700s there were several prominent

By the 1930s South Carolina peaches were being shipped to markets up and down the eastern seaboard. WPA Photograph. Courtesy, South Caroliniana Library, University of South Carolina

accounts of peach cultivation in South Carolina. The native Indians cultivated peaches and preserved them by drying and pressing them into cakes. Henry William Ravenel of Aiken is credited as the first commercial grower to ship peaches outside the state in the 1850s.

At the start of the twenty-first century, peaches were the most widely grown commercial fruit crop in South Carolina, comprising more than seventeen thousand acres in the state and with an estimated annual farm value of between $30 million and $40 million. Peaches have been grown in three primary regions proceeding from the mountains to the coast: the Piedmont, "The Ridge" region between Columbia and Augusta, and the coastal plains. South Carolina ranks as the number-two peach producer in the United States, after California. In 1984 the peach was designated by the General Assembly as the state fruit of South Carolina.

More than forty commercial varieties of peaches are grown in South Carolina. In a normal year more than two hundred million pounds of peaches are harvested in the state. The peach harvest season begins in early May and ends in late September. The vast majority of the commercially grown South Carolina peaches are destined for fresh markets up the eastern seaboard of the United States. Local roadside markets are the second major outlet for fresh peaches. Some peaches are grown specifically for processing into baby food and other value-added processed products.

Most peach trees in South Carolina's commercial orchards actually begin in Tennessee nurseries. First a seedling rootstock is grown, and then a desirable fruiting cultivar is grafted onto that seedling. Trees are then dug bare-root and shipped to South Carolina for planting during the winter. Peach trees begin bearing fruit during their third year after planting, and peach orchards will remain in production for roughly fifteen years. A mature tree that is well cared for can produce up to eight bushels of fruit and may use up to forty gallons of water per day near harvest.

Peach cultivation in South Carolina can be very profitable, but several factors may negatively impact year-to-year profitability. Some of these include adverse environmental conditions (warm winters, spring freezes, hail, drought), pests and disease (peach tree short life, oak root rot disease), and economic factors (labor costs, urban encroachment). To diminish the impact of some of these factors, growers are utilizing newer technologies such as microsprinkler irrigation, integrated pest management, wind machines, and resistant rootstocks. In addition, they are constantly planting newer, high-quality varieties to expand their marketing opportunities. DESMOND R. LAYNE

Corbin, Mike. *Family Trees: The Peach Culture of the Piedmont.* Spartanburg, S.C.: Hub City Writers Project, 1998.

Peachtree Rock (Lexington County). Peachtree Rock is the namesake of a 305-acre South Carolina Nature Conservancy preserve located on the Sandhills of Lexington County, sixteen miles southwest of Columbia. The rock is a small, highly eroded remnant of sandstone perched on a small, tapered base. Peachtree Rock and the surrounding sandstones were formed in a marine environment during the Middle Eocene epoch. Walking from Peachtree Rock toward the dirt road at the entrance to the preserve, the observer traverses sediments of progressively younger ages: Upper Eocene marine sands, river-deposited sands from the Miocene epoch, and sand dunes from the Pliocene and Pleistocene epochs.

The geology of the Peachtree Rock preserve reflects the conditions that existed during the Eocene to the Pleistocene epochs. During the Eocene epoch the sea levels globally were much higher than they are in the twenty-first century, and the climate was warmer. Many species of marine animals swam in seas that covered what is now the coastal plains. The nature of the fossils found at Peachtree Rock give evidence that they were not formed in deep water, but rather in shallow water near shore. By the Pleistocene epoch the sea levels had fallen and the Peachtree Rock area was above water.

Other interesting features of Peachtree Rock preserve are found by a small waterfall that runs over sandstone preserved by a silicified caprock. The small Eocene marine fossils located near the falls consist of shell hash and shrimp burrows as trace fossils. The preserve also contains a wide diversity of plant life that can be observed by walking the trails that wind more than a mile through the ridges and dunes of the area. CAROLYN H. MURPHY

Able, Gene. *Exploring South Carolina: Wild and Natural Places.* Rock Hill, S.C.: Palmetto Byways, 1995.

Murphy, Carolyn H. *Carolina Rocks! The Geology of South Carolina.* Orangeburg, S.C.: Sandlapper, 1995.

Peanuts. Peanuts have been cultivated and consumed in South Carolina since colonial times. Native to South America, peanut culture was carried to Africa by European explorers. Later, slave ships often carried quantities of peanuts to feed enslaved Africans, and surplus nuts were sold on the docks. Thus, peanuts likely entered South Carolina as a by-product of slavery. Many South Carolinians raised peanuts for home consumption, but some were being exported for sale soon after the Revolution.

Peanuts were an important subsistence crop throughout the nineteenth century. The nuts were roasted or boiled for humans, while the shells and vines were sometimes fed to livestock. A growing market for peanut products encouraged peanut culture in the early twentieth century. In the 1910s, as the boll weevil crept ever closer, many South Carolina farmers planted peanuts as an alternative to cotton. Peanut culture was labor-intensive, however, and acreage expanded slowly. In the 1930s the federal government established a production control program for peanuts. Growers accepted land-bound acreage allotments in exchange for price supports and tariff protection. Later, poundage quotas were imposed as well.

Peanut culture underwent substantial changes after World War II. With profits virtually assured by the government commodity program, growers invested in tractors, cultivators, and harvesting machines. In the 1950s self-propelled peanut combines appeared. Moreover, improved seed stocks and chemical fertilizers multiplied yields dramatically. South Carolina production per acre passed one thousand pounds in 1956, two thousand pounds in 1971, and three thousand pounds in 1996. Predictably, given Georgia's leadership in peanut production, peanut culture in the Palmetto State prospered along the Savannah River. Allendale, Hampton, and Barnwell Counties have been big producers, as have Sumter and Lee Counties in the Midlands. In 2001 South Carolina growers received $8 million for about ten thousand acres of peanuts.

Like other government commodity plans, the peanut program came under careful scrutiny in the 1990s. Candy companies and other large-scale processors argued that the artificially high price of peanuts hobbled American industry and penalized consumers. In 2002 Congress approved a five-year buyout plan to end production controls. Since 1982 the town of Pelion has hosted the annual South Carolina Peanut Party, a celebration of the state's peanut culture. ELDRED E. PRINCE, JR.

Kirby, Jack Temple. *Rural Worlds Lost: The American South, 1920–1960.* Baton Rouge: Louisiana State University Press, 1987.

Pearson, David Gene (b. 1934). Racecar driver. A native of the mill town of Whitney in Spartanburg County, Pearson has been one of the greatest drivers in the history of National Association for Stock Car Auto Racing (NASCAR) Winston Cup racing. In a twenty-six-year career, Pearson amassed 105 career wins, second on the all-time list, and three season championships (1966, 1968, 1969). Pearson holds the NASCAR record for winning percentage (18.29 percent) and percentage of races started from the pole (20 percent).

Pearson was born on December 22, 1934. He quit school after the ninth grade and, like most young men in his community, followed his parents into the Whitney Cotton Mill. However, life in the mill was not for Pearson. He soon quit and went to work in his brother's body shop. Fortunately for Pearson, Spartanburg in the 1950s and 1960s was a hotbed of stock-car racing, and an opportunity opened for him to compete in local dirt-track events. Soon, Pearson became a regular at tracks in the upstate area. After winning the track championship at Greenville-Pickens Speedway in 1959, fans pooled their money to help Pearson buy a car to race at the NASCAR Grand National (which became Nextell Cup in 2004) level.

Pearson quickly demonstrated the talent to compete not only on the short dirt tracks but also on the growing number of high-banked, paved superspeedways. In his early years Pearson raced for such NASCAR legends as Ray Fox, Spartanburg's Cotton Owens, and the powerful Holman-Moody team. Pearson's most productive years as a driver came in the seven years he drove for the Wood Brothers (1972–1979). In the number 21 Mercury, Pearson won forty-three times and captured fifty-one poles. In 1973 Pearson had one of the most dominating seasons in NASCAR history, winning eleven times in only eighteen starts. Pearson had his greatest success at Darlington Raceway, South Carolina's only superspeedway. As of 1980 he still held the record of ten Winston Cup wins at the track.

Pearson has also been known for his longtime on-track rivalry with Richard Petty. Between 1963 and 1977 the pair finished first and second in sixty-three races, with Pearson winning thirty-three. In the 1976 Daytona 500, the pair had their most memorable duel in one of the greatest races in NASCAR history. On the backstretch of the final lap of the race, Pearson moved past Petty into first place. Petty attempted to regain the lead but cut in too quickly, sending Pearson into the wall and losing control of his own car. Both cars spun wildly into the infield only one hundred yards from the finish line. Pearson demonstrated his legendary cool as he kept the car running, while Petty's engine died. Pearson's car limped across the finish line at 20 mph to secure his first, and only, win in NASCAR's most prestigious event. Despite their on-track rivalry, Petty asserted, "David was the best I ever ran with." In 1988 Pearson retired to his home near Spartanburg, where he remained active for a time as a successful car owner. DANIEL S. PIERCE

Chapin, Kim. *Fast as White Lightning: The Story of Stock Car Racing.* Rev. ed. New York: Three Rivers, 1998.

Golenbock, Peter. *The Last Lap: The Life and Times of NASCAR's Legendary Heroes.* Rev. ed. New York: Hungry Minds, 2001.

Pee Dee River. The Pee Dee is a river system that drains northeastern South Carolina and central North Carolina. It is properly called the Great Pee Dee or more commonly the Big Pee Dee to distinguish it from one of its tributaries, the Little Pee Dee River. One of the Carolinas' principal rivers, the Pee Dee begins its journey in the mountains of North Carolina, where it is known as the Yadkin River, and travels 197 miles in South Carolina to meet the Atlantic Ocean in Georgetown's Winyah Bay. Along the way, the Pee Dee receives the outflow of several smaller streams, including the Black, Little Pee Dee, Lynches, and Waccamaw Rivers, and discharges about fifteen thousand cubic feet of water per second into Winyah Bay. The Pee Dee River was named for a Native American people of the same name who inhabited the region.

Until well into the twentieth century, riverboats carried freight and passengers on the Pee Dee River between Cheraw and Georgetown. Courtesy, South Caroliniana Library, University of South Carolina

For thousands of years people lived along the Pee Dee, and the river provided generously of fish, game, and waterfowl. The Native American kingdom of Cofitachiqui extended into the Pee Dee region and thrived for centuries before Europeans arrived. Spanish conquistadors entered the Pee Dee region during the 1540s–1560s, and Englishmen arrived in the early eighteenth century. By the 1730s the English had settled around Winyah Bay, and soon they were moving up the Pee Dee, establishing a village upstream at Cheraw.

The Pee Dee's first cash crop was naval stores: the tar, pitch, and turpentine produced by the region's pine trees and used on sailing vessels as wood preservatives and caulking. The Pee Dee backcountry was covered with ancient pine forests, and the naval-stores business thrived as thousands of barrels per year were rafted down the river bound for Europe. By the 1730s rice was replacing naval stores as the region's principal crop. Rice thrived in the swampy areas along the Pee Dee, and soon hundreds of fields were cleared and thousands of enslaved Africans were imported to work in them. By the 1740s blacks outnumbered whites in much of the region.

The coming of cotton about 1800 transformed the Pee Dee yet again. Thanks to cotton's low startup costs, the Pee Dee backcountry boomed, as large flatboats propelled by African slaves carried cotton bales to Georgetown and merchandise back to eager consumers at every landing along the way.

The maturation of the cotton economy and the advent of steamboats marked a golden age of the river. By the 1820s steam-powered barges were plowing the dark waters of the Pee Dee, and river towns such as Cheraw, Georgetown, and Society Hill flourished. Steamboats soon received fierce competition from railroads, which diverted freight from Georgetown to Charleston and Wilmington, North Carolina. Railroad expansion in the late nineteenth century and the advent of automobiles in the early twentieth century gradually replaced river transport altogether, but the Pee Dee's importance as a water and power source increased. Population growth and industrial expansion made increasing demands on the river, and development polluted the Pee Dee with silt, chemicals, and sewage. By the 1970s environmental legislation was in place, and by century's end the Pee Dee was much cleaner. ELDRED E. PRINCE, JR.

Kovacik, Charles F., and John J. Winberry. *South Carolina: The Making of a Landscape.* 1987. Reprint, Columbia: University of South Carolina Press, 1989.

Linder, Suzanne C., with Emily Linder Johnson. *A River in Time: The Yadkin–Pee Dee River System.* Spartanburg, S.C.: Palmetto Conservation Foundation, 2000.

Pellagra. The threat that pellagra once posed in the South is now largely and happily forgotten. But in the first three decades of the twentieth century it was on many southerners' minds. By the late 1920s, for no apparent reason, it was striking some 200,000 people a year, both white and black in about equal measure.

Though death claimed only about three percent of cases, pellagra's ravages would have made many victims wish for an end. Known as the sickness of the four D's—diarrhea, dermatitis, dementia, and death—its first sign was a reddening of areas commonly exposed to sun. Often confused with sunburn or poison oak, pellagra was indisputable when reddened skin crusted over and peeled, leaving splotched arms and telltale butterflylike lesions on the face. Over time, general malaise became serious depression and in the worst cases dementia, whose victims were commonly committed to (and often died in) asylums.

Such suffering, especially prevalent in textile mill villages, led to the convening in Columbia of three national conferences between 1909 and 1915, attended by health officers, scientists, and physicians. Their mission: discover pellagra's cause, which could open a way to prevent and perhaps even cure it. The disease had been known in Mediterranean Europe since the mid–eighteenth century, but no one could work out its etiology. The favored theory was that it was caused by eating spoiled corn. And certainly the heavy reliance on grits and cornmeal by mill hands seemed to give that theory confirmation. But by the 1900s other ideas also found favor. Some saw an insect origin, while many others, such as South Carolina health officer James A. Hayne, argued for the presence of some undiscovered bacterium.

But pellagra's root cause was not biological; it was economic. Southerners fell ill because they were poor and ate a diet heavy on salt pork, molasses, grits, and cornmeal but woefully deficient in foods known to prevent pellagra, such as eggs, milk and butter, fresh meat, and green vegetables. Chief advocate of this novel idea that the absence of something could cause disease was Joseph Goldberger, a Public Health Service epidemiologist and Hungarian immigrant. Because his notion assaulted southern pride and flew in the face of conventional wisdom, it faced a wall of opposition. But in a series of brilliant field researches in Mississippi and South Carolina from 1914 to 1916, his ideas won general, if grudging, acceptance.

Having shown pellagra's tie to diet, Goldberger turned to a group of Spartanburg County mill villages to establish that poverty was the ruling link between the two. The connection was tragically clear: mill hands earning top wages showed a disease rate of only three and a half cases per thousand, while those earning the least—too little to buy preventive foods—had twelve times more pellagra. Especially troubling was the ten-times-higher rate among nonworking women within the textile industry. Pregnancy, Goldberger reasoned, was partly to blame, for the developing fetus would have undermined most women's fragile nutritional stability. But the disparity also sprang from mill mothers' habit of deferring pellagra-preventive foods to family workers.

Goldberger's hypothesis became unarguable with America's entry into World War I, which brought an economic upturn so robust that it lifted even mill operatives' resources. By 1919 wages in the two Carolinas had vaulted 240 percent. Pellagra fell in equal measure, dropping by 1920 to its lowest level ever. Doctors in Spartanburg County, where Goldberger had worked, were so jubilant that they held a gala dinner to "bury pellagra." Goldberger rejected such optimism and warned that if bad times returned, so would pellagra. And that soon happened: 1920 began a national depression that, along with the boll weevil, hit the cotton South uniquely hard. As cotton profits, prices, and wages fell, pellagra returned with a vengeance. In 1921 it started a climb that would go on for nearly a decade.

Yet if economic stagnation and pellagra looked to be permanent burdens, history pulled an unexpected surprise. In 1925 Goldberger discovered the miraculous curative powers of cheap, abundant brewer's yeast. By the late 1920s an expanded network of local health departments was putting that discovery to use. South Carolina's effort was typical: the health officer James Hayne finally got behind Goldberger and from 1928 to 1929 oversaw the disbursement of six tons of yeast through county health units to cure some 34,000 people. In the 1930s, even as economic conditions worsened, pellagra's decline continued, thanks partly to Red Cross participation in yeast distribution but also (and ironically) to cotton's further collapse. Farmers, now forced to diversify, began raising those pellagra-preventive foods for which they previously allotted no acreage. By 1940 pellagra had almost vanished from the South.

Sadly, Goldberger died in 1929 before these final victories. He also did not witness the solution of pellagra's great mystery: its biological cause. In the late 1930s biochemists at the University of Wisconsin showed that it was the absence of niacin (a B vitamin) that unleashed the malady. Later work also proved the spoiled-corn theorists partly right. Corn diets lacked tryptophan, the vital ingredient in the body's production of niacin. ED BEARDSLEY

Beardsley, Edward H. *A History of Neglect: Health Care for Blacks and Mill Workers in the Twentieth-Century South.* Knoxville: University of Tennessee Press, 1987.

Etheridge, Elizabeth. *The Butterfly Caste: A Social History of Pellagra in the South.* Westport, Conn.: Greenwood, 1972.

Goldberger, Joseph, et al. "A Study of the Relation of Family Income and Other Economic Factors to Pellagra Incidence in Seven Cotton Mill Villages of South Carolina." *Public Health Reports* 35 (November 12, 1920): 2673–714.

Pelzer, Francis Joseph (1826–1916). Entrepreneur, textile manufacturer. Pelzer was born on April 9, 1826, in Charleston, the son of Anton Aloys Pelzer and Johanna M. Clarke. His father had emigrated from Aix-la-Chapelle, Germany, to Charleston, where he was a schoolteacher; Pelzer may have studied at his father's school, but the details of his education are not known. Pelzer began his business career in 1840 working as a clerk for his brother-in-law, E. H.

Rodgers, a cotton factor. In 1847 Rodgers took on Pelzer as a partner. When the elder Rodgers died in 1867, Pelzer reorganized the firm with Rodgers's son as Pelzer, Rodgers, and Company. The firm did as much as $3 million in cotton business annually.

In the years following the Civil War, Pelzer expanded his business interests into other areas connected to his cotton factoring business. He was at the forefront of two major South Carolina industries in the decades after the Civil War: phosphate and textiles. Using capital from his cotton factorage and commission merchant businesses, Pelzer became a director of the Wando Mining and Manufacturing Company in 1868. In May 1870 he was one of the organizers of the Atlantic Phosphate Company, and in 1872 he became its president. In 1878 Pelzer helped to organize the Charleston Bagging Manufacturing Company. He was also president of the Union Wharf and Compress Company of Charleston. Pelzer's connection to cotton also aided him when he organized the Pelzer Manufacturing Company in 1881, one of the first textile mills in the upstate financed by Charleston capitalists. Over the years Pelzer was also involved in many other textile mills and other businesses in the upstate and in Charleston.

In addition to his business pursuits, Pelzer was active in civic life in Charleston. He served as an alderman there twice during the 1870s and was harbor commissioner for a time. Pelzer was on the board of commissioners of the Charleston Orphan House for nearly forty years. He married Sarah Ann Keller on April 13, 1848. After she died in 1872, Pelzer married Eliza Ford de Saussure McIver on May 4, 1875. After a long period of declining health, Pelzer died in Charleston on March 31, 1916, and was buried in the cemetery of the Bethel Methodist Church. BRUCE E. BAKER AND SHEPHERD W. MCKINLEY

"Francis J. Pelzer Has Passed Away." Charleston *News and Courier,* April 1, 1916, p. 10.

Pember, Phoebe Yates (1823–1913). Confederate hospital matron, author. Born in Charleston on August 18, 1823, Pember was the fourth of six daughters born to Jacob Clavius Levy and Fanny Yates, a prosperous and cultured Jewish couple. The family moved to Savannah, Georgia, in 1848. In 1856 she married Thomas Pember, a Christian, and moved to his home in Boston, Massachusetts. He soon thereafter contracted tuberculosis, and the couple relocated to Aiken, South Carolina, where he died on July 9, 1861. Phoebe went to live in Savannah with her parents, who shortly thereafter "refugeed" to Marietta, Georgia.

In November 1862 Pember was approached by Mrs. George W. Randolph, wife of the Confederate secretary of war. She asked Pember to serve as matron in Chimborazo Hospital, a complex of military hospitals on the outskirts of Richmond, Virginia. Pember became chief matron of Hospital No. 2 and is believed to have been the first matron appointed at Chimborazo. In her autobiography Pember described her hospital duties as follows: "I have entire charge of my department, seeing that everything is cleanly, orderly and all prescriptions of physicians are given in the proper time, food properly prepared and so on." She overcame considerable opposition from her male counterparts in the other Chimborazo Hospitals, as well as from some patients, their families, and camp followers. The noted Civil War historian Bell Wiley described her as a "dynamic little woman." On one occasion she even brandished a cocked pistol to defend her supply of medicinal whiskey from an undeserving soldier. After Federal forces captured Richmond in 1865, Pember remained at Chimborazo until "all the sick were either convalescent or dead," caring for wounded Confederates during the transition marked by the Federal occupation.

After the war, Pember returned to Georgia. She traveled a great deal and wrote articles for several periodicals. In 1879 she published *A Southern Woman's Story,* which remains one of the best accounts of hospital care and conditions during the Civil War. She died in Pittsburgh, Pennsylvania, on March 4, 1913, and was buried in Savannah beside her husband in Laurel Grove Cemetery. In 1995 the U.S. Postal Service included Pember on a sheet of twenty stamps honoring persons and events associated with the Civil War. JANE MCCUTCHEN BROWN

Pember, Phoebe Yates. *A Southern Woman's Story: Life in Confederate Richmond.* 1879. Reprint, Columbia: University of South Carolina Press, 2002.

Rosen, Robert. "New Stamp Honors Charleston-Born Confederate Heroine." Charleston *Post and Courier,* June 19, 1995, p. A7.

Pendleton (Anderson County; 2000 pop. 2,966). The town of Pendleton was created in 1790 as the seat of Pendleton County. Situated on the Cherokee Path, it was named for Judge Henry Pendleton, a Virginian who fought in the Revolutionary War and remained in South Carolina. In 1800, when the county became Pendleton District, the General Assembly ordered commissioners to create a formal town plan. The resulting plat contained fifty-one town lots of one acre each and forty-three larger "outlots." One of the first to settle in the new town was William Steele, who opened a store and later became postmaster of what was then the westernmost post office in the United States.

Pendleton Farmers' Society building, 1826. Courtesy, Pendleton District Commission

Until the division of Pendleton District in 1826, the town was one of the most influential in the upper half of South Carolina. Initial settlement was by Scots-Irish veterans of the Revolutionary War, but by 1800 lowcountry planters had discovered the Pendleton area and built summer homes. Its mix of small farmers and educated, wealthy summer residents made Pendleton unusual among upstate communities during the antebellum era. A second courthouse was erected on the village green in 1800, and a circulating library was incorporated in 1811. The second decade of the nineteenth century found Pendleton flourishing. A new jail was built off the town square, the circulating library had its funds diverted for a male academy, and a Sunday school society was in operation. The Pendleton Farmers Society, organized in 1815, was still active entering the twenty-first century, making it one of the oldest agricultural societies in the nation. In 1826 Pendleton District was divided into Anderson and Pickens Districts, and the town of Pendleton lost its courthouse status. The Farmers Society bought another courthouse then under construction, completed it, and made it its headquarters.

Pendleton survived despite the loss of its courthouse status. Three miles from the town, John C. Calhoun established his beloved

Fort Hill plantation. Calhoun's son-in-law, Thomas Clemson, bequeathed the site to the state for an agricultural college that became Clemson University. In 1851 the Blue Ridge Railroad began construction of a track between Belton and Pendleton. The road was later extended to Walhalla but advanced no farther due to a lack of funds.

Industry arrived in the twentieth century. Two Milliken textile mills opened nearby, as did large manufacturing establishments operated by Michelin Tire Company, Westinghouse, and Allied Signal Laminates. With its proximity to Clemson University, Pendleton also became home to many of the school's faculty and staff. In 1970 much of the town was placed on the National Register of Historic Places, helping Pendleton become an upcountry tourist center attracting as many as 100,000 visitors annually. HURLEY E. BADDERS

Badders, Hurley E. *Historic Pendleton: A Survey.* Pendleton, S.C.: Foothills Printing, 1973.

Klosky, Beth Ann. *The Pendleton Legacy.* Columbia, S.C.: Sandlapper, 1971.

Simpson, R. W. *History of Old Pendleton District: With a Genealogy of the Leading Families of the District.* 1913. Reprint, Greenville, S.C.: Southern Historical Press, 1996.

Pendleton Messenger. The *Pendleton Messenger* began as *Miller's Weekly Messenger,* named for its publisher "Printer" John Miller (ca. 1744–1807), an early white settler in the Pendleton District. While connected with the *London Evening Post* from 1769 to 1780, Miller was charged with libel several times and imprisoned for six months for printing articles exposing corruption in the English government, including the famous "Junius Letters," which attacked corruption in Britain. He immigrated to Philadelphia, where he was invited to become South Carolina's state printer. Miller founded the *South-Carolina Gazette and General Advertiser* in Charleston in 1783. It became the state's first daily newspaper in November 1784.

That same year Miller moved to Pendleton District, where he was granted 640 acres of land. He may have attempted an earlier newspaper that failed. In 1807 he began publishing *Miller's Weekly Messenger,* the westernmost newspaper in the state at that time. Miller died later that year, and his son, John Miller, Jr. (later called John Miller, Sr.), continued publication of the paper. The name changed to the *Pendleton Messenger* around 1812. The newspaper's audience included lowcountry plantation owners who discovered Pendleton as a summer retreat in the early 1800s. The paper included notices of interest to both regions.

In 1826 John Miller was succeeded as editor by Frederick W. Symmes, a physician and writer from Pendleton. John C. Calhoun's famous "Fort Hill Address," in which he made his first public declaration in favor of nullification, was published as a letter to the editor of the *Pendleton Messenger* on July 26, 1831. For months afterward the newspaper was filled with favorable press notices for the address. Symmes published the *Pendleton Messenger* until the mid-1840s, and then it was taken over by Burt and Thompson until the 1850s. In 1858 the paper moved to Hartwell, Georgia, and became the *Hartwell Messenger.* SUSAN GIAIMO HIOTT

Klosky, Beth Ann. *The Pendleton Legacy.* Columbia, S.C.: Sandlapper, 1971.

McNeely, Patricia G. *The Palmetto Press: The History of South Carolina's Newspapers and the Press Association.* Columbia: South Carolina Press Association, 1998.

Moore, John Hammond, comp. and ed. *South Carolina Newspapers.* Columbia: University of South Carolina Press, 1988.

Penn Center. Located on St. Helena Island in Beaufort County, Penn Center, Inc., originated as the Penn Normal School. The school was established in 1862 on St. Helena by the northern missionaries Laura Towne and Ellen Murray. It was one of approximately thirty schools built on St. Helena as part of the Port Royal Experiment, an effort by northern missionaries to educate formerly enslaved Africans and prepare them for life after slavery. The leaders of the Port Royal Experiment were philanthropists, abolitionists, and Quaker missionaries from Pennsylvania who came to the Beaufort County area during the Civil War. They named the school in honor of their home state and for the Quaker activist William Penn.

Penn School at the turn of the twentieth century. Courtesy, South Caroliniana Library, University of South Carolina

Laura Towne arrived on St. Helena Island in April 1862 and was joined by Ellen Murray in June of the same year. The two began educating blacks in a one-room schoolhouse on the Oaks Plantation. As the number of students outgrew this space, they moved to the Brick Baptist Church. They remained there until 1864, when a prefabricated building was sent down from Pennsylvania. A fifty-acre tract of land was purchased from a freedman named Hastings Gantt so that the building could be erected.

In 1901 the school was chartered as the Penn Normal, Industrial, and Agricultural School. The Tuskegee Curriculum, developed by Booker T. Washington, was slowly incorporated into the Penn curriculum. So, in addition to reading, writing, and arithmetic, Penn started teaching classes in carpentry, basket making, harness making, cobbling, shoe lasting, midwifery, teacher training, and mechanics.

In 1948 the Penn School board decided that it was no longer economically feasible to keep the Penn School open as a private boarding school since public schools were now being brought onto St. Helena Island. As a result, the Penn School class of 1953 was the last one to graduate.

After becoming Penn Community Center in 1953, the institution began to focus on social issues affecting the well-being of the native islanders. This expanded to African Americans as a whole in the 1960s, when Dr. Martin Luther King, Jr., the Southern Christian Leadership Conference (SCLC), and other civil rights organizations began coming to the island to have meetings at the Frissell Community House, one of several buildings that students and community members had built on the campus.

Penn Center, Inc.'s programs and educational partnerships included the History and Culture Program, the Program for Academic and Cultural Enrichment (PACE), the Land Use and Environmental Education Program, and the Early Childhood / At-Risk Families Initiative. In 1974 the United States Department of the Interior designated the Penn Center's buildings and grounds a National Historic Landmark District. Exhibitions that focus on the history of Penn School and its connections to the native Gullah / Geechee culture of the Sea Islands are housed in the York W. Bailey

Museum, which serves as a major tourist attraction. QUEEN QUET MARQUETTA L. GOODWINE

Beal, Patricia A. "Penn Normal, Industrial, and Agricultural School, St. Helena Island, Beaufort County, S.C.: The World War II Years, 1940–1945." Master's thesis, University of South Carolina, 1992.

Goodwine, Marquetta L. *St. Helena's Serenity.* Brooklyn, N.Y.: Kinship, 1995.

Jordan, Francis Harold. "Across the Bridge: Penn School and Penn Center." Ph.D. diss., University of South Carolina, 1991.

Rose, Willie Lee. *Rehearsal for Reconstruction: The Port Royal Experiment.* 1964. Reprint, Athens: University of Georgia Press, 1999.

Wright, Roberta Hughes. *A Tribute to Charlotte Forten.* Southfield, Mich.: Charro, 1993.

Pentecostals. The New Testament book of Acts, chapter 2, reports that Christian disciples in Jerusalem were seized by the Holy Spirit on the Jewish festival of Pentecost and received the gift of glossolalia, or speaking in tongues. The modern Pentecostal movement, according to most historians, has its roots in 1906 revivals led by the African American Holiness preacher William J. Seymour at a small mission on Azusa Street in Los Angeles.

However, there is evidence of even earlier Pentecostal expression in South Carolina. As early as December 1896, for example, the Iowa Methodist evangelist Benjamin Hardin Irwin conducted meetings in the upstate, where his preaching emphasized not only salvation and sanctification but also the necessity of a third blessing or work of grace, "baptism with the Holy Ghost and Fire." Irwin was one of the founders of the Fire-Baptized Holiness Church, organized in Anderson in 1898.

When the Azusa Street revivals erupted in Los Angeles a decade later, word spread quickly in South Carolina. North Carolinian Gaston Barnabus Cashwell, who went to Azusa Street and subsequently had the experience of speaking in tongues, is responsible for bringing the Pentecostal movement to much of the upstate during a preaching tour in the area in 1907 after he returned from California. Popularly called the "apostle of Pentecost in the South," Cashwell helped convince onetime Presbyterian Nickels John Holmes of the validity of Pentecostal teaching. In turn, Holmes's Bible school and church in Greenville became centers of Pentecostal activity in South Carolina.

A popular periodical published in Columbia from 1890 to 1931, *The Way of Faith,* also helped spread the Pentecostal message throughout the state and region. That weekly carried eyewitness reports of the Azusa Street revivals every week for more than a year.

Among African Americans in the state, Anderson native William E. Fuller was a tireless advocate for the Pentecostal cause, first as an evangelist for the Fire-Baptized Holiness Association and then as bishop (later presiding bishop) of the (Colored) Fire-Baptized Holiness denomination. Fuller is credited with starting more than fifty predominantly African American churches in South Carolina and north Georgia that reflected Pentecostal styles.

In South Carolina in the early twenty-first century, there were several other flourishing denominations that represented Pentecostalism, many with roots in the earlier Holiness movement. Among them were the Pentecostal Holiness Church, the Church of God (Cleveland, Tennessee), the Church of God in Christ, and the Assemblies of God. Jim and Tammy Faye Bakker, popular televangelists of the 1970s and 1980s, were members of the Assemblies of God. In addition, Pentecostal expression has spread throughout other Christian groups in the state, from Roman Catholics to Southern Baptists, influencing worship styles as well as promoting spiritual gifts such as glossolalia, although Pentecostals remain a minority in these groups.

Although Pentecostals have been receptive to the idea of spiritual gifts, they have not been of a single mind on other theological issues. There has been considerable disagreement among Pentecostals, for example, over the doctrine of the Trinity. Denominations such as the Church of God (Cleveland, Tennessee) and the Assemblies of God are orthodox Trinitarian in orientation and baptize believers using the traditional formula that ends "in the name of the Father, Son, and Holy Ghost." Other, smaller groups with congregations in South Carolina, such as the United Pentecostal Church and the Pentecostal Assemblies of the World, have been referred to as "Oneness" or "Jesus only" groups because they do not use the Trinitarian formula but baptize only in the name of Jesus.

In addition, scores of independent congregations in the state have espoused a Pentecostal approach. Some of those have referred to themselves with the designation "Full Gospel" to denote that they believe adherents should expect to receive all the experiences reported in New Testament Christianity. As well, the few scattered congregations, mostly in the western mountain areas of the state, that have practiced serpent handling have affinities with the larger Pentecostal heritage. NANCY A. HARDESTY

Anderson, Robert Mapes. *Vision of the Disinherited: The Making of American Pentecostalism.* New York: Oxford University Press, 1979.

Hardesty, Nancy A. "The Holiness and Pentecostal Movements." In *Religion in South Carolina,* edited by Charles H. Lippy. Columbia: University of South Carolina Press, 1993.

Synan, Vinson. *The Holiness-Pentecostal Tradition: Charismatic Movements in the Twentieth Century.* 2d ed. Grand Rapids, Mich.: Eerdmans, 1997.

Periagua. A periagua was a long narrow canoe made from the hollowed trunk of a tree, sometimes widened by being built of two sections with a flat bottom inserted between. The addition of planks along the sides could deepen the vessel. The name derives from *piragua,* the Carib word for dugout canoe, which the Spanish adopted.

In colonial South Carolina the periagua was the workhorse of river travel. It took settlers to the backcountry and served as their main vehicle of transportation and supply. The commissioners of the Indian trade utilized periaguas to send trade goods such as cloth, blankets, tools, salt, gunpowder, guns, and rum to Indian nations and to bring back deerskins that were exported at great profit. The provincial legislature authorized periaguas as scout boats to patrol the inland passages south of Charleston to protect the colony against hostile Indians and Spanish raiders from St. Augustine.

Because individuals working independently constructed boats using available materials to serve their own needs, the sizes and shapes of boats classified broadly as periaguas differed widely. The builders used local cypress with a basic Indian dugout design enhanced by European boat-building techniques. Four to ten oarsmen supplied the motive power in narrow rivers, but some periaguas carried sails and removable masts for coastal bays or brief forays into open ocean. It is likely that a schooner rig was common, and the terms "schooner" and "periagua" were probably interchangeable because "schooner" describes the rigging and "periagua" refers to the hull. The average periagua had the capacity to carry thirty to fifty barrels of rice. SUZANNE LINDER

Braund, Kathryn E. Holland. *Deerskins and Duffels: The Creek Indian Trade with Anglo-America, 1685–1815.* Lincoln: University of Nebraska Press, 1993.

Crane, Verner. *The Southern Frontier, 1670–1732.* Durham, N.C.: Duke University Press, 1928.

Fleetwood, William C., Jr. *Tidecraft: The Boats of South Carolina, Georgia and Northeastern Florida, 1550–1950.* Tybee Island, Ga.: WBG Marine Press, 1995.

Ivers, Larry E. "Scouting the Inland Passage, 1685–1737." *South Carolina Historical Magazine* 73 (July 1972): 117–29.

Lawson, John. *A New Voyage to Carolina.* 1709. Reprint, Chapel Hill: University of North Carolina Press, 1967.

Linder, Suzanne C., with Emily Linder Johnson. *A River in Time: The Yadkin–Pee Dee River System.* Spartanburg, S.C.: Palmetto Conservation Foundation, 2000.

Perry, Benjamin Franklin (1805–1886). Journalist, governor. One of antebellum South Carolina's preeminent Unionist political leaders, Perry was born on November 20, 1805, in Pendleton District (now Oconee County), the son of Benjamin Perry and Anna Foster. Alternating farmwork with school, Perry was given complete management of the family farm by the age of fourteen. He attended one term, respectively, at the Asheville Academy in North Carolina in 1822 and the Greenville Male Academy in 1823. Perry began his legal studies in Greenville, which was to remain his lifelong residence, with the prominent state attorney Baylis J. Earle in March 1824. He was admitted to the bar on January 10, 1827. On April 27, 1837, Perry married Elizabeth Frances McCall of Charleston. They had seven children.

Perry's public career began with his editorship from 1830 to 1833 of the *Greenville Mountaineer,* an organ of the state's Unionists. Throughout his career Perry asserted that his political ideology rested on the principles of the *Federalist Papers* and Washington's *Farewell Address.* As a newspaper editor and political partisan, Perry frequently found himself embroiled in controversy. On August 16, 1832, he mortally wounded the pronullification newspaper editor Turner Bynum in a duel arising over a slanderous article. Elected to the 1832 nullification convention, Perry voted against the ordinance. He was an unsuccessful congressional candidate of the Unionist Democrats in 1834, 1835, and 1848. Perry served eleven terms in the state House of Representatives (1836–1841, 1848–1859, and 1862–1864), as well as two terms in the state Senate (1844–1847). In the General Assembly he advocated upcountry economic interests, democratization of state government, and legal and judiciary reform. Returning to journalism, from 1851 to 1858 he edited the *Southern Patriot,* and its successor the *Patriot and Mountaineer,* the only Unionist newspaper in the state at that time. A delegate to the 1860 national Democratic convention held in Charleston, Perry refused to join the state's delegation in its walkout from the convention, believing that the salvation of the Union and the South was inextricably bound to the survival of a united Democratic Party. While decrying secession as "madness and folly," Perry remained loyal to the state and the Confederacy, stating, "You are all now going to the devil and I will go with you." During the Civil War, Perry held the positions of district attorney (1862), assessment commissioner of impressed produce (1863), and district judge (1865) under the Confederate government. In 1863 Perry was commissioned a second lieutenant of the Greenville Mounted Riflemen, one of two companies he was instrumental in organizing for home defense.

Benjamin Franklin Perry. Courtesy, South Caroliniana Library, University of South Carolina

Perry's political career culminated with his appointment as provisional governor of South Carolina by President Andrew Johnson. Serving from June 30 to December 21, 1865, Perry was an energetic and able chief executive, whose ultimate success was oftentimes hampered by his legalist approach and misreading of northern public opinion and political objectives. He restored to office all state officials who occupied them when the Confederacy collapsed, permitted organization of volunteer militia companies, negotiated the abolition of trial by military tribunal for whites, and, to alleviate public distress, refused to levy taxes. He recommended passage of the controversial Black Codes, which severely restricted the rights of freed slaves, and ratification of the Thirteenth Amendment. Perry's greatest achievement was the creation of a new state constitution, which embodied such long-cherished personal goals as popular election of governor and presidential electors, more equitable representation in the Senate, and the abolition of property qualifications for members of the legislature. On October 30, 1865, Perry was elected to the U.S. Senate, but he was denied his seat by the Republican Congress. An ardent opponent of Reconstruction, Perry opposed black suffrage, ratification of the Fourteenth Amendment, and the calling of the 1868 constitutional convention. Defeated for election to Congress in 1872, Perry enthusiastically supported the candidacy of Wade Hampton III for governor in 1876.

Called by his admirers "the Old Roman" for his integrity and stoic adherence to principle, Perry had a reserved demeanor and brusque manner that masked a sensitive and emotional temperament. A passionate reader and prolific writer, in 1883 he published *Reminiscences of Public Men.* An irony of Perry's career was that while a devoted Unionist, he disliked the North, loathed abolitionists, and after the Civil War became a champion of states' rights when he judged them being usurped by extra-constitutional federal authority. Perry died on December 3, 1886, at his country estate Sans Souci and was buried in Greenville's Christ Episcopal Church Cemetary. PAUL R. BEGLEY

Bleser, Carol K. "The Perrys of Greenville: A Nineteenth-Century Marriage." In *The Web of Southern Social Relations: Women, Family, and Education,* edited by Walter J. Fraser, Jr., R. Frank Saunders, and Jon L. Wakelyn. Athens: University of Georgia Press, 1985.

Kibler, Lillian Adele. *Benjamin F. Perry: South Carolina Unionist.* Durham, N.C.: Duke University Press, 1946.

Meats, Stephen, and Edwin T. Arnold, eds. *The Writings of Benjamin F. Perry.* 3 vols. Spartanburg, S.C.: Reprint Company, 1980.

Perry, James Margrave (1894–1964). Attorney. "Miss Jim" Perry was the first woman admitted to the South Carolina Bar and a distinguished lawyer and civic leader for forty years. Born in Greenville on May 10, 1894, she was the third daughter of James Margrave Perry, an instructor at the Greenville Female College, who named her for himself, and Jeanne LeGal, a music teacher at the Due West

Female College. A delicate child, she was educated primarily at home before she entered the Greenville Female College in 1909. After receiving her bachelor of arts degree in 1913, she enrolled at the University of California at Berkeley, where she earned a second B.A. in 1915. That fall she entered Boalt Hall, the university's law school. In 1917 she received her J.D. and was admitted to the California Bar.

"Miss Jim," as she was called, returned to Greenville and joined the law firm of Haynsworth & Haynsworth. In 1918 she became the first woman admitted to the practice of law in South Carolina. She became a named partner in 1937, and the firm was renamed Haynsworth, Perry, Bryant, Marion & Johnstone. At first she practiced behind the scenes, doing legal research and briefing other attorneys on cases. As women became more accepted in the profession, she began to specialize in corporate and federal taxation law and wills, trusts, and estates.

A member of the South Carolina Bar Association, the National Association of Women Lawyers, and Kappa Beta Phi legal sorority, she served as president of the Greenville Bar Association in 1955. The American Bar Association appointed her to a committee to draft national marriage and divorce laws.

Active in civic affairs throughout her life, Perry volunteered with the Girl Scouts, helped begin the Hopewell Tuberculosis Hospital, and was a Greenville Library trustee. She was also a charter member of the Greenville Business and Professional Women's Club, serving as president from 1920 to 1922. Involved in the club's state federation, she was a member of its legislative and policy-making committees. Miss Jim was active in the League of Women Voters and Democratic politics, serving a term as vice president of the Greenville Democratic Party. She received the Mary Mildred Sullivan Award from Furman University in 1955 and was named Professional Woman of the Year in 1961.

Perry's most sustained civic contribution, however, was beginning the local humane society. An animal lover who had more than thirty cats and a dozen dogs, she worked almost single-handedly to establish the Greenville Animal Shelter. She was president and treasurer of the organization for many years and also served as a director of the American Humane Society. She was as proud of her contributions to the well-being of animals as she was of being a role model for young women. James Margrave Perry died on April 19, 1964, and was buried in Greenville's Christ Church Cemetery. JUDITH T. BAINBRIDGE

Cooper, Nancy Vance Ashmore. *Greenville: Woven from the Past.* Sun Valley, Calif.: American Historical Press, 2000.

"Miss Perry, Attorney, Dies Here." *Greenville News,* April 20, 1964, pp. 1–2.

Richardson, James M. *History of Greenville County, South Carolina, Narrative and Biographical.* 1930. Reprint, Spartanburg, S.C.: Reprint Company, 1980.

Perry, Matthew J., Jr. (b. 1921). Lawyer, jurist, civil rights activist. Perry was born in Columbia on August 3, 1921, the son of Matthew Perry and Jennie Lyles. Because of a disabling respiratory illness his father acquired during his service in World War I, Perry divided his early childhood between Columbia and Tuskegee, Alabama, where his father was treated at a Veterans Administration hospital. After his father's death when he was twelve, Perry was raised by his maternal grandfather, William Lyles, in Columbia while his mother sought to support the family as a seamstress in New York. Perry graduated from Booker T. Washington High School in Columbia, where he was heavily influenced by the school's principal J. Andrew Simmons.

After service in the United States Army (1943–1946), during which he once observed white American soldiers and Italian prisoners of war eating together in a railroad depot restaurant from which black soldiers were excluded, Perry resolved to study law as a means of combating racial injustice. He graduated from South Carolina State College with a B.S. in 1948 and was in the first graduating class of the South Carolina State Law School in 1951.

Perry married Hallie Bacote of Timmonsville in 1948, and they moved to Spartanburg in 1951 to open a law office. Perry devoted most of his efforts to the emerging and nonremunerative civil rights struggle, while the family was supported primarily by his wife's teaching salary. After practicing for a decade in Spartanburg, he returned to Columbia in 1961 to open a law office and assume the position of chief counsel of the South Carolina Conference of Branches of the National Association for the Advancement of Colored People (NAACP). From this position, which Perry held for fifteen years, he directed the civil rights movement's legal assault on segregation in South Carolina. He supervised various NAACP counsel within the state and worked closely with the NAACP's national legal counsel, including Thurgood Marshall, Constance Baker Motley, and Jack Greenberg.

Perry's most notable cases included his representation of Harvey Gantt in his admission as the first black student at Clemson University in 1963 and James Solomon and Henri Monteith in their admission that same year as the first African American students of the University of South Carolina in the twentieth century. He also served as the trial lawyer for some of the most significant U.S. Supreme Court cases of the modern civil rights era, including *Edwards v. South Carolina,* which established broad legal protections for civil rights marchers, and *Newman v. Piggy Park Enterprises,* one of the earliest interpretations of the 1964 Civil Rights Act. Perry's cases also led to the integration of South Carolina's public schools, state parks, beaches, and hospitals and his landmark 1974 voting rights case against the South Carolina General Assembly, which resulted in the creation of single-member districts and an end to the at-large election of legislators. In commenting on the impact of his civil rights work, Perry once stated, "I don't mean to be immodest, but my cases have turned South Carolina around."

Perry was nominated by President Gerald Ford as a judge on the United States Military Court of Appeals in 1976, making him the first African American from the Deep South nominated to the federal bench. He was sworn in by his longtime mentor and friend Associate Justice Thurgood Marshall. In 1979 President Jimmy Carter nominated Perry to be a United States district judge for the District of South Carolina, the first African American to serve in that position. Perry's service as a federal judge has been widely praised, with the *Almanac of the Federal Judiciary* noting his "excellent legal ability" and that his "unfailingly courteous and polite" demeanor "enhances the stature of the federal judiciary." Perry served as a district judge until 1995, when he assumed status as a senior United States district judge. Princeton University awarded Perry an honorary doctor of laws in 1998, noting that he was "a major force in the Civil Rights Movement in South Carolina" and "played a leading role in a number of significant legal cases." In 2000 ground was broken on the new Matthew J. Perry United States Courthouse in Columbia. See plate 37. RICHARD MARK GERGEL

Brinson, Claudia Smith. "Council Honors Judge for Key Role in Civil Rights History." Columbia *State,* June 14, 2001, pp. A1, A7.

Perry, Mattie Elmina (1868–1957). Healing evangelist. Perry was born on May 15, 1868, at Cheohee, Oconee County, the second of eight children. Her father, J. A. Perry, the son of Baptist parents, was a native of Oconee County and became a local Methodist preacher. Her mother, Jane Holden, was a Methodist and the daughter of William and Martha Holden of Rabun County, Georgia.

The family moved to Greenville County when Mattie was nine and later, in 1891, to Spartanburg. At age twelve she was converted at the Bethel camp meeting. In October 1887 she dedicated herself to God. She began her work at the Twelve Mile Campground in Pickens, praying and working with those seeking salvation. She studied at the Williamston Female College, completing her studies in June 1892.

Perry applied to the Methodist Church in 1893 to do city mission work but was told that there were no openings. She became an agent for J. M. Pike's periodical *Way of Faith* but was given no territory. She also applied to go as a missionary to China, but the Board of Missions turned her down. So she began to hold revivals with various Holiness evangelists around South Carolina and north Georgia. Her brother Samuel, an Asbury College graduate and Methodist minister, often accompanied her. During one of her meetings at Fitzgerald, Georgia, Fred F. Bosworth was healed. He would go on to become a prominent healing evangelist himself. Perry recorded meetings in Columbia, Dillon, Latta, Brownsville, and McColl, as well as elsewhere across the country.

From about 1898 to 1926 Perry ran the Elhanan orphanage and school for poor children in Marion, North Carolina. She may also have functioned during this period as a pioneer district superintendent for the fledgling Christian and Missionary Alliance. She spoke of her territory as including the Carolinas, Georgia, Florida, and Tennessee. The workload proved taxing, and for years she worked from a wheelchair. However, when fire damaged the school, she was forced to close it. She returned to preaching and regained her health, and she later offered the "Elhanan Bible Correspondence Course."

Even when Perry was bedridden, people would come to her, asking her to pray for them. In 1928 and 1929 she toured the Middle East. She also made two trips to Cuba. About 1937 she took up residence at God's Bible School in Cincinnati, Ohio, to teach the Old Testament and write for the *Revivalist*. In 1939 she published her autobiography, *Christ and Answered Prayer*. Although Perry lived in Atlanta for the final years of her life, she died in Aynor, South Carolina, on November 14, 1957, while visiting her sister. NANCY A. HARDESTY

Perry, Mattie E. *Christ and Answered Prayer: Autobiography of Mattie E. Perry.* Cincinnati, Ohio: by the author, 1939.

Stanley, Susie C. *Holy Boldness: Women Preachers' Autobiographies and the Sanctified Self.* Knoxville: University of Tennessee Press, 2002.

Perry, William Anthony (b. 1962). Football player. Perry was born in Aiken on December 16, 1962, the tenth of Hollie and Inez Perry's twelve children. Weighing more than thirteen pounds at birth, Perry seemed born to play football. He was introduced to the game in East Aiken by the elementary-school principal T. W. Williams. Perry worked for Williams doing various chores to earn money to pay the fee to play. As a teenager at Aiken High School, Perry excelled in football and also basketball. After graduating in 1981, Perry became the focus of nationwide collegiate football recruiting, and after rejecting offers from UCLA and Ohio State, he signed with Clemson University. At Clemson, Perry soon earned the nickname "G. E." from teammates and "Refrigerator" or "Fridge" from others because his six-foot, three-inch, 320-pound stature resembled the kitchen appliance. Playing middle guard, "Refrigerator" Perry earned the distinction of being Clemson's first three-time All American (1982–1984), setting team records in quarterback sacks that stood until his brother Michael Dean surpassed him in 1987. A first-round draft pick of the Chicago Bears in 1985, Perry played nine seasons with the Bears.

Although a professional-bowl-caliber defensive lineman, Perry became a national media sensation when head coach Mike Ditka began using the massive rookie as a running back. During a nationally televised *Monday Night Football* game against the Green Bay Packers, Perry opened the way for two touchdowns by teammate Walter Payton and then scored one himself. His nationwide popularity was secured when he scored the final touchdown in the Bears' 46–10 rout of the New England Patriots in Super Bowl XX. Perry remained with the Bears until 1993, when he signed with the Philadelphia Eagles. He retired from the National Football League in 1995 but nine months later signed with the World Football League to play in Europe for the London Monarchs. In 1996 Perry left the Monarchs and returned to Aiken to run a family business. He resided there with his wife, Sherry, and their four children. D. S. TAYLOR

Hewitt, Brian. *"The Refrigerator" and the Monsters of the Midway: William Perry and the Chicago Bears.* New York: New American Library, 1985.

Murphy, Austin. "Chillin' with the Fridge." *Sports Illustrated* 93 (July 31, 2000): 84–90.

Smith, Chris. "The Perry Clan and Its Roots." *Greenville News,* July 29, 1984, pp. C1, C10.

Telander, Rick. "Monster of the Midway." *Sports Illustrated* 63 (November 4, 1985): 42–49.

Peterkin, Julia Mood (1880–1961). Author, Pulitzer Prize winner. Peterkin was born on October 31, 1880, in Laurens County, the youngest daughter of Julius Mood, a schoolteacher, and his wife, Alma Archer. Julius Mood went on to become a doctor and to practice medicine in Sumter. Alma Mood died of tuberculosis when Peterkin was eighteen months old, and Julius Mood soon remarried. Peterkin was sent to live with her paternal grandparents, while her older sisters stayed with their father and his new wife. The loss of her mother and the sense that she had been "given away" would later become a haunting refrain in Peterkin's fiction.

Peterkin graduated from Converse College in 1896 and went on to earn a master's degree from Converse a year later. She taught in a one-room school in Fort Motte; married the cotton planter William George Peterkin on June 3, 1903; and moved to Lang Syne Plantation near St. Matthews, where she would live for the rest of her life.

Julia Mood Peterkin. Courtesy, Calhoun County Museum

Peterkin had one son, William George Peterkin, Jr., and spent the first twenty years of her marriage trying to fill the archaic role of plantation mistress.

Peterkin did not begin to write until she was forty years old. She began by telling tales of plantation life to her piano teacher, Henry Bellamann, a poet with literary leanings who encouraged her to write them down. Ambition soon led her to approach famous writers and critics, notably Joel Spingarn, Carl Sandburg, and H. L. Mencken, even while secretly taking a correspondence course on magazine writing. Her stories found a home in Emily Clark's new magazine the *Reviewer* and in Mencken's more widely read *Smart Set.* Within two years Peterkin had contracted to publish a book with Alfred A. Knopf, then just beginning to establish a distinguished reputation. The result was *Green Thursday* (1924), a collection of linked short stories about a black farm laborer named Killdee; his wife, Rose; and their foster daughter, Missie. Peterkin drew on what she knew about the lives of real people at Lang Syne, rendering some of them so acutely that the portraits are recognizable to their descendants. Yet the emotional force of many of the tales comes from her own life experience, especially the trauma of losing her mother and growing up apart from her father.

Peterkin's stark, poignant stories about black country folk were among the first flowerings in the movement toward ironic, realistic regional fiction later known as the Southern Renaissance. In 1929 she became the first southern writer to win the Pulitzer Prize for fiction, for the novel *Scarlet Sister Mary* (1928). Two of her books, *Black April* (1927) and *Scarlet Sister Mary,* became best-sellers, and her last, *Roll, Jordan, Roll* (1933), with photographs by her friend Doris Ulmann, was one of the groundbreaking documentaries of the 1930s.

White southerners found Peterkin's early stories offensive and considered her a traitor to her race, though their animosity faded as her celebrity grew. Her mature work gained international fame and was unlike anything that had come before it. Peterkin had the gift of luring mainstream white audiences into what was to them a strange new world: the community of black farmworkers who lived by traditions that were largely African in origin. Whites seldom appear in her work, except in trivial roles. Peterkin had a great ear for language and eventually worked out a literary rendering of the difficult Gullah dialect that was true to the cadences and flavor of the original but understandable to ordinary Americans. Her novels were considered racy and subversive, partly for their frank celebration of sex but also because they dared to reveal hard truths about how blacks were forced to live in the Jim Crow South. Taken together, *Green Thursday, Black April, Scarlet Sister Mary,* and *Bright Skin* (1932) chronicle the decline of the plantation economy and the wrenching personal and social forces that drove African Americans to leave the rural South.

Peterkin's stories won high praise from black writers and scholars associated with the Harlem Renaissance, including W. E. B. Du Bois, Walter White, Alain Locke, and Countee Cullen. African American novelists who emerged soon after, including Zora Neale Hurston, show clear signs of Peterkin's influence. During the Depression, Peterkin's fiction fell out of fashion, and it was largely ignored during the 1970s and 1980s, when the works of many other women writers were resurrected and appreciated. Yet her best work has the timeless quality of great literature and seems as fresh and vibrant in the twenty-first century as it did in the 1920s.

Peterkin died in Orangeburg on August 10, 1961, of congestive heart failure. She was buried in the family plot at the Episcopal Church near Fort Motte. SUSAN MILLAR WILLIAMS

Perry, Carolyn, and Mary Louise Weaks, eds. *The History of Southern Women's Literature.* Baton Rouge: Louisiana State University Press, 2002.

Williams, Susan Millar. *A Devil and a Good Woman, Too: The Lives of Julia Peterkin.* Athens: University of Georgia Press, 1997.

Petigru, James Louis (1789–1863). Lawyer, politician. Petigru was born near Abbeville on May 10, 1789, the eldest child of William Pettigrew, a farmer, and his wife, Louise Gibert, a well-educated Huguenot. He attended Moses Waddel's Willington Academy, graduated from South Carolina College in 1809, and taught at Beaufort College while he read law. Admitted to the bar in 1812 shortly after changing the spelling of his name, he served as Beaufort District's solicitor from 1816 to 1822. In 1816 he married Jane Amelia Postell, with whom he had four children: Alfred, Caroline, Daniel, and Susan.

James L. Petigru. Courtesy, South Carolina Historical Society

In 1819 Petigru moved to Charleston, where he became James Hamilton's law partner. Appointed South Carolina attorney general in 1822, he prosecuted all Charleston District civil and criminal cases, represented the state in appeals courts and federal courts, and advised the legislature. Upholding state authority, even as he strove to curtail the excesses of public officials, he also appealed to federal over state law when defending an army officer on slave-related charges. In addition, after a federal judge refused to rule on the state law that required free black sailors aboard vessels in Charleston harbor to be jailed, Petigru made no effort to enforce it.

In 1830 Petigru, a leader of the Unionist faction, resigned as attorney general and was elected to the state House of Representatives. Despite defeat in 1832, he remained a major spokesmen for his party until the repeal of nullification in 1833. In 1834, arguing for the plaintiff in *McCready v. Hunt,* he won a state appeals court decision that the nullifier-imposed test oath for all state officials violated South Carolina's constitutional ban on such oaths. Months later he framed the legislative compromise subordinating state to national allegiance. Despite a second term (1836–1837) in the legislature, Petigru's political career was destroyed by his loyalty to the checks and balances in the United States Constitution that restrained legislative power by judicial power and state government by federal government.

It was his preeminence as a lawyer that made Petigru a public man after 1840. Although he believed that common law must change in response to new social and economic conditions, his state's limited industrialization restricted his contribution to such change to a few transportation and banking cases. In *Pell v. Ball* (1845), however, he argued successfully that plantation property did not differ from other forms and must be distributed among heirs by the same principles.

In the 1850s Petigru's most distinctive equity practice relied heavily on arbitration and mediation to avoid erratic decisions from judges he considered inept. In court he appeared twice as often for the defendant as for the plaintiff. In cases involving abusive husbands, he served both rich and poor women, but his most visible representation of the legally disadvantaged served free people of color. As adviser to the British consul's campaign to thwart the incarceration of black seamen and when he rescued the free children of George Broad from slavery, he acted both behind the scenes and in court. And though he never challenged the institution of slavery, he defied public opinion when he successfully represented Reuben Smalle, an itinerant Yankee believed to be an abolitionist. In recognition of his legal expertise rather than political conformity, in 1859 the legislature appointed Petigru to codify South Carolina civil law, a task he finished in 1862. His code, whose only significant substantive changes benefited free blacks, was not adopted until 1872, and then only in a reorganized form. Torn between conflicting allegiances to federal constitution and to southern culture, Petigru had an unchanging commitment to justice and order through law. His loyalty to a constitutionally defined balance of power never wavered, whether it was defending minority rights from majority incursions, checking legislative excess by judicial action, or contending that knowledgeable judges shape juries' findings within the confines of the law.

Never backtracking in his condemnation of South Carolina's April 1861 attack on Fort Sumter for having set "a blazing torch to the temple of constitutional liberty," Petigru went to court to block the Confederacy's confiscation of absentee Carolinians' property and its requirement that lawyers, like other citizens, inform against such owners. Although he scorned the Richmond government and deplored war-time civilian dislocation, Petigru mourned Southern battlefield disasters, especially those injuring or killing his young kinsmen. He died in Charleston on March 9, 1863. In an impressive tribute, city and state officials as well as Charleston's Confederate officer corps followed his coffin to St. Michael's cemetery. WILLIAM H. PEASE AND JANE H. PEASE

Carson, James Petigru, ed. *Life, Letters and Speeches of James Louis Petigru, the Union Man of South Carolina.* Washington, D.C.: W. H. Lowdermilk, 1920.

Ford, Lacy K., Jr. "James Louis Petigru: The Last South Carolina Federalist." In *Intellectual Life in Antebellum Charleston,* edited by Michael O'Brien and David Moltke-Hansen. Knoxville: University of Tennessee Press, 1986.

Pease, William H., and Jane H. Pease. *James Louis Petigru: Southern Conservative, Southern Dissenter.* 1995. Reprint, Columbia: University of South Carolina Press, 2002.

Petroglyphs. Petroglyphs (rock carvings) and pictographs (drawings or painting on rock) are collectively referred to as "rock art." The first example of rock art reported in South Carolina was a petroglyph discovered in Greenville County in 1979. In 1983 two additional carvings were reported, one each in Lexington and Oconee Counties. Ultimately, these early reports were the catalyst for a survey conducted by the South Carolina Institute of Archaeology and Anthropology at the University of South Carolina to search for and record other examples of rock art in the state. The survey was begun in 1996 and resulted in the discovery of forty-four additional petroglyph sites, thirty-three portable carvings, and three pictographs.

Rock art has been discovered in Kershaw, Lexington, and Richland Counties, but the great majority occurs in Greenville, Laurens, Oconee, Pickens, and Spartanburg Counties. There is little rock

Rendering of petroglyphs found in Pickens County. Courtesy, South Carolina Institute of Archaeology and Anthropology

amenable to the carving of petroglyphs on the coastal plain, and no rock art has been recorded there.

A petroglyph site may contain one or several hundred carvings. Most of the carvings are highly eroded, difficult to see, and therefore hard to find. Although far from conclusive, data indicate that the optimum locations where prehistoric petroglyphs may occur are two vastly different landforms. One is westward-oriented bald rock near mountain crests, and the other is on or near the mountain foothills, where petroglyphs are found near streams and springs.

Petroglyph motifs on the two landforms differ consistently. The lowland petroglyphs are much more varied in form than those found near mountain crests. Petroglyphs near mountain crests are predominately circles, boldly carved, variable in size, and often asymmetrical. A few have radiating lines in a sunburst manner. Occasionally a triangle or square is carved among the circles, but the great majority are circles without any elaboration. Petroglyphs found on the foothills sites vary from simple circles to complex geometric and abstract forms. Several petroglyphs that might be construed as anthropomorphic (representing humans) have been recorded, but only a single carving has been found that clearly represents the human form. Two zoomorphic (representing animals) petroglyphs, perhaps representing deer or buffalo, have been recorded. Historic rock art is widespread and usually consists of modern graffiti, carved initials, names, and dates.

Modern graffiti is abundant, but only three pictograph sites believed to be prehistoric have been discovered in South Carolina. The fact that they survive is probably because they are located in rock shelters that have protected them from the elements. Drawn with red and orange ochre, the drawings at each site are different. One consists of simple circles, another has eight animal figures, and one has a sun-circle with seven radiating lines and animal-like figures drawn at the end of each line.

The ages of South Carolina's prehistoric rock art have not been established. Not amenable to radiocarbon dating, their cultural placement remains speculative. The oldest historic rock art in the state dates to the late eighteenth century. TOMMY CHARLES

Charles, Tommy. "The Rock Art of South Carolina." In *The Rock-Art of Eastern North America,* edited by Carol Diaz-Granados and James R. Duncan. Tuscaloosa: University of Alabama Press, 2004.

Peurifoy, John Emil (1907–1955). Diplomat. "Jack" Peurifoy was born in Walterboro on August 9, 1907, the son of John H. Peurifoy and Emily Wright. After graduating from high school in Walterboro in 1926, he joined the cadet corps at the U.S. Military Academy, but chronic ill-health forced him to withdraw two years later. For the next several years Peurifoy resided in various states, holding a variety of jobs. By 1934 he was living in Washington, D.C., employed as an elevator operator in the U.S. Senate Office Building. He married Betty Jane Cox, a schoolteacher from Kansas City, in 1936. Their marriage produced two sons.

Upon passing civil service examinations in 1938, Peurifoy gained employment at the U.S. State Department within the office processing export licenses. Although he attended American University and George Washington University, he never graduated from either institution. After the outbreak of World War II, he became a staff assistant with the Board of Economic Warfare. By 1942 he was a special assistant to the Office of Public Affairs at the State Department. Secretary of State Edward R. Stettinius in 1945 assigned him to coordinate logistical support for the United Nations Conference in San Francisco. In March 1946 he became special assistant to Undersecretary of State Dean Acheson. On Acheson's recommendation, in March 1947 Secretary of State George C. Marshall appointed Peurifoy assistant secretary of state for administration. Foremost among his many duties was assuring that State Department employees were not participating in subversive political activities.

In July 1950 President Harry S. Truman nominated Peurifoy to be U.S. ambassador to Greece. Since a major civil war recently had concluded, he found that Greece's domestic politics were highly unstable. Accordingly, he intervened repeatedly to strengthen anti-Communist political parties and to enhance the constitutional authority of the Greek monarchy. Peurifoy was also a consistent promoter of American interests throughout the eastern Mediterranean. During his tenure in Greece, Peurifoy gained a reputation for being a dedicated "Cold Warrior."

Although a lifelong Democrat, Peurifoy was retained in January 1953 when President Dwight D. Eisenhower took office. The following October, Secretary of State John Foster Dulles appointed Peurifoy to be U.S. ambassador to Guatemala. The Eisenhower administration was openly hostile to the left-wing policies of President Jacobo Arbenz Guzmán. Peurifoy alleged that Arbenz was attempting to secure closer ties with the Soviet Union. He cooperated closely with the Central Intelligence Agency (CIA) to organize a coup to overthrow Arbenz's democratically elected government. In June 1954 Peurifoy's influence was paramount in uniting the rebel forces behind Colonel Carlos Castillo Armas, the Eisenhower administration's chosen leader.

By September 1954 Peurifoy had become U.S. ambassador to Thailand. His arrival in Bangkok coincided with the growing influence of the United States within Southeast Asia, especially Indochina. Secretary Dulles expected Peurifoy to assume a lead role in combating Communism within that region. But on August 12, 1955, Peurifoy was killed after his car collided with a truck on a rural highway near Hua Hun, Thailand. His younger son, David Peurifoy, also died in the accident. Although these deaths were officially ruled accidental, rumors persisted that the two had been assassinated. They were both interred in Arlington National Cemetery. MILES S. RICHARDS

Lewis, Flora. "Ambassador Extraordinary: John Peurifoy." *New York Times Magazine,* July 18, 1954, pp. 9, 23, 26.

Schlesinger, Stephen C., and Stephen Kinzer. *Bitter Fruit: The Untold Story of the American Coup in Guatemala.* Garden City, N.Y.: Doubleday, 1982.

Phifer, Mary Hardy (1879–1962). Journalist. Phifer was born in Spartanburg on August 25, 1879, the daughter of Washington Hardy and Rebecca Carson. Both parents died when she was a toddler, so she was raised by her grandmother, an aunt, and an uncle. She attended Converse College, graduating in 1898. After teaching school for a year, she married the Spartanburg hardware store owner Moulton Phifer in July 1899. The couple had seven children. Phifer was an active member of Spartanburg's Episcopal Church of the Advent.

Once all her children were enrolled in school, Phifer became a journalist. She began as society editor for the Spartanburg *Herald,* a position she held for nearly twenty years. She continued to write a weekly column for the paper well into the 1950s. She also worked as a freelance journalist, interviewing literary figures for *Holland's Magazine* and writing gardening articles for various other magazines, including *House Beautiful.*

In the 1930s the Phifers moved to a farm in a rural section of southern Spartanburg County, where Mary developed a large garden. Eventually she opened a cannery to produce her own peach sauce, which was marketed at specialty stores in New York City and around the country. The business closed during World War II due to a shortage of labor and sugar.

During World War II a Spartan Mills executive asked her to edit its new employee newsletter, entitled the *Beaumont E.* She also produced a series of radio programs during the war. "Miss Mary" became famous among the Beaumont mill operatives for her lively interviews with workers and her "Phiferisms," the morale-boosting aphorisms she published in the newsletter. Among them was one that described her own philosophy: "I am an old lady who has looked at life a long time, and have learned that happiness dwells most securely with those who work. Taking it by and large working people are the happiest people in the world."

Phifer retired at the end of the war and devoted her time to gardening, canning, weaving, and her family. In 1951 Converse College awarded her its Mary Mildred Sullivan Award for her service to the community. Throughout her retirement Phifer continued to write and to speak to community groups. She published her own memoir and a biography of South Carolina bishop Kirkman George Finley. She was also elected an honorary member of Delta Kappa

Gamma, an organization of women educators. Phifer died at her home near Clifton on February 20, 1962, and was buried at Greenlawn Memorial Gardens. MELISSA WALKER

Dodge, Susan. "Mary Hardy Phifer." In *The Lives They Lived: A Look at Women in the History of Spartanburg County,* edited by Linda Powers Bilanchone. Spartanburg, S.C.: Spartanburg Sesquicentennial Focus on Women Committee, 1981.

Phoenix Riot. The Phoenix Riot occurred on November 8, 1898, in the small town of Phoenix in Greenwood County when a group of local Democrats attempted to stop a Republican election official from taking the affidavits of African Americans who had been denied the right to vote. The riot reflected the ongoing tension not only between Democrats and Republicans but also between whites and the county's African American population. In Greenwood County black men outnumbered white men, but few blacks had voted since Democrats regained power in the state following the 1876 elections.

The riot originated in front of Watson and Lake's general store, which was serving as an election site. Thomas Tolbert, a white man and brother of Republican congressional candidate Robert Red Tolbert, was sitting outside the store and collecting affidavits from blacks who had been prevented from casting ballots. He was approached by a group of local Democrats, including J. I. "Bose" Ethridge, the local party boss. The men ordered Tolbert to leave. When he refused, they overturned the box of affidavits and began to beat Tolbert. Tolbert responded in kind by hitting Ethridge over the head with a wagon axle. A larger fight erupted between the supporters of Tolbert and those of Ethridge. Shots rang out, though their source was not clear, and Ethridge was killed (his grave marker states that "He Died for his Country"). The Democrats retaliated by opening fire on the crowd of African American men gathered outside the store; Thomas Tolbert was shot in the neck, arms, and side, but he survived.

White retribution was swift and severe. In the days that followed, between six hundred and one thousand white men gathered in Phoenix, where they burned the Tolberts' homes and forced the Republicans into exile. Several local black men were not so fortunate; four were lynched outside of Rehoboth Church. Over the next several days the white mob killed at least eight black men, though the exact number is not known. No one was ever charged with any of these murders. The Phoenix Riot is usually overshadowed in larger historical narratives by the Wilmington, North Carolina, race riot that began on November 10, 1898, and resulted in the triumph of Democrats over Republicans and Populists in North Carolina's government. The Phoenix Riot occurred in an area that was already under Democratic control. Robert Red Tolbert, the Republican, lost the 1898 election to Democrat A. C. Latimer by a 996 to 107 margin.

The Phoenix Riot is best understood as an exaggerated example of the everyday violence that faced late nineteenth-century African Americans in South Carolina. African Americans in rural Greenwood County faced crippling debt and white terrorism routinely; any attempt to fight the system of white supremacy was met with violence by white enforcers drawn from surrounding areas. The Tolberts continued to fight for black political rights at the state and federal levels, despite the fact that their houses were continually set aflame by unknown arsonists. Phoenix was also home to a remarkably resilient African American population. The black community there maintained churches and schools even in the face of violence, and the civil rights activist Benjamin Mays was born there in 1894. MATTHEW H. JENNINGS

Hoyt, James A. *The Phoenix Riot: November 8, 1898.* N.p., 1935.

Prather, H. Leon, Sr. "The Origins of the Phoenix Racial Massacre of 1898." In *Developing Dixie: Modernization in a Traditional Society,* edited by Winfred B. Moore, Jr., Joseph F. Tripp, and Lyon G. Tyler, Jr. Westport, Conn.: Greenwood, 1988.

Wells, Tom Henderson. "The Phoenix Election Riot." *Phylon* 31 (spring 1970): 58–69.

Wilk, Daniel Levinson. "The Phoenix Riot and the Memories of Greenwood County." *Southern Cultures* 8 (winter 2002): 29–55.

Phosphate. The South Carolina phosphate mining industry began after the Civil War and dominated world production in the 1880s. Mining began in late 1867 on plantations near Charleston after the gentlemen-scientists Francis S. Holmes and St. Julien Ravenel and the chemists N. A. Pratt and C. U. Shepard discovered that local "stinking stones" contained unusually high amounts of bone phosphate of lime (BPL). Agricultural chemists had recently discovered that high-BPL phosphate rock was ideal for modern fertilizers, and South Carolina had the largest supply in the Southeast. Holmes and Pratt established the Charleston Mining and Manufacturing Company (CMMC) and quickly bought mining rights to several Ashley River plantations. Although CMMC would remain the largest land-mining company, many local firms competed. Entrepreneurs such as C. C. Pinckney, Jr., C. H. Drayton, and Williams Middleton mined phosphate from their own plantations.

In 1870 the legislature began granting river-mining rights to companies that each paid a royalty of one dollar per ton. Many of the early companies proved unprofitable, including a firm founded by the Reconstruction-era politicians Timothy Hurley and Franklin J. Moses, Jr., and the black leaders Robert B. Elliott, Alonzo J. Ransier, and Robert Smalls. As other companies joined the industry, mining spread to the Ashley, Stono, Edisto, Coosaw, Morgan, and Broad Rivers. By the mid-1870s the Coosaw Mining Company emerged as the dominant river miner. Controlled by the Adger family of Charleston, Coosaw mined the state's best territory and shipped its rock to Europe, where "Carolina river rock" enjoyed an excellent reputation.

Most miners were young black males in their twenties or thirties. Dissatisfied with the work habits of the former slaves, mine owners imported Italians and Germans and tried convict labor but were unsuccessful in displacing the freedmen's labor monopoly. Freed people in Charleston, Colleton, and Beaufort Counties incorporated mining into a two-day system that included sharecropping, farming their own land, hunting, fishing, and odd jobs. By 1880 more than sixteen hundred men mined the land, which paid well (about $1.75 per day) but was grueling work. Ankle-deep in mud and under the hot

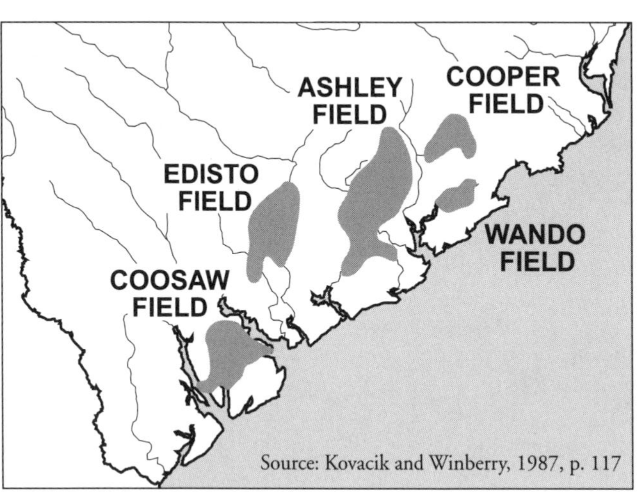

South Carolina phosphate fields

Wando Mining and Manufacturing Plant. Courtesy, South Carolina Historical Society

sun, freedmen with shovels and picks excavated several feet of overburden before reaching the twelve-inch phosphate layer. Miners pushed the rock in trams toward the river, where others dried the rock in the sun or on burning timber before shipping it to Charleston or beyond. Only in the 1890s would steam shovels and locomotives ease burdens. Although river-mining freedmen initially dove for, or collected, rocks at low tide, most worked on floating dredges or river flats. At least 1,000 miners dredged the rivers in the early 1880s. By 1892 the number of land and river miners had reached 5,242.

Phosphate mining helped to jump-start, and remained an integral part of, the lowcountry fertilizer industry. Ravenel and others established the Wando Fertilizer Company in 1867, while Pratt and Christopher G. Memminger began what became the Etiwan Phosphate Company a year later. CMMC supplied Etiwan with rock, while Wando and Boston-based Pacific Guano Company mined rock and manufactured fertilizers. During the 1870s phosphate-driven fertilizer mills crowded out farmers on the Charleston Neck, and fertilizer production increased rapidly. Hundreds of men were employed in Beaufort and Charleston, and many new firms emerged as demand for fertilizer soared among southern farmers in the 1880s. By the 1890s Charleston had displaced Baltimore as the nation's largest fertilizer-producing city. From 1869 to the 1940s South Carolina was one of the top five fertilizer-producing states in the nation.

South Carolina's phosphate industry was the world leader until the 1890s, when bad politics, bad luck, and bad weather brought on a rapid decline. Although the river industry contributed over $2,805,000 to the treasury between 1870 and 1892, Governor Benjamin Tillman—no friend of the Charleston elite—sought greater income from, and control over, the state's largest producer, the Coosaw Mining Company. The ensuing "war" reached the U.S. Supreme Court and caused Coosaw to suspend mining from 1891 to 1892. While Coosaw was in court, Florida's higher-BPL river and land rock gained a foothold in the international phosphate market. The 1893 hurricane crippled South Carolina's river-mining industry, and Florida displaced the Palmetto State as the nation's top producer the following year. The three blows sent South Carolina's phosphate industry into a steep decline, with its national market share falling from ninety-five percent in 1889 to twenty-two percent in 1900 and seven percent in 1910. River mining ended in 1909, followed by land mining in 1925. While the economic impact of the industry diminished, its environmental legacy was still felt. A farmer's 1881 lawsuit concerning Etiwan's sulfuric acid fumes foreshadowed the phosphate fertilizer industry's "legacy of contamination." At the dawning of the twenty-first century, officials of the federal Environmental Protection Agency (EPA) described the Charleston Neck as "one of the most concentrated areas of contamination in the nation," and former fertilizer mill locations emerged as EPA Superfund candidates. SHEPHERD W. MCKINLEY

Chazal, Philip E. *The Century in Phosphates and Fertilizers: A Sketch of the South Carolina Phosphate Industry.* Charleston, S.C.: Lucas-Richardson, 1904.

McKinley, Shepherd W. *Charleston Museum Collection Guide: The Edward Willis Scrapbooks.* Charleston, S.C.: Charleston Museum, 1999.

Shick, Tom W., and Don H. Doyle. "The South Carolina Phosphate Boom and the Stillbirth of the New South, 1867–1920." *South Carolina Historical Magazine* 86 (January 1986): 1–31.

Pickens (Pickens County; 2000 pop. 3,012). The upcountry city of Pickens, named for Revolutionary War general Andrew Pickens, was chartered on July 22, 1868, as the seat of government for the newly created Pickens County. It was the second town by that name, replacing Old Pickens, which had been the courthouse seat for the old Pickens District. Some of the structures in Old Pickens, including the jail, were dismantled and rebuilt in the new town.

The area was poor and rural in the years after the Civil War. In 1869 the Pickens population was less than one hundred, but within a year the town claimed two general stores, two barrooms, two boardinghouses, the courthouse, and several nearby dwellings. Court week was a big event each October. In 1871 the first hotel opened, and a school with sixty students operated as well. The *Pickens Sentinel* published its first issue that same year. The first house of worship was built by the African American congregation of the Griffin Ebenezer Baptist Church (1871). However, many town lots remained vacant, some of which were used to grow corn, cotton, or oats.

The last two decades of the nineteenth century were years of growth for Pickens, with new businesses developing westward along Main Street away from the original business district surrounding the courthouse. The Young Men's Christian Association was active in the 1880s, as was a Masonic Lodge. As the seat of county justice, Pickens also had lawyers' offices. In 1882 the Pickens Institute Joint Stock Company financed the building of an academy on Main Street, which was dedicated on April 20, 1883, and operated until financial troubles closed it in late 1888. There were several schemes to get a railroad to serve the town before the Pickens Railroad Company was chartered on December 24, 1890. The train derailed on its maiden run in 1898, to the dismay of investors. The 9.6-mile track led to Easley. In the early years of its operation, the tracks did not allow turning around, so the train had to run backward returning to Pickens. Locals named it the "Pickens Doodle" because its action reminded them of a doodlebug backing into its hole. The National Railway Utilization Company bought the line in 1973.

Pickens remained a small town throughout the twentieth century, although improvements continued. In 1947 Dr. Gaine E. Cannon began Cannon Memorial Hospital as a clinic, which expanded to a forty-seven-bed hospital in 1949 and moved to new facilities in 1982. A jail built in 1902 became the county museum in 1975. In the early 1980s city businesses produced textiles, aluminum die castings, electrical capacitors, and electric hand tools. The town had a radio station, and the *Pickens Sentinel* continued as a weekly newspaper. Although the Pickens County population grew considerably, the town population remained at just over three thousand from 1980 through most of the 1990s. The 2000 census showed a population of just over three thousand and a low unemployment rate. Pickens remained a pleasant, small town in the foothills, convenient to urban areas but without the attendant problems of a larger city. DONNA K. ROPER

Morris, Jane Boroughs. *Pickens: The Town and the First Baptist Church.* Pickens, S.C.: Pickens First Baptist Church, 1991.

Pickens County Heritage Book Committee. *Pickens County Heritage, South Carolina, 1995.* Waynesville, N.C.: Don Mills, 1995.

Pickens, Andrew (1739–1817). Soldier, legislator, congressman. Pickens was born in Paxtang Township, Pennsylvania, on September 19, 1739, the son of Andrew Pickens and Ann Davis. His family was among the Huguenots and Scots-Irish that settled in Northern Ireland and then migrated to Pennsylvania. After moving southward, the Pickens family eventually settled on Waxhaw Creek, South Carolina, by 1752. The young Pickens commenced his military service as a company grade officer in the Cherokee War of 1759–1761. After the hostilities, he moved to the Long Canes area of western South Carolina and married Rebecca Calhoun on March 19, 1765. The couple had twelve children. This marriage formed ties with several prominent upcountry families.

Andrew Pickens. Courtesy, South Carolina State Museum

During the Revolutionary War, Pickens became one of the most significant leaders of patriot forces in the South Carolina backcountry. He initially served as a militia company commander for Ninety Six District and campaigned against Tories in late 1775. By 1778 he had attained the rank of colonel of the Upper Ninety Six Regiment and had participated in expeditions against the British-allied Cherokees and the unsuccessful American invasion of East Florida. The most severe check of the Loyalists in the backcountry came on February 14, 1779, when patriots crushed the Loyalist force at Kettle Creek, Georgia. After the surrender of Charleston, Pickens took British protection and was paroled to his home. He renounced protection, however, when the British failed to prevent a Loyalist band from plundering his plantation. At the Battle of Cowpens on January 17, 1781, Pickens was in charge of the South Carolina militia during the decisive victory over Lieutenant Colonel Banastre Tarleton's British forces. Afterward, Pickens was named a brigadier general by Governor John Rutledge and cooperated with General Nathanael Greene's objective of isolating British posts in the South Carolina interior. Wounded at the Battle of Eutaw Springs in September 1781, Pickens recovered to wage two more punitive campaigns against the Cherokees in mid-1782.

After the war, Pickens served as both a legislator and a negotiator with the Native Americans. He represented Ninety Six District in the state House of Representatives from 1776 to 1788 and Pendleton District in the state Senate from 1790 to 1793. He resigned his Senate seat upon his election to the U.S. House of Representatives, where he served from 1793 to 1795. As a legislator, Pickens worked to establish schools, churches, and a legal system for the South Carolina backcountry. A recognized expert on Indian affairs, Pickens served as a federal commissioner to negotiate peace independently with the Cherokees, Chickasaws, Choctaws, and Creeks in the late 1780s and eventually negotiated a firm peace with the Treaty of Coleraine in 1796. The following year he and Benjamin Hawkins surveyed most of the southern boundary line between the United States and the Indian nations.

Pickens served two more terms in the General Assembly from 1796 to 1799, representing Pendleton District. He retired to his plantation Tamassee in 1805, coming out only briefly in 1812 when elected to a final term in the General Assembly to prepare South Carolina for war. He died at Tamassee on August 11, 1817, and was buried at the Old Stone Presbyterian Church. SAMUEL K. FORE

Ferguson, Clyde R. "General Andrew Pickens." Ph.D. diss., Duke University, 1960.

Skelton, Lynda Worley, ed. *General Andrew Pickens: An Autobiography.* Pendleton, S.C.: Pendleton District Historical and Recreational Commission, 1976.

Waring, Alice Noble. *The Fighting Elder: Andrew Pickens (1739–1817).* Columbia: University of South Carolina Press, 1962.

Pickens, Andrew, Jr. (1779–1838). Governor. Andrew Pickens, Jr., was born on November 13, 1779 in Ninety Six District, the son of Rebecca Calhoun and Revolutionary War hero and general Andrew Pickens. He attended Rhode Island College (later Brown University), graduating in 1801. Upon his election to Phi Beta Kappa, his father advised him, "Your improvements in learning . . . are gratifying . . . but you must remember that many, under tutors and governors, perform well, but after they come to act for themselves doe not act so well." Returning to South Carolina, Pickens married Susan Smith Wilkinson on April 19, 1804. The couple had two children. Pickens studied law in Charleston before settling in Pendleton District, where he took up farming on a portion of his father's plantation Hopewell. Following the death of his first wife in 1810, Pickens married Mary Nelson of Virginia. They had no children.

Pickens's political career began at the local level, where he served in minor public posts, such as commissioner for building the Pendleton District courthouse (1806) and commissioner of the Pendleton Circulating Library Society (1808–1814). In 1810 the voters of Pendleton District sent Pickens to the state House of Representatives, where he served a single term. Following the outbreak of war between Great Britain and the United States in 1812, Pickens was commissioned as a lieutenant colonel and served with the U.S. Tenth Infantry and the Forty-third Infantry. He resigned his U.S. Army commission on June 15, 1814, and returned to South Carolina, where he was made a colonel in the state militia.

On December 5, 1816, Pickens was elected governor of South Carolina, the first person from above the state's fall line to serve in that office. As an upcountry planter, Pickens sympathized with calls from the state's upper districts to improve transportation links between Charleston and the interior. The need was all the more urgent with cotton prices at all-time highs in the antebellum era. Pickens urged that public funds be spent to create a system of state-owned roads and canals, and in 1818 the legislature appropriated the unprecedented sum of $1 million to implement a statewide program of internal improvements.

Shortly after the end of his term in December 1818, Pickens moved to Alabama, where he acquired large landholdings and took up cotton planting. In 1820 John C. Calhoun, a cousin and longtime friend, helped secure Pickens a commission as U.S. negotiator with the Creek Indians, but he declined to serve. Returning to South Carolina in the early 1830s, Pickens resumed cotton planting at Oatlands plantation in Edgefield District. He died in Mississippi on June 24, 1838, and was buried at Old Stone Churchyard in Pendleton District. JAMES SPADY

Bailey, N. Louise, ed. *Biographical Directory of the South Carolina House of Representatives.* Vol. 4, *1791–1815.* Columbia: University of South Carolina Press, 1984.

Waring, Alice Noble. *The Fighting Elder: Andrew Pickens (1739–1817).* Columbia: University of South Carolina Press, 1962.

Pickens, Francis Wilkinson (1807–1869). Congressman, diplomat, governor. Born on April 7, 1807, in St. Paul's Parish, Pickens was the son of Governor Andrew Pickens, Jr., and Susan Smith Wilkinson. Reared among his father's extensive landholdings in South Carolina and Alabama, Pickens attended Franklin College in Georgia before entering South Carolina College as a sophomore. He was active at the latter in the Clariosophic Society and was known for his oratory skills. He left college in 1827 without graduating following a student revolt over compulsory mess attendance. On October 18, 1827, he married Margaret Eliza Simkins. After reading law with her father, Eldred Simkins, Pickens was admitted to the bar on December 2, 1828. Pickens amassed considerable property, including land in South Carolina, Alabama, and Mississippi, as well as a sizable number of slaves. The 1860 census lists him as the owner of $45,400 in real estate and $244,206 in personal property, including 276 slaves. Although heavily encumbered with debts, he still had considerable landholdings at the time of his death. Pickens's first wife died on August 12, 1842. He was married on January 9, 1845, to Marion Antoinette Dearing, and that marriage lasted until her death on August 14, 1853. On April 26, 1858, he married Lucy Petway Holcombe of Texas. His three marriages produced nine children.

Pickens's public career began in college when he authored a series of articles in the *Charleston Mercury* espousing state sovereignty and questioning the legality of a protective tariff. Later articles in the Columbia and Edgefield newspapers marked Pickens as a leading proponent of nullification. From 1832 to 1833 he represented Edgefield District in the General Assembly. He rose quickly to chair the committees on federal relations and the judiciary, playing an instrumental role in the passage of the test oath law. He was commissioned as a lieutenant colonel in the state militia and helped raise volunteers to defend against threatened federal military coercion.

Elected to fill the unexpired term of George McDuffie in the U.S. House of Representatives, Pickens took his seat in the Twenty-third Congress on December 8, 1834. He was a strong supporter of slavery, states' rights, and an independent national treasury. He was an ally and confidant of John C. Calhoun, with whom he had close family ties. He often served as Calhoun's chief lieutenant in the House, although the rise of rivals for Calhoun's favor led to a troubled relationship by the latter part of the decade. In 1839 Pickens's bid to be elected Speaker of the U.S. House was thwarted by his rivals in the South Carolina delegation, Robert B. Rhett and Franklin Elmore. The sectional bickering in the House led him not to seek reelection in 1842. He declined an appointment as minister to France, but he assisted Calhoun's unsuccessful attempt at the presidency in 1844 and was active at both the state and national Democratic conventions. Elected to the state Senate in the fall of 1844, he also harbored hopes of a U.S. Senate seat. In 1845 he again refused a diplomatic appointment, this time to Great Britain. He retired to Edgefield after serving one term in the state Senate.

Pickens attended the 1850 Southern Rights Convention in Nashville and advocated southern unity as the only means of stopping northern agitation over slavery. The failure of southern cooperation pushed him toward the radical position of separate state action. He lost a close vote for governor in December 1850 but was elected to the state convention held in 1852 to consider secession. The state had swung toward a more conservative position, and he lost subsequent bids for the U.S. Senate and for his old seat in the House. He renewed his activities with the national Democratic Party, which he now considered the best hope of preserving the southern cause within the Union. He attended the 1856 Democratic convention in Cincinnati and actively campaigned for James Buchanan, who, after his election as president, offered Pickens the position of minister to Russia. Although he initially declined, Pickens accepted the post after he lost a race for the Senate in 1857, and he sailed for St. Petersburg on May 28, 1858. Aware that he was being considered as a compromise presidential candidate and with a complaining wife and the growing political crisis, Pickens resigned his post on April 17, 1860. However, it was early November before he returned to the United States. He entered the contest for governor and prevailed after close balloting on December 16, 1860.

South Carolina seceded on December 20, 1860, placing Pickens in a difficult situation. Under intense local pressure to dislodge the Federal military presence in Charleston harbor despite the lack of military preparedness, Pickens adopted a cautious approach that sought a negotiated surrender. Except for shots fired on the *Star of the West* as the ship attempted to resupply Fort Sumter in January, Pickens avoided hostilities. The eventual bombardment and capture of Fort Sumter came after the Confederate government took control of events in the harbor.

Pickens's administration was dominated by military problems, including raising troops and supplies for defending the coast and assisting the war effort in Virginia. The lack of military resources became apparent when Union forces seized Port Royal Sound in November 1861. Confidence in Pickens's leadership reached a low point soon thereafter when large parts of Charleston were destroyed by fire. The Secession Convention reacted to these disasters and Pickens's perceived deficiencies by forming a five-member council to exercise executive authority. Although he was a member of the council, the usurpation of his authority created an antagonistic relationship between Pickens and the members elected by the convention. Conscription, slave impressments, and other measures enacted produced widespread disapproval of the council but increased Pickens's reputation. The council was abolished in December 1862, shortly after Pickens's term as governor ended. Pickens retired to his plantation in Edgefield. Aside from participating in the 1865 constitutional convention, he held no other office or political role. He died at his home on January 25, 1869, and was buried at Willowbrook Cemetery in Edgefield County. PATRICK MCCAWLEY

Edmunds, John B. *Francis W. Pickens and the Politics of Destruction.* Chapel Hill: University of North Carolina Press, 1986.

Pickens, William (1881–1954). Educator, author, civil rights advocate. Pickens was born in Anderson County on January 15, 1881, to Jacob Pickens and Fannie Porter. The family migrated to Arkansas, where the young boy worked in cotton fields and sawmills. In 1902 he graduated from Talladega College in Alabama. He went on to attend Yale University, which required two additional years of study for graduates of historically black colleges. Among his many academic honors, Pickens was elected Phi Beta Kappa before returning to teach foreign languages at Talladega from 1904 until 1914. Teaching at Talladega and at Morgan College in Baltimore, Pickens grew more radical in his views, speaking against accommodationist stances of Negro leader Booker T. Washington.

In 1910 Pickens began his forty-year affiliation with the National Association for the Advancement of Colored People

(NAACP), serving almost twenty of those years as director of branches, in the tradition of fellow intellectuals and activists W. E. B. Du Bois and James Weldon Johnson. In *New Negro* (1916), Pickens stressed belief in the debt the nation owed to African Americans and advocated integration, black economic cooperation, political activism, and nonviolent social protest. As a onetime supporter of the controversial black separatist Marcus Garvey, Pickens defied NAACP leaders and condemned the organization for supporting the Communist Party's defense of the infamous Scottsboro Boys. Ironically, in his last major controversy, Pickens was accused in 1943 by the House Un-American Activities Committee (HUAC) of being a Communist Party member. From 1942 to 1950 Pickens served with the U.S. Treasury Department, where he was responsible for the promotion and sale of savings bonds among African Americans. He ended his very public career respected as a loyal American willing to disagree with individuals and groups, of any color, he felt were unmindful of the full burden that race played in the country. As was the case with many civil rights activists of his era, the duality of being both black and an American during war years provoked difficult stances on the issue of patriotism.

Pickens used his intellectual talents as a method of protest, especially during his years as a full-time educator. His best-known work is his autobiography, *Bursting Bonds* (1923), but several of his lectures carried titles that articulated the expanding consciousness of African Americans: "Frederick Douglas and the Spirit of Freedom" (1912), "The Ultimate Effects of Segregation and Discrimination" (1915), and "American Aesop" (1926).

Pickens married Minnie Cooper McAlpine in 1905. The second of their three children, Harriet Ida Pickens, was a New Deal administrator and the first black woman commissioned as an officer in the WAVES during World War II. While cruising off the coast of South America, Pickens died on April 6, 1954, just one month before the Supreme Court handed down its famous *Brown v. Board of Education* ruling, which would begin to dismantle the discriminatory practices he had fought against throughout his life. MILLICENT ELLISON BROWN

Avery, Sheldon. *Up from Washington: William Pickens and the Negro Struggle for Equality, 1900–1954.* Newark: University of Delaware Press, 1989.

Pickens County (497 sq. miles; 2000 pop. 110,757). Located in South Carolina's northwest corner, Pickens County is an area of lakes and mountains, including the state's highest peak, Sassafras Mountain. The county was named for Revolutionary War general Andrew Pickens, as was its predecessor, Pickens District (created in 1826). In 1868 delegates took to the state constitutional convention in Charleston a petition to divide Pickens District. The inconvenient location of the old courthouse was the major reason for division, which had also been attempted in 1851, 1860, and 1866. The renewed request was granted on January 29, 1868, and a bill presented to create Pickens and Oconee Counties was ratified as part of the new state constitution on April 14–16, 1868. A new courthouse town, also named Pickens, was chosen at a location fourteen miles east of the former courthouse.

Although the upcountry largely escaped the destruction of the Civil War, the establishment and operation of the new county had their difficulties, coming as they did during the postwar economic crisis and a volatile political climate. In this rural, isolated area of small farmers (few of whom had owned slaves before the war), the citizens of Pickens County nevertheless moved ahead, organizing the first Board of Commissioners on October 10, 1868. The board promptly ordered male citizens to begin work on the roads, especially the one to the new Pickens Court House. In March 1869 the first county court was held. Conditions in the early years of the county stabilized, and Pickens had an excellent record of meeting its tax obligations. And while Republicans controlled state government during this era, Democrats dominated politics in Pickens County, and local "political clubs" contributed to the election of Wade Hampton III as governor in 1876.

The early emphasis on roads was an indication of the county's preoccupation with transportation, which soon focused on railroad development. With agriculture the main occupation of Pickens County residents, transporting crops quickly and cheaply to market was almost as important to farm profits as weather and soil conditions. Several attempts were made to attract a railroad line throughout the latter years of the nineteenth century. In 1870 voters approved a $100,000 bond subscription to the Atlanta and Charlotte Air Line Railroad, believing that it would serve the town of Pickens as well as other parts of the county. The line eventually passed through Pickens County, and towns quickly sprang up along its route (Easley, Liberty, and Garvon Stations in 1873 and Calhoun in 1892). However, the benefits of this early railroad were mixed since it came only to within a few miles of the county seat. Also, the small African American population of Pickens County used the line to leave the county for opportunities elsewhere. Plans for a Sassafras Gap railroad in the mid-1870s failed, as did those in the 1880s for the line known as the Atlantic and French Broad Valley Railroad. It was not until 1890 that the Pickens Railroad Company was finally chartered, and in 1898 the first train ran the line from Easley to Pickens. From 1927 to 1929 the Appalachian Lumber Company built and operated a logging rail line from Pickens to Eastatoe.

Agriculture suffered through several years of bad crops in the 1870s and 1880s, and farmers began to look for ways to improve their lot. The Pickens County Agricultural and Mechanical Association was formed in 1885 and encouraged its members to use their combined political influence. Local voters supported the election of Benjamin R. Tillman as governor in 1890. Of particular interest to Pickens County, "Pitchfork Ben" supported the establishment of Clemson Agricultural College, later Clemson University. The college was founded in 1889 on property that had been John C. Calhoun's plantation and then was willed to the state by Calhoun's son-in-law,

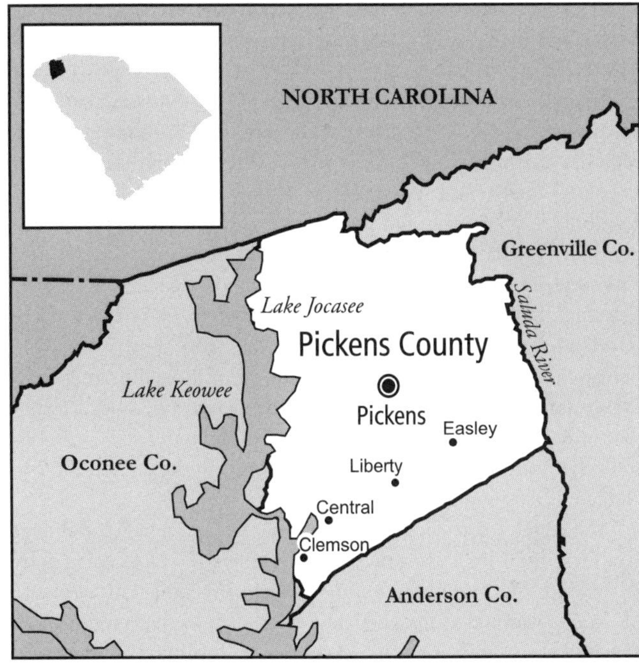

Thomas G. Clemson. Classes began in 1893, and Clemson quickly became a great asset to Pickens County and the state at large.

Industry in Pickens County expanded at the end of the nineteenth century, beginning with construction of the Norris Cotton Mill at Cateechee in 1895. By 1900 there were three cotton mills, two railroads, three banks, three roller mills, thirty-seven sawmills, ten shingle mills, and four brickyards. Despite these, the county remained predominantly rural throughout the first half of the twentieth century, with the majority of workers either raising crops or turning the cotton into cloth in local mill villages.

As with most of the upstate, the post–World War II economy in Pickens County reduced its reliance on the textile industry. By 1972 there were 99 manufacturing plants, and this number grew to approximately 150 by 1999. From 1985 to 1998 the county attracted more than $406 million in capital investments, which created more than 2,800 jobs. In addition to manufacturing, Pickens County's modern economy relied on education, especially Clemson University and Southern Wesleyan University (created in 1906 in the town of Central), as well as tourists attracted to the county's natural and historical resources. Landscape altering hydroelectric projects of the 1960s and 1970s covered many historic sites associated with Native Americans but resulted in Lakes Hartwell, Jocassee, and Keowee, which provided recreational opportunities. A long list of attractions drew visitors from across the country, including Table Rock State Park (built by the Civilian Conservation Corps in 1933), the Pickens County Museum (located in the 1902 county jail), and Fort Hill, the former Calhoun-Clemson mansion on the Clemson campus. Other historical resources include Old Stone Presbyterian Church (1800), where Andrew Pickens served as elder and now rests in the family plot, and the 1826 Hagood Grist Mill. The climate, natural beauty, historic sites, and Clemson University all made tourism a vital part of Pickens County's economy in the early twenty-first century. DONNA K. ROPER

Aheron, Piper Peters. *Pickens County.* Charleston, S.C.: Arcadia, 2000.

Morris, Jane Boroughs. *Pickens: The Town and the First Baptist Church.* Pickens, S.C.: Pickens First Baptist Church, 1991.

Piedmont. One of six landform regions in South Carolina, the Piedmont is defined by high hills to the north that give way to rolling hills at the center of the state. This region is part of the larger Piedmont Plateau that spreads southwest from Maryland through Virginia, North Carolina, South Carolina, and northern Georgia before ending in Alabama.

Spanning the state in a broad northeast to southwest band, the Piedmont is the second-largest of South Carolina's landform regions, encompassing 10,500 square miles, nearly one-third of the state's total area. It runs from the Blue Ridge in the north to the Sandhills in the south and includes all or portions of twenty-two counties: Abbeville, Anderson, Cherokee, Chester, Chesterfield, Edgefield, Fairfield, Greenville, Greenwood, Kershaw, Lancaster, Laurens, Lexington, McCormick, Newberry, Oconee, Pickens, Richland, Saluda, Spartanburg, Union, and York. Elevation increases markedly across the Piedmont, from three hundred feet at the eastern boundary, where Richland, Lexington, and Kershaw Counties straddle the line between the Sandhills and the Piedmont, to twelve hundred feet at its northwest border at the base of the Blue Ridge in Oconee and Pickens Counties.

The region experienced frequent periods of great geologic change. Land was built up and eroded away, leaving signs of geologic activity behind. Six hundred million years ago the land that forms the Piedmont was a land mass separate from the North American continent. Then, about 470 million years ago, this mass collided with the edge of the continent, changing the soils of the region through extensive folding, faulting, and metamorphism. Another, larger collision with the continent of Africa had similar effects. Before this, the Piedmont was the coast. With the retreat of the Atlantic Ocean, its sandy border became the Sandhills region that divides the Piedmont from the coastal plain region.

The result of these collisions is that most Piedmont rocks are metamorphic, originally sandstone and shale changed to gneiss and schist, with igneous intrusions of granite formed deep in the earth's crust during the tectonic activity associated with the continental collisions.

Despite the active tectonic history, the Piedmont is relatively flat. Like its predecessors, the most recent mountain range, formed ten million years ago during the Miocene epoch, began eroding as it was formed, flattening the landscape and covering it with red clay soil colored by iron-rich minerals. Remnants of techtonic activity in the form of monadnocks (mostly granite outcrops that resist weathering) remained as the softer rocks were eroded away. Good examples of this type of geological formation include Forty-Acre Rock in Lancaster County, Paris Mountain in Greenville County, and Kings Mountain in York County.

The geography and geology of the region determined its settlement and use by humans. Three major Piedmont river systems, the Santee, the Savannah, and the Pee Dee, filled with sediment from the eroding mountains, created the rich floodplains so attractive to the area's early settlers and later transported their produce downriver to the coast. During the colonial period, Scots-Irish, English, and German immigrants from Virginia and Pennsylvania poured into the region, establishing small farms. Place names such as York, Lancaster, and Chester reflect these settlers' connections to Pennsylvania, and Chesterfield suggests ties to piedmont Virginia.

Subsistence farmers at first, these rugged settlers after the 1790s changed to cotton, which became the upstate's principal commercial crop. Wheat and tobacco produced additional income as northerners moved into the area with expertise in cultivating these crops. In 1830 Piedmont districts of Abbeville, Edgefield, Fairfield, and Laurens produced almost one-half of the state's cotton crop. Better transportation in the form of canals and then railroads improved the demand for Piedmont cotton into the early 1900s. Railroads out of Columbia connected to Piedmont cities, including Anderson, Laurens, Greenville, and Spartanburg. By 1940 the upper Piedmont was producing only one-third of the state's cotton using tenant-farmer or sharecropper systems. Dropping prices, boll weevils, and poor land conservation practices caused the decline of cotton during the 1910s through the 1930s. The red clay soils of the Piedmont made water absorption difficult, leading to rapid runoff of rain and therefore high erosion potential. This and heavy demand on the soils produced severe erosion and depleted the topsoil. Most of the Piedmont lost up to ten percent of topsoil to erosion, and some places lost more.

The Piedmont is also a source of economically important rocks and minerals, primarily granite and gold. Lancaster, Chesterfield, and Fairfield Counties all have active gold mines, making the state one of the most productive gold-mining states east of the Mississippi. Other mining activities in the region have included clay (for brick), kyanite, kaolin, and some gemstones.

Most settlers in the Piedmont, however, were not miners but farmers. As constant farming began to deplete the soils and severe erosion made farming conditions worse, the Piedmont began changing from agriculture to industry, especially textiles. This transition was eased by readily available waterpower. Throughout the late nineteenth and early twentieth centuries, almost all significant Piedmont rivers and streams were dammed, first to provide power to cotton mills and then for creation of hydroelectricity.

Mill towns flourished as the textile industry grew through the early twentieth century and soon dominated the social and economic landscapes of the Piedmont. Railroads spread rapidly across the region to carry cotton to the coast, and towns sprang up along major routes. Cotton mills soon produced a way of life, as farming had before them. Along with textile factories, mill owners also built housing near the mill sites. With significant increases in hydroelectric power, the textile industry boomed in the state. In 1880 about forty percent of textile mills in the state were located in the upper Piedmont counties of Oconee, Anderson, Greenville, and Spartanburg. By the 1910s more than seventy percent of mills lay in the Piedmont between Anderson and York. However, more recent decades saw the decline of the textile industry in the South Carolina Piedmont, mostly as a result of cheaper overseas production.

In the early twenty-first century the Piedmont area still contained much rural land, which supported some farming, including cattle and forest production. These rural patches rested between the region's rapidly growing cities of Greenville, Spartanburg, Anderson, and Rock Hill. New industry, especially along the Interstate 85 corridor, had been heavily and successfully recruited in the area, resulting in rapid development. Future plans called for careful land-use planning to handle the rapid growth. CAROLINE FOSTER

Fairey, Daniel A. *South Carolina's Land Resources: A Regional Overview.* Rev. ed. Columbia: South Carolina Land Resources Commission, 1992.

Jones, Lewis P. *South Carolina: One of the Fifty States.* Orangeburg, S.C.: Sandlapper, 1985.

Kovacik, Charles F., and John J. Winberry. *South Carolina: The Making of a Landscape.* 1987. Reprint, Columbia: University of South Carolina Press, 1989.

South Carolina Maps and Aerial Photographic Systems. 4th ed. Columbia: South Carolina Department of Natural Resources, 2000.

Piedmont and Northern Railway. James B. Duke planned the Piedmont and Northern (P&N) electric railway to assist in the industrialization of the Piedmont region of the Carolinas. The line was envisioned as eventually connecting Greenwood, South Carolina, with Norfolk, Virginia. An initial twenty-four-mile line between Charlotte and Gastonia, North Carolina, and an eighty-nine-mile line between Spartanburg and Greenwood, South Carolina (connecting with Duke's existing twelve-mile electric line between Belton and Anderson), were built between 1911 and 1914. World War I and the federal takeover of the nation's railroads intervened, and it was 1924 before the P&N was ready to construct the fifty-one-mile line between Spartanburg and Gastonia. Although interurbans were exempt from the jurisdiction of the Interstate Commerce Commission (ICC), the Southern Railway successfully argued that the P&N, because of its extensive freight business, should be treated as a Class I railway and placed under ICC jurisdiction. The Southern management then successfully blocked any further construction by "that God-damned trolley line."

Throughout the 1920s and 1930s "The Electric" or "The Poor and Needy," as it was variously known to local citizens, carried workers to their jobs in the mills, shoppers to the larger cities, families on picnics and excursions, and freight to the mills, among other business activities. Passenger traffic peaked in 1921 and then began to decline. The last passenger train on the South Carolina section, consisting of car 2102 and the business car "Carolina," ran from Greenwood to Spartanburg on October 31, 1951. These two cars were preserved in a museum in Greenwood.

Between 1950 and 1954 the P&N was converted to diesel power to avoid the expensive replacement of the forty-year-old electric system. Two electric engines were retained until 1958 to serve several Charlotte industries that could be reached only via a section of weak track in the center of Mint Street. One of these engines, the only surviving P&N electric engine, is in the collection of the North Carolina Museum of Transport. In 1969 the P&N was acquired, over the protests of the Southern Railway, by the Seaboard Coast Line Railway (now part of CSX). Many of the Piedmont and Northern's yellow-brick and red-tile-roofed stations, although used for other purposes, continued to be valued by their respective communities in the early twenty-first century. DEWITT BOYD STONE, JR.

Fetters, Thomas T., and Peter W. Swanson, Jr. *Piedmont and Northern: The Great Electric System of the South.* San Marino, Calif.: Golden West, 1974.

Pike, John Martin (1840–1932). Clergyman, editor, publisher. Pike was born in Newfoundland, Canada, in June 1840, the son and brother of Arctic explorers. Educated in Newfoundland and Nova Scotia, he graduated from Mount Allison Wesleyan College and Seminary in Sackville, Nova Scotia. Ordained in 1868, Pike served Wesleyan Methodist and Methodist Church of Canada parishes in the Maritime Provinces. About 1873 he married Marry S. Pike, a Nova Scotia native. The couple had seven children.

In the mid-1880s the Methodist bishop of South Carolina invited Pike to preach at the Washington Street Methodist Episcopal Church, South in Columbia. Pike subsequently moved to the state and spent most of the rest of his life in South Carolina. He pastored Methodist Episcopal Church, South congregations in Lynchburg, Sumter, Summerville, and Charleston. For health reasons, he moved briefly to Florida, where he served several churches and also edited the *Florida Sunbeam* in Ocala.

Pike returned to Columbia in 1890 at the invitation of Methodist minister Robert C. Oliver, who was starting a periodical, *The Way of Faith,* in addition to his work at what became the Oliver Gospel Mission. Pike became assistant editor of the weekly publication, assuming responsibilities as editor when Oliver died in 1893. Pike remained as editor for twenty-five years and wrote occasional articles for the weekly for another five years after retiring. *The Way of Faith* ceased publication in 1931.

Through this periodical and his involvement with the Oliver Gospel Mission, Pike exercised pivotal influence on the planting of Holiness and Pentecostal strains of Protestantism in South Carolina. *The Way of Faith* carried reports of revivals led by Pentecostal Holiness Church founder A. B. Crumpler. The Christian and Missionary Alliance credits Pike with facilitating that organization's entry into the state, and Pike also made it possible for Nickels John Holmes's Bible Institute to use the Oliver Gospel Mission facilities for its classes between 1903 and 1905.

In addition, after the Pentecostal revivals at the Azusa Street mission in Los Angeles erupted in 1906, Pike and *The Way of Faith* became major conduits in publicizing the new movement not only in South Carolina but also throughout the region. Frank Bartleman sent Pike eyewitness reports of the Azusa Street events, and those reports first appeared in *The Way of Faith* and later were collected in Bartleman's *My Story: "The Latter Day Rain"* (1908), which was published by Pike.

Pike was also instrumental in publishing numerous other Holiness and Pentecostal books, including the Holiness writer Mary

Mabbette Anderson's *Lights and Shadows of the Life in Canaan* (1906) and the collected letters of Dr. Lilian B. Yeomans and her mother, Dr. Amelia Yeomans. These collected letters, *Pentecostal Papers,* contained a major account of the nature of Pentecostal religious experience and its relevance to women. Pike contributed occasional pieces to other Holiness periodicals, including Carrie Judd Montgomery's *Triumphs of Faith* in Oakland, California.

In his later years Pike added a significant social component to his work in Columbia, founding the Door of Hope, a ministry to women victimized by sexual predators, poverty, and domestic violence. Pike was a tireless fund-raiser for the agency, which was headed for many years by Anna Finnstrom. Pike died in Columbia on May 16, 1932. His funeral was held at the Washington Street Methodist Episcopal Church, South. NANCY A. HARDESTY

"Aged Minister Goes to Reward." Columbia *State,* May 17, 1932, pp. 1, 2.

Synan, Vinson. *The Holiness-Pentecostal Tradition: Charismatic Movements in the Twentieth Century.* 2d ed. Grand Rapids, Mich.: Eerdmans, 1997.

Pinckney, Charles (1757–1824). Planter, legislator, governor, statesman. Pinckney was born in Charleston on October 26, 1757, the son of Charles Pinckney and Frances Brewton. Little is known of his childhood. In 1773, while still in his teens, he enrolled in the Middle Temple in London, but the Revolution prevented him from attending. As a result, he received most of his education in Charleston, first under the tutelage of Dr. David Oliphant and later in the law office of his father.

Charles Pinckney. Courtesy, South Caroliniana Library, University of South Carolina

In 1779 Pinckney entered public service as a representative to the General Assembly from Christ Church Parish, home of his family's country estate, Snee Farm. During the Revolution he joined the Charleston militia and saw action at the siege of Savannah (September–October 1779) and was captured at the fall of Charleston in May 1780. After being confined on board the prison ship *Pack Horse,* Pinckney was eventually paroled in a general prisoner exchange in the summer of 1781. Following his release, he went to Philadelphia. After his father died in September 1782, Pinckney returned to South Carolina the following year to assist his mother in settling the estate and to resume his political career. In 1784 Pinckney reentered the General Assembly and, later that year, was elected to the Confederation Congress.

In Congress, Pinckney quickly made a name for himself. He became friends with James Monroe and served with the Virginian on a committee responsible for presenting Thomas Jefferson's ordinances regarding the Northwest Territory. Pinckney also spoke forcefully regarding negotiations with Spain, stressing that securing navigation rights to the Mississippi River for the United States was imperative to southern interests. In 1786 Pinckney was one of three members appointed to persuade the New Jersey assembly to pay their share of Confederation taxes. In his address, Pinckney suggested that if they did not agree with the operation of the government, they should call a convention to try to make necessary improvements. Making a similar call two months later in the Confederation Congress, Pinckney submitted a plan for amending the Articles of Confederation to give more power to the national government, especially in the regulation of commerce. His plan was put aside, however, when word came from Annapolis that a call had been made for a convention of the states to reconsider the powers of the federal government. Because of his outspoken belief that the Articles of Confederation were defective and his eloquence regarding the subject, the South Carolina General Assembly elected Pinckney as one of the five South Carolinians to attend the May 1787 constitutional convention in Philadelphia, where he became one of the convention's most active delegates.

On the third day of the convention he submitted what came to be known as "The Pinckney Draft," which was similar to the "Virginia Plan" of Edmund Randolph. Pinckney's proposal called for a strong central government consisting of three "separate and distinct" branches. The legislative branch would consist of a Senate and a House of Delegates. The House would be elected proportionately to the white population, with slaves being counted as three-fifths of a person toward representation. To fill the Senate, the states would be divided into districts according to size. The larger the size of the state, the more senators it would have. The legislature would be responsible for national defense, "regulating the Trade with the several States as well with Foreign Nations as with each other," forming a post office, regulating Indian affairs, coining money, "ordering the Militia of any State to any Place within the U.S.," choosing the president, and "instituting a federal judicial Court." The president would serve for a term of seven years and be responsible for informing the legislature "at every session of the condition of the United States." In other words, the president would deliver what have come to be known as "State of the Union Addresses." The president would also be the commander in chief of the military and would inspect the various departments within the government. He would have the power to call members of the legislature into emergency session and to dismiss them "when they cannot agree as to the time of their adjournment." The House of Delegates would have power of impeachment, with senators and federal judges holding the power to try the executive. The judicial branch, appointed by the legislature, would hear cases brought against United States officers and settle matters between states and between a state and the federal government. There would also be a court of admiralty. Judges would be appointed for a term of "good Behavior," although the manner of appointment was not specified. Pinckney even attached a small "Bill of Rights" to his document, which provided for "the privilege of the writ of habeas corpus—the trial by jury in all cases, criminal as well as civil—the freedom of the press and the prevention of religious tests as qualifications to offices of trust or emolument." Although his plan was not adopted in its entirety, dozens of Pinckney's proposals found their way into what would become the United States Constitution.

One of the most important moments for Pinckney during the convention came on June 25. Speaking to his fellow delegates, he made a forceful case for the unique quality of America and the importance of seeking original solutions for a new government. The address was redolent with republican ideology, such as calling for a nation led by an aristocracy based on merit, not birth, as well as themes that influenced Jacksonian democracy in the next century.

After the convention, Pinckney returned to South Carolina and married Mary Eleanor Laurens, daughter of Henry Laurens, on April 27, 1788. The following month he served at the state ratifying convention, speaking in support of the new constitution he had helped to create and reiterating the themes of his June 25, 1787, speech in Philadelphia. In doing so, he sought to placate backcountry delegates, who feared that the document would benefit the state's lowcountry elite and the northern states at the expense of their liberty. Supporters of the document, however, outweighed the opposition, and South Carolina ratified the Constitution by a vote of 149 to 73.

Pinckney was elected governor in 1789 and became the first to serve at the new capital of Columbia, basing his political operations from his plantation Greenwich, on the Congaree River just south of town. He also presided over the state constitutional convention of 1790. Using his considerable political influence, he organized backcountry dissidents into a voting bloc that, ten years later, would back his support of Thomas Jefferson's bid for the presidency. In supporting Jefferson, Pinckney broke with his economic base, his geographic roots in the lowcountry, and his family (his cousin Charles Cotesworth Pinckney was Jefferson's opponent) in order to unite the state and insure the election of his ideological peer.

When U.S. Senator John Hunter resigned from Congress in November 1798, Pinckney was appointed to serve out his term. However, after Jefferson's election as president in 1800, Pinckney was named minister plenipotentiary to Spain. From 1801 to 1805 he attempted to conduct foreign affairs but found himself hampered by an arrogant Spanish court and a secretary of state, James Madison, who believed Pinckney to be inept in diplomatic matters. Returning to South Carolina in 1806, Pinckney was reelected governor in December and served a record fourth term. Although he may have alienated his family and his socioeconomic peers, as well as some in his own party, the majority of the people in South Carolina respected his ability and his willingness to reach across class and geographic lines in order to unite the state. He served in various state offices until 1814, when he retired from public life. The respite was brief, however, and in 1819 Pinckney was elected to the U.S. House of Representatives. There he spoke in opposition to the Missouri Compromise, claiming that it threatened southern interests, particularly slavery, and paving the way for later southern advocates such as John C. Calhoun. Declining reelection in 1821, Pinckney left the public arena for good.

On October 29, 1824, Pinckney died in Charleston, and he was buried in the graveyard at St. Philip's Church. He was survived by a daughter, Mary Eleanor Pinckney, and a son, Henry Laurens Pinckney, whose birth had claimed the life of his mother in 1794. Another daughter, Frances Henrietta Pinckney, had predeceased her father. Scorned by his class and his family for much of his latter life, Pinckney was also dismissed by some historians as vain, arrogant, and too willing to take credit for the work of others. He was actually an important transitional figure at both the state and national levels. He succeeded in uniting his state across class and geographic lines to insure Jefferson's election in 1800 and, in doing so, earned distinction as a founder of the Democratic Party in South Carolina. On a national level, he bridged the generation gap between the founding fathers of the revolutionary period and their successors in the age of Andrew Jackson. MARTY D. MATTHEWS

Kaplanoff, Mark D. "Charles Pinckney and the American Republican Tradition." In *Intellectual Life in Antebellum Charleston,* edited by Michael O'Brien and David Moltke-Hansen. Knoxville: University of Tennessee Press, 1986.

Matthews, Marty D. *Forgotten Founder: The Life and Times of Charles Pinckney.* Columbia: University of South Carolina Press, 2004.

Williams, Frances Leigh. *A Founding Family: The Pinckneys of South Carolina.* New York: Harcourt Brace Jovanovich, 1978.

Pinckney, Charles Cotesworth (1746–1825). Soldier, statesman, diplomat. Pinckney was born in Charleston on February 14, 1746, to Charles Pinckney, a lawyer and member of the provincial council, and Elizabeth Lucas, who helped introduce indigo cultivation in South Carolina. In 1753 Pinckney accompanied his family to London, where his father served as the colony's agent until 1758. Young Pinckney received private tutoring before entering the prestigious Westminster School in 1761. Three years later he matriculated at both Christ Church College, Oxford, and at the Middle Temple, the London legal training ground. While at Oxford he attended lectures by the famed legal scholar Sir William Blackstone and listened to debates in the House of Commons pertaining to the American colonies. Pinckney was admitted to the English Bar in January 1769. Following a tour of Europe, he returned to South Carolina, where he began a successful legal practice.

Pinckney entered public service in 1769 with election to the Commons House of Assembly, where he represented St. John's Colleton Parish during the remainder of royal rule. Pinckney also served in the local militia, eventually attaining the rank of colonel. In 1773 he was made attorney general for the judicial districts of Camden, Cheraws, and Georgetown. That same year, on September 28, he married Sarah Middleton, daughter of the wealthy and well-connected Henry Middleton. The marriage produced four children. Through this marriage Pinckney became closely affiliated with some of the province's leading radicals in America's contest with Great Britain, such as Arthur Middleton, Edward Rutledge, and William Henry Drayton. By early 1775 Pinckney was a member of all the

Charles Cotesworth Pinckney. Courtesy, South Carolina Historical Society

important revolutionary committees, from which he advocated aggressive measures, including stealing royal arms from the Statehouse, penning inflammatory epistles to backcountry inhabitants, and planning the defense of Charleston against a possible British attack. At the same time, Pinckney served in the extralegal Provincial Congress, where he assisted in creating and training a rebel army and chaired the committee responsible for drafting a temporary frame of government for the province.

Once hostilities erupted with Britain, Pinckney switched his role as a politician to that of a soldier. Appointed commander of the First Regiment of South Carolina troops, he assisted in the successful defense of Charleston at the Battle of Sullivan's Island in June 1776. When the British moved north following this defeat, Pinckney followed to serve as an aide-de-camp to General George Washington. He participated at the battles of Brandywine and Germantown before rejoining the southern army to command a regiment in the expedition to East Florida and at the siege of Savannah. During the defense of Charleston he commanded Fort Moultrie and made a futile attempt to convince General Benjamin Lincoln, commander of the southern army, to defend the capital at all costs. When Charleston fell, the British placed Pinckney under house arrest and made a hapless attempt to lure him away from the American cause. The British later sent Pinckney to Philadelphia, where he was exchanged in 1782. He rejoined the southern army but saw no further action. Pinckney's first wife, Sarah Middleton, died in 1784, and he married Mary Stead in 1786.

Following the war, Pinckney devoted his efforts toward rebuilding his law practice and his rice plantations. In 1787 he served as a delegate to the constitutional convention, where he ardently and ably defended the exporting and slaveholding interests of southern planters. A staunch Federalist, Pinckney was important in South Carolina's ratification of the federal Constitution in 1788. He later helped draft the state's 1790 constitution. Over the next several years Pinckney rejected President Washington's numerous offers to serve in federal office—as commander of the army, as associate justice of the Supreme Court, as secretary of war, and as secretary of state—explaining that he needed to remain at home to restore his fortune. However, in 1796 Pinckney accepted Washington's offer to serve as minister to France. The next year President John Adams appointed him as one of three commissioners to negotiate a treaty with the French government. When French diplomats demanded a bribe from their American counterparts to facilitate discussions, Pinckney is credited as having exclaimed "NO! NO! Not a sixpense" and urged his government to raise "millions for defence but not one cent for tribute." In 1798 President Adams, anticipating war with France, appointed Pinckney commander of the southern department of the United States Army. He was discharged from military service in 1800.

Pinckney returned to politics in the election of 1800 as the Federalist Party's vice-presidential candidate. In 1804 and 1808 he was the Federalist candidate for president, but realizing that he had little chance of winning, he never actively campaigned. Instead, Pinckney devoted the remainder of his life to agricultural experiments (he was a member of the South Carolina Agricultural Society) and civic service. He helped establish South Carolina College in 1801 and served on its first board of trustees. He also busied himself as president of numerous organizations, including the South Carolina Jockey Club, the Society for the Relief of Widows and Orphans of South Carolina, the Charleston Bible Society, the Charleston Library Society, the South Carolina Society of the Cincinnati, and the national Society of the Cincinnati. Near the end of his life Pinckney campaigned against dueling in South Carolina. He died in Charleston on August 16, 1825, and was buried in the cemetery of St. Michael's Church. KEITH KRAWCZYNSKI

Rogers, George C. *Charleston in the Age of the Pinckneys.* Rev. ed. Columbia: University of South Carolina Press, 1980.

Williams, Francis Leigh. *A Founding Family: The Pinckneys of South Carolina.* New York: Harcourt Brace Jovanovich, 1978.

Zahniser, Marvin R. *Charles Cotesworth Pinckney: Founding Father.* Chapel Hill: University of North Carolina Press, 1967.

Pinckney, Eliza Lucas (ca. 1722–1793). Planter, matriarch. Born on December 28, ca. 1722, in the West Indies, probably Antigua, Eliza was the oldest of four children of George Lucas and Anne Milldrum. Her father was a sugar baron of fluctuating fortune who later served that island in its military forces and as lieutenant governor. At an early age, Eliza was sent from the remote plantation there to attend school in London. After she briefly rejoined her family in Antigua, they moved to the Lucas family's property on Wappoo Creek near Charleston. When George Lucas returned to the West Indies in 1739, Eliza was left in charge of the Wappoo plantation.

With the world rice market declining and Britain's New World supply sources disrupted by wars with Spain and France, George Lucas, from Antigua, sent his daughter a variety of seeds from the West Indies, hoping that Wappoo would provide a profitable crop. In the case of indigo, fresh seed of a desirable type was essential. In 1740 young Eliza wrote her father that she "had greater hopes from the Indigo (if I could have the seed earlier next year from the West India's) than any of the rest of the things I had tryd." George Lucas sent Nicolas Cromwell, an experienced dye maker from Montserrat, to South Carolina to construct an indigo "works" at Wappoo. In the fifth year of experimentation, the plantation could make use of its own seed supply and produced a crop worthy of marketing. "We please ourselves," Eliza wrote her father, "with the prospect of exporting in a few years a good quantity from home and supplying the Mother Country with a manufacture for which she is now supplied from the French Colony and many thousand pounds pr annum thereby lost to the nation which she might be as well supplied here if the matter was applied to in earnest." The six pounds of the finished dyestuff were sent to England "to try how tis approved there." A London broker "tried it against some of the best FRENCH, and in his opinion it is AS GOOD."

Indigo had been considered to be a potentially valuable crop for Carolina since the earliest colonizing, and stands of it were regularly included on many plantations. In the 1740s Eliza was the link in demonstrating that Carolina could produce a superior type. Her efforts were instrumental in alerting other planters to greater profitability, and she gave away indigo seeds "in small quantities to a great number of people" in the area. By July 1744 she was able to write to her father of "the prospect of exporting in a few years a good quantity from hence and supplying our mother country with a manufacture for which she has so great a demand."

On May 27, 1744, Eliza Lucas married Charles Pinckney, a widowed Charleston attorney and member of the Royal Council twenty-four years her senior. The Pinckneys settled into his Belmont plantation near Charleston on the Cooper River. During the next five years Eliza had four children, including the future soldier, diplomat, and Federalist Party leader Charles Cotesworth Pinckney and the future governor, diplomat, and congressman Thomas Pinckney. At Belmont, Eliza experimented with silk culture, producing in her "factory" enough thread to be woven later in England into three different patterns.

In 1753 the Pinckneys moved to London, where Charles represented South Carolina at the Board of Trade and the boys could be established in suitable schools. Leaving the two boys enrolled in schools there, the Pinckneys returned to Charleston in May 1758. When Charles died of malaria on July 12, Eliza readjusted to the role of directing plantations and spent increasingly more time with her daughter Harriott Horry's family at Hampton Plantation on the Santee River. Both sons returned from England in time to take up arms against the mother country. Eliza rode out the Revolutionary War at Charleston, Belmont, and Hampton. During the final stresses of British occupation, she wrote to an English friend, "I have been rob[b]ed and deserted by my slaves; my property pulled to pieces, burnt and destroyed; my money of no value, my Children sick and prisoners." But with victory, the fortunes of the area were reversed. Eliza Pinckney died on May 26, 1793, in Philadelphia, where she had gone for cancer treatments. She was buried in St. Peter's Churchyard, Philadelphia. ELISE PINCKNEY

Coon, David L. "Eliza Lucas Pinckney and the Reintroduction of Indigo Culture in South Carolina." *Journal of Southern History* 42 (February 1976): 61–76.

Pinckney, Elise. "The World of Eliza Lucas Pinckney." *Carologue* 13 (spring 1997): 8–12.

Pinckney, Eliza Lucas. *The Letterbook of Eliza Lucas Pinckney, 1739–1762.* 1972. Reprint, Columbia: University of South Carolina Press, 1997.

Ramagosa, Carol Walter. "Eliza Lucas Pinckney's Family in Antigua, 1668–1747." *South Carolina Historical Magazine* 99 (July 1998): 238–58.

Treckel, Paula A. "Eliza Lucas Pinckney: 'Dutiful, Affectionate, and Obedient Daughter.'" In *Developing Dixie: Modernization in a Traditional Society,* edited by Winfred B. Moore, Jr., Joseph F. Tripp, and Lyon G. Tyler, Jr. New York: Greenwood, 1988.

Williams, Frances Leigh. *A Founding Family: The Pinckneys of South Carolina.* New York: Harcourt Brace Jovanovich, 1978.

Williams, Harriet Simons. "Eliza Lucas and Her Family: Before the Letterbook." *South Carolina Historical Magazine* 99 (July 1998): 259–79.

Pinckney, Henry Laurens (1794–1863). Legislator, congressman, editor. Pinckney was born on September 24, 1794, the son of Charles Pinckney (1757–1824) and Mary Eleanor Laurens and the grandson of Henry Laurens. Descended from two of the state's most prestigious families, Pinckney enjoyed a privileged upbringing. Schooled by the Reverend George Buist in Charleston, he later entered South Carolina College. After graduating in 1812, Pinckney studied law with his brother-in-law, Robert Y. Hayne, but did not pursue a legal profession.

Pinckney launched a stellar legislative career in 1816 when St. Philip's and St. Michael's Parishes elected him to the South Carolina House of Representatives. He served from 1816 to 1828, including two terms as Speaker of the House (1824–1828). Returned to the House in 1830, Pinckney was chosen as Speaker again in 1832. As editor of the *Charleston Mercury* (1822–1832), Pinckney made the newspaper one of the most influential states' rights and proslavery organs in the South. An ardent ally of John C. Calhoun and a supporter of nullification, he was elected to the U.S. House of Representatives at the end of 1832.

Taking his seat in March 1833, Pinckney worked with Calhoun in the Senate and James Henry Hammond in the House to counter the influx of abolitionist petitions that inundated Congress in the early 1830s and which called for the abolition of the slave trade and slavery in the District of Columbia. Calhoun and Hammond maintained that Congress had no constitutional authority to interfere with slavery in the District of Columbia and that it should reject all such petitions without consideration. In 1836, in the midst of his second term in Congress, Pinckney suddenly and dramatically split with Calhoun and Hammond by introducing a series of resolutions in the House declaring that Congress had no right to interfere with slavery in the South, that Congress "ought not" to interfere with slavery in the District of Columbia, and that all abolitionist petitions should be tabled immediately following their reception. The motives for Pinckney's actions remain unclear, but he defended them as the South's best course of action against the rising tide of abolition in the North. Calhoun, Hammond, and most of South Carolina, however, denounced Pinckney. By stating that Congress "ought not" interfere with slavery, Pinckney was believed by his critics to have ceded a crucial constitutional point by tacitly implying that Congress had the authority to interfere if it chose to do so. Accepting and tabling abolitionist petitions likewise implied that Congress could act on them if it so desired. Despite the lack of support from his state, the Pinckney resolutions passed the House by wide margins and would become the basis of the infamous "gag rule" that would evoke years of bitter debate in Congress.

Fire-eaters and nullifiers in South Carolina organized to defeat Pinckney's reelection to Congress in 1837 and were successful. Returning to Charleston, he was elected mayor of the city in 1837, largely through the support of the city's working class, among whom he remained popular. He had also served as intendant (mayor) of Charleston from 1830 to 1832. An energetic civic leader, Pinckney began construction of White Point Gardens (the Battery), transformed the College of Charleston into America's first municipal college, and lobbied for the erection of a poorhouse for slaves and free African Americans.

Pinckney married twice. In 1814 he married Rebecca Pinckney Elliott. They had three children. Following Rebecca Pinckney's death in 1821, he married Sabina Elliott Ramsay. They had no children. Henry Laurens Pinckney died in Charleston on February 3, 1863, and was buried at the Independent Congregational Church. ALEXIA JONES HELSLEY

Ford, Lacy K., Jr. *Origins of Southern Radicalism: The South Carolina Upcountry, 1800–1860.* New York: Oxford University Press, 1988.

Freehling, William W. *Prelude to Civil War: The Nullification Controversy in South Carolina, 1816–1836.* New York: Harper & Row, 1965.

Moore, Alexander, ed. *Biographical Directory of the South Carolina House of Representatives.* Vol. 5, *1816–1828.* Columbia: South Carolina Department of Archives and History, 1992.

Pinckney Island National Wildlife Refuge. Pinckney Island National Wildlife Refuge is in Beaufort County between Skull Creek and Mackay Creek, with the island's northern tip facing Port Royal Sound. The entrance is one-half mile west of Hilton Head Island on South Carolina Highway 278. The refuge was established on December 4, 1975, and was opened to the public in 1985. It is comprised of four islands: Corn, Little Harry, Big Harry, and Pinckney. The largest island, Pinckney Island (twelve hundred acres), is the only one open to the public. From 1736 to 1936 the refuge was owned by the family and descendants of Charles Cotesworth Pinckney and managed as a cotton plantation. Other crops planted include corn, lentils, sweet potatoes, Irish potatoes, and grain. From 1937 to 1975 the island was managed as a game preserve.

Nearly two-thirds of the refuge consists of salt marsh and tidal creeks. Pinckney Island has a large variety of habitats including forestland, brushland, fallow field, salt marsh, and freshwater ponds. Management of the refuge focuses primarily on wading birds. During spring and summer, the freshwater ponds host large concentrations of nesting ibis, herons, and egrets. Waterfowl, shorebirds, raptors, and neotropical migrants such as the colorful painted bunting also are commonly seen. There are active osprey and bald eagle nests. American alligators bask on the banks of the ponds during spring and fall, while deer and fox squirrels may be encountered any time of the year. The refuge provides hiking and biking trails excellent for wildlife observation and photography. DIANA CHURCHILL

Pinckney, Josephine Lyons Scott (1895–1957). Poet, novelist, civic leader. Josephine Pinckney was born on January 25, 1895, in Charleston into a family long prominent in the state's history. She was a direct descendant of Eliza Lucas Pinckney and Governor Thomas Pinckney. Her parents were Thomas Pinckney, one of South Carolina's last great rice planters, and Camilla Scott of Virginia. In 1912 she graduated from Ashley Hall School, where she helped establish a literary magazine, and later attended the College of Charleston, Radcliffe College, and Columbia University. She received an honorary degree from the College of Charleston in 1935 and was named an honorary member of the William and Mary Chapter of Phi Beta Kappa in 1934. She received numerous honors for her writing, including the Southern Authors Award in 1946.

Pinckney played a key role in the literary revival that swept through the South after World War I. She worked closely with DuBose Heyward, Hervey Allen, and John Bennett in founding the Poetry Society of South Carolina in 1920. During the following decade, Pinckney emerged as a poet of national reputation when her work, often evocative eulogies to a vanishing way of southern life, appeared in influential journals such as the *Saturday Review of Literature and Poetry,* as well as in numerous anthologies. Her only book of poems, *Sea-Drinking Cities* (1927), received praise from Donald Davidson for "a luxuriance of phrase, a quiet humor controlling deep emotion."

Pinckney participated in other aspects of the Charleston Renaissance through her dedicated involvement in local cultural institutions, such as the Carolina Art Association, the Charleston Museum, and Dock Street Theatre. Active in the Society for the Preservation of Spirituals from its inception in 1922, Pinckney helped with the transcriptions and musical annotations for the African American songs included in *The Carolina Lowcountry* (1931). She also worked quietly behind the scenes of the historic preservation movement in Charleston and was posthumously honored by the American Scenic and Historic Preservation Society for the manner in which she "tactfully and persuasively, firmly and wisely" helped to restore the city's neighborhoods and notable buildings.

Josephine Pinckney with (left to right) Albert Simons, Harold A. Mouzon, and George C. Rogers of Charleston. Courtesy, South Carolina Historical Society

During the 1930s Pinckney embraced a modernist sensibility and turned her writing talents to prose. The *Virginia Quarterly Review* published her two short stories "They Shall Return as Strangers" (1934) and "The Marchant of London and the Treacherous Don" (1936). Her essay "Bulwarks against Change," which appeared in *Culture in the South,* edited by W. T. Couch (1934), remains an insightful commentary on the evolving South. In 1941 Pinckney published her first novel, *Hilton Head,* followed by the best-selling social comedy *Three O'Clock Dinner* (1945), which made her one of America's best-known women fiction writers. Her third novel, *Great Mischief* (1948), a Book-of-the-Month Club selection, was followed by *My Son and Foe* (1952) and *Splendid in Ashes* (1958). Her editor at Viking Press remembered Pinckney "more warmly" than any other of his distinguished writers of the day for the "charm and grace of her character, the intelligence of her insights into people, the delights of her Charleston ambiance tempered by her cosmopolitan ways and her irony."

Although Pinckney traveled widely, she maintained a home in Charleston and her family plantation on the Santee River, El Dorado. Josephine Pinckney died on October 4, 1957, and was buried in Magnolia Cemetery, Charleston. BARBARA L. BELLOWS

Kibler, James E., Jr. "Josephine Pinckney." In *Dictionary of Literary Biography.* Vol. 6, *American Novelists since World War II, Second Series,* edited by James E. Kibler, Jr. Detroit: Gale, 1980.

Pinckney, Josephine. Papers. South Carolina Historical Society, Charleston.

———. *Three O'Clock Dinner.* 1945. Reprint, Columbia: University of South Carolina Press, 2001.

Shippey, Herbert P. "Josephine Pinckney." In *South Carolina Women Writers,* edited by James B. Meriwether. Spartanburg, S.C.: Reprint Company, 1979.

Pinckney, Maria Henrietta (?–1836). Writer. Maria Pinckney was the eldest daughter of Charles Cotesworth Pinckney and Sarah "Sally" Middleton. She is notable for writing a defense of nullification entitled *The Quintessence of Long Speeches, Arranged as a Political Catechism.* Pinckney published the "Nullification Catechism" in Charleston in 1830, two years after the South Carolina General Assembly issued John C. Calhoun's "Exposition and Protest." The declaration asserted that the states had the right to nullify "unconstitutional, unequal, and oppressive" laws enacted by the federal government, in particular the 1828 "Tariff of Abominations."

In her tract Pinckney posed a series of thirty-four questions and answers designed to summarize the southern case for nullification, which she defined as "the Veto of a Sovereign State on an unconstitutional law of Congress." Pinckney asked, "Did the States, in forming the Constitution, divest themselves of any part of their Sovereignty?" and she answered firmly, "Of not a particle." The refusal of the southern states to accept unjust tariffs was not rebellion because rebellion "is the resistance of an *inferior* to the lawful authority of a *superior.* A child may rebel against a parent—a slave against his master—citizens against the government, and colonies against the mother-country—but a State cannot rebel; because one sovereign cannot rebel against another, for all Sovereigns are equal." States and federal governments should be able to coexist, she argued, but Washington, D.C., personified by "Daniel Webster & Co.," was "continually wandering out of the sphere of its legitimacy, and usurping powers" previously understood to be held by the states. Pinckney did not think, however, that South Carolina's assertion of her sovereignty would lead to civil war. "The General Government would not put itself so completely in the wrong," she stated, "as to consecrate its Usurpation by the blood of those it shall have attempted to oppress." In its "hour of peril," she called on South Carolinians to follow the example of "the patriot band who achieved the Revolution" of 1776 and their descendants.

Pinckney never married. After the death of her father's second wife, Mary Stead, in 1812, Pinckney and her sister Harriott took on the role of hostess for him. Maria Pinckney died on May 13, 1836, and was buried in St. Michael's Churchyard in Charleston. HUGH DAVIS

Pinckney, Maria. *The Quintessence of Long Speeches, Arranged as a Political Catechism.* Charleston, S.C.: A. E. Miller, 1830.

Pinckney, Thomas (1750–1828). Governor, diplomat, congressman, soldier. Pinckney was born in Charleston on October 23, 1750, the son of Charles Pinckney and Elizabeth "Eliza" Lucas, and the brother of Charles Cotesworth Pinckney. In 1753 the Pinckneys sailed to England to educate their sons. When their parents returned to South Carolina in 1758, the boys remained behind. Thomas Pinckney received a liberal education at Westminster School and Christ College, Oxford, and studied law at the Middle Temple in the Inns of Court. In addition, he briefly attended the Royal Military Academy in Caen, France, where he studied military science. After his return to Charleston in December 1774, he was admitted to the South Carolina Bar and commenced his law practice.

At the outbreak of war in 1775, Pinckney became a captain in the First South Carolina Continental regiment and was later promoted to major. He traveled to North Carolina and Virginia on recruiting missions and supervised the construction of fortifications. Much of his early service involved tedious garrison duty in Charleston harbor. At one point he wryly reassured his sister Harriott that she need not worry "for you may depend upon their being no fighting wherever I am." Pinckney subsequently participated in the failed invasion of East Florida in 1778. When the British invaded South Carolina in May 1779, they burned Pinckney's Aukland Plantation on the Ashepoo River. That fall Pinckney served as a liaison between American and French forces at the siege of Savannah. During a lull in the fighting, he married Elizabeth Motte on July 22, 1779. Their union produced six children. Three years after Elizabeth's death, he married her sister, Frances, on October 19, 1797. Pinckney's second marriage produced two children.

When the British laid siege to Charleston in 1780, Pinckney urged that the city be defended. Because General Benjamin Lincoln sent him to search for expected reinforcements, he avoided capture when the city surrendered in May. He then joined the remaining Continental troops in the Carolinas and became General Horatio Gates's aide-de-camp. At the Battle of Camden on August 16, 1780, Pinckney's leg was shattered by a musket ball and he was captured, ending his active service in the war. The British paroled him, and he spent time in Philadelphia and Virginia before returning to South Carolina. After the war, he publicly defended Gates's strategic and tactical decisions.

Pinckney shifted his attention from practicing law to planting and politics. He represented the city parishes of St. Philip's and St. Michael's in the state House of Representatives from 1776 until 1791. He was elected governor of South Carolina on February 20, 1787, and served two years. He submitted the federal Constitution to the state legislature and presided over the ratification convention that met in Charleston in 1788. Three years after leaving office in 1789, Pinckney accepted the prestigious and challenging appointment as U.S. minister to Great Britain on January 16, 1792.

Gen. Thomas Pinckney, by Charles Fraser, watercolor on ivory. Courtesy, Gibbes Museum of Art / Carolina Art Association

As a diplomat, Pinckney was competent rather than brilliant. To his frustration, he was unable to secure compensation for slaves removed by the British or resolve disputes over British fortifications in the Northwest and American fishing rights off Newfoundland. When Britain and France went to war in 1793, the United States found its neutrality threatened. Hoping to avert war, President George Washington sent John Jay in 1794 on a special mission to Britain. Despite his disappointment at being temporarily superseded, Pinckney charitably supported the mission and approved the controversial treaty that Jay negotiated.

Pinckney's moment did come, however, for in November 1794 he was appointed envoy extraordinary to Spain. From June to October 1795 Pinckney worked to settle territorial and commercial disputes between the United States and Spain. He considered indispensable the American right to deposit and ship goods from the mouth of the Mississippi River. To secure this point and end the diplomatic stalemate, he demanded his passport, which caused his counterpart, Manuel de Godoy, the prince of peace, to concede. The Treaty of San Lorenzo, signed on October 27, 1795, granted Americans the privilege (rather than the right) to use the port of New Orleans and established a clear boundary between the United States and West Florida. Pinckney's mission to Spain proved to be the high point of a long public career. The treaty he negotiated paved the way for American settlement of the Southeast and for future territorial acquisitions from the French and the Spanish.

In 1796 Pinckney resigned his European post and returned to South Carolina. Before he arrived, the Federalists nominated him as their candidate for vice president. Because of political maneuvering, Pinckney finished behind Thomas Jefferson in the voting. In November 1797 Pinckney was elected to the U.S. House of Representatives to complete William Smith's unexpired term. In Congress he generally supported the Adams administration's preparations for war with France, but he opposed the Sedition Act. He left Congress in 1801 and, except for another term in the General Assembly from 1802 to 1804, withdrew from public life.

His retirement ended during the War of 1812, when he was commissioned a major general and given command of the Southern Division of the U.S. Army. He worked to strengthen coastal fortifications and held overall command during the war with the Creeks, but he saw no action. After the war, Pinckney retired to his plantation on the Santee River, which he named El Dorado. Noted for his agricultural innovations, which included using dikes to reclaim saltwater marshes for rice cultivation and importing choice cattle from Europe, he contributed articles to the *Southern Agriculturist* and reports to the Agricultural Society. In 1825 he became president general of the national Society of the Cincinnati. On November 2, 1828, Pinckney died in Charleston. He was buried in St. Philip's Churchyard. GREGORY D. MASSEY

Bemis, Samuel Flagg. "The London Mission of Thomas Pinckney, 1792–1796." *American Historical Review* 27 (January 1923): 228–47.

———. *Pinckney's Treaty: America's Advantage from Europe's Distress, 1783–1800.* Rev. ed. New Haven, Conn.: Yale University Press, 1960.

Pinckney, Charles Cotesworth. *Life of General Thomas Pinckney.* Boston: Houghton, Mifflin, 1895.

Williams, Frances Leigh. *A Founding Family: The Pinckneys of South Carolina.* New York: Harcourt Brace Jovanovich, 1978.

Pine bark stew. "Communal stew" is the name the southern cooking authority Stan Woodward gives stews made in big batches and cooked over open fires in large cast-iron pots also used for washing clothes. Thought to be a fisherman's stew cooked on the banks of the Pee Dee River, pine bark stew had just such humble beginnings.

In the 1930 edition of *Two Hundred Years of Charleston Cooking,* Blanche Rhett credits the pine bark stew recipe to Captain John A. Kelly, of Kingstree, who made it a favorite dish of the Otranto Hunting Club in the Goose Creek area. *Charleston Receipts,* the renowned Junior League cookbook first published in 1950, agrees, titling its recipe "Otranto Pine Bark Stew," as relayed to the club's president Louis Y. Dawson, Jr., by his father.

The reason for the name "pine bark stew" is speculative. Was the stew dark in color? Seasoned with a sprig of pine? Based on oral history documented while researching Brunswick stew, Woodward concluded that the name came from colonists observing coastal Indians in Virginia and North Carolina eating fish stew, called "fish muddle," with pine bark servers or utensils. The most common conjecture is simply that the stew was cooked over a fire kindled with pine bark.

Most authorities agree on the ingredients: bacon, onions, potatoes, and several kinds of firm freshwater fish, which are layered and simmered slowly. In the recipe in his book *Southern Food,* however, John Egerton adds tomatoes. The seasonings vary slightly; curry, saffron, thyme, butter, ketchup, and Worcestershire sauce are all mentioned. In the *Charleston Receipts* recipe, the seasoning is provided in a separate sauce poured on top of the stew, which, as may be expected in Charleston, is served over rice. MARION B. SULLIVAN

Egerton, John. *Southern Food: At Home, on the Road, in History.* New York: Knopf, 1987.

Junior League of Charleston. *Charleston Receipts.* Charleston, S.C.: Walker, Evans and Cogswell, 1950.

Rhett, Blanche Salley. *Two Hundred Years of Charleston Cooking.* 1930. Reprint, Columbia: University of South Carolina Press, 1976.

Southern Stews: A Taste of the South. Produced and directed by Stan Woodward. Greenville, S.C.: Woodward Studio, 2002. Videocassette.

Pines. Nine native pine species are found within South Carolina. Three species are restricted to the upper Piedmont and mountain regions, three are found nearly throughout the state, and three are found primarily within the coastal plain. Pines are extremely important economically and ecologically within South Carolina. More than 5,750,000 acres of state forestland contain pine as important or dominant cover. Pines form the basis of the timber industry in South Carolina and make up the number-one cash crop in the state with approximately $900 million in receipts annually and employing more than 35,000 people.

South Carolina pines can be divided into two general groups, white pines and yellow pines. Yellow pines have needles in groups of two or three, while white pines have needles in groups of five. The only member of the white pine group found within South Carolina is the eastern white pine (*Pinus strobus*). It is restricted to the mountains and upper Piedmont but is planted as an ornamental throughout much of the state.

Among the yellow pines, the loblolly is the most abundant. This species, along with the similar slash pine (*Pinus elliottii*), is preferred for use on pine plantations. More than 4 million acres of forest in the state are classified as loblolly pine forest, while 2.4 million acres are in loblolly pine plantation. The loblolly pine was historically found in the lower Piedmont and coastal plain but has spread throughout the state through timber planting. Slash pine is native to the southern portions of the coastal plain but is planted throughout the coastal regions.

Historically, the most abundant species in the coastal plain region was the longleaf pine (*Pinus palustris*). This species is well known for its extremely long needles and large cones. It requires low-intensity ground fires to persist and has declined dramatically over the last century due to fire suppression and conversion of longleaf pine forest into loblolly pine plantations and agricultural fields. Longleaf pine is a keystone species in the longleaf pine savannas and flat woods that are home to some of the state's most unusual and endangered plant and animal species.

Virginia pine (*Pinus virginiana*) and shortleaf pine (*Pinus echinata*) are two species that are most abundant in the Piedmont region. These species are similar in that they both produce short needles and small cones. The Virginia pine produces needles that are usually less than two and one-half inches long and are twisted, while shortleaf pine produces needles that are typically three to five inches long and are straight.

Pitch pine (*Pinus rigida*) and pond pine (*Pinus serotina*) both have the characteristic of sprouting new growth from the branches or trunk. These species can survive a forest fire by resprouting after the branches are burnt off. Pitch pine is found in the mountain region, and pond pine is found in the acidic shrub bogs (pocosins) of the coastal plain and the Sandhills.

Table mountain pine (*Pinus pungens*) is an uncommon species found on exposed ridges and rock outcrops in the mountains and upper Piedmont. The species produces large, spiny cones that are closed until they are heated by fire. In order to successfully reproduce, stands of table mountain pine must be burned.

Spruce pine (*Pinus glabra*) is unique among yellow pine species in that it is tolerant of shade. This species is not abundant but is found in bottomland forests in the coastal plain. The smooth upper bark and soft foliage of this species are distinctive. PATRICK MCMILLAN

Porcher, Richard D., and Douglas A. Rayner. *A Guide to the Wildflowers of South Carolina.* Columbia: University of South Carolina Press, 2001.

Radford, Albert E., Harry E. Ahles, and C. Ritchie Bell. *Manual of the Vascular Flora of the Carolinas.* Chapel Hill: University of North Carolina Press, 1968.

Pinkney, Bill (b. 1925). Musician. Born on August 15, 1925, in Dalzell, Sumter County, Pinkney began singing gospel songs as a child while working in South Carolina's cotton fields. He would go on to a stellar career performing around the globe as an original member of the Drifters. The group became a rhythm and blues (R&B) pioneer, and in 1988 members of the Drifters were inducted into the Rock and Roll Hall of Fame.

The young Pinkney mixed his love of music with baseball, earning a pitching position with the New York Blue Sox in the Negro Baseball League. In 1949, while singing in gospel quartets, he met Clyde McPhatter, a young gospel singer who at the time was performing with Billy Ward and the Dominoes. Within two years McPhatter recruited Pinkney and brothers Gerhardt and Andrew Thrasher to form a new musical group, the Drifters. In 1953 the Drifters were offered a contract with Atlantic Records, and they eventually became, according to the label's founder, Ahmet Ertegun, "the all time greatest Atlantic recording group."

Moving beyond their gospel origins, the Drifters became internationally famous, creating a unique sweet soul sound that expanded the R&B genre. Later members, also inducted into the Rock and Roll Hall of Fame, included Johnny Moore, Ben E. King, Rudy Lewis, and Charlie Thomas. The Drifters' best-selling song, "White Christmas," was recorded in 1954 and featured Pinkney as lead bass singer. In 2002, in his seventy-seventh year, Pinkney continued to perform with the Original Drifters, a permutation of the legendary group.

Though the Drifters are closely associated with Carolina beach music, Pinkney disputes the notion that the state's popular beach sound is any different from the gospel-influenced R&B fare enjoyed in other regions. "The backbone of all R&B was created from gospel. Sam Cook did both, Otis Redding did both, and I did both," said Pinkney. "Beach music (in the Carolinas) is a mind thing," he said. "A song that might be called a beach song here is just R&B someplace else." FRANK BEACHAM

Piracy. Piracy flourished on the South Carolina coast chiefly in two periods: the early proprietary years (1670–1700) and at the end of the "Golden Age of Piracy" (1716–1720). Settled in 1670, Charleston soon became the chief port of Carolina, a region contested by the Spanish, French, and English in the frequent wars of the era. The proprietary government was often weak and sometimes was headed by corrupt officials. Pirates, most of whom began their commerce raiding as legal war-time privateers, thrived in such an uncertain and turbulent setting. The growing trade of Charleston also attracted raids by foreign privateers who were perceived by the local citizens as pirates.

Like merchants in all of the colonies, Charleston's traders were accustomed to dealing with smugglers and therefore welcomed the cheap goods and specie that the pirates brought. Customs officers were not above taking bribes to smooth illegal trade, and "consorting with pirates" was not an uncommon charge levied against governors by their opponents. When the colony's notorious reputation for "harbouring and encouraging of Pirates" reached the Privy Council in England in 1684, the provincial assembly was admonished to pass an act to suppress piracy. Open dealing with pirates caused the expulsion of council member John Boone in 1686 and peaked in the 1690s under Governors Seth Sothel and Philip Ludwell.

Throughout the colonial period Spanish and French privateers presented Charleston with a constant threat that reached its zenith during Queen Anne's War (1701–1713). In August 1706 a combined French and Spanish expedition of privateers and naval vessels raided the environs of Charleston but were driven off by a provincial flotilla led by Colonel William Rhett. At the end of the war many of the thousands of unemployed privateers in the West Indies flocked to the new center of piracy, New Providence Island in the Bahamas. South Carolina had just survived a devastating war with the Yamassee Indians in 1715 that left the colony unable to cope with the pirates swarming along the coast in 1717–1718. Among the most notorious of the pirates sailing off South Carolina were Blackbeard, Stede Bonnet, Charles Vane, Christopher Moody, Richard Worley, and Anne Bonney, who was from Charleston. Escalating piratical attacks peaked in May 1718 in a raid by Charles Vane and a brazen blockade by Blackbeard and Stede Bonnet. These incidents finally aroused the city to take action, and by the end of the year South Carolinians had rid themselves of the worst of their tormentors.

There had been several individual ships taken off Charleston in the previous year, but in mid-May 1718 Blackbeard and Stede Bonnet brought a four-ship fleet mounting about sixty guns to blockade the port. During the course of a week, numerous ships were plundered of goods and specie, trade came to a standstill, and hostages were ransomed for valuable medicines. This humiliating incident was preceded by Charles Vane's seizure of several ships off the harbor entrance. When Vane returned later in the summer for a brief blockade of Charleston, Colonel Rhett was sent with armed sloops to capture him. Vane eluded the pursuit, but Rhett found Stede Bonnet's fleet at Cape Fear, defeated him in a vicious battle, and

The pirate Stede Bonnet was hanged in Charleston on December 10, 1718. Copy of an engraving from the 1725 Dutch edition of Daniel Defoe's *History of the Pirates.* Courtesy, South Caroliniana Library, University of South Carolina

returned him and his crew to Charleston for execution. Christopher Moody's audacious taking of prizes in sight of Charleston in October led Governor Robert Johnson to organize another punitive expedition of four armed vessels. On November 5 Johnson's flotilla clashed with two pirate sloops in a bloody action at the harbor's mouth in sight of the port. When one of the sloops dashed for open sea, the governor gave chase and ultimately succeeded in taking the prize. The pirate captain, who was killed in the action, turned out to be Richard Worley. The battles fought by Rhett and Governor Johnson and the subsequent mass executions of pirates virtually ended the presence of pirates on the South Carolina coast.

Piracy in the province slowly died out in the 1720s. Among the few pirates who briefly appeared in that decade were George Lowther and Edward Low. Lowther attempted to take an armed merchantman off Charleston in 1722 but was defeated and driven off. The following year Edward Low ravaged five vessels off the harbor and escaped, but the Royal Navy soon captured him. Although an occasional rumor of a pirate sighting would reach Charleston, the "Golden Age of Piracy" was over. LINDLEY S. BUTLER

Coker, P. C., III. *Charleston's Maritime Heritage, 1670–1865: An Illustrated History.* Charleston, S.C.: CokerCraft, 1987.

Hughson, Shirley Carter. *The Carolina Pirates and Colonial Commerce, 1670–1740.* 1894. Reprint, New York: Johnson Reprint Company, 1973.

McCrady, Edward. *The History of South Carolina under the Proprietary Government, 1670–1719.* New York: Macmillan, 1897.

Sherman, Richard P. *Robert Johnson: Proprietary & Royal Governor of South Carolina.* Columbia: University of South Carolina Press, 1966.

Pisé de terre. Pisé de terre, or "rammed earth," is an ancient form of building construction. Clay is the basic material in rammed earth buildings. After a foundation of brick or stone is laid, clay is poured into wooden molds and then tamped until solid. Additional layers are added until the walls reach the desired height, and the finished walls are coated with stucco. In the mid–nineteenth century Dr. William W. Anderson, a Maryland native who settled in Stateburg in 1810, used it to create two of South Carolina's most distinctive works of architecture: the Borough House and the Church of the Holy Cross. He was influenced by S. W. Johnson, who introduced methods of rammed earth construction to America through his book *Rural Economy* (1806). In 1821 Anderson used the technique to rebuild the wings of the Borough House, the main building at his Hill Crest Plantation, and several outbuildings. In 1850 Anderson persuaded the Episcopal congregation of Stateburg to use pisé de terre in constructing the Church of the Holy Cross, a Gothic-revival structure designed by the Charleston architect Edward C. Jones. The Borough House and its outbuildings constitute the largest complex of pisé de terre buildings in the United States. The U.S. Department of the Interior designated the Church of the Holy Cross and the Borough House as National Historic Landmarks in 1973 and 1978, respectively. DANIEL J. VIVIAN

"Dr. William W. Anderson's Use of an Ancient Building Material in Stateburg." *South Carolina Historical Magazine* 85 (January 1984): 71–77.

Church of the Holy Cross, Stateburg, is an example of the pisé de terre construction technique. Courtesy, South Carolina Department of Archives and History

Plank roads. Plank roads enjoyed a brief popularity in the early 1850s, touted as an inexpensive and effective means of improving short-distance travel. Thick planks were laid across wood stringers in a roadbed, creating a level, smooth surface for wagons and other road traffic. Russia was the first country to construct plank roads, and the roads made their initial appearance in Canada and New York in the 1830s and 1840s. By the early 1850s South Carolina had joined the mania for plank roads. The textile manufacturer William Gregg became an effective early advocate, arguing that plank roads would be cheaper to build and easier to maintain than roads built of gravel and stone. In an 1851 essay Gregg called on the state to construct a nine-foot track from Abbeville to Charleston, a distance of 160 miles, estimating that the expense would be around $1,700 to $1,800 a mile. This amount, he assured, would easily be covered by tolls collected from plank-road travelers.

Between 1849 and 1853 the General Assembly chartered no fewer than ten plank-road companies in South Carolina. By 1850 legislators permitted plank-road companies to bypass the assembly and to receive charters directly from the governor and the secretary of state, one of the first general incorporation acts passed in South Carolina. Several roads were built. The longest, the Edgefield and Hamburg plank road, extended twenty-six miles. Others included the Cheraw and Anson plank road, which extended up the Charleston Neck, and a short road running north from Edgefield to the village of Cheatham. But despite the initial promise, the plank-road mania quickly subsided. They were expensive to build and even more costly to maintain, requiring constant maintenance to replace worn planks. In addition, farmers generally used plank roads only with full wagons, preferring to use free dirt roads for their return home once their cargoes had been sold—and thus denying plank roads return tolls. Plank-road companies soon found themselves deeply in debt, and most were out of business by the start of the Civil War. LLOYD JOHNSON

Downey, Tom. *Planting a Capitalist South: Masters, Merchants, and Manufacturers in the Southern Interior, 1790–1860.* Baton Rouge: Louisiana State University Press, 2005.

Gregg, William. *Essay on Plank Roads.* Charleston, S.C.: Walker and James, 1851.

Moore, John Hammond. *The South Carolina Highway Department, 1917–1987.* Columbia: University of South Carolina Press, 1987.

Plantations. In the seventeenth century the term "plantation," which formerly referred to any colonial outpost, evolved to refer specifically to large agricultural estates whose land was farmed by a sizable number of workers, usually slaves, for export crops. Englishmen initially created plantation societies in the West Indies, and in the 1670s South Carolina became a northern extension of this empire.

Plantations distinguished themselves from smaller farms not only by the sheer size of their landholdings and workforce but in other ways as well. There was a distinct separation between owners, overseers (managers), and the labor force. Evidence of this separation could be found in plantation housing patterns. Laborers were housed in often shoddy, crowded cabins clustered in a village or "street" at some remove from the owner's residence. While plantation "big houses" were mostly modest affairs, they sometimes reached uncharacteristic levels of opulence. These more elaborate residences became fixtures in an enduring plantation mythology. The Georgian and Greek-revival mansions popularized in romantic fiction were more the exception than the rule.

An additional defining element of plantations was their focus on one commercial crop. Although South Carolina planters grew a little tobacco in the early years, rice became the colony's most important staple, and in the years prior to the Revolutionary War, a full-scale plantation culture worked by African slaves emerged along the rivers of the Carolina lowcountry. The success of rice culture was due in large part to the agricultural skills of the slaves, many of whom hailed from rice-growing regions of Africa. An innovative development in rice culture was tidal irrigation. Water was drawn on and off the crop through an elaborate system of dams, canals, and gates. The landscape was dramatically altered, profits soared, and rice planters became some of the wealthiest people in North America. Planters typically divided their time between their country seats and residences in "town," moving to Charleston, Georgetown, or Beaufort for a winter social season and relief from the threat of malaria in summer.

The plantation system, in a modified form, spread inland, with cotton fueling the expansion. In the early 1800s cotton culture was lucrative, and many planters plowed their profits into acquiring more land and slaves. Thus, medium-sized farms could grow into plantations within a few years. By 1820 South Carolina was producing more than half the nation's total output of cotton. Although "King Cotton" continued to rule the state's economy in the antebellum decades, the center of cotton culture in America gradually moved west into Georgia, Alabama, Mississippi, Arkansas, and Texas.

The North's opposition to the continued expansion of slavery was the primary factor compelling South Carolina's secession from the Union, which set in motion the Civil War. Southern defeat resulted in the emancipation of the slaves and profound changes in southern agriculture. A common misconception is that when slavery ended, the plantation system collapsed. In reality, plantations were defined more by the size of their workforce than the status of the workers. Many South Carolina plantations survived the postwar years in a modified form dubbed "fragmented plantations" by geographers. These surviving plantations differed from antebellum properties in important ways. Sharecropping and tenantry replaced slavery as a labor system, and laborers were disbursed across the property rather than concentrated in a central location. Despite this reconfiguration brought about by the end of slavery, many freed people noticed little difference between their former and current living standards. Indeed, they frequently continued to live and work on the property of their former masters.

From the 1870s through the 1890s, southern agriculture entered a long decline and in most cases never regained antebellum levels of prosperity. South Carolina plantations met a variety of fates. As taxes and maintenance costs outpaced profits, many properties were sold off piecemeal by descendants unable to maintain them. But from the fertile soil of others, emblems of the New South sprang forth. Wealthy northerners purchased many former rice plantations in the late nineteenth and early twentieth centuries, transforming them into hunting preserves. Since the 1970s other former rice plantations have become upscale housing developments and golf communities. Further inland, abandoned plantation lands have frequently been harvested for their timber rather than cotton. Due to preservation and restoration efforts, however, in the early twenty-first century some 150 antebellum plantation houses remained in the lowcountry alone, and these estates, still an evocative symbol of the Old South, continued to be a powerful draw for the state's tourist industry.
ROBERT STEVENS

Aiken, Charles S. *The Cotton Plantation South since the Civil War.* Baltimore: Johns Hopkins University Press, 1998.

Chaplin, Joyce E. "Creating a Cotton South in Georgia and South Carolina, 1760–1815." *Journal of Southern History* 57 (May 1991): 171–200.

———. "Tidal Rice Cultivation and the Problem of Slavery in South Carolina and Georgia, 1760–1815." *William and Mary Quarterly,* 3d ser., 49 (January 1992): 29–61.

Iseley, N. Jane, and William P. Baldwin. *Lowcountry Plantations Today.* Greensboro, N.C.: Legacy Publications, 2002.

Iseley, N. Jane, William P. Baldwin, and Agnes L. Baldwin. *Plantations of the Low Country: South Carolina 1697–1865.* Greensboro, N.C.: Legacy Publications, 1997.

Kovacik, Charles F., and John J. Winberry. *South Carolina: The Making of a Landscape.* 1987. Reprint, Columbia: University of South Carolina Press, 1989.

Prunty, Merle, Jr. "The Renaissance of the Southern Plantation." *Geographical Review* 45 (October 1955): 459–91.

Plants. The vegetation of a particular region consists of all of its native plant species, as well as those that are introduced and naturalized. The term "flora" is used in a slightly different sense and refers only to naturally occurring plant species. As a rule, plant life, whether in terms of "vegetation" or "flora," refers to vascular plants, those containing vascular tissue. In South Carolina, these include the ferns (vascular plants reproducing by spores) and their relatives (horsetails and club mosses); gymnosperms, represented by conifers such as pines and cypresses (plants producing seeds but not flowers); and the largest group, by far, the flowering plants.

South Carolina's vegetation consists of approximately three thousand species. Considering the geographic size of the state, this is one of the most diverse parts of the entire nation. Georgia and North Carolina each boast greater numbers of species, which would be expected for their larger geographic sizes. The apparent high amount of botanical diversity within South Carolina may be explained through its extraordinary representation of natural habitats, which accounts for naturally occurring vegetation, but also through the easy influx of new introductions, many of which become permanent residents. Unfortunately, the influx of alien plant species into South Carolina, which is mostly the result of human activities, accounts for some serious weedy species that have had dramatic economic impacts on the state.

South Carolina may conveniently be divided into four major physiographic provinces, and these are more or less consistent with characteristic vegetation types. The smallest province is that of the Blue Ridge Escarpment, limited to the highest portions of Oconee, Pickens, and Greenville Counties. This area shows considerable affinity toward the vegetation of the Blue Ridge and Appalachian Mountains and even New England, thus affording habitat for southern extensions of many "northern" plant species. Steep topography and dramatic relief are featured in many sites. Elevation ranges vary from river bottoms upward to open granitic domes and, in some places, sheer cliffs. Among the characteristic species at the state's highest mesic sites are assemblages of white pine (*Pinus strobus*) and hemlock (*Tsuga canadensis*), often with diverse mixtures of oaks, hickories, deciduous magnolias, and other hardwoods. Other sites in the mountains, especially those on southern (warmer and drier) exposures, may be dominated by low, shrubby vegetation consisting of many species in the heath (or blueberry) family. Although this is the smallest province, it harbors the state's highest localized areas of rare species. One of the rarest orchids in North America, *Isotria medeoloides,* is known from a few spots in the state's mountains.

The Piedmont consists of a broad band of counties between the mountains and the central part of the state. This area is dominated by gently sloping landscapes, punctuated in places by isolated monadnocks, which suggest small mountain "islands" on a flatter landscape. The soils of the Piedmont were largely ravaged by the excesses of cotton farming throughout the nineteenth century. On the other hand, some excellent examples of naturally occurring Piedmont natural communities remain, countering the notion that this province is of little botanical interest. Strong evidence exists for the existence of southeastern grass-dominated prairies in parts of the Piedmont, these harboring many examples of rare and threatened species. One of these plants is a native sunflower (*Helianthus schweinitzii*), which is known in the world only from the two Carolinas. As well, significant stands of bottomland hardwood forest exist along various stretches of Piedmont rivers, these commonly dominated by sycamore (*Platanus occidentalis*) as well as an assortment of ash species, birches, oaks, and maples.

The Sandhill region is a relatively narrow strip of land stretching from Aiken County northeast through Chesterfield County. This region embraces the fall zone, a geologically distinctive phenomenon representing the first rapids (and boulders) encountered along rivers from the coast, while traveling inland. The Sandhills have a historic reputation of being barren and uninteresting botanically; recent studies have proved much the contrary. Although characterized by deep sandy deposits, the Sandhills contain fascinating wetland ecosystems as well. Fort Jackson Military Installation in Richland County, for instance, features uncommon diversity and rare plant species, somewhat paradoxical given its proximity to a large metropolitan area. In the early 1990s botanists discovered a large population of one of the world's most restricted species, rough-leaved loosestrife (*Lysimachia asperulaefolia*), within an open sandhill seepage bog in Richland County. Prior to this discovery, the plant had been known, and apparently extirpated, from a single site in Florence County.

The largest province is that of the coastal plain. This is a relatively recent formation of gently sloping terraces, dominated by sandy, acidic soils. The coastal plain is deeply cut through by a series of river channels, and extraordinary examples of historically known bottomland hardwood ecosystems are known. Characteristic tree components of these swamps and bottomlands are bald cypress (*Taxodium distichum*) and water tupelo (*Nyssa aquatica*). Bottomland forests can be highly diverse: the old-growth portions of Congaree National Park boasts some of the highest tree and woody vine diversity, for its size, in North America, easily rivaling the rainforests of the Pacific Northwest. Much of the coastal plain has been developed for agriculture, but significant natural vegetation remains. Many of these ecosystems developed as a response to periodic fires. For example, most of the area now represented by the coastal plain was historically dominated by longleaf pine (*Pinus palustris*), a fire-dependent species. Naturally occurring longleaf flatwoods and savannas dominated extensive portions of the outer coastal plain. Sadly, few intact examples of these extremely diverse habitats remain, largely due to urbanization and fire suppression. Additional and recent research has demonstrated intact ecosystems and rare plant species remaining in good examples of Carolina bays, as well as the pocosins. Plant communities of the latter depend on periodic fire and tend to be dominated by pond pine (*Pinus serotina*), hollies (especially the gallberries, *Ilex coriacea* and *I. glabra*), blueberries, and other members of the heath family. Pocosin systems in South Carolina are largely restricted to the Pee Dee portion of the coastal plain, with excellent intact examples at Lewis Ocean Bay Heritage Preserve, near Myrtle Beach. This site is also noteworthy as one of the few remaining localities in the state for Venus's-flytrap (*Dionaea muscipula*). The outer edges of the coastal plain deserve special consideration: these areas include the estuaries, sounds, maritime forests, and barrier islands that are increasingly threatened by human activity and development. Along the state's upper coastline, within the Grand Strand, dwarf pigweed (*Amaranthus pumilus*) may be found on fore dunes, an example of a threatened species that reaches its southern geographic limit in South Carolina.

Any consideration of South Carolina's naturally occurring flora must include some treatment of the threats to its integrity. These threats come from two sources. First, human development and manipulation of existing natural areas have constituted an ever-increasing threat to stable natural ecosystems since the seventeenth century. Urbanization has clearly resulted in significant loss of many naturally occurring plant communities and, thereby, a resultant loss of plant diversity. The second threat to the state's flora comes from aggressive, introduced plant species from other parts of the world. These aliens, once naturalized, essentially become a part of the surrounding landscapes and are then considered "naturalized." Naturalization of such invaders is sometimes a seemingly irreversible situation. For instance, Japanese honeysuckle (*Lonicera japonica*) was introduced into North America as an ornamental vine, probably numerous times, beginning in the early nineteenth century. This species is particularly troublesome in the Southeast, and in every county of South Carolina, due to its aggressive ability to cover vegetation and eventually shade out (and kill) its neighbors. There are many other examples of such unwelcome invaders, some of which are notorious as agricultural weeds, causing much damage from the standpoint of expensive control measures, which are often based on herbicides or chemical treatments. Initial establishment of a noxious weedy species is almost invariably the result of human activity, but secondary invasions may occur as well. In the case of Japanese honeysuckle, enough notoriety has been generated about it that gardeners tend not to grow it intentionally, but birds readily move the seeds from place to place after eating the fruits.

Despite the past botanical studies in South Carolina, new species continue to be discovered in the wild. For instance, a new species of native ragweed has recently been discovered on granitic rocks in a few places in the state's mountains. In the Sandhills an unusual aster that deserves recognition as a new species has been located along some black-water streams. The discovery and description of species new to science seems paradoxical, in light of the enormous effects of human development throughout the state. Nevertheless, the fact that new species continue to be described suggests a diverse and resilient flora. JOHN NELSON

Barry, John M. *Natural Vegetation of South Carolina.* Columbia: University of South Carolina Press, 1980.

Nelson, John B. *The Natural Communities of South Carolina.* Columbia: South Carolina Wildlife and Marine Resources Department, 1986.

Radford, Albert E., Harry E. Ahles, and C. Ritchie Bell. *Manual of the Vascular Flora of the Carolinas.* Chapel Hill: University of North Carolina Press, 1968.

Pocotaligo, Battle of (October 22, 1862). In the fall of 1862, the Union commander of the Department of the South, General Ormsby McKnight Mitchel, planned an operation to break the railroad connections between Charleston and Savannah at the headwaters of the Broad River near the towns of Pocotaligo and Coosawhatchie. If the railroad could be cut and a base of operations established, Federal forces could then move overland against Charleston or Savannah.

On the night of October 21, under the protection of a naval squadron and guided by former slave pilots and scouts, a Union force of 4,500 men sailed up the Broad River. The next morning a division of 4,200 men under General John M. Brannan landed on Mackey's Neck between the Pocotaligo and Tulifinny Rivers and moved inland toward Pocotaligo. The Confederates, under the overall command of Colonel William S. Walker, tried to slow Brannan's advance while awaiting reinforcements. The Federals pushed through Confederate defenses and drove the Southerners across the Pocotaligo River.

While Brannan's division dueled with the Confederates at Pocotaligo, a second Union force of 350 soldiers of the Forty-eighth New York Infantry and New York Engineers landed near Coosawhatchie. The Federals occupied the town, fired on a passing Confederate troop train, and destroyed some track. By late afternoon the Confederates received reinforcements, and both Federal columns withdrew. The battle cost the Federals 340 casualties, while the Confederates lost 163 men of the approximately 1,000 engaged.

Though the damage to the railroad was quickly repaired, Mitchel was elated by the attack's initial success. He planned new assaults, but before they could be launched, Mitchel died in Beaufort of yellow fever on October 30, 1862. General David Hunter replaced Mitchel, and the plans for renewed operations against the railroad were suspended. Union forces began organizing combined operations against Charleston. STEPHEN R. WISE

Carse, Robert. *Department of the South: Hilton Head Island in the Civil War.* 1961. Reprint, Hilton Head Island, S.C.: Impressions Printing, 1987.

Schmidt, Lewis G. *The Battle of Pocotaligo: October 22, 1862.* Allentown, Pa.: Lewis G. Schmidt, 1993.

Poellnitz, Baron Frederick Carl Hans Bruno (1734–1801). Nobleman, horticulturist, inventor. Born on December 30, 1734, in Gotha, Prussia, Poellnitz spent his early adult years in Europe, where he served as chamberlain in the court of Frederick the Great. He immigrated to the United States, arriving in Edenton, North Carolina, in 1782. He soon thereafter moved to New York City, where he bought a twenty-two-acre estate, Minto, on which stood a four-story brick house, the home of the last British governor of New York. There, Poellnitz pursued his interest in horticulture, conducted agricultural experiments, and grew a wide variety of fruit trees and other plants. He also focused his inventive interests on developing new types of farm implements. In 1790 President George Washington visited Minto and bought a plow for use at Mount Vernon. Poellnitz and his threshing machine appeared in a 1788 parade in New York to celebrate the ratification of the U.S. Constitution. In 1790 Poellnitz wrote to Washington outlining an ambitious plan for a federal demonstration farm to develop new agricultural techniques. Washington proposed the idea in his inaugural address, but no further action was taken.

Restless by nature, Poellnitz in 1790 exchanged his Minto estate for a 2,991-acre plantation, Wraggtown (later Ragtown), on the Great Pee Dee River in Marlboro County, South Carolina. At Wraggtown, the baron built a brick house on elevated ground, plans for which included an original design for bringing running water into the house from a nearby creek. No trace of the plantation house remains, but some of the canals he dug for irrigation and his experiments with crop rotation remain on the property.

The first federal census in 1790 listed Poellnitz's household as including three white males over sixteen, four white males under sixteen, three white females, and fifteen slaves. In 1792 Poellnitz purchased an additional 578 acres, giving him a total of 3,568 acres. Although a slaveholder, Poellnitz nevertheless expressed strong views about the need to abolish the practice and to give full citizenship to African Americans. In essays published in the *Gazette of the United States* in 1790, he wrote that slavery was a "contradiction to the laws of free government and to those of a well-regulated monarchy." He continued to correspond with President Washington, setting forth a broad range of views about agriculture, education, and the organization of society, with frequent reference to the law of nature. He again expressed his ideas about the importance of agriculture, commerce, and trade to the life of the nation.

Poellnitz died on April 7, 1801, and was buried at Wraggtown. An oak tree was planted atop his grave so that his ashes would become part of the tree and its acorns could be a reminder of his life and home in South Carolina for generations to come. In 1960 descendants placed a granite marker to his memory in Rogers Cemetery near his plantation. In 1976 the Marlboro County Historical Commission erected a South Carolina Historical Marker to Baron Poellnitz and Ragtown on South Carolina Highway 38 in Brownsville. JOHN L. NAPIER AND WILLIAM LIGHT KINNEY, JR.

Johnston, Henry Poellnitz. *Little Acorns from the Mighty Oak.* Birmingham, Ala.: Featon, 1962.

Kinney, William L., Jr. "The Baron of Marlboro County." *Carologue* 19 (winter 2003): 14–18.

Meador, Daniel J. *Rembert Hills and Myrtlewood.* Charlottesville, Va.: by the author, 2000.

Thomas, J. A. W. *A History of Marlboro County, with Traditions and Sketches of Numerous Families.* 1897. Reprint, Baltimore: Regional Publishing, 1971.

Poetry Society of South Carolina. This cultural organization helped revive the arts, not just in Charleston and South Carolina, but in the South in general. During the 1920s it had a national

DuBose Heyward with Gertrude Stein and his wife Dorothy on Stein's visit to Charleston for a reading sponsored by the Poetry Society. Courtesy, South Carolina Historical Society

audience and was credited with sparking one of the first flowerings of what was subsequently called the Southern Literary Renaissance.

Although incorporated in Charleston on November 17, 1920, the movement spearheaded by the Poetry Society had been developing for years. One key player was John Bennett of Ohio, who upon settling in Charleston in 1902 encouraged the use of local motifs and lore in the creative arts. It was not until after World War I, however, that his ideas caught on. The younger DuBose Heyward turned to Bennett for writing advice, as did Hervey Allen of Pittsburgh, who moved south following military service. For several years the three met together to discuss literature and art. At the same time, Laura Bragg of the Charleston Museum, another nonnative, mentored a group of women, including Helen von Kolnitz (later Hyer) and Josephine Pinckney. Meeting together, the two groups worked on Heyward's idea to found a local organization, based on the Poetry Society of America, with its aim to encourage all southern poets. This was a novel idea at the time, for the South was lagging behind culturally, a lingering result of the Civil War. The region was openly ridiculed by the Baltimore journalist Henry Mencken, who wrote of the area's sterility in his famous essay "The Sahara of the Bozart." The Charlestonians did not know of the essay when they founded their organization and had their first meeting in January 1921. By the time of their first annual yearbook, however, they had proved Mencken wrong.

The society continued to prosper for the entire decade, bringing in nationally and internationally known speakers and critics and giving large cash awards for poetry, the largest one being the Blindman Prize, named for a poem by Hervey Allen. Critics and poets turned to the group as the leader of the literary arts revival in the South; many states soon founded similar societies. Although other southern groups and schools, such as the Fugitive poets of Nashville, outstripped and eclipsed the Poetry Society of South Carolina, it nevertheless had a profound impact on the decade. Writers affiliated with it won two Pulitzer Prizes (Julia Peterkin for fiction and Robert Lathan for editorial writing) and became the ranking poets of their day, later moving on to prose and drama. The impact of the society was greater than literary, however. As an umbrella organization, it fostered the cultural rebirth of the area and stimulated the growth and development of many other agencies, such as the Preservation Society of Charleston and the Society for the Preservation of Spirituals. The society declined in national prominence by the end of the 1920s, and over the following years its fortunes waxed and waned. However, it continued into the twenty-first century as a viable group encouraging poets and the writing of poetry. HARLAN GREENE

Greene, Harlan. *Mr. Skylark: John Bennett and the Charleston Renaissance.* Athens: University of Georgia Press, 2001.

Harrison, James G. *The Poetry Society of South Carolina.* Charleston: Poetry Society of South Carolina, 1972.

Poets laureate. A poet laureate is a poetry writer who is honored, officially or unofficially, as the most distinguished or representative poet of a country or region. The South Carolina General Assembly made the title of state poet laureate official in 1934, proclaiming that "the Governor may name and appoint some outstanding and distinguished man of letters as poet laureate for the State of South Carolina." That same year Governor Ibra Blackwood appointed Archibald Rutledge as the first official poet laureate of South Carolina. Born near McClellanville in 1883, Rutledge held the title until his death in 1973. During his almost forty-year tenure, he attained almost legendary stature among his fellow South Carolinians.

Altogether, South Carolina has had six poets laureate since 1934: Archibald Rutledge (1934–1973), Helen von Kolnitz Hyer (1974–1983), Ennis Rees (1984–1985), Grace Beacham Freeman (1985–1986), Bennie Lee Sinclair (1986–2000), and Marjory Wentworth (2003–). Poets laureate do not have a strictly delineated job description, beyond the expectation that they will present poetry at a few state occasions. Nor is the position meant to be a lucrative one. It carried a small annual stipend until 2003, when Governor Mark Sanford vetoed funding for the position. Despite the absence of actual duties, however, the poet laureate has the unique responsibility of bringing poetry out of the classroom and into the places where South Carolinians are living their lives. JULIA ARRANTS

Poinsett, Joel Roberts (1779–1851). Congressman, diplomat, U.S. secretary of war. Poinsett was born on March 2, 1779, in Charleston, son of the Huguenot physician Elisha Poinsett and his English wife, Ann Roberts. As a child, Poinsett spent six years in England, where his formal education probably began. In 1794 he entered the Greenfield Hill, Connecticut, academy of Dr. Timothy

Joel Roberts Poinsett. Courtesy, South Carolina Historical Society

Dwight but stayed only two years because of his frail health. Returning to England, Poinsett attended private school at Wandsworth, where he excelled in languages. In 1797 he began medical school in Edinburgh, Scotland, but remained only one year. Returning to Charleston, Poinsett briefly studied law in 1800, but his interest quickly waned. In 1801 Poinsett set out for Europe, where he would spend most of the next seven years traveling across the continent. His fluency in foreign languages helped him form associations with several powerful European leaders, including Napoleon I, the French financier Jacques Necker, and Czar Alexander I of Russia.

Poinsett returned home in 1808 as war between Britain and the United States loomed. He hoped to secure a military appointment but instead in 1810 was named U.S. trade envoy to South America, where British forces regarded him as a "suspicious character." An ardent republican who long wanted a military career, Poinsett was soon promoting rebellion among South American countries. Failing to persuade Buenos Aires to break with Spain, in 1811 he crossed the Andes to Chile. Despite Washington's neutrality, Poinsett urged Chile to rebel and helped organize an army. But by 1814 Royalists had crushed the rebellion, and he was forced to flee.

Returning to South Carolina, Poinsett was elected in 1816 to the General Assembly, where he became a strong advocate of internal improvements. In 1819 Poinsett became president of the state Board of Public Works, actively supervising canals and roads built to link Charleston with the undeveloped interior, including a road through the Saluda Gap that brought trade from North Carolina and Tennessee.

In 1821 Poinsett won a seat in Congress, where he represented the Charleston congressional district until 1825. Although he seldom participated in floor debates, Poinsett opposed tariff increases, supported expansion of the military, and favored recognition of South American republics. In 1825 President James Monroe appointed Poinsett as the first U.S. ambassador to Mexico. Britain's influence there was strong, and Poinsett urged independence from Europe under America's Monroe Doctrine. He tried unsuccessfully to purchase Texas for the United States, thereby antagonizing Mexico. He failed to win a commercial treaty but succeeded in promoting trade along America's southwestern border. His meddling in local political affairs made him unpopular in Mexico, especially among British commercial interests and the country's monarchists. The Mexican government requested his recall, and Poinsett left the country in January 1830.

Poinsett returned to South Carolina at the height of the nullification crisis and eventually became one of the state's leading Unionists, even serving as President Andrew Jackson's confidential local agent in opposing the nullifiers and secretly organizing Unionist militias. Poinsett's efforts were praised in the North, but his influence in South Carolina waned before the states' rights doctrine put forth by his political nemesis, John C. Calhoun. After the crisis ended, on October 24, 1833, Poinsett married Mary Izard Pringle, the widow of a wealthy rice planter. The marriage produced no children.

In 1837 President Martin Van Buren named Poinsett secretary of war. He quickly set out to improve and expand the nation's paltry army of eight thousand poorly trained soldiers. He raised standards and sent officers to Europe for instruction. His artillery improvements made him one of America's foremost nineteenth-century military reformers. In 1838 Congress enlarged the army to 12,577 men. As secretary, Poinsett also presided over removal of more Indians from east of the Mississippi than any other of his predecessors. In an 1841 report, Poinsett said that 40,000 Indians had been pushed west of the Mississippi. He also encouraged exploration, authorizing the western expedition of John C. Fremont and Jean Nicollet as well as the Pacific voyages of Charles Wilkes.

Leaving office in March 1841, Poinsett spent his last decade on his Greenville District farm and his wife's Santee plantation near Georgetown. In retirement, he promoted education, economic development, and weaning of southern life from slavery. In 1844 Poinsett was elected president of the National Institute, a forerunner of the Smithsonian Institution. He served on the board of visitors of South Carolina College. He studied animal husbandry, agriculture, and botany. A red-leafed plant he introduced from Mexico, the poinsettia, was named in his honor. When secession again threatened the nation in 1850, Poinsett's friends sought his leadership in opposing the movement, but he declined. Poinsett died in Stateburg on December 12, 1851, while traveling from Charleston to his Greenville home. He was buried in the cemetery of the Church of the Holy Cross, Stateburg. JAMES T. HAMMOND

Poinsett, Joel Roberts. Papers. Historical Society of Pennsylvania, Philadelphia.

Putnam, Herbert Everett. *Joel Roberts Poinsett: A Political Biography.* Washington, D.C.: Mimeoform, 1935.

Rippy, J. Fred. *Joel Poinsett, Versatile American.* Durham, N.C.: Duke University Press, 1935.

Stillé, C. J. "The Life and Services of Joel R. Poinsett." *Pennsylvania Magazine of History and Biography* 12 (July 1888): 129–64; (October 1888): 257–303.

Poinsett Bridge. Named for Joel Roberts Poinsett, president of the Board of Public Works between 1819 and 1821, the Poinsett Bridge over Little Gap Creek was built during the construction of the state highway from Columbia to Saluda Mountain in 1820. Still intact and in good repair in the early twenty-first century, the bridge may be the oldest in the state. Located on Highway 42 just off Old Highway 25 in northern Greenville County, it was one of three Gothic-style arched bridges and forty-four smaller and simpler ones that spanned creeks and rivers along the ridge between the Tyger and Enoree Rivers.

In 1817 John Wilson, the state's civil and military engineer, proposed a toll road through the Saluda Gap in order to "attract a great portion of the trade of East Tennessee to this state." Construction through Greenville District did not begin until the summer of 1820; it was completed in October. Working with Abram Blanding, who was acting commissioner of public works, Poinsett personally supervised the construction of the seventeen-feet-wide state road over the mountain.

Poinsett Bridge. Courtesy, South Carolina Department of Archives and History

The bridge over Little Gap Creek extends 130 feet across the shallow stream. The Gothic arch at its center is 15 feet high and 7 feet wide. Poinsett, who had traveled widely and was trained as an engineer, is credited with its unusual Gothic design. The Poinsett Bridge was listed in the National Register of Historic Places in 1970 and is protected by Greenville County. JUDITH T. BAINBRIDGE

Cooper, Nancy Vance Ashmore. *Greenville, S.C.: Woven from the Past.* Sun Valley, Calif.: American Historical Press, 2000.

Huff, Archie Vernon, Jr. *Greenville: The History of the City and County in the South Carolina Piedmont.* Columbia: University of South Carolina Press, 1995.

Pollitzer sisters. Educators, suffragists, reformers. Born in Charleston, Carrie, Mabel, and Anita Pollitzer were the daughters of Gustave M. Pollitzer and Clara Guinzburg.

Carrie Teller Pollitzer (December 5, 1881–October 22, 1974), the oldest of the siblings, graduated from Memminger Normal School in Charleston in 1901. She studied at, and later directed, the South Carolina Kindergarten Training School in Charleston, where she established public health programs, home visits, kindergarten lunches, and parental-involvement programs. Carrie was active in the community, holding offices in the Charleston Federation of Women's Clubs and the Free Kindergarten Association. She was a founder and organizer of the Annual Community Children's Festival in Charleston and served as its director for twenty-three years. A tireless campaigner for women's rights, Carrie was a charter member of the Charleston Equal Suffrage League and was active in the National Woman's Party (NWP). On behalf of Charleston's City Federation of Women's Clubs, she launched the petition drive that led to the admission of women to the College of Charleston in 1918. When told that $1,200 was needed to effect coeducation, Pollitzer organized a mass meeting at the Chamber of Commerce and raised more than $1,500. In 1973 Carrie and sister Mabel were recognized by the Charleston chapter of the National Organization of Women (NOW) in appreciation of their "contributions towards women's equality."

Anita Pollitzer in Nashville, lobbying for the Nineteenth Amendment. Courtesy, South Carolina Historical Society

Mabel Louise Pollitzer (January 11, 1885–April 27, 1979) graduated from Memminger Normal School in Charleston in 1901 and from Teachers College, Columbia University, in 1906 with a major in biology. She returned to Charleston and organized the biology department at Memminger, where she taught for forty-four years. To encourage student interest in gardens, she organized a "Plant Exchange Day" in March 1915. The Civic Club helped sponsor what became an annual citywide event. She instituted nutritious lunches for schoolchildren and formed student honor organizations known as "No Cheating Clubs." In 1920 she was elected president of the Charleston County Teachers' Association. In 1929 she obtained legislation establishing the Charleston County Free Library. A charter member of the Charleston Equal Suffrage League, Pollitzer served as its publicity chair for many years. She was South Carolina state chairperson for the National Woman's Party, campaigning first for suffrage and then for the Equal Rights Amendment (ERA). In 1965 Mabel was named to the Hall of Fame of the Charleston Federation of Women's Clubs. At age ninety-three Mabel was still writing letters on behalf of the ERA.

Anita Lily Pollitzer (October 31, 1894–July 3, 1975), the youngest of the Pollitzer sisters, graduated from Memminger Normal School in Charleston in 1913, earned her B.S. in fine arts from Columbia University in 1916, and received her master's in international relations from Columbia in 1933. While a student at Columbia, she met Alfred Stieglitz, who became her "mentor in modernism." It was Pollitzer who showed him drawings by a young, unknown artist named Georgia O'Keeffe. Stieglitz consequently organized an exhibition of O'Keeffe's works, sparking her successful career as an artist. As a student, Anita became involved in the radical wing of the women's movement. Beginning in 1918 she held numerous National Woman's Party offices, including national chair from 1945 to 1949. She represented South Carolina at the International Feminists Conference at the Sorbonne in Paris in 1926 and the NWP at the first session of the United Nations in San Francisco in 1945. According to her nephew, Anita had dinner with Representative Harry Burn on the eve of Tennessee's crucial vote on the Nineteenth Amendment (which granted women the right to vote) and convinced him to support the measure. From suffrage she turned to other women's issues, including the right of married women to keep their U.S. citizenship and their government jobs and for gender equity in the National Fair Labor Standards Act. She fought tirelessly for the Equal Rights Amendment. Anita once told a reporter, "The day of chivalry is past. . . . We want to stand on our own feet." Pollitzer's biography of O'Keeffe, *A Woman on Paper,* was published posthumously in 1988, as was her selected correspondence with O'Keeffe in 1990. AMY THOMPSON MCCANDLESS

Giboire, Clive, ed. *Lovingly, Georgia: The Complete Correspondence of Georgia O'Keeffe & Anita Pollitzer.* New York: Simon & Schuster, 1990.

McCandless, Amy Thompson. "Anita Pollitzer: South Carolina Advocate for Equal Rights." *Proceedings of the South Carolina Historical Association* (2000): 1–10.

Pollitzer, Anita. Papers. South Carolina Historical Society, Charleston.

———. Papers. South Caroliniana Library, University of South Carolina, Columbia.

Pollitzer, Gustave M. Papers. South Carolina Historical Society, Charleston.

Pollitzer, Mabel L. Interview by Constance Ashton Myers. Tape and transcript, September 5, 1973. Constance Ashton Myers Collection, South Caroliniana Library, University of South Carolina, Columbia.

———. Papers. South Carolina Historical Society, Charleston.

Pollitzer, William Sprott. Interview by Dale Rosengarten and Barbara Karesh Stender. Tape and transcript, September 24, 1999. Jewish History Project, Special Collections, Robert Scott Small Library, College of Charleston, Charleston, South Carolina.

Pollock, William Pegues (1870–1922). U.S. senator. Pollock was born near Cheraw in Chesterfield County on December 9, 1870, the son of Alexander A. Pollock and Rebecca Pegues. He attended local schools before entering law school at the University of South Carolina, where he graduated in 1891. Two years later Pollock won an appointment to the U.S. Military Academy at West Point, but he failed the physical examination. He married Bessie Salley of Orangeburg.

From 1891 to 1893 Pollock served as clerk of the Committee on the District of Columbia in the U.S. House of Representatives. Returning to South Carolina, he was admitted to the bar in 1893 and elected to the state House of Representatives the following year, where he represented Chesterfield County until 1898. He was a presidential elector on the Democratic ticket in 1900. He returned to the state House in 1902 and served through 1906. In 1910 he made an unsuccessful run for the U.S. House of Representatives. Four years later Pollock participated in a spirited U.S. Senate campaign against Ellison D. Smith, Lang Jennings, and Cole Blease. Although unsuccessful, his energetic campaign made Pollock a statewide figure. In 1918 the General Assembly elected Pollock to fill the vacancy in the U.S. Senate after the death of Benjamin Tillman. Taking his seat on December 2, 1918, Pollock chaired the Committee on National Banks and participated in the vote for the enfranchisement of women, which he supported. Following the end of his short interim term on March 3, 1919, he resumed his law practice. Pollock died on June 2, 1922, in Cheraw. He was buried in St. David's Cemetery. VERONICA BRUCE MCCONNELL

"Former Senator Dies in Cheraw." Columbia *State,* June 3, 1922, p. 1.

Polo. Polo has been played in South Carolina nearly as long as it has existed in the United States. Polo began in modern-day Iran sometime between 500 B.C.E. and 100 C.E. The sport spread east and was encountered by the British military in India in the 1860s. In 1876 the sport was brought to the United States.

The first polo game in South Carolina was played on March 27, 1882, in Aiken, which has remained a major center for the sport. Attracted to South Carolina's congenial winter climate, American polo pioneers such as Thomas Hitchcock, W. C. Eustis, and Harry Payne Whitney made Aiken their winter home. Whitney Field in Aiken, built by Hitchcock and sold to Whitney, may be the oldest polo field in America in continuous use. Aiken has also been a training center for polo ponies since the 1910s. The Aiken Polo Club, founded in 1882, is one of the nation's oldest. The Camden Polo Club was founded in 1900.

During what was known as "the golden age of polo," through the 1950s, Aiken was the winter capital of polo in the United States. During this time polo was also an active sport in Columbia and Camden, with regular Sunday afternoon matches.

Polo continued to have a strong showing in the early twenty-first century. In 2004 there were fourteen polo fields in Aiken, which hosted sixteen- and twenty-goal tournaments during the fall and spring, some drawing entries from throughout the United States. Thirty polo professionals made their home in Aiken in that year, and there were active United States Polo Association clubs in Aiken, Charleston, and Columbia. DON BARTON

Daniels, John H. *Nothing Could Be Finer.* Camden, S.C.: John Culler, 1996.

Pomaria Nursery. Established in Newberry District in 1840 by William Summer (1815–1878), Pomaria Nursery was one of the most influential and prestigious nurseries of the antebellum South. Engaged in pomology (fruit cultivation) by the age of seventeen, Summer was selling fruit stock as early as 1838. An advocate of scientific agriculture and a distinguished journalist, Summer was a major contributor to the southern agricultural press.

Primarily interested in testing and developing fruit varieties suitable for southern orchards, Summer introduced the Pomaria Greening, Ferdinand, Fixlin, and Aromatic Carolina apples; the Pomaria Gage plum; the Pomaria Seedling strawberry; Pomaria Hebe and Upper Crust pears; and Poinsett and Mrs. Poinsett peaches. From 1852 to 1857 emphasis was placed on expanding Pomaria's inventory of ornamentals. It offered 1,091 varieties of trees, plants, and shrubs in 1858 and increased that number to 1,906 in 1862. Pomaria's greatest prosperity was from 1860 to 1862. In 1860 the nursery covered thirty-five acres, and its orchards were valued at $10,000. In October 1861 Pomaria opened a Columbia branch. Located on thirty acres, the facility was landscaped in the English natural style, had several glass houses, and was devoted exclusively to ornamentals. Summer also operated a rose nursery at Alston, Fairfield District. In 1865 Federal cavalrymen ransacked Pomaria, while the Columbia plant was totally destroyed at a loss of $114,000. Despite declaring bankruptcy, Summer continued to operate Pomaria, although his 1878 catalog, the last that was issued, offered only 338 varieties of plants. At Summer's death in 1878 the nursery was inherited by his nephew, but it closed in 1879. PAUL R. BEGLEY

Howard, William Herbert. "William Summer: Nineteenth-Century South Carolina Horticulturist." Master's thesis, University of South Carolina, 1984.

Kibler, James. "On Reclaiming a Southern Antebellum Garden Heritage: An Introduction to Pomaria Nurseries, 1840–1879." *Magnolia: Bulletin of the Southern Garden History Society* 10 (fall 1993): 1–12.

Pompion Hill Chapel (Berkeley County). Built in 1763, Pompion Hill Chapel is among the finest remaining examples of the Anglican parish churches of the lowcountry. Situated near Huger, the chapel stands on a bluff along the eastern branch of the Cooper River. It was built to replace a decaying wooden building erected sixty years earlier as a place of worship for plantations in the surrounding area. The cost of the new chapel was estimated at £570 sterling. The colonial government provided £200; the remaining funds came from private contributions. The chapel may have been designed by Zachariah Villepontoux, who supplied the bricks for its construction and marked his handiwork by carving his initials on the north and south doors.

The chapel is built on a rectangular plan and features Georgian styling. Its exterior features include a steeply pitched, slate-covered jerkinhead (clipped gable) roof; arched windows; and a projecting chancel with a Palladian window. The interior is finished with white plaster walls, a cove ceiling, and a floor of red brick laid in a herringbone pattern. The dais-style pulpit, carved from native red cedar by the Charleston cabinetmaker William Axson, Jr., was modeled on the one at St. Michael's. The chancel is trimmed with Doric pilasters supporting a full entablature and is enclosed by a balustrade. The

Palladian window is set in a recessed arch and trimmed with Doric colonettes with a full entablature above.

A fine example of colonial American architecture, Pompion Hill Chapel is one of only a handful of surviving eighteenth-century ecclesiastical buildings in the lowcountry. It was designated a National Historic Landmark by the U.S. Department of the Interior in 1970. DANIEL J. VIVIAN

Lane, Mills. *Architecture of the Old South: South Carolina.* Savannah, Ga.: Beehive, 1984.

Pope, Thomas Harrington, Jr. (1913–1999). Attorney, legislator, historian. Pope was born in Kinards, Newberry County, on July 28, 1913, to Thomas Harrington Pope and Marie Gary. His father, a physician, moved the family to the town of Newberry in 1920. Pope graduated from the Citadel in 1935 and took his law degree at the University of South Carolina in 1938. In 1936, at the end of his first year in law school, he won his first election to the state House of Representatives from Newberry. In the House he immediately gained a reputation for independence, supporting bills to restructure state government, to create a state police system and a board of regents for state colleges, and to end child labor. He supported Solomon Blatt's candidacy for Speaker, and Blatt took a special interest in Pope's career. Reelected in 1938, Pope resigned his seat in 1939 when he was named counsel to the state Unemployment Compensation Commission.

With America's entry into World War II, Pope, a National Guard captain, was called to active duty. He served in North Africa and Italy with the 107th Antiaircraft Battalion. By the end of the war, he had earned a promotion to lieutenant colonel. When one of Newberry's seats in the General Assembly became vacant in the spring of 1945, local supporters arranged his election in his absence. Pope returned to take his seat in time for the 1946 session, putting him one step ahead of the large number of veterans elected that summer. Speaker Blatt had come under fire in the gubernatorial campaign that summer, and under pressure, he stepped aside from the Speaker's chair after several challengers, including Pope, stepped forward.

When the legislature convened in January 1947, Pope faced Spartanburg attorney Bruce Littlejohn in a contest for Speaker of the House. Newly elected governor Strom Thurmond campaigned openly for Littlejohn, who won the election. Two years later, when Littlejohn left the House to become a judge, Pope succeeded him as Speaker. His tenure was short as well, for he left the House to run for governor in 1950. Soon after Pope announced, James F. Byrnes entered the race, and Pope lost badly to the senior statesman. He never again ran for public office.

Pope resumed his law practice and remained active in legal, business, and military circles. He retired as a brigadier general in the National Guard in 1957 and served as president of the South Carolina National Guard Association. A supporter of Newberry College, he chaired the state Foundation of Independent Colleges. He was president of the South Carolina Bar Association in 1964 and served on the State Ports Authority from 1958 to 1965 and on the Commission on Archives and History from 1965 to 1975. His interest in local history led him to write the two-volume *History of Newberry County* (1973, 1992).

Pope was married to Mary Waties Lumpkin on January 3, 1940. They had three children. Pope died on August 23, 1999, and was buried in Rosemont Cemetery, Newberry. R. PHILLIP STONE II

Pope, Thomas H., Jr. *History of Newberry County.* 2 vols. Columbia: University of South Carolina Press, 1973, 1992.

Poppenheim, Mary Barnett (1866–1936), and **Louisa Bouknight Poppenheim** (1868–1957). Clubwomen, social reformers. Born in Charleston on September 4, 1866, and December 13, 1868, respectively, Mary and Louisa Poppenheim were the eldest daughters of Christopher Pritchard Poppenheim and Mary Elinor Bouknight. The son of a rice planter, their father moved to Charleston after the Civil War and opened a successful dry goods store. After preparatory work at Charleston Female Seminary, Mary and Louisa attended Vassar College in Poughkeepsie, New York, graduating in 1888 and 1889, respectively. They returned to Charleston with leadership skills and a desire to promote women's education.

The Poppenheims helped bring the burgeoning women's club movement to Charleston, as founding members and officers of the Century Club, the Civic Club, the Intercollegiate Club, and the Charleston City Federation of Clubs. Louisa attended the organizational meeting of the South Carolina Federation of Women's Clubs (SCFWC) and became its second president. As a clubwoman, Louisa entreated South Carolina women to take up social reform in addition to literary study, which was initially favored by most clubs. Her interests included working to improve schools and libraries and to fund higher education for women. Louisa also prevailed upon Charleston politicians to appoint a matron to aid female prisoners and chaired the Municipal Playground Commission, the first municipal commission to have female members.

Beyond South Carolina, Louisa played a key role in bringing southern women into the national club movement. She attended meetings all over the South, where she helped organize other state federations. More importantly, Louisa persuaded southern women that they had an important role to play in the national movement, especially in the General Federation of Women's Clubs. She attended national conventions and was corresponding secretary and an honorary vice president of the General Federation. Louisa also used the *Keystone,* a monthly journal that she and her sister owned and edited from 1899 to 1913, to encourage southern clubwomen's activities. The journal eventually became the official organ for clubwomen and the United Daughters of the Confederacy (UDC) in several states, including North Carolina, Mississippi, Florida, and Virginia. The *Keystone* contained editorials, club news, short fiction, book reviews, and assorted articles on southern life, women's organizations, education, and social reform.

While Louisa embraced women's clubs, Mary focused on the UDC. She was president of the South Carolina division and then president-general of the national organization from 1917 to 1919. Mary was most interested in preserving history and was one of the editors of the first two volumes of *South Carolina Women in the Confederacy,* a collection of personal reminiscences published by the state UDC in 1903 and 1907. She also led South Carolina's fund-raising efforts for a UDC monument at Shiloh. Under her guidance, the UDC endowed seventy hospital beds at an American military hospital in Neuilly, France, during World War I.

The Poppenheim sisters lived at their parents' home at 31 Meeting Street until their deaths, Mary on February 12, 1936, and Louisa on March 4, 1957. Both were buried at Magnolia Cemetery. JOAN MARIE JOHNSON

Alumnae Biographical Files. Alumnae House, Vassar College, Poughkeepsie, New York.

Johnson, Joan M. "'This Wonderful Dream Nation!': Black and White South Carolina Women and the Creation of the New South, 1898–1930." Ph.D. diss., University of California at Los Angeles, 1997.

South Carolina Federation of Women's Clubs. Papers. Special Collections, Dacus Library, Winthrop University, Rock Hill, South Carolina.

Population. According to the 2000 census, South Carolina ranked twenty-sixth among the states, with a population of 4,012,012 persons. The demographic history of South Carolina reveals a slow and erratic pattern of growth. For most decades since the 1790 census, its growth rate lagged behind the national average. Only since 1970 has South Carolina shown consistent population growth (see table below).

An accurate assessment of South Carolina's population prior to the first federal decennial census in 1790 is difficult. Estimates, however, show that the colony grew slowly from 1670 to 1730 and that most people were concentrated around Charleston. The approximately 150 colonists increased to only about 4,000 whites and 3,000 slaves by 1700. Largely because of the developing rice industry, the population grew to about 30,000 in 1730, including a slave population of approximately 20,000. From 1730 to 1760 the population grew more rapidly as rice became established as the staple crop and the township system encouraged settlement of the interior. The colony's population reached about 180,000 in the 1770s as white yeoman farmers moved into the backcountry.

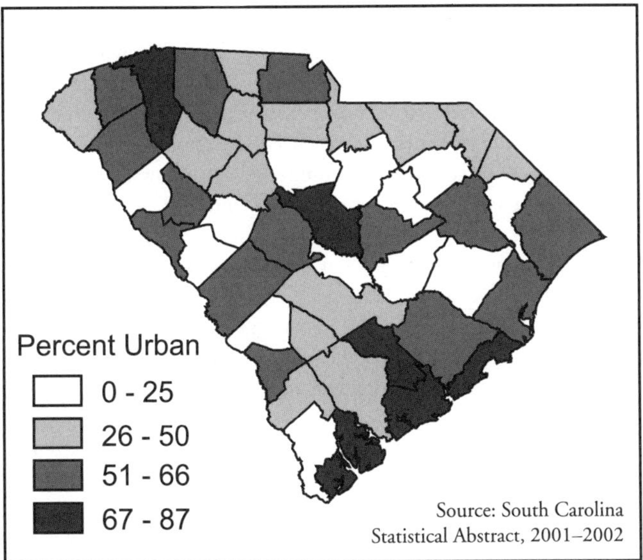

Increasing urbanization of the state

The state's population doubled between 1790 and 1820 as upland cotton spurred development in the Piedmont. Most low-country counties experienced little growth. During the next forty years, 1820 to 1860, just over 200,000 people were added to the state, for an increase of only forty percent, well behind the national population growth rate. This reflected a stagnating economy and a large out-migration of planters, farmers, and slaves. Push factors of this migration largely were declining soil fertility and productivity, while available and inexpensive land in Georgia, Alabama, and Mississippi acted as pull factors.

Few of the European immigrants who swelled population growth in the mid-Atlantic and midwestern states came to South Carolina during the antebellum period. The state also was unable to attract native-born migrants to any significant degree. South Carolina had a total free population of 301,302 in 1860, ninety-two percent of whom were native to the state. About three percent of the population was foreign-born, and only five percent came from other states.

In the decades between 1870 and 1940, South Carolina grew from just over 700,000 to about 1.9 million persons. The state's growth rate lagged far behind that of the nation and exceeded the national growth rate only twice during this period. The greatest wave of European immigration to the United States occurred between 1890 and 1920, when millions of immigrants flocked to the burgeoning industrial cities of the Northeast and the Midwest. South Carolina, however, did not receive any sizable foreign immigration because of its stagnant economy, entrenched tenant system, small cities, and limited industrial development. This absence of European immigrants left South Carolina and most other southern states outside of what traditionally is known as the "melting pot." Well-established white ethnic neighborhoods have been relatively rare in South Carolina's cities, nor have there been rural areas or small towns that are dominated by European people or customs. There was more of a European "melting pot" during the colonial period than during the first half of the twentieth century. Ethnicity in South Carolina usually means blacks and whites, and the white population is relatively homogeneous.

At the turn of the century, out-migration was decidedly to the north and consisted mostly of rural blacks. This caused a major demographic shift from a black population majority between 1820 and 1920 to a white majority since 1920. Push factors behind this out-migration among rural blacks were the lack of economic opportunity, the grinding poverty of tenancy, and the social and economic discrimination characteristic of a segregated society, while the major pull factor was a great labor demand in the rapidly growing industrial cities of the North. Between 1900 and 1940 more than 500,000 blacks left the state, with an additional estimate of 400,000 black out-migrants during the 1950s and 1960s. The major losses of black population occurred in the rural counties of the lower Piedmont and portions of the coastal plain. This loss was not as strong in the rural Pee Dee region, however, where the labor-intensive tobacco industry increased in significance.

The decade of the 1970s marked a significant milestone in South Carolina's population history. During the 1950s and 1960s a concerted effort by the state to attract manufacturing industries and societal changes associated with the civil rights movement set the stage for population changes that characterized the "Sunbelt South." Population growth during the 1970s exceeded the growth rates for every decade since 1880, and it exceeded the national average for only the second time during the twentieth century. More people were added to the state's population in the 1970s than were added during the twenty years between 1950 and 1970. An in-migration began as people from other parts of the country and foreign-born moved to South Carolina. The nonwhite population grew faster than at any other time during the twentieth century, as out-migration slowed and a return migration occurred among some blacks who previously had moved north. The nonwhite proportion of the total population increased for the first time since 1880. Also during the 1970s the number of urban dwellers first outnumbered rural residents. In addition, ethnic patterns began to change as Asians and especially Hispanics migrated to both urban and rural South Carolina.

There also has been a significant redistribution of population in South Carolina since the 1970s. Most of the change occurred in the metropolitan areas, as urban dwellers increased from just over forty percent in 1960 to sixty percent in 2000. The small, compact cities of the 1950s and 1960s have given way to more sprawling metropolitan patterns. Largely because of improved access to the state's larger cities provided by the expansion of the interstate highway system, it was the suburban fringe and not the central cities that grew the fastest. Some coastal counties, especially Horry and Beaufort, joined the suburban counties as high-growth areas because of the expansion of the tourism industry. A growing component of the growth along the coast has been retirees who are relocating from the North to the Myrtle Beach and Hilton Head Island areas.

Rural counties have not shared in this expansion, however, and many lost population throughout the twentieth century. Many small towns that once were thriving service centers for a more densely populated countryside now are characterized by empty streets and abandoned buildings. Despite the rapid growth in suburban and coastal counties, South Carolina at the turn of the twenty-first century still had a sizable rural population. Importantly, however, few people who lived in rural South Carolina were farmers. Most of this rural nonfarm population traded off the cost of commuting to jobs in nonagricultural activities for the economies of living in a rural area, but many remained because of strong feelings about place, land, and family. CHARLES F. KOVACIK

Total, Nonwhite, and Urban Population: 1790–2000

	Total SC Population	*Percent Change S.C.*	*Percent Change U.S.A.*	*Percent Nonwhite*	*Percent Urban*
1790	249,073			43.7	6.6
1800	345,591	38.8	35.1	43.2	5.4
1810	415,115	20.1	36.4	48.4	6.0
1820	502,741	21.1	33.1	52.8	4.9
1830	581,185	15.6	33.5	55.6	5.8
1840	594,398	2.3	32.7	56.4	5.7
1850	668,507	12.5	35.9	58.9	7.3
1860	703,708	5.3	35.6	58.6	6.9
1870	705,606	0.3	22.6	58.9	8.6
1880	995,577	41.1	30.2	60.7	7.5
1890	1,151,149	15.6	25.5	59.9	10.1
1900	1,340,316	16.4	21.0	58.4	12.8
1910	1,515,400	13.1	21.0	55.2	14.8
1920	1,683,724	11.1	14.9	51.4	17.5
1930	1,738,765	3.3	16.1	45.7	21.3
1940	1,899,804	9.3	7.2	42.9	24.5
1950	2,117,027	11.4	14.5	38.9	36.7
1960	2,382,594	12.5	19.0	34.9	41.2
1970	2,590,713	8.7	13.3	30.7	48.3
1980	3,122,814	20.5	11.5	31.2	54.1
1990	3,486,703	11.7	9.8	31.0	54.6
2000	4,012,012	15.3	13.2	32.8	60.5

Source: U.S. Census Bureau and South Carolina Statistical Abstract.

Kovacik, Charles F., and John J. Winberry. *South Carolina: The Making of a Landscape.* 1987. Reprint, Columbia: University of South Carolina Press, 1989.

Petty, Julian J. *The Growth and Distribution of Population in South Carolina.* Columbia, S.C.: State Council for Defense, 1943.

———. *Twentieth Century Changes in South Carolina Population.* Columbia: School of Business Administration, University of South Carolina, 1962.

South Carolina Statistical Abstract. Annual publication. Columbia: South Carolina State Budget and Control Board, Division of Research and Statistics.

Porcher, Francis Peyre (1824–1895). Physician, botanist. Porcher was born in St. John's Berkeley Parish on December 14, 1824, the son of William Porcher, a physician and planter, and his wife Isabella Sarah Peyre.

Porcher completed his preparatory education in Winnsboro at the Mt. Zion Academy, where he excelled in Latin and the Greek classics. In 1844 he graduated with honors from South Carolina College and entered the Medical College of the State of South Carolina in Charleston. Awarded the M.D. degree in 1847, Porcher received the first prize for his thesis, an exemplary scientific work that was published in the *Southern Journal of Medicine and Pharmacy* as "A Medico-Botanical Catalogue of the Plants and Ferns of St. John's, Berkeley, South Carolina."

In 1849 Porcher became coeditor of the *Charleston Medical Journal and Review,* and three years later he went abroad to study medical procedures in France and Italy. Upon returning to Charleston in 1854, he again became the journal's coeditor, serving through 1855. Meanwhile, in 1852, before he left for Europe, Porcher helped to establish the Charleston Preparatory Medical School, and he taught materia medica (medical remedies) and therapeutics there from 1854 until 1860. In 1855 he and a colleague established a hospital for African Americans, and three years later Porcher accepted appointment as physician to the Marine Hospital in Charleston, where he also served as a clinical professor for the medical college. Already the author of several articles, Porcher completed a forward-looking treatise in 1860 that was published the following year by the South Carolina Medical Association as *Illustrations of Disease with the Microscope.*

A slaveowner and supporter of secession, Porcher volunteered as a surgeon for the Confederate army in 1861, serving first in an army hospital in Norfolk, Virginia, and later in Petersburg, Virginia. In 1862 Samuel Preston Moore, the surgeon general of the Confederate states, commissioned Porcher to compile a work on the useful botanical resources of the South. A year later Porcher produced a large volume titled *Resources of the Southern Fields and Forests,* which won considerable praise as a contribution to the war effort. Porcher later revised the book and reissued it in 1869.

After the war, Porcher returned to private practice and continued to write medical articles. He was appointed as professor of clinical medicine at the Medical College of the State of South Carolina in 1872, and in 1874 he was made professor of materia medica and therapeutics. He held these positions until 1891, when he resigned over a dispute with the dean. Meanwhile, Porcher published many more articles, made contributions to the state medical society and the American Medical Association, once again served as a coeditor of the *Charleston Medical Journal and Review* (1874–1876), and wrote numerous columns for newspapers. Long interested in yellow fever, he advanced knowledge of that disease and promoted understanding of public hygiene.

Porcher married Virginia Leigh on April 25, 1855. Eleven years after her death in 1866, he married Margaret Bentley Ward on March 2, 1877. He had five children with his first wife and four with his second. The University of South Carolina awarded Porcher the LL.D. degree in 1891. Porcher died in Charleston on November 19, 1895, and was buried in Trinity "Black Oak" Cemetery, Berkeley County. His remains were later reburied in St. Stephen's Protestant Episcopal Cemetery. LESTER D. STEPHENS

Townsend, John F. "Francis Peyre Porcher, M.D. (1824–1895)." *Annals of Medical History,* 3d ser., 1 (March 1939): 177–88.

Waring, Joseph I. *A History of Medicine in South Carolina.* Vol. 2, *1825–1900.* Columbia: South Carolina Medical Association, 1967.

Port Royal (Beaufort County; 2000 pop. 3,950). Founded as a town and railroad terminus in 1874, Port Royal has a history of French (1562), Spanish (1565–1587), Scots (1684), and English (1670) settlement. In 1869 the Union army veteran Stephen Caldwell Millett began construction of the Port Royal Railroad between Augusta, Georgia, and Battery Point on the southern end of Port Royal Island. Town, railroad, and harbor facilities followed, and Port Royal was incorporated on March 9, 1874.

Between 1875 and 1900 Port Royal surpassed Beaufort in importance in both shipping and commercial activities. In 1880 some southeastern railroads pooled their lines "to establish a through traffic from the Ohio River to Savannah, Charleston and Port Royal." Two years later Congress authorized construction of a coaling dock and naval storehouse at Port Royal, followed by a naval dry dock and a large, brick sail loft on nearby Parris Island.

Commercial development of phosphate deposits in the Port Royal vicinity attracted shipping to load processed phosphate, as well as area lumber and cotton. The 1880s and 1890s saw the town establish regular railroad connections with inland cities, as well as passenger ship service to New York, Liverpool, and Bremen. Before the 1893 hurricane damaged phosphate boats and installations, it was said that more ships loaded phosphate in and near Port Royal than in Charleston and Savannah combined. Nearby Parris Island and the U.S. Naval Station also aided the local economy, and by 1883 Port Royal's population stood at 389.

When the phosphate industry declined in South Carolina, so did much of Port Royal's prosperity. A series of disastrous storms in the 1890s severely injured phosphate operations, as did state tax increases and the development of new phosphate deposits in Florida. An even greater blow came to Port Royal in 1902 with the relocation of the navy yard to Charleston. In addition, local cotton cultivation plummeted with the arrival of the boll weevil in 1919.

But as phosphate mining and cotton farming dwindled, other economic activities stepped in to revitalize Port Royal. Military training during World War I by army aviators and U.S. Marines, followed by the growth of fishing and shrimping in the 1930s spurred an economic revival in Port Royal. World War II and postwar Marine Corps training on Parris Island further contributed to growth. In 1958 Port Royal saw the dedication of a state port installation, which led to renewed shipping and railroad activities. Development of the town's waterfront, the expansion of residential housing, the continued existence of the Marine Corps Training Depot, and a vibrant seafood and tourist industry all promised a bright future for Port Royal at the end of the twentieth century. The arrival was a long time in coming. As the 1991 *History of the South Carolina State Ports Authority* sagely observed, "of South Carolina's three ports, the Port of Port Royal was the first to be visited by European colonial powers, but it was the last of the three to decide just what kind of a port it was suited to be." GERHARD SPIELER

Beaufort County Joint Planning Commission. *Port Royal Development Plan.* Beaufort, S.C.: Planning Commission, 1975.

McTeer, J. E. *Adventure in the Woods and Waters of the Lowcountry.* Beaufort, S.C.: Beaufort Book Company, 1972.

South Carolina State Ports Authority. *History of the South Carolina State Ports Authority.* Charleston: South Carolina State Ports Authority, 1991.

Port Royal, Battle of (November 7, 1861). The Battle of Port Royal culminated an amphibious operation designed to establish a United States military depot on the southeastern coast to carry out land and sea operations against the Confederacy. On October 29, 1861, a naval squadron organized for the capture of Port Royal Sound left Hampton Roads, Virginia, under the command of Flag Officer Samuel F. Du Pont. It consisted of seventeen warships, twenty-five coaling schooners, and thirty-three transports, which carried approximately thirteen hundred soldiers commanded by Brigadier General Thomas W. Sherman.

Fort Walker on Hilton Head and Fort Beauregard on Bay Point defended Port Royal Sound. Together they mounted thirty-nine guns and were manned by 2,400 men under the command of General Thomas Drayton. Assisting the fortifications was a small squadron of makeshift gunboats under Captain Josiah Tattnall. The Federal forces rendezvoused off the sound on November 3. Four days later, on November 7, Du Pont, on board his flagship, the USS *Wabash,* led his warships into the sound. Tattnall's gunboats were chased off, and while the *Wabash, Susquehanna,* and *Bienville* maneuvered in front of Fort Walker, the rest of the squadron took up position off the fort's northwest flank enfilading the work. Later the Federal gunboat *Pocahontas* arrived off Fort Walker's seaward flank and added her guns to the bombardment, completing the crossfire. In charge of the *Pocahontas* was Captain Percival Drayton, brother of the Confederate commander. After nearly five hours of fighting, the Confederates evacuated Fort Walker and Fort Beauregard and fled inland, abandoning Beaufort and the Sea Islands.

The battle cost Union forces eight killed and twenty-three wounded, while the Confederates on Hilton Head had eleven killed and forty-eight wounded. At Fort Beauregard, the Southerners suffered thirteen wounded. In a short time the Northern army and navy established a huge military installation that served as headquarters for the South Atlantic Blockading Squadron and the Department of the South. The capture of Port Royal provided the North with an important political and morale-boosting victory. It also heralded a new era of naval warfare by demonstrating that steam-powered warships with heavy ordnance could attack and defeat fixed fortifications. In addition to its effect on the war effort and military science, the battle at Port Royal began a social and economic revolution, for Du Pont's victory brought freedom to the thousands of slaves who lived in the Port Royal area. STEPHEN R. WISE

Ammen, Daniel. "Du Pont and the Port Royal Expedition." In *Battles and Leaders of the Civil War,* edited by Robert U. Johnson and Clarence C. Buel. Vol. 1. New York: Thomas Yoseloff, 1956.

Rowland, Lawrence S., Alexander Moore, and George C. Rogers. *The History of Beaufort County, South Carolina.* Vol. 1, *1514–1861.* Columbia: University of South Carolina Press, 1996.

Wise, Stephen. "The Battle of Port Royal." *Beaufort Magazine* (fall holiday 1994): 57–61.

Port Royal Experiment. The Port Royal Experiment, also called the Sea Island Experiment, was an early humanitarian effort to prepare the former slaves of the South Carolina Sea Islands for inclusion as free citizens in American public life. The Port Royal Experiment was made possible by the U.S. Navy's conquest of the Sea Islands of Beaufort District after the naval victory at the Battle of Port Royal on November 7, 1861. The islands remained in Union hands until the end of the war. The conquest was so swift that Beaufort District planters abandoned most of their property and hurriedly evacuated inland. Most importantly, nearly ten thousand slaves were abandoned on island plantations. Still not legally considered free, the abandoned slaves were declared "contraband of war" and placed under the jurisdiction of the U.S. Department of the Treasury. Treasury Secretary Salmon P. Chase sent his friend Edward L. Pierce of Boston to Port Royal to recommend measures to the federal government for dealing with the Sea Island "contrabands." Reverend Mansfield French was dispatched to Port Royal at the same time as agent of the New York–based American Missionary Association to ascertain what help was needed for the Sea Island blacks. Both men arrived at Port Royal in January 1862.

The combination of federal efforts to assist and employ the Sea Island blacks and the efforts of several philanthropic and missionary organizations to prepare the "contrabands" for emancipation led to the Port Royal Experiment. While the federal government concentrated on employing the "contrabands" to harvest and process the valuable Sea Island cotton, philanthropic organizations and religious missionaries assumed the task of providing education, which the Sea Island blacks eagerly sought. Both the government and private charities provided food, clothing, and medical assistance. In February 1862 Pierce returned to Boston and helped organize the Educational Commission and to seek volunteers for this "experiment" in the Sea Islands. At the same time, the National Freedmen's Relief Association in New York was collecting donations and enlisting volunteers to assist as well.

In March 1862 the steamer *Atlantic* brought the first contingent of these Boston and New York volunteers and philanthropists to Port Royal. Dubbed "Gideonites" by contemptuous Union soldiers, the volunteers were a mixed group of missionaries intent on teaching, organizing, evangelizing, or doing whatever good they could at Port Royal. Although diverse in their makeup, they were united by their fervent opposition to slavery and determination to help guide the liberated slaves of the Sea Islands. In April 1862 a second contingent of "Gideonites" arrived from Philadelphia, sponsored by that city's Port Royal Relief Committee. Prominent among this contingent was Laura Towne, who would found the Penn School on St. Helena Island. These groups were the vanguard of scores of missionaries who came to the Sea Islands of Beaufort District during the Civil War.

The partnership between the federal government and various philanthropic agencies to carry out humanitarian enterprises among the Sea Island blacks continued throughout the war. Notable among their achievements was the establishment of private freedmen's schools that continued a century and a half after the Port Royal Experiment ended. The Mather School on Port Royal Island survived until the 1960s, and the Penn School on St. Helena Island continued into the twenty-first century as the Penn Community Center.

On January 1, 1863, Lincoln's Emancipation Proclamation went into effect for the "contrabands" of the Sea Islands. Thereafter they were "freedmen" and entitled to many rights and responsibilities as citizens. This was the pinnacle of the Port Royal Experiment and a day of jubilation for Sea Island blacks.

Following emancipation, another effort of the Port Royal Experiment was the redistribution of abandoned plantation lands to the former slaves. Under the authority of the U.S. Direct Tax Act of 1862, most of the Sea Island plantations in Beaufort District were seized for nonpayment of taxes. Leaders of the Port Royal Experiment lobbied the federal government to distribute this land in small parcels to the freedmen. Of the 101,930 acres seized, approximately one-third was purchased on favorable terms by the freedmen. Much of Beaufort County retained the character of small black landholding into the twenty-first century.

On March 3, 1865, the federal government established the Bureau of Refugees, Freedmen and Abandoned Lands within the War Department to deal with the humanitarian problems across the South at the close of the Civil War. Better known as the Freedmen's Bureau, it was responsible for food, clothing, and medical relief as well as educational services for the freedmen. The first Freedmen's Bureau office in South Carolina was opened in Beaufort in 1865, and many volunteers of the Port Royal Experiment became leaders of the agency. General Rufus Saxton, the military governor of the Sea Islands and a major supporter of the Port Royal Experiment, was the Freedman's Bureau director for South Carolina, Georgia, and Florida. The Freedman's Bureau was the first humanitarian, or "welfare," agency established by the U.S. government. The Freedman's Bureau was officially disbanded in 1872, but the lingering influence of the Port Royal Experiment survived in Beaufort County's unique landownership patterns and educational institutions. LAWRENCE S. ROWLAND

Abbott, Martin. *The Freedmen's Bureau in South Carolina, 1865–1872.* Chapel Hill: University of North Carolina Press, 1967.

Forten, Charlotte L. *The Journal of Charlotte Forten: A Free Negro in the Slave Era.* 1953. Reprint, New York: Norton, 1981.

Holland, Rupert Sargent, ed. *Letters and Diary of Laura Towne: Written from the Sea Islands of South Carolina, 1862–1884.* 1912. Reprint, New York: Negro Universities Press, 1969.

Pearson, Elizabeth Ware, ed. *Letters from Port Royal: Written at the Time of the Civil War.* 1906. Reprint, New York: Arno, 1969.

Rose, Willie Lee. *Rehearsal for Reconstruction: The Port Royal Experiment.* 1964. Reprint, Athens: University of Georgia Press, 1999.

Port Royal Island, Battle of (February 3, 1779). The Battle of Port Royal Island was part of a larger campaign designed by the British to cover their operations against Augusta, Georgia. On February 2, 1779, while British units were marching on Augusta from Savannah, an amphibious expedition consisting of 150 light infantrymen on four transports, the twenty-four-gun ship *Vigilant,* and the smaller warship *Germaine* left Tybee Island, Georgia, for Port Royal. The approach of the British warships forced the patriots to destroy Fort Lyttleton at Beaufort. But instead of occupying Beaufort, the British continued into the Broad River and destroyed the homes of Stephen Bull and Thomas Heyward, Sr.

The next day, February 3, the British continued up the Broad River and landed the light infantrymen under Major William Gardner on Port Royal Island. The soldiers marched to Port Royal Ferry but found it well protected. While returning to their transports, the British discovered a force of four hundred militiamen and some Continental artillerymen under Generals Stephen Bull and William Moultrie drawn up across the road on a rise known as Grey's Hill. Though outnumbered, the British attacked. In a sharp fight lasting forty-five minutes, the Americans suffered about thirty casualties, while the British lost about seventy-five men. At the end of the battle both sides withdrew. The British remained in the area and gathered up slaves and were joined by Loyalists before returning to Savannah. Though the campaign was inconclusive, it did demonstrate the ability of the British to use their command of the waterways to strike at both military and civilian targets and to strengthen the resolve of South Carolina Loyalists. STEPHEN R. WISE

Butler, Lewis W. G. *Annals of the King's Rifle Corps.* Vol. 1. London: J. Murray, 1913.

Ripley, Warren. *Battleground: South Carolina in the Revolution.* Charleston, S.C.: Post-Courier, 1983.

Rowland, Lawrence S., Alexander Moore, and George C. Rogers. *The History of Beaufort County, South Carolina.* Vol. 1, *1514–1861.* Columbia: University of South Carolina Press, 1996.

Ward, Christopher. *The War of the Revolution.* 2 vols. New York: Macmillan, 1952.

Port Royal Naval Station. The conquest of the Sea Islands by a Union fleet in November 1861 was the beginning of more than a century of U.S. naval involvement with Port Royal Sound. With nearly thirty feet of water over the bar at all tides, Port Royal Sound is the deepest natural harbor on the Atlantic seaboard south of New York. With the completion of the Port Royal and Augusta Railroad to the harbor in 1873, the U.S. Navy was able to stockpile coal for its new steam-powered warships. In 1876 many of the capital ships of the U.S. Navy's Atlantic Fleet spent the winter in Port Royal Sound to escape ice in northern ports. In 1877 Port Royal Sound was officially designated as a fourth-class naval station and dubbed "United States Naval Station, Port Royal, South Carolina." In 1883 the navy began purchasing land on Parris Island in Port Royal Sound to build wharves and shoreside facilities. In 1890 the U.S. Navy appropriated more than $500,000 to build the largest dry dock in the United States on Parris Island. The dry dock was completed in 1895 and was the centerpiece of the Port Royal Naval Shipyard. During the Spanish American War, the Port Royal Naval Station was one of the principal support stations for U.S. naval actions around Cuba.

In 1901 Ben Tillman, an influential member of the Senate Naval Affairs Committee, arranged to have the annual appropriation for the Port Royal Naval Station removed to Charleston. This marked the end of the Port Royal Naval Station and the beginning of the Charleston Naval Shipyard. In 1903 a company of U.S. Marines was sent to oversee the government facilities on Parris Island, which later reemerged as the U.S. Marine Corps Recruit Depot, Parris Island, South Carolina. LAWRENCE S. ROWLAND

McNeil, Jim. *Charleston's Navy Yard: A Pictorial History.* Charleston, S.C.: CokerCraft, 1985.

Report of the Hearings before the Committee on Naval Affairs Relative to the Proposed Transfer of the Naval Station from Port Royal, South Carolina to Charleston, South Carolina. 56th Congress, Senate Document No. 156. Washington, D.C.: Government Printing Office, 1901.

Porter-Gaud School. Located in Charleston, Porter-Gaud had its beginning just after the Civil War. In 1867 the Reverend Anthony Toomer Porter launched the Episcopal Holy Communion Church Institute, a school for white boys. The school required a modest tuition for most students but subsidized the cost for orphans and indigents with private gifts, some from the northern states and Europe. Called Porter Academy after 1882, the school added a military department in 1887. At Porter's death in 1902, drills in military tactics and football were part of the curriculum along with Latin, modern languages, science, and mathematics. In 1913 the football team held the college boys of the Citadel to a scoreless tie.

In the 1950s, after years of declining enrollments as public schools gained broad acceptance, Porter Academy faced a grave crisis. Officials sold off assets such as football uniforms and jettisoned the military and high school departments just to survive. But fortunes changed quickly with the aggressive new leadership of Charles Owens. Porter achieved dramatic improvements in buildings and programs, making the school a viable option just as the *Brown v. Board of Education* decision increased demand for private schooling among white parents. In 1964 Porter merged with Gaud, a well-regarded secondary school founded in 1908 by Canadian-born William S. Gaud, and Watt, a primary feeder into Gaud's fourth grade. During the tenure of Berkeley Grimball as headmaster (1964–1988), the merged school, still an Episcopal affiliate, entered an era of financial security, full academic and extracurricular programs, a refurbished suburban campus, growing enrollments (including females and blacks after 1972), and a restored regional reputation. LAYLON WAYNE JORDAN

Greene, Karen. *Porter-Gaud School: The Next Step.* Easley, S.C.: Southern Historical Press, 1982.

Porter, A. Toomer. *Led On! Step by Step: Scenes from Clerical, Military, Educational, and Plantation Life in the South, 1828–1898.* 1898. Reprint, New York: Arno, 1967.

Ports and harbors. South Carolina is blessed with several deep-water harbors—Winyah Bay (Georgetown), Charleston harbor, and Port Royal Sound. As early as the sixteenth century, Spanish and French explorers sailed into Port Royal—"one of the finest natural harbors in the world"—and attempted settlements there before the English arrived. In 1670 the first English immigrants chose to settle at Charleston.

Besides harbors, scores of inlets and bays—Murrells Inlet, North Santee River Inlet, South Santee River Inlet, Bulls Bay, Stono Inlet, St. Helena Sound, Calibogue Sound, and others—cut the South Carolina coast. These outlets for the great rivers of South Carolina facilitated the development of an active coasting trade. South Carolina's waterways were the principal transportation arteries of the new colony and directly influenced the location of early settlements.

Trade was the lifeblood of the fledgling colony, and Charleston began enjoying a brisk business in the early seventeenth century, receiving as many as eighty ships annually. By 1704 the city had two wharves. Thousands of pounds of deerskins and naval stores traveled to London in exchange for manufactured goods. In later years rice, indigo, and cotton were the cash crops that drew world trade to South Carolina's ports.

The port of Charleston welcomed thousands of voluntary and involuntary immigrants. British, French, Swiss, and German immigrants entered South Carolina through the port of Charleston. Scholars have estimated that forty percent of the enslaved Africans imported into North America passed through the port of Charleston. The quarantine station on Sullivan's Island was the "Ellis Island" of African Americans.

Besides being commercial entrepôts, South Carolina's ports have had military and strategic value. During the Revolutionary War, the port of Charleston was home to the South Carolina navy before the city fell to the British in 1780. It remained in British hands until 1782. During the War of 1812, the British blockaded Charleston, Port Royal, and other east-coast ports. In ensuing years the federal government worked to strengthen harbor defenses in the state. The firing on Fort Sumter in the mouth of Charleston harbor began the Civil War in April 1861. South Carolina seized Union ships in the harbor to form the nucleus of her navy. Later that year Union forces captured Port Royal harbor and transformed it into the primary supply station for the Federal naval blockade of the southern coast. The capture of Port Royal was a serious setback for the Confederacy. During the war, Charleston was a center for Southern blockade-runners and was also the home of at least three ironclads—*Palmetto State, Chicora,* and *Charleston.* In addition, Charleston harbor became the site of the first successful submarine attack, when on February 17, 1864, the CSS *H. L. Hunley* sank the USS *Housatonic.* The *Hunley* then disappeared beneath the waves and was not raised until a century later. In 1901 the United States Naval Station relocated from Port Royal to Charleston. During World War II and the cold war, the Navy Yard brought an economic boom to the city, while its subsequent closing in the 1990s brought economic dislocation. Nevertheless, the commercial port in Charleston continued to thrive.

At the start of the twenty-first century, the South Carolina State Ports Authority operated, without state appropriations, three ports in the state: Charleston, Georgetown, and Port Royal. The modern port of Charleston, a container port, is South Carolina's busiest, handling trade with 140 nations. Trade with northern Europe accounts for thirty-seven percent of Charleston's trade. In dollar value of cargo, Charleston ranks sixth among United States customs districts. Charleston is the second-busiest container port on the east and gulf coasts and the fourth-busiest nationally. In 2001, 1,370,000 tons of cargo passed through the port of Georgetown, while Port Royal handled 162,000 tons. More than 2,500 ships and other vessels entered the Charleston, Georgetown, and Port Royal port terminals in 2001. From naval stores and deerskins, to indigo, rice, and cotton, and most recently to containers of fertilizer, cement, foodstuffs, and consumer goods, the trade through South Carolina's ports mirrors the commercial vitality of the state's economy. ALEXIA JONES HELSLEY

Post and Courier (2003 circulation: 98,896 daily and 109,457 Sunday). Published in Charleston, the *Post and Courier* is the oldest daily newspaper in South Carolina. The publication's lineage can be traced through three newspapers. The oldest, the *Charleston Courier,* began publication on January 10, 1803. It was founded by Massachusetts native Aaron Smith Willington and several partners. The newspaper opposed nullification in the 1830s and secession in the 1850s, ensuring that it would remain in conflict with its chief rival, the pro-states'-rights *Charleston Mercury.* The *Charleston Courier* advocated secession in 1860 but counseled moderation during the Civil War. The newspaper was seized by William T. Sherman's army at the close of the war and was briefly published by two Union war correspondents. In November 1865 control of the paper was turned over to Charleston native Thomas Y. Simons under the auspices of A. S. Willington & Co.

The *Charleston Daily News* was the second ancestor of the *Post and Courier.* James W. McMillian of Charleston and two other partners started the newspaper on August 14, 1865, and it was sold to Bartholomew R. Riordan, Francis Warrington Dawson, and Henry Evans two years later. Although Evans soon dropped out, Riordan and Dawson remained connected to the newspaper. On April 3, 1873, they purchased the *Courier,* and the first issue of the *News and Courier* was published on April 7, 1873. Robert Lathan became editor of the *News and Courier* in 1910. Fourteen years later he was awarded the Pulitzer Prize for his editorial "The Plight of the South."

The third newspaper in the *Post and Courier*'s lineage, the *Evening Post,* was founded by a group headed by Hartwell M. Ayer on October 1, 1894. It established itself as a newspaper opposed to Ben Tillman and his political followers. The newspaper was purchased by the *News and Courier* in 1926.

The *Evening Post* and the *News and Courier* continued to publish separately through most of the twentieth century. The newspapers also expanded, with the *News and Courier* climbing to third in circulation among South Carolina's daily newspapers under the editorship of William Watts Ball in the 1930s and 1940s. After World War II, the company spent millions on a new plant and then millions more on expanding it. In the aftermath of Hurricane Hugo in September 1989, the newspaper published a single daily issue and powered its plants for four days with generators.

Flagging circulation at the *Evening Post* led the two newspapers to combine their staffs in the 1980s. The papers formally merged on October 1, 1991, as the *Post and Courier,* a morning newspaper. The *Post and Courier* is part of the Evening Post Publishing Company, which operates several newspapers in the lowcountry as well as papers in Kingstree, Aiken, North Carolina, Texas, and Argentina. The company also operates television stations in Arizona, Colorado, Kentucky, Louisiana, Montana, and Texas. AARON W. MARRS

McNeely, Patricia G. *The Palmetto Press: The History of South Carolina's Newspapers and the Press Association.* Columbia: South Carolina Press Association, 1998.

Sass, Herbert Ravenel. *Outspoken: 150 Years of the News and Courier.* Columbia: University of South Carolina Press, 1953.

Potter's Raid (April 5–21, 1865). General Edward E. Potter's raid into lowcountry and central South Carolina in April 1865 was neither massive nor particularly crucial to Union victory. But coming as it did on the heels of William T. Sherman's "March to the Sea" and his destruction of Columbia, the raid witnessed some of the last engagements of the Civil War. The raid also underscored the unchallenged ability of the Union army to reach any part of the Confederacy. Among South Carolinians, the raid produced a rich collection of folklore and reminiscence that still resonates in the state.

In March 1865, while the rest of Sherman's army marched into North Carolina, a detachment of Union soldiers drove toward Darlington in hopes of breaking the area's railroad connections. Meeting resistance, they fell back. The failure irked Sherman, who called for a heavier force to finish the job. "[T]he food supplies in that section should be exhausted," he wrote Major General Quincy A. Gillmore. "I don't feel disposed to feel overgenerous. . . . Those cars and locomotives should be destroyed if to do it costs you 500 men." Gillmore obliged, ordering Potter with 2,500 men, including detachments from the 32d and 102d U.S. Colored Troops, to move inland from Georgetown and "make all the display possible."

Although hampered somewhat by Confederate guerrillas and slowed by supply difficulties, Potter encountered little to stop him. He raided as far as Sumter District before news of Sherman's armistice with Confederate general Joseph E. Johnston brought a cease-fire that eventually resulted in Confederate surrender. By then, Potter reported the destruction of trestles, lines, rolling stock, and 51,000 bales of cotton. When Potter returned to his base on the coast, according to one authority, five thousand newly liberated slaves followed him. PAUL CHRISTOPHER ANDERSON

Thigpen, Allan D., ed. *The Illustrated Recollections of Potter's Raid, April 5–21, 1865.* Sumter, S.C.: Gamecock City Printing, 1998.

Pottersville. Pottersville originated in Edgefield District between 1819 and 1820 around the stoneware factory of Abner Landrum a mile and a half north of the town of Edgefield. Landrum's was the first significant stoneware factory in Edgefield District. The owner established the community for the factory's free tradesmen and enslaved workers, but other craftsmen whose trades supported the wares' manufacture and transportation lived in the village. In 1826 Robert Mills estimated that the village, which he called Landrumsville, had "sixteen or seventeen houses, and as many families." By 1832 the village may have grown to 150 persons.

Pottersville workers produced strong, utilitarian stoneware vessels with a unique alkaline glaze that Landrum is thought to have introduced to South Carolina. The factory sold the vessels to local plantations, which needed large containers for food and household supplies. The ready market and local clays encouraged the growth of other stoneware factories in Edgefield District. Landrum family members and other investors established pottery factories on Turkey Creek near Pottersville and in the Horse Creek Valley. Perhaps the most recognized craftsman from Pottersville is the slave potter named Dave, whose ceramic work is recognized for its enormous size and strength and for the verses he wrote on the vessels.

In 1828 Landrum sold the factory and his property in the village. Different investors continued operations there, but by the time the local stoneware industry peaked in 1850, Pottersville had declined, and many tradesmen moved on to other factories. MARY SHERRER

Baldwin, Cinda K. *Great and Noble Jar: Traditional Stoneware of South Carolina.* Athens: University of Georgia Press, 1993.

Holcombe, Joe L., and Fred E. Holcombe. "South Carolina Potters and Their Wares: The Landrums of Pottersville." *South Carolina Antiquities* 18, nos. 1–2 (1986): 47–62.

Poultry. The humble chicken has risen from the obscurity of the barnyard to the summit of South Carolina agriculture. In the late twentieth century the poultry industry (broilers, turkeys, and eggs) became the state's leading agribusiness, contributing $500 million annually to the state's economy. But before chickens and turkeys were cash crops, they were part of the culture. Native Americans raised turkeys long before Europeans and Africans came to South Carolina, and chickens arrived with the first settlers. Soon chickens were the most common domestic animal in South Carolina, and virtually every farm family raised poultry for its own table and sold surplus eggs and fowl to townsfolk. This pattern of husbandry persisted nearly three centuries. Predictably, poultry earned an honored place in the region's cuisine: fried chicken, chicken and dumplings, chicken bog, and pilau became celebrated staples of the Carolina diet.

Poultry evolved from a subsistence activity to a business in the 1930s. Farmers fleeing boll-weevil-infested cotton fields experimented with poultry as a cash crop. Production of broilers (chickens ten to twelve weeks of age at processing) rose from a mere 300,000 head in 1934 to 14 million by 1952 and to 48 million by the 1980s. The South Carolina poultry industry followed the pattern developed in Georgia by J. D. Jewell in the 1940s. Farmers entered partnerships with poultry processors, providing land, buildings, and equipment; processors furnished baby chicks, feed, vaccines, and veterinary services. Farmers fed and cared for the chicks until market weight was achieved. Processors collected the fowl and paid farmers based on weight gain. Processors then slaughtered, dressed, packaged, and delivered birds to market. Farmers typically raised four broods each per year.

The poultry industry experienced phenomenal growth in the 1980s and 1990s. In the ten-year period from 1982 to 1992, receipts from chickens and turkeys tripled, rising to $206 million. In the 1990s poultry sales tripled again, topping $620 million and accounting for thirty-seven percent of the state's agribusiness income. Observers credit automation and mass production for keeping consumer prices low, making poultry a bargain. Cultural influences were also factors. Health-conscience consumers made chicken and turkey centerpieces of the trendy low-fat cuisine that swept the country in the 1990s. In 2001 broilers, turkeys, and eggs ranked first, fifth, and seventh, respectively, of South Carolina's top-ten commodities.

The state's largest poultry processors in the mid-1990s were Columbia Farms, headquartered in Lexington County; Prestage Farms, with plants in Kershaw and Newberry; and Perdue Farms, Dillon County's largest employer. Sumter County is home to Manchester Farms, the nation's largest producer of farm-raised quail. Poultry has affected the landscape as well. The high-tech chicken house has replaced cotton sheds and tobacco barns on many South Carolina farms. ELDRED E. PRINCE, JR.

Gray, Lewis C. *History of Agriculture in the Southern United States to 1860.* 2 vols. Washington, D.C.: Carnegie Institute, 1933.

Kirby, Jack Temple. *Rural Worlds Lost: The American South, 1920–1960.* Baton Rouge: Louisiana State University Press, 1987.

Kovacik, Charles F., and John J. Winberry. *South Carolina: The Making of a Landscape.* 1987. Columbia: University of South Carolina Press, 1989.

Rogers, Aida. "Poultry in Motion." *Sandlapper* 6 (spring 1995): 20–24.

Powder Magazine (Charleston). In 1703 the colonial assembly authorized the construction of a storehouse for gunpowder as part of the defenses of Charleston. The Powder Magazine was built on the northern edge of the walled city by 1713. Currently located at 21 Cumberland Street, it is considered to be the oldest surviving secular building in the Carolinas. The one-story brick structure has a pyramidal tile roof with cross gables and a single room measuring approximately twenty-seven feet square. The walls are thirty-six inches thick. Proprietary governor Nathaniel Johnson most likely oversaw its construction. Although replaced by a new magazine in 1748, it continued to be used for powder storage through the Revolutionary War. After 1820 the building reverted to the Izard and Manigault families, the owners of the property before 1703, who used it variously as a livery stable, a printing shop, and a wine cellar. The National Society of the Colonial Dames in South Carolina purchased the building in 1902 to save it from demolition and turned it into a museum. In 1993 Historic Charleston Foundation obtained a long-term lease from the Colonial Dames, restored the building to its mid-nineteenth-century appearance, and reopened it as a museum of early Charleston history. The Powder Magazine was designated a National Historic Landmark by the U.S. Department of the Interior in 1989. DANIEL J. VIVIAN

Poston, Jonathan H. *The Buildings of Charleston: A Guide to the City's Architecture.* Columbia: University of South Carolina Press, 1997.

Weyeneth, Robert R. *Historic Preservation for a Living City: Historic Charleston Foundation, 1947–1997.* Columbia: University of South Carolina Press, 2000.

Praise houses. "Praise houses" (sometimes called "prayer houses") functioned on antebellum South Carolina plantations as both the epitome of slave culture and symbols of resistance to slaveholders' oppressive version of Christianity. Generally simple, clapboard structures built by the slaves themselves, praise houses were erected with the knowledge, if not always the complete approval, of the master class. Meetings in the praise house usually occurred on week nights rather than on Sunday mornings. Pious masters preferred that their slaves be in attendance at white-dominated churches where sermons buttressed the slave system with carefully chosen scriptural texts.

The simple architectural aesthetic of the praise house mirrored the nonliturgical style of slave religion. Enslaved Christians favored empty space over altars, kneelers, pulpits, and sometimes even chairs and pews. The resulting sparseness provided the slaves more room for "ring shouts" during often all-night sessions of prayer and song. Frederick Law Olmsted recalled visiting one South Carolina rice plantation where the master had attempted to provide the plantation praise house with "seats having a back-rail," only to be informed by the slaves that this would not "leave them room enough to pray."

Weddings, funerals, and other activities centered on the praise house. Following emancipation, some of these structures continued to serve the freedmen, providing them with a place for schools and public meetings.

The very existence of praise houses in South Carolina indicates that masters failed in their attempt to make the plantation a completely closed system. Even under the degrading conditions of slavery, religious life and practice strengthened and sustained the slave community. The building of the praise houses reveals the struggle of the enslaved to maintain their humanity in the midst of an inhuman system. W. SCOTT POOLE

Carawan, Guy, and Candie Carawan. *Ain't You Got a Right to the Tree of Life? The People of Johns Island, South Carolina—Their Faces, Their Words, and Their Songs.* Rev. ed. Athens: University of Georgia Press, 1989.

Cooper, Nancy Ashmore. "Where Everybody Is Somebody: African American Churches in South Carolina." In *Religion in South Carolina,* edited by Charles H. Lippy. Columbia: University of South Carolina Press, 1993.

Pratt, Nathaniel Alpheus (1834–1906). Chemist, engineer, inventor. Pratt was born in Darien, Georgia, on January 25, 1834, the third of ten children of the Reverend Nathaniel Alpheus Pratt and Catherine Barrington King. He attended school at Roswell, Georgia; graduated from Oglethorpe University with an A.M. degree in 1852; and earned his M.D. from Savannah Medical College in 1856. On November 14, 1855, Pratt married Julia Eliza Stubbs at Milledgeville, Georgia. The couple had seven children. Pratt did not practice medicine but followed up with scientific studies at Harvard University. From 1858 to 1861 he was professor of chemistry at Savannah Medical College, followed by a brief tenure as a professor of chemistry and geology at Oglethorpe University.

At the outbreak of the Civil War, Pratt organized the "Jordan Grays" and was mustered into service of the state of Georgia in November 1861. Within a few months Pratt's scientific abilities were recognized, and he was named assistant chief of the Confederate States Nitre and Mining Bureau at Augusta, Georgia. He was responsible for securing domestic supplies of raw materials for munitions (nitre being an essential component of gunpowder manufacturing). At the end of the war, Pratt was acting chief of the Nitrate Bureau, although he had earlier been bureau chemist and superintendent in charge of nitre service for the Second Division (Georgia, Alabama, and South Carolina).

Pratt moved to Charleston at the end of the war with plans to construct a chemical plant to manufacture fertilizers. In his earlier search for materials to manufacture gunpowder, Pratt realized that the rocky nodules he had discovered around Charleston Neck were phosphate of lime. After completing an analysis of this rock from the Ashley River basin and determining that it was the highest grade and most extensive, he organized the Charleston Mining and Manufacturing Company in October 1867, backed by George T. Lewis of Philadelphia. In 1868 Pratt organized the Sulphuric Acid and Super-Phosphate Company (also known as the Etiwan Phosphate Company), with C. C. Memminger as president. That same year Pratt published a pamphlet, *Ashley River Phosphates History of the Marls of South Carolina and of the Discovery and Development of Native Bone Phosphates of the Charleston Basin.*

His reputation as a scientist having been established, in 1870 Pratt left Charleston to become professor of applied science at Washington and Lee University in Virginia, a position he held until 1876. In 1872 Pratt received three patents for improvements in treating phosphate of lime, phosphatic rocks, and the manufacture of fertilizers with lime.

Pratt went on to discover halloysites and bauxite in Georgia and Alabama and the lithia waters near Austell, Georgia. He was also active in the organization of several fertilizer and mining companies. He served as Georgia's state chemist (1879–1880) and geologist for the Georgia Department of Agriculture (1885–1889) and then went on to locate and develop phosphate deposits in Florida. On October 31, 1906, Pratt was killed in a train accident at Decatur, Georgia. MARY S. MILLER

Donnelly, Ralph W. "Scientists of the Confederate Nitre and Mining Bureau." *Civil War History* 2 (December 1956): 69–92.

Northen, William Jonathan. *Men of Mark in Georgia.* 6 vols. Atlanta: A. B. Caldwell, 1907–1912.

Prehistoric South Carolina. Sometime during the last Ice Age human groups made their way to what became South Carolina. Current debate about the continent of origin of these immigrants suggests Asia, Africa, and Europe. Recent evidence, although scant, has suggested the possibility of humans in South Carolina as early as 18,000 years ago, but a time frame beginning by about 13,000 years ago is widely accepted by archaeologists. At that time the climate of South Carolina was similar to that of upstate New York today. With well-fashioned, stone-tipped spears, the people, dubbed Paleo-Indians, hunted now-extinct animals such as woolly mammoths, giant sloths, mastodons, giant land tortoises, and saber-toothed tigers as well as elk, deer, and other smaller game. Preservation of the skeletons of these extinct animals in association with artifacts has yet to be discovered in South Carolina, and contexts for such preservation may be limited to Carolina bays or the bottom of the ocean. One rib bone discovered out of context on Edisto Island exhibits what appear to be intentional cut marks. Due to acidic soils, moist climate, and the ravages of time, stone tools are the only artifacts from this time, and interpretations are largely related to the manufacture, use, and discard behavior of such tools.

Only a handful of Paleo-Indian spear points have been excavated from in situ (undisturbed) deposits by professional archaeologists in

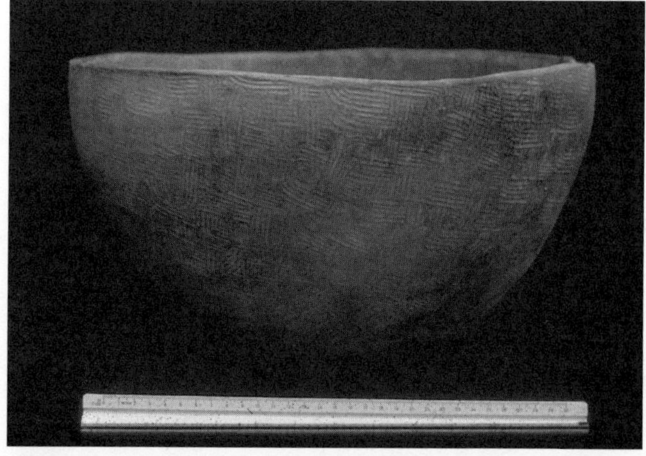

Mississippian pottery from the Mulberry archaeological site (Cofitachiqui). Photograph by Chris Judge. Courtesy, South Carolina Department of Natural Resources

Allendale, Aiken, Darlington, and Lexington Counties. Lancelet shaped, fluted and unfluted spearheads similar to ones found across the United States have been found mostly by the public and have been recorded by the archaeologist Tommy Charles of the University of South Carolina. The spear points are found in a variety of locations, but places where large streams entered major rivers appear to have been favored by Paleo-Indians. These spear points have been made of a variety of local and nonlocal stone materials such as chert, quartz, rhyolite, and sandstone. Other common Paleo-Indian stone tools include scrapers, knives, and bola stones. Toward the end of the Paleo-Indian period during the Dalton phase, chipped stone axes appear to suggest large woodworking activities. The lack of preservation of organic items such as bone, wood, leather, cordage, and food remains hinders an exact interpretation of lifeways. Highly mobile, kin-based groups of hunter/gatherers foraging along the margins of large rivers are theorized.

At the end of the Ice Age about ten thousand years ago, climatic, faunal, and landscape changes affected societies, as evidenced by significant changes in weaponry. The period between ten thousand and eight thousand years ago is known as the Early Archaic period. During this time, the fluted point gave way to side-notched and corner-notched forms, and a spear-throwing device known as the atlatl was introduced to facilitate hunting smaller, faster game such as white-tailed deer. A seasonal movement strategy along the state's major river systems is hypothesized from excavations along the Savannah River. This scheme began at the coast in spring to take advantage of earlier plant growth as well as trips made to stone quarries in the lower coastal plain to replenish tool kits, followed by summer in the upper coastal plain. Groups spent fall in the Piedmont, taking advantage of mast foods (nuts), persimmons, and deer and bear that reached maximum weight due to persimmon and mast-food consumption. Mast foods may have been gathered and stored in anticipation of winter shortages and larger group sizes. Winter was spent at the fall line, the divide between the coastal plain and the Piedmont, aggregating with similar groups to increase the size of the gene pool for potential mates, schedule movements, and hold ceremonies. Positioning settlement on the fall line during winter allowed exploitation of resources in coastal plain and Piedmont habitats at times of limited or marginal resource availability.

Starting about eight thousand years ago and continuing for three thousand years or so, human groups appear to have experienced a population explosion and also began to occupy habitats away from the major rivers. Up until this period, known as the Middle Archaic, stone tools were well made and resharpened for extended use. Expediently made stemmed spear points replaced notched forms at this time, and careful curation and resharpening of tools to extend their use life went by the wayside. Mobility was more than likely restricted by the establishment of territories and boundaries as populations became dispersed across the landscape. A worldwide increase in temperature about six thousand years ago likely also affected the lifestyle of prehistoric people.

A period from five thousand to three thousand years ago is called the Late Archaic by archaeologists and is known for important innovations, including tribal societies, clay pottery vessels, shell rings, and soapstone disks and vessels. Soapstone disks have been interpreted as cooking stones, which were heated and dropped into water to cook food or extract oil from nuts or used as charcoal briquettes are used in modern times. Polished stone artifacts such as winged atlatl weights, often referred to as "bannerstones," and three-quarter grooved axes are found in artifact assemblages from this time period.

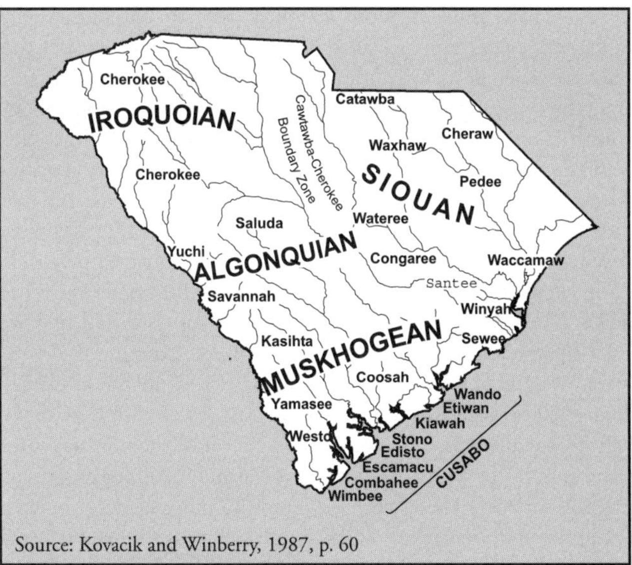

Source: Kovacik and Winberry, 1987, p. 60

Indian nations at the time of European contact

Humans again focused their settlement along rivers as well as along the Atlantic coast, which during this time was about twelve feet below its modern position. The earliest house in South Carolina was discovered from this period at a site on Hilton Head Island. The structure is D-shaped, similar to others in Georgia and Florida. Fiber and sand tempered clay pots made their appearance and indicate a semi-sedentary settlement perhaps by season. These pots were molded or coiled with forms that included conical jars and semi-hemispherical bowls. Surfaces of clay vessels were left plain or decorated with various types of punctuations, including periwinkle shells at the coast. Shell middens (garbage piles made predominantly of shellfish remains but also containing other rubbish) accumulated around sites, giving further credence to extended-stay settlement. The middens were also used as architectural materials to construct fifteen rather impressive shell ring complexes along the outer coastal plain. Whether these were habitation sites, ceremonial sites, dance rings, or signs of conspicuous consumption has yet to be resolved. However, these sites remain important ecological as well as cultural time capsules due to the enhanced preservation afforded by the calcium in shell. Plant remains and animal bones, including carved bone pins and carved antler, have been recovered.

By three thousand years ago, at the beginning of the Woodland period, pottery began to spread and be made into different forms tempered with a variety of materials, including sand, crushed stone, crushed pottery fragments known as grog, and pulverized sandstone. Vessel surfaces were decorated with an ever-increasing number of techniques, including check stamped designs carved into a wooden paddle and applied to the outer surface of vessels in a process to meld together coils. Other effects include cord-marked, fabric-impressed, finger-pinched, and other decorations.

The bow and the arrow were introduced and the first small triangular-shaped points made their appearance in the archaeological record. Evidence of horticultural activities was preserved at the Pumpkin site in the Piedmont region, where goosefoot and maygrass seeds—oily, starchy grains—point toward human manipulation of natural species. Polished stone gorgets, drilled for suspension and often notched along the edges, suggest a nonutilitarian personal adornment function. The gorgets also might have been wrist protectors for archers, or they might have been fitted with cordage and then twirled to make noises.

The final period of South Carolina prior to European exploration and colonization is called Mississippian, due to the fact that the earliest manifestation of this culture appears in the midcontinent along the Mississippi River. The period is defined by temple mound construction, full-scale floodplain agriculture, fortified villages, and complex chiefdom-level societies. Temple mound sites are generally found along rivers that drain from the mountains to the sea. The mounds were built in stages, and the house of the chief and often temples were erected on the summits of these truncated pyramids. Early explorers noted that when a chief died, his home was burnt down, a new layer of earth was added to the mound, and the new chief's home was built on top of the new layer. Extensive trade networks were established for status items such as marine shell and copper. These materials were fashioned into jewelry worn by members of the upper class. Nonmound sites are also common across the state, as noted by the presence of carved, paddle-stamped designs on exterior surfaces. These were fashioned by the societies that were encountered by Spanish explorers in the early to mid–sixteenth century, which marked the beginning of the end for the progression of native culture.

With the arrival of the Spanish, French, and English during the sixteenth and seventeenth centuries, there followed the great destruction of native society through the introduction of European disease and the devastating effects of slavery, abuse by traders, and warfare. Many aspects of Indian culture survive in modern culture, such as grits, and tribal names have been given to rivers and roads. Catawba potters still fire hand-built pottery in open fires, and some ten thousand South Carolinians claimed native ancestry in the 2000 census. Thirteen tribal groups were recently represented on an ad hoc committee on Native American affairs. CHRISTOPHER JUDGE

Anderson, David G., Kenneth E. Sassaman, and Christopher Judge, eds. *Paleoindian and Early Archaic Period Research in the Lower Southeast: A South Carolina Perspective.* Columbia: Council of South Carolina Professional Archaeologists, 1992.

Bense, Judith A. *Archaeology of the Southeastern United States: Paleoindian to World War I.* San Diego: Academic Press, 1994.

Goodyear, Albert C., III, and Glen T. Hanson, eds. *Studies in South Carolina Archaeology: Essays in Honor of Robert L. Stephenson.* Columbia: Institute of Archaeology and Anthropology, University of South Carolina, 1989.

South Carolina Antiquities 25, nos. 1–2, special anniversary issue (1993).

Presbyterian Church in America. The Presbyterian Church in America (PCA) organized in 1973 when 215 churches withdrew from the Southern Presbyterian Church (Presbyterian Church, U.S. [PCUS]), charging that Southern Presbyterians "denied the deity of Jesus Christ and the inerrancy and authority of Scripture." In addition, they rejected the position of the PCUS that allowed women to be ordained as elders and ministers.

While calling itself at first the National Presbyterian Church, the new denomination was clearly a movement within the states of the old Confederacy. Its leaders were vigorous opponents of the approaching union between Northern Presbyterians and Southern Presbyterians. In announcing its birth, the PCA deliberately adopted the language and format of an address written by James Henley Thornwell in 1861 at the formation of the Presbyterian Church in the Confederate States of America. The name of the denomination was changed in 1974 to the Presbyterian Church in America.

While large and historic congregations joined the PCA in other southern states, none did in South Carolina. No congregation in the lowcountry (Charleston Presbytery) joined. Nevertheless, during the coming years the PCA had substantial growth throughout the state fueled by a vigorous program of evangelism and by theological and social conservatism. The social web that connected South Carolina Presbyterians for generations was not broken by the formation of the PCA; members of the PCA have continued to support historic Presbyterian institutions in the state such as Presbyterian College and the Presbyterian retirement homes. ERSKINE CLARKE

Clarke, Erskine. *Our Southern Zion: A History of Calvinism in the South Carolina Low Country, 1690–1990.* Tuscaloosa: University of Alabama Press, 1996.

Smith, Frank Joseph. *The History of the Presbyterian Church in America.* 2d. ed. Lawrenceville, Ga.: Presbyterian Scholars Press, 1999.

Thompson, Ernest Trice. *Presbyterians in the South.* 3 vols. Richmond, Va.: John Knox, 1963–1973.

Presbyterian College. A liberal arts college affiliated with the Presbyterian Church (USA) and located in Clinton, Presbyterian College was founded in 1880 by William Plumer Jacobs, minister of the town's First Presbyterian Church. Jacobs established the college as the means of furthering the education of youth in Thornwell Orphanage, which he had begun in Clinton five years earlier.

Originally known as Clinton College, the institution became the Presbyterian College of South Carolina in 1890, when oversight of the college was increased to include all presbyteries in the Synod of South Carolina. In 1904 a new charter replaced local control with a board of trustees largely elected by the state presbyteries. This governing structure ended a decade of uncertainty about the institution's future and cemented the college's relationship with the church. This relationship grew stronger in 1928 when Presbyterians in the Synod of Georgia joined in support of the institution, now named Presbyterian College.

Growth marked the tenures of Presidents William G. Neville (1904–1907) and Davison M. Douglas (1911–1926). From a student body of 58 and six faculty members in 1904, the college expanded to 276 students and a faculty of twenty. In 1923 the college gained full accreditation by the Southern Association of Colleges and Secondary Schools. Over the next twenty years, however, Presbyterian College faced serious challenges. The decline in South Carolina's agricultural economy in the 1920s and the national economic depression that followed diminished college support and led to operating deficits and increased financial liabilities. In 1935 the college lost full accreditation due to its precarious financial position. Presbyterian College survived through the careful management of President John McSween (1928–1935) and the promotional efforts of President William P. Jacobs II (1935–1945), a grandson of the college's founder.

The years following World War II brought renewed growth. Now debt free, Presbyterian College regained full accreditation in 1949, and enrollment approached five hundred. Under the presidency of Marshall Brown (1945–1963) the physical plant was expanded to accommodate larger enrollments, the endowment substantially increased, and the academic program modernized.

In 1965, during the presidency of Marc Weersing (1963–1979), Presbyterian College began admitting women as residential students. From its inception the college had welcomed women, but only as commuting students. With the addition of residential women students, enrollment increased to 850 by 1971. In the next two decades Presbyterian College solidified its position as a leading liberal arts college in the state. During the presidency of Kenneth Orr (1979–1997) careful planning, successful financial campaigns, and the inclusion of Florida Presbyterians in the governance of the institution led the college to grow to more than 1,000 students. Under President John Griffith, Presbyterian College began the new century with a strategic plan to integrate its academic program, diversify its student body, and emphasize living-learning opportunities on its campus.

In the early twenty-first century, Presbyterian College maintained its close connection to the Presbyterian Church. The institution prided itself on providing a liberal arts education "within a community of faith, learning, and intellectual freedom." Presbyterian College's community spirit, seen in the personal relationships among students and faculty, was exemplified in the school's honor code and its dedication to service. PETER H. HOBBIE

Hammet, Ben Hay. *The Spirit of PC: A Centennial History of Presbyterian College.* Clinton, S.C.: Jacobs, 1982.

Presbyterians. Presbyterianism is a movement within Christianity that traces its distinctive character to the Swiss Reformation of the sixteenth century and in particular to the theological and social thought of John Calvin. Presbyterianism in South Carolina represents a complex interaction of this distinct religious tradition with the social and cultural lives of the state over a three-hundred-year period.

At the heart of Presbyterian theology and piety is an insistence that in all of life one is confronted by the God of Israel, the high and holy One, who is revealed most clearly and fully, most graciously and compassionately, in Jesus Christ. The doctrine of predestination, often associated with Presbyterianism, is an attempt to acknowledge that salvation is a gift of this gracious, sovereign God's own holy, just, and loving purposes.

A theological emphasis on the sovereignty of a gracious God has encouraged among Presbyterians an ethic that emphasizes the importance of ordinary work that is for the common good of the community and a sense of vocation that is a calling to such work. Presbyterians have emphasized that faithful living involves frugality, simplicity, delay of gratification, and control of impulses. The theology and ethic of Presbyterians have frequently created a distinct personality type marked by a consciousness of personal worth, a vocation to reform society, and a sense of undeserved privilege and substantial responsibility. Presbyterianism has traditionally honored the life of the mind and has insisted that only a life of love exceeds it as a means of praise to God.

Presbyterians were among the Calvinists who, beginning in the late seventeenth century, came to South Carolina. By the time of the Revolutionary War, the Presbyterian Church was the largest denomination in the colony. In the lowcountry Presbyterianism was closely linked with the Congregationalism of New England. In Charleston, Presbyterians at first, together with many Huguenots, worshiped with Congregationalists at the White Meeting House. In 1731 Scottish Presbyterians left the Meeting House to form the First (Scots) Presbyterian Church in Charleston. The islands south of Charleston—James, Johns, Wadmalaw, and Edisto—had strong Presbyterian congregations from the early colonial period with growing numbers of African American members.

Presbyterianism came to the upcountry primarily by way of Philadelphia and the Great Wagon Road. Scots-Irish immigrants established Presbyterian churches at Waxhaw in Lancaster, at Nazareth on the Tyger River, at Old Greenville at Donalds, at Upper Long Cane in Abbeville County, and at a host of other places. Associate Reformed Presbyterians settled around Due West. Presbyterian congregations throughout the state, except for the Scots in Charleston, were deeply identified with the patriot cause during the Revolution.

Presbyterianism after the Revolution—while losing its numerical leadership to Methodist and Baptist churches—grew rapidly and entered a period of significant social and intellectual strength. Most notable was the strength of the Presbyterian churches in the lowcountry, where, with the Congregationalists, they remained the largest religious community among the whites. In Columbia a circle of Presbyterian intellectuals—including James H. Thornwell, Benjamin Morgan Palmer, George Howe, Joseph LeConte, and Louisa Cheves McCord—gained national influence.

Following the Civil War, most Congregational churches became Presbyterian. Strong African American congregations, with roots going back to the colonial period, emerged from white-dominated churches in the lowcountry. They established an extensive school system, including four boarding schools, which nurtured a tight-knit African American community that was deeply Presbyterian in its ethos and ethic.

From 1865 to 1945 Presbyterianism in South Carolina was marked by significant social cohesion and theological conservatism. Institutions of the church—especially Presbyterian College and Columbia Theological Seminary—played a part in nurturing this cohesion, but it was rooted in a dynamic interaction between religious traditions and the social and cultural character of the state, especially the state's poverty and intensified provincialism.

An influx of people into the state after 1945 changed the character of Presbyterianism as it once again grew rapidly and developed internal tensions. No longer composed primarily of "old Presbyterian families," Presbyterianism experienced a split in 1973 with the formation of the Presbyterian Church in America. This new denomination, lodged primarily in the states of the old Confederacy, identified closely with the most conservative theological traditions of Presbyterianism and long-established patterns of social life in the state. A union in 1983 of the "Northern" United Presbyterian Church and the "Southern" Presbyterian Church in the U.S. brought together into the Presbyterian Church (USA) the great majority of Presbyterians in the state. ERSKINE CLARKE

Clarke, Erskine. *Our Southern Zion: A History of Calvinism in the South Carolina Low Country, 1690–1990.* Tuscaloosa: University of Alabama Press, 1996.

Howe, George. *History of the Presbyterian Church in South Carolina.* 2 vols. Columbia, S.C.: Duffie and Chapman, 1870–1883.

Thompson, Ernest Trice. *Presbyterians in the South.* 3 vols. Richmond, Va.: John Knox, 1963–1973.

Preservation Society of Charleston. Founded in 1920, the Preservation Society of Charleston is the oldest community-based historic preservation organization in the United States. Originally called the Society for the Preservation of Old Dwellings, it was founded by Susan Pringle Frost and a small group of individuals who were concerned about the future of the Joseph Manigault House, a ca. 1802 dwelling that was eventually restored. Frost, an active suffragette and thought to be the first woman realtor in Charleston, sought to create an organization dedicated to the preservation of historic dwellings. In 1931 the society was instrumental in persuading the Charleston City Council to pass the nation's first historic district zoning law, which established a board of architectural review and designated a 138-acre "Old and Historic District." The district has since been expanded to include more than 4,800 historic structures.

The adoption of the society's current name in 1957 reflected the organization's expanded mission to protect not only dwellings but all sites and structures of historic significance or aesthetic value. The society has sought to fulfill its mission through programs that focus on preservation education, advocacy, and planning. One such effort is the organization's Carolopolis Award program, begun in 1953 to recognize outstanding achievement in exterior preservation, exterior restoration, exterior rehabilitation, and new construction in the city. As of 2003 the Preservation Society of Charleston had given more than twelve hundred Carolopolis plaques. In 1956 the society began publishing its award-winning quarterly newsletter, *Preservation Progress,* to better inform its members of historic preservation issues. In the 1970s it was one of the first organizations in South Carolina to accept exterior and interior preservation easements. The society's preservation easement program offers owners of historic properties an effective way to protect the architectural integrity of their historic properties and receive state and federal tax deductions.

As of 2002 the society had more than two thousand members from South Carolina and thirty-five other states who are concerned about the future of Charleston's historic district. The Preservation Society of Charleston is a volunteer organization administered by a volunteer board and seven paid staff members. As an advocacy organization, the society has fought to encourage developers and private homeowners to use appropriate techniques to preserve historic buildings and to ensure that new construction is compatible with and respectful of the city's existing historic architecture. It has also worked closely with Charleston's historic neighborhood associations to support the concerns of citizens who seek to maintain a livable historic city. In recognition of its efforts, the American Institute of Architects presented the Preservation Society of Charleston with its 1996 Institute Honor Award, recognizing that by "being as much a part of Charleston, South Carolina history as protector of it, this Society has wrought a standard of commitment to community befitting the beauty and rich legacy of the city it has served for over 75 years." ROBERT GURLEY

Bland, Sidney R. *Preserving Charleston's Past, Shaping Its Future: The Life and Times of Susan Pringle Frost.* 2d ed. Columbia: University of South Carolina Press, 1999.

Preston, William Campbell (1794–1860). U.S. senator. William C. Preston was born on December 27, 1794, in Philadelphia, Pennsylvania, where his father, Francis Smith Preston, served as a member from Virginia in the U.S. House of Representatives. He was the grandson of two notable Virginia frontiersmen, William Preston and William Campbell, and a great-nephew of Patrick Henry. At fourteen, Preston entered Washington College in Lexington, Virginia, but poor health forced him to leave the school. He was later sent by his family to South Carolina College in Columbia, where he graduated in 1812.

Preston returned to Virginia and studied law in Richmond under William Wirt. However, illness again plagued Preston, and he traveled for his health. After traveling through several states, in 1817 he went to the university in Edinburgh, Scotland, where he continued his legal education, matriculating on November 3, 1818. While at Edinburgh, he became close friends with Hugh Swinton Legaré of South Carolina and the author Washington Irving. Preston returned to Virginia in 1820 to continue his law practice in Abingdon and was appointed a justice of Washington County in 1821. In 1822 he traveled to Missouri and married Maria Eliza Coalter, whose father lived in Columbia, South Carolina. Preston's first wife died in 1829, and he married Louise Penelope Davis of Columbia in 1831. Preston and his first wife had two children; he and his second wife had one.

In 1824 Preston moved from Virginia to Columbia and entered a law partnership with William Harper, who had married Preston's sister-in-law. Preston was elected to the South Carolina House of Representatives in 1828 and served until 1833, representing Richland District. He championed free trade, states' rights, and nullification but disagreed with more radical nullifiers on the issue of the test oath. In 1833 Preston was elected by the South Carolina legislature to fill the U.S. Senate seat of Stephen D. Miller, who had resigned. Preston was reelected in 1837.

In the Senate, he was considered by many to be an eloquent orator. Skilled in delivering a prepared text, he was also an able extemporaneous speaker. Preston introduced a resolution for the annexation of Texas right after Texas had won its independence from Mexico in 1836. He supported the "Gag Rule" and opposed the sending of abolition literature through the U.S. mail. He was an active critic of President Andrew Jackson, voting to censure Jackson in 1834. His opposition to Jackson led him into the emerging Whig Party.

Nor was Preston a supporter of Martin Van Buren when the latter became president in 1837. Unlike his colleague John C. Calhoun, Preston opposed Van Buren's subtreasury proposal. His failure to support Van Buren's proposal widened the political breach that already existed between Preston and Calhoun. Between 1837 and 1840 Preston had the political support of many South Carolinians. However, Calhoun exerted considerable political pressure against Preston and his supporters. By 1840 Preston and the fledgling South Carolina Whig Party crumbled under the Democratic attack led by Calhoun, resulting in a one-party state. In 1842 the South Carolina legislature instructed him to vote for the subtreasury. Preston refused, angering the legislature and Calhoun. Politically isolated, he resigned instead. Despite his political defeat, Preston remained personally popular with many in South Carolina. When he returned home, the Democratic-turned-Whig was given a public dinner that was attended mostly by Democrats.

Returning to Columbia to resume his law practice, Preston was appointed president and professor of belles lettres of South Carolina College in 1845 and assumed his post on January 1, 1846. Preston was an able scholar and a successful college administrator. He undertook efforts to improve the college, including the creation of a board of visitors, and advocated university status for the school. Admired and respected by the students, Preston had to retire from the position in 1851 after he suffered a stroke. He remained a trustee of South Carolina College until he resigned on November 29, 1857. Preston founded the Columbia Lyceum, endowing it with his three-thousand-volume library. He died in Columbia on May 22, 1860, and was buried in the Trinity Episcopal Churchyard. TRENTON HIZER

Lander, Ernest M., Jr. "The Calhoun-Preston Feud, 1836–1842." *South Carolina Historical Magazine* 59 (January 1958): 24–37.

Preston, William Campbell. *The Reminiscences of William C. Preston.* Chapel Hill: University of North Carolina Press, 1933.

Rion, James H. *William C. Preston, LL.D., as President, and Belles-Lettres Professor, of South Carolina College: An Address Delivered before the Class of 1850, at Their Second Quinquennial Meeting, December, 1860.* Columbia, S.C.: R. W. Gibbes, 1861.

Primitive Baptists. Primitive Baptists comprised one early nineteenth-century form of the "antimission" movement protesting the development of Baptist organizations in the South. Emanating from the Kehukee Association in North Carolina, this particular brand of protest in South Carolina was found most commonly in the upcountry. These Primitive or Old School Baptist churches, and

Huspah Primitive Baptist Church, Hampton. Photograph by Walker Evans for the Farm Security Administration. Courtesy, South Caroliniana Library, University of South Carolina

the later loosely organized denomination by the same name, were strongly Calvinistic, especially emphasizing predestination. However, they would argue that their doctrine was derived from the Bible and the "primitive" church, not Calvin. This belief, along with a general dislike for institutional structures that were assumed to drain local congregations of their money and their autonomy, led Primitive Baptists to "abandon all creature power" and reject missionary societies, Sunday schools, seminaries, and even a paid clergy. Distinctive practices then and in the early twenty-first century often included unaccompanied singing in a style said to resemble that of New England Puritans, foot washing, segregated seating for men and women, and the rejection of both instrumental music and the collection of offerings in the context of worship. Officers of the church included elders, deacons, and ministers, who were untrained because God both calls and "qualifies" preachers. Like other Baptists, they baptized the converted by immersion, but unlike other Baptists, sinners were not exhorted to accept Christ or join the church. In the early twenty-first century the churches identified by this name, though scattered across the United States, were few and tended to be in isolated areas, most commonly in Appalachia. Most of the few congregations remaining in South Carolina were in the foothills. HELEN LEE TURNER

McBeth, H. Leon. *The Baptist Heritage.* Nashville, Tenn.: Broadman, 1987.

Piepkorn, Arthur C. "The Primitive Baptists of North America." *Baptist History and Heritage* 7 (January 1972): 33–51.

Primus Plot (May–June 1720). The Primus Plot was South Carolina's first alleged slave conspiracy. Word of this conspiracy surfaced while the colony's atmosphere was tense. A Waccamaw Indian attack had recently been repelled. South Carolina was suffering from economic problems. After expelling the proprietary government in 1719, the colonists were awaiting an official response from England. Anxieties were further heightened by Spanish privateer attacks against Carolina shipping and rumors that Spain would invade South Carolina and, in the process, arm the colony's slaves against its white inhabitants. All this occurred as South Carolina's enslaved black majority, spurred by labor demands for rice cultivation, had quickly grown to nearly twice the number of its white population.

The colonists first learned of this purported slave conspiracy on May 20, 1720, when a black man named Andrew addressed the South Carolina Commons House. What Andrew said is unknown. Apparently it concerned an attempt by at least fourteen slaves from the upper Ashley River to run away to St. Augustine, which was the capital of Spanish Florida. In the ensuing panic, it was said that the runaways, who were led by a slave named Primus, conspired to destroy isolated plantations, recruit more followers, and then attack Charleston. What these would-be insurgents were going to do after seizing Charleston is unknown. As the slaves fled toward Florida, and away from Charleston, the South Carolina Commons House of Assembly authorized all whites, blacks, and Native Americans to pursue them and offered a reward of £20 for each slave taken—dead or alive. Then, in the midst of this purported slave uprising, the Commons House adjourned for two weeks.

By the time the assembly reconvened on June 7, the supposed plot had been suppressed. On June 9 Governor James Moore notified the Commons House that three slaves, Primus, Nero, and Robin, had been captured and were being held at Savannah Town. Moore wanted the accused rebels summarily executed. However, at the insistence of the Commons House, the slaves were taken to Charleston, where they were publicly executed, with Primus being hung alive in chains.

While existing evidence suggests that the Primus Plot was an effort by a group of slaves to reach freedom in Florida, rather than a planned rebellion, white South Carolinians regarded it as an insurrection in the making. The Commons House obviously believed that these slaves posed an immediate danger to the colony's white inhabitants. Once recaptured, the slaves were punished as if they were insurgents. Even after the accused conspirators were executed, white South Carolinians would continue to worry about slave conspiracies into the 1730s and beyond. KEVIN DAWSON

Aptheker, Herbert. *Negro Slave Revolts in the United States, 1526–1850.* Rev. ed. New York: International, 1974.

Moore, John Alexander. "Royalizing South Carolina: The Revolution of 1719 and the Evolution of Early South Carolina Government." Ph.D. diss., University of South Carolina, 1991.

Prince Frederick's Parish. Established on April 9, 1734, Prince Frederick's Parish stretched like an elongated triangle from the Santee River northward "to the utmost bounds of the Province," encompassing all or part of modern Dillon, Marion, Florence, Horry, Georgetown, and Williamsburg Counties. Prior to 1730 European settlement north of the Santee was sparse. Still, in 1721 the assembly organized the area into Prince George Winyah Parish, and by 1734 a wooden parish church had been completed on the Black River approximately thirteen miles upstream from its mouth. By then, however, the port of Georgetown had been founded, rice cultivation had surpassed the Indian trade and naval stores in the local economy, and the fast-growing coastal population needed its own church. In 1734 the assembly divided Prince George Winyah and its inland portion became Prince Frederick's Parish, which was granted two representatives. Because the Black River Church fell within the bounds of the new parish, it became the parish church of

Prince Frederick's. A major indigo producer, the parish flourished until foreign competition and the end of British bounties forced its decline in the last decades of the eighteenth century.

A new brick parish church near Plantersville was authorized in 1857, but due to the Civil War, it was not completed until 1878. Known locally as the "Gunn Church" for a building contractor who fell to his death from its roof, the structure stood as a ruin in the early twenty-first century. Prince Frederick's Parish lost its status as an election district in 1790 and was divided into Liberty (Marion) and Williamsburg Counties. MATTHEW A. LOCKHART

Linder, Suzanne Cameron. *Anglican Churches in Colonial South Carolina: Their History and Architecture.* Charleston, S.C.: Wyrick, 2000.

Lumpkin, Robert L., and Sarah Parker Lumpkin. *Minutes of the Vestry, Prince Frederick's Parish, April 9, 1827–March 29, 1880.* N.p., n.d.

Pringle, Elizabeth W. Allston, ed. *The Register Book for the Parish Prince Frederick Winyaw.* 1916. Reprint, Easley, S.C.: Southern Historical Press, 1982.

Rogers, George C. *The History of Georgetown County, South Carolina.* Columbia: University of South Carolina Press, 1970.

Prince George Winyah Parish. Comprising portions of modern Georgetown, Horry, Marion, and Dillon Counties, Prince George Winyah Parish was established on March 10, 1721, to accommodate a wave of European settlers who had taken up residence north of the Santee River following the Yamassee War. One year earlier the inhabitants of "Winyaw," a burgeoning settlement on "Sampeet Creek," had petitioned the assembly for parish organization because they were "so far distant from the next parish church to them" that they received "no benefit from the same." A wooden parish church for Prince George was completed on the Black River in 1734, but by then rice cultivation had begun to dominate the local economy, the port of Georgetown had been founded, and the parish's center of population had shifted toward the coast. Once again many found themselves unable to "attend the publick worship . . . by reason of the great distance." The cornerstone of a new brick parish church was laid in Georgetown in 1745.

The perfection of tidal culture in the late eighteenth century transformed Georgetown and its environs into the principal rice-producing area in the United States, with African slaves approaching ninety percent of the population of Prince George Winyah by 1810. As one observer noted, "The Planters here all got rich." In 1860 free residents of the parish were among the wealthiest per capita in the nation. With the abolition of the parish system in 1865, Prince George Winyah Parish became part of Georgetown, Horry, and Marion Counties. MATTHEW A. LOCKHART

Holcomb, Brent H., ed. *Parish Registers of Prince George Winyah Church, Georgetown, South Carolina, 1815–1936.* Columbia, S.C.: SCMAR, 1996.

Linder, Suzanne Cameron. *Anglican Churches in Colonial South Carolina: Their History and Architecture.* Charleston, S.C.: Wyrick, 2000.

Lumpkin, Sarah Parker. *Heritage Passed On: History of Prince George, Winyah, Parish.* Columbia, S.C.: R. L. Bryan, 1992.

Rogers, George C. *The History of Georgetown County, South Carolina.* Columbia: University of South Carolina Press, 1970.

Prince William's Parish. On May 25, 1745, the Commons House of Assembly passed an act creating Prince William's Parish. The parish was named for William, duke of Cumberland, the son of King George II, and encompassed the mainland region between the Combahee and Coosawhatchie Rivers, located in modern Beaufort and Jasper Counties. Previously part of St. Helena's Parish, the new parish was created because the increasingly prosperous rice planters in the region found traveling to the town of Beaufort, located on Port Royal Island, to be too difficult.

The parish church was completed near William Bull's Sheldon Plantation in 1753. The original church was burned during the Revolutionary War, rebuilt, and burned again during the Civil War, with the ruins of the second church surviving into the twenty-first century. Aside from its suitability for cotton cultivation, Prince William's Parish was also the principal rice-growing region in the Beaufort area and was home to several large slaveholders. At his death in 1851, Nathaniel Heyward owned 1,800 slaves and 35,000 acres of land, with 4,400 of those acres planted in rice principally in Prince William's Parish. In 1850 Beaufort District, which included Prince William's and the surrounding parishes, had a population of 38,805. Of that total, 32,279, or eighty-three percent, were slaves.

The whites of Prince William's Parish overwhelmingly supported the nullification movement in 1832, and the region continued to be a center of secession sentiment throughout the antebellum period. The parish system was abolished with the adoption of the new state constitution in 1865, and Prince William's Parish was incorporated into Beaufort District. See plate 15. MICHAEL S. REYNOLDS

Linder, Suzanne Cameron. *Anglican Churches in Colonial South Carolina: Their History and Architecture.* Charleston, S.C.: Wyrick, 2000.

———. *Historical Atlas of the Rice Plantations of the ACE River Basin—1860.* Columbia: South Carolina Department of Archives and History, 1995.

Rowland, Lawrence S., Alexander Moore, and George C. Rogers. *The History of Beaufort County, South Carolina.* Vol. 1, *1514–1861.* Columbia: University of South Carolina Press, 1996.

Pringle, Elizabeth Waties Allston (1845–1921). Rice planter, author. Pringle was born on May 29, 1845, on Pawleys Island at her family's summer home at Canaan Seashore. Her parents were Robert Francis Withers Allston and Adele Petigru. Her father, a state legislator and governor, owned 630 slaves and more than fourteen hundred acres planted in rice or covered by timber. The Allstons' home, Chicora Wood, was by the Pee Dee River near Georgetown. A governess tutored Pringle until she was nine, when she was sent to Madame Acelie Togno's Charleston boarding school.

The Civil War disrupted Pringle's education. She sought shelter in various places. After her father died in 1864, Pringle endured economic hardships because he had mortgaged most of his possessions. She taught in a Charleston boarding school her mother established until her dower's rights to Chicora Wood were legally recognized and the Allston family members were reinstated in their home. She married her neighbor John Julius Pringle on April 26, 1870, and they lived at nearby White House. The couple's only son died as an infant. In 1876 Pringle's husband succumbed to malaria.

By 1880 Pringle was able to buy her home and fields from her husband's family, and she later acquired Chicora Wood after her mother's death in 1896. Pringle relied on her land yielding profitable rice crops to pay her mortgages and taxes. She wanted her family to regain its prestige and affluence lost during the Civil War, and she persevered to overcome obstacles in the patriarchal society. Her brother and other men questioned Pringle's ability because she lacked agricultural experience. With minimal assistance from family and friends, Pringle oversaw both farms, utilized scientific agriculture methods, and decided to plant fruits such as peaches and rent property to hunters to supplement her income. She refused to sell her land.

Desperate because rice production in the lowcountry faced decreased profits, Pringle convinced the New York *Sun* editor to buy

Elizabeth Allston Pringle in the yard at Chicora Wood. From *Chronicles of Chicora Wood* (1922). Courtesy, South Caroliniana Library, University of South Carolina

weekly articles she wrote about being a female rice-plantation owner. Under the pseudonym "Patience Pennington," Pringle's essays were printed from 1904 to 1907. In 1913 her articles were collected in a single volume, *A Woman Rice Planter.* Pringle edited her previous pieces to resemble a diary, with vignettes that describe plantation life from a sentimental, aristocratic point of view that is often patronizing and racist. She included insightful details about African American folklife, white-black relationships, and racial attitudes. As the book's narrator, Pringle subtly criticizes contemporary popular opinion that southern women should be passive.

Pringle's best-selling book eased her financial worries. By 1920 she began writing another book to tell about her childhood and how women fared during the Civil War and Reconstruction. She died on December 5, 1921, at her family home and was buried in Magnolia Cemetery. Her manuscript was published posthumously the next year. Like her first book, *Chronicles of Chicora Wood* depicts an aristocratic view; the book gives the impression that white southerners heroically endured traumatic social changes and, incorrectly, assumes that slaves enjoyed their servitude. ELIZABETH D. SCHAFER

Blythe, Anne Montague. "Elizabeth Allston Pringle's 'The Woman Rice Planter': The New York Sun Letters, 1903–1912." Ph.D. diss., University of South Carolina, 1987.

Pringle, Elizabeth Allston. *Chronicles of Chicora Wood.* New York: Scribner's, 1922.

———. *A Woman Rice Planter.* 1913. Reprint, Columbia: University of South Carolina Press, 1992.

Pringle, Robert (1702–1776). Merchant, planter, legislator, jurist. Pringle was born in Symington in the county of Edinburgh, Scotland, in 1702. He came to South Carolina in 1725 from London, where he had been a clerk in a West Indian merchant firm. He first established himself in Charleston as a factor to London and New England merchants but soon became a merchant himself. He sold a variety of imported dry goods from his shop on Tradd Street and exported domestic produce. During the 1740s Pringle briefly participated in business partnerships, but in general he preferred to conduct his trade independently. An amateur botanist, Pringle was enthusiastic about the production of Carolina indigo and supported efforts to discover new cash crops. He personally experimented with the cultivation of olives and mahogany, and he grew oranges in sufficient quantities for exportation.

Robert Pringle. Courtesy, Mrs. McColl Pringle, Charleston, S.C.

Pringle's marriage on July 18, 1734, to Jane Allen, daughter of the wealthy Charleston merchant Andrew Allen, further enhanced his social standing and increased his property holdings. The marriage produced one son, who died in infancy. By the middle of the eighteenth century, Robert Pringle became one of the most prosperous merchants in the city. He built two elegant town houses on Tradd Street, in 1741 and 1774 respectively, both of which survived into the twenty-first century.

Following Jane's death in 1746, Pringle left Charleston for his only journey back to Britain. Shortly after he departed in August 1747, a Spanish privateer captured his ship, and he was briefly imprisoned at St. Augustine, Florida. After his release, he traveled to England and Scotland, where in September 1748 the Council of Edinburgh Burgesses and Guild Bretheren awarded Pringle an honorary membership. He returned to Charleston in 1749. On April 19, 1751, Pringle married Judith Mayrant Bull, the widow of Stephen Bull, and the couple eventually had three children.

Back in Charleston, Pringle turned his energies from trade to public service. Early in his career he had served on the vestry of St. Philip's Church, and as churchwarden he oversaw the distribution of aid after the disastrous Charleston fire of 1740. He was among the commissioners who oversaw the construction of St. Michael's Church during the 1750s, and he served as its first churchwarden when it opened in 1761. More significantly, Pringle was recommended for a seat on the Royal Council in 1751, but he chose instead to serve in the Commons House of Assembly. He represented Prince William's Parish during the 1752–1754 session and then St. James Santee Parish from 1755 to 1762. Although not trained in the law, Pringle was named an assistant judge of the Court of Common Pleas and General Sessions in 1761. For several years he was the lone assistant judge serving under the unpopular chief justice Charles Shinner. During the Stamp Act crisis of 1765–1766, Pringle and three newly appointed assistant judges attempted to subvert Shinner and open the courts without stamped paper. Following this effort and Pringle's later support of the Non-Importation Association, he was removed from the bench in 1770 and retired from public life. He died in Charleston on January 13, 1776. The surviving records of his business and political activities provide a valuable example of life in colonial South Carolina. NICHOLAS MICHAEL BUTLER

Edgar, Walter B., ed. *The Letterbook of Robert Pringle.* 2 vols. Columbia: University of South Carolina Press, 1972.

———. "Robert Pringle's World." *South Carolina Historical Magazine* 76 (January 1975): 1–11.

Edgar, Walter, and N. Louise Bailey, eds. *Biographical Directory of the South Carolina House of Representatives.* Vol. 2, *The Commons House of Assembly, 1692–1775.* Columbia: University of South Carolina Press, 1977.

Pringle-Garden Family. Papers. South Carolina Historical Society, Charleston.

Prisons and penitentiaries. The first significant jail in South Carolina, a twelve-foot square designed to accommodate sixteen prisoners, was built in Charleston in 1769. Additional jails were built following the division of South Carolina into judicial districts. According to one account, "These jails were forbidding structures, reared to prevent escape and make life gloomy for their inmates." South Carolina was slow to join the national penal reform movement taking place in antebellum America, and prison confinement as punishment remained relatively rare in the state. As late as 1813 the death penalty remained the standard punishment for no fewer than 165 crimes, although this harsh sentence was seldom carried out. Fines were by far the most popular method of punishment, followed by corporal punishments such as whipping or branding. Confinement in county jails seldom exceeded thirty days, and prison terms of more than three years were extremely rare. Overcrowding in county jails was the rule, and escapes were frequent. Nor were criminals sorted by offense, and offenders ranging from petty thieves to murderers could frequently be found in the same cell.

Although calls to reform the criminal code and establish a state penitentiary were commonplace in antebellum South Carolina, the General Assembly failed to take any concrete action until after the Civil War. In September 1866 the General Assembly passed an act establishing a state penitentiary. Situated on the banks of the Columbia Canal in the capital city, the facility began accepting prisoners in April 1868. Renamed in 1965 as the Central Correctional Institution (CCI), it became the most notorious of the state's prisons. At the time of its construction, the new state penitentiary was considered revolutionary in its humanity, despite the fact that the original tiered cell block did not have a roof. Inmates slept on straw and climbed to their cells on ladders. The most infamous characteristic of the prison was a quarter-mile-long tunnel that started at the chapel and ended at the living areas. It was necessary to use this tunnel to move to any location within the prison. The inmates referred to it as "purgatory" because it was between "heaven" (the chapel) and "hell" (the living quarters). This area saw frequent outbreaks of violence, including a near riot between 200 black and white inmates in 1981. Another significant feature was the death house, which operated between 1912 and 1986. During that time 195 blacks and

Central Correctional Institute (CCI) in Columbia. Courtesy, South Carolina Department of Archives and History

48 whites were put to death in the electric chair. The original Cell Block One was still in use at the time of the prison's closure. Since the building did not meet state fire codes, inmates had to volunteer to be housed in the five-feet by eight-feet cells that were locked with large padlocks. CCI was closed in 1994 when it was replaced by the 1,468-bed, $45 million Lee Correctional Institution in Bishopville. During 127 years of operation CCI housed 80,000 inmates and had 243 executions performed within its walls.

As of 2002, the South Carolina Department of Corrections (established in 1960) operated twenty-nine prisons. Combined, they housed more than 21,000 inmates. Each facility is categorized into one of four divisions. Division I institutions are minimum security, meaning that inmates are housed in double-bunk cubicles or open-bay wards and the perimeters of the facility are not fenced. These institutions are usually for inmates who have been convicted of nonviolent offenses and who have been given relatively short sentences. There are two varieties of this type of institution—prerelease centers and prisons. Prerelease centers prepare inmates for the transition back into society through specialized programs. Inmates are usually transferred from another prison to the prerelease center no more than thirty-six months prior to their scheduled release. There are seven of these centers scattered among Aiken, Florence, Richland, York, Charleston, and Spartanburg Counties. Additionally, there are four minimum-security prisons variously located in both Richland and Spartanburg Counties.

Division II institutions are considered to be medium security. This means that most of the facilities double bunk inmates in cells, while a few use double-bunk cubicles. Usually there is a single fence around the perimeter of the institution. The seven Division II prisons are in Clarendon, Dorchester, Edgefield, Jasper, Richland, Spartanburg, and Sumter Counties. The highest security levels are Division III prisons, in which violent offenders with long sentences are housed. The inmates are single or double bunked with close supervision and limited movement. The perimeters of these facilities are double fenced and staffed with armed guards and electronic security. There are nine such institutions in the state in Allendale, Anderson, Dorchester, Lancaster, Lee, Marlboro, McCormick, and Richland Counties.

Women's facilities constitute a separate division (IV) but have the same security levels as the men's facilities. There are two maximum-security facilities for women: the Camille Griffin Graham Correctional Institution, located at the Broad River correctional complex in Columbia; and Leath Correctional Institution in Greenwood. A third facility, Goodman Correctional Institution, is minimum security and is in Columbia. In addition to state prisons, the Federal Bureau of Prisons has two facilities in the state, one in Edgefield and one in Estill. These prisons house inmates who have been convicted of federal crimes. REID C. TOTH

Allard, John. "Changing of the Guard." Columbia *State,* February 13, 1994, pp. D1, D6–D7.

Thomas, John Charles. "The Development of 'An Institution': The Establishment and First Years of the South Carolina Penitentiary, 1795–1881." Master's thesis, University of South Carolina, 1983.

Progressive Democratic Party. Aware that many white Democrats in South Carolina opposed President Franklin D. Roosevelt's reelection to a fourth term in 1944, African American activists sought to demonstrate their loyalty to the national party by mobilizing black support for the president. In January 1944 Samuel J. McDonald, Sr., of Sumter proposed the creation of a statewide network of "Fourth Term for Roosevelt Democratic Clubs." John H. McCray, editor of the Columbia *Lighthouse and Informer,* an influential black newspaper, endorsed the plan in a February editorial. Within a month a rudimentary network of clubs existed throughout South Carolina, which McCray thought foreshadowed a new black political party. On March 18 McCray ran another editorial proposing the creation of the South Carolina Negro Democratic Party. The following day the *Columbia Record,* a white newspaper, reprinted this piece and placed it on the Associated Press wire service, giving national exposure to McCray's proposal.

For much of the twentieth century, the Columbia Women's Club was one of many women's organizations that were instrumental in the passage of laws relating to child labor, education, and public health. The group is seen here hosting a reception during World War II. Courtesy, South Caroliniana Library, University of South Carolina

McCray envisioned an independent party possessing an organizational structure comparable to that of the existing Democratic Party. Consequently, the Negro Democrats' structural backbone was local clubs, organized by county, situated throughout South Carolina. Although they planned to finance their activities by raising funds in-state, donations also were sought from outside supporters. The initial independent contribution of $5 was made on March 22 by Mrs. Margaret Howe, an elderly white widow from Columbia. She later suggested that the party's name be changed to the Progressive Democrats, to underscore the goal of achieving an interracial membership. By May 1944 the organization was known formally as the Progressive Democratic Party (PDP).

The PDP convened its first state convention on May 24, 1944, at the Negro Masonic Temple in Columbia. As acting state secretary, McCray presided over 172 delegates from thirty-nine counties. When white Democrats refused to consider an integrated South Carolina delegation at the upcoming Democratic National Convention in Chicago, the PDP chose its own eighteen representatives and two alternates. They were expected to contest the seating of the rival white contingent as the state's official delegation.

Prior to the convention, national Democratic leaders attempted to dissuade the Progressive Democrats from pursuing their challenge. Progressive Democratic representatives, including McCray, held two meetings in Washington with Robert E. Hannegan, the Democratic Party's national chairman. On July 17 Hannegan assigned the PDP's challenge to a special subcommittee. Although complimentary of the Progressive Democratic spokesmen, that panel ruled that the regular white delegation legally represented South Carolina.

Several PDP delegates sought to mount a formal seating challenge. However, McCray and other leaders believed that it was imperative to demonstrate their commitment to Roosevelt's reelection by not publicly contesting the adverse ruling. Nevertheless, the Progressive Democrats had mounted the first modern, concerted attempt by a southern African American organization to win official recognition at a Democratic National Convention.

In August 1944 the Progressive Democratic State Committee resolved to run Osceola E. McKaine as the PDP candidate in the upcoming U.S. Senate race against Governor Olin D. Johnston, a noted white supremacist. Despite allegations of vote fraud, McKaine was accorded 3,214 votes. But PDP poll watchers around the state claimed that he had actually received a much larger total. Over the next fifteen years the PDP ran African American candidates for various public offices within South Carolina.

In July 1948 the Progressive Democrats sent a delegation of twenty-eight members to seek official representation at the Democratic National Convention in Philadelphia. A bitter fight with the regular white delegates before the Credentials Committee on July 13 lasted nearly five hours. Despite their best oratorical efforts, the Progressive Democrats' challenge again was thwarted. However, the Progressive Democrats remained fiercely loyal to the national Democrats, repudiating suggestions that they affiliate with Henry A. Wallace's Progressive Party. They also were among the South Carolina Democratic factions to support President Harry Truman's 1948 reelection campaign.

During the 1950s the Progressive Democrats experienced a steady erosion in strength, due in part to McCray's frequent absences from the state. By 1958 the organization had become formally known as the Progressive Democratic Caucus. McCray later claimed that the Progressive Democrats in 1960 had helped carry South Carolina for John F. Kennedy. However, within four years the Progressive Democratic organization had been disbanded. MILES S. RICHARDS

Frederickson, Kari. *The Dixiecrat Revolt and the End of the Solid South, 1932–1968.* Chapel Hill: University of North Carolina Press, 2001.

Richards, Miles S. "The Progressive Democrats in Chicago, July 1944." *South Carolina Historical Magazine* 102 (July 2001): 219–37.

Progressive movement. In the early twentieth century, South Carolina's interrelated economic and social problems defied easy solutions due to their sheer magnitude. Taken together, South Carolina's poorly educated population, its low per capita wealth, and its cotton-dependent economy left the state saddled with a small tax base. The inadequate tax base made mustering political support for programs or policies that strained South Carolina's limited financial resources an arduous task. Yet, a small portion of South Carolinians recognized the need to reverse these long-standing, economically distressing trends. Confronted with South Carolina's economic and social "backwardness," an active cohort of progressive reformers worked to move South Carolina from the bottom tier of many lists that evaluated economic well-being and satisfactory standard of living.

South Carolina progressives, like reformers throughout the nation, emerged primarily from the town-based middle class, which included lawyers, journalists, professors, educators, ministers, businessmen, doctors, civic leaders, agricultural scientists, agricultural extension agents, and others. These progressives pushed for economic and social improvement in their state from roughly 1900 through the 1920s. As a loosely knit group of individuals who shared a broad and variously articulated vision for the future of their state and region, South Carolina progressives dreamed of an economically prosperous state that could ease human suffering. Like their national counterparts, South Carolina reformers were imbued with notions linking efficiency and progress and with a belief that the appropriate expertise could remedy any of society's economic, political, and social ills. They wanted to bring order and efficiency to government and business. But implementation of the progressives' agenda for South Carolina required a more activist state government than many South Carolinians believed to be acceptable. Consequently, progressives constantly faced entrenched conservative opposition to their reform agenda.

Civic Associations were active proponents of progressive ideas and civic improvement. This park in Anderson was the result of the efforts of the local civic improvement association. Courtesy, South Caroliniana Library, University of South Carolina

Fundamentally, progressives deemed an educated population to be essential to all other reform endeavors. From grade school to college, educational improvement received attention from reformers because of South Carolina's manifest deficiencies at all levels. Progressives advocated improving the economy with commercial and industrial development. Moreover, they focused on strengthening the economy with improved agriculture by helping South Carolina diversify its agriculture, decrease its dependence on cotton, and encourage scientific agricultural methods. Most progressives advocated construction of a state network of highways, believing that improved transportation facilitated all other economic development strategies. Since additional revenue was central to any reform, revising South Carolina's tax structure loomed large on the reformers' agenda. To improve humanitarian institutions, some progressives highlighted as serious social ills South Carolina's horrendous prison conditions, its inadequate reformatories for errant youths, its labor-exploitative chain gangs, and the employment of children in the textile industry. Others crusaded for improvement in public health, better mental health facilities, county almshouses for indigent elderly people, and restrictions on child labor in industry. Like their counterparts in other southern states, some South Carolina progressives crusaded for an improved system of criminal justice and against extralegal violence, including the practice of lynching. But as southerners, South Carolina progressives remained firmly committed to segregation and white dominance. They insisted on carefully devised reform efforts to insure that proposed reforms benefited whites first and foremost.

Most of the progressives' legislative successes came after 1915, when Richard I. Manning succeeded Cole Blease, an ardent opponent of reform, as governor. Blease, who enjoyed the solid political support of mill operatives, had used his veto power to thwart middle-class reforms desired by progressives but deemed intrusive by mill operatives. During Manning's governorship, South Carolina progressives proudly included among their accomplishments state prohibition, child labor restrictions, compulsory school attendance, creation of the state tax commission, a reorganized state mental hospital, and most importantly, state aid for public schools. Yet even the reforms undertaken during Manning's administration only partially remedied the state's problems. For example, a loophole remained in prohibition that allowed each South Carolinian to obtain a "gallon-a-month" of alcohol for medicinal purposes. Child labor laws restricted employment only of children less than twelve years old (later raised to fourteen years old), and compulsory school attendance remained "optional," with few districts opting for it. In the 1920s progressives managed significant tax reform that began taxing income to ease the fiscal burden on non-income-generating property. This new revenue helped fund enormous increases in education and highway spending. Conservative opposition and a lumbering economy remained formidable obstacles for progressives well into the 1920s. The onset of the Great Depression in the 1930s finally halted a generation of reform. Given the state's limited resources, the constraints of white supremacy, and extensive conservative opposition, South Carolina progressives made respectable gains in public education, infrastructure improvement, and tax equalization, building a foundation for later generations interested in bringing South Carolina into the educational and economic mainstream. JANET G. HUDSON

Burts, Robert Milton. *Richard Irvine Manning and the Progressive Movement in South Carolina.* Columbia: University of South Carolina Press, 1974.

Carlton, David L. *Mill and Town in South Carolina, 1880–1920.* Baton Rouge: Louisiana State University Press, 1982.

Mitchell, Sandra Corley. "Conservative Reform: South Carolina's Progressive Movement, 1915–1929." Master's thesis, University of South Carolina, 1979.

Promised Land (Greenwood and Abbeville Counties; 2000 pop. 559). Located just off S.C. Highway 10 south of Greenwood, this rural African American community was created by freed slaves in the early 1870s. Before Promised Land, the 2,742-acre tract of land belonged to the estate of Samuel Marshall, a white plantation owner. Marshall's heirs sold the land to the South Carolina Land Commission in 1869 at a rate of $10 per acre. The commission divided the property into fifty lots of approximately fifty acres each and then sold them to freed African Americans. Eleven families purchased lots in Promised Land in 1870; by 1872 some forty-eight families resided in the community. The name derived from their "promise" to pay the commission for the land. The sale of the Marshall property gave blacks in the upstate a rare opportunity to acquire land, which to most symbolized the essence of freedom in the post–Civil War years. Descendents of these original purchasers occupied the land continually throughout the twentieth century and into the twenty-first century.

From its inception, residents of Promised Land exerted a significant influence over the political, economic, and social life of rural Abbeville and Greenwood Counties. During Reconstruction many of the men served as Republican Party officials. Seven Promised Land residents were delegates to a county Republican convention in 1872. Two men served on Abbeville County's first integrated jury. Many of Promised Land's residents shared family or kin ties, and few households were untouched by an overlapping network of in-laws and cousins. Churches provided the foundation for the community's leadership. Leadership within the churches was carefully controlled from each generation within the same kin groups.

World War I, the boll weevil, and the Depression stimulated migration from Promised Land. Begun as a push by landless youths, migration was an outgrowth of community dynamics, peonage agriculture, and the maturation of blacks. The trend began to reverse itself by the end of the twentieth century, as new residents moved to the community. Many residents remained, however, tied to the land and community that had provided independence for hundreds of African Americans in the upstate for more than a century. ROBERT ASHTON COBB

Bethel, Elizabeth Rauh. *Promiseland: A Century of Life in a Negro Community.* Philadelphia: Temple University Press, 1981.

Bleser, Carol K. *The Promised Land: The History of the South Carolina Land Commission, 1869–1890.* Columbia: University of South Carolina Press, 1969.

Wideman, John Edgar. *Fatheralong: A Meditation on Fathers and Sons, Race and Society.* New York: Pantheon, 1994.

Provincials. With tensions between Great Britain and her North American colonists coming to a boil, the crown found itself mobilizing for war in 1775. In addition to regular British soldiers and German mercenaries, British officials organized loyal Americans into conventional fighting units commonly referred to as provincials. A provincial soldier was a volunteer subject to the same control, benefits, and hardships as a British soldier but was ineligible for allowances and perquisites equal to those received by regular troops.

In South Carolina, Loyalists stepped forward in reaction to the actions of the Committee of Safety during the summer of 1775. However, British field commanders and civil administrators, expecting the war to be over quickly, did not raise many provincial units. By 1778 events in the northern theater caused the British high command to reexamine its strategy and turn its attention southward.

Emboldened by successes in Georgia in 1778 and 1779, the British army launched a major offensive against the patriot stronghold of Charleston, which surrendered on May 12, 1780. The South Carolina Royalists (a unit actually formed in East Florida from loyal refugees who were chiefly from Ninety Six District), the King's American Regiment, and the British Legion were provincial units instrumental in the royal victory. Moving into the backcountry, Lord Cornwallis actively sought to recruit provincial units in South Carolina. One such regiment, raised by John Harrison of the Pee Dee region, became known as the South Carolina Rangers.

Beset by decentralized leadership, unreliable support, and the determination of the patriots, provincials were not utilized to their full potential in the conflict. With the end of hostilities, the officers and men of the various provincial units chose to relocate to Canada, Britain, and the West Indies. SAMUEL K. FORE

Allen, Robert S., ed. *The Loyal Americans: The Military Role of the Loyalist Provincial Corps and Their Settlement in British North America, 1775–1784.* Ottawa, Canada: National Museums of Canada, 1983.

Bass, Robert D. "A Forgotten Loyalist Regiment: The South Carolina Rangers." *Proceedings of the South Carolina Historical Association* (1977): 64–71.

Lambert, Robert Stansbury. *South Carolina Loyalists in the American Revolution.* Columbia: University of South Carolina Press, 1987.

Shy, John. "British Strategy for Pacifying the Southern Colonies, 1778–1781." In *The Southern Experience in the American Revolution,* edited by Jeffery J. Crow and Larry E. Tise. Chapel Hill: University of North Carolina Press, 1978.

PTL Club. Based first in Charlotte, North Carolina, and then in Fort Mill, South Carolina, the PTL Club was one of the most successful ventures in televangelism for much of the 1970s and 1980s. PTL stood for both "Praise the Lord" and "People That Love." Jim Bakker (b. January 2, 1940) and his wife Tammy Faye (b. March 7, 1942) used the popular program as a springboard to develop a Pentecostally oriented resort, theme park, shopping mall, cable network, and entertainment center called Heritage USA in Fort Mill.

The complex drew more than five million visitors annually by the mid-1980s.

Bakker, once affiliated with the Assemblies of God, began his career in religious television in 1966 working with Pat Robertson. After leaving Robertson's employ in 1972, Bakker helped form the Trinity Broadcasting System in California. In January 1974 the PTL Club was launched in Charlotte. The Bakkers combined the traditional talk-show format with lively religious entertainment, personal testimonies, and frequent pitches for financial support. Personal religious experience, usually of an emotional nature, was touted as the panacea for all problems.

The Bakker empire endured several run-ins with tax authorities, but when a sex scandal involving Bakker erupted in 1986 and 1987, he resigned in disgrace. Bakker turned over the PTL Club and Heritage USA to Jerry Falwell, who remained at the helm only briefly. Bakker later served a prison term for income tax evasion. His wife divorced him and married one of his associates. Parts of Heritage USA endured, but by the 1990s it had ceased to be a monument to televangelism and evangelical popular culture. CHARLES H. LIPPY

Fore, William F. *Television and Religion.* Minneapolis: Augsburg, 1987.

Frankl, Razelle. *Televangelism: The Marketing of Popular Religion.* Carbondale: Southern Illinois University Press, 1987.

White, Cecile Holmes. "Jim and Tammy Bakker." In *Twentieth-Century Shapers of American Popular Religion,* edited by Charles H. Lippy. Westport, Conn.: Greenwood, 1989.

Public health. The historian Edward H. Beardsley concluded that the story of public health in South Carolina is a "history of neglect." Indeed, since 1914, when data on vital statistics in South Carolina were first collected, the state's residents have been significantly less healthy than most Americans. A confluence of poverty, racism, close alliances between government and industry, and adherence to states' rights and limited government worked to prevent significant improvements in public health throughout much of South Carolina's history. When improvements finally came, they did so for the most part due to federal largesse and changes in the workplace (air conditioning in textile mills, for example) undertaken largely to increase efficiency (machinery broke down less often and could be run at higher speeds with less humidity).

South Carolina's doctors enforced medical segregation, ignored occupational health issues, and fought perceived encroachments on private practice by public health officials who offered free or low-cost clinics and vaccinations. Public health officials rarely questioned the legacy of paternalism and social practices that led to ill health among both whites and blacks. Even the state's few black physicians were slow to challenge medical segregation and second-class care. The advent of the civil rights movement of the 1950s and 1960s pushed most southern black physicians into the battle for health and medical equality, although most did so as followers, not leaders.

Despite the history of neglect, South Carolina's public health history contains its share of heroic practitioners and public-spirited health officers who fought against great odds to improve the health of their communities. As early as 1796 a Charleston ordinance permitted any one of three commissioners of health to order ships removed, cleaned, aired, and fumigated if deemed dangerous. Residents of the city established quarantine stations shortly after the turn of the nineteenth century and a Board of Health in 1815. Beginning in 1813 a Ladies Benevolent Society provided nursing services for "such persons as suffer under the anguish of disease and penury." Early public health efforts in Charleston focused on the removal of decomposing animal and vegetable matter that was thought to spread disease. According to popular beliefs that attributed illness to "marsh miasmas," disturbing the soil led to epidemics of yellow fever and malaria. As late as 1910 critics condemned the city's health department for digging sewer lines during hot South Carolina summers. Still, under the direction of Dr. John Mercier Green, Charleston built a water-filtering plant, piped clean water into the city from Goose Creek, and inspected food and milk by the 1910s.

The delivery of public health services in the rest of the state was slowed by the dominance of plantation-based agriculture. Large landholders controlled the scope and quality of medical services provided to those in their employ as well as to those held as slaves. Small farmers and their families were left to fend for themselves. As was the case with public schools, statewide public health efforts did not begin until after the Civil War. The General Assembly established a State Board of Health in 1878. From the beginning it was poorly funded and overextended—its four employees were charged with developing and implementing a thorough sanitary program for the state. Early efforts of the State Board of Health included campaigns to encourage smallpox vaccinations, school sanitation, and ventilation.

By the twentieth century working-class whites and blacks had separate profiles of poor health. Due in large part to laws that excluded blacks from most categories of textile work, whites had higher rates of industrial diseases associated with hot, dusty environments, especially byssinosis ("brown lung"). Textile hands also suffered more from hookworm and pellagra than did blacks. African Americans incurred venereal disease and tuberculosis at higher rates than whites, and black maternal and infant mortality rates were among the highest in the nation throughout most of the twentieth century.

Securing state appropriations proved to be an ongoing obstacle to public health efforts. In 1915 the Red Cross agreed to pay the salary of one supervising field nurse, grants from the Rockefeller foundation gave impetus to the establishment of county health departments and initiated efforts to eradicate hookworm, and the U.S. Children's Bureau sent a physician and a nurse to conduct a survey of infant and child health problems in Orangeburg County. Ruth Dodd, the Children's Bureau nurse in South Carolina, authored a 1919 report that recommended the establishment of a Bureau of Child Hygiene. The legislature appropriated $10,000 to do so, making Dodd its first director and hiring two additional nurses. The same session of the General Assembly created a Division of Venereal Disease Control.

Between 1922 and 1929 federal funds made available under the Sheppard-Towner Act added a midwife supervisor and a nutritionist to the State Board of Health's payroll, financed a demonstration unit in child health education, employed four traveling public health nurses, and sponsored midwife training institutes, nutrition camps, and child health conferences. The Federal Maternity Infancy Fund sponsored clinics for diphtheria immunization throughout the state. In counties where there was no health department, public health nurses helped private physicians give the inoculations.

Congress discontinued Sheppard-Towner funding in 1929. Since the South Carolina General Assembly made no appropriations for child health and private donations were not forthcoming during the Great Depression, the Bureau of Child Hygiene was abolished in 1933. According to the State Board of Health, infant and maternal mortality rates and tuberculosis rates increased in South Carolina for the first time since 1915.

Many of South Carolina's public health programs suffered from a lack of state support, however, well before the onset of the Great

Depression. The tuberculosis sanatorium program failed to serve many of those in need throughout the 1920s due to insufficient funding and racism that limited access by African Americans to treatment. By the end of the decade, ninety percent of the 230 patients at the Columbia facility were white. Despite the prevalence of tuberculosis among black children, white youngsters at the sanatorium outnumbered black children by fifty percent. Routinely, blacks waited longer for treatment and when finally hospitalized died at close to four times the rate of whites.

Federal funds for venereal disease control stopped in 1923. Within a year state appropriations ended and programs designed to prevent and treat venereal diseases were shelved. Despite the appeals of public health officers, the General Assembly refused to resume funding venereal disease work. When the State Board of Health presented venereal disease programs again fourteen years later, it was supported with federal funds released as part of the Social Security Act.

South Carolina was seen as a poor risk by Public Health Service officials, who viewed federal dollars as seed money. In addition to recalcitrant politicians, James A. Hayne, who served as the state's health officer between 1911 and 1944, refused to advocate for programs that would assist blacks disproportionally. Like most of the state's private physicians and public health officials, Hayne was a South Carolina native who did not question segregation and believed that the state's embarrassing health record was due to the presence of so many blacks. After Hayne's retirement, Dr. Hilla Sheriff was able to parlay her position as director of the Division of Maternal and Child Health (between 1941 and 1967) and connections in the U.S. Children's Bureau into increased funding for prenatal clinics, well-baby clinics, toxoid distribution, midwife training and supervision, nutrition programs, postgraduate scholarships for physicians in obstetrics and pediatrics, mortality studies, dental clinics for indigent schoolchildren, motion pictures on public health topics, and a rural home project to decrease the likelihood of premature births. Sheriff's reports emphasized that state services were meant for all citizens: "the aim of the Division is to have every woman under medical care as early in pregnancy as possible and to see that she has a safe delivery in an environment that offers the least risk possible to both mother and baby." Sheriff made presentations to mixed-race audiences of public health nurses, physicians, and teachers, and the number of clinics in primarily black areas increased under her tenure.

After World War II public health programs expanded to include vision screening, accident prevention, a migrant laborers' project, PKU (phenylketonuria) testing for all infants born in hospitals, child abuse prevention programs, school nurses, and statewide family planning services. Still, much of the increased work was paid for with federal funds. In relatively prosperous times and with infant and maternal mortality rates still well above national averages, the State Board of Health's budget increased by just over $500,000 between 1950 and 1960 (from $3,355,115.52 to $3,891,503.75). Federal grants for venereal disease control and hospital construction and improvement, however, totaled more than $3.5 million—almost as much as the Board of Health's entire annual budget.

In 1968 public health services provided by county health departments were consolidated into thirteen statewide health districts. Both Sheriff and the new state health officer Kenneth Aycock had experience as county health officers and understood that programs dependent on federal funds could be more efficiently administered at a district level by a generation of public health officials less opposed to integrated programs and facilities. The establishment of state health districts motivated some veteran county health officers to retire and hastened South Carolina's dismantling of segregated public health and medical services.

Calls for limited government still prevailed in South Carolina, and public medicine remained suspect at the start of the twenty-first century. Despite significant improvements in the past thirty years, South Carolinians compared poorly to residents of other states in most health categories—a legacy of the state's history of neglecting the health care needs of those unable to afford or without access to private physicians. PATRICIA EVRIDGE HILL

Banov, Leon. *A Quarter Century of Public Health in Charleston, South Carolina.* Charleston, S.C.: Charleston County Department of Health, [1945?].

Beardsley, Edward H. *A History of Neglect: Health Care for Blacks and Mill Workers in the Twentieth-Century South.* Knoxville: University of Tennessee Press, 1987.

Free, Mary Louise. "History and Development of Services to Mothers and Children in South Carolina." Typescript in Hilla Sheriff Papers, South Caroliniana Library, University of South Carolina, Columbia.

Hill, Patricia Evridge. "Hilla Sheriff (1903–1988)." In *Doctors, Nurses, and Medical Practitioners: A Bio-Bibliographical Sourcebook,* edited by Lois N. Magner. Westport, Conn.: Greenwood, 1997.

Sheriff, Hilla. Papers. South Caroliniana Library, University of South Carolina, Columbia.

Punches. Punches have been prominent at South Carolina social gatherings from the state's beginnings. When Eliza Lucas Pinckney recorded her favorite receipts (recipes) in 1756 at her plantation north of Charleston, she included one for the Duke of Norfolk Punch, made with twelve pounds of sugar, thirty oranges plus five and one-half quarts of juice, thirty lemons plus three and one-half quarts of juice, and a gallon of rum. Though men often drank rum, "slings," "flipps," "toddies," beer, and claret at home, they also enjoyed drinking in the rowdy atmosphere of the city's many taverns. Women also drank socially, at the parties and balls that were frequent in Charleston town houses, on the neighboring plantations, and in the elegant buildings that were built by the numerous private "societies." Women drank imported wines, including fortified sherry, Madeira, and port, but they also made their own liqueurs such as ratafia from peach kernels, brandy, and sugar. Punches, which were favored throughout the colonies, were made to serve a crowd, and individual recipes were named for particular social clubs, such as the St. Cecilia Society or the Cotillion Club. The tradition continued for three hundred years. When the Junior League of Charleston published its fund-raiser cookbook *Charleston Receipts* in 1950, it began with sixteen pages of recipes for beverages, many of them for punches that serve hundreds. The book has been the most successful of its kind and has remained in print after more than fifty years. Some of the recipes begin with a base of tea, long a favorite in the lowcountry, and most include tropical fruit such as citrus or pineapple. Some are variations of eggnog, such as "Flip," which was popular in seventeenth-century England. With changes in both social structure and liquor laws in South Carolina, punches have fallen out of favor. JOHN MARTIN TAYLOR

Fraser, Walter J. *Charleston! Charleston! The History of a Southern City.* Columbia: University of South Carolina Press, 1989.

Junior League of Charleston. *Charleston Receipts.* Charleston, S.C.: Walker, Evans and Cogswell, 1950.

Pinckney, Eliza Lucas. *Recipe Book of Eliza Lucas Pinckney, 1756.* Charleston, S.C.: J. Furlong, 1936.

Purrysburg (Jasper County). The town of Purrysburg, located on the Savannah River in present-day Jasper County, was named after its founder, Jean-Pierre Purry (1675–1736). Born in Neuchâtel, Switzerland, Purry was a wine merchant who, after traveling to South Africa, Indonesia, and Australia, developed colonization plans based on meteorological theories that highlighted certain areas of the world as having an ideal climate for agriculture. After unsuccessfully submitting his projects to the Dutch and the French, Purry approached British authorities in the 1720s. A first attempt to send Swiss settlers to South Carolina failed in 1724–1726 due to the uncertain political status of the colony following the revolution of 1719 and the proprietors' sudden withdrawal of their financial pledge. The township plan, initiated in 1731 under Governor Robert Johnson, provided the necessary impetus for the foundation of Purrysburg the following year. This new policy was designed to encourage the immigration of continental Protestants who would settle together in a string of townships along the colony's frontier and develop the hoped-to-be lucrative production of silk, indigo, and wine. In 1732 and 1733 possibly three hundred French-Swiss and German-Swiss colonists arrived in South Carolina with Purry to settle the 48,000-acre township promised by the colony's authorities.

Although the Swiss settlement experienced some degree of economic success, at least in terms of silk production, the inhospitable terrain and severe climate, land encroachments by British settlers, bickering between French- and German-speaking settlers over linguistic matters, and most importantly, the relocation of many enterprising Purrysburgers to Charleston and Savannah condemned Purrysburg to remaining a marginal southern frontier town. DeSaussure, Beaufain, Huguenin, Verdier, Borquine, Mengersdorff, Holzendorf, and Mayerhoffer are among well-known South Carolina surnames from Purrysburg. BERTRAND VAN RUYMBEKE

Crane, Verner W. *The Southern Frontier, 1670–1732.* Durham, N.C.: Duke University Press, 1928.

Hirsch, Arthur H. *The Huguenots of Colonial South Carolina.* 1928. Reprint, Columbia: University of South Carolina Press, 1999.

Meriwether, Robert L. *The Expansion of South Carolina, 1729–1765.* Kingsport, Tenn.: Southern Publishers, 1940.

Migliazzo, Arlin C. "Ethnic Diversity on the Southern Frontier: A Social History of Purrysburgh, South Carolina, 1732–1792." Ph.D. diss., Washington State University, 1982.

———. "A Tarnished Legacy Revisited: Jean Pierre Purry and the Settlement of the Southern Frontier, 1718–1736." *South Carolina Historical Magazine* 92 (October 1991): 232–52.

Rowland, Lawrence S., Alexander Moore, and George C. Rogers. *The History of Beaufort County, South Carolina.* Vol. 1, *1514–1861.* Columbia: University of South Carolina Press, 1996.

Smith, Henry A. M. "Purrysburgh." *South Carolina Historical and Genealogical Magazine* 10 (October 1909): 187–219.

Purvis, Melvin Horace, Jr. (1903–1960). Federal agent. Purvis was born in Timmonsville on October 24, 1903. He gained national fame during the 1930s as the nation's "ace G-man," credited with gunning down the notorious outlaws John Dillinger and Charles "Pretty Boy" Floyd—although throughout his life Purvis maintained that each event was a team project.

Purvis earned a law degree from the University of South Carolina in 1925 and then practiced law in Florence for two years. Frustrated in his efforts to enter diplomatic service, in February 1927 he joined the Justice Department's Bureau of Investigation, the forerunner of the Federal Bureau of Investigation (FBI). Purvis quickly came to the attention of bureau director J. Edgar Hoover, who offered Purvis opportunities to earn rapid promotion. In 1932 Purvis was named senior agent in charge of the bureau's Chicago field office, where he orchestrated the capture of the bank robber and murderer John Dillinger, America's "Public Enemy Number One." On July 22, 1934, acting on a tip from a Chicago brothel operator, Purvis and his team of agents surrounded the Biograph Theater, where Dillinger was attending a movie. When Dillinger walked out, Purvis lit his cigar, signaling other agents that he had spotted the fugitive. Purvis reportedly said to Dillinger, "Stick'em up, Johnny, we have you surrounded," but Dillinger pulled his gun and ran. Agents fired, and Dillinger died at the scene. Purvis refused to take personal credit for Dillinger's death, nor did he identify the agents who shot Dillinger. Three months later, on October 22, Purvis led the collection of federal agents and local police that tracked down and killed the outlaw Charles "Pretty Boy" Floyd in a field near Clarkson, Ohio.

Reporters took an instant liking to the modest Purvis, and the mild-mannered G-man quickly became a national celebrity. Hoover, however, was jealous of Purvis's publicity. He assigned Purvis to bad cases and subjected him to close review. In 1935, just a year after he had captured Dillinger, Purvis resigned from the FBI. Hoover undermined his efforts to find work in law enforcement, despite numerous job offers. Moving to California, Purvis practiced law and capitalized on his celebrity, endorsing products such as Dodge automobiles and Post Toasties cereal and publishing an autobiography, *American Agent* (1936).

In 1938 Purvis returned to Florence County, where he married Rosanne Willcox on September 14. They had three sons. He published a daily newspaper, the *Florence Evening Star,* and then became a partner in the ownership of local radio station WOLS in 1941. During World War II he served in the provost general's office, attaining the rank of colonel by 1945. After the war, Purvis was appointed deputy director of the War Crimes Office of the War Department. Purvis died of a gunshot wound at his home in Florence on February 29, 1960. The FBI initially reported his death as a suicide, but later reports stated that he died accidentally. He was buried in Mt. Hope Cemetery, Florence. BOB FORD

Purvis, Melvin H. *American Agent.* New York: Doubleday, Doran, 1936.

Quakers. The Society of Friends (more commonly known as the Quakers) experienced a fragmented history in South Carolina. This was due in large part to the isolation they faced living as antislavery pacifists in a slave economy and their distance geographically from more prominent Quaker settlements in the North. Ties were maintained, however, through visitation by Friends ministers (several of them women) from Europe and elsewhere in America.

Founded in England in 1652, the Religious Society of Friends emphasized a personal religious experience and the presence of God in every individual, which encouraged a belief in the equality of all regardless of sex, race, or economic status. Other characteristics of this radical Christian group that have continued to hold value to many Friends include opposition to all forms of violence and living one's life with simplicity and integrity.

Quakerism came to South Carolina in the 1670s, and a meeting, the organizational unit of the Society of Friends, was established in Charleston by 1682. John Archdale, Quaker governor of Carolina from 1695 to 1696, promoted religious toleration and peace with the Native Americans. However, Friends' involvement in and influence on South Carolina politics came to an end with oath requirements for officeholders mandated by the Church Act of 1706. Quakers testified against the taking of oaths due to their belief, based on the teachings of Jesus, that individuals should be truthful in all matters and affirm rather than swear to an oath.

Charleston Friends held ties to London and Philadelphia Yearly Meetings and remained separate from the other South Carolina Quaker settlements, which were affiliated with North Carolina Yearly Meeting. A group of Irish Quakers settled along the Wateree River near Camden about 1750. Also in the mid-seventeenth century, Friends from Quaker communities elsewhere in the American colonies migrated to the areas of Marlboro and Newberry Counties. Bush River was by far the largest and most influential of the Piedmont South Carolina meetings, with attendance reportedly as high as five hundred. The Quaker population in South Carolina peaked by 1800, however, and suffered dramatic decline due to out-migration to slave-free Ohio. By 1822 only a weak Charleston Meeting remained, and it too ceased to exist by the time of the Civil War. Except for some northern Quaker women caring for newly freed slaves during the Reconstruction period, South Carolina was without a Quaker presence for more than one hundred years.

Beginning with Columbia Meeting in 1967, several small worship groups formed in South Carolina during the late twentieth century. By 2003 there were an estimated eighty-five meeting members and regular attendees. South Carolina Friends have met annually since 1999 for the Palmetto Friends Gathering. Three of the seven small meetings are affiliated with the Southern Appalachian Yearly Meeting, and all practice the distinctive silent worship traditionally associated with Quakers. GWENDOLYN GOSNEY ERICKSON

Hinshaw, William Wade. *Encyclopedia of American Quaker Genealogy.* Vol. 1, *North Carolina.* 1936. Reprint, Baltimore, Md.: Genealogical Publishing, 1969.

Webber, Mabel L., ed. "The Records of the Quakers in Charles Town." *South Carolina Historical and Genealogical Magazine* 28 (January 1927): 22–43; (April 1927): 94–107; (July 1927): 176–97.

Weeks, Stephen B. *Southern Quakers and Slavery: A Study in Institutional History.* Baltimore, Md.: Johns Hopkins University Press, 1896.

Quary, Robert (1644?–1712). Governor. If he is the same Robert Quary who married Mary Cocker of St. Margaret's, Westminster, in 1670, Robert Quary was born in 1644 and attended the Inns of Court at Middle Temple. In any case, he immigrated to South Carolina from England in 1684 with his (second?) wife "Madm Sarah Quary" and eleven servants. He arrived bearing commissions as clerk of court and deputy of the new proprietor Thomas Amy of London. The Lords Proprietors of Carolina also referred to Quary as "Capt." and urged Sir Richard Kyrle, their governor, to leave him militarily in charge of Charleston when the governor was absent. In 1685 they commissioned Quary as the colony's receiver and escheater (the proprietary agent responsible for collecting rents, fines, and probated estates) and secretary (the colony's chief recording officer for government business).

Governor Kyrle died less than a month after his arrival in 1684 and was succeeded by former governor Joseph West. Quary briefly became governor on July 12, 1685, when Governor West left the province to recoup his own precarious health. The Grand Council elected Quary interim governor, but he served only three months before former governor Joseph Morton assumed the office on specific instructions from the proprietors.

In 1686 the Lords Proprietors ordered an investigation of charges that Quary had aided pirates while serving as governor. Three times in the following years the proprietors gave their governors the power to remove Quary because of charges that he withheld and altered proprietary instructions, failed to send copies of land records to England, and continued to deal with pirates. An order removing him from all offices arrived in February 1688. His actions, if true, would have aided the colony's antiproprietary Goose Creek faction. In 1690 Quary joined members of that faction in supporting a coup d'état led by Seth Sothel, who claimed the governor's office on the basis of a proprietary share that he had purchased. In the same year Sothel appointed Quary chief justice of the colony's only functioning civil and criminal court. Quary fled to Philadelphia in 1693 after the other proprietors deposed Sothel.

With the patronage of Governor Francis Nicholson of Maryland, Quary became judge of the Vice-Admiralty Court of Pennsylvania, the Lower Counties and West New Jersey in 1697, and he succeeded Edward Randolph as Her Majesty's surveyor general of customs in America in 1702. In 1709 this position was divided into two, with a surveyor for the northern colonies and another for the southern ones, the latter of which Quary retained. Quary also served on the councils of New Jersey, Maryland, and Virginia. A strong supporter of the royal prerogative and opponent of proprietary governments, Quary has been described in a dissertation as "a political man on the make." Quary died on October 19, 1712, in Virginia, where he was awaiting the next fleet for a visit back to England. Aside from some charitable bequests, he left his widow Sarah as his sole heir. CHARLES H. LESSER

Lesser, Charles H. *South Carolina Begins: The Records of a Proprietary Colony, 1663–1721.* Columbia: South Carolina Department of Archives and History, 1995.

Papenfuse, Edward C., et al. *A Biographical Dictionary of the Maryland Legislature, 1635–1789.* 2 vols. Baltimore, Md.: Johns Hopkins University Press, 1979–1985.

Ronda, James P. "Robert Quary in America." Ph.D. diss., University of Nebraska, 1970.

Quillen, Robert (1887–1948). Editor, syndicated columnist. For more than a quarter of a century Robert Quillen was one of America's best-known homespun philosophers. As editor and publisher of the *Fountain Inn Tribune,* his syndicated editorials, letters, cartoons, and paragraphs—as well as much-loved, pungent one-liners—brightened the Depression era for millions. Quillen was born in Syracuse, Kansas, on March 25, 1887, and grew up in a village near Topeka, where his father published a local weekly. After a brief stint in the U.S. Army, he worked as a printer in various communities before settling down in Fountain Inn, the hometown of his wife Donnie Cox. After her death, Quillen married Marcelle Babb in 1922.

As owner of the *Tribune,* Quillen struggled to make the weekly profitable, to improve daily life in the rural market town, and also to become an established writer. Although two novels elicited little attention, by 1920 his small-town, "folksy" wit was appearing in publications such as the *Baltimore Sun.* This success led to ties with a Chicago syndicate that teamed him up with a professional artist to produce "Folks Back Home," which gave birth to "Willie Willis" and "Aunt Het," his best-known creations. Quillen also is widely remembered for engaging letters written to his adopted daughter, Louise.

On two occasions he sold the *Tribune*—once for $1—only to buy it back. He realized he needed the paper to provide fodder for his syndicated material. In time, he referred to his Chicago employers as "the old ball and chain." Nevertheless, by the early 1930s his words were seen each day by twelve million readers in more than four hundred newspapers throughout the United States, Canada, Europe, and the Far East.

Although viewed by his neighbors as a grand success, Quillen battled recurrent bouts of frustration. He failed as a novelist, and his attempts to launch a monthly magazine also foundered. In a sense, he was trapped by Fountain Inn, the *Tribune,* and his own words. Try as he might, he could not sever ties to the rural scene he so eloquently described. "I stick to the sticks," he once wrote. "The peace and quiet of a small town furnishes me inspiration. It is a wise general who keeps his army close to his base of supplies." Quillen died on December 9, 1948, in Hendersonville, North Carolina. He was interred in the family crypt at Cannon's Memorial Mausoleum, Fountain Inn. JOHN H. MOORE

Cann, Marvin L. "The Wit and Wisdom of Robert Quillen, 1887–1948." *South Carolina Historical Magazine* 102 (April 2001): 110–34.

Moore, John H. "The Sage of Fountain Inn." *Sandlapper* 12 (spring 2001): 25–28.

Quilt-making. Quilt-making describes the process used by individuals and groups to sew decorative bed covers from layers of fabric, either for personal use or for sale. South Carolina quilts have changed over time, reflecting the influences of geography, historical events, technological innovations, economic circumstances, ethnic traditions, and personal aesthetics.

The earliest settlers in South Carolina depended on transoceanic trade for their household goods. Bedcovers were among the most common household textiles in the American colonies. As quilts became popular in Western Europe during the late eighteenth century, they also appeared in South Carolina. Only wealthy families could afford the expensive fabrics used for quilts during this time. Among the earliest styles was the whole-cloth quilt, which was made from two large sheets of silk or cotton fabric with a layer of loose cotton between them often sewn together with a decorative pattern of stitches.

Early South Carolina quilts were also made from printed cotton fabrics imported from India or Europe. Quilt makers cut out the individual floral motifs from printed chintzes and sewed them to plain foundations in pleasing arrangements. Another European needlework technique popular in Charleston in the early nineteenth century was English-template piecing, or mosaic patchwork. In this technique, small geometric shapes—often hexagons—were cut from paper and covered fabric, and then the covered motifs were sewn together to form a design. Many fine early-nineteenth-century chintz and mosaic patchwork quilts survive from coastal South Carolina.

African Americans, both enslaved and free, made quilts. Some slaveowners supplied families with purchased blankets, while others directed the production of thick, homemade, whole-cloth comforters. Skillful seamstresses made fine quilts for their owners or clients, and some acquired fabrics to make quilts for their own use. While most surviving nineteenth-century quilts made by African Americans resemble those made by European Americans, there is some evidence of the survival of African design elements.

During the first half of the nineteenth century, distinctly American styles of patchwork quilts developed in the Delaware Valley. Combining British needlework techniques with German decorative traditions to produce bold geometric designs in contrasting colors, the new styles entered South Carolina through coastal cities and inland routes into the backcountry. In the same period, New England textile mills produced affordable fabrics, replacing imports for everyday clothing and household needs. Quilt-making became popular among middle-class women, and South Carolina quilts made in the second half of the nineteenth century display a wide variety of techniques, patterns, and color combinations.

Quilt pattern diagrams were published in popular periodicals in the 1890s. As a result, regional patterns were distributed nationally, many new patterns emerged, and some old patterns were given names for the first time. The development of textile mills in South Carolina near the end of the century made fabric more available, and even poor families could afford cloth for quilts.

Although by 1900 quilts were considered old-fashioned and quaint, and upper- and middle-class women turned to other types of needlework, within a few years the country experienced the colonial revival movement, which encouraged Americans to emulate the activities and values of their colonial ancestors. Urban middle-class women took up quilt-making as a hobby, although the designs they produced were influenced more by contemporary styles than by actual historical quilts. The popularity of quilt-making during the 1920s and 1930s was fueled by women's magazines and mail-order pattern companies.

Quilt-making declined during World War II. During the 1950s quilt-making continued as a low-profile activity without attention from popular media. A renewed interest in quilt-making emerged in the late 1960s and spread rapidly during the late twentieth century. Throughout South Carolina quilt clubs, called "guilds," formed during the 1980s. Quilt guilds provided opportunities for their members to meet and to learn, and they sponsored public quilt shows and raised money for charitable causes.

One widespread misconception is that the earliest American quilts were made by frontier settlers from fabric scraps in the absence of other bedcovers and that quilts only later developed decorative properties. During the late twentieth century, as scholars examined historic quilts and supporting documents they published books and curated exhibitions that more accurately portray the history of quilt-making. In 1983–1985 McKissick Museum and the South Carolina State Museum sponsored a survey of South Carolina quilts. Exhibitions and publications by South Carolina museums have provided the public with a better understanding of the state's quilts.

South Carolina quilt-makers continue to make quilts for the same reasons as those of earlier generations: to engage in a satisfying creative activity, to produce beautiful objects of lasting value for family and friends, and to make connections with other people. See plates 14 and 35. LAUREL HORTON

Charleston Museum. *Mosaic Quilts: Paper Template Piecing in the South Carolina Lowcountry.* Greenville and Charleston, S.C.: Curious Works Press and The Charleston Museum, 2002.

Horton, Laurel, and Lynn Robertson Myers. *Social Fabric: South Carolina's Traditional Quilts.* Columbia, S.C.: McKissick Museum, 1985.

Quitrents. Quitrents were annual land payments made originally to the Lords Proprietors and later to the British crown that permitted tenants to own, deed, bequeath, or transfer acreage in colonial South Carolina. The rents were synonymous with those that free English peasants had been paying since the Middle Ages and exempted their payers from all feudal obligations except allegiance. They were brought to North America by Sir Humphrey Gilbert in 1578, required of Virginia's colonists by 1624, and introduced into North Carolina by the Carolina Proprietors in 1663. Six years later these rents, now incorporated into the Fundamental Constitutions of Carolina, were charged to South Carolina as well.

Quitrents in South Carolina were designed to encourage immediate colonization by taking into account settlers' lack of money. Quitrents were not due until 1689, and the system provided settlers with land immediately while the proprietors retained allegiance and indirect ownership through a perpetual lease. Rent could be as little as a penny an acre. Although the Fundamental Constitutions permitted the collection of these fees in kind (indigo, pork, rice, beef, cotton, silk, and peas), the proprietors insisted on payment in sterling, or silver. Attempts to enforce this decree, however, were futile, and the proprietors were eventually forced to recognize payment in kind, to remit select rents in arrears, and even to resort to the outright sale of their land to settlers for one shilling per twenty-five acres, excepting one shilling per one hundred acres for rents. In 1731, after South Carolina had become a royal colony, the crown mandated three shillings sterling or four shillings proclamation (paper) money for each one hundred acres granted, but the declining value of paper money made profits elusive.

During the colonial period, the proprietors and the crown appointed quitrent collectors called receiver generals, who received a percentage of what they collected. In South Carolina, however, the holders of this office were unable to raise more than a fraction of the amounts owed. Colonial officials and landholders, in order to protect their holdings, conspired to undermine the compilation of an accurate rent roll. The quitrents that were collected were used to pay the salaries of important officials, such as the chief justice, the attorney general, and the provost marshal. The Revolutionary War ended the quitrent system. LOUIS P. TOWLES

Ackerman, Robert K. *South Carolina Colonial Land Policies.* Columbia: University of South Carolina Press, 1977.

Bond, Beverley W. *The Quit-Rent System in the American Colonies.* New Haven, Conn.: Yale University Press, 1919.

Watson, Alan D. "The Quitrent System in Royal South Carolina." Ph.D. diss., University of South Carolina, 1971.

R

R. L. Bryan Company. The publishing firm of R. L. Bryan Company is Columbia's oldest industry. It began in 1844, when Richard Lathan Bryan of Charleston began to operate a newsstand and stationery shop on Richardson Street in Columbia that was owned by his brother-in-law, James J. McCarter. The business of Bryan & McCarter was ravaged by fire on February 18, 1865, but quickly resumed operations at a temporary location.

When McCarter died in 1872, Bryan continued the concern under his own name until he retired in 1882. His nephew, Thomas S. Bryan, and his son, R. Berkeley Bryan, assumed control and changed the firm's name to the R. L Bryan Company. In 1884 the company added a printing department. It began printing bills and journals for the General Assembly in 1898, triggering a long association. In 1922 the printing operation moved to a new two-story facility on Sumter Street. At the turn of the twentieth century, the company became the state's textbook distributor, and it had to expand its depository storage several times over the years. The firm entered the office-furniture market in 1910 and in time became involved in interior design and health-care design. A fire that destroyed the office at 1440 Main Street in 1915 stymied the firm only briefly. In 1969, on its 125th anniversary, R. L. Bryan began a move to the Greystone Complex, consolidating all operations. The corporation, previously closely held, in 1985 established an employee stock ownership plan. The firm became one hundred percent employee owned in 1991.

In 2004 the company employed two hundred people and had offices in Columbia, Charleston, and Greenville in South Carolina, and in Raleigh and Charlotte in North Carolina. The firm, ever reshaped by technology, maintained a core business of printing, office furniture and design, and children's books. The General Assembly cited R. L. Bryan as a major economic contributor to the state, and in 1990 the Richland County Council hailed R. L. Bryan as the county's oldest industry. ROBERT A. PIERCE

Barberousse, Deborah. *The History of the R. L. Bryan Company.* Columbia, S.C.: R. L. Bryan, 1994.

Railroads. Although South Carolina never developed a railroad network comparable to those in most northern states, it nevertheless gained recognition as a railroad pioneer in the United States. Chartered in 1827, the South Carolina Canal and Rail Road Company (SCC&RR) ran its first train on Christmas Day in 1830, the initial railroad line in the South. When its 136-mile line between Charleston and Hamburg was completed in 1833, it was the longest continuous railroad line under single management in the world. Although not an immediate success, the SCC&RR (later reorganized as the South Carolina Railroad) touched off a railroad mania in antebellum South Carolina. Several new railroads were chartered by the General Assembly, including the ambitious Louisville, Cincinnati, and Charleston Railroad, but a chronic lack of investment capital and a generally stagnant economy dampened most railroad efforts in South Carolina throughout most of the 1830s and 1840s.

To stimulate additional railroad development, in 1847 the General Assembly established a revolving fund to provide state aid to railroad construction. This aid, coupled with a revived economy, created a railroad boom in South Carolina in the 1850s, with railroad mileage increasing during the decade from 289 to 973, representing a capital investment of more than $22 million in public and private funds. By 1860 there were eleven railroads operating in the state, including two major arteries: the Charlotte and South Carolina Railroad, which connected Columbia with Charlotte, North Carolina; and the Greenville and Columbia Railroad. Railroads, and the accompanying economic boom of the 1850s, helped transform the state's upcountry. Existing towns along the railroads grew, and new towns, such as Rock Hill and Belton, came into existence. With a vastly improved transportation system, commerce and cotton production in the upstate soared.

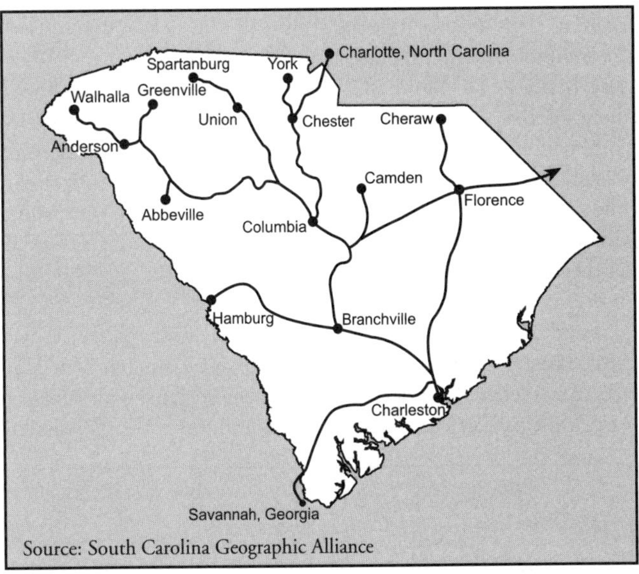

Railroads, 1860

The Civil War seriously damaged railroads. Hundreds of miles of track were worn out or destroyed by Union forces, as were engines and rolling stock. New construction all but ceased during the war. Antebellum railroad companies emerged from the war deeply in debt, with most either failing or consolidating in the ensuing years. Reconstruction-era legislatures eagerly used the credit of the state to put South Carolina's railroads back in order, which also created a series of postwar scandals involving railroad managers and corrupt legislators who bilked the state treasury of millions of dollars. Nevertheless, by 1877 more than 350 miles of new track had been added to prewar totals.

The last decades of the nineteenth century saw considerable railroad development. By the end of the century, South Carolina boasted nearly four thousand miles of track. These new lines, which reached every county, resulted from several railroad-building strategies. Interstate "system building," which swept the region in the 1880s and 1890s, became the most important. Three outside companies, the result of an array of corporate mergers, leases, and construction, became dominant: Atlantic Coast Line (ACL), Seaboard Air Line (SAL), and Southern (SRR). By World War I the ACL covered the lowcountry, with its main line connecting Wilmington, North Carolina, with Savannah, Georgia, and serving Charleston and Florence. The SAL operated its principal stem between Hamlet, North Carolina, and Savannah, which served Columbia. This busy artery, made possible by the construction of ninety-one miles of new track between Cheraw and Columbia in 1900, largely superseded the earlier SAL route via Charleston. The main line of the Southern between Charlotte, North Carolina, and Atlanta, Georgia, sliced through the upstate with major facilities at Greenville and Spartanburg. But the SRR controlled a web of additional track that included the South Carolina Railroad and a Charlotte-Savannah line via Columbia.

Even though system building dominated, some earlier and even later short-lines remained outside the orbits of the "Big Three." The Pickens Railroad, for example, chartered in 1892 to build a nineteen-mile road between Easley and Olenoy Gap via Pickens, in 1898 completed only a ten-mile segment between Pickens and Easley, where it connected with the SRR. The Pickens remains an independent short-line. Another illustration is the Lancaster & Chester Railway. This twenty-nine-mile short-line, which still served the communities of its corporate name as of the early twenty-first century, began in 1873 as the Cheraw & Chester Railway, one of only three narrow-gauge common carriers built in South Carolina. Although planned as a fifty-five-mile route between Lancaster and Cheraw, the company, like the Pickens Railroad, failed to realize its intended goals. After it was reorganized in 1896 as the Lancaster & Chester Railway, its owners wisely converted their property to standard gauge six years later and benefited from traffic generated from local cotton mills.

South Carolina experienced another type of short-line, the "tap" road. These pikes were usually not common carriers but were affiliates of a single industrial operation, likely associated with timber or turpentine production. Examples abound. In order to serve its mill in Summerville, the D. W. Taylor Lumber Company in 1880 built a fourteen-mile private railroad to reach stands of trees in the Wassamassaw Swamp of Berkeley County. Until abandonment in mid-1920s, this tap road expanded and contracted under various corporate banners.

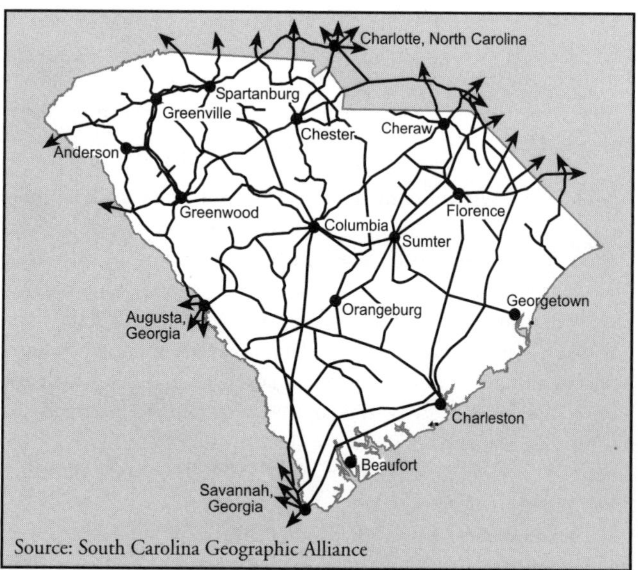

Railroads, 1925

The "Railway Age" in South Carolina lasted until after World War I. With greater usage of automobiles, buses, and trucks, which traveled over ever-improving public roads, the need for freight and passenger trains diminished. Yet, mileage did not shrink dramatically until the 1960s, eventually declining to fewer than 2,400 miles. The difficulty of winning regulatory permission to abandon lessened with the Transportation Act of 1958 and other legislative measures. Moreover, appendages and even secondary and main lines became less desired by major carriers as a result of corporate mergers, which affected every one of the state's three primary railroads. In 1967 the ACL and SAL combined to form the Seaboard Coast Line (SCL), and in 1980 SCL joined with the Chesapeake & Ohio system to create CSX. Then in 1982 the Southern merged with Norfolk & Southern, producing Norfolk Southern (NS). With development of two dominant carriers in South Carolina, CSX and NS, hundreds of unwanted miles were either abandoned or sold to existing or new short-line operators. The Waccamaw Coast Line Railroad is an example. In 1984 CSX wished to dispose of its fourteen-mile branch between Conway and Myrtle Beach. In order to continue movement of forest products and other bulk commodities, Horry County bought the line and leased it to the newly formed Horry County Railroad. Three years later the county leased the property to the Waccamaw Coast Line.

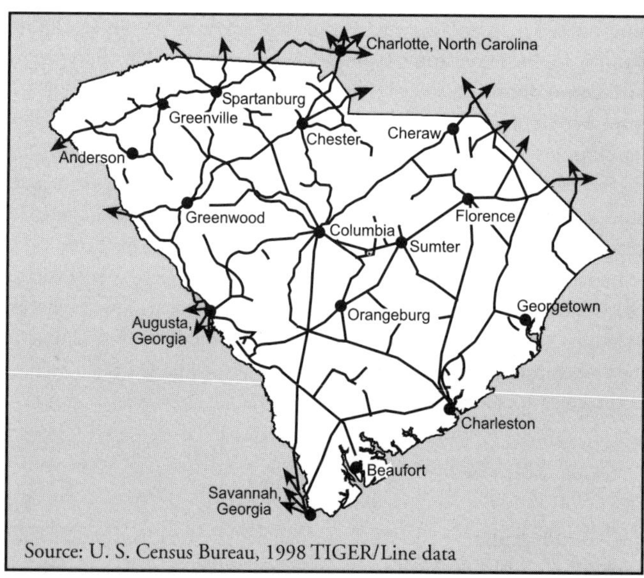

Railroads, 1998

In the twenty-first century, railroads in South Carolina remained vital arteries of freight transport. The few remaining passenger trains, operated by the National Railroad Passenger Corporation (Amtrak), created in 1971, served principal stations along the former ACL, SCL, and SRR. H. ROGER GRANT

Derrick, Samuel M. *Centennial History of South Carolina Railroad.* 1930. Reprint, Spartanburg, S.C.: Reprint Company, 1975.

Ford, Lacy K., Jr. *Origins of Southern Radicalism: The South Carolina Upcountry, 1800–1860.* New York: Oxford University Press, 1988.

Hilton, George W. *American Narrow Gauge Railroads.* Stanford, Calif.: Stanford University Press, 1990.

Lewis, Edward A. *American Shortline Railway Guide.* 5th ed. Waukesha, Wis.: Kalmbach, 1996.

Nelson, Scott. *Iron Confederacies: Southern Railways, Klan Violence, and Reconstruction.* Chapel Hill: University of North Carolina Press, 1999.

Saunders, Richard, Jr. *Merging Lines: American Railroads, 1900–1970.* DeKalb: Northern Illinois University Press, 2001.

Simkins, Francis Butler, and Robert Hilliard Woody. *South Carolina during Reconstruction.* Chapel Hill: University of North Carolina Press, 1932.

Stover, John F. *Iron Road to the West: American Railroads of the 1850s.* New York: Columbia University Press, 1978.

Vivian, Daniel J. "Railroad Development and Community Change in the New South: A Social History of the Seaboard Air Line Railway in the South Carolina Midlands, 1898–1915." Master's thesis, University of South Carolina, 1997.

Rain porch. A sheltered exterior residential living area, the rain porch consists of a roof structure with freestanding supports, in an anterior arrangement to a pier-supported, balustraded deck. This vernacular form typically occurs on houses from ca. 1820 to ca. 1860 in the South Carolina counties located north of the Santee River and east of the Wateree and Catawba Rivers. Isolated examples have also been identified in Berkeley, Chester, Fairfield, Lexington, Newberry, and York Counties, as well as in central and eastern North Carolina counties along the South Carolina border. Westward migration during the antebellum period transplanted this vernacular building tradition to Florida's north-central region, where it became an important element within the classic "Cracker-style" architecture of the area, and to lower-south areas of Georgia, Alabama, Mississippi, and Louisiana, where the form is referred to as a "Carolina porch."

The Evander Gregg House in Florence County has an excellent example of a rain porch. Courtesy, South Carolina Department of Archives and History

Typically, the form occurs in association with provincial interpretations of the Greek-revival style—that is, attached to classic Carolina plantation houses (extended I-houses) or raised cottages with either hall-and-parlor or central hall plans. Examples can be found, however, on Federal-style farmhouses built before 1800, as well as on modest late nineteenth-century and turn-of-the-twentieth-century folk Victorian residences. In all occurrences the elongated roof supports produce an optical illusion of additional height and grandeur.

While some architectural historians theorize West Indian origins, others speculate an indigenous origin within an area settled by a variety of ethnicities—English, Scots, Scots-Irish, Welsh, French, and African Americans—each with different building traditions. Because it does not appear on the region's earliest houses, the rain porch more than likely emerged in South Carolina from assimilated building traditions, and as a means to preserve a much-used outdoor living space from decay by exposure in a subtropical to temperate climate. It remains an architectural phenomenon worthy of continued research and investigation.

Notable examples of the form within South Carolina include the ca. 1840 Red Doe (Evander Gregg House) in Florence County; Tanglewood (ca. 1831) and Bloomsbury (ca. 1850) in Camden; the Zachariah Cantey House (ca. 1795) near Boykin in Kershaw County; Magnolia (1853) in Bennettsville; Myrtle Moor (ca. 1830) in Sumter County; and New Market (ca. 1820), the Salters Plantation House (ca. 1830), the John Calvin Wilson House (ca. 1847), and the Samuel Itly Wilson House (ca. 1850) in Williamsburg County. ANDREW W. CHANDLER

Noble, Allen G. *Wood, Brick, and Stone: The North American Settlement Landscape.* Vol. 1, *Houses.* Amherst: University of Massachusetts Press, 1984.

Sweet, Ethel Wylly. *Camden Homes and Heritage.* Camden, S.C.: Kershaw County Historical Society, 1978.

Upton, Dell, and John Michael Vlach. *Common Places: Readings in American Vernacular Architecture.* Athens: University of Georgia Press, 1986.

Rainbow Row. The vibrant pastel paint colors applied to the exterior of neglected buildings between 79 and 107 East Bay Street became one of the earliest and most potent symbols of Charleston's emerging preservation movement. In 1931 the decorator and preservationist Dorothy Haskell Porcher Legge purchased and began renovating a house at 99–101 East Bay Street. Legge's house stood amid a row of buildings that dated from the early eighteenth century and had originally served as the businesses and residences of prosperous merchants. The ground floors were used as stores and counting rooms; living quarters occupied the upper floors. Once located along the wharves of Charleston harbor, these buildings became neglected after the docks silted and mercantile activities moved elsewhere. Inspired by the bright pastel colors associated with colonial Caribbean architecture, Legge's nonhistorical, attention-grabbing paint scheme sought to encourage their rehabilitation. As the buildings along East Bay Street were restored in the 1930s, 1940s, and 1950s, the block became known as Rainbow Row. In the early twenty-first century this picturesque collection of buildings was among the most widely recognized images of Charleston and symbolized the role of preservation as a stimulus for urban revitalization. DANIEL J. VIVIAN

Poston, Jonathan H. *The Buildings of Charleston: A Guide to the City's Architecture.* Columbia: University of South Carolina Press, 1997.

Stockton, Robert. "The Evolution of Rainbow Row." Master's thesis, University of South Carolina, 1979.

Rainey, Joseph Hayne (1832–1887). Congressman. Rainey was born a slave in Georgetown to Edward L. Rainey and his wife Gracia on June 21, 1832. His father, a barber, purchased the family's freedom, and they moved to Charleston about 1846. The elder Rainey also purchased two slaves. By 1860 Joseph Rainey had become a barber at Charleston's fashionable Mills House hotel.

In 1859 Rainey traveled to Philadelphia, where he married Susan (maiden name unknown). During the Civil War, Rainey was compelled to serve as a steward on a blockade-runner and then to work on Confederate fortifications. He fled with his wife to Bermuda in 1862 on a blockade-runner and resumed barbering, first in St. George and then in Hamilton. In 1865 he returned to Charleston and—accompanied by his elder brother Edward—participated in the Colored People's Convention at Zion Presbyterian Church. Attendees sought ways in which to advance "the interests of our people." Rainey was also elected to represent Georgetown in the 1868 constitutional convention.

Rainey was one of the more conservative black leaders during Reconstruction. He favored implementing a poll tax as a requirement for voting if the revenues were devoted to public education. He also supported an effort to legalize the collection of debts contracted before the Civil War, including debts incurred in the purchase of slaves. Neither measure passed in the 1868 state constitution. In 1870 Georgetown voters elected Rainey to the state Senate, where he became chair of the Finance Committee. He was also a brigadier general in the state militia, and he served as an agent with the ill-fated State Land Commission. He attended the 1869 State Labor Convention, which lobbied the General Assembly for prolabor legislation to protect black workers.

Rainey was the first black man to serve in the U.S. House of Representatives. He took his seat in December 1870, filling the unexpired term of Benjamin F. Whittemore. He was reelected four times to the First District seat, serving from 1870 to 1879. In Congress, Rainey advocated passage of the 1872 Ku Klux Klan Act as a means to rid the state of that terrorist organization. He supported an amnesty bill to remove remaining liabilities on former Confederates while simultaneously promoting a civil rights bill sponsored by Massachusetts senator Charles Sumner. The amnesty bill passed in 1874, and the civil rights bill was enacted in 1875.

From 1879 to 1881 Rainey was an agent with the Internal Revenue Service in South Carolina. An active entrepreneur, he invested in the Columbia and Greenville Railroad and was a director of the Enterprise Railroad, a black-owned corporation organized in 1870 to transport freight by horse-drawn street railway between the Charleston wharves and the railroad depot. In the early 1880s Rainey attempted unsuccessfully to manage a brokerage and banking business in Washington, D.C. He died in Georgetown on August 2, 1887, and was buried in the Baptist Cemetery. WILLIAM C. HINE

Christopher, Maurine. *Black Americans in Congress.* Rev. ed. New York: Crowell, 1976.

Holt, Thomas. *Black over White: Negro Political Leadership in South Carolina during Reconstruction.* Urbana: University of Illinois Press, 1977.

Packwood, Cyril O. *Detour–Bermuda, Destination–U.S. House of Representatives: The Life of Joseph Hayne Rainey.* Hamilton, Bermuda: Baxter's, 1977.

Rogers, George C. *The History of Georgetown County, South Carolina.* Columbia: University of South Carolina Press, 1970.

Williamson, Joel. *After Slavery: The Negro in South Carolina during Reconstruction, 1861–1877.* Chapel Hill: University of North Carolina Press, 1965.

Ramsay, David (1749–1815). Physician, legislator, historian. Ramsay was born on April 2, 1749, in Lancaster County, Pennsylvania, the son of the Irish immigrant James Ramsay, a farmer, and Jane Montgomery. Intellectually precocious, Ramsay learned to read at an early age. As a youth, he tutored boys much older than himself. He graduated from the College of New Jersey (Princeton) in 1765 and received a bachelor of physic degree from the College of Philadelphia in 1773. He was later awarded an honorary doctor of medicine degree from Yale in 1803. After a brief practice in Maryland, Ramsay moved to Charleston in 1773 on the recommendation of his close friend and confidant Dr. Benjamin Rush. A Presbyterian, Ramsay quickly associated himself with the Independent Congregational Church in Charleston.

Ramsay's rise to position and influence in Charleston was rapid, and it was soon apparent that his activities would not be confined to medicine. He was an ardent supporter of the American Revolution and delivered a stirring speech in support of the American cause on July 4, 1778, at an anniversary celebration of the Declaration of Independence. Ramsay served as a military surgeon early in the war and was imprisoned in St. Augustine, Florida, by the British for eleven months with other patriots after the fall of Charleston in May 1780.

First elected to the South Carolina legislature by St. Philip's and St. Michael's Parishes in 1776, Ramsay was active in colonial and state politics during and after the war, eventually serving a total of twenty-three years in the South Carolina legislature, including six years as president of the Senate from 1791 to 1797. He was elected to the Confederation Congress in 1782 and served until 1786, serving as president pro tempore during his final term. He strongly supported the ratification of the U.S. Constitution and was morally opposed to slavery, but he saw no practical solution in the political, economic, and social climate of the times. His liberal views on slavery and his well-known friendship with northern abolitionists such as Benjamin Rush contributed to his failed bids for election to the U.S. House of Representatives in 1788 and the U.S. Senate in 1794.

In 1789 Ramsay was among the founders of the Medical Society of South Carolina, and he was elected its president in 1797. He was one of the first advocates of formal medical education in South Carolina, which came to fruition with the first graduating class of the Medical College of South Carolina ten years after his death. He was also the originator of many innovative measures for the improvement of the public health, including the successful introduction of a smallpox vaccination in South Carolina.

Ramsay's most lasting legacy, however, was as a historian, in which role he gained national and international renown. He produced six major works of history, including *History of the American Revolution* (1789), which went through six American editions by 1865 and was also published in English, French, Irish, German, and Dutch editions. Ramsay's *History* is recognized as a pioneering scholarly treatise on the war and has secured his place as one of the originators of the American historical consciousness. His other significant works include *History of the Revolution of South Carolina* (2 vols., 1785), *Review of the Improvements, Progress and the State of Medicine in the XVIIITH Century* (1801), *Life of George Washington* (1807), *History of South Carolina from Its First Settlement in 1670 to 1808* (2 vols., 1809), and a posthumously published three-volume *History of the United States* (1816–1817) and a twelve-volume *Universal History Americanized* (1819).

Ramsay's successes as a physician, legislator, and historian contrasted sharply with his lack of financial success. He was a visionary with little aptitude for business, and his investments almost never produced the expected return. He nevertheless figured prominently in such commercial and financial institutions as the Santee Canal, the Reciprocal Insurance Company, the Bank of the United States, the Catawba Company, the South Carolina Homespun Company, and the Hamilton Steamship Company.

Ramsay was married and widowed three times. He married Sabina Ellis on February 9, 1775. After her death in 1776, Ramsay on March 18, 1783, married Frances Witherspoon, the daughter of John Witherspoon, a signer of the Declaration of Independence and president of the College of New Jersey. She died in 1784 after giving birth to a son. His third marriage, on January 28, 1787, was to Martha Laurens, daughter of Henry Laurens. The couple had eleven children, eight of whom survived infancy, before Martha's death in

1811. Ramsay died on May 8, 1815, from gunshot wounds inflicted by a deranged patient. He was buried in the Circular Congregational Churchyard in Charleston. W. CURTIS WORTHINGTON

Shaffer, Arthur H. *To Be an American: David Ramsay and the Making of the American Consciousness.* Columbia: University of South Carolina Press, 1991.

Waring, Joseph I. *A History of Medicine in South Carolina.* Vol. 1, *1670–1825.* Columbia: South Carolina Medical Association, 1964.

Randolph, Benjamin Franklin (ca. 1820–1868). Legislator, clergyman. Randolph was born free in Kentucky to parents who may have been of mixed race. He grew up in Morrow County, Ohio, where he received a primary education. He attended preparatory school at Oberlin College and graduated from its collegiate program in 1862. Shortly thereafter he was ordained as a Methodist Episcopal minister, but he served as a Presbyterian chaplain with the Twenty-sixth U.S. Colored Troops at Hilton Head. After the war he returned to the Methodist fold.

Randolph settled in Charleston in 1865 and worked for the American Missionary Association and then the Freedmen's Bureau as assistant superintendent of schools. He participated in the Colored People's Convention at Charleston's Zion Presbyterian Church. In 1866 he coedited, with the Rev. E. J. Adams, the Charleston *Journal.* By 1867 he was the associate editor of the *Charleston Advocate,* a Methodist publication.

With the introduction of universal manhood suffrage in 1867, Randolph joined in Reconstruction politics as an active Republican. He rose rapidly through the leadership ranks. He represented Orangeburg County in the 1868 constitutional convention. He dismayed many black and white Republicans when he strongly supported measures disfranchising illiterate voters and those who failed to pay poll taxes. He also endorsed a constitutional ban on racial discrimination. He spoke in favor of the integration of public schools: "The time has come when we shall have to meet things squarely, and we must meet them now or never. The day is coming when we must decide whether the two races shall live together or not." However, none of the constitutional proposals that Randolph endorsed passed.

In 1868 Randolph was elected to represent Orangeburg County in the state Senate. He also served as a county school commissioner. The state Republican convention elected him chair of the state central committee. One white Republican leader, John Morris, declared that Randolph was "quite a speaker and a good man" but was "totally unfit for that position." On October 16, 1868, while campaigning on behalf of the Republican Party, Randolph was assassinated after he stepped off a train at Hodges station in Abbeville County. There were allegations that the Ku Klux Klan was responsible for his murder, but no one was convicted of the crime. Randolph was one of four Republican leaders—Solomon G. W. Dill, James Martin, and Lee Nance were the others—slain during 1868. He was buried in Columbia in the cemetery that now bears his name. WILLIAM C. HINE

Holt, Thomas. *Black over White: Negro Political Leadership in South Carolina during Reconstruction.* Urbana: University of Illinois Press, 1977.

Powers, Bernard E. *Black Charlestonians: A Social History, 1822–1885.* Fayetteville: University of Arkansas Press, 1994.

Williamson, Joel. *After Slavery: The Negro in South Carolina during Reconstruction, 1861–1877.* Chapel Hill: University of North Carolina Press, 1965.

Ransier, Alonzo Jacob (1834–1882). Lieutenant governor, congressman. Ransier was born free in Charleston on January 3, 1834, to parents who may have been immigrants from Haiti. He acquired the equivalent of a common school education and worked as a clerk at a Charleston shipping firm prior to the Civil War.

Ransier attended the 1865 Colored People's Convention at Charleston's Zion Presbyterian Church, a gathering of freedmen held in order to "advance the interests of our people." He spoke in defense of the competence of black people and commended the black men who had fought with the Union army. He served as associate editor of the Charleston *Leader,* a postwar black newspaper.

In 1868 Ransier represented Charleston County in the constitutional convention. He pursued a moderate course, favoring the Reverend Richard H. Cain's petition to Congress appealing for funds to provide land to the freedmen. He successfully opposed a literacy requirement for voters and supported efforts to have in the new constitution a civil rights provision that would prohibit racial discrimination. He perplexed many delegates when he called for the creation of a public school system in which the race and color of students would not be mentioned.

Ransier was elected to the South Carolina House of Representatives from Charleston in 1868. He was also a presidential elector pledged to Ulysses S. Grant, and he served as a trustee to the State Orphan Asylum. He was Charleston county auditor from 1868 to 1870. Following the assassination of Benjamin F. Randolph in 1868, Ransier succeeded him as chair of the Republican State Executive Committee. Ransier supported the right of women to vote and participated in the 1870 Women's Suffrage Convention in Columbia. He also attended the 1869 State Labor Convention, an assembly of black politicians and labor leaders that lobbied the General Assembly for prolabor legislation.

In 1870 Ransier was elected to a two-year term as the state's first black lieutenant governor, serving during the second administration of Governor Robert K. Scott. Ransier was active in several black organizations in Charleston, including the Amateur Literary and Fraternal Association and Centenary Methodist Episcopal Church. He was also secretary to the Enterprise Railroad, a black corporation founded to operate a horse-drawn street railway to haul freight between the city's wharves and the railroad terminal.

Ransier was elected to the U.S. House of Representatives in 1872 from the Second District, and he served one term from 1873 to 1875. He declined to vote for the 1875 Civil Rights Act because a section banning discrimination in education had been removed from the final bill. From 1875 to 1877 he was a collector for the U.S. Internal Revenue Service. Ransier's political career declined rapidly after Reconstruction ended in 1877. He worked for a time as a night watchman at the Charleston Custom House and as a street laborer.

Ransier married Louisa Ann Carroll in 1856, and they were the parents of eleven children. She died in 1875, and he married Mary Louisa McKinlay in 1876. Ransier died in obscurity in Charleston on August 17, 1882. WILLIAM C. HINE

Christopher, Maurine. *Black Americans in Congress.* Rev. ed. New York: Crowell, 1976.

Holt, Thomas. *Black over White: Negro Political Leadership in South Carolina during Reconstruction.* Urbana: University of Illinois Press, 1977.

Powers, Bernard E. *Black Charlestonians: A Social History, 1822–1885.* Fayetteville: University of Arkansas Press, 1994.

Williamson, Joel. *After Slavery: The Negro in South Carolina during Reconstruction, 1861–1877.* Chapel Hill: University of North Carolina Press, 1965.

Rash, Ron (b. 1953). Poet, novelist. Rash was born in Chester on September 23, 1953, the son of James Hubert Rash and Sue Holder. He earned a B.A. in English at Gardner-Webb College in North Carolina and then received his M.A. in English from Clemson University. He has taught writing and literature at Tri-County Technical College in Pendleton and in the master of fine arts program at Queens University in Charlotte, North Carolina. In 2003 he was named John A. Parris, Jr., and Dorothy Luxton Parris Distinguished Professor in Appalachian Cultural Studies at Western Carolina University in Cullowhee, North Carolina. He and his wife, Ann, and their two children live in Clemson.

Rash's family has lived in the southern Appalachian Mountains and in the Piedmont of the Carolinas since the mid-1700s. He uses the agrarian life in the mountains as a main theme in much of his poetry and fiction, showing the humor and tragedy of farm people struggling against the vagaries of weather and unstable farm prices on isolated, hardscrabble patches of land.

Rash's third book of poems, *Raising the Dead* (2002), and his novel *One Foot in Eden* (2002) take as their central theme the plight of mountain people who are about to be displaced from their family lands by the waters of a lake built by an electric power company. Generations of people tied to ancestral soil undergo the anxieties of removal into the textile mill towns of the Piedmont.

These mill towns serve as the locales for three of Rash's books: his first book of stories, *The Night the New Jesus Fell to Earth and Other Stories from Cliffside, North Carolina* (1994); his book of stories *Casualties* (2000); and his book of poems *Eureka Mill* (1998). These poems and stories center on the lives of those who have left their mountain homes in search of stable wages and security in the mills. All too often they find hardship and poverty instead.

Rash's fiction and poetry about the people of Appalachia and the mill towns are filled with gentle humor, family strife, and economic problems. Although the people in his work are beset by drought, floods, and layoffs, Rash focuses on their enduring and universal qualities. He tells of their everyday joys and sorrows, of their disappointing religious yearnings, of their strengths, weaknesses, and foibles. CHARLES ISRAEL

Ratification of the U.S. Constitution. South Carolina's ratification of the United States Constitution in May 1788 was never in doubt. Had there ever been any suspense, it ended in January when the General Assembly, by a 76 to 75 vote, selected Charleston as the site of the ratifying convention, with the backcountry voting 57 to 2 for the losing side. Ratification opponent Aedanus Burke credited the unity of the city, its newspapers, and the open houses kept by merchants to treat delegates for the failure to prevent ratification. But location only determined the size of the Federalist victory. On several occasions during the 1780s, factions from across the state and political spectrum had supported strengthening the national government's power to regulate foreign commerce. In January 1788 David Ramsay predicted that the Constitution would be "accepted by a very great majority." Indeed, in the final ratification vote, Federalists (supporters of ratification) routed their Anti-Federalist opponents by more than a two-to-one margin, 149 to 73.

The South Carolina delegation played an active role at the 1787 constitutional convention in Philadelphia. Politically experienced and influential, Charles Pinckney, Charles Cotesworth Pinckney, Pierce Butler, and John Rutledge helped to broker numerous compromises and ensured that the final document would serve the state's economic interests, especially slavery. They secured protections for slave property, the continuation of the slave trade for at least twenty years, and the return of fugitive slaves. In addition, representation in the U.S. House of Representatives would be based on the number of free people and three-fifths the number of slaves. The South Carolina delegation was also unanimous in supporting provisions that prohibited states from impairing the obligation of contracts. Such "debtor relief" had been a fixture in the politics of South Carolina and other states during the years following the Revolution. Federalists had benefited greatly from debt-relief measures in the mid-1780s but would eschew such actions once their crisis had passed.

Since the state's economic interests were well served by the new document, the most serious debate in South Carolina over ratification would revolve around the contested meaning of the American Revolution, which reflected the political conflicts that had divided the state since independence. In simplest terms, Federalists saw the Constitution as a way to complete the Revolution; Anti-Federalists saw it as a threat to their emerging power. James Lincoln, an Anti-Federalist from Ninety Six District, warned about a change from a "well-formed democratic" government to an aristocratic one and asked what people had been "contending for these ten years past?" In contrast, the lowcountry Federalist Francis Kinloch welcomed the proposed government precisely because he believed that Americans lacked the virtue necessary to maintain a "free form of government."

Anti-Federalists probably would have opposed any government supported by South Carolina's delegates at the constitutional convention. The state's delegation was dominated by influential lowcountry figures. Working behind closed doors in Philadelphia, they had tried to limit the role of the people at large and successfully opposed the popular election of U.S. senators. Anti-Federalists objected to the election of senators by state legislatures and the absence of enforced rotation of officeholders, a principle that had been applied to the state's delegates to the Confederation Congress and to the South Carolina governor. Federalists countered that under the new government the people were better represented than they had been under the Articles of Confederation. They neglected to add, however, that the Articles had left the central government so weak that it had hardly mattered who was represented.

However predictable the Federalist victory, Anti-Federalists undoubtedly represented a majority of the state's white population. Representation in the ratifying convention, however, was the same as in the General Assembly, which was skewed in favor of coastal areas. With fewer than 30,000 white inhabitants in 1790, Charleston, Georgetown, and Beaufort were allowed 143 delegates. In contrast, the backcountry had only 93 delegates, even though the region had almost four times the number of white inhabitants. The vote over ratification followed those geographic lines. Support for the Constitution radiated out from the coastal centers of the three lowcountry districts. Parishes around Beaufort supported the Constitution 14 to 0, those around Georgetown by 12 to 1, and Charleston and the surrounding parishes by a vote of 73 to 0. In six other lowcountry parishes the vote was 22 to 15, putting the total lowcountry vote at 121 to 16 in favor of ratification. The backcountry voted 57 to 28 against ratification. Seventeen of the 28 backcountry votes for ratification and only 1 of the 57 votes against came from four election units bordering lowcountry parishes.

The delegates opposed to the Constitution represented about fifty-two percent of the population, those in favor represented about thirty-nine percent, and those not voting about nine percent. Aedanus Burke complained that the Constitution had been ratified even though "4/5 of the people do from their souls detest it." In addition to the geographic division over the Constitution, there was an economic one. The wealthier the delegate to the ratifying convention, the more likely he was to support the Constitution. The split between Federalists and Anti-Federalists was even greater outside the convention. Backcountry settlers invariably sent the same people to the convention as they sent to the General Assembly, for which there was a property qualification, which meant that many relatively poor people had to vote for people who were better off.

Politically speaking, opposition to the Constitution came from areas that were gaining political power since the Revolution, and for the first time seemed poised to dominate the state. Conversely, support for the Constitution came from those uncomfortable with the political forces unleashed by independence and the defeat of the British. Fearful of additional change, of chaos, and even of anarchy, supporters of ratification saw a strengthened central government as a means to limit further damage. JEROME J. NADELHAFT

Bradford, M. E. "Preserving the Birthright: The Intention of South Carolina in Adopting the U.S. Constitution." *South Carolina Historical Magazine* 89 (April 1988): 90–101.

Nadelhaft, Jerome J. *The Disorders of War: The Revolution in South Carolina.* Orono: University of Maine Press, 1981.

Weir, Robert M. "South Carolina: Slavery and the Structure of the Union." In *Ratifying the Constitution,* edited by Michael Allen Gillespie and Michael Lienesch. Lawrence: University Press of Kansas, 1989.

———. "South Carolinians and the Adoption of the U.S. Constitution." *South Carolina Historical Magazine* 89 (April 1988): 73–89.

Ravenel, Beatrice (1870–1956). Poet, journalist. Born in Charleston on August 24, 1870, Beatrice Ravenel was one of six daughters of Charlotte Sophia Reeves of Charleston and Charles Otto Witte of Hanover, Germany. She and her sisters, who married into many elite lowcountry families, grew up in the mansion subsequently turned into the private girls' school Ashley Hall. Finishing her education at Miss Kelly's School in Charleston, Ravenel entered the Harvard Annex (later Radcliffe College) as a special student in 1889. She studied for three years, left, and then returned in 1895 for two more years. She published a few short stories and poems and was considered a bright intellect, equal to many of the men at Harvard.

Forsaking that, Beatrice Witte returned to Charleston and in 1900 married Francis Gualdo Ravenel, son of Mrs. St. Julien Ravenel, author of the classic *Charleston: The Place and the People* (1906). Francis Ravenel invested much of his wife's inheritance, lost it, and died in 1920, leaving her to care for their daughter, also named Beatrice (later the author of *Architects of Charleston*). Turning to writing to support herself, Beatrice Ravenel produced poetry, some of it splendid, and short stories, mostly derivative and plot-heavy, although one, "The High Cost of Conscience," was published in the first volume of the *O. Henry Memorial Short Stories.*

Ravenel is possibly the best example of the influence of the Poetry Society of South Carolina on local writers; its founding in the year of her husband's death brought her into a poetry-conscious environment. Here she met the poet Amy Lowell when Lowell lectured in Charleston in 1922. Lowell and the Imagist school were strong influences on Ravenel, prompting great changes in her work, which Lowell encouraged and championed. The poetry that Ravenel wrote in the 1920s reveals a broad intellectual outlook and a warm sensual glow. She wrote of outsiders and the dispossessed, such as the Yamassee Indians who lost their land to the whites, and a young actress, soon to die, musing on her young son. The latter, "Poe's Mother," was her most reprinted work and shows her difference from other Charleston poets, who often celebrated local lore, while

Beatrice Ravenel (1892). Courtesy, South Carolina Historical Society

Ravenel examined subtle subconscious states and philosophic points. This was perhaps due to her having been a student of William James, George Santayana, George Baker, and others.

In 1919 Ravenel also began to write editorials, mostly on foreign affairs, and reviews for her brother-in-law William Watts Ball, editor of the Columbia *State.* Her one volume of poems, *The Arrow of Lightning,* came out in 1925, with Ravenel paying part of the cost. She married Samuel Prioleau Ravenel, a distant cousin of her first husband, in 1926 and, no longer needing to support herself, slowed her production. She traveled widely and still wrote arresting and sensual lyrics, which were not published in her lifetime. Ravenel died on March 15, 1956, and was buried in Charleston's Magnolia Cemetery, all but forgotten. In 1969 a book of her poems, edited by the Charlestonian Louis Rubin, was published, and in the ensuing years scholars and critics began to claim her as the best poet of the Charleston Literary Renaissance and the author of some excellent individual works. HARLAN GREENE

Heyward, DuBose. "Beatrice Ravenel." In *The Library of Southern Literature,* supplement 1, edited by Edwin Anderson Alderman and Charles Alphonso Smith. Atlanta: Martin and Hoyt, 1923.

"Mrs. S. Prioleau Ravenel, Author and Poet, Dies." *Charleston Evening Post,* March 15, 1956, p. A2.

Rubin, Louis. *The Yemassee Lands: Poems of Beatrice Ravenel.* Chapel Hill: University of North Carolina Press, 1969.

Ravenel, Charles Dufort (b. 1938). Politician, businessman. Charles "Pug" Ravenel was born in Charleston on February 14, 1938, the son of Charles F. Ravenel and Yvonne Marie Michel. A football standout in high school in Charleston, he graduated from Bishop England (1956), Philips Exeter Academy (1957), Harvard

University (1961), and Harvard Business School (M.B.A., 1964). He was first marshall (president) of Harvard's graduating class and corecipient of the Bingham Award for most outstanding athlete. He worked on Wall Street from 1964 to 1972 and as a White House fellow at the U.S. Treasury Department (1966–1967). Ravenel returned to Charleston and established a merchant-banking firm. He married Mary Curtis on December 26, 1963. They have three children. Following a divorce, he married Susan Gibbes Woodward on November 30, 1991.

In 1974 Ravenel won the Democratic Party's nomination for governor on a platform emphasizing a new South Carolina. He criticized the state Senate establishment for opposing ethics, home rule, and campaign reform. He openly opposed the death penalty, supported the right of collective bargaining by public employees, openly reported his campaign expenditures, and conducted the first sophisticated media campaign in South Carolina. Ravenel led the first primary and defeated Congressman William Jennings Bryan Dorn in a runoff. Despite a circuit court ruling before his campaign that he met state residency requirements, some disgruntled Democrats challenged Ravenel's residency status. On September 23, 1974, the state Supreme Court reversed the circuit court, issuing an injunction against his candidacy. The Democratic Party then selected Dorn as its gubernatorial candidate. This schism resulted in the election of James B. Edwards as the first Republican governor of South Carolina since Reconstruction.

In 1978 Ravenel ran against Republican incumbent Strom Thurmond for the U.S. Senate. Thurmond was reelected, but by the narrowest victory margin since he became a senator in 1954. In 1980 Ravenel served as U.S. associate deputy secretary of commerce and was the Democratic Party's candidate for the First Congressional District seat. He was narrowly defeated by Republican Tommy Hartnett.

In 1981 Ravenel withdrew from political life for a career combining public service and banking. He was a trustee of Philips Exeter Academy, a member of the Harvard College Board of Overseers Visitors' Committee, a trustee for Historic Charleston Foundation, president of Spoleto Festival USA, and chair of the Governor's State Employment and Training Council. In business he was chair of Capital South Corporation, specializing in capitalizing smaller companies, as well as a board member of numerous other corporations.

In 1996 Ravenel pleaded guilty to bank fraud conspiracy involving Citadel Federal Savings Bank and was sentenced to eleven months and seventeen days in a federal prison. Following completion of his sentence, Ravenel returned to Charleston, where he continued his work in the community and in real estate. In January 2001 Ravenel was officially pardoned by the president of the United States. WILLIAM V. MOORE

Bass, Jack, and Walter DeVries. *The Transformation of Southern Politics: Social Change and Political Consequence since 1945.* 1976. Reprint, Athens: University of Georgia Press, 1995.

Ravenel, Charles D. Papers. Modern Political Collections, South Caroliniana Library, University of South Carolina, Columbia.

Ravenel, Edmund (1797–1871). Physician, naturalist. Ravenel was born in Charleston on December 8, 1797, sixth of the nine children of the planter Daniel Ravenel and his wife, Catherine Prioleau. Little information exists on the early years and education of Ravenel, but it is known that he completed the medical program of the University of Pennsylvania and received the M.D. degree in 1819. Soon thereafter Ravenel established a medical practice in Charleston. On April 16, 1823, he married Charlotte Matilda Ford, who died three years later after giving birth to their only child. In 1829 Ravenel married Charlotte's half sister, Louisa Catherine Ford, with whom he had seven children.

After helping to establish the Medical College of South Carolina in 1824, Ravenel served as its professor of chemistry and pharmacy and, later, as dean. Following a controversy over control of the institution, Ravenel participated in the formation of the Medical College of the State of South Carolina in 1834 and served on its faculty until 1835, when he moved to a plantation called the Grove, north of Charleston on the Cooper River. Although he was a highly successful planter, Ravenel became better known for his work in natural history.

Initially interested in fish, Ravenel soon turned his attention to conchology (the study of mollusks) and, later, to paleontology. In due course, he amassed a huge collection of mollusk shells, and in 1834 he published a catalog, or list, of his specimens, which included more than seven hundred living and fossil species and contained the first description of the lettered olive (*Oliva sayana*). Through exchanges, Ravenel also built a large collection of shells from elsewhere. By the 1840s he was collecting invertebrate marine fossils uncovered from marl beds on his plantation. Especially interested in fossil echinoderms, Ravenel discovered several species new to science. As he enhanced his reputation, he was called upon by some of the world's most noted scientists, including Charles Lyell and Louis Agassiz.

During the 1850s Ravenel resumed his interest in shells and contributed several articles to scientific journals. By the outbreak of the Civil War, his collection included nearly 3,300 species of mollusk shells, and a noted American contemporary referred to Ravenel as a leading conchologist who possessed "a valuable cabinet, rich in marine and other species." Eventually, Ravenel's great collection went to the Charleston Museum, and it continues to be an important source for modern malacologists.

Meanwhile, Ravenel continued to practice medicine, mainly during the summers when he was at his home on Sullivan's Island. During the 1850s he served as physician to the indigent on the island. A vigorous proponent of secession, Ravenel strongly defended the notion of states' rights and the institution of slavery, but virtual blindness and advancing age prevented him from assisting the Confederacy. Although his record of scientific publications is comparatively modest, Ravenel did much to advance knowledge of conchology and paleontology in South Carolina, and he earned deserved recognition for his promotion of scientific research in the region. He died in Charleston on July 27, 1871, from injuries received from a fall down a staircase in his home. LESTER D. STEPHENS

Stephens, Lester D. *Science, Race, and Religion in the American South: John Bachman and the Charleston Circle of Naturalists, 1815–1895.* Chapel Hill: University of North Carolina Press, 2000.

Ravenel, Harriott Horry Rutledge (1832–1912). Novelist, biographer, historian. Ravenel was born on August 12, 1832, in Charleston, the daughter of Edward Cotesworth Rutledge and Rebecca Motte Lowndes. In her youth, she received private tutoring at her home in Charleston and attended Madame Talvande's prestigious female academy. On March 20, 1851, she married a prominent physician, St. Julien Ravenel, with whom she would have nine children. During the Civil War her husband oversaw a Confederate hospital and medical laboratory, and she accompanied him to Columbia. While her husband was away on Confederate business, Ravenel resisted Sherman's soldiers and protected her home from fire, prompting Mary Chesnut to write in her diary, "Mrs. St. Julien

. . . actually awed the Yankees into civil behavior." Ravenel's brief memoir, "When Columbia Burned," was presented as a speech to the Daughters of the Confederacy and appeared several years later in *South Carolina Women in the Confederacy.*

Though she wrote poetry, brief essays, and stories on other subjects, Ravenel's major works focused on southern history and manners. Her most successful piece of fiction, *Ashurst; or "The Days That Are Not,"* fondly depicted antebellum lifestyles and landscapes. The novelette was featured as the prize story in the Charleston *Weekly News* under the pen name Mrs. H. Hilton Broom before being published in book form in 1879. Ravenel's other major works were born of her interest in preserving state and family history. A descendant of the statesmen John Rutledge and William Lowndes and a relative of the famed Charles Cotesworth Pinckney, Ravenel drew on her "intimate knowledge of family history and traditions" as well as letters, journals, and archives to shape her writings.

In 1896, as part of a national series entitled "Women of Colonial and Revolutionary Times," Ravenel published a brief biography, *Eliza Pinckney,* to preserve the achievements of her great-great-grandmother. Five years later she published *Life and Times of William Lowndes of South Carolina, 1782–1822* as a tribute to her maternal grandfather, who served in Congress with John Calhoun and Langdon Cheves. Her final work, *Charleston: The Place and the People,* appeared in 1906, tracing the history of her native city from its lively colonial past to the Civil War era. While Ravenel's works received many favorable contemporary reviews, her books were also noted for reflecting a "sympathetic interest" and "uncritical" perspective. Ravenel observed the difficulty of writing history that held such deeply personal meaning for the author. In her recollection of Columbia's burning, she humbly offered her vantage point as one of many that sought to contribute "a real and correct picture in true and perfect proportions." Characterized as "a great lady of the Old South," Ravenel worked devotedly on her last publication even while in feeble health. She died in Charleston on July 2, 1912, and was buried in Magnolia Cemetery. SANDRA BARRETT MOORE

Ravenel, Harriott Horry. *Ashurst; or, "The Days That Are Not": The Prize Story from the Charleston Weekly News.* Charleston, S.C.: News and Courier Book Presses, 1879.

———. *Charleston: The Place and the People.* New York: Macmillan, 1906.

———. Papers. South Carolina Historical Society, Charleston.

———. "When Columbia Burned." In *South Carolina Women in the Confederacy,* edited by Mrs. Thomas Taylor. Vol. 1. Columbia, S.C.: State Company, 1903.

Ravenel, Henry William (1814–1887). Botanist, diarist. Ravenel was born at his grandfather's plantation, Pooshee, in St. John's Berkeley Parish on May 19, 1814. His parents, Dr. Henry Ravenel, a physician and planter, and Catherine Stevens, were both descended from prominent Huguenot families. As was the case with other children of planters, Henry's early education was with private tutors and at private academies, but it also included exploring the lowcountry's natural environment and enjoying the stories and folklore told by the plantation slaves, by his family, and most certainly by visiting naturalists.

In January 1829 Ravenel left Pooshee to attend the school of James M. Daniels in Columbia to prepare for admission to South Carolina College that fall. At college he was active in the Clariosophic Society and graduated in December 1832. Returning to the lowcountry, he married Elizabeth Galliard Snowden on December 1, 1835. The marriage produced five daughters and one son. Ravenel's father dissuaded him from a medical career, so he followed family tradition and acquired Northampton Plantation from his father.

At Northampton, Ravenel developed his interest in collecting, identifying, and pressing/preserving plants, which included all levels of plants from fungi to flowering plants. During this period he developed many of his lifelong collaborations with other botanists, including Asa Gray, Moses Curtis, Edward Tuckerman, and Miles Berkeley. In 1851 Ravenel's health began to decline and he decided to move to Aiken, which was only a day's train ride to Charleston. In 1853 Ravenel sold Northampton and built a house just west of Aiken called Hampton Hills. His wife Elizabeth died in 1855, and on August 12, 1858, he married Mary Huger Dawson. His second marriage produced five daughters.

One of Ravenel's major legacies is the journal that he began keeping on December 19, 1859, and in which he faithfully made daily entries until July 2, 1887, fifteen days before his death. They reveal his deep southern patriotism and that he invested heavily in the Confederacy, but his age and frail health prevented any active service in the Confederate army. After the Civil War he kept detailed records of his botanical collecting and correspondence. His observations have proven to be a rich resource to both historians and botanists.

Ravenel's other major contribution was in the field of botany, primarily mycology: the study of fungi. He was a well-established botanist before the Civil War and remained so until his death. In his honor, several genera bear the species name *ravenelii* and one genus of fungal rust was named *Ravenelia.* He published two major works of mycology, *Fungi Caroliniani Exsiccati,* published in five volumes in Charleston between 1852 and 1860, and *Fungi Americani Exsiccati,* published in eight parts in London with the English mycologist M. C. Cooke between 1878 and 1882. Together, these works afforded mycologists in America and in Europe a unique opportunity to see fungi native to the southeastern United States. Ravenel died in Aiken on July 17, 1887, and was buried at St. Thaddeus Episcopal Church cemetery there. HARRY E. SHEALY, JR.

Childs, Arney Robinson, ed. *The Private Journal of Henry William Ravenel, 1859–1887.* Columbia: University of South Carolina Press, 1947.

Haygood, Tamara Miner. *Henry William Ravenel 1814–1887, South Carolina Scientist in the Civil War Era.* Tuscaloosa: University of Alabama Press, 1987.

Ravenel, St. Julien (1819–1882). Physician, chemist, inventor. Ravenel was born in Charleston on December 15, 1819, son of the merchant John Ravenel and Anna Elizabeth Ford. He was educated at schools in Charleston and Morristown, New Jersey. He then persuaded his father to let him read on his own for two years rather than attend college. During that period he made the acquaintance of Dr. John E. Holbrook, a professor at the Medical College of South Carolina. Ravenel began the study of medicine in the office of Drs. Holbrook and Thomas L. Ogier. He graduated from the Medical College of South Carolina in 1840 and then studied in Philadelphia and Paris before returning to Charleston. Ravenel was appointed a demonstrator of anatomy at the Medical College, but his mentors, Holbrook and Louis Agassiz, encouraged his interest in natural history and physiology as well as agricultural chemistry. He married Harriott Horry Rutledge on March 20, 1851, and the couple had four daughters and five sons. He withdrew from the active medical practice in 1851.

Investigating the marl deposits along the Cooper River, Ravenel ascertained that the marl could be converted into lime. In 1856 he secured a patent to use carbonate of lime for the production of artificial stone, and a year later he established the first stone lime works in the state at Stony Landing, which would go on to supply most of the lime used by the Confederacy. During the Civil War, Ravenel served with the Phoenix Rifles at Fort Sumter and then was commissioned a surgeon. He was placed in charge of the Confederate hospital at Columbia in 1862 and later headed the laboratory that prepared drugs and medical stores for the army. Ravenel also helped design the semisubmersible torpedo boat *David,* which in October 1863 attacked the Federal warship *New Ironsides.*

After the war, Ravenel returned to Charleston and experimented with the phosphate deposits along the Ashley and Cooper Rivers for the purpose of producing fertilizers. In 1868 he and several other investors organized the Wando Mining and Manufacturing Company to manufacture fertilizers with a process that made phosphate rocks soluble with the addition of ammonia to animal matter. Ravenel next produced phosphate fertilizers without ammonia and developed a process for adding marl to counteract the acid, which had previously destroyed the bags in which the fertilizer was shipped. Ravenel also helped establish the Charleston Agricultural Lime Company at Woodstock. While working as a chemist at this lime works, he found that using lime made from marl combined with silica prevented caustic action on the plants it was fertilizing. In April 1871 Ravenel received a second patent for an improvement in an apparatus used to produce sulfuric acid used in fertilizers.

Ravenel also directed the drilling of a system of artesian wells in and around Charleston, which greatly improved the quality of the city's water supply. At the time of his death he was working on plans to irrigate abandoned rice fields and use the lands to cultivate grasses for hay. Ravenel's work had an enormous impact on the health and economy of the South Carolina lowcountry. He died in Charleston on March 16, 1882, and was buried in the cemetery of the Huguenot Church. MARY S. MILLER

"Dr. St. Julien Ravenel." Charleston *News and Courier,* March 18, 1882, p. 2.

State Agricultural Society of South Carolina. *Memorial to Dr. St. Julien Ravenel, April 13, 1882.* Charleston, S.C., 1882.

Ravenel, Shannon. (b. 1938). Editor. Ravenel was born in Charlotte, North Carolina, on August 13, 1938, the daughter of Elias Prioleau and Harriet Steedman. She was reared in Charleston and Camden. On May 25, 1968, she married neurobiologist Dale Purves, and they have two children. Ravenel holds a B.A. from Hollins College (1960). She began her publishing career in Houghton Mifflin's trade department as a secretary but soon moved into an editorial position. She worked at Houghton Mifflin's Boston offices from 1961 to 1971, and during that time she edited the work of Pat Conroy, Willie Morris, Anne Sexton, C. K. Williams, and Jonathan Kozol.

In 1977 Ravenel was asked to serve as series editor of *The Best American Short Stories.* She edited thirteen volumes of the anthology (1978–90) as well as the retrospective *Best American Short Stories of the Eighties* (1990). Ravenel was a lecturer in creative writing at Washington University in St. Louis from 1983 to 1985. She has been a juror and panelist for numerous organizations including the National Endowment for the Arts, the DeWitt and Lila Wallace Literary Marketing Grants, and the Rea Award for the Short Story. In 1990 Ravenel was the recipient of the Council of Literary Magazines and Presses Distinguished Achievement Award.

It is her work at Algonquin Books, however, for which Ravenel is renowned in American letters. In 1982 she and her former teacher Louis Rubin established Algonquin in Chapel Hill. Her first position there was senior editor and member of the board of directors; through the years she progressed to editorial director and vice president. During her tenure at Algonquin, Ravenel brought attention to writers such as Larry Brown, Julia Alvarez, Jill McCorkle, A. J. Verdelle, Lewis Nordan, Clyde Edgerton, Robert Morgan, Tony Earley, and Lee Smith.

In January 2001 Ravenel stepped down as Algonquin's editorial director to select books for her own imprint, Shannon Ravenel Books with Algonquin, which is now a division of Workman Publishing. Her work continues on the *New Stories from the South: The Year's Best* series, which began in 1986. These yearly volumes feature some twenty works of short fiction chosen each year from hundreds of southern stories published in literary publications as well as national magazines and provide exposure both to emerging writers and often to emerging literary journals. When asked what she considers to be her chief contribution to southern letters, Ravenel replied, "Simply making certain that those writers who don't have connections are given a way to become better known." ELLEN MALPHRUS

Ravenel, Shannon. "'I Want You to Think about Something:' Louis D. Rubin Jr. and the Establishment of Algonquin Books of Chapel Hill." *Southern Review* 38 (Autumn 2002): 704–11.

———. "The State of the Story." *Literary Review* 35 (Summer 1992): 619–22.

———. "The Thrill of Discovery." *Five Points* (Spring 2004).

Rea, Paul Marshall (1878–1948). Biologist, educator, museologist. Rea was born in Cotuit, Massachusetts, on February 13, 1878, the son of the Reverend John T. Rea and S. Helen Rea. He graduated from Williams College in 1899; did additional academic work at the Marine Biological Laboratory at Woods Hole, Massachusetts, and at Columbia University; and for a time was an assistant in biology at Williams. He married Carolyn Morse of Medford, Massachusetts, in 1904. The couple had one son before Carolyn died from typhoid fever in 1913. On June 25, 1919, Rea married Marian Goddard Hussey, with whom he had a daughter.

In 1903 Rea became professor of biology and geology and curator of the museum at the College of Charleston. He would remain at the college until 1914. He assumed his position as curator of the museum at a time when it needed a leader with vision and a commitment to increasing the educational and research potentials of the collections. Assisted by his first wife, Rea set out to make the museum more visible, presenting public lectures on natural history, publishing a museum bulletin sent to leaders of the city, and founding the Charleston Natural History Society (which later would become a chapter of the National Audubon Society). In March 1906 Rea negotiated a change in his title from curator to director of the museum, and in December 1906 he arranged for the name of the museum to be changed from the College of Charleston Museum to the Charleston Museum. Through Rea's efforts the museum was moved from the college, where it had been housed for many years, into the vacant Thomson Auditorium, which had been built for the 1899 reunion of Confederate Veterans. In order to adequately handle the collections, Thomson Auditorium was remodeled, and by the middle of 1911 the move of the museum holdings to their new quarters was essentially complete. In 1915 the Charleston Museum was chartered as an independent organization with its own board of trustees and with Paul Rea continuing as director until 1920. In addition to his other duties, Rea taught embryology and physiology at the Medical College of the State of South Carolina in Charleston from 1911 to 1920.

Rea served as secretary of the American Association of Museums from 1907 to 1917 and later served as president of that organization from 1919 to 1921. He wrote *Directory of American Museums* (1910), *The Museum and the Community* (1932), and numerous articles on museum work.

In 1920 Rea moved to Ohio to become director of the Cleveland Museum of Natural History, a position he held until 1928. Later he was executive officer of the Philadelphia Museum of Art (1929), consultant to an advisory group on museums established by the Carnegie Corporation of New York (1930–1932), and director of the Santa Barbara Museum of Natural History (1933–1936). Rea died suddenly at his home in Santa Barbara, California, on January 15, 1948. WILLIAM D. ANDERSON, JR.

Sanders, Albert E., and William D. Anderson, Jr. *Natural History Investigations in South Carolina from Colonial Times to the Present.* Columbia: University of South Carolina Press, 1999.

Read, Jacob (ca. 1752–1816). Lawyer, U.S. senator. Born around 1752 in Christ Church Parish, Read was the eldest son of the Charleston merchant James Read and Rebecca Bond. About 1759 Read's parents settled in Savannah, where he received his early education at a local boarding school. He began the study of law in 1768, and although admitted to the South Carolina Bar in 1773, he went on to Gray's Inn in London to further his legal studies. While there, Read joined other Americans in the British capital in petitioning against the Coercive Acts of 1774. Upon his return to South Carolina two years later, he assumed a captaincy in the Charleston militia. After the fall of the city in 1780, Read was one of sixty-five South Carolina patriots exiled by the British to St. Augustine, Florida. There, he landed in solitary confinement for twelve days as a result of "some imprudent expressions" in his correspondence. Refusing to admit any wrongdoing, he remained a prisoner in St. Mark's Castle for five months, until his exchange in July 1781.

With the restoration of civil government in South Carolina, Read in January 1782 took a seat in the Jacksonborough Assembly, where he represented the city parishes of St. Philip's and St. Michael's. He remained a member of the House of Representatives until 1794. During his first term, he served on the committee for the amercement of Loyalists and helped lead the opposition to the arming of blacks. The following year, on February 12, 1783, the General Assembly elected him to Congress. A delegate for two years, Read played an active part in deliberations that culminated in the Northwest Ordinance of 1787. He also lobbied to have the federal capital placed in a southerly location. Toward the end of his congressional tenure, on October 13, 1785, Read married Catherine Van Horne, daughter of the wealthy New York merchant David Van Horne. The couple had four children.

Read's time in Congress led him to chafe at the impotence of the federal government under the Articles of Confederation. "To be respected [Congress] must be enabled to enforce an Obedience to their Ordinance. . . . If this is denied Congress is I think an Unnecessary & Useless Burden." In the January 1788 debates on the Constitution in the state House of Representatives, Read spoke strongly in favor of the new plan of government. Representing Christ Church Parish at the state ratification convention the following May, Read also voted for it.

Chosen Speaker of the South Carolina House of Representatives in 1789, Read repeatedly offered himself for higher office without success. Finally, in 1794, he won election to the U.S. Senate, where he sat from 1795 to 1801. A Federalist with close ties to the mercantile community, Read cast the crucial vote necessary for ratification of the Jay Treaty, for which a Charleston mob opposing the accord hung him in effigy and threatened his home. Despite having been treated "exceedingly Cruelly" by John Rutledge in the wrangle over the treaty, Read struggled to get his fellow South Carolinian confirmed as chief justice of the United States Supreme Court, although he was unsuccessful. Through patronage, Read gained influence over local customs and excise services and the Charleston branch of the Bank of the United States, agencies of particular importance to his merchant allies. At the peak of his public career in the late 1790s, Read, with James Simons, headed the most powerful faction in state politics. In 1800, however, he narrowly lost a reelection bid to John Ewing Colhoun, with Read apparently "sacrificed" for his support of the administration of John Adams. Appointed a federal district judge by Adams under the Judiciary Act of 1801, Read never served, as the authorizing legislation was repealed before he could take office.

As a lawyer, Read achieved distinction at both the state and the federal bars. From 1776 to 1779 he acted as counsel for South Carolina. In 1786 he joined the defense in the sensational trial of William Clay Snipes for the dueling murder of Maurice Simons. In the mid-1790s he litigated a series of sensitive cases for the British vice consuls in Charleston and Savannah, who sought to use American courts to recover British vessels captured by French privateers. Despite his experiences during the Revolution, Read often represented British interests, which likely cemented his reputation for being "decidedly anti-Gallican." In 1795 Read became the first South Carolinian to argue before the U.S. Supreme Court.

Although given to "wonderful pomposity," Read was deemed "a sensible, as well as a very good natured man." He died in Charleston on July 17, 1816, survived by his wife and children. ROBERT F. KARACHUK

Bailey, N. Louise, and Elizabeth Ivey Cooper, eds. *Biographical Directory of the South Carolina House of Representatives.* Vol. 3, *1775–1790.* Columbia: University of South Carolina Press, 1981.

Reconstruction. The final defeat of the Confederacy in 1865 brought an important and difficult problem for the federal government: how were the defeated states to be brought back into the Union? Most agreed that this should be accomplished as rapidly as possible, but not so rapidly that the planter elite that had led the South in secession would be able to renew the rebellion or reverse the results of the war. The South would have to remain under federal

The Zion School in Charleston was one of many that came into existence to provide educational opportunities for black Carolinians of all ages. Courtesy, South Carolina Historical Society

control until it was deemed safe to leave matters to the southern state governments. This probationary period of federal control was termed "Reconstruction." To some contemporaries, the reconstruction of the Union was complete, and Reconstruction ended when the South's representatives were readmitted to Congress in 1868. In modern parlance, however, the period of President Andrew Johnson's control of the process of readmission is termed "provisional Reconstruction" or "Presidential Reconstruction." The following period, marked by the control of southern policy by Congress, is termed "Congressional Reconstruction" or "Radical Reconstruction," after the Radical Republicans who dominated Congress. The duration of the Reconstruction period varied among southern states, depending on when they were readmitted to the Union by Congress, or when they reestablished Democratic rule. In South Carolina, Reconstruction lasted from 1865 to 1877, with the break between Presidential and Congressional control occurring in 1867 when the freedmen were registered to vote for delegates to a constitutional convention.

President Johnson's plan for Reconstruction would have left the antebellum elite in control of the southern states and would not have included black suffrage. It did, however, require that southern whites accept the results of the war—in particular the abolition of slavery. The plan did not sit well with Republicans in Congress, who considered it too lenient. Northerners blamed the war on southern planters, who used their control of black labor to control their states. In a serious miscalculation of northern sentiment, southern leaders passed Black Codes, laws restricting the activities and occupations of African Americans and remanding them to the control of their former owners. South Carolina's code, enacted in December 1865, was typical: there were stringent regulations on work and travel that applied only to African Americans and a system of courts that tried only African Americans. The Black Codes were invalidated by the state's military governor, who saw them as reestablishing slavery in everything but name. South Carolinians then lost their last chance to avoid Congressional Reconstruction by refusing to ratify the Fourteenth Amendment, which among other provisions would have made African Americans citizens of the state and punished the state if it did not give them the vote.

Congressional Republicans capitalized on northern outrage in 1867 by passing the Reconstruction Acts, which mandated the registration of all adult males in the South as voters and the holding of elections for delegates to a constitutional convention. In South Carolina, of 124 delegates to the 1868 convention, 73 were black or of mixed ancestry, and all were Republicans. The constitution they wrote was modeled on those of northern states on matters such as local government, women's rights, and public education, but it surpassed them in its commitment to racial equality. It extended voting rights to all men; proposals to limit voting to the literate, the educated, or those who paid a poll tax were all voted down overwhelmingly.

Under the new constitution the state's African Americans, who comprised sixty percent of the voting population, had the voting strength to ensure Republican control of the state government. This domination allowed the passage of more legislation to improve the condition of the freedmen than was accomplished in any other state. An example was the creation in 1869 of the South Carolina Land Commission, an institution unique to the state, whose purpose was to make landownership possible for poor blacks. Unfortunately, one-party domination also led to a lack of accountability on the part of many Republican officeholders. Corruption flourished in the state legislature and in the executive offices of the state. In one instance in 1870–1871, the state's financial board secured the authority to print and sell $1 million in state bonds; there were to be $1,000 bonds numbered 1 to 1,000. Members of the board printed two sets—both numbered 1 to 1,000—and sold both sets. They kept no records of their transactions and were caught only when a New York investment firm came into possession of two bonds with the same number on both. Partly as a result of such malfeasance, and partly because of legitimate increases in expenditures such as the creation of a public school system from scratch, state budgets skyrocketed during Reconstruction and the state slipped further and further into debt.

Most white South Carolinians never admitted the legitimacy of the Republican government. Claiming that Republican leaders lacked the wealth, education, and intelligence to govern the state, the former planter-elite derided their opponents in vituperative and bitter language. Often they did worse. Organizations such as the Ku Klux Klan were formed to intimidate Republicans, especially Republican leaders; they whipped or beat hundreds of victims and murdered scores. Some of those killed were Republican legislators, such as Solomon Dill, Benjamin Franklin Randolph, and James Martin, all assassinated in 1868. From that year until 1871 South Carolina Republicans operated in a climate of terror. Some were able to defend themselves; others were able to move. Most had to be vigilant and try to stay one step ahead of the Ku-Klux, as it was then called. Almost all Republicans had the experience of spending nights in the woods to avoid attack.

President Ulysses S. Grant, elected in 1868, was much more sympathetic to Congress's view of Reconstruction than Johnson had been. In 1871 Grant's administration undertook an extensive effort to crack down on terrorism, and South Carolina in particular was under scrutiny. Congress passed the Ku-Klux Act, making it a federal crime to "conspire or go in disguise . . . for the purpose of depriving . . . any person or class of persons of the equal protection of the laws." Nine upcountry counties were placed under martial law, and hundreds of arrests were made. Convictions were few since the federal prosecutors were overwhelmed by the number of cases and since most of the attacks had occurred before the passage of the Ku-Klux Act. Federal intervention certainly reduced the scale of terrorism, and the Ku-Klux as an organization was destroyed as many of its leaders fled the state. Nevertheless, the government's assault on political violence was not a complete success. Attacks on leading Republicans continued throughout Reconstruction and beyond.

White Democrats often claimed that violence was a response to corrupt government. Simple chronology disproves this assertion—terrorism began well before the first frauds were committed—but it was accepted as truth by much of the northern press. Perhaps the most important example is the reporting of James S. Pike, first in the pages of the *New York Tribune* and then in a widely read book, *The Prostrate State.* In the book, Pike portrayed the South Carolina government as a sink of corruption and ignorance, and he placed the blame squarely on blacks. Most of his accusations were unfair and many were entirely fictitious, but the northern public believed them. Such writings undermined northern will to maintain the southern Republican governments in power.

White Democrats attempted to achieve some level of influence in state politics by several means. In the 1870, 1872, and 1874 elections, they joined with disaffected Republicans to create fusion tickets. These all went down to failure, but the last one did increase the number of Democrats in the legislature and in some county governments. In 1871 and 1874 they orchestrated "Taxpayers' Conventions," which met to decry the government's extravagance and

Although the vote in the disputed election of 1876 was very close, it was clear to outside observers that the real power in the state rested with Wade Hampton and the Democrats—not with Daniel Chamberlain and the Republicans. Courtesy, South Carolina Historical Society

investigate its finances; these too had only limited results. The means by which they recaptured the state was simply the assertion of force. This strategy, pioneered in 1875 by Mississippi whites, was put into effect in 1876. In the election of that year, the Democrats ran a full statewide ticket for the first time since 1868. Wade Hampton III, South Carolina's highest-ranking Confederate officer, accepted the nomination for governor, and the other Democrats on the ticket were also former Confederates. The Democrats used a dual strategy: Hampton portrayed himself as a moderate and made appeals for black support, while his lieutenants practiced strong-arm tactics of intimidation and violence. Combined with massive fraud, the strategy propelled the Democrats to victory, at least on the face of the returns; but the returns were clearly fraudulent.

Hampton and the Republican incumbent, Daniel H. Chamberlain, each claimed to be governor. Both parties claimed control of the state legislature. And both parties claimed to have carried the state for their candidates in the 1876 presidential election. Republican Rutherford Hayes was awarded the presidency by a bipartisan election commission, but after meeting with Hampton and Chamberlain he decided not to use federal power to protect Chamberlain's government. Chamberlain knew that spelled the end of Republican government in South Carolina. Hampton commanded the loyalty of almost all white South Carolinians, giving him the largest taxpayers of the state and a superior military force of trained Confederate veterans. Chamberlain resigned in April 1877, thus ending Reconstruction in South Carolina. With the Democrats in control of the state, the election system was altered to prevent most blacks from voting. By the 1890s there were almost no black or Republican officeholders in the state, a condition that continued for more than half a century. HYMAN S. RUBIN III

Holt, Thomas. *Black over White: Negro Political Leadership in South Carolina during Reconstruction.* Urbana: University of Illinois Press, 1977.

Reynolds, John S. *Reconstruction in South Carolina, 1865–1877.* 1905. Reprint, New York: Negro Universities Press, 1969.

Simkins, Francis Butler, and Robert Hilliard Woody. *South Carolina during Reconstruction.* Chapel Hill: University of North Carolina Press, 1932.

Williamson, Joel. *After Slavery: The Negro in South Carolina during Reconstruction, 1861–1877.* Chapel Hill: University of North Carolina Press, 1965.

Zuczek, Richard. *State of Rebellion: Reconstruction in South Carolina.* Columbia: University of South Carolina Press, 1996.

Red dots. A phenomenon that piques the curiosity of both visitors and lifelong residents: why do South Carolina liquor stores display red dots? The answer lies in a heated battle between drys and wets that developed when liquor sales became legal again in 1935 after Prohibition. During the ensuing decade those selling booze, diehard Prohibitionists, and the State Tax Commission (given the task of regulating this revived trade) wrangled constantly over on-site advertising.

Storefront ads so infuriated upcountry drys that in 1938 authorities decreed that only a discreet "Retail Liquor Dealer" sign could be displayed. Seven years later, with creation of the Alcoholic Beverage Control Board (ABC), they decided to reduce any such sign to letters only a few inches high placed in the lower right-hand corner of a display window or on the front door. Liquor stores of that era had no *back* door.

Under these circumstances, Jesse J. Fabian, a successful Charleston liquor dealer, hired "Doc" Wansley to create a legal sign for one of his shops. When it was completed, Wansley realized that few would notice such minuscule lettering and, inspired by a design then found on every pack of Lucky Strike cigarettes, drew a bright red circle around his masterpiece. Thus was born South Carolina's famous red dot.

These now-familiar circles grew and prospered until January 1968, when the ABC suddenly ruled that these constituted advertising and should be banished from the landscape. The General Assembly voted instead to save the dot, although members agreed that on each exterior wall of a store there could be only one dot, not to exceed thirty-six inches in diameter. These subsequent rules have been relaxed somewhat, but into the twenty-first century the red dot remained a faithful beacon for those seeking liquor, as well as a warning sign for those determined to avoid it. JOHN H. MOORE

Moore, John H. "Solving the Red Dot Mystery." *Sandlapper* (spring 2000): 32–34.

Red Shirts. The Red Shirts, named for their distinctive uniforms, were the horsemen who accompanied Wade Hampton III and other Democratic candidates on their tour around South Carolina in the tumultuous election of 1876. They executed a Democratic strategy euphemistically termed "force without violence" to defeat the much more numerous Republicans and thereby reestablish white supremacy in South Carolina.

The Red Shirts were simply a more organized version of the "rifle clubs" or "sabre clubs" that had proliferated in South Carolina after the breakup of the Ku Klux Klan by federal forces in 1871. These clubs, ostensibly social in nature, were in fact local paramilitary forces loyal to the Democratic Party. Composed of hundreds of rifle clubs totaling fifteen thousand or more men, the Red Shirts were much more numerous than the detachment of U.S. troops in the state at that time. Memoirs of former Red Shirts indicate that the uniform was originally a mockery of the Republican practice of "waving the bloody shirt," a slang term for efforts to arouse sectional passions among voters. Given their purpose of securing home rule, the Red

Shirts may also have been a reference to Garibaldi's Italian nationalist organization of that name.

Organized as Red Shirt brigades, they intimidated and sometimes attacked Republicans during the 1876 campaign. "Force without violence" was a slogan, not a binding policy, and Red Shirt groups sometimes used deadly violence. The worst instance was the Ellenton Riot, in which Edgefield Red Shirts killed thirty black militiamen and a state senator, many in cold blood. Red Shirts all over the state stuffed ballot boxes and committed other frauds to ensure Hampton's election. In the traditional mythology of Reconstruction, these unsavory aspects of the campaign were forgotten, and the Red Shirts—Hampton first among them—became the noble saviors of the state. The editors of the *State* newspaper commented in 1905: "Wade Hampton and the men who wore red shirts in the broad light of day and the women who blessed them redeemed South Carolina from negro rule." Although they were overwhelmingly white and were committed to white supremacy, the Red Shirts did count some African Americans in their number. These black Democrats often retained the right to vote after most African Americans were disfranchised. HYMAN S. RUBIN III

Drago, Edmund L. *Hurrah for Hampton! Black Red Shirts in South Carolina during Reconstruction.* Fayetteville: University of Arkansas Press, 1998.

Jarrell, Hampton M. *Wade Hampton and the Negro: The Road Not Taken.* Columbia: University of South Carolina Press, 1949.

Sheppard, William Arthur. *Red Shirts Remembered: Southern Brigadiers of the Reconstruction Period.* Atlanta: Ruralist Press, 1940.

Williams, Alfred B. *Hampton and His Red Shirts: South Carolina's Deliverance in 1876.* Charleston, S.C.: Walker, Evans, and Cogswell, 1935.

Zuczek, Richard. *State of Rebellion: Reconstruction in South Carolina.* Columbia: University of South Carolina Press, 1996.

Redcliffe (Aiken County). Constructed between 1857 and 1859, Redcliffe was the home place of South Carolina governor James Henry Hammond and three generations of his descendants. Located in western Aiken County near Beech Island, Redcliffe served as an architectural and horticultural showplace, as well as the center of domestic life for the Hammond family. By 1860 it functioned primarily as a headquarters for Hammond's extensive cotton plantations, which were sustained by more than three hundred slaves.

Hammond worked closely with the contractor William Henry Goodrich to design and build the two-story, frame mansion at Redcliffe. Transitional Greek revival in style, the house also displays restrained Italianate elements, unusual in South Carolina. Greek-revival features include a series of rectangular frieze-band windows; exterior doors with transoms and sidelights; Doric porch columns; square, two-story paneled corner pilasters; and pedimented windows. An Italianate cupola, or observatory, once capped the mansion's hipped roof. A spectacular center hall, fifty-three feet long and twenty feet wide, dominates the interior. Much of the interior woodwork, including doors, library shelves, banisters, and mantles, was crafted from local sycamore trees. The grounds were designed by the landscape architect Louis Berckmans and include terraced hillsides. One of Redcliffe's most dramatic features is a long avenue of southern magnolias.

In 1935 John Shaw Billings, a Hammond descendant and an editor of *Time* and *Life* magazines, purchased Redcliffe and began extensive restoration. Shortly before his death he donated the property to the South Carolina Department of Parks, Recreation, and Tourism. In 1975 Redcliffe State Historic Site was opened to the public as a house museum. AL HESTER

Bleser, Carol, ed. *The Hammonds of Redcliffe.* New York: Oxford University Press, 1981.

Faust, Drew Gilpin. *James Henry Hammond and the Old South: A Design for Mastery.* Baton Rouge: Louisiana State University Press, 1982.

Nylund, Rowena. *Redcliffe Plantation State Park: A Visitors' Guide.* Columbia: South Carolina Department of Parks, Recreation, and Tourism, 1991.

Redfern, Paul Rinaldo (1902–1927). Aviator. Redfern was born on February 24, 1902, in Rochester, New York, the son of Frederick and Blanche Redfern. The family moved to Columbia, South Carolina, in 1910 after Paul's father accepted a teaching position at Benedict College. From an early age the younger Redfern displayed considerable interest in aviation. In 1916, during his second year at Columbia High School, Redfern constructed a standard-sized wooden airplane, lacking only an engine. The following year he worked for the Army Air Corps as a production inspector at Standard Aircraft Company's plant in Elizabeth, New Jersey. In February 1919 he returned to Columbia to complete high school.

With several helpers, Redfern assembled an airplane and transported passengers on day trips around the Carolinas. He became a noted stunt pilot at air exhibitions held throughout the Southeast. In 1925 Redfern met Gertrude Hildebrandt in Toledo, Ohio, while working for her father, and they were married that same year.

In 1926 the U.S. Customs Service in Savannah, Georgia, hired Redfern to be an aerial scout. However, he was ambitious to gain fame and fortune by undertaking an international solo air flight. In 1927 a group of prominent businessmen in Brunswick, Georgia, agreed to underwrite a flight from their city to Rio de Janeiro, Brazil. In June 1927 Redfern supervised the construction of a monoplane by the Stinson Aircraft Corporation of Detroit, Michigan. This aircraft, known as the *Port of Brunswick,* was painted primarily green and yellow—Brazil's national colors.

At 12:45 P.M. on August 25 Redfern took off from Brunswick. Five hours later a seaplane spotted him approximately three hundred miles east of the Bahamas. At 3:30 P.M. on August 26 a Norwegian freighter, the *Christian Krogh,* sailing west of Trinidad encountered Redfern's aircraft. The pilot dropped a canister into the water containing a handwritten note, which requested that the crewmen indicate the direction and the approximate distance to Venezuela's northern coastline. Subsequently, Redfern was seen by numerous eyewitnesses when the plane passed over the Orinoco delta in Venezuela. Various craft sailing south along the Orinoco River noted the monoplane flying overhead. Additional sightings occurred at Ciudad Bolivar, a town deep in the Venezuelan interior. Several observers noted a conspicuous trail of black smoke coming from the aircraft. The last definitive sighting of Redfern was approximately one hundred miles south of Ciudad Bolivar, only two flying hours from northern Brazil.

By August 29 Redfern had failed to reach any of his proposed destinations in Brazil. Reports that he had landed at various Brazilian locales proved false. Rumors circulated for more than two decades that he was alive and being held prisoner by Indians within a remote locale along the upper Amazon River. Despite several search-and-rescue missions, Redfern and his airplane have never been found.

In an attempt to capitalize on the public fascination with Redfern, MGM Studio included his saga as a subplot within the 1938 adventure movie *Too Hot to Handle.* A street in Rio de Janeiro was named in Redfern's honor. Although Redfern failed in his ultimate goal, he did achieve the first solo flight over the Caribbean. He also successfully completed the first nonstop air voyage between North and South America. MILES S. RICHARDS

Dennison, Leonidas R. *Devil Mountain.* New York: Hastings House, 1942.
Holdridge, Desmond. *Escape to the Tropics.* New York: Harcourt, Brace, 1937.
Richards, Miles S. "Paul R. Redfern, the Daring Lost Airman." *Carologue* 13 (winter 1997): 14–19.
Titler, Dale Milton. *Wings of Mystery: True Stories of Aviation History.* New York: Dodd, Mead, 1966.

Reform Party. During the Reconstruction era, South Carolina's voting population was about sixty percent African American, the vast majority of whom normally voted for the Republican Party. Democrats could not carry a statewide election unless, by persuasion or by force, they convinced numerous black voters to side with them. As a result, the statewide elections of 1870, 1872, and 1874 saw Democrats attempt to cooperate with disaffected Republicans to defeat the regular Republican Party. The Conservative Party of 1870 was widely viewed as a disguised Democratic party, and few Republicans voted for it. The Liberal Republicans of 1872 were perceived as truly Republican and received few Democrats' votes. In 1874, however, the coalition, this time called the "Reform Party," attracted a high turnout among Democrats and substantial defections from the Republicans; the result was the closest election of the three. The Republicans won, however, their candidate for governor prevailing by a margin of 80,403 votes to 68,818.

The Reform Party ran on the same platform as the regular Republicans, and for their nominees for governor and lieutenant governor the Reformers chose the runners-up for those offices from the regular Republican convention. John T. Green, the Reform nominee for governor, was a white native of Sumter County who had served as a circuit judge and was considered a man of integrity and honesty. The Reformers strove to make these traits the issue of the campaign. Financial scandals in nearly every branch of government had made South Carolina nationally famous for graft, and Democrats argued that the Republican Party could not be trusted to remedy the situation. The Republican candidate, Daniel H. Chamberlain, was a Harvard graduate and a Massachusetts native who had served as attorney general two years previously. He was not untouched by scandal, but he also promised that if elected he would undertake "reform," by which he meant both greater honesty in government and financial retrenchment.

The campaign was dominated by two sets of accusations: the Reformers accused the Republicans of being dishonest, and the Republicans accused the Reformers of being Democrats. In bolstering their claim, the Reformers noted that two years earlier the Republicans had promised reform but failed to rein in corruption and overspending. Meanwhile, Republicans accused Democrats of following a "possum policy" of pretending to be indifferent to the Reform movement while secretly bankrolling it; one Republican leader called the Reform Party "a white league ku klux possum." Indeed, white conservatives resorted to economic pressure and even violence in an attempt to carry the election for the Reform Party.

In the balloting, however, enough Republicans held firm that the party continued in power. But the fusion strategy was not a total failure for Democrats. Democrats and Reform Republicans together won 53 of 124 seats in the state House of Representatives and 15 of 33 seats in the state Senate—both numbers represent the best showing for the Democrats since the advent of black suffrage. These results were achieved largely through cooperation with Reform Republicans at the local level, and they illustrate that the potential existed for Democrats to retake the state through (mostly) peaceful means. Whether that potential would have become reality will never be known, as Democrats in 1876 abandoned fusion politics and regained control of the state by force. HYMAN S. RUBIN III

Rubin, Hyman S., III. "The South Carolina Scalawags." Ph.D. diss., Emory University, 2001.
Zuczek, Richard. *State of Rebellion: Reconstruction in South Carolina.* Columbia: University of South Carolina Press, 1996.

Reformed Episcopal Church. This small denomination (approximately six thousand members nationwide in 2000) was organized in New York City on December 2, 1873, by eight clergy and twenty laypersons who had been members of the Protestant Episcopal Church. It emerged out of the low-church / high-church controversy of the mid–nineteenth century. Assistant Bishop George Cummins of Kentucky and Charles Edward Cheney, rector of Christ Church, Chicago, were both opposed to the ritualism and ecclesiasticism of the high-church party and especially to the doctrine of baptismal regeneration, which taught that at baptism a person is not only initiated into the Christian community but is also truly "born again," regenerated, made new. The immediate cause of the division was Cummins's participation in a joint communion service with Presbyterians and Methodists at the Fifth Avenue Presbyterian Church in New York City, a service at which the Episcopal *Book of Common Prayer* was not used. Cummins was criticized for this and withdrew from the Episcopal Church.

The Reformed Episcopal Church in South Carolina is part of the Diocese of the Southeast, which also has churches in Tennessee and Florida. In the early twenty-first century there were approximately thirty-one parishes and missions in South Carolina with about 2,500 members, and they were about evenly divided between whites and blacks. Many blacks who joined the Reformed Episcopal Church had left the Protestant Episcopal Church. The Reformed Episcopal Church has three theological seminaries, one of which is the Cummins Memorial Theological Seminary in Summerville, which was established in 1876. The office of the Diocese of the Southeast is located at the seminary. DONALD S. ARMENTROUT

Guelzo, Allen C. *For the Union of Evangelical Christendom: The Irony of the Reformed Episcopalians.* University Park: Pennsylvania State University Press, 1994.
McCarriar, Herbert Geer, Jr. "A History of the Missionary Jurisdiction of the South of the Reformed Episcopal Church, 1874–1970." *Historical Magazine of the Protestant Episcopal Church* 41 (June 1972): 197–220; (September 1972): 287–324.
Price, Annie D. *A History of the Formation and Growth of the Reformed Episcopal Church, 1873–1902.* Philadelphia, 1902.

Reformed Methodist Union Episcopal Church. The Reformed Methodist Union Episcopal Church was organized in Charleston in 1885 after seceding from the African Methodist Episcopal Church (AME). As the two major black Methodist bodies, the AME and AME Zion churches, established themselves in the South during the post–Civil War era, they found that some adherents became dissatisfied with the governance or rules of their bodies. The beginning of the Reformed Methodists has been attributed to two possible causes. According to one view, the separation occurred because of differences over the selection of representatives to an annual conference. The other view holds that the Reverend William E. Johnson and some erstwhile congregants of the famed Morris Brown AME

Church sought ownership of the church's property. The court battle between the Johnson contingent and the AME Church resulted in a ruling that each party could use the facilities provided that it kept membership in the denomination. Nonetheless, sometime later the Johnson faction withdrew and organized the Reformed Methodist Church. Possibly, each of these accounts is a constituent element of the whole story. It is clear, however, that the Reformed party initially sought a more congregationally based, less episcopal-style church governance.

The denomination is Methodist in theology, doctrine, and practice, with love feasts and class meetings. One hundred years after its establishment, the church had eighteen congregations, twenty-six clergy, and 3,800 members. Headquartered in Charleston, the church publishes *The Doctrines and Discipline.* SANDY DWAYNE MARTIN

Murphy, Larry G., J. Gordon Melton, and Gary L. Ward, eds. *Encyclopedia of African American Religions.* New York and London: Garland, 1993.

Regular Baptists. Though in no way a full-blown organization, this largely eighteenth-century movement identified with the 1742 Philadelphia Baptist Confession of Faith and at earlier times with the 1689 London Confession, both of which reflected the modified Calvinism of English Particular Baptists. William Screven of Massachusetts Bay is said to be largely responsible for bringing this form of Baptist life to South Carolina when he settled in Charleston in 1696, but Oliver Hart gave the movement its lasting influence when he brought to Charleston in 1749 the values of the Philadelphia Baptist Association. Throughout the eighteenth century the coast and the lowcountry continued to be the center of the movement in the state, and the Charleston Association was formative for the movement in the South. "Regulars" favored the limited use of confessions of faith, orderly worship, formal hymns, educated pastors, and women who kept silent in worship. In all of these things they differentiated themselves from the Separate Baptists, who in the colonial South emanated from Sandy Creek, North Carolina, and who in South Carolina tended to be backcountry and rural. In 1787 in Dover, Virginia, there was a formal union between the groups that mirrored what was already happening less formally in South Carolina. Merger of the groups in South Carolina was instigated by persons such as Richard Furman, who had friends and sympathies on both sides of the divide. By 1790, as associations of Baptists were formed across the state, little mention of "Separates" and "Regulars" appears in the histories of these organizations. HELEN LEE TURNER

King, Joe M. *A History of South Carolina Baptists.* Columbia: General Board of the South Carolina Baptist Convention, 1964.

Owens, Loulie Latimer. *Saints of Clay: The Shaping of South Carolina Baptists.* Columbia, S.C.: R. L. Bryan, 1971.

Turner, Helen Lee. "The Evangelical Traditions I: Baptists." In *Religion in South Carolina,* edited by Charles H. Lippy. Columbia: University of South Carolina Press, 1993.

Regulators. The Regulators were backcountry settlers who banded together in 1767 in response to a wave of crime that swept their region in the aftermath of a disruptive war with the Cherokee Indians (1759–1761). Bandit gangs, including women as well as escaped slaves, roamed the country with little fear of capture. Lacking local sheriffs, courts, or jails and frustrated by the distance and leniency of the colony's judicial system, Regulators took the law into their own hands. They punished suspected bandits by whipping them, carrying them to the Charleston jail, or escorting them out of the colony. Gradually they expanded their activities to include the regulation of household order. They whipped unruly women and forced the idle to work. Regulators also struggled to control the wandering hunters whose activities threatened farmers. From a backcountry population that included about 35,000 settlers in the mid-1760s, it is likely that between 3,000 and 6,000 men participated in the Regulator uprising.

Protection of lives and property was the primary impetus behind Regulator activities, but the movement also grew out of tensions between frontier settlers and the colonial administration. South Carolina's backcountry, which included the entire area beyond the coastal parishes, did not have any organized local government apart from justices of the peace whose judicial authority was minimal. On the eve of the uprising, the region had only two representatives in the Commons House of Assembly from the single backcountry parish of St. Mark's. In 1767 men who identified themselves as Regulators presented a remonstrance to the assembly in which they enumerated long-standing regional grievances. They demanded local courts, jails, and other mechanisms for suppressing crime. They also requested local mechanisms for processing land warrants and increased representation in the assembly. Regulators took steps to win influence in the government and to dramatize their political grievances. During the election of 1768, hundreds of Regulators marched to three lowcountry polling places, where they claimed the right to vote. The following year Patrick Calhoun (the father of John C. Calhoun) traveled to the polls at Prince William's Parish with a group of armed men, who elected him to the assembly. It is likely that Calhoun was a Regulator.

On the basis of the 118 clearly identifiable Regulators, certain generalizations can be made about the social composition of the movement. Regulators were farmers and small-scale planters. At least thirty-one known Regulators eventually acquired slaves, and at least seventeen eventually owned ten slaves or more. At least two leading Regulators were surveyors—a position that offered significant commercial advantages—and five operated ferries. Five Regulators later participated in the state convention that ratified the United States Constitution. Although the wealthiest and most prominent men in the backcountry were not Regulators, they did sympathize with the movement. In sum, Regulators were ambitious yeomen and aspiring planters who sought to make their region safe for planting, slavery, and commercial activities.

The Regulation provoked a sympathetic and restrained response from Charleston authorities. In November 1767, within a week of receiving the remonstrance, the assembly effectively legalized Regulator activities by establishing two backcountry ranger companies consisting of men who were already active in the uprising. During the same session, legislators began work on circuit court and vagrancy acts. Tensions mounted in early 1768 when several victims of Regulator violence sued the perpetrators in the Charleston court. It was only when colonial officials attempted to deliver court processes that they became embroiled in several violent clashes with the insurgents.

The angriest response to the Regulators came from within the backcountry. Early in 1769 a group of men who called themselves "Moderators" organized themselves in opposition to the uprising. Like their rivals, leading Moderators were prosperous, commercially oriented settlers. They were not adverse to demands laid out in the remonstrance, but they resented the Regulators' increasingly precipitous use of violence. A truce between Moderators and Regulators, negotiated by leading backcountry men on March 25, 1769, signaled the end of the Regulator movement.

By that time Regulators had achieved significant victories. The Circuit Court Act, passed in March 1769, established a system of courts, jails, and sheriffs in four new judicial districts. Had it not been for a protracted dispute with Parliament, the act would have passed earlier. Backcountry men had elected representatives to the assembly, and the colonial government had placed new restrictions on hunters. In 1771 Governor Lord Charles Montagu issued general Regulator pardons. The Regulator uprising signaled regional tensions that would divide South Carolina for years to come, but it also initiated processes of integration that would accelerate with the cotton boom and culminate with the reform of the state constitution in 1808. RACHEL N. KLEIN

Brown, Richard Maxwell. *The South Carolina Regulators.* Cambridge: Belknap Press of Harvard University Press, 1963.

Klein, Rachel N. *Unification of a Slave State: The Rise of the Planter Class in the South Carolina Backcountry, 1760–1808.* Chapel Hill: University of North Carolina Press, 1990.

Woodmason, Charles. *The Carolina Backcountry on the Eve of the Revolution: The Journal and Other Writings of Charles Woodmason, Anglican Itinerant.* Edited by Richard J. Hooker. Chapel Hill: University of North Carolina Press, 1953.

Reno, Donald Wesley (1927–1984). Musician. Don Reno probably ranks second only to Earl Scruggs in prestige among bluegrass banjo pickers. He composed many original songs in the early days of bluegrass, most of which he recorded on the King label with his longtime partner Arthur "Red" Smiley. Born on February 21, 1927, in Spartanburg, Reno grew up in Haywood County, North Carolina, where he learned to play banjo from local musicians and indirectly from the radio artist "Snuffy" Jenkins. He spent his early professional days working with both Arthur Smith's Crackerjacks and the team of Wiley and Zeke Morris, both at WSPA radio in Spartanburg.

Enlisting in the army in World War II, Reno saw combat in Burma as a member of the unit that became known as Merrill's Marauders. Back in civilian life, the young man spent a year in Nashville with Bill Monroe's Blue Grass Boys as a replacement for Earl Scruggs. In 1949 he joined Tommy Magness and the Tennessee Buddies, through which he met the guitarist and lead-vocalist Red Smiley. As members of this band, they did their first recordings together on Federal in March 1951. Later that year they formed a partnership. They made the first sixteen of more than two hundred recordings for King in January 1952, including Reno's classic gospel original "I'm Using My Bible for a Roadmap." They had trouble getting show dates for a time even though their records did well. Meanwhile, Reno went to work for Arthur Smith at WBT radio in Charlotte. During that time Reno and Smith composed and recorded their noted instrumental "Feuding Banjos."

In the spring of 1955 the Reno and Smiley team finally got to work together on a regular basis at WDBJ-TV in Roanoke, Virginia, with their Tennessee Cutups band that included John Palmer and Mack Magaha. This group performed together for nearly a decade, dissolving their partnership in the fall of 1964. They continued their periodic sessions for King, producing such classic songs as "I Know You're Married (But I Love You Still)," "Trail of Sorrow," and "Let's Live for Tonight," as well as original Reno banjo tunes such as "Banjo Signal" and "Choking the Strings."

Reno had a short partnership with the fiddler Benny Martin and then formed another team effort with the singer-guitarist Bill Harrell that lasted for a decade and resulted in many more recordings for King, Rural Rhythm, CMH, and other labels as well as numerous appearances at bluegrass festivals. He also made two more albums with Red Smiley, who died in 1972. After that Reno formed a group that included his sons Ronnie, Don Wayne, and Dale. They made numerous recordings, but Reno's health began to fail. Heart problems ended his life on October 16, 1984. His sons continued to perform as the Reno Brothers for some fifteen years until they split into two groups at the end of 2001. ABBY GAIL GOODNITE AND IVAN M. TRIBE

"Don Reno." *Bluegrass Unlimited* 19 (December 1984): 8.

Kuykendall, Pete. "Don Reno." *Bluegrass Unlimited* 6 (July 1971): 11–16.

Smith, Michael B. *Carolina Dreams: The Musical Legacy of Upstate South Carolina.* Beverly Hills, Calif.: Marshall Tucker Entertainment, 1997.

Republican Party. The origins of the Republican Party in South Carolina date back to the Reconstruction era. During Reconstruction, the only citizens allowed to register to vote were black and white males twenty-one years of age or older who had not aided the Confederacy. These voters participated in choosing delegates to a convention that drew up a new state constitution of 1868. Under this constitution a new Republican Party–dominated government, from governor to town councils, emerged. Robert K. Scott, a white Republican from Ohio, was elected governor in 1868 and reelected in 1870. Two more white Republicans, Franklin J. Moses, Jr., and Daniel H. Chamberlain, were elected governor in 1872 and 1874 respectively.

Black South Carolinians dominated the Republican Party in this era. In the General Assembly election of 1868, 109 of 124 House members (75 black, 34 white) and 25 of 32 Senate members (10 black, 15 white) were Republican. Black Republicans were also elected to Congress and to several statewide offices, including lieutenant governor, adjutant general, secretary of state, and state treasurer. Overall, between 1867 and 1876 blacks won 255 of the 487 elections for state or federal offices in South Carolina.

By 1875 white South Carolinians began to react to black Republican domination, and a policy of voting only for Democrats began to evolve. The disputed election of 1876 eventually resulted in Democrat Wade Hampton III becoming governor. By 1877, because of new elections, resignations, and expulsions, the Democratic Party gained control of the General Assembly. After 1878 the Republican Party did not even nominate a candidate for governor. While some Republicans continued to be elected to office during

The popularity of President Dwight D. Eisenhower (here flanked by pioneering Republicans William D. Workman, Jr., and Floyd Spence) gave a real boost to the party in what had traditionally been one of the most solidly Democratic states of the "Solid South." Courtesy, Modern Political Collections, University of South Carolina the last twenty years of the nineteenth century, the party generally ceased to be a viable political entity in South Carolina, especially after African Americans were disfranchised in 1895. For example, between 1920 and 1950 no Republican candidate for governor or the U.S. Senate received as much as five percent of the popular vote.

The resurrection of the Republican Party in South Carolina during the second half of the twentieth century was a top-down phenomenon. The first major victory for the Republican Party occurred in 1964. In 1961 Republican U.S. senator Barry Goldwater of Arizona, referring to conservative white southerners, stated, "we're not going to get the Negro vote as a bloc in 1964 and 1968 so we ought to go hunting where the ducks are." Conservative white South Carolinians supported Goldwater for president in 1964 and his states' rights message, and he carried the state, receiving 58.9 percent of the popular vote. From 1964 to the end of the twentieth century, South Carolina voted Republican in every presidential election except 1976, when Jimmy Carter won the state.

The Goldwater campaign provided an impetus for Republican Party development in the state. In 1964 U.S. Senator Strom Thurmond switched to the Republican Party. One year later Congressman Albert Watson resigned from Congress and switched to the Republican Party after the House Democratic caucus stripped him of his congressional seniority because of his support of Goldwater in 1964. Watson became the first Republican congressman from South Carolina in the twentieth century when he was reelected in a special election in June 1965. Republicans also began to successfully contest state legislature races in the 1960s. Their support, however, was limited primarily to a few urban districts. By 1970 Republicans held just five seats in the state House and three in the Senate.

While much of the support for the Republican Party in the 1960s was linked to racial politics, the party was beginning to attract supporters from the rapidly growing urban middle class in the state, which supported the conservative economic philosophy of the Republicans. The party also benefited by the influx of business executives and retirees into South Carolina. In 1974 James Edwards became the first Republican governor since Reconstruction. While Edwards's victory was a result of a Democratic Party split, it was a symbolic triumph.

The major growth of the state's Republican Party occurred in the 1980s and 1990s as conservative whites switched to the Republicans. In 1986 Republican Carroll Campbell was elected governor in a close contest, but he was reelected in a landslide in 1990. Republican David Beasley succeeded him in 1994. Beasley was a former Democrat who had switched to the Republican Party in 1991. In the same election the Republican Party also won seven of the state's nine constitutional offices. The Republican Party also became increasingly successful in winning state legislative seats. In the General Assembly, Republican membership in the House increased from 17 in 1981 to 42 in 1991, and in 1995 the Republican Party held a majority of the House seats for the first time since Reconstruction. The Republican Party experienced a similar growth in the state Senate. In 1981 there were only 5 Republican state senators. This figure increased to 12 by 1991. Following the 2000 elections, the Republican Party held a majority in both the House and the Senate, making South Carolina the only Deep South state to have both legislative houses controlled by Republicans. In 2002 the Republican Party held 69 of the 124 House seats and 25 of the 46 Senate positions.

A 1990 Mason-Dixon poll illustrated the growth of the Republican Party in South Carolina. In that poll fifty-one percent of the state's white voters considered themselves Republicans while only twenty-seven percent considered themselves Democrats. In contrast, seventy-eight percent of African Americans considered themselves Democrats. Thus, since Reconstruction the Republican Party in South Carolina has changed from being a liberal party dominated by African Americans to a conservative party dominated by whites. At the beginning of the twenty-first century South Carolina had become the most Republican of the Deep South states. WILLIAM V. MOORE

Bass, Jack, and Walter DeVries. *The Transformation of Southern Politics: Social Change and Political Consequence since 1945.* 1976. Reprint, Athens: University of Georgia Press, 1995.

Moore, William V. "Parties and Elections in South Carolina." In *South Carolina Government: An Introduction,* edited by Charlie B. Tyer. Columbia: Institute for Public Service and Policy Research, University of South Carolina, 2002.

Revolution of 1719. A popular, almost bloodless coup led by Arthur Middleton and a host of prominent colonists, the Revolution of 1719 ended proprietary rule in South Carolina. Proprietary governor Robert Johnson was deposed on December 21 and James Moore, Jr., a respected landowner and war hero, was proclaimed provisional governor, setting the stage for South Carolina's transformation into a British royal colony.

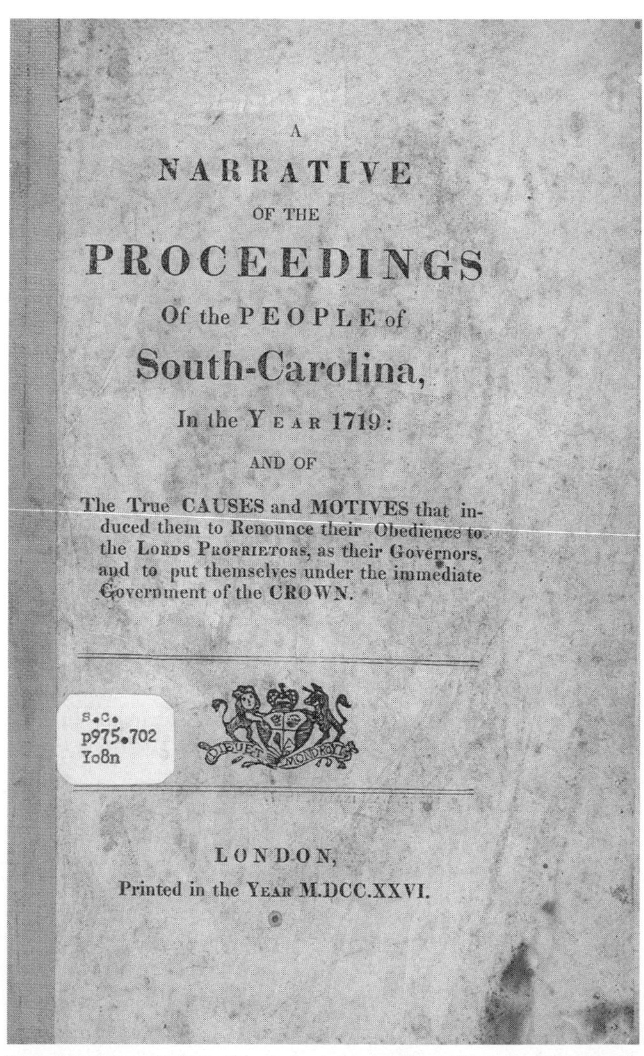

A
NARRATIVE
OF THE
PROCEEDINGS
Of the PEOPLE of
South-Carolina,
In the YEAR 1719:
AND OF
The True CAUSES and MOTIVES that induced them to Renounce their Obedience to the LORDS PROPRIETORS, as their Governors, and to put themselves under the immediate Government of the CROWN.

LONDON,
Printed in the YEAR M.DCC.XXVI.

When the colonists rebelled against the Lords Proprietors in 1719, they passed a "Resolution of Grievances" justifying their actions. Courtesy, South Carolina Department of Archives and History

The Lords Proprietors of Carolina intended their colony to be a money-making proposition from the outset. With the bottom line as their top priority, they governed Carolina erratically and ineffectively, and always with economic expediency in mind. Initially the proprietors resisted representative government and incited bitter factionalism in the colony. When they failed to see any return on their investment after several decades, their overbearing leadership turned to outright neglect. The failure of the proprietors to assist South Carolina during and after the devastating Yamassee War (1715–1718) and against pirates (1718–1719) provided colonists with galling evidence that the men in London had placed personal profit above the public welfare. Interference in land-settlement policies and the vetoing of key legislation, seemingly guaranteed by Archdale's Law (1696), brought the province to confrontation with the proprietors. The Commons House of Assembly, representing the colonists, responded by appointing officials, raising new taxes, and revising the quitrent law in open defiance of proprietary authority. In November 1719 Johnson was informed by members of the legislature that they were "unanimously of Opinion that they would have no *Proprietors'* Government."

Johnson, who had tried to moderate the escalating quarrel, was forced to dissolve the assembly. When a new assembly convened in December 1719, assembly members ignored Johnson's authority and deemed themselves a "Convention of the People." As such, they elected Moore governor and petitioned the British crown to be made a royal colony. Even though the first royal governor, Francis Nicholson, was not sent for a year and a half, the provisional government maintained the reins of power, blocked two attempts by Johnson to overthrow them, and maintained a sound economy.
LOUIS P. TOWLES

Moore, John Alexander. "Royalizing South Carolina: The Revolution of 1719 and the Evolution of Early South Carolina Government." Ph.D. diss., University of South Carolina, 1991.

Sirmans, M. Eugene. *Colonial South Carolina: A Political History, 1663–1763.* Chapel Hill: University of North Carolina Press, 1966.

Revolutionary War (1775–1782). The decision of South Carolinians to leave the British Empire was as much the result of local grievances as it was of changes in imperial policy that occurred after the French and Indian War. At the beginning of the 1770s, the Commons House of Assembly was embroiled in the latest in a series of fierce power struggles with royal officials, known as the Wilkes Fund Controversy. Coupled with new imperial initiatives, these clashes convinced the colony's elite that if it wanted to control the political destiny of South Carolina, then separation was the only answer.

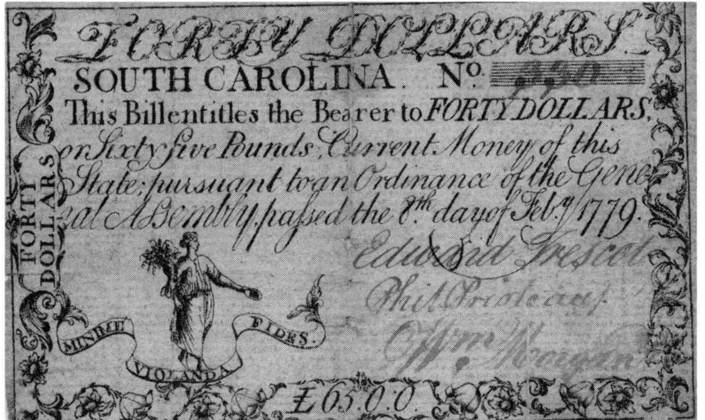

The General Assembly issued paper money to finance the Revolution. Note that the amount on the bill is for forty dollars or sixty-five pounds current money. Courtesy, South Carolina Department of Archives and History

While the Wilkes Fund Controversy was still boiling, news arrived of the Tea Act granting a monopoly to the British East India Company. In late 1773 the arrival of a ship with a cargo of tea led to the call for a "Mass Meeting" of the populace on December 3. At the meeting, all present agreed to boycott the tea and to establish a committee to enforce the boycott.

The Mass Meeting laid the groundwork for an independent government in South Carolina. At subsequent gatherings, the Mass Meeting established a General Committee to enforce its resolutions and the nonimportation association. When word arrived of the Intolerable Acts—Parliament's response to the Boston Tea Party—South Carolina had in place an organization that could react.

Martha Bratton of York District courted death by refusing to reveal the whereabouts of her husband's band of partisans. Courtesy, Historical Center of York County

When the Boston town meeting asked for assistance and the New York General Assembly suggested an intercolonial congress, the General Committee issued a call for a "General Meeting" of delegates from all corners of the province. The General Meeting, in Charleston on July 6, 1774, adopted a series of resolutions, elected five delegates to the First Continental Congress, and created a Committee of 99 to act on behalf of the General Meeting. This committee quickly became the de facto government of South Carolina as lowcountry residents responded to the Committee of 99—not the king's appointees. The Commons House fully supported the actions of the General Meeting and appropriated funds for the congressional delegation.

In November 1774 the General Meeting called for the election of a Provincial Congress, which convened in Charleston in January 1775. Over the next nine months, the Provincial Congress and its committees consolidated their hold on the colony. It authorized the seizure of arms and ammunition from royal powder magazines and the Statehouse, the issuing of paper currency to support its operations, the raising of three regiments to defend the colony, and the creation of a Council of Safety with unlimited authority.

Although a majority of congress approved these actions, it was a slim one. Not everyone was ready to make the break with the empire in the summer of 1775; however, the new revolutionary government was in no mood to tolerate dissent. Those who disagreed with congress were dealt with harshly.

The backcountry was a real concern. Nearly two-thirds of the colony's white population resided there, and backcountry residents had more of a beef with the provincial government in Charleston than they did with the British. After backcountry Loyalists ambushed a revolutionary raiding party, congress sent William Henry Drayton and a delegation to the interior settlements, and they achieved an uneasy truce.

While Drayton and his team were in the backcountry, Lord William Campbell, the last royal governor, arrived. He refused to recognize the Provincial Congress as a legitimate body, and a meeting with the Commons House accomplished nothing. In September 1775 Campbell officially dissolved the assembly and fled for his life to a British warship in Charleston harbor. There was no one now to challenge the authority of the Provincial Congress, and it moved swiftly to suppress any opposition.

Renewed tensions in the backcountry led to the mobilization of both Loyalist and patriot militia units. In November 1775, at Ninety Six, there was a skirmish and the first blood of the Revolution in the state was shed. In retaliation, Colonel Richard Richardson raised a force of more than four thousand patriot militiamen to subdue backcountry Loyalists. In what became known as the "Snow Campaign," he defeated the Loyalist militia and tracked down and captured those who had fled.

The new year began with the Provincial Congress in control of all of South Carolina. The backcountry was quiet, and British warships had left Charleston harbor. In March 1776 South Carolina became the first southern colony and the second of the thirteen to draft a state constitution. The Provincial Congress declared itself to be the new General Assembly of South Carolina and elected John Rutledge as president of the state.

South Carolina's new government was concerned with the defense of the state—and with good reason. There were incessant rumors that the British intended to attack Charleston and to incite the Cherokees to invade the frontier settlements. On June 28 a British invasion force launched a combined naval and amphibious assault against revolutionary forces on Sullivan's Island. Led by William Moultrie and William Thomson, the revolutionaries repulsed a British landing force and the sand and palmetto-log fort rendered the naval bombardment ineffective. At the end of the day American casualties were light, and the British withdrew in disarray. The Battle of Sullivan's Island gave a tremendous boost to the revolutionary cause and the upper hand to those who favored a more resolute course of action.

The British fleet remained off Charleston until August. Its presence, and the urging of northern Indian nations, spurred the Cherokees and some Tories to launch a series of raids in July. The response was immediate and brutal. Andrew Williamson led backcountry militia units against the Native Americans, destroyed most of their towns east of the mountains, and then joined with the North Carolina militia to do the same in that state and Georgia. For the remainder of the war, the Cherokees were not a factor.

While the backcountry was subduing the Cherokees, news arrived on August 2 of the Declaration of Independence. That, however, may have been the high tide of revolutionary fervor for a while. After the twin threats of invasion and Indian war had been defeated, the state entered a two-year period of calm that bordered on apathy.

After independence the state needed a new constitution, and a new one was adopted without fanfare in March 1778. Maintaining zeal for the revolution was difficult. So many legislators absented themselves that it was difficult for the General Assembly to meet a quorum. Enlistments declined, and in order to fill its quotas for the Continental army, the legislature offered land and cash bonuses to volunteers. In 1778 the militia law was revised so that one-third of the militia could be slaves (only in support roles). Some black Carolinians, however, were more than engineers or sailors. There were black soldiers in Francis Marion's partisan band and in militia units at King's Mountain and Cowpens.

The lull in the war in the South ended in autumn 1778 when the British captured Savannah. With a base of operations, they could now execute their "southern strategy" to roll up the southern colonies one by one. Throughout 1779 the British made a series of probing attacks against South Carolina almost to the walls of Charleston. In September a French fleet arrived, and the next month the allies launched an unsuccessful attack on Savannah. After the battle the French sailed away, leaving the Americans to fend for themselves.

The new year did not bode well for the American cause in the South. The already thin ranks of the Continentals had been further depleted at Savannah. Benjamin Lincoln, the commander of American forces, under pressure from South Carolina politicians, let himself be convinced that he should move his army behind the walls of Charleston.

Sir Henry Clinton, commander of British forces, brought a large, well-supplied army and a powerful fleet to South Carolina in February 1780. By the end of March, the British army had begun a siege of Charleston and the Royal Navy a blockade by sea. Lincoln's army was trapped.

On April 13 Governor John Rutledge and several members of his council slipped out of the city so that state government could continue. Two months earlier he had been granted extraordinary powers by the General Assembly to prosecute the war. On May 12, 1780, Lincoln surrendered his army of more than 5,500 men. When word of the capitulation reached interior garrisons, they too surrendered.

The capture of Charleston was celebrated throughout the British Empire. But within weeks, blunders by Clinton and his subordinates led to the undoing of his victory. Under the terms of surrender, which applied to civilians as well as military personnel, all adult males were paroled. They agreed that they would not take up arms against the British, and in turn they would not be molested. That suited many Carolinians who simply wanted to go back to their farms and families. However, on June 3 Clinton abrogated the parole of most Carolinians and issued a proclamation that they must take a new oath of allegiance that would require them to take up arms against their fellow Carolinians—something most were loath to do. He then announced the confiscation of the estates of leading revolutionaries and looked the other way as his army plundered the lowcountry. Encouraged, Tories launched a campaign of retribution.

To solidify his hold on the province, Clinton dispatched units to occupy Ninety Six and Camden. He then left South Carolina for New York, placing Lord Charles Cornwallis in command. Cornwallis ordered his men to "take the most *vigorous* measures to *extinguish the rebellion.*" As they moved into the interior, British troops followed his orders. They executed individuals almost at whim and harassed and maltreated virtually everyone. One commander declared that Presbyterian meetinghouses were "sedition shops" and burned those he encountered. Rather than cowing the populace, these wanton acts of cruelty roused them.

In less than three months, the British and their Tory allies turned what appeared to be a brilliant triumph into a dicey situation. In the northern districts along the North Carolina border, hundreds of Scots-Irish settlers flocked to join partisan bands headed by Thomas Sumter, William Hill, and others. On July 12, 1780, at Williamson's Plantation, partisans defeated elements of the hated British Legion. Over the next ninety days there were sixteen engagements in the northern districts. With the exception of defeats at Camden and Fishing Creek, the remainder were all partisan victories culminating in the smashing victory at King's Mountain. Losing more than one thousand soldiers killed, wounded, or captured so unnerved the British that Cornwallis delayed a planned invasion of North Carolina.

The situation deteriorated throughout the remainder of the year as partisans attacked isolated outposts and supply trains. Francis Marion operated at will in the northeastern portion of the state. Andrew Pickens led forces in the Savannah River Valley, and William Harden did the same in the lowcountry south of Charleston. Thomas Sumter continued his operations in the central and northern districts.

In December, Nathanael Greene appeared with a new Continental army. It was a turning point in the war. Unlike most regular military men who disliked and dismissed partisans, Greene coordinated their efforts with his own and kept the British continually off balance. By trading space for time, he planned a war of attrition that would eventually defeat a superior enemy force.

Shortly after his arrival in South Carolina, he divided his command, sending a large detachment under Daniel Morgan toward Ninety Six. As he had hoped, Cornwallis divided his army. On January 17, 1781, Morgan made a stand on the Broad River in Spartan District at Hiram Sanders's cowpens. For the first time in the Revolution, a regular British force broke and ran. Nearly one thousand of the enemy were killed or captured along with most of their supplies. The successful partisan operations, coupled with the victories at King's Mountain and Cowpens, had turned the tide in South Carolina in the Americans' favor. But the war had not yet been won.

On December 14, 1782, Gen. Nathanael Greene led patriot forces into Charleston, ending a brutal British occupation of thirty-one months. Courtesy, South Carolina Historical Society

After Cowpens, Morgan moved swiftly into North Carolina to rejoin Greene's main army with Cornwallis right behind him. Eventually, after racing to the Dan River, Greene doubled back to Guilford Courthouse, where he engaged the British. When the fighting ended, the British held the field, but they had suffered heavy casualties. Cornwallis withdrew his tattered army to Wilmington and from there marched north to Virginia.

Greene headed back to South Carolina. Facing him was a combined regular-Loyalist force of about eight thousand stationed in Charleston and at outposts from Georgetown to Ninety Six. The British may have controlled the strong points, but the countryside belonged to the partisans. With Greene's army to keep the main British forces occupied, the partisans picked off the enemy garrisons one by one.

During the spring and summer of 1781 there were three major battles in the state. On April 25 at Hobkirk's Hill, the British won the battle but withdrew their garrison from Camden. At Ninety Six,

A nineteenth-century engraving of the Battle of Eutaw Springs, the last major engagement of the Revolution in South Carolina. Courtesy, South Carolina Historical Society

Greene conducted an unsuccessful siege from May 22 to June 19, but the British abandoned the fort in June. At Eutaw Springs on September 8, in what was the bloodiest battle of the southern campaign, Greene initially held the field, but the British counterattacked and, at the end of the day, drove the Americans back. There were other battles after Eutaw Springs, but none of any strategic significance. On November 14, 1782, the last of the 137 battles fought in South Carolina and the last battle of the American Revolution occurred on Johns Island.

Because the British still occupied Charleston in January 1782, the General Assembly met in Jacksonborough. Under the protection of Greene's army, the legislature elected a new governor and passed two acts identifying and punishing Loyalists. The state was able to reassert its authority everywhere except for James Island and the Charleston peninsula.

In September 1782 a British fleet sailed into Charleston harbor to transport the remaining troops and the 4,200 Loyalists who wished to leave the state. On December 14, 1782, the last of the occupying troops withdrew block by block, and the city was turned over to Greene's army. At 3:00 P.M. Greene escorted Governor John Mathewes and other officials into the city. For South Carolina, the war was over.

After thirty months of bloody fighting and brutal occupation, South Carolinians were once again in control of their own affairs—thanks to Nathanael Greene and local partisan leaders. The war may have begun and ended in Charleston, but it was won in the forests and swamps of the backcountry.

From Ninety Six to Charleston the countryside was in ruins. Dwellings, farm buildings, and mills had been burned. Fields had been abandoned and had become overgrown. Livestock had been taken by one side or the other. There were thirty thousand fewer slaves in the state than there had been in 1775. The state's economy was in shambles.

Not only were the means of production damaged or destroyed, but individuals and the state faced huge debts. South Carolina, with a white population of less than 100,000, had spent $5.4 million on the war effort. In spite of the difficulties facing it, the state had regularly met its financial obligations to the Continental Congress. In 1783 it was the only state to pay its requisition in full. The financial losses were nothing compared to the personal ones. In 1783 a visitor noted the large number of widows in Charleston, but there were far more in the backcountry. In Ninety Six District it was estimated that there were at least twelve hundred widows.

The American Revolution in South Carolina was a bloody, desperate struggle—America's first civil war. Because of the nature of the conflict, it is impossible to know exactly how many Carolinians perished. However, of the total number of American casualties for the entire war, eighteen percent of those killed and thirty-one percent of those wounded fell in South Carolina during the last two years of fighting. Given the material and human losses, it is no small wonder that the American historian George Bancroft would write: "Left mainly to her own resources, it was through the depths of wretchedness that her sons were to bring her back to her place in the republic . . . having suffered more, and dared more, and achieved more than the men of any other state." WALTER EDGAR

Buchanan, John. *The Road to Guilford Courthouse: The American Revolution in the Carolinas.* New York: Wiley, 1997.

Edgar, Walter. *Partisans and Redcoats: The Southern Conflict That Turned the Tide of the American Revolution.* New York: Morrow, 2001.

McCrady, Edward. *The History of South Carolina in the Revolution.* 2 vols. New York: Macmillan, 1901–1902.

Rhett, Robert Barnwell (1800–1876). Congressman, U.S. senator. Rhett was born Robert Barnwell Smith in Beaufort on December 21, 1800, the eighth child of James Smith and Marianna Gough. The Smith sons changed their surname to Rhett in 1837 to honor their ancestor Colonel William Rhett. Robert Barnwell Rhett attended Beaufort College and later read law in the Charleston office of Thomas Grimké. Rhett was admitted to the bar in 1821 and two years later formed a law partnership in Colleton District with his cousin Robert W. Barnwell. On February 21, 1827, he married Elizabeth Washington Burnet. The couple had eleven children. After the death of his first wife in 1852, Rhett married Catherine Herbert Dent on April 25, 1854. His second marriage produced three more children.

Robert Barnwell Rhett. Courtesy, South Carolina Department of Archives and History

Rhett was elected to the state House of Representative by the voters of St. Bartholomew's Parish in 1826. He proved himself an active, promising legislator and was returned to the next three sessions. Rhett also earned a reputation as one of South Carolina's most vehement critics of the Tariff of 1828, the so-called "Tariff of Abominations." In 1832 Rhett was elected to the nullification convention, which initially nullified the federal tariff law but rescinded the resolution after a compromise was worked out that reduced tariff schedules. Rhett opposed the compromise, believing that it failed to recognize state sovereignty. "A people, owning slaves, are mad, or worse than mad," he declared, "who do not hold their destinies in their own hands."

Rhett resigned from the legislature after his election as South Carolina attorney general in November 1832. His reputation as a passionate defender of state interests helped him in 1837 win a seat in the U.S. House Representatives, where he followed the political leadership of John C. Calhoun. However, as Rhett grew more radical, he broke with the more moderate Calhoun on several occasions. In 1844 Rhett led what became known as the Bluffton Movement, which called for state action against the tariff and the unwillingness of northern congressmen to admit Texas to the Union. The movement failed but left Rhett as the recognized leader of the immediate secessionists, or "fire-eaters," in South Carolina. Rhett's career in the House of Representatives ended in 1849 when he chose not to seek reelection.

After leaving Congress, Rhett attended the Nashville Convention of 1850, where he denounced the Compromise of 1850 and again called on South Carolinians to leave the Union. The convention accomplished little, but radical majorities in the South Carolina legislature elected Rhett to the U.S. Senate in December 1850. With strong initial support at home, Rhett again called for South Carolina and the other slaveholding states to secede if their grievances were not addressed. However, in elections held in October 1851 for delegates to yet another southern congress, the secession faction in South Carolina was soundly defeated by cooperationists, and Rhett resigned his Senate seat on May 7, 1852.

For the next seven years Rhett tended his private affairs and kept his distance from politics. Together with his son Barnwell Rhett, Jr., he acquired the *Charleston Mercury,* which became a leading advocate of secession. On July 4, 1859, at Grahamville, Rhett made his first public speech in seven years and called upon his state to secede if a Republican won the 1860 presidential election. After South Carolina left the Union on December 20, 1860, it was Rhett who suggested that the remaining southern states meet in Montgomery, Alabama, to establish a new nation. Rhett played a prominent role at the Montgomery Convention, serving as chair of the foreign affairs committee and actively participating in the creation of the Confederate constitution. He introduced the six-year presidential term and sections banning protective tariffs and most government-sponsored internal improvements. But other proposals were not adopted, including recognition of the right of secession and the requirement that future Confederate states must permit slavery within their borders. Rhett also failed to remove the section that declared the foreign slave trade illegal.

After the Provisional Confederate Congress adjourned in 1862, Rhett never again held public office. Even before he left the congress, Rhett began a concerted campaign against Jefferson Davis and his administration. Through the *Mercury,* Rhett attacked Davis with the same vitriol he used against the national Democrats before the war. The war ruined Rhett financially, and he was physically weakened by skin cancer. He died at the plantation of his son-in-law near New Orleans on September 14, 1876. In an obituary, the Charleston *News and Courier* described Rhett as "the paramount advocate of that secession of South Carolina which, through him, more than any other, became an accomplished fact." Rhett was buried at Magnolia Cemetery, Charleston. MICHAEL S. REYNOLDS

Davis, William C. *Rhett: The Turbulent Life and Times of a Fire-Eater.* Columbia: University of South Carolina Press, 2001.

Rhett, Robert Barnwell. *A Fire-Eater Remembers: The Confederate Memoir of Robert Barnwell Rhett.* Edited by William C. Davis. Columbia: University of South Carolina Press, 2000.

Walther, Eric H. *The Fire-Eaters.* Baton Rouge: Louisiana State University Press, 1992.

White, Laura A. *Robert Barnwell Rhett: Father of Secession.* 1931. Reprint, Gloucester, Mass.: Peter Smith, 1965.

Ribault (Ribaut), Jean (ca. 1515–1565). Explorer, mariner. Ribault established the short-lived colonial outpost of Charlesfort, the earliest French settlement in the present-day United States, in Port Royal Sound. A native of the port city of Dieppe, in upper Normandy, France, Ribault sailed with Norman merchant fleets in European waters from his teenage years, establishing a reputation as one of France's most accomplished mariners. For much of the 1540s and 1550s, Ribault resided in England, working with Sebastian Cabot for the English Admiralty in planning voyages of discovery. During these years he also gathered military intelligence for both France and England. In the late 1550s Ribault, by then a Protestant, returned to Dieppe and resumed his maritime career in both military and commercial roles.

On the eve of the outbreak of the French Wars of Religion in early 1562, Admiral of France Gaspard Coligny de Châtillon, a leader of the early French Protestant (Huguenot) movement, commissioned Ribault to lead an expedition to North America. Commanding a small force of two ships and about 150 men, Ribault departed from Dieppe in February and landed six weeks later near modern Jacksonville, Florida. He then explored north along the coast, claiming a section of it for France. Before returning across the Atlantic in June he left about two dozen men in a small garrison, Charlesfort, named for King Charles IX, in Port Royal Sound.

However, due to the outbreak of civil war in France, Ribault was unable to resupply Charlesfort as intended, and eventually the men who had been left there abandoned the settlement and sailed back to Europe. In the meantime, Ribault, having fled to England during the siege of Dieppe in late 1562, had solicited English support for his fledgling colony and in the process unintentionally alerted Spanish officials to the French presence in America. As diplomatic relations between France and England deteriorated over other matters in 1563, English authorities imprisoned Ribault in the Tower of London on charges of espionage, making him unavailable to lead the French expedition that established Fort Caroline on the St. John's River in Florida in 1564.

When Ribault was released from English custody in late 1564, Coligny assigned him to lead a large relief fleet to Fort Caroline to defend it from an impending Spanish attack. Shortly after Ribault's arrival in Florida in the late summer of 1565, Spanish forces led by Admiral Pedro Menéndez de Avilès inflicted a crushing defeat on the French, killing Ribault along with hundreds of soldiers and civilians. As a result of this catastrophe, and also due to continuing domestic turmoil, French authorities abandoned their colonial designs in North America for several decades. French Protestant writers and publishers soon memorialized Ribault as a Huguenot martyr, and in later years his name became attached to several places in the Port Royal Sound area. JOHN T. MCGRATH

Laudonnière, René Goulaine de. *Three Voyages.* Gainesville: University Presses of Florida, 1975.

Lyon, Eugene. *The Enterprise of Florida: Pedro Menéndez de Avilès and the Spanish Conquest of 1565–1568.* Gainesville: University Presses of Florida, 1976.

McGrath, John T. *The French in Early Florida: In the Eye of the Hurricane.* Gainesville: University Press of Florida, 2000.

Rice. South Carolina's first great agricultural staple, rice dominated the lowcountry's economy for almost two hundred years, influencing almost every aspect of life in the region from the early eighteenth century to the early twentieth century. Rice was responsible for the area's rise to prominence in the colonial era. But the commercial rice industry collapsed in the late nineteenth century, leaving much of the lowcountry with few viable economic options for a half-century or more. It was only in the second half of the twentieth century that the economic and social legacy of rice began to recede into history.

Domestication of rice began in Asia between seven thousand and ten thousand years ago and spread gradually to other parts of Eurasia and Africa. The cereal arrived in the Western Hemisphere along with Europeans and Africans as part of the "Columbian exchange" of plants, animals, and germs that began in the late fifteenth century. Although rice accompanied Europeans and Africans to the Western Hemisphere, the cereal did not become an important cash crop in

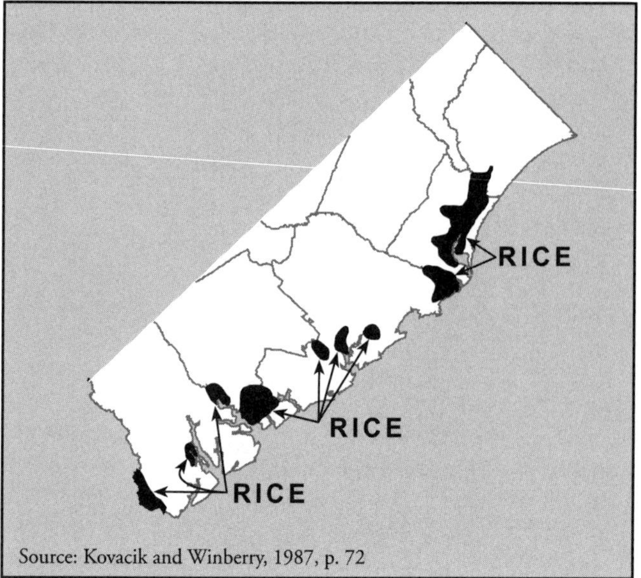

Areas of rice cultivation

the Americas until the South Carolina rice complex was developed in the eighteenth century. Carolinians, both Europeans and Africans, had likely grown small amounts of rice to eat, but not until the 1710s or 1720s were local capital, labor, and entrepreneurship sufficient to support significant commercial production.

The origin of the South Carolina rice industry is complex and controversial. Until relatively recently historians accorded Europeans primary credit for originating rice production in South Carolina. During the past few decades, however, some scholars have amassed evidence suggesting instead that Africans were the prime movers in the earliest days of rice cultivation in South Carolina. In a technical (and technological) sense, the "black rice" view of the origins of rice cultivation may be correct. It is important to note, however, that there were several other plausible routes of transmission, and that there is a big difference between rice production and a rice industry. Regardless of the origins of rice cultivation in the colony, the South Carolina rice industry was informed by European and Euro-American aspirations and entrepreneurship along with African technology and labor.

Despite considerable research, little is known about early rice production techniques or even sites. Some "wet" rice may have been grown from the start, but scholars generally agree that the first rice crops were produced "dry," that is, without irrigation and on relatively "high" ground. Throughout its history in South Carolina, most rice cultivation took place in the lowcountry, but production was distributed quite unevenly within this region.

By the 1720s a rice industry had begun to develop. Production became better established and systematic, and cultivation relocated from "high" ground to inland, freshwater swamps, where rudimentary water-control mechanisms—such as impoundments—could be employed. After 1750 the locus of production shifted again, this time to drained swamps on or adjacent to South Carolina's major tidal rivers. The so-called tidal rice zone, which was to constitute the heart of the lowcountry rice industry, developed within narrow geographical and hydrological limits. The idea behind tidal cultivation was to harness daily river tides to draw water onto and off the fields, which irrigated the crop and otherwise reduced labor requirements. The trick was to find places where tidal action was strong enough to raise and lower water sufficiently without being too brackish or salty. Over time such places were found, and tidal cultivation flourished from about ten to twenty miles inland along the tidewater rivers of the lowcountry: the Waccamaw, Santee, Cooper, Ashley, Combahee, and Savannah in particular.

Rice cultivation under any circumstances is arduous, but this is particularly true when it is cultivated under "wet" conditions, as was the norm by the early eighteenth century. Moreover, because populations working in the swamps of the lowcountry were also subject to mosquito-borne diseases, morbidity and mortality rates in rice areas were extremely high. As a result of the rigorous labor demands and unhealthy conditions of rice culture, it proved difficult to attract sufficient numbers of white laborers. Moreover, because many West Africans were already familiar with rice culture and had greater immunities to mosquito-borne diseases, it is not surprising that the rice industry in South Carolina quickly became—and remained—dominated by black labor.

It is difficult to appreciate how much labor was involved in building and maintaining the "wet rice" regime in the lowcountry. Although only about 80,000 to 120,000 acres were devoted to rice in South Carolina at its pre–Civil War peak, the amount of engineering and construction needed to render this land suitable for commercial rice cultivation was staggering. Before planting could begin, swamps had to be drained, cleared of trees, and leveled. Next, the elaborate irrigation system needed to regulate the tidal flow was constructed. For the rice plantations of the lowcountry, this meant miles of levees, ditches, and culverts, interspersed with assorted floodgates, trunks, and drains.

Furthermore, rice was a row crop that needed considerable attention during the growing season. Thus, rice workers endured a rigorous year-long labor regimen: repairing irrigation facilities, readying the fields for cultivation, planting, flooding, draining, hoeing, harvesting, processing, and transporting it for further milling or marketing. Africans and African Americans provided the vast majority of this labor, although draft animals sometimes supplemented human labor, and inanimate power sources—water, wind, and steam—were employed as well.

Unlike in most areas of the slave South, the labor system in the South Carolina lowcountry—in rice and other activities—was dominated by the task system rather than the gang system. Under the latter, slaves worked in groups, were subject to close supervision, and worked for set periods of time ("sunup to sundown"). The task system was quite different. In this scheme a slave was responsible for a set amount of work: a daily "task" or "tasks." Once complete, the slave was relieved of any further labor responsibilities to the master for the rest of the day and could do as he or she chose. Further, the close supervision associated with the gang system was generally absent from the task system. Therefore, slaves in the lowcountry enjoyed somewhat greater independence and autonomy within the context of slavery. The persistence of the task system was evident in the lowcountry even after emancipation, as free black workers often contracted with landowners not for a calendar year or a growing season, but for specific tasks such as sowing, hoeing, or harvesting.

Rice cultivation in the South Carolina lowcountry is often associated with large plantations worked by many slaves in specialized tasks. Such units of production were often highly capitalized, marked by economies of scale, and owned (if not directly operated) by white men and women of great wealth. This image is not so much wrong as incomplete. To be sure, rice planters were often wealthy, and many planter families were more or less stereotypical grandees. It is important to note, however, that rice plantations, even large ones, were not always extremely profitable (particularly by the late antebellum period), and that many small lowcountry farmers grew some rice. It is also worth remembering that rice cultivation was concentrated in certain parts of the lowcountry and that only a minority of lowcountry farmers grew rice. For example, according to the Census of Agriculture of 1859, less than forty percent of lowcountry farms grew any rice at all.

South Carolina was unquestionably the leading North American rice producer for almost two centuries, from the late 1600s until the 1880s, when Louisiana surpassed the Palmetto State in rice production. Although data on total rice output are lacking until 1839, good data on rice exports existed from the start, and the broad parameters of the early rice period can be spoken of with confidence. Rice exports from "Carolina"—South Carolina and North Carolina combined—averaged 268,602 pounds annually between 1698 and 1702, growing to more than 30 million pounds annually between 1738 and1742 and more than 66 million pounds annually between 1768 and 1772. The vast majority of these "Carolina" exports originated in South Carolina, but a small amount of "Carolina" rice exports during the late colonial period originated in the Cape Fear region of North Carolina.

After rice was cut, it was loaded onto barges such as this one and transported to the plantation yard for processing. Courtesy, South Carolina Historical Society

Except for small quantities grown in Louisiana and Florida, almost all North American rice came from "Carolina" and Georgia in the eighteenth century, and these two areas constituted the two largest producing regions until the Civil War. American rice production grew substantially during the eighty-five years between the Revolution and the Civil War, although rice exports stagnated after about 1800. Throughout this period South Carolina dominated production and exports, constituting roughly three-quarters of total U.S. rice production in both 1839 and 1849, and about sixty-four percent of a much higher total in 1859.

While the American rice industry continued to expand in the nineteenth century, its position in world markets became increasingly untenable. In the eighteenth century virtually all American rice was exported. Most exports went to northern Europe, where rice was welcomed as a cheap and versatile food source. Before American rice entered European markets, Italy supplied most of Europe's demand for rice. By the mid–eighteenth century, however, rice from South Carolina (and, to a lesser extent, Georgia) had supplanted Italian rice, and it would dominate European markets for the rest of the century.

The expansion of European trade with Asia changed things. As early as the 1790s European merchants were importing large quantities of cheaper Asian rice, and thus making inroads into South Carolina's markets. This development intensified throughout the nineteenth century. Between 1800 and 1860 cheap Burmese, Javanese, and Indian rice came to dominate European markets, and South Carolina rice was gradually forced out of Europe and into the Caribbean (especially Cuba) or into the domestic market of the United States. Despite increasing European demand for rice, U.S. rice exports to Europe were far lower in the 1850s than they had been in the 1790s, demonstrating that American rice was becoming uncompetitive as global market integration proceeded.

With the coming of the Civil War, the competitive decline in the South Carolina rice industry became precipitous. Indeed, the United States as a whole actually became a net importer of rice from the time of the Civil War until well into the twentieth century. There are several reasons for this. Asian rice continued to undermine the position of American rice—including that produced in South Carolina—in global markets, as improving transportation and communications facilities increasingly linked low-cost producers in Asia to consumers in Europe and elsewhere. As a high-cost producer of a basic commodity, South Carolina's rice industry was probably doomed even without the Civil War. Even so, the war-time destruction of infrastructure, emancipation of the labor force, and the postbellum transformation of agriculture doubtless hastened its demise.

International competition cost the rice industry in South Carolina and Georgia not only its export markets, but ultimately its domestic customers as well. In the 1880s and 1890s American rice production shifted to Louisiana, Arkansas, and Texas. In these states, and later in the Sacramento Valley of California, rice producers attempted to meet low-cost Asian competition by replacing labor with machinery. In so doing, growers in these areas—aided by tariff protection—rebuilt the U.S. rice industry.

These solutions were unavailable to South Carolina rice producers. The swampy lowcountry could not bear the weight of the new equipment, and investor interest and capital were short in any case. With the loss of its export markets and the establishment of more efficient domestic competitors, the southern Atlantic rice industry simply collapsed in the 1870s and 1880s. South Carolina, which produced almost 120 million pounds in 1859, saw its rice output fall to about 30 million pounds in 1889, a decline of seventy-five percent. Nature had a hand in things as well. Between 1893 and 1906 a series of hurricanes struck the rice coast, further damaging the decaying infrastructure. By 1919 the state's rice production had dropped to about 4 million pounds, about three percent of its annual antebellum output. As a commercial activity, South Carolina rice was dead and gone.

The rice legacy lived on for a long time, however. Throughout its long history, rice production was synonymous with the lowcountry. Although other crops were grown there—Sea Island cotton, indigo, naval stores—this ecologically fragile and economically limited region was built by and for rice, with the building done largely by blacks and largely for whites. Without rice, the heavily black population of the lowcountry had few viable options, and the once-wealthy region withered into one of the poorest in the nation. Only with the onset of World War II did the region begin to rise again. The lowcountry's economy in the early twenty-first century was based largely on tourism, forest products, military installations, and service-sector employment in Charleston. See plate 28. PETER A. COCLANIS

Carney, Judith A. *Black Rice: The African Origins of Rice Cultivation in the Americas.* Cambridge: Harvard University Press, 2001.

Chaplin, Joyce E. *An Anxious Pursuit: Agricultural Innovation and Modernity in the Lower South, 1730–1815.* Chapel Hill: University of North Carolina Press, 1993.

Coclanis, Peter A. "Distant Thunder: The Creation of a World Market in Rice and the Transformations It Wrought." *American Historical Review* 98 (October 1993): 1050–78.

———. *The Shadow of a Dream: Economic Life and Death in the South Carolina Low Country, 1670–1920.* New York: Oxford University Press, 1989.

Littlefield, Daniel C. *Rice and Slaves: Ethnicity and the Slave Trade in Colonial South Carolina.* Baton Rouge: Louisiana State University Press, 1981.

Morgan, Philip D. *Slave Counterpoint: Black Culture in the Eighteenth-Century Chesapeake and Lowcountry.* Chapel Hill: University of North Carolina Press, 1998.

Rice, James Henry, Jr. (1868–1935). Conservationist, writer. Born near Ninety Six on July 2, 1868, Rice distinguished himself as an early proponent of wildlife conservation, environmentally sound farming, preservation of wetlands, and an end to lynching. His parents, James Henry Rice, Sr., and Anna Bolling Lawton, lived at Riverlands Plantation at the time of his birth, although Rice later became well known as the resident and owner of Brick House Plantation in Wiggins.

After Rice graduated from Ninety Six High School and South Carolina College, he began a career in high school teaching. He married Jennie Maner of Allendale on April 30, 1892. They had seven children. Rice left teaching in 1895 to begin a career in journalism and writing. That year he became editor of the Columbia *Evening News* and of a monograph, *Colonial Records of South Carolina.* He also served as an editorial writer for the *State* newspaper in Columbia, and he contributed editorial columns to the Charleston *News and Courier.* Typically, his writing concerned the flora and fauna of South Carolina, farming practices, and environmental issues. Rice served as chief game warden of South Carolina (1911–1913) and as an inspector for the U.S. Biological Survey (1913–1917). Among many groups and associations in which he was active were the Audubon Society, the American Forestry Association, and the Conservation Society of South Carolina.

Rice wrote two notable books. *Glories of the Carolina Coast* (1925) is an enthusiastic celebration of the South Carolina coast that includes descriptions of its early history, inhabitants, economy, culture, and environment. *The Aftermath of Glory* (1934) describes the key people and events involved in the early twentieth-century history of coastal development in and around Myrtle Beach, Charleston, Georgetown, Beaufort, and other locations. His narrative also discusses the impact of this development on the native flora and fauna. Most notable among the poems he published were "The Poet and the City" and "Hampton: Salutem." Rice died at Brick House Plantation on March 24, 1935, and was buried in Magnolia Cemetery, Charleston. KATHERINE REYNOLDS CHADDOCK

Rice, James Henry. Papers. South Caroliniana Library, University of South Carolina, Columbia.

Wauchope, George. *Writers of South Carolina.* Columbia, S.C.: State Company, 1910.

Rice, John Andrew, Jr. (1888–1968). Educator, author. A prominent figure in U.S. higher education, Rice was born at Tanglewood Plantation in Lynchburg (Lee County) on February 1, 1888. He was the eldest son of John Andrew Rice, a Methodist minister, and Anna Bell Smith, the sister of U.S. Senator Ellison D. "Cotton Ed" Smith.

During Rice's early childhood, his family lived in several South Carolina towns as his father moved from one Methodist congregation to another, finally securing the presidency of Columbia Female College in 1894. After his mother died in 1899, Rice lived with relatives near Varnville in Colleton County. He left South Carolina in 1905, when his stepmother, Launa Darnell Rice, urged him to attend the Webb School, a highly regarded preparatory academy in Bell Buckle, Tennessee.

After graduating with a B.A. from Tulane University in 1911, Rice won a Rhodes Scholarship. He graduated from Oxford with first honors in jurisprudence in 1914 and in the same year married Nell Aydelotte. They had two children. He later attended the University of Chicago but left before completing his Ph.D. in classical Greek and Latin philosophy and language. During a succession of faculty appointments, Rice developed a reputation as an expert classics scholar and brilliant Socratic teacher. He also became known as critical and candid, railing openly at the administration of his own institutions and others. In widely published articles he chastised American higher education for teaching unconnected course subjects with pedagogy that still emphasized lecture and response.

In 1933 Rice first gained nationwide attention when the demand for his resignation from Rollins College sparked a highly publicized investigation by the American Association of University Professors (AAUP). Although the AAUP exonerated Rice and censured Rollins, Rice had already made plans to start Black Mountain College, near Asheville, North Carolina. Black Mountain became a renowned site of experimental and progressive education, especially known for Rice's commitment to experiential learning, artistic expression in support of learning in any discipline, democratic governance among faculty and students, and the absence of outside trustees. As founder and first rector of the college, Rice recruited faculty talent that included Josef and Anni Albers, Buckminster Fuller, and Dante Fiorello. Other visitors who frequented the classrooms included John Dewey, Thornton Wilder, Aldous Huxley, Henry Miller, and Marcel Breuer.

Rice, ever unable to check his stinging candor, left Black Mountain College in 1940 at the insistence of his colleagues. He divorced and returned to South Carolina and began a second career in writing with his memoir, *I Came Out of the Eighteenth Century* (1942). With his second wife, Dikka Moen, and their two children, he lived in the Charleston area from 1945 to 1948, writing short stories for the *New Yorker, Collier's,* the *Saturday Evening Post,* and other periodicals, largely on themes about life and race relations in the South. These appeared in anthologies and were collected as *Local Color* (1955). Later, Rice and his family moved to Maryland, where he died on November 17, 1968. KATHERINE REYNOLDS CHADDOCK

Duberman, Martin. *Black Mountain: An Exploration in Community.* New York: Dutton, 1972.

Reynolds, Katherine C. *Visions and Vanities: John Andrew Rice of Black Mountain College.* Baton Rouge: Louisiana State University Press, 1998.

Rice, John Andrew. *I Came Out of the Eighteenth Century.* New York: Harper and Brothers, 1942.

Rice dishes. Rice dishes are legion in South Carolina, where the grain was the major crop for nearly two hundred years. Based on the stew-pot dishes of West Africa, whence came the rice-plantation slaves, lowcountry rice cookery is the highlight of South Carolina's Creole cuisine.

By the middle of the eighteenth century, Charleston had become one of the richest and most cosmopolitan cities in the New World.

While rice exports brought fabulous wealth to a handful of planters and merchants, its consumption provided sustenance for all. Exotic fruits from the Caribbean, cookbooks from England, and fresh herbs from local gardens were regularly advertised in newspapers. Wealthy Charleston ladies tried the latest cooking fads from European courts, while their black cooks added dishes from their homelands, such as collards, gumbo, and benne (sesame) candy. Rice was served in some form at every meal, most often as the accompaniment to the main course. Nowhere else in the country were people growing or cooking the grain (it was not introduced into other states until after the Civil War).

The recipe for cooking rice that Eliza Pinckney recorded on her plantation north of Charleston in 1756 is archetypically Carolinian, following the African method, so that each grain stands by itself. She warned, "Be sure to avoid stirring the rice . . . for one turn with a spoon will spoil all." The grain appeared in both yeast breads and quick breads such as hoecakes and waffles, in fritters, in soups, pureed to thicken sauces, and in desserts. But the pilau, a one-pot dish filled with meats, vegetables, and/or shellfish, is the defining rice dish of Carolina, a precursor to Louisiana's jambalaya, and a direct descendant of the pilafs of the Middle East. JOHN MARTIN TAYLOR

Hess, Karen. *The Carolina Rice Kitchen: The African Connection.* Columbia: University of South Carolina Press, 1992.

Pinckney, Eliza Lucas. *Recipe Book of Eliza Lucas Pinckney, 1756.* Charleston, S.C.: J. Furlong, 1936.

Rice milling. Booming rice production created a problem for colonial-era planters: how to efficiently process the large quantities of rice they were producing. Although attempts at mechanization dated back to the 1690s, planters remained largely dependent on slave labor and West African technology for this physically exhausting task.

One of the chief difficulties facing would-be innovators was the fact that rice required delicate handling. On the one hand, the hull had to be removed in order for rice to be digestible; on the other hand, rice could not simply be pounded indiscriminately since whole rice commanded much higher prices than broken rice did. These demands were met by a three-step milling process done by hand until the end of the eighteenth century. This method used West African mortar-and-pestle technology and the particular expertise of female slaves. First, grains were separated from stalks in the threshing process. The last two steps occurred in tandem. The second step, winnowing, separated the empty husks from the grain when the rice was shaken in a flat basket. The final step, pounding, involved using a mortar and pestle to remove hulls from rice and polish it. Milling by hand required substantial skill to prevent the grain from breaking. The milling process was also extremely labor-intensive. As late as 1794 the rice planter Peter Manigault told his overseer that "[i]f the Rice made at Goose-Creek is not yet beat out, I wd. wish to have it sold in the rough, to save Labour to the Negroes." Yet slaves were not spared labor after mechanization was introduced into the rice industry.

Early eighteenth-century patents for rice-milling machinery focused on powering the pestle, or multiple pestles. A 1744 design featured a treadmill operated by slaves; other designs incorporated horse power. By the time of the Revolutionary War, millers were beginning to fully exploit waterpower to drive the mills. Planters focused on tidal estuaries, using irrigation systems already in place in order to control water flow as necessary. Jonathan Lucas and Jonathan Lucas, Jr., established one of the first toll rice mills in South Carolina in 1801. Other planters followed suit in order to recoup their investments in machinery.

By the middle of the nineteenth century, rice milling was well established in Charleston. Cannonborough Mills began operation in 1825 under the direction of Thomas Bennett. The mill included twenty-two pestles driven by steam and fourteen driven by the tides of the Ashley River. Jonathan Lucas III built an even larger mill, the West Point Mills, in 1839. The mill featured forty pestles and employed eighty-nine slaves in 1860. These Charleston mills as well as several mills in Georgetown helped establish South Carolina as the premier state for rice milling prior to the Civil War.

As war approached, however, the industry went into decline. One of the Cannonsborough Mills and the West Point Mills both burned in 1860. Chisholm's Rice Mills in Charleston also burned in 1859. Although the proprietors rebuilt a larger operation that would have employed 150 laborers, the rice industry in South Carolina was not well-positioned to recover after the combined effects of the Civil War and an international shift in the supply sources of rice. AARON W. MARRS

Carney, Judith. "Rice Milling, Gender, and Slave Labour in Colonial South Carolina." *Past and Present* 153 (November 1996): 108–34.

Chaplin, Joyce E. *An Anxious Pursuit: Agricultural Innovation and Modernity in the Lower South, 1730–1815.* Chapel Hill: University of North Carolina Press, 1993.

Lander, Ernest M., Jr. "Charleston: Manufacturing Center of the Old South." *Journal of Southern History* 26 (August 1960): 330–51.

Rice trunks. The rice trunk was an ingenious, yet simple apparatus that made large-scale planting and irrigation control possible in the South Carolina lowcountry. Rice trunks are wooden sluices installed in "banks" or dikes of rice fields for irrigation or flood control. They are long, narrow, wooden boxes made of thick planks, and each has a door at each end. Hung on uprights, the swinging doors, called gates, may be raised or lowered to drain or flood a field. When the gate on the river end of a trunk is raised, the water in the field runs into the river at low tide. As the tide turns, the rising water exerts pressure on the river gate and swings it tightly shut, preventing water from returning to the field. To flood the field, the process is reversed.

It is possible that early settlers who had seen trunks used in the freshwater marshes of England brought the practice to America. As early as the thirteenth century, both the English and the French used tide-operated mills for grinding grain. Swinging gates allowed the incoming tide to flood ponds, and when the tide turned, the pressure of the water inside automatically closed the gates. When the pond was full, the miller opened the gates and escaping water drove the mill wheels. Before the advent of steam, South Carolina planters also used tide-operated rice mills.

In the early colonial period, planters used hollow cypress logs, each with a vertical plug at one end, as sluices. David Doar, rice planter and historian, believed that this practice was the origin of the term "trunk." In rice fields located in West African mangrove swamps it was customary to use tree trunks with plugs, and it seems evident that Africans brought this method of controlling irrigation to America. Archaeology at Drayton Hall plantation near Charleston in 1996 revealed an intermediate form that indicated a step in evolution from the plug trunk to the hanging gate sluice. Dating to the early 1800s, the excavated device was a sixteen-foot-long wooden box, about two feet wide and twelve inches high, with grooved ends containing a rectangular gate that moved up and down to control the flow of water. The rice historian Judith Carney called

Rice trunks were used to control the level of water in the fields. Courtesy, South Carolina Historical Society

the Drayton gate "the hybridized product of both African and European inventiveness." SUZANNE LINDER

Carney, Judith A. *Black Rice: The African Origins of Rice Cultivation in the Americas.* Cambridge: Harvard University Press, 2001.

Chaplin, Joyce E. *An Anxious Pursuit: Agricultural Innovation and Modernity in the Lower South, 1730–1815.* Chapel Hill: University of North Carolina Press, 1993.

Doar, David. *Rice and Rice Planting in the South Carolina Low Country.* 1936. Reprint, Charleston, S.C.: Charleston Museum, 1970.

Heyward, Duncan Clinch. *Seed from Madagascar.* 1937. Reprint, Columbia: University of South Carolina Press, 1993.

Richards, James Prioleau (1894–1979). Congressman, diplomat. Richards was born on August 31, 1894, in Liberty Hill, the oldest of nine children born to Norman Smith Richards and Phoebe Gibbes. His roots were planted in the agricultural hamlet of Liberty Hill. However, more than two decades of service in Congress and as an envoy to the Middle East would place him on an international stage in a rapidly changing world.

In 1911 Richards earned a scholarship to Clemson College. He attended classes for two years and then transferred to the University of South Carolina. A lackadaisical student, Richards returned to Liberty Hill in 1915 without a degree. He enlisted in the U.S. Army in April 1917 and saw combat in France during World War I. Returning to South Carolina, Richards entered law school at the University of South Carolina in 1919 and received his law degree two years later. On November 4, 1925, Richards married Katherine Wiley of Lancaster County. They had three children.

In 1922 Richards won election to the Lancaster County probate judgeship, serving until 1933. This was the beginning of a distinguished political career that would last more than thirty years. He would never taste defeat at the ballot box.

With the Great Depression ravaging South Carolina's Fifth Congressional District, in 1932 Richards challenged the incumbent representative, William Francis Stevenson, who had been in Congress since 1917. On the stump, the youthful veteran stressed his military service (Stevenson had none) and the need for a change in Washington. In that summer's Democratic Party primary (the only election that mattered), Richards ousted Stevenson.

Richards entered Congress in 1933 as a New Deal Democrat. He was an enthusiastic supporter of President Franklin D. Roosevelt's domestic and foreign policies until 1941, when the congressman, now a member of the House Foreign Affairs Committee, raised serious questions about Roosevelt's request for a watered-down Neutrality Act. In a congressional speech that November, Richards recalled his own World War I experiences and noted that FDR was trying to get America into another conflict "through the back door." Richards adamantly vowed, "America comes first with me."

When Pearl Harbor was attacked by the Japanese the following month, Richards tried to enlist in the military, but the administration requested that he remain in Congress. By the end of the war, Richards was a senior member of the House, visiting numerous countries to witness the war's destruction and rebuilding efforts. By 1950 Richards had become a vigilant cold warrior, urging a steadfast stand against Communist encroachment abroad. He chaired the House Foreign Affairs Committee twice (1951–1953 and 1955–1957), working closely with Presidents Harry Truman and Dwight Eisenhower.

After retiring from Congress in early 1957, Richards was called back into service by the Eisenhower administration as a special ambassador to the Middle East. From March to June 1957 Richards toured that region, meeting with leaders to discuss the threat of "International Communism." He dispensed $200 million in financial aid on the mission, visited fifteen nations, traveled thirty thousand miles, and persuaded leaders of the strategic region to remain friendly to the United States.

Richards worked as a consultant for the American Tobacco Institute after his diplomatic mission and practiced law in Lancaster with his son. He retained a keen interest in international affairs, corresponding with Presidents John Kennedy, Richard Nixon, and Gerald Ford. He died in Lancaster on February 21, 1979, and was buried in the Liberty Hill Presbyterian Church Cemetery. JOSEPH EDWARD LEE

Lee, Joseph Edward. "'America Comes First with Me': The Political Career of Congressman James P. Richards, 1932–1957." Ph.D. diss., University of South Carolina, 1987.

———. "A South Carolinian in the Middle East: Ambassador James P. Richards's 1957 Mission." *Proceedings of the South Carolina Historical Association* (1988): 103–11.

Richards, James Prioleau. Papers. Modern Political Collections, South Caroliniana Library, University of South Carolina, Columbia.

Richards, John Gardiner, Jr. (1864–1941). Governor. Born in Liberty Hill, Kershaw County, on September 11, 1864, Richards was the son of John G. Richards and Sophia Edwards Smith. According to one scholar, Richards experienced "a relatively serene childhood" and enjoyed such genteel pursuits as lancing tournaments and fox hunting. He attended the common schools of Liberty Hill and spent two years at Bingham Military Institute in Mebane, North Carolina, before returning home at age nineteen to manage the family farm. In June 1888 Richards married Betty Coates Workman. The couple had eleven children.

In 1890 Richards supported "Pitchfork Ben" Tillman in his agrarian crusade against the conservative leaders of the Democratic Party, the so-called "Bourbons." Tillman triumphed, and Richards became a Kershaw County magistrate. After serving for eight years, he won a seat in the state House of Representatives in 1898. Over the next twelve years Richards championed agriculture, conservative budgets, public education for whites, and liquor control. The son of a Presbyterian minister, Richards was a staunch advocate of prohibition.

After an unsuccessful bid for the governorship in 1910, Richards was appointed to the state Railroad Commission, where he sat for twelve years between 1910 and 1926. During that time he shifted his political allegiance from Tillman to Coleman Blease, the victor in the 1910 gubernatorial election. Richards failed to succeed Blease as governor in 1914 and lost a third run for the office in 1918. Finally, in his fourth attempt, Richards won the governorship in 1926.

In office Richards declared war on the board of public welfare, evolution, and the highway and tax commissions, proclaiming the latter to be "a veiled effort to establish an oligarchy." He urged strict adherence to the Ten Commandments, ordering the state constabulary to close businesses that violated the Sabbath, and he even had golfers arrested for ignoring state blue laws. Appalled, the *New York Times* editorialized in March 1927, "There is another sport in South Carolina which is not seriously interfered with. This is lynching." A month later a *Columbia Record* poll revealed that 249 respondents favored the governor's position on Sunday activities while 3,943 opposed his interpretation of the Ten Commandments. The legislature and the state supreme court responded by curtailing Richards's authority, while popular opinion rejected his actions.

By 1928 the governor had abandoned his persecution of golfers and concentrated on rallying support for a $65 million road construction project and the upgrading of public schools. Both of these endeavors were tremendously successful under Richards's stewardship but were overshadowed by his zealous moral crusade. By the time he left office in 1931, South Carolinians enduring the Great Depression were far more concerned with obtaining the basic necessities of this life than with the narrow moral code of their governor. Retiring to his farm in Liberty Hill, Richards remained a loyal Democrat and supported Franklin Roosevelt in the 1932 presidential campaign, although he simultaneously led opposition in the state to the repeal of national prohibition. Richards died on October 9, 1941, and was buried in Liberty Hill Cemetery. JOSEPH EDWARD LEE

Cann, Katherine D. "John G. Richards and the Moral Majority." *Proceedings of the South Carolina Historical Association* (1983): 15–28.

McClure, Charles F. "The Public Career of John G. Richards." M.A. thesis, University of South Carolina, 1972.

Richardson, Dorcas Nelson (ca. 1741–1834). Revolutionary War heroine. Richardson was the daughter of Jared Nelson (Neilson), who operated Nelson's Ferry on the Santee River in what later became Sumter District. In 1761 she married Richard Richardson, Jr. (1741–ca. 1816), son of Richard Richardson and Mary Cantey. The couple had ten children.

Dorcas Richardson's husband was the captain of a militia company and was taken prisoner after the surrender of Charleston. The British held him at Johns Island, where he became ill with smallpox. After recovering, he escaped and hid out in the swamps of the Santee River near his home. Meanwhile, British colonel Banastre Tarleton had made the Richardson house a cavalry station. Richardson's family was confined to a few rooms of their house and received little to eat. Nevertheless, Dorcas Richardson managed to send food and even a horse into the swamp for her husband while the British troops hunted for him. The British allegedly taunted Richardson with what they would do to her husband when they captured him.

After her husband succeeded in joining Francis Marion's troops, the British changed their tactics on Richardson. Using flattery and promises of wealth and promotion, they tried to persuade Dorcas to convince her husband to change to the British side. She defiantly refused their advances, however, "and refused to be made instrumental to their purposes." While the reports of British cruelty to Dorcas Richardson may have been exaggerated, they and other similar stories became anti-British propaganda to rally South Carolinians to the patriot cause. Richardson died in 1834. BRENDA THOMPSON SCHOOLFIELD

Bailey, N. Louise, and Elizabeth Ivey Cooper, eds. *Biographical Directory of the South Carolina House of Representatives.* Vol. 3, *1775–1790.* Columbia: University of South Carolina Press, 1981.

Ellet, Elizabeth F. *The Women of the American Revolution.* 2 vols. New York: Baker and Scribner, 1848.

Richardson, Eudora Ramsay (1891–1973). Feminist, author, lecturer. Born in Versailles, Kentucky, on August 13, 1891, Richardson was the daughter of the Reverend David Marshall Ramsay and Mary Woolfolk. She grew up in Charleston, South Carolina, and Richmond, Virginia, where her father held pastorates at leading Baptist churches. She received bachelor's degrees from Hollins College and the University of Richmond (1911) and an M.A. degree from Columbia University (1914).

From 1912 to 1914 Richardson headed the English department at the Greenville Female College (renamed the Greenville Woman's College in 1914), a South Carolina institution for which her father served as president from 1911 to 1930. Popular as a teacher, Richardson named the literary societies that played a significant part of campus life. She also became noted for her promotion of women's suffrage, with her stated goal at the Greenville Woman's College being to educate "girls who are staunch advocates of women's rights." Such a view was perhaps shocking to some but was accepted with good grace at the conservative Baptist institution, which would merge with the all-male Furman University during the Great Depression.

Leaving the Greenville Woman's College in 1914, Richardson embarked on a three-year speaking career as field director of the National American Woman Suffrage Association. She worked closely with the suffragist Carrie Chapman Catt. She met her future husband, Fitzhugh Briggs Richardson of Richmond, while campaigning for votes for women. The couple married on December 13, 1917. The union produced one daughter, Eudora (Dolly).

During much of her married life, Richardson devoted herself to lecturing and writing. In the 1920s she spoke frequently at the Greenville Woman's College, became affiliated with the Southern Women's Educational Alliance, and served as president of the Richmond branch of the American Association of University Women. She published *Little Aleck; A Life of Alexander H. Stephens* (1932), *The Woman Speaker; A Hand-book and Study Course on Public Speaking* (1936), and *The Influence of Men—Incurable* (1936). In much of her speaking and writing, Richardson's goal was to further her feminist agenda and to have women taken seriously as political leaders, community activists, and employees. She opposing protective legislation, seeing it as an attempt to take away from women the legal equality they had fought so long and hard to achieve.

In 1938 Richardson was selected to serve as director of the Federal Writers' Project in Virginia and the state supervisor of the Virginia Writers' Project. Her efforts led to a variety of publications, including *Virginia; A Guide to the Old Dominion* (1940) and *The Negro in Virginia* (1940). When her agency was abolished in 1943, Richardson found employment as a writer for the Quartermaster

Technical Training Service at Camp Lee, Virginia. She retired in 1950 with a meritorious service commendation.

After retirement, Richardson continued to write and remained dedicated to her feminist views. Critical of the "women's lib" movement of the early 1970s, she stated in an interview, "Not too much has changed since we got the vote. . . . We were effective but they're not accomplishing anything much now." She died in Richmond, Virginia, on October 6, 1973, and was buried in Hollywood Cemetery. MARIAN ELIZABETH STROBEL

Garner, Anita M. "Richmond's Own Eudora." *Richmond Quarterly* 7 (winter 1984): 15–19.

Martin-Perdue, Nancy J., and Charles L. Perdue. *Talk about Trouble: A New Deal Portrait of Virginians in the Great Depression.* Chapel Hill: University of North Carolina Press, 1996.

Richardson, Eudora Ramsay. Papers. Special Collections Department, Alderman Memorial Library, University of Virginia, Charlottesville.

"What Happened to . . . Eudora R. Richardson." *Richmond Times-Dispatch,* July 12, 1971.

Richardson, James Burchell (1770–1836). Governor. Richardson, the son of Richard Richardson and Dorothy Sinkler, was born on October 28, 1770, in St. Mark's Parish. His father immigrated to South Carolina from Virginia in the 1730s and became one of the backcountry's leading planters and political figures. Richardson grew up on his family's plantation and married Anne Cantey Sinkler on May 10, 1791. Twelve children were born to their marriage. The upland cotton boom hit the South Carolina interior when Richardson was in his early twenties. Capitalizing on his family's extensive resources, he quickly became one of the state's wealthiest planters. He owned five plantations totaling more than five thousand acres in Sumter District and St. John's Berkeley and St. James Santee Parishes, plus nearly seven thousand acres of unimproved land scattered from Charleston to Columbia. At death he owned 395 slaves.

In 1792 Richardson was elected by Clarendon County to the state House of Representatives, where he remained until his election as governor on December 8, 1802. Richardson became the first backcountry resident—indeed the first non-Charlestonian—to hold the office, and his election reflected the increasing political and economic solidification of the state based on cotton, slavery, and the plantation system. Richardson also was the first of six lineal descendants of Richard Richardson to serve as governor. A Democratic-Republican with an ear to his inland constituents, Richardson turned his attention to demands from interior districts to reopen the slave trade in South Carolina. Since the early 1790s the General Assembly had banned the importation of slaves from both foreign and domestic sources. With the spread of cotton into the backcountry in the 1790s, however, demand for agricultural labor soared. Richardson argued that prohibition of the trade was unenforceable and unfair, "for in the present state of things, the citizens in the frontier and seacoast districts do accrue late this property without the possibility of being detected, while those of the interior and middle districts only experience the operation of that law." In 1803, at his urging, the General Assembly repealed all laws against the slave trade; only the importation of slaves from the West Indies remained illegal, as did importing male slaves over fifteen years of age from other states without certification of prior good behavior. During his tenure Richardson supported backcountry demands for increased representation in the legislature. A bill to reapportion the General Assembly to more accurately reflect the growing wealth and population of interior districts passed the House but was defeated in the Senate.

After Richardson's successor was chosen on December 7, 1804, he was immediately returned by Sumter to the General Assembly, where he represented the district in the House from 1804 to 1805 and then in the Senate from 1806 to 1813. In 1812 Richardson was named a director of the Bank of the State of South Carolina. He served one final term for Sumter in the House (1816–1817) before retiring from public life. Richardson died on April 28, 1836, and was buried in Richardson Cemetery, Sumter District. MATTHEW A. LOCKHART

Bailey, N. Louise, Mary L. Morgan, and Carolyn R. Taylor, eds. *Biographical Directory of the South Carolina Senate, 1776–1985.* 3 vols. Columbia: University of South Carolina Press, 1986.

Richardson, John Peter (1801–1864). Congressman, governor. Born in Sumter District on April 14, 1801, Richardson was the son of John Peter Richardson and Floride Bonneau Peyre. He attended Willington Academy and South Carolina College, but he withdrew from the latter in 1819 during his senior year. On October 16, 1827, Richardson married his first cousin Juliana Augusta Manning. They had at least five children. A successful planter, Richardson owned a large plantation in Sumter District and at least 194 slaves by 1860.

In 1825 Richardson was elected to the state House of Representatives, where he served until 1833. A Unionist, Richardson opposed the nullification movement in South Carolina, doubting that federal laws could be nullified by the individual states. In November 1832 Sumter District sent Richardson to the state nullification convention in Columbia, where he voted against the ordinance that declared the federal tariffs of 1828 and 1832 null and void in South Carolina.

In 1834 Richardson was elected to the South Carolina Senate and served a two-year term. As a senator, Richardson debated the Test Oath Bill with Governor James Hamilton, the recognized leader of the nullification movement. Richardson opposed the bill, which required all civil and military officers to pledge their ultimate allegiance to South Carolina over the nation. Richardson resigned from the state Senate upon his election to the U.S. House of Representatives. Chosen to complete the term of his late brother-in-law, Richard I. Manning, Richardson took his seat in Congress on December 19, 1836, and served until 1839.

Shortly after his return to South Carolina, Richardson's name was put forward as a candidate for governor in January 1840. His nomination represented an attempt to reconcile Unionists and nullifiers in the state, with his election allowing nullifiers to woo Unionists by giving one of their own the prestigious, but largely ceremonial, office of governor. When the General Assembly convened, Richardson was easily elected governor on December 9, 1840. In office, Richardson supported a statewide agricultural and geologic survey in order to improve agriculture and halt the migration of planters and farmers from the state. The impact of this out-migration was made clear in the 1840 federal reapportionment, in which South Carolina lost two congressional districts. Richardson was also an advocate of military education and played a key role in establishing the Citadel in Charleston and Arsenal Academy in Columbia.

After Richardson left office in December 1842, his Unionist sympathies gradually eroded as he observed the growing abolitionist movement in the North. He served as a deputy to the Nashville Convention in 1850. He served as president of the state Southern Rights Association the following year and as a delegate to the

Southern Rights state convention in 1852. Clarendon District sent Richardson to the Secession Convention of 1860, where he joined his fellow delegates in their unanimous support for the Ordinance of Secession. Richardson died on January 24, 1864, and was buried in the family cemetery in Clarendon District. MATTHEW A. BYRON

Bailey, N. Louise, Mary L. Morgan, and Carolyn R. Taylor, eds. *Biographical Directory of the South Carolina Senate, 1776–1985.* 3 vols. Columbia: University of South Carolina Press, 1986.

Richardson, John Peter, III (1831–1899). Governor. Last of the conservative-era governors, Richardson was born in Sumter District (later Clarendon) on September 25, 1831, the son of Governor John Peter Richardson and Juliana Augusta Manning. Educated by private tutors, he graduated third in his class from South Carolina College in 1849. By profession a planter, Richardson had extensive agricultural interests in the Panola section of northwestern Clarendon District. On December 3, 1868, he married Eleanora Norvelle Richardson. After her death in 1874, he wed Juliana Augusta Manning Richardson on February 13, 1877. Both marriages were childless.

Richardson represented Clarendon District in the state House of Representatives from 1856 to 1861. He entered Confederate service in 1862, serving first as brigade and later as division inspector general on the staff of his first cousin Brigadier General James Cantey. Active politically after the war, Richardson served as a delegate to the 1865 state constitutional convention, again represented Clarendon District in the House in 1865 and from 1878 to 1880, and also had a brief tenure in the state Senate from 1865 to 1866. He served three consecutive terms as state treasurer from 1880 until 1886. After a skillful campaign managed by the newspaperman Narciso G. Gonzales, Richardson won the Democratic nomination for governor over the incumbent John C. Sheppard. Inaugurated on November 30, 1886, Richardson utilized all of the influence of his office to secure passage of a bill reorganizing South Carolina College into a university. Faced with a severe agricultural depression, in 1887 he recommended postponement of the tax deadline to help prevent farm forfeitures. Although strongly opposed by the Farmers' Association and its leader Benjamin R. Tillman, "Clarendon's Silver Tongued Orator" was renominated in 1888. His second term was dominated by the founding of Clemson College. Richardson opposed acceptance of the Clemson bequest on the grounds that the state would not have ultimate control of the college, its establishment would siphon funds from the University of South Carolina (which already had an agricultural department), and the uncertainty over court challenges to the bequest. After the Clemson will was validated by a federal court on May 21, 1889, he reluctantly signed the bill creating the college into law in November 1889. Richardson stated his racial policy in 1889: "We believe that the whites must dominate, but at the same time we do not refuse local offices to blacks." In that same year he recommended alteration of the state's civil rights law to permit racially separate but equal accommodations on railroad cars, and he ordered the state militia to York to prevent the lynching of black prisoners.

Characterized as "a man of sense and a most lovable gentleman," Richardson continued to be active in conservative Democratic politics and in civic and business affairs after relinquishing public office. He divided his time between residence at his Clarendon County plantation, Elmswooe, and Columbia's Hotel Jerome. He died at the latter place on July 5, 1899, and was buried at the Quaker Cemetery in Camden, South Carolina. PAUL R. BEGLEY

Bailey, N. Louise, Mary L. Morgan, and Carolyn R. Taylor, eds. *Biographical Directory of the South Carolina Senate, 1776–1985.* 3 vols. Columbia: University of South Carolina Press, 1986.

Begley, Paul R. "Governor Richardson Faces the Tillman Challenge." *South Carolina Historical Magazine* 89 (April 1988): 119–26.

Cooper, William J., Jr. *The Conservative Regime: South Carolina, 1877–1890.* Baltimore: Johns Hopkins Press, 1968.

Richardson, Richard (ca. 1705–1780). Legislator, soldier. Richardson was born in Virginia and immigrated to South Carolina in the 1730s, settling on the upper Santee River in Prince Frederick's Parish. Through grants he amassed substantial landholdings and became a prosperous planter. On October 11, 1738, he married Mary Cantey. The couple had seven children. Mary died in 1767, and Richardson then married Dorothy Sinkler. His second marriage produced four sons. Richardson would be the founder of one of South Carolina's leading political families, with six of his descendants becoming governor of the state.

In the 1750s and 1760s Richardson emerged as a leading political figure in the backcountry, regularly representing Prince Frederick's and St. Mark's Parishes in the Commons House of Assembly from 1754 to 1765. In 1768 Richardson was instrumental in negotiating an end to the violent Regulator movement in the backcountry. He was a member of the First and Second Provincial Congresses of South Carolina and was a well-respected militia officer at the start of the Revolutionary War.

In November 1775 Richardson and Colonel William Thomson were given command of 2,500 men and ordered to scatter the large concentration of Loyalists gathering in the South Carolina backcountry. As Richardson and his men advanced through the Loyalist stronghold between the Broad and Saluda Rivers, Loyalists put up brief stands along the way but kept retreating in front of the patriot force. Richardson continued his pursuit, pushing four miles beyond the Cherokee tribal boundary to the Great Cane Break on Reedy River. When he learned that the Tories were encamped there, Richardson sent Thomson to attack them. On December 22, 1775, a sharp fight ensued after the rebels nearly surrounded the Tories. Although the Tory leader Patrick Cunningham managed to escape, the patriot mission of dispersing the Loyalists had been an unquestionable success. Without a leader to guide them, Loyalist resistance fell apart. After Richardson dismissed his men and started on his march home, a heavy snow fell, lending the nickname "Snow Campaign" to the venture.

The Snow Campaign was Richardson's first and last active duty during the Revolutionary War. He was promoted to brigadier general, but his advanced age led him to resign his commission in late 1779. He was captured by the British at the fall of Charleston in May 1780. After several months of harsh treatment at the hands of his British captors, Richardson died at his home plantation, Big Home, in September 1780, and was buried there. KENDRA DEBANY

Buchanan, John. *The Road to Guilford Courthouse: The American Revolution in the Carolinas.* New York: Wiley, 1997.

Edgar, Walter, and N. Louise Bailey, eds. *Biographical Directory of the South Carolina House of Representatives.* Vol. 2, *The Commons House of Assembly, 1692–1775.* Columbia: University of South Carolina Press, 1977.

Lumpkin, Henry. *From Savannah to Yorktown: The American Revolution in the South.* Columbia: University of South Carolina Press, 1981.

Richardson, Robert Clinton (b. 1935). Baseball player. "Bobby" Richardson has been a major league baseball star, a college baseball coach, and a leader for youth and evangelism. Born in Sumter on

Bobby Richardson. Courtesy, University of South Carolina Athletic Department

August 19, 1935, Richardson played sandlot, high school, and American Legion baseball in his hometown before signing with the New York Yankees in 1953. After playing on several minor league teams, Richardson made his debut with the Yankees in 1955. Richardson went on to be New York's regular second baseman from 1957 to 1966, an era in which the Yankees dominated major league baseball.

Richardson earned national attention when he hit a grand slam in Game Six of the 1960 World Series, in which he set a Series record of twelve runs batted in and was voted the Series MVP. Richardson again gained national acclaim during the final play of Game Seven of the 1962 World Series. With the Yankees leading 1–0 in the ninth inning, and with two San Francisco Giants in scoring position, Richardson was perfectly positioned to catch Willie McCovey's line drive to end the game and the World Series. The *Sporting News* ranked the dramatic catch as the thirteenth-greatest moment in baseball history. The 1962 World Series capped Richardson's best season, in which he hit .302 and finished second in American League MVP voting to his Yankee teammate Mickey Mantle. Still in his prime as a player, Richardson retired in 1966 to enter youth and evangelical work. In his major league career he hit .266 with 34 home runs and 390 runs batted in. A seven-time All-Star (1957, 1959, 1962–1966), Richardson also won the American League Gold Glove Award for the best fielding second baseman five consecutive years (1961–1965).

In 1970 Richardson became the first full-time head baseball coach at the University of South Carolina. Attracting many quality recruits, Richardson increased the popularity and prestige of the Gamecock baseball program as record crowds attended games to watch his often stellar teams. His 51–6 team of 1975 was his best, which lost 2–0 to Texas in the championship game of the College World Series in Omaha. Richardson left the USC baseball team after the 1976 season with a 220–90–2 overall record and a .702 winning percentage.

In 1976 Richardson ran for Congress as a Republican, losing to incumbent Ken Holland but earning forty-nine percent of the vote. After his political venture, he continued in youth and evangelical work and later returned to college coaching at Coastal Carolina University and Liberty University in Virginia, where he retired as athletic director in 1990. Returning to his hometown of Sumter, Richardson remained active in the Fellowship of Christian Athletes and served for ten years as president of Baseball Chapel, an organization providing church services for baseball players before Sunday games. DAN G. RUFF

Golenbock, Peter. *Dynasty, the New York Yankees, 1949–1964.* Englewood Cliffs, N.J.: Prentice-Hall, 1975.

Price, Tom. *A Century of Gamecocks: Memorable Baseball Moments.* Columbia, S.C.: Summerhouse, 1996.

Richardson, Bobby. *The Bobby Richardson Story.* Westwood, N.J.: Revell, 1965.

"Richardson Waltz." State waltz. The "Richardson Waltz" was designated South Carolina's official state waltz in legislation signed by Governor James Hodges on July 21, 2000. The General Assembly noted that this "beautiful and soulful" dance music had been created and preserved for generations by members of the Richardson family, "descendants of General Richard Richardson . . . who came from Virginia as a surveyor to settle in South Carolina." Richard Richardson was a colonial legislator and important military leader during the Revolutionary War who pacified the backcountry Tories in 1775 and then served with General Benjamin Lincoln at Purrysburgh in 1778. He founded an important political family and was the lineal ancestor of six governors of South Carolina.

Since the eighteenth century, members of the Richardson family were known in Clarendon and Sumter Counties, and elsewhere in South Carolina, for their hospitality, entertainments, and love of dancing. A family member whose identity has been forgotten composed the waltz, which was played at family balls and passed down "by ear" for more than two centuries.

In 1985 the music was written down by Mary Richardson Briggs of Summerton in order to insure its preservation. Briggs copyrighted the melody in 1986. Its adoption as the state waltz was successfully promoted by the Elizabeth Peyre Richardson Manning Chapter of the Daughters of the American Revolution. On the day that Governor Hodges signed the bill before a large audience in the State House rotunda, the waltz was played and danced. DAVID C. R. HEISSER

Richland County (756 sq. miles; 2000 pop. 320,677). Richland County was created in 1785 when sprawling Camden District was divided. The original boundaries of Richland—named either for the fertile land along the banks of the Congaree or a plantation owned by Thomas Taylor—were described in this manner: "beginning at

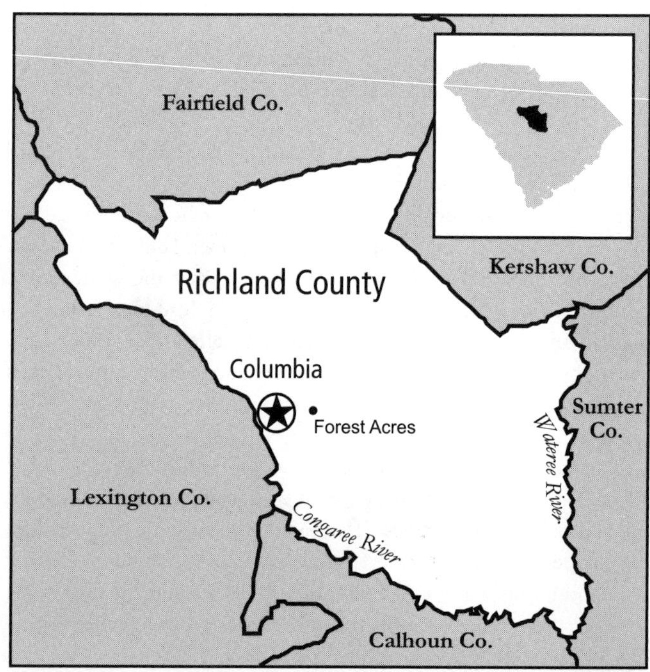

the corner of Clarendon county line, at Person's Island, thence up the Congaree river to the mouth of Cedar creek, thence on a strait line to the mouth of Twenty-Five Mile creek, thence down the Wateree river to the beginning, and shall be called Richland county." Not everyone was pleased, for during the decade that followed, the northern and eastern borders were altered slightly. By 1799 Richland County assumed its modern form, at the same time becoming a "district" (the area served by a district court), the official designation of all South Carolina counties until 1868.

This region, part of what geographers call an "inner" coastal plain, has an elevation above sea level that varies from 80 to 550 feet as one proceeds inland. The most obvious physical features are the Sandhills, a disjointed band of gentle slopes marking the fall line, and the Congaree and Wateree Rivers, which unite to form the Santee River at the extreme southeast corner of the county. This landscape can be divided into three major areas. Lower Richland, stretching from the Congaree Swamp north to the Sumter Highway (U.S. Highway 76), is by far the best farmland. Here large-scale agriculture and substantial estates developed during the early nineteenth century. A line drawn from Columbia (seat of local and state government) to the northeast corner of the county splits the upper two-thirds into two triangles: Sandhills and an area akin to the Piedmont. The former generally defines Fort Jackson's domain, with soil less fertile than found elsewhere and never farmed extensively. The Piedmont triangle bordering various rivers—traditionally home to small farms—eventually became something of a suburban-industrial maze.

Before Europeans ventured inland from Charleston and south from Virginia, this region was a Native American hunting ground, as well as a no-man's-land between two hostile tribes, the Wateree and the Congaree. However, their ranks dwindled, and by the time permanent settlers appeared in 1740, both groups had moved northward and merged with the more numerous Catawbas, leaving only the names of local rivers as their legacy.

Richland's colonial history was much like that of many frontier outposts. Explorers, fur traders, and cowboys were followed by restless pioneers seeking cheap land and opportunity to prosper, first by growing essential foodstuffs and then by producing money crops such as wheat, indigo, tobacco, and eventually cotton. The warfare of those decades, even the Revolution, had limited impact, for this was no colonial crossroads. Trade, for the most part, went up the west bank of the Congaree into the lands of the Cherokee, one of the Southeast's most powerful tribes. But change was in the air, largely because of the flow of settlers into the backcountry, their demand for more representative local government, and the concept of centrality—a belief that authority should be exercised from a central site easily accessible to the governed.

The result was Richland County and the city of Columbia, a new, more centralized seat of state government. Ironically, local residents tried briefly to make Horrell Hill, located about a dozen miles east of Columbia, the new county's "capital," but to no avail. Lawyers refused to cooperate, and legislation passed in 1799 stipulated that the local district court would meet in Columbia. Originally home to a minuscule gaggle of government officials, hundreds of farm-plantation households, and a few shops and stores tied closely to agriculture, Richland County has experienced steady growth. Only in the 1850s did the population decline due to outmigration of slaves, worn-out soil, and the lure of other regions. From 1800 to 1920 a majority of residents were black.

Not surprisingly, Richland's story mirrors that of similar communities. By turns, it embraced canal travel, railroads, textiles, and a variety of commercial ventures, and the county even dreamed of becoming the site of an inland seaport. Yet, as this tale unfolded, it became apparent that the region's well-being—especially since 1950—depended for the most part on state government, the University of South Carolina, and Fort Jackson. These giant enterprises annually pumped millions into the local economy and supported a metropolitan complex of some 500,000 people, which included not just Richland County but also scores of outlying villages, towns, and cities. By the early twenty-first century it was virtually impossible to imagine the region without this threesome, which, in turn, have attracted and fostered many related activities. And it was equally difficult to separate county and city—Richland and Columbia. The result was an entity sometimes referred to as "the capital of the Midlands," a vague grouping of communities located between the upcountry and the lowcountry.

Nevertheless, this concept possesses some degree of political, economic, and social reality, for Columbia, Richland County, and their neighbors frequently charted a "middle" way between extremes advocated by other regions. And, because of the presence of state authority, they often are seen as spokesmen, especially on sectional and national matters, for virtually all South Carolinians. Born of compromise in the 1780s, this community has spent much of its life balancing contending forces—rural and urban, farm and factory, upland and coastal. This conciliatory stance, an attitude some would label "pragmatic," was of paramount importance during the integration crisis of the 1960s and may serve equally well in years to come.

Over half a century ago this state's well-known Works Progress Administration guide characterized the typical South Carolinian as having "fire in his head, comfort in his middle, and a little lead in his feet." In the early twenty-first century concern for comfort remained as strong as ever in Richland County and throughout the Midlands, but to achieve that ease, fire and lead were transformed—the former tempered by several wars and profound social change and the latter by a desire to realize more fully the American dream.

JOHN H. MOORE

Freeman, James W., comp. *Greater Columbia Data Book.* Columbia, S.C.: Economic Development Commission of Greater Columbia, Richland and Lexington Counties, 1976.

Green, Edwin L. *A History of Richland County.* Vol. 1, *1732–1805.* Columbia, S.C.: R. L. Bryan, 1932.

Moore, John Hammond. *Columbia and Richland County: A South Carolina Community, 1740–1990.* Columbia: University of South Carolina Press, 1993.

Ridgeland (Jasper County; 2000 pop. 2,518). The town of Ridgeland grew around a depot established by the Charleston and Savannah Railroad, which was completed in 1860. Ridgeland might never have existed had the citizens of the village of Grahamville, about one mile east, not objected to the railroad being routed through their community. The small railroad station began to attract homes and small businesses. The community was first named Gopher Hill for the "burrowing" tortoise that inhabited the area.

The depot was burned during the Civil War and was rebuilt almost a mile north of its initial location. Because the station was on the highest ridge between Charleston and Savannah, the railroad named it Ridgeland. The small town was incorporated on December 24, 1894, with a population of 271. The railroad separated Beaufort and Hampton Counties, with Ridgeland astride that line. The charter stipulated that the town limits included all property within a one-mile rectangle surrounding the railroad depot. When

Jasper County was formed by the state in 1912 from parts of Beaufort and Hampton Counties, Ridgeland, the largest and most central town in the new county, became the county seat. Its courthouse was completed in 1915 and remained in use at the beginning of the twenty-first century. The town's city limits have been extended several times over the years by annexations.

After the Civil War, Ridgeland and the surrounding area were left in abject poverty. Most former rice and indigo plantations passed into "yankee" ownership and became hunting preserves, while small farmers began raising cotton and corn. Ridgeland catered to both the hunting clubs and area farms. Sawmills contributed to the early growth of the town, but the railroad, by then the Atlantic Coastline Railroad, remained at the center of town. As the automobile became more prevalent, Ridgeland's location on U.S. Highway 17, the main route between New York and Florida, made the town a natural stopping place for travelers. The railroad dwindled in importance after World War II, and the Ridgeland depot closed in 1972. Railroad-related businesses, such as the cotton gin, sawmills, and the small hotels that faced the tracks, have long since disappeared.

The 1970s brought Interstate 95, while the 1980s brought a new interchange and shopping center. Ridgeland's three interstate exits attracted motels, restaurants, service stations, and numerous small businesses. In the 1990s several new industries came to Ridgeland along with an expansion of Palmetto Electric Cooperative's offices and maintenance facility. Major beautification projects costing in excess of $500,000 revitalized Main Street. The short commute from Ridgeland to Beaufort, Hilton Head, and Savannah made Ridgeland an increasingly popular location for many to live. The 1995 opening of the Ridgeland Correctional Institution, a medium-security prison, added some one thousand residents to Ridgeland's population in the 1990s. New projects in the Ridgeland vicinity at the start of the twenty-first century, such as the SCANA Generating Plant, a planned University of South Carolina campus on the Beaufort-Jasper county line, a new hospital, and a proposed new seaport at the mouth of the Savannah River, promised additional growth. WOFFORD MALPHRUS

Harvey, Bruce G. *An Architectural and Historical Survey of Jasper County, South Carolina.* Atlanta: Brockington and Associates, 1996.

Perry, Grace Fox. *Moving Finger of Jasper.* [Ridgeland, S.C., 1962].

Right-to-work law. Section 14(b) of the Taft-Hartley Act, passed in 1947 over the veto of President Harry Truman, enabled states to pass so-called "right-to-work" laws, which prohibit union security agreements, or "closed shops." The laws vary widely from state to state, but generally they forbid companies and unions from agreeing to contracts that require workers to belong to a union as a provision of employment. As of 2004 twenty-two states, predominately in the Southeast and the West, had right-to-work laws.

South Carolina's General Assembly passed such legislation in 1954 after more than a dozen other states had done so. While South Carolina had traditionally been viewed as an anti-union state, the state's adoption of a right-to-work law was controversial. Spartanburg representative Raymond C. Eubanks, a railway conductor and representative of the Brother of Railway Trainmen, led a pro-union faction in the House in a fight against the law. In an eight-hour debate that featured a five-hour, twenty-five-minute filibuster by Eubanks and fifteen proposed amendments, the pro-union faction was unable to amend the bill or prevent its passage. An effort to repeal the law the next year also failed.

The effects of right-to-work laws on levels of unionization, wages, and cost of living are still being debated. Opponents of the laws derisively term them "right-to-work for less" laws and point out that right-to-work states have lower levels of unionization and, consequently, lower average wages than non-right-to-work states. Proponents maintain that right-to-work states have lower levels of unemployment and a lower cost of living that results in higher disposable income. Economic scholars have split along similar lines regarding the effects of right-to-work laws. Eager to bring new industries to the state, South Carolina business leaders frequently cite the law as an example of the state's probusiness atmosphere when courting companies.

The law remained a subject of debate in the early twenty-first century. In 1997 lawmakers proposed strengthening the law by imposing stiffer penalties for offenders and offering the ability to sue to workers who feel unfairly pressured by unions. The law passed in 2002, prompting an unsuccessful attempt by pro-union lawmakers to repeal the law the following year. BENJAMIN PETERSEN

Riley, Joseph P., Jr. (b. 1943). Legislator, mayor of Charleston. Riley was born in Charleston on January 19, 1943, the son of Joseph P. Riley, Sr., and Helen Schachte. He graduated from Bishop England High School in Charleston in 1960. He received his undergraduate degree in political science from the Citadel in 1964 and his law degree from the University of South Carolina in 1967. On August 20, 1966, he married Charlotte Douglas deLoach. They have two sons.

Riley was first elected to the South Carolina House of Representatives in 1968. He served three terms as a legislator and earned a reputation as a reformer. He also served as a member of the State Reorganization Commission.

In 1975 Riley was elected mayor of Charleston. After continuous reelections, in 2002 he was serving his seventh term as mayor. In 1994 he was a Democratic candidate for governor, but he was narrowly defeated in the Democratic Party runoff primary.

Under Riley's leadership, Charleston experienced significant revival and growth that brought national and international recognition. This included revitalization of its historical residential and business areas, including the rebirth of King Street, its main street. The city also renovated Hampton Park and developed new parks and recreational attractions, including a waterfront park on the Cooper River, the Charleston Maritime Center, the South Carolina Aquarium, and the Joseph P. Riley, Jr., Baseball Stadium. A major tennis facility seating approximately ten thousand spectators was built on Daniel Island, and the Women's Family Circle Tennis tournament relocated from Hilton Head to Charleston.

During the Riley administration Charleston also experienced a cultural renaissance through the initiation of several arts festivals. These included the internationally acclaimed Spoleto Festival USA, Piccolo Spoleto, and the MOJA African American Arts Festival. With the revitalization of the historic district and the development of these new facilities and events, Charleston has become one of the top tourist destinations in the United States.

The Riley administration also significantly improved race relations in the city through a variety of programs. Riley was a leader in the effort to create affordable housing in Charleston. He established the Mayors Council on Homelessness and Affordable Housing. Charleston's scattered-site housing program received a Presidential Design Award as well as three HUD Blue Ribbon Awards for Best Practices. Other programs established include a Minor Home Repair program, the Parent Program, Home (an owner-occupied and rental rehabilitation program), and the Charleston Bank Consortium, a program designed to assist low- and moderate-income families in obtaining mortgages.

Riley served as president of the U.S. Conference on Mayors (1986–1987) and as president of the National Association of Democratic Mayors (1988–1992). He was named the 1991 Municipal Leader of the Year by *American City and County.* In 2000 he was awarded the first President's Award from the U.S. Conference of Mayors and was the first recipient of the Urban Land Institute J. C. Nichols Prize for Visionary Urban Development. WILLIAM V. MOORE

Riley, Richard Wilson (b. 1933). Governor, U.S. secretary of education. Riley was born on January 2, 1933, in Greenville, the son of Edward Patterson Riley and Martha Dixon. He attended public grade schools in Greenville and was graduated from Furman University in 1954. After college Riley entered the U.S. Navy, serving from 1954 to 1956. While in the navy he was diagnosed with spondylitis, a painful bone disease that caused his spine to curve forward and left him unable to turn his neck. He was determined to pursue an active career, however, and in 1956 entered law school at the University of South Carolina, graduating in 1959. In 1957 he married Ann Osteen Yarborough, with whom he later had four children. In 1960 he joined his father's Greenville law firm.

Richard Wilson Riley. Courtesy, Modern Political Collections, University of South Carolina

In 1962 Riley was elected to the state House of Representatives as a Democrat from Greenville. He served until 1966, when he won election to the state Senate. During his ten years in the Senate, Riley was considered a "young Turk," one of a group of progressive, reform-minded legislators who pushed causes such as judicial reorganization, home rule, constitutional revision, equitable financing for school districts, and peaceful desegregation of public schools. Riley declined to seek reelection in 1976, but he captured the 1978 Democratic gubernatorial nomination in a runoff and won the general election with sixty-one percent of the vote.

After assuming office on January 10, 1979, Riley pressed reform causes such as merit selection of the state's Public Service Commission, limitation of nuclear waste dumping in South Carolina, aid for the medically indigent, and a change to the state constitution that would allow a sitting governor to serve a second term. The latter change gained legislative and public approval. As a result, Riley became the first South Carolina governor in history to serve consecutive four-year terms. Reelected on November 2, 1982, with some seventy percent of the vote, Riley capitalized on his popularity to launch his most ambitious reform, a comprehensive effort to overhaul the state's public school system.

Long an advocate of public schools, Riley made education reform the priority of his second term. After the General Assembly rejected his first legislative package in 1983, Riley changed his approach and sought the ideas of thousands of South Carolinians who turned out at forums designed to solicit public input. Through intense lobbying he gained the support of business leaders and educators for a longer school day, merit pay for teachers, and school accountability measures. A keystone of the plan, which came to be known as the Education Improvement Act (EIA), was a one-cent hike in the state's sales tax to fund the reforms. Riley's sweeping education package received grassroots support across the state. Despite determined opposition, the General Assembly approved the EIA in June 1984. It was acclaimed as the most comprehensive school reform package ever enacted at one time and a model of education reform.

After leaving the governor's office in early 1987, Riley joined the influential law firm Nelson, Mullins, Riley and Scarborough of Columbia, Greenville, and Myrtle Beach. However, the success of his education reform efforts cemented his reputation as one of the nation's leading public school advocates. Following the election of former Arkansas governor Bill Clinton as president in 1992, Riley was named U.S. secretary of education.

President Clinton charged Riley with launching a national school reform effort similar to that enacted in South Carolina. He unveiled a legislative package designed to set national standards for students and teachers and provide incentives for schools to meet them. It included improvements in federal school aid for needy children, direct loans for college-bound students, and a program to encourage parental involvement in their children's schooling. When Republicans gained control of Congress in 1994, they set out to eliminate the Department of Education. But Riley's efforts and popular support for public education ultimately strengthened the department. By the end of Clinton's second term, Riley had helped the Department of Education reach record levels of federal education spending. After eight years in the post of secretary of education, Riley was hailed in the national press as "one of the great statesmen of education" in the twentieth century and "one of the most decent and honorable men in public life." In 2001 he returned to South Carolina, where he continued to advance education issues through professorships at Furman University and the University of South Carolina. HENRY H. LESESNE

Anderson, Nick. "With a Gift for Dialogue, Education Chief Gets Congress Talking." *Los Angeles Times,* July 6, 1999, p. A5.

Bagwell, Benjamin Prince. *Riley: A Story of Hope.* Pickens, S.C.: Pickens County Publishing, 1986.

Bailey, N. Louise, Mary L. Morgan, and Carolyn R. Taylor, eds. *Biographical Directory of the South Carolina Senate, 1776–1985.* 3 vols. Columbia: University of South Carolina Press, 1986.

Broder, David S. "Under Riley, a Reversal of Fortune at Education." *Washington Post,* January 19, 2001, p. A35.

Ring shout. In West and Central Africa dances done in a circular formation are widespread. The most important are performed on sacred occasions such as marriage ceremonies, at burials, and to honor the spirits of departed ancestors. Africans in Togo, West Africa, have been observed carrying the bodies of deceased persons around their homes to gather the ancestral spirits before going to the burial ceremonies. In Central Africa the BaKongo people participate in an ancestral ceremony whereby a cross inside a circle depicts four phases of human life between birth and death, similar to the phases of the sun's daily movement from dawn to night. In these dances participants move in a counterclockwise manner accompanied by drumming, clapping, and singing. In Africa certain dances are considered forms of worship designed to summon ancestral spirits or deities into the celebrants' midst.

As enslaved people adopted Christianity in the South Carolina and Georgia lowcountry, the foregoing rituals became a profound aspect of the Africanized Christianity they practiced. No longer accompanied by drums (which were prohibited), the singing, hand clapping, and counterclockwise movements remained part of ecstatic worship services, where the "Holy Spirit" frequently entered the celebrants. The ring shout, as the practice was known, evoked controversy because black and white religious leaders sometimes denounced it as the vestige of "paganism." Aside from its strictly religious function, during the slave era as Africans from various ethnic groups joined together in the ring shout, it became an important mechanism through which a new common African American identity was formed. The ring shout was still practiced in the early twenty-first century, but comparatively rarely. BERNARD E. POWERS, JR.

Parrish, Lydia. *Slave Songs of the Georgia Sea Islands.* New York: Creative Age, 1942.

Stuckey, Sterling. *Slave Culture: Nationalist Theory and the Foundations of Black America.* New York: Oxford University Press, 1987.

Ripley, Alexandra Braid (1934–2004). Writer. Ripley was born in Charleston on January 8, 1934, the daughter of Alexander and Elizabeth Braid. After graduating from Ashley Hall, she attended Vassar College on a United Daughters of the Confederacy scholarship. After receiving a B.A. in Russian in 1955, Ripley worked a succession of jobs, living in New York City, Washington, D.C., and Florence, Italy. In 1963 she returned to Charleston, where she held various positions from travel agent to tour guide to ghost writer. She returned to New York and began working in publishing and then moved to Virginia in the early 1970s to pursue a writing career. Ripley published her first historical novel, *Charleston,* in 1981 while working at a bookstore. She followed with a sequel, *On Leaving Charleston* (1984), and then two more works of historical fiction, *The Time Returns* (1985) and *New Orleans Legacy* (1987), the latter of which became a Literary Guild alternative and a Reader's Digest Condensed Book selection.

In 1986 Ripley was chosen to write a sequel to Margaret Mitchell's Pulitzer Prize–winning classic, *Gone With the Wind* (1936), by Mitchell's estate. In 1988 Warner Books successfully bid $4,940,000 for the publishing rights. On September 25, 1991, *Scarlett: The Sequel to Margaret Mitchell's Gone With the Wind* appeared in bookstores. It spent sixteen weeks on the *New York Times* best-seller list, selling two million copies by the end of the year. The book follows Scarlett O'Hara Hamilton Kennedy Butler as she makes her way from Charleston to Savannah, Georgia, and finally to Ireland, where she restores her ancestral estate, raises her daughter, joins an insurrectionist movement, and marries an English earl before finally reuniting with Rhett Butler. Despite the heady sales figures and intense, if brief, popularity of *Scarlett,* reviewers uniformly panned the book. Ripley shrugged off the criticism, however, and continued to write after the hoopla over *Scarlett* subsided. She published two more historical novels, *From Fields of Gold* (1994) and *A Love Divine* (1996), which were both well received.

Ripley was married to Leonard Ripley from 1958 until their divorce in 1963. In 1981 she married John Graham, a rhetoric professor at the University of Virginia. Ripley had two daughters from her first marriage. She died at her home in Richmond, Virginia, on January 10, 2004. R. F. STALVEY

Ripley, Clements (1892–1954), and **Katharine Ball Ripley** (1898–1955). Writers. "Believe it or not, the Ripleys—Clements and Katharine—are Charleston's most prolific and best known national authors," asserted the *Charleston Evening Post* on September 5, 1949. Between 1923 and 1953 the couple published ten books—including novels and memoirs—and dozens of short stories and nonfiction pieces. Furthermore, they became successful collaborative screenwriters during the 1930s and 1940s, traveling between Charleston and Hollywood to fulfill contract obligations under Clements's name. In a letter of February 17, 1940, Ripley wrote Louis F. Edelman, his contact man at Warner Brothers Pictures: "You must realize that anybody who deals with me is getting the services of two trained writers—my wife and myself."

Born on August 26, 1892, in Tacoma, Washington, Clements "Clem" Ripley was the son of the offspring of two old Vermont families, Thomas Emerson Ripley and Charlotte Howard Clement. Katharine "Kattie" Ball Ripley, the daughter of the legendary newspaperman William Watts Ball and Fay Witte, was born in Charleston on March 20, 1898. Clem was educated at the Taft School at Watertown, Connecticut, and graduated from Yale in 1916. Kattie attended Chatham Episcopal Institute (Virginia), where in 1914 she saw her work published in the school's student literary journal. They met while Clem was stationed as an army officer during World War I at Camp Jackson, near Columbia. They were married in 1919. Their son, William Y. "Warren" Ripley, was born in 1921.

In the early 1920s Clem resigned his commission and, with a $30,000 advance on his inheritance, invested in a hundred acres in the sandhills of North Carolina, where for seven years he and Kattie tried their hands at peach farming (the subject of her first book, *Sand in My Shoes,* 1931). In order to augment the farm income, Clem also tried his hand at writing, selling a story for $110 in 1922. By 1927, when they decided to give up the farm, Clem had sold his novel *Dust and Sun* to *Adventure* for $3,000. From 1924 to 1953 his adventure yarns and action tales—as either serialized novels, novelettes, or short stories—appeared in magazines and newspapers across the nation. In addition to *Dust and Sun* (1929), Clem published six other novels: *Devil Drums* (1930), *Black Moon* (1933), *Murder Walks Alone* (1935), *Gold Is Where You Find It* (1936), *Clear for Action* (1940), and *Mississippi Belle* (1942).

In 1932 the *Atlantic Monthly* published three of Kattie's stories. Her second book, *Sand Dollars* (1933), was a memoir written out of the experience of the stock market crash. In 1936 Doubleday Doran published her novel of modern Charleston manners, *Crowded House.* DuBose Heyward, remarking on its universality, wrote: "There is such a family in every community inviting at once our contempt and our sympathy. It is a tribute to Mrs. Ripley's sure characterizations that we think of them with an anger that has become positively a pleasure."

During his Hollywood years, Clem worked as a contract writer, producing scenarios of his own writings or adapting the works of others for the screen. His story "Voodoo Moon," released in 1934 under the title *Black Moon,* starred Jack Holt and Fay Wray. *Gold Is Where You Find It,* a vehicle for George Brent and Olivia de Havilland, was released by Warner Brothers in 1938. *Love, Honor, and Behave,* based on writing by Stephen Vincent Benet, appeared in 1936, and *Buffalo Bill,* an adaptation of a story by Frank Winch, in

1944. Clem also received top billing for the screen adaptation of Owen Davis's play *Jezebel* (1938), for which Bette Davis won an Academy Award.

Clements Ripley died in Charleston on July 22, 1954, and Katharine Ball Ripley died on July 24, 1955. Both are buried in Magnolia Cemetery. In 1990 Warren Ripley published a paperback selection of his parents' short fiction entitled *Cities of Fear and Other Adventure Stories.* Five years later Down Home Press published a paperback edition of Kattie's first nonfiction book, *Sand in My Shoes,* as one in its Carolina Classics series. THOMAS L. JOHNSON

Ripley, Clements, and Katharine Ball Ripley. Papers. South Caroliniana Library, University of South Carolina, Columbia.

River travel. River travel was a necessity in early South Carolina. Usable roads—those wide enough for a wagon—were almost nonexistent in the seventeenth and early part of the eighteenth centuries. Those present were not roads but rather Native American trails that were hard to find and harder to follow. One writer noted that in 1697 the "woods, swamps, rivers, creeks and runs" made overland travel difficult, frequently leaving horses, stock, and travelers up "to the[ir] knees in mud, or the ankles in sand." It was easier, faster, cheaper, and safer to move goods by water. In addition, since the colony often lacked resources to build and maintain roads, settlers from the earliest times sought to obtain land on waterways—the ocean, rivers, streams, or creeks—with either a private or a public landing that gave them access to the water road.

The vessels used in this travel and trade varied. The smallest and most convenient were canoes made from hollowed-out tree trunks. They were easy to maneuver, were shallow draft, and could be managed by one or two paddlers. A few were large enough for sails and major cargo, although none was as big as the periagua, which had a flat bottom, a sail, and room for multiple oars on either side. Shallops, ketches, yawls, pinks, and small sloops resembled the larger periaguas in their ability to carry cargo and in their shallow bottoms. These smaller vessels were propelled by one or more sails and were largely used in the coasting trade and on the lower rivers where wind and draft permitted. In the same category as the periagua, although smaller and poled rather than paddled or rowed, was the scow, flat, or flatboat. In general, however, periaguas and large canoes were the transportation of choice as far north as the fall line. There, rocks and rapids forced travelers and goods to depart from the waterways or to portage them. Towns such as Augusta, Hamburg, Columbia, Camden, and Cheraw frequently grew up along the rivers at these transportation bottlenecks.

Until after World War I, riverboats on the Pee Dee River continued to be an important means of transportation for passengers and cargo between Cheraw and Georgetown. Courtesy, South Carolina Historical Society

Trade and travel saw only limited change until the middle of the nineteenth century. In 1700 John Lawson left Charleston to explore the coast and the Santee River in a ten-man canoe handled by four Indians. By sail and hard rowing his small vessel managed to reach the upper Santee, and from there he crossed into North Carolina on foot. Thirty-three years later an English gentleman shipped from Charleston to Savannah by schooner engaged a canoe manned by four blacks to Purrysburg and then returned by periagua to Charleston.

The addition of a state turnpike from Charleston to Columbia, canals on the upstate rivers, and small steamboats on the lower rivers in the 1820s and 1830s improved transportation networks in South Carolina. But poor construction and high costs diminished the benefits provided by these improvements, forcing many Carolinians to continue to rely on poorly maintained roads and perilous rivers for their transportation needs. The construction of railroads in the nineteenth century and a modern highway system in the twentieth century brought about the demise of most river travel in South Carolina. LOUIS P. TOWLES

Clonts, F. W. "Travel and Transportation in Colonial North Carolina." *North Carolina Historical Review* 3 (January 1926): 16–35.

Meriwether, Robert L. *The Expansion of South Carolina, 1729–1765.* Kingsport, Tenn.: Southern Publishers, 1940.

Merrens, H. Roy, ed. *The Colonial South Carolina Scene, 1697–1774: Contemporary Views.* Columbia: University of South Carolina Press, 1977.

Moore, John Hammond. *The South Carolina Highway Department, 1917–1987.* Columbia: University of South Carolina Press, 1987.

Taylor, George Rogers. *The Transportation Revolution, 1815–1860.* New York: Rinehart, 1951.

Riverbanks Zoo and Garden (Columbia). The South Carolina General Assembly established the Riverbanks Park Special Purpose District in 1969 to "plan, establish, develop . . . and protect public recreation and zoo facilities within . . . Richland and Lexington Counties." The district is governed by the seven-member Riverbanks Park Commission, which is comprised of appointed representatives of the two counties and the city of Columbia.

Riverbanks Zoo opened on April 24, 1974, and was an instant hit with residents of the Midlands. Soon after opening, the new zoo experienced some controversy when visitor-generated income did not support the operating budget. This ended when Richland and Lexington Counties voted to supplement the zoo's budget by levying a dedicated tax. The Riverbanks Society, a private, nonprofit organization, was formed in 1978 so that individuals could demonstrate their support for the zoo. Public bond issues and private fund campaigns resulted in major expansions of the zoo in 1989 and 2002. A similar funding plan was used to build a botanical garden in 1995.

Riverbanks Zoo has repeatedly been recognized as one of America's most successful zoological parks, with nearly one million annual visitors. The zoo and garden maintains 573 animal and 6,536 plant species. Riverbanks has garnered prestigious awards, twice wining the American Zoo and Aquarium Association's highest conservation honor, the Edward H. Bean Award. In response to a major expansion program and its status as South Carolina's largest tourist attraction, Riverbanks received the Governor's Cup as South Carolina's Most Outstanding Attraction and the Southeast Tourism Society's

Shining Example Award as Travel Attraction of the Year in 2002. PALMER KRANTZ

Rivers. South Carolina has an abundance of rivers that originate from within the state or that enter from North Carolina and Georgia and drain land as far away as Virginia. These rivers flow generally from the northwest to the southeast, following the geography from high elevations in the Blue Ridge and Piedmont to the lower elevations of the coastal plain. The Blue Ridge and Piedmont contain narrow drainage divides between river tributaries, some only a few miles wide. The result is a landscape that is almost completely dissected by streams and rivers. Some rivers begin at the base of the Sandhills and cross over the coastal plain to the Atlantic Ocean. Others begin outside of the state and flow into South Carolina, forming three large river systems: the Santee, the Savannah, and the Pee Dee.

The Santee River system is the largest on the east coast. It drains water from North Carolina and carries it through South Carolina through three major rivers (Saluda, Catawba, Broad) and through smaller tributaries (Enoree, Tyger, Reedy). The Broad and the Saluda join at Columbia to form the Congaree River. Geomorphic features of interest on the Congaree floodplain include oxbow lakes and an extensive series of meanders. In the north, the Catawba River enters South Carolina near Rock Hill and is renamed the Wateree as it flows south to form Lake Wateree. Further downstream just above Lake Marion, the Wateree and the Congaree join to form the Santee River, which then flows into the Atlantic Ocean, forming the Santee Delta just south of Georgetown.

During the 1930s and 1940s the Santee River system was dammed in several places to form lakes for flood control, hydroelectric power, and recreation. A major geological and ecological change resulted. The sediment load previously carried by the river water was diverted as the water passed into the lakes. As the river water slowed, the sediments fell and collected on lake bottoms and behind dams, instead of flowing down the river to the coast. After 1942, when the dams and lakes opened, there was a marked decrease in water and sediment flow down the Santee River. This decrease in turn prevented the long-shore ocean currents from moving the sand up and down the coast to nourish the barrier islands, which has resulted in their erosion. Silting of Charleston harbor also became a problem. Since 1985 a rediversion canal has diverted some of the water and sediment back into the Santee River. This has lessened the sedimentation of the harbor.

The Savannah River system forms the western boundary of South Carolina and drains water from portions of North Carolina

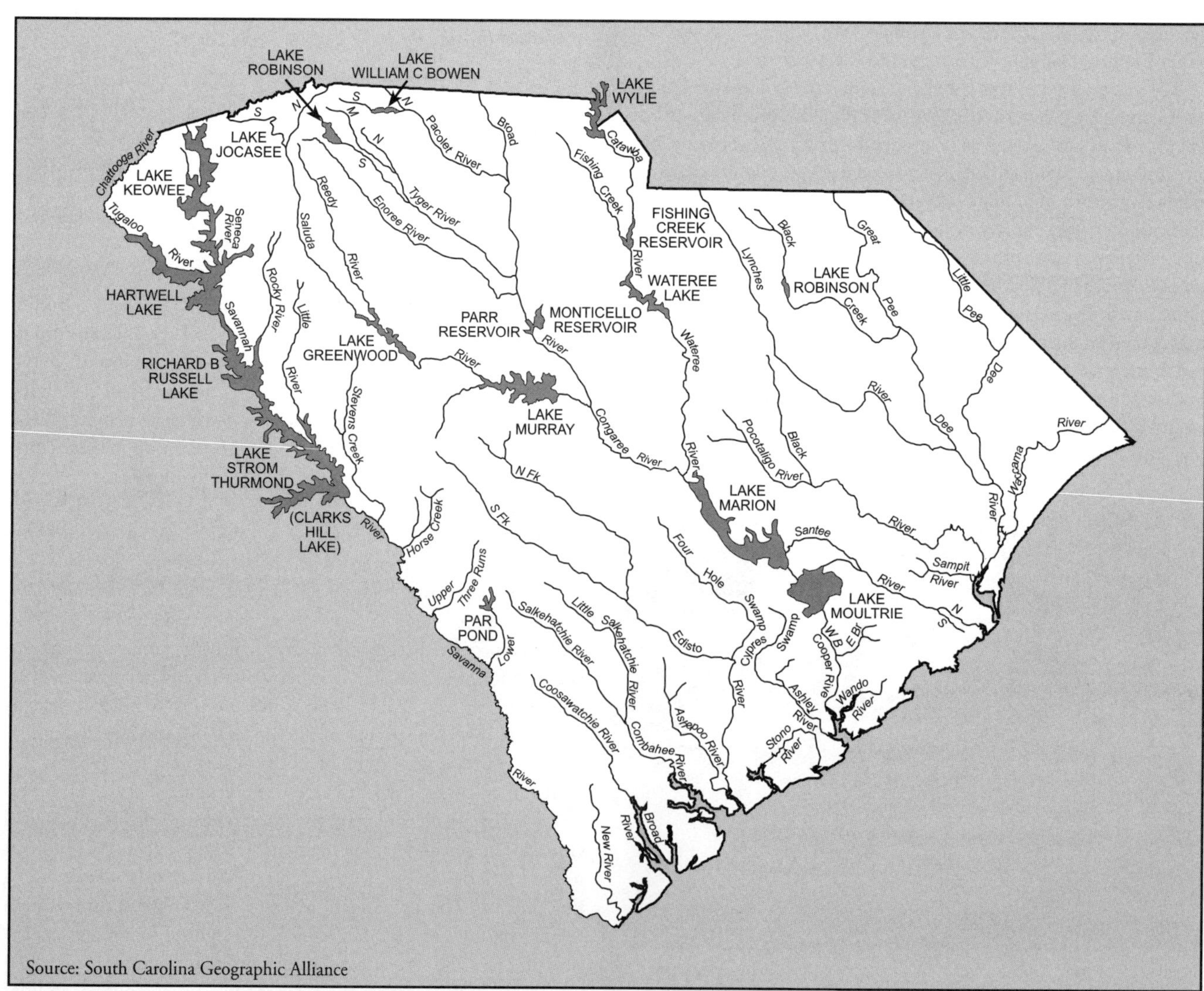

The rivers and lakes of South Carolina

and Georgia as well as South Carolina. Rivers that help to form it are the Chattooga, Tugaloo, and Keowee. The Savannah River empties into the Atlantic Ocean at Savannah, Georgia. Like the Santee, the Savannah River system has been dammed in several places, forming massive man-made lakes. The Savannah is the only river system in South Carolina in which large ships can travel upstream for any distance.

The third river system in South Carolina is the Pee Dee, which is the only system in the state left undammed. Rivers that form the Pee Dee system include the Great Pee Dee, Little Pee Dee, Waccamaw, Black, and Lynches. Two smaller rivers, the Sampit and Pocotaligo, are also part of the Pee Dee system, which enters the Atlantic Ocean at Winyah Bay in Georgetown.

Some of the most beautiful rivers in the state are those that begin on the coastal plain. Because they move slowly over the low relief of the coastal plain to the Atlantic, they do not transport large amounts of sediment. As a result, they are clearer than the rivers that cross the Piedmont. Tannic acid in the organic matter found in these rivers gives them a dark cast, and so they are known as "black rivers." The North and South Forks of the Edisto River begin in the Sandhills in Lexington and Aiken Counties and end at the Atlantic at Edisto Island. The Edisto is the largest of the black rivers in South Carolina and one of the most pristine. Several state parks have been built along its banks to accommodate recreational uses. Other black rivers include the Waccamaw, Black, Pocotaligo, Salkahatchie, Combahee, Coosawhatchie, Ashley, Cooper, and Ashepoo.

Other rivers of importance in South Carolina include those relatively small mountain streams that provide the scenic beauty of rapids and waterfalls. South Carolina has a favorable climate with sufficient rainfall and a high relief, which has endowed it with natural waterfalls in the upstate. There are more than fifty waterfalls in the state, primarily in the Blue Ridge and upper Piedmont in Oconee, Greenville, and Pickens Counties. The spectacular Whitewater Falls in Oconee County has the highest series of falls in eastern North America. Many of the falls have been protected through the establishment of state and county parks. CAROLYN H. MURPHY

Kovacik, Charles F., and John J. Winberry. *South Carolina: The Making of a Landscape.* 1987. Reprint, Columbia: University of South Carolina Press, 1989.

Murphy, Carolyn H. *Carolina Rocks! The Geology of South Carolina.* Orangeburg, S.C.: Sandlapper, 1995.

Rivers, John Minott (1903–1988). Broadcasting executive. Born in Charleston on July 22, 1903, Rivers was the son of Moultrie Rutledge Rivers and Eliza Ingraham Buist. He graduated from the public and private schools of Charleston and attended the College of Charleston for two years. In 1924 he received an economics degree from the Wharton School of the University of Pennsylvania. On December 7, 1929, Rivers married Martha Robinson of Gastonia, North Carolina. They had three children.

After graduation Rivers was employed as a runner by the Bank of Charleston (later South Carolina National Bank [SCNB]). Later he became manager of SCNB's Greenville branch and then assistant vice president of SCNB. In 1936 he became vice president of the Charleston office of McAlister, Smith & Pate, a securities firm based in Greenville. Rivers entered the broadcasting business two years later at the urging of W. Frank Hipp, president of Liberty Life Insurance Company, which operated radio stations in Columbia and Charleston. On January 1, 1938, Rivers became president of South Carolina Broadcasting Company, which operated WCSC radio at Charleston. In 1939 he was named president and manager. When Hipp died, his successors—two sons and their uncle—honored Hipp's unsigned memorandum allowing Rivers to buy the station if he made it successful. Rivers purchased the property for $144,000.

In 1948 Rivers began operation of an FM radio station. In June 1953 he put WCSC-TV, South Carolina's first VHF television station, on the air. He served as president and manager of the AM/FM radio stations and the TV property. Rivers's company, WCSC, Inc., eventually became involved in background music, long distance and cellular telephones, security systems, and other enterprises. In 1972 Rivers became chairman of the board of WCSC and turned over his other titles and the responsibilities of running the stations to his son, John M. Rivers, Jr.

The elder Rivers served as president of the South Carolina Association of Broadcasters, which he helped found in 1952. In 1974 he became the second person to be inducted into the Broadcasters Hall of Fame. Rivers was inducted into the South Carolina Business Hall of Fame in 1997. One of Rivers's daughters, Martha R. Ingram, was also in the South Carolina and National Business Halls of Fame.

At thirty-three, Rivers was the youngest person ever to be elected president of the Charleston Chamber of Commerce. He served as chairman of the South Carolina Chamber of Commerce in 1969 and was named Businessman of the Year for 1966. Rivers was on the South Carolina Educational Television Commission from 1966 to 1982. In 1989 the College of Charleston's John M. Rivers Communications Museum was established through an endowment from the Rivers family. Rivers was active in the community through the St. Andrews Society, St. Philip's Church, and Ashley Hall School. He died on January 24, 1988, in Charleston. ROBERT A. PIERCE

Lunan, Bert, and Robert A. Pierce. *Legacy of Leadership.* Columbia: South Carolina Business Hall of Fame, 1999.

Rivers, Lucius Mendel (1905–1970). Congressman. Mendel Rivers was born on September 28, 1905, in the rural Berkeley County community of Gumville. He was the fifth child and second son of Lucius Hampton Rivers, a turpentine still operator, and Henrietta McCay. The family moved to North Charleston in 1916 following the death of Lucius Rivers and the subsequent loss of the family farm. Rivers attended the College of Charleston from 1926 to 1929. After his third year, he was admitted to the University of South Carolina School of Law. At the end of his second year he was last in his class and not invited back. Despite his lack of a degree, he passed the bar exam in 1932 by reading the law.

Rivers first ran for the state House of Representatives in 1932 but lost in the Democratic primary runoff. In 1933 he was elected in a

L. Mendel Rivers. Courtesy, South Carolina Historical Society

special election to the state House. In 1934 he became chair of the Charleston County House Delegation because he received more votes than any other candidate. In 1936 he left the political arena and went to work for the United States Department of Justice in its taxes and penalties division. Rivers married Margaret Middleton 1938. They had one son and two daughters.

Rivers returned to politics following the death of First District congressman Tom McMillan in 1939. In August 1940 he won the Democratic primary, successfully defeating the Charleston "Ring" headed by Burnet Maybank. He was subsequently reelected to Congress fifteen times with only minor opposition.

As a freshman congressman, Rivers was appointed to the Public Buildings and Grounds Committee and the Merchant Marines and Fisheries Committee. In March 1941, however, he was appointed to the Naval Affairs Committee headed by Carl Vinson of Georgia. There, Mendel Rivers developed a career as a staunch supporter of the military and national defense. Following Vinson's retirement in 1965, Rivers became chair of the House Armed Services Committee, a position he held until his death.

Rivers was a conservative Democrat who was often at odds with his party. He frequently criticized American foreign policy, foreign aid, and the United Nations. He was a strong supporter of increased military spending and the establishment of a nuclear navy. During his years in Congress, the First Congressional District was a major benefactor of military spending. Major installations in the district included the Charleston Naval Base and Shipyard, the Charleston Air Force Base, the Navy Minecraft Base, the Ordnance Depot, the Marine Corps facilities at Beaufort and Parris Island, and a Veterans Administration Hospital. Vinson once told Rivers that if he put another thing down in his district it was going to sink.

While Rivers was seen as an advocate of the little man, he was also a segregationist. He supported the States' Rights Democratic Party in 1948 and called the 1954 *Brown v. Board of Education* decision unconstitutional, immoral, illegal, and outrageous. He asserted that the National Association for the Advancement of Colored People was under Communist influence or infiltration, and he opposed the major civil rights bills of the 1960s.

Rivers died following surgery in Birmingham, Alabama, on December 28, 1970. The man servicemen often called their champion was buried in the St. Stephens Episcopal Churchyard in Berkeley County. WILLIAM V. MOORE

Huntley, Will F. "Mighty Rivers of Charleston." Ph.D. diss., University of South Carolina, 1993.

Rivers, Prince (ca. 1824–1887). Soldier, statesman. Born a slave in the coastal town of Beaufort, Prince Rivers had training as an artisan and was frequently hired out by his owners as a coachman. Rivers's precocious nature soon became apparent. He learned to read and write despite the legal and customary barriers to slave literacy. Following the Union occupation of Beaufort in November 1861, Rivers's white owners, the Stuart family, fled to the upcountry district of Edgefield. Making use of the dislocations of war, Rivers escaped Edgefield for the safety of Union lines on the coast. There he joined the First South Carolina Volunteers, one of the first African American Union regiments, reorganized later in the war as the Thirty-third U.S. Colored Troops.

By late 1862 Rivers served as a sergeant in the First South Carolina, holding the position of provost of the guard. Rivers's obvious leadership skills soon received notice. His commanding officer, Thomas Wentworth Higginson, later wrote, "If there should ever be a black monarchy in South Carolina, he will be its King." A clearly impressed General David Hunter, commander of Union forces along the southern coast of South Carolina and one of the early proponents of black enlistment, took Rivers along on a recruiting trip to New York City in 1862. Working-class New York whites, filled with a combination of antiwar and racist sentiment, hurled stones and racial epithets at Rivers. The indomitable Rivers refused to back down and physically held off his attackers until military police arrived to provide him safe escort.

Following the war, Rivers resided in Edgefield and the new county of Aiken. He was a representative at the 1868 constitutional convention and then represented Edgefield County in the state House of Representatives from 1868 to 1872. After Aiken County had been created in 1871, Rivers served as its representative in the House until 1874.

After completing his tenure in the General Assembly, Rivers served as a trial justice in Aiken County. In this capacity he became embroiled in an incident in the town of Hamburg that would lead to the infamous Hamburg Massacre. Rivers attempted to mediate the situation, both trying to quell white intransigence and encouraging the black militiamen to turn over their weapons in order to prevent a bloodbath. The white Red Shirts clearly wanted battle, evidenced in part by their bringing of cannons from nearby Augusta, Georgia. Seven African Americans died in the Hamburg Massacre, and the Red Shirts ransacked and destroyed the homes of black leaders, including that of trial justice Rivers.

The end of Reconstruction in 1876, hard on the heels of the destruction of his property, forced Rivers to find work as a house painter and, as in antebellum times, a carriage driver. Rivers lost much of his savings in the 1880s during an extended illness. He died in Aiken in 1887. W. SCOTT POOLE

Higginson, Thomas Wentworth. *Army Life in a Black Regiment.* 1870. Reprint, New York: Norton, 1984.

Holt, Thomas. *Black over White: Negro Political Leadership in South Carolina during Reconstruction.* Urbana: University of Illinois Press, 1979.

Rivers Bridge, Battle of (February 2–3, 1865). Rivers Bridge, in southern Bamberg County, is the site of a Civil War battle fought on February 2 and 3, 1865. The battle pitted about twelve hundred Confederates against some seven thousand Union soldiers and marked the only major resistance to the march of General William T. Sherman through South Carolina.

Sherman led his army of sixty thousand veterans into the state late in January 1865. On February 2 soldiers of the right wing of Sherman's army—the First Division, Seventeenth Army Corps, commanded by Major General Joseph A. Mower—attempted to seize one of several strategic crossings of the Salkehatchie River. Failing to take the crossing at Broxton's Bridge, Mower's troops advanced upstream to Rivers Bridge, which was defended by a Confederate brigade under Colonel George P. Harrison. Harrison's strongly entrenched force repulsed a direct Union assault down the narrow causeway that spanned the thick Salkehatchie swamp. On February 3 Union soldiers crossed the swamp upstream of Rivers Bridge, leading Mower to launch a major assault on the Confederate right. Another Union division crossed the river downstream at the same time, flanking the thin Confederate line and forcing Harrison to retreat. The battle cost each side about one hundred casualties, gave Union forces possession of the countryside north of the Salkehatchie, and led to the cutting of the South Carolina Railroad.

In 1876 men from nearby communities reburied the Confederate dead from Rivers Bridge in a mass grave about a mile from the battlefield and began a tradition of annually commemorating the battle. The Rivers Bridge Memorial Association eventually obtained the battlefield and in 1945 turned the site over to South Carolina for a state park. Rivers Bridge State Historic Site preserves the battlefield and its earthen fortifications and interprets the Civil War and its changing commemoration. DANIEL BELL

Power, J. Tracy, and Daniel J. Bell. *Rivers Bridge State Park Visitors Guide.* Columbia: South Carolina Department of Parks, Recreation, and Tourism, Division of State Parks, 1992.

Roads and highways. Until the War of 1812, South Carolina's roads were secondary to water transportation. The British blockade during the war, however, increased interest in overland travel. During the internal improvement campaign in the 1820s, the General Assembly commissioned the State Road to connect Charleston with western North Carolina.

In 1825 the General Assembly enacted the first traffic regulations but left road maintenance and construction to local road commissioners. Local residents, or their slaves, were required to labor a set number of days each year on road construction or repair. Conflicting state and local interests were, and remain, a constant in highway maintenance and construction. In 1883 U.S. Senator Matthew C. Butler urged a tax in lieu of roadwork and the use of prison labor. His ideas were later adopted. Legislation in 1894 created county supervisors with general oversight for the roads and other administrative matters. The period from 1891 to 1911 was the era of the "good roads" movement in South Carolina as citizens lobbied for better roads.

State interest coincided with federal interest in improved road construction. By 1910 federal supervision and local manpower had completed seventeen South Carolina road projects. U.S. Senator Asbury C. Latimer and Congressman James F. Byrnes pushed for a nationally funded program of coordinated road construction. In 1909 state agriculture commissioner E. J. Watson urged the creation of a South Carolina public highway department.

These efforts produced the Federal Aid Road Act in 1916. To access federal highway dollars, the General Assembly created the State Highway Commission the following year. Within seventy years this small commission became one of South Carolina's largest state agencies. The commission levied the first license fee and created a two-division department—the Engineering Division and the Division of Automobile Licensing and Registration.

This 1956 photograph shows work on the Horse Range Creek Bridge on U.S. 176 in Orangeburg/Calhoun Counties. Courtesy, South Carolina Department of Archives and History

World War I limited road construction, but following the war the highway department obtained surplus property for its first motorized equipment. In 1922 federal highways and the first gasoline tax arrived. Governor Thomas G. McLeod signed the Pay-As-You-Go Highway Act in 1924.

In 1925 the commission named Samuel P. McGowan as its first chief highway commissioner. His successor, Ben Sawyer, lobbied for the General Reimbursement Act of 1926, which authorized counties to issue bonds for highway construction. In 1929 Governor John G. Richards signed the State Highway Bond Act, which enabled the highway department to fund construction of a statewide highway system by issuing bonds, allowing the agency to abandon its pay-as-you-go formula.

Under Sawyer's leadership the commission created the State Highway Patrol in 1930 and developed a system of driver licensing. Sawyer defended the commission from Governor Olin D. Johnston's efforts to replace him (and the other commissioners) and successfully fended off Governor Burnet Maybank's efforts to divert highway funds for other purposes. In 1940 the South Carolina Supreme Court issued a "permanent injunction" barring the use of highway funds for nonhighway-related expenses.

World War II brought national security concerns to highway design. In 1944 legislation created the National System of Interstate and Defense Highways, a joint federal and state project. The postwar period brought heightened highway construction, the classification of primary and secondary roads, and in 1956 the Interstate Highway System.

In 1964 Interstate 85 became the first interstate highway completed in South Carolina. In 1965 Governor Robert McNair signed landmark legislation requiring photographs on drivers' licenses, vision checks, and state aid for driver's training. Speed limits came in 1966, welcome centers in 1968, and Breathalyzer tests for suspected drunken drivers in 1969.

In 1980 the department was renamed the Department of Highways and Public Transportation. The commission facilitated local planning but lacked a firm commitment to public transportation. Funding for the department, despite allocated resources, was a perennial challenge. In 1981 efforts for another gasoline tax increase triggered conflicts about the independence of highway funding, the construction of new roads in lieu of maintaining existing ones, and the need to match federal appropriations. Governor Richard Riley complained that funds were not being used as intended to resurface secondary roads and that the highway department continued "to construct new roads when it is clear that revenues are not sufficient to maintain our present system." Also in 1981 the Legislative Audit Council released a report that criticized personnel practices and highway maintenance.

Despite the challenges, the Department of Transportation, as it became in 1993, maintained one of the largest state highway systems in the nation. Interstates 26, 20, 77, and 95 joined Interstate 85. The department continued to revisit the tensions between construction and maintenance as it sought to develop a transportation system for the twenty-first century. ALEXIA JONES HELSLEY

Moore, John Hammond. *The South Carolina Highway Department, 1917–1987.* Columbia: University of South Carolina Press, 1987.

Robert, Henry Martyn (1837–1923). Engineer, author. Born May 2, 1837, on his grandfather's plantation near Robertville in Jasper County, Henry Martyn Robert was the second son of the Reverend Joseph Thomas Robert, an educator and Baptist minister, and Adeline Elizabeth Lawton. Members of the Robert family were slave owners; however, a cousin, William Henry Brisbane, opposed slavery, freed his slaves, and moved north where he became an outspoken abolitionist. Robert's father apparently shared his cousin's views, and in 1851 he relocated his family to Ohio, where he also spoke out against slavery.

In 1853 Robert was appointed to the U.S. Military Academy at West Point, New York. He graduated fourth in his class in 1857 and was commissioned as a second lieutenant assigned to the Corps of Engineers. After a year of teaching at the academy, he was sent into the field in the fall of 1858 to build fortifications in the Washington Territory and explore westward routes for wagon roads. From 1867 until his retirement in 1901, he crossed the country, working as an engineer on federal construction and improvement projects involving river systems in Oregon and Washington; fortifications in Puget Sound; ports and lighthouses on the Great Lakes and the St. Lawrence River; harbors in the Philadelphia area, Delaware Bay, and Long Island Sound; a deep-sea port at Galveston Island, Texas; and dams and locks on the Tennessee and Cumberland rivers. After the 1900 Galveston hurricane, Robert helped design a concrete seawall to protect against future tidal waves. Prior to his retirement on May 2, 1901, he was promoted to brigadier general, chief of engineers, U.S. Army.

Robert is best remembered, however, not as an engineer, but as an author. During the Civil War, Robert worked on fortification projects to strengthen defenses in several northern cities. While assigned to duty in New Bedford, Massachusetts, he was asked to preside at a local public meeting. Embarrassed by knowing nothing about how to run a meeting, Robert used this experience to begin collecting bits of information about parliamentary procedure that he scribbled on note cards and carried around with him for several years. Finally, in 1876, he put his notes together into a self-published manuscript titled *Pocket Manual of Rules of Order for Deliberative Assemblies,* better known by its short title, *Robert's Rules of Order.* The work was immediately popular. Of the four thousand copies printed at his expense, Robert freely distributed one thousand to legislators and civic leaders across the country. The remainder sold in four months. In the years that followed, Robert updated and revised the manual several times. More than a half million copies had been sold by 1915. *Robert's Rules of Order* has never been out of print and remains the definitive voice of parliamentary procedure in meeting rooms worldwide.

Robert married twice, first to Helen M. Thresher on December 24, 1860, and, following her death in 1895, to Isabel Livingstone Hoagland on May 8, 1901. Only the first marriage produced children, four daughters and one son. Robert died on May 11, 1923, in Hornell, New York. He is buried in Arlington National Cemetery. ELLEN CHAMBERLAIN

Doyle, Don H. "Rules of Order: Henry Martyn Robert and the Popularization of American Parliamentary Law." *American Quarterly* 32 (Spring 1980): 3–18.

Hendricks, George Brian. "Rules of Order: A Biography of Henry Martyn Robert, Soldier, Engineer, Churchman, Parliamentarian." Master's thesis, Georgia Southern University, 1998.

Lawton, Thomas O., Jr. "Our People: Henry Martyn Robert; Robert's Rules of Order." *Carologue* 16 (Winter 2000): 3.

Robert Mills House (Columbia). A National Historic Landmark, Columbia's Robert Mills House is most noted for its association with the first American-trained architect and the first federal architect of the United States. Of further significance is the building's role as a regionally important religious institution and as an example of the grassroots historic preservation movement of the 1960s.

The Robert Mills House in Columbia after restoration by the Historic Columbia Foundation in the 1960s. Courtesy, South Caroliniana Library, University of South Carolina

Originally intended as a private home for the Columbia merchant Ainsley Hall, the three-story mansion ultimately would serve solely in a public capacity. Equally ironic is that the building's namesake, the Charlestonian Robert Mills, was an architect best known for public works, such as courthouses and jails, throughout South Carolina, rather than private structures. Architecturally, the Robert Mills House exemplifies early nineteenth-century classical revival design and reflects Mills's association with Thomas Jefferson, James Hoban, Charles Bulfinch, and Benjamin Latrobe. During the building's construction in 1823, however, Ainsley Hall died prematurely, leaving behind an ill-managed estate, which spawned years of legal suits that eventually resulted in the property's liquidation in 1829. Purchased by the Presbyterian Synod, the building and its four-acre tract became the Columbia Theological Seminary, an institution that prepared religious leaders from 1830 until 1927.

Following a seven-year campaign for its restoration, the Robert Mills House opened to the public in 1967 as a historic house museum showcasing the neoclassical architecture and decorative arts of the early nineteenth century. Since 1967 the house has been chiefly operated by the Historic Columbia Foundation. JOHN M. SHERRER III

Doescher, Kirsten L. "A Home for a Seminary: The Columbia Theological Seminary and the Hall's House." Master's thesis, University of South Carolina, 2001.

Lipscomb, Terry W. "The Legacy of Ainsley Hall." *South Carolina Historical Magazine* 99 (April 1998): 158–79.

Marsh, Blanche. *Robert Mills: Architect in South Carolina.* Columbia, S.C.: R. L. Bryan, 1970.

Robertson, Benjamin Franklin, Jr. (1903–1943). Journalist. Ben Robertson was born on June 22, 1903, in Clemson. His father, a member of the first graduating class of Clemson College, was a chemist for the Agricultural Extension Service. His mother, Mary Bowen, died when he was ten years old, and his stepmother, Hattie Boggs, died in the 1918 influenza pandemic. Robertson was a respected and well-traveled journalist and war correspondent and the author of three books, including a memoir of his youth in the South Carolina upcountry.

After graduating in 1923 from Clemson, where he edited the student newspaper, Robertson attended the School of Journalism at the University of Missouri and, after a year with the Charleston *News and Courier,* took his second bachelor's degree in 1926. That same year he landed a job with the *Honolulu Star-Bulletin,* leaving soon afterward to write for the *News* in Adelaide, Australia. After a few months with the U.S. Consulate in Java, he returned home to South Carolina by way of India and Europe.

In 1929 Robertson became a reporter for the *New York Herald-Tribune.* He moved to Washington, D.C., in 1934 to cover the New Deal for the Associated Press but resigned after two years. He then returned to Pickens County to write a novel. *Travelers' Rest,* published privately in 1938, was neither a critical nor a popular success, and Robertson went back to journalism, covering South Carolina politics for the *Anderson Independent.* In 1940 he was hired by *PM,* an innovative left-liberal newspaper published by the former *Fortune* editor Ralph Ingersoll, as its London correspondent during the battle of Britain. During a two-month furlough in early 1941, he wrote *I Saw England,* a well-received account of British resolve in the face of constant bombardment by the German Luftwaffe that reached a wide audience after being condensed by *Reader's Digest.*

Ben Robertson. Courtesy, Special Collections, Clemson University Libraries

After another stint in London, Robertson returned to Clemson in August 1941 and began work on *Red Hills and Cotton: An Upcountry Memory,* which he finished in January 1942. A celebration of Scots-Irish folkways and the agrarian lifestyle, *Red Hills and Cotton* evokes a simpler time in rural South Carolina through a nostalgic portrayal of several generations of Robertson kin. While proudly asserting his heritage—"Honor is at the base of our personal attitude toward life"—he also looks to the future: "The South is our South and it must progress." An outspoken, if idiosyncratic, liberal during the 1930s, Robertson, who once said, "What we need is a man with the heart and mind of Jefferson and the tactics of Huey Long," may have softened his politics in *Red Hills and Cotton* in anticipation of a run for public office.

Over the course of 1942 Robertson covered World War II from Libya, the Soviet Union, and India for *PM.* In January 1943 he was hired again by the *New York Herald-Tribune,* this time to run its London Bureau. He never made it back to England. On February 22, 1943, the flying boat *Yankee Clipper* crashed into the Tagus River on its approach to Lisbon, Portugal, killing Robertson at the age of thirty-nine. His remains were returned to South Carolina and buried in the family burial plot near Liberty in Pickens County. The Liberty Ship SS *Ben Robertson* was launched in Savannah, Georgia, in January 1944 and supported the invasion of Normandy later that year. HUGH DAVIS

Ford, Lacy K., Jr. "The Affable Journalist as Social Critic: Ben Robertson and the Early Twentieth-Century South." *Southern Cultures* 2 (winter 1996): 353–73.

Robertson, Ben. *Red Hills and Cotton: An Upcountry Memory.* 1942. Reprint, Columbia: University of South Carolina Press, 1991.

Robertson, Thomas James (1823–1897). U.S. senator. Robertson was born near Winnsboro on August 3, 1823, son of the War of 1812 veteran John Robertson. He was graduated from South Carolina College in 1843. Three years later he married Mary C. Caldwell, whose father later became president of the South Carolina Railroad. A prominent planter, Robertson was appointed aide-de-camp to Governor R. F. W. Allston in 1858. During the Civil War, however, Robertson sided with the Union and was said to have entertained General William T. Sherman in his Columbia home.

After the war, Robertson joined the Republicans. As one of the leading native South Carolinians in the party, he won election as a delegate from Richland County to the 1868 constitutional convention. In that body, of which he was the wealthiest member, Robertson advocated two principles: that former Confederates should be punished; and that conservative financial measures should be adopted in order to win the confidence of northern financiers. Thus, he opposed a "stay law" to prevent the collection of debts, arguing that the "largest debtors in this State are those who staked their all on secession."

In return for his loyalty to the Union and the Republican Party, Robertson was bitterly condemned by most white Carolinians. In particular, the *Charleston Mercury* denounced him as a harsh taskmaster whose embrace of racial equality was motivated by self-interest. In Republican circles, however, he was considered one of the best men the party had to offer, both because of his private wealth and because of his political moderation. As a result, the state legislature elected him to the U.S. Senate in 1868. He was reelected in 1870 and served until 1877.

In the Senate, Robertson served as chairman of the Committee on Manufactures. On the issues surrounding Reconstruction, his stance softened somewhat during his time in office. Soon after arriving he proposed a bill designed to punish former Confederates by continuing to deny them most of their political rights. In 1871, however, he opposed the Ku Klux Klan Act, which attempted to punish Democratic violence, as well as an attempt by Massachusetts senator Charles Sumner to link amnesty for former Confederates with a civil rights bill. In the summer of 1874 he assailed the corruption of South Carolina Republicans and predicted that if better men were not elected, "the President will refuse to recognize the Government by withholding the aid it will require in the enforcement and collection of taxes, in which case it is bound to fall through." By 1877, with his commitment to Reconstruction eroded, he advised President Ulysses S. Grant to allow the election of the Democrat Wade Hampton III as governor, which effectively ended Reconstruction.

During his time in the Senate, Robertson seems to have been plagued by poor health. When his term ended in 1877, he retired from public life and private business for health reasons. For the next twenty years he was almost entirely paralyzed and in constant discomfort, but he died peacefully in Columbia on October 13, 1897. He was buried in Elmwood Cemetery. HYMAN S. RUBIN III

Reynolds, John S. *Reconstruction in South Carolina, 1865–1877.* 1905. Reprint, New York: Negro Universities Press, 1969.

Robertson, Thomas James. Papers. South Caroliniana Library, University of South Carolina, Columbia.

Seip, Terry L. *The South Returns to Congress: Men, Economic Measures, and Intersectional Relationships, 1868–1879.* Baton Rouge: Louisiana State University Press, 1983.

Robinson, Bernice Violanthe (1914–1994). Educator, civil rights activist. Robinson was born in Charleston on February 7, 1914. Her father was a bricklayer, plasterer, and tile setter, which made the family financially independent. As such, Robinson's parents discouraged their nine children from seeking jobs as domestic workers in white Charleston homes. Robinson grew to realize the value of education, a lesson that served her well. She married in the 1930s and had a daughter, Jacquelyn, but her husband left to find work and never returned. During the 1940s Robinson left Charleston for New York City with intentions of becoming a musician. Instead she worked in garment factories, as a beautician, and eventually as a civil servant. In New York she enjoyed the privilege of living in a non-segregated community.

Returning to Charleston in 1947 to help care for her parents, Robinson joined the National Association for the Advancement of Colored People (NAACP) and became involved with voter-registration drives. Self-employed as a beautician, Robinson could undertake civil rights work without fear of economic reprisal from the white community. In 1954 Septima Clark convinced Robinson to attend a workshop at the Highlander Folk School in Monteagle, Tennessee, where she met activists such as Rosa Parks and Esau Jenkins. Persuaded by Jenkins, who was dedicated to the social and political advancement of the black population of the South Carolina Sea Islands, Robinson returned from the Highlander workshop with a commitment to educating African Americans in her community.

In January 1957, with financial support from the Field Foundation and the Highlander School, Jenkins opened the first of what became known as the Citizenship Schools on Johns Island and asked Robinson to become its first teacher. Basing her curriculum on the practical needs of the people, she achieved great success with her first class. At the end of the five-month school period all fourteen pupils could read and write their own names and do arithmetic. More importantly, they had received voter-registration cards. The success of the Johns Island school led to the opening of additional schools on Wadmalaw and Edisto Islands. Robinson recruited teachers for these schools to be trained at Highlander.

In 1961 Robinson was chosen by Highlander and the Southern Christian Leadership Conference (SCLC) to set up voter-registration workshops across the racially charged South. These workshops helped transform the political and economic status of thousands of disenfranchised blacks. Robinson left the SCLC in 1970 and was hired by the South Carolina Commission of Farm Workers (SCCFW), for which she supervised Volunteers in Service to America (VISTA) volunteers in Charleston. In 1972 she ran for the state House of Representatives, the first African American woman to do so, but was defeated. Afterward Robinson returned to the SCCFW, where she worked with migrant workers until 1977. She died on September 3, 1994. PATRICIA H. SIMPSON

Fairclough, Adam. *Better Day Coming: Blacks and Equality, 1890–2000.* New York: Viking, 2001.

Wigginton, Eliot, ed. *Refuse to Stand Silently By: An Oral History of Grass Roots Social Activism in America, 1921–1964.* New York: Doubleday, 1992.

Rock Hill (York County; 2000 pop. 41,643). Rock Hill began in 1852 as a depot and watering station on the Charlotte and South Carolina Railroad. The name came from a notation on a construction supervisor's map marking a spot where the road encountered a small, flinty knoll. The railroad had planned to run its line through nearby Ebenezer, the second-largest settlement in York District. However, Ebenezer citizens objected to the smoke and noise a train would produce and forced the railroad to be built elsewhere. A plantation owner, Alexander Templeton Black, allowed the railroad to pass through his property and consequently became known as the founding father of Rock Hill. The original town plan encompassed twenty-three lots laid out along a single street labeled "Main." The establishment of a post office on April 17, 1852, became the unofficial birth date of Rock Hill. In 1869 a group of citizens petitioned the legislature to incorporate the town, stating that Rock Hill contained "over three hundred inhabitants, two churches, eleven stores, two bar rooms, two hotels, one male and one female school." Opponents protested, arguing that Rock Hill was only a railroad town with half of its population "of a transient and floating character." The debate postponed the incorporation of Rock Hill by the General Assembly until February 26, 1870.

Through the efforts of the local entrepreneur James Morrow Ivy in the 1870s, Rock Hill developed into a booming cotton market. In 1872 Ivy founded a newspaper, the *Lantern,* which became the *Herald* two years later. He was also active in the drive that established the first steam-powered textile mill in the upcountry, the Rock Hill Cotton Factory, in 1880. Rock Hill had four cotton mills by 1890 and added two more in 1896, the Arcade Mills and Manchester Mills. The corporate limits of Rock Hill were extended in 1890, and it was rechartered as a city on December 24, 1892. The 1890s also saw the city make a successful bid to become the new home of the Winthrop Normal and Industrial College, which opened in Rock Hill in 1895. Two black junior colleges were established in the same period: Friendship in 1891 and Clinton College in 1894. In 1915 Rock Hill became the second town in South Carolina to adopt the city-manager form of government.

In the early twentieth century Rock Hill expanded its industrial base beyond the cotton textile industry. In 1916 the carriage maker John Gary Anderson organized the Anderson Motor Company, which produced as many as thirty-five automobiles per day before its failure in 1924. In 1929 the Lowenstein Corporation of New York converted the automobile plant into its Rock Hill Printing and Finishing Company (known locally as the Bleachery). Other major industries to locate in Rock Hill were the fiber maker Celanese Corporation of America in 1948 and the paper manufacturer Bowaters Carolina Corporation in 1959. The presence of these three giants—a bleachery, a major acetate yarn plant, and one of the world's largest paper mills—helped Rock Hill weather the departure of several textile plants in the early 1970s.

During the 1970s, in an effort to revitalize the city center, officials roofed over a block of the downtown and converted it into a mall. But most local shoppers continued to shun downtown in favor of a new shopping complex on Cherry Road (U.S. Highway 21), the city's main connector with Charlotte, North Carolina. The expanding metropolis just across the state line also attracted a growing number of Rock Hill shoppers and commuters, an attraction accelerated by the completion of Interstate 77 in 1982.

In 1986 Betty Jo Rhea, a former councilwoman, became Rock Hill's first woman mayor. Her twelve-year tenure initiated numerous changes that beautified Rock Hill. The roof was removed from downtown, and major revitalization projects began. The Downtown Rock Hill Association was formed in 1993. A gateway to the city was incorporated into Dave Lyle Boulevard (named for a former mayor), and city boundaries were enlarged through annexation. During the 1990s Rock Hill experienced an influx of new business and industry, including the chemical producer Atotech in 1996 and

Tyco Electronics in 1997. The Rock Hill Industrial Park, established in 1963, continued to thrive and eventually contained twenty businesses employing some fourteen hundred people. The city's remarkable success in attracting foreign investment and promoting economic growth prompted former governor Carroll Campbell to proclaim, "Every city in this state should look to Rock Hill to see the formula for success in action." MATTHEW A. LOCKHART

Brown, Douglas Summers. *A City without Cobwebs: A History of Rock Hill, South Carolina.* Columbia: University of South Carolina Press, 1953.

Hildebrand, Jack D. *Rock Hill: Reflections.* Chatsworth, Calif.: Windsor, 1989.

Lee, J. Edward, and Anne E. Beard, eds. *Rock Hill, South Carolina: Gateway to the New South.* Charleston, S.C.: Arcadia, 1999.

Shankman, Arnold, et al. *York County, South Carolina: Its People and Its Heritage.* Norfolk, Va.: Donning, 1983.

We the People . . . E Pluribus Unum: A Study in the Processes of Local Government. Rock Hill, S.C.: Rock Hill School District No. 3, 1971.

Rock Hill movement. Following the 1955 bus boycott in Montgomery, Alabama, and the 1960 Woolworth lunch-counter sit-ins by North Carolina A&T students in Greensboro, African Americans in Rock Hill took the lead in energizing the civil rights movement in South Carolina. Led by the politically charged student body of Friendship Junior College, the Rock Hill movement signaled a major change in protest tactics by black Carolinians, supplementing traditional legal challenges with direct, large-scale demonstrations against segregation laws and customs.

From July to December 1957 black Rock Hill residents protested the segregated seating policies of the Star Transit Authority bus lines. Local members of the National Association for the Advancement of Colored People (NAACP), led by the Reverend Cecil Ivory, and the Council of Human Relations (a chapter of the integrated Southern Regional Council) led the nonviolent protests. The boycott forced Star Transit out of business, leading local African Americans to establish an alternative service consisting of two buses purchased with community donations, which remained in operation until 1961. No city-sponsored bus services were available to the black community until 1965, but the new services were integrated. The experience during the bus boycott created a foundation for the stepped-up confrontations of the 1960s.

Just days after the "A&T Four" sought service at a North Carolina lunch counter on February 1, 1960, almost all of the 224 students at Rock Hill's Friendship Junior College organized into the Friendly Student Civic Committee, choosing Martin Johnson, Abe Plummer, and John Moore as leaders. The first South Carolina sit-ins were held on February 12 (Abraham Lincoln's birthday) at the Woolworth and McCrory variety stores as well as at Good's and Philip's drugstores. Approximately one hundred student demonstrators sought service at the stores' lunch counters. Additional sit-ins and demonstrations continued intermittently for a year.

Inspired in part by a workshop held in December 1960 by the Congress of Racial Equality (CORE) field secretary Thomas Gaither, who touted the effectiveness of jail-ins as opposed to paying fines or accepting bail, the sit-ins and protests intensified in Rock Hill. On January 31, 1961, Gaither and nine Friendship students sat at the McCrory's lunch counter and were immediately arrested. Rather than paying $100 fines, Gaither and eight of the students chose to serve thirty days' hard labor in the county jail. Their action was the first "jail, no bail" declaration of the civil rights movement and brought the Rock Hill demonstrators national attention. Hundreds of relatives, friends, and sympathizers visited the students in jail. Their actions inspired four Atlanta students affiliated with the Student Non-Violent Coordinating Committee (SNCC) to travel to Rock Hill, where they likewise sat in at McCrory's, were arrested, and chose to serve their time in jail. The "jail, no bail" tactic switched the financial burden of protests from the limited means of African American demonstrators to white authorities, who had to pay for jail space and feeding the prisoners.

The sit-ins that began at Rock Hill soon spread across the state, with demonstrations occurring in most large communities in South Carolina. Meanwhile in Rock Hill, picketing of segregated businesses continued, and other students and NAACP members attempted "kneel-ins" at six white churches. Friendship Junior College, with its politicized group of young people ready to sacrifice school for their beliefs, was by then the center for student activism. Adults negotiated for the creation of a biracial committee through which to negotiate the demands for desegregated facilities throughout the city, but the mayor and city officials refused. Resolution came only after federally imposed civil rights legislation. The forced desegregation of the city's Trailways Bus Station in 1962 foreshadowed the dismantling of discrimination in Rock Hill and throughout South Carolina.

Although the Rock Hill movement failed in its immediate effort to desegregate downtown businesses, its participants influenced activists across the South. The historian Taylor Branch called the events at Rock Hill "an emotional breakthrough for the civil rights movement." The student-prisoners set a new standard of commitment to the movement and made the "jail-in" an integral means of civil rights protest. In January 2001 members of the "Friendship Nine" reunited in Rock Hill at an NAACP-sponsored program honoring the role these men played in the fight to end segregation. MILLICENT ELLISON BROWN

Amick, Dorothy. "The Direct Action by Rock Hill Negroes in Protest against Segregation." Master's thesis, Winthrop University, 1970.

Branch, Taylor. *Parting the Waters: America in the King Years, 1954–63.* New York: Simon and Schuster, 1988.

Meier, August, and Elliott Rudwick. *CORE: A Study in the Civil Rights Movement, 1942–1968.* New York: Oxford University Press, 1973.

Newby, I. A. *Black Carolinians: A History of Blacks in South Carolina from 1895 to 1968.* Columbia: University of South Carolina Press, 1973.

Peck, James. *Freedom Ride.* New York: Simon and Schuster, 1962.

Rock music. South Carolina has been the birthplace of numerous rock music pioneers and nationally and internationally known acts. South Carolinians, particularly African American artists, were instrumental in the development of early rock and roll. The Dixie Hummingbirds, founded in Greenville in the late 1920s, were among the various African American gospel groups who influenced early rhythm and blues and emerging rock and roll of the 1950s. (The Hummingbirds had their own pop hit in 1973, appearing on Paul Simon's "Loves Me Like a Rock"). In 1953 South Carolinian Bill Pinkney helped the Drifters pioneer the rhythm and blues "doo-wop" style, later labeled "beach music," and in 1960 Ernest Evans of Spring Gully changed his name to Chubby Checker and introduced the nation to "the twist." However, the South Carolinian with the greatest influence on popular music since the 1950s was the Barnwell native James Brown. Merging his gospel roots with a polyrhythmic beat, blaring staccato horns, and a vocal style that moaned, groaned, shrieked, and wailed, the "Godfather of Soul" created a performance style whose influence spread internationally; laid the foundations for funk, disco, and hip-hop; and inspired later rock musicians in both sound and spectacle. Brown was one of the first performers inducted into the Rock and Roll Hall of Fame in 1986. He was later joined by Pinkney's Drifters and Charleston-born James Jamerson, a bassist for Motown records in the 1960s and a member of Motown's famous in-house group known as "the Funk Brothers."

Joe Bennett and the Sparkletones were the first white rock and roll artists from South Carolina to reach national attention. Their sound was strongly influenced by the country and blues-based rockabilly style of Jerry Lee Lewis, Carl Perkins, and the early Elvis Presley. In 1957 the Sparkletones, a group of teenagers from the Cowpens area, released their million-selling hit "Black Slacks." Though years of successful touring and appearances on *The Ed Sullivan Show* and *American Bandstand* followed, the Sparkletones failed to generate a second hit. Likewise, the Swinging Medallions of Greenwood are best known for a single million-seller. Their 1966 hit "Double Shot (of My Baby's Love)" has been labeled beach, frat rock, garage rock, and even protopunk and earned the band the title "party band of the South."

The emergence of southern rock in the early 1970s brought to national attention the Marshall Tucker Band, a Spartanburg-based group whose semi-Western swing sound included multiple guitars and a flute. Signed to the successful Capricorn Records label, the home of southern rock pioneers the Allman Brothers, Marshall Tucker released a string of gold and platinum records and scored such hits as "Can't You See," "Fire on the Mountain," and "Heard It in a Love Song." Spartanburg was also the home of Marshall Chapman, who began her career as a country-rock singer and guitarist in the early 1970s but is best known as a songwriter, penning songs for Jimmy Buffet, Crystal Gale, Joe Cocker, and others.

The most successful South Carolina–based rock act, in terms of both sales and Grammy awards, to emerge in the latter part of the twentieth century was Hootie and the Blowfish. Like the Swinging Medallions, Hootie and the Blowfish began as a frat-party and bar band. In 1994 the quartet, led by singer Darius Rucker, released their debut album, *Cracked Rear View,* on Atlantic records. The album sold more than seventeen million copies and earned the group Best New Artist awards from both MTV and the Grammies. The group won a second Grammy for the single "Let Her Cry." The success of Hootie prompted record companies to scout South Carolina for other possible superstars. Atlantic Records signed Charleston native Edwin McCain, who scored hits with the power ballads "Solitude" (1995) and "I'll Be" (1997). Atlantic also partnered with members of Hootie and the Blowfish to establish the short-lived Breaking Records label. Among the first bands signed to the label were Charleston's Jump! Little Children and Columbia's Treadmill Trackstar. After Atlantic dropped the label in 2001, Hootie and the Blowfish established Handpicked Records, an independent label based in Columbia, and released two compilation albums featuring the South Carolina acts Five Way Friday, Danielle Howle and the Tantrums, Moviestar, and Tootie and the Jones. STEPHEN CRISWELL

DeCurtis, Anthony, and James Henke. *The Rolling Stone Illustrated History of Rock and Roll.* 3d ed. New York: Random House, 1992.

Smith, Michael B. *Carolina Dreams: The Musical Legacy of Upstate South Carolina.* Beverly Hills, Calif.: Marshall Tucker Entertainment, 1997.

Rogers, Frank Mandeville (1857–1945). Farmer, businessman. Rogers was born to a prominent planter family near Mars Bluff on March 26, 1857. He received a private education in Charleston and returned to Mars Bluff to manage his family's agrarian interests. By the mid-1880s cotton prices had fallen to 8¢ a pound. Dismayed by the poor prospects for cotton, Rogers began experimenting with bright leaf (flue-cured) tobacco. Relying heavily on printed instructions, Rogers planted three acres of Orinoco tobacco and built a log barn to cure his crop. His tobacco profits were more than ten times greater per acre than returns for cotton at prevailing prices.

Rogers publicized his success in area newspapers and encouraged others to plant tobacco. He recruited young men from the North Carolina–Virginia tobacco belt to advise and instruct novice growers in cultivating and curing the new crop. In 1885 Rogers began corresponding with Francis W. Dawson, editor of the Charleston *News and Courier.* Citing Rogers's success, the paper urged South Carolina farmers to reduce their cotton acreage in favor of bright leaf. Aware that further expansion of tobacco culture was hindered by the lack of local markets, Rogers led a group of area businessmen to found the state's first bright leaf market in Florence in 1891. Rogers remained active in agribusiness affairs until his death on June 9, 1945. He was buried in Mt. Hope Cemetery, Florence. ELDRED E. PRINCE, JR.

Prince, Eldred E., and Robert R. Simpson. *Long Green: The Rise and Fall of Tobacco in South Carolina.* Athens: University of Georgia Press, 2000.

Rogers, F. M. Papers. Darlington County Historical Commission, Darlington, South Carolina.

Rogers, George Calvin, Jr. (1922–1997). Author, historian. Rogers was born on June 15, 1922, in Charleston, the son of George Calvin Rogers, a school administrator, and Helen Bean. He attended the Craft School and the High School of Charleston. After receiving an A.B. degree from the College of Charleston in 1943, Rogers enlisted in the army and served during World War II as a meteorologist. His tour of duty in Great Britain nurtured his interest in the study of history. After his discharge, Rogers enrolled in the University of Chicago to study American and British history. He earned an M.A. degree in 1948 and a doctorate in history in 1953. His interest in and affection for English ways influenced his choice of research topics throughout his life.

Rogers began teaching at the University of Pennsylvania in 1953. In 1958 he joined the history department of the University of South Carolina (USC), where he remained for the rest of his career. Rogers's first book, *Evolution of a Federalist: William Loughton Smith of Charleston (1758–1812),* published in 1962, was a biography of a prominent South Carolina planter-politician. This study demonstrated Rogers's knowledge of political biography, elite culture, and the politics of the new American nation, subjects that informed his life's work. In 1965 he joined a documentary editing project, the *Papers of Henry Laurens,* which was sponsored by the South Carolina Historical Society and housed at the USC history department. From 1971 to 1981 Rogers was chief editor, and the project published nine volumes of Laurens's letters, business papers, and political records. In addition to the Laurens volumes, Rogers published *Charleston in the Age of the Pinckneys* in 1969. His *History of Georgetown County, South Carolina* (1970) was the first modern history of a South Carolina county. It received an award for merit from the American Association of State and Local History and has been a model for other county histories. In addition to these and other books, Rogers published more than forty articles, essays, and introductions. The *South Carolina Historical Magazine* was his main vehicle of scholarly publication. He published twelve articles in the magazine and was its editor from 1965 to 1970. One of his articles,

"Names Not Numbers," published in a 1988 issue of the *William and Mary Quarterly,* voiced his lifelong scholarly interest in personalities and events and admonished historians not to neglect the human and idiosyncratic elements of their subjects in favor of statistics and thesis-driven studies.

Rogers was a distinguished teacher and administrator. He was chair of the USC history department from 1983 to 1986 and served on the boards of the South Carolina Tricentennial Commission, the South Carolina Archives and History Commission, and the South Carolina Historical Society. Rogers retired from USC in 1986 and continued to write and publish on South Carolina history for another decade. He was awarded an honorary doctor of letters from the College of Charleston, was a member of the American Antiquarian Society, and in 1997 was inducted into the South Carolina Academy of Authors. He died on October 7, 1997, and was buried in Charleston's Magnolia Cemetery, the resting place of the South Carolina historians William Gilmore Simms, William James Rivers, Yates Snowden, and Anna Wells Rutledge. ALEXANDER MOORE

Chesnutt, David R., and Clyde N. Wilson, Jr., eds. *The Meaning of South Carolina History: Essays in Honor of George C. Rogers, Jr.* Columbia: University of South Carolina Press, 1991.
Obituary. Charleston *Post and Courier,* October 9, 1997, pp. B1, B6.
———. *Journal of Southern History* 64 (February 1998): 187–88.

Rogers, George Washington, Jr. (b. 1958). Football player. Rogers was born in Atlanta, Georgia, on December 8, 1958, to George Washington Rogers and Grady Ann Rogers. He struggled through childhood in poverty. His father spent much of his son's youth serving a prison term, and his mother labored to raise five children. Raised largely by his aunt in Duluth, Georgia, Rogers became a prominent high school football player under the coach Cecil Morris. Encouraged and driven by Morris, Rogers overcame early academic deficiencies to qualify for a college grant-in-aid.

Rogers became the prize catch of University of South Carolina (USC) coach Jim Carlen in 1977 and had the best rushing day of his career, 237 yards and two touchdowns against Wake Forest, on November 18, 1978. He would finish with twenty-seven 100-yard-plus games out of the forty-six in which he participated, closing his college career with twenty-two straight. The 1979 and 1980 seasons would be the brightest of Rogers's career. In 1979 he rushed for a then USC record 1,681 yards and averaged 5.4 yards per carry as the Gamecocks finished with an 8–4 record. He earned all-America honors from the Associated Press. The following year Rogers broke his own school single-season rushing record with 1,894 yards on 324 carries for a 5.8 average per carry. His yardage led the Division I runners nationally and earned him the Heisman Trophy, the most prestigious of college football's individual honors. As of the early twenty-first century he remained the only winner from a South Carolina school. Rogers closed his college career with a school record 5,204 career yards and a staggering 954 carries.

George Rogers. Courtesy, University of South Carolina Athletic Department

The New Orleans Saints made Rogers the top selection in the 1980 professional draft, and he did not disappoint, rushing for 1,674 yards on 378 carries and scoring thirteen touchdowns to lead the National Football League in rushing and clinch Rookie of the Year honors. He played four seasons for the Saints before going to the Washington Redskins for three seasons. His best year in Washington produced 1,203 yards on 303 carries and eighteen touchdowns in 1986. He earned a Super Bowl ring with Washington in 1987, his last season as a player.

Rogers admitted to alcohol and drug abuse while playing in New Orleans, and a cocaine arrest in Columbia in 1990 cost him his first job with USC. He did twenty-eight days of rehab, reversed his lifestyle, and returned to work with USC. Rogers channeled much of his effort through the George Rogers Foundation, which provides scholarship aid to students who have overcome obstacles to achieve. An annual golf tournament of celebrities, former teammates, and other athletes helps fund the project. Rogers is a member of the South Carolina Athletic Hall of Fame (1981), the University of South Carolina Athletic Hall of Fame (1987), and the National Football Foundation Hall of Fame (1997). W. K. MITCHELL

Gillespie, Bob. "Rogers and the Heisman, 20 Years After." Columbia *State,* May 9, 2000, pp. C1, C2.

Rollin sisters. The five Rollin sisters were born in Charleston; they included Frances Anne (November 19, 1845–October 17, 1901), Charlotte "Lottie" (1849–?), Kate (1851–March 4, 1876), Louisa (1858–?), and Florence (1861–?). Descendants of émigrés who fled the St. Domingue Revolution in the late eighteenth century, the Rollins were free people of color living prosperously in South Carolina during the era of slavery. The political and social influence and activism of Frances, Lottie, and Louisa within the Reconstruction state government made them the three most notable Rollin sisters.

Before the Civil War the sisters lived in an elegant mansion in Charleston on America Street with their parents, William and Margaretta Rollin. Their father was a devout Catholic who operated a prosperous lumber business. The girls attended private Catholic schools in Charleston, and the three eldest were sent to the Institute for Colored Youth in Philadelphia for secondary education. The Civil War damaged the family's wealth, and the sisters living in the North were temporarily stranded with family friends. Shortly after the end of the war, they returned to South Carolina and established Columbia as their base of political activity. Known for their grace, intelligence, and charm, the Rollin sisters were active participants in the highest social circles, and their Columbia home became an important, if informal, venue for Republican Party leaders in South Carolina.

During Reconstruction, Frances, Lottie, Louisa, and Kate were active in South Carolina politics. Lottie and Kate taught in Freedmen's Bureau schools in Columbia and attempted to raise money to establish a Rollin family school. Later they each bought property in Columbia. Lottie Rollin became well known in South Carolina Reconstruction government as a clerk in the office of Congressman Robert Brown Elliott. She was also active in the American Woman Suffrage Association (AWSA) and in 1870 was elected secretary of the South Carolina Woman's Rights Association. In 1871 Lottie led a rally at the State House to promote woman suffrage. Her younger sister Louisa had addressed the South Carolina House of Representatives on the subject in 1869. By 1872 Louisa and the sisters' mother, Margaretta, shared Lottie's home in Columbia. However, following the death of their father in 1880, Lottie and Louisa Rollin moved their mother to Brooklyn, New York. Little else is known of their activities.

Frances Rollin, the most prominent of the sisters, became a writer, educator, law clerk, and civil rights activist. In 1868, while living in Boston, she wrote a biography of the black abolitionist and emigrationist Martin R. Delany, *The Life and Times of Martin R. Delany,* which she published under the name Frank A. Rollin. The only one of the sisters to marry, Frances wed William J. Whipper, an influential black legislator and later a judge, on September 17, 1868. The marriage produced five children but did not last. In 1880 Frances and her surviving children moved to Washington, D.C. She took a job with the federal government and by the 1890s was helping her youngest daughter, Ionia Rollin Whipper, to finance her studies at the Howard University School of Medicine, where she earned a degree. Returning to Beaufort, South Carolina, with failing health a few years later, Frances died there in 1901. ROSALYN TERBORG-PENN

Gatewood, Willard B. "'The Remarkable Misses Rollin': Black Women in Reconstruction South Carolina." *South Carolina Historical Magazine* 92 (July 1991): 172–88.

Ione, Carole. *Pride of Family: Four Generations of American Women of Color.* New York: Summit, 1991.

Terborg-Penn, Rosalyn. "Nineteenth-Century Black Women and Woman Suffrage." *Potomac Review* 7 (spring–summer 1977): 13–23.

Roper Hospital. Roper Hospital originated with an 1845 bequest by Colonel Thomas Roper to the Medical Society of South Carolina, which he charged with creating a hospital to treat "all such sick, maimed and diseased paupers as need surgical or medical aid . . . without regard to complexion, religion or nation." Additional funding from the city, district, and state as well as private contributions supplemented the Roper bequest. Construction began in Charleston on the corner of Queen and Mazyck Streets in 1850, and Roper Hospital admitted its first regular patients on February 12, 1856. The facility also served as the teaching hospital for the Medical College and the summer medical schools of the city.

During the Civil War, Roper Hospital unofficially became a Confederate hospital over the protests of its trustees, who demanded that the hospital remain open to treat lunatics and the sick poor. In February 1865 the federal government seized the Roper building for its own use, occupying it until November 11, 1865.

In 1873 the city council leased Roper for use as a city hospital. The building was severely damaged by a cyclone in 1885 and then was wrecked by an earthquake the following year. The building was eventually repaired in 1891, but inadequate finances prevented its operation. The city withdrew its support in favor of building its own hospital, Memorial Hospital, in 1888.

A second Roper Hospital building opened on the corner of Calhoun and Lucas Streets on February 19, 1906, and was operated by the Medical Society under contract with Charleston City Council. The Medical Society assumed full ownership in 1932. A third Roper Hospital was constructed on Calhoun Street and opened on April 15, 1946. Roper Hospital continued to expand and refine its patient care and medical services, including the addition of a rehabilitation hospital and a doctors' office building. In 1998 Roper Hospital affiliated with CareAlliance Health Services, a corporation that manages Roper and St. Francis Hospitals. JANE MCCUTCHEN BROWN

Waring, Joseph I. *A Brief History of Roper Hospital.* Charleston, S.C.: Board of Commissioners of Roper Hospital, 1964.

Rose Hill Plantation (Union County). Rose Hill Plantation was the home of South Carolina governor William Henry Gist. A wealthy upcountry cotton planter, Gist is best remembered as one of the South's "fire-eaters," a group of antebellum politicians who actively sought secession.

Constructed between 1828 and 1832, the Gist mansion at Rose Hill is a large but simple house with a symmetrical plan and solid masonry walls. Federal-style fanlights, slender fluted columns flanking entries and hearths, delicate carved rope molding, and a graceful curving staircase combine to create "more refined ornamentation than usual in upcountry houses of the period." The two-story front and rear classical porticoes and stucco cladding were added later, possibly around 1860. During a 1940s restoration, owner Clyde Franks added the square columns on the porticoes. Franks also created the majority of the formal rose gardens that surround the house, though the surrounding wall, ironwork, magnolias, and some of the boxwood hedges may date to the nineteenth century. No slave quarters from the plantation survived, though a historic kitchen building and several reconstructed outbuildings were extant in the early twenty-first century.

The plantation, built and worked by hundreds of slaves, consisted of more than eight thousand acres in 1860. Following Gist's death in 1874, his wife, Mary E. Gist, managed the property until 1889. By the 1930s the house had seriously deteriorated. Concerned citizens purchased the former plantation in the hopes of preserving it as a Confederate shrine. In 1960 the state of South Carolina purchased the property and opened it to the public as a state historic site. AL HESTER

Bell, Daniel J. "Interpretive Booklets for Local Historic Sites: Rose Hill State Park, Union, South Carolina: As a Model." Master's thesis, University of South Carolina, 1983.

Rosemond, James R. (1820–1902). Clergyman. Rosemond was born as Jim on February 1, 1820, the son of Abraham and Peggy, slaves belonging to Waddy Thompson, Jr., of Greenville. When Jim was six, his parents were sent to Alabama as a wedding present with one of Thompson's sons. Jim remained in Greenville and was sold to Vardry McBee, the largest landowner and entrepreneur in the area. Known as Jim McBee, he lived with a family of white Methodists under whose influence he was baptized in 1844. The following year he was appointed a class leader in the Greenville Methodist Episcopal Church, South. He became an exhorter, and in 1851 the church granted him permission to travel with Gabriel Poole, a black Baptist minister. On September 12, 1854, Jim was licensed to preach and delivered his first sermon at Salem Church near the Saluda River. He was a regular preacher at Sharon Church in Anderson District, and the congregation collected $500 to purchase his freedom. However, Jim's owner set the price at $800, and he remained in bondage.

Emancipated after the Civil War, Jim took the name of James R. Rosemond, and he gathered a group of black Methodists to establish a separate congregation in Greenville. At first the group paid the Greenville church $100 annually to worship there, but when the Freedmen's Bureau school opened under the leadership of Charles Hopkins, a black missionary of the northern Methodist Episcopal

Church, the congregation moved to the school. In 1866 the Methodist Episcopal Church purchased a lot, and in 1869 the Silver Hill Church (now John Wesley Church) opened. Meanwhile, in 1867 Rosemond entered the Baker Theological Institute in Charleston, and after one term he was ordained a deacon.

Rosemond returned to the upstate and began to establish churches. In 1868 he was ordained an elder, and he eventually established fifty churches in the area stretching from Oconee to York Counties. Recognized as one of the pioneers of the Methodist Episcopal Church in South Carolina, he was commonly referred to as Father Rosemond. He died in 1902 was buried at St. Matthew Church near Greenville. A. V. HUFF, JR.

Huff, A. V., Jr. "A History of South Carolina United Methodism." In *United Methodist Ministers in South Carolina.* Columbia: South Carolina Conference of the United Methodist Church, 1984.

Tolbert, James A. *Christ in Black, or the Life and Times of Rev. James R. Rosemond.* Greenville, S.C.: Shannon, 1902.

Rosenwald schools. In the early twentieth century, schooling for southern blacks was neither well planned nor well supported. Classes were held in vacant buildings, and teaching was frequently done by older children who had perhaps completed elementary school. Through his friendship with the African American educator Booker T. Washington, Julius Rosenwald, a Chicago merchant and philanthropist, made the most significant contribution to the education of southern rural blacks of the time through construction of school buildings. From 1913 to 1932, 5,357 schools, shops, and teachers' homes were built in fifteen states through contributions from Rosenwald. Believing that schooling should be a collaborative effort, Rosenwald required that all parties give toward the community schools. Of the $28 million spent from 1913 to 1932, 16.5 percent was given by Rosenwald, 19 percent by blacks, 4.5 percent by whites, and 60 percent by state and local governments.

Four hundred and fifty Rosenwald schools were built in South Carolina between 1913 and 1940 at a cost of $2,892,360. Fourteen of these were built under the supervision of Washington's Tuskegee Institute in Alabama prior to the incorporation of the Rosenwald Fund in 1917. More than 74,000 black students were educated in these buildings. Mt. Zion Rosenwald School in Florence, Liberty Colored High School in Pickens County, and Walhalla Graded School in Walhalla are listed in the National Register of Historic Places. Rosenwald / St. David's Elementary in Society Hill was still used as an elementary school as of the early twenty-first century. As the needs of schools changed, some of the buildings were used for other purposes. Roebuck School in Spartanburg became a school for white children. The Felton Teacherage was used by South Carolina State University. Many buildings, when no longer needed as schools, were sold to neighboring churches. Other buildings deteriorated and were destroyed. TAMARA S. POWELL

The Rosenwald School in Barnwell. Courtesy, South Carolina Department of Archives and History

Bullock, Henry Allen. *A History of Negro Education in the South, from 1619 to the Present.* Cambridge: Harvard University Press, 1967.

Embree, Edwin R., and Julia Waxman. *Investment in People: The Story of the Julius Rosenwald Fund.* New York: Harper, 1949.

Hawkins, Andy. "The Rosenwald Schools: The Chicago Connection." *Mid-Carolina Journal* (winter 1988–1989): 20–21.

Royal Council. The Royal Council, the linear heir of the council under the Lords Proprietors, was a twelve-man governing board created in 1720 to serve as an adviser to the governor, as a court of appeals, and as an upper house of the legislature. Throughout royal rule, the council was dominated by a relatively equal number of planters, merchants, and lawyer/placemen who were nominated by the governor and approved by the London-based Board of Trade for their wealth, political connections, and willingness to support English policies. Legislative experience was not an important criterion for appointment to the council. Its members served without pay, and its meetings were held irregularly at the call of the governor.

During the first several decades of royal rule, the council enjoyed a significant increase in its political autonomy and authority. Members were no longer subjected to the frequent arbitrary dismissals that they had experienced at the hands of the Lords Proprietors. A series of weak governors who deferred to the council added to its power and independence, allowing it to elect its own president and permitting it to compile a list of men suitable for replacements. The upper house soon likened itself, in both prestige and power, to the English House of Lords. This comparison was flawed, however, for councillors were not members of the hereditary nobility who held their political posts for life. Still, the councillors vigorously and successfully fought encroachments on their authority in the 1740s and 1750s by both the Commons House of Assembly and governors. The council did make one concession in this political power struggle in 1739, however, when it surrendered its claim to amend money bills in exchange for the right to exclude the governor from its legislative sessions. Nevertheless, by the mid-1750s South Carolina's upper house carried considerable power and prestige, a highly unusual circumstance at a time when most colonial councils were becoming political nonentities.

The council's stature dropped precipitously after 1756, however, when Governor William Henry Lyttleton arbitrarily suspended William Wragg from that body for opposing the governor's unwillingness to defend the council's right over partial control of the colonial agent. Wragg's dismissal led to a wave of resignations in the upper house, which quickly gained a reputation for being a "dependent body" whose members were "removable at pleasure." Consequently, most men of fortune found the council a "contemptible" body, and no amount of inducement could persuade them to serve on it. Instead, the English ministry, in an attempt to create an absolutely subservient upper legislative body that would give unwavering support of its measures during the Anglo-American dispute, selected men to the council who were financially dependent on the crown. Generally these appointees were British bureaucrats (placemen) of mediocre abilities who were more interested in upholding the crown's prerogative than preserving the colony's welfare. Their conduct in the council became increasingly counterproductive to effective government. With encouragement from King George III, the placemen-dominated upper house attempted to force the assembly to rescind a £1,500 donation given in 1769 to John Wilkes, an English opponent of the king, by refusing to approve any legislation until the lower house returned the "Wilkes fund" to the provincial treasury. The assembly refused to budge on the issue. This political standoff lasted until February 1775, when the upper house, under enormous political pressure, finally approved a tax bill, the last measure enacted under royal government. For all intents and purposes, though, royal rule had ended in South Carolina in 1770. In its place emerged illegal governing committees organized by leading men increasingly frustrated by the council's obstructionist behavior. Indeed, William Henry Drayton in his "Freeman" letter of 1774 to the Continental Congress listed the decline of the council as one of his seven major grievances against the crown. When America declared its independence from Britain in 1776, these de facto governing bodies enabled South Carolina to make a smooth transition from royal rule to self-government. KEITH KRAWCZYNSKI

Greene, Jack P. "The Role of the Lower Houses of Assembly in Eighteenth-Century Politics." *Journal of Southern History* 27 (November 1961): 451–74.

Krawczynski, Keith. *William Henry Drayton: South Carolina Revolutionary Patriot.* Baton Rouge: Louisiana State University Press, 2001.

Sirmans, M. Eugene. "The South Carolina Royal Council, 1720–1763." *William and Mary Quarterly,* 3d ser., 18 (July 1961): 373–91.

Weir, Robert M. *Colonial South Carolina: A History.* 1983. Reprint, Columbia: University of South Carolina Press, 1997.

Rubin, Louis Decimus, Jr. (b. 1923). Teacher, author, editor, publisher. Rubin was born in Charleston on November 19, 1923, the son of Louis D. Rubin, an electrical contractor, and his wife, Janet Weinstein. He was a third-generation Charlestonian, his Grandfather Hyman having immigrated to the city from Russia in 1886. Rubin would live his first nineteen years in Charleston, attending the College of Charleston from 1940 to 1942. He never resided permanently in the city after 1942; but he would return to it for setting and inspiration in his novels *The Golden Weather* (1961), *Surfaces of a Diamond* (1981), and *The Heat of the Sun* (1995), and in evocative nonfictional works such as *Small Craft Advisory* (1991), *Seaports of the South* (1998), and *My Father's People* (2002).

After serving in the United States Army during World War II, Rubin received his B.A. in history from the University of Richmond in 1946, and he went on to earn a Ph.D. in aesthetics of literature from Johns Hopkins in 1954. He was an instructor in English and editor of the *Hopkins Review* from 1950 to 1954 and assistant professor of American civilization at the University of Pennsylvania from 1954 to 1956. During the years Rubin pursued his graduate studies, he also worked in newspapers as an editor and staff writer, and from 1956 to 1957 he served as associate editor of the Richmond, Virginia, *News-Leader.* Years later he would publish a vivid account of these work experiences in *An Honorable Estate: My Time in the Working Press* (2001).

In 1957 Rubin turned permanently to teaching. For ten years he served on the faculty of Hollins College in Virginia. At Hollins he chaired the English department, taught the future writers Annie Dillard and Lee Smith, and continued his impressive scholarship and editing with works such as *Southern Renascence* (1953) and *Thomas Wolfe: The Weather of His Youth* (1955). In 1967 he joined the English faculty at the University of North Carolina at Chapel Hill. He taught at North Carolina for twenty-two years, guiding students and future teachers of southern literature and culture; mentoring noted southern writers such as Clyde Edgerton, Jill McCorkle, and Kaye Gibbons; and continuing an impressive academic career

Louis D. Rubin, Jr. © David G. Spielman-97, New Orleans

that would result in his authoring or editing more than fifty books. He retired from teaching in 1989 and continued to live in Chapel Hill with his wife, Eva Redfield Rubin, whom he married on June 2, 1951.

Rubin left teaching in order to concentrate all of his energies on Algonquin Books of Chapel Hill, a press that he had founded in 1983 to encourage talented young writers. By any measure Rubin's publishing house has been an impressive success, launching the careers of McCorkle and Edgerton as well as Larry Brown, Dori Sanders, and many other authors.

Rubin's distinguished career as teacher, scholar, editor, and novelist has brought him numerous awards and honors, including honorary degrees from the University of Richmond, the College of Charleston, and Clemson University. He has been named to the South Carolina Academy of Authors and has received the North Carolina Award for Literature and the R. Hunt Parker Memorial Award for his lifetime contributions to the literary heritage of North Carolina. These distinctions are appropriate for a man who during the course of a long and extraordinarily productive career has acquired, in the words of the critic Leonard Rogoff, "a cultural mantle . . . as Dean of Southern Literature." RITCHIE DEVON WATSON

Weaver, Teresa K. "Southern Fiction's Father Figure." *Atlanta Journal-Constitution,* December 29, 2002, pp. M1–M3.

Rugeley, Rowland (1738–1776). Author. One of South Carolina's earliest writers, Rowland Rugeley was born in England on August 25, 1738, the son of a linen draper of St. Ives. In 1763 his *Miscellaneous Poems: Translations from La Fontaine and Others* was published in Cambridge. Containing translations from Horace; "Belphagon, or The Devil's Marriage" by La Fontaine, and several short poems, the book showed Rugeley to be a writer of some learning, modest talent, and real wit.

In 1765 Rugeley immigrated to South Carolina with a loan from his father and the promise of help from the colonial governor, Lord Charles Montagu. Montagu awarded Rugeley the office of register, and in 1769 Rugeley became a member of the Royal Council. He purchased several large tracts of land around Charleston for planting but never had the funds to develop them. The lands, bought on credit, were eventually lost. In 1774 *The Story of Aeneas and Dido: Burlesqu'd from the Fourth Book of the Aeneid of Virgil* was published in Charleston. This work, which has been called the first classical burlesque written in America, has a lengthy preface satirizing the pretensions of poets in the New World, witty footnotes in Latin, and a wildly comic spirit. Rugeley showed himself to be comfortable with neoclassical forms and a content that mixes the classical with the contemporary.

Rugeley married Harriet Dawson on March 27, 1775, but she died in December 1776, a week after the death of their infant daughter. Rugeley died shortly thereafter on December 23, 1776. In his obituary in the *South-Carolina and American General Gazette* of January 2, 1777, Rugeley was praised for his "integrity and philanthropy" as well as for his wit, learning, and charm. Rugeley's works have never been reprinted. Copies are extant in the special collections of the South Caroliniana Library, University of South Carolina. THORNE COMPTON

Rugeley, Rowland. *Miscellaneous Poems: Translations from La Fontaine and Others.* Cambridge, U.K.: Fletcher and Hodson, 1763.

———. *The Story of Aeneas and Dido: Burlesqu'd from the Fourth Book of the Aeneid of Virgil.* Charleston, S.C.: Robert Wells, 1774.

Rugeleys in America. 2 vols. Austin, Tex.: Rugeley Family Association, 1995–1997.

Russell, Donald Stewart (1906–1998). University president, governor, U.S. senator, jurist. Russell was born in Lafayette Springs, Mississippi, on February 22, 1906, the son of Jesse Russell, a farmer, and his wife Lula Russell. At the age of four, the death of his father doomed the family farm, and Russell moved with his mother to Chester, South Carolina. At age fifteen Russell entered the University of South Carolina, where he graduated first in his class in 1925. He then entered the University of South Carolina's law school, where he graduated at the head of his class in 1928. On June 15, 1929, Russell married Virginia Faire Utsey of St. George. They remained married for nearly seventy years and raised four children.

Donald and Virginia Russell in the garden at the President's House, University of South Carolina. Courtesy, University of South Carolina Archives

After a year of graduate study in law at the University of Michigan, Russell entered private practice in Union in 1929. In 1930 he moved to Spartanburg and joined the influential law firm of Nicholls, Wyche and Byrnes, where he began a close working relationship with James F. Byrnes. By late 1937 Sam J. Nicholls had died, C. C. Wyche was appointed to the Federal District Court, and James F. Byrnes was appointed to the U.S. Supreme Court, so Russell ran the practice alone. After the Japanese attack on Pearl Harbor, Russell moved to Washington, D.C., where, as Byrnes's protégé, he served in Franklin Roosevelt's White House as assistant to the director of economic stabilization and later as assistant to the director of war mobilization. In 1944 he entered the U.S. Army with the rank of major and served on the staff of General Dwight D. Eisenhower in France. In early 1945 he returned to the White House, where he served under Byrnes as deputy director of war mobilization and reconversion. After Byrnes became secretary of state in July 1945, Russell was named assistant secretary of state for administration. He traveled with Byrnes to the Potsdam conference and sat in on the discussions that led to the dropping of the atomic bombs on Japan.

After Byrnes resigned as secretary of state in January 1947, Russell joined him in a Washington, D.C., law office affiliated with the powerful firm of Hogan & Hartson. He also entered several commercial ventures in the Carolinas, principally the short-term, high-interest-loan business, which soon made him a millionaire. Following Byrnes's election as governor in 1950, Russell was named president of the University of South Carolina (USC) in late 1951. During his five-year tenure Russell updated the curriculum, attracted nationally respected faculty, and modernized the campus. His administration is remembered as one of the most successful in university history.

Russell resigned as USC's president in late 1957 to run for governor. A usually quiet, unassuming, and scholarly man, he entered a bitter political campaign and lost the 1958 Democratic Party primary to Ernest F. Hollings. Four years later Russell again ran for governor and was elected. His term was marked by several milestones in race relations. He celebrated his inauguration with an integrated picnic on the grounds of the Governor's Mansion. It was the first integrated public social event in South Carolina since Reconstruction. A few weeks later Clemson Agricultural College was desegregated, with Russell calling on the state to face the issue "peacefully, without violence, without disorder and with proper regard for the good name of our state and our people." Nonetheless, Governor Russell continued the state's legal efforts to prevent the desegregation of other schools and colleges in the state, and he called the landmark federal Civil Rights Act of 1964 "unfortunate."

On April 18, 1965, U.S. Senator Olin D. Johnston died in office. Four days later, citing his own extensive Washington experience, Governor Russell resigned his office and the state's new governor, Robert E. McNair, appointed him to fill Johnston's seat in the Senate until the next statewide election. As senator, Russell opposed the Voting Rights Act of 1965. He served in the Senate until 1966, when Ernest F. Hollings defeated him in a special election. The following year President Lyndon B. Johnson named Russell to the U.S. District Court for the Western District of South Carolina. Four years later, in 1971, Richard Nixon elevated Russell to the U.S. Court of Appeals for the Fourth Circuit. While on that court, Russell wrote nearly 475 published opinions and earned a reputation as a thoughtful conservative. He served on the Fourth Circuit for more than twenty-five years and never took "senior status," working full-time until his death in Spartanburg on his ninety-second birthday, February 22, 1998. HENRY H. LESESNE

Moylan, John C., III. "Donald Stuart Russell—In Memoriam." *South Carolina Law Review* 49 (spring 1998): 353–57.

Obituary. *New York Times,* February 25, 1998, p. B8.

Widener, H. Emory, Jr. "Honorable Donald Stewart Russell (1971–1998)." *Washington and Lee Law Review* 55 (spring 1998): 474–76.

Russell's Magazine (1857–1860). *Russell's Magazine* was the last of the southern antebellum literary magazines and arguably the best. It should be credited for a desire to keep politics out of literary assessments, although in practice this objectivity applied only as long as slavery was not in any way attacked or "falsely" portrayed. It was also the home base for two of the best poets in antebellum South Carolina, Paul Hamilton Hayne (its editor) and Henry Timrod, poet and critic. *Russell's* was the magazine of the professional middle class—lawyers, college faculty, and doctors. In Charleston the magazine had the support of two literary groups. The first, the Wigwam, met at William Gilmore Simms's town residence for little suppers, while the second and larger group met in John Russell's Charleston bookstore. They were confirmed conservatives, Charleston's most literary and literate professionals, and all males.

Hayne promised to publish "undiscovered genius" in the South, largely due to the reluctance of northern editors to publish southern writers. The only undiscovered genius, however, turned out to be Henry Timrod. George C. Hurlbut was added as assistant editor to help Hayne, but no one could solve either the financial problems or the political ones as secession and war drew nearer. At another time *Russell's* might have succeeded, but the clock had run too late. Its last issue appeared in March 1860.

Hayne did coax Timrod into writing his version of "What Is Poetry?" (October 1857), presenting a case for romanticism as opposed to the conservative taste for neoclassicism evidenced in the literary opinions of William J. Grayson, author of *The Hireling and the Slave.* The result was a version of the ancients versus the moderns and the neoclassicists versus the romantics that reveals much about the hesitancy of Charleston professional men to accept change in literature. It was, however, the works published by the South Carolina triumvirate of Timrod, Hayne, and Simms that distinguished *Russell's Magazine.* RICHARD CALHOUN

Calhoun, Richard J. "The Ante-Bellum Literary Twilight: *Russell's Magazine.*" *Southern Literary Journal* 3 (fall 1970): 89–110.

Longton, William Henry. "*Russell's Magazine* 1857–1860." In *The Conservative Press in Eighteenth and Nineteenth Century America,* edited by Ronald Lora and William Henry Longton. Westport, Conn.: Greenwood, 1999.

Rutledge, Archibald (1883–1973). Poet, writer. Rutledge was born in McClellanville on October 23, 1883, the son of Henry Middleton Rutledge III, an army officer, and Margaret Hamilton. Descended from a lineage of notable South Carolinians, Rutledge included among his ancestors John Rutledge, Edward Rutledge, Arthur Middleton, Charles Cotesworth Pinckney, and Thomas Pinckney.

Rutledge grew up in Georgetown County at Hampton Plantation, built in 1730 on a two-thousand-acre tract secured by his Huguenot ancestor Daniel Horry in 1686. Rutledge claimed that had it not been for his parents' insistence that he obtain an education, he might never have left the Santee River delta. In 1900 he graduated as salutatorian from Porter Military Academy in Charleston and was subsequently packed off to Union College in Schenectady, New York, where he earned both bachelor's (1904) and master's (1907) degrees. For nearly thirty-two years Rutledge headed the English department at Mercersburg Academy, a college preparatory school in south-central Pennsylvania. On December 19, 1907, he married Florence Hart, who died in 1934. She was the mother of his three sons. In 1936 Rutledge married Alice Lucas.

Rutledge began publishing poetry in 1907, but he did not earn recognition until 1918, when his memoir of youth, *Tom and I on the Old Plantation,* was published. While teaching, Rutledge published many books, poems, and articles in national magazines, including the *Saturday Evening Post* and *Good Housekeeping.* In 1934 the South Carolina General Assembly named Rutledge the state's first poet laureate, an honor he held for the remainder of his life.

As the title of his 1918 memoir suggests, Rutledge took life at Hampton as his literary subject, but to his national audience he spoke as the ambassador for an increasingly anachronistic Deep South. When treating the abundant natural beauty and wildlife of the Santee River delta, Rutledge crafted lyrical, engaging prose, but his homespun depictions of "my black henchmen" and their "happy blending with the plantation landscape" reflected what one colleague described as his "unreconstructed views on white supremacy." Rutledge wore the mantle of planter paternalism, a habit of mind mirrored in his alternate reverence and ridicule of the black men and women he "inherited" at Hampton. *Home by the River* (1941) and *God's Children* (1947) are particularly noteworthy for this tendency, which Rutledge discussed under the rubric of "dusky dilemmas."

Rutledge retired from Mercersburg Academy in 1937 and returned to Hampton, which he had inherited from his father in 1923. With the help of the plantation's black laborers, he lovingly restored the house and grounds, which once had played host to Francis Marion and George Washington. Rutledge died on September 15, 1973, at Little Hampton, his home in McClellanville. He is buried with his sons Archibald Jr. and Henry Middleton at Hampton Plantation, which he bequeathed to the state of South Carolina. Located sixteen miles south of Georgetown on U.S. Highway 17, it is open to the public as Hampton Plantation State Historic Site. ELIZABETH ROBESON

Casada, Jim. *Hunting and Home in the Southern Heartland: The Best of Archibald Rutledge.* Columbia: University of South Carolina Press, 1992.

Rutledge, Archibald. *Home by the River.* Indianapolis: Bobbs-Merrill, 1941.

Wheeler, Mary B., and Genon H. Neblett. *Hidden Glory: The Life and Times of Hampton Plantation, Legend of the South Santee.* Nashville, Tenn.: Rutledge Hill, 1983.

Rutledge, Edward (1749–1800). Lawyer, governor. Edward Rutledge, the youngest son of Dr. John Rutledge and Sarah Hext, was born on November 23, 1749. He studied law under the direction of his older brother, John, and then continued his studies at the Middle Temple in London. He was admitted to the South Carolina Bar in January 1773. His marriage on March 1, 1774, to Henrietta Middleton produced three children. After Henrietta's death in 1792, he married Mary Shubrick Eveleigh on October 28, 1792.

One of Rutledge's first cases in 1773 involved a successful habeas corpus petition that freed a printer jailed for contempt by the upper house of assembly. The reputation he gained in this politically charged case paved the way for his election to the Continental Congress in 1774. At first he hoped to achieve a settlement with Britain that would preserve colonial rights within the British Empire. Events, particularly the beginning of the war, moved him to support independence in principle by February 1776. In June, however, he opposed a formal declaration of independence because he believed that the colonies should first agree on a confederation and secure foreign aid. But when the final vote in favor of independence came,

Edward Rutledge. Courtesy, South Carolina Historical Society

Rutledge swayed his South Carolina colleagues to support it "for the sake of unanimity." He became the youngest signer of the Declaration of Independence.

Rutledge returned to South Carolina in December 1776 to assume his post as a captain in the Charleston Artillery. He also took his seat in the South Carolina House of Representatives, where he worked with some success for a strong executive, military preparedness, and harsh sanctions against Loyalists. When the British captured Charleston in 1780, Rutledge became a prisoner of war on parole. Later that year he and other Charlestonians were arrested for allegedly plotting to organize resistance, a charge that Rutledge denied. The alleged plotters were held prisoner in St. Augustine, Florida, and their property was sequestered for the support of the British army. His war-time experience left Rutledge with a lasting bitterness toward Britain.

Rutledge was freed in a prisoner exchange in July 1781. The following January he returned to the state House of Representatives, where he served for the next thirteen years and became one of South Carolina's most influential political leaders. Rutledge worked in the 1780s to promote the economic recovery of the state and to maintain the political dominance of lowcountry gentlemen. Both goals required concessions. A skilled conciliator, Rutledge found those concessions easier to make than did many of his compatriots. He played an important role in the postwar confiscation and amercement of Loyalist property and unsuccessfully opposed removal of the state capital from Charleston to Columbia. He later argued against constitutional revision and then helped to devise limited concessions to the upcountry that still preserved lowcountry control in the state constitution of 1790. Rutledge also supported what he considered to be the least objectionable of various plans for paper money and debt relief in order to pacify popular discontent.

As a delegate to the South Carolina ratifying convention in 1788, Rutledge was a leader in supporting ratification of the U.S. Constitution. He moved successfully for the endorsement of proposed constitutional amendments to conciliate the opposition. President George Washington twice asked Rutledge if he would accept appointment to the U.S. Supreme Court in the 1790s and also considered him for secretary of state and minister to France, but Rutledge's personal and family circumstances prevented him from leaving South Carolina. Unable for the same reasons to seek election to Congress, he nevertheless had some influence in national politics because of his ties to national leaders and his power in his state. Rutledge supported Alexander Hamilton's financial program but remained strongly anti-British in foreign affairs. He did not align himself completely with either of the two emerging national political parties during Washington's administration.

Rutledge's long tenure in the South Carolina House of Representatives ended in 1796, when he was elected to the state Senate. There Rutledge worked for military preparedness in the undeclared naval war with France that followed the XYZ Affair. He was now aligned with the Federalist Party, but his freedom from British attachments made him more acceptable to Democratic-Republicans than were most Federalists. Rutledge was elected governor in 1798 and continued to strengthen his state's defenses in that capacity. He died in office during the night of January 23–24, 1800, after suffering a stroke. He was buried in St. Philip's Churchyard, Charleston.
JAMES HAW

Clow, Richard Brent. "Edward Rutledge of South Carolina, 1749–1800: Unproclaimed Statesman." Ph.D. diss., University of Georgia, 1976.

Haw, James. *John and Edward Rutledge of South Carolina.* Athens: University of Georgia Press, 1997.

Smith, Dorothy Caroline. "The Revolutionary War Service of Edward Rutledge, 1774–1782." M.A. thesis, University of South Carolina, 1947.

Rutledge, John (ca. 1739–1800). Lawyer, jurist, governor. Rutledge's exact date of birth is unknown. The eldest son of Dr. John Rutledge and Sarah Hext, he studied law with his uncle Andrew Rutledge and with James Parsons in Charleston before attending the Middle Temple in London. Admitted to the South Carolina Bar in 1761, he quickly became one of the most successful attorneys in the colony. On May 1, 1763, he married Elizabeth Grimké. They had ten children, eight of whom survived to adulthood.

Rutledge served in the Commons House of Assembly from 1761 to 1775 and became one of its leaders. He upheld the rights of the "country" in a series of disputes with successive royal governors and firmly opposed the Stamp, Townshend, and Tea Acts, representing his colony at the Stamp Act Congress in 1765. As a delegate to the First and Second Continental Congresses, he advocated a steadfast defense of American rights, but by means that would not impede reconciliation with the mother country. When events made reconciliation impossible, he reluctantly accepted independence as a necessity.

John Rutledge. Courtesy, South Carolina Historical Society

In the meantime, as royal authority dissolved in his own and other colonies, Rutledge supported a congressional resolution for the creation of new governments based on constitutions created by the people, not royal charters, until the crisis was resolved. He left Congress in November 1775 to carry that resolution to South Carolina. Rutledge was one of the drafters of the state constitution of 1776 and was elected president (governor) of South Carolina in March of the same year. Under his energetic leadership, the new state repulsed a British attack on Charleston in June 1776 and suppressed a Cherokee uprising later that summer.

Rutledge resigned as president in March 1778 to protest the adoption of a new state constitution of which he disapproved, but he was elected governor under that constitution in February 1779. When the British captured Charleston and overran South Carolina in 1780, Rutledge escaped to function as a one-man government in exile. He twice visited Philadelphia to seek increased aid for the South from Congress but spent most of his time with the southern Continental army organizing and trying to supply his state's militia for continued resistance. Eventual military successes in the South allowed him to restore state government and turn over the governorship to his elected successor, John Mathewes, in January 1782.

After serving again in Congress from 1782 to 1783, Rutledge accepted appointment to the South Carolina Court of Chancery, and he remained a leader in the state legislature in the 1780s. His experience in Congress convinced him that the United States needed a stronger central government. He was chosen as one of South Carolina's delegates to the constitutional convention in 1787.

Rutledge played a prominent role in writing the federal Constitution. He advocated a national government of greatly increased but still limited powers and entrusted to an executive and a Congress designed to consist of gentlemen made relatively independent of public opinion. As chairman of the committee of detail, he had a major role in the enumeration of congressional powers, the provision forbidding taxation of exports, and the ban on national prohibition of slave imports until 1808. Rutledge also promoted the constitution's adoption as a member of the South Carolina ratifying convention.

In 1789 Rutledge reluctantly accepted appointment as one of the first justices of the United States Supreme Court. He resigned from that position in 1791 to become chief justice of South Carolina, an office he held until 1795. Since the Supreme Court was just getting organized during his tenure, he made no important rulings on the federal bench.

In the early 1790s John Rutledge became an emotionally troubled man. Large debts threatened the loss of all of his property. A serious illness in 1781, coupled with gout, had severely damaged his health. His wife's sudden death in 1792 was the final blow, plunging him into deep depression.

Apparently unaware of Rutledge's problems, President George Washington appointed him chief justice of the United States Supreme Court in 1795. However, before learning of his nomination, Rutledge made a speech denouncing the recently negotiated Jay Treaty with Britain. This speech outraged Federalists and, combined with reports of his "derangement" and financial problems, caused the Federalist-dominated Senate to reject his nomination. Probably before hearing of the rejection, a despondent Rutledge attempted suicide and then resigned from the South Carolina Supreme Court for reasons of health. Except for one term in the South Carolina House of Representatives, Rutledge remained in retirement until his death on July 18, 1800. JAMES HAW

Haw, James. *John and Edward Rutledge of South Carolina.* Athens: University of Georgia Press, 1997.

St. Andrew's Parish. On November 30, 1706, St. Andrew's Day, the South Carolina Commons House of Assembly passed an act establishing the Church of England in South Carolina. St. Andrew's Parish was one of the ten parishes created by that act. The parish included the mainland region south and west of Charleston along the Ashley River and James Island. The parish church was completed around 1706 and still accommodated Episcopal worshipers at the turn of the twenty-first century, making it the oldest Episcopal Church building in South Carolina. Due to the growing profitability of rice cultivation and subsequent population growth, the parish was divided in 1717, with the territory surrounding the upper Ashley River becoming St. George's Dorchester Parish.

St. Andrew's Parish Church. Courtesy, South Caroliniana Library, University of South Carolina

The rice plantations along the Ashley River in St. Andrew's Parish prospered during the colonial era. White planters displayed their wealth by building elaborate plantation homes such as Magnolia, Drayton Hall, and Middleton Place and increasing the number of African slaves to work the fields. In 1728 it was estimated that there were about eight hundred whites and eighteen hundred slaves in the parish.

During the late colonial period, tidal lands better suited for rice production drew many planters away from the Ashley River and St. Andrew's Parish. Nevertheless rice production continued to dominate the parish economy throughout the antebellum era. After the parish system was abolished by the constitution of 1865, St. Andrew's Parish was incorporated into Charleston District. MICHAEL S. REYNOLDS

Linder, Suzanne Cameron. *Anglican Churches in Colonial South Carolina: Their History and Architecture.* Charleston, S.C.: Wyrick, 2000.

St. Andrew's Society of Charleston. The St. Andrew's Society is a social and benevolent organization that was founded in Charleston on November 30, 1729. Its founders were men, mostly of Scottish descent, who came together to celebrate St. Andrew's Day. Its membership was never limited to Scotsmen, however, so it quickly grew to include some of South Carolina's foremost merchants, politicians, lawyers, doctors, and planters. The society's stated purpose was to provide for the relief of the indigent and poor. It generated substantial revenue for that purpose through admission fees, dues, gifts, and bequests. The society was incorporated in 1798, and on January 9, 1804, it opened a school for the education of the poor and the children of members who had fallen on hard times. The school operated until after passage of the State Free School Act of 1811. The society began construction of a hall in 1814 and completed it the following year. It was the scene of numerous social events during its forty-five-year existence. The hall also was the meeting place for the Secession Convention, which passed the Ordinance of Secession there on December 20, 1860. St. Andrew's Hall burned on December 11, 1861, in a fire that consumed much of Charleston. Thereafter, the St. Andrew's Society met in the South Carolina Society Hall at the invitation of that organization. In the early twenty-first century, the society's membership was capped at 250. Meetings of the organization are held monthly except for July and August, with the annual celebration of St. Andrew's Day being the highlight of its calendar. In keeping with its original purpose, the society annually contributed to twelve charities and four schools. W. ERIC EMERSON

Easterby, J. H. *History of the St. Andrew's Society of Charleston, South Carolina, 1729–1929.* Charleston, S.C.: The Society, 1929.

St. Bartholomew's Parish. One of the ten original parishes established by the Church Act of 1706, St. Bartholomew's Parish, located in modern Colleton County, included the territory between the Edisto and Combahee Rivers. With the spread of rice cultivation, St. Bartholomew's numerous tidal rivers attracted planters who brought large numbers of African slaves to work their fields. During the second half of the eighteenth century the production of indigo further increased their wealth and demand for slaves.

The whites of St. Bartholomew's Parish could not agree on a location for a parish church, so several Anglican chapels of ease were built. In 1725 a chapel was authorized at Pon Pon, a neighborhood near where the Charleston road crossed the Edisto River. A second was authorized in 1745 at Edmundsbury, a village on the Ashepoo River.

During the antebellum era, the fertile soil and optimum growing conditions made the ACE (Ashepoo, Combahee, Edisto) River Basin a center of rice production in the state. In 1820 Colleton District, which included St. Bartholomew's Parish, had a population that was 83.6 percent African slaves. The planters of St. Bartholomew's were known for their political radicalism, electing the outspoken fire-eater Robert Barnwell Rhett to represent them in the General Assembly and Congress. When a new state constitution was adopted in 1865, the parish system was abolished and St. Bartholomew's Parish was incorporated into Colleton District. MICHAEL S. REYNOLDS

Linder, Suzanne Cameron. *Anglican Churches in Colonial South Carolina: Their History and Architecture.* Charleston, S.C.: Wyrick, 2000.

———. *Historical Atlas of the Rice Plantations of the ACE River Basin—1860.* Columbia: South Carolina Department of Archives and History, 1995.

St. Cecilia Society. Named for the patron saint of music, the St. Cecilia Society of Charleston was formed in 1766 as a private subscription concert organization. Its musical patronage ended in 1820, but the society continued to flourish into the twenty-first century as one of South Carolina's oldest and most exclusive social institutions.

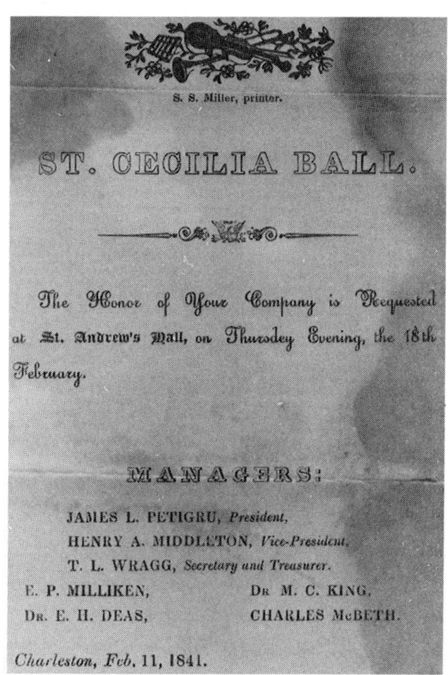
S. S. Miller, printer.

ST. CECILIA BALL.

The Honor of Your Company is Requested at St. Andrew's Hall, on Thursdey Evening, the 18th February.

MANAGERS:

JAMES L. PETIGRU, *President*,
HENRY A. MIDDLETON, *Vice-President*,
T. L. WRAGG, *Secretary and Treasurer*.
E. P. MILLIKEN, Dr M. C. KING,
Dr. E. H. DEAS, CHARLES McBETH.

Charleston, Feb. 11, 1841.

An invitation to the St. Cecilia Ball, 1841. Courtesy, South Carolina Historical Society

The society's importance as a musical institution is considerable. Modeled on concert organizations in contemporary Britain, it was the earliest musical society in America. For fifty-four years it maintained an annual series of private concerts and balls, which generally commenced in mid-autumn and continued fortnightly through early spring. While the society's existence is not unknown to music historians, few details of its concert activity have heretofore been available. A recent reconstruction of the society's musical era reveals it to be the most significant example of concert patronage in the United States before the advent of the New York Philharmonic in 1842.

Music at the society's concerts was performed by gentlemen amateurs and hired professionals. Lady amateurs and professionals appeared occasionally as instrumental or vocal soloists. The repertory included orchestral, chamber, and vocal works by European masters and was modeled largely on British musical fashions. The society seems to have made no effort to encourage local composers. Similarly, it never owned or built its own performance space. In its first century the society employed ten different venues in Charleston, ranging from tavern long rooms to the South Carolina Statehouse. Since the early 1880s its events have been held at Hibernian Hall.

The termination of the St. Cecilia Society's concert series was motivated by several factors. By 1815 musical fashions in Charleston were changing and enthusiasm for the society's concerts was in decline. In 1817 the Charleston Theatre company initiated a touring circuit that disrupted the society's practice of sharing musicians with the local theater. In addition, the Panic of 1819 unraveled the local economy and induced the society to curtail its activities. After the meager 1819–1820 season, the society abandoned its concert series and in subsequent years presented a greatly reduced number of dancing assemblies.

The society's early records were lost in 1865. Memories of its musical heritage soon faded, and observers have since focused on the society's social activities and its annual debutante ball. By the end of the nineteenth century the St. Cecilia Society was recognized as an important link to Charleston's former "golden age" of prosperity. To many, it was also a symbol of the city's rigid social insularity and its resistance to new socioeconomic realities. Despite this friction, in the early twenty-first century inclusion in the society's activities was still widely believed to confer upon participants the ultimate insider status in Charleston. Its membership has always been limited to gentlemen of the city's elite, long-established families, though ladies of the members' families and invited guests have been admitted since 1767. Desiring to remain above controversy, the St. Cecilia Society has for the past century sought to eschew public notice while it discreetly carries on a social tradition unbroken for nearly two and a half centuries. NICHOLAS MICHAEL BUTLER

Butler, Nicholas Michael. "Votaries of Apollo: The St. Cecilia Society and the Patronage of Concert Music in Charleston, South Carolina, 1766–1820." Ph.D. diss., Indiana University, 2004.

Doyle, Don H. *New Men, New Cities, New South: Atlanta, Nashville, Charleston, Mobile, 1860–1910.* Chapel Hill: University of North Carolina Press, 1990.

"Rules of the St. Cecilia Society." *South Carolina Historical and Genealogical Magazine* 1 (July 1900): 223–27.

St. David's Church (Cheraw). Old St. David's was the parish church for St. David's Parish, established in 1768 from portions of St. Mark's and Prince Frederick's Parishes, or modern-day Chesterfield, Marlboro, Darlington, and portions of Florence Counties. Construction on the church began in 1770, and the building was in use by 1773. Thomas Bingham was the carpenter.

Similar to other colonial churches, although less ornate, the original frame church was fifty-three feet long and thirty feet wide with a jerkin-head roof. During the Revolutionary War, the British used the church as a hospital, and several British soldiers are buried in the churchyard. Following the war the Anglican Church was disestablished, clergy were scarce, and the church was used only occasionally by other denominations.

In 1819 the Episcopal Church, successor to the Anglican Church, sent the Reverend Andrew Fowler to hold services in St. David's. In 1826 the congregation added a vestibule and a steeple and relocated the stairs to the gallery. A vestry room was later added to the east end.

During the Civil War the church was in the path of both General William Hardee's retreating Confederates and General William Sherman's advancing Union army. One of the first Confederate monuments in the country was erected in the church graveyard in 1867.

In need of more space, the congregation completed a new church on Market Street in 1916, and Old St. David's was used only sporadically thereafter. Old St. David's was listed in the National Register of Historic Places in 1971. Four years later St. David's Parish gave the old church building to the Chesterfield County Historic Preservation Commission. The commission restored the building to the period of 1826. It is frequently visited and used for weddings and civic events. SARAH CAIN SPRUILL

Godfrey, William. *An Historical Sketch of Old St. David's Church, Cheraw, South Carolina from 1768 to 1916.* Cheraw, S.C., 1916.

Gregg, Alexander. *History of the Old Cheraws.* 1867. Reprint, Greenville, S.C.: Southern Historical Press, 1991.

Holcomb, Brent H., ed. *St. David's Parish, South Carolina: Minutes of the Vestry, 1768–1832, Parish Register, 1819–1924.* Easley, S.C.: Southern Historical Press, 1979.

Waddill, Helen Brackett, et al. *Old St. David's, Cheraw, South Carolina, 1770–1947.* N.p., n.d.

St. David's Parish. The backcountry parish of St. David's was established on April 12, 1768, and included the area of modern Marlboro, Darlington, and Chesterfield Counties, plus a small portion of northwestern Florence County. Among the earliest settlers in the upper Pee Dee region were Welsh Baptists from Pennsylvania drawn to South Carolina in the 1730s by the colonial government's promise of free land in Queensboro Township. Indigo planters from the coast began arriving in the 1750s, and by 1760 the "Welsh Tract" contained approximately 3,500 people, 300 of whom were slaves. In the late 1760s the area became a target for "Out Laws and Fugitives from the Colonies of Virginia and North Carolina" and subsequently a hotbed of Regulator activity. In 1767 the visiting Reverend Charles Woodmason drew up "a Petition to the Legislature for this Part of the Province to be rais'd into a Parish," which the residents "cheerfully sign'd." Local support for parish organization came more from a desire to establish law and order than from a desire for a church, however.

The assembly authorized St. David's the following year. Since British imperial policy had forbidden the enlargement of colonial legislatures, it was given one of the two representatives from neighboring St. Mark's. A parish church at Cheraw was opened in 1773, and in 1778 the St. David's Society was incorporated to support schooling in the area. When counties became the basis for backcountry representation in 1785, St. David's Parish was divided into Marlboro, Darlington, and Chesterfield Counties. MATTHEW A. LOCKHART

Gregg, Alexander. *History of the Old Cheraws.* 1867. Reprint, Greenville, S.C.: Southern Historical Press, 1991.

Holcomb, Brent H. *St. David's Parish, South Carolina: Minutes of the Vestry, 1768–1832, Parish Register, 1819–1924.* Easley, S.C.: Southern Historical Press, 1979.

Johnson, George Lloyd, Jr. *The Frontier in the Colonial South: South Carolina Backcountry, 1736–1800.* Westport, Conn.: Greenwood, 1997.

Linder, Suzanne Cameron. *Anglican Churches in Colonial South Carolina: Their History and Architecture.* Charleston, S.C.: Wyrick, 2000.

Woodmason, Charles. *The Carolina Backcountry on the Eve of the American Revolution: The Journal and Other Writings of Charles Woodmason, Anglican Itinerant.* Edited by Richard J. Hooker. Chapel Hill: University of North Carolina Press, 1953.

St. George's Dorchester Parish. The South Carolina Commons House of Assembly passed an act creating St. George's Dorchester Parish on December 11, 1717. The new parish was previously part of St. Andrew's Parish and was created to accommodate the growing number of colonists along the upper Ashley River. In 1695 a group of Congregationalists from Dorchester, Massachusetts, established a New England–style township twenty-six miles upriver from Charleston and named it in honor of their former home. These religious dissenters formed the core of the parish's early population.

An Anglican church was completed in the town in 1720, and a 1726 census found 537 whites and about 1,300 slaves in the parish. In 1759, due to unrest caused by the French and Indian War, Fort Dorchester, a brick powder magazine surrounded by earthen works, was completed. Most of the descendants of the Congregationalists left the parish for Georgia beginning in 1752, but Dorchester remained an economically important town until the Revolutionary War.

The British burned Dorchester in 1781, and the town was subsequently abandoned. After the war the town of Summerville replaced Dorchester as the regional market. Rice plantations along the upper Ashley River dominated the parish's early economy and continued to be an important source of wealth into the nineteenth century. During the antebellum era planters from St. George's and surrounding parishes built summer homes in Summerville to escape their plantations during the malarial season. After the constitution of 1865 abolished the parish system, St. George's Dorchester Parish was incorporated into Colleton District. MICHAEL S. REYNOLDS

Linder, Suzanne Cameron. *Anglican Churches in Colonial South Carolina: Their History and Architecture.* Charleston, S.C.: Wyrick, 2000.

Sigmon, Daniel Ray. "Dorchester, St. George's Parish, South Carolina: The Rise and Decline of a Colonial Frontier Village." Master's thesis, University of South Carolina, 1992.

St. Helena's Parish. On June 7, 1712, the South Carolina Commons House of Assembly passed an act designating all of the land between the Combahee and Savannah Rivers (most of modern Beaufort and Jasper Counties) as the parish of St. Helena. The new parish consisted of the mainland between the two rivers and the numerous Sea Islands off Port Royal and St. Helena Sounds. British settlers anglicized the name given to the area by early Spanish settlers, Santa Elena. Although the town of Beaufort on Port Royal Island was chartered in 1711, the town and parish did not grow substantially until after the Yamassee uprising was suppressed in the 1720s. The St. Helena's Parish church was built in 1724 in Beaufort.

In 1745 Prince William's Parish was created out of St. Helena's Parish because of complaints by rice planters about the difficulty of traveling to Beaufort. Similar complaints led to the creation of St. Peter's Parish in 1747 and St. Luke's Parish in 1767. By 1767 St. Helena's Parish consisted of only Port Royal, Ladys, and St. Helena Islands.

Indigo was the major cash crop grown on the islands before the American Revolution, but it was replaced by Sea Island cotton in the 1790s. Large numbers of slaves were brought to the parish to work the plantations. In 1830 there were 1,063 whites and 7,725 blacks in the parish, all but 65 of the latter of whom were slaves. The parish system was abolished by the South Carolina constitution of 1865, and St. Helena's Parish fell under the jurisdiction of Beaufort District. MICHAEL S. REYNOLDS

Linder, Suzanne Cameron. *Anglican Churches in Colonial South Carolina: Their History and Architecture.* Charleston, S.C.: Wyrick, 2000.

Rosengarten, Theodore. *Tombee: Portrait of a Cotton Planter.* New York: Morrow, 1986.

Rowland, Lawrence S., Alexander Moore, and George C. Rogers. *The History of Beaufort County, South Carolina.* Vol. 1, *1514–1861.* Columbia: University of South Carolina Press, 1996.

St. James Goose Creek Parish. A long, narrow rectangle extending northwestward from the Cooper River through modern Charleston, Berkeley, and Orangeburg Counties, St. James Goose Creek was one of the ten original parishes created by the Church Act of 1706. Although few English Barbadians participated in the founding of Charleston in 1670, within two years new arrivals from the island had pushed their numbers to half of Carolina's white population. The colonists at Charleston soon began to take up "the scent of better land," and by 1672 a group of Barbadians had settled with their slaves on nearby Goose Creek, a meandering tributary of the Cooper River. The "Goose Creek Men" were experienced colonists and accomplished planters, and they quickly came to dominate the colony politically and economically. Among their allies were Huguenots who arrived in the area in the 1680s and were readily absorbed into the local Anglican establishment. As the "Neighbourhood" became more affluent, working plantations gave way to fashionable country seats, and the banks of Goose Creek became home to "many persons of considerable note," including governors, members of the council and the assembly, and wealthy Charleston merchants.

Colonial Goose Creek was the most prosperous and populous community outside of Charleston, attributes that are reflected in its ornate parish church. St. James Episcopal Church was completed in 1719 and is located near the modern town of Goose Creek. With the abolition of the parish system in 1865, St. James Goose Creek Parish became part of Berkeley County. MATTHEW A. LOCKHART

Heitzler, Michael J. *Historic Goose Creek, South Carolina, 1670–1980.* Easley, S.C.: Southern Historical Press, 1983.

Klingberg, Frank, ed. *The Carolina Chronicle of Dr. Francis Le Jau, 1706–1717.* 1956. Reprint, Millwood, N.Y.: Kraus, 1980.

Linder, Suzanne Cameron. *Anglican Churches in Colonial South Carolina: Their History and Architecture.* Charleston, S.C.: Wyrick, 2000.

St. James Santee Parish. The parish of St. James Santee was established on April 9, 1706, and included the northeastern portions of modern Berkeley and Charleston Counties. The earliest Europeans to settle along the southern bank of the lower Santee River were Huguenots attracted to South Carolina in the 1680s by the promise of religious and political freedom. Although the exact date is unknown, the Huguenots built their first church, a small frame structure overlooking the river, shortly after arriving, and by 1699 it contained 111 members. In 1706 a village called Jamestown was laid out around the church, and that same year the one hundred French families and sixty English families living in the vicinity successfully petitioned the assembly for parish status. Unlike Jamestown, which never prospered and soon disappeared, the church was able to persevere despite circumstances that one early rector described as "very strange." Because of the language barrier within the congregation, for decades St. James Santee required a minister who could "Preach to the French in French and ye English in English." The present church, located near McClellanville, was the fourth to serve the parish. Built in 1768, it is known locally as "The Brick Church."

Early experiments with silk, grapes, and olives were unsuccessful, but in the eighteenth century rice and indigo "poured streams of wealth into the pockets of the French planters." With the abolition of the parish system in 1865, St. James Santee Parish became part of Berkeley County. MATTHEW A. LOCKHART

Bridges, Anne Baker Leland, and Roy Williams III. *St. James Santee, Plantation Parish: History and Records, 1685–1925.* Spartanburg, S.C.: Reprint Company, 1997.

Hirsch, Arthur Henry. *The Huguenots of Colonial South Carolina.* 1928. Reprint, Columbia: University of South Carolina Press, 1999.

Linder, Suzanne Cameron. *Anglican Churches in Colonial South Carolina: Their History and Architecture.* Charleston, S.C.: Wyrick, 2000.

St. John's Berkeley Parish. One of the ten original parishes created by the Church Act of 1706, the parish of St. John's Berkeley stretched northwestward from the upper reaches of the Cooper River to the Santee River through modern Berkeley and Orangeburg Counties. European settlement began in earnest in the early 1690s when Huguenots who had taken up residence along the lower Santee the previous decade were forced upriver by frequent floods. They were soon joined by English, Irish, and Barbadian settlers following the Cooper up from Charleston. In 1705, just prior to becoming a parish, St. John's had an approximate population of 315 whites and 180 blacks. By 1720 those numbers had increased to 437 and 1,439, respectively. The explosion in the parish's black population corresponded to a general shift in South Carolina from growing rice in dry, upland fields to cultivating it in freshwater inland swamps, of which St. John's had an abundance. African slave laborers were imported to clear, dike, and cultivate the swamps, and rice became the "Source of infinite Wealth" for local planters.

The parish church of St. John's Berkeley, called Biggin Church, was erected in 1712 on Biggin Swamp near modern Moncks Corner. The church burned twice in the eighteenth century and was restored. Burned again in a forest fire ca. 1886, it stands as a brick ruin. With the abolition of the parish system in 1865, St. John's Berkeley Parish became part of Berkeley County. MATTHEW A. LOCKHART

Linder, Suzanne Cameron. *Anglican Churches in Colonial South Carolina: Their History and Architecture.* Charleston, S.C.: Wyrick, 2000.

Terry, George D. "'Champaign Country': A Social History of an Eighteenth Century Lowcountry Parish in South Carolina, St. Johns Berkeley County." Ph.D. diss., University of South Carolina, 1981.

St. John's Colleton Parish. Previously a part of St. Paul's Parish, St. John's Colleton Parish was established by the South Carolina Commons House of Assembly on April 9, 1734. The new parish consisted of Johns, Wadmalaw, Edisto, Seabrook, and Kiawah Islands. The population grew as wealthy planters from the Charleston area looked to expand their agricultural interests, prompting the establishment of the new parish. The parish church, completed in 1742, was on Johns Island overlooking Bohicket Creek and the Wadmalaw River.

Indigo and rice were the cash crops that brought great wealth to the planters of St. John's Colleton during the colonial period. Johns and Wadmalaw Islands, with their access to freshwater, contained most of the rice plantations, while indigo was grown profitably on all of the islands in the parish. After the Revolutionary War, indigo was replaced by Sea Island cotton, and by 1849 cotton was grown on almost all of the 104 plantations in the parish.

The planters of St. John's Colleton bought large numbers of African slaves to work their plantations. The 1790 census found 600 whites, 4,660 slaves, and 40 free blacks living in the parish. Of the white households, ninety-five percent owned slaves. Due to increased investment in human property and natural increase, the number of slaves more than doubled in the sixty years between 1790 and 1850. The 1850 census recorded 10,332 slaves for an average of seventy-five per white household. The parish system was abolished in 1865 when a new state constitution was adopted, and St. John's Colleton Parish was subsequently incorporated into Charleston County. MICHAEL S. REYNOLDS

Jordan, Laylon Wayne, and Elizabeth Stringfellow. *A Place Called St. John's.* Spartanburg, S.C.: Reprint Company, 1998.

St. Luke's Parish. The South Carolina Commons House of Assembly passed an act creating St. Luke's Parish from St. Helena's Parish on May 23, 1767. The new parish, located in modern Beaufort and Jasper Counties, included the mainland region between the New and Broad Rivers, known as Euhaws, and Hilton Head Island. The British Board of Trade disallowed the act creating St. Luke's in 1772. After the Revolutionary War the parish was reestablished, and the Church of the Holy Trinity at Grahamville was completed about 1786.

During the colonial period, indigo was the major crop on Hilton Head Island and the lower mainland portion of the parish, while rice plantations became increasingly profitable in the upper section along the New and Coosawhatchie Rivers. In the 1790s Sea Island cotton replaced indigo as the major staple grown in the lower part of St. Luke's, while rice cultivation continued to expand in the upper part. African American slaves dominated the parish demographically for most of the colonial and all of the antebellum period. In 1850 slaves made up over eighty-three percent of the parish population.

Antebellum planters in St. Luke's Parish were in the vanguard of political radicalism in the state. The 1844 Bluffton Movement was initiated in the parish town of the same name, and the region was a hotbed of secession sentiment in the 1850s and 1860. After the parish system was abolished by the new state constitution adopted in 1865, St. Luke's Parish was incorporated into Beaufort District. MICHAEL S. REYNOLDS

Linder, Suzanne Cameron. *Anglican Churches in Colonial South Carolina: Their History and Architecture.* Charleston, S.C.: Wyrick, 2000.

Rowland, Lawrence S., Alexander Moore, and George C. Rogers. *The History of Beaufort County, South Carolina.* Vol. 1, *1514–1861.* Columbia: University of South Carolina Press, 1996.

St. Mark's Parish. South Carolina's first backcountry parish and by far its largest in land area, St. Mark's was established on May 21, 1757, and included the entire country between the Great Pee Dee and Santee Rivers from the modern Clarendon-Williamsburg county line northward to North Carolina and westward as far "as it shall be inhabited by his Majesty's subjects." The parish was originally a part of the even more vast and vaguely defined parish of Prince George Winyah, and coastal planters, mainly English and Huguenots, started moving into the eastern extent of what later became St. Mark's in the 1730s. In 1734 they secured the organization of the expansive inland portion of Prince George as Prince Frederick's Parish. Around 1750 a second, more substantial wave of settlers, mostly Scots-Irish from Virginia and Pennsylvania, began to pour into the back parts of the parish. The tide of western immigration was so great that within a few years the old planters of Prince Frederick's found themselves being outvoted by the frontiersmen. Therefore, when St. Mark's Parish was created in 1757 and was granted two representatives of its own, it was as much to protect established lowcountry interests as to promote those of the emerging backcountry.

St. Mark's has been served by four churches. All of them, including the present edifice near Pinewood, which was completed in 1855, have been located in the extreme southeastern corner of the parish. St. Mark's Parish lost its status as an election district in 1785 and was divided into eleven counties. MATTHEW A. LOCKHART

Burgess, James M. *Chronicles of St. Mark's Parish, Santee Circuit and Williamsburg Township, South Carolina, 1731–1885.* 1888. Reprint, Greenville, S.C.: Southern Historical Press, 1991.

Linder, Suzanne Cameron. *Anglican Churches in Colonial South Carolina: Their History and Architecture.* Charleston, S.C.: Wyrick, 2000.

Woodmason, Charles. *The Carolina Backcountry on the Eve of the Revolution: The Journal and Other Writings of Charles Woodmason, Anglican Itinerant.* Edited by Richard J. Hooker. Chapel Hill: University of North Carolina Press, 1953.

St. Matthew's Parish. Comprising the southern and eastern portions of modern Calhoun and Orangeburg Counties, St. Matthew's Parish was established on April 12, 1768, in what was then the South Carolina backcountry. European settlement of the area began in the 1730s when the colonial government created two abutting frontier townships, Orangeburg and Amelia, between the North Edisto and Santee Rivers. German immigrants rapidly peopled the townships and in 1748 petitioned the assembly for parish status, but it was not until the 1760s, when large indigo planters of English stock began arriving from the coast, that the request finally caught the ear of the legislature.

On August 9, 1765, the assembly joined Orangeburg and Amelia to form St. Matthew's, allowing the new parish two representatives. A small, wooden parish church was built on Halfway Swamp near present Lone Star in Calhoun County that same year. However, King George III contended that only he could change the size of colonial legislatures and disallowed the parish in 1767. Due in part to the agitation of the Regulators, the assembly reestablished St. Matthew's in 1768, this time circumventing royal displeasure by granting it one representative taken from the lowcountry parish of St. James Goose Creek.

The original church building was the first of four to serve the parish, each on a different site. The present St. Matthew's Episcopal Church at Fort Motte was built in 1852. With the abolition of the parish system in 1865, St. Matthew's Parish became part of Orangeburg County. MATTHEW A. LOCKHART

Culler, Daniel Marchant. *Orangeburgh District, 1768–1868: History and Records.* Spartanburg, S.C.: Reprint Company, 1995.

Linder, Suzanne Cameron. *Anglican Churches in Colonial South Carolina: Their History and Architecture.* Charleston, S.C.: Wyrick, 2000.

Salley, A. S., ed. *Minutes of the Vestry of St. Matthew's Parish, South Carolina, 1767–1838.* Columbia, S.C.: State Company, 1939.

St. Michael's Church (Charleston). In 1751 the General Assembly divided Charleston into two Anglican parishes and authorized construction of a new church on the southeast corner of Broad and Meeting Streets, at the center of the civic square platted on the Grand Modell plan of the 1680s and opposite the site selected for the colony's first statehouse. Royal governor James Glenn laid the cornerstone in February 1752. The exterior was largely complete by 1756, and the church opened for services in 1761. Modern historians consider St. Michael's Church to be one of the most sophisticated ecclesiastical buildings erected in the American colonies.

The design of St. Michael's was influenced by contemporary English churches and is reminiscent of the London designs of Sir Christopher Wren and James Gibbs, but it cannot be definitively attributed to a single source or an architect. Samuel Cardy, an Irish builder, oversaw construction. The church is built of brick finished in stucco and fronted by a monumental portico. Its dominant feature is a 186-foot steeple that rises from a rusticated base in three octagonal sections before tapering to a peak, where it is surmounted by a weather vane with a gilt ball. Tuscan pilasters and arched windows with rusticated surrounds run the length of the side elevations. The congregation hall is richly ornamented. Suspended from a pendant in the center of the cove ceiling is a forty-two-light brass chandelier imported from England in 1803. The case of the original Snetzler organ, which was installed in 1768, occupies the rear wall of the gallery. The box pews, columns, gallery facings, and soffits are carved from red cedar. Placed on the walls in various locations are marble memorial plaques. The chancel is trimmed with Corinthian pilasters supporting a full entablature with a modillion cornice and foliated frieze moldings. A Tiffany stained glass window modeled on Raphael's painting of St. Michael slaying the dragon is surrounded by eight small plaster columns. The English wrought-iron altar rail was installed in 1772.

The bells of St. Michael's were imported from England in 1764. They were stolen by the British in 1782 and later returned. The church was damaged by Federal shelling during the Civil War. The bells were sent to Columbia for safekeeping but were severely damaged when that city burned in February 1865. After the war they were shipped to the Whitechapel Foundry, the original manufacturer, to be recast.

St. Michael's is one of Charleston's most enduring landmarks. It has inspired artists and writers for centuries, and its bells are featured in the musical score of the opera *Porgy and Bess.* The church was designated a National Historic Landmark by the U.S. Department of the Interior in 1960. DANIEL J. VIVIAN

Lane, Mills. *Architecture of the Old South: South Carolina.* Savannah, Ga.: Beehive, 1984.

Poston, Jonathan H. *The Buildings of Charleston: A Guide to the City's Architecture.* Columbia: University of South Carolina Press, 1997.

Severens, Kenneth. *Charleston Antebellum Architecture and Civic Destiny.* Knoxville: University of Tennessee Press, 1988.

St. Michael's Parish. On June 14, 1751, the South Carolina Commons House of Assembly passed an act dividing the city of Charleston into two parishes. St. Philip's Parish previously encompassed the entire city, but because of steady growth St. Philip's Church could no longer accommodate the city's Anglican worshipers. The new parish, St. Michael's, included the city of Charleston south of Broad Street. The cornerstone of the parish church was laid on February 17, 1752, at the corner of Broad and Meeting Streets, and construction was completed nine years later. The new church, boasting a 185-foot steeple with a clock and bells, continued to be a landmark in downtown Charleston at the beginning of the twenty-first century.

Charleston was the capital of South Carolina until 1790 and was the cultural and social center for the people of the surrounding parishes. Many planters had homes in the city, living in Charleston during the social season and during the summer when their country homes were deemed too unhealthy for habitation. Charleston was also a major port, shipping rice and cotton grown throughout the state to the North and to Europe.

A census taken in the city in 1848 recorded 26,451 residents, of whom 1,492 were free blacks and 10,772 were slaves. Unlike the other lowcountry parishes, St. Michael's and St. Philip's Parishes were combined for the purpose of electing the city's delegation to the General Assembly, and they jointly elected two senators since each parish and district was allotted one delegate to the state Senate. After the parish system was abolished by the constitution of 1865, St. Michael's Parish was incorporated into Charleston District. MICHAEL S. REYNOLDS

Fraser, Walter J., Jr. *Charleston! Charleston!: The History of a Southern City.* Columbia: University of South Carolina Press, 1989.

Linder, Suzanne Cameron. *Anglican Churches in Colonial South Carolina: Their History and Architecture.* Charleston, S.C.: Wyrick, 2000.

St. Paul's Parish. St. Paul's Parish was one of the original ten parishes created in South Carolina by the Church Act of 1706. The parish included a mainland region between the South Edisto and Stono Rivers as well as the adjacent Sea Islands. However as the population of the parish grew, the Sea Islands were separated from St. Paul's in 1734 and became St. John's Colleton Parish. The parish church was completed in November 1707 near the south branch of the Stono River but was relocated further inland in 1737.

Rice and indigo production dominated St. Paul's during the colonial period, bringing large numbers of African slaves to work parish plantations. By 1720 the parish contained 1,634 slaves, over sixty percent of the population. The Stono Rebellion, the most successful slave uprising in the state's history, began in St. Paul's Parish on September 9, 1739, and was suppressed only after about twenty white and black colonists had been killed.

After the Revolutionary War, Sea Island cotton replaced indigo as a staple crop in the parish, and rice cultivation continued to flourish. In Colleton District, which included St. Paul's and the surrounding parishes, slaves made up over eighty percent of the population by 1820. The planters of St. Paul's Parish were vocal supporters of states' rights during the antebellum period and overwhelmingly backed secession in 1860. The parish system was abolished by the state constitution of 1865, and St. Paul's Parish was incorporated into Colleton District. MICHAEL S. REYNOLDS

Linder, Suzanne Cameron. *Anglican Churches in Colonial South Carolina: Their History and Architecture.* Charleston, S.C.: Wyrick, 2000.

———. *Historical Atlas of the Rice Plantations of the ACE River Basin—1860.* Columbia: South Carolina Department of Archives and History, 1995.

Wood, Peter H. *Black Majority: Negroes in Colonial South Carolina from 1670 through the Stono Rebellion.* New York: Knopf, 1974.

St. Peter's Parish. In 1747 the South Carolina Commons House of Assembly established St. Peter's Parish, bounded on the west by the Savannah River and on the east by the New River. The parish, consisting of most of modern Jasper County, was formerly part of St. Helena's Parish. In 1733 a group of Swiss Protestants led by Jean Pierre Purry was granted 24,000 acres along the lower Savannah River. The new immigrants established the town of Purrysburg, and the community initially prospered, prompting the establishment of the new parish. The parish church was located in Purrysburg, and the town served as a way station along the Savannah River.

In the 1760s the fortunes of the people of St. Peter's Parish began to decline, and many of the original Swiss and French inhabitants migrated to Georgia and more settled areas of South Carolina. Before the Revolutionary War, a few wealthy planters established rice plantations along the lower Savannah River, but development in the area expanded greatly in the 1820s, and lower St. Peter's Parish eventually became an important rice-growing region.

Upper St. Peter's Parish was much different from the lower part of St. Peter's. Few large planters resided in the area, and the main crops included short-staple cotton, corn, and sweet potatoes. Nevertheless, the growth of rice plantations in the lower Savannah region swelled the slave population of St. Peter's to 8,999, making it the largest slaveowning parish in Beaufort District. After a new state constitution was adopted in 1865, the parish system was abolished, and St. Peter's Parish was incorporated into Beaufort District. MICHAEL S. REYNOLDS

Linder, Suzanne Cameron. *Anglican Churches in Colonial South Carolina: Their History and Architecture.* Charleston, S.C.: Wyrick, 2000.

McCurry, Stephanie. *Masters of Small Worlds: Yeoman Households, Gender Relations, and the Political Culture of the Antebellum South Carolina Low Country.* New York: Oxford University Press, 1995.

Rowland, Lawrence S., Alexander Moore, and George C. Rogers. *The History of Beaufort County, South Carolina.* Vol. 1, *1514–1861.* Columbia: University of South Carolina Press, 1996.

St. Philip's Church (Charleston). Located at 146 Church Street, St. Philip's was the first English church established in South Carolina. In 1680 Originall and Millicent Jackson, "being excited with a pious zeal," donated four acres of land for a house of worship. Sometime between 1681 and 1692 settlers built a "large and stately" church of black cypress on a brick foundation at the southeast corner of Broad and Meeting Streets, the site originally designated for it in the model of the town. A 1697 deed refers to the church as "St. Philip's." In 1698 the assembly provided a salary of £150 per year and directed that a slave and cows be purchased for the use of the minister. In the same year Afra Coming, widow of John Coming, donated seventeen acres adjoining the town for a glebe (farm) for the minister.

St. Philip's Church. Courtesy, South Carolina Department of Archives and History

In 1704 and 1706 the South Carolina Assembly passed church acts that established the Anglican Church in the colony. Because it was the seat of the commissary (the representative of the bishop of London in South Carolina), St. Philip's was the center of Anglican activity in the colony. Under the leadership of Commissary Gideon Johnston, church members began a new building on Church Street between Queen and Cumberland in 1711. Completed in 1733, the building was of brick and later was covered with stucco. It was in the form of a cross and was crowned by an octagonal tower containing bells, a clock, and a lantern topped by a weather vane. An English writer in 1753 called the new St. Philip's Church building "one of the most regular and complete structures of the kind in America."

The colonial church building burned in 1835, but members replaced it with a similar structure that was completed by 1838. The new St. Philip's Church retained many of the design elements of its predecessor, including its triple Tuscan portico. The prominent steeple, designed by Edward Brickell White, was completed in 1850. The steeple housed a chime of bells and a musical clock that played tunes at three different intervals in each twenty-four hours. The selections were "Welcome Sweet Day of Rest," "Greenland's Icy Mount," and "Home, Sweet Home."

At the beginning of the Civil War, St. Philip's Church donated its bells to the Confederate government to be cast into cannons. During the bombardment of Charleston, shells hit St. Philip's ten times, piercing the roof and destroying the chancel and the organ. Repair work was finally completed in 1877, but the church was heavily damaged again in the 1886 earthquake. By arrangement with the federal government, the steeple served as a beacon to guide ships into the harbor from 1893 to 1915 and again briefly in 1921. Repairs and expansions in the 1920s provided additional space for the choir and organ. A new marble altar and wooden reredos as well as the "All Saints" window by Clement Heaton enhanced the beauty of the interior. The church was designated a National Historic Landmark in 1973. Restored in 1993–1994, St. Philip's has retained its importance as a historical landmark while continuing its ministry with an active congregation. Its churchyard is the burial site for several notable South Carolinians, including John C. Calhoun.
SUZANNE LINDER

Bolton, S. Charles. *Southern Anglicanism: The Church of England in Colonial South Carolina.* Westport, Conn.: Greenwood, 1982.

Linder, Suzanne Cameron. *Anglican Churches in Colonial South Carolina: Their History and Architecture.* Charleston, S.C.: Wyrick, 2000.

Thomas, Albert Sidney. *A Historical Account of the Protestant Episcopal Church in South Carolina, 1820–1957.* Columbia, S.C.: R. L. Bryan, 1957.

St. Philip's Parish. St. Philip's was one of the ten original parishes created by the Church Act of 1706. The parish consisted of the city of Charleston and was served by St. Philip's Church, built between 1683 and 1692, which sat at the corner of Broad and Meeting Streets. The rapid growth of the city made it necessary to build a larger church. The first services held at the new St. Philip's Church on Church Street took place sometime in the mid-1720s. In 1751 the city was divided into two parishes, with everything south of Broad Street in the new parish of St. Michael's. St. Philip's Church burned in February 1835, and the rebuilding project was completed in 1850. The 1850 church continues to serve Charleston's Episcopal worshipers into the twenty-first century.

Charleston was the cultural and social center of the lowcountry, and the city's parishes were the most demographically diverse in the state. Along with the planters, free blacks, and slaves in the city there were also many ethnic Germans and Sephardic Jews who worked in a variety of trades. Nevertheless, Charleston was dominated socially and economically by planters and the businessmen who shipped their staple crops. In 1847 over seventy-four percent of the U.S. rice crop was exported from the city.

St. Philip's and St. Michael's Parishes were combined into one voting district for the purpose of electing the city's legislative delegation, and they jointly elected two senators since each parish and district was allotted one delegate to the state Senate. The parish system was abolished with the adoption of the constitution of 1865, and St. Philip's Parish was incorporated into Charleston District. MICHAEL S. REYNOLDS

Fraser, Walter J., Jr. *Charleston! Charleston! The History of a Southern City.* Columbia: University of South Carolina Press, 1989.

Linder, Suzanne Cameron. *Anglican Churches in Colonial South Carolina: Their History and Architecture.* Charleston, S.C.: Wyrick, 2000.

St. Stephen's Parish. Established on May 11, 1754, St. Stephen's Parish was located on the south side of the Santee River in modern Berkeley County. Huguenots attracted to South Carolina in the 1680s by the promise of religious and political freedom were the earliest Europeans to take up residence along the lower Santee, and in 1706 their settlement centered at Jamestown was erected into the parish of St. James Santee. But the area around Jamestown was given to frequent flooding "that ruined the plantations," and in succeeding decades many families were forced upriver in search of higher ground. The high ground they discovered was ideally suited to indigo cultivation, and soon the French planters were joined by English planters from the coast, who quickly came to predominate. Consequently, the upper part of St. James became known unofficially as "English Santee" and the lower part as "French Santee." The division became official in 1754 when English Santee was organized as St. Stephen's Parish and granted one representative.

A chapel of ease at Echaw in St. James Santee that fell within the new parish became the church of St. Stephen's. The chapel was old and in disrepair, however, and the prosperous indigo planters set out to erect a brick building more suited to their status. The present St. Stephen's Episcopal Church, located in the town of St. Stephen, was completed in 1769. With the abolition of the parish system in 1865, St. Stephen's Parish became part of Berkeley County. MATTHEW A. LOCKHART

Linder, Suzanne Cameron. *Anglican Churches in Colonial South Carolina: Their History and Architecture.* Charleston, S.C.: Wyrick, 2000.

Misenhelter, Jane Searles. *St. Stephen's Episcopal Church, St. Stephen, S.C., Including Church of the Epiphany, Upper St. John's, Berkeley and Chapel of Ease, Pineville, S.C.: History and Registers.* Columbia, S.C.: State Printing, 1977.

St. Thomas and St. Denis Parish. Located on the peninsula formed by the Cooper and Wando Rivers in modern Berkeley County, St. Thomas and St. Denis were two of the ten original parishes created by the Church Act of 1706 and constituted colonial South Carolina's only parish within a parish. Huguenots settled on the neck in the 1680s and constructed a small wooden church in what became known as the French, or Orange, Quarter. English settlers soon followed, took up the surrounding lands, and built their own house of worship. Pompion Hill Chapel on the Cooper River, the oldest Anglican edifice in the colony outside of Charleston, was erected in 1703. Despite speaking different languages and attending different churches, the two "nations" followed the same formula for success. Both parishes became home to slaveholding planters, and by the early eighteenth century both were "much improved in their fortunes."

In 1706 the entire peninsula with its English-speaking majority was organized as St. Thomas Parish, but in order to accommodate the French of Orange Quarter, the parish of St. Denis was established "in ye middle of it." By the mid–eighteenth century intermingling and intermarriage had made the English and French "one and the same people," and St. Thomas and St. Denis officially became one parish in 1784. St. Thomas Episcopal Church, constructed in 1708 near modern Cainhoy, was made the parish church. With the abolition of the parish system in 1865, St. Thomas and St. Denis Parish became part of Berkeley County. MATTHEW A. LOCKHART

Clute, Robert F., ed. *The Annals and Parish Register of St. Thomas and St. Denis Parish, in South Carolina, from 1680 to 1884.* 1884. Reprint, Baltimore: Genealogical Publishing, 1974.

Hirsch, Arthur Henry. *The Huguenots of Colonial South Carolina.* 1928. Reprint, Columbia: University of South Carolina Press, 1999.

Linder, Suzanne Cameron. *Anglican Churches in Colonial South Carolina: Their History and Architecture.* Charleston, S.C.: Wyrick, 2000.

Salkehatchie/Combahee Rivers. The Salkehatchie and Combahee River system extends more than one hundred miles through the southeastern quarter of South Carolina. The Salkehatchie consists of two blackwater river-swamps: the Big Salkehatchie, with headwaters in Barnwell County near Williston; and the Little Salkehatchie, with headwaters near Blackville. The two meet north of Yemassee to form the Combahee River. The Combahee becomes tidal freshwater, brackish water, and then salt as it feeds into the Atlantic Ocean at St. Helena Sound. The Salkehatchie was once known as the "salt ketcher," while the Combahee takes its name from an area Indian group.

The Combahee became an important river in lowcountry rice culture beginning with significant plantation development in the 1730s. The last rice cultivation on the Combahee ended in 1929. However, plantation landholdings remained largely intact and in private hands. Carolinians engaged in timber extraction, turpentine production, and farming along its banks. Commercial shell fishing took place in the brackish and salt parts of the river. After it divides into two branches further inland near Yemassee, the Combahee becomes more of a swamp and is usable only by shallow draft boats.

Through the late nineteenth century little timber harvesting took place along the Salkehatchie because of the difficulty of bringing logs out of the swamp. The first major commercial effort came in the twentieth century with the Big Salkehatchie Cypress Company. This company, formed in Varnville in 1915, logged the old-growth cypress from the Salkehatchie until 1929. Others followed, and the region has subsequently been heavily logged for pine, cypress, and hardwoods. Still, in the early twenty-first century the watershed remained forested and mostly undeveloped. It is home to a wide range of fish, birds, and game animals. JAMES H. TUTEN

Linder, Suzanne Cameron. *Historical Atlas of the Rice Plantations of the ACE River Basin—1860.* Columbia: South Carolina Department of Archives and History, 1995.

Williams, Rose-Marie Eltzroth. *Railroads and Sawmills, Varnville, S.C., 1872–1997: The Making of a Low Country Town in the New South.* Varnville, S.C.: Varnville Community Council, 1998.

Salley, Alexander Samuel (1871–1961). Historian. Alexander Samuel Salley, son of Alexander McQueen Salley and Sallie McMichael, was born on June 16, 1871, on his father's plantation in Orangeburg County. He attended primary schools in Orangeburg and, from 1881 to 1887, Sheridan's Classical School in the same city. He entered the Citadel in Charleston on October 1, 1887, and graduated from that institution on July 8, 1892. Late in 1892 Salley undertook the study of law, gaining admission to the South Carolina Bar in 1899. While studying law, he worked for the editorial department of the Charleston *News and Courier.* Fascinated by history, he also investigated local records and other primary sources, preparing his first monograph based on research in 1897. From that time forward he wrote continuously on South Carolina historical topics, producing countless articles and over one hundred monographs.

On October 1, 1899, Salley assumed the position of secretary, treasurer, and librarian at the South Carolina Historical Society in Charleston, a private organization concerned with the preservation of the state's past. Simultaneously, the discovery in the State House of Revolutionary War records previously believed to be lost spurred Salley to advocate their preservation. His Sunday *News and Courier* articles included all sorts of historical matters, as well as plans for the custody and care of the newly found State House records. A South Carolina Historical Society–sponsored bill six years later passed the General Assembly, creating the funding and a full-time secretary for the previously nonfunded, functionless State Historical Commission and legislatively making the agency responsible for all state public records. Salley began as that secretary on April 1, 1905. For the next forty-five years Salley organized, filed, and wrote about South Carolina's documentary heritage, the beginning of what is now the South Carolina Department of Archives and History. A pioneer in the nationwide archives movement, he was renowned for being a source of information that assisted scholars and citizens. Salley's lasting contribution to South Carolina is the state's rich historical traditions preserved in her priceless documents.

Salley died on February 19, 1961, and was buried at Sunnyside Cemetery in Orangeburg. He was survived by his wife, Harriet Gresham Milledge, whom he had married on July 11, 1918. ROBERTA V. H. COPP

Salley, Eulalie Chafee (1883–1975). Suffragist, realtor. Salley was born in Augusta, Georgia, on December 11, 1883, the daughter of Marguerite Eulalie Gamble and George Kinloch Chafee. Her father was in the kaolin (porcelain clay) business, and her mother was an accomplished pianist and product of one of Baltimore's finest finishing schools. Salley spent an enjoyable but sickly youth, often with rheumatic fever, on her maternal grandparents' plantation in Louisville, Georgia, before moving to Aiken in 1892. Her economic status and social class insured schooling by governesses, private tutors, and a year each at Mary Baldwin College in Virginia and at Converse College in Spartanburg, South Carolina. In 1906 she married the prominent lawyer Julian Booth Salley, then mayor of Aiken. She then bore two children and appeared headed for the life of a traditional southern lady.

Salley's interest in women's rights was sparked by the plight of Lucy Dugas Tillman, granddaughter of Lucy Pickens and wife of Ben Tillman, Jr., son of the prominent South Carolina senator. During Lucy's illness, her husband had her two children deeded away to his mother. When she recovered, Lucy spent virtually everything she had in an unsuccessful bid to regain them in a case that called attention to women's legal inequities.

Eulalie Chafee Salley. Courtesy, Sara S. Wood, Aiken, S.C.

Salley soon immersed herself in the woman suffrage movement. Claiming that it was "the best dollar I ever spent," she responded to a newspaper advertisement to join the South Carolina Equal Suffrage League (SCESL). Salley then got five women together around 1912 and organized the Aiken County Equal Suffrage League, serving as its first president. Salley was an aggressive and innovative suffrage campaigner, traveling on unpaved county roads to canvass door-to-door, staging a myriad of fund-raisers (she once took boxing lessons and performed in a prizefight as a "Gold Dust Twin"), and riding in an airplane with a pilot scattering suffrage pamphlets over the town. Some, including her husband, regarded her actions as scandalous. Salley knew firsthand and greatly admired Carrie Chapman Catt and Anna Howard Shaw, leaders of the National American Woman Suffrage Association, and she had little regard for the "unladylike" militant wing of the movement. In 1919 Salley became SCESL president. Once suffrage was achieved, she joined in the formation of the South Carolina League of Women Voters (later serving as regional vice president), and she worked tirelessly to achieve its goal of ending discrimination against women. Salley was invited to stand behind the governor when he finally signed the Nineteenth Amendment into law in the state in 1969. Scolding Democrats by pointing out that it took a Republican senator to insure that the amendment was finally approved in South Carolina, the eighty-five-year-old Eulalie Salley remarked: "Boys, I've been waiting 50 years to tell you what I think of you."

To fund her suffrage work, Salley applied for and received a real estate license in 1915, becoming the first woman realtor in the state and launching a career that helped put Aiken on the map and made her something of a legend. Her style of real estate catered to the needs of the growing numbers of wealthy people who came south for the winter between the two world wars. Clients found flowers in full bloom, well-trained servants, and a Salley-owned antique shop from which to furnish spacious "cottages," with meals awaiting them on their arrival—all dovetailing with her slogan, "We do everything but brush your teeth." In addition to selling at one time or another virtually "every large piece of property in Aiken," Salley maintained an office in Beaufort and sold numerous large hunting preserves in the lowcountry. She knew personally many of the wealthy and famous who seasonally visited. Salley was among the founders of the Aiken Board of Realtors, vice president of the South Carolina Association of Real Estate Boards, and in 1959 was chosen the "First Lady of South Carolina Realtors." Eulalie Salley and Company continued to thrive as a successful real estate company in Aiken after her death.

Long enamored with the life, beauty, and stories of Lucy Pickens, and disturbed at finding the historic Pickens house, Edgewood (near Edgefield), falling into disrepair, Salley impulsively purchased it. During the Great Depression it was moved piece by piece to Salley's grandfather's first homesite in Aiken and remained the Salley home until their deaths. Salley died on March 8, 1975, after a short bout with cancer. Ever the individualist, South Carolina's "First Lady of Real Estate" insisted on burial, not with her husband, but in a "second-hand section" of St. Thaddeus Episcopal Cemetery, with only a single white camellia to mark her remains. SIDNEY R. BLAND

Bull, Emily L. *Eulalie.* Aiken, S.C.: Kalmia, 1973.

"Mrs. Salley, Leader of Suffrage, Dies." *Aiken Standard,* March 10, 1975, p. 1.
Salley, Eulalie Chafee. Interview by Constance B. Myers. Tape recording. Winthrop University Archives, Rock Hill, South Carolina.
———. Papers. South Caroliniana Library, University of South Carolina, Columbia.

Saluda (Saluda County; 2000 pop. 3,066). In 1895 the ordinance that created Saluda County mandated that voters choose a site for the county seat "within three miles of the geographical centre of the County." Three communities vied for the seat. After much controversy, voters chose Red Bank, where Mine Creek and Red Bank Creek converge to form Little Saluda River. Trees were removed and streets and lots laid out. Town limits extended one-half mile in each direction from the courthouse. On July 28, 1896, the cornerstone was laid for the courthouse, and the first town lots sold shortly thereafter. By late 1896 a dispensary, drug store, and general store had been built. After the town was incorporated in 1897, officers were elected, the first court session was held, two hotels opened, and country people moved to town or came for business. The town had a newspaper (the *Saluda Sentinel*), two churches, five attorneys, two doctors, and a dentist. By 1912 the population topped eight hundred and the economy was booming. The town had a railroad, a dozen stores, the three-story Able Building, two banks, two hotels, three lumber mills, two brick plants, cotton gins, a newspaper, three churches, two livery stables, two drugstores, many private homes, and a school that offered a high school diploma. In 1918 the town dedicated a new courthouse to replace the original structure.

In the 1920s the boll weevil, deflation, droughts, and floods weakened Saluda's cotton-based economy. In the 1930s prices continued to drop, jobs were scarce, and banks failed. However, during the same period a sewing plant and a hosiery mill opened and were among the first employers in town to offer jobs to women. In addition, streets were paved, water and sewage systems completed, a swimming pool constructed, and a new school built—all with federal funds. Also, the Saluda Theater opened on July 4, 1936. Unfortunately, after the advent of new highways, the train became unprofitable and ceased operation in 1941.

After World War II, Saluda showed signs of new prosperity. In the 1950s many new businesses opened and additional garment manufacturers arrived. In 1966 the textile giant Deering Millikin built its Saluda plant, and South Carolina Helicopters, with its heliport in town, became a leader in helicopter flight training. New school buildings accommodated all students in Saluda School District One, and in 1970 black and white schools merged.

At the end of the twentieth century, businesses still lined Main and Church Streets and were elsewhere throughout the town. When new high school and middle school facilities opened in 2001, older buildings served elementary students. In the past, few tourists visited Saluda, but the restored Saluda Theater and a museum—both on the courthouse square—began to attract visitors. In 2000 Saluda faced challenges to meet the needs of all its citizens—African American, white, and Hispanic. With the influx of Hispanics working in the county's poultry industry, the Saluda population increased from 2,831 in 1990 to 3,234 in 1998, and Spanish was heard on the streets and taught in the schools. BELA P. HERLONG

Herlong, Bela, ed. *Scraps of Interesting History and Other Writings: From the Papers of Benjamin West Crouch.* Saluda, S.C.: Saluda County Historical Society, 1996.
Herlong, Bela, and Gloria Caldwell, eds. *Breaking New Ground: A Pictorial History of Saluda County.* Saluda, S.C.: Saluda County Centennial Commission, 1995.

Saluda County (452 sq. miles; 2000 pop. 19,181). Saluda County, created in 1895 by an ordinance of the South Carolina Constitutional Convention, encompasses 288,877 acres in west-central South Carolina. It is bordered by Lexington, Aiken, Edgefield, McCormick, Newberry, and Greenwood Counties. Big Saluda River flows along the northern edge, where it is joined by the Little Saluda River a few miles above the Lexington County line. In 1929, when Lake Murray was created, Saluda County gained one hundred miles of shoreline and found 5,120 acres of its territory underwater.

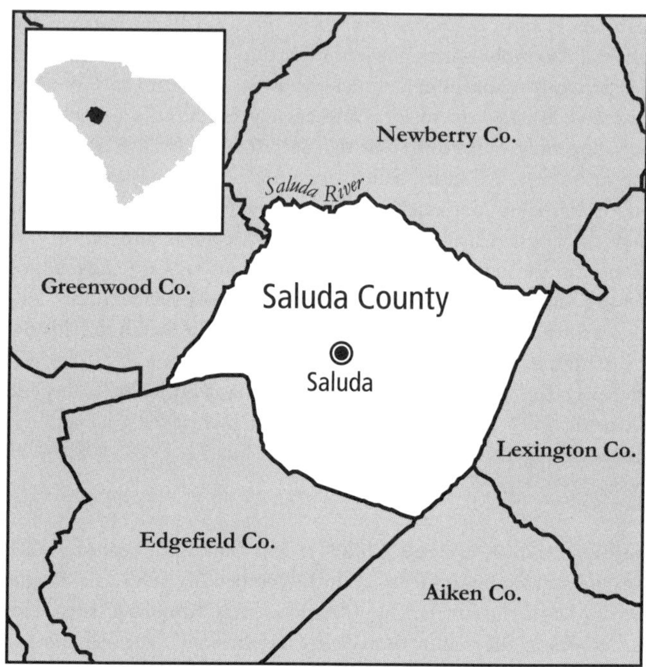

The county was once part of Ninety Six District, then of Edgefield District, and finally of Edgefield County and therefore shares its early history with these entities. After the 1755 Saluda Old Town Treaty brought peace with the Indians, settlers from Pennsylvania and Virginia came to the Carolina backcountry. According to Benjamin W. Crouch, the "Father of Saluda County," the first settlers to the Saluda area were the "Cavalier, the Scots-Irish, and the Dutch. The Dutch element predominates in the Delmar section—formerly called Germanville. The Cavalier and Scots-Irish in the other parts of the county." State and national leaders from the Saluda side of Edgefield District included General William Butler of Revolutionary War fame; Andrew P. Butler, judge and U.S. senator; Pierce M. Butler, governor and colonel of the Palmetto Regiment; Milledge Luke Bonham, general and governor, and the Alamo martyrs James Butler Bonham and William Barret Travis.

Agriculture has historically dominated the economy of Saluda County, which has soil consisting of deep, well-drained loams and clays with sand along the "Ridge" section. Hills are low and easily adapted to cultivation. Abundant rainfall enabled early settlers to grow a variety of crops. They also raised livestock on the native grasses flourishing in the mild climate, which has a year-round average of sixty-two degrees. With the introduction of the cotton gin at the end of the eighteenth century, cotton quickly became the dominant crop. African American slaves came into the area along with whites, who purchased more slaves as cotton production increased. By 1860 more than forty-six percent of household heads in Edgefield District owned slaves, with surviving records showing that white farmers on the Saluda side shared in the antebellum prosperity as well. Between the Civil War and the creation of Saluda County, the effects of war, emancipation, and Reconstruction altered the economic and social order and brought great changes. Cotton was still the most important crop, but with a sharecropping system in place to provide land, capital, and labor.

With the creation of Saluda County in 1895, Red Bank became the site of Saluda, the county seat. County officers were elected, and on December 1, 1896, the county began functioning as a legal entity. Three towns were already present: Ridge Spring, Ward, and Monetta (part of which lay in Aiken County).

In the 1900 census Saluda County had a population of 18,966, with 46.5 percent whites and 53.5 percent African Americans. By 1920 the population had grown to 22,088. Then, in the 1920s, the destruction of cotton crops by the boll weevil led to the migration of African Americans to northern cities. By 1970 the population had decreased to 14,528. In 1990 it had risen to 16,357, but with whites now comprising two-thirds of the county population. In the 1990s the county gained about nine hundred Hispanics, who worked in the poultry industry.

In 1902 the county's dual school system had more than thirty school districts, with forty-nine buildings for whites and forty-eight for African Americans. There were 2,563 white and 2,825 African American students in 1907. The one- and two-teacher country schools ran for five or six months during the year. By 1912 the county had two accredited high schools. In the 1950s country schools were closed and students were transported to town schools. At this time one section of the county became a part of Lexington District Three and another became a part of Aiken County Schools. In 2000 only the 2,300 students living in Saluda School District One attended school within the county. In 1970 Saluda School District One schools were integrated, and after 1972, when the African American Hollywood High School was closed, all high school students in the district attended Saluda High School. New facilities for all Saluda middle and high schools students opened in 2001. One private school, King Academy, has operated since the 1970s. In 1998 Piedmont Technical College opened a center in Saluda County to provide technical and core courses for local students.

At the end of the twentieth century, agriculture still dominated the Saluda County economy, but cotton was replaced by the poultry industry, cattle farms, dairy production, and tree farming in most of the county, and there were peach orchards along the "Ridge." In 1998 Saluda County ranked ninth in the state in sales of agricultural products, third in livestock, and nineteenth in timber sales. That same year found 271 business establishments in the county. Amick Farms, a poultry producer, had the most employees with 1,100, followed by Knight Industries, a textile firm, with 730. Also in 1998, however, 4,790 Saluda residents commuted to jobs outside the county, and median household income in Saluda County lagged considerably behind the state average.

Despite such statistics, Saluda County remained optimistic about its economic future at the end of the twentieth century. In the early 1990s the county established an industrial park and built new law enforcement facilities. County officials likewise sought funding to complete a proposed four-lane highway from Columbia to Greenwood to improve Saluda's access to outside markets. Recognition of the county's cultural resources has led to the preservation of county landmarks and the establishment of a museum. The Economic Development Board and the Chamber of Commerce actively promoted the county's unique assets in an attempt to attract industry, tourists, and retirees. With recent improvements in county water and sewer service, new schools, the county industrial park, opportunities for recreation, and emphasis on education and cultural resources, Saluda County joined others in South Carolina in building on its past to enhance its future. BELA P. HERLONG

Herlong, Bela, ed. *Scraps of Interesting History and Other Writings from the Papers of Benjamin West Crouch.* Saluda, S.C.: Saluda County Historical Society, 1996.

Herlong, Bela, and Gloria Caldwell, eds. *Breaking New Ground: A Pictorial History of Saluda County.* Saluda, S.C.: Saluda County Centennial Commission, 1995.

Saluda County Planning Commission. *Saluda County New Millennium Plan.* Saluda, S.C.: Saluda County Planning Commission, 1999.

Saluda River. In the Blue Ridge Mountains of Greenville County near the North Carolina / South Carolina state line, the North and South Saluda Rivers meet to form the Saluda River. Its major tributaries are the Reedy, Little, Bush, and Little Saluda Rivers and Rabon Creek. One of the principal rivers of the Santee River Basin, the Saluda River flows southeasterly 170 miles through the Piedmont, joining the Broad River just below the fall line in Columbia to form the Congaree River.

The native settlers were primarily Cherokees who farmed along the river and named it "river of corn." Along the west side of the Saluda River was one of the tribe's major trading paths. In the 1700s European settlers, primarily Germans, began to settle along the Saluda River. Because transportation on the river was difficult due to the rock outcrops and rapids at the fall line, the state legislature appropriated funds in the early 1800s for improving roads and building canals.

Of the eight canals planned, two were constructed on the Saluda River, enabling cotton from the backcountry to be transported to Charleston. The largest cotton mill in the state, the Saluda Factory, was built on the river in the 1830s. In order to meet the demand for hydroelectricity in the 1930s and 1940s, dams and hydroelectric facilities were built creating Lake Greenwood and Lake Murray.

The Saluda River offers industrial, commercial, residential, and recreational activities. Two sections of the Saluda River have become part of South Carolina's Scenic Rivers Programs: Middle Saluda was designated a Natural River on August 14, 1978; and Lower Saluda was designated a State Scenic River on August 31, 1991. MICHELINE BROWN

Lower Saluda River Task Force. *The Lower Saluda River Corridor Plan.* Columbia: South Carolina Water Resources Commission, South Carolina Department of Parks, Recreation and Tourism, 1990.

Salvador, Francis (ca. 1747–1776). Legislator, patriot. Salvador was born in London, son of the wealthy merchant Jacob Salvador. Members of the prominent Sephardic Salvador family left Portugal in the late seventeenth century after the Inquisition, settling first in Holland and then in England, where they became one of the country's wealthiest Jewish families. After he had been educated on the Continent, the family lost its fortune with the failure of the Dutch East India Company. The family coat of arms is in the possession of the College of Charleston.

Salvador came to South Carolina in an attempt to restore the family fortune, arriving in Charleston on December 6, 1773. His indigo plantation in Ninety Six District along Coronaca Creek, known as Corn Acre, was the remnant of more than 200,000 acres that had been acquired earlier by his uncle and father-in-law, Joseph Salvador. That property covered more than half of present-day Greenwood County and until the 1920s was often called "Jews

Lands." He acquired roughly thirty slaves and with his social polish quickly made friends and won acceptance among the leading planters in this upcountry region.

In the events leading to the Revolutionary War, Salvador quickly identified with the patriot cause. Its leaders, impressed with his education and ability, accepted him into their ranks. Slightly over a year after arriving in Charleston, he was elected on December 19, 1774, to the First Provincial Congress of South Carolina, along with Patrick Calhoun and eight other representatives from Ninety Six District. Salvador was the first person of the Jewish faith elected to the South Carolina legislature, while the Jewish historian Barnett Elzas claimed that he was "the first Jew in America to represent the masses in a popular assembly."

Salvador served on important committees for the First and Second Provincial Congresses and for South Carolina's first General Assembly. On August 1, 1776, he died during an official mission aimed at consolidating backcountry support. A force of Cherokee Indians and Loyalists ambushed his unit at night. Salvador died after being shot and scalped. His death three weeks after the signing of the Declaration of Independence made him the first Jew to die for the patriot cause. Chief Justice William Henry Drayton of the South Carolina Supreme Court wrote in his memoirs that Salvador's death "excited universal regret. . . . His manners were those of a polished gentleman." In 1950 a plaque in Charleston's City Hall Park was dedicated to his memory. JACK BASS

Elzas, Barnett A. *The Jews of South Carolina from the Earliest Times to the Present Day.* 1905. Reprint, Spartanburg, S.C.: Reprint Company, 1972.

Herd, E. Don, Jr. *The South Carolina Upcountry: Historical and Biographical Sketches.* Vol. 1. Greenwood, S.C.: Attic Press, 1981.

Sampson. Slave, medical practitioner. Although little is known about him, Sampson was a healer of some renown in colonial South Carolina, with an apparent specialty in curing those who had been poisoned. Reports circulated that he frequently went about with rattlesnakes on his person, placing them in his pockets, against his chest, or even in his mouth without being bitten. To demonstrate the effectiveness of his snakebite remedies, however, "he several Times suffered himself to be bitten by the most venomous Snakes" and then cured himself with his own herbal concoctions.

In January 1754 the Commons House of Assembly appointed a committee to investigate "the most effectual way to procure . . . a Cure for the Bite of Rattle Snakes from Sampson, a Negro fellow belonging to Mr. Robert Hume." Several days later the committee reported that Sampson had successfully treated "several Negroes at different times, for many Years past" and were assured that "he has always had good success in such Cures, and have not heard he ever failed in such Attempts." In addition, some slaveowners testified that "their Negroes have been perfectly cured by the said Sampson." Deeming the discovery of a snakebite cure to be "a General benefit to Mankind," the committee recommended that Sampson be freed and given an annual allowance in exchange for "the Cure of such Bites." When committee members were satisfied with the effectiveness of his treatment, Sampson was freed by the Commons House in 1755 and awarded an annual annuity of £50 Currency. His master was paid £300 in compensation for Sampson's manumission. The cure was ordered to be printed in the *South-Carolina Gazette* and appeared there on April 8, 1756.

Colonial South Carolinians greatly feared the rattlesnake, and poisoning in general, and the lack of effective treatments had only magnified their anxiety. Such uneasiness helps explain the generosity of the Commons House toward slave healers such as Sampson and his contemporary Caesar, a fellow slave healer who had been freed several years earlier in exchange for his poison and snakebite cures. Sampson's cure differed somewhat from Caesar's in composition but not in efficacy: "Take *Heart Snake-Root,* both Root and Leaves, two Handfuls, *Polipody* Leaves, one Handful, bruise them in a Mortar, press out a Spoonful of the Juice, and give it as soon as possible after the Bite; scarify the Wound, and take the Root of the Herb *Avens,* bruise it, pour a little Rum over it, and apply to the Part, over which is to be put the Heart Snake-Root and Polipody, which remains after the Juice is squeezed out. These Medicines and Applications must be repeated according to the Violence of the Symptoms, so as in some dangerous Cases it must be given to the Quantity of eight Spoonfuls in an Hour, and the Wound dressed two or three Times in a Day." VENNIE DEAS-MOORE

Lipscomb, Terry W., ed. *The Journal of the Commons House of Assembly.* Vol. 12, *November 21, 1752–September 6, 1754.* Columbia: University of South Carolina Press, 1983.

———. *The Journal of the Commons House of Assembly.* Vol. 13, *November 12, 1754–September 23, 1755.* Columbia: University of South Carolina Press, 1986.

San Miguel de Gualdape. Founded in September 1526 by Lucas Vázquez de Ayllón, San Miguel de Gualdape was the first Spanish town in the territory of the present-day United States. The town's name likely came from its founding on or around September 29, the feast day of St. Michael the Archangel. "Gualdape" appears to refer to the region where the town was located. Scholars place San Miguel at various sites along the coast of present South Carolina and Georgia, but only an archaeological discovery will resolve this debate. San Miguel de Gualdape initially had some six hundred residents, among them sailors, Spanish colonists (including women and children), several priests, and an unknown number of African slaves. The group constructed houses and a church and established the institutions of government there. Supplies in the colony were scarce, due to the loss of the expedition's flagship and its cargo. In these harsh conditions, San Miguel's residents soon began to sicken and die. Ayllón was among those who perished in the town's first weeks. After his death, some of the Spaniards mutinied and imprisoned the town's authorities. The African slaves set fire to the mutiny leader's house, and nearby Indians killed some colonists who attempted to steal their food. By mid-November 1526 the Spaniards had abandoned San Miguel. Of the expedition's initial 600 participants, only 150 survived. Even with these disastrous results, some Europeans could still see the promise this land held. KAREN L. PAAR

Hoffman, Paul E. *A New Andalucia and a Way to the Orient: The American Southeast during the Sixteenth Century.* Baton Rouge: Louisiana State University Press, 1990.

Quattlebaum, Paul. *The Land Called Chicora: The Carolinas under Spanish Rule with French Intrusions, 1520–1670.* Gainesville: University of Florida Press, 1956.

Quinn, David B., ed. *New American World: A Documentary History of North America to 1612.* Vol. 1, *America from Concept to Discovery: Early Exploration of North America.* New York: Arno, 1979.

Sand Hills State Forest. Located in Chesterfield and Darlington Counties, Sand Hills State Forest is characterized by generally arid, infertile, sandy soils. Ninety-two thousand acres of this land were purchased by the federal government in the 1930s as part of the Federal Resettlement Administration's program to move families from worn-out farms to more productive land. Half of this tract became the Carolina Sandhills National Wildlife Refuge, while half was leased to South Carolina for use as a state forest.

Between 1939 and 1991 the South Carolina Forestry Commission managed the 46,000-acre state forest and handled timber practices on the adjacent wildlife refuge as well. Through the early 1940s the Civilian Conservation Corps contributed manpower and expertise to develop the property. In 1991 the Forestry Commission was granted fee-simple title to the forest.

From its outset, Sand Hills State Forest has been operated as "a demonstration conservation area, embodying the principles and objectives of multiple-use management." Part of the long-range goal was to provide local jobs and stimulate local industry through forest production. Throughout the years traditional forest products such as sawlogs, poles, and pulpwood have been harvested from the forest. Other products, including pine tar, turpentine, fence posts, and pine straw, have played important economic roles at various times since 1939.

Sand Hills State Forest has been totally self-supporting since 1967. As was the case with all South Carolina state forests into the early twenty-first century, twenty-five percent of the income generated from Sand Hills was paid to the county school system in lieu of property taxes. SOUTH CAROLINA FORESTRY COMMISSION

Sanders, Dorinda (Sua) Watsee (b. 1934). Farmer, novelist. Dori Sanders was born in Filbert, York County, on June 8, 1934, the eighth of ten children born to Marion Sylvester Sanders, a rural elementary school principal and landowner, and his wife, Cazetta Sylvia Patton. The novelist's middle name reflects the Native American heritage of her paternal grandmother. During her childhood Sanders saw herself as an underachiever in the family but also as its most popular storyteller. Her family's more than two-hundred-acre farm, where fourteen varieties of peaches are grown, is one of the oldest African American–owned farms in York County.

Dori Sanders. © David G. Spielman-97, New Orleans

Sanders attended Fairview Elementary School in Filbert and Roosevelt High School in Clover. For about a year in the early 1950s, she attended community colleges in Prince George's and Montgomery Counties in Maryland. She married in 1956; the marriage did not end officially until 1989. During the winter months she worked, especially when crops had failed, as an associate banquet manager in Camp Springs, near Andrews Air Force Base, and did some of her early writing there. During the growing season she was still helping farm the family land in the early twenty-first century, and in the summer she often helped staff Sanders' Peach Shed, an open-air produce stand on U.S. Highway 321.

After years of farming, Sanders tried writing, but her first literary effort (a Gothic romance about sharecroppers) was considered too melodramatic by Louis D. Rubin, Jr., her later publisher, and was not accepted for publication. Her first published novel, *Clover* (1990), gave a child's-eye view of racial differences in a fictional South Carolina town in the 1980s. When her father dies only hours after his interracial wedding, Clover is left with a white stepmother. The novel shows how stepmother and child are met with resentment by both races, but it also suggests that people can overcome the racial barriers of the rural and small-town South. The perceptive ten-year-old black girl resolves cultural and racial crises in the lives of several people. The lyrical and insightful novel drew rave reviews, stayed on the *Washington Post* best-seller list for ten weeks, and won the coveted Lillian Smith Book Award. Sanders's second novel, *Her Own Place* (1993), has an indomitable African American heroine who is abandoned by her husband, learns about life as a single mother of five, works her own South Carolina farm, and copes with things as they come. Sanders's direct approach to the changing racial and gender situation did not disappoint.

Sanders also published *Dori Sanders' Country Cooking: Recipes and Stories from the Family Stand* (1995), a cookbook and storybook. On Interstate 85 southwest of Charlotte, North Carolina, this book was advertised on a fourteen-foot, hand-painted roadside billboard showing her likeness marketing "Fine Produce and Books." On September 10, 1997, Sanders was awarded the Order of the Palmetto for her creative writing by Governor David Beasley. On the same date a movie version of *Clover* by USA Pictures TV was first aired. JAN NORDBY GRETLUND

Powell, Dannye Romine. *Parting the Curtains: Interviews with Southern Writers.* Winston-Salem, N.C.: John F. Blair, 1994.

Sanders, Dori. "'After Freedom'—Blacks and Whites in the 1990s: The Facts and the Fiction." In *The Southern State of Mind,* edited by Jan Nordby Gretlund. Columbia: University of South Carolina Press, 1999.

Tate, Linda. *A Southern Weave of Women: Fiction of the Contemporary South.* Athens: University of Georgia Press, 1994.

Sandhills. The Sandhills are gently rolling hills that form the uppermost portion of the coastal plain in South Carolina. They continue beyond South Carolina westward into Georgia and northward into Virginia. The Sandhills are composed of discontinuous bands of clay and sand that cut the state diagonally in a northeast to southwest direction, forming approximately twelve percent of the state. The Sandhills lie within many counties, including Richland and Lexington (which form the Columbia metropolitan area), Aiken, Barnwell, Kershaw, Chesterfield, and portions of Bamburg, Orangeburg, Sumter, Lancaster, Marlboro, and Darlington. There are many elevated locations throughout the Sandhills from which to view the rolling terrain, especially along ridges in northeastern Columbia, Edmund in the high dunes in Lexington County, Manchester State Forest in Sumter County, and McBee and Sand Hills State Forest in Chesterfield County.

The name "Sandhills" can be misleading, for the sediments that compose the region include tremendous amounts of clay as well as sand. The underlying geology of the Sandhills begins in some areas with Cretaceous clays that form the lowest visible layers. They are well exposed in sites throughout the region that have been cut by streams and rivers. These clays often have a maroon and pink, mottled color. Where thick beds of Cretaceous clays are accessible, as in

Aiken County, they are often mined. In other portions of the Sandhills the sediments sit directly atop Piedmont rocks, where because the Cretaceous had previously eroded away, they form unconformites. Within the Sandhills many other clay and sand formations of interest to the geologist and hobbyist are found. Some interesting locations include sediments of Paleocene age found in eastern Richland County near Fort Jackson and the sandstones and varieties of sand found at Peachtree Rock in Lexington County near Edmund.

The clay and sands of the Sandhills came from the Blue Ridge and Piedmont Mountains that stood to the north and northwest. The sand was derived primarily from granites, gneisses, and schists, rocks that formed the cores of these mountains. Because the chemical weathering process altered the micas and feldspars in these rocks to clay that then leached out of the rock, over millions of years the more stable and harder quartz was freed to become sand. These sands and clays were then carried downstream to the coast, which, due to the rising and falling of the sea, was then located in what is now the middle of South Carolina. The currents of the sea worked and shaped the sands into ridges, and winds blew the sand into dunes. Some of these dunes are mined for their relatively pure silica content, particularly in Lexington County. As water moved through the sand, it carried minerals in solution, including silica and iron that helped to cement sand to form sandstones. Remnants of these sandstones are not common in the Sandhills but can be seen in a few sites, including Sugarloaf Mountain. A large amount of the clays that were also brought downstream by rivers was deposited with the sand to form the Sandhills. These clays and sands eroded further as the sea regressed and exposed the surface to more recent erosion. The geology of the Sandhills, then, is primarily a story of rising and falling sea levels, of erosion and deposition.

The geology of the Sandhills has shaped the use of the land. Quartz sand ($SiO2$), abundant in the Sandhills, contains few nutrients, and the consequent absence of organic matter in the soil causes great permeability. Therefore, rainwater drains rapidly through the sandy soil, further leaching it and leaving a relatively acidic, infertile topsoil. In addition, the clays often bake into hardpans in which plants have difficulty growing. As a result, the Sandhills support a tenacious and in places desertlike, or xerophytic, plant life that includes scrub turkey oak, longleaf pine, briars, berries, and cactus. The Carolina Sandhills National Wildlife Refuge in Chesterfield County provides examples of relatively undisturbed and mature Sandhills ecosystems. These poor growing conditions led farmers in the eighteenth and early nineteenth centuries to avoid the Sandhills. Some crops, however, were found to do well in the sandy soils. Peaches are grown in many parts of the Sandhills, including Saluda, Edgefield, and Lexington Counties, and small truck farms are common.

The Sandhills overlap both the hard rock of the Piedmont and the sediments of the upper coastal plain. As rivers cut through the Piedmont rock and meet the coastal-plain sediments, they form a fall zone that is up to a mile and a half wide in places. The sharp differences in elevation between rock and sediment at the fall zone produce river rapids, which were key to the social and economic development of South Carolina. The fall-zone rapids provided energy that powered mills that facilitated industrial growth. The rapids of the fall zone also created a barrier to inland navigation, and many of South Carolina's significant inland towns were located at these heads of navigation, including Columbia, Hamburg (North Augusta), Camden, and Cheraw. CAROLYN H. MURPHY

Kovacik, Charles F., and John J. Winberry. *South Carolina: The Making of a Landscape.* 1987. Reprint, Columbia: University of South Carolina Press, 1989.

Murphy, Carolyn H. *Carolina Rocks! The Geology of South Carolina.* Orangeburg, S.C.: Sandlapper, 1995.

Sandlapper. *Sandlapper, the Magazine of South Carolina,* was established in 1968 by the Lexington lawyer Robert P. Wilkins and his wife Rose. Concerned about South Carolina's image, Wilkins began promoting the state's beauty, citizens, and history through the magazine. The first issue appeared in January 1968 with a portrait of Governor James F. Byrnes on the cover. Robert P. Wilkins and Delmar L. Roberts were editors from 1968 through 1972.

Wilkins continued the magazine until 1973, when he ceased his activity. It was continued by others until 1982, when it was merged with *Tarheel,* a North Carolina magazine, to form *Carolina Lifestyle.* That magazine ceased publication in 1983.

Wilkins revived *Sandlapper* in 1990 as a glossy, bimonthly magazine, publishing it through RPW Publishing Company. In 1991 Wilkins began publishing the magazine twice a year in a hard-back format. A year later he returned to the soft-cover format and began printing it quarterly. In 1994 Sandlapper Society, Inc., was formed to publish the magazine as a nonprofit, advertising-free publication. The society's mission was to educate readers about South Carolina's people, places, history, and culture. The magazine has been circulated throughout the state, the nation, and overseas. Since 1990 Wilkins has been the editor and Daniel E. Harmon and Aida Rogers have served as managing and associate editors.

Sandlapper uses a variety of South Carolina photographers and writers to showcase the best of the state. Columns about restaurants, bed-and-breakfasts, and recipes are included with articles about towns, counties, history, and trends. As of 2002, Sandlapper Society had more than eight thousand members, and ten thousand copies of *Sandlapper* were distributed each quarter. AIDA ROGERS

Sanford, Marshall Clement, Jr. (b. 1960). Real estate developer, congressman, governor. Mark Sanford was born on May 28, 1960, in Fort Lauderdale, Florida, the eldest of four children born to Marshall C. Sanford, Sr., a cardiologist, and his wife, Margaret, a Juilliard-trained pianist. Sanford's father bought property on St. Helena Island in the 1950s and then Coosaw Plantation in Beaufort County in 1965. The family spent holidays and summers there, where the children learned to do farm chores such as running tractors, building dikes, and castrating bulls. The family moved to Coosaw in 1978—Sanford's senior year in high school—when his father was diagnosed with Lou Gehrig's disease. Sanford earned a business degree in 1983 from Furman University, where he was student body president. He worked for real estate firms in Charleston until he attended the Darden Graduate School of Business Administration at the University of Virginia, graduating with a master's degree in 1988. He met his future wife, Jennifer Sullivan, while participating in a summer training program at Goldman Sachs in New York City. Sullivan, whose family owned the company that made Skil Saws, was in mergers and acquisitions at Lazard Freres & Co. After two years working in New York, Sanford returned to South Carolina in 1990 and ultimately established a leasing and brokerage company in Charleston.

Sanford, a Republican, was elected to Congress from South Carolina's First District in 1994 with the promise that he would serve only three terms. He became known as a fiscal conservative and voted against bills that would provide funding for his district, including money for a bridge over the Cooper River in Charleston. Notoriously frugal despite personal wealth estimated at $3 million, Sanford slept in his office, showered at the gym, and gave back $250,000 from his office allowance—almost a third of the budget—to the federal government each year. Despite being elected in 1998 with ninety-one percent of the vote, he ended his service after three terms as promised.

In 2002 Sanford was elected governor, ousting Governor Jim Hodges. Jenny Sanford served as his campaign manager and as an adviser in the governor's office. Sanford set up panels to review government operations, one of which streamlined operations at the Department of Motor Vehicles. He had less success realizing his central campaign promise of eliminating property taxes over eighteen years and replacing them with a higher gas tax. By 2006 the General Assembly had not passed such legislation. Sanford billed himself as an "outsider," and the Republican-controlled General Assembly treated him as such. When he vetoed numerous provisions in the 2004 state budget, the General Assembly overrode the vetoes easily and without much discussion. Sanford, in turn, brought pigs to the State House to criticize what he called the legislature's "pork barrel" spending. Sanford and his wife have four sons and make their home on Sullivan's Island. LYN RIDDLE

Eichel, Henry. "Outsider Sanford Pushing Change." *Charlotte (N.C.) Observer,* May 10, 2002, pp. Y1, Y6.

Smith-Brinson, Claudia. "Anti-politics Sanford Stresses Family, Land." Columbia *State,* October 13, 2002, pp. A1, A11.

Santa Elena. Founded in April 1566 by Pedro Menéndez de Avilés on present-day Parris Island, Santa Elena was the northernmost settlement of the Spanish province of La Florida. At that time La Florida in theory extended from the Florida Keys north to Newfoundland. Spaniards had used the name "Santa Elena" for the area around Port Royal Sound south to Tybee Island, Georgia, since 1526, when Lucas Vázquez de Ayllón's expedition explored these lands on August 18, the feast day of St. Helena, mother of the emperor Constantine. Fear that the French would claim the excellent harbor at Port Royal Sound led Menéndez to the Parris Island site, where in 1562 Captain Jean Ribault had built the short-lived Charlesfort in the name of France's king. Challenges from the French and, later, the English shaped Santa Elena's history in important ways.

Santa Elena was the capital of La Florida for much of its first ten years, during which time the growing settlement conducted political and religious outreach to the native population of a broad region.

An archaeologist's rendering of Spanish dwellings in Santa Elena. The round building is thought to have been a servant's quarters behind Governor Miranda's house. Drawings by Darby Erd. Courtesy, South Carolina Institute of Archaeology and Anthropology

As part of these interactions, the Spaniards also sought to extract food and labor from the Indians for this growing colony, which chronically faced supply shortages. The company of Captain Juan Pardo arrived at Santa Elena in July 1566 to strengthen the Spanish presence there after a mutiny took most of the initial one hundred soldiers from the fort. Efforts to bring native peoples inland under Spanish rule began when Pardo led expeditions from Santa Elena northwest through present South Carolina into North Carolina and eastern Tennessee in 1566 and 1567. The Spaniards' goal of evangelizing the Indians gained more attention when Jesuit priests arrived in La Florida in 1566. They attempted to found missions in the Santa Elena area and, when those failed, one on the Chesapeake Bay. This effort resulted in the massacre of several priests and the withdrawal of the Jesuits from La Florida in 1572. Members of the Franciscan order arrived the next year and continued this work in the area of Santa Elena. The Spaniards' demands on the Indians grew as families arrived in the town, beginning with a 1569 expedition of nearly two hundred colonists. Pedro Menéndez de Avilés brought his own wife and household to Santa Elena in 1571. Conflict between the settlers and members of Menéndez's extended family, who governed during his frequent absences from La Florida, soon tore this small community as each group sought to assert its privileges. War with the Orista, Guale, and Escamazu tribes eclipsed these concerns in 1576, as these peoples—angered by years of Spanish demands and abuses—united to drive the Spaniards from their lands.

Indians destroyed Santa Elena in 1576, but one year later Spaniards rebuilt there by order of their king, who feared that the French would learn of their absence and occupy this site. The French had indeed returned to Port Royal Sound, where the ship *Le Prince* wrecked crossing the bar. Many of the survivors perished when Indians attacked them in the belief that they were Spaniards. Those whom the Indians spared became valuable allies to the Orista and Guale chiefdoms. With the combined French and Indian threat that continued into the early 1580s, military concerns dominated the second period of Santa Elena's Spanish occupation. St. Augustine became the colony's capital under Pedro Menéndez Marqués, whom Philip II appointed to replace his now-deceased uncle Pedro Menéndez de Avilés as governor. Spaniards rebuilt the town of Santa Elena, and families occupied it once more, but they lived under military rule with no municipal institutions through which to assert their rights. A guarded peace returned in early 1583, after Pedro Menéndez Marqués launched a war of fire and blood against the Orista and Guale chiefdoms, which was followed by a severe drought. Santa Elena was once again a thriving community—albeit one supported by the Spanish crown—when Philip II ordered the town's abandonment following Sir Francis Drake's 1586 raid on St. Augustine. The English attack raised yet again the issue of the Florida settlements' vulnerability. In August 1587 Pedro Menéndez Marqués arrived at Santa Elena and carried out the command to destroy the Spanish fort and town and relocate its inhabitants to St. Augustine. In 1979 the archaeologist Stanley South verified that Parris Island was Santa Elena's location, and since then he and others have conducted excavations there. The National Park Service designated the Charlesfort–Santa Elena site a National Historic Landmark in January 2001. KAREN L. PAAR

Lyon, Eugene. *Santa Elena: A Brief History of the Colony, 1566–1587.* Columbia: South Carolina Institute of Archaeology and Anthropology, University of South Carolina, 1984.

Paar, Karen L. "'To Settle Is to Conquer': Spaniards, Native Americans, and the Colonization of Santa Elena in Sixteenth-Century Florida." Ph.D. diss., University of North Carolina at Chapel Hill, 1999.

South, Stanley, Russell K. Skowronek, and Richard E. Johnson. *Spanish Artifacts from Santa Elena.* Columbia: South Carolina Institute of Archaeology and Anthropology, University of South Carolina, 1988.

Santee Canal. A canal to connect the Santee and Cooper Rivers had been conceived as early as 1770, but the Revolutionary War intervened and plans for the canal were postponed until the mid-1780s. By linking the Santee and Cooper Rivers, investors hoped to create a trade route that would bring prosperity to the state in general and Charleston in particular. The canal would be quicker and cheaper than overland travel and avoid the long and frequently treacherous ocean passage from the mouth of the Santee to the city. In March 1786 the General Assembly chartered the "Company for the Inland Navigation from Santee to Cooper River," giving the company full responsibility for the canal, from construction to maintenance. Financing the canal was achieved privately through selling stock and holding lotteries to raise capital. After a route from White Oak Landing on the Santee to Biggin Creek, a Cooper River tributary, was selected, work commenced in 1793. Completed in 1800, the Santee Canal cost $650,667, more than twice original estimates. The canal consisted of two double locks and eight single locks; was twenty-two miles long, thirty-five feet wide at the surface, and twenty feet at the bottom; and drew four feet of water. Tolls ranged from $10 to $30 depending on the size of the boat.

Although hailed as one of the great internal improvements of its day, the Santee Canal was not a success. Financial problems, lawsuits, poor design and construction, lack of traffic, and droughts all contributed to the canal's disappointing results. With the rise of railroad competition in the 1840s, investors pulled out of the project, and the General Assembly canceled the canal company's charter in 1853. Portions of the canal were used sporadically until about 1865 and then were abandoned entirely. Proposals to reopen the Santee Canal in the late nineteenth and early twentieth centuries went nowhere. In the 1940s most of the canal was inundated by the waters of Lake Moultrie. In 1989 the state of South Carolina converted the surviving portion of the canal into Old Santee Canal Park. Management of the park was transferred to Santee Cooper in 1999. JANE W. SQUIRES

Bennett, Robert B. "The Santee Canal, 1785–1939." Master's thesis, University of South Carolina, 1988.

Santee Cooper. The history of the Santee Cooper project can be traced to 1785, when a group of wealthy investors petitioned the General Assembly to construct a canal connecting the Santee and Cooper Rivers in order to improve inland navigation between Charleston and Columbia. The twenty-two-mile canal opened in

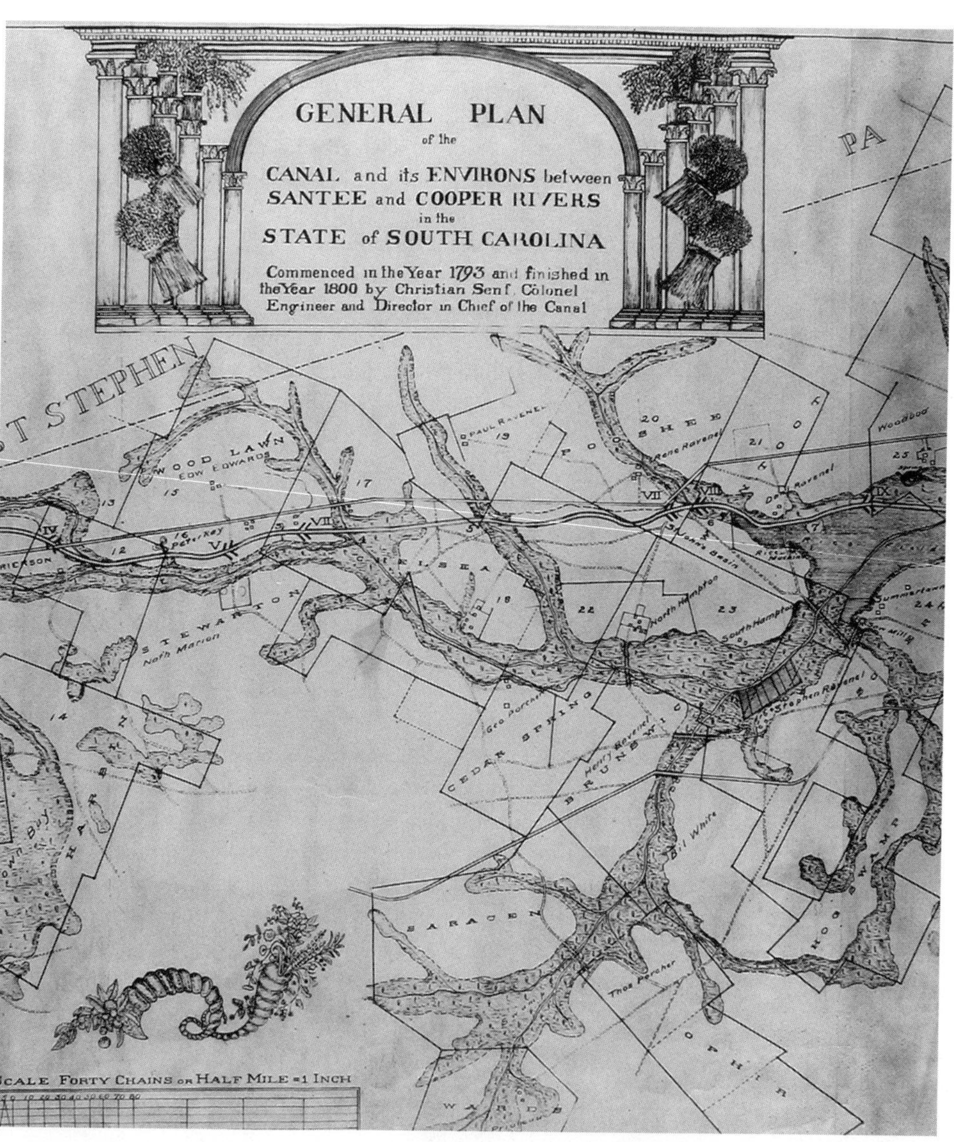

The general plan of the Santee Canal, 1800. Courtesy, South Caroliniana Library, University of South Carolina

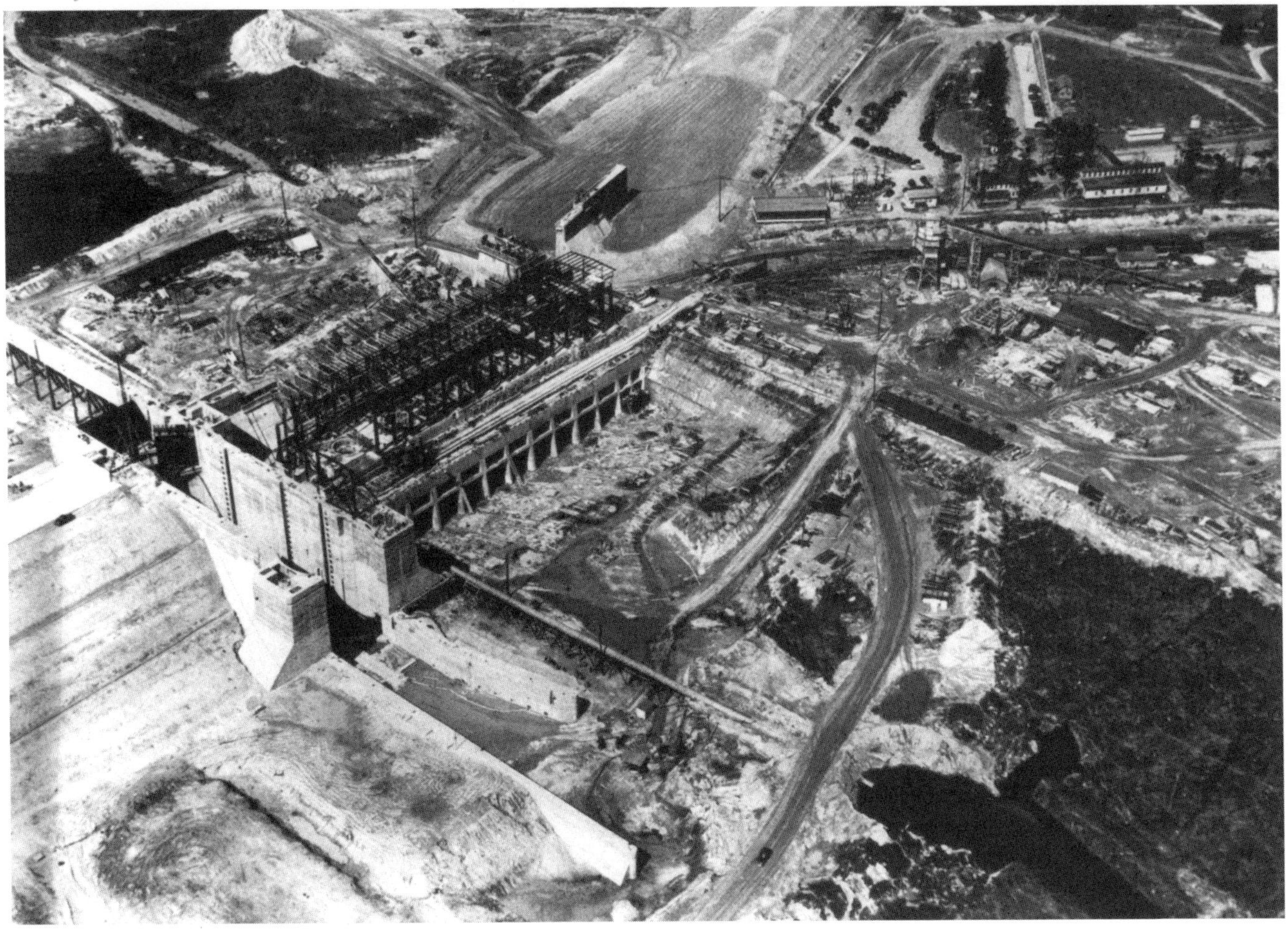

Construction of the lock and dam at Pinopolis, the Santee Cooper Project. Courtesy, Calhoun County Museum

1800 and for the next fifty years allowed planters to ship cotton, rice, and timber to Charleston. By the mid–nineteenth century, however, railroads virtually eliminated the need for the inland waterway, and swampy vines reclaimed the canal. During the 1920s Thomas C. Williams, an engineer and steamboat operator, gained rights to rebuild the canal and reopen the area to inland navigation. Williams's Columbia Railroad and Navigation Company retained the rights to this project for eight years, but financial concerns frustrated construction efforts.

In 1934 Governor Ibra Blackwood signed a bill creating the South Carolina Public Service Authority and granting it permission to dam the Santee River, divert its water into the Cooper River, clear land for two large reservoirs, construct a hydroelectric plant at Pinopolis, and sell electricity to residents in surrounding counties. A year later President Franklin Delano Roosevelt gave the Public Service Authority approval to draw on funding from the Public Works Administration, making the Santee Cooper project (as it was quickly dubbed) the largest New Deal program in the Palmetto State. Santee Cooper had several purposes. The project would provide economic relief to the area by drawing the majority of its workforce from relief rolls; the hydroelectric plant would contribute to the electrification of rural farms; the creation of two reservoirs would reopen navigation from Charleston to Columbia; and the regulation of the Santee River would prevent future flooding and eliminate malarial outbreaks. This combination of cheap power, efficient transportation, and a healthy environment would attract industry to the impoverished agricultural region of the state. Santee Cooper received support from the prominent U.S. senator James F. Byrnes, who was largely responsible for persuading President Roosevelt to support the project, and Charleston mayor Burnet Maybank, who spearheaded the campaign for public and political support within the state.

Construction, however, was not a foregone conclusion. The Santee Cooper project met opposition from several groups. In Washington, Secretary of the Interior Harold Ickes, for personal and political motives, opposed federal funding of the project. In South Carolina, private utility companies denounced what they saw as a government monopoly on production and sale of power. In the Santee Cooper area, private landowners fought the dislocation of families living in the new flood basins and the inundation of historic homes, churches, and battlefields. In addition, environmentalists voiced disapproval over the destruction of wildlife habitat in the Santee Swamp and the elimination of thousands of acres of virgin hardwood forest.

Following a four-year court battle, construction began in 1939. At its peak, the project employed nearly fifteen thousand workers, most of whom came from Depression relief rolls. Living in military-style camps scattered throughout the Santee and Pinopolis basins, the laborers cleared more than 160,000 acres with handsaws and mule-drawn wagons. They hauled dirt and clay to dam sites, built railroads, relocated cemeteries, and aided in the construction of the diversion and tail-race canals and the new power plant. Sight-seers from across the state came by the thousands to witness the massive undertaking that became the largest land-clearing project in United States history and created the largest single-lift lock in the world. In

1941 President Roosevelt declared the Santee Cooper a defense project, and one year later the power plant in Pinopolis began generating power. Within two decades it was providing electricity to the majority of the state's farms as well as industries in surrounding counties. More surprisingly, the new reservoirs, renamed Lake Marion and Lake Moultrie, attracted sport fishermen from across the country. Soon vacation homes, state parks, and fish camps dotted the 450-mile perimeter of the lakes. By the end of the twentieth century fishing, boating, and other recreational activities brought more than $200 million in annual revenue to Santee Cooper country.

By the end of the twentieth century, the Public Service Authority sold wholesale electricity to twenty cooperatives and two municipalities that served approximately 600,000 customers, and it directly retailed electricity to more than 130,000 additional in-state customers. One of the largest state-owned utilities in the nation, Santee Cooper operates in all forty-six counties in South Carolina. In the 1990s the Public Service Authority expanded its operations and created the Santee Cooper Regional Water System to treat and transport water from Lake Moultrie and provide water for much of the South Carolina lowcountry. T. ROBERT HART

Edgar, Walter B. *History of Santee Cooper: 1934–1984.* Columbia, S.C.: R. L. Bryan, 1984.

Hayes, Jack Irby. *South Carolina and the New Deal.* Columbia: University of South Carolina Press, 2001.

Santee National Wildlife Refuge. Established in 1942, Santee National Wildlife Refuge (NWR) was created to alleviate the loss of natural waterfowl and wildlife habitat caused by the construction of hydroelectric projects on the Santee and Cooper Rivers. Management and protection are provided for 15,095 acres that stretch for eighteen miles along the northern shore of Lake Marion in Clarendon County.

The area includes more than ten thousand acres of open water and freshwater marsh along with mixed hardwoods and pines, croplands, old fields, ponds, and managed impoundments. Significant waterfowl concentrations winter on the refuge, as do other birds of interest. Santee Refuge overwinters the largest group of Canada geese belonging to the Southern James Bay population in South Carolina. With recorded observations of 296 species, the refuge is one of the best inland birding areas in the state.

Santee NWR includes four units, each with its own unique characteristics. The Bluff Unit is home to the Santee Indian Mound, which dates back more than 3,500 years. The mound is also the site of Fort Watson, which was an important British encampment during the Revolutionary War. Dingle Pond is home to a Carolina bay and provides unique habitat for several wetland species including alligators, wood ducks, mallards, great blue herons, and other wading and song birds. Pine Island provides protection and habitat for American alligators, numerous species of wading birds, and nesting bald eagles and is home to thousands of wintering ducks, geese, and swans. The Cuddo Unit includes mixed hardwood and pine woodlands, numerous freshwater impoundments and marshes, and several old-field and cropland sites. Bird life is abundant, as are alligators and many other native species.

Santee NWR promotes conservation and stewardship by providing wildlife-dependent recreational opportunities and offers environmental education programs. Interpretive exhibits in the visitors' center provide an orientation to the refuge. Visitors can explore the refuge on several miles of hiking trails or on an auto drive. Fishing and hunting are permitted during designated seasons in accordance with special refuge regulations. KAY W. MCCUTCHEON

Santee River. The 143-mile-long Santee River is formed by the confluence of the Congaree and Wateree Rivers. The Santee flows southeast and meets the Atlantic Ocean between the cities of Georgetown and Charleston. Near its mouth, the river forms a delta created by the large amount of sediment picked up by the waters of the Santee and its tributaries as they pass from origins in the Appalachian Mountains of North Carolina through the Piedmont of North and South Carolina. About twenty miles from the coast, the river splits into the North and South Santee.

The Native American groups that inhabited the region near the river before the presence of Europeans came from a common Siouan origin and included the Seewee, Winyah, Congaree, Catawba, and Santee tribes. It is believed that "Santee" translated to "people of the river." Europeans, led by Huguenots, began settling along the river in the late seventeenth century. The village of Jamestown was established thirty miles from the river's mouth, and it was estimated that by 1700 seventy families lived in the vicinity. Huguenots so dominated the lower section of the river that the area was called the French Santee, and the upper section of the river was known as the English Santee. The river helped to facilitate a brisk trade in deerskins and other goods between Europeans and Native Americans. As the result of white encroachment and dwindling numbers, the Santee and other tribes in the region moved north, eventually merging with the Catawbas.

The Huguenot families of the lower Santee prospered, allowing many such as the Manigaults and Hugers to expand their landholdings and purchase large numbers of African slaves. This massive labor force was needed to work the tidal rice plantations established along the banks of the Santee. Before the Revolutionary War, indigo was also an important cash crop. The Huguenot descendant and Revolutionary War hero Francis Marion used his knowledge of the Santee and Pee Dee River regions to conduct his partisan campaign against the British.

The need to improve the state's transportation infrastructure brought significant changes to the Santee River. The mouth of the Santee was too shallow to be an effective harbor, so beginning in the 1780s a plan was developed to link the Santee and Cooper Rivers. The plan brought together the reach into the backcountry of the Santee and its tributaries with the Cooper River's outlet in Charleston harbor. The Santee Canal, completed in 1800, was twenty-two miles long and thirty-five feet wide. At its height in 1830 seventeen thousand boats passed through the Santee Canal, but by the end of the 1840s it was out of use because cargo could be more efficiently transported by railroad.

The Santee River faced its next major transformation when from 1939 to 1942 the Santee Cooper project saw two hydroelectric dams built on the river, creating the reservoirs that became Lake Marion and Lake Moultrie. The South Carolina Public Service Authority provided electricity for homes and businesses across South Carolina, but the majority of the Santee's water flow was diverted through the lakes to the Cooper River. After dramatically altering the Santee River region, the state, through Santee Cooper and the Department of Natural Resources, has sought to protect the environment by establishing the 15,000-acre Santee National Wildlife Refuge and an 18,250-acre wildlife-management area. MICHAEL S. REYNOLDS

Kovacik, Charles F., and John J. Winberry. *South Carolina: The Making of a Landscape.* 1987. Reprint, Columbia: University of South Carolina Press, 1989.

Savage, Henry. *River of the Carolinas: The Santee.* Rev. ed. Chapel Hill: University of North Carolina Press, 1968.

Sapp, Claud Napoleon (1886–1947). Legislator, U.S. district attorney, education advocate. Sapp was born in Lancaster County on February 11, 1886, the son of Daniel F. Sapp and Mittie Fulp. Proud of his rural roots from Sapp's Crossings in Lancaster County, Claud Sapp championed progressive causes in the first half of the twentieth century that he envisioned would improve the lives of ordinary white South Carolinians. Gifted with a strong, analytical mind, Sapp earned his A.B. degree from Wofford College in 1907 and graduated from the University of South Carolina Law School in 1911, the same year he was admitted to the South Carolina Bar. He began his law career in Lancaster, serving as city attorney and later as county attorney. Sapp represented Lancaster County in the state House of Representatives in the 1913–1914 term. In 1916 he married Mary Davis of Lancaster. The marriage produced two sons. Shortly after their wedding, the couple moved to Columbia, where Sapp became assistant attorney general, an office he held until 1919. As South Carolina's first assistant attorney general, Sapp developed a reputation for writing legal opinions with clarity, force, and thoroughness.

After World War I, Sapp returned to the State House, this time representing Richland County from 1921 to 1924. As a progressive leader, Sapp envisioned a prosperous South Carolina that would educate its citizens, modernize its infrastructure, and integrate itself more fully into the economic mainstream of the nation. He tirelessly advocated for improved public education and generous public spending to broaden educational opportunities for South Carolina's rural white population. When he became chair of the powerful House Ways and Means Committee, Sapp used his influence to pass the 6–0–1 Law, landmark legislation that dramatically increased state spending on and responsibility for education. When Sapp encountered resistance from those who preferred local funding or lower taxes, he regularly repeated his mantra: "Tax property wherever you find it to educate children wherever they may be." Sapp also worked to build roads and create a tax structure that would enhance state revenue and tax wealth fairly.

Sapp's political activity continued through leadership in the Democratic Party, which gained him state and national attention. Sapp chaired the South Carolina Democratic Executive Committee from 1930 to 1934. Throughout the 1930s he served as a strong and loyal supporter of Franklin Roosevelt and garnered support among South Carolinians for Roosevelt's New Deal policies. In 1934 Roosevelt appointed Sapp as United States district attorney for the Eastern District of South Carolina, a position he held for the remainder of his life. From 1911 to 1947 Sapp practiced law both as a prosecutor and as a criminal defense attorney. Contemporaries readily acknowledged his zeal, persuasive powers, and disarming wit. After twelve years as U.S. district attorney, Sapp died on February 3, 1947, in Columbia from a heart condition. He was buried at Elmwood Cemetery in Columbia. JANET G. HUDSON

"Claud N. Sapp Dies, Rites to Be Held Today." Columbia *State,* February 4, 1947, pp. 1, 9.

History of the Bar of Richland County 1790–1948. Columbia, S.C.: Sloane, 1948.

Sass, Herbert Ravenel (1884–1958). Journalist, naturalist, novelist. Sass was born in Charleston on November 2, 1884, son of the poet George Herbert Sass and Anna Ravenel, daughter of Dr. and Mrs. St. Julien Ravenel. His grandfather was the creator of submarines for the Confederacy, and his grandmother was the author of the classic *Charleston: The Place and the People.* Taking his inheritance seriously and rarely leaving the city, Sass graduated from the College of Charleston with a B.A. in 1905, an M.A. in 1906, and an honorary Litt.D. in 1922. Starting to work for the *News and Courier* in 1908, he used his love of the lowcountry as the basis of his long-running column, "Woods and Waters." The nature artist and writer Charles Livingston Bull convinced him to send similar work to the *Saturday Evening Post,* which, along with other national magazines, published his nature stories. National publication enabled Sass to give up newspaper work in 1924, having served as both city editor and assistant editor.

Sass's collections of nature stories, showing his lush use of language and intimate knowledge of bird and animal life, include *The Way of the Wild* (1925), *Adventures in Green Places* (1926; enlarged, 1935), *Gray Eagle* (1927), and *On the Wings of a Bird* (1929). His fascination with lowcountry and Native American history is displayed in his historical novels *War Drums* (1928), *Hear Me, My Chiefs* (1940), *Emperor Brims* (1941), and most especially in his best work, *Look Back to Glory* (1933), a tale of the Civil War. A chapter was published in *Fort Sumter* (1938) with a chapter from DuBose Heyward's novel *Peter Ashley.* In Heyward's novel the title character debated between his head and heart in throwing in his lot with the South; but Sass and his characters supported secession and the South wholeheartedly. The author saw no reason to doubt the rightness of the "lost cause" and argued passionately for the political principals of John C. Calhoun, in both his fiction and his magazine pieces. Believing that history should be colored with romance, he used his lyric talents to celebrate the lowcountry and a past he saw as fabled and tragic. This showed in his nonfiction works: *A Carolina Rice Plantation of the Fifties,* with Alice R. H. Smith watercolors (1936); *Outspoken: 150 Years of the News and Courier* (1953), whose conservative racial views he championed (most especially in his 1956 *Atlantic Monthly* article "Mixed Schools and Mixed Blood"); and *The Story of the Carolina Lowcountry* (1956), in which he argued that the role of the lowcountry and that of the South in shaping the country had not been adequately acknowledged by historians. He was so adamant in this in his magazine pieces that the historian Bernard De Voto answered him in the pages of the *Saturday Evening Post.*

Shy, redheaded, tall, lean, and gracious, Sass was nicknamed "Hobo" for his wandering ways in the lowcountry and his hobbling together of income to support his wife, Marion Hutson, and three children. At least two of his short stories became the basis of films; *The Raid* came from his "Affair at St. Albans," and *Anne of the Indies* was drawn from his story of the same name. He died on February 18, 1958, and was buried in Charleston's St. Philip's Episcopal Cemetery. While all could not agree with him politically, none could deny his love or loyalty for the Carolina lowcountry. HARLAN GREENE

"Charleston Author Tells of Wild Life in Woods and of His Native Heath." Charleston *News and Courier,* December 4, 1938, 9-iii.

Coit, Margaret. "Tribute to Herbert R. Sass." Charleston *News and Courier,* March 2, 1958, p. A12.

"H. R. Sass Dies after Long Illness." Charleston *News and Courier,* February 19, 1958, pp. A1, A11.

"Myth, Says Devoto of Sass' Charges." Charleston *News and Courier,* January 12, 1954, p. A10.

Sassafras Mountain (Pickens County). Sassafras Mountain, which lies along the South Carolina / North Carolina border, rises to 3,554 feet above sea level and is the highest point in South Carolina. While the summit is privately owned, it is included in the Appalachian Trail system and is a prime site for hikers. The mountain and surrounding areas contain miles of trails from which to view majestic mountain streams, waterfalls, and exposed rocks that give evidence of the area's geologic history.

The geology of Sassafras Mountain reflects millions of years of plate tectonics. It lies within the inner Piedmont belt and is thought to be part of a continental fragment that attached or even reattached North America during the Middle Ordovician at a time of continental collision and mountain building called the Taconic Orogeny (mountain-building episode). Metamorphism continued during subsequent collisions in the Devonian period (Acadian Orogeny) and in the Pennsylvania to Permian periods (Alleghenian Orogeny). During these episodes North America collided with the European plate (Baltica) and the African plate, respectively. These collisions, which generated tremendous heat and pressure, transformed sedimentary and igneous rocks into schists and the distinctive Henderson gneiss that underlies Sassafras Mountain. The gneiss is a large, lens-shaped igneous intrusion, or pluton, containing folds and textures that reflect a long history of intense pressure and heat from the collision of these landmasses. The region is also thought to have undergone extensive Mesozoic extensional faulting and later isostatic uplift from the Oligocene to the Miocene. These geologic processes caused active stream down-cutting and the resultant modern scenic gorges and waterfalls that surround Sassafras Mountain. CAROLYN H. MURPHY

Kovacik, Charles F., and John J. Winberry. *South Carolina: The Making of a Landscape.* 1987. Reprint, Columbia: University of South Carolina Press, 1989.

Murphy, Carolyn H. *Carolina Rocks! The Geology of South Carolina.* Orangeburg, S.C.: Sandlapper, 1995.

Savannah National Wildlife Refuge. Savannah National Wildlife Refuge (NWR) is located on the lower Savannah River eighteen miles upstream from the city of Savannah. Established in 1927, the Savannah NWR habitats include freshwater marshes, more than sixty-three miles of tidal rivers and creeks, as well as bottomland hardwoods composed primarily of cypress, gum, and maple species. A three-thousand-acre freshwater impoundment system, which by the early twenty-first century was managed for the benefit of wading birds and migratory waterfowl, makes use of dikes and trunk gates built in the eighteenth century for the cultivation of rice.

The refuge offers a variety of public-use opportunities, including wildlife observation, photography, interpretation, hiking, bicycling, fishing, and hunting (deer, turkeys, feral hogs, squirrels, and waterfowl). Laurel Hill Wildlife Drive (entrance on S.C. Highway 170 six miles south of Hardeeville) follows a four-mile route along the former rice-field dikes and is open to vehicular traffic from sunrise to sunset seven days a week. The refuge is home to a large variety of wildlife—especially waterbirds such as ducks, egrets, herons, and ibises. It provides excellent habitat for the American alligator, the refuge resident attracting by far the most public attention. Hardwood hammocks provide resting areas for neotropical migratory songbirds including tanagers, warblers, and thrushes. Several threatened or endangered species make use of the refuge, including bald eagles, wood storks, manatees, and short-nosed sturgeon. DIANA CHURCHILL

Savannah River. The headwaters of the Savannah River originate in the mountains near the border where the states of South Carolina, Georgia, and North Carolina meet. The 314-mile-long river is formed by the confluence of the Tugaloo and Seneca Rivers, and along with the lower section of the Tugaloo, the Savannah forms the western boundary between South Carolina and Georgia. The Savannah drains a basin of 10,577 square miles, with 4,581 being in South Carolina.

The Savannah River Valley was home to large numbers of indigenous peoples, who were no doubt attracted to the area by fertile soil, abundant game, and the easy transportation afforded by the river. By the time the English had established their colony in 1670, the Westo Indian nation was an important presence in the river valley. The Cherokees also had established villages along the northern section of the river and its tributaries. A brisk trade developed between the English colonists and the Indians. The Savannah River was an important trade route, with thousand of deerskins and other goods being floated down the river annually in canoes.

In the early 1680s the Westos were driven out of the area by the Savannahs, a branch of the Shawnee nation. By the end of the Yamassee War (1715–1718), the English colonists built both Fort Moore and Fort Prince George along the river, extending their influence and establishing important trading centers. The town of Purrysburg was established by Swiss immigrants along the lower Savannah River in 1732, and after the port town of Savannah, Georgia, was settled the next year, Purrysburg became an important link on the trade route between that city and Charleston.

By the late eighteenth century the majority of the Indian population of the Savannah River Valley had moved to the west, opening the region to white settlers. Tidal rice cultivation came to dominate the lower Savannah, and planters brought thousands of slaves to the area to grow the staple crop. After cotton cultivation spread, the Savannah served as an important transportation link between the interior and the coast. Large flat-bottom boats carried cotton from the Piedmont of South Carolina and Georgia to the port at Savannah, Georgia. By the early decades of the nineteenth century, steamboats were in use on the river ferrying people and cargo to the coast.

The town of Hamburg, established across the river from Augusta, Georgia, was an important center for trade during the antebellum era. The South Carolina Railroad, completed in 1833, enabled traders to tap into the upcountry market by floating cargo to Hamburg on the river and then sending it by rail to Charleston. By the turn of the twentieth century modern technology, such as the railroad and the automobile, diminished the need to use the river for transportation, but the people of the region continued to find uses for the river. Hydroelectric dams were built to harness the power of the river, resulting in significant geographic changes including the creation of three lakes.

The Savannah River Site (SRS), a nuclear weapons facility, began operation on a 310-square-mile tract of land along the river in Aiken, Barnwell, and Allendale Counties in 1952. As population and industrial development increased in the Savannah River Valley, pollution became a problem for the river, with the high level of mercury posing the most danger. The Savannah National Wildlife Refuge along the lower Savannah and much of the SRS land are environmentally protected and are home to endangered animals including alligators, manatees, short-nosed sturgeon, bald eagles, and red-cockaded woodpeckers. In South Carolina the Savannah River serves as the water source for Hilton Head, Beaufort, and smaller communities. MICHAEL S. REYNOLDS

Anderson, David G. *The Savannah River Chiefdoms: Political Change in the Late Prehistoric Southeast.* Tuscaloosa: University of Alabama Press, 1994.

Kovacik, Charles F., and John J. Winberry. *South Carolina: The Making of a Landscape.* 1987. Reprint, Columbia: University of South Carolina Press, 1989.

Stokes, Thomas L. *The Savannah.* 1951. Reprint, Athens: University of Georgia Press, 1982.

Savannah River Scenic Highway. The Savannah River Scenic Highway stretches over one hundred miles from Oakway in Oconee County to the Georgia border in Edgefield County just south of Clarks Hill. It incorporates four state highways: 24, 187, 81, and 28. The highway is also a part of the South Carolina Natural Heritage Corridor, which extends from Charleston to Oconee County. Running along the Savannah River, the highway passes near numerous recreational and historical sites.

State parks near the scenic highway include Lake Hartwell, Sadlers Creek, Calhoun Falls, Hickory Knob, Baker Creek, and Hamilton Branch. These parks, situated on Hartwell Lake, Richard J. Russell Lake, and J. Strom Thurmond Lake, offer visitors camping, fishing, and numerous other recreational opportunities. Near Thurmond Lake the road passes through Sumter National Forest.

The scenic highway also incorporates several sites of historic interest. The restored Abbeville Opera House and Ninety Six National Historic Site, which features a museum and Revolutionary War battlefield, are both within reach of the road. Historic markers stand in the place of Willington Academy in McCormick County. The highway also passes through McCormick, which boasts a recently refurbished downtown including an art gallery, a diner, and a historic railroad depot. AARON W. MARRS

Savannah River Site. The Savannah River Site (SRS) processes and stores nuclear materials in support of national defense efforts. SRS covers 310 square miles that border the Savannah River and encompass parts of Aiken, Barnwell, and Allendale Counties. Owned by the U.S. Department of Energy (DOE), it has been operated since 1989 by Westinghouse Savannah River Company. In 2002 SRS had a budget of nearly $1.3 billion and employed about 13,800 people.

Following World War II, the federal government was interested in establishing sites for the creation of nuclear weapons. SRS was selected from an initial list of over one hundred potential sites in eighteen states as a facility to produce materials for nuclear and thermonuclear weapons. The materials produced at SRS would then be shipped to other locations where the actual weapons were manufactured. The site was chosen in 1950, and the Atomic Energy Commission (AEC) asked E. I. DuPont de Nemours and Company to design, construct, and manage the facility. Construction began on February 1, 1951, and the heavy water plant began operation on August 17, 1952. Construction was fully complete in 1956. Because of security concerns, SRS was protected by U.S. Army anti-aircraft battalions from 1955 to 1959.

The construction of the plant precipitated two major population shifts. First, workers moved to South Carolina to construct and operate the plant. Building the plant required 35,000 workers, who came from across the country. After construction, duPont employees arrived to manage the SRS operations. The nearby town of Aiken became inundated with this influx of new workers. Although the workers overwhelmed public services and drove off some of the visitors who used Aiken as a winter colony, the construction project put about $1 million per day into the area's economy.

The second demographic shift affected the six thousand residents of several small communities, including Ellenton and Dunbarton, which were located in the area to be taken over by SRS. For security and safety reasons, these townspeople were required to leave by March 1, 1952, only fifteen months after the AEC's announcement that the SRS would be built. The government appraised the value of homes, farms, and other real estate of Ellenton and Dunbarton; owners received government payment for their properties but no assistance in finding new homes and relocating. The federal government played no role in designing or creating a government town to serve the needs of residents, as they had with other nuclear projects at Oak Ridge, Tennessee, and Hanford Washington. Hardest hit were renters, who received no compensation at all but still had the cost and inconvenience of the mandatory and permanent evacuation. Many of these displaced residents moved just north of the plant site and formed a new community called New Ellenton.

During the 1950s five reactors were built, and SRS began to produce nuclear materials, primarily tritium and plutonium-239. Radioactive materials were moved from the reactors to one of two chemical separations plants, known as "canyons," where the highly refined nuclear products of tritium and plutonium were chemically separated from waste by-products. SRS produced about thirty-six metric tons of plutonium (along with its accompanying nuclear waste by-products) from 1953 to 1988, at which time the K, L, and P reactors were shut down. In 1988 DuPont notified the DOE that it would cease operating and managing the site. In 1989 SRS was officially placed on the National Priority List (the Environmental Protection Agency's [EPA] Superfund List) and became regulated by the EPA.

Through these changes SRS remained a primary DOE site. SRS's work with tritium was crucial since tritium, with a half-life of 12.5 years, must be replenished constantly in the nation's nuclear weapons stockpile. SRS also focused on the disposition of legacy materials, a euphemism for radioactive wastes. Spent nuclear fuel primarily from the site's production reactors was stored at SRS in water-filled concrete basins, awaiting processing. SRS had two processing (separations) canyons, F canyon and H canyon, which stabilized and managed most of the remaining inventory of plutonium-bearing materials at SRS. In 2000 there was a public announcement that SRS would be the site for three new plutonium missions: a mixed oxide fuel fabrication facility, a pit disassembly and conversion facility, and a plutonium immobilization facility. In 2002 F canyon was shut down after completing its last production run to process legacy materials.

Ecologically rich in rare species of flora and fauna, SRS operates an environmental remediation program. Restoration of this ecology is essential as SRS is home to the bald eagle and the red-cockaded woodpecker and is visited by the peregrine falcon and the wood stork, all of which are endangered species. Alligators, wild turkeys, white-tailed deer, otters, and short-nosed sturgeon also find their homes at SRS. As of March 2002, 340 of 500 acres had been remediated. Although more than four billion gallons of groundwater had been treated and about one million pounds of solvents removed, the cleanup process was expected to take decades at a dollar cost that could not be accurately estimated. RICK D. BOULWARE

Brooks, Richard David, and David Colin Crass. *A Desperate Poor Country: History and Settlement Patterning on the Savannah River Site, Aiken and Barnwell Counties, South Carolina.* Columbia: Savannah River Archaeological Research Program, South Carolina Institute of Archaeology and Anthropology, University of South Carolina, 1991.

Browder, Tonya, David Colin Crass, and Richard David Brooks. "Oral History at the Savannah River Site." *Proceedings of the South Carolina Historical Association* (1994): 138–42.

Farmer, James O., Jr. "A Collision of Cultures: Aiken, South Carolina, Meets the Nuclear Age." *Proceedings of the South Carolina Historical Association* (1995): 40–49.

Mori, Mark, and Susan Robinson. *Building Bombs.* Oakland, Calif.: The Video Project, 1989. Videocassette.

Reed, Mary Beth, et al. *Savannah River Site at Fifty.* Washington, D.C.: U.S. Department of Energy, 2002.

Sawyer, Benjamin Mack (1890–1940). Public official. Born in Aiken County near Salley on October 22, 1890, Sawyer received undergraduate and graduate degrees from the University of South Carolina. After a brief teaching stint, he enlisted in the army in 1917 and rose to the rank of first lieutenant before his discharge in 1919. In 1918 he married Ruth Louise Simmons, and they eventually had three children. After departing the army, Sawyer became the first secretary of the State Budget Commission. In 1921 he also became clerk of the South Carolina House of Representatives Ways and Means Committee. In 1925 Sawyer became secretary-treasurer of the Highway Commission.

Politically astute, Sawyer became chief highway commissioner in 1926. During his remarkable tenure in office, Sawyer survived many political controversies while superintending the steady growth of the Highway Department. In his fourteen years as chief commissioner, Sawyer successfully laid the underpinnings for the modern State Highway Department. He lobbied for bond funding to construct a statewide network of highways, survived the ensuing controversy, resisted the efforts of Governor Olin D. Johnston to deprive him and his commissioners of their offices, and defended the highway fund from diversion by Governor Burnet Maybank.

The 1929 bond controversy concerned legislation that made the state of South Carolina one district for issuing highway construction bonds. Moving from local funding to statewide funding was a quantum leap for highway construction in South Carolina. Bond bill opponent Olin D. Johnston became governor in 1935. Johnston initiated a lengthy period of unrest when he attempted to remove commission members, used the National Guard to bar Sawyer from office, declared the department in a state of "insurrection," and tried to replace Sawyer and the commissioners with his own appointees. Numerous court challenges and legislative maneuverings left Sawyer in office and local districts electing the members of the commission.

With the dust barely settled from the Johnston challenge, in 1939 Governor Burnet Maybank and the General Assembly attempted to divert highway funds to pay teachers, balance the state budget, and fund other New Deal projects. Twice the legislature enacted such legislation, and twice the South Carolina Supreme Court ruled that the highway fund was a special fund created by license fees and gasoline taxes paid by users of the highways and could not be diverted to the general fund.

Despite these challenges, Sawyer remained focused on his department and on improving South Carolina roads. During his tenure, the miles of roadways doubled and two out of three of those miles were paved.

As a lieutenant colonel in the U.S. Army Reserve, Sawyer was on active service in 1940 at Fort Jackson as an ordnance officer. Despite his military duties, Sawyer continued to serve as chief highway commissioner. On December 22, 1940, Sawyer, pursuing a weight-loss regimen in the office of a Columbia chiropractor, was accidentally asphyxiated. He was buried in Elmwood Cemetery. ALEXIA JONES HELSLEY

Moore, John Hammond. *The South Carolina Highway Department, 1917–1987.* Columbia: University of South Carolina Press, 1987.

Sawyer, Frederick Adolphus (1822–1891). U.S. senator. Sawyer was born in Bolton, Massachusetts, on December 12, 1822. After graduating from Harvard University in 1844, he taught school in Maine, New Hampshire, and Massachusetts until 1859. While in New Hampshire he met and married Delia Gay of Nashua in 1854. In 1859 he accepted an offer to create a normal school for women in Charleston, South Carolina.

After the state seceded, Sawyer remained aloof from the Confederate effort until forced to join the Home Guards in 1864. At that point he secured a pass for himself and his family through the lines to a Union outpost. They returned to the North, where Sawyer campaigned for Abraham Lincoln's reelection in 1864. In February 1865 he returned to Charleston and became active in advancing Reconstruction measures. Later that year he was appointed as a collector of internal revenue for South Carolina. He was elected to the 1868 constitutional convention but did not attend.

In 1868 Sawyer was elected as a Republican to the U.S. Senate, narrowly defeating Albert G. Mackey, a native white Republican. Sawyer then engineered the removal of Mackey from his post as collector of customs at the port of Charleston. For the rest of his term Sawyer and Congressman Christopher C. Bowen were considered the leaders of the "customs-house faction" of the Republican Party, which often opposed party regulars headed by Governor Robert K. Scott.

In the Senate, Sawyer gained a reputation as a conservative Republican and an active legislator. While he affirmed the right of blacks to vote and hold office, he also favored amnesty for former Confederates. Much of his energy was spent appealing for federal aid to the devastated South, including railroad appropriations, patronage appointments, and circulating currency. On issues relating to Reconstruction, Sawyer strongly opposed Republican corruption in South Carolina. In 1872 he returned to the state with an alleged message from President Ulysses Grant calling for an honest man to receive the Republican nomination for governor. When it went to the notoriously corrupt Franklin J. Moses, Jr., Sawyer and other moderates bolted the party and set up a rival convention, making their own nominations for state offices.

If Sawyer's conservatism won him support in Washington, it hurt him in South Carolina. Regular Republicans first complained against Sawyer in 1870, when he was accused by a prominent black leader of failing to appoint enough African Americans to customhouse jobs. It was his participation in the bolters' movement in 1872, however, that led to his replacement in the Senate. His four-year term ended that year, and he was not a serious candidate for reelection. The state legislature instead elected John J. Patterson.

After leaving the Senate, Sawyer remained in government for many years, serving in the U.S. Treasury Department, the Coast Survey, and the War Department. Retiring in 1887, he taught for a time in Ithaca, New York, and then moved to Tennessee to engage in the real estate business. Sawyer died suddenly in Shawnee, Tennessee, on July 31, 1891. He was buried on his property, Sawyer Heights, near East Cumberland Gap. HYMAN S. RUBIN III

Reynolds, John S. *Reconstruction in South Carolina, 1865–1877.* 1905. Reprint, New York: Negro Universities Press, 1969.

Sawyer, Frederick Adolphus. Papers. South Caroliniana Library, University of South Carolina, Columbia.

Seip, Terry L. *The South Returns to Congress: Men, Economic Measures, and Intersectional Relationships, 1868–1879.* Baton Rouge: Louisiana State University Press, 1983.

Saxe-Gotha Township. Originally laid out in 1733 as Congarees Township, Saxe-Gotha Township was located southwest of the confluence of the Broad and Saluda Rivers. Named to honor the marriage of the then Prince of Wales, Frederick Louis Hannover, to Augusta, Princess of Saxe-Gotha-Altenburg, the settlement contained "few, if any" Germans from Saxe-Gotha. German-speaking Swiss in Charleston petitioned for and received land grants in February 1735, were provisioned and transported by boat at the colony's expense, and by May were reported to be actively engaged in settlement. The first organized immigration of German-speaking Swiss, led by John Jacob Riemensperger, arrived in 1737, increasing the township's population by some twenty-nine families, including the Swiss Reformed minister Christian Theus. Riemensperger returned to Switzerland in 1740 and 1748, promoted immigration to Saxe-Gotha, and succeeded in enticing some six hundred Palatines and Württembergers to the township. Other immigration agents brought in some fifteen hundred Germans, so that by 1750 both Saxe-Gotha Township and the area to the northeast, known as the "Dutch Fork," were soon populated with a mix of German-speaking small farmers and redemptioners (indentured servants). During the Revolutionary War many sided with the British, both out of fear that their land grants would be rescinded and out of a sense of appreciation for the courtesies shown them by the crown. In 1785 the township's name was changed to Lexington County to honor the patriots of Massachusetts. MICHAEL EVERETTE BELL

Meriwether, Robert L. *The Expansion of South Carolina, 1729–1765.* Kingsport, Tenn.: Southern Publishers, 1940.

Moore, John Hammond. *Columbia and Richland County: A South Carolina Community, 1740–1990.* Columbia: University of South Carolina Press, 1993.

Salley, Alexander S. *The History of Orangeburg County, South Carolina from Its First Settlement to the Close of the Revolutionary War.* 1898. Reprint, Baltimore: Regional Publishing, 1969.

Sayers, Valerie (b. 1952). Author. Sayers was born on August 8, 1952, in Beaufort, the daughter of Paul Sayers and Janet Hogan. She grew up in Beaufort and was educated in local schools. She earned a B.A. from Fordham University and an M.F.A. from Columbia University and has taught creative writing at the City University of New York. In 1993 she joined the English department faculty at the University of Notre Dame, where she became director of the master of fine arts program in creative writing. She married Christian Jara on June 29, 1974. The couple has two children.

Sayers is the author of five novels and several short stories. Her first novel, *Due East* (1987), serves as an anchor work for her subsequent four novels. Due East is the name Sayers gives to the thinly disguised Beaufort of her youth and adolescence. She has said, "I was raised in a little coastal town—Beaufort, South Carolina—suspiciously like Due East. I moved to New York at seventeen, but evidently have a compunction to return to that particular southern landscape." In part, her return to Beaufort is an imaginative return to her past life and to the past life of her large family. Her second novel, *How I Got Him Back* (1989), and her third novel, *Who Do You Love* (1991), are also set in Due East. She wrote, "Every time I write about Due East—which is mostly every time I write—I am trying to come to terms with South Carolina, with how that place has seeped into my being."

Sayers's fiction centers on the family and its discontents. Daughters are alienated from fathers, husbands are alienated from wives, and children struggle to find clear paths out of the maze of family conflicts. In their search for certitude, Sayers's characters sometimes feel isolated and disappointed, and frequently they are forced to settle for small victories of reconciliation and affection.

Sayers's fiction is wholeheartedly unsentimental. Its narrative force is carried by the author's strong display of comic irony. Several critics have suggested that Sayers's ironic stance is tempered by her self-declared Catholic religious faith, placing her in a way in the southern tradition of Flannery O'Connor and Walker Percy.

Valerie Sayers was the 1992 National Endowment for the Arts literature fellow, and she has served on the fellowship panel for the National Endowment for the Arts and on the fellowship panel for the South Carolina Arts Commission. She is a frequent book reviewer for the *New York Times* and the *Washington Post.* CHARLES ISRAEL

"Valerie Sayers." In *Contemporary Authors, New Revision Series.* Vol. 61. Edited by Daniel Jones and John D. Jorgenson. Detroit: Gale, 1998.

Sayle, William (?–1671). Governor. Sayle was likely born in England in the early 1590s, though his exact place of origin, date of birth, and ancestry are unknown. Married, he fathered three sons named Thomas, Nathaniel, and James.

Sayle served as governor of English colonies in both Bermuda and South Carolina. He was first appointed governor of Bermuda on September 15, 1641, and occupied this office intermittently for the next two decades. In 1646 Sayle and William Rener purchased one-half share in a ship sent to explore the Bahama Islands. By July 1647 Sayle and a "Company of Adventurers for the Plantation of the Islands of Eleutheria" may have obtained a patent to settle one hundred Bermuda Independents in the Bahamas. Sayle departed Bermuda with about seventy adventurers and reached the Bahama Islands before October 1648. The challenges of establishing a new colony, coupled with infighting among the settlers and the inadequacy of provisions, forced Sayle to appeal to other colonies for aid. Sayle, accompanied by his wife and three children, returned to Bermuda in March 1657. Reappointed governor the following year, Sayle held this position until 1662.

In 1663 the Lords Proprietors received the right to settle and govern thousands of acres in a land called "Carolina" from Charles II of England. In August 1669 three ships carrying more than one hundred colonists departed England, under the command first of Captain Joseph West and later of Sir John Yeamans. Sailing by way of Barbados, two vessels were lost to Atlantic storms, another was blown off course to Bermuda, and a replacement ship was blown to Virginia. Returning to Barbados, Yeamans appointed William Sayle governor of the intended colony just as the sole remaining vessel set sail from Bermuda for its final destination in February 1670. Possibly nearly eighty years old at the time, Sayle was described by Yeamans as "a man of noe great sufficiency yett the ablest I could then meete with." Arriving first in Port Royal, Sayle and the colonists eventually chose to settle on the western side of the Ashley River. This later proved an undesirable site. In 1670 Sayle reserved six hundred acres on a neck of land called "Oyster Point" located at the convergence of the Ashley and Cooper Rivers. Colonial officials relocated the government to this land in 1680 and designated the property "Charles Town."

As in Bermuda and the Bahamas, political strife plagued Sayle's administration. In letters to the proprietors several prominent colonists blamed Sayle's puritan religious outlook, advanced age, and failing health for many of the colony's problems. One observer described Sayle as "a persone verie anchant or Aged and verie feble" and so riddled by illness that "what small reason he had is almost taken." A faction led by William Owen tried unsuccessfully to unseat the governor. Sayle died shortly thereafter on March 4, 1671. A copy of an addendum to his will and its proof by his successor Joseph West remain the earliest surviving probate documents in South Carolina. He bequeathed all his property to his sons Nathaniel and James. MEAGHAN N. DUFF

Cheves, Langdon, ed. *The Shaftesbury Papers.* 1897. Reprint, Charleston, S.C.: Tempus, 2000.

Miller, W. Hubert. "The Colonization of the Bahamas, 1647–1670." *William and Mary Quarterly,* 3d ser., 2 (January 1945): 33–46.

Salley, A. S., Jr., ed. *Records of the Secretary of the Province and the Register of the Province of South Carolina, 1671–1675.* Columbia: Historical Commission of South Carolina, 1944.

Sayre, Christopher Gadsden (1876–ca. 1935). Architect. Christopher G. Sayre made a career out of designing public buildings throughout the Carolinas during the first three decades of the twentieth century. Born in Mount Pleasant, he graduated with a degree in civil engineering from South Carolina College in 1897. He spent the next several years working on surveying and engineering projects across the upstate. In 1908 Sayre established an architectural practice in Anderson with James J. Baldwin. The firm's designs included commercial buildings, numerous residences, and schools in small communities throughout the state. By about 1915 the towns of North, St. George, Central, Chester, Woodruff, Holly Hill, Dillon, and Latta all had schools designed by Sayre & Baldwin. Ultimately more than twenty schools in South Carolina were designed by Sayre & Baldwin or independently by Sayre.

As their business expanded, Sayre & Baldwin opened an office in Raleigh, North Carolina, in 1914, but Baldwin left the following year to establish an independent practice. Sayre continued to pursue work in the Carolinas and Georgia. After about 1918 he worked almost exclusively in North Carolina. Sayre's most important independent projects in South Carolina include the Bamberg City Hall (1908–1909), the Saluda County Courthouse (1917), the First Baptist Church in Abbeville (1911), and the Washington Street Baptist Church (1913) in Sumter. DANIEL J. VIVIAN

Wells, John E., and Robert E. Dalton. *The South Carolina Architects, 1885–1935: A Biographical Directory.* Richmond, Va.: New South Architectural Press, 1992.

Scarborough, William Harrison (1812–1871). Painter. Scarborough was born on March 7, 1812, in Dover, Tennessee, into a family that had emigrated from England two generations previously. His earliest studies were in art and medicine, first in Nashville and then with Horace Harding in Cincinnati, an emerging art center. Portraiture was the dominant art form at the time, and Scarborough developed a proficiency in rendering sober likenesses of statesmen, planters, and merchants.

Scarborough moved to South Carolina, arriving in 1836 in Charleston, where he would have faced competition with well-established painters. He spent the early years of his career as an itinerant, advertising in local newspapers and often staying with his clients while he painted their portraits. For example, in 1836 he was in Cheraw; three years later, in 1839, he moved to Darlington, where he remained until 1846, when he made Columbia his permanent home. He spent summers at Caesars Head and made regular trips to New York to purchase art supplies. In 1857 he made a grand tour to Europe, visiting Paris, Rome, and Naples, and he even climbed Mount Vesuvius. In Florence he frequented the studio of the noted expatriate sculptor Hiram Powers and the picture galleries of the Uffizi and Pitti palaces, where he commented on the "excellent paintings."

After his return he aspired to establish an art gallery in Columbia. As an antebellum portraitist Scarborough achieved considerable success, and at his heyday he charged $125 per portrait. The majority of his portraits were oils on canvas, although he produced miniatures, small portraits done in watercolor on ivory. He also painted a few landscapes, including views of the falls of the Reedy River in Greenville and Geiger's Pond near Columbia. His portraits followed the artistic conventions of the day, with individuals shown facing the viewer and placed against plain backgrounds. Men wear dark suits, while women are often depicted with bonnets and dresses trimmed with lace. His roster of clients included many statesmen: John C. Calhoun, Governors Thomas Bennett and James H. Hammond, and Governor and Mrs. William Henry Gist. He also painted noted residents of Columbia: Mr. and Mrs. Benjamin Franklin Taylor, Dr. Robert W. Gibbes, and William C. Preston.

Scarborough married twice. On October 8, 1833, he married Sarah Ann Grimes, who died in 1835. Three years later, on November 28, 1838, he married Miranda Eliza Miller. The marriages produced four children. During the Civil War, Scarborough suffered serious financial reversals because of the decline in art patronage and his significant investments in Confederate enterprises. Examples of his work are found at the South Carolina State Museum, the Columbia Museum of Art, the Gibbes Museum of Art in Charleston, the Greenville County Museum of Art, and the South Carolina State House. Scarborough died in Columbia on August 16, 1871, and was buried in Trinity Episcopal Churchyard, Columbia. His remains were later relocated to a cemetery near Ridge Spring. See plate 20. MARTHA R. SEVERENS

Hennig, Helen Kohn. *William Harrison Scarborough: Portraitist and Miniaturist.* Columbia, S.C.: R. L. Bryan, 1937.

Schofield, Martha (1839–1916). Educator. Schofield was born in Newtown, Pennsylvania, on February 1, 1839, the daughter of Oliver Schofield and Mary Jackson. Both parents came from Quaker families that had opposed slavery for two generations, and

Martha Schofield. Courtesy, South Carolina Historical Society

her mother served as a minister who traveled to Quaker meetings in Maryland and Virginia opposing slavery. Schofield was educated at home and by friends and relatives in the Philadelphia area.

Schofield began a teaching career in 1858 at the age of nineteen in New York and during the Civil War taught in a Quaker school for African American students in Philadelphia. In 1865 she received an appointment from the Pennsylvania Freedmen's Relief Association to teach at Wadmalaw Island in South Carolina. The first year was difficult with almost no supplies, but conditions improved in 1866 when she moved to schools in the Charleston and Edisto areas. In 1867 she worked with Laura Towne on St. Helena Island, but illness, probably malaria, caused her to request an assignment in higher country. In 1868 she went to Aiken to a Freedmen's Bureau School, and she remained in Aiken until her death forty-eight years later. She initially had few social contacts with the white community, which shunned her because she encouraged the former slaves to become politically active.

When the Freedmen's Bureau School was closed in 1871, a small inheritance enabled Schofield to purchase land and construct a larger private residential school, which was later known as the Schofield Normal and Industrial School. The school had a ten-year academic program and a ten-month school year, which was longer than that for public schools for either race in South Carolina. It soon developed a good reputation for its academic standards and for its agricultural, home economics, industrial, and craft training programs. It eventually contained dormitories for boys and girls, ten classrooms, a library, a chapel, a farm, and craft areas. Many graduates went into teaching and were certified by the state as college graduates upon completion of the ten-year program. Funding came from tuition, products sold, and charitable contributions that Schofield solicited on annual trips to the North.

Schofield was also interested in women's rights and waged a campaign in the 1890s for women to be selected as speakers at the annual National Education Association conventions. She worked for women's suffrage and prohibition vigorously and became nationally known. Although initially resented by Aiken white families, she gained acceptance in the community when her fund-raising brought in donations from wealthy northerners, including the industrialist Andrew Carnegie. She was pleased to be appointed a director of the Aiken bank in recognition of her financial success.

Schofield died on February 1, 1916, her seventy-seventh birthday. The Aiken public high school for African American students was named for her. After school integration, it became a middle school, which continued to use her name as well as the bell that had rung on her campus since 1886. ALICE H. HENDERSON

Smedley, Katherine. *Martha Schofield and the Re-education of the South, 1839–1916.* Lewiston, N.Y.: Edwin Mellen, 1987.

Schofield Normal and Industrial School. Founded in 1871 by Martha Schofield, a Pennsylvania Quaker, this Aiken school for freed slaves remained a center of education for black South Carolinians for more than seventy years. The school's initial financial support came from Schofield, the John F. Slater Fund, and other Quakers from Pennsylvania. Unfortunately, these contributions proved to be inadequate, and the financial burden fell entirely to Schofield, who used her personal fortune to sustain the school until she resigned in 1912. The school operated in the original Freedman's Bureau school building until 1882, when a new building was constructed. The school began as a day school, and from its beginning the goal was to prepare teachers who were desperately needed in the state's rural black schools. As with most freedmen's schools, the curriculum was a simplified version of the classical course of study.

Schofield was also the site for a summer Colored Teachers' Institute where teaching methods, teacher qualifications, and community-school relations were discussed. With more than twenty years of training teachers, the state board of education recognized the school's success by granting it university status in 1908, and later graduates were automatically licensed to teach without taking county or state examinations. Initially vocal in their animosity toward the school and its students, the white community eventually came to praise the students for their dependability and skills. The school joined the Aiken school system in 1953 as a public high school for blacks. Since integration in the 1960s, Schofield has served Aiken County as a public middle school, and the bell tower from the original building still sat on the Sumter Street campus in the early twenty-first century. LOUISE ALLEN

Smedley, Katherine. *Martha Schofield and the Re-education of the South, 1839–1916.* Lewiston, N.Y.: Edwin Mellen, 1987.

———. "Martha Schofield and the Rights of Women." *South Carolina Historical Magazine* 85 (July 1984): 195–210.

Toole, Gasper Loren. *Ninety Years in Aiken County: Memoirs of Aiken County and Its People.* N.p., n.d.

Scots. The first Scot to visit South Carolina was John Crafford, supercargo aboard the *James of Erwin* in 1682. The *James* was charting sites for a proposed Scottish colony, and Crafford, probably under commission of the Lords Proprietors, published a glowing review titled *A New and Most Exact Account of the Fertiles and Famous Colony of Carolina.* Carolina, Crafford said, was "the most healthfull and fertile of His Majesties territories." Over the coming centuries many Scots would make their names, fortunes, or at least better lives in Carolina. Time would show, though, that the Carolina climate was certainly not healthful to expatriate Scots, nor were the rewards of colonization always equal to its costs.

For Scots, one of the attractions of Carolina was religious liberty. The proprietors guaranteed it, and Scottish Covenanters stood ready to emigrate for it. The Covenanters were rigid Presbyterians, opposed to the authority of royally appointed bishops and loyal to the proscribed Covenant of 1638. Through the 1670s several Covenanting leaders, among them William Dunlop and Henry Erskine, Lord Cardross, hoped to establish a Presbyterian haven abroad. Cardross and Dunlop opened negotiations with the proprietors in 1680, arranged for the *James* to reconnoiter, and planted their new colony, Stuart's Town, in October 1684.

Unfortunately for the Scots, Port Royal Sound was claimed by Spain, and in August 1686 the Spanish dispatched an expedition against them that destroyed the settlement. Most of the colonists survived, but the demise of Stuart's Town ensured that South Carolina would henceforth be an English colony, under English law, with its center of gravity at Charleston.

The 1707 Treaty of Union allowed Scots free access to the British Empire, and large numbers made their way to the southern colonies. Scottish immigration to South Carolina was distinctive, however, for while Georgia and North Carolina received waves of poor highlanders, South Carolina attracted lowlanders, the educated younger sons of the landed and professional classes. A self-conscious Scottish elite of merchants, planters, and professionals coalesced in the cities. They founded churches, schools, and a Charleston-based St. Andrew's Society, creating a social network that attracted still more of their countrymen and countrywomen. Representative of these was Dr.

John Moultrie, who in 1728 brought his Scottish medical training—then the world's best—to Carolina, the first of several generations of Edinburgh-schooled Moultries to practice medicine in Charleston. Another was Robert Pringle, who arrived in South Carolina in 1725 as a merchant's agent but made good on his own through trade in land, slaves, rice, and indigo. Perhaps the most prominent Scot in colonial South Carolina was Governor James Glen. Appointed in 1738, Glen combined ironclad integrity and conservative financial policy—if not modesty. He boasted that he found the colony "in ashes, defenceless and declining" and left it "fortified and flourishing." By 1790, even after significant war-time departures, more than 21,000 South Carolinians—about fifteen percent of the state's white population—were ethnic or immigrant Scots.

The Revolutionary War transformed the Scottish community in British North America. Scottish networks of influence and authority collapsed as many, especially highlanders, refused to tolerate rebellion against British sovereignty. The watershed for South Carolina Scots came in 1782, when British forces evacuated Charleston. Four thousand Loyalists, largely but not exclusively Scottish, left with the redcoats. Those who remained and those who came later no longer proclaimed their Scottish identity so openly. As the historian William Brock noted, they "ceased to be Scots resident in America, and became Americans of Scottish descent." Even a man such as George Buist, principal of Charleston College, found it necessary to lose his accent to avoid the "Tory" taint. Scottish immigration gradually resumed, rising to a peak in the 1820s, but industrial-era migrants were more often the displaced and the dispossessed, people less enamored of Scotland and determined to assimilate in America.

The Scottish legacy in South Carolina is mixed. The American tradition of religious liberty is affirmed in South Carolina by the experiment at Stuart's Town. Scots were instrumental in the development of the colony's first staples: rice and indigo. Staples, however, require labor, and Scots were enthusiastic slavers, turning to Africans after royal governors forbade kidnapping Indians. Another double-edged blessing is the Scottish tradition of bellicose independence and distrust of central authority, invoked triumphantly by some in 1776 and tragically by others in 1860. More recently, that curious Fifeshire pastime golf has become a bulwark of the Carolina economy, and highland games are as popular in the lowcountry as they are in the upstate. In the twenty-first century Scots remain one visible component of the ethnic stew that is South Carolina. ROBERT H. LANDRUM

Brock, William R. *Scotus Americanus: A Survey of the Sources for the Links between Scotland and America in the Eighteenth Century.* Edinburgh: Edinburgh University Press, 1982.

Dobson, David. *Directory of Scottish Settlers in North America, 1625–1825.* 6 vols. Baltimore: Genealogical Publishing, 1986.

Donaldson, Gordon. *The Scots Overseas.* London: Robert Hale, 1966.

Scott, Robert Kingston (1826–1900). Governor. Scott was born on July 8, 1826, in Armstrong County, Pennsylvania, the son of John Scott, a farmer, and Jane Hamilton. At age sixteen he moved to Ohio, where he attended Central College and Sterling Medical College. He joined the gold rush to California in 1850 but returned to Ohio the following year and settled in Henry County, where he prospered as a physician, real estate speculator, and retailer. Sometime in the 1850s he married Rebecca Jane Lowry, and the couple eventually had two children. During the Civil War, Scott organized the Sixty-eighth Ohio Volunteers and eventually rose to the rank of brigadier general. In 1866 Scott was appointed assistant commissioner of the Freedmen's Bureau in South Carolina. He struggled diligently to provide food for freedmen and destitute whites but was dismayed by the opposition and cruelty of many whites toward the former slaves.

Scott reluctantly accepted the Republican Party's nomination for governor in 1868 and was elected with support derived largely from newly enfranchised black male voters. With most white South Carolinians regarding his administration as illegitimate, Scott instead cultivated a working but sometimes uneasy relationship with black political leaders. In his 1868 inaugural address he urged reconciliation and advocated the establishment of segregated public schools, and then he failed to invite any African Americans to a reception that followed. In 1870 he supported the election of the black congressmen Robert Brown Elliott and Robert DeLarge, and Alonzo Ransier served as the state's first black lieutenant governor during Scott's second term.

In 1868 and 1869 white violence and terror erupted as dozens of black and white Republicans were threatened, beaten, and assassinated. Scott signed a bill in 1869 organizing a state militia composed largely of black men. The violence continued unabated in several upcountry counties until President Ulysses S. Grant dispatched federal troops and suspended the writ of habeas corpus in 1871 in nine counties. Scott's administration was further tarnished by the corruption that contaminated Republican and Democratic leaders during Reconstruction. Though he adamantly denied it, Scott was alleged to have participated in a bribery scheme involving the sale of railroad bonds. Reelected in 1870, Scott avoided impeachment in 1872 when several legislators allegedly accepted bribes to defeat the resolution. John J. Patterson defeated both Scott and Robert Brown Elliott for a U.S. Senate seat in 1872 amid further allegations of bribery.

Well intentioned but ineffective, Scott was unable to sustain the confidence of many Republicans and was thoroughly despised by almost every Democrat. Worth more than $300,000 before he became governor, Scott added to his wealth through a series of Columbia real estate transactions. He frequently loaned money to less prosperous black and white politicians as well as to impoverished white planters. He remained in Columbia until 1878 and then returned to Ohio rather than face indictment on charges of corruption. In 1880 Scott was charged with killing a Napoleon, Ohio, drugstore clerk but was acquitted of accidental homicide. He suffered a stroke in 1899 and died on August 12, 1900. He was buried in Henry County, Ohio. WILLIAM C. HINE

Current, Richard Nelson. *Those Terrible Carpetbaggers.* New York: Oxford University Press, 1988.

Scott, Robert K. Governors' Papers. South Carolina Department of Archives and History, Columbia.

———. Papers. Ohio Historical Society, Columbus.

Sea Islands. Scattered along the state's approximately 185 miles of coastline, South Carolina's Sea Islands shelter the mainland from storms and erosion. But this ever-changing string of islands, battered by ocean tides as well as by man's influences, is more than just a physical buffer. The islands' borders also protect a way of life, a unique cultural identity nurtured by the nearby warm Gulf Stream waters that provided the climate that has defined life on the Sea Islands.

The islands differ considerably in formation, size, and land use. Within this string of more than one hundred islands stretching from South Carolina to northern Florida, geologists describe two distinct types: active barriers and erosion remnants. Active barrier islands

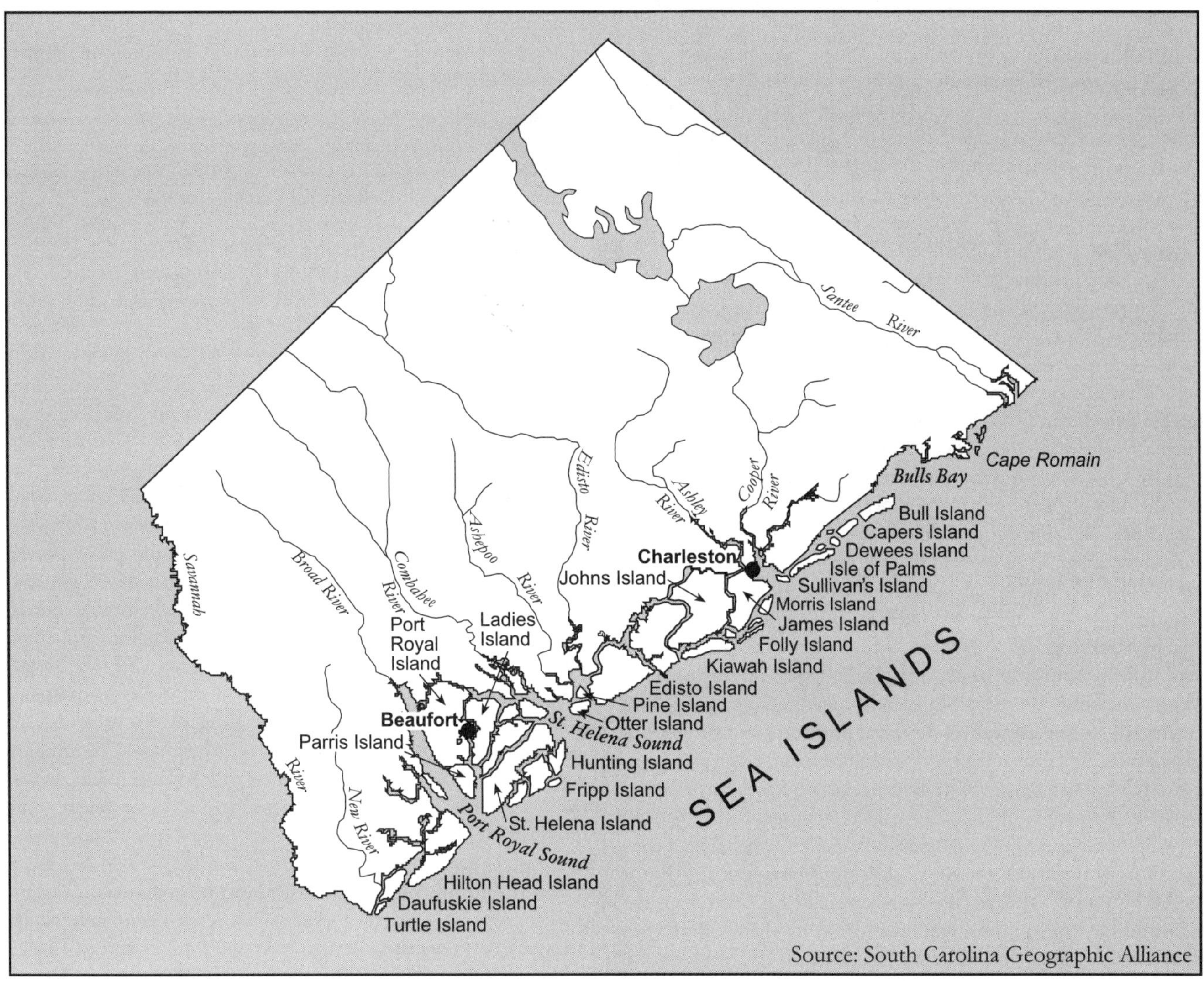

The coastal zone and the sea islands

developed as currents and storms moved sand into beach ridges and dunes, held in place by persistent vegetation. These islands are the least stable of the two types and are subject to significant alteration by natural forces or wind and sea currents. Hunting and Fripp Islands are examples of this type.

Once part of the mainland, erosion remnant islands separated as the sea level declined during the Pleistocene epoch, forming valleys that were then flooded when the sea level rose again at the end of the most recent ice age. Richer and more stable, this type includes some of the larger barrier islands such as Hilton Head.

The islands vary in size from small enough to toss a stone across to large enough to lose sight of the bordering ocean or estuary. Traditionally focused on agriculture, many of the Sea Islands in the twenty-first century face problems associated with heavy development pressure, while some lie in areas shielded by state or national laws preventing development. The islands associated with the Cape Romain National Wildlife Refuge and other protected areas along the coast remain pristine and natural. In some areas islands still support significant agriculture and development has been slower in coming. Wadmalaw Island, outside of Charleston, is one example.

Development on some of the islands was made more difficult by the passing of the 1983 Barrier Islands Act, which removed them from federal flood insurance programs and disallowed subsidies for the building of infrastructure needed for development, including roads and sewers. In spite of this, development has still occurred on some of the islands covered under this act.

Sea Island natural and cultural character can in large part be traced to the nearby Gulf Stream, which warms the air as well as the water as it passes the South Carolina coast. Many islands still feature the maritime forest vegetation that thrives only in the semitropical temperatures allowed by warm, humid salt air and sandy soils. This distinct type of forest includes live oak, palmetto, wax myrtle, groundsel, salt-tolerant slash pines, and yaupon holly. This jungle-like forest provides cover for a variety of wildlife species, including many insects, reptiles, crustaceans, birds, and mammals. For this reason, early settlers in the lowcountry called the islands "hunting islands," where they went to pursue the plentiful game.

Warmth from the Gulf Stream also provided the long growing season—290 days—in the early days for cultivation of indigo. When the Revolutionary War ended trade with England, and thus indigo profits, planters turned to long staple, or "Sea Island" cotton, for which the area became famous. Sea Island cotton thrived in the long growing season, humidity, salty air, and arid conditions. As demand for Sea Island cotton grew, the plantation system flourished, dependent on large holdings and slave labor. Farmers made rich by raising the staple planted every available foot of land in Sea

Island cotton. A planter elite grew out of the wealth produced on the Sea Island plantations. But with a limited amount of suitable land, plantations stopped expanding, and acres planted in cotton stabilized by the 1830s. With cotton land on the islands at a premium, cotton growers made extensive efforts to sustain and restore the soil, which became depleted during the antebellum period. They used soil, crushed oyster shells, and decayed vegetation for fertilizer. They drained low-lying areas to create more growing acreage and reclaimed some salt-marsh areas by diking and draining.

Plantation life during the heyday of Sea Island cotton was good for planters and their families. Plantation owners built large houses of tabby, a locally available building material of sand, lime, oyster shells, and water mixed to form the consistency of concrete and poured into forms to construct walls. Tabby ruins left throughout the Sea Islands testify to the popularity of this material, which was often covered with stucco. Game and seafood were plentiful, and wealthy families often left plantations for summer retreats on the islands, forming summer communities at places such as Eddingsville, Rockville, and Isle of Palms to avoid the diseases associated with hot weather. They believed that the sea air was healthy and prevented diseases, but it was actually the breezes keeping disease-carrying mosquitoes at bay that likely kept them healthy.

The cultivation of Sea Island cotton was done by hand and depended on a vast slave labor force. Slave populations surpassed the white populations on many Sea Islands, sometimes by a ratio of as much as ten to one. Africans and African Americans living in the Sea Islands passed on elements of African culture, from crafts and cooking to music and language. The influence of African culture remains apparent. Remnants of the slave Creole language, called Gullah, show up in the speech of longtime Sea Island residents. Gullah consists of a vocabulary of mostly English words arranged in African sentence structure. Because the islands remained isolated from the mainland for so long, these and other elements of the unique Sea Island culture remained long after the end of slavery. Slave culture and the Gullah language made indelible marks on the islands, and efforts are in place to preserve the remnants of this way of life.

Eighty years after the reign of Sea Island cotton began, the Civil War erupted. The Union occupation of the Port Royal region in the fall of 1861 led many island landowners to abandon their plantations. The Sea Island way of life never recovered after the Civil War. Many of the plantations were divided up among former slaves, who grew subsistence crops for food rather than for cash. Plantations that remained intact faced disabling labor problems. Sea Island cotton production struggled on for a short time after the war but continued to dwindle until the early 1920s, when it collapsed under the combined weight of hurricanes, the boll weevil, and competition from other cotton-growing regions.

After the demise of "King Cotton," the Sea Islands residents continued to rely on the fruits of the land and sea. Truck farming provided staples: potatoes, tomatoes, cucumbers, and corn, much of which is still grown on small Sea Island farms. Commercial fishing, including oystering, crabbing, and shrimping, also provided food and cash during the lean years. Shrimp remained the most valuable seafood product as of the early twenty-first century.

The development of Hilton Head Island in the 1960s paved the way for high-end residential and resort communities on other Sea Islands, such as Kiawah, Fripp, and Daufuskie. With changes from rural agricultural land to developed land that welcomes new residents by the thousands and visitors by the millions each year, tourism has become the economic mainstay. Despite dramatic demographic and environmental changes, the Sea Islands remain among the most unique natural and cultural attractions on the eastern coast. CAROLINE FOSTER

Danielson, Michael N. *Profits and Politics in Paradise: The Development of Hilton Head Island.* Columbia: University of South Carolina Press, 1995.

Fairey, Daniel A. *South Carolina's Geologic Framework.* Columbia: South Carolina Land Resources Conservation Commission, 1977.

Jordan, Laylon Wayne, and Elizabeth Stringfellow. *A Place Called St. John's.* Spartanburg, S.C.: Reprint Company, 1998.

Kovacik, Charles F., and John J. Winberry. *South Carolina: The Making of a Landscape.* 1987. Reprint, Columbia: University of South Carolina Press, 1989.

Rhyne, Nancy. *Chronicles of the South Carolina Sea Islands.* Winston-Salem, N.C.: John F. Blair, 1998.

Sea Pines Company. The Sea Pines Plantation Company was incorporated in 1957 by Charles E. Fraser of Georgia to develop the southern third of Hilton Head Island into a residential, recreational, and resort community. By 2000 the project had blossomed into a hugely influential and extremely profitable venture encompassing 5,200 acres, five miles of Atlantic Ocean shoreline, a nature preserve, private villas, hotels, a beach club, conference centers, golf courses, tennis courts, both a marina and a yacht basin, walking and equestrian trails, restaurants, and one of South Carolina's five largest real estate companies, averaging more than $1 million per day in transactions.

Fraser's plans for Sea Pines were influenced in part by Sea Island, Georgia, and Pebble Beach, California, where some community master planning had been implemented with positive results. Fraser, however, controlled the development of Sea Pines much more tightly, in the process introducing many profitable innovations that have been widely emulated. The new community would be unique in its environmental sensitivity, with beaches, golf courses, resorts, and shopping all discreetly tucked into a seven-square-mile nature preserve. Quiet understatement would result from extremely detailed restrictions on land use. He insisted on building the very best in order to attract the very wealthiest customers in order to maximize the inevitable increase in land values. By weaving home sites in and around golf courses, he was able to create a different kind of premium home site market, and by removing roads to a location further inland and connecting home sites to the beach via paved paths, Fraser increased the number of "waterfront" lots that could be sold at prestige prices.

In the early 1960s Sea Pines struggled financially, but its explosive growth in the second half of that decade and throughout the rest of the century testified to Fraser's foresight. Developments following the Sea Pines model later occupied all of Hilton Head Island and can be found widely throughout the United States. MARGARET A. SHANNON

Danielson, Michael N. *Profits and Politics in Paradise: The Development of Hilton Head Island.* Columbia: University of South Carolina Press, 1995.

Seabrook, Whitemarsh Benjamin (1793–1855). Governor. Seabrook was born in Colleton District on June 30, 1793, son of the Edisto Island planter Benjamin Seabrook and Elizabeth Meggett. After graduating from the College of New Jersey (Princeton) in 1812, Seabrook returned to Colleton District, where he established himself as a cotton planter and a leading advocate of agricultural reform. A prolific writer on agricultural subjects, Seabrook urged South Carolina planters to diversify their agricultural pursuits and adopt scientific farming techniques. A member of several agricultural organizations, he also led the successful effort to create the State

Agricultural Society in 1839. On February 7, 1815, Seabrook married Margaret Wilkinson Hamilton. The couple had eleven children.

Along with his zeal in promoting agriculture, Seabrook was one of South Carolina's most vocal defenders of slavery and states' rights. His political service included representing St. John's Colleton Parish in the state House of Representatives (1814–1819) and the state Senate (1826–1833), as well as a term as lieutenant governor (1834–1836). In the 1830s and 1840s Seabrook allied himself with the state's most radical political movements, including nullification in the early 1830s and the Bluffton Movement of 1844. Seabrook penned several proslavery works that upheld the institution and warned slaveholders of the growing threat of abolitionism from the North and Great Britain.

An unsuccessful candidate for governor in 1844, Seabrook was narrowly elected to the office by the General Assembly on December 12, 1848. His tenure came in the stormy wake of the Wilmot Proviso controversy, in which northern members of Congress attempted to prohibit slavery in territories gained by the United States in the Mexican War. Believing that "there is to be no peace for the slaveholder" while South Carolina remained in the Union, Governor Seabrook urged his state to prepare for secession and the defense of its institutions. He asked legislators for appropriations to purchase arms and build armories, while also urging a reorganization of the state militia. Seabrook demanded that the distribution of abolitionist writings "be declared an offence punishable with severe and definite penalties." Failing to act on Seabrook's demands in its 1849 session, the legislature passed an act to strengthen the state's defenses the following year after Congress passed the so-called Compromise of 1850, which Seabrook denounced as "another triumph over the South by the fell spirit of abolitionism."

Following the end of his term in December 1850, Seabrook joined other radicals in canvassing the state to drum up popular support for secession as the only viable defense against northern aggression. These efforts were thwarted in 1851 when voters in an election for delegates to a "Southern Convention" opted for the more moderate cooperationists, who called for secession only if joined by other southern states. Seabrook remained an ardent secessionist for the remaining few years of his life. He died on April 16, 1855, at Strawberry Hill plantation in St. Luke's Parish, Beaufort District, and was buried at Gun Bluff plantation on Edisto Island. TOM DOWNEY

Bailey, N. Louise, Mary L. Morgan, and Carolyn R. Taylor, eds. *Biographical Directory of the South Carolina Senate, 1776–1985.* 3 vols. Columbia: University of South Carolina Press, 1986.

Barnwell, John. *Love of Order: South Carolina's First Secession Crisis.* Chapel Hill: University of North Carolina Press, 1982.

Secession. December 20, 1860, the day in Charleston on which delegates at the South Carolina state convention voted unanimously to secede from the Union, is arguably the decisive moment in the state's history. On that day the representatives of the people of South Carolina committed themselves to leading other slave states out of the federal Union. It was not the first time South Carolinians had contemplated secession.

To understand those momentous events of December 1860, as well as the people and their ideals, requires a foray into the state's past, into developments surrounding the making of that perilous dissent from the Union. South Carolinians, from the first decades of settlement, had displayed a willingness to rebel against outside forces they viewed as dangerous to their way of life. In the "Revolution of 1719," the colonists mounted the only successful colonial rebellion when they overthrew the regime of the Lords Proprietors. When Carolinians rebelled in the 1770s, they hearkened back to the events of 1719. Similarly, when South Carolina's leaders promoted secession in 1860, they considered themselves the political heirs of the men of 1776.

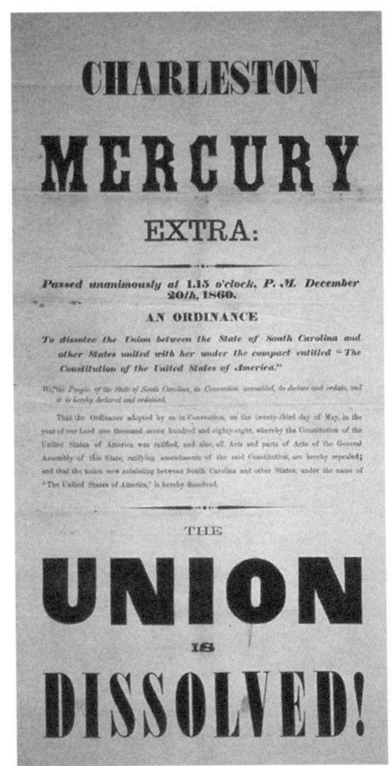
CHARLESTON

MERCURY

EXTRA:

Passed unanimously at 1.15 o'clock, P. M. December 20th, 1860.

AN ORDINANCE

To dissolve the Union between the State of South Carolina and other States united with her under the compact entitled "The Constitution of the United States of America."

We, the People of the State of South Carolina, in Convention assembled, do declare and ordain, and it is hereby declared and ordained,

That the Ordinance adopted by us in Convention, on the twenty-third day of May, in the year of our Lord one thousand seven hundred and eighty-eight, whereby the Constitution of the United States of America was ratified, and also, all Acts and parts of Acts of the General Assembly of this State, ratifying amendments of the said Constitution, are hereby repealed; and that the union now subsisting between South Carolina and other States, under the name of "The United States of America," is hereby dissolved.

THE

UNION

IS

DISSOLVED!

"The Union Is Dissolved" was the banner headline in the prosecessionist newspaper the *Charleston Mercury.* Courtesy, South Carolina Historical Society

Although South Carolinians played a major role in the creation of the new federal Constitution, there were those in the state who feared the power of a strong central government. These men, including Aedanus Burke, Wade Hampton I, and Rawlins Lowndes, questioned whether slave-state interests could possibly gain support from the more populous northern free states who would control the new government.

By the 1820s South Carolina had become, through the use of slave labor, the largest and wealthiest cotton-producing and -exporting state. But the desire of northern states for tariff protection for its manufacturers threatened South Carolina's and other slave states' dependence on a free market for the exportation of cotton. Vice President John C. Calhoun took the covert, and later overt, lead in the antitariff struggle. His 1832 nullification doctrine of state interposition of the federal tariff delivered the state's first threat of secession from the Union.

During the nullification crisis of 1832–1833, South Carolina failed to persuade other slave states of the graveness of the situation, and its leaders were divided over how to defend the state's interests without support from the rest of the South. The crisis subsided shortly thereafter, but tensions over the need to protect slavery did not end. During the 1840s state leaders such as Governor James Henry Hammond and Robert Barnwell Rhett, with his organ the radical *Charleston Mercury,* once again advocated the secession of South Carolina. Rhett's secessionist so-called Bluffton Movement of 1844 failed to convince either South Carolinians or other southern states of the dangers to their way of life.

During the 1848–1852 sectional crisis over creating new slave and free states, another secessionist movement began in South Carolina. Once again Calhoun eloquently called for southern unity and threatened secession to ward off the threat posed by northern states to slave society. Calhoun's famous March 4, 1850, speech in Congress has been regarded as a major defense of the right of secession to protect the interests of a political minority. With Calhoun's death later that year, the mantle of sectionalist leadership passed to Rhett and Hammond. They attempted to arouse other slave states to the northern threat to their way of life. Once again they failed, as moderate Unionists in the state and in the South, such as James L. Orr and Benjamin F. Perry, succeeded in quelling the secession fervor. Hammond, tempering his rhetoric, attended a southern convention in 1850 held in Nashville, Tennessee. There he asked the other slave states to unite with South Carolina to resist what he called northern aggression against their "peculiar institution." But the Nashville convention failed to unite either other slave states or all South Carolinians.

South Carolina's secession movement appeared dormant in the late 1850s, although some state leaders continued to talk to allies in other slave states about the necessity of secession. The fledgling Republican Party, founded in 1854, was anathema to virtually all white Carolinians. Early in 1860 the moderate South Carolinian Christopher G. Memminger traveled to Virginia to persuade its legislature of the Republican danger to the interests of all of the slave states. Though Memminger seemingly failed in his task, his speech before the Virginia legislature stands alongside Calhoun's as an eloquent statement of the right of secession. Printed in pamphlet form and circulated throughout South Carolina and the other slave states, Memminger's justification of secession called for the unity of all slave states. When the national Democratic convention, held in Charleston in April 1860, failed to nominate a presidential candidate, Memminger and others held out hope for a southern Democratic candidate who would unite the slave states. It was not to be. With the Democrats hopelessly divided, it appeared almost certain that the Republican candidate, Abraham Lincoln, would be elected president in November.

In September a group calling itself the "1860 Association" came into being. It represented South Carolinians of all political persuasions, but the bulk of its membership came from longtime cooperationists—men who believed in secession if the other southern states would follow suit. The 1860 Association, foreseeing Lincoln's election, determined that secession was the only way for white Carolinians to preserve their way of life. The group was also determined that they, and not radicals such as Rhett, would lead the state out of the Union and into a new nation.

While not totally of one mind, South Carolina was the least divided of all slave states. Years of fear propaganda preached from pulpit and political platform, published in newspapers and journals, and presented in fiction and poetry left little room for dialogue over how the state should defend itself. In addition, the state's wealth resided in the slave economy and related enterprises. The dependence of the economy on slave labor and of the political system on slavery united slaveholder and yeoman farmer alike in defense of their interests. All felt that the federal government threatened the rights of those who believed in the authority of local government in a republic. When material interests and political and cultural values united with fear of slave insurrection, few leaders and citizens questioned the need for South Carolina to leave the Union.

When the General Assembly met in November to vote for presidential electors, it remained in Columbia until the results of the election were known. Upon receiving the news of Lincoln's victory, the legislators voted to hold an election for delegates to a special state convention. At about the same time the state's congressional delegation resigned. In addition, Governor William Gist and his successor Francis W. Pickens had been in touch with governors of Alabama, Mississippi, Florida, and Georgia, all of whom had promised that their legislatures would call for conventions to consider a response to Lincoln's election. On December 6 the state's citizens voted for representatives to the South Carolina convention. The delegates, made up largely of planters committed to secession, met in Columbia on December 17, 1860. An outbreak of smallpox caused the convention to relocate to Charleston, and on December 20, 1860, the 169 delegates present voted unanimously to secede from the federal Union. The city erupted in a wild celebration with bonfires, parades, and the pealing of church bells.

In Institute Hall on Meeting Street in Charleston, South Carolina voted to secede from the Union. Courtesy, South Caroliniana Library, University of South Carolina

Just as their forebears had justified their rebellions in 1719 and 1776, so too the men of 1860 left a rationale for their actions. The Secession Convention delegates named Rhett and Memminger to write up the reasons for secession. Rhett wrote "The Address to the Slave-Holding States," and his central argument was based on the right to self-government. He wrote of the history of the North's desire to control the South and thus focused on the struggles for a free government. His political argument was also laced with a discussion of how the North and the South had become two peoples. Memminger, in his "Declaration of the Causes of Secession," took a more direct approach to the defense of slavery. He listed the northern states' violation of the fugitive slave law, their personal liberty laws claiming that slavery was unjust, and the election of an antislavery Republican president as the reasons why South Carolina seceded, and he stated that the rest of the slave states should follow suit.

Values, ideals, needs, and fear all came together in South Carolinians' defense of their way of life. There was no choice, said a united white South Carolina, but to leave the Union they had once embraced and helped to create. See plate 22. JON L. WAKELYN

Boucher, Chauncey S. "The Annexation of Texas and the Bluffton Movement in South Carolina." *Mississippi Valley Historical Review* 6 (June 1919): 3–33.

Channing, Steven A. *Crisis of Fear: Secession in South Carolina.* New York: Simon and Schuster, 1970.

Ford, Lacy K, Jr. *Origins of Southern Radicalism: The South Carolina Upcountry, 1800–1860.* New York: Oxford University Press, 1988.

Freehling, William W. *Prelude to Civil War: The Nullification Controversy in South Carolina, 1816–1836.* New York: Harper & Row, 1965.

Hamer, Philip M. *The Secession Movement in South Carolina, 1847–1852.* 1918. Reprint, New York: Da Capo, 1971.

Schultz, Harold S. *Nationalism and Sectionalism in South Carolina, 1852–1860: A Study of the Movement for Southern Independence.* Durham, N.C.: Duke University Press, 1950.

Sinha, Manisha. *The Counterrevolution of Slavery: Politics and Ideology in Antebellum South Carolina.* Chapel Hill: University of North Carolina Press, 2000.

Wakelyn, Jon L., ed. *Southern Pamphlets on Secession, November 1860–April 1861.* Chapel Hill: University of North Carolina Press, 1996.

Secession crisis of 1850–1851. In the late 1840s the escalating sectional controversy over the expansion of slavery into the territory acquired from Mexico set in motion South Carolina's secession crisis of 1850–1851. In response to the Wilmot Proviso, a congressional proposal to ban slavery in the territory gained in the Mexican War, and the so-called Compromise of 1850, a series of measures maneuvered through Congress in an attempt to pacify both northern and southern interests, South Carolina secessionists brought their state to the brink of disunion. Palmetto secessionists, however, were disappointed by the growing acceptance of the Compromise of 1850 across the South. Procompromise Whigs and Democrats successfully played on party loyalty to wean southern states away from the notion of a southern party committed solely to the defense of slavery—a goal to which much of South Carolina was committed.

With the death of John C. Calhoun in March 1850, radical secessionists, including Robert Barnwell Rhett, Maxcy Gregg, James H. Adams, David F. Jamison, and Daniel Wallace, demanded that South Carolina secede, regardless of the course adopted by other slaveholding states. Cooperationists, meanwhile, professed their willingness to secede but argued that separate secession would leave South Carolina isolated and impotent.

Secessionists constituted a majority when the General Assembly met in December 1850. They elected the secessionist John H. Means governor, sent Rhett to the U.S. Senate, and levied new taxes to fund increased appropriations for a board of ordinance and other military measures. Competing secessionist and cooperationist plans for future action resulted in compromise. Cooperationists supported and won a measure calling for elections in October 1851 to choose two delegates to a proposed southern congress. Secessionists obtained a bill providing for elections in February 1851 to choose representatives to a state convention, but they could not get the cooperationists' agreement on setting a date for these elections.

Secessionist candidates prevailed in the February elections, but voter turnout was low. To quicken support for their cause, secessionists employed local Southern Rights Associations and multiplied their number. Throughout the first five months of 1851, secessionists enjoyed an organizational advantage over cooperationists and propounded a clear and definitive message: secession would protect slavery permanently in South Carolina and lead to unparalleled prosperity for its producers of stable crops. The May 1851 statewide convention of Southern Rights Associations called for secession alone and against any odds.

Cooperationists countered that separate secession would bring economic disaster and ruin efforts at forming a united southern defense of slavery. In Charleston cooperationists launched their own newspaper, the *Southern Standard,* to counter the *Mercury's* powerful voice for secession. Led by James L. Orr, John S. Preston, and James Chesnut in the midstate and the upcountry, and by Langdon Cheves, Robert W. Barnwell, Isaac Hayne, and Christopher G. Memminger in Charleston and the lowcountry, the cooperationists by October 1851 matched or exceeded the local organizations of their opponents, especially in the middle and upper districts of the state. The October 1851 elections for the now chimerical Southern Congress became a referendum on separate secession. In that election cooperationists were aided in the upcountry by a tacit alliance with the followers of Benjamin Perry's conditional Unionists. Statewide, cooperationist candidates won 58.8 percent of the vote. Only in the Seventh Congressional District, where the slave majority of the population reached or exceeded 80 percent in lowcountry parishes, did the secessionists prevail. Secession was thwarted for the time being but would rise again following the election of Abraham Lincoln in the fall of 1860. JOHN BARNWELL

Barnwell, John. *Love of Order: South Carolina's First Secession Crisis.* Chapel Hill: University of North Carolina Press, 1982.

Ford, Lacy K., Jr. *Origins of Southern Radicalism: The South Carolina Upcountry, 1800–1860.* New York: Oxford University Press, 1988.

Secessionville, Battle of (June 16, 1862). In April 1862 Union generals David Hunter and Henry Benham decided to assault Charleston by marching one wing across Johns Island and sailing another for Battery Island. From there the combined columns would rush across James Island, establish batteries at Charleston harbor, and batter the city into submission.

Battle of Secessionville. Courtesy, South Carolina Historical Society

Union forces occupied Battery Island and Johns Island during the first week of June, but they were surprised at the spirited resistance of Confederate forces. Before Hunter returned to Hilton Head on June 11, he warned Benham not to attack. Benham, however, used Hunter's absence to organize an assault on the Confederate Tower Battery near the planter village of Secessionville, an operation he launched on the morning of June 16. One hundred infantrymen and two artillery companies under Colonel Thomas G. Lamar recoiled before the first Federal assault, but the battery's defenders, supported by the timely arrival of reinforcements, threw back the Union troops in hand-to-hand fighting. A second Northern wave crashed against the battery's left flank, but the Confederates again withstood the storm. Meanwhile, Lamar's artillery turned the expanse west of the battery into a killing field.

Unbeknownst to the Northerners, the battery stood at the choke point of a telescoping peninsula. The marshy terrain forced the Federal attackers into the mouths of the Confederate guns, and the impassable "pluff mud" prevented Benham's second wing from attacking the fort's northern flank. These Federals established a firing line just 125 yards away, but Colonel Johnson Hagood directed a Confederate attack on the Union position from the north, while another Confederate battalion confronted the Federals from the south. Aided by nearby artillery, the Confederates repelled the Northerners with a ring of fire. After three frustrating hours, Benham withdrew his forces.

Of the 4,500 Federal attackers, nearly 700 became casualties. Confederate forces totaled only about 1,000, with a loss of fewer than 200 men. Secessionville blunted what proved to be the North's best chance to capture Charleston. The Civil War may have produced larger engagements with heavier casualties, but the battle at Secessionville remains one of South Carolina's most important. PAT BRENNAN

Brennan, Patrick. *Secessionville: Assault on Charleston.* Campbell, Calif.: Savas, 1996.

Segregation. Segregation, the residential, political, and social isolation of African Americans, was accomplished in South Carolina by a long and varying effort in the aftermath of slavery. The de facto, or socially based, segregation of the races was channeled in the late nineteenth and early twentieth centuries into a rigid legal, or de jure, system that effectively enforced the second-class citizenship of African Americans. As all-encompassing as the system of "Jim Crow" came to be in South Carolina, it was constructed through a slow and halting process, which black Carolinians contested at every turn.

The legalized segregation of the races in South Carolina arose as a part of white Carolinians' long reaction to emancipation and Reconstruction. Though it emerged as a response to a particular political and social reality—the psychological and material threat posed by black Carolinians' anticipation of equality—segregation resonated deeply with southern culture and history. In the aftermath of emancipation, perennial white southern fears of slave insurrection were transformed into the dread specter of black political domination, as exemplified by the mythologized "tragedy" of Reconstruction. The goal of preventing African American power came with the Black Codes, enacted in 1865. The codes created many legal impediments to the progress of the freedmen. Taken as a whole, however, they were much more concerned with controlling African Americans as a labor force and maintaining the plantation economy. The intent of the Black Codes, then, was the retention of white supremacy but not the legal segregation of the races.

Reconstruction after 1868 represented a radical shift in the racial politics of South Carolina. After the state's readmission to the Union that year, African Americans increased their political participation both as voters and as politicians. South Carolina counted African Americans among high-ranking members of the state government, as well as its United States congressional delegation. Outside of politics, African Americans did not hesitate to assert their new rights. When Charleston established a streetcar system in December 1866,

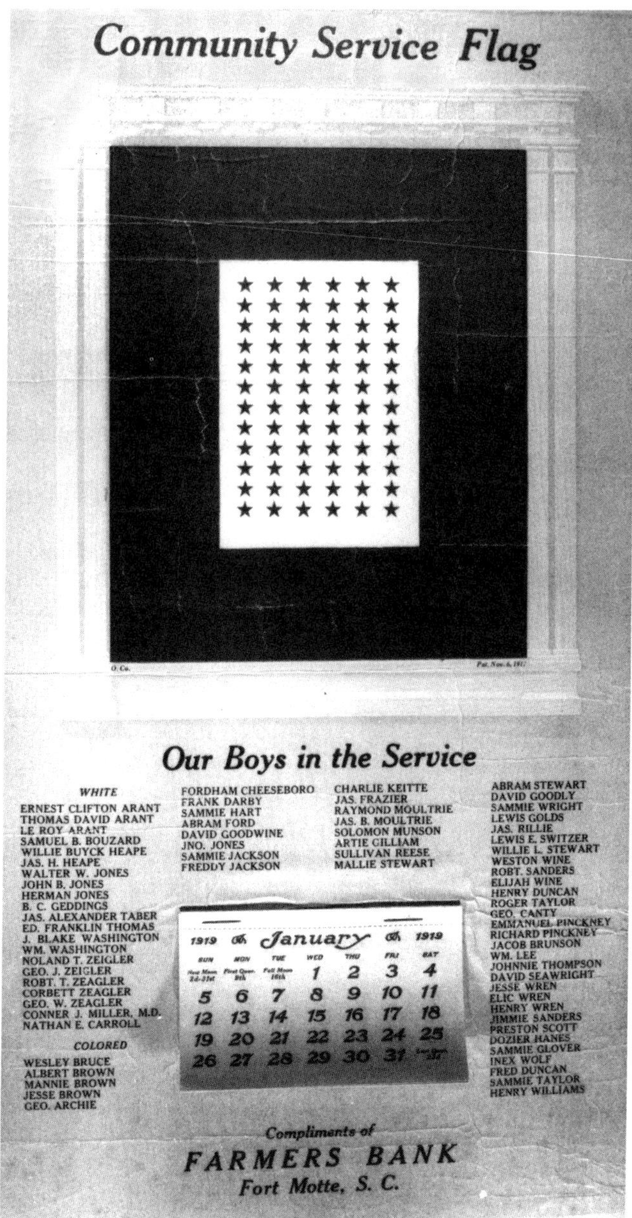

Jim Crow customs dictated the segregation of the names of a town's young men in uniform fighting "to make the world safe for democracy," Courtesy, Calhoun County Museum

African Americans immediately demanded equal accommodation. Protest eventually led to federal intervention, and in May 1867 blacks were granted equal access to streetcars. Change came in education as well: from 1873 to 1877 African Americans were admitted to the University of South Carolina, and the school was tuition-free.

These freedoms, however, were brief, and the transition to full-scale de jure segregation occurred after the end of Reconstruction in 1877. Wade Hampton III and Benjamin Ryan Tillman provide appropriate touch points for this evolution. Hampton's election to the governorship in 1876 marked an ambiguous beginning to the "redemption" effort. On the one hand, Hampton had campaigned unequivocally for the return of white rule in South Carolina. As a Confederate hero, he could offer his war credentials as proof of his commitment to the legacy of the Old South. On the other hand, Hampton—out of personal commitment or political savvy—offered the significant remaining number of the state's black voters some reason to believe that he would not completely overturn the gains of

Reconstruction. His message of moderation was juxtaposed with the violently antiblack rhetoric emanating from figures in the upstate such as Martin Gary, who advocated the so-called "Mississippi Plan" of disfranchisement by extralegal means. In the end, Hampton benefited from all of these factors, as well as the activities of the vigilante group known as the Red Shirts, who used intimidation and violence to keep blacks from voting, especially in the upstate. Despite Hampton's proclaimed moderation, the movement toward de jure segregation proceeded apace: in 1879 South Carolina passed a law prohibiting interracial marriage.

The election of Tillman in 1890 represented the end of any semblance of racial moderation in South Carolina. Tillman was completely open in sanctioning illegal means of disfranchising the remaining black voters. White Carolinians' campaign of fraud and intimidation was successful enough by 1895 that the constitutional convention of that year counted among its members only a handful of African Americans, despite the state's significant black majority. In silencing the once-powerful black vote, the way was paved for the next step in the campaign for white supremacy, the legal separation of the races. Accordingly, the 1895 constitution defined a black person as anyone having "one eighth or more negro blood." The U.S. Supreme Court's ruling in favor of "separate but equal" accommodations in the 1896 *Plessy v. Ferguson* case gave federal sanction to the Jim Crow ordinances and laws that had already begun popping up across the South.

Why segregation? The redeemers' call for a return to the rule of white men invoked the antebellum status quo, in which African Americans certainly played a subservient role but which did not necessarily feature the separation of the races. The slave regime's ideology ordered the world hierarchically, with white plantation owners unquestionably on the top rung. In plantation society there was no question as to whether blacks were subordinate to whites. The system of slavery, as a matter of course, placed whites and blacks in intimate contact with one another on a daily basis; indeed, the planters' claims to superiority in many ways depended on ready comparison to the lowest members of society. In this way segregation was antithetical to the ruling ideology of the antebellum South. One of the early precedents for the 1896 *Plessy v. Ferguson* ruling was the case of *Roberts v. City of Boston* (1850), in which the Massachusetts high court affirmed the right of local school boards to discriminate between students on the basis of race. Before the Civil War, segregation was not solely a southern issue.

With the passage of the Fourteenth and Fifteenth Amendments to the U.S. Constitution, the racial hierarchy was upset, creating the need in the minds of many whites for a legal system that would ensure the second-class status of African Americans. In the absence of slavery, segregation would prove an effective means of demonstrating the inferiority of African Americans and enforcing social inequality in South Carolina.

The period around the turn of the century brought about a flurry of laws and ordinances specifically designed to segregate the races. As before, these actions were not uncontested. When Columbia ordered streetcars segregated in 1903, the African American community organized a boycott, although it ultimately proved ineffective. Segregation legislation quickly grew into a labyrinth of city ordinances and state laws that covered the entire state. Residential segregation was accomplished by a complex network of city ordinances, banking practices, and social agreements. In the mills black and white workers by law worked in different rooms with different entrances and toilets.

Not surprisingly, the great migration of African Americans from the South coincided with the completion of Jim Crow segregation. The advent of World War I provided some economic opportunities for blacks in the industrialized North, and many took advantage of their remaining freedom to migrate. Their second-class status now a matter of law in South Carolina, many African Americans saw little reason to remain in the state.

For the majority who remained, the experience of life in a segregated society was often traumatic. A wide range of laws set African Americans apart from whites. Blacks sat in the balconies of movie theaters, drank from separate water fountains, waited for trains in separate waiting rooms, and sat in the backs of buses. Even when African Americans could use the same facility as whites—as at a post office—they would wait until all whites had been served. African Americans had separate parks and swimming pools in Charleston, and the beaches at the Isle of Palms, Sullivan's Island, and Folly Beach were off-limits. A separate school system for blacks was established in the constitution of 1895, and the pervasive inequality of the system eventually sparked a legal protest that would bring the entire system of de jure segregation crashing down.

Jim Crow Laws required that restroom and all other public facilities be labeled for "colored" and "white" use. Photograph by Cecil Williams

The legal proscriptions were generally accompanied by a socially enforced system of etiquette, which was felt in intensely personal and painful ways by black Carolinians. This system, while never codified, could still be quite rigid: African Americans were never given the title of "Mr." or "Mrs."; they were expected to give up the sidewalk upon encountering whites; and blacks were to enter white homes always through the back doors. The ever-present threat of vigilante lynch mobs added a particularly devastating level of terror to the everyday lives of blacks, particularly those who dared to transgress even the most minor points of the social order. Taken as a whole, de facto segregation provided an effective complement to the legal system of Jim Crow in enforcing white supremacy.

Maintaining a segregated society required a great deal of material and psychological effort on the part of the white community. In the face of internal ironies and perceived threats from without, the general trend moving into the mid–twentieth century was an intensification of commitment to racism and Jim Crow. In 1951 the General Assembly established an official legislative committee (the Gressette Committee) to monitor and fight all efforts at desegregation and equal rights for blacks. As the storm and thunder surrounding its demise indicates, segregation was not accomplished or maintained in South Carolina without a struggle. Blacks fought city ordinances and state laws as best they could. In establishing an alternate economy supported and run by the African American community, they maintained a certain quality of life and a semblance of self-determination. Day-to-day encounters provided numerous informal opportunities to resist the white power structure. Black Carolinians kept up their pressure on the system of segregation, never fully relinquishing their hopes for equality. In 1950 the attorney Harold Boulware of Columbia filed suit on behalf of twenty African American parents in Clarendon County challenging the segregation of schools there. The case of *Briggs v. Elliott* eventually folded into *Brown v. Board of Education* and overturned the precedent of "separate but equal" on which legalized segregation was built. Public schools were to be desegregated "with all deliberate speed."

The Scott's Branch School that was built in the early 1950s to provide a "separate but equal" school for the black children of Clarendon School District 22 (Summerton). Photograph by Cecil Williams

There was swift and determined opposition to the *Brown* ruling. Most southern political and civic leaders joined force and organized and endorsed the "Declaration of Southern Principles," or "Southern Manifesto," coauthored by Strom Thurmond. The ruling was seen as "judicial encroachment." The manifesto clearly advocated white southerners' universal contempt for and defiance of the U.S. Supreme Court. White resistance took several forms: legislative action under the banner of states' rights; school closings; and new organizations such as white Citizen Councils, which organized and raised funds for local resistance efforts. The impact on education was immediate. In 1955 the General Assembly repealed the compulsory school attendance law, allowing white parents to keep their children out of integrated schools. Private schools only for white children sprang up in many communities. In 1956 the legislature passed a law that prohibited state employees from joining the National Association for the Advancement of Colored People (NAACP). South Carolina's congressional delegation opposed every civil rights bill proposed in Congress from 1957 to 1965. Thurmond, known nationally for his prosegregation views, attempted to thwart passage of the 1957 Civil Rights Act with a record-setting filibuster lasting more than twenty-four hours.

Segregation had long been a defining feature of South Carolina life. In 1963, when outgoing governor Ernest Hollings concluded, "South Carolina is running out of courts," a peaceful desegregation took place at the University of South Carolina and Clemson. The end of segregation in secondary schools would take longer. Desegregation of the public schools began in Charleston in the fall of 1963, but progress was slow: in 1965 ninety-five percent of African American children across the state still attended segregated schools. Only in the early 1970s was there widespread desegregation of public education. Although *Brown* marked the end of de jure segregation, resistance to the decision demonstrated that ending de facto segregation continued to be a work in progress. CLEVELAND L. SELLERS, JR.

Dailey, Jane, Glenda Elizabeth Gilmore, and Bryant Simon, eds. *Jumpin' Jim Crow: Southern Politics from Civil War to Civil Rights.* Princeton, N.J.: Princeton University Press, 2000.

Hale, Grace E. *Making Whiteness: The Culture of Segregation in the South, 1890–1940.* New York: Pantheon, 1998.

Litwack, Leon F. *Trouble in Mind: Black Southerners in the Age of Jim Crow.* New York: Knopf, 1998.

Meier, August, and Elliott Rudwick. "The Boycott Movement against Jim Crow Streetcars in the South, 1900–1906." *Journal of American History* 55 (March 1969): 756–75.

Perman, Michael. *Struggle for Mastery: Disfranchisement in the South, 1888–1908.* Chapel Hill: University of North Carolina Press, 2001.

Powers, Bernard E. *Black Charlestonians: A Social History, 1822–1885.* Fayetteville: University of Arkansas Press, 1994.

Smyth, William D. "Segregation in Charleston in the 1950s: A Decade in Transition." *South Carolina Historical Magazine* 92 (April 1991): 99–123.

Tindall, George. *South Carolina Negroes, 1877–1900.* 1952. Reprint, Columbia: University of South Carolina Press, 2003.

Woodward, C. Vann. *The Strange Career of Jim Crow.* 3d ed. New York: Oxford University Press, 1974.

Seibels Bruce Group, Inc. Seibels Bruce, a provider of property and casualty insurance products and related services, was founded in Columbia in 1869 by Edwin W. Seibels and J. B. Ezell and evolved into one of the South's largest insurance firms. It first occupied the shambles of a small single-story brick building on Columbia's Main Street that had burned during the Civil War. The firm grossed only $5,000 in premiums for the first year but began operations as a general agency in 1897. The company was incorporated in 1908 under the name of Edwin G. Seibels, Manager, Inc., named for the son of the founder. In 1919 the business became Seibels, Bruce and Company—a salute to the work of Charles J. Bruce, a longtime member of the firm. In 1969 Seibels Bruce began development of an on-line insurance data processing system, which it marketed to more than 125 companies in the United States and Canada by 1974. This resulted in an increase in staff from 265 in 1969 to 1,200 in 1979. At the close of the twentieth century, Seibels Bruce operated on a smaller scale, and in February 2004 the company's management moved to make Seibels Bruce a private company. ROBERT A. PIERCE

Seigler, Marie Samuella Cromer (1882–1964). Educator, girls' club founder. Seigler was born on November 9, 1882, in rural Abbeville County, the daughter of William Cromer and Ella Cox. Her doting father, who called her "Beaut," instilled in her confidence and ambition beyond the norm for girls of that era. After graduation from Abbeville High School in 1898, she attended college in North Carolina. In 1907 she moved to Aiken County to teach in a one-teacher school.

The main focus of Seigler's career began in late 1909 when she heard a representative of the U.S. Department of Agriculture extol the virtues of the Boys' Corn Clubs of America at a state teachers' meeting. He catalyzed her hopes of doing something to broaden the vision and self-confidence of rural girls. "I was born in the country," she explained, "and I know something of its lonesomeness and sleepy-spiritedness. It is because I love the country and its people that I want to do something for the young girls—to help them keep the thinking up when school is over." In a few months Seigler had created the Aiken County Girls' Tomato Club, the first such group in the nation, and was attracting favorable attention from government and philanthropic groups.

Seigler began by recruiting members with the promise of a scholarship to Winthrop College for the girl whose one-tenth-acre garden was the most productive, taking on the task of raising the $140 cost of the scholarship as well. By 1910 she had forty-seven girls from several Aiken County schools enrolled. The Columbia office of the U.S. Farm Demonstration Service took note and awarded the project $5,000, which provided canning equipment and experienced operators to teach canning to the girls. A demonstration of the machinery took place in front of the Aiken County Court House. Each can was labeled "Put up by the Girls' Tomato Club of Aiken County" and bore the autograph of the grower. During the first summer, in 1910, Katie Gunter put up 512 cans of tomatoes and netted $40 from her tenth of an acre, thus gaining the Winthrop scholarship, for which funds were still being raised. Thomas Hitchcock, a wealthy New Yorker and leader of Aiken's winter colony, responded to Seigler's plea and funded the scholarship. On August 16, 1910, Seigler was made a special agent of the U.S. Department of Agriculture.

By 1913 some twenty thousand girls in the southern states were participating. The General Education Board of New York City awarded the clubs $25,000 for equipment, and the U.S. Department of Agriculture took over the publicity and distribution of instructional literature. The federal Smith-Lever Act of 1914 consolidated all such efforts and funded them through land-grant colleges, including Clemson College.

On April 24, 1912, Marie Cromer married Cecil Seigler, the superintendent of Aiken County schools. Soon she was raising children and moving to the background of the movement. It continued to grow and evolved into the 4-H Clubs, which in the early twenty-first century still offered practical instruction and social opportunities to children in rural America. In 1953, at the national 4-H camp, President Dwight D. Eisenhower honored Seigler for her role as a founder of 4-H. She died on June 14, 1964, and was buried in the Seigler family cemetery near Johnston, South Carolina. JAMES O. FARMER, JR.

Bodie, Idella. *South Carolina Women.* Orangeburg, S.C.: Sandlapper, 1991.

Martin, Oscar Baker. *The Demonstration Work: Dr. Seaman A. Knapp's Contribution to Civilization.* 3d ed. San Antonio, Tex.: Naylor, 1941.

Self, James Cuthbert (1876–1955). Textile manufacturer, philanthropist. Self was born in the Bowles Mountain section of Edgefield County (now part of Greenwood County) on July 1, 1876, the middle of three sons of James Anderson Self, a doctor, and Mary California "Callie" Holloway, a former schoolteacher. Self briefly attended Wofford Fitting School and was a member of Clemson College's first class in 1893 before leaving for financial reasons. He worked as a country store clerk in Greenwood County and completed a course at Smithdeal Business College in Richmond, Virginia. In 1899 Self was hired as a bookkeeper in the Bank of Greenwood. Even after becoming president and treasurer of Greenwood Cotton Mill in 1908, he continued as cashier at the bank until 1916.

James Cuthbert Self. Courtesy, Archives Department, The Self Family Foundation

Greenwood Cotton Mill, chartered in 1889, comprised two plants (one closed) and 250 employees when Self became president in 1908. It housed obsolete equipment and was mired in debt. Self purchased new looms on credit, hired skilled associates, and improved working and living conditions for employees. In 1916 Self became one of the first mill owners to add a night shift. He reopened the second plant around 1912 and purchased Ninety Six Cotton Mill in 1921 and Grendel Mill No. 2 (Mathews Mill) in 1930. In 1935, with his mills operating three shifts a day in the midst of the Great Depression, Self purchased all outstanding stock to become sole owner of Greenwood Cotton Mill.

After winning awards for providing special textiles for the armed forces during World War II, Self established Greenwood Mills Inc., with offices in New York City, as his own selling house in 1946. The mills eventually were merged into a new corporate structure under the name Greenwood Mills. Self opened the Harris Plant in 1950 and Durst Plant in 1953, and he modernized the other plants in the early 1950s. All improvements took place without outside financial assistance. By 1955 Greenwood Mills was "reported to be one of the largest privately owned textile empires in the world," employing approximately six thousand workers.

Self was known for his commitment to his employees and to the Greenwood community. The Greenwood Mills construction division built sturdy, modern employee houses in attractive, landscaped communities. Self also provided schools, churches, and recreational facilities. In 1927 he founded Greenwood Country Club for mill employees. Self also started the private Self Foundation in 1942. One of the foundation's first projects was Self Memorial Hospital, which was completed in 1951 and was funded by the foundation for many years. The foundation continued in the early twenty-first century to provide grants to projects that improved the quality of life in Greenwood and South Carolina.

Among his numerous recognitions, Self was the first South Carolinian to win the Man of the South award (1952) from the magazine *Dixie Business,* and he received the national Horatio Alger Award in 1955. He married Lura Mathews in 1916, and they had one son, James C. Self, Jr. (1919–1998), who took charge of Greenwood Mills after his father's death. Self died on July 21, 1955, and was buried in Edgewood Cemetery in Greenwood. SUSAN GIAIMO HIOTT

Klosky, Beth Ann. "Greenwood Mills: A Self Enterprise." *Sandlapper* 7 (April 1974): 24–30.

Robinson, G. O. *The Character of Quality: The Story of Greenwood Mills.* Rev. ed. Columbia, S.C.: R. L. Bryan, 1975.

Sellers, Cleveland Louis, Jr. (b. 1944). Civil rights activist, educator. Sellers was born in Denmark, South Carolina, on November 8, 1944, to the successful businessman Cleveland L. Sellers, Sr., and Pauline Taggart, an educator. Due to the success of his parents, Sellers lived a fairly privileged life as an African American growing up in the segregated town of Denmark. Even though he experienced segregation and lived in a "black world," according to his autobiography, he did not experience the harsher aspects of racial segregation and discrimination that typically confronted African Americans. Nevertheless, he was aware of racial divisions and as a teenager participated in a sit-in movement in downtown Denmark in the spring of 1960. While attending the high school program at Voorhees Junior College, he participated in student protests. Sellers also organized a Youth Chapter of the National Association for the Advancement of Colored People in Denmark. But he was forced to resign from the organization at his father's insistence.

After graduating from high school, Sellers left South Carolina in 1962 to attend Howard University in Washington, D.C. At Howard he met several student activists, including Stokely Carmichael, who would later become chairman of the Student Nonviolent Coordinating Committee (SNCC). Through these contacts, Sellers began a lifelong commitment to activism and social justice. From 1962 to 1964 he participated in demonstrations, marches, and protests organized by Howard's student organization, Nonviolent Action Group (NAG), as well as those of other organizations in the Washington, D.C., area. In August 1963 he served on the planning committee for and participated in the monumental march on Washington led by SNCC and other civil rights organizations. In the spring of 1964 he worked with Gloria Richardson's Cambridge Nonviolent Action Committee to organize demonstrations protesting the poor economic conditions of African Americans in Cambridge, Maryland.

Sellers's role in SNCC earned him his reputation for activism. In the summer of 1964 he helped to organize and participate in SNCC's Freedom Summer voter registration project in Mississippi. He recruited college students for the project and served as an organizer in Holly Springs, Mississippi. Following the 1964 summer project, Sellers remained in the Deep South as an organizer for SNCC and eventually became its national program secretary. He was also present at many of the key events of the civil rights movement, including the 1965 march at Selma, Alabama, and the Lowndes County (Alabama) Freedom Organization political campaign in 1966.

Returning to South Carolina in 1967, Sellers sought to organize students at the state's historically black colleges—Benedict, Allen, Morris, and South Carolina State—to address problems that poor blacks faced. Sellers spent most of his time working with South Carolina State's Black Awareness Coordinating Committee (BACC). While Sellers was working with BACC, other students began demonstrations to desegregate a bowling alley in downtown Orangeburg. Beginning on February 5, 1968, a group of students who were not members of the BACC launched demonstrations to force the bowling alley to open its facilities to black students. As the confrontations between the students and the Orangeburg police escalated, several students were beaten and arrested, and white-owned property near the bowling alley and the campus was damaged. Sellers acted as an adviser to the students involved in the protests and sought to maintain calm. Despite his efforts, on the night of February 8, 1968, police and state troopers opened fire on South Carolina State and Claflin College students, wounding twenty-seven and killing three.

In the aftermath of what was termed the "Orangeburg Massacre," Sellers was blamed for inciting a riot, indicted, and convicted. He served seven months in prison. At the end of his prison term he left the state and earned graduate degrees at Harvard and the University of North Carolina at Greensboro. In 1990 he returned to South Carolina to teach at the University of South Carolina. In 1996 he received a pardon for his conviction in connection with the Orangeburg shootings. Since 2000 he has served as director of the African American Studies Program at the University of South Carolina. W. MARVIN DULANEY

Bass, Jack, and Jack Nelson. *The Orangeburg Massacre.* 2d ed. Macon, Ga.: Mercer University Press, 1996.

Sellers, Cleveland L., Jr. Papers. Avery Research Center for African American History and Culture, College of Charleston, Charleston, South Carolina.

Sellers, Cleveland L., Jr., with Robert Terrell. *The River of No Return: The Autobiography of a Black Militant and the Life and Death of SNCC.* 1973. Reprint, Jackson: University Press of Mississippi, 1990.

Selvy, Franklin Delano (b. 1932). Basketball player. Selvy was born on November 9, 1932, in Corbin, Kentucky, to Ira and John Robert Selvy. From 1951 to 1954 he played basketball at Furman University and is best known for his high-scoring performances that made national headlines, including 100 points in a 149–95 victory over Newberry College. The Newberry game was only one highlight near the end of a record-breaking college career. Selvy led all college players in scoring during the 1952–1953 (29.5 points per game) and 1953–1954 (41.7 points per game) seasons. He was the first college player to average more than 40 points per game in a single season and the first to score more than 1,000 points in a single season (1,209 in 1953–1954). Selvy's scoring prowess helped the Paladins to defeat larger schools, including a combined seven victories versus in-state rivals Clemson and South Carolina, and a victory over nationally ranked Duke.

The media recognized Selvy with three All-American awards and the United Press National Player of the Year award in 1954. His honors brought unprecedented national attention to the tiny Baptist school in Greenville. Furman supporters and opponents alike admired his humble nature and work ethic as much as his playing

Frank Selvy. Courtesy, *Greenville News*

ability. A writer for the Furman student newspaper in 1952 said that basketball as played by Selvy and his teammates was "fine art." The Baltimore Bullets of the National Basketball Association took notice of Selvy's skills and made him the first overall pick of the 1954 draft. Selvy played with several teams, including the St. Louis Hawks (with whom he won a World Championship in 1957) and the Los Angeles Lakers. After Selvy's professional career ended in 1964, he returned to Furman as an assistant coach with the men's basketball team. In 1966 Furman named Selvy the head coach, and he directed the men's team for four seasons. He then entered the business world and worked for St. Joe Paper Company in Laurens for twenty-five years. Selvy retired in 1995 and lives with his wife, Barbara, in Simpsonville. BRADLEY S. SAULS

Black, Art. "Frank Selvy Made Basketball History." *Greenville News,* January 14, 1976, Furman sesquicentennial section, pp. 24–25.

Foster, Dan. "Selvy to Resign Monday as Paladins' Head Coach." *Greenville News,* March 2, 1970, p. 12.

Reid, Alfred Sandlin. *Furman University: Toward a New Identity, 1925–1975.* Durham, N.C.: Duke University Press, 1976.

Seneca (Oconee County; 2000 pop. 7,652). Founded on August 14, 1873, as Seneca City, the town's name was taken from an earlier Indian village and the nearby Seneca River. As was the case with several other upcountry towns, the arrival of the Atlanta and Charlotte Air Line Railroad was responsible for Seneca's establishment. The Air Line route intersected the Blue Ridge Railroad on land purchased from Joseph Newton Brown of Anderson. Town lots went on sale on August 30, 1873, and the state legislature granted the town a charter on March 14, 1874. In its first year the town had a population of two hundred, half black and half white. One of the first structures was a union church used by all denominations, to which the town contributed $500 toward its construction. By 1880 census takers counted 382 residents in Seneca City, including 15 merchants. On February 19, 1908, the original charter was given up and the town was reincorporated simply as Seneca.

Most trains stopped at Seneca, and it quickly became a commercial center, especially for marketing the area's cotton crop. Although the town suffered three fires in its first forty years, Seneca recovered without any lasting ill effects. At the cotton weighing platform at the railroad freight station, wagons often lined up for several blocks waiting to unload the year's cotton harvest. The Keowee Hotel had a fine reputation for food and hospitality among railroad passengers. In the early twentieth century a popular public park was developed across from the railroad station, with a gazebo, landscaping, and even a colony of prairie dogs brought in by a local resident who had traveled in the West.

The town built its first school building in 1874, with the upstairs used by local Masons for meetings. From 1898 to 1939 Seneca was also the site of the Seneca Institute, a well-known African American college.

The economy was based on agriculture until cotton mills appeared at the nearby villages of Newry and Lonsdale, which drew their workforces from the surrounding countryside. Seneca benefited from the change, and in 1911 a newspaper reported that the town's population had grown to fifteen hundred and declared Seneca to be "the commercial center of Oconee County." New businesses continued to appear, including in 1898 the Oconee Telephone Company, which Southern Bell purchased in 1919 when there were 102 telephones in Seneca. By 1924 Seneca even had its own airport, Tribble Field.

Manufacturing continued to replace farming during the second half of the twentieth century. In August 1973 Seneca celebrated its centennial with parades, exhibits, and other public events. Even after centennial celebrations dwindled, Seneca did not forgot its heritage. A seven-block area was designated a National Register Historic District in 1975. The Episcopal Church of the Ascension, consecrated in 1882, was converted into the headquarters of the Blue Ridge Arts Council. The 1909 house of Dr. William J. Lunney was deeded to Oconee County in 1970 and soon thereafter became the Lunney Museum. DONNA K. ROPER

Holleman, Frances. *The City of Seneca, South Carolina.* Greenville, S.C.: Creative Printers, 1973.

Sewees. The Sewees were a Native American nation based along the Santee River and the Sea Islands. Nicholas Carteret, an early settler, noted that when the English came to Carolina in 1670, the Sewees showed them the best harbors and gave them ritual greetings of friendship.

The Sewees helped the Carolinians militarily against the Spanish in Florida and with food when the colony ran short. Living in close proximity to Europeans, the Sewees fell victim to a variety of plagues, including smallpox. Interested in trade from the beginning, the Sewees noticed that various middlemen made profits on their trade with Charleston and that certain goods, such as furs and pelts, were sold for high profit back in England.

The Sewees determined to make direct trade contact with English merchants. Seeing ships from England appear on the horizon, they believed that their own sturdy canoes could easily traverse the seas to England, a voyage they imagined as very short. A large number of the nation set to work on this plan and, when ready, loaded their canoes with supplies and trade goods. On open sea they ran into storms that wrecked the fleet, and many Sewees drowned. A passing English slave ship picked up survivors, who were then sold in the West Indies. By 1700 only a handful of this tribe remained alive in the colony. Other tribes absorbed them, and they ceased to exist as a distinct group by the early eighteenth century. MICHAEL P. MORRIS

Josephy, Alvin M. *500 Nations: An Illustrated History of North American Indians.* New York: Knopf, 1994.

Milling, Chapman J. *Red Carolinians.* 1940. Reprint, Columbia: University of South Carolina Press, 1969.

Shag. State dance. South Carolina's official state dance since 1984, the "Shag" is southern swing tempered by the influences of jazz, blues, and gospel music. Though few agree on its exact origins, pioneering dancers in the Shag Hall of Fame (all Caucasians) credit the dance's modern evolution to a taboo collaboration with African Americans that occurred in the segregated Carolinas during the late 1940s.

Called "jitterbugs" for the jazz-based acrobatic dance they performed along the Carolina coast, the white dancers found that the emerging "race" music (soon to be renamed "rhythm and blues") slowed and smoothed their movements. "The shag is the jitterbug on Quaaludes . . .[,] the jitterbug slowed down," noted the veteran Myrtle Beach dancer Dino Thompson.

A key site of the biracial dance collaboration was a black nightclub in Myrtle Beach owned by the black impresario Charlie Fitzgerald. "I first heard the term shag at Charlie's Place," said George Lineberry, a shag pioneer who left the beach in 1948. "I think the shag and dirty shag came out of Charlie's nightclub."

In black clubs the white dancers discovered and adapted erotic dance movements that mimicked the act of copulation. Called the "dirty shag," this cruder dance reflected the very definition of the word "shag," which, according to *The Oxford Dictionary of Modern Slang,* means "to have sex with." The belly roll, often cited as the ultimate shag step, originated from the dirty version of the dance.

Blacks, said the shag innovator Harry Driver, had a huge impact on how the dance evolved. "What we learned from the blacks was their rhythm and tempo. We emulated what they did. Everybody claims to have started the shag. Nobody started it. It evolved from one dance to another in a big melting pot." Fifty years later dozens of shag clubs remained active throughout the South, while thousands of shaggers converged each year in North Myrtle Beach, a community that preserved its dance legacy. FRANK BEACHAM

Rogers, Aida. "Shaggin'." *Sandlapper* 1 (July/August 1990): 12–18.

Shand, Gadsden Edwards (1868–1948). Architect, engineer. Shand was born in Columbia on March 21, 1868, the son of Robert Shand and Louisa Edwards. He received a B.S. in civil engineering from South Carolina College in 1888 and also studied architecture at Columbia College in New York. He and Patience Griffin Bonham had five children.

Shand became known for his public and commercial building designs and played a significant role in the development of the textile industry in South Carolina during the early twentieth century. He served as superintendent of construction of the South Carolina State House from 1888 to 1890, under the direction of the architect Frank Niernsee, and established an independent engineering practice in Columbia in 1891. The Canal Dime Savings Bank (1893), a Romanesque-revival building on Main Street, was among his early architectural work. In 1895 Shand joined the firm of W. B. Smith Whaley & Company, which built textile mills across the state, including such major complexes as Olympia, Granby, and Richland mills in Columbia. Shand and George E. Lafaye provided most of the firm's architectural services. When Whaley left Columbia in 1903, Shand and Lafaye established their own architectural and engineering practice. Their most important works included the Clarendon County Courthouse in Manning (1908), the Ottaray Hotel in Greenville (1907–1908), the rebuilding of the Columbia College campus in Columbia (1909), and the seven-story Fulton Bag and Cotton Mills Warehouse in Atlanta, Georgia (1909). Shand also drew the original plans for Shandon, the fashionable suburb in Columbia developed by his father and other investors in the Columbia Land and Investment Company.

Shand ended his partnership with Lafaye in 1912 to focus solely on his engineering company, which worked mainly on industrial and engineering projects. The firm was also a major supplier of structural steel and ornamental iron for building projects throughout the state in the 1920s. In 1933 he went to work for the South Carolina Public Service Commission, first as the director of the agency and later as a valuation engineer. His son, Gadsden E. Shand, Jr., continued to manage the Shand Engineering Company. Shand died in Columbia on April 17, 1948, and was buried in the Trinity Episcopal Churchyard. DANIEL J. VIVIAN

Moore, John Hammond. *Columbia and Richland County: A South Carolina Community, 1740–1990.* Columbia: University of South Carolina Press, 1993.

Power, J. Tracy. "'The Brightest of the Lot': W. B. Smith Whaley and the Rise of the South Carolina Textile Industry, 1893–1903." *South Carolina Historical Magazine* 93 (April 1992): 126–38.

Wells, John E., and Robert E. Dalton. *The South Carolina Architects, 1885–1935: A Biographical Directory.* Richmond, Va.: New South Architectural Press, 1992.

Shaw Air Force Base. Established in 1941 on the outskirts of Sumter to train pilots for World War II, Shaw Air Force Base later evolved into a home for U.S. Air Force tactical units. The facility was named after Sumter native Ervin Shaw, a pilot shot down over France in July 1918. Shaw Airfield originally consisted of less than three thousand acres and three 4,500-foot runways. Work began on the army flying school in May 1941 at an estimated cost of $2.5 million. Its first class of pilot cadets began training in December 1941 with BT-13s for basic flight training, the second of three training phases in earning a pilot's commission. During the latter stages of World War II, Shaw was also the site of a German prisoner-of-war camp of about four hundred prisoners. Before the Axis surrendered in 1945, more than 8,600 American, British, Canadian, and French cadets received training at Shaw. After the war the airfield became a separation center for thousands of soldiers being discharged from the military. At about the same time it was also designated as the headquarters for training Nationalist Chinese crews to fly B-25 aircraft.

By 1948 the U.S. Air Force considered deactivating the facility but chose instead to rename it Shaw Air Force Base. It became part of its Tactical Air Command and home to the Ninth Air Force two years later. Its planes played an active role in the cold war, including reconnaissance patrols over Cuba during the 1962 Missile Crisis. Its units were involved in combat and reconnaissance tours in the Vietnam conflict and played pivotal roles in the Gulf War (1990–1991) and the Balkans crises. In 1993 Shaw became the permanent home of the Twentieth Fighter Wing, comprised of four fighter squadrons. Following the September 2001 attacks on New York and the Pentagon, Shaw AFB had personnel and planes assigned to action against Taliban and Al Qaeda forces in Afghanistan. As of 2002 Shaw AFB had 5,800 active-duty personnel, employed 1,000 civilians, and housed 6,500 dependents. The base and its payrolls injected more than $500 million into the local economy. FRITZ HAMER

50th Anniversary: Shaw Air Force Base, S.C. 1941–1991. [Sumter, S.C.]: 363d Tactical Fighter Wing, Office of History, 1991.

University of South Carolina Legacy Project. *The Cold War in South Carolina, 1945–1991: An Inventory of Department of Defense Cold War Era Cultural and Historical Resources in the State of South Carolina; Final Report.* Vol. 3, *The Department of the Air Force in South Carolina.* Aberdeen Proving Ground, Md.: Legacy Resource Management Program, United States Department of Defense, 1995.

She-crab soup. She-crab soup is uniquely Charlestonian—a silky, seafood chowder with a European heritage. The dish helped put Charleston on the regional culinary road map as surely as Philadelphia's cheese steaks or Chicago's deep-dish pizzas did the same for those locations. Shrimp and grits are perhaps the only items appearing more often on the menus of Charleston restaurants than this elegant appetizer. "There's nothing quite like it on this side of the Atlantic," said John Martin Taylor (known as "Hoppin' John"), cookbook author and the notorious arbiter of lowcountry cuisine. Although some Charleston-area restaurateurs bemoan it as nothing more than a novelty item slurped by the gallon by gullible tourists, Taylor maintained that the soup is an example of a delightfully distinct regional cuisine that at times has been bred into mediocrity by chefs taking shortcuts such as thickening it with flour ("wallpaper paste," he says with disgust).

Food historians believe that she-crab soup is based on the Scottish seafood bisque *partan bree,* which was brought by settlers to the New World in the early 1700s and was localized in Charleston with the addition of boiled and pureed long-grain rice and the roe of blue crabs. During a 1909 visit to Charleston, President William Howard Taft supped on she-crab soup at the home of Mayor R. Goodwyn Rhett. The recipe for the soup calls for the meat of a dozen female crabs, fish stock, milk, spices, and heavy cream. A blending of the New and Old Worlds and served hot, she-crab soup's finishing touches often include a sprinkling of the orange crab eggs across the surface of the thick soup, followed by a dollop of a fine, dry sherry such as amontillado. DAN HUNTLEY

Sheheen, Robert Joseph (b. 1943). Lawyer, legislator. Sheheen was born on January 21, 1943, in Camden, one of four sons of Austin M. Sheheen and Lucile Roukos. Sheheen graduated from Camden High School in 1961, received a B.A. degree from Duke University in 1965, and earned a J.D. from the University of South Carolina Law School in 1968. He was admitted to the South Carolina Bar in 1968 and was first elected to the South Carolina House of Representatives from Kershaw County in 1976. During his early career in the House, he served as chairman of the Judiciary Committee (1981–1986) and championed causes including freedom-of-information legislation, the strengthening of local government powers, and the periodic review of state agency regulatory functions popularly known as "sunset" laws.

Sheheen was elected Speaker of the House of Representatives in 1986. Four years later he presided over the South Carolina House during one of the state's major political scandals, a Federal Bureau of Investigation (FBI) sting operation called "Operation Lost Trust." Speaker Sheheen led efforts to restore public trust by enacting strong ethics legislation. In 1991 the General Assembly adopted the Ethics Reform Act, which included a $25 limit on lobbyists' spending on legislators, dubbed the "cup of coffee" provision. Other parts of the bill banned campaign donations by lobbyists, enlarged the State Ethics Commission, and expanded that commission's authority.

Sheheen also worked to close the facility for the storage of low-level radioactive waste materials at Barnwell. Sheheen and his environmentally oriented colleagues fought to have the Barnwell facility closed on schedule, and a compromise reached on the final day of the 1992–1993 session gave the Barnwell facility an additional four years of operation, but with significant restrictions and limitations.

As Speaker, Sheheen devoted much of his time to organizational and procedural issues at a time when South Carolina's two-party system was growing increasingly partisan and competitive. Sheheen's eight years as Speaker ended in 1994 when Republicans took control of the House for the first time in the twentieth century. Sheheen served three more terms in the House before retiring at the end of the 1999–2000 session. He was replaced by his nephew, Vincent A. Sheheen. After his legislative service, Sheheen continued his legal career as a member of the firm of Savage, Royall & Sheheen in Camden. PHILIP G. GROSE, JR.

Sheldon Church (Beaufort County). Moss-draped live oak trees shade the quiet burial ground that surrounds the ruined Sheldon Church of Prince William's Parish. Its molded brick columns support a nonexistent portico and continue between arched openings along the side walls to lend a sense of enclosure to the unroofed building. Even in ruins, Sheldon Church symbolizes Beaufort County's prosperity during South Carolina's early years as a royal colony. Sophisticated in its architecture and craftsmanship, this isolated brick edifice was among the first examples of the temple design in the English-speaking world.

In the 1730s influential planters began moving to the former Indian lands, bringing their slaves and creating wealth, and in 1745 the Commons House of Assembly established Prince William's Parish. No longer was it necessary to travel to St. Helena's Parish for worship or voting. So that a church could be built, Elizabeth Bellinger donated a fifty-acre tract of Tomotley Barony, next to William Bull's Sheldon Plantation. Construction was funded largely by the Bulls, supplemented by legislative appropriations. The result, completed in 1757, was "esteem'd a more beautiful Building than St. Philip's. It is far more elegant than St. Michael's."

This emblem of English political and religious organization was burned in 1779 by a band of Beaufort Tories. Not until 1825 did commissioners advertise for estimates "to cover the Ruins of the Sheldon Church . . . with a plain strong wooden Roof, putting Doors, Windows, Benches, and a Floor to the same." The rebuilt church was consecrated in 1826, but in 1865 both the church and its summer chapel at McPhersonville were burned. A replacement chapel was constructed in 1898. Sheldon Church has never been rebuilt. It was listed in the National Register of Historic Places in 1970. See plate 15. SARAH FICK

Linder, Suzanne Cameron. *Anglican Churches in Colonial South Carolina: Their History and Architecture.* Charleston, S.C.: Wyrick, 2000.

Rowland, Lawrence S., Alexander Moore, and George C. Rogers. *The History of Beaufort County, South Carolina.* Vol. 1, *1514–1861.* Columbia: University of South Carolina Press, 1996.

Stoney, Samuel G. *Plantations of the South Carolina Low Country.* 5th ed. Charleston, S.C.: Carolina Art Association, 1964.

Todd, John R., and Francis M. Hutson. *Prince William's Parish and Plantations.* Richmond, Va.: Garrett and Massie, 1935.

Shell, Arthur (b. 1946). Football player, coach. Art Shell was born in Charleston on November 26, 1946, the eldest child of Arthur Sr. and Gertrude Shell. Shell's mother died of heart failure in 1961 at age thirty-five. His father, a paper mill employee, died in 1989 of complications from diabetes. During his youth Shell resided in the Daniel Jenkins housing project and attended Bonds-Wilson High School, excelling in football and basketball and graduating in 1964. He starred in football at Maryland State College (now University of Maryland Eastern Shore) and graduated in 1968. Shell played both offensive and defensive tackle and was named to several All-American teams. The Oakland Raiders of the American Football League selected him in the third round of the 1968 draft. A fixture at left tackle from 1968 to 1982, Shell became one of the most dominating offensive linemen in professional football history. He earned Pro Bowl honors eight times, played for National Football League (NFL) championship teams in 1976 and 1980, and was inducted into the Professional Football Hall of Fame in 1989.

Immediately after retiring, Shell became a scout and assistant coach for the Raiders. In 1989 the team named Art Shell head coach, the first African American NFL head coach in the modern era. Prior to Shell, the only African American head coach had been Fritz Pollard, coaching a Hammond, Indiana, team (1923–1925). As head coach (1989–1994), Shell amassed a 56–41 record. He left the Raiders in 1995, serving as offensive line coach for the Kansas City Chiefs (1995–1996) and the Atlanta Falcons (1996–2000). Shell then worked in the office of NFL commissioner Paul Tagliabue (2000–2004), adjudicating player disciplinary appeals, representing the NFL in relationships with colleges, and writing a regular column for the NFL Web site. In 2004 he became head of football operations for the NFL and NFL representative on the USA Football Board of Directors. JOHN F. JAKUBS

Porter, David L. *African-American Sports Greats: A Biographical Dictionary.* Westport, Conn.: Greenwood, 1995.

Shepard, Charles Upham (1804–1886). Chemist, mineralogist, naturalist. Shepard was born in Little Compton, Rhode Island, on June 29, 1804, the son of the Reverend Mase Shepard and Deborah Haskins. As a schoolboy Shepard became interested in mineralogy from reading Benjamin Silliman's *Journal of Travels* and began his first mineralogical cabinet while a student at Providence Grammar School. When Shepard was fifteen years old, his father died and his mother moved the family to Amherst, Massachusetts. He graduated from Amherst College in 1824 and then studied botany and mineralogy in nearby Cambridge with the mineralogist Thomas Nuttall. He returned to Boston, where he taught botany and mineralogy and corresponded with Silliman. In 1827 he became Silliman's assistant at Yale College. On September 23, 1831, he married Silliman's adoptive daughter, Harriet Taylor. The couple had three children.

A prolific author, Shepard wrote dozens of papers reporting on his mineral observations, many of which were published in the *American Journal of Science,* which Silliman edited. From 1832 to 1833 Shepard visited and surveyed areas in Louisiana, Florida, and Georgia as part of Silliman's investigation of sugar production requested by the secretary of the treasury. He also published his *Treatise on Mineralogy* (1832–1835), was a lecturer at Yale College from 1833 to 1847, and then taught at Amherst College from 1847 until his retirement in 1877.

In 1834, acting on a recommendation from Silliman, the Medical College of South Carolina in Charleston appointed Shepard professor of chemistry. He taught during the colder months at the Medical College until 1861, returning to New Haven each spring. A highly respected and popular teacher at the Medical College, Shepard also arranged mineralogical collections and botanical facilities on the campus with specimens gathered from across the United States and Europe. Together with his students, he also explored the state's mineral deposits, with his findings frequently becoming the subject of papers and publications. Perhaps his greatest contribution was the investigations in the late 1850s of the vast phosphate deposits in the South Carolina lowcountry. Benjamin Silliman, Jr., the son of his mentor, remarked, "No observation or original research of Dr. Shepard has been fruitful of so much good in its consequences" as the discovery of these deposits "and the distinct recognition of the fact of its great value for agriculture." Shepard published three pamphlets on these investigations: *On the Development and Extent of the Fertilizer Industry, Charleston Phosphates* (1869) and *Guano as a Fertilizer* (1869).

Shepard left Charleston in 1861 at the onset of the Civil War but returned in 1865 to resume teaching at the Medical College. He resigned his professorship at Charleston in 1869 and was succeeded by his son, Charles Jr., though he continued to lecture at the Medical College for several years afterward. Shepard died in Charleston on May 1, 1886, following an extended illness. MARY S. MILLER

Wilson, Leonard G., ed. *Benjamin Silliman and His Circle: Studies in the Influence of Benjamin Silliman on Science in America.* New York: Science History Publications, 1979.

Sheriff, Hilla (1903–1988). Physician, public health official. Born on May 29, 1903, in Pickens County, Sheriff was the fifth of seven children of John Washington Sheriff and Mary Lenora Smith. The family moved to Orangeburg when Hilla was still in elementary school. She attended the College of Charleston for two years before transferring to the Medical College of the State of South Carolina, where she received the M.D. in 1926. After an internship at the Hospital of the Women's Medical College of Pennsylvania, Sheriff completed residencies in Washington, D.C., and New York City. She opened a pediatrics practice in Spartanburg, South Carolina, in 1929.

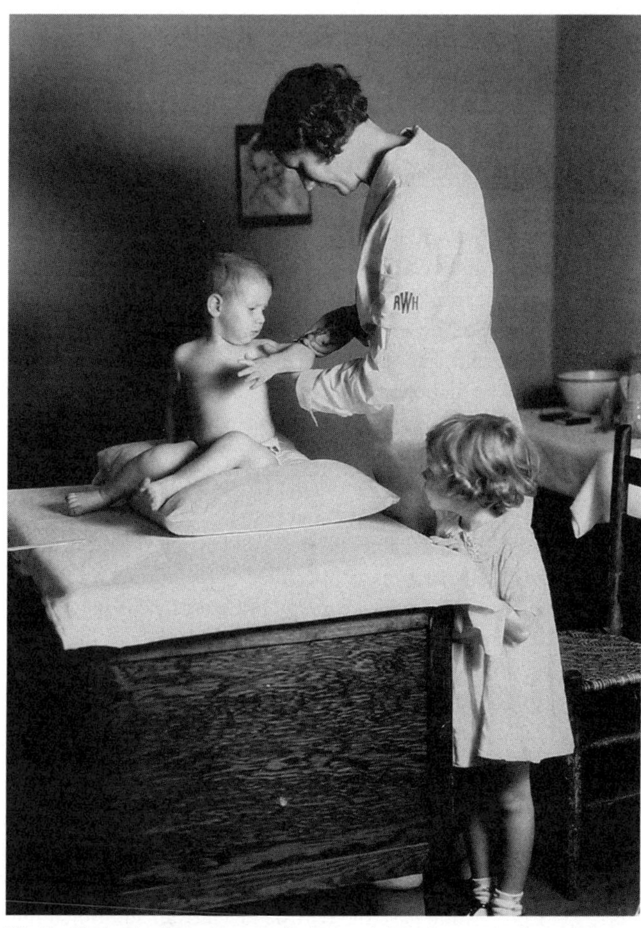

Hilla Sheriff administering an immunization in a rural clinic. Courtesy, South Caroliniana Library, University of South Carolina

The poverty of her patients and an offer in 1931 to direct the first American units of the American Women's Hospitals resulted in Sheriff's move from private practice to the field of public health. Sheriff served as deputy and later chief health officer for Spartanburg County between 1933 and 1940, during which time her responses to endemic diphtheria, pellagra, and tuberculosis; her innovative maternal and child health campaigns; and her contraceptive research for the Milbank Memorial Fund spawned programs throughout the South based on her models. She established the first family-planning clinic associated with a county health department in the United States. Health departments around the state followed Sheriff's lead after 1936, and by 1939 South Carolina became the second state to make birth control an official public health service (North Carolina was the first).

In 1936 Sheriff received a fellowship to study public health at Harvard University. She became the first American woman to receive the M.P.H. (master of public health) degree from Harvard the next year. In 1940 Sheriff moved to Columbia to become the assistant director of the Board of Health's Division of Maternal and Child Health. She advanced to director the following year and continued to administer programs for women and children until 1967, when she was promoted to deputy commissioner of the State Board of Health and chief of the Bureau of Community Health Services. She held these positions until retiring in 1974. In 1940 Sheriff married George Henry Zerbst, an ophthalmologist and public health officer who had been one of her medical school instructors eighteen years earlier.

Sheriff's efforts to train and license lay midwives in South Carolina during the postwar decades reveal the pragmatism that guided her public health policies. Most South Carolina midwives were African American women whose patients were denied the option of an attending physician by poverty and segregation. Sheriff argued that outlawing lay midwifery would not end the practice but would ensure that midwives remained beyond the reach of health officials. She sanctioned the use of licensed midwives during routine deliveries, which raised their status and ensured high levels of participation in the state's training programs. Sheriff also linked lay practitioners with local nurse midwives and physicians willing to attend difficult births.

After the use of antibiotics controlled many contagious diseases, Sheriff focused state resources on accident prevention, poison control, family planning, and the elimination of child abuse. In 1968 Sheriff used her professional and personal skills to win support for consolidation of county health departments into the state health districts that remain her legacy. After a brief illness, Sheriff died in Columbia on September 10, 1988, and was buried in Greenlawn Memorial Park. PATRICIA EVRIDGE HILL

Buice, Allison. "Dr. Sheriff: Health Pioneer." Spartanburg *Herald-Journal,* June 22, 1986, pp. B1, B11.

"Dr. Hilla Sheriff, Honored Health Professional in S.C." Columbia *State,* September 12, 1988, p. A4.

Hill, Patricia Evridge. "Go Tell It on the Mountain: Hilla Sheriff and Public Health in the South Carolina Piedmont, 1929 to 1940." *American Journal of Public Health* 85 (April 1995): 578–84.

———. "Invisible Labours: Mill Work and Motherhood in the American South." *Social History of Medicine* 9 (August 1996): 235–51.

Sheriff, Hilla. Papers. South Caroliniana Library, University of South Carolina, Columbia.

Whitten, Kathleen. "The More I Did, the More I Saw the Need." Columbia *State Magazine,* February 16, 1986, pp. 8–11.

Sherman's march. This Union campaign is one of the most controversial of the Civil War because of the damage it wrought to civilian property and the questions it raised about fair play in war. Arriving at Savannah, Georgia, in December 1864, General William T. Sherman planned to advance his Union army north through the Carolinas into Virginia, where armies under Robert E. Lee and Ulysses Grant remained deadlocked in trench combat. As Sherman had done in Georgia, he also hoped in South Carolina to destroy railroads, supplies, and morale. He saw poetic justice in unleashing his forces upon the state that seceded first and had been the site of the war's first shots. "The whole army is burning with an insatiable desire to wreak vengeance upon South Carolina," Sherman wrote. "I almost tremble at her fate, but feel that she deserves all that seems in store for her."

After a month's preparation, operations began on February 1, 1865. Sherman organized his 60,079 men into left and right wings, commanded by General Henry Slocum and General Oliver Howard, respectively, and a cavalry force under General Judson Kilpatrick. The right wing (Fifteenth and Seventeenth Corps) feinted toward Charleston. The Union naval blockade and occupation of the Sea Islands had reduced the city's usefulness as a port, but Charleston had remained a haven for blockade-runners, a munitions center, and a target of rich symbolic value. Meanwhile, the left wing of Sherman's army (Fourteenth and Twentieth Corps) angled toward Augusta, which contained important munitions and gunpowder factories. After several days, however, Sherman brought the wings together and advanced north toward Columbia.

Confederate general P. G. T. Beauregard responded as Sherman hoped by concentrating his defenses at Charleston and Augusta. This Union deception aside, the Confederate leadership suffered from personnel shortages and disunity of command. Beauregard had

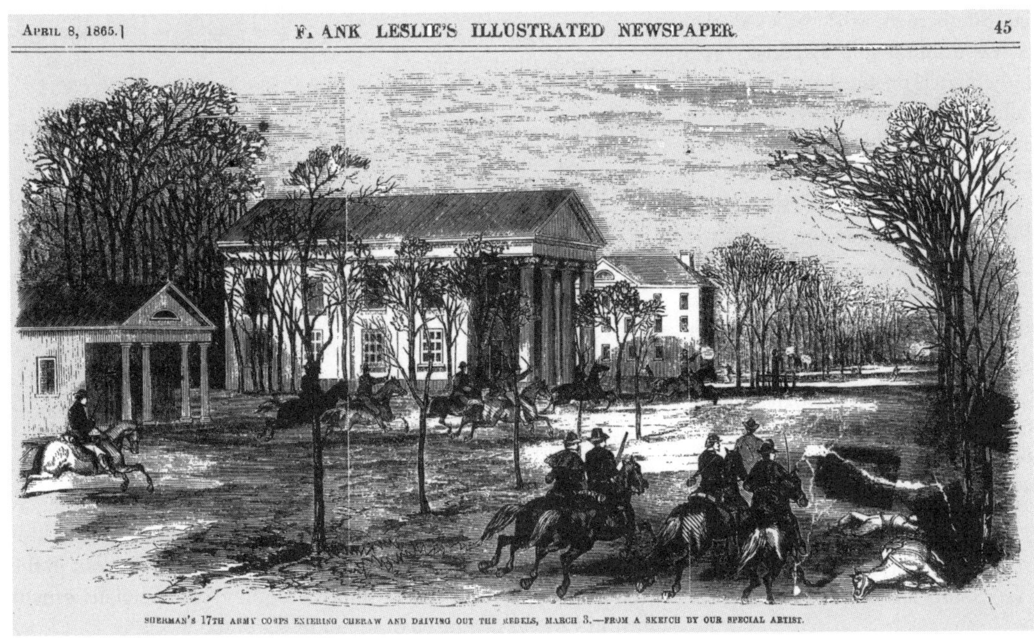
APRIL 8, 1865.] FRANK LESLIE'S ILLUSTRATED NEWSPAPER. 45

SHERMAN'S 17TH ARMY CORPS ENTERING CHERAW AND DRIVING OUT THE REBELS, MARCH 3.—FROM A SKETCH BY OUR SPECIAL ARTIST.

Union forces enter Cheraw (Chesterfield County), March 3, 1865, on Sherman's march through the state. *Frank Leslie's Illustrated Newspaper,* April 8, 1865. Courtesy, South Caroliniana Library, University of South Carolina twenty thousand soldiers, many of whom were poorly trained boys and old men. From Virginia, Lee sent a depleted infantry brigade under John Doby Kennedy, a Georgia cavalry brigade, and a small cavalry detachment commanded by two South Carolinians, Matthew Butler and Wade Hampton III. These officers mainly added to the confusion. The only general to successfully engage Sherman was Joseph Wheeler. On February 11 Wheeler's cavalry achieved one of the few Confederate victories of the campaign by ambushing Kilpatrick's cavalry at Aiken.

Few people thought that the Union army could cross the swamps and rivers that formed a natural barrier to Columbia. Winter rains made lowcountry roads impassable. Sherman's scouts used canoes, and his engineers navigated the obstacles with portable pontoon bridges and "corduroy roads" of logs. Despite skirmishes with Wheeler's cavalry and occasional Confederate attempts to defend key terrain (as happened at Rivers Bridge from February 2 to February 4), the Union forces averaged almost ten miles daily. On February 15 they reached Columbia's outskirts. Confederate forces under Hampton resisted briefly before evacuating and leaving the mayor to surrender on February 17.

That night a fire destroyed one-third of Columbia. In the accusations that followed, Sherman blamed Hampton for leaving burning cotton bales in the streets, a northern wind for helping to spread the blaze, and civilians for giving his troops alcohol. Sherman's detractors accused him at best of failing to control his soldiers, at worst of planning arson. Vengeful former slaves and ex-Union prisoners of war held at nearby Camp Sorghum have also been named as possible culprits.

The Columbia conflagration was unusual only for its size. Barnwell, Orangeburg, and smaller places along Sherman's thirty-mile-wide path also suffered. Railroads and anything of military value were destroyed. Residents went hungry after losing winter food supplies to foragers, both Union and Confederate. Although rape and murder were unreported, civilians endured theft of valuables, humiliation of women, and destruction of homes and private property at the hands of opportunistic Union "bummers." After burning portions of Winnsboro, Camden, and Cheraw (Florence was spared after a successful defense on March 5 by cavalry general Beverly Robertson), Sherman ordered his army to behave less vindictively when it crossed into North Carolina at the beginning of March.

Sherman's march embittered Southerners who believed that making war on noncombatants was dishonorable. Especially as it passed through South Carolina, the march presaged the "total war" that would become common during the twentieth century. For slaves, however, it meant freedom. Although Sherman called African Americans the "inevitable Sambo" and used his black soldiers as laborers, he did, with the approval of Secretary of War Edwin Stanton, order that the coastline and thirty miles inland from Charleston to northern Florida be reserved for former slaves, introducing the idea of "forty acres and a mule" as compensation. Sherman's order was later overturned, but it would become the subject of still more controversy during Reconstruction. ANDREW H. MYERS

Barrett, John G. *Sherman's March through the Carolinas.* Chapel Hill: University of North Carolina Press, 1956.

Glatthaar, Joseph T. *The March to the Sea and Beyond: Sherman's Troops in the Savannah and Carolinas Campaigns.* New York: New York University Press, 1985.

Lucas, Marion Brunson. *Sherman and the Burning of Columbia.* 1976. Reprint, Columbia: University of South Carolina Press, 2000.

Nelson, Larry E. "Sherman at Cheraw." *South Carolina Historical Magazine* 100 (October 1999): 328–54.

Royster, Charles. *The Destructive War: William Tecumseh Sherman, Stonewall Jackson, and the Americas.* New York: Knopf, 1991.

Sherman, William Tecumseh. *Memoirs of General W. T. Sherman.* 1875. Reprint, New York: Library of America, 1990.

Sherrill, Homer Lee (1915–2001). Musician. "Pappy" Sherrill, a traditional fiddler, is known primarily to South Carolinians for his long musical association with the banjoist DeWitt "Snuffy" Jenkins that dated back to 1939. Although the two made few recordings together during their prime, later albums preserve much of their music. According to the Nashville deejay and music historian Eddie Stubbs, Pappy Sherrill "was a wonderful old-time fiddle player . . . his playing had so much life in it."

Sherrill was born near Hickory, North Carolina, on March 23, 1915. He started playing fiddle at age seven and made his radio debut at thirteen in Gastonia. Through the mid-to-late 1930s Sherrill played with several groups that worked for the Crazy Water Crystals Company, including the East Hickory String Band, the Crazy Hickory Nuts, Mack and Shorty, Mainer's Mountaineers, the Morris Brothers—with whom he recorded as Wiley, Zeke, and Homer—and the Blue Sky Boys, with whom he made some radio transcriptions. They worked at WWNC Asheville, WGST Atlanta, WPTF Raleigh, and WBT Charlotte. In October 1939 Sherrill came to Columbia, South Carolina, and joined Byron Parker's Hillbillies (or Mountaineers), recording with them on Bluebird in 1940 and DeLuxe in 1946. Homer acquired the nickname "Pappy" in July 1940, when his wife presented him with a son.

From 1939 until 1990 the musical career of Pappy Sherrill was closely entwined with that of Snuffy Jenkins. They recorded later albums for Folk-Lyric, Rounder, and Old Homestead. In addition, Sherrill made a reunion album with the Morris Brothers on Rounder. On one of the Rounder albums he got to record his signature tune "Cherry Blossom Waltz." After Jenkins died in 1990, Sherrill made some appearances with the WBT Briarhoppers and received such honors as the South Carolina Folk Heritage Award and the North Carolina "Order of the Long Leaf Pine." Sherrill remained active almost to the time of his death in Columbia on November 30, 2001. ABBY GAIL GOODNITE

Ahrens, Pat J. *A History of the Musical Careers of DeWitt "Snuffy" Jenkins, Banjoist, and Homer "Pappy" Sherrill, Fiddler.* Columbia, S.C., 1970.

Hinshaw, Dawn. "Bluegrass Legend Pappy Sherrill, 86." Columbia *State,* December 1, 2001, pp. A1, A4.

Shrimp. South Carolina shrimp are considered among the best in the world and are part of the foundation of lowcountry cooking. The Gulf and South Atlantic are renowned for commercially landed brown (*Penaeus aztecus*), pink (*Penaeus duorarum*), and white (*Penaeus setiferus*) shrimp. The common names do not clearly describe these shrimp since most shrimp change color relative to bottom type and water clarity. Some farm-raised shrimp are considered close in quality to wild caught shrimp.

Although many larger shrimp trawlers that are out of port for a week or more freeze shrimp shortly after being caught—sometimes even cooking them on the boat—most commercial boats sell them fresh. Many South Carolinians catch their own shrimp, usually by pulling a seine or by casting a circular net (which takes training as well as strength). Small creek shrimp caught in shallow, brackish waters are thought to be sweeter than those caught further out in the rivers and ocean. It is rare to find any of these commercially caught shrimp very far off the coast in South Carolina.

The standard practice for most is to purchase shrimp headless. Some lowcountry cooks prefer to cook shrimp with the head on, sucking the juices out of the head as one would a crawfish. Aficionados of the creek shrimp may even eat the softer parts of the shell. The shell may be removed before or after cooking, although it is preferable to cook shrimp with the shell on to get the fullest flavor and a more tender texture. Some prefer to remove the vein along the back of the shrimp (the digestive tract). Shrimp are not eaten raw and are best cooked quickly, a few minutes at most, with the cooking stopped as soon as the shell turns red. Overcooked shrimp are tough and tasteless. The head and shell of the shrimp can be used to make a shrimp stock usable in sauces and broths. Shrimp can be sautéed, fried (without the shell), poached (called "boiled"), grilled, baked, or steamed. In the 1800s shrimp mousses made with butter or cream (also called "shrimp butter") were fashionable. In the late twentieth century shrimp and grits became popular, as did lowcountry shrimp boil, which is also called many other names.

No laws govern standard market sizes of shrimp. They are usually graded commercially by the number of whole shrimp or shrimp tails there are to a pound. A rule of thumb would be jumbo shrimp, twenty-one to twenty-five shrimp tails per pound; large, from thirty-one to thirty-five per pound; and medium, from thirty-six to forty per pound. However, the grading varies according to the seller. NATHALIE DUPREE

Davidson, Alan. *Seafood: A Connoisseur's Guide and Cookbook.* New York: Simon and Schuster, 1989.

Peterson, James. *Fish and Shellfish.* New York: Morrow, 1996.

Silver. From the late seventeenth century through the early nineteenth century, the center of South Carolina silver production, importation, and consumption was Charleston. Populated with an oligarchy of planters and merchants, the city had the highest per capita income in British North America. British culture dominated Charleston society, and British goods, including silver, were in great demand. In a society known for its conspicuous consumption, owning silver was a practical way to both display and preserve one's wealth.

A silver coffeepot (circa 1750–1760) by the Charleston silversmith Alexander Petrie. Courtesy, Collection of the Museum of Early Southern Decorative Arts, Winston-Salem, N.C.

The early colonists imported all silver or plate from England, but by the early 1700s colonial silversmiths began to compete with imported British wares. A surviving chalice dated 1711 and attributed to the Charleston goldsmith Miles Brewton (1675–1745) indicates early silver production in the city. Charleston silversmiths, such as Alexander Petrie and Thomas You, as well as most American silversmiths, usually marked their wares with either their initials or their last names. Pseudohallmarks similar to British hallmarks were sometimes added to give the appearance of English wares.

The Revolutionary War called a temporary halt to the importation of silver and curtailed the work of many South Carolina silversmiths. Reportedly British soldiers carried off large loads of silver when they evacuated Charleston. After the war members of Charleston society continued their close ties to England but also supported local silversmiths as well as other artisans living in the city.

The popularity of owning silver grew, as indicated by the high number of silversmiths and jewelers working in the Charleston area between 1780 and 1820. Domestic silver, especially pieces associated with the serving of tea, was the mainstay of these Charleston artisans. They also were commissioned by churches, fraternal organizations, and civic groups to produce silver for ceremonies and awards. Notable silversmiths of the era included Heloise and Louis Boudo and John Ewan.

By the early 1800s emerging inland communities such as Columbia and Camden could boast several working silversmiths. William Glaze initially began his career as a silversmith but later established the Palmetto Armory in Columbia to provide weapons for the defense of the state. William Gregg is known more for starting one of the state's first cotton mills than he is as a master silversmith in Columbia. A Camden silversmith, Alexander Young, operated a bookstore in his shop and also sold items from military goods to patent medicine.

Less is known about silversmiths working in the upstate. By the mid–nineteenth century, when many communities had the populations to support silversmiths, silver manufactured in the Northeast was easy to obtain and more fashionable than locally made wares. The popularity of imports lessened the demand for South Carolina artisans. Flatware, however, does exist bearing the marks of upstate jewelers and silversmiths, indicating that at least some silver continued to be produced in Chester, York, and Greenville up until the Civil War.

Little silver was produced in South Carolina after the Civil War. The exception was the Eastern Carolina Silver Company, which operated in Hartsville from 1907 to 1909. The company was one of the few southern ventures in the mass production of silver-plated wares. KAREN SWAGER

Bivens, John, and Forsyth Alexander. *The Regional Arts of the Early South.* Winston-Salem, N.C.: Museum of Early Southern Decorative Arts, 1991.

Burton, E. Milby. *South Carolina Silversmiths 1690–1860.* Revised and edited by Warren Ripley. Charleston, S.C.: Charleston Museum, 1991.

Wilmot, Patricia J. *Hartsville's Eastern Carolina Silver Company.* Hartsville, S.C.: Hartsville Museum, 1988.

Silver Bluff Baptist Church (Beech Island). Located near the South Carolina–Georgia state line, Silver Bluff Baptist Church is one of the oldest independent African American Christian congregations in the United States. Traditional accounts have dated the organization of Silver Bluff Church to around 1775, though some type of religious association among area slaves may have developed as early as the 1750s. Silver Bluff, as was the case with other black congregations, began in a context of the Revolutionary-era emphasis on the "rights of man" and evangelical revivalist preaching. Revivalist preaching during the era seemed most successful in attracting people, black and nonblack, to Christianity. Also, many evangelicals held antislavery sentiments, or at least were sympathetic to interracial ideals.

The Indian trader and planter George Galphin was a crucial element in the origins and growth of Silver Bluff because he permitted black and white preachers to minister on his plantation. George Liele, a Virginia native living in Georgia, was converted around 1773 and later manumitted so that he might preach to plantation blacks in the vicinity, including those at the Galphin plantation. A white New England minister, Wait Palmer, also preached in Silver Bluff around the same time and organized a church, eventually placing David George, a Virginia native and runaway slave, in charge. Church members were temporarily scattered during the Revolutionary War. Reunited, Liele and George ministered in the area. Liele eventually journeyed to Jamaica, where he established the first Baptist church on the island. He also converted Andrew Bryan, who established what is regarded as the oldest continuous black congregation in Savannah. George ultimately settled in Sierra Leone, where he established the first Baptist church on the African continent. Jesse Galphin (sometimes called Jesse Peters) reorganized the Silver Bluff church and then later moved with most of its members to Augusta, where they founded what would become Springfield Baptist Church. A smaller party remained in the Silver Bluff area. The current church building dates to 1873 and houses the Silver Bluff Missionary Baptist Church. In 2001 the congregation received a $250,000 grant to restore the site. SANDY DWAYNE MARTIN

Billingsley, Andrew. *Mighty Like a River: The Black Church and Social Reform.* New York: Oxford University Press, 1999.

Brooks, Walter Henderson. "The Priority of the Silver Bluff Church and Its Promoters." *Journal of Negro History* 7 (April 1922): 172–96.

———. *The Silver Bluff Church: A History of Negro Baptist Churches in America.* Washington, D.C.: R. L. Pendleton, 1910.

Gordon, Grant. *From Slavery to Freedom: The Life of David George, Pioneer Black Baptist Minister.* Hantsport, Nova Scotia: Lancelot, 1992.

Sernett, Milton C., ed. *African American Religious History: A Documentary Witness.* 2d ed. Durham, N.C.: Duke University Press, 1999.

Simkins, Francis Butler (1897–1966). Historian. Simkins was born on December 14, 1897, in Edgefield, the son of Samuel McGowan Simkins and Sarah Raven Lewis. He attended school in Edgefield and in 1918 received his B.A. from the University of South Carolina. He attended Columbia University in New York City and earned his M.A. in 1920 and a Ph.D. in 1926. In 1928 he accepted a position at Longwood College in Farmville, Virginia, and remained there until his retirement in 1966, except for various positions at other institutions as a visiting professor. He built a reputation as an excellent teacher by challenging his students to think for themselves. On August 16, 1930, Simkins married Edna Chandler, and they later divorced. On June 7, 1942, he married Margaret Robinson Lawrence. The marriage produced one son, Francis Butler Simkins, Jr.

Simkins's contributions to the field of southern history were enormous. Two themes recurred in his writing: the South ought to be treated on its own terms; and the South possessed cultural characteristics that were different from those of the rest of the nation. In the 1927 *Journal of Negro History,* Simkins exposed the violence and pretensions of "chivalry" in the Ku Klux Klan. In 1932 he won the Dunning Prize for *South Carolina during Reconstruction,* in which he and his coauthor Robert Woody argued that during Reconstruction, although African Americans were allowed to exercise their right to vote, whites continued to dominate the majority of southern institutions. In 1936, well in advance of other gender studies, Simkins wrote *The Women of the Confederacy* in collaboration with James Patton. In 1938 Simkins delivered a provocative paper, "New Viewpoints of Southern Reconstruction," to the Southern Historical Association, in which he exhorted the cultivation of "more moderate, saner, perhaps newer views of [t]his period." Hints of this attitude came as early as 1921 in the *South Atlantic Quarterly* article "Race Legislation in South Carolina," which stated that Republican legislators "instituted radical reforms in education, which South Carolina, radical or conservative, has never seen fit to repudiate." In this early paper he contradicted the prevailing assumption of innate African American inferiority. In *Pitchfork Ben Tillman,* completed in 1944, Simkins presented the extreme racism of Tillman without judgment, despite his disagreement with it. In 1947 Simkins wrote *The South, Old and New: A History, 1820–1947,* which became a major textbook for southern history. It was revised in 1953 as *A History of the South.* In 1954 the profession honored Simkins for his scholarship by electing him president of the Southern Historical Association.

While Simkins was intellectually progressive, he nevertheless maintained emotional ties to white southern traditionalism. He looked with disapproval on the shameful treatment of African Americans, but liberal critics thought that he did not move fast enough. He felt that the South should arrive at its own solution for race and criticized federal activism in securing civil rights, but conservatives attacked him as a revisionist. When the momentous events of the 1950s and 1960s challenged the traditional order in the American South, Simkins rediscovered much in the old to be conserved and became a spokesperson for the status quo. Therein lies an irony in the full circle of his life. For decades Simkins worked to revise the face of the South in history. His pioneering work on race relations was one of the major intellectual forces that helped set in motion the civil rights movement. In the end, Simkins was unable to keep pace with the very changes that he had helped engineer. He died on February 9, 1966, in Farmville, Virginia. ORVILLE VERNON BURTON AND BEATRICE BURTON

McWhiney, Grady. "Historians as Southerners." *Continuity* 9 (fall 1984): 1–31.

Obituary. *Journal of American History* 53 (September 1966): 439.

Obituary. *Journal of Southern History* 32 (August 1966): 435.

Simkins, Modjeska Monteith (1899–1992). Educator, civil rights organizer, community activist. Simkins was born in Columbia on December 5, 1899, the eldest child of Henry Clarence Monteith and Rachel Evelyn Hall. The family lived on a small farm outside of the city. Henry Monteith worked as a brick mason, while Rachel and the children contributed to the family's income by selling surplus produce from the family farm.

Modjeska Monteith Simkins. Watercolor by Larry Lebby. Courtesy, South Caroliniana Library, University of South Carolina

Simkins's home environment fostered religious growth, independence, compassion, pride, and civic duty. Henry Monteith especially encouraged his children to support Columbia's black community. He demonstrated his own commitment by patronizing the city's black establishments and acting as one of the earliest depositors at Victory Savings Bank, the state's first black-owned bank. Much of Simkins's inspiration to become an advocate for the black community came from her parents.

Simkins was educated at Benedict College in Columbia, a school designed to accommodate primary-, secondary-, and college-level students. She began Benedict College in the second grade in 1905 and remained there until she received her teaching degree in 1921. Following graduation, she taught mathematics at Booker T. Washington School in Columbia until her marriage to the businessman Andrew Whitfield Simkins in December 1929.

Once married, Simkins was no longer eligible to teach in Columbia since the school system refused to employ married women. She accepted a position with the South Carolina Tuberculosis Association as director of the Negro Program from 1931 to 1942. As director, she worked diligently to increase education and awareness of tuberculosis and other health-related threats prevalent in the state's black community. She proved highly successful in the position but was forced to leave the association because of her increased involvement with the National Association for the Advancement of Colored People (NAACP).

Simkins joined the NAACP with encouragement from her mother and two aunts, all of whom were members. In the late 1930s she was elected chairperson of the Columbia branch's program committee and a member of the executive board. Simkins was also present at the founding meeting of the South Carolina Conference of the NAACP, a forum that allowed local chapters to function as a cohesive unit to represent the state. During Simkins's years with the NAACP, she assisted the organization in making great strides in the fight against inequality. She encouraged Charleston and Columbia teachers to fight for equal pay, which they earned in 1944 and 1945, respectively. She was also involved in the cases that challenged the legality of South Carolina's whites-only Democratic primaries, *Elmore v. Rice* and *Brown v. Baskins.*

Simkins's most noted involvement came in her work in the 1950s with the case of *Briggs v. Elliott,* which sought to end segregation in Clarendon County Schools. *Briggs v. Elliott,* along with *Brown v. Board of Education,* was one of the five NAACP desegregation cases to go before the U.S. Supreme Court. The nature of *Briggs v. Elliott* led to extensive economic reprisals for families involved in the suit. For those affected, Simkins functioned as a liaison between the black community of Clarendon County and organizations willing to provide them with aid.

Even after years of involvement with the NAACP's State Conference, Simkins remained committed to civic action. She continued her work with many local activities and authored numerous letters and appeals on topics concerning the black community. Her organizational affiliations ranged from local improvement clubs to national efforts with groups such as the Civil Rights Congress and the National Negro Congress. In addition to her civic activism, she returned to full-time employment in 1956, accepting a job at Victory Savings Bank as public relations director.

Simkins's life embodied many of the ideals set forth by her parents. She proved herself as an independent leader and advocate for the black community. Her diligent work contributed to successful local, state, and national campaigns on topics ranging from health care to racial equality. Simkins died in Columbia on April 9, 1992. She was buried in Columbia's Palmetto Cemetery. CAROLYN L. KIMBRELL

Aba-Mecha, Barbara Woods. "Black Woman Activist in Twentieth Century South Carolina: Modjeska Monteith Simkins." Ph.D. diss., Emory University, 1978.

Simkins, Modjeska Monteith. Papers. South Caroliniana Library, University of South Carolina, Columbia.

Woods, Barbara A. "Modjeska Simkins and the South Carolina Conference of the NAACP, 1939–1957." In *Women in the Civil Rights Movement: Trailblazers and Torchbearers 1941–1965,* edited by Vicki L. Crawford, Jacqueline Anne Rouse, and Barbara Woods. Brooklyn, N.Y.: Carlson, 1990.

Simmons, Philip (b. 1912). Blacksmith. Born on June 9, 1912, on Daniel Island in a Gullah-speaking community just a few miles from Charleston, Simmons moved to the port city in 1925. He soon apprenticed himself to an elderly African American wheelwright named Peter Simmons (no relation), a man who was born in slavery on a plantation near St. Stephen and whose father and grandfather had also worked as blacksmiths. Under Peter's watchful eye Philip would initiate an illustrious career. From Peter the thirteen-year-old apprentice was exposed to so many branches of ironworking that Philip Simmons would later describe himself as a "general blacksmith" since he could shoe horses, repair wagons, fashion iron fittings for boats, make and mend tools, and fabricate structural iron for buildings. When motorized trucks began to replace the horses and wagons that were mainstays of his business, he began to try his hand at making decorative wrought-iron gates and balconies. He quickly found that he could do that sort of work since he "could mash out a leaf the same as a horseshoe." Shifting from the pragmatic to the artistic branch of blacksmithing, Philip Simmons would establish himself as an artistic force in Charleston.

Simmons's most elaborate ironworks were created for homes in the celebrated Battery District near the harbor. Between 1938 and 1990 he produced more than two hundred commissions, which included gates, fences, railings, and balconies. Among the most visible of his works are the gates made for the Christopher Gadsden House on East Bay Street, which feature a pair of threatening rattlesnakes that commemorate Gadsden's "Don't Tread on Me" flag designed during the Revolutionary War.

Coming to the notice of the Smithsonian Institution in 1976, Simmons was invited to demonstrate his skills at the Festival of American Folklife held on the Mall in Washington, D.C. There, at the foot of the Lincoln Memorial, he crafted a gate filled with a variety of images intended to show the range of his abilities. This work came to be known as the "Star and Fish" gate and was acquired by the National Museum of American History in 1982. This was the same year that the National Endowment for the Arts began to recognize and honor American folk artists with the title of National Heritage Fellow. As a member of the initial class of Fellows, Simmons was widely lauded, and he began to receive commissions from various museums.

The work that will probably stand as his masterpiece is a gate created in 1987 for the South Carolina State Museum in Columbia. It features two large egrets surrounded by numerous scrolls and is topped with an image of a palmetto tree. While Simmons was fashioning this gate he often referred to it as "the gate for the state," but after it was installed, the museum chose to honor its creator by naming it "The Philip Simmons Gate" and placing it at the entrance to the history galleries.

While he turned his shop over to his former apprentices, Simmons continued to design decorative pieces and receive accolades into the twenty-first century. In addition to his induction into the South Carolina Hall of Fame and a lifetime achievement award from the state for his efforts in historic preservation, he has had a public garden, two parks, and the blacksmithing studio in the School for the Building Arts named for him. JOHN MICHAEL VLACH

Vlach, John Michael. *Charleston Blacksmith: The Work of Philip Simmons.* Rev. ed. Columbia: University of South Carolina Press, 1992.

Simms, William Gilmore (1806–1870). Poet, historian, novelist. Simms was born on April 17, 1806, in Charleston, the son of the Irish immigrant William Gilmore Simms and Harriet Ann Singleton. His mother died when Simms was an infant. His distraught father moved west, leaving his son to be reared by a grandmother who told him stories of Charleston during the Revolutionary War and the exploits of his ancestors. In 1818 Simms's father sent a representative to Charleston to bring his son west. The twelve-year-old boy refused his father's entreaties and chose to remain in Charleston.

William Gilmore Simms. Courtesy, South Caroliniana Library, University of South Carolina

Lacking much formal education, Simms was a voracious reader and an acute observer. From his reading and his travel he absorbed history as well as local legends and acquired material for the volumes he would later write. In 1825 he took up the study of law in Charleston. Literature, however, remained his passion, and in that same year he helped found and edit *The Album,* which characterized itself as "a weekly literary miscellany." He married Anna Malcolm Giles on October 19, 1826. That same year he was admitted to the bar. The birth of his daughter Anna added to the young family's joy even as it stretched their meager finances and reduced the time available for literary pursuits. In 1829 Simms became editor of the *City Gazette,* a Charleston newspaper through which he railed against nullification and John C. Calhoun's doctrine of state interposition.

In the early 1830s Simms experienced a series of devastating personal setbacks. In 1830 both his father and his grandmother died. His house in Summerville burned to the ground. In February 1832 his wife succumbed to a lingering illness. Alone but for his four-year-old daughter, Simms resigned his editorship and went north to explore new opportunities. In New York he met James Lawson, a young Scots businessman and occasional poet. Through Lawson, Simms was introduced to a group of young writers and critics and their publishers. For the rest of his life he would engage in a lively correspondence with these new friends, and he would make almost annual visits to New York to renew and deepen their friendships.

Buoyed by the success of his trip, Simms returned to Charleston determined to make a living as a professional writer. During the next three years he published *Martin Faber* (1833), a ghost story and his first work of fiction; *Guy Rivers* (1834), the first of his "border tales" set in the Georgia frontier; *The Yemassee* (1835), a colonial romance based on an Indian uprising in 1715; and *The Partisan* (1835), the first of his Revolutionary War romances. Published by Harper and Brothers of New York, these works were widely and warmly reviewed and established Simms as one of his country's leading literary lights.

In 1836 Simms's life took another propitious turn with his marriage to Chevillette Roach, the nineteen-year-old daughter of a wealthy planter. The newlyweds made their home at Woodlands, one of the Roach plantations on the Edisto River near Orangeburg. Simms savored life at Woodlands and the setting it provided for his literary endeavors. Though he spent his summers in Charleston, Woodlands would be his home for the remainder of his life.

Despite the delights of plantation living, Simms felt himself a "man marked for the scourge." Of the fourteen children borne by Chevillette, only five would live to adulthood. His father-in-law's poor management of the plantation kept the family's financial situation precarious and forced on Simms a pace of composition that occasionally affected his health and morale.

Simms believed that "to be national in literature, one must needs be sectional." Indeed, he continued, "he who shall depict one *section* faithfully, has made his proper and sufficient contribution to the great work of *national* illustration." Though occasionally annoyed by an inaccurately perceived sense of neglect in his home state, and prompted at times to consider removing to what he hoped might be a more hospitable literary climate in New York, Simms remained a South Carolinian and devoted his professional life to telling the Palmetto State's story. His efforts varied widely. He edited numerous literary journals, engaged in a rich and voluminous correspondence, and lectured widely. He wrote stories about the southern frontier, essays on literary and social topics, and reviews of newly published works.

But Simms's principal contributions to a broader understanding of South Carolina may be found in his poetry, his history, his biographies, and perhaps most notably, his fiction. Simms's best poetry, such as "Maid of Congaree" and "Dark-Eyed Maid of Edisto," conveyed the beauty and mystery of South Carolina. After the Civil War he collected and published *War Poetry of the South,* a valuable document of the Confederate experience. A committed historian, Simms possessed one of the finest private libraries of historical materials in the South. He published a history of South Carolina in 1840 (versions revised by his granddaughter Mary Simms Oliphant would become a staple for schoolchildren in the twentieth century), followed by biographies of Francis Marion and Nathanael Greene. His beloved Woodlands was put to the torch by Union troops in 1865 (though later rebuilt), and his entire library was destroyed. Simms retreated inland, where he witnessed the burning and devastation there, which he later described in *Sack and Destruction of the City of Columbia, S.C.*

In his fiction Simms was a master of the "romance," which he likened more to epic poetry. He covered the entire sweep of Carolina history, from the earliest years of French and Spanish settlement (*The Lily and the Totem* and *Vasconselos*), through the period of English colonization (*The Yemassee*), through the Revolution (a "cycle" of seven romances, most notably *The Partisan* and *Woodcraft*), up to Simms's own time, where a distinctive American character began to emerge (*Guy Rivers*).

Keeping nation and section in balance became increasingly difficult for Simms during the 1850s. Some critics have read *Woodcraft,* with its view of a coherent, hierarchical plantation society, as a rebuttal to *Uncle Tom's Cabin.* More certain was Simms's growing sense of alienation from the North, which came to a climax during a lecture tour in New York in 1856. Speaking on "South Carolina in the Revolution," he asserted his native state's contributions to the country's history and attacked the antislavery movement for its "defamation" of South Carolina. So negative were the reviews of his first lecture that Simms cancelled the remainder of his engagements and returned home. From that point on he became an advocate of southern secession.

Broken by the war and enfeebled by illness, Simms attempted in 1865 to revive his literary career, but the result was undistinguished. He died in Charleston on June 11, 1870, and was buried in Magnolia Cemetery. JOHN M. MCCARDELL, JR.

Guilds, John C. *Simms: A Literary Life.* Fayetteville: University of Arkansas Press, 1992.

McCardell, John. "William Gilmore Simms and Antebellum Southern Literature." In *The Oxford Encyclopedia of American Literature,* vol. 4, edited by Jay Parini. New York: Oxford University Press, 2004.

Oliphant, Mary C. Simms, Alfred Taylor Odell, and T. C. Duncan Eaves, eds. *The Letters of William Gilmore Simms.* 6 vols. Columbia: University of South Carolina Press, 1952–1982.

Simons, Katherine Drayton Mayrant (1890–1969). Poet, novelist, playwright, historian. Simons was born on January 21, 1890, in Charleston, the daughter of Sedgewick Lewis Simons and Katherine Drayton Mayrant. She spent her early years in and around Summerville in Dorchester County. She was educated at local schools and at Converse College in Spartanburg, where she earned a bachelor of letters degree in 1909. Converse awarded her an honorary doctor of literature degree in 1952 for "brilliant contributions" to the literary traditions of her state and nation.

Interested in literary pursuits since girlhood, Simons began writing seriously while in college. Her primary love was poetry, with a focus on lyrical verse, sonnets, and nature poems. The first of her three books of poetry, *Shadow Songs,* appeared in 1912 under the pen name "Kadra Maysi" (created from the first few letters of each unit of her full name). A decade later she became a charter member of the Poetry Society of South Carolina. She would go on to win every award given by the Poetry Society, and at the time of her death she was the only woman ever to have been elected its president. Her other books of poetry were *The Patteran* (1925) and *White Horse Leaping,* which the University of South Carolina Press published in 1951.

Katherine Drayton Mayrant Simmons at a signing for her novel *A Sword from Galway.* Courtesy, South Carolina Historical Society

Simons later created a national reputation for herself in the field of fiction. Her serious interests in travel, the equestrian arts, and South Carolina history are reflected in the eight historical (sometimes labeled "romantic" or "dramatic") novels she published under the pseudonym "Drayton Mayrant" between 1948 and 1960: *A Sword from Galway* (1948), *The Running Thread* (1949), *First the Blade* (1950), *Courage Is Not Given* (1952), *The Red Doe* (1953), *Always a River* (1956), *Lamp in Jerusalem* (1957), and *The Land beyond the Tempest* (1960). Seven of these were chosen as book club selections. Critics alluded to her "genius for description" and described her work as "superlatively well written" and "warmly imaginative." "Perhaps because she was first a poet," one reviewer wrote, Simons "created sentences and paragraphs one returns to again and again for their beauty."

The author of numerous short stories, Simons also wrote or cowrote five plays and a sketch for the ballet *The Lost Atlantis,* which was presented by the Charleston Civic Ballet Company in 1964. Furthermore, she wrote many articles or essays for newspapers and magazines. Between 1955 and 1967 she contributed regularly to the popular onomastic journal *Names in South Carolina.* Two small nonfiction books attest to her love for Charleston and the Summerville area: *Roads of Romance and Historic Spots near Summerville* (1925) and *Stories of Charleston Harbor* (1930).

Simons died on March 31, 1969, and was buried in Magnolia Cemetery in Charleston. In 1997 she was inducted into the South Carolina Academy of Authors. THOMAS L. JOHNSON

LaBorde, Rene. "In Memoriam: Katherine Drayton Mayrant Simons (1890–1969)." *Names in South Carolina* 16 (winter 1969): 4.

Pinckney, Elise. "A Huguenot Writer." Columbia *State Magazine,* September 28, 1952, p. 10.

Simons, Katherine Drayton Mayrant. Papers. South Caroliniana Library, University of South Carolina, Columbia.

Telfair, Nancy. "Katherine Drayton Mayrant Simons." *South Carolina Magazine* 12 (November 1949): 8, 34.

Simons & Lapham. The architectural firm of Simons & Lapham was formed by Albert Simons (1890–1980) and Samuel Lapham (1892–1972) on July 8, 1920. The firm received both local and national acclaim for their work in the areas of architectural design and preservation. Responsible for the design of traditional buildings, especially houses, churches, and schools, and for renovations to many of the historic houses in Charleston, the firm was based in that city. In addition to their architectural work, both partners were involved in detailed historic research on the architecture of Charleston. They coedited *The Octagon Library of Early American Architecture, Volume I: Charleston, South Carolina* (1927) and *Plantations of the Carolina Low Country* (1939), along with numerous well-researched articles.

Albert Simons descended from a long line of Charleston families. He studied at the College of Charleston and completed his B.S. and M.S. degrees in architecture at the University of Pennsylvania. Following his graduation, he traveled through Europe and Northern Africa studying architecture through measurements, drawings, and notes. He then studied at the Atelier Hebrard in Paris, which was connected with the École des Beaux-Arts. He was one of the first instructors of architecture at Clemson University, teaching there from 1915 to 1916, and was then briefly a partner in the firm of Todd, Simons and Todd. After serving in the U.S. Army during World War I, Simons returned to Charleston and formed the firm with Samuel Lapham.

Samuel Lapham VI was the son of a prominent ice manufacturer and city councilman in Charleston. He graduated from the College of Charleston in 1913 and proceeded from there to earn a B.S. degree in architecture from the Massachusetts Institute of Technology in 1916. Lapham served in the U.S. Army during World War I before returning to Charleston, where he joined with Albert Simons.

In the 1920s Simons and Lapham were busy with commissions for new houses and restorations, including thirteen houses in the elite neighborhood called Yeaman's Hall. They also added a wing to the main building of the College of Charleston and consulted on the restoration of Charleston's famous "Rainbow Row." During this decade both partners taught at the College of Charleston. During the Great Depression the firm thrived on federally sponsored work, especially housing. Both partners worked extensively with the federally sponsored Historic American Building Survey. The firm worked on the renovation of the Planter's Hotel on Church Street into Dock Street Theatre and designed the new Memminger Auditorium in the manner of Robert Mills. The firm also completed new plantation houses and restored many others.

In addition to restoring downtown houses, Simons and Lapham worked actively with the Charleston city government to protect historic buildings. Simons helped create the first historic district in America and the first Board of Architectural Review. He also served on the planning commissions for the city of Charleston and Charleston County. Both partners worked on a survey of Charleston architecture that led to a book, *This Is Charleston* (1944).

After World War II the firm grew as postwar commissions flowed in, including the Charleston Municipal Airport, the Law School building at the University of South Carolina, and the restoration of two buildings designed by Robert Mills: the Fireproof Building and Ainsley Hall House. Through the admission of new partners, the business survived the deaths of Simons and Lapham as the architectural firm of Mitchell & Small. RALPH MULDROW

Blevins, Ernest. "The Architecture of Simons & Lapham." Master's thesis, Savannah College of Art and Design, 2002.

Simons, Albert. Papers. South Carolina Historical Society, Charleston.

Simons, Albert, and Simon Lapham. *The Early Architecture of Charleston.* Columbia: University of South Carolina Press, 1970.

Stoney, Samuel G. *Plantations of the South Carolina Low Country.* 5th ed. Charleston, S.C.: Carolina Art Association, 1964.

———. *This Is Charleston: A Survey of the Architectural Heritage of a Unique American City.* Rev. ed. Charleston, S.C.: Carolina Art Association, 1976.

Simpsonville (Greenville County; 2000 pop. 14,352). Incorporated on August 13, 1901, Simpsonville began many decades earlier as a crossroads hamlet where the Old Stage Road intersected a former Cherokee trail, later named the Georgia Road. Residents of northeast Laurens County became Simpsonville's first businessmen. In 1838 the farmer Peter Simpson arrived and established a blacksmithing operation, followed shortly thereafter by the merchant Silas Gilbert, who opened a general store. In that same year the locale was assigned a post office called Plain. As Simpson's services grew in popularity, the crossroads became known as Simpsonville. However, in 1853 the Greenville and Columbia Railroad was completed several miles east of Simpsonville and siphoned off wagon trade and brought growth in the village to a standstill through Reconstruction.

After the war members of the local African American population left the churches of former slaveowners and organized Cedar Grove Baptist Church in 1870, the first church within the modern city limits. Completion of the Greenville and Laurens Railroad near Simpsonville in the mid-1880s brought further change. A high school was built, and a merchant, Sidney J. Wilson, surveyed land for a town and began selling lots. In 1886 the Plain post office officially became Simpsonville. Soon the town became a cotton-processing hub, claiming three gins and a cottonseed oil mill by 1900. That same year the Simpsonville population reached four hundred. In 1907 town representatives solicited the brothers John and Edward Woodside to build the Simpsonville Cotton Mill, which remained the town's largest employer until after World War II.

Schools enjoyed a great deal of attention. In 1911 the Simpsonville Music College was established, and in 1915 the high school issued the first state diplomas in Greenville County. Also, between 1921 and 1940, the Simpsonville High School girls' basketball team, the "Whirlwind," amassed 303 wins and four state championships.

During the Depression of the 1930s, the Farmer's Bank of Simpsonville was one of the few banks in Greenville County that did not fail, but Simpsonville remained a stagnant agricultural center until 1953, when the Greenville Water Works extended its system through the towns of Mauldin, Simpsonville, and Fountain Inn. The towns served by this new water line, dubbed the "Golden Strip" by a local reporter, became attractive locations for industrial development in the early 1960s. A simultaneous demand for new housing and the widening of U.S. Highway 276 in 1956 laid the foundation for further expansion. In the 1980s Simpsonville began attracting residential overflow from the Greenville-Spartanburg metropolitan area. Industry accelerated on Simpsonville's periphery along Interstate 385, and houses were purchased by employees in the larger urban areas as well as by local workers. Between 1970 and 1990 Simpsonville's population grew 254 percent. An additional increase of more than 13 percent from 1990 to 1992 made Simpsonville the fastest-growing city in the state. As Simpsonville responded to the effects of suburban sprawl, city officials worked to combine efforts to encourage growth while preserving the ambient appeal of the small town core. STEVE RICHARDSON

Huff, Archie Vernon, Jr. *Greenville: The History of the City and County in the South Carolina Piedmont.* Columbia: University of South Carolina Press, 1995.

Richardson, Lawrence R., and Robert L. Richardson. *Simpsonville: A Community Study.* Simpsonville, S.C., 1939.

Sims, James Marion (1813–1883). Gynecologist, surgeon. Sims was born near Hanging Rock Creek, Lancaster District, on January 25, 1813, and named Marion in honor of General Francis Marion, the famous "Swamp Fox" of the Revolutionary War. He pursued a bachelor's degree at South Carolina College, graduating in 1832. His father, John Sims, despite disapproving of his son's decision to study medicine, arranged for him to be an apprentice under the preceptor Dr. Churchill Jones before enrollment at the Medical College of South Carolina in Charleston in 1833. After another short spell as an apprentice, Sims completed the requirements for the M.D. at Jefferson Medical College, Philadelphia, in May 1835. Returning to Lancaster District, he married Eliza Theresa Jones in 1836. The couple had at least five children. Sims had a disastrous start to his medical career with the death of his first two infant patients. Disheartened, he migrated to Alabama, where he eventually established a successful practice in Montgomery and gained a reputation for bold surgical interventions in cases of cross-eye, clubfoot, harelip, and tumors of the jaw.

Between 1844 and 1849, a time he described as his "memorable era," Sims developed a surgical method for the repair of a debilitating condition known as vesico-vaginal fistula. Having previously shunned the practice of obstetrics and gynecology, Sims encountered his first case of vesico-vaginal fistula following his assistance at the protracted labor and childbirth of a seventeen-year-old slave girl named Anarcha in 1845. During the same period he located other female slaves with the same condition, expanding the capacity of his back-yard slave hospital from eight to sixteen beds to cope with this increase in patients. During the performance of more than thirty operations on Anarcha alone, Sims designed various instruments, the most notable of which were his speculum and wire sutures, and operative procedures including the eponymous genupectoral or "Sims" position.

Having perfected his surgery in the repeated experiments on his slave patients, Sims sought to make his breakthrough known to the wider medical profession and available to lucrative paying patients. Despite debilitating bouts of diarrhea, he managed to dictate an article detailing his surgical research on vesico-vaginal fistula, which was published in the *American Journal of Medical Sciences* in 1853. In that same year Sims and his family moved from Montgomery to New York and set up home on Madison Avenue. Building a successful medical practice was another matter, for as he recorded in his autobiography, in New York he "had no friends, no influence, no health and nothing to recommend me to business." Sims's solution to this situation came in repeating one of the keys to his professional self-making in Montgomery: establishing a charity hospital under his control for the instruction of fellow physicians. The Woman's Hospital opened at 83 Madison Avenue on May 4, 1855, and later expanded to new premises on Forty-ninth and Fiftieth Streets and chartered as the Woman's Hospital of the State of New York.

In 1861 Sims left the United States for Europe, allegedly because of the discomfort he felt as a southerner in New York during the Civil War. Visiting medical centers such as Edinburgh, London, and Paris, Sims displayed his "peculiar method of operation" to many observers. He also acquired an elite referral practice that included members of the aristocracy, such as the duchess of Hamilton, the empress Eugenie, and the empress of Austria. Sims returned to New York in 1868 but maintained consultation rooms in Paris and London. In Paris in 1870, he was appointed chief surgeon of the Anglo-American Ambulance Corps for treating casualties in the Franco-Prussian War. He was made president of the American Medical Association in 1875, became a founding member of the American Gynecological Society in 1877, and was made that society's president in 1880. Sims died in New York on November 13, 1883, of coronary artery disease and was buried in Greenwood Cemetery.

Up until the 1970s historical narratives of Sims's career were largely favorable. Indeed, it would be fair to say that Sims was celebrated and revered in medical histories in much the same way as he was memorialized in the numerous monuments erected after his death, as both the "Father of Gynecology" and the savior of suffering womanhood. However, with the rise of women's history, the social history of medicine, and African American history in the early 1970s, Sims's career received a thorough reconsideration from the perspective of his slave, pauper, and female patients. While traditional medical historians continued their attempts to minimize the damage to Sims's reputation, the overwhelming academic historiographical consensus became that Sims was self-serving, exploitative, dangerous, and unethical in many of his surgical experiments.
STEPHEN C. KENNY

Harris, Seale. *Woman's Surgeon: The Story of J. Marion Sims.* New York: Macmillan, 1950.

McGregor, Deborah Kuhn. *Sexual Surgery and the Origins of Gynecology: J. Marion Sims, His Hospital, and His Patients.* New York: Garland, 1989.

Sims, James Marion. *The Story of My Life.* 1884. Reprint, New York: Da Capo, 1968.

Sinclair, Bennie Lee (1939–2000). Novelist, poet. Sinclair was born on April 15, 1939, in Greenville to Graham Sinclair and Bennie Ward. While she was in the first grade, her first published poem appeared in a teachers' magazine. Overwhelmed by the attention she received, she stopped writing poetry and returned to it only after the deaths of her father and her brother. A 1956 graduate of Greenville High School, Sinclair entered Furman University, where she received her B.A. in English and later received the Distinguished Alumni Award in 1996. In 1957 she married Thomas Donald Lewis.

Governor Richard Riley appointed Sinclair as poet laureate of South Carolina in 1986. The state's fifth poet laureate and the third woman to serve in the role, she held the position for the remainder of her life. She taught writing at Furman University and gave workshops at the University of Notre Dame, Western Carolina University, and Brevard College. Her commitment to teaching poetry included a twenty-eight-year connection with the South Carolina Arts Commission through its Artists-in-the-Schools program. Additionally, she taught poetry at the Governor's School for the Arts and Humanities. Sinclair promoted public appreciation for poetry via educational radio programs during National Poetry Month each April. She composed Coastal Carolina University's alma mater in 1994 and wrote poems for formal state functions, most notably one for Governor Jim Hodges's inauguration in 1999, a poem that also celebrated the end of the millennium.

In addition to four books of poetry, Sinclair published short stories as well as a novel, *The Lynching* (1992), which was based on the state's last lynching in 1947. She composed poems in her mind before writing them down and amazed everyone with her capacity for memorization. Sinclair died of a heart attack at her home, Wildernesse, near Cleveland, South Carolina, on May 22, 2000.
REBECCA TOLLEY-STOKES

Sirrine, Joseph Emory (1872–1947). Architect, engineer. Sirrine, an important industrial architect and engineer practicing in South Carolina, was born on December 9, 1872, in Americus, Georgia, the son of George W. Sirrine and Sarah Rylander. When his father was appointed superintendent of the Gower, Cox, and Markley Coach Factory in 1876, he moved to Greenville, South Carolina, with his family. Sirrine was educated at Furman University, where he earned his B.S. degree in 1890. After working for several years as a rodman on railroad surveys, he was hired in 1895 by Lockwood, Greene & Company, a New England textile engineering firm, to be resident engineer for two Greenville projects: cotton mills for American Spinning Company and Poe Manufacturing Company.

In 1899 Lockwood, Greene appointed Sirrine as its southern representative, responsible for all of the company's textile construction (twenty-two mills and villages between 1895 and 1902) in the region. Although he was poised to be a partner in the firm, in February 1903 he left the company and opened his own business, J. E. Sirrine, Architects and Engineers. His first commission was designing a mill and village for Chicola Manufacturing Company in Honea Path.

During the next five decades most of the company's business was in southeastern textile construction. By 1920 they had engineered sixty-four mills, twenty-two mill expansions, and sixteen hundred village houses. But Sirrine and his associates also designed schools, hospitals, churches, tobacco and paper factories, bridges and sewer systems, colleges and military camps. The company designed and supervised the engineering for Greenville's Masonic Building; Furman, Clemson, and North Carolina State college buildings; Greenville Country Club; Parker and Greenville high schools; the Chamber of Commerce headquarters in Greenville; and the Poinsett Hotel in downtown Greenville. R. J. Reynolds & Co. employed the firm to build tobacco factories in Winston-Salem, North Carolina. Sirrine helped construct Camp Sevier in Greenville County and Fort Bragg in North Carolina during World War I. During the Great Depression, when textile mills suffered, Sirrine and his associates became experts in engineering for pulp and paper plants.

Perhaps Sirrine's greatest contribution to Greenville was his work on the Southern Textile Manufacturing Exposition. As an organizer of the event, he was so involved in its arrangements that *Cotton* magazine called him the exposition's "godfather." The first show in November 1915 confirmed Greenville's textile importance, and the exposition's board commissioned him to build a permanent home for the biennial event. Textile Hall opened in December 1917 and served as Greenville's convention/exposition center and auditorium/arena until the 1960s. Named to the National Register of Historic Places because of its design and innovative engineering, it was demolished in 1992.

Sirrine was president of the Brandon Corporation; vice president of four other mills and director of nineteen others; a board member of Liberty Life, First National Bank, and the Greenville News-Piedmont; and a Clemson trustee. Although he and his wife, Jane Pinckney Henry, had no children, he and his brother donated the building that served as the pediatric ward of the Greenville Hospital. At his death on August 9, 1947, he left his estate to establish Sirrine Scholarships for Greenville high school graduates. He was buried at Christ Episcopal Church, Greenville. JUDITH T. BAINBRIDGE

Cooper, Nancy Vance Ashmore. *Greenville: Woven from the Past.* Sun Valley, Calif.: American Historical Press, 2000.

Huff, Archie Vernon, Jr. *Greenville: The History of the City and County in the South Carolina Piedmont.* Columbia: University of South Carolina Press, 1995.

Wells, John E., and Robert E. Dalton. *The South Carolina Architects, 1885–1935: A Biographical Directory.* Richmond, Va.: New South Architectural Press, 1992.

Sisters of Charity of Our Lady of Mercy. The Catholic bishop John England founded the Sisters of Charity of Our Lady of Mercy in Charleston in 1829, using the Sisters of Charity in Emmitsburg, Maryland, as a model for the new religious community. By the 1840s the congregation operated an orphanage, an academy, and a free school for girls and a school for free children of color, and it attended the sick during cholera and yellow fever epidemics.

During the Civil War members staffed a Confederate hospital in Virginia and visited men of both armies in Charleston's hospitals and prisons. In 1863 they moved the orphans to Sumter, where they established St. Joseph's Academy. Grateful for the care given to Union soldiers, Congress appropriated $12,000 in 1871 to rebuild the motherhouse and orphanage in Charleston.

The community expanded its ministries in the twentieth century. St. Francis Xavier Hospital, Charleston, established in 1882, added a nursing school in 1900 and a social service agency, known as the Neighborhood House, in 1915. In York the Sisters opened Divine Savior Hospital in 1938 and erected a nursing home in 1963. Although the academies in Sumter and Charleston closed in 1929 and 1930, respectively, the congregation operated St. Angela in Aiken until 1988. Sisters have also taught in parochial schools and religious education programs throughout South Carolina and in New Jersey.

In 1989 the congregation transferred ownership of its hospitals to the Bon Secours Health System and opened a community center to provide education, housing, and outreach services to the residents of James, Johns, and Wadmalaw Islands. Sisters also worked in a variety of parish programs in the Diocese of Charleston. The motherhouse is located on James Island. SISTER ANNE FRANCIS CAMPBELL

Campbell, Sister M. Anne Francis, OLM. "Bishop England's Sisterhood, 1829–1929." Ph.D. diss., St. Louis University, 1968.

Guilday, Peter. *The Life and Times of John England.* 2 vols. 1927. Reprint, New York: Arno, 1969.

Sisters of Charity of Our Lady of Mercy. Archives. Charleston, South Carolina.

6–0–1 Law (1924). In his 1925 inaugural address, Governor Thomas McLeod proudly proclaimed the 6–0–1 Law to be "the most progressive step . . . South Carolina had taken on educational lines since the establishment of the public school system." Passed by the General Assembly on March 21, 1924, the 6–0–1 Law was hailed as a landmark in education reform. In essence, the law guaranteed at least a seven-month school term for all white children. Additionally, it shifted the financial responsibility away from local districts, which often lacked resources, to the state. Although in many ways progressive, the 6–0–1 Law nevertheless reinforced South Carolina's commitment to a racially segregated education system because its provisions did not apply to African Americans.

Reform advocates imbedded the formula for funding the guaranteed seven-month school term in the law's title. The state paid all teacher salaries for six months ("6") provided that local school districts paid for one month ("1"). Counties were encouraged, but not required, to supply additional funding to further expand the school term ("0"). Prior to this act, local districts funded their own schools largely from property taxes. Consequently, school terms varied widely depending on the resources and property values in individual districts. Equalizing educational opportunities for rural white children was the primary objective of 6–0–1 Law advocates. Representative Claud Sapp of Richland County, a supporter of the law, regularly expressed the sentiment that "every white child in the state should be given the opportunity to be educated" and that the only way to accomplish this was to "tax all the property of the state for that purpose, eradicate the county lines, and make the state the unit of education." JANET G. HUDSON

Hudson, Janet Goodrum. "Maintaining White Supremacy: Race, Class, and Reform in South Carolina, 1917–1924." Ph.D. diss., University of South Carolina, 1996.

———. "South Carolina's 6–0–1 Law of 1924: A Study of Educational Reform." Master's thesis, University of South Carolina, 1992.

Slave badges. Slave badges served as the physical proof required to demonstrate the legal status of slaves hired out by their masters. Laws controlling such hiring began early, and badges or "tickets" were mentioned by 1751, with wearing them mandated by 1764. With its 1783 incorporation, Charleston immediately passed badge laws. Although other cities had similar laws, only Charleston badges have survived, suggesting that it may have been the only city to manufacture and sell them and to police their wearing. In 1800 laws became more uniform, and the earliest surviving badges known date

After 1788 the city of Charleston required all slaves hired out by their masters to wear badges as proof of their status. This 1821 Charleston badge was number 508. Courtesy, South Carolina State Museum

from this year. By around 1806 badges were valid for a calendar year and were sold, at varying fees, in specific categories: mechanics, fruiterers (hucksters), fishers, porters, and servants. Most badges bore the geographic locator "Charleston." All sported a category, a number, and a year. Surviving badges have holes for suspension since all slaves, except servants, had to wear them. Badges were made of copper of various shapes, depending on the design of the badge makers, who were appointed annually by the city council. Round, diamond, and square badges in differing sizes are known. Enforced until the end of slavery in 1865, badge laws required the keeping of records and the swearing of oaths by those purchasing them, and the laws stipulated punishments for failure to wear, produce, or buy badges. As many as one-quarter of Charleston's slaves wore them in some years, and the income from badge sales added significantly to city coffers. By the end of the twentieth century, these throw-away items had become highly collectible, often selling for thousands of dollars. HARLAN GREENE

Greene, Harlan, and Harry Hutchins, Jr. *Slave Badges and the Slave-Hire System in Charleston, South Carolina, 1783–1865.* Jefferson, N.C.: McFarland, 2004.

Singleton, Theresa. "The Slave Tag: An Artifact of Urban Slavery." *South Carolina Antiquities* 16, nos. 1–2 (1984): 41–65.

Slave codes. South Carolina's earliest formal code of law regarding slaves, established in 1690, borrowed heavily from the statutes governing slavery on the Caribbean island of Barbados, which were enacted in 1661 as a measure to protect a small white elite from a large, restive African labor force. As they evolved throughout the colonial and antebellum years, the codes reflected the fears of the planting class and the racial character of slavery in the New World.

The 1690 "Act for the Better Ordering of Slaves," which was quickly disallowed by the Lords Proprietors (who mistrusted the intentions of the colony's Barbadian planters), codified the institution of chattel slavery in South Carolina. Slaves were required to get written passes from their masters to travel from the plantations. The act provided for corporal punishment of slaves through branding, nose-slitting, and emasculation. Following the disallowance by the proprietors, a new slave code, again based on Barbadian principles, was enacted in 1696 even though slaves constituted a minority of the population at the time. The situation of the colony's nascent planting class during this time, however, made rigid enforcement of a slave code difficult. Fledgling planters often labored alongside their slaves and servants to clear land and raise livestock. In addition, slaves, many of them armed, frequently traveled unsupervised between plantations and to Charleston.

In the first decade of the eighteenth century, the African population surpassed the white population. Shortly thereafter a new slave code went into effect. The act of 1712 covered much of the same ground as the 1690 act. Under the new act, children followed the conditions of their mothers, thereby making slavery a perpetual status for the offspring of whites and slave women. Slaves who believed that they were held unjustly could sue for their freedom, but they did so against overwhelming legal odds. The 1712 act also levied a penalty if the ratio of unfree laborers to overseers exceeded six to one. It further provided, as a measure against slave insurrection and rowdiness, that slaves who came from the countryside to Charleston could be whipped for visiting the town to gamble or to engage in "any wicked designs." As with earlier statutes, enforcement of the revised code was difficult and frequently haphazard. Slaves still found the means to move about with a level of freedom that many planters found disconcerting. And while the codes sanctioned and enforced the awesome power that planters as a class wielded over the slave population, individual slaves and slaveowners nevertheless negotiated for power on a daily basis on the plantations and elsewhere.

The Stono Rebellion in 1739 resulted in a more rigid slave code that would remain the basis for South Carolina slavery until its end in 1865, and which would influence slave codes throughout the South. The 1740 "Bill for the better ordering and governing of Negroes and other Slaves in this Province," or the Negro Act, laid out the legal basis for a mature colonial society based on enslaved labor. It codified the slaves' lack of access to the rights of English common law and constructed them as legal nonentities. They could not testify under oath, and the testimonies of whites continued to trump those of slaves. The murder of a slave by a white person was reduced to a misdemeanor, punishable by a fine. Interestingly, a slave could strike a white man to defend his master's life but was forbidden from doing so to protect his own life. Penalties for slave crimes increased: execution was sanctioned for plotting rebellion (or running away), committing arson, or instructing other slaves in the use of poisonous plants. Any white person, not just slaveowners, was given the authority to arrest and punish blacks found in violation of the law. Almost every aspect of slave life came under tightened legal scrutiny. Slave writing was prohibited, as were drumming and playing horns for fear that these activities might awaken some revolutionary impulse. The Negro Act legislated slave clothing, suggesting that slaves should not dress above their social status, and proscribed certain fabrics. Slaves could not hire their own time or keep firearms.

In the aftermath of the Revolutionary War, the Negro Act was upheld by the General Assembly and "made perpetual." Though the document was occasionally revised, it survived the years leading up to the Civil War basically intact. In 1822, following the Denmark Vesey scare, contact between slaves and free black sailors was prohibited as part of the Negro Seaman Acts, which also jailed free black sailors while their ships were in South Carolina ports. In 1841 the General Assembly outlawed manumission as a measure to cut down on the number of free people of color in the state. Slave codes, however, were never as all-encompassing as they appeared to be on paper. Even in the face of stifling legislation throughout the colonial and antebellum periods, slaves worked hard to maintain what little autonomy they could. MATTHEW H. JENNINGS

Henry, Howell M. *The Police Control of the Slave in South Carolina.* 1914. Reprint, New York: Negro Universities Press, 1968.

Higginbotham, A. Leon, Jr. *In the Matter of Color: The Colonial Period.* New York: Oxford University Press, 1978.

Olwell, Robert. *Masters, Slaves, and Subjects: The Culture of Power in the South Carolina Low Country, 1740–1790.* Ithaca, N.Y.: Cornell University Press, 1998.

Sirmans, M. Eugene. "The Legal Status of the Slave in South Carolina, 1670–1740." *Journal of Southern History* 28 (November 1962): 462–73.

Wood, Peter H. *Black Majority: Negroes in Colonial South Carolina from 1670 through the Stono Rebellion.* New York: Knopf, 1974.

Slave labor. Slavery was work, and for most slaves it was monotonous and relatively undifferentiated labor. Lowcountry South Carolina plantations were distinguished by the use of the task system rather than gang labor. Under this system a slave cultivated a certain measure of land, normally a quarter of an acre, and had the rest of the day to him- or herself when the task was completed. How the task system developed in Carolina is not entirely clear. Some scholars believe that tasking was best suited to hardy crops, such as rice, that did not require minute supervision, or in cases when a production schedule was not urgent, or when the labor force was scattered, which made close supervision difficult. Gang labor, in which slaves worked in unison, from dawn to dusk, under the direction of an overseer, was needed where close supervision was required. Whatever the precise lines of evolution, the procedure became highly identified with, though not exclusive to, the South Carolina–Georgia lowcountry; and it was used with Sea Island (long staple) cotton as with rice.

The task system benefited planters by encouraging slaves to complete an assignment quickly and well and by attaching them to the plantation. As one planter proclaimed, "no Negro with a well-stocked poultry house, a small crop advancing, a canoe partly finished or a few tubs unsold, all of which he calculates soon to enjoy, will ever run away." Slaves worked on their own garden plots and were allowed to sell or trade the produce. In this way slaves could accumulate money and personal property and validate their sense of self-worth. Of course, some slaves complained that masters did not properly honor the task arrangement and routinely created tasks that most slaves could not easily, or quickly, complete. Some planters roundly resented the independence the system provided and attempted various ways to constrain it. But the consequences were so disruptive of plantation harmony, in particular of a productive work regimen, that few planters attempted for long to alter an accepted custom. By the nineteenth century most slaves probably worked ten hours or so daily.

Black foremen, or "drivers," were also important in the region and exercised considerable authority. The driver was distinguished not so much by his ability to use the whip as by his power to assign tasks. An effective driver accurately measured the task to the capacity of the laborer and ensured that work ran smoothly. He had an influence in the white community as well as the black one. If a white overseer was present, he ignored the driver at his peril, for these men could determine the success or failure of the enterprise. Because drivers had the free time earned by industrious laborers who completed their tasks early, they were entitled to help from other members of the slave community in their private endeavors, such as raising supplemental goods. They often retained their positions of leadership at emancipation.

Fifty miles inland the choice between tasking or gang labor depended largely on the size of the estate. Small farmers with few slaves could usually not afford the task system as too much needed to be done. Slaves were usually compensated, however, by some small plot for their own cultivation. In the middle region most planters probably used tasking, though not all liked it. James Henry Hammond tried diligently to bend his slaves from tasking to gang labor but eventually had to acquiesce. In the upcountry gang labor prevailed, with slaves working the traditional routine of sunup to sundown. Many of the dynamics of slavery were different on small as opposed to large units of production, and in cotton as opposed to rice production. Upcountry slaves were less likely to have their own garden plots, for example. But even in the upcountry, early features of slavery as established on the coast, particularly in terms of the task system, had to be taken into account. For example, some might use gang labor in cultivating cotton but the task system in harvesting.

Though the majority of plantation laborers worked in the fields, the important minority that exercised skills was crucial to the profitable management of a plantation. Carpenters, coopers, blacksmiths, boatmen, coachmen, and even jockeys who raced their masters' horses were all in positions that afforded the enslaved a degree of status and responsibility. In the domestic arena, women might engage in sewing, washing (which, considering the requirements of heavy pots, scalding water, and corrosive soaps, demanded strength as well as skill), and cooking (which a man might do also). Men or women might be personal servants of one kind or another (as valets), obliging sensitivity, perception, and presence perhaps as much as skill. Domestic and field slaves on a plantation would have different work routines. Domestic slaves were "on call" at all hours, unlike their field-hand counterparts. The close proximity of domestic slaves to their owners meant that they could easily become the victims of displaced aggression and be reprimanded readily. But the division between house servants and field hands should not be overdrawn, for the people in the "Big House" had ties of blood and marriage to those in the fields.

Urban slavery also had its special demands and labor practices. Particularly in Charleston, ironworking was a specialized profession, and much of the decorative work that graces the city was done by enslaved Africans. Charleston slaves also worked as bricklayers, plasterers, coopers, tailors, and in other trades. In 1860 the West Point Rice Mills on the Ashley River owned 160 slaves who worked in a variety of positions. Masters also hired out slave labor to others. Although slaves could not legally hire themselves out, the law was widely violated, and some urban slaves were left free to negotiate their own wages and hours.

Slave labor affected slave women differently than male slaves. Whether raising rice or cotton, women were disadvantaged in that they were less likely to be trained as artisans and more likely than men to be confined to fieldwork. They also had the additional responsibilities of motherhood and the care of families, within the limits permitted by their other duties. On some estates they were responsible for sewing clothes as well as preparing daily meals for their own families. Children had little time for childhood, performing light chores beginning at age five or six and were introduced to the fields between the ages of ten and twelve. While labor was constant, slavery was not the monolithic institution it is sometimes made out to be. It changed over time and across regions. DANIEL C. LITTLEFIELD

Carney, Judith A. *Black Rice: The African Origins of Rice Cultivation in the Americas.* Cambridge: Harvard University Press, 2001.

Hudson, Larry E., Jr. *To Have and to Hold: Slave Work and Family Life in Antebellum South Carolina.* Athens: University of Georgia Press, 1997.

Joyner, Charles W. *Down by the Riverside: A South Carolina Slave Community.* Urbana: University of Illinois Press, 1984.

King, Wilma. *Stolen Childhood: Slave Youth in Nineteenth-Century America.* Bloomington: Indiana University Press, 1995.

Littlefield, Daniel C. *Rice and Slaves: Ethnicity and the Slave Trade in Colonial South Carolina.* Baton Rouge: Louisiana State University Press, 1981.

Morgan, Phillip D. "Work and Culture: The Task System and the World of Lowcountry Blacks, 1700 to 1880." *William and Mary Quarterly*, 3d ser., 39 (October 1982): 563–99.

White, Deborah G. *Ar'n't I a Woman?: Female Slaves in the Plantation South.* Rev. ed. New York: Norton, 1999.

Slave patrols. Slave patrols were a crucial mechanism of slave control in the colonial and antebellum periods of South Carolina's history. From their experimental colonial beginnings, slave patrols bound elite planters to less wealthy white farmers and helped white South Carolinians enforce their perceived racial superiority.

Like South Carolina's earliest slave codes, the earliest slave patrol systems were based on Barbadian models. Trapped by the paradox of enslaving native peoples and employing them as slave catchers, white South Carolinians took matters into their own hands; they provided for official slave patrols beginning in 1704. The slave patrol and the local militia both drew from the same pool of able-bodied men, but in times of invasion patrollers were to stay away from combat and police the slave population. In the early years of the eighteenth century, gentlemen served alongside poorer white farmers in the patrols. From 1734 to 1737, in an effort to improve the quality of patrols, patrollers were paid for their services. Following the Stono Rebellion in 1739, the Commons House of Assembly passed the Negro Act of 1740, which provided for constant, regular patrols. Patrol captains divided their beats systematically, and the Charleston night watch patrolled the streets of the colony's only city of any significance. The system of patrols established in 1740 would last, with minor revision, until the end of the Civil War.

The popular conception of slave patrollers has often conflated them with professional slave catchers. In South Carolina all plantation owners were called upon to serve in patrols, and specific rules were instituted so that women and exempted men (men in ill health, firemen, and military officers who had served more than seven years) could provide substitutes. As the nineteenth century progressed and local militias lost power, city councils and other governing bodies took responsibility for slave patrols. Patrol beats were not large; most ranged between ten and fifteen miles. Slave patrols served social functions as well, providing patrollers from different social classes a chance to share liquor or compete for leadership in an exclusively male arena. Such interaction strengthened the idea of white solidarity across class lines.

Former slaves often recalled the patrollers as drunken, rowdy men from the lowest rungs of society, but men of property did serve as patrol captains, particularly during the colonial period. In the antebellum period overseers and other nonslaveowning whites rode on patrol. The typical antebellum patrol consisted of a handful of men on horseback with three principal tasks: to search slave quarters, to disperse slave gatherings, and to guard roads and towns from delinquent slaves. During times of heightened tension, such as rebellions or wars, patrols stayed out all night and were invested with increased authority to disrupt the lives of slaves. Following the Civil War, official slave patrols ended. Unfortunately for recently freed slaves, however, white South Carolinians were bent on maintaining their racial superiority. Paramilitary groups, such as the Ku Klux Klan, terrorized the state's African American population in ways that reflected the long tradition of the slave patrol. MATTHEW H. JENNINGS

Hadden, Sally E. *Slave Patrols: Law and Violence in Virginia and the Carolinas.* Cambridge: Harvard University Press, 2001.

Henry, Howell M. *The Police Control of the Slave in South Carolina.* 1914. Reprint, New York: Negro Universities Press, 1968.

Jones, Norrece. *Born a Child of Freedom, yet a Slave: Mechanisms of Control and Strategies of Resistance in Antebellum South Carolina.* Middletown, Conn.: Wesleyan University Press, 1989.

Slave religion. Enslaved Africans arriving in South Carolina brought their traditional belief systems with them, and until the early nineteenth century, Christianity only marginally affected them and their descendants. Little effort was made to Christianize them because some planters initially believed that conversion required emancipation. Others feared that Christianity would lead to literacy or make their slaves less tractable. In addition, language barriers and African resistance to the faith of their oppressors, combined with South Carolina's high percentage of Africans, ensured that African religion would survive tenaciously.

West and South Central Africans shared many sacred beliefs—for instance, in an omnipotent and omniscient creator God who remained at some distance from life's daily affairs. Theirs was a pantheistic world containing lesser deities, the spirits of natural forces, nonbiological objects, and the spirits of ancestors. No sharp demarcation existed between the spiritual and the corporeal. Ancestors were considered the "living dead" because their spirits could affect the material, corporeal world. Ritual homage was regularly shown to them through sacrifices. Problems in life such as illness or bad fortune were considered to have spiritual as well as physical causes. Priests, diviners, or medical specialists were consulted to identify the genesis of these problems and to apply sacred medicines or perform rituals to counteract "bad magic." These and related ways of conceptualizing the world were persistent and informed the spiritual beliefs of enslaved Carolinians.

Beginning in the late 1820s, faced by the rising abolitionist threat and convinced by white missionaries that Christianity would make their bondsmen more docile, slaveholders allowed and even supported a sustained missionary effort to evangelize the slaves. By the 1840s support for the plantation missions was widespread throughout South Carolina. When the slaves did not attend their owners' churches, masters hired local preachers or utilized trustworthy slaves or free blacks to lead religious services. Conversions occurred because eventually the power of African spirits diminished in the new environment. Furthermore, Christianity offered an explanation of the suffering plight of the enslaved and a hope for ultimate redemption that traditional beliefs did not. In addition, for all their differences, traditional African beliefs and Christianity had important points of convergence, making the latter more easily understood. A creator God was present in both, and the Christian Trinity and angels were suggestive of a multiplicity of deities. Also, the story of death and resurrection was familiar to West and South Central Africans who believed in reincarnation.

The brand of Christianity that enslaved Carolinians practiced was highly Africanized; they did not passively accept the faith as given but reshaped and embellished it according to their own culture. This occurred throughout the state and especially in the lowcountry where Gullah culture was prominent. West African religious ceremonies frequently included sacred dances that evoked the presence of ancestral spirits, as the supplicants moved in a counterclockwise motion to the accompaniment of music. The ring shout, as it was known, was a frequent part of Carolina slave worship services. Some slave religious practices derived from South Central Africa's BaKongo culture. Baptism by immersion was especially important for enslaved Carolinians. BaKongo people believed that the most powerful ancestors reside in the "land of all things white," below the water of the sea and rivers; their priests used crosslike staffs to perform important water rituals. When Carolina slaves were baptized, the participants were usually dressed in white and crosses were often part of the ceremonies, and when the preachers immersed the candidates below the water, the persons were placed in spiritual contact with powerful ancestral spirits. Thus, the baptismal ceremony that appeared fully Christian to the untrained eye might have derived much of its spiritual force from African ceremonial analogs. Funerary rites were important, and in the African tradition, Carolina slaves were frequently buried with objects they cherished in this world, or grave sites were decorated with objects last used by those deceased. This honored and placated the spirits, preventing them from becoming wandering, vengeful ghosts.

Baptisms, funerals, and ring shouts involved the slaves in spiritual communities whose members provided mutual support that reinforced their humanity and worth. These bonds were strengthened when they gathered secretly at their "prayin' grounds" or bush arbors in isolated wooded areas. These services were led by men who frequently lacked white sanction but whom the slave communities chose as their informal leaders for their rhetorical ability, their literacy, or their scriptural discernment. Their unique biblical understanding led the enslaved to develop their own eschatology. Enslaved Carolinians believed that the Bible condemned bondage, and many viewed themselves as morally superior to their depraved owners. The God they worshiped aided the downtrodden, and so the Old Testament Book of Exodus had special appeal. Collectively singing spirituals with titles and lyrics such as "No Man Can Hinder Me" and "the Lord shall bear his children home" reinforced the idea of ultimate delivery despite slaveowners' contrary efforts. In myriad ways slave religion thus created a vital psychic buffer, enabling black Carolinians to survive slavery's potentially devastating impact. BERNARD E. POWERS, JR.

Creel, Margaret W. *A Peculiar People: Slave Religion and Community-Culture among the Gullahs.* New York: New York University Press, 1988.

Gomez, Michael A. *Exchanging Our Country Marks: The Transformation of African Identities in the Colonial and Antebellum South.* Chapel Hill: University of North Carolina Press, 1998.

Jones, Norrece T. *Born a Child of Freedom, yet a Slave: Mechanisms of Control and Strategies of Resistance in Antebellum South Carolina.* Middletown, Conn.: Wesleyan University Press, 1989.

Raboteau, Albert. *Slave Religion: The "Invisible Institution" in the Antebellum South.* New York: Oxford University Press, 1978.

Stuckey, Sterling. *Slave Culture: Nationalist Theory and the Foundations of Black America.* New York: Oxford University Press, 1987.

Slave trade. The Atlantic slave trade was one of the most important demographic, social, and economic events of the modern era. It extended across four centuries and fostered the involuntary migration of millions of African peoples from their homelands to forced labor in the Americas and elsewhere around the globe. In the process, it reshaped African societies and provided much of the raw material for constructing new social, economic, and political structures in the New World. It also left an unfortunate legacy of racism by establishing a connection between servility, barbarity, and peoples of African descent.

The major stream of African labor went to sugar-producing regions in the West Indies or Latin America. Britain's North American colonies were different. They did not grow sugar and therefore did not command much of the slave trade. Over the course of the trade's existence, Britain's North American colonies absorbed no more than about five percent of Africans brought into the New World. But South Carolina, where by 1715 blacks exceeded whites by about forty percent, resembled plantation societies such as Barbados or Jamaica more than it resembled Virginia or Maryland. Eighteenth-century South Carolina was the continent's leading importer of slaves, importing approximately 100,000 Africans. Not all of these people remained within the colony. Many were transshipped to other regions along the southeastern coast between the Chesapeake and Florida. Beaufort and Georgetown received small cargoes, but the major and most dependable trade was in Charleston.

Three kinds of trade brought Africans to South Carolina: direct trade with Africa; trade with the West Indies; and trade with other North American colonies. Only the first was strictly a slave trade; the other two involved different exchanges in which slaves were occasionally included. No more than twenty percent of slaves brought into Carolina in the eighteenth century stopped first in the Caribbean. No more than one percent came from other continental colonies. The contrast between these two figures underscores South Carolina's closer relationship with the islands, and the colony was sometimes referred to as part of the West Indies. Slavers brought more slaves (around two hundred or so per voyage) to the colony and also used larger ships than those involved in coastal or local West Indian trade. The average size of slavers frequenting South Carolina was about one hundred tons, while coastal or West Indian trading vessels averaged about half as much.

Crowded and unsanitary conditions, poor food and inadequate supplies, insufficient drinking water, epidemic diseases, and long voyages conspired to make slave ships legendary for their foul smell and high death rates. These rates decreased from a seventeenth-century average of as high as twenty-four percent to an average range in the eighteenth and nineteenth centuries of from ten to fifteen percent. Despite harsh conditions, ship captains had to have reasonable consideration for their cargoes as their wages and commissions often depended on the number delivered safely to port. To guard against the importation of epidemic diseases, incoming ships were quarantined on Sullivan's Island until the cargoes could be certified as safe.

European profits ranged from as low as three percent to as high as fifty-seven percent in the eighteenth century. A slave that cost £9.43 in Africa in the 1720s fetched £25 in South Carolina in the same period. Prices rose during the century, and a similar slave in the 1760s cost £14.10 and sold in South Carolina for £35. Since costs included the price of trade goods and customs, tolls, and taxes paid to the African potentates who controlled the African coast, the percentage profit on any one transaction is not easy to calculate.

To avoid loss by sudden weather change, the slave trade was largely a seasonal affair, with Carolina's optimum period of trade running between March and September. The largest number of slaves, carried in vessels from Africa, arrived in the span between May and November. Planters normally asked for slaves in proportion of two men for every woman, and slave ships generally approximated this ratio. The reason that slave cargoes indicated a pattern of twice as many men as women has as much to do with African desires as American demands. African sellers proved reluctant to part with women and children. They could absorb these individuals into their own societies. They were more willing to sell men, who could prove dangerous to have on hand.

South Carolina joined with other colonies to forbid the trade during the Revolutionary era and was the only state to reopen it at the war's conclusion. The state's delegates prevented the trade's abolition during the 1787 constitutional convention in Philadelphia, effecting a compromise guaranteeing its continuation for twenty years. In the five years before federal prohibition in 1808, almost forty thousand Africans entered the port of Charleston. Many of these slaves were transported beyond the limits of the state to newly developing regions in the West. Sullivan's Island has been styled the black man's Ellis Island because large numbers, perhaps even the majority, of enslaved Africans who settled in the American South passed through the island.

The internal slave trade in the colonies and later the United States began in earnest during the late eighteenth century as frontier areas in the old Southwest opened up to settlement and labor was needed to clear and cultivate the virgin soil. Once fields were cleared and large-scale planting began, the demand for slave labor increased exponentially.

Ending the Atlantic slave trade ensured that the internal slave trade would become increasingly profitable. Some Africans were smuggled into the United States after the ban, but the labor demands of these developing plantation regions were filled by the sale and transportation of slaves from east (especially the Chesapeake) to west. While the number of slaves sold to traders and taken out of South Carolina is unknown, the practice was common, and by the 1820s the state became a net exporter of slaves.

Transportation improvements made it easier and quicker for traders to ship their human cargoes, and by the 1830s traders regularly shipped slaves by railroad. Most towns of any size in South Carolina had slave jails or pens where traders could temporarily keep their human property, and cities such as Columbia and Charleston had larger auction and jail complexes. Many Charleston traders centered their operations downtown around Chalmers Street. Slave trading was big business in South Carolina, as a casual perusal of any antebellum newspaper will attest.

The impact of the slave trade on the slaves themselves was considerable. At a master's whim family and friends could be permanently separated by sale. The former slave Jacob Stroyer, describing the scene after a railroad car had been loaded with the purchased slaves, wrote, "As the cars moved away we heard the weeping and wailing from the slaves as far as the human voice could be heard; and from that time to the present I have neither seen nor heard from my two sisters." This drama was played out thousands of times in South Carolina and across the South as slaveowners and slave traders went about the business of selling people. Abolitionists pointed to the slave trade as one of the most reprehensible aspects of slavery, and writers made it a central theme of their works—for example, Harriet Beecher Stowe in her novel *Uncle Tom's Cabin.* It is impossible to understand the impact of slavery as a whole without understanding the legacy of the internal and external slave trade. DANIEL C. LITTLEFIELD

Bancroft, Frederic. *Slave Trading in the Old South.* 1931. Reprint, Columbia: University of South Carolina Press, 1996.

Drago, Edmund L., ed. *Broke by the War: Letters of a Slave Trader.* Columbia: University of South Carolina Press, 1991.

Eltis, David. "Free and Coerced Transatlantic Migrations: Some Comparisons." *American Historical Review* 88 (April 1983): 251–80.

———. *The Rise of African Slavery in America.* Cambridge: Cambridge University Press, 2000.

Littlefield, Daniel C. "Charleston and Internal Slave Redistribution." *South Carolina Historical Magazine* 87 (April 1986): 93–105.

———. "The Colonial Slave Trade to South Carolina: A Profile." *South Carolina Historical Magazine* 91 (April 1990): 68–99.

———. *Rice and Slaves: Ethnicity and the Slave Trade in Colonial South Carolina.* Baton Rouge: Louisiana State University Press, 1981.

Manning, Patrick. *Slavery and African Life: Occidental, Oriental, and African Slave Trades.* New York: Cambridge University Press, 1990.

Rothman, Adam. "The Expansion of Slavery in the Deep South, 1790–1820." Ph.D. diss., Columbia University, 2000.

Shugerman, Jed. "The Louisiana Purchase and South Carolina's Reopening of the Slave Trade in 1803." *Journal of the Early Republic* 22 (summer 2002): 263–90.

Tadman, Michael. *Speculators and Slaves: Masters, Traders, and Slaves in the Old South.* Madison: University of Wisconsin Press, 1989.

Slavery. Africans were present at the founding of the English colony in South Carolina and within several decades became a majority. The first governor, William Sayle, brought three blacks in the founding fleet in 1670 and another a few months later. The Fundamental Constitutions (1669) envisioned slavery among other forms of servitude and social hierarchy at the colony's inception. In fact, in their "Declarations and Proposals to all that will Plant in Carolina" (1663), the Lords Proprietors had not mentioned black slavery, merely offering land under a "head-right" system for every servant transported to the Carolina coast. But the proprietors soon acquiesced to the desires of the Barbadians they sought to attract and who wanted to bring their slaves. For in plantation colonies African slaves came to be the universal solution to problems of labor when other solutions, including white indentured servitude and bound Native American labor, proved inadequate. South Carolina was distinctive, however, in that it was alone among England's

TO BE SOLD on Wedneſday the 19th Inſtant, a Cargoe of about *Three Hundred* and *Fifty* choice healthy Negroes, juſt imported in the Ship *Loango*, *Thomas Dolman* Commander from the Coaſt of *Angola* directly, by *Benj. Savage* and Comp.

N. B. *Great regard will be had for preſent Pay in Rice or Currency.*

To be Sold 2 compleat Sawyers, not exceeding 24 Years of Age, apply to *John Watſone.*

Run away from on board the Snow *Molley*, lying at *Stone's* Bridge, the 3d Inſtant at Night, an indented Servant, named *Wm. Bridge*, aged about 19, of a ſhort Stature, pale Complexion and low voic'd, without any Beard, and his hair off, had on a blue pea or dark Kearſey Jacket, a blue or ſtrip'd Swan skin Waſtcoat : Whoever ſecures him ſo that he may be had again, ſhall have 5 l: reward paid by me *John Howell.*

Be it to their Peril that conceal him.

To be Sold

ON Thurſday the 3d of *February* next, by *Roger Saunders* ſurviving Executor of the laſt Will and Teſtament of *Thomas Smith* Eſq; formerly deceaſed, at the Plantation of ſaid *Tho: Smith* on *Aſhley* River, the perſonal Eſtate of the ſaid *Smith*, conſiſting of between twenty and thirty choice Negro Slaves, moſt this Country born, with a Team of very good Oxen and Ox Cart, and ſundry other Things : The Sale to begin at one o'Clock in the Forenoon, Credit will be given till the 1ſt of *May* next following, on giving ſuch Security as will be approved of by *Roger Saunders*

Colonial advertisements for the sale of slaves. The top advertisement is for a sale of 350 "just imported" Angolans and the bottom one for slaves "this Country born." *South Carolina Gazette,* 22 January 1737. Courtesy, Charleston Library Society colonies in continental North America in preferring African labor to the former.

Africans were imported in significant numbers from about the 1690s, and by 1715 the black population made up about sixty percent of the colony's total population. This marked another distinctive feature of South Carolina, for it was the only colony in English North America where this proportion existed. As in Virginia, many slaves in seventeenth-century South Carolina came from the West Indies. Although the colder winters on the coast created for them some disadvantages, they were better equipped epidemiologically (in terms of resistance to malaria and yellow fever) and pharmacologically (in terms of their ability to make use of native plants) to cope with South Carolina's semitropical environment. In this early period of Carolina's history, then, Africans had some advantages over Europeans. Their familiarity with tropical herbs, ability to move along inland waterways using canoes or pirogues, and skill in fishing enabled them to live off the land much more easily than their masters could. Similar outlooks toward land and nature, and comparable facets of material culture, facilitated their contact with native peoples. Both had basket-weaving traditions, and both were skilled in the use of small watercraft on inland rivers. Africans were among the first to appropriate native languages and were often used as translators. These conditions facilitated African adjustment and appropriation of local skills. Often, Africans were the mediators of knowledge between red men and white men. African expertise as well as rough pioneer conditions of a new settlement facilitated a degree of "sawbuck equality" in the seventeenth century—a term derived from the image of a slaveowner working all day sawing wood with his slave, each facing the other on opposite sides of a sawbuck. The South Carolina slave code of 1696, based on the Barbadian code of 1688, announced an end to this relatively benign period.

Beginning in the eighteenth century the colony increasingly embraced rice as a staple, and by 1740 indigo joined the grain as a lucrative but subordinate staple crop. The English colonists benefited from the knowledge of their African bondsmen, many of whom came from rice-growing regions in Africa and knew more about the cultivation of the crop than did Englishmen. Indeed, when buying slaves, Carolinians adopted a preference for people from the rice-producing Senegambia region, and this preference lasted through most of the colonial period, though the vagaries of trade prevented that region's ethnic groups from always dominating importation statistics. Various Senegambians were associated with the African cattle complex and brought expertise in that endeavor, perhaps accentuating the planters' regional preference. For while colonists searched for a staple, South Carolina was "the colony of a colony," providing beef, hides, and other foodstuffs to Barbados. The practice of free grazing, night-time penning for cattle protection, and seasonal burning to freshen pastures all had West African antecedents. The historian Peter Wood suggested that the "cowboy," prominently connected with the nineteenth-century American West, may well have found its first usage in South Carolina.

The demographic disproportion continued. Of 17,000 people in South Carolina in 1720, 12,000 were black; by 1740 only 15,000 of the 45,000 people in South Carolina were white. It is no wonder, then, that a Swiss immigrant remarked in 1737 that "Carolina looks more like a Negro country than a country settled by white people." Although the proportion was not as great as that in the West Indies, where blacks sometimes outnumbered whites by as many as ten or more to one, the disequilibrium was more than sufficient to make the colony unique on the mainland. In 1765 blacks outnumbered whites by more than two to one (90,000 to 40,000), and Charleston imported more slaves than did any other North American port.

These surroundings could not help but affect the perceptions and attitudes of white South Carolinians, and these and other circumstances relate them more closely than other British North Americans to their compatriots in the West Indies. The extent of African diversity in South Carolina did not prevent but may have inhibited the thinking about Africans in solely racial terms. English ethnocentrism was such that the English assumed superiority in the face of practically everyone they met, and Africans were no exception. But if a distinction can be made between ethnocentrism and racism, then it might be suggested that eighteenth-century attitudes toward Africans partook as much of the former as of the latter.

ſtreet, Orange, Anniſeed, Clove, Lime and Tanſie Waters at 40 *s.* *per* Gallon, Lemon Water at 3 *l.* Cinamon Water at 5 *l.* Citron Water at 6 *l.* fine Uſquebaugh at 8 *l.* and Spirits of Wine at 3 *l.* 10 *s.* *per* Gallon, Bitters at 40 *s.* *per* Quart.

Run away on the 13th of *March* laſt, a Muſtee Fellow named *Cyrus*, who lately belonged to Meſſrs. *Mulryne* and *Williams* of *Port-Royal*. Whoever ſecures, or brings the ſaid Fellow to me, or to Mr. *David Brown* of *Charles-Town* Shipwright, ſhall have TWENTY POUNDS Reward, and the Charges allow'd by Law. And whoever gives me Information of his being employed by any Perſon, ſo that he may be convicted thereof, ſhall, upon ſuch Conviction, have THIRTY POUNDS current Money paid him, by *David Linn*.

A bay ſtray Horſe, about 13 Hands and an half high, branded WT in one on the mounting Shoulder, taken up at *Aſhepoo*. The Owner may have him by applying to *J. Hutchinſon*.

South-Carolina. Whereas *John Griffin*

Runaway slave advertisements described the slave and generally offered a reward. *South Carolina Gazette,* 11 June 1747. Courtesy, Charleston Library Society

Reacting to the Stono Rebellion, the colony in 1740 passed its most comprehensive slave law, which made it illegal for more than seven adult male slaves to travel together except in the company of a white person. The 1740 code was the basis for all slave laws subsequently passed in the colonial and antebellum eras. During the second half of the eighteenth century, and especially during the Revolutionary crisis, racial attitudes in South Carolina hardened. This harsher attitude can be seen in the increasingly restrictive laws passed to regulate the slave and free-black population. Burglary, arson, and running away, inter alia, were all capital offenses punishable by death. Slaves were not to be away from a plantation between sunset and sunrise and at no time without the permission of the master or they could be taken up and whipped.

In the early years South Carolinians grew rice on dry upland soils, but planters soon switched to inland swamps. At the end of the eighteenth century rice cultivation was adapted to the tide flow, and rice fields were constructed out of low-lying regions fronting rivers. For slaves, this meant that the workload was increased. These fields required the building of massive dikes, levees, and canals by hand with picks and shovels, working in the mud with snakes, alligators, and other vermin. Slaves worked much harder under this new system, especially when new plantations were being formed, though they had less weeding to do once the plantations were established. Moreover, these constructions had to be maintained. All of these things meant that the external attributes of slavery in South Carolina were harsh.

Psychologically, though, slaves in Carolina may have had an easier time than those in, say, Virginia because they were much more likely to come and remain in contact with people from their own ethnic groups. Thus, slaves could provide each other with moral, spiritual, and sometimes cultural support. In addition, the greatest number of Africanisms surviving in British North American can be found in the Carolina region—in the Sea Islands off the coast of South Carolina and Georgia. One historian suggested that early South Carolina was effectively bilingual, with slaves speaking a patois or dialect that masters could not understand. The pidgin English concocted as a means of communication between and among masters and various African ethnic groups became more regularized and evolved into a separate Creole language among Gullah and Geechee speakers along the coast.

Few African material artifacts survived the middle passage intact, but African artistic and functional values found material expression in African-made pottery and the work baskets and other implements that accompanied rice cultivation. Africanisms more often abided in underlying assumptions about life—in folkways, folktales, and a cosmology that placed greater emphasis on kin—and extended family relationships were no doubt strengthened by the fragility of family life under slavery. Extended kin, fictive or otherwise, helped ease the burden of children separated from parents, of wives removed from husbands. Naming practices, particularly sons after fathers (and less often daughters after mothers), served to memorialize connections that might easily be physically sundered by forces over which those enslaved had no control.

Natural increase began in the decades between 1710 and 1730, though it was interrupted by increasing imports into the lowcountry after 1720. The growth of a Creole, or native-born, population signaled formation of a Creole culture that was neither African nor European but contained elements of both, modified by the attributes of a new environment and the input of Native Americans. In many parts of South Carolina these Creole slaves had the critical mass to develop societies apart from whites.

Lowcountry South Carolina was distinguished by the task system of labor organization, which allowed slaves time to work for themselves after completion of their daily assignments and permitted some to accumulate property. Partly as an offshoot of the task system, slaves organized an internal marketing system. Goods they acquired or produced in their spare time they sold or exchanged with other slaves and with whites. As in Africa and the West Indies, these markets were dominated by women. They sold everything from oysters to peaches, cake to cloth and were not above organizing to control prices. Masters acquiesced to slaves participating in this informal economy because it would have been difficult to prevent and the existence of a market for fresh vegetables and slave-made crafts provided a convenient and relatively cheap source for food and other goods. It is perhaps true that many masters resented the self-confidence and relative independence such a system permitted and that some were more successful than others at limiting the slaves' possibilities, but all masters made concessions.

South Carolina was an anomaly to other continental colonies in British North America in that it was the only one where slave concubinage was almost instituted in open practice, in imitation of English customs in the West Indies. Race mixture occurred in every colony where people of different races met. Distinctions developed in terms of the degree to which it was embraced. In the islands, the black population highly outnumbered the white population, and there an English planter was practically expected to take a black mistress.

There was some degree of public opinion in the colony opposed to such liaisons. When miscegenation occurred, it was usually a one-way affair involving a white man and a black (slave) woman. The white woman was put on a pedestal and was expected to stay there. The historian Winthrop Jordan argued that in perhaps no other area was the prohibition on interracial sex involving a white woman and a black man so early and strictly established and maintained. This attitude is thought to be related to the sex ratio and the density of the black population. Where there was a great disproportion of blacks to whites, black concubinage seemed to be more often acceptable. In areas where the black population was less dense, the practical result was more equality between white males and females in terms of miscegenation, although it was never entirely acceptable, and nearly everywhere white females were punished by the eighteenth century.

Along with rice, cotton was also planted in colonial South Carolina, but mostly for domestic consumption and often by black slaves. During the Revolutionary period when protest and war hindered commercial production, many plantations were given over more fully to food crops for domestic consumption and to cotton for local textile manufacture. In this era of unrest, plantations were often run entirely by slaves for their own use. Planters were entirely satisfied with this arrangement if it encouraged the slaves to stay put.

In the aftermath of the war, as the economy slowly recovered, planters produced cotton for export. Eli Whitney's 1793 introduction of an improved cotton gin led to the rapid extension of cotton production into upland South Carolina and elsewhere. As transportation improved, more land was given over to cotton and less to foodstuffs, which could be imported. The mechanics of cotton production were closer to those of tobacco than to those of rice. Cotton production was not as labor intensive as rice production and could be carried out by a man and his family. These considerations facilitated the spread of slavery by making it more accessible to the successful farmer. He could start off slowly and gradually acquire bondspeople to expand cultivation. This process could be seen clearly in South Carolina, where people who settled the upcountry did not have the wherewithal to compete in the coastal rice economy. In 1790 these upland counties operated essentially in a free-labor society, fifteen thousand slaves amounting to no more than a fifth of the population. The onset of cotton production contributed to a substantial increase in the slave population, and by 1830 the slave population was almost equal to the white population. This was in contrast to the lowcountry, where blacks had outnumbered whites since the beginning of the eighteenth century.

The expansion of slavery throughout the state led to the full maturity of the slave society in South Carolina. By 1860, 45.8 percent of white families in the state owned slaves, giving the state one of the highest percentages of slaveholders in the country. During the antebellum era the majority of slaves lived on plantations claiming more than twenty slaves, while the majority of slaveholders owned far fewer than twenty slaves. Largely concentrated in places such as the rice regions of the lowcountry and fertile cotton regions such as Sumter District, slaves created communities shaped as much by their own interactions as by their relationships with whites. Slave cabins on large plantations were often built in rows on either side of dirt roads or "streets" relatively close to the fields but some distance from the masters' houses. This arrangement provided both physical and to some extent psychological distance between masters and slaves, allowing slaves some autonomy once the workday was over, a luxury that was often denied house servants and those living on small farms. The slave family was generally made up of a mother and a father living in a cabin with their children and perhaps extended kin.

Slave men and women were often married and lived in monogamous relationships, although strictures against premarital sex were

Slave auction, Charleston, 1856. *Illustrated London News,* Courtesy, South Carolina Historical Society

often not closely adhered to in the slave communities. Despite the real possibility that a husband or wife could be sold, large numbers of slave couples lived in long-term marriages, and most slaves lived in double-headed households. When suitable husbands could not be found on plantations, masters often allowed "abroad" marriages uniting men and women from neighboring plantations. It was in a master's financial interest to allow these unions because the more children a slave woman had, the more slaves the master could claim as his property. The average age of child bearing among slave women in the antebellum South was nineteen years old, while the average age for white women was twenty-one.

Once weaned from their mothers, and sometimes even before, slave children on large plantations were usually cared for and watched after by older slave women while their mothers went back to work in the fields. Children were initiated to work at the age of five or six, learning how to take orders and fulfill small tasks, and on cotton plantations they helped with the labor-intensive job of picking cotton. By the age of ten or twelve they were fully initiated into the world of adult work, although they were not expected to do the work of a full hand until about age sixteen.

While the slave's work regime was intensive, slaves by no means passively acquiesced to the whims of masters. The many ways that slaves resisted the institution of slavery have been major themes of historical literature over the years. Over time, slaves negotiated rights and customs that allowed them to build close-knit communities and develop family bonds. These informal customs were recognized by masters who wanted to keep slaves as productive as possible. Everyday forms of resistance such as work slowdowns and breaking tools were used by slaves in this complicated negotiating system. Slaves customarily received part of the day Saturday and all day Sunday off from work in the fields, using this time to cultivate their own provision grounds, worship with family and friends, and court the opposite sex, among myriad other activities.

The most extreme form of resistance, open revolt, was not common in antebellum South Carolina, but slave violence against whites was a common occurrence, despite the fact that slaves convicted of committing such acts faced extreme punishments ranging from death to severe whipping. Slave runaways, those who in effect stole themselves, were numerous, as the ubiquitous advertisements in antebellum newspapers posting rewards for their capture attest. The goal of many was to escape to the North and freedom, but this was a difficult journey that only the fittest and most determined successfully completed. Many runaways fled temporarily, hiding close by with the support of the slave communities, in order to escape punishment or to protest actions taken by their masters.

Freedom came for all slaves in South Carolina as a result of the Union invasion of the state during the Civil War. The hard times associated with the slave regime did not end with emancipation for the state's freedmen and freedwomen, but the family and community bonds forged during slavery proved invaluable assets during the Reconstruction era. DANIEL C. LITTLEFIELD

Ball, Edward. *Slaves in the Family.* New York: Farrar, Straus and Giroux, 1998.

Ferguson, Leland. *Uncommon Ground: Archaeology and Early African America, 1650–1800.* Washington, D.C.: Smithsonian Institution Press, 1992.

Jordan, Winthrop D. *White over Black: American Attitudes toward the Negro, 1550–1812.* Chapel Hill: University of North Carolina Press, 1968.

Joyner, Charles W. *Down by the Riverside: A South Carolina Slave Community.* Urbana: University of Illinois Press, 1984.

Koger, Larry. *Black Slaveowners: Free Black Slave Masters in South Carolina, 1790–1860.* 1985. Reprint, Columbia: University of South Carolina Press, 1995.

Littlefield, Daniel C. *Rice and Slaves: Ethnicity and the Slave Trade in Colonial South Carolina.* Baton Rouge: Louisiana State University Press, 1981.

Olwell, Robert. *Masters, Slaves, and Subjects: The Culture of Power in the South Carolina Low Country, 1740–1790.* Ithaca, N.Y.: Cornell University Press, 1998.

Ramsey, William L. "A Coat for 'Indian Cuffy': Mapping the Boundary between Freedom and Slavery in Colonial South Carolina." *South Carolina Historical Magazine* 103 (January 2002): 48–66.

Wood, Peter H. *Black Majority: Negroes in Colonial South Carolina from 1670 through the Stono Rebellion.* New York: Knopf, 1974.

Smallpox. An acute, highly contagious viral disease, smallpox was a major threat in South Carolina from the late seventeenth century until the late nineteenth century. Worldwide, smallpox killed and disfigured untold millions of people before it was effectively eradicated by 1977 through a combination of vaccination and isolation of those infected. Its characteristic symptoms included fever, skin and throat eruptions with pustules ("pox"), sloughing, and scarring of skin. Fatalities generally occurred when it attacked internal organs and/or caused internal and external hemorrhaging. No cure was ever discovered. During the sixteenth century an extremely virulent form of smallpox (*variola major*) developed in the Old World and gradually spread to the New. It was one of the most feared diseases in the world, not only because it often killed upward of twenty percent of the infected, but also because it often left survivors scarred with facial "pock marks" and sometimes blinded them in one or both eyes.

Smallpox was endemic (always present) in some large European cities by the eighteenth century, but it was an occasional epidemic import into South Carolina. It arrived via ships from the Old World or the Caribbean, or by sea or land from other parts of eastern North America. Many epidemics of smallpox struck South Carolina between 1697 and 1897. Those of 1697–1698, 1711, 1738, and 1759–1760 were particularly deadly. Each killed hundreds of Europeans and Africans and devastated local Native American populations.

The epidemic of 1738 was significant as the first occasion in South Carolina when doctors resorted to widespread inoculation as a smallpox preventive. According to one of the main Charleston inoculators at the time, James Kilpatrick, between 800 and 1,000 people were inoculated and 8 died. The editor of the *South-Carolina Gazette,* who was unfriendly to inoculation, claimed that 437 were inoculated and 16 died. Inoculation had previously been used in epidemics in Boston and Philadelphia, but the numbers inoculated there were much smaller. Methods of inoculation varied but generally involved placing matter from the pustules of smallpox victims under the skin of the uninfected in hopes of producing a mild infection and immunity. Although this practice occasionally produced a serious infection and death, contemporary statistics show that it was far less likely to kill or disfigure than a natural infection was. Although widely employed throughout the eighteenth century in South Carolina, it was highly controversial. Opponents accused inoculators of needlessly spreading the disease or interfering with Divine Providence.

In the early nineteenth century inoculation was gradually replaced by vaccination. The method developed and publicized by the English physician Edward Jenner in the late 1790s involved placing matter from what he claimed was cowpox, a related but mild disease, under the skin in the same manner as inoculation. Vaccination (from the Latin *vacca,* or "cow") was safer than inoculation. But it was soon discovered that the immunity it provided was only temporary and that periodic revaccination was required. By 1802 several South Carolina physicians were promoting vaccination. One of them, David Ramsay, confidently predicted the imminent demise of smallpox through vaccination. But many people opposed it for much the same reasons that they had opposed inoculation. The state did not make vaccination compulsory until 1905. Several major smallpox epidemics occurred in the late nineteenth century, but by 1930 the disease had been eradicated from South Carolina. PETER MCCANDLESS

Banov, Leon. *As I Recall: The Story of the Charleston County Health Department.* Columbia, S.C.: R. L. Bryan, 1970.

Duffy, John. *Epidemics in Colonial America.* Baton Rouge: Louisiana State University Press, 1953.

Hopkins, Donald R. *The Greatest Killer.* Chicago: University of Chicago Press, 2002.

Kirkpatrick, James. *An Essay on Inoculation Occasioned by the Smallpox Being Brought into South Carolina in the Year 1738.* London: J. Huggonsohn, 1743.

Waring, Joseph I. *A History of Medicine in South Carolina.* 3 vols. Columbia: South Carolina Medical Association, 1964–1971.

Wood, Peter. "The Impact of Smallpox on the Native Population of the 18th Century South." *New York State Journal of Medicine* 87 (January 1987): 30–36.

Smalls, Robert (1839–1915). Legislator, congressman. Smalls was born in Beaufort on April 5, 1839, the son of Lydia Smalls, a house slave, and possibly her master, John McKee. In 1851 Smalls was inherited by Henry McKee, who hired him out as a laborer in Charleston. Smalls worked as a waiter, a lamplighter, a stevedore, and eventually a ship rigger and sailor on coastal vessels. On December 24, 1858, Smalls married Hannah Jones, a slave woman fourteen years his senior. The couple had at least three children. After the 1883 death of his first wife, Smalls married Annie Elizabeth Wigg on April 9, 1890. They had one child.

At the start of the Civil War, Smalls was employed as a pilot on the cotton steamer *Planter,* which was impressed into Confederate service as an armed courier. Early on the morning of May 13, 1862, in the absence of the vessel's white officers, Smalls led the takeover of the *Planter* by its slave crew, sailed past the harbor's formidable defenses, and surrendered the vessel to the Federal blockading force. The daring act made Smalls famous, and the information he provided on Confederate defenses was valuable in planning Union operations. Congress voted prize money to the crew for their deed, with Smalls receiving $1,500.

Robert Smalls. Courtesy, South Caroliniana Library, University of South Carolina

As Smalls was a knowledgeable pilot, his services were in demand. On December 1, 1863, he was piloting the *Planter* near Secessionville when severe enemy fire caused the white captain to abandon his post. Smalls brought the vessel out of danger and was awarded with an army contract as captain of the *Planter.* He was the first black man to command a ship in U.S. service and remained captain of the *Planter* until it was sold in 1866. By his own count, Smalls was involved in seventeen military engagements during the war.

After the war Smalls settled in his native Beaufort, where he purchased the house of his former master. Smalls's war-time accomplishments made him a political force in the Sea Islands, with its overwhelmingly black population. In 1867 Smalls was one of the founders of the Republican Party in South Carolina, an organization to which he remained loyal all his life. In 1868 he was a delegate to the state constitutional convention and won election to the state House of Representatives, where he represented Beaufort County until 1870. That same year Beaufort voters sent Smalls to the state Senate, and in 1873 he was promoted to major general in the militia. In the Senate, Smalls was made chairman of the printing committee, an assignment with the potential for graft. In 1877 he was tried and convicted of accepting a bribe and was sentenced to three years, but he was pardoned in an amnesty that also quashed proceedings against Democrats for election irregularities. Even Smalls's enemies at the time said that the case against him was not strong, and it was likely part of the campaign to remove African Americans from public office.

In 1874 Smalls was elected to the U.S. House of Representatives. He was reelected to the following Congress and served intermittently until 1886. With the return of Democratic rule in South Carolina after 1876, Smalls had increasing difficulty winning reelection. He lost to George D. Tillman in 1878 and 1880 but successfully contested the results of the latter election and took Tillman's seat in July 1882. Two years later Smalls failed to secure renomination, losing to Edmund W. M. Mackey, who died soon after taking office. Smalls was elected to fill the vacancy and returned to Washington in March 1884, but he lost a bid for another term in 1886. While in Congress, Smalls earned a reputation as an effective speaker. He secured appropriations for harbor improvements at Port Royal and was a vocal opponent of the removal of federal troops from the South.

After returning to South Carolina, Smalls successfully lobbied his old congressional colleagues for a veteran's pension and more compensation for the *Planter.* His last major political role was as one of six black members of the 1895 state constitutional convention, where he unsuccessfully opposed efforts to disenfranchise African Americans. In 1889 President Benjamin Harrison appointed Smalls as collector of customs for the port of Beaufort, an office he held, except during President Grover Cleveland's second term, until June 1913, when he was forced out by South Carolina's senators. Smalls died on February 22, 1915, at his home in Beaufort. He was buried in Tabernacle Baptist Churchyard. EDWARD A. MILLER, JR.

Miller, Edward A., Jr. *Gullah Statesman: Robert Smalls from Slavery to Congress, 1839–1915.* Columbia: University of South Carolina Press, 1995.

Uya, Okon Edet. *From Slavery to Public Service: Robert Smalls, 1839–1915.* New York: Oxford University Press, 1971.

Smith, Alice Ravenel Huger (1876–1958). Artist. Smith was born in Charleston on July 14, 1876, the daughter of Daniel Elliott Huger Smith and Caroline Ravenel. Although largely self-taught, Smith emerged as the leading artist of the Charleston Renaissance. Through her writings and art she helped to disseminate the history and charm of her native lowcountry to a national audience.

Reticent and claiming to be too poor to seek training away from Charleston, Smith received her only formal art education as a young girl in classes offered by the Carolina Art Association. Louise Fery, a Frenchwoman, instructed her students in the basics and, most importantly for Smith, in the technique of watercolor. Smith's initial output was modest: fans, dance programs, cards painted with flowers, small sketches of African Americans, and occasional portraits of family members. She sought lessons from the tonalist landscape painter and teacher Birge Harrison, from Woodstock, New York, who sojourned several winters in Charleston beginning in 1908. Harrison, while refusing to give formal instruction, offered guidance and served as her mentor until his death.

Beginning about 1917, Smith undertook an intense study of Japanese color wood-block prints, largely from the ukiyo-e school, which had been collected by her friend Motte Alston Read. Smith cataloged the collection and, experimenting with actual blocks, taught herself how to print in the traditional Japanese manner. Synthesizing the methods of the Japanese with lowcountry imagery, Smith invented a visual language that would remain with her throughout her life. In 1923 Smith spearheaded the founding of the Charleston Etchers Club, a collaborative group that jointly acquired a press and shared expertise and criticism. By the late 1920s Smith abandoned prints and began to concentrate on watercolor.

Through her evocative imagery Smith fueled the Charleston Renaissance, the cultural and economic renewal of the city. During the 1920s paintings and prints by Smith were included in forty-two exhibitions, mostly one-artist presentations. For example, in 1924 she sent sixty-eight paintings to the Philadelphia Art Alliance; entitled "Watercolors of the Carolina Coast," the selection included typical southern flora and fauna—lotus, magnolias, ibises, and egrets. Of the thirty-one works listed in her ledger for that year, she sold twelve works to Philadelphians. Her account books from throughout her career record a widespread national clientele, many of whom visited Smith in her studio.

Smith was also active in the field of publishing. She provided the illustrations for Elizabeth Allston Pringle's *A Woman Rice Planter* (1913) and in 1914 issued *Twenty Drawings of the Pringle House,* a portfolio of drawings of the historic Miles Brewton House. In *The Dwelling Houses of Charleston, South Carolina* (1917) Smith's illustrations accompany her father's house histories. This volume was critical to the evolution of the city's preservation movement; it not only instilled pride among Charlestonians for their architectural heritage but also brought national attention to the city. Smith's most ambitious volume was *A Carolina Rice Plantation of the Fifties* (1936), which combined an essay on rice cultivation by Herbert Ravenel Sass, her father's recollections of growing up on a rice plantation, and thirty color reproductions of her watercolors. In 1940 she authored an introduction and oversaw the publication of *A Charleston Sketchbook, 1796–1806,* by the nineteenth-century artist Charles Fraser. Always keenly interested in heritage, architecture, and preservation, Smith was a member of the committee that researched and published *This Is Charleston* (1944), an inventory of Charleston architecture.

Around 1950 Smith began to write her reminiscences. In them she traces her family's history, recollections of the earthquake of 1886 and later hurricanes, comments on social mores, and her view of art. The Gibbes Museum of Art in Charleston is the major repository of her work. Other South Carolina museums have representative examples of her paintings. Smith died in Charleston on February 3, 1958, and was buried in Magnolia Cemetery. See plate 28. MARTHA R. SEVERENS

Alice Ravenel Huger Smith of Charleston, South Carolina: An Appreciation on the Occasion of Her Eightieth Birthday. Charleston, S.C., 1956.

Severens, Martha R. *Alice Ravenel Huger Smith: An Artist, a Place and a Time.* Charleston, S.C.: Carolina Art Association / Gibbes Museum of Art, 1993.

Smith, Arthur (b. 1921). Musician. Thanks to the widespread popularity of his instrumental hit "Guitar Boogie," Arthur Smith became one of the better-known guitarists in country music. Born in Clinton on April 1, 1921, Smith also played fiddle and other instruments and is sometimes confused with central Tennessee's Fiddlin' Arthur Smith and the eastern Tennessee songwriter Arthur Q. Smith.

Like many other South Carolina musicians, Smith was a product of the textile mills, where his father worked as a loom fixer and musical director in the town of Kershaw. Smith followed his father into mill work at an early age and also shared his musical interests. His initial interest had been in horn music, but he also learned guitar and turned to electric instruments early in his career. He started a Dixieland jazz band and played at WSPA Spartanburg, but the group had little success until switching to country music—although still somewhat jazz influenced—as Smith's Carolina Crackerjacks. In the fall of 1938 they had a record session for Bluebird at Rock Hill, where they waxed their best-known song, "Going Back to Old Carolina."

Midway through World War II, Smith transferred his radio base to WBT Charlotte, where he filled in with both the Briarhoppers and the Tennessee Ramblers. He made the first recording of "Guitar Boogie" with the Ramblers about 1945. Reforming the Crackerjacks after the war, Smith and his band became regulars on radio for many years and from 1951 on WBTV as well, recording periodically for MGM, Dot, Starday, Monument, and CMH. In addition to "Guitar Boogie," he had major hits with "Banjo Boogie" and "Boomerang," all in 1948.

During the1950s and 1960s Smith became the dominant figure on the Charlotte music scene with both daily and weekly television programs. His shows were syndicated in several markets. In addition to showcasing his own talents, *The Arthur Smith Show* featured other artists, including his brothers, Ralph and Sonny Smith; Ray and Lois Atkins; the banjoists Don Reno, a native of Spartanburg, and David

Deese; and the singer-guitarist Tommy Faile, a native of Lancaster, South Carolina. Ironically, he enjoyed only one hit in this era, a comic parody of the Australian song "Tie Me Kangaroo Down, Sport," rewritten as "Tie My Hunting Dog Down, Jed," in 1963.

Smith's compositions had a way of reappearing in modified form years later. "Guitar Boogie" became a pop hit for the Virtues in 1959 as "Guitar Boogie Shuffle" and again for the Ventures in 1962 as "Guitar Twist." The British guitarist Bert Weedon had a hit with it in the United Kingdom. A lesser number at the time in 1955, "Feudin' Banjos," by Smith and Don Reno, reappeared as "Mocking Banjos" in 1957 and as "Dueling Banjos" by Eric Weisberg and Steve Mandel in the 1972 hit film *Deliverance.* Smith and Reno went to court and received royalties.

In 1959 Smith started a recording studio in Charlotte, which produced jingles and commercials for regional radio and television. His studio also recorded numerous country, sacred, and bluegrass titles and even a soul hit for James Brown. Smith's musical and business career enabled him to retire in relative comfort as "a leading citizen of the Charlotte community." Nonetheless, he remains best remembered for his jazz-influenced electric-guitar dexterity. ABBY GAIL GOODNITE

Smith, Michael B. *Carolina Dreams: The Musical Legacy of Upstate South Carolina.* Beverly Hills, Calif.: Marshall Tucker Entertainment, 1997.

Smith, Benjamin (1717–1770). Merchant, politician, planter. Smith was born in South Carolina in 1717, the eldest child of the planter and politician Thomas Smith (?–1724) and Sabina Smith. At age eighteen Smith inherited a two-thousand-acre plantation in St. James Goose Creek Parish. Smith's real interest, however, was in trade. In 1735 he began a twenty-seven-year mercantile career with several partners in both London and Charleston. His heavy involvement in the lucrative trade in slaves and furs made him one of the wealthiest factors in South Carolina by midcentury.

Financially secure and civic-minded, Smith entered public service in 1746 when St. Philip's Parish elected him to the Commons House of Assembly. He became an active and prominent legislator, serving on important committees and as Speaker of the House from 1755 to 1763. He provided nearly continuous service in the assembly until his death in 1770. But legislative work did not satisfy Smith's thirst for public service. He also served as an assistant judge, as a justice of the peace, as a fire-master for Charleston, and as a commissioner for sundry public projects. His wealth, prominence, and dedication to public service earned him a recommendation from Lieutenant Governor William Bull in 1760 to a position in the Royal Council. Smith declined the position, perhaps because the council and its members had lost considerable power and prestige during the preceding decade. As rebellion against England increased, Smith generally supported the patriots' cause. As an assistant judge, for example, he advocated the opening of the courts during the Stamp Act controversy in 1765. After his death his estate lent the South Carolina government nearly £275,000.

Smith was also prominent in Charleston's active fraternal societies. He served as master of Solomon's Lodge and provincial grand master of the Masons, and he was a member of the South Carolina Society, the St. Andrew's Society, and the Charleston Library Society. In 1760 he was elected an American member of the Society for Encouraging Arts, Manufactures, and Commerce in London. He owned pews in St. Michael's Church, which he helped to establish, and St. Philip's Church, where he served as vestryman and warden. A philanthropic man, Smith donated money to the Ludlam School and to a local school for African Americans, an ironic contribution, considering his deep involvement in the slave trade. Upon his death he left bequests of £1,000 to the Charleston Library Society,£1,000 to Charleston's poor, £1,000 to the South Carolina Society, £500 to the proposed College of Charleston, and £50 for the purchase of an organ for St. Philip's Church.

Smith married twice, first in 1740 to Anne Loughton, daughter of William Loughton and Mary Griffith. Their union produced seven children, four of whom lived to adulthood. Anne Loughton Smith died in 1760 from a smallpox inoculation. Eight months later Smith married Mary Wragg, daughter of Joseph Wragg and Judith DuBosc. His second marriage produced six children. Smith died on July 29, 1770, while vacationing with his family in Newport, Rhode Island. He was buried in Trinity Churchyard in Newport, Rhode Island, but was reinterred in St. Philip's Churchyard in Charleston later that year. KEITH KRAWCZYNSKI

Edgar, Walter, and N. Louise Bailey, eds. *Biographical Directory of the South Carolina House of Representatives.* Vol. 2, *The Commons House of Assembly, 1692–1775.* Columbia: University of South Carolina Press, 1977.

Smith, Ellison Durant (1864–1944). U.S. senator. Smith was born in Sumter District (later Lee County) on August 1, 1864, one of ten children born to William H. Smith, a Methodist minister, and his wife, Mary Isabella McLeod. After attending schools in nearby Lynchburg and taking college preparatory work at Stewart's School in Charleston, Smith entered South Carolina College as a sophomore in 1885. A year later he transferred to Wofford College, where he received an A.B. degree in 1889. In 1892 Smith married Martha Cornelia Moorer, who died of childbirth complications the following year. The son survived until 1912, when he died of an accidental gunshot wound. Smith married Annie Brunson Farley in 1906, and from this union four children were born.

Ellison D. "Cotton Ed" Smith. Courtesy, South Carolina Historical Society

Smith represented Sumter County in the state legislature from 1897 to 1901. After losing a bid for Congress in 1901, Smith began working with several agricultural organizations. In 1905, as an executive committee member of the Southern Cotton Association, Smith traveled the Southeast organizing cotton growers and polishing his oratorical skills. In 1908 Smith stunned the political establishment by winning election to the United States Senate. He remained there for thirty-six years.

Although an advocate for southern farmers, Smith was not a Populist. Rather, he entered the Senate as a southern progressive who favored government regulation of commodity markets and extension of credit for farmers. Smith's passionate defense of cotton growers led a reporter in *Colliers* to describe him as a "press agent for King Cotton." In South Carolina constituents dubbed him "Cotton Ed" Smith. Smith's legislative agenda sought to expand farm credit and use the federal government to regulate in the interest of fair prices. He wanted the Department of Agriculture to keep statistics, expose fraud, and promote good farm practices. Although such programs expanded the functions of government, Smith nevertheless looked upon federal bureaucrats with suspicion, particularly when they meddled in state affairs beyond cotton.

Throughout his six terms in the Senate, Smith emphasized his consistent belief in tariff reduction, states' rights, and white supremacy. However, to accommodate his interest in agriculture, he remained pragmatic on states' rights. During World War I he supported federal takeover of private railroads, government purchase of nitrates for farmers, and price controls for all commodities except cotton. During the agricultural depression of the early 1920s, he wanted the federal government to buy cotton and give it to European textile firms. He even gave reluctant support to the Agricultural Adjustment Act in 1933, although only after he and other conservatives reworked the legislation to ignore inequities in southern agriculture that left many black and white farm laborers in virtual peonage to large landowners.

While identified with cotton for his first four terms, Smith became best known as a champion of racial segregation later in his career. In his early Senate campaigns he seldom mentioned race. But in the 1930s Smith earned a national reputation as a southern demagogue. By mid-decade Smith was among the most vocal opponents of federal New Deal legislation, arguing that it went too far in expanding the size and influence of the federal government. Smith denounced bills to establish a national minimum wage and regulate work-place conditions. A Georgia newspaper columnist said that Smith possessed "the courage of his prejudices and a vocabulary which runs the gamut from invective to invective." *Time* magazine called him a "conscientious objector to the 20th century." Smith was especially alarmed at the growing influence of African Americans in the national Democratic Party. He vehemently opposed federal antilynching legislation and enjoyed telling crowds of white voters about his walkout at the 1936 Democratic National Convention after a black minister led the benediction. Smith castigated President Franklin Roosevelt for his attempt to pack the Supreme Court and for seeking third and fourth presidential terms. Roosevelt campaigned against Smith in his 1938 reelection campaign, which probably aided Smith's victory. The New Deal and Roosevelt were popular in South Carolina, but presidential intervention was resented.

In August 1944 Governor Olin D. Johnston defeated the aging "Cotton Ed" in the state Democratic primary. Despite assertions by Smith that if he lost, the headlines would read "A Victory for the Brother in Black," Johnston posed no threat to the racial status quo, and white supremacy was not a casualty of Smith's defeat. Just months after losing his bid for a seventh term, the eighty-year-old senator died of coronary thrombosis at his home near Lynchburg on November 17, 1944. SELDEN K. SMITH

Bouknight, Martha Nelle. "The Senatorial Campaigns of Ellison Durant ('Cotton Ed') Smith of South Carolina." Master's thesis, Florida State University, 1961.

Gehring, Mary Louise. "'Cotton Ed' Smith: The South Carolina Farmer in the United States Senate." In *The Oratory of Southern Demagogues,* edited by Cal M. Logue and Howard Dorgan. Baton Rouge: Louisiana State University Press, 1981.

Hollis, Daniel W. "'Cotton Ed Smith'—Showman or Statesman?" *South Carolina Historical Magazine* 71 (October 1970): 235–56.

Simon, Bryant. *A Fabric of Defeat: The Politics of South Carolina Millhands, 1910–1948.* Chapel Hill: University of North Carolina Press, 1998.

Smith, Selden K. "Ellison Durant Smith: A Southern Progressive, 1909–1929." Ph.D. diss., University of North Carolina, 1970.

Smith, Nell Whitley (b. 1929). Legislator, educator, businesswoman. Smith, the daughter of Arthur Hugh Smith and Alice Beryl Whitley, was born in Washington, North Carolina, on November 12, 1929. After attending Salem College in Winston-Salem, North Carolina, Smith received a B.S. degree in chemistry and biology at the University of North Carolina in Greensboro in 1951. She married Harris Page Smith on April 18, 1952, and moved to Easley, South Carolina, where she taught junior high school science and later owned the House Antiques and Gifts. The mother of four children, Smith was a well-known figure in the community and served on various Pickens County boards and commissions, including those related to the public library, the arts commission, and home health care.

Harris Smith, a state senator from Pickens County since 1971, died on July 12, 1981. The following November voters in Senate District No. 1 (Abbeville, Anderson, Oconee, and Pickens) elected Nell Whitley Smith, a Democrat, to serve out his unexpired term. At the time of her election, Smith was just the sixth woman to be elected to the South Carolina Senate. Upon taking office in January 1982, Smith joined Elizabeth J. Patterson and Norma Russell in the Senate, as well as Lieutenant Governor Nancy Stevenson. As a result of redistricting, in 1985 Smith's district changed to District No. 2 (Pickens), and voters from that district elected her to full terms in 1984 and 1988. She retired from the Senate at the end of the 1992 legislative session. Smith was chair of the Rules Committee, the first woman to serve as chair of a standing Senate committee. As chair of the Joint Legislative Committee on Children and Families, Smith worked on issues such as licensing day-care centers that resulted from more women entering the workforce. Following her retirement from the Senate, Smith continued to serve the community on a volunteer basis through membership on numerous boards and commissions. KATHERINE CANN

Bailey, N. Louise, Mary L. Morgan, and Carolyn R. Taylor, eds. *Biographical Directory of the South Carolina Senate, 1776–1985.* 3 vols. Columbia: University of South Carolina Press, 1986.

Smith, Thomas (ca. 1648–1694). Governor. Born in England around 1648, Smith immigrated with his family to Carolina in 1683, likely as a member of a great Dissenter migration to the province that occurred during the 1680s. His first wife was Barbara Atkins, whom he wed in England. The couple had two sons, Thomas and George, both of whom were born in England and went on to careers in early Carolina politics. Smith obtained a landgrave's grant, which secured for him 48,000 acres of land in the new Carolina colony. His holdings were collectively called Wiskinboo Barony. He augmented his wealth with influence during the 1680s and on May 4, 1688, was named a commissioner of customs by the Lords Proprietors. Later he was named to the Grand Council. While he was a member, the General Assembly met at his house in Charleston.

When Governor Philip Ludwell departed Carolina in May 1693, he appointed Smith to be deputy governor. The proprietors issued a commission to Smith to hold that post on November 29, 1693, seven months after he had assumed the office. Smith's Dissenter connections gave him some political security, but the conflict between Dissenters and Anglicans and between proprietary supporters and opponents kept the province in turmoil. Smith had a few successes that reduced tensions. In 1694 the Commons House passed a quitrent law that formally enrolled land grants and assessed quitrent payments that were to be made to the proprietors. Smith also sought to end the Indian slave trade and reduce commerce with pirates.

Landgrave Smith's connections with Medway Plantation, on the Back River, a Cooper River tributary, were a significant aspect of his political career and represent the degree to which landownership and local power meshed in early Carolina. On March 22, 1688, Smith wed Sabina de Vignon van Arsens, widow of Johan Wernhout van Arsens, a Netherlands Huguenot who had secured a barony of twelve hundred acres in 1686. He and his servants had named the plantation Medway. Upon his marriage, Smith petitioned the proprietors to assume control of van Arsens's barony and to take over his title as landgrave. The petition was granted in 1691, and Smith assumed ownership of Medway. Smith died on November 16, 1694, and was buried at Medway. In his will he bequeathed his medical instruments to his son George, his landgrave's patent to Joseph Blake, and the property of Medway to his son Thomas. The house that the van Arsens family had inhabited was sold by Smith's son. It burned in 1704 and was rebuilt by its new owners, the Hyrne family. In the early twenty-first century the second Medway house still stood on a large tract of land protected from development by strong conservation and preservation easements. ALEXANDER MOORE

Beach, Virginia. *Medway.* Charleston, S.C.: Wyrick, 1999.

Smith, William (ca. 1762–1840). U.S. senator. Born near the North Carolina border, Smith spent most of his life in York District. After studying with the Reverend Joseph Alexander and attending Mount Zion College in Winnsboro, Smith opened his own legal practice in the late 1780s. He was also a successful planter, with landholdings across the state and at least seventy-one slaves by 1810. By 1820 he began acquiring land in Alabama and Louisiana for sugar and cotton cultivation. Around 1781 Smith married Margaret Duff. They had one daughter.

Smith was one of the most prominent political leaders in early nineteenth-century South Carolina. A Jeffersonian of the purest stripe, Smith espoused strict-constructionist and states' rights principles well before such views came to dominate southern politics. He represented York District in the South Carolina House of Representatives from 1796 to 1797 and then from 1803 to 1808 in the state Senate, where he served as president from 1806 until 1808. In June 1808 he was elected to a judgeship on the Court of General Sessions and Common Pleas. On December 4, 1816, Smith was selected by the General Assembly to fill the unexpired term of John Taylor in the United States Senate. That same day he was elected to a full term, defeating the Charlestonian James Pringle.

In the U.S. Senate, Smith gained notoriety in both state and national politics. His style was boisterous, and his speeches were laden with sarcasm and invective against anyone who happened to be his unfortunate opponent. Smith's defense of his section during the controversy over Missouri's admission to the Union also placed him in the vanguard of proslavery ideology. During a Senate speech in January 1820, Smith became one of the first to defend slavery as a positive good, arguing that slaves "are so domesticated, or so kindly treated by their masters, and their situations so improved" that few would express discontent with their condition. Appealing to both states' rights principles and biblical texts in framing this argument, Smith anticipated the path that the South's defense of slavery would later take in the antebellum period.

Smith's rigorous adherence to states' rights principles and a strict interpretation of the Constitution made him the implacable enemy of the nationalist John C. Calhoun, twenty years his junior. The Smith-Calhoun rivalry dominated South Carolina political culture for much of the 1820s, as the two men and their factions jockeyed for supremacy. Calhoun seemed to gain the upper hand in 1822, when Smith was defeated in his reelection bid by the Calhounite Robert Y. Hayne. But returned to the state House of Representative in 1824, Smith took advantage of South Carolina's fear of federal power—inspired by the Missouri crisis, the Denmark Vesey rebellion, and the protective Tariff of 1824. In partnership with his colleague Stephen Miller, in 1825 Smith pushed through the General Assembly a set of resolutions declaring the protective tariff unconstitutional and stating that all powers not *expressly* delegated to Congress by the Constitution were the domain of the states. The principles embodied in the Smith-Miller Resolutions signaled South Carolina's decisive retreat from Calhoun-style nationalism and toward the doctrine of states' rights.

Smith returned to the U.S. Senate in 1826 and reemerged as a leading spokesman for Jeffersonian principles and the nascent Jacksonian movement. But these same principles also led to a bitter controversy back home with the emergence of the nullification movement. Although he agreed that the Tariff of 1828 was unconstitutional, Smith's strict-constructionist beliefs prevented him from accepting nullification as a legitimate constitutional recourse since he believed that the doctrine threatened states' rights with its broad interpretation of the Constitution. But South Carolina politics had little room for two competing states' rights factions. Calhoun and the nullifiers, aided by many former Smithites, achieved political ascendancy in the state. In his bid for reelection to the Senate in 1830, Smith lost to his former ally Stephen Miller. He was elected to the state Senate the next year but had grown tired of South Carolina politics. To Smith, the dominance that Calhoun and his followers now enjoyed presented a humiliating spectacle and the subversion of the states' rights principles for which he had fought his entire career.

In late 1831 Smith left South Carolina and moved to his lands in Madison County, Alabama. Unable to remain outside of politics for long, he became the county's representative in the Alabama legislature in 1836, professing his "Old Republican" principles as loudly as ever. On June 26, 1840, Smith died of congestive fever in Huntsville. He was buried at his plantation in Madison County. KEVIN M. GANNON

Ford, Lacy K., Jr. *Origins of Southern Radicalism: The South Carolina Upcountry, 1800–1860.* New York: Oxford University Press, 1988.

Freehling, William W. *Prelude to Civil War: The Nullification Controversy in South Carolina, 1816–1836.* New York: Harper & Row, 1965.

Hardin, Richard L. "William Smith and the Rise of Sectionalism in South Carolina." Master's thesis, University of South Carolina, 1971.

Smith, Caroline P. "Jacksonian Conservative: The Later Years of William Smith, 1826–1840." Ph.D. diss., Auburn University, 1977.

———. "South Carolina Radical: The Political Career of William Smith to 1826." Master's thesis, Auburn University, 1971.

Smith, William Loughton (1758–1812). Lawyer, congressman, diplomat. Smith was born on October 2, 1758, the son of the prominent merchant Benjamin Smith and Anne Loughton. In 1804 the younger Smith added Loughton to his name. Prior to his father's death in July 1770, Smith went to Europe for schooling. He studied

William Loughton Smith (1755–1828) by Gilbert Stuart, oil on canvas. Courtesy, Gibbes Museum of Art / Carolina Art Association

under private tutors in London and in Geneva. In January 1779 he began studying law at the Middle Temple in the Inns of Court. He remained in Britain throughout the Revolutionary War and did not return to Charleston until November 21, 1783.

Admitted to the bar in 1784, Smith promptly began a successful law career and formed important ties with British merchants. On May 1, 1786, he married Charlotte Izard, daughter of the wealthy planter Ralph Izard. The couple had two children before Charlotte's death in 1792. Smith and his father-in-law became allies in South Carolina and national politics. Despite his extended sojourn in Europe, Smith moved successfully into state politics, representing St. James Goose Creek Parish in the state House of Representatives from 1785 until 1789. He voted to ratify the federal Constitution.

Smith announced his candidacy for the United States House of Representatives in November 1788 and won election easily but not without controversy. During the campaign and later in a petition, his opponent David Ramsay charged that Smith's long absence from South Carolina made him ineligible for national office. Smith countered by emphasizing Ramsay's northern birth and his liberal views on slavery. The House voted overwhelmingly to seat Smith.

An outspoken representative, Smith vehemently opposed the introduction of antislavery petitions. His support for a stronger central government placed him squarely in the Federalist Party. He forcefully advocated treasury secretary Alexander Hamilton's proposals that the central government fund the national debt, assume state debts, and form a national bank. Smith speculated in public securities, prompting opponents to charge that he used inside information for personal profit. These charges surfaced throughout Smith's public career but did not prevent him from serving four terms in Congress. Though Smith's strong pro-British stance ran counter to public opinion in South Carolina, his consistent support of commercial interests endeared him to Charleston's mercantile community.

During the 1796 presidential campaign, he published a satirical series of articles under the pseudonym "Phocion" entitled *The Pretensions of Thomas Jefferson.* In 1797 Smith was appointed minister to Portugal, where he served until 1801. Hardly a plum position, the assignment befitted his public stature. In Hamilton's words, Smith was an able man, but "popular with no description of men, from a certain *hardness* of character."

In 1803 Smith returned to Charleston, where he resumed his law practice and successfully invested in land. On December 19, 1805, he married Charlotte Wragg, and their union produced two children. Despite private success, Smith failed to win election to Congress in 1806 as the Federalists had fallen out of fashion. Two years later, in a remarkable about-face, he embraced Jefferson's Embargo Act, arguing that the legislation provided an opportunity to develop American self-sufficiency. His shift from Federalist to Jeffersonian alienated former supporters. After a brief illness, Smith died on December 19, 1812, and was buried in St. Philip's Churchyard, Charleston. GREGORY D. MASSEY

Rogers, George C. *Evolution of a Federalist: William Loughton Smith of Charleston (1758–1812).* Columbia: University of South Carolina Press, 1962.

Smyth, Ellison Adger (1847–1942). Industrialist. Smyth was born on October 26, 1847, in Charleston, the son of the Reverend Thomas Smyth and Margaret M. Adger. Smyth attended the South Carolina Military Academy, leaving it in 1864 to join the Confederate army. On February 17, 1869, he married Julia Gambrill. During Reconstruction, Smyth was one of the founders of the Carolina Rifle Club, and during the 1876 election campaign that brought Reconstruction to an end, he was captain of the Washington Artillery Rifle Club.

Smyth's business career began immediately after the Civil War with a position as a junior clerk in the firm of J. E. Adger and Company, a hardware wholesaler. During the 1860s and 1870s, however, Charleston began to lose its dominance over wholesale trade due to unfavorable freight rates and the proliferation of wholesalers in inland towns once supplied by Charleston merchants. By the end of the 1870s Smyth became convinced that it was better to invest in the emerging textile industry of the upstate. In cooperation with the Charleston capitalist Francis J. Pelzer, Smyth decided to organize a cotton mill on the Saluda River in Anderson County. The first mill of the Pelzer Manufacturing Company was built in 1881, and over the next fifteen years three more mills would be added to Pelzer. Smyth served as the president of Pelzer Manufacturing Company for forty-three years until he sold it to Lockwood, Green, and Company in 1923.

The mill at Pelzer had a profound effect on the development of the textile industry in upstate South Carolina. From the beginning, Pelzer Mill took advantage of the newest technology available. Pelzer Mill was the first cotton mill to use incandescent lights. In 1895 Pelzer installed the first Draper Automatic Looms ever sold. The Number Four mill, built in 1896, drew its electrical power from a generating station four miles down the river. The mill later used some of the first automatic tying-in machines, and it was the first to use electric drives rather than the more dangerous belt systems. This progressive bent carried over to the company's relations with its workers. Smyth never established a company store in Pelzer, and he established Chicora Savings Bank for the workers. The Pelzer mill also served as an informal training center for many workers who went on to be foremen and superintendents at other mills.

Although Pelzer was Smyth's greatest accomplishment, it was not his only one. He also organized Belton Mills in 1899 and served as its president until 1920. Smyth was involved with many other mills, including Dunean and Brandon, both named for towns in Ulster where his ancestors had operated textile mills. He owned a controlling interest in the *Greenville News* from 1912 to 1923. Smyth helped found the Cotton Manufacturers Association of South Carolina and was active with the American Cotton Manufacturers Association. He served from 1896 to 1898 on the United States Industrial Commission. Smyth died at his home, Connemara, in Flat Rock, North Carolina, on August 3, 1942. He was buried in the Second Presbyterian Church cemetery, Charleston. BRUCE E. BAKER

"Capt. E. A. Smyth Dies at Age of 94." *Greenville News,* August 4, 1942, pp. 1, 8.

Jacobs, William Plumer. *The Pioneer.* Clinton, S.C.: Jacobs, 1935.

Smyth, Thomas (1808–1873). Clergyman, author. Smyth was born on June 14, 1808, in Belfast, Ireland, the son of Samuel Smyth, a merchant, and Ann Magee. Thomas's father, who had prospered in the "grocery and commission and tobacco manufacturing business," lost much of his wealth in an economic depression in 1825. Thomas graduated with honors from Belfast College in 1829 and entered Highbury College, London, in order to prepare for the Presbyterian ministry. His attendance at a theater in London caused a scandal, and he was forced to leave Highbury shortly after his arrival. Immigrating with his parents to the United States in 1830, he entered the senior class of Princeton Theological Seminary, where he came under the influence of Charles Hodge and other conservative Presbyterian theologians. In 1831, on the recommendation of Hodge, Smyth was called to be the supply pastor of the Second Presbyterian Church, Charleston, South Carolina. Three years later he was called to be the congregation's duly installed pastor, a position he held until 1870. On July 9, 1832, he married Margaret Milligan Adger, a parishioner and the daughter of James Adger, an elder of the congregation and one of Charleston's wealthiest citizens. The couple had nine children.

Smyth moved in a circle of conservative Presbyterian scholars that included Charles Hodge and Archibald Alexander of Princeton and James Henley Thornwell and George Howe of the Presbyterian Theological Seminary in Columbia. Their theological and social perspectives were deeply influenced by Protestant Scholasticism, the philosophical school of Scottish Common Sense Realism, and their social location in the midst of conservative and affluent elements of American society. They sought to avoid extremes in theology, ethics, and politics, believing that extremes led to disorder in thought and life.

Smyth was a great collector of books and made trips to Great Britain seeking rare volumes, especially those connected with the history of Calvinism. His personal library numbered almost twenty thousand volumes, most of which he eventually sold to Columbia Theological Seminary. Smyth was a compulsive writer, and the ten volumes of his *Collected Works* showed him to be a person of wide interests but not the deep learning of Thornwell or Hodge. For his studies in church history he received an honorary doctor of divinity from the College of New Jersey (Princeton). Perhaps his most important book was *The Unity of the Human Races,* in which he defended the full humanity of Africans and the sophistication of their past civilizations. In this study he attacked the claims of Louis Agassiz and southern radicals who were arguing that physiologically whites and blacks were so different that they must have had separate origins.

Smyth sought reforms within the system of slavery for more humane treatment of slaves, but he never challenged the system itself. He was a Unionist until the shots were fired on Fort Sumter. He then became an ardent Confederate and a bitter opponent of his old colleagues in the North. He died in Charleston on August 20, 1873. ERSKINE CLARKE

Clarke, Erskine. *Our Southern Zion: A History of Calvinism in the South Carolina Low Country, 1690–1990.* Tuscaloosa: University of Alabama Press, 1996.

Smyth, Thomas. *Autobiographical Notes, Letters and Reflections.* Edited by Louisa Cheves Stoney. Charleston, S.C.: Walker, Evans & Cogswell, 1914.

Snowden, Mary Amarinthia (1819–1898). Philanthropist. Snowden was born in Charleston on September 10, 1819, the daughter of Joseph Yates and Elizabeth Saylor. Her father, who ran a successful cooperage, died in 1821, and Snowden's mother moved the family to Philadelphia for five years. After returning to South Carolina, Snowden attended a school at Barhamville, near Columbia, run by Dr. Elias Marks. As a young woman she worked with her brother, Dr. William B. Yates, on the first of her many philanthropic ventures, a home where the poor could receive an education and also be trained for work as sailors. She married Dr. William Snowden in 1857, but he died in the Civil War. They had two children, including the future historian Yates Snowden.

Snowden was a close acquaintance of John C. Calhoun. After he died, she organized the Ladies' Calhoun Monument Association in Charleston in 1854. By 1861 the organization had raised nearly $40,000. Snowden protected the funds during the Civil War, even sewing them into the skirt she was wearing when she fled Columbia in February 1865. It was not until April 1887, however, that a monument to Calhoun was finally erected on Marion Square in Charleston.

Snowden was involved in many charitable activities to help Confederate soldiers. In July 1861 she founded the Soldiers Relief Association of Charleston to provide clothing and hospital stores to the men at the front. After Second Manassas, she traveled to Warrenton, Virginia, near the battlefield, to tend the wounded. Snowden took refuge in Columbia during the siege of Charleston. When Columbia fell, she remained to nurse hundreds of soldiers until they were well enough to return to their homes.

Late in 1865 Snowden returned to Charleston and continued her work for Confederate soldiers. In 1866 she formed the Ladies Memorial Association of Charleston, widely considered to be the first of hundreds of such organizations that were formed in the South after the Civil War to commemorate the Confederate dead. She was also instrumental in returning the remains of South Carolina soldiers who were interred at battlefields in other states. The Ladies Memorial Association established May 10 as Memorial Day and erected one of the first monuments in the South to the Confederate dead at Magnolia Cemetery in Charleston.

Snowden helped the living as well as the dead in the years after the Civil War. As she cared for wounded soldiers during the war, she became concerned about the fate of their families. In 1867, along with her sister Isabella, Snowden founded the Home for the Mothers, Widows, and Daughters of Confederate Soldiers (usually called simply the Confederate Home) in Charleston, the first of its kind in the southern states. Snowden and her sister mortgaged their own house to pay the first year's rent for the building on Broad Street. At the home, housing was provided for poor female dependents of Confederate soldiers, and a school was established for their children. Snowden served as president of the board of control of the home until her death in Charleston on February 23, 1898. BRUCE E. BAKER

Historical Sketch of the Confederate Home and College, Charleston, South Carolina, 1867–1921. Charleston, S.C.: Walker, Evans & Cogswell, [1921?].

Holmes, James G., ed. *Memorials to the Memory of Mrs. Mary Amarinthia Snowden Offered by Societies, Associations, and Confederate Camps.* Charleston, S.C.: Walker, Evans & Cogswell, 1898.

Snowden, Mary Amarinthia Yates. Papers. South Caroliniana Library, University of South Carolina, Columbia.

Snow's Island (Florence County). Snow's Island, in the southeast corner of Florence County, was the legendary campsite of the

Revolutionary War general Francis Marion, the "Swamp Fox." The island consists of highland marsh surrounded by the Pee Dee River, Lynches Creek, and Clarks Creek. Marion occupied Snow's Island from late December 1780 through January 1781, and it is possible that he camped there as early as August 1780. That August he took command of a band of Williamsburg County Whigs who were camped along Lynches Creek at Witherspoon's Ferry, just upstream from Snow's Island. After January 1781 Marion used the island as a supply base, although he was seldom, if ever, there himself. In March 1781 British forces under the command of Colonel Welborn Ellis Doyle raided and destroyed the campsite. In the raid, seven of Marion's men were killed and fifteen were wounded, and British prisoners held at the camp escaped to the safety of British forces at Georgetown. While the campsite was being destroyed, Marion's main forces were fighting another British force under the command of Colonel John Watson, who had the same objective of destroying Marion and his camp. Marion did not rebuild the camp. The exact location of the camp is not known, but it is believed to have been at William Goddard's plantation on the northern part of the island. It is possible that Marion's occupation actually consisted of several temporary camps on and near the island, instead of a single permanent campsite. STEVEN D. SMITH

Bass, Robert. *Swamp Fox: The Life and Campaigns of General Francis Marion.* New York: Holt, 1959.

James, William Dobein. *A Sketch of the Life of Brig. Gen. Francis Marion.* 1821. Reprint, Marietta, Ga.: Continental Book Company, 1948.

Rankin, Hugh F. *Francis Marion: The Swamp Fox.* New York: Crowell, 1973.

Society for the Preservation of Spirituals. The city of Charleston was incorporated in 1783 with the motto "Aedes Mors Juraque Curat" (She guards her buildings, customs, and laws). By the 1920s members of her elite class feared that her cultural and physical landscapes were beginning to erode, so they protected her buildings through the Society for the Preservation of Old Dwellings (1920) and the first historic-district zoning ordinance (1931). Protecting her customs was more complicated, but a group of city leaders decided that they could contribute by collecting the spirituals that were so much a part of their surroundings. Every plantation had its own repertoire of spirituals, so the project was immense. The Society for the Preservation of Spirituals was founded in 1921 with the triple purpose of "the preservation of the Negro Spirituals and Folk Songs, the education of the rising generation in their character and rendition, and the maintenance of a social organization for the pleasure of the members."

The society flourished, touring the East Coast with its concerts, which it performed in antebellum dress. George Gershwin consulted the society when he was working on *Porgy and Bess* (DuBose Heyward was a member). It even performed for President Franklin Roosevelt.

In 1931, to raise money for local blacks hard-hit by the Depression, the society published *The Carolina Low-Country,* which has articles and illustrations by Charlestonians. The book is certainly a period piece, but Robert W. Gordon's article on the spiritual is still considered an important treatment of the topic. The reputation of the society, like that of the creator of "Uncle Remus," Joel Chandler Harris, has waxed and waned through the years, but no one can deny that the Society for the Preservation of Spirituals has completely fulfilled its stated goals. The society no longer gave public concerts in the early twenty-first century, but it sold recordings and gave private concerts and continued to use its profits for charity. DALE VOLBERG REED

Greene, Harlan. *Mr. Skylark: John Bennett and the Charleston Renaissance.* Athens: University of Georgia Press, 2001.

Hutchisson, James M. *DuBose Heyward: A Charleston Gentleman and the World of* Porgy and Bess. Jackson: University Press of Mississippi, 2000.

Society for the Preservation of Spirituals. *The Carolina Low-Country.* New York: Macmillan, 1931.

Soils. Soils are the products of natural processes occurring on or near Earth's surface. Water accumulation and movement, oxygen levels, plant and animal life, underlying rock types, and varying temperatures on rock materials determine the nature and quality of soils. Soils vary from place to place according to the materials and processes that form them. More than 180 soil series have been recognized in South Carolina. Soil associations have been named after the most common soil series occurring in a landscape. The Soil Conservation Service of South Carolina has divided the state into six land resource areas according to soil associations and topographic settings.

About two percent of South Carolina's total land area is contained within the Blue Ridge Mountain region, which includes 387,000 acres in the northwest corner of the state. Acid-rich soils of the Blue Ridge are of a mesic temperature class. Most are naturally suitable for forestry and can become agriculturally prolific with the treatment of fertilizers and lime. Seventy percent of the area is forested with a mixture of oak-hickory and pine. Ten percent of the region is used for farming, primarily truck crops, hay, and corn.

Linking the Blue Ridge province to the Sandhills is the Piedmont. Extending westward from the fall line, the Piedmont area covers nearly seven million acres encompassing almost thirty-five percent of the state. Topography of the region is gently sloping to moderately steep with broad ridge tops and narrow stream valleys. Soils are of a thermic class and have suffered severe erosion due to years of farming. At least thirty percent of the region has been used for farming, while two-thirds is forested.

At the edge of the Piedmont, the Sandhills lie adjacent to the fall line in a belt five to thirty miles wide and covering more than two million acres of South Carolina. Soils have formed from unconsolidated sands and undergone slight to moderate erosion. Dry, sandy soils found in this region are strongly acidic and classified in a thermic family. Organic matter content and inherent fertility are low due to poor retention of water and plant nutrients. Two-thirds of the area is forested, with significant acreage in cash crops, predominantly cotton, corn, and soybeans.

Flanking the Sandhills, the coastal plain is a ten-to-forty-mile-wide belt encompassing nearly three million acres of South Carolina. Topography is slightly rolling near the Midlands, flattening to a nearly level coastline. Soils have developed from unconsolidated sands and clays and undergone slight to moderate erosion. Many soils in this region are poorly drained, although some well-drained soils occur along sandy slopes and ridges. Soils are strongly acidic and loamy in texture (moderately textured), underlain with slightly coarse clayey and sandy subsoils. Soils are of a thermic classification. Inherent fertility and organic matter content is moderate. The area, dominated by the state's agricultural belt, is well suited for farming. About one-half is forested, with significant acreage of cash crops.

Spanning from the coastal plain to the seashore, the Atlantic coast flat-woods area is a thirty-to-seventy-mile-wide land strip encompassing more than six million acres. Meandering streams carve broad valleys through the virtually flat topography. Highest elevations are 125 feet above sea level. Four general soil groups are found in the flat-woods region: loamy, clayey soils of the wet lowlands; wet, sandy soils found in strips near the coast; well-mixed soils of river floodplains, underlain with sandy, loamy sediments; and clayey, sandy soils of coastal-area salt marshes and dunes. Most soils are strongly acidic. About two-thirds of the area is forested, with major farm crops and pastures occupying the remaining portion. BETH PLEMING

Craddoc, Garnet R., and C. M. Ellerbe. *Land Resource Map of South Carolina.* Clemson, S.C., 1966.

Ellerbe, Clarence. *South Carolina Soils and Their Interpretations for Selected Uses.* Columbia: South Carolina Land Resources Conservation Commission, 1974.

Kovacik, Charles F., and John J. Winberry. *South Carolina: The Making of a Landscape.* 1987. Reprint, Columbia: University of South Carolina Press, 1989.

Smith, Bill R., and D. C. Hallbrick. *General Soil Map of South Carolina.* Clemson: South Carolina Agricultural Experiment Station, 1979.

South Carolina Water Resources Commission. *South Carolina Water Assessment.* Columbia: by the author, 1983.

Sonoco. This Hartsville-based international packaging manufacturer had its beginnings in the late nineteenth century, when Major James Lide Coker and his son James Jr. became the first to successfully produce paper from pine wood pulp. Following the success of their Carolina Fiber Company, the Cokers made a modest investment in equipment and began making cones for the southern textile industry from the paper produced by their pulp mill. W. F. Smith, who had experience in cone manufacturing with a Massachusetts firm, was employed to help the family set up operations. The paper cones were used in mills to wind cotton yarn at a time when the textile industry was growing rapidly in the South. On May 10, 1899, the cone-making enterprise was formally organized as the Southern Novelty Company with Major Coker as president.

The Southern Novelty Company Plant, Hartsville, in the 1920s. Courtesy, South Caroliniana Library, University of South Carolina

While Coker's eldest son, James Jr., focused on the management of Carolina Fiber, a younger son, Charles, joined his father at Southern Novelty. Charles Coker began as the firm's first treasurer and chief salesman and succeeded as company president upon his father's death in 1918. The company would continue to be headed by a member of the Coker family until 1998. Under Charles Coker's leadership, modern industrial practices were implemented. In a field driven by price and technological change, Coker introduced a research department to constantly improve production efficiency and quality, a professional sales staff, and the concept of long-range planning to the company.

Southern Novelty, while closely affiliated with its sister company Carolina Fiber, expanded into producing an array of packaging materials, including cones, bags, boxes, and tubes, to meet the needs of developing southern, and later national, industries. In the company's early years its products and prosperity were closely tied to the textile industry in the Carolinas. During the 1920s efforts to diversify into providing packaging solutions for industries besides textiles were intensified. The company changed its name to Sonoco Products Company in 1923, and Carolina Fiber merged into it in 1941. By the time of Charles Coker's sudden death in 1931, company sales reached $1.6 million in the depth of the Depression.

Charles Coker's sons, James Lide Coker III (president, 1931–1961) and Charles W. Coker (president, 1961–1970), and grandson "Charlie" Coker (president, 1970–1998) led Sonoco in the years that followed. These years saw Sonoco become a vertically integrated paper company, expand into foreign markets, and diversify into further packaging-product lines. It became the leader in composite cans for products such as frozen juice concentrate and in 1980 introduced the plastic grocery bags that have since become predominant in the supermarket industry. In the early twenty-first century the company was packaging products ranging from potato chips to trash. Sonoco is one of the world's largest packaging companies, with annual sales that grew from $17,000 in 1900 to $2.6 billion a century later. NED L. IRWIN

Coker, Charles W. *The Story of Sonoco Products Company.* New York: Newcomen Society in North America, 1976.

Simpson, George Lee, Jr. *The Cokers of Carolina: A Social Biography of a Family.* Chapel Hill: University of North Carolina Press, 1956.

Sothel, Seth (?–1694). Governor. Nothing is known of Sothel's early life except that he was "a discrete [*sic*] sober gentleman" of "considerable estate" in England. In 1675 Anthony Ashley Cooper (later the earl of Shaftesbury), the leader of the Lords Proprietors of Carolina, granted Sothel twelve thousand acres near Charleston to establish a settlement. Before this transpired, Ashley recruited Sothel as a proprietor, convincing him to purchase the Clarendon proprietorship in 1677 and undertake the government of North Carolina, which was deeply divided by Culpeper's Rebellion (1675–1680). Unfortunately, Algerian pirates captured Sothel on his journey to the colony, and he did not reach his destination until late 1682.

For the next six years Governor Sothel ruled northern Carolina, or Albemarle, as it was called, with considerable skill. He chose his advisers from among all factions but preferred men who were experienced, moderate, and Anglican. He avoided controversial issues that might create problems, tried to enforce proprietary law, and managed to train a cadre of new men, including two future governors, to rule the colony.

Nevertheless, conflict with Lord Ashley's successor Lord Craven and with local leaders led to problems. In 1679 Craven assumed control, and the style of proprietary administration changed. Ashley permitted flexibility and independence among his lieutenants as long as they did their jobs, but Craven discouraged initiative, preferring to dictate from London. Sothel, the only proprietor in Carolina, possessed powers equal to those of Lord Craven and was entitled to use his own judgment. In doing so, he increasingly displeased London.

Yet, it was not Craven but a coup engineered from within that brought the governor down. Thomas Pollock, a merchant and deputy to two of the eight Lords Proprietors, took control of the North Carolina colony in late 1689 and forced Sothel into exile. Francis Nicholson, Virginia's governor and a knowledgeable observer, blamed it on "ye Mob out of North Carolina," who were "very mutinous people."

In the meantime other "mutinous people" in Charleston were threatening Governor James Colleton. The governor had alienated the Commons House of Assembly by questioning its legislative authority. In addition, his zealous enforcement of Craven's rules, including limits on local liberty, the Indian and pirate trades, and land-granting and-taxing policies, brought Colleton into conflict with the antiproprietary party, many of whom were old Ashley adherents. This faction, known as the Goose Creek Men, outmaneuvered the governor and discredited him in London. When Colleton declared martial law in 1690, the Goose Creek Men prepared to oust him.

At this juncture Sothel unexpectedly arrived in the city. In the days that followed, members of the Goose Creek faction circulated a petition calling on Sothel to claim the governorship of South Carolina. At first Colleton ignored Sothel, and then Colleton threatened him with arrest or expulsion. In early October, Sothel, on the basis of his position as a proprietor, assumed the governorship with the support of the assembly and the Goose Creek Men.

In December 1690 Sothel appointed new, moderate deputies and summoned the Commons, which had not met for over two years. This body, with Sothel's assent, reaffirmed laws necessary to govern the colony, dealt with the Indian trade, excluded Colleton and his allies from office, and enfranchised recent French immigrants. Finally, a representative was dispatched to London to explain the sequence of events. As governor, Sothel pushed through laws to regulate the Indian trade in South Carolina by prohibiting trade with interior tribes. In addition, the governor was authorized to collect one-third of all fines levied as well as one-third of newly imposed duties on furs and skins. While these actions ran counter to the interests of many of his supporters, Sothel's toleration of the pirate trade reopened the lucrative business to the Goose Creek Men and moderated their opposition to being cut off from the interior Indian trade.

Such policies ran counter to the reform agenda of Lord Craven, who nevertheless accepted Sothel as our "governor for the time being." However, the proprietors soon thereafter reappointed all of Governor Colleton's supporters to office and dispatched Philip Ludwell, governor of North Carolina, to assume jurisdiction over all of Carolina. Sothel and a handful of supporters ignored these proprietary instructions and refused to accept Ludwell's commission when he arrived in the spring of 1692. Divided authority and Craven's refusal to permit key reforms tied Ludwell's hands, and he withdrew in May 1693. Sothel, possibly already ill, departed five months later and died at his home in North Carolina in 1694. LOUIS P. TOWLES

Sirmans, M. Eugene. *Colonial South Carolina: A Political History, 1663–1763.* Chapel Hill: University of North Carolina Press, 1966.

Towles, Louis. "Seth Sothel: Colonial Governor." *Journal of North Carolina Historians* 2 (1995): 52–82.

South Carolina. Warship. At the beginning of the Revolutionary War, patriot leaders of South Carolina worried about threats from the sea. Local officials dealt with this problem by creating a state navy—the most famous component of which was the frigate *South Carolina,* the largest warship under American command during the war. The ship was 168 feet long and 47 feet wide, sported forty guns, and carried 550 men. To obtain such a ship, the state sent Commodore Alexander Gillon to Europe in 1778. A successful merchant, Gillon spoke fluent French and Dutch, had extensive sea experience, and possessed marriage ties to influential Charleston families.

Surplus warships were scarce, but a nearly completed French frigate called *L'Indien* existed in Amsterdam. Through personal connections, Gillon secured a three-year lease of the ship in 1780 but did not get to sea until August 1781. The *South Carolina* arrived off Charleston in December, only to find the city occupied by the British. The commodore then took the ship south to Havana, where he received supplies from the Spanish government. In return, Gillon assisted the captain-general of Havana in capturing New Providence in the Bahamas in May 1782. After a dispute among allies over the spoils of war, the frigate headed north to Philadelphia. The *South Carolina* was refitted during autumn 1782 and left on her second cruise in December, only to fall captive to three British cruisers at the mouth of the Delaware River.

Since the *South Carolina* failed to benefit Gillon's state, the frigate generated considerable controversy. Some questioned as impracticable the idea of defending the state's coast. Many challenged the choice of Gillon to command, particularly since John Paul Jones also wanted the frigate. Most telling of all, the mass of confusing debts generated by the ship remained unsettled until 1856 and clouded the reputation of all tied to the enterprise. JAMES A. LEWIS

Grimball, Berkeley. "Commodore Alexander Gillon, South Carolina, 1741–1794." Master's thesis, Duke University, 1951.

Lewis, James A. *The Final Campaign of the American Revolution: Rise and Fall of the Spanish Bahamas.* Columbia: University of South Carolina Press, 1991.

———. *Neptune's Militia: The Frigate* South Carolina *during the American Revolution.* Kent, Ohio: Kent State University Press, 1999.

Middlebrook, Louis E. *The Frigate "South Carolina": A Famous Revolutionary War Ship.* Salem, Mass.: Essex Institute, 1929.

Smith, D. E. Huger. "Commodore Alexander Gillon and the Frigate South Carolina." *South Carolina Historical and Genealogical Magazine* 9 (October 1908): 189–219.

South Carolina Arts Commission. The South Carolina Arts Commission (SCAC) was established in 1967 as a state agency to create and operate a statewide program to advance the arts in South Carolina. SCAC directs its resources toward making the arts a part of the life experience of every citizen. Funding comes from the General Assembly, federal grants, private foundations, and community sponsors. The SCAC Board of Commissioners is comprised of nine volunteer citizens appointed at large for three-year terms by the governor and confirmed by the state Senate.

Since its inception, SCAC has offered a range of support to artists, arts organizations, educators, and local communities through programs, grants and fellowships, and technical assistance. By the mid-1970s SCAC programs had reached forty-five of the state's forty-six counties. In 1980 SCAC conducted its first "Canvas of the People," a long-range public planning process that was repeated in 1984, 1987, 1992, and 2001. The late 1980s brought the creation of South Carolina's Arts in the Basic Curriculum (ABC) Plan, which focused on the incorporation of the arts as basic elements in the curricula of South Carolina schools. Beginning in the early 1990s, the Cultural Visions for Rural Communities program promoted links between the arts and economic development. Other collaborations led to the development of the South Carolina Design Arts Partnership and the SCAC Folklife program. In 1999 a comprehensive ten-year evaluation of the Arts in the Basic Curriculum project was published, calling for expansion throughout the state. A legislative

Arts Caucus was formed the following year to inform legislators about issues affecting the arts and to advocate for arts funding. JAYNE DARKE

South Carolina Baptist State Convention. The South Carolina Baptist State Convention became the first Baptist convention in the South when it was founded in 1821 at First Baptist Church, Columbia, under the leadership of Richard Furman. The convention headquarters was still in Columbia as of 2004. From the beginning, the convention followed an organizational form brought to the state from Philadelphia by the Baptist minister Oliver Hart. In 2004 there were approximately two thousand churches affiliated with, but not governed by, the convention. Most, but not all, affiliated churches were also members of the Southern Baptist Convention and local associations of Baptists. Identification with any of these bodies was primarily to facilitate cooperation in missions and ministry, and not ecclesiastical control. Messengers, appointed members of affiliate churches who can be either clergy or laypersons and who are free to vote their own convictions at convention meetings, convene annually to do business and debate resolutions of contemporary importance.

Through the contribution of funds, member churches of the S.C. Baptist Convention engaged in missions and shared in the work of seven institutions. In 2004 the list of institutions included three colleges: Anderson College (Anderson, 1911), Charleston Southern University (Charleston, 1964), and North Greenville College (Tigerville, 1892). Previously, from its founding until 1990, Furman University was also associated with the convention. In addition to the colleges, the convention operated Connie Maxwell Children's Home (Greenwood, 1892), and through the South Carolina Baptist Ministries for the Aging, it supports two facilities for the elderly: Bethea Baptist Retirement Community and Health Center in Darlington; and Martha Franks Retirement Center in Laurens. A newspaper, the *Baptist Courier* (Greenville, 1869), and the South Carolina Baptist Foundation are also operated by the convention. Each institution has its own board of trustees, which are appointed by the convention. Other ministries of the convention include a variety of evangelistic programs, the camps LaVida and McCall for children, White Oak Conference Center, various college ministries, the distribution of spiritual and practical resources, assistance in "church planting," résumé services for ministers, migrant and other social ministries, and internship programs.

The historical significance of the South Carolina Baptist State Convention in the formation of the Southern Baptist Convention and other state conventions should not be ignored. Major architects of Baptist life in America—Oliver Hart, Richard Furman, Basil Manly, and William Bullein Johnson, among others—did their creative work in South Carolina. Here, national models for sending missionaries and providing education for clergy were developed. In South Carolina the state convention that became the paradigm for all others in the South was so strong and stable that it was virtually unscathed by nineteenth-century and early twentieth-century Baptist controversies that were quite destructive elsewhere—the antimission controversy, the Landmark controversy, and the Whitsitt controversy. Indeed, not until the fundamentalist controversy of the late twentieth century, which resulted in the formation of the South Carolina Cooperative Baptist Fellowship in response to growing fundamentalism among convention leadership, was there a major division, and even that did not result in significant decline in convention membership. HELEN LEE TURNER

Baker, Robert A. "The Contributions of South Carolina Baptists to the Rise and Development of the Southern Baptist Convention." *Baptist History and Heritage* 17 (July 1982): 2–9.

Clayton, J. Glenn. "South Carolina Shapers of Southern Baptists." *Baptist History and Heritage* 17 (July 1982): 10–19.

South Carolina Baptist Convention. http://www.scbaptist.org.

South Carolina Botanical Garden. The South Carolina Botanical Garden (SCBG) was dedicated in 1992. Located on the Clemson University campus, the SCBG was formed by merging two Clemson departmental outdoor laboratories. The horticultural portion of the garden was established in 1958 to preserve a camellia collection on the Clemson College campus.

The garden's mission, programs, and festivals focus on both environmental and cultural conservation. The 295-acre garden is comprised of woodlands, streams, ponds, trails, and continually evolving specialty areas such as a wildflower garden, a butterfly garden, a flower and turf display garden, a Xeriscape garden, a hosta garden, a piedmont prairie meadow, and heritage gardens. Encompassing one of America's largest daffodil, camellia, and nature-based sculpture collections, the garden is open 365 days a year from dawn to dusk, and admission is free of charge.

SCBG hosts an outstanding collection of nature-based sculpture built by artists working with Clemson University faculty and students. Educational outreach is also achieved through Sprouting Wings, an after-school program for children. Research and display gardens provide study of environmental issues including water conservation, pesticide reduction, plant breeding, turf-grass management, and sustainable and heirloom vegetable production. Buildings such as a geology and natural history museum, the Hanover House (a French colonial plantation home built in 1716 in Berkeley County and moved to Clemson in 1941), and a discovery center located in the garden provide insight into natural, cultural, and historic treasures of the Palmetto State. MARY TAYLOR HAQUE

South Carolina Budget and Control Board. South Carolina has historically been a "legislative state" with a tradition of a "commission" approach to government that goes at least as far back as the State Sinking Fund Commission of 1870. Joining legislators with executive-branch decision makers challenges the doctrine of separation of powers expressed in Article I, section 8 of the modern state constitution.

In 1919 the General Assembly created a three-member State Budget Commission (SBC) to soften its political tensions with the governor over taxation issues. The SBC's objective was to connect the governor with the chairs of the Senate Finance Committee and the House Ways and Means Committee during the budget preparation process. Advance endorsement by key legislators before a proposed budget was sent to the General Assembly was intended to encourage easier adoption.

Act 621, passed in 1948, expanded the SBC into a State Budget and Control Board (SBCB). The act added the treasurer and comptroller general to the new board and consolidated several other administrative units of state government. Since budget preparation is an "executive" rather than a "legislative" power, legal and political challenges to the continued membership of the two legislators have questioned whether the SBCB is actually an executive agency. With a majority of three executive-branch officers, the five-member board composition has survived. Some pressure on its budget preparation role has been reduced by legislation, beginning with fiscal year 1995, that authorized the governor's office to propose an "executive budget."

In 1977 the General Assembly created an executive director's position to replace the state auditor who had acted informally for almost two decades as the board's secretary. The board is reorganized internally on a fairly frequent basis and in 2003 had eight divisions: General Services, Budget, Retirement, Insurance and Grants, Procurement, Chief Information Officer, Strategic Planning & Operations, and Internal Audit & Performance Review. The SBCB employs approximately eleven hundred people who function as the central management agency for state government; who provide selected staff support for the governor's office, the General Assembly, and the judiciary; and who assist local governments and public groups such as state retirees. COLE BLEASE GRAHAM, JR.

South Carolina Chamber of Commerce. The South Carolina Chamber of Commerce is an association organized mainly to promote and lobby the interests of business. The chamber was formed as Organized Business, Inc., of South Carolina in 1940 under the leadership of C. Norwood Hastie of Charleston, a vice president of the C&S National Bank. The first board meeting was held on September 30, 1941, and the group began with 142 directors from a range of business concerns. Membership grew from 2,965 in October 1940 to 4,941 in September 1941 and was over 11,000 by 1950.

The chamber soon addressed issues of importance to the business community, such as reorganizing state government and urging the state to increase education funding. After several name changes, the group became the South Carolina Chamber of Commerce in 1972. By then, the organization was involved in a range of issues: industrial relations, travel protection, tourism, occupational safety and health, economic education, human relations, and environmental control.

During the 1970s the chamber joined with the South Carolina Department of Parks, Recreation, and Tourism to create the South Carolina Council on Tourism. In the next decade the chamber cultivated closer working relationships with local chambers of commerce and established the *South Carolina Business Journal* and *South Carolina Business* magazine. In the late twentieth century the state chamber expanded its business lobbying role by taking stands on such controversial issues as eliminating video poker and removing the Confederate flag from the State House. ROBERT A. PIERCE

South Carolina Christian Action Council. The South Carolina Christian Action Council is a statewide ecumenical agency embracing many of the state's major Christian denominations. It provides educational programs for its constituents and a Christian witness in public affairs. Its origins can be traced to 1933 and the formation of the South Carolina Federated Forces for Temperance and Law Observance. Temperance education and alcohol control provided the focus of activity in the early years. Reorganization in 1951 formally established the Christian Action Council and set forth a broader understanding of the agency's mission. The council became involved in race relations, world peace, and ministry to the handicapped. In the 1950s several black denominations joined the council, creating the state's first racially inclusive organization supported by both black and white denominations. Its collective voice in response to school desegregation was deemed a positive force for peaceful change.

Over the years the council's work expanded, and membership included Roman Catholic as well as Protestant denominations. It addressed a range of issues, including human rights, public education, empowerment of women, hunger, opposition to the death penalty, faith and health, and AIDS ministry. The council's approach to abortion affirmed the sanctity of human life and encouraged member denominations to work out more specific positions. The South Carolina Southern Baptist Convention objected that the position was not staunchly antiabortion and withdrew from council membership in 1997. The council promoted ways to facilitate cooperation between churches on membership, baptism, and other faith and order issues. Through its interchurch cooperation and linkage with other groups, the council's programs pursued a vision of justice for all of the state's citizens. CARL D. EVANS

Spears, R. Wright. *Journey toward Unity: The Christian Action Council in South Carolina.* Columbia, S.C.: Christian Action Council, 1983.

South Carolina Coastal Conservation League. Established in 1989, the South Carolina Coastal Conservation League has been a leading voice in the campaign to protect and preserve the coastal plain of the state. The grassroots, nonprofit organization is officiated by a staff and board of directors with offices in Columbia, Georgetown, Charleston, and Beaufort. Its mission is to "protect the threatened resources of the coastal plain—its natural landscapes, abundant wildlife, clean water, and traditional communities—by working with citizens and government on pro-active, comprehensive solutions to environmental challenges."

League initiatives are aimed at three separate categories: land and communities, clean water, and forests and wildlife. A variety of methods, ranging from research to litigation, are used to accomplish its mission in addition to educational programs and sponsorship of environmental control. Working with businesses and communities, the league has formed alliances with other conservation groups on both the state and national levels.

As advocates for conservative land development, members of the league help citizens and public officials find alternate approaches to community expansion that preserve the essence of the lowcountry and minimize problems caused by urban sprawl. The league has been a source of professional aid and technical insight to commercial enterprises and residents of coastal communities. It also has worked alongside state and federal land managers to combat the threat of suburban sprawl to rural communities by reenforcing long-sighted forest management programs and restoring diminishing forest ecosystems native to the coastal plain. The league has also played a role in helping protect coastal waters and fisheries, representing South Carolina's coastline and waterways in national campaigns for environmental control. BETH PLEMING

South Carolina Coastal Conservation League. http://www.scccl.org.

South Carolina Commission on Government Restructuring. In March 1991 Governor Carroll Campbell appointed the thirty-eight-member Commission on Government Restructuring to devise a blueprint for enhancing the powers of the state's weak chief executive. While reform had often been studied in South Carolina, this effort came in the wake of the shocking "Lost Trust" legislative scandal, which provided a clear pretext for fundamental change. Subsequently, the *State* newspaper published the ambitious "Power Failure" series, which placed the blame for the corruption on the 1895 S.C. Constitution, which permitted the 170 members of the General Assembly to control state agencies by naming the boards that ran them. When scandals broke, the governor was usually powerless to do anything about them.

The report, issued in September 1991, called for a dramatic shift to a cabinet form of government similar to that used in forty states. Almost all agencies and boards would be reorganized into fifteen cabinet departments with directors appointed by the governor. Citing Theodore Roosevelt, the report called for "a strong executive leader, [and] clear lines of authority and responsibility." It would allow the power of the state's executive to match the perception held by voters that the governor is the key mover in government.

Reelected in a landslide on a reform platform, Campbell was in a good position to push for reform. However, the determination of lawmakers to maintain their power and agencies to maintain their independence combined to scuttle the plan in 1992. As key business leaders continued to insist on a government overhaul, a weakened version of the plan passed the following year after efforts were dropped to place restructuring in the constitution. On July 1, 1993, Campbell was given a cabinet of thirteen departments, with the ability to hire and fire at will eleven of those agency's leaders. However, key agencies in charge of highways, mental health, and the environment remained beyond the governor's full control. MICHAEL SPONHOUR

South Carolina Commission on Government Restructuring. *Modernizing South Carolina State Government for the Twenty-First Century.* Columbia: South Carolina Commission on Government Restructuring, 1991.

Young, Richard D. *State Reorganization in South Carolina: Theories, History, Practices and Further Implications.* Columbia: University of South Carolina Institute for Public Service and Policy Research, 2002.

South Carolina Commission on Higher Education. The South Carolina Commission on Higher Education was created by the General Assembly in 1967. It replaced the Advisory Council on Higher Education, which had been created in 1962. The Commission on Higher Education serves as a statewide higher education coordinating body. There are fourteen board members, who are appointed by the governor and approved by the General Assembly. The staff is led by an executive director who is hired by the board. The mission states, "The South Carolina Commission on Higher Education will promote quality and efficiency in the State system of higher education with the goal of fostering economic growth and human development in South Carolina." The primary functions of the commission include: to promote access to higher education; to develop and maintain a process by which annual appropriation requests are based on institutional performance; to review and approve new degree-program proposals and evaluate existing academic programs; to examine and license nonpublic educational institutions; to maintain statewide higher education data collection; and to establish procedures for the transferability of courses at the undergraduate level between two-year and four-year institutions. In 1996 legislation was enacted by the General Assembly to require the Commission on Higher Education to develop a system for the funding of public colleges and universities based on performance in areas identified by the General Assembly. By the 1999–2000 and 2000–2001 fiscal years, all funding was to be based on the performance funding formula. However, for the 2000–2001 fiscal year, only three percent of funding for public colleges and universities was determined by performance scores. JOHN WESLEY LOWERY

Sheheen, Fred R. "Higher Education in South Carolina." In *The Organization of Public Education in South Carolina,* edited by John H. Walker, Michael D. Richardson, and Thomas I. Parks. Dubuque, Iowa: Kendall/Hunt, 1992.

South Carolina Department of Archives and History. Located in Columbia, the South Carolina Department of Archives and History (SCDAH) is a state agency responsible for collecting the valuable public records of South Carolina. The General Assembly established the Public Records Commission in 1891 to obtain copies of South Carolina records in the British Public Records Office and created the South Carolina Historical Commission in 1894 to preserve them. In 1905 the General Assembly expanded the mission of the Historical Commission, making it responsible for the state's archives, and authorized the hiring of a full-time secretary to take charge of all noncurrent state government records. In 1935 the Historical Commission relocated from the State House to the World War Memorial Building in Columbia. Twenty-five years later, in 1960, the commission moved into a facility at the corner of Senate and Bull Streets. The name of the agency was changed to the South Carolina Department of Archives and History in 1967. Since 1998 the department has occupied a state-of-the-art building at 8301 Parklane Road, the Archives and History Center, which also houses the state's Historic Preservation Office.

Services of the SCDAH encompass historic preservation, history education, historical research, publications, records management, and records conservation. As of 2006 the archives held over 27,000 cubic feet of records that spanned more than three hundred years of South Carolina history. In addition to state funding, the SCDAH receives support from a private nonprofit organization, the S.C. Archives and History Foundation. WILLIAM P. MORRIS

South Carolina Department of Commerce. The South Carolina Department of Commerce administers South Carolina's economic development program. Created by the General Assembly in 1945 as the Department of Research, Planning, and Development and later known as the State Development Board, it had five governor-appointed members.

During the late 1940s and 1950s the board sponsored industrial recruitment missions through which governors and state businessmen cultivated relationships with northern corporate executives. It also provided site location data and coordinated state and local development efforts. In early years the board lacked funding and staffing and held extraneous responsibilities for geological studies and promoting tourism.

Governor Ernest Hollings was the first governor to make economic development a central concern. He increased board membership to fourteen, and it began concentrating its efforts on industry recruitment. Board directors and chairmen began working more closely with governors.

In 1993 the Development Board became the S.C. Department of Commerce. Since then, economic development has remained a priority of governors, who have helped create a modernized state economy supported by knowledge-based industries. Today the department has divisions dedicated to industry recruitment, export development, existing industry and small business support, community and rural development, and workforce development. The South Carolina Film Commission and the Public Railways and Aeronautics Divisions are housed within the department.

The department maintains several overseas offices to aide international recruiting and to help state companies reach foreign markets. The South Carolina Japan Office opened in Tokyo in 1983 and is the longest continually operating state office there. The South Carolina European Office opened in Brussels in 1974, moving to Frankfurt, Germany, in the 1980s and then to Munich in 1999. In 2005 the state established the South Carolina China Office in Shanghai. R. PHILLIP STONE II

South Carolina. Preparedness for Peace Commission. *Report to the Governor and Members of the General Assembly.* [Columbia, S.C.], 1945.

South Carolina Department of Education. The South Carolina Department of Education is the administrative arm of the State Board of Education. The department promulgates and oversees state educational policies for the state's schools, as well as providing services, technical assistance, and assessments. The agency head is the state superintendent of education. South Carolina is one of only fourteen states that elect the state superintendent, or chief state school officer. The superintendent is responsible for administering school policy and operating the state's school system. The superintendent is secretary to the State Board of Education, a body of seventeen members appointed by the state legislators and the governor, which acts as the policy-making body for public elementary and secondary education in South Carolina.

The Department of Education was established in 1868 when the General Assembly ratified "An Act to Provide for the Temporary Organization of the Educational Department of the State." The 1868 constitution provided for an elected state superintendent of education, a school commissioner in each county, and an eventual system of public school districts. Justus K. Jillson, who had come to South Carolina from Massachusetts, was the first state superintendent. One year later the General Assembly passed the School Act of 1869–1870, which established state adoption of textbooks and the examination and certification of teachers.

Throughout the early twentieth century, the Department of Education increasingly sought uniformity and equality of standards throughout the state. The first compulsory attendance law, passed in 1919, required that children aged eight to fourteen attend at least four consecutive months annually. Although the law was not generally enforced for some time, schools grew rapidly in number in the coming years.

As the federal government's involvement in education policy accelerated in the 1950s and 1960s, the department increasingly took on a role of administering federal funds earmarked for the state in education. In 1966 the department moved into the new fifteen-story Rutledge Building, two blocks from the state capitol. During the last decades of the twentieth century, the department's programs and services greatly expanded, increasing the scope of its mission. Increased public policy focus on education saw implementation of significant new legislation administered statewide by the department, including the Education Finance Act of 1977, the Education Improvement Act of 1984, and the Education Accountability Act of 1998. In the late 1990s the department took the unprecedented move of taking over a school district, Allendale County, as prescribed by performance standards under statutes.

In the early twenty-first century the Department of Education administered State Board of Education policies in concerns ranging from textbook approval and teacher certification to adoption of education standards and curriculum requirements. The department's stated policy is to "provide leadership and services to ensure a system of public education through which all students will become educated, responsible, and contributing citizens." DAN G. RUFF

McDaniel, Thomas R., ed. *Public Education in South Carolina: Historical, Political, and Legal Perspectives.* Spartanburg, S.C.: Converse College, 1984.

Thomason, John Furman. *Foundations of the Public Schools of South Carolina.* Columbia, S.C.: State Company, 1925.

South Carolina Department of Natural Resources. Officially formed on July 1, 1994, the South Carolina Department of Natural Resources (SCDNR) combined the nonregulatory programs of the South Carolina Water Resources Commission and Land Resources Commission, the State Geological Survey, the South Carolina Migratory Waterfowl Committee, and the South Carolina Wildlife and Marine Resources Department. According to the agency's mission statement, SCDNR is "the advocate for and steward of the state's natural resources."

The General Assembly established the agency to provide for conservation, management, utilization, and protection of the state's natural resources. To accomplish these goals, the agency is divided into several divisions covering different areas of responsibility: Outreach and Support Services includes graphics/duplicating, education, a magazine, and news/video/media; Wildlife and Freshwater Fisheries includes wildlife management, freshwater fisheries, and wildlife diversity; Marine Resources includes policy and operations, fisheries management, public affairs, the Marine Resources Research Institute, budget and finance, and environmental management; Land, Water and Conservation includes conservation districts, environmental conservation, climatology, regional climate center, hydrology/geology, and natural resource information management and analysis; and Law Enforcement covers law enforcement districts around the state.

SCDNR is governed by a policy-making board of directors consisting of seven members who are appointed by and serve at the will of the governor. The board appoints the agency director. The agency's programs receive funding through several sources, including state appropriated funds, revenue (earned from things such as license and magazine sales), and federal grants. CAROLINE FOSTER

South Carolina Department of Parks, Recreation, and Tourism. Created by the General Assembly in 1967, the South Carolina Department of Parks, Recreation, and Tourism (SCPRT) is charged with promoting tourism in the state, operating a system of state parks, and assisting local governments in the development of recreational facilities and programs. Initially governed by a twelve-member commission, SCPRT in the early twenty-first century was a cabinet-level agency with a director appointed by the governor. As of 2002 the agency oversaw forty-six state parks, nine state welcome centers, the South Carolina Heritage Corridor discovery centers, and a wide variety of tourism, economic development, and recreation programs.

The establishment of SCPRT coincided with the dramatic expansion of South Carolina's tourism industry that occurred in the 1970s. Travelers to the state more than doubled, increasing from approximately eleven million in 1966 to twenty-two million in 1974. Tourism quickly became one of the state's leading areas of economic growth, providing an economic impact equivalent to more than eight percent of South Carolina's gross state product in 2002. SCPRT helped to support this growth through a variety of tourism promotion programs, which ranged from technical assistance for private industry and local governments to the operation of a system of state welcome centers.

SCPRT has supported recreational development in South Carolina through its management of the state park system, as well as through planning, technical assistance, and grant programs. It is responsible for preparing and coordinating the State Comprehensive Outdoor Recreation Plan (SCORP), which has been updated every five years since 1965. The agency also oversees the distribution of grants from the Recreation Land Trust Fund, the Land and Water Conservation Fund, and the Park and Recreation Development Program for the planning, acquisition, and development of local recreation facilities. AL HESTER

South Carolina. Department of Parks, Recreation, and Tourism. *South Carolina Comprehensive Outdoor Recreation Plan, 2002.* Columbia: South Carolina Department of Parks, Recreation, and Tourism, 2002.

South Carolina Educational Television Network. The South Carolina Educational Television Network (SCETV) is a state agency providing educational, cultural, and historical programming to South Carolinians through telecommunications. SCETV began in 1957 with a resolution by the General Assembly calling for a study of the use of television in the public schools. A pilot project began with a studio built at Dreher High School in Columbia in 1958. Following the success of the pilot project, the General Assembly established the South Carolina Educational Television Commission in 1960 and named R. Lynn Kalmbach general manager. By 1963 the SCETV closed-circuit network had reached schools in all forty-six counties, public school teachers and state agency employees had begun using SCETV for continuing professional education, and the first open-circuit broadcast station was added to the system, WNTV in Greenville.

The staff of South Carolina ETV, 1960. Courtesy, South Carolina Department of Archives and History

After Kalmbach's death, Henry J. Cauthen became the executive director of the network in 1965 and served as its leader until his retirement in 1997. Under Cauthen's leadership SCETV grew to seven open circuit stations, began the South Carolina Education Radio Network (now SCETV-Radio), built a state-of-the-art satellite broadcasting system, vastly expanded program offerings (including children's programming), began offering higher-education courses for credit over the closed circuit network, and began providing teleconferences for state agencies.

At the start of the twenty-first century, SCETV operated twelve regional stations, which were overseen by an eight-member commission. Since 1977 the ETV Endowment has subsidized state funding with private contributions from corporations and individual donors. The SCETV network began a conversion to digital broadcasting in 1999, and in 2000 WRLK-DT in Columbia became the first digital television station in the state. WILLIAM P. MORRIS

South Carolina Educational Television-Radio. The South Carolina Educational Television-Radio Network (SCETV-Radio) began broadcasting in 1972 when WETR (90.1) Greenville signed on the air, the first transmitter site of what became an eight-transmitter, statewide public radio network. As of 2006 transmitter sites included Beaufort, Charleston, Columbia, Greenville, Sumter, Aiken, Conway, and Rock Hill. These sites have allowed SCETV-Radio to fulfill its mission of providing continuous public radio programming to more than three hundred thousand people per week in three states.

SCETV-Radio began as a unit of the South Carolina Educational Television (SCETV) commission, under the guidance of Vice President William D. Hay, and continued into the twenty-first century to be governed and licensed by this commission. SCETV-Radio has benefited from its association with SCETV since, as each SCETV-Radio transmitter site began operations, SCETV transmission towers and engineers were in place to support SCETV-Radio transmissions, allowing SCETV-Radio to offer statewide public radio service before most states were able to do so. Since 1995 SCETV-Radio has used computer automation systems and content partnerships to offer NPR news, various music formats, and entertainment programming. Automation allowed SCETV-Radio to move to a twenty-four-hour operation day in 1996. Popular, locally produced programs include *Arts Daily, Southern Read, Walter Edgar's Journal,* and *Your Day.* In addition, SCETV-Radio is home to *Marian McPartland's Piano Jazz,* the recipient of two Peabody awards. The program debuted in 1980 and is currently the longest-running jazz series on public radio. The majority of funding for SCETV-Radio is secured through listener memberships to the ETV Endowment of South Carolina. Remaining funding is secured through corporate underwriting and an annual grant from the Corporation for Public Broadcasting. MICHELLE MAHER

South Carolina Electric & Gas Company. South Carolina Electric & Gas Company (SCE&G), primarily an energy firm, was formed by the merger of dozens of companies over the nineteenth and early twentieth centuries. The first, the Charleston Gas Light Company, was formed in 1846. During the nineteenth century SCE&G's predecessor companies engaged in electric lighting and electric streetcars. In 1894 a powerhouse owned by a predecessor company (Columbia Water Power Company) drove the world's first electrically powered textile mill.

In 1930 the Lexington Power Company completed a dam on the Saluda River, which was the world's largest man-made barrier built for power production. The Broad River Power Company adopted the name South Carolina Electric & Gas Company in 1937, and five years later Lexington Water Power Company merged with SCE&G.

SCE&G became fully independent in 1946 after briefly being held by the General Public Utilities Corporation, and it became the first South Carolina corporation to be listed on the New York Stock Exchange. In the post–World War II years, the company built major plants and established a natural gas company. In 1959 SCE&G joined with three other utilities to build the first electricity-producing nuclear power plant in the Southeast at Parr, South Carolina. In 1971 erstwhile archrivals SCE&G and Santee Cooper began a licensing process to build the V. C. Summer Nuclear Station.

SCANA Corporation, a diversified holding company, was born on December 31, 1984, with SCE&G as the flagship company. Although SCANA has ventured into such enterprises as telecommunications, natural gas exploration, and power-plant management, its primary business in the twenty-first century continued to be providing electricity and natural gas for commercial and residential customers. ROBERT A. PIERCE

Pierce, Robert A. *SCANA's First 150 Years: Building on Success.* Columbia, S.C.: SCANA, 1996.

South Carolina Equal Suffrage League. The South Carolina Equal Suffrage League (SCESL) was formed by the Spartanburg New Era Club and other members of the white South Carolina Federation of Women's Clubs in Spartanburg in 1914. Hannah Hemphill Coleman was elected the first president of the organization, which was affiliated with the National American Woman Suffrage Association. The league sought to win over the South Carolina public through suffrage literature, petitions, speakers, and parades. By 1917 the membership of the SCESL had grown to twenty-five clubs with about three thousand members. The formation of a South Carolina branch of the more militant National Woman's Party in that year presented a challenge to the mainstream SCESL, but most of the state's suffragists remained with the league. From 1919 to 1920 the capable leadership of SCESL president Eulalie Chafee Salley enabled the league to actively inform more than ten thousand South Carolinians of the arguments for woman suffrage. The SCESL lobbied the Democratic Party and the General Assembly to put the question of woman suffrage before the voters and later to ratify the Susan B. Anthony Amendment. Although one U.S. senator and a few state legislators sided with the suffragists, the state failed to pass any resolutions supporting woman suffrage. South Carolina did not ratify the Nineteenth Amendment until 1969, but when the amendment became part of the U.S. Constitution in 1920, South Carolina women began voting and the SCESL became the South Carolina League of Women Voters. MONICA MARIA TETZLAFF

Taylor, Antoinette Elizabeth. "South Carolina and the Enfranchisement of Women: The Later Years." *South Carolina Historical Magazine* 80 (October 1979): 298–310.

South Carolina Federation of Museums. Museum professionals who saw the need for museum staff and volunteers to work together to strengthen South Carolina's museums founded the South Carolina Federation of Museums (SCFM) in 1971. Incorporated in 1984, SCFM is a nonprofit professional association that represents and promotes the state's museums. Governed by an executive board elected by institutional and professional members, SCFM sponsors workshops and meetings each year that provide members with specialized skills and knowledge applicable to all areas of museum expertise. The annual conference of the SCFM is held in communities throughout the state, providing members an opportunity to visit and emulate the best of South Carolina's local museums. In addition, members willingly share their expertise with other professionals and institutions through a formal volunteer consultancy service aimed at increasing the quality of museum exhibits, programs, and collections preservation.

In its advocacy role, SCFM worked successfully with the South Carolina General Assembly in 1987 to pass the Abandoned Cultural Property Act, one of the first in the nation. This legislation enables all governmental and nonprofit organizations to claim ownership of artifacts and property in their possession for which they may not have adequate documentation. As of 2006 SCFM had 261 members, including both institutions and professionals. RODGER E. STROUP

South-Carolina Gazette. The publication of a newspaper in colonial South Carolina received its impetus from the General Assembly. The need for a printer in the colony led the General Assembly in 1731 to offer £1,000 to a printer who would move to South Carolina and open for business. George Webb, Eleazer Phillips, and Thomas Whitmarsh moved to Charleston to vie for the money; Phillips and Whitmarsh began publishing newspapers soon after they arrived. No copies of Phillips's paper, the *South-Carolina Weekly Journal,* have survived, and publication stopped after his death in July 1732. Whitmarsh's paper, the *South-Carolina Gazette,* began publication on January 8, 1732, and continued with some interruptions for more than four decades. Whitmarsh was a native of England and a former employee of Benjamin Franklin in Philadelphia. After Whitmarsh died in September 1733, the paper was published by the Timothy family. Lewis Timothy, a journeyman printer

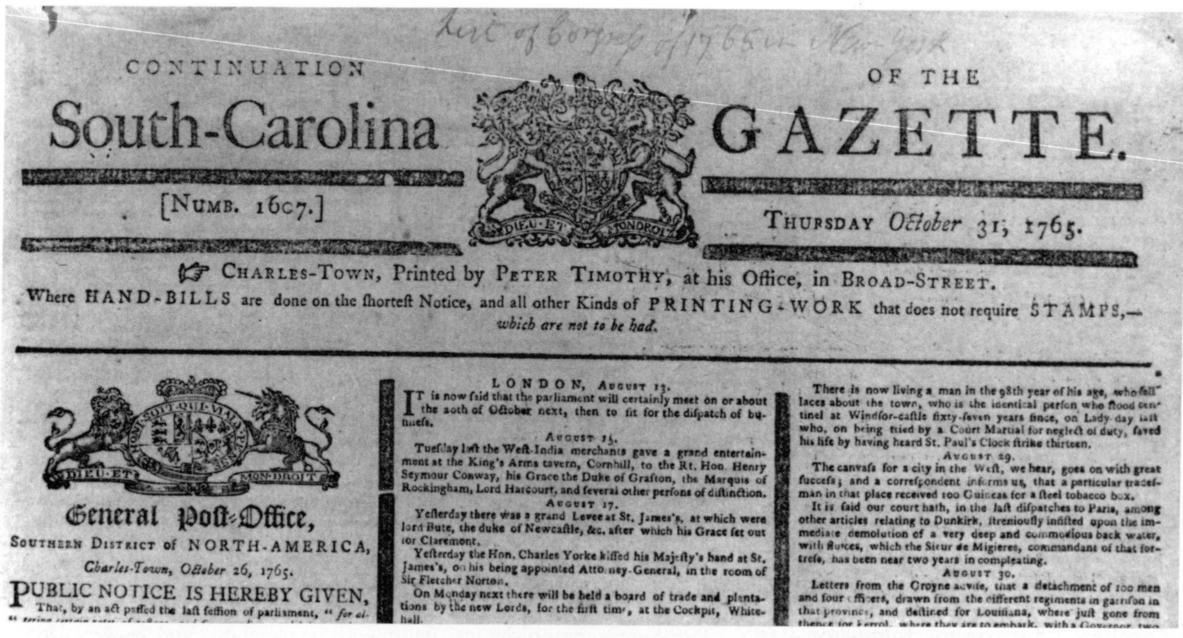

CONTINUATION OF THE South-Carolina GAZETTE.

[NUMB. 1607.] THURSDAY *October* 31, 1765.

CHARLES-TOWN, Printed by PETER TIMOTHY, at his Office, in BROAD-STREET.
Where HAND-BILLS are done on the ſhorteſt Notice, and all other Kinds of PRINTING-WORK that does not require STAMPS,—
which are not to be had.

DIEU ET MON DROIT

General Poſt-Office,
SOUTHERN DISTRICT of NORTH-AMERICA,
Charles-Town, October 26, 1765.

PUBLIC NOTICE IS HEREBY GIVEN,
That, by an act paſſed the laſt ſeſſion of parliament, "*for al-*

LONDON, AUGUST 13.

IT is now ſaid that the parliament will certainly meet on or about the 20th of October next, then to ſit for the diſpatch of buſineſs.

AUGUST 15.

Tueſday laſt the Weſt-India merchants gave a grand entertainment at the King's Arms tavern, Cornhill, to the Rt. Hon. Henry Seymour Conway, his Grace the Duke of Grafton, the Marquis of Rockingham, Lord Harcourt, and ſeveral other perſons of diſtinction.

AUGUST 17.

Yeſterday there was a grand Levee at St. James's, at which were lord Bute, the duke of Newcaſtle, &c. after which his Grace ſet out for Claremont.

Yeſterday the Hon. Charles Yorke kiſſed his Majeſty's hand at St. James's, on his being appointed Attorney-General, in the room of Sir Fletcher Norton.

On Monday next there will be held a board of trade and plantations by the new Lords, for the firſt time, at the Cockpit, Whitehall.

There is now living a man in the 98th year of his age, who ſells laces about the town, who is the identical perſon who ſtood centinel at Windſor-caſtle ſixty-ſeven years ſince, on Lady-day laſt who, on being tried by a Court Martial for neglect of duty, ſaved his life by having heard St. Paul's Clock ſtrike thirteen.

AUGUST 29.

The canvaſs for a city in the Weſt, we hear, goes on with great ſucceſs; and a correſpondent informs us, that a particular tradeſman in that place received 100 Guineas for a ſteel tobacco box.

It is ſaid our court hath, in the laſt diſpatches to Paris, among other articles relating to Dunkirk, ſtrenuouſly inſiſted upon the immediate demolution of a very deep and commodious back water, with ſluces, which the Sieur de Migieres, commandant of that fortreſs, has been near two years in compleating.

AUGUST 30.

Letters from the Groyne advise, that a detachment of 100 men and four officers, drawn from the different regiments in garriſon in that province, and deſtined for Louiſiana, where juſt gone from

The last issue of the *South Carolina Gazette* (October 31, 1765) before the Stamp Act went into effect. Courtesy, Charleston Library Society from France who had also worked for Franklin, restarted the newspaper in 1734. His young son Peter was designated as his successor. When Lewis died in 1738, his Dutch-born wife Elizabeth ran the paper under Peter's name; Peter took over shortly thereafter and continued to publish the paper until the end of 1775.

By 1764 the *Gazette* had subscription agents in North and South Carolina, Georgia, and Florida. The newspaper had a typical mix of news items, advertisements, reprinted material from other periodicals, and literature. Small woodcuts were published from 1735 onward; the publication of higher-quality images was aided by the acquisition of a new press in 1747. Although the newspaper was generally apolitical, Timothy eventually became a vocal supporter of the Revolutionary cause. The Boston Massacre and blockade of Boston were both announced in the newspaper with heavy black borders. The newspaper printed the names of those who violated nonimportation, and Timothy remained in close contact with Benjamin Franklin and the Boston patriot leader Samuel Adams. The *Gazette* continued to be a strong supporter of the rebel cause until it ceased publication in December 1775. AARON W. MARRS

Cohen, Hennig. *The South Carolina Gazette, 1732–1775.* Columbia: University of South Carolina Press, 1953.

Smith, Jeffery A. "Impartiality and Revolutionary Ideology: Editorial Policies of the *South-Carolina Gazette,* 1732–1775." *Journal of Southern History* 49 (November 1983): 511–26.

South Carolina–Georgia border. On June 29, 1977, an altercation between Georgia law enforcement officers and a South Carolina shrimp boat captain attracted national press and rekindled a controversy that would not be resolved until 1990. South Carolina and Georgia disagreed over the exact location of the boundary in the lower Savannah River, as well as ownership of several islands in that region. At stake in this border dispute was not only tax dollars but also potentially millions of dollars in federal aid. A 1976 amendment to the Coastal Zone Management Act of 1972 allowed grants and loans to coastal states to offset damage expected from the production of offshore oil. This appeal for federal aid forced South Carolina and Georgia to settle a border dispute that had been simmering for two centuries.

Since Georgia's chartering in 1733, the boundary for the southernmost tip of South Carolina had been in constant question. The original boundaries for Carolina stretched as far south as the St. Mary's River, in Florida, and westward to the Pacific Ocean. Georgia's founding charter established the colony as bounding Savannah's "northern stream" south to the Altamaha's "southern stream." During the 1750s South Carolina and Georgia, as well as Spain, laid claim to lands along the Altamaha River. In 1763, at the end of the Seven Years' War, the St. Mary's River became Georgia's southern boundary opposite the new British colony of East Florida.

Border controversies continued, and three commissioners from each state met in Beaufort on April 28, 1787, "to establish and permanently fix a Boundary between the two states." Charles Pinckney, Andrew Pickens, and Pierce Butler represented South Carolina in this convention; John Houstoun, James Habersham, and Lachlan McIntosh represented Georgia. The Treaty of Beaufort was ratified with the following provisions: the Savannah River served as the common boundary with navigation "equally free to the citizens of both States"; the area of land between the Tugaloo and Keowee Rivers (roughly modern Oconee County) was guaranteed to South Carolina; and all of the islands in the Savannah River belonged to Georgia.

Uncertainties remained, as shifting sands and waters contributed to an enormous amount of morphological change in the lower Savannah region, affecting several strips of land including Barnwell Island, Jones Island, and Oyster Bed Island. Also, between 1855 and 1900 the U.S. Army Corps of Engineers and other organizations significantly altered the lower region of the Savannah River to ensure safe navigation for deep-draft vessels. As boundary questions continued between the two states, a 1922 U.S. Supreme Court ruling placed the line at the Savannah "midway between the main banks of the river." On June 25, 1990, the U.S. Supreme Court ruled in favor of South Carolina and awarded ownership of most of the islands in the Savannah, adding three thousand acres of land and seven thousand acres of water to the Palmetto State. DONALD O. STEWART

De Vorsey, Louis, Jr. *The Georgia–South Carolina Boundary: A Problem in Historical Geography.* Athens: University of Georgia Press, 1982.

Georgia v. South Carolina, 497 U.S. 376 (1990).

South Carolina Good Roads Association. The South Carolina Good Roads Association (SCGRA) was a catalyst for change in transportation policy and road construction in the late 1890s and the first four decades of the twentieth century. Seventy promoters of good roads from all parts of the state founded the organization at Columbia on November 10, 1897. General Roy Stone, director of the U.S. Office of Road Inquiry, encouraged its formation, as he did similar organizations in other states. The SCGRA originally emphasized the construction and maintenance of quality sand-clay, stone, or macadam farm-to-market roads, and it had strong backing from various railroads, especially the Southern Railway. But by the 1920s it focused more on the promotion of professionally built and maintained hard-surfaced intrastate and interstate trunk-line highways.

The SCGRA chose Colonel Jonathan P. Thomas and C. C. Wilson, a civil engineer from Columbia, as its first president and its first secretary, respectively. The association met at least annually in January or February, usually in Columbia, with the governor, state legislators, and other state and national officials often attending and actively participating in the program, especially in its early years. Good-roads promoters, civil engineers, and dealers connected with road-materials and road-building equipment were prominent members.

The SCGRA was among the first South Carolina organizations to advocate professionally built and maintained roads, a state highway commission, and a powerful state highway department at a time when the general public was slow to accept these innovations. The SCGRA had strong ties to other South Carolina and regional good-roads organizations, the U.S. Department of Agriculture's Bureau of Public Roads (founded in 1893), American Automobile Association (founded in 1902), American Association for Highway Improvement (1910–1917), and the American Association of State Highway Officials (founded in 1914). KENNETH E. PETERS

Hilles, William C. "The Good Roads Movement in the United States, 1880–1916." Master's thesis, Duke University, 1958.

Moore, John Hammond. *The South Carolina Highway Department, 1917–1987.* Columbia: University of South Carolina Press, 1987.

Preston, Howard Lawrence. *Dirt Roads to Dixie: Accessibility and Modernization in the South, 1885–1935.* Knoxville: University of Tennessee Press, 1991.

Suttles, William L. "The Struggle for State Control of Highways in South Carolina, 1908–1930." Master's thesis, University of South Carolina, 1971.

South Carolina Highway Patrol. Operating under the South Carolina Department of Public Safety, the South Carolina Highway Patrol is a law enforcement organization that concentrates on traffic violations. The State Highway Patrol was originally a field unit of the State Highway Department's Motor Vehicle Division. The patrol began operation in 1930 with a sixty-nine-person staff, including forty-nine patrolmen. Originally troopers were given uniforms, badges, guns, summons books, and motorcycles. They received their first formal training in 1932. Motorcycles were soon replaced by cars, and in 1953 the patrol became a separate division in the department.

The existence and duties of the patrol were contentious almost from its founding. Governor Olin D. Johnston sought to replace the patrol with a state police force, as did Governor Burnet Maybank. Chief Commissioner Claude McMillian outlined plans to reorganize the patrol after pressure from Governor Strom Thurmond, but adroit legislative maneuvering by Thurmond led to legislation that gave patrolmen the same enforcement powers as deputies and required them to help sheriffs when asked.

The patrol also was under federal pressure to integrate racially. In 1967 a Newberry County native, U.S. Marine Corps veteran Israel Brooks, Jr., became the first African American trooper. Within five years six more blacks were sworn in. In 1974 the U.S. Department of Justice urged the patrol to revise its testing and recruiting program, and three years later the patrol accepted female troopers for assignment.

In 1993 the Department of Public Safety was created, and the patrol became part of it. By the first years of the twenty-first century there were more than nine hundred troopers patrolling the state's highways. Patrol persons underwent extensive training at the State Criminal Justice Academy for hazardous duties. ROBERT A. PIERCE

Moore, John Hammond. *The South Carolina Highway Department, 1919–1987.* Columbia: University of South Carolina Press, 1987.

Smith, Michael George. "A Historical Perspective of the S.C. Highway Patrol." Master's thesis, University of South Carolina, 1997.

South Carolina Historical Society. Located in Charleston, the South Carolina Historical Society is the state's oldest historical society and one of South Carolina's largest private manuscript archives. James Louis Petigru and several prominent Charleston residents founded the organization in 1855 with the mission "to collect information respecting every portion of our State, to preserve it, and when deemed advisable to publish it." To this end the organization's founders established a noncirculating research library.

In 1901 Mabel Webber was the society's secretary, treasurer, and librarian, and its collections were housed in the Charleston Library Society's building. Courtesy, South Carolina Historical Society

The society held its first formal meeting on Carolina Day, June 28, 1855, and was incorporated in 1856. In 1860 it moved a portion of its collections to the Robert Mills Fireproof Building on Meeting Street. This compilation was lost during or immediately following the Civil War. Frederick A. Porcher, the society's first recording secretary, saved much of the organization's collection by storing it at the College of Charleston's library. The society met once between 1861 and 1875, when it resumed regular meetings and moved its collection to the Charleston Library Society, where it remained until 1943. The society leased portions of the Robert Mills Fireproof Building from Charleston County for its operations during that year and in 1968 became the sole occupant of the building. Charleston County deeded the building to the society in 1980, and as of 2006 that location remained its headquarters.

In 1857 the organization began publishing manuscripts related to South Carolina history. That year it issued the *Collections of the South Carolina Historical Society, Volume I,* the first in a series of five volumes published. In 1900 the society began publication of the *South Carolina Historical and Genealogical Magazine,* and in 1952 the word "genealogical" was dropped from the title. For more than one hundred years the *South Carolina Historical Magazine* has published original scholarship and edited documents concerning South Carolina history. In 1985 the society began publication of *Carologue,* a general-interest magazine distributed to its approximately 3,800 members. W. ERIC EMERSON

South Carolina Inter-State and West Indian Exposition. Held in Charleston from December 1, 1901, to June 20, 1902, the West Indian Exposition followed world's fairs in other southern cities such as Atlanta (1881, 1895), New Orleans (1884–1886), and Nashville (1897). While many of the city's traditional merchants and bankers were uninterested, the idea gained support from the city's progressive young businessmen. Under the leadership of Frederick C. Wagener, Charleston's Exposition Company raised money through private and corporate subscriptions to stock, a municipal bond issue, state government, and donations of convict labor. The company acquired the lands of the old Washington Race Course and the adjacent Lowndes farm, lying north of the city along the Ashley River. The company hired Bradford Lee Gilbert, a New York–based architect and the supervising architect of Atlanta's Cotton States Exposition (1895), to oversee the design and construction of the landscape and buildings.

The goal of the exposition was to stimulate trade through the city's harbor, where traffic had steadily decreased since the Civil War. In the wake of the Spanish-American War, the exposition's

The South Carolina Pavilion at the South Carolina Inter-State and West Indian Exposition. Courtesy, South Carolina Historical Society

proponents sought to position Charleston as the principal port of exchange between the United States and the Caribbean and Latin America. However, the federal government did not give the exposition its formal approval until just before the start, and no foreign governments sent official exhibits. Poor weather, a late installation of many exhibits, and a chronic shortage of funds all contributed to the poor financial results of the exposition.

After the end of the exposition, the city of Charleston acquired the eastern portion of the grounds containing the formal court and main buildings for use as Hampton Park. In the 1910s the state acquired the western portion of the grounds along the Ashley River for the new campus of the Citadel. BRUCE G. HARVEY

Harvey, Bruce G. "An Old City in the New South: Urban Progressivism and Charleston's West Indian Exposition, 1901–1902." Master's thesis, University of South Carolina, 1988.

———. "World's Fairs in a Southern Accent: Atlanta, Nashville, Charleston, 1895–1902." Ph.D. diss., Vanderbilt University, 1998.

South Carolina Jockey Club. Horse racing has been a favorite sport in England since the sixteenth century and naturally found its way to the North American colonies not long after their settlement. The earliest record of horse racing in South Carolina surfaces in the *South-Carolina Gazette* of February 1734. During the next two decades the sport increased in popularity in the colony, but it became organized when a group of lowcountry gentlemen founded the South Carolina Jockey Club in 1758.

By the early 1770s race week became the most important time of the year for many South Carolinians. Troubles with the mother country, however, interrupted horse racing, and the South Carolina Jockey Club agreed to suspend its activities for the duration of the Revolutionary War. In December 1783, one year after the British evacuated Charleston, the Jockey Club revived anew with increased membership. During the economic turbulence of the postwar period, the association disbanded in 1788 and 1791 but was reestablished each time.

At the turn of the new century, the South Carolina Jockey Club ushered in what would be called the "golden age of racing." Not only did the club's annual races, usually held in January or February, serve as the high point of the Charleston social season, but they also served as a common meeting place for members of the planter class from across the state. In the ensuing years the races grew considerably and drew the attention of spectators and horse breeders from other states, who entered their horses in the competition. The loss of thoroughbreds during the Civil War and the economic decline that followed led to the demise of horse racing in the state. Efforts by the Jockey Club to revive the sport failed, and the club disbanded on December 28, 1899. Its assets were donated to the Charleston Library Society. SAMUEL K. FORE

Irving, John Beaufain. *The South Carolina Jockey Club*. 1857. Reprint, Spartanburg, S.C.: Reprint Company, 1975.

Sparks, Randy J. "Gentleman's Sport: Horse Racing in Antebellum Charleston." *South Carolina Historical Magazine* 93 (January 1992): 15–30.

South Carolina Land Commission. After the Civil War, South Carolina's Republican politicians recognized that the lack of access to land by former slaves was a serious impediment to the full enjoyment of their newly earned freedom. At the constitutional convention of January 1868, delegates proposed to petition Congress for a loan of $1 million to purchase some of the state's largest plantations for subdivision and sale to landless persons. Finding little support in Washington, Republican leaders pursued a different course. Promoted by the Reverend Richard H. Cain, a black delegate from Charleston and the convention's most vociferous advocate of land reform, the new constitution included a provision for a state land commission. The Republican-dominated General Assembly established the South Carolina Land Commission on March 27, 1869. It was administered by an advisory board consisting of the governor, secretary of state, state treasurer, attorney general, and state comptroller. This body also chose the land commissioner. The commission's goal was to purchase land for sale in plots of between twenty-five and one hundred acres, which would then be sold to landless blacks on favorable terms. South Carolina thus embarked on a unique experiment, using its authority to assist the freedmen in acquiring land.

From the beginning the S.C. Land Commission was plagued by organizational and other problems. The first commissioner, Charles P. Leslie, was corrupt and incompetent. His agents typically failed to inspect the tracts they recommended for purchase. This, combined with bribery and falsification of records, led the state to pay inflated prices for land that was frequently of low quality. Republicans forced Leslie from office in 1870, but his successor, Robert C. DeLarge, was equally disappointing. In addition, the operation of the Land Commission was commonly dictated by politics more than economics. For example, in 1870 the commission purchased land in Newberry County at a premium price to prevent freedmen there from becoming dependent on Democratic landowners. By 1871 approximately one-half of the commission land was in the black-majority counties of Charleston, Colleton, Georgetown, and Beaufort.

Following an 1872 legislative investigation, the secretary of state, Francis Cardozo, was given authority over the Land Commission. Cardozo removed corrupt officials, streamlined the agency's operations, reorganized its records, and introduced many innovations. Ironically, while Governor Franklin Moses's administration was being denounced for pervasive corruption, under Cardozo's leadership the Land Commission began achieving recognition for honesty and efficiency. Even so, a Democratically controlled investigation in 1876 soundly condemned the agency based on its earlier failings, without recognizing the reforms. In his bid to portray himself as a reformer and attract Democrats in the 1876 campaign, Republican governor Daniel Chamberlain (a former member of the commission's advisory board) condemned the Land Commission as ill conceived.

After 1877 the state's white politicians moved the Land Commission away from its original intent, viewing it purely as a source of state revenue. Land was sold in large parcels, and eviction rules were vigorously enforced. Perhaps as many as 14,000 African American families had been settled on commission lands by 1890. Most were unable to purchase these plots, but at least 960 received titles to 44,579 of the commission's 118,436 acres by 1890. Most of the remainder was acquired by whites. Commission lands were largely sold by 1890, and its activities ended shortly thereafter. Promised Land, in Abbeville and Greenwood Counties, is an example of an extant African American community organized around Land Commission plots acquired during Reconstruction. BERNARD E. POWERS, JR.

Abbott, Martin. *The Freedmen's Bureau in South Carolina, 1865–1872*. Chapel Hill: University of North Carolina Press, 1967.

Bethel, Elizabeth Rauh. *Promiseland: A Century of Life in a Negro Community*. Philadelphia: Temple University Press, 1981.

Bleser, Carol K. Rothrock. *The Promised Land: The History of the South Carolina Land Commission, 1869–1890.* Columbia: University of South Carolina Press, 1969.

Williamson, Joel. *After Slavery: The Negro in South Carolina during Reconstruction, 1861–1877.* Chapel Hill: University of North Carolina Press, 1965.

South Carolina Law Enforcement Division. The South Carolina Law Enforcement Division (SLED) is a highly visible investigative agency with origins that date back to 1947. Then governor Strom Thurmond issued an executive order creating the crime-fighting organization with statewide authority. Although no attesting records apparently exist, the acronym "SLED" reportedly was coined by a police reporter for a Columbia newspaper. Thurmond's decision to create SLED came at the behest of sheriffs and police chiefs seeking a centralized agency fashioned after the Federal Bureau of Investigation (FBI), whereby manpower, technical support, and expertise could be utilized. Thurmond's order creating SLED replaced the South Carolina State Constabulary, a controversial quasi-police agency. From its fledgling beginnings of approximately fifteen employees, SLED grew into a state-of-the-art agency with more than five hundred sworn and civilian employees.

SLED's first chief was Joel Townsend, who served for approximately two years (1947–1949) before being replaced by O. L. Brady in 1949. In 1954 veteran SLED agent J. P. "Pete" Strom began serving as interim chief until 1956, when he was named permanent chief, serving at the pleasure of the governor. Considered a national law enforcement pioneer, Strom served as SLED chief until his death in December 1987. Appointed by Governor Carroll Campbell, Robert Stewart took over as SLED chief in 1988. SLED's overall mission is to provide assistance to sheriffs and police departments statewide. SLED is nationally accredited by the Commission on Accreditation of Law Enforcement Agencies (CALEA) and the American Society of Crime Lab Directors / Laboratory Accreditation Board (ASCLD/LAB).

SLED provides investigative and technical assistance to law enforcement agencies on major felony crimes. The agency also provides support services in regulatory functions involving alcohol and gambling enforcement, concealed weapons permits, and private security registration. In addition, SLED maintains a seventy-thousand-square-foot crime lab and provides a centralized repository for criminal records. HUGH MUNN

South Carolina Lunatic Asylum / State Hospital. The South Carolina Lunatic Asylum, located in Columbia, was established by the General Assembly in 1821. It did not open, however, until 1828 due to delays and cost overruns. Its founding was the work of a small group of lawyers, legislators, and doctors, among them Samuel Farrow, William Crafts, and Dr. James Davis, who became its first visiting physician. It is the third-oldest state mental institution in the United States. The original building, named after its architect, Robert Mills, is the nation's oldest surviving state mental hospital structure and a National Historical Landmark. In the early twenty-first century it was occupied by the Department of Health and Environmental Control.

The asylum's founders, influenced by early nineteenth-century British and French ideas of moral treatment and therapeutic optimism, hoped to create a curative institution for patients of all classes. At first, however, the asylum had difficulty attracting patients, and it nearly shut down after a few years. Finances were also a problem. The fees of wealthy patients were intended to subsidize the care of the poorer ones, and counties paid for the care of their pauper (indigent) patients. But this system never worked particularly well, and the state had to provide subsidies periodically. Before the 1860s the number of resident patients was small, never exceeding two hundred. Nearly all were white, and in general nearly half were able to pay for their care. In 1849 the General Assembly passed an act allowing the admission of black patients, both slave and free, but the act had minimal effect. In 1865 only five black patients were in residence.

After the Civil War blacks were admitted to the asylum on the same basis as whites, and widespread poverty greatly increased indigent admissions. From 1871 the state paid the costs of the care of pauper (now called state "beneficiary") patients, which led to a large increase in their numbers. The number of patients was more than one thousand by 1900 and more than two thousand by 1920; nearly all were beneficiaries, and nearly half were African Americans. The asylum changed in other important ways after 1865. Without openly abandoning its curative goals (indeed, in 1892 it opened a training school for nurses, and in 1896 it was renamed the South Carolina State Hospital for the Insane), it gradually adopted a custodial function, caring for large numbers of patients deemed primarily chronic and incurable. Conditions at the hospital deteriorated badly around the turn of the century due to grossly inadequate funding and an unworkable administrative structure. Two major legislative investigations, in 1909 and 1914, revealed many of the problems, which included unsanitary conditions and horrific mortality rates, especially for black patients. In 1915 Governor Richard I. Manning instituted major reforms at the hospital, which modernized it and reduced mortality rates considerably. Like many other state hospitals, however, South Carolina's continued to suffer from underfunding, unsanitary and overcrowded facilities, and a custodial culture.

In 1913 the state began to build a separate hospital for black patients several miles from downtown Columbia at State Park. The black patients were transferred to this facility by 1930. The patients remained segregated until the mid-1960s, when State Park became a geriatric facility and was renamed Crafts-Farrow State Hospital. Meanwhile, the Depression of the 1930s and World War II worsened overcrowding and understaffing. By the 1950s, however, when the patient census had reached almost four thousand, new drugs, the phenothiazines, provided hope that many patients could function outside the hospital. By the 1960s and 1970s the antipsychiatry and civil rights movements, community care initiatives, and Medicaid led to deinstitutionalization, a gradual process by which the number of patients in the hospital dropped markedly. In 1996 the hospital was down to 410 beds. By 2003 the average hospital census was under 200, and the Department of Mental Health announced plans to close the facility. PETER MCCANDLESS

Craft, Susan. *Changing Minds, Opening Doors: A South Carolina Perspective on Mental Health Care.* Columbia: South Carolina Department of Mental Health, 1994.

McCandless, Peter. *Moonlight, Magnolias, and Madness: Insanity in South Carolina from the Colonial Period to the Progressive Era.* Chapel Hill: University of North Carolina Press, 1996.

South Carolina Manufacturers Alliance. The South Carolina Manufacturers Alliance (SCMA), a powerful networking, information, and lobbying group for the state's varied manufacturing industries, began as an organization for cotton mill owners in 1902. The mill owners, who began meeting informally to discuss common problems, such as production, availability of labor, and work hours, eventually formed the Cotton Manufacturers Association of South Carolina. The association launched a membership drive in 1926 and soon boasted twenty-one working committees, including the Cotton Committee, which sponsored the popular annual Maid of Cotton contest. The group's first paid lobbyist was hired in the late 1920s, and the association eventually became a visible and powerful voice for the textile industry. The organization supported laws for compulsory education, encouraged reduction of taxes on mills, opposed employing children under age fourteen, and opposed a legislated forty-hour workweek during the 1930s. During World War II the association launched a publicity campaign touting the importance of textiles for the war effort.

In 1951 the organization became the South Carolina Textile Manufacturers Association (SCTMA). SCTMA leaders, particularly John K. Cauthen, who served as executive vice president from 1945 to 1970, helped transform postwar South Carolina from an agricultural economy to an industrial economy. They guided state leaders in developing plans to attract new and diverse industry. Additional concerns of SCTMA in the latter half of the twentieth century included improving education, particularly the state's technical-school system; reducing taxes on mills; reducing power rates; environmental issues; and increasing tariff duties on imported products. In addition to lobbying, SCTMA continued to provide forums for the exchange of ideas among managers of the industry.

In 1996 SCTMA transformed itself into the broader-based South Carolina Manufacturers Alliance, whose members represented all manufacturing industries in the state. By 2001 forty-three percent of SCMA's approximately 85,000 members were managers from nontextile industries. SUSAN GIAIMO HIOTT

"SCMA 100th Anniversary." *Southern Textile News* 58 (May 13, 2002).

South Carolina Medical Association. Members of the Medical Society of South Carolina, largely a Charleston organization, founded the South Carolina Medical Association on February 14, 1848, in an effort to organize physicians from across the state. The object of the new association was to advance "the common interests of the medical profession in South Carolina, by promoting union, harmony, and good government among the members, and stimulating their zeal for the cultivation of Medical Science and literature." Dr. James Moultrie was elected its first president. At the original meeting there were delegates from fifteen of the twenty-nine districts of the state. SCMA developed rather slowly both before and after the Civil War, but twentieth-century advances in medical science and public health concerns heightened the need for an effective statewide organization.

SCMA evolved into an influential professional body, providing leadership and support in statewide efforts to combat epidemic and endemic disease, build hospitals, provide vaccinations/inoculations and school examinations for children, improve medical and nursing education, and educate the profession and the public on medical matters. Additional interests have included ethics, medical education, licensure, vital statistics, and the general improvement in the public image of the medical profession. Since 1905 SCMA has published the *Journal of the South Carolina Medical Association,* the oldest state medical journal in the South. In 2000 more than seventy percent of the licensed physicians in South Carolina were SCMA members. JANE MCCUTCHEN BROWN

South Carolina Medical Association. Minutes. Waring Historical Library, Medical University of South Carolina, Charleston.

Waring, Joseph I. *A Brief History of the South Carolina Medical Association.* Charleston: South Carolina Medical Association, 1948.

———. *A History of Medicine in South Carolina.* Vol. 2, *1825–1900.* Columbia: South Carolina Medical Association, 1967.

South Carolina National Heritage Corridor. The South Carolina National Heritage Corridor is a grassroots-led heritage tourism initiative that brings together communities throughout a fourteen-county region from the Blue Ridge Mountains of Oconee County to the Atlantic Ocean along Charleston and Colleton Counties. Receiving congressional designation in 1996 as a "national heritage area" and funded in part through the National Park Service, the Heritage Corridor is more than a regional tourism promotion effort. Using heritage tourism principals, communities build on an existing amenity base through packaging their natural, cultural, and historic resources. Through regional cooperation, communities collectively reap the economic benefit of increased tourism, which serves as a catalyst for business growth while providing greater awareness and incentive to conserve, preserve, and protect heritage resources. In addition to Discovery Centers that help interpret and guide visitors to designated sites within each of the four regions of the Heritage Corridor, two parallel automotive routes run its length and tie together related attractions. The Discovery Route links many significant historic sites and settlements, including mill villages, courthouse towns, battlefields, and military sites. The Nature Route begins with the waterfalls and mountains of Table Rock and the Mountain Bridge Wilderness Area and winds along the western part of the state, including Lakes Russell and Thurmond, and the Savannah and Edisto Rivers, down to the ACE Basin and the coastal plain. The project is managed by the South Carolina Department of Parks, Recreation, and Tourism under an agreement with a nonprofit board of directors. CURT COTTLE

South Carolina–North Carolina border. The histories of the two Carolinas are intertwined and yet distinct. Because of this, historians have pointed to different dates to signify their split. In his early eighteenth century history of the British Empire, John Oldmixon observed: "Tis very well known, that the Province of Carolina has been a long time divided into two separate Governments, the one being call'd North Carolina, and the other South Carolina; but the latter being more populous, goes generally under the Denomination of Carolina."

In 1665 Charles II issued the second Carolina charter that created a vast province stretching from the southern boundary of Virginia (36°30′ N latitude) to near present-day Daytona Beach, Florida (29° N latitude), and extending from the Atlantic to the Pacific. The 1669 version of the Fundamental Constitutions created four counties in the province: Colleton (between the Stono and Combahee Rivers); Berkeley (from the Stono River to Sewee Bay); Craven (from Sewee Bay to the Roanoke River in what is now North Carolina); and Albemarle (between the Roanoke River and the southern boundary of Virginia).

In 1689 the Lords Proprietors instructed Governor Philip Ludwell to call for elections to a legislative body that would meet in Charleston, the provincial capital of the entire province. If delegates from Albemarle County could not participate, he was to apportion their number among the other three counties; the northern boundary of Craven County was to be moved southward to Cape Fear; and he was to appoint a "deputy governor" for "North Carolina." The first meeting of the Commons House of Assembly occurred in 1692 with only delegates from the three southern counties attending. This year and 1712 (when a separate governor was appointed for North Carolina) are dates to which some historians point as the official division of the province.

In 1719 the colonists in South Carolina overthrew the proprietary government and petitioned the crown to become a royal colony. By 1729 South Carolina and North Carolina had become officially separated as royal colonies. Separation led to boundary disputes that were settled fairly amicably (unlike those with Georgia that lasted until late in the twentieth century).

In 1735 the two colonies appointed a joint boundary commission that agreed the boundary should begin at a point thirty miles south of the Cape Fear River. From there a straight line would be run northwest until it reached the 35th parallel, and from that juncture the line would proceed due west to the Pacific. Because of surveying errors, South Carolina's northern boundary was eleven miles south of where it should have been. To correct this mistake, the boundary was extended seventeen miles north of the 35th parallel and westward to the crest of the Saluda Mountains. The final section of the boundary was a straight line from the mountains to the point where the Chatooga River crosses the 35th parallel at the South Carolina–Georgia border. By 1815 the boundary between the Carolinas had largely taken its present shape. DONALD O. STEWART

Edgar, Walter. *South Carolina: A History.* Columbia: University of South Carolina Press, 1998.

Kovacik, Charles F., and John J. Winberry. *South Carolina: The Making of a Landscape.* 1987. Reprint, Columbia: University of South Carolina Press, 1989.

Salley, Alexander S. *The Boundary Line between North Carolina and South Carolina.* Columbia, S.C.: State Company, 1929.

"South Carolina on My Mind." State song. "South Carolina on My Mind" became an official state song in legislation approved by Governor Richard Riley on March 8, 1984. The General Assembly's intention was "to help inspire pride in our State and improve the quality of life among all South Carolinians." The ballad was composed by Hank Martin and performed and recorded by him and his partner Buzz Arledge. Both were native South Carolinians and professional musicians in Nashville, Tennessee, and New York City. Words and music were published in 1979. Martin and Arledge included it in their album *South Carolina on My Mind.*

Henry Grieshaber "Hank" Martin III was born in Columbia in 1944, brought up in Bishopville, and attended high school in Sumter. Nun Ellsworth "Buzz" Arledge, Jr., was born in 1944 in Sumter. The two began singing together while in high school. Beginning in the late 1970s they worked together in Nashville as performers and established Marledge, a music publishing company. Martin worked with the singer Dolly Parton and made national radio and television commercials in Nashville and New York City. He was inspired to write the state song in part by the poem "A Carolina Love Song," composed by his father-in-law, the Reverend Riley Munday, a Baptist minister, humorist, and sometime poet-in-residence at Columbia College. The lyrics evoke the state's natural beauty: "I've got South Carolina on my mind, / Remembering all those sunshine Summertimes, / And the Autumns in the Smokies / When the leaves turn to gold / Touches my heart and thrills my soul / To have South Carolina on my mind, / With those clean snow-covered Wintertimes / And the white sand of the beaches, / And those Carolina peaches. I've got South Carolina on my mind." DAVID C. R. HEISSER

Hladczuk, John, and Sharon Schneider Hladczuk. *State Songs: Anthems and Their Origins.* Lanham, Md.: Scarecrow, 2000.

South Carolina Plan (1944). On April 3, 1944, the U.S. Supreme Court ruled in *Smith v. Allwright* that the white primary in Texas was unconstitutional, stating that when primaries are an integral part of the state election machinery by law or when primaries predetermine the outcome of general elections, they are considered elections under the U.S. Constitution and the right to participate in them is protected by federal law.

In response to the *Smith* decision, South Carolina governor Olin Johnston called a special session of the General Assembly on April 12, 1944. Johnston urged the legislature to repeal all primary laws from the statute books in order to maintain white supremacy in the state's primaries. His reasoning was that if political parties were considered private organizations as opposed to public entities, then their primaries would not be subject to federal law. The General Assembly responded by passing 147 bills in six days separating party primaries from the control of state government. The legislators also approved a resolution proposing an amendment to the state constitution that would delete a section stating that the General Assembly would provide for the regulation of party primary elections. That amendment was approved by the voters in the fall elections and ratified by the legislature in 1945. When the state Democratic convention convened, it adopted a new set of rules for the conduct of primaries that excluded African Americans from voting. This exclusion of African Americans from the Democratic primary would continue until it was ruled unconstitutional by the *Elmore v. Rice* decision of Judge J. Waties Waring in 1947. WILLIAM V. MOORE

Lander, Ernest McPherson. *A History of South Carolina, 1865–1960.* 2d ed. Columbia: University of South Carolina Press, 1970.

Underwood, James L. *The Constitution of South Carolina.* Vol. 4, *The Struggle for Political Equality.* Columbia: University of South Carolina Press, 1994.

South Carolina Public Service Authority. The South Carolina Public Service Authority was established by the General Assembly in 1934 with the power to provide for navigation and flood control on the Santee, Congaree, and Cooper Rivers; to generate electricity; to reclaim swampland; and to reforest the state's watersheds. The prospect of using New Deal funds to build a hydroelectric generating station in the lowcountry excited many of that area's powerful legislators. These men envisioned a small industrial empire in the lowcountry, supplied with Santee Cooper power. They created the Public Service Authority to negotiate with and receive funding from the federal government.

Recognizing that the Public Service Authority's primary mission was to produce cheap electricity, privately owned power companies tried to block the construction of the massive Santee Cooper hydroelectric project in court. In what was just the first shot in a protracted battle between advocates of public power and those in favor of private power in South Carolina, they delayed the start of construction until 1939. During the early 1940s the Public Service Authority purchased several small power companies and began serving residential customers in Berkeley, Georgetown, and Horry Counties. Its attempt to buy the Lexington Water Power Company was blocked when the state Supreme Court ruled that it could not operate above the Congaree River. Courts, however, did side with the Public Service Authority's attempts in the 1950s to sell power to the state's electric cooperatives. A $7.5 million federal loan allowed the Central Electric Power Cooperative to build transmission lines between the Santee Cooper station and the cooperatives.

Relations between public and private power sources gradually became more amicable, and in 1973 the Public Service Authority purchased a one-third interest in South Carolina Electric and Gas's Summer Nuclear Plant. The Territories Act of 1973 limits the areas in which the Public Service Authority can operate. It generates the electricity for fifteen of the state's twenty electric cooperatives and some industrial customers. By 2001 Santee Cooper–generated power had reached all forty-six South Carolina counties. A board of eleven members appointed by the governor administers the Public Service Authority. R. PHILLIP STONE II

Edgar, Walter B. *History of Santee Cooper, 1934–1984.* Columbia, S.C.: R. L. Bryan, 1984.

Pushing Back the Darkness: The Story of Santee Cooper. Moncks Corner, S.C.: Santee Cooper, 1998.

South Carolina Railroad. In the early decades of the nineteenth century, Charleston sought to bolster its economy by attempting to attract trade from the west. One portion of this effort was the South Carolina Railroad, a pioneering part of American railroad history. First proposed in 1821, the railroad was chartered as the South Carolina Canal and Rail Road Company on December 19, 1827. Construction began in Charleston in January 1830; the entire road was built upon piles in an effort to avoid the cost of expensive embanking. The company let contracts to construct the road, and much of the labor was performed by slaves. In later years the railroad owned dozens of slaves to work on maintaining the line.

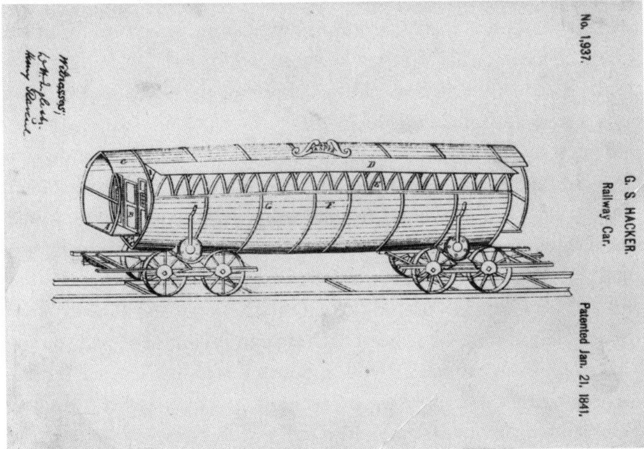

From its inception the South Carolina Railroad experimented with technology and innovation as seen in this design for a barrel-shaped car. Courtesy, South Carolina Historical Society

Despite being an entirely new transportation development, there was little resistance to the railroad's introduction in the state. The vast majority of landowners along its route granted the company a free right-of-way and gladly hired out their slaves to work for the railroad. The city of Charleston, however, initially did not allow the company to use steam power south of Line Street, feeling that the noise was disturbing and fearful of the danger from sparks. When completed on October 3, 1833, the road stretched for 136 miles, from Charleston to Summerville, Branchville, Blackville, Aiken, and ending in Hamburg. At the time, it was the longest railroad under single management in the world.

Although the operators briefly experimented with trains driven by horse, steam was finally selected to power the engines. The first engine built in America for railroad service, the *Best Friend of Charleston,* was built by the West Point Foundry in New York City and made its formal debut on Christmas Day in 1830. The *Best Friend*'s boiler exploded several months later, killing a fireman, but the road remained fully committed to steam.

Buoyed by its initial success, the South Carolina Railroad continued to spend money on improvements and additional track. The piling system proved ineffective, and the entire road had to be embanked. Branches to Columbia and Camden, both part of the original charter, were completed in 1842 and 1848, respectively. The Columbia branch departed the main line at Branchville and passed through Orangeburg, St. Matthews, and Hopkins. The Camden branch departed the Columbia branch near Kingville and included extensive trestlework over the Wateree Swamp. In 1853 the road was allowed to reach into Augusta, Georgia, and in 1858 the road was permitted to join its track to the Georgia Railroad, finally completing the western link desired for decades.

The South Carolina Railroad's track, buildings, and rolling stock were thoroughly destroyed during the Civil War. Rebuilding began immediately, and Columbia and Charleston were reconnected in January 1866. The company, however, quickly became mired in debt, and after a protracted court battle, the company was sold in 1881 to a committee of New York stock and bond holders. The new owners acquired several wharves in Charleston and built or bought additional track. But they were also unsuccessful in making the road profitable, and the company passed into receivership in 1889. It was sold in 1894 to another group of New York capitalists, who operated it as the South Carolina and Georgia Railroad Company. Five years later the road was leased to the Southern Railway. It was then consolidated into the Southern Railway–Carolina division in 1902, ending the South Carolina Railroad's existence as an independent company. AARON W. MARRS

Derrick, Samuel M. *Centennial History of South Carolina Railroad.* 1930. Reprint, Spartanburg, S.C.: Reprint Company, 1975.

Grinde, Donald A., Jr. "Building the South Carolina Railroad." *South Carolina Historical Magazine* 77 (April 1976): 84–96.

Phillips, Ulrich Bonnell. *History of Transportation in the Eastern Cotton Belt to 1860.* 1908. Reprint, New York: Octagon, 1968.

South Carolina Review. The *South Carolina Review* is a literary miscellany featuring short fiction, poetry, critical essays, interviews, and book reviews. Founded at Furman University in 1968, the *Review* was edited and published there until June 1973, when it moved to Clemson University under the leadership of Richard J. Calhoun, who became editor. Other members of Clemson's English department followed him as editor, and selected English department faculty members there served as advisers. For more than three decades the *South Carolina Review* had maintained its role as a vehicle for fiction writers and poets launching their careers, for critics and scholars desiring to share their insights and discoveries, and for reviewers intent on assessing the achievements of creative writers and outspoken scholars.

Among authors whose stories, poems, and letters have appeared in the *South Carolina Review* are Joyce Carol Oates, Fred Chappell, Mark Steadman, and Thomas Wolfe. Critical essays and reviews have ranged widely, from such grammatical issues as the spelling of alright / all right to the legacies of Robert Frost and James Dickey. In between, scholarly essays have examined such writers as Samuel

Beckett, Gerard Manley Hopkins, William Gilmore Simms, and John Milton.

Special issues dedicated to single authors represent the special efforts of the *South Carolina Review* to promote the exchange of ideas and discoveries. Since its move to Clemson, the magazine has devoted issues to James Dickey, Robert Frost, William Butler Yeats, and Virginia Woolf. Entering the new millennium, a special issue, *Ireland in the Arts and Humanities,* signaled the journal's aspiration to embrace both national and international literature. Yet the focus of the magazine remains southern and American literature. JOHN L. IDOL, JR.

South Carolina School for the Deaf and the Blind. This state institution is charged with the education of students with deafness, blindness, or sensory multidisabilities. It began in 1849 as a private school in the home of the Reverend and Mrs. Newton Pinckney Walker in the community of Cedar Spring, near Spartanburg. The first class included five deaf children. By the end of the first year the Walkers decided to devote the school exclusively to the education of deaf students. The first blind students were accepted in 1854. The state bought the school and 157 acres of land in 1856 for $10,759.

By the early twenty-first century the school had grown to about four hundred students with deafness, blindness, or multiple sensory disabilities enrolled in preschool through high school as well as vocational and postsecondary programs. Numerous others have been served through outreach and support services. While the main campus remains at the original location in Spartanburg, regional outreach centers are maintained in Charleston, Columbia, Conway, Florence, and Rock Hill. The school is governed by twelve commissioners, ten of whom are appointed, with the state superintendent of education and the state health commissioner acting as ex-officio members. Besides providing quality educational, vocational, and developmental services to its students, the school provides leadership information and technical assistance to organizations and individuals concerned with services to people with sensory disabilities. HANNAH JOYNER AND WILLIAM P. MORRIS

Brasington, JoAnn Mitchell. *The South Carolina School for the Deaf and the Blind: 1849–1999.* Spartanburg, S.C.: South Carolina School for the Deaf and the Blind, 2000.

Earle, Marie. "A History of the First Fifty Years of the South Carolina School for the Deaf and Blind at Cedar Spring, 1849–1900." Master's thesis, University of South Carolina, 1930.

Saunders, Martha Marshall, et al. *150 Years at Cedar Springs: The Pictorial History, 1849–1999.* Spartanburg, S.C., 1999.

South Carolina Society. The South Carolina Society is a social and benevolent organization established in Charleston in 1737. Its membership has included gentlemen of the highest rank in the history of both the city and the state.

The society was founded by Huguenots, mostly artisans and small merchants, who gathered weekly at a local tavern and collected funds for the relief of their distressed countrymen. From this practice they earned the title "Two Bit Club," but the present name was adopted in 1737 along with its first set of rules. Within a few years the French character of the society was diluted by the admission of English, Scots-Irish, and Scots members. The society's stock steadily increased through the collection of fees, interest on loans, rents on leased property, and donations. It was incorporated in 1751. In the mid-1740s the society began funding the primary education of orphans among its ranks, and by the 1760s it employed its own schoolmaster for this purpose. In 1804 the organization built its own hall on Meeting Street, which was designed for use as both a school and a social hall. After the state established free primary education in 1811, the society closed its classroom, but it opened male and female secondary schools in 1827. The society's principal era of activity came to an end around 1840, when the advent of public secondary education rendered these academies unnecessary. Despite its withdrawal from educational endeavors, the organization continued to extend monetary assistance to the families of members in need.

During the Civil War the society's hall was severely damaged, its records burned, and much of its invested funds lost. Reorganization and repairs were gradual, hampered by economic difficulties and natural disasters. During the early twentieth century the society scaled back its membership, and public programs gradually superceded its tradition of extending charitable assistance. The South Carolina Society is now primarily a social organization. Due to the great demand for inclusion, only descendants of early members are admitted. NICHOLAS MICHAEL BUTLER

South Carolina Society. *The Rules of the South Carolina Society . . . Containing . . . an Historical Sketch of the Institution from the Date of Its Foundation to the Year 1937.* Baltimore: Waverly, 1937.

South Carolina State Library. An independent state agency on Senate Street in Columbia, the South Carolina State Library assists libraries throughout the state in meeting the informational, educational, cultural, and recreational needs of citizens and to ensure adequate access for all. The State Library began in 1929 when the General Assembly created the State Public Library Association and the State Library Board to assist in establishing quality countywide library services across the state. No state funds were available, but grants were obtained to hire a field agent to assist communities interested in starting libraries. The federal Works Project Administration (WPA) was instrumental in establishing a measure of public library service to all counties between 1935 and 1943. The State Library Board inherited the library assets of the WPA and received its first state appropriation in 1943.

The responsibilities of the State Library Board expanded. In 1969 the General Assembly renamed it the South Carolina State Library, with the expanded responsibility to provide public library development, services to the vision impaired and physically disabled, and library services to state institutions and agencies. Since 1990, when Congress passed the Library Services and Construction Act, the State Library has been actively employing new technologies to provide information. DISCUS, South Carolina's Virtual Library, was created in 1998 to provide a wide range of on-line information to users in public, academic, and school libraries. WILLIAM P. MORRIS

South Carolina State Museum. South Carolina's multidisciplinary State Museum opened on October 29, 1988, in the renovated Mount Vernon Mill at 301 Gervais Street in Columbia's Congaree Vista. The development of a museum was initiated in 1973 when the state legislature formed the South Carolina Museum Commission and charged it with "the creation and operation of a State Museum reflecting the *history, fine arts and natural history and the scientific and industrial resources of the state.*" To that end, the State Museum provides displays in the Mount Vernon Mill building as well as traveling exhibitions. It also offers seminars and technical and staff support for museums throughout the state. Permanent exhibitions reflect the central themes of its charge: the geology, flora, and fauna of South Carolina; depictions of the everyday life of ordinary South Carolinians throughout history; the arts and crafts of

South Carolinians; the scientific and technological contributions of South Carolinians; and the impact of developments in such fields as transportation, communication, and manufacturing on the lives of South Carolinians. Additional galleries house short-term exhibitions and small, temporary exhibits—typically offering further explorations of central themes. The museum's "teaching collection" provides expendable materials for active learning related to the exhibits and further enhances the museum's effort to provide a "hands-on" experience to its visitors. The museum derives its funding from state appropriations and self-generated income and is accredited by the American Association of Museums. ROBERT P. GREEN, JR.

The Anderson Automobile exhibit attracts visitors at the South Carolina State Museum. Courtesy, South Carolina State Museum

Bryan, John M., and Hunter L. Clarkson. *The South Carolina State Museum: A History and Highlights from the Collection.* Columbia: South Carolina Museum Foundation, 2000.

South Carolina State Ports Authority. The South Carolina State Ports Authority is a state-owned enterprise established by the General Assembly in 1942 to create and operate seaports in Charleston, Georgetown, and Port Royal. Charleston is South Carolina's principal seaport, with five terminals and a sixth planned for the city's former U.S. Navy Base. As of 2004 Charleston ranked fourth in the United States for the number of containers handled and sixth for the value of its cargo, with $90 million worth of cargo crossing its docks on average every day.

Georgetown's cargoes consist mainly of cement, salt, and steel. Port Royal has also handled bulk commodities but has increasingly become less viable as a port. In 2004 the General Assembly directed the State Ports Authority to sell the Port Royal property and use the proceeds to help pay for the new terminal in Charleston.

Port of Charleston. Courtesy, South Carolina State Ports Authority

The State Ports Authority is governed by a board of nine members appointed by the governor and approved by the state Senate for seven-year terms. It does not receive an annual appropriation from the state, although it can petition the assembly for state support through general obligation bonds for major capital projects.

The economic impact of the state's port facilities has been immense. A 2002 study showed employment tied to the port of 281,000 jobs across the state and $23 billion in total annual economic impact. Each year people in port-related jobs earn $9.4 billion in personal income. Tax revenues annually total $2.5 billion. More than seven hundred businesses, representing every county in the state, use the port system. While many of the companies using the port are large international companies, two-thirds are small entrepreneurs.

The South Carolina State Ports Authority manages its own facilities with its own employees, who are state employees. It operates its own equipment and works through its sales force to attract cargo and steamship lines. As a public port, many transportation businesses such as freight forwarders, stevedoring firms, and trucking companies benefit from being able to enter port facilities as part of their daily work.

The port of Charleston has earned a reputation for efficiency and service. Major steamship lines have been attracted by the port's high productivity and offer regular and frequent service to all parts of the world. This service serves as an economic development tool for attracting new businesses to the state and as a boon to companies already operating in South Carolina. ANNE M. MOISE

South Carolina State Ports Authority. *History of the South Carolina State Ports Authority.* Charleston, S.C.: by the author, 1991.

South Carolina State University. The institution was founded in 1896 in Orangeburg as the Colored Normal, Industrial, Agricultural and Mechanical College of South Carolina. It was and remains, as of the early twenty-first century, the only state-assisted, historically black, land-grant institution in South Carolina. In 1872 the General Assembly had established the South Carolina Agricultural and Mechanical (A&M) Institute under the provisions of the 1862 Morrill Land-Grant Act. For twenty-four years the A&M school was attached to Claflin University, a Methodist institution. Following the separation from Claflin, the new school was supported in part by funds provided by the 1890 Morrill Land-Grant Act.

When the first students and faculty arrived in 1896, the campus was a sparse and unattractive place. The main building, Morrill Hall, was still under construction. There were no paved roads, no running water, and no electricity. During its early years the college was devoted to training black youngsters to be teachers, farmers, homemakers, and skilled artisans. The institution offered instruction in subjects such as poultry science, carpentry, harness making, cheese making, and sewing as well as academic courses including literature, history, and Latin. Most students were enrolled in primary and secondary grades. Few students earned college degrees. All students were required to work. Some were employed on the campus farm, and others worked in the laundry or the dining hall. Many of the early campus buildings were constructed by students under the supervision of faculty.

Thomas E. Miller, the first president of the college, was a lawyer, state legislator, and former member of the U.S. House of Representatives. Under Miller's leadership the college grew steadily despite considerable adversity and hostility to its existence. Among its earliest graduates were the acclaimed research biologist Ernest E. Just and Benjamin E. Mays, who later became president of Morehouse College and a mentor of Dr. Martin Luther King, Jr.

From its inception the institution offered advice and instruction to rural black families through farmers' institutes held on campus and in off-campus programs supervised by the Cooperative Extension Service of the U.S. Department of Agriculture. By 1929 the college had twenty black agents—twelve men and eight women—providing information on crop management, livestock production, insect eradication, canning fruits and vegetables, sewing, and health.

In the 1920s the number of college students increased, while the numbers enrolled in primary and secondary grades decreased. In 1933 the campus high school closed. The Great Depression caused severe hardship on faculty and staff as salaries were slashed and employees sometimes went without pay. New Deal programs combined with private philanthropy helped alleviate some of the worst effects of the economic crisis. Presidents Robert Shaw Wilkinson and Miller F. Whittaker were able to secure federal funds through such agencies as the Works Projects Administration and the National Youth Administration (in which the black leader Mary McLeod Bethune played a pivotal role) to keep the college functioning. The Rosenwald Foundation and the General Education Board (which was sponsored by the Rockefeller Foundation) provided funds to assist in teacher training, to support faculty enrolled in graduate schools, and in constructing the first separate library building, Wilkinson Hall.

The 1940s and 1950s brought dramatic changes to the campus. The college purchased 153 acres of land about two miles from the campus for additional space for farming and livestock. With World War II, large numbers of male students were drafted or enlisted. Following the conflict, veterans flocked to the college, determined to get an education under the G.I. Bill of Rights. The college lacked sufficient classroom and dormitory space to house the flood of students. In 1947 the U.S. Army established a Reserve Officers' Training Corps detachment, and participation was mandatory for male students until 1969. The military science program became a major source of black military officers.

In 1946 the U.S. Army Air Corps veteran and South Carolina State student John Wrighten was denied admission to the University of South Carolina Law School because of his race. With the assistance of the National Association for the Advancement of Colored People and its legal counsel Thurgood Marshall, Wrighten sued for admission. As a consequence of federal district judge J. Waties Waring's decision the following year, the General Assembly hastily created a graduate program and a law school at South Carolina State rather than admit black students to the state's white institutions. Among the graduates of the law school were federal judge Matthew Perry and South Carolina Supreme Court chief justice Ernest Finney. The school was closed in 1966 after the University of South Carolina Law School began to admit black students.

The legislature increased appropriations to South Carolina State in the 1950s in an attempt to create facilities "equal" to those at the state's white institutions and thereby preserve a segregated system of higher education. With additional financial assistance from the General Education Board, new classrooms, dormitories, and a student center were added and other improvements were made to the campus. In 1954 the name was legally changed to South Carolina State College. The institution was fully accredited for the first time in 1960.

South Carolina State students played a key role in the sit-ins, marches, and demonstrations that marked the early 1960s. Hundreds of students were teargassed, fire-hosed, and/or arrested during the protests against segregation. On February 8, 1968, in what has become known as the Orangeburg Massacre, three young men—Henry Smith, Delano Middleton, and Samuel Hammond—were shot and killed by highway patrolmen on the campus. The twenty-seven who were injured were among the students who had been protesting for several days over the persistence of segregation in Orangeburg, particularly at the All-Star Bowling Lanes.

During the last three decades of the twentieth century, the campus population became more diverse with a gradual increase in the number of white and international students and faculty. The program in agriculture was eliminated in 1971, and the campus farm was transformed into a city recreation facility for golf, tennis, and baseball. As of the early twenty-first century, however, the institution maintained its land-grant mission and received federal funds for research and extension projects. It has developed programs in agribusiness, speech pathology and audiology, and criminal justice, among others. There are also graduate programs leading to master's degrees, an educational specialist degree, and a doctorate in educational administration. The institution has added a museum and planetarium, dormitories, classroom buildings, and a campus plaza. In 1992 the legislature designated South Carolina State a university.

WILLIAM C. HINE

Hine, William C. "Civil Rights and Campus Wrongs: South Carolina State College Students Protest, 1955–1968." *South Carolina Historical Magazine* 97 (October 1996): 310–31.

———. "South Carolina State College: A Legacy of Education and Public Service." *Agricultural History* 65 (spring 1991): 149–67.

Potts, John F. *A History of South Carolina State College.* Orangeburg: South Carolina State College, 1978.

South Carolina Wildlife Federation. Founded in 1931, the South Carolina Wildlife Federation (SCWF) was established by outdoor enthusiasts concerned with protecting and preserving the natural heritage of their state. In partnership with the National Wildlife Federation, the nonprofit organization strives to facilitate cooperative efforts of sportsmen and conservationists to advocate sound environmental stewardship and enhance wildlife habitats. Governed by an elected board of officials, SCWF is funded by its own membership and applies all resources to support South Carolina.

Educational programs and alliances with other conservation groups have enabled SCWF to broaden public awareness and establish policies that protect South Carolina's natural assets. It retains a role in assessing agency permits and public policies, investigating resource problems, instigating open forums, offering suggestions for resource supervision, promoting land protection for public access, and assisting groups and individuals with an interest in the outdoors to insure that the activities they enjoy remain available.

Working alongside private and corporate landowners, schools, and communities, SCWF has helped to create and preserve natural wildlife habitats throughout the state. Through the Backyard Wildlife Habitat Certification program, South Carolina claims more certified wildlife habitats than any other state by encouraging private homeowners to create backyard environments in compliance with "natural habitat" specifications. Another SCWF-sponsored program, Schoolyard Habitats and Habitat Stewards, promotes habitat-based learning sites on school grounds. Tokens of the state's cultural and natural history were added to the scenery through a system of landscaping techniques, and large corporations were encouraged to consider the needs of wildlife habitats in land-management decisions through Wildlife and Industry Together (WAIT), a project unique to South Carolina. BETH PLEMING

South Carolina Wildlife Federation. http://www.scwf.org.

South Caroliniana Library. The South Caroliniana Library building was completed in 1840 as the central library building for South Carolina College (later the University of South Carolina). It was the first freestanding college library building in the United States, predating those of Harvard (1841), Yale (1846), and Princeton (1873). The structure contains design elements from several architects, most notably the South Carolina native and federal architect Robert Mills. A typical Mills architectural feature is the curved stairway leading to the second-floor reading room, which was closely modeled after the original Library of Congress. By 1850 the library's collections were considered among the best in the nation. After the Civil War the library's fortunes rose and fell through several decades of unsteady funding. Its collections continued to grow, however, necessitating the addition of two fireproof wings in 1927. Although the collections contained materials relating to South Carolina, there had been no concerted effort to acquire the state's historical documents until 1931, when the Caroliniana Committee was formed in order to develop the "greatest" collection of South Carolina materials and prevent such collections from being placed in out-of-state repositories. The term "Caroliniana" means "things pertaining to Carolina." In 1937 the committee was replaced by the University South Caroliniana Society. In 1940 the university's general library collection was moved into a new facility at the head of the Horseshoe, McKissick Memorial Library, and the Caroliniana collections remained in the old library. Thus, after serving as the university library for one hundred years, the historic building became the South Caroliniana Library—a repository for published and unpublished materials relating to the history, literature, and culture of South Carolina. ELIZABETH CASSIDY WEST

Bryan, John Morrill. *An Architectural History of the South Carolina College, 1801–1855.* Columbia: University of South Carolina Press, 1976.

Hollis, Daniel Walker. *University of South Carolina.* 2 vols. Columbia: University of South Carolina Press, 1951–1956.

South Caroliniana Library. *A Guide to the Manuscript Collection of the South Caroliniana Library.* Columbia: South Caroliniana Library, University of South Carolina, 1982.

South Carolinians for Eisenhower. South Carolinians for Eisenhower was formed by Columbia attorney Douglas McKay to support the candidacy of the Republican presidential nominee Dwight Eisenhower. Its ranks included anti-Truman Democrats, independents, and former Dixiecrats. It secured fifty thousand signatures on petitions to place on the ballot a slate of electors pledged to Eisenhower that was separate from that of the regular Republican Party. The McKay-led organization was joined by another group of Eisenhower supporters headed by William A. Kimbel of Myrtle Beach, who was the state's liaison with the Republican-oriented national Citizens for Eisenhower.

Well financed, South Carolinians for Eisenhower sought with some success to organize the state down to the precinct level. In many counties local Democratic officials worked for the independent slate. When Governor James F. Byrnes endorsed Eisenhower and the candidate addressed 55,000 spectators from the steps of the State House on September 30, 1952, South Carolinians for Eisenhower gained enormous impetus. It looked for a time as if the Eisenhower independents might carry the state.

The outcome of the presidential election was indeed close. Forty-six percent of the state's vote was cast for Eisenhower by way of the independent slate and three percent on the regular Republican ticket, giving Eisenhower forty-nine percent of the vote. The Democrats won a narrow fifty-one percent statewide victory. The near triumph of South Carolinians for Eisenhower in 1952 provided undisputed evidence that the possibility existed of establishing a competitive Republican Party in the state in the years thereafter. NEAL D. THIGPEN

David, Paul T., Malcolm Moos, and Ralph M. Goldman, eds. *Presidential Nominating Politics in 1952.* Vol. 3, *The South.* Baltimore: Johns Hopkins University Press, 1954.

Fowler, Donald L. *Presidential Voting in South Carolina 1948–1964.* Columbia: Bureau of Governmental Research and Service, University of South Carolina, 1966.

Kalk, Bruce H. *The Origins of the Southern Strategy: Two-Party Competition in South Carolina, 1950–1972.* Lanham, Md.: Lexington, 2001.

South Carolinians for Eisenhower. Records. Modern Political Collections, South Caroliniana Library, University of South Carolina, Columbia.

South of the Border. Located just south of the North Carolina border near the South Carolina town of Hamer, South of the Border has long captured the attention of travelers on U.S. Highway 301 and Interstate 95. The beer distributor Alan Schafer (1915–2001) opened a one-room beer depot on the border in January 1950 to sell beer to dry Robeson County, North Carolina. Construction materials for the new business were delivered to "Schafer project: south of the border," inspiring the name "South of the Border."

South of the Border became a welcome first stop in South Carolina for Florida-bound travelers. The expansion of the beer depot to include a twenty-four-hour diner and the opening of the South of the Border Motel in 1954 capitalized on growing tourist business. Amusement-park-style attractions such as Pedro's Plantation, a small zoo, and Confederateland were added, and shops including the Mexico Shop and Pedro's Arsenal (a fireworks store) were opened. Embracing a Mexican theme, Schafer adorned buildings, menus, and advertisements with yellow sombreros and served Mexican-style food. He also created "Pedro," a sombrero-clad cartoon spokesman who advertised South of the Border on billboards stretching from Virginia to Florida. Pedro drew business with puns such as "Pedro's Weather Report: Chili Today—Hot Tamale."

In 1964 North Carolina announced that Interstate 95 would cross the border and intersect with Highway 301 at South of the Border. Expansions aimed at attracting faster interstate traffic began. A ninety-seven-foot-tall neon sign in the shape of "Pedro" was constructed and was later joined by the twenty-two-story Sombrero Tower and the Pedroland amusement park. At Alan Schafer's death in 2001, the South of the Border entertainment complex covered 350 acres and included five restaurants, fourteen stores, three hundred motel rooms, a campground, an indoor miniature golf course, two fireworks outlets, and hundreds of larger-than-life statues. LAURA E. KOSER

Sass, Herbert Ravenel. *The Story of the South Carolina Lowcountry.* West Columbia, S.C.: J. F. Hyer, 1956.

South of the Border. Produced by Lisa Napoli. Columbia: South Carolina Educational Television, 1991. Videocassette.

Stokes, Durward T. *The History of Dillon County, South Carolina.* Columbia: University of South Carolina Press, 1978.

Southern 500. The Southern 500 at Darlington Raceway was the oldest and one of the most storied races on the National Association for Stock Car Auto Racing's (NASCAR) Winston Cup circuit. With a seventy-five-car field, the first race was held on Labor Day 1950. The Californian Johnny Mantz won the six-and-one-half-hour event. It was the first Grand National (later Winston Cup) race contested on a paved superspeedway and NASCAR's first five-hundred-mile race. The list of winners of this Labor Day weekend tradition reads like a who's who of stock car racing: Curtis Turner, Glen "Fireball" Roberts, Richard Petty, Bobby Allison, Bill Elliott, Dale Earnhardt, Jeff Gordon, and South Carolina racing legends Elzie "Buck" Baker (three victories), David Pearson (three victories), and Cale Yarborough (five victories).

The Southern 500 was the ultimate test of both human and machine. The heat and humidity of South Carolina in early September regularly sent temperatures inside the cars well into the triple digits. The unique egg-shaped configuration of the track increased the challenge. Few drivers left the track without the signature "Darlington Stripe" due to contact with the wall.

While the Southern 500 was an important event on the NASCAR calendar, it was also an important happening on the social calendars of many South Carolinians. Since the first Southern 500, when the first Mrs. Strom Thurmond cut the ceremonial ribbon to open the track, the race regularly attracted a sizable contingent of South Carolina politicians.

Perhaps the most storied aspect of the Southern 500, however, was the Darlington infield. In the early days of the race, race organizers encouraged fans to camp out in the infield due to the lack of accommodations in the area. Activities in the infield soon took on legendary status, with makeshift viewing stands flying the ubiquitous Confederate battle flag, all-night partying, numerous fights, and one woman doing her impression of Lady Godiva (using a motorcycle instead of a horse).

Although activities in the infield at the Southern 500 became considerably tamer in later years, the event remained a fan favorite, and a victory in the race was one of the most coveted prizes for Winston Cup drivers. In 2004, however, financial considerations led NASCAR to move the traditional Labor Day–weekend date of the Southern 500 to November. It would be the last Southern 500. The following year NASCAR officials dropped the fall race at Darlington from the Nextel Cup schedule. DANIEL S. PIERCE

Bledsoe, Jerry. *The World's Number One, Flat-Out, All-Time Great Stock Car Racing Book.* Garden City, N.Y.: Doubleday, 1975.

Fielden, Greg. *Forty Years of Stock Car Racing.* 4 vols. Ormond Beach, Fla.: Galfield, 1987–1990.

Southern Aviation School. The Southern Aviation School in Camden, founded in November 1940 by Frank W. Hulse and Ike F. Jones of Augusta, Georgia, trained military pilots between March 1941 and August 1944. In 1940 Hulse and Jones obtained contracts to provide flight training in Greenville and Anderson for students at Clemson and Furman. The program's success led Hulse to seek authorization to provide primary training for U.S. Army Air Corps student pilots. Assisted by S.C. aviation commissioner Dexter C. Martin and the Camden and Kershaw County Airport Commission, Hulse leased Woodward Airport in Camden and obtained an army contract.

In ninety days the company built classrooms, barracks, and additional hangars, and employed civilian pilots and ground-school instructors. Training of army fliers began on March 22, 1941. Among the two American cadet classes of 1941 was Robert K. Morgan, who later flew the famed B-17 bomber *Memphis Belle.* Between June 7, 1941, and February 16, 1942, the school trained 297 Royal Air Force (RAF) pilots, including the late John P. Moss, who became air vice marshal, second in command of the Rhodesian Air Force. After the RAF program ended, American cadets resumed training in Camden.

Paved runways, additional buildings, and new auxiliary fields were developed during the war years, and more than six thousand pilots were graduated. Shortly after the school closed in August 1944, its flying field was covered with surplus U.S. Navy warplanes, and German prisoners of war occupied its barracks. Later the school's war-time facilities were sold, and the Camden Military Academy came into existence. GILBERT S. GUINN

Wiener, Willard. *Two Hundred Thousand Flyers.* Washington, D.C.: Infantry Journal, 1945.

Southern Methodist Church. In 1934 white Methodists in the southern states who opposed the unification of the Methodist Episcopal Church, South and the Methodist Episcopal Church, which had split over slavery in 1844 along with the Methodist Protestant Church, formed the Laymen's Organization for the Preservation of the Southern Methodist Church. They feared northern domination as well as racial integration.

When the reunited denomination was established in May 1939, some four hundred opponents to union met in Columbia on June 7, 1940, to form the South Carolina Conference of the Methodist Episcopal Church, South. They created a denomination without bishops and added to the Methodist Articles of Religion statements on creationism, premillennialism, Satan, and racial segregation. Based on its control of Pine Grove Church in Turbeville, the conference entered suit against the Methodist Church for ownership of the Methodist Episcopal Church, South's church property. On March 12, 1945, federal judge George Bell Timmerman issued a ruling declaring that the bishops of the Methodist Church were the legal representatives of the new denomination and that it both controlled church property and had legal title to the former name of the denomination.

Consequently, the withdrawing group adopted as its name the Southern Methodist Church and established in Orangeburg both its national headquarters and Southern Methodist College. In 1999 the denomination listed 7,686 members in 117 churches stretching from Virginia to Texas. A. V. HUFF, JR.

Southern Quarterly Review. The *Southern Quarterly Review* (*SQR*) originated in January 1842 in New Orleans but moved to Charleston later that year, where it remained until October 1854. It relocated to Baltimore in 1855 and then returned to South Carolina and was published in Columbia from 1856 to 1857. It had the advantage of being not a literary magazine but rather a magazine open to any branch of knowledge. It also had experienced editors in Daniel K. Whitaker (1842–1847), transplanted from New England, and South Carolina's man of letters William Gilmore Simms (1849–1854). It survived longer than any other important magazine except the *Southern Literary Messenger.*

The *Review* was unabashedly a conservative southern magazine, advocating classicism in literature, agrarianism and slavery in economy, and Protestantism in religion. The antagonists were French philosophy, Voltaire, and the leaders of the French Revolution, all of whom were viewed as dangerous to government and to the South's predominant Protestantism. New England transcendentalism was considered the latest heresy imported from German idealism in an attempt to deny the literal truth of the Bible.

Agrarianism was a recurrent topic. George Frederick Holmes advocated plantation economy as promoting simplicity, moderation, patriotism, reverence for the past, and the classical virtues (October 1844). Holmes recognized that the mental discipline gained from the study of the classics was of great value to the professional man. Because it covered such a wide range of subjects, *SQR* had a large number of contributors, including William J. Grayson, Robert Barnwell Rhett, James Warley Miles, Frederick A. Porcher, Beverly Tucker, and J. D. W. DeBow. Authorities to whom it paid homage included Adam Smith, Edmund Burke, Samuel Taylor Coleridge, Walter Scott, and John C. Calhoun. No magazine sketched better the idea of the southern gentleman with his "polished manners" and "moral excellences" (January 1853). More than any other periodical, the *Southern Quarterly Review* sought to define the incompatibilities that would necessitate the South's becoming a separate nation. Its last issue appeared in February 1857. RICHARD CALHOUN

Ryan, Frank W. "*Southern Quarterly Review.*" In *The Conservative Press in Eighteenth and Nineteenth Century America,* edited by Ronald Lora and William Henry Longton. Westport, Conn.: Greenwood, 1999.

Southern Textile Exposition. First envisioned in Atlanta, Georgia, by members of the Southern Textile Association (STA), the Southern Textile Exposition invited local textile representatives to exhibit their machinery, products, and services. Unable to hold the show in Atlanta, the STA urged business leaders in Greenville, South Carolina, to sponsor the event in 1915. Soon a Greenville committee, led by Milton Smith, rented space at a local warehouse, initially attracting 169 exhibitors and more than 40,000 people. With the exposition's overwhelming success, a "Textile Hall" was constructed in 1917 for $130,000 by the J. E. Sirrine Company to host the event. Aided by the influx of northern textile companies, the Southern Textile Exposition soon became a symbol of the state's growing industrial economy.

By 1946 Greenville was quickly becoming the "Textile Capital of the World." Bertha Green, an assistant to William G. Sirrine, advised moving the exposition to a larger facility. With the opening of the spacious new Textile Hall in 1964 and the enormous growth of the Piedmont's textile industry, Greenville soon attracted its first international exhibitors. In 1969 the STA joined with the New Jersey–based American Textile Machinery Association (ATMA) to sponsor the American Textile Machinery Exhibition (ATME), the largest textile machinery show ever held in the United States. By 1973 the ATME became a two-show format every three years. Each show included a variety of exhibits and workshops featuring machinery, supplies, and services. In 2004 ATME met for the first complete exhibition in thirty years and for the final time at Greenville's Palmetto Expo Center. DARREN GREM

Huff, Archie Vernon, Jr. *Greenville: A History of the City and County in the South Carolina Piedmont.* Columbia: University of South Carolina Press, 1995.

Southern Wesleyan University. Southern Wesleyan University (SWU) is a private Christian liberal arts institution located in the town of Central in Pickens County. Founded in 1906 as Wesleyan Methodist Bible Institute, the university is affiliated with the Wesleyan Church, an evangelical denomination with Methodist roots in the American Holiness tradition. The Bible Institute was chartered as Wesleyan Methodist College in 1909 and in 1959 became Central Wesleyan College. Under President David Spittal, the institution changed its name to Southern Wesleyan University in 1995 and entered a period of unprecedented growth.

Regionally accredited, the university offers bachelor's degrees in disciplines ranging from the sciences to the humanities and graduate programs in business, education, and religion. A significant percentage of public- and private-school teachers in the surrounding area are SWU alumni, and the music program carries a high profile in the community as well. In 2000 Southern Wesleyan became the first school in the nation to offer a major in Internet computing. Athletic teams compete on the National Association of Intercollegiate Athletics level and in the National Christian College Athletic Association. In 2002 many of the 2,200 students were in nontraditional programs that offer evening and weekend classes to working adults at teaching sites across South Carolina.

Throughout its history, Southern Wesleyan's Christian mission has been central. Among its distinguished alumni are three who served the sponsoring denomination in its highest office, two of whom (Dr. Roy S. Nicholson, Sr., of Walhalla and Dr. Virgil A. Mitchell of Six Mile) are native South Carolinians. Southern Wesleyan is a member of the Coalition for Christian Colleges and Universities.

The university's Rickman Library specializes in Wesleyana and in upstate genealogical records, including an extensive family database. Also located on the Central campus is Freedom's Hill Church, the first Wesleyan meetinghouse built in the South (1847–1848) and, as a southern abolitionist church, a designated stop on South Carolina's National Heritage Corridor. ROBERT BLACK

Soybeans. An important cash crop widely grown in South Carolina, soybeans were first cultivated as a soil builder and animal fodder. Farmers simply broadcast the seeds and turned livestock into the fields to forage. In the early twentieth century, however, the famed agricultural scientist George Washington Carver discovered the high oil and protein content of soybeans and thus the crop's greater market value. Recognizing the crop's potential to free the state's farmers from "King Cotton," the agriculturalist John Edward Wannamaker worked to develop soybean varieties that would thrive in South Carolina.

Soybeans became a cash crop in South Carolina in the late 1940s. Farmers liked the crop's low fertilizer requirements, soil-building character, and market strength. Moreover, soybeans are a good rotational crop and thus a good fit in both cotton and tobacco cultures. Beans could be planted in spring or early summer and harvested from October to December. The advent of reliable harvesting combines hastened the spread of soybean culture. As the crop could be planted, cultivated, and harvested entirely by machine, labor requirements were few. Low production costs coupled with increasing demand for a broad range of soy products afforded dependable profits for growers. By the early 1960s soybeans were an important part of the state's agricultural economy. In some areas soybean acreage superseded cotton acreage.

South Carolina soybean production peaked in 1982 at 1.8 million acres. But rising costs of fuel, fertilizer, and equipment squeezed soy profits, while competing culture areas in the Midwest softened demand. Added to these trends was the declining real value of soybeans. In 2000 soybeans sold for about half their 1982 inflation-adjusted price. By the end of the twentieth century South Carolina soybean production had fallen to about 450,000 acres worth about

$48 million to growers and ranked tenth in cash value to South Carolina farmers. ELDRED E. PRINCE, JR.

Fite, Gilbert C. *Cotton Fields No More: Southern Agriculture, 1865–1980.* Lexington: University Press of Kentucky, 1984.

Kirby, Jack Temple. *Rural Worlds Lost: The American South, 1920–1960.* Baton Rouge: Louisiana State University Press, 1987.

Kovacik, Charles F., and John J. Winberry. *South Carolina: The Making of a Landscape.* 1987. Reprint, Columbia: University of South Carolina Press, 1989.

Spanish. On a monument at the tip of Parris Island, a tile plaque proclaims, "Aquí estuvo España" ("Here was Spain"). The plaque refers to the colony of Santa Elena, located at this site from 1566 to 1587, but the Spanish presence in South Carolina extended much longer than those twenty-one years. Some of Spain's earliest efforts at exploration, evangelization, and settlement in the present-day United States Southeast took place within South Carolina's boundaries. The Spaniards' activities in South Carolina became more sporadic after their withdrawal from Santa Elena in 1587, although they did not formally relinquish their claim to these lands. In the seventeenth and eighteenth centuries, South Carolina was the launching ground for challenges by the English and their Indian allies to Spanish rule in the Southeast. Spain's presence in South Carolina effectively ended in the seventeenth century, but the late twentieth century saw an influx of people of Hispanic descent into parts of the state once ruled by Spain.

Spanish ships likely had sailed along the present-day South Carolina coast since early in the sixteenth century, but the first documented appearance of Spaniards in these lands took place in 1521, when Pedro de Quejo and Francisco Gordillo stopped in the area of Winyah Bay on a slave-raiding expedition. This visit would have an important influence on later Spanish efforts to conquer and settle the American Southeast, for among their captives was a young man the Spaniards called Francisco de Chicora. Francisco's description of his homeland inspired Lucas Vázquez de Ayllón, a royal official who became his owner in Hispaniola, to request a contract to conquer and settle these lands for Spain. Francisco's stories entered the written record when he and Ayllón visited Spain and spoke with two of the main chroniclers of that age. Ayllón's expedition departed Hispaniola with some six hundred participants, including Francisco, in 1526. Its ships landed first in the area of Winyah Bay, where Francisco and the other Indian interpreters fled from the Spaniards. Ayllón ultimately founded the town of San Miguel de Gualdape on the coast of present-day South Carolina or Georgia. Due to death and dissent, the settlement lasted only a matter of weeks, but despite the grim accounts given by the survivors, the tales told by Francisco de Chicora and Lucas Vázquez de Ayllón inspired European interest in this land for years to come.

Spain's next major expedition to present-day South Carolina brought the Spanish into the interior of the state. Hernando De Soto and his army of six hundred crossed the Savannah River from present Georgia in April 1540 in the area of the Clark Hill Reservoir. The expedition came in search of the chiefdom of Cofitachiqui and its reported wealth. The Spaniards found one of the chiefdom's main towns after they traveled southeast to the confluence of the Congaree and Wateree Rivers and then north along the Wateree to present-day Camden. At a mortuary house in Cofitachiqui, De Soto and his men found Spanish artifacts that they believed had come from the Ayllón expedition, perhaps as tribute or through trade with coastal peoples. More than twenty-five years later the Juan Pardo expeditions that departed from the Spanish town of Santa Elena in 1566 and 1567 and headed northwest across present South Carolina into North Carolina and Tennessee visited some of the same towns and found that memories of the De Soto expedition endured there. The De Soto and Pardo expeditions provided valuable glimpses into the lives and cultures of these inland peoples, even as contact with the Spaniards had a devastating effect on them.

The settlement of Santa Elena, founded in 1566 on Parris Island, was Spain's most significant venture in South Carolina. Its influence lingered after Spaniards abandoned the town in 1587. Occupation of Santa Elena was key to Spain's struggle with France over control of North America's Atlantic coast. Santa Elena was also central to the Spaniards' outreach to the native peoples from a broad region. It served as the launching point for exploration and evangelization efforts, as well as the extraction of labor and tribute. Indians visited and even lived at Santa Elena, where they encountered not just Spanish soldiers but also families. Spaniards and Indians battled one another repeatedly during Santa Elena's Spanish occupation, although its last several years brought a period of relative peace. After Spaniards withdrew from Parris Island, Indians came to live at this site. In the mid–seventeenth century they and the nearby Escamazu sold corn to the St. Augustine garrison, but they never converted to Catholicism or moved into Franciscan missions such as the Guale of present Georgia. Spaniards traveled to the South Carolina coast to conduct this trade, but inland journeys were more rare. In 1628 Ensign Pedro de Torres visited Cofitachiqui to verify reports of white horsemen seen in the interior. His expedition found no such men, whom the Spaniards believed were Englishmen from Jamestown, but they did find an abundance of pearls at Cofitachiqui, as the De Soto expedition had more than eighty years before. Spaniards' fears of English colonization grew more immediate with the founding of Charles Town in 1670 and Stuart's Town in 1684 on Port Royal Sound. A Spanish raid destroyed Stuart's Town and attacked the homes of some of Charles Town's prominent citizens in 1686, but the Carolinas remained in English hands. Spanish influence gradually receded into peninsular Florida until Spain's final withdrawal from these lands in 1821.

The last decade of the twentieth century brought an interesting postscript to the story of the Spanish in South Carolina, as emigrants from countries once part of Spain's American empire entered the state in record numbers. Among the areas with the largest Hispanic population in the 2000 United States Census was Beaufort County, the land where Spaniards once built Santa Elena, a little piece of Spain. KAREN L. PAAR

Bushnell, Amy. *Situado and Sabana: Spain's Support System for the Presidio and Mission Provinces of Florida.* Athens: University of Georgia Press, 1994.

Gannon, Michael, ed. *The New History of Florida.* Gainesville: University Press of Florida, 1996.

Hoffman, Paul E. *A New Andalucia and a Way to the Orient: The American Southeast during the Sixteenth Century.* Baton Rouge: Louisiana State University Press, 1990.

Hudson, Charles. *The Juan Pardo Expeditions: Exploration of the Carolinas and Tennessee, 1566–1568.* Washington, D.C.: Smithsonian Institution Press, 1990.

———. *Knights of Spain, Warriors of the Sun: Hernando de Soto and the South's Ancient Chiefdoms.* Athens: University of Georgia Press, 1997.

Hudson, Charles, and Carmen Chaves Tesser, eds. *The Forgotten Centuries: Indians and Europeans in the American South, 1521–1704.* Athens: University of Georgia Press, 1994.

Lyon, Eugene, ed. *Pedro Menéndez de Avilés.* New York: Garland, 1995.

Spanish moss. Spanish moss (*Tillandsia usneoides*) is a gray tree-borne epiphyte native to the coastal plain of the southeastern United States. As an epiphyte, Spanish moss gets water and food from the air and does not harm the host tree. It is not a true moss but a relative of the pineapple family in the genus *Bromeliaceae.* Spanish moss produces small, yellow-green, three-petaled flowers in the spring and early summer. In mid- to late summer seedpods burst and rely on the wind for distribution. Typically they lodge in the bark of rough-barked trees, especially live oaks and cypress. The plants are a tangle of long stems and slender leaves. The individual mosses can extend over twenty feet in length and are host to red bugs and spiders.

The moss-draped oaks at the Tomotley plantation, Beaufort County. Courtesy, South Caroliniana Library, University of South Carolina

Lowcountry colonists sometimes used Spanish moss as insulation in chinking log houses. Its largest commercial use came as a stuffing for furniture after the Civil War, when it was called vegetable horsehair. In the early twentieth century South Carolina had several moss gins. In 1973 scientists studied Spanish moss taken from along U.S. Highway 17 to determine the levels of pollutants in the lowcountry air. Spanish moss declined dramatically in the state during the 1970s from the effects of a deadly mold, but it has since recovered.

Draped in live oaks and cypress, Spanish moss is a familiar and evocative symbol of the lowcountry. Some find it restful and comforting, while to others it suggests more sinister feelings. JAMES H. TUTEN

Dakin, Patricia L. "A Fragment of Americana: The Last Moss Gin." *Louisiana Review* 10 (winter 1981): 173–81.

Foshee, Anne Gometz. "Vegetable Hair: The Spanish Moss Industry in Florida." *Florida Historical Quarterly* 66 (January 1988): 265–79.

Spartan Mills. Organized in 1888 by the industrialist John H. Montgomery, the home builder W. C. Burnett, and other upcountry business leaders, Spartan Mills was the first textile mill built within Spartanburg city limits. In 1889 Spartan Mills merged with Whitfield Mills of Newburyport, Massachusetts, in an agreement whereby all machinery from Whitfield was shipped to Spartanburg. The first mill began operations in 1890 with thirty thousand spindles and eleven hundred looms, making it the largest mill in the state at that time. In addition to the factory, 150 mill homes were built in a surrounding village called Montgomeryville. The *Carolina Spartan* compared the mills to "a city on a hill, or rather several of them," and residents in and around the city began to keep track of time by the sound of the Spartan Mills whistle.

In 1896 a second mill was constructed with a capacity of 40,000 spindles and the new capability of producing narrow print cloth. Walter S. Montgomery succeeded his father as president of the company in 1902, and he was succeeded by his son, Walter, in 1929. Spartan Mills later absorbed South Carolina factories including Whitney, Tucapau, Beaumont, Powell Mill, and Niagra. In the 1970s, under the presidency of Walter S. Montgomery, Jr., Spartan Mills grew to include thirteen plants and five thousand employees. The company was renamed Spartan International in 2000 and ceased operations in 2001. BRUCE W. EELMAN

Carlton, David L. *Mill and Town in South Carolina, 1880–1920.* Baton Rouge: Louisiana State University Press, 1982.

Stokes, Allen H. "John H. Montgomery: A Pioneer Southern Industrialist." Master's thesis, University of South Carolina, 1967.

Teter, Betsy Wakefield, ed. *Textile Town: Spartanburg County, South Carolina.* Spartanburg, S.C.: Hub City Writers Project, 2002.

Spartanburg (Spartanburg County; 2000 pop. 39,673). The town of Spartanburg was incorporated in 1831, its name originating from a local Revolutionary War regiment: the Spartan Rifles. Its placement was determined in 1789 by the action of Spartanburg County officials, who chose a location for a jail and courthouse on Williamson's plantation in the center of the county. The town was built around an open rectangle of land, which became known as Morgan Square after a statue of Revolutionary War hero Daniel Morgan was erected in 1881.

During the antebellum years, the village of Spartanburg was the commercial center of an overwhelmingly agricultural district in which cotton and corn were the major crops. In 1860 the population of the village stood at about 2,000 in a district with a population of about 26,919, about one-third of whom were African American slaves. The city grew rapidly in the post–Civil War period. A bequest from the Methodist minister Benjamin Wofford led to the opening of Wofford College in 1854. Spartanburg became the terminus of the city's first railroad, the Spartanburg and Union, in 1859. In the succeeding decades several railroads, including the Charleston and Western Carolina, the Southern, and the Piedmont and Northern, made stops in Spartanburg and gave residents rail access to all points of the compass.

The city's commercial and financial role expanded further following a flurry of cotton mill building. The first mill in the city limits was Spartan Mills, built in 1888. By 1909 there were nine mills in or near the city of Spartanburg. The city's growing prosperity was evident in the elegant Victorian homes lining Magnolia, Main, and Pine Streets. Morgan Square was paved and electric street lamps were added by 1890. Several new banks spurred investment, and the Home Water Supply Company opened in 1888, supplying water to fifty hydrants in the city. Other improvements included a street railway system that connected all major parts of the city and many of the outlying mill villages, as well as the construction of two skyscrapers: the Chapman Building in 1912 and the Montgomery Building in 1923. In addition, in 1889 Converse College was founded, adding a second institution of higher learning to the city. A third followed in 1911 with the founding of the Textile Industrial Institute, which later became Spartanburg Methodist College. However, such progress was marked by increasing tensions between the middle-class citizens of the city and the working-class residents of surrounding mill villages. Social and economic strains grew as mill hands came to resent interference in their lives from urban "do-gooders." This friction led mill village voters to support politicians such as Cole Blease, who spouted racism and denounced progressive efforts to reform labor conditions and public health.

In 1917 the War Department built Camp Wadsworth on the edge of the city. The famed Twenty-seventh Division, made up mostly of white New York soldiers, trained at the camp. Despite protests from the city's Chamber of Commerce, the Department of the Army sent the Fifteenth Negro Infantry and the 330th (African American) Labor Battalion to the camp, where they trained in spite of minor racial incidents. Between the wars, Spartanburg remained the legal, financial, and commercial center of the county but was severely impacted by the Depression of the 1930s. With native sons such as Governor Ibra Blackwood, Governor and U.S. Senator Olin D. Johnston, and U.S. Senator James F. Byrnes cast in leading roles in state and national politics, Spartanburg acquired enviable political prestige during the 1930s and 1940s.

In 1928 the first plane bringing mail to South Carolina made its stop in Spartanburg, and in 1930 the first commercial radio station in the state, WSPA, went on the air. But the decade of the 1930s was mostly one of trial. In 1934 Spartanburg was the center of one of the largest strikes in the history of the textile industry. The organized-labor movement never recovered from the disastrous attempt to unionize southern mill hands. In 1940 the War Department decided to locate another army training camp, Camp Croft, just outside the city. Its positive impact on the local economy and its role in spreading the city's name across the nation were even greater than that of Camp Wadsworth during World War I.

After World War II, the city Chamber of Commerce, working in conjunction with state officials, endeavored to diversify the area's industry beyond its dependence on textiles. Although the effort was considered a success, most new plants and businesses located outside the city limits. During the last half of the twentieth century, opposition to annexation severely limited the growth of the city and reduced its tax base. In 1950 county schools were divided into seven districts, with the city comprising District 7. Spartanburg peacefully integrated its schools in 1970 due to cooperation between black and white communities. However, town planners could do little to prevent the growth of suburbs and the subsequent movement of retail businesses from the city's downtown to suburban shopping malls. The city of Spartanburg continued as the area's primary legal and financial center at the same time that it lost its commercial prosperity. Since the late 1960s several attempts have been made to revitalize the downtown, all of which failed. Hopes rested on a 1991 decision by Spartan Food Corporation to locate its headquarters in a new skyscraper in downtown Spartanburg. The effects from the completion of that project had yet to be fully realized by the turn of the twenty-first century. PHILIP N. RACINE

Racine, Philip N. *Seeing Spartanburg: A History in Images.* Spartanburg, S.C.: Hub City Writers Project, 1999.

Spartanburg County (811 sq. miles; 2000 pop. 253,791). Spartanburg County is located in the northwestern section of South Carolina in the foothills of the Blue Ridge Mountains. The area was originally occupied by the Cherokees, who because of the region's abundant wildlife, used it as a hunting ground. Probably the first Europeans to pass through were the Spanish. In 1934 a stone that is believed to have been left by the Spanish explorer Juan Pardo in 1567 was unearthed in a field. After the founding of Charleston in 1670, the land that became Spartanburg County remained outside the permissible area of British settlement for almost another century. The signing of a treaty with the Cherokees in 1755 made land grants available to British settlers, and the subsequent defeat of the Cherokees in 1761 made settlement more secure. At about the same time Scots-Irish settlers from Pennsylvania entered the region, settling along the bottomlands of the Tyger, Enoree, and Pacolet Rivers. Neglected by colonial authorities in Charleston and without an organized government of their own, these early settlers endured sporadic Indian attacks and unrestrained lawlessness.

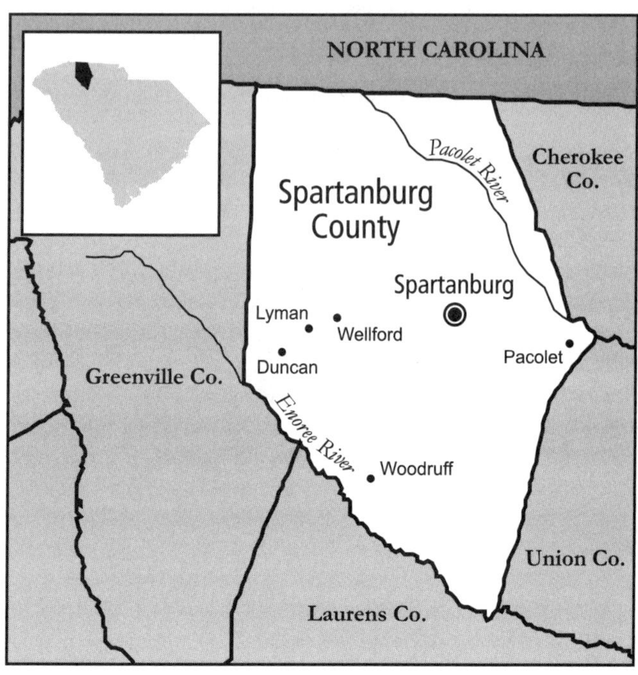

During the Revolutionary War many settlers remained loyal to Britain. They were the recipients of royal land grants and lacked the grievances of coastal planters and merchants. Fighting in the area resembled a civil war between patriots and Loyalists, with each side burning the farms of the other. Members of the Spartan Regiment, organized by Colonel John Thomas, were prominent fighters for the cause of independence. As fighting in the state moved into the backcountry in 1780, the second Battle of Cedar Spring and the Battle of Musgrove's Mill instilled new life into the patriot cause at a critical time. Still more important was the Battle of Cowpens in January 1781, where American forces defeated an army of British regulars and altered the course of the war in the South.

In 1785 Spartanburg was one of six counties established in the South Carolina interior by the General Assembly. Its name was likely taken from the famed Spartan Regiment. Thomas Williamson, a local resident, donated two acres of land in the middle of the county for the site of Spartanburg's first courthouse and jail. Spartanburg was designated a district in 1800 and remained so until the state constitution of 1868 changed all districts into counties. A final change came in 1897, when Spartanburg County lost its northeastern corner to the newly created Cherokee County.

Early settlers were mostly farmers with small landholdings who engaged in subsistence agriculture. They raised grains and vegetables. Hogs were the principal livestock and source of meat. Iron making was one of the earliest industrial efforts. The largest ironworks was probably the Wofford/Berwick Iron Works located at present-day Glendale on Lawson's Fork Creek. The area became part of what later was dubbed the "Old Iron District."

During the first half of the nineteenth century, short-staple cotton dominated the county's agricultural life. Although there were some large plantations, most of the cotton producers were small farmers with few or no slaves. The number of slaves rose as the century progressed, however, and by 1850 almost one-third of the county population was African American. During the same half-century the county's mild summers attracted lowcountry visitors to hotels at Limestone Springs and Glenn Springs. Access to the county was made easier in 1859 with the completion of the Spartanburg and Union Railroad. The antebellum years also saw educational opportunities grow and diversify. In 1849 the Cedar Spring School for the Deaf was founded, with instruction for the blind added in 1855. Higher education for men arrived with the opening of Wofford College in 1854. The Reidville Male and Female High Schools were established in 1857 and 1859, respectively.

No major battles were fought in Spartanburg District during the Civil War, but many of its citizens fought and died in the conflict. In the aftermath of the war, cotton farming and the textile industry came to dominate the economy. In the 1830s Dr. James Bivings had established the Bivingsville Cotton Factory on Lawson's Fork Creek. D. E. Converse acquired controlling interest in the Bivingsville factory in 1870 and later changed the name of the community to Glendale. Between 1870 and 1900 large mills were built throughout the county, making Spartanburg an important textile center in the state and the nation. Growth in manufacturing was accompanied by a rapid increase in population. In the midst of this expansion, some county leaders lamented the lack of higher education opportunities for women and founded Converse College in 1889.

During World War I, Spartanburg County benefited from the location of an infantry training center at Camp Wadsworth. Following the war, cotton declined as a major crop because of changing market demands, land exhaustion, and the boll weevil. In time peaches replaced cotton as the county's major cash crop. The textile industry also entered a slump in the 1920s, which was exacerbated by the Great Depression in the 1930s. World War II gave the county another army training base, Camp Croft, and rejuvenated the textile industry. Unfortunately, the boom was not to last, and textile production in Spartanburg experienced a steady decline throughout the remainder of the century. The demise in textiles was offset in part by industrial diversification, beginning with the arrival of the Kohler Company in 1957 and followed by the Milliken Research Center in 1958 and W. R. Grace and Company in 1963. The arrival of several German and Swiss industries soon gave Spartanburg a significant international community.

Expansion was also aided by further educational advances. Three new institutions were founded in the twentieth century: Spartanburg Methodist College in 1911, Spartanburg Technical College in 1963, and the University of South Carolina at Spartanburg in 1967 (which became USC–Upstate in 2004). Cultural and intellectual life revolved around an active Artists' Guild, the Spartanburg Music Foundation, and a newly organized Arts Center. The Spartanburg County Historical Association was founded in 1958 and established the Regional Museum of Spartanburg County in 1961. The founding of the Arts Partnership of Greater Spartanburg in 1994 and the Hub City Writers Project in 1995 assured that cultural activity kept pace with economic development. JEFFREY R. WILLIS

Foster, Vernon, ed. *Spartanburg: Facts, Reminiscences, Folklore.* Spartanburg, S.C.: Reprint Company, 1998.
Landrum, John B. O. *History of Spartanburg County, South Carolina.* 1900. Reprint, Spartanburg, S.C.: Reprint Company, 1977.
Racine, Philip N. *Seeing Spartanburg: A History in Images.* Spartanburg, S.C.: Hub City Writers Project, 1999.
South Carolina. Writers' Program. *A History of Spartanburg County.* 1940. Reprint, Spartanburg, S.C.: Reprint Company, 1976.
Willis, Jeffrey R. *Spartanburg, South Carolina.* Charleston, S.C.: Arcadia, 1999.

Spartanburg County Museum of Art. Located on South Spring Street in Spartanburg, the Spartanburg County Museum of Art was founded in 1907 with the acquisition of *The Girl with Red Hair,* an oil on canvas by the Ashcan school artist Robert Henri. Two Spartanburg artists and former students of Henri, Margaret M. Law and Josephine Sibley Couper, organized an exhibition in Spartanburg of leading American contemporary artists. Henri's painting was chosen as the first piece of a permanent collection for the city, which has now grown to more than 250 pieces of fine art and sculpture. Many well-known artists with ties to the upstate are represented in the collection, including August Cook, Margaret Law, Josephine Sibley Couper, and Grace DuPre. Contemporary artists in the collection include Carl Blair, MacArthur Goodwin, Daniel Cromer, and David Benson.

The museum offers a changing series of local, regional, and national artists every eight weeks. Other programs include the Museum Art School, the Art Lecture series, the annual Sidewalk Art Show, the biennial Hub City Art Competition, and the museum gift shop, which features fine arts and crafts by local artists. The museum also offers the Colors Program, a free after-school art studio program for at-risk youths. THERESA MANN

Spartanburg Methodist College. Spartanburg Methodist College is a two-year institution related to the United Methodist Church and located on 110 acres in western Spartanburg County. Enrollment in the fall of 2001 was 635.

The college traces its origins to the Textile Industrial Institute (TII), founded in 1911 by David English Camak (1880–1967), then pastor of Duncan Memorial Methodist Episcopal Church, South in the Spartan Mill village. While he was a student, Camak was inspired by the description by Dr. Henry Nelson Snyder, president of Wofford College, of the plight of southern cotton textile workers and determined to devote his life to ministry among mill workers. Camak persuaded Walter S. Montgomery, president of Spartan Mill, to provide space in a vacant house near the church for an elementary and secondary school. Camak began with one student and $100 in borrowed funds. In a unique arrangement, Camak's students alternately attended school one week, then worked in the mill one week.

In 1912 the school was adopted as a mission of the South Carolina Conference of the Methodist Episcopal Church, South. The following year the present campus was purchased, and students began to erect Charles P. Hammond Hall, which at the beginning of the twenty-first century was still in use as a residence hall. In 1927 TII began to offer the first two years of college-level work, preparing students for transfer to four-year institutions or for immediate employment.

Because of the increasing availability of public schools to the families of textile workers, TII dropped high school courses in 1940. In 1942 the institution became Spartanburg Junior College, a name it retained until 1974, when it became Spartanburg Methodist College. Perhaps its most distinguished alumnus is Olin D. Johnston, a former South Carolina governor and U.S. senator. A. V. HUFF, JR.

Camak, David English. *Human Gold from Southern Hills.* Greer, S.C., 1960.

Spartanburg Pellagra Hospital. The pellagra hospital in Spartanburg was the nation's first facility dedicated to discovering the cause of that baffling and serious disorder. Established in 1914 with a special congressional appropriation to the U.S. Public Health Service (PHS) and set up primarily for research, the hospital was the result of mutually reinforcing factors. One was pellagra's growing threat: 1,306 reported pellagra deaths in South Carolina during the first ten months of 1915; 100,000 southerners infected in 1916. Another was the need of the PHS—and of the rising epidemiologist Joseph Goldberger—for a clinic to conduct metabolic studies on pellagra to establish its probable dietary origin. Goldberger ultimately proved that preventive foods would stymie the disease. In addition, there was the enlightened influence of interested parties, notably Spartanburg civic leaders and South Carolina's congressional delegation, who were willing to have that city linked publicly to pellagra in order to obtain federal help in curbing what had become an epidemic of threatening proportions. By the time the hospital shut down in 1921, owing to optimistic but erroneous predictions of pellagra's imminent demise, the Spartanburg facility had helped scientists prove the dietary basis of pellagra and enabled hundreds of upstate South Carolinians to rid themselves—at government expense—of a life-threatening disease. ED BEARDSLEY

"Annual Report of the State Board of Health." In *Reports and Resolutions of the General Assembly of the State of South Carolina, Regular Session Commencing January 11, 1916.* Vol. 4. Columbia, S.C.: Gonzales and Bryan, 1915–1916.

Spence, Floyd Davidson (1928–2001). Legislator, congressman. Spence was born in Columbia on April 9, 1928, the son of J. W. and Addie Jane Spence of Lexington. He graduated from Lexington High School, where he was an all-state football player. He was a Korean War veteran and served in the U.S. Navy Reserve from 1947 until 1988, when he retired with the rank of captain. Spence attended the University of South Carolina on a football scholarship. He received his undergraduate degree in English in 1952 and his law degree in 1956 from the University of South Carolina. He then set up a law practice in West Columbia. His first wife, Lula Hancock Drake, whom he married on December 22, 1952, died in 1978. They had four sons. On July 3, 1988, he married Deborah E. Williams of Lexington.

In 1956 Spence was elected as a Democrat to the South Carolina House of Representatives. During his three terms, he served on the Judiciary and Ways and Means Committees. In 1962 Spence switched to the Republican Party, one of the first legislators in South Carolina to do so, and lost a close race for the U.S. House of Representatives to Democrat Albert Watson (who also later became a Republican). Four years later, in 1966, Spence returned to the state Senate, where he served as minority party leader.

In November 1970 Spence was elected to the U.S. Congress representing the Second Congressional District. He served in Congress from 1971 until his death in 2001. As a congressman, Spence was known for his conservative views. He was a strong supporter of the military as well as an advocate for limited government. He began his service on the House Armed Services Committee in 1971. From 1995 to 2001 he was chair of the Armed Services Committee, which was known as the National Security Committee during most of the six-year period. Upon the completion of his six-year term as chair he became chair of the Armed Services subcommittee on military procurement, where he served until his death. He was also a senior member of the Committee on Veterans' Affairs.

Spence considered defense and national security as the first priority of the United States. During his term as chair, he argued that cuts in the defense budget and manpower had jeopardized national security. He was also an early supporter of a national missile defense system. In 2000 he was recognized as Legislator of the Year by the Association of the United States Army. The Army Reserve Center at Fort Jackson, South Carolina, is named in his honor.

While Spence was a strong advocate of defense spending, he was a conservative in terms of domestic programs. In the 1990s he opposed the Clinton health care program, stating that the government could not be expected to succeed in providing health care since the government had been a failure in just about everything else.

In 2001 Floyd Spence underwent surgery for Bell's palsy and Ramsay Hunt syndrome, two disorders that attack facial nerves. Following surgery he developed a blood clot and died on August 16, 2001, in Jackson, Mississippi. He was buried in St. Peter's Lutheran Cemetery in Lexington, South Carolina. WILLIAM V. MOORE

Spencer, James Alexander (1850–1911). Legislator, educator. Spencer was born in Charleston on October 23, 1850, the eldest son of James A. Spencer, a porter, and his wife, Ellen Blondeau. The Spencers were free persons of color. Spencer's father was literate and a leader of Charleston's black Catholics.

Spencer acquired a good education, and, like his parents, he was a practicing Catholic. In 1870 he was a schoolteacher in Marion County. In 1872 he lived in Columbia, where he was chief clerk in the office of the South Carolina Land Commission. Again a schoolmaster, he represented Abbeville County in the state House of Representatives from 1874 to 1876. A contemporary said that Spencer "looks with an Evil eye on any exclusive works for the Negroes since he wants all blacks & whites to stand on an equal footing." He introduced and worked for legislation to improve funding for public education.

Spencer returned to Charleston in 1877. After working briefly as a porter, he was employed for a quarter-century as a messenger and then a clerk in the U.S. Lighthouse Engineer's Office. In 1875 or 1876 he married Ella Walton, a Charleston dressmaker (her family name appears as "Wragg" in some records). They had ten children, three of whom died in early childhood. The Spencers were members of St. Peter's Church, established in 1867 by Bishop Patrick Lynch as a parish for African Americans. Spencer became the principal black Catholic leader in Charleston. He was resolute in his conviction that blacks and whites should be treated equally in church. Denied membership in the white-dominated Charleston branch of the Catholic Knights of America, he organized a separate chapter for blacks. In 1888 Bishop Henry P. Northrop asked white Catholics to attend only segregated parishes, to which Spencer responded by asking the bishop if blacks were to be excluded from white churches. His actions galvanized African American parishioners in efforts to resist strict segregation in the church.

Spencer played a leading role in the national black Catholic lay congresses held from 1889 to 1894. He presided over the third congress in Philadelphia in 1892, making an impassioned plea for education and saying that no more churches for blacks need be built but that schools were needed: "[T]he Catholic Church has . . . no more sacred mission from its ruler and its God than to educate this race and lift it to spiritual and social liberty." He was president of the fourth Catholic lay congress, held in Chicago in 1893. There he deplored the establishment of special churches for blacks, which "had proven itself detrimental to the faith as the opportunity is thus offered for discrimination, thereby disturbing the peace and unity of the Church and destroying charity among her members." The Negro Catholic congresses were important in giving black Catholics a voice and a sense of unity and pride. They resulted in the founding of St. Peter Claver's Catholic Union, a national organization to promote churches, schools, and orphanages for blacks, and Spencer served as its first treasurer.

In his later years Spencer developed Bright's disease. He died in Charleston on July 27, 1911, and was buried in the Humane & Friendly Society Cemetery, Charleston. DAVID C. R. HEISSER

Davis, Cyprian. *The History of Black Catholics in the United States.* New York: Crossroad, 1990.

———. "The Holy See and American Black Catholics. A Forgotten Chapter in the History of the American Church." *U.S. Catholic Historian* 7 (spring/summer 1988): 157–81.

Spalding, David. "The Catholic Negro Congresses, 1889–1894." *Catholic Historical Review* 55 (October 1969): 337–57.

Spillane, Frank Morrison (1918–2006). Author. Nicknamed "Mickey" by his Irish Catholic father, Spillane was born in Brooklyn, New York, on March 9, 1918, the only child of John Joseph Spillane and his wife, Catherine Anne. Graduated from Brooklyn's Erasmus High School in 1935, he attended Kansas State College in 1939, intending to study law, although he dropped out that year. In 1940 he began work as a scripter and assistant editor for Funnies, Inc., a Manhattan comic-books producer. He joined the U.S. Army Air Force in December 1941, spending four years as a cadet flight instructor in Mississippi and Florida.

Mickey Spillane. © David G. Spielman-97, New Orleans

Spillane married Mary Anne Pearce in Greenwood, Mississippi, in 1945. Discharged from service as a captain, he returned to New York and the comic-book business. Needing money for a house, he turned out his first novel, *I, the Jury* (1947), in three weeks. The protagonist, Mike Hammer, a hard-drinking private investigator fond of buxom women and vigilante justice, became a household name by 1953, with five more Hammer novels selling millions of paperbacks. His hard-boiled plots and characters inspired the "Girl Hunt" production number with Fred Astaire and Cyd Charisse in the MGM musical *The Band Wagon* (1953).

Spillane became interested in the Grand Strand after judging the Myrtle Beach Sun-Fun Festival beauty contest, and in 1953 he moved his wife and four children to Murrells Inlet, where he has resided ever since. The twice-divorced Spillane married the actress Sherri Malinou in 1965 and then the former Miss South Carolina Jane Rodgers Johnson in 1983.

The Mike Hammer character was developed for radio, movies, and TV, including a 1980s series starring Stacy Keach. Spillane portrayed the character in the 1963 movie *The Girl Hunters* and starred as himself in *Ring of Fear* (1954). His TV credits include *The Milton Berle Show* and a 1974 episode of *Columbo.* During the 1970s and 1980s he was featured in commercials for Miller Lite Beer.

The author created another series character, espionage agent Tiger Mann, introduced in *Day of the Guns* (1964). Spillane's many magazine short stories have been collected in multiple volumes, and one of his children's books, *The Day the Sea Rolled Back* (1979), earned a Junior Literary Guild award. Mike Hammer resurfaces in *Black Alley* (1996), where he emerges from a coma and tracks down a missing fortune. *Something's Down There* (2003), a thriller set in the Caribbean, features Mako Hooker, a former U.S. government operative working as a fishing-boat captain.

As of the early twenty-first century Spillane's books had sold more than 140 million copies. He received the Grand Master Award of the Mystery Writers of America in 1995. Although his books proved to be a pervasive guilty pleasure during the first two decades of his career, they were almost universally panned by mainstream critics for their then-graphic depictions of sex and violence, as well as Hammer's "eye for an eye" sense of justice. Nevertheless, Spillane has accrued the respect attendant to his authorial longevity and the ongoing popularity of Mike Hammer, with the *New York Times* stating, "There's a kind of power about Mickey Spillane that no other writer can imitate." Spillane died on July 17, 2006. DAVID MARSHALL JAMES

Spielman, David G., and William W. Starr. *Southern Writers.* Columbia: University of South Carolina Press, 1997.

Spillane, Mickey. *The Hammer Strikes Again.* New York: Avenel, 1989.

Spirituals. South Carolina can boast a remarkably dynamic musical landscape. Gospel, bluegrass, blues, and string band all have a long history in the state. While these music forms might seem unrelated, they spring from common roots and share many similarities. South Carolina religious music is community-based, learned and played in the family room, church, or community center. With both sacred and secular influences, this music reflects the strong interplay between African American cultural traditions and those of European Americans.

Like other regional traditions, music can be closely tied to migration patterns. Scots-Irish moving into the Appalachians and English and French settlers making their homes on the coast introduced a rich variety of church hymnody. Slaves and freedmen introduced West African music styles markedly different from European forms. These disparate music traditions converged, traditions were shared, and new music styles formed. Most religious music performed in the twenty-first century is a product of this early synthesis.

Spirituals have subsequently influenced a range of contemporary music styles. Gospel and blues draw significantly from early African American spirituals. Most early blues musicians started out playing or singing in a religious context. A fairly recent form of musical expression, gospel emerged in the 1930s as a powerful combination of spirituals and secular forms such as ragtime and blues. In the late 1940s bluegrass incorporated string band, blues, and gospel into a tight, high-energy popular music phenomenon.

One of the primary features of both black and white spiritual music rests with an emphasis on group participation and improvisation. Spiritual music has many stylistic variations: three- and four-part harmony, shape note, common meter hymn choir, call and response, and praise house are all a part of this foundation. Spiritual music can employ polyrhythms, hand clapping, foot stomping, and the shouting style associated with the call-and-response tradition. An improvisational form of music, call and response involves one person "calling" a verse, with the remainder of the choir repeating the line in unison.

All of these sacred music styles have been practiced in South Carolina into the twenty-first-century. While shape-note, call-and-response, and multiple-part harmony groups can be found throughout the state, few regions in the South retain the vitality of the hymn choir, or common meter, tradition. Emerging in the 1700s from English Calvinist worship and African ritual practices, hymn choir traditions took root in slave communities in South Carolina. The tradition has been fairly localized in the York County area. Likewise, praise-house spirituals were an early form of African American folk music that can be found in the lowcountry and Sea Islands. Praise houses, which were small, single-room structures built by slaves, provided sites for some of the first worship services in the early African American community.

The invention of the shape-note method of reading music was an important thread in American musical history. Introduced at the end of the eighteenth century, shape-note books printed music with a different shaped note for each degree of the scale. Associated with the revivals of the Second Great Awakening in the early nineteenth century, shape-note hymnals were printed throughout the eastern United States, and the method was taught by itinerant singing schoolmasters. In the South, shape-note singing was adopted by both European American and African American congregations. Large shape-note singing conventions were still quite popular in several regions of the state in the early twenty-first century.

This music, whether shape-note or praise-house, has deep roots in the religious, social, and economic history of South Carolina. Much of it was forged through untold hardship, and the result is a highly emotional expression that carries intense personal and collective meaning. SADDLER TAYLOR

Allen, William Francis. *Slave Songs of the United States.* 1867. Reprint, New York: Dover, 1995.

Jackson, George Pullen. *White Spirituals in the Southern Uplands: The Story of the Fasola Folk, Their Songs, Singings, and "Buckwheat Notes."* 1933. Reprint, New York: Dover, 1965.

Johnson, Alonzo, and Paul Jersild, eds. *"Ain't Gonna Lay My 'Ligion Down": African American Religion in the South.* Columbia: University of South Carolina Press, 1996.

Joyner, Charles W. *Shared Traditions: Southern History and Folk Culture.* Urbana: University of Illinois Press, 1999.

Lomax, Alan. *The Folk Songs of North America, in the English Language.* Garden City, N.Y.: Doubleday, 1960.

Rosenberg, Neil V. *Bluegrass: A History.* Urbana: University of Illinois Press, 1985.

Spoleto. In the mid-1970s no one could have imagined staid, conservative Charleston welcoming an invasion by more than 150,000 people for seventeen days each year. That they should come for the arts seemed entirely fitting. Charleston, after all, was the site of the first ballet performance and one of the first theaters in the colonies. The modern city possessed the oldest museum and the oldest musical society. But who would have expected Charleston to welcome a French hip-hop ensemble or drama performed by one-inch ninja turtles?

In 1977 the composer Gian Carlo Menotti, backed by the National Endowment for the Arts, chose Charleston as the home for the American counterpart of his festival in Spoleto, Italy. He ran the festival himself. When he angrily pulled out in 1993, few thought that the festival would survive. It nearly did not. By 1995 it had only three employees, and by 1996 it was $3 million in debt.

The opening ceremony of the annual Spoleto Festival in Charleston is always a gala event. Photograph by Bill Murtin. Courtesy, City of Charleston

But by the start of the twenty-first century, Spoleto was flourishing. It developed a substantial endowment and an even more substantial reputation for quality, variety, innovation, and, not least, for nurturing young artists. It offered more than 120 performances, and its companion festival, Piccolo Spoleto, run by the city, added more than 700 events, most of them inexpensive or free. Performances frequently have included the offbeat, but there has been enough opera and ballet to satisfy the most traditional tastes. In 2000 visitors to these festivals spent $43.1 million in the Charleston area and generated $67.8 million in economic output in South Carolina. DALE VOLBERG REED

Hetzler, Sidney. "Two Town Festivals: Signs of a Theater of Power." Ph.D. diss., Emory University, 1990.

Kinzer, Stephen. "Still Setting the Tone in the Southeast." *New York Times,* June 5, 2001, pp. E1, E6.

Walsh, Michael. "Carolina's Grand New Opry." *Time* 145 (June 12, 1995): 66–67.

Spotted salamander. State amphibian. The spotted salamander (*Ambystoma maculatum*) became the official state amphibian by a law signed by Governor Jim Hodges on June 11, 1999. The designation resulted from the interest and activity of children in the third-grade class at Woodlands Heights Elementary School, Spartanburg, taught by Lynn K. Burgess. Students conducted research and a letter-writing campaign to get an amphibian adopted, enlisting support from scientists, public officials, and other third-graders in the state.

The spotted salamander is a six-to-eight-inch-long cold-blooded amphibian marked by two rows of yellow or yellowish-orange spots on its black or steel-gray back. The animal ranges from southeastern Canada throughout the eastern United States and is found across South Carolina. It lives mostly in bottomland deciduous forests but can also be found in coniferous forests and mountainous areas.

Born with gills, the spotted salamander later develops lungs. The female lays eggs mainly in springtime ponds. Salamanders are seldom seen by people because they live mostly underground, in or beneath rotting wood or leaf litter. All salamanders are predators; they play an important ecological role by consuming vast quantities of earthworms, mollusks, spiders, and insect larvae. They can live twenty-five years or more.

Some legislators and scientists had preferred designating a rare South Carolina species, the pine-barrens tree frog, found in the Sandhills, as state amphibian, but there is agreement that the spotted salamander is a beautiful and important animal. Salamanders are used extensively in scientific research, such as medical studies of limb and tissue regeneration. Scientists consider them important indicators of overall environmental health. DAVID C. R. HEISSER

Bishop, Sherman C. *Handbook of Salamanders.* Ithaca, N.Y.: Comstock, 1943.

Graves, Rachel. "Amphibian Approaches New Status." Charleston *Post and Courier,* April 25, 1999, pp. B1, B7.

Petranka, James W. *Salamanders of the United States and Canada.* Washington, D.C.: Smithsonian Institution Press, 1998.

Spratt, John McKee, Jr. (b. 1942). Congressman, lawyer. Spratt was born on November 1, 1942, in Charlotte, North Carolina, the son of John Spratt and Jane Bratton. He grew up in York, South Carolina, where his father practiced law and was an influential figure in state politics. At York High School, John Jr. played football and served as president of the student body in his senior year. In 1964 he received a bachelor's degree in history from Davidson College, where he served as student body president. He continued his studies in philosophy, politics, and economics at Oxford University in England, where he was a Marshall Scholar and earned a master's degree in 1966. Returning to the United States, he received his law degree from Yale Law School three years later. While attending Yale, Spratt married Jane Stacy on May 30, 1968. They are the parents of three daughters.

From 1969 to 1971 Spratt served on the staff of the assistant secretary of defense, the Pentagon's chief budget officer. During his military service, he worked primarily with budget problems in weapons procurement. He received the army's Meritorious Service Medal and left active duty with the rank of captain. Returning to York in 1971, Spratt immersed himself in the law firm of Spratt, McKeown and Spratt, and he became an influential figure in the economic and social life of the community.

In 1982 Spratt ran for the U.S. House of Representatives, seeking the congressional seat being vacated by retiring Fifth District representative Kenneth Holland. Victorious in his first attempt at elective office, Spratt entered Congress in 1983 and garnered seats on three key House committees: Budget, Armed Services, and Government Reform and Oversight. During the 1980s Spratt gained recognition by chairing the Armed Services' Military Application of Nuclear Energy Panel (1989–1994) and the Strategic Defense Initiative Panel (1988). The voters of his district reelected him in 1984, 1986, 1988, 1990, and 1992.

The shifting political landscape of the Fifth Congressional District, which has never elected a Republican, gave Spratt a stiff challenge in 1994 when the Republican Party candidate nearly defeated Spratt. Spratt kept his seat, however, and easily won reelection in 1996, 1998, 2000, 2002, and 2004.

Accumulating seniority, Spratt concentrated on the debate over the national budget. By 1997 he was the ranking Democrat on the House Budget Committee and was a key negotiator of a balanced budget agreement passed that year. He also continued as the second-ranking Democrat on the Armed Services Committee.

In early 2003 Spratt was chosen by his fellow Democrats as assistant to House minority leader Nancy Pelosi of California. He has frequently spoken to the nation, through the media and before a wide range of audiences, on fiscal matters and issues of national defense. His two decades of congressional service have earned for him honorary degrees from the University of South Carolina, Winthrop University, Presbyterian College, Newberry College, and Limestone College. He has also received the Governor's Award in the Humanities and the Order of the Palmetto. JOSEPH EDWARD LEE

Springdale (Lexington County; 2000 pop. 2,877). One of the youngest towns in the Midlands, until World War II this was a farming community with daily life dominated by crops, weather, seasons, church activities, and classes at Long Branch School. Creation of a U.S. Army Air Base and Columbia's municipal airport wrought profound change, as did the growth of postwar suburbia in general. The paving of Platt Springs Road in 1948—the "main street" of this thriving town—and designation of a former sand trail as S.C. Highway 602 tended to foster communal spirit.

In March 1955, reacting to fears of annexation by nearby West Columbia and Cayce, twenty residents informed state officials of tentative plans to establish the town of Sherwood. Its proposed boundaries included Boston Avenue, Columbia Airport, Watling Road, Black Snake Road, Rainbow Drive, and Route 215. None of the land, they stated, was "more than one mile from the center of the said area." However, on June 17, by a vote of thirty-five to twenty-four, a slightly larger region two-and-one-half miles long and one-and-one-half miles wide became the town of Springdale.

Those casting ballots were asked to do three things: approve or reject incorporation; if approved, choose a governing body (an intendant [mayor] and four wardens); and name their new town. Along the way the name Sherwood lost out to rival suggestions including Long Branch, Granby, and Springdale. The winning name was apparently inspired by numerous springs in the area, or as one resident observed, "perhaps they just liked the sound of the name."

At the time of its incorporation, Springdale had only three hundred inhabitants. By the 1990s it had about ten times that number. The 2.7-square-mile town is governed by a mayor and a six-member council, with the assistance of a full-time town administrator. Despite suburban growth, about half the land area remains undeveloped. Town offices are located on Platt Springs Road adjacent to an attractive park-playground honoring the memory of Felton C. Benton, town administrator (1981–1993). Near this site, lacking formal facilities, town officials held their first meeting in a parked automobile.

Long Branch School, which served the community for many decades, closed in January 1953 when students were transferred to Brookland-Cayce #3. Since then numerous other schools have appeared: Airport Junior High (1958), Fulmer Middle School (1954), and Springdale School (1967). The Will Lou Gray Opportunity School, a state agency, also is located in Springdale.

A key element in recent history has been the work of the Springdale Woman's Club. When local businessmen contributed materials to build town offices, these women held a barbecue to raise money for bathroom fixtures and were so successful that they added a kitchen sink. They bought the land that became Benton Park in 1960 and the following year, after an intensive drive, paid for streetlights.

A thirty-six-page *History Book,* published in 1995 to celebrate Springdale's fortieth birthday, describes still other bits of local lore and notes with obvious pride that area businesses recorded a new high of $45 million in gross sales that year. The authors also boast of three hotels, numerous restaurants, and many services available to both residents and visitors. Their town is, they conclude, "a stable, serene community which affords a quiet, friendly atmosphere with strong family values and excellent schools, [as well] as all the comforts of true southern living." JOHN H. MOORE

Springs. The springs of South Carolina became popular destinations for the citizens of the state from the late eighteenth century through the nineteenth century. There were scores of mineral springs in South Carolina. Some of them were local watering holes, while others were on the grounds of country homes built by wealthy planters to escape the sickly season.

The hotel at Glenn Springs was one of many such resorts in the state. Courtesy, South Caroliniana Library, University of South Carolina

Mineral spring water was considered to have curative properties. The water from Glenn Springs in Spartanburg County was described as having an odor of sulphur and a bitter saline taste. South Carolinians traveled to the springs to drink the water but also to visit with each other and to enjoy the community. The pace was slow as people took the time to heal.

Large resort hotels were built to take advantage of the popularity of the mineral springs. The hotel at Glenn Springs, built in 1838, was open until it was destroyed by fire in 1941. Stagecoaches carried visitors from nearby railroad lines until a narrow-gauge railroad was built in the late nineteenth century. Since the South Carolina Constitution of 1790 prohibited state officers from leaving the state while in office, Glenn Springs Hotel became known as the summer capital of South Carolina as the governor stayed there for a few weeks every summer.

During the 1870s Glenn Springs Hotel entertained over one thousand guests each summer, including prominent South Carolinians such as the Civil War generals Wade Hampton and M. C. Butler. The hotel offered more than a daily regimen of healing waters. Guests enjoyed midnight banquets and danced away the languor of South Carolina evenings to the music of orchestras imported from Italy. The hotel had tenpin alleys, billiard tables, and croquet grounds.

Other notable springs in South Carolina included Abbeville Springs in Abbeville District and Boiling Springs and Healing Springs in Barnwell District. Poplar Springs was in Orangeburg District, and Platt Springs was in Lexington District. Lonamsville Springs and Lightwood Knot Springs were both near Columbia, and Rice Creek Springs was halfway between Columbia and Camden. Cool Springs in the Kershaw District was a summer retreat for Wateree planters who also made their summer homes at Spring Hill in Marlboro District. Bradford Springs was in the High Hills of Santee. There were numerous springs in Spartanburg District, including Limekiln Spring, Cedar Spring, Chalybeate Springs, Cherokee Springs, Pacolet Springs, and Patterson's Spring. Hanging Rock Springs was in Lancaster District, and Williamston Springs was in Anderson District.

Springs and related resorts declined as vacation destinations in the early twentieth century when the automobile allowed people to travel farther afield and the Great Depression discouraged vacationing. Still, the water from the springs continued to be popular well into the 1940s. Water was bottled and sold in containers ranging from twelve-ounce bottles to five-gallon demijohns.

By the early twenty-first century some springs were dry. Glenn Springs no longer existed. Other springs in South Carolina were still open to the public, and people continued to visit in order to fill milk jugs and water bottles, but the social benefits of mineral water consumption in South Carolina had ended. DAVID HODGES

Brewster, Lawrence Fay. *Summer Migrations and Resorts of the South Carolina Low-Country Planters.* Durham, N.C.: Duke University Press, 1947.

Springs, Elliott White (1896–1959). Businessman, aviator, author. Springs was born in Lancaster on July 31, 1896, the son of Leroy Springs, a wealthy textile manufacturer, and Grace Allison White. He graduated from Culver Military Academy in Indiana in 1913 and received an A.B. from Princeton University in 1917. On October 4, 1922, he married Frances Hubbard Ley of Massachusetts. They had one daughter, Anne Kingsley Springs, who married H. William Close, and one son, Leroy "Sonny" Springs II, who was killed in an airplane crash in 1946.

Elliott White Springs in a Springmaid Print Shirt. Courtesy, the White Homestead Archives

Elliott Springs was one of the most daring pilots of World War I. Following his enlistment, Springs was sent to England for training with the Royal Flying Corps. Selected for the prestigious British 85th Squadron, Springs racked up four kills before he was wounded after crash-landing on June 26, 1918. Upon his recovery, he was promoted to captain and transferred to the 148th Squadron of the U.S. Army. He became an "ace" (five kills) on August 3. By the end of the war, Springs had shot down eleven planes (other likely "kills" were not confirmed) and was the fifth-ranking American ace of World War I. He was awarded the British Distinguished Flying Cross and the American Distinguished Service Cross. He would return to military service in 1941 during World War II and retired as a lieutenant colonel.

After World War I, Springs briefly worked as a test pilot for the LWF Engineering Company of New York. He then went back to South Carolina to work in the family's textile business. His demanding father put him to work in a variety of jobs to learn the family business, but the work did not suit Springs. To relieve the tedium, Springs took to writing accounts of his war-time experiences. He began by publishing short stories and then wrote *War Birds: The Diary of an Unknown Aviator,* a thinly disguised account of his time in England and France during World War I. Published in 1926, the book was an instant critical and commercial success. From 1927 to 1931 Springs published dozens of short stories and seven more books, mostly about his flying experiences. Although his later works fell far short of the acclaim garnered by *War Birds,* Springs nevertheless earned $250,000 from his writings. He was inducted into the South Carolina Academy of Authors in 2000.

After his father died in 1931, Springs defied predictions that he would quickly run through the estate (supposedly valued at $5 million) and took over his father's textile company. At the time, Springs Cotton Mills consisted of six aging plants in Chester, Lancaster, and York Counties. Springs mastered technical details as well as business principles, working on a loom in his basement to test proposals of his workers and supervisors. He found that "for a man who loves machines, a cotton mill beats an airplane." He learned to tell by sound whether a machine was running properly.

During the 1930s and 1940s Springs consolidated his mills into one company, built a finishing plant, established a sales arm, and modernized the business. By 1958, the last full year he managed the company, he had built assets to $138.5 million, compared to $13 million when he became president. Sales were $163 million, more than nineteen times greater than in 1933. Springs was the seventh-largest textile company in the nation but led the industry in profitability. The company had become the world's largest producer of sheets and pillowcases. In particular, Springs won acclaim (as well as criticism) for his humorous and risqué advertisements promoting his company's "Springmaid" sheets. He was also known for special benefits he provided employees, including medical care, profit sharing, and recreational facilities.

Springs died on October 15, 1959, in New York City. His remains were cremated and returned to Fort Mill for interment in the White family plot of the Presbyterian cemetery. He was named to the South Carolina Business Hall of Fame in 1985. ROBERT A. PIERCE

Davis, Burke. *War Bird: The Life and Times of Elliott White Springs.* Chapel Hill: University of North Carolina Press, 1987.

Springs, Leroy (1861–1931). Merchant, entrepreneur, manufacturer. Springs was born in Fort Mill on November 12, 1861, the seventh of eight children of Andrew Baxter Springs and Blandina Baxter. Aggressive as a youth, Springs found college life too confining. At the age of twenty, after completing only two years at the University of North Carolina, he became a traveling merchant for Burwell and Springs of Charlotte, North Carolina, selling groceries from a wagon. He opened his first business, Leroy Springs & Company, in Lancaster, South Carolina, when he was twenty-two. In 1886 Springs founded a lucrative cotton-shipping firm, and he established the Bank of Lancaster in 1889. By 1892 he was worth $1 million. He founded Lancaster Cotton Mills in 1895. With these ventures, Springs laid the foundation of the family fortune. On December 28, 1892, Springs married Grace Allison White, the daughter of Samuel Elliott White, also a textile mill owner. The couple had one son, Elliott White Springs, who would eventually succeed his father as head of the family's textile business.

Grace White Springs died in 1907. By this time Springs was heavily involved as a partner or sole proprietor in numerous businesses. Leroy Springs & Company now had five South Carolina branches and one in North Carolina. Springs was the president of five mercantile companies, four cotton mills, two banks, a railroad, a power company, and a cotton-compress company serving cotton shippers in South Carolina and Georgia. He sat on the boards of directors for Southern Railroad and eight South Carolina banks and held seats on cotton exchanges in New York and New Orleans.

A volatile personality caused Springs problems during his lifetime. In 1885 he shot and killed a man in Lancaster after an altercation. He claimed self-defense, and his case was never brought to trial. His relationship with his son, Elliott, was tempestuous at best, marked by frequent disagreements and confrontations. In 1928 Springs was shot by one of his employees, whom he had recently fired.

In 1913 Springs married Lena Jones Wade, a widow who was head of the English department at Queen's College in Charlotte. He died of respiratory failure on April 9, 1931, in Charlotte. Elliott Springs directed that his father be buried next to the enormous Lancaster Cotton Mill No. 3, where thousands of mourners attended the funeral. Elliott later expanded the plant over the grave of his father, allegedly commenting, "It's what he would have wanted."
RICK D. BOULWARE

Davis, Burke. *War Bird: The Life and Times of Elliott White Springs.* Chapel Hill: University of North Carolina Press, 1987.

Pettus, Louise, and Martha Bishop. *The Springs Story: Our First Hundred Years.* Fort Mill, S.C.: Springs Industries, 1987.

Springs Industries. Springs Industries, a cotton textile company, was founded in 1887 by Samuel Elliott White of Fort Mill. Originally named Fort Mill Manufacturing Company, the company soon became a leading textile manufacturer in South Carolina. After White's death in 1911, ownership transferred to "Colonel" Leroy Springs. In 1922 Springs organized a company—Springs Mills, Inc.—to centralize control over his various holdings in Lancaster County. But his aggressive management style had drawbacks. Laborers threatened strikes over low wages, and the disgruntled cotton buyer Eldred Griffith shot Springs in Charlotte, North Carolina, over a questionable business deal. Though wounded in the head, Springs recovered, but he decided to manage his mills remotely from his office in New York City. On April 9, 1931, Leroy Springs died of respiratory failure during a visit to Charlotte.

Elliott White Springs, his son, inherited his father's six cotton mills, 7,500 looms, and 300,000 spindles, all valued at $7.25 million. In his first months as mill president, Elliott Springs purchased used equipment from New England industries, and the recently renamed Springs Cotton Mills began to manufacture a variety of new fabrics—pillowcases, towels, dress goods, and spun rayon fabrics. But Elliott continued his father's administrative style, particularly his antipathy toward organized labor. Only under direct pressure from federal New Deal agencies did Elliott reluctantly increase wages and reduce the workweek from fifty-five to forty hours.

After World War II, Springs again expanded corporate holdings with an effective "Springmaid" advertising campaign and the construction of the $15 million Grace Bleachery. At the time of Elliott Springs's death in 1959, Springs Industries included assets worth $138.5 million, 17,800 looms, and 836,000 spindles. Management transferred to his son-in-law, H. W. Close.

The 1960s treated Springs well. In 1962 Springs built a twenty-one-story office building in midtown New York. The next year Close's mills began producing polyester-cotton fabrics. In 1969 Springs completed a ten-year, $230 million expansion program, but national economic slowdowns and foreign competition hindered profits during the following decade. At the same time, turnover rates soared as a younger generation chose not to work in the mills or live in their parents' communities. New federal environmental regulations in the 1970s forced a $1.8 million expansion of Grace Finishing Plant's waste-treatment facility, while a government recall in 1976 of Springs fabric treated with the carcinogenic chemical "Tris" cost the company millions of dollars in lost revenue and perhaps even more in bad publicity.

H. W. Close died of heart failure in 1983. Under new management, the company was renamed Springs Industries and in 1985 acquired a major competitor, Lowenstein Corporation, for $286 million. Additional acquisitions came a decade later, allowing the company to reorganize into three production groups: bed fashions, bath fashions, and diversified products. In 1998 Springs elected Crandall Close Bowles, daughter of H. W. Close, as company president. Net sales for Springs Industries in 2000 were $2.3 billion. DARREN GREM

Davis, Burke. *War Bird: The Life and Times of Elliott White Springs.* Chapel Hill: University of North Carolina Press, 1987.

Pettus, Louise, and Martha Bishop. *The Springs Story: Our First Hundred Years.* Fort Mill, S.C.: Springs Industries, 1987.

Stackhouse, Eunice Temple Ford (1885–1980). Educator, clubwoman. Stackhouse was born at Blenheim in Marlboro County on December 14, 1885, to the Baptist minister Rufus Ford and Harriet Temple. She graduated from the Bennettsville high school at age fourteen. An honors graduate of Limestone College in 1904, Stackhouse received both A.B. and A.M. degrees and a diploma from the Winnie Davis School of History. At the University of Chicago, Stackhouse earned a Ph.B. in 1914 and an M.A. in 1927. Beginning in 1906, she taught education, psychology, and philosophy and ethics at Limestone College. From 1920 until her marriage in June 1932, Stackhouse served as dean of the faculty. In recognition of her twenty-six years of service, the college bestowed on her an honorary doctorate in education (Ed.D.) in 1932, dedicated a dormitory in her name in 1939, and made her dean emerita in 1969. Her husband, Thomas Bascom Stackhouse (1857–1939), a widower, had been a teacher, a farmer, a cotton mill executive, and a banker. Having no children, they adopted as a daughter Eunice Stackhouse's niece, Jacqueline Roper Stackhouse, who later taught social work at Winthrop University.

With his wife's concurrence, T. B. Stackhouse bequeathed his Columbia home to the South Carolina Federation of Women's Clubs. Eunice Stackhouse, a federation vice president, chaired its department of education (1936), its adult education section (1939), and its division of community service and correctional institutions (1943). Honored as "the fairy godmother of the Federation," Stackhouse, who lived in an upstairs apartment, donated space in her home for its headquarters and purchased office equipment. When the South Carolina Citizens Committee on Children and Youth was organized in 1947, she turned her dining room into a conference room for a biracial meeting of twenty-seven statewide organizations.

In 1942 Governor Richard M. Jefferies appointed Stackhouse as the first woman to serve on the South Carolina Probation, Pardon and Parole Board. In 1946, while in Washington, D.C., participating in a panel on preventing juvenile delinquency, she shared a table in the Justice Department's cafeteria with the black woman president of the Parent-Teachers Association of New Jersey. Progressive on race relations, Stackhouse said that this felt "no different" than eating with a white woman since they were "both professional women, interested in the same questions." In a letter to the editor of the *State* published on August 23, 1955, Stackhouse described her biracial activities that included organizing a woman's club for black women. She belonged to several biracial groups, among them the South Carolina Council on Human Relations, and also worked to improve conditions at the Colored Boys Industrial School. After the Supreme Court's 1954 *Brown v. Board of Education* decision, Stackhouse urged whites to find ways of cooperating with blacks rather than blocking desegregation. The racial problem, she said, was "fundamentally more a question of culture than it is of color."

In the June 1957 issue of the South Carolina *Clubwoman,* her longtime friend Alice Spearman described Stackhouse as "definitely a pioneer," particularly in race relations and care of the elderly. Stackhouse was named woman of the year by the National Society of the Colonial Dames in 1969, and in April 1972 she received the Two Thousand Women of Achievement award in London. A prolific author, she wrote essays, pamphlets, and three books, including a biography of her father, *The Beloved Divine* (1948), completed with the assistance of her brother. Stackhouse died at the Methodist Home in Orangeburg on February 2, 1980. MARCIA G. SYNNOTT

"Dr. Stackhouse, Dean, Civic Leader, Dies." Columbia *State,* February 3, 1980, p. C14.

McMillan, Montague. *Limestone College, a History: 1845–1970.* Gaffney, S.C.: Limestone College, 1970.

"Mrs. Stackhouse Suggests Fields for Racial Cooperation." Columbia *State,* August 23, 1955, p. B12.

"Women's Federation Pays Tribute to Mrs. Stackhouse." Columbia *State,* May 5, 1959, p. B2.

***State,* the** (2003 circulation: 114,442 daily and 148,820 Sunday). The *State* is a morning daily newspaper published weekdays and Sundays in the city of Columbia. The paper was born in 1891 of a bitter political struggle that pitted three brothers against leaders of an agrarian movement that was spearheaded by Governor Benjamin "Pitchfork Ben" Tillman and threatened the state's political establishment. Narciso and Ambrose Gonzales, the main founders of the newspaper, were joined by their youngest brother, William. All three had worked for the Charleston *News and Courier* and were supported by the state's conservative leaders in their fight against Tillman and his organ, the *Columbia Register.*

The first issue of the *State* was printed on February 18, 1891, in the basement of the old Columbia City Hall building. The circulation was 2,300, and the pressrun was 3,000. Ambrose raised and borrowed money to keep the newspaper afloat, and in 1893 the *State* became the first newspaper in the Carolinas to use Linotype machines. Meanwhile, the editor, the feisty Narciso, battled Tillman and his pet project, the state whiskey dispensary system, which the *State* charged with spawning corruption in general and a bloody riot in Darlington in particular. The *State* also decried lynching and championed various Progressive causes. Narciso's opposition to Ben Tillman's nephew, James H. Tillman, proved fatal. James Tillman was soundly defeated in a race for governor in 1902. Several weeks later, on January 15, 1903, Tillman fatally shot Gonzales as he strolled down Columbia's main street across from the State House. Maintaining that he thought the unarmed Gonzales was reaching for a pistol, Tillman was acquitted. A monument was erected to the martyred Gonzales on Senate Street in Columbia. The other two Gonzales brothers continued to campaign for the Progressive wing of the Democratic Party, Ambrose as publisher and William as editor.

In the first editorial cartoon to appear in a South Carolina newspaper, the *State* depicted gubernatorial candidate Coleman L. Blease as a corrupt vulture ready to ravish the virtue of South Carolina. A number of political observers credited a voters' backlash to this cartoon as instrumental in Blease's 1910 victory. Courtesy, South Caroliniana Library, University of South Carolina

The *State* overtook the *News and Courier* as the largest newspaper in South Carolina by 1910 but lost this position to the *Greenville News* by 1927. By 1939 the *State* regained the top spot and held it into the twenty-first century. In contrast to its fiery early days, however, the *State* became blander and stabilized financially under publisher William Elliott, editor-publisher S. L. Latimer, Jr., and president-publisher J. M. Blalock. In 1945 the State Company bought the *Columbia Record.* In the 1950s descendants of the Gonzales family returned to more active roles. Ambrose Gonzales Hampton, a son of the founders' sister, joined the company in 1955, becoming president in 1962 and publisher in 1963. His brother Harry R. E. Hampton served as coeditor, and another brother, Frank, was chairman of the board. Ben R. Morris succeeded his father-in-law, Ambrose Hampton, as president in 1972 and as publisher in 1980. Under Morris, the newspaper successfully campaigned for liquor-law reform and battled for state government debt limitations.

For two decades beginning in the mid-1960s, the State Company embarked on an expansion program, buying and selling out-of-state television stations and newspapers. During this period the *State* was basically conservative, tending to endorse Republican candidates and causes. The *State* and its properties were purchased in 1986 by Knight Ridder for $311 million. The daily circulation reached 119,194 in 1987 after topping 150,000 on Sundays in 1984. The new owners closed the *Columbia Record* in 1988 but beefed up the *State*'s staff. On the positive side, the *State* was a Pulitzer Prize finalist for its reporting in 1989 on Hurricane Hugo. On the negative side, it was criticized for its passive coverage of scandals involving University of South Carolina president James B. Holderman, who resigned in disgrace. The newspaper campaigned for the restructuring of state government after public officials were convicted of bribery in Operation Lost Trust. ROBERT A. PIERCE

Pierce, Robert A. *Palmettos and Oaks: A Centennial History of* The State, *1891–1991.* Columbia, S.C.: State-Record Company, 1991.

State Council of Defense. The State Council of Defense was South Carolina's major public relations and propaganda arm during World War I. Created in 1917 to replace the Civic Preparedness Commission, the council was the "citizens' army" in South Carolina. Each county also had a county council of defense with a chairman and committee that oversaw activities on the local level. Governor Richard I. Manning named his energetic political ally David R. Coker as chairman of the State Council of Defense.

Among the council's activities were promoting support for President Woodrow Wilson and the war in Europe, conscription, conservation of resources, and cooperation with other patriotic organizations, as well as alleviating the distress of families with members on active duty. The council also worked with federal authorities to suppress the antiwar press in South Carolina.

The State Council of Defense was so successful throughout 1917—for example, suppressing the dissident voice of the *Charleston American*—that Dr. James A. B. Scherer of the Council of National Defense commended South Carolina. No state in the South, he noted, gave "greater encouragement . . . in the management of the council of defense."

In 1918 the council was reorganized and chapters were established in communities across the state. With reorganization, council efforts to curb criticism of the war achieved their zenith. For example, Ben L. Abney, Columbia counsel for the Southern Railway, lost his job due to accusations that he did not support the Red Cross. By the middle of 1918 Coker wrote that South Carolina "is probably as near 100% loyal as any in the Union." The State Council of Defense ended its duties with the war's end.

In February 1941 South Carolina again organized a State Council of Defense, which operated until the end of June 1945. Under the leadership of executive directors G. Heyward Mahon and John A. Brockman, the reconstituted council focused on press coverage of the war and disseminating information on civilian defense and disaster planning. The council also oversaw a network of child-care facilities in major cities and towns across the state. ALEXIA JONES HELSLEY AND TERRY LYNN HELSLEY

Helsley, Terry Lynn. "'Voices of Dissent': The Antiwar Movement and the State Council of Defense in South Carolina, 1916–1918." Master's thesis, University of South Carolina, 1974.

South Carolina. State Council of Defense. "Addenda to Historical Account of the Activities of the South Carolina State Council of Defense, July 1, 1944 through June 30, 1945." Typescript. South Caroliniana Library, University of South Carolina, Columbia.

———. State Council of Defense. *Report of South Carolina State Council of Defense.* Columbia, S.C.: State Company, 1918–1919.

State Fair. The South Carolina State Fair, formally the State Agricultural and Mechanical Society of South Carolina, was established in 1869 "to promote the material, educational, agricultural and industrial interest of the State." Two antebellum organizations, both known as the State Agricultural Society of South Carolina, preceded the modern organization. The first operated from 1839 through 1849, and the second operated from 1855 through 1861. Following the November 1861 fair, Confederate authorities occupied the fairgrounds on Elmwood Avenue in Columbia. These fairgrounds buildings were destroyed during the February 1865 burning of the city.

The third society traces its origins to April 28, 1869, when a group of citizens gathered in Columbia to improve the state's agricultural conditions and methodologies. Members sought to build support for reestablishing the State Fair by organizing statewide lectures. This grassroots campaign succeeded, and the society held its first postwar fair in November 1869 on the Elmwood Avenue site. By 1903 it had outgrown its Elmwood home, and the society purchased a one-hundred-acre tract south of the city for $15,000. The first fair on the modern fairgrounds opened on October 25, 1904. In 1912 the society purchased the Hippodrome Building. Used during the 1907 Jamestown Exposition in Virginia and then moved to Greensboro, North Carolina, to the meeting site of the 1908 National Republican Convention, the exhibit hall was finally moved to Columbia and served as the venue for the 1912 National Corn Show. Fire destroyed the Hippodrome in 1966, and the Hampton and Ruff steel buildings were constructed in its place.

For more than sixty years the State Fair was linked with the "Big Thursday" football classic between the University of South Carolina and Clemson University. The last Big Thursday game was played on November 12, 1959. Although best known for its annual eleven-day autumn carnival with amusement rides, exhibits, live entertainment, juried competitions, and food, the modern State Fair operates year-round. Trade shows, conventions, exhibitions, and special events are held on the society's 110-acre fairgrounds and in its six permanent buildings with more than 125,000 square feet of exhibit space. The State Fair receives no state appropriations and is wholly owned and operated by dues-paying life members. Revenue supports ongoing operations, capital improvements, a scholarship program, and contributions to nonprofit and charitable organizations throughout the state. J. CANTEY HEATH, JR.

Moore, Paul V. *A Brief History of the State Agricultural and Mechanical Society of South Carolina.* N.p., 1957.

State Agricultural and Mechanical Society of South Carolina. *History of the State Agricultural Society of South Carolina from 1839 to 1845, Inclusive, of the State Agricultural Society of South Carolina from 1855 to 1861, Inclusive, of the State Agricultural and Mechanical Society of South Carolina from 1869 to 1916, Inclusive.* Columbia, S.C.: R. L. Bryan, 1916.

State Farmers Market. The State Farmers Market is a three-site system of state-sponsored facilities designed to bring growers and consumers of agricultural products together. Operated by the South Carolina Department of Agriculture, markets in Columbia, Greenville, and the Pee Dee provide leased spaces to wholesale and retail vendors. All three markets have offered South Carolina fruits, vegetables, nuts, and other commodities. Some out-of-state produce has also been offered. Beginning in the late twentieth century, ornamental plants have been marketed, and annual floral festivals have drawn thousands of buyers.

The markets' economic impact has been considerable. For example, Columbia's Bluff Road market generated $275 million in annual sales in 2000. Vendors provided employment to one thousand full-time and another one thousand part-time employees. The Greenville and Pee Dee markets, though not as large as the Columbia site, have added significantly to the economies of their respective regions.

The facilities in all three cities grew from earlier public markets. Indeed, the Columbia market was among the first enterprises organized in the capital city. Until the 1860s the market was located in the basement of the city hall. Later the market moved to Assembly Street, where it remained for eight decades. The influence of the market may still be seen in the street's wide medians. Years of growth led to the creation of a new, fifty-four-acre facility off Bluff Road, which opened in 1951. "The Million Dollar Market" initially consisted of five sheds and four warehouses and was a vast improvement over the former downtown location. In 1974 the South Carolina Department of Agriculture assumed control of the facility. The Bluff Road site has been slated for replacement by 2010.

The Greenville market moved from the city hall to a separate agricultural complex in 1949. Nearly doubling in size, the operation remained under the direction of Greenville County until 1979, when the State Department of Agriculture assumed ownership.

In 1983 the Pee Dee market moved from downtown Florence to the site of the former Tobacco Experiment Station, located on U.S. Highway 52 between Florence and Darlington. The facility has had wholesale and retail facilities and a horticulture center. The newest of the three state-owned farmers markets has provided a place for the buyers and sellers of yet another South Carolina region to come together, to the benefit of both. BARRY A. PRICE

"It's Big Business When S.C. Farmers Come to the State Farmers Market." *South Carolina Magazine* 19 (May 1955): 16–17, 37.

State flag. South Carolina's blue flag with its white crescent moon rising above the white palmetto tree is simple in design but profoundly symbolic of a long history. Born for practicality, South Carolina's first state flag was a signal device used in the opening days of the Revolutionary War. In 1776 the Council of Safety ordered Colonel William Moultrie to produce a signal flag and supplied blue cloth for that purpose. Moultrie used the silver crescent worn on his troop's hats, placing this device in the upper-corner flagstaff side on the blue cloth.

This flag signaled victory to Charleston following Moultrie's repulse of the British fleet from the hastily erected palmetto log fort on Sullivan's Island. The palmetto tree immediately became a popular symbol. Though not incorporated into the flag during the Revolution, the palmetto tree did become part of the new state seal, firmly establishing it as a state emblem.

The Palmetto Regiment, South Carolina's volunteer unit raised for Mexican War duty in 1846, carried a banner of blue. These colors were the first American banners to be raised over Mexico City upon its capture. After the war, a medal presented to the regimental veterans clearly depicted this flag with a palmetto tree in the center of an oval.

In December 1860, when South Carolina seceded from the Union, Representative Plowden C. J. Weston called for the appointment of a joint committee to devise a South Carolina national flag or ensign. Exactly one month later the committee introduced a resolution creating a white flag with a green palmetto tree in the center and a blue union with a white crescent. Representative Robert Barnwell Rhett, Jr., amended the resolution to read "the National Flag or Ensign of South Carolina shall be blue with a white palmetto tree upright thereon, and a white crescent in the upper corner." Rhett reasoned that the colonial flag of blue with a white crescent and the white palmetto tree addition created a simple, beautiful flag. Not all of the legislators agreed with Rhett, however, and for seven days debate occurred in the House, the Senate, and the newspapers. Finally, on January 28, 1861, Rhett's design was approved, and the blue flag with a white palmetto tree centered and a white crescent with horns pointing upward in the corner became the official state flag. In April, when Fort Sumter was taken, this flag flew beside the flag of the Confederacy.

In 1869 the Reconstruction government raised the flag issue again. A resolution passed by the General Assembly provided that a United States flag and the 1861 state flag would wave over the State House. Thirty years later the legislature hotly debated the proposal of changing the flag's color from blue to purple to symbolize the blue flag being soaked with gallant South Carolina red blood. This gesture to honor the Confederate dead and the "Lost Cause" was overwhelmingly defeated; the flag remained blue.

In 1906 Senator Benjamin R. Tillman suggested that the state's coat of arms be incorporated with two shields leaning against the palmetto tree's base. Alexander Salley, secretary of the Historical Commission, quickly pointed out that the flag adhered to statutory law. Following the statutes, Salley and Governor Martin F. Ansel produced a lovely state flag in honor of President William Howard Taft's 1909 visit to the state. This effort spurred the passage of a 1910 General Assembly act providing for the display of the flag over public buildings. Clemson College was directed to manufacture the flags as prescribed by an 1861 General Assembly resolution. The act also stipulated that the secretary of the Historical Commission approve the design, so Salley carefully supervised every detail, even selecting the shade of blue. The only major change made was to place the crescent closer to the flagstaff with the horns turned to the staff rather than upward.

Manufactured by commercial firms in the twenty-first century, the state flag has changed little since 1910. With its simple design and long history, the flag has been an outstanding representation of South Carolina. ROBERTA V. H. COPP

Wates, Wylma A. *A Flag Worthy of Your State and People: The History of the South Carolina State Flag.* 2d ed. Columbia: South Carolina Department of Archives and History, 1996.

State House. Three different buildings have served as the capitol of South Carolina. Construction of the first statehouse began in June 1753 in Charleston. Authorities first occupied the building three years later, but the interior was not fully finished until the late 1760s. Located at the northwest corner of Broad and Meeting Streets, the Statehouse in Charleston was among the most sophisticated public buildings in the American colonies. It stood two stories tall and was built of brick finished with stucco. A central pavilion with four Composite-order columns dominated its broad, symmetrical facade. The building burned in 1788. Officials decided to rebuild immediately and returned it to service in the early 1790s as the Charleston County Courthouse.

The destruction of the Charleston building occurred as work on a new statehouse was already under way in Columbia. In 1786 the General Assembly had decided to move the capital from Charleston

The colonial State House. Courtesy, South Carolina Historical Society

and chose Columbia as the seat of government. The new statehouse stood at the southeast corner of Senate and Richardson (now Main) Streets and was first used for the legislative session of 1790. Built of wood with a base of stuccoed brick, its distinguishing feature was a projecting central portico. Offices occupied the ground floor; the legislative halls were located upstairs. Evidence suggests that the building was poorly constructed and deteriorated quickly. In the 1840s the legislature made frequent appropriations for repairs.

The 1791 State House, Columbia. Courtesy, South Caroliniana Library, University of South Carolina

As the limitations of the statehouse became increasingly apparent, efforts to secure funding for a new capitol building gained momentum. The mounting cost of repairs and concerns about the preservation of official records ultimately compelled the General Assembly to authorize construction of a new capitol. In 1849 Governor Whitemarsh B. Seabrook decried the poor conditions under which the state's early records and official documents were stored on the ground floor of the statehouse. The following year the General Assembly decided to build a fireproof building adjacent to the statehouse for archival storage and required that it be designed to serve, if needed, as the basement story for a wing of a new capitol. Construction began in December 1851, and the following year the General Assembly decided to proceed with construction of a new capitol.

The General Assembly declared its intent that the new statehouse was to be a monumental building "comparing in convenience and magnificence to any in the Union," but the chances of fulfilling such ambitions were cast in doubt when the project got off to a troubled start. The architect Peter H. Hammarskold was dismissed in June 1854 after the legislative commission overseeing the project discovered structural flaws in the foundations erected under his supervision. His replacement, George E. Walker, lasted only eight months before the commissioners grew tired of his temperamental outbursts, political ineptitude, and managerial shortcomings. Only after the Baltimore architect John R. Niernsee took charge of the project in 1855 did construction proceed swiftly. His design combined classicism with the central-block-and-wings form that had become virtually standard for capitol buildings in the antebellum republic.

The Civil War brought work to a standstill and ensured a different outcome than had been originally planned. By the fall of 1861 the exterior walls were nearly complete but the building had no roof or interior finishes. The fire that swept through Columbia on the night of February 17, 1865, destroyed the old statehouse but did not seriously damage the new capitol building. Almost entirely ruined, however, were the building materials stored at the site, which included massive quantities of cut marble and granite intended for the lobby and legislative halls. In preparation for the legislative session of 1869, authorities installed a temporary roof and interior finishes, but the statehouse would not be completed for another thirty years.

Work resumed in 1885 when Niernsee returned to Columbia to complete the project he had started three decades earlier. By then his health was failing, and he barely finished drafting construction plans before his death on June 7, 1885. Authorities then hired J. Crawford Neilson, Niernsee's former partner. Neilson completed the legislative halls before rising tensions with state officials led to his dismissal. In 1888 Niernsee's son Frank, an architect and engineer with a growing practice in Columbia, took charge. Under his supervision, workmen installed galvanized metal ceilings, fireproof floors, and cast-iron staircases, galleries, and balconies. The interior was substantially complete by the fall of 1890. The architect Frank P. Milburn finished the exterior by adding porticoes and a dome between 1900 and 1903.

The State House has undergone remarkably few changes since its completion more than a century ago. The legislature considered proposals to enlarge the building in the 1910s, in 1946, and again in 1995, but each was rejected because of financial considerations and respect for the historic design. Instead, the building underwent a series of cosmetic and functional alterations during the twentieth century: remodeling of the Senate in 1913, the House in 1937, and the governor's office in 1966; installation of air conditioning in 1959–1960; and renovation of the lobby in 1962. In 1992 work began on the first full-scale renovation in the building's history. With a total cost of more than $40 million, this project installed new mechanical systems, refurbished the interior, and made the building handicapped-accessible and compliant with current fire and safety codes. Also installed was a seismic protection system designed to minimize damage in the event of a major earthquake similar to the one that devastated Charleston in 1886. Completed in 1998, the renovation preserved the building's historic appearance and modernized it to meet the needs of state government well into the twenty-first century. See plates 38 and 40. DANIEL J. VIVIAN

Bryan, John M. *Creating the South Carolina State House.* Columbia: University of South Carolina Press, 1999.

Lounsbury, Carl. *From Statehouse to Courthouse: An Architectural History of South Carolina's Colonial Capitol and Charleston County Courthouse.* Columbia: University of South Carolina Press, 2001.

State mottoes. South Carolina has two official mottoes. These were engraved on the original great seal in 1777. ANIMIS OPIBUSQUE PARATI (Prepared in Mind and Resources) is on the rim of the seal obverse (front), accompanying a picture of a palmetto tree. The motto had earlier appeared on a £50 South Carolina banknote issued in 1776. The words were taken from the second book of Virgil's *Aeneid,* at the point in the story where Aeneas joined his band of followers who had escaped from the burning city of Troy and had gathered on the beach. Aeneas said that he found his Trojans armed, equipped, ready, and willing to follow him into exile. They were about to set forth on the great voyage of adventure that would ultimately lead to the founding of Rome. Revolutionary South Carolina's use of this motto expressed confidence in the state's destiny.

DUM SPIRO SPERO (While I Breathe, I Hope) appeared on the reverse (back) of the great seal, along with an image of the Roman goddess Spes (Hope). The phrase was popular in the British Isles, where it was borne as a motto by over fifty families. It had also been used as a personal motto by King Charles I and appeared on coins he minted during the English civil war. The words were probably chosen for South Carolina's seal as an expression of optimism that fit well with the picture of Hope. No special connection with Charles I or any of the various families that employed the motto is known. DAVID C. R. HEISSER

Heisser, David C. R. *The State Seal of South Carolina: A Short History.* Columbia: South Carolina Department of Archives and History, 1992.

Pinches, Rosemary, ed. *Elvin's Handbook of Mottoes.* Rev. ed. London: Heraldry Today, 1971.

State Normal School. In 1873 the South Carolina General Assembly, recognizing a need for trained teachers to educate African American citizens following the Civil War, passed "an act to provide for the establishment and support of a State Normal School." The legislators appropriated $25,000 for the school's support and directed the governor to appoint its board of regents. Although the turmoil of Reconstruction politics and the poverty of the state treasury combined to leave the State Normal School underfunded and short-lived, the institution managed to offer a significant example of public teacher training for African Americans and to educate dozens of students who later influenced several generations of schoolchildren.

The school's board of regents leased a building on the campus of the University of South Carolina and hired as principal Mortimer Warren, a well-regarded educator and former principal of the Avery Institute in Charleston. The State Normal School opened with seventeen students on September 1, 1874. Warren quickly realized that only a small portion of the appropriated funding would ever become available. He used encyclopedias donated by Shaw School in Charleston and maps borrowed from the University of South Carolina to establish a full curriculum of teaching theory and practice, history, geography, mathematics, geometry, English, and the constitution of South Carolina. While principal of the State Normal School, Warren also founded and edited the first journal for South Carolina teachers, the *Carolina Teacher,* which was printed on a press operated by students at the school.

The demand for teachers of African American youths prompted most students at the growing State Normal School to begin teaching in South Carolina schools before graduating. By 1877, however, the return of the Democratic Party to state leadership signaled the end of public education for future African American teachers, and the legislature refused to provide any funding for the State Normal School. One of the eight women who graduated in Rutledge Chapel on the closing day of the school on May 31, 1877, was Celia Emma Dial (1857–1935). As Celia Dial Saxon, she pursued a noteworthy fifty-five-year career in teaching and civic leadership in and around Columbia and was inducted into the South Carolina Black Hall of Fame in 1995. KATHERINE REYNOLDS CHADDOCK

Thomason, John Furman. *The Foundations of the Public Schools of South Carolina.* Columbia, S.C.: State Company, 1925.

United States. Bureau of Education. *Report of the Commissioner of Education Made to the Secretary of the Interior for the Year 1874 with Accompanying Papers.* Washington, D.C.: Government Printing Office, 1875.

State parks. As of 2004, South Carolina's system of state parks consisted of forty-six properties totaling more than eighty thousand acres of land. Its genesis came in the 1930s with the development of sixteen state parks under the auspices of the Civilian Conservation Corps (CCC), a Depression-era federal conservation and employment program. These early parks, which included recreation facilities such as lodges, cabins, campgrounds, swimming lakes, and trails, also provided access to some of the state's most scenic natural areas.

Poinsett State Park, like many other state parks, was a WPA project. Courtesy, South Caroliniana Library, University of South Carolina

With the dissolution of the CCC in 1942, state parks came under the management of the State Commission of Forestry, which operated the parks for the next twenty-five years. In the 1950s park attendance dramatically expanded as road improvements, the abundance of automobiles, and relative affluence brought about increased mobility and leisure time. During this period coastal parks at Hunting Island, Edisto Beach, and Myrtle Beach became popular recreation destinations for local residents and out-of-state tourists alike. Until the 1960s South Carolina's state parks were segregated, and though the state provided separate recreational facilities for whites and blacks, they were never equal as claimed. In 1961 a class-action suit was filed to integrate the parks, and in 1963 an order was issued for the state parks to comply with the Civil Rights Act of 1954. Rather than integrate the system, the state attorney general responded by closing the parks to all South Carolinians, regardless of race. However, in response to public demand, all of the parks were reopened on a desegregated basis by 1966.

In 1967 management of the state park system moved from the Forestry Commission to the newly created Department of Parks, Recreation, and Tourism (PRT). This agency was charged with promoting travel and tourism, operating the system of state parks, and assisting local governments in the development of recreational facilities and programs. Though PRT continued to operate parks that had natural and historical significance, a new emphasis was placed on serving local recreational needs. During this period the state added sixteen parks to the system, including several state resort parks. This ambitious acquisition program was made possible largely through massive infusions of federal funding for recreation granted in the 1970s.

At the start of the twenty-first century, PRT managed the state parks in accordance with two primary guiding principles: stewardship of the natural and cultural resources of the state; and service to the citizens and visitors of South Carolina. Consistent with this service mission, the parks provide resource-based recreational opportunities, as well as numerous educational programs. The state park system also embraces a large number of significant natural and cultural resources, including two National Historic Landmarks, eighteen properties listed in the National Register of Historic Places, ten Heritage Trust Sites, and thousands of acres that protect important archaeological sites, rare habitats, and endangered species. AL HESTER

Cox, Stephen Lewis. "The History of Negro State Parks in South Carolina: 1940–1963." Master's thesis, University of South Carolina, 1992.

South Carolina State Planning Board. *Parks and Recreational Areas of South Carolina.* Columbia, S.C.: State Council of Defense, 1941.

State Road. South Carolina's early road system could best be described as "local option." The roads were generally poor and were designed to facilitate local travel. But after the end of the War of 1812, the expansion of cotton production in the South Carolina interior fueled a demand for easy transportation to Charleston. In December 1818 the General Assembly responded by appropriating funds for internal improvements to the state and creating a board of public works to oversee improvement projects. As part of this larger effort, the board began construction on a 110-mile State Road, which would connect Charleston with Columbia. In addition, the board began construction of a road from Columbia to Buncombe County, North Carolina, to accommodate the importation of foodstuffs for South Carolina cotton farmers. This section of the State Road was better known as the Buncombe Road (not to be confused with the city of Greenville's own Buncombe Road). Only an eighteen-mile stretch of this section, running south from Saluda Mountain, was built by the state.

The State Road was not designed to connect towns in the state and, except for Charleston, did not enter a single county seat. The project was a true state enterprise, and for the first four years the laborers on the road were direct state employees. That method was abandoned in 1823, and the work was contracted out. The expensive undertaking was to be paid for with tolls. Plagued by high costs and low income from tolls, the State Road project was a failure. Poor maintenance and high tolls ensured that the road attracted little traffic. The General Assembly halted funding for the road in 1829 and turned over authority for its operation to local commissioners and private interests. More than a century later, Interstate 26 would essentially retrace the route of the original State Road. ALLAN D. CHARLES

Charles, Allan D. "The State's First Try at Building Highways." *Carolina Highways* 33 (February 1978): 23.

Kohn, David, and Bess Glenn. *Internal Improvement in South Carolina, 1817–1828.* Washington, D.C., 1938.

Moore, John Hammond. *The South Carolina Highway Department, 1917–1987.* Columbia: University of South Carolina Press, 1987.

Smith, Alfred G. *Economic Readjustment of an Old Cotton State: South Carolina, 1820–1860.* Columbia: University of South Carolina Press, 1958.

State seal. The great seal of South Carolina was first used on a document dated May 22, 1777. It was a double-sided, circular device impressed on wax and appended to documents by cords or ribbons. Its principal designers were William Henry Drayton and Arthur Middleton. Drayton was mainly responsible for the design of the obverse (front), and Middleton for the reverse (back).

The inspiration for the design came from the Battle of Sullivan's Island, June 28, 1776, when troops under Colonel William Moultrie, manning a palmetto-log fort, defeated a Royal Navy squadron. The seal obverse showed a palmetto on the shore representing the fort, at the base of which was a blasted oak representing the oak-timbered ships. From the tree hung shields inscribed "March 26," the date of ratification of the state constitution in 1776, and "July 4," for the Declaration of Independence. Twelve spears representing the sister states were bound to the palmetto's trunk by a ribbon. In the palm hung with shields, the seal's designers chose an ancient Roman emblem of victory. The reverse depicted the Roman goddess Spes (Hope) walking on the beach at dawn over discarded weapons

The silver matrix for the State Seal. Courtesy, South Carolina Department of Archives and History

and holding a laurel blossom. Spes symbolized the patriots' optimism. The two state mottoes appeared on the seal.

The original pendant seal was cumbersome to make and affix to documents, so sometime in the mid-1780s a small, one-sided seal with the pictures from the great seal compressed into ovals was introduced. Small seals have mostly been used ever since. The original great seal was used for the last time on the Ordinance of Secession (1860).

The state also uses a picture of the two faces of the great seal in ovals on a grassy compartment. On the viewer's left is the goddess Liberty in a long flowing gown bearing a *pileus,* or cap of freedom, on a spear. She holds a wreath of laurel in her outstretched left hand. On the right is an army officer of the Revolutionary War with a tricorn hat and a sword. Overhead the winged figure of Fame emerges from the clouds. She blows one trumpet and carries another. The design first appeared on the nameplate of the *State Gazette of South Carolina* in 1785. The identity of the designer is unknown, and the emblem was not adopted in any legislative enactment. Tradition, however, calls the design the coat of arms, and it frequently decorates state publications and stationery. DAVID C. R. HEISSER

Heisser, David C. R. *The State Seal of South Carolina: A Short History.* Columbia: South Carolina Department of Archives and History, 1992.

Salley, Alexander S., Jr. *The Seal of the State of South Carolina.* Columbia, S.C.: State Company, 1907.

Seals and Symbols of South Carolina Government through Three Centuries. Columbia, S.C.: Columbia Museums of Art and Science, 1982.

State symbols. As sovereign political entities, all fifty states have adopted special symbols. In every state the first emblem was a seal, to be affixed to official documents. In Europe, since ancient times, the seal was deemed an essential instrument of government and a special mark of sovereignty. American state seals were devised and put to use at the time of independence or when the state was admitted to the Union. The design for South Carolina's state seal was inspired by a Revolutionary victory, and the seal was put into service in the spring of 1777.

The practice of flying a state flag was not widely followed in the early years of the Republic. State flags came into use mainly as a result of the Civil War, when Southern states needed banners to replace the United States flag and Northern states required new regimental colors to identify state troops. South Carolina's state flag was adopted on January 26, 1861, shortly after secession. Official state flags came into common use in the decades following the Civil War.

All the states use seals and flags. Sometimes the seal depicts a state coat of arms, a design centered on a shield and more or less in accord with the traditions of European heraldry. In a few cases, such as Alabama, North Dakota, Texas, Vermont, and Virginia, the state uses a coat of arms in addition to, and different from, the seal design.

The tradition of designating flowers, trees, and birds as state symbols came into vogue in the late nineteenth and early twentieth centuries. South Carolina adopted the yellow jessamine as its state flower in 1924. American states' floral emblems have their counterparts in the British Isles, Canada, Australia, and other countries of the Commonwealth of Nations, as well as in Latin America. England's rose, Ireland's shamrock, and the thistle of Scotland are well known.

American state flowers have sometimes been designated by legislatures in recognition of agricultural and economic importance—for example, Florida's orange blossom (1909), Michigan's apple blossom (1897), and the pinecone and tassel of Maine (1895). Usually, however, blossoms have been chosen for their beauty and as particularly characteristic of the state—for example, Mississippi's *Magnolia grandiflora* (unofficially the state flower since 1900), North Carolina's dogwood (1941), Hawaii's hibiscus (1923), and the mayflower of Massachusetts (1918), which also recalls the ship that carried its first English settlers.

In 1926 Kentucky became the first to designate a state bird (the cardinal), and the avian emblems were chosen mainly in the 1920s–1940s. The Carolina wren became South Carolina's official bird in 1948. Texas was the first state to adopt a state tree (the pecan tree) in 1919. In some instances trees have figured early as state emblems—for example, South Carolina's *Sabal palmetto* (adopted in 1939) and Maine's white pine (1959), which appear on the respective state seals. Connecticut chose the white oak in commemoration of its Charter Oak, venerated as the hiding place, in 1687, of its colonial charter, which was rescinded by King James II. In general, legislatures have designated trees specially characteristic and beloved, such as Georgia's live oak (1937) and the southern pine shared by Alabama (1949), Arkansas (1939), and North Carolina (1963).

State songs may be popular or little known. Legislatures of many states have designated two or more musical expressions. As of 2002 Tennessee had five. Some state songs originated in the eighteenth and nineteenth centuries and only later were officially adopted, such as "Yankee Doodle" (Connecticut), two Stephen Foster favorites chosen by Florida ("The Swanee River [Old Folks at Home]") and Kentucky ("My Old Kentucky Home"), and "Maryland, My Maryland," popular during the Civil War. Official legislative designations began in 1911, when South Carolina and Iowa chose state songs.

After World War II, states began to name a great variety of special symbols, starting with California's official fish (the golden trout, 1947) and South Dakota's state animal (the coyote, 1949). Special symbols proliferated beginning in the 1970s. Legislatures named numerous official state fossils, insects, reptiles, shells, rocks and stones, fruits, beverages, grasses, dogs, and cats. Over a dozen states have designated the honeybee as their official state insect. Somewhat unusual are the state muffins of Massachusetts (corn muffin, 1986) and New York (apple muffin, 1987), Vermont's state pie (apple pie, 1999), and New Mexico's official state cookie (bizochito, 1989). DAVID C. R. HEISSER

South Carolina's official state emblems (as of December 2004) are:

American folk dance: Square dance. Adopted in Act No. 329, signed on April 20, 1994, by Governor Carroll Campbell. The General Assembly wanted to recognize a popular, traditional form of family recreation enjoyed by South Carolinians of all ages.

Amphibian: Spotted salamander (*Ambystoma maculatum*). Adopted in Act No. 79, approved by Governor Jim Hodges on June 11, 1999. The salamander was promoted by schoolchildren who found it to be important in the ecological system and an interesting example of wildlife to study.

Animal: White-tailed deer (*Odocoileus virginianus*). Designated by Act No. 1334, signed by Governor John C. West on June 2, 1972. The deer is one of the state's most popular game animals.

Beverage: Milk. Adopted in Act No. 360, signed by Governor Richard Riley on May 8, 1984. The legislation promoted public health and the state's dairy industry.

Bird: Carolina wren (*Thyrothorus ludovicianus* [Latham]). Adopted in Act No. 693, signed by Governor Strom Thurmond on April 3, 1948. The wren is a songbird found in all parts of the state throughout the year.

Butterfly: Eastern tiger swallowtail (*Papilio glaucus*). Designated by Act No. 319, signed by Governor Carroll Campbell on March 29, 1994. One of America's largest and most popular butterflies, it adds beauty to South Carolina gardens from early spring and through much of the year.

Dance: The shag. Declared by Act No. 329, approved by Governor Richard Riley on April 10, 1984. The dance, performed to rhythm and blues, originated in South Carolina and is one of the most popular cultural expressions of the state.

Dog: Boykin spaniel. Recognized by Act No. 31, signed by Governor Richard Riley on March 26, 1985. The spaniel is the only dog originally bred in South Carolina for the state's hunters. The General Assembly recognized the popular breed's superb hunting instincts and friendly personality.

Fish: Striped bass (*Morone saxatilis*). Adopted by the General Assembly in Act No. 1333, approved by Governor John C. West on June 2, 1972. The General Assembly recognized the state's most famous game fish, popular with anglers and caught in both freshwater and saltwater.

Flower: Yellow jessamine (*Gelsemium sempervirens*). Adopted by the General Assembly on February 1, 1924, approved by Governor Thomas Gordon McLeod. The assembly recognized the beautiful harbinger of spring found in all parts of the state.

Fruit: Peach. Recognized by Act No. 360, signed into law by Governor Richard Riley on May 8, 1984. Legislators acted to recognize the economic importance of the peach, as South Carolina is the leading producer of peaches in the eastern United States.

Gemstone: Amethyst. Adopted in Act No. 345, signed by Governor Robert McNair on June 24, 1969. The legislature recognized that South Carolina is one of the few states of the Union where high-quality amethyst is found, noting that a fine specimen was exhibited at the National Museum of Natural History.

Grass: Indian grass (*Sorghastrum nutans*). Named in Act No. 94, approved by Governor Jim Hodges in 2001. The General Assembly recognized Indian grass as a native plant beneficial to the environment.

Hospitality beverage: South Carolina–grown tea. Designated by Act No. 31, approved by Governor David Beasley on April 10, 1995. Tea was grown at Middleton Place near Charleston. Plants descended from Middleton tea are grown in the lowcountry.

Insect: Carolina mantid (*Stagmomantis carolina*), also called the praying mantis. Adopted by Act No. 591, signed by Governor Carroll Campbell on June 1, 1988. The mantis is a predator that consumes great quantities of insects and is therefore an important biological control agent. It is popular with schoolchildren as a living subject of study.

Music: Spiritual. Recognized by Act No. 64, approved by Governor Jim Hodges on June 11, 1999. The General Assembly acted to celebrate the song that originated in South Carolina in the era of slavery as an expression of religious faith and hope.

Opera: *Porgy and Bess.* Proclaimed by Act No. 94, signed into law by Governor Jim Hodges in 2001. The opera *Porgy and Bess,* with music by George Gershwin (1898–1937) and words by DuBose Heyward (1885–1940), is set in Charleston and is based on Heyward's novel *Porgy* (1925), about a crippled African American beggar. The opera premiered in 1935 and became the most popular American opera.

Popular music: Beach music. Acknowledged by Act No. 15, signed by Governor Jim Hodges on March 27, 2001. This favorite music among South Carolinians has become almost synonymous with the state dance, the shag.

Reptile: Loggerhead turtle (*Caretta caretta*). Declared by Act No. 588, signed by Governor Carroll Campbell on June 1, 1988. The General Assembly's action was an effort to protect the loggerhead turtle, a threatened species, from extinction. The South Carolina coastal beaches are among the turtles' favorite nesting places.

Songs (2): "Carolina." Adopted by the General Assembly on February 11, 1911, and approved by Governor Coleman L. Blease. The words of the Civil War patriotic poem "Carolina" by Henry Timrod were set to music by Anne Custis Burgess.

"South Carolina on My Mind." Declared by Act No. 302, signed into law by Governor Richard Riley on March 8, 1984. The ballad, composed by Hank Martin and performed and recorded by Martin and his partner Buzz Arledge, evokes the natural beauty of the state.

Shell: Lettered olive (*Oliva sayana*). Adopted by Act No. 360, signed by Governor Richard Riley on May 8, 1984. The General Assembly praised the beautiful lettered olive, a collector's favorite, and honored Charleston's pioneer conchologist Dr. Edmund Ravenel.

Spider: Carolina wolf spider (*Hogna carolinensis*). Approved by Act No. 389, Pt. II, signed by Governor Jim Hodges on July 21, 2000. South Carolina became the first state to adopt an official state spider. The Carolina wolf spider is important in the state's ecology as it preys on many insects. Skyler B. Hutto, a third-grade student at Sheridan Elementary School, Orangeburg, originally suggested the designation.

Stone: Blue granite. Declared by Act No. 345, signed by Governor Robert McNair on June 24, 1969. Winnsboro blue granite has been used in South Carolina and elsewhere in construction and for ornamental purposes for two centuries.

Tapestry: From the Mountains to the Sea. Designated by Act No. 354, approved by Governor Jim Hodges on June 14, 2000. The great tapestry *From the Mountains to the Sea,* measuring fifty-four by seventy-two inches, was designed by and woven in cotton for the South Carolina Cotton Museum in Bishopville. It includes pictures representing different regions of the state and various state emblems.

Tree: Palmetto (*Sabal palmetto*). Formally adopted in Act No. 63, signed by Governor Burnet R. Maybank on March 17, 1939. The palmetto has graced the state seal since 1777 and the state flag since 1861. It commemorates the Battle of Sullivan's Island, when South Carolina troops manning a palmetto-log fort defeated a British navy squadron on June 28, 1776.

Waltz: "Richardson Waltz." Declared in Act No. 389, Pt. I, approved by Governor Jim Hodges on July 21, 2000. The beautiful dance melody was composed by a member of the Richardson family, played at balls in Clarendon and Sumter Counties, and handed down for over two centuries. It was written down and copyrighted by Mary Richardson Briggs of Summerton.

Wild game bird: Wild turkey (*Meleagris gallopavo*). Recognized by Act No. 508, approved by Governor James Edwards on March 30, 1976. The General Assembly acted to honor the state's most popular game bird, prized as a table delicacy by generations of South Carolinians.

Shearer, Benjamin F., and Barbara S. Shearer. *State Names, Seals, Flags, and Symbols: A Historical Guide.* 3d ed. Westport, Conn.: Greenwood, 2002.

Smith, Whitney. *The Flag Book of the United States.* Rev. ed. New York: Morrow, 1975.

Stateburg. The name of this town, located in western Sumter County in the High Hills of Santee, reflects Stateburg's raison d'être. A group of speculators headed by Thomas Sumter founded Stateburg in 1783 in hopes that it would be named the new state capital of South Carolina. By the time the General Assembly took up the matter of capital relocation three years later, Stateburg had become a bustling village and seat of the newly established Claremont County. But Sumter lacked the popularity and political connections in the assembly necessary to make his capital dream a reality. Legislators gave Stateburg no serious consideration.

With the creation of Sumter District in 1800, Stateburg lost its status as a county seat, and the tiny town soon stagnated. The rural community that remained, however, prospered. Since the time of the Revolutionary War, wealthy lowcountry planters and their families had summered in the neighborhood. When intensive, inland cotton cultivation became lucrative in the early nineteenth century, some planters became year-round residents and replaced their rustic retreats crowning the hills with fine, permanent homes. The noted architect and engineer Robert Mills wrote in the mid-1820s that "there is not a more desirable place for residence, either for health or society, in any part of the state." The "affluence and hospitality" of those who resort and reside at Stateburg, he continued, "give to the place a character of ease and dignity."

For more than a century after the Civil War, Stateburg lost little of its refined, bucolic aura, and in 1971 the Stateburg Historic District was listed in the National Register of Historic Places. Because of its proximity to Shaw Air Force Base and the growing city of Sumter, by the turn of the twenty-first century the community's pastoral landscape, unprotected by local zoning ordinances, was fast becoming suburbanized. MATTHEW A. LOCKHART

Gregorie, Anne King. *History of Sumter County, South Carolina.* Sumter, S.C.: Library Board of Sumter County, 1954.

———. *Thomas Sumter.* Columbia, S.C.: R. L. Bryan, 1931.

Lockhart, Matthew A. "'Under the Wings of Columbia': John Lewis Gervais as Architect of South Carolina's 1786 Capital Relocation Legislation." *South Carolina Historical Magazine* 104 (July 2003): 176–97.

Sumter, Thomas S. *Stateburg and Its People.* 3d ed. Columbia, S.C.: State Printing, 1982.

Tisdale, Thomas. *A Lady of the High Hills: Natalie Delage Sumter.* Columbia: University of South Carolina Press, 2001.

States' rights. The doctrine of states' rights, a recurring theme of South Carolina political thought, is composed of two elements: a belief that the U.S. Constitution is a compact formed by states that retained their sovereign status; and a belief that powers not specifically granted by the Constitution to the national government remain in state hands. The second principle derives from the Tenth Amendment of the U.S. Constitution, which states that "the powers not delegated to the United States by the Constitution, nor prohibited it to the states, are reserved to the states respectively, or to the people." State-reserved powers were designed to discourage undue concentrations of power in a distant national government. On May 23, 1788, the South Carolina ratification convention strongly recommended passage of such an amendment.

During the sectional controversies before the Civil War, John C. Calhoun contended that states as sovereigns could nullify federal laws that exceeded the powers granted to the national government by the compact. Calhoun cautioned that this powerful instrument of interposition should be used only as a last resort when an unconstitutional act of the national government was "clear and palpable" and "highly dangerous." On November 24, 1832, a South Carolina convention declared the federal tariffs of 1828 and 1832 "null and void" amid charges that they would be economically devastating to the South by protecting northern manufacturers by raising levies on imported goods. This interposition was rescinded following a compromise tariff negotiated by Calhoun, but an 1833 convention nullified the "Force Bill," which President Andrew Jackson had lobbied through Congress to back enforcement of federal laws.

Much of the battle over federal power versus states' rights was fought over slavery and racial equality. In 1850–1851 South Carolina opposed congressional attempts to block the spread of slavery

An election ballot from the hotly contested 1832 election. Courtesy, South Carolina Historical Society

to new territories by arguing that power over slavery was reserved to the states. After the Compromise of 1850 admitted California as a free state, a South Carolina convention claimed the right to secede but declined to exercise that right when it became clear that other states would not follow.

Secession finally came on December 20, 1860. The Constitution of the Confederate States of America (March 11, 1861) was permeated with states' rights provisions. The preamble, announcing that each state was "acting in its sovereign and independent character," implied that states did not surrender their sovereignty to the new body. An extreme states' rights provision permitted a state to impeach Confederate officials whose duties were confined to that state. State officials frustrated Confederate attempts to control state troops and slave labor by contending that the power was reserved to them. States' rights were an inspiration for the birth of the Confederacy and a bane of its existence.

The presidential election of 1876 and subsequent Compromise of 1877, the end of Reconstruction, and narrow court interpretations of the Fourteenth and Fifteenth Amendments led to federal abandonment of civil rights enforcement and a corresponding reduction in states' rights rhetoric. States' rights forces took the field in 1948 when fears of President Harry Truman's advocacy of legislation to prevent racial discrimination in employment and voting spawned the States' Rights Democratic Party, or Dixiecrats. The Dixiecrats ran South Carolina governor Strom Thurmond for president, but Truman prevailed. The Dixiecrats carried only Alabama, Louisiana, Mississippi, and South Carolina, but the campaign created forces that undermined the Democratic Party's dominance and eventually led to a two-party South.

The Supreme Court's 1954 decision in *Brown v. Board of Education* (including *Briggs v. Elliott* from South Carolina) outlawed racial segregation in the public schools and again provoked states' rights arguments. In 1956 southern congressmen, led by Thurmond, issued the "Southern Manifesto," declaring, "we decry the Supreme Court's encroachment on the rights reserved to the States and to the people, contrary to established law, and to the Constitution." That same year a resolution of the South Carolina General Assembly charged that the Supreme Court had usurped the states' role in the constitutional amendment process by fashioning new principles to declare separate but equal schools invalid. The resolution proclaimed that South Carolina as a "loyal and sovereign State of the Union will exercise the powers reserved to it under the Constitution to judge for itself of the infractions [of the Constitution by the Supreme Court]." Although this could be interpreted as asserting a right to defy the Supreme Court's ruling, the resolution stopped short of declaring it null and void.

Such states' rights maneuvers stiffened resistance but did not halt desegregation. Interposition had become more of a relic in the museum of constitutional curiosities than an effective weapon against encroaching federal power. The right to political equality also became a galvanic force. In *South Carolina v. Katzenbach* (1966), states' rights arguments failed to convince the Supreme Court that federal laws implementing the constitutional prohibition of racial discrimination in voter qualifications violated power reserved to the state. Equal protection for all races prevailed as the supreme law of the land. JAMES L. UNDERWOOD

McDonald, Forrest. *States' Rights and the Union: Imperium in Imperio, 1776–1876.* Lawrence: University of Kansas Press, 2000.

Owsley, Frank Lawrence. *State Rights in the Confederacy.* 1925. Reprint, Gloucester, Mass.: Peter Smith, 1961.

Sinha, Manisha. *The Counterrevolution of Slavery: Politics and Ideology in Antebellum South Carolina.* Chapel Hill: University of North Carolina Press, 2000.

Steadman, Mark (b. 1930). Novelist. Steadman was born in Statesboro, Georgia, on July 2, 1930, the son of Mark Sidney Steadman, Sr., an engineer with the highway department, and Marie Hopkins. The family lived in Decatur from 1940 until 1947. After his father died, Steadman moved with his family to Savannah, where they had kin. He attended Armstrong Junior College (A.A., 1949) and Emory University (B.A. in English, 1951). He married Joan Anderson, a school librarian, on March 29, 1952. They have three sons: Clayton, Todd, and Wade.

Steadman served in the U.S. Navy as a naval air cadet from 1951 to 1953. From June 1953 he worked as a copywriter for the publishing company W. R. C. Smith in Atlanta. He then went back to school, at Florida State University (M.A. in English, 1956). In July 1957 he took a job as an instructor at Clemson College, and since then his life has been centered in rural Pickens County. He received his Ph.D. from Florida State University in 1963 for a thesis on "Modern American Humor." The subject reflects his permanent preoccupation.

Steadman taught humor and the American novel at Clemson for forty years. From 1980 until 1997 he was also writer in residence there. In 1968 he took a year's leave of absence and accepted a position as visiting professor at the American University in Cairo, Egypt, where he "found his voice" as a writer of fiction. By the time he left Cairo in June 1969 he had written six stories, and back in South Carolina he added seven more. They were published in 1971 as *McAfee County: A Chronicle.* It is set in an imaginary coastal county with a population of 6,254, fifty-eight percent of whom are African American. The county serves as a microcosm of a southern coastal city around 1960. With a Gothic sense of the comic and with much compassion, Steadman shows the grotesqueness in most lives. The book did well and was brought out in British, French, and German editions.

In 1976 *A Lion's Share* was published. The novel is about the greatest southern high school football player of all time. But we see more than his triumph; we also witness the hero's tragic failure in college, in his job, and in his marriage. As William Koon put it, Steadman "moves from comedy to genuine tragedy" in this novel. The book was not a public or critical success, and Steadman came to regret that he had not made the football part of it a separate novel. So fourteen years later he rewrote the funny and nostalgic part and published it as *Bang-Up Season.*

In 1983 Steadman was Fulbright lecturer at Leningrad State University and began work on his third novel, which became *Angel Child* (1987). It is a hilarious story about Langston James's "misformative years," but it is also about a grotesque-looking young southerner's dreams and troubled longing. In 1991 Steadman wrote the entry on "Humor" in the *Encyclopedia of Southern Culture.* Since leaving Clemson in 1997, he has been working on some "autobiographical fiction" and enjoying his retirement in Pickens County. JAN NORDBY GRETLUND

Boyd, Molly. "Rural Identity in the Southern Gothic Novels of Mark Steadman." *Studies in the Literary Imagination* 27 (1994): 41–54.

Greiner, Donald J. "The Southern Fiction of Mark Steadman." *South Carolina Review* 9 (November 1976): 5–11.

Koon, William. "Mark Steadman." In *Dictionary of Literary Biography.* Vol. 6, *American Novelists since World War II, Second Series,* edited by James E. Kibler. Detroit: Gale, 1980.

Nuwer, Hank. "Mark Steadman's Comedy of Ethos: An Interview." *Rendezvous: Journal of Arts and Letters* 21 (1985): 92–99.

Steele, Henry Maxwell (1922–2005). Writer, educator. Max Steele was born in Greenville on March 30, 1922, the son of John M. Steele and Minnie Russell. He attended Furman University for two years and Vanderbilt University while serving in the U.S. Air Force. He received a B.A. degree from the University of North Carolina at Chapel Hill in 1946. He did further study at the Academie Jullienne and the Sorbonne in Paris. On December 31, 1960, Steele married Dianna Whittinghill. They have two sons.

Steele's first published story, "Grandfather and Chow Dog: A Story," appeared in *Harper's* in 1944. His novel *Debby* was published in 1950, when it won the Harper prize of the year. It also received the Eugene F. Saxon Memorial Award and the Mayflower Cup for best book by a North Carolinian in 1950. *Debby* was reprinted by Perennial Library in 1960 as *The Goblins Must Go Barefoot* and by Louisiana State University Press in 1997 as *Debby.*

Steele is best known for his short stories, which have appeared in *Harper's* and other magazines including *Atlantic Monthly, New Yorker, Cosmopolitan, Esquire, Mademoiselle,* and *Quarterly Review of Literature.* Several stories have been included in anthologies used by teachers in middle- and high-school English classes, and Funk and Wagnall's selected "The Cat and the Coffee Drinkers" for its *Great Short Stories of the World* textbook. Three volumes of Steele's stories have been published: *Where She Brushed Her Hair and Other Short Stories* (1968); *The Cat and the Coffee Drinkers* (1969); and *The Hat of My Mother: Stories* (1988).

Steele began teaching in 1956 at the University of North Carolina (UNC), where he later served as writer in residence, professor, and director of the creative writing program. Under his leadership, the writing program produced some of the nation's most promising young writers. He retired from UNC in 1988 as professor emeritus. He also taught at the University of California at San Francisco, Bennington College, South Carolina Governor's School for the Arts, Bread Loaf Writers' Conference, and Squaw Valley Writers' Conference. He was an advisory editor of the *Paris Review* from 1952 to 1954 and has been an editor of *Story* magazine since 1988. He has received two O. Henry prizes, two National Endowment for the Arts and Humanities grants, the Standard Oil Award for Excellence in Undergraduate Teaching, and honorary degrees from Belmont Abby and Furman University.

In 1992 Steele was inducted into the South Carolina Academy of Authors. In his acceptance speech he said, "All of my work was written away from home but with an unbreakable tie to it." Since his eightieth birthday he has been concentrating on writing short-short stories, published in *Harper's* and the *Washington Post,* and lecturing in Paris, London, and Chapel Hill to University of North Carolina students. MARGUERITE HAYS

Nostrandt, Jeanne R. "Max Steele." In *Contemporary Southern Writers,* edited by Roger Mautz. Detroit: St. James, 1999.

"Postwar Paris: Chronicles of a Literary Life." *Paris Review* 41 (spring 1999): 302–4.

Stevenson, Ferdinan Backer (1928–2001). Lieutenant governor, civic leader, author. "Nancy" Stevenson was born on June 8, 1928, in New Rochelle, New York, the daughter of William Bryant Backer and Fernanda Legare. Upon the death of her husband, Fernanda, who was descended from several prominent Charleston families, returned in 1932 to her Charleston home with Nancy and her brother. Nancy attended Ashley Hall School and was awarded a bachelor of arts degree from Smith College in 1949. From 1950 to 1954 she was married to Olav Moltke-Hansen, a Norwegian diplomat, and lived in Norway and New York City with their two sons.

Ferdinan "Nancy" Stevenson. Courtesy, South Carolina Department of Archives and History

From 1952 to 1954 she worked for the *New York Herald Tribune,* writing book reviews and doing overseas reporting. After a divorce, she returned to Charleston with her sons and taught junior high school. From 1956 to 1980 she was married to Norman Williams Stevenson of Charleston, an attorney and state legislator. They had three children. She continued her interest in writing and, using a pseudonym, cowrote three mystery novels.

Stevenson was an active civic leader during the 1960s and 1970s, with a special interest in drama and historic preservation. Between 1965 and 1978 she was a trustee of the Historic Charleston Foundation, cochair of the Save Charleston Foundation, trustee and secretary of the College of Charleston Foundation, president of Footlight Players, and vice president of the South Carolina Historical Society. Frustrated by the lack of support for historic preservation from the General Assembly, she decided to run for office in 1974 and won Charleston's House District 110 seat. She was reelected in 1976. Her two major legislative interests were the Fiscal Accountability Act, which mandated a more uniform fiscal reporting system, and the Water Reporting Act, designed to report water usage and allocate water in times of drought.

In 1978 Stevenson successfully ran for lieutenant governor, becoming the first woman to serve in a statewide office in South Carolina. As lieutenant governor, she worked with Governor Richard Riley to pass significant legislation designed to improve South Carolina schools. Colleagues described her as an effective leader of the Senate and an active participant in the governor's policy discussions. She instituted the Lieutenant Governor's Writing Awards Program, which presented awards to fifth-graders and eighth-graders for creative writing, and the Public Assistance Line (PAL), a toll-free line designed to help citizens find out which agency or organization to call for assistance with personal and public problems.

Although not an active member of women's organizations, Stevenson demonstrated that women could be effective political leaders and work well with men. She set up the public hearings in the Senate devoted to the ultimately unsuccessful attempt to achieve South Carolina ratification of the Equal Rights Amendment. She also worked to increase public awareness and support for victims of domestic violence. She chose not to run for reelection in 1982 but served in 1983–1984 as cochair of the steering committee for Ernest Hollings's presidential campaign and as a member of the national Democratic platform accountability and steering committee. In 1984 she ran unsuccessfully for the Second Congressional District seat held by Republican congressman Floyd Spence.

Stevenson moved to the Washington, D.C., area in 1985 and turned her major efforts from politics to art. She established the Winston Gallery in Washington, which specialized in contemporary art. After a long struggle with breast cancer, Stevenson died at her home in Floyd, Virginia, on May 31, 2001. ALICE H. HENDERSON

Bailey, N. Louise, Mary L. Morgan, and Carolyn R. Taylor, eds. *Biographical Directory of the South Carolina Senate, 1776–1785.* 3 vols. Columbia: University of South Carolina Press, 1986.

Stewart, Thomas McCants (1853–1923). Lawyer, civil rights leader. Born in Charleston on December 28, 1853, to free black parents, George Gilchrist Stewart and Anna Morris, T. McCants Stewart achieved national distinction as an African American leader in the late nineteenth century. He attended the Avery Normal Institute before enrolling in Howard University in Washington, D.C., in 1869. There, Stewart distinguished himself as a student and contributed articles to the Washington *New National Era,* an African American newspaper. Dissatisfied with the quality of instruction at Howard, he enrolled in the University of South Carolina in 1874. In December 1875 Stewart graduated with B.A. and LL.B. degrees. In 1876 Stewart married Charlotte Pearl Harris, the daughter of Reverend W. D. Harris, a Methodist minister. The couple had two sons and a daughter before the marriage ended in divorce. In 1893 he married Alice Franklin. Stewart's second marriage produced three daughters.

Stewart taught mathematics at the State Agricultural and Mechanical College in Orangeburg between 1877 and 1878, and shortly thereafter he joined the law firm of South Carolina congressman Robert Brown Elliott. In 1877 Stewart also became an ordained minister in the African Methodist Episcopal Church, and the following year he was admitted to the Princeton Theological Seminary. Although Stewart did not graduate from the seminary, he became pastor of the Bethel AME Church in New York in 1880.

In New York, Stewart emerged as a national civil rights leader, a respected attorney, and a writer. He argued several important civil rights cases before the New York courts, served on the Brooklyn Board of Education, and contributed to the New York *Freeman,* an important African American newspaper. Stewart also organized the African American vote for the Democratic Party, making him one of the most visible black Democrats in the nation. In 1883 he migrated to Liberia to serve as a professor at Liberia College and to encourage African American immigration to the young republic. By 1885 Stewart returned to New York. Although disillusioned about the future of immigration to Africa, he wrote about his experience in a book, *Liberia: The Americo-African Republic* (1886).

Restless, but also struggling to earn a living as an attorney in New York, Stewart relocated to Hawaii in 1898. There he hoped to advance his legal practice and organize the Republican Party, which he supported after having renounced his Democratic sympathies several years earlier. After achieving little success, Stewart relocated to London in 1905 and in 1906 returned to Liberia, where he was appointed an associate justice on the Liberian Supreme Court in 1911. His outspokenness and criticism of Liberia's president resulted in his removal from the court in 1914.

Stewart returned to London, where he hoped to live out his life. But in 1921 he relocated to the Virgin Islands, a newly acquired United States territory. Regarded as an elder statesman, Stewart established a legal practice with Christopher Payne, one of the most experienced attorneys on the islands. One year after his arrival, Stewart supported a delegation of Virgin Islanders who petitioned the U.S. Congress to provide greater freedom to the inhabitants. On his return voyage to St. Thomas in December 1922, he contracted pneumonia. Stewart died in St. Thomas on January 7, 1923. ALBERT S. BROUSSARD

Broussard, Albert S. *African American Odyssey: The Stewarts, 1853–1963.* Lawrence: University Press of Kansas, 1998.

Wynes, Charles E. "T. McCants Stewart: Peripatetic Black South Carolinian." *South Carolina Historical Magazine* 80 (October 1979): 311–17.

Stoneman's Raid (May 1865). This minor cavalry raid through the South Carolina upstate occurred in the weeks following the assassination of President Abraham Lincoln and the flight of Confederate president Jefferson Davis and his cabinet from Richmond, Virginia. In mid-April 1865 General William T. Sherman ordered two brigades of General George Stoneman's federal cavalry, under the command of Colonels W. J. Palmer and S. B. Brown, into South Carolina to search for Davis and the fugitive Confederate government.

During the first week of May 1865, Palmer's brigade entered South Carolina from Hendersonville, North Carolina, and moved toward Spartanburg, which fell without significant resistance or damage on May 2. Moving into Greenville, Palmer was joined by Brown's brigade. Palmer then moved across the Tugaloo River into Georgia, while elements of Brown's brigade occupied Greenville and seized Anderson. In each case the raid came almost as a complete surprise, as the upstate had been largely isolated from news of the conflict since the destruction of Columbia in February 1865. In Greenville physical damage and civilian casualties were minimal, but cavalrymen plundered shops and warehouses along Main Street throughout the day. The Soldier's Rest Hospital, stripped of scarce medical supplies, served as a temporary headquarters for the raiders. However, apart from the plundering, it appears that the raiders did not inflict significant destruction or terror upon the town or its people.

In Anderson resistance to the raiders seems to have been sharper. Accounts indicate that Colonel Brown failed to maintain discipline among his soldiers, resulting in the harassment and beating of many citizens, the plundering of homes and businesses, and at least two casualties. As was the case in Greenville and Spartanburg, however, Anderson was spared burning.

Anderson was evacuated the day following its capture, and the federal units remaining in upper South Carolina were ordered back to Tennessee. Though Davis eluded capture in the Palmetto State, he eventually fell into Union hands on May 9, 1865, in Irwinville, Georgia. WILLIAM SHAUN ALEXANDER

Cooper, Nancy Vance Ashmore. *Greenville: Woven from the Past.* Sun Valley, Calif.: American Historical Press, 2000.

Huff, Archie Vernon, Jr. *Greenville: The History of the City and County in the South Carolina Piedmont.* Columbia: University of South Carolina Press, 1995.

Keys, Thomas Bland. "The Federal Pillage of Anderson, South Carolina: Brown's Raid." *South Carolina Historical Magazine* 76 (April 1975): 80–86.

Mason, Frank H. "General Stoneman's Last Campaign and the Pursuit of Jefferson Davis." In *Sketches of War History, 1861–1865: Papers Prepared for the Ohio Commandery of the Military Order of the Loyal Legion of the United States, 1888–1890.* Vol. 3 Cincinnati, Ohio: Robert Clarke, 1890.

Stoney, Samuel Gaillard (1891–1968). Architect, author, historian, preservationist. Stoney is considered by many to be the quintessential Charlestonian. Born in Charleston on August 29, 1891, son of the planter Samuel Stoney, Sr., and Louisa Cheves Smythe, he was descended on his mother's side from the antebellum writer Louisa McCord and was also related to the writer John Bennett and the preservation architect Albert Simons. After graduating from the College of Charleston, he saw service on the Mexican border. And although he was also an officer in the 318th Field Artillery, 81st Division in France, he never saw combat. A degree in architecture from the Georgia Institute of Technology led to work in Atlanta and New York, where his charm and knowledge brought him into contact with artists and scholars. His interest in Gullah enabled him to serve as a dialogue coach for actors in *Porgy* and so piqued the interest of the author Gertrude Mathews Shelby that she convinced Stoney to coauthor two books with her: a collection of creation tales told in Gullah, *Black Genesis* (1930); and a novel on the tragedy of miscegenation, *Po' Buckra* (1930).

In 1933, at the MacDowell Colony in New Hampshire, Stoney met and married the New England poet (and later novelist) Frances Frost. They moved to Charleston, and the marriage ended in divorce. Stoney then began a frank love affair with his native city. President of the South Carolina Historical Society, the Preservation Society, Historic Charleston Foundation, the Huguenot Society, and other organizations, Stoney helped document the city's past while fighting to save much of its architecture. His stubborn stands gained him both detractors and devotees. Living simply, he became a familiar sight on Charleston's streets, where he was known as much for his sandals and shirtsleeves as his curiosity, knowledge, and wit. He was a frequent and popular speaker on numerous topics, all colored with his affection for his city. He wrote the text to accompany Bayard Wootten's book of photographs, *Charleston: Azaleas and Old Brick* (1937), and contributed substantially to seminal works on area architecture: *Plantations of the Carolina Low Country* (1938) and *This Is Charleston* (1944), an architectural survey that has been key to the preservation of the physical city. Minor works include *The Story of South Carolina's Senior Bank: The Bank of Charleston* and *The Dulles Family in South Carolina* (both published in 1955).

As author of numerous historical articles, aide to scholars, and contributor to the intellectual life of the city, Stoney built a scholarly foundation for the documentation and study of Charleston, which, in turn, treated him as a favorite son. In May 1968 he was awarded a doctor of letters from the College of Charleston, where he had lectured from 1949 to 1966. He died at his own hand on July 30, 1968. His death, the *News and Courier* noted, "removes a Charleston landmark as real as the architectural treasures he spent his life fighting to preserve." He was buried at St. James Goose Creek Episcopal Church, which he had served as senior (and sole) warden for forty years. HARLAN GREENE

"Article Features Stoney and City." Charleston *News and Courier,* April 12, 1964, p. C11.

Bowles, Billy E. "Stoney's Death Takes Away City Landmark." Charleston *News and Courier,* August 4, 1968, p. C12.

Greene, Harlan. *Mr. Skylark: John Bennett and the Charleston Renaissance.* Athens: University of Georgia Press, 2001.

Leland, Jack. "Samuel Gaillard Stoney: 1891–1968." *Preservation Progress* 13 (November 1968): 1, 6.

Rigney, Harriet Stoney Popham. "Samuel Gaillard Stoney: 'If I Were a House. . . .'" *Carologue* 8 (autumn 1992): 6–7, 18–19.

Stono Rebellion (September 1739). The Stono Rebellion was a violent albeit failed attempt by as many as one hundred slaves to reach St. Augustine and claim freedom in Spanish-controlled Florida. The uprising was South Carolina's largest and bloodiest slave insurrection. While not a direct challenge to the authority of the state, the Stono Rebellion nevertheless alerted white authorities to the dangers of slave revolt, caused a good deal of angst among planters, and resulted in legislation designed to control slaves and lessen the chances of insurrection by the colony's black majority population.

The revolt began on Sunday, September 9, 1739, on a branch of the Stono River in St. Paul's Parish, near Charleston. Several factors influenced slaves' timing of the rebellion, including a suspicious visit to Charleston by a priest who contemporaries thought was "employed by the Spaniards to procure a general Insurrection of the Negroes," a yellow fever epidemic that swept the area in August and September, and rumors of war between Spain and England. It is also probable that the Stono rebels timed their revolt to take place before September 29, when a provision requiring all white men to carry firearms to Sunday church services was to go into effect. In addition, several of the insurgents originated from the heavily Catholic Kongo, and their religious beliefs influenced the timing of the uprising.

Whatever the slaves' reasoning, the revolt began early on Sunday when the conspirators met at the Stono River. From there, they moved to Stono Bridge, broke into a store, equipped themselves with guns and powder, and killed two men. Guns in hand, they burned a house, killed three people, and then turned southward, reaching a tavern before sunup. There the insurgents discriminated, sparing the innkeeper because they considered him "a good man and kind to his slaves." The innkeeper's neighbors were less fortunate; the rebels burned four of their houses, ransacked another, and killed all the whites they found. Other slaves joined the rebellion, and some sources suggest that at this point the insurgents used drums, raised a flag or banner, and shouted "Liberty!" during their march southward.

At about eleven o'clock, Lieutenant Governor William Bull encountered the insurgents on his way to Charleston. Bull and his four companions "escaped & raised the Countrey." As the rebels proceeded southward, their ranks increased from sixty to as many as one hundred participants. According to a contemporary account, they then "halted in a field and set to dancing, Singing and beating Drums to draw more Negroes to them."

By late afternoon the original insurgents had covered ten miles. Some were undoubtedly tired, and others were likely drunk on stolen liquor. Confident in their numbers and Kongolese military training, the rebels paused in an open field near the Jacksonborough ferry in broad daylight. To rest and also to draw more slaves to their ranks, they decided to delay crossing the Edisto River.

By four o'clock between twenty and one hundred armed planters and militiamen, possibly alerted to the revolt by Bull's party, confronted the rebels in what was thereafter known as "the battlefield." The rebels distinguished themselves as courageous, even in the eyes of their enemies, but white firepower won the day. Some slaves who had been forced to join the rebellion were released, others were shot, and some were decapitated and their heads set on posts. Thirty members of the rebel force escaped, many of whom were hunted down the following week.

Whites perceived the Stono insurrection to have continued at least until the following Sunday, when militiamen encountered the largest group of disbanded rebels another thirty miles south. A second battle ensued, this one effectively ending the insurrection. Yet white fears echoed for months. Militia companies in the area remained on guard, and some planters deserted the Stono region in November "for their better Security and Defence against those Negroes which were concerned in that Insurrection who were not yet taken." Some of the rebels were rounded up in the spring of 1740, and one leader was not captured until 1742.

The rebellion resulted in efforts to curtail the activities of slaves and free blacks. The 1740 Negro Act made the manumission of slaves dependent on a special act of the assembly and mandated patrol service for every militiaman. The colony also imposed a prohibitive duty on the importation of new slaves in 1741 in an effort to stem the growth of South Carolina's majority black population.

About forty whites and probably as many blacks were killed during the Stono insurrection. The willingness of slaves to strike out for freedom with such force heightened anxieties among whites over internal security in the South Carolina slaveholding society for years to come. MARK M. SMITH

Pearson, Edward A. "'A Countryside Full of Flames': A Reconsideration of the Stono Rebellion and Slave Rebelliousness in the Early Eighteenth-Century South Carolina Lowcountry." *Slavery and Abolition* 17 (August 1996): 22–50.

Smith, Mark M. *Stono: Documenting and Interpreting a Southern Slave Revolt.* Columbia: University of South Carolina Press, 2005.

Thornton, John K. "African Dimensions of the Stono Rebellion." *American Historical Review* 96 (October 1991): 1101–13.

Wood, Peter H. *Black Majority: Negroes in Colonial South Carolina from 1670 through the Stono Rebellion.* New York: Knopf, 1975.

Stowers, Freddie (ca. 1896–1918). Soldier, Medal of Honor recipient. This Anderson County native was the nation's only African American from World War I to be awarded the Medal of Honor, the military's highest decoration for heroism. The fourth of ten children born to Wylie and Annie Stowers, he grew up on a farm near Sandy Springs. He had a wife, Pearl, and a daughter, Minnie Lee. He was drafted in October 1917 and underwent initial training at Camp Jackson. All U.S. armed forces were segregated during this time, and few African Americans had the opportunity to become officers. Violent incidents during the summer of 1917 between black troops and white civilians in Houston, Texas, and in Spartanburg, South Carolina, strained race relations still more. Like many other African American draftees from South Carolina, Stowers served in the 371st Infantry Regiment, which had been formed at Camp Jackson. The army sent this regiment overseas in April 1918 as part of the all-black 93d Infantry Division, but because few U.S. generals wanted to command African American troops, the 371st and the three other regiments that comprised the 93d were attached to the French army. Although the American soldiers kept their khaki uniforms, they carried French weapons and equipment. France would later recognize the 371st for its World War I service by awarding the organization the *Croix de Guerre* with Palm for its "superb spirit and admirable disregard for danger."

Having attained the rank of private first class in December 1917, Stowers was promoted to corporal the following May. He served as a squad leader in Company C of the 371st and spent the summer in the Lorraine sector. Corporal Stowers distinguished himself in action and lost his life on September 28, 1918, during the Meuse-Argonne offensive. More than half of his company was killed after the Germans lured the Americans onto open ground by pretending to surrender. The enemy soldiers then jumped back into their trenches and opened fire with rifles, mortars, and machine guns. Stowers led the survivors of his squad in an attack on the machine gun that most threatened his company. After destroying the nest and killing the occupants, the corporal kept crawling forward until machine gun bullets from another position struck him. Though badly wounded, he continued encouraging his squad until he died. Stowers's actions and inspirational bravery contributed to the capture of an important hill and the infliction of a high number of casualties on the Germans.

Stowers's commander recommended him for the Medal of Honor, but whether through administrative oversight or racism, the award was not processed. Because the recommendation had been made within two years of the battle, however, military regulations allowed for the process to resume when the paperwork was discovered more than seventy years later after several congressmen questioned why no African Americans had been awarded the Medal of Honor during World War I. On April 24, 1991, President George Bush presented the medal to the hero's surviving sisters, Georgiana Palmer and Mary Bowens. Stowers is buried in the Meuse-Argonne American Cemetery in France. ANDREW H. MYERS

"A Medal of Honor for a Black Soldier from World War I." *New York Times,* April 6, 1991, p. 6.

Megginson, W. J. *Black Soldiers in World War I: Anderson, Pickens, and Oconee Counties, South Carolina.* Seneca, S.C.: Oconee County Historical Society, 1994.

Radcliffe, Donnie. "At Last, a Black Badge of Courage." *Washington Post,* April 25, 1991, p. C3.

Stuart, Bob. "Medal of Honor Presentation Seeks to Rectify Slight of World War I Hero." Columbia *State,* April 24, 1991, pp. B1, B2.

Strawberry Chapel (Berkeley County). James Child, founder of Childsbury Town on the Cooper River in St. John's Berkeley Parish, bequeathed an acre and a half for a chapel. The building was complete by 1725, when the South Carolina legislature passed an act establishing a parochial chapel of ease at the site. Chapels of ease made services more accessible to those who lived far from the parish centers, but most had to share ministers with the parish churches. The minister in 1726, Brian Hunt, reported that he preached at Childsbury once a month, every second Sunday afternoon. In addition to being at the intersection of two Indian trading paths, Childsbury was located at the farthest point that oceangoing vessels could travel up the west branch of the Cooper River. The town boasted a school, a chapel, a tavern, and a ferry.

The plan of Strawberry Chapel is typical of Anglican churches in colonial South Carolina: rectangular with entrances on the north, south, and west sides. The roof is called "jerkin-head" style because the beveled gable resembles a hooded jacket or jerkin. Bull's-eye windows ornament both gable ends, while single windows flank the doorways and the altar.

In addition to inhabitants of Childsbury, Strawberry Chapel served families from prosperous Cooper River rice plantations. The churchyard at Strawberry contains a special enclosure for the Ball family. The elaborate kinship network of the Balls included people of other names as well, and Strawberry Chapel became a symbol of family continuity in the area. Although no longer in regular use, services were still held at Strawberry Chapel several times per year into the twenty-first century. It was listed in the National Register of Historic Places in 1972. SUZANNE LINDER

Linder, Suzanne Cameron. *Anglican Churches in Colonial South Carolina: Their History and Architecture.* Charleston, S.C.: Wyrick, 2000.

Terry, George D. "'Champaign Country': A Social History of an Eighteenth Century Lowcountry Parish in South Carolina, St. Johns Berkeley County." Ph.D. diss., University of South Carolina, 1981.

Stretch-out. In the aftermath of World War I, with pressure to maintain profit margins in the face of increasing competition and falling demand for southern textiles, mill owners began looking for ways to cut operating costs and improve efficiency. The resulting strategies, collectively known as the "stretch-out," not only changed the way the workplace functioned, but also undermined the employer-employee relationship and led to a series of bitter strikes, culminating in the massive General Strike of 1934.

The techniques employed in the stretch-out originated with the time-and-motion studies of Frederick Winslow Taylor in the 1880s. The efficiency expert Gordon Johnstone is credited with introducing the study of time management to the southern textile industry. South Carolina mill owners quickly followed suit. World War I had forced wages to unprecedented highs. With the postwar recession, managers sought to cut back production costs and preserve profits, but workers understandably resisted wage cuts. Weavers were particularly targeted by the new reformers because they were among the highest-paid workers and because new technology was available to automate much of the weaving process. Managers turned to the "multiple-loom" system, which spread the duties of a weaver over an entire room of machines in a "standard patrol" fashion while delegating some of the simpler weaving tasks to lower-paid doffers and cleaners. When the efficiency experts arrived at Saxon Mills outside Spartanburg in 1927, the veteran weaver Charles Putnam found himself responsible for *three times* his previous workload of twenty-six looms. The new system also docked workers for quality defects, despite workers' insistence that the defects were due to machinery operating too fast. Putnam recalled that by 1930, despite the increasing workload, his wages had dropped substantially due to fines for defects.

Another approach to cost cutting came from eliminating "wasted time," and the techniques used in this approach created the greatest resentment among workers. Consulting firms such as Greenville's J. E. Sirrine Company offered their services to identify such wasted time and propose ways of eliminating it, with the goal of standardizing tasks and thus making individual workers interchangeable. Workers at Saxon Mills recalled that the efficiency experts—dubbed "minute men" by the workers for their obsession with stopwatches—timed every move, from knotting a broken thread to eating lunch, from going to the bathroom to drinking a glass of water. Workdays were extended, many types of breaks were banned, workers were forced to tend a larger number of machines, and they were fired if they could not keep up the pace. The workday was extended without additional pay. Scheduled meal breaks were eliminated, and "dope wagons" sold sandwiches and caffeinated colas to keep workers on the job and productive even while they ate. Pay scales were based on production quotas. While managers regarded the new system as scientifically justified, workers referred to it as the "pick pocket system" and compared it to slavery. Whatever trust the paternalistic management style of the earlier period had engendered between workers and owners the new system undermined.

By 1929 South Carolina workers began organizing to protest the effects of the stretch-out. Beginning at Ware Shoals in March 1929—led mostly by lifelong mill hands who appealed to the supposed paternalism of the mill owners—a wave of strikes swept South Carolina textile mills. The strikes often achieved a reduction of the workload and some alterations to the pay scale, but some of those who protested were punished for doing so. The General Assembly appointed a special committee to investigate textile workers' grievances. The committee concluded that the strikes were due to "deplorable living conditions in the villages" and "so-called efficiency measures" that put "more work on the employees than they can do." It also absolved unions of any complicity in the strikes. However, the legislature took no further action and the efficiency experts became a permanent factor of mill life. STEPHEN WALLACE TAYLOR

Hall, Jacquelyn Dowd, et al. *Like a Family: The Making of a Southern Cotton Mill World.* Chapel Hill: University of North Carolina Press, 1987.

Mitchell, Broadus, and George Sinclair Mitchell. *The Industrial Revolution in the South.* 1930. Reprint, New York: Greenwood, 1968.

Simon, Bryant. *A Fabric of Defeat: The Politics of South Carolina Millhands, 1910–1948.* Chapel Hill: University of North Carolina Press, 1998.

Tullos, Allen. *Habits of Industry: White Culture and the Transformation of the Carolina Piedmont.* Chapel Hill: University of North Carolina Press, 1989.

Strickland, Lily (1884–1958). Composer, writer, artist. Strickland was born in 1884 in Anderson, the only daughter of Charlton Hines Strickland, an insurance salesman, and Teresa Hammond Reed. Her father died when she was young, leaving Lily and her brothers to grow up in the Anderson home of their maternal grandparents, Judge and Mrs. J. Pinckney Reed. Lily attended Anderson schools and began studying piano at the age of six. Encouraged by her family to pursue her musical ambitions, she published her first composition while still in her teens and studied piano and composition at Converse College from 1901 to 1904. In 1905 she received a scholarship for study at the Institute of Musical Arts in New York (the forerunner to Juilliard). In New York she met Joseph Courtenay Anderson, a fellow South Carolinian and a Wofford graduate who taught English at Columbia University. The two married in 1912. They never had children.

Lily Strickland. Courtesy, South Caroliniana Library, University of South Carolina

Strickland (who used her maiden name professionally) spent the rest of her life composing, writing, and painting all over the world as she followed her husband to his various jobs. In 1920 Courtenay Anderson became manager of the Calcutta branch of an American company. The couple spent most of the next ten years in India. During these years Strickland journeyed all over Africa and Asia, composing, painting, and writing. Her travel essays appeared in numerous American magazines, and her watercolors graced the covers of her sheet music.

Strickland enjoyed breaking free of traditional restraints on women imposed by southern culture. After one five-week journey in India, she wrote to her goddaughter about a treacherous trip on a mountain road with a reckless driver: "Strange to say, I enjoyed it. . . . [A]fter so many years of repression and narrow-minded negations, I have just 'busted lose' [*sic*] and become a Fatalist."

A prolific composer, Strickland published 395 musical works for popular, church, and children's performances. Her early works displayed the influences of life in the Jim Crow South, incorporating numerous elements of African American spirituals and folk music and the rhythms of southern speech. Her later compositions were inspired by the music she heard in Asia and Africa. She enjoyed wide popularity, an unusual accomplishment for a female composer in the early twentieth century. Numerous ensembles, including the New York Philharmonic, the Charleston Symphony, and the Metropolitan Opera Orchestra, performed her work, as did such artists as Burl Ives and Paul Robeson. Her most famous composition was a popular piece with a southern flavor, "Mah Lindy Lou." In recognition of her accomplishments as a composer, Converse College conferred an honorary doctor of music degree on her in 1924.

After returning to the United States, Strickland and her husband lived in New York until 1948, when they retired to a farm near Hendersonville, North Carolina. Strickland continued to compose and write until her death of a stroke on June 6, 1958. MELISSA WALKER

Howe, Ann Whitworth. *Lily Strickland: South Carolina's Gift to American Music.* Columbia, S.C.: R. L. Bryan, 1970.

Kinscella, Hazel Gertrude. "An American Composer at Home." *Better Homes and Gardens* 16 (September 1937): 60, 94–97.

Strickland, Lily. Papers. Converse College Archives, Spartanburg, South Carolina.

Striped bass. State fish. The striped bass, or ocean rockfish (*Morone saxatilis*), became the official state fish in legislation signed by Governor John C. West on June 2, 1972. It is one of America's most popular game fish. Anglers appreciate the striper's large size and fierce nature, and it is a table delicacy. Rockfish are caught year-round in South Carolina, being most plentiful in the state's rivers during the spring spawning season.

Striped bass. Photograph by Philip Jones. Courtesy, South Carolina Department of Natural Resources

The mature fish often weighs 25 to 30 pounds. The largest recorded catch was 125 pounds, with a maximum length of six feet. The rockfish is pink or brown with a silver belly and seven or eight longitudinal stripes on the sides. Stripers eat shrimp, crab, and smaller fish. The fish is anadromous—that is, an ocean fish that spawns inland in freshwater. However, it adapts easily to a freshwater environment and can live and successfully reproduce in inland rivers, lakes, and reservoirs. Since the 1940s stripers have proliferated in Lakes Moultrie and Marion of the Santee Cooper system.

The striped bass was highly valued as a food fish by English colonists, beginning in the seventeenth century, from Maine to Georgia. In the colonial era bass were caught mainly in the Atlantic with nets. By the nineteenth century fly fishermen were landing them, and the fish became a popular catch for sportsmen. In the nineteenth century Americans introduced stripers to Pacific coast waters and western rivers. During the 1950s they were introduced into inland lakes and reservoirs nationwide. Popularity led to overfishing, threatening the population and bringing federal legislation to limit catches in order to save the species. DAVID C. R. HEISSER

Audubon Society Field Guide to North American Fishes, Whales, and Dolphins. New York: Knopf, 1983.

Hogan, Austin. "The Historic Striped Bass—A Brief Introduction." *American Fly Fisher* 2, no. 3 (1975): 7–8.

Wongrey, Jan. "The Fish That Made a State Famous." *South Carolina Wildlife* 18 (May–June 1971): 8–10.

Yates, Nancy. "It's Official: A State Animal and Fish." *Sandlapper* 6 (January 1973): 36–39.

Stroyer, Jacob (ca. 1846–ca. 1908). Clergyman, author. Stroyer was born and raised a slave in antebellum South Carolina. After emancipation, he authored an engrossing autobiographical narrative, *My Life in the South,* first published in 1879. Subsequently revised and expanded, the book is a collection of incidents that provides an intimate view of Stroyer's life as a slave. The slaves' struggle for survival, the constant task of having to shift loyalties, and the brutality of

Jacob Stroyer. Frontispiece from his autobiography, *My Life in the South.* Courtesy, South Caroliniana Library, University of South Carolina

day-to-day life are frankly shared by Stroyer in his narrative, as are the ethics, morality, and religious adherence of slave life.

By Stroyer's own account, he was born in 1846 (later editions of his autobiography state 1849) on the Singleton family's extensive Kensington Plantation, near Columbia. His mother and her parents were owned by the Singleton family, as was his father, who was transported from Africa as a young boy. Stroyer's father was married twice in "mutual agreement" slave marriages, which resulted in fifteen children. Jacob was the third son from his father's second marriage.

Like his father, Stroyer labored as a hostler (a keeper of horses and mules) on the Singleton plantation. Colonel M. R. Singleton kept race horses, including the notable prizewinners Capt. Miner and Inspector, which Stroyer, after becoming a legitimate certified rider, rode in many practice races. The death of Colonel Singleton put an end to Stroyer's care and racing of the family's sporting horses, and all of the men and boys who had been hostlers and riders were placed to labor in the cotton fields. Stroyer was small and seemingly not suitable for fieldwork. He was placed there anyway and suffered many brutal whippings before becoming acclimated to his new station.

After emancipation, Stroyer went to school in Columbia and Charleston and then moved north to Worcester, Massachusetts, in 1870. After attending evening schools, Stroyer went to Worcester Academy, where he studied for two years. During this time he was licensed as a preacher of the African Methodist Episcopal Church, and he later was ordained as a deacon at Newport, Rhode Island. Soon thereafter Stroyer was sent to Salem, Massachusetts, where he remained to "preach the gospel." During this period Stroyer became a much-sought-after speaker regarding his life as a slave, and he was encouraged to write and publish these accounts. He did so with the idea and purpose to raise means that would enable him to add to his education and devote his services and attainments to the good of his race. DEBORAH WRIGHT

Stroyer, Jacob. *My Life in the South, Part I.* Salem, Mass.: Salem Press, 1879.

Stuart, John (1718–1779). Soldier, colonial official. Stuart was born on September 25, 1718, in Inverness, Scotland, the son of John and Christian Stuart. As a youth, he joined the Royal Navy, and his ship circumnavigated the globe between 1740 and 1744. By 1748 Stuart had amassed sufficient capital to relocate to Britain's North American colonies, and he eventually settled in Charleston. During his time in South Carolina, he served as a fire master, a tax assessor, and an assemblyman. As a militia captain, in 1759 Stuart was assigned to Fort Loudoun in East Tennessee among the Overhill Cherokees, and he was the only officer spared following the capitulation of the fort to the Cherokees in August 1760.

Having gained notoriety by his escape, Stuart was named superintendent of Indian affairs for the Southern District by General Edward Braddock in January 1762. At first Stuart operated out of Charleston. His initial job was to familiarize the southern Indians with the Proclamation Line of 1763, which was supposed to keep English settlers east of the Appalachian Mountains. Stuart met with leaders of the various tribes at Augusta, Georgia, in December 1763. The Treaty of Augusta both recognized the eastern boundary of the Cherokees and established a 225-square-mile reservation for the Catawbas.

In response to the unfair practices employed in the highly competitive Indian trade, Stuart pursued policies designed to promote Anglo-Indian stability. Stuart's new position and authority placed both the licensure of Indian traders and the transfer of Indian lands under his control, superceding four decades of control by South Carolina's colonial government. Some officials complained about Stuart's enlarged powers. Thomas Boone, governor of South Carolina, wrote to the Board of Trade in 1764 with the suggestion that Stuart should be made subordinate to the governor and council of each colony. The biographer J. Russell Snapp noted that Stuart's Indian policies, often made at the expense of profitable trade or land acquisition, insured that colonial Americans and their British rulers would eventually clash.

The advent of the Revolutionary War made Stuart's job more difficult. The Charleston Sons of Liberty suspected that Stuart, a Loyalist, opposed their agenda and was using the southern tribes against patriots as early as the summer of 1775. Carolina patriots forced Stuart out of his Charleston base to Florida, although they kept his family as hostages to ensure Stuart's good behavior.

During the war, the patriots organized their own Indian agents, one of which, George Galphin, came into conflict with Stuart regularly. In the fall of 1775 Galphin met with Creeks and told them that their friend John Stuart was old and sick and could not be counted on by them for much longer. By late 1775 Stuart authorized his own Indian agents to treat patriot agents such as Galphin as rebels and to arrest them when possible. He also began organizing Indian tribes for war, an action that solidified opposition to the

British and further escalated the conflict in the southern interior. But Stuart did not live to see the end of the war. He died on March 21, 1779, in Pensacola, West Florida. MICHAEL P. MORRIS

Alden, John Richard. *John Stuart and the Southern Colonial Frontier: A Study of Indian Relations, War, Trade, and Land Problems in the Southern Wilderness, 1754–1775.* 1944. Reprint, New York: Gordian, 1966.

Snapp, J. Russell. *John Stuart and the Struggle for Empire on the Southern Frontier.* Baton Rouge: Louisiana State University Press, 1996.

Stuart's Town. Stuart's Town was a Scottish colony founded in 1684 and envisioned by the Lords Proprietors as a counterweight to the somewhat ungovernable English settlement at Charleston. Establishing New World colonies was difficult and dangerous work, but when the proprietors sought new settlers in 1680, they found willing recruits among Scots Covenanters (Presbyterians facing persecution for their adherence to the Covenant of 1638). The Covenanters wanted political autonomy and freedom of worship, and after securing guarantees from the Lords Proprietors, the new colonists set sail in March 1684.

The Scots disembarked near present-day Beaufort, calling their settlement Stuart's Town. The site was promising, but Stuart's Town lay on the disputed frontier between rival Spanish and English claims. It was also occupied by several feuding Indian nations. The colonists negotiated an alliance with one local nation, the Yamassee, and thereby inherited the Yamassees' ongoing conflict with the Timucuans, who were under Spanish protection. Peace held for a few months, but in March 1685 several Scots accompanied a Yamassee raid against the Timucuans at Santa Catalina. The incursion earned little more than a few slaves but generated considerable Spanish wrath.

Retribution arrived in August 1686. Three Spanish galleys and some 150 troops overran Scottish defenses. The Spanish allowed the colonists to escape but thoroughly plundered the town before burning it. Their ships then headed north, toward the English settlements on the Ashley, which survived thanks to a providential storm that scattered the Spanish fleet. Charleston was saved, but Stuart's Town—the first Covenanting colony—was not rebuilt. ROBERT H. LANDRUM

Insh, George Pratt. *Scottish Colonial Schemes, 1620–1686.* Glasgow: Maclehose, Jackson, 1922.

Rowland, Lawrence S., Alexander Moore, and George C. Rogers. *The History of Beaufort County, South Carolina.* Vol. 1, *1514–1861.* Columbia: University of South Carolina Press, 1996.

Stumphouse Mountain Tunnel. The Stumphouse Mountain Tunnel is an unfinished nineteenth-century railroad tunnel located near Walhalla. The variation of the name "Stump House" was drawn from the legend of a Cherokee woman who lived on the mountain with her white husband. Rejected by both their respective communities, the couple lived on the mountain in a log home built atop stumps.

In the 1850s Stumphouse Mountain played a key role in South Carolina's attempt to participate in antebellum America's commercial revolution. Planners contemplated cutting a one-and-one-half-mile railroad tunnel through the heart of the mountain in order to link the state's rail lines with the Blue Ridge Railroad coming from Knoxville, Tennessee. This enterprise, if successful, would have linked Charleston with the commercial heartland of the young nation. Unfortunately, the price of tunneling through Stumphouse Mountain proved prohibitive. The state government spent $1 million, and workers (ten of whom died) dynamited and drilled for three years before funds ran out in 1859. Two years later, with the outbreak of the Civil War, state planners abandoned the project, still one thousand feet short of completion. Briefly revived in 1876 and 1900, and discussed as late as 1940, the Stumphouse Mountain Tunnel was never completed.

Stumphouse Mountain Tunnel. Courtesy, Clemson University Photograph Collection, Special Collections, Clemson University Libraries

In 1951 Clemson College purchased the tunnel and for several years experimented with curing blue cheese in its cool, damp environment. Clemson leased the tunnel to the Pendleton Historic District in 1970, and it was listed in the National Register of Historic Places the following year. The tunnel became a popular tourist attraction but was closed to visitors following a rock slide in the mid-1990s. After rigorous safety testing, the tunnel reopened as a public park in 2000. W. SCOTT POOLE

Brown, George Dewitt. "A History of the Blue Ridge Railroad, 1852–1874." Master's thesis, University of South Carolina, 1967.

Federal Writers' Project. South Carolina. *South Carolina: The WPA Guide to the Palmetto State.* 1941. Reprint, Columbia: University of South Carolina Press, 1988.

Ford, Lacy K., Jr. *Origins of Southern Radicalism: The South Carolina Upcountry, 1800–1860.* New York: Oxford University Press, 1988.

Sugarloaf Mountain (Chesterfield County). Sugarloaf Mountain is an erosional remnant located in the Sand Hills State Forest within the upper coastal plain of South Carolina. It lies 513 feet above sea level and 100 feet above the surrounding terrain. From this position and elevation, Sugarloaf offers a wide view of the surrounding landscape. Sugarloaf Mountain is made up of sands, clays, and a sandstone that is capped in places by an ironstone that formed as iron-rich water percolated through the sands, forming a hard, almost impermeable layer. Sugarloaf is one of the few sites where abundant ironstone is found in the Sandhills.

The sand dunes and clays that make up Sugarloaf Mountain were originally rocks of the various high mountain ranges that formed beginning in the Ordovician period and continuing during the Devonian and Permian periods and then wore away. These mountains were located to the north and west of the Sandhills. They were made of rocks such as granite, gneiss, and schist. The minerals found in these rocks included feldspar and mica that chemically weathered into clay, and quartz that physically weathered into sand. Over millions of years these clays and sands were, in turn, carried and deposited by rivers to form unconsolidated sediments, clay deposits, and sandstone that are clearly visible at the surface at Sugarloaf Mountain.

During the Eocene to Miocene epochs, the sea rose to the level of the modern Sandhills, running as an embayment up the river valleys including the Congaree and the Wateree. Sugarloaf Mountain at that time would have formed part of a beach and dune system at the back of the coastline. Over millions of years the ocean has retreated to its present location at the coast. CAROLYN H. MURPHY

Kovacik, Charles F., and John J. Winberry. *South Carolina: The Making of a Landscape.* 1987. Reprint, Columbia: University of South Carolina Press, 1989.

Murphy, Carolyn H. *Carolina Rocks! The Geology of South Carolina.* Orangeburg, S.C.: Sandlapper, 1995.

Sullivan's Island (Charleston County; 2000 pop. 1,911). Sullivan's Island was discovered in 1666 by Captain Robert Sandford and named for Captain Florence O'Sullivan, a former Irish soldier and one of South Carolina's first colonists. On May 30, 1674, O'Sullivan was given the responsibility of manning the signal cannon on the island at the entrance to Charleston harbor. Thus began the island's relationship with military defense as well as the name "O'Sullivan's Island." Throughout the history of Sullivan's Island, military defense and summer recreation would be the two most important factors in its economic development.

A quarantine station was built on Sullivan's Island in 1707 and served as the primary line of defense against infectious disease reaching Charleston via newly arriving immigrants, primarily African slaves. On June 28, 1776, the first major defeat suffered by the British forces in the Revolutionary War took place at the Battle of Sullivan's Island, where the American fort on the island forced the withdrawal of British warships threatening the city. Beginning in 1791, private citizens "who thought it beneficial to their health" began spending summers on the island, making Sullivan's perhaps the state's original seaside resort. In 1817 the incorporation of the town of Moultrieville reflected the increase in summer and year-round residents. From 1827 to 1828 the resident Edgar Allan Poe, then a young army recruit, was stationed at Fort Moultrie. Years later Poe's story "The Gold Bug" drew on his time spent on Sullivan's Island. On January 30, 1838, the imprisoned chief Osceola of the Seminole Indians died and was buried at Fort Moultrie. Taking part in the opening shots of the Civil War on April 12, 1861, Confederate gunners at Fort Moultrie and three other batteries on Sullivan's Island participated in the bombardment of Fort Sumter.

Sullivan's Island's few businesses—boardinghouses, entertainment halls, grocery stores, drugstores, churches, and post offices—served residents and the military over the years. In 1906 the General Assembly revoked the charter for the town of Moultrieville, replacing it with a township government and creating the town of Sullivan's Island. Fort Moultrie was deactivated in 1947 and turned over to the National Park Service. A navigation beacon or lighthouse is the only remaining defensive fixture on Sullivan's Island from the days of Florence O'Sullivan. Sullivan's Island is prone to natural disasters, such as Hurricane Hugo, which hit on September 21, 1989, but still the island remains a desirable place for residents and guests, whether for a few days or all year long. CATHERINE FITZGERALD

Miles, Suzannah Smith. *Island of History: Sullivan's Island from 1670 to 1860 with Reminiscences of Moultrieville and Fort Moultrie.* Mount Pleasant, S.C.: Historic Views, 1994.

Rhyne, Nancy. *Chronicles of the South Carolina Sea Islands.* Winston-Salem, N.C.: John F. Blair, 1998.

Sullivan's Island, Battle of (June 28, 1776). The Battle of Sullivan's Island was the first major patriot victory in the Revolutionary War. In February 1776, after British plans to capture Charleston were revealed, South Carolina patriots began construction of a fort on Sullivan's Island close to the main shipping channel at the mouth of Charleston harbor. Colonel William Moultrie was given command of the island's forces and ordered to supervise the fort's construction.

The unnamed fort was to be a square with five-hundred-foot-long walls and a bastion at each corner. It was built of thousands of palmetto trees cut to make two parallel log walls sixteen feet apart and more than ten feet high. The space between the walls was filled with sand. By late June only the two walls and bastions facing the channel were complete; thirty-one cannons were in place, and fewer than four hundred soldiers garrisoned the incomplete fort. At the other end of Sullivan's Island, three hundred soldiers were positioned at Breach Inlet to block the British from crossing from Long Island (Isle of Palms) and attacking the fort from the rear.

A British fleet, which arrived on June 1, included nine men-of-war mounting almost three hundred cannons. On June 8 a British surrender demand was rejected, and the next day British infantrymen landed on Long Island. On June 28 the British ships advanced to attack the Sullivan's Island fort. By 11:30 A.M. six warships were in position and opened fire. The fort's guns soon responded. Not long after the bombardment began, three more British warships attempted to move into position between Sullivan's Island and the mainland, fire into the fort's unprotected rear, and block patriot troops from reinforcing the fort. But the movement failed when all three ran aground on the sandbanks in the harbor's mouth. Two later freed themselves, while the third remained hard aground.

The bombardment continued into the evening, but the fort withstood the pounding from the British heavy guns. Its palmetto-log and sand walls absorbed the solid shot and shells, resulting in little structural damage. At the same time, patriot rounds tore into the wooden warships. During the afternoon when the British on Long Island attempted to cross Breach Inlet, patriots on Sullivan's Island were able to turn them back.

At 9:00 P.M. the British ceased their attack and pulled out of the fort's range. Several warships had been damaged, and more than two hundred sailors were casualties. Inside the fort fewer than forty patriots had suffered the same fate. The next day the British set the grounded ship on fire, which exploded when the flames reached the powder magazine. The British soon withdrew, leaving Charleston free from attack until 1780.

Shortly after the battle, the fort was named Fort Moultrie in honor of its commander. Fort Moultrie is administered as part of Fort Sumter National Monument, a unit of the National Park Service. RICHARD W. HATCHER III

Stokeley, Jim. *Fort Moultrie: Constant Defender.* Washington, D.C.: Department of the Interior, 1985.

Sully, Thomas (1783–1872). Portraitist. Sully was born on June 8 or 9, 1783, in Horncastle, Lincolnshire, England, to Matthew Sully and Sarah Chester, both stage actors. In 1792 the entire Sully family immigrated to the United States, and two years later they settled in Charleston. Sully obtained his American citizenship in 1809 and emerged as this country's preeminent portrait painter of the nineteenth century.

In Charleston, Sully attended Reverend Robert Smith's school, where he met Charles Fraser, his first artistic mentor. William Dunlap, this country's earliest art historian, later quoted Sully as saying that Fraser "was the first person that ever took the pains to instruct me in the rudiments of the art, and although a mere tyro, his kindness, and the progress made in consequence of it, determined the course of my future life." Sully studied under the French miniature painter M. Belzons before leaving Charleston in 1799. For the next decade Sully lived an unsettled existence with short periods in Richmond, Norfolk, New York, Hartford, Boston, and Philadelphia. On June 27, 1806, Sully married Sarah Annis Sully, the widow of his brother Lawrence. The marriage produced nine children. From July 1809 until March 1810 he was in England, where the noted expatriate artist Benjamin West encouraged him to study anatomy. While in London, Sully copied canvases by West and old masters painters, the standard practice for aspiring artists of the day.

After his return, Sully made Philadelphia his base for the rest of his career, with short sojourns to East Coast cities in pursuit of portrait commissions. In 1837–1838 he was in London to paint a full-length likeness of a youthful Queen Victoria, an undertaking regarded as the highlight of his career. Quite businesslike, Sully maintained a register of his paintings that documents the fact that he painted more than two thousand canvases during his long life, along with six hundred additional "fancy pieces" consisting of genre and mythological subjects and copies of old masters.

Sully's success rests in his facile technique and ability to capture likenesses while flattering his sitters. He painted statesmen and military figures, successful merchants, and their wives and children. In 1841 and 1845 he made trips to Charleston; during the first one he completed seventeen portraits, and on the second he painted twenty-two canvases. Among his sitters were James Louis Petigru (1842) and his daughter Caroline Carson (1841), whose portraits belong to the Gibbes Museum of Art in Charleston. Over the years Sully painted other Charlestonians living elsewhere, including Charles Izard Manigault (1817) and Sarah Reeve Ladson Gilmor (1823). The latter, painted in Baltimore, belongs to the Gibbes Museum of Art and is considered to be one of Sully's most appealing portraits. A quiet and reflective Mrs. Gilmor stands dressed in a colorful turban, a gauzy white dress, and a lusciously textured silk green wrap trimmed in ermine. Sully died in Philadelphia on November 5, 1872, and was buried in Laurel Hill Cemetery. MARTHA R. SEVERENS

Biddle, Edward, and Mantle Fielding. *The Life and Works of Thomas Sully (1783–1872).* 1921. Reprint, Charleston, S.C.: Garnier, 1969.

Fabian, Monroe H. *Mr. Sully, Portrait Painter.* Washington, D.C.: Smithsonian Institution Press, 1983.

Summers, Eliza Ann (1844–1900). Educator. Summers was born on January 17, 1844, at Spruce Bank Farm near Woodbury, Connecticut. She was the youngest daughter of David Summers and Sarah Maria Upson. Throughout her youth Summers remained in Woodbury, where she was educated in the public school system. In 1863 she began teaching in various grammar schools in the vicinity of her hometown, where she gained a reputation for being a competent instructor. In December 1866 she submitted her resignation and volunteered her services to the American Missionary Association to teach emancipated slaves in South Carolina.

Although a member of the First Congregational Church in Woodbury, Summers was neither notably devout nor prone to religious fervor. However, her maternal uncle, Alvin Upson, had performed extensive fieldwork for the American Missionary Association a decade earlier. Summers was joined by her childhood friend Julia Benedict, and together they departed New York City on January 12, 1867, and arrived at Hilton Head Island six days later.

Following an orientation, Summers and Benedict were conducted to quarters in Mitchellville, a hamlet comprised of numerous small wooden houses built for the former slaves. Most of these freedmen once had been slaves at Drayton Plantation, a landholding abandoned by its owners since 1861. Five hundred families occupied Mitchellville. Three churches were utilized as freedmen schools. The majority of the teachers were affiliated with the American Missionary Association. Throughout her service on the island, Summers recorded her daily experiences in a diary. She also wrote many detailed letters to her older sister, Sarah. Her various writings provide detailed descriptions of life among the Hilton Head freedmen in 1867. Summers's correspondence was published many years after her death.

Eventually, Summers and Benedict were transferred to Lawton Plantation, another abandoned estate comprising eighteen hundred acres. Throughout the next six months they conducted both day and evening schools for approximately seventy-six pupils of all ages. The two teachers maintained a Sunday school program as well. Most of their classes were held within the "Praise House," the plantation building where the freedmen held religious services.

On June 20, 1867, Summers and Benedict resigned their positions and returned to Connecticut. Neither ever returned to South Carolina. On June 10, 1869, Summers married Floyd Frost Hitchcock in Woodbury. Upon her marriage she retired from teaching, except for educating her three children (a fourth child died in infancy). Summers died in Woodbury on July 30, 1900. MILES S. RICHARDS

Summers, Eliza Ann. *"Dear Sister": Letters Written on Hilton Head Island, 1867.* Edited by Josephine W. Martin. Beaufort, S.C.: Beaufort Book Company, 1977.

Summerville (Dorchester County; 2000 pop. 27,752). Summerville, the "Flower Town in the Pines," was established as a summer refuge for plantation owners of St. George's Dorchester and St. Paul's Parishes. The decline of the colonial town of Dorchester on the Ashley River was another source of population for the village. As Dorchester lost population, St. George's Dorchester Episcopal Church and the Presbyterian White Meeting House congregation relocated to Summerville. Prior to 1831 Summerville had few year-round residents, but the population swelled in the summers as lowcountry planters sought the breezes and pine forests that were deemed healthier than their swampland rice plantations. In 1831 the South Carolina Canal and Rail Road Company constructed a railway from Charleston to Hamburg. Summerville was one of the first stops along the route. The company laid out town lots in a grid pattern near the tracks, which it called New Summerville to distinguish it from the rambling arrangement of the old village.

Summerville was incorporated in 1847, and one of its first ordinances restricted the cutting of trees in the town limits. From its beginnings it was a resort, and much of its history has been tied to tourism and temporary residence. After the railroad was built, some antebellum residents of Summerville commuted to work in Charleston. The South Carolina writer William Gilmore Simms lived for a few years in Summerville and traveled on the train to his editor's job in Charleston. This early commuter traffic was a precursor to the bedroom-community character of Summerville in the twentieth century. During the Civil War the town was a refuge for lowcountry planter families, who moved away from the coast to escape Union attacks. The epicenter of the 1886 Charleston earthquake was near Summerville.

Toward the beginning of the twentieth century Summerville was promoted as a health resort and vacation destination. Large inns, the most notable being the Pine Forest Inn, provided accommodations for summer visitors. Sanatoriums were built for persons recuperating from tuberculosis and other pulmonary illnesses. As Charleston became home to an increasing number of United States military bases in the twentieth century, Summerville grew. For the first half of the twentieth century the town's population was stable. In 1910 the population was 2,355, and it had grown to only 3,028 in 1940. In 1960, just before the Sun Belt population explosion, the population was 3,633, but by 1990 the residents numbered 22,519. Five years later the population within the town limits was about 25,000, with an additional 50,000 residents in nearby areas. Summerville is a key element in the Charleston–North Charleston Metropolitan Statistical Area. Seven buildings and historic sites in and around Summerville are on the National Register of Historic Places.

Summerville is governed by a mayor and an elected city council. The Timrod Library Society, a private subscription library, was founded in 1897 and continues to be active. The Summerville-Dorchester Museum opened its doors in 1992 and exhibits photographs, artifacts, and other historical materials relating to the town and Dorchester County. ALEXANDER MOORE

Foster, Clarice, and Lang Foster, eds. *Beth's Pineland Village.* Columbia, S.C.: Summerville Preservation Society, 1988.

Hill, Barbara Lynch. *Summerville: A Sesquicentennial Edition of the History of the Flower Town in the Pines.* Summerville, S.C.: Town of Summerville, 1998.

Kwist, Margaret Scott. *Porch Rocker Recollections of Summerville, South Carolina.* Summerville, S.C.: Linwood, 1980.

Sumter (Sumter County; 2000 pop. 39,643). When the South Carolina legislature created Sumter District in 1800, they also established the crossroads village of Sumterville as the courthouse seat. Named after the area's most prominent resident, the Revolutionary War general and United States senator Thomas Sumter, Sumterville's growth was painfully slowly during its early years. Justices held trials in John Gayle's plantation home until the district erected the first courthouse and jail in 1806. The settlement was still quite small by 1812, with just one store, a tavern, and a few homes.

In the 1820s Sumterville enjoyed a growth spurt that saw the erection of several new buildings, including a courthouse designed by Robert Mills. The town was incorporated in 1845. Five years later Sumterville had ninety homes and a population of 840, including 330 African Americans. Following the arrival of the railroad, town leaders shortened the name to Sumter in 1855. During the Civil War citizens set up hospitals throughout the city for Confederate wounded. Due to the railroad and Sumter's central location, the Confederate army turned Sumter into a distribution center for military supplies. This led to Union general Edward E. Potter's raid through Sumter District in April 1865, during which he set up headquarters in Sumter.

Sumter swiftly recovered from the depredations of war, again due in large part to the railroads. The city built the Sumter Opera House in 1872, which quickly became both Town Hall and a cultural center. In the 1880s the city was a busy cotton market and shipping center. At the turn of the twentieth century Sumter was a major cotton and tobacco market and home to several industries, including a textile mill and an ice-manufacturing company. In 1912 the city became the first in the country to use the council-manager form of municipal government, which consisted of four elected officials (a mayor and three councillors) and a professional city manager chosen by the council. By 2001 the city retained the same model but had enlarged the council from three to six members.

As was the case in many rural towns in the second half of the twentieth century, Sumter's downtown experienced a period of decline. For four decades citizens attempted to revitalize Sumter's historic Main Street area. Efforts proved ineffective until the creation of the Downtown Sumter Revitalization Committee in 1997, which appointed a downtown manager, sponsored a performing-arts program, and improved parking, landscaping, and building facades. The efforts of Downtown Sumter, the city government, and residents contributed to Sumter's strong economic and cultural base. Other institutions contributing to the city's revitalization include the Sumter County Museum, Patriot Hall, and the Sumter Gallery of Art. RICKIE A. GOOD

Gregorie, Anne King. *History of Sumter County, South Carolina.* Sumter, S.C.: Sumter County Library Board, 1954.

Sumter, Thomas (1734–1832). Soldier, congressman, U.S. senator. Sumter was born on August 14, 1734, in Hanover County, Virginia. His father, William, was a miller and former indentured servant, while his mother, Patience, was a midwife. Most of Thomas Sumter's early years were spent tending livestock and helping his father at the mill, not in school. He joined the provincial militia at the outbreak of the French and Indian War and rose to the rank of sergeant. In 1761 Sumter was selected to participate in a diplomatic mission to the Cherokee nation and escorted an Indian delegation to London the following year. After returning to Virginia via Charleston, he was imprisoned for indebtedness but escaped and fled to South Carolina. Around 1764 Sumter settled in St. John's Berkeley Parish near the Santee River (Orangeburg County) and opened a country store. The mercantile venture prospered, and Sumter soon owned considerable property. In 1767 he married Mary Cantey Jameson, a wealthy, crippled widow eleven years his senior. Sumter and his wife moved to her plantation, Great Savannah, across the Santee in St. Mark's Parish. The couple had two children.

The Revolutionary War interrupted Sumter's comfortable life, and he found himself again a soldier. After being elected a delegate to the First and Second Provincial Congresses, Sumter participated

Thomas Sumter. Courtesy, South Caroliniana Library, University of South Carolina

in the Snow Campaign (December 1775), the Battle of Fort Moultrie (June 28, 1776), the Cherokee campaign (July–October 1776), and engagements in Georgia (1777, 1778). On September 19, 1778, Sumter left the army with the rank of colonel and returned to private life. He was in retirement when the British captured Charleston in May 1780. It was during this stage of the war, when the patriot tide in the state was at its lowest ebb, that Sumter made his greatest mark.

With South Carolina apparently subdued, the British were poised to push north and end the war in short order. They raided and burned Sumter's home in May 1780, an attack that Sumter took personally. He immediately returned to the field and organized local militiamen into an army of backcountry partisans who informally elected him their general. In the summer of 1780 "Sumter's Brigade" was the only organized opposition to the British in South Carolina. Though the brigade met with mixed success in engagements at Rocky Mount (July 30, 1780), Hanging Rock (August 6, 1780), and Fishing Creek (August 18, 1780), Sumter's exploits in the upper part of the state injected beleaguered South Carolina patriots with a renewed energy to resist, earning Sumter the nickname "Gamecock" for his daring and tenacious resistance. After four months of invaluable but unofficial service, Sumter was commissioned as a brigadier general of the South Carolina militia on October 6, 1780. His force fought well at Fishdam Ford (November 9, 1780) and Blackstock's (November 20, 1780), where Sumter was severely wounded. Incapacitated for several months, he returned to action in February 1781 and led his troops in additional encounters at Fort Granby (February 19–21, May 15, 1781) and Orangeburg (May 10–11, 1781).

Sumter's pride and rash manner made him ill-suited to accept command from others. When the Continental army returned to South Carolina in the spring of 1781, Sumter was less than cooperative with General Nathanael Greene. Sumter attempted to resign as early as May 1781, but Greene refused to allow it. Maintaining his independent command, Sumter finally joined Greene in July 1781 and led "the raid of the dog days" into the lowcountry. Still smarting over command changes and militia reorganization, Sumter resigned in February 1782 and closed his military career.

The remainder of Sumter's public life was spent in politics. He served eight terms in the General Assembly between 1776 and 1790. In 1783 he helped found the town of Stateburg, which he promoted for the new state capital. Elected by Camden District to the U.S. House of Representatives, he served five terms in Congress between 1789 and 1801. Sumter resigned from Congress on December 15, 1801, upon learning of his election to the U.S. Senate, where he served until December 16, 1810. In Washington, Sumter was a staunch Jeffersonian who remained devoted to the backcountry republican values he had known since childhood. Sumter died on June 1, 1832, at the age of ninety-seven. He was the last surviving general of the Revolutionary War. Sumter County and Fort Sumter were named in his honor. MATTHEW A. LOCKHART

Bass, Robert D. *Gamecock: The Life and Campaigns of General Thomas Sumter.* New York: Holt, Rinehart and Winston, 1961.

Gregorie, Anne King. *History of Sumter County.* Sumter, S.C.: Library Board of Sumter County, 1954.

———. *Thomas Sumter.* Columbia, S.C.: R. L. Bryan, 1931.

Sumter County (665 sq. miles; 2000 pop. 104,646). Located in central South Carolina, Sumter County is bounded by the Santee and Wateree Rivers on the west and Lynches River on the east. Prior to European colonization, the area was home to the Wateree and Santee Indians. After their defeat in the Yamassee War of 1715, both tribes left the area, opening the door for European settlement. In 1739 the colonial government reserved land on the east bank of the Wateree and Santee Rivers for an anticipated immigration of Scots settlers. While these particular Scots never arrived, in the 1740s Scots-Irish colonists from the Williamsburg area settled on the Black River in the eastern portion of the future county. In the 1750s an influx of settlers from Virginia and Pennsylvania settled along the Wateree in the High Hills of Santee.

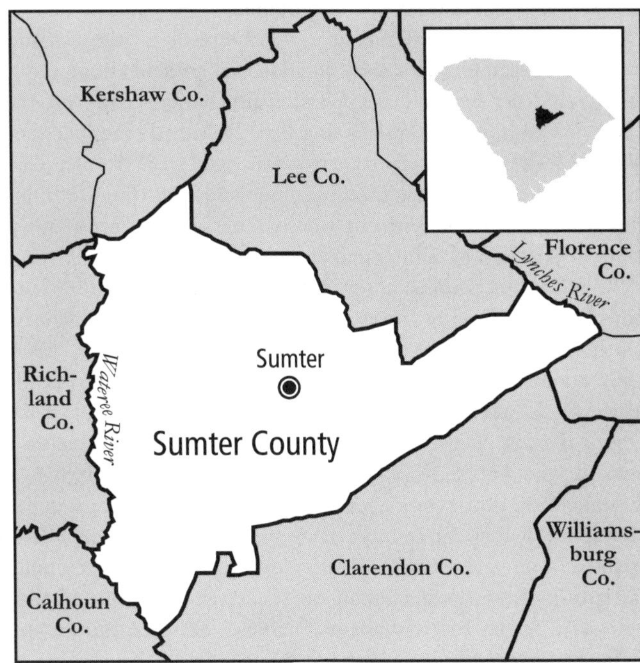

After the Revolutionary War, the South Carolina legislature decided to move the state capital from Charleston to a central location. General Thomas Sumter lobbied unsuccessfully for the relocation of the capital to Stateburg. According to local legend, Sumter's proposal lost by one vote. However, his name was later affixed to the district upon its creation in 1800.

Most eighteenth-century residents were small farmers who planted a variety of crops. But with the arrival of the cotton gin, cotton culture spread. Farmers planted Sumter's first commercial cotton crops in 1796. The success of these plantings convinced more and more Sumterites to engage in cotton cultivation. For the next six decades Sumter's fortunes rose and fell with the price of cotton. When cotton prices rose, the crop made fortunes. When they fell, many Sumter farmers migrated to new lands in the Southwest. Even the few manufacturing facilities in the district depended on cotton. William Ellison, one of the wealthiest free blacks in antebellum South Carolina, was a Stateburg gin wright who began making and repairing gins as early as 1817. William Mayrant, also of Stateburg, in 1815 established a cotton factory, which he sold in 1821. In the 1840s the planter Jeptha Dyson built a cotton factory in the southern portion of the district near the modern town of Pinewood.

The arrival of railroads in the 1840s and 1850s brought prosperity to communities in Sumter District. Manchester, a junction with lines running to Camden and to Wilmington, North Carolina, boomed. The district seat of Sumterville enjoyed such economic success that when the town reincorporated in 1855, it shortened its name to the more urban-sounding "Sumter." Mayesville grew up around another station located on the plantation of Matthew P. Mayes. Lynchburg also began as a railroad station but quickly grew to boast schools, a carriage and buggy shop, and a dry goods store. The town was incorporated in 1859.

In 1855 the General Assembly divided Sumter District, with the eastern portion becoming Clarendon District. That same year several misfortunes visited Sumter. The price of cotton plummeted, and many residents lost their property in sheriff sales, while the communities of Manchester and Sumter experienced several devastating fires. After secession in 1860, Sumter District prepared for war. James D. Blanding organized the Sumter Volunteers. Women formed relief associations and contributed to Wayside Homes to assist traveling soldiers. Residents set up hospitals for the sick and wounded. Because of its central location and railroad connections, Sumter District became an important distribution center for the Confederacy. In April 1865 Union general William T. Sherman sent General Edward E. Potter to destroy war matériel in Sumter District. Potter's Raid through the area culminated in the Battle of Dingle's Mill on April 9. With the Confederates defeat, Potter set up camp in the town of Sumter and occupied the district.

When South Carolina adopted a new constitution in 1868, the district became Sumter County. A county board of commissioners gained jurisdiction over taxes, schools, and public works. Financially, Sumter was in better shape than other counties during Reconstruction. Nonetheless, there were several charges of malfeasance against the county commissioners, and by 1873 the county closed some of the public schools and suspended currency payments. Repeated crop failures brought many Sumter residents to ruin in the 1880s, but by then the county's economic base no longer depended exclusively on agriculture. Industries included seventy-three flour and grist mills, thirty-one lumber mills, and ten turpentine companies. And thanks to its substantial railroad network, Sumter remained a busy cotton market and shipping center.

Sumter County entered the twentieth century with less land area (Lee County was created from the northeastern portion of Sumter in 1902) but with an increasingly vibrant economy. Farmers produced cotton, tobacco, grains, legumes, onions, peaches, and dairy products. New industries included brick manufactories and lumber mills. In addition to the railroads that crisscrossed the county, by 1924 the county completed a hard-surfaced highway system that radiated throughout the area. The county received another boost when the U.S. Army established Shaw Field in 1941. The county leased the land to the government for $1 a year for ninety-nine years. Renamed as Shaw Air Force Base, it became an integral part of the Sumter community and became the county's largest employer with more than seven thousand military and civilian personnel.

At the dawn of the twenty-first century, Sumter's economy was a blend of agriculture and manufacturing along with the strong military presence of Shaw Air Force Base. The county ranked third in the state in the sale of agricultural products, which included peanuts, corn, winter wheat, broilers and turkeys, soybeans, and tobacco. More than one hundred different industries operated in eighty manufacturing plants and five industrial parks. The county also contained a strong cultural base, with the Sumter Opera House, Sumter County Museum, Sumter Little Theatre, Patriot Hall, and several artists' guilds. Five public golf courses, Manchester State Forest, and Poinsett State Park provided recreation, and the county had five institutions of higher learning: University of South Carolina–Sumter, Morris College, Central Carolina Technical College, St. Leo College, and Troy State University.

A few of Sumter County's notable citizens include the African American educator Mary McLeod Bethune, the opera singer Clara Louise Kellogg, Reconstruction governor Franklin J. Moses, Confederate general Richard H. Anderson, and the artists Elizabeth White and Charles Mason Crowson. RICKIE A. GOOD

Gregorie, Anne King. *History of Sumter County, South Carolina.* Sumter, S.C.: Library Board of Sumter County, 1954.

Sumter National Forest. Named for Thomas Sumter, famed partisan of the American Revolution, Sumter National Forest encompasses over 350,000 acres in the Piedmont and mountains of South Carolina. The forest is divided into three ranger districts spread across eleven counties: Andrew Pickens (Oconee County); Enoree (Chester, Fairfield, Laurens, Newberry, and Union Counties); and Long Cane (Abbeville, Edgefield, Greenwood, McCormick, and Saluda Counties). Both Sumter National Forest and the lowcountry's Francis Marion National Forest are administered from a central supervisor's office in Columbia.

With the country's vital wood supply dwindling, Congress created the U.S. Forest Service in 1905 to manage the federal forest reserves (renamed as "national forests" in 1907) and provide quality timber to meet the long-term needs of the American people. Under the authority of the Weeks Law of 1911 and subsequent bolstering legislation, the Forest Service expanded the national forest system through the early decades of the twentieth century by purchasing millions of worn-out, cut-over acres in the eastern United States. One historian referred to these as the "lands nobody wanted," and when it came to abused, abandoned agricultural lands, by the 1930s northwestern South Carolina had an abundance. By executive order, President Franklin D. Roosevelt authorized the purchase of millions more acres for the eastern national forests, and in July 1936 he signed a proclamation establishing Sumter National Forest, much of it on infertile red hills eroded and exhausted from decades of intensive cotton cultivation. The Civilian Conservation Corps (CCC) was employed to terrace hillsides and plant trees. By the onset of World War II, the CCC had accomplished much of the spadework needed to bring the forest back into productivity. Reflecting a Forest Service–wide shift in policy, in the 1960s Sumter moved from managing the forest solely for timber to multiple uses including outdoor recreation and wilderness. MATTHEW A. LOCKHART

Clark, Thomas D. *The Greening of the South: The Recovery of Land and Forest.* Lexington: University Press of Kentucky, 1984.

Hayes, Jack Irby. *South Carolina and the New Deal.* Columbia: University of South Carolina Press, 2001.

Steen, Harold K. *The U.S. Forest Service: A History.* Rev. ed. Seattle: University of Washington Press, 2004.

Sun News (2003 circulation: 49,001 daily and 59,253 Sunday). A morning newspaper published daily and Sunday in Myrtle Beach, the *Sun News* was founded in 1935 as a weekly, the *News,* by C. L. Phillips and J. Clarence Macklen. They sold it in 1946 to William A. Kimbel, who moved the newspaper to a new plant on West Broadway Street. The Mullins publisher James L. Platt bought the *News* in 1949 and then five years later sold it to W. Leroy Harrelson. After that the *News* was purchased by Chicora Publishing Company, followed by the Grand Strand Publishing Company. In 1961 Mark Garner, owner of the weekly *Myrtle Beach Sun,* bought the *News* and merged the two newspapers into the *Sun-News.*

Garner sold the *Sun-News,* by then a three-times-a-week newspaper with a circulation of 6,600, to the State Record Company in Columbia in October 1973. It was made a daily within two months. Buoyed by a tourism boom on the Grand Strand, the *Sun-News* prospered. A new building was erected in 1976, and a Sunday publication was added in 1977. Knight-Ridder bought the State Record Company in 1986.

By 1995 the *Sun News* (which had dropped the hyphen from its name) had a circulation of 54,401. The principals at the *Sun News* included Jerry Ausband, editor; A. G. "Mike" Pate, publisher; and Gil Thelen, editor. In 2003 Paula Ellis was publisher and Trisha O'Conner was editor. ROBERT A. PIERCE

McNeely, Patricia G. *The Palmetto Press: The History of South Carolina's Newspapers and the Press Association.* Columbia: South Carolina Press Association, 1998.

Sunset Lodge. An internationally known brothel, the Sunset Lodge, founded about 1936, was located in a white frame house adorned by neon on U.S. Highway 17 originally three miles south of Georgetown's limits. The business was reportedly encouraged by business leaders, including Tom Yawkey, a Massachusetts millionaire who owned a resort home near Georgetown. They wanted to divert the attentions of workers building the International Paper Company mill at Georgetown from their local women.

Sunset Lodge, ca. 1969. Courtesy, private collection

The lodge's past is cloaked in legend and myth, but researchers generally agree that the clientele included servicemen, merchant seamen, college students, millionaires, and reportedly members of Yawkey's Boston Red Sox baseball team, which passed through en route to spring training in Florida. State legislators were also frequent visitors.

Hazel Weiss, who was said to be a former schoolteacher and was born Hazel Bennett in Indiana, owned Sunset Lodge for most of its life. She retained doctors to ensure that her employees were disease-free. According to Georgetown residents, Weiss was the largest yearly donor to the major organized charity in Georgetown. A reporter said that she ruled her business with an iron hand, refusing to tolerate drunks or rowdies and insisting on standards of behavior and dress.

Sunset Lodge developed such traditions as the baseball stopover, the dispensing of Christmas funds to deputies and patrolmen at Thanksgiving, the spring week when the lodge was open only to state legislators, and Hazel's birthday party, when Georgetown's socially elite (men only) were invited.

Sheriff Woodrow Carter closed the lodge, which had been protected by officers and granted anonymity by the press, in December 1969. Weiss moved to Charleston and then returned to Indiana, where she reportedly died in the 1970s. The structure housing the business burned in the late 1990s. ROBERT A. PIERCE

Leland, Jack. "Sun Sets on Sunset Lodge." Charleston *News and Courier,* December 24, 1969, p. A9.

Pierce, Robert A. *South Carolina and Me.* Columbia, S.C.: State Printing, 1992.

Surfside Beach (Horry County; 2000 pop. 4,425). This popular resort town lies south of Myrtle Beach along South Carolina's Grand Strand. The area was originally part of a rice plantation called "The Ark" by its owner John M. Tillman. The 1850 census valued the 3,200 acres, with its one and one-half miles of oceanfront, at $5,000. After Tillman's death in 1865, the tract passed to the Roach family and was variously known as Roach's Beach and Ark Beach. Until well into the twentieth century, local farmers came in covered wagons to camp among the dunes, fish, and enjoy the surf.

In the 1920s the property was acquired by George J. Holliday of Galivants Ferry. He renamed it Floral Beach to honor his wife, Flora. The Hollidays built a pavilion, a general store, and a few small rental cottages for summer visitors. Later a fishing pier was built. Little more was done to promote Floral Beach, however, and the area languished until the early 1950s.

In 1952 local investors including James Calhoun, Craig Wall, Ervin E. Dargan, and Collins Spivey purchased most of the original property, including a tract owned by the Burroughs family, for about $200,000. The new owners renamed the property Surfside Beach after a Florida town. In 1954 Hurricane Hazel caused significant damage to many Surfside residences, but the area was spared general devastation.

By the early 1960s the development of Surfside Beach was under way in earnest. The developers planned a mixed community of middle-class permanent residents and mostly single family resort housing for tourists. Growth increased the need for municipal services, and Surfside Beach was incorporated on March 14, 1964, with T. J. Harrison as mayor. City government wisely acted to limit housing density and commercial sprawl, avoiding some problems encountered by less prudent resort communities.

The 1970s and 1980s witnessed unprecedented growth. Although a few large hotels were constructed, single family units remained the norm. Commercial development flourished along U.S. Highway 17 parallel to the coast. As Surfside became a popular retirement destination, the influx of population from the North and the Midwest caused ripples in local politics. Nevertheless, Surfside's mayors and councils typically acted with wisdom and foresight in balancing growth with conservation. For example, a beautiful park graces the center of Surfside, and the town boasts magnificent live oaks well over a century old.

In 1989 Hurricane Hugo slammed into Surfside, causing major damage to hundreds of buildings. Cleanup and repairs disrupted the community for months. The storm accelerated drainage problems and beach erosion. In the early 1990s Surfside expanded the city's storm water system, although drainage problems remain. A comprehensive beach renourishment program was undertaken in 1998 and 1999. But lost sand can be replaced more easily than lost culture. By the late 1990s much of Surfside's architectural appeal had been sacrificed by developers who replaced charming, eclectic beach homes with monotonous tract housing. ELDRED E. PRINCE, JR.

Lewis, Catherine H. *Horry County, South Carolina, 1730–1993.* Columbia: University of South Carolina Press, 1998.

Swamp Angel. "Swamp Angel" was the nickname given to a 16,500-pound rifled Parrott cannon with an eight-inch bore that briefly shelled the city of Charleston in August 1863. The massive gun was positioned near Morris Island in a sandbagged earthwork known as the Marsh Battery. The construction of the Marsh Battery, which virtually floated on the marsh, was considered to be one of the greatest engineering feats of the war. The battery was completed by mid-August 1863, and by August 21 the Swamp Angel was mounted and ready to fire incendiary shells 7,900 yards into Charleston. Before the first shot was fired, the Union commander Quincy A. Gillmore demanded that the Confederates evacuate Morris Island and Fort Sumter or he would fire on the city. The request was refused, and early on the morning of August 22, directed by a compass reading on St. Michael's steeple, the first shell was fired into Charleston. The shelling continued until daylight and then resumed on the evening of August 23, when the Swamp Angel exploded while firing its thirty-sixth round. The bombardment of the city would continue from other batteries and new guns mounted in the Marsh Battery throughout the war. Though only a few people were killed or injured by the shelling, it did force the civilian evacuation of Charleston south of Broad Street. The Swamp Angel's damaged gun tube was later recovered and was mounted in Cadwallader Park in Trenton, New Jersey. STEPHEN R. WISE

Johnson, John. *The Defense of Charleston Harbor, Including Fort Sumter and the Adjacent Islands, 1863–1865.* 1890. Reprint, Germantown, Tenn.: Guild Bindery Press, 1994.

Olmstead, Edwin, Wayne E. Stark, and Spencer C. Tucker. *The Big Guns.* Bloomfield, Ont.: Museum Restoration Service, 1997.

Ripley, Warren. *Artillery and Ammunition of the Civil War.* 4th ed. Charleston, S.C.: Battery Press, 1984.

Wise, Stephen R. *Gate of Hell: Campaign for Charleston Harbor, 1863.* Columbia: University of South Carolina Press, 1994.

Swansea Veneer and Basket Works. Founded in 1914 by Washington Bartow Rast, the Swansea Veneer and Basket Works was an expansion of Rast's veneer mill that he had started in 1896. One of the first trade factories in South Carolina, it was for many years Swansea's only industry.

Initially the factory made banana drums, barrels, furniture, and fine veneers. By 1903 production was expanded to include wooden crates, boxes, and baskets used by the burgeoning truck-farming industry in South Carolina for shipping fruits and vegetables. By 1920 Swansea's location as a railroad stop on the main line of the Columbia-Savannah Railroad (now the Coastline Railroad) enabled the factory's products to be used for shipping from Lexington County to points all over the eastern seaboard and into Canada.

When Rast's son, Lewis Oliver Rast, joined his father in the business, it became known as W. B. Rast's Son's Company. After Washington Bartow Rast died, his son continued operating the company until it ceased operations in 1964. MICHELINE BROWN

Woody, Howard, and Thomas L. Johnson. *South Carolina Postcards.* Vol. 4, *Lexington County and Lake Murray.* Charleston, S.C.: Arcadia, 2000.

Swearingen, John Eldred (1875–1957). Educator. Swearingen was born in Trenton, Edgefield County, on January 9, 1875, the son of John Cloud Swearingen and Anna Tillman. Blinded in a hunting accident in 1888, Swearingen, along with his family, insisted that he receive the same education as that of a sighted student. Originally sent to the Georgia Academy for the Blind in 1888, Swearingen attended the Cedar Spring School for the Blind and Deaf from 1889 to 1894. After making a personal appeal to college officials, Swearingen was allowed to enroll in South Carolina College in 1895. He graduated with an A.B. in 1899 as the highest honor graduate of the Clariosophic Literary Society. He began his career in education at Cedar Spring as a teacher and principal of the blind department from 1899 through 1908. In 1916 Swearingen married Mary Hough. The marriage produced three children.

In 1908 Swearingen was elected state superintendent of education, a position he would hold unopposed for fourteen years. He was quick to state that he was not political but was interested in education and saw the position as an opportunity to serve the state. Progressive and pragmatic, Swearingen oversaw the significant expansion and improvement of public schools in South Carolina, thanks in large measure to the good relationships he fostered with progressive governors Richard Manning and Robert Cooper. Swearingen did, however, have an oppositional relationship with controversial governor Coleman Blease.

Swearingen was instrumental in getting several acts of educational legislation passed. Financial aid to school districts was raised several times, and local school tax laws were enacted. Swearingen expanded the minimum length of the school term and set size requirements for schools to encourage consolidation. New regulations for certifying teachers and a state-mandated curriculum with appropriate state-approved textbooks were also part of Swearingen's legacy. He enacted a statewide system of creating and inspecting public high schools. Swearingen was instrumental in the implementation and enforcement of the federal Smith-Hughes Act, which provided federal dollars for agricultural and vocational education.

Swearingen also used his office for broader reforms. He was a proponent of mill schools across the state. Though shackled by segregation, Swearingen worked with private funding organizations to foster education for African Americans. Working with Wil Lou Gray, he helped implement a series of night schools to combat adult illiteracy under the slogan "Let South Carolina secede from illiteracy." Outside the office, Swearingen was one of the charter members of the South Carolina Association for the Blind, which he used to promote education and industrial training for blind students, black and white, across South Carolina.

In 1922 Swearingen was encouraged to run for governor by the county superintendents of education, who wished to remove him from office. A friend left an anonymous note in his office to this effect, and once Swearingen realized his mistake, he reentered the race for state superintendent. His Bleasite opponents, however, embarked on a statewide smear campaign to ensure Swearingen's defeat. After losing the election, Swearingen retired from public life. He devoted himself to farming and lumbering family lands in South Carolina and Florida. He died in Columbia on September 24, 1957, and was buried in Greenlawn Memorial Park. EDWARD JANAK

Dreyfuss, James Vernon. *John Eldred Swearingen: Superintendent of Education in South Carolina 1909–1922.* Columbia: College of Education, University of South Carolina, 1997.

Janak, Edward. "John Eldred Swearingen and the Development of the Public High School in South Carolina." Ph.D. diss., University of South Carolina, 2003.

Swearingen, John Eldred. Papers. South Caroliniana Library, University of South Carolina, Columbia.

Swearingen, John Eldred, and Wil Lou Gray. *Midsummer Drive against Illiteracy, for White Schools.* Columbia, S.C.: State Superintendent of Education, 1920.

Swearingen, Mary Hough. *A Gallant Journey: Mr. Swearingen and His Family.* Columbia: University of South Carolina Press, 1959.

Swearingen, John Eldred, Jr. (b. 1918). Businessman. Swearingen was born in Columbia on September 7, 1918, to State Superintendent of Education John Eldred Swearingen, Sr., and his wife, Mary Hough. He married Roly George "Polly" Osterberger of New Orleans in 1942. Divorced in 1969, he married Bonnie Bolding of Birmingham, Alabama, and together they had three daughters: Marcia, Sally, and Linda.

From 1934 to 1938 Swearingen attended the University of South Carolina. Inducted into Phi Beta Kappa in 1938, he graduated magna cum laude with a bachelor's degree in chemical engineering. Swearingen attended the Carnegie Institution of Technology in Pittsburgh (later Carnegie-Mellon University) from 1938 to 1939, earning a master's degree in chemical engineering and the title Industrial Fellow. He would be honored with fifteen honorary degrees over his lifetime.

Swearingen accepted a position with Standard Oil of Indiana's (later BP-Amoco) Oklahoma City branch. In 1947 he received a patent for a catalytic conversion system. In 1952 Standard transferred him to Chicago, where he was made a director and then was elected president in 1958. In 1960 Swearingen assisted with the corporate overhaul of the company and was named chief executive officer.

In 1965 Swearingen became chairman of Standard Oil, a position he would fill until he retired on his birthday in 1983. During his tenure Swearingen, an outspoken opponent of government interference in private industry, streamlined Standard's operations and expanded the company's oil operations into forty nations, eventually becoming decorated by the governments of Egypt, Italy, and Iran. He also directed the exploration of other fuel resources, such as natural gas, coal, and chemicals. During Swearingen's tenure, Standard Oil became a multi-billion-dollar company and the nation's sixth-largest corporation in net income.

Swearingen served as chair of the national Petroleum Council from 1974 to 1975 and the American Petroleum Institute from 1978 to 1979. A longtime Republican supporter, Swearingen used these positions to appear on many television programs to oppose President Jimmy Carter's plans for solving the fuel crisis, eventually becoming the national face of "Mr. Big Oil." After supporting Ronald Reagan in the 1980 presidential election, Swearingen served on the presidential task force on the arts and humanities in 1981.

In 1984 Swearingen, at the request of the Federal Deposit Insurance Corporation, became chairman of the Continental Bank of Chicago (later Continental Illinois Corporation), holding this position until 1987 and then retiring as a board member in 1989. He took the institution from insolvency and a $4.5 billion bailout to profitability. Swearingen has held a variety of professional memberships, educational trusteeships, and corporate board positions.

From the 1950s through the 1980s Swearingen gave a variety of addresses throughout South Carolina. In 1965 he was awarded an honorary law degree from the University of South Carolina, which in 1987 dedicated its new College of Engineering facility as the John E. Swearingen Engineering Center. He was inducted into the South Carolina Business Hall of Fame in 1988. EDWARD JANAK

Crittenden, Ann. "At Home with John and Bonnie." *New York Times,* August 25, 1980, p. D1.

Janak, Edward. "John Eldred Swearingen and the Development of the Public High School in South Carolina." Ph.D. diss., University of South Carolina, 2003.

Lunan, Bert, and Robert A. Pierce. *Legacy of Leadership.* Columbia: South Carolina Business Hall of Fame, 1999.

Martin, Douglas. "The Special State of Indiana Standard." *New York Times,* December 13, 1981, sec. 3, p. 4.

Sword of State. The Sword of State is a special symbol of the South Carolina Senate. At the start of each legislative day, the sergeant at arms places the sword in a cradle at the front of the president's podium, where it rests whenever the Senate is in session. The ceremonial weapon is made of steel and gold and is thirty-nine inches long. The blade is etched with sprigs of yellow jessamine and has a picture of the state coat of arms on one side. The hilt has a pommel decorated with rosettes, and the grip is wrapped with gold braid. The scabbard is covered in burgundy leather, with brass fittings. Manufactured by Wilkinson Sword, Ltd., of London, England, the sword was presented to the state in 1951, the gift of the first earl of Halifax, the British ambassador to the United States during World War II, as a replacement for the original Sword of State stolen from the State House.

Sword of State. Courtesy, the Senate of South Carolina

South Carolina's first Sword of State was introduced in about 1704 at the behest of Governor Sir Nathaniel Johnson. In the eighteenth century it was carried in processions on special occasions such as solemn declarations of war and the installations of royal governors. After the Revolutionary War, the sword continued to be displayed at gubernatorial inaugurations and was eventually put to daily use by the Senate. The first sword was fifty inches in length and had a wavy blade, thought to have been made of imported steel. Tradition holds that the silver hilt was made in Charleston. This weapon disappeared from the State House in 1941. Lord Halifax learned of the theft during a 1944 visit to Columbia and promised to secure a British blade as a replacement after the war. For some years a cavalry sword belonging to the Charleston Museum was used by the Senate before the arrival of Halifax's gift sword. DAVID C. R. HEISSER

T

Tabby. Along the coasts of Florida, Alabama, Georgia, and the Carolinas, tabby was introduced by the Spanish in the seventeenth century as a low-cost and accessible building material. It was manufactured following methods long practiced throughout southern Spain by mixing various compounds including earth, limestone, and clay with lime and then pounding or pouring the resultant mix between boards positioned to define the required building shape. Once the cast was set, the form work was dismantled, repositioned, and refilled with the mix at successively higher building levels.

Tabby in North America is distinguished by the use of oyster shell aggregates and lime derived by burning shells. As with the earlier manufacture along the Mediterranean, the lime and the aggregate were mixed with sand and water and tamped into reusable wooden forms, usually made of horizontal tongue-and-groove timbers. The French Duc de La Rochefoucauld-Liancourt provides a late eighteenth-century observation of the casting process he saw in Beaufort County: "Mortar is poured into frames the length and thickness of the wall to be constructed. These forms have no bottoms but their sides are joined at certain intervals at top and bottom by pieces of wood. The mortar is pounded in with force and when brim full left for two or three days."

Although no tabby structure securely dated before 1730 survives above ground in South Carolina or Georgia, it is clear that tabby played an important role in shelter and defenses for early Europeans. Other durable building materials, such as brick and stone, were not easily available, especially in the Sea Islands, which lacked outcrops of clay and rock.

Recent research indicates that tabby manufacture was understood around Charleston before 1726, but it did not appear in Beaufort County until construction began in 1731 at Fort Frederick on the Beaufort River. Eventually it became ubiquitous to Beaufort County, where it was used in fortifications, houses, stores, and a variety of outbuildings. It is now represented by a handful of structures in the city of Beaufort (including the Barnwell-Gough House, Tabby Manse, and the Saltus House) and on Spring, St. Helena, Callawassie, and Hilton Head Islands. MAXINE LUTZ

Gritzner, Janet Bigbee Hazen. "Tabby in the Coastal Southeast: The Cultural History of an American Building Material." Ph.D. diss., Louisiana State University, 1978.

Table Rock (Greenville County). Table Rock is a small mountain that rises dramatically above the surrounding landscape northwest of Greenville. It rises to 3,197 feet above sea level with a relatively broad summit shaped like a table, a characteristic that is said to have inspired the name given to it by Native Americans of the region long ago. Table Rock, located in the inner Piedmont belt, is just south of the Mountain Bridge Wilderness and Recreation Area, including Caesars Head and Jones Gap, both of which share a similar geologic history.

Like Caesars Head and Sassafras Mountain, Table Rock formed through the process of plate tectonics. Geologists believe that a continental fragment or island arc moved, as one plate slid under another, and then collided with ancient North America during the Ordovician period about 430 million years ago. The force of this collision generated heat and produced magma. This formed a large batholith miles underground that later cooled and hardened to form granite. Today the exposed rock of this batholith is found from Virginia to Alabama. During later collisions in the Devonian and Pennsylvanian to Permian periods, this granite was squeezed and reheated in a metamorphic process that turned the granite into a metagranite, or granitic gneiss. Over millions of years the land was uplifted, the ancient mountains eroded, and so the intrusive igneous rock of Table Rock was exposed at the surface.

Table Rock. Photograph by Michael Foster. Courtesy, South Carolina Department of Natural Resources

At the base of Table Rock and visible along the trails at Table Rock State Park lies another interesting rock, amphibolite, which is metamorphic basalt derived from the ocean crust that was also emplaced during collision. These amphibolite schists and metavolcanics of the surrounding area have eroded faster than the harder metagranite of Table Rock, and so it has weathered to form an isolated hill called a monadnock. CAROLYN H. MURPHY

Kovacik, Charles F., and John J. Winberry. *South Carolina: The Making of a Landscape.* 1987. Reprint, Columbia: University of South Carolina Press, 1989.

Murphy, Carolyn H. *Carolina Rocks! The Geology of South Carolina.* Orangeburg, S.C.: Sandlapper, 1995.

Talvande, Madame Rose (ca. 1790–ca. 1840), and **Madame Ann Marsan (Mason) Talvande** (ca. 1807–1850). Educators. Between approximately 1816 and 1850, Madame Talvande's Ladies Boarding School in Charleston educated the daughters of the elite families of South Carolina, including the diarist Mary Chesnut and the novelist Susan Petigru King. The school provided a typical finishing-school education for girls, including lessons in French, music, and dancing. In the early nineteenth century, however, a new idea of women's citizenship had emerged that required the future mothers of the republic to be educated, particularly the daughters of the elite classes. The Talvande academy followed this trend by offering instruction in rhetoric and the sciences, courses in which girls seldom received training otherwise. The curriculum reflected the high expectations of the Talvande academy's clientele, who paid dearly for the school's services. Talvande's was considered exclusive enough not to have to advertise for students.

Little is known about Madame Talvande, however, beyond the stories told of her by her most renowned pupil, Mary Chesnut. According to Chesnut, who attended the school between 1835 and 1840, Madame Talvande was Ann Marsan Talvande. Another student, Harriott Horry Ravenel, remembered that Talvande ran the girls' school with her aunt, a Mademoiselle Daty. Both women believed their teachers to have been refugees from Santo Domingo.

The stories written by Chestnut about her years at Talvande's school, while helpful in reconstructing Talvande's life, are problematic. Chesnut's descriptions appear in fictional stories based on her childhood, for which she may have taken a certain extent of literary license. She also wrote the stories set at the Talvande school later in her life, when time may have distorted some of her impressions. Certainly Ravenel had confused some of her own memories because "Mademoiselle Daty" was actually Julia Datty, who ran a different girls' school across Legare Street from Talvande's.

According to city directories and census information, two women assumed the professional name of "Madame Talvande." The elder, Rose Talvande, a widow by 1835, may actually have been the refugee from Haiti. She had moved to Charleston by 1806, when she first appeared in the city directory, and took a federal naturalization oath in Charleston in 1835. In 1816 "M. Talvande's Ladies School" opened at 32 Broad Street. The location changed to 51 Meeting Street before the school settled at 24 Legare Street in a large mansion that adjoined the lot containing the Talvande home on Tradd Street. By 1819 the proprietors of the school were Rose Talvande and Andrew Talvande (1787–1834), probably a younger relative. Andrew continued his involvement with the school into the 1830s.

During that decade the younger "Madame Talvande," Ann Marsan Talvande, joined the faculty through her marriage to Andrew. Sometime in the 1840s, she took over proprietorship of the school. Ann Talvande was certainly the "Tyrant of Legare St." as remembered by Chesnut. She does not seem to have lived in the school as "Madame Talvande" at the same time as Rose Talvande, but some of her students seem to have transferred to Ann many of the stories surrounding Rose. Ann was an immigrant from Santo Domingo and, like Rose Talvande, took a naturalization oath in 1835. After the death of the elder two Talvandes, Ann ran the school with Ann Johnston until about 1850, at which time the school no longer operated. Ann Talvande died on November 16, 1850, after a residence in Charleston of forty-three years. She was buried in St. Patrick's Churchyard. LEIGH FOUGHT

Muhlenfeld, Elisabeth. *Mary Boykin Chesnut: A Biography.* Baton Rouge: Louisiana State University Press, 1981.

Ravenel, Harriott Horry. *Charleston: The Place and the People.* New York: Macmillan, 1906.

Tarleton, Banastre (1754–1833). British soldier. Few other figures in South Carolina history have been labeled as villainous as Banastre Tarleton has. He was born in Liverpool, England, on August 21, 1754, the third child of John Tarleton and Jane Parker. John Tarleton, who served as mayor of Liverpool, wished for the popular and athletic Banastre to study law and enrolled him at Oxford. When his father died in 1773, Banastre first used the legacy he received to further his study of the law, but on April 20, 1775, he purchased a cornet's commission in the First Dragoon Guards.

Banastre Tarleton. Courtesy, South Carolina Historical Society

Tarleton sailed for America in February 1776 and was part of the British force that attacked Charleston in June 1776, although he played no major role in operations against the fort on Sullivan's Island. In the northern theater, Tarleton served with Lieutenant Colonel William Harcourt of the Sixteenth Regiment of Light Dragoons and played a key role in the capture of General Charles Lee in December 1776. Impressing his superior officers, Tarleton rose steadily through the ranks, and on August 1, 1778, he was appointed lieutenant colonel of Lord Cathcart's Legion, a mixed unit of cavalry and infantry comprised primarily of Loyalists. Tarleton led this unit, which was usually referred to as the British Legion or simply the Legion, when it sailed from New York southward in December 1779. Most of the British cavalry horses perished in the long and stormy voyage from New York to Georgia, so General Sir Henry Clinton sent Tarleton and his dragoons to the Beaufort area to collect new mounts. Tarleton shined in the ensuing Charleston campaign. His dragoons completely overwhelmed the American cavalry at Biggin's Bridge near Moncks Corner on April 14, 1780, and then surprised and beat them again at Lenud's Ferry on the Santee River on May 6.

Tarleton gained his greatest notoriety in the aftermath of Charleston's surrender. Lord Cornwallis dispatched his Legion to overtake Colonel Abraham Buford and the last remaining detachment of Continental troops in South Carolina after Charleston's fall. Aware of the British pursuit, Buford retreated toward North Carolina. Covering 105 miles in fifty-four hours, Tarleton's force caught up with the Americans on May 29, 1780, at the Waxhaws (near the North Carolina / South Carolina border in modern-day Lancaster County). Tarleton's cavalry smashed through Buford's infantry, and slaughter then ensued. In the charge, Tarleton's horse was shot out from under him. According to Tarleton, his men, believing they had lost their commander, were "stimulated . . . to a vindictive asperity not easily restrained." His dragoons cut down men with their sabers as those soldiers tried to surrender or run away. Tarleton reported that 113 American soldiers "were killed on the spot" while 150 others were so badly wounded that Tarleton had to leave them behind on parole. The British had only 5 killed and 14 wounded. Word of the massacre spread quickly. The action at the Waxhaws established Tarleton as a ruthless and bloodthirsty villain in the minds of South

Carolina patriots, and the phrase "Tarleton's quarter" came to mean "no quarter."

Following the American defeat at Camden, Tarleton's dragoons again chased down fleeing soldiers. On August 18, 1780, he surprised and routed a detachment under General Thomas Sumter at Fishing Creek. At Blackstock's plantation on November 20, 1780, Tarleton again attacked Sumter, but this time Sumter held a strong fortified position from which his men inflicted over one hundred casualties upon the British troops. Both sides claimed victory in the action. Tarleton also had troubles with Francis Marion. Ordered by Cornwallis to "get at Mr. Marion," Tarleton pursued his force through the swamps of the Pee Dee region but was unable to catch him. At the Battle of Cowpens (January 17, 1781), Tarleton suffered one of the most critical defeats of the Revolutionary War when his troops crumbled before the ragtag army of General Daniel Morgan. It was Tarleton's last hurrah in South Carolina. In the wake of the defeat, General Cornwallis determined to drive Nathanael Greene into North Carolina; Tarleton and the Legion went with him. In March 1781 Tarleton fought in the Battle of Guilford Courthouse, North Carolina, where an American musket ball mangled his right hand, and he was captured with the British army at Yorktown.

After the war Tarleton returned to England and served in Parliament. He died on January 16, 1833, and was buried in the churchyard at Leintwardine, England. While portrayed by many historians as cruel and inhumane, one cannot deny Tarleton his success. He excelled at quick-strike, surprise attacks that overwhelmed his enemy. Until Blackstock's and Cowpens, his methods were brutally effective against South Carolina patriots. CARL BORICK

Bass, Robert D. *The Green Dragoon: The Lives of Banastre Tarleton and Mary Robinson.* New York: Holt, 1957.

Pancake, John S. *This Destructive War: The British Campaign in the Carolinas, 1780–1782.* University: University of Alabama Press, 1985.

Tarleton, Banastre. *A History of the Campaigns of 1780 and 1781, in the Southern Provinces of North America.* 1787. Reprint, Spartanburg, S.C.: Reprint Company, 1967.

Taxpayers' Conventions (1871, 1874). In 1871 and 1874 white Democrats in South Carolina, frustrated with high taxes and the Republicans' domination of the state government, held statewide conventions to register their protests. The 1871 convention met in Columbia to protest that year's tax increase to the unheard-of level of eleven mills on the dollar. William D. Porter of Charleston presided, and the leading members of the convention were Matthew C. Butler and Martin W. Gary of Edgefield. The delegates undertook a rather cursory review of the state's finances and (erroneously) pronounced the state's debt to be entirely legitimate. They also advocated a scheme for "cumulative voting," which would have increased the representation of the minority party (the Democrats) in the legislature.

In 1873 widespread reports of profligate spending and financial malfeasance by the Republican state government surfaced, accompanied by the highest taxes of the Reconstruction era (twelve mills). A second Taxpayers' Convention therefore met in February of 1874, with William D. Porter again presiding. Martin Gary again played a leading role, this time proposing to solve the problems of white South Carolinians by recruiting white immigrants into the state in order to outnumber blacks. The convention submitted a petition to President Ulysses Grant and to Congress complaining of "taxation without representation," by which they meant that the class that paid the bulk of the taxes—white Democrats—was unable to win elective office. Neither Congress nor the president was impressed by this logic.

The 1874 convention, like its predecessor in 1871, achieved its most important results indirectly: by shining a light on the financial situation of the state, both conventions shamed the Republican government into conducting its own investigation. The second investigation, completed in June 1874, provided the most revealing picture yet of Republican financial mismanagement and laid the foundation for the rapid improvements that took place during Governor Daniel Chamberlain's administration. HYMAN S. RUBIN III

Proceedings of the Tax-Payers' Convention of South Carolina, Held at Columbia, Beginning May 9th, and Ending May 12th, 1871. Charleston, S.C.: Edward Perry, 1871.

Proceedings of the Tax-Payers' Convention of South Carolina, Held at Columbia, Beginning February 17, and Ending February 20, 1874. Charleston, S.C.: News and Courier, 1874.

Rubin, Hyman S., III. "The South Carolina Scalawags." Ph.D. diss., Emory University, 2001.

Taylor, Anna Heyward (1879–1956). Artist. Born in Columbia on November 13, 1879, Taylor was the daughter of Dr. Benjamin Taylor and Marianna Heyward, both members of prominent South Carolina families. In 1897 she graduated from the South Carolina Presbyterian Institute for Young Ladies.

After sojourns in New York and Boston, Taylor spent the summers of 1903 and 1904 studying abroad with the noted art instructor William Merritt Chase, first in Holland and then in London. In 1908 and 1909 she traveled extensively in Europe, followed by travels to the Far East in 1914. She spent the summers of 1915 and 1916 in Provincetown, Massachusetts, an emerging artists' colony where printmakers were experimenting with wood-block prints. In 1916 and 1920 she joined expeditions led by William Beebe to British Guiana, where she studied and rendered tropical vegetation. During World War I she was the first woman from South Carolina to serve with the American Red Cross in France. Taylor resided in New York through the 1920s until 1929, when she moved to Charleston permanently.

Already a charter member of the Columbia Art Association since 1915, she soon became identified as a leading member of the Charleston Renaissance along with Alice Ravenel Huger Smith, Elizabeth O'Neill Verner, and Alfred Hutty. Unlike her colleagues, Taylor was well traveled, and she continued to explore new locales. For fifteen months in 1935 and 1936 she traveled extensively in Mexico. Taylor was accomplished in a variety of mediums, including watercolor, linoleum and wood-block prints, batik on silk, and the design of screens. She excelled, however, in color wood-block prints using the white-line method, which she had learned in Provincetown from B. J. O. Nordfeldt during the summer of 1916. In this technique, artists carve grooves between separate color areas, allowing the use of only one wood block, instead of the many required in the more traditional Japanese manner. Taylor's subjects were often Charleston street scenes or exotic flowers seen at close range, which she printed in bright, solid colors. Her black and white prints are distinctive for broad areas of flat black or plain white. Many served as illustrations for *This Our Land* (1949), a volume published by the Agricultural Society of South Carolina with a text by Chalmers S. Murray. One of her black and white prints, *Harvesting Rice,* was selected for inclusion at the 1939 New York World's Fair.

In 1950 Taylor's art was the focus of a retrospective exhibition, the first one-artist undertaking at the Columbia Museum of Art.

Examples of Taylor's work can be found in numerous private collections and at the Gibbes Museum of Art in Charleston, the Columbia Museum of Art, the South Carolina State Museum, and the Greenville County Museum of Art. Taylor died at her Charleston residence on March 4, 1956. See plate 26. MARTHA R. SEVERENS

Burgess, Lana Ann. "Anna Heyward Taylor: 'Her Work Which Is of Enduring Quality Will Remain to Attest to Her Reputation as an Artist and Her Generosity as a Citizen.'" Master's thesis, University of South Carolina, 1994.

Murray, Chalmers S. *This Our Land: The Story of the Agricultural Society of South Carolina.* Charleston, S.C.: Carolina Art Association, 1949.

Severens, Martha R. *Anna Heyward Taylor: Printmaker.* Greenville, S.C.: Greenville County Museum of Art, 1987.

Taylor, John (1770–1832). Congressman, governor, U.S. senator. Born near Granby on May 4, 1770, Taylor was the eldest son of the upcountry planter Thomas Taylor and Ann Wyche. Taylor attended academies in Camden and Winnsboro for three years prior to entering the College of New Jersey (Princeton University) as a sophomore in 1788. Graduated second in his class two years later, he returned to South Carolina. There, he read law under the Charleston attorney Charles Cotesworth Pinckney from January 1791 until his own admission to the bar in June 1793. Toward the end of his legal apprenticeship, on March 17, 1793, Taylor married Sarah Cantey Chesnut, daughter of the Camden merchant John Chesnut. The couple settled in Columbia and went on to have sixteen children, seven of whom survived to adulthood.

Although Taylor practiced law for several years and enjoyed success as a planter, his long career in public office began well before he proved himself in either of his private callings. In December 1793 he entered the South Carolina House of Representatives, where he served as a member first from Saxe Gotha (1793–1794), then from his home district of Richland (1794–1801), and again from Saxe Gotha (1804–1805). Attentive to upcountry interests, Taylor supported the abolition of plural voting, the reapportionment of representation, the improvement of inland navigation, and the perpetuation of slave importation. He was deemed one of the "ablest" and "most active" members of the House.

In 1806 Taylor won election to the U.S. House of Representatives, where he sat from 1807 to 1810. Defeated for reelection by William Lowndes, Taylor was subsequently elected to the U.S. Senate, where he served from 1810 to 1816, when he resigned for personal reasons. A Democratic-Republican, Taylor became a key player in congressional efforts to make economic sanctions an effective deterrent against British and French violations of American neutral trading rights. The author of Macon's Bill No. 2, the last of the sanctions acts, which passed in 1810, Taylor continued to believe in economic coercion at least until Congress declared war against Britain in June 1812, when he voted in favor of hostilities. By the return of peace in 1815, he had renounced sanctions altogether. While in Congress, Taylor also played a leading role in the unsuccessful campaign to renew the charter of the Bank of the United States before its expiration in 1811. Refuting allegations that the bank was unconstitutional despite its twenty years of service to the nation, Taylor declined to be "a stickler" for states' rights: "Preserve your Constitution without abandoning its legitimate powers, such as you have prospered in the exercise of, and I fear not this hobgoblin [consolidation]."

After a two-year hiatus, Taylor returned to public life as a member of the South Carolina Senate, where he represented Richland District from 1818 to 1825. During this period Taylor's political views, like those of the state in general, shifted from nationalist to states' rights. In 1824 Taylor joined in passing a set of resolutions that placed a state law intended to help prevent slave insurrections above a federal treaty guaranteed as supreme under the Constitution. Later that year and again the next, he voted for resolutions denying congressional authority to enact protective tariffs or sponsor internal improvements and reserving to the states any power that the Constitution did not explicitly delegate to the federal government.

In October 1826 Taylor lost a reelection bid to Wade Hampton II, only to become governor of South Carolina two months later on December 9, 1826. Throughout his two-year term, Taylor used his position to rally opposition against Congress, whose continued sanction of protective tariffs and internal improvements he denounced as unconstitutional and inequitable. Taylor urged resort to every lawful means of redress but refused to go so far as to question the value of the Union: "If I have any firmness, it will be exerted to preserve the union—to preserve, protect, and defend the constitution of this state and of the United States."

After the expiration of his term on December 10, 1828, Taylor remained politically active for at least another two years, during which time his antipathy for tariffs drove him to increasingly radical stances. In the late summer of 1830, he presided over a pair of public meetings called to advance a state convention to consider nullification of the 1828 Tariff of Abominations. And, in an exchange of letters with U.S. Supreme Court justice William Johnson, he not only declared his preference for secession over submission but also implied that the time to choose was drawing near. On April 16, 1832, Taylor died unexpectedly in Camden. He was buried in his family cemetery in Columbia. ROBERT F. KARACHUK

Culler, Justine Bond. "John Taylor: neglected South Carolinian." Master's thesis, University of South Carolina, 1970.

Taylor, Susie King (ca. 1848–?). Nurse, teacher. Born into slavery as Susan Baker near Savannah, Georgia, Taylor became free at the age of fourteen when her uncle led her and some of her other family members out of bondage. A federal gunboat plying the waters near the Confederate coastal defense of Fort Pulaski became her ride to freedom.

Taylor found herself one of thousands of refugees on the South Carolina Sea Islands. She soon attached herself to the First South Carolina Volunteers, the first black regiment in the United States Army. First organized under Major General David Hunter, the military governor Rufus Saxton would become the driving force behind the unit's creation.

Taylor originally worked as the regimental laundress and throughout the war would perform the essential duties of cooking and washing. However, her other talents—especially her ability to read and write—soon gave her a wider scope of responsibility. Her knowledge of folk remedies and what she learned of more conventional medicine enabled her to nurse the regiment's sick and wounded. She also served as the reading instructor for the regiment of former slaves. This would make her a beloved figure in the First South Carolina. The unit's white abolitionist colonel, Thomas Wentworth Higginson, would later write of them, "Their love of the spelling-book is perfectly inexhaustible."

Taylor married Sergeant Edward King of the First South Carolina sometime in 1862. Together they would remain with the unit (later in the war designated as the Thirty-third United States Colored Troops) until it was mustered out of service in 1866. During that time Taylor apparently developed into a dead shot, possibly even serving on picket duty. Some accounts describe her as having a ready capacity with the mechanism and the use of rifled muskets.

The Kings moved to Savannah, Georgia, in February of 1866. Susie hoped to continue her teaching career and opened a private school for the children of freedmen. Unfortunately, Edward King developed a fatal illness in the summer of that year and died in September. Soon afterward her private school failed when a free public school for former slaves opened. By 1868 Taylor had been forced to find work as a domestic servant, work she continued after her move to Boston in 1872. In 1879 she married Russell Taylor. She devoted much of the rest of her life to work with the Woman's Relief Corps, a national organization for female Civil War veterans. In 1902 she published a memoir of her Civil War service, in which she wrote of her continued interest and love for "the boys in blue." The date and circumstances of Susie King Taylor's death are unknown. W. SCOTT POOLE

Higginson, Thomas Wentworth. *Army Life in a Black Regiment.* 1870. Reprint, New York: Norton, 1984.

Taylor, Susie King. *A Black Woman's Civil War Memoirs: Reminiscences of My Life in Camp with the 33rd U.S. Colored Troops.* 1902. Reprint, New York: M. Wiener, 1988.

Technical education. Technical education in South Carolina has a lengthy history, dating back to John de la Howe's 1797 bequest of land to a school that would provide practical instruction for the needy children of Abbeville District. Systematic technical education, however, would have to wait until the post–World War II era, when political leaders realized that South Carolina's ability to attract new industry hinged on the availability of an educated workforce.

The South Carolina technical education system was founded at a time when the economic outlook of South Carolina was depressed. Farm employment opportunities were rapidly diminishing, and the state was faced with an underskilled labor force and no adequate means of training them for the rapidly changing job market. The idea for a technical education system began with Governor Ernest F. Hollings. Hollings appointed a joint legislative study committee of three senators and three representatives under the chairmanship of state senator John C. West. The committee's purpose was to develop a training system that would attract new and diversified industry to the state. After careful study, the Committee recommended a "crash" program to provide immediate training for established industries and a technical training program to train high school graduates for initial employment as technicians in industry. The first step the South Carolina General Assembly took to initiate a technical education system was to establish the Advisory Committee for Technical Training in May 1961.

The short-term training program became known as Special Schools (renamed the Center for Accelerated Technology Training in 2001). The Special Schools program worked in coordination with the South Carolina Development Board. After an industry indicated that it would locate in South Carolina, Special Schools staff determined training needs and recruited and trained potential employees. After the Special Schools training program was implemented, the Advisory Committee established permanent regional technical education centers. Greenville County was the first to apply for a technical center in September 1961, and the center opened the following year. Sixteen centers were established from that time until 1972, insuring that ninety-five percent of the state's population was within a twenty-five-mile commuting distance of the nearest center.

In 1972 seven of the centers were authorized to offer college transfer associate degrees. Upon accreditation by the Southern Association of Colleges and Schools (SACS), technical education centers became two-year comprehensive community colleges known as technical colleges. By 1990 the remaining nine centers were also authorized to offer college transfer associate degrees.

Throughout the closing decades of the twentieth century the technical colleges continued to pursue innovative means of educating South Carolinians. In 1981 the technical colleges began developing closer relationships with local high schools to prepare students for technical careers. Several universities and colleges collaborated with Greenville Technical College to create the University Center of Greenville and allow Greenville-area residents to take advantage of the resources of each school. A similar center was later established in Hilton Head. In 1988 Greenville Technical College broke ground on a new facility that would allow instruction to be offered via satellite. Classes were also taught via videocassette. With the advent of the Internet, technical college courses were offered on-line as well.

In 2004 sixteen technical colleges still served the state. The colleges enrolled 230,485 South Carolinians in all programs in 2003. Sixty-four percent of the students were women in 2003, and thirty-eight percent of all students were minority students. Technical colleges continue to provide learning opportunities that promote the economic and human resource development of the state. The technical education system has played a significant role in transforming a workforce formerly based in agriculture and textiles into a skilled workforce for highly diversified industries. GEMMA K. FROCK

Barton, Thomas E., Jr. "Technical and Vocational Education in South Carolina." In *The Organization of Public Education in South Carolina,* edited by John Walker, Michael D. Richardson, and Thomas I. Parks. Dubuque, Iowa: Kendall/Hunt, 1992.

Frock, Gemma K. "Historical Case Study: Developmental Influences and Political Processes Surrounding the Founding of the South Carolina Technical Education System." Ph.D. diss., University of South Carolina, 2002.

Tega Cay (York County; 2000 pop. 4,044). A recreation-oriented community on Lake Wylie with stronger ties to North Carolina than South Carolina, Tega Cay came into being in 1970 when Duke Power Company sold sixteen hundred acres in northwestern Fort Mill Township to the Ervin Company of Charlotte. The name allegedly comes from an obscure Polynesian dialect and means "Lovely Peninsula." Historically, the site was identified as India Hook Hills, which aptly described the red clay spur of land that jutted like a fishhook into the Catawba River. The unique landscape blends a mountainlike atmosphere with a man-made lake created in 1904, when the Catawba River was dammed by Duke Power at India Hook Shoals. The resulting peninsula contained more than sixteen miles of shoreline, with Gold Hill Road serving as the land access to the city.

The Ervin Company and several later companies folded before completing their development plans. In 1982 Tega Cay citizens chose to incorporate in the hope that they would achieve greater control over growth and services. Why choose to be a city instead of a town? One citizen reported that the application papers sent from the secretary of state's office in Columbia allowed them to check whether they wished to be a city rather than a town. Since nearby Fort Mill was a town, they decided to become a city. On July 4, 1982, Tega Cay became a South Carolina municipality. Every year since then, city residents have made the Fourth of July the city's birthday party. Fireworks, block parties, a boat parade, and other events are coordinated by Tega Cay's Property Owners Association.

From the beginning of the Catawba Indian suit against the property owners of the area in 1976 until the settlement in 1993, Tega Cay, to a greater degree than other municipalities in the suit area, was handicapped by the cloud over land titles. With the successful conclusion of the Catawba suit led by Congressman John Spratt (who for five years served as attorney for Tega Cay), the city was freed to attract further developers. However, like their predecessors, several of the new developers also went bankrupt.

The 1990 census revealed that the Tega Cay population was not typical of South Carolina municipalities. The city had no African American residents. More than one-third of the adult population held college degrees (in contrast to 16.6 percent of adults statewide). The city's per capita income of $23,207 was the third-highest among all South Carolina cities and towns. There were far fewer senior citizens than the statewide average (and none over age eighty-five), with most of the population between twenty-five and sixty-four years of age. A high percentage were employed in North Carolina.

In 2000 a massive new development, Stonecrest, was announced by Coldwell Banker / Tuttle Company, which anticipated 119 acres of town houses and apartments along with a second entrance to Tega Cay. Such expansion plans seem to indicate that Tega Cay's growth and prosperity will continue well into the new century. LOUISE PETTUS

Television. Snowy black-and-white television pictures first flickered into South Carolina on a regular basis on July 15, 1949, when WBTV Channel 3 signed on the air in Charlotte, North Carolina. However, it would be four more years before a station in South Carolina would go on the air because of a nationwide freeze on new construction imposed by the Federal Communications Commission (FCC). With just twelve VHF (Very High Frequency) channels in use, the FCC was concerned about interference, so new construction was stopped while sixty-nine new UHF (Ultra High Frequency) channels were created.

After the freeze was lifted in 1952, six South Carolina stations raced to go on the air: three in Columbia, two in Charleston, and one in Greenville. The first was WCOS-TV in Columbia, which began airing a test pattern on April 23, 1953. With no competition, the new station could choose shows from all four networks—NBC, CBS, ABC, and Dumont—and began broadcasting May 1, 1953, with *The Life of Riley, The Dennis Day Show, Famous Playhouse,* and boxing. The station was located in a Quonset hut, and chief engineer Robert Lambert said that viewers could hear water beating against the metal roof when it rained.

With call letters that stood for "Wonderful Charleston South Carolina," WCSC-TV made its debut June 19, 1953. The original owner, John M. Rivers, Sr., passed the station to his son John M. Rivers, Jr., who sold it to General Electric in 1987. It has been owned by Jefferson Pilot since 1992.

In Columbia, WNOK-TV began broadcasting on September 1, 1953, as another CBS affiliate on UHF Channel 67. Dick Laughridge, who joined the station the next month, said that pine trees swaying in the wind caused UHF pictures to wiggle in those days. The station later moved to Channel 19 and changed its call letters to WLTX-TV. It is one of the oldest UHF stations in the country. Both WNOK-TV and WCSC-TV bought cameras from the Allen B. Dumont Company in New Jersey. Dumont's chief engineer Thomas T. Goldsmith was a Greenville native and a pioneer of American television who helped develop the cathode ray tube, television circuitry, and transmission standards for the industry. The Fox affiliate WTTG-TV Channel 5, the former Dumont station in Washington, D.C., is still identified by Goldsmith's initials.

In the early days of television, VHF stations had a considerable advantage over their UHF counterparts because their signals were stronger and their pictures better. So it was not surprising that two radio stations fought for a valuable VHF channel allocated to Columbia. Under the direction of G. Richard Shafto, WIS joined with WMSC to go on the air November 7, 1953, on Channel 10 with a live broadcast of a University of South Carolina football game. As an NBC radio affiliate, WIS (which stood for "Wonderful Iodine State") carried over the affiliation to television. This spelled the beginning of the end for WCOS -TV, which was left with ABC, then a struggling network. The station signed off January 21, 1956. Five years later Channel 25 was reallocated to WCCA-TV, and in 1964 the station was purchased by Cy N. Bahakel of Charlotte and became WOLO-TV.

South Carolina's fifth and sixth television stations were in the upstate. WAIM-TV Channel 40 (now WBSC-TV) began broadcasting in Anderson on December 1, 1953, and WFBC-TV Channel 4 went on the air in Greenville at midnight on December 31, 1953, its next-door position obliterating the Charlotte signal that had dominated the area for four years. WFBC-TV was the brainchild of Roger Peace, who owned WFBC radio, and R. A. Jolley, Sr., who owned WMRC radio. WFBC's first program arrived by freight just hours before sign-on at midnight on December 31, 1953. The engineers did not have time to check the film before air time, so the first show was broadcast upside down and backward. WFBC-TV was renamed WYFF-TV ("Your Friend Four") when it was bought by Pulitzer Broadcasting in 1983.

By the end of 1953, every home in South Carolina with a television set could receive at least one of those stations. The South Carolina Educational Television network began broadcasting on closed circuits from a studio at Dreher High School in Columbia in 1958, and the first open-circuit educational television station, WNTV, began broadcasting in Greenville on September 15, 1963. By the beginning of the twenty-first century, eleven noncommercial channels were licensed to South Carolina. SCETV and more than twenty commercial television stations were broadcasting in South Carolina. PATRICIA G. MCNEELY

Pendleton, Nat. "The Start of Television in South Carolina." *Proceedings to the South Carolina Historical Association* (2001): 83–90.

Tenantry. Dating back to the colonial era, tenantry played a significant role in the agrarian society of South Carolina. Tenant farming was a system designed to allow people without capital to gain access to land and work it as their own. In return for the privilege of pursuing the Jeffersonian ideal of the independent yeoman, tenant farmers paid the owners of the land in cash or in part of their crops. In antebellum South Carolina, there were both white and free African American tenant farmers. After the Civil War tenant farming became more racially divided. Although there were still white tenants, the majority of tenants in South Carolina were African American.

In the years immediately following the Civil War, white landowners hired African American laborers and worked them in gangs as under slavery. However, laborers rebelled against this system. The two groups had different goals, with the crucial issue being control:

who would control the labor, the laborer or the landowner? African Americans released from slavery considered farm tenancy a step up. As tenants, African Americans had some control of the land and their own lives. They could nurture their strong desire for landownership. Amid negotiation and compromise, white landowners became more accepting of sharecropping and tenantry. Nevertheless, while the number of African American family tenant farmers increased dramatically, less than half of all African American household heads operated farms as late as 1880. The more typical African American household was not operating a farm as either renter or sharecropper but was still dependent on whites for wage-labor income.

A nineteenth-century landowner meeting with his tenants. Courtesy, South Carolina Historical Society

Part of the reason more successful former slaves could climb the agricultural ladder from the hired-labor rung to the sharecropping/tenantry rung during the 1870s was due to politics working in tandem with economics in two distinct phases. During one phase, African Americans held tremendous political power in the Republican Party, economic independence was possible, and tenantry meant autonomy. During the second phase, when conservative Democrats again seized political control, economic gains became less substantive. African Americans could still climb the economic ladder up to tenantry, but tenantry no longer necessarily meant autonomy.

The tenantry system had strong political implications. During slavery, living arrangements in slave quarters fostered a slave community; during Reconstruction, this same living pattern facilitated political and military organization among African Americans. By dispersing African American farmers into the countryside, tenantry made political and military organization more difficult for them. In addition, African Americans isolated on thirty- to sixty-acre plots were more vulnerable to white vigilantes and terrorist groups than were African Americans living nearer one another. The tenantry system, then, helped white Democrats to wrest control of the government. By 1900 South Carolina had close to 95,000 tenant farmers, 66,000 of which were African American.

During World War I cotton prices skyrocketed and, for the first time, tenant farmers and sharecroppers had significant disposable income. Cotton prices continued to rise briefly following the war, but the prosperity was fleeting. Competition and overproduction in

Mechanization on the farms spurred rural out-migrations, leaving abandoned tenant houses along country roads. Courtesy, South Caroliniana Library, University of South Carolina

the textile mills led to a sharp decline in demand, and cotton prices plummeted. Tenant farmers, along with sharecroppers, landlords, operatives, and mill owners, all found themselves without the ready cash to which they had grown accustomed. Their plight only worsened throughout the remainder of the 1920s and the onset of the Great Depression in the 1930s.

The New Deal programs of the Franklin Roosevelt administration had a tremendous impact on tenantry in South Carolina and the rest of the South. Crop reduction and soil conservation programs took a large percentage of farm acreage out of production, which greatly reduced the need for tenants and their labor. Between 1930 and 1940 the number of tenants on South Carolina farms dropped by almost twenty-five percent. Manpower shortages during World War II brought full employment to tenant farmers, but the decline in farm tenancy continued with renewed vigor after the war as farms became increasingly mechanized, reducing the need for farm labor even further. In 1950 about 63,000 of the 140,000 farms were worked by tenants. The decline accelerated in the decades that followed, until by 1992 just 7.4 percent of South Carolina farms were tenant operated. Once an omnipresent feature of the South Carolina landscape, tenantry has become largely a thing of the past.
ORVILLE VERNON BURTON, BEATRICE BURTON, AND MATTHEW CHENEY

Tenant Farms as Percentage of All Farms in South Carolina

Year	*Total Number of Farms*	*Total Number Tenant Operated*	*Percentage Tenant Operated*
1880	93,864	47,219	50.3
1890	115,000	862,168	54.1
1900	155,355	94,884	61.1
1910	176,434	111,221	63.0
1920	192,693	124,231	64.5
1930	157,931	102,768	65.1
1940	137,558	77,184	56.1
1950	139,364	63,186	45.3
1959	78,172	24,109	30.8
1969	39,559	4,897	12.3
1982	24,929	2,160	8.7
1992	20,242	1,495	7.4

Burton, Orville Vernon. "African American Status and Identity in a Postbellum Community: An Analysis of the Manuscript Census Returns." *Agricultural History* 72 (spring 1998): 213–40.

Kovacik, Charles F., and John J. Winberry. *South Carolina: The Making of a Landscape.* 1987. Reprint, Columbia: University of South Carolina Press, 1989.

Test Oath Controversy (1832–1834). A dispute between supporters and opponents of nullification over state loyalty oaths, the Test Oath Controversy erupted into violence as nullifiers sought to guarantee that only those who shared their views on state sovereignty could serve in certain state offices or as militia officers.

The Ordinance of Nullification, adopted November 24, 1832, authorized the General Assembly to require that all civil and military state officials (except legislators) "take an oath well and truly to obey, execute, and enforce" the ordinance and related legislation The legislature adopted such a test oath in December. It essentially barred conscientious Unionists, who considered nullification unconstitutional, from holding designated offices. Although the March 1833 state convention repealed the Ordinance of Nullification and thus rescinded the legal authority for the oath, it empowered the legislature to create, by a simple majority, another test oath. With the ordinance dead, any new oath would punish Unionists for having opposed the nullifiers during the crisis with the federal government.

In December 1833 the legislature passed a test oath requiring all militia officers to swear "true allegiance" to South Carolina. Because the oath's framers clearly intended this to mean exclusive allegiance to the state, Unionists, who believed they owed allegiance to the federal government as well, could not serve in good conscience.

Unionists challenged this militia test oath. Encouraged by the new, militantly Unionist editor of the *Greenville Mountaineer,* William Lowndes Yancey (who ironically later became a rabid secessionist), upcountry militiamen who opposed nullification refused to obey orders of anyone swearing the oath. In addition, the refusal of Unionists Edward McCready of Charleston and James McDonald of Lancaster to take the oath led to legal disputes that ended up before the state Court of Appeals in May 1834. The Unionist majority of the three-man court, John Belton O'Neall and David Johnson, struck down the oath. Dissenting was William Harper, the court's sole nullifier and the author of the Ordinance of Nullification, which had included the original test oath provision. Nullifiers responded by pledging to win a two-thirds majority in the fall legislative elections so they could incorporate a test oath directly into the state constitution.

During the fall 1834 legislative campaign, angry words—and more—passed between Unionists and nullifiers. In one incident, a group of unruly Charleston nullifiers—reportedly three or four hundred strong—attacked the city's Unionist headquarters, where their opponents greeted them with buckshot. As nullifiers threatened reprisals, only the intervention of Governor Robert Hayne and former governor James Hamilton, both leading nullifiers, prevented further violence.

After an overwhelming nullifier victory at the polls, the legislature gathered in December 1834 to pass a constitutional amendment containing a new test oath. To avoid further conflict, Hamilton worked out a deal with Unionist leader James L. Petigru, his former law partner. They agreed that the General Assembly should adopt a report declaring that "the allegiance required by the oath . . . is the allegiance which every citizen owes to the State consistently with the Constitution of the United States." That formulation satisfied most members of both parties and resolved the issue. ROBERT TINKLER

Freehling, William W. *Prelude to Civil War: The Nullification Controversy in South Carolina, 1816–1836.* New York: Harper & Row, 1965.

Textile Hall (Greenville). Greenville and Spartanburg were still vying for dominance of South Carolina's textile industry when local representatives of northern textile machine manufacturers began planning a Greenville trade show in December 1914. A committee including Greenville natives Joseph E. Sirrine and James F. Richardson worked feverishly for ten months, and on November 2, 1915, they welcomed the first of forty thousand visitors to the first Southern Textile Exposition, held in a railroad warehouse.

Textile Hall. Courtesy, South Carolina Department of Archives and History

The show was so successful that immediately after it closed, a new committee began planning for a permanent hall. Bennette Geer chaired the fund-raising committee; J. E. Sirrine designed and supervised construction of the $130,000 state-of-the-art exhibition space. When the second exposition opened on December 10, 1917, its construction was, according to the editor of *Cotton Magazine,* "a fitting monument" to the committee's work, "mute evidence of what the proper cooperative spirit can accomplish when suitably inspired." Located on West Washington Street, the massive red brick building immediately became the center of Greenville life. Armistice Day celebrations, the Southern Piedmont Textile Basketball Tournament, automobile shows, concerts, lectures by dignitaries such as William Jennings Bryan, Chamber of Commerce dinners, and movies were scheduled for its flexible space. Textile Hall expanded three times, nearly doubling its original space. The Southern Textile Exposition proclaimed Greenville the center of the southern textile industry; by the 1960s it was the world center. But the aging building was inadequate, and Textile Hall Corporation decided to replace it. In 1962 Old Textile Hall hosted its last trade show, and in 1964 the Piedmont Exposition Center opened. In 1992 the building, a victim of neglect, was condemned and demolished. JUDITH T. BAINBRIDGE

Gilkerson, Yancy S. "Textile Hall's First Sixty Years." *Proceedings and Papers of the Greenville County Historical Society* 5 (1971–1975): 79–83.

Huff, Archie Vernon, Jr. *Greenville: The History of the City and County in the South Carolina Piedmont.* Columbia: University of South Carolina Press, 1995.

Textile industry. From the late nineteenth century through most of the twentieth century, the textile industry dominated South Carolina manufacturing. It employed the majority of all manufacturing workers, and its company towns set the terms of life for thousands

The Saluda Factory near Columbia was one of the few textile mills in the state prior to the Civil War. Courtesy, South Carolina Historical Society

of white Carolinians. Upcountry cities such as Greenville, Spartanburg, and Rock Hill rose to prominence as textile manufacturing centers. The industry, however, has also been charged with poor treatment of workers, hostility to progressive social and economic change, and failure to prepare for the global economy of the twenty-first century. For better or worse, its impact on the state's history has been enormous.

Factory production of textiles in South Carolina commenced in fits and starts shortly after the Revolutionary War. After 1814 a handful of mainly northern-born manufacturers migrated into the state and set up spinning mills on the rapidly flowing watercourses of Spartanburg, Greenville, and Pendleton Districts, taking advantage of the natural monopolies afforded by the upcountry's inaccessibility to outside competitors. Their mills were typically tiny, employing on average one to two dozen workers, who were frequently the children and older daughters of local farmers. The coarse yarn they produced was sold from wagons or distributed to upcountry stores. The major market was farmers' wives and daughters, who would weave it into clothing.

Several more ambitious enterprises, frequently using slave labor, grew up around the fall zone. The state's most important antebellum cotton mill, the Graniteville Manufacturing Company, began operations in 1849 on Horse Creek in present-day Aiken County. Its developer, William Gregg, was one of the South's leading advocates of industrial development, and he organized Graniteville to put his ideas into effect. Gregg modeled his mill on the great integrated operations of Lowell, Massachusetts, engaging in bulk production for both local sale and export. He employed some four hundred workers, by design virtually all white, drawn mainly from the immediate vicinity and housed in an especially elaborate mill village. In many respects Graniteville set the pattern for what came later.

The antebellum textile industry was always small. In 1860 it employed fewer than one thousand workers (around forty percent of them at Graniteville alone), compared to nearly forty thousand in Massachusetts. While the war years saw little military destruction (just one mill was burned by Sherman's troops), the mills ran full-out to supply the Confederacy and entered the postwar era with worn-out equipment. But the industry quickly recovered, and its nucleus of "mill men" carried their experience forward into postbellum times, when a convergence of events revolutionized the industry.

During and after Reconstruction, the national economy opened up to the state's industrial producers. Large rail systems came into existence and dramatically reduced transportation costs. The shift from slavery to sharecropping, and a major movement by small white upcountry farmers into cotton growing, opened opportunities for an expanding group of interior merchants. Many of these clustered in the numerous towns growing up along the new rail lines, each of which boasted its own set of "boosters" casting about for means of putting their community on the map.

For many, the manufacture of cotton textiles seemed an ideal growth strategy. While small-town merchants and bankers lacked manufacturing experience, the antebellum industry had accumulated experience on which they could draw. Also, by the late nineteenth century the technology and business of the American cotton textile industry had matured. A network of commission merchants, mill architects, and machinery makers had arisen to serve the industry, all of whom were eager to develop new markets outside the industrialized Northeast. Textile technology was highly portable and designed to compensate for low levels of skill. Ring spinning frames could be worked by young girls standing on crates, and the automatic loom allowed for low-cost bulk production by inexperienced weavers.

With national markets open to them, and outside technology and expertise available to substitute for local inadequacies of skill and experience, South Carolina mill men could exploit their major advantage over their northeastern competitors: low labor costs. Set by the deepening poverty of the southern countryside, wage rates were as much as fifty percent lower than in New England, and until the early twentieth century the lack of labor laws allowed mills to run sixty-six or more hours a week. Manufacturers were also able to make extensive use of child labor, commonly hiring entire families. In 1900 the U.S. Census reported that thirty percent of South Carolina mill hands were between the ages of ten and sixteen.

After 1880 the South Carolina textile industry grew rapidly, as local boosters and outside investors built large, state-of-the-art plants. By 1900 South Carolina was second only to Massachusetts as a cotton-textile-producing state, and by 1930 the state passed the Bay State to rank second behind North Carolina. Clustered in the upper Piedmont in a belt centered on the rising industrial cities of Greenville and Spartanburg, textile mills attracted not only nearby rural white inhabitants but also migrants from Appalachia. By the 1920s the culture of mill village life had become central to some one-sixth of white South Carolinians (from the postbellum years to the 1960s, black Carolinians were largely barred from mill work). Companies controlled not only housing but frequently also retailing, schooling, religion, recreation (notably mill league baseball), and other aspects of community life.

In the 1920s and 1930s, however, the industry began to experience progressively greater increasing difficulties. While they vanquished their competitors in New England, southern mills increasingly found themselves competing among themselves in a stagnating textile market, which added to the pressure to find ways to cut costs. The Great Depression worsened the problems, as competition became cutthroat and efforts at cooperative action to stabilize prices and output, such as those undertaken under the National Recovery Administration of 1933–1935, came to naught.

Most manufacturers' costs were accounted for by raw materials and labor. With no real control over the former, they increasingly sought to get more out of the latter by intensifying the work pace. Workers responded to the hated "stretch-out" with unprecedented resistance. A period of intense, if sporadic, labor conflict began in 1929, peaking with the General Textile Strike of 1934—up to that point the largest strike in American labor history. Nonetheless, unions never made significant headway in the industry. The general lack of skill among workers and the decentralized, disintegrated structure of the industry left them at a chronic disadvantage against employers willing to go to sometimes enormous lengths to maintain their control. The failure of the Congress of Industrial Organizations' "Operation Dixie" in the late 1940s effectively ended the challenge from organized labor.

The industry revived with World War II and in the immediate postwar years prospered from pent-up consumer demand. The 1940s and 1950s saw the consolidation of many of the industry's numerous independent units into vertically integrated giants such as J. P. Stevens and Company, M. Lowenstein and Company, and Deering, Milliken and Company. A major homegrown firm, the Springs Cotton Mills of Fort Mill, established a national brand name in home furnishings, thanks in part to the racy advertising campaigns launched by its eccentric chief Elliott White Springs. While the industry consolidated, it also divorced itself from the worker communities it had called into being. A movement, begun in the 1930s, to sell the company-owned mill villages was largely carried through by the end of the 1950s. Workers could now own their own homes, but this increasingly scattered workers and broke the link between work and neighborhood.

Following the initial burst of postwar prosperity, the industry's troubles resumed. As early as the 1930s, southern manufacturers had suffered from Japanese competition. In a postwar world committed to freer trade, pressure from imports worsened. The 1960s saw a last burst of prosperity, tied in part to the rise of synthetic fibers, many of which were made in large, capital-intensive plants within the state. From the 1970s onward, however, South Carolina producers found developing countries increasingly beating them at their own low-cost game. Like Springs, some firms held their own with brand recognition, or like Milliken, they developed niche markets and new, sophisticated products. Many others, though, began to go under. Among the numerous smaller mill towns of the Piedmont, the closings frequently devastated communities and left workers lacking the skills with which to adapt to a changing economy. After 1997 the process of decline accelerated, and by 2001 the industry was approaching collapse, the century-old brick mills not only abandoned but increasingly dismantled. With the onset of the twenty-first century, the curtain had evidently rung down on the textile era of South Carolina history. DAVID L. CARLTON

Carlton, David L. *Mill and Town in South Carolina, 1880–1920.* Baton Rouge: Louisiana State University Press, 1982.

———. "The Revolution from Above: The National Market and the Beginnings of Industrialization in North Carolina." *Journal of American History* 77 (September 1990): 445–75.

Hall, Jacquelyn D., et al. *Like a Family: The Making of a Southern Cotton Mill World.* Chapel Hill: University of North Carolina Press, 1987.

Lander, Ernest McPherson, Jr. *The Textile Industry in Antebellum South Carolina.* Baton Rouge: Louisiana State University Press, 1969.

Leiter, Jeffrey, et al., eds. *Hanging by a Thread: Social Change in Southern Textiles.* Ithaca, N.Y.: ILR Press, 1991.

Simon, Bryant. *A Fabric of Defeat: The Politics of South Carolina Millhands, 1910–1948.* Chapel Hill: University of North Carolina Press, 1998.

Teter, Betsy Wakefield, ed. *Textile Town: Spartanburg County, South Carolina.* Spartanburg, S.C.: Hub City Writers Project, 2002.

Textile Workers Organizing Committee. The Textile Workers Organizing Committee (TWOC) was formed as part of the attempt by the Congress of Industrial Organizations (CIO) to use the provisions of the 1935 National Labor Relations Act to organize all the mass production industries in America. In the aftermath of the disastrous General Textile Strike of 1934, the United Textile Workers of America (UTWA) essentially collapsed, and in 1937 it reorganized as a subordinate branch of the CIO with Sidney Hillman of the Amalgamated Clothing Workers of America as chairman. By patiently building local union membership before holding a National Labor Relations Board (NLRB) election, the TWOC hoped to establish strong locals before any potential conflict with employers began and to avoid a repeat of the 1934 strike.

The TWOC organizing campaign officially began on March 19, 1937, but the recession of 1937–1938 and employer opposition limited the union's success. Among the few mills successfully organized was Pacific Mills in Columbia. After a period of infighting between the TWOC and some remnants of the UTWA, the TWOC reorganized as the Textile Workers Union of America (TWUA) in May 1939. World War II, and the protection offered workers and their unions by the National War Labor Board in order to keep production uninterrupted, allowed the TWOC to make substantial advances in organizing southern textile mills and increasing wages.

Immediately after the war, the CIO began an intense organizing drive throughout the South, called "Operation Dixie," so that the South's lower wages and pool of nonunion workers would not continue to weaken the labor movement at the national level. The first phase of Operation Dixie tried to organize the largest mills and chains of mills in the largest centers of textile production, including the Greenville and Spartanburg area. This phase began in July 1946 and was largely abandoned by November 1946. By the time a new round of organizing attempts began in 1947, the Tart-Hartley Act, which reduced government protection of organized labor, and anticommunist red-baiting had hindered the effectiveness of the NLRB in supporting fledgling unions. CIO organizers often saw improvement in labor relations as inextricable from social change in other areas, especially race relations and civil rights. Employers often used this commitment to civil rights against the TWOC, especially in campaigns in Fair Forest and Rock Hill. In some instances, the Ku Klux Klan also worked for textile manufacturers against union efforts. A strike at Gaffney Manufacturing Company from 1945 to 1947 demonstrated that determined employers could outlast the union, especially since an increasing number of mills were part of chains with considerable resources. The local at Gaffney simply ceased to exist after the strike, as did one in Rock Hill after a similar experience.

The last gasp of Operation Dixie was the 1951 general strike. Driven more by national concerns with increasing wages than by agitation from the South, the 1951 strike was nonetheless the second-largest strike the South had ever seen. The strike began on April 1, 1951, but it came to a quick end as employers argued that wages had already risen significantly since the war, and union solidarity fell apart at crucial locations. The TWOC never fully recovered from the failure of the 1951 strike, which greatly reduced its organizing activities. BRUCE E. BAKER

Kennedy, John W. "A History of the Textile Workers Union of America, C.I.O." Ph.D. diss., University of North Carolina, 1950.

Minchin, Timothy J. *What Do We Need a Union For? The TWUA in the South, 1945–1955.* Chapel Hill: University of North Carolina Press, 1997.

Waldrep, George Calvin. *Southern Workers and the Search for Community: Spartanburg County, South Carolina.* Urbana: University of Illinois Press, 2000.

Theological education. Theological education in South Carolina, as elsewhere, is typically conducted by theological schools or seminaries. They are graduate institutions requiring a bachelor's degree for admission and offer degrees at the master's and doctoral levels. Although some theological schools are integral parts of private universities, such as the divinity schools of Duke University and the University of Chicago, most are freestanding institutions founded by a particular church or group of churches. Their primary purpose is to educate persons to serve churches in ordained ministry or some other professional capacity. Seminaries, like law schools and medical schools, are educational institutions with a strong professional identity, providing constituencies with the educated leadership they need.

There have been numerous efforts at conducting theological education in South Carolina. The need for an educated ministry motivated the establishment of colleges, which were invariably church-related. Education for ministry was central to the early curriculum of Furman University, which served the Southern Baptist Convention until the 1859 founding of the Southern Baptist Theological Seminary in Greenville, a school that moved to Louisville, Kentucky, in 1877. Newberry College offered the theological program for Lutheran ministerial candidates in the 1880s and 1890s until the seminary moved to its own campus. Presbyterians opened a seminary in Columbia in 1830 that was housed in a residence designed by the architect Robert Mills until it relocated to the Atlanta suburb of Decatur in 1927.

South Carolina hosts four Protestant theological schools, representing different theological traditions: Reformed (Presbyterian), evangelical/fundamentalist, and Lutheran. These four are Lutheran Theological Southern Seminary in Columbia (Evangelical Lutheran Church in America), Erskine Theological Seminary in Due West (Associate Reformed Presbyterian), Greenville Theological Seminary (Presbyterian Church in America), and Columbia Biblical Seminary and School of Missions (unaffiliated). The primary accrediting agencies for such schools are the Southern Association of Colleges and Schools and the Association of Theological Schools in the United States and Canada. In addition to these four, more informal efforts at theological education, with varying concern for educational standards, have prepared those of European and African descent for ministerial careers. They include, for example, Bob Jones University and Holmes College of the Bible, both in Greenville.

With some individual variation, the faculties and curricula of theological seminaries reflect a common organizing principle. There are typically three academic areas of study: Bible, church history and theology, and ministry (formally called "practical theology"). The last addresses more intentionally the professional tasks of the pastor, including leadership roles in worship and education, preaching, and pastoral counseling. The latter half of the twentieth century witnessed renewed emphasis on such professional responsibilities in curricula; some seminaries required a year-long internship that placed the student under supervision in a congregational or institutional setting. Most seminaries require a summer of clinical pastoral education (CPE), usually conducted at a hospital and involving ministry to patients as well as intensive, small-group sessions. Optional off-campus activities introduce students to other facets of ministry or expose them to cross-cultural settings.

Methods used in studying the Bible constitute a continuing fault line in theological education. The hermeneutical or interpretive task in explicating documents dating to ancient times and reflecting culture different from our own represents a major challenge. Seminaries of mainline or "oldline" denominations (e.g., Episcopal, Presbyterian, Lutheran, Methodist) inform study of scripture with historical and literary scholarship. Seminaries oriented to a fundamentalist or conservative evangelical perspective tend to resist the application of these methods. Literal interpretations of the biblical narrative and suspicion of those unable to accept everything in the Bible "as it stands" characterize their approach. A theory of verbal inerrancy undergirds this stance as a way to guarantee the truth of the biblical record. These two understandings of scripture involve basic assumptions so antithetical to each other that scholars on opposing sides find it virtually impossible to conduct meaningful biblical and theological dialogue.

Although the four seminaries in the state do not have significant cooperative programs, arrangements between Lutheran and Erskine and between Columbia and Erskine facilitate transfer of credits for students taking courses at both schools. Lutheran and Erskine are also members of the Atlanta Theological Association, linking their programs to Candler School of Theology at Emory University, Columbia Seminary in Decatur, and the African American seminaries constituting the Interdenominational Theological Center in Atlanta.

The two largest Protestant denominations in South Carolina, the Southern Baptist Convention and the United Methodist Church, do not maintain seminaries in the state. The Methodists, however, have certified both the Lutheran seminary and the Associate Reformed Presbyterian seminary as institutions where their pastoral candidates may receive training. PAUL JERSILD

Theus, Jeremiah (1716–1774). Portrait painter. Born on April 5, 1716, in Chur, Switzerland, Theus immigrated to Orangeburg Township, Carolina, in 1735 with other Protestants seeking refuge from persecution. He moved to Charleston in 1740 and advertised his services in the local press as a limner (portraitist), as well as a painter of signs, crests, and coats of arms. The nature of his training, if any, is unknown. Eager to please, he advertised his willingness to travel to area plantations. Despite his lack of training, he modeled his likenesses after fashionable English portraits of the day. Like his better-known Boston counterpart, John Singleton Copley, Theus studied mezzotints derived from portraits of the English gentry. After his death, his will revealed that he owned a selection of such prints.

The large majority of Theus's portraits are half-lengths, with sitters standing erect and shown without their hands. While the men wear sober street clothes and hold their hands in their waistcoats, women are dressed in great finery consisting of lace, fabric, pearls, and even ermine. His most ambitious portraits are the three-quarter-length portrayals of Colonel and Mrs. Barnard Elliott (Gibbes Museum of Art in Charleston) and Mrs. Peter Manigault (Charleston Museum). For the high-style dresses of many female sitters Theus copied outfits worn in contemporary English portraits. For example, Mrs. Elliott is modeled after a portrait of Lady Ann Fortescu by Francis Cotes and engraved by Thomas Watson. The portraits of Mrs. Thomas Lynch (Reynolda House, Winston-Salem, North Carolina), Mrs. Charles Lowndes (Gibbes Museum of Art), and Susannah Holmes (Charleston Museum) all derive from the same mezzotint of the Duchess of Hamilton's portrait by Francis Cotes.

It seems that both Theus and his clientele aspired to be as fashionable as their London counterparts. Over a career that exceeded three decades, Theus created a veritable social register of Charleston's merchants, plantation owners, and their wives and children. Among his sitters were members of the Elliott, Grimball, Heyward, Izard, Manigault, Mazyck, and Ravenel families. While the frames for most of Theus's paintings are simple moldings painted black, many portraits retain original frames designed by the Charleston furniture maker Thomas Elfe. Portraits by Theus can be found in the collections sited above and in the Columbia Museum of Art; the Telfair Museum of Art in Savannah, Georgia; the Greenville County Museum of Art; the Museum of Early Southern Decorative Arts in Winston-Salem, North Carolina; the Brooklyn Museum of Art; the Boston Museum of Fine Arts; and the Metropolitan Museum of Art in New York City. Theus died on May 17, 1774, in Charleston. See plate 3. MARTHA R. SEVERENS

Middleton, Margaret Simons. *Jeremiah Theus: Colonial Artist of Charles Town.* Columbia: University of South Carolina Press, 1953.

Severens, Martha R. "Jeremiah Theus of Charleston: Plagiarist or Pundit?" *Southern Quarterly* 24 (fall–winter 1985): 56–70.

Thompson, Hugh Smith (1836–1904). Educator, governor. Father of South Carolina's modern public school system and the only professional educator to serve as governor, Thompson was born in Charleston on January 24, 1836, the son of Henry Tazewell Thompson and Agnes Smith. Reared on his father's farm in Greenville District, Thompson entered the Citadel in 1852, graduating in 1856. On January 1, 1858, he was elected second lieutenant and assistant professor of mathematics and French at the Arsenal Academy in Columbia. In October 1861 he was transferred to the Citadel as captain-professor of French and belles lettres. Thompson married Elizabeth Anderson Clarkson on April 6, 1858. The couple had nine children.

During the Civil War, Thompson continued to teach and served as captain of a battalion of state cadets, which saw service defending Charleston harbor and other areas of the state. Returning to Columbia after the war, Thompson served as principal of the Columbia Male Academy from 1865 until 1880. During his tenure, he forged the institution into one of the state's premier preparatory schools, and it became universally known as "Thompson's school."

First elected state superintendent of education in 1876, and reelected in 1878 and 1880, Thompson laid the foundations for the development of the state's public school system. As superintendent, he helped win passage of the 1878 school law that centralized management of the school system in a state board of commissioners. He worked to equalize expenditures for white and black schools, established summer teachers' institutes in 1880, and was responsible for the creation of the State Teachers' Association in 1881. His greatest achievement was in winning support for public education in general and for blacks in particular against a tradition of public hostility, apathy, and prejudice.

Thompson agreed to accept the presidency of South Carolina College in 1882 but reversed his decision (an action he regretted for the rest of his life) when he was nominated by a deadlocked Democratic convention as a compromise candidate for governor. Inaugurated on December 5, 1882, Thompson continued his advocacy of educational improvement, supported civil service and tax reform, and called for rigid economy in government. Reelected without opposition in 1884, he was appointed assistant secretary of the U.S. Treasury by President Grover Cleveland on June 28, 1886, and resigned the governorship on July 10. Lieutenant Governor John C. Sheppard completed the remainder of Thompson's term. Frequently in charge of the Treasury Department, Thompson's timely actions were credited with averting a financial crisis on more than one occasion. On May 7, 1889, President Benjamin Harrison nominated him as a member of the U.S. Civil service Commission, on which he served with Theodore Roosevelt. He resigned in April 1892 to become comptroller of the New York Life Insurance Company, a position he held until his death.

Affectionately known as "the Captain" by his students, Thompson was described as "a man of charming personality, distinguished address and eloquent speech." He died at his residence in New York City on November 20, 1904, the last surviving member of Wade Hampton's original 1876 cabinet, and was buried in Columbia's Trinity Episcopal Churchyard. Theodore Roosevelt said of Thompson: "I never met a braver, gentler or more upright man." PAUL R. BEGLEY

Hennig, Helen Kohn. *Great South Carolinians of a Later Date.* Chapel Hill: University of North Carolina Press, 1949.

Thompson, Henry T. *The Establishment of the Public School System of South Carolina.* Columbia, S.C.: R. L. Bryan, 1927.

Thompson, Waddy, Jr. (1798–1868). Congressman, diplomat. Thompson was born in Pickensville on January 8, 1798, the son of Waddy Thompson, Sr., and Eliza Blackburn. When he was an infant his family moved to Greenville. He entered the sophomore class of South Carolina College in 1811, graduating in 1814. Admitted to the bar in 1819, Thompson established a lucrative legal practice in Greenville and engaged in planting. In 1819 Thompson married Emmala Elizabeth Butler, who died in 1848. In 1851 he wed Cornelia Jones. Thompson had two children by his first wife and one by his second.

Thompson represented Greenville District in the South Carolina House of Representatives from 1826 to 1829. A supporter of John C. Calhoun, he opposed the protective tariffs of 1824 and 1828 and was a proponent of the principle of nullification. As a nullifier in a Unionist district, Thompson did not seek reelection in 1830. The General Assembly elected Thompson solicitor of the western circuit in 1830 and brigadier general of the first brigade of militia in 1832. With nullification sentiment ascendant in the state, Thompson was elected as an anti-Jacksonian to the Twenty-fourth Congress in September 1835. Twice reelected, Thompson served in Congress until March 1841. He was instrumental in obtaining congressional recognition of Texas independence in 1837 and was an advocate of Texas statehood. Also in 1837, Thompson broke with Calhoun over his return to the Democratic Party and support of the subtreasury plan.

President John Tyler rewarded Thompson's loyalty to the Whig Party by appointing him as minister to Mexico, where he served from 1842 to 1844. To facilitate his mission, Thompson learned Spanish, and although he recalled being initially "regarded with distrust and dislike" by Mexicans for his support of Texas, his ministry was a signal success. He established a rapport with Mexican president Santa Anna, negotiated the release of 300 Texan prisoners and saved 159 from execution, persuaded Mexico to permit American immigration to California, concluded some commercial agreements, and seriously attempted to negotiate the peaceful cession of California to the United States.

After returning to Greenville, Thompson retired from public life. In 1846 *Recollections of Mexico,* Thompson's valuable memoir of his ministry, was published. He opposed the Mexican War, which he judged "not only inexpedient, but unjust." Conflicted about secession, he opposed unilateral action by South Carolina in 1850, and in 1852 he cofounded the *Southern Patriot,* a Unionist newspaper in Greenville. Thompson's friend Benjamin F. Perry described him as "a man of rare talents, tact and energy of character." In later years Thompson became a devotee of spiritualism and a participant in séances. In early 1867, with his Greenville property ruined as a result of the Civil War, Thompson moved to Madison, Florida, where he owned a cotton plantation, and served briefly in 1868 as a circuit solicitor general. Thompson died on November 23, 1868, while visiting Tallahassee, and was buried there in the churchyard of St. John's Episcopal. PAUL R. BEGLEY

Lander, Ernest M., Jr. "General Waddy Thompson, a Friend of Mexico during the Mexican War." *South Carolina Historical Magazine* 78 (January 1977): 32–42.

Thompson, Henry T. *Waddy Thompson, Jr.: Member of Congress, 1835–41: Minister to Mexico, 1842–44.* N.p., 1929.

Thornwell, James Henley (1812–1862). Theologian, college president. Thornwell was born on December 9, 1812, in Marlboro District, the son of James Thornwell, a plantation overseer, and Martha Terrell. When his father died in 1820, the family was left in distress, but two neighbors assumed financial responsibility for his education. After studying at Cheraw Academy, in 1830 he entered the junior class of South Carolina College, where he was influenced by the philosophical school of Scottish commonsense realism. After graduating at the top of his class in 1831, Thornwell taught school and immersed himself in the Westminster Confession of Faith, which he found congenial to his logical mind. He wrote in his journal, "My understanding assents [to the doctrines of Christianity], but my feelings are dead. My religion seems to be all in the head. Would to God it were otherwise." A conversion experience finally stirred his feelings, and he determined to become a minister.

In 1834 Thornwell enrolled in Andover Theological Seminary in Massachusetts, but New England weather, manners, and theology did not appeal to him. He tried Harvard Divinity School but found Boston Unitarians even less to his liking, and he was soon back in South Carolina. Ordained in 1835, he became pastor of the Presbyterian Church in Lancaster. On December 3, 1835, he married Nancy Witherspoon, whose father had served as lieutenant governor of the state. The marriage produced nine children.

Thornwell was elected professor of belle lettres and logic at the South Carolina College in 1837. He acquired a reputation as a brilliant young professor, and his fame soon spread. He served briefly as pastor of the Presbyterian Church in Columbia but returned to the college as professor of sacred literature and evidences of Christianity. He accepted a call to a Presbyterian church in Charleston in 1851 but was called the next year to the college, this time as president. In 1855 he became professor of theology at Columbia Theological Seminary, a position he held until his death.

A popular professor, Thornwell could control the often-rowdy students at the college as no one else of his generation could. He was also an influential advocate for a public school system in the state. Thornwell was at the center of a circle of Presbyterian intellectuals in Columbia that included Benjamin Morgan Palmer, George Howe, Joseph LeConte, and Louisa Cheves McCord. He advocated a middle way between extremes in matters social, political, and theological. In a sermon opening a church for blacks in Charleston, he championed what he called "regulated liberty" for slaves.

Thornwell was a Unionist until 1860, but when secession came, he became an ardent supporter of the southern cause. His theological and political thought provided a powerful ideological prop for the Confederacy. In 1861 he wrote a theological justification for slavery unsurpassed in its startling brilliance. He believed that industrial capitalism was moving toward social anarchy. He died on August 1, 1862, in Charlotte, North Carolina, of tuberculosis and was buried in Columbia's Elmwood Cemetery. His understanding of the church's relationship to social issues dominated Presbyterian thought in the South until the 1930s. ERSKINE CLARKE

Clarke, Erskine. *Our Southern Zion: A History of Calvinism in the South Carolina Low Country, 1690–1990.* Tuscaloosa: University of Alabama Press, 1996.

Farmer, James O. *The Metaphysical Confederacy: James Henley Thornwell and the Synthesis of Southern Values.* Macon, Ga.: Mercer University Press, 1986.

Palmer, Benjamin Morgan. *The Life and Letters of James Henley Thornwell.* Richmond, Va.: Whittet & Shepperson, 1875.

Thurmond, James Strom (1902–2003). U.S. senator, governor. Thurmond was born in Edgefield on December 5, 1902, to John William Thurmond and Eleanor Gertrude Strom. His father was a community leader of some repute and notoriety (he killed a man in a fight in 1897, claiming self-defense). James Strom was the second of six children. His parents immediately dropped "James," and from then on he was known as "Strom."

Senator Strom Thurmond (1964). Courtesy, Strom Thurmond Collection, Special Collections, Clemson University Libraries

Thurmond got an early taste for politics. The family home was a gathering place for the political elite, and Thurmond listened attentively to the lively discussions over Sunday dinner. When he was nine, he watched a gubernatorial debate. Entranced with the energy of the moment, he resolved that one day he would be governor. Thurmond earned a bachelor of science degree from Clemson College in 1923. His first job was teaching at the white school in McCormick. In 1928 he won his first political office as superintendent of the Edgefield County schools. Shortly after he started his work, he began studying law with his father. He passed the state bar in December 1930. Early the next year, he was appointed Edgefield's town attorney and combined those duties with private law practice.

Thurmond won a seat in the state Senate in 1932, where he served until 1938. In his first term, he championed legislation to improve the public schools, which earned him a commendation from state teachers. His continuing efforts on behalf of education won him a seat on the Winthrop College Board of Trustees. Years later the college named a building after him.

In 1937 Thurmond ran for an open judicial seat against the better-known George B. Timmerman. The state legislature elected judges, and Thurmond brazenly asked House speaker Sol Blatt and Senator Edgar Brown, both pledged to Timmerman, to stay neutral. When the lawmakers met on January 13, 1938, Thurmond had corralled so many votes that Timmerman withdrew his name. The *Anderson Independent* called Thurmond's victory "a political upset of major proportions, which stunned even those who usually feel that they know what is going to happen."

Thurmond was reelected to a full judicial term in 1940 without challenge. He volunteered for the army in World War II, although he was old enough to avoid service. As a member of the 82d Airborne Division, he was wounded during the D-day landing in France when his glider crashed behind German lines. In the meantime at home, Thurmond had been reelected without opposition, and after he left the army he resumed his judicial duties.

Seven months after returning, on May 15, 1946, Thurmond resigned from the bench to run for governor. Thurmond campaigned unapologetically against the "Barnwell Ring," the powerful group of legislators headed by Blatt and Brown, and promised to bring a new spirit to South Carolina governance. Thurmond ran first in the August primary and easily defeated James McLeod in the September runoff.

Inaugurated on January 21, 1947, Thurmond introduced a progressive agenda championing more money for education, including the impoverished black schools, and encouraging women to serve in government. He garnered positive national attention for dispatching a government prosecutor to Greenville to try the brutal Willie Earle lynching case. On November 7, 1947, he took time out to marry Jean Crouch, one of his secretaries and twenty-three years his junior. He infamously posed for *Life* magazine standing on his head in front of Jean with the caption "VIRILE GOVERNOR." Jean Thurmond died in 1960 of a brain tumor. They had no children.

The most significant moment of Thurmond's governorship occurred outside of South Carolina and was directly related to the growing national ferment over race. Up to this moment Thurmond had stayed clear of any direct racial disputes, but now he was drawn into the debate between southern Democrats and the national party over civil rights. Though relatively inexperienced and less well known than long-serving southern senators, Thurmond emerged as a leader in the states' rights movement. A central tenet was the belief that the states had complete freedom to regulate social affairs within their borders—"custom and tradition" in Thurmond's benign euphemism for segregation.

While delegates from Mississippi and Alabama bolted the July 1948 Democratic convention in Philadelphia, Thurmond held the South Carolina delegates in check. A few days later he went to the states' rights gathering in Birmingham. Responding to urgent entreaties, he agreed to carry the group's banner in the presidential election. In a racially charged speech accepting the nomination as the States' Rights Democratic Party candidate, Thurmond said, "I want to tell you that there's not enough troops in the army to force the southern people to break down segregation and admit the Negro race into our theaters, into our swimming pools, into our homes, and into our churches." Thurmond and his running mate, Mississippi governor Fielding Wright (dubbed the "Dixiecrats"), carried only Alabama, Louisiana, Mississippi, and South Carolina.

In 1950 Thurmond challenged incumbent U.S. senator Olin D. Johnson but was defeated in the Democratic primary. It was the only election Thurmond ever lost. He returned to his law practice after his gubernatorial term, but politics beckoned again in 1954. After the unexpected death of U.S. Senator Burnet Maybank barely two months before the next election, Democratic Party leaders selected Edgar Brown to be his replacement over objections from those who favored a more open process. Thurmond was cajoled into running as a write-in candidate and prevailed over Brown in the November election with a stunning 63.1 percent of the votes. Despite the events of 1948, Thurmond promised that he would participate in the Senate's Democratic caucus. He had also promised to resign and run for a full term in 1956.

Though friends urged Thurmond to ignore his resignation promise, he refused. He came back to South Carolina and coasted to reelection in 1956 when no one filed to run against him. In the meantime Thurmond burnished his segregationist credentials. He was the major force behind the "Southern Manifesto" in 1956, a broadside that counseled resistance to the Supreme Court's *Brown v. Board of Education* decision that mandated the desegregation of public schools. The next year Thurmond set the record for a filibuster (twenty-four hours, eighteen minutes) when he spoke against a civil rights bill that eventually passed. The election of John F. Kennedy in 1960 and Kennedy's subsequent moves on civil rights created renewed disaffection. When Lyndon Johnson assumed the White House after Kennedy's assassination and pressed civil rights legislation with even more vigor, Thurmond, though not the architect of the southern resistance, was a vocal and consistent opponent of every new bill.

Unhappy with the Democrats' political drift and acting against the advice of friends and associates, Thurmond switched parties when Arizona Republican Barry Goldwater secured the 1964 GOP nomination for president. Thurmond claimed, "The Democratic Party has abandoned the people." Though he would not be the most important southern Republican in the decades to come, he was at the forefront of the region's political realignment, and in 1968 he was an important part of Richard Nixon's vaunted "southern strategy." The emerging political realignment in the South was fueled in large part by the transformation of the electorate from all-white to white and black. The critical element was the 1965 Voting Rights Act, which Thurmond, like every other Deep South senator, opposed.

But time would demonstrate Thurmond's ability to adjust to new realities. He was first to hire a black man, Thomas Moss, to his Senate staff. Thurmond also began to court the growing number of black politicians in the state and paid more attention to black communities seeking federal help. In a changed electorate, he should have been a prime target for defeat, but even as a Republican he won easy reelection in 1966, 1972, and 1978. On December 22, 1968, Thurmond married Nancy Moore, a former Miss South Carolina forty-four years his junior. They had four children by 1977, and the family proved to be an asset in his successful race in 1978 against an accomplished and much younger opponent, Charles "Pug" Ravenel.

The election of Ronald Reagan in 1980 and the return of the Senate to Republican control gave Thurmond his first committee chairmanship, of the Judiciary Committee, and at a dramatic moment. The man with a reputation as the standard-bearer for segregation now headed the committee that handled the renewal of the all-important Voting Rights Act. Thurmond chose not to play obstructionist politics and ended up supporting the renewal bill. The next year he backed a federal holiday honoring Martin Luther King, Jr.

Democrats regained control of the Senate from 1987 to 1994. When Republicans took over again after the 1994 election, Thurmond became chairman of the Armed services Committee and president pro tempore of the Senate. But at age ninety-two, he was a figurehead; the day-to-day work was done by others. Reelected to a seventh term in 1996, he relinquished the chairmanship at the end of 1998, a concession to his advancing age and infirmities. Thurmond focused on his ceremonial role as Senate president, but his frail condition required him to give up those duties early in 2001.

Nevertheless, he remained in office: the oldest senator ever and the longest-serving. He completed his final Senate term and then retired to a special suite in the Edgefield County Hospital. He died in Edgefield on June 26, 2003, and was buried in Willowbrook Cemetery.

Six months after Thurmond died, Essie Mae Washington-Williams, a seventy-eight-year-old woman who lived in Los Angeles, came forward to say that she was the child of Thurmond and Carrie Butler, who in 1925 had been a sixteen-year-old black maid working for the Thurmonds in Edgefield. Thurmond had long been rumored to have fathered a black child, but he always denied it, as did Williams, saying for years that she was simply a family friend. When she came forward in December 2003, Williams said that Thurmond had maintained a private relationship with her, helping financially over the years. Thurmond's son, J. Strom Jr., said that the family would not contest Williams's claim. NADINE COHODAS

Banks, James G. "Strom Thurmond and the Revolt against Modernity." Ph.D. diss., Kent State University, 1970.

Bass, Jack, and Marilyn W. Thompson. *Ol' Strom: An Unauthorized Biography of Strom Thurmond.* Atlanta: Longstreet, 1998.

Cohodas, Nadine. *Strom Thurmond and the Politics of Southern Change.* New York: Simon and Schuster, 1993.

Lachicotte, Alberta. *Rebel Senator: Strom Thurmond of South Carolina.* New York: Devon-Adair, 1966.

"Strom Thurmond, S.C. Legend, Dies." Columbia *State,* June 27, 2003, pp. A1, A4.

Thompson, Marilyn W. "What a Family Secret Begat: Essie, Strom, and Me." *Washington Post,* December 21, 2003, p. D1.

Thurmond, Strom. Papers. Clemson University Library Special Collections, Clemson.

Tillman, Benjamin Ryan (1847–1918). U.S. senator, governor. Tillman was born in Edgefield District on August 11, 1847, to Benjamin and Sophia Tillman. The family was wealthy in land and slaves, and Ben Tillman was educated in local schoolhouses and on the family's acres. A serious illness at the age of sixteen cost him his left eye, and his convalescence kept him out of Confederate service. In 1868 he married Sallie Starke. They had seven children.

Benjamin Ryan Tillman. Courtesy, South Caroliniana Library, University of South Carolina

In the mid-1870s Tillman joined the Sweetwater Sabre Club and became part of the paramilitary rifle-club movement, through which white landowners challenged the Republican state government. He took part in the Hamburg Massacre (July 1876), in which rifle-club members (known thereafter as "Red Shirts") besieged a black militia unit and murdered several captives. Tillman later explained that "the leading white men of Edgefield" had determined "to seize the first opportunity that the negroes might offer them to provoke a riot and teach the negroes a lesson." The massacre fractured compromise arrangements between state Democrats and Republicans and helped create the electoral crisis of 1876–1877.

Over the next few years, the failure of Democratic leaders to address the impoverishment of most white households inspired challenges from Martin Gary, who portrayed the Red Shirts as the latest upcountrymen to be treated unfairly by lowcountry leaders, and from the interracial Greenback-Republican alliance, comprised of whites discontented with elite control of the Democratic Party and black Republicans. In 1882 this alliance posed a serious enough challenge that the Democrats responded with paramilitary force. Tillman, an active member of the Red Shirt "Edgefield Hussars," learned two lessons from these campaigns: that the Democratic Party, having failed to meet the needs of most white men, remained vulnerable to interracial political alliances; and that the tradition of conflict between upcountry and lowcountry offered Tillman a platform for uniting a majority of white South Carolinians against both conservative Democratic leadership and African Americans voters.

During the mid-1880s Tillman presented himself as the champion of "the farmers" against lawyers, politicians, merchants, "aristocrats," and "Bourbons," whom he blamed for the hardship common to white agricultural households. Through the meetings of his Farmers' Association, he called for reform in education, agriculture, taxation, and legislative apportionment. The centerpiece of his agenda became the establishment of a "farmers college," and in 1886 he and other proponents of practical agricultural education met with Thomas Green Clemson, heir to John C. Calhoun's estate, and encouraged Clemson to use his will to help further this project.

Though Tillman was the leader of the "Farmers" movement (also known as the "Reform" or "Tillman" movement), he was most effective as a gadfly. In newspapers and on the stump, Tillman denounced the state's leadership as a "ring" of "broken-down politicians and old superannuated Bourbon aristocrats, who are thoroughly incompetent, who worship the past, and are incapable of progress of any sort, but who boldly assume to govern us by divine right." Their educational institutions demonstrated their uselessness: South Carolina College produced "helpless beings," while the Citadel was "a military dude factory." Further, he charged elected officials with malfeasance and corruption, often insinuating that particular men were to blame but then denying having done so.

Tillman's efforts soon bore political fruit. In 1888 Clemson's bequest came before the legislature just as the Farmers Alliance, a protest vehicle for hard-pressed farmers, arrived in South Carolina. Tillman presented himself as the champion of both the college and the alliance, and in 1890, despite significant opposition and a bitter convention fight, he won the Democratic nomination for governor. He then faced a challenge from disgruntled conservative Alexander C. Haskell, who appealed for black electoral support. This betrayal of white supremacy made Haskell unappealing even to those who opposed Tillman's policies and methods. Tillman was also able to use racial fears to defeat radical alliance members who supported the People's Party, better known as the Populists. He argued that Populists' insistence on federal intervention in the economy, coupled with their support for black voting rights, threatened a return to the political, economic, and racial evils of Reconstruction. By 1892, when he ran for reelection, Tillman offered himself to white farmers as a sensible alternative to President Grover Cleveland's economic conservatism on one side and the Populists' radicalism on the other.

As governor, Tillman made reforms that were more symbolic than substantive. He oversaw the establishment of Clemson College for white men and Winthrop College for white women, but he remained less committed to the practice of higher education than to the principle of white supremacy. In 1891 he refused federal aid for Clemson if that would require him to accept a proportionate amount of aid for black higher education at Claflin. He took popular but economically inconsequential stands against railroads and the state-chartered phosphate monopoly. He established a state liquor monopoly, the "Dispensary," which provided him with unprecedented patronage power. Conflicts over the law and its enforcement by state-appointed constables led to a showdown and political crisis in the town of Darlington in 1893, the "Darlington Riot."

Tillman's most important contribution to South Carolina's political life came with the Constitutional Convention of 1895. Tillman argued that only a revision of the laws regarding electoral qualification could safeguard the state from a potential black Republican resurgence. His promise that no white man would lose his vote was greeted with skepticism. The 1894 referendum on whether to call a convention was fiercely contested, as Sampson Pope, formerly a Tillmanite, left the Democratic Party to run an independent campaign for governor and against the convention referendum. While Pope earned only about thirty percent of the vote, the convention referendum was much closer and proconvention forces won their narrow victory amid accusations of electoral fraud.

Tillman helped draft a constitution under which men had to own substantial taxable property, prove their literacy, or demonstrate "understanding" of the constitution in order to register to vote. The "understanding" clause was adopted in order to allow white Democratic officials to discriminate on racial and partisan grounds. Like most of his colleagues, Tillman also rejected arguments made by some white female suffragists that granting voting rights to women could establish a less obviously fraudulent electoral bulwark for white supremacy. Politics, Tillman believed, ought to remain the province of white men.

In 1895 Tillman entered the U.S. Senate, where he achieved notoriety for his rhetorical attacks on racial equality, corporate power, and imperial expansion. Tillman's lifelong hostility to black freedom gained particular infamy. Though Tillman frequently condemned lynching as an assault on the authority of the state, he made one great exception in 1892, when he publicly pledged that in cases in which a black man was accused of raping a white woman, he would lead the lynch mob. Tillman never actually put his pledge into practice, but he did on occasion collude with lynch mobs. In one 1893 case, Tillman sent a black rape suspect, protected by only a single guard, to face a crowd of many hundreds. The man was lynched. Tillman argued that white male violence toward accused black rapists was a product of their instinct for "race preservation," a force so powerful that it could cause "the very highest and best men we have [to] lose all semblance of Christian human beings."

Tillman made his "race problem" speech before hundreds of audiences nationwide. He also spoke against "trusts and monopolies" and U.S. imperialism. In his maiden Senate speech, "Bimetallism or Industrial Slavery," and countless sequels he suggested that the "money power" was hard at work against the interests of farmers and workers. In his view, Republicans conspired with corporations to raise prices on imported goods, lower the wages of industrial workers, and subordinate the southern economy. Imperial expansion would benefit corporations while undermining democracy, either through the corruptions of empire or by incorporating millions of nonwhites into a nation where white supremacy had been under siege since 1865.

Nationally most journalists and public officials initially perceived Tillman as a "wild man." This impression drew credibility from many sources: Tillman's frequent boast that in 1876 "we shot negroes and stuffed ballot boxes"; his threat to stick a pitchfork into Grover Cleveland; his part in the successful defense of his nephew James Tillman, who murdered the journalist Narciso Gonzales; and his 1902 fistfight on the Senate floor with fellow South Carolina senator John McLaurin. But in 1906 Tillman's reputation began to soften. In an attempt to derail a railroad rate bill, congressional Republicans put it in Tillman's hands and assumed that the erratic senator would be unable to accomplish anything. However, despite the final bill's shortcomings, Tillman emerged from the fight with a reputation as an effective reformer. During his last decade, the formerly ardent foe of federal power and champion of "the farmers" helped steer millions of federal military dollars to South Carolina. He also denounced the language and character of his former ally Coleman L. Blease, whose popularity caused Tillman—later lauded as "the friend and leader of the common people"—to question the capacity of men, even white men, for self-government.

In 1908 Tillman endured the first of several debilitating strokes. Shortly before his seventy-first birthday, he suffered a cerebral hemorrhage. Tillman died in Washington, D.C., on July 3, 1918, and was buried in Ebenezer Cemetery in Trenton, South Carolina. STEPHEN KANTROWITZ

Kantrowitz, Stephen. *Ben Tillman and the Reconstruction of White Supremacy.* Chapel Hill: University of North Carolina Press, 2000.

Simkins, Francis Butler. *Pitchfork Ben Tillman: South Carolinian.* Baton Rouge: Louisiana State University Press, 1944.

Tillman, Benjamin Ryan. Governor's Papers. South Carolina Department of Archives and History, Columbia.

———. Papers. Clemson University Library Special Collections, Clemson.

———. *The Struggles of 1876—How South Carolina Was Delivered from Carpet-Bag and Negro Rule.* N.p., 1909.

Tillman, James Hammond (1868–1911). Lieutenant governor. Born on June 27, 1868, in Clarks Hill (now McCormick County), Tillman was the son of George D. Tillman and Margaret Jones. After his education at Georgetown University, Tillman read law in Winnsboro and was admitted to the bar in 1891. Instead of the law, however, Tillman pursued journalism and began writing for the Winnsboro *News and Herald.* Writing under the name "Fair Play," Tillman countered the attacks of Narciso G. Gonzales, editor of the *State* newspaper in Columbia and one of the state's most ardent critics of Tillman's uncle, U.S. Senator Benjamin "Pitchfork Ben" Tillman. From 1893 to 1894 Tillman also served as a correspondent for the *Atlanta Constitution* and the *Columbia Journal.* He married Mamie Norris on June 25, 1896. They had one daughter.

Arrogant, bombastic, and a notorious drinker and gambler, Tillman nevertheless rose to political prominence during the 1890s. He was active in the state militia and commanded one of South Carolina's regiments that served in the Spanish-American War in 1898. That same year Edgefield County elected Tillman as a delegate to the South Carolina Democratic convention. Appealing to racial prejudices and capitalizing on his family name, Tillman was elected lieutenant governor in 1900. Soon afterward, however, he would again cross swords with Gonzales.

In 1902 Tillman ran for governor of South Carolina, a campaign that Gonzales and the *State* opposed with a series of scathing newspaper reports denouncing the candidate. The *State* referred to Tillman as "a proven liar, defaulter, gambler and drunkard." Gonzales

The members of the Lexington County jury that acquitted the lieutenant governor of the murder of N. G. Gonzales. Courtesy, South Caroliniana Library, University of South Carolina

accused Tillman (with just cause) of falsifying Senate records, disgraceful military conduct, and fiscal improprieties. When Tillman refused to invite President Theodore Roosevelt to visit South Carolina because Roosevelt had refused to invite his uncle to a state dinner, Gonzales castigated the lieutenant governor's "boorishness." Disgraced before the public, Tillman was defeated in his campaign for governor, a defeat he blamed on "the brutal, false and malicious newspaper attacks headed by N. G. Gonzales."

The Tillman-Gonzales feud ended on January 15, 1903. As the two men passed each other on the sidewalk at the corner of Main and Gervais Streets in Columbia, Tillman pulled out a pistol and shot the unarmed Gonzales once through the abdomen. The editor staggered back to his office and then was taken to Columbia Hospital, where he died on January 19. Tillman was arrested and charged with murder. His defense team succeeded in having his trial moved from Columbia (where the martyred editor was revered) to Lexington County (a center of pro-Tillman support). The trial opened on September 28, 1903. Tillman's lawyers argued that their client was not guilty on grounds of self-defense, claiming that Gonzales, whose hands were in his pockets at the time of the attack, had moved them in a menacing way before Tillman shot him. The defense also introduced editorials from the *State* as evidence that such inflammatory attacks justified Tillman's actions. Such arguments found favor with the pro-Tillman jury. On October 15, 1903, it brought in a verdict of not guilty, ruling that the shooting was self-defense. The state and national press condemned Tillman and the "farce" of his trial.

Tillman retired from public life disgraced and in poor health. He died in Asheville, North Carolina, on April 1, 1911, and was buried in Edgefield. ALEXIA JONES HELSLEY

Bailey, N. Louise, Mary L. Morgan, and Carolyn R. Taylor, eds. *Biographical Directory of the South Carolina Senate, 1776–1985.* 3 vols. Columbia: University of South Carolina Press, 1986.

Jones, Lewis P. *Stormy Petrel: N. G. Gonzales and His State.* Columbia: University of South Carolina Press, 1973.

Sewell, Michael. "The Gonzales-Tillman Affair: The Public Conflict of a Politician and a Crusading newspaper Editor." Master's thesis, University of South Carolina, 1967.

Tillman Hall (Clemson). Other than the famous Tiger Paw, Tillman Hall is the most recognizable symbol associated with Clemson University. Its brick clock tower rises above the tree line, making it the most prominent of the original campus buildings. Originally known as the Main Building, this three-story brick structure was intended to be the centerpiece of the college located at the top of a hill near the home of John C. Calhoun, whose plantation was given to the state by his son-in-law, Thomas G. Clemson. The building was designed by the architects Alexander C. Bruce and Thomas H. Morgan of Atlanta, and construction began in late 1890 and was complete when the school opened in 1893. On May 22, 1894, a fire in a third-floor laboratory spread to the rest of the building, destroying everything but its brick walls. Bruce and Morgan returned to oversee the reconstruction, which began immediately and was completed in 1895. Connected to the Main Building was Memorial Hall, an all-purpose assembly space that served as chapel, meeting hall, and entertainment venue. It was also the setting for early graduation exercises. The building officially became known as Tillman Hall on the fiftieth anniversary of Clemson's first graduating class in 1946, when it was renamed in memory of Benjamin Ryan Tillman, the former South Carolina governor, U.S. senator, and ardent voice for the establishment of the college. In 1963 Tillman Hall was the site where the architecture student Harvey Gantt peacefully enrolled in school, the first African American to be admitted to Clemson. Since the late 1960s Tillman Hall has been the home of the university's School of Education, and its auditorium hosts lectures, concerts, and other events. BRADLEY S. SAULS

Bryan, Wright. *Clemson: An Informal History of the University, 1889–1979.* Columbia, S.C.: R. L. Bryan, 1979.

Timber. Timber has been part of South Carolina's economy since the late seventeenth century. Over time, timber grew into a major employer with millions of dollars in invested capital that, in the process, altered the landscape of South Carolina.

Colonists saw Carolina's magnificent virgin forests as a prime resource ripe for the taking. Many of the uses they found continue today: lumber and shingles for buildings, posts and rails for fences, firewood, and tool handles. Other uses from the preindustrial era, such as barrel staves, are less common today. For shipbuilders, live oaks were especially valued for use as ships' knees and mast trees. England and her Caribbean colonies needed wood in all its forms during the eighteenth century, and South Carolina exported a steady supply.

During the antebellum era the timber industry remained a relatively small portion of the economy. Lumbermen, not infrequently slaves, chopped trees down with axes and used horses, mules, or oxen to drag the sawed logs to a river for floating or all the way to a mill. The mills used waterwheels to power their saws until the 1850s, when steam engines took hold. The industry also spread further into the interior of the state to places such as Aiken, while the ports remained vital in finish milling and exporting. Antebellum South Carolina timber products went to the West Indies, Europe, and to the major ports of the North.

After the Civil War, South Carolina briefly became the center of the naval stores industry. North Carolinians had exhausted their timber resources and moved their enterprises south. However, turpentine and tar burning exhaust a stand of pines in a decade or less, and by the 1920s the industry had declined substantially. The decline of the wooden shipbuilding industry brought an end to demand for live oak.

The greatest transformation came with the rise of industrial timber operations at the turn of the twentieth century. Big industrial timber mills set up company housing and stores, and used vertical integration to control everything: land, harvesting, transportation, and milling. In the late nineteenth century and the early twentieth century much new railroad construction was to move harvested timber from forest to mill and from mill to customer. The Atlantic

Coast Lumber Company of Georgetown serves as a particularly good example. Organized in 1899, the ACL, as it was known, came to dominate its region of the state, owning or leasing timber rights to 250,000 acres by 1916. It held the prime harbor-front land in Georgetown, produced its own electrical power to run multiple mills, and had its own railroad (the Georgetown and Western), over which it could move its six mobile lumber camps.

In the second half of the twentieth century, vertical integration continued. Companies such as Westvaco and Georgia Pacific had mills for converting pulp into paper and for making board lumber. They employed foresters, cutting crews, tree planters, and fleets of tractor-trailers and owned tens of thousands of acres of land. Alongside these larger corporations was a wide range of smaller mills, timber crews, foresters, and landowners. The entire industry mechanized to a higher degree using log skidders to cut trees down and log loaders to quickly strip off limbs and stack logs on tractor-trailers.

The most important aspect of the industrial timber era began in the 1930s with the arrival of the pulpwood industry. The opening of the state's first pulp paper mill in Georgetown "revivified the community, which holds its nose and discounts the price of prosperity . . . the repellent odor" emanating from the mill. Decades elapsed until improved technologies reduced the pungent smell associated with the pulp paper mills. A half-dozen such mills are spread from the coast to the Pee Dee and Midlands. The pulpwood industry, based mostly on harvesting pine trees, accounts for a large majority of the state's timber resources.

The environmental impact of foresting in South Carolina has been significant. By the end of the twentieth century, very little virgin or old-growth timber existed in the Palmetto State. However, despite the continued harvesting of timber, South Carolina remained more than fifty percent wooded. Several factors are responsible. First, with the overall decline in row-crop agriculture in the state, landowners converted those acres to timber production. The quality of South Carolina forests also changed as they came to be seen as a slow-growing row crop. The widespread long-leaf pines, cut early in the twentieth century, were replaced with forests of planted slash or loblolly pines, which grow to maturity much faster. The forests also took on a regularized rowlike pattern. Control burning and regularly maintained firebreaks crisscrossed the pine forests in efforts to suppress wildfires.

In 1993 South Carolina had more than twelve million acres of commercial timberland. State or federal government owned nine percent of the land, timber companies held nineteen percent, and seventy-two percent was in the hands of private owners. At the end of the twentieth century timber was the most valuable crop in the state. In more than half of South Carolina's counties, timber was worth more than all other crops combined. JAMES H. TUTEN

Clark, Thomas D. *The Greening of the South: The Recovery of Land and Forest.* Lexington: University Press of Kentucky, 1984.

Eisterhold, John A. "Charleston: Lumber and Trade in a Declining Southern Port." *South Carolina Historical Magazine* 74 (April 1973): 61–72.

Fetters, Thomas. *Logging Railroads of South Carolina.* Forest Park, Ill.: Heimburger House, 1990.

Times and Democrat (2003 circulation: 18,103 daily and 17,871 Sunday). The *Times and Democrat* is a daily newspaper that serves the city of Orangeburg and the surrounding community. It was formed in 1881, the result of a merger between the *Orangeburg Times* and the *Orangeburg Democrat.* These two papers were formed from mergers of several post–Civil War newspapers.

The *Orangeburg Times* was a weekly paper founded in 1872 under the editorship of J. S. Heyward and F. P. Beard. It merged with the *Orangeburg News* (founded in 1867) in 1875 and was briefly called the *Orangeburg News and Times* before reverting to *Orangeburg Times* in 1877. James L. Sims purchased the *Edisto Clarion* in 1878 and changed the name to the *Orangeburg Democrat.* The next year the *Orangeburg Democrat* appeared as a weekly under the editorship of Sims and H. G. Sheridan.

The *Times and Democrat* began publishing twice a week in 1908 and by 1953 was publishing every day including Sunday. The newspaper became the first daily newspaper in the state to convert to offset printing in 1965. In October 1972 the newspaper's printing facility was destroyed by fire, but with the help of other newspapers the *Times and Democrat* continued to publish on schedule. The newspaper was able to repay the favors after Hurricane Hugo in 1989, when it assisted the Sumter *Item* after that newspaper's plant was without power. In 1981 the *Times and Democrat* was purchased by Howard Publications of Oceanside, California, and in 2002 Howard Publications was acquired by Lee Enterprises, based in Davenport, Iowa. AARON W. MARRS

McNeely, Patricia G. *The Palmetto Press: The History of South Carolina's newspapers and the Press Association.* Columbia: South Carolina Press Association, 1998.

Timmerman, George Bell, Jr. (1912–1994). Governor. Timmerman was born in Anderson on August 11, 1912, the son of George Bell Timmerman and Mary Vandiver Sullivan. The family moved to Batesburg when Timmerman was a child. He attended the Citadel from 1930 to 1933 and earned a bachelor of laws degree from the University of South Carolina in 1937. In 1935 Timmerman married Helen DuPre, but the union would produce no children. During World War II, he served in the U.S. Navy. After returning home, Timmerman practiced law in Lexington and became involved in politics. He was elected lieutenant governor in 1946 and was reelected in 1950.

In 1954 Timmerman planned to do what no previous lieutenant governor had ever accomplished: advance to the governor's office by the election route. Seven earlier aspirants had failed to win the governorship in this manner. Timmerman, who had served as lieutenant governor longer than anyone else in the state's history, triumphed in a landslide, carrying forty-one of the state's forty-six counties.

Timmerman took office at a crucial juncture in South Carolina history. In 1954 the U.S. Supreme Court unanimously issued its landmark *Brown v. Board of Education* decision, which ruled that racially segregated schools were "inherently unequal." Assuming his office in 1955, Timmerman was presented with the opportunity to lead the state forward in the area of race relations. However, Timmerman resolutely opposed integration, as had Strom Thurmond and James Byrnes, his predecessors as governor. Reaffirming the status quo, he told the state Senate in 1954 that "the 'separate-but-equal' policy provides a fair and practicable basis for race relations in South Carolina." The 1956 session of the legislature has been called the "Segregation Session" for its hostile posture on civil rights, including legislation barring National Association for the Advancement of Colored People members from public employment.

While Timmerman did nothing as dramatic as standing in the schoolhouse door to block entry by African Americans, he certainly did nothing to ease the transition to integration. He ordered Clemson to reject a $350,000 grant from the Atomic Energy Commission because that agency required a nondiscrimination commitment. Timmerman denounced the widely read publication *South Carolinians Speak* and its call for moderation in race relations. He criticized Billy Graham for endorsing "racial mixing" and forced the evangelist to relocate a crusade slated for the State House. He pressured three African American educational institutions (S.C. State College, Allen University, and Benedict College) to reject integration. Timmerman also urged the S.C. Department of Education to revoke accreditation for Allen's education program. Ironically, when the department submitted to the governor's demands, it gave African Americans legal grounds to seek admission to the University of South Carolina.

After his term as governor ended in 1959, Timmerman returned to private life and resumed his law practice. In 1967 the legislature elected him judge of the Eleventh Circuit Court, where he served until 1984. In September 1994 Timmerman was involved in an automobile accident, and he succumbed to his injuries on November 29, 1994. JOSEPH EDWARD LEE

Bailey, N. Louise, Mary L. Morgan, and Carolyn R. Taylor, eds. *Biographical Directory of the South Carolina Senate, 1776–1985.* 3 vols. Columbia: University of South Carolina Press, 1986.

Jordan, Frank E. *The Primary State: A History of the Democratic Party in South Carolina, 1876–1962.* N.p., n.d.

Quint, Howard H. *Profile in Black and White: A Frank Portrait of South Carolina.* Washington, D.C.: Public Affairs, 1958.

Timothy, Elizabeth (?–1757). Newspaper publisher. Little is known of Elizabeth Timothy's origins and early life. Benjamin Franklin described her as "born and bred in Holland." She was married to Louis Timothée, a French-born immigrant from Rotterdam. Together with their four young children, the couple sailed to Philadelphia in 1731. Louis worked as a French instructor and soon after established an association with Franklin, who helped him become a journeyman printer for the *Pennsylvania Gazette.* In November 1733 Franklin established Louis in a six-year business partnership as the new printer of the *South-Carolina Gazette.* While Louis prepared the first issue of his Charleston newspaper, Elizabeth settled family business in Philadelphia before moving her family to South Carolina in March 1734. The family became established members of lowcountry society. The name Louis was anglicized to "Lewis" and Timothée became "Timothy," and the family was registered at St. Philip's Church. By 1736 Lewis Timothy prospered as a landholder and printer, serving as the official colonial printer for South Carolina. In December 1738 Lewis died as the result of "an unhappy Accident," leaving Elizabeth in the care of "six small Children and another hourly expected." She had already mourned the loss of two of her children by 1737.

According to the arrangement between her husband and Franklin, Elizabeth's eldest son, Peter, was to carry on the business in the event of his father's death. But because of Peter's youth, she assumed control of the printing office as well as responsibility for her family. The newly widowed Elizabeth published the next issue of the *Gazette* on January 4, 1739, pledging "to make it as entertaining and correct as may be reasonably expected." By the end of the year, she bought out Franklin's interest in the partnership and became the first woman in the American colonies to own and publish a newspaper. Franklin praised her regular and exact accounting and commended her for both raising a family and purchasing the printing operation from him.

Elizabeth gradually relinquished control of printing operations when Peter came of age in 1746. Requests for payment from the South Carolina Commons House of Assembly from 1740 to 1743 in Elizabeth's name show her reliance on the revenues as public printer. In addition to publishing the *Gazette* and colonial laws, she sold legal blanks, broadsides, and stationery and established a bookstore adjacent to her son's printing office.

Elizabeth drafted her will on April 2, 1757, and was buried two days later at St. Philip's Church. She bequeathed to her children personal property, eight slaves, and household items. In Peter's care she also left a silver watch belonging to her late husband, with the intent that he leave it to his son. Through her son Peter, daughter-in-law Ann, and grandson Benjamin Franklin Timothy, Elizabeth ensured that the Timothy printing legacy in South Carolina would continue for three generations. MARTHA J. KING

Baker, Ira L. "Elizabeth Timothy: America's First Woman Editor." *Journalism Quarterly* 54 (summer 1977): 280–85.

Cohen, Hennig. *The South Carolina Gazette, 1732–1775.* Columbia: University of South Carolina Press, 1953.

King, Martha J. "Making an Impression: Women Printers of the Southern Colonies in the Revolutionary Era." Ph.D. diss., College of William and Mary, 1992.

Timothy, Lewis (?–1738). Newspaper printer. Timothy was born Louis Timothée, the son of a Huguenot who took refuge in Holland following the revocation of the Edict of Nantes. With his Dutch-born wife, Elizabeth, and their four small children, Lewis sailed onboard the *Britannia* from Rotterdam to Philadelphia in 1731. Shortly after his arrival in North America, he anglicized his name to Lewis Timothy, swore a loyalty oath to King George II, and placed an ad in the *Pennsylvania Gazette* (October 14, 1731) seeking employment as a French instructor. He found work, however, in the printing business. In May 1732 Lewis assisted Benjamin Franklin with the production of the short-lived German language newspaper called the *Philadelphische Zeitung.* He later became a journeyman printer for the *Pennsylvania Gazette* and the first librarian of the Library Company of Philadelphia.

In 1731 Franklin had sent Thomas Whitmarsh to South Carolina to establish a newspaper for the colony. When Whitmarsh died in September 1733, Timothy was invited to succeed him. On November 26, 1733, Timothy entered a six-year publishing agreement with Franklin whereby he would maintain a two-thirds interest as the new printer of the *South-Carolina Gazette.* The Timothy family moved to Charleston, where Lewis maintained a print shop on Church Street. The *South-Carolina Gazette* resumed weekly publication under Timothy's name on February 2, 1734. Of Timothy, Franklin wrote, "He was a man of learning and honest, but ignorant in matters of account; and tho' he sometimes made me remittances, I could get no account from him nor any satisfactory state of our partnership while he lived."

The Timothy family achieved prominence in South Carolina society. Lewis became the official colonial printer. He and his family were members of St. Philip's Church in Charleston. Lewis became a founder and officer of the South Carolina Society, a social and charitable organization made up of Huguenots. By 1736 he obtained land grants totaling six hundred acres and a town lot in Charleston.

In the October 12, 1738, issue of the *Gazette,* Timothy explained a delay in publication "by reason of Sickness, myself and Son having been visited with this Fever, that reigns at present, so that neither of us hath been capable for some time of working much at the Press." Timothy died as the result of "an unhappy Accident" in December 1738 and was buried in the St. Philip's Church cemetery on December 30. He left his widow, Elizabeth, to continue the printing business and to serve out the contract with Franklin until his eldest son, Peter, reached his majority. Peter Timothy was to carry on the business in the event of his father's death and "to keep & improve ye materials of printing" until the expiration of the original partnership. The Timothy printing enterprise would last in South Carolina for three generations. MARTHA J. KING

Cohen, Hennig. *The South Carolina Gazette, 1732–1775.* Columbia: University of South Carolina Press, 1953.

Labaree, Leonard W., and Whitefield, J. Bell, Jr., eds. *The Papers of Benjamin Franklin.* Vol. 1, *January 6, 1706 through December 31, 1734.* New Haven, Conn.: Yale University Press, 1959.

Timothy, Peter (ca. 1725–1782). Newspaper printer, patriot. Timothy was born in Holland to Louis and Elizabeth Timothée before they immigrated to Philadelphia in 1731 and anglicized their name to Timothy. His father was a business partner of Benjamin Franklin, and in 1733 Lewis Timothy settled in Charleston and became printer of the *South-Carolina Gazette.* After his father's death in 1738, Peter's mother, Elizabeth, continued the contract. In 1739 Elizabeth bought out Franklin's interest in the partnership for her son. By 1746 Peter reached his legal majority and assumed the family business. The previous year, on December 8, 1745, he married Ann Donavan. The marriage produced at least twelve children.

Peter Timothy was the official printer to the Commons House of Assembly and maintained a monopoly on the South Carolina printing business until 1758, when Robert Wells began publishing the *South-Carolina Weekly Gazette.* Timothy became postmaster general for Charleston in 1756, and during the Stamp Act Crisis he became deputy postmaster of the southern colonies and acting postmaster of the district in 1766. The *South-Carolina Gazette* under Timothy became increasingly partisan in the colonial crisis. It published critiques of Governor James Glen, expressed support of the Wilkes Fund and American manufactures, and roundly condemned the Boston Massacre and the blockade of the port of Boston.

Timothy's interests extended beyond printing. He was elected to the Twentieth Royal Assembly (1751–1754) by St. Peter's Parish. Active in the Sons of Liberty, he was a member of the General Committee of Correspondence in 1774 and chairman of the Committee of Observation and clerk of the Council of Safety in 1775. He served on the Committee of Ninety-Nine for Charleston and in the First and Second Provincial Congresses (1775–1776) for St. Philip's and St. Michael's Parishes. In 1776 the House elected him clerk of the First General Assembly. He offered to resign when members protested his dual office holding and yet was retained. Timothy was also secretary of the Grand Lodge of Free Masons, a founding member of the Charleston Library Society, a member of the South Carolina Society, a pewholder in St. Philip's Church, and a landholder in Orangeburg and Berkeley Counties.

Timothy was an ardent patriot. During the siege of Charleston, he was a military observer and watched the British fleet from atop St. Michael's steeple. Following the fall of Charleston in May 1780, Timothy refused to take a loyalty oath and was exiled to St. Augustine with other prominent city patriots. After a ten-month imprisonment he was exchanged but forbidden to return to Charleston. Reunited with family in Philadelphia, Timothy in autumn 1782 accompanied two daughters and a grandchild on a ship bound for the West Indies. Intending to visit his daughter in Antigua, and perhaps plot a return to South Carolina, Timothy and some members of his family perished in a storm off the coast of Delaware. His will, proved on May 2, 1783, left all his property to his wife, an unmarried daughter named Sarah, his invalid son Robert, and his son Benjamin Franklin, who would eventually continue the family printing enterprise after his mother's death. MARTHA J. KING

Cohen, Hennig. *The South Carolina Gazette, 1732–1775.* Columbia: University of South Carolina Press, 1953.

Edgar, Walter, and N. Louise Bailey, eds. *Biographical Directory of the South Carolina House of Representatives.* Vol. 2, *The Commons House of Assembly, 1692–1775.* Columbia: University of South Carolina Press, 1977.

McMurtrie, Douglas C. "The Correspondence of Peter Timothy, Printer of Charlestown, with Benjamin Franklin." *South Carolina Historical and Genealogical Magazine* 35 (October 1934): 123–29.

Timrod, Henry (1828–1867). Poet, essayist. Timrod was born on December 8, 1828, in Charleston, the only son of a bookbinder, William Henry Timrod, and his wife, Thyrza Prince. Hedged by poverty, frail health, and the cataclysm of the Civil War, Timrod led a brief tubercular life that bore the stamp of the romantic tradition that he revered and defended among his neoclassical contemporaries in Charleston's antebellum literary circles.

Henry Timrod. Courtesy, South Carolina Historical Society

Timrod attended the prestigious Classical School, where he befriended his lifelong ally and fellow poet Paul Hamilton Hayne. As a young man, Timrod enjoyed solitude, nature, and the contemplation of romantic love and death. William Gilmore Simms found Timrod "morbid," but the ever-loyal Hayne memorialized him as "passionate, impulsive, [and] eagerly ambitious." When scant resources precluded his graduation from the University of Georgia, Timrod returned to Charleston in 1846 to study law with James L. Petigru. However, as one contemporary put it, Timrod "was too wholly a poet" to find the regimen compatible. Until the outbreak of the Civil War, he tutored the children of lowcountry planters while publishing his poetry and essays in *Russell's Magazine* (which he helped to found in 1857 with Hayne), the *Southern Literary Messenger,* and the Charleston newspapers. *Harper's* magazine hailed "the true poetical genius" of Timrod's *Poems* (1860), the only collection published in his lifetime.

Scholars generally concur that slavery and its ideological defense retarded the intellectual evolution of the antebellum South, particularly in the realm of letters. Timrod's 1859 essay "Literature in the South" buttresses this point of view. Southern readers at best, he wrote, were indifferent to southern writers, but more often criticized them "as not sufficiently Southern in spirit." According to Timrod, literature served merely as "epicurean amusement" for the South's "provincial" people. Even among the most learned, said Timrod, the "fossil theory of [classical] criticism" remained de rigueur. A devotee of romanticism, Timrod argued that the embracement of new modes of expression was not inherently subversive. In his other notable essay, an exchange with William J. Grayson titled "What Is Poetry?" (1859), Timrod vehemently rebutted Grayson's defense of verse as simply "form and order." Precisely for its disavowal and articulation of the modern sensibility in southern voices, the literary scholar Richard J. Calhoun has called this exchange "one of the more interesting critical debates in antebellum literary history."

Although Timrod opposed secession, the opening of the Confederate Congress in February 1861 elicited from him the exultant "Ethnogenesis," which prophesied the world made over in the image of a utopian South free "from want and crime." But as the war dragged on, Timrod's poems—"The Cotton Boll" (1861), "Carolina" (1862), "Charleston" (1862), "Christmas" (1862), "The Unknown Dead" (1863), and the postwar "Ode" (1866)—turned from ardor to apprehension and gloom, earning for him the sobriquet "Poet Laureate of the Confederacy." Lauding the "controlled eloquence" of his wartime compositions, the literary scholar Louis D. Rubin has written, "Nothing in Timrod's pre-secession verse really prepares us for this sudden maturation as a poet. It is as if the advent of secession and the war had jarred him loose from his preoccupation with his own personality, the obsessive self-consciousness of his role as sensitive spokesman for aesthetic Ideality, into an abrupt confrontation with his identity as a member of the civil community." Even so harsh a critic as Ralph Waldo Emerson chose to read Timrod's war poetry to New England audiences after the Civil War, a tribute to his artistry and evocation of the sectional crisis.

Timrod enlisted in the Confederate service several times, but his chronic tuberculosis led to repeated discharges. In the spring of 1862, as a war correspondent for the *Charleston Mercury,* Timrod witnessed the retreat of the Confederate army from Shiloh. Overwhelmed by the horror, he returned home and in January 1864 assumed the editorship of the *South Carolinian,* a daily newspaper published in Columbia. He married his long-betrothed Kate Goodwin, the English sister of his brother-in-law, and on Christmas Eve their son Willie was born. Timrod remained at his desk while Sherman's troops destroyed the capital city, issuing "thumbsheets" until the occupation forced him into hiding. Facing ruin and starvation, Timrod futilely sought employment, depending on the charity of friends and the sale of his meager possessions for survival. The poet's bloodstained manuscripts still attest to his precipitous physical decline after the death of Willie, "our little boy beneath the sod," in October 1865. Henry Timrod died from tubercular hemorrhages on October 7, 1867, and was buried in the cemetery at Trinity Episcopal Cathedral in Columbia. In 1911 the South Carolina General Assembly adopted Timrod's "Carolina" as the state song. ELIZABETH ROBESON

Parks, Edd Winfield, ed. *The Essays of Henry Timrod.* Athens: University of Georgia Press, 1942.

———. *Henry Timrod.* New York: Twayne, 1964.

Parks, Edd Winfield, and Aileen Wells Parks, eds. *The Collected Poems of Henry Timrod.* Athens: University of Georgia Press, 1965.

Rubin, Louis D. *The Edge of the Swamp: A Study in the Literature and Society of the Old South.* Baton Rouge: Louisiana State University Press, 1989.

Tindall, George Brown (b. 1921). Historian, educator. A meticulous scholar, eloquent writer, and engaging teacher, Tindall is one of the nation's most distinguished historians. Born in Greenville on February 26, 1921, Tindall developed a love of writing and current events at an early age. A self-described "newspaper junkie and current events buff," he graduated from Greenville High School in 1938. As an undergraduate at Furman University, Tindall coedited the *Echo,* the student literary magazine, and he also authored a column on world events that appeared in the school newspaper. After graduating from Furman in 1942 with a degree in English, Tindall enlisted in the U.S. Air Force, where he served in the Pacific theater.

On June 29, 1946, Tindall married a Furman classmate, Blossom McGarrity of Charleston. The marriage produced two children. Soon after his marriage, he enrolled as a graduate student at the University of North Carolina at Chapel Hill. He received a doctoral degree in history in 1951. During a teaching career that would span more than forty years, Tindall served on the faculties at Eastern Kentucky State College, the University of Mississippi, and Louisiana State University. He joined the history department at the University of North Carolina at Chapel Hill in 1958 and remained there until retiring in 1990.

Tindall's first book, *South Carolina Negroes, 1877–1900,* was published in 1952 by the University of South Carolina Press. It details the living conditions among South Carolina blacks after Reconstruction. The book served as an important source for C. Vann Woodward's pathbreaking study *The Strange Career of Jim Crow* (1955). In 1957 he was awarded a Guggenheim Fellowship. He was a member of the Institute for Advanced Study at Princeton in 1963–1964, a Fulbright Guest Professor at the University of Vienna in 1967–1968, and a fellow at the Institute for Advanced Study in the Behavioral Sciences at Stanford in 1979–1980.

The Emergence of the New South, 1913–1945, published in 1967 by Louisiana State University Press, is Tindall's signature work. A magisterial study more than seven hundred pages in length, the book analyzes the South's struggle to adapt to a rapidly changing world during the years between the two world wars. *The Emergence of the New South* is remarkable for its balance, grace, and objectivity. It was awarded the first Lillian Smith Book Award, named for the Georgia writer known for her outspoken views against segregation, and it received the Charles Sydnor Award from the Southern Historical Association. Tindall's growing stature led the Southern Historical Association to elect him as its president in 1973.

Throughout the 1970s Tindall lectured widely and authored several important books, including *The Disruption of the Solid South* (1972), *The Persistent Tradition in New South Politics* (1975), and *The Ethnic Southerner,* a collection of essays published in 1976. In 1984 he completed *America: A Narrative History,* a distinctive survey textbook featuring a seamless narrative written by a single author. *America* quickly became one of the most popular American history textbooks. Tindall lives in Chapel Hill and remains active as a visiting lecturer and a lucid writer. DAVID E. SHI

Ashmore, Susan Youngblood. "Continuity and Change: George Brown Tindall and the Post-Reconstruction South." In *Reading Southern History: Essays on Interpreters and Interpretations,* edited by Glenn Feldman. Tuscaloosa: University of Alabama Press, 2001.

Carter, Dan T. "Introduction: The Adaptable South." In *The Adaptable South: Essays in Honor of George Brown Tindall,* edited by Elizabeth Jacoway et al. Baton Rouge: Louisiana State University Press, 1991.

Toal, Jean Hoefer (b. 1943). Lawyer, jurist. Toal was born in Columbia on August 11, 1943, the daughter of Herbert W. Hoefer and Lilla Farrell. She attended parochial and public schools before

Jean Toal. Courtesy, the Hon. Jean Hoeffer Toal, Columbia, S.C.

enrolling in Agnes Scott College. As an undergraduate she served on the Judicial Council National Supervisory Board of the U.S. National Student Association and was a member of Phi Beta Kappa. In 1965 she graduated with a degree in philosophy. Toal received her J.D. degree in 1968 from the University of South Carolina Law School, where she served as managing editor, leading articles editor, and book review editor of the *South Carolina Law Review.* Because of her high academic achievement she was a member of the Order of the Coif and Mortar Board. In 1967 she married her law school classmate William Thomas Toal. They have two daughters.

Toal became the ninetieth woman admitted to the South Carolina Bar on October 3, 1968. Professionally, she was first associated with the Haynsworth firm of Greenville. Toal then returned to Columbia, first as an associate and then as a partner in the firm of Belser, Baker, Barwick, Ravenel, Toal, and Bender. Here she gained substantial experience as a litigator in the state and federal courts. Toal represented the law student Victoria Eslinger in her effort to serve as page in the South Carolina Senate. Toal won the case when the Fourth Circuit Court of Appeals held that the practice of hiring only males as pages was unconstitutional.

In 1975 Toal began thirteen years of service as a member of the South Carolina House of Representatives representing Richland County. She was the first woman to be appointed chair of a standing committee and became a floor leader for legislation important to the judicial system. After working for Jimmy Carter's 1976 presidential campaign, Toal was asked to consider a judgeship. Although she declined, she remained open to the idea, and on March 16, 1988, she was elected to serve as an associate justice of the Supreme Court of South Carolina. She was the first female justice, the first Roman Catholic justice, and the first native of Columbia to serve on the state's highest court. While serving as associate justice, Toal maintained her interest in legal education, presenting over seventy professional lectures and papers on various topics of the law. With two of her law clerks, she authored a text on appellate practice in South Carolina. Toal became the first female chief justice of the Supreme Court of South Carolina on March 23, 2000.

Toal was awarded the South Carolina Trial Lawyers Outstanding Contribution to Justice Award in 1995. She has received honorary degrees from the University of South Carolina, Francis Marion University, the Citadel, Columbia College, and the College of Charleston. RUTH W. CUPP

Cupp, Ruth Williams. *Portia Steps up to the Bar: The First Women Lawyers of South Carolina.* Raleigh, N.C.: Ivy House, 2003.

Tobacco. Three times in the history of South Carolina, tobacco has risen to the status of a major cash crop, and three times it has declined. Early settlers planted tobacco around Charleston in the 1670s, forging the colony's first links to world markets. But overproduction in Virginia and Maryland kept leaf prices low, and South Carolinians soon embraced rice as a more profitable staple. By the 1690s rice had supplanted tobacco as the colony's leading export, and the weed all but disappeared in South Carolina.

Tobacco reemerged in the backcountry in the 1760s. Too far from the coast for tidewater rice culture, frontier farmers needed a moneymaker to supplement their corncribs and smokehouses. An uptick in leaf prices encouraged backcountry farmers to cultivate tobacco. The Revolutionary War disrupted commerce for several years, but after the war a lively demand for tobacco revived the culture. The state government established several "inspection warehouses" around the state to handle the trade. Production peaked at ten million pounds in 1799. But the cotton boom of the early 1800s quickly drove tobacco from the red hills of the backcountry, and by the 1810s leaf culture had again vanished in the Palmetto State.

South Carolina's most important tobacco period began in the Pee Dee region in the 1880s. Although cotton had been the focus of agrarian life for eight decades, profits had fallen below $15 per acre. The cotton depression coincided with the spectacular rise of cigarette smoking in the United States and Europe. By the 1880s highly addictive cigarettes made of mild, aromatic, flue-cured tobacco (also called bright leaf) were being mass-produced and aggressively marketed. Demand for cigarette tobaccos increased apace. In the mid-1880s

Bright leaf tobacco ready for auction, Dixie Warehouse, Florence. Courtesy, South Caroliniana Library, University of South Carolina

farmers in the Mars Bluff community near Florence planted experimental bright leaf crops that yielded profits of nearly $150 per acre—ten times the value of cotton. Soon, beleaguered cotton farmers in Darlington, Florence, Horry, Marion, Clarendon, and Williamsburg Counties were learning tobacco culture. By 1900 local entrepreneurs had established leaf markets in several Pee Dee towns, and flue-cured tobacco was an integral part of the state's agricultural economy.

The labor-intensive nature of flue-cured tobacco culture increased tenancy, and small, wood-frame tenant houses became as commonplace as curing barns on the Pee Dee landscape. With virtually all tasks performed by hand, much of the crop's value went into the wages of laborers and thence to local merchants. The tobacco trade revived older towns such as Conway and Darlington and grew new ones such as Mullins and Lake City. Indeed, the rhythm of life in many Pee Dee communities followed the cycle of tobacco culture.

By the 1920s, however, tobacco growers were falling on hard times. The tendency of growers to overproduce coupled with the monopolistic practices of cigarette manufacturers drove leaf prices down. In an attempt to strengthen their marketing position, growers in the Carolinas and Virginia formed a cooperative. Although the co-op succeeded in raising leaf prices for a few years, manufacturers destroyed it by refusing to buy co-op leaf and subverting grower confidence through propaganda. Leaf prices—and the fortunes of the Pee Dee—entered a long decline.

The Great Depression of the 1930s hit the Pee Dee hard. Crop prices plunged to record lows, forcing many farmers into foreclosure. Market towns suffered as merchants and banks failed. The Agricultural Adjustment Act (AAA) of 1933 rescued tobacco farmers and revived the Pee Dee economy. The AAA solved the dual problems of overproduction and grower disunity; growers agreed to reduce their tobacco acreage and join a government-sponsored marketing group. The production control plan balanced supply with demand, leaf prices rose, and the Pee Dee began a sustained recovery.

After World War II the production control program was expanded to include price supports. Tobacco leaves failing to bring the parity price at auction were purchased by the marketing group and later resold to manufacturers. Operations were subsidized by government loans. The combination of production controls and price supports raised growers' incomes, and the land-bound tobacco quota became a valuable franchise for landowners. Moreover, government oversight of tobacco marketing protected growers from exploitation by manufacturers. Pee Dee market towns prospered as well. The federal tobacco program became the cornerstone of the Pee Dee economy in the 1950s. South Carolina's leaf production peaked in 1955 at 197 million pounds.

By 1970, however, mounting evidence of smoking-related illness was reducing demand for cigarette tobaccos. Concurrently, cigarette manufacturers began fostering tobacco production abroad, further eroding demand for American leaves. Culture methods were changing as well. The development of mechanical harvesters and bulk curing barns sharply reduced labor requirements, and many growers quickly replaced people with machines. Thousands of tenants left farming to seek employment elsewhere. Market towns felt the pinch as wages formerly spent with local merchants went instead to out-of-state equipment manufacturers. Rising capital requirements for modern harvesting and curing equipment pressured many small farmers to rent or sell their leaf quotas. Thus, Pee Dee tobacco farms became fewer and larger. From 1974 to 1992 the number of tobacco farms declined seventy percent, and the traditional agrarian culture of the Pee Dee passed from the scene.

At century's end, South Carolina's tobacco industry was in retreat. Health concerns and leaf imports continued to undermine demand for American tobaccos, and quotas were cut substantially in the 1990s. Moreover, leaf prices fell behind the inflation curve and did not recover. Quota cuts and lower profit margins accelerated the consolidation of smaller farms into ever larger ones. Manufacturers, seeking to eliminate the competitive auction system and remove government supervision from tobacco marketing, began purchasing leaves directly from growers. In 2001 production fell to sixty-eight million pounds, and eighty percent of the crop was sold outside the auction system. While tobacco remains an important cash crop in South Carolina, its decline has been dramatic and its future is uncertain. ELDRED E. PRINCE, JR.

Prince, Eldred E., and Robert R. Simpson. *Long Green: The Rise and Fall of Tobacco in South Carolina.* Athens: University of Georgia Press, 2000.

Tobacco barns. Tobacco curing barns have helped to define the Pee Dee landscape since the 1880s. Unlike in Burley-tobacco regions such as Kentucky, where ventilated air-drying sheds were used, in South Carolina bright leaf tobacco was flue-cured by artificial heat. Thus, curing barns were tightly constructed to maintain high temperatures during the four- to five-day curing process. A brick furnace circulated heat through a network of stove pipes (flues) that ran parallel to and a few inches above the floor. Tobacco leaves were strung on wooden sticks and hung overhead on rows of tier poles. Early tobacco barns were generally sixteen feet square and twenty feet high with four "rooms" of tier poles. As crop yields increased in the 1940s and 1950s, twenty-foot square, five-room barns became the norm. Typically, the outside walls were skirted by a shed roof that sheltered hanging and stringing.

Tobacco barn, ca. 1938. Courtesy, South Caroliniana Library, University of South Carolina

Curing-barn architecture evolved slowly. Until the 1940s most farmers built their barns from homegrown materials: stout logs chinked with clay and roofed with hand-hewn shingles. Tier poles were fashioned from slender pine saplings. Later, farmers purchased dressed lumber and covered it with store-bought asphalt sheathing. Handmade shingles bowed to tin roofing. In the 1950s and 1960s a few farmers invested in cement block construction. Curing fuels and technologies also evolved. At first, tobacco growers fueled their brick furnaces with firewood cut from their own forests. By the 1950s, however, kerosene and propane gas burners were commonplace in the Pee Dee.

As tobacco culture mechanized in the late 1960s, all-metal, rectangular "bulk" barns began replacing traditional barns. Bulk curing eliminated several labor-intensive tasks and cured more leaves with less fuel. Automated controls greatly simplified curing. By 1990 essentially all of the state's tobacco crop was bulk cured. At century's end, a few examples of wooden tobacco barns were being preserved as heritage assets in the Pee Dee. ELDRED E. PRINCE, JR.

Daniel, Pete. *Breaking the Land: The Transformation of Cotton, Tobacco, and Rice Cultures since 1880.* Urbana: University of Illinois Press, 1985.

Kirby, Jack Temple. *Rural Worlds Lost: The American South, 1920–1960.* Baton Rouge: Louisiana State University Press, 1987.

Kovacik, Charles F., and John J. Winberry. *South Carolina: The Making of a Landscape.* 1987. Reprint, Columbia: University of South Carolina Press, 1989.

Prince, Eldred E., and Robert R. Simpson. *Long Green: The Rise and Fall of Tobacco in South Carolina.* Athens: University of Georgia Press, 2000.

Tobler, John (?–1765). Promoter, publisher. Born in Appenzell, Switzerland, Tobler became that canton's governor until he was removed from office in a power struggle. He then worked with other prominent members of his community to bring Swiss settlers to South Carolina. After some delays in Europe, Tobler and about 190 Swiss arrived in Charleston in February 1737. Leading the first twenty-five settlers from the coast, Tobler took the group across the province to settle the township of New Windsor on the South Carolina side of the Savannah River. The Swiss native established a store in the township and probably had a small farm. But his abilities were much broader than just working the land. In 1744 he claimed to have invented a machine to clean rice that, with three slaves, could do three barrels in a day. He wrote promotional pieces about South Carolina to attract more settlers, including detailed accounts of his travels and observations about life on the colonial frontier.

In the early 1750s Tobler began to publish an annual almanac, the *South Carolina Almanack.* The reference work included information on diverse subjects ranging from details on phases of the moon and eclipses, advice on bleeding, a garden calendar, cures for poison, and a description of the roads in the southern colonies. After his death, Tobler's son John continued to publish the work until 1790. John Tobler, Sr., also published a Pennsylvania almanac briefly during his lifetime. The Swiss patriarch brought a new level of culture to the colonial frontier that included a "house" or chamber organ and several books in German. Tobler married sometime before his arrival in the New World and had at least four children. He died on April 19, 1765. FRITZ HAMER

Cordle, Charles G., ed. "The John Tobler Manuscripts: An Account of German-Swiss Emigrants in South Carolina, 1737." *Journal of Southern History* 5 (February 1939): 83–97.

Meriwether, Robert L. *The Expansion of South Carolina, 1729–1765.* Kingsport, Tenn.: Southern Publishers, 1940.

Robbins, Walter L., ed. and trans. "John Tobler's Description of South Carolina (1753)." *South Carolina Historical Magazine* 71 (July 1970): 141–61.

———. "John Tobler's Description of South Carolina (1754)." *South Carolina Historical Magazine* 71 (October 1970): 257–65.

Webber, Mabel L. "South Carolina Almanacs to 1800." *South Carolina Historical and Genealogical Magazine* 15 (April 1914): 73–81.

Tombee (Beaufort County). Tombee Plantation House was built by Thomas Benjamin Chaplin, for whom ("Tom B.") it was named. A member of an established St. Helena Island family, Chaplin was among the early planters of Sea Island cotton and probably built the house with his first profits. Raised on a tabby foundation, the two-story frame dwelling faces Station Creek with a wide, two-tiered veranda. Although its exact construction date is unknown, the house was most likely built between 1795 and 1810. The narrow scale of the lateral gable core and the restrained but finely carved interior trim suggest a late eighteenth-century date. The early attribution is supported by the T-shaped plan, which provides three windows in each of the six major rooms, and which had become characteristic of Beaufort construction by the 1790s.

Tombee is celebrated as one of a handful of Beaufort County cotton plantation dwellings that survived into the twenty-first century, but it is better known as the home of the diarist Thomas B. Chaplin. His journal from 1845 to 1861, with an afterword dated 1886, depicts agricultural, domestic, and social activities from the personal viewpoint of a moderately successful planter whose neighbors had more land, more slaves, more houses, and more money than he did—and who were mostly his relatives. Tombee is a private residence and was listed in the National Register of Historic Places in 1975. SARAH FICK

Isely, N. Jane, William P. Baldwin, and Agnes L. Baldwin. *Plantations of the Low Country: South Carolina 1697–1865.* Greensboro, N.C.: Legacy Publications, 1985.

Rosengarten, Theodore. *Tombee: Portrait of a Cotton Planter.* New York: Morrow, 1986.

Rowland, Lawrence S., Alexander Moore, and George C. Rogers. *The History of Beaufort County, South Carolina.* Vol. 1, *1514–1861.* Columbia: University of South Carolina Press, 1996.

Tompkins, Daniel Augustus (1851–1914). Industrialist, journalist. Tompkins was born in Edgefield on October 12, 1851, the eldest child of Dewitt Clinton Tompkins and Hannah Virginia Smyly. Tompkins began his education in schools around Edgefield, including Long Cane School and Dr. Luther Rice Gwaltney's Academy. By the time he was ready for college, South Carolina had just emerged from the Civil War. Tompkins spent two years at South Carolina College, but in 1869 he traveled north to study civil engineering at Rensselaer Polytechnic Institute in Troy, New York, where he graduated in 1873. While in college, Tompkins began to work in the John A. Griswold and Company steel plant in Troy, and after graduating he went to work for Alexander L. Holley's engineering office in Brooklyn designing and setting up steel plants, including the J. Edgar Thompson Iron Works at Bessemer, Pennsylvania, and Bethlehem Iron Works in Bethlehem, Pennsylvania.

Tompkins spent ten years working in industries in the North, but he always intended to return to the South to put his experience to work there. In 1883 he took a position as a representative of Westinghouse Machine Company. Establishing the D. A. Tompkins Company with headquarters in Charlotte, North Carolina, Tompkins sold and installed electrical equipment all over the South. He soon expanded his business to include building facilities to serve the cotton industry, such as cottonseed oil mills. By 1892 Tompkins expanded his interests to include the construction of cotton textile mills. The first mill he was involved with was the Catawba Manufacturing Company in Chester, South Carolina. Until the D. A. Tompkins Company was reorganized in 1907, it helped promote, finance, design, and build more than 250 cottonseed oil mills and 100 cotton textile mills, many of them in North Carolina and South Carolina.

At least as important as Tompkins's efforts to build industry in the South was his role as a spokesman and leader for that industry. He bought the *Charlotte (N.C.) Observer* in 1891 and used it to express his views about the place of industry in southern society. He also bought a controlling interest in the *Greenville News* in 1905. In 1900 Tompkins became a member of the United States Industrial Commission and the National Association of Manufacturers. In all these capacities, he was one of the leading opponents of child labor legislation in the nation. For several years he successfully blocked the implementation of child labor laws at both the state and national levels. He also opposed compulsory education and supported bringing European immigrants to the South to augment the industrial workforce.

Tompkins died at his summer home in Montreat, North Carolina, on October 18, 1914. He was buried in Elmwood Cemetery in Charlotte. BRUCE E. BAKER

Clay, Howard Bunyan. "Daniel Augustus Tompkins: An American Bourbon." Ph.D. diss., University of North Carolina at Chapel Hill, 1950.

Sutherland, Daniel E. *The Confederate Carpetbaggers.* Baton Rouge: Louisiana State University Press, 1988.

Tompkins, Daniel Augustus. *A Builder of the New South: Being the Story of the Life Work of Daniel Augustus Tompkins.* Garden City, N.Y.: Doubleday, Page, 1920.

Tourism. Tourism solidified its place in South Carolina's economy during the twentieth century, but people have long flocked to the Palmetto State. Numerous travel accounts from before the Civil War show that northerners enjoyed the sights and sounds of South Carolina. Near Charleston, northerners went to see the races, visited sites of the Revolutionary War, and wrote home that they had caught a glimpse of a "genuine" plantation. Charleston also served as the rail gateway to points west from 1830 to 1860, and many travelers saw the landscape between Charleston and present-day North Augusta from the windows of a train. Tourists marveled at the railroad's inclined plane and stationary steam engine near Aiken. In Columbia, visitors hoped to meet the city's elite and tour South Carolina College, particularly its famous library. Although travel in the upstate was rarer, natural sites such as Table Rock also drew visitors.

Tourism got a slow start after the Civil War. While some believed that Charleston would be a natural for attracting the convention trade, the hotel business in the city was wholly inadequate in the late nineteenth century. Charleston's city council rejected the idea of hosting a national Confederate veterans reunion in 1896, but in 1899 Charleston did host the convention after the city quickly built an auditorium to accommodate eight thousand spectators, and local residents opened their homes when hotels were unable to handle the crowd.

In the 1920s and 1930s tourism took off in Charleston, coinciding with the growth of interest in preserving the city's historic architecture. This required a delicate balance: city leaders pushed for modern buildings and infrastructure to serve the visitors, while historic preservationists fought to maintain the city's buildings and charm that attracted travelers.

Before the creation of the United States Interstate Highway System in 1954, South Carolina served as a transportation corridor for tourists traveling from the Northeast and Midwest to Florida because of the state's position between northern tourism origins and southern destinations. Major routes included U.S. Highways 1, 17, and 301, and these pathways provided intermediate destinations that had vehicular services, accommodations, food, and local handicrafts. Small towns were relatively uniformly distributed along the roadways and railroads and included a wide variety of locally owned tourist-oriented services, such as service stations, truck stops, motor courts, campgrounds, regional restaurants, retail stores, and community festivals.

Following World War II increased population, disposable income, mobility, and leisure time resulted in the rapid growth of tourists passing through and vacationing in the state. Interstate Highways 95, 85, 77, 26, and 20 greatly improved accessibility. Investments in accommodations, restaurants, retail outlets, golf courses, and entertainment—especially in the three coastal destinations of Myrtle Beach, Charleston, and Hilton Head Island—amplified the value of the state to visitors because travel time and distance to South Carolina were shorter than to Florida. The Palmetto State was also less expensive. Also of importance were long, unspoiled beaches and marshes; water-related activities such as swimming, sunbathing, boating, and excellent fresh and saltwater fishing; beautiful scenery; and a pleasant climate with warm, moist summers and moderate, dry winters.

At the beginning of the twenty-first century, South Carolina was attracting thirty million tourists annually, of whom twenty-two percent originated within the state. The majority of out-of-state visitors came from North Carolina, Georgia, Florida, and Virginia.

The state's forty-six counties have been divided into nine tourism regions by the South Carolina Department of Parks, Recreation and Tourism for promotional materials, especially at eight Welcome Centers, as a method of enticing tourists to tour the entire state. For those who visit any of the nine tourism regions, shopping is the most highly ranked activity followed in order by visits to the ocean or the many lakes and rivers; visits to historical sites and museums; fishing, hunting, or hiking at state parks, state forests, or national wildlife refuges; attending festivals held throughout the state; and playing golf. South Carolina is known as a golfing paradise and had one of the country's largest shares of the tourism golf market in 2001. By 2004 the state had approximately four hundred courses, with the largest concentration in the Grand Strand and a secondary cluster in and near Hilton Head Island.

In the 2002–2003 fiscal year tourism produced $9.4 billion in gross state product. Almost 340,000 individuals, or about twelve percent of the state's total workforce, were employed by tourism, which made it the number one employer in the state. The substantial role that tourism played in South Carolina's economy led the National Association for the Advancement of Colored People (NAACP) in 1999 to urge tourists to boycott South Carolina because of the Confederate flag's presence on top of the State House.

As tourism has grown in South Carolina, the focus of the tourism industry has also embraced wider culture. Whereas in the early twentieth century promoters of Charleston emphasized a romanticized antebellum past, in the early twenty-first century tourists could encounter a richer African American history and culture. This expansion has brought new tensions: while expanding tourism has brought jobs and economic benefits to areas such as the Sea Islands, it has also presented challenges to preserving the natural and social environments. LISLE S. MITCHELL

Washburn, Meika R. "Resident Attitudes and Beliefs towards Sustainable Tourism on Edisto Island: An African American Residents' Perspective." Master's thesis, University of South Carolina, 2004.

Yuhl, Stephanie Eileen. "High Culture in the Low Country: Arts, Identity and Tourism in Charleston, South Carolina, 1920–1940." Ph.D. diss., Duke University, 1998.

Town Theatre (Columbia). Columbia's Town Theatre is the longest continuously operating community theater in America. The theater got its start in June 1919, when Daniel Reed, a former professional actor and producer stationed at Camp Jackson, joined forces with the Columbia Drama League, a group of prominent citizens interested in promoting live theater in the city. Together, they formed the Columbia Stage Society as a producing entity for Town Theatre, with Reed serving as its first director. The opening production, *Joint Owners in Spain,* was presented on October 9, 1919, in Columbia High School auditorium.

After presenting plays at venues all around the city (including an athletic field at the University of South Carolina), the Stage Society acquired an old residence at 1012 Sumter Street. Plays were performed there on a makeshift stage until December 18, 1924, when a production of *The Torchbearers* opened in an actual theater built on the site. Although it has undergone renovation and modernization, Town Theatre continues production in what is essentially the same building, which was listed on the National Register of Historic Places in 1974.

Fed by talent from Fort Jackson and the University of South Carolina, as well as the larger community, Town Theatre flourished under the series of professional directors who succeeded Reed. Town Theatre alumni who have gone on to national success in the performing arts include Oscar winners Delbert Mann and Stanley Donen and twotime Emmy winner Fred Coe.

The theater usually produces between five and eight shows a year, ranging from original musicals to Shakespeare. Theater arts classes and productions for young people have always been an integral part of the organization. Because of its combination of a long production history and a focus on stimulating young people in the performing arts, Town Theatre has had a major impact on theatrical development both in Columbia and across the state. MALIE HEIDER

Brown, Adger. "Columbia's Town Theatre." *Sandlapper* 1 (November 1968): 48–52.

Rogers, Aida. "This 'Town's' Alive." *Sandlapper* 9 (summer 1998): 53–55.

"Town Theater Makes Bow as Columbia's Playhouse." Columbia *State,* December 16, 1920, p. 2.

Towne, Laura Matilda (1825–1901). Educator. Towne was born on May 3, 1825, in Pittsburgh, Pennsylvania, to John Towne and Sarah Robinson. During her childhood the family relocated to Philadelphia. The Townes regularly attended the First Unitarian Church of Philadelphia, where the minister William Henry Furness strongly influenced Towne's development into a militant abolitionist. When the Civil War commenced in April 1861, she was working as a teacher in Newport, Rhode Island.

By December 1861 Federal forces had occupied St. Helena Island, as well as other barrier islands on the South Carolina coast. White planters fled to the mainland, abandoning thousands of African American slaves. Federal military authorities called upon physicians and teachers to volunteer and provide vital aid for nearly ten thousand freedmen. Among the earliest to offer her services was Towne, who arrived in April 1862 at Port Royal. She was the official representative of the Port Royal Relief Committee of Philadelphia.

From her arrival Towne was determined to ensure that the "Port Royal Experiment" would be a success. Initially, she concentrated on dispensing supplies, including medicines, to St. Helena's black residents. Her primary accomplishment, however, was the founding of Penn School, the earliest educational facility on the island. By September 1862, with her longtime friend from Philadelphia, Ellen Murray, Towne had started teaching in a local Baptist church sanctuary. But the arrival of prefabricated building materials from Pennsylvania enabled the two women to move into a new schoolhouse.

At first, Penn School was the only local facility providing African Americans with secondary education. After 1870 it also served as a normal school, training black teachers to serve throughout South Carolina. Along with her educational duties, for many years Towne served as the local public health officer. She led long-standing temperance efforts to eliminate the liquor trade within the Sea Islands. Although not an attorney, Towne often provided sound legal advice to numerous African American families seeking to purchase land on St. Helena.

During her forty years of residency on the Sea Islands, Towne became conversant in Gullah and was a perceptive observer of African American folk culture. In 1867 she purchased and renovated Frogmore, an abandoned St. Helena plantation, where she lived with Murray until her death. Despite her lengthy residence, Towne seldom ventured to the mainland. Consequently, her contacts with white South Carolinians were negligible. Throughout adulthood Towne remained a staunch Republican Party partisan.

During her final two decades Towne experienced recurring bouts of malaria, which seriously undermined her health. She died of influenza on February 22, 1901, at Frogmore. Numerous African Americans, including many former pupils, followed the mule cart that conveyed Towne's remains to the Port Royal ferry. She was interred in her family plot in Laurel Hill Cemetery, Philadelphia. MILES S. RICHARDS

Rose, Willie Lee. *Rehearsal for Reconstruction: The Port Royal Experiment.* 1964. Reprint, Athens: University of Georgia Press, 1999.

Townes, Charles Hard (b. 1915). Physicist, Nobel laureate. Townes was born in Greenville on July 28, 1915, the second of six children born to Henry Keith Townes, an attorney, and Ellen Hard. He grew up on a farm and was interested in natural history from an early age. Townes visited the collections of the Charleston Museum and was fascinated by the differences in plants and animals he saw on the shore and in tidal inlets and those of his own Piedmont region. He attended Greenville public schools and Furman University, where he received a bachelor of science in physics and a bachelor of arts in modern languages, graduating summa cum laude in 1935. Townes completed work for a master of arts in physics at Duke University in 1936 and entered graduate school at the California Institute of Technology, where he received his doctorate in 1939. He married Frances H. Brown of New Hampshire on May 4, 1941. The couple has four daughters.

As a member of the technical staff of Bell Telephone Laboratories from 1939 to 1947, Townes designed radar bombing systems during World War II. He subsequently joined the faculty of Columbia University, where he served successively as associate professor, professor, and chairman of the physics department from 1948 to 1961. From 1959 to 1961 Townes was vice president and director of research of the Institute for Defense Analysis in Washington, D.C., and then served as provost and institute professor at the Massachusetts Institute of Technology from 1961 to 1966. Since 1967 Townes has been a professor at the University of California, Berkeley.

He became university professor emeritus in 1986 and professor in the Graduate School in 1994.

Townes's principal scientific work has been in microwave spectroscopy, nuclear and molecular structure, quantum electronics, radio astronomy, and infrared astronomy. He holds the original patents for the maser and the laser, the latter of which he shares with his brother-in-law, Arthur L. Schawlow. Townes conceived the idea of the "maser" (an acronym for "microwave amplification by stimulated emission of radiation") in 1951 and achieved the first amplification and generation of electromagnetic waves by stimulated emission in 1954. Four years later Townes and Schawlow suggested that masers could be made to function in the optical and infrared region. They dubbed these optical and infrared masers "lasers" ("light amplification by stimulated emission of radiation"). His pioneering work with masers and lasers earned Townes the Nobel Prize in physics in 1964.

During much of his career Townes has been a government adviser. In 1960 he was a founding member of the Jasons, a group of scientists who provide advice to the government regarding national issues that involve science and technology. Townes served on the President's Science Advisory Committee from 1966 to 1970 and was chairman of the technical advisory committee for the Apollo Program until shortly after the lunar landing. He chaired committees on strategic weapons and the MX missile and has been an active member in the National Academy of Science. Additionally, he has been active in helping to formulate advice given by the Papal Academy to the pope on issues of peace and the control of nuclear weapons.

Townes is the author of three books: *Microwave Spectroscopy* (with Arthur Schawlow, 1955), *Making Waves* (1995), and *How the Laser Happened: Adventures of a Scientist* (1999), as well as numerous articles. His achievements have been recognized with numerous awards and honors, including the National Medal of Science (1982) and no fewer than twenty-seven honorary degrees. MARY S. MILLER

Townes, Charles Hard. *How the Laser Happened: Adventures of a Scientist.* New York: Oxford University Press, 1999.

———. "A Life in Physics: Bell Telephone Laboratories and World War II, Columbia University and the Laser, M.I.T. and Government service, California and Research in Astrophysics." Interview by Suzanne B. Riess. 1991–1992. Regional Oral History Office, Bancroft Library, University of California, Berkeley.

Township plan. For three decades following the founding of Charleston in 1670, population growth in South Carolina was painfully slow. Settlement remained concentrated close to the capital along the Ashley, Cooper, and Edisto Rivers. As late as 1715, probably ninety percent of South Carolina's population lived within thirty miles of Charleston. With the development of rice as a staple crop early in the eighteenth century, the importation of African slaves increased rapidly, giving South Carolina a black majority population by 1710. By 1730 African slaves outnumbered whites by a margin of two to one. For colonial officials and the minority white population, slave insurrections were a perpetual threat, as were attacks from the Spanish at St. Augustine and Indians on the frontier.

In an attempt to rectify South Carolina's racial imbalance with mass white immigration and to provide a front line of defense against the Spanish and the Indians, Governor Robert Johnson suggested a "Scheem . . . for Settling Townships" in 1731. The plan involved the establishment of eleven townships sixty or more miles north and west of Charleston but south and east of the fall line.

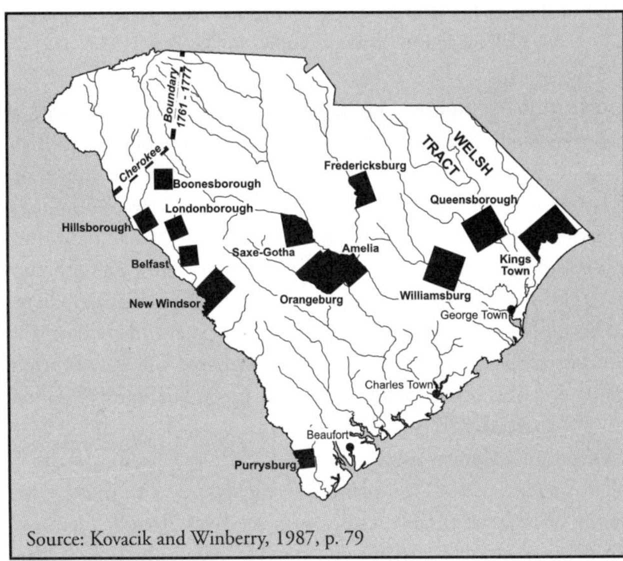

Source: Kovacik and Winberry, 1987, p. 79

Townships, 1731–1765

These townships were to be located on key South Carolina waterways and were to receive an initial grant of twenty thousand acres each, with all land six miles or less from the town reserved for future colonists. Each family of settlers was to be given fifty acres per family member and a town lot. Three hundred acres in each town were reserved for a commons, with additional acreage set aside for schools, churches, and public buildings. To finance the plan, which included equipment, seed, and provisions, the governor was authorized to make use of the colony's sinking fund that was earmarked to retire paper money.

Backed by imperial authorities in England, in 1732 Governor Johnson began laying out the new settlements. Although his death in 1735, war, and colonial bickering delayed the project, thirteen towns were completed by 1765: Amelia on the Santee River, Boonesborough and Hillsborough on Long Cane Creek, Queensboro and Welsh Tract on the Pee Dee, Kingston on the Waccamaw, Londonborough on Hard Labor Creek, Purrysburg and New Windsor on the Savannah, Orangeburg on the Edisto, Fredricksburg on the Wateree, Saxe Gotha on the Congaree, and Williamsburg on the Black. Two townships, Purrysburg and Hillsborough, were French. German or mostly German townships included Amelia, Londonborough, Orangeburg, New Windsor, and Saxe Gotha. Welsh Tract and Queensboro were mostly Welsh, and Boonesborough, Kingston, and Williamsburg were predominantly Irish or Scots-Irish. Even though the colony tapped its sinking fund in support of the township plan, the amount was insufficient for the task. To complete the project, a tax was placed on imported slaves, a means that raised nearly £60,000 by 1775. According to one authority, "the aid to settlements . . . had no counterpart in any other English continental colony."

Settlement, however, was slow. Many township sites were poorly laid out. Only Orangeburg and Williamsburg survived the Revolutionary War. Still, the project was considered a success. The township plan attracted between ten and fifteen thousand settlers from Europe or Virginia to South Carolina, where they became permanent assets and helped to populate both the Midlands and the upcountry. LOUIS P. TOWLES

Meriwether, Robert L. *The Expansion of South Carolina, 1729–1765.* Kingsport, Tenn.: Southern Publishers, 1940.

Sherman, Richard P. *Robert Johnson: Proprietary & Royal Governor of South Carolina.* Columbia: University of South Carolina Press, 1966.

Traditional medicine. Traditional medicine, although viewed as unconventional and often in contradiction to established medical practices, was once commonplace in South Carolina. Since the founding of the colony in the late seventeenth century, South Carolina suffered from a lack of trained medical professionals, and until their widespread availability in the latter half of the twentieth century, traditional medicine met that need. Combining ingredients that could be purchased at the general store, patent medicines, and common herbs, traditional medicine was based on the common healing practices of the three cultures that resided in South Carolina: Native American, African, and European.

European colonists were impressed with the healing skills of Indians, whose use of local plants to treat sickness and injuries frequently brought admirable results. African slaves brought their own treatments to the New World and quickly added practices learned from the Indians. Slaves became so proficient in the use of traditional medicine that it became rare for a plantation not to have a midwife or doctor-woman to care for the sick. A drawback, at least for slaveowners, was the knowledge of natural poisons that slaves also possessed. The threat of poisoning constantly worried slaveowners and prompted the Commons House of Assembly in 1751 to pass a law condemning to death any slave who passed on knowledge of poison-making.

While Native American and African remedies may not have been much more effective than those of the Old World, European colonists were willing to try them when their own remedies failed. In the mid-1700s the *South-Carolina Gazette* published the respective cures for rattlesnake poison by two slaves, Caesar and Sampson. Legislators were so grateful for the cures that they purchased the slaves' freedom and gave each a pension. In some instances effective traditional treatments were adopted by medical professionals in both Europe and America, such as the use of Indian pinkroot by the Cherokees as a cure for worms.

Traditional medicine practices were distributed throughout the population orally or in print. newspapers often featured home cures for a variety of common ailments. By the latter half of the eighteenth century, books such as William Buchan's *Domestic Medicine* and John Wesley's *Primitive Physick* were sources of readily available treatments. Perhaps the most famous collection of traditional medicine remedies was Dr. Francis Porcher's *Resources of the Southern Fields and Forests.* Published in Charleston in 1863 at the request of the Confederate government, this book detailed the medicinal uses of more than six hundred species of southern plants and eased the effects of the Union blockade on medical supplies.

The practice of traditional medicine persisted in South Carolina for decades after the publication of Porcher's book. The use of traditional medicine waned, however, with the increasing availability of professional medical care in the twentieth century. VENNIE DEAS-MOORE

Morton, Julia F. *Folk Remedies of the Low Country.* Miami, Fla.: E. A. Seemann, 1974.

Moss, Kay K. *Southern Folk Medicine, 1750–1820.* Columbia: University of South Carolina Press, 1999.

Waring, Joseph I. *A History of Medicine in South Carolina.* Vol. 1, *1670–1825.* Columbia: South Carolina Medical Association, 1964.

Wood, Peter. "People's Medicine in the Early South." *Southern Exposure* 6, no. 2 (1978): 50–53.

Transportation. In its broadest sense, transportation pertains to the movement or conveyance of people and products, as well as the various techniques and means utilized in traversing distances. Much of transportation's story in South Carolina is about the movement of peoples and their different forms of contact with each other. Towns and cities, frequently with distinctive architectural features of a specific transportation component, emerged along various connecting routes. Often economic progress was determined by the availability of transportation. Over the centuries, transportation needs have regularly determined political decisions; and government participation, at all levels, has resulted in an enormous number of bills and acts pertaining to transportation. Building transportation arteries has had an impact on the environment, determined recreation access, and affected the state's fiscal success or failure. The melding of cultures to create today's South Carolina was certainly a result of transportation.

The origins of transportation networks in the area now called South Carolina began with the earliest settlers. Native Americans entering the area as early as 15,000 years ago probably utilized animal trails and river banks as they walked from place to place. Over time, marginal trails became significant connector paths for trade and communication. Landforms, waterways, soil, and climate determined not only transportation routes but also who and what passed over them. By 1150 C.E., the Mississippian Culture connected peoples throughout the Southeast via the transportation routes that had emerged. In South Carolina the most important tracks included the Occanoochee Trail, which followed the fall zone throughout the Southeast (in South Carolina from present-day Silver Bluff to Camden and Cheraw); the Cherokee Path (from Keowee, near Clemson, along the Saluda River to present-day Columbia, then along the Congaree/Santee Rivers to the coast); and a coastal trail paralleling the ocean but inland from the tidewater areas (roughly the route of U.S. Highway 17).

The earliest European contacts with native Carolinians were made by oceangoing ships seeking harbors for the establishment of colonies, forts, and trading posts or by explorers following Native American highways. In the age of sail, westerly winds encouraged sea routes from Europe to the southeastern coast of North America. In the sixteenth century coastal bases were established near Beaufort and perhaps near present-day Georgetown. The Spanish explorer Hernando De Soto (1540) followed the Occanoochee Trail, while the Spaniard Juan Pardo (1567) utilized parts of the Cherokee Path in his quest for silver. Although a lasting European settlement was not founded until 1670, the transportation routes created by the first Americans established the basic configuration of subsequent overland transportation networks, while the harbors and rivers explored by Europeans provided a foundation for coastal and international connections.

After the arrival of British settlers in 1670, the network of roads, bridges, ferries, and fords for overland travel expanded to allow people and commodities quick and easy mobility throughout the lowcountry. The importance of creating and maintaining an adequate transportation infrastructure is evidenced by "An Act for Making and Mending High-ways and Paths, and, for Cutting of Creeks and Water Cour[s]es" (1698). The Commons House created a self-perpetuating Commission of the High Roads in every parish that was primarily responsible for the maintenance of roads once they had been constructed by separate legislative act. Other commissions were created to keep rivers navigable and to widen channels. The riverine networks provided by the Salkehatchie, Edisto, Santee, and Pee Dee Rivers also added to the ease of colonial transportation.

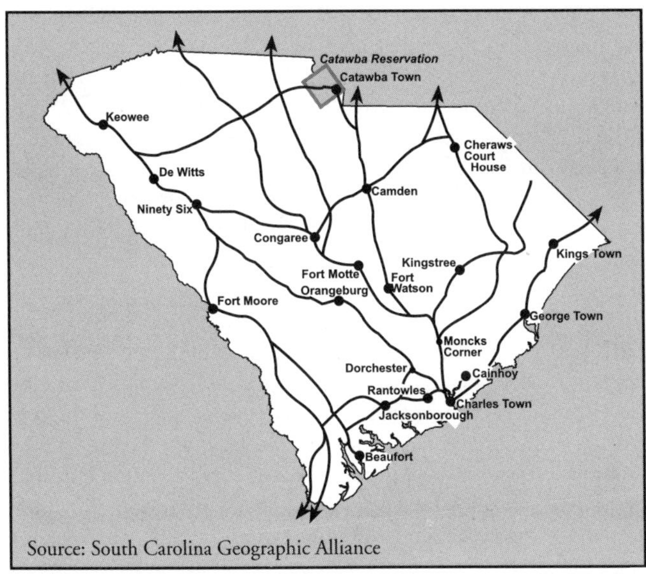

Source: South Carolina Geographic Alliance

Colonial roads, 1775

Extending one hundred miles or more from the fall line to the ocean, these rivers provided cheap, convenient transportation for bulk crops. Periaguas, canoes, dugouts, flatboats, and rafts brought furs, indigo, grain, and other commodities to coastal piers. There, the wooden vessels were often dismantled, and the goods were transferred to bay boats or to Bermuda sloops for their journey to Charleston, Georgetown, or Port Royal / Beaufort.

As the scale of exports rose, port facilities, such as Gadsden's Wharf in Charleston, and government facilities, such as the Exchange (built 1767–1771), were constructed. During this period as many as three hundred ships might be in Charleston harbor, ranging from oceangoing sailing vessels, to bay boats, to Native American canoes. Beaufort and Charleston developed significant ship-building industries that constructed vessels for coastal as well as international trade.

While many European groups immigrated to South Carolina, the Scots-Irish were particularly significant in developing South Carolina's transportation network. Many were Presbyterian and came primarily from the north of Ireland (Ulster) and the Scottish Lowlands. They followed the Great Philadelphia Wagon Road down the Shenandoah Valley of Virginia through backcountry North Carolina, entering upcountry South Carolina at one of the most significant river crossings: Nations Ford, near modern-day Rock Hill. By trading guns, metal pots, alcoholic beverages, and other supplies for furs, these settlers above the fall zone established themselves in virtually the same areas and along virtually the same transportation routes used by the Native Americans they displaced.

River transportation in the upcountry was of less significance because numerous rapids and swift-flowing currents made such travel hazardous. In place of river highways, Native American paths and fords were adapted to horse and wagon trails; horse-, oxen-, and mule-drawn wagons, carts, and carriages transferred commodities from the upcountry to the fall line, where they could then be transferred to river craft. Wainwrighting thus emerged as a significant craft in backwoods Carolina. Town location was usually associated with major transportation features. Crossroads, fords, and ferry sites frequently supported stores or taverns around which other dwellings would emerge. Ferries were considered especially important and were provided with special protection by the colonial legislature. Many ferries—such as Garner's near Columbia, Shockley near Anderson, and Givhans near Summerville—were granted monopolies by the legislature, protecting them from competition. These same acts, however, also set ferry standards and the prices that operators could charge for their services.

By 1776 a highway connected Boston with Savannah, the Great Wagon Road crossed the backcountry, and postal roads connected the coast with the interior, but virtually none of the roads were paved. With the exception of the coastal region, a view of South Carolina's transportation grid at the time of the American Revolution would show a virtual mirror image of Native American paths and trails. During the next fifty years, two developments resulted in a transportation revolution in South Carolina. The first was the invention of the cotton gin in 1793, which made the growing of short staple cotton not only feasible but also highly profitable. Upcountry farmers were quick to demand more effective transportation routes to the coast to transport their lucrative, but bulky, commodity. The second event was Alexander Hamilton's 1791 "Report on Manufactures," which proposed a network of internal improvements at government expense. Successful roads such as the National Road (authorized by Congress in 1806) and canals such as New York's Erie Canal (built 1817–1825) spurred similar efforts throughout the states, including South Carolina.

Although the Santee Canal (1785–1800) predated much of South Carolina's internal improvements boom, the twenty-one-mile link between the Santee and Cooper Rivers opened Charleston to upcountry traffic. The General Assembly authorized a Board of Internal Improvements (1818) and a Board of Public Works (1819); these agencies began the process of creating a more comprehensive transportation network for the state. Robert Mills, a member of the Board of Public Works, wrote *Inland Navigation & Internal Improvements* (a pamphlet for transportation improvement) in 1821. Mills and John Wilson, the civil and military engineer of South Carolina, produced the 1822 map of South Carolina, which was used to develop transportation links throughout the state. In 1824 the State Road, a corduroy road from Charleston to Columbia, and later extended to Saluda Gap above Greenville, was authorized. Other types of roads, such as toll roads, turnpikes, and causeways, also made their appearance. Another road built during this period was the Great Western Road & Mail Route, which followed the fall line between Columbia and Cheraw. Covered bridges, such as the Augusta-Hamburg Bridge built by Henry Schulz in 1814, facilitated travel greatly. Stagecoach lines began running regular routes between major towns, carrying passengers and mail.

Of much greater importance to South Carolina's cotton growers, however, was the construction of canals around rapids, waterfalls, and other river obstructions along the Catawba, Broad, Wateree, and Saluda Rivers. About twenty-five miles of canals—including the Columbia, Wateree, Catawba, and Landsford canals—opened virtually the entire upper part of the state to the shipping of bulk cargo by water. The introduction of steam boats on rivers below the fall zone further facilitated this trend. Shipbuilding continued to be a significant industry, as typified by the success of Charleston's Pregnall & Company in building 130-foot-long pilot boats and coastal schooners.

Despite these successes, Charleston's rank as a significant American port continued to decline in relation to northeastern and other southern ports. Some of the city's businessmen saw another transportation innovation as an answer to their problem. On December 19, 1827, the General Assembly chartered the South Carolina Canal and Rail Road Company (later the South Carolina Railroad

Company). William Aiken and Alfred Andrew Dexter proposed to build a rail connection from Charleston to Hamburg on the South Carolina side of the Savannah River across from Augusta. In October 1833 the 136-mile connection was completed. South Carolina cotton was now transported by rail to Charleston instead of by steamship to Savannah. As other lines in South Carolina were constructed, rail mileage grew to almost 1,000 miles by 1860. Charleston was connected to Savannah, Augusta, Charlotte, and Wilmington and from those points to the rest of the United States. An important feature of the railroad boom was the appearance of numerous new towns along the rail lines, each focused on the train station that was its commercial hub.

The Civil War was a catastrophe for South Carolina's transportation infrastructure and equipment. For four years the rail system was relentlessly used with minimal repair or maintenance; overland and riverine links suffered the same fate. Shipping, except for the few vessels that evaded the Union blockade, ceased; port and docking facilities deteriorated or were destroyed. William T. Sherman's march through the state in 1865 ruined bridges, railroad tracks, stations, warehouses, and cotton. With Confederate bonds and money worthless, the state under martial law, and Reconstruction preoccupied by a myriad of political and social issues, the transportation system could best be described as only marginally adequate.

Although railroad mileage increase by thirty-seven percent during Reconstruction, the rest of the system was only slowly improved. Typifying the malaise facing South Carolina's rail system was the demise of the South Carolina Railroad Company. After thirteen years of financial struggle, the company went into receivership. In 1881 it was purchased by a group of New York capitalists and reconstituted as the South Carolina Railway Company. Charleston's port reopened, but the dilapidated facilities and the loss of cotton markets overseas made recovery slow at best. Steamship lines connected Charleston with northern and European ports, but the glory days of antebellum Charleston were gone.

The latter decades of the nineteenth century witnessed the beginnings of a transportation transformation in South Carolina not unlike that of the 1820s. Road improvement, rail mergers, port facility upgrading, and the introduction of public transportation greatly facilitated the movement of people and products within and without the state. With virtually none of the state roads paved, M. C. Butler, state senator from Edgefield, called for constructing and maintaining all-weather roads, especially for farmers, in 1883. There were only about three hundred miles of paved roads in the state by 1925, but major United States highways (1, 17, 21, 25, 29, 76, and 78) traversed the state, and more than two hundred bridges had been constructed.

South Carolina's railroads were linked nationally when Southern Railway, the Atlantic Coast Line Railroad, and the Seaboard Railroad incorporated the most important rail links in the state into their systems. They dominated South Carolina's rail system until after World War II, although local lines continued to serve local needs and specific industries that were not on the main routes, such as textiles and timber. Charleston's status as a ship-building location was enhanced by its selection as a navy yard in 1901, but the port still lagged behind in cargo tonnage and facilities. A Port Utilities Commission was established in 1920, and the Charleston Port Survey of 1921, done by Edwin J. Clapp, issued fifty-five specific findings and recommendations for improving the port. This was the genesis of Charleston's real rebirth as a significant port.

Prior to the Depression of the 1930s, virtually all transportation matters were state-sponsored and state-funded. Since the 1930s, however, federal initiatives and projects have dramatically altered all aspects of transportation in South Carolina. Federally sponsored programs aided in the construction of roads, bridges, dams, port facilities, and airports. Maintenance or anticipatory actions, such as dredging or wetlands preservation, are often done under federal oversight. At the same time, federal guidelines and regulations increasingly changed the nature of transportation, and federal agencies became an integral part of how the transportation industries were monitored and maintained. Federal money usually required matching state funding, and transportation issues often meant political fights over how best to raise money and, often more importantly, over which county got the most benefits. Moreover, as the transportation grid expanded, secondary transportation industries, especially those affiliated with business and tourism—motels, service stations, and eating establishments—emerged as significant economic components. Transportation industries such as freight hauling and construction companies greatly benefited from the integration of South Carolina's diverse transportation components within the state and with the rest of the nation. Indeed, virtually all

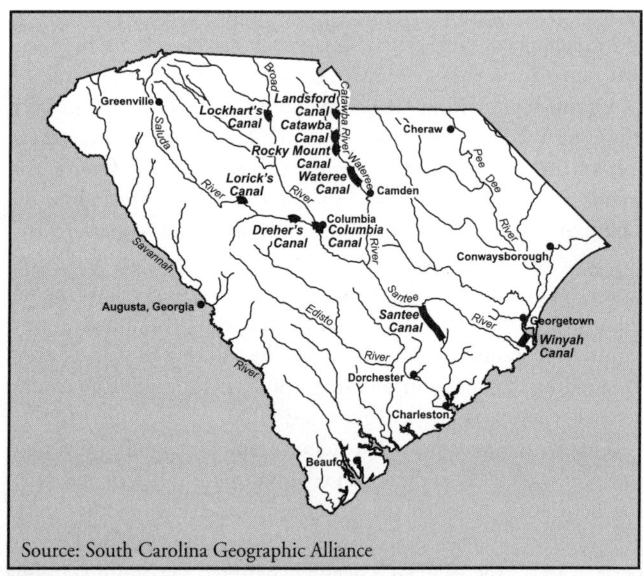

Antebellum canals, 1860

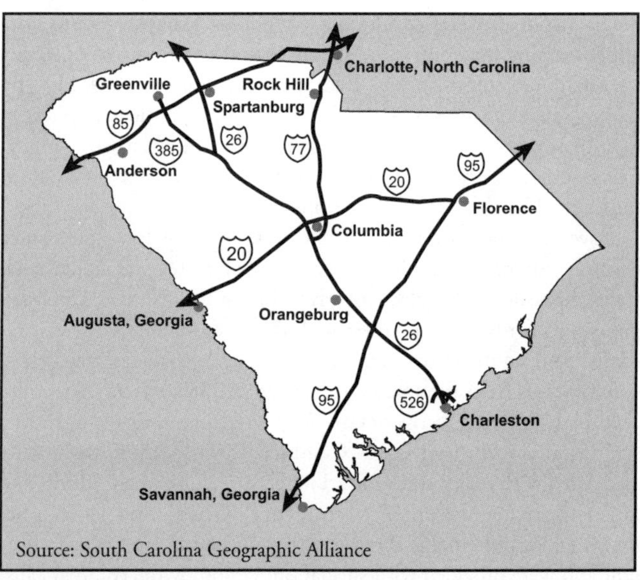

Interstate highway system, 2000

South Carolinians benefited from, and were challenged by, the transportation revolution that took place from the 1930s through the early twenty-first century.

Perhaps the most visible element in South Carolina's early twenty-first-century transportation network is its highway system. As of 2004, South Carolina had the fourth-largest state-maintained highway system in the United States, with more than 41,000 miles of state highway (sixty-five percent of the state's total road mileage), over 8,250 bridges, 35 rest areas and welcome centers, 500,000 traffic signs, and a multitude of driveways, ditches, and guardrails managed and maintained by the South Carolina Department of Transportation. While federal funding provided eighty percent of the original cost of building the roads, all maintenance, as well as construction of required safety structures, is the state's responsibility.

Water transportation has also witnessed a transformation. Where once rivers flowed freely, there are now more than 50,000 dams throughout the state, including 34 federally regulated dams and more than 2,250 state-regulated dams. River transportation is more for recreational purposes than for economic reasons, although the service industries for recreation are thriving. Ocean transportation is still funneled primarily through Charleston. Robert M. Figg, Jr.'s 1941 report calling for State Ports Authority (SPA) resulted in legislation creating the South Carolina State Ports Authority in 1942. The SPA spent millions on improving and upgrading the port's facilities. The Atlantic Intracoastal Waterway was established by four federal bills during the 1930s and is the water highway from Maine to the Florida Keys.

The latest transportation revolution witnessed the decline of one major transportation link and the creation of a new one. In 1924 South Carolina rail mileage was about 3,800 miles, most of which was externally owned and operated. Despite rail's pivotal role in winning World War II and the introduction of diesel locomotives to improve rail transportation, highways became the preferred mode of travel for Americans by midcentury. Except for two Amtrak train routes through the state, passenger traffic on trains has almost disappeared. By 2000 track mileage had dwindled to less than 2,600 miles. Freight traffic remained an important segment of rail profitability, and the introduction of container cargo carriers assisted rail's continued significance to the state.

The advent of air transportation led to the establishment of the South Carolina Aeronautics Commission in 1935. Pioneers such as Paul R. Redfern, Caroline Hembel, and Jimmie L. Hamilton helped to popularize aviation in the state, which eventually came to be the home of six commercial airports and fifty-four general aviation airports. Charleston International is the busiest passenger airport, and Columbia Metropolitan Airport is the busiest cargo airport. All in all, South Carolina is an integral part of a global transportation network that connects South Carolinians to the world. WILLIAM S. BROCKINGTON, JR.

Easterby, J. H., ed. *Transportation in the Ante-Bellum Period.* Columbia: Historical Commission of South Carolina, 1951.

Ford, Ralph Watson. "The Changing Geographic Pattern of South Carolina's Railroad System, 1860–1902." Master's thesis, University of South Carolina, 1986.

Kovacik, Charles F., and John J. Winberry. *South Carolina: The Making of a Landscape.* 1987. Reprint, Columbia: University of South Carolina Press, 1989.

Moore, John Hammond. *The South Carolina Highway Department, 1917–1987.* Columbia: University of South Carolina Press, 1987.

South Carolina State Ports Authority. *History of the South Carolina State Ports Authority.* Charleston: South Carolina State Ports Authority, 1991.

Travelers Rest (Greenville County; 2000 pop. 4,099). The modern city developed in northern Greenville County near the intersection of the Buncombe Road and the road to Jones Gap. After the completion of the new wagon road to Asheville and Knoxville in 1794, drovers crowded the Buncombe Road in the fall, camping and staying overnight at local farmhouses and taverns. The Travelers Rest post office was established in 1808 to serve the largely farming community, and the mail was delivered by stage, which ran from Asheville, North Carolina, to Greenville. Churches nearby included Reedy River Baptist Church (ca. 1778), an early Separate Baptist congregation, and Jackson Grove Methodist Church (1832), the latter created at the site of a camp meeting. Local one-room schools were operated in the area, and in 1883 the Travelers Rest Academy (later High School) opened.

In 1888 the Carolina, Knoxville, and Western Railway began construction of a line along the Reedy River from Greenville north to River Falls. The train was commonly known as the "Swamp Rabbit." Summer visitors from the lowcountry boarded at the spacious home of Robert W. Anderson, later known as Spring Park Inn. A rivalry developed between residents in the lower and upper sections of Travelers Rest over access to the rail line, and two railroad stations were constructed. After the town was incorporated by the legislature in 1891, the residents of the upper section secured incorporation as the town of Athens in 1893. In 1900, when Athens ceased to function as a town, it had a population of 107, just one more person than inhabited Travelers Rest.

Churches were established as the village grew, including Travelers Rest Methodist Church in 1893 and First Baptist Church in 1913. Trinity Presbyterian Church was established in 1933 in Renfrew. The first major industry came in 1929, when Brandon Mills began production at Renfrew Bleachery. In 1946 it became a part of Abney Mills. After changing hands several times, it closed in 1988. After World War II other industries located in Travelers Rest, including the Zonolite Division of W. R. Grace (1946), two garment plants, Curtron Curtains, and two embroidery plants: EMB-TEX and Kemco. By 1960 the population of Travelers Rest had risen to 1,973. An international business, Ernst Diamond, which produces grinding wheels, opened in 1982. In the final decades of the twentieth century, the town's population expanded as it increasingly became a bedroom community within the flourishing Greenville-Spartanburg metropolitan area. A. V. HUFF, JR.

Goodlett, Mildred W. *Travelers Rest at Mountain's Foot; The History of Travelers Rest.* N.p., 1966.

Huff, Archie Vernon, Jr. *Greenville: The History of the City and County in the South Carolina Piedmont.* Columbia: University of South Carolina Press, 1995.

Travis, William Barret (1809–1836). Soldier. Travis was born on August 9, 1809, in Edgefield District, the son of Mark Travis and Jemima Stallworth. In 1818 the family migrated to Conecuh County, Alabama. Travis moved to nearby Claiborne while still in his teens, teaching school and studying law under Judge James Dellett. Seeking respectability, Travis became a Mason, was commissioned in the local militia, and published a small newspaper, the Claiborne *Herald.* On October 26, 1828, he married Rosanna Cato. Perennially in debt, Travis abandoned his pregnant wife and infant son early in 1831 and fled to Texas.

Travis set up a law practice in Anahuac, Texas, in 1831 and began a life of drinking, gambling, and womanizing, all of which he faithfully recorded in his diary. He was heavily involved in resistance to

Mexican rule, playing a major role in the "Anahuac War" of 1832 and the capture of the Anahuac garrison in January 1835. When the Texas revolution broke out in September 1835, Travis was commissioned a major of artillery, and he became a lieutenant colonel of cavalry on December 24.

In January 1836 Governor Henry Smith ordered Travis to reinforce Lieutenant Colonel James C. Neill's garrison at San Antonio de Béxer. Travis and his detachment of thirty men arrived about February 2, and shortly thereafter Travis was placed in command when Neill left on furlough because of sickness in his family. This brought Travis into conflict with Colonel James Bowie, commander of the volunteers, who technically outranked Travis. The issue was resolved when the two agreed on a joint command, and it became moot when Bowie fell ill. Travis moved the garrison into the Alamo on February 23, just ahead of Santa Anna's army. On the morning of March 6, 1836, Travis was killed by a bullet to the head as the Mexican army began its final assault. JACK ALLEN MEYER

Groneman, Bill. *Alamo Defenders: A Genealogy, the People and Their Words.* Austin, Tex.: Eakin, 1990.

Long, Jeff. *Duel of Eagles: The Mexican and U.S. Fight for the Alamo.* New York: Morrow, 1990.

McDonald, Archie P. *Travis.* Austin, Tex.: Jenkins, 1976.

Roberts, Randy, and James S. Olson. *A Line in the Sand: The Alamo in Blood and Memory.* New York: Free Press, 2001.

Treaty of Augusta (1763). At the end of the French and Indian War, John Stuart, the superintendent of Indian affairs in South Carolina, negotiated this critical treaty at an Anglo-Indian conference held in Augusta, Georgia, in November 1763. The meeting was to inform the southeastern Indian tribes about the royal Proclamation Line of 1763 and to end permanently wars between the southern tribes and the English colonies. The dividing line was supposed to keep English colonists east of the Appalachian Mountains and reserve the land to the west for native peoples.

Stuart, along with governors from the southern colonies, met in Augusta with nearly one thousand native peoples from the Cherokee, Creek, Catawba, Chickasaw, and Choctaw Nations. The governors preferred to meet in Charleston, but the Creek Indians pressed for Augusta, which they considered their town as much as did the English. As a result of the treaty, South Carolina recognized the eastern boundary of the Cherokees. The agreement also established a 225-square-mile reservation for the Catawbas in present-day York County.

Over the next few years, various tribes aligned with South Carolina participated in defining the line as it passed through their lands. In 1766 the Cherokees hammered out the location of the dividing line in North Carolina and their leader, Ustenaka, laid down a string of beads across the proposed border. In 1768 Cherokee and South Carolina officials signed the Treaty of Hard Labor Creek, which demarcated a fifty-foot-wide line in South Carolina marked on nearby trees. The line in South Carolina ran from the Savannah River to White Oak Mountain on the North Carolina border. Most of present-day Anderson, Pickens, Greenville, and Oconee Counties lay to the west of the line and were part of Indian territory.

The Treaty of Augusta was one of many initiatives used by British authorities in their efforts to gain complete control over Indian affairs. The treaty failed, however, to keep white settlers from encroaching on Indian lands. With the onset of the Revolutionary War, British officials no longer mediated between the two sides, and conflict again broke out between the Cherokees and South Carolina by 1776. MICHAEL P. MORRIS

Cashin, Edward J. *The Story of Augusta.* Augusta, Ga.: Richmond County Board of Education, 1980.

Hatley, M. Thomas. *The Dividing Paths: Cherokees and South Carolinians through the Era of the Revolution.* New York: Oxford University Press, 1993.

Merrell, James H. *The Indians' New World: Catawbas and Their Neighbors from European Contact through the Era of Removal.* Chapel Hill: University of North Carolina Press, 1989.

Trenholm, George Alfred (1807–1876). Merchant, financier. Trenholm was born on February 25, 1807, in Charleston, the son of William and Irene Trenholm. His father was a merchant, and his mother was the daughter of the Comte de Greffin, a French landowner on the island of San Domingue (now Haiti). Following the death of his father, a teenaged George Trenholm left school and went to work for John Fraser & Company, a well-established and respected Charleston firm that specialized in trading Sea Island cotton. Displaying a remarkable talent for business, Trenholm advanced rapidly, becoming a partner in Fraser & Company as well as a prominent business leader in the city. By the early 1850s Trenholm was the senior partner in the firm, which had become the leading commercial house in Charleston and one of the most prominent in the entire South, with branches in New York (Trenholm Brothers) and Liverpool, England (Fraser, Trenholm, & Company). The success of the firm made Trenholm an immensely rich and influential businessman whose diversified interests included warehouses, ships, wharves, hotels, plantations, and slaves. He represented Charleston in the General Assembly four times during the 1850s and 1860s (1852–1855, 1860–1863). In 1828 he married Anna Lee Holmes. They had thirteen children.

When the Civil War began, Trenholm placed the ample financial and transportation resources of Fraser & Company at the disposal of the Confederate government. The firm's Liverpool branch became the overseas depository for the Confederate treasury, from which it advanced credit to purchasing agents and arranged for the payment and shipment of vital supplies to the South. Early in the war, when most Southern leaders favored withholding cotton from the market in the belief that it would force Britain to recognize southern independence, Trenholm urged Confederate leaders to ship as much cotton as possible in exchange for weapons, ammunition, and other war materials. Trenholm's shipping interests played a vital role in running the Union naval blockade of the Southern coast, an activity that earned Trenholm justifiable praise for his patriotism as well as substantial profits for his company.

Throughout the first years of the war, Trenholm was a valued adviser to the Confederate secretary of the treasury, Christopher Memminger, a fellow Charlestonian and close friend. When Memminger resigned in June 1864, President Jefferson Davis appointed Trenholm to the post. As secretary, Trenholm urged that the Confederate government strengthen its financial position through direct taxation, reducing the supply of paper currency in circulation, and purchasing its own line of blockade-runners rather than continuing to rely on private shippers. Despite receiving Davis's endorsement, Trenholm's recommendations were rejected by the Confederate Congress. He continued in his position, however, doing what he could to counter the rapidly deteriorating state of Confederate finance. When Davis and his cabinet fled Richmond in April 1865, Trenholm remained in the city until finally resigning his position on April 27.

Shortly after his resignation, Trenholm was imprisoned by federal authorities for several months before being paroled by President

Andrew Johnson in October 1865. Pardoned the following year, Trenholm set about to rebuild his business empire. Although forced to declare bankruptcy in 1867, he soon thereafter regained a large measure of his former wealth through the creation of a new cotton brokerage firm, George A. Trenholm & Son, and timely investments in the state's postwar phosphate mining boom. In 1874 he was returned to the General Assembly, one of the few Democrats elected that year. He died in Charleston on December 9, 1876. TOM DOWNEY

Loy, Wesley. "10 Rumford Place: Doing Confederate Business in Liverpool." *South Carolina Historical Magazine* 98 (October 1997): 349–74.

Nepveux, Ethel Trenholm Seabrook. *George Alfred Trenholm and the Company That Went to War.* Charleston, S.C., 1973.

Todd, Richard Cecil. *Confederate Finance.* Athens: University of Georgia Press, 1954.

Wise, Stephen R. *Lifeline of the Confederacy: Blockade Running during the Civil War.* Columbia: University of South Carolina Press, 1988.

Trescot, William Henry (1822–1898). Writer, diplomat, historian. Trescot was born on November 10, 1822, in Charleston, the son of Henry Trescot and Sarah McCrady. Trescot studied at the College of Charleston, graduating in 1841, and then pursued legal studies with Edward McCrady and Mitchell King. He was admitted to the bar in 1843. Through his 1848 marriage to Eliza Natalie Cuthbert, he assumed the proprietorship of Barnwell Island, a self-sustaining Sea Island cotton plantation bordering the Broad River in Beaufort District. His marriage produced seven children.

An astute and productive writer, Trescot produced a series of addresses, essays, and pamphlets to define the culture of the planter class, defend its social hegemony, and put forth an essentially conservative case for southern nationalism. As a result, he developed a distinctive rationale for secession, extended through a broad campaign of correspondence with younger leaders of the landed interest from Virginia to the Gulf of Mexico. With the collapse of the first secession movement in 1852, he turned to writing essays on the diplomatic history of the Revolution and early republic, along with published critiques of foreign policy issues of the day. These writings brought him a posting to the U.S. embassy in London in 1852 and appointment as assistant secretary of state in 1860 under President James Buchanan.

Still loyal to the secession cause, by the end of 1860 Trescot found himself in a crucially informed position in the U.S. government at the very moment when South Carolina was moving against it and the embryonic Confederacy was beginning to arm. Corresponding with the conservative wing of the secession movement, Trescot effectively kept them apprised of secret military action or inactivity on the part of the central government and seems materially to have assisted in the transfer of arms to situations that would fall outside Union control.

Trescot's Civil War career was a quiet one. He served on the state Executive Council, in the General Assembly (1862–1866), and on the staff of General Roswell Ripley. Trescot drew on his special knowledge of the state's race laws to become involved in cases affecting the status of captured troops from the Union's black regiments. And from first blood forth, he was called upon to eulogize the Confederate dead. He wrote eloquent, widely published memorials in one form or another for the rest of his life. Elaborate, affectionate, but clear-eyed portraits of plantation culture, these justifications of the social and moral relations of the Old South are his most important legacy.

With the end of the war, Trescot allied himself with the old "Union and Cooperation" forces of the upcountry. He served as agent for Governors Benjamin Perry and James Orr as a lobbyist in Washington, particularly for the recovery of confiscated land. Both there and in the pages of the press, Trescot argued for a cooperative approach to reordering the economic and social relations of the South, a system based on race separation and property privilege. With the implementation of congressional Reconstruction in South Carolina in 1868, such questions become moot, and Trescot's remaining career was devoted to a series of diplomatic missions, from China to Chile to Mexico. In 1889 Trescot was especially instrumental in the formation of the Pan American Union. While he lived most of his last years in Washington, he maintained the family's old summer residence in Pendleton, where he died on May 4, 1898. He was buried in the cemetery of St. Paul's Episcopal Church, Pendleton. R. NICHOLAS OLSBERG

Betts, Rose Miller. "William Henry Trescot." Master's thesis, University of South Carolina, 1929.

Farley, M. Foster, ed. "Three Letters of William Henry Trescot to Howell Cobb, 1861." *South Carolina Historical Magazine* 68 (January 1967): 22–30.

Hunt, Gaillard. "Narrative and Letter of William Henry Trescot, Concerning the Negotiations between South Carolina and President Buchanan in December 1860." *American Historical Review* 13 (April 1908): 528–56.

Moltke-Hansen, David. "A Beaufort Planter's Rhetorical World: The Contexts and Contents of William Henry Trescot's Orations." *Proceedings of the South Carolina Historical Association* (1981): 120–32.

Olsberg, R. Nicolas. "A Government of Class and Race: William Henry Trescot and the South Carolina Chivalry, 1860–1865." Doctoral diss., University of South Carolina, 1972.

———. "William Henry Trescot: The Crisis of 1860." Master's thesis, University of South Carolina, 1967.

Trott, Nicholas (1663–1740). Jurist, scholar. Trott was born in London on January 19, 1663. His father, Samuel Trott, was a London merchant, but his mother's name is unknown. Members of the family were closely involved with the Somers Island Company, the proprietors of Bermuda. His uncle, also named Nicholas and with whom he has sometimes been confused, was a governor of the Bahamas notorious for his dealings with pirates. Through marriage, this other Nicholas acquired a share in the Carolina proprietorship. Trott was educated at Merchant Taylors School in London and admitted to Inner Temple in 1695.

Trott arrived in South Carolina in 1699 with appointments as attorney general and naval officer after earlier service as attorney general of Bermuda, where he had married Jane Willis on September 23, 1694. In 1703 he became chief justice. The earliest South Carolina official to have been trained at the Inns of Court, Trott was both a scholar and a political power whose offices at various times also included proprietor's deputy on council, secretary and register of the province, elected member of the Lower House of Assembly, and judge of vice admiralty. A contentious man, he reached the height of his power in 1714 when, during a visit to London, the proprietors gave him a veto over the colony's laws and required his presence for a quorum of council. Colonial protests quickly ended this extraordinary authority given to a man who was never governor, but he and William Rhett, whose son had married Trott's daughter Mary, continued to monopolize many of the South Carolina government offices until the revolution against proprietary government in 1719. Both men had strong ties with Richard Shelton, the long-term secretary to the proprietary board in London.

Part of Trott's political difficulties arose from his strong support of an established Anglican church and the exclusion of dissenters from office. Trott began a codification of South Carolina law shortly after he became chief justice, but his first legal publication was a compilation of colonial laws relating to religion for the Society for the Propagation of the Gospel in 1721. His South Carolina code did not see print until 1736, when it became the first book printed in South Carolina. He published (at Oxford) a work on the Psalms in 1719 and was at work on a translation of the Hebrew text of the New Testament at the time of his death. Both Oxford University and the University of Aberdeen granted him doctorates for his publications. As vice admiralty judge, he presided over the trial of the pirate Stede Bonnet. The published proceedings of this trial became a foundation document of the literature on piracy.

After the death of his first wife, Trott married Sarah Cooke, the widow of his political ally William Rhett, on March 4, 1728. Trott died in Charleston on January 21, 1740, and was buried in St. Philip's Churchyard. CHARLES H. LESSER

Hogue, L. Lynn. "Nicholas Trott: Man of Law and Letters." *South Carolina Historical Magazine* 76 (January 1975): 25–34.

Lesser, Charles H. *South Carolina Begins: The Records of a Proprietary Colony, 1663–1721.* Columbia: South Carolina Department of Archives and History, 1995.

Truck farming. Truck farming is the production of annual fruit and vegetable crops to be sold fresh. Truck farming began after the Civil War as cities grew and the spread of railroads made transport faster and more efficient. In 1868 William Geraty and Frank Towles began farming on Yonges and Wadmalaw Islands, where the soil and long growing season were ideal for truck crops. In 1889 farmers in Charleston, Colleton, Beaufort, Horry, and Berkeley Counties planted 2,103 acres of produce for market. By 1900 the acreage had more than doubled, to 4,928 acres. They grew cabbages, Irish potatoes, asparagus, turnips, string beans, lettuce, and cabbage plants. The area around Meggett in Charleston County became the world leader in the production of cabbages and potatoes.

Truck farming helped fill an agricultural niche in the lowcountry as the commercial production of rice ended. A 1907 report on agriculture in South Carolina described the Sea Islands as crisscrossed with rail lines, rail spurs, packing sheds, and icehouses to service the industry: "at every mile, and in some instances at a less distance, are station platforms filled with barrels, crates and baskets of vegetables for shipping." On Yonges Island, in an area known as Barrelville, barrels were made to supply the farmers' demands. Several hundred rail cars a day shipped out of Meggett, headed for eastern and western markets.

While it was a boon to the Sea Islands, truck farming was not yet a major factor in South Carolina agriculture. The 1920s and 1930s were disastrous for South Carolina agriculture as a whole. In 1932, at the urging of the Agricultural Society of South Carolina, Clemson College opened the South Carolina Truck Experiment Station (renamed the Coastal Research and Education Center in the mid-1980s) to solve problems affecting truck crops. By then some large truck farmers farmed from a distance, not living on the farms and using African Americans from South Carolina and Florida as laborers.

By the late 1970s truck farming had come into its own, and as the twenty-first century dawned, truck crops were an important contributor to South Carolina agriculture, valued at over $60 million. While many Sea Islands may appear to be wilderness from the highway, on the back roads the cotton and rice fields have given way to fields of tomatoes, melons, and other truck crops, which are harvested by migrant and resident Mexican labor. KAREN NICKLESS

Murray, Chalmers S. *This Our Land: The Story of the Agricultural Society of South Carolina.* Charleston, S.C.: Carolina Art Association, 1949.

South Carolina. Department of Agriculture. *Handbook of South Carolina: Resources, Institutions and Industries of the State.* Columbia, S.C.: State Company, 1907.

Tuberculosis. In any historic survey of tuberculosis (TB) in the South, two things stand out. First, until about the 1920s it was one of the region's leading causes of death, mostly brought on by slow destruction of the lungs. Second, it killed—and was allowed to kill—African Americans three times more often than whites. In 1900 in South Carolina it claimed the lives of 219 blacks per every 100,000 of population, while the white rate was just above 70.

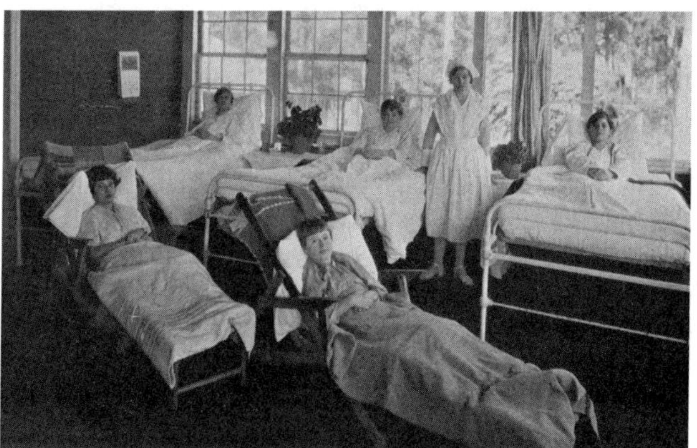

The children's cottage at Ridgewood, the state's tuberculosis facility. Courtesy, Richland Tuberculosis Board of Directors, 2005

While its immediate cause was the germ *Mycobacterium tuberculosis,* contributing factors were multiple and generally the same for both races, though all affected blacks much more severely. Malnutrition was one, for the long absence of key vitamins lessened the body's ability to resist infection. But infection's greatest spur was overcrowding: in close quarters one active case could infect many. The culprit, epidemiologists would discover, was the dried remains of bacteria-laden droplets called "droplet nuclei." Sprayed into the air as a fine mist by cough or sneeze, droplet nuclei could hang in the air for long periods—even after the infected source had departed—and were small enough to be inhaled into terminal air passages where TB could begin. The one predisposing cause unique to blacks was their lack of historic experience with TB. Exposed to it on first encountering whites, usually in New World slave societies, blacks as late as the twentieth century had not had time to acquire whites' immunity level.

A final factor, bearing on both races but putting blacks at special disadvantage during segregation, was insufficient medical care and treatment. Until chemotherapy emerged in the late 1940s, the one fairly sure—if slow—cure for TB was the sanatorium, which offered not medicine but bed rest on open-air porches. Blacks, however, had no access to them until the 1920s, many years after white care began; and even when sanatoriums were built for blacks, they were woefully inadequate. South Carolina was typical: the white facility opened in 1916; blacks had none until 1921, and they had to raise much of its funding themselves. Moreover, the state's blacks had only a fraction of needed beds. The standard was one for every TB death. In 1934, 844 blacks died, but their sanatorium accommodated only 148 patients. The hospital for whites met the standard.

Although TB continued to be a problem for blacks until the 1960s, increased federal funding after 1945 for added beds and TB control (which searched out victims and got them into treatment) helped blacks disproportionately. Then in the 1950s improved chemotherapy offered a sure and speedy cure without hospitalization. Once black pressure and civil rights law ended medical segregation in the 1960s, blacks gained equal access to such therapy. By 1970 all those factors, plus rising income, finally brought blacks' TB under control. In 1945 their mortality in South Carolina was 56 cases per 100,000; twenty years later it was just over 6. Though that was still three times the rate for whites, in the interval blacks' progress had slightly surpassed whites', and their long struggle against TB was over. ED BEARDSLEY

Beardsley, Edward H. *A History of Neglect: Health Care for Blacks and Mill Workers in the Twentieth-Century South.* Knoxville: University of Tennessee Press, 1987.

Lerner, Gerda. "Early Community Work of Black Club Women." *Journal of Negro History* 59 (April 1974): 158–67.

Scheele, Leonard A. "The Health Status and Health Education of Negroes in the United States." *Journal of Negro Education* 18 (summer 1949): 200–208.

Wyngaardan, James, Lloyd Smith, and J. Claude Bennett, eds. *Cecil Textbook of Medicine.* 19th ed. Philadelphia: W. B. Saunders, 1992.

Tucker, Cornelia Dabney (1881–1970). Political activist. Tucker was born on October 15, 1881, in Charlotte, North Carolina, the daughter of Harvey Mayfield Ramseur and Mary Cosby Badham. She graduated at the age of sixteen from Synodical Presbyterian College in Tennessee. The following year she moved to Charleston to teach French. In 1899 she married the businessman Robert Pinckney Tucker. The couple had five children. After her husband's death in 1920 and financial setbacks, she rented out her Charleston home and moved to Flat Rock, North Carolina. She returned to Charleston six years later and began working in an antique shop.

Although she had shown no previous interest in politics, Tucker suddenly began working to oppose New Deal policies. President Franklin Roosevelt's plan to expand the U.S. Supreme Court led Tucker to launch a personal letter-writing and petition-passing campaign. She set up a small Charleston women's organization called the Supreme Court Security League, which gathered petition signatures and sent copies to all U.S. senators in 1937. She joined the South Carolina Republican Party and was named chair of publicity, a position for which she was well suited. An attractive woman from a socially prominent family, she succeeded in getting her picture and story in newspapers at a time when women in her position usually avoided public attention.

In 1940 South Carolina was the only state that did not provide a single ballot with the names of candidates of both parties. Instead, voters at the polling place had to state publicly which party's ballot they wanted and could not split their ticket. Tucker believed that this procedure hurt the Republican Party, and she began a vigorous public campaign to get it changed. She spoke uninvited to the South Carolina General Assembly on the issue, reading her speech while the Speaker and the sergeant of arms tried to remove her. She regularly picketed the State House wearing a banner across her chest demanding the secret ballot. Finally, in 1951 her campaign was successful, after she got the support of women's groups and the S.C. Chamber of Commerce.

Tucker continued to push her conservative views and remained politically active well into her seventies. She worked for relief for China and against the right of workers to strike during wartime. In 1954 and 1955 she vigorously opposed the Supreme Court's desegregation decision, which she charged was a Communist plot, and worked to change the procedure for appointing Supreme Court justices. Continuing her opposition to the civil rights movement, Tucker backed legislation to deny state employees the right to join the National Association for the Advancement of Colored People. She lobbied for a requirement that all state high school students successfully complete courses in American government and the free enterprise system before graduation. She supported the John Birch Society and opposed the National Council of Churches, which she believed was a front for Communist activities. She also denounced the 1962 Supreme Court decision against prayer in public schools. Tucker's picture and her letters to the editor were regular features of South Carolina newspapers. Her personally typed letters and telegrams appeared frequently on the desks of state and national political leaders. In the last two years of her life, she moved to Atlanta to be with her son. She died in Atlanta on October 28, 1970. ALICE H. HENDERSON

Kittel, Mary Radham. *The First Republican Southern Belle.* Columbia, S.C.: R. L. Bryan, 1969.

Workman, William D. "Cornelia Dabney Tucker." *South Carolina Magazine* 11 (May 1948): 5, 17.

Tugaloo River. The Tugaloo River is formed by the Chattooga and Tallulah Rivers near the juncture of Georgia, North Carolina, and South Carolina. It flows along the Georgia border through Oconee and Anderson Counties, accepting drainage from the Chauga River and other smaller streams before joining the Seneca River to form the Savannah River. Power plants erected along the Tugaloo River beginning in the 1910s formed Lake Yonah and Lake Tugaloo.

Hartwell Dam, completed in 1963 at the juncture of the Seneca, Tugaloo, and Savannah Rivers, caused the waters in the Savannah River basin upstream to swell and form Lake Hartwell. The lake covers nearly 56,000 acres and has 962 miles of shoreline that stretch 49 miles up the Tugaloo River and 45 miles up the Seneca River.

The name "Tugaloo" is likely of Native American origin, probably meaning "two." The first settlements along the Tugaloo River were Cherokee. After the Revolutionary War, white settlers received land grants along the river in modern Oconee County. The early white settlers built several small blockhouses or forts along the Tugaloo River, including Fort Madison. SUSAN GIAIMO HIOTT

Oconee County Historical Society. *Historic Sites of Oconee County, S.C.* 2d ed. N.p.: Oconee County Historical Society, 1991.

Tukey, Richard Ellery (1918–1979). Civic leader. Richard "Dick" Tukey was a crucial figure in the post–World War II economic development of the South Carolina Piedmont, especially Spartanburg County. As executive vice president of the Spartanburg Chamber of Commerce, Tukey helped to transform the region's economy by international recruitment, by expansion away from textiles, and by taking a decidedly global outlook on economic development.

Tukey was born on July 9, 1918, in Brooklyn, New York, and raised in White Plains. After graduating cum laude from Maine's Bowdoin College, Tukey thought about becoming a journalist, working as a reporter for the International News service in New York between 1940 and 1941. During World War II, Tukey served as an army staff specialist at Fort Benning, Georgia. After his release from the army in 1946, Tukey stayed in Georgia to become the director of the Columbus Chamber of Commerce. Tukey returned to New York in 1948, where he worked as an executive director of the Cigar Institute of America and a vice president of operations for the Ettinger Company, a New York City public relations firm. In 1954 he married Virginia Walker Ligon. The couple had two sons.

In May 1951 Tukey became the executive vice president of the Spartanburg Chamber of Commerce, a position he held until his death. He rapidly became one of Spartanburg's leading economic decision makers. Expansive, persistent, and demanding, Tukey's style and personality made him an effective salesman for Spartanburg. Depending on the situation, he could use either gentle persuasion or stern enforcement to unite the community behind the ruling boosters' vision and recruitment efforts.

During the 1960s and 1970s Tukey's vision of Spartanburg's and South Carolina's economic future became increasingly global. International economic developments made foreign investment in the United States increasingly profitable. From early on, Tukey understood the potential of luring foreign direct investments to Spartanburg. He started to direct a growing portion of his time to recruiting foreign companies. The first big success was the decision by the German chemical company Hoechst to build a large factory in northern Spartanburg County in 1965.

Tukey's and Spartanburg's efforts soon gained attention throughout South Carolina. During their visit to Basel, Switzerland, to attend an International Textile Machinery Show in 1967, Tukey shared his "reverse investment" plan with South Carolina's then lieutenant governor, John C. West. West later adopted the key elements of Tukey's international recruitment plan in his run for governor of South Carolina in 1970. Instead of using the South's traditional sales pitch of cheap and docile labor, Tukey emphasized Spartanburg's cooperative business environment, effective transportation network, and well-trained workforce. He was largely successful in his attempts to modernize and delocalize the South Carolina Piedmont's business culture, making it more amenable for post–World War II economic realities. One of Tukey's favorite slogans was "We don't sell South Carolina's magnolias and moonlight. We sell economic justification."

By the time of Tukey's death, Spartanburg and the South Carolina Piedmont had become an international success story of economic globalization. By the late 1970s approximately thirty percent of South Carolina's industrial investment capital came from abroad. Tukey died from cancer in July 25, 1979, and was buried at Greenlawn Memorial Gardens in Spartanburg. MARKO MAUNULA

"Richard Tukey Mourned Here." *Spartanburg Journal,* July 26, 1979, p. A1.

Tunley, Roul. "In Spartanburg, the Accent Is on Business." *South Carolina Magazine* 37, no. 3 (1973): 10–13.

Tuomey, Michael (1805–1857). Geologist. Tuomey was born in county Cork, Ireland, on September 29, 1805, the son of Thomas Tuomey and Nora Foley. In his early twenties Tuomey joined a Friends teaching school in Yorkshire, England. He soon immigrated to the United States, arriving in New York in 1830. Circumstances allowed Tuomey to study in Troy, New York, and in 1835 he received a bachelor of natural science degree from the prestigious Rensselaer School (now Rensselaer Polytechnic Institute). He married Sarah Handy in 1838, and the couple had two daughters. In 1841 Tuomey moved to Petersburg, Virginia, where the agricultural reformer Edmund Ruffin assisted him in establishing a private school. Tuomey began a long-standing correspondence with Dr. Lewis R. Gibbes of the College of Charleston, who introduced Tuomey to the scientific activities of the "cultivators of science" in South Carolina, including Francis S. Holmes, Edmund Ravenel, Robert W. Gibbes, and John P. Barratt.

Acting on a recommendation by Ruffin, Governor James H. Hammond appointed Tuomey "State Geological Surveyor" in 1844 to succeed Ruffin in completing an agricultural survey of South Carolina. Tuomey redirected the emphasis of the survey from an agricultural interest to that of geology, with a focus on economically valuable mineral deposits. His *Report on the Geological and Agricultural Survey of the State of South Carolina* (1844) provided an overview of the rocks and minerals in the state with a discussion of soils and contributed appendixes on agriculture and marl deposits. The report stimulated interest in the mineral deposits of the state and provided the first detailed scientific descriptions of potential economic mineral resources in South Carolina.

The South Carolina legislature provided support in 1845 to continue the survey for two additional years. Tuomey undertook a wide-ranging investigation of the state, again with an emphasis on geology with obligatory attention to agriculture, soils, and marl deposits. His work represented the first systematic geological survey of the state, but legislative discontent with requested extensions to complete the survey forced an early end to Tuomey's work as "Geologist to the State." Tuomey's final report while in this position was *Report on the Geology of South Carolina* (1848), which was widely received as one of the most creditable and detailed geologic studies made in the antebellum South.

Tuomey departed South Carolina in 1847 when he was elected professor of the newly established chair of geology, mineralogy, and agricultural chemistry at the University of Alabama, and he was subsequently appointed the first state geologist in Alabama. During this time Tuomey completed an impressive paleontological monograph, *Pleiocene Fossils of South-Carolina* (1857), with Francis S. Holmes of the College of Charleston. This taxonomic work on marine fossils was subsidized by the South Carolina legislature to make amends for deleting the paleontological illustrations from Tuomey's 1848 report. The collaboration of Tuomey and Holmes on this private report contributed significantly to the advancement of geologic research during a period when Charleston was recognized as the center of scientific activity in the Old South. Tuomey died on March 30, 1857, in Tuscaloosa, Alabama, where he was also buried. LEWIS S. DEAN

Stephens, Lester D. *Ancient Animals and Other Wondrous Things: The Story of Francis Simmons Holmes, Paleontologist and Curator of the Charleston Museum.* Charleston, S.C.: Charleston Museum, 1988.

Tuomey, Michael. *The Papers of Michael Tuomey.* Edited by Lewis S. Dean. Spartanburg, S.C.: Reprint Company, 2001.

Turner, Henry McNeal (1834–1915). Clergyman, politician. Turner was born in Newberry on February 1, 1834, the son of Hardy Turner and Sarah Greer. Turner, a light-skinned African American, was born free. His mother hired a tutor, but South Carolina law forbade education of black children, so the tutor was let go. His father died while he was still young. After his mother married Jabez Story, the family moved to Abbeville in 1848. There lawyers hired Turner as a janitor and, in defiance of the law, educated him in many subjects, including history, law, and theology. In July 1849 Turner experienced an emotional conversion on a campground outside Abbeville due to the evangelism of a white Methodist preacher, C. A. Crowell, and he joined the Methodist Episcopal Church, South. In 1853 he was licensed to preach, and he traveled throughout South Carolina and other southern states preaching to both black and white audiences and achieving considerable renown. In 1856 he married Eliza Peacher of Columbia. He was widowed three times and was remarried each time: in 1893 to Martha DeWitt, in 1900 to Harriet Wayman, and in 1907 to Laura Lemon.

Turner enjoyed his acceptance as a Methodist preacher, but he abhorred the proslavery politics of antebellum South Carolina. One event that shocked him was Representative Preston Brooks's 1856 caning of Massachusetts senator Charles Sumner on the floor of the U.S. Senate, an event that later prompted Turner to refer to South Carolina as "the pestiferous State of my nativity." In 1858 Henry and Eliza Turner moved to Baltimore, Maryland, where Turner joined the African Methodist Episcopal Church. From 1863 to 1865 Turner served as a chaplain to the First U.S. Colored Troops, a regiment he helped to recruit. In 1865 he moved to Georgia and helped organize both the AME Church and the Republican Party. He served as a member of the Georgia House of Representatives and also briefly as a U.S. postmaster in Macon. After 1865 he made his home in Georgia.

During the last four decades of his life, Turner became a vocal supporter of the emigration of African Americans to Africa. He personally attended the sailing of the ship *Azor* from Charleston to Liberia in April 1878 with two hundred emigrants aboard. Turner believed that African Americans needed "a theater of manhood and activity established somewhere for our young men and women," where their abilities in such areas as politics and economics could be developed without fear of white supremacist violence. Furthermore, he believed that African Americans should play a leading role in Christianizing Africa. In the 1890s he made four trips to West and South Africa to build up the AME Church.

In 1880 Turner was elected a bishop in the AME Church. When AME churches in South Carolina threatened to separate from the denomination in 1884 and 1891, Turner reduced the extent of the schism by skillfully mediating the disputes. He was, however, increasingly critical of the United States. In 1906, after riots in Atlanta devastated the black community, Turner declared that "hell is an improvement upon the United States where the Negro is concerned." Turner said that he did not want to die in the United States because of its denial of human rights to African Americans, and he did not. On his way to an AME Church conference in Canada, he suffered a massive stroke as he disembarked the ferry at Windsor, Ontario, and he died several hours later on May 8, 1915. He was buried in Atlanta. STEPHEN W. ANGELL

Angell, Stephen W. *Bishop Henry McNeal Turner and African-American Religion in the South.* Knoxville: University of Tennessee Press, 1992.

———. "Black Methodist Preachers in the South Carolina Upcountry, 1840–1866." In *"Ain't Gonna Lay My 'Ligion Down": African American Religion in the South,* edited by Alonzo Johnson and Paul Jersild. Columbia: University of South Carolina Press, 1996.

Redkey, Edwin S. *Black Exodus: Black Nationalist and Back-to-Africa Movements, 1890–1910.* New Haven, Conn.: Yale University Press, 1969.

Turner, Henry McNeal. *Respect Black: The Writings and Speeches of Henry McNeal Turner.* Edited by Edwin S. Redkey. New York: Arno, 1971.

Tuscarora War (1711–1713). In the first decade of the eighteenth century the Tuscaroras, an Iroquoian tribe, inhabited eastern North Carolina in fifteen towns with 1,200 warriors and a population of about 4,800 people. Increased European settlement threatened Tuscarora autonomy and put great pressure on resources. In 1710 Baron Christophe von Graffenreid established a settlement of Swiss and Palatine Germans at New Bern, in territory formerly reserved for the Tuscaroras and smaller eastern tribes. In addition, during 1711 the political insurrection called Cary's Rebellion preoccupied the attentions of white Carolinians. Chief Hancock and other Tuscarora leaders seized the opportunity to raid white settlements. They struck on September 22, 1711, killing more than 120 settlers and capturing von Graffenreid and John Lawson, explorer and author of *A New Voyage to Carolina.* Lawson was tortured and killed, but Graffenreid was released. He and Chief Hancock negotiated a treaty that would spare the Swiss and German settlers but offered no full guarantees of peace. North Carolina governor Edward Hyde called upon Virginia and South Carolina for assistance.

South Carolina dispatched Colonel John Barnwell and a force of about five hundred European and Indian troops to defeat the Tuscaroras. In January 1712 Barnwell and his force converged on Narhantes, also called Fort Hancock, west of New Bern. The Tuscaroras' fort was well constructed, using approved European engineering techniques (one source reported that the fort had been designed and built under the direction of a fugitive South Carolina slave named Harry). Barnwell's force established a siege in March. They isolated the fort, dug trenches, and engaged the Tuscarora defenders in skirmishes. The siege lasted until April 17, when Hancock's warriors capitulated. The fort was demolished, the Tuscaroras agreed to pay annual tribute, and the hunting ranges of their tribal lands were diminished. Barnwell returned to South Carolina, but on the march his troops encountered and attacked a group of Tuscaroras. More than fifty were killed, and nearly two hundred Tuscarora women and children were carried back to Charleston and enslaved. This action broke the peace, and the Tuscaroras resumed their warfare.

A second South Carolina expedition, led by Colonel James Moore, Jr., future governor of the colony, arrived in North Carolina in March 1713. This force attacked Fort Nohoroco (Neoheroka), capturing the fort and Chief Hancock. He was executed, and the Tuscaroras were forced to sign a treaty that restricted them to a small reservation on the Roanoke River. In 1715 remnants of the Tuscarora tribe migrated to New York. They joined the Iroquois Confederacy and in 1722 became the sixth nation of that famous Native American confederation. ALEXANDER MOORE

[Barnwell, John.] "The Tuscarora Expedition: Letters of Colonel John Barnwell." *South Carolina Historical and Genealogical Magazine* 9 (January 1908): 28–54.

Barnwell, Joseph W. "The Second Tuscarora Expedition." *South Carolina Historical and Genealogical Magazine* 10 (January 1909): 33–48.

Lawson, John. *A New Voyage to Carolina.* 1709. Reprint, Chapel Hill: University of North Carolina Press, 1967.

Parramore, Thomas C. "Tuscarora War (1711–1713)." In *Colonial Wars of North America, 1512–1763: An Encyclopedia,* edited by Alan Gallay. New York: Garland, 1996.

———. "With Tuscarora Jack on the Back Path to Bath." *North Carolina Historical Review* 64 (April 1987): 115–38.

Two Seed in the Spirit Baptists. Two Seed in the Spirit Baptists are one of several so-called "hardshell" Baptist groups of the early nineteenth century. Like other churches in the movement, these Baptists were highly predestinarian, antimissionary Calvinists, who saw no need for "new-fangled" missionary societies or what they believed to be the corrupting influence of higher education to advance God's kingdom. This particular group, influenced by the ideas of Daniel Parker, who lived and worked primarily in Tennessee, believed that people are born with either a good seed planted by God or an evil seed planted by the devil. Like Primitive Baptists, who are associated with the same school, these Baptists practiced foot washing and opposed the idea of a paid clergy. Some even rejected the idea of Sunday schools. Few if any such Baptists exist in

South Carolina today, and their numbers are extremely small worldwide. HELEN LEE TURNER

Parker, Daniel. *Views on the Two Seeds.* Vandalia, Ill.: Robert Blackwell, 1826.

Tybee Island National Wildlife Refuge. Located in Jasper County at the mouth of the Savannah River, across the river from the Georgia town of Tybee Island, the refuge was created under an executive order of President Franklin D. Roosevelt in 1938 as a breeding area for migratory birds and other wildlife. It began as a one-acre oyster shoal, Oyster Bed Island, which was used by the U.S. Army Corps of Engineers for harbor dredge disposal. The refuge-enabling legislation granted control of the one-acre Oyster Bed Lighthouse Reservation to the U.S. Coast Guard, with the Corps of Engineers retaining soil deposition rights. On February 17, 1960, the lighthouse tract was transferred to the U.S. Fish and Wildlife service. In the late nineteenth century the island was the site of a quarantine station for the city of Savannah and a residence for customhouse officials.

The refuge's acreage has expanded due to dredge disposal activity related to river and harbor improvements. This refuge is primarily managed for the benefit of migrating and nesting shorebirds and is closed to the public. Visitor use is not compatible with the nesting, feeding, and resting use of the small refuge by birds. Sandy portions of the island have only sparse vegetation, while more stable areas may support eastern red cedar, wax myrtle, salt cedar, and groundsel bush. Least terns, black skimmers, and Wilson's plovers have nested on the soil deposits, while brown pelicans, gulls, terns, and many other species use it as a resting area. DIANA CHURCHILL

Tyger River. The North, Middle, and South Tyger Rivers begin in Spartanburg County and join to form the Tyger River near the city of Woodruff. The river flows through Union County, including twenty-four miles through Sumter National Forest, to join the Broad River at the juncture of Union, Newberry, and Fairfield Counties. The last six miles of the river form the boundary between Union and Newberry Counties. The Tyger River basin covers 807.9 square miles. It includes six watersheds and 517,056 acres. There are approximately 938 stream miles and 2,889 acres of lake waters in the basin.

The Tyger River is generally shallow and narrow, ranging from two to six feet deep and forty to seventy feet wide. There is some white water in the upper sections, but most of the river is brisk flat water. The surrounding landscape is pine-hardwood-mix forest and some marshy bogs.

Two theories exist about the river's name. One says it refers to a French trader named Tygert who visited the area around 1755. Another cites a legend about a wild cat (tiger) and a bear that fought on the river's banks, with the cat winning. The Cherokees called the river Amoyescheck. SUSAN GIAIMO HIOTT

Herd, E. Don, Jr. *The South Carolina Upcountry: Historical and Biographical Sketches.* Vol. 1. Greenwood, S.C.: Attic Press, 1981.

Tynte, Edward (?–1710). Governor. Tynte was from a Somerset, England, family that had recently risen to a baronetcy, but neither his parents nor his date of birth are known. His family connection is established through the arms on a large seal that he used to ratify legislative acts in South Carolina. Surviving documents refer to Tynte variously as major or colonel. Other family members attended Oxford, and many of the men who came to South Carolina with Tynte to serve in his administration were lawyers. In a Latin poem expressing high hopes for Tynte's administration, the Tory writer William King implies that Tynte was also a man of culture: "Tynte was the man who first, from British shore, / Palladian arts to Carolina bore; / His tuneful harp attending Muses strung, / And Phoebus' skill inspired the lays he sung."

Frustrated by nearly a decade of paralyzing factionalism between the church and dissenter parties in their colony, the Lords Proprietors decided to institute a wholesale change of government and began by commissioning Tynte as the new governor on December 9, 1708. After almost a year's delay, Tynte arrived in Charleston and was proclaimed governor on November 26, 1709. Unfortunately, he had little opportunity to realize the proprietors' ambitions. Tynte died on June 26, 1710, after only seven months in office. The first of the acts that would eventually establish a free school system in the colony was the only notable legislation of his administration. By the terms of his will, Tynte left his entire estate to Frances Killner, spinster of London. CHARLES H. LESSER

Lesser, Charles H. *South Carolina Begins: The Records of a Proprietary Colony, 1663–1721.* Columbia: South Carolina Department of Archives and History, 1995.

Union (Union County; 2000 pop. 8,793). Although European settlers first arrived in the 1750s to the area that became Union, it was not until the General Assembly created the county in 1785 that the town of Union began to take shape. Colonel Thomas Brandon, the area's greatest Revolutionary War hero, donated two acres to locate a courthouse and jail on the top of what came to be known as Jail Hill. Brandon was held in such high regard that there was a movement to name the county seat Brandonburgh in his honor. But nothing came of the effort, and the town was named Unionville. The original 1789 brick courthouse was replaced in 1823 with a stone building designed by Robert Mills. It was demolished in 1911 to make room for the current courthouse, but Mills's 1823 stone jail next door survived and continued to be used for government offices. In 1817 the first church (Presbyterian) was built in the village, and by the 1830s a business district had grown up on Jail Hill around the courthouse. Through the decades the business district stretched eastward away from the hill, reaching Church Street four blocks away by the end of the century. The town was incorporated in 1837 as Union, although Unionville continued in popular usage until the 1870s.

Starting in the 1890s, Union began a transition from small farming town to industrial city. The first textile mill was Union Mill, built a block behind the courthouse in 1893 by Thomas Duncan. Expanded in 1896, Union Mill was joined by Excelsior Mill in 1897, which produced knitwear in the undeveloped southwestern part of town. Together the two mills employed 1,317 workers by 1900, almost ninety percent of whom were from nearby rural areas. In 1890 there were 1,609 people living in Union. By 1900 the population had grown to 5,400. The trend continued through the next decade with the development of two mill village suburbs: Buffalo (built by Thomas Duncan three miles northwest of Union in 1900) and Monarch Mills (founded by John A. Fant just east of town in 1900).

Union's rapid growth stalled by 1910. Little expansion or alteration of the downtown area occurred in the twentieth century, and Main Street continued to look much as it had in the late nineteenth century. By 2000, however, Union's historic downtown had become a cherished asset. Most of the new development that occurred in the city took place on the U.S. Highway 176 bypass. Constructed in 1955, the route was widened to five lanes in the early 1970s and soon became a clogged artery. By the early 1990s there were four shopping centers, a six-screen theater, and many separate stores and offices lining the bypass. Although the population of the town had grown little since 1910, the burgeoning businesses along the bypass demonstrated that modern Unionites were much better off per capita than those of their grandparents' day. ALLAN D. CHARLES

Charles, Allan D. *The Narrative History of Union County, South Carolina.* 3d ed. Greenville, S.C.: A Press, 1997.

Mabry, Mannie Lee, ed. *Union County Heritage, 1981.* Union, S.C.: Union County Heritage Committee, 1981.

Union County (514 sq. miles; 2000 pop. 29,881). A Union County of 540 square miles was created by the state legislature in 1785. A century later, in 1897, the county lost its two northernmost townships in the creation of Cherokee County, reducing Union County to 514 square miles and establishing its modern boundaries. Probably the first white settlers in the area were James McIlwaine and a party of Scots-Irish Protestants who arrived from Virginia and Pennsylvania about 1751. Others followed and were soon joined by large numbers of Quakers. Baptists were also among the early settlers, and an entire congregation settled on lower Fairforest Creek around 1760. To save effort, inhabitants of various denominations in the Brown's Creek area built a common house of worship and called it a "union" church. The generic name became a given name, and in 1785 Union County was named in honor of that early church.

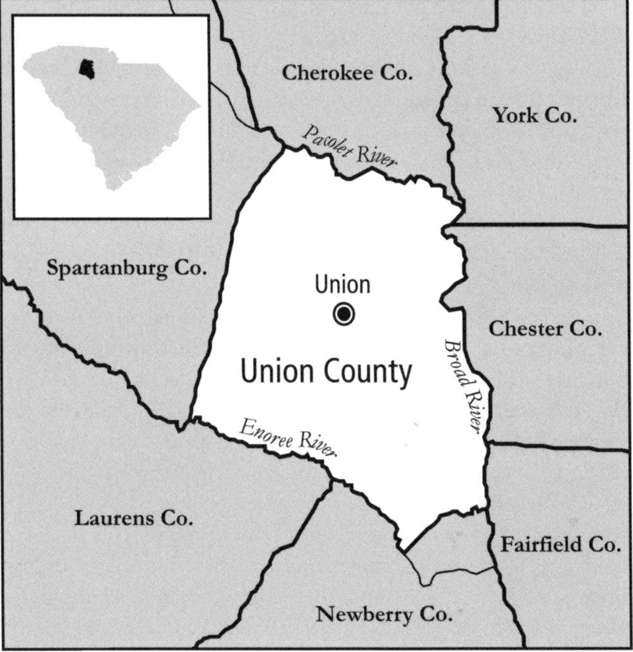

During the Revolutionary War residents were active on both sides of the conflict and a civil war raged in what was to become Union County, while the pacifist Quakers hunkered down and rode out the storm as best they could. Probably no other county in South Carolina was as evenly divided between Tories and patriots as Union County was. At least five Revolutionary War battles occurred within or exactly on the later boundaries of the county. The most important battle took place at Blackstock's on November 20, 1780, when state militiamen under Thomas Sumter defeated a British force commanded by the notorious Banastre Tarleton.

After the return of peace and the creation of the actual county, a log courthouse and a log jail were built in 1786. Space for the public buildings had been donated by the county's greatest Revolutionary War hero, Colonel Thomas Brandon. In May 1788 Brandon also led Union County representatives at the state's ratification convention, where the entire delegation opposed adoption of the new national Constitution.

Cotton became king soon after 1800, and large plantations appeared in the fertile southern parts of Union County, where numerous slaves worked under the eyes of the overseers. Area Quakers felt uncomfortable with this sudden increase in the slave population and abandoned Union in the first decade of the nineteenth century, resettling north of the Ohio River, primarily in southwestern Ohio. Poor soil conservation practices left fields eroded and red by the 1830s, sparking a second exodus from the county as people left for new lands in the Southwest. Although many emigrants took their slaves with them, established plantations grew larger as the slave population increased and the white population declined. Slaves became a majority in the county in the 1840s, and blacks continued to outnumber whites until about 1915. Efforts were made to restore prosperity to the county in the 1850s. In 1858 John L. Young, a local merchant and railroad entrepreneur, succeeded in linking Union to the outside world with a railroad, the Spartanburg and Union. The following year he pushed the line to Spartanburg, which remained the terminus of the line until after the Civil War.

In 1860 the governor of South Carolina was William H. Gist of Union. On October 5, 1860, Gist dispatched his Union County first cousin, States Rights Gist, as special envoy to the governors of other southern states to sound them out on the question of secession. When States Rights sent back letters assuring the governor that the Deep South would follow a secession move by South Carolina, Gist called a special session of the legislature to convene on November 5, the day before it was expected that Lincoln would be elected. When their worst fear was realized, the legislators voted to call a state convention. That convention on December 20, 1860, unanimously signed the Ordinance of Secession, an instrument written in the hand of convention secretary Benjamin F. Arthur of Union. Many Union County men fought in the Confederate army, and after the war they were especially active in resisting what they considered to be the tyranny of Reconstruction. The Union County Ku Klux Klan was among the most active in the state, and in February 1871 the county was the scene of the largest KKK raid that ever occurred in the South. "Carpetbag" rule was ended in the county in 1872, four years before the Democratic "redemption" of 1876 brought Reconstruction to an end in the state as a whole.

Trapped in postwar poverty, most Union County residents, black and white, were small cotton farmers or sharecroppers in the late nineteenth century. Not until 1893 did a measure of prosperity return in the form of cotton mills. Thomas Cary Duncan was the county's preeminent industrialist, and his Union Cotton Mill was the first in the county to go into production. Lockhart Mill and others soon followed, and by 1907 some 4,075 workers were tending 7,645 looms and 285,800 spindles in the county. In an era of segregation African Americans were not employed inside the mills, and whites from the North Carolina mountains filled many mill jobs. During the period between the world wars, many blacks left the county and migrated north in search of better lives.

Following World War II, Union County entered a second phase of industrial development and by the 1990s possessed metal working plants, such as those operated by Torrington and Webb Forging, although most manufacturing remained textile-related. Cotton growing declined after the 1920s and all but disappeared by the 1970s, being replaced by forestry, cattle raising, and soybean farming. With the return of forests, deer reappeared in the 1960s and eventually drove out soybeans, which were regarded as a delicacy. At the end of the twentieth century the taking of deer by both local and out-of-county hunters had become an industry in itself, and deer coolers (to process the meat) and hunt camps sprang up all over the county. Throughout the twentieth century, economic growth balanced with economic difficulties, and thus the county's population remained almost exactly the same for some ninety years, hovering just above the thirty-thousand level. Despite changes, history remained a real presence in the county, with many Union inhabitants descended from longtime residents. ALLAN D. CHARLES

Charles, Allan D. *The Narrative History of Union County, South Carolina.* 3d ed. Greenville, S.C.: A Press, 1997.

Mabry, Mannie Lee, ed . *Union County Heritage, 1981.* Union, S.C.: Union County Heritage Committee, 1981.

Union Daily Times (2003 circulation: 6,355 daily). An evening newspaper, daily except Sunday, published in the city of Union. The *Union Daily Times* claims to be Union County's oldest enterprise. Its ancestor was the *Unionville Journal,* a weekly founded on May 3, 1850, with B. F. Arthur as editor and Robert McKnight as publisher. The name was changed to the *Unionville Times* in 1859 and carried the states' rights banner: "The Constitution as our fathers gave it, or separate independence." After the Civil War the name was changed to the *Weekly Union Times* in 1869 and to the *Union Times* in 1894. The Reverend Lewis Malone Rice purchased the *Union Times* in 1906, converting it to a daily in 1917 and renaming it the *Union Daily Times.*

Rice died in 1946, and his grandson William R. Feaster served as editor and publisher until his death in 1967. Feaster's widow, Dorothy, succeeded him as editor and publisher. In 1974 Mid-South Management Company bought the newspaper. When Dorothy Feaster retired, Donald E. Wilder served as publisher until 1995, when he was succeeded by David M. "Mike" Pippin. In 2002 Anthony Summerlin was the publisher.

The newspaper occupied various buildings, dating from the first site when it had offices in a structure known as the "old police station," but was printed in a livery stable. The daily survived a fire in 1912 and eventually moved into a fourteen-thousand-square-foot building in the county's industrial park in 1992. In 1996 the *Times* began complete pagination, integrating editorial and classified advertising layouts. ROBERT A. PIERCE

McNeely, Patricia G. *The Palmetto Press: The History of South Carolina's newspapers and the Press Association.* Columbia: South Carolina Press Association, 1998.

Union Leagues. Union Leagues sprang into existence across South Carolina and the South in the years immediately following the end of the Civil War. Sometimes called Loyal Leagues, the postwar league descended from the Union League of America, a patriotic club formed in the North by hard-core Republicans during the war. The organization spread south during and after the war, attracting some members from the southern Unionist faction but mostly from among the millions of newly freed African Americans. The attraction of the Union Leagues was partly fraternal, with meetings marked by elaborate rituals, singing, and patriotic proclamations. The primary mission of the leagues, however, was the political education of the freedmen. League meetings discussed the leading issues of the day, such as public education, voting rights, land reform, labor contracts, and debt relief. League leaders also recommended candidates for public office who best pursued the interests of league members. These activities were vital in attracting newly enfranchised black voters to the ranks of the Republican Party.

Union Leagues were active in South Carolina as early as late 1866 and played a significant role in state politics in 1867 and 1868. In October 1867 the *Charleston Daily News* reported the presence of no fewer than eighty-eight league organizations in South Carolina, which had enrolled "every Negro almost in the state." This network of Union Leagues was key to the election of Republican Robert K. Scott to the governor's chair in 1868. Almost as quickly as it had come into existence, however, the Union League movement rapidly faded from the state's political landscape. With the establishment of the Republican Party in South Carolina, grassroots organizations such as the league were no longer needed to build party strength. In addition, Union Leagues became a particular target of the Ku Klux Klan in the years following 1868, which further hastened their demise. Although they had largely disappeared from South Carolina by 1870, Union Leagues nevertheless had been an important means by which freedmen entered politics and staked their claim to citizenship in the postbellum South. TOM DOWNEY

Foner, Eric. *Reconstruction: America's Unfinished Revolution, 1863–1877.* New York: Harper & Row, 1988.

Silvestro, Clement Mario. "None but Patriots: The Union Leagues in Civil War and Reconstruction." Ph.D. diss., University of Wisconsin, 1959.

Simkins, Francis Butler, and Robert Hilliard Woody. *South Carolina during Reconstruction.* Chapel Hill: University of North Carolina Press, 1932.

Sweat, Edward F. "The Union Leagues and the South Carolina Election of 1870." *Journal of Negro History* 61 (AprÈl 1976): 200–214.

Unionists. Unionists were antisecessionists and supporters of the federal Union during the pre–Civil War decades, particularly during the nullification controversy of the early 1830s and the secession crises of the early 1850s and 1860.

A pro-Union political organization, the Union and State Rights Party, developed in 1830 in response to calls for nullification of the federal tariff in South Carolina. Fearing that nullification would spawn secession, Unionists opposed the doctrine by running candidates for city offices in Charleston and for legislative seats throughout the state in 1830. Initially strong in Charleston, where leaders included James L. Petigru and Joel R. Poinsett, the party lost influence there in the face of a relentless nullifier political organization. More reliably Unionist areas included heavily yeoman districts such as Greenville, Horry, Pickens, and Spartanburg.

Unionists continued to frustrate nullifiers after failing to prevent the adoption of the Ordinance of Nullification in November 1832. In December the party created a statewide network of militia units, called Union societies, headed by Poinsett, who was in contact with President Andrew Jackson. Upcountry Unionists responded to the call to arms with particular enthusiasm. Greenville's Paris Mountain Union Society expressed its members' resolve: "in defence of the Federal Union, *we have drawn our swords and flung away the scabbards* . . . we have but two words by way of reply to the Nullifiers, which are these: '*Come on.*'" In Charleston, Poinsett reported enrolling more than eleven hundred Unionist militiamen. In part because of this determined Unionist resistance, nullifier leaders sought compromise rather than armed confrontation with federal authorities.

The rise of abolitionism and fears of its influence in the federal government weakened Unionists in South Carolina after the mid-1830s. Although a few hardy Unionists, such as Petigru and Greenville's Benjamin Perry, persistently opposed calls for secession, they were ultimately unsuccessful in their efforts. ROBERT TINKLER

Freehling, William W. *Prelude to Civil War: The Nullification Controversy in South Carolina, 1816–1836.* New York: Harper & Row, 1965.

Pease, Jane H., and William H. Pease. "The Economics and Politics of Charleston's Nullification Crisis." *Journal of Southern History* 47 (August 1981): 335–62.

Tinkler, Robert. "Against the Grain: Unionists and Whigs in Calhoun's South Carolina." Senior thesis, Princeton University, 1984.

Unitarian Church (Charleston). Located at 6 Archdale Street in Charleston, the Unitarian Church has long been considered one of the city's most exceptional buildings. In 1772 construction began on a new church building to serve as a house of worship for the city's Unitarian congregation, which had grown out of the Congregational Church on Meeting Street. In 1852 the noted architect Francis D. Lee was commissioned to enhance the building with Gothic-revival features. Constructed of stuccoed brick, the church features a three-bay facade, a crenellated tower, false buttresses, tracery, and compound piers. The central bay of the west facade facing Archdale Street boasts an expansive lancet-arched window with hood mold. Lee's design for the interior includes exquisite fan vaulting, which is said to have been inspired by the interior of the Henry VII chapel at Westminster Abbey.

Unitarian Church, Charleston. Courtesy, South Carolina Historical Society

Gothic architecture gained popularity in Charleston during the mid–nineteenth century, following the lead of the romantic and picturesque movements in England. Buildings such as the Unitarian Church were altered to reflect the emotional mood of the times. When threats of slave insurrection increased in Charleston after 1820, the fortresslike appearance of Gothicized architecture was reassuring to the wealthy elite as it evoked a sense of control. Gothic design also afforded the wealthy elite an opportunity to display their familiarity with historic architectural styles.

Notable design elements accompanying the Unitarian Church site include a historic garden and graveyard featuring a Gothic monument to Dr. Samuel Gilman and his wife, Caroline. Gilman was the pastor of the Unitarian Church from 1819 to 1858 and is most noted for writing the song "Fair Harvard," the anthem of that university.

The Unitarian Church was designated a National Historic Landmark in 1973. LINDSEY GERTZ

Jacoby, Mary Moore, ed. *The Churches of Charleston and the lowcountry.* Columbia: University of South Carolina Press, 1993.

Poston, Jonathan H. *The Buildings of Charleston: A Guide to the City's Architecture.* Columbia: University of South Carolina Press, 1997.

Sellers, Hazel Crowson. *Old South Carolina Churches.* Columbia, S.C.: Crowson Printing, 1941.

Unitarians. Unitarians in South Carolina boast a legacy of professional distinction and influence disproportionate to their size and numbers. Throughout the nineteenth century, Unitarians filled the top ranks of the growing urban professional classes and forged a respectable place for rational Christianity alongside an increasing evangelical culture.

Unitarianism in South Carolina had several religious and philosophical sources: an indigenous Arminianism, commonsense realism, Anglican latitudinarianism, and English and New England Unitarianism. During the antebellum period, southern Unitarians neutralized the more radical elements in all of these sources and created a core of "rational Christianity" that many within southern orthodoxy embraced. As "Christians," they maintained that the Bible was the Word of God and believed in the virgin birth, the Resurrection, and the miracles and divinity of Christ, although they stressed the Unity of God as opposed to the Trinity. They believed that Christ was the Son of God but, as the Son, was not as divine as the Father. For this, many within orthodoxy rejected their claim as "Christians." Unitarian theology was broad and liberal at its foundation and ecumenical in nature. For Unitarians, theology was a reasonable and rational enterprise designed to commend the Christian faith to an ever expanding class of educated southerners who, like them, wanted to reform and purify the church while keeping separate the elements of church and state.

The Second Independent Church of Charleston was incorporated in 1817 under the guidance of its minister Anthony Forster. Its origins, however, are tied to the Independent or Congregational Church of Charleston. Founded in the 1680s, the Independent Church originally gathered a broad faction of dissenting religious groups in Charleston: Huguenots, Scots and Irish Presbyterians, and Old and New Englanders. By the time Forster became copastor, the church had a sizable "Unitarian" constituency. Though trained as a Presbyterian, Forster was soon swayed by the arguments of the English Unitarian Joseph Priestley. Without assuming the name Unitarian, Forster began to preach on the common elements of Christianity and salvation.

Following Forster's untimely death, the congregation took the name Second Independent or Congregational Church of Charleston and hired Samuel Gilman, a young Harvard tutor and an avowed Unitarian. His ministry in Charleston has been called the "golden age" of Unitarianism in South Carolina. Though he was faced with increasing opposition from evangelical circles, Gilman's poise, conciliatory spirit, character, and intellect soon became apparent to many in the city. Both he and his liberal constituency rose within the ranks of the city's literary, mercantile, and professional elite, which helped to place their church among the most respected in Charleston despite the unpopularity of their beliefs and the initial hostilities from the community at large. The congregation soon formed the Charleston Unitarian Book and Tract Society, the first organization in the United States for the circulation of Unitarian literature, and established the Association of Southern Unitarians with Charleston as its center. By the early 1840s the initiative for establishing and supporting Unitarian churches in the South rested almost entirely on the Charleston congregation as it helped found churches in Augusta and Savannah, Georgia, and Mobile, Alabama.

On the eve of the Civil War, like other denominational divisions, the congregation broke from the American Unitarian Association in Boston. Since then, Unitarianism has evolved and changed in South Carolina. As part of the Unitarian-Universalist Association, contemporary Unitarianism embraces a broad spectrum of both Eastern and Western philosophies, including Buddhism, humanism, earth-centered traditions, and Judeo-Christian teachings. Fundamentally, Unitarians profess a belief in the dignity and worth of every human being and uphold justice, equity, and compassion in human relations. They stress that personal experience, conscience, and reason should be the final authorities in all religious matters. With more than twelve hundred members scattered across South Carolina, Unitarian congregations can be found in Aiken, Beaufort, Charleston, Clemson, Columbia, Florence, Greenville, Hilton Head Island, Newberry, Pawleys Island, and Spartanburg. JOHN ALLEN MACAULAY

Edwards, George N. *A History of the Independent or Congregational Church of Charleston, South Carolina.* Boston, Mass.: Pilgrim Press, 1947.

Gibson, George H. "Unitarian Congregations in the Ante-Bellum South." *Proceedings of the Unitarian Historical Society* 12, pt. 2 (1959): 53–78.

Gohdes, Clarence. "Some Notes on the Unitarian Church in the Ante-Bellum South: A Contribution to the History of Southern Liberalism." In *American Studies in Honor of William Kenneth Boyd by Members of the Americana Club of Duke University,* edited by David Kelly Jackson. Durham, N.C.: Duke University Press, 1940.

Howe, Daniel Walker. "A Massachusetts Yankee in Senator Calhoun's Court: Samuel Gilman in South Carolina." *New England Quarterly* 44 (June 1971): 197–220.

Macaulay, John A. *Unitarianism in the Antebellum South: The Other Invisible Institution.* Tuscaloosa: University of Alabama Press, 2001.

Stange, Douglas C. "Abolitionism as Malfeasance: Southern Unitarians Versus 'Puritan Fanaticism'—1831–1860." *Harvard Library Bulletin* 26 (April 1978): 146–71.

Wright, Conrad. "The Theological World of Samuel Gilman." *Proceedings of the Unitarian Historical Society* 17, pt. 2 (1973–75): 54–72.

United Church of Christ. In 1957 the United Church of Christ was established through the union of Congregational Christian churches and congregations of the German Reformed tradition. Churches that called themselves Congregational were organized in America when the Pilgrims of Plymouth Plantation (1620) and the Puritans of the Massachusetts Bay Colony (1630) acknowledged their unity in the Cambridge Platform of 1648.

Congregational churches were established during the colonial period throughout the South Carolina lowcountry. The Congregational Meeting House in Charleston (later known as the Circular Congregational Church) included some of the city's wealthiest and most influential citizens, such as Miles Brewton, Josiah Smith, Daniel DeSaussure, Solomon Legarè, and Henry Perroneau. South Carolina Congregationalists overwhelmingly supported the patriot side during the Revolutionary War. During the antebellum period, the Congregationalists became more closely tied to Presbyterian congregations. Circular Congregational at that time had a particularly powerful association of political leaders including U.S. Senator Robert Young Hayne, U.S. Congressman Henry Laurens Pinckney, and U.S. Secretary of State Hugh Swinton Legarè.

After the Civil War most Congregational churches in South Carolina became Presbyterian. Congregationalists' greatest contributions to the life of the state in the twentieth century were through its African American members and through the Avery Normal Institute that educated many of the political and social leaders of Charleston's black community until the 1950s. The name United Church of Christ was adopted in 1957 at the time of the union with the German Reformed Church. ERSKINE CLARKE

Clarke, Erskine. *Our Southern Zion: A History of Calvinism in the South Carolina Low Country, 1690–1990.* Tuscaloosa: University of Alabama Press, 1996.

"Congregationalists." In *The Westminster Dictionary of Church History,* edited by Jerald C. Brauer. Philadelphia, Pa.: Westminster, 1971.

Drago, Edmund L. *Initiative, Paternalism, and Race Relations: Charleston's Avery Normal Institute.* Athens: University of Georgia Press, 1990.

United Citizens Party. The United Citizens Party (UCP) is a political party unique to South Carolina. Its purpose is to promote, through the electoral process, human, civil, workers,' and reproductive rights, in addition to advocating environmental protection and governmental reform. Organized in 1969 primarily by the civil rights activist John Roy Harper, the UCP grew largely from disquieted Democrats angered by their party's refusal to nominate African American candidates for public offices. Harper, who later led the National Association for the Advancement of Colored People in the 1980s, formed the UCP.

In the aftermath of sit-ins and boycotts, civil rights took a more political approach through the UCP. It relied less on protests and more on direct action through representation. Perhaps the biggest impetus for the movement came from South Carolina's total failure at electing black politicians during most of the twentieth century. In the years before the UCP was founded, South Carolina was one of only three southern states—Alabama and Arkansas were the other two—with an all-white legislature.

The party's strategy was to run candidates for the General Assembly and local government in counties with black majority populations. The party ran candidates in the elections of 1970 and 1972. In its first campaign, UCP support succeeded in getting three black candidates (I. S. Leevy Johnson, James Felder, and Herbert Fielding) elected as Democrats to the S.C. House of Representatives.

During the 1970s the Democratic Party diversified its racial makeup, and the UCP subsequently lost prominence as a third party for black candidates. African American anger over political subordination subsided with the emergence of electoral clout. Many black leaders made reapportionment of congressional and state legislative districts into a key issue since their candidates were being elected by predominantly black constituencies.

By the early twenty-first century the UCP plotted a resurgence in response to the internal cohesiveness of the Democratic and Republican Parties, which UCP leaders asserted were not responsive enough to the needs and interests of all South Carolina citizens. In August 2000 the UCP held a convention in Columbia that advocated expanded rights for the working class, gays and lesbians, racial minorities, citizens without health insurance, and the disabled. Attendees also promoted structural changes in government, such as campaign finance reform. At the same convention the party nominated the consumer advocate Ralph Nader for president of the United States. The UCP also continued to advocate economic, social, and environmental justice. In 2002 the party ran candidates for a variety of national and state offices and succeeded in electing five candidates that it endorsed to the General Assembly. KEVIN FELLNER

Bethea, Margaret Berry. "Alienation and Third Parties: A Study of the United Citizens Party in South Carolina." Master's thesis, University of South Carolina, 1973.

United Methodist Church. Formed in 1968 by a union of the former Evangelical United Brethren Church (EUB) and the Methodist Church, the United Methodist Church was born in South Carolina against the backdrop of the civil rights movement. There were no EUB churches in the state, but after the unification of the Methodist Church in 1939, black Methodists from the South Carolina Conference of the former Methodist Episcopal Church were members of the all-black Central Jurisdiction and white Methodists from the South Carolina Conference of the former Methodist Episcopal Church, South, were members of the all-white Southeastern Jurisdiction. In 1964 the General Conference of the Methodist Church set the goal of a racially inclusive United Methodist Church. No reference to the Central Jurisdiction appeared in the Plan of Union, and 1972 was set as the date for eliminating racial structures altogether.

In 1966 the white South Carolina Conference approved the transfer of black Central Jurisdiction conferences into the Southeastern Jurisdiction and requested Bishop Paul Hardin, Jr., to appoint merger committees to plan the creation of a single, interracial South Carolina Conference. In 1968 the Central Jurisdiction was abolished, and the white conference was designated the "South Carolina Conference (1785)" and the black conference was designated the "South Carolina Conference (1866)." Both became part of the Columbia Episcopal Area, with Hardin as resident bishop. The two groups held joint pastors' schools and leadership training programs.

However, creating an interracial structure proved difficult. Merger committees of the two conferences proposed a plan in 1970. While in June 1971 the 1866 conference adopted it, the 1785 group defeated it. Bishop Hardin then appointed a smaller committee of six of the 1785 conference. Their plan was adopted by the white group and defeated by the black group. New committees of six from each group presented a final plan, which was adopted in January 1972. On June 5, 1972, the two conferences met separately for the last time in Spartanburg, and that evening the merged conference convened.

At first there were separate black and white districts within the conference. In 1974 Bishop Edward Tullis created twelve interracial districts, and in 1984 Bishop Roy Clark announced his intention of making interracial pastoral appointments, a process that moved slowly. In 1988 native son Joseph Bethea was the first black bishop appointed to South Carolina since the merger.

Issues other than race occupied the attention of United Methodists in the state. Attacks on the National Council of Churches (NCC) in the 1960s led to a conference study of NCC structure and policies. By the mid-1970s women entered the ordained ministry in increasing numbers but were slowly accepted by the churches. There were sharp debates over the Vietnam War in the 1970s. In the 1980s and 1990s conservative evangelicalism made increasing inroads among clergy and laity. Successive conference resolutions deplored the flying of the Confederate flag over the State House in Columbia and the adoption of a state lottery. A. V. HUFF, JR.

Huff, A. V., Jr. "The Evangelical Traditions II: Methodists." In *Religion in South Carolina,* edited by Charles H. Lippy. Columbia: University of South Carolina Press, 1993.

———. "A History of South Carolina United Methodism." In Morgan David Arant and Nancy McCracken Arant, eds., *United Methodist Ministers in South Carolina.* Columbia: South Carolina Conference of the United Methodist Church, 1984.

United Presbyterian Church in the U.S.A. The denomination was formed in 1958 with the union of the Presbyterian Church in the United States of America and the United Presbyterian Church of North America. The United Presbyterian Church was widely known in South Carolina as the "Northern Presbyterian Church" to distinguish it from the Presbyterian Church in the United States (PCUS), which was known as the "Southern Presbyterian Church." Long-established black congregations in South Carolina, primarily in the lowcountry, were part of the United Presbyterian Church.

In 1861 southern Presbyterians broke with the Presbyterian Church in the United States of America and formed a Southern Presbyterian Church. After 1865 African American members of congregations dominated by whites withdrew and organized separate congregations that were part of the Presbyterian Church in the United States of America. They took with them an African American Presbyterian tradition that reached back to the colonial period. With the help of northern missionaries and money, local black church leaders organized an extensive school system built around their congregations. By 1917 they had a network of forty-seven Presbyterian schools in South Carolina, such as Larimer High School on Edisto Island and boarding schools in Aiken, Cheraw, Chester, and Irmo. Many graduates went to Johnson C. Smith University in Charlotte. The schools nurtured a tight, well-educated community that contributed significant leadership to the social and political life of the state. In 1983 the "Northern" and "Southern" churches united to form the Presbyterian Church (USA). ERSKINE CLARKE

Clarke, Erskine. *Our Southern Zion: A History of Calvinism in the South Carolina Low Country, 1690–1990.* Tuscaloosa: University of Alabama Press, 1996.

Leith, John. *An Introduction to the Reformed Tradition: A Way of Being the Christian Community.* Rev. ed. Atlanta: John Knox, 1981.

Parker, Inez Moore. *The Rise and Decline of the Program of Education for Black Presbyterians of the United Presbyterian Church, U. S. A., 1865–1970.* San Antonio, Tex.: Trinity University Press, 1977.

United Textile Workers of America. The United Textile Workers of America (UTWA) formed as an affiliate of the American Federation of Labor (AFL) in 1901. It aimed to bring all textile workers in the country into one union instead of being separated into different unions by trade. The UTWA first appeared in South Carolina during a wave of labor unrest between 1898 and 1902. After losing a strike in Augusta, Georgia, in 1902, the UTWA virtually disappeared from South Carolina for the next ten years, except for a few local chapters that existed briefly in the Horse Creek Valley and Columbia. Taking advantage of the expansion of production during World War I, the UTWA became active again in 1915, with strikes in Greenville, Anderson, Westminster, and Columbia. In 1919 the UTWA demanded a forty-eight-hour week for textile workers, which led to a series of strikes starting in February and continuing sporadically through 1920. Despite limited success in reducing hours, these strikes were generally failures and ground to a halt with the onset of the depression of the textile industry in 1921.

In the 1920s, as southern textile mills faced tight competition with New England manufacturers, scientific management spread and individual operatives found themselves tending more machines for the same pay, a system that became known as the "stretch-out." In March 1929 workers in Ware Shoals and Pelzer struck briefly against the stretch-out, and at the end of the month a more serious strike occurred in Greenville. Central, Anderson, and Union also saw strikes. The UTWA had minimal involvement in these spontaneous strikes of 1929, but they did show that textile workers were ready to organize.

When the National Industrial Recovery Act was enacted in summer 1933, section 7(a) specifically provided workers the right to organize their own unions. Other sections established a board to oversee industry practices. South Carolina mill hands responded with a flurry of organizing, and by spring 1934 three-quarters of mill villages had a UTWA local. The oversight board did not live up to workers' expectations, however, and during the summer of 1934 it approved a reduction in work hours and a corresponding cut in wages in many mills across the South. South Carolina mill workers mounted wildcat strikes in July, pushing the UTWA into action that resulted in the General Textile Strike of September 1934, which involved tens of thousands of South Carolinians and shut down more than 120 mills. This massive disruption led to violence, including a shooting at Chiquola Mills in Honea Path that left seven union members dead. The UTWA was not prepared to support a strike of this magnitude, and by October the general strike—the largest in South Carolina and the South, and the second largest in the United States—ended with an agreement that gave workers little. The UTWA collapsed in the wake of the strike's failure. Locals fell apart, and union members were blacklisted for years. The entire strike and its aftermath influenced generations of South Carolina workers, souring them on the idea of unions and leaving them suspicious of government promises of protection. BRUCE E. BAKER

Hall, Jacquelyn Dowd, et al. *Like a Family: The Making of a Southern Cotton Mill World.* Chapel Hill: University of North Carolina Press, 1987.

Irons, Janet. *Testing the New Deal: The General Textile Strike of 1934 in the American South.* Urbana: University of Illinois Press, 2000.

Mitchell, George S. *Textile Unionism and the South.* Chapel Hill: University of North Carolina Press, 1931.

Simon, Bryant. *A Fabric of Defeat: The Politics of South Carolina Millhands, 1910–1948.* Chapel Hill: University of North Carolina Press, 1998.

Waldrep, George Calvin. *Southern Workers and the Search for Community: Spartanburg County, South Carolina.* Urbana: University of Illinois Press, 2000.

Universal Fellowship of Metropolitan Community Churches. This Protestant denomination was founded in Los Angeles, California, in 1968 by the Reverend Troy Perry. A former Pentecostal pastor in Georgia and Florida, Perry was ousted from his pulpit when he announced that he was gay. Perry from the first sought to create a church that would welcome those who felt excluded from most Christian churches. Convinced that labeling homosexuality as a sin distorted the meaning of the Christian gospel, the denomination has given particular emphasis to including gays, lesbians, bisexuals, and transgendered persons in its ministry.

Affirming the historic creeds of Protestant Christianity, UFMCC maintains a strong commitment to social action, particularly in areas of discrimination on the basis of race, ethnicity, gender, age, and health. Consequently, the denomination boasts an extraordinarily high proportion of women clergy. Worship styles vary among congregations and range from the charismatic to the liturgical. All churches affiliated with UFMCC, however, celebrate the Eucharist weekly.

Within five years of the denomination's founding, churches had been established in the South in Atlanta, Miami, and Dallas. In South Carolina there are UFMCC congregations in Charleston, Columbia, and Greenville. Churches in Charlotte, North Carolina, and Augusta, Georgia, also include members from South Carolina.

In 1999 UFMCC opened an international headquarters in Los Angeles. An elected board of elders provides global leadership between biannual general conferences. Starting in 2002 oversight of local congregations came through geographic regions. International membership in 2001 was 42,000, but estimates hold that at least twice as many persons have some association with the denomination. CHARLES H. LIPPY

Perry, Troy. *The Lord Is My Shepherd and He Knows I'm Gay.* Los Angeles, Calif.: Nash, 1972.

Perry, Troy, with Thomas L. P. Swicegood. *Don't Be Afraid Anymore: The Story of Reverend Troy Perry and the Metropolitan Community Churches.* New York: St. Martin's, 1990.

University Center of Greenville. Chartered as the Greenville Higher Education Center by the South Carolina Commission on Higher Education on July 1, 1987, this nonprofit consortium of higher education institutions is dedicated to increasing access to adult educational opportunities in metropolitan Greenville. The center offers more than forty-five undergraduate and graduate degrees and provides adults with educational opportunities from eight institutions: Clemson University, Furman University, Lander University, Medical University of South Carolina, South Carolina State University, University of South Carolina, University of South Carolina–Upstate, and Greenville Technical College. By offering day, evening, and distance education classes, the center permits adults to work while attending college at their own pace.

Originating in a suite on the Greenville Tech campus, the center changed locations as its popularity increased. In April 2001 the center completed renovations on 123,000 square feet of the former McAlister Square shopping mall. The effort created new classrooms, office space, a library, and an auditorium needed to meet the anticipated growth in enrollment. Operating with Clemson University as its fiduciary agent for budget and personnel, the center is supported by credit-hour charges, membership fees, and state appropriations. The presidents of participating institutions comprise a board of directors that oversees the center. An administrative staff manages the facility, headed by a chief executive officer. An advisory council consisting of local civic, business, and political leaders provides additional leadership. TONY W. CAWTHON

University Center of Greenville. *Moving at the Speed of Knowledge.* Greenville, S.C.: by the author, 2001.

University of South Carolina. The institution was originally chartered as South Carolina College on December 19, 1801. Its establishment was a response to the changing political landscape in the Palmetto State at the outset of the nineteenth century. South Carolina's political leaders saw a new college as a way of bringing together the sons of the Federalist elite of the lowcountry with the sons of the upcountry Jeffersonians in order, in the words of the college charter, to "promote the good order and harmony" of the state. It was intentionally sited in the relatively new capital city of Columbia to demonstrate independence from the influence of Charleston interests. Chartered by the General Assembly with an initial appropriation of $50,000, South Carolina College got under way remarkably quickly. In little more than three years of planning and preparation, the board of trustees hired a distinguished president and a faculty, established a curriculum, and constructed the first building on the new campus. Located a short distance southeast of the State House, the college opened on January 10, 1805, and in subsequent years enjoyed the generous annual support of the General Assembly, an unusual luxury for a state college in that era.

South Carolina College provided students a cosmopolitan education. Many early faculty members, as well as the college's curriculum and rules governing student behavior, were drawn from the leading New England universities of the time. Early faculty included renowned European scholars such as Thomas Cooper and Francis Lieber, as well as respected American scientists such as John and Joseph LeConte.

By the end of the antebellum era, the institution stood as a bulwark of conservatism. The curriculum was a traditional classical one, focusing primarily on the study of literary works in Latin and ancient Greek and emphasizing the mastery of oratory. "The object of College education," said trustee William Harper, "is not to advance the student in any particular profession, but to give him that liberal knowledge of general intelligence which is equally valuable in every profession." Boasting a distinguished faculty, a handsome campus, the latest scientific equipment, a large library, and generous public funding, South Carolina College ranked as one of the nation's premier institutions of higher education, and it educated most of the state's antebellum elite.

Then disaster struck. South Carolina's secession unleashed the devastation of the Civil War, and South Carolina College paid dearly. In 1862 the institution was forced to close for want of students, and its buildings served as a military hospital during wartime. In 1866 state leaders revived the institution with ambitious plans for a diverse University of South Carolina. However, with a nearly empty state treasury, the university that emerged was barely a shadow of its former self. For the next century the institution struggled to regain the status it had once held.

After the war the political controversies of Reconstruction buffeted the university. In 1869 the Republican General Assembly elected the first African American trustees, and in 1873, when Republicans insisted that black students be admitted, influential faculty resigned and the state's white elite largely abandoned the institution. The school's first black students enrolled that year, as did the first black faculty member, Harvard graduate Richard T. Greener. Between 1873 and 1877 the institution was racially integrated and was the only southern state university to admit and grant degrees to black students during Reconstruction.

In 1877, members of South Carolina's white leadership, led by Governor Wade Hampton, closed the institution to purge it of the Republican influences that they believed had sullied it. They reopened it in 1880 as an all-white Morrill Land Grant Institution: the South Carolina College of Agriculture and Mechanics. This institution thereafter became caught in the political upheaval of the last two decades of the nineteenth century. It went through several reorganizations in which the curriculum frequently changed and its status shifted from college to university and back again. During a brief period in the mid-1880s, it made significant strides toward regaining its antebellum glory, but again outside forces intervened to lower the college's status.

The low point came in the late 1880s when Benjamin R. Tillman harshly attacked the institution. Tillman was the champion of those in South Carolina who thought the state should support an agricultural college, not a liberal arts university. Tillman convinced the state to establish Clemson Agricultural College in 1889 as an alternative to the University of South Carolina. In 1890 South Carolina's voters elected him governor. Tillman stirred up class resentments and made attacking the university a central part of his program, calling it "the seedbed of the aristocracy" and promising to close it forever. Although he never followed through on his threats, the attacks crippled the institution. Enrollment fell to just sixty-eight students in 1893–1894, and in 1895 the institution's entire book budget was only $71.

By the late 1890s the institution, again with the name South Carolina College, began a slow recovery from neglect. Women were admitted for the first time in 1895, and in the first decade of the twentieth century the curriculum was broadened. Enrollment began a slow rise, and the state rechartered the college as a university for the final time in 1906.

In the early part of the new century, the University of South Carolina struggled to compete for funding with five other state colleges (Clemson, Winthrop, the Citadel, the State Medical College, and the Colored Normal, Industrial, Agricultural and Mechanical College—later known as South Carolina State). A small, poor state, South Carolina simply could not afford to support six separate colleges and maintain a high standard of scholarship at any of them. When the Southern Association of Colleges and Schools (SACS) was founded in 1895, not a single college in South Carolina—public or private—qualified for membership. The University of South Carolina became the first state-supported institution in South Carolina to qualify for SACS membership in 1917.

During the 1920s there was a brief revival at Carolina. The student body more than doubled (from 621 to 1,419), state appropriations grew, and the university added academic programs in music, art, and electrical engineering; Ph.D. programs in history, English, and education; and new schools for pharmacy and journalism.

For all the successes of the 1920s, serious problems remained, largely owing to the persistent poverty in South Carolina. For example, in 1925 the annual appropriation for the University of North Carolina exceeded that for all of South Carolina's state colleges combined. The Great Depression ended the brief period of promise of the 1920s. State appropriations plummeted, and the hard times forced the state to pay faculty salaries, already woefully inadequate, in scrip. The administration raised student tuition and severely curtailed graduate programs.

The outbreak of World War II revived and transformed the university. As students left school in droves to enter the armed forces, the university initiated programs to help train civilians for defense-related industries. In 1943 the campus became home to officer training programs of the U.S. Navy and the trainees filled the dormitories, outnumbering civilian students. In the aftermath of the war veterans filled the campus, expanding the student body to new records and taxing the capacity of campus facilities.

However, the state continued to provide inadequate resources, and the University of South Carolina ranked at or near the bottom in comparisons with its peers in other states. In 1951 trustees named Donald Russell president, and he began a reform program that put the university on the road to recovery. He recruited prestigious faculty, established new academic programs, and revived old ones. With the support of the General Assembly, Carolina began a wide-scale construction program that modernized the campus. To meet the growing demand for higher education, in the late 1950s the institution began establishing regional campuses in communities such as Florence, Conway, and Beaufort.

With increasing levels of state funding and the arrival of the baby boom generation during the 1960s and early 1970s, Carolina grew from a student body of about 5,000 to nearly 25,000. Degree offerings expanded likewise, and under the leadership of President Thomas Jones, graduate education and research received growing emphasis.

Change was constant. The increasing size of the student body was matched with changes in the nature of those students. As the result of a federal court order, on September 11, 1963, Henrie D. Monteith, Robert Anderson, and James Solomon became the first of an ever-growing number of African American students to enroll at the university in the late twentieth century. Increasing numbers of international students came to Columbia as well.

In the late 1970s and 1980s, the university's physical growth slowed but new degree programs and schools and colleges such as the College of Criminal Justice, the medical school, the College of Library Science, and the undergraduate Honors College helped expand educational opportunities. Renovations of older areas such as the Horseshoe ensured that the historic heart of the campus survived. Private fund-raising became a priority as state funding continued to lag behind growth, and the university emphasized international programs that attracted national attention. The quest for national recognition briefly stumbled when the university's aggressive president James B. Holderman was driven from office in 1990 in the wake of a highly publicized spending scandal.

In the 1990s the University of South Carolina continued the drive for national recognition, emphasizing increased levels of faculty research and outside research funding. In 2001 the institution celebrated a legacy of two hundred years of educating South Carolinians by dedicating itself to continued improvements in the quality of service it offers to the Palmetto State. HENRY H. LESESNE

Burke, W. Lewis, Jr. "The Radical Law School: The University of South Carolina School of Law and Its African American Graduates, 1873–1877." In *At Freedom's Door: African American Founding Fathers and Lawyers in Reconstruction South Carolina,* edited by James Lowell Underwood and W. Lewis Burke, Jr. Columbia: University of South Carolina Press, 2000.

Green, Edwin L. *A History of the University of South Carolina.* Columbia, S.C.: The State Company, 1916.

Hollis, Daniel Walker. *University of South Carolina.* 2 vols. Columbia: University of South Carolina Press, 1951–1956.

La Borde, Maximilian. *History of the South Carolina College.* Charleston, S.C.: Walker, Evans & Cogswell, 1874.

Lesesne, Henry H. *A History of the University of South Carolina, 1940–2000.* Columbia: University of South Carolina Press, 2001.

Sugrue, Michael. "South Carolina College: The Education of an Antebellum Elite." Ph.D. diss., Columbia University, 1992.

White, Pamela Mercedes. "'Free and Open': The Radical University of South Carolina, 1873–1877." Master's thesis, University of South Carolina, 1975.

Urbanization. Like other southern states, South Carolina became urban at a far slower rate than did the northeastern and midwestern regions of the United States. Although Charleston had been the fourth largest city in North America in the eighteenth century, during the antebellum period a mature plantation economy and dispersed backcountry settlement led to a pattern of rural agriculture with scattered courthouse and market towns. After Reconstruction, railroads and textile mills gradually stimulated the growth of urban centers, but nevertheless the majority of South Carolina's population remained rural until 1980. Much of the new urban population, however, lived in suburban and coastal communities that did not resemble traditional cities.

After early settlers relocated to Oyster Point in 1680, Charleston became one of the wealthiest and fastest-growing cities in the colonies, with twelve thousand residents by 1775. About one-quarter of all

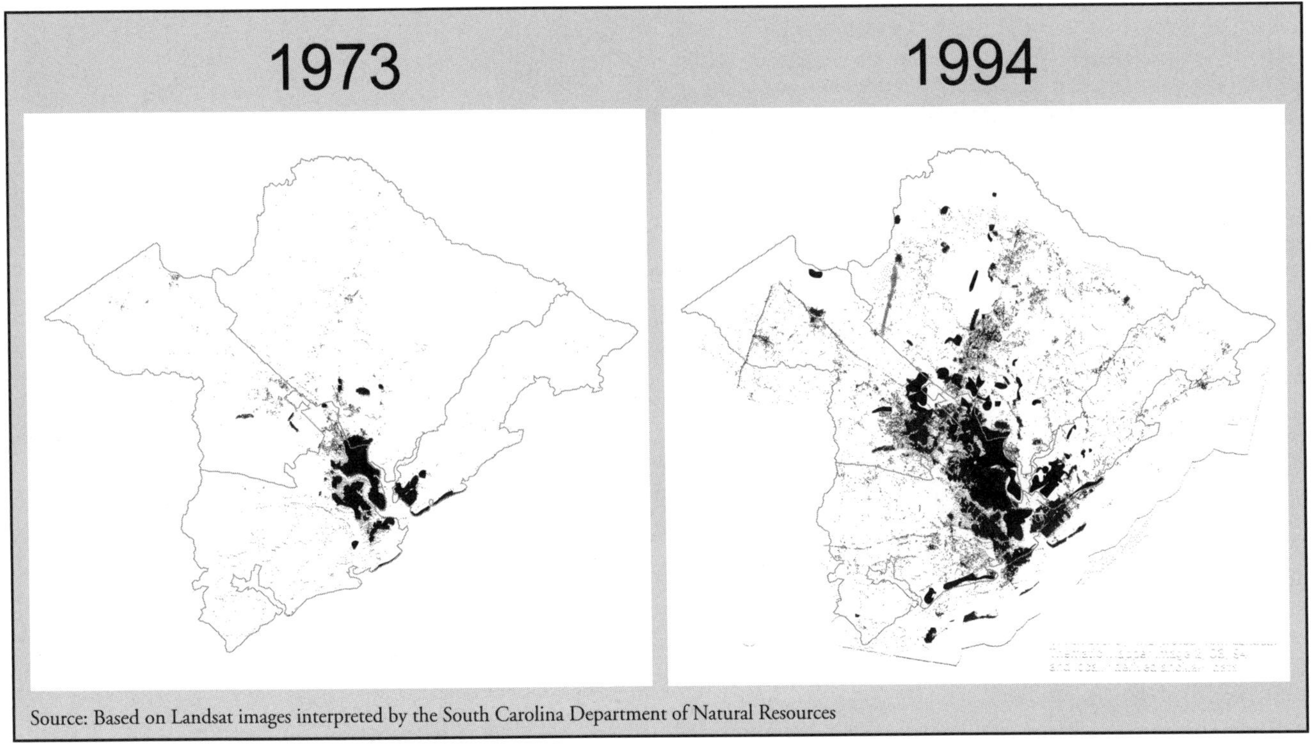

Urban sprawl—the encroachment of cities on farmland and forests—as seen in these two maps of the greater Charleston area

white South Carolinians lived there; no other colony had such a population concentration. Fine homes, grand churches, diverse shops, skilled craftsmen, and cultural institutions made the bustling seaport and colonial capital an urban and urbane center.

After Columbia was chosen as the state capital in 1786, it grew steadily, reaching 4,340 residents by 1840 and 6,060 in 1850. It officially (and symbolically) changed its name to the "City of Columbia" in 1855. Despite Columbia's steady growth, Charleston remained larger until well into the twentieth century. At the time of the Civil War, they were the only true cities in the state. They were still the largest in 2000.

South Carolina's devotion to agriculture worked against the development of cities and towns for much of its history. Antebellum plantations and farms stressed self-sufficiency and sought the marketing and distribution services of urban centers only during relatively confined portions of the year, especially in the months after the harvest. The state's large slave population kept consumer demand low, with many large planters preferring to order supplies in bulk from northern merchants rather than patronize smaller, local establishments. In addition, the devotion of South Carolina whites to the rural way of life made them deeply suspicious of cities, seeing them as breeding grounds of vice, crime, fanaticism, and—especially in northern states—abolitionism.

The state's courthouse towns were tiny urban centers. Most were busy on court days, but their permanent populations remained small. The expansion of railroads beginning in the 1850s, however, sparked a noticeable increase in the number and population of towns in South Carolina. Existing courthouse towns, such as York and Laurens, saw dramatic increases in their populations following the arrival of railroads, while new towns, such as Rock Hill and Blackville, emerged from depots and turnouts erected along railroad lines.

The Civil War devastated Charleston and Columbia and depopulated coastal plantation areas. Railroads recovered rapidly afterward, however, bringing hope to towns along their tracks. Sumter, for example, invested in several railroads at once in order to create its own destiny as a rail hub. After 1873 the Charlotte and Atlanta Air Line railroad provided reliable and faster transportation to the markets of the Northeast.

In 1876 the state's first postbellum textile mills were built in the upper Piedmont. Most were small, backed by local capital, and shipped finished goods north. As larger mills were established across the state at the end of the century, former tenant and subsistence farmers flocked to their mill villages. While textile employees were poorly paid and considered a low social class, the mills economically supported an expanding urban middle class. Few of the European immigrants who fueled the growth of northern cities settled in the South.

Cotton mills made the upcountry more urban. Greenville reached 10,000 people by 1900, 20,000 before 1920, and a peak of 66,188 in 1960. Spartanburg, Anderson, and Rock Hill kept pace, frequently jostling for numerical supremacy. Although Florence, Orangeburg, and Sumter became regional railroad and industrial hubs, the population center of the state was shifting north and west.

With larger urban populations the availability of goods, services, schools, entertainment, and libraries also improved, leading to a way of city life that was markedly different from that in the countryside and small towns. In the 1910s and 1920s the appearance of cities changed. The first skyscrapers were erected, including the Palmetto Building in Columbia and the Woodside Building in Greenville. First trolleys and then automobiles encouraged the growth of middle-class neighborhoods outside downtown. In 1918 Columbia's street railway carried eleven million passengers.

The growth of cities slowed but did not stop during the Great Depression. Federal programs employed city dwellers; some worked for new businesses, especially the life insurance industry. Many farmers abandoned their land and sought refuge and hope in the cities. By 1940 about one-fourth of the population was considered

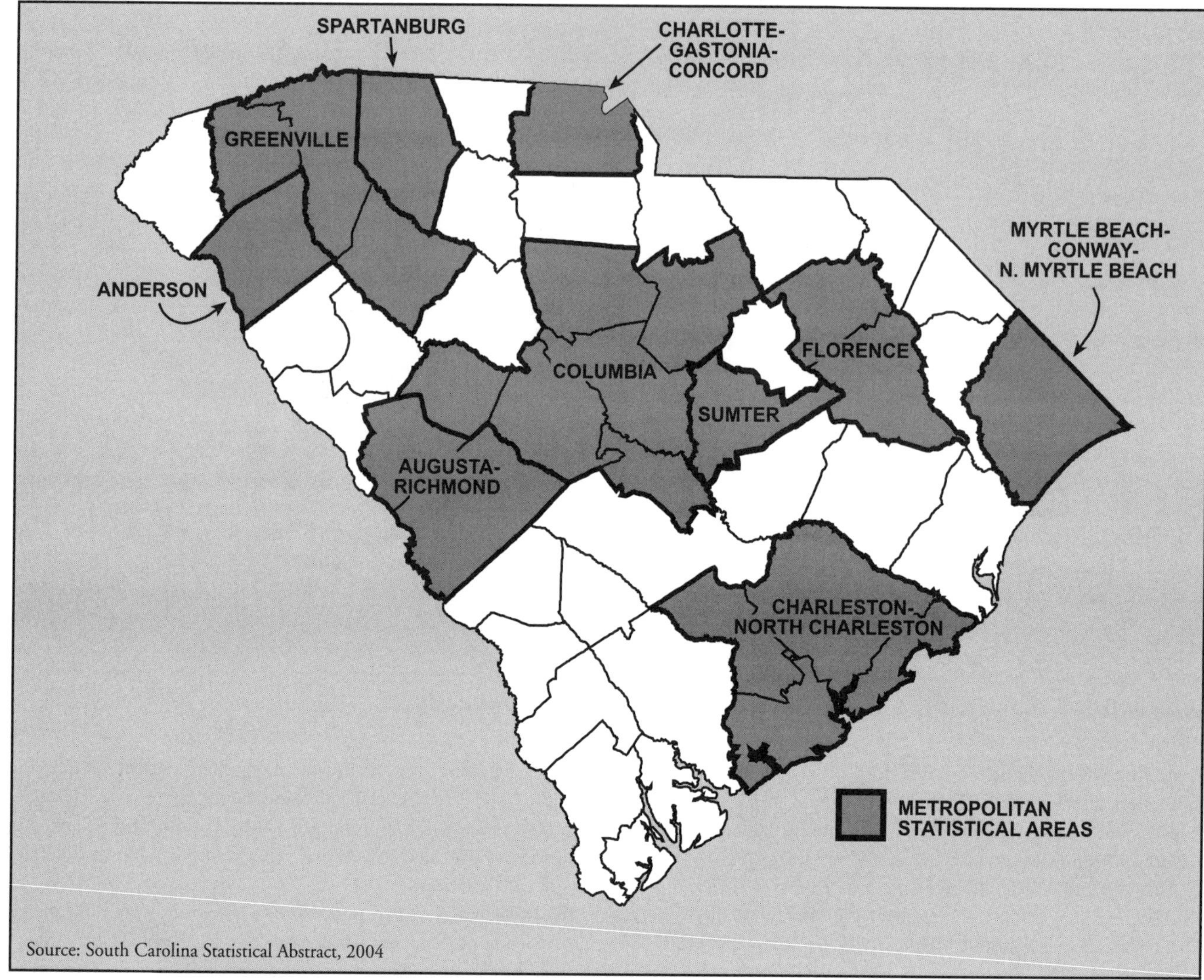

Metropolitan statistical areas, 2004

urban as compared to one-twelfth in 1870. South Carolina was becoming more urban, but at rates that lagged behind the national averages by about fifty years. As late as 1950 only ten cities had more than ten thousand residents.

World War II brought military mobilization; cities grew from the influx of military personnel at air bases in Sumter and Greenville, the army base at Fort Jackson in Columbia, and the navy base in Charleston. Many soldiers, sailors, and airmen made their first visits to South Carolina during the war; some stayed or returned later to retire.

Following the war, South Carolina shared the national explosion of new automobile-oriented suburbs. As early as the 1950s, this new growth spilled across city boundaries into unincorporated areas. Because of restrictive annexation laws, many cities could not expand, and their population growth slowed or stopped while suburbs flourished. Overall, the state's urban population grew from 36.7 percent in 1950 to 54.1 percent in 1980.

The formation of the South Carolina Development Board in 1954 marked a new era of industrial recruitment that began to take South Carolina beyond the textile age. While the new jobs were concentrated in the upstate, Columbia, Charleston, and smaller regional centers such as Florence, Sumter, Orangeburg, and Greenwood expanded as well. International companies began to move into the state. By 1973 Spartanburg had twenty-four foreign corporations employing four thousand workers.

The Development Board also made the first intensive study of the potential for resort and tourism development along the coast. With Sea Pines Plantation, Hilton Head Island developer Charles Fraser provided a new model for growth that changed the state and influenced the nation. Large-scale gated retirement communities on the Fraser model, with accompanying commercial centers, spread across the lowcountry. The population of the coastal region, virtually stagnant since the Civil War, climbed dramatically. Prosperity returned to languishing coastal communities such as Beaufort. Between 1950 and 1980 the population of Hilton Head Island grew from a few hundred to 11,344. Tourists and retirees prompted rapid growth in Myrtle Beach and the surrounding Grand Strand as well. Charleston, long too poor to tear down and replace its old buildings, became a world leader in historic preservation and heritage tourism.

While railroads shaped the state in the nineteenth century, highways dominated the twentieth century. The interstate highway system especially benefited larger cities. The authorizing legislation, passed in the 1950s as a defense measure, mandated the connection of all metropolitan areas with populations of more than fifty thousand. Charleston, Greenville, Columbia, Florence, and Spartanburg made the list, as did Charlotte, Savannah, and Augusta just across the state lines. Cities such as Myrtle Beach, Sumter, Orangeburg, and Greenwood did not, retarding their growth. By 1980 the seven metropolitan areas of the state, including Rock Hill / Charlotte and Augusta/Aiken, led the state in population growth and prosperity.

While South Carolina officially became an urban state in 1980, in reality it was a predominantly *suburban* state. In Greenville County, for example, the city population has remained near 60,000 since 1960, while the county population has climbed to nearly 400,000 by 2000. The trends were similar in Columbia and Charleston. North Charleston, Goose Creek, and Hanahan were unincorporated communities in 1950. By 1980 their populations respectively reached 79,641, 29,208, and 12,937. Mount Pleasant grew from fewer than 5,000 people in the 1940s to 47,609 in 2000.

Suburban growth benefited small towns near urban centers. Lexington, Cayce, and Irmo grew faster than Columbia. Easley, Greer, Mauldin, and Simpsonville outpaced Greenville. In the upstate the area between Anderson, Spartanburg, and Fountain Inn became an almost continuous urban region. The seven-county upstate region passed one million people by 2000.

Suburban residents helped make emerging metropolitan areas more sophisticated by promoting new office buildings, live theater companies, symphonies, museums, and arenas. Charleston and Greenville dramatically revitalized their downtowns. Charleston, Columbia, Greenville, Florence, and Myrtle Beach sponsored minor-league sports teams.

Rapid suburban growth led to increasing concern about sprawl and the loss of community identity. In the 1990s South Carolina ranked within the top five states in the conversion of rural land to urban uses. "New Urbanism," an alternative to sprawl pioneered by Andres Duany and Elizabeth Plater-Zyberk at Seaside, Florida, inspired similar projects in South Carolina. In Beaufort County the Village at Port Royal, New Point, and Habersham became compact walkable developments based on traditional small towns. The I'On and Daniel Island communities became competitive with traditional suburbs near Charleston.

By 2000 South Carolina had become increasingly urban and more closely tied to national trends. However, it remained more rural than the nation as a whole. Its towns and cities developed at a rate similar to those of other states in the Old South, suggesting that this lag in urbanization was a regional phenomenon. ROBERT W. BAINBRIDGE

Caldwell, Wilber W. *The Courthouse and the Depot: The Architecture of Hope in an Age of Despair.* Macon, Ga.: Mercer University Press, 2001.

Carlton, David L. *Mill and Town in South Carolina, 1880–1920.* Baton Rouge: Louisiana State University Press, 1982.

Ernst, Joseph A., and H. Roy Merrens. "'Camden's Turrets Pierce the Skies!': The Urban Process in the Southern Colonies during the Eighteenth Century." *William and Mary Quarterly,* 3d ser., 30 (October 1973): 549–74.

Glaab, Charles N., and A. Theodore Brown. *A History of Urban America.* 2d ed. New York: Macmillan, 1976.

Huff, Archie Vernon, Jr. *Greenville: The History of the City and County in the South Carolina Piedmont.* Columbia: University of South Carolina Press, 1995.

Kovacik, Charles F., and John J. Winberry. *South Carolina: The Making of a Landscape.* 1987. Reprint, Columbia: University of South Carolina Press, 1989.

Moore, John Hammond. *Columbia and Richland County: A South Carolina Community, 1740–1990.* Columbia: University of South Carolina Press, 1993.

V

Vanderhorst, Arnoldus (1748–1815). Governor. Vanderhorst, the son of Arnoldus Vanderhorst and Elizabeth Simons, was born on March 21, 1748, in Christ Church Parish. He wed Elizabeth Raven on March 5, 1771, and the union produced at least six children. A successful planter and slaveholder, Vanderhorst owned a 1,350-acre plantation on Kiawah Island as well as substantial landholdings elsewhere in South Carolina.

Vanderhorst's public career began in 1772 when he was elected to the Thirtieth Royal Assembly by Christ Church Parish. He was reelected three times before that body was dissolved in 1775. As the Revolutionary War approached, he demonstrated his patriotic sympathies by serving on the Committee of Ninety-Nine (1774) and representing his home parish in the First (1775) and Second (1775–1776) Provincial Congresses. During the war, Vanderhorst served as a militia captain at Haddrell's Point (1776) and as a colonel under General Francis Marion (1782).

Following the war, Vanderhorst spent most of his time in Charleston. He operated a mercantile firm and came to own considerable property around the city. He also became an active figure in civic affairs, serving twice as intendant mayor for Charleston (1785–1786, 1791) and as a trustee for the College of Charleston (1785–1791). Still a landowner in Christ Church, he represented that parish in the General Assembly nine times between 1776 and 1794, twice in the House and seven times in the Senate. Aligning himself with Charleston's strong Federalist contingent, Vanderhorst joined his lowcountry colleagues in resisting upcountry demands for legislative reapportionment and opposing the relocation of the capital from Charleston to Columbia, which he sarcastically dubbed "Town of Refuge," believing that the remote inland location would make the new capital a haven for outlaws.

Vanderhorst's Federalist connections, particularly the powerful Rutledge-Pinckney faction, led to his election as governor on December 17, 1794. Although serving as governor of a state rife with sectionalism and partisanship, Vanderhorst managed to set aside his personal biases and provide South Carolina with positive leadership. He requested improvement of state jail facilities and sought revision of the criminal code, proposing "instead of the indiscriminate punishment of death . . . inflict a long or short term of solitary confinement on the offenders, in some measure proportionate to their crime." An advocate of public education, Vanderhorst urged the General Assembly to establish schools throughout the state to diffuse "knowledge and information" so that "morals and virtue" might "adorn and characterize the citizens of South Carolina." Also, with Indian troubles in the West and the threat of war with Britain and France looming over the state and nation, Vanderhorst pushed the state to attend to its defenses, placing a priority on the protection of both Charleston and the frontier. At the close of his term as governor in 1796, Vanderhorst still held his party's favor and was selected to act as a presidential elector for John Adams.

Following his gubernatorial term, Vanderhorst served a final term in the House as a representative for St. Philip's and St. Michael's Parishes (1798–1799). He died in Charleston on January 29, 1815, and was buried in St. Michael's Churchyard. MATTHEW A. LOCKHART

Bailey, N. Louise, Mary L. Morgan, and Carolyn R. Taylor, eds. *Biographical Directory of the South Carolina Senate, 1776–1985.* 3 vols. Columbia: University of South Carolina Press, 1986.

Venus flytrap. Often described as the most unusual plant on earth, the Venus flytrap (*Dionaea muscipula* Ellis) is a terrestrial insectivorous (bug-eating) plant native to a small section of South Carolina and North Carolina within an approximately one-hundred-mile radius of Wilmington, North Carolina. The plant produces highly modified leaves that act as active trapping mechanisms, which snap shut when small insects crawl across the leaf. The surfaces of the leaves contain nectar glands along the margins that produce a sweet substance to attract insects. Small hairs on the leaf surfaces act as triggering mechanisms. A prey must touch more than one hair or a single hair twice within a twenty-second interval for the trap to close. This adaptation allows the plant to differentiate between a meal and a raindrop or other object dropping on the leaf. Once the trap is triggered, it closes within a half-second, trapping the insect inside. Special glands on the leaf surface "digest" the insect and then the leaf may open again. Each leaf can close approximately three times before dying or becoming inactive.

Venus flytrap. Photograph by Robert Clark. Courtesy, South Carolina Department of Natural Resources

This unusual plant is found in longleaf pine savannas and on margins of pocosins (shrub bogs), where light is abundant and soils are sandy and acidic. These areas are kept open by frequent low-intensity ground fires that have traditionally burned through the area in intervals from two to seven years. In South Carolina this species is currently found only in Horry and Georgetown Counties and is threatened by development, overcollection, and lack of fire. Large populations occur in the Lewis Ocean Bay Heritage Preserve and Cartwheel Bay Heritage Preserve, both in Horry County. PATRICK MCMILLAN

Fagerberg, Wayne R., and Dawn Allain. "A Quantitative Study of Tissue Dynamics during Closure in the Traps of Venus's Flytrap *Dionaea muscipula* Ellis." *American Journal of Botany* 78 (May 1991): 647–57.
Porcher, Richard D. *A Guide to the Wildflowers of the South Carolina Lowcountry and Lower Pee Dee.* Columbia: University of South Carolina Press, 1996.
Porcher, Richard D., and Douglas A. Rayner. *A Guide to the Wildflowers of South Carolina.* Columbia: University of South Carolina Press, 2001.
Sibaoka, Takao. "Rapid Plant Movements Triggered by Action Potentials." *Botanical Magazine* [Tokyo] 104 (March 1991): 73–95.

Verner, Elizabeth O'Neill (1883–1979). Artist. Verner was born in Charleston on December 21, 1883, the daughter of Henry John O'Neill and his wife, Mollie. A 1902 graduate of Ursuline Academy in Columbia, she attended the Pennsylvania Academy of the Fine Arts for two years (1903–1904), where she studied with Thomas Anshutz. After teaching for a year in Aiken, she took up residence in Charleston, where she married E. Pettigrew Verner on April 24, 1907. The couple had two children. She was active in numerous art organizations, as a founder of the Charleston Sketch Club, the Charleston Etchers' Club, and the Southern States Art League, on whose board she served from 1922 to 1933.

Elizabeth O'Neill Verner. Courtesy, South Carolina Historical Society

Verner emerged as a leading figure of the Charleston Renaissance alongside her mentor, Alice Ravenel Huger Smith. Early in her career, she focused on etchings of Charleston street scenes that depicted the city's architectural heritage and African American residents. Attached to her birthplace, she felt obligated to portray its picturesque charm: "I owe my native city incalculably much, and so it is in this spirit that this collection of my etchings has been gathered together," she declared in *Prints and Impressions of Charleston.* Over a long and productive career she created about 260 etchings in a variety of sizes, including miniatures that measure two by two inches. Edition sizes ranged from fifty to one hundred. In the mid-1930s she began to work in pastel, a medium that allowed her to introduce color. After a 1937 trip to Japan she perfected rendering pastel on silk mounted to board. In her pastels she frequently portrayed flower vendors, a Charleston tradition that she helped to preserve when a new ordinance threatened their activities. She was a charter member of the Society for the Preservation of Old Dwellings and was a strong advocate for preservation in Charleston.

Verner avidly produced books and articles, using her etchings and drawings to disseminate the charms of Charleston. These include *Prints and Impressions of Charleston* (1939), *Mellowed by Time: A Charleston Notebook* (1941), and *Other Places* (1946). She opened her studio to visitors and frequently served as a tour guide for groups such as the Art Institute of Chicago. In return, these tourists bought examples of her work. She traveled to Europe in 1930 and to Japan in 1937. In 1947 both the University of South Carolina and the University of North Carolina awarded her honorary degrees. Her work is represented in the following museums: Gibbes Museum of Art, Columbia Museum of Art, Greenville County Museum of Art, South Carolina State Museum, and Metropolitan Museum of Art, New York. Verner died on April 27, 1979, in Charleston. See plate 29. MARTHA R. SEVERENS

Bussman, Marlo Pease. *Born Charlestonian: The Story of Elizabeth O'Neill Verner.* Columbia, S.C.: State Printing, 1969.
Myers, Lynn Robertson, ed. *Mirror of Time: Elizabeth O'Neill Verner's Charleston.* Columbia: McKissick Museum, University of South Carolina, 1983.
Verner, Elizabeth O'Neill. *Prints and Impressions of Charleston.* Columbia, S.C.: Bostick & Thornley, 1939.
———. *Mellowed by Time: A Charleston Notebook.* Columbia, S.C.: Bostick & Thornley, 1941.

Vesey, Denmark (ca. 1767–1822). Slave, artisan, abolitionist. Vesey was probably born on the Danish Caribbean sugar island of St. Thomas around 1767; the names and nationality of his parents are unknown. In 1781 he was purchased by Captain Joseph Vesey, a slave trader, who trained him as a cabin boy during the short voyage to the French colony of Saint Domingue. Captain Vesey sold the boy as one of 390 slaves in the city of Cap François but was forced to purchase him back on April 23, 1782, because the child had displayed "epileptic fits." These were perhaps feigned, for they ceased once the boy reboarded Captain Vesey's vessel. This time Joseph Vesey kept him and renamed him Telemaque, after the mythical son of Odysseus. Over time fellow slaves corrupted or punned the name into Telmack and then into Denmark, after the Danish-owned island of his birth.

In the late spring of 1783 Joseph Vesey established himself in Charleston as a ship chandler. Denmark evidently lived with the Vesey family on 281 King Street. For the next seventeen years the literate and multilingual Denmark was responsible for helping to receive imported goods from incoming ships, cataloging items in Captain Vesey's East Bay Street office, and even conducting minor transactions in his master's absence. At some point during this time Denmark married an enslaved woman named Beck, who gave birth to at least three of his children: Sandy, Polydore, and Robert. But Denmark and Beck never lived in the same home, and their relationship was further strained in 1796 when Joseph Vesey, now a widower, moved his household to the Grove, an Ashley River plantation.

Denmark's luck changed on November 9, 1799, when he won $1,500 in the "East-Bay Lottery." The captain and his wealthy mistress—who by then was Denmark's legal owner—agreed to let him purchase his freedom for $600. On December 31, 1799, Denmark handed over a portion of his winnings in exchange for his freedom papers. Because he intended to stay in Charleston and learn carpentry, he adopted the surname of Vesey, which was well known among the white businessmen who would be his main clients as the city expanded north up the peninsula.

Vesey rented a modest home at 20 Bull Street. Thomas Bennett, a merchant and politician, constructed his lumber mill at the west end of the avenue on the Ashley River, which made the street a natural home for men who earned their livelihoods in construction. There, following the collapse of his relationship with Beck, Vesey married the much younger Susan, who was born a slave around

1795 but gained her freedom early in the nineteenth century. Despite modern allegations that Vesey practiced polygamy, no evidence exists to support the theory. As the only woman to bear Denmark's adopted surname, Susan Vesey may have married her husband in one of the city's churches. To help supplement the family's meager income, Susan took in laundry and ironing from her white neighbors. Despite later assertions that Vesey died a wealthy man worth more than $7,000, there is no evidence that he ever owned property.

Vesey may have had his marriage to Susan solemnized in the Second Presbyterian Church, which he attended as late as April 1817. But perhaps infuriated by the proslavery brand of Christianity heard within that church's walls, Vesey became an early member (and lay preacher) in the city's African Methodist Episcopal Church on Anson Street, commonly dubbed the "African Church." Although the Reverend Morris Brown's Sunday sermons included a creative melding of African and Christian elements, Vesey's nightly Bible lessons turned to "the stern and Nemesis-like God of the Old Testament." Embittered by the continuing bondage of Beck and his children, Vesey turned his back on the New Testament and what he regarded as its false promise of universal brotherhood.

Recognizing the dangers that the African Church posed to white control, city authorities briefly closed its doors in 1818 and then again in late 1820 and in January 1821. In response, Vesey began to consider a plan by which he might lead his children and disciples into freedom in Haiti. What made his conspiracy unique was not merely the advanced age of its leader (fifty-four years), but that Vesey planned a mass exodus of families out of Charleston. The plot called for urban slaves and bondmen across the Ashley and Cooper Rivers to slay their masters on the morning of Sunday, July 14, 1822, and fight their way toward the city docks. Although Vesey employed several enslaved blacksmiths to forge weapons, the leading conspirators wisely decided not to stockpile weapons nor to recruit thousands of soldiers before mid-July. "Let us assemble a sufficient number to commence the work with spirit," Vesey remarked, "and we'll not want men, [as] they'll fall in behind fast enough."

On May 22 William Paul, one of Vesey's chief recruiters, made a fatal mistake. While at the Market Wharf, he spoke of the plan to Peter, a mulatto cook, who passed the alarm to his master Colonel John C. Prioleau. At about the same time another mulatto slave, George Wilson, gave information about the plan to his master, who hurried with the news to Intendant (Mayor) James Hamilton and Governor Thomas Bennett. Exactly one month later, on June 22, Vesey was arrested at the "house of one of his wives," probably Beck. Four days after his capture, the aged carpenter was brought before two magistrates and five freeholders in the city workhouse. The tribunal found Vesey guilty and sentenced him to hang "on Tuesday next, the 2d July, between six and eight in the morning." On that morning Warden John Gordon loaded Vesey and five other abolitionists into a "cart" for the two-mile ride north to Blake's Lands. Before "immense crowds of whites and blacks," the six men hobbled up the gallows stairs. According to Intendant Hamilton, they collectively "met their fate with the fortitude of Martyrs."

In all, related to Vesey's plan, the Charleston courts arrested 131 slaves and free blacks. Thirty were released without trial. Of the 101 men who appeared before the tribunals, the magistrates ordered 35 hanged and 37, including Vesey's daughter Sandy, transported to Spanish Cuba. Twenty-three were acquitted, 2 more died while in custody, 3 were found not guilty but were whipped, and 1 free black was released on condition that he leave the state. City authorities exiled the Reverend Morris Brown of the AME Church to Philadelphia and razed the building. Vesey's son Robert rebuilt it in October 1865 at the end of the Civil War. DOUGLAS R. EGERTON

Egerton, Douglas R. *He Shall Go Out Free: The Lives of Denmark Vesey.* Madison, Wis.: Madison House, 1999.

Paquette, Robert L., and Douglas R. Egerton. "Of Facts and Fables: New Light on the Denmark Vesey Affair." *South Carolina Historical Magazine* 105 (January 2004): 8–48.

Powers, Bernard E. *Black Charlestonians: A Social History, 1822–1885.* Fayetteville: University of Arkansas Press, 1994.

Vesta Mills. By the close of the nineteenth century, the concentration of textile factories in the upstate manufacturing centers of Greenville and Spartanburg caused manufacturers to become concerned about supplies of local cotton and labor. Spartanburg mill owner John Montgomery and New York commission merchant Seth Milliken ventured far afield in 1899 with a controversial purchase of a mill in Charleston, which the partners intended to operate with African American labor.

Montgomery and Milliken purchased the Charleston Cotton Mills not long after the National Union of Textile Workers launched an organizational campaign in South Carolina. The experiment with African American labor in Charleston also occurred at a time when mill owners and industrial boosters were responding to critics who voiced concerns about the "cotton mill problem."

The Charleston Cotton Mills had failed in 1898 after a period of labor unrest between former white employees and the African American operatives who replaced them. Montgomery and Milliken acquired the property at auction for $100,000 in 1899 and renamed it Vesta Mills. Montgomery's correspondence does not reveal the extent of his financial involvement in the "coon mill" in Charleston, but he did identify Milliken as the "back bone" of the acquisition.

At the outset of operations Vesta Mills did not employ African American labor throughout the mill. Approximately forty white operatives worked in the weave room, but Montgomery was convinced that in time blacks would be employed in all departments. Managerial problems, rather than the operatives, were a major concern to Montgomery, who on more than one occasion complained to the mill's manager about the cost of production.

At a meeting of Vesta's stockholders in autumn 1900, there was discussion and contention about the mill's future. A decision was postponed, and Montgomery advised Milliken, "I would rather lose fifteen thousand dollars invested some where else than to have that mill fail." The stockholders' decision to close the mill in January 1901 chilled relations between Montgomery and Milliken. Public comment in the press generally attributed the mill's closing to failure of the African American labor, but Montgomery would likely have concurred with the view of William Bird, a Charleston businessman and Vesta stockholder, who faulted Milliken, accusing him of taking "every means to show the colored labor unprofitable. Those negro women could tie a knot at a spindle as well as white women could." ALLEN STOKES

Stokes, Allen H. "Black and White Labor and the Development of the Southern Textile Industry, 1800–1920." Ph.D. diss., University of South Carolina, 1977.

———. "John H. Montgomery: A Pioneer Southern Industrialist." Master's thesis, University of South Carolina, 1967.

Voorhees College. Located in Denmark, Voorhees College is a four-year liberal arts undergraduate institution. Founded in 1897 by Elizabeth Evelyn Wright and Jessie Dorsey, the school was first

Vorhees College in the early twentieth century. Courtesy, South Caroliniana Library, University of South Carolina

known as the Denmark Industrial School and was based on Booker T. Washington's Tuskegee Institute. Wright was Washington's protégée and had determined that she wanted to "be the same type of woman as Mr. Washington was of a man." On graduation she set out for South Carolina to develop a second Tuskegee.

Wright's first efforts at Govan and in Hampton County were thwarted by a hostile white community, which burned buildings and building materials. Undaunted, Wright approached state senator Stanwix G. Mayfield of Bamberg County, who sold her twenty acres of land after she obtained an endorsement from Washington and collected pennies and nickels from black churches. The Denmark Industrial School became a reality when Wright and Dorsey taught 14 boarders and 236 pupils in the upstairs of an abandoned store. The curriculum included the basics of reading, writing, and arithmetic, but the school's primary mission was to develop students through an industrial-vocational system modeled after Tuskegee.

By 1902 Wright had successfully persuaded a New Jersey industrialist, Ralph Voorhees, to donate money that was used to purchase land and construct buildings. The institution was renamed for its benefactor, and the state legislature incorporated the school in 1904 as the Voorhees Industrial School for Colored Youths. The school now had almost 350 students and 17 faculty members and was supported by the local black community as well as through solicitation campaigns. Though Wright died in 1906, the school continued to prosper. By the end of World War I, however, Voorhees faced a financial crisis when gifts and grants decreased. In 1924 the school was taken over by the Episcopal Church's American Institute for Negroes and remains affiliated with the Diocese of South Carolina.

The school's name was changed in 1947 to Voorhees School and Junior College, and in 1962 it became Voorhees College. Earning full accreditation as a four-year school from the Southern Association of Colleges and Schools in 1968, Voorhees faced student unrest over civil rights and personnel issues. Voorhees students objected to the lack of blacks serving on the school's board of trustees as well as student living conditions, wage scales for nonacademic workers, few black history courses, and a poorly equipped library. With tempers rising and protests growing, armed students took over the library in April 1969. The demonstration was reported in the national press but ended quickly when the National Guard was called to the campus by President John Potts and J. Kenneth Morris, chairman of the board of trustees.

Potts's tenure as president of Voorhees from 1954 to 1970 was marked by both progress and protest. During that time the institution dropped its high school component and became a four-year college. Other accomplishments included increased enrollment, an improvement in the quality of the faculty, and an upgrading of the curriculum and programs. Several presidents who succeeded Potts did not prove to be as visionary in dealing with programs, finances, or students and were dismissed from office. Enrollment reached a high of one thousand students in 1976. In 2001 Voorhees had seven hundred students when it welcomed its seventh president, Dr. Lee Monroe. The college offers a traditional liberal arts program and awards bachelor's degrees in eleven majors. LOUISE ALLEN

"Academic Freedom and Tenure: Voorhees College (South Carolina)." *AAUP Bulletin* 60 (March 1974): 82–89.

Blanton, Robert J. *The Story of Voorhees College: From 1897 to 1982.* Smithtown, N.Y.: Exposition, 1983.

Jabs, Albert Emil. "The Mission of Voorhees College: Its Roots and Its Future." Ph.D. diss., University of South Carolina, 1983.

Robinson, James C. "South Carolina's Black Colleges: A Strategy for Survival." Ph.D. diss., University of Massachusetts, 1973.

Stoops, Barbara H. "Changes in Courses, Administration Planned." Columbia *State,* August 23, 1970, p. B1.

Wickenberg, Margaret. "Borrowed Bell and Two Chairs: Voorhees College's Beginnings." Columbia *State,* July 24, 1966, pp. D2, D12.

Voting Rights Act (1965). The Voting Rights Act of 1965 was enacted to reverse the effects of state disfranchisement and secure equal voting rights for all citizens. The legislation was a victory for racial minorities, especially African Americans in the South, because many had experienced social opposition to their voting.

After Reconstruction, the Ku Klux Klan and other organizations used violence and intimidation to limit African American voter turnout. South Carolina's African Americans faced legal challenges as well. Beginning in 1882, the Eight Box Law functioned effectively as a literacy test. In 1896 statewide party primaries that barred African American participation were introduced. With South Carolina firmly under white Democratic control, African Americans were excluded from politics, and voter registration plummeted: in October 1896 only 5,500 African Americans were registered to vote in the state.

In the presence of a growing national civil rights movement, President Lyndon Johnson issued a call for strong voting rights laws in 1965. The Voting Rights Act, signed into law in August 1965, suspended literacy tests and provided for the appointment of federal examiners with the power to register qualified citizens to vote. South Carolina immediately challenged the law's constitutionality in *South Carolina v. Katzenbach.* South Carolina, supported by briefs from other states, argued that Congress could not authorize federal officials to impose themselves on state affairs in the manner outlined by the act. The United States Supreme Court rejected that argument by an eight-to-one vote, declaring that Congress acted within its authority to enforce the goals of the Fifteenth Amendment. For the court's majority, widespread discrimination constituted "exceptional conditions" that allowed Congress to pass legislation to protect voting rights.

On being signed into law, the act had an almost immediate impact. In South Carolina the number of American Americans registered to vote rose dramatically. In 1964, 38.7 percent of voting-age African Americans were registered. Four years later that number climbed to 50.8 percent. There were also gains in African American political participation. Twelve black South Carolinians attended the 1968 Democratic National Convention as delegates. In 1970 three African Americans were elected to the General Assembly, the first black legislators since the 1890s. Less than a decade after the passage of the act, the number of African American legislators had risen to thirteen.

According to the United States Justice Department, the Voting Rights Act of 1965, as extended in 1970, 1975, and 1982, may be the most significant civil rights legislation passed by the United States Congress. Now blacks in South Carolina register to vote at about the same rate as whites. Enforcement of the act provides opportunities to challenge election methods that may weaken majority voting strength—for example, at-large elections, racially gerrymandered districting plans, or runoff requirements. Recently, leading civil rights organizations, through the National Commission on the Voting Rights Act, conducted hearings across the nation about the status of African American, Latino, Native American, and Asian American voters. Its report, presented to Congress in February 2006, documented the act's achievements as well as the need for the reauthorization of those portions of the act due to expire in 2007. KEVIN FELLNER

Davidson, Chandler, and Bernard Grofman, eds. *Quiet Revolution in the South: The Impact of the Voting Rights Act, 1965–1990.* Princeton: Princeton University Press, 1994.

Grofman, Bernard. *Minority Representation and the Quest for Voting Equality.* New York: Cambridge University Press, 1992.

Hudson, David M. *Along Racial Lines: Consequences of the 1965 Voting Rights Act.* New York: Peter Lang, 1998.

Waccamaw National Wildlife Refuge. Waccamaw National Wildlife Refuge (NWR) was established on December 1, 1997, to protect and manage diverse habitat components within an important coastal river ecosystem. Located in portions of Horry, Georgetown, and Marion Counties, Waccamaw NWR's acquisition boundary spans 55,000 acres and includes large sections of the Waccamaw and Great Pee Dee Rivers and a small section of the Little Pee Dee River. The U.S. Fish and Wildlife service continues to acquire lands within this acquisition boundary from willing sellers. As of 2002, refuge lands purchased totaled just under 8,000 acres.

Habitats within Waccamaw NWR's acquisition boundary include 6,166 acres of upland forest, located primarily on Sandy Island, with the remaining acreage being made up primarily of wetlands. The wetland diversity of this refuge sets it apart from most others found along the East Coast. Wetland habitats range from historic, broken tidal rice fields, to actively managed rice fields, to blackwater and alluvial floodplain forested wetlands of the Waccamaw and Great Pee Dee Rivers. These tidal freshwater wetlands are some of the most diverse of their type found in North America and offer many important habitats for migratory birds, fish, and resident wildlife. Swallow-tailed kites, ospreys, wood storks, white ibis, prothonotary warblers, and many species of waterfowl can be observed on a seasonal basis. Additionally, these wetlands play a critical role in the filtration and storm-water retention of the primary drinking water resource for the greater Grand Strand region.

Waccamaw NWR is one in a complex of four refuges administered by Cape Romain NWR. Public use opportunities include hunting, fishing, canoeing, and nature observation. MARSHALL SASSER

Waccamaw River. The Waccamaw River, named for the Waccamaw nation of Native Americans, begins at Lake Waccamaw in North Carolina. The river runs parallel to the coast through Horry and Georgetown Counties, never straying more than fifteen miles from the Atlantic Ocean. In Horry County the river runs through the county seat of Conway. The river is navigable from Georgetown to Conway, but its upper reaches become shallow and swampy.

The Waccamaw became the focus of a boundary dispute between South Carolina and North Carolina in 1729. In that year British officials declared that the river was to delimit part of the boundary line between the two colonies. Since officials were unfamiliar with the Waccamaw's course, however, the instructions proved ambiguous. The dispute was resolved in 1735, with South Carolina retaining Waccamaw Neck and what later became known as the Grand Strand.

From its mouth at Winyah Bay to the end of its tidal influence, the Waccamaw River once boasted the most successful rice plantations in South Carolina, which used the twice-daily tides to perfect tidal rice culture in the late eighteenth century. Rice remained king of the Waccamaw until early in the twentieth century.

Only two towns besides Conway ever bordered on the Waccamaw: Bucksport and Bucksville, both founded by Maine lumberman Henry Buck. Buck migrated to the Waccamaw in the 1830s and established sawmills around which these communities grew. After the Civil War his sons attempted a shipbuilding venture, and they turned out the only clipper ship built in South Carolina, the *Henrietta,* in 1875. The Buck ventures ultimately failed. Today the river is used for recreation and as part of the Intracoastal Waterway. Some former rice plantations, such as those making up Bernard Baruch's Hobcaw Barony, remain intact as nature preserves. A few, such as Brookgreen, have been transformed into tourist sites, while most have followed the pattern of Willbrook and Wachesaw and been developed for luxury housing and golf courses. JAMES H. TUTEN

Burroughs, Franklin. *The River Home: A Return to the Carolina Low Country.* 1992. Reprint, Athens: University of Georgia Press, 1998.

Joyner, Charles W. *Down by the Riverside: A South Carolina Slave Community.* Urbana: University of Illinois Press, 1984.

Linder, Suzanne Cameron, and Marta Leslie Thacker. *Historical Atlas of the Rice Plantations of Georgetown County and the Santee River.* Columbia: South Carolina Department of Archives and History for the Historic Ricefields Association, 2001.

Walhalla (Oconee County; 2000 pop. 3,801). Founded in 1850, Walhalla was a carefully planned German settlement that became the seat of Oconee County. Its settlers were members of the German Colonization Society, formed in Charleston by John A. Wagner, a German immigrant who had become a successful newspaper editor and businessman. Society members wanted suitable land to pursue their agrarian avocation. After advertising, the group was approached by Colonel Joseph Grisham of Pickens District, who offered to sell a tract of land. On December 24, 1849, the society purchased 17,859 acres from Grisham for $27,000. The town remained distinctly German until it became the courthouse seat in 1868. Its name, pronounced "Valhalla," was taken from Norse mythology and means "Garden of the Gods."

The town was laid out on a ridge at the foot of Stumphouse Mountain in eight four-acre sections on either side of a long and wide Main Street. Each society member received a half-acre lot on Main Street and an acre on either North or South Broad Street. Opposite those streets fifty-acre farms were laid out, and a meeting to draw lots for the property was held in Charleston on March 26, 1850. The first German immigrants arrived shortly thereafter. By 1854 Walhalla had a German population of some four hundred. The town was incorporated on December 19, 1855. One of the first structures was what became St. John's Lutheran Church, placed on the National Register of Historic Places in 1980.

At the outset of the Civil War, the Walhalla Riflemen, first organized in 1852, was among the first militia units to volunteer for Confederate service. During the war the town became a haven for lowcountry refugees, and nonresidents had to have certificates issued by the town council to remain within the town limits. The relative isolation of the region surrounding Walhalla attracted deserters and other men attempting to avoid military service. After the Confederate surrender, a small contingent of federal troops occupied the town.

After Walhalla was selected as the seat for Oconee County in 1868, the predominant German population was diluted by an influx of new settlers, including many from Pickens Court House, the former seat of the old Pickens District. The *Keowee Courier* likewise migrated from Pickens to Walhalla in 1868.

Walhalla had three colleges in its early history. Newberry College moved to Walhalla in 1856, remaining until 1877 when it returned to the town of Newberry. Citizens then organized Adger College under the Presbytery of South Carolina, which was discontinued in 1886. Walhalla Female College opened in 1877 but failed ten years later.

Known as the gateway to the Blue Ridge Mountains, Walhalla has maintained a steady population, but the German influence is all but gone. Drawing on its heritage, however, the town has held an annual Octoberfest celebration since 1979. The German Colonization Society no longer exists, and newer arrivals have been attracted to the town's growing manufacturing sector. Twentieth-century industries included Avondale Mills, Nason (which manufactured electrical switches), Oxford Industries, and Torrington Bearings. HURLEY E. BADDERS

Shealy, George Benet. *Walhalla: A German Settlement in Upstate South Carolina, "The Garden of the Gods."* Seneca, S.C.: Blue Ridge Art Association, 1990.

Walker, George Edward (ca. 1827–1863). Architect, engineer. Walker was among the first generation of architects to work professionally in South Carolina. He began practicing architecture in Charleston about 1850. His designs for Free School No. 6 and the library building at the College of Charleston garnered attention. His career took a sharp turn upward after he began serving under the direction of Edward B. White, the leading Charleston architect of the era, as superintending architect of the new customhouse.

In August 1854 Walker became the architect of the new state capitol at Columbia. He replaced Peter H. Hammarskold, who was dismissed when the half-completed foundations built under his direction were found to be crumbling. The appointment appeared to confirm Walker's emerging talent, but he proved unable to work productively with the commissioners and consulting architect John R. Niernsee. Walker oversaw the demolition of Hammarskold's failed foundations, but thereafter the project came to a standstill. In April 1855, after eight months of delays, the commissioners dismissed Walker and hired Niernsee to take his place, having recognized that Walker lacked the administrative skills and political acumen necessary to move the troubled project forward.

Despite his ill-fated tenure with the new state capitol, Walker was a competent architect of smaller buildings and designed Trinity Episcopal Church in Abbeville, Christ Church in Columbia, and buildings for educational institutions such as Columbia Female College and Newberry College. Walker enlisted in the Confederate army in April 1861 and supervised the construction of fortifications near Charleston and Savannah. His career came to a premature end when he died in Columbus, Georgia, of a sudden illness on September 16, 1863, at the age of thirty-six. DANIEL J. VIVIAN

Ravenel, Beatrice St. Julien. *Architects of Charleston.* 1945. Reprint, Columbia: University of South Carolina Press, 1992.

Vivian, Daniel J. "South Carolina's Architectural Ambition: The Effort to Erect the New State Capitol, 1851–1855." *South Carolina Historical Magazine* 100 (April 1999): 98–123.

Walker, William (1809–1875). Teacher, composer, author. Walker was born on May 6, 1809, near Cross Keys, Union District, the son of Absalom Walker and Susan Jackson. The family moved to the Cedar Springs section of Spartanburg District when he was seventeen. In 1832 Walker joined the Cedar Springs Baptist Church. About 1835 he married Amy Golightly, a member of the same congregation. The couple moved to the town of Spartanburg in the same year. They were the parents of five sons and five daughters.

In September 1835 Walker published *Southern Harmony,* a shaped-note hymnal using a four-shape (fa-so-la) system. The shaped-note style is a simplified musical notation developed to make it easier for untrained congregations to sing in harmony without instrumental accompaniment. Shapes (triangle=fa, oval=so, rectangle=la, and diamond=mi) were added to the note heads to help singers find pitches within major and minor scales. *Southern Harmony* included some of Walker's own compositions and the first publication of the tune "New Britain" with the words "Amazing Grace." Some older hymns and psalms in standard usage at the time were included as well as new compositions by other southern composers. The work was immensely popular across the South, going through several editions and selling more than 600,000 copies by 1854. When he signed his name, Walker added the initials "A.S.H." ("Author of Southern Harmony"), and he was affectionately known as "Singing Billy" Walker.

In 1846 Walker published *Southern and Western Pocket Harmonist.* Twenty years later he brought out a publication in the seven-shape (or do-re-mi) system entitled *Christian Harmony.* It contained many of the same hymns and psalms as his earlier publications, but with the addition of several modern tunes "more suitable to church use." A second and enlarged edition was published in 1873 and underwent printings as late as 1979. Other editions of his *Christian Harmony* and reprints of *Southern Harmony* are still available and remain in use. His last publication was *Fruits and Flowers* for use in Sunday schools. Some groups remain dedicated to continuing the tradition of singing Walker's *Southern Harmony* and the shaped-note style. The "Big Singing" is an annual event, held continually since 1884, on the fourth Sunday in May in Benton, Kentucky. The music group The Black Crowes named their 1992 album *The Southern Harmony and Musical Companion* after Walker's work. In May 2002 Wofford College in Spartanburg hosted a gathering of *Southern Harmony* enthusiasts.

In addition to his musical publications, Walker traveled over the South conducting singing schools. As early as 1849 he was an agent for the *Spartan,* the weekly newspaper in the town of Spartanburg. In June 1862 he was sent to Richmond to nurse Confederate soldiers. He maintained a bookstore for a time in Spartanburg. Walker died in Spartanburg on September 24, 1875, and was buried in that city's Magnolia Cemetery. BRENT HOLCOMB

Eskew, Harry L. "*Southern Harmony* and Its Era." *The Hymn* 41 (1990): 28–34.

Landrum, John B. O. *History of Spartanburg County, South Carolina.* 1900. Reprint, Spartanburg, S.C.: Reprint Company, 1977.

Walker, William. *The Southern Harmony and Musical Companion.* Edited by Glenn L. Wilcox. Lexington: University Press of Kentucky, 1987.

Walker, William Aiken (1839–1921). Painter. Walker was born in Charleston on March 11, 1839, the son of John Falls Walker and Mary Elizabeth Flint. Raised in Charleston and Baltimore, Maryland, Walker probably first exhibited a painting at the South Carolina Institute Fair of 1850. Early in the Civil War he enlisted in the Hampton Legion and was wounded at the Battle of Seven Pines. After a lengthy recuperation he returned to service as a cartographer. Following the war, Walker moved to Baltimore but returned to Charleston often to visit friends on nearby plantations, sketching their homes and the African Americans who worked for them.

Walker's name became practically synonymous with painting in the South by the end of the century, so popular were his images of African Americans, their cabins, and their way of life. During the 1870s Walker spent the summers in Baltimore, lived part of each autumn in Charleston, and then headed further south for the winter months, either to New Orleans or to Saint Augustine or Ponce Park, Florida. He developed a particular affinity for New Orleans, which he visited again and again over a thirty-year period. He often set up his easel at the corner of Royal and Dumaine Streets and sold freshly painted boards to tourists.

Walker was a serious and accomplished artist. Nevertheless, he used an assembly-line method to generate a prodigious output of postcard-size portraits that he sold to northern tourists as souvenirs of the Old South. Walker would take a large piece of academy board, mark it off into eight-by-four-inch sections, and then go over the whole with his ground color, usually sienna. Next he would paint in the sky, then the landscape, and finally he would place a figure in each rectangular space. He would then divide the board along the lines previously drawn into nearly pocket-size compositions. What he did not sell to passersby he consigned to local galleries, photography studios, and gift shops, which found a steady stream of purchasers.

Describing his style and output, Walker once said, "I am like the machine: I paint and repaint these subjects so that many can share the feelings I have for this magnificent world of ours. Art is not only for the artist, it is for all and I shall do my best to see that all can afford it, to the extent that I shall paint and paint and paint until the brush runs dry." Lesser-known aspects of his career include his topographical drawings, which include a series of careful renderings of Florida's east coast, and his trompe l'oeil (a technique that creates an illusion of three-dimensionality) paintings of fish and game.

Walker died in Charleston on January 3, 1921, and was buried with other members of his family at Magnolia Cemetery. His work is held in the collections of the Gibbes Museum of Art in Charleston, the Columbia Museum of Art, and the Greenville County Museum of Art as well as in numerous private collections. ROBERT M. HICKLIN, JR.

Seibels, Cynthia. *The Sunny South: The Life and Art of William Aiken Walker.* Spartanburg, S.C.: Saraland, 1995.

Trovaioli, August P., and Roulhac B. Toledana. *William Aiken Walker, Southern Genre Painter.* Baton Rouge: Louisiana State University Press, 1972.

Wallace, David Duncan (1874–1951). Historian. Wallace was born in Columbia on May 23, 1874, the son of William Henry Wallace and Alice Amanda Lomax Wallace. Wallace pursued his education at Newberry College, Wofford College, and Vanderbilt University. Wofford awarded him a B.A. in 1894 and an M.A. in 1895. He earned his Ph.D. from Vanderbilt in 1899. Both Presbyterian College and the University of South Carolina later recognized him with honorary degrees. On January 10, 1900, Wallace married Sophie W. Adam of Spartanburg. They were the parents of four children. Following Sophie Wallace's death in 1933, Wallace married Maud Orr on October 6, 1937.

David Duncan Wallace. Photograph by J. F. Sofge. Courtesy, James F. Sofge, Jr.

Wallace left a dual legacy for the study of South Carolina history. As a professor of history and economics for more than four decades at Wofford College, he challenged hundreds of students to love history and to value citizenship. As a writer, Wallace's magnum opus, the multivolume *History of South Carolina,* was the premier history of the state for more than six decades after its publication in 1935. In 1951 the University of North Carolina published an abridged version of Wallace's history entitled *South Carolina: A Short History, 1520–1948,* which became the college text for many future teachers and practitioners of South Carolina history.

In addition to the *History of South Carolina,* Wallace wrote *Constitutional History of South Carolina, 1727–1775* (1899), *Civil Government of South Carolina and the United States* (1906), *Life of Henry Laurens* (1915), *The Government of England* (1925), *South Carolina Constitution of 1895* (1927), and *History of Wofford College* (1951). He also produced scholarly articles and was a regular contributor to the *Southern Christian Advocate.*

Wallace considered his *History of South Carolina* and *Life of Henry Laurens* to be his best historical works. While "holding the most exacting standards of scientific accuracy," Wallace also believed that "all history should be written to be read." Thus, while advocating the scientific history of the nineteenth century, Wallace in his writing style looked toward the twenty-first century. Considered progressive at the time of its publication, Wallace's *History* nevertheless reflected the attitudes and biases that prevailed in the South Carolina of his day.

A historian who valued public service, Wallace was active in the Methodist Church, served on the State Board of Charities and Corrections (later the State Board of Public Welfare), and was a trustee for the South Carolina Boys' Industrial School. He was also elected to Phi Beta Kappa. Wallace died on April 29, 1951, in Spartanburg and was buried in Oakland Cemetery. ALEXIA JONES HELSLEY

Wallace, David Duncan. *The History of South Carolina.* 4 vols. New York: American Historical Society, 1935.

Walter, Thomas (ca. 1740–1789). Botanist, planter, patriot, politician. Walter was probably born in Hampshire, England. His aunt Frances Knight died there in 1784. She left a house to Walter from which he received rents until his death. His parents' names, his place and time of birth, and his education are not known. By 1769 Walter was in Charleston and remained in the lowcountry for the next twenty years. He acquired 4,500 acres through purchase and royal grants.

During this period Walter produced a manuscript for *Flora Caroliniana* that stands as a hallmark in its genre. It was the first flora document of a region of North America to utilize the Linnaean system of classification. For years Walter had collected plants in the coastal plain of South Carolina and cultivated many in his garden. He also received many specimens from the plant collector John Fraser. Fraser, a Scot, had traveled to South Carolina and, after meeting Walter, agreed to collect plants in the Piedmont and foothills for him. Walter added four hundred plants from Fraser to his own collection of approximately six hundred. His Latin descriptions of these species became the basis for the *Flora*. More than one thousand species are described, many of which were new to science, including Walter's pine (*Pinus glabra*) from the coastal plain and a magnolia (*Magnolia fraseri*) from the Carolina mountains that Walter named for Fraser. The plant collections, along with Walter's manuscript, were taken by Fraser to London in 1788. The *Flora* was published that year, and the collection remains housed in the British Museum of Natural History.

Walter collected plants and wrote descriptions while operating as a merchant and planter in the Carolina lowcountry. Active in the community, he could not escape the Revolutionary War. As a member of the committee for the Continental Association, Walter actively recruited for the patriot cause. In 1779 he received a commission as deputy paymaster of the state militia. After the war Walter became involved with planning the Santee Canal. Although the canal was constructed after his death, he did serve as a member of a company organized in 1786 to investigate the possibility of connecting the Santee and Cooper Rivers. The president of this company was General William Moultrie, and the vice president was John Rutledge. In addition to Walter, members of the board included Generals Thomas Sumter, Francis Marion, and Charles Cotesworth Pinckney.

Walter married Ann Lesesne of Daniels Island on March 26, 1769. She died without issue that same year. On March 20, 1777, he married Ann Peyre. The union produced three daughters and a son before Ann died in 1780. Walter was married for a third time the next year, to Dorothy Cooper. This final marriage produced one daughter.

Walter was elected to the General Assembly in the fall of 1788 but died in January 1789 before he was able to serve. He was buried in his garden on the south side of the Santee River in Berkeley County, near the old St. Stephen / St. John Parish line. DAVID H. REMBERT, JR.

Coker, W. C. "A Visit to the Grave of Thomas Walter." *Journal of Elisha Mitchell Scientific Society* 26 (April 1910): 31–42.

Maxon, William R. *Thomas Walter, Botanist.* Washington, D.C.: Smithsonian Institution, 1936.

Rembert, David. *Thomas Walter, Carolina Botanist.* Columbia: South Carolina Museum Commission, 1980.

Thomas, John Peyre, Jr. *Thomas Walter, Botanist.* Columbia: Historical Commission of South Carolina, 1946.

Walterboro (Colleton County; 2000 pop. 5,153). Just after the Revolutionary War, rice planters along the Edisto, Combahee, and Ashepoo Rivers, tired of an annual summer jaunt of fifty miles to Charleston, created an alternate refuge from the malarial swamps closer to home. By the 1790s, among local forests and freshwater springs, they built a village of about twenty log houses, which they called Walterboro, after two brothers whose retreat was prominent among them. A parish house for the conduct of public business was authorized in 1796, a sign that the healthy landscape had attracted permanent residents. Owing to the skill and labor of black slaves and the profits from rice and indigo, the planters and town both prospered. In 1817 centrally located Walterboro succeeded Jacksonboro as the Colleton District seat. An elegant brick courthouse designed by Robert Mills entered service in 1822, followed in quick succession by stores, a tavern, and a library. In 1826 Walterboro was incorporated, with boundaries extending "3/4 of a mile in every direction from the Walterborough Library" and a municipal government consisting of an elected council and intendant (mayor).

Walterboro was a hotbed of states' rights sentiment in the antebellum years when the North and the South dueled over tariffs, western expansion, and slavery. In 1828 Robert Barnwell Rhett launched the nullification movement at the Walterboro Courthouse. In 1861 the white men of Walterboro shouldered rifles and went to war to defend their beliefs and interests. Four years later the vanquished remnant came home to find slavery dead, agriculture in decline, whites poorer, and freed slaves accounting for more than half the Walterboro population of 834. Despite a short boom in phosphate mining from the 1880s through 1910s and the rise of more durable forest industries, prosperity proved elusive. In the 1880s, when house lots were still fenced to contain livestock and baseball and brass bands were the rage, the town got a railroad spur that connected Walterboro to the Atlantic Coast Line Railroad. Town councils passed laws protecting pine trees and Sundays and also installed oil lamps before switching to electric lights in 1915, about the time gasoline cars appeared. The two primary streets were paved in 1921.

In the latter decades of the twentieth century, Walterboro added population and wealth as it developed jobs in construction and light industry as well as public services, such as the $28 million Department of Veteran's Affairs Nursing Home. The high school was integrated and established itself as a football power in the 1970s, just as Colleton County was traversed by a new federal highway, Interstate 95. But if the old town was fading, links to the past survived. The farmers' market was still a central institution. Townspeople held fast to traditional ties of family and church. Hunting was a favored pastime. LAYLON WAYNE JORDAN

Glover, Beulah. *Narratives of Colleton County.* N.p., 1963.

Jordan, Laylon Wayne, and Elizabeth Stringfellow. *A Place Called St. John's.* Spartanburg, S.C.: Reprint Company, 1998.

Wanderer. The *Wanderer* was a schooner built in New York and initially intended to be a racing yacht. It was later sold to Captain William C. Corrie, who represented a group of investors in Savannah, Georgia, led by Charles A. L. Lamar. After a successful slave-trade voyage to Africa, the *Wanderer* landed near Brunswick, Georgia, in December 1858 with 420 Africans aboard. Most of the Africans were shipped up the Savannah River and put ashore in South Carolina near Augusta, Georgia, where they were sold into slavery. Many southerners, especially South Carolinians, applauded Lamar's bold venture and triumphantly proclaimed that the successful voyage of the *Wanderer* had reopened the slave trade. The venture also brought forth cries of protest from abolitionists in the North. Publicity of the *Wanderer*'s voyage prompted federal authorities, led by the U.S. attorney for the district of Georgia, to investigate the ship for violation of the 1820 federal statute that outlawed the slave trade. During the investigation, the ship was condemned and repurchased by Lamar at a Savannah auction.

Lamar sold part interest in the *Wanderer* to a captain named Martin, and the two planned another slave-trading expedition. Martin, who apparently never paid nor intended to pay Lamar, gathered a crew and with no notice left Savannah before the ship was fully loaded. The crew was not informed that they were serving on a slave-trading voyage until the ship was out of the harbor, and then they were threatened with death if they tried to leave the ship. When Captain Martin boarded a French boat to obtain more provisions and directions, the crew on the *Wanderer,* under the direction of the first mate, quickly raised the sail and headed for Boston. When they reached Boston late in 1859, they turned the ship over to federal authorities and claimed it in lieu of their wages and for its salvage value. Federal authorities at the same time began proceedings against the *Wanderer* under federal piracy statutes.

While proceedings were under way in federal court in Boston, South Carolina federal district court judge Andrew Magrath, at the April 1860 term of court in Charleston, addressed the charges that the U.S. attorney for the district of Georgia had brought against William C. Corrie, who had been the captain of the *Wanderer* on the voyage in which slaves were brought to South Carolina and Georgia. Magrath threw the case out of court, ruling that the foreign slave trade was not considered piracy, in spite of the 1820 federal statute that made it illegal. Magrath's extraordinary ruling did not render the statute null and void, but it did send a strong message to federal authorities that they could not successfully prosecute slave traders in South Carolina's federal district court. In June 1860, only a couple of months after Magrath announced his ruling, a federal judge in Boston condemned the *Wanderer* as a slave-trading ship. MICHAEL ROBERT MOUNTER

Bancroft, Frederic. *Slave Trading in the Old South.* 1931. Reprint, Columbia: University of South Carolina Press, 1996.
Finkelman, Paul. *Slavery in the Courtroom: An Annotated Bibliography of American Cases.* Washington, D.C.: Library of Congress, 1985.
Sinha, Manisha. *The Counterrevolution of Slavery: Politics and Ideology in Antebellum South Carolina.* Chapel Hill: University of North Carolina Press, 2000.

Wannamaker, John Edward (1851–1935). Agriculturalist, civic leader. Wannamaker was born on September 12, 1851, at Poplar Spring, Orangeburg District (now Calhoun County). He was the son of John Jacob Wannamaker and his second wife, Mary Salley. The Wannamakers were substantial planters and slaveowners. Educated at home by private tutors, Wannamaker earned a bachelor of arts from Wofford College in 1872. He married Martha Duncan on January 31, 1878, with whom he eventually had eight children.

After graduating from Wofford, Wannamaker assumed management of his father's farming interests. In 1873 he established his own property, Aeolian Hill Farm, near St. Matthews. Wannamaker was keenly interested in agricultural improvement, and he applied his considerable resources to agrarian research and innovation. He practiced crop rotation, scientific livestock breeding, and seed development. Dismayed that many farmers stubbornly continued to grow cotton for ruinously low prices, Wannamaker sought to break the tradition of dependence on the old staple. In the 1930s he experimented with soybeans, seeking to develop a seed stock suitable to South Carolina soils and climate.

A leading advocate of comprehensive agricultural education, Wannamaker lobbied for the establishment of an agricultural college in South Carolina. When Thomas Green Clemson bequeathed his land to the state for that purpose in 1888, Wannamaker was appointed one of seven lifetime trustees of Clemson College. He eventually served as chairman.

During World War I, Wannamaker headed several bond drives to finance the war effort. He was active in community affairs and served his church in several capacities. Wannamaker died at Aeolian Hill Farm on March 5, 1935. He was buried in St. Paul's Methodist Church cemetery in St. Matthews. LAWRENCE J. KENT

"J. E. Wannamaker Dies at Home." Columbia *State,* March 6, 1935, pp. 1, 3.
Snowden, Yates, ed. *History of South Carolina.* 5 vols. Chicago: Lewis, 1920.
Wallace, David Duncan. *The History of South Carolina.* 4 vols. New York: American Historical Society, 1934.

Waring, Joseph Ioor (1897–1977). Pediatrician, medical historian. Waring was born in Charleston on September 4, 1897, the son of Joseph Ioor Waring and Emma Taber. He attended Porter Military Academy, graduating in 1912, followed by the Episcopal High School of Virginia, where he finished in 1914. In 1917 he graduated from the College of Charleston with an A.B. degree, and in 1921 he was the first honor graduate of the Medical College of the State of South Carolina (which became the Medical University of South Carolina). Between 1924 and 1927 Waring was the director of pediatric service at Rutherford County Child Health Demonstration, Murfreesboro, Tennessee. Waring returned to South Carolina in 1927 and began the private practice of pediatrics, while also becoming an assistant in the department of pediatrics in the Medical College of the State of South Carolina, where he eventually rose to the rank of clinical professor of pediatrics. Among the original medical articles published by Waring were those on the subject of "Beriberi in Infants," "Syphilis as a Factor in Infant Mortality in South Carolina," and "Mongolism in One of Twins." While the majority of Waring's medical publications appeared in the *Journal of the South Carolina Medical Association,* his influence in pediatrics was also felt on a national level with publication credits in the *Journal of Pediatrics* and the *American Journal of Medical Sciences.* In 1935 he married Ferdinanda Legare Backer, a widow with three children. The couple had no children of their own.

Waring's career as a medical historian began in 1929 with the publication of a short paper titled "An Incident in Early South Carolina Medicine" and later included articles in the nation's leading professional journals in the field, *Bulletin of the History of Medicine* and the *Journal of the History of Medicine and Allied Sciences.* Waring was elected librarian of the Medical Society of South Carolina in 1949, and during his term as director he greatly expanded the collection of rare books, manuscripts, and museum artifacts informing the subject of medical history in South Carolina. Located in a distinctive octagonal-shaped brick building on the campus of the Medical University of South Carolina, this valuable archive was renamed the Waring Historical Library in 1969 in honor of the first director.

Waring was an active member of the South Carolina Historical Society, serving as a curator of the society (1934–1945, 1959), a member of the publications committee, vice president in 1960, and as president from 1961 to 1963. He also published short articles and edited documents in the society's journal, the *South Carolina Historical Magazine,* and served as editor from 1969 and 1974. Following retirement from clinical practice in 1961, Waring intensified his activities as a medical historian and produced his greatest achievement, the three-volume *History of Medicine in South Carolina* (1964–1971), the first general and comprehensive history of medicine in the state. He died at his home, Old Town Plantation, on December 21, 1977, and was buried at St. James Episcopal Church, Goose Creek. STEPHEN C. KENNY

Donato, Anne K., and Jane Oxner Waring, eds. *Joseph Ioor Waring: A True Physician.* Charleston, S.C.: Medical University Press, 1997.

Waring, Julius Waties (1880–1968). Jurist. Waring was born in Charleston on July 27, 1880, the son of Edward Perry Waring, Charleston County superintendent of education, and Anna Thomasine Waties. Following primary and secondary schooling at Charleston's private University School and an undergraduate education at the College of Charleston, he read law with the trial attorney J. P. Kennedy Bryan, a friend of his father. Waring passed the bar and began law practice in his native city. On October 30, 1913, Waring married Annie Gammell, a well-connected woman a year his senior. Two years later they moved into Annie Waring's house at 61 Meeting Street in the elite section of Charleston south of Broad Street. The marriage produced one daughter.

Waring's involvement in Democratic politics earned him an appointment in 1914 as assistant U.S. attorney for South Carolina's eastern district, a post he held for the balance of the Woodrow Wilson administration. He then formed a law partnership with David A. Brockinton, which thrived in the 1920s but fell on relatively hard times during the Depression. Following the election of his political ally Burnet Rhett Maybank as Charleston's mayor in 1931, Waring won appointment as corporation counsel, or city attorney.

In that position, Waring continued to maintain close political ties with Maybank, U.S. senator Ellison D. "Cotton Ed" Smith, and other powerful Democratic politicians. In late 1941, when the U.S. district judgeship became vacant in Charleston, Maybank, by now a U.S. senator, helped to engineer President Franklin Roosevelt's nomination of Waring for the position. "Cotton Ed" also supported Waring, and on January 20, 1942, the Senate confirmed the choice without objection.

Waring's first two years as judge of the federal district court for South Carolina's eastern district were largely uneventful. In 1944, however, he began handing down decisions equalizing the salaries of black and white teachers, ordering the state to desegregate its law school or create an equal facility for blacks, and rebuffing South Carolina's efforts to salvage its all-white Democratic primary. The judge's rulings angered white South Carolinians. In addition, his 1945 divorce from his wife of more than thirty years, followed almost immediately by his marriage to Elizabeth Hoffman, a twice-divorced northern matron, enraged his family and former friends.

Waring later attributed what he called his growing "passion for justice" to his new wife's liberalizing influence and the increased awareness of southern racism he acquired on the federal bench. But white Charlestonians, including his nephew Tom, the editor of the Charleston *News and Courier,* contended that the judge was simply seeking revenge against a society that had refused to accept his divorce and second wife.

Whatever Waring's motivation, he and Elizabeth broke completely with his segregationist past. They entertained prominent blacks in the Meeting Street house the judge had purchased from Annie Waring, spoke to African American and racially mixed audiences in Charleston and throughout the nation, and scorned the "decadence" of the white southern "slavocracy." Unabashed racists were not the only targets of their wrath. Most southern liberals favored improvement in the economic conditions of blacks as a prelude to desegregation. Such "gradualists," the Warings charged, were even worse than avowed segregationists. When two members of a three-judge district court, in *Briggs v. Elliott* (1951), rejected a challenge to South Carolina's segregated public schools, Judge Waring registered a vehement dissent, declaring, several years before the Supreme Court's *Brown* ruling, that segregation was "*per se inequality.*"

Well before his *Briggs* dissent, the Warings had become pariahs in his native state. Responding to petitions from thousands of constituents, L. Mendel Rivers and other members of South Carolina's congressional delegation campaigned unsuccessfully for the judge's impeachment. A cross was burned on their lawn and their house stoned in incidents that white Charlestonians attributed to teenage pranksters but that the judge and Elizabeth—taunted as the "witch of Meeting Street" by locals—declared to be the work of the Ku Klux Klan.

In 1952 Judge Waring—eligible for retirement at full pay and increasingly disenchanted at the prospects for southern racial reform—retired from the bench, and he and Elizabeth departed Charleston for a life of "exile" in New York City. There they enjoyed for a time the adulation denied them by most white South Carolinians and were active in a variety of civil rights efforts. But they also remained contemptuous of the fainthearted in such struggles.

Judge Waring died on January 11, 1968. Elizabeth died in late October of that year. His body was returned to Charleston for burial, which was attended by more than two hundred blacks but fewer than a dozen whites. But time and politics healed wounds and blurred memories. White politicians began vying for black votes, and some of the Warings' African American friends became active in the community's civic affairs. In 1981 a sculpture honoring Judge Waring's memory was placed in the city council chamber, overlooking the federal courthouse in which he had once presided. TINSLEY E. YARBROUGH

Waring, J. Waties. Papers. Moreland-Spingarn Research Center, Howard University, Washington, D.C.

Yarbrough, Tinsley E. *A Passion for Justice: J. Waties Waring and Civil Rights.* New York: Oxford University Press, 1987.

Waring Historical Library. A department of the main library of the Medical University of South Carolina, the Waring Historical Library is the primary medical history collection in South Carolina. The nucleus of the Waring collections is the library of the Medical Society of South Carolina, which contains books, periodicals, artifacts, manuscripts, and medical art. The Medical Society's library was created in 1791 to allow physicians to share current medical literature. In 1813 the book committee of the Medical Society was instructed to purchase "all periodical publications now publishing in the U. States, which in their opinion are of value." Many medical classics were added through the years, and the library prospered. However, between 1860 and 1949 the library was seriously neglected until Joseph I. Waring, M.D., became librarian of the Medical Society of South Carolina. His interest resulted in the Medical Society library moving to the Medical College of South Carolina in 1964. The collections are housed in a building that was once the library of Porter Military Academy and was acquired by the Medical College in 1966. In 1969 the library was named for Dr. Waring. Since then, its collections have expanded to include twelve thousand books, physicians' papers, biographical files on South Carolina physicians, theses of Medical College students from 1825 to 1860, minutes of the Board of Trustees (1847–1978) and the faculty, minutes of the Medical Society of South Carolina (1789–1986), records of the trustees of the Shirras Dispensary (1813–1931) and Roper Hospital (1856–1868), medical caricatures, oral histories, photographs, and archival materials related to the Medical University of South Carolina. The Waring Library Society is a "Friends of the Library" group founded in 1977 to honor Dr. Waring and perpetuate the library and interest in the history of the health sciences. JANE MCCUTCHEN BROWN

Washington, William (1752–1810). Soldier. Washington was born on February 28, 1752, in Overwharton Parish, Stafford County, Virginia, the son of Bailey Washington and Catherine Storke, and he was a second cousin of President George Washington. Having no middle name, he is often confused in history with his distant cousin William Augustine Washington (1757–1810). At the outbreak of the Revolutionary War, in 1775 he was elected a captain of Stafford County Minutemen, which was integrated into the Third Virginia Regiment in 1776. After marching north with his unit later in the year, Captain Washington led a successful charge against a Hessian artillery battery at the Battle of Trenton on December 26, 1776. Wounded in this action, he was rewarded with a promotion to major of the Fourth Regiment of Continental Light Dragoons.

By the end of 1779 Washington had advanced to the rank of lieutenant colonel, commanding the Third Regiment of Continental Light Dragoons, and was ordered to join the patriot forces of General Benjamin Lincoln in Charleston, South Carolina. By March 1780 Washington's regiment was detached with the light forces near Moncks Corner to reconnoiter and screen against the advancing enemy. On March 26, 1780, he had his first encounter with British Lieutenant Colonel Banastre Tarleton near Rantowle's Bridge. Washington's command was soundly defeated by Tarleton at Moncks Corner on April 14 and again at Lenud's Ferry on May 5. After refitting in North Carolina, Washington captured Rugeley's Fort near Camden and then defeated a marauding band of Tories at Hammond's Old Store in the Little River District later in the year. On January 17, 1781, Washington commanded a combined cavalry force at the Battle of Cowpens that was instrumental in the victory there. For his intrepidity in this engagement, Congress awarded him a silver medal. Always at the head of his regiment, Washington fought valiantly at Guilford Courthouse, North Carolina, in March and, on returning to South Carolina, at Hobkirk Hill in April. At the Battle of Eutaw Springs on September 8, 1781, he was seriously wounded while leading a charge and was subsequently captured by the enemy. The British commander in the South, Lord Cornwallis, would later comment that "there could be no more formidable antagonist in a charge, at the head of his cavalry, than Colonel William Washington."

As a prisoner of war, Washington spent the remaining war years in Charleston. There he married Jane Reily Elliott on April 21, 1782, and consequently gained Sandy Hill plantation and other properties in St. Paul's Parish. The marriage produced two children. Pursuing the life of a successful lowcountry planter, Washington represented the parish in the General Assembly from 1787 to 1804. He also accepted a post as brigadier general commanding the Seventh Brigade of state militia in 1794. During the anticipated hostilities with France in 1798, he was appointed a brigadier general in the U.S. Army commanding South Carolina and Georgia, serving until 1800. After a lingering illness, Washington died on March 16, 1810. SAMUEL K. FORE

Bailey, N. Louise, Mary L. Morgan, and Carolyn R. Taylor, eds. *Biographical Directory of the South Carolina Senate, 1776–1985.* 3 vols. Columbia: University of South Carolina Press, 1986.

Haller, Stephen E. *William Washington: Cavalryman of the Revolution.* Bowie, Md.: Heritage Books, 2001.

Lumpkin, Henry. *From Savannah to Yorktown: The American Revolution in the South.* Columbia: University of South Carolina Press, 1981.

Warley, Felix B. *An Oration, Delivered in Saint Michael's Church, in the City of Charleston, South Carolina, on Tuesday, the 19th June, 1810, on the Death of the Late Gen. William Washington.* Charleston, S.C.: W. P. Young, 1810.

Wateree River. The Catawba River enters central South Carolina, flows into Wateree Lake, and after passing through Wateree Dam in Kershaw County, becomes the Wateree River. Approximately seventy-five miles in length, the remote Wateree follows a meandering path south through the upper coastal plain past Camden and then into several swamps including Betty Neck Swamp, White Marsh Swamp, and Gum Swamp. Along the way it receives the tributary waters of nine creeks before terminating at its junction with the Congaree River. The Wateree marks a heavily traveled path that has played a significant role in the prehistory and history of South Carolina.

Several Native American settlements, including the Mississippian capital of Cofitachequi, existed in close proximity to the Wateree River over seven hundred years ago. Later, various settlements of Siouan Indians (including the Wateree tribe, for whom the river was named) thrived along its banks. The first European settlement along the Wateree was Camden, which soon became an interior trading center for wheat, tobacco, indigo, and later cotton. Interestingly, most travel through the area during the colonial years was along the ancient Catawba path—also called the King's Highway—that ran parallel to the river. This was to change. By the early nineteenth century the backcountry planters needed the Wateree to transport cotton from inland plantations to market in Charleston. To improve communication and transportation links with the coast, the Wateree Canal was begun north of Camden in 1821. For several years cotton barges were common sights along the Wateree. With the coming of railroads in the 1850s, river transport became less important, and the Wateree resumed its traditional role of supplying food and water to residents along its banks. ROBERT STEVENS

Ernst, Joseph A., and H. Roy Merrens. "'Camden's Turrets Pierce the Skies!': The Urban Process in the Southern Colonies during the Eighteenth Century." *William and Mary Quarterly,* 3d ser., 30 (October 1973): 549–74.

Kovacik, Charles F., and John J. Winberry. *South Carolina: The Making of a Landscape.* 1987. Reprint, Columbia: University of South Carolina Press, 1989.

Watermelons. Watermelons (*Citrullus lanatus*) are members of the gourd family native to Africa. Both African slaves and European colonists were probably responsible for first introducing the fruit to South Carolina. In colonial times watermelons were generally much smaller than most modern-day varieties. Eating watermelon was considered an effective remedy for fevers. Watermelons were also crushed for their juice, some of which was fermented to make watermelon wine. The rinds were often pickled.

According to the South Carolina Watermelon Board, watermelons can be grown all across South Carolina, but modern commercial production is concentrated in the southern portion of the state (Bamberg, Barnwell, Colleton, Allendale, Hampton, and Aiken Counties). Historically, the Sandhills region was celebrated for its watermelon production, and Chesterfield County is still a significant producer. Although production has declined in recent years, in 2002 watermelons were still planted in nine thousand acres of farmland, with a harvest valued at $7,878,000. The watermelon season in South Carolina begins with planting in March and April and ends with the harvest in June, July, and August. Watermelon festivals are held annually in Hampton and Pageland.

In 1954 C. Fred Andrus of the U.S. Vegetable Laboratory in Charleston revolutionized watermelon production with the development of the Charleston Gray watermelon. The Charleston Gray was bred to resist disease and to better withstand the rigors of being transported. By the 1960s it was estimated that the Charleston Gray variety of watermelon made up ninety-five percent of the U.S. watermelon crop. Although the Charleston Gray has more recently lost ground to newer watermelon varieties such as the seedless watermelon, many of these newer varieties owe part of their lineage to the Charleston Gray. ALLISON FAIX

Adams, Sean. "That Gray Melon from Charleston." *Agricultural Research* 42 (October 1994): 23–25.

Allred, Amy J., and Gary Lucier. *The U.S. Watermelon Industry.* Washington, D.C.: Government Printing Office, 1990.

Rupp, Rebecca. *Blue Corn and Square Tomatoes: Unusual Facts about Common Vegetables.* Pownal, Vt.: Storey, 1987.

South Carolina Watermelon Board. http://www.scwatermelon.com/

Watson, Albert William (1922–1994). Legislator, congressman. Watson was born in Sumter on August 30, 1922, the son of Claude A. Watson and Eva Clark. He attended public schools in Columbia, North Greenville Junior College, and the University of South Carolina. During World War II he served in the U.S. Army Air Force as a weather specialist in the Mediterranean theater of operations from 1942 to 1946. He married Lillian Audrey Williams of Walterboro on May 24, 1948. They had three children. He earned a law degree from the University of South Carolina School of Law in 1950 and began practicing law in Columbia the following year.

Watson was first elected to the South Carolina General Assembly in 1954 and served from 1955 to 1958 and from 1961 to 1962. He was also an unsuccessful candidate for lieutenant governor. In 1957 he served as national chairman for the Voice of Democracy Program for the United States Junior Chamber of Commerce.

In 1962 Watson was elected as a Democrat to the U.S. House of Representatives from the Second Congressional District. He was reelected in 1964 but resigned from Congress on February 1, 1965, after he was stripped of his seniority by the House Democratic Caucus for his support of Republican candidate Barry Goldwater in the 1964 presidential election. Watson then switched to the Republican Party and was reelected in a special election on June 15, 1965. Watson was reelected to Congress in 1966 and in 1968.

In 1970 Watson ran for governor against John West, one of his former law school teachers. Watson, an opponent of school integration, made a speech in Darlington County during the campaign urging residents to "use every means at your disposal to defend" the state against what he considered an illegal federal court order on school desegregation. Nine days later a white mob attacked three buses carrying African American children to school in the Darlington County town of Lamar, overturning one of them. While no one was injured, many of Watson's critics blamed the incident on his speech. He was also criticized during the campaign for a commercial showing African Americans rioting in Los Angeles. Although Watson received a majority of the white vote, he received only forty-six percent of the total vote to his opponent's fifty-two percent and was defeated in the gubernatorial election.

After Watson was defeated, President Richard Nixon nominated him to the United States Military Court of Appeals, a civilian court that reviews courts-martial. However, protests from civil rights groups and others resulted in Nixon withdrawing the nomination. In 1973 Watson was appointed as a federal administrative law judge for the U.S. Social Security Administration. He died on September 25, 1994, in Columbia and was buried in Crescent Hill Memorial Gardens. WILLIAM V. MOORE

Hathorn, Billy B. "The Changing Politics of Race: Congressman Albert William Watson and the S.C. Republican Party, 1965–1970." *South Carolina Historical Magazine* 89 (October 1988): 227–41.

Kalk, Bruce H. *The Origins of the Southern Strategy: Two-Party Competition in South Carolina, 1950–1972.* Lanham, Md.: Lexington, 2001.

Watson, Ebbie Julian (1869–1917). "Good Roads" pioneer. Watson was born in Ridge Spring on June 29, 1869, to Tillman Watson, a contractor, and Helen O'Neall Mauldin. Watson graduated from the University of South Carolina in 1889. Two years later he joined the staff of Columbia's *State* newspaper. He married Margaret Smith Miller on December 17, 1896. In 1904 Governor Duncan Clinch Heyward appointed him head of the redesigned Department of Agriculture, Commerce and Immigration.

As commissioner, Watson advocated the diversification of agriculture. He tracked the progress of the boll weevil across the South and wanted to end South Carolina's dependence on cotton. Watson had other ideas for improving life in South Carolina. A "good roads" exponent, he led his department into the highway business. When the department was reorganized in 1909, he recommended creating a highway department within the Department of Agriculture and espoused sand-clay surfaced roads as the wave of the future. In 1911 Watson reported that only ten percent of South Carolina's roads were treated, and five years later he warned in his annual report that recent federal legislation would force South Carolina to address the state of her roads.

The acme of Watson's efforts to improve highway transportation was the publication of free route map brochures beginning in 1912. These brochures included directions, maps, and traffic regulations. A New York City magazine for travelers applauded the effort as the first by any state. During his tenure with the Department of Agriculture, Watson's staff produced state highway maps in 1914 and 1916. These maps included primary and secondary roads with distances between destinations. In 1916 he reported that the maps were so popular that the print run of 3,500 was exhausted by September. The map featured color-coded markings that matched signs posted on the highways, guiding travelers to their destinations.

In 1916 Watson reported the completion of the Appalachian highway that ran from Columbia to the mountains. Watson also spearheaded a campaign to rehabilitate the historic State Road from Columbia to Charleston. When the commissioner's position became an elected one in 1916, he faced no opposition in the election.

Despite these achievements, good highway construction in South Carolina was a rarity. For eight years Watson lobbied for the registration of motor vehicles and the establishment of a highway department staff with capable engineers. When the Highway Commission was created on March 10, 1917, Governor Richard I. Manning took a small step toward those goals. On October 27, 1917, Watson died of asthma in Columbia, and he was buried in Ridge Spring. ALEXIA JONES HELSLEY

Moore, John Hammond. *The South Carolina Highway Department, 1917–1987.* Columbia: University of South Carolina Press, 1987.

Waxhaws. Waxhaws are an extinct nation of Native Americans that once lived in present-day Lancaster County. Like many South Carolina Indian nations, the Waxhaws spoke a Siouan language. The origin of their name is uncertain. Some believe it means "people of the cane." The first known contact between the Waxhaws and Europeans occurred in 1566, when a party of about one hundred Spanish explorers passed through the Waxhaw lands. Juan Pardo, the commander of this expedition, noted that their villages were composed of long lodges, which were typical of eastern Woodland Indians. The next mention of the Waxhaws is in 1670. John Lederer, who was passing through the area, called them the "Wisacky" in his journal. He also noted that they were subordinate to the larger Catawba tribe, their neighbors to the north. The English explorer John Lawson left a detailed description of the Waxhaws after he encountered them in his travels across the Carolinas in 1701. He described their lodges as large, comfortable buildings and wrote that they were gracious hosts. He also noted their practice of flattening their foreheads in the belief that this made them better hunters. The Waxhaw Indians fought against the colonists in the Yamassee War, and this action along with disease caused the dispersion of the nation. The Waxhaws that survived the war are believed to have been absorbed by the Catawbas and Seminoles. RHETT A. ADAMS

Milling, Chapman J. *Red Carolinians.* 1940. Reprint, Columbia: University of South Carolina Press, 1969.

Pettus, Louise. *The Waxhaws.* Rock Hill, S.C.: Regal Graphics, 1993.

Waxhaws. The Waxhaws is an area of vague borders in the lower South Carolina Piedmont. It was named for the Waxhaws, an extinct nation of Native Americans who once lived in the area. The center of the Waxhaws was known as the Waxhaw Settlement, consisting of the general area of Lancaster County south of Twelve Mile Creek and north of Cane Creek. The actual boundaries of the Waxhaws, however, are hard to define. Most authors agree that land in Chester and Lancaster Counties makes up what was once the domain of the Waxhaws, so this area still retains the name.

The Waxhaws area was settled by Scots-Irish who came from Virginia and Pennsylvania. They brought the Presbyterian faith with them and founded Old Waxhaw Church, the oldest in the upcountry, around 1750. This church became the center of Presbyterian influence in the backcountry, and with the founding of the Waxhaw Academy, it became the intellectual center as well.

The area was a stronghold of patriot sentiment during the Revolutionary War. The Battle of the Waxhaws (May 29, 1780) was fought here, while the Battle of Hanging Rock (August 6, 1780) took place just south of the Waxhaws. It was here that future president Andrew Jackson, the region's most distinguished native son, first saw combat. Besides Jackson, other notable statesmen hailed from the Waxhaws, including Governor Stephen D. Miller, Congressman James Blair, U.S. Senator William Smith, and the Revolutionary War hero William R. Davie. RHETT A. ADAMS

Booraem, Hendrik. *Young Hickory: The Making of Andrew Jackson.* Dallas, Tex.: Taylor Publishing, 2001.

Moore, Peter N. "Family Dynamics and the Great Revival: Religious Conversion in the South Carolina Piedmont." *Journal of Southern History* 70 (February 2004): 35–62.

———. "This World of Toil and Strife: Land, Labor, and the Making of an American Community, 1750–1805." Ph.D. diss., University of Georgia, 2001.

Pettus, Louise. *The Waxhaws.* Rock Hill, S.C.: Regal Graphics, 1993.

Waxhaws, Battle of the (May 29, 1780). The Battle of the Waxhaws, also known as Buford's Massacre, was one of several incidents in the backcountry that helped turn the Revolutionary War in the South into a bloody civil war. Most of Georgia and South Carolina fell under British and Loyalist control after the fall of Savannah in late 1779 and the surrender of Charleston, along with 5,500 Continentals and militiamen, on May 12, 1780.

In late May, Colonel Abraham Buford's patriot force of 350 to 400 Virginians, primarily infantry and the only significant body of Continentals remaining in the South, retreated toward North Carolina intending to join militia units there and help rebuild the American army in the Carolinas. Colonel Banastre Tarleton pursued him with a force of about 250 to 300 British regulars and Loyalists made up of cavalry, mounted infantry, and dragoons. He overtook Buford on May 29 just south of the North Carolina–South Carolina border (in present-day Lancaster County) and demanded his immediate surrender. Buford refused, and Tarleton charged the Americans, routing them. Though some Americans tried to surrender, others kept fighting, and the British and Loyalists shot or bayoneted many of them, with more than 250 killed or wounded and more than 50 taken prisoner. Tarleton later boasted, "I have cut 170 Off[ice]rs and Men to pieces." American accounts claimed that the British and Loyalists "killed at least 200 men in a most Cruel & Inhumane manner."

Most Americans considered Buford's defeat a massacre rather than a battle, and a British history of the Revolution published a few years after the war commented, "the virtue of humanity was totally forgot." This bloody action inspired many in South Carolina and elsewhere to continue, or in some cases to join, the fight against the British and Loyalists in spite of the immense odds against them. "Tarleton's Quarter!" and "Remember Buford!" became watchwords among the patriots in the southern backcountry for the rest of the war. J. TRACY POWER

Edgar, Walter. *Partisans and Redcoats: The Southern Conflict That Turned the Tide of the American Revolution.* New York: Morrow, 2001.

Lumpkin, Henry. *From Savannah to Yorktown: The American Revolution in the South.* Columbia: University of South Carolina Press, 1981.

Power, J. Tracy. "'The Virtue of Humanity Was Totally Forgot': Buford's Massacre, May 29, 1780." *South Carolina Historical Magazine* 93 (January 1992): 5–14.

Wayne, Arthur Trezevant (1863–1930). Ornithologist. Wayne was born in Blackville on January 1, 1863, where his parents, Daniel Gabriel Wayne and Harriott Ward, had moved from Charleston with hopes of escaping the dangers of the Civil War. Shortly after the war his family returned to Charleston, where Wayne attended private school for several years and then entered high school, graduating with honors in 1880. He married Maria L. Porcher on June 6, 1889.

Around 1874 Wayne began visiting the Charleston Museum regularly after school, displaying great interest in birds. Gabriel Manigault, museum curator, introduced him to John Dancer, a local taxidermist, who taught Wayne how to prepare bird skins. Soon he was collecting birds, nests, and eggs, and at age fifteen he donated the first of many specimens he would contribute to the museum. The well-known ornithologist William Brewster visited Charleston in 1883, and Manigault introduced him to Wayne, who was then employed by a cotton dealer while continuing to study birds in his spare time. Influenced by Brewster and having an extreme dislike for his work ("he hated business pursuits with a cordiality that increased daily"), Wayne quit his job and dedicated his waking hours to the study of birds.

For the rest of his life Wayne hewed to the same course, eking out an existence for his wife and himself by collecting birds and selling their skins to other ornithologists. In 1906 Wayne became honorary curator of birds at the museum, a position that carried no salary but allowed access to the collections in return for assistance in their care. First meeting Wayne at about the age of fourteen, Burnham Chamberlain, who became an accomplished ornithologist, recollected many years later that Arthur Wayne had slightly reddish hair and was small, little more than five feet, seven inches tall: "It was a combination that you didn't tangle with unnecessarily," and "we early learned that unless you knew what you were talking about you'd better keep a zipped-up mouth."

Wayne frequently published his observations in *The Auk* (the journal of the American Ornithologists' Union). His careful work made him the most knowledgeable student of his day on South Carolina birds. Encouraged by Paul M. Rea, then director of the Charleston Museum, and others, Wayne wrote *Birds of South Carolina,* published in 1910 by the museum. Wayne's book established him as a leading American ornithologist and stimulated interest in the ornithology of South Carolina. He died at his home at Porcher's Bluff near Mount Pleasant on May 5, 1930. WILLIAM D. ANDERSON, JR.

Sanders, Albert E., and William D. Anderson, Jr. *Natural History Investigations in South Carolina from Colonial Times to the Present.* Columbia: University of South Carolina Press, 1999.

Sprunt, Alexander, Jr. "In Memoriam: Arthur Trezevant Wayne, 1863–1930." *Auk* 48 (January 1931): 1–16.

Sprunt, Alexander, Jr., and E. Burnham Chamberlain. *South Carolina Bird Life.* Rev. ed. Columbia: University of South Carolina Press, 1970.

Wayne, Arthur T. *Birds of South Carolina.* Charleston, S.C.: [Daggett], 1910.

Wayside hospitals. Wayside hospitals were formed across South Carolina during the Civil War as means to care for sick and wounded Confederate soldiers traveling throughout the state. Usually situated at depots or other railroad stopping points, wayside facilities provided a range of services to soldiers in transit. Most offered meals and basic nursing, while larger wayside hospitals contained overnight accommodations and were staffed with physicians or surgeons. All wayside hospitals in the state originated through private means, usually the efforts of local women and relief organizations. Although a few larger facilities were eventually placed under the supervision of Confederate medical authorities, all wayside hospitals depended in large measure on private donations of food, clothing, bandages, medicine, and labor.

Charleston opened the first wayside hospital in South Carolina in November 1861. Shortly thereafter the Young Ladies Hospital Association of Columbia organized its own wayside facility in the capital city. Relocating to the South Carolina Railroad depot in March 1862, the Columbia Wayside Hospital became the largest and most frequented facility of that type in the state, serving some 75,000 soldiers before being disbanded in February 1865. Other wayside hospital locations included Florence, Orangeburg, Sumter, and Greenville. While varying in size and scope, all wayside facilities were recognized for providing valuable services to the Confederacy, and thousands of soldiers blessed the memory of the care and comfort they received there. Sarah Rowe of Orangeburg received the official thanks of the General Assembly for her ceaseless attention to the sick and wounded traveling across the state, while Mary Amarinthia Snowden of Charleston was given a "just and hearty tribute" by the Confederate Congress for the hospital work of her and her colleagues. By the end of the war, wayside hospitals had become one of the most visible, and important, contributions of South Carolina women to the war effort. TOM DOWNEY

Downey, Thomas More. "A Call to Duty: Confederate Hospitals in South Carolina." Master's thesis, University of South Carolina, 1992.

Wellford (Spartanburg County; 2000 pop. 2,030). Located in west-central Spartanburg County between the North and Middle Tyger Rivers, Wellford was once part of the hunting grounds of the Cherokee Nation. Cherokees called the area "Tucapau," meaning "strong cloth." Tucapau later became the name of a single community. European settlers, mostly Scots-Irish, began arriving from Pennsylvania and Virginia in the late 1750s. Attracted by the fertile farmland and ample wildlife, they settled along the North and Middle Tyger Rivers, which became known as the "upper settlement." Fort Prince, approximately a mile and a half from Wellford's future location, provided early settlers with protection from Native Americans and British during the Revolutionary War.

Following the war, the area became part of Spartanburg County. For most of the nineteenth century, the future site of Wellford remained a settlement of scattered farms associated with Beech Springs Township. Businesses developed after the Danville and Richmond Railroad arrived in 1876. A depot was built along with a wooden water tower from which the steam locomotives could fill their tanks. The emerging village was named for C. P. A. Wellford, a railway surveyor and a director of the Danville and Richmond. Several general merchandise stores, a post office, and the Wellford Bank were built near the depot. This section of Main Street became known as "Merchants' Row." The first homes in the village were also built along Main Street, and churches and an academy soon followed. In 1881 a group of African Americans established Sunny Graded School for the education of the former slave population. In 1882 Wellford received a town charter and elected its first intendant (mayor) and town wardens.

During the early twentieth century, Wellford remained an agricultural community with a few small textile factories. In 1922 Jackson Mills opened a plant just outside the town. The only source of electrical power for the community was the power plants at the mills. In the 1950s Wellford became a more diversified industrial area, with additional firms arriving to take advantage of electric service provided by Duke Power Company. Jackson Mills was joined by Leigh Fibers, Sybron/Tanatex Chemical Corporation, and International Paper Company, which built plants just beyond the town's limits. With this new growth, Wellford was incorporated as a city in 1976. Wellford benefited from its location along a rapidly growing corridor paralleling U.S. Highway 29 and Interstate 85 between the cities of Spartanburg and Greenville. In 1970 the population was 1,298. Two decades later the population had almost doubled. JEFFREY R. WILLIS

Leonard, Michael. *Our Heritage: A Community History of Spartanburg County, S.C.* Spartanburg, S.C.: Band & White, 1986.

Wells, Helena (?–1824). Author. Wells was born in Charleston, the daughter of Scottish immigrants Robert Wells and Mary

Rowand. Her father was a successful Charleston bookseller and newspaper publisher. Although she received no formal education, Wells was raised in the privileged atmosphere of Charleston society. Her father espoused the cultural life of the city. He was an accomplished Latinist who wrote poetry. He was also an outspoken Loyalist who published his views in his newspaper. By 1775 he had earned the enmity of the Charleston community, and in 1777–1778 he responded by moving his family to London. Helena never returned to the land of her birth. Nevertheless, in her writings her attitudes appear to have been shaped by her experiences growing up during the Revolutionary War period as a young female member of the Charleston merchant class.

Not long after settling in England, the Wells family fell upon hard times and Helena was forced to seek employment. During the 1780s she worked as a teacher and perhaps as a governess and opened a boardinghouse for "young gentlewomen of fortune" with her sister. Wells also turned to writing, possibly to supplement her meager income. Although strongly conservative in her views, she sought to convey the somewhat revolutionary idea that gentlewomen should be schooled for employment as well as for marriage. She believed that to succeed, however, they had to remain within the norms of society, never surrendering their integrity, modesty, or virtue, no matter what the cost.

The two novels Wells wrote played on this theme. The first, *The Step-Mother: A Domestic Tale from Real Life,* was published in England in 1798. A second edition, identifying the author as "Helena Wells of Charles Town, S.C.," was published in Charleston the next year. The book was well received at the time, although later critics found it to be didactic and overly sentimental. It was followed in 1799 by *Letters on Subjects of Importance to the Happiness of Young Females,* cautionary letters written to impressionable young female pupils and imploring them to keep their emotions in check by avoiding excessive novel reading and by using proper English. The letters also stressed the importance of upright manners and sound religious principles and warned against luxury, laziness, godlessness, gossiping, uncleanliness, and snobbery toward, or familiarity with, servants. In 1800 Wells published a second novel, *Constantia Neville: or The West Indian.* More than one thousand pages long, this work of fiction, like her earlier novel, was well received by contemporary reviewers but later criticized by twentieth-century scholars for its thin plot, weak characterization, and cloying sentimentality.

In 1801 Wells married Edward Whitford and bore four children in quick succession. In 1809 she published *Thoughts and Remarks on Establishing an Institution for the Education of Unportioned Respectable Females,* in which she proposed a teacher-training school that would provide young gentlewomen with academic training, proper health care, and spiritual guidance while expecting them to help maintain the premises and charging them according to their ability to pay. This last work received little critical attention. Ahead of her time in her views on educating and supporting single or widowed women without means, Wells faded from public view and died in London on July 6, 1824. ELLEN CHAMBERLAIN

Hamelman, Steven. "Helena Wells." In *Dictionary of Literary Biography.* Vol. 200, *American Women Prose Writers to 1820,* edited by Carla Mulford, Angela Vietto, and Amy E. Winans. Detroit: Gale, 1999.

Moltke-Hansen, David. "A World Introduced: The Writings of Helena Wells of Charles Town, South Carolina's First Novelist." In *South Carolina Women Writers: Proceedings of the Reynolds Conference, University of South Carolina, October 24–25, 1975,* edited by James B. Meriwether. Spartanburg, S.C.: Reprint Company, 1979.

Ponick, Frances M. "Helena Wells and Her Family: Loyalist Writers and Printers of Colonial Charleston." Master's thesis, University of South Carolina, 1975.

Welsh. Settlers of Welsh descent played an important role in settling the South Carolina backcountry in the 1730s and 1740s. Many of these early Welsh migrated from Pencader Hundred Baptist Church in New Castle County, Pennsylvania (later Delaware). Most migrated to South Carolina for religious and economic reasons. Arminian practices associated with the first Great Awakening were entering northern Baptist churches, which may have offended the more Calvinistic traditions of early Welsh Baptists. Land shortages and tensions with Quakers over slavery may have inspired other Welsh immigrants to forsake Pennsylvania for the southern colonies. A few of the Welsh brought slaves with them to South Carolina.

In 1736 Welsh Baptists in Pennsylvania petitioned South Carolina officials for a grant of 10,000 acres of land in Queensborough Township and all the land above it for eight miles straddling the Pee Dee River. The request was approved, and petitioners received a generous grant of 173,040 acres, situated in present-day Darlington, Chesterfield, and Marlboro Counties. The land became known as the Welsh Tract and quickly became one of the most populated and prosperous sections of the South Carolina backcountry. Most early settlers here received grants of land through the head-right system and until 1745 held the prerogative to choose whom they wanted to settle in the community. Welsh Tract inhabitants raised grain, indigo, and cattle and constructed mills on several Pee Dee River tributaries to grind flour for the Charleston market. At least three Welsh Tract settlers, William Hughes, James Price, and Job Edwards, came from Wales in 1746. With the exception of these men, however, there does not appear to have been a direct migration from Wales to the Welsh Tract.

In 1738 some families with Welsh surnames founded the Welsh Neck Baptist Church. Members of this church were bilingual, and some used the *Cyd Gordiad,* the first Welsh Bible published in Philadelphia in 1730. John Fordyce, a minister with the Society for the Propagation of the Gospel who visited the area in the 1740s, noted that these people were speaking both Welsh and English. The Welsh Neck Baptist Church became a center of Baptist influence in colonial South Carolina, serving as the mother church for more than thirty Baptist congregations established between 1738 and 1800.

Many settlers in the Welsh Tract were Baptists, and they managed to keep a distinct cultural identity for several decades. The aftermath of the Cherokee War in the 1760s, however, altered the distinctive ethnic composition of this community. Settlers of Scots-Irish descent migrated by way of the Great Wagon Road into the Welsh Tract. Between 1760 and 1768 the population increased from about 3,500 whites and 300 slaves to more than 5,000 whites and 1,276 slaves. In 1768 the Welsh Tract became St. David's Parish, and in 1777 residents established St. David's Society and Academy to promote learning in the parish. This institution continued to function into the twenty-first century.

The Welsh influence in South Carolina could also be found in Charleston. In 1736 the St. David's Society, named for the patron saint of Wales and celebrated by local inhabitants of Welsh descent, was first organized in Charleston. Some indentured servants who came to the colony were Welsh. The *South-Carolina Gazette* in 1744 offered a reward for a runaway indentured servant named Thomas Edwards who spoke "Welshy." A 1771 advertisement in the *Gazette* for the St. David's Day festivities in Charleston appeared in Welsh, although the annual celebration was interrupted by 1774 due to the rising tensions between the colonies and England.

By 1790 persons of Welsh descent represented just over six percent of South Carolina's white population. Some prominent South Carolinians of Welsh descent in the eighteenth and early nineteenth centuries included the Reverend Evan Pugh and David Rogerson Williams, who served as governor from 1812 to 1814. From 1783 to 1800 several members of the Welsh Neck Baptist Church served in the General Assembly. LLOYD JOHNSON

Edgar, Walter. *South Carolina: A History.* Columbia: University of South Carolina Press, 1998.

Johnson, George Lloyd, Jr. *The Frontier in the Colonial South: South Carolina Backcountry, 1736–1800.* Westport, Conn.: Greenwood, 1997.

Meriwether, Robert L. *The Expansion of South Carolina, 1729–1765.* Kingsport, Tenn.: Southern Publishers, 1940.

Wentworth, Marjory Heath (b. 1958). Poet. Born in Lynn, Massachusetts, on June 3, 1958, Wentworth is the daughter of John Heath and Mary Tully. She received a bachelor's degree from Mount Holyoke College in anthropology and political science in 1980 and an M.A. in literature and creative writing from New York University in 1984. On June 27, 1981, she married the filmmaker Peter Wentworth. They have three sons. Wentworth went to work as a book and film publicist soon after graduate school and has been involved in publicity and marketing ever since.

In 1989 the Wentworth family moved to Sullivan's Island, South Carolina. In 1992 Wentworth began conducting poetry workshops for schoolchildren in the Charleston area, and a year later she became adjunct instructor of English at Trident Technical College. Since then, Wentworth has taught creative writing to children and adults in a variety of settings across the state. She taught creative writing at the Charleston County School of the Arts and directs a poetry program for cancer patients and their families. Her poetry has been published in numerous journals and anthologies and has been incorporated into three novels. Collections of her poetry include a chapbook, *Nightjars* (1995); *What the Water Gives Me* (2002), a collaboration with the artist Mary Edna Fraser; and *Noticing Eden* (2003). Her poems have also been included in several museum and gallery exhibitions, and they have twice been nominated for the Pushcart Prize, an annual collection of the best literary work published by small presses.

Wentworth read her poem "Rivers of Wind" at the inauguration of Governor Mark Sanford in January 2003. She was named South Carolina's poet laureate later the same year. As poet laureate, she has initiated projects designed to bring the enjoyment and writing of poetry into the lives of South Carolinians. JULIA ARRANTS

Watts, Judy. "Hard Times Have Inspired New Poet Laureate of South Carolina to Become an Advocate for Writing." Charleston *Post and Courier,* August 30, 2003, pp. F1, F3.

West, John Carl (1922–2004). Governor, diplomat. Born in Camden on August 27, 1922, to Shelton J. West and Mattie Ratterree West, West was reared in the Charlotte Thompson community near Camden. West's father was killed in the Cleveland School fire of 1923, and his mother then gave up teaching to run the family farm. West graduated from The Citadel in May 1942 and shortly thereafter entered the military. Later that year, on August 29, he married his longtime sweetheart, Lois Rhame. The couple had three children. West was selected for intelligence work in the Pentagon, where he deciphered Japanese signals. He went overseas after the war as part of the U.S. Strategic Bomb Survey. On his return to South Carolina, West enrolled in the University of South Carolina (USC) School of Law. He passed the bar exam while in law school, entered into a partnership with the attorney Allen Murchison of Camden, and completed his course work at USC while teaching in the political science department. He received his LL.B. degree in 1948.

John C. West. Courtesy, Modern Political Collections, University of South Carolina

West's political career began with his election in 1948 to the State Highway Commission. He won election to the state Senate in 1954 campaigning on the need for better health care. He represented Kershaw County in the Senate from 1955 until November 1966, when he was elected lieutenant governor.

The hotly contested 1970 gubernatorial general election featured candidates with clear and important differences in their visions for South Carolina's future. West defeated Republican congressman Albert Watson with 53.2 percent of the major party vote. His humane and progressive administration, from January 19, 1971, to January 21, 1975, assured a peaceful improvement of affairs for most South Carolinians. Among his major accomplishments were passage of mandatory automobile insurance for all drivers and the creation of the Coastal Zone Planning and Management Council, the Housing Authority, the Health Policy and Planning Council, the Social Development Council, and the Commission on Human Relations. West also reorganized the governor's office and Departments of Labor and Wildlife and Marine Resources. When asked what gave him the greatest satisfaction as governor, West cited improved race relations and noted that "in a fairly critical period we made a transition and changed a lot of attitudes."

After leaving office, West returned to his law practice with the goal of building it into a statewide firm with national and international interests. The election of his friend Jimmy Carter as president brought rumors that West might return to public life. West accepted an appointment as ambassador to Saudi Arabia, which administration officials called "the key diplomatic post in the world." West served as ambassador from 1977 to 1981, a tense period in the Middle East.

After retiring from public life, West served on several corporate boards, including a term as chairman of the board of the Seibels Bruce Insurance Company; lectured on government and international studies; and remained active in service to the community. After a year-long battle with liver cancer, West died at his home on Hilton Head Island on March 21, 2004. He was buried at Forest Lawn Memorial Park in Camden. HERBERT J. HARTSOOK

Carlisle, Douglas H. *The Administration of John Carl West, Governor of South Carolina 1971–1975.* Columbia, S.C., 1975.

Hartsook, Herbert. "Elect a Good Man Governor." *Ex Libris* (1996): 26–29.

Sheinin, Aaron Gould. "'Colorblind' Governor Championed Racial Reform." Columbia *State,* March 22, 2004, pp. A1, A4–A5.

West, John C. Oral History. Modern Political Collections, South Caroliniana Library, University of South Carolina, Columbia.
———. Papers. Modern Political Collections, South Caroliniana Library, University of South Carolina, Columbia.

West, Joseph (?–1691). Governor. Nothing is known of the birth and parentage of Joseph West, who commanded the fleet that brought the first permanent European settlers to South Carolina and whose service as governor was crucial to the survival of the settlement. The first definite reference to West is a 1667 commission as a lieutenant on His Majesty's ship *Jersey* during the Second Anglo-Dutch War. West served in the West Indies in 1667 and 1668 under Captain James Carteret, a son of Sir George Carteret, who was one of the eight original Lords Proprietors of Carolina. After participation in victories over Dutch and allied French naval forces off Martinique, Guyana, and Surinam, West returned to England. By the time of his departure for Carolina, he was styled "Capt. Joseph West, of the sd City of London, Merchant."

In 1669 Anthony Ashley Cooper, who later became the first Earl of Shaftesbury, convinced the other Carolina proprietors to send settlers from England to their floundering colonial enterprise. Joseph West was commissioned to command the proprietors' three-ship fleet. Sir Peter Colleton and Sir George Carteret were the other proprietors most actively supporting Ashley Cooper in the settlement venture, and the three men projected a joint private plantation there. When the fleet left England in August 1669, West was also charged with managing that private plantation and serving as storekeeper for the colony's vital foodstuffs and other supplies.

A large proportion of the initial settlers were indentured servants. West's orders emphasized prevention of their running away. Violent storms during and after a planned stop in Barbados destroyed the fleet's two smaller ships. When the largest ship, the *Carolina,* was forced to spend time on repairs in Bermuda, it took two proclamations from the governor there threatening lengthened terms of service to round up the settlers.

West was not South Carolina's first governor, but he held that office for ten of the colony's first fifteen years and took a leading role in managing the colony from the beginning. The proprietors had originally authorized the Barbadian Sir John Yeamans either to serve as governor or to name another in his stead. Yeamans named the Bermudan William Sayle, who was nearly eighty and survived less than a year as the settlers built a fortified town. As a proprietor's deputy, Joseph West took a leading role on the governing Grand Council. As early as September 1670 West warned Ashley Cooper that Sayle was "very aged, and hath much lost himselfe in his Governmt." Sayle recognized West's leadership in the colony and on his deathbed on March 4, 1671, named West as his interim successor, as did the Grand Council.

Before the harvest in 1673, the colonists barely survived on imported food supplies. At the beginning, West emphasized subsistence crops while experimenting with more tropical products to provide future wealth for both the colonists and the colony's proprietary owners. A practical man, West was both worldly and religious. In urging a replacement for the dying Governor Sayle, West asked Ashley Cooper for a man who would "feare God above all worldly Interest" and "root out evill and wickedness." Yet West owned a diamond watch and had already by 1673 laid out a formal garden at the private proprietary plantation where he then resided. When his wife Joanna (about whom nothing else is known) joined him from England in August 1671, she brought additional indentured servants to further his colonial ventures as merchant and planter. While successful, West was not rapacious, but it was his fate to govern a colony that had attracted some rapacious men.

The proprietors' Fundamental Constitutions provided for a hereditary aristocracy of landgraves and cassiques. In the absence of a commissioned governor, the senior resident landgrave was to take office. When Sir John Yeamans arrived in South Carolina in the summer of 1671, he claimed the office of governor by virtue of his patent as a landgrave. West and the Grand Council initially refused Yeamans the office but acquiesced when orders arrived from England in April 1672. When Yeamans died in August 1674, West was elevated to landgrave and served as governor for the next eight years, the period in which the colony became firmly established. Proprietary dissatisfaction with lack of profits prompted major initiatives to encourage immigration and reform the colony in 1682. West was replaced as governor by Joseph Morton in 1682 but resumed the office in August 1684 on the death of Sir Richard Kyrle, who died of malaria after serving only one month in office.

West became gravely ill with malaria and dry gripes (a form of lead poisoning caused by drinking rum) and resigned in early summer 1685. He went to Boston to recoup his health, leaving powers of attorney over 1,630 acres, a town house, ten African and two Indian slaves, and two indentured servants. West returned to South Carolina in 1686 but stayed only about a year and sold his property there. Governor Joseph West died in New York City at the home of the Quaker merchant Miles Forster between May 6, 1691, when he made out his will, and July 1 of the same year, when it was probated. After bequests to the Forsters, three kinsmen in England, and others, West left the remainder of his sizable estate to the Quaker poor of London. His slave Will received his freedom and "such cloathing and Apparell of mine as my Executor shall think fitt." CHARLES H. LESSER

Cheves, Langdon, ed. *The Shaftesbury Papers.* 1897. Reprint, Charleston, S.C.: Tempus, 2000.
Childs, St. Julien R. "The Naval Career of Joseph West." *South Carolina Historical Magazine* 71 (April 1970): 109–16.
Lesser, Charles H. *South Carolina Begins: The Records of a Proprietary Colony, 1663–1721.* Columbia: South Carolina Department of Archives and History, 1995.
Sirmans, M. Eugene. *Colonial South Carolina: A Political History, 1663–1763.* Chapel Hill: University of North Carolina Press, 1966.

West Columbia (Lexington County; 2000 pop. 13,064). Although never home to textile operations, Columbia's western suburbs were influenced by industrial activity throughout the nineteenth century: the Guignard Brick Works, the Saluda Factory, and the much larger cotton mills of the 1890s, most notably Columbia's "Duck Mill." Soon several hundred workers and their families were living in Aretasville, named for Aretas Blood, president of Columbia Mills. Their presence on the west bank of the Congaree River gave birth to stores, shops, and taverns. In December 1894 the growing community, essentially a mill village, was incorporated as the town of Brookland. Since several South Carolina cities of that era referred to their outskirts as Brooklyn or Jersey City (an obvious reference to Manhattan), this probably explains the term: an emerging suburb separated from an older, more established entity by water. In fact, state records initially cited this upstart as Brooklyn. However, since a black settlement on the Wateree River already bore that name, hence the spelling change. Despite a devastating fire in 1905 and annexation bids by Columbia, this community prospered and gradually assumed the more familiar name of New Brookland. This designation, in turn, gave way to West Columbia in 1938, and in 1964 that town became a city.

Governed by a mayor and an eight-member council and possessing a land area of 11.45 square miles, West Columbia is home to several hotels and motels, three hospitals, sixty churches, and fifteen public schools. It is served by three interstates, and some five thousand area residents work for such major manufacturing concerns as Allied-Signal, Michelin Tire, NCR, SMI, Union Switch & Signal, and Fairmont Tamper.

For most of its history, West Columbia spread westward along U.S. Highway 1 and Platt Springs Road and far north of the original mill village. However, in recent decades the old riverfront has garnered renewed interest, largely because of the development of Columbia's upscale Vista. Ironically, in the early 1900s New Brookland was considered the urban pioneer. Almost from the outset it boasted a park, a school, and a lyceum hall, amenities provided by farsighted industrialists who created what was hailed as "the finest mill village south of New England." The homes sold to workers in 1947 constitute the heart of the New Brookland Historic District. This twenty-one-block area is filled with three distinct types of structures: an L-shaped overseer's residence; an eight-room duplex; and four-room, single-family houses. In the 1990s, as restaurants, cafés, and antique shops appeared along Meeting and State Streets, West Columbia's leaders became aware of the region's commercial potential. The result was the West Vista Festival, first held in September 1999 in cooperation with the State Museum and the South Carolina Department of Archives and History.

In a turnabout that would puzzle residents a century ago, New Brookland's historic past is being analyzed and extolled, thus bridging the Congaree in a manner none could have anticipated. Thanks to the concept of the Vista, two distinct communities are gradually blending into one. JOHN H. MOORE

Wilhelm, Jody Bierer. *West Columbia, U.S.A.* West Columbia, S.C.: J. B. Wilhelm, 1986.

West Committee (1966–1969). Created in 1966 at the urging of young reformers in the General Assembly, the Committee to Make a Study of the South Carolina Constitution of 1895 was known as the "West Committee," after its chairman, state senator (later governor) John C. West. It performed a major overhaul on the state's fundamental political document and gradually weakened legislative dominance of state government.

Despite some sentiment that South Carolina should call a constitutional convention, the West Committee embarked upon three years of intense study and revision. The final report, issued in 1969, proposed seventeen new articles. But this was just the beginning of a laborious process. Each amendment required a two-thirds vote by the legislature to be placed on the statewide ballot, then legislative ratification and the passage of legislation to implement the new constitutional provisions.

Though their power was waning, the old barons of the General Assembly were able to slow many of the changes via a legislative steering committee that guided the amendments through the legislature. One key amendment passed in 1973 prohibited bills involving just one county, a direct effort to end legislative delegation rule of local government. Not until 1975 was home rule legislation approved, freeing county governments from daily micromanagement by legislators in Columbia.

The committee also called for abolishing the system of county courts, through which old-time lawyers and state senators had exerted extreme influence over court operations. However, only in 1984 would the chief justice gain full power to set rules and procedures for the state's courts. A recommendation to allow governors to run for reelection was not enacted until 1981.

While reform prevailed, the committee stopped short of other symbolic changes. It recommended keeping language permitting a literacy test for voters, even though the practice had been outlawed by the 1965 Voting Rights Act. Nor did it strike defunct language banning interracial marriages, which remained until 1998. MICHAEL SPONHOUR

Graham, Cole Blease, Jr., and William V. Moore. *South Carolina Politics and Government.* Lincoln: University of Nebraska Press, 1994.

South Carolina. Committee to Make a Study of the South Carolina Constitution of 1895. *Final Report of the Committee to Make a Study of the South Carolina Constitution of 1895.* Columbia, S.C., 1969.

Underwood, James L. *The Constitution of South Carolina.* Vol. 1, *The Relationship of the Legislative, Executive, and Judicial Branches.* Columbia: University of South Carolina Press, 1986.

Westminster (Oconee County; 2000 pop. 2,743). Founded in 1874, Westminster was a child of the railroad. The Atlanta and Charlotte Railroad came through, and the water stop evolved into a town, as did others along the new rail line. A post office was established on June 22, 1874, and the town was chartered on March 17, 1875. The first intendant (mayor) was Albert Zimmerman, and the wardens were R. A. Mattheson, J. D. Sheldon. J. H. Ligon, and R. T. Murphy.

Beacon Manufacturing Company, a division of Pillow-tex, has been a mainstay of the local economy since its establishment in 1899, employing as many as six hundred people in the manufacture of blankets, bedspreads, and draperies. Surrounding the mill are many of the original company-owned homes that housed the workers. Far from being a one-mill town, Westminster has benefited from a diversification of industry. At the edge of town, the Dunlop Sporting Goods factory has produced golf balls and tennis rackets. Other companies locating near the town include BMI (metal components), Lift Technologies (forklifts), Steel Heddle (wire), and U.S. Engine Valves.

More than one hundred homes unique to the late nineteenth and early twentieth centuries remain in Westminster. Old Main Street, now bypassed by U.S. Highways 76 and 123, attracted an influx of private investment that restored most of its buildings, which have drawn both shoppers and tourists. Passenger railroad service ceased in the 1970s, and the restored depot in the town center became a chamber of commerce. As the gateway to the Long Creek apple country to its west, Westminster hosts the South Carolina Apple Festival each September. HURLEY E. BADDERS

Westminster in the South Carolina Foot Hills of the Blue Ridge. Westminster, S.C.: Westminster Board of Trade, [1904].

Westmoreland, William Childs (1914–2005). Soldier. Westmoreland was born in Saxon on March 26, 1914, the son of James Ripley Westmoreland and Eugenia Talley Childs. Raised in Pacolet, Westmoreland was a good student, an Eagle Scout, and a competent athlete. After one year at the Citadel, he transferred to West Point, and in 1936 he graduated as first captain of the cadet corps, ranking 112 in a class of 275. The ambitious graduate was commissioned a second lieutenant in the field artillery and assigned to Fort Sill, Oklahoma. He was later transferred to Schofield Barracks, Hawaii.

In Vietnam, General William C. Westmoreland meets with Congressman Mendel Rivers of Charleston, chairman of the House Armed Services Committee. Courtesy, South Carolina Historical Society

Prior to World War II he was ordered to the Ninth Infantry Division at Fort Bragg, North Carolina. In late December 1942 he landed in North Africa for his first combat experience. He later served in the Normandy invasion (June 1944), the Huertgen Forest (fall 1944), the Battle of the Bulge (December 1944–January 1945), and at the Remagen Bridge (March 1945). After the war, Westmoreland, now a colonel, was appointed regimental commander in the Eighty-second Airborne Division, followed by an assignment as instructor to the Command and General Staff College at Fort Leavenworth, Kansas. On May 3, 1947, he married Katherine Van Deusen. They had three children. In mid-1952 he was assigned to Korea as commander of the 187th Regimental Combat Team. Before returning to the United States, Westmoreland was promoted to brigadier general at the age of thirty-eight. Then came appointments to the Pentagon, followed by command of the crack 101st Airborne Division. In 1960 Westmoreland was named superintendent of West Point, one of his most cherished assignments. He persuaded the president to double the size of the cadet corps to 4,417 and broadened the curriculum.

In 1964 Westmoreland was assigned to Vietnam as deputy to General Paul Harkins, commander of U.S. Military Assistance Command, Vietnam. Westmoreland landed in Saigon on January 27 and in March was appointed to succeed Harkins, in part because President Lyndon Johnson and his advisers thought he had a more realistic understanding of the obstacles faced in Indochina. During his command, Westmoreland oversaw the U.S. military commitment rise from 20,000 troops to more than 500,000. Along with the Pentagon, he supported the intensive bombing of North Vietnam and oversaw the search-and-destroy tactics against the enemy. According to his biographer Samuel Zaffiri, Westmoreland did this reluctantly after Johnson stated that one of his goals was to "Kill enemy soldiers faster than they could be replaced."

Although *Time* magazine named him Man of the Year for 1965, Westmoreland's star gradually tarnished as American casualties mounted and a conclusion to the war seemed no closer than when he assumed command. In the wake of the Tet Offensive in February 1968, criticism became ever greater even though the enemy attacks were soundly defeated. Although there is uncertainty as to the exact motives for relieving Westmoreland, in 1968 he was brought home to a promotion as army chief of staff. Even this position was fraught with controversy as he tried shoring up the public perception of the military. He supervised the establishment of the all-volunteer force and elimination of the draft and worked for other changes in the army command structure before retiring in June 1972.

Returning to South Carolina, Westmoreland settled in Charleston. Encouraged in part by a "Draft Westmoreland" campaign, he entered the Republican primary for governor in 1974. But the career military man had little political acumen and fell victim to his opponent's better grasp of politics. When he lost the primary to James Edwards, he was relieved. Westmoreland returned to writing his memoirs, published in 1976. But the controversy over his Vietnam tenure did not disappear. In 1982 in an interview with Westmoreland, the television show *CBS Reports* accused him of misrepresenting enemy strength to President Johnson and his advisers in 1967. The libel suit that Westmoreland brought against the network was inconclusive, although both sides claimed victory. Westmoreland spent his remaining years out of the public eye. He died in Charleston on July 18, 2005, and was interred in the cemetery at West Point, New York. FRITZ HAMER

Westmoreland, William C. Papers. South Caroliniana Library, University of South Carolina, Columbia.

———. *A Soldier Reports.* Garden City, N.Y.: Doubleday, 1976.

Zaffiri, Samuel. *Westmoreland: A Biography of General William C. Westmoreland.* New York: Morrow, 1994.

Westos. Carolina colonists learned of this powerful Native American Savannah River nation soon after their arrival. Most lowcountry Indians feared the Westos, who had a warlike reputation. In early 1674 the earl of Shaftesbury instructed Dr. Henry Woodward to build a trade relationship with either the Westos or the Cussitaws. When a group of Westos appeared at St. Giles, a plantation at the head of the Ashley River, in the fall of 1674, Woodward returned with them to their village on the Savannah River. He noted that the Westos gave him both ritual friendship greetings as well as a lengthy discourse about their strength. From this visit, Woodward forged an alliance that launched a lucrative trade in skins and Indian slaves. Between 1674 and 1680 Carolina officials supplied the Westos with weapons in return for protection against the Spanish and any other enemies. The deerskin and slave trades made Indian traders wealthy, and the Westos became the best-armed Indian nation in the Southeast. They used their power to capture hundreds of neighboring Indians for the slave trade.

From 1674 to 1677 the trade with the Westos was conducted by private entrepreneurs. Troubled by the trade in slaves, however, as well as seeking to claim the lucrative business for themselves, the Lords Proprietors initiated a seven-year monopoly over the Westos' trade beginning in 1677. Some disgruntled Carolinians continued a private trade with other Indians, some of whom were enemies of the Westos. Now unsure of their position with the Carolina government, the Westos killed two English subjects, and as a result the government forbade them from entering Charleston. The Westos also stole colonists' cattle and raided other tribal allies of Carolina. Some sources indicate that private traders deliberately provoked hostilities with the Westos, hoping to profit in war with them from the sale of Indian slaves.

In spring 1680 the Carolina government dispatched the agents John Boone and James Moore to improve relations with the tribe. This effort failed. The Carolina Grand Council then placed a trade embargo on the Westos. Ultimately war erupted from 1680 to 1683 and the colonists secured the military service of the Savannahs, a new area tribe who desired Westo territory, and of the Creeks. The

Westo War broke the power of the Westos, without "much Blood shed, or Money spilt" by the colony, as one source noted. Most of the Westos were killed or captured. The survivors at first moved north to join the Iroquois, then relocated to the Ocmulgee River in Georgia, where they were eventually absorbed by the Creek Confederacy. MICHAEL P. MORRIS

Crane, Verner. *The Southern Frontier, 1670–1732.* Durham, N.C.: Duke University Press, 1928.

Milling, Chapman J. *Red Carolinians.* 1940. Reprint, Columbia: University of South Carolina Press, 1969.

Whaley, William Burroughs Smith (1866–1929). Architect, engineer. W. B. Smith Whaley was born on May 24, 1866, in Charleston, the son of William Baynard Whaley, a prominent Charleston cotton broker, and Helen Smith. He studied engineering at Bingham Military Institute in North Carolina, as well as Stevens Institute of Technology in Hoboken, New Jersey, before earning a degree in mechanical engineering from Cornell University in 1888. He soon joined the Providence, Rhode Island, architectural and engineering firm of Thompson & Nagle, the major partner of which, D. M. Thompson, was a textile designer and developer in New England. In 1892 Whaley visited Columbia, South Carolina, to study the potential for hydroelectric-powered textile mills on the Columbia Canal. Impressed by the industrial promise of Columbia, Whaley returned there later that same year, opening an office as a cotton mill engineer. He produced his first South Carolina design in 1893, the ten-thousand-spindle Union Cotton Mill, for Union County textile entrepreneur Thomas C. Duncan.

In January 1894 Smith forged a partnership with the local architect and civil engineer Gadsden E. Shand. Known as W. B. Smith Whaley & Company, the firm became the state's premier architectural and engineering concern specializing in textile mill design, innovation, and development. With designs to its credit in Massachusetts, Alabama, Georgia, North Carolina, and South Carolina, Whaley & Company earned both regional and national reputations. In South Carolina alone, from 1894 to 1903 the firm designed and built sixteen mills, including four that Whaley owned and managed himself in Columbia—Richland (1894–1895), Granby (1896), Capital City (1899), and Olympia (1899–1900). Other textile mills included the Courtenay Mill in Newry (1893–1894), the Enterprise Mill in Orangeburg (1896), the Warrenville Mill in Aiken County (1897), the Buffalo Mill in Union County (1899), the Lancaster Mills for the textile magnate Leroy Springs (1900), the DeKalb Mill in Camden (1900), and the Glenn-Lowry Mill in Whitmire (1900). In 1899–1900 Whaley built his masterpiece, the 2,400-loom, 104,000-spindle, four-story Olympia Mill near Columbia. As the largest, most expensive, and most technologically and architecturally advanced textile mill under one roof in the world, Olympia Mill, Whaley hoped, would establish Columbia as "the greatest cotton manufacturing city in the south."

In 1900 Whaley expanded his operations by opening an office in Boston and hiring the young architect George E. Lafaye of New Orleans to take charge in Columbia. As chief draftsman, Lafaye designed and executed, under Shand's direction, much of the firm's work in the state after 1900. Apart from textile mills, Whaley & Company's designs included the Columbia *State* newspaper building (1897) and Columbia's YMCA building (1898–1899), as well as some large residences. Because indebtedness and labor disputes threatened the existence of his four Columbia mills, their board of directors reorganized operations, and Whaley resigned as president in November 1903. Despite his genius for mill design and promotion of industrial development, his company could not avoid bankruptcy.

Whaley's Columbia office reorganized as Shand & Lafaye, Architects and Engineers, as Whaley relocated to Boston in December 1903 to pursue textile mill design and engineering in New England. He later moved to New York, where he developed and perfected an internal combustion engine, touted by numerous engineers as an improvement over the diesel engine. Whaley died in New Rochelle, New York, on April 17, 1929, and was buried at Larchmont, New York. ANDREW W. CHANDLER

Power, J. Tracy. "'The Brightest of the Lot': W. B. Smith Whaley and the Rise of the South Carolina Textile Industry, 1893–1903." *South Carolina Historical Magazine* 93 (April 1992): 126–38.

Smith, Fenelon DeVere. "The Economic Development of the Textile Industry in the Columbia, South Carolina Area, from 1790 through 1916." Ph.D. diss., University of Kentucky, 1952.

Wells, John E., and Robert E. Dalton. *The South Carolina Architects, 1885–1935: A Biographical Directory.* Richmond, Va.: New South Architectural Press, 1992.

Whig Party. One of the two major political parties in the United States from approximately 1834 to 1856, the Whig Party had few South Carolina supporters during most of its existence. Nevertheless, South Carolina nullifiers were among the first to adopt this Anglo-American term connoting hostility to tyranny in order to signify their opposition to President Andrew Jackson, leader of the Democratic Party.

Led by John C. Calhoun, nullifiers joined other anti-Jackson men from across the country and across the ideological spectrum to form the national Whig Party in the early 1830s. However, Calhoun soon realized that his alliance with politicians such as Henry Clay and Daniel Webster, who supported far greater federal power than he did, could not work. He therefore used the issue of banking policy to take his followers out of the national Whig fold in 1837.

Not all South Carolina Whigs, however, agreed to leave the party. Calhoun's own Senate colleague William Campbell Preston remained a loyal Whig. With their numbers seriously depleted by the defection of Calhoun and most of his followers, South Carolina Whigs mounted effective campaigns in only a few areas. As in other southern states, Whigs in South Carolina stressed economic issues and enjoyed their greatest support among commercially oriented planters, merchants, and professionals.

After 1837 a remnant of planters in upcountry cotton districts such as Laurens and especially the Anderson section of Pendleton continued to support Whig financial policy. Democratic destruction of the Second Bank of the United States and the creation of the "pet bank" system had led, Whigs charged, to the depression of the late 1830s. The *Highland Sentinel,* a Pendleton Whig newspaper founded in 1840, declared that once the Democrats stopped "tampering with the business and currency of the country, our planters will pay their debts, and be found again marching forward in a train of uninterrupted prosperity and happiness." Upcountry Whigs looked forward to the reestablishment of a national bank, for, as a Whig kinsman of Calhoun said, "we have always had a better currency with, than without" such a bank.

Although most of these planters had supported nullification, not all Whigs were former nullifiers. Some nullification-era Unionists found the Whig economic program appealing. These included merchants and professionals in Charleston, such as the lawyer James L.

Petigru. The *Charleston Courier,* a major Unionist voice in the early 1830s, became one of the South's foremost Whig newspapers.

Whigs never overcame Calhoun's strong appeal and efficient political organization. Moreover, the national party's inability to deliver on its financial program during the presidency of John Tyler (1841–1845) demoralized state party members. Whigs won a few legislative seats before disappearing from ballots after 1844. During the party's brief life, it succeeded best in Pendleton District—ironically, Calhoun's home. In 1840 Pendleton voters elected Whigs to the state Senate seat and to six of its seven state House seats. The Greenville-Pendleton congressional district elected the only two Whigs the state sent to Congress following Calhoun's defection, Waddy Thompson, Jr., and William Butler. ROBERT TINKLER

Ford, Lacy K., Jr. *Origins of Southern Radicalism: The South Carolina Upcountry, 1800–1860.* New York: Oxford University Press, 1988.

Holt, Michael F. *The Rise and Fall of the American Whig Party: Jacksonian Politics and the Onset of the Civil War.* New York: Oxford University Press, 1999.

Tinkler, Robert. "Whiggery in the South Carolina Upcountry: Jacksonian Politics in the Greenville-Pendleton Congressional District." Master's thesis, University of North Carolina at Chapel Hill, 1992.

Whipper, Lucille Simmons (b. 1928). Educator, legislator. Whipper was born in Charleston on June 6, 1928, the daughter of Joseph Simmons and Sarah Marie Washington. When her mother later married Edward A. Stroud, she spent her childhood on the east side of Charleston and in the Liberty Hill section of North Charleston. Her first exposure to the costs of social activism came when her stepfather attempted to organize a labor union and lost his job.

Whipper graduated from Avery Normal Institute in 1944. She then went to Talladega College in Alabama, where she earned a degree in sociology and economics and married her first husband. After his untimely death, she returned home with an infant son and taught social studies in the public schools. She was awarded a scholarship to the University of Chicago and in 1955 graduated with a master's degree in political science.

While encouraged by her professors to remain in Chicago, Whipper again chose Charleston and became the director of guidance services at two prominent black high schools, Burke High and Bonds-Wilson. In 1957 she married the Reverend Benjamin Whipper, a widower with five children. The family grew when the Whippers had a daughter, raising the number of children in their household to seven.

In 1972 Whipper became the director of human relations at the College of Charleston, serving for four years before being enticed back to the public schools. She directed a multi-million-dollar federal project, the Elementary and Secondary School Act, which set up model school programs across Charleston County. Finding the position to be more paperwork than action, she returned to the College of Charleston, officially retiring in 1981. Her respite was not long-lived as she devoted her efforts to reclaiming and preserving the building that had housed Avery Normal Institute for more than one hundred years. Fearing that it would be sold to developers, she worked with officials at the College of Charleston to secure a National Endowment for the Humanities grant. Ultimately her work led to Avery becoming a research center and archive focusing on the history and culture of lowcountry African Americans.

During this same time period (1978–1982), Whipper was also a member of the school board for District 20 of Charleston County Schools, her first real experience with politics. She sought greater public service when a state House of Representatives seat for Mount Pleasant became open in autumn 1986. After a family conference, the Whippers decided to move into an upscale suburb in Mount Pleasant. This action gave her legal residence in the district, a requirement before her name could be placed on the ballot. Winning the election, she became Charleston's first black woman legislator and represented House District 109 until 1996. She was inducted into the South Carolina Black Hall of Fame in 1995. LOUISE ALLEN

Brazell, Dawn. "Lucille Whipper: House Representative with a Cause." Charleston *Post and Courier,* April 20, 1991, pp. C1, C3.

Simms, Lois. *Profiles of African American Females in the Low Country of South Carolina.* Charleston, S.C.: Avery Research Center, 1992.

Whipper, William J. (?–1907). Legislator. Whipper was one of the most influential African American politicians in South Carolina's Reconstruction government. He was born free in Philadelphia, the son of a prominent lumber merchant who was an active Pennsylvania abolitionist. Early in the Civil War, Whipper was working as a clerk in an attorney's office. During the war he joined a Michigan volunteer regiment. At the end of the war Whipper was among the federal occupation forces in South Carolina. He read law and passed the South Carolina Bar to enter practice in Charleston in 1865. He then moved to Beaufort and became the town's most prominent Reconstruction lawyer. Along with Robert Smalls and Richard Howell Gleaves, he founded the Beaufort Republican Club at the Steven's House in Beaufort on March 26, 1867. This was the first Republican political organization in South Carolina.

In autumn 1867 Whipper was elected as a delegate to the state constitutional convention of 1868, where he took a leading role. He was among the most progressive delegates, supporting free public education for all South Carolinians and the widest possible voting franchise. Whipper even introduced a resolution to add a woman-suffrage provision to the state constitution, declaring, "The systems of legislation have been laid on insecure foundations, and they will never be permanent until women are recognized as the equal of men and . . . permitted to enjoy the privileges which appertain to the citizen." However, this provision was too extreme even for the "radical" convention of 1868 and was defeated.

Whipper represented Beaufort County in the South Carolina House of Representatives from 1868 to 1872 and from 1875 to 1876. While he was in Columbia, his talent and intellect made him one of the most influential members of the Reconstruction legislature. In 1872 Whipper challenged Robert Smalls for the state Senate. Whipper was soundly defeated, and the spirited campaign divided the loyalties of Beaufort County freedmen and began a lasting rivalry between the two men. In 1875 Whipper was elected a circuit judge by the legislature but fell victim to the corruption scandals of the state government. Governor Daniel Chamberlain refused to sign his commission, blocking him from taking his seat on the bench. Whipper returned to Beaufort and served for twelve years as Beaufort County probate judge. He was finally ousted by a white Democratic office seeker in 1888 as part of the "People's Ticket," a fusion government compromise between Beaufort County's black Republicans led by Robert Smalls and white Democrats led by William Elliott and William J. Verdier.

Part of Whipper's special influence in the Reconstruction state government derived from his marriage on September 17, 1868, to Frances Ann Rollin, the daughter of a wealthy and prominent free-black family of Charleston. Whipper's last political duty was as a delegate from Beaufort County to the state constitutional convention of

1895, where he tried to head off moves by Democrats to disenfranchise African American voters. When their efforts failed, Whipper and the entire Beaufort County delegation refused to sign the new constitution. He retired from politics and died in Beaufort in 1907. LAWRENCE S. ROWLAND

Holt, Thomas. *Black over White: Negro Political Leadership in South Carolina during Reconstruction.* Urbana: University of Illinois Press, 1977.

Miller, Edward A. *Gullah Statesman: Robert Smalls from Slavery to Congress, 1839–1915.* Columbia: University of South Carolina Press, 1995.

Powers, Bernard E. *Black Charlestonians: A Social History, 1822–1885.* Fayetteville: University of Arkansas Press, 1994.

Taylor, Alrutheus A. *The Negro in South Carolina during the Reconstruction.* 1924. Reprint, New York: Russell and Russell, 1969.

Tindall, George Brown. *South Carolina Negroes, 1877–1900.* 1952. Reprint, Columbia: University of South Carolina Press, 2003.

Underwood, James L. *The Constitution of South Carolina.* 4 vols. Columbia: University of South Carolina Press, 1986–1994.

White, Benjamin Franklin (1800–1879). Composer, author. White was born on September 10, 1800, in the Padgett's Creek section of Union District, the youngest of fourteen children born to Robert White and Mildred Whitehead. He attended school for only a short time but inherited a musical inclination from his father. On December 30, 1825, he married Thurza Golightly, the sister of Amy Golightly, the wife of the shaped-note composer William Walker. The Whites were the parents of fourteen children, nine of whom reached adulthood. The family moved to Harris County, Georgia, about 1842.

White was probably a contributor to Walker's *Southern Harmony,* though he received no credit. While earning his livelihood as a farmer in Georgia, in 1844 he published *The Sacred Harp,* a shaped-note singing book, in conjunction with E. J. King. Shaped-note singing in the South evolved from the eighteenth-century New England singing-school movement. Itinerant music teachers taught the shaped-note system to church congregations. The easy-to-learn system made it possible for congregations to sing in harmony without musical accompaniment and also without the singers having to be trained to read formal sheet music. Shapes (triangle=fa, oval=so, rectangle=la, and diamond=mi) were added to the note heads to help singers find pitches within major and minor scales. The 1850 census lists White's occupation as "music teacher," but by 1860 he identified himself to census takers simply as "Author of Sacred Harp." White used the four-shape (or fa-so-la) system and became one of the most prominent figures in the movement of that method. While some others changed to a seven-shape (or do-re-mi) system, White admonished his followers to "Ask for the old paths and walk therein." He composed the tunes and harmony to many hymns in his book. *The Sacred Harp* went through many printings and remains in use, with its most recent republication occurring in 1991. Singers across the South have kept the *Sacred Harp* tradition of shaped-note singing alive into the twenty-first century.

In 1852 White began the first newspaper in Harris County, the *Organ,* and served as the county's clerk of the inferior court in 1858. He formed the Southern Musical Convention in Upson County, Georgia, in 1857 and served as its president until 1862. In 1865 he served as mayor of Hamilton, Georgia. He died on December 6, 1879, in Atlanta, Georgia, and was buried in that city's Oakland Cemetery. *The Sacred Harp* tradition remains prominent in upstate South Carolina, western North Carolina, eastern Texas, and parts of Kentucky. BRENT HOLCOMB

Chase, Gilbert. *America's Music.* 3d ed. Urbana: University of Illinois Press, 1992.

Cobb, Buell. *The Sacred Harp: A Tradition and Its Music.* Athens: University of Georgia Press, 1978.

Coleman, Kenneth, and Charles Stephen Gurr, eds. *Dictionary of Georgia Biography.* 2 vols. Athens: University of Georgia Press, 1983.

White, Edward Brickell (1806–1882). Architect. Known for his Gothic-revival designs and knowledge of Greek and Roman architecture, White was the preeminent Charleston architect of the 1840s and 1850s. He was born on January 29, 1806, to John Blake White, a planter, artist, and playwright, and his first wife, Elizabeth Allston White, at Chapel Hill plantation in St. John's Berkeley Parish. He studied engineering at the United States Military Academy at West Point and, after graduating in 1826, served in the army as an artillery officer. On April 18, 1832, he married Delia Adams in her hometown of New London, Connecticut. He left military service in 1836 to survey routes for several proposed railroads, including the Louisville, Cincinnati and Charleston. By 1839 White had settled in Charleston and was working as a civil engineer, architect, and surveyor. During the following decade, he became one of the most successful architects in South Carolina.

White's first major commission was Market Hall (1840–1841), a monumental building erected to serve as the center of Charleston's public markets, which had been devastated by fire in 1838. White designed the building in the form of a Roman temple, possibly using the Temple of Fortuna Virilis as a model, and symbolized its purpose with an entablature ornamented with bucrania and rams' skulls. Behind the hall he erected a series of sheds to provide space for vendors. The project showed White to be a careful student of Roman architecture and added significantly to his reputation.

White's early projects included several ecclesiastical buildings that demonstrated the breadth of his stylistic vocabulary. His designs for St. Johannes Lutheran Church (1841–1842) and the Centenary Methodist Episcopal Church (1842) displayed his mastery of the Greek-revival style. He introduced the Gothic-revival style to Charleston with the Huguenot Church (1844–1845) and also used the same style for Grace Church (1847–1848), Trinity Episcopal Church (1847) in Columbia, and the Chapel of the Cross (1854–1857) in Bluffton. White's other major projects of the era included the Charleston High School (1840–1842), the James Louis Petigru law office (1848), and a steeple for St. Philip's Church (1848–1850). In 1849 he designed wings and a third story for the South Carolina Military College, and the following year he added wings and a portico to the main building at the College of Charleston.

White's general approach to architecture was eclectic. Neither impulsive nor dogmatic in his stylistic choices, he believed that each commission warranted a design specifically crafted to suit its particular circumstances. Indeed, White's greatest talent was his flexibility as a designer. Because he was at ease with classicism and the rising tide of romanticism, he was able to accommodate both Charleston's traditional conservatism and its taste for the flamboyant new architecture from Europe. In addition, his background in engineering provided an advantage that many of his competitors lacked, and he excelled at creating successful designs on limited budgets.

About 1850 White was selected as the superintending architect of the new Custom House. The plans for this monumental building, furnished by the Boston architect Ammi Burnham Young, called for an imposing edifice with a dome and four porticos. Construction progressed slowly and was plagued by cost overruns. Amid the escalating sectional crisis, many northern congressmen questioned the need for such an opulent customhouse in a city known for its distaste of federal authority. In 1859 Congress refused to appropriate additional funding for the project, which left White with no choice but to halt construction. The total cost of the building, originally estimated at $370,000, eventually reached $3 million. It was finally completed in 1879 without the dome and side porticos and with a somewhat diminished interior plan.

As the Civil War approached, White suspended his architectural practice and devoted himself to the Confederate cause. He had been active in the state militia since leaving military service in 1836 and, with war nearing, helped organize the Palmetto Battalion. He served initially at the rank of major and was later promoted to lieutenant colonel. During the war he saw action on James Island and also in North Carolina. At the end of hostilities in 1865, White returned to Charleston and resumed his practice, but obtaining commissions in the war-devastated city proved difficult. In 1866 he oversaw repairs to St. Michael's Church, which had sustained damage during the siege of Charleston, and he later designed a small office building for the Charleston Gas and Light Company (1876–1878). By 1879 he had moved to New York, where he died on May 10, 1882. He was buried in St. Michael's Churchyard in Charleston. DANIEL J. VIVIAN

Lane, Mills. *Architecture of the Old South: South Carolina.* Savannah, Ga.: Beehive, 1984.

Poston, Jonathan H. *The Buildings of Charleston: A Guide to the City's Architecture.* Columbia: University of South Carolina Press, 1997.

Ravenel, Beatrice St. Julien. *Architects of Charleston.* 1945. Reprint, Columbia: University of South Carolina Press, 1992.

Severens, Kenneth. *Charleston Antebellum Architecture and Civic Destiny.* Knoxville: University of Tennessee Press, 1988.

White, John Blake (1781–1859). Playwright, painter. White was born on September 2, 1781, near Eutaw Springs at Whitehall Plantation, St. John's Berkeley Parish, to Blake Leay White and Elizabeth Borquin. A pioneer in early American painting and literature, White was a leading figure in both art forms in antebellum South Carolina.

After growing up at Whitehall and reading law in Columbia, in 1800 White sailed for England, where he studied painting under Benjamin West, the American-born official historical painter to King George III. In 1803 White returned to South Carolina and settled in Charleston. Finding little market for the grand historical subjects he wished to execute, he applied to the bar and attempted to make a living painting portraits. In 1806 his first two plays, *Foscari, or the Venetian Exile* and *The Mysteries of the Castle,* were performed at the Charleston Theatre. He was admitted to the bar in 1808, greatly improving his financial and social standing. In 1818 he was elected by the city parishes of St. Philip's and St. Michael's to the General Assembly, where he served one term. He became a director of the South Carolina Academy of Fine Arts the year it was chartered in 1821. Beginning in 1826, he was engaged in running the state's only paper mill, in Lexington District, but he moved back to Charleston in 1832 after a fire destroyed the plant. There he took a position at the U.S. Custom House, where he worked for the next twenty-five years. In 1845 he was made an honorary member of the National Academy of Design. He was married twice, first to Elizabeth (Eliza) Allston on March 28, 1805, and then to Anna Rachel O'Driscoll on October 2, 1819, two years after Eliza's death. His first marriage produced four children, and his second produced eight.

Although White's earliest plays are Gothic romantic tragedies set in Europe, his other dramas are notable for addressing contemporary American concerns. *Modern Honor,* which opened at the Charleston Theatre in 1812, was the first antidueling play in American literature and attacked the practice as "sanctioned murder." Unafraid of controversy, White also spoke out against capital punishment and allied himself with opponents of nullification. *The Forgers,* written in 1829 and published in 1837, was one of America's first temperance plays. *The Triumph of Liberty, or Louisiana Preserved* ostensibly celebrated Andrew Jackson's victory at the Battle of New Orleans during the War of 1812. But the play, published in 1819, also attempted to justify the execution in 1818 of two British citizens convicted of inciting Indians during the Seminole War.

Both of White's parents served in the Revolutionary War, his father at Fort Moultrie and his mother as a spy for Francis Marion. Some of his paintings depict dramatic scenes from the conflict. Four of these, *General Marion Inviting a British Officer to Share His Meal, Sergeants Jasper and Newton Rescuing American Prisoners from the British, Mrs. Motte Directing Generals Marion and Lee to Burn Her Mansion to Dislodge the British,* and *The Defense of Fort Moultrie,* all painted between 1810 and 1815, hang in the U.S. Capitol. Among his portraits are those of South Carolina luminaries John C. Calhoun, Charles Cotesworth Pinckney, and Henry Middleton. White died on August 24, 1859, in Charleston and was buried in the family plot at St. Philip's Church. HUGH DAVIS

Moore, Alexander, ed. *Biographical Directory of the South Carolina House of Representatives.* Vol. 5, *1816–1828.* Columbia: South Carolina Department of Archives and History, 1992.

Partridge, Paul W., Jr. "John Blake White: Southern Romantic Painter and Playwright." Ph.D. diss., University of Pennsylvania, 1951.

Turner, Mary Ellen. "John Blake White: An Introduction." *Journal of Early Southern Decorative Arts* 16 (May 1990): 1–17.

Watson, Charles S. *Antebellum Charleston Dramatists.* University: University of Alabama Press, 1976.

White, Joshua Daniel (1914–1969). Musician. White was born in Greenville on February 11, 1914. A sophisticated guitarist and singer, Broadway actor, and favorite of the New York City folk music and leftist political scenes of the 1940s, Josh White played a major role in introducing the African American blues tradition to white audiences and establishing the blues singer as an American cultural icon. While his repertoire spanned pop tunes, protest songs, and folk ballads, White remained rooted in the blues and spirituals he learned while growing up in Greenville. The son of a Baptist minister, White got his start as a "lead boy" for a succession of itinerant blues musicians and made his recording debut with the guitar evangelist Blind Joe Taggart in 1928. After graduating from high school in Greenville, he moved to New York City and became established in the early 1930s as a popular recording artist among African American audiences in both blues (as "Pinewood Tom") and gospel. White's early blues records relied on the double-entendre lyrics typical of the era as well as the elaborate finger-picked guitar style that characterized the East Coast school of blues. In the early 1940s White began branching out musically and reaching new audiences as an integral figure in the burgeoning New York folk scene. He debuted on Broadway with Paul Robeson, performed with the Almanac Singers (a group that included Pete Seeger and Woody Guthrie), and sang at the invitation of President Franklin Delano Roosevelt. In 1941 he recorded *Chain Gang,* a pioneering album that commented explicitly on civil rights. Although his career declined during the 1950s, White found new fans during the folk revival of the early 1960s. White died of a heart attack in Manhasset, New York, on

September 5, 1969. He is buried in Cypress Hills Cemetery, Brooklyn, New York. DAVID NELSON

Wald, Elijah. *Josh White: Society Blues.* Amherst: University of Massachusetts Press, 2000.

White, Vanna (b. 1957). Television personality. White was born Vanna Marie Rosich in Conway on February 18, 1957, the daughter of Miguel Angel Rosich and Joan Marie Rosich. Her parents divorced when she was less than one year old, and she was raised in North Myrtle Beach by her mother and her stepfather, Herbert Stackley White, Jr. She graduated from North Myrtle Beach High School, then attended Atlanta School for Fashion and Design. After gaining some modeling experience, she moved to Los Angeles to pursue her lifetime ambition of an acting career. White landed a few minor acting roles in Hollywood, but her career stalled and she worked part-time as a waitress to help make ends meet.

White's big break came in 1982, when the television producer Merv Griffin added her to his NBC game show creation *Wheel of Fortune,* hosted by Pat Sajak. At the call of the contestants attempting to solve word puzzles, White turned letters on a giant board. The show was a hit and soon entered national syndication. As a result, the attractive and spirited letter-turner from South Carolina became a household name and pop icon. Always cheering on the contestants, White was recognized by the *Guinness Book of World Records* in 1992 as TV's most frequent clapper. She averaged 720 claps per show and more than 28,000 per season. She won endorsement contracts, marketed her own fragrance, and got a starring role in the 1988 movie *Goddess of Love.* Her autobiography, *Vanna Speaks,* was published in 1987.

On December 31, 1990, White married the restaurateur George Santo Pietro. They had two children. The couple filed for divorce in 2002. ROBERT A. PIERCE

White, Vanna. *Vanna Speaks.* New York: Warner, 1987.

White lightning. White lightning, a white whiskey made surreptitiously and illegally, was once produced in great quantities in South Carolina. It got its name from its color and the kick it delivers when consumed.

The beverage achieved popularity in South Carolina and the rest of the South largely because of the high taxes on legal whiskey, the ready availability of the major raw material—traditionally corn—and the region's poverty, which made moonshining an attractive industry for many farmers. Production mushroomed between 1915, when South Carolina went legally dry, and 1933, when national prohibition ended. White lightning became part of the culture of some rural areas, including parts of southern Appalachia.

The potable, often referred to as "moonshine" because it was usually produced at night, is often made under conditions so primitive that it has proved lethal. But its "proper" manufacture is considered an art form by some backwoods connoisseurs.

The whiskey is produced from mash, which is a mixture of grain, sugar, water, and yeast that ferments to produce the alcohol. Lack of aging leaves the whiskey with a clean "white" look. Distilleries are commonly made of copper for the most part, which, the producers think, helps maintain the flavor. Manufacturers usually make their own stills.

Agents from the Bureau of Alcohol, Tobacco, and Firearms, humorously called "revenooers" by the moonshiners, have sharply curtailed the illegal operations. In 2003 a South Carolina law

After a raid on an illegal still, Allendale law enforcement officers disposed of confiscated white lightning. L-R: Police Officer Jimmy Grubbs, Chief of Police Harold Bennett, and Officer Counsel Dunbar; Deputy Sheriff Joe Stack and Sheriff G. C. Forrester. Courtesy, the collection of Samuel Bennett, Allendale, S.C.

enforcement official said the last distillery raid had probably occurred just three months earlier. But isolated moonshiners still ply their art in South Carolina, and many of their customers wax ecstatic when they are lucky enough to purchase a batch they consider safe and savory. ROBERT A. PIERCE

"SLED," *Sandlapper* (Winter 2003–4): 20.

White primary. Party primary elections were introduced in the nineteenth century. They were touted as a more democratic means of nominating candidates for state office than the traditional party convention. The final choice of a candidate for office is made in the general election, which is generally contested by candidates from opposing parties. But in the "Solid South" of 1876–1960, where Democrats were the only viable party, the primary was the only opportunity for meaningful participation by voters. In essence, the candidate who won the Democratic primary was also the de facto winner of the general election since there was almost never a viable candidate from another party to oppose him.

Democratic primaries spread across South Carolina in the last quarter of the nineteenth century, beginning with Pickens County in 1876. In 1896 the state became the first in which all elected officials were nominated in primaries. However, followers of Ben Tillman imposed a "whites only" rule in the primary in an effort to eliminate African Americans from the state's political life. A few blacks who had supported Wade Hampton for governor in 1876 were permitted to vote in the primaries. But with the effective disenfranchisement of the state's black majority by the constitution of 1895, politics were closed to African Americans for the next fifty years.

Beginning in the 1920s, black plaintiffs from across the South challenged the white primary in the courts. Success came in 1944 in the Texas case of *Smith v. Allwright,* in which the U.S. Supreme Court concluded that the primary was an integral part of the election process and that, at least in Texas, the Democratic Party was an arm of the state in its exclusion of voters based on race. Thus, the Fourteenth and Fifteenth Amendments to the U.S. Constitution required an end to the white primary.

South Carolina's small contingent of civil rights activists took heart from the ruling but were under no illusions about its immediate impact in their state. Indeed, while Democratic officials in most of the South yielded reluctantly to the inevitable, Governor Olin

Johnston and the General Assembly defiantly refused to concede defeat. With state control of voting at stake and fearing the return of the "black rule" of Reconstruction, they maneuvered to circumvent the ruling, or at least to delay its implementation as long as possible. In a one-week special session in April 1944, the General Assembly repealed 147 laws relating to the primaries in hopes that the courts would allow the Democratic Party, now as a private club, to continue to exclude African Americans.

The efforts were to no avail because blacks in the state, including George Elmore of Columbia, courageously pressed their right to vote in the primaries. In 1947 the federal judge J. Waties Waring of Charleston, applying the *Smith* ruling to Elmore's suit against a Richland County Democratic official, ruled in *Elmore v. Rice* that African Americans must be permitted to enroll in the party. One last attempt at evasion, a "loyalty oath" that required would-be voters to swear that they supported white supremacy, was shot down by Waring in *Brown v. Baskin* in 1948. As a result, some fifty thousand blacks voted in the 1948 Democratic primary. While the final overthrow of the old political order would come only with the federal Voting Rights Act of 1965, the fall of the white primary was a major step in undermining the status quo. JAMES O. FARMER, JR.

Burton, Orville Vernon. "The Black Squint of the Law: Racism in South Carolina." In *The Meaning of South Carolina History: Essays in Honor of George C. Rogers, Jr.,* edited by David R. Chesnutt and Clyde N. Wilson. Columbia: University of South Carolina Press, 1991.

Hine, Darlene Clark. *Black Victory: The Rise and Fall of the White Primary in Texas.* Millwood, N.Y.: KTO, 1979.

Lawson, Steven F. *Black Ballots: Voting Rights in the South, 1944–1969.* New York: Columbia University Press, 1976.

White-tailed deer. State animal. Found throughout North America, the white-tailed deer (*Odocoileus virginianus*) was adopted as South Carolina's state animal in 1972. The trade and exportation of deerskins was vital to the economy of colonial South Carolina, and the species remains one of the state's most popular game animals. Elusive white-tails, which may run as fast as thirty miles per hour, inhabit every county in South Carolina. The underside of this deer's body and tail are completely white, a color particularly noticeable as the animal "flags" its tail when alarmed. Adult does (female deer) average between 100 and 110 pounds; adult males, or bucks, average 140 pounds. The heaviest doe recorded in South Carolina weighed 175 pounds; the heaviest buck, 316 pounds. Bucks begin growing antlers in April. As antlers consist of growing bone, they remain covered with blood vessels and nerves, or "velvet" skin, until the antlers harden in late August. Bucks generally shed their antlers in January and February. Deer have a reddish coat in the summer and a thicker, gray or dark brown coat during winter. The primary breeding season for deer takes place between mid-October and mid-November. Deer prefer a fertile, diverse habitat. Since natural predators no longer present a serious threat to deer, recreational hunting provides a check for overpopulation and disease. Deer hunting has the ancillary benefit of generating some $200 million annually in the state. Overpopulation became a growing concern in the last decades of the twentieth century, however, with crop damage and deer vehicle accidents showing significant increases by the end of the century. FORD WALPOLE

Whitehead, G. Kenneth. *Deer of the World.* London: Constable, 1972.

Whitefield, George (1714–1770). Clergyman. Whitefield was born on December 16, 1714, in Gloucester, England, the son of Thomas Whitefield and Elizabeth Edwards, innkeepers. After studying at the local grammar school, he worked in the inn with his widowed mother. Enrolling at Pembroke College, Oxford, in 1732, he worked as a servant and came under the influence of the Holy Club led by John and Charles Wesley. The following year he had a deeply moving religious experience. Attracting the attention of Selina, Countess of Huntingdon, a leader in the evangelical revival, he was ordained deacon in the Church of England in June 1736, shortly before receiving a B.A. degree. Personally winsome and spellbinding as a preacher, he began to attract large crowds. David Garrick, the London actor, once commented that Whitefield could make his hearers weep by pronouncing the word "Mesopotamia."

George Whitefield. Courtesy, South Carolina Historical Society

Whitefield succeeded John Wesley as chaplain to Georgia in 1738 and made plans to establish Bethesda Orphan House, patterned after the one built in Halle by the German pietist August Francke. He sailed to England from Charleston to collect money for Bethesda and to be ordained a priest in the Church of England (January 1739). On this first visit to Charleston, Whitefield was received hospitably by Alexander Garden, the rector of St. Philip's and commissary of the Bishop of London. In England, where many pulpits were closed to him because of his criticism of the clergy and accusations against him of enthusiasm, Whitefield preached outdoors to large crowds in both London and Bristol. Before returning to Georgia, he persuaded Wesley to take up his field preaching appointments. Whitefield's increasing commitment to the doctrine of predestination, however, led to a break with Wesley, and although the two were personally reconciled, they never again worked together.

Whitefield sailed to America again in 1739, the second of seven trips, landing in Philadelphia in November. He attracted the support of Benjamin Franklin in Pennsylvania and Jonathan Edwards in Massachusetts. Returning to Georgia to oversee the construction of Bethesda, he stopped in South Carolina at a tavern near Little River on New Year's Day, 1740, and preached against the dancing that went on through the night. In Savannah he recognized the need for slave labor to build his orphan house and joined the campaign to legalize slavery. He eventually purchased a plantation he named Providence in St. Paul's Parish, South Carolina, for support.

Whitefield encountered his strongest opposition in America in South Carolina. On March 14, 1740, Commissary Garden summoned Whitefield to Charleston and charged him with enthusiasm and defamation of other clergy and suspended him from preaching. The following Sunday, Garden preached against Whitefield on the text "Those who have turned the world upside down have come hither also." Whitefield retaliated with a sermon in the Congregational church on the text "Alexander the coppersmith hath done me much evil; the Lord reward him according to his works." Garden subsequently published a pamphlet attacking the revivalist. When Whitefield returned to Charleston on July 6, Garden preached against Whitefield and denied him the Sacrament. The next day Garden summoned Whitefield to appear before a church court, but Whitefield appealed to the Bishop of London. A year later Garden again summoned Whitefield. When Whitefield failed to appear, Garden suspended him from his ministerial functions. Whitefield ignored the suspension.

On January 4, 1741, Whitefield arrived in Charleston to sail to England. He was served a warrant for revising for publication a letter written by one of his followers, the Beaufort planter Hugh Bryan. Bryan was jailed, and Whitefield was cited with "false, malicious, scandalous, and infamous libel against the clergy." Whitefield appeared in court, paid a fine, and sailed to London with the good wishes of his adherents. Beyond the controversy he incited, Whitefield had little lasting impact on South Carolina.

Back in England on November 14, 1741, Whitefield married a widow, Elizabeth James. Their one child, John, lived only four months.

On his final trip to America in 1770 Whitefield became ill in Boston and died in Newburyport, Massachusetts, on September 30. He was buried beneath the pulpit of the First Presbyterian Church. A. V. HUFF, JR.

Henry, Stuart C. *George Whitefield: Wayfaring Witness.* New York: Abingdon, 1957.

Huff, A.V., Jr. "A History of South Carolina United Methodism." In *United Methodist Ministers in South Carolina.* Columbia: South Carolina Conference of the United Methodist Church, 1984.

Jackson, Harvey H. "Hugh Bryan and the Evangelical Movement in South Carolina." *William and Mary Quarterly,* 3d ser., 43 (October 1986): 594–614.

Stout, Harry S. *The Divine Dramatist: George Whitefield and the Rise of Modern Evangelicalism.* Grand Rapids, Mich.: Eerdmans, 1991.

Whittaker, Johnson Chesnut (1858–1931). Slave, West Point cadet, lawyer, educator. Whittaker was born on August 23, 1858, on the Camden plantation of James Chesnut, Sr. He was the son of Maria Whitaker, a slave, and James Whitaker, a free black man. A student at the briefly integrated University of South Carolina (1874–1876), Whittaker gained a congressional appointment to the United States Military Academy at West Point in 1876. At first, he roomed with West Point's first black graduate, Henry O. Flipper. Following Flipper's graduation in 1877 and the later dismissal of another black cadet, Whittaker lived a solitary existence, ostracized by the white cadets because of his race. On April 6, 1880, at reveille he was found unconscious on the floor in his room, his legs secured to the rails of his bed, his arms tied in front of him, his ear lobes slashed, and his hair gouged. He told West Point authorities that three masked men had attacked him during the night. A court of inquiry found him guilty of self-mutilation to avoid an examination two months in the future. To exonerate himself, Whittaker demanded a court-martial, which in 1881 found him guilty again. The following year, however, the army's judge advocate general threw out the decision on procedural and factual grounds. But Secretary of the Army Robert T. Lincoln (the son of Abraham Lincoln) expelled Whittaker from the academy anyway, based, he said, on Whittaker's failure in an 1880 examination. The case was a national sensation, headlined in all the major journals of the day.

After a brief national tour, Whittaker became a teacher at Charleston's Avery Institute. In 1885 he was admitted to the South Carolina Bar and practiced briefly in Sumter. He married Page Harrison in 1890, and they had two sons, one of whom, Miller F. Whittaker, became president of Orangeburg's Colored Normal, Industrial, Agricultural and Mechanical College of South Carolina (which became South Carolina State University). During the 1890s Whittaker was principal of the first black school in Sumter, and from 1900 to 1908 he was principal of the academy at the Orangeburg black college. From 1908 to 1925 he served as teacher and principal at Douglass High School in Oklahoma City, where one of his students was the black novelist Ralph Ellison. Whittaker returned to Orangeburg in 1925 as teacher and administrator. He died there on January 14, 1931, and was buried in the local black cemetery. In 1995, in a White House ceremony, President Bill Clinton awarded Whittaker a posthumous U.S. Army commission. JOHN F. MARSZALEK

Marszalek, John F. "A Black Cadet at West Point." *American Heritage* 22 (August 1971): 30–37, 104–6.

———. *Assault at West Point: The Court-Martial of Johnson Whittaker.* New York: Collier, 1994.

Whittaker, Miller Fulton (1892–1949). Architect, college president. Whittaker was born on December 30, 1892, in Sumter, the son of Johnson Chesnut Whittaker and Page Harrison Whittaker. He attended school in Sumter and at the academy of the Colored Normal, Industrial, Agriclutural, and Mechanical College of South Carolina in Orangeburg, where his father had joined the faculty in 1900. In 1908 the family moved to Oklahoma City, where Whittaker graduated from Douglass High School in 1909. He earned a bachelor's degree in architecture from Kansas State College in 1913.

That year Whittaker joined the faculty of Colored Normal, Industrial, Agriclutural, and Mechanical College (which later became South Carolina State University) and taught mechanical drawing and physics. During World War I, Whittaker served as a second lieutenant with the 371st and 368th infantry regiments of the all-black 92d Division. In 1925 he became dean of the mechanical arts program at the college, but he devoted much time to architecture. He designed several campus buildings and supervised student labor in their construction. He was the architect for Hodge Hall, a facility for the science and agricultural programs. In 1928 Kansas State College awarded Whittaker a professional degree in architecture after he submitted as his thesis the drawings of Hodge Hall.

Whittaker was named the third president of South Carolina State College in 1932 following the death of Robert Shaw Wilkinson. He guided the college through the grim days of the Depression. Faculty salaries were slashed by one-third, and for a time there were doubts that the state could meet the college payroll. Enrollment declined to less than one thousand, and the high school program was terminated. With the assistance of New Deal programs, the financial support of the Rockefeller-sponsored General Education Board, and a 1937 state bond issue, two academic buildings and a dormitory were erected. Following World War II, enrollments surged and more than fourteen hundred students were admitted, including five hundred veterans. Another five hundred were rejected because of lack of space.

With the onset of the civil rights movement, Whittaker found himself caught between state officials defending segregation and a black community increasingly insistent on dismantling Jim Crowism. John Wrighten, an Army Air Force veteran and a graduate of South Carolina State, applied for admission to the University of South Carolina Law School and was rejected because of his race.

Alternatively state leaders prepared to establish a separate law school at South Carolina State. However, with the assistance of Thurgood Marshall and the NAACP, Wrighten sued the university. Whittaker was called to testify in federal court in 1947. Marshall bluntly asked Whittaker if the proposed law school in Orangeburg would be equal to that of the university. Whittaker replied, "I don't think so." Whittaker had already complained, "They are putting me in the middle between the plaintiff and the defendants in this law school business." Wrighten lost the suit, and Whittaker supervised the creation of the new black law school.

Whittaker died of heart failure on November 14, 1949. He had not married. He had continued his work as an architect in the 1930s and 1940s. His last project, designed in collaboration with John H. Blanche, was the Orangeburg Lutheran Church, which was completed in 1950. WILLIAM C. HINE

Hine, William C. "South Carolina State College: A Legacy of Education and Public service." *Agricultural History* 65 (spring 1991): 149–67.

Marszalek, John F. *Assault at West Point: The Court-Martial of Johnson Whittaker.* New York: Collier, 1994.

Potts, John F. *The History of South Carolina State College, 1896–1978.* Orangeburg: South Carolina State College, 1978.

Whitten, Benjamin Otis (1886–1970). Physician. Whitten was born on August 12, 1886, in Pendleton, one of six children born to Edward Whitten and Martha Douthis. As a teenager, he left home to work as a railroad telegrapher. Despite his parents' objections, Whitten decided to study medicine and enrolled in the Atlanta College of Physicians and Surgeons (later part of Emory University), paying his own way. He graduated with honors in 1913 and returned to South Carolina. In October 1913 he married Myra Ballenger. They had two daughters. After a short stint as a general practitioner in the small town of Cross Hill, Whitten worked as a company physician in the mill town of Newry. In 1916 he joined the staff of the South Carolina State Hospital for the Insane in Columbia.

Whitten joined the hospital staff at an opportune time, as the facility was undergoing an important transformation. As part of Governor Richard Manning's reform program, the facility was modernized and its new superintendent, Dr. C. Frederick Williams of Columbia, instituted many new treatment regimens. Part of Manning's reform package consisted of separating those individuals categorized as "feeble-minded" from those labeled as "insane." In 1918 the General Assembly, with Manning's prodding, established a separate facility designed to house South Carolina residents labeled as "feeble-minded" or "mentally defective." Setting aside land in the town of Clinton, the assembly appointed Whitten the first superintendent of the South Carolina State Training School for the Feeble-Minded. The institution admitted its first residents in September 1920.

Whitten fought a continuous battle with a frugal legislature, which consistently underfunded his facility. He developed a national reputation as a skilled institutional administrator, adept at running a large facility, instituting training programs for residents, and advocating his facility throughout the state. In the 1920s Whitten established "colonies" within the Training School. These were small, self-contained facilities away from the institution's main buildings and were designed to house higher functioning residents and teach them self-sufficiency and independent living skills. By 1931 the Training School housed more than five hundred white residents (state law prohibited the admission of blacks), with close to one hundred in colony settings. In that same year, the state of Utah hired Whitten to establish a similar training school. Whitten spent the better part of 1931 and 1932 in Utah before returning to Clinton and his position at the Training School. He entertained offers from other states but never again left Clinton.

In 1937 Whitten achieved the pinnacle of his profession when he was elected president of the American Association on Mental Deficiency. By the 1940s and 1950s Whitten oversaw an institution that rapidly grew in size and numbers. With increased state and federal funding, Whitten Village (as it was called by then; in 1972 it became Whitten Center) reached a resident population of 2,500 by 1965. He retired that same year. Whitten received many awards for his dedicated service, including an award from the Joseph P. Kennedy Foundation and an honorary doctorate from Presbyterian College in Clinton in 1965. He died in Clinton on November 5, 1970, and was buried in the cemetery of the First Presbyterian Church. STEVEN NOLL

McCandless, Peter. *Moonlight, Magnolias, and Madness: Insanity in South Carolina from the Colonial Period to the Progressive Era.* Chapel Hill: University of North Carolina Press, 1996.

Noll, Steven. *Feeble-Minded in Our Midst: Institutions for the Mentally Retarded in the South, 1900–1940.* Chapel Hill: University of North Carolina Press, 1995.

Sloan, William, and Harvey Stevens. *A Century of Concern: A History of the American Association on Mental Deficiency, 1876–1976.* Washington, D.C.: American Association on Mental Deficiency, 1976.

Whitten, Benjamin O. *A History of Whitten Village.* Clinton, S.C.: Jacobs, 1967.

Whitten Center. Whitten Center was South Carolina's first and largest institution housing persons labeled as mentally handicapped or developmentally disabled. Located in Clinton, the facility was chartered in 1918 and admitted its first patients in September 1920. Initially called the South Carolina State Training School for the Feeble-Minded, the facility was designed to protect South Carolina's citizens from the "menace of the feeble-minded."

The Training School's first superintendent was Benjamin Whitten, a medical doctor who had been the assistant superintendent of the South Carolina State Hospital for the Insane in Columbia. Whitten remained as superintendent of the Training School for forty-seven years, retiring in 1965. At its opening, the institution housed approximately fifty male and female patients, mostly in their teens and early twenties. The facility did not admit black residents until 1965. Chronically underfunded and understaffed throughout Whitten's tenure, the institution nevertheless managed to serve an increasing population of individuals with a range of problems.

The facility was renamed Whitten Village in 1952 and became Whitten Center in 1972. By the 1950s, with improved funding on the state level and the influx of federal funds, Whitten's facilities and population increased dramatically. In 1965 Whitten Village served more than 2,500 residents. However, as society moved to a different understanding of mental retardation, the number of patients began to decline. With federal funding going toward public school special education and parents increasingly caring for their children at home, Whitten Center's population continues to both decline and age. As of January 2002 Whitten Center, under the auspices of the South Carolina Department of Disabilities and Special Needs, housed 372 residents. STEVEN NOLL

Noll, Steven. *Feeble-Minded in Our Midst: Institutions for the Mentally Retarded in the South, 1900–1940.* Chapel Hill: University of North Carolina Press, 1995.

Whitten, Benjamin O. *A History of Whitten Village.* Clinton, S.C.: Jacobs, 1967.

Wigfall, Louis Trezevant (1816–1874). U.S. senator. Lewis Trezevant Wigfall was born in Edgefield District on April 21, 1816, the son of Levi Durand Wigfall and Eliza Thompson. Orphaned by age thirteen, he attended local academies and the University of Virginia before finishing his education at South Carolina College. Rebellious, Wigfall often skipped classes, but he excelled in the debates of the college's Euphradian Society, absorbing the school's ardent nullification and states' rights philosophy. He briefly left school in 1836 to volunteer for the Seminole War, attaining the rank of lieutenant.

Graduating in 1837, Wigfall studied law in Edgefield, passing the bar in 1839. Financially irresponsible, he squandered his moderate inheritance on gambling, liquor, and prostitutes. Politics soon drew his interest and gave him an arena for his oratorical skills. He briefly gained control of the *Edgefield Advertiser* newspaper and, despite his own nullification leanings, used it to support the Unionist John P. Richardson for governor in 1840. Wigfall's strident attacks and personal differences with his opponents led to numerous disputes, including a duel that left Wigfall and Preston Brooks severely injured. Marriage to Charlotte Cross in November 1841 brought some stability to his life and eventually produced five children.

A proponent of the expansion of slavery and opponent of tariffs, Wigfall viewed secession as a means of settling sectional differences. His early extremism kept him from attaining political office. Financial difficulties continued to plague Wigfall, and in 1846 he lost his home and property at a sheriff's auction. That same year Wigfall's eldest son died and the family moved to Texas to start over, including altering the spelling of his first name to Louis.

Settling in Marshall, Wigfall served in the Texas House from 1849 to 1850 and the Texas Senate from 1857 to 1859. His vigorous opposition to the Unionist politics then prevalent in Texas burnished his reputation as a fire-eater. Reaction to the John Brown raid propelled Wigfall into the U.S. Senate in 1859, where he actively fought proposals to ease the political crisis.

Despite the secession of Texas in February 1861, Wigfall remained in Washington, gathering information and opening a Confederate recruiting station in Baltimore. He traveled to Charleston in April, where he recklessly visited Fort Sumter during the bombardment in an unauthorized attempt to negotiate its surrender. He represented Texas in the Confederate Provisional Senate, served as a military aide to Confederate president Jefferson Davis, and accepted a commission as brigadier general in December 1861. He resigned in 1862, prior to taking his seat in the Confederate Senate, where he proposed the first conscription law in American history. He clashed with President Davis over military policy and became a leading opponent of the administration, which mitigated his influence for the rest of the war.

Following Appomattox, he fled to Texas and then to London, where he lived in exile until 1872. He lived briefly in Baltimore before returning to Texas in 1874 with plans to reopen his law practice. He died in Galveston, Texas, on February 18, 1874, and was buried in that city's Episcopal Cemetery. PATRICK MCCAWLEY

King, Alvy L. *Louis T. Wigfall: Southern Fire-Eater.* Baton Rouge: Louisiana State University Press, 1970.

Lord, C. W. "Young Louis Wigfall: South Carolina Politician and Duelist." *South Carolina Historical Magazine* 59 (April 1958): 96–112.

Walther, Eric H. *The Fire-Eaters.* Baton Rouge: Louisiana State University Press, 1992.

Wigg, James (ca. 1850–?). Legislator. Wigg was born a slave in Beaufort County around 1850. As a young boy during the Union occupation of the Sea Islands, he earned money waiting on the U.S. Army officers stationed on Hilton Head Island. He was evidently a clever youngster and gained the favor of the abolitionist General David Hunter. After the war, Hunter took Wigg to Washington and enrolled him in the Whalen Institute. Wigg proved to be an apt student of theology and was described as "an earnest follower of Swedenborg," the eighteenth-century Swedish scientist and mystic.

Wigg returned to Beaufort County after his formal education. He became a large landowner and prosperous cotton farmer on St. Helena Island during the 1880s. In 1888 he was elected school commissioner for Beaufort County on the "People's Ticket," a fusionist political movement comprised of moderate black Republicans and moderate white Democrats. Wigg was elected to the South Carolina House of Representatives from Beaufort County for the Fifty-ninth General Assembly, serving one term from 1890 to 1891. During the election of 1892, Wigg fell out with the "People's Ticket" and ran as a Republican for Beaufort County sheriff against a black fusionist candidate, George A. Reed. He lost to Reed by 107 votes. During the 1892 election campaign, Wigg was described as a "very uninfluential yellow man" by the Beaufort newspaper, the *Palmetto Post,* a Democratic organ and fusionist mouthpiece.

When the Tillman wing of the South Carolina Democratic Party called for a constitutional convention in 1895 to disfranchise African Americans, Wigg was selected as a delegate from Beaufort County. During the convention Wigg, along with Robert Smalls, William J. Whipper, Thomas E. Miller, and Isaiah R. Reed, maintained a heroic but futile rearguard action against the dominant Democratic majority. Wigg, described as "an adroit needler of white delegates," made his most telling points at the convention by challenging the Democrats to impose a true property test and true literacy test for voting in South Carolina. He claimed that such tests would produce only a small majority of white votes in South Carolina. Such tests honestly applied would have retained an overwhelming black majority in Beaufort County. Wigg's amendments were rejected by the convention. In the end, the Beaufort delegates refused to sign the South Carolina Constitution of 1895.

Political opportunity for Beaufort's black leadership gradually disappeared after 1895, and the Sea Island cotton economy declined as well. Wigg disappeared from the public record, and his date of death is not known. LAWRENCE S. ROWLAND

Miller, Edward A. *Gullah Statesman: Robert Smalls from Slavery to Congress, 1839–1915.* Columbia: University of South Carolina Press, 1995.

South Carolina. Constitutional Convention, 1895. *Journal of the Constitutional Convention of the State of South Carolina.* Columbia, S.C.: C. A. Calvo, 1895.

Tindall, George Brown. *South Carolina Negroes, 1877–1900.* 1952. Reprint, Columbia: University of South Carolina Press, 2003.

Wild turkey. A wild turkey (*Meleagris gallapavo*) is a large galliform (chickenlike) bird. Males weigh up to twenty pounds, and females weigh about half as much. The turkey is characterized by its large size, iridescent plumage, and large fan-shaped tail. The head and neck are blue-gray with pink wattles and caruncles. Males and occasionally females have beards, which are brushlike clusters of keratinous fibers that hang from midbreast. Turkeys are adept at running. During the day turkeys spend most of their time on the ground, obtaining fruits, seeds, and tubers, especially acorns, chufa (sedge), black gum, and sabal palmetto and hickory nuts. They are also strong fliers and attain speeds approaching sixty miles per hour. At night they roost in the tops of tall trees, usually in swamps.

In springtime high-ranking males guard harems of females. These males accomplish most of the breeding. Nesting in South Carolina occurs from late March to late May. Turkeys nest on the ground and lay ten to twelve eggs each. The incubation period averages twenty-eight days. The young (poults) leave the nest soon after hatching and are able to fly in ten days. The average life span of a wild turkey is about two years, but one bird is known to have survived for thirteen years. Wild turkeys are hunted in the spring, when males can be lured by imitations of their mating call (gobble).

Before European settlement, wild turkeys were relatively abundant in eastern North America and were a common food of Indians. During the nineteenth century the eastern population was greatly reduced by habitat destruction and by hunting. In South Carolina the species survived mainly in coastal areas on large plantations, where they were protected and managed as game. The wild turkey population in the eastern United States fell to about thirty thousand by the early 1900s. Subsequently, the species made a dramatic recovery due the enactment of hunting laws and to programs that transplanted wild-caught birds to proper habitats. The eastern populations had increased to about 1.3 million by 1980 and topped 6.4 million as of 2004. Turkeys now are found throughout South Carolina in suitable habitats such as heavy woods. They have even colonized wooded areas in the suburbs, where they have become relatively tame. The National Wild Turkey Federation, which sponsors significant educational and conservation programs, is located in Edgefield. WILLIAM POST

Hewitt, Oliver H. *The Wild Turkey and Its Management.* Washington, D.C.: Wildlife Society, 1967.

Latham, Roger. *The Complete Book of the Wild Turkey.* Harrisburg, Pa.: Stackpole, 1956.

Williams, Lovett E. *The Book of the Wild Turkey.* Tulsa, Okla.: Winchester, 1981.

Wilkes Fund Controversy. The 1770s Wilkes Fund Controversy forced South Carolina to recognize that its own view of the imperial constitution and the British Parliament's view were fundamentally at odds. The British radical John Wilkes, celebrated in the 1760s for his opposition to prerogative government, became a popular hero for Americans resisting parliamentary taxes with cries of "Wilkes and Liberty!" In the October 1768 legislative elections, Charleston's mechanics, the Sons of Liberty, made some official show of support for Wilkes a campaign issue. Carolina's elite leadership, although anxious to show bold support for American rights, was skeptical of Wilkes's brand of radical constitutional reform. The compromise, a December 8, 1769, resolution to vote £1,500 toward Wilkes's debts, passed hastily through the Commons House, the last motion of the last day before Christmas adjournment. The moderate Whig Henry Laurens, who was absent, opposed it, while House Speaker Peter Manigault, who was present, later regretted it.

Their bold gesture had unintended consequences. Through long practice, the Commons House had gained financial control by issuing money from the public treasury without the consent of the governor or his council, repaying it from the next year's tax bill. The practice implicitly denied the power to frame money bills to any chamber but the elected one. This unusual constitutional tradition was unknown in London until the passage of the Wilkes Fund resolution. Whitehall responded on April 14, 1770, with a "Special Instruction" forbidding the treasury to issue any money, including the £1,500 Wilkes donation, without the governor's signature. The House, regarding the instruction as an attack on its customary rights, refused to comply. Legislative government effectively came to a halt. No annual tax bill was passed in South Carolina after 1769, and no legislation at all after 1771. The Wilkes Fund "gesture" generated a constitutional crisis that first polarized and then broke the back of royal government in South Carolina. REBECCA STARR

Greene, Jack P. "Bridge to Revolution: The Wilkes Fund Controversy in South Carolina, 1769–1775." *Journal of Southern History* 29 (February 1963): 19–52.

———, ed. *The Nature of Colony Constitutions: Two Pamphlets on the Wilkes Fund Controversy in South Carolina.* Columbia: University of South Carolina Press, 1970.

Wilkinson, Eliza Yonge (1757–?). Chronicler, letter writer. Born on February 7, 1757, on Yonge's Island, St. Paul's Parish, Eliza Wilkerson was the third child of Francis Yonge, Sr., and his first wife, Sarah Clifford. While still in her teens, ca. 1774, she married Joseph Wilkinson, a descendent of another prominent planter family in the region. He died within the year. Their son, born in 1775, died soon after birth. Widowed and without resources, Eliza returned to Yonge's Island, where her father put her in charge of one of his plantations, ensuring her independence and wealth.

Wilkinson is remembered principally for her letters, twelve of which were edited from her original letter book and published by Caroline Gilman in 1839. The letters cover a two-year period from the spring of 1779 until sometime following the surrender of Lord Cornwallis in October 1781. Arranged, edited, and perhaps enhanced by Gilman, the letters form a continuous narrative, "a most living picture," leaving the reader with the impression of having been an eyewitness to events taking place.

Of the twelve published letters, letters I and II describe events leading up to the British invasion of the lowcountry, a time of nervous anticipation and waiting. Letters III–VII deal with direct experiences with the enemy in wartime: the confrontations and threats as homes are invaded and pillaged, and forced flights to safety made in the dead of night. Letters VIII–XII describe daily life as experienced against the backdrop of enemy occupation, and the surreal reality of an uneasy truce in the middle of wartime.

Wilkinson's letters are addressed to a "Miss M—P" or "my dear Mary." This is likely Mary Porcher, the daughter of a Huguenot family in a neighboring parish and half sister to Wilkinson's second husband-to-be, Peter Porcher, whom she married after the war on January 4, 1786. The letters reveal a young woman who is self-assured, somewhat feisty, obviously charming and attractive, and possessed of a ready wit and engaging personality. She is high-spirited and on the way to becoming an ardent rebel. In fact, her writings are historically significant not only because of the day-to-day descriptions they provide but also because they show how subjects loyal to the British crown could turn into American patriots.

Wilkinson's letters are also memorable for their emotional impact and dramatic flair. She displayed a good ear for re-creating conversations and capturing dialogues, weaving them into suspenseful scenes of action. She seemed to realize that she was potentially writing for a wider audience and frequently injected her own viewpoints and asides into the narrative. Wilkinson chafed at the restrictions her society placed on women by not allowing them to speak out on political and public issues. The letters became her soapbox, and she took good-humored advantage of the opportunity to expound on social issues near and dear to her young heart.

No further writings by Wilkinson survive. Following her marriage to Porcher, she moved to his plantation at Black Swamp near the Savannah River. Together they had four children, and perhaps her attention was redirected to more pressing family matters. The actual date of her death is undocumented but is thought to be between 1812 and 1820. ELLEN CHAMBERLAIN

Arnold, Edwin T. "Women Diarists and Letter Writers of 18th Century South Carolina." In *South Carolina Women Writers: Proceedings of the Reynolds Conference, University of South Carolina, October 24–25, 1975,* edited by James B. Meriwether. Spartanburg, S.C.: Reprint Company, 1979.

Letters of Eliza Wilkinson, during the Invasion and Possession of Charlestown, S.C., by the British in the Revolutionary War, arranged by Caroline Gilman. New York: S. Colman, 1839.

Wilkinson, C. P. Seabrook. "Eliza Yonge Wilkinson." In *Dictionary of Literary Biography.* Vol. 200, *American Women Prose Writers to 1820,* edited by Carla Mulford, Angela Vietto, and Amy E. Winans. Detroit: Gale, 1999.

Wilkinson, Marion Birnie (1870–1956). Social reformer, black women's club leader. Wilkinson was born in Charleston on June 23, 1870, to Richard Birnie and Anna Frost. Both of her parents were descendants of antebellum free black families and members of Charleston's black elite. Her father and her uncle Charles Birnie were wealthy cotton shipping agents. She attended the Avery Normal Institute, graduating with honors in 1888, then taught at the institute for nine years. On June 29, 1897, she married Robert Shaw Wilkinson, the second president of the South Carolina Colored Normal, Industrial, Agriclutural, and Mechanical College.

Marion Birnie Wilkinson. Courtesy, South Carolina State University Historical Collection

From an early age Wilkinson was interested in social reform efforts in South Carolina and encouraged educated, middle-class African American women to share their knowledge and material resources with those less fortunate. While at South Carolina State, she served as chief Young Women's Christian Association (YWCA) adviser and headed the boarding department. By 1928 her leadership had resulted in the construction of the only YWCA building on a historically African American college campus. Wilkinson also served on the South Carolina Interracial Commission, the county executive committee of the Red Cross, and the board of trustees of Voorhees Institute in Denmark. To further facilitate her reform efforts, she was a charter member and president of the South Carolina Federation of Colored Women's Clubs (SCFCWC). Organized in 1909, the SCFCWC became a vehicle by which black women could use their knowledge and skills to improve social and racial conditions. She was also a trustee of the Marion Birnie Wilkinson Home for Girls in Cayce, created to house destitute young black women. Wilkinson founded the Sunlight Club in Orangeburg in addition to organizing the first Rosenwald School in South Carolina to help improve educational facilities for African Americans.

Wilkinson's influence carried beyond the borders of South Carolina. During World War I, she and other black club women organized recreation centers for black soldiers. During the 1930s she advised the Hoover administration on child welfare programs and helped establish a Works Progress Administration training school and nursery. Wilkinson was also the third president of the National Association of Colored Women's Clubs, which was founded in 1896 and spearheaded the national black women's club movement. Known by the students at South Carolina State as "Mother Wilkinson," she encapsulated the efforts of educated, middle-class black women for social and racial reform. Wilkinson died in Orangeburg on September 19, 1956. CHERISSE R. JONES

Gordon, Asa H. *Sketches of Negro Life and History in South Carolina.* 2d ed. Columbia: University of South Carolina Press, 1971.

Johnson, Joan M. "'This Wonderful Dream Nation!': Black and White South Carolina Women and the Creation of the New South, 1898–1930." Ph.D. diss., University of California, Los Angeles, 1997.

Jones, Cherisse Renee. "'Loyal Women of Palmetto': Black Women's Clubs in Charleston, South Carolina, 1916–1965." Master's thesis, University of Charleston and The Citadel, 1997.

Wilkinson, Robert Shaw (1865–1932). College president. Wilkinson was born on February 18, 1865, in Charleston, the son of Charles Henry Wilkinson and Lavinia Smith Wilkinson. He attended Shaw Memorial School and Avery Institute in Charleston. He received an appointment to the U.S. Military Academy but was unable to meet the physical requirements and did not attend. In 1884 he entered the preparatory program at Oberlin College and subsequently earned a bachelor's degree in 1891.

Wilkinson joined the faculty of the State University of Kentucky at Louisville in 1891 and taught Latin, Greek, and political science at the black institution. When the South Carolina Colored Normal, Industrial, Agriclutural, and Mechanical College (later South Carolina State University) was established in 1896 in Orangeburg, Wilkinson became one of its first faculty members. He was a professor of physics and chemistry until 1911. In 1898 he was granted a Ph.D. from the State University in Louisville.

After Governor Coleman Blease forced Thomas E. Miller to resign in 1911, Wilkinson was named the second president of South Carolina State. During the two decades that he led the institution, the college made the transition from essentially a primary and secondary school to a genuine college. Enrollment in the college program increased from 23 in 1917 to 224 in 1926. The basic mission of the black land-grant college in its early decades was to prepare students to teach agriculture, trades, and domestic sciences in South Carolina's black public schools. In the 1920s Wilkinson was instrumental in gaining philanthropic support from the Julius Rosenwald Foundation and Rockefeller-sponsored General Education Board that provided funds for the construction of a teacher-training school and Hodge Hall, a facility to house the science and agricultural programs.

Following the passage of the Smith-Lever Agricultural Extension Act in 1914, Wilkinson helped create and supervise a cooperative extension program for the state's black farm families. The program was administered by the state's white land-grant institution Clemson College, but Wilkinson hired, fired, and directed the black agents. By 1929 there were twenty black agents—twelve men and eight women—imparting information on crop management, livestock production, the canning of fruits and vegetables, and health and hygiene to rural and often impoverished black people. Though

Wilkinson did not challenge the racial status quo, when black farmers complained in the early 1930s that they were unable to secure applications for federal loans, Wilkinson promptly contacted Clemson officials to ask "that Negroes are given a fair consideration in this respect."

Wilkinson served on several community organizations and was on the boards of Voorhees Industrial College in Denmark and Victory Savings Bank in Columbia. He was an active Episcopalian. Wilkinson married Marion Raven Birnie on June 29, 1897, and they were the parents of two sons and two daughters. He died of pneumonia on March 13, 1932. WILLIAM C. HINE

Hine, William C. "South Carolina State College: A Legacy of Education and Public service." *Agricultural History* 65 (spring 1991): 149–67.

Potts, John F. *A History of South Carolina State College, 1896–1978.* Orangeburg: South Carolina State College, 1978.

Williams, David Rogerson (1776–1830). Congressman, governor. Williams was born in Cheraw (later Darlington) District on March 8, 1776, the son of David Williams, a planter, and Anne Rogerson. Williams traveled north for most of his education, attending school at Wrentham, Massachusetts, before enrolling at Rhode Island College in 1792. Three years later Williams returned to South Carolina to redeem his inheritance, which was encumbered with debt. Between 1796 and 1800 he still spent much of his time in Rhode Island, where he studied law and was admitted to the bar. On August 14, 1796, Williams married Sarah Power of Providence. The couple had two children. Following Sarah's death in 1803, Williams married Elizabeth Witherspoon in November 1809. They had no children.

At the start of 1801, Williams formed partnerships with John McIver and then Peter Freneau to publish two Charleston newspapers, the *City Gazette* and the *Weekly Carolina Gazette.* In 1804 Williams returned to his plantations near Society Hill, Darlington District, and thereafter made planting his chief occupation. Williams was a progressive farmer and was perhaps the first to introduce mules into South Carolina. He also engaged in other business ventures. About 1812 he built one of the first cotton mills in the state and operated its machinery with slave labor. He later experimented with other manufacturing activities and was actively involved in the state militia, internal improvements, and literary and educational activities.

Williams entered public service in 1805, when he was elected to the U.S. House of Representatives, serving from 1805 to 1809 and 1811 to 1813. A Democratic-Republican, Williams supported President Thomas Jefferson's Embargo Act of 1807 and later joined three prominent South Carolina "War Hawks" (John C. Calhoun, Langdon Cheves, and William Lowndes) in calling for war with Great Britain. In his final term in the House, Williams served as chairman of the Military Affairs Committee.

In 1813, with the War of 1812 under way, President James Madison commissioned Williams a brigadier general, and Williams briefly saw service on the Canadian frontier. He resigned his commission in December 1813 and returned to South Carolina, where he was elected governor on December 10, 1814. His was a vigorous administration. The recent war made Williams a vocal advocate of military preparedness, and he pushed hard for state and federal funds to strengthen South Carolina's militia and coastal defenses. Williams's tenure also saw the settlement of the state's boundary dispute with North Carolina and the acquisition of the Cherokee strip in northwestern South Carolina.

After his term ended on December 5, 1816, Williams retired to his home plantation, Centre Hall, near Society Hill. Except for a brief stint as Darlington District's representative in the state Senate (1824–1828), he refused public office. However, he remained politically active. Although he opposed the tariff of 1828, Williams rejected nullification as a danger to the Union. He instead advocated that South Carolina develop its own manufacturing and reduce its reliance on northern-made goods. He probably would have been a Unionist leader but for his untimely death on November 17, 1830. While building a bridge on Lynches Creek, he was struck by a falling timber and died the following day. ERNEST MCPHERSON LANDER, JR.

Bailey, N. Louise, Mary L. Morgan, and Carolyn R. Taylor, eds. *Biographical Directory of the South Carolina Senate, 1776–1985.* 3 vols. Columbia: University of South Carolina Press, 1986.

Cook, Harvey Toliver. *The Life and Legacy of David Rogerson Williams.* New York, 1916.

Lander, Ernest McPherson, Jr. *The Textile Industry in Antebellum South Carolina.* Baton Rouge: Louisiana State University Press, 1969.

Williams, Hannah English (?–1722). Naturalist. Not much has been recorded about Hannah English Williams's early life. Her birth date, birthplace, and parents' names are unknown. She lived in Charleston. Williams was the first female in the American British colonies to gather plant and animal specimens for scientific collections. Her work aided the cataloging of many of South Carolina's natural resources and contributed to advancing botanical and zoological awareness and understanding in that colony and in England, where people were intrigued by the unfamiliar organisms indigenous to the New World.

Using vessels under the command of the South Carolina shipmaster Major William Halstead, Williams shipped specimens to James Petiver of the Royal Society in London. Williams and Petiver corresponded from 1701 to 1713, and he listed those items he wished her to procure when she joined his network of collectors. Petiver encouraged her interest in natural history, declaring Williams the "discoverer" of unique butterflies and describing her as "my generous benefactress." He instructed Williams how to preserve specimens for shipping, with "each stuck on a pin or in a little viall drowned in Rum or Brandy." Petiver described Williams's contributions in his published serial booklets entitled *Musei Petiveriani Centuria Prima Rariora Naturae.*

A February 6, 1704, letter from Williams to Petiver accompanied a shipment of "Some of Our Vipers and Severall Sorts of Snakes Scorpions and Lizzards" in addition to shells, a bee nest, and a "few Other Insex." She promised to send "some Mockin birds and Red birds" in the spring because, "If I should send you any Now the Could would Kill them." She also enclosed a "Westo Kings Tobacco pipe and a Queens Petticoat made off Moss" and asked for newspapers and "medisons." Williams's son met Petiver in England to discuss collections his mother had been gathering until she heard false reports of Petiver's death.

Petiver expressed his respect for Williams by naming some butterfly species for her. In 1767 Petiver's *Gazophylacium Naturae et Artis* included illustrations of Williams's orange girdled Carolina butterfly (also called the viceroy, which mimics monarch butterflies), Williams's yellow tipt Carolina butterfly (popularly called dog's head), and Williams's selvedge-eyed Carolina butterfly (known as creole pearly eye).

Sources do not specify when Williams settled in South Carolina. With her first husband, believed to have been named Mathew

English, she gave birth to two children. When her first husband died, as "Hannah English, Widow" she was warranted five hundred acres located in the proximity of Stony Point in November 1692. She then married a neighboring planter, William Williams. Three years later, as "Mrs. Hannah English alias Williams" she doubled her land holdings when she acquired an additional five hundred acres north of the Ashley River at Stony Point. Williams collected plants, shells, insects, birds, and reptiles on her property.

Williams asked Petiver for medical advice and pharmaceuticals because "I am Very much Troubled with the splene." Records indicate that Williams was buried on December 16, 1722, in St. Philip's Churchyard, Charleston. ELIZABETH D. SCHAFER

"An Account of Animals and Shells Sent from Carolina to Mr. James Petiver, F.R.S." *Philosophical Transactions* [of the Royal Society of London] 24 (1704–1705): 1952–60.

Smith, Beatrice Scheer. "Hannah English Williams: America's First Woman Natural History Collector." *South Carolina Historical Magazine* 87 (April 1986): 83–92.

Stearns, Raymond P. "James Petiver, Promoter of Natural Science, c. 1663–1718." *Proceedings of the American Antiquarian Society,* n.s., 62 (October 1952): 243–365.

———. *Science in the British Colonies of America.* Urbana: University of Illinois Press, 1970.

Williams Brice Stadium. Dominating Columbia's southern skyline is the largest of the University of South Carolina's athletics facilities, Williams Brice Stadium. From a distance the football stadium's shape, with its angled lighting supports extending over doubled tiered decks, has been likened to a trap ready to spring on unsuspecting prey.

Williams Brice Stadium, home of the Gamecocks of the University of South Carolina. Courtesy, USC Athletics Department

Williams Brice Stadium's grandeur belies the facility's modest beginnings in the 1930s. Prior to 1934, the Carolina football team typically played at Melton Field on campus. With a crowd capacity of only 7,000, this venue proved insufficient for special games such as "Big Thursday" between USC and Clemson College. For this annual showdown the teams would battle one another at the state's fairgrounds, which boasted seating for 15,000 at its old wooden bowl. Seeking improvement, alumni and city of Columbia officials began a movement to erect a new stadium. Their efforts came to fruition by October 1934 as Municipal Stadium with a capacity of 18,200 opened. In 1941 the city deeded the property to the university and the facility subsequently was renamed Carolina Stadium.

Following years of sporadic enlargement and improvement, Carolina Stadium became known thirty-one years later as Williams Brice Stadium in honor of Martha Williams Brice, whose bequest of $2.75 million enabled the structure to seat 72,440 fans, while featuring a VIP lounge, a president's box, a modern press box, and improved locker room, training, and medical facilities. Additions followed in 1995 and 1996 that included updated executive suites and press boxes, a football office complex, and increased seating that has allowed Williams Brice Stadium to hold as many as 85,000 spectators. JOHN M. SHERRER III

Edens, Ruth J. *It Took an Act of Congress: Martha Williams Brice Bequest for the Williams Brice Stadium.* N.p., 1995.

Griffin, John Chandler. *The First Hundred Years: A History of South Carolina Football.* Atlanta: Longstreet, 1992.

Williamsburg County (937 sq. miles; 2000 pop. 37,217). Williamsburg County, located in the outer coastal plain and in the southern tip of the Pee Dee area, dates from Governor Robert Johnson's Township Plan of the 1730s, which included the creation of Williamsburg Township on the Black River. Named for King William III of England, Williamsburg became part of Prince Frederick's Parish in 1734. It became a district in 1804 and a county in 1868. A small area of Williamsburg became part of Florence County in 1888.

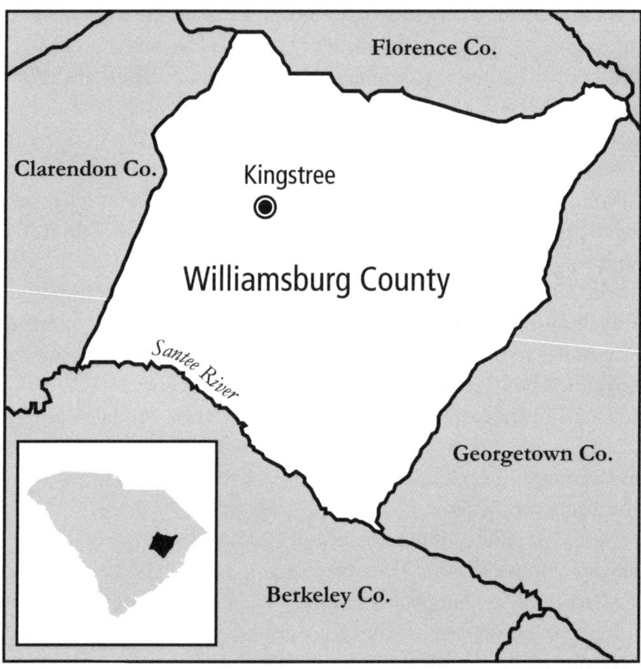

Native Americans, believed to be tribes of Mingoes, Wee Nees, and Wee Tees, had largely abandoned the area before the first whites arrived. A small number of settlers arrived in the area as early as 1710, forming a colony called Winyaw. But the focal point of settlement was Williamsburg Township, first settled by forty Scots-Irish in 1732. Scots-Irish and Huguenots dominated the early population, although English, Scots, Irish, Welsh, German, and Swedish settlers could be found as well.

The first house of worship was a brick meetinghouse erected for dissenters in 1726 at Black Mingo (later known as Willtown). The Williamsburg Presbyterian congregation, formed in 1736, secured land for the Williamsburg Meeting House two years later, and it remained the largest building in the township until the Revolutionary

War. A second Presbyterian congregation, the Indiantown Presbyterian Church, was organized in 1757.

People of the area, called "poor Protestants" by outsiders, raised livestock, flax, and cotton and exported deerskins, pork, and lard. Most produce was carried down the Black River to Georgetown, which served as the area's main center of trade. In the late 1740s indigo was introduced, which enriched many farmers and led to the widespread introduction of plantation slavery.

Williamsburg's white planters had become prosperous by the outbreak of the Revolutionary War. After Charleston fell in 1780, Williamsburg men made up the nucleus of General Francis Marion's brigade, and the "Swamp Fox" often headquartered at nearby Snow Island. Williamsburg skirmishes included the battles of Kings Tree (August 27, 1780), Black Mingo (September 28–29, 1780), Mount Hope Swamp (March 1781), and Lower Bridge (March 1781).

In 1804 Williamsburg became a separate district with the seat at Kingstree. By then, Williamsburg District was prosperous again, raising cattle and growing cotton, tobacco, and other crops. White farmers depended heavily on slave labor. Most herdsmen and planters each owned a few slaves, although by 1790 eighty men in the county owned more than 20 slaves each. The largest slaveholder, Theodore Gourdin, had 150. By 1830 blacks outnumbered whites by a margin of three to one.

Willtown, now vanished, reached its zenith about 1800 when it got its own post office. Ten years later Kingstree had a post office, and in 1823 the noted South Carolina architect Robert Mills designed the district courthouse. A later boon was the building of the Northeastern Railway from Charleston northward through Williamsburg in 1856. The line allowed planters to ship their products more easily to Charleston, which soon replaced Georgetown as the district's trading seat. The railroad line benefited innkeepers and spawned the production of naval stores and lumber. R. C. Logan founded the first newspaper, the *Kingstree Star,* in 1856.

On December 16, 1860, a "Secession flag" was raised in Kingstree. A year later more men from Williamsburg were in the Confederate military than on the voter rolls. The county historian William Boddie claimed that half of Williamsburg's male population was "sacrificed to the god of war" during the conflict.

With defeat, white residents tried to adjust economically to the end of slavery and politically to rule by blacks and non-native white Republicans. Only one member of the ruling Republican Party was white and native-born in 1876. With the end of Reconstruction and demise of Republican rule, Democrats would elect every officeholder in the county until 1986.

The turpentine and naval stores business persisted during Reconstruction while cotton prices fell. Tobacco reemerged around 1900 as an important addition to the county's agricultural economy. At first, tobacco was marketed in Florence and Lake City, but by 1909 two local warehouses were operating on the site of the county fairgrounds. In 1918 the county produced eleven million pounds of tobacco, which sold at an average price of $33.20 per hundred pounds. As the economy expanded, the Bank of Kingstree opened in 1901. Other banks opened at Greeleyville, Lane, Cades, and Hemingway. After World War I, tobacco and cotton continued to provide cash to area farmers, but the Williamsburg economy would suffer greatly during the Great Depression of the 1930s. The downturn continued until World War II.

In the postwar decades, major changes occurred in Williamsburg's political, social, and economic landscape. Blacks regained voting rights in the 1960s and in 1971 elected the first black officeholder since Reconstruction, a county councilman. In response, white voters withdrew support for the Democratic Party, which had dominated the county since Reconstruction. The county backed Republican candidates in 1960, 1964, and 1972 but returned to the Democratic fold in later years as blacks flexed their newfound voting muscle. By the start of the twenty-first century, black officeholders had become commonplace. The changes were generally peaceful, but racial tensions periodically arose. The burning of the Mount Zion AME Church in 1995 prompted Governor David Beasley to create a statewide Commission on Race Relations.

Heavily agricultural, Williamsburg in 2001 had the state's second-highest amount of acreage in farmland, most of which was devoted to cotton (29,000 acres), soybeans (20,500 acres), and corn (12,600 acres). Beginning in the 1980s tobacco production began a steady decline, wilting under the combined pressure of the courts, growing health concerns, higher taxes, and direct marketing schemes. At the beginning of the twenty-first century, Williamsburg remained a "poor Protestant" rural county, somewhat as it began. Per capita income was only $12,794 in 1999, compared to $18,795 in the state as a whole. Twenty-eight percent of the population lived below the poverty level. The county's single institution of higher learning, Williamsburg Technical College, worked to fight the poverty cycle in the area.

Despite its problems, Williamsburg has retained a rustic charm and is known to many as a "Sportsman's Paradise," with plentiful wildlife and hunting preserves. Local celebrations such as Hemingway's annual Bar-B-Q Shag Day Festival and Greeleyville's Flag Day draw large crowds annually. ROBERT A. PIERCE

Boddie, William Willis. *History of Williamsburg.* 1923. Reprint, Spartanburg, S.C.: Reprint Company, 1980.

Williamsburg County Historical Society. *Williamsburg County, South Carolina: A Pictorial History.* Dallas, Tex.: Taylor Publishing, 1991.

Williamson, Andrew (ca. 1730–1786). Soldier. Williamson immigrated to Ninety Six District from his native Scotland. He was earning a living as a cattle driver by 1758 and was commissioned as a lieutenant in the South Carolina Provincial Regiment of Foot during the Cherokee War of 1760–1761. At the end of the war he was awarded the contract to supply provisions to backcountry garrisons. By 1767 he had acquired a large plantation, White Hall, on Hard Labor Creek (present-day Greenwood County) and lived there with his family.

An ardent patriot at the outbreak of the Revolutionary War, Williamson held the rank of major in the militia of Ninety Six District and represented the area in the First and Second Provincial Congresses. Williamson's arrest of the Tory leader Robert Cunningham provoked British sympathizers in the region, and on November 19, 1775, a large Loyalist force attacked his patriot force, who had thrown up a hastily constructed fort at Ninety Six. After several days of intermittent fighting, both sides agreed to a truce. Reinforced by patriot soldiers under Colonel Richard Richardson, Williamson continued to pursue and detain Loyalist leaders in the following weeks in what was to become the Snow Campaign.

At the behest of William Henry Drayton, Williamson was promoted to the rank of colonel in 1776 and charged with conducting a punitive expedition against British-allied Native Americans on the frontier. The campaign subdued the Cherokees, who signed a treaty at DeWitt's Corner on May 20, 1777, that ceded practically all of their lands in South Carolina. Williamson had been promoted to the rank of brigadier general by 1778 and commanded the South

Carolina militia in Major General Robert Howe's disastrous Florida expedition that summer. In September–October of the following year he participated in the unsuccessful siege of Savannah.

Williamson's actions in the days surrounding the capture of Charleston led many to conclude that he had "turned coat." He accepted British protection and retired to White Hall. Though pressed on two occasions to renounce his parole, Williamson feared for his family and accepted British protection in Charleston, where he did serve as a double agent for Continental forces. Because of this, Williamson was allowed to stay in South Carolina after the war. He died at his plantation in St. Paul's Parish, near Charleston, on March 21, 1786. SAMUEL K. FORE

Cann, Marvin L. "Prelude to War: The First Battle of Ninety-Six, November 19–21, 1775." *South Carolina Historical Magazine* 76 (October 1975): 197–214.

Johnson, Joseph. *Traditions and Reminiscences, Chiefly of the American Revolution in the South.* 1851. Reprint, Spartanburg, S.C.: Reprint Company, 1972.

Lumpkin, Henry. *From Savannah to Yorktown: The American Revolution in the South.* Columbia: University of South Carolina Press, 1981.

Williamson's Plantation, Battle of (July 12, 1780). After the British capture of Charleston in May 1780, many Whigs took protection and withdrew to their homes. The New Acquisition District in present-day York County was reputedly the only district in South Carolina where virtually no one took such protection from the British. In June partisan bands formed in the district and struck a Loyalist muster at Alexander's Old Fields and a garrison of Tories at Mobley's Meeting House. Lieutenant Colonel George Turnbull, commanding the British garrison at Rocky Mount, dispatched Captain Christian Huck with a detachment of the British Legion, the New York Volunteers, and some local militia in response to these incursions. Captain Huck responded vigorously by insulting the inhabitants and pillaging the countryside. On July 11, 1780, he captured two young rebels melting pewter dishes to make bullets in the home of Captain John McClure and sentenced them to be hanged at sunrise the next day. That evening the British force encamped at the abandoned plantation of James Williamson in the community now known as Brattonsville. The location of the royal encampment reached the patriot forces that same evening. A Whig force of 133 men under the command of Colonels William Bratton, William Hill, Edward Lacey, and Andrew Neel and Captain James McClure resolved to march on the British camp and attack at first light. Dividing their forces in two, the rebels encircled the enemy camp and attacked. Caught by surprise, Huck's force of about 120 troops offered little resistance. An American sharpshooter felled Captain Huck. Casualties were fairly high for the British troops. However, the Americans only suffered one killed. Popularly known as Huck's Defeat, the Battle of Williamson's Plantation was the first significant check on the British advance since their victory at Charleston. SAMUEL K. FORE

Edgar, Walter. *Partisans and Redcoats: The Southern Conflict That Turned the Tide of the American Revolution.* New York: Morrow, 2001.

Scoggins, Michael. "Huck's Defeat: The Battle of Williamson's Plantation." Serialized in *York County Genealogical & Historical Society Quarterly* 13–14 (September 2001–March 2003).

Thomas, Samuel N. *The Dye Is Cast: The Scots-Irish and Revolution in the Carolina Back Country.* Columbia, S.C.: Palmetto Conservation Foundation, 1997.

Williamston (Anderson County; 2000 pop. 3,791). Around 1842 West Allen Williams discovered the mineral spring on his property that gave rise to the town named for him. Stories of the spring's healing properties attracted people to try the waters. By 1845 an article in the *Anderson Gazette* on "Williams' Spring" reported visitors living in tents around the spring, with a boardinghouse almost completed by Mr. Williams and plans to construct cabins. Another catalyst for development came in 1849 when the Greenville and Columbia Railroad announced plans to run near the famous spring. The first post office for the new village was established in 1850 as "Mineral Spring" but was changed to Williamston on February 9, 1852. By 1851 the population was 275. The town's charter was granted on December 16, 1852.

By 1852 W. J. Cobb's Williamston Hotel was completed, the first of several catering to the visitors attracted by the spring. Williamston seemed well on its way to becoming a fashionable resort, but a fire in 1860 destroyed the hotels and leveled most of the business district. Difficult years during the Civil War and Reconstruction further slowed the town's development. One of the last skirmishes of the Civil War took place near Williamston on May 1, 1865, when cadets from the Arsenal Academy at Columbia had a brush with Stoneman's Raiders.

At the start of the twentieth century, Williamston businesses included a variety of shops as well as a lumber mill, a cottonseed oil and fertilizer company, the Bank of Williamston, and the Gossett Cotton Mill (originally the Williamston Print Cloth Mill). Ransom's Williamston Carbonating Company produced 2,400 bottles of spring-based celery cola and ginger ale daily. Development in the second half of the twentieth century included Duke Power's Lee Steam Plant, built near the town in 1951. The cotton mill changed ownership, becoming Textron-Southern in 1946 and one of the Mount Vernon Mills in 1957. In the early 1950s Textron built the Cushman Plant, which housed a variety of textile operations. Later, as part of the Milliken Company, Cushman became the largest employer in Williamston, supplying filament yarns to thirty Milliken locations and used in more than twenty-five businesses.

Between the World Wars, a city waterworks was built, roads and bridges were improved, and a new high school was constructed. In 1947 Battery D of the South Carolina National Guard began calling Williamston home. A variety of small businesses came to town during the last decade of the twentieth century. Dr. Dwight Smith came to Williamston in 1949 and established a sixteen-room clinic that expanded to become the Williamston Hospital, classified as a "general hospital" by the State Board of Health in 1958. Sold to the Anderson Hospital System in 1988, it became a substance-abuse treatment center in 1989. And although visitors could still take a sip from the historic spring, Williamston State Park became more famous as the annual decorated Christmas Park, attracting thousands of visitors each holiday season for the past fifty years. DONNA K. ROPER

Welborn, Gene. *A Town Springs Forth: The Story of Williamston, South Carolina.* Bountiful, Utah: Family History Publishers, 2000.

Willington Academy. The Willington Academy of Doctor Moses Waddel, a log-constructed classical school for boys, was perhaps the most prestigious preparatory school in antebellum South Carolina. Waddel, a Presbyterian minister, moved his academy from Vienna on the Georgia side of the Savannah River to Willington (near the modern town of McCormick) around 1804 at the urging of Huguenot settlers who desired rigorous Calvinist teaching.

The school was a collection of student-built study cabins arrayed on a dirt street with a log-constructed recitation hall that doubled as a chapel. Boys boarded with nearby planters or in small cabins near the school. Ambitious youths, from the red hills of the upcountry to the tidelands of the coast, flocked to Willington, so named because the Huguenot worshipers in the region were "willing to" merge their Calvinist worship with the local Scots-Irish Presbyterians at Waddel's urging.

Waddel's teaching of the classics, especially by the recitation method, attracted the attention of educators throughout the nation. Students learned to read ancient Greek and Latin and studied the great classical works. They also honed their oratorical skills, which were vital to politically ambitious members of society. Students were called to class by Waddel's hunting horn, and recitations were not complete until he was satisfied. With such thorough preparation, Willington graduates entered colleges such as Yale and Princeton as juniors. The academy's distinguished graduates included John C. Calhoun, Augustus B. Longstreet, Hugh Swinton Legaré, George McDuffie, and James Louis Petigru.

Waddel ran Willington from 1804 to 1819, when he left to become president of Franklin College (later the University of Georgia). With Waddel's departure, the school closed until 1830, when his sons James and John Waddel revived the institution and recaptured much of its earlier prestige. With the arrival of the Civil War, Willington Academy closed in 1861. THOMAS B. HORTON

Horton, Thomas B. "Moses Waddel: Nineteenth-Century South Carolina Educator." Ph.D. diss., University of South Carolina, 1992.

Lyon, Ralph M. "Moses Waddel and the Willington Academy." *North Carolina Historical Review* 8 (July 1931): 284–99.

Waddel, John N. *Memorials of Academic Life: Being an Historical Sketch of the Waddel Family.* Richmond, Va.: Presbyterian Committee of Publication, 1891.

Williston (Barnwell County; 2000 pop. 3,307). Williston, located on U.S. Highway 78 in Barnwell County, is named for early settlers, the Willis family. In 1830 the railroad from Charleston to Hamburg was begun, and small towns grew up along its route. In 1832 Elijah Willis, a well-to-do planter, donated land for a church, a post office, and a depot. On December 21, 1858, the South Carolina General Assembly issued a charter for Williston.

A private school was opened in 1853. A second private school was established and operated until after the Civil War. In 1873 Elijah Willis donated land on which to build a school. The Williston Graded School District received a charter from the General Assembly in 1888. Because of its strategic location on the railroad line, in February 1865 federal troops under General Hugh Judson Kilpatrick occupied Williston, destroying the railroad tracks and burning more than thirty homes.

Agriculture and associated businesses helped Williston to recover from the Civil War. Cotton, a chief crop, continued to fare well, although local farmers discovered that the climate and soil were also well suited for growing asparagus. The town experienced moderate growth throughout the first half of the twentieth century, including the establishment of a telephone system (1905), a water system (1917), and electricity provided by the Edisto Public service Company (1919). In 1921 Austin Lattimore established a newspaper, the *Williston Way,* which continued publication until 1989, when it merged with the *Barnwell People-Sentinel.*

On November 8, 1950, the Atomic Energy Commission announced the coming of the Savannah River Site. The population of Williston rose from 869 in 1950 to an estimated 10,000 or more for the town and outlying area during the peak of "The Bomb Plant" construction. The population decreased to 2,722 in 1960, with many construction workers remaining to work for DuPont in operating the plant.

Williston enjoyed a blend of old and new entering the twenty-first century. Though some downtown storefronts have been destroyed and the railroad tracks removed, new buildings and industries helped the town maintain its vibrancy. Industries have filled the industrial park developed by Williston and the Barnwell County Economic Development Commission. In July 2001 the Economic Development Commission bought 161 acres for a second industrial park. The old railroad bed paralleling Main Street has undergone a beautification project, and the town's annual celebration, Wonderful Williston Weekend, draws visitors from around the state. The festival begins with a beauty pageant and continues with events in the town park and a street dance at night. ELLEN BUSH JENKINS AND POSEY BELCHER

Barnwell County Heritage Book Committee. *Barnwell County Heritage, South Carolina.* Marceline, Mo.: Walsworth, 1994.

Chapman, Mrs. C. C., Mrs. F. L. Harper, and Mrs. M. F. Maxon. "History of Williston." South Carolina Tricentennial Edition. *Barnwell People-Sentinel,* June 25, 1970, pp. 22–26.

Wilson, Charles Coker (1864–1933). Architect. Wilson was born on November 20, 1864, in Hartsville to Dr. Furman Edwards Wilson and Jane Lide Coker. He earned an A.B. in civil engineering in 1886 and the C.E. degree in 1888 from South Carolina College. Beginning his career as a railroad engineer in Columbia and Roanoke, Virginia, Wilson entered architectural practice in 1891 in Roanoke. By 1896 he had returned to Columbia to enter into partnership with William Augustus Edwards. Wilson & Edwards's designs included the Masonic Temple of Columbia (1898–1900), the People's Bank of Anderson (1899), and the First Baptist Church of Sumter (1900–1901). From 1896 to 1899 Wilson also served as Columbia's city engineer and superintendent of the waterworks. He completed a course of architectural study in 1900 in the Atelier H. Duray at the École des Beaux-Arts in Paris. He returned to Columbia that year to an expanded private practice that included such notable design projects as the Darlington Graded School. Wilson and Edwards dissolved their partnership in 1901.

Between 1904 and 1907 Wilson made repairs to and rebuilt parts of the South Carolina State House, which had been substantially completed by Frank P. Milburn in 1903. From 1905 to 1907 his collaboration with Henry Ten Eyck Wendell produced Coppin Hall at Allen University (1906–1907), First Baptist Church of Hartsville (1906–1907), and Neville Hall at Presbyterian College (1906–1907). Wilson's association with Edwin D. Sompayrac (1907–1918) and James B. Urquhart (1907–1910) was arguably the state's most successful partnership prior to World War I and coincided with Wilson's tenure as architect for the University of South Carolina (USC). The firm's designs included Davis (1908) and LeConte (1909–1910) Colleges at USC, Davidson Hall at Coker College (1908–1910), the J. L. Coker & Company Department Store in Hartsville (1909–1910), the Gresham Hotel in Columbia (1912), construction supervision of the Palmetto Building in Columbia (1912–1913), Camden's Carnegie Library (1915), and the Darlington High School (1915). Wilson took George R. Berryman and J. Robie Kennedy as associates in 1923 and 1924, respectively, only to end that partnership as early as 1927. Important works by Wilson, Berryman & Kennedy included several buildings at Limestone College, Greenwood High School (1925), and the Andrew Jackson Hotel of Rock Hill (1925–1926). Harold Tatum joined Wilson as his final associate in 1929 and remained until Wilson's death in 1933. Wilson & Tatum were credited with the design of Sumter's Tuomey Hospital (1929–1930) and the Cheraw Post Office (1931–1932).

Wilson was arguably the state's most significant and influential early twentieth-century architect. His practice was both regional and varied in nature, and his office was perhaps the first in the state to encompass all disciplines involved in building construction and thereby reflected more than most the complexities of modern architectural practice. In 1914 Wilson became the first twentieth-century South Carolinian to be named a Fellow of the American Institute of Architects, after having been elected the South Carolina chapter's charter president the previous year. He served as the first chairman of the South Carolina Board of Architectural Examiners from 1917 to 1933 and helped draft the state's first building codes.

Wilson married Adeline McKenzie Selby on December 23, 1889. The couple had two daughters. He died in Columbia on January 26, 1933, and was buried in Elmwood Cemetery. ANDREW W. CHANDLER

Wells, John E., and Robert E. Dalton. *The South Carolina Architects, 1885–1935: A Biographical Directory.* Richmond, Va.: New South Architectural Press, 1992.

Withey, Henry F., and Elsie Rathburn Withey. *Biographical Dictionary of American Architects (Deceased).* 1956. Reprint, Los Angeles: Hennessey and Ingalls, 1970.

Wilson, John Lyde (1784–1849). Governor. Wilson was born in Cheraw District in May 1784 to John Wilson and Mary Lyde. He studied law in Baltimore and was admitted to the South Carolina Bar in 1807. Two years later, on December 31, 1809, Wilson married Charlotte Alston. The marriage produced two daughters. Charlotte died in 1817, and Wilson married Rebecca Eden of New York in October 1825. Together they had three children.

Attracted to politics at an early age, Wilson entered public life as a Democratic-Republican. He served four terms in the General Assembly from 1806 to 1817. During the War of 1812 he edited a short-lived, prowar Charleston newspaper. In 1817 Prince George Winyah Parish elected Wilson to the state Senate, where he served until 1822. During his last term he served as president of the Senate for several days until he was elected governor on December 7, 1822.

As governor, Wilson demonstrated himself to be an ardent advocate of states' rights. He denied that Congress had the power to make internal improvements. Legislative resolutions during Wilson's tenure declared that protective tariffs were unconstitutional and that Congress was without authority to tax the citizens of one state to pay for improvements within another. Another accomplishment during his term was the abolishment of the state Court of Equity. He also advocated, unsuccessfully, a more humane revision in laws affecting South Carolina's black population. Simultaneously, Wilson warned his constituents to guard against antislavery influence in Congress and the northern states, insisting on "a firm determination to resist, at the threshold, every invasion of our domestic tranquility." Wilson proved less diligent in maintaining the financial records of his office, however, and he was threatened with impeachment for failing to account for his contingent funds in a timely manner.

After his term ended, Wilson returned to the Senate, serving from 1826 to 1829. In late 1832 Charleston voters sent him to the Nullification Convention in Columbia, where he was one of the more ardent proponents of nullification. Afterward he retired from public office to concentrate on his writing and his somewhat radical positions involving public affairs. In 1835 he became head of "The Lynch Club" and supported mob action in Charleston regarding the seizure of abolitionist mailings.

In 1838 Wilson published *Code of Honor: or Rules for the Government of Principals and Seconds in Duelling.* He was reportedly experienced in the practice and believed himself qualified to codify its regulations. By doing so, he hoped to prevent needless encounters and perhaps to save lives. The *Code's* provisions addressed such topics as responses to insults, appropriate time between an insult and the duel, weapons, paces, roles of a participant's "second," and even the wording to be used. Despite assertions that his code would save lives, it required that any man refusing to fight be publicly labeled a coward. *Code of Honor* was so popular that it was reprinted in 1858 and again in 1878. Indeed, Wilson wished that his code of honor would be employed by gentlemen "until the advent of the millennium."

Wilson died in Charleston on February 13, 1849, and was buried in St. Paul's churchyard. MARTY D. MATTHEWS

Bailey, N. Louise, Mary L. Morgan, and Carolyn R. Taylor, eds. *Biographical Directory of the South Carolina Senate.* 3 vols. Columbia: University of South Carolina Press, 1986.

Wilson, Robert (1867–1946). Physician, educator. Wilson was born at Stateburg on August 23, 1867, the son of the Reverend Robert Wilson, M.D., and Ann Jane Shand. His father was a graduate of the Medical College of the State of South Carolina and a surgeon in the Confederate army but had given up medicine after the death of his first wife. Wilson grew up on the Eastern Shore of Maryland, where his father was parish priest. He attended the College of Charleston and graduated from South Carolina College in 1887. After traveling in Europe and teaching school, he entered the Medical College of the State of South Carolina, graduating in 1892. He married Harriet Chisolm Cain of Pinopolis on November 27, 1895. They had three children.

After attending the New York Postgraduate Medical School, Wilson joined the faculty of the Medical College of the State of South Carolina in 1893. He served the school for fifty-one years, first as instructor in bacteriology, then as professor of medicine and nervous diseases, and later as professor of medicine and head of the medicine department. He became dean (president) in 1908 and held this position until 1943. He was also physician in chief of the Roper Hospital staff from 1913 to 1943. As a teacher, Wilson emphasized a conservative approach to medicine, which encouraged a meticulous physical examination and a close analysis of the findings to arrive at an accurate diagnosis. In the first half of the twentieth century his service, example, and accomplishments had a lasting influence on the physicians of the state as well as the lives of those who were associated with him.

As the first bacteriologist for the city of Charleston (1897–1912), Wilson worked to improve the quality of the city's water supply. Possessing a deep interest in public health matters, he was a member of the state Board of Health from 1898 until 1935, serving as chairman from 1907 until 1935. Following the 1909 publication of the landmark Flexner Report, which harshly criticized almost all medical schools in the United States, Wilson realized the need to find a source of regular funding for the Medical College. He established an unlikely relationship with Governor Coleman L. Blease. In 1913 they persuaded the General Assembly to assume ownership of the Medical College and provide financial support. The Charleston business community raised funds for a new building, which was built on Lucas Street near Roper Hospital.

Wilson also served as president of the South Carolina Medical Association (1905), the Medical Society of South Carolina (1920–1922), the Tri-State Medical Association, and the Southern Medical Association. He was an early editor of the *Journal of the South Carolina Medical Association* and organized the Medical History Club that now bears his name. He received honorary LL.D. degrees from the University of South Carolina in 1918 and from the College of Charleston in 1922, and the doctor of civil laws degree from the University of the South, Sewanee, in 1926. He died in Charleston on May 20, 1946, and was buried in Magnolia Cemetery. JANE MCCUTCHEN BROWN

Biographical files. Waring Historical Library, Medical University of South Carolina, Charleston.

Waring, Joseph I. *A History of Medicine in South Carolina.* Vol. 3, *1900–1970.* Columbia: South Carolina Medical Association, 1971.

Winnsboro (Fairfield County; 2000 pop. 3,599). Winnsboro, the seat of Fairfield County, lies in the Piedmont on a ridge between the Broad and Wateree Rivers. In 1768 John Winn began acquiring the land that would become Winnsboro. At the time of the Revolutionary War, Winnsboro was a small village with few residents and only twenty houses. The British general Lord Cornwallis occupied the town from October 1780 through early January 1781. Prior to 1785 Winn had a master plan drawn for Winnsboro, and he sold more than one hundred lots between 1785 and 1787.

Incorporated in 1832 and named for the Revolutionary War hero Richard Winn, Winnsboro became a religious and educational center.

Granite quarry, Winnsboro, 1939. Photograph by Carl T. Julien for the WPA. Courtesy, South Caroliniana Library, University of South Carolina

During the 1780s the Mount Zion Society opened a school for boys, which enjoyed a reputation for educational excellence and eventually became a public school by 1878. Furman Academy and Theological Institution operated near Winnsboro from 1837 until 1850. This institution produced both Furman University in Greenville and Southern Baptist Theological Seminary in Louisville, Kentucky. The Reverend James Jenkins and John Buchanan, a Revolutionary War veteran, established First United Methodist Church in Winnsboro in 1808. An Associate Reformed Presbyterian church, Bethel, was incorporated in 1823.

Cotton brought prosperity to Winnsboro and Fairfield County. Many lowcountry planters came to Winnsboro in search of healthier environs. Construction of the Winnsboro courthouse began around 1822 under a design by William Jay, but the structure was later redesigned by Robert Mills. Another striking architectural feature of Winnsboro is the town clock, a two-story rectangular brick structure built between 1835 and 1837.

During the Civil War many lowcountry planter families sought refuge in Winnsboro. On February 19, 1865, Confederate forces under General P. G. T. Beauregard moved through Winnsboro after abandoning Columbia. Shortly afterward, on February 21, the Union general John W. Geary, commanding the left wing of William T. Sherman's Union army, arrived at Winnsboro. An earlier wave of "bummers" had already ravaged the town and set fire to some of its buildings. Federal troops destroyed twenty to thirty buildings. When federal troops left on February 22, Geary detached two mounted troopers to guard the town against stragglers.

After the Civil War, Winnsboro recovered more quickly than did the countryside. Most of the refugees returned home, trade resumed, and merchants prospered. Reconstruction, however, was a time of economic and social adjustment for Winnsboro. In 1869 northern Presbyterians established Fairfield Institute, a school for newly freed African Americans. Kelly Miller, later a nationally known African American educator, attended the institute. Fairfield Institute closed in 1888 to merge with Brainerd Institute in Chester. In 1873 African Americans organized their first church in Winnsboro, St. Paul Baptist Church.

Industry arrived in earnest at the end of the nineteenth century. Winnsboro merchants financed various industries, including the Fairfield Cotton Mills in 1896. Later renamed the Winnsboro Cotton Mills, this plant became an economic mainstay of the town throughout the twentieth century. Additional factories opened after World War II, including plants operated by Salant Corporation, Mack Trucks, and Fuji-Copian Corporation. Uniroyal Goodrich, the successor of the Winnsboro Cotton Mills, celebrated the centennial anniversary of the Winnsboro plant in 1998, but layoffs at the plant and the departure of Mack Truck challenged Winnsboro at the start of the twenty-first century. ALEXIA JONES HELSLEY

Bellardo, Lewis. "A Social and Economic History of Fairfield County, South Carolina, 1865–1871." Ph.D. diss., University of Kentucky, 1979.

Chappell, Buford S. *The Winns of Fairfield County: Colonel John Winn, William Winn, General Richard Winn.* Columbia, S.C.: R. L. Bryan, 1975.

McMaster, Fitz Hugh. *History of Fairfield County, South Carolina: From "Before the White Man Came" to 1942.* 1946. Reprint, Spartanburg, S.C.: Reprint Company, 1980.

Winthrop University. Located in Rock Hill, Winthrop University traces its roots to Reconstruction. David Bancroft Johnson, superintendent of the Columbia City School System, lobbied Robert C.

Winthrop, president of the Board of Trustees of the Peabody Education Fund, for money to start a teacher-training institution in 1886. Impressed by the need for teachers in South Carolina, Winthrop provided $1,500 of Peabody funds, plus $50 from his own pocket. On November 15, 1886, Winthrop Training School opened its doors in Columbia to nineteen students. Despite name changes, Winthrop University asserted its "century-old heritage as the pre-eminent teacher preparation program in the Southeast."

In 1891 the General Assembly passed an act creating "The Winthrop Normal and Industrial College of South Carolina for the education of white girls." Support came in the form of scholarships; each county was granted two. The act's intent proclaimed that the college be "good enough for the richest and cheap enough for the poorest." In 1900 it was argued that "South Carolina generously maintains three institutions for the higher education of men. The women in the State are greater in numbers than the men, and the State's welfare is more dependent upon them. To educate the mother assures the education of the children."

Winthrop graduates on the balcony of Byrnes Auditorium, 1963. Photograph by Joel Nichols, university photographer. Courtesy, Winthrop University

Winthrop did not remain in the state's capital; three towns competed for a new Winthrop facility. In 1895 the institution was moved to Rock Hill. The state pledged buildings, equipment, and the "labor of 100 convicts for three years." By 1920 the name was changed again, this time to Winthrop College, the South Carolina College for Women. By 1929 Winthrop's board of trustees proudly presented data to the General Assembly bragging of the college's production of teachers. To that date the college had produced 2,601 graduates with certificates to teach. Their nearest competitor had produced 396.

Leadership in the early years was consistent. Dr. D. B. Johnson served as the college's president from 1886 until 1928. Typical of southern women's colleges, Winthrop did not have a female president until 1986. Martha Kims Piper served only two years before she died in office in 1988.

Throughout its history, the college retained its roots in the liberal arts. As a women's institution, Winthrop observed the social conventions of the times. Female students wore uniforms until 1955, and they remained under the care of the college until they returned home. As early as 1900 more than five hundred students were enrolled, and the campus grew to accommodate its growing population. By the 1940s the "College Farm" was producing vegetables, dairy, and poultry in support of the institution.

Integration came before coeducation. In 1964 the first African American student enrolled. By 2002–2003 African Americans accounted for approximately one-quarter of the student body. In 1974 the governor authorized the board of trustees to pursue coeducation.

By the end of the twentieth century, Winthrop was awarding both bachelor's and master's degrees and enrolled more than six thousand undergraduate and graduate students. The college houses the South Carolina Center for Teacher Recruitment, the nation's oldest teacher recruitment program, although business management has replaced education as Winthrop's largest program. JULIE A. ROTHOLZ

Chepesiuk, Ronald, and Magdalena Chepesiuk. *Winthrop University.* Charleston, S.C.: Arcadia, 2000.

WIS Radio and Television. WIS Radio and Television stations in Columbia played an influential role in the development of South Carolina's media as a result of being among the state's pioneer commercial broadcasters and locating their studios in the state's capital city. The last station in the country to be granted a three-letter call sign, WIS Radio signed on the air on the evening of July 10, 1930, from a one-room studio in the Jefferson Hotel in Columbia with speeches by Governor John G. Richards and Mayor L. B. Owens and performances by live musicians. The call sign initials stood for "Wonderful Iodine State"—a slogan born when the station's initial owners envisioned the ability to advertise South Carolina's iodine-rich vegetable crop to listeners. In 1931 the station was acquired by Liberty Life Insurance Company.

In its early years the Columbia television station regularly featured local musical talent shows. Courtesy, WIS Television

In 1953 the owners of a few South Carolina commercial radio stations, including WIS, were awarded licenses by the Federal Communications Commission to operate commercial television stations. WIS Television was assigned Channel 10, the only VHF channel in central South Carolina, an advantage that the station maintained for years. Its first broadcast on November 7, 1953, was a live telecast of a University of South Carolina football game in Columbia.

WIS Radio, after an ownership change in 1987, changed its call letters to WVOC (Voice Of Columbia) but continued broadcasting at 560 kilocycles on the AM radio band. RUSS MCKINNEY, JR.

Jarrells, Ralph. "History of Broadcasting in South Carolina: WSPA, WCSC, and WIS." Unpublished manuscript. South Caroliniana Library, University of South Carolina, Columbia.

Lang, Louis DeSaussure. "So Rich a Heritage—Contributions of WIS to Broadcasting Industry." Louis DeSaussure Lang Papers. South Caroliniana Library, University of South Carolina, Columbia.

McNeely, Patricia G. *Fighting Words: The History of the Media in South Carolina.* Columbia: South Carolina Press Association, 1998.

Wofford College. A four-year liberal arts college in Spartanburg, Wofford College was founded with a bequest from the Methodist minister and Spartanburg County native Benjamin Wofford. After only a few years in the active ministry, Wofford spent his life concentrating on his investments, and at his death in 1850 he left $100,000 to establish "a college for literary, classical and scientific education." Half of the bequest was used for the construction of buildings and the other half for the endowment. Edward C. Jones, a Charleston architect, designed Wofford's Main Building in the Italianate or Tuscan Villa style. Four houses flanked the Main Building, all of which remain in use. The General Assembly granted the trustees a charter in 1851, and the college opened on August 1, 1854, with three faculty members and seven students.

Old Main at Wofford is still the focal point of the college's campus. Courtesy, South Caroliniana Library, University of South Carolina

In addition to their studies in Latin, Greek, literature, and mathematics, the students participated in debating societies. The first graduate, Samuel Dibble, took his diploma in 1856 and went on to become a congressman during the 1880s. Enrollment grew each year, and by 1861 sixty-five men had taken their degrees. With the outbreak of the Civil War, most of the student body joined the Confederate army. The college's trustees invested the entire endowment in Confederate bonds and bank securities. A long period of rebuilding the endowment followed the war. While the college remained open through the period, only in 1872 did the number of graduates exceed prewar levels.

During this period, one faculty member stood above all others as the college's "spiritual endowment." James Henry Carlisle began teaching mathematics at the institution in 1854 and became its third president in 1875. During his presidency the student body remained small and the faculty concentrated on producing alumni of character who could provide leadership for their home communities. Other significant developments in the Carlisle era included the first intercollegiate football game in South Carolina, between Wofford and Furman in 1889; the rise of fraternities on campus; and participation by Wofford faculty members in the founding of the Association of Southern Colleges and Secondary Schools in 1895.

On Carlisle's retirement in 1902, Henry Nelson Snyder, a professor of English, began a forty-year term as president. He presided over a faculty of distinguished teaching scholars, including the eminent South Carolina historian David Duncan Wallace. Snyder was an influential Methodist layman, serving on the commission that reunified the Methodist Church in 1939 and on other church boards. He saw a Reserve Officers' Training Corps unit established at the college during World War I. Early in his tenure, Snyder secured funds to construct four new buildings, including a library and a science building. The faculty's work to improve Wofford's academic reputation culminated in 1941 with the awarding of a chapter of Phi Beta Kappa.

The outbreak of World War II saw many students leave college, and early in 1943 the U.S. Army Air Corps began using the campus as a training facility. After the war ended, there was a marked increase in the number of students and a commensurate increase in the size of the faculty. These new, young professors formed the core of the teaching staff for the next generation. During the 1960s there was continued growth in facilities and there were some important social developments. The trustees voted to desegregate in May 1964, and in September, Wofford became the first private college in the state to enroll an African American student. The college had a few women students as early as 1897, but only with the approval of full residential coeducation in 1975 did large numbers of women enroll.

The 1960s and 1970s saw changes in student life and the college curriculum. A new code of conduct gave students more responsibility for enforcing campus rules. The Interim, a four-week period of intensive study or travel, was implemented in 1968. During the administration of Joab M. Lesesne, Jr. (1972–2000), more students participated in study-abroad programs and the Presidential International Scholarship allowed one student annually to travel extensively in the developing world. Also during the Lesesne presidency, the college was named the best southern liberal arts college by *U.S. News and World Report* and the college's athletics program began to compete in the NCAA Division I Southern Conference. Lesesne, a historian, became the first southerner to serve as president of the National Association of Independent Colleges and Universities, and he was a leader in state and national educational organizations. As president, he led the college through a period of strategic planning that brought a major grant from the Olin Foundation, an increased endowment, and eight new buildings. R. PHILLIP STONE II

Norrell, Thomas Harmon. "The History of Wofford College: A Small College in the Context of Change." Ph.D. diss., University of South Carolina, 1993.

Snyder, Henry Nelson. *An Educational Odyssey.* Nashville, Tenn.: Abingdon-Cokesbury, 1947.

Wallace, David Duncan. *History of Wofford College, 1854–1949.* Nashville, Tenn.: Vanderbilt University Press, 1951.

Wofford, Kate Vixon (1894–1954). Educator. Wofford was born on October 20, 1894, in Laurens, the eldest of ten children of John Albert Wofford and Cleo Cunningham. She received an A.B. with honors in 1916 from Winthrop College and soon after started teaching at Laurens High School. She served briefly in the Washington office of U.S. Senator Ben Tillman and then joined the navy as a yeoman during World War I. Wofford returned to teach at Laurens High and in 1922 was elected to the first of two terms as county superintendent of schools, the first female school superintendent in South Carolina and the first woman elected to public office in the state. The support of women, with their newly granted suffrage rights, was important to Wofford's election success. In addition to bringing needed change to the county's rural schools, Wofford focused on improving conditions and standards for African American schools as well, a choice thrown at her in the second campaign but a challenge she overcame. Active in the South Carolina State

Teachers Association, she was elected president for the 1926–1927 term and was the first woman to serve in this office as well.

In 1930 Wofford continued her education, receiving her A.M. from Cornell University (1931) and her Ph.D. from Columbia University (1934). Her dissertation was published in 1935 as *An History of the Status and Training of Elementary Rural Teachers of the United States, 1860–1930.*

Wofford became head professor and director of rural education at State Teachers College, Buffalo, New York, where she authored two books, *Modern Education in the Small Rural School* (1938) and *Teaching in Small Schools* (1946), and became widely known and respected for her expertise on education in rural schools. In 1935 Wofford was offered the position of dean at the University of South Carolina, but she declined because it would take her out of the field of rural education.

Wofford's expertise led to many accomplishments and honors, including visiting professorships across the United States and internationally. She held positions within the rural education department of the National Education Association and wrote for and edited some of the association's yearbooks.

In 1947 Wofford became director of elementary education at the University of Florida in Gainesville, where she gained further distinction. In 1952 she organized a program fulfilling a recommendation to the Turkish Ministry of Education. With her colleagues, Wofford gained funding and then directed a course of study for twenty-five Turkish educators. Her report of this success, *The Workshop Way with Foreign Students,* was published in 1954. Wofford died of cancer at her home in Gainesville on October 31, 1954. She was buried in the New Prospect Baptist Church Cemetery near Laurens, South Carolina. MARGARET MEGGS

"Dr. K. V. Wofford, Florida Educator." *New York Times,* November 1, 1954, p. 27.

Wofford, Kate Vixon. Papers. South Caroliniana Library, University of South Carolina, Columbia.

Women. Although women constitute a majority of South Carolina's population, they have had to overcome many of the same barriers to equality as have women across the nation. During the colonial and antebellum periods and for many years after, South Carolina women lacked legal rights, had little access to education, and had few means available to support themselves other than depending on husbands, fathers, or other male relatives. By the twenty-first century South Carolina women had knocked down many of these barriers but still lagged on many indicators, including education, employment, income, and health care. This may be attributed at least in part to the state's conservative culture, in which change comes slowly and women have been seen first and foremost as wives and mothers. Nonwhite women have also had to overcome racial discrimination. A portrait of the state in 2000 would show that South Carolina had a smaller percentage of white women (65.6) and a larger percentage of African American (30.4) and other nonwhite women (4) than did the nation as a whole. The percentage of Hispanic women (1.9) was low but growing.

The story of South Carolina's women is one of slow progress. While women could inherit money and property in colonial and antebellum South Carolina, only single women and widows could own property and sign contracts. When a woman married, her husband gained the ownership of her property unless her family had set up a trust or some other kind of legal settlement. Married women had no other legal protection for their property until 1868 when the delegates at the state constitutional convention gave them the right to make contracts and to control property. Protecting women's property was in part a recognition that some husbands were not good stewards of their family's affairs.

In the domestic sphere, the power of the husband was generally unchecked by the law. With the exception of a brief period in the late 1860s, South Carolina had no provision for divorce until 1949. A woman who sought an out-of-state divorce might lose custody of her children. By the late 1970s, however, state laws required that decisions about child custody and support be made based on the best interests of the child and the ability of the parents to provide support. The state did not recognize marital rape as a crime until 1991. In 2000, in acknowledgment of the state's number one ranking in the rate at which women were killed by men, Governor James Hodges appointed a task force to address the issue of domestic violence. In 2001 the General Assembly passed a bill adding a $20 fee to marriage licenses, with revenues earmarked for women's shelters. The state began to increase prosecutions of men charged with domestic violence, which became a felony in 2003. As of 2002 South Carolina ranked third in the nation in the rates at which men killed their wives and female partners.

During the colonial and antebellum periods, education for women focused on skills considered appropriate to make them good wives and mothers. The abolitionist Sarah Grimké of Charleston described the women of her class in her "Letters on the Equality of the Sexes" as "butterflies of the fashionable world" whose "education is miserably deficient." By the 1840s some private schools existed around the state, making a classical education available to upper-class women. But few educational opportunities were available for the poor through most of the 1800s and early 1900s. As late as 1900 only fifty-four percent of South Carolina girls under age fifteen were attending school.

In the 1850s several religious denominations established women's colleges. But much of the impetus for the establishment of women's colleges came in the latter part of the nineteenth century and grew out of a need for teachers to staff the public schools that had been provided for under the 1868 constitution. Columbia school superintendent D. B. Johnson obtained a grant to set up a one-year training course in 1886 at what became Winthrop Training School. The school in 1891 became a state-supported institution emphasizing vocational training for white women and eventually expanded into a four-year teachers' college. Many of the private and church-related women's colleges of the era did not offer vocational courses, providing instead a more traditional liberal arts program as well as religion, art, music, and ethics courses for the "genteel" southern woman.

There were no private colleges for African American women. Many attended coeducational African American institutions such as Claflin College, founded in 1869. In the pre–civil rights era, public colleges in the state were segregated by race. Although the University of South Carolina began admitting white women in the mid-1890s, it was 1963 before Henrie Monteith became the first African American woman to attend that university. By the end of the twentieth century the percentage of African Americans attending public universities remained low compared to the percentage of African Americans residing in the state.

In the late twentieth century women in South Carolina were still less likely than women in the nation as a whole to have completed a four-year college degree or even to have finished high school. The state's women were legally entitled to the same educational opportunities and scholarships as the state's men, but cultural barriers still remained.

With Shannon Faulkner's admission to the Citadel in 1995 and Nancy Mace's graduation from that institution in 1999, women breached the state's most ardent bastion of all-male higher education.

Employment opportunities were limited for women prior to the twentieth century. In early South Carolina, especially in Charleston, some women (known as "femme sole traders") ran shops or other businesses. But by the early 1800s cultural expectations in American society dictated that women should remain in the private, or domestic, sphere away from the world of government and commerce, although middle- and upper-class women were expected to act as hostesses for their husbands, run their households, and, in the South, supervise slaves. The southern lady became a cultural icon, placed on a pedestal where she would not soil her hands with hard labor. She was described by the scholar Anne Firor Scott as "a submissive wife whose reason for being was to love, honor, obey, and occasionally amuse her husband, to bring up his children, and to manage his household." The pedestal, however, was never an option for poor white women in the state. By the late 1840s around thirteen percent of South Carolina's white labor force consisted of women who had to work for a living. Nor was the pedestal an option for African American women in South Carolina. Most were enslaved in the period prior to the Civil War and lived in poverty in the years after. By 1900 about thirty-eight percent of all South Carolina women were employed outside of the home. About fourteen percent of all white women worked, while about two-thirds of all African American women were employed, a majority in the fields. Others were likely to hold jobs as mill workers if they were white, or as maids or laundresses if they were black.

More women joined the labor force in the twentieth century. About three-fifths of all South Carolina women were employed outside of the home by 2000, and the state ranked sixteenth in the nation in terms of the percentage of women who held professional and managerial positions. Women owned more than 64,000 South Carolina businesses.

Few professions were open to South Carolina women prior to the twentieth century. In 1918 the General Assembly passed legislation permitting women to practice law, and James M. "Miss Jim" Perry became the state's first woman lawyer that same year. More than fifty years later, in 1983, Judy Cone Bridges became the state's first female judge with her election by the General Assembly to the family court. In 1988 Jean Toal became the first woman to serve on the South Carolina Supreme Court (becoming chief justice in 2000) and also in 1988 Carol Connor became the first woman to serve on the state circuit court. Connor became the first female judge on the state court of appeals in 1993, and Kay Hearn became its first female chief justice in 2000. South Carolina's first woman physician, Sara Campbell Allen, began to practice in 1894. In 1900 less than five percent of the state's physicians were women. By 2000 women comprised nearly twenty percent of the total.

Despite the limitations that attitudes and law placed on women's roles, South Carolina women were actively involved in charitable and religious organizations throughout the 1800s. In the antebellum period, women's organizations in communities across the state helped the poor. The Ladies Benevolent Association in Charleston, for example, raised money and went into the slums to help those in need. In the late 1800s, through the efforts of the Women's Christian Temperance Union and other groups, the sale of liquor was outlawed in much of the state. Members of this group were among those who brought the debate over suffrage to the forefront. A tradition of activism continued into the next century. In the early 1900s women's groups provided an outlet for women to sell their crafts in Charleston, lobbied for a public health nurse in Dillon County, and supported the building of libraries. White women's groups also raised money for statues and other Confederate memorials. The League of Women Voters emerged after women gained the vote in 1920. The state league supported "Peace . . . education, better babies . . . good roads," and other progressive causes. African American women formed their own groups in a segregated society. They set up an umbrella organization, the South Carolina Federation of Colored Women's Clubs, in 1910. During much of the twentieth century, women such as Septima Poinsette Clark and Modjeska Simkins worked for civil rights through the National Association for the Advancement of Colored People (NAACP).

Like most American women, South Carolina's women lacked the right to vote until passage of the Nineteenth Amendment to the U.S. Constitution in 1920. Although South Carolina women were among the officers of the Equal Rights Association as early as 1869, there was little active support from the state's women. Delegates to South Carolina's 1895 constitutional convention defeated a proposal to allow women to vote, with the state senator John T. Sloan, Jr., declaring that God "never intended her to be put on an equality with man in any respect." By the early 1900s woman suffrage was becoming a mainstream issue, with support from some middle-class women's organizations. White women organized suffrage leagues around the state under the leadership of such women as Eulalie Salley and Susan Pringle Frost. Black women were excluded from these organizations. The Nineteenth Amendment was passed into law without the support of South Carolina's General Assembly, which did not ratify it until 1969. The General Assembly did pass a law giving women the right to vote once the Nineteenth Amendment became law, and some women registered and began to vote. At the same time, the legislature passed a law excluding women from jury duty. This exclusion remained in effect until 1967. The legislature did not ratify the Equal Rights Amendment in the 1970s.

Following suffrage, a few women began to run for political office, often based on an interest in improving education. Kate Vixon Wofford, elected as superintendent of education in Laurens County in 1922, was the first woman elected to office in South Carolina. In 1928 Mary Gordon Ellis of Jasper County became the first woman elected to the state Senate. Harriet Frazier Johnson of York County became the first woman elected to the S.C. House of Representatives in 1945. Both of these legislators were interested in improving education and in improving the lives of African Americans. With her 1978 election as lieutenant governor, Nancy Stevenson became the first woman elected to a statewide office in South Carolina. By 2003 two women had held the office of state superintendent of education, Barbara Nielson and Inez Tenenbaum. At the national level, in 1938 Elizabeth Hawley Gasque of Florence became the first of five South Carolina women to be elected to Congress. With the exception of Elizabeth Patterson, however, all were chosen to complete their late husbands' terms under the "widow's mandate."

By 2000 fifty-six percent of the state's registered voters were female, ranking first in the South Atlantic region in both registration and turnout. South Carolina was one of only fifteen states with a women's caucus in both houses of its legislature as well as a commission on women. But women in the state have not seen themselves as an interest group or a voting bloc. As the political analyst Whit Ayres noted, "Party is a whole lot more important than gender when it comes to voting." Prior to 1970 only nine women had been elected to the General Assembly. In 2003 sixteen members of the legislature were women, the smallest percentage of female state legislators in the country. With the exception of Democrat Gilda Cobb-Hunter, who had served as House minority leader, women had held virtually no leadership positions in the General Assembly. With just a handful of women legislators, the Women's Caucus, founded in 1982, was unable to bring about change or even develop a consensus on many legislative priorities. The state's governors had appointed only a few women to cabinet positions or to positions on boards and commissions. In 2003, during a time of tight budgets, Governor Mark Sanford vetoed funding for the state's Commission on Women, stating that he would cover its functions with part-time support from staff in his office.

Despite substantial gains, South Carolina's women by 2000 still had not achieved parity. The poverty rate for South Carolina women was almost thirteen percent in 1999, and twenty-six percent for African American women. More than thirty percent of households headed by women where no husband was present fell below the poverty level in 2000. Women lagged behind men of any race in terms of income, earning less than seventy-one percent of what men earned in 1999. They ranked thirty-seventh in the nation in terms of women's median annual earnings.

Health care presented a mixed picture, pointing to a need for intervention to improve women's health. Participants at a series of statewide forums on women's health held in 2000 concluded that women needed more access to birth control, mental health services, protection from domestic violence, and HIV care. In one study the state ranked fortieth overall for women's health care and forty-eighth on women's life expectancy. As with other indicators, white women generally did better than nonwhites in the rankings. At the beginning of the twenty-first century women in South Carolina were more likely than women in the nation as a whole to have health insurance, although nearly eleven percent of all South Carolina women had none. Women comprised a majority of the state's elderly population, the age cohort that makes the most demands on an overburdened health care system.

In many respects, life is dramatically better for the South Carolina woman of the twenty-first century than it was for her counterpart in history. Women have far more legal protections than in the past. With passage of the 1972 South Carolina Human Affairs Law and its subsequent amendments, the General Assembly created the Human Affairs Commission to investigate complaints of discrimination in employment, including those based on sex. The South Carolina Fair Housing Law passed in 1989 gave the commission the power to investigate sex-based fair housing complaints. With changes in laws and attitudes, South Carolina's women should continue to see their educational and economic status improve throughout the century. CAROL SEARS BOTSCH

Botsch, Carol Sears. "Women in South Carolina Politics." In *South Carolina Government: A Policy Perspective,* edited by Charlie B. Tyer. Columbia, S.C.: Institute for Public service and Policy Research, 2003.

Caiazza, Amy B., ed. *The Status of Women in South Carolina.* Washington, D.C.: Institute for Women's Policy Research, 2002.

Fox-Genovese, Elizabeth. *Within the Plantation Household: Black and White Women of the Old South.* Chapel Hill: University of North Carolina Press, 1988.

Hornsby, Benjamin F., Jr. *South Carolina Women: A Timeline.* Columbia: South Carolina Department of Archives and History, 1995.

McCandless, Amy Thompson. *The Past in the Present: Women's Higher Education in the Twentieth-Century American South.* Tuscaloosa: University of Alabama Press, 1999.

McSwain, Gayla S. L. *The Legal Status of Women: An Analysis of the NOW Report and Comparison of Laws in South Carolina to Laws in Other States.* Columbia: South Carolina Commission on Women, 1990.

Scott, Anne Firor. *The Southern Lady from Pedestal to Politics, 1830–1930.* Chicago: University of Chicago Press, 1970.

Women's clubs. The South Carolina women's club movement was a powerful force for social change. It challenged the landscape of the state's conventionalism and supported social reform for all South Carolinians. The core organizations of this movement were the South Carolina Federation of Women's Clubs (SCFWC) and the South Carolina Federation of Colored Women's Clubs (SCFCWC), organized in 1898 and 1909, respectively. Like state federated organizations around the nation, SCFWC and SCFCWC members often held membership in numerous organizations. Most of the clubs in these organizations initially formed for women's self-improvement. However, over time the focus of both organizations shifted to social reform, and in the case of the SCFCWC, to racial reform. Although segregated in membership, similarities between the SCFWC and the SCFCWC were nevertheless present. Like women's organizations throughout the nation, both groups emphasized community uplift and better educational access for black and white South Carolinians.

The Tuesday Afternoon Club, Columbia, was one of many literary, civic, and cultural organizations formed by South Carolina women at the turn of the twentieth century. Courtesy, South Caroliniana Library, University of South Carolina

Nationally, the white General Federation of Women's Clubs was founded in 1890, claiming 100,000 members in five hundred women's clubs across the nation. Initially its purpose was the intellectual advancement of women, but its mission gradually expanded to include philanthropy and education. When the SCFWC formed in South Carolina in 1898, it did so with only thirty-two delegates from nineteen clubs. Such members as Louisa Poppenheim, onetime president of the SCFWC, officer in the General Federation of Women's Clubs, and member of the Century Club, focused not only on educational access but also on school conditions. In doing this, and because Poppenheim and many other white southern clubwomen were members of the United Daughters of the Confederacy, white clubwomen placed great emphasis on teaching white southern homogeneity—that is, teaching children southern history and southern values. In cosmopolitan places such as Charleston, the SCFWC reflected a degree of religious and ethnic diversity. When the Charleston City Federation of Women's Clubs formed in 1899, it was affiliated with such organizations as the Council of Catholic

Women and the Council of Jewish Women. However, interracial cooperation with the SCFCWC would remain limited.

In the late nineteenth century most southern African Americans were only a few decades removed from the institution of American slavery. Many had firsthand experience with white-on-black violence, poverty, and few economic opportunities that resulted from the racial segregation dominating southern society. The national black women's club movement, which resulted in the formation of the National Association of Colored Women in 1896, represented efforts by African American women to improve conditions by providing assistance to African American communities. In South Carolina, such prominent black women as Marion Birnie Wilkinson, also founder of the Sunlight Club in Orangeburg, created a coalition of black women's organizations when they founded the South Carolina Federation of Colored Women's Clubs in May 1909 at Sidney Park CME Church in Columbia. Using the motto of the national black women's club movement, "Lifting as We Climb," as well as their own song "Loyal Women of Palmetto," set to the tune of the "Battle Hymn of the Republic," black women committed themselves to uplifting African Americans in South Carolina.

Like members of progressive organizations elsewhere, black and white clubwomen fought for prohibition, the sanctity of the home, educational opportunities, suffrage, health, and community improvement. However, unlike those in white women's progressive organizations, South Carolina's black clubwomen also fought to protect black women from sexual exploitation and racial discrimination by forming such institutions as the Fairwold School for Delinquent Negro Girls (later the Marion Birnie Wilkinson School for Girls) in 1917 in Cayce.

Through the SCFWC and the SCFCWC, the South Carolina women's club movement provided much needed assistance to white and black communities. Despite these organizations' successes in social activism, membership in both declined in the 1960s and 1970s as older members passed on and a younger generation expressed little interest in joining women's clubs. In the case of the SCFCWC, national and local civil rights advances negated the importance of African American women's clubs as a force for racial change. Yet the legacy of the SCFWC, the SCFCWC, and the women's club movement clearly revealed the commitment of white and black women in South Carolina to community uplift, social reform, and access to better educational opportunities, while simultaneously perpetuating pride in a distinctive southern identity. CHERISSE R. JONES

Johnson, Joan M. "'This Wonderful Dream Nation!' Black and White South Carolina Women and the Creation of the New South, 1898–1930." Ph.D., diss., University of California, Los Angeles, 1997.

Jones, Cherisse R. "'Loyal Women of Palmetto': Black Women's Clubs in Charleston, South Carolina, 1916–1965." Master's thesis, University of Charleston and The Citadel, 1997.

Newby, I. A. *Black Carolinians: A History of Blacks in South Carolina from 1895 to 1968.* Columbia: University of South Carolina Press, 1973.

Women's suffrage. The enfranchisement of women in South Carolina was first discussed publicly during the Reconstruction period. A women's rights convention held in Columbia in December 1870 received a warm letter of support from Governor R. K. Scott. In 1872 the General Assembly endorsed a petition of the American Woman Suffrage Association to grant women political rights, but it adjourned without taking any specific action. The earliest suffrage clubs in the state were not organized until the 1890s, but suffragists were beginning to receive notice. Writing for the Charleston *News and Courier* in 1882, the journalist N. G. Gonzales described the typical suffragist as "thirty to sixty, a majority of considerable embonpoint, a majority passable looking, a majority with gray hair and a majority wearing bright colors."

Virginia Durant Young of Fairfax almost single-handedly transformed the South Carolina woman suffrage climate in the 1890s. Wife of a country town doctor who supported her endeavors, Young came to the suffrage cause via church work and the Women's Christian Temperance Union. She championed both prohibition and votes for women in her weekly, the *Fairfax Enterprise.* Together with a "little knot of (temperance) women," in April 1890 in Greenville, Young formed the South Carolina Equal Rights Association (SCERA), which soon claimed memberships from places as small as Frogmore (Beaufort County) and Chitty (Barnwell County) to cities such as Charleston and Columbia. Young soon aligned the SCERA with the National American Woman Suffrage Association (NAWSA), which constituted a committee for the southern states in 1892 and named Young a vice president for South Carolina.

Columbia College students were active in the women's suffrage movement. Courtesy, Columbia College

Young found a crucial suffrage ally in Robert R. Hemphill, editor of the *Abbeville Medium* and a longtime member of the South Carolina Senate. In December 1892 she persuaded Hemphill to introduce a joint resolution to allow women to vote and hold office, although this was unsuccessful. The next year Young got Hemphill to introduce a petition claiming that the state was violating her civil rights as a tax-paying citizen by denying her the ballot, but no debate resulted.

Suffragists became increasingly active in 1895. Several, including Young and Senator Hemphill, attended the NAWSA convention in Atlanta in 1895 and hosted Susan B. Anthony on her return north. They vigorously lobbied legislators at the 1895 constitutional convention, hoping to get educated, property-owning women enfranchised. In so doing, they argued giving white women the vote could achieve the goal of restricting black political power. Young, the prominent suffragist Laura Clay, and several other enthusiasts visited twenty-three towns in the spring of 1895 hoping to gain converts and start new suffrage clubs. Numerous factors, however, including the influence of conservative religious groups and ties of the suffrage movement to abolitionism and the controversial Grimké sisters, coupled with the widely held view that the women's rights movement was "against Scripture, against nature, and against commonsense," insured legislative failure. Following rejection of an amendment to extend the franchise to women possessing three hundred dollars worth of taxable property, the South Carolina woman suffrage movement entered a near twenty-year period of dormancy. The SCERA disintegrated with Young's death in 1906.

The September 1912 formation in Spartanburg of the New Era Club, which was committed to advancing "the industrial, legal and educational rights of women and children," signaled a revival of the cause in the state. The pace quickened in spring 1914 when visits to Columbia and Charleston by Lila Meade Valentine, founder of the Equal Suffrage League of Virginia, resulted in leagues in those cities and, in May 1914, formation of the South Carolina Equal Suffrage League (SCESL). There were twenty-five leagues and a membership of three thousand by the time of the convention of 1917. Aligned with NAWSA, the SCESL carefully distanced itself from the English-style militancy of the National Woman's Party (NWP), supporters of a federal suffrage amendment.

Recognizing the uphill battle before it, the SCESL initially kept its legislative work on a small scale and focused on organization and education. The league distributed literature at state and county fairs, clubs, and schools. Outside speakers, including NAWSA leader Dr. Anna Howard Shaw, were brought to the state. The first suffrage parade was held during the 1914 State Fair. An overall plan to organize counties, towns, and wards was drafted.

Foremost leaders in the final suffrage drive were Susan Pringle Frost of Charleston and Eulalie Chaffee Salley of Aiken, both professional realtors and arguably the state's most controversial feminists. An eighth-generation Charlestonian and grande dame of that city's historic preservation movement, Frost headed the Charleston Equal Suffrage League (CESL) until December 1917, when she narrowly failed to align it with Alice Paul's NWP and resigned to form a Woman's Party branch, one of three in the state. Frost and her small group of Paul partisans, including Anita Pollitzer, later head of the national organization, continued to promote woman suffrage during the war years, and Frost joined one of the demonstrations against President Wilson in Washington. Eulalie Salley was organizer and president of the Aiken Equal Suffrage League and, in 1919, SCESL president. An aggressive and innovative suffrage campaigner, Salley once boxed in a prizefight to raise money and scattered suffrage pamphlets over Aiken while hanging out of an airplane.

With the death of Ben Tillman in 1918, South Carolina suffragists concentrated lobby efforts on his interim replacement in the U.S. Senate, William Pollock of Cheraw. With the Senate only two votes shy of passing the Anthony amendment in October 1918, an intense and successful "Helping Pollock to Declare" campaign was waged. However, his was the only additional vote in favor of the amendment. Although his replacement voted against the Nineteenth Amendment, it was passed in 1919.

The journalist William Watts Ball observed in January 1920 that "legions of suffragists . . . painfully excited" had descended on the state capitol in Columbia as ratification was debated in the General Assembly. Despite the heroic support of Beaufort legislator Neils Christensen, however, the cause was hopeless. The S.C. House rejected the amendment 93 to 21, the S.C. Senate 32 to 3. Following national ratification of the Nineteenth Amendment, the South Carolina General Assembly reluctantly passed a law giving women the right to vote but simultaneously passed another statute excluding women from jury duty. Patriarchal and recalcitrant to the end, the state finally ratified the Nineteenth Amendment in 1969. Standing behind the governor on the occasion, eighty-six-year-old Eulalie Salley reputedly had the last word, remarking, "Boys, I've been waiting fifty years to tell you what I think of you." SIDNEY R. BLAND

Bland, Sidney R. *Preserving Charleston's Past, Shaping Its Future: The Life and Times of Susan Pringle Frost.* 2d ed. Columbia: University of South Carolina Press, 1999.

Bull, Emily L. *Eulalie.* Aiken, S.C.: Kalmia, 1973.

Herndon, Eliza. "Woman Suffrage in South Carolina: 1872–1920." Master's thesis, University of South Carolina, 1953.

Taylor, Antoinette Elizabeth. "South Carolina and the Enfranchisement of Women: The Early Years." *South Carolina Historical Magazine* 77 (April 1976): 115–26.

———. "South Carolina and the Enfranchisement of Women: The Later Years." *South Carolina Historical Magazine* 80 (October 1979): 298–310.

Ulmer, Barbara Bellows. "Virginia Durant Young: New South Suffragist." Master's thesis, University of South Carolina, 1979.

Woodmason, Charles (ca. 1720–?). Clergyman. Little is known about Woodmason before he came to South Carolina. He was born in England and was probably of the gentry class. While his place of birth remains uncertain, he probably grew up in London. In his writings Woodmason says nothing about parents, brothers, sisters, or other relatives. Around 1752 he came to South Carolina. At some point an injury received from a horse's kick left him unfit for "Nuptial Rites," and his wife remained in England. She never joined him in South Carolina.

Soon after his arrival in Charleston, Woodmason began buying land in the Pee Dee River area. For about ten years he lived in Prince Frederick's Parish, becoming church warden for the parish in 1756. In the absence of a rector, he read prayers and a sermon each Sunday. He was elected to the parish vestry in 1757 and was appointed justice of the peace the following year, serving for seven years in Craven County and Charleston. In 1762 Woodmason returned to England, and later that year or early in 1763 he came back to South Carolina and settled in Charleston. After he applied for the office of stamp distributor for the unpopular Stamp Act of 1765, he was hated and fell into disrepute.

Late in 1765 Woodmason applied for the position of itinerant Anglican minister in St. Mark's Parish in the South Carolina backcountry. Since there was no Church of England bishop in the colonies, he had to go to England for ordination. He returned to South Carolina an ordained Anglican priest and was licensed to work in St. Mark's. The backcountry was religiously diverse, with Anglicans, German Lutherans and Reformed, Huguenots, Scots and Ulster Irish Presbyterians, Quakers, Dunkards, Seventh-day Baptists, Regular Baptists, and Separate Baptists. As a gentleman, an Anglican, and an Englishman, Woodmason had little initial sympathy or understanding of backcountry residents or their religious habits.

Over time, Woodmason became a supporter of the Regulator movement, whose participants in 1768 protested the backcountry's lack of political and judicial representation. The longer he lived among the backcountry's inhabitants, the more Woodmason supported them and worked for their improvement. He labored for the relief of the poor, the needy, the stranger, the traveler, the sick, and the orphan. He was committed to the advancement of religion, the good of the church, and the suppression of idleness, beggary, profaneness, and lewdness. With the Separate Baptists outgrowing the Anglicans, Woodmason moved to Virginia in 1773 and then to Maryland. Later, in 1774, he returned to England and sought aid as a Loyalist refugee. After November 1776 nothing is known about him, including his death and place of burial. Woodmason's major literary contribution is his *Journal of C. W. Clerk, Itinerant Minister in South Carolina, 1766, 1767, 1768,* in which he accurately described life in the backcountry and defended the Regulators. DONALD S. ARMENTROUT

Woodmason, Charles. *The Carolina Backcountry on the Eve of the Revolution: The Journal and Other Writings of Charles Woodmason, Anglican Itinerant.* Edited by Richard J. Hooker. Chapel Hill: University of North Carolina Press, 1953.

Woodrow, James (1828–1907). Scientist, educator, college president. Born in Carlisle, England, on May 30, 1828, James Woodrow, son of Reverend Thomas Woodrow and Marion Williamson, moved with his family to Chillicothe, Ohio, in 1837. After graduating in 1849 with highest honors from Jefferson College in Canonsburg, Pennsylvania, and teaching in academies in Alabama, in 1853 he became a professor at Oglethorpe University in Georgia. In the summer of 1853 Woodrow studied under Louis Agassiz at Harvard and then used a leave of absence to study at Heidelberg, receiving his Ph.D. in 1856. On August 4, 1857, he married Felie S. Baker, daughter of a Georgia clergyman. Declining an offer to lecture at Heidelberg, Woodrow returned to Oglethorpe, teaching there until 1861. While at Oglethorpe, he studied Hebrew and theology and eventually became an ordained Presbyterian minister.

During the Civil War, Woodrow was chief of the Confederacy's chemical laboratory in Columbia. In 1861 he accepted the newly founded "Perkins Professorship of Natural Sciences in Connexion with Revelation" at Columbia Theological Seminary, a Presbyterian institution. Woodrow edited and published the *Southern Presbyterian Review,* a quarterly journal, from 1861 until 1885 and the *Southern Presbyterian,* a weekly periodical, from 1865 until 1893. He also operated a commercial printing business. In addition to teaching at the seminary, he was a professor (1869–1872, 1880–1897) at South Carolina College, where he later served as president from 1891 to 1897.

Despite possessing superb scientific credentials, Woodrow in his chief publications dealt with religious topics. He became embroiled in a dispute that developed in the Presbyterian Church in 1884 and attracted nationwide interest. Even though he had not accepted Darwinism, some influential Presbyterians considered him suspect in that regard. As a result, the seminary's board of directors asked him to publish his views on evolution. Woodrow reviewed the evidence and changed his position. In May 1884 he gave an address in support of Darwinian theory, and it was published in the *Southern Presbyterian Review* (July 1884). In September 1884 the board debated the way to handle the presentation of such ideas in the seminary. Woodrow won the first battle in what became known as the "Woodrow War." Nevertheless, conservatives in the church persisted in their attempts to have him removed, and he was dismissed from his professorship in December 1884. Reinstated in December 1885, Woodrow was again dismissed by the board in December 1886. Woodrow appealed to the Southern Presbyterian Church's highest court, the General Assembly, which rejected his plea in May 1888. The Woodrow War did not influence his standing in the church, had no effect on his faculty position at South Carolina College, and was not an issue when he was chosen president of the college in 1891. He was awarded four honorary degrees, and in 1914 a new dormitory was named for him at the University of South Carolina. Survived by his wife and three daughters, Woodrow died on January 17, 1907, and was buried in Elmwood Cemetery in Columbia. WILLIAM D. ANDERSON, JR.

Anderson, William D., Jr. "Andrew C. Moore's 'Evolution Once More': The Evolution-Creationism Controversy from an Early 1920s Perspective." *Bulletin* [Alabama Museum of Natural History] 22 (November 2002): iii–iv, 1–35.

Eaton, Clement. "Professor James Woodrow and the Freedom of Teaching in the South." *Journal of Southern History* 28 (February 1962): 3–17.

Elder, Fred Kingsley. "James Woodrow." *South Atlantic Quarterly* 46 (October 1947): 483–95.

Sanders, Albert E., and William D. Anderson, Jr. *Natural History Investigations in South Carolina from Colonial Times to the Present.* Columbia: University of South Carolina Press, 1999.

Woodruff (Spartanburg County; 2000 pop. 4,229). Located at the intersection of S.C. Highway 101 and State Road 50 in southern Spartanburg County, the junction that became the town of Woodruff originated at the meeting of the Buncombe Road, which ran from Charleston to the mountains, and the Georgia Road. In 1787 Joseph Woodruff, his brothers, and other family were listed as members and deacons in the earliest minutes of the Church of Christ at Jamey's Creek, which would later become Woodruff Baptist Church. As early as 1789 Woodruff purchased two hundred acres of land on Jamey's Creek, including the present site of Woodruff. By 1825 Woodruff post office (which took its name from the postmaster Thomas Woodruff, Joseph's son) and Woodruff's Tavern dominated the crossroads.

Situated in the midst of an expanding cotton region, Woodruff developed as a trade center for the rural farming communities. By the 1850s the town was hosting substantial fairs for the exchange of livestock and domestic manufactures. Woodruff was incorporated in 1874 with a population estimated at 150, but with the coming of the railroad in 1885 the population had grown to an estimated 1,600 by 1886. As a terminus on the rail line, the station at Woodruff included a turntable that would return trains to Augusta, Georgia.

A fair that began in the 1870s grew into a major annual event by the 1890s, drawing visitors from as far away as North Carolina. During the 1880s and 1890s construction steadily progressed along Main Street, with the popular Leatherwood Hotel as the focal point. Industry came to town in 1898 with the arrival of Woodruff Cotton Oil Company, and within three years the newly chartered Woodruff Cotton Mill began operation. By 1907 the W. S. Gray Cotton Mill was established, further expanding Woodruff's residential base with additional mill houses. Until World War II the major diversion from textiles in the area was peaches, with more than 200,000 trees within a ten-mile radius. During the 1950s, with industries settling near large cities, Woodruff saw a four percent drop in population. But with the 1962 opening of the Jeffery Manufacturing Company, an industrial equipment maker, the town's industrial base grew and diversified. New jobs attracted residents, and Woodruff's population reached 4,576 by 1970.

Woodruff probably gained its greatest recognition in the postwar decades due to the success that the coach W. L. "Willie" Varner brought to Woodruff High School athletics, especially football. Under Coach Varner, the Wolverines won ten state football championships.

A change to a council/manager city government coincided with revitalization efforts in the mid-1980s to combat revenue shortfalls brought on by a stagnant local economy. This resulted in an eight percent drop in population between 1970 and 2000. In 2001, however, grant funding initiated a $1.1 million revitalization of downtown to replace sidewalks, add decorative lighting, and bury overhead wires. STEVE RICHARDSON

Irby, Hannah Burton. *Woodruff: An Historical View.* N.p., 1974.

Woods, Sylvia Pressley (b. 1926). Restaurateur, author, businesswoman. Woods was born in Brooklyn, New York, on February 2, 1926, the only child of Van and Julia Pressley. Her father died three days later, and Sylvia and her mother moved to Hemingway, South Carolina, to live with her maternal grandparents on their thirty-five-acre farm. It was here that Woods learned to cook traditional southern and African American food.

Sylvia married Herbert Woods in Hemingway on January 18, 1944. They started a family, which would eventually grow to include four children, and she owned a beauty parlor. In 1950 the family moved to Harlem, and in 1954 she began waiting tables at Johnson's Restaurant. Eight years later she bought the eatery with a $20,000 loan from her mother, who mortgaged the family farm to raise the money, and renamed it Sylvia's.

Sylvia's became a popular neighborhood restaurant, but it was not until *New York* magazine's food critic Gael Greene wrote a 1979 article dubbing Woods "the queen of soul food" that the business gained worldwide attention. Her simple southern dishes—many of which were created by Hemingway native Ruth Gully, who ran the restaurant's kitchen from 1975 until her death in 1995—attracted throngs of tourists each year and have spawned a multi-million-dollar empire, Sylvia Woods Enterprises. The company includes the Harlem restaurant, an Atlanta branch, cookbooks, and a successful line of packaged food products sold in stores across the country.

By the early twenty-first century Wood's four children ran the business, and she divided her time between Hemingway and Harlem (Herbert Woods died in June 2001). Her 1999 cookbook, *Sylvia's Family Soul Food Cookbook,* is an homage to her childhood in Hemingway, a town that, she wrote, "has more great cooks per square inch than you would find in most cooking schools." BRUCE LANE AND SCOTT WYATT

Woods, Sylvia. *Sylvia's Family Soul Food Cookbook: From Hemingway, South Carolina, to Harlem.* New York: Morrow, 1999.

Woods, Sylvia, and Christopher Styler. *Sylvia's Soul Food: Recipes from Harlem's World-Famous Restaurant.* New York: Morrow, 1992.

Woodside, John Thomas (1864–1946). Textile mill owner, entrepreneur. Woodside was born in Greenville County on May 9, 1864, the son of John Lawrence Woodside, a prominent landowner, and Ellen Permelia Charles. As a merchant, manufacturer, banker, and real estate developer, Woodside personified South Carolina's transformation to a modern economy. He grew up working on his father's farm in Woodville, near the southern tip of Greenville County. The elder Woodside also owned a general store and served the area with a gristmill, saw mill, tannery, and cotton gin. Ellen Woodside was one of the area's leading churchwomen, founding Lickville Presbyterian Church in 1882.

Woodside received his education first under private tutors and later at a nearby school. In 1883 he left home to teach school in Greer. The following year he went to work for his uncle at the Reedy River Factory, a cotton mill south of Greenville. He remained there seven years and gained experience in every aspect of cotton manufacturing. In 1891 Woodside struck out on his own and opened a grocery store in Pelzer. He moved to Greenville in 1894 and opened another grocery store on Main Street. On April 25, 1894, he married Lou A. Carpenter. The marriage produced no children.

In upstate South Carolina, textile mills were the order of the day. Woodside followed the lead of several other local entrepreneurs and built Woodside Mill in Greenville's west-side industrial district. He began operations with eleven thousand spindles in 1902. The mill was an instant success and underwent several expansions in the following decade. Woodside also purchased additional plants in Easley, Liberty, Simpsonville, and Fountain Inn, merging them into a single firm, Woodside Cotton Mills, in 1911. In 1912 he expanded Woodside Mill to 112,000 spindles, making it the largest complete cotton mill under one roof in America.

Woodside Cotton Mills was the centerpiece of John T. Woodside's entrepreneurial empire. Courtesy, South Caroliniana Library, University of South Carolina

In addition to textile manufacturing, Woodside ventured into banking and real estate. He established the Farmers and Merchants Bank in 1907 and eventually served as director of five upstate banks. In 1923 he constructed his Greenville headquarters, the seventeen-story Woodside Building. In 1926 Woodside purchased 66,000 acres in Horry County, where he began the first large-scale development along the Grand Strand. He completed a championship golf course and the Ocean Forest Hotel in Myrtle Beach in 1929.

The 1929 crash on Wall Street devastated Woodside's fortune. Within five years his banks failed, his Myrtle Beach venture collapsed, and he lost control of Woodside Cotton Mills to creditors. He spent the remainder of his life in Greenville in modest circumstances and largely forgotten. Unique among his fellow textile manufacturers, Woodside completed an extensive autobiography, although it was not published. Woodside died in Greenville on January 5, 1946. JAMES A. DUNLAP III

Dunlap, James A., III. "Victims of Neglect: The Career and Creations of John T. Woodside, 1865–1986." Master's thesis, University of South Carolina, 1986.

Huff, Archie Vernon, Jr. *Greenville: The History of the City and County in the South Carolina Piedmont.* Columbia: University of South Carolina Press, 1995.

Woodside, John T. Autobiography. Southern Historical Collection, University of North Carolina, Chapel Hill.

Woodside Building (Greenville). The Woodside Building was constructed on Main Street in Greenville in 1923. At seventeen stories, it was Greenville's first skyscraper and the tallest building in either North or South Carolina. It served as banking headquarters for the entrepreneur John T. Woodside, a central figure in the upstate cotton mill boom. In 1929 a local observer described the Woodside Building as a "silent sentinel that bespeaks for Greenville's enterprise." The neoclassical structure with its white marble exterior stood as a Greenville landmark for a half-century. The marble lobby contained Ionic columns and French plate mirrors, while a rooftop garden offered a splendid vista of the upcountry metropolis. At Christmas, office lights were left burning on each floor so that the illuminated windows formed a cross on all four sides. For two generations the windows "became as much a part of the Christmas tradition as breaking out the family ornaments." The South Carolina National Bank purchased the Woodside Building in 1950. The large, round letters "SCN" placed along the roof became an additional city landmark.

By 1974 two modern structures overshadowed the Woodside Building. The Daniel Building, a gleaming monument to the construction magnate Charles E. Daniel, was the architectural expression of a new age of "soaring aspirations . . . far from the fields of cotton and the 'mill towns' of the early twentieth century." The new Greenville City Hall had a dark bronze facade that bore a striking resemblance to Manhattan's Seagram Building. By contrast, the Woodside Building seemed hopelessly out of date. The structure was demolished in 1974 to make way for a new building for South Carolina National Bank. JAMES A. DUNLAP III

Dunlap, James A., III. "Victims of Neglect: The Career and Creations of John T. Woodside, 1865–1986." Master's thesis, University of South Carolina, 1986.

Marsh, Kenneth Frederick, and Blanche Marsh. *The New South: Greenville, South Carolina.* Columbia, S.C.: R. L. Bryan, 1965.

Woodward, Henry (ca. 1646–ca. 1686). Physician, Indian agent. Woodward was among the earliest English settlers of South Carolina. Little is known about his formative years, although he was apparently well educated. In the summer of 1666, the young Woodward was a part of the expedition of Robert Sandford, who came to Port Royal to explore the region for the Lords Proprietors. When Sandford left, Woodward remained among the tribes there, studying the culture of its peoples and learning their language. A Spanish expedition learned of his presence, however, and captured Woodward, imprisoning him in St. Augustine. When the English privateer Robert Searle attacked that city in 1668, Woodward escaped and sailed with Searle as a ship's surgeon. Around 1669 he married a woman known only as Margaret.

Woodward returned to South Carolina by 1670, where the proprietors, particularly Lord Ashley, valued him as a highly useful agent, Indian trader, and diplomat. In 1670 he helped to negotiate support from surrounding Indians against a possible conflict with the Spanish. For his services, the proprietors rewarded him with a gift of £100. He also undertook secret missions at the behest of Lord Ashley Cooper and Governor Sir John Yeamans to explore the frontier for precious metals and potential Indian trading partners.

In the spring of 1674 the proprietors directed him to establish peaceful relations and regular trade with either the Cussitaws or the Westos, for which he would receive one-fifth of the profit. That autumn Woodward traveled with a visiting group of Westos to their village on the Savannah. The visit opened a lucrative trade in skins and slaves, and the ensuring treaty with the Westos opened the way for the expansion of English settlement beyond Charleston. From a military standpoint, the Westos were to provide support against attacks launched from Spanish Florida. In 1680 a group of southeastern tribes, including the Westos, launched attacks into Spanish territory under English direction. As a direct result of the relationship, the Westos became the most heavily armed tribe in the Southeast, free to terrorize other Indians for the ever-lucrative slave trade. Warfare among Indians continued and by 1680 degenerated into the Westo War, which ultimately destroyed that nation. Woodward was fined by the government for providing the Westos with weapons (which they later used against pro-English tribes), and he was subsequently censured by the proprietors. He traveled to England to defend his actions, however, and was pardoned. Returning to Carolina, he resumed his position as Indian agent.

In 1681 Woodward married a wealthy member of the South Carolina elite, Mary Godfrey. The marriage produced three children. The following year the Lords Proprietors commissioned Woodward to explore the backcountry of Carolina and to find a passage through the bordering Appalachian Mountains. In the summer of 1685 Woodward made contact with the Lower Creeks, previously allied with the Spanish. He forged an alliance with this nation, much to the displeasure of the Spanish, who scoured the backcountry for Woodward. He returned to Charleston in 1686 gravely ill and accompanied by a large party of Creeks. Woodward died sometime before March 1690. MICHAEL P. MORRIS

Crane, Verner. *The Southern Frontier, 1670–1732.* Durham, N.C.: Duke University Press, 1928.

Salley, Alexander S. *Narratives of Early Carolina 1650–1708.* New York: Scribner's, 1911.

Woodward, Isaac, beating of (February 1946). Isaac Woodward was discharged on February 12, 1946, after four years of active army service. A native of Winnsboro, Woodward was returning from Camp Gordon, Georgia, to his hometown when he got into an argument with the driver of his bus after requesting a stop to use the restroom. When the bus pulled into Batesburg, South Carolina, the driver asked two local police officers to take Woodward into custody for his "very abusive" attitude. Officer Elliot Long and Police Chief Lynwood L. Shull later testified that Woodward was drunk and had resisted arrest for disorderly conduct. In a scuffle with the officers, Woodward had tried to defend himself by taking the chief's nightstick. "I hit him across the front of the head," Chief Shull later recalled, "after he attempted to take away my blackjack."

According to Woodward, he had been trying to explain his argument with the bus driver when the Batesburg officers told him to "shut up" and began beating him with their blackjacks. He admitted having taken Shull's nightstick in the struggle but said that he had been forced to drop it when the other officer pulled his pistol. Woodward alleged that the officers tried to gouge out his eyes as retribution for his resisting arrest. In court the next day, he denied that he had been drinking or that he had instigated the argument with the bus driver. The court sentenced him to pay a $50 fine or serve thirty days in jail, and then he was taken to the Veterans' Administration hospital in Aiken, where he was treated for bleeding in both eyeballs and a ruptured cornea in the right eye. The beating left him blind for the remainder of his life.

On learning of the attack on a black veteran, Walter White, the head of the National Association for the Advancement of Colored People (NAACP), petitioned President Harry Truman and the Justice Department to redress Woodward's grievances and pursue criminal charges against the Batesburg officers. A benefit for Woodward, hosted by heavyweight boxing champion Joe Louis, was held in New York City in August. Several entertainers spoke or performed, including Woody Guthrie, who penned and sang "The Blinding of Isaac Woodward" for the event.

The Justice Department eventually filed a suit against Chief Lynwood Shull for violating Isaac Woodward's civil rights, but an all-white federal court jury in Columbia took just thirty minutes to return a verdict of not guilty in November 1946. A civil suit filed the next year was also unsuccessful, but Woodward took the money raised from the benefit concert and moved to New York to start a new life.

Woodward's case gained national recognition as one of several incidents of racial discrimination against black veterans returning from service after World War II. These incidents and the important contributions of African Americans during the war inspired the NAACP's "Double V" campaign for victory over oppression abroad and at home at the conclusion of the war. STEVE ESTES

Hampton, Henry, Steve Fayer, and Sarah Flynn. *Voices of Freedom: An Oral History of the Civil Rights Movement from the 1950s through the 1980s.* New York: Bantam, 1990.

O'Brien, Gail Williams. *The Color of the Law: Race, Violence, and Justice in the Post–World War II South.* Chapel Hill: University of North Carolina Press, 1999.

Wynn, Neil A. *The Afro-American and the Second World War.* Rev. ed. New York: Holmes & Meier, 1993.

Workman, William Douglas, Jr. (1914–1990). Journalist, author. Workman was born on August 10, 1914, in Greenwood, the son of William D. Workman and Vivian Watkins. Following his 1935 graduation from the Citadel, he was a reporter for the *News and Courier* in Charleston. On June 10, 1939, he married Rhea Thomas of Walterboro. They had two children. Workman entered the U.S. Army in 1941 and was on active duty for five years during World War II.

William D. Workman campaigning for the U.S. Senate in 1962. Courtesy, Modern Political Collections, University of South Carolina

After military service, Workman returned to the *News and Courier* and was the paper's Columbia-based capital correspondent from 1946 until 1962. By the late 1950s, as a result of his reporting on government, politics, and racial issues throughout the South; his widely syndicated columns; and his frequent appearances as a television commentator, his name recognition in the state was so great that his newspaper byline was simply his initials, "W.D.W." His conservative political attitudes were similarly known, especially with the 1960 publication of his first book, *The Case for the South,* which asserted his own views of the constitutionality and wisdom of maintaining racial segregation in the southern states.

In 1962 leaders of the state's fledgling Republican Party, especially J. Drake Edens, Jr., persuaded Workman to run as a Republican for the U.S. Senate seat held by Democrat Olin D. Johnston. South Carolina Republicans had only rarely nominated candidates for local office, much less statewide. Johnston, a staunch segregationist, was not directly vulnerable on the race issue. Consequently, Workman painted him as a supporter of President John F. Kennedy and intimated that a vote for Johnston was a vote for the invasion of Mississippi by federal troops. Johnston held on to win the election, but Workman's remarkable forty-four percent of the vote was a clear sign that the Republican Party in South Carolina had become a viable force.

Workman returned to journalistic duties when he joined the editorial department of the Columbia *State* in 1963, and he served as the paper's editor from 1966 to 1972. He remained with the *State* until his retirement in 1979. In 1982 Workman, to the surprise of friends and contrary to the advice of his 1962 campaign manager, Drake Edens, announced his candidacy for the Republican nomination for governor to face the Democratic governor Richard W. Riley. Suffering from a mild form of Parkinson's disease, Workman waged a lackluster campaign in which he acknowledged that there were few issues. Riley was overwhelmingly reelected, and Workman failed to win any of the state's forty-six counties.

The 1982 contest marked Workman's final quest for office, and thereafter his progressive illness began to worsen. He died in Greenville on November 23, 1990, and was buried in Greenlawn Memorial Park in Columbia. His obituary in the *State* called Workman "a singular influence in establishing a two-party political system in the state." NEAL D. THIGPEN

Merritt, Russell. "The Senatorial Election of 1962 and the Rise of Two-Party Politics in South Carolina." *South Carolina Historical Magazine* 98 (July 1997): 281–301.

Wickenberg, Charles, Jr. "Journalist, GOP Crusader William Workman Dies." Columbia *State,* November 24, 1990, pp. A1, A7.

Workman, William D., Jr. Papers. Modern Political Collections, South Caroliniana Library, University of South Carolina, Columbia.

World War I (1917–1918). When Congress declared war on Germany in April 1917, part of South Carolina was already on a war footing. Charleston buzzed with rumors and fear on February 1917 when a German freighter, interned since 1914, tried to block the Navy Yard channel. The ship's skeleton crew failed, and all were convicted and imprisoned. Inland, the cities of Greenville, Spartanburg, and Columbia had started lobbying for army training centers in their communities, for both economic and patriotic reasons. Led by Governor Richard I. Manning, this patriotic zeal grew stronger after the United States entered the war. However, not all of the state's leaders agreed with the nationalistic fervor. During the spring and summer of 1917, former governor Coleman Blease publicly spoke out against the war, trying to garner support among textile workers. His efforts drew few supporters.

More than 65,000 South Carolinians served in the armed forces, while others supported the war effort through liberty bond drives, home gardens, and meatless and wheatless days. Through the Women's Committee of the South Carolina State Council of Defense, many women made significant, but often unrecognized contributions. With the onset of war-time food shortages, the committee provided

A Liberty Loan parade in Spartanburg promoting the purchase of bonds to support the war effort. Courtesy, South Caroliniana Library, University of South Carolina

A platoon of the 188th Regiment, 30th (Old Hickory) Division in the streets of St. Martin-Rivière, France, October 1918. Courtesy, South Caroliniana Library, University of South Carolina

instructions on how to can and preserve foods and methods to grow "Liberty Gardens." Women also entered the workforce as young men went to war. A few joined the army nurse corps. Patriotism cut across racial boundaries in broad support of bond drives and the Red Cross.

The war revitalized the state's main livelihoods—agriculture and textiles. Total farm incomes in South Carolina rose from an average of $121 million in 1916 to $446 million during the war. The value of textile production doubled between 1916 and 1918, from $168 million to $326 million. New military installations also improved the economic outlook of many South Carolina communities. Camp Sevier in Greenville, Camp Jackson in Columbia, and the Charleston Navy Yard sparked large population increases, from the arrival of both armed forces personnel and civilian employees.

Portrait of an unknown black soldier from Calhoun County. Courtesy, Calhoun County Museum

However, most of the changes wrought by World War I in South Carolina would not survive the war. With Germany's surrender in November 1918, military and naval bases quickly demobilized, with most closed by the early 1920s. Only the Charleston Navy Yard and the Parris Island Marine installations remained active, but at severely reduced levels. These closings foreshadowed an economic tailspin throughout the state in other important areas. War-time food and cotton surpluses after 1918 saw farm prices drop precipitously. Cotton prices fell from a war-time high of 40¢ a pound to less than half that by the early 1920s. Textile mills slashed war-time wages, which mill hands protested in a series of massive, yet unsuccessful strikes. Although race relations had relaxed somewhat during the war, they regressed in the postwar period. Many returning African American servicemen were greeted with race riots across the United States, including one in Charleston in 1919. Segregation grew more pronounced, and opportunities for African Americans returned to the more limited prewar levels, leading to their mass exodus to northern cities in the following two decades. FRITZ HAMER

Hemmingway, Theodore. "Prelude to Change: Black Carolinians in the War Years, 1914–1920." *Journal of Negro History* 65 (summer 1980): 212–27.

Moore, John H. "Charleston in World War I: Seeds of Change." *South Carolina Historical Magazine* 86 (January 1985): 39–49.

South Carolina. Adjutant-General's Office. *Official Roster of South Carolina Soldiers, Sailors, and Marines in the World War, 1917–1918.* 2 vols. Columbia, S.C.: Joint Committee on Printing, 1929.

West, Elizabeth C. "'Yours for Home and Country': The War Work of the South Carolina Woman's Committee." *Proceedings of the South Carolina Historical Association* (2001): 59–68.

World War II (1941–1945). Prior to the entry of the United States into World War II, the depressed South Carolina economy had already started to recover. Federal money constructed or expanded military and naval installations across the state, including Camp Croft in Spartanburg, Fort Jackson in Columbia, the Charleston Navy Yard, and several smaller bases. Economic expansion centered in major urban centers. Large population increases occurred during the war years in Charleston County (thirty-three percent), Richland County (eleven percent), and Greenville County (three percent). But South Carolina's total population changed little from 1940 to 1944, remaining about 1,890,000. While thousands left the state for military duty or jobs in other states, an equal number of outsiders came to South Carolina.

The war brought a much-needed boost to South Carolina's agricultural sector, which had struggled since the early 1920s. Agricultural wages in the state more than doubled between 1939 and 1943

On completion of pilot training at Hawthorne field in Orangeburg, Thomas D. Hammond of rural Greenville County flew thirty-five missions in a B-17 bomber over Germany. Courtesy, James T. Hammond, Columbia, S.C.

as state farmers tried to keep up with war-time demands for cotton and produce. Despite the dramatic increase, farm wages in South Carolina still lagged behind those in the rest of the country, and many farmers faced significant labor shortages. These shortages were partially alleviated by employing German prisoners of war (POWs) on farms in such counties as Aiken, Greenwood, and Marlboro. Seasonal camps of from two hundred to four hundred POWs were constructed in these and other counties between 1943 and 1945, with a central camp for nearly two thousand prisoners placed at Fort Jackson in 1944.

In the textile industry, increases in production and the labor force occurred as manufacturers successfully met war-time production goals. Cotton consumption by textile mills increased more than sixty percent between 1939 and 1943. But heavy war industries, such as aircraft plants in Georgia and weapons plants in North Carolina, did not exist in South Carolina. The closest to such industries in the state was the Charleston Navy Yard, which produced more than three hundred medium-size and small vessels while repairing numerous others. Aiding the yard were small steelworks, such as Kline Iron and Steel in Columbia and Carolina Industries of Sumter, which built ship components and then delivered them to Charleston for assembly. Military bases across the state also gave employment to civilians, who provided services, repairs, and construction expertise.

Major Billy McNulty of Columbia fought with the First Marine Division on Peleliu, New Britain, and Guadalcanal in the South Pacific. Courtesy, Katherine McNulty Hubbard

Estimates are imprecise, but at least 900,000 men received military training in South Carolina during the war. More than 180,000 South Carolinians, including 2,500 women, entered the armed services. More were willing to serve, but forty-one percent of those examined statewide were rejected for various mental or physical problems, making the recruit rejection rate in South Carolina the second highest in the nation. Civilian defense began to organize in South Carolina more than a year before Pearl Harbor. By summer 1941 the State Council of Defense was soliciting 12,500 aircraft spotters for eight hundred posts across South Carolina. In the last months of the war, the council claimed that more than 250,000 South Carolinians had volunteered for duties ranging from serving as nurses' aides and salvage workers to providing war bond activities and aircraft spotting.

South Carolinians contributed to the war effort in other ways as well, especially through rationing. Tire rationing began less than a month after Pearl Harbor, with just 2,921 tires allotted the entire state for January 1942. Six months later gas rationing began on the East Coast, and many in South Carolina grumbled about bearing the brunt of this war measure. By 1943 the entire nation was under the same restrictions. This system reduced gas consumption for private cars to between three and four gallons every two weeks for the remainder of the war. In March 1943 nationwide food rationing began. Under the mandatory system coordinated through the federal Office of Price Administration, all canned and processed foods were severely rationed, as were red meat, sugar, and coffee. Foods exempted by the rationing board were fresh vegetables and fruits as well as seafood. Victory gardens were successfully promoted in cities and towns to supplement family needs, so that by 1943 more than 330,000 plots were reported across the state.

With housing rents rising even before Pearl Harbor, many cities and towns had to impose rent controls early in the war. While Columbia imposed them less than a year after the Japanese attack, the housing shortage in Charleston became so acute by 1940 that the navy established a city clearinghouse. This helped, but housing remained scarce and complaints grew that local landlords and residents were gouging the public. The housing shortage along with problems in food distribution and labor needs forced the federal government to list Charleston as one of eighteen cities in the nation considered Congested Production Areas that needed special assistance. Greenville and Spartanburg also faced shortages, but to a lesser degree.

Spann Watson of Johnston (second row, second from left) and Willie Ashley, Jr., of Sumter (second row, third from left) were among the 996 black pilots known as the Tuskeegee Airmen. Courtesy, Sumter County Museum and Archives

Amid war-time conditions, segregation laws came under pressure. The influx of non–South Carolinians with different ideas on social customs led to temporary changes, especially on military bases. Nevertheless, African Americans remained at the bottom rung of the social ladder. Although some minorities gained promotions to skilled jobs, most of these went to recent arrivals. Segregated United Service Organizations, restaurants, and movie houses remained standard throughout the war. When reports reached South Carolina congressmen about "violations" of southern traditions on military installations, those congressmen did not hesitate to protest. U.S. Senator Burnet Maybank wrote a strong objection to the captain of the Charleston Navy Yard after a constituent protested that blacks were working alongside whites and that some minorities were getting promotions above whites. Although segregation would remain entrenched in the early postwar period, seeds of change were planted during the war, particularly through landmark court decisions. In

1944 the federal district court ordered South Carolina to provide equal salaries to black and white teachers. In the same year, in the case of *Smith v. Allright,* the U.S. Supreme Court ruled the all-white primary unconstitutional. Politicians in the state, led by Governor Olin D. Johnston, fought these and subsequent court rulings, but African Americans in South Carolina were slowly but steadily gaining voting rights by the end of the war. Between 1940 and 1946 the number of registered African American voters in the state increased from fifteen hundred to fifty thousand.

As the war ended, most white South Carolinians expected prewar social customs to remain. These hopes were mixed with fears of an economic depression like the one that followed World War I. Fortunately, although some military bases closed and others downsized, the GI Bill helped maintain a strong economy by providing low-interest loans and free education to former servicemen. Thousands of veterans entered the University of South Carolina and other state schools in the immediate postwar years. As the cold war accelerated by the early 1950s, several bases on the verge of closing gained new life and expanded as the nation retooled to confront the threat of global communism. FRITZ HAMER

Callcott, W. H., ed. *South Carolina: Economic and Social Conditions in 1944.* Columbia: University of South Carolina Press, 1945.

Downey, Tom. "'The Situation Has Been Badly Fumbled': South Carolina's Response to Gas Rationing during World War II." *South Carolina Historical Magazine* 95 (April 1994): 156–71.

Hamer, Fritz. "A Southern City Enters the Twentieth Century: Charleston, Its Navy Yard, and World War II, 1940–1948." Ph.D. diss., University of South Carolina, 1998.

Moore, John H. "Nazi Troopers in South Carolina." *South Carolina Historical Magazine* 81 (October 1980): 306–15.

———. "No Room, No Rice, No Grits: Charleston's Time of Trouble, 1942–1944." *South Atlantic Quarterly* 85 (winter 1986): 23–31.

South Carolina. Adjutant-General's Office. *The Official Roster of South Carolina Servicemen and Servicewomen in World War II, 1941–1946.* 5 vols. Columbia, S.C., 1967–1972.

Springs, Holmes B. *Selective service in South Carolina, 1940–1947.* Columbia, S.C.: Vogue, 1948.

Wragg, William (ca. 1714–1777). Loyalist. Wragg was born in South Carolina, the son of Samuel Wragg and Marie DuBosc. His father was a prosperous merchant and influential member of the Royal Council. William benefited from his father's wealth and influence and was educated in England at Westminster, St. John's College, Oxford, and the Middle Temple. Called to the English Bar in 1733, he practiced law until he returned to South Carolina about the time of his father's death. In England he married Mary Wood, and the union produced one son. Mary Wragg died in 1767, and William married his cousin Henrietta Wragg on February 5, 1769. His second marriage produced four children.

When Samuel Wragg died in 1750, William inherited substantial property, including the 6,000-acre Ashley Barony, a Charleston townhouse, 6,900 acres on the Pee Dee River, and three plantations: River Settlement, Middle Settlement, and Wampee. In 1777 Wragg's estate included 7,100 acres and 256 slaves with an appraised value of £36,359 sterling.

Wragg continued his father's tradition of public service. Named to the Royal Council in 1753, he supported the council in its controversies with the Commons House over the tax bill. Wragg became the spokesman for the council and for the crown as the ultimate source of authority. Ironically, in an attempt to appease the Commons House, Governor William Henry Lyttleton asked the crown to suspend Wragg because of his vociferous support of the crown. On December 6, 1757, Wragg was suspended, and he was later removed.

In 1758 St. John's Colleton Parish elected Wragg to the Commons House of Assembly, where he would represent the parish until 1768. He declined further service because he did not support the Massachusetts and Virginia Resolutions. St. Helena's Parish elected him in 1773, but again he refused to serve. During his time in the Commons House, Wragg consistently supported the prerogatives of the British crown. He opposed the actions of the Stamp Act Congress. In 1769 he published "Reasons for Not Concurring in the Non-Importation Resolution" in the *South-Carolina Gazette.* He also protested the erection of a statue honoring William Pitt, suggesting one of King George III instead. In 1769 Wragg declined appointment as chief justice for South Carolina because he did not wish to profit from his devotion to the crown. He also declined reappointment to the Royal Council.

In 1775 Wragg refused to sign the Non-Importation Association or to recognize the authority of the Continental Congress. Confined to his plantation, Wragg refused to take an oath of abjuration in 1777. Banished from South Carolina, Wragg left his wife and daughters and sailed for Amsterdam in July. On September 2, 1777, his ship, the *Commerce,* foundered off the coast of Holland. Wragg drowned trying to save the life of his son.

The English honored Wragg's loyalty with a tablet in his memory—the first erected for an American. Now in Westminster Abbey, the inscription is a fitting tribute to his devotion to England: "In Him, Strong natural Parts, improved by Education, together with Love of Justice and Humanity, Formed the compleat character of A Good Man." ALEXIA JONES HELSLEY

Edgar, Walter B., and N. Louise Bailey, eds. *Biographical Directory of the South Carolina House of Representatives.* Vol. 2, *The Commons House of Assembly, 1692–1775.* Columbia: University of South Carolina Press, 1977.

Wright, Alice Buck Norwood Spearman (1902–1989). Human relations activist. Born in Marion on March 12, 1902, Wright was the first child of the banker Samuel Wilkins Norwood and Albertine Buck, granddaughter of one of South Carolina's largest slaveowners. After attending Marion private and public schools, Alice earned a bachelor of arts degree in history and literature from Converse College in 1923. Participation in student activities of the Young Women's Christian Association channeled her liberal Baptist religious beliefs into social service.

Wright taught school in South Carolina before moving to New York City in 1926. After earning a master's degree in religious education from Columbia Teachers' College and taking courses at the YWCA National Training School and Union Theological Seminary, she worked for the Germantown, Pennsylvania, YWCA. In 1930 she began a three-year journey around the world, attending conferences in England, the Soviet Union, India, and China and studying Asian culture in Japan. She also taught school in the Philippines and China. Through her contacts with cultured people of different races, she developed a cosmopolitan outlook.

Returning home, Wright became the first South Carolina woman appointed to administer a county relief program, in Marion. She set up relief during the 1934 strike of the United Textile Workers of America. Though she openly expressed sympathy for the strikers, her family's prominence prevented her from being fired. Promoted to district supervisor of eight counties, Wright later directed the

Alice Spearman Wright. Courtesy, Nichols Studio, 1311 Main Street, Newberry, S.C.

rural rehabilitation survey. Eventually she served as state supervisor of education for federal programs in adult and worker education.

In November 1936 Wright married Eugene H. Spearman and moved to his Newberry farm. They had one son. A partner in marriage, she helped her husband write his campaign speeches for the position of county supervisor. Drawn to civil rights, Wright in 1943 helped to organize the South Carolina Division of the Southern Regional Council (SRC). Needing a paying job in 1951, she became executive director of the South Carolina Federation of Women's Clubs and associate editor of *Clubwoman* magazine. Then, in October 1954, she was chosen executive director of the South Carolina Council on Human Relations, the new name of this SRC affiliate. Holding her position until 1967, she worked to build a biracial community committed to racial justice.

Wright's strategy was to encourage open discussion of the U.S. Supreme Court's 1954 *Brown v. Board of Education* decision. But she found that most whites, particularly clubwomen, closed their minds to desegregation during the state's massive resistance period. By 1963, however, the South Carolina Council and its Student Council on Human Relations helped prepare campus opinion for peaceful desegregation at Clemson College and the University of South Carolina. Under her direction the council participated in a Voter Education Project, encouraged compliance with the 1964 Civil Rights Act, and developed programs targeting illiteracy, lack of job skills, and rural and urban poverty. An appointee to the South Carolina Advisory Committee to the U.S. Civil Rights Commission, Wright in 1964 was awarded an honorary doctorate in humanities by Morris College in Sumter.

Wright showed that an upper-middle-class white woman could break free from the traditional feminine role and racial prejudices of her society. In 1970 she married the attorney and former Southern Regional Council president Marion A. Wright (Eugene Spearman had died in 1962). The North Carolina Civil Liberties Union bestowed the Frank P. Graham Award on Alice Spearman Wright in 1973. She died in Columbia on March 12, 1989. MARCIA G. SYNNOTT

"Alice N. Wright, worked to better human relations." Columbia *State,* March 13, 1989, p. A6.

Bass, Jack. "South Carolinian Doesn't Pussy-Foot about Life." *Charlotte (N.C.) Observer,* January 3, 1967, p. A8.

Synnott, Marcia G. "Alice Norwood Spearman Wright: Civil Rights Apostle to South Carolinians." In *Beyond Image and Convention: Explorations in Southern Women's History,* edited by Janet Lee Coryell et al. Columbia: University of Missouri Press, 1998.

Wright, Elizabeth Evelyn (1872–1906). Educator. Wright was born in Talbotton, Georgia, on April 3, 1872, the seventh of twenty-one children born to the African American carpenter John Wesley Wright and his full-blooded Cherokee wife, Virginia Rolfe. She spent her youth in a three-room cabin built by her father and learned to read at an all-grades school held in a church basement. At age sixteen she read a flyer about the Tuskegee Institute, founded in Alabama by Booker T. Washington to provide African Americans with vocational skills aimed at improving economic opportunities. After scraping together enough money for train fare, she arrived at Tuskegee in 1888 as a night student who would pay her way by working on campus during the day. After two years at Tuskegee, she moved to McNeill's, a sawmill town in Hampton County, South Carolina, to help in a school for rural African Americans founded by Tuskegee trustee Almira S. Steele. When the school was burned down by local white citizens, Wright returned to Tuskegee to graduate. She then moved back to South Carolina, determined to start an institution that would replace the school in McNeill's.

Several of Wright's lowcountry schools fell victim to white arsonists and to the objections of county and state education officials. She managed to find funding by campaigning at local churches and tapping northern benefactors willing to support education for African Americans. In 1895, determined to teach basic math and literacy to mill and farm workers, she founded in Hampton County the state's first night school for African American men. Although she later organized two additional all-grades schools for African Americans in Hampton County, her goal was a large institute on the Tuskegee model, with acreage enough for a demonstration farm.

In 1897 Wright relocated to the town of Denmark, opened a school over a grocery store, and began raising money for her larger venture, Denmark Industrial Institute. Her most generous benefactor was Ralph Voorhees of Clinton, New Jersey, who provided $5,000 for the purchase of 280 acres and construction of a schoolhouse. Voorhees Industrial School opened its first building to African American male and female students from elementary to high school ages in 1902. By 1903 the student population numbered 252. They learned math, reading, and writing, as well as farming, cooking, sewing, cleaning, leather working, carpentry, and other vocational skills. In a February 18, 1904, letter to Booker T. Washington, Wright summarized her curricular motivations: "As most of the people in the South live by tilling the soil, if they have a knowledge of agriculture they will soon become independent men."

Wright married Tuskegee graduate Martin A. Menafee in 1906. Within a month she became terminally ill with intestinal problems that had plagued her since childhood. She traveled to Battle Creek, Michigan, for surgery and died there on December 14, 1906. In 1929 Voorhees Industrial School opened a junior college, which became the first junior college for African Americans to be accredited by the Southern Association of Colleges and Schools. It later became Voorhees College, a private four-year college. KATHERINE REYNOLDS CHADDOCK

Coleman, J. *Tuskegee to Voorhees.* Columbia, S.C.: R. L. Bryan, 1922.

Morris, J. Kenneth. *Elizabeth Evelyn Wright, 1872–1906: Founder of Voorhees College.* Sewanee, Tenn.: University of the South Press, 1983.

Wright, Jonathan Jasper (1840–1885). Attorney, legislator, jurist. Wright was born in Luzerne County, Pennsylvania, on February 11, 1840, the son of Samuel Wright, a runaway slave, and his wife, Jane. He was raised on a family farm in Springville, Pennsylvania, and came under the influence of a local minister and antislavery advocate, Dr. William Wells Pride. Wright studied privately with Pride for three years and thereafter attended Lancasterian Academy near Ithaca, New York, graduating in 1860. Wright then began teaching, first in Montrose and later in Wilkes-Barre, Pennsylvania. In addition to his teaching duties, Wright began reading law.

Wright's first attempt in 1864 to be licensed to practice law in Pennsylvania was rebuffed, apparently due to his race. He then took a position with the American Missionary Association teaching black federal soldiers, many recently freed slaves, stationed on the Sea Islands near Beaufort, South Carolina. Wright arrived in April 1865 and soon became involved in the civic and political affairs of the community. He returned briefly to Pennsylvania in 1866 in a successful effort to be licensed to practice law, making him the first black attorney in that state. He returned to South Carolina in January 1867 as an employee of the Freedman's Bureau, officially described as an "agent assisting free people in legal affairs." As such, Wright became the first black attorney to practice in South Carolina.

Wright returned to South Carolina just as the state's black majority was poised to receive the right to vote. He was elected a delegate and a vice chair of the 1868 constitutional convention. Wright was a vocal and successful advocate of constitutional provisions for public education and a broad homestead exemption. Wright's prominent role in the state constitutional convention won him wide praise. After narrowly losing the Republican nomination for lieutenant governor at the party's 1868 convention, Wright was elected to the state Senate from Beaufort County, making him among the state's first African American legislators.

When an opening occurred on the state's supreme court in 1870, Wright found broad support for his candidacy across party lines. Elected by the General Assembly as an associate justice on February 1, 1870, Wright became the first black man elected to a state or federal appellate judgeship in the United States. His election sparked celebration in the state's black community, and the *Charleston Daily News* observed that Wright now sat in "the highest position held by a colored man in the United States."

Wright served on the court for nearly seven years and wrote some ninety opinions. Most dealt with routine legal matters, but several notable cases addressed legal issues arising out of slavery or claims related to the recently concluded war. In one decision Wright recognized the liability of a railroad for the racially discriminatory act of its employee, and in another opinion he voided the corporate charter of a company incorporated during the war as a blockade-runner because this was "an act of hostility to the United States."

Wright's tenure on the court ended following the election of the Democrat Wade Hampton as governor. The election disputes eventually reached the state's supreme court, and Wright angered Hampton supporters when he issued an opinion refusing to recognize Hampton's legal status as governor. One Democratic newspaper wrote that Wright had made an "ass of himself. . . . Condemn him!" Shortly after Democrats began impeachment proceedings against him, Wright resigned from the court in August 1877.

Wright moved to Charleston, where he opened a law practice at 84 Queen Street and trained young lawyers in his office as the chair of the Claflin College law department. He encountered significant health problems with tuberculosis, however, and died on February 19, 1885. He was buried in the cemetery of the Calvary Episcopal Church, Charleston. RICHARD MARK GERGEL

Gergel, Richard, and Belinda Gergel. "'To Vindicate the Cause of the Downtrodden': Associate Justice Jonathan Jasper Wright and Reconstruction in South Carolina." In *At Freedom's Door: African American Founding Fathers and Lawyers in Reconstruction South Carolina,* edited by James Lowell Underwood and W. Lewis Burke, Jr. Columbia: University of South Carolina Press, 2000.

Woody, R. H. "Jonathan Jasper Wright, Associate Justice of the Supreme Court of South Carolina, 1870–77." *Journal of Negro History* 18 (April 1933): 114–31.

Wright, Louis Booker (1899–1984). Historian, library administrator. Wright was born on March 1, 1899, in the crossroads village of Phoenix in Greenwood County, the son of Thomas F. Wright, a country schoolmaster, and Lena Booker. He studied chemistry at Wofford College (B.A., 1920) and English literary history at the University of North Carolina, Chapel Hill (M.A., 1924; Ph.D., 1926). He was a newspaper correspondent and an editor of the Greenwood *Index-Journal* before turning to the academic life. After graduate school, he remained at Chapel Hill as an instructor and associate professor of English; then he became a member of the research staff of the Huntington Library in San Marino, California. He remained at the Huntington Library until 1948, when he was appointed director of the Folger Shakespeare Library in Washington, D.C., whence he retired in 1968. During his tenure at the Folger Library, he arranged major acquisitions of rare early imprints and the library became a world-class research institution.

Wright was a superb scholar and a prolific writer whose graceful style made the prodigious research that went into his articles, which were published in professional journals, appear deceptively easy. Perhaps his best books were *Middle-Class Culture in Elizabethan England* (1935) and *Gold, Glory, and the Gospel: Adventurous Lives and Times of Renaissance Explorers* (1970). He was coeditor (with Elaine W. Fowler) of *West and by North: North America Seen through Eyes of Its Seafaring Discoverers* (1971) and *Moving Frontier: North America Seen through Eyes of Its Pioneer Discoverers* (1972). He was also author of a charming pair of memoirs: *Barefoot in Arcadia: Memories of a More Innocent Era* (1974), about coming of age in South Carolina; and *Of Books and Men* (1976). In addition he wrote *South Carolina: A Bicentennial History* (1976). His paperback annotated editions of Shakespeare's works were for many years standard fare for high school and college students. He served as associate editor of the *Journal of the History of Ideas* (1940–1955), *William & Mary Quarterly* (1944–1945), and *Pacific Spectator* (1947–1948). He frequently delivered distinguished lectures and occasionally served as resident scholar or as a visiting professor. He was a consultant historian of the National Geographic Society, chairman of the Guggenheim Memorial Foundation advisory board, vice chairman of the Council of Library Resources board of directors, a member of the board of directors of the Harry S. Truman Library Institute of National and International Affairs, and vice chairman of the board of the American Council of Learned Societies. Because of his prominent position in these learned societies, he influenced the course of scholarship in America for decades.

Wright was a member of the Modern Language Association of America, the American Historical Association, the American Philosophical Society, and the American Academy of Arts and Sciences, and he was a fellow of the Royal Historical Society. He was awarded twenty-nine honorary degrees from United States and foreign universities; Queen Elizabeth II made him an officer in the Order of the British Empire; and the Royal Society of Arts presented him with the Benjamin Franklin Gold Medal.

Wright married Frances Marion Black on June 10, 1925. They had one son. Wright died on February 26, 1984, at his home in Chevy Chase, Maryland. JACKSON C. BOSWELL

Wright, Mary Honor Farrow (1862–1946). Educator. Born into slavery on August 11, 1862, in Spartanburg, Wright was the youngest of three daughters of Lott and Adeline Farrow. She was educated by northern teachers who came south to teach Spartanburg's freed persons after the Civil War. Of them, Wright said, "They were Yankees, but they were not carpetbaggers. Their aim was to give the South something rather than to take away." Wright went on to study at the Asheville Normal School and the Scotia Seminary in Concord, North Carolina. She graduated from Claflin University. In August 1879 she accepted her first teaching position in Inman, where she held classes in a brush arbor. She later organized schools and taught in mill villages and churches in Spartanburg and Saxon.

In 1884 she married William Corbeth Wright, a house painter. They had ten children, two of whom died in infancy. She continued teaching after her marriage, and in 1904 she organized a school in her home for black children who were too young to walk to the nearest black school. This institution eventually became a public school, and Wright went on to become the leading black educator in Spartanburg during her sixty-four-year teaching career.

Wright was also active in professional and community activities. For over fifty years she served as chair of the Palmetto State Teachers Association Department of Primary Teachers (the state association for black teachers). She organized a first-aid school for African Americans during World War I. She also founded the Home for Aged Negro Women in Spartanburg. In 1925 she began the Charity Christmas Tree program for underprivileged black children. A member of Silver Hill Methodist Church, she was also an active member of the Household of Ruth and other mutual aid organizations. Wright was well respected by blacks and whites alike, as evidenced by the Spartanburg *Daily Herald*'s front-page tribute to her in June 1937.

Wright retired in 1943 at the age of eighty-one and died on August 25, 1946. Carrier Street School, the institution that began in her home, was later renamed Mary Wright Elementary School in her memory. MELISSA WALKER

Boler, Gail. "Mary Honor Farrow Wright." In *The Lives They Lived: A Look at Women in the History of Spartanburg,* edited by Linda Powers Bilanchone. Spartanburg, S.C., 1981.

Button, Jack. "Negro Teacher Has Won Respect of County through 58 Years of Service." Spartanburg *Daily Herald,* June 20, 1937, pp. 13, 24.

WSPA. WSPA in Spartanburg became South Carolina's first commercial radio station when it signed on the air at 6:45 P.M. on February 13, 1930. It was the beginning of many broadcasting "firsts" that would distinguish WSPA.

Over the years the station established a standard of providing diverse programming to its upstate audience. This was reflected from the first night when it broadcast a speech by Governor John G. Richards as well as musical performances by a classical violinist and a local yodeler live from its studios atop the Montgomery Building. In November 1931 WSPA was the first station in the state to broadcast play-by-play coverage of a sporting event, a football game between Spartanburg High School and Georgia Military Academy. By 1935 the station had established a commitment to upstate news coverage. Regularly scheduled live musical programming became a staple of WSPA. Earl Scruggs, one of country music's greatest banjo players and a member of the nationally known bluegrass group Flatt and Scruggs, played from the studios. The Blue Ridge Quartet and Arthur Smith and the Crackerjacks were also names synonymous with the station.

In 1977 CBS news anchor Walter Cronkite (with shovel) assisted Walter J. Brown (left), the founder and president of Spartan Radiocasting Company, with the groundbreaking for a new television facility in Spartanburg. Courtesy, Watson-Brown Foundation

WSPA launched the state's first FM station in 1947, and in 1958—combining both its AM and FM signals—aired the first broadcast in stereo. In 1961 WSPA FM became the first FM station in the Southeast to broadcast in true multiplex stereo. WSPA Television (Channel 7) went on the air on April 29, 1956. The station was the first in South Carolina to broadcast live in color from its studio. RUSS MCKINNEY, JR.

Jarrells, Ralph. "History of Broadcasting in South Carolina: WSPA, WCSC, and WIS." Unpublished manuscript. South Caroliniana Library, University of South Carolina, Columbia.

McNeely, Patricia G. *Fighting Words: The History of the Media in South Carolina.* Columbia: South Carolina Press Association, 1998.

XYZ Affair. When South Carolinian Charles Cotesworth Pinckney arrived in France in November 1796 to serve as his young country's minister to France, he immediately found himself embroiled in controversy between the two nations. The French—angered by the 1794 Jay Treaty, which brought improved relations between the United States and Great Britain—had begun to attack American merchant ships. After Pinckney's arrival, the French government continued to be hostile to the United States: France determined that it had no need for an American minister on its soil and demanded that Pinckney leave in January 1797.

When President John Adams learned of the troubles that Pinckney was facing, he appointed two commissioners to join Pinckney in France and attempt to defuse the situation: John Marshall and Elbridge Gerry. They met with the French minister of foreign relations, Charles Maurice de Talleyrand-Périgord, who was initially cordial to the three men but refused to negotiate with them in any official capacity. Instead, a series of unofficial envoys met with the American representatives. These envoys soon made it clear that the French government expected to be bribed in return for improved relations with the United States. Despite being rebuffed by the Americans, the French envoys persisted, and, in response to another demand for a bribe, Pinckney is claimed to have responded "NO! NO! Not a sixpense!"

Further negotiations were fruitless, and in the United States a firestorm of anger against France broke out when the dispatches from the American negotiators were published (the names of the French envoys were replaced with the letters *X, Y,* and *Z,* thus giving the scandal its name). Tensions remained high—in what historians term the "Quasi-War"—until a settlement with France was finally concluded in the Convention of 1800. AARON W. MARRS

Stinchcombe, William C. *The XYZ Affair.* Westport, Conn.: Greenwood Press, 1980.

Yamassee War (1715–1718). The Yamassee War was a major eighteenth-century conflict between the colony of Carolina and its trade partners the Yamassees. Based along the Savannah River, this tribe had established strong trade ties with Carolina, at first exchanging deerskins for trade items. As commercial hunters, however, the Yamassees and other tribes heavily depleted their deer supplies. Consequently, the Yamassees began raiding Florida tribes, such as the Apalachees, and trading those they kidnapped as slaves to Carolina merchants.

Governor Charles Craven and the Yamasee War. "The gruesome attack of the Indians on the English in Carolina, West Indies, on April 19, 1715, and some days after, in which action the Barbarians gruesomely tortured many human beings." Peter Schenk, Amsterdam, 1716. Courtesy, South Caroliniana Library

Unscrupulous traders overextended credit to tribes such as the Yamassees, hoping to force land concessions from them when they could not pay their trade bills. In 1707 the South Carolina government created the Board of Indian Commissioners to regulate trade and enforce fair trade practices. The board, however, and its Indian agent Thomas Nairne had little success in reining in the traders. The Yamassee trade debt continued to increase and eventually required at least two years' labor from every adult male Yamassee. The Yamassees were further angered by the intrusion of white settlers onto their lands.

In spring 1715 Charleston heard rumors of an uprising by the Yamassees. On April 14, 1715, William Bray, Samuel Warner, and Nairne met at Pocotaligo Town, southwest of modern Charleston, in an attempt to defuse the violence. Having exhausted their deer and slave supplies, the Yamassees decided to resolve their trade debt by killing their creditors and attacking white settlements along Carolina's southern frontier on Good Friday, April 15, 1715. Intending to kill not only their traders and creditors but most Euro-Americans in their area, they immediately killed Bray and Warner. Nairne died after several days of ritual torture. The Yamassees then struck against plantations near the coast.

Despite its name, the Yamassee War also involved the Cherokees, Creeks, and Choctaws in a far-ranging rebellion from the Savannah River to Charleston. Just as Nairne was put to death, other ally tribes, such as the Creeks, Choctaws, Apalachees, Saraws, Santees, and Waccamaws, also executed their traders, ninety percent of whom were killed by June 1715. Initial Yamassee attacks along plantations near Port Royal killed one hundred colonists. Some three hundred lucky planter families boarded a ship seized for smuggling and made their escape while the Yamassees attacked their farms and killed their livestock.

White inhabitants fled the countryside for the relative safety of Charleston. There colonists struggled to achieve a defense perimeter around the city. Charles Craven, the governor, utilized all white males and even armed black slaves for the colony's defense. Surrounding southern colonies sent little or no assistance, although Massachusetts did send weapons to South Carolina. Rumors swirled around the city that either the Spanish or the French had encouraged the uprising.

The turning point in the conflict came at the battles of Port Royal and Salkehatchie, where the Yamassees were defeated and driven south of the Savannah River. The Yamassee allies, however, remained a potent force. One historian described this alliance as the greatest in colonial American history because it could have destroyed the Carolinas and Virginia. The alliance continued to attack Carolina settlements until 1716, when the Carolinians managed to convince the Lower Cherokees to side with them against the Creeks, launching a deadly war between these two groups that continued for the next forty years.

The worst of the Yamassee War was over by April 1716, and South Carolina officials finally brought the conflict to a close by 1718. The damage inflicted by the war was tremendous. The former prosperity of the trade in deerskins was not reached again until 1722. Carolina farmers had been driven from half the cultivated land in the colony. Approximately four hundred settlers had been killed, and property damage stood at £236,000 sterling. Military costs to defend the colony rested at £116,000 sterling, more than three times the combined value of all exports. No English colony came as close to eradication by a native population as South Carolina did during the Yamassee War.

As a result of this trade-based war, South Carolina government assumed a direct monopoly over the Indian trade in 1716, replacing private Indian traders with government agents charged with obeying stringent new trade guidelines. A company of rangers was created to patrol the backcountry, and scout boats regularly sailed along the southern coastline of South Carolina. The failure of the Lords Proprietors to assist the colony in this time of crisis further added to the dissatisfaction with them and helped to hasten the demise of the proprietary regime in 1719. MICHAEL P. MORRIS

Crane, Verner. *The Southern Frontier.* Durham, N.C.: Duke University Press, 1928.

Edgar, Walter. *South Carolina: A History.* Columbia: University of South Carolina Press, 1998.
Hudson, Charles. *The Southeastern Indians.* Knoxville: University of Tennessee Press, 1976.
Moore, Alexander, ed. *Nairne's Muskhogean Journals: The 1708 Expedition to the Mississippi River.* Jackson: University of Mississippi Press, 1988.
Morris, Michael P. *The Bringing of Wonder: Trade and the Indians of the Southeast, 1700–1783.* Westport, Conn.: Greenwood Press, 1999.

Yarborough, William Caleb (b. 1940). Race-car driver. Born on March 27, 1940, in the Florence County town of Sardis, Yarborough is a National Association for Stock Car Auto Racing (NASCAR) legend with a driving career that lasted from 1957 to 1988. As of 2004 he was the only driver to win three consecutive Winston Cup Championships (1976–1978), and his eighty-three victories placed him fifth on the all-time win list. Yarborough had a reputation as one of the toughest, most aggressive drivers in the history of Winston Cup racing. The legendary driver and car owner Junior Johnson asserted that Yarborough was "a great competitor . . . I've seen him drive cars I couldn't believe he could drive—wrecked up, patched up, tore up, no way a human being could drive something like that—but he was tough and strong, did not give up, had an attitude that was unbelievable."

Cale Yarborough. Photograph by Dorsey Patrick. Courtesy, Yarborough Family

Yarborough craved adventure, even danger, from an early age. He once wrestled an alligator, was bitten by a rattlesnake, was struck by lightning, was shot accidentally, had considerable success as a Golden Gloves boxer and semiprofessional running back, and even fell out of an airplane (his parachute opened just in time to save his life). Yarborough's daredevil nature led him to early success on local dirt tracks. In 1957 he lied about his age and raced in his first Grand National (which became Nextel Cup in 2004) race, the Southern 500 at nearby Darlington, which later became the site of Yarborough's greatest career success—a record five victories.

Yarborough had his most productive years driving for Junior Johnson from 1973 to 1980. During that eight-year period Yarborough won fifty-five races—including the Daytona 500 and three victories in the Southern 500—won three consecutive Winston Cup championships, and finished second in the championship race three times.

However, Yarborough's most famous race ended not in a trip to victory lane but in an infield brawl. In the 1979 Daytona 500, Yarborough and Donnie Allison came into the final lap in a door-to-door battle. On the backstretch the two cars collided repeatedly, crashed into the third turn wall, and came to rest in the infield, opening the door for Richard Petty to claim the victory. CBS cameras, televising the race for the first time flag-to-flag, turned their attention away from Petty (as he headed for victory) and toward a fight that had erupted in the infield between Yarborough and the Allison brothers, Donnie and Bobby (Bobby had stopped to check on his younger brother). The excitement and drama of the race/fight brought national attention to an essentially regional sport and helped lay the groundwork for the later national popularity of NASCAR.

In 1981 Yarborough left Johnson for a part-time driving position with M. C. Anderson. Despite his success and fame, Yarborough longed to spend more time on his farm in Sardis with his wife Betty Jo and his three daughters. Even though he generally raced only half of the schedule over the next eight years, Yarborough still won an impressive fourteen races. In 1988 he retired as a driver, although he remained active as a race-car owner. DANIEL S. PIERCE

Higgins, Tom, and Steve Waid. *Junior Johnson: Brave in Life.* Phoenix, Ariz.: David Bull Publishing, 1999.
Yarborough, Cale, with William Neely. *Cale: The Hazardous Life and Times of America's Greatest Stock Car Driver.* New York: Times Books, 1986.

Yeamans, Sir John (1611–1674). Governor. Yeamans was born in Bristol, England, in 1611, a younger son of John Yeamans, a brewer. A Royalist soldier, Yeamans rose to the rank of colonel during the English Civil War (1642–51). In 1650 he joined other Royalists in immigrating to Barbados, where he became a large landowner, judge, and member of council. Yeamans's first wife, a daughter of a Mr. Limp, apparently died in Barbados in the late 1650s. Yeamans once held some land in Barbados in partnership with Benjamin Berringer. Before Berringer died under suspicious circumstances in January 1661, his wife Margaret Forster Berringer transferred her affections to Yeamans. The Barbadian Assembly was among those who thought that Yeamans had hired someone to murder Berringer. Yeamans married the new widow ten weeks later.

Eight English noblemen acquired Carolina as a proprietary colony in 1663. Soon thereafter Yeamans's eldest son, William, negotiated with the new proprietors to establish a Barbadian settlement there. The proprietors named John Yeamans governor of the projected settlement and arranged his elevation to the lesser aristocracy as a baronet. Sir John led the Barbadians to Cape Fear in 1665 but did not stay there long. The settlement was abandoned in 1667. When Anthony Ashley Cooper, who later became the first earl of Shaftesbury, convinced the other proprietors to send settlers from England in 1669, Yeamans was given the choice of becoming governor or naming another to lead the new settlement. Although he initially joined the settlers, he changed his mind and named for that task an aged Bermudan, William Sayle, who died a year later.

The proprietors' Fundamental Constitutions for their colony established a hereditary aristocracy of landgraves and cassiques and provided that the senior resident landgrave should become governor in the event of a vacancy. They named Yeamans as the third landgrave of Carolina in April 1671. When Yeamans belatedly came to South Carolina in the summer of that year, he claimed the office of governor. Interim governor Joseph West and the Grand Council initially rejected his claim, but they accepted Yeamans as governor when a proprietary commission arrived in April 1672.

The Grand Council had earlier opposed Yeamans's appointment with the argument that he had abandoned both the Cape Fear and South Carolina settlements to pursue his own interests. They noted that he departed the latter after a storm near Bermuda left it in "bleeding condition"—a result of the fact that the struggling colony was still dependent on imported provisions. In the slightly more than two years that he was governor, Yeamans sold food at inflated prices for his own profit. At the time he died, proprietary orders removing him from office were on their way across the Atlantic.

Yeamans died between August 3, when he was present at a meeting of the Grand Council, and August 14, 1674, when that body elected Joseph West as his temporary replacement. In addition to his second wife, Margaret, who returned to Barbados and remarried, Yeamans's will named eight children. CHARLES H. LESSER

Campbell, P[eter] F. *Some Early Barbadian History.* St. Michael, Barbados: by the author, 1993.

Cheves, Langdon, ed. *The Shaftesbury Papers and Other Records Relating to Carolina and the First Settlement on Ashley River prior to the Year 1676.* 1897. Reprint, Charleston, S.C.: Tempus, 2000.

Yellow fever. Yellow fever was one of the most dreaded diseases in South Carolina during the eighteenth and nineteenth centuries. Along with malaria, it helped establish the reputation of the South Carolina lowcountry as a dangerously unhealthy place for whites and was used to justify African slavery. Like malaria, yellow fever is transmitted by mosquitoes and strikes in warm weather. Unlike malaria, which spread over most of the state, yellow fever was largely restricted to seaports by the habits of the *Aedes aegypti* mosquito. Yellow fever is caused by a flavivirus. Its name derives from one of its common symptoms, a jaundice produced by the virus's attacks on the liver. Other symptoms include high fever, vomiting, exhaustion, convulsions, delirium, severe body aches, and bleeding from the nose, mouth, stomach, rectum, and skin. Gastric acid turns the blood in the stomach black, and when vomited it resembles coffee grounds, which led the Spanish to call the disease the "black vomit." Yellow fever generally runs its course in a week to ten days. Victims often die of kidney failure, but patients who survive are henceforth immune. As a result, in places where the disease is common most victims are newcomers or small children. Yellow fever's predilection for these victims gave rise to yet another name for the disease, "stranger's fever." Yellow fever kills many of the infected, but establishing accurate case mortality rates is extremely difficult. Many cases, especially among children, present mild symptoms and may not be diagnosed as yellow fever. Moreover, dengue fever and malaria, which have much lower case mortality rates, have often been misdiagnosed as yellow fever.

Yellow fever, like falciparum malaria, was introduced into South Carolina as a result of the African slave trade. The first major epidemic struck Charleston in 1699, killing about fifteen percent of the population, including many officials. At least five and perhaps as many as eight major epidemics occurred between 1706 and 1748. The disease was probably present in several other years as well. For several decades after 1748 no large epidemics occurred, although it appeared sporadically in some years. Between the 1790s and 1850s Charleston hosted numerous epidemics. The victims were primarily white "strangers": immigrants, travelers, upcountry folk, and children. Few "natives" of Charleston, black or white, died from the disease. Some antebellum proslavery writers misleadingly claimed that Africans were immune to yellow fever. This was not true, as modern epidemics in Africa attest, although some Africans may have inherited resistance to it. Although primarily a disease of seaport towns, yellow fever occasionally penetrated inland as far as Augusta, Georgia. Yellow fever was sporadically present in Charleston during the Civil War and killed about two hundred people there in 1871. The state's last recorded epidemic took place in Beaufort in 1878. Concern with yellow fever remained high until the early twentieth century, when the disease retreated from the United States altogether.

Yellow fever was dreaded not only for the horrible deaths it caused, but also because it could have a devastating impact on public business and commerce. Epidemics often prevented the sitting of the colonial assembly in the eighteenth century, and they had the potential of bringing trade to a virtual standstill for months. Because of the disease's economic impact and the need to establish an effective public policy to deal with it, theories about its origins and transmission aroused enormous controversy until 1900, when American army physicians in Cuba demonstrated the role of the mosquito as its vector. Before then, advocates of the idea that yellow fever was contagious and/or imported demanded strict quarantine regulations. Others, who argued that the disease was noncontagious and produced by heat acting upon accumulated filth, pressed for sanitary measures. Both ideas aroused opposition. Enforcing strict quarantine regulations to avoid an epidemic disrupted trade; but sanitary improvements were expensive and interfered with property rights. PETER MCCANDLESS

Carrigan, Jo Ann. "Yellow Fever: Scourge of the South." In *Disease and Distinctiveness in the American South,* edited by Todd L. Savitt and James Harvey Young. Knoxville: University of Tennessee Press, 1988.

Carter, Henry Rose. *Yellow Fever: An Epidemiological and Historical Study of Its Place of Origin.* Baltimore, Md.: Williams and Wilkins, 1931.

Harris, Tucker. "Facts and Observations, Chiefly Relative to the Yellow Fever, as It Has Appeared at Different Times, in Charleston, South Carolina." *Philadelphia Medical and Physical Journal* 2 (1805): 21–34.

Humphreys, Margaret. "Yellow Fever: The Yellow Jack" and "Dengue Fever: Breakbone Fever." In *Plague, Pox and Pestilence: Disease in History,* edited by Kenneth F. Kiple. London: Weidenfeld & Nicolson, 1997.

Kiple, Kenneth F., and Virginia H. Kiple. "Black Yellow Fever Immunities, Innate and Acquired, as Revealed in the American South." *Social Science History* 1 (summer 1977): 419–36.

Waring, Joseph I. *A History of Medicine in South Carolina.* 3 vols. Columbia: South Carolina Medical Association, 1964–1971.

Yellow jessamine. State flower. The yellow, or Carolina, jessamine (*Gelsemium sempervirens*) was chosen as state flower by the General Assembly in 1924. In 1923 the legislature appointed a commission to select a floral emblem. Senator Thomas B. Butler and Representatives George B. Ellison and Thomas Savage Heyward recommended the yellow jessamine to the senate and house on February 1, 1924, and it was promptly adopted by both chambers.

The legislators observed that the jessamine was "the unanimous selection of . . . the great majority of the ladies of the State who expressed a preference." Four specific reasons were given for the designation: "(1) It is indigenous to every nook and corner of the State. (2) It is the first premonitor of coming spring. (3) Its fragrance greets us first in the woodland and its delicate flower suggests the pureness of gold. (4) Its perpetual return out of the dead winter suggests the lesson of constancy in, loyalty to, and patriotism in the service of the State."

The yellow jessamine is a twining woody vine with pointed, evergreen leaves. It climbs over bushes, fences, and even tree limbs. Five-petaled, star-shaped yellow flowers bloom from February or March through early May, and the capsule-like fruit matures from September to November. It is common in the South Carolina Piedmont and Sandhills and in the coastal plain from Virginia to Florida, as well as west to Texas and Arkansas. All parts of the plant are poisonous, and even touching it can cause dermatitis. The drug gelsemium was formerly made from the plant and dispensed for the treatment of malaria, but overdoses could be fatal and it is no longer used. Sprigs of jessamine are etched on the steel blade of the Sword of State used by the South Carolina Senate. DAVID C. R. HEISSER

Causey, Beth G. "Yellow Jessamine." *Sandlapper* 3 (March 1970): 80.
Porcher, Richard D., and Douglas A. Rayner. *A Guide to the Wildflowers of South Carolina.* Columbia: University of South Carolina Press, 2001.

York (York County; 2000 pop. 6,985). The courthouse town of York was originally known as Fergus' Cross Roads, lying at the intersection of two stagecoach lines. The Fergus family operated a popular tavern at the site, but William Hill, the proprietor of an ironwork, owned the crossroads and a large tract of surrounding land. In 1786 Yorkville was laid out with the crossroads becoming Liberty and Congress Streets. In the early 1800s the name was changed to York, but the town was incorporated as Yorkville in 1849. The first intendant (mayor) was I. W. Clawson. In 1915 the name was changed back to York.

The earliest Europeans in the region were mostly Scots-Irish who came via Virginia and Pennsylvania. Yorkville served as the social center and market for antebellum York County's farmers and was also a popular site for lowcountry planters escaping the malarial season. Sometimes called the "Charleston of the Upcountry," antebellum Yorkville boasted macadamized streets and gas lighting, as well as a theater group and an opera house. In 1852 both the Rose Hotel and the Kings Mountain Railroad (which ran from Yorkville to Chester) were completed. A year later the Yorkville Female College began operation, and in 1855 Citadel graduates Micah Jenkins and Asbury Coward opened the Kings Mountain Military School. By 1861 only Charleston exceeded Yorkville in per capita income.

Yorkville's voters supported secession in 1860 and, while little military action took place in the region during the Civil War, the violence in York during Reconstruction was unparalleled in any other S.C. county. The Ku Klux Klan organized in Yorkville as early as 1868, and it took two companies of federal troops stationed in the town to quell the violence. After President Ulysses Grant declared martial law in 1871, some 195 York County whites were imprisoned for crimes related to Klan activity.

In the late nineteenth century, Yorkville experienced the same forces of industrialization as the rest of York County and the southern Piedmont. Cheap labor combined with low tax rates encouraged a cotton mill boom, and many poor farmers came to town in search of work. Several mills were built in the town in the 1890s, but nearby Rock Hill quickly became the economic center of the county, greatly outpacing Yorkville in population and economic development. By 1900 the population of Yorkville was 2,012 while Rock Hill had 5,485 residents. After several cotton mills closed in the 1970s and 1980s, many workers sought employment in Rock Hill and Charlotte, North Carolina.

York has remained a relatively small town. In 1970 the population was 5,081, and thirty years later it had grown to slightly less than 7,000. The city's large historic district includes many antebellum homes that attract visitors and help retain a sense of the town's long history. MICHAEL S. REYNOLDS

Judge, Peter. "'Charleston of the Upcountry,' Yorkville Offered Genteel Living." Rock Hill *Evening Herald,* March 4, 1985, p. C4.
Shankman, Arnold, et al. *York County South Carolina: Its People and Its Heritage.* Norfolk, Va.: Donning, 1983.

York County (682 sq. miles; 2000 pop. 164,614). Located in the north-central part of the state, York County was one of seven counties created in 1785 from the judicial district of Camden. The Catawba Nation was the dominant Native American group in the region during the colonial period. The first European settlers were Scots-Irish from Virginia and Pennsylvania. The county was named for York, Pennsylvania, and the county seat was situated at a place known as Fergus' Cross Roads. The town of Yorkville (later shortened to York) was laid out at the site and incorporated in 1849.

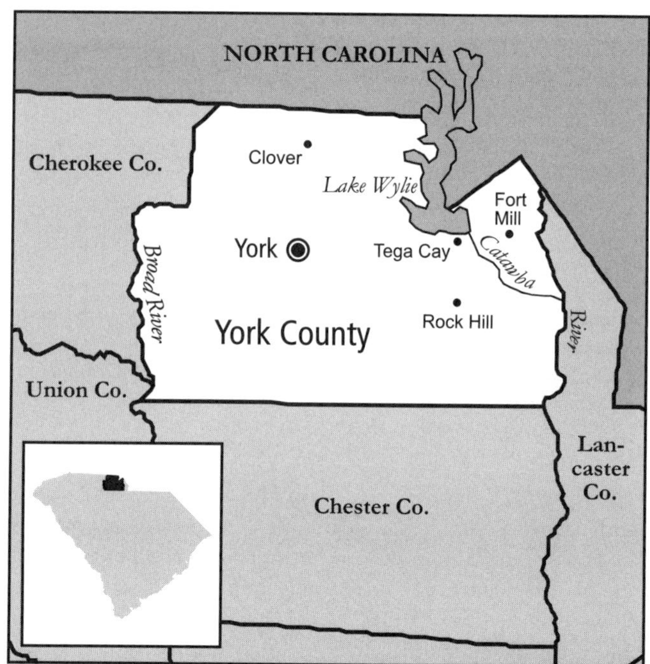

In 1763, as a part of the peace settlement ending the French and Indian War, the Catawbas were granted a fifteen-square-mile territory, with most of the acreage in York County. Two Revolutionary War battles were fought in York in the summer and fall of 1780. Patriots routed the Loyalist force of Captain Christian Huck on July 12 in a skirmish that came to be known as "Huck's Defeat." Later that year, on October 7, American forces won a decisive victory at the Battle of Kings Mountain. Two of York County's leading tourist attractions are associated with the Revolutionary War: Kings Mountain National Military Park and Historic Brattonsville, the site of Huck's Defeat and home of Colonel William Bratton, a patriot officer and prominent local citizen.

Of the 6,604 people who lived in York County in 1790 only 14 percent were slaves. Most whites lived modest lives growing grains and raising livestock. While almost one-third of York's white families owned slaves, only 4 of the 227 masters listed in the 1790 census owned more than 20 slaves, the typical designation of a planter. The expansion of short-staple cotton into the southern Piedmont had a profound impact on York's economy and society. By 1860 the district's population had tripled to 21,502, with slaves making up almost half (46.4 percent) of that number. In 1850 York produced almost four million pounds of cotton, the most grown in South Carolina's upper Piedmont and a testament to the vital role cotton played in York's antebellum economy.

Besides Yorkville, the only other population center in the district before the 1850s was the village of Ebenezer. The towns of Rock Hill and Fort Mill began as railroad depots for the Charlotte and South Carolina Railroad in 1852. York's voters supported the nullification movement by a slim majority in 1832 but opposed the 1851 secession movement by a two-to-one margin. Nevertheless they supported secession in response to Abraham Lincoln's election in 1860.

At the end of the Civil War, Jefferson Davis and his cabinet traveled through York District, fleeing south from Richmond after the Confederate capitol fell. There was also a military skirmish (Stoneman's Raid) in which the railroad crossing over Nation Ford was burned.

After the Civil War most poor whites and newly freed slaves became sharecroppers. In 1890 almost sixty percent of the farms in York County were rented for cash or shares. While economic prospects after the Civil War were bleak, conflict ensued over the role that the newly freed slaves would play in society. The Ku Klux Klan organized as early as 1868 in York, and both rich and poor white citizens joined in order to keep blacks from voting and also to disarm black militia companies in the region. By spring 1871 about 1,800 of the 2,300 adult white males in the county were members of the Klan, which was estimated to have committed eleven murders and six hundred whippings, beatings, and aggravated assaults. Federal troops were stationed in Yorkville to quell the violence, but order was not restored until President Ulysses Grant declared martial law, suspending the writ of habeas corpus in nine counties including York in October 1871.

Industrial development in the late nineteenth century dramatically changed York County. Rock Hill was home to the first steam-driven cotton mill in South Carolina, the Rock Hill Cotton Factory, which began operation in 1880. At Fort Mill in 1888 the Fort Mill Manufacturing Company commenced production, the first unit in what would become Springs Industries. The town of Clover was incorporated in 1887 and also benefited from the booming cotton textile industry when the Clover Spinning Mill opened in 1890. By 1900 there were 108 factories of various types in the county employing 2,285 workers. Four years later the first hydroelectric project on the Catawba River and the second in South Carolina began operations. The India Hook hydroelectric plant contained one powerhouse generating 8,000 horsepower that was distributed along forty miles of lines serving Rock Hill, Fort Mill, and Charlotte, North Carolina. Industrialization brought farmers to town in search of jobs, and Rock Hill quickly became the industrial center of the county.

In 1895 Winthrop Normal and Industrial College was moved from Columbia to Rock Hill. Under the leadership of David Bancroft Johnson, Winthrop grew to become the state's premier teacher training college. Friendship College and Clinton College were established as schools for African Americans respectively in 1891 and 1894. Higher education in York County continued to improve well into the twentieth century with the establishment of York Technical College in 1964 and expansion of Winthrop into a coeducational institution in 1974.

After World War II, York County's economy diversified and continued to grow. While still dependent on cotton textile mills, York County residents found jobs in other industries. In 1959 Bowater began producing newsprint and pulpwood, and in the 1980s Duke Power Company completed construction of its $3.9 billion Catawba Nuclear Station near Clover, providing power to many in both North and South Carolina. The short commute to Charlotte, North Carolina, was made easier after Interstate 77 was completed in 1973. Its proximity to Charlotte prompted continued growth for York County as both businesses and people moved south in order to take advantage of South Carolina's lower tax rates and cheaper land prices. Interstate 77 was widened to eight lanes between Rock Hill and Charlotte in autumn 2000 to facilitate the increasing traffic.

Beginning in the 1990s the York County Council began addressing problems associated with urban development by offering tax incentives to property owners to set aside areas of green space in perpetuity. The program, called "York County Forever," proved successful and, coupled with numerous projects emanating from the Anne Springs Close Greenway and the Nation Ford Land Trust, earned York County a reputation as a statewide leader in environmental protection. MICHAEL S. REYNOLDS

Ford, Lacy K. "One Southern Profile: Modernization and the Development of White Terror in York County, 1856–1876." Master's thesis, University of South Carolina, 1976.

Shankman, Arnold, et al. *York County South Carolina: Its People and Its Heritage.* Norfolk, Va.: Donning, 1983.

Young, Anne Austin (1892–1989). Physician. Young was born on January 15, 1892, in the Cross Hill community of Laurens County to Robert Austin and Clara Nabers. When she was fourteen years old, she enrolled at Presbyterian College in Clinton, where she graduated with honors. Young briefly taught school and then moved to Philadelphia in 1911 to study at the Woman's Medical College of Pennsylvania. After one year the college presented Young with a scholarship recognizing that she had attained the highest scholastic average among students. Young's professional specialty was obstetrics and gynecology.

After graduation in 1915, Young declined a fellowship offered by the University of Edinburgh in Scotland. Instead she returned home to focus her energies on providing quality medical care for the people of South Carolina. Young took the South Carolina Medical Board and achieved the highest score ever tallied on the examination up to that time. On March 31, 1918, she married the physician Charles Henry Young. The couple had one daughter.

The Youngs settled in Anderson County, where they devoted their careers to the Anderson Memorial Hospital, practicing medicine together. During more than sixty years of providing medical services, Young assisted in the delivery of an estimated eleven thousand infants and received praise for her patient care and her service as a mental retardation clinician.

Young promoted philanthropy. In Clinton she led efforts to create Whitten Village, a facility for mentally retarded patients. She donated money to build a medical clinic in Zaire, Africa. Young also wanted to assist the civic advancement of communities in Zaire and gave money to construct three schools and three churches there.

In 1981 Young became the second woman inducted into the South Carolina Hall of Fame. She received numerous other awards and honors, including an honorary doctorate from Columbia College. After her husband died in 1966, Young continued her medical services as long as possible. She died in Anderson on January 25, 1989, and was buried in Forest Lawn Memorial Park. ELIZABETH D. SCHAFER

Klosky, Beth Ann. *Daring Venture: A Biography of Anne Austin Young, Pioneer Woman Doctor.* Anderson, S.C.: by the author, 1978.

Obituary. *Anderson Independent-Mail,* January 26, 1989, p. A1.

Young, Virginia Durant Covington (1842–1906). Suffragist, editor, author. Young was born in Georgetown on March 10, 1842, the daughter of William Wallace Durant and his second wife, Julia. Shortly after Virginia's birth, the family moved to Marion District, where her father became a prosperous planter and active politician. At age sixteen Virginia married Benjamin H. Covington. During the Civil War she began writing short stories and novellas under various pseudonyms for magazines such as *Southern Field and Fireside* and *The XIX Century.* In 1874 she moved with her husband to a farm in DeSoto County, Mississippi, where he died in 1879.

Returning to Marion, she married Dr. William Jasper Young of Fairfax on December 22, 1880.

Young's career followed the pattern of many suffragists. After active participation in Baptist missionary societies, she joined the Woman's Christian Temperance Union (WCTU) in 1886. Suffrage appealed as an avenue to temperance goals. Young moved onto the national reform stage by writing magazine articles and lecturing at temperance forums across the country. After writing columns in several state newspapers, she became the editor of the *Fairfax Enterprise,* becoming its sole owner in 1899. Her weekly was said to be like Mrs. Young, a "charming medley of politics, women's rights and good natured wit and humor."

In 1890 Young and Adelaide Viola Neblett founded the South Carolina Equal Rights Association (SCERA), which became an affiliate of the National American Woman Suffrage Association (NAWSA). As president of the SCERA from 1892 to 1895, Young worked to break down prejudices against southern women among northern suffragists and at the same time tried (futilely) to win the vote in South Carolina.

Young found an ally in Abbeville legislator and editor Robert R. Hemphill. In 1892 he introduced a joint resolution to the General Assembly granting women the right to vote and hold office. The resolution was rejected. Young then petitioned the legislature for her personal enfranchisement. When a constitutional convention was called in 1895, Young and the SCERA campaigned vigorously for a woman-suffrage amendment. In an address to the convention, she advocated a strategy first put forward by northern suffragists. Enfranchising women with a property or educational requirement would assure white supremacy without the oppressive Jim Crow laws being proposed to disenfranchise African Americans. The amendment to enfranchise women with $300 worth of taxable property went down to defeat 121 to 26.

Young's proposal in 1896 to allow women to vote in presidential elections found no support. The SCERA fell into disarray. NAWSA leaders criticized Young for not developing a more broad-based movement. She suffered from criticism at home for sullying women with politics. Voting rights for South Carolina women came through federal amendment in 1919.

Young also wrote three novels. *Beholding as in a Glass* (1895) and *A Tower in the Desert* (1896) were essentially vehicles for her temperance and suffrage messages. The third, *One of the Blue Hen's Chickens* (1902), reflected her interest in the "positive thinking" movement called "Mental Science," which was popular among suffragists. Young died at her home in Fairfax on November 2, 1906, as one of the best-known women in the state. BARBARA L. BELLOWS

Taylor, Antoinette Elizabeth. "South Carolina and the Enfranchisement of Women: The Early Years." *South Carolina Historical Magazine* 77 (April 1976): 115–26.

Ulmer, Barbara Bellows. "Virginia Durant Young: New South Suffragist." Master's thesis, University of South Carolina, 1979.

Z

Zubly, John Joachim (August 27, 1724–July 23, 1781). Minister. John J. Zubly was born in St. Gall, Switzerland, to Reformed Protestants David and Helena Zubly. While Zubly was still a gymnasium student, his parents left in 1736 for the Swiss immigrant enclave at Purrysburg in South Carolina before settling in Georgia. Zubly set out to join them after his ordination at London's German Reformed Church on August 19, 1744.

Zubly preached for a time among the Salzburger community, where he met Anna Tobler, whom he married on November 12, 1746. They had one child, who died. His second wife was Ann (Pye?). The Reformed congregation in Vernonsburg, near Savannah, petitioned the Georgia trustees to appoint Zubly as their pastor; the congregation then chose another, who remained even after the trustees finally approved Zubly's appointment. Zubly then traveled among German communities in the South Carolina lowcountry and Georgia, preaching whenever possible there and among the German Lutheran community in Orangeburg. In 1757 he accepted a call to pastor the Wappetaw Church on Wando Neck northeast of Charleston. Known for his erudition, Zubly occasionally lectured at the Independent Meeting House in Charleston and in 1759 published a collection of sermons dealing with a Calvinist understanding of the meaning of death. Later he wrote in opposition to the appointment of an Anglican bishop for the colonies. His learning led the College of New Jersey (Princeton) to confer on him both M.A. and D.D. degrees.

AN

HUMBLE ENQUIRY

INTO

The NATURE of the DEPENDENCY of the *AMERICAN* COLONIES upon the PARLIAMENT of *GREAT-BRITAIN*,

AND

The RIGHT of PARLIAMENT to lay TAXES on the ſaid COLONIES.

By a FREEHOLDER of *SOUTH-CAROLINA*.

A Houſe divided againſt itſelf cannot ſtand.

When people heard ſhip money demanded *as a right*, and found it by ſworn judges of the law adjudged ſo, upon ſuch grounds and reaſons as every ſtander-by was able to ſwear was not law, and ſo had loſt the pleaſure and delight of being kind and dutiful to the King, and, inſtead [illegible] GIVING, were required to PAY, and by a logick that left no man any thing [illegible] he might call his own, they no more looked upon it as the caſe of one man, [illegible] the caſe of the kingdom, nor as an impoſition laid upon them by the King, but by the judges, which they thought themſelves bound in publick juſtice not to ſubmit to. It was an obſervation long ago of *Thucydides*, "That men are much more paſſionate for injuſtice "than for violence, becauſe (ſaith he) the one proceeding as from an equal ſeems "rapine, when the other proceeding from a ſtranger is [illegible] the effect of neceſſity." —When they ſaw reaſon of ſtate urged as elements of law, judges as ſharp-ſighted as ſecretaries of ſtate, judgment of law grounded upo[illegible] matter of fact of which there was neither enquiry nor proof, and no reaſon given for the payment but what included all the eſtates of the ſtanders-by, they had no reaſon to hope that doctrine, or the promoters of it, would be contained wi[illegible]n any bounds; and it is no wonder that they who had ſo little reaſon to be plea[illegible] own condition were no leſs ſolicitous for, or apprehenſive of the in[illegible] attend any alteration.—*Hiſtory of the long Rebellion*, vol. 1

PRINTED in the YEAR M,DCC,LXIX.

[Price Twelve Shillings and Sixpence.]

"An Humble Enquiry" was one of several pamphlets Zubly wrote that discussed the strained relationship between the colonies and the Mother Country. Although published after he had moved to Georgia, the author identified himself as "A Freeholder of South-Carolina." Courtesy, South Caroliniana Library, University of South Carolina

Zubly, however, is noted more for his political writings and involvement in public affairs, which came in 1760 after he accepted a call to the Independent Church in Savannah. There he also acquired considerable land and slaves. As tension between the colonies and Britain intensified following passage of the Stamp Act in 1765, Zubly penned several tracts sketching for a Georgia audience inclined to Loyalist sentiment various perspectives emerging in colonial political circles. Consequently, in July 1775 he was elected to the Georgia provincial congress and then selected to represent Georgia in the Continental Congress.

Although Zubly appreciated colonial opposition to British imperial policy, some of which he believed was oppressive, he remained convinced that nothing should sever ties between colonies and mother country. Hence he opposed moves toward independence, returning to Savannah in October 1775. With independence sentiment in Georgia growing, Zubly was branded a Loyalist, taken into custody by the Georgia Committee of Public Safety, and in late 1777 banished from Georgia, with much of his estate confiscated. Zubly came to South Carolina, but he returned to Savannah in 1779 after the reestablishment of a royal colonial government. Distrusted by both ardent patriots and Loyalists, Zubly remained in Savannah until his death. He is buried in Savannah's Colonial Park.

CHARLES LIPPY

Hawes, Lilla Mills, ed. *Journal of the Reverend John Joachim Zubly, A.M. D.D., March 5, 1770 through June 22, 1781.* Savannah: Georgia Historical Society, 1989.

Martin, Roger A. "John J. Zubly: Preacher, Planter, and Politician." Ph.D. diss., University of Georgia, 1976.

Miller, Randall M., ed. *"A Warm & Zealous Spirit": John J. Zubly and the American Revolution, a Selection of His Writings.* Macon, Ga.: Mercer University Press, 1982.

Seamon, Janice Louise. "John Joachim Zubly: A Voice for Liberty and Principle." M.A. thesis, University of South Carolina, 1982.

Index